# THE COMPLETE RECORD OF THE FA CUP

MIKE COLLETT

SPORTSBOOKS

# THE AUTHOR

Mike Collett missed the 1953 Matthews FA Cup final only because he was born 12 days too late. Since then he has travelled to all five continents mainly covering football as a journalist.
The greatest moment in his sporting lifetime came when Ricky Villa scored the winning goal for Spurs in the replayed FA Cup final against Manchester City in 1981.
That was on his birthday and he made sure he was at Wembley for that one.
He is the World Football Editor at Reuters, the international news agency, lives in London and is married with three children.
Previous published work: The Guinness Record of the FA Cup (1993).

Published by SportsBooks Ltd
SportsBooks Limited
PO Box 422
Cheltenham
GL50 2YN
United Kingdom
Tel: 08700 713 965
Fax: 08700 750 888
e-mail randall@sportsbooks.ltd.uk
Website www.sportsbooks.ltd.uk



ISBN 1899807 19 5
Cover design: Katherine Northam

Printed in China by Midas Printing International Ltd
on behalf of Compass Press Ltd

# CONTENTS



## Part One – The History



## Part Two – Club by Club Results

## Part Three – Head to Heads



## Part Four – Facts & Feats

# INTRODUCTION

IT IS now 10 years since the first version of this book appeared and very little in the world of football has remained the same as it was then. In the autumn of 1993 the second seasons of both the FA Premier League and the Champions League were just getting underway – as was the 113th season of the FA Cup.

It would be churlish to deny that both the Premier League and the Champions League have gone from strength to strength since then capturing the focus of media attention. In contrast, the FA Cup, the oldest and greatest annual knockout competition in world football, has suffered somewhat in comparison.

But it is still in there and fighting back after coming through the most turbulent period in its long and glorious history.

In 1993 it would have been hard to imagine that any club could think of fielding a weakened side in the FA Cup, or that the third round would be played in December, or that the holders would not compete the following season, or that the cup final would not be played under Wembley's twin towers.

All those things have happened – and all of them have taken some gloss off the competition. But there is absolutely no denying the fact either that the FA Cup still retains a special place in the hearts of millions of fans worldwide and it is still special for the thousands of players who have played in it – whether they now come from Senegal or Solihull.

For a handful of coaches and players at the very peak of the English game winning the FA Cup might not mean quite what it once did. Finishing third or fourth in the Premier League is now considered by some to be more important than winning the FA Cup because those league positions offer a route into the Champions League.

Perhaps the time has come for the FA to strike a special deal with UEFA and propose the FA Cup winners are offered a Champions League place. As UEFA president Lennart Johansson has said in the past: "It is not a league of champions, but it is a league which produces the Champions of Europe."

If the FA Cup offered a route into that land of riches, it is doubtful whether too many managers would risk playing weakened teams in the future.

Sir Bobby Robson, Ipswich Town's manager when they won the cup in 1978 and the guest of honour in 2003 says: "The FA Cup final is the greatest single match outside the World Cup final – and its ours".

It has to be carefully nurtured and not taken for granted because it still means enough to enough fans to guarantee its place at the very heart of English soccer's body politic for generations to come.

The reason for that is that every season the FA Cup produces romance, drama, shocks and intrigue in a way that a season-long league programme cannot do. Perhaps real acts of giant-killing are less frequent than there once were, but when they do happen, our love affair with the FA Cup is re-kindled. Obviously not for the beaten giants and their supporters... but for everyone else at least.

And there are still great occasions every season when the FA Cup lifts the spirits of even the most jaded fan and re-affirms one's faith in the game – and these occasions do not even have to occur when the big clubs are involved in the later stages.

Was any true fan unaware of the progress of Team Bath through the later rounds of the qualifying competition last season, when they became the first student team to reach the Competition Proper for more than a century ? I doubt it.

Team Bath's match against Mansfield Town was shown live on Sky TV and the students were far from discredited despite losing 4-2 to the Third Division side. Team Bath also collected a total of £146,000 in prize money and for their appearance on live TV – another reason why the appeal of the FA Cup is so great for the smaller clubs.

Even the winners of the 45 extra-preliminary round ties in 2002-03 collected £500 each – enough to pay for a new set of kit. In all last season's prize fund was £11.5 million with the winners guaranteed £2 million and the runners-up £1 million.

And while Team Bath might have captured the public's imagination on a cold winter's day in November, even the most passionate Arsenal fan would agree that Southampton were the popular choice to win the cup last May. In the end Arsenal won the cup fair and square, but it was left to Saints' manager Gordon Strachan to sum up exactly what the cup still means to most people afterwards.

"They say that the FA Cup has had its day, but I don't agree with that – the big clubs are still entering the competition, and still winning it, so they must be taking it seriously. But the FA Cup is special because it gives players who are not the best in the world, the taste of what its like to be a champion.

"Hopefully my players who were beaten today can go on and become champions. The League determines the best players and the best team – but the FA Cup has a romance which allows people who have had hard times to have a moment when they feel like champions."

Or perhaps Graeme Souness summed it up best of all after a third round tie in January 2003 when his Blackburn side had won 4-1 at Aston Villa, the latest meeting in a cup rivalry that goes back to 1889.

"The FA Cup is the best cup competition in the world and has been since the day it started. I can say that today because we've won!"

And that ultimately, is what it is all about. Winning the FA Cup still remains the dream of millions as either a player or a fan. Last season 624 clubs – a record in modern times - took part and more than 700 matches were watched by over two million people. An estimated 400 million TV viewers in over 50 countries worldwide watched the final live and saw Robert Pires become the latest (French) man to score the winner in the final.

But the beauty of the cup is that there are heroes in every round – and there always have been since the competition started in 1871-72.

The stories of many of them are told in the following pages – George Mutch, Stanley Matthews, Jim Montgomery, to name just three, but for me, one story captures the magic of the FA Cup like no other.

In November 1965 Wigan Athletic, then in the Cheshire County League, beat fourth division Doncaster Rovers 3-1 in a first round replay. Somehow a report of this obscure FA Cup match was carried by *The Times* and it makes astonishing reading:

"H Lyon was the toast of Wigan last night. Carried off on a stretcher after 20 minutes of the FA Cup first round replay against Doncaster Rovers at Wigan, he defied the pain of *sprained ankle ligaments* (my italics) to score three goals.

"Lyon spent 15 minutes in the Wigan dressing room while a doctor plied him with whisky and tablets to ease the pain.

"The prescription worked wonders. Lyon's *flashing header* found the back of Doncaster's net in the 57th minute. This was followed up by a *volley* with his strapped up foot 15 minutes later, and then three minutes from the end he scored with another header.

"After being chaired off the field by jubilant supporters, Lyon said: "I could hardly walk when I got back on the pitch, but when the first goal went in I was chuffed. I forgot all about the pain. It just didn't seem to hurt any more."

The man was a solid gold cup hero. This book is for him and the thousands of others who have made the FA Cup the greatest annual knockout competition in the world.

**Mike Collett**
**London, August 2003**

# BIBLIOGRAPHY

*AFS Book of Cup Final Players*, Paul Marsh, 1992
*Association Football*, FNS Creek 1937
*Association Football*, 4 volumes, Caxton, editors Fabian & Green 1960
*Association Football & The Men Who Made It*, Gibson & Pickford 1906
*Athletic News Football Annuals*, various
*Book of Football*, 12 volumes, 1905
*Book of Football*, 5 Volumes, 1972
*By The Book*, Clive Thomas, 1984
*Corinthians & Cricketers*, Edward Grayson 1957
*Cup Final Extra!*, Martin Tyler, 1981
*Cup Final Story, 1946-1965*, David Prole, 1966
*Denied FC, The Football League Election Struggles*, Dave Twydell, 2001
*Encyclopaedia of Association Football*, Maurice Golesworthy, various editions
*England Football Fact Book*, Cris Freddi, 1991
*English Football Internationalists Who's Who*, Douglas Lamming, 1990
*FA Cup Complete Results*, Tony Brown, 1999
*FA Cup Final, a Post-War History*, Ivan Ponting, 1994
*FA Cup Giant Killers*, Geoff Tibballs, 1994
*FA Official Yearbooks*, from 1948
*Father of Modern Sport – The Life and Times of Charles W Alcock*, Keith Booth, 2002
*Finney – A Football Legend*, Paul Agnew, 1989
*Football From the Goalmouth*, Frank Swift, 1949
*Football in Sheffield*, Percy M Young, 1981
*Football League Players Records*, 1888-1939, Michael Joyce
*Football League Players Records*, 1946-1998, Barry Hugman
*Football League 1888-1988, The Official Illustrated History*, Bryon Butler, 1987
*Football Worlds*, Stanley Rous, 1978
*For the Good of the Game, The Official History of the PFA*, John Harding, 1991
*Forward Arsenal*, Bernard Joy, 1952
*Giantkillers, The*, Bryon Butler, 1982
*Glorious Wembley*, Howard Bass, 1982
*Gone But Not Forgotten* series, Dave Twydell, various
*Grounds for a Change*, Dave Twydell, 1992
*Guinness Book of Soccer Facts and Feats*, various editions, Jack Rollin
*History of the FA Amateur Cup*, Bob Barton, 1984
*History of Non-League Football Grounds*, Kerry Miller, 1996
*History of the Wembley FA Cup Final*, Daily Mail publications, 1994
*Hotbed of Soccer, The Story of Football in the North East*, Arthur Appleton, 1961
*Jackie Milburn In Black and White*, Mike Kirkup, 1990
*Ninety Years of the Blues*, Ron Hockings, 1995
*Non League*, Bob Barton, 1985
*Non-League Club Directory*, publisher Tony Williams, various
*Northern Goalfields, The official History of the Northern League*, Brian Hunt, 1988
*Official Centenary History of the Southern League*, Leigh Edwards, 1994
*Official Illustrated History of the FA Cup*, Bryon Butler 1996
*Official History of the Football Association*, Bryon Butler, 1991
*Official History of the FA Cup*, Geoffrey Green, 1949, 1960
*One Hundred Years of the FA Cup*, Tony Pawson, 1972
*Pictorial History of Soccer*, Dennis Signy, 1968
*Shanks, The Authorised Biography of Bill Shankly*, Dave Bowler, 1996
*Soccer: A Panorama*, Brian Glanville, 1969
*Soccer at War 1939-1945*, Jack Rollin 1985
*Southern League Football, The First 50 years*, Paul Harrison 1989
*Southern League Football, the Post War Years*, Paul Harrison 1987
*Spurs Supreme*, Ralph L Finn, 1961
*Stanley Matthews – The Authorised Biography*, David Miller, 1989
*Strange Kind of Glory*, Eamon Dunphy, 1991
*The Double*, Ken Ferris, 1996
*The Double and Before*, Danny Blanchflower, 1961
*There's Only One United*, Geoffrey Green, 1978
*To The Palace for the Cup*, Ian Bevan, Stuart Hibberd & Michael Gilbert, 1999
*We Won The Cup!* David Barber, 1981
*Wembley: The Greatest Stage*, Tom Watt & Kevin Palmer, 1998

As well as the above books, information has been obtained from many other sources including all Rothmans Football Yearbooks from 1970-71, Athletic News Football Annuals, News of the World Annuals, club yearbooks, programmes and official club magazines, etc. I have also consulted every club record history published by Breedon Books as well as thousands of match programmes.

A major source of information covering the 1871-1925 period was published in four volumes by the Association of Football Statisticians between 1985-87.

# ACKNOWLEDGEMENTS

Thanks are due to many people who helped in the production of this book either by loaning historical or reference books or programmes, offering advice, general guidance or hard facts and figures.

I am indebted to two people in particular, my long-suffering wife Siobhan and Paul Radford, my Nottingham Forest-supporting Sports Editor at Reuters. They know more than anyone of the countless problems that had to be overcome before this book could be completed. Without their support it probably wouldn't have been.

I would also like to thank David Davies, who has been Chief Executive of the Football Association more times than most teams have ever won the cup, for his initial encouragement in the project. Thanks are also due to David Barber, the FA's incomparable historian and FA executives Paul Mullen and Marc Armstrong.

Among Fleet Street's finest particular thanks are due to Glenn Moore of *The Independent* for his painstakingly helpful checking of stats, Walter Gammie of The Times for his help in checking the Non-League section and most especially Richard Whitehead of *The Times*, a constant source of help and inspiration. I've only just stopped buzzing after the caffeine intake at Waterloo Station in February.

On the technical side special thanks are due to Tony Brown, a veritable giant among football statisticians, who allowed us the use of his Head-to-Head records from his own *FA Cup Complete Results* book and whose other statistical publications provide the font of so much statistical knowledge now.

The original version of this book appeared a decade ago as *The Guinness Record of the FA Cup* and I would like to thank William Morgan for the months of work he put in converting results from an old computer into a modern data-based format.

Thanks are also due to the following, some of whom helped with original source material and without whom: Mihir Bose, Neil Bruce, Ian Chadband, Tim Collings, Simon Evans, Simon's dad David Evans, Ken Ferris, Bernard Gallagher of *Claret and Blue* magazine, Caroline Helly, Trevor Huggins, John Ley, Angus Loughran, Pat McCarty, David Meek, Kevin Mitchell, Nick Mulvenney, Ed Osmond, Mitch Phillips, Jack Rollin, Chas Sumner, Martin Tyler and Robert Woodward.

To Steve Crisp and Alexia Singh of the Reuters Photographic desk and to Reuters for the use of their photographs.

My publisher Randall Northam has been a constant source of support who lives in hope that perhaps this will be the season Plymouth Argyle finally win the old trophy. Keep dreaming Randall.

I would also like to thank Bob Dylan for some of the finest music known to humanity. Listening to old Bob was especially soothing while having to compile Arsenal's recent list of successes.

Last but not least a big thank you too to Ryan, Hannah and Melissa ... in case you were wondering, this is what Dad was doing in the basement for the last year!

# THE HISTORY OF THE FA CUP

# AMATEUR HOUR 1872-1882

ON NOVEMBER 11, 1871 four football matches took place that were unlike any other that had ever been played before. In west London, a team from the Civil Service turned up for their game against Barnes with only eight men. In south London, Crystal Palace laid out the welcome mat for the men from Hitchin, who had travelled across Hertfordshire and the metropolis. Out in east London, Upton Park were playing Clapham Rovers, while in rural Berkshire, Maidenhead and Marlow, two clubs who are still rivals to this day, were meeting competitively for the first time.

Those eight teams, all of them from the south and all of them amateur, were playing themselves into history. They were taking part in the very first FA Cup matches of all.

The balls that were sent rolling across those muddy fields when those matches kicked off, have long since disappeared but the passions, emotions and frenzies that were first set in motion on that distant Victorian afternoon, remain as strong as ever.

These games were also the first truly 'competitive' soccer matches. A prize, a tangible reward, was waiting for the winners of this competition. It could be argued that modern soccer really began that afternoon.

**Huge Impact**

Could anyone living then possibly have imagined the impact the FA Cup was going to have on the development of soccer? Probably not. Could anyone in the middle of the 19th century ever have imagined the impact soccer was going to have on the national, and later the global consciousness? Definitely not. The men who formed the Football Association were not great social reformers like William Wilberforce or the Earl of Shaftesbury. But, by their deeds they would, indirectly, have a huge impact on the social life of the nation – an impact felt to this day.

Football of course has been with us probably for as long as men have had feet with which to kick things. The Chinese were the first to formalise the game in any way with their ancient game of T'su Chi which was more of an individual ball control game than a team effort. The Greeks played a game called 'episkyres' and the Romans one called 'harpustum' – both more like rugby than soccer. In the Middle Ages, in Florence, Italy, the game of 'calcio' developed – a brawling, violent, colourful spectacle which is still enacted in Renaissance costumes today.

Various forms of the 'foote-ball' had been known in rural Olde Englande since long before the Middle Ages. The annual Shrove Tuesday match in Derbyshire is said to date back to AD 217 when the men of Derby drove out a number of Roman soldiers from the town. From ancient times there was a Shrovetide match played in Chester, and there were others at Corfe Castle in Dorset and Scone in Perthshire. The Shrove Tuesday match at Ashbourne in Derbyshire is played to this day between the 'uppers' and 'downers' while every January 6 in north Lincolnshire the villagers of Haxey and Westwoodside engage in a brawling, heaving scrum for up to six or seven hours until one side scores a 'goal' – getting the 'ball' through the doors of the nearest pub.

Most of these ancient rural traditions have survived unaltered from the earliest times – even surviving King Edward II's proclamation early in the 14th Century which banned the playing of this type of football altogether.

"Forasmuch as there is great noise in the city caused by Hustling over large balls, from which many evils may arise, which God forbid, we command and forbid on behalf of the King, on pain of imprisonment, such game to be used in the city in future".

Two hundred years later nothing much had changed. In 1531 Sir Thomas Elyot said that football was "nothing but beastlie furie and extreme violence deserving only to be put in perpetual silence". And the author of *Anatomic of Abuses in the Realme of England,* published in 1583, was of the same mind: "As concerning football playing, I proteste unto you that it may rather be called a friendlie kind of fight than a play or recreation... a bloody murthering practice than a fellowly sport or pastime".

As late as 1829 a report of a 'match' in Derbyshire told of people "falling, bleeding beneath the feet of the surrounding mob".

Clearly the gap between matches of that kind, the only kind of their day, and the type of football being played just 42 years later had been closed extremely quickly, even if the football being played on that November day in 1871 may seem hugely outdated to us today, we clearly have far more in common, in terms of playing the game at least, with our relatively athletic Victorian friends, rather than with the brawling mob in Derby. Well, some of us, at least.

By 1871 there was a clearly defined pitch, with recognisable goals, a referee and umpires, teams of 11-a-side and distinct strips. But there were no crossbars or goal-nets; free-kicks and penalties had yet to be invented and there were no markings on the pitch except for the touchlines. When the ball was kicked out of play the team who "touched it down" first, rugby style, took the throw-in.

This revolutionary change in little more than a generation was brought about by the public schools who helped calm down the game, taking the basic structure and purpose of the urban, folkloric working-class pastime, and codifying it into a sport. It was within the courtyards and libraries, the assembly halls and dormitories, but most importantly on the playing fields, where football as we know and understand it today, first put down its roots.

### Catalyst Game Needed

There was a major change of attitude towards education for the privileged in the early part of the 19th century. The boys who went to these schools had no time for the pastimes of a country squire. They did not go horse-riding or hunting at school, and while they may have rowed later at Oxford or Cambridge, their main outdoor pursuits until then were to be found on convenient playing fields, or cloisters, or any open space within the school grounds. All that was needed was enough boys to make two teams and a ball.

The catalyst the game needed at this stage was Dr Thomas Arnold, the reforming educationalist at Rugby School. He helped the youngsters organise themselves and impose some discipline on the embryonic football they were playing, an adaptation of the town and village games that had been around for centuries.

So by the second or third decade of the 19th century, various forms of football had now come into being in the major public schools. At Winchester the playing field was about 80 yards long and 80-feet wide; at Eton they changed ends at half-time, but at other schools they changed ends after every goal was scored. The art of dribbling with the ball was much favoured by the boys at Charterhouse and Harrow where the goals were known as 'bases' – and stood 150 yards apart. At Cheltenham College, the game was played with the precursor of the modern-day throw-in. Outside of the public schools, the game was also developing in other isolated pockets like Sheffield. Some rules permitted the use of hands, others did not. Some allowed hacking, others did not. Quite clearly out of this Tower of Babel there could only be one result – chaos.

### The Simplest Game

It was not until 1848 that the first attempt was made to unify all of these different strands. In that year 14 old boys from Rugby, Winchester, Eton, Harrow and Shrewsbury met at Cambridge and after much vexing and argument, 'The Cambridge Rules' were drafted. But the knot the old boys tied that year was not a secure one, and soon unravelled with each school and club soon playing by its own rules again.

In 1862, and with the game still a decade away from capturing even a twinkle of the public's imagination, another attempt was made to unite the nation's footballers. In that year Mr JC Thring of Uppingham School in Rutland drafted another set of 10 rules, for what he called 'The Simplest Game'. These rules allowed no kicking of the ball in the air, and no violence. Tripping was outlawed – so was kicking at your opponent's heels. These rules, also contained the birth of the concept of today's goal-kick. They also contained what can now be seen to be an embryonic rugby offside law... nevertheless, they were widely circulated, provoked interest and some schools adopted them.

In November 1862 a match took place at Cambridge between Cambridge Old Etonians and Cambridge Old Harrovians. These young Victorian gentlemen had each played by one set of rules at school – now they were meeting on a level playing field to a set of rules most of us could recognise today; 11-a-side, with an umpire from each side plus a neutral referee. The goals were 12ft across and up to 20ft high, and the match had a set time limit of 75 minutes. What is more – the rules worked. And they provided the basis for the revised Cambridge Rules of 1863 which in turn, were the basis of the first laws of the Football Association.

In one of soccer's great masterworks, *The Book of Football*, published in 1905, one writer calculated that 5,905 years previously football began with Cain and Abel kicking apples about in the Garden of Eden. By his reckoning, the formation of the Football Association was long overdue.

It did, in fact, come into being at a meeting at the Freemasons' Tavern, in Great Queen Street, Lincoln's Inn Fields, on Monday, October 26, 1863. The meeting was suggested by Ebenezer Cobb Morley, a fine player in his day and the founder of the Barnes Club in 1862. He became the FA's first secretary in 1863 and lived to see the first FA Cup final at Wembley in 1923, dying the following year at the age of 93.

### Sixth Meeting

Representatives of a dozen London and suburban clubs accepted Morley's invitation. They came from Barnes, Blackheath, Blackheath Proprietory School, Charterhouse School, Crystal Palace, Crusaders, Forest of Leytonstone, Kensington School, No Names of Kilburn, Percival House, Surbiton and the War Office. There were many more clubs and schools playing football by now than those represented in that upstairs oak-panelled room in the heart of Victorian London. There were no representatives of the game being played in Sheffield and Nottingham; none, surprisingly, from Cambridge, or from public schools like Harrow, Eton or Winchester. Eleven of the 12 clubs enrolled themselves as founder members – Charterhouse bided their time – and Arthur Pember of the No Names Club was elected as chairman. The main business of the evening was to "form an Association with the object of establishing a definite code of rules for the regulation of the game".

Over the next six weeks the FA met six times and it was in that sixth meeting that football and rugby finally branched apart from the trunk that had given birth to them both. The Blackheath Club played their game by the Rugby rules – and they were adamant that they would not sanction any proposal that outlawed the thorny old problem of 'hacking' or tripping. The football men would not budge, and so Blackheath left the FA. In 1871 they became founder-members of the Rugby Union, probably the only sports club in the world, which, playing basically the same game, became founder-members of two different sporting bodies.

At first the FA did not attempt to impose its new 'unified' Laws. Rather, it saw itself as exerting an influence on the growth of the game. By 1865, for example, its membership was still small and it had only one member in the provinces. That was the Sheffield Club, founded in 1855, the oldest football club in the world, and still in existence today.

But change was not long in coming. Inter-city and inter-county representative matches were starting up, and in 1870 an event that can now be seen as being as important as anything that had happened on the playing field up to then took place in the committee rooms of the Football Association.

Charles William Alcock was appointed as the Secretary of the Football Association. It was a post he was to hold for the next 25 years. Alcock had two brilliant ideas. He was the man who invented the FA Cup, and can rightly be regarded as the father of international soccer because he proposed the first internationals between England and Scotland, starting with the unofficial games in 1870 and the first official matches two years later.

### Strong Hunch

Alcock, barely 30 years old and still playing for the Wanderers club, which had evolved from Forest FC of Leytonstone, was an Old Harrovian. During his time at the school from 1855-1859 he had played in the 'Cock House' game – a sudden-death inter-house football competition. Alcock took the concept of that game and imagined it on a national scale – a knockout cup competition between the FA's member clubs. He probably had a very strong hunch that his proposal would be accepted by the FA Committee when he proposed it to them on the summer evening of July 20, 1871.

The meeting had been convened in the offices of *The Sportsman* newspaper, long since demolished, but which then stood down the hill from St Paul's Cathedral at the bottom of Ludgate Hill, just off Fleet Street and not far from the first headquarters of the FA at 51 Holburn Viadect.

He put his proposal to the FA's Honorary Treasurer, A Stair of the Upton Park Club; CW Stephenson of Westminster School; JH Giffard of the Civil Service Club, D Allport of the Crystal Palace club; MP Betts of Harrow and to Captain Francis Marindin, an officer of the Royal Engineers.

After the usual formalities had been taken care of, Charles William Alcock delivered the words that would guarantee him a place in soccer history. He asked the committee to agree "that it is desirable that a Challenge Cup should be established in connection with the Association for which all clubs belonging to the Association should be invited to compete".

**Three Teams Scratched**

The tweaking of Victorian moustaches was brief and the committee agreed to the idea almost immediately. Three months later, on October 16, 1871, the 18 rules were drafted but there was a disappointing response from the FA's members. By now almost 50 clubs had affiliated themselves to the FA, but only 15 wanted to take part in this latest fad. Many stayed away preferring to play friendlies, to play the game for the game's sake.

The 15 clubs that entered – and were accepted – were Barnes, Wanderers, Harrow Chequers, Civil Service, Crystal Palace, Upton Park, Clapham Rovers and Hampstead Heathens from the London area. From around the Home Counties came Hitchin, Royal Engineers, Reigate Priory, Maidenhead and Marlow, while only two clubs came from north of Hertfordshire – Queens Park from Glasgow, and Donington Grammar School from Spalding in Lincolnshire.

It was not much, but it was a start even though three teams scratched before they played a match – Harrow Chequers, Reigate Priory and Donington School. One Harrow Chequer was still to play a major part in this first FA Cup competition but his club, formed by Harrow Old Boys, was to have something of a love-hate relationship with the FA Cup.

Three times, in 1871, 1874 and again in 1875, Harrow Chequers entered the competition, and three times they scratched without ever playing a match. But the main concern to the committee in the autumn of 1871 was not the problem of scratching, but the purchase of their new FA Cup trophy. The firm of Martin, Hall and Company manufactured one in silver for a cost of £20. It stood about 18 inches high, had a footballer figurine on its lid and became known in time as, "the little tin idol".

So the stage was set for the first round of the first FA Cup. The first goal that day was scored by Jarvis Kenrick of Clapham in their match at Upton Park. He also scored another that afternoon as Clapham duly went through to the second round by winning 3-0, while Barnes beat the Civil Service 2-0 and Maidenhead beat Marlow by the same score. In south London Crystal Palace and Hitchin drew 0-0, and, under the laws of this new, haphazard tournament, both teams were allowed through to the second round.

To illustrate even further just how odd this first competition was in a modern context among the handful of clubs taking part were Queen's Park of Glasgow. The Scottish FA not yet formed, there seemed nothing unusual then about the Glasgow side taking part in the 'English Cup'. The FA, recognising how far Queen's Park had to travel and how much it was going to cost them, exempted them until the semi-finals where they were drawn against the Wanderers. Queen's Park had been formed in 1867 and although playing nothing like the number of matches clubs play today, they turned up for their semi-final at Kennington Oval, the home of the Surrey County Cricket Club on March 4, 1872 with an amazing record. They had never conceded a goal since they were founded five years previously a record that in all lasted for the first seven years of their existence.

**Eliminated by Default**

And by the end of that afternoon, their defence still had not been breached. The teams drew 0-0 but as Queen's Park had only £4 in the bank before the journey to London – which was only made possible by passing the hat around – they had to return to Glasgow, unbeaten, but eliminated by default.

The rules of the time stated that all matches after the second round had to take place at Kennington and that didn't help their cause either. The thought was probably never entertained that the Wanderers should go to Glasgow for a replay, Instead, the Wanderers were in the final on a walkover, after a 1-0 win over Clapham and a 0-0 draw with Crystal Palace with both teams advancing.

Another quirk of this competition was that Royal Engineers also reached the final after playing Crystal Palace – but the FA ruled that the Engineers and Crystal Palace would have to replay after their 0-0 draw in the semi-final. This first competition may have been weird but not even the FA could handle the concept of three teams playing each other in the cup final. In the event, the Royal Engineers won their replay 3-0 – and that was to be the nearest any side called Crystal Palace got to the cup final until the modern club reached Wembley 118 years later.

**Odds-on Favourites**

The first FA Cup final took place at Kennington Oval on March 16, 1872 in front of a largely middle class crowd of 2,000 people who had each paid the then princely sum of one shilling (5p) to be there.

The Royal Engineers – officers to a man – were the odds-on favourites. They had not been beaten for two years and as *The Sporting Life* reported, that "by better organisation and concentration" they ought to be able to beat the Wanderers, "despite the acknowledged superiority of the latter... in individual excellence and skill".

The Engineers – two captains and nine lieutenants – must have taken the field feeling confident in their red and blue outfits. The Wanderers had all but backed into the final with a narrow win over Clapham and goalless draws against Crystal Palace (who the Engineers had beaten 3-0) and Queen's Park. But it took only a quarter of an hour for the game to be decided. As has happened so many times since this first final – the Engineers were depleted by injury – and could not come back after the underdogs opened the scoring. Lieutenant Edmund Cresswell earned himself a place in the record books when he became the first player to be injured in a cup final – falling awkwardly after 10 minutes and breaking his collar bone. He limped out to the wing and manfully "stayed at his post" as it was reported at the time, but the Engineers never recovered from that setback – or the next five minutes later.

Robert Walpole Sealey-Vidal, who had learned his soccer at Westminster School and was known as "the prince of the dribblers" fed the ball to Morton Peto Betts. His shot beat Capt. William Merriman in the "military goal" and the Wanderers were 1-0 up. As was then the vogue, the teams changed ends, and soon after CW Alcock himself had the ball in the net – but the goal was disallowed for handball.

For many years the records showed that the Wanderers goal was scored by 'AH Chequer'– a thinly disguised 'nom de guerre' used by Betts for reasons that are no longer obvious. Betts was a member of the Harrow Chequers club which scratched against the Wanderers in the first round, and was clearly well known to everyone in footballing circles at the time, and was one of the committee members who agreed to the formation of the FA Cup. One of the first rules drawn up to govern the new competition was that a player could only play for one club in any one season. Although he was a Harrow player, they had scratched without playing a match, so there was no risk of him being 'cup-tied' or falling foul of the authorities – especially as 'the authorities' in the person of CW Alcock, the FA's secretary, was also a team-mate.

**Little Tin Idol**

The cup was not presented to the winning team on the day. Instead the presentation took place three weeks later at the Wanderers annual dinner in the Pall Mall Restaraunt, Charing Cross. Alcock received the cup at seven o'clock that evening from EC Morley, now the president of the FA. The ceremony took place barely a mile away from the offices of *The Sportsman* where Alcock had first proposed the competition nine months before.

The Wanderers name was the first to be inscribed on the little tin idol, and it was also the second. This was the only time when the holders, under one of the original rules of the competition were exempt until the final – the Challenge round.

While the Wanderers bided their time playing friendlies, Oxford University made it through to the final which was played at the Amateur Athletic Ground at Lillie Bridge in West Brompton, London, not far from where Earls Court now stands. The choice of venue was also, for this season only, the prerogative of the cup holders – but the kickoff time was not.

The match was due to start at 11 o'clock, and as *The Sporting Life* reported in the week before the match, "this arrangement will give those anxious to see the boat race ample time to reach Putney, Hammersmith or any other places on the line of the race". Clearly, the FA Cup final still had some way to go before it won its place in the heart of the nation.

And imagine how anxious some of the 3,000-crowd at Lillie Bridge must have been feeling that morning as the final kicked off half-an-hour behind schedule due to the late arrival of some of the players. Goals from Charles Wollaston and Arthur Kinnaird, of the long red beard and white trousers, gave the Wanderers a 2-0 victory, and secured for both men the first of the five winners' medals each was to win over the next few years. Overall it wasn't a great day for the Dark Blues – Cambridge won the boat race by three lengths.

**Strongest Team in the Land**

Lord Kinnaird, as he later became, played in a record nine finals, making six appearances for the Old Etonians and three for the Wanderers. He was also President of the Football Association for 33 years until his death at the age of 77 shortly before the opening of Wembley in 1923.

The first seven finals were all fought out by just four teams – the Wanderers, the Royal Engineers, Oxford University and the Old Etonians, with players like RWS Vidal and CJ Ottaway seemingly changing sides back and forth from season to season.

The Royal Engineers, based at Chatham, were probably the strongest team in the land, losing only three matches of the 86 they played between 1871 and 1875. Two of the games they did lose were the cup finals of 1872 and 1874, but they finally won the cup in 1875, for the first, and only time, with a 2-0 win over the Old Etonians after the competition's first drawn Final.

Absent that day was another colossus of the era, Sir Francis Marindin, known as 'The Major'. While Lord Kinnaird sported a dazzling full red beard, Marindin was also a man of his times, with a full 'Empire' moustache and a wide, expanding pair of sideburns. He was the inspiration behind the Royal Engineers, led them into the FA in 1869 and also played in their losing finals of 1872 and 1874.

He sat on the committee that inaugurated the cup in 1871 and he also helped found, and later play for, the Old Etonians. So he faced a dilemma in 1875 when the Engineers met the Old Etonians in the final. He chose the only way out – and played for neither. Major Marindin also holds another record unlikely to be beaten of refereeing nine cup finals in 1880, 1884-90 and the replayed game of 1886. He was president of the FA from 1874-90 and in his 'spare' time he became the Inspector of Railways for England and also had a hand in developing London's electric lighting system.

By the mid-1870s, the number of teams entering the competition was growing. If it was not exactly the 'cup fever' of a decade later, it was certainly a move in the right direction. Sheffield became the first team from the north, apart from Queen's Park, to enter in 1874, while in 1876 Druids became the first Welsh club to take part. Between 1876 and 1878 the number of entries grew from 32 to 43 – but the Wanderers remained invincible. They became the first team to win three successive cup finals, and under the prevailing rules they were allowed to keep the trophy. But they handed it back to the Football Association with the proviso that no other team winning it three times in succession in the future could keep it either. Since then only Blackburn Rovers have done so – and they have a shield in their boadroom to mark their rare achivement.

**No Fourth Successive Victory**

It may not have been immediately obvious when the Wanderers were presented with the cup after beating the Royal Engineers 3-1 at the Oval that March afternoon in 1878 that their domination of the trophy was coming to an end. The Wanderers had always drawn their best players from public school old boys – but now the public schools themselves were beginning to take more and more notice of the cup and began forming their own teams. The Wanderers began their bid for a fourth successive victory with a match against their old rivals, the Old Etonians, who they had last met, and beaten in the replayed final of 1876. This time the old boys handed out the lesson with a 7-2 hiding. The following season, on January 24, 1879, the Old Etonians beat them again in the third round. That was the last FA Cup match the Wanderers ever played. They scratched when drawn to play against Rangers FC of London in 1880, and scratched again when they could not raise a team to play against a side from St Bart's Hospital in 1881. It was a sad end for "the celebrated Wanderers" as Major Marindin used to call them.

The competition of 1878-79 is notable for three events that help illustrate the growth of the cup. For the first time one of the finalists – Clapham Rovers – came from outside the "big four" of the Wanderers, the Royal Engineers, the Old Etonians and Oxford University. Secondly, a team from the provinces – Nottingham Forest – reached the semi-finals for the first time, and thirdly, a team of young working men from the Lancashire mill town of Darwen gave the Old Etonians, the eventual winners, a run for their money in the fourth round.

**Beyond Recognition**

Given the impact teams from Lancashire were to have on the cup in the years to come, its ironic that the first seeds of interest in Lancashire were sown by a team from a town with a population of about 30,000 people; which was to have a team in the Football League for only eight seasons and which, half-a-century later, were to lose a cup match to Arsenal at Highbury 11-1.

But Darwen's exploits in 1879 were important not just because they awakened Lancastrians to the idea of cup football – but also because they had a couple of Scotsmen in their team who were no doubt being paid to be there – in strict contravention of the rules of the day. Fergie Suter, a stonemason by trade, and Jimmy Love moved from Glasgow to play football in Lancashire and it is inconceivable to think they were not paid for doing so. It was to be another six years before the FA legalised professionalism, but by then the nature of the cup and whole shape of football in England had changed beyond recognition from the way it looked in 1872, and certainly 1863. Suter himself was to go on to play in four finals for Blackburn Rovers and pick up three winner's medals.

Darwen also helped changed the rules and composition of the FA Cup. They had reached round four – the last six teams under the still evolving draw system – with a walkover against Birch of Manchester and wins over Eagley of Bolton and Remnants, an amateur side from Berkshire. In the fourth round they were drawn to play the Old Etonians at the Oval. Trailing 1-5 with just 15 minutes to play they scored four times in the last 15 minutes to force a 5-5 draw – a performance that still ranks as one of the cup's greatest comebacks.

Three weeks later, after a public collection had raised nearly £200, the men from Darwen were back in the capital – and again refused to be beaten, forcing their more illustrious rivals to a 2-2 draw. The decent thing would surely have been for the Old Etonians to agree to play the third match in Lancashire – or at least somewhere closer to Darwen than the manicured lawns of the Kennington Oval. But, invoking the rule at the time which stated that all matches after the second round should be played at Kennington, the Old Etonians stood firm. A week later Darwen made a third, exhausting trip to London and were beaten 6-2. But they had made their point. From the following season, the earlier rounds of the cup were regionalised, and although all semi-finals and finals were still played at the Oval until 1882, more cup matches began to be played all over the country.

**Youngest Finalist**

Old Etonians went on to beat Clapham Rovers 1-0 in the Final on March 29, the match in which the youngest finalist of all time made his first appearance. James Frederick McLeod Prinsep was his name and he was 17 years 245 days old when he played for Clapham Rovers – 11 days younger than Paul Allen was when he played for West Ham in the cup final 101 years later. Described by the writer W Unite Jones as "one of the prettiest half-backs that ever did duty for the Rose", Prinsep was born in India on July 27, 1861. He played his one and only game for England against Scotland on April 5, 1879 when aged 17 years 252 days to become England's youngest ever international, exactly a week after playing in the cup final. Prinsep had left Clapham by the time they won the cup the following season but picked up a winner's medal when Old Carthusians beat the Old Etonians 3-0 in 1881, the last of the all-amateur finals.

On March 25, 1882, almost 10 years to the day since the Wanderers first won the first FA Cup final, Old Etonians brought the curtain down on the success of the southern amateurs. They beat Blackburn Rovers 1-0 at the Oval and after the presentations Lord Kinnaird celebrated his fifth winners medal in his eighth final by standing on his head in front of the dignitaries in the grandstand. There were those watching who felt that the whole world as they knew it was about to be turned upside down.

# THE NORTH COMES TO TOWN 1883-1892

ALTHOUGH KINNAIRD and his Old Etonian team-mates returned to the Oval the following year with a team that included six England internationals, they were beaten by Blackburn Olympic, the first northern side to win the cup. The professions of the men who made up the Olympic team that day are worth noting. Three of them were weavers, one was a spinner, one a cotton worker, another an iron worker; there was a picture framer, a dentist's assistant, a plumber, and two who were clearly professionals. These were not men of leisure, they were working class. The balance had tilted away from the amateurs for ever.

### Cup Fever

Blackburn Olympic were one of a number of clubs from that town that competed in the cup around this time, and although they were soon eclipsed by the success of Blackburn Rovers, they nevertheless have a secure place in the history of the cup. Their supporters – and there were thousands of them swelling the attendance at the Oval to a record 7,000 – descended on London like a conquering army – the first time the capital had seriously been struck by an attack of 'cup fever'. In the week before the final the team itself had spent time "in strict training in Blackpool", noted *The Sportsman*.

Olympic had settled into their hotel in Richmond on the Thursday before the Final to make sure they had recovered from the long rail journey in good time – general principles of preparing for a cup final still used by teams today.

And clearly they served them well. Legend has it that when someone in the crowd saw the cup they shouted out, "is that t'Coop, why it looks like a tea kettle". Sam Warburton, the Olympic captain, replied, "Ay, it might do, but its very welcome to Lancashire and it'll never go back to London". If only Warburton knew how prophetic his words were. In the next 12 years it never went south of Birmingham, where in 1895 it was stolen from a sports shop and never recovered.

The cup finals of the early and mid-1880s were played out against a background of fierce feuding over the increase in, and eventual legalisation of, paying players to play football. For a while it seemed as though the FA would split on the whole argument of professionalism, with one body administering a professional game in the north and another body administering an amateur game in the south – the situation in which the breakaway sport of rugby found itself a few years later. There was even a very strong move to form a British Football Association, but it came to nothing. Football today would be very different if it had.

### Common in the North

In November 1883 Accrington had been disqualified from the cup, accused of professionalism – and they were disqualified a year later on the same charge too. The whole issue was the subject of a heated debate in January 1884 after Preston North End drew 1-1 with the amateurs of Upton Park, one of the original 15 entrants in 1872. Upton Park protested to the FA that some of Preston's players were obviously professional. That much was true and the Preston chairman Major William Suddell admitted it to the FA. He also told them the practice was common in the north and although Preston were disqualified from that season's competition, his argument convinced some of the more enlightened FA officials – including Charles Alcock – that nothing would stop the rise of the professional game.

The FA took another 18 months to legalise professionalism and ride out a ferocious storm that seriously threatened to sink them. The 14th cup competition that began in the autumn of 1885, the first after professionalism was allowed, was a very different affair than the almost local get-togethers between southern gentlemen which it had been for much of its early existence.

While Blackburn Olympic had taken the cup north for the first time in 1883, the first northern side to really make a lasting impact were Blackburn Rovers. They played in six finals in 10 seasons between 1882 and 1891 and won five of them – three in successive years in 1884-85-86 and the other two in succession in 1890 and 1891.

### Three Times Running

Blackburn Rovers and the Wanderers are still the only clubs to have won the cup three times running and the former still hold the record for the longest unbeaten run in the competition's history. After losing 1-0 at neighbours Darwen in a second round match on December 2, 1882, they went 23 games (not including walkovers) before losing at home to the Scottish club Renton on November 27, 1886.

Perhaps Renton felt they were exacting some revenge for footballers north of the border, for two of Blackburn's three cup final victories in both 1884 and 1885 were over Queen's Park. By the start of the 1883-84 competition, Queens Park had entered the English cup eight times, but they had played only one match in the tournament, the 0-0 draw with the Wanderers in the 1872 semi-final. They had scratched from the competition seven times, but when they decided to play they made their mark.

Their opening two matches, against Crewe Alexandra and Manchester Football Club resulted in wins of 10-0, and 15-0 and they carried on towards the final with wins over Oswestry (7-1), Aston Villa (6-1), Old Westminsters (1-0), and the holders Blackburn Olympic 4-1 in the semi-final. Before the kickoff they were the 6-4 favourites to win the cup, but goals from Joe Sowerbutts and James Forrest gave Rovers a 2-1 victory. Forrest, who shares with CWR Wollaston of the Wanderers and Lord Kinnaird the record of five winners' medals, scored against the Scots again the following year when Blackburn beat them 2-0 at The Oval. In the entire history of the competition this remains the only time the same two finalists met each other in successive years.

It was also Queen's Park's swansong. Two years later, after Glasgow Rangers almost became the second Scottish side to reach the final, failing only against Aston Villa in the semis, the Scottish FA, formed in 1873 now banned their clubs from taking part in the English Cup. The Irish FA, whose leading teams like Distillery, Crusaders and Linfield had all competed in the past, followed their lead, but Welsh clubs were not withdrawn by the FA of Wales and still compete to this day.

In 1886 Blackburn Rovers completed their hat-trick of victories with a replayed 2-0 win over West Bromwich Albion in the first final contested by clubs who are still in existence and members of the Football or Premier Leagues. It was also the first time the final had been decided away from London, with the replay taking place in Derby. A snowstorm on the morning of the replay threatened the game, but by lunchtime the snow had melted. By 5 o'clock West Brom's resistance had melted too, beaten 2-0.

Thousands of fans had made the trip from Birmingham to Derby for the match and according to one eyewitness account, "the Albion supporters had in their hats a large blue card, upon which was a throstle and the words `Play Up Throstles` Before the termination of the match however the spirits of these ardent enthusiasts were dampened to such an extent that they were glad to put the cards out of sight, their appearance being a subject more of ridicule than anything else". After losing in 1886 to Blackburn and 1887 to Aston Villa in the first all-Midlands final, Albion were back for a third successive final in 1888 – and this time they won it, the first club to do so with an all-English team.

### Villa's Glory Years

The first 15 finals were won by clubs from just two cities – London and Blackburn, but now teams from the Midlands and Yorkshire were beginning to make an impact.

Aston Villa first entered the cup in 1879-80, but after beating Stafford Road, a railway works team from Wolverhampton, they scratched rather than face the then mighty Oxford University. But seven years later things were very different. By general consensus the club's glory years in the later part of the 19th century and early part of the 20th were founded on a rock laid by three Scots – George Ramsay and Archie Hunter, who were players, and an official, William McGregor, the father of the Football League.

It was Aston Villa who succeeded Blackburn as cup holders and in the 11 seasons from 1887 until 1897 they appeared in four finals winning three times, in 1887,

1895 and 1897 when they became the last team for 64 years to win the league and cup double. Their 3-2 win over Everton in 1897 still ranks as one of the best finals of all time. This was Villa's golden era. They won the League title five times in the last seven years of the century and in 1957 they won the competition for what was then a record seventh time.

Aston Villa's double of 1897 was the second. The first team to achieve that feat was Preston North End, 'The Invincibles' of 1889 whose record in winning the first ever Football League championship without losing a match and winning the cup without conceding a goal are unlikely ever to be equalled.

**Confident of Victory**

The previous year Preston had also reached the final and on their way set another record unlikely to be beaten. Their 26-0 win over Hyde on October 15, 1887 is the biggest victory ever recorded in the nearly 60,000 matches which have been played in the FA Cup since the competition began.

In fact, Preston seemed certain to win in 1888. Including their win over Hyde they scored a total of 55 goals in seven cup matches and they were so confident of victory over West Bromwich Albion in the final they asked Major Marindin whether they could be pictured with the trophy before the match.

Major Marindin's shrewd rejoinder has entered football folklore. "Had you better not win it first?" he asked – and of course after that, how could they. West Brom beat them 2-1.

But the next season, 1888-89, the first of the Football League and the first when the FA Cup had a qualifying competition, not even West Bromwich Albion could stop them.

Among West Brom's ranks at this time was one of the finest wingers of the day – William Isiah 'Billy' Bassett. He was only 5ft 5½ins tall, but was so tricky on the right wing he won 16 caps for England and spent 13 years in the West Brom first team. He served the Albion for 50 years as a player, director and chairman and was at Wembley to see them beat Birmingham in the 1931 cup final.

But back in 1889 even his undoubted brilliance on the flank could do nothing to slow Preston's march. After disposing of Bootle (3-0), Grimsby Town (2-0), and Birmingham St George's (2-0), Preston gained their revenge over the holders with a 1-0 semi-final win at Bramall Lane, Sheffield. Their opponents in the final were Wolverhampton Wanderers, making the first of their eight appearances. While Preston had won the league, Wolves had done well too, finishing third, but they had lost 4-0 at home to Preston the previous September and 5-2 away in the October.

In the final, watched by a record crowd of 22,000, Preston were once again too hard to handle. Major Marindin not only refereed the game, he presented the cup to Preston too – something he had rightly refused to do before the final the previous year.

The Preston team, containing as it did such giants of the day as Jack Gordon, Jimmy Ross and the mesmerising John Goodall, succeeded in retaining the League Championship the following season – but this was their last appearance in the cup final for 33 years, and they would not win the cup again until 1938.

The start of the last decade of the 19th century witnessed the first 'Roses' final. Blackburn, with three survivors of the cup-winning teams of the mid-Eighties were back stronger than ever and opposing them were Sheffield Wednesday – or The Wednesday as they were known until the 1920s.

**Completely Outplayed**

Wednesday then played in the Football Alliance, a short-lived league formed a year after the Football League and one which was absorbed into the Football League as its Second Division in 1892. And in 1890 Wednesday came to the final looking for what would have been a unique 'double' – Football Alliance champions and FA Cup winners.

But on the afternoon of March 29, 1890, Wednesday were completely outplayed and lost by the then record cup final margin of 6-1. William Townley scored the first hat-trick in a final – something done only twice in more than a century since.

But The Wednesday did set one record that year. They became the first team to reach the final after losing a match on the way, although this happened again in 1946 when Charlton Athletic reached the final after losing the second leg of their two-legged third round tie against Fulham.

Where The Wednesday's record differs is that they were actually 'knocked out' after losing 3-2 to Notts County in a replayed quarter-final. The first quarter-final had ended in a 5-0 win for Wednesday but the match was replayed after a Notts County protest. The replay ended 3-2 to County – then Wednesday protested. So with each side having won once and protested once a third game was played. Sheffield Wednesday concluded this farce with a 2-1 win.

But both teams were to have their honour satisfied before the turn of the century. Notts County became the first team from the Second Division to win the cup when they surprisingly beat First Division Bolton Wanderers in 1894 and Wednesday won the cup for the first time in 1896.

A year after their record win over The Wednesday, Blackburn were back at the Oval to win the cup for a fifth time, to equal the record set by the Wanderers back in 1878. William Townley, who had scored three goals in the final the previous year, added another in the 3-1 win over Notts County while James Forrest collected his fifth winner's medal.

Blackburn's bid for what would have been a unique second hat-trick of victories came to an abrupt end in the second round of the following season's competition. They began the defence of the cup with a 4-1 win over Derby with Jack Southworth, an England international and a cup winner in both 1890 and 1891, scoring all four goals.

Southworth's other great love was music and after injury forced an early retirement he became a violinist with the Halle Orchestra. No doubt he was playing a mournful tune on the night of January 30, 1892 after Blackburn were dumped out of the cup by West Bromwich Albion. But there was going to be nothing but sweet music for Albion in 1892, the last time the Oval was used as the venue for the cup final.

By this time football had established itself as the premier sport in the land. The Oval was bursting at the seams and could no longer cope with the huge crowds coming to watch the match. The first final in 1872 was watched by just 2,000. By 1892 this had increased to more than 32,000. It was clear a bigger venue was needed. Even the timing of the Boat Race had become an irrelevance.

Aston Villa started as the favourites to win the 1892 final, and repeat their victory of 1887 over the Albion. In the end it was a one-sided contest with Albion, inspired by Billy Bassett, winning 3-0. Albion's third goal came from John Reynolds who was to achieve an odd double of his own three years later when he played for Aston Villa in their third final against West Bromwich Albion.

Fittingly it was Lord Kinnaird who presented what was now known as "the paltry pot" to Albion's captain Charles Perry, one of five brothers from the same family who played for WBA in the 1880s and 1890s.

Ten years previously Kinnaird stood on his head at the end of the cup final. All he was left to do after the 1892 game was close the Oval door and follow the road to Manchester.

# TO MANCHESTER AND BACK 1893-1915

THE FIRST FA Cup final played in Manchester did not take place at Old Trafford or Maine Road. It was held at the Manchester Athletic Club in Fallowfield in 1893 when Wolverhampton Wanderers won the competition for the first time.

Their 1-0 win over Everton, played in front of a record crowd of 45,000 and in brilliant spring sunshine, made headlines in the days that followed for reasons that echo down through the years.

Apart from the replayed final of 1886, which was staged in Derby, this was the first final scheduled to be played outside London, which did not have a stadium thought secure and safe enough to accomodate the growing numbers who wanted to see the game.

Neither, it is obvious, was Fallowfield the ideal place to hold the match. A photograph taken on the day, somewhat similiar to the scenes at Wembley exactly 30 years later, shows the crowd standing around the touchlines, with thousands hardly able to see a thing.

According to a report in *The Sporting Chronicle*, it was only the good-natured behaviour of the crowd that prevented what would have been football's first disaster. The newspaper was critical of the small number of police on hand to control the numbers and reports, "as it was, there were several small encounters between individual policemen and the crowd and some of the latter went home with cracked heads". At one point Lord Kinnaird and the referee CJ Hughes were debating whether to call off the game and play it as a friendly.

By all accounts it was not a brilliant match, Wolves winning it by the only goal scored after about an hour by their skipper Harry Allen. His high, dipping long range shot apparently blinding Dick Williams in the Everton goal as the ball dropped out of the sunshine.

Everton were the strong favourites – especially as the week before the final they had fielded their reserves and beaten Wolves 4-2 in a Division One match.

The following year Everton's new Goodison Park ground was the venue for the final. Wolves succumbed to Aston Villa 4-2 in their first defence of the trophy, while Everton also went out in the first round to Stoke. But these were the days when the north reigned supreme. The only southern clubs to make it through the qualifying rounds to the competition proper were Luton Town, Woolwich Arsenal and Reading but the northern clubs soon confirmed their authority. Luton went out 2-1 to Middlesbrough Ironopolis, Arsenal were beaten 2-1 by The Wednesday while Preston North End created another record when they beat Reading 18-0 – the highest victory ever by a Football League club over a Non-League club. The gap between the northern professionals and the amateurs in the south was as wide as ever.

### Prisoner on the Run

The match at Deepdale was played in deep mud, but Preston had coated their boots with a form of treacly black lead and hammered in long bars or studs to their boots to secure some kind of foothold in the awful conditions. Reading had not prepared so methodically and were literally swept off their feet. Seven goals went in in the first half, 11 in the second. It was Reading's worst-ever defeat.

But Reading, in 1894, also added a lighter footnote to the history of the cup because earlier in the competition they became the only club ever to have won a cup match with the winning goal being scored by a prisoner on the run from his jailers!

The player in question was called Jimmy Stewart who, when not playing for Reading, served as a private in the King's Own Regiment at Aldershot. He was in detention in the guardroom for a breach of discipline, but Reading desperately needed him to play in their third round qualifying match against Southampton St Mary's.

Reading's secretary at the time, Horace Walker, decided to persuade the Army authorities to release Stewart for the match, and turned up at the barracks with a couple of bottles of scotch. After the officer watching Stewart got thoroughly inebriated, he agreed Stewart could return to Reading for the afternoon. All went well, Stewart played, scored the winner, and returned to barracks under cover of darkness that night. But the story leaked out... Southampton were informed and immediately protested to the FA to have the match replayed. But as there was nothing in the FA rules specifically mentioning the fact that escaped prisoners were not allowed to play for affiliated teams, the protest was rejected! In light of what happened at Preston though, perhaps Reading got their just deserts after all.

### Move to Crystal Palace

After thumping Reading, Preston lost to Liverpool in the next round, and by the time the field had thinned out to the last four there were two previous winners left – Blackburn Rovers and The Wednesday – and two previous finalists – Bolton Wanderers and Second Division Notts County, who became the first team from outside the First Division to win the cup. Notts County, formed in 1862, pre-date the FA itself by a year. But in all that long history, winning the FA Cup in 1894 is their only major honour. James Logan became the second man to score a hat-trick in the final as Notts County beat Bolton 4-1.

After two years in Lancashire, at Fallowfield and Goodison, the final returned to London, where, between 1895 and 2000 when Wembley Stadium closed, it was decided every year with only six exceptions: (the 1915 final and replays of 1901, 1910, 1911, 1912 and 1970).

Its new home was at Crystal Palace, the equivalent then of a late 19th-century theme park. Victorians went there for a ride on the famous 'Switchback' roller-coaster railway; there were also other recreation facilities; they took picnics and they rode bikes. For many years at Crystal Palace the final was played after the crowd had eaten their lunch or had a few beers. The stadium was situated not far from where the modern National Sports Centre is and should not be confused with Crystal Palace's ground at Selhurst Park.

All through the history of the cup there are strange twists and ironies, and it seems entirely fitting that the two teams who brought the Oval era to a close in 1892 should be the same two that opened the Crystal Palace era in 1895.

### Best Ever Played?

And it took only about 40 seconds for that era to open with a goal. The 1895 final brought together Birmingham's two greatest clubs for the third time – West Bromwich Albion and Aston Villa. Until Arsenal played Newcastle United in 1998 and Liverpool met Arsenal in 2001 they were the only two clubs to have met each other in three cup finals.

They went into the game with both sides having beaten the other once in the final, Villa winning in 1887 and West Brom in 1892, and the 1895 final can still be described as one of the best ever played. Villa won it 1-0 with a goal from inside-right Bob Chatt whose shot on the turn hit the legs of West Brom's keeper and spun into the goal. No-one will ever know for sure exactly how soon after the kickoff the goal came because some reports have the goal being scored after 30 seconds, others after 35 and 40. The only thing that does seem certain is that it was scored faster than Roberto Di Matteo's 43-second strike for Chelsea in the 2000 final against Middlesbrough and that it is the fastest ever goal scored in the history of the cup final. And it came while thousands of the 42,000 crowd were still taking their places. Despite a tremendous onslaught for the next 89 minutes, Aston Villa's defence stood firm and John Reynolds, who gained a winner's medal playing for WBA against Aston Villa in 1892, now picked up another, playing for Villa against his old side.

And it was in 1895 that an old prophecy was about to come true. Back in 1883, Sam Warburton, the skipper of Blackburn Olympic declared when he took the cup back to the north for the first time, that it would never go back to London. Well of course, the cup did physically go back to London to be presented to the winners at the end of the Final, but that first cup, 'the little tin idol', never was won again by a London team.

Aston Villa exhibited it in the shop window of William Shillcock, a boot and shoe manufacturer of Newtown Row, Birmingham and on the night of September 11, 1895 it was stolen and never recovered.

Over half-a-century later, in February 1958, the *Sunday Pictorial* led their front page with a story from a man called Harry Burge, who had spent 46 of his 83 years in and out of jail. He confessed to stealing the cup with two accomplices and melting it down that night to make counterfeit half-crowns. Forty years later, another, more credible, version of events was published after investigations by local reporters. (see 'The FA Cup Trophies') The theft was national news. Although it had been heavily insured and an exact replica was made in time for the 1896 final, the Football Association fined Aston Villa £25.

### Enthusiastic Supporters

The new cup also had a new home – Yorkshire. The Wednesday, now in the League, took it back to Sheffield for the first time with a 2-1 win over Wolves – and bedlam greeted its arrival. The cup was paraded through the streets after the party got off the train from London, but the *Sheffield Daily Telegraph* were very upset about the chaotic arrangements made for the cup's homecoming.

"There was no method... no knowledge of what was to be done... It is easy to see how all this could have been avoided. Clubs such as the gay and gallant Rovers from Blackburn, with all their cup-holding experience would never have made such an error, and when Wednesday have won the trophy a few more times perhaps we shall have a settled programme to work to, and enthusiastic supporters of the club have a better knowledge of where to go to see their favourites".

There was plenty of opportunity to get the logistics worked out over the next few years with Sheffield United winning the cup in 1899, 1902, and 1915, and Wednesday following their initial success with another victory in 1907. Between them the two sides also won the League three times in the six seasons between 1898 and 1904.

But while the Sheffield sides had undoubted success at the turn of the century the giants of this era were Aston Villa and the peak of their achievements came on April 10, 1897 when they beat Everton 3-2 to become the second club in history to win the double.

Apart from a dip in their form in the 1897-98 season, Villa could have won the League Championship for five successive seasons. They took the title in 1896 and 1897, and then again in 1899 and 1900 and only finished outside the top three once in seven years between 1894 and the turn of the century.

Their 1897 double-winning side contained five men from the cup-winning team of 1895 – the England internationals Howard Spencer (full-back), John Reynolds (half-back), Charlie Athersmith (winger – who, legend has it, once played a whole match taking cover from the rain under an umbrella) – John Devey (centre-forward) and the Scottish international defender James Cowan. But the Everton side was a strong one too, having finished as runners-up in the league to Sunderland in 1895 and third behind Villa and Derby County in 1896.

John Bell, Edgar Chadwick and Johnny Holt knew all about the Crystal Palace atmosphere, having played there the week previously for England against Scotland. And in 1897, when Villa won the double, they lost only four out of their 30 league games – and one of those had been to Everton. The record crowd of 65,891 knew they might be in for something special – and they were not disappointed. But what the crowd could not have known was that the Villa and Everton players had already seen each other for breakfast that morning. Both teams had booked – purely by chance – into the same hotel!

### Delightful Goal

All the goals in Villa's 3-2 win came in a 25-minute spell in the first half. Villa took the lead after 18 minutes when Athersmith and Devey combined to set up John Campbell. The Scot's shot swerved on the wind, deceiving goalkeeper Bob Menham as it flashed inside his post.

Everton replied within minutes with a delightful goal, when Scottish international John Bell drew Jimmy Whitehouse from his goal and then slipped the ball into the net as the goalkeeper charged him down.

On the half hour, with the pace increasing on the field and the tension mounting in the crowd, Everton were ahead with a free-kick from Richard Boyle leaving Whitehouse beaten. The Everton fans were cheering in delight, but almost as soon as the caps and hats thrown in the air had come back down to earth Villa were level... and almost immediately back in front.

Fred Wheldon, another of Villa's internationals, made it 2-2 and soon after that there was another goal when Jimmy Crabtree headed what proved to be the winner for Villa two minutes before half-time. The second half was just as passionate and only a series of outstanding saves from Whitehouse stopped Everton from scoring. Never before had a team scored twice in the cup final and lost, and apart from Sheffield United, who lost the 1901 final after a replay, Everton were to be the last team for 38 years to score as many as two goals in the Final and return home empty-handed.

### Finest Final

The next edition of *Association Football* magazine was lavish in its praises. "It was the finest final that has ever been fought," it declared. Naturally Villa were greeted by thousands of ecstatic fans when they brought the cup back to Birmingham the following day, but when Everton returned to Lime Street they were given a cordial, polite round of applause by a handful of well-wishers. Everton still had another decade to wait until their turn for cup glory while babies being born at the time would be grandparents by the time Liverpool first came home with the cup.

There is a curious symmetry to the cup finals at the turn of the century, largely involving four clubs – Bury, Derby County, Sheffield United and Southampton none of whom it must be said, have made a lasting impact on the cup since then.

This odd sequence really begins in 1898 when Derby County lost to Nottingham Forest in an East Midlands derby, and then returned the following year to lose again, to Sheffield United in front of a then world record crowd of 73,883. There was said to be a curse on Derby, given to them by gypsies the club had ordered off land that was to become the Baseball Ground. They lost all three finals they reached in those six years and were not to win the cup until 1946.

In 1900 Bury enter the picture with a 4-0 win over Southampton, the first southern club to have been in the final since the Old Etonians in 1883. Sheffield United returned in 1901 to lose to Tottenham Hotspur – and then came back again in 1902 to beat Southampton. In 1903, to round this whole period off, Bury were back in the final for a second, and last time, to see off Derby County 6-0 – the biggest ever cup final winning margin.

In fact Bury's winning aggregate margin of 10-0 is something of a record in itself although when they won the cup in 1900 against Southampton, Bury's local paper did not consider the event worthy of its front page! Bury had finished 12th in the First Division that season, and the paper complained, on an inside page, "Bury's Cup win was only some consolation for their poor League performance this season".

### World Record Crowd

The 1901 final is one of the most famous in history. The principal reason for this is that for the first, and only time since the formation of the Football League in 1888, a Non-League team won the competition. Tottenham, like Southampton, had benefited enormously from the formation of the Southern League in 1894 which enabled them to attract a higher standard of player from around the country, rather than rely on merely local talent.

The Tottenham cup-winning team of 1901 included five Scots, two Welshmen, one Irishman and three English players – and none of them came from south of the Trent. They were the first southern club to have won the cup for 19 years – but they were hardly a southern team. Tottenham had knocked out three First Division teams, including cup-holders Bury, on the way to the final, but it was Sheffield United who started the day as favourites. Although they had finished only five places off the bottom of the First Division, United, fielding nine internationals were still capable of excellent football on their day.

They had won the championship in 1898, won the cup in 1899 and been runners-up in the League in 1900. And they had two of the game's all-time great characters in their side, the 22-stone goalkeeper Billy 'Fatty' Foulke in goal and Ernest 'Nudger' Needham at wing-half.

The interest in the match was so great it attracted a world record crowd of 110,820 people to the Crystal Palace and is the first cup final of which there is surviving newsreel footage. And more than 100 years after it was played, the fourth goal remains as one of the most controversial ever scored in a final.

The first half ended 1-1 and five minutes into the second half, Spurs centre-forward Sandy Brown, who in scoring the first goal had become the first man ever to score in every round of the competition in the same season, added a second to make it 2-1. Within a minute United were level after a mysterious decision by the referee, A Kingscott of Derby.

There are almost as many accounts of what happened next as there were spectators at the match, but according to the most reliable, United's Bert Lipsham shot, and George Clawley, the Spurs' keeper fumbled his catch. The ball dropped behind Clawley who scrambled the ball away just as United's Walter Bennett came rushing in to challenge him. The linesman immediatley signalled for a corner, but the referee over-ruled him and gave a goal-kick. The referee then, inexplicably, changed his mind, and before the kick was taken, awarded a goal to Sheffield United which has entered the record books as Bennett's goal. Both teams seem to have been affected by the decision, and the match ended in a tame 2-2 draw. The general feeling was that the referee was at fault and that he should have consulted his linesman, which he never did.

### Late-Victorian Sportsmen

But he was back in charge the following week when the match was replayed at Burnden Park, Bolton, a strange choice and one that was never properly explained. Whereas more than 110,000 watched the first game, only 20,470 saw the replay – the lowest attendance for a cup final in the 20th century. Spurs won that game 3-1 to begin their sequence of winning something when the year ends in a '1' and Sandy Brown's goal in the replay took his tally that year to 15.

At Tottenham's post-match banquet, the wife of the club's vice-chairman tied blue-and-white ribbons onto the cup, often cited as the start of that particular cup final tradition. But was it? Notts County's 1894 cup winning side, as fine a looking collection of late-Victorian sportsmen as you could wish to see, clearly have black-and-white ribbons tied to the cup handles in their winning team group shot.

As we've seen, Tottenham's victory was the first by a southern club for 19 years – and the last by a southern club until they themselves won it again 20 years later. They were the only London club to play in the cup final at both Crystal Palace and Stamford Bridge, the two London venues used in the 20th century before Wembley was built in 1923. The domination of the competition by northern and midland teams was so great at this time that between Tottenham's two victories, only three teams from the south – Southampton (1902), Bristol City (1909) and Chelsea (1915) even reached the final.

Southern League Southampton, who knocked out cup-holding Spurs in 1902, were the last Non-League team to reach the final. Even though they beat the reigning champions Liverpool 4-1 in the second round and had in CB Fry one of the most outstanding footballers and all-round sportsmen of all time (England international at both football and cricket, world record holder in the long jump), at full-back, they were beaten 2-1 by Sheffield United after a drawn game at the Crystal Palace.

Bristol City's one and only cup final appearance ended in more disappointment for the South. They had drawn in every round but one to get to the final, which was their tenth cup match of the season. Manchester United, also playing in their first cup final won it 1-0 with a Sandy Turnbull goal.

And Chelsea's appearance, in the 'Khaki Cup Final' – the only one played during a World War on April 24, 1915 also ended in defeat, beaten 3-0 by Sheffield United at Old Trafford. At the end of the game, Lord Derby, who presented the trophy, told the players, "you have played with one another, and against one another for the cup; now go and play with one another for England".

### Beating the Record

In this great period of northern and midland domination two great teams stand out – one for what they achieved, the other for what they did not.

The achievers were Aston Villa, who continued in the new century where they left off in the old one. After two more triumphs in 1905 and 1913, they won the cup for the sixth time in 1920, beating the record of five wins previously held by the Wanderers and Blackburn Rovers.

Their 2-0 victory over Newcastle on April 15, 1905, was watched by another huge crowd of 101,117. Newcastle started the match as favourites. They were League Champions and 10 days before the final had beaten Villa for the second time that season, 2-0 at home. They were also bidding, in their first cup final, to become the first team since Villa eight years previously, to win the double.

But Villa's cup-fighting tradition was legendary. After just two minutes they were a goal up through Harry Hampton, who added a second 14 minutes from time. For Newcastle, the hoodoo of playing at the Crystal Palace ground had begun.

They returned again in 1906 and lost 1-0 to Everton. In 1907 they won the championship again – and lost 1-0 at home in the first round of the cup to Crystal Palace then in the Southern League.

In 1908 Newcastle were back at Crystal Palace for their third cup final in four seasons – and lost 3-1 to Wolves, who had finished the season half-way down the Second Division. There seemed to be no end to the curse. In 1910 they reached the final again. Again they played a moderate Second Division side – Barnsley – and again they failed to win. But at least this time – just – they did not lose either.

### Deliberate Kicking

Barnsley had reached the final by avoiding First Division opposition until they beat Everton, after a replay, in the semi-final. Now with seven minutes to go in the final, the 77,000 crowd must have thought they were about to see yet another huge upset. Barnsley had gone ahead in the 38th minute with a goal from Harry Tufnell. But with time running out on a poor game, Jack Rutherford, with a collection of loser's medals from 1905, 1906 and 1908, headed the equaliser. There was no extra time then, Barnsley and Newcastle shook hands on a 1-1 draw and the final was replayed the following week at Goodison Park.

And here Newcastle finally became cup holders for the first time with two goals from

Albert Sheppard, the second from the penalty spot was the first goal from a penalty in a Cup Final. According to the *Daily Mirror* though, Newcastle were desperate men, kicking anything that moved. "It really seemed as if some of the players had deliberately gone onto the field to win at all costs," intoned the *Mirror*, adding, "there were cases of deliberate kicking today". After what they had been through in the previous few years, one can understand their desperation.

Newcastle's was the last name to be inscribed on the trophy. Its design had been pirated and a similar cup was being used for a tournament in Manchester, so the FA commissioned a new design – the one in use today – and presented the old cup to Lord Kinnaird to mark his 21 years as President of the FA.

So in 1911 a new cup, made by the Bradford silversmiths Fattorini and Sons, was used for the first time. By one of those inexplicable coincidences that pepper its history, the cup was won that year by Bradford City – the only time either of Bradford's sides came anywhere near the cup final. It almost goes without saying they beat Newcastle in the final.

### Long, Slow Fight to the Death

If there was an omen that Bradford were going to win it came two weeks before the final when they beat Newcastle 1-0 in the First Division. The final at the Crystal Palace was a dour affair, and ended in a 0-0 draw. Newcastle, back on their old 'bogey' ground were without their star centre forward Albert Sheppard who had a broken arm, and Peter McWilliam, one of the best inside forwards of the time, and their attacks floundered on City's solid defence. Four days later they could find no way through in the replay at Old Trafford either, as Jimmy Speirs scored after only 15 minutes to give Bradford City, who had been formed only eight years previously, victory. Amazingly, the day after winning the cup, City, with four changes, beat Middlesbrough 1-0 in a First Division match.

Until 1911 only two cup finals, those of 1876 and 1886, had ended goalless. Now, in 1912, it was about to happen for the second successive year. But no-one should have been too surprised. Barnsley, an average Second Division team but one that clearly relished a long, slow fight to the death, were back to keep the cup in Yorkshire for a second successive season – after a record number of six goalless draws. Three of those had been against the cup-holders Bradford City.

The opposition was West Bromwich Albion, back in the final for the first time since losing their last duel with Aston Villa 17 years previously. The first game at the Palace ended 0-0 and after 90 minutes of the replay at Bramall Lane, it was still 0-0. An unprecedented second replay looked certain, but with only two minutes of extra time to go, the Barnsley winger Harry Tufnell evaded the WBA defenders caught out at the halfway line, and chased half the length of the field to score the winner. Like Bradford before them, Barnsley have not been back to the final since.

While Newcastle had reached five finals in seven seasons, their north-east rivals Sunderland had never been further than the last four. Sunderland's 'Team of all the Talents' had won the League Championship three times in the 1890s, but since they first entered the FA Cup in 1884, their best performances had been in reaching the semi-finals in 1891 and 1895.

### Penalty Miss

Despite another championship in 1902, Sunderland's cup record continued to be uninspiring until 1913, when they, like Newcastle in 1905, came close to winning the double only to be denied by Aston Villa in the cup final. In fact the 1913 final was the only one until Liverpool met Everton in 1986 in which the top two teams at the end of the season also met in the cup final.

In 1905 Newcastle, then League champions, lost out on the double when Aston Villa beat them in the cup final. Now, eight years later, Sunderland were to be denied by Villa too. Villa's reappearance and Sunderland's first final swelled the crowd at Crystal Palace to another world record – 120,081. Fans climbed up trees, balanced precariously on poles and climbed onto roofs to see the match that fully lived up to expectation.

Aston Villa's Charlie Wallace became the first player – and the last until John Aldridge in 1988 – to miss a penalty in the final, but his team won 1-0 with a header from Tommy Barber – exactly as Clem Stephenson, the Villa inside-right, had dreamed the night before the match.

Four days later the teams met again at Villa Park in the league. Sunderland's dream of the double had died, but their championship hopes were very much alive. Charlie Buchan, a legend on Wearside, rallied his men who drew 1-1 with the new cup holders and stayed unbeaten to the end of the season to win the title from Villa by four points.

Sunderland's reign as holders lasted until a replayed fourth round match the following March. Their conquerors were Burnley, who went on to record their first cup success in the first final witnessed by a reigning monarch.

The previous year King George V had been linked with another great sporting event but in altogether different circumstances when the suffragette Emily Davison threw herself under his horse in the Derby and died as a result of her injuries. But there were very few women at the 1914 cup final, just about 72,000 hats and caps sitting on the tops of 72,000 men's heads. The King, in a bowler, watched Burnley beat Liverpool 1-0 in the first final for both clubs and the first all-Lancashire final since 1904.

### Bigger Battle

A year later the final was to be played in very different circumstances on a wet and cold day in Manchester when Sheffield United beat Chelsea, and in a way Manchester is the apt venue to bring this, 'the Crystal Palace era' of the cup's history to a close, because it was during this period that both Manchester City and Manchester United won the cup for the first time.

Oddly, their wins were both inspired by the same man – the legendary Welsh wizard of the right-wing, Billy Meredith. Meredith, who always chewed a tooth-pick when he played, is often compared to Stanley Matthews as one of the greatest outside rights of all-time but he was a better finisher than Matthews and scored almost 200 league and cup goals in more than 700 matches in his 30-year career. One of those goals won the FA Cup for Manchester City when they beat Bolton 1-0 in 1904. That was his first cup winner's medal, and his second came five years later when he played in the Manchester United team which beat Bristol City 1-0. He played in his last cup match, a semi-final during his second spell with Manchester City in 1924 when he was 49 years and eight months old and is the oldest player ever to appear in the competition proper. His international career lasted 25 years and he won 48 Welsh caps.

Meredith may have been a legend on the field, but he was a constant thorn in the side of authority off it. In 1905 he was the major protagonist in first a bribes and then illegal payment scandal that led to him being suspended by the FA with several others and Manchester City almost destroyed as a club.

Eighteen months after helping City win the cup, he went to United. In 1909 United won the cup with a goal from Sandy Turnbull, who together with Meredith had played in Manchester City's Cup winning side five years previously. By now Meredith, and the United skipper Charlie Roberts were active members in the fight to get the Players Union accepted by the FA and Football League. The argument raged on for 18 months and during the summer of 1909, just weeks after winning the cup, those same players were briefly suspended by the FA, although they were all re-instated by the time the 1909-10 season began.

But for Sandy Turnbull, and for millions of other young men like him who had grown up at exactly the same time as football had also reached its manhood, another far bigger battle was soon raging. Turnbull, twice a Cup winning hero, was one of those who died in the war, killed in action in France on May 3, 1917.

# BRIDGE-BUILDING 1920-1922

THE LAST cup final before the competition came to a halt for the First World War was played on April 24, 1915. The first one after the end of the war was exactly five years to the day later, on April 24, 1920, and Aston Villa's presence seemed to suggest that nothing much had changed in the intervening time.

If you had casually said at the time that Aston Villa would win the League Championship and the FA Cup just once more in the next 80 years your sanity would probably have been called into question. But since 1920 Aston Villa have been back to the final only three times, losing to Newcastle in

1924, beating Manchester United in 1957 and losing again to Chelsea in 2000.

Villa's victory over Huddersfield at Stamford Bridge was the swansong to their golden era which began in 1894. They were consistently successful, winning the League Championship six times, finishing as runners-up five times in that period, appearing in five cup finals between 1895 and 1920 – winning each one. Their achievement in winning the double in 1897 was not to be equalled for 64 years, and they could trace their first cup success all the way back to 1887.

So when Villa battled through to the final again, there was no real surprise. The team that ran out to play Huddersfield Town at the FA Cup's temporary home of Stamford Bridge that April afternoon included four men who had played in Villa's last cup final in 1913 – goalkeeper Sam Hardy, first capped by England in 1907, full-back Tommy Weston, and wingers Charlie Wallace, who missed the penalty in 1913, and Clem Stephenson.

Also in their line-up was a 23-year-old, born a few months after Villa won the double, who was destined for unique 'double' success of his own later in life. He was Billy Walker, who was still playing for England as late as 1933 and who is the only man to have managed two different FA Cup winning teams – Sheffield Wednesday in 1935 and Nottingham Forest in 1959.

**Temporary Home**

That day, as a future international, he picked up his first major honour as Aston Villa beat Huddersfield 1-0 after extra time. The only goal came after 100 minutes when Billy Kirton scored with a header from a corner – but he didn't realise that he was the scorer until the referee told him after the match.

Or was he? More than 70 years after that game, one of Huddersfield's players was still alive and even though he was in his late 90s, he remembered that match perfectly. Jack Swann wore the no. 10 shirt for Huddersfield in that final, and, talking over a pint of Guinness in an Ex-Serviceman's Club in north London in 1990, he described the goal. "We scored the only goal of the game and lost," Swann recalled. "The ball came over from the right and about four of us went up to head it... I got a touch but the ball went the wrong way right into the back of our net. The Villa players started celebrating the goal and I wasn't going to put my hand up and say it came off me, but I always thought it did".

This was the first final played at Chelsea's Stamford Bridge home and as the competition progressed it looked more and more likely that the FA were going to be faced with a very awkward problem.

Crystal Palace was still requisitioned for use by the War Office, and the plan was for the FA to play the final back there as soon as possible. In the meantime though, a temporary home had to be found and Stamford Bridge, just a stone's throw from the site of the old Lillie Bridge ground used for the 1873 final, was chosen.

The competition's rules state that the final has to be played on a neutral ground – but Chelsea, beaten finalists in the 1915 final and now riding high in the League, had made it through to the semi-finals. Plans were too far advanced to change the venue, which meant that Chelsea, if they beat Villa in the semi-final at Bramall Lane, would be very much at home in the cup final. Villa saved the FA a huge dilemma, beating Chelsea 3-1.

But what about Huddersfield's 'unfair' advantage? Their semi-final against Bristol City was at Stamford Bridge – the last time – until Tottenham in 1991 – that one team played the semi-final and final at the same venue. For Huddersfield reaching their first final was an inspiring achievement by a club that faced liquidation earlier in the season. Their day would soon come, but Aston Villa took the cup back to Birmingham that year.

**Slippery Surface**

The second of the three Stamford Bridge finals was played on a quagmire of a pitch just after a cloudburst. It had been 20 years since a London club had won the competition and that same London club was back in the final. Since their triumph as a Non-League side in 1901, Spurs had risen from the Southern League to the First Division and were strong favourites to beat Second Division Wolves. For once, the favourites lived up their billing. The winning goal came after 55 minutes when Jimmy Dimmock maintained his balance on the slippery surface, sending his fast, low angled shot into the far corner of the net, always out of reach of goalkeeper Noel George.

It has often been said that the three finals at Stamford Bridge are the 'forgotten finals'.

Although at the time they were as keenly fought as any other match, in hindsight they tend to be overlooked because of the opening of Wembley in 1923, and also perhaps because they all ended 1-0, and because the last one of the three has gone down in history as the worst final of all time.

It ended in a win for Huddersfield who beat Preston 1-0 thanks to a penalty scored by Billy Smith after 67 minutes. The only reason the match is ever mentioned at all today, is that it served as a prequel for the 1938 final which was also between Huddersfield and Preston, and also ended 1-0 – although Preston won that game with George Mutch's famous penalty in the last minute of extra time.

The only other curiosity value about 1922 was that Preston's goalkeeper Jim Mitchell was an amateur who wore glasses and whose antics as Smith ran up to take the penalty – "acting like a circus clown" according to the match reports by waving his arms and jumping up and down, led to the law being changed whereby a goalkeeper must keep still until the kick is taken.

### Grander Stage

The FA Cup competition itself was something of a dog's dinner, too, by the early 1920s. While the basic concept of the cup itself had never changed from CW Alcock's original sudden-death idea, the competition had grown enormously. The first competition in 1871-72 had consisted of 15 teams – only 12 of whom actually played. Ten years later that figure had grown to 73, and by 1891-92 to 163. When Tottenham won the cup for the second time in 1921, 674 clubs entered the tournament, an all-time record. These days the number of clubs accepted by the FA is around the 550-mark. So naturally the organisation of the tournament has undergone periodic changes.

Between 1896 and 1925 there were all kinds of anomalies with league clubs playing in the qualifying round so the FA reorganised the competition for the start of the 1925-26 season, exempting all league clubs until the Competition Proper starts with the First Round in November. The rules have been amended slightly now and again since then, but in the last 80 years only one current league club has played a significant part in the Qualifying Competition.

In 1932-33 Brighton & Hove Albion, then in the Third Division South, forgot to claim their exemption until the first round. So they went into the hat for the first qualifying round along with Courage Sports & Social FC; Leavesden Mental Hospital FC and Shoreham FC who they despatched 12-0. They then beat Worthing, Hastings and Barnet and made it all the way to the fifth round where they lost 1-0 to Second Division West Ham after a replay. They played 11 cup matches that season, scored 43 goals – and did not even reach the quarter-finals. When they did reach the cup final for the first time, exactly 50 years later, they played only six games, and scored only 11 goals!

When Brighton's turn did eventually come, it came, of course at Wembley, which, by 1983 had been the home of the cup final for 60 years.

Stamford Bridge's temporary role as the home of the cup final was now over, but the FA never did take the match back to Crystal Palace. Instead a much grander stage was being prepared for what was now the greatest day in the sporting life of the nation – Wembley Stadium.

# WEMBLEY – HOME OF LEGENDS 1923-1939

IF A man called Edward Watkin had succeeded in a half-baked idea he dreamt up in 1901 it is unlikely that Wembley Stadium would ever have been built. No twin towers, no 'Abide With Me', no walk up Wembley Way, no 'Ossie's going to Wembley, his knees have gone all trembly'.

Of course something else would have taken its place, but the only reason Wembley Stadium got built in the first place was because Edward Watkin failed with a plan to turn himself into England's answer to Gustav Eiffel.

Mr Watkin attempted to build a 1,150-foot (350m) high tower to rival the Eiffel Tower in Paris. It reached a height of 200-ft (61m) before the concrete foundations collapsed and the project was abandoned. Still, 'Watkin's Folly' as it became known, towered above the largely open countryside that was then Wembley for another 20 years. It stood exactly on the site later occupied by the stadium.

In the early 1920s the government decided to hold a British Empire Exhibition in 1924 and chose Wembley as the site with a great stadium as the centrepiece. Watkin's Folly was pulled down and work started on the stadium. It took just 300 working days to build, at a cost of £750,000.

The Duke of York, who later became King George VI, cut the first turf to the right of what was the royal entrance tunnel in January 1922 and just over a year later the final workmen moved out. An infantry battalion and hundreds of local volunteers then marched up and down the terraces to test their strength and safety. In hindsight it was a strange thing to volunteer for. How did anyone know for sure the terracing would not collapse?

### Grave Error

The stadium opened on April 28, 1923, a year before the exhibition. Its official title was The Empire Stadium and the first event ever staged there was the FA Cup final between Bolton Wanderers and Second Division West Ham United. At the time it was built Wembley was the biggest and most dramatic sports stadium in the world. And its opening day was be unlike any other in its history.

The authorities estimated that Wembley would hold 127,000 people, but, incredibly, they were also convinced that because only 53,000 had watched the previous year's final at the spartan and unwelcoming Stamford Bridge, nothing like that six-figure number would come to the match. Therefore they decided that whoever did show up would be allowed to pay at the turnstiles and be allowed in.

It was a grave, and almost tragic error of judgement. Cup final day dawned bright and sunny. About a quarter of a million people woke up, saw the weather and soon got the same idea into their heads – "let's go to that new stadium at Wembley and see the cup final".

The match was due to kickoff at 3pm, and by 1.45pm the doors were shut with more than 126,000 people inside. But still they came... swarming over railings, scaling walls and climbing over the little turnstile barriers. At 2 o'clock police stations for miles around were being mobilised, but by the time those police reinforcements arrived, they could hardly do anything to stop the chaos or flow of people into the stadium. Never before have so many people ever turned up to see a match. There were anywhere between 200,000-250,000 inside Wembley – and probably almost as many outside. And while the stadium was being over-run, tens of thousands more people were still arriving. The roads for miles around were jammed solid and the Bolton team were forced to abandon their coach a mile away and push and shove their way into the stadium.

King George V somehow arrived on time at 2.45, and when he got to the Royal Box and looked out he must have thought his entire empire had turned up for the match. There were thousands of people on the pitch. THEY didn't think it was all over ... for them it hadn't even started.

### The White Horse

More than three-quarters of the playing area was covered by the crowd and it looked unlikely that the match could be played. But out of the mayhem there emerged a saviour – as much a part of England's equine sporting mythology as Arkle, Red Rum or Desert Orchid – a 13-year-old white horse called Billy.

Billy was not the only horse in Wembley, but he was the only white one, and that was the crucial factor. Ridden by PC George Scorey he began gradually moving the crowd back around the touchlines.

It was a slow process, but the crowd responded and inch by inch the playing area was cleared. A few years later PC Scorey explained in an interview to the BBC how he had managed it. "As my horse picked his way onto the field, I saw nothing but a sea of heads. I thought, `We can't do it. It's impossible.` But I happened to see an opening near one of the goals and the horse was very good – easing them back with his nose and tail until we got a goal-line cleared. I told them in front to join hands and heave and they went back step by step until we reached the line. Then they sat down and we went on like that... it was mainly due to the horse. Perhaps because he was white he commanded more attention. But more than that, he seemed to understand what was required of him. The other helpful thing was the good nature of the crowd".

Eventually the playing area was cleared, but thousands in the crowd, 20 deep in places, could hardly see a thing. It was a miracle that no-one was killed, and that there were only a few injuries.

An inquiry was held into the near-disaster and the FA returned money to ticket holders who claimed never to have reached their seats. Officials also publicly said that if it had not been for PC Scorey and the white horse, the final would never have gone ahead that afternoon. But PC Scorey, who lived to be 82, was not a football fan. Thirty years after he saved the cup final he admitted, "I never went to another game in my life".

### Goal in Two Minutes

The match eventually started 40 minutes late and after only two minutes Bolton were ahead. David Jack, destined to become the first £10,000 player when he moved to Arsenal in October 1928, hammered in a shot so hard that it not only beat Ted Hufton in the West Ham goal but knocked down a spectator standing right behind him. He in turn brought down a section of the crowd around him like ninepins. While that goal was being scored, West Ham's right-half Jack Tresadern was trapped in the crowd, unable to get back onto the pitch after a throw-in that led to the goal.

The players stayed on the field at half-time, and eight minutes after the re-start Bolton went 2-0 up when Ted Vizard crossed for John Smith to volley past Hufton, but the goal was controversial for two reasons. First, it appeared the ball had hit the woodwork because it immediately bounced back into play, but referee David Asson, ruled that the ball had hit the spectators behind the goal and not the crossbar and the goal stood. West Ham then pointed to a Bolton fan they alleged had kicked the ball back out of touch into Vizard's path as he dribbled down the wing before crossing. Mr Asson pointed to the centre circle. West Ham's captain George Kay then asked the referee to abandon the match, but Bolton's skipper chimed in, "we're doing fine, ref, We'll play until dark to finish the match if necessary".

There were no more goals and Bolton, founder members of the Football League in 1888, and beaten in their two previous finals in 1894 and 1904, had won their first major honour. They came back to win at Wembley with unerring regularity in 1926, and again in 1929. They won all three finals without conceding a goal and used only 17 players to do so.

West Ham, who gained some consolation for their defeat by winning promotion to the First Division the following week, would not return until 1964. And any of the crowd who wished to return to Wembley for the following year's cup final would have to buy a ticket in advance. From then on, with the exception of the replayed 1982 final between Spurs and Queens Park Rangers, every cup final and replay at Wembley was all-ticket.

Familiar colours filled Wembley in the 1920s. There were the black-and-white stripes of Newcastle, the claret-and-blue of Aston Villa, the red-and-white stripes of Sheffield United and the blue-and-white halves of Blackburn. And there were new colours too – the red and white of Arsenal, not yet the all-conquering giants of the 1930s, and the blue-and-white of Cardiff and Portsmouth.

Old scores were settled in 1924 and 1926. First Newcastle avenged their 2-0 loss to Aston Villa in the 1905 final with a 2-0 win at Wembley. Whereas the Magpies never won a cup final at the Crystal Palace, Wembley was a venue they loved. Newcastle won in 1924, 1932, 1951, 1952 and 1955. They eventually lost their unbeaten record on their sixth appearance in 1974, and then counter-balanced their back-to-back victories of 1951 and 1952 with successive defeats in 1998 and 1999.

### Talk of Demolishing Wembley

But Bolton were the first club to have a love affair with the old place. After winning in 1923, Bolton returned in 1926 and, in the first final played under the new off-side law, avenged their 1904 defeat to Manchester City with a 1-0 win in Wembley's first all-Lancashire final. David Jack, the scorer of Wembley's first ever Wembley goal, returned to score the winner again.

For a time though, it looked as if the 1926 cup final might be the last at Wembley, for in circumstances entirely different from those at the end of the 20$^{th}$ century, there was talk of demolishing Wembley and moving the final to a new, 150,000-capacity stadium which was to be built a few miles away at White City.

Wembley had been built as part of the 1924 Empire Exhibition which closed in October 1925 after suffering heavy losses. Author Tom Watt describes in his 75th anniversary history of the stadium, *Wembley, The Greatest Stage* how the buildings comprising the exhibition were gradually sold off and removed to become different facilities around the country. Eventually the stadium stood alone in the vast empty complex and as Watt states: "Once the Exhibition had closed, the stadium itself was no longer a commercial proposition, and with only a cup final every year and an international every other year on the books, its demolition too, was privately and publicly discussed".

Finally the stadium was saved from the bulldozers by the intervention of Arthur Elvin, then a young entrepreneur, who secured the stadium's future in 1927 and who retained control of it for much of the rest of his life.

Appropriately then that the most famous win in the 1920s came on April 23, 1927 when Cardiff beat Arsenal 1-0 to become the only team from outside England to win the cup.

### Heady Times

These were heady times when the Cardiff bluebird soared higher than ever before – or since. In 1924 Cardiff had missed out on the League championship to Huddersfield on the old goal-average rule of 0.24 of a goal. They came back from that disappointment to reach the 1925 cup final only to be beaten 1-0 by Sheffield United after a solitary mistake by their wing-half Henry Wake. The headlines then were as predictable as they would be today, "Wake Not Awake" moaned one.

But Cardiff were back again two years later and this time there was to be no slip. The sound of 'Abide with Me' – sung at the final for the first time – and 'Land of My Fathers' – sung for the last time – rolled down the Wembley terraces and across the stadium and inspired the Cardiff team to victory. Four of the side – but not the unfortunate Wake – had played in 1925, they had knocked cup holders Bolton out along the way, and they were about to make history.

The match, dubbed 'The Married Men's Final' because only three players were single, was not a classic – but it was settled by one of the most famous goals in Wembley's history. Herbert Chapman, who had masterminded Huddersfield Town's hat-trick of League wins between 1924-26, was in his first season in charge at Arsenal, who had never won a major honour.

They, of course, became world-famous in the next decade initially under Chapman, but in Wembley in 1927 they were relying on a player from a bygone age to bring them success. Fourteen years previously Charlie Buchan had been in the Sunderland team beaten by Villa. Now at Wembley, in the twilight of his career, he gave one final heroic display. Tall, elegant and still blessed with exquisite touch, he inspired Arsenal all afternoon, but it was all to no avail.

With 17 minutes to go, Cardiff's Scottish centre-forward Hugh Ferguson sent a first time shot at goal which Arsenal's (ironically) Welsh international goalkeeper – Dan Lewis had covered. Lewis dropped to his knees to gather the ball with Len Davies and Sam Irving running in to challenge. At that moment Lewis turned his back, the ball slid across his chest, under his left armpit and rolled across the goalline as he desperately tried to snatch at it. The Welsh side leapt for joy, thousands of Welshmen screamed in delight – but one Welshman just held his head in his hands.

### Scale the Heights

Tom Whittaker, the Arsenal trainer, believed the ball slipped under Lewis's arm because of the sheen on the goalkeeper's new jersey. From that day it has been an Arsenal tradition that every new goalkeeper's jersey is softened up in the wash before being worn.

That match was the turning point for both clubs. Cardiff disappeared down a valley so deep they would have to apply for re-election to the League just seven years later. Arsenal were to scale the heights no other side had ever reached – and few have matched since.

Their first major success came in 1930 when Herbert Chapman's old club, Huddersfield, met Herbert Chapman's new club Arsenal in the final. To mark Chapman's affiliation with both clubs, it was decided that both teams would walk out together for the final – the first time that had happened.

Huddersfield had been to Wembley two years previously and had come close to the double that season – finishing second in the

League to Everton and runners-up in the cup final to Blackburn, whose 3-1 victory took them level with Aston Villa's record number of six wins.

James Roscamp's opening goal for Blackburn that day – about 50 seconds after the kickoff – was the fastest yet scored in a Wembley final. Only two goals – Jackie Milburn's opener after 45 seconds for Newcastle in 1955 and Roberto Di Matteo's 43-second goal for Chelsea in 1997 were scored faster than that in the final at Wembley.

When they met Arsenal in 1930, Huddersfield had five survivors from 1928, Arsenal four from 1927, but it was Arsenal's new signings, the men who would carry them to greatness over the next decade, who decided the issue.

This was the Arsenal of Tom Parker, Eddie Hapgood, Alex James of the baggy shorts, and David Jack, who had already won two finals with Bolton. It was the Arsenal of Joe Hulme, Cliff 'Boy' Bastin, who won every honour in the game by the time he was 21, and 'Honest Jack' Lambert and that afternoon they were too clever for Huddersfield Town. Alex James rarely scored – but he got the opener after 16 minutes and provided the pass for Lambert to make it 2-0 two minutes from time.

### Clinched Promotion

It was Arsenal's first major honour and the first cup win by a London side since Tottenham in 1921. The new decade had begun with a new name on the cup – and a new shape in the sky. During this match the German Graf Zeppelin flew over Wembley, casting the only shadow on an otherwise perfect afternoon – for one half of north London, at least.

The following year's final was played in a downpour. Wembley had witnessed its first all-Lancashire final in 1926 and now it had its first all-Midlands affair. It had to wait until 1967 for the first all-London final, while the White Rose county never provided both teams for the cup final beneath the twin towers.

West Bromwich Albion, who had already played three finals against local rivals Aston Villa, now met another team from down the road – Birmingham, who did not add 'City' to their name until 1945. That spring Albion entered the record books by becoming the only team to win the cup and promotion from the old Second Division in the same season. They actually clinched promotion the Saturday after winning the cup final when they beat Charlton 3-2 in front of a then-record crowd at the Hawthorns of 52,415.

When the Baggies last played in the final in 1912 they lost to Barnsley in a replay. Their goalkeeper was Hubert Pearson, who naturally was rather disappointed with his losers' medal. His four-year-old son Harry probably didn't appreciate the full significance of what losing in a cup final meant then – but he did now.

Harry had followed his father's footsteps into the Albion goal and now faced Birmingham across a rain-lashed Wembley in the final of 1931. Lining up in Birmingham's goal was his cousin – the great England international Harry Hibbs – but it was to be the Pearson branch of the family rejoicing that night.

Albion scored twice through William 'Ginger' Richardson to take the cup back to the Hawthorns for the third time. 'WG' – best remembered for the four goals in five minutes he scored against West Ham the following November – hit the winner in the final less than a minute after Joe Bradford had equalised for Birmingham. West Brom returned to Wembley four years later as a First Division team, but lost 4-2 to Sheffield Wednesday. They clinched the match with two goals from Ellis Rimmer in the last five minutes which made him the fifth player to have scored in every round of the competition.

### Huge Win

There had been controversial goals before in the cup final – but there had never been anything like the controversy that surrounded Newcastle's opening goal in 1932. Their opponents, Arsenal, had powered their way back to Wembley for the third time in five years, winning every game without the need for a replay. They started their advance as they meant to go on, beating Darwen, those cup fighters of old now playing in the Lancashire Combination, 11-1 at Highbury.

Arsenal, who became the first London side to win the League title the previous year with a record haul of 66 points under the old system of two points for a win, finished as runners-up to Everton in 1932 and were to be champions again in 1933, 1934 and 1935, but they were to finish second best to the Magpies on this occasion. Newcastle had also had a huge win on their way to the final, beating Third Division Southport 9-0 after two draws in the fourth round. But they had had a moderate season in the League, finishing 11th. Like so many teams before them and since, they had reserved their best for the cup.

Arsenal were without the injured Alex James, but their side was full of stars and contained six survivors from the cup-winning side of 1930. The defence looked secure with future England internationals Eddie Hapgood and George Male at the back and 'Police Constable' Herbert Roberts, the king of the stopper centre-halves, in the middle. There was Parker, Lambert and Jack, there was Bastin and James's replacement, Bob John. In contrast Newcastle looked an ordinary side, although fullback Jimmy Nelson had played for Cardiff when they beat Arsenal in 1927.

No-one was too surprised when Bob John put Arsenal ahead after 15 minutes, but then six minutes before half-time came perhaps the most controversial goal ever scored in the cup final.

**'Over the Line Goal'**

Newcastle inside-right Jimmy Richardson chased a long clearance down the right, slithered onto the ball and crossed it in one movement, just as it appeared to have gone a foot over the bye-line. The Arsenal defence instinctively relaxed as Richardson's cross found the unmarked Jack Allen who put it past Frank Moss and into the goal. But to the horror of the Arsenal players, the referee Percy Harper pointed to the centre-spot and awarded a goal. The players protested but captain Tom Parker waved them back to their positions. The goal stood. Later that day newsreel film and still photos seemed to prove the ball was out of play when Richardson crossed. The incident made the front pages of the newspapers – a rare thing for a sports story in 1932 – and arguments about the 'over-the-line goal' have raged ever since. The match was a classic, but Arsenal never recovered from that demoralising setback. Allen scored a second as Arsenal became the first team to score first in a Wembley cup final and lose.

In 1952 the two sides again met in the final with Newcastle winning. It was not until 1998 and their third final encounter that Arsenal finally laid the old ghost to rest when they beat Newcastle 2-0 to clinch the double for the second time in their history.

Whatever injustice Arsenal may have felt about the 1932 final did not hold them back for long and they had far more to celebrate than console themselves for throughout the decade – with one notable exception.

Arsenal were champions five times in the 1930s and won the cup again in 1936 when they beat Sheffield United 1-0 with a goal from Ted Drake. But in January 1933 Arsenal were humbled in what must be regarded as the biggest upset in the history of the competition.

By January 1933 the team that Chapman had built was so good it was almost unbeatable. It had been 36 years since Aston Villa last achieved the double – but no-one doubted that this Arsenal team could emulate them. And when the draw for the third round of the cup was made nobody thought Walsall, halfway down the Third Division North table, would give them a moment's trouble. Arsenal won their last match before the cup-tie 9-2 against Sheffield United in the First Division. Walsall hadn't won for a month.

But Arsenal's manager Herbert Chapman was guilty of a rare yet costly error that wintry day in the middle of the Depression. He under-estimated the opposition. Arsenal took the field without four regulars – Eddie Hapgood, Bob John, Jack Lambert and Tim Coleman, missing through injury or illness. England winger Joe Hulme was also out of the side after a loss of form, but Chapman called in four reserves, only one of whom, Norman Sidey, had played in the first team before.

**Sensation**

Arsenal, the southern aristocrats, who, it was said, had spent more on their bootlaces than Walsall had on their team, were outfought by the poor provincial underdogs. Walsall battled for every ball, Arsenal men went flying over the surrounding wall after robust tackles, and in the end the Gunners were simply played off the park.

On the hour Gilbert Alsop put Walsall 1-0 up, heading home a corner. Five minutes later Tommy Black, who was never to play another game for Arsenal and was transferred to Plymouth the following week, aimed a kick at Alsop in the box and Bill Sheppard scored from a penalty. The final score was Walsall 2, Arsenal 0. It was a sensation.

Walsall's glory did not last long – they were knocked out in the next round by Manchester City, while Arsenal went on to win the championship. Arsenal have had a few bad days in the cup since then – losing to Northampton Town (1958), Peterborough (1965), York City (1985) and Wrexham (1992), but they've never had a day as black as that one in the Black Country in 1933.

The final that year was the first in which the teams were numbered – with Everton playing in 1-11 and Manchester City 12-22 and it was also the year Everton achieved what is an often over-looked treble. In 1931 they won the Second Division title, in 1932 they won the League Championship, and in 1933 they won the cup. It is a unique achievement and although the team was an outstanding one much of its success was due to the goalscoring brilliance of Dixie Dean who in those three years played in 126 league and cup matches for Everton – scoring 123 goals including the second in Everton's 3-0 win over City in 1933.

### Tragedy and Glory

City returned to win the cup the following year with a 2-1 win over Portsmouth. Matt Busby, later to know both tragedy and glory with Manchester United, had been in the team beaten by Everton and this time picked up a winner's medal. The great Frank Swift, later to lose his life in the Munich air crash that almost cost Busby his life too, was then a 19-year-old bundle of nerves in the City goal. He fainted with relief at the final whistle.

Both of City's goals came from Fred Tilson, who had scored four in the semi-final when City beat Aston Villa 6-1. Tilson's winning goal was made by Alec Herd, whose son David was to play for the United side managed by Busby in the 1963 Cup Final.

But one of the most famous people on the field in that 1934 final was not a player. He was the referee, Stanley Rous. As Sir Stanley he would become the secretary of the FA and eventually the president of FIFA. His previous involvement with the cup final had been as a linesman in the 1926 game between Bolton and Manchester City, but now he was in charge, and very nearly came close to making history of a different kind.

In his book, *Football Worlds*, published in 1978, Sir Stanley revealed how close he came in 1934 to sending off a player for the first time in the history of the final – something that did not happen until Durham referee Peter Willis dismissed Kevin Moran of Manchester United 51 years later.

Portsmouth were struggling against City and Rous noticed that John Mackie, their Northern Ireland full-back was threatening City's England winger Eric Brook. "I warned Mackie that he would be sent off if he carried out his threats," wrote Sir Stanley. "He answered me back, 'Sure. You'll never send me off at Wembley, Mr Rous'. 'Try it once more and you will find I will' I told him in a tone that seemed to convince him. Certainly he gave me no more trouble, and certainly I would have sent him off if he had".

City were to repeat their feat of losing and then winning in successive finals in the mid-1950s, but before then two other teams were going to return as winners the year after losing. The second was Charlton, losers in 1946, winners in 1947, but first it was Preston's turn, beaten by Sunderland in 1937 and winners over Huddersfield in 1938.

In 1937, with the final being played in May for the first time, Sunderland, inspired by Raich Carter, won the cup for the first time in their history with an emphatic 3-1 win over Preston whose Frank O'Donnell scored to at least have the consolation of scoring in every round. But Preston were back the following spring to beat Huddersfield Town in a repeat of the 1922 final at Stamford Bridge.

It was Preston's first cup success since the days of the 'Invincibles' half-a-century previously. In the side was a man, like Busby, who would have a profound influence on football in the 1960s.

### Close Your Eyes and Blast it

Bill Shankly was one of four men in the Preston line-up who had lost to Sunderland in 1937, but by the end of almost two hours play that afternoon he seemed no nearer a winner's medal. The match, much like the previous final between the two clubs in 1922 was a drab and uneventful affair. Goalless at 90 minutes, it was still goalless a minute from the end of extra time and the first replay in a final since 1912 looked inevitable. But the fates had one card still to play. Huddersfield had beaten Preston by a penalty in 1922 – now Preston were to do the same to them. With a minute of extra time remaining, Huddersfield's captain and centre-half Alf Young was adjudged to have tripped George Mutch as he came through for one last attack on goal. The foul happened at the very edge of the box – perhaps even outside – but the referee pointed to the spot. A bemused

Mutch was handed the ball, and legend has it that Shankly went up to him and told him to close his eyes and blast it. Mutch said after the game, "I thought it was funny they gave the ball to me ... an injured man. As I took my run I wondered what I was doing and why. I don't remember aiming at goal". But his aim was true enough, the ball going in off the underside of the bar.

That match closed the book on Preston's cup success, although they returned for the finals of 1954 and 1964. It also brought to a close the career of Joe Hulme, now playing for Huddersfield after moving from Arsenal. That day he made his fifth final appearance at Wembley – a feat not equalled until Johnny Giles played for Leeds United in the 1973 final.

But if a chapter had closed for Preston, and for Hulme in 1938, it was an era that ended in 1939. There had been major upsets in the cup final before, and in the last final played before the outbreak of the Second World War, there was to be another.

Portsmouth had struggled all season against relegation while Wolves, managed by Major Frank Buckley and inspired by their future manager Stan Cullis, the skipper in those days, were in contention for the championship. Portsmouth had only won three games away from home all season – at Derby and Sunderland in the league and at Highbury in the FA Cup where they had beaten Huddersfield, the previous season's beaten finalists, 2-1 in the semi-final. What was more, exactly a month before the final, they had been trounced 8-2 by Middlesbrough in the First Division. In contrast, Wolves had stormed into the final. Dennis Westcott had scored 11 goals on the way to Wembley including four in the 5-0 semi-final victory over Grimsby at Old Trafford.

### Shaky Signatures

Portsmouth had lost on both their previous Wembley appearances, to Bolton in 1929 and Manchester City in 1934, and no-one except their fans gave them a chance of making it third time lucky. Maybe the influence of their manager Jack Tinn's lucky spats helped settled their nerves, perhaps they took heart when they saw the almost unrecognisably shaky signatures of the Wolves players in the Wembley visitors book when they went to sign it.

Whatever happened, it was the biggest upset since Blackburn beat Huddersfield 11 years previously. Wolves never got going and gave their worst display of the season. Bert Barlow, a Wolves player until two months previously, scored against his old side to put Portsmouth ahead and the final was decided either side of halftime. Just before the interval John Anderson made it 2-0 and a minute after they re-started Barlow made it 3-0. Dickie Dorsett, not yet 20, became the youngest ever player to score in a Wembley final up until that time when he pulled a goal back for Wolves, but Cliff Parker completed the rout, heading in Portsmouth's fourth with 18 minutes to play.

The Wolves players reportedly took a potion made of monkey-glands to boost their energy before the match. It is a famous cup tale, but one strongly denied by Stan Cullis many years later. "It was a publicity stunt, and it never happened. Major Buckley was always interested in getting publicity for himself and for the club and that is all it was".

The match was played in front of a crowd of 99,370, the largest at Wembley since the first final in 1923. Portsmouth became the first club from south of London to win the cup – and they also became the holders of the trophy for the longest time in its history. It stayed in their safe-keeping until the end of the war in 1945, even surviving an enemy bombing raid.

# MATTHEWS, MORTENSEN AND THE GEORDIE BOYS 1946-1956

IN JUNE 1945, just three weeks after the end of the Second World War, the FA Cup organising committee met and agreed that the competition should be re-started the following autumn.

The Football League was not resurrected until the following year, and the FA Cup had an unusual flavour in that transitional first season after the war. From round one until the quarter-finals, ties would be played over two-legs, while matches in the qualifying round, the semi-finals and final, would, as usual be played on a regular, one-off knock-out basis.

So on September 1, 1945, just as it had back in November 1871, the FA Cup kicked off with just four matches in the Extra Preliminary round. Aylesbury United beat Chesham 5-0, Banbury Spencer beat Headington United (later to become Oxford United), 8-1; Pressed Steel beat Morris Motors 1-0 while Uxbridge scored an 11-0 win over Lyons FC. The FA Cup was rolling again.

There were 294 entries less than half the number that had taken part in the last pre-war competition, but the important thing for millions was that at last life after wartime was slowly returning to normal – and that there was once more some real, competitive football to watch.

**Quirky Results**

There were certainly some quirky results as the competition progressed. Aldershot beat Reading 8-6 on aggregate in the first round, and Newport from the Isle of Wight 12-0 on aggregate in the second. Middlesbrough beat Leeds 11-6 on aggregate in the third round, while Bradford Park Avenue lost 3-1 at home to Manchester City as expected in the fourth round – then won the second leg 8-2 at Maine Road! Derby, the eventual winners, beat Brighton 10-1 on aggregate in their fifth round tie, while Charlton, the eventual runners-up, beat Brentford 9-4 on aggregate in the quarter-finals. A staggering total of 859 goals were scored in the cup that season at an average of almost four goals a game – but one team did not score any.

Portsmouth, the 1939 winners and the club who looked after the FA Cup itself all through the war lost 1-0 on aggregate to Birmingham City.

And thousands came to every match with ground records being broken almost weekly. More than 76,000 saw the sixth round tie between Derby and Aston Villa, while in the semi-finals, 80,483 watched Derby play Birmingham at Maine Road and 70,819 watched Charlton play Bolton at Villa Park. But many of the grounds were in disrepair and simply not equipped to handle such huge masses of people. On March 9, 1946, 65,419 squeezed into every available inch of space at Burnden Park to watch Bolton's sixth round, second-leg tie with Stanley Matthews' Stoke, a wall collapsed and 33 people were crushed to death. It was the worst football disaster in English history, and remained so until the Bradford fire in 1985.

The competition – comprising a record number of 229 matches in the competition proper – ultimately reached its climax on April 27 when the nation turned its gaze back to Wembley, turned on its wireless sets, and heard the familiar voice of Raymond Glendenning commentating on the first cup final for seven years.

Charlton, in fact, were no strangers to Wembley although this was their first appearance in the cup final. They had played in the League South Wartime Cup Finals of 1943 and 1944 and six of the team to face Derby had played in at least one of those matches. Goalkeeper Sam Bartram was in the middle of a spell in which he played in four Wembley finals in four years. He missed the 1943 Final, but played in 1944, as a guest for Millwall in the 1945 match and for Charlton in their two FA Cup finals of 1946 and 1947.

And the first final after the war was one of Wembley's great finals. Nine years previously Raich Carter helped one famous old club win the cup for the first time when he scored one of Sunderland's goals against Preston, now he was to help another, Derby County.

**First Goal for Both Sides**

Derby scored 33 goals on the way to Wembley with Carter scoring 12 and the great Peter Doherty nine. By the end of the afternoon, Derby's tally was 37, Doherty had also reached double figures and The Rams were cup holders. The Carter-Doherty partnership in attack was the cornerstone of Derby's success, but it was almost a Charlton player that gave them the cup as with only five minutes to play defender Bert Turner deflected the ball into his own goal and for a moment that seemed to have settled it. But a minute later at the other end Charlton won a free-kick. Turner blasted the ball, it took a deflection off Peter Doherty and Charlton were level. Turner became the first man – and the last until Tommy Hutchison of Manchester City in 1981 – to score for both sides in the final.

But even before extra-time began there was another surprise when the ball burst. In one of those weird cup coincidences the referee ED Smith of Cumberland, had said on the BBC the night before that he thought the odds of the ball bursting were a million to one. Someone should have had some money on it. Five days after the Wembley final, Derby met Charlton in a league match and the ball burst again, and when Charlton played Burnley in the 1947 final, it burst again too.

If new balls in cricket make things easier for bowlers, the new ball in the cup final certainly helped Derby who scored three times without reply in extra-time.

It was actually Charlton's second defeat in the cup that season, as they had lost 2-1 to Fulham in the second leg of their third round match but gone through 4-3 on aggregate. Only one other side had ever lost a completed match before and still made it to the final – Sheffield Wednesday back in 1890. But perhaps Derby's name was always destined to be on the cup that year.

**The Curse Lifted**

A few days before the final an enterprising Fleet Street journalist remembered the old story about the gypsy curse on Derby dating back to the 1890s. The journalist, sensing a good yarn, took Jack Nicholas, the Derby skipper, to a gypsy a few days before the final. He crossed her palm, she lifted the curse, and Derby won the cup.

But Charlton, like Manchester City and Preston before them, and as Manchester City, Manchester United, Arsenal and Liverpool did later, returned to Wembley a year after losing and lifted the cup.

Their opponents in 1947 were Second Division Burnley, whose manager Cliff Britton was a member of Everton's winning team 14 years previously. Charlton's manager Jimmy Seed had also had a winner's medal as a player, with Tottenham, in 1921, and it was Seed who drank champagne at the end as Charlton won a dour match 1-0 with a goal from Chris Duffy. Again the ball burst, again the game went into extra-time, but this was not one of Wembley's gala occasions.

The cup final of 1948, however, was and is still regarded, as one of the best finals of all times, with perhaps only 1953 beating it for drama and excitement. And in fact there are similarities between both games. They both featured Blackpool and Stanley Matthews, and in both finals the eventual winners had to come from behind.

In 1948, Manchester United came from 0-1 and then 1-2 down to beat Blackpool 4-2, while in 1953, Blackpool came from 1-3 down to beat Bolton 4-3. In 1948 Manchester United became the first side to be behind twice in the cup final and win it.

The 1953 game, "The Matthews Final" has a special place in the history books, taking place as it did in the same year as Elizabeth II was crowned, Everest was climbed and Gordon Richards won the Derby. But in 1948 it must have seemed like the match between United and Blackpool could never be bettered.

United reached the final by having to play every match away from Old Trafford which was still being repaired after war-time bombing. They shared Maine Road with Manchester City but when both City and United were drawn at home in the fourth and fifth rounds, United had to find another ground. They beat Liverpool 3-0 at Goodison Park, and Charlton 2-0 at Huddersfield before they disposed of Preston 4-1 at Maine Road, and Derby 3-1 in the semi-final at Hillsborough.

The biggest obstacle Blackpool overcame was in the semi-final at Villa Park when a Stanley Mortensen hat-trick gave them a 3-1 win over Spurs after extra time.

And with 20 minutes to go at Wembley, Blackpool looked to have done enough to have won the cup. Eddie Shimwell had put them ahead from the penalty spot after Allenby Chilton fouled Mortensen after 15 minutes, even though the trip looked well outside the area. Thirteen minutes later United were level when Jack Rowley scored, but seven minutes later Mortensen turned in his stride and cracked the ball past Jack Crompton in the United goal to maintain his record of scoring in every round, the first player to do so since O'Donnell of Preston in 1937.

**Most Famous Comeback**

Both teams continued to play dazzling soccer in the second half, with Blackpool in command of the match. But then came the incident on which the match turned. Hugh Kelly, Blackpool's left-half clashed with John Morris on the right of the penalty area. Blackpool's defence hesitated, but Morris quickly took the free-kick, and Rowley equalised. With the score still 2-2, Mortensen thought he had won it for Blackpool, but his powerful shot, heading for the corner of the net, was tipped away at the last second by Crompton. A minute later Stan Pearson scored for United at the other end to make it 3-2 and when John Anderson drilled the ball past Joe Robinson in the Blackpool goal from 30 yards seven minutes from time, it was all over.

Blackpool returned in 1951 and lost 2-0 to Newcastle United and two Jackie Milburn goals, but the tangerine ribbons were finally tied to the cup in 1953 when they pulled off the most famous comeback in the competition's history.

The whole country – apart from Bolton fans of course – wanted Blackpool to win the 1953 Cup Final – even those who had never seen a football match. At 38, and after the disappointments of 1948 and 1951, surely this was Stanley Matthews' last chance for his lifelong ambition – a cup winner's medal. The only people who were not feeling quite so magnanimous towards Blackpool's ambitions were the Bolton team, and their fans. They were to be cast in a similar role in 1958 when they met a Manchester United team carried to the final on a wave of post-Munich sympathy. But whereas in 1958 Bolton won, this time they lost.

### 'The Matthews Final'

The match of course has gone down in history as 'The Matthews Final' and while his influence grew to almost mythical heights in the last 20 minutes after his marker Ralph Banks was suffering from cramp, Stan Mortensen had every right to claim the final as his, too, after scoring Wembley's first and only cup final hat-trick under the twin towers.

With only 75 seconds played however, it was Bolton who took the lead, when the Blackpool goalkeeper George Farm let a Nat Lofthouse shot squeeze under his body. Lofthouse followed Jackie Milburn as the second man in three years to have scored in every round. But 15 minutes later Bolton's left-half Eric Bell pulled a muscle and went out to play on the wing – Harry Hassall, the inside-left was pulled back to left-half, and Bob Langton, was moved across from the wing into the centre of the attack. Despite going 3-1 ahead the Bolton side looked unbalanced and as the hot afternoon wore on and the turf sapped the energy, it was Blackpool who rose to the occasion.

Mortensen had pulled Blackpool level at 1-1 in the 35th minute, but five minutes later Bolton were back in front when Farm made another hash of a save from Bill Moir. Then when Bell, jumping off his one good leg, headed Bolton 3-1 ahead 10 minutes after halftime, the match appeared to be over.

But Mortensen pulled another goal back after 68 minutes. With Banks crippled by cramp, Matthews had the right wing to himself, sending in cross after cross. Many sailed harmlessly over the bar, but finally one did some damage.

Stan Hanson went up for yet another high ball – and dropped it. Mortensen whipped it into the back of the net despite colliding with the post. Blackpool 2, Bolton 3.

### Exhausted and Confounded

Now Matthews swerved and feinted his way through the Bolton defence ... but time was running out. With three minutes to go Bolton, exhausted and confounded by the wizard on the wing, were hanging on to the cup by their fingertips. But then their grasp was prised away. Referee Mervyn Griffiths awarded a free kick on the edge of the penalty area. Mortensen blasted the ball high into the net. It was 3-3, with a minute or two of injury time left.

For the last time, Matthews went down the line, going inside the helpless Banks, before rounding centre-half Malcolm Barrass. He pushed the ball to within four yards of the goal-line and then passed to Bill Perry who had made space for himself on the edge of the six-yard box. He turned and shot the ball home. Almost immediately it was all over. Blackpool 4, Bolton Wanderers 3... Matthews had his medal. And so at last did Eddie Shimwell, skipper Harry Johnston and Stan Mortensen who also played in the losing finals of 1948 and 1951.

The afternoon was a special one, too, for Blackpool's manager Joe Smith who joined that select band of men to have played in and later managed, cup winning teams. He had been to Wembley twice before – as a winner with Bolton in 1923 and 1926.

Sandwiched between Blackpool's first cup final in 1948 and their last in 1953 were the exploits of two very different clubs which captured the nation's imagination. The first was Yeovil Town, the second Newcastle United. Yeovil's cup run of 1949 really is the stuff of legend and their giant-killing acts through the years since help define the FA Cup as the greatest knockout competition in the world.

Yeovil had been claiming league scalps since 1924, but their only cup match against a First Division side had ended in a crushing 6-2 defeat by Liverpool on their famous sloping pitch at The Huish in 1935. In 1949 they had reached the fourth round for the first time and been drawn at home against First Division Sunderland. At the time Yeovil were sixth from bottom of the Southern League, Sunderland were eighth in Division One.

**Plenty of Laughter**

More than 15,000 watched the match and more than 100 journalists went to cover it. There was nowhere to put them, so the club borrowed some desks from the local junior school, put the desks down one touchline and told Fleet Street's finest to sit in them. They did – causing plenty of laughter as they squeezed into seats usually used by seven-year-olds.

And what a story they had to file. Yeovil took the lead with a goal from player-manager Alec Stock after 28 minutes, then Sunderland equalised through Barney Ramsden after 62 minutes. In the Sunderland side was Len Shackleton, the most expensive signing in England, but not even he could conjure up a goal – for Sunderland at least – that afternoon. After 90 minutes it was 1-1 and as cup-ties were still then being played under the Government's austerity measures to save energy and avoid lost working days following the war, extra time was played.

Just before the end of the first period, Shackleton, "the clown prince of football" tried one trick too many. Juggling the ball on the halfway line, he sent it back towards his own goal by mistake. Ray Wright, Yeovil's inside-left pounced on it, and passed it to Eric Bryant who scored what proved to be the winner. In the next round Yeovil's part-timers went off to face Cup holders Manchester United, and an 80,000 crowd turned up to see if they could pull off another miracle. They didn't. Manchester United won 8-0, but Yeovil's win over Sunderland is still remembered as one of the greatest upsets of all time.

Even today, more than half a century on from that win, Yeovil are still lowering reputations in the cup, and had knocked out more league teams than any other Non-League side, although that will stop for the time being at least as they won promotion to the Football League in 2003 when they topped The Conference.

In the days before automatic promotion from The Conference, Non-League clubs would lobby for votes and between 1960 and 1972, Peterborough and Hereford United both gained League status largely through their cup exploits, whereas Yeovil, the most famous Non-League cup team of the late twentieth century, never did.

Peterborough, "The Posh" took few prisoners in the 1950s, beating Second Division Ipswich and Lincoln among others. Between 1949 and 1972, when they were voted into the League, Hereford only once failed to reach the first round. Their greatest victory came in February 1972 when they beat First Division Newcastle United at their Edgar Street ground in a third round replay with a winning goal from Ronnie Radford, as famous a goal today as many that have won the cup at Wembley.

In the 1970s and 1980s there were famous Non-League wins for Wimbledon, Altrincham, Telford and Blyth Spartans. In 1989 Sutton United of the Vauxhall Conference knocked out Coventry, cup winners less than two years before. Giant-killing is a vital ingredient of the cup's endless magic. And there has to be some magic. How else could you explain Woking's 4-2 win at a club like West Bromwich Albion, whose history is older than the tournament itself? How else could a club like Chorley take apart a club like Wolves? How else could works teams like Birmingham Corporation Tramways and Farnham United Breweries get through qualifying rounds and reach the competition proper?

**Corinthians Legend**

But one of the greatest of all Non-League clubs provides only a footnote to this story. The legendary Corinthians, formed in 1882 and at one time able to provide every player for the England side, never played in the FA Cup during their hey-day because their rules prevented them from taking part in any competitive matches.

But the Corinthians were more than a match for the leading professional teams of the late 19th and early 20th centuries. In March 1904, Bury, who the previous year had won the cup by a record margin of 6-0 over Derby County came to London to play the Corinthians for the Sheriff of London's Shield at the Queen's Club. The Bury team contained ten of their cup winning players – and the Corinthians beat them 10-3.

In 1884 Blackburn Rovers won the first of their three successive finals. Corinthians beat them 8-1. When Blackburn won the cup the following year, Corinthians beat them 6-0. The Corinthians finally entered the cup for the first time in 1922 – and two years later were still good enough to beat Blackburn Rovers, then of the First Division, 1-0. Their final season in the cup was in the last competition before the Second World War, but by then their time had passed. The history of the FA Cup would have been very different if they had taken part from the time of their formation.

So the Corinthians legend is something of a lost one. But while Yeovil were busy creating one of their own, Newcastle United were adding to theirs.

After never being able to win a cup final at the old Crystal Palace, it was a different matter at Wembley. In 1924 they beat Aston Villa 2-0, and in 1932 they scored their controversial 2-1 win over Arsenal.

### History Made

And in 1952 they became the first team since Blackburn Rovers (1890 and 1891) to win the cup in successive seasons. A gauge of their dominance in the competition, only matched at various times since by Manchester United, Spurs and Arsenal, was that in the five years from January 1951 to February 1956 they played 35 cup matches, won it three times – and lost only three games.

Since then they have appeared in three finals – losing their 100 per cent record at Wembley to Liverpool in 1974 and beaten again by both Arsenal in 1998 and Manchester United in 1999 – but in the days of 'Wor' Jackie Milburn, the Robledo brothers, Joe Harvey and Bobby Mitchell, Newcastle were the best cup team in the land.

The 1951 win was largely due to Milburn who scored in every round including both the goals in a five-minute spell in the 2-0 win over Blackpool in the final.

The move that led to the second goal, one of the best scored in a cup final, started after a mistake by Stanley Matthews. He hit an aimless pass which was picked up by Tommy Walker who fed Ernie Taylor. Taylor back-heeled the ball into the path of Milburn, who, sprinting at full tilt, blasted the ball home on the run from 25 yards. Stan Seymour, the Newcastle manager, also made history that afternoon by becoming the first man to play for and then manage the same club in a winning cup final. He was a member of the Newcastle side that beat Villa in 1924.

But if 1953 was the "Matthews Final" it is surprising that 1951 never became known as "Milburn's Final".

"It was definitely Milburn's match," said Matthews a few years later, "and his second goal was right out of this world. It was the greatest goal I have ever seen and certainly the finest ever scored at Wembley. A goal that every player dreams about... but how many other players would have chanced such a shot, especially in a Wembley final? Very few would have had the courage".

The following year Newcastle were back and faced their old adversaries Arsenal, playing in their second final in three years. In 1950 Arsenal beat Liverpool 2-0 with the oldest cup team of all time – an average age of 30 years 2 months. The 1950 final was also the first since the Bolton-West Ham match to have a 100,000 attendance.

### Series of Injuries

The Arsenal side of 1952 was younger and fitter, but was reduced to 10 men after an early injury to Welsh international defender Walley Barnes, the first in a series of injuries in the 1950s and early 1960s that became known as the "Wembley hoodoo".

Twenty years previously Newcastle had beaten Arsenal with the controversial "over-the-line" goal, and Arsenal could not exact revenge now. Newcastle won 1-0 with George Robledo, their Chilean born inside-left, scoring the only goal six minutes from time.

Newcastle's League form at this time never matched their cup displays. Although they never finished out of the top 10 from 1949 until 1952, they slipped below mid-table in 1953 and 1954 and their league form was only moderate again when they returned to Wembley to win the cup for the third time in five years in 1955.

In between the wins for Matthews and Milburn there was a cup final defeat for another giant of that era, Tom Finney. 'The Preston Plumber' is still regarded by many people as the best player that ever lived – better than George Best, better than Pele. That may or may not be so, but he did something in his career that neither Best – nor Pele – managed in theirs – playing in the cup final at Wembley.

### Support for Tom Finney

If the country had willed Matthews to his winner's medal in 1953, there was just as much neutral support for Finney in 1954. Preston had twice got to the sixth round since Finney had made his debut for Preston in 1946, but in 1954 they finally made it to Wembley. The previous season they had lost the title to Arsenal on goal average and their league form had slumped during the 1953-54 season. They had finished 11th, while their opponents in the final, West Bromwich Albion, had finished second, behind Wolves.

Although West Brom started as the favourites, everyone expected Finney to dictate the play on the Wembley wings he knew so well. Instead he had, by his own admission, the worst match he ever played for his club.

Biographer Paul Agnew, in his book *Finney – A Football Legend* quotes Finney's memories of the final. "Whatever the reason," remembered Finney, "May 1st, 1954 will always remain my worst performance. I could do little right on the day when I wanted everything to go better than ever before".

Finney, the Preston skipper, had a nightmare and Len Millard, his marker, virtually played him out of the game. Even so, Preston led after 51 minutes when Charlie Wayman rounded Jim Saunders in the Albion goal to put his side 2-1 up to become the third player in four years to score in every round. But Preston's cheers were short-lived. Just after an hour, Ronnie Allen scored his second of the match from the penalty spot after Tommy Docherty was judged to have pulled down Johnny Nicholls. Three minutes from time West Brom won the match with a goal from Frank Griffin. Preston, and Finney in particular, plumbed the depths of despair that day.

And there was an eerie corollary to that final almost exactly 10 years later. Preston, by then in the old Second Division, reached Wembley again in 1964. Again they were involved in a five goal thriller and again they lost after being 2-1 up during the middle period of the match.

Preston were, in fact, only denied victory by two West Ham goals in the last two minutes. The Hammers had not played in the cup final since the first one at Wembley in 1923. Now they were back – with seven men in the team whose surnames began with the letter B, and led by a man named Bobby who was to make Wembley his second home.

Preston included a young wing-half called Howard Kendall, who, 20 days before his 18th birthday was to become the youngest player to appear in a Wembley cup final. But they had some old campaigners too. Doug Holden played in the Bolton side beaten by Blackpool in 1953 and Alex Dawson was in the makeshift Manchester United team of 1958. And it was Holden who gave Preston the lead after 10 minutes. A minute later another teenager, 18-year-old Johnny Sissons, became the youngest scorer at Wembley when he equalised for the Hammers. Five minutes before the interval Dawson headed Preston ahead... and that is how it stayed until the 89th minute when Geoff Hurst headed West Ham level. With only seconds remaining West Ham won it when Ronnie Boyce, running in unmarked at the far post, headed in a cross from Peter Brabrook – then ran around the back of the goal in delight.

### End of an Era

Tom Finney had retired four years earlier in 1960 and the following season Newcastle and Preston were both relegated from the First Division. It was an end of an era, Preston have never been back in the top flight since, and Newcastle never won another major domestic honour by the time the 20th century ended.

But back in 1955, Newcastle were still the team to fear in the FA Cup. Before reaching Wembley though, they had a nasty fright in the semi-final against Third Division York City, only the third side from that division after Millwall (1937) and Port Vale (1954) to make it to the last four. Newcastle beat them after a replay.

Another tie earlier in the competition that year looked as if it was going to last all the way until cup final day itself. The third round tie between Stoke and Bury lasted for a record playing time for the competition proper of 9 hours 22 minutes, over five matches, one of which was abandoned. Stoke finally won through after a 3-2 extra time win in the fourth replay at Old Trafford – and were promptly beaten by Swansea in the fourth round five days later.

Jackie Milburn said before the eve of the 1955 final against Manchester City, "It seems like playing a tie at home" and he obviously felt comfortable there – within 45 seconds of the kickoff he headed Newcastle ahead – the fastest Wembley cup final goal until Roberto Di Matteo's 43-second strike for Chelsea in 1997.

But it was Manchester City, despite the early loss of Jimmy Meadows, but inspired by their Footballer of the Year Don Revie, who played the better football and deservedly equalised through Bobby Johnstone just before half-time. But then two goals in six minutes from Bobby Mitchell and George Hannah gave United the cup. It was their sixth win to equal the record of Aston Villa and Blackburn and their 10th final – more than any other club.

At the end City's captain Roy Paul vowed that his side would return the following year and win the trophy – and they did. This time the Revie-plan, borrowed from the Hungarians and involving the use of the player as a deep-lying centre-forward, worked to perfection and Birmingham City were outplayed and out-fought 3-1.

Bert Trautman, once a German prisoner-of-war, but now Manchester City's fearless goalkeeper, unknowingly played out the last 20 minutes of the match with a broken neck.

# CHASING THE DOUBLE 1957-1972

MANCHESTER CITY'S successive appearances were now to be equalled by two in a row by their rivals Manchester United, the "Busby Babes", in circumstances that were unparalleled in the history of the game. In 1957 Aston Villa won the cup for a record seventh time with a 2-1 win over United, who started the final as league champions looking for the first double since Villa in 1897. But the match was marked by a controversy over the sixth minute injury to United goalkeeper Ray Wood, who was barged so heavily by Villa's outside left Peter McParland that he broke his jaw and went off. He came back later as a passenger on the wing. Centre-half Jackie Blanchflower took over in goal and Duncan Edwards replaced Blanchflower in the middle of the defence. For more than an hour United did well to hold Villa, especially Blanchflower, who pulled off some important saves. But two goals from McParland midway through the second half finally settled the match, Tommy Taylor's late goal for United not being enough.

Although United had lost the final and the double, the feeling was this young, exciting team, champions in both 1956 and 1957, had time on its side and could win more honours in the years ahead. They had reached the semi-finals of the European Cup a few months previously and although they had lost to Real Madrid, manager Matt Busby was confident he was on the verge of producing the greatest British club side of all time. "The only difference between us and Real Madrid was in their experience, and we shall soon acquire that," he said.

But nine months later, on February 6, 1958, the plane bringing United back from a European Cup match in Belgrade crashed on take-off after a refuelling stop at Munich and six of the side that faced Villa were killed outright or died later in hospital from their injuries – the captain Roger Byrne, Eddie Colman, Duncan Edwards, Billy Whelan, Tommy Taylor and David Pegg.

Jackie Blanchflower and Johnny Berry never played again, and goalkeeper Ray Wood's career was effectively over.

Bobby Charlton and Bill Foulkes both survived the crash and were in the side that reached the final again, on a wave of unprecedented public emotion, a year later.

United's first match after the disaster was on February 19, 1958 when they beat Sheffield Wednesday 3-0 in a fifth round tie before 60,000 emotional souls at Old Trafford. United reached Wembley with further wins over West Brom and Second Division Fulham who they beat 5-3 in the semi-final after a 2-2 draw. They played in that final with Stan Crowther, hurriedly signed from Aston Villa, and Ernie Taylor, a cup winner with Newcastle in 1951 and Blackpool in 1953, who were given permission to play for United by the FA even though they were cup-tied. Crowther in fact had played against United in the 1957 final.

But Bolton were the better team on the day and two goals from Nat Lofthouse finally brought a sad end to United's emotional journey that had captured the heart of the nation – everywhere outside Bolton of course. Bolton's 2-0 win at Wembley was their fourth and, so far, last FA Cup final victory. Bolton had used only 17 players winning their three finals in the 1920s. United had used 20 players in successive finals. They would have to wait a few more years for their next cup success.

By the late 1950s and early 1960s football was undergoing one of its periodic moultings, shedding one skin and growing another. Equipment was changing, balls and boots were being made of lighter materials; shorts were getting shorter; the maximum wage was abolished, balls had stopped bursting like party balloons and Johnny Haynes started earning £100 a week. There had always been great characters in the game, but now they seemed to be more famous, advertising products like breakfast cereals and turning up on TV. Footballers were beginning to receive the kind of adulation until now reserved for film stars. There were great teams to watch too – Wolves won the League in 1958 and 1959 scoring more than 100 goals each time. The race for the title in 1960 was the closest for years with Burnley pipping Wolves to the title by a point – and so depriving Wolves of the double as well.

Wolves beat Blackburn Rovers, reduced to 10-men after Dave Whelan broke his leg, 3-0 in one of the poorest cup finals five days later. Whelan may have been a loser on the day, but he had spectacular success later in life with his sports clothing business and stayed in football as chairman of Wigan Athletic.

**Double Done**

If the 1960 final was a poor match the 1961 final between Tottenham Hotspur and Leicester City was not much better – but it created soccer history, because by winning it 2-0 Spurs became the first team in the 20th century to do the double and win both trophies in the same season since Aston Villa in 1897.

Spurs created record after record that season which they opened with 11 straight wins. They were not beaten until their 17th match and won 31 of their 42 League games. They won a record number of 16 away matches and lost only seven games – two of those in the last three matches with the championship already sown up and the cup final approaching.

In goal for Leicester that afternoon of May 6, 1961 was a young man named Gordon Banks. He was to have his moments of glory under the twin towers – but he was powerless to stop goals from Bobby Smith and Terry Dyson midway through the second half winning the match for Spurs.

And so at the end of 90 minutes Danny Blanchflower climbed the 39 steps to the Royal Box and took the cup from the Duchess of Kent. He had already had one memorable little chat with her before the match started.

After she had been introduced to the Leicester players, she came across to meet the Spurs team. She then turned to Blanchflower and said to him "the other team have their names on their tracksuits".

**'Chessboard Final'**

Blanchflower, quick as a flash replied, "yes, but *we* know each other". It was quite a day for Blanchflower. He ended it looking down Shirley Bassey's throat after she claimed she couldn't sing at their Savoy reception because of tonsillitis.

Spurs returned in 1962 to emulate Newcastle's feat of a decade earlier by winning the cup in successive seasons. The final against Burnley was an altogether different affair from the match against Leicester and is sometimes known as the "Chessboard final" because every player knew his place – and it became a fascinating battle of wills and tactics before Spurs triumphed.

Spurs had beaten Burnley in the semi-final on the way to Wembley in 1961, and in 1962 the two teams had been locked in a battle for the championship with Alf Ramsey's Ipswich who eventually beat them both to the title.

But now the old rivals were facing each other in the final, the last to be played in the "unmodernised" Wembley before the roof went on in 1963.

The Tottenham team showed two changes from the double-winning side, Les Allen and Terry Dyson making way for Terry Medwin and Jimmy Greaves, who had joined Tottenham the previous December in a £99,999 move back to England from AC Milan. Greaves had already scored 21 goals in 22 league games for Tottenham and another eight goals in six cup matches. Within three minutes of the start he had made it nine in seven.

Burnley were a fine side, captained by Jimmy Adamson and with the cultured Irish genius Jimmy McIlroy – being watched by the Sampdoria manager – always capable of creating a chance out of nothing. But the game was won and lost five minutes after half-time when Jimmy Robson equalised for Burnley with the 100th cup final goal at Wembley – and a minute later Bobby Smith made it 2-1 for Tottenham with the 101st. He was to be the last player for 40 years to score in successive finals until Freddie Ljungberg scored for Arsenal in 2001 and 2002.

Ten minutes from time Blanchflower sent Adam Blacklaw the wrong way from the penalty spot and soon after that made his familiar walk up the steps to receive the cup, this time from the Queen.

**The Big Freeze**

Remarkably for the third time in three seasons, the two sides were drawn together in the third round in 1963. But now it was Burnley's turn, and on a snowbound White Hart Lane pitch the following January Burnley, the 3-0 victors, became the first team to beat Spurs in the cup for three years.

That match was played on a Wednesday afternoon during the longest round in the history of the competition. The "big freeze" winter of 1963 virtually brought football to a standstill for two months. The third round took from January 5 until March 11 – 66 days – to complete and included 261 postponements. For the only time the cup final, originally due to be played on May 4, 1963 was moved back until May 25.

And after all the postponements and disruptions two teams emerged from the Wembley tunnel – one team in form and one "ragged rabble" as one newspaper described them. The form team were Leicester City, fourth-placed finishers in Division One. The rabble were Manchester United – who had narrowly avoided relegation to Division Two.

But United won the cup in 1963, the first played under the new roof built as part of the refurbishment of the stadium for the 1966 World Cup finals, largely because Denis Law had the type of game that earned him the nickname "The King". He opened the scoring after half-an-hour and then terrorised a Leicester defence in which Gordon Banks had a rare off-day.

**Start of Golden Era**

David Herd, whose father Alec had played with the United manager Matt Busby for Manchester City in the finals of 1933 and 1934, scored twice to give United their first honour of the 1960s, a decade that would climax for them on this same Wembley pitch five years later with a win over Benfica in the European Cup Final. Bobby Charlton and Bill Foulkes, the only men who played in both the 1957 and 1958 finals, gained cup-winners medals against Leicester. It was the start of a golden era for Busby's latest team.

In the 68 competitions played from the end of the amateur era in 1882 until Tottenham won the double in 1961, London clubs had won the cup just seven times, Spurs and Arsenal winning it three times, and Charlton once. Compare that with 24 Lancashire victories, 19 from the Midlands, 10 from Yorkshire, seven from the North East and one each from Wales and Hampshire.

But in the 42 finals since 1961, London clubs have been more successful than those from Lancashire. From Spurs' victory over Leicester in 1961 until Arsenal's win over Southampton in 2003, London clubs won the cup 19 times, Lancashire clubs 18 times. In the corresponding period it has only been won by midlands sides twice (WBA 1968, Coventry 1987), and once each by a club from Yorkshire (Leeds 1972), the north east (Sunderland 1973), Hampshire (Southampton 1976) and East Anglia (Ipswich 1978).

For four seasons from 1979 to 1982 the cup never moved out of the capital with two wins for Spurs and one each for Arsenal and West Ham.

If the trend started with Tottenham in the early 1960s, it was maintained by West Ham, who beat Second Division Preston 3-2 in the thrilling final of 1964. Tottenham won again when they beat Chelsea 2-1 in the first all-London final at Wembley in 1967. Chelsea maintained the capital's momentum with their first Cup victory over Leeds in 1970.

The West Ham win in 1964 was the start of a remarkable hat-trick for the Hammers' skipper Bobby Moore, who in 1964 lifted the FA Cup at Wembley, in 1965 the European Cup Winners Cup and in 1966 the World Cup itself with England.

But it was a little Cornishman playing for a team from Lancashire who was responsible for the most thrilling win of that decade – Everton's 3-2 win over Sheffield Wednesday in 1966. It was the first time since Blackpool in 1953 that a team had come from two goals down to win the cup. No-one has done it since.

But before examining Everton's win it is worth turning the clock back a year to 1965 and Liverpool's first FA Cup final victory.

### Liverpool's Reign

This was the start of Liverpool's 20-year plus reign as the kings of English, and ultimately, if briefly, European soccer. Bill Shankly, who went to Anfield in 1959, re-built a Liverpool side that had sunk into the Second Division in 1954. By the time it re-emerged in 1962 it was nearly ready to take on the world.

In 1964 Liverpool won the title for the first time since 1947 and in 1965 Ian St John headed the extra-time goal that gave them a 2-1 extra time win over Leeds for their first cup success. A new chant was now boomed by Kopites around Wembley, "Ee-ay-adio, we've won the cup".

But in 1966 it was Everton's turn, and it had been a very long wait. Everton had won the League in 1963, Liverpool the League in 1964. Liverpool had won the cup in 1965, and had already clinched the championship by the time Everton faced Sheffield Wednesday at a Wembley soon to host the World Cup finals.

No Yorkshire side had won the cup since Wednesday in 1935. Everton had not won it since 1933, but after 57 minutes it looked as though Wednesday had done enough to settle the argument. Goals from Jim McCalliog, after only four minutes, and David Ford (57) left Everton trailing 2-0.

But suddenly Everton hit back. Before the match, the Everton manager Harry Catterick caused a major surprise when he dropped centre-forward Fred Pickering, a crowd favourite, and played instead a young reserve called Mike Trebilcock, signed from Plymouth on New Years' Eve 1965.

Trebilcock, whose name and profile were not even in the cup final programme, had only played in seven League matches for Everton and one cup match – the semi-final against Manchester United, but Catterick thought he would do a better job than Pickering.

Later Catterick explained, "Fred was popular and could score goals but he'd been injured and had gone off the boil a bit. Trebilcock was a first rate goal-poacher. I always felt his sharpness would show".

And it did. For almost an hour Everton had been second best with the Wednesday defence totally in control. But a minute after Wednesday's second, their armour was breached when Trebilcock drove past Ron Springett who had just blocked a Derek Temple header. One of the greatest ever cup fightbacks had begun.

Five minutes later it was 2-2. Sam Ellis, the Wednesday centre-half weakly headed at an Alex Scott free-kick, and Trebilcock lashed the ball into the net.

And then 10 minutes from time, came another of those cup final goals that defy belief. A long punt upfield should have been easily trapped by left-half Gerry Young standing near the halfway line. But the ball rolled under his foot and Temple was onto it in an instant. Springett advanced, it was one-against-one, Temple shot and the ball flashed into the corner of the net. Everton had won 3-2.

From 1964 when West Ham beat Preston, all the finals for the next nine years were won by just one-goal margins.

### Youngest Goalkeeper

Following Liverpool's win in 1965, Everton's in 1966 and Spurs in 1967, West Bromwich Albion maintained the sequence with a 1-0 extra time win over Everton in 1968. Manchester City, champions the previous year, sent Leicester to their fourth final defeat at Wembley with a solitary Neil Young goal. It was all gloom for Leicester that year. They were relegated to the Second Division as well.

It was an odd coincidence that two of England's greatest ever goalkeepers – Gordon Banks (1961 and 1963) and Peter Shilton (1969) both played in losing cup finals for Leicester in the Sixties. Shilton is the youngest goalkeeper ever to play in a Wembley FA Cup final, but despite a career that brought him a world record number of

125 England caps and almost every other honour in the game, that was his one and only cup final.

The sequence of single-goal margins continued well into the Seventies. In 1970 Chelsea beat Leeds 2-1 in a replay at Old Trafford after Wembley's first drawn final; in 1971 Arsenal beat Liverpool 2-1 to win the double; in the Centenary final of 1972 Leeds beat Arsenal 1-0 and then the following year Sunderland beat Leeds 1-0 to become the first Second Division winners since 1931. The sequence ended in 1974 when Liverpool beat Newcastle 3-0.

But there was another coincidental thread running through the finals at this time, besides the obvious involvement of Leeds United, a club which had never even played in the final until 1965.

### Montgomery's Brilliance

It was more a question of wise heads on still sprightly shoulders. In 1969 Manchester City's win was master-minded by manager Joe Mercer, a cup-winner with Arsenal in 1950. Don Revie, a winner as a player with Manchester City in 1956, became a winning manager with Leeds in 1972, while in 1973 Bob Stokoe joined their ranks.

He was in the Newcastle team that won the cup in 1955, now he made another run across the Wembley turf to embrace Jim Montgomery his goalkeeper whose brilliance had preserved his side's hold on the cup after Ian Porterfield's famous goal.

Oddly however, the man that masterminded only the second double of the century was never a professional player. Bertie Mee had become Arsenal's manager in the mid-Sixties after serving as the team's physiotherapist. Together with his first lieutenant at Highbury, Don Howe, they built a team that never knew when it was beaten.

That point was never better illustrated than in the semi-final against Stoke at Hillsborough on March 27, 1971. Arsenal were trailing 0-2 at half-time and Stoke seemed set for the cup final for the first time in their 108-year history. But Arsenal fought back. With a minute to play they were still 2-1 down when Peter Storey beat Gordon Banks with a penalty. Arsenal destroyed Stoke in the replay. A year later they met Stoke again in the semi-final, and again beat them in a replay after a draw.

Arsenal knew all about chasing lost causes that spring. On March 20, with only eight league games to play Leeds were six points clear in the championship race. But Leeds faltered on the run-in, Arsenal picked up 27 points out of a possible 30 from their last 15 matches and clinched the title at Tottenham of all places five days before the cup final.

Suddenly the double looked a possibility, but there could be hardly be a tougher obstacle to doing it. Liverpool had also reached Wembley the hard way, pulling a goal back against Everton in the semi-final at Old Trafford. This Liverpool team gave little away, they had conceded just one goal on their way to the final and with Ray Clemence in goal, Tommy Smith in defence and youngsters like Larry Lloyd, Steve Heighway and the experienced John Toshack and Ian Callaghan up front they were a formidable force.

But Arsenal were just as uncompromising. Goals from Ray Kennedy, later to join Liverpool, John Radford and George Graham had carried Arsenal to the title, while their captain Frank McLintock, a loser with Leicester in the cup finals of 1961 and 1963, and a loser with Arsenal in the League Cup Finals of 1968 and 1969, inspired his team to the heights.

### First Substitute to Score

It was goalless after 90 minutes, but Liverpool struck the opening goal in extra time when Steve Heighway beat Bob Wilson with a left-foot drive. Bill Shankly said before the match that if Liverpool scored first they would win – but he was wrong. Arsenal equalised with an untidy goal 10 minutes later – at first credited to Graham but after TV replays, given to Eddie Kelly, who became the first substitute to score in the final.

Just when it appeared that for the second successive year the final would end in a draw, Charlie George gave the ghosts of Herbert Chapman, Alex James and David Jack something to cheer. He cracked home the winner past a despairing, diving Ray Clemence from just inside the penalty area. The double belonged to Highbury. George lay down on the Wembley turf, arms aloft, and soaked up the adulation.

Arsenal were back in 1972, the Centenary Year of the FA Cup, with Geoff Barnett in goal for Bob Wilson and Alan Ball, signed for Everton for a then record fee of £200,000, taking Ray Kennedy's place. A poor start to the season had ultimately cost them their title and they finished fifth in the league – which was still unfinished by cup final day.

Leeds were in with a chance of repeating Arsenal's double achievement but their final First Division match was not until 48 hours after the final, at Wolverhampton on the Monday night. Liverpool were also in contention for the title. Their final game was at Arsenal, also on the Monday. Derby, top of the table, had finished their fixtures and were already relaxing on holiday on the beach in Spain.

So the 1972 final was played out against the intriguing possibility that Arsenal could emulate Newcastle and Tottenham by returning to Wembley to retain the trophy – or that Leeds United could clinch the first half of the double.

In the event a poor final was settled by a solitary goal from Allan Clarke, a loser with Leicester in 1969 and Leeds in 1970. Instead of emulating Newcastle and Spurs, Arsenal became the first team to return to Wembley as cup holders and lose.

So Leeds had completed one half of the double... but could they also join the immortals? Manager Don Revie banned all celebrations after the final and allowed them to drink only orange juice. They went to Wolverhampton needing just a draw for the title – and lost 2-1. On the same night Liverpool's 0-0 draw at Arsenal cost them the title – so Derby, sunbathing in Spain, became English champions for the first time.

Leeds' best chance of winning the double had gone – and their disappointments, in the cup at least, were to continue.

# UNDERDOGS ON TOP 1973-1980

THE LEEDS team built by Don Revie was the most powerful in the country in the late 1960s and early 1970s. From the time of their first cup final appearance in 1965 until Revie left to become the England manager in July 1974 they were always in contention for the major prizes, but too often finished second best.

Their second cup final appearance in 1970 ended in disappointment, just as their first had done against Liverpool. Leeds met Chelsea on April 11, 1970, the earliest date for a cup final for 73 years, to help world champions England prepare for their defence of the trophy in Mexico where the World Cup started on May 31. The fact the final was not resolved until April 29 rather defeated the object however.

The first game was played on a Wembley pitch that looked more like the Sahara than Wembley as it was largely covered in sand. The Horse of the Year Show the previous year had badly damaged the turf.

### High Drama

The first game ended in a 2-2 draw with Jack Charlton and Peter Houseman scoring first half goals to make it 1-1 and then Mick Jones of Leeds and Ian Hutchison of Chelsea scoring in the last six minutes of normal time. It was an excellent match. Jones put Leeds ahead in the replay at Old Trafford too but on a night of high drama and tension Chelsea fought back to equalise with a magnificent diving header from Peter Osgood – who joined the select band of men to have scored in every round – and then win with a late second from David Webb after one of Ian Hutchison's famous long throws, right into the jaws of the Leeds defence.

But Leeds came back time and again... in the cup, in Europe and in the league. In 1974 Revie took them to the championship for the second time in five seasons, and the year after he left they reached the European Cup Final, but lost to Bayern Munich in Paris.

Losing to the Germans, then in the middle of their hat-trick of European Cup wins, was always a possibility and could not be classed as a major upset. But Leeds were involved in two major cup upsets in the early Seventies. The first ranks as one of the biggest shocks in the competition's history. It happened on February 13, 1971 and ended Colchester United 3, Leeds United 2. At the time Leeds were three points clear at the top of the First Division and Colchester were in the middle of Division Four. Six of the Colchester team were over 30 including Ray Crawford, 34, a member of the Ipswich side that won the title in 1962 but now fast approaching retirement. He predicted before the match he would score – and he did – twice – while Colchester's manager Dick Graham said if his side won he would scale the walls of Colchester Castle afterwards. A few days later, he kept his word. Colchester were given absolutely no hope against the likes of Norman Hunter, Jack Charlton, Johnny Giles, Allan Clarke et al. Billy Bremner was injured and missed the debacle and could only watch in amazement as Colchester led 3-0 after 55 minutes with two goals from Crawford and the other from Dave Simmons. Leeds pulled two back in the last half-an-hour through Hunter and Giles, but Colchester held on for a memorable victory.

### Outstanding Achievement

Leeds' second cup failure came on a far grander stage than Layer Road in Colchester. It happened at Wembley Stadium where they lost to Second Division Sunderland in the 1973 cup final. The result also ranks as one of the greatest cup shocks of all time, and possibly the greatest upset in the final.

Leeds, appearing in the final for the third time in four years, had finished third in the First Division and no-one – save a few romantics on Wearside – gave Sunderland the faintest hope of winning. Earlier in the season they had been faced with relegation to the Third Division, but their season had changed around with the appointment as manager of Bob Stokoe, a cup winner with Newcastle in 1955. Their outstanding achievement before the final was beating Arsenal in the semi-final at Hillsborough. The fans knew Stokoe had turned their club around. They refused to leave the ground until he came back on the pitch after the final and took their salute.

The Leeds team was full of international stars – Billy Bremner, Johnny Giles – playing in his fifth Wembley cup final – Norman Hunter, Allan Clarke, Peter Lorimer et al... revered names, cup holders, and surely destined, in Wembley's 50th anniversary year, to match Newcastle and Tottenham by winning the cup in successive seasons.

But they didn't. After 30 minutes they went 1-0 down to a goal scored by Ian Porterfield who killed a clearance on his left thigh and then swung to crack the ball into the roof of the net with his right foot.

Leeds surged back but were denied time and time again by the Sunderland defence, at the heart of which the future England international Dave Watson towered majestically. None of the Sunderland team had a full cap.

### Just as Incredible

With 20 minutes to go came the moment Leeds probably realised they would never win the match, the moment that Jim Montgomery made his 'double save', now more famous than many a cup winning goal.

Paul Reaney centered from the right, and Trevor Cherry dived to head the cross home. Montgomery made a diving save, but the ball flew to Peter Lorimer, the man reputed to have the hardest shot in soccer.

He blasted the ball for what seemed a certain goal, but Montgomery changed direction, twisted himself in mid-air, and diverted the ball onto the underside of the bar. It then bounced clear and Sunderland held on to win the cup for the first time since 1937. No Second Division had won the cup for 42 years. When Sunderland next reached the cup final in 1992, again as a Second Division club, the save was replayed countless times on television. It looked just as incredible almost 20 years later.

The north east were represented the following year but Newcastle were unable to match Sunderland's success when they surrendered their record of never having lost at Wembley. This was Newcastle's 11th final and a record at the time, but it is an afternoon Geordies would rather forget.

Opposing them were Liverpool – and Newcastle hardly got a look-in. Malcolm Macdonald came to Wembley looking to become only the 13$^{th}$ player to score in every round – but never had a shot on goal until 12 minutes from the end of a game that by then Newcastle were losing 2-0 after goals from Kevin Keegan and Steve Heighway. Keegan, later to become a Geordie hero as both a player and manager, added another two minutes from time to give Liverpool the biggest final win for 14 years.

Playing out on the turf that day was the third great side that Bill Shankly had created at Liverpool. It included Ray Clemence, Larry Lloyd, Keegan and Heighway, Emlyn Hughes, John Toshack and Ian Callaghan but was to be the last that Shankly put together. A few weeks after the final he suddenly announced his retirement as manager. At the end of the final two fans got down on their hands and knees and kissed Shankly's feet. They had a lot to thank him for.

### Trend Changed

During the first 41 years at Wembley there had only ever been six teams from the old Second Division in the cup final but in the 1970s, when it appeared for a while that the gap between the top divisions was narrowing, that trend changed.

Sunderland were the first side to make their mark when they beat Leeds in 1973. In 1975 Second Division Fulham reached the final, losing to West Ham, but the following year Second Division Southampton emulated Sunderland's achievment by winning the cup when they beat Manchester United and in 1980 West Ham did the same when they beat Arsenal. All of those games ended 1-0.

Since then Queens Park Rangers in 1982 and Sunderland in 1992 have both reached the final only to lose, but it is West Ham's cup record that is intertwined with clubs outside the top division – including themselves.

In 1923 they reached the final as a Second Division team. In 1964, in their second final, they played Second Division Preston. In 1975 West Ham won the cup for a second time, beating Second Division Fulham, and in 1980, their third victory, they themselves were in the Second Division.

Fulham, perhaps, were the most surprising cup finalists of the last three decades – and they needed 11 matches to get to Wembley which included three against Hull in the third round, four against Nottingham Forest in the fourth round and two against Birmingham City in the semi-final. In fact Fulham reached the final without winning a game on their own pitch.

This was only the second all-London final at Wembley, and it contained some of the great characters of the capital's soccer scene. Billy Bonds, Frank Lampard and Trevor Brooking were in the Hammers side, while playing for Fulham were two men in the twilight of their careers – Bobby Moore, 34, who had led West Ham to their previous Cup Final victory in 1964 and Alan Mullery, 33, who had been in the Tottenham side which won the cup in 1967. Fulham were managed by a man who knew all about cup romance – Alec Stock, the player-manager when Yeovil dumped mighty Sunderland out of the cup in 1949. But there was not much romance about the 1975 final, an uneventful match which ended 2-0 to West Ham. Both goals were scored by Alan Taylor, who had been playing for Fourth Division Rochdale the previous Christmas.

### Top Cup-Fighters

It was the last final in which neither side used a substitute. Just one per team was allowed then, and the man wearing the No. 12 shirt for West Ham, Bobby Gould, would have to wait another 13 years for his day in the sun. He was to manage Wimbledon to Cup glory in 1988.

The Seventies ended with some familiar names doing battle at Wembley – Liverpool, Arsenal and Manchester United – but two clubs who had never won the trophy before finally got their names inscribed on the silver plinth.

At the turn of the century Southampton were one of the top cup-fighters in the country, reaching the final as a Southern League team, but losing in both 1900 and 1902. It had been a long wait for their next appearance. Lawrie McMenemy had built a side that really was the right blend of that old football cliche – youth and experience. Mick Channon, Peter Osgood, Peter Rodrigues and Jim McCalliog provided some of the experience, and three of them had played in the cup final before.

Osgood scored Chelsea's opening goal in the replayed final of 1970, Rodrigues was in the Leicester side beaten by Manchester City in 1969, while McCalliog, a former Manchester United player, had scored for Sheffield Wednesday when they lost the 1966 final to Everton.

Tommy Docherty, the manager of the Chelsea team beaten by Tottenham in 1967, was in the process of building a fine, attacking side at Old Trafford with Gordon Hill and Steve Coppell playing like old-fashioned wingers. The side was an inexperienced one with an average age of only 24, but were still odds-on favourites to dispense with the South Coast underdogs. But, as so often, the giant was slain. A goal seven minutes from time from Bobby Stokes, who was to die aged just 44 in 1995 in sad, broken circumstances, settled the match.

United who had chased cup and league honours all season were left empty-handed.

For now.

Docherty's side were back a year later with eight of the team that faced Southampton – nine if substitute David McCreery, the only teenager to play in two Wembley finals, is included. And while they had been odds-on favourites to beat Southampton in 1976, this time Liverpool were not only expected to beat them, but also clinch a unique treble of league, FA Cup and European Cup.

**One of the Great Finals**

This was one of the great finals that was decided in a five minute spell just after half-time. Stuart Pearson scored for United, Jimmy Case equalised with a tremendous shot from the edge of the box two minutes later – and while the Liverpool fans were still roaring and cheering, United went back in front with an untidy goal, a shot from Lou Macari taking a widely arcing deflection off Jimmy Greenhoff to plant itself in the back of Ray Clemence's net.

Ray Kennedy hit the post for Liverpool late in the game, but Liverpool, the champions, were going to have to wait for the league and cup double. And when Martin Buchan went up to collect the cup he also wrote his name into the record books as the first player to captain Scottish and English FA Cup winning teams. He had previously captained Aberdeen when they won the Scottish Cup in 1970.

This was United's day – and more poignantly Tommy Docherty's day. He had lost as a player with Preston in 1954 and as a manager with Chelsea in 1967 and Manchester United in 1976 – but now, in his eighth Wembley match including internationals for Scotland, he was a winner for the first time.

Early the following morning the Doc went for a jog in Hyde Park and apparently, just by Speakers' Corner, it hit him. He had finally won the cup, and started to do cartwheels in celebration. It was his final hurrah as United's manager. On July 3, just six weeks later, Docherty was sacked for "a breach of contract". He had been having an affair with the wife of the club's physio. "I must be the first football manager to be sacked for falling in love," mused Docherty afterwards.

Liverpool may have been devastated by that cup final defeat, but they rallied. Four days after losing to United at Wembley the club had one of its greatest nights. Fielding the side that lost in the final they beat Borussia Moenchengladbach 3-1 in Rome to become only the second English side to become the champions of Europe. The first? Manchester United of course.

**Superb Display**

A young man in a blue-and-white stripped shirt, who would create history for United in the 1980s and 1990s, helped knock Manchester United out of the cup the following season. Bryan Robson was then playing for West Bromwich Albion and was in the side that beat United 3-2 in a replayed fourth round match. West Brom reached the semi-final for a record 18th time, but they went down 3-1 to Ipswich at Highbury.

Ipswich had never been in the final before. Only once had they ever reached the semi-final, but managed by the future England manager Bobby Robson and inspired by a brilliant display from Clive Woods, Ipswich "murdered" Arsenal 1-0 with the winning goal scored by Roger Osborne 13 minutes from time. He was so overcome by "sunstroke and emotion" after scoring, he had to go off. Ipswich hit the woodwork three times, and were denied further goals by a superb display in goal by Pat Jennings.

It was another dreadful disappointment for Arsenal's Malcolm Macdonald, a loser with Newcastle in 1974, and also a loser in the Newcastle team beaten by Manchester City in the 1976 League Cup Final. But there was a defiant – and accurate – message from Arsenal's manager Terry Neill at the end of the game.

"We are a young team, we've got a bright future and we will be back," said Neill afterwards and he was right. Arsenal became the first club to play in a three successive Wembley finals. They came back in 1979 to beat Manchester United 3-2 and returned again in 1980 when they went down to a Trevor Brooking goal in a 1-0 defeat to West Ham.

One man in Arsenal's 1979 team was making history of his own. Brian Talbot played for the winning Ipswich team against Arsenal in 1978 and then played for the winning Arsenal team in 1979 to become the first man in the 20th century to play for different winning teams in successive years.

He was also involved in one of the game's mysteries – the identity of Arsenal's first goalscorer – but he, rather than Alan Sunderland, was ultimately credited with the shot that put Arsenal 1-0 ahead. Although this was another of Wembley's great, emotional occasions, most of the emotion was contained in the last five minutes when three of the goals were scored. The match itself was rather ordinary until then – despite it sometimes being included in a "Best Cup Finals of All Time" lists. It wasn't. It just had a great finale.

Frank Stapleton, later to win winners' medals with United, had doubled Arsenal's lead just before half-time to 2-0 and with only five minutes to play neither side had added to the scoreline. Arsenal looked safe. Terry Neill, who always denied this was a mistake, then took off David Price and brought on the youngster Steve Walford. Arsenal, as their defenders had done back in 1932, collectively seemed to relax believing their task was over and that Neill had sent Walford on for a sentimental run-out.

**Utter Despair**

At that moment Arsenal's concentration went. Joe Jordan turned Steve Coppell's free kick back into the middle and Gordon McQueen scored. Two minutes later United, unbelievably, were level. Sammy McIlroy, took a pass from Coppell, shimmied past David O'Leary and Walford and scored the equaliser. It was 2-2. The Arsenal players looked at each other in utter despair and bewilderement. Wembley was a sea of Manchester United red and white. Surely United had saved themselves and forced extra time.

There was less than one minute to play when Arsenal scored the winner straight from the kickoff. The goal was made by Liam Brady who gave a magnificent midfield performance and said later, "I was so tired I dreaded the thought of extra time so I tried to take the ball into their half". He succeeded, pushing the ball through to Graham Rix whose cross was slid home by Alan Sunderland.

It was an astonishing finale, and McIlroy summed up the awful feeling for the United players and supporters. "It was like picking eight draws and then finding the pools coupon still in your pocket," he said.

The following day was the hottest day of the year with the mercury hitting 75f in London. Arsenal paraded the cup through Islington in front of around 200,000 people and that evening when Terry Neill brought home football's most famous trophy his young daughters said to him, "What's that grubby old thing?" Soon afterwards they were giving the FA Cup a good wash – in their neighbour's swimming pool.

Civic receptions for London cup winners now became something of a habit. West Ham had theirs the following year when they beat Arsenal with a Trevor Brooking header at Wembley – only about the third goal Brooking ever remembered getting with his head.

But Arsenal were just about physically and mentally exhausted by the time that final was played on May 10.

Between April 12 and May 1 Arsenal had met Liverpool four times in what seemed to be a never-ending semi-final series. After drawing 0-0 at Hillsborough and 1-1 twice after extra time at Villa Park, Arsenal at last made it through to the final with a 1-0 win in the third replay at Coventry thanks to a Brian Talbot goal.

At the same time Arsenal were advancing in the European Cup Winners Cup and were due to face Valencia in Brussels four days after the final.

A few weeks before the 1980 cup final Brian Clough wrote in an article, that "Trevor Brooking floats like a butterfly – and stings like one...". but it was Brooking that delivered the knockout blow to Arsenal heading home in the 13th minute. Paul Allen, at 17 years 256 days became the youngest player to have played in a Wembley final – and the youngest cup finalist for 101 years. He cried tears of joy at the end.

But unlike Liverpool who three years before had lost in the cup final and then gone on to win a prize in Europe, Arsenal were a spent force. Their long season had taken its toll and Valencia beat them on penalties to win the Cup Winners Cup four days later. Arsenal re-wrote the record books with their five finals between 1971 and 1980. Only the Wanderers in the 1870s and Newcastle United between 1905 and 1911 had ever appeared in so many finals in a shorter time-span. Pat Rice became the first, and so far only, man to play in five Wembley finals for the same team and Arsenal equalled Newcastle's record of 11 final appearances.

But for the next two years the other side of north London were going to be doing the crowing.

# REPLAY ON THURSDAY 1981-1983

IN 1978, just after the World Cup finals in Argentina, Tottenham pulled off one of the most audacious transfer coups in British soccer history when they signed the Argentinians Osvaldo Ardiles and Ricardo Villa from Huracan and Racing Club respectively. Ardiles had played in the World Cup winning team, while Villa had made a couple of appearances as Argentina fought their way to the final.

On the day he signed for Tottenham, Ardiles said, "my big ambition is to play for Tottingham (as he always pronounced it) in the cup final at Wembley". Three years later Ossie's dream came true.

Tottenham, in fact, played at Wembley seven times in 15 months between May 1981 and August 1982, but it was their performance in the replayed centenary final against Manchester City that lives brightest in the memory.

All the omens pointed to a Spurs victory. The year ended in a '1', and it was the Chinese Year of the Cockerel. It had been 14 years since their last cup final appearance, and apart from a difficult semi-final against their old cup rivals Wolves, which they won after a replay at Highbury with Villa scoring with a stunning 25-yard shot in their 3-0 win, their path to Wembley was a relatively smooth one. Their new strike force of Steve Archibald and Garth Crooks had scored 46 goals between them going into the final and, inspired by Ardiles and Glenn Hoddle in midfield and with the driving force of skipper Steve Perryman behind them, Tottenham, managed by the dour Yorkshireman Keith Burkinshaw, could match any team in the country on their day. But Manchester City would be no pushovers. They had also powered their way into the final with wins over Crystal Palace (4-0), Norwich (6-0) and Peterborough (1-0) setting them on their course. They took Everton apart in a sixth round replay in front of 52,000 at Maine Road and then reached Wembley by beating Ipswich 1-0 in the semi-final at Villa Park.

### Thinking of Europe

But while Burkinshaw had been building his team at Tottenham for almost three years, Manchester City had been transformed in half a season. The previous October, City chairman Peter Swales sacked manager Malcolm Allison and coach Tony Book – City's captain the last time they won the cup in 1969 – and four days later the Norwich manager John Bond moved to Maine Road.

In his first match in charge City lost 1-0 at home to Birmingham and were bottom of the table without a win in 12 matches. Curiously their revival started in their next match – a 3-1 win over Spurs. City were revitalised as Bond strengthened his side by signing Bobby McDonald and Tommy Hutchison from Coventry and the tenacious Gerry Gow from Bristol City. By the time of the cup final all thoughts of relegation had disappeared – now they were thinking of Europe.

The first match on a grey, overcast day was something of an anti-climax for both teams and supporters and ended in Wembley's first drawn final for 11 years. Tommy Hutchison scored with a header for City in the first half and then late in the game deflected a Glenn Hoddle free kick past Joe Corrigan for Spurs equaliser.

Not since Bert Turner in 1946 had the same player scored for both sides in the final. There was no breakthrough in extra time and so the teams would meet again in the first replay at Wembley the following Thursday.

One feature of that first match had been the substitution of Villa after 68 minutes and his long mournful walk back to the dressing room, reminiscent of another long slow walk taken by the Argentinian captain Antonio Rattin, sent off at Wembley playing against England in the 1966 World Cup quarter final. But Rattin never got another chance at Wembley. Villa did – and how he took it. The replay was only seven minutes old when Villa lashed in the opening goal to put Tottenham 1-0 up. But three minutes later City were level with a superb shot by Steve Mackenzie giving Tottenham's goalkeeper Milija Aleksic no chance. Today it is largely forgotten and rarely shown on television. But it was a goal good enough to win any match.

Five minutes after halftime, City took the

lead for the second time over the two games when Dave Bennett was sandwiched between two Tottenham defenders and referee Keith Hackett awarded a penalty. No penalty had ever been missed in a Wembley final – and Kevin Reeves ensured he was not going to be the first to do so, placing his kick wide of Aleksic.

It was now that Tottenham began to play their best football of the final and with 20 minutes left they drew level. Hoddle lofted a pass that caught the City players coming out and Archibald onside and moving in on goal. But he couldn't control it properly and the ball ran to Crooks who equalised.

**Place in History**

With 76 minutes played Ricky Villa not only played himself into Tottenham folklore but guaranteed himself a place in the history of the competition. It was the kind of goal that would look dazzling scored in a Sunday League parks match – but to decide the 100th Cup Final, under the floodlights in the first ever Wembley replay, it was as magical a moment as any in the history of the FA Cup.

The goal was begun by Tony Galvin who took a long ball out of the Spurs defence and found Villa with a 20-yard pass 35 yards from goal. He was a long way out and anyway the route to goal was well policed by City defenders. But Villa was not to be deterred. Inside him, Hoddle, and then Archibald were screaming for the ball. But the tall bearded Argentinian ignored them,

He closed in on the penalty area, with Garth Crooks stepping back out of his way. Then he quickened his pace, going past Tommy Caton and then swerving past Ray Ranson. He cut back inside, and beat the covering Caton and Ranson again. With Nicky Reid chasing back to cover and Corrigan and Caton converging on him, Villa still had control of the ball. At the precise moment Corrigan spread himself to smother the ball, Villa shot, the ball went through the goalkeeper's legs and into the net. Villa – who had just run 35 yards with the ball, then ran 60 yards without it – sprinting across to the Spurs bench in ecstacy. Manchester City were a beaten team and Spurs were cup holders for the sixth time in their sixth appearance, a new unbeaten record.

In 1951 and 1952 Newcastle won the cup, in 1961 and 1962 Spurs won it. And in 1982 Spurs again retained it. Their opponents in 1982 were Second Division Queens Park Rangers, managed by Terry Venables, who had played for Spurs when they won in 1967 and who would manage Spurs to victory in 1991.

But Tottenham took the field without the two Argentinians who had done so much to inspire the victory 12 months previously.

**Hot Favourites**

Tottenham had already played in one final at Wembley that season when they were beaten 3-1 in the League Cup Final by Liverpool, and in fact for most of the season they were chasing four trophies – the League Championship, the FA Cup, the European Cup Winners Cup and the League Cup.

But by the time they reached the cup final on May 22, it was the only trophy they still had a chance of capturing. A combination of the Falklands' War and Argentina's preparations for the 1982 World Cup finals meant that neither Ardiles or Villa played in the final. Ray Clemence, who joined Spurs from Liverpool the previous summer, was now in goal and Spurs started as the hot favourites.

But after a goalless 90 minutes the game went into extra time. Hoddle broke the deadlock with only 10 minutes of extra time remaining – and Terry Fenwick, later to become a Spurs player himself, headed the equaliser.

A Glenn Hoddle penalty after only six minutes of the replay settled the 1982 final. Hoddle, like the five Wembley penalty takers before him, converted his spot-kick, but the match never reached the heights attained in the 1981 replay.

The 1982 cup final also saw the start of an unhappy sequence, which prompted the FA to later change their rules in an attempt to prevent it happening again.

Three times in three years the captain of one of the finalists was suspended from the match. In 1982 the QPR captain Glenn Roeder played in the first match, but was suspended from the replay. In 1983 Steve Foster, the Brighton captain, was ruled out of the final, but played in the replay, while in 1984 Watford's skipper Wilf Rostron missed his team's match against Everton. In each case the team with the suspended skipper failed to win the cup.

After Spurs had won in 1961 and 1962, Manchester United followed them as winners in 1963. Now history was to repeat itself. Spurs' reign as cup-holders ended in a fifth round match at Everton who in turn lost to Manchester United, and it was United who went all the way to victory in 1983.

United had three survivors from the team that lost to Arsenal in 1979 – goalkeeper Gary Bailey and defenders Gordon McQueen and Arthur Albiston. They also now had Frank Stapleton, who played against them in 1979, leading their attack. With the England captain Bryan Robson, his international teammate Ray Wilkins and the Irish international teenager Norman Whiteside in their ranks, they were far too strong for Brighton and Hove Albion who ended the season relegated to the Second Division.

**Unorthodox Way**

United had only conceded one goal on the way to Wembley – against Arsenal in a 2-1 semi-final win at Villa Park, but Brighton had proved they could raise their game when it mattered. They beat Liverpool 2-1 at Anfield in the fifth round – the winning goal coming from Jimmy Case, for so long a Liverpool player.

Brighton flew high on the way to Wembley in another, more unorthodox way too. At the time their main sponsor was the airline company British Caledonian and they flew from Brighton to Wembley and back by helicopter.

Manchester United were well and truly brought down to earth too by the high-flying Seagulls when Gordon Smith headed Brighton ahead after only 14 minutes.

The Brighton fans, in keeping with the "inflatables" craze at the time, had a penchant for sporting huge outsize foam hands and thousands of these were raised in triumph as Wembley braced itself for yet another upset.

But United, who had lost in the League Cup final to Liverpool a few weeks previously, rallied and started to control the match. They deservedly equalised after 55 minutes through Frank Stapleton and went ahead with a wonderful curling shot from Ray Wilkins with 18 minutes to play. With only three minutes to go, and Brighton seemingly beaten, Gary Stevens saved them when he made it 2-2. But the greatest drama was still to come. There were only seconds left to play when Brighton got one last golden opportunity to win the match. Michael Robinson forced his way through the defence to set what looked like an easy chance for Smith. Surely he was going to score the winner.

The radio commentator thought so too, "...and Smith must score..". he said... but Smith didn't. Gary Bailey saved his shot with his legs and Manchester United were reprieved.

Smith played in six cup finals for Glasgow Rangers and in 1978 scored the winner against Celtic in the last minute of extra time in the Scottish League Cup. But south of the border, and especially on the South Coast it is that miss that has made him famous. Naturally, a Brighton fanzine was born entitled, "And Smith Must Score".

Smith recalls: "I remember going off at half-time and seeing my name on the scoreboard with the score at 1-0 and thinking to myself that if we were going to win it, it would have to stay like that. The underdogs only ever won 1-0 in the final.

"That would have been great. People said to me later, 'if only you had done the business at the end,' but these things happen. For me the main thing was to have taken part. It was the highlight of my career, despite playing in six cup finals for Rangers in Scotland".

And so for the third successive year, the cup final went to a replay. Brighton had their skipper Steve Foster back after suspension but they were never really in the game.

Two goals from Bryan Robson and another before the break from Norman Whiteside gave United the biggest half-time lead in a cup final since 1900. And a second-half penalty from the Dutchman Arnold Muhren – the third penalty in three years – was converted to give United a 4-0 victory, the biggest ever cup final win at Wembley.

Whiteside became the youngest player to score in a Wembley final and for one sprightly old man there was good cause to celebrate. On Sir Matt Busby's 74th birthday, United had won the cup for the fifth time .

# MERSEYSIDE AT WEMBLEY 1984-1989

IF SIR MATT BUSBY was the man who built United, then future England manager Graham Taylor was the man who put Watford on the footballing map – with more than a little help from his rock star chairman Elton John.

Elton, born Reginald Dwight just a stone's throw from Wembley in Pinner in 1947, was not the first member of his family to be connected with the cup final. In 1959 his cousin Roy Dwight was a member of the Nottingham Forest team which beat Luton 2-1 to win the cup.

Young Reg from Pinner grew up a Watford fan, but it wasn't until the mid-1970s when he was already established as one of the world's great rock stars that he began to get involved with his favourite club, now well established as Fourth Division also-rans.

Elton's masterstroke was persuading Graham Taylor to come to Vicarage Road as manager and between them they helped transform not only the team but the club as well. With the experience of Bertie Mee, the man who led Arsenal to the double in 1971, Watford had made rapid progress and in 1983 they finished second behind Liverpool in the title race.

Now they were in their first ever cup final. Their previous best in the cup was a semi-final appearance against Chelsea in 1970 which they lost 5-1.

But in the 1984 semi, Watford themselves were the hot favourites against Third Division Plymouth Argyle. They duly won that game 1-0 at Villa Park to face an Everton team who had also undergone something of a transformation.

The season had started poorly for Everton but once they signed the Scottish international striker Andy Gray from Wolves the previous November for £250,000, things began to happen at Goodison Park.

"That was the turning point of our season," remembered Everton manager Howard Kendall, "he set the whole place bubbling and gave the team's confidence a boost".

Like Tottenham in 1982 and Manchester United in 1983, Everton also reached the League Cup final a few weeks before playing in the cup final, and like Tottenham and United, Everton had lost to Liverpool. Everton though had gone down to Liverpool only after a replay at Maine Road. Now they were to go one better and win the cup for the first time since 1966. Goals from Graeme Sharp and Andy Gray gave Everton a deserved 2-0 victory. Elton, who had cried tears of emotion at the start of the aternoon, was left in tears at the end too... but he would be back, and so would Everton. He returned for a concert at the stadium on June 30 – Everton came back to play in the cup finals of 1985 and 1986 but lost both times.

Everton returned to Wembley the following year as league champions, looking for the first double since 1971 and also in the hunt for the never-achieved treble of English cup and league and European trophy in the same season.

In 1977 Liverpool won the league and the European Cup, but were beaten in the cup final by Manchester United, thus dashing their hopes of the treble. Now Manchester United were to do the same to Everton. Howard Kendall's side had stormed to their first championship for 15 years by finishing 13 points clear of the field. Three days before the cup final they won the European Cup Winners Cup final beating Rapid Vienna 3-1 in Rotterdam. For good measure they had played Manchester United three times already that season without losing and had beaten them 5-0 in the league the previous October.

This Everton side of Peter Reid and Paul Bracewell, Andy Gray and Kevin Ratcliffe, simply never knew when they were beaten. With five minutes left of their semi-final against Luton at Villa Park, Everton, who had not been beaten for 20 matches, were trailing 1-0. Then Kevin Sheedy drove in a free-kick to equalise and Derek Mountfield scored the winner in extra-time.

United had had a relatively easy passage to the semi-finals with wins over Bournemouth, Coventry, Blackburn and West Ham. But then came two titanic struggles with Liverpool, first at Goodison Park and then at Maine Road. Goals from Bryan Robson and Mark Hughes gave United a 2-1 win to spoil the possibility of the first all-Merseyside final – for a year at least.

So the two Lancashire giants converged on Wembley for what everyone hoped would be a classic between two of the finest teams in the country. And everyone needed something to revive their faith and hope in the sport. The previous week the Bradford fire disaster had claimed more than 50 lives.

### First Sending Off

But the match turned out to be a disappointment for the fans and an even greater one for Manchester United defender Kevin Moran. After 78 minutes referee Peter Willis of County Durham, a retired police inspector, sent Moran off for a late tackle on Reid. It was the first time in 116 Cup Final matches stretching back 113 years that anyone had been sent off. United were down to 10 men – and suddenly started playing like 20.

The game went into extra time and then with only 10 minutes to play, Norman Whiteside, still only 18, scored a cup final goal for the second time in three years. His long curling shot deceived Neville Southall in the Everton goal and United had achieved a famous, if muted, 1-0 victory. Moran had to wait several weeks before getting his winners' medal.

Eight of the United team, including substitute Mike Duxbury, had played in the winning team against Brighton two years previously, but a year later six Everton players were back at Wembley for their third successive Cup Final – Kevin Ratcliffe, Gary Stevens – whose namesake had played for Brighton – Derek Mountfield, Peter Reid, Trevor Steven and Graeme Sharp.

Only Arsenal had played in three successive Wembley finals before and they had only emerged as winners once. Everton had to overcome fairly formidable opposition to go one better than that. They had to beat the league champions and they happened to be Liverpool.

Liverpool had been through a difficult year. On May 29, 1985 their supporters had rioted before the European Cup final against Juventus at the Heysel Stadium in Brussels where 39 innocent people died, almost all of them Juventus fans. The incident brought worldwide condemnation for England and the English game. The FA withdrew all English clubs from European competition, UEFA later banned them as well, and the Heysel Stadium disaster coming as it did just 18 days after the Bradford fire, caused many people to question the state of the game.

The day after the tragedy, Liverpool announced that Kenny Dalglish was taking over from Joe Fagan as the club's player-manager, and it was Dalglish's inspiration as both a man and a player that helped Liverpool regain their self-respect.

At the start of the 1985-86 season though it looked as though the title race was going to be all over by Christmas and that Manchester United were going to win it. The cup holders opened the season with 10 straight wins. By the second week of January they were the only team that had topped the table all season, but then they started to falter.

### First All-Merseyside Final

Everton then led the standings in February and March, until Liverpool went top for the first time as late as March 31. But once there, they never left. If United started the season in invincible form, Liverpool ended it the same way, winning 11 of their last 12 matches, winning the last seven in a row and clinching the title with the only goal in a 1-0 win over Chelsea at Stamford Bridge. The scorer of the only goal – player-manager Kenny Dalglish.

So a week later, and for the first time since 1913 the teams that had finished first and second in the championship met in the cup final, the first all-Merseyside cup final, between Liverpool and Everton. It was not the first time the teams had met at Wembley though.

Their first meeting had come in the 1984 League Cup final which ended in a 0-0 draw and they had also met at Wembley in August 1984 in the Charity Shield which Everton won 1-0.

And now, after 57 minutes of what was dubbed 'The Friendly Final' it looked as though Everton were going to maintain their unbeaten record at Wembley against Liverpool. There had never been any segregation between the fans in derby matches at either Anfield or Goodison and now at Wembley the red and blue colours mixed into one another all around the ground.

Unlike in Manchester or London where familes are usually united behind either City or United or Spurs or Arsenal, in Liverpool, families are often divided in their support of Everton and Liverpoool.

Cars left Liverpool on the morning of the match and drove down the M6 and M1 with red scarves flying out of one window and blue ones out of the other. Fathers and sons, brothers and sisters went their separate ways at the top of Wembley Way... meeting back at the car park afterwards.

Just a year on from the Heysel disaster, more than 400 million people watching around the world in 40 countries got a different view of English soccer. The fans chanted in unison "Merseyside, Merseyside" and there was only a handful of arrests. A 40-a-side match between the fans in the stadium car park provided an interesting appetiser before the main event.

And for most of the first hour of the match it was the Everton fans who looked like celebrating. A mistake by Dalglish had allowed Peter Reid to feed Gary Lineker after 28 minutes and the England striker duly put Everton ahead.

### Destined to Make History

But suddenly, as so often happens in this story, the ghostly vision of Lord Kinnaird standing on his head floated across the decades – and turned this game upside down too.

As Hugh McIlvanney wrote in the following day's *Observer*: "Everton are obliged to believe that Liverpool were simply destined to make history at Wembley yesterday by becoming only the third club this century to complete the double of the League Championship and victory in the FA Cup final. How else can the losers rationalise a match in which they went a goal ahead and achieved an almost disdainful superiority for nearly an hour and yet finished the day comprehensively beaten and all but demoralised?"

Once Ian Rush had scored the equaliser after 57 minutes, Everton must have known the fates were against them. In the six years since he had joined Liverpool from Chester in April 1980 Rush had scored in 120 matches for Liverpool – and they had not lost any of them. This was Goalscoring Match No. 121 and they did not lose this one either. Further goals from Rush and the South African-born Craig Johnston finally sealed Liverpool's historic victory, while the architect of the whole performance had been the Danish brick outhouse, otherwise known as Jan Molby.

Dalglish became the first player-manager in history to take his side to the double. Everton had had their chances to win, but had been denied them. At the end Liverpool fans chanted, "we love you Everton, we do". It was small consolation.

In 1989 the two teams met in the final again. The 1986 final had been an emotional occasion played out against the memory of the Heysel Disaster the previous year, but cup final day in 1989 was to be unlike any other day in English soccer's history. Hopefully there will never be another day like it in the future.

### Hillsborough Disaster

On April 15, 1989 Liverpool were due to play Nottingham Forest for the second straight year in the cup semi-final at Hillsborough. In 1988 Liverpool beat Nottingham Forest 2-1 to reach the cup final where they lost to Wimbledon. Now a year later were back in the semi again, against Nottingham Forest at Hillsborough again.

In 1988 Liverpool came close to another double but Wimbledon ended those dreams with their unexpected victory in the cup final. Now there was more talk of another double. But it ended as the disaster at the Leppings Lane end of Hillsborough unfolded. Ultimately 96 lost their lives in the worst disaster in British sporting history.

The semi-final between Nottingham Forest and Liverpool had actually been in progress for six minutes but was immediately abandoned as the full horror of what was happening behind the wretched fences became known.

Liverpool did not play another match until May 3. The players and the relatives of the victims were united in a sorrow that not only enveloped the city but the entire nation. Anfield was turned into a shrine of remembrance with the penalty area at the Kop End covered in thousands and thousands of bouquets of flowers. It was moving, terrible, time.

The semi-final was replayed on May 7 at Old Trafford and there was only ever going to be one winner. Liverpool beat Nottingham Forest 3-1 and would play Everton in the final.

But a major decision had to be taken – whether or not to postpone the final to the start of the following season, or whether in fact, to play it at all. In the end, the FA, in consultation with Liverpool, decided the match should go ahead as scheduled. The programme for the match on May 20 carried a black-bordered message from Bert Millichip, the chairman of the FA, who wrote: "In years to come the memory of today's match, and in a sense the importance attached to its outcome, will pale to insignificance when compared to the memory of the day when 95 supporters (one more died later) lost their lives at the semi-final tie at Hillsborough.

"The Football Association was faced with the choice of calling off the competition or continuing in what clearly would be difficult circumstances. We believe that we made the right decision, not only as a memorial to those who died, but as a means of providing concrete support for those left to grieve their passing".

**Force Extra Period**

John Aldridge gave Liverpool the lead after four minutes of the 1989 final, but the match really came to life in a brief period just before the end of normal time and just after the start of extra-time.

First, Everton substitute Stuart McCall equalised in the 89th minute to force the extra period. Then Ian Rush, who came on as a substitute for John Aldridge, made it 2-1 in the 94th minute, but eight minutes later McCall equalised again to become the first substitute to score twice in the cup final. He did not keep that unique record for long though because two minutes later Rush turned the Everton defence and fired past Neville Southall for the winner.

So Liverpool had won the cup – and six days later they met Arsenal in the championship decider. Liverpool had not lost in the league since New Year's Day and only needed a point, or at the very worst, a 1-0 home defeat, and they would be champions.

As if the nerves of all concerned with Liverpool had not been stretched and jangled enough over the previous six weeks, it was Arsenal who carried the championship crown out of Liverpool's grasp and back to London for the first time since they themselves won the double in 1971 when Michael Thomas's goal, with virtually the last kick of the last game of the season, gave Arsenal a 2-0 win.

Arsenal became the second London team to deny Liverpool the double in little over a year. Twelve months previously Liverpool went to Wembley as champions and the hottest favourites since Leeds in 1973 to win the cup against unfancied opposition.

And there were not many who fancied Wimbledon in any shape or form that spring. The Dons had risen from Non-League football to the First Division in only 11 seasons and in the main they had got there playing 'Route One' soccer – a rather less sophisticated brand of the POMO – position of maximum opportunity – system employed by Watford earlier in the decade. Basically it involved a big boot upfield, cutting out the pretty stuff in the middle with the intention of causing mayhem in the opposing defence. By and large it worked for the Dons whose team spirit was based on an "all for one and one for all" credo that really did bring it some unlikely victories.

They did not have many fans, and they did not have all that many admirers either. On the morning of the match *The Times* carried an hysterical headline that suggested the world as we know it would end if Wimbledon won the cup.

**Valid Goal**

The condemnation of Wimbledon's playing style was as biased and uninformed as it could be, with much of Fleet Street fawning pathetically to Liverpool. Wimbledon might not have been pretty to watch, but they deserved their famous victory.

They were lucky when Peter Beardsley had a valid goal ruled out by an impatient referee who blew too quickly after a trip when Beardsley clearly had maintained advantage, but apart from that the Dons made their own luck.

Lawrie Sanchez scored with a well-worked header shortly before half-time and even when Liverpool had a golden opportunity to pull themselves back into the match, they blew it. In the 61st minute the referee Brian Hill ruled that Clive Goodyear had tripped Aldridge in the penalty box – but TV replays clearly showed afterwards that Goodyear had played the ball and not touched the man.

But a penalty it was. All seven cup final penalties taken at Wembley had been converted. No-one had missed a cup final penalty since 1913. Aldridge, who usually put his penalties to the goalkeeper's left did so again. Dave Beasant, the first goalkeeper ever to captain a cup final side, had studied Aldridge's spot-kicks on video and knew just where this one was going. He dived low to his left and beat the ball away.

Half-an-hour later Beasant went up to get the cup. Wimbledon were the 42nd team to have won it. But there was a sad postscript to Wimbledon's victory. Just over a year later, on July 15, 1989, Laurie Cunningham, who came on as a second half substitute for Alan Cork, was killed in a car crash in Spain.

Wimbledon followed Coventry as a new name on the old trophy. In 1987 Coventry ended their 104-year wait for a major honour when they ended Tottenham's 100 per cent record in the cup final.

### Sartorial Ineptitude

Coventry had advanced to Wembley with wins over Bolton (3-0), Manchester United (1-0), Stoke (1-0), Sheffield Wednesday (3-1) and Leeds, then in the Second Division, who put up a determined fight in the semi-final at Hillsborough before Coventry won 3-2 in extra-time. The team had been put together by manager John Sillett and managing director George Curtis, who played more than 500 matches for Coventry in the 1950s and 1960s. Apart perhaps from Cyrille Regis, it was a team without stars, but with an indefatigable spirit which they were to prove conclusively on the afternoon of May 16, 1987.

Their opponents were Tottenham who had won all their seven cup finals. But from the moment they stripped off their tracksuits they could have been forgiven for thinking this was not going to be their day. Some of the players had shirts with their sponsor's name on the front – and others did not.

Still, Tottenham quickly forgot about their sartorial ineptitude and took the lead after only two minutes with a superb header from Clive Allen whose father Les had been in the Spurs team when they won the double in 1961. Clive Allen had briefly played against Spurs for QPR in the 1982 final but came off injured early in the match. That this was his 49th goal of the season. It seemed only a matter of time before he would get his 50th that afternoon. But it never came.

Instead Coventry pulled level through Dave Bennett seven minutes later. Bennett, like Allen, had played against Spurs in a cup final and lost when he was in the Manchester City team in 1981. Bennett would get his revenge later that afternoon by running round Wembley with the cup.

Tottenham had not gained their cup reputation stretching back 86 years for no reason. They had three survivors from the team that won the cup in 1982 – goalkeeper Ray Clemence playing in his fifth cup final, Chris Hughton and Glenn Hoddle, while Ardiles, Hughton and Hoddle had all been in the 1981 cup-winning team.

Also in the side was Clive's cousin Paul, the youngest Wembley cup finalist when he played with West Ham in 1980 and the England internationals Chris Waddle, Gary Mabbutt and Steve Hodge. And it was Mabbutt who put Tottenham back in front shortly before halftime with a mis-hit pass that took a deflection off Brian Kilcline on the way into the goal.

Hoddle, the most skillful player England had produced in a generation, was playing in his last match for Tottenham after a 12-year career at White Hart Lane but had a poor game, tightly marshalled by Lloyd McGrath. Tottenham may have been leading, but they were never truly in control and when Keith Houchen equalised for Coventry midway through the second half with a fabulous diving header, the writing was on the wall for Spurs, even if it was not on most of their shirts.

The final moved into extra time and was decided six minutes later when a speculative cross-cum-shot from Lloyd McGrath took a deflection off Mabbutt and flew over Clemence into the back of the Spurs goal. History could not save Spurs now and Coventry held on for the final 24 minutes to take the cup back to the midlands for the first time since West Bromwich Albion 19 years previously.

# A BRAND NEW BALL GAME 1990-1995

IF THE first-time successes of Coventry City in 1987 and Wimbledon in 1988 suggested the competition was about to become a far more egalitarian affair than ever before, it was an illusion.

It almost goes without saying that new names will be added to the list of the 42 winners over time, but by the end of the 1980s and beginning of the 1990s the most powerful clubs were beginning to flex their financial muscles and demanding more power, more say in running the game – and a bigger slice of the riches available.

The successful way they have accomplished their aims are all too obvious today. The Premier League itself, set up in 1992, has itself splintered into a handful of clubs who can realistically win the title and those whose ambitions are less grand. And FA Cup finals over the last decade and a half or so have also mirrored this trend.

Indeed Arsenal's late-late win over Sheffield Wednesday in 1993 represents another turning point in the story of the FA Cup. The day after Arsenal's 2-1 victory every headline focused on Andy Linighan's winning header in the 119th minute of extra-time – the latest cup final goal ever scored.

Sheffield Wednesday had also lost to Arsenal in the League Cup final a few weeks earlier as the two clubs became the first, and so far only ones to play each other in both major domestic finals in the same season. Arsenal also became the first club to win the League and the FA Cup 'double' in the same season.

### Turbulent Period

But what was perhaps not fully realised at the time was that Arsenal's success – over a club looking to lift the FA Cup for the first time since 1935 – was a significant nail in the coffin of the less glamorous clubs looking for glory in the FA Cup.

It also marked the beginning of a new chapter in English football with the introduction of the Premier League the previous August. Along with the increasing financial rewards and prestige offered by the Champions League and the mis-management of the FA Cup competition later in the decade, the competition was entering the most turbulent period in its long history.

This new ball game began rolling in the 1992-93 season when the elite clubs took their places in the Premier League and the European Champions Cup metamorphosised into the European Champions' League.

At the end of this season of change, Manchester United emerged as English champions for the first time since 1967 and Arsenal triumphed in the FA Cup to set the pattern for much of the following decade. The game was changing, the big clubs were becoming more powerful and the FA Cup was in real danger of being over-shadowed by the push for premier league and Champions League cash and glory.

### Turning Point

It is a myth to think there was ever a "golden age" when smaller clubs regularly triumphed in the cup – but there was a time when the competition was far more open than it now appears to be – and a look at the winners since the late 1980s proves this age has passed – at least for now and possibly for the foreseeable future.

In the 1970s and 1980s clubs like Fulham, Southampton and West Ham, all made it to the final and were capable of winning it from outside the top flight as Southampton did in 1976 and the Hammers four years later. It appeared then that the gap might be closing between the old first and second divisions.

But the creation of the Premier League blew that notion away. Wimbledon were the last 'first-time' winners – in 1988. And the last club from outside the top flight to get to the final were Sunderland in 1992 who were easily beaten 2-0 by Liverpool. That was Liverpool's second win in four seasons, while the other two winners immediately before the Premier League began were Manchester United (1990) and Tottenham (1991), who set a new record with their eighth win in the competition with a 2-1 win over Nottingham Forest. Little wonder that many say today that the romance has gone out of the cup. It has in some way, but there is plenty still there just under the surface.

United's win in 1990 marked a turning point in the club's history. Alex Ferguson had been in charge at Old Trafford for four years without a trophy, but despite calls from impatient fans for him to be sacked, the board kept faith with the ambitious Scotsman. He has duly repaid them for their trust in those early difficult years in ways they could only have dreamed of, but history might have taken a very different turn if Crystal Palace had held on to their 3-2 lead for another 18 minutes against Manchester United in the 1990 cup final.

A Mark Hughes equaliser seven minutes from time – not the last time he would do that for United at Wembley – earned United a 3-3 draw and they went on to win their first trophy under Ferguson when a Lee Martin goal gave them a 1-0 win in the replay five days later.

Twelve months later there was another familiar name on the trophy when Tottenham Hotspur won for a then-record eighth time. Although Spurs have been among the also-rans for much of the last decade, that victory was no less important to them because at the time they were facing the very real prospect of bankruptcy.

**Stupendous Free Kick**

In April 1991 Tottenham and Arsenal made history by playing in the first FA Cup semi-final at Wembley with Spurs winning 3-1 then returning the following month to win the cup with a 2-1 extra time win over Nottingham Forest.

It escaped no-one's attention that the year ended in '1' again, although for Paul Gascoigne, the brilliant, yet indisciplined, midfield genius whose stupendous free kick had set up Spurs victory in the semi-final, the day ended in hospital after his infamous challenge on Forest's Gary Charles. For Tottenham's captain Gary Mabbutt the final was especially poignant. It was his own goal that gave Coventry their 3-2 win in 1987 – now in 1991 his pressure had forced Forest's Des Walker to head into his own goal for Spurs' winner.

That match was the last first class game Gascoigne played in Tottenham's colours, and for a while it looked like being one of the last matches that Tottenham Hotspur might ever play. Faced with debts of around £20 million, they drifted close to extinction before being taken over by Terry Venables, their former manager and player and Alan Sugar, a wealthy businessman.

In 1992 Liverpool returned to Wembley after becoming the first side to reach the final by winning a penalty shoot-out in the semi-final against Second Division Portsmouth. Liverpool then had an almost routine 2-0 victory against Second Division Sunderland in the final, the Wearsiders unable to repeat the kind of heroics that brought their predecessors their famous win against Leeds in 1973. Liverpool won with goals from Michael Thomas, the player who denied Liverpool the league and cup double in 1989, and Ian Rush, whose fifth cup final goal was an all-time record. Their captain Mark Wright became the first man to hold up the new FA Cup after the victory – an exact replica of the trophy made in 1911.

In fact since Wimbledon's unlikely win over Liverpool only six different clubs won the FA Cup in the following 14 seasons while the first ten years of the premier league produced just five different winners: Arsenal (1993, 1998 and 2002), Manchester United (1994, 1996 and 1999), Chelsea (1997 and 2000), Everton (1995) and Liverpool (2001).

Never in the history of the competition had 10 successive seasons produced so few different winning teams. Even the first 10 competitions between 1872 and 1881, when the Wanderers won five times, produced six different winners – the Wanderers and five others.

And as if further proof was needed that the cup was losing its romance, four of the five clubs to win in the last few years have also reached the final and lost, Everton the only club to just reach the final once and win it.

Chelsea were beaten in 1994 and 2002, Manchester United in 1995, Liverpool in 1996 and Arsenal in 2001. All the other teams beaten in the same period were Premier League clubs too: Sheffield Wednesday (1993), Middlesbrough (1997), Newcastle United (1998 and 1999) and Aston Villa (2000).

**No Favours**

Arguably, none of this matters because the best teams in the land have traditionally done well in the competition and the true romantic cup tales have usually come in the earlier rounds anyway. No-one who plays for, or supports Mansfield Town or Hull City truly believes their club will win the FA Cup – but that will never stop them arguing that it is a possibility – while the chance of knocking out Manchester United, Arsenal, Spurs, Liverpool or Chelsea in the third round, is theoretically at least, something that can happen any old year. And sometimes does. But in other ways this polarisation of success, plus the demolition of Wembley, the abolition of multiple replays, and the irresistible pull of the Champions' League for the big clubs, has had a negative impact on the competition.

The FA also did themselves no favours either by tinkering with the format of the competition in the 1999-2000 season when the third round was played before Christmas – or when Manchester United were allowed to pull out of the FA Cup in the same season to take part in the inaugural Club World Championship in Brazil as part of some half-baked plan that this would curry favour with FIFA and help England secure the right to stage the 2006 World Cup finals. Those blunders harmed the integrity of the competition far more than the fact that Arsenal, United, Chelsea and Liverpool have dominated it for much of the past decade, but all those ingredients together have taken more than a little gloss off the trophy.

**Most Dramatic Winners**

But in this lies the greatest irony of all. When you are a fan and you are watching your team play for a place in the next round defending a one goal lead with five minutes to go -- whether the next round happens to be the first round proper or the final itself, your heart races like at no other match – and all you want is for the whistle to go and for your team's name to be in the draw for the next stage. That is the true magic of the cup and probably nothing will take that away.

Even though some of the romance may have diminished after the formation of the Premier League in 1992-93, the drama did not – and Arsenal won the FA Cup in 1993 with the latest and one of the most dramatic victories ever.

Arsenal began their successful campaign at Non-League Yeovil, a good omen for the Gunners despite Yeovil's giant-killing reputation.

When Arsenal won the first of their League and FA Cup doubles in 1971, they began their cup campaign with a 3-0 win in Somerset – and history repeated itself in January 1993 when an Ian Wright hat-trick secured Arsenal a 3-1 win back at The Huish. Still, the Gunners were taking nothing for granted before the match. Their previous seven league games had produced five defeats and two draws and their shock defeat at Wrexham at the same stage the previous season was still fresh in their minds. As skipper Tony Adams said the day before the game: "We are all well aware of the stick we will get if things go wrong at Yeovil. Nobody will ever forget the defeat at Wrexham and we certainly don't intend to let the same thing happen again". In the event Wright had put Arsenal three goals clear by the 68th minute. The Gunners were on their way to Wembley.

And so too were Sheffield Wednesday – and for that matter, Sheffield United and Spurs. While Arsenal progressed to the last four with wins over Leeds, Nottingham Forest and Ipswich, Sheffield Wednesday had acquired the stomach for a cup battle too. In 1991 they won promotion from the old second division and beat Manchester United 1-0 to win the League Cup. Two seasons later, manager Trevor Francis guided them back into the League Cup final – and also into their first FA Cup final since their heartbreaking loss to Everton in 1966. FA Cup wins over Cambridge United, Sunderland, Southend and Derby County saw them through to the last four along with Sheffield United, Spurs and Arsenal.

Spurs and Arsenal had of course met at Wembley in the 1991 semi-final – at the time regarded as a one-off. But once they were drawn together again in 1993 and with the two Sheffield clubs meeting in the other semi, playing both matches at Wembley was the only logical decision the FA could make.

Sheffield Wednesday sealed their place in the final first when they beat Sheffield United 2-1 after extra time on the Saturday afternoon. The following day Arsenal avenged their 1991 defeat when a Tony Adams header gave them a 1-0 win over Tottenham.

**Bitter-Sweet Afternoon**

Arsenal and Sheffield Wednesday returned to Wembley just two weekends after the FA Cup semi-finals for the League Cup final on what turned out to be a bitter-sweet afternoon for Arsenal's Steve Morrow. He scored Arsenal's winner in their 2-1 win over the Yorkshire side – but then broke his arm when Tony Adams dropped him in the post-match celebrations. That fracture kept him out of the cup final itself a month later and, more significantly for the Ulsterman, curtailed his long-term career at Highbury where he never fully established himself in the team again.

But he did make one unique contribution to cup folklore. Presented with his League Cup winners' medal before the start of the FA Cup final, he remains the only player ever to be presented with a winner's medal before kickoff on cup final day.

The first match was a poor one, petering

out at 1-1, Ian Wright heading Arsenal ahead and David Hirst replying for Wednesday. The teams returned the following Thursday and until the dying seconds of that replay it seemed the FA Cup final would be decided on penalties for the first time.

Ian Wright, almost inevitably, had scored for Arsenal in the first half. Chris Waddle equalised with a deflected shot after 68 minutes, and the stalemate lasted until the very last minute of extra time. Then, with seconds left to play and the first ever penalty shoot-out looming, Andy Linighan, who had spent much of his Highbury career in the reserves and much of this match nursing a broken nose, headed the winner from a corner to take the cup back to Highbury for the first time for 14 years.

### New Chapter

The victory not only heralded the start of a new chapter in the saga of the competition, but it also marked the end of an era for Arsenal with David O'Leary, the only survivor of their 1979 FA Cup winning team, coming on as a substitute to make his record-extending 719th and final match for the club. Manager George Graham also savoured the moment, as he became the 13th man to win the cup as both a player and manager – and just the fourth to do so with the same club.

In contrast to the 1993 final which was so evenly balanced, there was never any doubt about the outcome the following year when Manchester United crushed Chelsea 4-0 to become the sixth English club to win the double. It was the biggest winning margin since United had beaten Brighton 4-0 in the 1983 replay – and the biggest win in the final itself since Bury beat Derby County 6-0 in 1903.

Arsenal had surprisingly crashed out 3-1 in a replayed fourth round tie at Highbury to that scourge of the cup holders, Bolton, but no-one could stop United as they reached the sixth round without conceding a goal after successively more emphatic victories over Sheffield United (1-0), Norwich (2-0) and Wimbledon (3-0). Charlton were brushed aside 3-1 in the quarter-finals leaving United to meet Oldham, who they had beaten at the same stage after a replay in 1990, in one semi-final.

Chelsea, emerging as a serious force under former Tottenham favourite Glenn Hoddle, despatched Barnet (4-0), the previous season's runners-up Sheffield Wednesday (3-1 after a draw), Oxford United (2-1) and Wolves (1-0) to reach the semi-finals for the first time in 24 years. Their opponents Luton were back in the last four for the third time in 10 years, but only ever had an outside hope of reaching their first final since 1959.

The FA decided, to not altogether universal acclaim, that both semi-finals would again take place at Wembley and Chelsea duly sealed their place in the cup final first with Gavin Peacock scoring both their goals in a 2-0 win over Luton on Saturday, April 9. One day later and Oldham thought they were heading for the cup final for the first time in their history.

### Momentary Lapse

A week previously Oldham battling, as it turned out, unsuccessfully against relegation, had narrowly lost 3-2 to Manchester United at Old Trafford in the league, and six days later at Wembley they again made a mockery of their poor league form. Neither side had produced a goal after 90 minutes and they remained deadlocked until the first minute of the second period of extra time when fullback Neil Pointon scored his first goal of the season to put Oldham ahead. It stayed that way until 40 seconds before the end when Mark Hughes took advantage of a momentary lapse in the Oldham defence to volley in a spectacular equaliser.

Three days later Pointon scored again for Oldham in the replay – but goals by Denis Irwin, against his former club, Andrei Kanchelskis, Bryan Robson and Ryan Giggs saw United comfortably through to their second final of the season.

A few weeks earlier United had been chasing a league, FA Cup and League Cup treble but that dream died when Aston Villa, managed by Ron Atkinson, United's FA Cup-winning manager of 1983 and 1985, surprisingly beat United 3-1 in the League Cup final.

That was one of only five domestic defeats United suffered all season. And two of those had been inflicted by Chelsea who had beaten United 1-0 at both Old Trafford at Stamford Bridge during the league campaign and who United now met in the FA Cup final on May 14, 1994.

Although it had been a season of almost unremitting joy for United on the field, it was marred by sadness off it. On January 20, Sir Matt Busby, aged 84 died after a long illness, just four short months before they finally won the double for the first time – something the Munich air disaster denied his Busby Babes the chance of achieving in the 1950s. But there was no doubt he was leaving the club he built in safe hands.

Alex Ferguson's men survived a scare after 26 minutes when Peacock, who scored the only goal in both of Chelsea's 1-0 league wins over United, shot against the crossbar – but Chelsea – with player-manager Glenn Hoddle one of the substitutes, could not take advantage of a jittery United defence when it mattered. Hoddle's influence might have changed the game but by the time he came on with 22 minutes left it was too late.

United finally wore Chelsea down and they struck three goals in nine minutes after an hour's play on a miserable overcast and rainy afternoon.

Two of them were penalties from the incomparable French midfielder Eric Cantona, who became the first man ever to score two penalties in the final. His goals after 60 and 66 minutes finally put United in command, while Mark Hughes took advantage of a mistake to make it 3-0 after 69 minutes and substitute Brian McClair added the fourth in stoppage time.

The victory crowned one of the greatest seasons in United's history as they equalled Arsenal's record of 12 cup final appearances, equalled Tottenham's record of eight FA Cup wins and took Ferguson's haul of trophies at Old Trafford to six in five seasons. Mark Hughes scored in all four matches United played at Wembley during the season including the Charity Shield game against Arsenal. They may have missed out on the domestic treble – but a far more notable treble was waiting for them before the end of the decade. Chelsea, too, would later have their place in the sun. But that afternoon Wembley belonged to United.

### Without Key Players

United returned a year later too but despite Ferguson's men starting the 50th post-war final as 7-4 on favourites, Everton did have cause for some optimism. United were without three key players: Eric Cantona, Andrei Kanchelskis and Andy Cole. Their talismanic Frenchman Cantona had been banned since his infamous kung-fu kick attack on a fan at Selhurst Park the previous January while Kanchelskis was injured and Cole, signed for a then-British record fee of £7million pounds from Newcastle in January, was cup-tied.

Twelve months previously United's victory over Chelsea secured them the double, but they had been deposed as champions a week before the final by Blackburn – and now Everton were to complete a remarkable season of their own by wresting the FA Cup from their grasp.

The fact Everton were in the final at all was a major achievement for Joe Royle, who took over at Goodison the previous November after Everton had made the worst start in their history drawing four and losing eight of their opening 12 league matches. Royle had taken Oldham to within 40 seconds of the cup final seven months earlier before losing to United. But not even he could have imagined how he would avenge that defeat by the end of the season. Gradually his team began to improve, but even so, by the time of the third round in January, Everton were only 20th in the table with only Leicester and Ipswich below them.

Still a 1-0 win over First Division Derby County put them on their way and they reached the semi-finals without conceding a goal against Bristol City (1-0), Norwich City (5-0) and Newcastle United (1-0).

United, perhaps never quite reaching their usual heights without Cantona's magic, were still far too good for almost everyone else and advanced almost effortlessly to the semi-finals with wins over Sheffield United (2-0), Wrexham (5-2), Leeds (3-1) and QPR (2-0).

### FA Cup Ban

So the penultimate stage was set with Everton meeting Tottenham in one semi-final at Elland Road and Manchester United facing Crystal Palace at Villa Park. If Everton were a surprise semi-finalist – at least based on their early season form – then Tottenham's place in the last four was even more incredible as at one point they had actually been banned from taking part in the 1994-95 FA Cup competition.

In June 1994, in the heaviest punishment ever handed out by the FA, Spurs had been fined £600,000, deducted 12 Premier League points from the start of the following season and banned from the FA Cup for a season because of "financial irregularities" involving loans to players under a previous administration at White Hart Lane.

On appeal the 12 point deduction was reduced to six and the fine increased to £1.5 million pounds – but the FA Cup ban stayed. Tottenham chairman Alan Sugar then took the case to an independent arbitration panel, arguing against the punishment and battling as hard as he could to get Spurs reinstated into the cup. Eventually he got his way – to a storm of protest from an angry media.

The case went on for almost six months and when the draw for the third round was made at the beginning of December 1994, Spurs' place in the competition was still uncertain. Famously, or infamously, depending on your point of view, FA chief executive Graham Kelly declared "Bye or Tottenham Hotspur" when Spurs' number was drawn out of the bag.

### Strange Feeling

A moment later Altrincham were paired with Spurs. What it meant was this: If Spurs won the appeal they would play the non-leaguers at White Hart Lane in the third round on the first weekend of January. If they lost it, Altrincham would go through to round four. Graham Heathcote, Altrincham's assistant manager, summed up the confusion. "It was a strange feeling to come out of the bag against Tottenham, or with a bye," he said. "It's left us in limbo, but we'd much prefer to play them from a football and financial point of view".

The following week Tottenham were duly re-instated. Fleet Street was furious and accused the FA of bungling their initial judgement against Spurs. As *The Times* put it: "The lawyers hired by Alan Sugar were able to drive a coach and horses through statutes framed half-a-century ago, a time when neither the money now swilling around in the pockets of chairmen, nor the ruthless attitudes of winning at all costs prevailed in what is still called a sport".

Henry Winter in the Daily Telegraph wrote: "Spurs are on their way to Wembley; the FA's gone and done it again. A club forever associated with great FA Cup results achieved another knockout success yesterday, trouncing Lancaster Gate (after extra time). The Guardian said: "If Spurs win the FA Cup, their chairman Alan Sugar, should lead the players up to collect it".

And they nearly did. Inspired by German star Jürgen Klinsmann, Spurs duly played and beat Altrincham 3-0 and went all the way to the semi-finals with astonishing away wins over Southampton (6-2 at The Dell in a fifth round replay) and 2-1 over Liverpool at Anfield in the quarter-finals setting up their last four clash with Everton at Elland Road. But Everton succeeded where the FA failed. They removed Spurs from the FA Cup with an emphatic 4-1 win, with the Nigerian Daniel Amokachi coming on as a 70$^{th}$ minute substitute to score twice in the last eight minutes and seal Everton's place.

With Everton secure in the final, Manchester United and Crystal Palace kicked off at Villa Park to decide who would meet them. But this semi-final was marred by murder off the field and thuggery on it.

### Savage Attack

Bad blood had simmered between rival Palace and United fans since Eric Cantona's attack on a Palace fan after being sent off against the Londonders at Selhurst Park at the end of January. Cantona was originally jailed and later given a lesser sentence for the attack as well as being banned from playing for eight months, and the clubs clash in the semi-finals was their first since the incident.

Before the kickoff rival fans had been drinking together at the New Fullbrook pub in Walsall, but taunts over Cantona sparked a savage attack by United fans on Palace supporters just as the Palace fans were leaving the pub to board their coach for the match. After what many eye-witnesses described as "savage fighting and total carnage" one Palace fan, 35-year-old Paul Nixon from Surrey, was dead, another was seriously injured, four fans were taken to hospital and 50 detectives were involved in a murder investigation.

The match went ahead as scheduled ending in a 2-2 draw after Palace had led twice – and the replay took place back at Villa Park three days later. Managers Alex Ferguson of United and Alan Smith of Palace called for calm from players and supporters before the match and both teams and officials lined up for a minute's silence as a mark of respect to the murdered fan before the kickoff.

Villa Park was less than half-full for the replay with only 17,000 fans present after the Palace club had asked their fans to stay away from the game in deference to the murdered fan. But the 17,000 who did turn up saw a dreadful, cynical game, littered with fouls, five yellow cards, two red cards and a second half brawl between the players, sparked by Roy Keane.

Already 2-0 ahead and coasting towards the final thanks to headers from Steve Bruce and Gary Pallister, Keane stamped on Palace's prone skipper Gareth Southgate who had caught Keane's ankles with a late, lunging tackle. Keane, who had had stitches put in a gash in the ankle at half-time, was immediately shown the red card by referee David Elleray but within seconds Palace players went for him.

The first to arrive was Darren Patterson, who lunged at the Irishman's throat, sending him crashing into an advertising hoarding. Patterson was then sent off for his trouble. Keane was banned for three matches and despite calls for him to be banned for the final, he was there at Wembley for United's record 13th cup final appearance five weeks later.

**Keeping it in Perspective**

But there was to be no happy ending to the 1994-95 season for United and their fans. A 30th minute header from Everton striker Paul Rideout was the only goal of the game and brought Everton, inspired by a superb performance by Swede Anders Limpar among others, their fifth FA Cup final success and also avenged their 1985 final defeat to United. It was something of a double triumph fot the city of Liverpool too. For the first time the FA Cup had a sponsor, and Littlewoods Pools, based in Liverpool, expressed their delight after the first year of their £14m four-year sponsorship.

For manager Joe Royle the moment was particularly sweet. As a 19-year-old he had been in the Everton side beaten in the 1968 final by West Brom and had twice lost to United in the semi-finals while at Oldham. But it was left to one of Everton's all-time heroes, goalkeeper Neville Southall, to keep it all in perspective.

After yet another great performance for Everton which included a double-save from Paul Scholes near the end, Southall missed the celebration party afterwards, going home immediately after the match to have a night out with his wife and daughter instead. "When you've been with these lads as long as I have, you'd want to go home," he joked afterwards.

For Alex Ferguson, left to rue the loss of United's title and the cup, it was no laughing matter. "The Cantona situation cost us everything," he said afterwards, "it hit us very hard". But 12 months later, Ferguson would have much to thank the Frenchman for.

# THE CUP GOES CONTINENTAL 1996-1997

ERIC CANTONA returned after his ban for Manchester United's home league match against Liverpool on October 1, 1995. During his eight month absence United had lost both the league title and the FA Cup to finish runners-up in both competitions.

It took him exactly 67 seconds to mark his comeback in style by spinning in a high cross from the left for Nicky Butt to lift the ball over David James to score. The Frenchman got himself on the scoresheet after 70 minutes when he made it 2-2 from the penalty spot, and, as the now defunct *Today* newspaper saw it: "Old Trafford's Theatre of Dreams was turned into a temple of worship. For the United faithful this was the second coming and Eric, The Messiah, had not disappointed".

Prophetic words indeed for 'Le Roi' was about to lead United from the desert of failure in 1995 to the promised land of glorious success in 1996 when they became the first English club to win the FA Cup and league double for a second time.

For much of the season Kevin Keegan's exciting Newcastle United side had set the pace in the title race and by the end of January had established a 12-point lead over Alex Ferguson's side.

The turning point came at St James' Park on March 4 when the Reds became the first team to beat Newcastle at home all season with Cantona scoring the winner in their 1-0 win. That narrowed the gap at the top from seven points to four – and in the end a thrilling race for the title saw Manchester United finish four points clear.

A key feature of their run-in was Cantona's astonishing goalscoring record – not exactly prolific, but absolutely lethal. Following the 1-0 win over Newcastle, United then drew 1-1 with QPR before beating Arsenal 1-0 and Spurs 1-0. Cantona was the only scorer in every match. He scored for the fifth successive match with a penalty in a 3-2 win over Manchester City and then got the only goal in the 1-0 win over Coventry City. His single match-winning or equalising goals alone secured United 16 premier league points in the run-in.

He was also finding the net regularly in the FA Cup as well as Manchester progressed to Wembley for the third successive year – a feat only Arsenal (1978-79-80) and Everton (1984-85-86) had previously managed.

**Rich in Quality Football**

In fact, the only round in which he did not score was in a classic semi-final against Chelsea at Villa Park where United came from behind to beat Glenn Hoddle's side 2-1. It was a match rich in quality football and intrigue. Ruud Gullit, who would make FA Cup history of his own a little more than a year later, put Chelsea ahead after converting a cross from ex-United legend Mark Hughes after 35 minutes – but two goals in four minutes early in the second half from Andy Cole and David Beckham turned the match United's way.

Standing in the way of United achieving a second double in three seasons on May 11, 1996 were Liverpool – who had not only finished third but had drawn and beaten United in the league campaign.

Liverpool started on the cup trail with a 7-0 demolition of Third Division Rochdale in the third round and then saw off Shrewsbury (4-0), Charlton (2-1) and Leeds United (3-0) before beating Aston Villa 3-0 in their semi-final at Old Trafford.

Today, Liverpool are mainly remembered for the white suits they wore before the 1996 cup final kicked off rather than for anything they did on the pitch. A much-hyped match turned out to be a poor one which seemed to be grinding interminably towards extra time before newly crowned Footballer of the Year Eric Cantona produced one absolutely brilliant moment of genius to win the game and a double double for United and crown his comeback season in the best possible way.

With 85 minutes played Beckham sent over an out-swinging corner which Liverpool goalkeeper David James fumbled. The ball fell to Cantona on the edge of the penalty area, who, in an instant, re-positioned his body to crack a swerving right-footed volley through a crowd of players and into the back of the net. 1-0 to General De Goals. Liverpool were beaten. United, in a record 14th final had won the cup for a record ninth time.

It was Cantona's third cup final goal following the two penalties he scored against Chelsea in 1994 and maintained his incredible record of success in the cup with United. That was his 14th match in the competition for the club and he had not lost any of them, winning 13 and drawing one. By the time he announced his retirement from the game a year later, he had played in 17 FA Cup matches and only lost one – the last one of all, a 1-0 defeat the following season in a fourth round replay at Wimbledon.

But there was poignancy surrounding that winning goal too. Ian Rush, who scored 44 goals in the FA Cup – the 20th century record – had replaced the ineffective Stan Collymore with 16 minutes to go to try and save the game for Liverpool. But he could not add to that tally, or his all-time record of five FA Cup final goals, and Liverpool lost.

**Most Open for Years**

United retained the title in 1997, but not the FA Cup, when the final, for the first time since 1975, featured none of the old 'Big Five' – Manchester United, Liverpool, Arsenal, Tottenham or Everton. All of them were eliminated by the fourth round and the 1996-97 competition became one of the most open for years.

In the end, Chelsea, about to embark on the most successful period in their history, won the FA Cup for the first time since 1970 – while Middlesbrough not only lost their first-ever FA Cup final but were relegated as well. It was a heart-breaking season for the club as they were also beaten by Leicester

City in the replayed League Cup final – after being just two minutes away from victory in the original match at Wembley before a late Emile Heskey equaliser cancelled out Fabrizio Ravanelli's 95th minute goal.

Middlesbrough were more than a little fortunate in being back at Wembley in any case. While no-one could deny their appearance in the final added some much needed romance to the cup, there was a widespread feeling that Second Division Chesterfield should really have been lining up against Chelsea under the twin towers that afternoon.

Chesterfield had captured the nation's imagination with an unlikely run from the first round to the semi-finals which started with a 1-0 win over Bury, also of the Second Division, the previous November. Victories over Third Division Scarborough (2-0) and Second Division Bristol City (2-0) in the second and third rounds followed with nothing more than tepid nation-wide media interest.

But all that changed after their 3-2 fourth round win at First Division Bolton Wanderers thanks to a hat-trick from 20-year-old Kevin Davies. Chesterfield were in the fifth round for only the fourth time, and for the first time in 47 years.

**Deservedly Winning**

They were drawn against Premier League Nottingham Forest who had won 2-1 at Newcastle in the fourth round. No-one gave manager John Duncan's Second Division battlers much hope of reaching the sixth round, but they out-played Forest on the day, deservedly winning 1-0 with a Tom Curtis penalty after 54 minutes.

While Chesterfield were progressing, so too were Second Division Wrexham, whose greatest-ever moment in the cup had come in 1992 when they knocked out reigning champions Arsenal. Now the Welsh team, who had despatched Premier League West Ham in a replayed third round tie at Upton Park, had their focus set on the final itself.

Just like Chesterfield, they had progressed from the first round and had caused one of the shocks of the season with their 3-1 away win at Birmingham in the fifth round.

One of the two Second Division sides were guaranteed a place in the semi-finals after they were drawn together in the sixth round – and it was Chesterfield who triumphed.

Their team, assembled for a modest £340,000 put the club into the semi-finals for the first time in their 131-year history thanks to Chris Beaumont who took advantage of confusion in the Wrexham defence to score the only goal at their modest Saltergate ground after 58 minutes.

Chesterfield had become only the seventh club from the third tier of English soccer to reach the last four. And it was not inconceivable they could beat Middlesbrough too.

Boro were having the most bizarre of seasons. After a bright start to the campaign in which they lost just once (to Chelsea) in their opening six matches, their form slumped and they won just one of their next 16 league games. Then on December 21 they refused to play their scheduled match at Blackburn claiming illness in the camp and were deducted three points by the FA.

Losing those points proved crucial as they were relegated at the end of the season with 39 points. Finishing with 42 points would have been enough for 16th spot and survival. But at least in the cups they were unstoppable.

Progressing to the League Cup final on one front, they were unbeatable in the FA Cup as well and reached the FA Cup semi-final for the first time in their history when they won 2-0 at Derby County in the sixth round thanks to goals from their Brazilian hero Juninho and their goalscoring Italian Fabrizio Ravanelli.

So at Old Trafford on Sunday, April 13 the most unlikely of cup semi-finalists, Chesterfield and Middlesbrough came out to do battle for a place in the cup final. Just over an hour later it looked as though Chesterfield were there.

Chesterfield were given a boost eight minutes before half-time when Vladimir Kinder, playing in only his fifth match for Middlesbrough since signing from Slovan Bratislava in January, was sent off by referee David Elleray for a second yellow card offence.

**Disallowed Goal**

And the Second Division side, harassing Middlesbrough at every turn, eventually made their numerical advantage pay early in the second half. First Andy Morris followed up a Kevin Davies shot to tap-in their opener after 54 minutes. Six minutes later skipper

Sean Dyche made it 2-0 from the spot after Morris had been brought down by 'Boro keeper Ben Roberts. Chesterfield were 36 minutes away from the cup final.

At last Middlesbrough began to play and pulled a goal back through Ravanelli four minutes later. But then came the turning point of the entire tie – and the issue which is still talked about in the pubs of Chesterfield today. With 69 minutes gone and leading 2-1, Chesterfield attacked again. Jonathan Howard turned defender Neil Cox on the six-yard line and lashed the ball past Roberts. It flew off the underside of the bar and landed a foot over the goal-line. But instead of celebrating a 3-1 lead, Chesterfield were stunned as Elleray disallowed the goal. No-one in the ground saw Howard foul Cox – but Elleray was adamant. The goal did not stand.

"I accept the ball crossed the line," the referee said later, "but I made a decision for an infringement before the shot". A minute later Elleray proved to be Middlesbrough's saviour again when he awarded them a highly controversial penalty after ruling that Dyche brought down Juninho inside the penalty area.

**Everlasting Mark**

TV replays clearly showed that the foul took place outside the box, and that Juninho's theatrically dramatic fall bore no relation to the amout of contact Dyche made on the little Brazilian. But Craig Hignett brought the score back to 2-2 to force extra time.

Middlesbrough, clearly now favourites to win the tie, eventually took the lead for the first time when Gianluca Festa made it 3-2 after 100 minutes. But still Chesterfield were not finished and sent the tie into a replay when Jamie Hewitt, the only Chesterfield-born player in the team, headed the equaliser to make it 3-3 in the 119th minute.

Three days later Middlesbrough lost 1-0 to Leicester in the replayed League Cup final and relegation looked even more likely after losing 1-0 at home to Sunderland in the league. But they finally had something to celebrate when they beat Chesterfield 3-0 in the semi-final replay at Hillsborough. But Chesterfield had made an everlasting mark on the cup, putting their small town – previously only famous for its crooked church spire – onto the FA Cup map.

In comparison to Middlesbrough, Chelsea had an almost trouble-free ride to the final, apart from their fourth round match against Liverpool – one of the great cup matches of the Nineties. Liverpool had raced into a 2-0 lead after 21 minutes at Stamford Bridge with goals from Robbie Fowler and Stan Collymore – but Chelsea stormed back to win 4-2 with second half-goals from Gianfranco Zola, Mark Hughes and two from Gianluca Vialli. From that moment on, Chelsea's name seemed to be on the cup.

Victories over Leicester, Portsmouth and Wimbledon in the semi-finals saw Chelsea through to their second cup final in four seasons. And there was little doubt they were going to win it after Italian Roberto Di Matteo put them 1-0 up against 'Boro after 43 seconds – the fastest ever FA Cup final goal at Wembley, two seconds quicker than Jackie Milburn's 45-second goal for Newcastle against Manchester City in 1955.

It was another bad day for Middlesbrough. Ravanelli had been their saviour with 31 goals in all competitions, but he limped off with a hamstring injury after 22 minutes, followed by a limping Robbie Mustoe six minutes later. Gianluca Festa had an equaliser disallowed on the stroke of half-time, and Chelsea duly wrapped up their first FA Cup win at Wembley and only the second in their history with an Eddie Newton goal seven minutes from time. Middlesbrough's despair was compounded. A week before the final they were relegated.

But 1997 made more than just club history for Chelsea. In his first season in charge at Stamford Bridge Dutchman Ruud Gullit became the first foreign coach to win the FA Cup in the first truly cosmopolitan – or "least English" final played. It featured five Italians, two Brazilians, a Slovak, a Dane, a Frenchman, a Romanian and a Norwegian – as well as assorted Englishmen and one very special Welshman.

Mark Hughes, appearing in his fifth FA Cup final, became the first player in the 20th century to collect four winners' medals following his earlier successes with Manchester United in 1985, 1990 and 1994 when he played and scored against Chelsea.

He also became the sixth man to have played in five Wembley finals: Joe Hulme, Johnny Giles, Pat Rice, Frank Stapleton and Ray Clemence being the others. Since then, John Barnes and Roy Keane have added their names to the club.

# THE CURTAIN FALLS ON WEMBLEY 1998-2000

CHELSEA HAD not known anything like this since the old days when Osgood and Hudson were lording it over the King's Road in their flares. Chelsea followed their 1997 success with two more trophies in 1998. They beat Middlesbrough again, 2-0 after extra time, to win the League Cup final back at Wembley and then won the European Cup Winners' Cup two months later with a 1-0 win over VfB Stuttgart in Stockholm.

But their grip on the FA Cup was wrenched apart in bright sunshine on the first Sunday of 1998 when Manchester United thumped them 5-3 at Stamford Bridge after going 5-0 up with two goals each from David Beckham and Andy Cole and one from Teddy Sheringham. Chelsea gave the scoreline a modicum of respectability with three goals in the last 12 minutes, but the defence of their trophy was over.

It was not to be United's year either as they went out in a replayed fifth round tie at Barnsley. United had, by their own high standards, a disappointing season in 1997-98, the first without Eric Cantona who announced his retirement at the end of the previous campaign.

Instead the season was going to be a triumph for another Frenchman seemingly possessed of magic powers – Arsene Wenger, who marked his first full season at Highbury by winning the double. At the beginning of January though, there were no thoughts of trophies at Highbury with Arsenal sixth in the table having won just two of their eight league games before Christmas. The gloom deepened when lowly First Division side Port Vale held Arsenal to a 0-0 draw at Highbury in the third round of the FA Cup, but appearances were deceptive.

Wenger, with his scholarly looks and professorial air, was close to finding the right formula for success – and even though they needed a penalty shootout to despatch Port Vale after a 1-1 draw in the replay, Arsenal's roll had begun.

Between December 13 and May 3, the day they clinched the title with a 4-0 win over Everton at Highbury, Arsenal did not lose in the league for 18 matches – including a run of 10 successive wins which included a 1-0 win at Old Trafford against Manchester United on March 14 which turned the season around. Had United won that match they would have gone 12 points clear of Arsenal with seven matches to play.

Instead the victory moved Arsenal to within six points of United – with three matches in hand. In the end Arsenal, inspired by their dynamic midfield French partnership of Patrick Vieira and Emmanuel Petit who would win the World Cup with France that summer, pipped United to the title by a point. Oddly their progress in the cup was more problematic. After the penalty shoot-out win over Port Vale, Arsenal won 2-1 at Middlesbrough, but then were held to another goalless draw at home by Crystal Palace in the fifth round before winning the replay 2-1.

West Ham were the sixth round visitors to Highbury and again prevented Arsenal from winning at home by securing a 1-1 draw. The replay at Upton Park ended in a 1-1 draw too, but again Arsenal held their nerve in the shootout to come through 4-3 for a semi-final against First Division Wolves at Villa Park. An early goal from Christopher Wreh separated the teams at the end and Arsenal were back in the final for the 13th time.

Their opponents were Kenny Dalglish's Newcastle United, who reached Wembley despite a poor run of league form that saw them slip into the relegation dogfight for a while during a long mediocre spell when wins were hard to come by.

Their toughest obstacle in the cup proved to be Conference side Stevenage Borough, who fought out a 1-1 draw with the Magpies at home in the fourth round, before losing 2-1 at St James' Park in the replay.

Alan Shearer, now restored to full health after missing the first half of the season through injury, scored all three goals in the tie, and also got the winner in the 1-0 fifth round win over Tranmere Rovers. Although he failed to score in the 3-1 victory over Barnsley in the sixth round, he sealed Newcastle's place in the final with the only goal in the 1-0 win in the semi-final over Sheffield United.

But Newcastle's cup run was also significant for Ian Rush. Now nearing the end of his career, Rush had joined Newcastle on a free transfer from Leeds at the start of the season. He made only 14 appearances for Newcastle in all, and five of those were brief ones as a substitute, but he did score in the only FA Cup match he played for Newcastle – a 67th minute winner in the 1-0 win over his old nemesis Everton in the third round at Goodison Park. It was his 44th and final FA Cup goal, a 20th century record.

Arsenal had something to avenge in the 1998 cup final, the third between the clubs with Newcastle winning the previous two finals in 1932 and 1952. The champions were hot favourites on a blisteringly hot day and even though Footballer of the Year Dennis Bergkamp missed the match because of a hamstring injury, there was never much doubt about the outcome.

### Ragged Defence

Newcastle, looking for their first honour since lifting the old Inter Cities Fairs Cup in 1969 and their first domestic honour since winning the FA Cup in 1955, were negative and uninspired – and once Arsenal's Marc Overmars shot between Shay Given's legs for the opening goal in the 24th minute, there was only going to be one winner.

Newcastle hit the woodwork twice in the second half through Nikos Dabizas and Alan Shearer, but Arsenal wrapped up the match – and the double – in the 70th minute when Ray Parlour's through ball allowed Nicolas Anelka to break free of the ragged Newcastle defence and run on before firing past Given into the bottom left-hand corner.

Some Arsenal fans were upset that their record scorer and cult hero Ian Wright, involved in his last match for the club, was never called off the bench, even for a farewell appearance in the last few minutes with the match won.

But one old-timer did make a brief appearance when Newcastle manager Kenny Dalglish sent on John Barnes for the last five minutes. That short appearance earned Barnes a place in the history books as he became only the third man in history to play for three different teams in the final after his appearances with Watford in 1984 (lost), Liverpool in 1988 (lost), 1989 (won) and 1996 (lost). He also became the first man to lose with three different clubs – and the seventh to play in five Wembley finals.

So, two years after Manchester United had become the first English side to win a second double, Arsenal matched them. In 1971 Bertie Mee's side had hauled back Leeds United in the title run-in and come from behind to beat Liverpool in the cup final to win the double for the first time. This time Wenger's men had shown similar strength of character, especially in the League with their 10 successive wins. But good as 1998 was for Arsenal, 1999 was going to be even better for Manchester United.

Newcastle were back in the final the following year – bidding to become the seventh team in post-war Wembley finals to win the cup 12 months after losing it. But they had one major problem. They were playing Manchester United.

### Incredible Season

Books have already been written about Manchester United's incredible season which reached its climax in Barcelona on May 26, 1999 when they scored two goals in injury time to beat Bayern Munich 2-1 in the European Cup final to become the first English club to win the treble.

After losing at home to Middlesbrough on December 19, Manchester United arrived at Wembley for the cup final on May 22 unbeaten for 31 cup and league matches. The run included away wins by 6-2 at Leicester and 8-1 at Nottingham Forest in the Premier League and an incredible 3-2 away win at Juventus in the Champions League where they came back from 2-0 down to clinch their place in the final 4-3 on aggregate.

United's personnel had changed remarkably little since their last FA Cup final appearance in 1996 when they also clinched the double for the second time. Eric Cantona and Gary Pallister had retired but the other 11 players who appeared in the 1996 match were all still part of the regular first team squad.

With one eye on the European Cup final just four days later, Alex Ferguson's selection contained some surprises with Dwight Yorke and Jaap Stam on the bench and Nicky Butt not even among the substitutes. But there was no mystery over Ryan Giggs' place.

Already a United legend, a wonderous goal from the Welshman sealed United's place in the FA Cup final when he scored the winner 10 minutes from the end of extra time in their semi-final replay against holders Arsenal at Villa Park five weeks earlier.

It was a shame the two had met then. An Arsenal-United final in 1999 would have provided the perfect finale to the 20th century between two clubs who had won three doubles between them in the previous five seasons.

For the semi-final replay was really the highlight of that season's competition. David Beckham put United ahead with a superb goal after just 17 minutes and the tempo of the match never dropped as Arsenal battled for the equaliser which duly came from Dennis Bergkamp with 21 minutes to play.

United, on top for so long, suffered a huge blow when Roy Keane was sent off five minutes later – and they looked to be heading out of the cup altogether when Arsenal were awarded a penalty in injury time. But for once Bergkamp's clinical finishing let him down with Peter Schmeichel saving his spot-kick to send the match into extra time. It needed something special to separate them and that moment duly arrived in the 109th minute. Ryan Giggs, picking up a wayward Arsenal ball in his own half, set off on a 70-yard run towards the Arsenal goal. Weaving in and out of Arsenal defenders and getting closer to his target all the while, he finally unleashed an unstoppable left-foot shot that flew into the roof of David Seaman's net. Giggs' goal celebration revealing a hairy chest when he ripped off his shirt, is also well-remembered as 25,000 United fans went absolutely wild with delight cheering his goal of the season.

### FA Agree to Replay

Unlike the previous year when they struggled to find their true momentum in the cup, Arsenal, until they met United, had few problems seeing off the challengers to their trophy in 1999 – but they were involved in an incident unique in FA Cup history in the fifth round.

It occurred on February 13 when first division Sheffield United went to Highbury with a place in the quarter-finals at stake. Instead the match became the first to be declared void for 'sporting' reasons in the competition's 127-year history.

With the scores level at 1-1 after 76 minutes and with United's Lee Morris lying injured, United goalkeeper Alan Kelly kicked the ball out of play so that he could be treated by the United physiotherapist. A minute or so later Ray Parlour's throw-in return to the United players was seized upon by Arsenal substitute Nwankwo Kanu, making his Gunners' debut and who had only been on the field for 10 minutes.

Kanu later claimed he had no idea of the convention of playing the ball harmlessly back to the opposition to get the action re-started. What he did instead was cross the ball to Marc Overmars, with the United defenders reacting too late to what was going on.

### Eight Days of Argument

Overmars duly scored to make it 2-1 to unleash a tirade of anger from United that took almost five minutes to pacify. There were no further goals and Arsenal had won 2-1. However, within minutes of the finish, Arsene Wenger offered to replay the match in the interests of "fair play" and the FA duly agreed. But not everyone was happy – and that included FIFA, soccer's worldwide governing body.

Instead of welcoming the decision, FIFA took a dim view. They maintained that as no law had actually been broken – only an 'understanding' between players, there was nothing wrong with the result and they initially ruled the result should stand.

After eight days of argument, FIFA finally agreed the match could be replayed – but with one bizarre proviso. FIFA ordered that both clubs had to sign a declaration, for legal reasons, that the winner of the rematch or any replay would advance to the next round even though Arsenal won the original match 2-1 and the result of that game remained in the record books.

The thinking behind FIFA's decision was that if Arsenal subsequently lost the replayed match, they would protest about the out-come. Which was an odd way of looking at things as Arsenal had called for the match to be replayed in the first place. In the event, the replayed match back at Highbury 10 days later ended with Arsenal winning 2-1 again. It was not the last time FIFA were to become involved in the FA Cup though.

Newcastle, now under the control of ex-Chelsea boss Ruud Gullit after replacing Kenny Dalglish just two weeks into the season, were making steady progress of their own to their second successive final and after wins over Crystal Palace, Bradford City, Blackburn Rovers and Everton. They now found themselves paired with Tottenham in the semi-final at Old Trafford.

The London side were back in the semi-finals for the fourth time in nine seasons, and with the prospect of an Arsenal-Spurs final a real possibility, Spurs were determined to put the disappointment of their losing semi-finals of 1993 and 1995 behind them. But in the end luck, and two Alan Shearer extra time goals went against them as Newcastle won 2-0. The Geordies were back at Wembley, vowing to their fans they would definitely improve on the previous season's supine performance against Arsenal.

They were wrong. Although Newcastle did play better in 1999 than 1998, Manchester United were simply too good for them – despite losing Roy Keane, playing in his fifth Wembley final, after only nine minutes when a strong challenge from Gary Speed left the Irishman with a badly bruised and swollen ankle.

### Careless Clearance

But instead of Keane's absence tipping the game Newcastle's way, a brilliant tactical switch by Alex Ferguson secured United victory. He brought Ole Gunnar Solskjaer back into the right side of midfield, moved David Beckham into the centre and brought on Teddy Sheringham to link up with Paul Scholes in attack.

Within 100 seconds of leaving the bench, Sheringham shot past Steve Harper after a perfect return from Paul Scholes to put United 1-0 up. United sealed their 10$^{th}$ Cup win after 53 minutes when Newcastle's Greek defender Nikos Dabizas played a careless clearance straight to Solskjaer. Sheringham then found Scholes who scored with a left-footed shot from the edge of the box.

United swarmed forward and could have had three or four more – a great Sheringham chip hit the bar – and for the second year running Newcastle left Wembley empty-handed. Four days later United were crowned champions of Europe, but no-one could have known then that this was to be the last FA Cup match Manchester United would play for nearly 20 months.

For while United's players were taking their summer breaks, officials from the club, the FA and senior government politicians were meeting to discuss a somewhat tricky problem that United's European Cup victory had created for them.

### Massive Problem

The FA, with the full support of first John Major's government and then Tony Blair's, were bidding to bring the 2006 World Cup finals to England. But one massive problem stood in the way of this dream ever becoming a reality. UEFA backed Germany's rival bid and all seven of UEFA's members who were also on FIFA's 24-man Executive Committee would vote for Germany when the decision on hosting the finals would be taken in Zurich in the summer of 2000.

The only European on the FIFA executive backing England's bid was David Will of Scotland in his role as the British vice-president. But despite this huge obstacle, England pressed ahead with their bid to host the finals – and this is where Manchester United came in.

FIFA had organised their first Club World Championship for continental champions for January 2000 in Brazil, and as European champions United were obliged to take part. The view of the FA was simple enough, even if the fan in the street saw things very, very differently. The FA view was: how can we expect to ask for the right to host FIFA's World Cup, if we refuse to take part in a competition FIFA is organising?

The FA and the government were adamant. United could not pull out of the competition in Brazil. What no-one expected was that United would pull out of the FA Cup instead, a decision which has tarnished the competition ever since.

The crisis became public on June 21, four weeks after United had won the cup, when reports hinted that United might have to play a weakened team – or possibly even withdraw from the competition completely.

A week later David Davies, the acting FA chief executive, said they were looking at ways to "find a window" for United to compete in both the FA Cup and the tournament in Brazil, but on June 30, United's chairman Martin Edwards revealed United would not enter the FA Cup in January. "We had to consider that England's World Cup bid may have been at stake if we do not go to Brazil – we are in a no-win situation".

The point was though: England were never in a situation likely to win the World Cup vote. As senior FIFA officials said privately at the time, "Manchester United going to Brazil will have absolutely no impact on England's World Cup bid. If they go or if they don't will not sway the people who vote one way or another".

The affair rumbled on for months but key questions was never adequately answered by anyone. Why could not a postponement of United's fourth round tie be accommodated for a week or so? Who really decided that United would not compete in the FA Cup? And why? Everyone involved passed the buck – and still does.

Still, it was not all doom and gloom for United that summer as Alex Ferguson went to the Palace to get knighted by the Queen after lifting the treble.

While the government, the FA and even United themselves were damaging the prestige of the FA Cup on the one hand, other key elements of the FA Cup's magical appeal were also being tampered with on the other.

**Rightful Place**

The first was the FA's decision to schedule the third round – one of the highlights of every season and almost always played on the first weekend of the New Year – for the second week of December. This decision, following in the wake of United's exit, was hugely unpopular with everyone and lasted for just one season before the FA came to their senses and restored the third round to its rightful place in the calendar.

While the FA were allowing United to take the season off and tampering with the competition's traditions, long-awaited plans for the demolition and re-building of Wembley Stadium were finally unveiled in the last summer of the old century. And the twin towers had no place in the plans for the new stadium. The 2000 final would bring the curtain down on those famous landmarks.

Roberto Di Matteo, who had scored the fastest–ever goal in a Wembley FA Cup final in 1997, scored the last-ever goal under the twin towers in 2000. He had also scored Chelsea's second in their 2-0 win over Middlesbrough in the 1998 League Cup final, and as he said after securing Chelsea's second Cup win in four seasons: "It's a shame they are knocking the stadium down, I always seem to do well here, its a lucky stadium for me".

**Final Disappointment**

But the last final at Wembley between Chelsea and Aston Villa, in the final for the first time since 1957, was a disappointment, settled by Di Matteo 17 minutes from time.

Villa goalkeeper David James, who had bad memories of the 1996 final when he lost with Liverpool, should have done better than just flapping at a Gianfranco Zola free-kick. The ball rebounded off the chest of Gareth Southgate and fell to Di Matteo who crashed it into the roof of the Villa net.

Villa had been involved in a little bit of cup history earlier in the campaign when they knocked Darlington out of the cup 2-1 in the third round. Darlington, in a sense were the only real beneficiaries of Manchester United's absence from the competition and won through to the third round as the "lucky losers" from the second round.

Darlington beat Southport 2-1 in the first round but lost 3-1 at Gillingham in the second before being given a second chance in the "lucky loser" draw. It was history of a sort. But there was no glory attached to it and apart from Chelsea's delighted players and fans who thoroughly deserved their success, the 1999-2000 competition is best forgotten.

As a postscript though, it is worth noting just how successful Manchester United's visit to Brazil was in January. Well after a public relations disaster when United were perceived to have snubbed the locals by training behind closed doors, they had David Beckham sent off in their first match: a 1-1 draw against CONCACAF champions Necaxa of Mexico. They then lost 3-1 to Vasco da Gama of Brazil and were eliminated from the 8-team competition in the group stage before a consolation 2-0 win over mighty South Melbourne of Australia, the Oceania champions.

And of course, Germany won the right to stage the 2006 World Cup. England polled just two votes as the Germans beat South Africa 12-11 in the final round of voting.

# THE CUP LEAVES FOR CARDIFF AGAIN – 2001-2003

CARDIFF CITY are famously the only club from outside England to win the FA Cup. Now, 74 years after the Welsh side's 1927 FA Cup victory over Arsenal, the famous trophy was returning to Wales.

It would be leaving again soon afterwards though to be placed into either Liverpool's or Arsenal's trophy room as the 2001 FA Cup final became the first since the 1922 game between Huddersfield Town and Preston North End at Stamford Bridge not to take place at Wembley Stadium.

The irony of course was that Wembley could have staged the 2001 final – and the 2002 final for that matter, because the demolition of the old stadium was delayed for more than two years while first one scheme, then another collapsed for either financial or political reasons.

The FA briefly contemplated holding the final at Twickenham but opposition from tweedy locals and the fact that Twickenham's rugby pitch was too narrow for football quickly ended that debate.

Eventually Cardiff's magnificent new Millennium Stadium was chosen for the showpiece match of the English soccer season. And, as so often happens in the history of the FA Cup, fate again appeared to play a hand as an English hero with a Welsh surname wrote his name into the competition's folklore by scoring both of Liverpool's goals in their 2-1 come-from-behind win over Arsenal in the Welsh capital.

It was the third time the clubs had met in the final following Arsenal's victories in 1950 and 1971, and just when it seemed the Gunners were going to make it three out of three, Michael Owen changed the game around with two goals scored after 83 and 88 minutes which cancelled out Freddie Ljungberg's 71st minute opener for Arsenal.

The Gunners had reached the final, coming from behind to outclass arch-rivals Spurs 2-1 in the all-North London semi-final, which, with Wembley no longer viable, was held 250 miles away from the Seven Sisters Road at Old Trafford.

Spurs, who had controversially replaced George Graham as manager with Tottenham idol Glenn Hoddle less than two weeks before the match, had taken an early lead through Gary Doherty, but the game was already going Arsenal's way when Tottenham skipper Sol Campbell limped off towards the end of the first half after colliding with Arsenal's Ray Parlour. Goals from Patrick Vieira and Robert Pires saw Arsenal through.

That was Campbell's last-ever action after 10 years as a Spurs player. Less than three months later he joined Arsenal and little over a year on was celebrating another Arsenal double with Parlour and his new team-mates. Funny game football.

Liverpool also won their semi-final 2-1, beating Second Division Wycombe Wanderers, only the eighth side in cup history from outside the top two divisions to have reached the semi-finals.

Wycombe, coached by Lawrie Sanchez, who headed the winning goal for Wimbledon against Liverpool in 1988, had knocked out Premier League Wimbledon on their way to the last eight when they served up one of the real fairytales of the FA Cup story.

### Teletext Striker

With an injury crisis mounting, Sanchez put out an appeal on TV's Teletext for a striker to contact him to make up the numbers in his depleted squad. Step forward, much-travelled 25-year-old Northern Irish journeyman Roy Essandoh. Sanchez immediately played him in the league match at Port Vale on March 3 and a week later named him among the substitutes for the sixth round tie against Premier League Leicester at Filbert Street. A script-writer could not have made up what happened next – or perhaps only a script-writer could… Essandoh headed the stoppage time winner to give Wycombe an unbelievable 2-1 victory.

He came on again in the semi-final against Liverpool at Villa Park too, but although

*More than Law, more than Rush, more than anyone. No-one has scored more goals in the history of the FA Cup than Henry 'Harry' Cursham, who hit 49 for Notts County between 1877 and 1888 – 48 in the Competition Proper and one in a qualifying round match. He also scored five goals in eight internationals for England, including the first hat-trick in the Home International series.*

*The first giants of the English game 'the Invincibles' of Preston North End who won the double in 1889, winning the FA Cup without conceding a goal and winning the first-ever league championship without losing a match. Back row (l to r): George Drummond, Rob Howarth, Right Hon. RW Hanbury, Sir WEM Tomlinson, David Russell, Bob Holmes, Major William Sudell (manager), Johnny Graham, Dr Robert Mills-Roberts. Front row: Jack Gordon, Jimmy Ross, John Goodall, Fred Dewhurst, Sam Thomson. (National Football Museum)*

*Billy Meredith, one of the greatest players of pre-First World War football. He played for Manchester City in the 1904 FA Cup final, scoring the only goal against Bolton Wanderers, and neighbours United in 1909 when they beat Bristol City to notch their first ever FA Cup win.* (Action Images)

*Part of the vast crowd at the first Wembley cup final in 1923. PC George Scorey on his white horse Billy helped get the crowd under control and behind the touchlines so the match between Bolton Wanderers and West Ham could go ahead. Scorey was no football lover and never went to another match. The official attendance is recorded as 126,000 but there were probably nearer to 200,000 people in the stadium on the day. A rather bedraggled police band looks decidedly out of tune too.*
*(Action Images)*

*The 1933 final was the first in which the players were numbered. Everton wore 1-11, Manchester City 12-22 – but there was nothing much that No.22, Manchester City goalkeeper Len Langford could do to stop Everton winning with some ease. Dixie Dean has just put Everton two-up on their way to a 3-0 win and a hat-trick of successes following the Second Division title in 1931 and the League championship in 1932. (Action Images)*

*The Matthews Final. Wembley 1953 and (top) Bill Perry scores the final goal in Blackpool's 4-3 win against Bolton, a goal created by Stan Matthews. (Below) Matthews (right) is chaired alongside skipper Harry Johnston. (Empics)*

*West Bromwich Albion goalkeeper Jim Sanders cannot bear to watch as Ronnie Allen's penalty brings WBA level at 2-2 in the 1954 cup final against Preston North End. Sanders and his teammates eventually won 3-2. (Action Images)*

*Who'd be a goalkeeper? Manchester City's Bert Trautmann (above) receives treatment for a broken neck in 1956, although he continued playing, while Peter Murphy (10) of Birmingham City is also in need of the magic sponge. But City won 3-1, whereas (below) Jackie Blanchflower, normally a centre-half but here a stand-in for Ray Wood, can only watch as Peter McParland scores Aston Villa's second goal against Manchester United in their 2-1 victory a year later. (Empics)*

there was to be no repeat performance – Liverpool were made to battle all the way for their victory with late goals from Emile Heskey and Michael Owen in the last 12 minutes finally ending Wycombe's glory run. Even then, Wycombe were not finished, sending the match into a barnstorming finish thanks to Keith Ryan's 88th minute goal.

So on a blazing hot May afternoon Liverpool and Arsenal met in the 120th English FA Cup final in Wales.

Arsenal totally dominated the first 80 minutes creating chance after chance which Thierry Henry or Sylvain Wiltord failed to convert. But it was Owen, a largely peripheral figure while Arsenal dominated, who was going to turn the final on its head.

His first was an instinctive close-range volley and his second a goal of stunning brilliance. Owen, still only 21, left Arsenal veterans Lee Dixon (aged 37) and Tony Adams (35) for dead before firing an angled shot past David Seaman (37) for the winner.

### Unique Record

The cup was back with the red half of Merseyside for the sixth time – and the first since 1992 when Owen was a 12-year-old Everton fan. The victory meant Liverpool, who had won the League Cup by beating Birmingham City on penalties in Cardiff three months previously, had equalled Arsenal's unique record of winning both major cups in the same season. Liverpool were not finished there though because four days later in Dortmund, Germany, they beat Alaves of Spain 5-4 to lift the UEFA Cup, their first European trophy since winning the European Cup in 1984.

The 2001 final was the first in which both managers were from overseas, or at least, from across the English Channel. Arsene Wenger had totally transformed Arsenal since his arrival at Highbury in 1996 winning the double in his first full season in 1998. And Gerard Houllier, since assuming sole control of the team after a brief spell sharing the job with Roy Evans, had restored Liverpool's pride and was in the middle of an incredible spell of success. From February to August in 2001 Liverpool picked up five pieces of silverware: the League Cup, the FA Cup, the UEFA Cup, the Charity Shield and the European Supercup. Scousers certainly had lots to celebrate – and look forward to – as they crawled out of Cardiff in some of the slowest moving traffic jams of all time that hot spring afternoon.

### No-one was Listening

But what of Manchester United in 2001? Clearly, someone was punishing them for 2000. After a gap of nearly 20 months they returned to the competition on January 7 and beat Fulham 2-1 at Craven Cottage with an 89th minute Teddy Sheringham goal sealing their victory. But they were not involved for long. Three weeks later West Ham went to Old Trafford and won 1-0 with a 76th minute winner from Paolo di Canio whose arrowed angled shot sped past goalkeeper Fabian Barthez who had his arm raised appealing for offside at the time. He might have been appealing, but no-one was listening.

Arsenal though did not have to wait long to avenge their 2001 cup final defeat to Liverpol, beating them 1-0 at Highbury in the fourth round the following January with Dennis Bergkamp's first-half goal ending Liverpool's reign as holders.

With Robert Pires in such blistering form he was named Footballer of the Year despite missing the last six weeks of the season with a leg injury, and with Thierry Henry lethal in front of goal, Arsenal were simply unstoppable in the second half of the 2001-02 season.

And once Manchester United were knocked out of the competition by Middlesbrough in the fourth round, it was hard to see who was going to stop Arsenal in either the cup or the League.

The answer, basically, was that nobody could. Arsenal re-wrote the record books as they ended the season with 13 straight league wins, by scoring in every league match they played and by becoming the first team since Preston North End in 1888-89 to go undefeated away in their league campaign.

After knocking out Watford (4-2) and Liverpool (1-0) they steamrollered their way to the cup final with victories over Gillingham (5-2), Newcastle (3-0 after a 1-1 draw) and Middlesbrough (1-0) in the semi-final at Old Trafford.

### All-London Final Again

The second Millennium Stadium cup final between Arsenal and Chelsea was the setting for the first all-London final for 20 years.

Chelsea reached their fourth final in nine seasons by seeing off London rivals West

Ham (3-2 after a 1-1 draw), Tottenham (4-0) and Fulham (1-0) in the semi-finals on the way to Cardiff as well as Norwich (4-0 after a 0-0 draw) and Preston (3-1), but they were always second best to Arsenal on another scorching hot cup final day.

For the second successive year neither manager was British with Claudio Ranieri sitting on the Chelsea bench opposite Arsene Wenger. Ranieri was the fourth different helmsman to steer Chelsea to the final since they emerged as a cup-fighting team in the early 1990s, following Glenn Hoddle (1994), Ruud Gullit (1997) and Gianluca Vialli (2000).

But neither Ranieri, or Emmanuel Petit, who won the double with Arsenal in 1998, or anyone else in a blue shirt were going to stop Arsenal that afternoon – even though it took them 70 minutes to break down Chelsea's resistance.

The opening goal was outstanding and came from one of the few home-grown players to make an impact at Highbury in recent seasons. Ray Parlour, the villain 12 months previously after giving away the free-kick which led to Michael Owen's opening goal for Liverpool in the 2001 final, was now Arsenal's hero with his stunning 70th minute 30-yard shot on the run which Chelsea keeper Carlo Cudicini could only get a hand to.

Ten minutes later Arsenal sealed their victory when Ljungberg forged his way through the Chelsea defence before curling home a well-struck shot from the edge of the box to become the first player since Bobby Smith of Spurs 40 years previously to score in successive finals.

### Equalling Record

Chelsea were hampered by a calf injury to striker Jimmy Floyd Hasselbaink who had an ineffective, immobile match, and how they could have done with their former cup final winning hero, Roberto Di Matteo.

The Italian, who scored in both the 1997 and 2000 finals, led out the Chelsea side following his untimely retirement earlier in the season following a serious leg fracture. Not even he could sprinkle some magic dust as his former team-mates were defeated by the better side and it was left to Tony Adams, making his 669th and what was to be his last appearance for Arsenal, to equal Bryan Robson's record by lifting the FA Cup for the third time as the winning captain.

Arsenal broke with precedent in 2002 when they equalled Manchester United's feat of winning the double for a third time – because they became the first team of the ten teams which have won the double to do so by winning the FA Cup first. Four days after beating Chelsea they went to Old Trafford and clinched the title with a 1-0 victory over Manchester United who ended the campaign without a trophy for only the third time in 13 seasons.

Another victory for Arsenal – their ninth in a record 16th FA Cup final appearance, might on the surface suggest that the 2002-03 FA Cup just followed the same old pattern ending in a routine victory for one of the big clubs.

But nothing could be further from the truth. True, their eventual 1-0 win over Southampton in the third FA Cup final in Cardiff may have been predictable, but the competition did re-capture some of its old magic during the season.

### Tournament Reaffirmed

Paul Jackson, for one, certainly thought so. On August 31, four months before Arsenal even thought about having their first kick in the tournament, he equalled the all-time FA Cup individual scoring record with 10 goals as Stocksbridge Park Steels of Sheffield, who play in the Northern Premier League, beat Oldham Town of the North West Counties League 17-1 in a preliminary round match.

Try telling the 110 people who watched that match on that bright summer's day that there is no magic left in the cup. Well, the one's that were not involved with Oldham Town, anyway.

And try telling that to the students of Team Bath, too, because when a team of students from Bath University can move to within two matches of playing the likes of Manchester United, Arsenal or any other premiership club in a competitive match, the universal appeal of the 130-year-old tournament must be reaffirmed.

Team Bath, who were only formed in 2000, battled through five qualifying rounds to earn their first round tie against Second Division Mansfield Town and become the first student side since Oxford and

Cambridge Universities in 1880 to take part in the competition proper.

Oxford University actually won the FA Cup in 1874 – with six England internationals in their side – and reached the final four times in all, losing in 1873, 1877 and 1880 – but while Team Bath are never going to win the cup, they were hugely successful in their own right.

### Heads Held High

As manager Ged Roddy said after their penalty shoot-out win over Horsham in their replayed fourth qualifying round game: "Our target was not to disgrace ourselves. All through the cup run we were positive and I told the players to play without fear. We were ambassadors for university football as a whole and have shown to people the standard it has reached."

As far as most football fans are concerned, Team Bath will now be forever associated with the FA Cup. And not just something you jump into to wash the mud off after a match.

The students left the cup with their heads held high after a 4-2 home defeat to Mansfield, to concentrate on their league matches and a memorable season ended with them winning the Western League championship in May.

They might not have reached the minnows' Mecca of the Third Round, but among those that did were Shrewsbury Town of the Third Division and Farnborough Town, Dagenham & Redbridge and Morecambe from The Conference.

Shrewsbury pulled off the biggest shock of the season with a stunning 2-1 win over Everton, delighting Shrews' boss Kevin Ratcliffe, the former Everton player, and Nigel Jemson, now nearing the autumn of his career after service with 13 different clubs. Jemson scored twice as Shrewsbury stunned the Premier League side being rejuvenated by David Moyes.

It proved to be the highlight of a season that was to end in such disappointment when they were relegated from the Football League after a woeful run of form in the spring. Chelsea had ended their cup run in the fourth round with a 4-0 win at the end of January.

Arsenal and Southampton, the two clubs destined to meet in the final in May, both had relatively easy starts to their campaigns. Southampton, who had had to battle all the way to beat a determined Tottenham side 1-0 in the league at St Mary's on New Years Day, met Spurs there again three days later – and played them off the park with an emphatic 4-0 drubbing. There was an air of inevitability linking the Saints to the final after that.

Arsenal began their defence with a straight-forward 2-0 win over Oxford United at Highbury, but for sheer drama no third round tie matched the game at Molineux where Wolves beat Newcastle United 3-2 in an atmosphere that was also a throwback to days gone by.

### Cast-iron Guarantees

Arsenal also had it easy in the fourth round – although their match against Farnborough, who had beaten Darlington 3-2 away in the third round, was not without controversy in that it was taking place at Highbury rather than Farnborough who sacrificed the slight possibility of an upset against the reigning champions by switching the match to North London for a guaranteed bumper pay-cheque.

They got that – and a 5-1 thumping for their trouble after defender Christian Lee was unfortunate to be sent off in the first half when they were already 2-0 down – but the FA have decided that ties can no longer be switched for the money.

In future senior Non-League clubs must have cast-iron guarantees from their local authorities and police that FA Cup matches against major clubs can go ahead at their home stadiums with a pre-set capacity crowd limit.

While Arsenal were coasting against Farnborough, Southampton were made to battle hard by Millwall and needed two matches to get past the First Division side. Millwall, were in fact just minutes away from a victory at St Mary's before Kevin Davies scored a late equaliser to force a 1-1 draw – and Southampton needed an extra-time goal at the New Den from Matt Oakley to go through 2-1 to round five.

Manchester United also flexed their muscles by crushing West Ham 6-0 at Old Trafford – a record cup defeat for the London side – while Rochdale reached the fifth round for the first time in 32 years with a 2-0 win over first division Coventry City.

And so the serious business really began and these days nothing in England comes bigger than Manchester United v Arsenal. More than 67,000 packed into Old Trafford to see the biggest game of the competition outside the final, and once Arsenal had emerged as the 2-0 winners thanks to a deflected free-kick from Edu which flew in off David Beckham's shoulder, and a second from Sylvain Wiltord early in the second half, United were out. It could have been very different indeed if Ryan Giggs had not wasted a golden chance to score with an open goal at his mercy just before Arsenal took the lead.

The repercussions of the defeat did not end there either for Beckham or United. It was after this match that a furious Alex Ferguson kicked a football boot across the dressing room which cut Beckham's eyebrow. There was no a public apology from the manager who dismissed it as "a million-to-one freak chance" and it must be seen as the catalyst for the final breakdown in their relationship which saw Beckham join Real Madrid in a £25 million deal in 2003.

Southampton also went through after winning 2-0 against Norwich City at St Mary's and welcomed Wolves – and former Saints manager David Jones – in the quarter-finals. Former Wolves player Chris Marsden opening the scoring with an overhead kick after 56 minutes and Saints wrapped it up 2-0 when Wolves skipper Paul Butler scored an own goal near the end.

### Slightly Below Superb

As if beating Manchester United was not hard enough, Arsenal now had to face Chelsea in a repeat of last season's final. A thriller at Highbury ended in a 2-2 draw, but Arsenal appear to have as much of an Indian sign over Chelsea as Chelsea do over Spurs. Chelsea have not beaten Arsenal in the FA Cup since 1947 and even though Arsenal finished the replay with 10 men after having Pascal Cygan sent off after 66 minutes, they also finished as 3-1 winners at Stamford Bridge.

Arsenal boss Arsene Wenger had steered his side into a record-equalling 23rd semi-final where they would meet First Division promotion hopefuls Sheffield United. Southampton would face Watford, also of the First Division, in the other semi – and it seemed just a question of when for Arsenal and not if. How long, that is, would they have to wait for a second successive double.

Arsenal had, however, gone out of the Champions League after a 2-1 defeat to Valencia in the middle of March, as their form dipped to slightly below superb.

They faltered in the title run-in with draws against Aston Villa, Manchester United – when a red card for Sol Campbell earned him a suspension that would keep him out of the cup final – and Bolton Wanderers before losing 3-2 at home to Leeds United when they finally lost the title race. They never looked entirely happy in their FA Cup semi-final against Sheffield United either, even though Freddie Ljungberg had put them ahead in the 34th minute with what proved to be the only goal of the game.

### Save of the Season

In the end they needed the Save of the Season from David Seaman who somehow defied his 39 years to reach a goal-bound header from Paul Peschisolido while he appeared stranded in no-man's land in the centre of his goal to preserve their 1-0 win. It was a fitting way to mark his 1,000th first team appearance and guaranteed Arsenal a place in the FA Cup final for the third successive season.

Southampton won the other semi against Watford 2-1 at Villa Park with goals from Brett Ormerod just before half-time and a Paul Robinson own goal 10 minutes from time. Marcus Gayle gave Watford some hope when he pulled the score back to 2-1 with three minutes remaining, but Saints held on to reach the final for the first time since 1976.

By the time FA Cup final day arrived, Arsenal's dreams of a double double had died. Arsenal had been top from the middle of November, but Manchester United, winning match after match, moved into first place on April 12 – and stayed there for good.

Arsenal went to Cardiff looking to salvage their season by winning the cup, but without the suspended Campbell and injured skipper Patrick Vieira. After a somewhat nervous start they were just a little too street-wise and savvy for Southampton. In all 10 of the Arsenal players had had previous experience of an FA Cup final. None of the

Saints had played in the final before and Northern Ireland Under-21 international Chris Baird, Gordon Strachan's surprise choice on the right, had only ever played three first team matches – two of those were as a substitute.

And once Arsenal took the lead with a well-executed goal from Frenchman Robert Pires seven minutes before half-time, Southampton were always chasing the game. Arsenal in fact could have gone ahead after just 24 seconds with what would have been the fastest FA Cup final goal of all time when Thierry Henry burst clear, stayed on his feet rather than fall after being hauled back by Claus Lundekvam only to fire straight at Finnish goalkeeper Antti Niemi. Niemi pulled a muscle in the second half and was replaced by Welsh international goalie Paul Jones – the first substitute goalkeeper in an FA Cup final.

### Select Band

Freddie Ljungberg started the match looking to become the first player ever to score in three successive finals – and went close to doing so in the second half – while Seaman, playing what turned out to be his last match for the Gunners after 13 years at the club, became the oldest goalkeeper ever to play in the final and the third oldest of all time – and only the second keeper to captain a team in the final following Dave Beasant's achievement in 1988.

Southampton had their chances and went close to an equaliser seconds from the end when Ashley Cole cleared a James Beattie header off the line, but in the end Arsenal became the first club since their old rivals Spurs (1961 and 1962, and 1981 and 1982) to win the cup in successive seasons – and Arsene Wenger joined the select band of managers to win the trophy three times, following the victories in 1998 and 2002.

All this happened under the closed roof of the Millennium Stadium – another first.

For Arsenal it was just another successful day out in Cardiff, for the Saints fans their first chance for 27 years to shine on the big stage and shine they did. They were a credit to their club and to the sport and even stayed at the end to applaud Arsenal who collected the cup for the ninth time in their history – just one less than the all-time record 10 wins established by Manchester United in 1999.

Wenger said afterwards: "We were under immense pressure today. We would have been sad to finish the season without a trophy. We were disappointed not to win the championship because we came so close to a double double." Still, there is always 2004 when Arsenal will attempt to become the first club to play in four successive cup finals – and the first since Blackburn in 1886 to complete a hat-trick of wins.

And while almost 70,000 fans were making their way home from Cardiff to London, or Southampton and all other points in between along the slow moving M4, a patch of ground in north London lay silent and empty, its bulldozers still, its 450-strong work force at home, probably watching the cup final on television.

Wembley's twin towers have been demolished and all trace of the old stadium gone. In its place in May 2003 was a barren patch of land with concrete and steel towers being excavated into place to support the new steel skeleton for the new Wembley that is due to open in 2006.

### Timeless Link

And when the FA Cup final returns to its traditional Wembley home, thousands of fans will, as thousands of fans have done in the past, take the tube or over-ground train home or drive away along the North Circular Road, sad or elated at the afternoon's events.

But probably none of them, except for those who might live there, will ever take three Metropolitan Line stops north to Harrow-on-the-Hill station and make the short walk to Harrow School.

But it was there, just a couple of miles from Wembley Stadium, that Charles Alcock, the man who invented the FA Cup, went to school and first got the idea for the cup based on Harrow's Cock House knockout game.

If the wind was blowing in the right direction you could hear the noise of the Wembley cup final crowd in Harrow – a natural, timeless link to the very birthplace of what is still the world's greatest knockout competition. Could Alcock ever have imagined what he was starting? Probably not. But millions of people are very glad he took the trouble.

# LIST OF ABBREVIATIONS

TO SIMPLIFY the identification of the leagues, the original name of the competition has been used throughout. Isthmian League clubs, for example, are always designated as IL irrespective of the sponsor's name or the name of the league in any given season. Although there was no Football League competition in the 1945-46 season, the clubs have been designated to the League division they were in for the 1939-40 season which was curtailed when World War II began.

Note that the abbreviation 'Conf' has been used as the abbreviation throughout for the various guises of The Conference since 1986-87 (Gola League, GM Vauxhall Conference, the Nationwide Conference and finally The Conference) The abbreviation APL refers to the competition from 1979-80 until 1985-86.

PL..............................Premier League
D1............Football League Division 1
D2............Football League Division 2
D3............Football League Division 3
D4............Football League Division 4
3N.......Football League Division 3 (N)
3S........Football League Division 3 (S)
APL............................Alliance Premier League
AL.............................Athenian League
BC............Birmingham Combination
BDL....Birmingham & District League
CA...............................Central Alliance
CC...............Cheshire County League
CL................................Central League
CML...........Central Midlands League
Conf...........................The Conference
CRN.......................Corinthian League
Cumb.................Cumberland League
DEL..........................Delphian League
DSL...........Derbyshire Senior League
ECL...........Eastern Counties League
FAll............................Football Alliance
HEL...........................Hellenic League
HL........................Hampshire League
IL..............................Isthmian League
KL...................................Kent League
LC...............Lancashire Combination
LCC...Liverpool County Combination
Lincs..................Lincolnshire League
LL..........................Lancashire League
Lon............................London League
MAN....Manchester & District League
MC....................Midland Combination
MET....................Metropolitan League
ML.............................Midland League
NAll..........................Northern Alliance
N&S............Norfolk & Suffolk League
NCO.........Northern Counties League
NCOE..........Northern Counties (East) League
N&D...............................Nottingham & Derbyshire Senior League
NEL..................North Eastern League
NELC.....NE Lancashire Combination
NL.............................Northern League
NPL...........Northern Premier League
NRL..........Northern Regional League
NWC....North West Counties League
NWAC..North Wales Coastal League
PDL..Peterborough & District League
SAL......Sheffield Association League
SCL..............Sussex County League
SL...........................Southern League
SML.............South Midlands League
SPT.............................Spartan League
SSL...................Surrey Senior League
SFCL.............Suffolk County League
SWL..............South Western League
TC............................The Combination
TSL.........................Tees-side League
UCL............United Counties League
UL................................United League
WCL..........West Cumberland League
Wear.........................Wearside League
Welsh............................Welsh League
WL............................Western League
WMRL.........West Midlands Regional League
WS .....................West Surrey League
WYL..............West Yorkshire League
YL............................Yorkshire League

Country Abbreviations: ARG-Argentina; AUT-Austria; BEL-Belgium; BRA-Brazil; CAM-Cameroon; CH-Chile; CIS-Commonwealth of Independent States; CIV-Ivory Coast; CRO-Croatia; CZ-Czech Republic; DEN-Denmark; E-England; FIN-Finland; F-France; GEO-Georgia; GER-Germany; GRE-Greece; IRE-Ireland; ISL-Iceland; ITA-Italy; JAM-Jamaica; LIB-Liberia; NETH-Netherlands, NI-Northern Ireland; NIG-Nigeria; NOR-Norway; PER-Peru; RI-Republic of Ireland, ROM-Romania; RUS-Russia; S-Scotland; SVK-Slovakia; SWE-Sweden; SWI-Switzerland; TT-Trinidad & Tobago; UKR-Ukraine; URU-Uruguay; USA-United States of America; W-Wales; YUG-Yugoslavia (from February 2003 renamed Republic of Serbia and Montenegro).

# An explanation of the Club v Club Record section

THE CLUBS listed in the main results section are those who have been included in the draw for the First Round proper of the FA Cup since the competition began in 1871-72.

A number of clubs like Donington School, Harrow Chequers and Preston Zingari, for example, never played a match but were in the draw and so are included in this list.

With a listing as exhaustive as this going back more than 130 years, some anomalies inevitably occur. It was decided to include qualifying round match results of present day League clubs were practical but, generally speaking the records for former Football League clubs list only the matches they have played in the Competition Proper.

The listings for the majority of the Non-League clubs are, in most cases, their complete records in the Competition Proper, but occasionally some of their qualifying round matches have been included. This is usually where they have beaten a Football League club in one qualifying round, before being knocked out in another before reaching the Competition Proper.

Generally speaking the organisation of the FA Cup falls into three periods.

The first from 1871-72 until 1887-88 consisted of the Competition Proper with no qualifying rounds.

From 1888-89 until 1924-25 there was an exhaustive qualifying competition which involved Football League clubs, but which, by the 1920s had become too unwieldy following the creation of the third division (north and south) of the Football League.

The 'modern' era began in 1925-26 when the competition was re-organised basically along the lines still used today.

The only change since then was in the 'transitional' 1945-46 season, when all ties in the Competition Proper from the First Round to the quarter-finals were played over two legs.

# CLUB-BY-CLUB FA CUP RESULTS

## 105TH REGIMENT

*Entered the FA Cup: 1875-76 – 1878-79. Also known as the Madras Light Infantry, they combined with the 51st Regiment in 1881 to form the King's Own Yorkshire Light Infantry.*

| | | | | | | | |
|---|---|---|---|---|---|---|---|
| 1875-76 | 1 | 06.11.75 | **Crystal Palace** (1861) | H | D | 0-0 | |
| | 1r | 20.11.15 | **Crystal Palace** (1861) | A | L | 0-3 | |
| 1876-77 | 1 | 11.11.76 | **1st Surrey Rifles** | H | W | 3-0 | |
| | 2 | 14.12.76 | **Oxford University** | A | L | 1-6 | |
| 1877-78 | 1 | 07.11.77 | **Old Harrovians** | H | L | 0-2 | |
| 1878-79 | 1 | | Minerva | - | | | |
| | | | *105th Regiment scratched. Minerva walkover* | | | | |

## 1ST SURREY RIFLES

*Formed 1869. Entered FA Cup: 1872-73 – 1886-87. Played their home matches at their Flodden Road headquarters in Camberwell.*

| | | | | | | | |
|---|---|---|---|---|---|---|---|
| 1872-73 | 1 | 26.10.72 | **Upton Park** | H | W | 2-0 | Allport, Hastie |
| | 2 | 23.11.72 | **Maidenhead** | A | L | 0-3 | |
| 1873-74 | 1 | 25.10.73 | **Barnes** | H | D | 0-0 | |
| | 1r | 08.11.73 | **Barnes** | A | L | 0-1 | |
| 1875-76 | 1 | 23.10.75 | **Wanderers** | A | L | 0-5 | |
| 1876-77 | 1 | 11.11.76 | **105th Regiment** | A | L | 0-3 | |
| 1877-78 | 1 | 07.11.77 | **Forest School** | H | W | 1-0 | Kirkpatrick |
| | 2 | 22.12.77 | **Old Harrovians** | A | L | 0-6 | |
| 1885-86 | 1 | 31.10.85 | **Clapham Rovers** | A | L | 0-12 | |
| 1886-87 | 1 | 23.10.86 | **Upton Park** | A | L | 0-9 | |

## 93rd HIGHLANDERS

*Formed 1872. Played in the FA Cup in 1890-91 and the following season when they were eliminated in the qualifying competition.*

| | | | | | | | |
|---|---|---|---|---|---|---|---|
| 1890-91 | 1 | 17.01.91 | **Sunderland Albion** | A | L | 0-2 | |

## ABERDARE ATHLETIC

*Formed 1893 as Aberdare Town; Reformed as Aberdare Athletic 1920. Amalgamated with Aberaman Athletic 1927 to form Aberdare & Aberaman Athletic. Entered FA Cup: 1911-12 – 1947-48. Members of the Football League 1922-27. Club later reformed with separate identities: Aberaman Athletic continued in the Welsh League until 1950. Aberdare Town competed in the Welsh League between 1934-47.*

| | | | | | | | |
|---|---|---|---|---|---|---|---|
| 1922-23 (3S) | | | 5q Newport County (H) 1-1; 5qr Newport County (A) 1-1aet; Newport County at Ninian Park 2-1; 6q Carlisle Utd (H) 0-0; 6qr Carlisle Utd (A) 2-1 | | | | |
| | 1 | 13.01.23 | **Preston North End** (D1) | H | L | 1-3 | Brown |
| 1923-24 (3S) | | | 4q Torquay Utd (A) 0-0; 4qr Torquay Utd (H) 4-0; 5q Reading (H) 1-0; 6q Walsall (H) 1-0 | | | | |
| | 1 | 12.01.24 | **West Ham Utd** (D1) | A | L | 0-5 | |
| 1924-25 (3S) | | | 4q Newport County (H) 0-0; 4qr Newport County (A) 0-3 | | | | |
| 1925-26 (3S) | 1 | 28.11.25 | **Bristol Rovers** (3S) | H | W | 4-1 | Barwood, Barnham 3 |
| | 2 | 12.12.25 | **Luton Town** (3S) | H | W | 1-0 | Smith |
| | 3 | 09.01.26 | **Newcastle Utd** (D1) | A | L | 1-4 | Taylor |
| 1926-27 (3S) | 1 | 27.11.26 | **Exeter City** (3S) | A | L | 0-3 | |
| 1927-28 (SL) | 1 | 26.11.27 | **Exeter City** | A | L | 1-9 | Watts |

## ACCRINGTON FC

*Formed 1876. Founder members of the Football League 1888. Disbanded January 1896. Accrington FC was a separate club from Accrington Stanley.*

| | | | | | | | |
|---|---|---|---|---|---|---|---|
| 1881-82 | 1 | | Queen's Park, Glasgow | | | - | |
| | | | *Queen's Park scratched. Accrington FC walkover* | | | | |
| | 2 | 26.11.81 | **Darwen** | A | L | 1-3 | Yates |
| 1882-83 | 1 | 04.11.82 | **Blackburn Olympic** | A | L | 3-6 | Brown, Bamber, Yates |
| 1883-84 | 1 | 10.11.83 | **Blackpool St John's** | H | W | 4-0 | Hacking, Bryce 2, Hargreaves |
| | 2 | 26.11.83 | **Blackburn Park Road** | A | W | 3-2 | Harper og, Hargreaves, MacBeth |
| | | | *Accrington disqualified for professionalism, Park Road declined re-instatement* | | | | |
| 1884-85 | 1 | 11.10.84 | **Southport** | H | W | 3-0 | |
| | | | *Accrington disqualified for professionalism, Southport reinstated* | | | | |
| 1885-86 | 1 | 17.10.85 | **Witton** | H | W | 5-4 | F Wood 2, Deakin, Hargreaves, Wade |
| | 2 | 21.11.85 | **Darwen Old Wanderers** | A | L | 1-2 | Whittaker |
| 1886-87 | 1 | 30.10.86 | **Renton** | A | L | 0-1 | |

| | | | | | | | |
|---|---|---|---|---|---|---|---|
| 1887-88 | 1 | 15.10.87 | **Rossendale FC** | H | W | 11-0 | Fecitt 4, Lofthouse 3, Conway 2, Bonar, Yates |
| | 2 | 05.11.87 | **Burnley** | H | W | 3-2 | Conway, Bonar, Lofthouse |
| | 3 | 26.11.87 | **Blackburn Rovers** | H | L | 1-3 | Yates |
| 1888-89 (D1) | 1 | 02.02.89 | **Blackburn Rovers** (D1) | H | D | 1-1 | Wilkinson |
| | 1r | 09.02.89 | **Blackburn Rovers** ) | A | L | 0-5 | |
| 1889-90 (D1) | 1 | 25.01.90 | **WBA** (D1) | H | W | 3-0 | Entwistle 2, Barbour |
| | | | *FA ordered match to be replayed after protest* | | | | |
| | 1 | 18.01.90 | **WBA** | H | W | 3-1 | |
| | 2 | 01.02.90 | **Sheffield Wed** (FAll) | A | L | 1-2 | A Wilkinson |
| 1890-91 (D1) | 1 | 17.01.91 | **Bolton Wanderers** (D1) | H | D | 2-2 | Whitehead, Kirkham |
| | 1r | 24.01.91 | **Bolton Wanderers** | H | W | 5-1 | Gallocher, Kirkham, Whitehead, Pendergast, AN Other |
| | 2 | 31.01.91 | **Wolverhampton W** (D1) | H | L | 2-3aet | Pendergast, Kirkham |
| 1891-92 (D1) | 1 | 16.01.92 | **Crusaders** | A | W | 4-1 | Haworth, Thomson, Kirkham, Whitehead |
| | 2 | 30.01.92 | **Sunderland** (D1) | H | W | 1-0 | |
| | | | *FA declared match void after protests and ordered a replay* | | | | |
| | 2r | 06.02.92 | **Sunderland** | H | L | 1-3 | Whitehead |
| 1892-93 (D1) | 1 | 21.01.93 | **Stoke** (D1) | H | W | 2-1 | Cookson, H Lea |
| | 2 | 04.02.93 | **Preston North End** (D1) | H | L | 1-4 | H Lea |
| 1893-94 (LL) | 1 | 27.01.94 | **Sunderland** (D1) | A | L | 0-3 | |
| 1894-95 (LC) | | | 1q Bacup (H) 0-4 | | | | |
| 1895-96 (LC) | | | P West Manchester (A) 1-5 | | | | |

# ACCRINGTON STANLEY

*Formed 1893. A separate club from Accrington. 1921 Reformed and admitted to the Football League when Division Three North was created in 1921-22. Resigned from Football League March 1962 but were legally not wound up until December 1963. Briefly reformed as Accrington FC December 1963, wound-up January 1966. In 1968 were reformed as Accrington Stanley (1968). Best FA Cup Performance: 4th round 1927, 1937, 1959. Members of The Conference.*

| | | | | | | | |
|---|---|---|---|---|---|---|---|
| 1896-97 (NELC) | | | 1q Carlisle City walkover; 2q Chorley (H) 0-5 | | | | |
| 1897-98 (NELC) | | | 1q Carlisle City (A) 4-0; 2q Horwich (A) 1-3 | | | | |
| 1898-99 (NELC) | | | 1q Oswaldtwistle R (A) 4-2; 2q Frizington White Star (H) 8-0; 3q South Shore (A) 1-5 | | | | |
| 1899-00 (NELC) | | | P Blackburn Park Road (A) 0-3 | | | | |
| 1900-01 (LC) | | | did not enter | | | | |
| 1901-02 (LC) | | | 1q Nelson (H) 2-1; 2q Oswaldtwistle R (H) 1-1; 2qr Oswaldtwistle R (A) 2-0; 3q Darwen (A) 1-2 | | | | |
| 1902-03 (LC) | | | 1q Bacup (H) 5-0; 2q Rossendale Utd (H) 1-0; 3q Manchester Utd (A) 0-7 | | | | |
| 1903-04 (LC) | | | 1q Padiham (A) 0-0; 1qr Padiham (H) 4-0; 2q Nelson (H) 2-1; 3q Southport (H) 0-1 | | | | |
| 1904-05 (LC) | | | 3q Blackpool (H) 1-4 | | | | |
| 1905-06 (LC) | | | P Nelson (H) 7-0; 1q Burnley Belvedere (H) 5-0; 2q Padiham (A) 4-1; Int. Burton Utd (A) 0-3 | | | | |
| 1906-07 (LC) | | | 5q West Norwood (A) 9-1 | | | | |
| | 1 | 12.01.07 | **Crewe Alexandra** (BDL) | A | D | 1-1 | Randall |
| | 1r | 16.01.07 | **Crewe Alexandra** | H | W | 1-0 | Sheridan |
| | 2 | 02.02.07 | **Bradford City** (D2) | A | L | 0-1 | |
| 1907-08 (LC) | | | P Chorley (A) 1-2 | | | | |
| 1908-09 (LC) | | | P Rochdale (A) 5-3; 1q Rossendale U (H) 2-0; 2q Darwen (H) 3-1; 3q Colne (H) 1-1; 3qr Colne (A) 2-2aet abandoned – bad light; 3q 2r Colne 1-0 (at Burnley); 4q Northern Nomads (H) 0-2 | | | | |
| 1909-10 (LC) | | | 4q Haslingden (A) 4-3; 5q Brentford (H) 1-0 | | | | |
| | 1 | 15.01.10 | **Blackburn Rovers** (D1) | A | L | 1-7 | Bradley |
| 1910-11 (LC) | | | 4q Haslingden (A) 1-0; 5q Torquay T (H) 4-0 | | | | |
| | 1 | 14.01.11 | **Wolverhampton W** (D2) | A | L | 0-2 | |
| 1911-12 (LC) | | | 4q Carlisle Utd (H) 3-0; 5q Walsall (A) 1-2 | | | | |
| 1912-13 (LC) | | | 4q Rochdale (A) 1-6 | | | | |
| 1913-14 (LC) | | | 4q Stalybridge Celtic (A) 0-2 | | | | |
| 1914-15 (LC) | | | P Adlington (H) 1-1; Pr Adlington (H) 2-3 | | | | |
| 1919-20 (LC) | | | 1q Nelson (A) 1-2 | | | | |
| 1920-21 (LC) | | | 1q Fleetwood (A) 0-8 | | | | |
| 1921-22 (3N) | | | 4q Nelson (H) 0-1 | | | | |

| | | | | | | | | | |
|---|---|---|---|---|---|---|---|---|---|
| 1922-23 | (3N) | | | 5q Halifax Town (H) 1-1; 5qr Halifax Town (A) 0-1 | | | | | |
| 1923-24 | (3N) | | | 5q Rochdale (H) 1-0; 6q Wrexham (H) 1-0 | | | | | |
| | | 1 | 12.01.24 | **Charlton Athletic** | (3S) | H | D | 0-0 | |
| | | 1r | 16.01.24 | **Charlton Athletic** | (3S) | A | L | 0-1 | |
| 1924-25 | (3N) | | | 5q New Brighton (A) 0-0; 5qr New Brighton (H) 3-2; 6q Chesterfield (H) 1-0 | | | | | |
| | | 1 | 10.01.25 | **Portsmouth** | (D2) | H | L | 2-5 | R Thompson 2 (1p) |
| 1925-26 | (3N) | 1 | 28.11.25 | **Wrexham** | (3N) | H | W | 4-0 | Jepson 3, Rooks |
| | | 2 | 12.12.25 | **Blyth Spartans** | (NEL) | H | W | 5-0 | Gummery, Jepson 3, Powell |
| | | 3 | 09.01.26 | **Bolton Wanderers** | (D1) | A | L | 0-1 | |
| 1926-27 | (3N) | 1 | 27.11.26 | **Rochdale** | (3N) | H | W | 4-3 | Gee (p), Clarkson 2, Martin |
| | | 2 | 11.12.26 | **Chilton Coll** | (NEL) | A | W | 3-0 | Gee, Clarkson, Martin |
| | | 3 | 08.01.27 | **Exeter City** | (3S) | A | W | 2-0 | Clarkson, Martin |
| | | 4 | 29.01.27 | **Chelsea** | (D2) | A | L | 2-7 | Powell, Wyper |
| 1927-28 | (3N) | 1 | 26.11.27 | **Lincoln City** | (3N) | H | L | 2-5 | Clarkson, Parkin |
| 1928-29 | (3N) | 1 | 24.11.28 | **South Shields** | (3N) | H | W | 2-1 | Parkin, Parry |
| | | 2 | 08.12.28 | **Spennymoor Utd** | (NEL) | H | W | 7-0 | Jepson 3, Parry 2, McLoughlin 2 |
| | | 3 | 12.01.29 | **Bournemouth** | (3S) | H | D | 1-1 | Jepson |
| | | 3r | 16.01.29 | **Bournemouth** | | A | L | 0-2 | |
| 1929-30 | (3N) | 1 | 30.11.29 | **Rochdale** | (3N) | H | W | 3-1 | Jepson 2, Armstrong (p) |
| | | 2 | 14.12.29 | **Bristol Rovers** | (3S) | A | L | 1-4 | Ferguson |
| 1930-31 | (3N) | 1 | 29.11.30 | **Lancaster Town** | (LC) | H | W | 3-1 | Agar 2, Abel |
| | | 2 | 13.12.30 | **Torquay Utd** | (3S) | H | L | 0-1 | |
| 1931-32 | (3N) | 1 | 28.11.31 | **Rotherham Utd** | (3N) | A | D | 0-0 | |
| | | 1r | 02.12.31 | **Rotherham Utd** | | H | W | 5-0 | Williamson 3, Watson, Agar |
| | | 2 | 12.12.31 | **Halifax Town** | (3N) | A | L | 0-3 | |
| 1932-33 | (3N) | 1 | 26.11.32 | **Hereford Utd** | (BDL) | H | W | 2-1 | Maycock, Price (p) |
| | | 2 | 10.12.32 | **Aldershot** | (3S) | H | L | 1-2 | Johnson |
| 1933-34 | (3N) | 1 | 25.11.33 | **Scunthorpe Utd** | (ML) | A | D | 1-1 | Kelly |
| | | 1r | 29.11.33 | **Scunthorpe Utd** | | H | W | 3-0 | Lennox, Cheetham 2 |
| | | 2 | 09.12.33 | **Bristol Rovers** | (3S) | H | W | 1-0 | Cheetham |
| | | 3 | 13.01.34 | **Millwall** | (D2) | A | L | 0-3 | |
| 1934-35 | (3N) | 1 | 24.11.34 | **Mansfield Town** | (3N) | A | L | 1-6 | Brown |
| 1935-36 | (3N) | 1 | 30.11.35 | **Darlington** | (3N) | A | L | 2-4 | Reynolds, Brown |
| 1936-37 | (3N) | 1 | 28.11.36 | **Wellington Town** | (BDL) | H | W | 3-1 | Mortimer, Mee, Reynolds |
| | | 2 | 12.12.36 | **Tunbridge Wells R** | (KL) | H | W | 1-0 | Mee |
| | | 3 | 16.01.37 | **Blackburn Rovers** | (D2) | A | D | 2-2 | Mortimer 2 |
| | | 3r | 20.01.37 | **Blackburn Rovers** | | H | W | 3-1aet | Mortimer 2, Rivers |
| | | 4 | 30.01.37 | **Manchester City** | (D1) | A | L | 0-2 | |
| 1937-38 | (3N) | 1 | 27.11.37 | **Lancaster Town** | (LC) | H | D | 1-1 | Moir |
| | | 1r | 01.12.37 | **Lancaster Town** | | A | D | 1-1 | Curran |
| | | 1 2r | 06.12.37 | **Lancaster Town** | | | W | 4-0 | Curran 2, O'Grady, Andrews |
| | | | | *played at Deepdale, Preston* | | | | | |
| | | 2 | 11.12.37 | **Crystal Palace** | (3S) | H | L | 0-1 | |
| 1938-39 | (3N) | 1 | 26.11.38 | **Hartlepools Utd** | (3N) | A | L | 1-2 | Alexander |
| 1945-46 | (3N) | 1 1L | 17.11.45 | **Chorley** | (LC) | A | L | 1-2 | Keeley |
| | | 1 2L | 24.11.45 | **Chorley** | (LC) | H | W | 2-0 | Rothwell, Hudson |
| | | 2 1L | 08.12.45 | **Oldham Athletic** | (3N) | A | L | 1-2 | Hudson |
| | | 2 2L | 15.12.45 | **Oldham Athletic** | | H | W | 3-1 | Hudson, Shipman og, Rothwell |
| | | 3 1L | 05.01.46 | **Manchester Utd** | (D1) | H | D | 2-2 | Conroy, Keeley |
| | | 3 2L | 09.01.46 | **Manchester Utd** | | A | L | 1-5 | Keeley |
| | | | | *played at Maine Road* | | | | | |
| 1946-47 | (3N) | 1 | 30.11.46 | **Doncaster Rovers** | (3N) | A | D | 2-2 | Conroy, Keeley |
| | | 1r | 04.12.46 | **Doncaster Rovers** | | H | L | 0-5 | |
| 1947-48 | (3N) | 1 | 29.11.47 | **Stockport County** | (3N) | A | L | 1-3 | T Butler |
| 1948-49 | (3N) | 1 | 27.11.48 | **Hull City** | (3N) | A | L | 1-3 | Webster |
| 1949-50 | (3N) | 1 | 26.11.49 | **Hartlepools Utd** | (3N) | H | L | 0-1 | |
| 1950-51 | (3N) | 1 | 25.11.50 | **Wrexham** | (3N) | A | L | 0-1 | |
| 1951-52 | (3N) | 1 | 24.11.51 | **Chester** | (3N) | H | L | 1-2 | Watkinson |
| 1952-53 | (3N) | 1 | 22.11.52 | **Horden CW** | (NEL) | A | W | 2-1 | Watkinson |
| | | 2 | 06.12.52 | **Mansfield Town** | (3N) | H | L | 0-2 | |
| 1953-54 | (3N) | 1 | 21.11.53 | **Blyth Spartans** | (NEL) | A | W | 1-0 | Cocker |

| | | | | | | | | |
|---|---|---|---|---|---|---|---|---|
| | | 2 | 12.12.53 | **Tranmere Rovers** (3N) | H | D | 2-2 | Eastham, Musgrave (p) |
| | | 2r | 16.12.53 | **Tranmere Rovers** | A | L | 1-5 | Brydon |
| 1954-55 | (3N) | 1 | 20.11.54 | **Creswell Colliery** (CA) | H | W | 7-1 | Devlin 2, Scott 2, Wright, Brydon, Cocker |
| | | 2 | 11.12.54 | **Millwall** (3S) | A | L | 2-3 | Scott, Bodle |
| 1955-56 | (3N) | 1 | 19.11.55 | **Wrexham** (3N) | H | W | 3-1 | Stewart 2, Wright |
| | | 2 | 10.12.55 | **Darlington** (3N) | A | W | 1-0 | Dick |
| | | 3 | 07.01.56 | **Liverpool** (D2) | A | L | 0-2 | |
| 1956-57 | (3N) | 1 | 17.11.56 | **Morecambe** (LC) | H | W | 4-1 | Scott, Stones 2, Dick |
| | | 2 | 08.12.56 | **Oldham Athletic** (3N) | H | W | 2-1 | Stewart 2 |
| | | 3 | 05.01.57 | **Bournemouth** (3S) | A | L | 0-2 | |
| 1957-58 | (3N) | 1 | 16.11.57 | **Wrexham** (3N) | A | W | 1-0 | Stewart (p) |
| | | 2 | 07.12.57 | **Carlisle Utd** (3N) | A | D | 1-1 | Mulkerrin |
| | | 2r | 11.12.57 | **Carlisle Utd** | H | W | 3-2 | J Anders 3 |
| | | 3 | 04.01.58 | **Bristol City** (D2) | H | D | 2-2 | Stewart, Byrom |
| | | 3r | 07.01.58 | **Bristol City** | A | L | 1-3 | Sowden |
| 1958-59 | (D3) | 1 | 15.11.58 | **Workington** (D4) | H | W | 5-1 | Scott 3, H Anders, Stewart |
| | | 2 | 06.12.58 | **Buxton** (CC) | H | W | 6-1 | Scott 2, J Anders 3, Tighe |
| | | 3 | 10.01.59 | **Darlington** (D4) | H | W | 3-0 | J Anders, Stinson, Scott |
| | | 4 | 24.01.59 | **Portsmouth** (D1) | H | D | 0-0 | |
| | | 4r | 28.01.59 | **Portsmouth** | A | L | 1-4 | Scott |
| 1959-60 | (D3) | 1 | 14.11.59 | **Mansfield Town** (D3) | H | L | 1-2 | Tighe |
| 1960-61 | (D4) | 1 | 05.11.60 | **Barrow** (D4) | H | W | 2-1 | Swindells 2 |
| | | 2 | 30.11.60 | **Mansfield Town** (D4) | H | W | 3-0 | Swindells, Hudson, Duff |
| | | 3 | 07.01.61 | **Preston North End** (D1) | A | D | 1-1 | Duff |
| | | 3r | 09.01.61 | **Preston North End** | H | L | 0-4 | |
| 1961-62 | (D4) | 1 | 04.11.61 | **Stockport County** (D4) | A | W | 1-0 | Pickup |
| | | 2 | 25.11.61 | **Hartlepools Utd** (D4) | A | L | 1-2 | Irving |
| 1992-93 | (NPL) | 1 | 14.11.92 | **Gateshead** (Conf) | H | W | 3-2 | Beck 3 |
| | | 2 | 05.12.92 | **Crewe Alexandra** (D3) *played at Ewood Park* | H | L | 1-6 | Cooper |
| 1993-94 | (NPL) | 1 | 14.11.93 | **Scunthorpe Utd** (D3) | H | L | 2-3 | Connor, Wood |

## ACTON

*Formed 1874. Entered FA Cup: 1879-80 – 1885-86. Played their home matches at Gunnersbury Lane, Acton, west London. Used the King's Head pub as their dressing rooms.*

| | | | | | | | |
|---|---|---|---|---|---|---|---|
| 1879-80 | 1 | 08.11.79 | **Old Carthusians** | H | L | 0-4 | |
| 1880-81 | 1 | 13.11.80 | **Kildare FC** | H | D | 1-1 | |
| | 1r | 20.11.80 | **Kildare FC** | A | W | 5-0 | |
| | 2 | 11.12.80 | **Reading Abbey** | A | L | 1-2 | Lacey |
| 1881-82 | 1 | 29.10.81 | **Finchley** | H | D | 0-0 | |
| | 1r | 12.11.81 | **Finchley** | A | W | 4-0 | |
| | 2 | 03.12.81 | **Maidenhead** | A | L | 1-2aet | R Grey |
| 1882-83 | 1 | 04.11.82 | **Windsor Home Park** | A | L | 0-3 | |
| 1883-84 | 1 | 10.11.83 | **Upton Park** | A | L | 0-2 | |
| 1884-85 | 1 | 08.11.84 | **Old Carthusians** | H | L | 1-7 | |
| 1885-86 | 1 | 31.10.85 | **Old Brightonians** | A | L | 1-2 | |

## ADDLESTONE & WEYBRIDGE TOWN

*Formed 1979 by the merger of Addlestone (1885) and Weybridge FC. Addlestone first entered the FA Cup in 1924-25, Weybridge in 1914-15. The merged club folded in 1985.*

| | | | | | | | | |
|---|---|---|---|---|---|---|---|---|
| 1980-81 | (SL) | 1 | 22.11.80 | **Brentford** (D3) *played at Griffin Park* | H | D | 2-2 | Morris, Donaldson |
| | | 1r | 25.11.80 | **Brentford** (D3) | A | L | 0-2 | |

## AFC SUDBURY

*Formed 1999 by the merger of Sudbury Town (1885) and Sudbury Wanderers (1958). First entered FA Cup as AFC Sudbury 1999-2000. FA Vase Runners-up: 1989. Members of the Eastern Counties League. Competed in first round in 1996-97 as Sudbury Town.*

| | | | | | | | | |
|---|---|---|---|---|---|---|---|---|
| 1996-97 | (SL) | 1 | 16.11.96 | **Brighton** (D3) | H | D | 0-0 | |
| | | 1r | 26.11.96 | **Brighton** *Sudbury won 4-3 on penalties* | A | D | 1-1aet | Brown |

| | | | | | | | |
|---|---|---|---|---|---|---|---|
| | 2 | 07.12.96 | **Brentford** (D2) | H | L | 1-3 | McClean |
| | | | *played at Layer Road, Colchester* | | | | |
| 2000-01 (ECL) | 1 | 18.11.00 | **Darlington** (D3) | A | L | 1-6 | Claydon |

# ALDERSHOT

*Formed 1926 as Aldershot Town. Dropped the 'Town' from their name in 1931. In March 1992 became the first club since Accrington Stanley to fold and leave the Football League during the season. Reformed later in 1992 as Aldershot Town and re-entered senior football in the third division of the Isthmian League. First competed in the FA Cup 1927-28. Best FA Cup performance: 5th Round, 1933, 1979. Record FA Cup win: 11-1 v Kingstonian, 4th qualifying round, 1929-30. In Competition Proper: 7-0 v Chelmsford City, 1st round, 28.11.1931 and v Newport (IOW), 2nd rd, 1st leg, 8.12.1945 (Agg: 12-0); Record FA Cup defeat: 0-7 v Swindon Town, 3rd rd, 8.1.1983. Members of The Conference.*

**As Aldershot Town**

| | | | | | | | |
|---|---|---|---|---|---|---|---|
| 1927-28 (SL) | 1 | 26.11.27 | **QPR** (3S) | H | - | 0-1ab | |
| | | | *abandoned because of fog* | | | | |
| | 1 | 30.11.27 | **QPR** | H | W | 2-1 | Collins, Martin |
| | 2 | 10.12.27 | **Peterborough & F** (SL) | A | L | 1-2 | Martin |
| 1928-29 (SL) | | | 1q Wellington Works (H) 6-1, 2q Guildford C (H) 0-1 | | | | |
| 1929-30 (SL) | 1 | 30.11.29 | **Northampton Town** (3S) | H | L | 0-1 | |
| 1930-31 (SL) | 1 | 29.11.30 | **Peterborough & F** (SL) | H | W | 4-1 | Thorn 3, Williams |
| | 2 | 13.12.30 | **Gillingham** (3S) | A | W | 3-1 | Thorn 2, Edgar |
| | 3 | 10.01.31 | **Bradford Park A** (D2) | H | L | 0-1 | |

**as Aldershot**

| | | | | | | | |
|---|---|---|---|---|---|---|---|
| 1931-32 (SL) | 1 | 28.11.31 | **Chelmsford** (Lon) | H | W | 7-0 | Thorn 3, Hopkins, Stevenson, Middleton, McDougall |
| | 2 | 12.12.31 | **Crook Town** (NEL) | H | D | 1-1 | Thorn |
| | 2r | 16.12.31 | **Crook Town** | A | L | 0-1 | |
| 1932-33 (3S) | 1 | 26.11.32 | **Clapton Orient** (3S) | A | W | 1-0 | Fishlock |
| | 2 | 10.12.32 | **Accrington Stanley** (3N) | A | W | 2-1 | White, Lane |
| | 3 | 14.01.33 | **Bristol Rovers** (3S) | H | W | 1-0 | Lane |
| | 4 | 28.01.33 | **Millwall** (D2) | H | W | 1-0 | Fishlock |
| | 5 | 18.02.33 | **Derby County** (D1) | A | L | 0-2 | |
| 1933-34 (3S) | 1 | 25.11.33 | **Cardiff City** (3S) | A | D | 0-0 | |
| | 1r | 29.11.33 | **Cardiff City** | H | W | 3-1 | Lee, White, Smithson |
| | 2 | 09.12.33 | **Gainsborough T** (ML) | A | W | 2-0 | Proud, Lee |
| | 3 | 13.01.34 | **Crystal Palace** (3S) | A | L | 0-1 | |
| 1934-35 (3S) | 1 | 24.11.34 | **Bournemouth** (3S) | H | W | 4-0 | Williams, Bunch, Black, McDougall |
| | 2 | 08.12.34 | **Barrow** (3N) | A | W | 2-0 | Williams, Bunch |
| | 3 | 12.01.35 | **Reading** (3S) | H | D | 0-0 | |
| | 3r | 16.01.35 | **Reading** | A | L | 1-3 | G Summerbee |
| 1935-36 (3S) | 1 | 30.11.35 | **Clapton Orient** (3S) | A | D | 0-0 | |
| | 1r | 04.12.35 | **Clapton Orient** | H | L | 0-1 | |
| 1936-37 (3S) | 1 | 28.11.36 | **Millwall** (3S) | H | L | 1-6 | E Smith og |
| 1937-38 (3S) | 1 | 27.11.37 | **Dulwich Hamlet** (IL) | A | W | 2-1 | Court, Egan |
| | 2 | 11.12.37 | **Rotherham Utd** (3N) | A | W | 3-1 | Egan, Court, Kilsby |
| | 3 | 08.01.38 | **Notts County** (3S) | H | L | 1-3 | Court |
| 1938-39 (3S) | 1 | 26.11.38 | **Guildford City** (SL) | H | D | 1-1 | Egan |
| | 1r | 30.11.38 | **Guildford City** | A | W | 4-3 | Ray 2, Proud, Chalmers |
| | 2 | 10.12.38 | **Runcorn** (CC) | A | L | 1-3 | Ray |
| 1945-46 (3S) | 1 1L | 17.11.45 | **Reading** (3S) | A | L | 1-3 | Brooks |
| | 1 2L | 24.11.45 | **Reading** | H | W | 7-3 | Brooks 5, Glidden og, Fitzgerald |
| | 2 1L | 08.12.45 | **Newport (IOW)** (Hants) | H | W | 7-0 | Brooks 5, Hobbs, Hold |
| | 2 2L | 15.12.45 | **Newport (IOW)** | A | W | 5-0 | Brooks, Ray, Fitzgerald 2, Summerbee |
| | 3 1L | 05.01.46 | **Plymouth Argyle** (D2) | H | W | 2-0 | Hobbs, Brooks |
| | 3 2L | 09.01.46 | **Plymouth Argyle** | A | W | 1-0 | Hold |
| | 4 1L | 26.01.46 | **Brighton** (3S) | A | L | 0-3 | |
| | 4 2L | 30.01.46 | **Brighton** | H | L | 1-4 | White |
| 1946-47 (3S) | 1 | 30.11.46 | **Cheltenham Town** (SL) | H | W | 4-2 | Hobbs, Brooks, Hassell 2 |
| | 2 | 14.12.46 | **Bournemouth** (3S) | A | L | 2-4 | White, Griffiths |
| 1947-48 (3S) | 1 | 29.11.47 | **Bromsgrove Rovers** (BC) | H | W | 2-1 | Wainwright og, Sherwood |
| | 2 | 13.12.47 | **Swindon Town** (3S) | H | D | 0-0aet | |
| | 2r | 20.12.47 | **Swindon Town** | A | L | 0-2 | |

| | | | | | | | |
|---|---|---|---|---|---|---|---|
| 1948-49 (3S) | 1 | 27.11.48 | **Ipswich Town** (3S) | A | - | 0-1ab | |
| | | | *abandoned after 63 minutes – fog* | | | | |
| | 1 | 04.12.48 | **Ipswich Town** | A | W | 3-0 | Rawcliffe, Sherwood, White |
| | 2 | 11.12.48 | **Chester** (3N) | H | W | 1-0 | White |
| | 3 | 08.01.49 | **Gateshead AFC** (3N) | A | L | 1-3 | Sinclair |
| 1949-50 (3S) | 1 | 26.11.49 | **Weymouth** (SL) | A | D | 2-2 | Rogers, Sinclair |
| | 1r | 30.11.49 | **Weymouth** | H | L | 2-3 | McNichol, Rogers (p) |
| 1950-51 (3S) | 1 | 25.11.50 | **Bromley** (AL) | H | D | 2-2 | Menzies, Flint |
| | 1r | 29.11.50 | **Bromley** | A | W | 1-0 | Woodward |
| | 2 | 09.12.50 | **Bournemouth** (3S) | H | W | 3-0 | Flint, Gormley, Woodward |
| | 3 | 10.01.51 | **Bristol Rovers** (3S) | A | L | 1-5 | Woodward |
| 1951-52 (3S) | 1 | 24.11.51 | **Tonbridge** (SL) | A | D | 0-0 | |
| | 1r | 28.11.51 | **Tonbridge** | H | W | 3-2aet | Raine, Billington, Flint |
| | 2 | 15.12.51 | **Buxton** (CC) | A | L | 3-4 | Gormley, Jefferson, Flint |
| 1952-53 (3S) | 1 | 22.11.52 | **Millwall** (3S) | H | D | 0-0 | |
| | 1r | 27.11.52 | **Millwall** | A | L | 1-7 | Flint |
| 1953-54 (3S) | 1 | 21.11.53 | **Wellington Town** (CC) | H | W | 5-3 | McCulloch 2, Laird, Menzies, Gaynor |
| | 2 | 12.12.53 | **Peterborough Utd** (ML) | A | L | 1-2 | Lacey |
| 1954-55 (3S) | 1 | 20.11.54 | **Chelmsford City** (SL) | H | W | 3-1 | Menzies, Cheney 2 |
| | 2 | 11.12.54 | **Hartlepools Utd** (3N) | A | L | 0-4 | |
| 1955-56 (3S) | 1 | 19.11.55 | **Yeovil Town** (SL) | A | D | 1-1 | Lacey |
| | 1r | 23.11.55 | **Yeovil Town** | H | D | 1-1aet | Billington |
| | 1 2r | 28.11.55 | **Yeovil Town** | | W | 3-0 | L Gaynor, Lacey 2 |
| | | | *played at The Dell, Southampton* | | | | |
| | 2 | 10.12.55 | **Reading** (3S) | A | D | 2-2 | Billington, Menzies |
| | 2r | 14.12.55 | **Reading** | H | W | 3-0aet | J Gaynor, L Gaynor, Lacey |
| | 3 | 07.01.56 | **Barnsley** (D2) | H | L | 1-2 | Flint |
| 1956-57 (3S) | 1 | 17.11.56 | **Hereford Utd** (SL) | A | L | 2-3 | Costello 2 |
| 1957-58 (3S) | 1 | 16.11.57 | **Worcester City** (SL) | H | D | 0-0 | |
| | 1r | 21.11.57 | **Worcester City** | A | D | 2-2aet | Flint, Lacey |
| | 1 2r | 25.11.57 | **Worcester City** | | W | 3-2aet | Henry, Jackson, Lacey |
| | | | *played at St Andrews* | | | | |
| | 2 | 07.12.57 | **Coventry City** (3S) | H | W | 4-1 | Lacey 3, Walters |
| | 3 | 04.01.58 | **Portsmouth** (D1) | A | L | 1-5 | Lacey |
| 1958-59 (D4) | 1 | 15.11.58 | **Swindon Town** (D3) | A | L | 0-5 | |
| 1959-60 (D4) | 1 | 14.11.59 | **King's Lynn** (SL) | A | L | 1-3 | Mundy |
| 1960-61 (D4) | 1 | 05.11.60 | **Notts County** (D3) | H | W | 2-0 | Lawlor 2 |
| | 2 | 26.11.60 | **Colchester Utd** (D3) | H | W | 3-1 | Kirkup 3 |
| | 3 | 07.01.61 | **Shrewsbury Town** (D3) | H | D | 1-1 | Lawlor (p) |
| | 3r | 11.01.61 | **Shrewsbury Town** | A | D | 2-2aet | Tyrer, Stepney |
| | 3 2r | 16.01.61 | **Shrewsbury Town** | | W | 2-0 | Henry, Stepney |
| | | | *played at Villa Park* | | | | |
| | 4 | 28.01.61 | **Stoke City** (D2) | A | D | 0-0 | |
| | 4r | 01.02.61 | **Stoke City** | H | D | 0-0aet | |
| | 4 2r | 06.02.61 | **Stoke City** | | L | 0-3 | |
| | | | *played at Molineux* | | | | |
| 1961-62 (D4) | 1 | 04.11.61 | **Tunbridge Wells Utd** (SL) | H | W | 3-1 | Norris, Hasty 2 |
| | 2 | 25.11.61 | **Brentford** (D3) | H | D | 2-2 | Woan, Matthews |
| | 2r | 28.11.61 | **Brentford** | A | L | 0-2 | |
| 1962-63 (D4) | 1 | 03.11.62 | **Brentford** (D4) | H | W | 1-0 | Woan |
| | 2 | 24.11.62 | **Port Vale** (D3) | A | L | 0-2 | |
| 1963-64 (D4) | 1 | 16.11.63 | **Sutton Utd** (IL) | A | W | 4-0 | Fogg 2, Towers 2 |
| | 2 | 07.12.63 | **Torquay Utd** (D4) | A | W | 3-2 | Fogg, Priscott 2 |
| | 3 | 04.01.64 | **Aston Villa** (D1) | A | D | 0-0 | |
| | 3r | 08.01.64 | **Aston Villa** | H | W | 2-1 | Towers, Palethorpe |
| | 4 | 25.01.64 | **Swindon Town** (D2) | H | L | 1-2 | Priscott |
| 1964-65 (D4) | 1 | 14.11.64 | **Dartford** (SL) | A | D | 1-1 | Chamberlain |
| | 1r | 17.11.64 | **Dartford** | H | W | 1-0 | Kearns |
| | 2 | 05.12.64 | **Reading** (D3) | H | L | 1-3 | Burton |
| 1965-66 (D4) | 1 | 13.11.65 | **Wellingborough T** (UCL) | H | W | 2-1 | Priscott, Kearns |
| | 2 | 04.12.65 | **Walsall** (D3) | H | L | 0-2 | |

| | | | | | | | | |
|---|---|---|---|---|---|---|---|---|
| 1966-67 (D4) | 1 | 26.11.66 | **Torquay Utd** (D3) | H | W | 2-1 | Kearns, A Smith og |
| | 2 | 16.01.67 | **Reading** (D3) | H | W | 1-0 | Howarth |
| | 3 | 28.01.67 | **Brighton** (D3) | H | D | 0-0 | |
| | 3r | 01.02.67 | **Brighton** | A | L | 1-3 | Walton |
| 1967-68 (D4) | 1 | 13.12.67 | **Reading** (D3) | A | L | 2-6 | Walker, Howarth |
| 1968-69 (D4) | 1 | 16.11.68 | **Dartford** (SL) | A | L | 1-3 | Howarth |
| 1969-70 (D4) | 1 | 15.11.69 | **Margate** (SL) | A | W | 7-2 | Brown 3, Howarth 3, Gowans |
| | 2 | 06.12.69 | **Bristol Rovers** (D3) | H | W | 3-1 | Howarth 2, Brown |
| | 3 | 03.01.70 | **Huddersfield Town** (D2) | A | D | 1-1 | Walker |
| | 3r | 12.01.70 | **Huddersfield Town** | H | W | 3-1 | Melia 2 (1p), Gowans |
| | 4 | 24.01.70 | **Carlisle Utd** (D2) | A | D | 2-2 | Howarth, Jopling |
| | 4r | 28.01.70 | **Carlisle Utd** | H | L | 1-4 | Howarth |
| 1970-71 (D4) | 1 | 21.11.70 | **Hendon** (IL) | A | W | 2-0 | Howarth 2 |
| | 2 | 12.12.70 | **Bristol Rovers** (D3) | H | D | 1-1 | Brown |
| | 2r | 15.12.70 | **Bristol Rovers** | A | W | 3-1 | Howarth, Giles, Melia |
| | 3 | 02.01.71 | **Liverpool** (D1) | A | L | 0-1 | |
| 1971-72 (D4) | 1 | 24.11.71 | **Alvechurch** (MC) | H | W | 4-2 | Brodie 2, Hunt og, Sydenham |
| | 2 | 11.12.71 | **Reading** (D4) | A | L | 0-1 | |
| 1972-73 (D4) | 1 | 18.11.72 | **Southend Utd** (D3) | A | W | 2-0 | Melledew, Brodie |
| | 2 | 09.12.72 | **Watford** (D3) | A | L | 0-2 | |
| 1973-74 (D3) | 1 | 24.11.73 | **Dagenham** (IL) | A | W | 4-0 | Dean 2, Brodie, Howarth |
| | 2 | 15.12.73 | **Cambridge Utd** (D3) | H | L | 1-2 | Howarth |
| 1974-75 (D3) | 1 | 23.11.74 | **Brighton** (D3) | A | L | 1-3 | Brodie |
| 1975-76 (D3) | 1 | 22.11.75 | **Wealdstone** (SL) | H | W | 4-3 | Richardson, Morissey (p), Howarth 2 |
| | 2 | 13.12.75 | **Bishop's Stortford** (IL) | H | W | 2-0 | Warnock, Morrissey |
| | 3 | 03.01.76 | **Lincoln City** (D4) | H | L | 1-2 | Howarth |
| 1976-77 (D4) | 1 | 20.11.76 | **Portsmouth** (D3) | H | D | 1-1 | McGregor |
| | 1r | 23.11.76 | **Portsmouth** | A | L | 1-2 | McGregor |
| 1977-78 (D4) | 1 | 26.11.77 | **Reading** (D4) | A | L | 1-3 | McGregor |
| 1978-79 (D4) | 1 | 25.11.78 | **Weymouth** (SL) | H | D | 1-1 | Crosby |
| | 1r | 29.11.78 | **Weymouth** | A | W | 2-0 | Shanahan, Dungworth |
| | 2 | 16.12.78 | **Barking** (IL) | A | W | 2-1 | Dungworth, Shanahan |
| | 3 | 09.01.79 | **Sheffield Utd** (D2) | A | D | 0-0 | |
| | 3r | 15.01.79 | **Sheffield Utd** | H | W | 1-0 | Dungworth (p) |
| | 4 | 30.01.79 | **Swindon Town** (D3) | H | W | 2-1 | Dungworth 2 |
| | 5 | 20.02.79 | **Shrewsbury Town** (D3) | H | D | 2-2 | Dungworth 2 |
| | 5r | 26.02.79 | **Shrewsbury Town** | A | L | 1-3aet | Dungworth |
| 1979-80 (D4) | 1 | 24.11.79 | **Exeter City** (D3) | H | W | 4-1 | Crosby, Jopling, Brodie, Giles og |
| | 2 | 15.12.79 | **Hereford Utd** (D4) | A | W | 2-1 | Marshall og, Needham |
| | 3 | 05.01.80 | **Everton** (D1) | A | L | 1-4 | McGregor |
| 1980-81 (D4) | 1 | 22.11.80 | **Oxford Utd** (D3) | A | L | 0-1 | |
| 1981-82 (D4) | 1 | 21.11.81 | **Leytonstone-Ilford** (IL) | H | W | 2-0 | Garwood 2 |
| | 2 | 15.12.81 | **Oxford Utd** (D3) | H | D | 2-2 | Brodie, McDonald |
| | 2r | 30.12.81 | **Oxford Utd** | A | L | 2-4 | Robinson, French |
| 1982-83 (D4) | 1 | 20.11.82 | **Wimborne Town** (WL) | H | W | 4-0 | Banton 2 (1p), Sanford, Brodie |
| | 2 | 11.12.82 | **Portsmouth** (D3) | A | W | 3-1 | Briley, Banton 2 |
| | 3 | 08.01.83 | **Swindon Town** (D4) | A | L | 0-7 | |
| 1983-84 (D4) | 1 | 19.11.83 | **Worcester City** (APL) | H | D | 1-1 | Burvill |
| | 1r | 21.11.83 | **Worcester City** | A | L | 1-2 | Banton |
| 1984-85 (D4) | 1 | 17.11.84 | **Newport County** (D3) | A | D | 1-1 | McDonald (p) |
| | 1r | 20.11.84 | **Newport County** | H | W | 4-0 | Banton, Foley 2, McDonald (p) |
| | 2 | 08.12.84 | **Burton Albion** (NPL) | H | L | 0-2 | |
| 1985-86 (D4) | 1 | 16.11.85 | **Plymouth Argyle** (D3) | A | L | 0-1 | |
| 1986-87 (D4) | 1 | 15.11.86 | **Torquay Utd** (D4) | H | W | 1-0 | King (p) |
| | 2 | 06.12.86 | **Colchester Utd** (D4) | H | W | 3-2 | Wignall, Foyle 2 |
| | 3 | 10.01.87 | **Oxford Utd** (D1) | H | W | 3-0 | Smith, Burvill, Barnes |
| | 4 | 31.01.87 | **Barnsley** (D2) | H | D | 1-1 | Foyle |
| | 4r | 03.02.87 | **Barnsley** | A | L | 0-3 | |
| 1987-88 (D3) | 1 | 14.11.87 | **Sutton Utd** (Conf) | A | L | 0-3 | |
| 1988-89 (D3) | 1 | 19.11.88 | **Hayes** (IL) | H | W | 1-0 | McDonald |
| | 2 | 10.12.88 | **Bristol City** (D3) | H | D | 1-1 | McDonald (p) |

| | | | | | | | | |
|---|---|---|---|---|---|---|---|---|
| | | 2r | 13.12.88 | **Bristol City** | A | D | 0-0aet | |
| | | 2 2r | 20.12.88 | **Bristol City** | | D | 2-2aet | Randall, Claridge |
| | | 2 3r | 22.12.88 | **Bristol City** | A | L | 0-1 | |
| 1989-90 | (D4) | 1 | 18.11.89 | **Cambridge Utd** (D4) | H | L | 0-1 | |
| 1990-91 | (D4) | 1 | 17.11.90 | **Tiverton Town** (WL) | H | W | 6-2 | Stewart, Henry 2, Williams, Puckett, Randall |
| | | 2 | 08.12.90 | **Maidstone Utd** (D4) | H | W | 2-1 | Puckett, Stewart |
| | | 3 | 05.01.91 | **West Ham Utd** (D2) | H | D | 0-0 | |
| | | | | *played at Upton Park* | | | | |
| | | 3r | 16.01.91 | **West Ham Utd** (D2) | A | L | 1-6 | Randall |
| 1991-92 | (D4) | 1 | 16.11.91 | **Enfield** (IL) | H | L | 0-1 | |
| **As Aldershot Town** | | | | | | | | |
| 1999-00 | (IL) | 1 | 30.10.99 | **Hednesford Town** (Conf) | H | D | 1-1 | Abbott |
| | | 1r | 08.11.99 | **Hednesford Town** | A | W | 2-1 | Chewins, Abbott |
| | | 2 | 20.11.99 | **Exeter City** (D3) | A | L | 0-2 | |
| 2000-01 | (IL) | 1 | 18.11.00 | **Brighton** (D3) | H | L | 2-6 | Abbott 2 (1p) |
| 2001-02 | (IL) | 1 | 17.11.01 | **Bristol Rovers** (D3) | H | D | 0-0 | |
| | | 1r | 27.11.01 | **Bristol Rovers** | A | L | 0-1 | |

## ALFRETON TOWN

*Formed 1921. Reformed 1959. First entered FA Cup: 1921-22. Their one victory over a Football League club was against Lincoln City in the 5th qualifying round in the 1924-25 season. Members of the Northern Premier League.*

| | | | | | | | | |
|---|---|---|---|---|---|---|---|---|
| 1924-25 | (CA) | | 01.01.25 | 5q Lincoln City (3N) H 1-0; 6q Port Vale (D2) H 2-8 | | | | |
| 1969-70 | (ML) | 1 | 15.11.69 | **Barrow** (D3) | H | D | 1-1 | Bate |
| | | 1r | 17.11.69 | **Barrow** | A | D | 0-0aet | |
| | | 1 2r | 20.11.69 | **Barrow** | | D | 2-2aet | Ford, Woodward (p) |
| | | | | *played at Saltergate, Chesterfield* | | | | |
| | | 1 3r | 24.11.69 | **Barrow** | | L | 0-2 | |
| | | | | *played at Deepdale, Preston* | | | | |
| 1973-74 | (ML) | 1 | 24.11.73 | **Blyth Spartans** (NL) | H | D | 0-0 | |
| | | 1r | 28.11.73 | **Blyth Spartans** | A | L | 1-2 | Ford |

## ALTON TOWN

*First entered FA Cup: 1949-50. Hampshire League champions 2002. Members of the Wessex League.*

| | | | | | | | | |
|---|---|---|---|---|---|---|---|---|
| 1972-73 | (Hants) | 1 | 18.11.72 | **Newport County** (D4) | A | L | 1-5 | Morton |

## ALTRINCHAM

*Formed 1891. First entered FA Cup: 1905-06. FA Trophy winners: 1978, 1986. Runners-up: 1982. League clubs beaten: Birmingham City, Blackpool (2), Chester, Crewe Alexandra, Hartlepool United, Lincoln City, Rochdale (2), Rotherham United, Scunthorpe United (2), Sheffield United, Tranmere Rovers, York City, Wigan Athletic. Members of the Northern Premier League.*

| | | | | | | | | |
|---|---|---|---|---|---|---|---|---|
| 1921-22 | (CC) | | | 4q Tranmere Rovers (3N) H 4-4; 4qr Tranmere Rovers (A) 4-2; 5q Southport (3N) 0-3 | | | | |
| 1933-34 | (CC) | 1 | 25.11.33 | **Gainsborough T** (ML) | A | L | 0-1 | |
| 1963-64 | (CC) | 1 | 20.11.63 | **Wrexham** (D3) | H | D | 0-0 | |
| | | 1 | 16.11.63 | **Wrexham** | H | - | 1-2ab | Taberner |
| | | | | *abandoned after 76 minutes – fog* | | | | |
| | | 1r | 26.11.63 | **Wrexham** (D3) | A | L | 0-3 | |
| 1965-66 | (CC) | 1 | 13.11.65 | **Scarborough** (ML) | H | W | 6-0 | Swindells 5, Connolly |
| | | 2 | 08.12.65 | **Rochdale** (D4) | A | W | 3-1 | Swindells, Campbell, Connolly |
| | | 3 | 22.01.66 | **Wolverhampton W** (D2) | A | L | 0-5 | |
| 1967-68 | (CC) | 1 | 09.12.67 | **Grantham Town** (ML) | A | W | 3-0 | Peters, Lister, Farmer og |
| | | 2 | 06.01.68 | **Barrow** (D3) | H | L | 1-2 | Lister |
| 1968-69 | (NPL) | 1 | 16.11.68 | **Crewe Alexandra** (D3) | H | L | 0-1 | |
| 1971-72 | (NPL) | 1 | 23.11.71 | **Rossendale Utd** (CC) | A | L | 0-1 | |
| 1972-73 | (NPL) | 1 | 18.11.72 | **Notts County** (D3) | H | L | 0-1 | |
| 1973-74 | (NPL) | 1 | 24.11.73 | **Hartlepool** (D4) | H | W | 2-0 | Dickinson, Windsor |
| | | 2 | 15.12.73 | **Blackburn Rovers** (D3) | A | D | 0-0 | |
| | | 2r | 19.12.73 | **Blackburn Rovers** | H | L | 0-2 | |
| 1974-75 | (NPL) | 1 | 23.11.74 | **Scunthorpe Utd** (D4) | A | D | 1-1 | J Hughes |
| | | 1r | 25.11.74 | **Scunthorpe Utd** | H | W | 3-1 | Morris, Davison, J Hughes |

| | | | | | | | | |
|---|---|---|---|---|---|---|---|---|
| | | 2 | 14.12.74 | **Gateshead Utd** (NPL) | H | W | 3-0 | J Hughes, R Hughes, Morris |
| | | 3 | 04.01.75 | **Everton** (D1) | A | D | 1-1 | J Hughes |
| | | 3r | 07.01.75 | **Everton** | | L | 0-2 | |
| | | | | *played at Old Trafford* | | | | |
| 1975-76 | (NPL) | 1 | 22.11.75 | **Halifax Town** (D3) | A | L | 1-3 | Moore |
| 1976-77 | (NPL) | 1 | 20.11.76 | **Rotherham Utd** (D3) | A | L | 0-5 | |
| 1978-79 | (NPL) | 1 | 25.11.78 | **Southport** (NPL) | H | W | 4-3 | Johnson 2, Bailey, Rogers |
| | | 2 | 16.12.78 | **Droylesden** (CC) | A | W | 2-0 | Johnson, Brooke |
| | | 3 | 10.01.79 | **Tottenham Hotspur** (D1) | A | D | 1-1 | Johnson |
| | | 3r | 16.01.79 | **Tottenham Hotspur** | H | L | 0-3 | |
| | | | | *played at Maine Road* | | | | |
| 1979-80 | (APL) | 1 | 24.11.79 | **Crewe Alexandra** (D4) | H | W | 3-0 | Rogers, Whitbread, Wilson |
| | | 2 | 15.12.79 | **Rotherham Utd** (D3) | A | W | 2-0 | Bailey, Howard |
| | | 3 | 05.01.80 | **Orient** (D2) | H | D | 1-1 | Whitbread |
| | | 3r | 09.01.80 | **Orient** | A | L | 1-2 | Johnson |
| 1980-81 | (APL) | 1 | 22.11.80 | **Burscough** (CC) | A | W | 2-1 | Johnson, Rogers |
| | | 2 | 13.12.80 | **Scunthorpe Utd** (D4) | A | D | 0-0 | |
| | | 2r | 15.12.80 | **Scunthorpe Utd** | H | W | 1-0 | Davison (p) |
| | | 3 | 03.01.81 | **Liverpool** (D1) | A | L | 1-4 | Heathcote (p) |
| 1981-82 | (APL) | 1 | 21.11.81 | **Sheffield Utd** (D4) | A | D | 2-2 | Rogers 2 |
| | | 1r | 23.11.81 | **Sheffield Utd** | H | W | 3-0 | Howard 2, Heathcote |
| | | 2 | 12.12.81 | **York City** (D4) | A | D | 0-0 | |
| | | 2r | 02.01.82 | **York City** | H | W | 4-3 | Goulding, Rogers, Whitbread 2 |
| | | 3 | 18.01.82 | **Burnley** (D3) | A | L | 1-6 | Howard |
| 1982-83 | (APL) | 1 | 20.11.82 | **Rochdale** (D4) | H | W | 2-1 | Davison, Howard |
| | | 2 | 11.12.82 | **Huddersfield Town** (D3) | H | L | 0-1 | |
| 1983-84 | (APL) | 1 | 19.11.83 | **Frickley Athletic** (APL) | A | W | 1-0 | Gardner |
| | | 2 | 10.12.83 | **Darlington** (D4) | A | D | 0-0 | |
| | | 2r | 14.12.83 | **Darlington** | H | L | 0-2 | |
| 1984-85 | (APL) | 1 | 17.11.84 | **Blackpool** (D4) | A | W | 1-0 | Fagan |
| | | 2 | 08.12.84 | **Doncaster Rovers** (D3) | H | L | 1-3 | Bennett |
| 1985-86 | (APL) | 1 | 16.11.85 | **Chorley** (NPL) | A | W | 2-0 | Reid, Anderson |
| | | 2 | 07.12.85 | **Blackpool** (D3) | A | W | 2-1 | Reid, Anderson |
| | | 3 | 14.01.86 | **Birmingham City** (D1) | A | W | 2-1 | Ellis, Hopkins |
| | | 4 | 25.01.86 | **York City** (D3) | A | L | 0-2 | |
| 1986-87 | (Conf) | 1 | 15.11.86 | **Frickley Athletic** (Conf) | A | D | 0-0 | |
| | | 1r | 18.11.86 | **Frickley Athletic** | H | W | 4-0 | Anderson, Farrelly, Reid, Bishop |
| | | 2 | 06.12.86 | **Telford Utd** (Conf) | A | L | 0-1 | |
| 1987-88 | (Conf) | 1 | 14.11.87 | **Wigan Athletic** (D3) | H | L | 0-2 | |
| 1988-89 | (Conf) | 1 | 19.11.88 | **Lincoln City** (D4) | H | W | 3-2 | Timmons, Ellis 2 |
| | | 2 | 10.12.88 | **Halifax Town** (D4) | H | L | 0-3 | |
| 1990-91 | (Conf) | 1 | 18.11.90 | **Huddersfield Town** (D3) | H | L | 1-2 | Rowlands |
| 1992-93 | (Conf) | 1 | 14.11.92 | **Chester City** (D2) | A | D | 1-1 | Comstive og |
| | | 1r | 25.11.92 | **Chester City** | H | W | 2-0 | Harris, Freeman |
| | | 2 | 05.12.92 | **Port Vale** (D2) | H | L | 1-4 | Dyson |
| 1994-95 | (Conf) | 1 | 12.11.94 | **Southport** (Conf) | H | W | 3-2 | Green, Morton, France |
| | | 2 | 03.12.94 | **Wigan Athletic** (D3) | H | W | 1-0 | Sharratt |
| | | 3 | 07.01.95 | **Tottenham Hotspur** (PL) | A | L | 0-3 | |
| 1995-96 | (Conf) | 1 | 22.11.95 | **Crewe Alexandra** (D2) | H | L | 0-2 | |
| 1996-97 | (Conf) | 1 | 16.11.96 | **Preston North End** (D2) | A | L | 1-4 | Shepherd (p) |
| 2001-02 | (NPL) | 1 | 17.11.01 | **Lancaster City** (NPL) | H | D | 1-1 | Thornley (p) |
| | | 1r | 27.11.01 | **Lancaster City** | A | W | 4-1aet | Poland 3 (1p), Thornley (p) |
| | | 2 | 08.12.01 | **Darlington** (D3) | H | L | 1-2 | Maddox |

## ALVECHURCH

*Formed 1929. Folded 1992. Reformed 1994. First entered FA Cup: 1968-69. Alvechurch set an FA Cup record with Oxford City in 1971-72 when their fourth qualifying round tie needed six attempts before Alvechurch won 1-0. League club beaten: Exeter City. Members of the Midland Combination League.*

| | | | | | | | | |
|---|---|---|---|---|---|---|---|---|
| 1971-72 | (MC) | 1 | 24.11.71 | **Aldershot** (D4) | A | L | 2-4 | Palmer, Hope |
| 1973-74 | (WMRL) | 1 | 24.11.73 | **Exeter City** (D4) | A | W | 1-0 | Allner |
| | | 2 | 15.12.73 | **King's Lynn** (SL) | H | W | 6-1 | Lawrence 2, Palmer, Edwards 2, Lyne (p) |
| | | 3 | 05.01.74 | **Bradford City** (D4) | A | L | 2-4 | Lawrence, Horne |

## AMATEUR ATHLETIC CLUB (AAC)

*The AAC's home ground was Lillie Bridge, West Brompton, London, venue of the second FA Cup Final in 1873. However AAC never played an FA Cup match there themselves, entering the competition just once and scratching from their match against Clapham Rovers.*

| | | | | | | | | | |
|---|---|---|---|---|---|---|---|---|---|
| 1873-74 | | 1 | | Clapham Rovers | A | | - | |
| | | | | *AAC scratched. Clapham Rovers walkover* | | | | |

## ANDOVER

*Formed 1883. First entered FA Cup: 1898-99. Members of the Wessex League.*

| | | | | | | | | |
|---|---|---|---|---|---|---|---|---|
| 1962-63 | (SL) | 1 | 03.11.62 | **Gillingham** (D4) | H | L | 0-1 | |

## ANNFIELD PLAIN

*Formed 1890. First entered FA Cup: 1906-07. Record crowd of 7,200 v Southport, 1928. Exactly half that number – 3,600 – saw the match between the same two clubs 36 years later. Wearside League champions 1984-85. Based in Stanley, Co.Durham.*

| | | | | | | | | |
|---|---|---|---|---|---|---|---|---|
| 1926-27 | (NEL) | 1 | 27.11.26 | **Chilton Coll Rec A** (NEL) | H | L | 2-4 | Jones, Roots |
| 1928-29 | (NEL) | 1 | 24.11.28 | **Southport** (3N) | H | L | 1-4 | Ferguson |
| 1964-65 | (Wear) | 1 | 14.11.64 | **Southport** | H | L | 1-6 | Lawson |

## AP LEAMINGTON

*Formed 1945 as Lockheed Leamington. Changed name 1973 to AP Leamington when company changed their name to Automotive Products. First entered FA Cup: 1948-49. Became Leamington FC in 1985 when they lost the company's backing. Folded 1988.*

| | | | | | | | | |
|---|---|---|---|---|---|---|---|---|
| 1974-75 | (SL) | 1 | 23.11.74 | **Southend Utd** (D3) | H | L | 1-2 | Lee |
| 1975-76 | (SL) | 1 | 22.11.75 | **Stafford Rangers** (NPL) | H | L | 2-3 | Keeley 2 |
| 1977-78 | (SL) | 1 | 26.11.77 | **Enderby Town** (SL) | H | W | 6-1 | Stewart, Brown 3, Cavenagh (p), Keeley |
| | | 2 | 17.12.77 | **Southend Utd** (D4) | H | D | 0-0 | |
| | | 2r | 19.12.77 | **Southend Utd** | A | L | 0-4 | |
| 1978-79 | (SL) | 1 | 25.11.78 | **Dartford** (SL) | A | W | 2-1 | Gardner 2 |
| | | 2 | 16.12.78 | **Torquay Utd** (D4) | H | L | 0-1 | |
| 1979-80 | (APL) | 1 | 24.11.79 | **Tranmere Rovers** (D4) | A | L | 0-9 | |
| 1983-84 | (SL) | 1 | 19.11.83 | **Gillingham** (D3) | H | L | 0-1 | |

## APSLEY

*Formed 1885. Entered FA Cup: 1901-02 – 1946-47. Merged with Hemel Hempstead Utd in 1947 to create Hemel Hempstead Town. Have never reached Competition Proper as Hemel Hempstead. Hemel Hempstead are members of the Isthmian League.*

| | | | | | | | | |
|---|---|---|---|---|---|---|---|---|
| 1938-39 | (SPT) | 1 | 26.11.38 | **Bromley** (AL) | A | L | 1-2 | Hook |

## ARGONAUTS

*Amateur club who entered the FA Cup once. No relation to the later Argonauts 'club' which applied to join the Football League three times in 1928, 1929 and 1930 without ever playing a match.*

| | | | | | | | | |
|---|---|---|---|---|---|---|---|---|
| 1879-80 | | 1 | 08.11.79 | **Hotspur FC** | A | D | 1-1 | Gore |
| | | 1r | 15.11.79 | **Hotspur FC** | H | L | 0-1 | |

## ARNOLD TOWN

*Formed 1928 as Arnold St Mary's. First entered FA Cup: 1913-14. Merged with Arnold Kingswell (formed 1962) in1989 and became Arnold Town. Based in Nottinghamshire . Members of the Northern Counties East League.*

| | | | | | | | | |
|---|---|---|---|---|---|---|---|---|
| 1967-68 | (ML) | 1 | 09.12.67 | **Bristol Rovers** (D3) | H | L | 0-3 | |
| 1977-78 | (ML) | 1 | 26.11.77 | **Port Vale** (D3) | H | D | 0-0 | |
| | | 1r | 28.11.77 | **Port Vale** | A | L | 2-5 | Brockhurst, Livesey |

## ARSENAL

*Formed 1886 as Dial Square but soon changed their name to Royal Arsenal. 1886-1893 Royal Arsenal; 1893-1914 Woolwich Arsenal; 1914 Arsenal. FA Cup and League double 1971, 1998, 2002. Have appeared in a record 16 FA Cup finals. FA Cup winners (9 times): 1930, 1936, 1950, 1971, 1979, 1993, 1998, 2002, 2003. Runners-up (7 times): 1927, 1932, 1952, 1972, 1978, 1980, 2001; Hold joint-record (with Everton) of 23 semi-final appearances. Record FA Cup win: 12-0 v Ashford 1st qualifying round, 14.10.1893. In Competition Proper: 11-1 v Darwen, 3rd round, 9.1.1932. Record FA Cup defeat: 0-6 v Sunderland, 1st round, 21.1.1893; v Derby County, 1st round, 28.1.1899; v West Ham Utd, 3rd round, 1st leg, 5.1.1946 (Lost 1-6 on aggregate)*

**as Royal Arsenal**

| | | | | | | | |
|---|---|---|---|---|---|---|---|
| 1889-90 | | | 1q Lyndhurst (H) 11-0; 2q Thorpe, Norwich (A) 2-2aet; 2qr Thorpe, Norwich (H) walkover 3q Crusaders (H) 5-2aet; 4q Swifts (H) 1-5 | | | | |
| 1890-91 | 1 | 17.01.91 | **Derby County** (D1) | H | L | 1-2 | Offer |
| 1891-92 | 1 | 16.01.92 | **Small Heath** (FAll) | A | L | 1-5 | Davie |
| 1892-93 | | | 1q Highland Lt Infantry (H) 3-0; 2q City Ramblers (H) 10-1; 3q Millwall A (H) 3-2; 4q Clapton (H) 3-0 | | | | |
| | 1 | 21.01.93 | **Sunderland** (D1) | A | L | 0-6 | |

**as Woolwich Arsenal**

| | | | | | | | |
|---|---|---|---|---|---|---|---|
| 1893-94 (D2) | | | 1q Ashford U (H) 12-0; 2q Clapton Orient (H) 6-2; 3q Millwall A (H) 2-0; 4q 2nd Scots Guards (A) 2-1aet | | | | |
| | 1 | 27.01.94 | **Sheffield Wed** (D1) | H | L | 1-2 | Elliott |
| 1894-95 (D2) | 1 | 02.02.95 | **Bolton Wanderers** (D1) | A | L | 0-1 | |
| 1895-96 (D2) | 1 | 01.02.96 | **Burnley** (D1) | A | L | 1-6 | O'Brien |
| 1896-97 (D2) | | | 4q Leyton (H) 5-0; 5q Chatham (H) 4-0; Int Millwall (A) 2-4 | | | | |
| 1897-98 (D2) | | | 3q St Albans (H) 9-0; 4q Sheppey U (H) 3-0; 5q New Brompton (H) 4-2 | | | | |
| | 1 | 29.01.98 | **Burnley** (D2) | A | L | 1-3 | Brock |
| 1898-99 (D2) | 1 | 28.01.99 | **Derby County** (D1) | H | L | 0-6 | |
| 1899-00 (D2) | | | 3q New Brompton (H) 1-1; 3qr New Brompton (A) 0-0; 3q 2r New Brompton at Millwall 2-2; 3q 3r New Brompton at Tottenham 1-1; 3q 4r New Brompton at Gravesend 0-1 | | | | |
| 1900-01 (D2) | | | Int Darwen (A) 2-0 | | | | |
| | 1 | 09.02.01 | **Blackburn Rovers** (D1) | H | W | 2-0 | Tennant, Low |
| | 2 | 23.02.01 | **WBA** (D1) | H | L | 0-1 | |
| 1901-02 (D2) | | | Int Luton T (H) 1-1; Int R Luton T (A) 2-0 | | | | |
| | 1 | 25.01.02 | **Newcastle Utd** (D1) | H | L | 0-2 | |
| 1902-03 (D2) | | | Int Brentford (A) 1-1; Int R Brentford (H) 5-0 | | | | |
| | 1 | 07.02.03 | **Sheffield Utd** (D1) | H | L | 1-3 | W Anderson |
| 1903-04 (D2) | | | Int Bristol R (A) 1-1; Int R Bristol R (H) 1-1; Int 2r Bristol R (at White Hart Lane) 1-0 | | | | |
| | 1 | 06.02.04 | **Fulham** (SL) | H | W | 1-0 | Shanks |
| | 2 | 20.02.04 | **Manchester City** (D1) | H | L | 0-2 | |
| 1904-05 (D1) | 1 | 04.02.05 | **Bristol City** (D2) | H | D | 0-0 | |
| | 1r | 08.02.05 | **Bristol City** | A | L | 0-1 | |
| 1905-06 (D1) | 1 | 13.01.06 | **West Ham Utd** (SL) | H | D | 1-1 | Sharp (p) |
| | 1r | 18.01.06 | **West Ham Utd** | A | W | 3-2 | Ducat, Satterthwaite, Garbutt |
| | 2 | 03.02.06 | **Watford** (SL) | H | W | 3-0 | Freeman, Coleman, Fitchie |
| | 3 | 24.02.06 | **Sunderland** (D1) | H | W | 5-0 | Garbutt 2, Fitchie, Sands, Coleman |
| | 4 | 10.03.06 | **Manchester Utd** (D2) | A | W | 3-2 | Freeman 2, Coleman |
| | SF | 31.03.06 | **Newcastle Utd** (D1) | | L | 0-2 | |
| | | | *played at Victoria Ground, Stoke* | | | | |
| 1906-07 (D1) | 1 | 12.01.07 | **Grimsby Town** (D2) | | D | 1-1 | Garbutt |
| | 1r | 16.01.07 | **Grimsby Town** | H | W | 3-0 | Satterthwaite, Sands, Garbutt |
| | 2 | 02.02.07 | **Bristol City** (D1) | H | W | 2-1 | Hynds, Kyle |
| | 3 | 23.02.07 | **Bristol Rovers** (SL) | A | W | 1-0 | Neave |
| | 4 | 09.03.07 | **Barnsley** (D2) | A | W | 2-1 | Satterthwaite, Neave |
| | SF | 23.03.07 | **Sheffield Wed** (D1) | | L | 1-3 | Garbutt |
| | | | *played at St Andrews* | | | | |
| 1907-08 (D1) | 1 | 11.01.08 | **Hull City** (D2) | H | D | 0-0 | |
| | 1r | 16.01.08 | **Hull City** | A | L | 1-4 | Kyle |
| 1908-09 (D1) | 1 | 16.01.09 | **Croydon Common** (SL) | A | D | 1-1 | Fitchie |
| | 1r | 20.01.09 | **Croydon Common** | H | W | 2-0 | Raybould, Ducat |
| | 2 | 06.02.09 | **Millwall Athletic** (SL) | H | D | 1-1 | Lewis |
| | 2r | 10.02.09 | **Millwall Athletic** | A | L | 0-1 | |
| 1909-10 (D1) | 1 | 15.01.10 | **Watford** (SL) | H | W | 3-0 | Lewis 2, McKellar |
| | 2 | 05.02.10 | **Everton** (D1) | A | L | 0-5 | |
| 1910-11 (D1) | 1 | 14.01.11 | **Clapton Orient** (D2) | A | - | 1-0 | McEachrane |
| | | | *abandoned afer 55 minutes* | | | | |
| | 1 | 16.01.11 | **Clapton Orient** | A | W | 2-1 | Chalmers, Hoare |
| | 2 | 04.02.11 | **Swindon Town** (SL) | A | L | 0-1 | |
| 1911-12 (D1) | 1 | 13.01.12 | **Bolton Wanderers** (D1) | A | L | 0-1 | |
| 1912-13 (D1) | 1 | 11.01.13 | **Croydon Common** (SL) | A | D | 0-0 | |
| | 1r | 15.01.13 | **Croydon Common** | H | W | 2-1 | Duncan, Graham |

| | | | | | | | |
|---|---|---|---|---|---|---|---|
| | 2 | 01.02.13 | **Liverpool** (D1) | H | L | 1-4 | Lewis |
| 1913-14 (D1) | 1 | 10.01.14 | **Bradford City** (D1) | A | L | 0-2 | |
| **as Arsenal** | | | | | | | |
| 1914-15 (D2) | 1 | 09.01.15 | **Merthyr Town** (SL) | H | W | 3-0 | King 3 |
| | 2 | 30.01.15 | **Chelsea** (D1) | A | L | 0-1 | |
| 1919-20 (D1) | 1 | 10.01.20 | **Rochdale** (CL) | H | W | 4-2 | Rutherford, Groves, Graham, Pagnam |
| | 2 | 31.01.20 | **Bristol City** (D2) | A | L | 0-1 | |
| 1920-21 (D1) | 1 | 08.01.21 | **QPR** (D3) | A | L | 0-2 | |
| 1921-22 (D1) | 1 | 07.01.22 | **QPR** (3S) | H | D | 0-0 | |
| | 1r | 11.01.22 | **QPR** | A | W | 2-1 | Graham (p), Milne |
| | 2 | 28.01.22 | **Bradford Park A** (D2) | A | W | 3-2 | White 2, Blyth |
| | 3 | 18.02.22 | **Leicester City** (D2) | H | W | 3-0 | White 2, Rutherford |
| | 4 | 04.03.22 | **Preston North End** (D1) | H | D | 1-1 | White |
| | 4r | 08.03.22 | **Preston North End** | A | L | 1-2aet | Blyth |
| 1922-23 (D1) | 1 | 13.01.23 | **Liverpool** (D1) | A | D | 0-0 | |
| | 1r | 17.01.23 | **Liverpool** | H | L | 1-4 | Turnbull |
| 1923-24 (D1) | 1 | 12.01.24 | **Luton Town** (3S) | H | W | 4-1 | Blyth, Woods, Turnbull, Milne |
| | 2 | 02.02.24 | **Cardiff City** (D1) | A | L | 0-1 | |
| 1924-25 (D1) | 1 | 14.01.25 | **West Ham Utd** (D1) | A | D | 0-0 | |
| | 1r | 21.01.25 | **West Ham Utd** | H | D | 2-2aet | Brain 2 |
| | 1 2r | 26.01.25 | **West Ham Utd** | | L | 0-1 | |
| | | | *played at Stamford Bridge* | | | | |
| 1925-26 (D1) | 3 | 09.01.26 | **Wolverhampton W** (D2) | A | D | 1-1 | Brain |
| | 3r | 13.01.26 | **Wolverhampton W** | H | W | 1-0 | Baker |
| | 4 | 30.01.26 | **Blackburn Rovers** (D1) | H | W | 3-1 | Haden, Brain, Hope og |
| | 5 | 20.02.26 | **Aston Villa** (D1) | A | D | 1-1 | Buchan |
| | 5r | 24.02.26 | **Aston Villa** | H | W | 2-0 | Paterson, Brain |
| | 6 | 06.03.26 | **Swansea Town** (D2) | A | L | 1-2 | Mackie |
| 1926-27 (D1) | 3 | 08.01.27 | **Sheffield Utd** (D1) | A | W | 3-2 | Brain, Buchan, Hulme |
| | 4 | 29.01.27 | **Port Vale** (D2) | A | D | 2-2 | Buchan, Brain |
| | 4r | 02.02.27 | **Port Vale** | H | W | 1-0 | Buchan |
| | 5 | 19.02.27 | **Liverpool** (D1) | H | W | 2-0 | Brain, Buchan |
| | 6 | 05.03.27 | **Wolverhampton W** (D2) | H | W | 2-1 | Blyth, Butler |
| | SF | 26.03.27 | **Southampton** (D2) | | W | 2-1 | Hulme, Buchan |
| | | | *played at Stamford Bridge* | | | | |
| | F | 23.04.27 | **Cardiff City** (D1) | | L | 0-1 | |
| | | | *played at Wembley Stadium* | | | | |
| 1927-28 (D1) | 3 | 14.01.28 | **WBA** (D2) | H | W | 2-0 | Brain, Hulme |
| | 4 | 28.01.28 | **Everton** (D1) | H | W | 4-3 | Hulme 2, Brain, Buchan |
| | 5 | 18.02.28 | **Aston Villa** (D1) | H | W | 4-1 | Brain 2, Lambert, Hulme |
| | 6 | 03.03.28 | **Stoke City** (D2) | H | W | 4-1 | Blyth 2, Hoar 2 |
| | SF | 24.03.28 | **Blackburn Rovers** (D1) | | L | 0-1 | |
| | | | *played at Filbert Street* | | | | |
| 1928-29 (D1) | 3 | 12.01.29 | **Stoke City** (D2) | H | W | 2-1 | Brain, Hulme |
| | 4 | 26.01.29 | **Mansfield Town** (ML) | H | W | 2-0 | Jack, Peel |
| | 5 | 16.02.29 | **Swindon Town** (3S) | A | D | 0-0 | |
| | 5r | 20.02.29 | **Swindon Town** | H | W | 1-0 | Brain |
| | 6 | 02.03.29 | **Aston Villa** (D1) | A | L | 0-1 | |
| 1929-30 (D1) | 3 | 11.01.30 | **Chelsea** (D2) | H | W | 2-0 | Lambert, Bastin |
| | 4 | 25.01.30 | **Birmingham** (D1) | H | D | 2-2 | Bastin, Jack |
| | 4r | 29.01.30 | **Birmingham** | A | W | 1-0 | Baker (p) |
| | 5 | 15.02.30 | **Middlesbrough** (D1) | A | W | 2-0 | Lambert, Bastin |
| | 6 | 01.03.30 | **West Ham Utd** (D1) | A | W | 3-0 | Lambert 2, Baker |
| | SF | 22.03.30 | **Hull City** (D2) | | D | 2-2 | Jack, Bastin |
| | | | *played at Elland Road* | | | | |
| | SFr | 26.03.30 | **Hull City** | | W | 1-0 | Jack |
| | | | *played at Villa Park* | | | | |
| | F | 26.04.30 | **Huddersfield Town** (D1) | | W | 2-0 | James, Lambert |
| | | | *played at Wembley Stadium* | | | | |
| 1930-31 (D1) | 3 | 10.01.31 | **Aston Villa** (D1) | H | D | 2-2 | Lambert, Jack |
| | 3r | 14.01.31 | **Aston Villa** | A | W | 3-1 | Hulme 2, Jack |
| | 4 | 24.01.31 | **Chelsea** (D1) | A | L | 1-2 | Bastin |

| | | | | | | | |
|---|---|---|---|---|---|---|---|
| 1931-32 (D1) | 3 | 09.01.32 | **Darwen** (LC) | H | W | 11-1 | Bastin 4, Jack 3, Lambert 2, Hulme 2 |
| | 4 | 23.01.32 | **Plymouth Argyle** (D2) | H | W | 4-2 | Lambert 2, Hulme, Roberts og |
| | 5 | 13.02.32 | **Portsmouth** (D1) | A | W | 2-0 | Bastin, Hulme |
| | 6 | 27.02.32 | **Huddersfield Town** (D1) | A | W | 1-0 | Roberts |
| | SF | 12.03.32 | **Manchester City** (D1) | | W | 1-0 | Bastin |
| | | | *played at Villa Park* | | | | |
| | F | 23.04.32 | **Newcastle Utd** (D1) | | L | 1-2 | John |
| | | | *played at Wembley Stadium* | | | | |
| 1932-33 (D1) | 3 | 14.01.33 | **Walsall** (3N) | A | L | 0-2 | |
| 1933-34 (D1) | 3 | 13.01.34 | **Luton Town** (3S) | A | W | 1-0 | Dunne |
| | 4 | 27.01.34 | **Crystal Palace** (3S) | H | W | 7-0 | Dunne 2, Bastin 2, Beasley 2, Birkett |
| | 5 | 17.02.34 | **Derby County** (D1) | H | W | 1-0 | Jack |
| | 6 | 03.03.34 | **Aston Villa** (D1) | H | L | 1-2 | Dougall |
| 1934-35 (D1) | 3 | 12.01.35 | **Brighton** (3S) | A | W | 2-0 | Hulme, Drake |
| | 4 | 26.01.35 | **Leicester City** (D1) | A | W | 1-0 | Hulme |
| | 5 | 16.02.35 | **Reading** (3S) | A | W | 1-0 | Bastin |
| | 6 | 02.03.35 | **Sheffield Wed** (D1) | A | L | 1-2 | Catlin og |
| 1935-36 (D1) | 3 | 11.01.36 | **Bristol Rovers** (3S) | A | W | 5-1 | Bastin 2, Drake 2, Bowden |
| | 4 | 25.01.36 | **Liverpool** (D1) | A | W | 2-0 | Bowden, Hulme |
| | 5 | 15.02.36 | **Newcastle Utd** (D2) | A | D | 3-3 | Bowden 2, Hulme |
| | 5r | 19.02.36 | **Newcastle Utd** | H | W | 3-0 | Bastin 2 (2p), Beasley |
| | 6 | 29.02.36 | **Barnsley** (D2) | H | W | 4-1 | Beasley 2, Bowden, Bastin (p) |
| | SF | 21.03.36 | **Grimsby Town** (D1) | | W | 1-0 | Bastin |
| | | | *played at Leeds Road, Huddersfield* | | | | |
| | F | 25.04.36 | **Sheffield Utd** (D2) | | W | 1-0 | Drake |
| | | | *played at Wembley Stadium* | | | | |
| 1936-37 (D1) | 3 | 16.01.37 | **Chesterfield** (D2) | A | W | 5-1 | Drake 2, Kirchen 2, Davidson |
| | 4 | 30.01.37 | **Manchester Utd** (D1) | H | W | 5-0 | Bastin, Davidson, Drake, Kirchen, Brown og |
| | 5 | 20.02.37 | **Burnley** (D2) | A | W | 7-1 | Drake 4, Crayston, Bastin, Kirchen |
| | 6 | 06.03.37 | **WBA** (D1) | A | L | 1-3 | Bastin |
| 1937-38 (D1) | 3 | 08.01.38 | **Bolton Wanderers** (D1) | H | W | 3-1 | Bastin 2, Kirchen |
| | 4 | 22.01.38 | **Wolverhampton W** (D1) | A | W | 2-1 | Kirchen, Drake |
| | 5 | 12.02.38 | **Preston North End** (D1) | H | L | 0-1 | |
| 1938-39 (D1) | 3 | 07.01.39 | **Chelsea** (D1) | A | L | 1-2 | Bastin |
| 1945-46 (D1) | 3 1L | 05.01.46 | **West Ham Utd** (D2) | A | L | 0-6 | |
| | 3 2L | 09.01.46 | **West Ham Utd** | H | W | 1-0 | Cumner |
| 1946-47 (D1) | 3 | 11.01.47 | **Chelsea** (D1) | A | D | 1-1 | McPherson |
| | 3r | 15.01.47 | **Chelsea** | H | D | 1-1 | Rooke |
| | 3 2r | 20.01.47 | **Chelsea** | | L | 0-2 | |
| | | | *played at White Hart Lane* | | | | |
| 1947-48 (D1) | 3 | 10.01.48 | **Bradford Park A** (D2) | H | L | 0-1 | |
| 1948-49 (D1) | 3 | 08.01.49 | **Tottenham Hotspur** (D2) | H | W | 3-0 | McPherson, Roper, Lishman |
| | 4 | 29.01.49 | **Derby County** (D1) | A | L | 0-1 | |
| 1949-50 (D1) | 3 | 07.01.50 | **Sheffield Wed** (D2) | H | W | 1-0 | Lewis |
| | 4 | 28.01.50 | **Swansea Town** (D2) | H | W | 2-1 | Logie, Barnes (p) |
| | 5 | 11.02.50 | **Burnley** (D1) | H | W | 2-0 | Lewis, D Compton |
| | 6 | 04.03.50 | **Leeds Utd** (D2) | H | W | 1-0 | Lewis |
| | SF | 18.03.50 | **Chelsea** (D1) | | D | 2-2 | Cox, L Compton |
| | | | *played at White Hart Lane* | | | | |
| | SFr | 22.03.50 | **Chelsea** | | W | 1-0aet | Cox |
| | | | *played at White Hart Lane* | | | | |
| | F | 29.04.50 | **Liverpool** (D1) | | W | 2-0 | Lewis 2 |
| | | | *played at Wembley Stadium* | | | | |
| 1950-51 (D1) | 3 | 06.01.51 | **Carlisle Utd** (3N) | H | D | 0-0 | |
| | 3r | 11.01.51 | **Carlisle Utd** | A | W | 4-1 | Lewis 2, Logie, Goring |
| | 4 | 27.01.51 | **Northampton Town** (3S) | H | W | 3-2 | Lewis 2, Roper |
| | 5 | 10.02.51 | **Manchester Utd** (D1) | A | L | 0-1 | |
| 1951-52 (D1) | 3 | 12.01.52 | **Norwich City** (3S) | A | W | 5-0 | Lishman 2, Logie, Goring, Roper |
| | 4 | 02.02.52 | **Barnsley** (D2) | H | W | 4-0 | Lewis 3, Lishman |
| | 5 | 23.02.52 | **Leyton Orient** (3S) | A | W | 3-0 | Lishman 2, Lewis |

| | | | | | | | |
|---|---|---|---|---|---|---|---|
| | 6 | 08.03.52 | **Luton Town** (D2) | A | W | 3-2 | Cox 2, Milton |
| | SF | 05.04.52 | **Chelsea** (D1) | | D | 1-1 | Cox |
| | | | *played at White Hart Lane* | | | | |
| | SFr | 07.04.52 | **Chelsea** | | W | 3-0 | Cox 2, Lishman |
| | | | *played at White Hart Lane* | | | | |
| | F | 03.05.52 | **Newcastle Utd** (D1) | | L | 0-1 | |
| | | | *played at Wembley Stadium* | | | | |
| 1952-53 (D1) | 3 | 10.01.53 | **Doncaster Rovers** (D2) | H | W | 4-0 | Lishman, Holton, Logie, Roper |
| | 4 | 31.01.53 | **Bury** (D2) | H | W | 6-2 | Holton, Lishman, Logie, Milton, Roper, T Daniel og |
| | 5 | 14.02.53 | **Burnley** (D1) | A | W | 2-0 | Holton, Lishman |
| | 6 | 28.02.53 | **Blackpool** (D1) | H | L | 1-2 | Logie |
| 1953-54 (D1) | 3 | 09.01.54 | **Aston Villa** (D1) | H | W | 5-1 | Roper 2, Holton, Logie, Milton |
| | 4 | 30.01.54 | **Norwich City** (3S) | H | L | 1-2 | Logie |
| 1954-55 (D1) | 3 | 08.01.55 | **Cardiff City** (D1) | H | W | 1-0 | Lawton |
| | 4 | 29.01.55 | **Wolverhampton W** (D1) | A | L | 0-1 | |
| 1955-56 (D1) | 3 | 07.01.56 | **Bedford Town** (SL) | H | D | 2-2 | Tapscott, Groves |
| | 3r | 12.01.56 | **Bedford Town** | A | W | 2-1aet | Groves, Tapscott |
| | 4 | 28.01.56 | **Aston Villa** (D1) | H | W | 4-1 | Tapscott 2, Groves, Charlton |
| | 5 | 18.02.56 | **Charlton Athletic** (D1) | A | W | 2-0 | Groves, Bloomfield |
| | 6 | 03.03.56 | **Birmingham City** (D1) | H | L | 1-3 | Charlton |
| 1956-57 (D1) | 3 | 05.01.57 | **Stoke City** (D2) | H | W | 4-2 | Herd 2, Tapscott, Haverty |
| | 4 | 26.01.57 | **Newport County** (3S) | A | W | 2-0 | Tapscott, Herd |
| | 5 | 16.02.57 | **Preston North End** (D1) | A | D | 3-3 | Clapton, Herd, Dunn og |
| | 5r | 19.02.57 | **Preston North End** | H | W | 2-1 | Dodgin, Herd |
| | 6 | 02.03.57 | **WBA** (D1) | A | D | 2-2 | Herd, Charlton |
| | 6r | 05.03.57 | **WBA** | H | L | 1-2 | Holton |
| 1957-58 (D1) | 3 | 04.01.58 | **Northampton Town** (3S) | A | L | 1-3 | Clapton |
| 1958-59 (D1) | 3 | 10.01.59 | **Bury** (D3) | A | W | 1-0 | Herd |
| | 4 | 24.01.59 | **Colchester Utd** (D3) | A | D | 2-2 | Groves 2 |
| | 4r | 28.01.59 | **Colchester Utd** | H | W | 4-0 | Herd 2, Julians, Evans (p) |
| | 5 | 14.02.59 | **Sheffield Utd** (D2) | H | D | 2-2 | Evans (p), Julians |
| | 5r | 18.02.59 | **Sheffield Utd** | A | L | 0-3 | |
| 1959-60 (D1) | 3 | 09.01.60 | **Rotherham Utd** (D2) | A | D | 2-2 | Julians, Williams og |
| | 3r | 13.01.60 | **Rotherham Utd** | H | D | 1-1aet | Bloomfield |
| | 3 2r | 18.01.60 | **Rotherham Utd** | | L | 0-2 | |
| | | | *played at Hillsborough* | | | | |
| 1960-61 (D1) | 3 | 07.01.61 | **Sunderland** (D2) | A | L | 1-2 | Herd |
| 1961-62 (D1) | 3 | 06.01.62 | **Bradford City** (D4) | H | W | 3-0 | Charles 2, Lawlor og |
| | 4 | 31.01.62 | **Manchester Utd** (D1) | A | L | 0-1 | |
| 1962-63 (D1) | 3 | 30.01.63 | **Oxford Utd** (D4) | H | W | 5-1 | Baker 2, Strong 2, MacLeod |
| | 4 | 12.03.63 | **Sheffield Wed** (D1) | H | W | 2-0 | MacLeod, Strong |
| | 5 | 16.03.63 | **Liverpool** (D1) | H | L | 1-2 | MacLeod |
| 1963-64 (D1) | 3 | 04.01.64 | **Wolverhampton W** (D1) | H | W | 2-1 | Strong, Baker |
| | 4 | 25.01.64 | **WBA** (D1) | A | D | 3-3 | MacLeod, Armstrong, Baker |
| | 4r | 29.01.64 | **WBA** | H | W | 2-0 | Armstrong, Strong |
| | 5 | 15.02.64 | **Liverpool** (D1) | H | L | 0-1 | |
| 1964-65 (D1) | 3 | 09.01.65 | **Darlington** (D4) | A | W | 2-0 | Radford, Armstrong |
| | 4 | 30.01.65 | **Peterborough Utd** (D3) | A | L | 1-2 | Radford |
| 1965-66 (D1) | 3 | 22.01.66 | **Blackburn Rovers** (D1) | A | L | 0-3 | |
| 1966-67 (D1) | 3 | 28.01.67 | **Bristol Rovers** (D3) | A | W | 3-0 | Graham, Neilson, Armstrong |
| | 4 | 18.02.67 | **Bolton Wanderers** (D2) | A | D | 0-0 | |
| | 4r | 22.02.67 | **Bolton Wanderers** | H | W | 3-0 | Radford 3 |
| | 5 | 11.03.67 | **Birmingham City** (D2) | A | L | 0-1 | |
| 1967-68 (D1) | 3 | 27.01.68 | **Shrewsbury Town** (D3) | A | D | 1-1 | Radford |
| | 3r | 30.01.68 | **Shrewsbury Town** | H | W | 2-0 | Sammels, Jenkins |
| | 4 | 17.02.68 | **Swansea Town** (D4) | A | W | 1-0 | Gould |
| | 5 | 09.03.68 | **Birmingham City** (D2) | H | D | 1-1 | Radford |
| | 5r | 12.03.68 | **Birmingham City** | A | L | 1-2 | Gould |
| 1968-69 (D1) | 3 | 04.01.69 | **Cardiff City** (D2) | A | D | 0-0 | |
| | 3r | 07.01.69 | **Cardiff City** | H | W | 2-0 | Armstrong, Gould |

| | | | | | | | |
|---|---|---|---|---|---|---|---|
| | 4 | 25.01.69 | **Charlton Athletic** (D2) | H | W | 2-0 | Sammels, Robertson |
| | 5 | 12.02.69 | **WBA** (D1) | A | L | 0-1 | |
| 1969-70 (D1) | 3 | 03.01.70 | **Blackpool** (D2) | H | D | 1-1 | Radford |
| | 3r | 15.01.70 | **Blackpool** | A | L | 2-3 | Sammels, Radford |
| 1970-71 (D1) | 3 | 06.01.71 | **Yeovil Town** (SL) | A | W | 3-0 | Radford 2, Kennedy |
| | 4 | 23.01.71 | **Portsmouth** (D2) | A | D | 1-1 | Storey (p) |
| | 4r | 01.02.71 | **Portsmouth** | H | W | 3-2 | George, Simpson, Storey (p) |
| | 5 | 17.02.71 | **Manchester City** (D1) | A | W | 2-1 | George 2 |
| | 6 | 06.03.71 | **Leicester City** (D2) | A | D | 0-0 | |
| | 6r | 15.03.71 | **Leicester City** | H | W | 1-0 | George |
| | SF | 27.03.71 | **Stoke City** (D1) | | D | 2-2 | Storey 2 (1p) |
| | | | *played at Hillsborough* | | | | |
| | SFr | 31.03.71 | **Stoke City** | | W | 2-0 | Graham, Kennedy |
| | | | *played at Villa Park* | | | | |
| | F | 08.05.71 | **Liverpool** (D1) | | W | 2-1aet | Kelly, George |
| | | | *played at Wembley Stadium* | | | | |
| 1971-72 (D1) | 3 | 15.01.72 | **Swindon Town** (D2) | A | W | 2-0 | Armstrong, Ball |
| | 4 | 05.02.72 | **Reading** (D4) | A | W | 2-1 | Rice, Morgan og |
| | 5 | 26.02.72 | **Derby County** (D1) | A | D | 2-2 | George 2 |
| | 5r | 29.02.72 | **Derby County** | H | D | 0-0aet | |
| | 5 2r | 13.03.72 | **Derby County** | | W | 1-0 | Kennedy |
| | | | *played at Filbert Street* | | | | |
| | 6 | 18.03.72 | **Orient** (D2) | A | W | 1-0 | Ball |
| | SF | 15.04.72 | **Stoke City** (D1) | | D | 1-1 | Armstrong |
| | | | *played at Villa Park* | | | | |
| | SFr | 19.04.72 | **Stoke City** | | W | 2-1 | George, Radford |
| | | | *played at Goodison Park* | | | | |
| | F | 06.05.72 | **Leeds Utd** (D1) | | L | 0-1 | |
| | | | *played at Wembley Stadium* | | | | |
| 1972-73 (D1) | 3 | 13.01.73 | **Leicester City** (D1) | H | D | 2-2 | Kennedy, Armstrong |
| | 3r | 17.01.73 | **Leicester City** | A | W | 2-1 | Radford, Kelly |
| | 4 | 03.02.73 | **Bradford City** (D4) | H | W | 2-0 | Ball, George |
| | 5 | 24.02.73 | **Carlisle Utd** (D2) | A | W | 2-1 | Ball, McLintock |
| | 6 | 17.03.73 | **Chelsea** (D1) | A | D | 2-2 | Ball, George |
| | 6r | 20.03.73 | **Chelsea** | H | W | 2-1 | Ball (p), Kennedy |
| | SF | 07.04.73 | **Sunderland** (D2) | | L | 1-2 | George |
| | | | *played at Hillsborough* | | | | |
| | 3/4 | 18.08.73 | **Wolverhampton W** (D1) | H | L | 1-3 | Hornsby |
| 1973-74 (D1) | 3 | 05.01.74 | **Norwich City** (D1) | A | W | 1-0 | Kelly |
| | 4 | 26.01.74 | **Aston Villa** (D2) | H | D | 1-1 | Kennedy |
| | 4r | 30.01.74 | **Aston Villa** | A | L | 0-2 | |
| 1974-75 (D1) | 3 | 04.01.75 | **York City** (D2) | H | D | 1-1 | Kelly |
| | 3r | 07.01.75 | **York City** | A | W | 3-1aet | Kidd 3 |
| | 4 | 25.01.75 | **Coventry City** (D1) | A | D | 1-1 | Ball |
| | 4r | 29.01.75 | **Coventry City** | H | W | 3-0 | Armstrong 2, Matthews |
| | 5 | 15.02.75 | **Leicester City** (D1) | H | D | 0-0 | |
| | 5r | 19.02.75 | **Leicester City** | A | D | 1-1aet | Radford |
| | 5 2r | 24.02.75 | **Leicester City** | A | W | 1-0aet | Radford |
| | 6 | 08.03.75 | **West Ham Utd** (D1) | H | L | 0-2 | |
| 1975-76 (D1) | 3 | 03.01.76 | **Wolverhampton W** (D1) | A | L | 0-3 | |
| 1976-77 (D1) | 3 | 08.01.77 | **Notts County** (D2) | A | W | 1-0 | Ross |
| | 4 | 29.01.77 | **Coventry City** (D1) | H | W | 3-1 | Macdonald 2, Stapleton |
| | 5 | 26.02.77 | **Middlesbrough** (D1) | A | L | 1-4 | Macdonald |
| 1977-78 (D1) | 3 | 07.01.78 | **Sheffield Utd** (D2) | A | W | 5-0 | Macdonald 2, Stapleton 2, O'Leary |
| | 4 | 28.01.78 | **Wolverhampton W** (D1) | H | W | 2-1 | Sunderland, Macdonald |
| | 5 | 18.02.78 | **Walsall** (D3) | H | W | 4-1 | Stapleton 2, Macdonald, Sunderland |
| | 6 | 11.03.78 | **Wrexham** (D3) | A | W | 3-2 | Macdonald, Sunderland, Young |
| | SF | 08.04.78 | **Orient** (D2) | | W | 3-0 | Macdonald 2, Rix |
| | | | *played at Stamford Bridge* | | | | |
| | F | 06.05.78 | **Ipswich Town** (D1) | | L | 0-1 | |
| | | | *played at Wembley Stadium* | | | | |
| 1978-79 (D1) | 3 | 06.01.79 | **Sheffield Wed** (D3) | A | D | 1-1 | Sunderland |

| | | | | | | | |
|---|---|---|---|---|---|---|---|
| | 3r | 09.01.79 | **Sheffield Wed** | H | D | 1-1aet | Brady |
| | 3 2r | 15.01.79 | **Sheffield Wed** *played at Filbert Street* | | D | 2-2aet | Brady, Sunderland |
| | 3 3r | 17.01.79 | **Sheffield Wed** *played at Filbert Street* | | D | 3-3aet | Stapleton 2, Young |
| | 3 4r | 22.01.79 | **Sheffield Wed** *played at Filbert Street* | | W | 2-0 | Gatting, Stapleton |
| | 4 | 27.01.79 | **Notts County** (D2) | H | W | 2-0 | Young, Talbot |
| | 5 | 26.02.79 | **Nottingham Forest** (D1) | A | W | 1-0 | Stapleton |
| | 6 | 19.03.79 | **Southampton** (D1) | A | D | 1-1 | Price |
| | 6r | 21.03.79 | **Southampton** | H | W | 2-0 | Sunderland 2 |
| | SF | 31.03.79 | **Wolverhampton W** (D1) *played at Villa Park* | | W | 2-0 | Stapleton, Sunderland |
| | F | 12.05.79 | **Manchester Utd** (D1) *played at Wembley Stadium* | | W | 3-2 | Talbot, Stapleton, Sunderland |
| 1979-80 (D1) | 3 | 05.01.80 | **Cardiff City** (D2) | A | D | 0-0 | |
| | 3r | 08.01.80 | **Cardiff City** | H | W | 2-1 | Sunderland 2 |
| | 4 | 26.01.80 | **Brighton** (D1) | H | W | 2-0 | Nelson, Talbot |
| | 5 | 16.02.80 | **Bolton Wanderers** (D1) | A | D | 1-1 | Stapleton |
| | 5r | 19.02.80 | **Bolton Wanderers** | H | W | 3-0 | Sunderland 2, Stapleton |
| | 6 | 08.03.80 | **Watford** (D2) | A | W | 2-1 | Stapleton 2 |
| | SF | 12.04.80 | **Liverpool** (D1) *played at Hillsborough* | | D | 0-0 | |
| | SFr | 16.04.80 | **Liverpool** *played at Villa Park* | | D | 1-1aet | Sunderland |
| | SF 2r | 28.04.80 | **Liverpool** *played at Villa Park* | | D | 1-1aet | Sunderland |
| | SF 3r | 01.05.80 | **Liverpool** (D1) *played at Highfield Road, Coventry* | | W | 1-0 | Talbot |
| | F | 10.05.80 | **West Ham Utd** (D2) *played at Wembley Stadium* | | L | 0-1 | |
| 1980-81 (D1) | 3 | 03.01.81 | **Everton** (D1) | A | L | 0-2 | |
| 1981-82 (D1) | 3 | 02.01.82 | **Tottenham Hotspur** (D1) | A | L | 0-1 | |
| 1982-83 (D1) | 3 | 08.01.83 | **Bolton Wanderers** (D2) | H | W | 2-1 | Davis, Rix |
| | 4 | 29.01.83 | **Leeds Utd** (D2) | H | D | 1-1 | Sunderland |
| | 4r | 02.02.83 | **Leeds Utd** | A | D | 1-1aet | Rix |
| | 4 2r | 09.02.83 | **Leeds Utd** | H | W | 2-1 | Woodcock, Rix |
| | 5 | 19.02.83 | **Middlesbrough** (D2) | A | D | 1-1 | Rix |
| | 5r | 28.02.83 | **Middlesbrough** | H | W | 3-2 | Talbot, Woodcock, Davis |
| | 6 | 12.03.83 | **Aston Villa** (D1) | H | W | 2-0 | Woodcock, Petrovic |
| | SF | 16.04.83 | **Manchester Utd** (D1) *played at Villa Park* | | L | 1-2 | Woodcock |
| 1983-84 (D1) | 3 | 07.01.84 | **Middlesbrough** (D2) | A | L | 2-3 | Woodcock, Nicholas |
| 1984-85 (D1) | 3 | 05.01.85 | **Hereford Utd** (D4) | A | D | 1-1 | Woodcock |
| | 3r | 22.01.85 | **Hereford Utd** | H | W | 7-2 | Mariner 2, Talbot 2, Nicholas, Anderson, Woodcock |
| | 4 | 26.01.85 | **York City** (D3) | A | L | 0-1 | |
| 1985-86 (D1) | 3 | 04.01.86 | **Grimsby Town** (D2) | A | W | 4-3 | Nicholas 3, Rix |
| | 4 | 25.01.86 | **Rotherham Utd** (D3) | H | W | 5-1 | Allinson 2 (1p), Robson, Rix, Nicholas |
| | 5 | 15.02.86 | **Luton Town** (D1) | A | D | 2-2 | Allinson, Rocastle |
| | 5r | 03.03.86 | **Luton Town** | H | D | 0-0aet | |
| | 5 2r | 05.03.86 | **Luton Town** | A | L | 0-3 | |
| 1986-87 (D1) | 3 | 10.01.87 | **Reading** (D2) | A | W | 3-1 | Nicholas 2, Hayes (p) |
| | 4 | 31.01.87 | **Plymouth Argyle** (D2) | H | W | 6-1 | Anderson 2, Nicholas, Davis, Quinn, Rocastle |
| | 5 | 21.02.87 | **Barnsley** (D2) | H | W | 2-0 | Hayes (p), Nicholas |
| | 6 | 14.03.87 | **Watford** (D1) | H | L | 1-3 | Allinson |
| 1987-88 (D1) | 3 | 09.01.88 | **Millwall** (D2) | H | W | 2-0 | Hayes, Rocastle |
| | 4 | 30.01.88 | **Brighton** (D3) | A | W | 2-1 | Richardson, Groves |
| | 5 | 20.02.88 | **Manchester Utd** (D1) | H | W | 2-1 | Smith, Duxbury og |
| | 6 | 12.03.88 | **Nottingham Forest** (D1) | H | L | 1-2 | Rocastle |

| | | | | | | | |
|---|---|---|---|---|---|---|---|
| 1988-89 (D1) | 3 | 08.01.89 | **West Ham Utd** (D1) | A | D | 2-2 | Merson 2 |
| | 3r | 11.01.89 | **West Ham Utd** | H | L | 0-1 | |
| 1989-90 (D1) | 3 | 06.01.90 | **Stoke City** (D2) | A | W | 1-0 | Quinn |
| | 4 | 27.01.90 | **QPR** (D1) | H | D | 0-0 | |
| | 4r | 31.01.90 | **QPR** | A | L | 0-2 | |
| 1990-91 (D1) | 3 | 05.01.91 | **Sunderland** (D1) | H | W | 2-1 | Smith, Limpar |
| | 4 | 27.01.91 | **Leeds Utd** (D1) | H | D | 0-0 | |
| | 4r | 30.01.91 | **Leeds Utd** | A | D | 1-1aet | Limpar |
| | 4 2r | 13.02.91 | **Leeds Utd** | H | D | 0-0aet | |
| | 4 3r | 16.02.91 | **Leeds Utd** | A | W | 2-1 | Merson, Dixon |
| | 5 | 27.02.91 | **Shrewsbury Town** (D3) | A | W | 1-0 | Thomas |
| | 6 | 09.03.91 | **Cambridge Utd** (D3) | H | W | 2-1 | K Campbell, Adams |
| | SF | 14.04.91 | **Tottenham Hotspur** (D1) | | L | 1-3 | Smith |
| | | | *played at Wembley Stadium* | | | | |
| 1991-92 (D1) | 3 | 04.01.92 | **Wrexham** (D4) | A | L | 1-2 | Smith |
| 1992-93 (PL) | 3 | 03.01.93 | **Yeovil Town** (Conf) | A | W | 3-1 | Wright 3 |
| | 4 | 25.01.93 | **Leeds Utd** (PL) | H | D | 2-2 | Parlour, Merson |
| | 4r | 03.02.93 | **Leeds Utd** | A | W | 3-2aet | Wright 2, Smith |
| | 5 | 13.02.93 | **Nottingham Forest** (PL) | H | W | 2-0 | Wright 2 |
| | 6 | 06.03.93 | **Ipswich Town** (PL) | A | W | 4-2 | Adams, Wright (p), Whelan og, K Campbell |
| | SF | 04.04.93 | **Tottenham Hotspur** (PL) | | W | 1-0 | Adams |
| | | | *played at Wembley Stadium* | | | | |
| | F | 15.05.93 | **Sheffield Wed** (PL) | | D | 1-1aet | Wright |
| | | | *played at Wembley Stadium* | | | | |
| | Fr | 20.05.93 | **Sheffield Wed** | | W | 2-1aet | Wright, Linighan |
| | | | *played at Wembley Stadium* | | | | |
| 1993-94 (PL) | 3 | 09.01.94 | **Millwall** (D1) | A | W | 1-0 | Adams |
| | 4 | 31.01.94 | **Bolton Wanderers** (D1) | A | D | 2-2 | Wright, Adams |
| | 4r | 09.02.94 | **Bolton Wanderers** | H | L | 1-3aet | Smith |
| 1994-95 (PL) | 3 | 07.01.95 | **Millwall** (D1) | A | D | 0-0 | |
| | 3r | 18.01.95 | **Millwall** | H | L | 0-2 | |
| 1995-96 (PL) | 3 | 06.01.96 | **Sheffield Utd** (D1) | H | D | 1-1 | Wright |
| | 3r | 17.01.96 | **Sheffield Utd** | A | L | 0-1 | |
| 1996-97 (PL) | 3 | 04.01.97 | **Sunderland** (PL) | H | D | 1-1 | Hartson |
| | 3r | 15.01.97 | **Sunderland** | A | W | 2-0 | Bergkamp, Hughes |
| | 4 | 04.02.97 | **Leeds Utd** (PL) | H | L | 0-1 | |
| 1997-98 (PL) | | 03.01.98 | **Port Vale** (D1) | H | D | 0-0 | |
| | 3r | 14.01.98 | **Port Vale** | A | D | 1-1aet | Bergkamp |
| | | | *Arsenal won 4-3 on penalties* | | | | |
| | 4 | 24.01.98 | **Middlesbrough** (D1) | A | W | 2-1 | Overmars, Parlour |
| | 5 | 15.02.98 | **Crystal Palace** (PL) | H | D | 0-0 | |
| | 5r | 25.02.98 | **Crystal Palace** | A | W | 2-1 | Anelka, Bergkamp |
| | 6 | 08.03.98 | **West Ham Utd** (PL) | H | D | 1-1 | Bergkamp (p) |
| | 6r | 17.03.98 | **West Ham Utd** | A | D | 1-1aet | Anelka |
| | | | *Arsenal won 4-3 on penalties* | | | | |
| | SF | 05.04.98 | **Wolverhampton W** (D1) | | W | 1-0 | Wreh |
| | | | *played at Villa Park* | | | | |
| | F | 16.05.98 | **Newcastle Utd** (PL) | | W | 2-0 | Overmars, Anelka |
| | | | *played at Wembley Stadium* | | | | |
| 1998-99 (PL) | 3 | 04.01.99 | **Preston North End** (D2) | A | W | 4-2 | Boa Morte, Petit 2, Overmars |
| | 4 | 24.01.99 | **Wolverhampton W** (D1) | A | W | 2-1 | Overmars, Bergkamp |
| | 5 | 13.02.99 | **Sheffield Utd** (D1) | H | W | 2-1 | Vieira, Overmars |
| | | | *Result declared void* | | | | |
| | 5 | 23.02.99 | **Sheffield Utd** | H | W | 2-1 | Overmars, Bergkamp |
| | 6 | 06.03.99 | **Derby County** (PL) | H | W | 1-0 | Kanu |
| | SF | 11.04.99 | **Manchester Utd** (PL) | | D | 0-0aet | |
| | | | *played at Villa Park* | | | | |
| | SFr | 14.04.99 | **Manchester Utd** | | L | 1-2aet | Bergkamp |
| | | | *played at Villa Park* | | | | |
| 1999-00 (PL) | 3 | 13.12.99 | **Blackpool** (D2) | H | W | 3-1 | Grimandi, Adams, Overmars |
| | 4 | 09.01.00 | **Leicester City** (PL) | H | D | 0-0 | |

| | | | | | | | |
|---|---|---|---|---|---|---|---|
| | 4r | 19.01.00 | **Leicester City** | A | D | 0-0aet | |
| | | | *Leicester City won 6-5 on penalties* | | | | |
| 2000-01 (PL) | 3 | 06.01.01 | **Carlisle Utd** (D3) | A | W | 1-0 | Wiltord |
| | 4 | 27.01.01 | **QPR** (D1) | A | W | 6-0 | Plummer og, Wiltord 2, Rose og, Pires, Bergkamp |
| | 5 | 18.02.01 | **Chelsea** (PL) | H | W | 3-1 | Henry, Wiltord 2 |
| | 6 | 10.03.01 | **Blackburn Rovers** (D1) | H | W | 3-0 | Wiltord, Adams, Pires |
| | SF | 08.04.01 | **Tottenham Hotspur** (PL) | | W | 2-1 | Vieira, Pires |
| | | | *played at Old Trafford* | | | | |
| | F | 12.05.01 | **Liverpool** (PL) | | L | 1-2 | Ljungberg |
| | | | *played at Millennium Stadium, Cardiff* | | | | |
| 2001-02 (PL) | 3 | 05.01.02 | **Watford** (D1) | A | W | 4-2 | Henry, Ljungberg, Kanu, Bergkamp |
| | 4 | 27.01.02 | **Liverpool** (PL) | H | W | 1-0 | Bergkamp |
| | 5 | 16.02.02 | **Gillingham** (D1) | H | W | 5-2 | Wiltord 2, Kanu, Adams, Parlour |
| | 6 | 09.03.02 | **Newcastle Utd** (PL) | A | D | 1-1 | Edu |
| | 6r | 23.03.02 | **Newcastle Utd** | H | W | 3-0 | Pires, Bergkamp, Campbell |
| | SF | 14.04.02 | **Middlesbrough** (PL) | | W | 1-0 | Festa og |
| | | | *played at Old Trafford* | | | | |
| | F | 04.05.02 | **Chelsea** (PL) | | W | 2-0 | Parlour, Ljungberg |
| | | | *played at Millennium Stadium, Cardiff* | | | | |
| 2002-03 (PL) | 3 | 04.01.03 | **Oxford Utd** (D3) | H | W | 2-0 | Bergkamp, McNiven og |
| | 4 | 25.01.03 | **Farnborough T** (Conf) | A | W | 5-1 | Campbell, Jeffers 2, Bergkamp, Lauren |
| | | | *played at Highbury* | | | | |
| | 5 | 15.02.03 | **Manchester Utd** (PL) | A | W | 2-0 | Edu, Wiltord |
| | 6 | 08.03.03 | **Chelsea** (PL) | H | D | 2-2 | Jeffers, Henry |
| | 6r | 25.03.03 | **Chelsea** | A | W | 3-1 | Terry og, Wiltord, Lauren |
| | SF | 13.04.03 | **Sheffield Utd** (D1) | | W | 1-0 | Ljungberg |
| | | | *played at Old Trafford* | | | | |
| | F | 17.05.03 | **Southampton** (PL) | | W | 1-0 | Pires |
| | | | *played at Millennium Stadium, Cardiff* | | | | |

## ASHFORD TOWN

*Formed 1930. First entered FA Cup: 1930-31. Members of the Southern League.*

| | | | | | | | |
|---|---|---|---|---|---|---|---|
| 1934-35 (KL) | 1 | 24.11.34 | **Clapton Orient** (3S) | H | L | 1-4 | French |
| 1958-59 (KL) | 1 | 15.11.58 | **Crystal Palace** (D4) | H | L | 0-1 | |
| 1959-60 (SL) | 1 | 14.11.59 | **Brentford** (D3) | A | L | 0-5 | |
| 1960-61 (SL) | 1 | 05.11.60 | **Gillingham** (D4) | H | L | 1-2 | White |
| 1961-62 (SL) | 1 | 04.11.61 | **Wycombe W** (IL) | A | D | 0-0 | |
| | 1r | 08.11.61 | **Wycombe W** | H | W | 3-0 | White, Clayton, Shepherd |
| | 2 | 25.11.61 | **QPR** (D3) | H | L | 0-3 | |
| 1966-67 (SL) | 1 | 26.11.66 | **Cambridge City** (SL) | H | W | 4-1 | Soutar 2, Roberts 2 |
| | 2 | 10.01.67 | **Swindon Town** (D3) | A | L | 0-5 | |
| 1974-75 (SL) | 1 | 27.11.74 | **Walsall** (D3) | H | L | 1-3 | Hold |
| 1994-95 (SL) | 1 | 12.11.94 | **Fulham** (D3) | H | D | 2-2 | Arter, Dent |
| | 1r | 22.11.94 | **Fulham** | A | L | 3-5aet | Stanton 2, Dent |
| 1995-96 (SL) | 1 | 11.11.95 | **Bognor Regis Town** (IL) | A | D | 1-1 | Allon |
| | 1r | 21.11.95 | **Bognor Regis Town** | H | L | 0-1 | |
| 1996-97 (SL) | 1 | 16.11.96 | **Dagenham & Red** (IL) | H | D | 2-2 | Warrilow, Dent |
| | 1r | 25.11.96 | **Dagenham & Red** | A | D | 1-1aet | White |
| | | | *Ashford won 4-3 on penalties* | | | | |
| | 2 | 07.12.96 | **Watford** (D2) | A | L | 0-5 | |

## ASHINGTON

*Formed 1883. First entered FA Cup: 1888-89. Members of the Football league 1921-29. Ashington is the birthplace of Bobby and Jack Charlton and their cousin Jackie Milburn who played in nine FA Cup Finals between them. Members of the Northern League.*

| | | | | | | | |
|---|---|---|---|---|---|---|---|
| 1921-22 (3N) | | | 4q Close Works (H) 6-0; 5q Leadgate Park (H) 2-1; 6q Stalybridge Celtic (H) 1-0 | | | | |
| | 1 | 07.01.22 | **Millwall Athletic** (3S) | A | L | 2-4 | Robertson 2 |
| 1922-23 (3N) | | | 5q Blyth Spartans (A) 1-2 | | | | |
| 1923-24 (3N) | | | 4q Bishop Auckland (A) 2-1; 5q Carlisle Utd (H) 2-0; 6q Hartlepools Utd (H) 2-1 | | | | |
| | 1 | 12.01.24 | **Aston Villa** (D1) | H | L | 1-5 | Robertson |

| | | | | | | | |
|---|---|---|---|---|---|---|---|
| 1924-25 (3N) | | | 4q Hartlepools Utd (A) 0-0; 4qr Hartlepools Utd (H) 2-0. FA disqualified Ashington for fielding an ineligible player | | | | |
| 1925-26 (3N) | 1 | 02.12.25 | **Durham City** (3N) | A | L | 1-4 | Robertson |
| 1926-27 (3N) | 1 | 27.11.26 | **Stockton** (NL) | A | W | 2-1 | Watson, Randall |
| | 2 | 11.12.26 | **Nelson** (3N) | H | W | 2-1 | Randall, Johnson |
| | 3 | 08.01.27 | **Nottingham Forest** (D2) | H | L | 0-2 | |
| 1927-28 (3N) | 1 | 26.11.27 | **Crewe Alexandra** (3N) | A | D | 2-2 | Bell 2 |
| | 1r | 30.11.27 | **Crewe Alexandra** | H | L | 0-2 | |
| 1928-29 (3N) | 1 | 24.11.28 | **Wigan Borough** (3N) | A | L | 0-2 | |
| 1929-30 (NEL) | 1 | 30.11.29 | **Rotherham Utd** (3N) | A | L | 0-3 | |
| 1950-51 (NEL) | 1 | 25.11.50 | **Halifax Town** (3N) | A | W | 3-2 | Gibson, Simpson, Scott |
| | 2 | 09.12.50 | **Rochdale** (3N) | H | L | 1-2 | Skeen |
| 1952-53 (NEL) | 1 | 22.11.52 | **Tranmere Rovers** (3N) | A | L | 1-8 | Wort |
| 1961-62 (Nco) | 1 | 04.11.61 | **Chester** (D4) | A | L | 1-4 | Lackenby |

## ASHTON UNITED

*Formed 1878 as Hurst FC. First entered FA Cup as Hurst 1883-84. Changed name to Ashton United 1946. Based in Ashton-under-Lyne. Members of the Northern Premier League. See also Hurst FC.*

| | | | | | | | |
|---|---|---|---|---|---|---|---|
| 1952-53 (LC) | 1 | 22.11.52 | **Halifax Town** (3N) | A | D | 1-1 | Diamond |
| | 1r | 25.11.52 | **Halifax Town** | H | L | 1-2 | Diamond |
| 1955-56 (LC) | 1 | 19.11.55 | **Southport** (3N) | A | L | 1-6 | Mather |

## ASTLEY BRIDGE

*Played at Astley Bridge, Bolton. Entered FA Cup: 1880-81 – 1888-89. Used the Lamb Inn pub near the playing field as their dressing room. No direct links with Astley Bridge FC, formed in 1982 and which now plays in junior leagues in Lancashire.*

| | | | | | | | |
|---|---|---|---|---|---|---|---|
| 1880-81 | 1 | 30.10.80 | **Eagley** | H | W | 4-0 | Curran, Foole, Moore, Smith |
| | 2 | 18.12.80 | **Turton** | H | L | 0-3 | |
| 1881-82 | 1 | 29.10.81 | **Turton** | H | D | 2-2 | Smith, AN Other |
| | 1r | 12.11.81 | **Turton** | A | D | 1-1 | |
| | 1 2r | 19.11.81 | **Turton** *played at Great Lever* | | D | 3-3 | |
| | 1 3r | 26.11.81 | **Turton** | A | L | 0-2 | |
| 1882-83 | 1 | 28.10.82 | **Northwich Vtoria** | A | L | 2-3 | Swimby 2 |
| 1883-84 | 1 | 20.10.83 | **Great Lever** | A | L | 1-4 | |
| 1884-85 | 1 | | Bolton Association *Astley Bridge scratched. Bolton Association walkover* | | | - | |
| 1885-86 | 1 | 10.10.85 | **Southport** | H | W | 3-2 | |
| | 2 | 18.11.85 | **Preston North End** | A | L | 3-11 | |
| 1886-87 | 1 | 23.10.86 | **Burnley** | H | D | 3-3 | |
| | 1r | 30.10.86 | **Burnley** *FA disqualified Burnley after protest* | A | D | 2-2 | |
| | 2 | | Darwen *Astley Bridge scratched. Darwen walkover* | | | - | |
| 1887-88 | 1 | 15.10.87 | **Hurst** *FA disqualified Hurst after protest. Astley Bridge re-instated* | A | L | 3-5 | |
| | 2 | 05.11.87 | **Halliwell** | H | L | 0-4 | |

## ASTON SHAKESPEARE

*Short-lived amateur club based in Birmingham.*

| | | | | | | | |
|---|---|---|---|---|---|---|---|
| 1887-88 | 1 | 08.10.87 | **Burton Wanderers** *FA ordered replay after protest. Burton Wanderers scratched.* | H | L | 2-3 | |
| | 2 | 05.11.87 | **Wolverhampton W** | A | L | 0-3 | |

## ASTON UNITY

*Formed 1874 in the same year as Aston Villa, they were Aston Villa's first-ever opponents. Originally known as Aston Park Unity, a number of players appeared for both clubs. Played their home matches at the Lower Grounds, Aston, close to where Villa Park was later built.*

| | | | | | | | |
|---|---|---|---|---|---|---|---|
| 1882-83 | 1 | | bye | | | | |
| | 2 | 02.12.82 | **Birmingham St G** | H | W | 3-1 | |
| | 3 | 06.01.83 | **Aston Villa** | A | L | 1-3 | Wilson |
| 1883-84 | 1 | 10.11.83 | **Stafford Road** | A | L | 1-5 | |

| | | | | | | | |
|---|---|---|---|---|---|---|---|
| 1884-85 | 1 | 01.11.84 | **Birmingham St G** | H | L | 0-5 | |
| 1885-86 | 1 | 31.10.85 | **WBA** | A | L | 1-4 | |
| 1886-87 | 1 | 30.10.86 | **Derby County** | H | L | 1-4 | |
| 1887-88 | 1 | 15.10.87 | **Small Heath Alliance** | A | L | 1-6 | |

# ASTON VILLA

*Formed 1874. FA Cup and League double 1897. FA Cup winners: (7 times) 1887, 1895, 1897, 1905, 1913, 1920, 1957. FA Cup runners-up: 1892, 1924, 2000. Record FA Cup win: 13-0 v Wednesbury Old Athletic, 1st round, 30.10.1886; Record FA Cup defeat: 1-8 v Blackburn Rovers, 3rd round, 16.2.1889*

| | | | | | | | |
|---|---|---|---|---|---|---|---|
| 1879-80 | 2 | 13.12.79 | **Stafford Road** | A | D | 1-1 | Andy Hunter |
| | 2r | 24.01.80 | **Stafford Road** | H | W | 3-1 | Mason 2, Law |
| | 3 | | **Oxford University** | | | - | |
| | | | *Aston Villa scratched. Oxford University walkover* | | | | |
| 1880-81 | 1 | 30.10.80 | **Wednesbury Strollers** | H | W | 5-3 | |
| | 2 | 04.12.80 | **Nottingham Forest** | A | W | 2-1 | Andy Hunter, Vaughton |
| | 3 | 12.02.81 | **Notts County** | A | W | 3-1 | Andy Hunter 2, Archie Hunter |
| | 4 | 19.02.81 | **Stafford Road** | H | L | 2-3 | Vaughton 2 |
| 1881-82 | 1 | 05.11.81 | **Nottingham Forest** | H | W | 4-1 | Whateley 2, Brown 2 |
| | 2 | | bye | | | | |
| | 3 | 31.12.81 | **Notts County** | H | D | 2-2aet | Davis, Whateley |
| | 3r | 07.01.82 | **Notts County** | A | D | 2-2aet | Brown, Archie Hunter |
| | 3 2r | 14.01.82 | **Notts County** | H | W | 4-1 | Hunter, Whateley, Brown, Dawson |
| | 4 | 21.01.82 | **Wednesbury Old Ath** | A | L | 2-4 | Vaughton, Archie Hunter |
| 1882-83 | 1 | 21.10.82 | **Walsall Swifts** | H | W | 4-1 | Brown 2, Vaughton, Andy Hunter |
| | 2 | 18.11.82 | **Wednesbury Old Ath** | H | W | 4-1 | Harvey, Archie Hunter, Whateley, Vaughton |
| | 3 | 06.01.83 | **Aston Unity** | H | W | 3-1 | Davis, Vaughton, Archie Hunter |
| | 4 | 27.01.83 | **Walsall Town** | H | W | 2-1 | Vaughton, Brown |
| | 5 | 03.03.83 | **Notts County** | A | L | 3-4 | Archie Hunter, Whateley, Brown |
| 1883-84 | 1 | 10.11.83 | **Walsall Swifts** | A | W | 5-1 | Archie Hunter 2, Roberts, Phillips og, Vaughton |
| | 2 | 01.12.83 | **Stafford Road** | A | W | 5-1 | Brown 2, Archie Hunter 2, Whateley |
| | 3 | 29.12.83 | **Wednesbury Old Ath** | A | W | 7-4 | Brown 2, Whateley, Vaughton 3, Archie Hunter |
| | 4 | 19.01.84 | **Queen's Park, Glasgow** | A | L | 1-6 | Vaughton |
| 1884-85 | 1 | 03.11.84 | **Wednesbury Town** | H | W | 4-1 | Arthur Brown 2, Archie Hunter, Albert Brown |
| | 2 | 06.12.84 | **Walsall Town** | A | W | 2-0 | Whateley, Archie Hunter |
| | 3 | 03.01.85 | **WBA** | H | D | 0-0 | |
| | 3r | 10.01.85 | **WBA** | A | L | 0-3 | |
| 1885-86 | 1 | 17.10.85 | **Walsall Town** | A | W | 5-0 | Archie Hunter, Davis, Vaughton, Albert Brown, Arthur Brown |
| | 2 | 14.11.85 | **Derby County** | A | L | 0-2 | |
| 1886-87 | 1 | 30.10.86 | **Wednesbury Old Ath** | H | W | 13-0 | Hodgetts 3, Loach 2, Davis, Archie Hunter 3, Albert Brown 3, Burton |
| | 2 | 20.11.86 | **Derby Midland** | H | W | 6-1 | Loach 2, Hodgetts, Archie Hunter, Albert Brown 2 |
| | 3 | 11.12.86 | **Wolverhampton W** | H | D | 2-2 | Hunter, Hodgetts |
| | 3r | 15.01.87 | **Wolverhampton W** | A | D | 1-1aet | Albert Brown |
| | 3 2r | 22.01.87 | **Wolverhampton W** | A | D | 3-3aet | Vaughton, Davis, Albert Brown |
| | 3 3r | 29.01.87 | **Wolverhampton W** | H | W | 2-0 | Dawson, Hunter |
| | 4 | | bye | | | | |
| | 5 | 05.02.87 | **Horncastle** | H | W | 5-0 | Davis, Albert Brown 3, Hunter |
| | 6 | 12.02.87 | **Darwen** | H | W | 3-2 | Dawson, Hunter, Hodgetts |
| | SF | 05.03.87 | **Glasgow Rangers** | | W | 3-1 | Hunter 2, Albert Brown |
| | | | *played at Nantwich Road, Crewe* | | | | |
| | F | 02.04.87 | **WBA** | | W | 2-0 | Hodgetts, Hunter |
| | | | *played at Kennington Oval* | | | | |
| 1887-88 | 1 | 15.10.87 | **Oldbury Town** | A | W | 4-0 | Albert Brown 2, Hunter, Allen |
| | 2 | 05.11.87 | **Small Heath Alliance** | A | W | 4-0 | Green 2, Allen, Albert Brown |
| | 3 | | bye | | | | |

| | | | | | | | |
|---|---|---|---|---|---|---|---|
| | 4 | 17.12.87 | **Shankhouse** | A | W | 9-0 | Hunter 2, Hodgetts, Allen 2, Green 2, Albert Brown 2 |
| | 5 | 07.01.88 | **Preston North End** | H | L | 1-3 | Hunter |
| 1888-89 (D1) | 1 | 02.02.89 | **Witton** | H | W | 3-2 | Allen, Hunter, Green |
| | 2 | 16.02.89 | **Derby County** (D1) | H | W | 5-3 | Hunter 2, Hodgetts 2, Brown |
| | 3 | 02.03.89 | **Blackburn Rovers** (D1) | A | L | 1-8 | Hodgetts |
| 1889-90 (D1) | 1 | 18.01.90 | **South Shore** | A | W | 4-2 | Hodgetts 2, Allen, Dickson |
| | 2 | 01.02.90 | **Notts County** (D1) | A | L | 1-4 | Hodgetts |
| 1890-91 (D1) | 1 | 17.01.91 | **Casuals** | H | W | 13-1 | Hodgetts 4, L Campbell 3, McKnight 2, A Brown 2, Graham 2 |
| | 2 | 31.01.91 | **Stoke** (FAll) | A | L | 0-3 | |
| 1891-92 (D1) | 1 | 16.01.92 | **Heanor Town** | H | W | 4-1 | Hodgetts 3, J Devey |
| | 2 | 30.01.92 | **Darwen** (D1) | H | W | 2-0 | J Devey, Hodgetts |
| | 3 | 13.02.92 | **Wolverhampton W** (D1) | A | W | 3-1 | L Campbell, Athersmith, J Devey |
| | SF | 27.02.92 | **Sunderland** (D1) *played at Bramall Lane* | | W | 4-1 | J Devey 2, Hodgetts 2 |
| | F | 19.03.92 | **WBA** (D1) *played at Kennington Oval* | | L | 0-3 | |
| 1892-93 (D1) | 1 | 21.01.93 | **Darwen** (D2) | A | L | 4-5 | J Devey, Cowan, Athersmith, J Brown |
| 1893-94 (D1) | 1 | 27.01.94 | **Wolverhampton W** (D1) | H | W | 4-2 | J Devey 2, Chatt, Cowan |
| | 2 | 10.02.94 | **Sunderland** (D1) | A | D | 2-2aet | Cowan, Hodgetts |
| | 2r | 21.02.94 | **Sunderland** | H | W | 3-1 | Athersmith, Hodgetts, Chatt |
| | 3 | 24.02.94 | **Sheffield Wed** (D1) | A | L | 2-3aet | Chatt 2 |
| 1894-95 (D1) | 1 | 02.02.95 | **Derby County** (D1) | H | W | 2-1 | Devey, Smith |
| | 2 | 16.02.95 | **Newcastle Utd** (D2) | H | W | 7-1 | Dorrell 2, Russell, Devey 2, Athersmith 2 |
| | 3 | 02.03.95 | **Nottingham Forest** (D1) | H | W | 6-1 | Chatt 2, Smith 2, Russell, Cowan |
| | SF | 16.03.95 | **Sunderland** (D1) *played at Ewood Park* | H | W | 2-1 | Smith 2 |
| | F | 20.04.95 | **WBA** (D1) *played at Crystal Palace* | | W | 1-0 | Chatt |
| 1895-96 (D1) | 1 | 01.02.96 | **Derby County** (D1) | A | L | 2-4 | Burton, Hodgetts |
| 1896-97 (D1) | 1 | 30.01.97 | **Newcastle Utd** (D2) | H | W | 5-0 | Athersmith, Wheldon 2, Smith, White og |
| | 2 | 13.02.97 | **Notts County** (D2) | H | W | 2-1 | Wheldon, Campbell |
| | 3 | 27.02.97 | **Preston North End** (D1) | A | D | 1-1 | Campbell |
| | 3r | 03.03.97 | **Preston North End** | H | D | 0-0 | |
| | 3 2r | 10.03.97 | **Preston North End** *played at Bramall Lane* | | W | 3-2 | Athersmith 2, Campbell |
| | SF | 20.03.97 | **Liverpool** (D1) *played at Bramall Lane* | | W | 3-0 | Cowan 2, Athersmith |
| | F | 10.04.97 | **Everton** (D1) *played at Crystal Palace* | | W | 3-2 | Campbell, Wheldon, Crabtree |
| 1897-98 (D1) | 1 | 29.01.98 | **Derby County** (D1) | A | L | 0-1 | |
| 1898-99 (D1) | 1 | 28.01.99 | **Nottingham Forest** (D1) | A | L | 1-2 | Johnson |
| 1899-00 (D1) | 1 | 27.01.00 | **Manchester City** (D1) | A | D | 1-1 | Devey |
| | 1r | 31.01.00 | **Manchester City** | H | W | 3-0 | Garraty 2, Wheldon |
| | 2 | 10.02.00 | **Bristol City** (SL) | A | W | 5-1 | Devey 4, Garraty |
| | 3 | 24.02.00 | **Millwall Athletic** (SL) | A | D | 1-1 | Wheldon |
| | 3r | 28.02.00 | **Millwall Athletic** | H | D | 0-0aet | |
| | 3 2r | 05.03.00 | **Millwall Athletic** *played at Elm Park, Reading* | | L | 1-2 | Johnson |
| 1900-01 (D1) | 1 | 26.01.01 | **Millwall Athletic** (SL) | H | W | 5-0 | Johnson 3, Devey, Smith |
| | 2 | 23.02.01 | **Nottingham Forest** (D1) | H | D | 0-0 | |
| | 2r | 27.02.01 | **Nottingham Forest** | A | W | 3-1aet | Athersmith, Cowan, Garraty |
| | 3 | 23.03.01 | **Small Heath** (D2) | A | D | 0-0 | |
| | 3r | 27.03.01 | **Small Heath** | H | W | 1-0aet | Garraty |
| | SF | 06.04.01 | **Sheffield Utd** (D1) *played at City Ground, Nottingham* | | D | 2-2 | Garraty, Devey |
| | SFr | 11.04.01 | **Sheffield Utd** *played at Baseball Ground, Derby* | | L | 0-3 | |
| 1901-02 (D1) | 1 | 25.01.02 | **Stoke** (D1) | A | D | 2-2 | Garraty 2 |

| | | | | | | | |
|---|---|---|---|---|---|---|---|
| | 1r | 29.01.02 | **Stoke** | H | L | 1-2aet | Garraty |
| 1902-03 (D1) | 1 | 07.02.03 | **Sunderland** (D1) | H | W | 4-1 | Bache, Johnson 2, Pearson |
| | 2 | 21.02.03 | **Barnsley** (D2) | H | W | 4-1 | McLuckie 3, Johnson |
| | 3 | 07.03.03 | **Tottenham Hotspur** (SL) | A | W | 3-2 | McLuckie 2, Johnson |
| | SF | 21.03.03 | **Bury** (D1) | | L | 0-3 | |
| | | | *played at Goodison Park* | | | | |
| 1903-04 (D1) | 1 | 06.02.04 | **Stoke** (D1) | A | W | 3-2 | Brawn (p), Leake, Bache |
| | 2 | 20.02.04 | **Tottenham Hotspur** (SL) | A | - | 1-0ab | Bache |
| | | | *abandoned after 38 minutes following a pitch invasion* | | | | |
| | 2r | 25.02.04 | **Tottenham Hotspur** (SL) | H | L | 0-1 | |
| 1904-05 (D1) | 1 | 04.02.05 | **Leicester Fosse** (D2) | H | W | 5-1 | Bache 2, Hampton, Leake, Hall |
| | 2 | 18.02.05 | **Bury** (D1) | H | W | 3-2 | Bache, Garraty, Hampton |
| | 3 | 04.03.05 | **Fulham** (SL) | H | W | 5-0 | Pearson, Hampton 2, Bache, Hall |
| | SF | 25.03.05 | **Everton** (D1) | | D | 1-1 | Hall |
| | | | *played at Victoria Ground, Stoke* | | | | |
| | SFr | 29.03.05 | **Everton** (D1) | | W | 2-1 | Hampton, Garraty |
| | | | *played at Trent Bridge, Nottingham* | | | | |
| | F | 15.04.05 | **Newcastle Utd** (D1) | | W | 2-0 | Hampton 2 |
| | | | *played at Crystal Palace* | | | | |
| 1905-06 (D1) | 1 | 13.01.06 | **King's Lynn** (N&S) | H | W | 11-0 | Millington 4, Hall 3, Garraty 2, Pearson, Wilkes |
| | 2 | 03.02.06 | **Plymouth Argyle** (SL) | H | D | 0-0 | |
| | 2r | 07.02.06 | **Plymouth Argyle** | A | W | 5-1 | Garraty 2, Garratt, Bache, Hampton |
| | 3 | 24.02.06 | **Manchester Utd** (D2) | A | L | 1-5 | Hall |
| 1906-07 (D1) | 1 | 12.01.07 | **Burnley** (D2) | A | W | 3-1 | Bache 2, Cantrell |
| | 2 | 02.02.07 | **Bolton Wanderers** (D1) | A | L | 0-2 | |
| 1907-08 (D1) | 1 | 11.01.08 | **Stockport County** (D2) | H | W | 3-0 | Wallace, Bache, A Logan |
| | 2 | 01.02.08 | **Hull City** (D2) | H | W | 3-0 | Hall 2 (1p), Hampton |
| | 3 | 22.02.08 | **Manchester Utd** (D1) | H | L | 0-2 | |
| 1908-09 (D1) | 1 | 16.01.09 | **Nottingham Forest** (D1) | A | L | 0-2 | |
| 1909-10 (D1) | 1 | 15.01.10 | **Oldham Athletic** (D2) | A | W | 2-1 | Bache, Hall |
| | 2 | 05.02.10 | **Derby County** (D2) | H | W | 6-1 | Hampton 3, Wallace, Bache, Scattergood og |
| | 3 | 19.02.10 | **Manchester City** (D2) | H | L | 1-2 | Gerrish |
| 1910-11 (D1) | 1 | 14.01.11 | **Portsmouth** (SL) | A | W | 4-1 | Hampton 2, Bache, Thompson og |
| | 2 | 04.02.11 | **Manchester Utd** (D1) | A | L | 1-2 | Henshall |
| 1911-12 (D1) | 1 | 13.01.12 | **Walsall** (BDL) | H | W | 6-0 | Henshall 2, Hampton 2, Bache,Wallace |
| | 2 | 03.02.12 | **Reading** (SL) | H | D | 1-1 | Hampton |
| | 2r | 07.02.12 | **Reading** | A | L | 0-1 | |
| 1912-13 (D1) | 1 | 15.01.13 | **Derby County** (D1) | A | W | 3-1 | Halse 2, Hampton |
| | 2 | 01.02.13 | **West Ham Utd** (SL) | H | W | 5-0 | Halse 2, Morris, Hampton, Stephenson |
| | 3 | 22.02.13 | **Crystal Palace** (SL) | H | W | 5-0 | Halse 2, Stephenson 2, Bache |
| | 4 | 08.03.13 | **Bradford Park A** (D2) | A | W | 5-0 | Hampton 3, Halse, Stephenson |
| | SF | 29.03.13 | **Oldham Athletic** (D1) | | W | 1-0 | Stephenson |
| | | | *played at Ewood Park* | | | | |
| | F | 19.04.13 | **Sunderland** (D1) | | W | 1-0 | Barber |
| | | | *played at Crystal Palace* | | | | |
| 1913-14 (D1) | 1 | 10.01.14 | **Stoke** (SL) | H | W | 4-0 | Stephenson 2, Hampton 2 |
| | 2 | 31.01.14 | **Exeter City** (SL) | A | W | 2-1 | Hampton 2 |
| | 3 | 21.02.14 | **WBA** (D1) | H | W | 2-1 | Bache, Hampton |
| | 4 | 07.03.14 | **Sheffield Wed** (D1) | A | W | 1-0 | Edgley |
| | SF | 28.03.14 | **Liverpool** (D1) | | L | 0-2 | |
| | | | *played at White Hart Lane* | | | | |
| 1914-15 (D1) | 1 | 09.01.15 | **Exeter City** (SL) | H | W | 2-0 | C Stephenson, Bache |
| | 2 | 30.01.15 | **Manchester City** (D1) | A | L | 0-1 | |
| 1919-20 (D1) | 1 | 10.01.20 | **QPR** (SL) | H | W | 2-1 | Walker 2 |
| | 2 | 31.01.20 | **Manchester Utd** (D1) | A | W | 2-1 | Stephenson, Walker |
| | 3 | 21.02.20 | **Sunderland** (D1) | H | W | 1-0 | Stpehenson |
| | 4 | 06.03.20 | **Tottenham Hotspur** (D2) | A | W | 1-0 | Clay og |

| | | | | | | | | |
|---|---|---|---|---|---|---|---|---|
| | | SF | 27.03.20 | **Chelsea** (D1) | | W | 3-1 | Walker 2, Edgley |
| | | | | *played at Bramall Lane* | | | | |
| | | F | 24.04.20 | **Huddersfield Town** (D2) | | W | 1-0aet | Kirton |
| | | | | *played at Stamford Bridge* | | | | |
| 1920-21 | (D1) | 1 | 08.01.21 | **Bristol City** (D2) | H | W | 2-0 | C Stephenson (p), Walker |
| | | 2 | 29.01.21 | **Notts County** (D2) | A | D | 0-0 | |
| | | 2r | 02.02.21 | **Notts County** | H | W | 1-0 | Walker |
| | | 3 | 19.02.21 | **Huddersfield Town** (D1) | H | W | 2-0 | Walker 2 |
| | | 4 | 05.03.21 | **Tottenham Hotspur** (D1) | A | L | 0-1 | |
| 1921-22 | (D1) | 1 | 07.01.22 | **Derby County** (D2) | H | W | 6-1 | Walker 3, Kirton 2, Dickson |
| | | 2 | 28.01.22 | **Luton Town** (3S) | H | W | 1-0 | Walker |
| | | 3 | 18.02.22 | **Stoke** (D2) | A | D | 0-0 | |
| | | 3r | 22.02.22 | **Stoke** | H | W | 4-0 | Dickson 3, Walker |
| | | 4 | 04.03.22 | **Notts County** (D2) | A | D | 2-2 | Dickson 2 |
| | | 4r | 08.03.22 | **Notts County** | H | L | 3-4 | Dickson 2, Walker |
| 1922-23 | (D1) | 1 | 13.01.23 | **Blackburn Rovers** (D1) | H | L | 0-1 | |
| 1923-24 | (D1) | 1 | 12.01.24 | **Ashington** (3N) | A | W | 5-1 | Walker 2, Page og, Capewell, Blackburn |
| | | 2 | 02.02.24 | **Swansea Town** (3S) | A | W | 2-0 | Capewell 2 |
| | | 3 | 23.02.24 | **Leeds Utd** (D2) | H | W | 3-0 | Capewell 2, Walker |
| | | 4 | 08.03.24 | **WBA** (D1) | A | W | 2-0 | Capewell, Dorrell |
| | | SF | 29.03.24 | **Burnley** (D1) | | W | 3-0 | York 2, Kirton |
| | | | | *played at Bramall Lane* | | | | |
| | | F | 26.04.24 | **Newcastle Utd** (D1) | | L | 0-2 | |
| | | | | *played at Wembley Stadium* | | | | |
| 1924-25 | (D1) | 1 | 10.01.25 | **Port Vale** (D2) | H | W | 7-2 | Capewell 4, Walker 3 |
| | | 2 | 31.01.25 | **Swansea Town** (3S) | A | W | 3-1 | Walker 2, York |
| | | 3 | 21.02.25 | **WBA** (D1) | A | D | 1-1 | Walker |
| | | 3r | 25.02.25 | **WBA** | H | L | 1-2 | Phoenix |
| 1925-26 | (D1) | 3 | 09.01.26 | **Hull City** (D2) | A | W | 3-0 | Capewell 2, York |
| | | 4 | 29.01.26 | **WBA** (D1) | A | W | 2-1 | Walker, Kirton |
| | | 5 | 20.02.26 | **Arsenal** (D1) | H | D | 1-1 | Kirton |
| | | 5r | 24.02.26 | **Arsenal** | A | L | 0-2 | |
| 1926-27 | (D1) | 3 | 08.01.27 | **Cardiff City** (D1) | A | L | 1-2 | Dorrell |
| 1927-28 | (D1) | 3 | 14.01.28 | **Burnley** (D1) | A | W | 2-0 | Walker, Beresford |
| | | 4 | 28.01.28 | **Crewe Alexandra** (3N) | H | W | 3-0 | Cook 3 |
| | | 5 | 18.02.28 | **Arsenal** (D1) | A | L | 1-4 | Cook |
| 1928-29 | (D1) | 3 | 12.01.29 | **Cardiff City** (D1) | H | W | 6-1 | Beresford 2, Tate, Dorrell, Waring, York |
| | | 4 | 26.01.29 | **Clapton Orient** (D2) | H | D | 0-0 | |
| | | 4r | 30.01.29 | **Clapton Orient** | A | W | 8-0 | Waring 3, Swales, Dorrell, York, Cook, Beresford |
| | | 5 | 16.02.29 | **Reading** (D2) | A | W | 3-1 | Waring 2, Dorrell |
| | | 6 | 02.03.29 | **Arsenal** (D1) | H | W | 1-0 | Waring |
| | | SF | 23.03.29 | **Portsmouth** (D1) | | L | 0-1 | |
| | | | | *played at Highbury* | | | | |
| 1929-30 | (D1) | 3 | 11.01.30 | **Reading** (D2) | H | W | 5-1 | Houghton 2, Brown, Walker (p), York |
| | | 4 | 25.01.30 | **Walsall** (3S) | H | W | 3-1 | Walker 2, Brown |
| | | 5 | 15.02.30 | **Blackburn Rovers** (D1) | H | W | 4-1 | Brown 3 (1p), Beresford |
| | | 6 | 01.03.30 | **Huddersfield Town** (D1) | H | L | 1-2 | Brown (p) |
| 1930-31 | (D1) | 3 | 10.01.31 | **Arsenal** (D1) | A | D | 2-2 | Brown, Walker |
| | | 3r | 14.01.31 | **Arsenal** | H | L | 1-3 | Waring |
| 1931-32 | (D1) | 3 | 09.01.32 | **WBA** (D1) | A | W | 2-1 | Houghton, Brown |
| | | 4 | 23.01.32 | **Portsmouth** (D1) | A | D | 1-1 | Beresford |
| | | 4r | 27.01.32 | **Portsmouth** | H | L | 0-1 | |
| 1932-33 | (D1) | 3 | 14.01.33 | **Bradford City** (D2) | A | D | 2-2 | Mandley, Brown |
| | | 3r | 18.01.33 | **Bradford City** | H | W | 2-1 | Brown, Tate |
| | | 4 | 28.01.33 | **Sunderland** (D1) | H | L | 0-3 | |
| 1933-34 | (D1) | 3 | 13.01.34 | **Chesterfield** (3N) | A | D | 2-2 | Cunliffe 2 |
| | | 3r | 17.01.34 | **Chesterfield** | H | W | 2-0 | Astley, Beresford |
| | | 4 | 27.01.34 | **Sunderland** (D1) | H | W | 7-2 | Astley 4, Houghton 3 |
| | | 5 | 17.02.34 | **Tottenham Hotspur** (D1) | A | W | 1-0 | Astley |
| | | 6 | 03.03.34 | **Arsenal** (D1) | A | W | 2-1 | Astley, Houghton |

| | | | | | | | |
|---|---|---|---|---|---|---|---|
| | SF | 17.03.34 | **Manchester City** (D1) | | L | 1-6 | Astley |
| | | | *played at Leeds Road, Huddersfield* | | | | |
| 1934-35 (D1) | 3 | 12.01.35 | **Bradford City** (D2) | H | L | 1-3 | Hamilton og |
| 1935-36 (D1) | 3 | 11.01.36 | **Huddersfield Town** (D1) | H | L | 0-1 | |
| 1936-37 (D2) | 3 | 16.01.37 | **Burnley** (D2) | H | L | 2-3 | Houghton, Broome |
| 1937-38 (D2) | 3 | 08.01.38 | **Norwich City** (D2) | A | W | 3-2 | Houghton, Haycock, Iverson |
| | 4 | 22.01.38 | **Blackpool** (D1) | H | W | 4-0 | Houghton, Broome, Shell, Starling |
| | 5 | 12.02.38 | **Charlton Athletic** (D1) | A | D | 1-1 | Shell |
| | 5r | 16.02.38 | **Charlton Athletic** | H | D | 2-2 | Broome, Shell |
| | 5 2r | 21.02.38 | **Charlton Athletic** | | W | 4-1 | Broome 3, Haycock |
| | | | *played at Highbury* | | | | |
| | 6 | 06.03.38 | **Manchester City** (D1) | H | W | 3-2 | Shell, Broome, Haycock |
| | SF | 26.03.38 | **Preston North End** (D1) | | L | 1-2 | Shell |
| | | | *played at Bramall Lane* | | | | |
| 1938-39 (D1) | 3 | 07.01.39 | **Ipswich Town** (3S) | H | D | 1-1 | Allen |
| | 3r | 11.01.39 | **Ipswich Town** | A | W | 2-1 | Haycock 2 |
| | 4 | 21.01.39 | **Preston North End** (D1) | A | L | 0-2 | |
| 1945-46 (D1) | 3 1L | 05.01.46 | **Coventry City** (D2) | A | L | 1-2 | Smith |
| | 3 2L | 08.01.46 | **Coventry City** | H | W | 2-0 | Smith, Goffin |
| | 4 1L | 26.01.46 | **Millwall** (D2) | A | W | 4-2 | Edwards 2, Goffin, Smith |
| | 4 2L | 28.01.46 | **Millwall** | H | W | 9-1 | Broome 3, Goffin 2, Parkes, Edwards, Smith, Iverson |
| | 5 1L | 09.02.46 | **Chelsea** (D1) | A | W | 1-0 | Broome |
| | 5 2L | 12.02.46 | **Chelsea** | H | W | 1-0 | Goffin |
| | 6 1L | 02.03.46 | **Derby County** (D1) | H | L | 3-4 | Edwards, Iverson, Broome |
| | 6 2L | 09.03.46 | **Derby County** | A | D | 1-1 | Broome |
| 1946-47 (D1) | 3 | 11.01.47 | **Burnley** (D2) | A | L | 1-5 | Graham |
| 1947-48 (D1) | 3 | 10.01.48 | **Manchester Utd** (D1) | H | L | 4-6 | Edwards 2, Smith, Dorsett (p) |
| 1948-49 (D1) | 3 | 08.01.49 | **Bolton Wanderers** (D1) | H | D | 1-1aet | Ford |
| | 3r | 15.01.49 | **Bolton Wanderers** | A | D | 0-0aet | |
| | 3 2r | 17.01.49 | **Bolton Wanderers** | H | W | 2-1aet | Edwards, H Smith |
| | 4 | 29.01.49 | **Cardiff City** (D2) | H | L | 1-2 | Dorsett |
| 1949-50 (D1) | 3 | 07.01.50 | **Middlesbrough** (D1) | H | D | 2-2 | Gibson, Dorsett (p) |
| | 3r | 11.01.50 | **Middlesbrough** | A | D | 0-0aet | |
| | 3 2r | 16.01.50 | **Middlesbrough** | | L | 0-3 | |
| | | | *played at Elland Road* | | | | |
| 1950-51 (D1) | 3 | 06.01.51 | **Burnley** (D1) | H | W | 2-0 | Thompson, L Smith |
| | 4 | 27.01.51 | **Wolverhampton W** (D1) | A | L | 1-3 | Dixon |
| 1951-52 (D1) | 3 | 12.01.52 | **Newcastle Utd** (D1) | A | L | 2-4 | Dixon 2 |
| 1952-53 (D1) | 3 | 10.01.53 | **Middlesbrough** (D1) | H | W | 3-1 | Dixon, Thompson, Gibson |
| | 4 | 31.01.53 | **Brentford** (D2) | H | D | 0-0 | |
| | 4r | 04.02.53 | **Brentford** | A | W | 2-1 | Walsh, Thompson |
| | 5 | 14.02.53 | **Rotherham Utd** (D2) | A | W | 3-1 | Walsh 2, Goffin |
| | 6 | 28.02.53 | **Everton** (D2) | H | L | 0-1 | |
| 1953-54 (D1) | 3 | 09.01.54 | **Arsenal** (D1) | A | L | 1-5 | McParland |
| 1954-55 (D1) | 3 | 08.01.55 | **Brighton** (3S) | A | D | 2-2 | Thompson 2 |
| | 3r | 10.01.55 | **Brighton** | H | W | 4-2 | Lockhart 2, Southren, Thompson |
| | 4 | 29.01.55 | **Doncaster Rovers** (D2) | A | D | 0-0 | |
| | 4r | 02.02.55 | **Doncaster Rovers** | H | D | 2-2aet | Thompson 2 |
| | 4 2r | 07.02.55 | **Doncaster Rovers** | | D | 1-1aet | Thompson |
| | | | *played at Maine Road* | | | | |
| | 4 3r | 14.02.55 | **Doncaster Rovers** | | - | 0-0ab | |
| | | | *played at Hillsborough. Abandoned after 90 minutes – bad light* | | | | |
| | 4 4r | 15.02.55 | **Doncaster Rovers** | | L | 1-3 | Dixon |
| | | | *played at The Hawthorns* | | | | |
| 1955-56 (D1) | 3 | 07.01.56 | **Hull City** (D2) | H | D | 1-1 | McParland |
| | 3r | 12.01.56 | **Hull City** | A | W | 2-1 | Dixon, Sewell |
| | 4 | 28.01.56 | **Arsenal** (D1) | A | L | 1-4 | Dixon |
| 1956-57 (D1) | 3 | 05.01.57 | **Luton Town** (D1) | A | D | 2-2 | Dixon, McParland |
| | 3r | 07.01.57 | **Luton Town** | H | W | 2-0 | Dixon 2 |
| | 4 | 26.01.57 | **Middlesbrough** (D2) | A | W | 3-2 | Pace, Smith, Dixon |

| | | | | | | | | |
|---|---|---|---|---|---|---|---|---|
| | | 5 | 16.02.57 | **Bristol City** (D2) | H | W | 2-1 | Pace, Sewell |
| | | 6 | 02.03.57 | **Burnley** (D1) | A | D | 1-1 | McParland |
| | | 6r | 06.03.57 | **Burnley** | H | W | 2-0 | Dixon, McParland |
| | | SF | 23.03.57 | **WBA** (D1) *played at Molineux* | | D | 2-2 | McParland 2 |
| | | SFr | 28.03.57 | **WBA** *played at St Andrews* | | W | 1-0 | Myerscough |
| | | F | 04.05.57 | **Manchester Utd** (D1) *played at Wembley Stadium* | | W | 2-1 | McParland 2 |
| 1957-58 | (D1) | 3 | 04.01.58 | **Stoke City** (D2) | A | D | 1-1 | McParland |
| | | 3r | 08.01.58 | **Stoke City** | H | D | 3-3aet | Sewell, Lynn, Hitchens |
| | | 3 2r | 13.01.58 | **Stoke City** *played at Molineux* | | L | 0-2 | |
| 1958-59 | (D1) | 3 | 10.01.59 | **Rotherham Utd** (D2) | H | W | 2-1 | Sewell, Hitchens |
| | | 4 | 24.01.59 | **Chelsea** (D1) | A | W | 2-1 | Hitchens, Myerscough |
| | | 5 | 14.02.59 | **Everton** (D1) | A | W | 4-1 | Wylie 3, McParland |
| | | 6 | 28.02.59 | **Burnley** (D1) | H | D | 0-0 | |
| | | 6r | 03.03.59 | **Burnley** | A | W | 2-0 | McParland 2 |
| | | SF | 14.03.59 | **Nottingham Forest** (D1) *played at Hillsborough* | | L | 0-1 | |
| 1959-60 | (D2) | 3 | 09.01.60 | **Leeds Utd** (D1) | H | W | 2-1 | McParland, Wylie |
| | | 4 | 30.01.60 | **Chelsea** (D1) | A | W | 2-1 | McParland, Thompson |
| | | 5 | 20.02.60 | **Port Vale** (D3) | A | W | 2-1 | Hitchens, Thompson |
| | | 6 | 12.03.60 | **Preston North End** (D1) | H | W | 2-0 | Hitchens, McParland |
| | | SF | 26.03.60 | **Wolverhampton W** (D1) *played at The Hawthorns* | | L | 0-1 | |
| 1960-61 | (D1) | 3 | 07.01.61 | **Bristol Rovers** (D2) | A | D | 1-1 | Thompson |
| | | 3r | 09.01.61 | **Bristol Rovers** | H | W | 4-0 | Thompson 2, Hitchens 2 |
| | | 4 | 28.01.61 | **Peterborough Utd** (D4) | A | D | 1-1 | Banham og |
| | | 4r | 01.02.61 | **Peterborough Utd** | H | W | 2-1 | McParland 2 |
| | | 5 | 18.02.61 | **Tottenham Hotspur** (D1) | H | L | 0-2 | |
| 1961-62 | (D1) | 3 | 06.01.62 | **Crystal Palace** (D3) | H | W | 4-3 | Burrows 2, McParland, Dougan |
| | | 4 | 27.01.62 | **Huddersfield Town** (D2) | H | W | 2-1 | Hale, Crowe |
| | | 5 | 17.02.62 | **Charlton Athletic** (D2) | H | W | 2-1 | Dougan, Burrows |
| | | 6 | 10.03.62 | **Tottenham Hotspur** (D1) | A | L | 0-2 | |
| 1962-63 | (D1) | 3 | 16.01.63 | **Bristol City** (D3) | A | D | 1-1 | Burrows (p) |
| | | 3r | 07.03.63 | **Bristol City** | H | W | 3-2 | Burrows, Baker, Thompson |
| | | 4 | 11.03.63 | **Manchester Utd** (D1) | A | L | 0-1 | |
| 1963-64 | (D1) | 3 | 04.01.64 | **Aldershot** (D4) | H | D | 0-0 | |
| | | 3r | 08.01.64 | **Aldershot** | A | L | 1-2 | Hateley |
| 1964-65 | (D1) | 3 | 09.01.65 | **Coventry City** (D2) | H | W | 3-0 | Hateley 2, MacLeod |
| | | 4 | 30.01.65 | **Sheffield Utd** (D1) | A | W | 2-0 | Hateley, Stobart |
| | | 5 | 20.02.65 | **Wolverhampton W** (D1) | H | D | 1-1 | Hateley |
| | | 5r | 24.02.65 | **Wolverhampton W** | A | D | 0-0aet | |
| | | 5 2r | 01.03.65 | **Wolverhampton W** *played at The Hawthorns* | | L | 1-3 | Park |
| 1965-66 | (D1) | 3 | 22.01.66 | **Leicester City** (D1) | H | L | 1-2 | Woosnam |
| 1966-67 | (D1) | 3 | 28.01.67 | **Preston North End** (D2) | A | W | 1-0 | Roberts |
| | | 4 | 18.02.67 | **Liverpool** (D1) | A | L | 0-1 | |
| 1967-68 | (D2) | 3 | 27.01.68 | **Millwall** (D2) | H | W | 3-0 | Godfrey, Anderson, Woodward |
| | | 4 | 17.02.68 | **Rotherham Utd** (D2) | H | L | 0-1 | |
| 1968-69 | (D2) | 3 | 04.01.69 | **QPR** (D1) | H | W | 2-1 | Godfrey, Martin |
| | | 4 | 25.01.69 | **Southampton** (D1) | A | D | 2-2 | Godfrey, Hole |
| | | 4r | 29.01.69 | **Southampton** | H | W | 2-1 | Broadbent, Martin |
| | | 5 | 12.02.69 | **Tottenham Hotspur** (D1) | A | L | 2-3 | Hole, Broadbent |
| 1969-70 | (D2) | 3 | 03.01.70 | **Charlton Athletic** (D2) | H | D | 1-1 | Martin |
| | | 3r | 12.01.70 | **Charlton Athletic** | A | L | 0-1 | |
| 1970-71 | (D3) | 1 | 21.11.70 | **Torquay Utd** (D3) | A | L | 1-3 | Aitken |
| 1971-72 | (D3) | 1 | 20.11.71 | **Southend Utd** (D4) | A | L | 0-1 | |
| 1972-73 | (D2) | 3 | 13.01.73 | **Everton** (D1) | A | L | 2-3 | Vowden, Evans |
| 1973-74 | (D2) | 3 | 05.01.74 | **Chester** (D4) | H | W | 3-1 | Morgan 2, Nicholl |

| | | | | | | | | |
|---|---|---|---|---|---|---|---|---|
| | | 4 | 26.01.74 | **Arsenal** (D1) | A | D | 1-1 | Morgan |
| | | 4r | 30.01.74 | **Arsenal** | H | W | 2-0 | Morgan, Evans |
| | | 5 | 16.02.74 | **Burnley** (D1) | A | L | 0-1 | |
| 1974-75 | (D2) | 3 | 04.01.75 | **Oldham Athletic** (D2) | A | W | 3-0 | Little, Nicholl, Graydon |
| | | 4 | 25.01.75 | **Sheffield Utd** (D1) | H | W | 4-1 | Leonard 2, Nicholl, Graydon |
| | | 5 | 15.02.75 | **Ipswich Town** (D1) | A | L | 2-3 | McDonald, Evans |
| 1975-76 | (D1) | 3 | 03.01.76 | **Southampton** (D2) | A | D | 1-1 | Gray |
| | | 3r | 07.01.76 | **Southampton** | H | L | 1-2aet | Graydon |
| 1976-77 | (D1) | 3 | 08.01.77 | **Leicester City** (D1) | A | W | 1-0 | Gray |
| | | 4 | 29.01.77 | **West Ham Utd** (D1) | H | W | 3-0 | Deehan 2, Mortimer |
| | | 5 | 26.02.77 | **Port Vale** (D3) | H | W | 3-0 | Nicholl, Deehan, Little |
| | | 6 | 19.03.77 | **Manchester Utd** (D1) | A | L | 1-2 | Little |
| 1977-78 | (D1) | 3 | 07.01.78 | **Everton** (D1) | A | L | 1-4 | Gray |
| 1978-79 | (D1) | 3 | 10.01.79 | **Nottingham Forest** (D1) | A | L | 0-2 | |
| 1979-80 | (D1) | 3 | 04.01.80 | **Bristol Rovers** (D2) | A | W | 2-1 | Cowans, Shaw |
| | | 4 | 26.01.80 | **Cambridge Utd** (D2) | A | D | 1-1 | Donovan |
| | | 4r | 30.01.80 | **Cambridge Utd** | H | W | 4-1 | Donovan 2, Little, Evans |
| | | 5 | 16.02.80 | **Blackburn Rovers** (D3) | A | D | 1-1 | Geddis |
| | | 5r | 20.02.80 | **Blackburn Rovers** | H | W | 1-0 | Evans |
| | | 6 | 08.03.80 | **West Ham Utd** (D2) | A | L | 0-1 | |
| 1980-81 | (D1) | 3 | 03.01.81 | **Ipswich Town** (D1) | H | L | 0-1 | |
| 1981-82 | (D1) | 3 | 05.01.82 | **Notts County** (D1) | A | W | 6-0 | Geddis 3, Cowans (p), Shaw, Richards og |
| | | 4 | 23.01.82 | **Bristol City** (D3) | A | W | 1-0 | Shaw |
| | | 5 | 13.02.82 | **Tottenham Hotspur** (D1) | A | L | 0-1 | |
| 1982-83 | (D1) | 3 | 08.01.83 | **Northampton Town** (D4) | A | W | 1-0 | Walters |
| | | 4 | 29.01.83 | **Wolverhampton W** (D2) | H | W | 1-0 | Withe |
| | | 5 | 19.02.83 | **Watford** (D1) | H | W | 4-1 | Shaw, Morley, Gibson, Cowans |
| | | 6 | 12.03.83 | **Arsenal** (D1) | A | L | 0-2 | |
| 1983-84 | (D1) | 3 | 07.01.84 | **Norwich City** (D1) | H | D | 1-1 | Withe |
| | | 3r | 11.01.84 | **Norwich City** | A | L | 0-3 | |
| 1984-85 | (D1) | 3 | 05.01.85 | **Liverpool** (D1) | A | L | 0-3 | |
| 1985-86 | (D1) | 3 | 04.01.86 | **Portsmouth** (D2) | A | D | 2-2 | Birch, Kerr |
| | | 3r | 13.01.86 | **Portsmouth** | H | W | 3-2aet | Stainrod 2, Evans |
| | | 4 | 25.1.86 | **Millwall** (D2) | H | D | 1-1 | Hodge |
| | | 4r | 29.1.86 | **Millwall** | A | L | 0-1 | |
| 1986-87 | (D1) | 3 | 10.01.87 | **Chelsea** (D1) | H | D | 2-2 | Cooper, Hunt |
| | | 3r | 21.01.87 | **Chelsea** | A | L | 1-2aet | Hunt |
| 1987-88 | (D2) | 3 | 09.01.88 | **Leeds Utd** (D2) | A | W | 2-1 | Gray, McInally |
| | | 4 | 31.01.88 | **Liverpool** (D1) | H | L | 0-2 | |
| 1988-89 | (D1) | 3 | 07.01.89 | **Crewe Alexandra** (D4) | A | W | 3-2 | Platt, Gage, McInally |
| | | 4 | 28.01.89 | **Wimbledon** (D1) | H | L | 0-1 | |
| 1989-90 | (D1) | 3 | 06.01.90 | **Blackburn Rovers** (D2) | A | D | 2-2 | Olney, Ormondroyd |
| | | 3r | 10.01.90 | **Blackburn Rovers** | H | W | 3-1 | Ormondroyd, Daley, May og |
| | | 4 | 27.01.90 | **Port Vale** (D2) | H | W | 6-0 | Platt, Birch 2, Olney, Gray 2 |
| | | 5 | 17.02.90 | **WBA** (D2) | A | W | 2-0 | Mountfield, Daley |
| | | 6 | 14.03.90 | **Oldham Athletic** (D2) | A | L | 0-3 | |
| 1990-91 | (D1) | 3 | 05.01.91 | **Wimbledon** (D1) | H | D | 1-1 | Gray |
| | | 3r | 09.01.91 | **Wimbledon** | A | L | 0-1aet | |
| 1991-92 | (D1) | 3 | 05.01.92 | **Tottenham Hotspur** (D1) | H | D | 0-0 | |
| | | 3r | 14.01.92 | **Tottenham Hotspur** | A | W | 1-0 | Yorke |
| | | 4 | 05.02.92 | **Derby County** (D2) | A | W | 4-3 | Yorke 3, Parker |
| | | 5 | 16.02.92 | **Swindon Town** (D2) | A | W | 2-1 | Yorke, Froggatt |
| | | 6 | 08.03.92 | **Liverpool** (D1) | A | L | 0-1 | |
| 1992-93 | (PL) | 3 | 02.01.93 | **Bristol Rovers** (D1) | H | D | 1-1 | Cox |
| | | 3r | 20.01.93 | **Bristol Rovers** | A | W | 3-0 | Saunders 2, Houghton |
| | | 4 | 23.01.93 | **Wimbledon** (PL) | H | D | 1-1 | Yorke |
| | | 4r | 03.02.93 | **Wimbledon** | A | D | 0-0aet | |
| | | | | *Wimbledon won 6-5 on penalties* | | | | |
| 1993-94 | (PL) | 3 | 08.01.94 | **Exeter City** (D2) | A | W | 1-0 | Saunders (pen) |
| | | 4 | 29.01.94 | **Grimsby Town** (D1) | A | W | 2-1 | Houghton, Yorke |
| | | 5 | 20.02.94 | **Bolton Wanderers** (D1) | A | L | 0-1 | |
| 1994-95 | (PL) | 3 | 07.01.95 | **Barnsley** (D1) | A | W | 2-0 | Yorke, Saunders |

| | | | | | | | | |
|---|---|---|---|---|---|---|---|---|
| | | 4 | 28.01.95 | **Manchester City** (PL) | A | L | 0-1 | |
| 1995-96 | (PL) | 3 | 06.01.96 | **Gravesend & N** (SL) | A | W | 3-0 | Draper, Milosevic, Johnson |
| | | | | *played at Villa Park* | | | | |
| | | 4 | 28.01.96 | **Sheffield Utd** (D1) | A | W | 1-0 | Yorke (p) |
| | | 5 | 17.02.96 | **Ipswich Town** (D1) | A | W | 3-1 | Draper, Yorke, Taylor |
| | | 6 | 13.03.96 | **Nottingham Forest** (PL) | A | W | 1-0 | Carr |
| | | SF | 31.03.96 | **Liverpool** (PL) | | L | 0-3 | |
| | | | | *played at Old Trafford* | | | | |
| 1996-97 | (PL) | 3 | 14.01.97 | **Notts County** (D2) | A | D | 0-0 | |
| | | 3r | 22.01.97 | **Notts County** | H | W | 3-0 | Yorke 2, Ehiogu |
| | | 4 | 25.01.97 | **Derby County** (PL) | A | L | 1-3 | Curcic |
| 1997-98 | (PL) | 3 | 03.01.98 | **Portsmouth** (D1) | A | D | 2-2 | Staunton, Grayson |
| | | 3r | 14.01.98 | **Portsmouth** | H | W | 1-0 | Milosevic |
| | | 4 | 24.01.98 | **WBA** (D1) | H | W | 4-0 | Grayson, Yorke 2, Collymore |
| | | 5 | 14.02.98 | **Coventry City** (PL) | H | L | 0-1 | |
| 1998-99 | (PL) | 3 | 02.01.99 | **Hull City** (D3) | H | W | 3-0 | Collymore 2, Joachim |
| | | 4 | 23.01.99 | **Fulham** (D2) | H | L | 0-2 | |
| 1999-00 | (PL) | 3 | 11.12.99 | **Darlington** (D3) | H | W | 2-1 | Carbone, Dublin |
| | | 4 | 08.01.00 | **Southampton** (PL) | H | W | 1-0 | Southgate |
| | | 5 | 30.01.00 | **Leeds Utd** (PL) | H | W | 3-2 | Carbone 3 |
| | | 6 | 20.02.00 | **Everton** (PL) | A | W | 2-1 | Stone, Carbone |
| | | SF | 02.04.00 | **Bolton Wanderers** (D1) | | D | 0-0aet | |
| | | | | *played at Wembley Stadium – Aston Villa won 4-1 on penalties* | | | | |
| | | F | 20.05.00 | **Chelsea** (PL) | | L | 0-1 | |
| | | | | *played at Wembley Stadium* | | | | |
| 2000-01 | (PL) | 3 | 06.01.01 | **Newcastle Utd** (PL) | A | D | 1-1 | S Stone |
| | | 3r | 17.01.01 | **Newcastle Utd** | H | W | 1-0 | D Vassell |
| | | 4 | 27.01.01 | **Leicester City** (PL) | H | L | 1-2 | J Joachim |
| 2001-02 | (PL) | 3 | 06.01.02 | **Manchester Utd** (PL) | H | L | 2-3 | Taylor, Phil Neville og |
| 2002-03 | (PL) | 3 | 04.01.03 | **Blackburn Rovers** (PL) | H | L | 1-4 | Angel |

## ATHERSTONE UNITED

*Formed 1979. First competed in FA Cup:1979-80. Members of the Southern League.*

| | | | | | | | | |
|---|---|---|---|---|---|---|---|---|
| 1987-88 | (SL) | 1 | 14.11.87 | **VS Rugby** (SL) | A | D | 0-0 | |
| | | 1r | 17.11.87 | **VS Rugby** | H | L | 0-2 | |
| 1990-91 | (SL) | 1 | 17.11.90 | **Fleetwood** (NPL) | H | W | 3-1 | Parker 3 |
| | | 2 | 12.12.90 | **Crewe Alexandra** (D3) | A | L | 0-1 | |
| 1991-92 | (SL) | 1 | 16.11.91 | **Hereford Utd** (D4) | H | D | 0-0 | |
| | | 1r | 26.11.91 | **Hereford Utd** | A | L | 0-3 | |

## ATTERCLIFFE

*Formed 1870. Home matches played at Brightside Lane, Sheffield. Competed in the FA Cup until 1903-04.*

| | | | | | | | | |
|---|---|---|---|---|---|---|---|---|
| 1886-87 | | 1 | 30.10.86 | **Staveley** | A | L | 0-7 | |
| 1887-88 | | 1 | 15.10.87 | **Sheffield Heeley** | A | L | 0-9 | |

## AVELEY

*Formed 1927. First entered FA Cup: 1954-55. Members of the Isthmian League.*

| | | | | | | | | |
|---|---|---|---|---|---|---|---|---|
| 1970-71 | (AL) | 1 | 21.11.70 | **Yeovil Town** (SL) | A | L | 0-1 | |

## AYLESBURY UNITED

*Formed 1897 by merger of Aylesbury Night School FC and Aylesbury Printing Works. First entered FA Cup: 1896-97. League club beaten: Southend Utd. Members of the Isthmian League.*

| | | | | | | | | |
|---|---|---|---|---|---|---|---|---|
| 1951-52 | (Del) | 1 | 24.11.51 | **Watford** (3S) | H | L | 0-5 | |
| 1985-86 | (SL) | 1 | 16.11.85 | **Slough Town** (IL) | A | D | 2-2 | Botterill, Hercules |
| | | 1r | 19.11.85 | **Slough Town** | H | L | 2-5 | Campbell 2 |
| | | | | *played at Tring* | | | | |
| 1986-87 | (SL) | 1 | 15.11.86 | **Bath City** (Conf) | A | L | 2-3 | Hercules, Botterill (p) |
| 1987-88 | (SL) | 1 | 14.11.87 | **Bristol City** (D3) | A | L | 0-1 | |
| 1988-89 | (Conf) | 1 | 19.11.88 | **Waterlooville** (SL) | A | W | 4-1 | Hercules 2, Boyland 2 |
| | | 2 | 10.12.88 | **Sutton Utd** (Conf) | H | L | 0-1 | |
| 1989-90 | (IL) | 1 | 18.11.89 | **Southend Utd** (D4) | H | W | 1-0 | Donegal |
| | | 2 | 09.12.89 | **Northampton Town** (D3) | A | D | 0-0 | |

| | | | | | | | | |
|---|---|---|---|---|---|---|---|---|
| | | 2r | 13.12.89 | **Northampton Town** | H | L | 0-1aet | |
| 1990-91 | (IL) | 1 | 17.11.90 | **Walsall** (D4) | H | L | 0-1 | |
| 1991-92 | (IL) | 1 | 16.11.91 | **Kidderminster H** (Conf) | A | W | 1-0 | Davies |
| | | 2 | 07.12.91 | **Hereford Utd** (D4) | H | L | 2-3 | Hercules 2 |
| 1992-93 | (IL) | 1 | 14.11.92 | **WBA** (D2) | A | L | 0-8 | |
| 1994-95 | (IL) | 1 | 12.11.94 | **Newport** (IOW) (SL) | A | W | 3-2 | C Hercules 2, Pluckrose (p) |
| | | 2 | 03.12.94 | **Kingstonian** (IL) | A | W | 4-1 | C Hercules, Bashir, Pluckrose (p), Blencowe |
| | | 3 | 07.01.95 | **QPR** (PL) | H | L | 0-4 | |
| 2001-02 | (IL) | 1 | 17.11.01 | **Port Vale** (D2) | A | L | 0-3 | |

## BAMBER BRIDGE

*Formed 1952. First entered FA Cup: 1992-93. Based in Preston. Members of the Northern Premier League.*

| | | | | | | | | |
|---|---|---|---|---|---|---|---|---|
| 1999-00 | (NPL) | 1 | 30.10.99 | **St Albans City** (IL) | A | W | 2-0 | Whittaker, Carroll |
| | | 2 | 20.11.99 | **Cambridge Utd** (D2) | A | L | 0-1 | |

## BANBURY UNITED

*Formed 1933 as Banbury Spencer. First entered FA Cup: 1934. Reformed as Banbury United 1965. The club once proposed to the FA a competition for FA Cup first round losers with a final at Wembley Stadium. The FA declined the idea. Members of the Southern League.*

**as Banbury Spencer**

| | | | | | | | | |
|---|---|---|---|---|---|---|---|---|
| 1947-48 | (BC) | 1 | 29.11.47 | **Colchester Utd** (SL) | A | L | 1-2 | North |
| 1961-62 | (BDL) | 1 | 04.11.61 | **Shrewsbury Town** (D3) | A | L | 1-7 | Redding |

**as Banbury Utd**

| | | | | | | | | |
|---|---|---|---|---|---|---|---|---|
| 1972-73 | (SL) | 1 | 18.11.72 | **Barnet** (SL) | H | L | 0-2 | |
| 1973-74 | (SL) | 1 | 24.11.73 | **Northampton Town** (D4) | H | D | 0-0 | |
| | | 1r | 29.11.73 | **Northampton Town** | A | L | 2-3 | Gregory og, Haynes |

## BANGOR CITY

*Formed 1876. First entered FA Cup: 1896-97. FA Trophy: Runners-up 1984. Welsh FA Cup winners: 1889, 1896, 1962. League clubs beaten: Wrexham, Rochdale. Members of the League of Wales.*

| | | | | | | | | |
|---|---|---|---|---|---|---|---|---|
| 1951-52 | (CC) | 1 | 24.11.51 | **Southport** (3N) | H | D | 2-2 | Wyles, Higgins |
| | | 1r | 27.11.51 | **Southport** | A | L | 0-3 | |
| 1952-53 | (CC) | 1 | 22.11.52 | **Southport** (3N) | A | L | 1-3 | Glaister |
| 1960-61 | (CC) | 1 | 05.11.60 | **Wrexham** (D4) | H | W | 1-0 | D Jones |
| | | 2 | 26.11.60 | **Southport** (D4) | H | D | 1-1 | Hunt |
| | | 2r | 29.11.60 | **Southport** | A | L | 1-3 | Gryba |
| 1963-64 | (CC) | 1 | 16.11.63 | **Barrow** (D4) | A | L | 2-3 | Kinsella 2 |
| 1964-65 | (CC) | 1 | 14.11.64 | **York City** (D4) | A | L | 1-5 | Pitchford |
| 1966-67 | (CC) | 1 | 26.11.66 | **Mansfield Town** (D3) | A | L | 1-4 | Conde |
| 1968-69 | (NPL) | 1 | 16.11.68 | **Morecambe** (NPL) | H | L | 2-3 | Conde 2 |
| 1969-70 | (NPL) | 1 | 15.11.69 | **Kirkby Town** (LC) | H | W | 6-0 | Grant 2, Jackson, Morton, Broadhead, Lucas (p) |
| | | 2 | 06.12.69 | **York City** (D4) | H | D | 0-0 | |
| | | 2r | 9.12.69 | **York City** | A | L | 0-2 | |
| 1970-71 | (NPL) | 1 | 21.11.70 | **Darlington** (D4) | A | L | 1-5 | Grant |
| 1971-72 | (NPL) | 1 | 20.11.71 | **Bolton Wanderers** (D3) | A | L | 0-3 | |
| 1972-73 | (NPL) | 1 | 18.11.72 | **Rochdale** (D3) | A | W | 2-1 | Brodie, Marsden |
| | | 2 | 09.12.72 | **York City** (D4) | H | L | 2-3 | Marsden, Morton |
| 1983-84 | (APL) | 1 | 19.11.83 | **Northwich V** (APL) | A | D | 1-1 | Howat |
| | | 1r | 22.11.83 | **Northwich V** | H | W | 1-0 | Urquhart (p) |
| | | 2 | 10.12.83 | **Blackpool** (D4) | H | D | 1-1 | Urquhart |
| | | 2r | 13.12.83 | **Blackpool** | A | L | 1-2 | Urquhart (p) |
| 1984-85 | (NPL) | 1 | 17.11.84 | **Tranmere Rovers** (D4) | H | D | 1-1 | Urquhart (p) |
| | | 1r | 20.11.84 | **Tranmere Rovers** | A | L | 0-7 | |

## BARKING

*Formed 1880. First entered FA Cup: 1905-06. .FA Amateur Cup runners-up 1927. Merged with East Ham United to form Barking and East Ham United in 2001. League club beaten: Oxford United. Members of the Isthmian League.*

| | | | | | | | | |
|---|---|---|---|---|---|---|---|---|
| 1926-27 | (AL) | 1 | 27.11.26 | **Gillingham** (3S) | H | D | 0-0 | |
| | | 1r | 01.12.26 | **Gillingham** | A | L | 0-2 | |

| | | | | | | | |
|---|---|---|---|---|---|---|---|
| 1928-29 (AL) | 1 | 24.11.28 | **Exeter City** (3S) | A | L | 0-6 | |
| 1978-79 (IL) | 1 | 25.11.78 | **Yeovil Town** (SL) | A | W | 1-0 | Key |
| | 2 | 16.12.78 | **Aldershot** (D4) | H | L | 1-2 | Ashford |
| 1979-80 (IL) | 1 | 24.11.79 | **Oxford Utd** (D3) | H | W | 1-0 | Brothers |
| | 2 | 15.12.79 | **Reading** (D3) | A | L | 1-3 | Dingwall |
| 1981-82 (IL) | 1 | 21.11.81 | **Bideford** (WL) | A | W | 2-1 | Hillman, Key |
| | 2 | 15.12.81 | **Gillingham** (D3) | A | D | 1-1 | Hillman |
| | 2r | 02.01.82 | **Gillingham** | | L | 1-3aet | Anderson |
| | | | *played at Gillingham* | | | | |
| 1983-84 (IL) | 1 | 19.11.83 | **Farnborough Town** (IL) | H | W | 2-1 | Crown 2 |
| | 2 | 10.12.83 | **Plymouth Argyle** (D3) | A | L | 1-2 | Groom |

# BARNES

*Formed 1862 by Ebenezer Cobb Morley, the first secretary of the Football Association. One of the founding member clubs of the FA on October 26, 1863 and one of the original 15 entrants in the first FA Cup competition in 1871-72. Their home ground was a field near the White Hart pub. Entered FA Cup: 1871-72 – 1885-86. Surrey Senior Cup Winners 1884.*

| | | | | | | | |
|---|---|---|---|---|---|---|---|
| 1871-72 | 1 | 11.11.71 | **Civil Service** | H | W | 2-0 | Dunnage, P Weston |
| | 2 | 23.12.71 | **Hampstead Heathens** | H | D | 1-1 | AC Highton |
| | 2r | 06.01.72 | **Hampstead Heathens** | A | L | 0-1 | |
| 1872-73 | 1 | 19.10.72 | **South Norwood** | H | L | 0-1 | |
| 1873-74 | 1 | 25.10.73 | **1st Surrey Rifles** | A | D | 0-0 | |
| | 1r | 08.11.73 | **1st Surrey Rifles** | H | W | 1-0 | Hudson |
| | 2 | 22.11.73 | **Oxford University** | A | L | 0-2 | |
| 1874-75 | 1 | 24.10.74 | **Upton Park** | A | W | 3-0 | Hudson, Morice, Soden |
| | 2 | 21.11.74 | **Wanderers** | A | L | 0-5 | |
| 1875-76 | 1 | 30.10.75 | **Reigate Priory** | A | L | 0-1 | |
| 1876-77 | 1 | | Old Etonians | | | - | |
| | | | *Old Etonians scratched. Barnes walkover.* | | | | |
| | 2 | 09.12.76 | **Upton Park** | A | L | 0-1 | |
| 1877-78 | 1 | | St Mark's | | | - | |
| | | | *St Mark's scratched. Barnes walkover.* | | | | |
| | 2 | 15.12.77 | **Marlow** | H | W | 3-1 | Ainslie 2, Dorling |
| | 3 | 12.01.78 | **Wanderers** | A | D | 1-1 | Ainslie |
| | 3r | 26.01.78 | **Wanderers** | A | L | 1-4 | Weston |
| 1878-79 | 1 | 19.10.78 | **Maidenhead** | H | D | 1-1 | Dorling |
| | 1r | 09.11.78 | **Maidenhead** | A | W | 4-0 | Wylie 2, Chamberlain, Hudson |
| | 2 | 04.01.79 | **Upton Park** | H | W | 3-2 | Johnstone 2, Chamberlain |
| | 3 | 02.02.79 | **Oxford University** | A | L | 1-2 | Dorling |
| 1879-80 | 1 | | Old Etonians | | | - | |
| | | | *Barnes scratched. Old Etonians walkover* | | | | |
| 1880-81 | 1 | 06.11.80 | **Herts Rangers** | A | L | 0-6 | |
| 1881-82 | 1 | 05.11.81 | **Rochester** | H | W | 3-1 | |
| | 2 | 03.12.81 | **Old Carthusians** | A | L | 1-7 | Sibbs |
| 1882-83 | 1 | 28.10.82 | **Brentwood** | H | L | 2-4 | |
| *1883-84* | | | *did not enter* | | | | |
| 1884-85 | 1 | 08.11.84 | **Brentwood** | A | L | 0-2 | |
| 1885-86 | 1 | 31.10.85 | **Lancing Old Boys** | H | L | 1-7 | |

# BARNET

*Formed 1888. Known as Barnet Alston 1906-1919. First entered FA Cup: 1911-12. Football League 1991-2001. FA Trophy: runners-up: 1972. FA Amateur Cup: winners: 1946. Runners-up: 1948, 1959. League clubs beaten as a Non-League club: Newport County, Northampton Town. Record FA Cup win: 6-1 v Newport County, 1st round, 21.11.1970; Record FA Cup defeat: 2-9 v Southend Utd, 2nd round, 14.12.1946. Members of The Conference.*

| | | | | | | | |
|---|---|---|---|---|---|---|---|
| 1925-26 (AL) | 1 | 28.11.25 | **Brentford** (3S) | A | L | 1-3 | Donnelly og |
| 1926-27 (AL) | 1 | 27.11.26 | **Brighton** (3S) | A | L | 0-3 | |
| 1931-32 (AL) | 1 | 28.11.31 | **QPR** (3S) | H | L | 3-7 | Finch, Marchant, MacDonald |
| 1933-34 (AL) | 1 | 25.11.33 | **Cheltenham Town** (BC) | A | L | 1-5 | Richardson |
| 1945-46 (AL) | 1 1L | 17.11.45 | **QPR** (3S) | H | L | 2-6 | Reilly, Hawkins |
| | 1 2L | 24.11.45 | **QPR** | A | L | 1-2 | Finch |
| 1946-47 (AL) | 1 | 30.11.46 | **Sutton Utd** (AL) | H | W | 3-0 | Hawkes, Phipps, Finch (p) |
| | 2 | 14.12.46 | **Southend Utd** (3S) | H | L | 2-9 | Phipps 2 |

| | | | | | | | | |
|---|---|---|---|---|---|---|---|---|
| 1948-49 | (AL) | 1 | 04.12.48 | **Exeter City** (3S) | H | L | 2-6 | Kelleher, Phipps |
| 1954-55 | (AL) | 1 | 20.11.54 | **Southampton** (3S) | H | L | 1-4 | Rudolf |
| 1959-60 | (AL) | 1 | 14.11.59 | **Salisbury City** (WL) | A | L | 0-1 | |
| 1961-62 | (AL) | 1 | 04.11.61 | **Weymouth** (SL) | A | L | 0-1 | |
| 1963-64 | (AL) | 1 | 16.11.63 | **Torquay Utd** (D4) | A | L | 2-6 | Figg, Richards |
| 1964-65 | (AL) | 1 | 14.11.64 | **Cambridge Utd** (SL) | H | W | 2-1 | D Harding, Finch |
| | | 2 | 05.12.64 | **Enfield** (IL) | A | D | 4-4 | Figg 2 (1p), Morris, Finch |
| | | 2r | 08.12.64 | **Enfield** | H | W | 3-0 | Finch 2, Figg |
| | | 3 | 09.01.65 | **Preston North End** (D2) | H | L | 2-3 | Figg, White |
| 1965-66 | (SL) | 1 | 13.11.65 | **Dartford** (SL) | H | L | 0-2 | |
| 1967-68 | (SL) | 1 | 13.12.67 | **Hereford Utd** (SL) | A | L | 2-3 | Eason, Searle |
| 1968-69 | (SL) | 1 | 16.11.68 | **Brentwood Town** (SL) | H | D | 1-1 | Meadows |
| | | 1r | 18.11.68 | **Brentwood Town** | A | L | 0-1 | |
| 1969-70 | (SL) | 1 | 15.11.69 | **Walton & H** (AL) | A | W | 1-0 | Meadows |
| | | 2 | 06.12.69 | **Sutton Utd** (IL) | H | L | 0-2 | |
| 1970-71 | (SL) | 1 | 21.11.70 | **Newport County** (D4) | H | W | 6-1 | George 3, Ferguson og, Powell, Adams |
| | | 2 | 12.12.70 | **Slough Town** (AL) | A | W | 1-0 | Eason |
| | | 3 | 05.01.71 | **Colchester Utd** (D4) | H | L | 0-1 | |
| 1971-72 | (SL) | 1 | 20.11.71 | **Kettering Town** (SL) | A | W | 4-2 | Embery 2, Eason 2 |
| | | 2 | 11.12.71 | **Torquay Utd** (D3) | H | L | 1-4 | Flatt |
| 1972-73 | (SL) | 1 | 18.11.72 | **Banbury Utd** (SL) | A | W | 2-0 | Powell, Eason |
| | | 2 | 09.12.72 | **Bilston Town** (WMRL) | H | D | 1-1 | Fascione |
| | | 2r | 11.12.72 | **Bilston Town** | A | W | 1-0 | Powell |
| | | 3 | 13.01.73 | **QPR** (D2) | A | D | 0-0 | |
| | | 3r | 16.01.73 | **QPR** | H | L | 0-3 | |
| 1977-78 | (SL) | 1 | 26.11.77 | **Peterborough Utd** (D3) | H | L | 1-2 | Brown |
| 1978-79 | (SL) | 1 | 25.11.78 | **Woking** (IL) | H | D | 3-3 | Cleary 2 (1p), Oliver |
| | | 1r | 28.11.78 | **Woking** | A | D | 3-3aet | Fairbrother 2, Brown |
| | | 12r | 05.12.78 | **Woking** *played at Griffin Park* | | L | 0-3 | |
| 1980-81 | (APL) | 1 | 22.11.80 | **Minehead** (SL) | H | D | 2-2 | Walker og, Hughes (p) |
| | | 1r | 25.11.80 | **Minehead** | A | W | 2-1 | Roberts 2 |
| | | 2 | 13.12.80 | **Peterborough Utd** (D4) | H | L | 0-1 | |
| 1981-82 | (APL) | 1 | 21.11.81 | **Harlow Town** (IL) | A | D | 0-0 | |
| | | 1r | 24.11.81 | **Harlow Town** | H | W | 1-0 | Sargent |
| | | 2 | 15.12.81 | **Wycombe W** (IL) | H | W | 2-0 | Foody, Barnes |
| | | 3 | 02.01.82 | **Brighton** (D1) | H | D | 0-0 | |
| | | 3r | 05.01.82 | **Brighton** | A | L | 1-3 | Sargent |
| 1982-83 | (APL) | 1 | 20.11.82 | **Carshalton Athletic** (IL) | A | L | 0-4 | |
| 1983-84 | (APL) | 1 | 19.11.83 | **Bristol Rovers** (D3) | H | D | 0-0 | |
| | | 1r | 22.11.83 | **Bristol Rovers** | A | L | 1-3 | Evans |
| 1984-85 | (APL) | 1 | 17.11.84 | **Plymouth Argyle** (D3) | A | L | 0-3 | |
| 1987-88 | (Conf) | 1 | 14.11.87 | **Hereford Utd** (D4) | H | L | 0-1 | |
| 1989-90 | (Conf) | 1 | 18.11.89 | **Bristol City** (D3) | A | L | 0-2 | |
| 1990-91 | (Conf) | 1 | 17.11.90 | **Chelmsford City** (SL) | H | D | 2-2 | Bull, Willis |
| | | 1r | 21.11.90 | **Chelmsford City** | A | W | 2-0 | Clarke, Willis |
| | | 2 | 08.12.90 | **Northampton Town** (D4) | H | D | 0-0 | |
| | | 2r | 12.12.90 | **Northampton Town** | A | W | 1-0 | Clarke |
| | | 3 | 05.01.91 | **Portsmouth** (D2) | H | L | 0-5 | |
| 1991-92 | (D4) | 1 | 16.11.91 | **Tiverton Town** (WL) | H | W | 5-0 | Bull, Naylor, Carter, Evans, Showler |
| | | 2 | 07.12.91 | **Enfield** (IL) | A | W | 4-1 | Carter 3, Bull |
| | | 3 | 05.01.92 | **Charlton Athletic** (D2) | A | L | 1-3 | Carter |
| 1992-93 | (D3) | 1 | 14.11.92 | **Bournemouth** (D2) | A | D | 0-0 | |
| | | 1r | 25.11.92 | **Bournemouth** | H | L | 1-2 | Carter |
| 1993-94 | (D2) | 1 | 13.11.93 | **Carshalton Athletic** (IL) | H | W | 2-1 | Haag, Close |
| | | 2 | 04.12.93 | **Crawley Town** (SL) | A | W | 2-1 | Rowe, C Hoddle |
| | | 3 | 08.01.94 | **Chelsea** (PL) *played at Stamford Bridge* | H | D | 0-0 | |
| | | 3r | 19.01.94 | **Chelsea** | A | L | 0-4 | |
| 1994-95 | (D3) | 1 | 12.11.94 | **Woking** (Conf) | H | D | 4-4 | McMahon, Cooper 2, Hodges |

| | | | | | | | | |
|---|---|---|---|---|---|---|---|---|
| | | 1r | 22.11.94 | **Woking** | A | L | 0-1 | |
| 1995-96 | (D3) | 1 | 11.11.95 | **Woking** (Conf) | H | D | 2-2 | Primus, Devine |
| | | 1r | 21.11.95 | **Woking** | A | L | 1-2aet | Hodges |
| 1996-97 | (D3) | 1 | 16.11.96 | **Farnborough Town** (Conf) | A | D | 2-2 | Devine 2 |
| | | 1r | 26.11.96 | **Farnborough Town** | H | W | 1-0 | Devine |
| | | 2 | 07.12.96 | **Wycombe W** (D2) | H | D | 3-3 | Simpson, Hodges, Devine |
| | | 2r | 17.12.96 | **Wycombe W** | A | L | 2-3 | Campbell, Hodges |
| 1997-98 | (D3) | 1 | 15.11.97 | **Watford** (D2) | H | L | 1-2 | Charlerey |
| 1998-99 | (D3) | 1 | 14.11.98 | **Hednesford Town** (Conf) | A | L | 1-3 | Currie |
| 1999-00 | (D3) | 1 | 31.10.99 | **Burnley** (D2) | H | L | 0-1 | |
| 2000-01 | (D3) | 1 | 18.11.00 | **Hampton & R** (IL) | H | W | 2-1 | Richards, Currie |
| | | 2 | 08.12.00 | **Walsall** (D2) | A | L | 1-2 | Cottee |
| 2001-02 | (Conf) | 1 | 17.11.01 | **Carlisle Utd** (D3) | H | D | 0-0 | |
| | | 1r | 27.11.01 | **Carlisle Utd** | A | L | 0-1 | |

# BARNSLEY

*Formed 1887 as Barnsley St Peters. Barnsley 1899. First entered FA Cup: 1893-94. FA Cup winners: 1912; runners-up: 1910; Record FA Cup win: 8-0 v Leeds AFC 2nd qualifying round, 1894-95; In Competition Proper: 6-0 v Blackpool, 1st round replay, 20.01.1910; Record FA Cup defeat: 1-8 v Derby County, 1st round, 30.01.1897*

| | | | | | | | | |
|---|---|---|---|---|---|---|---|---|
| 1893-94 | | | | 1q Gainsborough T (H) 4-5 | | | | |
| 1894-95 | | | | 1q Grantham R (H) 3-1; 2q Leeds AFC (H) 8-0; 3q Mexborough T (A) 1-1; 3qr Mexborough T (H) 1-0 4q Worksop T (H) 3-1 | | | | |
| | | 1 | 02.02.95 | **Liverpool** (D1) | H | L | 1-2aet | Cutts |
| | | | | *FA ordered replay after protest* | | | | |
| | | 1r | 11.02.95 | **Liverpool** | A | L | 0-4 | |
| 1895-96 | (ML) | | | 1q Rotherham T (A) 1-1; 1qr Rotherham T (H) 3-7 | | | | |
| 1896-97 | (ML) | | | 3q Hunslet (H) 3-2; 4q Sheffield Club (H) 2-1; 5q Lincoln C (A) 2-1 | | | | |
| | | 1 | 30.01.97 | **Derby County** (D1) | A | L | 1-8 | Smith |
| 1897-98 | (ML) | | | 3q Mexborough T (A) 1-2 | | | | |
| 1898-99 | (D2) | | | 2q Wombwell (A) 1-0; 3q Gainsborough T (A) 2-2; 3qr Gainsborough T (H) 4-0; 4q Doncaster R (A) 1-2 | | | | |
| 1899-00 | (D2) | | | 3q Lincoln C (H) 1-0; 4q Grimsby T (A) 2-3 | | | | |
| 1900-01 | (D2) | | | 3q Doncaster R (H) 2-1; 4q Lincoln C (H) 1-0; 5q Chesterfield (H) 1-5 | | | | |
| 1901-02 | (D2) | | | 3q Gainsborough T (H) 1-0; 4q Ilkeston T (A) 4-2; 5q Lincoln C (H) 0-0; 5qr Lincoln C (A) 1-3aet | | | | |
| 1902-03 | (D2) | | | 3q Belper T (A) 4-1; 4q Chesterfield (H) 3-2; 5q Gainsborough T (H) 3-2; Int Swindon T (H) 4-0 | | | | |
| | | 1 | 07.02.03 | **Lincoln City** (D2) | H | W | 2-0 | Bennett, Welch |
| | | 2 | 21.02.03 | **Aston Villa** (D1) | A | L | 1-4 | Lees |
| 1903-04 | (D2) | | | Int Grimsby T (A) 0-2 | | | | |
| 1904-05 | (D2) | | | 6q Burslem PV (H) 0-0; 6qr Burslem PV (A) 2-1; Int Plymouth A (A) 0-2 | | | | |
| 1905-06 | (D2) | | | 4q Earlestown (A) 2-0 | | | | |
| | | 1 | 13.01.06 | **Crewe Alexandra** (BDL) | A | D | 1-1 | Stacey |
| | | 1r | 18.01.06 | **Crewe Alexandra** | H | W | 4-0 | Stacey, Wilkinson, Helliwell, Wall |
| | | 2 | 03.02.06 | **Liverpool** (D1) | A | L | 0-1 | |
| 1906-07 | (D2) | 1 | 12.01.07 | **Nottingham Forest** (D2) | A | D | 1-1 | Helliwell |
| | | 1r | 17.01.07 | **Nottingham Forest** | H | W | 2-1 | Helliwell, Hall |
| | | 2 | 02.02.07 | **Portsmouth** (SL) | H | W | 1-0 | O'Donnell |
| | | 3 | 23.02.07 | **Bury** (D1) | H | W | 1-0 | Powell |
| | | 4 | 09.03.07 | **Woolwich Arsenal** (D1) | H | L | 1-2 | O'Donnell |
| 1907-08 | (D2) | 1 | 11.01.08 | **Plymouth Argyle** (SL) | A | L | 0-1 | |
| 1908-09 | (D2) | 1 | 16.01.09 | **Everton** (D1) | A | L | 1-3 | Lillycrop |
| 1909-10 | (D2) | 1 | 15.01.10 | **Blackpool** (D2) | A | D | 1-1 | Tufnell |
| | | 1r | 20.01.10 | **Blackpool** | H | W | 6-0 | Lillycrop 2, Tufnell 2, Gadsby, Boyle |
| | | 2 | 05.02.10 | **Bristol Rovers** (SL) | H | W | 4-0 | Forman, Utley, Bartrop, Gadsby |
| | | 3 | 19.02.10 | **WBA** (D2) | H | W | 1-0 | Tufnell |
| | | 4 | 05.03.10 | **QPR** (SL) | H | W | 1-0 | Bartrop |
| | | SF | 26.03.10 | **Everton** (D1) | | D | 0-0 | |
| | | | | *played at Elland Road* | | | | |
| | | SFr | 31.03.10 | **Everton** | | W | 3-0 | Gadsby, Forman, Tufnell |
| | | | | *played at Old Trafford* | | | | |

| | | | | | | | |
|---|---|---|---|---|---|---|---|
| | F | 23.04.10 | **Newcastle Utd** (D1) | | D | 1-1 | Tufnell |
| | | | *played at Crystal Palace* | | | | |
| | Fr | 28.04.10 | **Newcastle Utd** | | L | 0-2 | |
| | | | *played at Goodison Park* | | | | |
| 1910-11 (D2) | 1 | 14.01.11 | **Watford** (SL) | A | W | 2-0 | Boyle, Lillycrop |
| | 2 | 04.02.11 | **Burnley** (D2) | A | L | 0-2 | |
| 1911-12 (D2) | 1 | 13.01.12 | **Birmingham** (D2) | A | D | 0-0 | |
| | 1r | 22.01.12 | **Birmingham** | H | W | 3-0 | Tufnell, Lillycrop 2 |
| | 2 | 03.02.12 | **Leicester Fosse** (D2) | H | W | 1-0 | Lillycrop |
| | 3 | 24.02.12 | **Bolton Wanderers** (D1) | A | W | 2-1 | Lillycrop, Whiteside og |
| | 4 | 09.03.12 | **Bradford City** (D1) | H | D | 0-0 | |
| | 4r | 13.03.12 | **Bradford City** | A | D | 0-0aet | |
| | | | *played at Elland Road* | | | | |
| | 42r | 18.03.12 | **Bradford City** | | D | 0-0aet | |
| | | | *played at Elland Road* | | | | |
| | 43r | 21.03.12 | **Bradford City** | | W | 3-2aet | Travers, Lillycrop 2 |
| | | | *played at Bramall Lane* | | | | |
| | SF | 30.03.12 | **Swindon Town** (SL) | | D | 0-0 | |
| | | | *played at Stamford Bridge* | | | | |
| | SFr | 03.04.12 | **Swindon Town** | | W | 1-0 | Bratley |
| | | | *played at Meadow Lane, Nottingham* | | | | |
| | F | 20.04.12 | **WBA** (D1) | | D | 0-0 | |
| | | | *played at Crystal Palace* | | | | |
| | Fr | 24.04.12 | **WBA** | | W | 1-0aet | Tufnell |
| | | | *played at Bramall Lane* | | | | |
| 1912-13 (D2) | 1 | 11.01.13 | **Gillingham** (SL) | A | D | 0-0 | |
| | 1r | 16.01.13 | **Gillingham** | H | W | 3-1 | Tufnell, Lillycrop 2 |
| | 2 | 01.02.13 | **Blackburn Rovers** (D1) | H | L | 2-3 | Moore, Tufnell |
| 1913-14 (D2) | 1 | 10.01.14 | **Liverpool** (D1) | A | D | 1-1 | Travers |
| | 1r | 15.01.14 | **Liverpool** | H | L | 0-1 | |
| 1914-15 (D2) | 1 | 09.01.15 | **Everton** (D1) | A | L | 0-3 | |
| 1919-20 (D2) | 1 | 10.01.20 | **WBA** (D1) | A | W | 1-0 | Fletcher |
| | 2 | 31.01.20 | **Plymouth Argyle** (SL) | A | L | 1-4 | Downs |
| 1920-21 (D2) | 1 | 08.01.21 | **Bradford City** (D1) | A | L | 1-3 | Fletcher |
| 1921-22 (D2) | 1 | 07.01.22 | **Norwich City** (D3) | H | D | 1-1 | Spoors |
| | 1r | 11.01.22 | **Norwich City** | A | W | 2-1 | Hine, Fletcher |
| | 2 | 28.01.22 | **Oldham Athletic** (D1) | H | W | 3-1 | Fletcher 2, Wainscoat |
| | 3 | 18.02.22 | **Preston North End** (D1) | H | D | 1-1 | Fletcher |
| | 3r | 22.02.22 | **Preston North End** | A | L | 0-3 | |
| 1922-23 (D2) | 1 | 13.01.23 | **Swindon Town** (3S) | A | D | 0-0 | |
| | 1r | 18.01.23 | **Swindon Town** | H | W | 2-0 | Hine, Wainscoat |
| | 2 | 03.02.23 | **Sheffield Wed** (D2) | A | L | 1-2 | Baines |
| 1923-24 (D2) | 1 | 12.01.24 | **Brighton** (3S) | H | D | 0-0 | |
| | 1r | 16.01.24 | **Brighton** | A | L | 0-1 | |
| 1924-25 (D2) | 1 | 10.01.25 | **Millwall Athletic** (3S) | A | D | 0-0 | |
| | 1r | 15.01.25 | **Millwall Athletic** | H | W | 2-1 | Fletcher, Kelly |
| | 2 | 31.01.25 | **Bradford City** (D2) | H | L | 0-3 | |
| 1925-26 (D2) | 1 | 28.11.25 | **Northampton Town** (3S) | A | L | 1-3 | Fletcher |
| 1926-27 (D2) | 3 | 08.01.27 | **Crewe Alexandra** (3N) | H | W | 6-1 | Tilson, Fletcher 3, Eaton, Curran |
| | 4 | 29.01.27 | **Swansea Town** (D2) | H | L | 1-3 | Eaton |
| 1927-28 (D2) | 3 | 14.01.28 | **Port Vale** (D2) | A | L | 0-3 | |
| 1928-29 (D2) | 3 | 12.01.29 | **Blackburn Rovers** (D1) | A | L | 0-1 | |
| 1929-30 (D2) | 3 | 11.01.30 | **Bradford Park A** (D2) | H | L | 0-1 | |
| 1930-31 (D2) | 3 | 10.01.31 | **Bristol City** (D2) | H | W | 4-1 | Proudfoot, Gibbs, Curran, Harvey |
| | 4 | 24.01.31 | **Sheffield Wed** (D1) | H | W | 2-1 | Harvey, Curran |
| | 5 | 14.02.31 | **Wolverhampton W** (D2) | H | L | 1-3 | Henderson |
| 1931-32 (D2) | 3 | 09.01.32 | **Southport** (3N) | H | D | 0-0 | |
| | 3r | 12.01.32 | **Southport** | A | L | 1-4 | Ashton |
| 1932-33 (3N) | 3 | 14.01.33 | **Luton Town** (3S) | H | D | 0-0 | |
| | 3r | 18.01.33 | **Luton Town** | A | L | 0-2 | |
| 1933-34 (3N) | 1 | 25.11.33 | **Halifax Town** (3N) | A | L | 2-3 | Andrews 2 |
| 1934-35 (D2) | 3 | 12.01.35 | **Preston North End** (D1) | A | D | 0-0 | |

| | | | | | | | | |
|---|---|---|---|---|---|---|---|---|
| | | 3r | 16.01.35 | **Preston North End** | H | L | 0-1 | |
| 1935-36 | (D2) | 3 | 11.01.36 | **Birmingham** (D1) | H | D | 3-3 | Hine 2, Ashton |
| | | 3r | 15.01.36 | **Birmingham** | A | W | 2-0 | Hine, Waring |
| | | 4 | 25.01.36 | **Tranmere Rovers** (3N) | A | W | 4-2 | Waring, Hine, Ashton, Fisher |
| | | 5 | 15.02.36 | **Stoke City** (D1) | H | W | 2-1 | Gallacher, Hine |
| | | 6 | 29.02.36 | **Arsenal** (D1) | A | L | 1-4 | Gallacher |
| 1936-37 | (D2) | 3 | 16.01.37 | **Walsall** (3S) | A | L | 1-3 | Hamill |
| 1937-38 | (D2) | 3 | 08.01.38 | **Southend Utd** (3S) | A | D | 2-2 | Asquith, Barlow |
| | | 3r | 12.01.38 | **Southend Utd** | H | W | 3-1 | Barlow, Hunt 2 |
| | | 4 | 22.01.38 | **Manchester Utd** (D2) | H | D | 2-2 | Bokas, Fisher |
| | | 4r | 26.01.38 | **Manchester Utd** | A | L | 0-1 | |
| 1938-39 | (3N) | 3 | 07.01.39 | **Stockport County** (3N) | H | L | 1-2 | McGarry |
| 1945-46 | (D2) | 3 1L | 05.01.46 | **Newcastle Utd** (D2) | A | L | 2-4 | Harvey og, Pallister |
| | | 3 2L | 09.01.46 | **Newcastle Utd** | H | W | 3-0 | Wilson, Smith, Baxter |
| | | 4 1L | 26.01.46 | **Rotherham Utd** (3N) | H | W | 3-0 | Kelly, Smith, G Robledo |
| | | 4 2L | 31.01.46 | **Rotherham Utd** | A | L | 1-2 | Pallister |
| | | 5 1L | 09.02.46 | **Bradford Park A** (D2) | H | L | 0-1 | |
| | | 5 2L | 13.02.46 | **Bradford Park A** | A | D | 1-1 | G Robledo |
| 1946-47 | (D2) | 3 | 11.01.47 | **Huddersfield Town** (D1) | A | W | 4-3 | Smith, Asquith, Bennett, Baxter |
| | | 4 | 25.01.47 | **Preston North End** (D1) | A | L | 0-6 | |
| 1947-48 | (D2) | 3 | 10.01.48 | **Manchester City** (D1) | A | L | 1-2 | Wright |
| 1948-49 | (D2) | 3 | 08.01.49 | **Blackpool** (D1) | H | L | 0-1 | |
| 1949-50 | (D2) | 3 | 07.01.50 | **Stockport County** (3N) | A | L | 2-4 | Wright, Griffiths |
| 1950-51 | (D2) | 3 | 06.01.51 | **Northampton Town** (3S) | A | L | 1-3 | McCormack |
| 1951-52 | (D2) | 3 | 12.01.52 | **Colchester Utd** (3S) | H | W | 3-0 | McMorran, Jarman, Wood |
| | | 4 | 02.02.52 | **Arsenal** (D1) | A | L | 0-4 | |
| 1952-53 | (D2) | 3 | 10.01.53 | **Brighton** (3S) | H | W | 4-3 | Kaye, Taylor 2, McMorran |
| | | 4 | 31.01.53 | **Plymouth Argyle** (D2) | A | L | 0-1 | |
| 1953-54 | (3N) | 1 | 21.11.53 | **York City** (3N) | H | W | 5-2 | Kaye, Lumley, Bartlett 2, Chappell |
| | | 2 | 12.12.53 | **Norwich City** (3S) | A | L | 1-2 | Brown |
| 1954-55 | (3N) | 1 | 20.11.54 | **Wigan Athletic** (LC) | H | W | 3-2 | Bartlett, Lumley 2 |
| | | 2 | 11.12.54 | **Gateshead AFC** (3N) | A | D | 3-3 | Wood, Kaye, Bartlett |
| | | 2r | 16.12.54 | **Gateshead AFC** | H | L | 0-1 | |
| 1955-56 | (D2) | 3 | 07.01.56 | **Aldershot** (3S) | A | W | 2-1 | Brown 2 |
| | | 4 | 28.01.56 | **Blackburn Rovers** (D2) | H | L | 0-1 | |
| 1956-57 | (D2) | 3 | 05.01.57 | **Port Vale** (D2) | H | D | 3-3 | Kaye 2, Bartlett |
| | | 3r | 07.01.57 | **Port Vale** | A | W | 1-0 | Hayward og |
| | | 4 | 26.01.57 | **Cardiff City** (D1) | A | W | 1-0 | Bartlett |
| | | 5 | 16.02.57 | **Nottingham Forest** (D2) | H | L | 1-2 | Kaye |
| 1957-58 | (D2) | 3 | 04.01.58 | **Hull City** (3N) | A | D | 1-1 | Smith |
| | | 3r | 08.01.58 | **Hull City** | H | L | 0-2 | |
| 1958-59 | (D2) | 3 | 10.01.59 | **Brentford** (D3) | A | L | 0-2 | |
| 1959-60 | (D3) | 1 | 14.11.59 | **Bradford City** (D3) | H | D | 3-3 | Barber, Bartlett, Beaumont (p) |
| | | 1r | 18.11.59 | **Bradford City** | A | L | 1-2 | Beaumont |
| 1960-61 | (D3) | 1 | 05.11.60 | **Gateshead AFC** (NCo) | A | D | 0-0 | |
| | | 1r | 09.11.60 | **Gateshead AFC** | H | W | 2-0 | Bartlett, Beaumont |
| | | 2 | 26.11.60 | **Bradford City** (D3) | A | W | 2-1 | Bartlett 2 |
| | | 3 | 07.01.61 | **Reading** (D3) | A | D | 1-1 | Tindill |
| | | 3r | 11.01.61 | **Reading** | H | W | 3-1 | Oliver, Tindill, Bartlett |
| | | 4 | 01.02.61 | **Huddersfield Town** (D2) | A | D | 1-1 | Oliver |
| | | 4r | 06.02.61 | **Huddersfield Town** | H | W | 1-0 | Wood |
| | | 5 | 18.02.61 | **Luton Town** (D2) | H | W | 1-0 | Lunn |
| | | 6 | 04.03.61 | **Leicester City** (D1) | A | D | 0-0 | |
| | | 6r | 08.03.61 | **Leicester City** | H | L | 1-2aet | Oliver |
| 1961-62 | (D3) | 1 | 04.11.61 | **West Auckland T** (NL) | A | D | 3-3 | Oliver 2, Swindells |
| | | 1r | 08.11.61 | **West Auckland T** | H | W | 2-0 | Swindells, Smillie |
| | | 2 | 25.11.61 | **Carlisle Utd** (D4) | H | L | 1-2 | Swindells |
| 1962-63 | (D3) | 1 | 03.11.62 | **Rhyl** (CC) | H | W | 4-0 | Kerr 2, Leighton, O'Hara (p) |
| | | 2 | 24.11.62 | **Chesterfield** (D4) | H | W | 2-1 | Oliver 2 |
| | | 3 | 15.01.63 | **Everton** (D1) | H | L | 0-3 | |
| 1963-64 | (D3) | 1 | 16.11.63 | **Stockport County** (D4) | H | W | 1-0 | Byrne |

| | | | | | | | |
|---|---|---|---|---|---|---|---|
| | 2 | 07.12.63 | **Rochdale** (D4) | H | W | 3-1 | Kerr 2, Leighton |
| | 3 | 04.01.64 | **Scunthorpe Utd** (D2) | A | D | 2-2 | O'Hara, Byrne |
| | 3r | 07.01.64 | **Scunthorpe Utd** | H | W | 3-2aet | O'Hara, Byrne 2 |
| | 4 | 25.01.64 | **Bury** (D2) | H | W | 2-1 | Gallagher og, Kerr |
| | 5 | 15.02.64 | **Manchester Utd** (D1) | H | L | 0-4 | |
| 1964-65 (D3) | 1 | 14.11.64 | **Netherfield** (LC) | A | W | 3-1 | Byrne, Kerr, Graham |
| | 2 | 05.12.64 | **Chester** (D4) | H | L | 2-5 | Byrne, Senior |
| 1965-66 (D4) | 1 | 13.11.65 | **Lincoln City** (D4) | A | W | 3-1 | Bettany, Kerr (p), Earnshaw |
| | 2 | 04.12.65 | **Grimsby Town** (D3) | H | D | 1-1 | Kerr |
| | 2r | 08.12.65 | **Grimsby Town** | A | L | 0-2aet | |
| 1966-67 (D4) | 1 | 26.11.66 | **Southport** (D4) | H | W | 3-1 | Evans, Thomas 2 |
| | 2 | 07.01.67 | **Port Vale** (D4) | H | D | 1-1 | Hewitt |
| | 2r | 16.01.67 | **Port Vale** | A | W | 3-0 | Sherrat og, Bettany, Hewitt (p) |
| | 3 | 28.01.67 | **Cardiff City** (D2) | H | D | 1-1 | Evans |
| | 3r | 31.01.67 | **Cardiff City** | A | L | 1-2 | Thomas |
| 1967-68 (D4) | 1 | 09.12.67 | **Chesterfield** (D4) | A | L | 0-2 | |
| 1968-69 (D3) | 1 | 09.11.68 | **Rochdale** (D4) | H | D | 0-0 | |
| | 1r | 18.11.68 | **Rochdale** | A | W | 1-0 | Dean |
| | 2 | 07.12.68 | **Darlington** (D4) | A | D | 0-0 | |
| | 2r | 10.12.68 | **Darlington** | H | W | 1-0aet | Winstanley |
| | 3 | 04.01.69 | **Leicester City** (D1) | H | D | 1-1 | Evans |
| | 3r | 08.01.69 | **Leicester City** | A | L | 1-2 | Layden (p) |
| 1969-70 (D3) | 1 | 15.11.69 | **Darlington** (D4) | A | D | 0-0 | |
| | 1r | 18.11.69 | **Darlington** | H | W | 2-0 | Dean, Graham |
| | 2 | 06.12.69 | **Barrow** (D3) | H | W | 3-0 | Loyden 2, Robson |
| | 3 | 03.01.70 | **Mansfield Town** (D3) | A | L | 2-3 | Dean, Evans |
| 1970-71 (D3) | 1 | 21.11.70 | **Bradford Park A** (NPL) | H | W | 1-0 | Dean (p) |
| | 2 | 12.12.70 | **Rhyl** (CC) | A | D | 0-0 | |
| | 2r | 15.12.70 | **Rhyl** | H | D | 1-1aet | Lea |
| | 22r | 21.12.70 | **Rhyl** | H | L | 0-2 | |
| 1971-72 (D3) | 1 | 20.11.71 | **Rochdale** (D3) | A | W | 3-1 | Winstanley 2, Seal |
| | 2 | 11.12.71 | **Chesterfield** (D3) | H | D | 0-0 | |
| | 2r | 15.12.71 | **Chesterfield** | A | L | 0-1 | |
| 1972-73 (D4) | 1 | 18.11.72 | **Halifax Town** (D3) | H | D | 1-1 | Lea |
| | 1r | 21.11.72 | **Halifax Town** | A | L | 1-2 | Kemp og |
| 1973-74 (D4) | 1 | 24.11.73 | **Chesterfield** (D3) | A | D | 0-0 | |
| | 1r | 28.11.73 | **Chesterfield** | H | W | 2-1 | Manning 2 |
| | 2 | 15.12.73 | **Bradford City** (D4) | H | D | 1-1 | Butler |
| | 2r | 19.12.73 | **Bradford City** | A | L | 1-2 | Brown |
| 1974-75 (D4) | 1 | 23.11.74 | **Halifax Town** (D3) | H | L | 1-2 | Brown |
| 1975-76 (D4) | 1 | 22.11.75 | **Marine** (CC) | A | L | 1-3 | Butler |
| 1976-77 (D4) | 1 | 20.11.76 | **Boston Town** (ML) | H | W | 3-1 | Joicey 3 (1p) |
| | 2 | 11.12.76 | **Port Vale** (D3) | A | L | 0-3 | |
| 1977-78 (D4) | 1 | 26.11.77 | **Huddersfield Town** (D4) | H | W | 1-0 | Warnock |
| | 2 | 17.12.77 | **Grimsby Town** (D4) | A | L | 0-2 | |
| 1978-79 (D4) | 1 | 25.11.78 | **Worksop Town** (NPL) | H | W | 5-1 | Clarke, Riley, Bell, Reed 2 |
| | 2 | 16.12.78 | **Rotherham Utd** (D3) | H | D | 1-1 | Clarke |
| | 2r | 09.01.79 | **Rotherham Utd** | A | L | 1-2 | Forrest og |
| 1979-80 (D3) | 1 | 24.11.79 | **Hartlepool Utd** (D4) | H | W | 5-2 | Clarke, Glavin 2, Aylott, Lester |
| | 2 | 18.12.79 | **Chester** (D3) | A | L | 0-1 | |
| 1980-81 (D3) | 1 | 22.11.80 | **Chester** (D3) | A | W | 2-1 | Cooper, Banks |
| | 2 | 13.12.80 | **Rotherham Utd** (D3) | A | W | 1-0 | Parker |
| | 3 | 03.01.81 | **Torquay Utd** (D4) | H | W | 2-1 | Parker 2 |
| | 4 | 24.01.81 | **Enfield** (IL) | H | D | 1-1 | Aylott |
| | 4r | 28.01.81 | **Enfield** | A | W | 3-0 | Aylott 2, Glavin |
| | | | *played at White Hart Lane* | | | | |
| | 5 | 14.02.81 | **Middlesbrough** (D1) | A | L | 1-2 | Lester |
| 1981-82 (D2) | 3 | 05.01.82 | **Blackpool** (D4) | H | L | 0-2 | |
| 1982-83 (D2) | 3 | 08.01.83 | **Bradford City** (D3) | A | W | 1-0 | Glavin |
| | 4 | 29.01.83 | **Cambridge Utd** (D2) | A | L | 0-1 | |
| 1983-84 (D2) | 3 | 07.01.84 | **Sheffield Wed** (D2) | A | L | 0-1 | |

| | | | | | | | | |
|---|---|---|---|---|---|---|---|---|
| 1984-85 | (D2) | 3 | 05.01.85 | **Reading** (D3) | H | W | 4-3 | R Futcher, Owen 2(1p), Joyce |
| | | 4 | 26.01.85 | **Brighton** (D2) | H | W | 2-1 | Owen, R Futcher |
| | | 5 | 04.03.85 | **Southampton** (D1) | A | W | 2-1 | Agnew, Owen (p) |
| | | 6 | 10.03.85 | **Liverpool** (D1) | H | L | 0-4 | |
| 1985-86 | (D2) | 3 | 13.01.86 | **Bury** (D3) | A | L | 0-2 | |
| 1986-87 | (D2) | 3 | 10.01.87 | **Caernarfon Town** (NPL) | A | D | 0-0 | |
| | | 3r | 26.01.87 | **Caernarfon Town** | H | W | 1-0 | Wylde |
| | | 4 | 31.01.87 | **Aldershot** (D4) | A | D | 1-1 | Agnew |
| | | 4r | 03.02.87 | **Aldershot** | H | W | 3-0 | May 2, Thomas |
| | | 5 | 21.02.87 | **Arsenal** (D1) | A | L | 0-2 | |
| 1987-88 | (D2) | 3 | 09.01.88 | **Bolton Wanderers** (D4) | H | W | 3-1 | Broddle 2, Beresford |
| | | 4 | 30.01.88 | **Birmingham City** (D2) | H | L | 0-2 | |
| 1988-89 | (D2) | 3 | 07.01.89 | **Chelsea** (D2) | H | W | 4-0 | Thomas, Agnew 2, Currie |
| | | 4 | 28.01.89 | **Stoke City** (D2) | A | D | 3-3 | Currie 2, MacDonald |
| | | 4r | 31.01.89 | **Stoke City** | H | W | 2-1 | MacDonald, Cooper |
| | | 5 | 19.02.89 | **Everton** | H | L | 0-1 | |
| 1989-90 | (D2) | 3 | 06.01.90 | **Leicester City** (D2) | A | W | 2-1 | Currie, Lowndes |
| | | 4 | 27.01.90 | **Ipswich Town** (D2) | H | W | 2-0 | Taggart, Cooper |
| | | 5 | 18.02.90 | **Sheffield Utd** (D2) | A | D | 2-2 | Smith, Cooper |
| | | 5r | 21.02.90 | **Sheffield Utd** | H | D | 0-0aet | |
| | | 5 2r | 05.03.90 | **Sheffield Utd** | H | L | 0-1aet | |
| 1990-91 | (D2) | 3 | 06.01.91 | **Leeds Utd** (D1) | H | D | 1-1 | Deehan |
| | | 3r | 09.01.91 | **Leeds Utd** | A | L | 0-4 | |
| 1991-92 | (D2) | 3 | 04.01.92 | **Norwich City** (D1) | A | L | 0-1 | |
| 1992-93 | (D1) | 3 | 13.01.93 | **Leicester City** (D1) | A | D | 2-2 | Whitlow og, Redfearn |
| | | 3r | 20.01.93 | **Leicester City** | H | D | 1-1aet | Archdeacon |
| | | | | *Barnsley won 5-4 on penalties* | | | | |
| | | 4 | 24.01.93 | **West Ham Utd** (D1) | H | W | 4-1 | Rammell 3, Refearn |
| | | 5 | 13.02.93 | **Manchester City** (PL) | A | L | 0-2 | |
| 1993-94 | (D1) | 3 | 08.01.94 | **Bromsgrove R** (Conf) | A | W | 2-1 | Rammell, O Archdeacon |
| | | 4 | 29.01.94 | **Plymouth Argyle** (D2) | A | D | 2-2 | Payton, Taggert |
| | | 4r | 09.02.94 | **Plymouth Argyle** | H | W | 1-0 | O'Connell |
| | | 5 | 19.02.94 | **Oldham Athletic** (PL) | A | L | 0-1 | |
| 1994-95 | (D1) | 3 | 07.01.95 | **Aston Villa** (PL) | H | L | 0-2 | |
| 1995-96 | (D1) | 3 | 06.01.96 | **Oldham Athletic** (D1) | H | D | 0-0 | |
| | | 3r | 23.01.96 | **Oldham Athletic** | A | L | 1-2 | Redfearn |
| 1996-97 | (D1) | 3 | 14.01.97 | **Oldham Athletic** (D1) | H | W | 2-0 | Bullock, Marcelle |
| | | 4 | 25.01.97 | **QPR** (D1) | A | L | 2-3 | Redfearn, Hendrie |
| 1997-98 | (PL) | 3 | 03.01.98 | **Bolton Wanderers** (PL) | H | W | 1-0 | Barnard |
| | | 4 | 24.01.98 | **Tottenham Hotspur** (PL) | A | D | 1-1 | Redfearn (p) |
| | | 4r | 04.02.98 | **Tottenham Hotspur** | H | W | 3-1 | Ward, Redfearn, Barnard |
| | | 5 | 15.02.98 | **Manchester Utd** (PL) | A | D | 1-1 | Hendrie |
| | | 5r | 25.02.98 | **Manchester Utd** | H | W | 3-2 | Hendrie, Jones 2 |
| | | 6 | 08.03.98 | **Newcastle Utd** (PL) | A | L | 1-3 | Liddell |
| 1998-99 | (D1) | 3 | 02.01.99 | **Swindon Town** (D1) | A | D | 0-0 | |
| | | 3r | 19.01.99 | **Swindon Town** | H | W | 3-1 | McClare, Bullock, Hignett |
| | | 4 | 23.01.99 | **Bournemouth** (D2) | H | W | 3-1 | Sheridan, Hignett, Bullock |
| | | 5 | 13.02.99 | **Bristol Rovers** (D2) | H | W | 4-1 | Hignett 3, Dyer |
| | | 6 | 16.03.99 | **Tottenham Hotspur** (PL) | H | L | 0-1 | |
| 1999-00 | (D1) | 3 | 11.12.99 | **Wimbledon** (PL) | A | L | 0-1 | |
| 2000-01 | (D1) | 3 | 06.01.01 | **Leeds Utd** (PL) | A | L | 0-1 | |
| 2001-02 | (D1) | 3 | 05.01.02 | **Blackburn Rovers** (PL) | H | D | 1-1 | Barnard |
| | | 3r | 16.01.02 | **Blackburn Rovers** | A | L | 1-3 | Dyer |
| 2002-03 | (D2) | 1 | 16.11.02 | **Blackpool** (D2) | H | L | 1-4 | Dyer |

# BARNSTAPLE TOWN

*Formed 1906. First entered FA Cup: 1948-49. Members of the Western League,*

| | | | | | | | | |
|---|---|---|---|---|---|---|---|---|
| 1951-52 | (WL) | 1 | 24.11.51 | **Folkestone** (KL) | H | D | 2-2 | Pickard, Godbeer |
| | | 1r | 28.11.51 | **Folkestone** | A | L | 2-5 | Hayward, Granville |
| 1954-55 | (WL) | 1 | 20.11.54 | **Bournemouth** (3S) | H | L | 1-4 | Stocker |
| 1959-60 | (WL) | 1 | 14.11.59 | **Exeter City** (D4) | A | L | 0-4 | |
| 1972-73 | (WL) | 1 | 18.11.72 | **Bilston Town** (WMRL) | H | L | 0-2 | |

# BARROW

*Formed 1901. First entered FA Cup: 1901-02. Members of the Football League: 1921-1972. FA Trophy winners: 1990. Best performances in FA Cup: 3rd round eight times. Members of the Northern Premier League.*

| | | | | | | | | |
|---|---|---|---|---|---|---|---|---|
| 1905-06 | (LC) | 1 | 13.01.06 | **Bradford City** (D2) | A | L | 2-3 | Lawrenson, McBeath |
| 1912-13 | (LC) | 1 | 15.01.13 | **Bradford Park A** (D2) | A | D | 1-1 | Pinkey |
| | | 1r | 22.01.13 | **Bradford Park A** | H | L | 0-1 | |
| | | | | *played at Bradford* | | | | |
| 1921-22 | (3N) | | | 4q Lancaster T (H) 2-2; 4qr Lancaster T (A) 0-1 | | | | |
| 1922-23 | (3N) | | | 4q Workington (H) 1-0; 5q Stockport Co (H) 3-2; 6q Bath C (H) 2-2; 6qr Bath C (A) 0-2 | | | | |
| 1923-24 | (3N) | | | 4q Carlisle U (H) 1-2 | | | | |
| 1924-25 | (3N) | | | 4q Darwen (H) 1-0; 5q Wrexham (H) 4-0; 6q Gillingham (A) 0-0; 6qr Gillingham (H) 1-1aet; 6q 2r Gillingham 1-1 (at Molineux); 6q 3r Gillingham 1-1 (at Highbury); 6q 4r Gillingham 2-1 (at Millwall) | | | | |
| | | 1 | 10.01.25 | **Blackpool** (D2) | A | D | 0-0 | |
| | | 1r | 14.01.25 | **Blackpool** | H | L | 0-2 | |
| 1925-26 | (3N) | 1 | 28.11.25 | **New Brighton** (3N) | A | L | 0-2 | |
| 1926-27 | (3N) | 1 | 01.12.26 | **Wigan Borough** (3N) | A | D | 2-2 | Tilbrook 2 |
| | | 1r | 06.12.26 | **Wigan Borough** | H | L | 0-1 | |
| 1927-28 | (3N) | | | 4q Workington (A) 1-3 | | | | |
| 1928-29 | (3N) | 1 | 24.11.28 | **York City** (ML) | A | W | 1-0 | Ferrari |
| | | 2 | 08.12.28 | **Mansfield Town** (ML) | H | L | 1-2 | Ferrari |
| 1929-30 | (3N) | 1 | 30.11.29 | **Newark Town** (ML) | H | W | 1-0 | Patton |
| | | 2 | 14.12.29 | **Stockport County** (3N) | A | L | 0-4 | |
| 1930-31 | (3N) | 1 | 29.11.30 | **Lincoln City** (3N) | A | L | 3-8 | Millar 2, Moon |
| 1931-32 | (3N) | 1 | 28.11.31 | **Doncaster Rovers** (3N) | H | D | 3-3 | Littler 2, Suggett |
| | | 1r | 03.12.31 | **Doncaster Rovers** | A | D | 1-1aet | Littler |
| | | 1 2r | 07.12.31 | **Doncaster Rovers** | | D | 1-1aet | Tinnion |
| | | | | *played at Maine Road* | | | | |
| | | 1 3r | 09.12.31 | **Doncaster Rovers** | | L | 0-1aet | |
| | | | | *played at Elland Road* | | | | |
| 1932-33 | (3N) | 1 | 26.11.32 | **Gateshead AFC** (3N) | H | L | 0-1 | |
| 1933-34 | (3N) | 1 | 25.11.33 | **Doncaster Rovers** (3N) | H | W | 4-2 | Shankly 3, Roberts |
| | | 2 | 09.12.33 | **Bristol City** (3S) | A | L | 1-3 | Murray |
| 1934-35 | (3N) | 1 | 24.11.34 | **Doncaster Rovers** (3N) | A | W | 2-0 | Robinson 2 |
| | | 2 | 08.12.34 | **Aldershot** (3S) | H | L | 0-2 | |
| 1935-36 | (3N) | 1 | 30.11.35 | **Wrexham** (3N) | H | W | 4-1 | Foster (p), Reid, Robinson, Dunkerle |
| | | 2 | 14.12.35 | **Bournemouth** (3S) | A | L | 2-5 | Reid 2 |
| 1936-37 | (3N) | 1 | 28.11.36 | **Mansfield Town** (3N) | H | L | 0-6 | |
| 1937-38 | (3N) | 1 | 27.11.37 | **Crewe Alexandra** (3N) | H | L | 0-1 | |
| 1938-39 | (3N) | 1 | 26.11.38 | **Lincoln City** (3N) | A | L | 1-4 | Harris |
| 1945-46 | (3N) | 1 1L | 17.11.45 | **Netherfield** (LC) | H | W | 1-0 | McIntosh |
| | | 1 2L | 24.11.45 | **Netherfield** | A | D | 2-2 | Clarke, Hull |
| | | 2 1L | 08.12.45 | **Carlisle Utd** (3N) | H | W | 4-2 | Clarke 3, Dunnigan |
| | | 2 2L | 15.12.45 | **Carlisle Utd** | A | W | 4-3 | Clarke 3, McIntosh |
| | | 3 1L | 05.01.46 | **Manchester City** (D2) | A | L | 2-6 | Clarke 2 |
| | | 3 2L | 10.01.46 | **Manchester City** | H | D | 2-2 | Clarkson, McIntosh |
| 1946-47 | (3N) | 1 | 30.11.46 | **Halifax Town** (3N) | H | D | 0-0 | |
| | | 1r | 04.12.46 | **Halifax Town** | A | L | 0-1aet | |
| 1947-48 | (3N) | 1 | 29.11.47 | **Carlisle Utd** (3N) | H | W | 3-2 | Mullen, Burnett 2 |
| | | 2 | 13.12.47 | **Runcorn** (CC) | A | W | 1-0 | Livingstone |
| | | 3 | 10.01.48 | **Chelsea** (D1) | A | L | 0-5 | |
| 1948-49 | (3N) | 1 | 27.11.48 | **Rochdale** (3N) | A | D | 1-1aet | McIntosh (p) |
| | | | | *played at Boundary Park, Oldham* | | | | |
| | | 1r | 04.12.48 | **Rochdale** | H | W | 2-0 | Collins, Livingstone |
| | | 2 | 11.12.48 | **Notts County** (3S) | A | L | 2-3 | Miller 2 |
| 1949-50 | (3N) | 1 | 26.11.49 | **Southport** (3N) | A | D | 1-1 | Gordon |
| | | 1r | 01.12.49 | **Southport** (3N) | H | L | 0-1 | |
| 1950-51 | (3N) | 1 | 25.11.50 | **Carlisle Utd** (3N) | A | L | 1-2 | King |
| 1951-52 | (3N) | 1 | 24.11.51 | **Chesterfield** (3N) | H | L | 0-2 | |
| 1952-53 | (3N) | 1 | 22.11.52 | **York City** (3N) | A | W | 2-1 | Hannah, Gordon |

| | | | | | | | | |
|---|---|---|---|---|---|---|---|---|
| | | 2 | 06.12.52 | **Millwall** (3S) | H | D | 2-2 | Gordon, McLaren |
| | | 2r | 10.12.52 | **Millwall** | A | L | 1-4 | Gordon |
| 1953-54 | (3N) | 1 | 21.11.53 | **Spennymoor Utd** (NEL) | A | W | 3-0 | Gordon 3 |
| | | 2 | 12.12.53 | **Great Yarmouth T** (ECL) | H | W | 5-2 | Gordon 2, A Keen, McLaren, Collins |
| | | 3 | 09.01.54 | **Swansea Town** (D2) | H | D | 2-2 | J Keen, McLaren |
| | | 3r | 14.01.54 | **Swansea Town** | A | L | 2-4 | Gordon, Collins |
| 1954-55 | (3N) | 1 | 20.11.54 | **Darlington** (3N) | H | D | 1-1 | Glover |
| | | 1r | 24.11.54 | **Darlington** | A | L | 1-2 | Ormond |
| 1955-56 | (3N) | 1 | 19.11.55 | **Crewe Alexandra** (3N) | H | D | 0-0 | |
| | | 1r | 23.11.55 | **Crewe Alexandra** | A | W | 3-2aet | Proctor, Godwin, Roberts |
| | | 2 | 10.12.55 | **Tranmere Rovers** (3N) | A | W | 3-0 | Roberts 2, Ormond |
| | | 3 | 07.01.56 | **Sheffield Utd** (D1) | A | L | 0-5 | |
| 1956-57 | (3N) | 1 | 17.11.56 | **Chester** (3N) | A | D | 0-0 | |
| | | 1r | 22.11.56 | **Chester** | H | W | 3-1 | Birch, J Keen, Callaghan |
| | | 2 | 08.12.56 | **Chesterfield** (3N) | A | L | 1-4 | J Keen |
| 1957-58 | (3N) | 1 | 16.11.57 | **Stockport County** (3N) | A | L | 1-2 | Callaghan |
| 1958-59 | (D4) | 1 | 15.11.58 | **Notts County** (D3) | A | W | 2-1 | Roberts, McCreadie |
| | | 2 | 06.12.58 | **Hartlepools Utd** (D4) | H | W | 2-0 | Robertson 2 |
| | | 3 | 10.01.59 | **Wolverhampton W** (D1) | H | L | 2-4 | Robertson, J Keen |
| 1959-60 | (D4) | 1 | 14.11.59 | **York City** (D3) | A | L | 1-3 | Murdoch |
| 1960-61 | (D4) | 1 | 05.11.60 | **Accrington Stanley** (D4) | A | L | 1-2 | Lowes |
| 1961-62 | (D4) | 1 | 04.11.61 | **Wrexham** (D4) | A | L | 2-3 | Dixon, Kemp |
| 1962-63 | (D4) | 1 | 03.11.62 | **Buxton** (CC) | A | D | 2-2 | Clark, Darwin (p) |
| | | 1r | 05.11.62 | **Buxton** | H | W | 3-1 | Darwin (p), Dixon, Hale |
| | | 2 | 24.11.62 | **Wrexham** (D3) | A | L | 2-5 | Wright, Dixon |
| 1963-64 | (D4) | 1 | 16.11.63 | **Bangor City** (CC) | H | W | 3-2 | Darwin, Thomson, Clark |
| | | 2 | 07.12.63 | **Chester** (D4) | A | W | 2-0 | Maddison, Hale |
| | | 3 | 04.01.64 | **Swansea Town** (D2) | A | L | 1-4 | Anderson |
| 1964-65 | (D4) | 1 | 14.11.64 | **Grimsby Town** (D3) | H | D | 1-1 | Clifton og |
| | | 1r | 17.11.64 | **Grimsby Town** | A | D | 2-2aet | Tait, Worthington |
| | | 12r | 23.11.64 | **Grimsby Town** | | L | 0-2 | |
| | | | | *played at Old Trafford* | | | | |
| 1965-66 | (D4) | 1 | 13.11.65 | **Grimsby Town** (D3) | H | L | 1-2 | Mulholland |
| 1966-67 | (D4) | 1 | 26.11.66 | **Rochdale** (D4) | A | W | 3-1 | Field 2, McCarthy |
| | | 2 | 07.01.67 | **Tranmere Rovers** (D4) | H | W | 2-1 | McAdams, J King (og) |
| | | 3 | 28.01.67 | **Southampton** (D1) | H | D | 2-2 | McAdams, Mulholland |
| | | 3r | 01.02.67 | **Southampton** | A | L | 0-3 | |
| 1967-68 | (D3) | 1 | 09.12.67 | **Oldham Athletic** (D3) | H | W | 2-0 | Harrison, Hartland |
| | | 2 | 06.01.68 | **Altrincham** (CC) | A | W | 2-1 | McGarry 2 |
| | | 3 | 27.01.68 | **Leicester City** (D1) | H | L | 1-2 | Storf |
| 1968-69 | (D3) | 1 | 16.11.68 | **Goole Town** (NPL) | A | W | 3-1 | Mulvaney 2, McLean |
| | | 2 | 07.12.68 | **Stockport County** (D3) | A | L | 0-2 | |
| 1969-70 | (D3) | 1 | 15.11.69 | **Alfreton Town** (ML) | A | D | 1-1 | Hartland |
| | | 1r | 17.11.69 | **Alfreton Town** | H | D | 0-0aet | |
| | | 12r | 20.11.69 | **Alfreton Town** | | D | 2-2aet | Garbett, Knox |
| | | | | *played at Saltergate, Chesterfield* | | | | |
| | | 13r | 24.11.69 | **Alfreton Town** | | W | 2-0 | Knox, Fletcher |
| | | | | *played at Deepdale, Preston* | | | | |
| | | 2 | 06.12.69 | **Barnsley** (D3) | A | L | 0-3 | |
| 1970-71 | (D4) | 1 | 21.11.70 | **Lincoln City** (D4) | A | L | 1-2 | Hartland |
| 1971-72 | (D4) | 1 | 20.11.71 | **Darlington** (D4) | H | L | 0-2 | |
| 1976-77 | (NPL) | 1 | 20.11.76 | **Goole Town** (NPL) | H | L | 0-2 | |
| 1988-89 | (NPL) | 1 | 19.11.88 | **Rotherham Utd** (D4) | A | L | 1-3 | Carroll |
| 1990-91 | (Conf) | 1 | 17.11.90 | **Bishop Auckland** (NPL) | A | W | 1-0 | Burgess |
| | | 2 | 12.12.90 | **Whitley Bay** (NPL) | A | W | 1-0 | Gilmour |
| | | 3 | 05.01.91 | **Bolton Wanderers** (D3) | A | L | 0-1 | |
| 1995-96 | (NPL) | 1 | 11.11.95 | **Nuneaton B** (SL) | H | W | 2-1 | Morton, Dobie |
| | | 2 | 02.12.95 | **Wigan Athletic** (D3) | H | L | 0-4 | |
| 2000-01 | (NPL) | 1 | 18.11.00 | **Leyton Orient** (D3) | H | L | 0-2 | |
| 2001-02 | (NPL) | 1 | 17.11.01 | **Oldham Athletic** (D2) | A | D | 1-1 | Housham |
| | | 1r | 27.11.01 | **Oldham Athletic** | H | L | 0-1 | |
| 2002-03 | (NPL) | 1 | 16.11.02 | **Moor Green** (SL) | H | W | 2-0 | Holt, Salmon |
| | | 2 | 07.12.02 | **Shrewsbury Town** (D3) | A | L | 1-3 | Housham |

## BARRY TOWN

*Formed 1912 as Barry AFC. Changed name to Barry Town 1945 and reverted back to Barry Town after a brief spell as Barri in the early 1990s. First entered FA Cup 1911-12. Welsh FA Cup winners: 1955, 1994,1998, 2001, 2002, 2003. Runners-up: 1996. League of Wales Champions 1995-96, 1996-97, 1997-98, 1998-99, 2001-02, 2002-03. Have also competed in the qualifying rounds of both the Champions League and UEFA Cup. Members of the League of Wales.*

| | | | | | | | |
|---|---|---|---|---|---|---|---|
| 1929-30 (SL) | 1 | 30.11.29 | **Dagenham Town** (Lon) | H | D | 0-0 | |
| | 1r | 04.12.29 | **Dagenham Town** | A | W | 1-0 | Jones |
| | | | *played at Upton Park* | | | | |
| | 2 | 14.12.29 | **Brighton** (3S) | A | L | 1-4 | Ward |
| 1934-35 (SL) | 1 | 24.11.34 | **Northampton Town** (3S) | H | L | 0-1 | |
| 1951-52 (SL) | 1 | 24.11.51 | **Newport County** (3S) | A | L | 0-4 | |
| 1961-62 (SL) | 1 | 04.11.61 | **QPR** (D3) | H | D | 1-1 | Sheffield |
| | 1r | 06.11.61 | **QPR** | A | L | 0-7 | |
| 1984-85 (Welsh) | 1 | 17.11.84 | **Reading** (D3) | H | L | 1-2 | Love |

## BARTON ROVERS

*Formed 1898. First entered FA Cup: 1976-77. FA Vase Runners-up 1978. Based in Bedford. Members of the Isthmian League.*

| | | | | | | | |
|---|---|---|---|---|---|---|---|
| 1980-81 (IL) | 1 | 22.11.80 | **Torquay Utd** (D4) | A | L | 0-2 | |

## BASFORD ROVERS

*Formed 1878. Home ground was at Marmion Road, Nottingham and the club used the Pear Tree Inn as their changing room.*

| | | | | | | | |
|---|---|---|---|---|---|---|---|
| 1886-87 | 1 | 30.10.86 | **Notts County** | A | L | 0-13 | |
| 1887-88 | 1 | 15.10.87 | **Lincoln Albion** | H | W | 3-2 | |
| | 2 | | Notts County | | | - | |
| | | | *Basford Rovers scratched. Notts County walkover* | | | | |

## BASHLEY

*Formed 1947. First entered FA Cup: 1988-89. Members of the Southern League.*

| | | | | | | | |
|---|---|---|---|---|---|---|---|
| 1994-95 (SL) | 1 | 12.11.94 | **Chesham Utd** (IL) | A | W | 1-0 | Paskins |
| | 2 | 04.12.94 | **Swansea City** (D2) | H | L | 0-1 | |

## BASINGSTOKE TOWN

*Formed 1896 when Aldsworth Utd and Basingstoke Albion amalgamated. First entered FA Cup: 1902-03. League club beaten: Wycombe Wanderers (on penalties). Members of the Isthmian League.*

| | | | | | | | |
|---|---|---|---|---|---|---|---|
| 1971-72 (SL) | 1 | 20.11.71 | **Northampton Town** (D4) | H | L | 1-5 | Brown |
| 1989-90 (IL) | 1 | 17.11.89 | **Bromsgrove Rovers** (SL) | H | W | 3-0 | Clarkson 2, Webb |
| | 2 | 09.12.89 | **Torquay Utd** (D4) | H | L | 2-3 | Blankley, Clarkson |
| 1997-98 (IL) | 1 | 15.11.97 | **Wycombe W** (D2) | A | D | 2-2 | Coombs, Wilkinson |
| | 1r | 25.11.97 | **Wycombe W** | H | D | 2-2aet | Coombs 2(1p) |
| | | | *Basingstoke won 5-4 on penalties* | | | | |
| | 2 | 06.12.97 | **Northampton Town** (D2) | A | D | 1-1 | Carey |
| | 2r | 16.12.97 | **Northampton Town** | H | D | 0-0aet | |
| | | | *Northampton won 4-3 on penalties* | | | | |
| 1998-99 (IL) | 1 | 14.11.98 | **Bournemouth** (D2) | H | L | 1-2 | Mancey |

## BATH CITY

*Formed 1889. First entered FA Cup: 1889-90. Record crowd: 18,020 v Brighton 3rd Round, January 1960. League clubs beaten: Barrow, Cardiff City, Crystal Palace , Exeter City (2), Hereford Utd, Merthyr Town, Millwall, Newport County, Notts County, Southend Utd. Their 9-0 win over Nunhead in 1931 is the joint-highest victory by one Non-League club over another since the competition was re-organised in 1925. Members of the Southern League.*

| | | | | | | | |
|---|---|---|---|---|---|---|---|
| 1920-21 (SL) | | | 5q Merthyr Town (3S) A 0-0; 5qr Merthyr Town H 1-0; 6q Leytonstone A 1-1, H 2-0 | | | | |
| | 1 | 08.01.21 | **Hull City** (D2) | A | L | 0-3 | 0-3 |
| 1922-23 (SL) | | | 5q Exeter C (3S) A 2-1; 6q Barrow (3N) A 2-2; 6qr Barrow H 2-0 | | | | |
| | 1 | 13.01.23 | **Wigan Borough** (3N) | A | L | 1-4 | Dore |
| 1927-28 (SL) | 1 | 26.11.27 | **Southall** (AL) | H | W | 2-0 | Shepherd 2 |
| | 2 | 10.12.27 | **London Cal** (IL) | A | L | 0-1 | |
| 1929-30 (SL) | 1 | 30.11.29 | **Tunbridge Wells R** (SL) | A | W | 3-1 | Brittain, Alsop, Compton |
| | 2 | 14.12.29 | **Coventry City** (3S) | A | L | 1-7 | Brittain |
| 1931-32 (SL) | 1 | 28.11.31 | **Nunhead** (IL) | H | W | 9-0 | Guyan 5, Rhodes og, Mulley og, Whipp, McCartney |

| | | | | | | | | |
|---|---|---|---|---|---|---|---|---|
| | | 2 | 12.12.31 | **Crystal Palace** (3S) | H | W | 2-1 | Rowson, McCartney |
| | | 3 | 09.01.32 | **Brentford** (3S) | A | L | 0-2 | |
| 1933-34 | (SL) | 1 | 25.11.33 | **Charlton Athletic** (3S) | H | D | 0-0 | |
| | | 1r | 29.11.33 | **Charlton Athletic** | A | L | 1-3 | McMillan |
| 1934-35 | (SL) | 1 | 24.11.34 | **Guildford City** (SL) | A | W | 2-1 | Coombs, McMillan |
| | | 2 | 08.12.34 | **Boston Utd** (ML) | H | W | 2-1 | Coombs, Prentice |
| | | 3 | 12.01.35 | **Norwich City** (D2) | A | L | 0-2 | |
| 1936-37 | (SL) | 1 | 28.11.36 | **Tunbridge Wells R** (KL) | H | L | 1-2 | Buckley |
| 1945-46 | (SL) | 1 1L | 17.11.45 | **Cheltenham Town** (SL) | H | W | 3-2 | Simmons, Browne, Farringdon |
| | | 1 2L | 24.11.45 | **Cheltenham Town** | A | W | 2-0 | Brown, McConnon |
| | | 2 1L | 08.12.45 | **Lovell's Athletic** (Welsh) | A | L | 1-2 | Woods |
| | | 2 2L | 15.12.45 | **Lovell's Athletic** | H | L | 2-5 | Farrington 2 |
| 1952-53 | (SL) | 1 | 22.11.52 | **Southend Utd** (3S) | H | W | 3-1 | Ellison, Snook 2 |
| | | 2 | 06.12.52 | **Grimsby Town** (3N) | A | L | 0-1 | |
| 1953-54 | (SL) | 1 | 21.11.53 | **Walsall** (3S) | H | L | 0-3 | |
| 1957-58 | (SL) | 1 | 16.11.57 | **Exeter City** (3S) | H | W | 2-1 | Boseley, Pickard |
| | | 2 | 07.12.57 | **Yeovil Town** (SL) | A | L | 0-2 | |
| 1958-59 | (SL) | 1 | 15.11.58 | **Colchester Utd** (D3) | A | L | 0-2 | |
| 1959-60 | (SL) | 1 | 14.11.59 | **Millwall** (D4) | H | W | 3-1 | Wilshire, Fleming, Meadows |
| | | 2 | 05.12.59 | **Notts County** (D4) | A | W | 1-0 | O'Neil |
| | | 3 | 09.01.60 | **Brighton** (D2) | H | L | 0-1 | |
| 1960-61 | (SL) | 1 | 05.11.60 | **Swindon Town** (D3) | A | D | 2-2 | Wilshire, Fleming |
| | | 1r | 10.11.60 | **Swindon Town** | H | L | 4-6 | Fleming 2, Book, O'Neil |
| 1963-64 | (SL) | 1 | 16.11.63 | **Maidenhead** (AL) | A | W | 2-0 | Cartwright, Sanderson |
| | | 2 | 07.12.63 | **Wimbledon** (IL) | A | D | 2-2 | Willis og, Cartwright |
| | | 2r | 12.12.63 | **Wimbledon** | H | W | 4-0 | Sanderson, Fleming, Owen, Cartwright |
| | | 3 | 04.01.64 | **Bolton Wanderers** (D1) | H | D | 1-1 | Owens |
| | | 3r | 08.01.64 | **Bolton Wanderers** | A | L | 0-3 | |
| 1964-65 | (SL) | 1 | 14.11.64 | **QPR** (D3) | A | L | 0-2 | |
| 1965-66 | (SL) | 1 | 13.11.65 | **Newport County** (D4) | H | W | 2-0 | Denton 2 |
| | | 2 | 04.12.65 | **Bournemouth** (D3) | A | L | 3-5 | Denton 2, Horton |
| 1966-67 | (SL) | 1 | 26.11.66 | **Sutton Utd** (IL) | H | W | 1-0 | Lofty |
| | | 2 | 07.01.67 | **Brighton** (D3) | H | L | 0-5 | |
| 1974-75 | (SL) | 1 | 23.11.74 | **Wimbledon** (SL) | A | L | 0-1 | |
| 1977-78 | (SL) | 1 | 26.11.77 | **Plymouth Argyle** (D3) | H | D | 0-0 | |
| | | 1r | 29.11.77 | **Plymouth Argyle** | A | L | 0-2 | |
| 1985-86 | (APL) | 1 | 16.11.85 | **Farnborough Town** (IL) | A | W | 4-0 | Chandler, Palmer (p), Ricketts, Bodin |
| | | 2 | 07.12.85 | **Peterborough Utd** (D4) | A | L | 0-1 | |
| 1986-87 | (Conf) | 1 | 15.11.86 | **Aylesbury Utd** (SL) | H | W | 3-2 | Bodin, Grimshaw, Adams |
| | | 2 | 06.12.86 | **Bristol City** (D3) | A | D | 1-1 | Bodin |
| | | 2r | 09.12.86 | **Bristol City** *played at Ashton Gate* | H | L | 0-3 | |
| 1987-88 | (Conf) | 1 | 14.11.87 | **Chelmsford City** (SL) | A | W | 2-1 | Payne, Grimshaw |
| | | 2 | 05.12.87 | **Welling Utd** (Conf) | A | W | 1-0 | Singleton |
| | | 3 | 09.01.88 | **Mansfield Town** (D3) | A | L | 0-4 | |
| 1988-89 | (SL) | 1 | 19.11.88 | **Grays Athletic** (IL) | H | W | 2-0 | Singleton 2 |
| | | 2 | 10.12.88 | **Welling Utd** (Conf) | H | D | 0-0 | |
| | | 2r | 14.12.88 | **Welling Utd** | A | L | 2-3 | |
| 1989-90 | (SL) | 1 | 19.11.89 | **Fulham** (D3) | H | D | 2-2 | Freegard, Randall |
| | | 1r | 22.11.89 | **Fulham** | A | L | 1-2 | Smart |
| 1992-93 | (Conf) | 1 | 14.11.92 | **Cardiff City** (D3) | A | W | 3-2 | Withey, Gill, Vernon |
| | | 2 | 06.12.92 | **Northampton Town** (D3) | H | D | 2-2 | Smart, Randall |
| | | 2r | 15.12.92 | **Northampton Town** | A | L | 0-3 | |
| 1993-94 | (Conf) | 1 | 13.11.93 | **Molesey** (IL) | A | W | 4-0 | Mings, Boyle, Adcock 2 |
| | | 2 | 05.12.93 | **Hereford Utd** (D3) | H | W | 2-1 | Brooks, Batty |
| | | 3 | 08.01.94 | **Stoke City** (D1) | A | D | 0-0 | |
| | | 3r | 18.01.94 | **Stoke City** | H | L | 1-4 | Chenoweth |
| 1994-95 | (Conf) | 1 | 12.11.94 | **Bristol Rovers** (D2) | H | L | 0-5 | |
| 1999-00 | (SL) | 1 | 30.10.99 | **Hendon** (IL) | H | L | 0-2 | |

## BEDFORD TOWN

*Originally formed 1908. Original Bedford Town folded with £15,000 debts in 1982. Reformed 1989. First entered FA Cup: 1910-11. Played at the famous Eyrie Ground until 1981. League clubs beaten: Brighton, Exeter City, Newcastle Utd, Norwich City, Oxford Utd, Watford. Held Arsenal to a 2-2 draw in a third round tie in 1956. Members of the Isthmian League.*

| | | | | | | | | |
|---|---|---|---|---|---|---|---|---|
| 1934-35 | (UCL) | 1 | 24.11.34 | **Dartford** (SL) | H | L | 2-3 | Carr 2 |
| 1951-52 | (SL) | 1 | 24.11.51 | **Swindon Town** (3S) | A | L | 0-2 | |
| 1953-54 | (SL) | 1 | 21.11.53 | **Weymouth** (SL) | A | L | 0-2 | |
| 1954-55 | (SL) | 1 | 20.11.54 | **Dorchester Town** (WL) | A | L | 0-2 | |
| 1955-56 | (SL) | 1 | 19.11.55 | **Leyton FC** (AL) | H | W | 3-0 | Farquhar, Adey, Staroscik |
| | | 2 | 10.12.55 | **Watford** (3S) | H | W | 3-2 | Steel, Staroscik 2 |
| | | 3 | 07.01.56 | **Arsenal** (D1) | A | D | 2-2 | Steel, Moore |
| | | 3r | 12.01.56 | **Arsenal** | H | L | 1-2aet | Yates |
| 1956-57 | (SL) | 1 | 17.11.56 | **Norwich City** (3S) | H | W | 4-2 | Chrichton, Murray 2, Reid |
| | | 2 | 08.12.56 | **Reading** (3S) | A | L | 0-1 | |
| 1959-60 | (SL) | 1 | 14.11.59 | **Gillingham** (D4) | H | L | 0-4 | |
| 1962-62 | (SL) | 1 | 03.11.62 | **Cambridge Utd** (SL) | H | W | 2-1 | Hukin, Wright |
| 1962-63 | (SL) | 2 | 24.11.62 | **Gillingham** (D4) | A | L | 0-3 | |
| 1963-64 | (SL) | 1 | 16.11.63 | **Weymouth** (SL) | A | D | 1-1 | Fahy |
| | | 1r | 21.11.63 | **Weymouth** | H | W | 1-0 | Miles |
| | | 2 | 07.12.63 | **Chelmsford City** (SL) | A | W | 1-0 | Miles |
| | | 3 | 04.01.64 | **Newcastle Utd** (D2) | A | W | 2-1 | Fahy, McKinney og |
| | | 4 | 25.01.64 | **Carlisle Utd** (D4) | H | L | 0-3 | |
| 1965-66 | (SL) | 1 | 13.11.65 | **Exeter City** (D3) | A | W | 2-1 | Hall, Bailey |
| | | 2 | 04.12.65 | **Brighton** (D3) | A | D | 1-1 | Brown |
| | | 2r | 06.12.65 | **Brighton** | H | W | 2-1 | Hall, Paton |
| | | 3 | 22.01.66 | **Hereford Utd** (SL) | H | W | 2-1 | Hall 2 |
| | | 4 | 12.02.66 | **Everton** (D1) | H | L | 0-3 | |
| 1966-67 | (SL) | 1 | 26.11.66 | **Wycombe W** (IL) | A | D | 1-1 | Fogg |
| | | 1r | 30.11.66 | **Wycombe W** | H | D | 3-3aet | Sturrock 2 (1p), Skinn |
| | | 12r | 05.12.66 | **Wycombe W** | A | - | 1-1ab | Paton |
| | | | | *abandoned after 90 minutes – ground unfit* | | | | |
| | | 13r | 08.12.66 | **Wycombe W** | H | W | 3-2 | Rundle og, Riley, Fogg |
| | | 2 | 11.01.67 | **Oxford Utd** (D3) | A | D | 1-1 | Fogg |
| | | 2r | 16.01.67 | **Oxford Utd** | H | W | 1-0 | Sturrock |
| | | 3 | 28.01.67 | **Peterborough Utd** (D3) | H | L | 2-6 | Cooley, Fogg |
| 1975-76 | (SL) | 1 | 22.11.75 | **Wycombe W** (IL) | A | D | 0-0 | |
| | | 1r | 24.11.75 | **Wycombe W** | H | D | 2-2aet | Phillips, Folds |
| | | 12r | 01.12.75 | **Wycombe W** | A | L | 1-2 | Markham |
| 1981-82 | (SL) | 1 | 21.11.81 | **Wimbledon** (D3) | H | L | 0-2 | |
| 2001-02 | (IL) | 1 | 17.11.01 | **Peterborough Utd** (D2) | H | D | 0-0 | |
| | | 1r | 27.11.01 | **Peterborough Utd** | A | L | 1-2 | Slinn |

## BEDLINGTON TERRIERS

*Formed 1949 as Bedlington Mechanics and after a number of name changes adopted their present title in 1974. Entered FA Cup as Bedlington Mechanics: 1959-60 – 1962-63. FA Vase Runners-up: 1999. Northumberland-based. League club beaten: Colchester United. Members of the Northern League.*

| | | | | | | | | |
|---|---|---|---|---|---|---|---|---|
| 1998-99 | (NL) | 1 | 14.11.98 | **Colchester Utd** (D2) | H | W | 4-1 | Ditchburn, Milner 2(1p), Cross |
| | | 2 | 05.12.98 | **Scunthorpe Utd** (D3) | A | L | 0-2 | |

## BEDLINGTON UNITED

*Northumberland-based club who competed in the FA Cup from 1908-1936. No connection to later Bedlington United, a former name of Bedlington Terriers, who were formed in 1949.*

| | | | | | | | | |
|---|---|---|---|---|---|---|---|---|
| 1926-27 | (NEL) | 1 | 27.11.26 | **Bishop Auckland** (NL) | H | W | 1-0 | Spry |
| | | 2 | 11.12.26 | **Carlisle Utd** (NEL) | A | L | 0-4 | |

## BEIGHTON MINERS WELFARE

*Competed in FA Cup 1948-1958, playing 25 matches in total, reaching the Competition Proper once.*

| | | | | | | | | |
|---|---|---|---|---|---|---|---|---|
| 1952-53 | (YL) | 1 | 22.11.52 | **Wrexham** (3N) | H | L | 0-3 | |
| | | | | *played at Millmoor, Rotherham* | | | | |

## BELPER TOWN

*Formed 1883. First competed in FA Cup: 1887-88. Best performance since 1888: 4th qualifying round 1957-58, 2000-01, 2001-02. Members of the Northern Premier League.*

| | | | | | | | | |
|---|---|---|---|---|---|---|---|---|
| 1887-88 | | 1 | 15.10.87 | **Sheffield Wed** | H | L | 2-3 | |

## BEXLEY UNITED

*Originally formed in 1917 – during World War One – as Bexleyheath Labour, the start of a convoluted Non-League history of soccer in Bexleyheath and its surrounding neighbourhoods. A series of name changes and reformed clubs came and went down the years: Bexleyheath Town (1922) , Bexleyheath & Welling (1931) until the name Bexley United was adopted in 1963. However that club was wound up in 1976 with debts of £30,000. Welling United now play on their Park View ground.*

| | | | | | | | | |
|---|---|---|---|---|---|---|---|---|
| 1963-64 | (SL) | 1 | 16.11.63 | **Wimbledon** (IL) | H | L | 1-5 | Johnson |

## BIDEFORD

*Originally formed as Bideford Town, adopted current title in 1949. First entered FA Cup: 1925-26. Members of the Western League.*

| | | | | | | | | |
|---|---|---|---|---|---|---|---|---|
| 1964-65 | (WL) | 1 | 14.11.64 | **Colchester Utd** (D3) | A | D | 3-3 | Court, Bennett, Penny (p) |
| | | 1r | 18.11.64 | **Colchester Utd** | H | L | 1-2 | Bennett |
| 1973-74 | (SL) | 1 | 24.11.73 | **Bristol Rovers** (D3) | H | L | 0-2 | |
| 1977-78 | (WL) | 1 | 26.11.77 | **Portsmouth** (D3) | A | L | 1-3 | Wingate |
| 1981-82 | (WL) | 1 | 21.11.81 | **Barking** (IL) | H | L | 1-2 | Brown |

## BILLERICAY TOWN

*Formed 1880. First entered FA Cup: 1977-78. FA Vase winners: 1976, 1977, 1979. Members of the Isthmian League.*

| | | | | | | | | |
|---|---|---|---|---|---|---|---|---|
| 1997-98 | (IL) | 1 | 15.11.97 | **Wisbech Town** (SL) | H | L | 2-3 | Battram, Moore |

## BILLINGHAM SYNTHONIA

*Formed 1923. First entered FA Cup: 1934-35. When Synthonia won the Northern League in 1951 they did not concede any goals at home, ending with a scoring record of 44-0 from their 13 games. Members of the Northern League.*

| | | | | | | | | |
|---|---|---|---|---|---|---|---|---|
| 1948-49 | (NL) | 1 | 27.11.48 | **Crewe Alexandra** (3N) | A | L | 0-5 | |
| 1949-50 | (NL) | 1 | 26.11.49 | **Stockport County** (3N) | A | L | 0-3 | |
| 1951-52 | (NL) | 1 | 24.11.51 | **Scunthorpe Utd** (3N) | A | L | 0-5 | |
| 1956-57 | (NL) | 1 | 17.11.56 | **Carlisle Utd** (3N) | A | L | 1-6 | Duffy |
| 1957-58 | (NL) | 1 | 16.11.57 | **Boston Utd** (ML) | A | L | 2-5 | Taylor 2 |
| 1987-88 | (NL) | 1 | 14.11.87 | **Halifax Town** (D4) | H | L | 2-4 | Allen, Hewitt |
| | | | | *played at Victoria Ground, Hartlepool* | | | | |
| 1989-90 | (NL) | 1 | 18.11.89 | **Lincoln City** (D4) | A | L | 0-1 | |

## BILSTON TOWN

*Formed 1895. First entered FA Cup: 1907-08. Former Bilston player Stan Crowther played in the 1957 and 1958 FA Cup finals for Aston Villa and Manchester Utd.*

| | | | | | | | | |
|---|---|---|---|---|---|---|---|---|
| 1968-69 | (WMRL) | 1 | 16.11.68 | **Halifax Town** (D4) | H | L | 1-3 | Silwood (p) |
| 1972-73 | (WMRL) | 1 | 18.11.72 | **Barnstaple Town** (WL) | A | W | 2-0 | Cooper, Cope |
| | | 2 | 09.12.72 | **Barnet** (SL) | A | D | 1-1 | Langford |
| | | 2r | 11.12.72 | **Barnet** | H | L | 0-1 | |

## BIRCH, MANCHESTER

| | | | | | | | | |
|---|---|---|---|---|---|---|---|---|
| 1878-79 | | 1 | | Darwen | | | - | |
| | | | | *Birch scratched. Darwen walkover* | | | | |

## BIRMINGHAM CALTHORPE

*Formed 1873. Played on fields at Bristol Road, Calthorpe, Birmingham*

| | | | | | | | | |
|---|---|---|---|---|---|---|---|---|
| 1879-80 | | 1 | 25.10.79 | **Maidenhead** | A | L | 1-3 | Rushell |
| 1880-81 | | 1 | 11.11.80 | **Grantham Town** | H | L | 1-2 | |
| 1881-82 | | 1 | | Notts County | | | - | |
| | | | | *Birmingham Calthorpe scratched. Notts County walkover* | | | | |
| 1882-83 | | 1 | 28.10.82 | **Birmingham St G** | A | L | 1-4 | |
| 1883-84 | | 1 | 10.11.83 | **Walsall Town** | H | L | 0-9 | |

## BIRMINGHAM CITY

*Formed 1875 as Small Heath Alliance. 1888 Small Heath. 1905 Birmingham. 1945 Birmingham City FA Cup runners-up: 1931, 1956. Record FA Cup win: 10-0 v Druids, 4th qualifying round, 9.11.1898; In Competition Proper: 9-2 v Burton Wanderers , 1st round, 31.10.1885. Record FA Cup defeat: 0-6 v Wednesbury OA, 2nd round, 03.12.1881; v Tottenham Hotspur, 6th round replay, 12.04.1967*

**as Small Heath Alliance**

| | | | | | | | | |
|---|---|---|---|---|---|---|---|---|
| 1881-82 | | 1 | 17.10.81 | **Derby Town** | H | W | 4-1 | Slater 2, Hards, A James |
| | | 2 | 03.12.81 | **Wednesbury Old Ath** | A | L | 0-6 | |
| 1882-83 | | 1 | | bye | | | | |
| 1882-83 | | 1 | 04.11.82 | **Stafford Road** | H | D | 3-3 | |
| | | 1r | 18.11.82 | **Stafford Road** | A | L | 2-6 | |
| 1883-84 | | 1 | 20.10.83 | **Birmingham Excelsior** | H | D | 1-1 | A James |
| | | 1r | 11.11.83 | **Birmingham Excelsior** | A | L | 2-3 | A James, Stanley |
| 1884-85 | | 1 | 08.11.84 | **Birmingham Excelsior** | A | L | 0-2 | |
| 1885-86 | | 1 | 31.10.85 | **Burton Wanderers** | H | W | 9-2 | Stanley 4, Davenport 2, Evetts, A James, Morris |
| | | 2 | 21.11.85 | **Darwen** | H | W | 3-1 | Felton, Morris, Stanley |
| | | 3 | 12.12.85 | **Derby County** | H | W | 4-2 | Stanley 2, Hill, Davenport |
| 1885-86 | | 4 | | bye | | | | |
| 1885-86 | | 5 | 16.01.86 | **Davenham** | A | W | 2-1 | Figures, Davenport |
| | | 6 | 13.02.86 | **Redcar** | H | W | 2-0 | Davenport 2 |
| | | SF | 06.03.86 | **WBA** | | L | 0-4 | |
| | | | | *played at Aston Lower Grounds, Birmingham* | | | | |
| 1886-87 | | 1 | 30.10.86 | **Birmingham St G** | H | L | 1-3 | Price |
| 1887-88 | | 1 | 15.10.87 | **Aston Unity** | H | W | 6-1 | Smith 2, W Dixon 2, Figures, Stanley |
| | | 2 | 05.11.87 | **Aston Villa** | H | L | 0-4 | |

**as Small Heath**

| | | | | | | | | |
|---|---|---|---|---|---|---|---|---|
| 1888-89 | | | | 1q bye; 2q Burslem PV (H) 3-2; 3q Leek (H) 4-0; 4q Burton W (H) 9-0 | | | | |
| 1888-89 | | 1 | 02.02.89 | **WBA** (D1) | H | L | 2-3 | Hill 2 |
| 1889-90 | (FAll) | | | 1q Hednesford Town (H) 8-0; 2q Wednesbury OA (A) 2-0 | | | | |
| 1889-90 | (FAll) | 1 | 18.01.90 | **Clapton** | H | W | 3-1 | Stanley 2, W Devey |
| | | 2 | 01.02.90 | **Wolverhampton W** (D1) | A | L | 1-2 | W Devey |
| 1890-91 | (FAll) | | | 1q Hednesford Town (H) 8-0; 2q Wednesbury OA (A) 2-0. FA disqualified Small Heath for fielding an unregistered player | | | | |
| 1891-92 | (FAll) | | | 1q Leicester Fosse (A) 6-2; 2q Burton Wanderers (A) 1-1; 2qr Burton Wanderers (H) 2-1; 3q Burton Swifts (H) 4-2; 4q Brierley Hill Alliance (H) 6-2 | | | | |
| 1891-92 | (FAll) | 1 | 16.01.92 | **Royal Arsenal** | H | W | 5-1 | Hallam 2, Weddon 2, Walton |
| | | 2 | 30.01.92 | **Sheffield Wed** (FAll) | A | L | 0-2 | |
| 1892-93 | (D2) | 1 | 21.01.93 | **Burnley** (D1) | A | L | 0-2 | |
| 1893-94 | (D2) | 1 | 27.01.94 | **Bolton Wanderers** (D1) | H | L | 3-4 | Hallam, Mobley, Wheddon |
| 1894-95 | (D1) | 1 | 02.02.95 | **WBA** (D1) | H | L | 1-2 | Walton |
| 1895-96 | (D1) | 1 | 01.02.96 | **Bury** (D1) | H | L | 1-4 | Lewis |
| 1896-97 | (D2) | 1 | 30.01.97 | **Notts County** (D2) | H | L | 1-2 | Walton |
| 1897-98 | (D2) | | | 3q Port Vale (A) 1-2 | | | | |
| 1898-99 | (D2) | | | 3q Chirk (H) 8-0; 4q Druids (H) 10-0; 5q Burslem PV (H) 7-0 | | | | |
| 1898-99 | (D2) | 1 | 28.01.99 | **Manchester City** (D2) | H | W | 3-2 | McRoberts 2, Abbott |
| | | 2 | 11.02.99 | **Stoke** (D1) | A | D | 2-2 | Robertson, Wharton |
| | | 2r | 15.02.99 | **Stoke** | H | L | 1-2 | Inglis |
| 1899-00 | (D2) | | | 3q Oswestry Utd (H) 10-2; 4q Wrexham (H) 6-1; 5q Walsall (H) 0-0; 5qr Walsall (A) 0-2 | | | | |
| 1900-01 | (D2) | 1 | 09.02.01 | **Stoke** (D1) | A | D | 1-1 | Main |
| | | 1r | 13.02.01 | **Stoke** | H | W | 2-1aet | Bennett, Wharton |
| | | 2 | 23.02.01 | **Burnley** (D2) | H | W | 1-0 | McMillan |
| | | 3 | 23.03.01 | **Aston Villa** (D1) | H | D | 0-0 | |
| | | 3r | 27.03.01 | **Aston Villa** | A | L | 0-1aet | |
| 1902-03 | (D2) | 1 | 07.02.03 | **Derby County** (D1) | A | L | 1-2 | Windridge |
| 1904-05 | (D1) | 1 | 04.02.05 | **Portsmouth** (SL) | H | L | 0-2 | |

**as Birmingham**

| | | | | | | | | |
|---|---|---|---|---|---|---|---|---|
| 1905-06 | (D1) | 1 | 13.01.06 | **Preston North End** (D1) | H | W | 1-0 | Beer |
| | | 2 | 03.02.06 | **Stoke** (D1) | A | W | 1-0 | WH Jones |
| | | 3 | 24.02.06 | **Tottenham Hotspur** (SL) | A | D | 1-1 | Harper |
| | | 3r | 28.02.06 | **Tottenham Hotspur** | H | W | 2-0aet | Green, Mounteney |
| | | 4 | 10.03.06 | **Newcastle Utd** (D1) | H | D | 2-2 | Green, WH Jones |
| | | 4r | 14.03.06 | **Newcastle Utd** | A | L | 0-3 | |
| 1906-07 | (D1) | 1 | 12.01.07 | **Liverpool** (D1) | A | L | 1-2 | Green (p) |
| 1907-08 | (D1) | 1 | 11.01.08 | **WBA** (D2) | A | D | 1-1 | W H Jones |
| | | 1r | 15.01.08 | **WBA** | H | L | 1-2 | Eyre |
| 1908-09 | (D2) | 1 | 16.01.09 | **Portsmouth** (SL) | H | L | 2-5 | Chapple (p), King |

| | | | | | | | |
|---|---|---|---|---|---|---|---|
| 1909-10 (D2) | 1 | 15.01.10 | **Leicester Fosse** (D2) | H | L | 1-4 | Lappin |
| 1910-11 (D2) | 1 | 14.01.11 | **Oldham Athletic** (D1) | H | D | 1-1 | Hall (p) |
| | 1r | 17.01.11 | **Oldham Athletic** | A | L | 0-2 | |
| 1911-12 (D2) | 1 | 13.01.12 | **Barnsley** (D2) | H | D | 0-0 | |
| | 1r | 22.01.12 | **Barnsley** | A | L | 0-3 | |
| 1912-13 (D2) | 1 | 11.01.13 | **Manchester City** (D1) | A | L | 0-4 | |
| 1913-14 (D2) | 1 | 10.01.14 | **Southend Utd** (SL) | H | W | 2-1 | Duncan 2 |
| | 2 | 31.01.14 | **Huddersfield Town** (D2) | H | W | 1-0 | Morgan |
| | 3 | 21.02.14 | **QPR** (SL) | H | L | 1-2 | Duncan |
| 1914-15 (D2) | 1 | 09.01.15 | **Crystal Palace** (SL) | H | D | 2-2 | AW Smith (p), Eyre |
| | 1r | 16.01.15 | **Crystal Palace** | A | W | 3-0 | Gibson, Tinkler, AW Smith |
| | | | *played at St Andrews* | | | | |
| | 2 | 30.01.15 | **Brighton** (SL) | A | D | 0-0 | |
| | 2r | 06.02.15 | **Brighton** | H | W | 3-0 | Gibson, Morgan, AW Smith |
| | 3 | 20.02.15 | **Oldham Athletic** (D1) | H | L | 2-3 | Gibson, Hodges |
| 1919-20 (D2) | 1 | 10.01.20 | **Everton** (D1) | H | W | 2-0 | Burkinshaw, Whitehouse |
| | 2 | 31.01.20 | **Darlington** (NEL) | H | W | 4-0 | Whitehouse 3, Millard |
| | 3 | 21.02.20 | **Liverpool** (D1) | A | L | 0-2 | |
| 1920-21 (D2) | 1 | 08.01.21 | **Luton Town** (3S) | A | L | 1-2 | Barton |
| 1921-22 (D2) | | | did not enter | | | | |
| 1922-23 (D1) | 1 | 13.01.23 | **Huddersfield Town** (D1) | A | L | 1-2 | Bradford |
| 1923-24 (D1) | 1 | 12.01.24 | **Huddersfield Town** | A | L | 0-1 | |
| 1924-25 (D1) | 1 | 10.01.25 | **Chelsea** (D2) | H | W | 2-0 | Briggs 2 |
| | 2 | 31.01.25 | **Stockport County** (D2) | H | W | 1-0 | Harris |
| | 3 | 21.02.25 | **Liverpool** (D1) | A | L | 1-2 | Briggs |
| 1925-26 (D1) | 3 | 09.01.26 | **Grimsby Town** (3N) | H | W | 2-0 | Russell, Briggs |
| | 4 | 30.01.26 | **South Shields** (D2) | A | L | 1-2 | Bradford (p) |
| 1926-27 (D1) | 3 | 08.01.27 | **Manchester City** (D2) | H | W | 4-1 | Bradford, Islip, Crosbie, Briggs |
| | 4 | 29.01.27 | **Southampton** (D2) | A | L | 1-4 | Briggs |
| 1927-28 (D1) | 3 | 14.01.28 | **Peterborough & F** (SL) | H | W | 4-3 | Bradford 3, Davies |
| | 4 | 28.01.28 | **Wrexham** (3N) | A | W | 3-1 | Davies 2, Randle (p) |
| | 5 | 18.02.28 | **Manchester Utd** (D1) | A | L | 0-1 | |
| 1928-29 (D1) | 3 | 12.01.29 | **Manchester City** (D1) | H | W | 3-1 | Bradford 2, Briggs |
| | 4 | 27.01.29 | **Chelsea** (D2) | A | L | 0-1 | |
| 1929-30 (D1) | 3 | 11.01.30 | **Bolton Wanderers** (D1) | H | W | 1-0 | Morrall |
| | 4 | 25.01.30 | **Arsenal** (D1) | A | D | 2-2 | Briggs 2 |
| | 4r | 29.01.30 | **Arsenal** | H | L | 0-1 | |
| 1930-31 (D1) | 3 | 10.01.31 | **Liverpool** (D1) | A | W | 2-0 | Curtis, Bradford |
| | 4 | 24.01.31 | **Port Vale** (D2) | H | W | 2-0 | Bradford 2 |
| | 5 | 14.02.31 | **Watford** (3S) | H | W | 3-0 | Curtis 2, Bradford |
| | 6 | 28.02.31 | **Chelsea** (D1) | H | D | 2-2 | Bradford, Curtis |
| | 6r | 04.03.31 | **Chelsea** | A | W | 3-0 | Bradford 2, Firth |
| | SF | 14.03.31 | **Sunderland** (D1) | | W | 2-0 | Curtis 2 |
| | | | *played at Elland Road* | | | | |
| | F | 25.04.31 | **WBA** (D2) | | L | 1-2 | Bradford |
| | | | *played at Wembley Stadium* | | | | |
| 1931-32 (D1) | 3 | 09.01.32 | **Bradford City** (D2) | H | W | 1-0 | Bradford |
| | 4 | 23.01.32 | **Grimsby Town** (D1) | A | L | 1-2 | Bradford |
| 1932-33 (D1) | 3 | 14.01.33 | **Preston North End** (D2) | H | W | 2-1 | Gregg, Grosvenor |
| | 4 | 28.01.33 | **Blackburn Rovers** (D1) | H | W | 3-0 | Curtis 2, Haywood |
| | 5 | 18.02.33 | **Middlesbrough** (D1) | A | D | 0-0 | |
| | 5r | 22.02.33 | **Middlesbrough** | H | W | 3-0 | Gregg, Haywood, Curtis |
| | 6 | 04.03.33 | **West Ham Utd** (D2) | A | L | 0-4 | |
| 1933-34 (D1) | 3 | 13.01.34 | **Sheffield Utd** (D1) | H | W | 2-1 | Robertson, Haywood |
| | 4 | 27.01.34 | **Charlton Athletic** (3S) | H | W | 1-0 | Morrall |
| | 5 | 17.02.34 | **Leicester City** (D1) | H | L | 1-2 | Haywood |
| 1934-35 (D1) | 3 | 12.01.35 | **Coventry City** (3S) | H | W | 5-1 | Harris 3, Mangnall, Guest |
| | 4 | 26.01.35 | **Southampton** (D2) | A | W | 3-0 | White, Fillingham, Guest |
| | 5 | 21.02.35 | **Blackburn Rovers** (D1) | A | W | 2-1 | White, Whiteside og |
| | 6 | 06.03.35 | **Burnley** (D2) | A | L | 2-3 | Jones, White |
| 1935-36 (D1) | 3 | 11.01.36 | **Barnsley** (D2) | A | D | 3-3 | White, Jones, Harris |
| | 3r | 15.01.36 | **Barnsley** | H | L | 0-2 | |

| | | | | | | | |
|---|---|---|---|---|---|---|---|
| 1936-37 (D1) | 3 | 16.01.37 | **Stoke City** (D1) | A | L | 1-4 | Morris |
| 1937-38 (D1) | 3 | 08.01.38 | **Blackpool** (D1) | H | L | 0-1 | |
| 1938-39 (D1) | 3 | 07.01.39 | **Halifax Town** (3N) | H | W | 2-0 | Jennings, Phillips |
| | 4 | 21.01.39 | **Chelmsford City** (SL) | H | W | 6-0 | Harris 2, Madden 2, Brown, Jennings |
| | 5 | 11.02.39 | **Everton** (D1) | H | D | 2-2 | Madden 2 |
| | 5r | 15.02.39 | **Everton** | A | L | 1-2 | Harris |
| **as Birmingham City** | | | | | | | |
| 1945-46 (D2) | 3 1L | 05.01.46 | **Portsmouth** (D2) | H | W | 1-0 | Flewin og |
| | 3 2L | 09.01.46 | **Portsmouth** | A | D | 0-0 | |
| | 4 1L | 26.01.46 | **Watford** (3S) | H | W | 5-0 | Mulraney 3, Jones, Bodle |
| | 4 2L | 30.01.46 | **Watford** | A | D | 1-1 | Jones |
| | 5 1L | 09.02.46 | **Sunderland** (D1) | A | L | 0-1 | |
| | 5 2L | 13.02.46 | **Sunderland** | H | W | 3-1 | Jones 2, Mulraney |
| | 6 1L | 02.03.46 | **Bradford Park A** (D2) | A | D | 2-2 | Dougall, Jones |
| | 6 2L | 09.03.46 | **Bradford Park A** | H | W | 6-0 | Dougall 2, Bodle 2, Mulaney 2 |
| | SF | 23.03.46 | **Derby County** (D1) | | D | 1-1 | Mulraney |
| | | | *played at Hillsborough* | | | | |
| | SFr | 27.03.46 | **Derby County** | | L | 0-4aet | |
| | | | *played at Maine Road* | | | | |
| 1946-47 (D2) | 3 | 11.01.47 | **Fulham** (D2) | A | W | 2-1 | Jones, Dorman |
| | 4 | 25.01.47 | **Portsmouth** (D1) | H | W | 1-0 | Harris |
| | 5 | 08.02.47 | **Manchester City** (D2) | H | W | 5-0 | Trigg 2, Bodle, Mitchell (p), Mulraney |
| | 6 | 01.03.47 | **Liverpool** (D1) | A | L | 1-4 | Mitchell (p) |
| 1947-48 (D2) | 3 | 10.01.48 | **Notts County** (3S) | H | L | 0-2 | |
| 1948-49 (D1) | 3 | 08.01.49 | **Leicester City** (D2) | H | D | 1-1aet | Roberts |
| | 3r | 15.01.49 | **Leicester City** | A | D | 1-1aet | Bodle |
| | 3 2r | 17.01.49 | **Leicester City** | H | L | 1-2 | Dorman |
| 1949-50 (D1) | 3 | 07.01.50 | **Swansea Town** (D2) | A | L | 0-3 | |
| 1950-51 (D2) | 3 | 06.01.51 | **Manchester City** (D2) | H | W | 2-0 | Stewart, Higgins |
| | 4 | 27.01.51 | **Derby County** (D1) | A | W | 3-1 | Stewart, Trigg, Smith |
| | 5 | 10.02.51 | **Bristol City** (3S) | H | W | 2-0 | Stewart, Trigg |
| | 6 | 24.02.51 | **Manchester Utd** (D1) | H | W | 1-0 | Higgins |
| | SF | 10.03.51 | **Blackpool** (D1) | | D | 0-0 | |
| | | | *played at Maine Road* | | | | |
| | SFr | 14.03.51 | **Blackpool** | | L | 1-2 | Smith |
| | | | *played at Goodison Park* | | | | |
| 1951-52 (D2) | 3 | 12.01.52 | **Fulham** (D1) | A | W | 1-0 | Briggs |
| | 4 | 02.02.52 | **Leyton Orient** (3S) | H | L | 0-1 | |
| 1952-53 (D2) | 3 | 10.01.53 | **Oldham Athletic** (3N) | A | W | 3-1 | Murphy 3 |
| | 4 | 31.01.53 | **Sheffield Utd** (D2) | A | D | 1-1 | Purdon |
| | 4r | 04.02.53 | **Sheffield Utd** | H | W | 3-1 | Murphy 2, Wardle |
| | 5 | 14.02.53 | **Chelsea** (D1) | A | W | 4-0 | Purdon 2, Trigg, Murphy |
| | 6 | 28.02.53 | **Tottenham Hotspur** (D1) | H | D | 1-1 | Wardle |
| | 6r | 04.03.53 | **Tottenham Hotspur** | A | D | 2-2aet | Ferris, Boyd |
| | 6 2r | 09.03.53 | **Tottenham Hotspur** | | L | 0-1 | |
| | | | *played at Molineux* | | | | |
| 1953-54 (D2) | 3 | 09.01.54 | **Wolverhampton W** (D1) | A | W | 2-1 | Murphy, Rowley |
| | 4 | 30.01.54 | **Ipswich Town** (3S) | A | L | 0-1 | |
| 1954-55 (D2) | 3 | 08.01.55 | **Hull City** (D2) | A | W | 2-0 | Kinsey, Brown |
| | 4 | 29.01.55 | **Bolton Wanderers** (D1) | H | W | 2-1 | Govan, og |
| | 5 | 19.02.55 | **Doncaster Rovers** (D2) | H | W | 2-1 | Brown 2 |
| | 6 | 12.03.55 | **Manchester City** (D1) | H | L | 0-1 | |
| 1955-56 (D1) | 3 | 07.01.56 | **Torquay Utd** (3S) | A | W | 7-1 | Brown 3, Murphy 2, Kinsey, Astall |
| | 4 | 28.01.56 | **Leyton Orient** (3S) | A | W | 4-0 | Brown 2, Murphy, Finney |
| | 5 | 18.02.56 | **WBA** (D1) | A | W | 1-0 | Murphy |
| | 6 | 03.03.56 | **Arsenal** (D1) | A | W | 3-1 | Astall, Murphy, Brown |
| | SF | 17.03.56 | **Sunderland** (D1) | | W | 3-0 | Kinsey, Astall, Brown |
| | | | *played at Hillsborough* | | | | |
| | F | 05.05.56 | **Manchester City** (D1) | | L | 1-3 | Kinsey |
| | | | *played at Wembley Stadium* | | | | |
| 1956-57 (D1) | 3 | 05.01.57 | **Carlisle Utd** (3N) | A | D | 0-0 | Murphy 2, Astall |

| | | | | | | | |
|---|---|---|---|---|---|---|---|
| | 3r | 09.01.57 | **Carlisle Utd** | H | W | 4-0 | Brown 2, Kinsey, Astall |
| | 4 | 26.01.57 | **Southend Utd** (3S) | A | W | 6-1 | Govan 3, Murphy, Cox, Lawler og |
| | 5 | 16.02.57 | **Millwall** (3S) | A | W | 4-1 | Kinsey 2, Govan, Brown |
| | 6 | 02.03.57 | **Nottingham Forest** (D2) | H | D | 0-0 | |
| | 6r | 07.03.57 | **Nottingham Forest** | A | W | 1-0 | Murphy |
| | SF | 23.03.57 | **Manchester Utd** (D1) | | L | 0-2 | |
| | | | *played at Hillsborough* | | | | |
| 1957-58 (D1) | 3 | 08.01.58 | **York City** (3N) | A | L | 0-3 | |
| 1958-59 (D1) | 3 | 24.01.59 | **Middlesbrough** (D2) | A | W | 1-0 | Harris og |
| | 4 | 28.01.59 | **Fulham** (D2) | H | D | 1-1 | Jackson |
| | 4r | 04.02.59 | **Fulham** | A | W | 3-2 | Hooper 2, Larkin |
| | 5 | 14.02.59 | **Nottingham Forest** (D1) | H | D | 1-1 | Astall |
| | 5r | 18.02.59 | **Nottingham Forest** | A | D | 1-1aet | Gordon |
| | 5 2r | 23.02.59 | **Nottingham Forest** | | L | 0-5 | |
| | | | *played at Filbert Street* | | | | |
| 1959-60 (D1) | 3 | 09.01.60 | **Watford** (D4) | A | L | 1-2 | Hooper |
| 1960-61 (D1) | 3 | 07.01.61 | **Nottingham Forest** (D1) | A | W | 2-0 | Singer 2 |
| | 4 | 28.01.61 | **Rotherham Utd** (D2) | H | W | 4-0 | Singer 2, Neal, Harris |
| | 5 | 18.02.61 | **Leicester City** (D1) | H | D | 1-1 | Harris (p) |
| | 5r | 22.02.61 | **Leicester City** | A | L | 1-2 | Harris |
| 1961-62 (D1) | 3 | 06.01.62 | **Tottenham Hotspur** (D1) | H | D | 3-3 | Harris 2, Leek |
| | 3r | 10.01.62 | **Tottenham Hotspur** | A | L | 2-4 | Harris, Leek |
| 1962-63 (D1) | 3 | 05.03.63 | **Bury** (D2) | H | D | 3-3 | Leek, Harris, Lynn (p) |
| | 3r | 07.03.63 | **Bury** | A | L | 0-2 | |
| 1963-64 (D1) | 3 | 04.01.64 | **Port Vale** (D3) | H | L | 1-2 | Beard |
| 1964-65 (D1) | 3 | 09.01.65 | **West Ham Utd** (D1) | A | L | 2-4 | Jackson, Thwaites |
| 1965-66 (D2) | 3 | 22.01.66 | **Bristol City** (D2) | H | W | 3-2 | Vowden 2, Thompson |
| | 4 | 12.02.66 | **Leicester City** (D1) | H | L | 1-2 | Thwaites |
| 1966-67 (D2) | 3 | 28.01.67 | **Blackpool** (D1) | H | W | 2-1 | Vowden, Thompson |
| | 4 | 18.02.67 | **Rotherham Utd** (D2) | A | D | 0-0 | |
| | 4r | 21.02.67 | **Rotherham Utd** | H | W | 2-1 | Hockey, Bridges |
| | 5 | 11.03.67 | **Arsenal** (D1) | H | W | 1-0 | Vowden |
| | 6 | 08.04.67 | **Tottenham Hotspur** (D1) | H | D | 0-0 | |
| | 6r | 12.04.67 | **Tottenham Hotspur** | A | L | 0-6 | |
| 1967-68 (D2) | 3 | 27.01.68 | **Halifax Town** (D4) | A | W | 4-2 | Pickering, Vowden, Bridges, Beard |
| | 4 | 17.02.68 | **Orient** (D3) | H | W | 3-0 | Vowden 2, Bridges |
| | 5 | 09.03.68 | **Arsenal** (D1) | A | D | 1-1 | Vowden |
| | 5r | 12.03.68 | **Arsenal** | H | W | 2-1 | Bridges 2 |
| | 6 | 30.03.68 | **Chelsea** (D1) | H | W | 1-0 | Pickering |
| | SF | 27.04.68 | **WBA** (D1) | | L | 0-2 | |
| | | | *played at Villa Park* | | | | |
| 1968-69 (D2) | 3 | 04.01.69 | **Lincoln City** (D4) | H | W | 2-1 | Pickering, Robinson |
| | 4 | 25.01.69 | **Sheffield Wed** (D1) | A | D | 0-0 | |
| | 4r | 28.01.69 | **Sheffield Wed** | H | W | 2-1 | Pickering, Beard |
| | 5 | 11.02.69 | **Manchester Utd** (D1) | H | D | 2-2 | Beard, Robinson (p) |
| | 5r | 24.02.69 | **Manchester Utd** | A | L | 2-6 | Greenhoff, Summerill |
| 1969-70 (D2) | 3 | 03.01.70 | **Chelsea** (D1) | A | L | 0-3 | |
| 1970-71 (D2) | 3 | 02.01.71 | **Huddersfield Town** (D1) | A | D | 1-1 | Summerill (p) |
| | 3r | 05.01.71 | **Huddersfield Town** | H | L | 0-2 | |
| 1971-72 (D2) | 3 | 15.01.72 | **Port Vale** (D3) | H | W | 3-0 | Francis 2, Hynd |
| | 4 | 05.02.72 | **Ipswich Town** (D1) | H | W | 1-0 | Latchford |
| | 5 | 26.02.72 | **Portsmouth** (D2) | H | W | 3-1 | Latchford 2 Hatton |
| | 6 | 18.03.72 | **Huddersfield Town** (D1) | H | W | 3-1 | Page, Latchford, Hatton |
| | SF | 15.04.72 | **Leeds Utd** (D1) | | L | 0-3 | |
| | | | *played at Hillsborough* | | | | |
| | 3/4 | 05.08.72 | **Stoke City** (D1) | H | D | 0-0 | |
| | | | *played at St Andrews – Birmingham won 4-3 on penalties* | | | | |
| 1972-73 (D1) | 3 | 13.01.73 | **Swindon Town** (D2) | A | L | 0-2 | |
| 1973-74 (D1) | 3 | 05.01.74 | **Cardiff City** (D2) | H | W | 5-2 | Latchford 2, Hatton 2, Francis |
| | 4 | 26.01.74 | **QPR** (D1) | A | L | 0-2 | |
| 1974-75 (D1) | 3 | 04.01.75 | **Luton Town** (D1) | A | W | 1-0 | Kendall |

| | | | | | | | |
|---|---|---|---|---|---|---|---|
| | 4 | 25.01.75 | **Chelsea** (D1) | A | W | 1-0 | Burns |
| | 5 | 15.02.75 | **Walsall** (D3) | H | W | 2-1 | Hatton, Burns |
| | 6 | 08.03.75 | **Middlesbrough** (D1) | H | W | 1-0 | Hatton |
| | SF | 05.04.75 | **Fulham** (D2) | | D | 1-1 | Gallagher |
| | | | *played at Hillsborough* | | | | |
| | SFr | 09.04.75 | **Fulham** | | L | 0-1aet | |
| | | | *played at Maine Road* | | | | |
| 1975-76 (D1) | 3 | 03.01.76 | **Portsmouth** (D2) | A | D | 1-1 | Francis |
| | 3r | 06.01.76 | **Portsmouth** | H | L | 0-1 | |
| 1976-77 (D1) | 3 | 08.01.77 | **Portsmouth** (D3) | H | W | 1-0 | Kendall |
| | 4 | 29.01.77 | **Leeds Utd** (D1) | H | L | 1-2 | Burns |
| 1977-78 (D1) | 3 | 07.01.78 | **Wigan Athletic** (NPL) | H | W | 4-0 | Francis 2, Bertschin 2 |
| | 4 | 01.02.78 | **Derby County** (D1) | A | L | 1-2 | Bertschin |
| 1978-79 (D1) | 3 | 09.01.79 | **Burnley** (D2) | H | L | 0-2 | |
| 1979-80 (D2) | 3 | 05.01.80 | **Southampton** (D1) | H | W | 2-1 | Bertschin, Gallagher |
| | 4 | 26.01.80 | **Middlesbrough** (D1) | H | W | 2-1 | Gemmill (p), Bertschin |
| | 5 | 16.02.80 | **Tottenham Hotspur** (D1) | A | L | 1-3 | Bertschin |
| 1980-81 (D1) | 3 | 03.01.81 | **Sunderland** (D1) | H | D | 1-1 | Bertschin |
| | 3r | 07.01.81 | **Sunderland** | A | W | 2-1aet | Bertschin, Evans |
| | 4 | 24.01.81 | **Coventry City** (D1) | A | L | 2-3 | Worthington (p), Ainscow |
| 1981-82 (D1) | 3 | 02.01.82 | **Ipswich Town** (D1) | H | L | 2-3 | Worthington (p), Curbishley |
| 1982-83 (D1) | 3 | 08.01.83 | **Walsall** (D3) | A | D | 0-0 | |
| | 3r | 11.01.83 | **Walsall** | H | W | 1-0aet | Summerfield |
| | 4 | 29.01.83 | **Crystal Palace** (D2) | A | L | 0-1 | |
| 1983-84 (D1) | 3 | 06.01.84 | **Sheffield Utd** (D3) | A | D | 1-1 | Wright (p) |
| | 3r | 10.01.84 | **Sheffield Utd** | H | W | 2-0 | Harford, Wright (p) |
| | 4 | 28.01.84 | **Sunderland** (D1) | A | W | 2-1 | Kuhl, Harford |
| | 5 | 18.02.84 | **West Ham Utd** (D1) | H | W | 3-0 | Hopkins, Rees, Wright (p) |
| | 6 | 10.03.84 | **Watford** (D1) | H | L | 1-3 | Terry og |
| 1984-85 (D2) | 3 | 05.01.85 | **Norwich City** (D1) | H | D | 0-0 | |
| | 3r | 23.01.85 | **Norwich City** | A | D | 1-1aet | Wright |
| | 3 2r | 26.01.85 | **Norwich City** | H | D | 1-1aet | Geddes |
| | 3 3r | 28.01.85 | **Norwich City** | A | L | 0-1 | |
| 1985-86 (D1) | 3 | 14.01.86 | **Altrincham** (APL) | H | L | 1-2 | Hopkins |
| 1986-87 (D2) | 3 | 10.01.87 | **Ipswich Town** (D2) | A | W | 1-0 | Mortimer |
| | 4 | 31.01.87 | **Walsall** (D3) | A | L | 0-1 | |
| 1987-88 (D2) | 3 | 09.01.88 | **Gillingham** (D3) | A | W | 3-0 | Williams, Handysides, og |
| | 4 | 30.01.88 | **Barnsley** (D2) | A | W | 2-0 | Rees, Wigley |
| | 5 | 20.02.88 | **Nottingham Forest** (D1) | H | L | 0-1 | |
| 1988-89 (D2) | 3 | 07.01.89 | **Wimbledon** (D1) | H | L | 0-1 | |
| 1989-90 (D3) | 1 | 17.11.89 | **Leyton Orient** (D3) | A | W | 1-0 | Sturridge |
| | 2 | 09.12.89 | **Colchester Utd** (D4) | A | W | 2-0 | Gleghorn 2 |
| | 3 | 06.01.90 | **Oldham Athletic** (D2) | H | D | 1-1 | Gleghorn |
| | 3r | 10.01.90 | **Oldham Athletic** | A | L | 0-1 | |
| 1990-91 (D3) | 1 | 17.11.90 | **Cheltenham Town** (Conf) | H | W | 1-0 | Sturridge |
| | 2 | 12.12.90 | **Brentford** (D3) | H | L | 1-3 | Aylott |
| 1991-92 (D3) | 1 | 16.11.91 | **Torquay Utd** (D3) | A | L | 0-3 | |
| 1992-93 (D1) | 1 | 15.11.92 | **Reading** (D2) | A | L | 0-1 | |
| 1993-94 (D1) | 3 | 08.01.94 | **Kidderminster H** (Conf) | H | L | 1-2 | Harding |
| 1994-95 (D2) | 1 | 12.11.94 | **Slough Town** (IL) | A | W | 4-0 | Shearer 2, McGavin 2 |
| | | | *played at St Andrews* | | | | |
| | 2 | 02.12.94 | **Scunthorpe Utd** (D3) | H | D | 0-0 | |
| | 2r | 14.12.94 | **Scunthorpe Utd** | A | W | 2-1 | McGavin, Cooper |
| | 3 | 07.01.95 | **Liverpool** (PL) | H | D | 0-0 | |
| | 3r | 18.01.95 | **Liverpool** | A | D | 1-1aet | Otto |
| | | | *Liverpool won 2-0 on penalties* | | | | |
| 1995-96 (D1) | 3 | 06.01.96 | **Wolverhampton W** (D1) | H | D | 1-1 | Poole |
| | 3r | 17.01.96 | **Wolverhampton W** | A | L | 1-2 | Hunt |
| 1996-97 (D1) | 3 | 04.01.97 | **Stevenage B** (Conf) | A | W | 2-0 | Francis, Devlin (p) |
| | | | *played at St Andrews* | | | | |
| | 4 | 25.01.97 | **Stockport County** (D2) | H | W | 3-1 | Furlong, Devlin, Francis |
| | 5 | 15.02.97 | **Wrexham** (D2) | H | L | 1-3 | Bruce |

| | | | | | | | | |
|---|---|---|---|---|---|---|---|---|
| 1997-98 (D1) | 3 | 03.01.98 | **Crewe Alexandra** (D1) | A | W | 2-1 | Furlong 3(1p) |
| | 4 | 24.01.98 | **Stockport County** (D1) | H | W | 2-1 | S Hughes 2 |
| | 5 | 14.02.98 | **Leeds Utd** (PL) | A | L | 2-3 | Ablett, Ndlovu |
| 1998-99 (D1) | 3 | 02.01.99 | **Leicester City** (PL) | A | L | 2-4 | Robinson, Adebola |
| 1999-00 (D1) | 3 | 11.12.99 | **Watford** (PL) | A | W | 1-0 | Rowett |
| | 4 | 08.01.00 | **Everton** (PL) | A | L | 0-2 | |
| 2000-01 (D1) | 3 | 06.01.01 | **Manchester City** (PL) | A | L | 2-3 | Grainger, Adebola |
| 2001-02 (D1) | 3 | 05.01.02 | **Liverpool** (PL) | A | L | 0-3 | |
| 2002-03 (PL) | 3 | 05.01.03 | **Fulham** (PL) | A | L | 1-3 | S John |

## BIRMINGHAM CLUB

*Amateur-based outfit with no links to Small Heath Alliance who later became Birmingham City.*

| | | | | | | | |
|---|---|---|---|---|---|---|---|
| 1879-80 | 1 | | Panthers | | | - | |
| | | | *Panthers scratched. Birmingham walkover* | | | | |
| | 2 | 19.01.80 | **Oxford University** | A | L | 0-6 | |

## BIRMINGHAM CORPORATION TRAMWAYS

*Works team that entered the FA Cup for nearly 40 years from 1911. Known as Birmingham City Transport FC 1938-1950.*

| | | | | | | | |
|---|---|---|---|---|---|---|---|
| 1934-35 (BC) | 1 | 24.11.34 | **Workington** (NEL) | A | L | 0-2 | |

## BIRMINGHAM EXCELSIOR

*Formed 1876. Played at Witton Fields, Birmingham. Excelsior's John and Harry Devey later played in four FA Cup finals between them for Aston Villa.*

| | | | | | | | |
|---|---|---|---|---|---|---|---|
| 1883-84 | 1 | 20.10.83 | **Small Heath Alliance** | A | D | 1-1 | |
| | 1r | 11.11.83 | **Small Heath Alliance** | H | W | 3-2 | |
| | 2 | 01.12.83 | **Derby Midland** | H | D | 1-1 | Barlow |
| | 2r | 15.12.83 | **Derby Midland** | A | L | 1-2 | |
| 1884-85 | 1 | 08.11.84 | **Small Heath Alliance** | H | W | 2-0 | J Devey, H Devey |
| | 2 | 06.12.84 | **Birmingham St G** | A | D | 2-2 | |
| | 2r | 20.12.84 | **Birmingham St G** | H | L | 0-2 | |
| 1885-86 | 1 | 31.10.85 | **Derby Midland** | A | L | 1-2 | |
| 1886-87 | 1 | 30.10.86 | **Derby Midland** | H | D | 3-3 | |
| | 1r | 13.11.86 | **Derby Midland** | A | L | 1-2 | |
| 1887-88 | 1 | 15.10.87 | **Warwick County** | H | W | 4-1 | |
| | | | *FA ordered replay after protest* | | | | |
| | 1r | 22.10.87 | **Warwick County** | A | W | 5-0 | |
| | 2 | | bye | | | | |
| | 3 | 26.11.87 | **Great Bridge Unity** | A | L | 1-2 | |

## BIRMINGHAM SOUTHFIELD

| | | | | | | | |
|---|---|---|---|---|---|---|---|
| 1887-88 | 1 | 15.10.87 | **Burton Swifts** | A | L | 0-7 | |

## BIRMINGHAM ST GEORGE'S

*Formed 1875. Also known as Mitchell St George's. Played at Fentham Road, Birchfield. Among former St Georges' players were Dennis Hodgetts and John Devey who both played in FA Cup finals for Aston Villa.*

| | | | | | | | |
|---|---|---|---|---|---|---|---|
| 1881-82 | 1 | 05.11.81 | **Wednesbury Old Ath** | A | L | 1-9 | |
| 1882-83 | 1 | 28.10.82 | **Birmingham Calthorpe** | H | W | 4-1 | |
| | 2 | 02.12.82 | **Aston Unity** | A | L | 1-3 | |
| 1883-84 | 1 | 10.11.83 | **Wednesbury Old Ath** | A | L | 0-5 | |
| 1884-85 | 1 | 01.11.84 | **Aston Unity** | A | W | 5-0 | Green 3, Hodgetts, AN Other |
| | 2 | 06.12.84 | **Birmingham Excelsior** | H | D | 2-2 | |
| | 2r | 20.12.84 | **Birmingham Excelsior** | A | W | 2-0 | |
| | 3 | 10.01.85 | **Walsall Swifts** | H | L | 2-3 | Hodgetts 2 |
| 1885-86 | 1 | 31.10.85 | **Derby County** | A | L | 0-3 | |
| 1886-87 | 1 | 30.10.86 | **Small Heath Alliance** | A | W | 3-1 | Meakin 2, Harrison |
| | 2 | 20.11.86 | **Derby County** | A | W | 2-1 | Rogers, AN Other |
| | 3 | 11.12.86 | **Walsall Town** | A | W | 7-2 | Brown 3, Breeze 2, Meakin, Rogers |
| | 4 | 15.01.87 | **WBA** | H | L | 0-1 | |
| 1887-88 | 1 | 15.10.87 | **Walsall Town** | A | W | 2-1 | Harrison, Hunt |
| | 2 | 05.11.87 | **WBA** | A | L | 0-1 | |
| 1888-89 | 1 | 02.02.89 | **Long Eaton Rangers** | H | W | 3-2 | Blackham, Harrison, J Devey |
| | 2 | 16.02.89 | **Halliwell** | A | W | 3-2 | J Devey 2, Harrison |
| | 3 | 02.03.89 | **Preston North End** (D1) | A | L | 0-2 | |

| | | | | | | | | |
|---|---|---|---|---|---|---|---|---|
| 1889-90 | (FAll) | 1 | 18.01.90 | **Notts County** (D1) | H | D | 4-4 | J Devey 3, Richards |
| | | 1r | 25.01.90 | **Notts County** | A | L | 2-6 | Marshall, Richards |
| 1890-91 | (FAll) | 1 | 24.01.91 | **Crusaders** | A | W | 2-0 | Davis, Shaw |
| | | 2 | 31.01.91 | **WBA** (D1) | H | L | 0-3 | |
| 1891-92 | (FAll) | 1 | 16.01.92 | **Sunderland Albion** (FAll) | A | W | 2-1 | Marshall, AN Other |
| | | | | *FA ordered replay, match only lasted one hour* | | | | |
| | | 1r | 23.01.92 | **Sunderland Albion** (FAll) | A | L | 0-4 | |

# BISHOP AUCKLAND

*Formed 1886 as Auckland Town. First entered FA Cup: 1889-90. The most successful and famous amateur cup team of the 20th century. Won the FA Amateur Cup 10 times and were runners-up eight times. Northern League Champions 19 times. League Clubs beaten: Crystal Palace, Ipswich Town, Tranmere Rovers. Members of the Northern Premier League.*

| | | | | | | | | |
|---|---|---|---|---|---|---|---|---|
| 1905-06 | (NL) | 1 | 13.01.06 | **Wolverhampton W** (D1) | H | L | 0-3 | |
| 1909-10 | (NL) | 1 | 15.01.10 | **Bradford Park A** (D2) | A | L | 0-8 | |
| 1926-27 | (NL) | 1 | 27.11.26 | **Bedlington Utd** (NEL) | A | L | 0-1 | |
| 1935-36 | (NL) | 1 | 30.11.35 | **Kidderminster H** (BDL) | A | L | 1-4 | Stephenson (p) |
| 1945-46 | (NL) | 1 1L | 17.11.45 | **Willington** (NL) | A | W | 5-0 | Clapham, Richardson 3, Anderson |
| | | 1 2L | 24.11.45 | **Willington** | H | L | 0-2 | |
| | | 2 1L | 08.12.45 | **York City** (3N) | H | L | 1-2 | Tait |
| | | 2 2L | 15.12.45 | **York City** | A | L | 0-3 | |
| 1946-47 | (NL) | 1 | 30.11.46 | **Rochdale** (3N) | A | L | 1-6 | Rutherford |
| 1947-48 | (NL) | 1 | 29.11.47 | **Chester** (3N) | A | L | 1-3 | Farrer |
| 1950-51 | (NL) | 1 | 25.11.50 | **York City** (3N) | H | D | 2-2 | Davison, Edwards |
| | | 1r | 29.11.50 | **York City** | A | L | 1-2 | McIlvenny |
| 1951-52 | (NL) | 1 | 24.11.51 | **Blyth Spartans** (NEL) | A | L | 1-2 | McIlvenny |
| 1952-53 | (NL) | 1 | 22.11.52 | **Selby Town** (YL) | A | W | 5-1 | Armstrong 2, McIlvenny 3 |
| | | 2 | 06.12.52 | **Coventry City** (3S) | H | L | 1-4 | Nimmins |
| 1954-55 | (NL) | 1 | 20.11.54 | **Kettering Town** (SL) | H | W | 5-1 | Major, Dickson 2, Oliver 2 |
| | | 2 | 11.12.54 | **Crystal Palace** (3S) | A | W | 4-2 | Edwards, Major 3 |
| | | 3 | 08.01.55 | **Ipswich Town** (D2) | A | D | 2-2 | Oliver, McKenna |
| | | 3r | 12.01.55 | **Ipswich Town** | H | W | 3-0 | McKenna 2, Major |
| | | 4 | 29.01.55 | **York City** (3N) | H | L | 1-3 | Edwards |
| 1955-56 | (NL) | 1 | 19.11.55 | **Durham City** (NL) | H | W | 3-1 | Barnwell, Oliver, Lewin |
| | | 2 | 10.12.55 | **Scunthorpe Utd** (3N) | H | D | 0-0 | |
| | | 2r | 15.12.55 | **Scunthorpe Utd** | A | L | 0-2 | |
| 1956-57 | (NL) | 1 | 17.11.56 | **Tranmere Rovers** (3N) | H | W | 2-1 | Edwards, Bradley |
| | | 2 | 08.12.56 | **Rhyl** (CC) | A | L | 1-3 | Thursby |
| 1957-58 | (NL) | 1 | 16.11.57 | **Bury** (3N) | H | D | 0-0 | |
| | | 1r | 19.11.57 | **Bury** | A | L | 1-4 | O'Connell |
| 1958-59 | (NL) | 1 | 15.11.58 | **Tranmere Rovers** (3N) | A | L | 1-8 | Brown |
| 1960-61 | (NL) | 1 | 05.11.60 | **Bridlington Town** (YL) | H | W | 3-2 | O'Connell, Gowland, Sharp |
| | | 2 | 26.11.60 | **Stockport County** (D4) | A | L | 0-2 | |
| 1966-67 | (NL) | 1 | 26.11.66 | **Blyth Spartans** (NL) | H | D | 1-1 | Siddle |
| | | 1r | 30.11.66 | **Blyth Spartans** | A | D | 0-0aet | |
| | | 1 2r | 05.12.66 | **Blyth Spartans** | | D | 3-3aet | Roughley, J Barker, McClelland |
| | | | | *played at Roker Park* | | | | |
| | | 1 3r | 08.12.66 | **Blyth Spartans** | | W | 4-1 | McClelland, J Barker, Armstrong 2 |
| | | | | *played at Roker Park* | | | | |
| | | 2 | 07.01.67 | **Halifax Town** (D4) | H | D | 0-0 | |
| | | 2r | 10.01.67 | **Halifax Town** | A | L | 0-7 | |
| 1974-75 | (NL) | 1 | 23.11.74 | **Morecambe** (NPL) | H | W | 5-0 | Boylan 3, Shoulder, Leigh og |
| | | 2 | 14.12.74 | **Preston North End** (D3) | H | L | 0-2 | |
| 1981-82 | (NL) | 1 | 21.11.81 | **Nuneaton B** (SL) | H | W | 4-1 | Cross 2, Foster, D Newton |
| | | 2 | 02.01.82 | **Carlisle Utd** (D3) | A | - | 0-0ab | |
| | | | | *abandoned after 69 minutes – waterlogged pitch* | | | | |
| | | 2 | 09.01.82 | **Carlisle Utd** | A | L | 0-1 | |
| | | | | *played at Workington* | | | | |
| 1987-88 | (NL) | 1 | 14.11.87 | **Blackpool** (D3) | H | L | 1-4 | Pearson |
| 1989-90 | (NPL) | 1 | 18.11.89 | **Tow Law Town** (NL) | H | W | 2-0 | Grant, Healey |
| | | 2 | 09.12.89 | **Crewe Alexandra** (D3) | A | D | 1-1 | Healey (p) |
| | | 2r | 13.12.89 | **Crewe Alexandra** | H | L | 0-2 | |

| | | | | | | | |
|---|---|---|---|---|---|---|---|
| 1990-91 (NPL) | 1 | 17.11.90 | **Barrow** (Conf) | H | L | 0-1 | |
| 1994-95 (NPL) | 1 | 12.11.94 | **Bury** (D3) | H | D | 0-0 | |
| | 1r | 22.11.94 | **Bury** | A | D | 1-1aet | Todd |
| | | | *Bury won 4-2 on penalties* | | | | |

# BISHOP AUCKLAND CHURCH INSTITUTE

*Formed 1882. Bishop Auckland Church Institute competed in the FA Cup between 1886 and 1890. Absorbed by Bishop Auckland in 1892.*

| | | | | | | | |
|---|---|---|---|---|---|---|---|
| 1886-87 | 1 | 23.10.86 | **Middlesbrough** | H | L | 0-1 | |
| 1887-88 | 1 | 15.10.87 | **Elswick Rangers** | A | D | 3-3aet | |
| | 1r | 22.10.87 | **Elswick Rangers** | H | L | 0-2 | |

# BISHOP'S STORTFORD

*Formed 1874. First entered FA Cup: 1924-25. Last winners of FA Amateur Cup: 1974. FA Trophy winners: 1981. League club beaten: Reading. John Radford, who played for Arsenal when they won the FA Cup in 1971, became the first player to subsequently win the FA Trophy when he played for Bishop's Stortford in 1981. Members of the Isthmian League.*

| | | | | | | | |
|---|---|---|---|---|---|---|---|
| 1970-71 (AL) | 1 | 21.11.70 | **Reading** (D3) | A | L | 1-6 | Deveaux |
| 1972-73 (IL) | 1 | 18.11.72 | **Enfield** (IL) | A | D | 1-1 | Francis |
| | 1r | 21.11.72 | **Enfield** | H | W | 1-0 | Dear |
| | 2 | 09.12.72 | **Peterborough Utd** (D4) | H | D | 2-2 | Leakey (p), Lawrence |
| | 2r | 11.12.72 | **Peterborough Utd** | A | L | 1-3 | Francis |
| 1974-75 (IL) | 1 | 23.11.74 | **Leatherhead** (IL) | H | D | 0-0 | |
| | 1r | 26.11.74 | **Leatherhead** | A | L | 0-2 | |
| 1975-76 (IL) | 1 | 22.11.75 | **Dartford** (SL) | A | W | 4-1 | P Watson 3, McKenzie |
| | 2 | 13.12.75 | **Aldershot** (D3) | A | L | 0-2 | |
| 1981-82 (IL) | 1 | 21.11.81 | **Sutton Utd** (IL) | H | D | 2-2 | Worrell, Clarke |
| | 1r | 24.11.81 | **Sutton Utd** | A | L | 1-2 | Clarke |
| 1982-83 (IL) | 1 | 20.11.82 | **Reading** (D3) | A | W | 2-1 | Sullivan, Worrell |
| | 2 | 11.12.82 | **Slough Town** (IL) | A | W | 4-1 | Lynch 3, Simmonds |
| | 3 | 08.01.83 | **Middlesbrough** (D2) | A | D | 2-2 | Bradford 2 |
| | 3r | 11.01.83 | **Middlesbrough** | H | L | 1-2 | Lynch |
| 1984-85 (IL) | 1 | 17.11.84 | **Brentford** (D3) | A | L | 0-4 | |
| 1985-86 (IL) | 1 | 16.11.85 | **Peterborough Utd** (D4) | H | D | 2-2 | Hardy 2 |
| | 1r | 20.11.85 | **Peterborough Utd** | A | L | 1-3 | Flynn |
| 1986-87 (IL) | 1 | 15.11.86 | **Colchester Utd** (D4) | H | D | 1-1 | Fergusson |
| | 1r | 18.11.86 | **Colchester Utd** | A | L | 0-2 | |

# BLACKBURN LAW

*Formed 1881. Played at the Raven's Wing Ground, Blackburn. This was the only FA Cup match they ever played.*

| | | | | | | | |
|---|---|---|---|---|---|---|---|
| 1881-82 | 1 | 05.11.81 | **Bootle** | A | L | 1-2 | |

# BLACKBURN OLYMPIC

*Formed 1876 and originally played at the Hole-In-The-Wall Ground, Blackburn. FA Cup winners: 1883. Did not compete in the FA Cup after 1888. They were the first Northern club to win the FA Cup.*

| | | | | | | | |
|---|---|---|---|---|---|---|---|
| 1880-81 | 1 | 30.10.80 | **Sheffield FC** | A | L | 3-4 | Lever, 2 others |
| 1881-82 | 1 | 29.10.81 | **Darwen** | A | L | 1-3 | Weseley |
| 1882-83 | 1 | 04.11.82 | **Accrington FC** | H | W | 6-3 | Wilson 3, J Yates 2, Weseley |
| | 2 | 09.12.82 | **Lower Darwen** | H | W | 8-1 | Wilson 2, Hunter, Matthews, 4 others |
| | 3 | 16.12.82 | **Darwen Ramblers** | H | W | 8-0 | Matthews, 7 others |
| | 4 | 03.02.83 | **Church FC** | H | W | 2-0 | Wilson, AN Other |
| | 5 | 24.02.83 | **Druids** | H | W | 4-1 | Costley 2, Yates, AN Other |
| | SF | 17.03.83 | **Old Carthusians** | | W | 4-0 | Dewhurst, Wilson, Matthews, Costley |
| | | | *played at Whalley Range, Manchester* | | | | |
| | F | 31.03.83 | **Old Etonians** | | W | 2-1aet | Matthews, Costley |
| | | | *played at Kennington Oval* | | | | |
| 1883-84 | 1 | 13.10.83 | **Darwen Ramblers** | H | W | 5-1 | Matthews 2, Yates 2, Dewhurst |
| | 2 | 01.12.83 | **Darwen** | A | W | 2-1aet | Matthews, AN Other |
| | 3 | | bye | | | | |
| | 4 | 19.01.84 | **Old Wykehamists** | H | W | 6-0 | Dewhurst 2, Yates, Costley, AN Other, og |
| | 5 | 09.02.84 | **Northwich V** | H | W | 9-1 | Matthews 2, Yates 2, Dewhurst, Parker, og, 2 others |

| | | | | | | | |
|---|---|---|---|---|---|---|---|
| | SF | 01.03.84 | **Queen's Park, Glasgow** | | L | 1-4 | Costley |
| | | | *played at Trent Bridge, Nottingham* | | | | |
| 1884-85 | 1 | 11.10.84 | **Oswaldtwistle Rovers** | H | W | 12-0 | Parker 4, Whitehead 3, Costley, Dewhurst, 3 others |
| | 2 | 06.12.84 | **Blackburn Rovers** | A | L | 2-3 | Parker, AN Other |
| 1885-86 | 1 | 31.10.85 | **Church FC** | H | L | 1-3 | |
| 1886-87 | 1 | 23.10.86 | **Partick Thistle** | H | L | 1-3 | |
| 1887-88 | 1 | | bye | | | | |
| | 2 | 05.11.87 | **Blackburn Rovers** | A | L | 1-5 | Hothersall |

# BLACKBURN PARK ROAD

*Formed 1875. Played at Audley Lane, Blackburn*

| | | | | | | | |
|---|---|---|---|---|---|---|---|
| 1881-82 | 1 | 29.10.81 | **Blackburn Rovers** | A | L | 1-9 | Nuttall |
| 1882-83 | 1 | 21.10.82 | **Darwen** | A | L | 1-4 | |
| 1883-84 | 1 | 27.10.83 | **Clitheroe Low Moor** | H | W | 6-0 | Holden 3, Grimshaw, Holt, Mackereth |
| | 2 | 26.11.83 | **Accrington FC** | H | L | 2-3 | Holden, Slater |
| | | | *Accrington disqualified for professionalism, Park Road declined re-instatement* | | | | |
| 1884-85 | 1 | | **Clitheroe Low Moor** | | | - | |
| | | | *Blackburn Park Road scratched. Clitheroe Low Moor walkover* | | | | |
| 1885-86 | 1 | 17.10.85 | **Third Lanark** | A | L | 2-4 | |
| 1886-87 | 1 | 09.10.86 | **Cliftonville** | H | D | 2-2 | Nuttall, Reynolds |
| | 1r | 23.10.86 | **Cliftonville** | A | L | 2-7 | |
| 1887-88 | 1 | 08.10.87 | **Distillery, Belfast** | H | W | 2-1 | Fish, Pomfrey |
| | | | *FA disqualified Park Road after a protest, Distillery re-instated* | | | | |

# BLACKBURN ROVERS

*Formed 1875. Founder members of the Football League 1888. FA Cup winners: (6 times) 1884, 1885, 1886, 1890, 1891, 1928; FA Cup runners-up: 1882, 1960. Record FA Cup win: 11-0 v Rossendale United, 1st round, 13.10.1884; Record FA Cup defeat: 0-6 v Nottingham Forest, 3rd round, 31.01.1880. Hold the record for the longest unbeaten run in the FA Cup: 23 matches from December 1883 until December 1886 during which time they won the FA Cup three years in succession in 1884, 1885 and 1886, the last club to do so.*

| | | | | | | | |
|---|---|---|---|---|---|---|---|
| 1879-80 | 1 | 01.11.79 | **Tyne Association** | H | W | 5-1 | Brown 2, Lewis, J Duckworth |
| | 2 | 06.12.79 | **Darwen** | H | W | 3-1 | Brown 2, J Hargreaves |
| | 3 | 31.01.80 | **Nottingham Forest** | A | L | 0-6 | |
| 1880-81 | 1 | 30.10.80 | **Sheffield Providence** | H | W | 6-2 | Hornby, Brown 2, R Birtwistle, A Birtwistle, J.Hargreaves |
| | 2 | 18.12.80 | **Sheffield Wed** | A | L | 0-4 | |
| 1881-82 | 1 | 29.10.81 | **Blackburn Park Road** | H | W | 9-1 | Brown 2, J Douglas, Wilson og, Avery, J Hargreaves, Strachan 2, AN Other og |
| | 2 | 19.11.81 | **Bolton Wanderers** | H | W | 6-2 | Avery, McIntyre 2, Brown 2, Sharples |
| | 3 | | bye | | | | |
| | 4 | 30.01.82 | **Darwen** | H | W | 5-1 | J Hargreaves 2, Brown, J Duckworth 2 |
| | 5 | 11.02.82 | **Wednesbury Old Ath** | H | W | 3-1 | Lofthouse, Avery, Strachan |
| | SF | 06.03.82 | **Sheffield Wed** | | D | 0-0 | |
| | | | *played at St John's Rugby Ground, Huddersfield* | | | | |
| | SFr | 15.03.82 | **Sheffield Wed** | | W | 5-1 | J Hargreaves, Avery, J Douglas, og, Suter |
| | | | *played at Whalley Range, Manchester* | | | | |
| | F | 25.03.82 | **Old Etonians** | | L | 0-1 | |
| | | | *played at Kennington Oval* | | | | |
| 1882-83 | 1 | 23.10.82 | **Blackpool St John's** | H | W | 11-1 | Brown 4, Barton 3, J Duckworth 2, Suter, Avery |
| | 2 | 02.12.82 | **Darwen** | A | L | 0-1 | |
| 1883-84 | 1 | 20.11.83 | **Southport** | H | W | 7-0 | J Douglas 2, Lofthouse, J Duckworth, Sowerbutts, Avery 2 |
| | 2 | 01.12.83 | **South Shore** | A | W | 7-0 | Avery 2, Suter, J Sowerbutts 2, J Douglas, McIntyre |
| | 3 | 24.12.83 | **Padiham** | H | W | 3-0 | Brown, Connell og, Strachan |
| | 4 | 19.01.84 | **Staveley** | H | W | 5-1 | Brown 4, Sowerbutts |
| | 5 | 09.02.84 | **Upton Park** | A | W | 3-0 | Inglis, Lofthouse 2 |
| | SF | 01.03.84 | **Notts County** | | W | 1-0 | Lofthouse |

| | | | | | | | | |
|---|---|---|---|---|---|---|---|---|
| | | | | *played at Aston Lower Grounds, Birmingham* | | | | |
| | | F | 29.03.84 | **Queen's Park, Glasgow** | | W | 2-1 | Sowerbutts, Forrest |
| | | | | *played at Kennington Oval* | | | | |
| 1884-85 | | 1 | 11.10.84 | **Rossendale FC** | H | W | 11-0 | Fecitt 4, Barton 3, Sowerbutts 2, Brown, A Birtwistle |
| | | 2 | 06.12.84 | **Blackburn Olympic** | H | W | 3-2 | Fecitt 2, Sowerbutts |
| | | 3 | 22.12.84 | **Witton** | H | W | 5-1 | Forrest, Brown, Sowerbutts, Lofthouse, Fecitt |
| | | 4 | 19.01.85 | **Romford (1876)** | H | W | 8-0 | Fecitt 2, Rostron, J Douglas, Sowerbutts 2, 2 ogs |
| | | 5 | | bye | | | | |
| | | 6 | 21.02.85 | **WBA** | A | W | 2-0 | Lofthouse, J Douglas |
| | | SF | 07.03.85 | **Old Carthusians** | | W | 5-1 | Brown 2, Sowerbutts 2, Lofthouse |
| | | | | *played at Trent Bridge, Nottingham* | | | | |
| | | F | 04.04.85 | **Queen's Park, Glasgow** | | W | 2-0 | Forrest, Brown |
| | | | | *played at Kennington Oval* | | | | |
| 1885-86 | | 1 | 24.10.85 | **Clitheroe** | A | W | 2-0 | J Douglas,AN Other |
| | | 2 | 21.11.85 | **Oswaldtwistle Rovers** | H | W | 1-0 | McIntyre |
| | | 3 | 05.12.85 | **Darwen Old Wanderers** | H | W | 6-1 | Sowerbutts 2, Brown 2, Fecitt, Lofthouse |
| | | 4 | 23.01.86 | **Staveley** | H | W | 7-1 | Lofthouse 2, Fecitt 2, Walton 2, Sowerbutts |
| | | 5 | | bye | | | | |
| | | 6 | 27.02.86 | **Brentwood** | A | W | 3-1 | Fecitt, Walton 2 |
| | | SF | 13.03.86 | **Swifts** | | W | 2-1 | Walton, Strachan |
| | | | | *played at Derby Cricket Ground* | | | | |
| | | F | 03.04.86 | **WBA** | | | D | 0-0 |
| | | | | *played at Kennington Oval* | | | | |
| | | Fr | 10.04.86 | **WBA** | | W | 2-0 | Sowerbutts, Brown |
| | | | | *played at Derby Racecourse Ground* | | | | |
| 1886-87 | | 1 | | Halliwell | | | - | |
| | | | | *Halliwell scratched. Blackburn Rovers walkover* | | | | |
| | | 2 | 20.11.86 | **Renton** | A | D | 2-2aet | Walton, AN Other |
| | | 2r | 04.12.86 | **Renton** | H | L | 0-2 | |
| 1887-88 | | 1 | | Bury | | | - | |
| | | | | *Bury scratched. Blackburn Rovers walkover* | | | | |
| | | 2 | 05.11.87 | **Blackburn Olympic** | H | W | 5-1 | Rushton, Chadwick, Gill og, Jack Southworth, Townley |
| | | 3 | 26.11.87 | **Accrington FC** | A | W | 3-1 | Chadwick 2, Walton |
| | | 5 | 07.01.88 | **Darwen** | A | W | 3-0 | Heyes, Jack Southworth, Townley |
| | | 6 | 28.01.88 | **Derby Junction** | A | L | 1-2 | Jack Southworth |
| 1888-89 | (D1) | 1 | 02.02.89 | **Accrington FC** (D1) | A | D | 1-1 | AN Other |
| | | 1r | 09.02.89 | **Accrington FC** | H | W | 5-0 | Haresnape 2, Walton, Townley, Barton |
| | | 2 | 16.02.89 | Swifts | | | - | |
| | | | | *Swifts scratched. Blackburn Rovers walkover* | | | | |
| | | 3 | 02.03.89 | **Aston Villa** (D1) | H | W | 8-1 | Haresnape 3, Jack Southworth 4, og |
| | | SF | 16.03.89 | **Wolverhampton W** (D1) | | D | 1-1 | Haresnape |
| | | | | *played at Alexandra Road, Crewe* | | | | |
| | | SFr | 23.03.89 | **Wolverhampton W** (D1) | | L | 1-3 | Townley |
| | | | | *played at Alexandra Road, Crewe* | | | | |
| 1889-90 | (D1) | 1 | 18.01.90 | **Sunderland** | H | W | 4-2aet | Townley 2, Campbell, Barton |
| | | 2 | 01.02.90 | **Grimsby Town** (FAll) | H | W | 3-0 | Arnold, Ogilvie og, Jack Southworth |
| | | 3 | 15.02.90 | **Bootle** (FAll) | A | W | 7-0 | Walton 3, Jack Southworth 2, Forbes, Townley |
| | | SF | 08.03.90 | **Wolverhampton W** (D1) | | W | 1-0 | Jack Southworth |
| | | | | *played at Derby Racecourse Ground* | | | | |
| | | F | 29.03.90 | **Sheffield Wed** (FAll) | | W | 6-1 | Townley 3, Walton, Jack Southworth, Lofthouse |
| | | | | *played at Kennington Oval* | | | | |
| 1890-91 | (D1) | 1 | 17.01.91 | **Middlesbrough Iron** (NL) | A | W | 2-1aet | Jack Southworth, Hall |
| | | | | *FA ordered replay after protest* | | | | |
| | | 1r | 24.01.91 | **Middlesbrough Iron** | A | W | 3-0 | Hall 2, Stevenson og |
| | | 2 | 31.01.91 | **Chester** (TC) | H | W | 7-0 | Jack Southworth 3, Hall, Townley, |

| | | | | | | | | |
|---|---|---|---|---|---|---|---|---|
| | | | | | | | | Taylor og, AN Other |
| | | 3 | 14.02.91 | **Wolverhampton W** (D1) | H | W | 2-0 | Baugh og, Fletcher og |
| | | SF | 28.02.91 | **WBA** (D1) | | W | 3-2 | Jack Southworth, Hall, AN Other |
| | | | | *played at Victoria Ground, Stoke* | | | | |
| | | F | 21.03.91 | **Notts County** (D1) | | W | 3-1 | Dewar, Jack Southworth, Townley |
| | | | | *played at Kennington Oval* | | | | |
| 1891-92 | (D1) | 1 | 16.01.92 | **Derby County** (D1) | H | W | 4-1 | Jack Southworth 4 |
| | | 2 | 30.01.92 | **WBA** (D1) | A | L | 1-3 | Townley |
| 1892-93 | (D1) | 1 | 21.01.93 | **Newton Heath** (D1) | H | W | 4-0 | Campbell 2, Sawers 2 |
| | | 2 | 04.02.93 | **Northwich V** (D2) | H | W | 4-1 | Bowdler, Campbell, Sawers, |
| | | | | | | | | Jack Southworth |
| | | 3 | 18.02.93 | **Sunderland** (D1) | H | W | 3-0 | Jack Southworth 2, Bowdler |
| | | SF | 04.03.93 | **Wolverhampton W** (D1) | | L | 1-2 | Taylor |
| | | | | *played at Town Ground, Nottingham* | | | | |
| 1893-94 | (D1) | 1 | 27.01.94 | **WBA** (D1) | A | W | 3-2 | Calvey, Chippendale, Forrest |
| | | 2 | 10.02.94 | **Newton Heath** (D1) | A | D | 0-0 | |
| | | 2r | 17.02.94 | **Newton Heath** | H | W | 5-1 | Calvey, Chippendale, Haydock, |
| | | | | | | | | Whitehead 2 |
| | | 3 | 24.02.94 | **Derby County** (D1) | A | W | 4-1 | Haydock 3, Townley |
| | | SF | 10.03.94 | **Notts County** (D2) | | L | 0-1 | |
| | | | | *played at Bramall Lane* | | | | |
| 1894-95 | (D1) | 1 | 02.02.95 | **Burton Wanderers** (D2) | A | W | 2-1 | Haydock 2 |
| | | 2 | 16.02.95 | **Everton** (D1) | A | D | 1-1 | Forrest |
| | | 2r | 20.02.95 | **Everton** | H | L | 2-3 | Keslo og, Gordon |
| 1895-96 | (D1) | 1 | 01.02.96 | **WBA** (D1) | H | L | 1-2 | Turnbull |
| 1896-97 | (D1) | 1 | 30.01.97 | **Sheffield Utd** (D1) | H | W | 2-1 | Booth, Dewar |
| | | 2 | 13.02.97 | **Wolverhampton W** (D1) | H | W | 2-1 | Wilkie, Dewar |
| | | 3 | 27.02.97 | **Everton** (D1) | A | L | 0-2 | |
| 1897-98 | (D1) | 1 | 29.01.98 | **Everton** | A | L | 0-1 | |
| 1898-99 | (D1) | 1 | 28.01.99 | **Liverpool** (D1) | A | L | 0-2 | |
| 1899-00 | (D1) | 1 | 27.01.00 | **Portsmouth** (SL) | A | D | 0-0 | |
| | | 1r | 01.02.00 | **Portsmouth** | H | D | 1-1aet | Hulse |
| | | 1 2r | 05.02.00 | **Portsmouth** | | W | 5-0 | Blackburn 3, Hulse 2 |
| | | | | *played at Villa Park* | | | | |
| | | 2 | 17.02.00 | **Preston North End** (D1) | A | L | 0-1 | |
| 1900-01 | (D1) | 1 | 09.02.01 | **Woolwich Arsenal** (D2) | A | L | 0-2 | |
| 1901-02 | (D1) | 1 | 01.02.02 | **Derby County** (D1) | H | L | 0-2 | |
| 1902-03 | (D1) | 1 | 07.02.03 | **Sheffield Wed** (D1) | A | D | 0-0 | |
| | | 1r | 12.02.03 | **Sheffield Wed** | H | W | 1-0 | Monks |
| | | 2 | 21.02.03 | **Derby County** (D1) | A | L | 0-2 | |
| 1903-04 | (D1) | 1 | 06.02.04 | **Liverpool** (D1) | H | W | 3-1 | Watson, Bowman, Dewhurst |
| | | 2 | 20.02.04 | **Nottingham Forest** (D1) | H | W | 3-1 | Dewhurst, Bowman, Blackburn |
| | | 3 | 05.03.04 | **Derby County** (D1) | A | L | 1-2 | Dewhurst |
| 1904-05 | (D1) | 1 | 04.02.05 | **Sheffield Wed** (D1) | H | L | 1-2 | Blackburn |
| 1905-06 | (D1) | 1 | 13.01.06 | **Stoke** (D1) | A | L | 0-1 | |
| 1906-07 | (D1) | 1 | 12.01.07 | **Manchester City** (D1) | H | D | 2-2 | Martin, Wolsenholme |
| | | 1r | 16.01.07 | **Manchester City** | A | W | 1-0 | Martin |
| | | 2 | 02.02.07 | **Tottenham Hotspur** (SL) | H | D | 1-1 | Martin |
| | | 2r | 07.02.07 | **Tottenham Hotspur** | A | D | 1-1aet | Bracegirdle |
| | | 2 2r | 11.02.07 | **Tottenham Hotspur** | | L | 1-2 | Latheron |
| | | | | *played at Villa Park* | | | | |
| 1907-08 | (D1) | 1 | 11.01.08 | **Leicester Fosse** (D2) | A | L | 0-2 | |
| 1908-09 | (D1) | 1 | 16.01.09 | **Notts County** (D1) | A | W | 1-0 | Latheron |
| | | 2 | 06.02.09 | **Chelsea** (D1) | H | W | 2-1 | Cameron, Latheron |
| | | 3 | 20.02.09 | **Manchester Utd** (D1) | A | L | 1-6 | Davies |
| 1909-10 | (D1) | 1 | 15.01.10 | **Accrington Stanley** (LC) | H | W | 7-1 | Chapman 2, Aitkenhead 2, Latheron 2, |
| | | | | | | | | Anthony |
| | | 2 | 05.02.10 | **Bradford City** (D1) | A | W | 2-1 | Aitkenhead 2 |
| | | 3 | 19.02.10 | **Newcastle Utd** (D1) | A | L | 1-3 | Anthony |
| 1910-11 | (D1) | 1 | 14.01.11 | **Southend Utd** (SL) | H | W | 5-1 | Latheron 2, Bradshaw (p), |
| | | | | | | | | Aitkenhead, Thompson og |

| | | | | | | | |
|---|---|---|---|---|---|---|---|
| | 2 | 04.02.11 | **Tottenham Hotspur** (D1) | H | D | 0-0 | |
| | 2r | 09.02.11 | **Tottenham Hotspur** | A | W | 2-0 | Bradshaw, Davies |
| | 3 | 25.02.11 | **Middlesbrough** (D1) | A | W | 3-0 | Simpson 2, Smith |
| | 4 | 11.03.11 | **West Ham Utd** (SL) | A | W | 3-2 | Latheron, Simpson, Davies |
| | SF | 25.03.11 | **Bradford City** (D1) | | L | 0-3 | |
| | | | *played at Bramall Lane* | | | | |
| 1911-12 (D1) | 1 | 13.01.12 | **Norwich City** (SL) | H | W | 4-1 | Simpson 2, Chapman 2 |
| | 2 | 03.02.12 | **Derby County** (D2) | A | W | 2-1 | Orr, Chapman |
| | 3 | 24.02.12 | **Wolverhampton W** (D2) | H | W | 3-2 | Chapman, Aitkenhead 2 |
| | 4 | 09.03.12 | **Manchester Utd** (D1) | A | D | 1-1 | Aitkenhead |
| | 4r | 14.03.12 | **Manchester Utd** | H | W | 4-2aet | Simpson, Aitkenhead, Chapman 2 |
| | SF | 30.03.12 | **WBA** (D1) | | D | 0-0 | |
| | | | *played at Anfield* | | | | |
| | SFr | 03.04.12 | **WBA** | | L | 0-1aet | |
| | | | *played at Hillsborough* | | | | |
| 1912-13 (D1) | 1 | 18.01.13 | **Northampton Town** (SL) | H | W | 7-2 | Simpson, Latheron, Aitkenhead 3,Orr 2 |
| | 2 | 01.02.13 | **Barnsley** (D2) | A | W | 3-2 | Shea, Bradshaw (p), Aitkenhead |
| | 3 | 22.02.13 | **Reading** (SL) | A | W | 2-1 | Latheron, Anthony |
| | 4 | 08.03.13 | **Burnley** (D2) | H | L | 0-1 | |
| 1913-14 (D1) | 1 | 10.01.14 | **Middlesbrough** (D1) | H | W | 3-0 | Aitkenhead 3 |
| | 2 | 31.01.14 | **Bury** (D2) | H | W | 2-0 | Shea 2 |
| | 3 | 21.02.14 | **Manchester City** (D1) | H | L | 1-2 | Aitkenhead |
| 1914-15 (D1) | 1 | 09.01.15 | **Swansea Town** (SL) | A | L | 0-1 | |
| 1919-20 (D1) | 1 | 10.01.20 | **Wolverhampton W** (D2) | H | D | 2-2 | Reilly, Dawson |
| | 1r | 15.01.20 | **Wolverhampton W** | A | L | 0-1 | |
| 1920-21 (D1) | 1 | 08.01.21 | **Fulham** (D2) | H | D | 1-1 | Dawson |
| | 1r | 13.01.21 | **Fulham** | A | L | 0-1 | |
| 1921-22 (D1) | 1 | 07.01.22 | **Southport** (3N) | H | D | 1-1 | Rodgers |
| | 1r | 12.01.22 | **Southport** | A | W | 2-0 | Rodgers 2 |
| | 2 | 28.01.22 | **Swindon Town** (3S) | A | W | 1-0 | Rollo (p) |
| | 3 | 18.02.22 | **Huddersfield Town** (D1) | H | D | 1-1 | Hodkinson |
| | 3r | 22.02.22 | **Huddersfield Town** | A | L | 0-5 | |
| 1922-23 (D1) | 1 | 13.01.23 | **Aston Villa** (D1) | A | W | 1-0 | Bond (p) |
| | 2 | 03.02.23 | **South Shields** (D2) | A | D | 0-0 | |
| | 2r | 08.02.23 | **South Shields** | H | L | 0-1 | |
| 1923-24 (D1) | 1 | 12.01.24 | **Corinthians** | A | L | 0-1 | |
| | | | *played at Crystal Palace* | | | | |
| 1924-25 (D1) | 1 | 10.01.25 | **Oldham Athletic** (D2) | H | W | 1-0 | McKay |
| | 2 | 31.01.25 | **Portsmouth** (D2) | H | D | 0-0 | |
| | 2r | 04.02.25 | **Portsmouth** | A | D | 0-0aet | |
| | 2 2r | 09.02.25 | **Portsmouth** | | W | 1-0 | Crisp |
| | | | *played at Highbury* | | | | |
| | 3 | 21.02.25 | **Tottenham Hotspur** (D1) | A | D | 2-2 | Hulme, McKay |
| | 3r | 26.02.25 | **Tottenham Hotspur** | H | W | 3-1 | Campbell, Puddefoot,Hulme |
| | 4 | 07.03.25 | **Blackpool** (D2) | H | W | 1-0 | Puddefoot |
| | SF | 28.03.25 | **Cardiff City** (D1) | | L | 1-3 | McKay |
| | | | *played at Meadow Lane, Nottingham* | | | | |
| 1925-26 (D1) | 3 | 09.01.26 | **Preston North End** (D2) | H | D | 1-1 | Holland |
| | 3r | 14.01.26 | **Preston North End** | A | W | 4-1 | Dixon 2, Rigby 2 |
| | 4 | 30.01.26 | **Arsenal** (D1) | A | L | 1-3 | Harper |
| 1926-27 (D1) | 3 | 08.01.27 | **Southport** (3N) | A | L | 0-2 | |
| 1927-28 (D1) | 3 | 14.01.28 | **Newcastle Utd** (D1) | H | W | 4-1 | Puddefoot, Mitchell 2, Thornewell |
| | 4 | 28.01.28 | **Exeter City** (3S) | A | D | 2-2 | Roscamp, Rigby |
| | 4r | 02.02.28 | **Exeter City** | H | W | 3-1aet | Roscamp, Mitchell, Puddefoot |
| | 5 | 18.02.28 | **Port Vale** (D2) | H | W | 2-1 | Roscamp, Mitchell |
| | 6 | 03.03.28 | **Manchester Utd** (D1) | H | W | 2-0 | Puddefoot 2 |
| | SF | 24.03.28 | **Arsenal** (D1) | | W | 1-0 | Roscamp |
| | | | *played at Filbert Street* | | | | |
| | F | 21.04.28 | **Huddersfield Town** (D1) | | W | 3-1 | Roscamp 2, McLean |
| | | | *played at Wembley Stadium* | | | | |

| | | | | | | | | |
|---|---|---|---|---|---|---|---|---|
| 1928-29 | (D1) | 3 | 12.01.29 | **Barnsley** (D2) | H | W | 1-0 | Healless |
| | | 4 | 26.01.29 | **Derby County** (D1) | H | D | 1-1 | Bourton |
| | | 4r | 30.01.29 | **Derby County** | A | W | 3-0 | Roscamp, Bourton, McLean |
| | | 5 | 16.02.29 | **Bury** (D1) | H | W | 1-0 | Bourton |
| | | 6 | 02.03.29 | **Bolton Wanderers** (D1) | H | D | 1-1 | Hutton |
| | | 6r | 06.03.29 | **Bolton Wanderers** | A | L | 1-2 | Campbell (p) |
| 1929-30 | (D1) | 3 | 11.01.30 | **Northampton Town** (3S) | H | W | 4-1 | Cunliffe, Imrie (p), McLean, J Bruton |
| | | 4 | 25.01.30 | **Everton** (D1) | H | W | 4-1 | McLean, Bourton, J Bruton, Cunliffe |
| | | 5 | 15.02.30 | **Aston Villa** (D1) | A | L | 1-4 | Bourton |
| 1930-31 | (D1) | 3 | 10.01.31 | **Walsall** (3S) | H | D | 1-1 | L Bruton |
| | | 3r | 15.01.31 | **Walsall** | A | W | 3-0 | Puddefoot, Cunliffe, L Bruton |
| | | 4 | 24.01.31 | **Bristol Rovers** (3S) | H | W | 5-1 | Puddefoot, J Bruton, L Bruton 3 |
| | | 5 | 14.02.31 | **Chelsea** (D1) | A | L | 0-3 | |
| 1931-32 | (D1) | 3 | 09.01.32 | **Burton Town** (BDL) | A | W | 4-0 | J Bruton 2, Cunliffe 2 |
| | | 4 | 23.01.32 | **Derby County** (D1) | A | L | 2-3 | Britton, Cunliffe |
| 1932-33 | (D1) | 3 | 14.01.33 | **Lincoln City** (D2) | A | W | 5-1 | Dix, T McLean (p), Cunliffe 2, Bruton |
| | | 4 | 28.01.33 | **Birmingham** (D1) | A | L | 0-3 | |
| 1933-34 | (D1) | 3 | 13.01.34 | **Manchester City** (D1) | A | L | 1-3 | J Bruton |
| 1934-35 | (D1) | 3 | 12.01.35 | **Middlesbrough** (D1) | A | D | 1-1 | Talbot |
| | | 3r | 17.01.35 | **Middlesbrough** | H | W | 1-0 | Milne |
| | | 4 | 26.01.35 | **Liverpool** (D1) | H | W | 1-0 | Milne |
| | | 5 | 21.02.35 | **Birmingham** (D1) | H | L | 1-2 | Beattie |
| 1935-36 | (D1) | 3 | 11.01.36 | **Bolton Wanderers** (D1) | H | D | 1-1 | Halsall |
| | | 3r | 15.01.36 | **Bolton Wanderers** | A | W | 1-0aet | Thompson |
| | | 4 | 03.02.36 | **Bradford City** (D2) | A | L | 1-3 | Thompson |
| 1936-37 | (D2) | 3 | 16.01.37 | **Accrington Stanley** (3N) | H | D | 2-2 | Craven og, Fraser |
| | | 3r | 20.01.37 | **Accrington Stanley** | A | L | 1-3aet | Calladine |
| 1937-38 | (D2) | 3 | 08.01.38 | **Tottenham Hotspur** (D2) | A | L | 2-3 | Sale, Guest |
| 1938-39 | (D2) | 3 | 07.01.39 | **Swansea Town** (D2) | H | W | 2-0 | Clarke, Chivers |
| | | 4 | 21.01.39 | **Southend Utd** (3N) | H | W | 4-2 | Butt 2, Clarke, Weddle |
| | | 5 | 11.02.39 | **Sunderland** (D1) | A | D | 1-1 | Butt |
| | | 5r | 16.02.39 | **Sunderland** | H | D | 0-0aet | |
| | | 5 2r | 20.02.39 | **Sunderland** *played at Hillsborough* | | W | 1-0aet | Guest |
| | | 6 | 04.03.39 | **Huddersfield Town** (D1) | A | D | 1-1 | Weddle |
| | | 6r | 09.03.39 | **Huddersfield Town** | H | L | 1-2 | Butt |
| 1945-46 | (D2) | 3 1L | 05.01.46 | **Bolton Wanderers** (D1) | A | L | 0-1 | |
| | | 3 2L | 09.01.46 | **Bolton Wanderers** | H | L | 1-3 | Wyles |
| 1946-47 | (D1) | 3 | 11.01.47 | **Hull City** (3N) | H | D | 1-1 | McClelland |
| | | 3r | 16.01.47 | **Hull City** | A | W | 3-0 | McClelland, Rogers 2 |
| | | 4 | 25.02.47 | **Port Vale** (3S) | H | W | 2-0 | Rogers, Baldwin |
| | | 5 | 08.02.47 | **Charlton Athletic** (D1) | A | L | 0-1 | |
| 1947-48 | (D1) | 3 | 10.01.48 | **West Ham Utd** (D2) | H | D | 0-0aet | |
| | | 3r | 17.01.48 | **West Ham Utd** | A | W | 4-2aet | McClelland 2, Murphy, Graham |
| | | 4 | 24.01.48 | **Southampton** (D2) | A | L | 2-3 | Campbell, McClelland |
| 1948-49 | (D2) | 3 | 08.01.49 | **Hull City** (3N) | A | L | 1-2aet | Graham |
| 1949-50 | (D2) | 3 | 07.01.50 | **Liverpool** (D1) | H | D | 0-0 | |
| | | 3r | 11.01.50 | **Liverpool** | A | L | 1-2 | Edds |
| 1950-51 | (D2) | 3 | 06.01.51 | **Bristol City** (3S) | A | L | 1-2 | Wharton |
| 1951-52 | (D2) | 3 | 12.01.52 | **Nottingham Forest** (D2) | A | D | 2-2 | Crossan, Holmes |
| | | 3r | 16.01.52 | **Nottingham Forest** | H | W | 2-0 | Holmes, Nightingale |
| | | 4 | 02.02.52 | **Hull City** (D2) | H | W | 2-0 | Nightingale, Wharton |
| | | 5 | 23.02.52 | **WBA** (D1) | H | W | 1-0 | Eckersley (p) |
| | | 6 | 08.03.52 | **Burnley** (D1) | H | W | 3-1 | Nightingale, Holmes, Glover |
| | | SF | 29.03.52 | **Newcastle Utd** (D1) *played at Hillsborough* | | D | 0-0aet | |
| | | SFr | 02.04.52 | **Newcastle Utd** *played at Elland Road* | | L | 1-2 | Quigley |
| 1952-53 | (D2) | 3 | 10.01.53 | **Luton Town** (D2) | A | L | 1-6 | McLuckie |
| 1953-54 | (D2) | 3 | 09.01.54 | **Bristol Rovers** (D2) | A | W | 1-0 | Quigley |
| | | 4 | 30.01.54 | **Hull City** (D2) | H | D | 2-2 | Berry og, Quigley |
| | | 4r | 04.02.54 | **Hull City** | A | L | 1-2 | Briggs |

| | | | | | | | | |
|---|---|---|---|---|---|---|---|---|
| 1954-55 | (D2) | 3 | 08.01.55 | **Swansea Town** (D2) | H | L | 0-2 | |
| 1955-56 | (D2) | 3 | 07.01.56 | **Northampton Town** (3S) | A | W | 2-1 | Briggs 2 |
| | | 4 | 28.01.56 | **Barnsley** (D2) | A | W | 1-0 | Smith |
| | | 5 | 18.02.56 | **West Ham Utd** (D2) | A | D | 0-0 | |
| | | 5r | 23.02.56 | **West Ham Utd** | H | L | 2-3 | Langton (p), Smith |
| 1956-57 | (D2) | 3 | 05.01.57 | **Everton** (D1) | A | L | 0-1 | |
| 1957-58 | (D2) | 3 | 04.01.58 | **Rotherham Utd** (D2) | A | W | 4-1 | Douglas, Dobing 3 |
| | | 4 | 29.01.58 | **Everton** (D1) | A | W | 2-1 | Dobing, Meagan og |
| | | 5 | 15.02.58 | **Cardiff City** (D2) | A | D | 0-0 | |
| | | 5r | 20.02.58 | **Cardiff City** | H | W | 2-1 | McGrath, Douglas |
| | | 6 | 01.03.58 | **Liverpool** (D2) | H | W | 2-1 | Clayton, MacLeod |
| | | SF | 22.03.58 | **Bolton Wanderers** (D1) | | L | 1-2 | Dobing |
| | | | | *played at Maine Road* | | | | |
| 1958-59 | (D1) | 3 | 10.01.59 | **Leyton Orient** (D2) | H | W | 4-2 | Johnston, MacLeod, Vernon, Dobing |
| | | 4 | 28.01.59 | **Burnley** (D1) | H | L | 1-2 | Dobing |
| 1959-60 | (D1) | 3 | 09.01.60 | **Sunderland** (D2) | A | D | 1-1 | Dobing |
| | | 3r | 13.01.60 | **Sunderland** | H | W | 4-1 | Vernon 2, MacLeod, Bimpson |
| | | 4 | 30.01.60 | **Blackpool** (D1) | H | D | 1-1 | McGrath |
| | | 4r | 03.02.60 | **Blackpool** | A | W | 3-0 | Dobing 2, Dougan |
| | | 5 | 20.02.60 | **Tottenham Hotspur** (D1) | A | W | 3-1 | Woods, Bimpson 2 |
| | | 6 | 12.03.60 | **Burnley** (D1) | A | D | 3-3 | Douglas (p), Dobing, McGrath |
| | | 6r | 16.03.60 | **Burnley** | H | W | 2-0 | Dobing, MacLeod |
| | | SF | 26.03.60 | **Sheffield Wed** (D1) | | W | 2-1 | Dougan 2 |
| | | | | *played at Maine Road* | | | | |
| | | F | 07.05.60 | **Wolverhampton W** (D1) | | L | 0-3 | |
| | | | | *played at Wembley Stadium* | | | | |
| 1960-61 | (D1) | 3 | 07.01.61 | **Chesterfield** (D3) | A | D | 0-0 | |
| | | 3r | 11.01.61 | **Chesterfield** | H | W | 3-0 | Douglas, Dobing 2 |
| | | 4 | 28.01.61 | **Bolton Wanderers** (D1) | A | D | 3-3 | MacLeod 2, Dougan |
| | | 4r | 01.02.61 | **Bolton Wanderers** | H | W | 4-0 | Dobing 2, Douglas 2 |
| | | 5 | 18.02.61 | **Sheffield Utd** (D2) | A | L | 1-2 | Crowe |
| 1961-62 | (D1) | 3 | 06.01.62 | **Brighton** (D2) | A | W | 3-0 | Byrom, Ratcliffe, Pickering |
| | | 4 | 27.01.62 | **Stoke City** (D2) | A | W | 1-0 | Douglas (p) |
| | | 5 | 17.02.62 | **Middlesbrough** (D2) | H | W | 2-1 | Pickering, Lawther |
| | | 6 | 10.03.62 | **Fulham** (D1) | A | D | 2-2 | Thomas, Douglas |
| | | 6r | 14.03.62 | **Fulham** | H | L | 0-1 | |
| 1962-63 | (D1) | 3 | 05.03.63 | **Middlesbrough** (D2) | H | D | 1-1 | Pickering |
| | | 3r | 11.03.63 | **Middlesbrough** | A | L | 1-3 | Byrom |
| 1963-64 | (D1) | 3 | 04.01.64 | **Grimsby Town** (D2) | H | W | 4-0 | Pickering, McEvoy 3 |
| | | 4 | 25.01.64 | **Fulham** (D1) | H | W | 2-0 | Pickering, McEvoy |
| | | 5 | 15.02.64 | **Oxford Utd** (D4) | A | L | 1-3 | Ferguson |
| 1964-65 | (D1) | 3 | 09.01.65 | **Leicester City** (D1) | A | D | 2-2 | Harrison, Douglas |
| | | 3r | 14.01.65 | **Leicester City** | H | L | 1-2 | Byrom |
| 1965-66 | (D1) | 3 | 22.01.66 | **Arsenal** (D1) | H | W | 3-0 | McEvoy 2, Byrom |
| | | 4 | 12.02.66 | **West Ham Utd** (D1) | A | D | 3-3 | Byrom 3 |
| | | 4r | 16.02.66 | **West Ham Utd** | H | W | 4-1 | McEvoy 3, Byrom |
| | | 5 | 05.03.66 | **Norwich City** (D2) | A | D | 2-2 | Byrom, Jones |
| | | 5r | 09.03.66 | **Norwich City** | H | W | 3-2 | McEvoy, Darling, Harrison |
| | | 6 | 26.03.66 | **Sheffield Wed** (D1) | H | L | 1-2 | Byrom |
| 1966-67 | (D2) | 3 | 28.01.67 | **Carlisle Utd** (D2) | H | L | 1-2 | Connelly |
| 1967-68 | (D2) | 3 | 27.01.68 | **Swindon Town** (D3) | A | L | 0-1 | |
| 1968-69 | (D2) | 3 | 04.01.69 | **Stockport County** (D3) | H | W | 2-0 | Connelly, Fryatt |
| | | 4 | 25.01.69 | **Portsmouth** (D2) | H | W | 4-0 | Fryatt, Darling 3 |
| | | 5 | 24.02.69 | **Manchester City** (D1) | H | L | 1-4 | Fryatt |
| 1969-70 | (D2) | 3 | 03.01.70 | **Swindon Town** (D2) | H | L | 0-4 | |
| 1970-71 | (D2) | 3 | 02.01.71 | **Everton** (D1) | A | L | 0-2 | |
| 1971-72 | (D3) | 1 | 20.11.71 | **Port Vale** (D3) | H | D | 1-1 | Fazackerley |
| | | 1r | 22.11.71 | **Port Vale** | A | L | 1-3 | Field (p) |
| 1972-73 | (D3) | 1 | 18.11.72 | **Lincoln City** (D4) | A | D | 2-2 | Napier, Field |
| | | 1r | 27.11.72 | **Lincoln City** | H | W | 4-1 | McNamee, Field 3 |
| | | 2 | 09.12.72 | **Crewe Alexandra** (D4) | H | L | 0-1 | |

| | | | | | | | |
|---|---|---|---|---|---|---|---|
| 1973-74 (D3) | 1 | 24.11.73 | **Willington** (NL) | A | D | 0-0 | |
| | 1r | 03.12.73 | **Willington** | H | W | 6-1 | Field, O'Mara 2, Napier, Garbett, Parkes |
| | 2 | 15.12.73 | **Altrincham** (NPL) | H | D | 0-0 | |
| | 2r | 19.12.73 | **Altrincham** | A | W | 2-0 | Napier, Field (p) |
| | 3 | 05.01.74 | **Everton** (D1) | A | L | 0-3 | |
| 1974-75 (D3) | 1 | 23.11.74 | **Matlock Town** (NPL) | A | W | 4-1 | Martin, Beamish 2, Parkes |
| | 2 | 14.12.74 | **Darlington** (D4) | H | W | 1-0 | Oates |
| | 3 | 04.01.75 | **Bristol Rovers** (D2) | H | L | 1-2 | Martin |
| 1975-76 (D2) | 3 | 03.01.76 | **Luton Town** (D2) | A | L | 0-2 | |
| 1976-77 (D2) | 3 | 08.01.77 | **Charlton Athletic** (D2) | A | D | 1-1 | Svarc |
| | 3r | 12.01.77 | **Charlton Athletic** | H | W | 2-0 | Byrom, Parkes |
| | 4 | 29.01.77 | **Orient** (D2) | H | W | 3-0 | Waddington, Parkes, Byrom |
| | 5 | 26.02.77 | **Derby County** (D1) | A | L | 1-3 | Todd og |
| 1977-78 (D2) | 3 | 07.01.78 | **Shrewsbury Town** (D3) | H | W | 2-1 | Mitchell, Brotherston |
| | 4 | 28.01.78 | **Orient** (D2) | A | L | 1-3 | Metcalfe |
| 1978-79 (D2) | 3 | 10.01.79 | **Millwall** (D2) | A | W | 2-1 | Brotherston, Radford |
| | 4 | 30.01.79 | **Liverpool** (D1) | A | L | 0-1 | |
| 1979-80 (D3) | 1 | 24.11.79 | **Kidderminster H** (SL) | A | W | 2-0 | Crawford, Craig |
| | 2 | 17.12.79 | **Stafford Rangers** (APL) | H | W | 2-0 | Crawford, McKenzie |
| | 3 | 05.01.80 | **Fulham** (D2) | H | D | 1-1 | Crawford |
| | 3r | 15.01.80 | **Fulham** | A | W | 1-0 | Crawford |
| | 4 | 26.01.80 | **Coventry City** (D1) | H | W | 1-0 | Crawford |
| | 5 | 16.02.80 | **Aston Villa** (D1) | H | D | 1-1 | Evans og |
| | 5r | 20.02.80 | **Aston Villa** | A | L | 0-1 | |
| 1980-81 (D2) | 3 | 03.01.81 | **Notts County** (D2) | A | L | 1-2 | Burke |
| 1981-82 (D2) | 3 | 02.01.82 | **WBA** (D1) | A | L | 2-3 | Garner 2 |
| 1982-83 (D2) | 3 | 08.01.83 | **Liverpool** (D1) | H | L | 1-2 | Garner |
| 1983-84 (D2) | 3 | 07.01.84 | **Chelsea** (D2) | H | W | 1-0 | Brotherston |
| | 4 | 28.01.84 | **Swindon Town** (D4) | A | W | 2-1 | Garner, Keeley |
| | 5 | 18.02.84 | **Southampton** (D1) | H | L | 0-1 | |
| 1984-85 (D2) | 3 | 04.01.85 | **Portsmouth** (D2) | A | D | 0-0 | |
| | 3r | 26.01.85 | **Portsmouth** | H | W | 2-1 | Quinn 2 |
| | 4 | 30.01.85 | **Oxford Utd** (D2) | A | W | 1-0 | Quinn |
| | 5 | 15.02.85 | **Manchester Utd** (D1) | H | L | 0-2 | |
| 1985-86 (D2) | 3 | 04.01.86 | **Nottingham Forest** (D1) | A | D | 1-1 | Thompson |
| | 3r | 13.01.86 | **Nottingham Forest** | H | W | 3-2 | Lowey, Brotherston, Thompson |
| | 4 | 25.01.86 | **Everton** (D1) | A | L | 1-3 | Van den Hauwe og |
| 1986-87 (D2) | 3 | 10.01.87 | **Portsmouth** (D2) | A | L | 0-2 | |
| 1987-88 (D2) | 3 | 09.01.88 | **Portsmouth** (D1) | H | L | 1-2 | Garner |
| 1988-89 (D2) | 3 | 07.01.89 | **Welling Utd** (Conf) | A | W | 1-0 | Hildersley |
| | 4 | 28.01.89 | **Sheffield Wed** (D1) | H | W | 2-1 | Garner, Finnigan |
| | 5 | 18.02.89 | **Brentford** (D3) | H | L | 0-2 | |
| 1989-90 (D2) | 3 | 06.01.90 | **Aston Villa** (D1) | H | D | 2-2 | Stapleton, Sellars |
| | 3r | 10.01.90 | **Aston Villa** | A | L | 1-3 | Kennedy |
| 1990-91 (D2) | 3 | 05.01.91 | **Liverpool** (D1) | H | D | 1-1 | Garner |
| | 3r | 08.01.91 | **Liverpool** | A | L | 0-3 | |
| 1991-92 (D2) | 3 | 04.01.92 | **Kettering Town** (Conf) | H | W | 4-1 | Speedie, Newell 2, Cowans |
| | 4 | 04.02.92 | **Notts County** (D1) | A | L | 1-2 | Newell |
| 1992-93 (PL) | 3 | 02.01.93 | **Bournemouth** (D2) | H | W | 3-1 | Ripley 2, Newell |
| | 4 | 23.01.93 | **Crewe Alexandra** (D3) | A | W | 3-0 | Wegerle, Newell, Moran |
| | 5 | 13.02.93 | **Newcastle Utd** (D1) | H | W | 1-0 | Wegerle |
| | 6 | 06.03.93 | **Sheffield Utd** (PL) | H | D | 0-0 | |
| | 6r | 16.03.93 | **Sheffield Utd** | A | D | 2-2aet | Livingstone, Newell |
| | | | *Sheffield Utd won 5-3 on penalties* | | | | |
| 1993-94 (PL) | 3 | 08.01.94 | **Portsmouth** (D1) | H | D | 3-3 | Shearer, Gallacher, Sherwood |
| | 3r | 19.01.94 | **Portsmouth** | A | W | 3-1 | Shearer, May, Wilcox |
| | 4 | 29.01.94 | **Charlton Athletic** (D1) | A | D | 0-0 | |
| | 4r | 08.02.94 | **Charlton Athletic** | H | L | 0-1 | |
| 1994-95 (PL) | 3 | 08.01.95 | **Newcastle Utd** (PL) | A | D | 1-1 | Sutton |
| | 3r | 18.01.95 | **Newcastle Utd** | H | L | 1-2 | Sutton |

| | | | | | | | | |
|---|---|---|---|---|---|---|---|---|
| 1995-96 | (PL) | 3 | 06.01.96 | **Ipswich Town** (D1) | A | D | 0-0 | |
| | | 3r | 16.01.96 | **Ipswich Town** | H | L | 0-1aet | |
| 1996-97 | (PL) | 3 | 04.01.97 | **Port Vale** (D1) | H | W | 1-0 | Bohinen |
| | | 4 | 15.02.97 | **Coventry City** (PL) | H | L | 1-2 | Sherwood |
| 1997-98 | (PL) | 3 | 03.01.98 | **Wigan Athletic** (D2) | H | W | 4-2 | McGibbon, Gallacher 2, Sherwood |
| | | 4 | 26.01.98 | **Sheffield Wed** (PL) | A | W | 3-0 | Sutton, Sherwood, Duff |
| | | 5 | 14.02.98 | **West Ham Utd** (PL) | A | D | 2-2 | Gallacher, Sutton |
| | | 5r | 25.02.98 | **West Ham Utd** | H | D | 1-1aet | Ripley |
| | | | | *West Ham won 5-4 on penalties* | | | | |
| 1998-99 | (PL) | 3 | 02.01.99 | **Charlton Athletic** (PL) | H | W | 2-0 | Davies, Wilcox |
| | | 4 | 23.01.99 | **Sunderland** (D1) | H | W | 1-0 | Gillespie |
| | | 5 | 14.02.99 | **Newcastle Utd** (PL) | A | D | 0-0 | |
| | | 5r | 24.02.99 | **Newcastle Utd** | H | L | 0-1 | |
| 1999-00 | (D1) | 3 | 11.12.99 | **WBA** (D1) | A | D | 2-2 | Frandsen, Blake |
| | | 3r | 22.12.99 | **WBA** | H | W | 2-0aet | Duff, Carsley (p) |
| | | 4 | 10.01.00 | **Liverpool** (PL) | A | W | 1-0 | Blake |
| | | 5 | 31.01.00 | **Newcastle Utd** (PL) | H | L | 1-2 | Jansen |
| 2000-01 | (D1) | 3 | 06.01.01 | **Chester City** (Conf) | H | W | 2-0 | Taylor, Bent |
| | | 4 | 27.01.01 | **Derby County** (PL) | H | D | 0-0 | |
| | | 4r | 07.02.01 | **Derby County** | A | W | 5-2 | Flitcroft, Bent 2, Dunn (p), Jansen |
| | | 5 | 17.02.01 | **Bolton Wanderers** (D1) | A | D | 1-1 | Dunn |
| | | 5r | 07.03.01 | **Bolton Wanderers** | H | W | 3-0 | Flitcroft, Hignett 2 |
| | | 6 | 10.03.01 | **Arsenal** (PL) | A | L | 0-3 | |
| 2001-02 | (PL) | 3 | 05.01.02 | **Barnsley** (D1) | A | D | 1-1 | Hignett |
| | | 3r | 16.01.02 | **Barnsley** | H | W | 3-1 | Grabbi, Dunn (p), Johansson |
| | | 4 | 26.01.02 | **Millwall** (D1) | A | W | 1-0 | Cole |
| | | 5 | 16.02.02 | **Middlesbrough** (PL) | A | L | 0-1 | |
| 2002-03 | (PL) | 3 | 04.01.03 | **Aston Villa** (PL) | A | W | 4-1 | Jansen 2, Yorke 2 |
| | | 4 | 25.01.03 | **Sunderland** (PL) | H | D | 3-3 | Cole 2, Yorke |
| | | 4r | 05.02.03 | **Sunderland** | A | D | 2-2aet | Flitcroft 2 |
| | | | | *Sunderland won 3-0 on penalties* | | | | |

## BLACKHALL COLLIERY

*Competed in the FA Cup from 1931-1958*

| | | | | | | | | |
|---|---|---|---|---|---|---|---|---|
| 1951-52 | (NEL) | 1 | 24.11.51 | **Workington** (3N) | H | L | 2-5 | Ford, Mason |

## BLACKPOOL

*Formed 1887. Merged with South Shore on December 12, 1899. FA Cup winners: 1953. Runners-up: 1948, 1951. Record FA Cup win: 8-1 v Oswaldtwistle Rovers, 2nd qualifying round, 1892; In Competition Proper: 5-0 v Colchester Utd, 5th round, 07.02.1948. Record FA Cup defeat: 0-6 v Barnsley, 1st round replay, 20.01.1910*

| | | | | | | | | |
|---|---|---|---|---|---|---|---|---|
| 1891-92 | (LL) | | | 1q Higher Walton (A) 5-4; 2q Fleetwood R (H) 4-2; 3q Bury (A) 3-3; 3qr Bury (H) 4-3; 4q Newton Heath (A) 4-3 | | | | |
| | | 1 | 16.01.92 | **Sheffield Utd** (NL) | H | L | 0-3 | |
| 1892-93 | (LL) | | | 1q Heywood Central (A) 4-3; 2q Oswaldtwistle R (H) 8-1; 3q Fleetwood R (A) 3-1; 4q Rossendale (H) 2-1 | | | | |
| | | 1 | 21.01.93 | **Sheffield Utd** (D2) | H | L | 1-3 | E Parkinson |
| 1893-94 | (LL) | | | 1q South Shore (A) 1-2 | | | | |
| 1894-95 | (LL) | | | 1q Chorley (H) 3-2; 2q Rossendale (A) 1-2 | | | | |
| 1895-96 | (LL) | | | 2q Bacup (A) 2-1; 3q South Shore (A) 2-1; 4q Rossendale (A) 4-2 | | | | |
| | | 1 | 01.02.96 | **Burton Swifts** (D2) | H | W | 4-1 | Martin, Stirzaker, Wallace, Wilson |
| | | 2 | 15.02.96 | **Bolton Wanderers** (D1) | H | L | 0-2 | |
| 1896-97 | (D2) | | | 3q Darwen (A) 0-1abnd; 3qr Darwen (A) 2-1; 4q Chorley (A) 1-0; 5q Newton Heath (A) 2-2; 5qr Newton Heath (H) 1-2 | | | | |
| 1897-98 | (D2) | | | 3q Darwen (A) 2-3 | | | | |
| 1898-99 | (D2) | | | 1q Southport Central (A) 2-2; 1qr Southport Central (H) 1-2 | | | | |
| 1899-00 | (LL) | | | 3q Southport Central (A) 0-2 | | | | |
| 1900-01 | (D2) | | | 3q Blackburn Park Road (A) 1-0; 4q Darwen (A) 1-2 | | | | |
| 1901-02 | (D2) | | | 3q Southport Central (A) 0-0; 3qr Southport Central (H) 0-0; 3q 2r Southport Central 1-2 at Preston | | | | |
| 1902-03 | (D2) | | | 1q Black Lane Temperance (H) 4-1; 2q Rochdale (H) 0-1 | | | | |
| 1903-04 | (D2) | | | 3q Workington (A) 4-2; 4q Southport Central (A) 0-3 | | | | |

*Today the double is almost commonplace but after Aston Villa won the FA Cup and League in 1897, no other club matched their achievement until Tottenham Hotspur in 1961. The first double of the 20th century was completed after Spurs beat Leicester City 2-0 to leave (l to r) Ron Henry, Bill Brown, Peter Baker, skipper Danny Blanchflower, Cliff Jones, Maurice Norman (partly obscured), Terry Dyson and Bobby Smith running around Wembley with the cup. Action Images)*

*The greatest cup final goal ever scored? Ricky Villa completes his mazy, devastating run through the Manchester City defence to send the ball past goalkeeper Joe Corrigan and into the net for Spurs' winner in the replayed 1981 centenary final at Wembley. Spurs' No. 8 Steve Archibald and City's No.5 Paul Power are among those who can only look on in awe as Villa clinches the 3-2 victory. (Action Images)*

*(Top) Leeds United made up for finishing second in the First Division in 1972 by recording their only FA Cup victory. (Empics) Leeds were back a year later (below) as odds-on favourites to retain the trophy against Second Division Sunderland and would probably have done so but for an astonishing double save from goalkeeper Jim Montgomery. He saved a header from Trevor Cherry and then pushed Peter Lorimer's shot onto the bar to be instrumental in Sunderland pulling off one of the great shocks of the competition when they beat Leeds 1-0. (Action Images)*

*Manchester United's Kevin Moran protests his innocence to referee Peter Willis after tripping Peter Reid of Everton in the 1985 cup final. Willis, though, had seen enough and showed Moran the first – and so far only – red card in an FA Cup final. (Action Images)*

*In 1997 Middlesbrough ended a 114-year wait to reach the cup final – and when they finally did so they found themselves a goal down within 42 seconds. Chelsea's Italian star Roberto Di Matteo cracked an unstoppable shot past 'Boro goalkeeper Ben Roberts for the fastest cup final goal scored under Wembley's Twin Towers. Chelsea never looked back and eventually won 2-0. (Action Images)*

*Matteo enjoyed playing at Wembley. As well as his rapid-fire goal in the 1997 cup final, he also scored for Chelsea against Middlesbrough in the 1998 League cup final and in 2000 scored the last-ever goal at the old stadium to give Chelsea a 1-0 win over Aston Villa. (Reuters)*

*Make mine a Double. An enigmatic Eric Cantona considers his achievement after his goals in the title run-in and his stunning late winner against Liverpool in the 1996 FA Cup final give Manchester United their second double in three seasons. (Action Images)*

*(Above) Michael Owen (right) gets a bird's eye view as his shot sneaks past David Seaman's despairing dive to give Liverpool a 2-1 victory over Arsenal in the first Millennium Stadium FA Cup final in 2001. (Action Images) (Below) Owen celebrates with (from left to right) Emile Heskey, Steven Gerrard and Robbie Fowler. (Reuters)*

*Robert Pires, scorer of Arsenal's goal in their 1-0 victory over Southampton in 2003 , prepares to take a corner in the first FA Cup final played 'indoors.' The Millennium Stadium roof was closed. (courtesy Reuters)*

*(Top) The old Wembley Twin Towers go under the wrecking ball in 2003. (Above) A model of the new Wembley, due to stage the FA Cup final in 2006. (courtesy Reuters)*

| | | | | | | | | |
|---|---|---|---|---|---|---|---|---|
| 1904-05 | (D2) | | | 3q Accrington Stanley (A) 4-1; 4q Southport Central (H) 3-0; 5q Nelson (H) 1-0; 6q Stafford R (H) 2-2; 6qr Stafford R (A) 3-0; Int Bristol C (A) 1-2 | | | | |
| 1905-06 | (D2) | 1 | 13.01.06 | **Crystal Palace** (SL) | H | D | 1-1 | Hancock |
| | | 1r | 17.01.06 | **Crystal Palace** | A | D | 1-1aet | Threlfall |
| | | 1 2r | 22.01.06 | **Crystal Palace** | | W | 1-0 | Francis |
| | | | | *played at Villa Park* | | | | |
| | | 2 | 03.02.06 | **Sheffield Utd** (D1) | A | W | 2-1 | Hancock 2 |
| | | 3 | 24.02.06 | **Newcastle Utd** (D1) | A | L | 0-5 | |
| 1906-07 | (D2) | 1 | 12.01.07 | **West Ham Utd** (SL) | A | L | 1-2 | Grundy |
| 1907-08 | (D2) | 1 | 11.01.08 | **Manchester Utd** (D1) | A | L | 1-3 | Grundy |
| 1908-09 | (D2) | 1 | 16.01.09 | **Hastings & St L** (SL) | H | W | 2-0 | Threlfall, Whalley |
| | | 2 | 06.02.09 | **Newcastle Utd** (D1) | A | L | 1-2 | Weston |
| 1909-10 | (D2) | 1 | 15.01.10 | **Barnsley** (D2) | H | D | 1-1 | Wolstenholme |
| | | 1r | 20.01.10 | **Barnsley** | A | L | 0-6 | |
| 1910-11 | (D2) | 1 | 14.01.11 | **Manchester Utd** (D1) | A | L | 1-2 | Clennell |
| 1911-12 | (D2) | 1 | 13.01.12 | **Crewe Alexandra (CL)** | A | D | 1-1 | Milne |
| | | 1r | 17.01.12 | **Crewe Alexandra** | H | - | 2-1ab | Cahill, Wolstenholme |
| | | | | *abandoned after 61 minutes – blizzard* | | | | |
| | | 1r | 22.01.12 | **Crewe Alexandra** | H | D | 2-2aet | Wolstenholme, Quinn |
| | | 1 2r | 25.01.12 | **Crewe Alexandra** | | W | 2-1 | Cowie, Bainbridge |
| | | | | *played at Maine Road* | | | | |
| | | 2 | 03.02.12 | **Bolton Wanderers** (D1) | A | L | 0-1 | |
| 1912-13 | (D2) | 1 | 11.01.13 | **Tottenham Hotspur** (D1) | A | D | 1-1 | Charles |
| | | 1r | 16.01.13 | **Tottenham Hotspur** | H | L | 1-6 | Charles |
| 1913-14 | (D2) | 1 | 10.01.14 | **Gillingham** (SL) | A | L | 0-1 | |
| 1914-15 | (D2) | 1 | 09.01.15 | **Sheffield Utd** (D1) | H | L | 1-2 | Sibbald |
| 1919-20 | (D2) | 1 | 10.01.20 | **Derby County** (D1) | H | D | 0-0 | |
| | | 1r | 14.01.20 | **Derby County** | A | W | 4-1 | Charles, Sibbald, Lane 2 |
| | | 2 | 31.01.20 | **Preston North End** (D1) | A | L | 1-2 | Quinn |
| 1920-21 | (D2) | 1 | 08.01.21 | **Darlington** (NEL) | A | D | 2-2 | Barrass, Ratcliffe |
| | | 1r | 12.01.21 | **Darlington** | H | W | 2-1 | McGinn, Ratcliffe |
| | | 2 | 29.01.21 | **Southend Utd** (D3) | A | L | 0-1 | |
| 1921-22 | (D2) | 1 | 07.01.22 | **Watford** (3S) | H | L | 1-2 | Bedford |
| 1922-23 | (D2) | 1 | 13.01.23 | **Derby County** (D2) | A | L | 0-2 | |
| 1923-24 | (D2) | 1 | 12.01.24 | **Sheffield Utd** (D1) | H | W | 1-0 | White |
| | | 2 | 02.02.24 | **Southampton** (D2) | A | L | 1-4 | Bedford |
| 1924-25 | (D2) | 1 | 10.01.25 | **Barrow** (3N) | H | D | 0-0 | |
| | | 1r | 14.01.25 | **Barrow** | A | W | 2-0 | Streets, Bedford |
| | | 2 | 31.01.25 | **Bradford Park A** (3N) | A | D | 1-1 | Meredith |
| | | 2r | 04.02.25 | **Bradford Park A** | H | W | 2-1 | Streets, Meredith |
| | | 3 | 21.02.25 | **West Ham Utd** (D1) | A | D | 1-1 | Bedford |
| | | 3r | 25.02.25 | **West Ham Utd** | H | W | 3-0 | Bedford 2, Meredith |
| | | 4 | 07.03.25 | **Blackburn Rovers** (D1) | A | L | 0-1 | |
| 1925-26 | (D2) | 3 | 09.01.26 | **Swansea Town** (D2) | H | L | 0-2 | |
| 1926-27 | (D2) | 3 | 08.01.27 | **Bolton Wanderers** (D1) | H | L | 1-3 | Tremelling |
| 1927-28 | (D2) | 3 | 14.01.28 | **Oldham Athletic** (D2) | H | L | 1-4 | Neal |
| 1928-29 | (D2) | 3 | 12.01.29 | **Plymouth Argyle** (3S) | A | L | 0-3 | |
| 1929-30 | (D2) | 3 | 11.01.30 | **Stockport County** (3N) | H | W | 2-1 | Browell 2 |
| | | 4 | 25.01.30 | **Hull City** (D2) | A | L | 1-3 | Hampson |
| 1930-31 | (D1) | 3 | 10.01.31 | **Hull City** | A | W | 2-1 | Hampson, Upton |
| | | 4 | 26.01.31 | **Southport** (3N) | A | L | 1-2 | Downes |
| 1931-32 | (D1) | 3 | 09.01.32 | **Newcastle Utd** (D1) | H | D | 1-1 | Hampson |
| | | 3r | 13.01.32 | **Newcastle Utd** | A | L | 0-1 | |
| 1932-33 | (D1) | 3 | 14.01.33 | **Port Vale** (D2) | H | W | 2-1 | McClelland, Hampson |
| | | 4 | 28.01.33 | **Huddersfield Town** (D1) | H | W | 2-0 | McClelland, Douglas |
| | | 5 | 18.02.33 | **Sunderland** (D1) | A | L | 0-1 | |
| 1933-34 | (D2) | 3 | 13.01.34 | **Cheltenham Town** (BC) | A | W | 3-1 | Bussey, Watson, Doherty |
| | | 4 | 27.01.34 | **Stoke City** (D1) | A | L | 0-3 | |
| 1934-35 | (D2) | 3 | 12.01.35 | **Leicester City** (D1) | A | L | 1-2 | Hall |
| 1935-36 | (D2) | 3 | 11.01.36 | **Margate** (SL) | H | W | 3-1 | Finan, Watmough, W Jones |
| | | 4 | 25.01.36 | **Fulham** (D2) | A | L | 2-5 | Finan 2 |
| 1936-37 | (D2) | 3 | 16.01.37 | **Luton Town** (3S) | A | D | 3-3 | Finan, Middleton, Watmough |

| | | | | | | | | |
|---|---|---|---|---|---|---|---|---|
| | | 3r | 20.01.37 | **Luton Town** | H | L | 1-2 | Finan |
| 1937-38 | (D1) | 3 | 08.01.38 | **Birmingham** (D1) | A | W | 1-0 | Jones |
| | | 4 | 22.01.38 | **Aston Villa** (D2) | A | L | 0-4 | |
| 1938-39 | (D1) | 3 | 07.01.39 | **Sheffield Utd** (D2) | H | L | 1-2 | Lewis |
| 1945-46 | (D1) | 3 1L | 05.01.46 | **Wrexham** (3N) | A | W | 4-1 | Buchan, Mortensen, Blair, Dodds |
| | | 3 2L | 09.01.46 | **Wrexham** | H | W | 4-1 | Dodds 3, O'Donnell |
| | | 4 1L | 26.01.46 | **Middlesbrough** (D1) | H | W | 3-2 | Mortensen 2, Dodds |
| | | 4 2L | 30.01.46 | **Middlesbrough** | A | L | 2-3 | H O'Donnell, Mortensen |
| | | 4r | 04.02.46 | **Middlesbrough** | | L | 0-1aet | |
| | | | | *played at Elland Road* | | | | |
| 1946-47 | (D1) | 3 | 11.01.47 | **Sheffield Wed** (D2) | A | L | 1-4 | Mortensen |
| 1947-48 | (D1) | 3 | 10.01.48 | **Leeds Utd** (D2) | H | W | 4-0 | Dick, McIntosh 2, Mortensen |
| | | 4 | 24.01.48 | **Chester** (3N) | H | W | 4-0 | Shimwell, Mortensen 2, Johnston |
| | | 5 | 07.02.48 | **Colchester Utd** (SL) | H | W | 5-0 | Munro, McIntosh 2, Mortensen 2 |
| | | 6 | 28.02.48 | **Fulham** (D2) | A | W | 2-0 | Mortensen, McIntosh |
| | | SF | 13.03.48 | **Tottenham Hotspur** (D2) | | W | 3-1aet | Mortensen 3 |
| | | | | *played at Villa Park* | | | | |
| | | F | 24.04.48 | **Manchester Utd** (D1) | | L | 2-4 | Shimwell (p), Mortensen |
| | | | | *played at Wembley Stadium* | | | | |
| 1948-49 | (D1) | 3 | 08.01.49 | **Barnsley** (D2) | A | W | 1-0 | Mortensen |
| | | 4 | 29.01.49 | **Stoke City** (D1) | A | D | 1-1aet | Mortensen |
| | | 4r | 05.02.49 | **Stoke City** | H | L | 0-1 | |
| 1949-50 | (D1) | 3 | 07.01.50 | **Southend Utd** (3S) | H | W | 4-0 | Slater 3, Mortensen |
| | | 4 | 28.01.50 | **Doncaster Rovers** (3N) | H | W | 2-1 | McIntosh, McKnight |
| | | 5 | 11.02.50 | **Wolverhampton W** (D1) | A | D | 0-0 | |
| | | 5r | 15.02.50 | **Wolverhampton W** | H | W | 1-0 | Mortensen |
| | | 6 | 04.03.50 | **Liverpool** (D1) | A | L | 1-2 | Mortensen |
| 1950-51 | (D1) | 3 | 06.01.51 | **Charlton Athletic** (D1) | A | D | 2-2 | Perry, Mortensen |
| | | 3r | 10.01.51 | **Charlton Athletic** | H | W | 3-0 | Mortensen 2, Mudie |
| | | 4 | 27.01.51 | **Stockport County** (3N) | H | W | 2-1 | Mortensen, Mudie |
| | | 5 | 10.02.51 | **Mansfield Town** (3N) | H | W | 2-0 | Mudie, Brown |
| | | 6 | 24.02.51 | **Fulham** (D1) | H | W | 1-0 | Brown (p) |
| | | SF | 10.03.51 | **Birmingham City** (D2) | | D | 0-0 | |
| | | | | *played at Maine Road* | | | | |
| | | SFr | 14.03.51 | **Birmingham City** | | W | 2-1 | Mortensen, Perry |
| | | | | *played at Goodison Park* | | | | |
| | | F | 28.04.51 | **Newcastle Utd** (D1) | | L | 0-2 | |
| | | | | *played at Wembley Stadium* | | | | |
| 1951-52 | (D1) | 3 | 12.01.52 | **West Ham Utd** (D2) | A | L | 1-2 | Johnston |
| 1952-53 | (D1) | 3 | 10.01.53 | **Sheffield Wed** (D1) | A | W | 2-1 | Matthews, Taylor |
| | | 4 | 31.01.53 | **Huddersfield Town** (D2) | H | W | 1-0 | Garrett |
| | | 5 | 14.02.53 | **Southampton** (D2) | H | D | 1-1 | Perry |
| | | 5r | 18.02.53 | **Southampton** | A | W | 2-1 | Brown, Horton og |
| | | 6 | 28.02.53 | **Arsenal** (D1) | A | W | 2-1 | Taylor, Brown |
| | | SF | 21.03.53 | **Tottenham Hotspur** (D1) | | W | 2-1 | Perry, Mudie |
| | | | | *played at Villa Park* | | | | |
| | | F | 02.05.53 | **Bolton Wanderers** (D1) | | W | 4-3 | Mortensen 3, Perry |
| | | | | *played at Wembley Stadium* | | | | |
| 1953-54 | (D1) | 3 | 09.01.54 | **Luton Town** (D2) | H | D | 1-1 | Mortensen |
| | | 3r | 13.01.54 | **Luton Town** | A | D | 0-0aet | |
| | | 3 2r | 18.01.54 | **Luton Town** | | D | 1-1aet | Johnston |
| | | | | *played at Villa Park* | | | | |
| | | 3 3r | 25.01.54 | **Luton Town** | | W | 2-0 | Perry, Stephenson |
| | | | | *played at Molineux* | | | | |
| | | 4 | 30.01.54 | **West Ham Utd** (D2) | A | D | 1-1 | Brown |
| | | 4r | 03.02.54 | **West Ham Utd** | H | W | 3-1 | Perry 2, Brown |
| | | 5 | 20.02.54 | **Port Vale** (D3) | A | L | 0-2 | |
| 1954-55 | (D1) | 3 | 08.01.55 | **York City** (3N) | H | L | 0-2 | |
| 1955-56 | (D1) | 3 | 07.01.56 | **Manchester City** (D1) | A | - | 1-1ab | Taylor |
| | | | | *abandoned after 56 minutes – fog* | | | | |

| | | | | | | | | |
|---|---|---|---|---|---|---|---|---|
| | | 3 | 11.01.56 | **Manchester City** | A | L | 1-2 | Perry |
| 1956-57 | (D1) | 3 | 05.01.57 | **Bolton Wanderers** (D1) | A | W | 3-2 | Mudie 2, Durie |
| | | 4 | 26.01.57 | **Fulham** (D2) | H | W | 6-2 | Mudie 4, Lampe og, Durie |
| | | 5 | 16.02.57 | **WBA** (D1) | H | D | 0-0 | |
| | | 5r | 20.02.57 | **WBA** | A | L | 1-2 | Perry |
| 1957-58 | (D1) | 3 | 04.01.58 | **West Ham Utd** (D2) | A | L | 1-5 | H Kelly (p) |
| 1958-59 | (D1) | 3 | 10.01.59 | **Southampton** (D2) | A | W | 2-1 | Charnley 2 |
| | | 4 | 24.01.59 | **Bristol City** (D2) | A | D | 1-1 | Charnley |
| | | 4r | 28.01.59 | **Bristol City** | H | W | 1-0 | Durie |
| | | 5 | 14.02.59 | **WBA** (D1) | H | W | 3-1 | Charnley 2, Durie |
| | | 6 | 28.02.59 | **Luton Town** (D1) | H | D | 1-1 | Charnley |
| | | 6r | 04.03.59 | **Luton Town** | A | L | 0-1 | |
| 1959-60 | (D1) | 3 | 09.01.60 | **Mansfield Town** (D3) | H | W | 3-0 | Durie 3 |
| | | 4 | 30.01.60 | **Blackburn Rovers** (D1) | A | D | 1-1 | Kaye |
| | | 4r | 03.02.60 | **Blackburn Rovers** | H | L | 0-3 | |
| 1960-61 | (D1) | 3 | 07.01.61 | **Scunthorpe Utd** (D2) | A | L | 2-6 | Mudie, Charnley |
| 1961-62 | (D1) | 3 | 06.01.62 | **WBA** (D1) | H | D | 0-0 | |
| | | 3r | 10.01.62 | **WBA** | A | L | 1-2 | Hauser |
| 1962-63 | (D1) | 3 | 04.03.63 | **Norwich City** (D2) | A | D | 1-1 | McPhee |
| | | 3r | 06.03.63 | **Norwich City** | H | L | 1-3aet | Quinn |
| 1963-64 | (D1) | 3 | 04.01.64 | **WBA** (D1) | A | D | 2-2 | Charnley, Jones og |
| | | 3r | 08.01.64 | **WBA** | H | L | 0-1 | |
| 1964-65 | (D1) | 3 | 11.01.65 | **Stoke City** (D1) | A | L | 1-4 | Ball |
| 1965-66 | (D1) | 3 | 22.01.66 | **Manchester City** (D2) | H | D | 1-1 | James |
| | | 3r | 24.01.66 | **Manchester City** | A | L | 1-3 | Charnley |
| 1966-67 | (D1) | 3 | 28.01.67 | **Birmingham City** (D2) | A | L | 1-2 | Vowden, Thomson |
| 1967-68 | (D2) | 3 | 27.01.68 | **Chesterfield** (D4) | H | W | 2-1 | Neale og, Green |
| | | 4 | 17.02.68 | **Sheffield Utd** (D1) | A | L | 1-2 | Skirton |
| 1968-69 | (D2) | 3 | 04.01.69 | **Coventry City** (D1) | A | L | 1-3 | Brown |
| 1969-70 | (D2) | 3 | 03.01.70 | **Arsenal** (D1) | A | D | 1-1 | Hutchison |
| | | 3r | 15.01.70 | **Arsenal** | H | W | 3-2 | Suddick, Pickering, Burns |
| | | 4 | 24.01.70 | **Mansfield Town** (D3) | H | L | 0-2 | |
| 1970-71 | (D1) | 3 | 02.01.71 | **West Ham Utd** (D1) | H | W | 4-0 | Green 2, Craven, Mowbray |
| | | 4 | 23.01.71 | **Hull City** (D2) | A | L | 0-2 | |
| 1971-72 | (D2) | 3 | 15.01.72 | **Chelsea** (D1) | H | L | 0-1 | |
| 1972-73 | (D2) | 3 | 13.01.73 | **Bradford City** (D4) | A | L | 1-2 | Suddick (p) |
| 1973-74 | (D2) | 3 | 05.01.74 | **Southampton** (D1) | A | L | 1-2 | Dyson |
| 1974-75 | (D2) | 3 | 04.01.75 | **Plymouth Argyle** (D3) | A | L | 0-2 | |
| 1975-76 | (D2) | 3 | 03.01.76 | **Burnley** (D1) | H | W | 1-0 | Bentley |
| | | 4 | 24.01.76 | **Southampton** (D2) | A | L | 1-3 | Alcock |
| 1976-77 | (D2) | 3 | 08.01.77 | **Derby County** (D1) | H | D | 0-0 | |
| | | 3r | 19.01.77 | **Derby County** | A | L | 2-3 | Walsh, Spence |
| 1977-78 | (D2) | 3 | 07.01.78 | **WBA** (D1) | A | L | 1-4 | Hatton |
| 1978-79 | (D3) | 1 | 25.11.78 | **Lincoln City** (D3) | H | W | 2-1 | McEwan (p), Chandler |
| | | 2 | 16.12.78 | **Bury** (D3) | A | L | 1-3 | Kellow |
| 1979-80 | (D3) | 1 | 24.11.79 | **Wigan Athletic** (D4) | H | D | 1-1 | McEwan |
| | | 1r | 28.11.79 | **Wigan Athletic** | A | L | 0-2 | |
| 1980-81 | (D3) | 1 | 22.11.80 | **Fleetwood Town** (CC) | H | W | 4-0 | Entwistle, Morris, Hockaday |
| | | 2 | 13.12.80 | **Doncaster Rovers** (D4) | A | L | 1-2 | Williams |
| 1981-82 | (D4) | 1 | 21.11.81 | **Horden CW** (NL) | A | W | 1-0 | Harrison |
| | | | | *played at Victoria Ground, Hartlepool* | | | | |
| | | 2 | 02.01.82 | **Kettering Town** (APL) | A | W | 3-0 | Harrison, Wann, Morris |
| | | 3 | 05.01.82 | **Barnsley** (D2) | A | W | 2-0 | Bamber, Morris |
| | | 4 | 23.01.82 | **QPR** (D2) | H | D | 0-0 | |
| | | 4r | 26.01.82 | **QPR** | A | L | 1-5 | Entwistle |
| 1982-83 | (D4) | 1 | 20.11.82 | **Horwich RMI** (NWC) | H | W | 3-0 | Pashley, Bamber, Deary (p) |
| | | 2 | 11.12.82 | **Preston North End** (D3) | A | L | 1-2 | Brockbank |
| 1983-84 | (D4) | 1 | 19.11.83 | **Gainsborough T** (NPL) | A | W | 2-0 | Mercer, McNiven |
| | | 2 | 10.12.83 | **Bangor City** (APL) | A | D | 1-1 | Mercer |
| | | 2r | 13.12.83 | **Bangor City** | H | W | 2-1 | Stewart, Deary |
| | | 3 | 07.01.84 | **Manchester City** (D2) | H | W | 2-1 | McNiven, McNab og |

| | | | | | | | | |
|---|---|---|---|---|---|---|---|---|
| | | 4 | 28.01.84 | **Oxford Utd** (D3) | A | L | 1-2 | Mercer |
| 1984-85 | (D4) | 1 | 17.11.84 | **Altrincham** (APL) | H | L | 0-1 | |
| 1985-86 | (D3) | 1 | 16.11.85 | **Lincoln City** (D3) | A | W | 1-0 | West og |
| | | 2 | 07.12.85 | **Altrincham** (APL) | H | L | 1-2 | Stewart |
| 1986-87 | (D3) | 1 | 15.11.86 | **Middlesbrough** (D3) | A | L | 0-3 | |
| 1987-88 | (D3) | 1 | 14.11.87 | **Bishop Auckland** (NL) | A | W | 4-1 | Morgan, Madden (p), Taylor 2 |
| | | 2 | 06.12.87 | **Northwich V** (Conf) | A | W | 2-0 | Madden, Walwyn |
| | | 3 | 09.01.88 | **Scunthorpe Utd** (D4) | A | D | 0-0 | |
| | | 3r | 12.01.88 | **Scunthorpe Utd** | H | W | 1-0 | Madden |
| | | 4 | 30.01.88 | **Manchester City** (D2) | H | D | 1-1 | Sendall |
| | | 4r | 03.02.88 | **Manchester City** | A | L | 1-2 | Deary |
| 1988-89 | (D3) | 1 | 19.11.88 | **Scunthorpe Utd** (D4) | H | W | 2-1 | Cunningham, Garner |
| | | 2 | 10.12.88 | **Bury** (D3) | H | W | 3-0 | Cunningham, Garner, Deary |
| | | 3 | 07.01.89 | **Bournemouth** (D2) | H | L | 0-1 | |
| 1989-90 | (D3) | 1 | 18.11.89 | **Bolton Wanderers** (D3) | H | W | 2-1 | Eyres, Garner |
| | | 2 | 09.12.89 | **Chester City** (D3) | H | W | 3-0 | Brook, Burgess, Owen |
| | | 3 | 06.01.90 | **Burnley** (D4) | H | W | 1-0 | Methven |
| | | 4 | 27.01.90 | **Torquay Utd** (D4) | H | W | 1-0 | Owen |
| | | 5 | 18.02.90 | **QPR** (D1) | H | D | 2-2 | Groves, Eyres |
| | | 5r | 21.02.90 | **QPR** | A | D | 0-0aet | |
| | | 5 2r | 26.02.90 | **QPR** | A | L | 0-3 | |
| 1990-91 | (D4) | 1 | 17.11.90 | **Grimsby Town** (D3) | H | W | 2-0 | Groves, Garner |
| | | 2 | 10.12.90 | **Huddersfield Town** (D3) | A | W | 2-0 | Groves, Jackson og |
| | | 3 | 05.01.91 | **Tottenham Hotspur** (D1) | H | L | 0-1 | |
| 1991-92 | (D4) | 1 | 16.11.91 | **Grimsby Town** (D2) | H | W | 2-1 | Groves, Bamber |
| | | 2 | 07.12.91 | **Hull City** (D3) | H | L | 0-1 | |
| 1992-93 | (D2) | 1 | 14.11.92 | **Rochdale** (D3) | H | D | 1-1 | Mitchell |
| | | 1r | 25.11.92 | **Rochdale** | A | L | 0-1aet | |
| 1993-94 | (D2) | 1 | 13.11.93 | **Port Vale** (D2) | A | L | 0-2 | |
| 1994-95 | (D2) | 1 | 14.11.94 | **Preston North End** (D3) | H | L | 0-1 | |
| 1995-96 | (D2) | 1 | 11.11.95 | **Chester City** (D3) | H | W | 2-1 | Quinn, Lydiate |
| | | 2 | 02.12.95 | **Colwyn Bay** (NPL) | H | W | 2-0 | Preece, Quinn |
| | | 3 | 06.01.96 | **Huddersfield Town** (D1) | A | L | 1-2 | Quinn |
| 1996-97 | (D2) | 1 | 16.11.96 | **Wigan Athletic** (D3) | H | W | 1-0 | Quinn (p) |
| | | 2 | 07.12.96 | **Hednesford Town** (Conf) | H | L | 0-1 | |
| 1997-98 | (D2) | 1 | 15.11.97 | **Blyth Spartans** (NPL) | H | W | 4-3 | Clarkson 2, Preece, Linighan |
| | | 2 | 06.12.97 | **Oldham Athletic** (D2) | A | L | 1-2 | Ellis |
| 1998-99 | (D2) | 1 | 14.11.98 | **Wigan Athletic** (D2) | A | L | 3-4 | Blint, Ormerod, Aldridge |
| 1999-00 | (D2) | 1 | 30.10.99 | **Stoke City** (D2) | H | W | 2-0 | Carlisle, Nowland |
| | | 2 | 20.11.99 | **Hendon** (IL) | H | W | 2-0 | Clarkson, Durnin |
| | | 3 | 13.12.99 | **Arsenal** (PL) | A | L | 1-3 | Clarkson |
| 2000-01 | (D2) | 1 | 18.11.00 | **Telford Utd** (Conf) | H | W | 3-1 | J Murphy, Ormerod |
| | | 2 | 10.12.00 | **Yeovil Town** (Conf) | H | L | 0-1 | |
| 2001-02 | (D2) | 1 | 17.11.01 | **Newport County** (SL) | H | D | 2-2 | Jaszczun, Mackenzie (p) |
| | | 1r | 28.11.01 | **Newport County** | A | W | 4-1aet | Ormerod 2, J Murphy, Benton og |
| | | 2 | 08.12.01 | **Rochdale** (D3) | H | W | 2-0 | J Murphy, Simpson |
| | | 3 | 05.01.02 | **Charlton Athletic** (PL) | A | L | 1-2 | Hills |
| 2002-03 | (D2) | 1 | 16.11.02 | **Barnsley** (D2) | A | W | 4-1 | Hills, J Murphy, Dalglish, Taylor |
| | | 2 | 07.12.02 | **Torquay Utd** (D3) | H | W | 3-1 | Hazell og, Taylor, J Murphy |
| | | 3 | 04.01.03 | **Crystal Palace** (D1) | H | L | 1-2 | Popovic og |

## BLACKPOOL ST JOHN'S

*Formed around 1877. A forerunner of Blackpool FC, played at Masheters Field.*

| | | | | | | | |
|---|---|---|---|---|---|---|---|
| 1882-83 | 1 | 23.10.82 | **Blackburn Rovers** | A | L | 1-11 | Whiteside |
| 1883-84 | 1 | 10.11.83 | **Accrington FC** | A | L | 0-4 | |

## BLUE STAR

*Formed 1930. Based in Newcastle. FA Vase winners: 1978. Now known as Newcastle Blue Star. Members of the Northern League.*

| | | | | | | | | |
|---|---|---|---|---|---|---|---|---|
| 1984-85 | (Wear) | 1 | 17.11.84 | **York City** (D3) | A | L | 0-2 | |

# BLYTH SPARTANS

*Formed 1899. First entered FA Cup: 1908-09. In 1979 became only the third Non-League club since World War Two to reach the Fifth Round, and the first to do so since Yeovil 29 years previously. League clubs beaten: Ashington, Bury, Chesterfield, Crewe Alexandra, Gillingham, Hartlepools United, Stockport County, Stoke City. Members of the Northern Premier League.*

| | | | | | | | | |
|---|---|---|---|---|---|---|---|---|
| 1922-23 | (NEL) | | | 5q Ashington (3N) (H) 2-1; 6q Gillingham (3S) (A) 4-1 | | | | |
| | | 1 | 13.01.23 | **Stoke** (D1) | H | L | 0-3 | |
| 1925-26 | (NEL) | 1 | 28.11.25 | **Hartlepools Utd** (3N) | H | D | 2-2 | Green, Park |
| | | 1r | 02.12.25 | **Hartlepools Utd** | A | D | 1-1aet | Fletcher |
| | | 1 2r | 07.12.25 | **Hartlepools Utd** | | D | 1-1aet | Bell |
| | | | | *played at St James' Park* | | | | |
| | | 1 3r | 09.12.25 | **Hartlepools Utd** | | W | 2-1 | Alf Fenwick 2 |
| | | | | *played at Roker Park* | | | | |
| | | 2 | 12.12.25 | **Accrington Stanley** (3N) | A | L | 0-5 | |
| 1931-32 | (NEL) | 1 | 28.11.31 | **Lancaster Town** (LC) | A | W | 3-0 | Bunch, Smith, Ellis |
| | | 2 | 12.12.31 | **Bournemouth** (3S) | A | L | 0-1 | |
| 1934-35 | (NEL) | 1 | 24.11.34 | **Stockport County** (3N) | H | D | 1-1 | Kennedy |
| | | 1r | 28.11.34 | **Stockport County** | A | L | 1-4 | Robinson |
| 1935-36 | (NEL) | 1 | 30.11.35 | **Gainsborough T** (ML) | A | L | 1-3 | Hickman |
| 1936-37 | (NEL) | 1 | 28.11.36 | **Wrexham** (3N) | H | L | 0-2 | |
| 1937-38 | (NEL) | 1 | 27.11.37 | **Doncaster Rovers** (3N) | A | L | 0-7 | |
| 1951-52 | (NEL) | 1 | 24.11.51 | **Bishop Auckland** (NL) | H | W | 2-1 | Herman, Turney |
| | | 2 | 15.12.51 | **Tranmere Rovers** (3N) | A | D | 1-1 | Penrose |
| | | 2r | 19.12.51 | **Tranmere Rovers** | H | - | 1-1ab | Scott |
| | | | | *abandoned after 115 minutes – bad light* | | | | |
| | | 2 2r | 03.01.52 | **Tranmere Rovers** | | D | 2-2aet | Fenwick, Scott |
| | | | | *played at Brunton Park, Carlisle* | | | | |
| | | 2 3r | 07.01.52 | **Tranmere Rovers** | | L | 1-5 | Turney |
| | | | | *played at Goodison Park* | | | | |
| 1953-54 | (NEL) | 1 | 21.11.53 | **Accrington Stanley** (3N) | H | L | 0-1 | |
| 1954-55 | (NEL) | 1 | 20.11.54 | **Boston Utd** (ML) | A | D | 1-1 | Hogg |
| | | 1r | 24.11.54 | **Boston Utd** | H | W | 5-4 | Hogg 2, Gair 2, Weatherspoon |
| | | 2 | 11.12.54 | **Torquay Utd** (3S) | H | L | 1-3 | Hogg |
| 1956-57 | (NEL) | 1 | 17.11.56 | **Ilkeston Town** (ML) | A | W | 5-1 | Linacre, McHale, Turney, Langland 2 |
| | | 2 | 08.12.56 | **Hartlepools Utd** (3N) | H | L | 0-1 | |
| 1958-59 | (ML) | 1 | 15.11.58 | **Morecambe** (LC) | A | W | 2-1 | Turney, Potts |
| | | 2 | 06.12.58 | **Stockport County** (D3) | H | L | 3-4 | Reay, F Potts, Clempson og |
| 1959-60 | (ML) | 1 | 14.11.59 | **Wrexham** (D3) | A | L | 1-2 | Turney |
| 1960-61 | (NCo) | 1 | 05.11.60 | **Mansfield Town** (D4) | A | L | 1-3 | Caronn |
| 1961-62 | (NCo) | 1 | 04.11.61 | **Hartlepools Utd** (D4) | A | L | 1-5 | Lodge |
| 1962-63 | (NEL) | 1 | 03.11.62 | **Morecambe** (LC) | H | W | 2-1 | R Smith, A Smith |
| | | 2 | 24.11.62 | **Carlisle Utd** (D3) | H | L | 0-2 | |
| 1963-64 | (NEL) | 1 | 16.11.63 | **Chester** (D4) | A | L | 2-3 | Robson, A Smith |
| 1966-67 | (NL) | 1 | 26.11.66 | **Bishop Auckland** (NL) | A | D | 1-1 | Mason |
| | | 1r | 30.11.66 | **Bishop Auckland** | H | D | 0-0aet | |
| | | 1 2r | 05.12.66 | **Bishop Auckland** | | D | 3-3aet | Evans 2, Orrick |
| | | | | *played at Roker Park* | | | | |
| | | 1 3r | 08.12.66 | **Bishop Auckland** | | L | 1-4 | Orrick |
| | | | | *played at Roker Park* | | | | |
| 1971-72 | (NL) | 1 | 20.11.71 | **Crewe Alexandra** (D4) | A | W | 1-0 | Slane |
| | | 2 | 11.12.71 | **Stockport County** (D4) | H | W | 1-0 | Young |
| | | 3 | 15.01.72 | **Reading** (D4) | H | D | 2-2 | Nixon, Alder |
| | | 3r | 19.01.72 | **Reading** | A | L | 1-6 | B Wagstaff og |
| 1973-74 | (NL) | 1 | 24.11.73 | **Alfreton Town** (ML) | A | D | 0-0 | |
| | | 1r | 28.11.73 | **Alfreton Town** | H | W | 2-1 | Pink, Alder |
| | | 2 | 15.12.73 | **Grimsby Town** (D3) | A | D | 1-1 | Slane |
| | | 2r | 18.12.73 | **Grimsby Town** | H | L | 0-2 | |
| 1974-75 | (NL) | 1 | 23.11.74 | **Preston North End** (D3) | H | D | 1-1 | Dagless |
| | | 1r | 26.11.74 | **Preston North End** | A | L | 1-5 | Scott |
| 1977-78 | (NL) | 1 | 26.11.77 | **Burscough** (CC) | H | W | 1-0 | Mutrie |
| | | 2 | 17.12.77 | **Chesterfield** (D3) | H | W | 1-0 | Jones |

| | | | | | | | | |
|---|---|---|---|---|---|---|---|---|
| | | 3 | 07.01.78 | **Enfield** (IL) | H | W | 1-0 | Shoulder |
| | | 4 | 06.02.78 | **Stoke City** (D2) | A | W | 3-2 | Johnson 2, S Carney |
| | | 5 | 18.02.78 | **Wrexham** (D3) | A | D | 1-1 | Johnson |
| | | 5r | 27.02.78 | **Wrexham** | | L | 1-2 | Johnson |
| | | | | *played at St James' Park* | | | | |
| 1978-79 | (NL) | 1 | 25.11.78 | **York City** (D4) | A | D | 1-1 | Johnson (p) |
| | | 1r | 28.11.78 | **York City** | H | L | 3-5 | Shoulder 2 (2p), Davies |
| 1979-80 | (NL) | 1 | 24.11.79 | **Mansfield Town** (D3) | H | L | 0-2 | |
| 1980-81 | (NL) | 1 | 22.11.80 | **Burton Albion** (NPL) | H | W | 2-1 | P Walker, Mutrie |
| | | 2 | 13.12.80 | **Hull City** (D3) | A | D | 1-1 | Mutrie |
| | | 2r | 16.12.80 | **Hull City** | H | D | 2-2aet | Mutrie, Young |
| | | 22r | 22.12.80 | **Hull City** | A | L | 1-2aet | Mutrie (p) |
| | | | | *played at Elland Road* | | | | |
| 1981-82 | (NL) | 1 | 21.11.81 | **Walsall** (D3) | H | L | 1-2 | Rafferty |
| 1992-93 | (NL) | 1 | 14.11.92 | **Southport** (NPL) | H | L | 1-2 | Howie |
| 1995-96 | (NPL) | | 11.11.95 | **Bury** (D3) | A | W | 2-0 | Bond, Ditchburn |
| | | 2 | 02.12.95 | **Stockport County** (D2) | A | L | 0-2 | |
| 1997-98 | (NPL) | 1 | 15.11.97 | **Blackpool** (D2) | A | L | 3-4 | Henderson, Di Lella, Atkinson |

## BOGNOR REGIS TOWN

*Formed 1883. First entered FA Cup: 1908-09. League clubs beaten: Swansea City, Exeter City. Members of the Isthmian League.*

| | | | | | | | | |
|---|---|---|---|---|---|---|---|---|
| 1972-73 | (SL) | 1 | 18.11.72 | **Colchester Utd** (D4) | A | L | 0-6 | |
| 1984-85 | (IL) | 1 | 17.11.84 | **Swansea City** (D3) | A | D | 1-1 | Cooper |
| | | 1r | 21.11.84 | **Swansea City** | H | W | 3-1 | P Pullen 2, Clements |
| | | 2 | 08.12.84 | **Reading** (D3) | A | L | 2-6 | Poole, P Pullen |
| 1985-86 | (IL) | 1 | 16.11.85 | **Enfield** (APL) | A | W | 2-0 | Cooper, Clements |
| | | 2 | 07.12.85 | **Gillingham** (D3) | A | L | 1-6 | Cooper (p) |
| 1986-87 | (IL) | 1 | 15.11.86 | **Slough Town** (IL) | A | D | 1-1 | Crumplin |
| | | 1r | 17.11.86 | **Slough Town** | H | L | 0-1 | |
| 1987-88 | (IL) | 1 | 14.11.87 | **Torquay Utd** (D4) | H | L | 0-3 | |
| 1988-89 | (IL) | 1 | 19.11.88 | **Exeter City** (D4) | H | W | 2-1 | P Pullen, Guille |
| | | 2 | 10.12.88 | **Cambridge Utd** (D4) | H | L | 0-1 | |
| 1995-96 | (IL) | 1 | 11.11.95 | **Ashford Town** (SL) | H | D | 1-1 | Birmingham |
| | | 1r | 21.11.95 | **Ashford Town** | A | W | 1-0 | D Pearce |
| | | 2 | 02.12.95 | **Peterborough Utd** (D2) | A | L | 0-4 | |

## BOLLINGTON

*Formed 1875. Played at the Garden Street Ground, and changed at the Royal Oak pub*

| | | | | | | | |
|---|---|---|---|---|---|---|---|
| 1885-86 | 1 | 24.10.85 | **Oswestry Town** | H | L | 0-5 | |
| 1886-87 | 1 | 30.10.86 | **Oswestry Town** | H | L | 2-8 | |

## BOLTON ASSOCIATION

| | | | | | | | |
|---|---|---|---|---|---|---|---|
| 1883-84 | 1 | 03.11.83 | **Bradshaw** | H | W | 5-1 | Bentley, Harper, Murray, Walker, AN Other |
| | 2 | 01.12.83 | **Bolton Wanderers** | A | L | 0-3 | |
| 1884-85 | 1 | | Astley Bridge | | | - | |
| | | | *Astley Bridge scratched. Bolton Association walkover* | | | | |
| | 2 | 29.11.84 | **Darwen Old Wanderers** | A | L | 2-7 | |

## BOLTON OLYMPIC

*Formed 1876. Played in the Tonge area of Bolton. Only ever played two FA Cup matches.*

| | | | | | | | |
|---|---|---|---|---|---|---|---|
| 1882-83 | 1 | 04.11.82 | **Eagley** | H | L | 4-7 | Haslam, Austin, og, AN Other |
| 1883-84 | 1 | 10.11.83 | **Bolton Wanderers** | A | L | 0-9 | |

## BOLTON WANDERERS

*Formed 1874. Founder Members of the Football League 1888. FA Cup winners: 1923, 1926, 1929, 1958. The first club to win the FA Cup at Wembley Stadium in 1923. FA Cup runners-up: 1894, 1904, 1953; Record FA Cup win: 13-0 v Sheffield Utd, 2nd round, 01.02.1890; Record FA Cup defeat: 1-9 v Preston North End, 2nd round, 10.12.1887*

| | | | | | | | |
|---|---|---|---|---|---|---|---|
| 1881-82 | 1 | 22.10.81 | **Eagley** | H | D | 5-5 | Atherton, Gleaves, Struthers, 2 ogs |
| | 1r | 12.11.81 | **Eagley** | A | W | 1-0 | Steel |
| | 2 | 19.11.81 | **Blackburn Rovers** | A | L | 2-6 | Atherton, Struthers |

| | | | | | | | | |
|---|---|---|---|---|---|---|---|---|
| 1882-83 | | 1 | 04.11.82 | **Bootle** | H | W | 6-1 | Struthers 5, Steel |
| | | 2 | 30.11.82 | **Liverpool Ramblers** | H | W | 3-0 | Struthers 2, og |
| | | 2 | 02.12.82 | **Liverpool Ramblers** | H | W | 3-0 | |
| | | 3 | 06.01.83 | **Druids** | A | D | 0-0 | |
| | | 3r | 22.01.83 | **Druids** | H | D | 1-1aet | Atherton |
| | | 3 2r | 29.01.83 | **Druids** | | L | 0-1 | |
| | | | | *played at Wrexham Racecourse* | | | | |
| 1883-84 | | 1 | 10.11.83 | **Bolton Olympic** | H | W | 9-0 | Struthers 3, Steel 2, Davenport, Gleaves, Howarth, Scholes |
| | | 2 | 01.12.83 | **Bolton Association** | H | W | 3-0 | Steel 2, Struthers |
| | | 3 | 29.12.83 | **Irwell Springs** | H | W | 8-1 | Davenport 2, Fallon 2, Steel 2, Struthers, og |
| | | 4 | 19.01.84 | **Notts County** | A | D | 2-2aet | Davenport, Fallon |
| | | 4r | 02.02.84 | **Notts County** | H | L | 1-2 | Vaughan |
| 1884-85 | | 1 | | **Preston Zingari** | | | - | |
| | | | | *Match not played, both teams withdrew* | | | | |
| 1885-86 | | 1 | 17.10.85 | **Eagley** | H | W | 6-0 | Fallon 2, Gregory, Hough, Bullough, og |
| | | 2 | 21.11.85 | **Rawtenstall** | A | D | 3-3 | |
| | | | | *FA disqualified Rawtenstall for professionalism, Bolton advanced* | | | | |
| | | 3 | 12.12.85 | **Preston North End** | H | L | 2-3 | Davenport, Struthers |
| | | | | *FA disqualified Preston for professionalism, Bolton re-instated* | | | | |
| | | | | bye | | | | |
| | | 5 | 01.02.86 | **Old Westminsters** | | | - | |
| | | | | *FA disqualified Bolton for professionalism, Old Westminsters advanced* | | | | |
| 1886-87 | | 1 | 30.10.86 | **South Shore** | H | W | 5-3 | Davenport 2, Hewitson, Struthers, Howarth |
| | | 2 | 13.11.86 | **Third Lanark** | A | W | 3-2 | Hewitson 2, Struthers |
| | | 3 | 11.12.86 | **Darwen** | A | L | 3-4 | Davenport, Howarth, Struthers |
| 1887-88 | | 1 | 15.10.87 | **Everton** | H | W | 1-0 | Roberts |
| | | | | *FA ordered replay after Bolton player declared ineligible* | | | | |
| | | 1r | 29.10.87 | **Everton** | A | D | 2-2 | Brogan, Roberts |
| | | 1 2r | 12.11.87 | **Everton** | H | D | 1-1 | Brogan |
| | | 1 3r | 19.11.87 | **Everton** | A | L | 1-2 | Davenport |
| | | | | *FA disqualified Everton for ineligible players. Bolton re-instated* | | | | |
| | | 2 | 10.12.87 | **Preston North End** | A | L | 1-9 | Howarth |
| 1888-89 | (D1) | | | 1q Hurst (A) 0-0; 1qr Hurst, walkover; 2q West Mannchester (H) 9-0; 3q Linfield, Belfast (A) 0-4 | | | | |
| 1889-90 | (D1) | 1 | 18.01.90 | **Distillery, Belfast** | H | W | 10-2 | Weir 4, Cassidy 2, Davenport 2, 2 scrimmages |
| | | 2 | 01.02.90 | **Sheffield Utd** | H | W | 13-0 | Cassidy 5, Weir 4, Brogan 3, Robinson |
| | | 3 | 15.02.90 | **Preston North End** (D1) | A | W | 3-2 | Weir 2, Brogan |
| | | SF | 08.03.90 | **Sheffield Wed** (FAll) | | L | 1-2 | McNee |
| | | | | *played at Perry Barr, Birmingham* | | | | |
| 1890-91 | (D1) | 1 | 17.01.91 | **Accrington FC** (D1) | A | D | 2-2 | |
| | | 1r | 24.01.91 | **Accrington FC** | A | L | 1-5 | Cassidy |
| 1891-92 | (D1) | 1 | 16.01.92 | **Sheffield Wed** (FAll) | A | L | 1-2 | Munro |
| | | | | *FA ordered replay following protests over ground conditions* | | | | |
| | | 1r | 23.01.92 | **Sheffield Wed** (FAll) | A | L | 1-4 | Jones |
| 1892-93 | (D1) | 1 | 21.01.93 | **Wolverhampton W** (D1) | H | D | 1-1aet | Wilson |
| | | 1r | 28.01.93 | **Wolverhampton W** | A | L | 1-2 | McNee |
| 1893-94 | (D1) | 1 | 27.01.94 | **Small Heath** (D2) | A | W | 4-3 | Cassidy 2, Wilson 2 |
| | | 2 | 10.02.94 | **Newcastle Utd** (D2) | A | W | 2-1 | Hughes, Turner |
| | | 3 | 24.02.94 | **Liverpool** (D2) | H | W | 3-0 | Dickenson 2, Cassidy |
| | | SF | 10.03.94 | **Sheffield Wed** (D1) | | W | 2-1 | Bentley 2 |
| | | | | *played at Fallowfield, Manchester* | | | | |
| | | F | 31.03.94 | **Notts County** (D2) | | L | 1-4 | Cassidy |
| | | | | *played at Goodison Park* | | | | |
| 1894-95 | (D1) | 1 | 02.02.95 | **Woolwich Arsenal** (D2) | H | W | 1-0 | Jones |
| | | 2 | 16.02.95 | **Bury** (D2) | H | W | 1-0 | Cassidy |
| | | 3 | 02.03.95 | **Sunderland** (D1) | A | L | 1-2 | Cassidy |

| | | | | | | | | |
|---|---|---|---|---|---|---|---|---|
| 1895-96 | (D1) | 1 | 01.02.96 | **Crewe Alexandra** (D2) | A | W | 4-0 | Brown, Gunn, Tannahill, Wright |
| | | 2 | 15.02.96 | **Blackpool** (LL) | A | W | 2-0 | Cassidy, Wright |
| | | 3 | 29.02.96 | **Bury** (D1) | H | W | 2-0 | Wright, Gunn |
| | | SF | 21.03.96 | **Sheffield Wed** (D1) | | D | 1-1 | Tannahill |
| | | | | *played at Goodison Park* | | | | |
| | | SFr | 28.03.96 | **Sheffield Wed** | | L | 1-3 | Tannahill |
| | | | | *played at Town Ground, Nottingham* | | | | |
| 1896-97 | (D1) | 1 | 30.01.97 | **Grimsby Town** (D2) | A | D | 0-0 | |
| | | 1r | 08.02.97 | **Grimsby Town** | H | D | 3-3aet | Cassidy, Thomson, Jones |
| | | 12r | 11.02.97 | **Grimsby Town** | | W | 3-2 | Joyce 2, Jones |
| | | | | *played at Bramall Lane* | | | | |
| | | 2 | 13.02.97 | **Derby County** (D1) | A | L | 1-4 | Brown |
| 1897-98 | (D1) | 1 | 29.01.98 | **Luton Town** (D2) | A | W | 1-0 | Cassidy |
| | | 2 | 12.02.98 | **Manchester City** (D2) | H | W | 1-0 | T Miller |
| | | 3 | 26.02.98 | **Southampton** (SL) | H | D | 0-0 | |
| | | 3r | 02.03.98 | **Southampton** | A | L | 0-4 | |
| 1898-99 | (D1) | 1 | 28.01.99 | **Wolverhampton W** (D1) | A | D | 0-0 | |
| | | 1r | 01.02.99 | **Wolverhampton W** | H | L | 0-1 | |
| 1899-00 | (D2) | 1 | 27.01.00 | **Sheffield Wed** (D2) | A | L | 0-1 | |
| 1900-01 | (D1) | 1 | 09.02.01 | **Derby County** (D1) | H | W | 1-0 | L Bell |
| | | 2 | 23.02.01 | **Reading** (SL) | H | L | 0-1 | |
| 1901-02 | (D1) | 1 | 25.01.02 | **Wolverhampton W** (D1) | A | W | 2-0 | Williams, og |
| | | 2 | 08.02.02 | **Sheffield Utd** (D1) | A | L | 1-2 | McKie |
| 1902-03 | (D1) | 1 | 07.12.02 | **Bristol City** (D2) | H | L | 0-5 | |
| 1903-04 | (D2) | 1 | 06.02.04 | **Reading** (SL) | A | D | 1-1 | Marsh |
| | | 1r | 10.02.04 | **Reading** | | W | 3-2 | Freebairn, Marsh, Yenson |
| | | 2 | 20.02.04 | **Southampton** (SL) | H | W | 4-1 | Marsh 2, White 2 |
| | | 3 | 05.03.04 | **Sheffield Utd** (D1) | A | W | 2-0 | Marsh, Yenson |
| | | SF | 19.03.04 | **Derby County** (D1) | | W | 1-0 | Taylor |
| | | | | *played at Molineux* | | | | |
| | | F | 23.04.04 | **Manchester City** (D1) | | L | 0-1 | |
| | | | | *played at Crystal Palace* | | | | |
| 1904-05 | (D2) | 1 | 04.02.05 | **Bristol Rovers** (SL) | H | D | 1-1 | Marsh |
| | | 1r | 08.02.05 | **Bristol Rovers** | A | W | 3-0 | Stokes, Shephard, og |
| | | 2 | 18.02.05 | **Manchester City** (D1) | A | W | 2-1 | Shepherd, White |
| | | 3 | 04.03.05 | **Newcastle Utd** (D1) | H | L | 0-2 | |
| 1905-06 | (D1) | 1 | 13.01.06 | **Middlesbrough** (D1) | A | L | 0-3 | |
| 1906-07 | (D1) | 1 | 12.01.07 | **Brighton** (SL) | H | W | 3-1 | Stokes, Clifford, Shepherd |
| | | 2 | 02.02.07 | **Aston Villa** (D1) | H | W | 2-0 | Shepherd 2 |
| | | 3 | 23.02.07 | **Everton** (D1) | A | D | 0-0 | |
| | | 3r | 27.02.07 | **Everton** | H | L | 0-3 | |
| 1907-08 | (D1) | 1 | 11.01.08 | **Woking** (WS) | H | W | 5-0 | Cameron, Stokes, Owen, White, McEwan |
| | | 2 | 01.02.08 | **Notts County** (D1) | A | D | 1-1 | McEwan |
| | | 2r | 05.02.08 | **Notts County** | H | W | 2-1aet | Cameron,White |
| | | 3 | 22.02.08 | **Everton** (D1) | H | D | 3-3 | Marsh 3 |
| | | 3r | 26.02.08 | **Everton** | A | L | 1-3aet | Greenhalgh |
| 1908-09 | (D2) | 1 | 16.01.09 | **WBA** (D2) | A | L | 1-3 | Hunter |
| 1909-10 | (D1) | 1 | 15.01.10 | **Stockport County** (D2) | A | L | 1-4 | Hogan |
| 1910-11 | (D2) | 1 | 14.01.11 | **Chesterfield** (ML) | H | L | 0-2 | |
| 1911-12 | (D1) | 1 | 13.01.12 | **Woolwich Arsenal** (D1) | H | W | 1-0 | Smith |
| | | 2 | 03.02.12 | **Blackpool** (D2) | H | W | 1-0 | Bentley |
| | | 3 | 24.02.12 | **Barnsley** (D2) | H | L | 1-2 | Smith |
| 1912-13 | (D1) | 1 | 11.01.13 | **Oldham Athletic** (D1) | A | L | 0-2 | |
| 1913-14 | (D1) | 1 | 10.01.14 | **Port Vale** (CL) | H | W | 3-0 | Smith, Donaldson, Lillycrop |
| | | 2 | 31.01.14 | **Swindon Town** (SL) | H | W | 4-2 | Smith 3, Jones |
| | | 3 | 21.02.14 | **Burnley** (D1) | A | L | 0-3 | |
| 1914-15 | (D1) | 1 | 09.01.15 | **Notts County** (D1) | H | W | 2-1 | Smith, Hilton |
| | | 2 | 30.01.15 | **Millwall Athletic** (SL) | H | D | 0-0 | |
| | | 2r | 06.02.15 | **Millwall Athletic** | A | D | 2-2aet | Vizard, Smith (p) |
| | | 22r | 13.02.15 | **Millwall Athletic** | H | W | 4-1 | Jones 2, Vizard 2 |

| | | | | | | | | |
|---|---|---|---|---|---|---|---|---|
| | 3 | 20.02.15 | **Burnley** (D1) | H | W | 2-1aet | Smith 2 |
| | 4 | 06.03.15 | **Hull City** (D2) | H | W | 4-2 | Smith 2 (2p), Vizard, Jones |
| | SF | 27.03.15 | **Sheffield Utd** (D1) | | L | 1-2 | Smith |
| | | | *played at Ewood Park* | | | | |
| 1919-20 (D1) | 1 | 10.01.20 | **Chelsea** (D1) | H | L | 0-1 | |
| 1920-21 (D1) | 1 | 08.01.21 | **Preston North End** (D1) | A | L | 0-2 | |
| 1921-22 (D1) | 1 | 07.01.22 | **Bury** (D2) | H | W | 1-0 | Vizard |
| | 2 | 28.01.22 | **Manchester City** (D1) | H | L | 1-3 | Roberts |
| 1922-23 (D1) | 1 | 13.01.23 | **Norwich City** (3S) | A | W | 2-0 | J Smith, JR Smith |
| | 2 | 03.02.23 | **Leeds Utd** (D2) | H | W | 3-1 | Jack 2, J Smith |
| | 3 | 24.02.23 | **Huddersfield Town** (D1) | A | D | 1-1 | Jack |
| | 3r | 28.02.23 | **Huddersfield Town** | H | W | 1-0 | Jack |
| | 4 | 10.03.23 | **Charlton Athletic** (3S) | A | W | 1-0 | Jack |
| | SF | 24.03.23 | **Sheffield Utd** (D1) | | W | 1-0 | Jack |
| | | | *played at Old Trafford* | | | | |
| | F | 28.04.23 | **West Ham Utd** (D2) | | W | 2-0 | Jack, JR Smith |
| | | | *played at Wembley Stadium* | | | | |
| 1923-24 (D1) | 1 | 12.01.24 | **Hull City** (D2) | A | D | 2-2 | JR Smith, Jack |
| | 2 | 16.01.24 | **Hull City** | H | W | 4-0 | JR Smith 2, Jack 2 |
| | 3 | 02.02.24 | **Liverpool** (D1) | H | L | 1-4 | JR Smith |
| 1924-25 (D1) | 1 | 10.01.25 | **Huddersfield Town** (D1) | H | W | 3-0 | Jack, J Smith (p), Vizard |
| | 2 | 31.01.25 | **Tottenham Hotspur** (D1) | A | D | 1-1 | J Smith |
| | 2r | 04.02.25 | **Tottenham Hotspur** | H | L | 0-1 | |
| 1925-26 (D1) | 3 | 09.01.26 | **Accrington Stanley** (3N) | H | W | 1-0 | Jack |
| | 4 | 30.01.26 | **Bournemouth** (3S) | A | D | 2-2 | JR Smith, Jack |
| | 4r | 03.02.26 | **Bournemouth** | H | W | 6-2 | J Smith 2, JR Smith 2, Boston, Jack |
| | 5 | 20.02.26 | **South Shields** (D2) | H | W | 3-0 | J Smith (p), Jack, JR Smith |
| | 6 | 06.03.26 | **Nottingham Forest** (D2) | A | D | 2-2 | Butler 2 |
| | 6r | 10.03.26 | **Nottingham Forest** | H | D | 0-0aet | |
| | 6 2r | 15.03.26 | **Nottingham Forest** | | W | 1-0 | J Smith |
| | | | *played at Old Trafford* | | | | |
| | SF | 27.03.26 | **Swansea Town** (D2) | | W | 3-0 | J Smith 2 (1p), Baggett |
| | | | *played at White Hart Lane* | | | | |
| | F | 24.04.26 | **Manchester City** (D1) | | W | 1-0 | Jack |
| | | | *played at Wembley Stadium* | | | | |
| 1926-27 (D1) | 3 | 08.01.27 | **Blackpool** (D2) | A | W | 3-1 | JR Smith 3 |
| | 4 | 29.01.27 | **Leeds Utd** (D1) | A | D | 0-0 | |
| | 4r | 02.02.27 | **Leeds Utd** | H | W | 3-0 | Wright, Jack, JR Smith |
| | 5 | 19.02.27 | **Cardiff City** (D1) | H | L | 0-3 | |
| 1927-28 (D1) | 3 | 14.01.28 | **Luton Town** (3S) | H | W | 2-1 | Butler, Smith |
| | 4 | 28.01.28 | **Stoke City** (D2) | A | L | 2-4 | Round, Murphy |
| 1928-29 (D1) | 3 | 12.01.29 | **Oldham Athletic** (D2) | H | W | 2-0 | Gibson, Blackmore |
| | 4 | 26.01.29 | **Liverpool** (D1) | A | D | 0-0 | |
| | 4r | 30.01.29 | **Liverpool** | H | W | 5-2aet | Blackmore 2, Butler, McClelland, Gibson |
| | 5 | 16.02.29 | **Leicester City** (D1) | A | W | 2-1 | Seddon, Blackmore |
| | 6 | 02.03.29 | **Blackburn Rovers** (D1) | A | D | 1-1 | Blackmore |
| | 6r | 06.03.29 | **Blackburn Rovers** | H | W | 2-1 | Butler 2 |
| | SF | 23.03.29 | **Huddersfield Town** (D1) | | W | 3-1 | Butler, Gibson, Blackmore |
| | | | *played at Anfield* | | | | |
| | F | 27.04.29 | **Portsmouth** (D1) | | W | 2-0 | Butler, Blackmore |
| | | | *played at Wembley Stadium* | | | | |
| 1929-30 (D1) | 3 | 11.01.30 | **Birmingham** (D1) | A | L | 0-1 | |
| 1930-31 (D1) | 3 | 10.01.31 | **Carlisle Utd** (3N) | H | W | 1-0 | Blackmore |
| | 4 | 24.01.31 | **Sunderland** (D1) | H | D | 1-1 | Blackmore |
| | 4r | 27.01.31 | **Sunderland** | A | L | 1-3 | Blackmore |
| 1931-32 (D1) | 3 | 09.01.32 | **Preston North End** (D2) | A | D | 0-0 | |
| | 3r | 13.01.32 | **Preston North End** | H | L | 2-5 | Blackmore, Gibson |
| 1932-33 (D1) | 3 | 14.01.33 | **Charlton Athletic** (D2) | A | W | 5-1 | Cook 2, T Griffiths, Gibson, Milsom |
| | 4 | 28.01.33 | **Grimsby Town** (D2) | H | W | 2-1 | T Griffiths, Butler |
| | 5 | 18.02.33 | **Manchester City** (D1) | H | L | 2-4 | Westwood, Milsom |

| | | | | | | | |
|---|---|---|---|---|---|---|---|
| 1933-34 (D2) | 3 | 13.01.34 | **Halifax Town** (3N) | H | W | 3-1 | Cook 2, Westwood |
| | 4 | 27.01.34 | **Brighton** (3S) | A | D | 1-1 | Westwood |
| | 4r | 31.01.34 | **Brighton** | H | W | 6-1 | Milsom 3, Westwood, GT Taylor, Cameron |
| | 5 | 17.02.34 | **Liverpool** (D1) | A | W | 3-0 | GT Taylor, Milsom, Westwood |
| | 6 | 03.03.34 | **Portsmouth** (D1) | H | L | 0-3 | |
| 1934-35 (D2) | 3 | 12.01.35 | **Northampton Town** (3S) | A | W | 2-0 | Milsom, Cook |
| | 4 | 26.01.35 | **Plymouth Argyle** (D2) | A | W | 4-1 | Milsom 2, Westwood, Rae og |
| | 5 | 16.02.35 | **Tottenham Hotspur** (D1) | A | D | 1-1 | Atkinson |
| | 5r | 20.02.35 | **Tottenham Hotspur** | H | D | 1-1aet | Westwood |
| | 5 2r | 25.02.35 | **Tottenham Hotspur** *played at Villa Park* | | W | 2-0 | Westwood, Walton |
| | 6 | 02.03.35 | **Everton** (D1) | A | W | 2-1 | Eastham, Milsom |
| | SF | 16.03.35 | **WBA** (D1) *played at Elland Road* | | D | 1-1 | Walton |
| | SFr | 20.03.35 | **WBA** *played at Victoria Ground, Stoke* | | L | 0-2 | |
| 1935-36 (D1) | 3 | 11.01.36 | **Blackburn Rovers** (D1) | A | D | 1-1 | Woods |
| | 3r | 15.01.36 | **Blackburn Rovers** | H | L | 0-1aet | |
| 1936-37 (D1) | 3 | 16.01.37 | **West Ham Utd** (D2) | A | D | 0-0 | |
| | 3r | 20.01.37 | **West Ham Utd** | H | W | 1-0 | Halford |
| | 4 | 30.01.37 | **Norwich City** (D2) | H | D | 1-1 | Westwood |
| | 4r | 04.02.37 | **Norwich City** | A | W | 2-1aet | Anderson, Milsom |
| | 5 | 20.02.37 | **Manchester City** (D1) | H | L | 0-5 | |
| 1937-38 (D1) | 3 | 08.01.38 | **Arsenal** (D1) | A | L | 1-3 | Carruthers |
| 1938-39 (D1) | 3 | 07.01.39 | **Middlesbrough** (D1) | A | D | 0-0 | |
| | 3r | 11.01.39 | **Middlesbrough** | H | D | 0-0aet | |
| | 3 2r | 16.01.39 | **Middlesbrough** *played at Elland Road* | | L | 0-1 | |
| 1945-46 (D1) | 3 1L | 05.01.46 | **Blackburn Rovers** (D2) | H | W | 1-0 | Moir |
| | 3 2L | 09.01.46 | **Blackburn Rovers** | A | W | 3-1 | Westwood 2, Hunt |
| | 4 1L | 26.01.46 | **Liverpool** (D1) | H | W | 5-0 | Westwood 3, Lofthouse 2 |
| | 4 2L | 30.01.46 | **Liverpool** | A | L | 0-2 | |
| | 5 1L | 09.02.46 | **Middlesbrough** (D1) | H | W | 1-0 | Westwood |
| | 5 2L | 13.02.46 | **Middlesbrough** | A | D | 1-1 | Hunt |
| | 6 1L | 02.03.46 | **Stoke City** (D1) | A | W | 2-0 | Westwood 2 |
| | 6 2L | 09.03.46 | **Stoke City** | H | D | 0-0 | |
| | SF | 23.03.46 | **Charlton Athletic** (D1) *played at Villa Park* | | L | 0-2 | |
| 1946-47 (D1) | 3 | 11.01.47 | **Stockport County** (3N) | H | W | 5-1 | Lofthouse 2, Geldard, Barrass, Woodward |
| | 4 | 25.01.47 | **Manchester City** (D2) | H | D | 3-3 | Lofthouse, Barrass, Wrigglesworth |
| | 4r | 29.01.47 | **Manchester City** | A | L | 0-1 | |
| 1947-48 (D1) | 3 | 10.01.48 | **Tottenham Hotspur** (D2) | H | L | 0-2aet | |
| 1948-49 (D1) | 3 | 08.01.49 | **Aston Villa** (D1) | A | D | 1-1aet | Bradley |
| | 3r | 15.01.49 | **Aston Villa** | H | D | 0-0aet | |
| | 3 2r | 17.01.49 | **Aston Villa** | A | L | 1-2aet | Lofthouse |
| 1949-50 (D1) | 3 | 07.01.50 | **Coventry City** (D2) | A | W | 2-1 | Lofthouse, Langton |
| | 4 | 28.01.50 | **Leeds Utd** (D2) | A | D | 1-1 | Lofthouse |
| | 4r | 01.02.50 | **Leeds Utd** | H | L | 2-3aet | Lofthouse, McShane |
| 1950-51 (D1) | 3 | 06.01.51 | **York City** (3N) | H | W | 2-0 | Lofthouse, Langton |
| | 4 | 27.01.51 | **Newcastle Utd** (D1) | A | L | 2-3 | Moir 2 |
| 1951-52 (D1) | 3 | 12.01.52 | **WBA** (D1) | A | L | 0-4 | |
| 1952-53 (D1) | 3 | 14.01.53 | **Fulham** (D2) | H | W | 3-1 | Holden, Moir, Lofthouse |
| | 4 | 31.01.53 | **Notts County** (D2) | H | D | 1-1 | Lofthouse |
| | 4r | 05.02.53 | **Notts County** | A | D | 2-2aet | Moir 2 |
| | 4 2r | 09.02.53 | **Notts County** *played at Hillsborough* | | W | 1-0 | Lofthouse |
| | 5 | 14.02.53 | **Luton Town** (D2) | A | W | 1-0 | Lofthouse |
| | 6 | 28.02.53 | **Gateshead AFC** (3N) | A | W | 1-0 | Lofthouse |

| | | | | | | | |
|---|---|---|---|---|---|---|---|
| | SF | 21.03.53 | **Everton** (D2) *played at Maine Road* | | W | 4-3 | Lofthouse 2, Moir, Holden |
| | F | 02.05.53 | **Blackpool** (D1) *played at Wembley Stadium* | | L | 3-4 | Moir, Bell, Lofthouse |
| 1953-54 (D1) | 3 | 09.01.54 | **Liverpool** (D1) | H | W | 1-0 | Moir |
| | 4 | 30.01.54 | **Headington Utd** (SL) | A | W | 4-2 | Moir, Parry, Lofthouse, Stevens |
| | 5 | 20.02.54 | **Portsmouth** (D1) | H | D | 0-0 | |
| | 5r | 24.02.54 | **Portsmouth** | A | W | 2-1 | Moir 2 |
| | 6 | 13.03.54 | **Sheffield Wed** (D1) | A | D | 1-1 | Moir (p) |
| | 6r | 17.03.54 | **Sheffield Wed** | H | L | 0-2 | |
| 1954-55 (D1) | 3 | 08.01.55 | **Millwall** (3S) | H | W | 3-1 | Moir 2 (1p), Parry |
| | 4 | 29.01.55 | **Birmingham City** (D2) | A | L | 1-2 | Moir |
| 1955-56 (D1) | 3 | 07.01.56 | **Huddersfield Town** (D1) *abandoned after 47 minutes* | H | - | 0-0ab | |
| | 3 | 11.01.56 | **Huddersfield Town** | H | W | 3-0 | Lofthouse, Stevens, Neill |
| | 4 | 28.01.56 | **Sheffield Utd** (D1) | H | L | 1-2 | Hartle |
| 1956-57 (D1) | 3 | 05.01.57 | **Blackpool** (D1) | H | L | 2-3 | Hennin (p), Gubbins |
| 1957-58 (D1) | 3 | 04.01.58 | **Preston North End** (D1) | A | W | 3-0 | Parry 2, Stevens |
| | 4 | 25.01.58 | **York City** (3N) | A | D | 0-0 | |
| | 4r | 29.01.58 | **York City** | H | W | 3-0 | Allcock 2, Birch |
| | 5 | 15.02.58 | **Stoke City** (D2) | H | W | 3-1 | Lofthouse, Stevens, Parry |
| | 6 | 01.03.58 | **Wolverhampton W** (D1) | H | W | 2-1 | Stevens, Parry |
| | SF | 22.03.58 | **Blackburn Rovers** (D2) *played at Maine Road* | | W | 2-1 | Gubbins 2 |
| | F | 03.05.58 | **Manchester Utd** (D1) *played at Wembley Stadium* | | W | 2-0 | Lofthouse 2 |
| 1958-59 (D1) | 3 | 10.01.59 | **Scunthorpe Utd** (D2) | A | W | 2-0 | Lofthouse 2 |
| | 4 | 24.01.59 | **Wolverhampton W** (D1) | A | W | 2-1 | Lofthouse, Parry (p) |
| | 5 | 14.02.59 | **Preston North End** (D1) | H | D | 2-2 | Birch, Parry |
| | 5r | 18.02.59 | **Preston North End** | A | D | 1-1aet | Holden |
| | 5 2r | 23.02.59 | **Preston North End** *played at Ewood Park* | | W | 1-0 | Lofthouse |
| | 6 | 28.02.59 | **Nottingham Forest** (D1) | A | L | 1-2 | Birch |
| 1959-60 (D1) | 3 | 09.01.60 | **Bury** (D3) | A | D | 1-1 | Parry |
| | 3r | 13.01.60 | **Bury** | H | W | 4-2aet | Parry 2, Stevens, Birch |
| | 4 | 30.01.60 | **WBA** (D1) | A | L | 0-2 | |
| 1960-61 (D1) | 3 | 07.01.61 | **Hull City** (D3) | A | W | 1-0 | Stevens |
| | 4 | 28.01.61 | **Blackburn Rovers** (D1) | H | D | 3-3 | Stanley (p), McAdams, Stevens |
| | 4r | 01.02.61 | **Blackburn Rovers** | A | L | 0-4 | |
| 1961-62 (D1) | 3 | 06.01.62 | **Manchester Utd** (D1) | A | L | 1-2 | Stevens |
| 1962-63 (D1) | 3 | 06.03.63 | **Sheffield Utd** (D1) | A | L | 1-3 | Lee |
| 1963-64 (D1) | 3 | 04.01.64 | **Bath City** (SL) | A | D | 1-1 | Lee |
| | 3r | 08.01.64 | **Bath City** | H | W | 3-0 | Taylor, Lee (p), Davies |
| | 4 | 25.01.64 | **Preston North End** (D2) | H | D | 2-2 | Deakin 2 |
| | 4r | 27.01.64 | **Preston North End** | A | L | 1-2 | Edwards |
| 1964-65 (D2) | 3 | 09.01.65 | **Workington** (D3) | H | W | 4-1 | Davies 2, Hill, Butler |
| | 4 | 30.01.65 | **Preston North End** (D2) | A | W | 2-1 | Lee (p), Davies |
| | 5 | 20.02.65 | **Liverpool** (D1) | H | L | 0-1 | |
| 1965-66 (D2) | 3 | 22.01.66 | **WBA** (D1) | H | W | 3-0 | Lee 2, Bromley |
| | 4 | 12.02.66 | **Preston North End** (D2) | H | D | 1-1 | Davies |
| | 4r | 14.02.66 | **Preston North End** | A | L | 2-3 | Lee, Davies |
| 1966-67 (D2) | 3 | 28.01.67 | **Crewe Alexandra** (D4) | H | W | 1-0 | Lee (p) |
| | 4 | 18.02.67 | **Arsenal** (D1) | H | D | 0-0 | |
| | 4r | 22.02.67 | **Arsenal** | A | L | 0-3 | |
| 1967-68 (D2) | 3 | 07.01.68 | **Nottingham Forest** (D1) | A | L | 2-4 | Taylor, Hulme |
| 1968-69 (D2) | 3 | 04.01.69 | **Northampton Town** (D3) | H | W | 2-1 | Fletcher, Greaves |
| | 4 | 25.01.69 | **Bristol Rovers** (D3) | H | L | 1-2 | Williams |
| 1969-70 (D2) | 3 | 03.01.70 | **Watford** (D2) | H | L | 1-2 | Greaves |
| 1970-71 (D2) | 3 | 02.01.71 | **York City** (D4) | A | L | 0-2 | |
| 1971-72 (D3) | 1 | 20.11.71 | **Bangor City** (NPL) | H | W | 3-0 | Ritson (p), Nicholson, Duffy |

| | | | | | | | |
|---|---|---|---|---|---|---|---|
| | 2 | 11.12.71 | **Rossendale Utd** (CC) | A | W | 4-1 | Greaves 3, Byrom |
| | | | *played at Gigg Lane, Bury* | | | | |
| | 3 | 15.01.72 | **Torquay Utd** (D3) | H | W | 2-1 | Hunt, Greaves |
| | 4 | 05.02.72 | **Chelsea** (D1) | A | L | 0-3 | |
| 1972-73 (D3) | 1 | 18.11.72 | **Chester** (D4) | H | D | 1-1 | Byrom |
| | 1r | 22.11.72 | **Chester** | A | W | 1-0 | G Jones |
| | 2 | 09.12.72 | **Shrewsbury Town** (D3) | H | W | 3-0 | Phllips, Lee, Ritson |
| | 3 | 13.01.73 | **Charlton Athletic** (D3) | A | D | 1-1 | Lee |
| | 3r | 17.01.73 | **Charlton Athletic** | H | W | 4-0 | Greaves 2, Nicholson, G Jones |
| | 4 | 03.02.73 | **Cardiff City** (D2) | H | D | 2-2 | G Jones, Ritson |
| | 4r | 07.02.73 | **Cardiff City** | A | D | 1-1aet | G Jones |
| | 4 2r | 12.02.73 | **Cardiff City** | | W | 1-0 | Lee |
| | | | *played at The Hawthorns* | | | | |
| | 5 | 24.02.73 | **Luton Town** (D2) | H | L | 0-1 | |
| 1973-74 (D2) | 3 | 05.01.74 | **Stoke City** (D1) | H | W | 3-2 | Byrom 3 |
| | 4 | 26.01.74 | **Southampton** (D1) | A | D | 3-3 | Byrom 2, G Jones (p) |
| | 4r | 30.01.74 | **Southampton** | H | L | 0-2aet | |
| 1974-75 (D2) | 3 | 04.01.75 | **WBA** (D2) | H | D | 0-0 | |
| | 3r | 08.01.75 | **WBA** | A | L | 0-4 | |
| 1975-76 (D2) | 3 | 03.01.76 | **Brentford** (D4) | A | D | 0-0 | |
| | 3r | 06.01.76 | **Brentford** | H | W | 2-0 | Whatmore 2 |
| | 4 | 24.01.76 | **Huddersfield Town** (D4) | A | W | 1-0 | Reid |
| | 5 | 14.02.76 | **Newcastle Utd** (D1) | H | D | 3-3 | G Jones, P Jones, Allardyce |
| | 5r | 18.02.76 | **Newcastle Utd** | A | D | 0-0aet | |
| | 5 2r | 23.02.76 | **Newcastle Utd** | | L | 1-2 | G Jones |
| | | | *played at Elland Road* | | | | |
| 1976-77 (D2) | 3 | 08.01.77 | **West Ham Utd** (D1) | A | L | 1-2 | Waldron |
| 1977-78 (D2) | 3 | 07.01.78 | **Tottenham Hotspur** (D2) | A | D | 2-2 | Greaves (p), Whatmore |
| | 3r | 10.01.78 | **Tottenham Hotspur** | H | W | 2-1aet | Ritson, G Jones |
| | 4 | 06.02.78 | **Mansfield Town** (D2) | H | W | 1-0 | Worthington |
| | 5 | 27.02.78 | **Middlesbrough** (D1) | A | L | 0-2 | |
| 1978-79 (D1) | 3 | 09.01.79 | **Bristol City** (D1) | A | L | 1-3 | Smith |
| 1979-80 (D1) | 3 | 05.01.80 | **Sunderland** (D2) | A | W | 1-0 | Whatmore |
| | 4 | 26.01.80 | **Halifax Town** (D4) | H | W | 2-0 | Greaves, Whatmore |
| | 5 | 16.02.80 | **Arsenal** (D1) | H | D | 1-1 | Allardyce |
| | 5r | 19.02.80 | **Arsenal** | A | L | 0-3 | |
| 1980-81 (D2) | 3 | 03.01.81 | **Nottingham Forest** (D1) | A | D | 3-3 | Hoggan 2, Whatmore |
| | 3r | 06.01.81 | **Nottingham Forest** | H | L | 0-1aet | |
| 1981-82 (D2) | 3 | 02.01.82 | **Derby County** (D2) | H | W | 3-1 | Gowling, Foster, Thompso |
| | 4 | 23.01.82 | **Crystal Palace** (D2) | A | L | 0-1 | |
| 1982-83 (D2) | 3 | 08.01.83 | **Arsenal** (D1) | A | L | 1-2 | Whatmore |
| 1983-84 (D3) | 1 | 19.11.83 | **Tranmere Rovers** (D4) | A | D | 2-2 | Joyce, Chandler (p) |
| | 1r | 22.11.83 | **Tranmere Rovers** | H | W | 4-1aet | Chandler 2(1p), Rudge, Caldwell |
| | 2 | 10.12.83 | **Mansfield Town** (D4) | H | W | 2-0 | Foster, Rudge |
| | 3 | 07.01.84 | **Sunderland** (D1) | H | L | 0-3 | |
| 1984-85 (D3) | 1 | 17.11.84 | **Hull City** (D3) | A | L | 1-2 | Foster |
| 1985-86 (D3) | 1 | 16.11.85 | **Wrexham** (D4) | A | L | 1-3 | Thompson (p) |
| 1986-87 (D3) | 1 | 15.11.86 | **Halifax Town** (D4) | A | D | 1-1 | Oghani |
| | 1r | 18.11.86 | **Halifax Town** | H | D | 1-1aet | Caldwell |
| | 1 2r | 24.11.86 | **Halifax Town** | A | W | 3-1 | Thompson, Caldwell, Gavin |
| | 2 | 06.12.86 | **Tranmere Rovers** (D4) | H | W | 2-0 | Caldwell, Thompson |
| | 3 | 10.01.87 | **Coventry City** (D1) | A | L | 0-3 | |
| 1987-88 (D4) | 1 | 14.11.87 | **Burnley** (D4) | A | W | 1-0 | Thomas (p) |
| | 2 | 05.12.87 | **Wrexham** (D4) | A | W | 2-1 | Thomas 2 |
| | 3 | 09.01.88 | **Barnsley** (D2) | A | L | 1-3 | Stevens |
| 1988-89 (D3) | 1 | 19.11.88 | **Chesterfield** (D3) | H | D | 0-0 | |
| | 1r | 28.11.88 | **Chesterfield** | A | W | 3-2 | Stevens, Storer, Darby |
| | 2 | 10.12.88 | **Port Vale** (D3) | H | L | 1-2 | Keeley |
| 1989-90 (D3) | 1 | 18.11.89 | **Blackpool** (D3) | A | L | 1-2 | Crombie |
| 1990-91 (D3) | 1 | 17.11.90 | **Witton Albion** (NPL) | A | W | 2-1 | Darby, Comstive |
| | 2 | 11.12.90 | **Chesterfield** (D4) | A | W | 4-3 | Reeves, Philliskirk, Thompson, Storer |

| | | | | | | | |
|---|---|---|---|---|---|---|---|
| | 3 | 05.01.91 | **Barrow** (Conf) | H | W | 1-0 | Philliskirk |
| | 4 | 26.01.91 | **Manchester Utd** (D1) | A | L | 0-1 | |
| 1991-92 (D3) | 1 | 17.11.91 | **Emley** (NPL) | A | W | 3-0 | Reeves 2, Philliskirk |
| | | | *played at Leeds Road, Huddersfield* | | | | |
| | 2 | 07.12.91 | **Bradford City** (D3) | H | W | 3-1 | Burke, Reeves, Philliskirk |
| | 3 | 04.01.92 | **Reading** (D3) | H | W | 2-0 | Philliskirk |
| | 4 | 25.01.92 | **Brighton** (D2) | H | W | 2-1 | Walker, Philliskirk (p) |
| | 5 | 16.02.92 | **Southampton** (D1) | H | D | 2-2 | Walker, Green |
| | 5r | 26.02.92 | **Southampton** | A | L | 2-3aet | Walker, Darby |
| 1992-93 (D2) | 1 | 14.11.92 | **Sutton Coldfield T** (SL) | H | W | 2-1 | Reeves, Walker |
| | 2 | 05.12.92 | **Rochdale** (D3) | H | W | 4-0 | McAteer, McGinlay 2, Walker |
| | 3 | 03.01.93 | **Liverpool** (PL) | H | D | 2-2 | McGinlay, Seagraves |
| | 3r | 15.01.93 | **Liverpool** | A | W | 2-0 | McGinlay, Walker |
| | 4 | 24.01.93 | **Wolverhampton W** (D1) | A | W | 2-0 | Green, McGinlay |
| | 5 | 13.02.93 | **Derby County** (D1) | A | L | 1-3 | Walker |
| 1993-94 (D1) | 1 | 13.11.93 | **Gretna** (NPL) | A | W | 3-2 | McGinlay (p), Coyle 2 |
| | 2 | 04.12.93 | **Lincoln City** (D3) | A | W | 3-1 | Thompson, Brown, Coyle |
| | 3 | 08.01.94 | **Everton** (PL) | H | D | 1-1 | Patterson |
| | 3r | 19.01.94 | **Everton** | A | W | 3-2aet | McGinlay, Stubbs, Coyle |
| | 4 | 31.01.94 | **Arsenal** (PL) | H | D | 2-2 | McAteer, Coyle |
| | 4r | 09.02.94 | **Arsenal** | A | W | 3-1aet | McGinlay, McAteer, Walker |
| | 5 | 20.02.94 | **Aston Villa** (PL) | H | W | 1-0 | Stubbs |
| | 6 | 12.03.94 | **Oldham Athletic** (PL) | H | L | 0-1 | |
| 1994-95 (D1) | 3 | 07.01.95 | **Portsmouth** (D1) | A | L | 1-3 | Sneekes |
| 1995-96 (PL) | 3 | 06.01.96 | **Bradford City** (D2) | A | W | 3-0 | McGinlay, Curcic 2 |
| | 4 | 14.02.96 | **Leeds Utd** (PL) | H | L | 0-1 | |
| 1996-97 (D1) | 3 | 21.01.97 | **Luton Town** (D2) | A | D | 1-1 | Pollock |
| | 3r | 25.01.97 | **Luton Town** | H | W | 6-2 | McGinlay, Blake 2, Thompson, Pollock, Green |
| | 4 | 04.02.97 | **Chesterfield** (D2) | H | L | 2-3 | Taylor, Green |
| 1997-98 (PL) | 3 | 03.01.98 | **Barnsley** (PL) | A | L | 0-1 | |
| 1998-99 (D1) | 3 | 02.01.99 | **Wolverhampton W** (D1) | H | L | 1-2 | Sellars |
| 1999-00 (D1) | 3 | 21.12.99 | **Cardiff City** (D2) | H | W | 1-0 | Gudjohnsen |
| | 4 | 08.01.00 | **Grimsby Town** (D1) | A | W | 2-0 | Gudjohnsen, Hansen |
| | 5 | 29.01.00 | **Cambridge Utd** (D2) | A | W | 3-1 | Taylor 2, Gudjohnsen |
| | 6 | 19.02.00 | **Charlton Athletic** (D1) | H | W | 1-0 | Gudjohnsen |
| | SF | 02.04.00 | **Aston Villa** (PL) | | D | 0-0aet | |
| | | | *played at Wembley Stadium – Aston Villa won 4-1 on penalties* | | | | |
| 2000-01 (D1) | 3 | 06.01.01 | **Yeovil Town** (Conf) | H | W | 2-1 | O'Kane, Ricketts |
| | 4 | 28.01.01 | **Scunthorpe Utd** (D3) | H | W | 5-1 | Holdsworth, Nolan |
| | 5 | 17.02.01 | **Blackburn Rovers** (D1) | H | D | 1-1 | Ricketts |
| | 5r | 07.03.01 | **Blackburn Rovers** | A | L | 0-3 | |
| 2001-02 (PL) | 3 | 16.01.02 | **Stockport County** (D2) | A | W | 4-1 | Bergsson, Norris, Pedersen, Ricketts |
| | 4 | 05.02.02 | **Tottenham Hotspur** (PL) | A | L | 0-4 | |
| 2002-03 (PL) | 3 | 04.01.03 | **Sunderland** (PL) | H | D | 1-1 | Ricketts |
| | 3r | 14.01.03 | **Sunderland** | A | L | 0-2aet | |

## BOOTLE

*Formed 1878 as Bootle St John's and were (very) briefly the top club on Merseyside in the 1880s. As a Second Division club in 1892-93 they beat amateurs Gorton Villa 10-0 in a qualifying round match. The current Bootle club in the North West Counties League dates from 1953.*

| | | | | | | | |
|---|---|---|---|---|---|---|---|
| 1881-82 | 1 | 05.11.81 | **Blackburn Law** | H | W | 2-1 | Smith, Turner |
| | 2 | 03.12.81 | **Turton** | A | L | 0-4 | |
| 1882-83 | 1 | 04.11.82 | **Bolton Wanderers** | A | L | 1-6 | Robertson |
| 1886-87 | 1 | 16.10.86 | **Great Lever** | H | L | 2-4 | |
| 1887-88 | 1 | 15.10.87 | **Workington** | H | W | 6-0 | Lewis 2, Wilding 2, Anderson, Morris |
| | 2 | 05.11.87 | **South Shore** | H | D | 1-1 | Veitch |
| | 2r | 12.11.87 | **South Shore** | A | W | 3-0 | Anderson, Hastings, Lewis |
| | 3 | 26.11.87 | **Higher Walton** | A | W | 6-1 | Hastings 4, Anderson, Morris |
| | 4 | 17.12.87 | **Great Bridge Unity** | A | W | 2-1 | |
| | 5 | 07.01.88 | **Old Carthusians** | A | L | 0-2 | |
| 1888-89 | 1 | 02.02.89 | **Preston North End** (D1) | H | L | 0-3 | |

| | | | | | | | | |
|---|---|---|---|---|---|---|---|---|
| 1889-90 | (FAll) | 1 | 18.01.90 | **Sunderland Albion** (FAll) | H | L | 1-3 | Jamieson |
| | | | | *FA disqualified Sunderland Albion for ineligible players and awarded tie to Bootle* | | | | |
| | | 2 | 01.02.90 | **Derby Midland** (ML) | H | W | 2-1 | Galbraith, Woods |
| | | 3 | 15.02.90 | **Blackburn Rovers** (D1) | H | L | 0-7 | |
| 1890-91 | (FAll) | | | 1q Carlisle (A) 6-1; 2q Newton Heath (H) 2-1; 3q Halliwell (A) 3-4 | | | | |
| 1891-92 | (FAll) | 1 | 16.01.92 | **Darwen** (D1) | H | L | 0-2 | |
| 1892-93 | (D2) | | | 1q Gorton Villa (H) 10-0; 2q Liverpool Caledonians (H) 2-3 | | | | |

# BOREHAMWOOD

*Formed 1948 by the merger of Borehamwood Rovers and the exotically named 'Royal Retournez'. First entered FA Cup: 1970-71. Members of the Isthmian League.*

| | | | | | | | | |
|---|---|---|---|---|---|---|---|---|
| 1973-74 | (AL) | 1 | 24.11.73 | **Southend Utd** (D3) | A | L | 0-3 | |
| 1977-78 | (AL) | 1 | 26.11.77 | **Swindon Town** (D3) | H | D | 0-0 | |
| | | 1r | 29.11.77 | **Swindon Town** | A | L | 0-2 | |
| 1996-97 | (IL) | 1 | 16.11.96 | **Rushden & D** (Conf) | H | D | 1-1 | Robbins |
| | | 1r | 26.11.96 | **Rushden & D** | A | W | 3-2 | Hefter, T Samuels, D Samuels |
| | | 2 | 07.12.96 | **Luton Town** (D2) | A | L | 1-2 | Robbins |
| 1997-98 | (IL) | 1 | 15.11.97 | **Hayes** (Conf) | A | W | 1-0 | Marshall |
| | | 2 | 06.12.97 | **Cheltenham Town** (Conf) | A | D | 1-1 | Marshall |
| | | 2r | 16.12.97 | **Cheltenham Town** | H | L | 0-2 | |
| 1998-99 | (IL) | 1 | 15.11.98 | **Luton Town** (D2) | H | L | 2-3 | Nisbet, Xavier |
| 2002-03 | (IL) | 1 | 16.11.02 | **Torquay Utd** (D3) | A | L | 0-5 | |

# BOSTON TOWN

*Originally formed 1870. Reformed 1963. Boston Town, known as 'FC' locally, play in the United Counties League. Boston United were previously known as both Boston FC and later Boston Town which has given rise to some historical confusion in the past. Boston Utd's records for the 1887-88, 1925-26, 1926-27 and 1932-33 seasons when they competed in the FA Cup as Boston Town, are shown under Boston Utd's entry. The current Boston Town first entered FA Cup: 1965-66.*

| | | | | | | | | |
|---|---|---|---|---|---|---|---|---|
| 1976-77 | (ML) | 1 | 20.11.76 | **Barnsley** (D4) | A | L | 1-3 | Daley |

# BOSTON UNITED

*Formed 1934. First entered FA Cup: 1934-35. FA Trophy Runners-up: 1985. League clubs beaten as a Non-League club: Bradford Park A, Crewe Alexandra, Derby County, Hartlepool, Southport. Promoted to Football League 2002.*

| | | | | | | | | |
|---|---|---|---|---|---|---|---|---|
| 1887-88 | | 1 | 15.10.87 | **Gainsborough T** | A | L | 0-9 | |
| 1925-26 | (ML) | 1 | 28.11.25 | **Mansfield Town** (ML) | H | W | 5-2 | Doran, Porter, Clarke, Jenkinson, Miller |
| | | 2 | 12.12.25 | **Bradford Park A** (3N) | H | W | 1-0 | Doran |
| | | 3 | 09.01.26 | **Sunderland** (D1) | A | L | 1-8 | Porter |
| 1926-27 | (ML) | 1 | 27.11.26 | **Northampton Town** (3S) | H | D | 1-1 | Wainwright |
| | | 1r | 02.12.26 | **Northampton Town** | A | L | 1-2 | Menlove |
| 1932-33 | (ML) | 1 | 26.11.32 | **Darlington** (3N) | A | L | 0-1 | |
| 1934-35 | (ML) | 1 | 24.11.34 | **Darwen** (LC) | A | W | 2-1 | Bungay, Marshall |
| | | 2 | 08.12.34 | **Bath City** (SL) | A | L | 1-2 | Bungay |
| 1935-36 | (ML) | 1 | 30.11.35 | **Crewe Alexandra** (3N) | A | L | 2-4 | McConnell, Bungay |
| 1936-37 | (ML) | 1 | 28.11.36 | **Spennymoor Utd** (NEL) | H | D | 1-1 | Nottey |
| | | 1r | 02.12.36 | **Spennymoor Utd** | A | L | 0-2 | |
| 1952-53 | (ML) | 1 | 22.11.52 | **Oldham Athletic** (3N) | H | L | 1-2 | Kurz |
| 1953-54 | (ML) | 1 | 21.11.53 | **Scunthorpe Utd** (3N) | A | L | 0-9 | |
| 1954-55 | (ML) | 1 | 20.11.54 | **Blyth Spartans** (NEL) | H | D | 1-1 | Wilkins |
| | | 1r | 24.11.54 | **Blyth Spartans** | A | L | 4-5 | Lowder 2, Hazeldine 2 |
| 1955-56 | (ML) | 1 | 19.11.55 | **Northwich V** (CC) | H | W | 3-2 | Whitfield 2, Wilkins |
| | | 2 | 10.12.55 | **Derby County** (3N) | A | W | 6-1 | Wilkins 2, Hazeldine 3, Birbeck |
| | | 3 | 07.01.56 | **Tottenham Hotspur** (D1) | A | L | 0-4 | |
| 1956-57 | (ML) | 1 | 17.11.56 | **Bradford Park A** (3N) | H | L | 0-2 | |
| 1957-58 | (ML) | 1 | 16.11.57 | **Billingham S** (NL) | H | W | 5-2 | Graver 4, Lewis |
| | | 2 | 07.12.57 | **Darlington** (3N) | A | L | 3-5 | Graver, Hukin 2 |
| 1958-59 | (SL) | 1 | 15.11.58 | **Chester** (D4) | A | L | 2-3 | Hukin 2 |
| 1962-63 | (ML) | 1 | 03.11.62 | **King's Lynn** (SL) | H | L | 1-2 | Bull |
| 1967-68 | (WMRL) | 1 | 09.12.67 | **Corby Town** (SL) | A | W | 3-0 | Bowers, Rayner, Robinson |
| | | 2 | 06.01.68 | **Orient** (D3) | H | D | 1-1 | Wood og |
| | | 2r | 15.01.68 | **Orient** | A | L | 1-2 | Thompson |

| | | | | | | | | |
|---|---|---|---|---|---|---|---|---|
| 1970-71 | (NPL) | 1 | 21.11.70 | **Southport** (D4) | A | W | 2-0 | Bates, Mackay |
| | | 2 | 12.12.70 | **York City** (D4) | H | L | 1-2 | Bates |
| 1971-72 | (NPL) | 1 | 20.11.71 | **Ellesmere Port T** (NPL) | A | W | 3-0 | Wilkinson, Svarc, Coates |
| | | 2 | 11.12.71 | **Hartlepool** (D4) | H | W | 2-1 | Smith, Froggart |
| | | 3 | 15.01.72 | **Portsmouth** (D2) | H | L | 0-1 | |
| 1972-73 | (NPL) | 1 | 18.11.72 | **Lancaster City** (NPL) | H | L | 1-2 | Froggart |
| 1973-74 | (NPL) | 1 | 24.11.73 | **Hayes** (IL) | H | D | 0-0 | |
| | | 1r | 28.11.73 | **Hayes** | A | W | 2-1aet | Tewley, Froggart |
| | | 2 | 15.12.73 | **Hitchin Town** (IL) | H | W | 1-0 | Conde |
| | | 3 | 05.01.74 | **Derby County** (D1) | A | D | 0-0 | |
| | | 3r | 09.01.74 | **Derby County** | H | L | 1-6 | Conde |
| 1974-75 | (NPL) | 1 | 23.11.74 | **Chesterfield** (D3) | A | L | 1-3 | Tewley |
| 1975-76 | (NPL) | 1 | 22.11.75 | **Lincoln City** (D4) | H | L | 0-1 | |
| 1978-79 | (NPL) | 1 | 25.11.78 | **Tranmere Rovers** (D3) | A | L | 1-2 | Mayes |
| 1980-81 | (APL) | 1 | 22.11.80 | **Rotherham Utd** (D3) | H | L | 0-4 | |
| 1981-82 | (APL) | 1 | 21.11.81 | **Kettering Town** (APL) | H | L | 0-1 | |
| 1982-83 | (APL) | 1 | 20.11.82 | **Crewe Alexandra** (D4) | H | W | 3-1 | Lumby, Cook 2 |
| 1983-84 | (APL) | 1 | 19.11.83 | **Bury** (D4) | H | L | 0-3 | |
| 1985-86 | (Conf) | 1 | 16.11.85 | **Runcorn** (Conf) | A | D | 2-2 | Casey, Nuttell |
| | | 1r | 20.11.85 | **Runcorn** | H | D | 1-1aet | Gilbert |
| | | 12r | 25.11.85 | **Runcorn** | A | L | 1-4 | Gilbert |
| 1986-87 | (Conf) | 1 | 15.11.86 | **Runcorn** (Conf) | A | D | 1-1 | Fee |
| | | 1r | 19.11.86 | **Runcorn** | H | L | 1-2aet | Lissaman (p) |
| 1990-91 | (Conf) | 1 | 17.11.90 | **Wycombe W** (Conf) | H | D | 1-1 | Cavell |
| | | 1r | 21.11.90 | **Wycombe W** | A | L | 0-4 | |
| 1996-97 | (NPL) | 1 | 16.11.96 | **Morecambe** (Conf) | H | W | 3-0 | L Chambers 2, S Chambers |
| | | 2 | 07.12.96 | **Chester City** (D3) | A | L | 0-1 | |
| 1997-98 | (NPL) | 1 | 15.11.97 | **Ilkeston Town** (SL) | A | L | 1-2 | Cavell |
| 2002-03 | (D3) | 1 | 16.11.02 | **Northampton Town** (D2) | A | L | 2-3 | Battersby (p), Higgins |

# BOTWELL MISSION (HAYES)

*Formed 1909 as Botwell Mission and provided the nucleus for the new, re-named Hayes 1930. First entered FA Cup: 1919-20. Middlesex Senior Cup winners 1920, 1921, 1926. See also Hayes.*

| | | | | | | | | |
|---|---|---|---|---|---|---|---|---|
| 1927-28 | (SPT) | 1 | 30.11.27 | **Peterborough & F** (SL) | H | L | 3-4 | Treasure 3 |

# BOURNEMOUTH

*Formed 1899. Played as Boscombe FC 1899-1923 and played against Bournemouth FC in the FA Cup. Became Bournemouth and Boscombe Athletic in 1923 and changed name to AFC Bournemouth in 1971. First competed in FA Cup: 1909-10; Best FA Cup performance: 6th round, 1957. Record FA Cup win: 11-0 v Margate 1st round, 20.11.1971 when Ted MacDougall scored an FA Cup Competition Proper record of nine goals in one match. Record FA Cup defeat: 0-7 v Sheffield Wed, 4th round, 23.01.1932 and v Burnley 3rd round replay, 25.01.1966.*

**as Boscombe FA**

| | | |
|---|---|---|
| 1909-10 | (Hants) | P Bournemouth Gasworks (A) 0-0; Pr Bournemouth Gasworks (A) 2-1; 1q Poole (A) 2-3 |
| 1910-11 | (Hants) | 1q Weymouth (A) 4-3; 2q Poole (A) 0-0; 2qr Poole (A) 4-1; 3q Torquay T (A) 0-1 |
| 1911-12 | (Hants) | did not enter |
| 1912-13 | (Hants) | P Portland (H) 6-0; 1q Gosport U (A) 1-1; 1qr Gosport (H) 7-1; 2q Basingstoke (H) 3-1; 3q 1st Kings Rifles (H) 0-0; 3qr 1st Kings Rifles (A) 0-1 |
| 1913-14 | (Hants) | P Royal Engineers, Aldershot (A) 2-0; 1q Cowes (A) 3-2; 2q Bournemouth FC (H) 0-1 |
| 1914-15 | (Hants) | P RC Artillery walkover; 1q Bournemouth Tramways (H) 3-0; 2q Thornycrofts Ath (A) 6-1; 3q Cowes (A) 1-0; 4q Welton R (H) 2-1; 5q Brentford (H) 0-0; 5qr Brentford (A) 1-0; 6q Bristol R (A) 0-3 |
| 1919-20 | (Hants) | P Poole & St Marys (H) 9-0; 1q Basingstoke (A) 0-1 |
| 1920-21 | (SL) | 1q Blandford (H) 1-1; 1qr Blandford (A) 1-2 |
| 1921-22 | (SL) | P Royal Artillery Gosport (H) 2-0; 1q Bournemouth FC (A) 0-0; 1qr Bournemouth FC (H) 6-0; 2q Thornycroft Woolston (H) 1-0; 3q Harland & Wolffs (A) 3-2; 4q Torquay U (A) 1-0; 5q Swansea T (A) 0-5 |
| 1922-23 | (SL) | P Blandford (H) 3-0; 1q Bournemouth Tramways (A) 2-1; 2q Sholing Ath (H) 2-1; 3q Gosport Ath (H) 4-0; 4q Exeter C (A) 0-0; 4qr Exeter C (H) 1-3 |

**as Bournemouth & Boscombe Athletic**

| | | |
|---|---|---|
| 1923-24 | (3S) | P Portsea Gas Company (H) scratched |

| | | | | | | | |
|---|---|---|---|---|---|---|---|
| 1924-25 (3S) | | | 4q Yeovil & Petters U (A) 2-3 | | | | |
| 1925-26 (3S) | 1 | 28.11.25 | **Merthyr Town** (3S) | H | W | 3-0 | Eyre, Maidment, Stringfellow |
| | 2 | 12.12.25 | **Brentford** (3S) | A | W | 2-1 | Stringfellow, Eyre |
| | 3 | 09.01.26 | **Reading** (3S) | H | W | 2-0 | Eyre 2 |
| | 4 | 30.01.26 | **Bolton Wanderers** (D1) | H | D | 2-2 | Stringfellow, Roberts |
| | 4r | 03.02.26 | **Bolton Wanderers** | A | L | 2-6 | Butt, Eyre |
| 1926-27 (3S) | 1 | 27.11.26 | **Swindon Town** (3S) | H | D | 1-1 | Hayward |
| | 1r | 29.11.26 | **Swindon Town** | A | W | 4-3 | Eyre 2, Taylor 2 |
| | 2 | 11.12.26 | **Bristol City** (3S) | A | D | 1-1 | Stringfellow |
| | 2r | 15.12.26 | **Bristol City** | H | W | 2-0 | Eyre 2 |
| | 3 | 08.01.27 | **Liverpool** (D1) | H | D | 1-1 | Taylor |
| | 3r | 12.01.27 | **Liverpool** | A | L | 1-4 | Eyre |
| 1927-28 (3S) | 1 | 26.11.27 | **Coventry City** (3S) | A | D | 2-2 | Pike 2 |
| | 1r | 30.11.27 | **Coventry City** | H | W | 2-0 | Pike, Eyre |
| | 2 | 10.12.27 | **Bristol Rovers** (3S) | H | W | 6-1 | Taylor 2, Clifford 2, Miles, Eyre |
| | 3 | 14.01.28 | **Sheffield Wed** (D1) | A | L | 0-3 | |
| 1928-29 (3S) | 1 | 24.11.28 | **Poole Town** (SL) | A | W | 4-1 | Clifford, Eyre 2, Cherrett |
| | 2 | 08.12.28 | **Guildford City** (SL) | A | W | 5-1 | Hayward, Eyre 4 |
| | 3 | 12.01.29 | **Accrington Stanley** (3N) | A | D | 1-1 | Clifford |
| | 3r | 16.01.29 | **Accrington Stanley** | H | W | 2-0 | Clifford, Bryce |
| | 4 | 26.01.29 | **Watford** (3S) | H | W | 6-4 | Bryce, Cherrett Eyre 3, Clifford |
| | 5 | 16.02.29 | **West Ham Utd** (D1) | H | D | 1-1 | Graham |
| | 5r | 20.02.29 | **West Ham Utd** | A | L | 1-3 | Hayward (p) |
| 1929-30 (3S) | 1 | 30.11.29 | **Torquay Utd** (3S) | H | W | 2-0 | Beswick, Eyre |
| | 2 | 14.12.29 | **Caernarfon Town** (Welsh) | A | D | 1-1 | Beswick |
| | 2r | 18.12.29 | **Caernarfon Town** | H | W | 5-2 | Edwards og, Eyre 2, Boswick, Price |
| | 3 | 11.01.30 | **Fulham** (3S) | A | D | 1-1 | Eyre |
| | 3r | 15.01.30 | **Fulham** | H | L | 0-2 | |
| 1930-31 (3S) | 1 | 29.11.30 | **Walsall** (3S) | A | L | 0-1 | |
| 1931-32 (3S) | 1 | 28.11.31 | **Northfleet Utd** (KL) | H | D | 1-1 | White |
| | 1r | 02.12.31 | **Northfleet Utd** | A | W | 1-0 | Webb |
| | 2 | 12.12.31 | **Blyth Spartans** (NEL) | H | W | 1-0 | Hayward |
| | 3 | 09.01.32 | **Halifax Town** (3N) | A | W | 3-1 | Beswick 2, Eyre |
| | 4 | 23.01.32 | **Sheffield Wed** (D1) | A | L | 0-7 | |
| 1932-33 (3S) | 1 | 26.11.32 | **Torquay Utd** (3S) | A | D | 0-0 | |
| | 1r | 30.11.32 | **Torquay Utd** | H | D | 2-2aet | Eyre 2 |
| | 12r | 05.12.32 | **Torquay Utd** *played at Ashton Gate* | | L | 2-3 | Tennant og, Russell |
| 1933-34 (3S) | 1 | 25.11.33 | **Hayes** (AL) | H | W | 3-0 | Surtees, White 2 |
| | 2 | 09.12.33 | **Tranmere Rovers** (3N) | H | L | 2-4 | Russell 2 |
| 1934-35 (3S) | 1 | 24.11.34 | **Aldershot** (3S) | A | L | 0-4 | |
| 1935-36 (3S) | 1 | 30.11.35 | **Walthamstow A** (AL) | A | D | 1-1 | Parris |
| | 1r | 04.12.35 | **Walthamstow A** | H | W | 8-1 | Chalmers 3, Parris 3, Barrow, Burgin |
| | 2 | 14.12.35 | **Barrow** (3N) | H | W | 5-2 | Parris 3, Barrow, Riley |
| | 3 | 11.01.36 | **Bradford City** (D2) | A | L | 0-1 | |
| 1936-37 (3S) | 1 | 28.11.36 | **Harwich & P** (ECL) | H | W | 5-1 | Marsden 2, Harris, Riley, Kilcar |
| | 2 | 12.12.36 | **Mansfield Town** (3N) | A | W | 3-0 | Parris 2, Riley |
| | 3 | 16.01.37 | **Everton** (D1) | A | L | 0-5 | |
| 1937-38 (3S) | 1 | 27.11.37 | **Dartford** (SL) | H | D | 0-0 | |
| | 1r | 01.12.37 | **Dartford** | A | W | 6-0 | Chalmers 2, Whittam 2, Millar, Collins og |
| | 2 | 11.12.37 | **Newport County** (3S) | A | L | 1-2 | Miller |
| 1938-39 (3S) | 1 | 26.11.38 | **Bristol City** (3S) | H | W | 2-1 | Elliott, Langley |
| | 2 | 10.12.38 | **Bristol Rovers** (3S) | A | W | 3-0 | Elliott, Langley 2 |
| | 3 | 17.01.39 | **Leeds Utd** (D1) | A | L | 1-3 | Fletcher |
| 1945-46 (3S) | 1 1L | 17.11.45 | **Lovell's Athletic** (Welsh) | A | L | 1-4 | Thomas |
| | 1 2L | 24.11.45 | **Lovell's Athletic** | H | W | 3-2 | Paton, J Thomas 2 |
| 1946-47 (3S) | 1 | 30.11.46 | **Exeter City** (3S) | H | W | 4-2 | Gallacher, Tunnicliffe, Kirkham (p), Paton |
| | 2 | 14.12.46 | **Aldershot** (3S) | H | W | 4-2 | Kirkham 2, Tagg, Mcdonald |
| | 3 | 11.01.47 | **Derby County** (D1) | H | L | 0-2 | |
| 1947-48 (3S) | 1 | 29.11.47 | **Guildford City** (SL) | H | W | 2-0 | Milligan, McDonald |

| | | | | | | | | |
|---|---|---|---|---|---|---|---|---|
| | | 2 | 13.12.47 | **Bradford City** (3N) | H | W | 1-0 | Blair |
| | | 3 | 10.01.48 | **Wolverhampton W** (D1) | H | L | 1-2 | Milligan |
| 1948-49 | (3S) | 3 | 08.01.49 | **Manchester Utd** (D1) | A | L | 0-6 | |
| 1949-50 | (3S) | 3 | 07.01.50 | **Bradford Park A** (D2) | A | W | 1-0 | Cross |
| | | 4 | 28.01.50 | **Northampton Town** (3S) | H | D | 1-1 | Weigh |
| | | 4r | 02.02.50 | **Northampton Town** | A | L | 1-2 | Cross |
| 1950-51 | (3S) | 1 | 25.11.50 | **Colchester Utd** (3S) | H | W | 1-0 | Boxshall |
| | | 2 | 09.12.50 | **Aldershot** (3S) | A | L | 0-3 | |
| 1951-52 | (3S) | 1 | 24.11.51 | **Southend Utd** (3S) | A | L | 1-6 | Stroud |
| 1952-53 | (3S) | 1 | 22.11.52 | **Ipswich Town** (3S) | A | D | 2-2 | Cheney, Harrison |
| | | 1r | 26.11.52 | **Ipswich Town** | H | D | 2-2aet | Rees og, Cross |
| | | 12r | 01.12.52 | **Ipswich Town** *played at Highbury* | | L | 2-3 | Eyre 2 |
| 1953-54 | (3S) | 1 | 21.11.53 | **Southampton** (3S) | A | D | 1-1 | Fidler |
| | | 1r | 25.11.53 | **Southampton** | H | W | 3-1 | Fidler, Stephens, Cheney |
| | | 2 | 12.12.53 | **Scunthorpe Utd** (3N) | A | L | 0-1 | |
| 1954-55 | (3S) | 1 | 20.11.54 | **Barnstaple Town** (WL) | A | W | 4-1 | Harrison 2, Hunt, Siddall |
| | | 2 | 11.12.54 | **Oldham Athletic** (3N) | H | W | 1-0 | Allen |
| | | 3 | 08.01.55 | **WBA** (D1) | H | L | 0-1 | |
| 1955-56 | (3S) | 1 | 19.11.55 | **Reading** (3S) | A | L | 0-1 | |
| 1956-57 | (3S) | 1 | 17.11.56 | **Burton Albion** (BDL) | H | W | 8-0 | Wright og, Lyons, Bedford, Norris 3, Newsham 2 |
| | | 2 | 08.12.56 | **Swindon Town** (3S) | A | W | 1-0 | Cutler |
| | | 3 | 05.01.57 | **Accrington Stanley** (3N) | H | W | 2-0 | Norris, Bedford |
| | | 4 | 26.01.57 | **Wolverhampton W** (D1) | A | W | 1-0 | Cutler |
| | | 5 | 16.02.57 | **Tottenham Hotspur** (D1) | H | W | 3-1 | Norris, Newsham, Stiffle |
| | | 6 | 02.03.57 | **Manchester Utd** (D1) | H | L | 1-2 | Bedford |
| 1957-58 | (3S) | 1 | 16.11.57 | **Oswestry Town** (BDL) | A | W | 5-1 | Bedford 3, Dowsett, Burgess |
| | | 2 | 07.12.57 | **Northampton Town** (3S) | A | L | 1-4 | Norris |
| 1958-59 | (D3) | 1 | 15.11.58 | **Tooting & M** (IL) | A | L | 1-3 | Burgess |
| 1959-60 | (D3) | 1 | 14.11.59 | **Walthamstow A** (IL) | A | W | 3-2 | Evans, Brown, Bumstead |
| | | 2 | 05.12.59 | **Enfield** (AL) | A | W | 5-1 | Bumstead 3, Dowsett, Arnott |
| | | 3 | 09.01.60 | **York City** (D3) | H | W | 1-0 | Southren |
| | | 4 | 30.01.60 | **Bradford City** (D3) | A | L | 1-3 | Lawlor og |
| 1960-61 | (D3) | 1 | 05.11.60 | **Exeter City** (D4) | A | D | 1-1 | Bumstead |
| | | 1r | 09.11.60 | **Exeter City** | H | W | 3-1 | Bolton, Bumstead, Evans |
| | | 2 | 26.11.60 | **Yeovil Town** (SL) | H | W | 3-1 | Bolton, Weller, Smith |
| | | 3 | 07.01.61 | **Burnley** (D1) | A | L | 0-1 | |
| 1961-62 | (D3) | 1 | 04.11.61 | **Margate** (SL) | H | L | 0-3 | |
| 1962-63 | (D3) | 1 | 03.11.62 | **Coventry City** (D3) | A | L | 0-1 | |
| 1963-64 | (D3) | 1 | 16.11.63 | **Bristol Rovers** (D3) | H | L | 1-3 | Crickmore |
| 1964-65 | (D3) | 1 | 14.11.64 | **Gravesend & N** (SL) | H | W | 7-0 | Hodgson 3, Bolton, Bumstead, Coxon, Groves |
| | | 2 | 05.12.64 | **Bristol City** (D3) | H | L | 0-3 | |
| 1965-66 | (D3) | 1 | 13.11.65 | **Weymouth** (SL) | H | D | 0-0 | |
| | | 1r | 17.11.65 | **Weymouth** | A | W | 4-1 | Crickmore, Archer (p), Coughlin 2 |
| | | 2 | 04.12.65 | **Bath City** (SL) | H | W | 5-3 | Naylor, Coughlin 3, Hodgson |
| | | 3 | 22.01.66 | **Burnley** (D1) | H | D | 1-1 | Archer |
| | | 3r | 25.01.66 | **Burnley** | A | L | 0-7 | |
| 1966-67 | (D3) | 1 | 26.11.66 | **Welton Rovers** (WL) | H | W | 3-0 | Weller 2, Hold |
| | | 2 | 07.01.67 | **QPR** (D3) | A | L | 0-2 | |
| 1967-68 | (D3) | 1 | 09.12.67 | **Northampton Town** (D3) | H | W | 2-0 | Bolton (p), Hole |
| | | 2 | 06.01.68 | **Walthamstow A** (IL) | A | W | 3-1 | K.White, Pound 2 |
| | | 3 | 27.01.68 | **Liverpool** (D1) | H | D | 0-0 | |
| | | 3r | 30.01.68 | **Liverpool** | A | L | 1-4 | Hughes og |
| 1968-69 | (D3) | 1 | 16.11.68 | **Bury Town** (Met) | A | D | 0-0 | |
| | | 1r | 20.11.68 | **Bury Town** | H | W | 3-0 | Hold, Bolton, Heffer og |
| | | 2 | 07.12.68 | **Bristol Rovers** (D3) | H | D | 0-0 | |
| | | 2r | 10.12.68 | **Bristol Rovers** | A | L | 0-1 | |
| 1969-70 | (D3) | 1 | 15.11.69 | **Luton Town** (D3) | H | D | 1-1 | Hartley |
| | | 1r | 18.11.69 | **Luton Town** | A | L | 1-3 | White |

| | | | | | | | | |
|---|---|---|---|---|---|---|---|---|
| 1970-71 (D4) | 1 | 21.11.70 | **Oxford City** (IL) | A | D | 1-1 | MacDougall |
| | 1r | 23.11.70 | **Oxford City** | H | W | 8-1 | Macdougall 6, Longhorn, Rowles |
| | 2 | 12.12.70 | **Yeovil Town** (SL) | H | L | 0-1 | |
| **as AFC Bournemouth** | | | | | | | |
| 1971-72 (D3) | 1 | 20.11.71 | **Margate** (SL) | H | W | 11-0 | MacDougall 9 (1p), Cave, Machin |
| | 2 | 11.12.71 | **Southend Utd** (D4) | H | W | 2-0 | Boyer, MacDougall |
| | 3 | 15.01.72 | **Walsall** (D3) | A | L | 0-1 | |
| 1972-73 (D3) | 1 | 18.11.72 | **Cambridge Utd** (D4) | H | W | 5-1 | Clark 2, Gibson, Groves, Boyer |
| | 2 | 09.12.72 | **Colchester Utd** (D4) | H | D | 0-0 | |
| | 2r | 11.12.72 | **Colchester Utd** | A | W | 2-0 | Clark, Boyer |
| | 3 | 13.01.73 | **Newcastle Utd** (D1) | A | L | 0-2 | |
| 1973-74 (D3) | 1 | 24.11.73 | **Charlton Athletic** (D3) | H | W | 1-0 | Boyer |
| | 2 | 15.12.73 | **Watford** (D3) | A | W | 1-0 | Cave |
| | 3 | 05.01.74 | **Orient** (D2) | A | L | 1-2 | Powell |
| 1974-75 (D3) | 1 | 23.11.74 | **Southwick** (SCL) | H | W | 5-0 | Goddard 3, Greenhalgh, Hague |
| | 2 | 14.12.74 | **Wycombe W** (IL) | A | D | 0-0 | |
| | 2r | 18.12.74 | **Wycombe W** | H | L | 1-2 | Goddard |
| 1975-76 (D4) | 1 | 22.11.75 | **Sutton Utd** (IL) | A | D | 1-1 | Ashworth |
| | 1r | 26.11.75 | **Sutton Utd** | H | W | 1-0 | Ashworth |
| | 2 | 13.12.75 | **Hereford Utd** (D3) | H | D | 2-2 | Ashworth, Goddard |
| | 2r | 17.12.75 | **Hereford Utd** | A | L | 0-2 | |
| 1976-77 (D4) | 1 | 20.11.76 | **Newport County** (D4) | H | D | 0-0 | |
| | 1r | 23.11.76 | **Newport County** | A | L | 0-3 | |
| 1977-78 (D4) | 1 | 26.11.77 | **Colchester Utd** (D3) | A | D | 1-1 | Howarth |
| | 1r | 29.11.77 | **Colchester Utd** | H | D | 0-0aet | |
| | 12r | 05.12.77 | **Colchester Utd** | H | L | 1-4 | Barton |
| 1978-79 (D4) | 1 | 25.11.78 | **Hitchin Town** (IL) | H | W | 2-1 | Massey (p), M.Butler |
| | 2 | 16.12.78 | **Wimbledon** (D4) | A | D | 1-1 | MacDougall |
| | 2r | 28.12.78 | **Wimbledon** | H | L | 1-2aet | MacDougall |
| 1979-80 (D4) | 1 | 24.11.79 | **Peterborough Utd** (D4) | A | W | 2-1 | Chard og, Evanson |
| | 2 | 15.12.79 | **Colchester Utd** (D3) | A | L | 0-1 | |
| 1980-81 (D4) | 1 | 22.11.80 | **Wycombe W** (IL) | A | W | 3-0 | Massey, Morgan 2 |
| | 2 | 13.12.80 | **Charlton Athletic** (D3) | A | L | 1-2 | Webb |
| 1981-82 (D4) | 1 | 21.11.81 | **Reading** (D3) | H | W | 1-0 | Funnell |
| | 2 | 12.12.81 | **Dorchester Town** (SL) | A | D | 1-1 | Funnell |
| | 2r | 15.12.81 | **Dorchester Town** | H | W | 2-1aet | Crawford, Williams |
| | 3 | 02.01.82 | **Oxford Utd** (D3) | H | L | 0-2 | |
| 1982-83 (D3) | 1 | 20.11.82 | **Southend Utd** (D3) | H | L | 0-2 | |
| 1983-84 (D3) | 1 | 19.11.83 | **Walsall** (D3) | H | W | 4-0 | Thompson, Beck, Morgan, Lee |
| | 2 | 13.12.83 | **Windsor & Eton** (IL) | A | D | 0-0 | |
| | 2r | 19.12.83 | **Windsor & Eton** | H | W | 2-0 | Beck, Thompson |
| | 3 | 07.01.84 | **Manchester Utd** (D1) | H | W | 2-0 | Graham, Thompson |
| | 4 | 31.01.84 | **Middlesbrough** (D2) | A | L | 0-2 | |
| 1984-85 (D3) | 1 | 17.11.84 | **Kettering Town** (APL) | A | D | 0-0 | |
| | 1r | 20.11.84 | **Kettering Town** | H | W | 3-2 | Savage, Russell, Thrower og |
| | 2 | 08.12.84 | **Dartford** (APL) | A | D | 1-1 | Savage |
| | 2r | 11.12.84 | **Dartford** | H | W | 4-1 | Williams, Savage (p), Russell, Rafferty |
| | 3 | 05.01.85 | **Manchester Utd** (D1) | H | L | 0-3 | |
| 1985-86 (D3) | 1 | 16.11.85 | **Dartford** (APL) | H | D | 0-0 | |
| | 1r | 19.11.85 | **Dartford** | A | W | 2-0 | Clarke, Newton |
| | 2 | 07.12.85 | **Dagenham** (APL) | H | W | 4-1 | O'Driscoll, Thompson, Brown, Clarke |
| | 3 | 04.01.86 | **Wigan Athletic** (D3) | A | L | 0-3 | |
| 1986-87 (D3) | 1 | 15.11.86 | **Fareham Town** (SL) | H | W | 7-2 | Aylott, Richards 2, Puckett 3, Davies og |
| | 2 | 06.12.86 | **Orient** (D4) | H | L | 0-1 | |
| 1987-88 (D2) | 3 | 09.01.88 | **Brighton** (D3) | A | L | 0-2 | |
| 1988-89 (D2) | 3 | 07.01.89 | **Blackpool** (D3) | A | W | 1-0 | Blissett |
| | 4 | 28.01.89 | **Hartlepool Utd** (D4) | A | D | 1-1 | Blissett (p) |
| | 4r | 31.01.89 | **Hartlepool Utd** | H | W | 5-2 | Baker og, Stokes og, Newson, Morrell, Cooke |
| | 5 | 18.02.89 | **Manchester Utd** (D1) | H | D | 1-1 | Aylott |
| | 5r | 22.02.89 | **Manchester Utd** | A | L | 0-1 | |
| 1989-90 (D2) | 3 | 06.01.90 | **Sheffield Utd** (D2) | A | L | 0-2 | |

| | | | | | | | | |
|---|---|---|---|---|---|---|---|---|
| 1990-91 (D3) | 1 | 17.11.90 | **Gillingham** (D4) | H | W | 2-1 | Teale, Jones |
| | 2 | 08.12.90 | **Hayes** (IL) | H | W | 1-0 | Brooks |
| | 3 | 05.01.91 | **Chester City** (D3) | A | W | 3-2 | Jones 2, Ekoku |
| | 4 | 26.01.91 | **Portsmouth** (D2) | A | L | 1-5 | Fereday |
| 1991-92 (D3) | 1 | 16.11.91 | **Bromsgrove Rovers** (SL) | H | W | 3-1 | Bond, Mundee 2 |
| | 2 | 07.12.91 | **Brentford** (D3) | H | W | 2-1 | Quinn 2 |
| | 3 | 04.01.92 | **Newcastle Utd** (D2) | H | D | 0-0 | |
| | 3r | 14.01.92 | **Newcastle Utd** | A | - | 0-0ab | |
| | | | *abandoned after 17 minutes – fog* | | | | |
| | 3r | 22.01.92 | **Newcastle Utd** | A | D | 2-2 | Wood, Bond |
| | | | *Bournemouth won 4-3 on penalties* | | | | |
| | 4 | 05.02.92 | **Ipswich Town** (D2) | A | L | 0-3 | |
| 1992-93 (D2) | 1 | 14.11.92 | **Barnet** (D3) | H | D | 0-0 | |
| | 1r | 25.11.92 | **Barnet** | A | W | 2-1 | Lovell, Mundee |
| | 2 | 05.12.92 | **Cheltenham Town** (SL) | A | D | 1-1 | Shearer |
| | 2r | 16.12.92 | **Cheltenham Town** | H | W | 3-0 | Mundee, McGorry, Morgan |
| | 3 | 02.01.93 | **Blackburn Rovers** (PL) | A | L | 1-3 | Ekoku |
| 1993-94 (D2) | 1 | 13.11.93 | **Brighton** (D2) | H | W | 4-2 | McGarry, Pennock, Masters, Wood |
| | 2 | 04.12.93 | **Nuneaton B** (SL) | H | D | 1-1 | Watson |
| | 2r | 15.12.93 | **Nuneaton B** | A | W | 1-0 | S Cotterill |
| | 3 | 08.01.94 | **Preston North End** (D3) | A | L | 1-2 | Aspinall (p) |
| 1994-95 (D2) | 1 | 12.11.94 | **Worthing** (IL) | H | W | 3-1 | Morris, Russell, McElhatton |
| | 2 | 03.12.94 | **Plymouth Argyle** (D2) | A | L | 1-2 | Jones |
| 1995-96 (D2) | 1 | 11.11.95 | **Bristol City** (D2) | H | D | 0-0 | |
| | 1r | 21.11.95 | **Bristol City** | A | W | 1-0 | Robinson |
| | 2 | 02.12.95 | **Brentford** (D2) | H | L | 0-1 | |
| 1996-97 (D2) | 1 | 16.11.96 | **Brentford** (D2) | A | L | 0-2 | |
| 1997-98 (D2) | 1 | 15.11.97 | **Heybridge Swifts** (IL) | H | W | 3-0 | Robinson 2, C Beardsmore |
| | 2 | 07.12.97 | **Bristol City** (D2) | H | W | 3-1 | Carey og, O'Neill, Fletcher |
| | 3 | 13.01.98 | **Huddersfield Town** (D1) | H | L | 0-1 | |
| 1998-99 (D2) | 1 | 14.11.98 | **Basingstoke Town** (IL) | A | W | 2-1 | O'Neill, Stein |
| | 2 | 05.12.98 | **Torquay Utd** (D3) | A | W | 1-0 | Robinson |
| | 3 | 02.01.99 | **WBA** (D1) | H | W | 1-0 | Howe |
| | 4 | 23.01.99 | **Barnsley** (D1) | A | L | 1-3 | Howe |
| 1999-00 (D2) | 1 | 30.10.99 | **Notts County** (D2) | A | D | 1-1 | Warren |
| | 1r | 09.11.99 | **Notts County** | H | W | 4-2 | S Fletcher 3, Stein |
| | 2 | 20.11.99 | **Bristol City** (D2) | H | L | 0-2 | |
| 2000-01 (D2) | 1 | 18.11.00 | **Swansea City** (D2) | H | W | 2-0 | Elliott, Hayter |
| | 2 | 09.12.00 | **Nuneaton B** (Conf) | H | W | 3-0 | S Hughes, Elliott, O'Connor |
| | 3 | 06.01.01 | **Gillingham** (D1) | H | L | 2-3 | Defoe, C Fletcher |
| 2001-02 (D2) | 1 | 17.11.01 | **Worksop Town** (NPL) | H | W | 3-0 | S Hughes, Hayter, S Fletcher |
| | 2 | 08.12.01 | **Peterborough Utd** (D2) | A | L | 0-1 | |
| 2002-03 (D2) | 1 | 16.11.02 | **Doncaster Rovers** (Conf) | H | W | 2-1 | Thomas, Elliot |
| | 2 | 07.12.02 | **Southend Utd** (D3) | A | D | 1-1 | Broadhurst |
| | 2r | 17.12.02 | **Southend Utd** | H | W | 3-2 | S Fletcher, Holmes, Browning |
| | 3 | 04.01.03 | **Crewe Alexandra** (D2) | H | D | 0-0 | |
| | 3r | 14.01.03 | **Crewe Alexandra** | A | D | 2-2aet | Hayter, S Fletcher |
| | | | *Bournemouth won 3-1 on penalties* | | | | |
| | 4 | 26.01.03 | **Stoke City** (D1) | A | L | 0-3 | |

## BOURNEMOUTH ROVERS

*Formed 1873. Played at Dean Park and Malmesbury Park, Bournemouth*

| | | | | | | | |
|---|---|---|---|---|---|---|---|
| 1884-85 | 1 | 01.11.84 | **Old Westminsters** | A | L | 0-6 |
| 1885-86 | 1 | | Old Etonians | | - | |
| | | | *Bournemouth Rovers scratched. Old Etonians walkover* | | | |
| 1886-87 | 1 | | Chatham | | - | |
| | | | *Bournemouth Rovers scratched. Chatham walkover* | | | |

## BRACKNELL TOWN

*Formed 1896. First entered FA Cup: 1965-66. Members of the Isthmian League*

| | | | | | | |
|---|---|---|---|---|---|---|
| 2000-01 (IL) | 1 | 18.11.00 | **Lincoln City** (D3) | A | L | 0-4 |

# BRADFORD CITY

*Formed 1903. Originally a Rugby League club known as Manningham. FA Cup winners: 1911. They were the first winners of the third FA Cup trophy which was made in Bradford. Record FA Cup win: 9-0 v Sunderland WE, 6th qualifying round 1904-05. In Competition Proper: 11-3 v Walker Celtic, 1st round replay, 01.12.1937; Record FA Cup defeat: 1-6 v Newcastle Utd, 3rd round, 07.03.1963. They have also suffered 0-5 defeats v Burnley, 5th round replay, 23.02.1960 and v Tottenham Hotspur, 3rd round replay, 07.01.1970.*

| | | | | | | | |
|---|---|---|---|---|---|---|---|
| 1903-04 (D2) | | | 1q Rockingham Colliery (H) 6-1; 2q Mirfield U (H) 3-1; 3q W orksop (H) 5-0; 4q Chesterfield (A) 1-2 | | | | |
| 1904-05 (D2) | | | 6q Sunderland WE (H) 9-0; Int Millwall Athletic (H) 1-4 | | | | |
| 1905-06 (D2) | | | Int Darlington (A) 4-0 | | | | |
| | 1 | 13.01.06 | **Barrow** (LC) | H | W | 3-2 | Smith 2, Bennett |
| | 2 | 03.02.06 | **Wolverhampton W** (D1) | H | W | 5-0 | Clarke, McGeachan, Robinson, Smith, Conlin |
| | 3 | 24.02.06 | **Everton** (D1) | A | L | 0-1 | |
| 1906-07 (D2) | 1 | 12.01.07 | **Reading** (SL) | H | W | 2-0 | Bartlett, Hall |
| | 2 | 02.02.07 | **Accrington Stanley** (LC) | H | W | 1-0 | Penman |
| | 3 | 23.02.07 | **Liverpool** (D1) | A | L | 0-1 | |
| 1907-08 (D2) | 1 | 11.01.08 | **Wolverhampton W** (D2) | H | D | 1-1 | Handley |
| | 1r | 15.01.08 | **Wolverhampton W** | A | L | 0-1 | |
| 1908-09 (D1) | 1 | 19.01.09 | **Workington** (NEL) | H | W | 2-0 | Robinson, Hanger |
| | 2 | 06.02.09 | **WBA** (D2) | A | W | 2-1 | Pennington og, Hardman |
| | 3 | 20.02.09 | **Sunderland** (D1) | H | L | 0-1 | |
| 1909-10 (D1) | 1 | 15.01.10 | **Notts County** (D1) | H | W | 4-2 | O'Rourke 2, Bond, Speirs |
| | 2 | 05.02.10 | **Blackburn Rovers** (D1) | H | L | 1-2 | O'Rourke |
| 1910-11 (D1) | 1 | 14.01.11 | **New Brompton** (SL) | A | W | 1-0 | Bond |
| | 2 | 04.02.11 | **Norwich City** (SL) | H | W | 2-1 | Speirs, Logan |
| | 3 | 25.02.11 | **Grimsby Town** (ML) | H | W | 1-0 | Bond |
| | 4 | 11.03.11 | **Burnley** (D2) | H | W | 1-0 | Thompson |
| | SF | 25.03.11 | **Blackburn Rovers** (D1) | | W | 3-0 | O'Rourke, Devine, Thompson |
| | | | *played at Bramall Lane* | | | | |
| | F | 22.04.11 | **Newcastle Utd** (D1) | | D | 0-0 | |
| | | | *played at Crystal Palace* | | | | |
| | Fr | 26.04.11 | **Newcastle Utd** (D1) | | W | 1-0 | Speirs |
| | | | *played at Old Trafford* | | | | |
| 1911-12 (D1) | 1 | 13.01.12 | **QPR** (SL) | A | D | 0-0 | |
| | 1r | 18.01.12 | **QPR** | H | W | 4-0 | Walden 3, Logan |
| | 2 | 03.02.12 | **Chelsea** (D2) | H | W | 2-0 | Bond, Logan |
| | 3 | 24.02.12 | **Bradford Park A** (D2) | A | W | 1-0 | O'Rourke |
| | 4 | 09.03.12 | **Barnsley** (D2) | A | D | 0-0 | |
| | 4r | 13.03.12 | **Barnsley** | H | D | 0-0aet | |
| | | | *played at Elland Road* | | | | |
| | 4 2r | 18.03.12 | **Barnsley** | | D | 0-0aet | |
| | | | *played at Elland Road* | | | | |
| | 4 3r | 21.03.12 | **Barnsley** | | L | 2-3aet | Speirs, Devine |
| | | | *played at Bramall Lane* | | | | |
| 1912-13 (D1) | 1 | 11.01.13 | **Newcastle Utd** (D1) | A | - | 0-0ab | |
| | | | *abandoned at half-time – gale* | | | | |
| | 1 | 16.01.13 | **Newcastle Utd** | A | L | 0-1 | |
| 1913-14 (D1) | 1 | 10.01.14 | **Woolwich Arsenal** (D1) | H | W | 2-0 | Bond 2 |
| | 2 | 31.01.14 | **Millwall Athletic** (SL) | A | L | 0-1 | |
| 1914-15 (D1) | 1 | 09.01.15 | **Darlington** (NEL) | A | W | 1-0 | Shepherd |
| | 2 | 30.01.15 | **Middlesbrough** (D1) | H | W | 1-0 | Bond |
| | 3 | 20.02.15 | **Norwich City** (SL) | H | D | 1-1aet | Shepherd |
| | 3r | 27.02.15 | **Norwich City** | A | D | 0-0aet | |
| | 3 2r | 03.03.15 | **Norwich City** | | W | 2-0 | McDonald, Bond (p) |
| | | | *played at Sincil Bank, Lincoln* | | | | |
| | 4 | 06.03.15 | **Everton** (D1) | H | L | 0-2 | |
| 1919-20 (D1) | 1 | 10.01.20 | **Portsmouth** (SL) | H | - | 2-2ab | Bond, McIlvenny |
| | | | *abandoned after 63 minutes – waterlogged pitch* | | | | |
| | 1 | 17.01.20 | **Portsmouth** | H | W | 2-0 | Fox, Goldthorpe |
| | 2 | 31.01.20 | **Sheffield Utd** (D1) | H | W | 2-1 | Goldthorpe, Logan |

| | | | | | | | | |
|---|---|---|---|---|---|---|---|---|
| | | 3 | 21.02.20 | **Preston North End** (D1) | A | W | 3-0 | Bond 2 (1p), Goldthorpe |
| | | 4 | 06.03.20 | **Bristol City** (D2) | A | L | 0-2 | |
| 1920-21 | (D1) | 1 | 08.01.21 | **Barnsley** (D2) | H | W | 3-1 | Howson, Bond (p), Marsh |
| | | 2 | 29.01.21 | **Tottenham Hotspur** (D1) | A | L | 0-4 | |
| 1921-22 | (D1) | 1 | 07.01.22 | **Walsall** (3N) | A | D | 3-3 | Howson 2, Hibbert |
| | | 1r | 11.01.22 | **Walsall** | H | W | 4-0 | Hibbert, Howson 2, Logan |
| | | 2 | 28.01.22 | **Notts County** (D2) | H | D | 1-1 | Bond (p) |
| | | 2r | 01.02.22 | **Notts County** | A | D | 0-0aet | |
| | | 2 3r | 06.02.22 | **Notts County** | | L | 0-1 | |
| | | | | *played at Bramall Lane* | | | | |
| 1922-23 | (D2) | 1 | 13.01.23 | **Manchester Utd** (D2) | H | D | 1-1 | Duckett (p) |
| | | 1r | 17.01.23 | **Manchester Utd** | A | L | 0-2 | |
| 1923-24 | (D2) | 1 | 12.01.24 | **Liverpool** (D1) | A | L | 1-2 | Logan |
| 1924-25 | (D2) | 1 | 10.01.25 | **Derby County** (D2) | A | W | 1-0 | Rhodes |
| | | 2 | 31.01.25 | **Barnsley** (D2) | A | W | 3-0 | Cheetham 2, Rigby |
| | | 3 | 21.02.25 | **Southampton** (D2) | A | L | 0-2 | |
| 1925-26 | (D2) | 3 | 09.01.26 | **Nottingham Forest** (D2) | A | L | 0-1 | |
| 1926-27 | (D2) | 3 | 08.01.27 | **Derby County** (D1) | H | L | 2-6 | Cheetham, McMillan |
| 1927-28 | (3N) | 1 | 26.11.27 | **Workington** (NEL) | H | W | 6-0 | Cairns, Moore, Richardson 2, Burkinshaw 2 |
| | | 2 | 10.12.27 | **Rotherham Utd** (3N) | H | L | 2-3 | Harvey, Richardson |
| 1928-29 | (3N) | 1 | 24.11.28 | **Doncaster Rovers** (3N) | H | W | 4-1 | Moore 3, Randall |
| | | 2 | 08.12.28 | **Tranmere Rovers** (3N) | A | W | 1-0 | Moore |
| | | 3 | 12.01.29 | **Stockport County** (3N) | H | W | 2-0 | Mitchell, Barkas |
| | | 4 | 26.01.29 | **Portsmouth** (D1) | A | L | 0-2 | |
| 1929-30 | (D2) | 3 | 11.01.30 | **Southampton** (D2) | H | W | 4-1 | Cairns, Cochrane 2, Moore |
| | | 4 | 25.01.30 | **Wrexham** (3N) | A | D | 0-0 | |
| | | 4r | 27.01.30 | **Wrexham** | H | W | 2-1 | Cochrane, Whitehurst |
| | | 5 | 15.02.30 | **Huddersfield Town** (D1) | A | L | 1-2 | Cochrane |
| 1930-31 | (D2) | 3 | 14.01.31 | **Middlesbrough** (D1) | A | D | 1-1 | Moore |
| | | 3r | 19.01.31 | **Middlesbrough** | H | W | 2-1 | Scrivens, Peel |
| | | 4 | 24.01.31 | **Wolverhampton W** (D2) | H | D | 0-0 | |
| | | 4r | 28.01.31 | **Wolverhampton W** | A | L | 2-4 | Cairns 2 |
| 1931-32 | (D2) | 3 | 09.01.32 | **Birmingham** (D1) | A | L | 0-1 | |
| 1932-33 | (D2) | 3 | 14.01.33 | **Aston Villa** (D1) | H | D | 2-2 | Watmough, Bauld |
| | | 3r | 18.01.33 | **Aston Villa** | A | L | 1-2 | Hallows |
| 1933-34 | (D2) | 3 | 13.01.34 | **West Ham Utd** (D2) | A | L | 2-3 | Hallows, Spence |
| 1934-35 | (D2) | 3 | 12.01.35 | **Aston Villa** (D1) | A | W | 3-1 | Hallows, Keetley 2 |
| | | 4 | 26.01.35 | **Stockport County** (3N) | H | D | 0-0 | |
| | | 4r | 31.01.35 | **Stockport County** | A | L | 2-3aet | Hallows, Spence |
| 1935-36 | (D2) | 3 | 11.01.36 | **Bournemouth** (3S) | H | W | 1-0 | Jeffries |
| | | 4 | 03.02.36 | **Blackburn Rovers** (D1) | H | W | 3-1 | Travis 2, Hallows |
| | | 5 | 15.02.36 | **Derby County** (D1) | H | L | 0-1 | |
| 1936-37 | (D2) | 3 | 16.01.37 | **York City** (3N) | H | D | 2-2 | Travis, Gallon |
| | | 3r | 20.01.37 | **York City** | A | L | 0-1 | |
| 1937-38 | (3N) | 1 | 27.11.37 | **Walker Celtic** (NEL) | A | D | 1-1 | Deakin |
| | | 1r | 01.12.37 | **Walker Celtic** | H | W | 11-3 | Deakin 4 (1p), Bartholomew 4, Bagley, Whittingham, Cooke |
| | | 2 | 11.12.37 | **Wrexham** (3N) | A | W | 2-1 | Bartholomew 2 |
| | | 3 | 08.01.38 | **Chesterfield** (D2) | H | D | 1-1 | Deakin |
| | | 3r | 12.01.38 | **Chesterfield** | A | D | 1-1aet | Bartholomew |
| | | 3 2r | 17.01.38 | **Chesterfield** | | L | 0-2 | |
| | | | | *played at Bramall Lane* | | | | |
| 1938-39 | (3N) | 1 | 26.11.38 | **Chester** (3N) | A | L | 1-3 | Hinsley |
| 1945-46 | (3N) | 1 1L | 17.11.45 | **Notts County** (3S) | A | D | 2-2 | Murphy 2 |
| | | 1 2L | 24.11.45 | **Notts County** | H | L | 1-2 | Pickles |
| 1946-47 | (3N) | 1 | 30.11.46 | **Gateshead AFC** (3N) | A | L | 1-3 | G Murphy |
| 1947-48 | (3N) | 1 | 29.11.47 | **Gateshead AFC** | A | W | 3-1 | McGill, Neilson 2 |
| | | 2 | 13.12.47 | **Bournemouth** (3S) | A | L | 0-1 | |
| 1948-49 | (3N) | 1 | 04.12.48 | **Doncaster Rovers** (3N) | H | W | 4-3 | Brown, Shearer 2 (1p), Hawksworth |
| | | 2 | 11.12.48 | **New Brighton** (3N) | H | D | 0-0 | |

| | | | | | | | | |
|---|---|---|---|---|---|---|---|---|
| | | 2r | 18.12.48 | **New Brighton** | A | L | 0-1 | |
| 1949-50 | (3N) | 1 | 26.11.49 | **Fleetwood** (LC) | H | W | 9-0 | Carr 4, W Price 3 (1p), McGill, Ward |
| | | 2 | 10.12.49 | **Southport** (3N) | A | L | 1-2 | W Price |
| 1950-51 | (3N) | 1 | 25.11.50 | **Oldham Athletic** (3N) | H | D | 2-2 | McGill, W Price |
| | | 1r | 28.11.50 | **Oldham Athletic** | A | L | 1-2 | Carr |
| 1951-52 | (3N) | 1 | 24.11.51 | **Carlisle Utd** (3N) | H | W | 6-1 | Millar 2, Carr 2, Williamson (p), Twentyman og |
| | | 2 | 15.12.51 | **Bradford Park A** (3N) | A | L | 2-3 | Millar, Greenhoff |
| 1952-53 | (3N) | 1 | 22.11.52 | **Rhyl** (CC) | H | W | 4-0 | Close 2, Ward 2 |
| | | 2 | 06.12.52 | **Ipswich Town** (3S) | H | D | 1-1 | Close |
| | | 2r | 10.12.52 | **Ipswich Town** | A | L | 1-5 | Williamson |
| 1953-54 | (3N) | 1 | 21.11.53 | **Crewe Alexandra** (3N) | A | D | 0-0 | |
| | | 1r | 25.11.53 | **Crewe Alexandra** | H | L | 0-1 | |
| 1954-55 | (3N) | 1 | 20.11.54 | **Mansfield Town** (3N) | H | W | 3-1 | Robb (p), Squires 2 |
| | | 2 | 11.12.54 | **Merthyr Tydfil** (SL) | H | W | 7-1 | Tunnicliffe 2, Chapman 2, Duthie 2, Chew |
| | | 3 | 08.01.55 | **Brentford** (3S) | A | D | 1-1 | Lambert |
| | | 3r | 12.01.55 | **Brentford** | H | D | 2-2aet | Robb, Bakes |
| | | 3 2r | 20.01.55 | **Brentford** *played at Highbury* | | L | 0-1 | |
| 1955-56 | (3N) | 1 | 19.11.55 | **Oldham Athletic** (3N) | H | W | 3-1 | Walsh, Kelly 2 |
| | | 2 | 10.12.55 | **Worksop Town** (ML) | H | D | 2-2 | Webb, Kelly |
| | | 2r | 15.12.55 | **Worksop Town** | A | L | 0-1 | |
| 1956-57 | (3N) | 1 | 17.11.56 | **Derby County** (3N) | A | L | 1-2 | Simm |
| 1957-58 | (3N) | 1 | 16.11.57 | **Scarborough** (ML) | H | W | 6-0 | Samuels, D.Jackson, Webb, Marshall 3 |
| | | 2 | 07.12.57 | **Chester** (3N) | A | D | 3-3 | D Jackson 2, Samuels |
| | | 2r | 11.12.57 | **Chester** | H | W | 3-1 | Boyle, Samuels, Lawlor |
| | | 3 | 04.01.58 | **Scunthorpe Utd** (3N) | A | L | 0-1 | |
| 1958-59 | (D3) | 1 | 15.11.58 | **Mansfield Town** (D3) | A | W | 4-3 | D Jackson, McCole 3 |
| | | 2 | 06.12.58 | **Bradford Park A** (D4) | A | W | 2-0 | McCole 2 |
| | | 3 | 10.01.59 | **Brighton** (D2) | A | W | 2-0 | D.Jackson, Stokes |
| | | 4 | 24.01.59 | **Preston North End** (D1) | A | L | 2-3 | McCole, Lawlor |
| 1959-60 | (D3) | 1 | 14.11.59 | **Barnsley** (D3) | A | D | 3-3 | Stokes 2, Reid |
| | | 1r | 18.11.59 | **Barnsley** | H | W | 2-1 | Rea, Stokes |
| | | 2 | 05.12.59 | **Rochdale** (D4) | A | D | 1-1 | Stokes |
| | | 2r | 09.12.59 | **Rochdale** | H | W | 2-1 | Stokes 2 |
| | | 3 | 09.01.60 | **Everton** (D1) | H | W | 3-0 | D Jackson, Reid, Stokes |
| | | 4 | 30.01.60 | **Bournemouth** (D3) | H | W | 3-1 | D Jackson, Stokes 2 |
| | | 5 | 20.02.60 | **Burnley** (D1) | H | D | 2-2 | Webb, Stokes |
| | | 5r | 23.02.60 | **Burnley** | A | L | 0-5 | |
| 1960-61 | (D3) | 1 | 05.11.60 | **Scarborough** (NCo) | H | D | 0-0 | |
| | | 1r | 09.11.60 | **Scarborough** | A | W | 3-1aet | Hockey, Smith 2 |
| | | 2 | 26.11.60 | **Barnsley** (D3) | H | L | 1-2 | Webb |
| 1961-62 | (D4) | 1 | 04.11.61 | **York City** (D4) | H | W | 1-0 | Layne |
| | | 2 | 25.11.61 | **Hull City** (D3) | A | W | 2-0 | Layne, Webb |
| | | 3 | 06.01.62 | **Arsenal** (D1) | A | L | 0-3 | |
| 1962-63 | (D4) | 1 | 03.11.62 | **Oldham Athletic** (D4) | A | W | 5-2 | P Bircumshaw 3, Devitt, Harland (p) |
| | | 2 | 24.11.62 | **Gateshead AFC** (NRL) | H | W | 3-2 | Harland, McCole, P Bircumshaw |
| | | 3 | 07.03.63 | **Newcastle Utd** (D2) | H | L | 1-6 | Kelly |
| 1963-64 | (D4) | 1 | 16.11.63 | **Port Vale** (D3) | H | L | 1-2 | D Price |
| 1964-65 | (D4) | 1 | 14.11.64 | **Scarborough** (ML) | A | L | 0-1 | |
| 1965-66 | (D4) | 1 | 13.11.65 | **Darlington** (D4) | A | L | 2-3 | Ellam, Rodon |
| 1966-67 | (D4) | 1 | 26.11.66 | **Port Vale** (D4) | H | L | 1-2 | Hall |
| 1967-68 | (D4) | 1 | 09.12.67 | **Wrexham** (D4) | H | W | 7-1 | Bannister 2, Aimson 2, Rackstraw, Swallow, Hall |
| | | 2 | 06.01.68 | **Bury** (D3) | H | L | 2-3 | Bannister, Hall |
| 1968-69 | (D4) | 1 | 16.11.68 | **Chester** (D4) | H | L | 1-2 | Bannister |
| 1969-70 | (D3) | 1 | 15.11.69 | **Grimsby Town** (D4) | H | W | 2-1 | Leighton, Corner |
| | | 2 | 06.12.69 | **Lincoln City** (D4) | H | W | 3-0 | Middleton 2, Hall |
| | | 3 | 03.01.70 | **Tottenham Hotspur** (D1) | H | D | 2-2 | England og, Stowell |
| | | 3r | 07.01.70 | **Tottenham Hotspur** | A | L | 0-5 | |

| | | | | | | | | |
|---|---|---|---|---|---|---|---|---|
| 1970-71 | (D3) | 1 | 21.11.70 | **Macclesfield T** (NPL) | H | W | 3-2 | Bannister (p), Middleton, Corner |
| | | 2 | 12.12.70 | **Lincoln City** (D4) | A | D | 2-2 | Bannister, Corner |
| | | 2r | 16.12.70 | **Lincoln City** | H | D | 2-2aet | Corner, Bannister |
| | | 22r | 21.12.70 | **Lincoln City** | | L | 1-4 | Corner |
| | | | | *played at Belle Vue, Doncaster* | | | | |
| 1971-72 | (D3) | 1 | 20.11.71 | **Wrexham** (D3) | A | L | 1-5 | O'Neill |
| 1972-73 | (D4) | 1 | 18.11.72 | **Grantham Town** (SL) | H | W | 3-0 | Ingram, Oates, Johnston |
| | | 2 | 09.12.72 | **Tranmere Rovers** (D3) | H | W | 2-1 | Gilliver, Brown |
| | | 3 | 13.01.73 | **Blackpool** (D2) | H | W | 2-1 | Ingram 2 |
| | | 4 | 03.02.73 | **Arsenal** (D1) | A | L | 0-2 | |
| 1973-74 | (D4) | 1 | 24.11.73 | **Workington** (D4) | H | W | 2-0 | Gilliver, Ingram (p) |
| | | 2 | 15.12.73 | **Barnsley** (D4) | A | D | 1-1 | Ingram |
| | | 2r | 19.12.73 | **Barnsley** | H | W | 2-1 | Cooke, Brown |
| | | 3 | 05.01.74 | **Alvechurch** (WMRL) | H | W | 4-2 | Ham, Baker, Oates, Ingram (p) |
| | | 4 | 26.01.74 | **Luton Town** (D2) | A | L | 0-3 | |
| 1974-75 | (D4) | 1 | 23.11.74 | **Hartlepool** (D4) | A | L | 0-1 | |
| 1975-76 | (D4) | 1 | 22.11.75 | **Chesterfield** (D3) | H | W | 1-0 | Hutchins |
| | | 2 | 13.12.75 | **Rotherham Utd** (D3) | A | W | 3-0 | Cooke, Ingram 2 |
| | | 3 | 03.01.76 | **Shrewsbury Town** (D3) | A | W | 2-1 | Cooke, Hutchins |
| | | 4 | 24.01.76 | **Tooting & M** (IL) | H | W | 3-1 | Hutchins 2, Middleton |
| | | 5 | 23.02.76 | **Norwich City** (D1) | A | W | 2-1 | Hutchins, McGinley |
| | | 6 | 06.03.76 | **Southampton** (D2) | H | L | 0-1 | |
| 1976-77 | (D4) | 1 | 20.11.76 | **Walsall** (D3) | A | D | 0-0 | |
| | | 1r | 24.11.76 | **Walsall** | H | L | 0-2 | |
| 1977-78 | (D3) | 1 | 26.11.77 | **Crewe Alexandra** (D4) | H | L | 0-1 | |
| 1978-79 | (D4) | 1 | 25.11.78 | **Port Vale** (D4) | H | W | 1-0 | Dolan (p) |
| | | 2 | 16.12.78 | **Stockport County** (D4) | A | L | 2-4 | Cooke, Dolan |
| 1979-80 | (D4) | 1 | 24.11.79 | **Brandon Utd** (NAII) | A | W | 3-0 | Gallagher, Martinez, McNiven |
| | | | | *played at Spennymoor* | | | | |
| | | 2 | 15.12.79 | **Darlington** (D4) | A | W | 1-0 | Baines |
| | | 3 | 05.01.80 | **Carlisle Utd** (D3) | A | L | 2-3 | Baines, Dolan (p) |
| 1980-81 | (D4) | 1 | 22.11.80 | **Port Vale** (D4) | A | L | 2-4 | Wood, Chapman |
| 1981-82 | (D4) | 1 | 21.11.81 | **Scunthorpe Utd** (D4) | A | L | 0-1 | |
| 1982-83 | (D3) | 1 | 20.11.82 | **Port Vale** (D4) | A | W | 1-0 | Campbell |
| | | 2 | 11.12.82 | **Mansfield Town** (D4) | A | D | 1-1 | Gray |
| | | 2r | 15.12.82 | **Mansfield Town** | H | W | 3-2 | Campbell, Lester, McNiven |
| | | 3 | 08.01.83 | **Barnsley** (D2) | H | L | 0-1 | |
| 1983-84 | (D3) | 1 | 19.11.83 | **Wigan Athletic** (D3) | H | D | 0-0 | |
| | | 1r | 28.11.83 | **Wigan Athletic** | A | L | 2-4 | Hawley, Haire |
| 1984-85 | (D3) | 1 | 17.11.84 | **Tow Law Town** (NL) | H | W | 7-2 | McCall, Hendrie, Campbell 2, Goodman 3 |
| | | 2 | 08.12.84 | **Mansfield Town** (D4) | H | W | 2-1 | Campbell, Abbott |
| | | 3 | 05.01.85 | **Telford Utd** (APL) | A | L | 1-2 | Haire |
| 1985-86 | (D2) | 3 | 04.01.86 | **Ipswich Town** (D1) | A | D | 4-4 | Goodman, Abbott 2 (1p), Hendrie |
| | | 3r | 13.01.86 | **Ipswich Town** | H | L | 0-1 | |
| | | | | *played at Elland Road* | | | | |
| 1986-87 | (D2) | 3 | 10.01.87 | **Oldham Athletic** (D2) | A | D | 1-1 | McCall |
| | | 3r | 19.01.87 | **Oldham Athletic** | H | W | 5-1 | Hendrie 2, Ormondroyd 2, Ellis |
| | | 4 | 31.01.87 | **Everton** (D1) | H | L | 0-1 | |
| 1987-88 | (D2) | 3 | 09.01.88 | **Wolverhampton W** (D4) | H | W | 2-1 | Hendrie, Ellis |
| | | 4 | 30.01.88 | **Oxford Utd** (D1) | H | W | 4-2 | Kennedy (p), McCall, Evans, Hendrie |
| | | 5 | 20.02.88 | **Portsmouth** (D1) | A | L | 0-3 | |
| 1988-89 | (D2) | 3 | 07.01.89 | **Tottenham Hotspur** (D1) | H | W | 1-0 | Mitchell |
| | | 4 | 28.01.89 | **Hull City** (D2) | H | L | 1-2 | Leonard |
| 1989-90 | (D2) | 3 | 07.01.90 | **Charlton Athletic** (D1) | A | D | 1-1 | Tinnion (p) |
| | | 3r | 10.01.90 | **Charlton Athletic** | H | L | 0-3 | |
| 1990-91 | (D3) | 1 | 17.11.90 | **Shrewsbury Town** (D3) | H | D | 0-0 | |
| | | 1r | 21.11.90 | **Shrewsbury Town** | A | L | 1-2 | Jewell |
| 1991-92 | (D3) | 1 | 16.11.91 | **Bury** (D3) | A | W | 1-0 | Tinnion |
| | | 2 | 07.12.91 | **Bolton Wanderers** (D3) | A | L | 1-3 | Tinnion |
| 1992-93 | (D2) | 1 | 14.11.92 | **Preston North End** (D2) | H | D | 1-1 | Jewell |

| | | | | | | | |
|---|---|---|---|---|---|---|---|
| | 1r | 25.11.92 | **Preston North End** | A | W | 5-4 | McCarthy 2, Blake, Tinnion (p), Jewell |
| | 2 | 06.12.92 | **Huddersfield Town** (D2) | H | L | 0-2 | |
| 1993-94 (D2) | 1 | 13.11.93 | **Chester City** (D3) | H | D | 0-0 | |
| | 1r | 30.11.93 | **Chester City** | A | L | 0-1 | |
| 1994-95 (D2) | 1 | 12.11.94 | **Scunthorpe Utd** (D3) | H | D | 1-1 | Tolson |
| | 1r | 22.11.94 | **Scunthorpe Utd** | A | L | 2-3aet | Power, Richards |
| 1995-96 (D2) | 1 | 11.11.95 | **Burton Albion** (SL) | H | W | 4-3 | Showler 2, Robson, Ormondroyd |
| | 2 | 02.12.95 | **Preston North End** (D3) | H | W | 2-1 | Jacobs 2 |
| | 3 | 06.01.96 | **Bolton Wanderers** (PL) | H | L | 0-3 | |
| 1996-97 (D1) | 3 | 05.01.97 | **Wycombe W** (D2) | A | W | 2-0 | Dreyer 2 |
| | 4 | 25.01.97 | **Everton** (PL) | A | W | 3-2 | Dreyer, C Waddle, Steiner |
| | 5 | 16.02.97 | **Sheffield Wed** (PL) | H | L | 0-1 | |
| 1997-98 (D1) | 3 | 03.01.98 | **Manchester City** (D1) | A | L | 0-2 | |
| 1998-99 (D1) | 3 | 02.01.99 | **Grimsby Town** (D1) | H | W | 2-1 | Mills, Lawrence |
| | 4 | 23.01.99 | **Newcastle Utd** (PL) | A | L | 0-3 | |
| 1999-00 (PL) | 3 | 11.12.99 | **Crewe Alexandra** (D1) | A | W | 2-1 | Blake, D Saunders |
| | 4 | 11.01.00 | **Gillingham** (D2) | A | L | 1-3 | D Saunders |
| 2000-01 (PL) | 3 | 08.01.01 | **Middlesbrough** (PL) | H | L | 0-1 | |
| 2001-02 (D1) | 3 | 08.01.02 | **Walsall** (D1) | A | L | 0-2 | |
| 2002-03 (D1) | 3 | 04.01.03 | **WBA** (PL) | A | L | 1-3 | Danks |

## BRADFORD PARK AVENUE

*Formed 1907. Members of the Football League 1908-1970. Disbanded 1974. Reformed 1988. Their record FA Cup victory – an 11-0 win over Denby Dale in a 2nd qualifying round tie in 1908 was achieved by their reserve side as the game was scheduled for the same day as a League match. The FA fined the club £50 for not fielding their strongest side in the FA Cup! Members of the Northern Premier League.*

| | | | | | | | |
|---|---|---|---|---|---|---|---|
| 1908-09 (D2) | | | 1q South Kirkby Coll. (H) 8-1; 2q Denby Dale (A) 11-0; 3q Heckmondwike walkover; 4q Mexborough (H) 6-0; 5q Croydon Common (H) 1-2 | | | | |
| 1909-10 (D2) | 1 | 15.01.10 | **Bishop Auckland** (NL) | H | W | 8-0 | Newton 3, McClarence, Smith 2, Reeves 2 |
| | 2 | 05.02.10 | **Sunderland** (D1) | A | L | 1-3 | Reeves |
| 1910-11 (D2) | 1 | 14.01.11 | **QPR** (SL) | H | W | 5-3 | Turnbull 2, Little 2, Logan |
| | 2 | 04.02.11 | **Darlington** (NEL) | A | L | 1-2 | Thackeray |
| 1911-12 (D2) | 1 | 13.01.12 | **Nottingham Forest** (D2) | A | W | 1-0 | Reeves |
| | 2 | 03.02.12 | **Portsmouth** (SL) | H | W | 2-0 | Reeves, Simpson |
| | 3 | 24.02.12 | **Bradford City** (D1) | H | L | 0-1 | |
| 1912-13 (D2) | 1 | 15.01.13 | **Barrow** (LC) | H | D | 1-1 | Smith |
| | 1r | 22.01.13 | **Barrow** *played at Bradford* | A | W | 1-0 | Smith |
| | 2 | 01.02.13 | **Wolverhampton W** (D2) | H | W | 3-0 | Smith 2, Little |
| | 3 | 22.02.13 | **Sheffield Wed** (D1) | H | W | 2-1 | Smith, Howie |
| | 4 | 08.03.13 | **Aston Villa** (D1) | H | L | 0-5 | |
| 1913-14 (D2) | 1 | 10.01.14 | **Reading** (SL) | H | W | 5-1 | Bauchop 3, Smith, McCandless |
| | 2 | 31.01.14 | **Sheffield Utd** (D1) | A | L | 1-3 | Smith |
| 1914-15 (D1) | 1 | 09.01.15 | **Portsmouth** (SL) | H | W | 1-0 | Smith |
| | 2 | 30.01.15 | **Bury** (D2) | A | W | 1-0 | Bauchop |
| | 3 | 20.02.15 | **Sheffield Utd** (D1) | A | L | 0-1aet | |
| 1919-20 (D1) | 1 | 10.01.20 | **Nottingham Forest** (D2) | H | W | 3-0 | McLean, Bauchop, Turnbull |
| | 2 | 31.01.20 | **Castleford Town** (ML) | H | W | 3-2 | Little, McLean 2 |
| | 3 | 23.02.20 | **Notts County** (D1) | A | W | 4-3 | McLean 2, McCandless, Bauchop |
| | 4 | 06.03.20 | **Chelsea** (D1) | A | L | 1-4 | Little |
| 1920-21 (D1) | 1 | 08.01.21 | **Clapton Orient** (D2) | H | W | 1-0 | Burkinshaw |
| | 2 | 29.01.21 | **Huddersfield Town** (D1) | H | L | 0-1 | |
| 1921-22 (D2) | 1 | 07.01.22 | **Sheffield Wed** (D2) | H | W | 1-0 | Batten |
| | 2 | 28.01.22 | **Arsenal** (D1) | H | L | 2-3 | McLean, Bauchop |
| 1922-23 (3N) | 1 | 13.01.23 | **Everton** (D1) | A | D | 1-1 | Peel |
| | 1r | 17.01.23 | **Everton** | H | W | 1-0 | McLean |
| | 2 | 03.02.23 | **Plymouth Argyle** (3S) | A | L | 1-4 | Fell |
| 1923-24 (3N) | 1 | 12.01.24 | **Swindon Town** (3S) | A | L | 0-4 | |
| 1924-25 (3N) | | | 5q Wigan Borough (A) 1-0; 6q Crook Town (A) 4-0 | | | | |
| | 1 | 10.01.25 | **Middlesbrough** (D2) | H | W | 1-0 | Turnbull |
| | 2 | 31.01.25 | **Blackpool** (D2) | H | D | 1-1 | Hubbert |

| | | | | | | | | |
|---|---|---|---|---|---|---|---|---|
| | | 2r | 04.02.25 | **Blackpool** | A | L | 1-2 | Scattergood (p) |
| 1925-26 | (3N) | 1 | 28.11.25 | **Lincoln City** (3N) | H | D | 2-2 | McDonald 2 |
| | | 1r | 02.12.25 | **Lincoln City** | A | D | 1-1aet | McDonald |
| | | 1 2r | 07.12.25 | **Lincoln City** | | W | 2-1 | Peel 2 |
| | | | | *played at Bramall Lane* | | | | |
| | | 2 | 12.12.25 | **Boston Utd** (ML) | A | L | 0-1 | |
| 1926-27 | (3N) | 1 | 27.11.26 | **Walsall** (3N) | A | L | 0-1 | |
| 1927-28 | (3N) | 1 | 26.11.27 | **Nelson FC** (3N) | A | W | 3-0 | Cartwright 2, Hawes |
| | | 2 | 10.12.27 | **Southport** (3N) | H | L | 0-2 | |
| 1928-29 | (D2) | 3 | 12.01.29 | **Hull City** (D2) | A | D | 1-1 | Parris |
| | | 3r | 16.01.29 | **Hull City** | H | W | 3-1 | Davis, Atherton, McLean |
| | | 4 | 26.01.29 | **Plymouth Argyle** (3S) | A | W | 1-0 | Davis |
| | | 5 | 16.02.29 | **WBA** (D2) | A | L | 0-6 | |
| 1929-30 | (D2) | 3 | 11.01.30 | **Barnsley** (D2) | A | W | 1-0 | Quantrill |
| | | 4 | 25.01.30 | **Derby County** (D1) | A | D | 1-1 | Harwood |
| | | 4r | 29.01.30 | **Derby County** | H | W | 2-1 | Millership, Davis |
| | | 5 | 15.02.30 | **Sheffield Wed** (D1) | A | L | 1-5 | McLean |
| 1930-31 | (D2) | 3 | 10.01.31 | **Aldershot Town** (SL) | A | W | 1-0 | Scott |
| | | 4 | 24.01.31 | **Burnley** (D2) | H | W | 2-0 | McMillan, Rhodes |
| | | 5 | 14.02.31 | **Southport** (3N) | A | L | 0-1 | |
| 1931-32 | (D2) | 3 | 09.01.32 | **Cardiff City** (3S) | H | W | 2-0 | Harwood, Rhodes |
| | | 4 | 23.01.32 | **Northampton Town** (3S) | H | W | 4-2 | Leedham, Harwood, Dickinson, Davis |
| | | 5 | 13.02.32 | **Watford** (3S) | A | L | 0-1 | |
| 1932-33 | (D2) | 3 | 14.01.33 | **Plymouth Argyle** (D2) | H | W | 5-1 | Dickinson, Robertson 2, Robson 2 |
| | | 4 | 28.01.33 | **Brighton** (3S) | A | L | 1-2 | Robson |
| 1933-34 | (D2) | 3 | 13.01.34 | **Stoke City** (D1) | A | L | 0-3 | |
| 1934-35 | (D2) | 3 | 12.01.35 | **Leeds Utd** (D1) | A | L | 1-4 | Suggett |
| 1935-36 | (D2) | 3 | 11.01.36 | **Workington** (NEL) | H | W | 3-2 | Lewis, Nolan, Doran |
| | | 4 | 29.01.36 | **WBA** (D1) | H | D | 1-1 | Wesley |
| | | 4r | 03.02.36 | **WBA** | A | D | 1-1aet | Meek |
| | | 4 2r | 10.02.36 | **WBA** | | W | 2-0 | Nolan, Doran |
| | | | | *played at Old Trafford* | | | | |
| | | 5 | 15.02.36 | **Tottenham Hotspur** (D2) | H | D | 0-0 | |
| | | 5r | 17.02.36 | **Tottenham Hotspur** | A | L | 1-2 | Nolan |
| 1936-37 | (D2) | 3 | 16.01.37 | **Derby County** (D1) | H | L | 0-4 | |
| 1937-38 | (D2) | 3 | 08.01.38 | **Newport County** (3S) | H | W | 7-4 | Martin, Henson 4, Lewis 2 |
| | | 4 | 22.01.38 | **Stoke City** (D1) | H | D | 1-1 | Wesley |
| | | 4r | 26.01.38 | **Stoke City** | A | W | 2-1 | Stabb, Henson |
| | | 5 | 12.02.38 | **Sunderland** (D1) | A | L | 0-1 | |
| 1938-39 | (D2) | 3 | 07.01.39 | **Wolverhampton W** (D1) | A | L | 1-3 | Gallon |
| 1945-46 | (D2) | 3 1L | 05.01.46 | **Port Vale** (3S) | H | W | 2-1 | Downie, Gibbons |
| | | 3 2L | 07.01.46 | **Port Vale** | A | D | 1-1 | Gibbons |
| | | 4 1L | 26.01.46 | **Manchester City** (D2) | H | L | 1-3 | Gibbons |
| | | 4 2L | 30.01.46 | **Manchester City** | A | W | 8-2 | Gibbons 4, Dix 2, Knott, Farrell |
| | | 5 1L | 09.02.46 | **Barnsley** (D2) | A | W | 1-0 | Shackleton |
| | | 5 2L | 13.02.46 | **Barnsley** | H | D | 1-1 | Gibbons |
| | | 6 1L | 02.03.46 | **Birmingham City** (D2) | H | D | 2-2 | Hallard, Dix |
| | | 6 2L | 09.03.46 | **Birmingham City** | A | L | 0-6 | |
| 1946-47 | (D2) | 3 | 11.01.47 | **Manchester Utd** (D1) | H | L | 0-3 | |
| 1947-48 | (D2) | 3 | 10.01.48 | **Arsenal** (D1) | A | W | 1-0 | Elliott |
| | | 4 | 24.01.48 | **Colchester Utd** (SL) | A | L | 2-3 | Elliott, Ainsley |
| 1948-49 | (D2) | 3 | 08.01.49 | **Newcastle Utd** (D1) | A | W | 2-0 | Downie, McIlvenny |
| | | 4 | 29.01.49 | **Manchester Utd** (D1) | A | D | 1-1aet | Henry |
| | | | | *played at Maine Road* | | | | |
| | | 4r | 05.02.49 | **Manchester Utd** | H | D | 1-1aet | Farrell |
| | | 4 2r | 07.02.49 | **Manchester Utd** | A | L | 0-5aet | |
| | | | | *played at Maine Road* | | | | |
| 1949-50 | (D2) | 3 | 07.01.50 | **Bournemouth** (3S) | H | L | 0-1 | |
| 1950-51 | (3N) | 1 | 25.11.50 | **Chester** (3N) | A | W | 2-1 | Elliott, Deplidge |
| | | 2 | 09.12.50 | **Millwall** (3S) | A | D | 1-1 | Crosbie |
| | | 2r | 13.12.50 | **Millwall** | H | L | 0-1 | |
| 1951-52 | (3N) | 1 | 24.11.51 | **York City** (3N) | A | D | 1-1 | Crosbie |

| | | | | | | | |
|---|---|---|---|---|---|---|---|
| | 1r | 28.11.51 | **York City** | H | D | 1-1aet | Lyons |
| | 12r | 03.12.51 | **York City** | | W | 4-0 | Haines 2, Turner, Crosbie |
| | | | *played at Elland Road* | | | | |
| | 2 | 15.12.51 | **Bradford City** (3N) | H | W | 3-2 | Turner 2, Lyons |
| | 3 | 12.01.52 | **Sheffield Wed** (D2) | H | W | 2-1 | Turner 2 |
| | 4 | 02.02.52 | **Leeds Utd** (D2) | A | L | 0-2 | |
| 1952-53 (3N) | 1 | 22.11.52 | **Rochdale** (3N) | H | W | 2-1 | Haines, Lyons |
| | 2 | 06.12.52 | **Gateshead AFC** (3N) | H | L | 1-2 | Smith |
| 1953-54 (3N) | 1 | 21.11.53 | **Selby Town** (YL) | A | W | 2-0 | Dunlop, Pickard |
| | 2 | 12.12.53 | **Cambridge Utd** (ECL) | A | W | 2-1 | Pickard, Whitaker |
| | 3 | 09.01.54 | **Manchester City** (D1) | H | L | 2-5 | Pickard, Beattie |
| 1954-55 (3N) | 1 | 20.11.54 | **Southport** (3N) | H | W | 2-0 | Adey, Wright |
| | 2 | 11.12.54 | **Southend Utd** (3S) | H | L | 2-3 | McLaren, Miles |
| 1955-56 (3N) | 1 | 19.11.55 | **Rhyl** (CC) | A | W | 3-0 | Brickley, Ward, Houghton |
| | 2 | 10.12.55 | **Workington** (3N) | H | W | 4-3 | Houghton 2, Whitaker, Ward |
| | 3 | 07.01.56 | **Middlesbrough** (D2) | H | L | 0-4 | |
| 1956-57 (3N) | 1 | 17.11.56 | **Boston Utd** (ML) | A | W | 2-0 | Kendall, Smith |
| | 2 | 08.12.56 | **Peterborough Utd** (ML) | A | L | 0-3 | |
| 1957-58 (3N) | 1 | 16.11.57 | **Oldham Athletic** (3N) | A | L | 0-2 | |
| 1958-59 (D4) | 1 | 15.11.58 | **Gateshead AFC** (D4) | A | W | 4-1 | Buchanan, Atkinson, Booth |
| | 2 | 06.12.58 | **Bradford City** (D3) | H | L | 0-2 | |
| 1959-60 (D4) | 1 | 14.11.59 | **Scarborough** (ML) | H | W | 6-1 | Buchanan 4, Allan 2 |
| | 2 | 05.12.59 | **S Shields (1936)** (ML) | A | W | 5-1 | Allan 2, Harvey 2, Buchanan |
| | 3 | 09.01.60 | **Chelsea** (D1) | A | L | 1-5 | Allan |
| 1960-61 (D4) | 1 | 05.11.60 | **York City** (D4) | A | D | 0-0 | |
| | 1r | 09.11.60 | **York City** | H | L | 0-2 | |
| 1961-62 (D3) | 1 | 04.11.61 | **Port Vale** (D3) | H | L | 0-1 | |
| 1962-63 (D3) | 1 | 03.11.62 | **Halifax Town** (D3) | A | L | 0-1 | |
| 1963-64 (D4) | 1 | 16.11.63 | **Heanor Town** (ML) | H | W | 3-1 | Evans, Atkinson, Flynn |
| | 2 | 07.12.63 | **Oldham Athletic** (D3) | A | L | 0-2 | |
| 1964-65 (D4) | 1 | 14.11.64 | **Doncaster Rovers** (D4) | H | L | 2-3 | Fryatt, Hector |
| 1965-66 (D4) | 1 | 13.11.65 | **Hull City** (D3) | H | L | 2-3 | Lightowler, Hector |
| 1966-67 (D4) | 1 | 26.11.66 | **Witton Albion** (CC) | H | W | 3-2 | Symonds, Robinson, Waddell |
| | 2 | 11.01.67 | **Workington** (D3) | H | W | 3-1 | Symonds 2, Madden |
| | 3 | 28.01.67 | **Fulham** (D1) | H | L | 1-3 | Robinson |
| 1967-68 (D4) | 1 | 09.12.67 | **Grimsby Town** (D3) | A | D | 1-1 | Down |
| | 1r | 11.12.67 | **Grimsby Town** | H | W | 4-1 | Lloyd 2, Ham, Down |
| | 2 | 06.01.68 | **Tranmere Rovers** (D3) | H | L | 2-3 | Ham, Pritchard og |
| 1968-69 (D4) | 1 | 16.11.68 | **Stockport County** (D3) | A | L | 0-3 | |
| 1969-70 (D4) | 1 | 15.11.69 | **S Shields (1936)** (NPL) | A | L | 1-2 | Brannan |
| 1970-71 (NPL) | | | 4q Washington (A) 3-0 | | | | |
| | 1 | 21.11.70 | **Barnsley** (D3) | A | L | 0-1 | |

## BRADSHAW

*Formed 1878. Played at Rigby Fields, Bradshaw, near Bolton.*

| | | | | | | |
|---|---|---|---|---|---|---|
| 1883-84 | 1 | 03.11.83 | **Bolton Association** | A | L | 1-5 |
| 1884-85 | 1 | 11.10.84 | **Darwen** | A | L | 0-11 |
| 1885-86 | 1 | 31.10.85 | **Hurst** | A | L | 1-3 |

## BRANDON UNITED

*Formed 1968 as Rostrons FC, a waste-paper company works team where most of the players were employed. Became Brandon United 1974. Based in Durham. Members of the Northern League.*

| | | | | | | | |
|---|---|---|---|---|---|---|---|
| 1979-80 (NAII) | 1 | 24.11.79 | **Bradford City** (D4) | H | L | 0-3 | |
| | | | *played at Spennymoor* | | | | |
| 1988-89 (NL) | 1 | 19.11.88 | **Doncaster Rovers** (D4) | A | D | 0-0 | |
| | 1r | 22.11.88 | **Doncaster Rovers** (D4) | H | L | 1-2 | Calvert |
| | | | *played at Belle Vue, Doncaster* | | | | |

## BRENTFORD

*Formed 1889. FA Cup best performance: 6th round, 1938, 1946, 1949, 1989; FA Cup record win: 7-0 v Windsor & Eton, 1st round, 20.11.1982; FA Cup record defeat: 1-7 v Manchester United, 3rd round, 14.1.1928*

| | |
|---|---|
| 1897-98 (Lon) | 1q 1st Coldstream Guards (H) 6-1; 2q 3rd Grenadier Guards (H) 1-1; 2qr 3rd Grenadier Guards (A) 1-4 |

| | | | | | | | | |
|---|---|---|---|---|---|---|---|---|
| 1898-99 | (SL) | | | 3q Clapton (A) 1-6 | | | | |
| 1899-00 | (SL) | | | 3q Richmond Association (H) 1-2 | | | | |
| 1900-01 | (SL) | | | 3q Maidenhead (A) 3-1; 4q Richmond Association (A) 0-1 | | | | |
| 1901-02 | (SL) | | | 3q Marlow (A) 3-0; 4q Shepherds Bush (H) 0-0 abandoned; 4q Shepherds Bush (H) 2-3 | | | | |
| 1902-03 | (SL) | | | 3q Oxford City (A) 2-2; 3qr Oxford City (H) 5-4; 4q Southall (H) 5-0; 5q Shepherds Bush (H) 2-2; 5qr Shepherds Bush (A) 1-1; 5q 2r Shepherds Bush 1-0 at Kensal Rise; Int Woolwich Arsenal (H) 1-1; Int r Woolwich Arsenal (A) 0-5 | | | | |
| 1903-04 | (SL) | | | 3q Uxbridge (H) 8-0; 4q Oxford City (A) 3-1; 5q Wycombe W (A) 4-1; Int Plymouth Argyle (H) 1-1; Int r Plymouth Argyle (A) 1-4 | | | | |
| 1904-05 | (SL) | | | 6q QPR (A) 2-1; Int Reading (H) 1-1; Int r Reading (A) 0-2 | | | | |
| 1905-06 | (SL) | | | 4q Wycombe W (H) 4-0 | | | | |
| | | 1 | 13.01.06 | **Bristol City** (D2) | H | W | 2-1 | Corbett 2 |
| | | 2 | 03.02.06 | **Lincoln City** (D2) | H | W | 3-0 | Parsonage, Underwood, Corbett |
| | | 3 | 24.02.06 | **Liverpool** (D1) | A | L | 0-2 | |
| 1906-07 | (SL) | 1 | 12.01.07 | **Glossop North End** (D2) | H | W | 2-1 | Corbett, Pentland (p) |
| | | 2 | 02.02.07 | **Middlesbrough** (D1) | H | W | 1-0 | Hagan |
| | | 3 | 23.02.07 | **Crystal Palace** (SL) | A | D | 1-1 | Hagan |
| | | 3r | 27.02.07 | **Crystal Palace** | H | L | 0-1 | |
| 1907-08 | (SL) | 1 | 11.01.08 | **Carlisle Utd** (LC) | A | D | 2-2 | Bowman, Corbett |
| | | 1r | 15.01.08 | **Carlisle Utd** | H | L | 1-3aet | Tomlinson |
| 1908-09 | (SL) | 1 | 16.01.09 | **Gainsborough T** (D2) | H | W | 2-0 | Richards 2 |
| | | 2 | 06.02.09 | **Nottingham Forest** (D1) | A | L | 0-1 | |
| 1909-10 | (SL) | | | 4q Luton Town (H) 2-1; 5q Accrington Stanley (A) 0-1 | | | | |
| 1910-11 | (SL) | 1 | 14.01.11 | **Preston North End** (D1) | H | L | 0-1 | |
| 1911-12 | (SL) | | | 4q Kings Royal Rifles (H) 1-1; 4qr Kings Royal Rifles (H) 4-1; 5q Southend U (A) 1-0 | | | | |
| | | 1 | 13.01.12 | **Crystal Palace** (SL) | H | D | 0-0 | |
| | | 1r | 17.01.12 | **Crystal Palace** | A | L | 0-4 | |
| 1912-13 | (SL) | | | 4q Watford (H) 0-0; 4qr Watford (A) 1-5 | | | | |
| 1913-14 | (SL) | | | 4q Luton Clarence (H) 1-0; 5q Southend U (H) 1-1; 5qr Southend U (A) 0-2 | | | | |
| 1914-15 | (SL) | | | 4q Nunhead (A) 1-0; 5q Boscombe (A) 0-0; 5qr Boscombe (H) 0-1 | | | | |
| 1919-20 | (SL) | 1 | 10.01.20 | **Huddersfield Town** (D2) | A | L | 1-5 | Morris |
| 1920-21 | (D3) | 1 | 08.01.21 | **Huddersfield Town** (D1) | H | L | 1-2 | King |
| 1921-22 | (3S) | | | 5q Dulwich Hamlet (H) 3-1; 6q Shildon (H) 1-0 | | | | |
| | | 1 | 07.01.22 | **Tottenham Hotspur** (D1) | H | L | 0-2 | |
| 1922-23 | (3S) | | | 5q Maidstone U (A) 0-0; 5qr Maidstone U (H) 4-0; 6q Merthyr Town (H) 0-1 | | | | |
| 1923-24 | (3S) | | | 5q Botwell Mission (A) 1-1; 5qr Botwell Mission (H) 2-0; 6q Portsmouth (H) 1-1; 6qr Portsmouth (A) 0-1aet | | | | |
| 1924-25 | (3S) | | | 5q St Albans City (A) 3-5 | | | | |
| 1925-26 | (3S) | 1 | 28.11.25 | **Barnet** (AL) | H | W | 3-1 | J Lane, Whitton, Graham |
| | | 2 | 12.12.25 | **Bournemouth** (3S) | H | L | 1-2 | Whitton |
| 1926-27 | (3S) | 1 | 27.11.26 | **Clapton** (IL) | A | D | 1-1 | Anderson |
| | | 1r | 01.12.26 | **Clapton** | H | W | 7-3 | Watkins 3, J Lane 2, Hendren 2 |
| | | 2 | 11.12.26 | **Gillingham** (3S) | A | D | 1-1 | Hendren |
| | | 2r | 15.12.26 | **Gillingham** | H | W | 1-0 | Dearn |
| | | 3 | 08.01.27 | **Oldham Athletic** (D2) | A | - | 1-2ab | Watkins |
| | | | | *abandoned after 73 minutes – fog* | | | | |
| | | 3 | 10.01.27 | **Oldham Athletic** | A | W | 4-2 | Allen 3, Watkins |
| | | 4 | 29.01.27 | **West Ham Utd** (D1) | A | D | 1-1 | J Lane |
| | | 4r | 02.02.27 | **West Ham Utd** | H | W | 2-0 | J Lane, Allen |
| | | 5 | 19.02.27 | **Reading** (D2) | A | L | 0-1 | |
| 1927-28 | (3S) | 3 | 14.01.28 | **Manchester Utd** (D1) | A | L | 1-7 | Jones og |
| 1928-29 | (3S) | 1 | 24.11.28 | **Brighton** (3S) | H | W | 4-1 | J Lane 2, Drinnan, Sherlaw |
| | | 2 | 08.12.28 | **Plymouth Argyle** (3S) | H | L | 0-1 | |
| 1929-30 | (3S) | 1 | 30.11.29 | **Southend Utd** (3S) | A | L | 0-1 | |
| 1930-31 | (3S) | 1 | 29.11.30 | **Ilford** (IL) | A | W | 6-1 | W Lane 3, J Lane 3 |
| | | 2 | 13.12.30 | **Norwich City** (3S) | H | W | 1-0 | J Lane |
| | | 3 | 10.01.31 | **Cardiff City** (D2) | H | D | 2-2 | Berry, W Lane |
| | | 3r | 14.01.31 | **Cardiff City** | A | W | 2-1 | W Lane, J Lane |
| | | 4 | 24.01.31 | **Portsmouth** (D1) | H | L | 0-1 | |

| | | | | | | | | |
|---|---|---|---|---|---|---|---|---|
| 1931-32 | (3S) | 1 | 28.11.31 | **Tunbridge Wells R** (KL) | A | D | 1-1 | Burns |
| | | 1r | 02.12.31 | **Tunbridge Wells R** | H | W | 2-1 | W Lane, Burns |
| | | 2 | 12.12.31 | **Norwich City** (3S) | H | W | 4-1 | W Lane 2, Robson, Berry |
| | | 3 | 09.01.32 | **Bath City** (SL) | H | W | 2-0 | W Lane, Berry |
| | | 4 | 23.01.32 | **Manchester City** (D1) | A | L | 1-6 | W Lane |
| 1932-33 | (3S) | 1 | 26.11.32 | **Reading** (3S) | A | L | 2-3 | Scott, Holliday |
| 1933-34 | (D2) | 3 | 13.01.34 | **Hull City** (D2) | A | L | 0-1 | |
| 1934-35 | (D2) | 3 | 12.01.35 | **Plymouth Argyle** (D2) | H | L | 0-1 | |
| 1935-36 | (D1) | 3 | 11.01.36 | **Leicester City** (D2) | A | L | 0-1 | |
| 1936-37 | (D1) | 3 | 16.01.37 | **Huddersfield Town** (D1) | H | W | 5-0 | Reid 2 (1p), McCulloch 2, Holliday |
| | | 4 | 30.01.37 | **Derby County** (D1) | A | L | 0-3 | |
| 1937-38 | (D1) | 3 | 08.01.38 | **Fulham** (D2) | H | W | 3-1 | Reid, Holliday, McCulloch |
| | | 4 | 22.01.38 | **Portsmouth** (D1) | H | W | 2-1 | Wilson (p), McCulloch |
| | | 5 | 12.02.38 | **Manchester Utd** (D2) | H | W | 2-0 | Holliday, Reid |
| | | 6 | 05.03.38 | **Preston North End** (D1) | H | L | 0-3 | |
| 1938-39 | (D1) | 3 | 07.01.39 | **Newcastle Utd** (D2) | H | L | 0-2 | |
| 1945-46 | (D1) | 3 1L | 05.01.46 | **Tottenham Hotspur** (D2) | A | D | 2-2 | Durrant, Thomas |
| | | 3 2L | 10.01.46 | **Tottenham Hotspur** | H | W | 2-0 | Hopkins 2 |
| | | 4 1L | 26.01.46 | **Bristol City** (3S) | A | L | 1-2 | Townsend |
| | | 4 2L | 31.01.46 | **Bristol City** | H | W | 5-0 | McAloon 3, Durran, og |
| | | 5 1L | 09.02.46 | **QPR** (3S) | A | W | 3-1 | McAloon, Durrant, Hopkins |
| | | 5 2L | 14.02.46 | **QPR** | H | D | 0-0 | |
| | | 6 1L | 02.03.46 | **Charlton Athletic** (D1) | A | L | 3-6 | McAloon 2, Durrant |
| | | 6 2L | 09.03.46 | **Charlton Athletic** | H | L | 1-3 | Scott |
| 1946-47 | (D1) | 3 | 11.01.47 | **Cardiff City** (3S) | H | W | 1-0 | Townsend |
| | | 4 | 25.01.47 | **Leicester City** (D2) | H | D | 0-0 | |
| | | 4r | 30.01.47 | **Leicester City** | A | D | 0-0aet | |
| | | 4 2r | 03.02.47 | **Leicester City** | | L | 1-4 | Scott |
| | | | | *played at Villa Park* | | | | |
| 1947-48 | (D2) | 3 | 10.01.48 | **Rotherham Utd** (3N) | A | W | 3-0 | Dawson, Gibbons, Buchanan |
| | | 4 | 24.01.48 | **Middlesbrough** (D1) | H | L | 1-2 | Girling |
| 1948-49 | (D2) | 3 | 08.01.49 | **Middlesbrough** | H | W | 3-2aet | Harper, Monk, McKennon |
| | | 4 | 29.01.49 | **Torquay Utd** (3S) | H | W | 1-0 | McKennan |
| | | 5 | 12.02.49 | **Burnley** (D1) | H | W | 4-2 | McKennan 2, Gibbons, Monk |
| | | 6 | 26.02.49 | **Leicester City** (D2) | H | L | 0-2 | |
| 1949-50 | (D2) | 3 | 07.01.50 | **Chelsea** (D1) | H | L | 0-1 | |
| 1950-51 | (D2) | 3 | 06.01.51 | **Stockport County** (3N) | A | L | 1-2 | Paton |
| 1951-52 | (D2) | 3 | 12.01.52 | **QPR** (D2) | H | W | 3-1 | Coote, Paton, Sperrin |
| | | 4 | 02.02.52 | **Luton Town** (D2) | A | D | 2-2 | Sperrin 2 |
| | | 4r | 06.02.52 | **Luton Town** | H | D | 0-0aet | |
| | | 4 2r | 18.02.52 | **Luton Town** | | L | 2-3aet | Dare 2 |
| | | | | *played at Highbury* | | | | |
| 1952-53 | (D2) | 3 | 10.01.53 | **Leeds Utd** (D2) | H | W | 2-1 | Ledgerton, Lawton |
| | | 4 | 31.01.53 | **Aston Villa** (D1) | A | D | 0-0 | |
| | | 4r | 04.02.53 | **Aston Villa** | H | L | 1-2 | Lawton |
| 1953-54 | (D2) | 3 | 09.01.54 | **Hull City** (D2) | H | D | 0-0 | |
| | | 3r | 14.01.54 | **Hull City** | A | D | 2-2aet | Dudley, Rainford |
| | | 3 2r | 18.01.54 | **Hull City** | | L | 2-5 | Sperrin, Bloomfield |
| | | | | *played at Belle Vue, Doncaster* | | | | |
| 1954-55 | (3S) | 1 | 20.11.54 | **Nuneaton B** (BDL) | H | W | 2-1 | Dare, Stobbart |
| | | 2 | 11.12.54 | **Crook Town** (NL) | H | W | 4-1 | Stobbart 2, Rainford, Towers |
| | | 3 | 08.01.55 | **Bradford City** (3N) | H | D | 1-1 | Dudley |
| | | 3r | 12.01.55 | **Bradford City** | A | D | 2-2aet | Dare, Dudley |
| | | 3 2r | 20.01.55 | **Bradford City** | | W | 1-0 | Dare |
| | | | | *played at Highbury* | | | | |
| | | 4 | 29.01.55 | **Newcastle Utd** (D1) | A | L | 2-3 | Stobbart, Rainford |
| 1955-56 | (3S) | 1 | 19.11.55 | **March Town Utd** (ECL) | H | W | 4-0 | Stobbart 2, Towers (p), Francis |
| | | 2 | 10.12.55 | **Leyton Orient** (3S) | A | L | 1-4 | Taylor |
| 1956-57 | (3S) | 1 | 17.11.56 | **Guildford City** (SL) | H | W | 3-0 | Taylor, 2ogs |
| | | 2 | 08.12.56 | **Crystal Palace** (3S) | H | D | 1-1 | Taylor |
| | | 2r | 12.12.56 | **Crystal Palace** | A | L | 2-3aet | Towers, Francis |

| | | | | | | | |
|---|---|---|---|---|---|---|---|
| 1957-58 (3S) | 1 | 16.11.57 | **Millwall** (3S) | A | L | 0-1 | |
| 1958-59 (D3) | 1 | 15.11.58 | **Exeter City** (D4) | H | W | 3-2 | Towers, Francis, Rainford |
| | 2 | 06.12.58 | **King's Lynn** (SL) | H | W | 3-1 | Towers 3 |
| | 3 | 10.01.59 | **Barnsley** (D2) | H | W | 2-0 | Towers, Francis |
| | 4 | 24.01.59 | **WBA** (D1) | A | L | 0-2 | |
| 1959-60 (D3) | 1 | 14.11.59 | **Ashford Town** (SL) | H | W | 5-0 | Francis 4, Towers |
| | 2 | 05.12.59 | **Exeter City** (D4) | A | L | 1-3 | Francis |
| 1960-61 (D3) | 1 | 05.11.60 | **Watford** (D3) | A | D | 2-2 | Francis 2 |
| | 1r | 08.11.60 | **Watford** | H | L | 0-2 | |
| 1961-62 (D3) | 1 | 04.11.61 | **Oxford Utd** (SL) | H | W | 3-0 | Edgley 2, Summers |
| | 2 | 25.11.61 | **Aldershot** (D4) | A | D | 2-2 | Edgley, Francis |
| | 2r | 28.11.61 | **Aldershot** | H | W | 2-0 | Edgley, Brooks |
| | 3 | 06.01.62 | **Leyton Orient** (D2) | H | D | 1-1 | Summers |
| | 3r | 08.01.62 | **Leyton Orient** | A | L | 1-2 | Higginson |
| 1962-63 (D4) | 1 | 03.11.62 | **Aldershot** (D4) | A | L | 0-1 | |
| 1963-64 (D3) | 1 | 16.11.63 | **Margate** (SL) | H | D | 2-2 | Block, Dick |
| | 1r | 20.11.63 | **Margate** | A | W | 2-0 | Ward 2 |
| | 2 | 07.12.63 | **Gravesend & N** (SL) | H | W | 1-0 | Block |
| | 3 | 04.01.64 | **Middlesbrough** (D2) | H | W | 2-1 | Dick, McAdams |
| | 4 | 25.01.64 | **Oxford Utd** (D4) | A | D | 2-2 | Block, Ward |
| | 4r | 28.01.64 | **Oxford Utd** | H | L | 1-2 | Mcadams |
| 1964-65 (D3) | 1 | 14.11.64 | **Wisbech Town** (SL) | A | W | 2-0 | Bonson, Cobb |
| | 2 | 05.12.64 | **Notts County** (D4) | H | W | 4-0 | Cobb 2, Bonson, Fielding |
| | 3 | 09.01.65 | **Burnley** (D1) | A | D | 1-1 | Lazarus |
| | 3r | 12.01.65 | **Burnley** | H | L | 0-2 | |
| 1965-66 (D3) | 1 | 13.11.65 | **Yeovil Town** (SL) | H | W | 2-1 | Fielding 2 |
| | 2 | 04.12.65 | **Reading** (D3) | A | L | 0-5 | |
| 1966-67 (D4) | 1 | 26.11.66 | **Chelmsford City** (SL) | H | W | 1-0 | Docherty (p) |
| | 2 | 07.01.67 | **Leyton Orient** (D3) | A | D | 0-0 | |
| | 2r | 10.01.67 | **Leyton Orient** | H | W | 3-1 | Docherty 2, Richardson |
| | 3 | 28.01.67 | **Sunderland** (D1) | A | L | 2-5 | Docherty 2 |
| 1967-68 (D4) | 1 | 09.12.67 | **Guildford City** (SL) | H | - | 1-2ab | |
| | | | *abandoned after 53 minutes – snow* | | | | |
| | 1 | 14.12.67 | **Guildford City** | H | D | 2-2 | Docherty, Myers |
| | 1r | 18.12.67 | **Guildford City** | A | L | 1-2 | Myers |
| 1968-69 (D4) | 1 | 16.11.68 | **Woking** (IL) | H | W | 2-0 | Fenton, Ross |
| | 2 | 07.12.68 | **Watford** (D3) | A | L | 0-1 | |
| 1969-70 (D4) | 1 | 15.11.69 | **Plymouth Argyle** (D3) | H | D | 0-0 | |
| | 1r | 19.11.69 | **Plymouth Argyle** | A | L | 0-2 | |
| 1970-71 (D4) | 1 | 21.11.70 | **Gillingham** (D3) | H | W | 2-1 | Docherty, Dawson |
| | 2 | 12.12.70 | **Walsall** (D3) | H | W | 1-0 | Cross |
| | 3 | 02.01.71 | **Workington** (D4) | A | W | 1-0 | Docherty |
| | 4 | 23.01.71 | **Cardiff City** (D2) | A | W | 2-0 | Graham, Docherty |
| | 5 | 13.02.71 | **Hull City** (D2) | A | L | 1-2 | Ross |
| 1971-72 (D4) | 1 | 20.11.71 | **Swansea City** (D3) | A | D | 1-1 | O'Mara |
| | 1r | 22.11.71 | **Swansea City** | H | L | 2-3 | Ross, O'Mara |
| 1972-73 (D3) | 1 | 18.11.72 | **Yeovil Town** (SL) | A | L | 1-2 | Allen |
| 1973-74 (D4) | 1 | 24.11.73 | **Plymouth Argyle** (D3) | A | L | 1-2 | Allen |
| 1974-75 (D4) | 1 | 23.11.74 | **Slough Town** (IL) | A | W | 4-1 | Woon 2, Graham, Simmons |
| | 2 | 14.12.74 | **Brighton** (D3) | A | L | 0-1 | |
| 1975-76 (D4) | 1 | 22.11.75 | **Northampton Town** (D4) | H | W | 2-0 | Sweetzer 2 |
| | 2 | 13.12.75 | **Wimbledon** (SL) | A | W | 2-0 | Johnson 2 (1p) |
| | 3 | 03.01.76 | **Bolton Wanderers** (D2) | H | D | 0-0 | |
| | 3r | 06.01.76 | **Bolton Wanderers** | A | L | 0-2 | |
| 1976-77 (D4) | 1 | 20.11.76 | **Chesham Utd** (IL) | H | W | 2-0 | French, Cross |
| | 2 | 11.12.76 | **Colchester Utd** (D4) | A | - | 0-0ab | |
| | | | *abandoned after 62 minutes – icebound pitch* | | | | |
| | 2 | 20.12.76 | **Colchester Utd** | A | L | 2-3 | Rolph, Fraser |
| 1977-78 (D4) | 1 | 26.11.77 | **Folkestone & Sh** (SL) | H | W | 2-0 | Phillips 2 |
| | 2 | 17.12.77 | **Swindon Town** (D3) | A | L | 1-2 | Phillips (p) |
| 1978-79 (D3) | 1 | 25.11.78 | **Exeter City** (D3) | A | L | 0-1 | |
| 1979-80 (D3) | 1 | 24.11.79 | **Swindon Town** (D3) | A | L | 1-4 | Smith |

| | | | | | | | | |
|---|---|---|---|---|---|---|---|---|
| 1980-81 | (D3) | 1 | 22.11.80 | **Addlestone & W** (SL) | A | D | 2-2 | Booker, Funnell (p) |
| | | | | *played at Griffin Park* | | | | |
| | | 1r | 25.11.80 | **Addlestone & W** | H | W | 2-0 | Crown, Funnell |
| | | 2 | 13.12.80 | **Fulham** (D3) | A | L | 0-1 | |
| 1981-82 | (D3) | 1 | 21.11.81 | **Exeter City** (D3) | H | W | 2-0 | Bowen 2 |
| | | 2 | 16.12.81 | **Colchester Utd** (D4) | H | D | 1-1 | G Roberts |
| | | 2r | 30.12.81 | **Colchester Utd** | A | L | 0-1 | |
| 1982-83 | (D3) | 1 | 20.11.82 | **Windsor & Eton** (IL) | A | W | 7-0 | Mahoney 3, Hurlock 2, McNichol, Joseph |
| | | | | *played at Griffin Park* | | | | |
| | | 2 | 11.12.82 | **Swindon Town** (D4) | A | D | 2-2 | Bowen, G Roberts |
| | | 2r | 14.12.82 | **Swindon Town** | H | L | 1-3aet | G Roberts |
| 1983-84 | (D3) | 1 | 19.11.83 | **Dagenham** (APL) | A | D | 2-2 | Joseph, P Roberts |
| | | 1r | 22.11.83 | **Dagenham** | H | W | 2-1 | Mahoney, G Roberts |
| | | 2 | 10.12.83 | **Wimbledon** (D3) | H | W | 3-2 | Kamara, G Roberts, Joseph |
| | | 3 | 07.01.84 | **Gillingham** (D3) | A | L | 3-5 | G Roberts, Hurlock, Cassells |
| 1984-85 | (D3) | 1 | 17.11.84 | **Bishop's Stortford** (IL) | H | W | 4-0 | Alexander 2, Cassells 2 |
| | | 2 | 08.12.84 | **Northampton Town** (D4) | H | D | 2-2 | Alexander, Cassells (p) |
| | | 2r | 11.12.84 | **Northampton Town** | A | - | 0-0ab | |
| | | | | *abandoned after 26 minutes – fog* | | | | |
| | | 2r | 17.12.84 | **Northampton Town** | A | W | 2-0 | Hurlock, Cassells |
| | | 3 | 05.01.85 | **Oldham Athletic** (D2) | A | L | 1-2 | Kamara |
| 1985-86 | (D3) | 1 | 16.11.85 | **Bristol Rovers** (D3) | H | L | 1-3 | Evans |
| 1986-87 | (D3) | 1 | 03.12.86 | **Bristol Rovers** (D3) | A | D | 0-0 | |
| | | 1r | 06.12.86 | **Bristol Rovers** | H | W | 2-0 | Stevens 2 |
| | | 2 | 09.12.86 | **Cardiff City** (D4) | A | L | 0-2 | |
| 1987-88 | (D3) | 1 | 14.11.87 | **Brighton** (D3) | H | L | 0-2 | |
| 1988-89 | (D3) | 1 | 19.11.88 | **Halesowen Town** (SL) | H | W | 2-0 | Evans, Sinton |
| | | 2 | 10.12.88 | **Peterborough Utd** (D4) | A | D | 0-0 | |
| | | 2r | 14.12.88 | **Peterborough Utd** | H | W | 3-2 | Cadette, Cockram, Smillie |
| | | 3 | 07.01.89 | **Walsall** (D2) | A | D | 1-1 | Jones |
| | | 3r | 10.01.89 | **Walsall** | H | W | 1-0 | Cockram |
| | | 4 | 28.01.89 | **Manchester City** (D2) | H | W | 3-1 | Blissett 2, Jones |
| | | 5 | 18.02.89 | **Blackburn Rovers** (D2) | A | W | 2-0 | Blissett 2 |
| | | 6 | 18.03.89 | **Liverpool** (D1) | A | L | 0-4 | |
| 1989-90 | (D3) | 1 | 18.11.89 | **Colchester Utd** (D4) | H | L | 0-1 | |
| 1990-91 | (D3) | 1 | 17.11.90 | **Yeovil Town** (Conf) | H | W | 5-0 | Holdsworth 2, Blissett, May, Jones |
| | | 2 | 12.12.90 | **Birmingham City** (D3) | A | W | 3-1 | Blissett, Godfrey, Jones |
| | | 3 | 05.01.91 | **Oldham Athletic** (D2) | A | L | 1-3 | Holdsworth |
| 1991-92 | (D3) | 1 | 18.11.91 | **Gillingham** (D3) | H | D | 3-3 | Holdsworth 2, Blissett |
| | | 1r | 26.11.91 | **Gillingham** | A | W | 3-1 | Holdsworth 2, Sealy |
| | | 2 | 07.12.91 | **Bournemouth** (D3) | A | L | 1-2 | Bates |
| 1992-93 | (D1) | 3 | 02.01.93 | **Grimsby Town** (D1) | H | L | 0-2 | |
| 1993-94 | (D2) | 1 | 13.11.93 | **VS Rugby** (SL) | A | W | 3-0 | Allon 2(1p), Gayle |
| | | 2 | 04.12.93 | **Cardiff City** (D2) | H | L | 1-3 | Gayle |
| 1994-95 | (D2) | 1 | 12.11.94 | **Cambridge Utd** (D2) | A | D | 2-2 | Annon, Taylor |
| | | 1r | 22.11.94 | **Cambridge Utd** | H | L | 1-2 | Grainger |
| 1995-96 | (D2) | 1 | 11.11.95 | **Farnborough Town** (Conf) | H | D | 1-1 | Bent |
| | | 1r | 22.11.95 | **Farnborough Town** | A | W | 4-0 | A Smith, Taylor 2, Bent |
| | | 2 | 02.12.95 | **Bournemouth** (D2) | A | W | 1-0 | Taylor |
| | | 3 | 06.01.96 | **Norwich City** (D1) | A | W | 2-1 | Newsome og, Bent |
| | | 4 | 07.02.96 | **Charlton Athletic** (D1) | A | L | 2-3 | Ashby, Smith |
| 1996-97 | (D2) | 1 | 16.11.96 | **Bournemouth** (D2) | H | W | 2-0 | Smith, Forster |
| | | 2 | 07.12.96 | **AFC Sudbury** (SL) | A | W | 3-1 | Taylor 2, McGhee |
| | | | | *played at Layer Road, Colchester* | | | | |
| | | 3 | 25.01.97 | **Manchester City** (D1) | H | L | 0-1 | |
| 1997-98 | (D2) | 1 | 15.11.97 | **Colchester Utd** (D3) | H | D | 2-2 | Taylor 2 |
| | | 1r | 25.11.97 | **Colchester Utd** | A | D | 0-0aet | |
| | | | | *Colchester Utd won 4-2 on penalties* | | | | |
| 1998-99 | (D3) | 1 | 14.11.98 | **Camberley Town** (IL) | H | W | 5-0 | Bates, Quinn, Folan 2, Hreidarsson |
| | | 2 | 05.12.98 | **Oldham Athletic** (D2) | A | D | 1-1 | Freeman (p) |

| | | | | | | | |
|---|---|---|---|---|---|---|---|
| | 2r | 15.12.98 | **Oldham Athletic** | H | D | 2-2aet | Owusu, Freeman |
| | | | *Oldham Athletic won 4-2 on penalties* | | | | |
| 1999-00 (D2) | 1 | 30.10.99 | **Plymouth Argyle** (D3) | H | D | 2-2 | Owusu, Marshall |
| | 1r | 09.11.99 | **Plymouth Argyle** | A | L | 1-2aet | Quinn |
| 2000-01 (D2) | 1 | 18.11.00 | **Kingstonian** (Conf) | H | L | 1-3 | Pinamonte |
| 2001-02 (D2) | 1 | 17.11.01 | **Morecambe** (Conf) | H | W | 1-0 | Gibbs |
| | 2 | 08.12.01 | **Scunthorpe Utd** (D3) | A | L | 2-3 | Dobson, Burgess |
| 2002-03 (D2) | 1 | 16.11.02 | **Wycombe W** (D2) | A | W | 4-2 | Vine 2, O'Connor, Somner |
| | 2 | 07.12.02 | **York City** (D3) | A | W | 2-1 | McCammon, Hunt |
| | 3 | 04.01.03 | **Derby County** (D1) | H | W | 1-0 | Hunt |
| | 4 | 25.01.03 | **Burnley** (D1) | H | L | 0-3 | |

# BRENTWOOD

*Essex-based amateur club which competed in the FA Cup between 1878-79 and 1885-86. No connection with later Brentwood Town.*

| | | | | | | | |
|---|---|---|---|---|---|---|---|
| 1878-79 | 1 | 09.11.78 | **Pilgrims** | H | L | 1-3 | Sparham |
| 1879-80 | 1 | 01.11.79 | **South Norwood** | A | L | 2-4 | Groves, Sparham |
| 1880-81 | 1 | 06.11.80 | **Old Etonians** | H | L | 0-10 | |
| 1881-82 | 1 | 17.10.81 | **Marlow** | A | L | 1-3 | Bowen |
| 1882-83 | 1 | 28.10.82 | **Barnes** | A | W | 4-2 | |
| | 2 | 02.12.82 | **Old Etonians** | A | L | 1-2 | Rumbal |
| 1883-84 | 1 | 03.11.83 | **Hanover Utd** | A | W | 6-1 | Abott, Evelyn, Morice, Powell 2 |
| | 2 | | bye | | | | |
| | 3 | 29.12.83 | **Romford (1876)** | A | W | 4-1 | Britten 3, Evelyn |
| | 4 | 19.01.84 | **Northwich V** | A | L | 0-3 | |
| 1884-85 | 1 | 08.11.84 | **Barnes** | H | W | 2-0 | Crossly, Evelyn |
| | 2 | 06.12.84 | **Old Etonians** | H | D | 2-2 | Evelyn, Rose |
| | 2r | 20.12.84 | **Old Etonians** | A | L | 1-6 | Bretton |
| 1885-86 | 1 | 31.10.85 | **Maidenhead** | H | W | 3-0 | |
| | 2 | 14.11.85 | **Lancing Old Boys** | H | W | 6-1 | |
| | 3 | | bye | | | | |
| | 4 | 02.01.86 | **South Reading** | A | W | 3-0 | Marchand 2, Morice |
| | 5 | 16.01.86 | **Burslem PV** | A | D | 1-1 | Evelyn |
| | 5r | 13.02.86 | **Burslem PV** | H | D | 3-3aet | Britten, Moore, AN Other |
| | | | *Port Vale scratched before second replay took place* | | | | |
| | 6 | 27.02.86 | **Blackburn Rovers** | H | L | 1-3 | Britten |

# BRENTWOOD TOWN

*Formed 1965. Folded 1970 after the FA refused to ratify a merger by directors with Chelmsford City. Their ground, The Hive, formerly the home of amateurs Brentwood & Warley was sold for re-development. League club beaten: Reading.*

| | | | | | | | |
|---|---|---|---|---|---|---|---|
| 1968-69 (SL) | 1 | 16.11.68 | **Barnet** (SL) | A | D | 1-1 | Stevenson |
| | 1r | 18.11.68 | **Barnet** | H | W | 1-0 | Stevenson |
| | 2 | 07.12.68 | **Southend Utd** (D4) | A | L | 1-10 | Stratton |
| 1969-70 (SL) | 1 | 15.11.69 | **Reading** (D3) | H | W | 1-0 | Halliday |
| | 2 | 06.12.69 | **Hendon** (IL) | A | W | 2-0 | O'Connell, Halliday |
| | 3 | 12.01.70 | **Northampton Town** (D4) | H | L | 0-1 | |

# BRIDGWATER TOWN

*Formed 1948. An earlier Bridgwater club first competed in the FA Cup in 1901. Bridgwater Town first entered FA Cup in 1948-49. Folded in 1983 but reformed a year later. Members of the Western League.*

| | | | | | | | |
|---|---|---|---|---|---|---|---|
| 1960-61 (WL) | 1 | 05.11.60 | **Hereford Utd** (SL) | H | W | 3-0 | Rice, Burr 2 |
| | 2 | 26.11.60 | **Oxford Utd** (SL) | A | L | 1-2 | Burr |
| 1961-62 (WL) | 1 | 04.11.61 | **Weston-super-Mare** (WL) | H | D | 0-0 | |
| | 1r | 09.11.61 | **Weston-super-Mare** | A | W | 1-0 | Irons |
| | 2 | 25.11.61 | **Crystal Palace** (D3) | H | L | 0-3 | |
| 1963-64 (WL) | 1 | 16.11.63 | **Luton Town** (D3) | H | L | 0-3 | |
| 1971-72 (WL) | 1 | 20.11.71 | **Reading** (D4) | H | L | 0-3 | |

## BRIDLINGTON TOWN

*Formed 1926. Known as Bridlington Central until 1959. FA Vase winners: 1993. Runners-up 1990. Members of the Northern Counties East League.*

| | | | | | | | |
|---|---|---|---|---|---|---|---|
| 1960-61 (YL) | 1 | 05.11.60 | **Bishop Auckland** (NL) | A | L | 2-3 | Pudsey, Head |
| 1991-92 (NPL) | 1 | 16.11.91 | **York City** (D4) | H | L | 1-2 | Stephenson |

## BRIERLEY HILL ALLIANCE

*First entered the FA Cup in 1891 and only made it to the competition proper once. Disbanded 1981*

| | | | | | | | |
|---|---|---|---|---|---|---|---|
| 1961-62 (BDL) | 1 | 04.11.61 | **Grantham Town** (ML) | H | W | 3-0 | Richardson, Thomas 2 |
| | 2 | 25.11.61 | **Shrewsbury Town** (D3) | A | L | 0-3 | |

## BRIGG BRITANNIA

| | | | | | | | |
|---|---|---|---|---|---|---|---|
| 1880-81 | 1 | 16.10.80 | **Turton** | A | L | 0-5 | |
| 1881-82 | 1 | 05.11.81 | **Sheffield FC** | A | L | 0-8 | |
| 1882-83 | 1 | | **Nottingham Forest** | | | - | |
| | | | *Brigg Britannia scratched. Nottingham Forest walkover* | | | | |

## BRIGG TOWN

*Formed 1864. First entered FA Cup: 1879-80. FA Vase winners: 1996, 2003. When they played Tranmere Rovers in the First Round in 2001, it was the first time they had played in the Competition Proper for 120 years. Lincolnshire-based club who currently play in the Northern Counties East League.*

| | | | | | | | |
|---|---|---|---|---|---|---|---|
| 1879-80 | 1 | 25.10.79 | **Turton** | A | L | 0-7 | |
| 1880-81 | 1 | 13.11.80 | **Darwen** | A | L | 0-8 | |
| 1881-82 | 1 | 05.11.81 | **Grantham Town** | A | L | 0-6 | |
| 1987-88 (NCoE) | 4Q | 24.10.87 | **Lincoln City** (Conf) | A | L | 1-4 | |
| 2001-02 (NCoE) | 1 | 17.11.01 | **Tranmere Rovers** (D2) | A | L | 1-4 | Leech |

## BRIGHTON & HOVE ALBION

*Formed 1900. First entered FA Cup: 1901-02. FA Cup runners-up: 1983. FA Cup record win: 14-2 v Brighton Athletic, 1st qualifying round, 1902-03. In Competition Proper: 10-1 v Wisbech Town, 1st round, 13.11.1965. FA Cup record defeat: 2-7 v Norwich City, 1st round, 30.11.1946. In 1932 the club forgot to claim their rightful exemption until the First Round and had to go into the qualifying competition .*

| | | | | | | | |
|---|---|---|---|---|---|---|---|
| 1901-02 | | | P Brighton Athletic (H) 6-2; 1q Eastbourne (H) 3-1; 2q Hastings (H) 5-0; 3q Clapton (H) 2-3 | | | | |
| 1902-03 | | | 1q Brighton Athletic (H) 14-2; 2q Shoreham (A) 2-0; 3q Grays U (H) 5-5; 3qr Grays U (A) 3-0; 4q Ilford (A) 0-1 | | | | |
| 1903-04 (SL) | | | 3q West Ham Utd (A) 0-4 | | | | |
| 1904-05 (SL) | | | 3q Shoreham (H) 7-1; 4q Gillingham (A) 1-0; 5q Ilford (H) 5-1; 6q West Ham Utd (A) 2-1; Int. Bristol R (H) 1-2 | | | | |
| 1905-06 (SL) | | | 4q Glossop North End (A) 1-0 | | | | |
| | 1 | 13.01.06 | **Swindon Town** (SL) | H | W | 3-0 | Hall, Yates 2 |
| | 2 | 03.02.06 | **Middlesbrough** (D1) | H | D | 1-1 | J Kennedy |
| | 2r | 07.02.06 | **Middlesbrough** | A | D | 1-1aet | Joynes |
| | 2 2r | 12.02.06 | **Middlesbrough** | | L | 1-3 | Hulme |
| | | | *played at Bramall Lane* | | | | |
| 1906-07 (SL) | 1 | 12.01.07 | **Bolton Wanderers** (D1) | A | L | 1-3 | Smith |
| 1907-08 (SL) | 1 | 11.01.08 | **Preston North End** (D1) | H | D | 1-1 | Hall |
| | 1r | 16.01.08 | **Preston North End** | A | - | 2-1ab | Hall 2 |
| | | | *abandoned after 112 minutes – fog* | | | | |
| | 1r | 20.01.08 | **Preston North End** (D1) | | W | 1-0 | Wombwell |
| | | | *played at Stamford Bridge* | | | | |
| | 2 | 01.02.08 | **Liverpool** (D1) | A | D | 1-1 | Hall |
| | 2r | 05.02.08 | **Liverpool** | H | L | 0-3 | |
| 1908-09 (SL) | 1 | 16.01.09 | **Manchester Utd** (D1) | A | L | 0-1 | |
| 1909-10 (SL) | 1 | 15.01.10 | **Southampton** (SL) | H | L | 0-1 | |
| 1910-11 (SL) | 1 | 14.01.11 | **Leeds City** (D2) | A | W | 3-1 | Jones 2, Smith |
| | 2 | 04.02.11 | **Coventry City** (SL) | H | D | 0-0 | |
| | 2r | 09.02.11 | **Coventry City** | A | L | 0-2 | |
| 1911-12 (SL) | 1 | 13.01.12 | **Darlington** (NEL) | A | L | 1-2 | Haworth |
| 1912-13 (SL) | 1 | 15.01.13 | **Portsmouth** (SL) | A | W | 2-1 | Higham, Webb |
| | 2 | 01.02.13 | **Everton** (D1) | H | D | 0-0 | |
| | 2r | 05.02.13 | **Everton** | A | L | 0-1 | |

| | | | | | | | | |
|---|---|---|---|---|---|---|---|---|
| 1913-14 | (SL) | 1 | 10.01.14 | **Oldham Athletic** (D1) | A | D | 1-1 | Jones |
| | | 1r | 14.01.14 | **Oldham Athletic** | H | W | 1-0aet | Booth |
| | | 2 | 31.01.14 | **Clapton Orient** (D2) | H | W | 3-1 | Webb 2, Jones |
| | | 3 | 24.02.14 | **Sheffield Wed** (D1) | A | L | 0-3 | |
| 1914-15 | (SL) | 1 | 09.01.15 | **Lincoln City** (D2) | H | W | 2-1 | Longstaff, Jones |
| | | 2 | 30.01.15 | **Birmingham** (D2) | H | D | 0-0 | |
| | | 2r | 06.02.15 | **Birmingham** | A | L | 0-3 | |
| 1919-20 | (SL) | | | 6q Luton Town (H) 0-1 | | | | |
| 1920-21 | (D3) | 1 | 08.01.21 | **Oldham Athletic** (D1) | H | W | 4-1 | Coomber, Marsh 2, Doran |
| | | 2 | 29.01.21 | **Cardiff City** (D2) | H | D | 0-0 | |
| | | 2r | 02.02.21 | **Cardiff City** | A | L | 0-1 | |
| 1921-22 | (3S) | 1 | 07.01.22 | **Sheffield Utd** (D1) | H | W | 1-0 | Little |
| | | 2 | 28.01.22 | **Huddersfield Town** (D1) | H | D | 0-0 | |
| | | 2r | 01.02.22 | **Huddersfield Town** | A | L | 0-2 | |
| 1922-23 | (3S) | 1 | 13.01.23 | **Corinthians** | H | D | 1-1 | Neil |
| | | 1r | 17.01.23 | **Corinthians** | A | D | 1-1aet | Cook |
| | | | | *played at Crystal Palace* | | | | |
| | | 12r | 22.01.23 | **Corinthians** | | W | 1-0 | Cook |
| | | | | *played at Stamford Bridge* | | | | |
| | | 2 | 03.02.23 | **West Ham Utd** (D2) | H | D | 1-1 | Cook |
| | | 2r | 07.02.23 | **West Ham Utd** | A | L | 0-1 | |
| 1923-24 | (3S) | 1 | 12.01.24 | **Barnsley** (D2) | A | D | 0-0 | |
| | | 1r | 16.01.24 | **Barnsley** | H | W | 1-0 | Hopkins |
| | | 2 | 02.02.24 | **Everton** (D1) | H | W | 5-2 | Little, Neil, Cook 3 |
| | | 3 | 23.02.24 | **Manchester City** (D1) | H | L | 1-5 | Little |
| 1924-25 | (3S) | 1 | 10.01.25 | **Watford** (3S) | A | D | 1-1 | Hopkins |
| | | 1r | 14.01.25 | **Watford** | H | W | 4-3 | Dennison 3, Hopkins |
| | | 2 | 31.01.25 | **Southampton** (D2) | A | L | 0-1 | |
| 1925-26 | (3S) | 1 | 28.11.25 | **Watford** (3S) | H | D | 1-1 | Little |
| | | 1r | 02.12.25 | **Watford** | A | L | 0-2 | |
| 1926-27 | (3S) | 1 | 27.11.26 | **Barnet** (AL) | H | W | 3-0 | Jennings 2, Cook |
| | | 2 | 11.12.26 | **Watford** (3S) | A | W | 1-0 | Cook |
| | | 3 | 08.01.27 | **Sheffield Wed** (D1) | A | L | 0-2 | |
| 1927-28 | (3S) | 1 | 30.11.27 | **Watford** (3S) | A | W | 2-1 | James, Cook |
| | | 2 | 10.12.27 | **Northampton Town** (3S) | A | L | 0-1 | |
| 1928-29 | (3S) | 1 | 24.11.28 | **Brentford** (3S) | A | L | 1-4 | Kirkwood |
| 1929-30 | (3S) | 1 | 30.11.29 | **Peterborough & F** (SL) | H | W | 4-0 | Farrell, Kirkwood 2, Smith |
| | | 2 | 14.12.29 | **Barry Town** (SL) | H | W | 4-1 | Smith 2, Kirkwood, Thompson |
| | | 3 | 11.01.30 | **Grimsby Town** (D1) | H | D | 1-1 | Dutton |
| | | 3r | 14.01.30 | **Grimsby Town** | A | W | 1-0 | Vallance |
| | | 4 | 25.01.30 | **Portsmouth** (D1) | A | W | 1-0 | Vallance |
| | | 5 | 15.02.30 | **Newcastle Utd** (D1) | A | L | 0-3 | |
| 1930-31 | (3S) | 3 | 10.01.31 | **Leicester City** (D1) | A | W | 2-1 | Smith 2 |
| | | 4 | 26.01.31 | **Watford** (3S) | A | L | 0-2 | |
| 1931-32 | (3S) | 1 | 28.11.31 | **Folkestone** (SL) | A | W | 5-2 | Farrwell, Wilson, Attwood, Smith, Kirkwood |
| | | 2 | 12.12.31 | **Doncaster Rovers** (3N) | H | W | 5-0 | Wilson, Kirkwood, Attwood 2, Farrell |
| | | 3 | 09.01.32 | **Port Vale** (D2) | H | L | 1-2 | Attwood |
| 1932-33 | (3S) | | | 1q Shoreham (H) 12-0; 2q Worthing (H) 7-1; 3q Hastings (A) 9-0; 4q Barnet (A) 4-0 | | | | |
| | | | | **Brighton failed to claim exemption* | | | | |
| | | 1 | 26.11.32 | **Crystal Palace** (3S) | A | W | 2-1 | Thompson, Attwood |
| | | 2 | 10.12.32 | **Wrexham** (3N) | H | D | 0-0 | |
| | | 2r | 14.12.32 | **Wrexham** | A | W | 3-2 | Smith, Walker, Farrell |
| | | 3 | 14.01.33 | **Chelsea** (D1) | H | W | 2-1 | Attwood, Wilson |
| | | 4 | 28.01.33 | **Bradford Park A** (D2) | H | W | 2-1 | Attwood, Smith |
| | | 5 | 18.02.33 | **West Ham Utd** (D2) | H | D | 2-2 | Wilkinson, Attwood |
| | | 5r | 22.02.33 | **West Ham Utd** | A | L | 0-1 | |
| 1933-34 | (3S) | 3 | 13.01.34 | **Swindon Town** (3S) | H | W | 3-1 | Short Walker, Farrell |
| | | 4 | 27.01.34 | **Bolton Wanderers** (D2) | H | D | 1-1 | Wilkinson |
| | | 4r | 31.01.34 | **Bolton Wanderers** | A | L | 1-6 | Finney og |
| 1934-35 | (3S) | 1 | 24.11.34 | **Folkestone** (SL) | H | W | 3-1 | Smith, Jepson, Brown |

| | | | | | | | |
|---|---|---|---|---|---|---|---|
| | 2 | 08.12.34 | **QPR** (3S) | A | W | 2-1 | Brown, Farrell |
| | 3 | 12.01.35 | **Arsenal** (D1) | H | L | 0-2 | |
| 1935-36 (3S) | 1 | 30.11.35 | **Cheltenham Town** (SL) | H | D | 0-0 | |
| | 1r | 04.12.35 | **Cheltenham Town** | A | W | 6-0 | Law 3, Stephens 2, Farrell |
| | 2 | 14.12.35 | **Scarborough** (ML) | A | D | 1-1 | Farrell |
| | 2r | 18.12.35 | **Scarborough** | H | W | 3-0 | Law, Farrell, Darling |
| | 3 | 11.01.36 | **Fulham** (D2) | A | L | 1-2 | Farrell |
| 1936-37 (3S) | 1 | 28.11.36 | **QPR** (3S) | A | L | 1-5 | Davie |
| 1937-38 (3S) | 1 | 27.11.37 | **Tunbridge Wells R** (KL) | H | W | 5-1 | Davie 3, Wilson, Farrell |
| | 2 | 11.12.37 | **South Liverpool** (LC) | A | D | 1-1 | Wilson |
| | 2r | 15.12.37 | **South Liverpool** | H | W | 6-0 | Davie 4, Stephens, Farrell |
| | 3 | 08.01.38 | **Bury** (D2) | A | L | 0-2 | |
| 1938-39 (3S) | 1 | 26.11.38 | **Yeovil & Petters Utd** (SL) | A | L | 1-2 | Marriott |
| 1945-46 (3S) | 1 1L | 17.11.45 | **Romford** (IL) | H | W | 3-1 | Davie 2, Hindley |
| | 1 2L | 24.11.45 | **Romford** | A | D | 1-1 | Stephens |
| | 2 1L | 08.12.45 | **Walthamstow A** (IL) | A | D | 1-1 | Longdon |
| | 2 2L | 15.12.45 | **Walthamstow A** | H | W | 4-2 | Longdon, Stephens, Wilson, Davie |
| | 3 1L | 05.01.46 | **Norwich City** (3S) | A | W | 2-1 | Stephens, Moore |
| | 3 2L | 09.01.46 | **Norwich City** | H | W | 4-1 | Chase, Davie (2), Stephens |
| | 4 1L | 26.01.46 | **Aldershot** (3S) | H | W | 3-0 | Davie 2, Chase, Stephens |
| | 4 2L | 30.01.46 | **Aldershot** | A | W | 4-1 | Davie 2, Chase, Stephens |
| | 5 1L | 09.02.46 | **Derby County** (D1) | H | L | 1-4 | Willems |
| | 5 2L | 13.02.46 | **Derby County** | A | L | 0-6 | |
| 1946-47 (3S) | 1 | 30.11.46 | **Norwich City** (3S) | A | L | 2-7 | Hindley, Darling |
| 1947-48 (3S) | 1 | 29.11.47 | **Trowbridge Town** (WL) | A | D | 1-1aet | Willard |
| | 1r | 06.12.47 | **Trowbridge Town** | H | W | 5-0 | Hacking, Sim, Chapman 2, James (p) |
| | 2 | 13.12.47 | **Hartlepools Utd** (3N) | A | D | 1-1aet | Hacking |
| | 2r | 20.12.47 | **Hartlepools Utd** | H | W | 2-1 | Willard, Sim |
| | 3 | 10.01.48 | **Portsmouth** (D1) | A | L | 1-4 | Booth |
| 1948-49 (3S) | 1 | 27.11.48 | **Newport County** (3S) | A | L | 1-3 | Tennant |
| 1949-50 (3S) | 1 | 26.11.49 | **Ipswich Town** (3S) | A | L | 1-2 | Tennant |
| 1950-51 (3S) | 1 | 25.11.50 | **Tooting & M** (AL) | A | W | 3-2 | Mansell, Tennant, McNicholl |
| | 2 | 09.12.50 | **Ipswich Town** (3S) | H | W | 2-0 | Mansell, Thompson |
| | 3 | 06.01.51 | **Chesterfield** (D2) | H | W | 2-1 | Bennett, McNichol |
| | 4 | 27.01.51 | **Bristol City** (3S) | A | L | 0-1 | |
| 1951-52 (3S) | 1 | 24.11.51 | **Bristoi City** (3S) | H | L | 1-2 | Bennett |
| 1952-53 (3S) | 1 | 22.11.52 | **Yeovil Town** (SL) | A | W | 4-1 | Howard, Owen 2, Tennant |
| | 2 | 06.12.52 | **Norwich City** (3S) | H | W | 2-0 | Bennett 2 |
| | 3 | 10.01.53 | **Barnsley** (D2) | A | L | 3-4 | Owens, Howard, Reed |
| 1953-54 (3S) | 1 | 21.11.53 | **Coventry City** (3S) | H | W | 5-1 | Addinall 2, Leadbetter, Howard, Tennant |
| | 2 | 12.12.53 | **Wrexham** (3N) | A | D | 1-1aet | Leadbetter |
| | 2r | 16.12.53 | **Wrexham** | H | D | 1-1aet | Gordon |
| | 2 2r | 21.12.53 | **Wrexham** *played at Selhurst Park* | | L | 1-3 | Sirrell |
| 1954-55 (3S) | 1 | 20.11.54 | **Tunbridge Wells Utd** (KL) | H | W | 5-0 | Leadbetter, Gordon, Gilberg 2, Tennant |
| | 2 | 11.12.54 | **Norwich City** (3S) | A | D | 0-0 | |
| | 2r | 15.12.54 | **Norwich City** | H | W | 5-1 | Tennant, Mundy 2, Leadbetter, Howard |
| | 3 | 08.01.55 | **Aston Villa** (D1) | H | D | 2-2 | Moore, Munday |
| | 3r | 10.01.55 | **Aston Villa** | A | L | 2-4 | Foreman, Wilson |
| 1955-56 (3S) | 1 | 19.11.55 | **Newport County** (3S) | H | W | 8-1 | Harburn 4, Foreman 3, Howard |
| | 2 | 10.12.55 | **Norwich City** (3S) | H | L | 1-2 | Langley |
| 1956-57 (3S) | 1 | 17.11.56 | **Millwall** (3S) | H | D | 1-1 | Wilson |
| | 1r | 19.11.56 | **Millwall** | A | L | 1-3 | Langley (p) |
| 1957-58 (3S) | 1 | 16.11.57 | **Walsall** (3S) | H | W | 2-1 | Sexton 2 |
| | 2 | 07.12.57 | **Norwich City** (3S) | A | D | 1-1 | Foreman |
| | 2r | 11.12.57 | **Norwich City** | H | L | 1-2 | Foreman |
| 1958-59 (D2) | 3 | 10.01.59 | **Bradford City** (D3) | H | L | 0-2 | |
| 1959-60 (D2) | 3 | 09.01.60 | **Bath City** (SL) | A | W | 1-0 | Tiddy |

| | | | | | | | | |
|---|---|---|---|---|---|---|---|---|
| | | 4 | 30.01.60 | **Rotherham Utd** (D2) | A | D | 1-1 | Thorne |
| | | 4r | 03.02.60 | **Rotherham Utd** | H | D | 1-1aet | Thorne |
| | | 4 2r | 08.02.60 | **Rotherham Utd** | | W | 6-0 | Curry 3, Jones, Thorne 2 |
| | | | | *played at Highbury* | | | | |
| | | 5 | 20.02.60 | **Preston North End** (D1) | A | L | 1-2 | Wilson (p) |
| 1960-61 | (D2) | 3 | 07.01.61 | **Derby County** (D2) | H | W | 3-1 | McNeill, Laverick, Windross |
| | | 4 | 28.01.61 | **Burnley** (D1) | H | D | 3-3 | Bertolini, McNicol, Windross |
| | | 4r | 31.01.61 | **Burnley** | A | L | 0-2 | |
| 1961-62 | (D2) | 3 | 06.01.62 | **Blackburn Rovers** (D1) | H | L | 0-3 | |
| 1962-63 | (D3) | 1 | 03.11.62 | **Southend Utd** (D3) | A | L | 1-2 | Cooper |
| 1963-64 | (D4) | 1 | 16.11.63 | **Colchester Utd** (D3) | H | L | 0-1 | |
| 1964-65 | (D4) | 1 | 14.11.64 | **Bristol City** (D3) | A | L | 0-1 | |
| 1965-66 | (D3) | 1 | 13.11.65 | **Wisbech Town** (SL) | H | W | 10-1 | Livesey 3, Smith 2, Cassidy 2, Howell og, Goodchild, Collins |
| | | 2 | 04.12.65 | **Bedford Town** (SL) | H | D | 1-1 | Gall |
| | | 2r | 06.12.65 | **Bedford Town** | A | L | 1-2 | Morgan og |
| 1966-67 | (D3) | 1 | 26.11.66 | **Newport County** (D4) | A | W | 2-1 | Turner, Whittington |
| | | 2 | 07.01.67 | **Bath City** (SL) | A | W | 5-0 | Turner, Whittington 2, Tawse 2 |
| | | 3 | 28.01.67 | **Aldershot** (D4) | A | D | 0-0 | |
| | | 3r | 01.02.67 | **Aldershot** | H | W | 3-1 | Whittington, K Napier, Livesey |
| | | 4 | 18.02.67 | **Chelsea** (D1) | H | D | 1-1 | Turner |
| | | 4r | 22.02.67 | **Chelsea** | A | L | 0-4 | |
| 1967-68 | (D3) | 1 | 13.12.67 | **Southend Utd** (D4) | H | W | 1-0 | K Napier |
| | | 2 | 06.01.68 | **Swansea Town** (D4) | A | L | 1-2 | Hickman |
| 1968-69 | (D3) | 1 | 16.11.68 | **Kidderminster H** (WMRL) | H | D | 2-2 | Livesey, Lawton |
| | | 1r | 20.11.68 | **Kidderminster H** | A | W | 1-0 | K Napier |
| | | 2 | 07.12.68 | **Northampton Town** (D3) | H | L | 1-2 | K Napier |
| 1969-70 | (D3) | 1 | 15.11.69 | **Enfield** (IL) | H | W | 2-1 | Gilliver 2 |
| | | 2 | 06.12.69 | **Walsall** (D3) | H | D | 1-1 | Dawson |
| | | 2r | 09.12.69 | **Walsall** | A | D | 1-1aet | Dawson |
| | | 2 2r | 15.12.69 | **Walsall** | | D | 0-0aet | |
| | | | | *played at Highfield Road* | | | | |
| | | 2 3r | 17.12.69 | **Walsall** | | L | 1-2 | Lawton |
| | | | | *played at Craven Cottage* | | | | |
| 1970-71 | (D3) | 1 | 21.11.70 | **Cheltenham Town** (SL) | H | W | 4-0 | Gilliver, O'Sullivan, K Napier (p), Woffinden |
| | | 2 | 12.12.70 | **Hereford Utd** (SL) | A | W | 2-1 | Lawton, K Napier |
| | | 3 | 02.01.71 | **Cardiff City** (D2) | A | L | 0-1 | |
| 1971-72 | (D3) | 1 | 20.11.71 | **Hillingdon Borough** (SL) | H | W | 7-1 | Spearitt, K Napier 2, O'Sullivan 2, Ryan og, Murray |
| | | 2 | 11.12.71 | **Walsall** (D3) | H | D | 1-1 | Irvine |
| | | 2r | 14.12.71 | **Walsall** | A | L | 1-2 | K Napier |
| 1972-73 | (D2) | 3 | 13.01.73 | **Chelsea** (D1) | H | L | 0-2 | |
| 1973-74 | (D3) | 1 | 24.11.73 | **Walton & H** (IL) | A | D | 0-0 | |
| | | 1r | 28.11.73 | **Walton & H** | H | L | 0-4 | |
| 1974-75 | (D3) | 1 | 23.11.74 | **Aldershot** (D3) | H | W | 3-1 | Binney 2, Mellor |
| | | 2 | 14.12.74 | **Brentford** (D4) | H | W | 1-0 | Binney |
| | | 3 | 04.01.75 | **Leatherhead** (IL) | H | L | 0-1 | |
| 1975-76 | (D3) | 1 | 22.11.75 | **Watford** (D4) | A | W | 3-0 | Martin, Binney 2 |
| | | 2 | 13.12.75 | **Gillingham** (D3) | A | W | 1-0 | Fell |
| | | 3 | 03.01.76 | **Southend Utd** (D3) | A | L | 1-2 | Binney |
| 1976-77 | (D3) | 1 | 20.11.76 | **Crystal Palace** (D3) | H | D | 2-2 | Ward, Mellor |
| | | 1r | 23.11.76 | **Crystal Palace** | A | D | 1-1aet | Mellor |
| | | 1 2r | 06.12.76 | **Crystal Palace** | | L | 0-1 | |
| | | | | *played at Stamford Bridge* | | | | |
| 1977-78 | (D2) | 3 | 07.01.78 | **Scarborough** (NPL) | H | W | 3-0 | Ward, Potts, Horton |
| | | 4 | 31.01.78 | **Notts County** (D2) | H | L | 1-2 | Towner |
| 1978-79 | (D2) | 3 | 09.01.79 | **Wolverhampton W** (D1) | H | L | 2-3 | Lawrence, Ryan |
| 1979-80 | (D1) | 3 | 05.01.80 | **Mansfield Town** (D3) | A | W | 2-0 | Ryan, Clarke |
| | | 4 | 26.01.80 | **Arsenal** (D1) | A | L | 0-2 | |
| 1980-81 | (D1) | 3 | 03.01.81 | **Manchester Utd** (D1) | A | D | 2-2 | Horton, Ritchie |

| | | | | | | | |
|---|---|---|---|---|---|---|---|
| | 3r | 07.01.81 | **Manchester Utd** | H | L | 0-2 | |
| 1981-82 (D1) | 3 | 02.01.82 | **Barnet** (APL) | A | D | 0-0 | |
| | 3r | 05.01.82 | **Barnet** | H | W | 3-1 | Thomas, Case, McNab (p) |
| | 4 | 23.01.82 | **Oxford Utd** (D3) | H | L | 0-3 | |
| 1982-83 (D1) | 3 | 08.01.83 | **Newcastle Utd** (D2) | H | D | 1-1 | Ritchie |
| | 3r | 12.01.83 | **Newcastle Utd** | A | W | 1-0 | Ward |
| | 4 | 29.01.83 | **Manchester City** (D1) | H | W | 4-0 | Case, Smillie, Robinson 2 |
| | 5 | 20.02.83 | **Liverpool** (D1) | A | W | 2-1 | Ryan, Case |
| | 6 | 12.03.83 | **Norwich City** (D1) | H | W | 1-0 | Case |
| | SF | 16.04.83 | **Sheffield Wed** (D2) | | W | 2-1 | Case, Robinson |
| | | | *played at Highbury* | | | | |
| | F | 21.05.83 | **Manchester Utd** (D1) | | D | 2-2aet | Smith, Stevens |
| | | | *played at Wembley Stadium* | | | | |
| | Fr | 26.05.83 | **Manchester Utd** | | L | 0-4 | |
| | | | *played at Wembley Stadium* | | | | |
| 1983-84 (D2) | 3 | 07.01.84 | **Swansea City** (D2) | H | W | 2-0 | McQuillan og, Connor |
| | 4 | 29.01.84 | **Liverpool** (D1) | H | W | 2-0 | Ryan, Connor |
| | 5 | 18.02.84 | **Watford** (D1) | A | L | 1-3 | Wilson (p) |
| 1984-85 (D2) | 3 | 05.01.85 | **Hull City** (D3) | H | W | 1-0 | Hutchings |
| | 4 | 26.01.85 | **Barnsley** (D2) | A | L | 1-2 | Ryan |
| 1985-86 (D2) | 3 | 04.01.86 | **Newcastle Utd** (D1) | A | W | 2-0 | Young, Saunders |
| | 4 | 25.01.86 | **Hull City** (D2) | A | W | 3-2 | Saunders, Connor 2 |
| | 5 | 15.02.86 | **Peterborough Utd** (D4) | A | D | 2-2 | Saunders, Jacobs |
| | 5r | 03.03.86 | **Peterborough Utd** | H | W | 1-0 | Saunders |
| | 6 | 08.03.86 | **Southampton** (D1) | H | L | 0-2 | |
| 1986-87 (D2) | 3 | 10.01.87 | **Sheffield Utd** (D2) | A | D | 0-0 | |
| | 3r | 21.01.87 | **Sheffield Utd** | H | L | 1-2 | Jasper |
| 1987-88 (D3) | 1 | 14.11.87 | **Brentford** (D3) | A | W | 2-0 | Nelson 2 (1p) |
| | 2 | 05.12.87 | **Northampton Town** (D3) | A | W | 2-1 | Bremner, Nelson |
| | 3 | 09.01.88 | **Bournemouth** (D2) | H | W | 2-0 | Rougvie, Nelson |
| | 4 | 30.01.88 | **Arsenal** (D1) | H | L | 1-2 | Nelson |
| 1988-89 (D2) | 3 | 07.01.89 | **Leeds Utd** (D2) | H | L | 1-2 | Curbishley (p) |
| 1989-90 (D2) | 3 | 06.01.90 | **Luton Town** (D1) | H | W | 4-1 | Dublin, Nelson, Codner, Curbishley |
| | 4 | 27.01.90 | **Oldham Athletic** (D2) | A | L | 1-2 | Barham |
| 1990-91 (D2) | 3 | 05.01.91 | **Scunthorpe Utd** (D4) | H | W | 3-2 | Barham 2, Gurinovich |
| | 4 | 26.01.91 | **Liverpool** (D1) | A | D | 2-2 | Small (p), Byrne |
| | 4r | 30.01.91 | **Liverpool** | H | L | 2-3aet | Small, Byrne |
| 1991-92 (D2) | 3 | 04.01.92 | **Crawley Town** (SL) | H | W | 5-0 | Gall, Walker, Chapman 2 (1p), Meade |
| | 4 | 25.01.92 | **Bolton Wanderers** (D3) | A | L | 1-2 | Meade |
| 1992-93 (D2) | 1 | 14.11.92 | **Hayes** (IL) | H | W | 2-0 | Kennedy, Codner |
| | 2 | 05.12.92 | **Woking** (Conf) | H | D | 1-1 | Kennedy |
| | 2r | 16.12.92 | **Woking** (Conf) | A | W | 2-1 | Codner, Crumplin |
| | 3 | 02.01.93 | **Portsmouth** (D1) | H | W | 1-0 | Edwards |
| | 4 | 23.01.93 | **Manchester Utd** (PL) | A | L | 0-1 | |
| 1993-94 (D2) | 1 | 13.11.93 | **Bournemouth** (D2) | A | L | 2-4 | Kennedy 2 |
| 1994-95 (D2) | 1 | 12.11.94 | **Kingstonian** (IL) | A | L | 1-2 | Codner |
| 1995-96 (D2) | 1 | 12.11.95 | **Canvey Island** (IL) | A | D | 2-2 | McDougald 2 |
| | 1r | 21.11.95 | **Canvey Island** | H | W | 4-1 | Byrne 2, McDougald, Smith |
| | 2 | 02.12.95 | **Fulham** (D3) | A | D | 0-0 | |
| | 2r | 14.12.95 | **Fulham** | H | D | 0-0aet | |
| | | | *Fulham won 4-1 on penalties* | | | | |
| 1996-97 (D3) | 1 | 16.11.96 | **AFC Sudbury** (SL) | A | D | 0-0 | |
| | 1r | 26.11.96 | **AFC Sudbury** | H | D | 1-1aet | Maskell |
| | | | *Sudbury won 4-3 on penalties* | | | | |
| 1997-98 (D3) | 1 | 15.11.97 | **Hereford Utd** (Conf) | A | L | 1-2 | Storer |
| 1998-99 (D3) | 1 | 14.11.98 | **Leyton Orient** (D3) | A | L | 2-4 | Barker, Mayo |
| 1999-00 (D3) | 1 | 30.10.99 | **Peterborough Utd** (D3) | A | D | 1-1 | Freeman |
| | 1r | 09.11.99 | **Peterborough Utd** | H | W | 3-0 | Rogers, Watson, Mayo |
| | 2 | 20.11.99 | **Plymouth Argyle** (D3) | A | D | 0-0 | |
| | 2r | 30.11.99 | **Plymouth Argyle** | H | L | 1-2 | Cullip |
| 2000-01 (D3) | 1 | 18.11.00 | **Aldershot Town** (IL) | A | W | 6-2 | Carpenter, Watson 2 (2p), Oatway, Zamora, Wicks |

| | | | | | | | | |
|---|---|---|---|---|---|---|---|---|
| | | 2 | 09.12.00 | **Scunthorpe Utd** (D3) | A | L | 1-2 | Zamora |
| 2001-02 | (D2) | 1 | 17.11.01 | **Shrewsbury Town** (D3) | H | W | 1-0 | Zamora |
| | | 2 | 08.12.01 | **Rushden & D** (D3) | H | W | 2-1 | Zamora, Cullip |
| | | 3 | 15.01.02 | **Preston North End** (D1) | H | L | 0-2 | |
| 2002-03 | (D1) | 3 | 14.01.03 | **Norwich City** (D1) | A | L | 1-3 | Pethick |

# BRISTOL CITY

*Formed 1894 as Bristol South End. Bristol City 1897. First entered FA Cup: 1895-96; FA Cup runners-up: 1909; FA Cup record win: 11-0 v Chichester City, 1st round, 05.11.1960; FA Cup record defeat: 1-6 v Sunderland, 4th round, 25.01.1964. They have also suffered 0-5 defeats v Preston North End, 5th round replay, 23.02.1935; v Brentford, 4th round, 2nd leg, 31.01.1946*

| | | | | | | | | |
|---|---|---|---|---|---|---|---|---|
| 1895-96 | | | | P Slough (H) 5-1; 1q Marlow (H) 0-1 | | | | |
| 1896-97 | | | | 1q Bedminster (H) 2-4 | | | | |
| 1897-98 | (SL) | | | 1q Clifton (H) 9-1; 2q Trowbridge Town (A) 5-2; 3q Southampton (A) 0-2 | | | | |
| 1898-99 | (SL) | | | 3q Cowes (A) 5-0; 4q Bristol St George (A) 1-0; 5q Reading (H) 3-2 | | | | |
| | | 1 | 28.01.99 | **Sunderland** (D1) | H | L | 2-4 | Finnerham, Langham |
| 1899-00 | (SL) | 1 | 27.01.00 | **Stalybridge Rovers** (LL) | H | W | 2-1 | Blessington, Jones |
| | | 2 | 10.02.00 | **Aston Villa** (D1) | H | L | 1-5 | Jones |
| 1900-01 | (SL) | | | Int Reading (A) 1-1; Int r Reading (H) 0-0aet; Int 2r Reading 1-2 at Swindon | | | | |
| 1901-02 | (D2) | | | 3q Bristol East (H) 5-1; 4q Bristol Rovers (A) 1-1aet; 4qr Bristol Rovers (H) 2-3 | | | | |
| 1902-03 | (D2) | | | Int Middlesbrough (H) 3-1 | | | | |
| | | 1 | 07.12.02 | **Bolton Wanderers** (D1) | A | W | 5-0 | Banks 3, Dean, Wombwell |
| | | 1 | 13.12.02 | **Middlesbrough** (D1) | H | W | 3-1 | |
| | | 2 | 21.02.03 | **Tottenham Hotspur** (SL) | A | L | 0-1 | |
| 1903-04 | (D2) | | | Int New Brompton (A) 1-1; Int r New Brompton (H) 5-2 | | | | |
| | | 1 | 06.02.04 | **Sheffield Utd** (D1) | H | L | 1-3 | Hosie |
| 1904-05 | (D2) | | | Int Blackpool (H) 2-1 | | | | |
| | | 1 | 04.02.05 | **Woolwich Arsenal** (D1) | A | D | 0-0 | |
| | | 1r | 08.02.05 | **Woolwich Arsenal** | H | W | 1-0 | Dean |
| | | 2 | 18.02.05 | **Preston North End** (D1) | H | D | 0-0 | |
| | | 2r | 23.02.05 | **Preston North End** | A | L | 0-1 | |
| 1905-06 | (D2) | 1 | 13.01.06 | **Brentford** (SL) | A | L | 1-2 | Maxwell |
| 1906-07 | (D1) | 1 | 12.01.07 | **Leeds City** (D2) | H | W | 4-1 | Gilligan 2, Maxwell 2 |
| | | 2 | 02.02.07 | **Woolwich Arsenal** (D1) | A | L | 1-2 | Gilligan |
| 1907-08 | (D1) | 1 | 11.01.08 | **Grimsby Town** (D2) | H | D | 0-0 | |
| | | 1r | 15.01.08 | **Grimsby Town** | A | L | 1-2 | Hilton |
| 1908-09 | (D1) | 1 | 16.01.09 | **Southampton** (SL) | H | D | 1-1 | Rippon |
| | | 1r | 20.01.09 | **Southampton** | A | W | 2-0 | Hardy, Rippon (p) |
| | | 2 | 06.02.09 | **Bury** (D1) | H | D | 2-2 | Burton, Gilligan |
| | | 2r | 10.02.09 | **Bury** | A | W | 1-0 | Gilligan |
| | | 3 | 20.02.09 | **Norwich City** (SL) | H | W | 2-0 | Burton, Rippon |
| | | 4 | 06.03.09 | **Glossop North End** (D2) | A | D | 0-0 | |
| | | 4r | 10.03.09 | **Glossop North End** | H | W | 1-0 | Gilligan |
| | | SF | 27.03.09 | **Derby County** (D2) *played at Stamford Bridge* | | D | 1-1 | Rippon (p) |
| | | SFr | 31.03.09 | **Derby County** *played at St Andrews* | | W | 2-1 | Hardy, Rippon |
| | | F | 24.04.09 | **Manchester Utd** (D1) *played at Crystal Palace* | | L | 0-1 | |
| 1909-10 | (D1) | 1 | 15.01.10 | **Liverpool** (D1) | H | W | 2-0 | Burton, Rippon |
| | | 2 | 05.02.10 | **WBA** (D2) | H | D | 1-1 | Gilligan |
| | | 2r | 09.02.10 | **WBA** | A | L | 2-4 | Gilligan, Staniforth |
| 1910-11 | (D1) | 1 | 14.01.11 | **Crewe Alexandra** (BDL) | H | L | 0-3 | |
| 1911-12 | (D2) | 1 | 13.01.12 | **Northampton Town** (SL) | A | L | 0-1 | |
| 1912-13 | (D2) | 1 | 15.01.13 | **Liverpool** (D1) | A | L | 0-3 | |
| 1913-14 | (D2) | 1 | 10.01.14 | **QPR** (SL) | A | D | 2-2 | Picken, Pullan (og) |
| | | 1r | 14.01.14 | **QPR** | H | L | 0-2aet | |
| 1914-15 | (D2) | 1 | 09.01.15 | **Cardiff City** (SL) | H | W | 2-0 | Burton 2 |
| | | 2 | 30.01.15 | **Everton** (D1) | A | L | 0-4 | |
| 1919-20 | (D2) | 1 | 10.01.20 | **Grimsby Town** (D2) | A | W | 2-1 | Howarth 2 |
| | | 2 | 31.01.20 | **Arsenal** (D1) | H | W | 1-0 | Howarth |
| | | 3 | 21.02.20 | **Cardiff City** (SL) | H | W | 2-1 | Howarth, Neesam |

| | | | | | | | | |
|---|---|---|---|---|---|---|---|---|
| | | 4 | 06.03.20 | **Bradford City** (D1) | H | W | 2-0 | Harris 2 |
| | | SF | 27.03.20 | **Huddersfield Town** (D2) | | L | 1-2 | Howarth |
| | | | | *played at Stamford Bridge* | | | | |
| 1920-21 | (D2) | 1 | 08.01.21 | **Aston Villa** (D1) | A | L | 0-2 | |
| 1921-22 | (D2) | 1 | 07.01.22 | **Nottingham Forest** (D2) | H | D | 0-0 | |
| | | 1r | 11.01.22 | **Nottingham Forest** | A | L | 1-3 | Bown |
| 1922-23 | (3S) | 1 | 13.01.23 | **Wrexham** (3N) | H | W | 5-1 | Fairclough 3, Paul, Walker |
| | | 2 | 03.02.23 | **Derby County** (D2) | H | L | 0-3 | |
| 1923-24 | (D2) | 1 | 12.01.24 | **Norwich City** (3S) | A | W | 1-0 | Smailes |
| | | 2 | 02.02.24 | **Sheffield Wed** (D2) | A | D | 1-1 | Pocock |
| | | 2r | 06.02.24 | **Sheffield Wed** | H | W | 2-0 | Walsh 2 |
| | | 3 | 23.02.24 | **Cardiff City** (D1) | A | L | 0-3 | |
| 1924-25 | (3S) | 1 | 10.01.25 | **Bristol Rovers** (3S) | A | W | 1-0 | Walsh |
| | | 2 | 31.01.25 | **Liverpool** (D1) | H | L | 0-1 | |
| 1925-26 | (3S) | 3 | 09.01.26 | **WBA** (D1) | A | L | 1-4 | Pocock |
| 1926-27 | (3S) | 1 | 27.11.26 | **Merthyr Town** (3S) | A | W | 2-0 | Foster, Paul |
| | | 2 | 11.12.26 | **Bournemouth** (3S) | H | D | 1-1 | Martin |
| | | 2r | 15.12.26 | **Bournemouth** | A | L | 0-2 | |
| 1927-28 | (D2) | 3 | 14.01.28 | **Tottenham Hotspur** (D1) | H | L | 1-2 | Martin |
| 1928-29 | (D2) | 3 | 12.01.29 | **Liverpool** (D1) | H | L | 0-2 | |
| 1929-30 | (D2) | 3 | 11.01.30 | **Derby County** (D1) | A | L | 1-5 | Williams |
| 1930-31 | (D2) | 3 | 10.01.31 | **Barnsley** (D2) | A | L | 1-4 | Vials |
| 1931-32 | (D2) | 3 | 09.01.32 | **Notts County** (D2) | A | D | 2-2 | Elliott 2 |
| | | 3r | 13.01.32 | **Notts County** | H | W | 3-2 | Williams 2, Elliott |
| | | 4 | 23.01.32 | **Watford** (3S) | A | L | 1-2 | Elliott |
| 1932-33 | (3S) | 1 | 26.11.32 | **Romford** (AL) | H | W | 4-0 | Bowen 3, Loftus |
| | | 2 | 10.12.32 | **Tranmere Rovers** (3N) | H | D | 2-2 | Keating, Loftus |
| | | 2r | 14.12.32 | **Tranmere Rovers** | A | L | 2-3 | Bowen, Loftus |
| 1933-34 | (3S) | 1 | 25.11.33 | **Kingstonian** (IL) | A | W | 7-1 | Brinton 2, Heale 2, Reed 2, Riley |
| | | 2 | 09.12.33 | **Barrow** (3N) | H | W | 3-1 | Cainey, Riley |
| | | 3 | 13.01.34 | **Derby County** (D1) | H | D | 1-1 | Scriven |
| | | 3r | 17.01.34 | **Derby County** | A | L | 0-1 | |
| 1934-35 | (3S) | 1 | 24.11.34 | **Gillingham** (3S) | H | W | 2-0 | Landells 2 |
| | | 2 | 08.12.34 | **Rotherham Utd** (3N) | A | W | 2-1 | Loftus |
| | | 3 | 12.01.35 | **Bury** (D2) | H | D | 1-1 | Harston |
| | | 3r | 16.01.35 | **Bury** | A | D | 2-2aet | Harston, Hodge |
| | | 3 2r | 21.01.35 | **Bury** | | W | 2-1 | Hodge 2 |
| | | | | *played at Villa Park* | | | | |
| | | 4 | 26.01.35 | **Portsmouth** (D1) | A | D | 0-0 | |
| | | 4r | 30.01.35 | **Portsmouth** | H | W | 2-0 | Harston, Hodge |
| | | 5 | 16.02.35 | **Preston North End** (D1) | H | D | 0-0 | |
| | | 5r | 25.02.35 | **Preston North End** | A | L | 0-5 | |
| 1935-36 | (3S) | 1 | 30.11.35 | **Crystal Palace** (3S) | H | L | 0-1 | |
| 1936-37 | (3S) | 1 | 28.11.36 | **Newport County** (3S) | A | L | 0-3 | |
| 1937-38 | (3S) | 1 | 27.11.37 | **Enfield** (AL) | H | W | 3-0 | Haycox 2, Hockaday (og) |
| | | 2 | 11.12.37 | **Cardiff City** (3S) | A | D | 1-1 | Brain (p) |
| | | 2r | 15.12.37 | **Cardiff City** | H | L | 0-2 | |
| 1938-39 | (3S) | 1 | 26.11.38 | **Bournemouth** (3S) | A | L | 1-2 | Peters |
| 1945-46 | (3S) | 1 1L | 17.11.45 | **Yeovil & Petters Utd** (SL) | A | D | 2-2 | Artus, Curran |
| | | 1 2L | 24.11.45 | **Yeovil & Petters Utd** | H | W | 3-0 | Chilcott 2, Curran |
| | | 2 1L | 08.12.45 | **Bristol Rovers** (3S) | H | W | 4-2 | Morgan 2, Clark, Williams |
| | | 2 2L | 15.12.45 | **Bristol Rovers** | A | W | 2-0 | Clark, Thomas |
| | | 3 1L | 05.01.46 | **Swansea Town** (D2) | H | W | 5-1 | Clark 3, Bentley, Chilcott |
| | | 3 2L | 10.01.46 | **Swansea Town** | A | D | 2-2 | Chilcott, Williams |
| | | 4 1L | 26.01.46 | **Brentford** (D1) | H | W | 2-1 | Hargreaves, Williams |
| | | 4 2L | 31.01.46 | **Brentford** | A | L | 0-5 | |
| 1946-47 | (3S) | 1 | 30.11.46 | **Hayes** (AL) | H | W | 9-3 | Clark 4, Williams 2, Chilcott, Hargreaves, Thomas |
| | | 2 | 14.12.46 | **Gillingham** (SL) | H | L | 1-2 | Clark |
| 1947-48 | (3S) | 1 | 29.11.47 | **Dartford** (SL) | A | D | 0-0aet | |
| | | 1r | 06.12.47 | **Dartford** | H | W | 9-2 | Clark 3, Townsend 3, Williams 3 |

| | | | | | | | |
|---|---|---|---|---|---|---|---|
| | 2 | 13.12.47 | **Crystal Palace** (3S) | H | L | 0-1aet | |
| 1948-49 (3S) | 1 | 27.11.48 | **Crystal Palace** | A | W | 1-0aet | Townsend |
| | 2 | 11.12.48 | **Swansea Town** (3S) | H | W | 3-1 | Barney, Boxshall, Townsend |
| | 3 | 08.01.49 | **Chelsea** (D1) | H | L | 1-3 | Clark |
| 1949-50 (3S) | 1 | 26.11.49 | **Nottingham Forest** (3S) | A | L | 0-1 | |
| 1950-51 (3S) | 1 | 25.11.50 | **Gloucester City** (SL) | H | W | 4-0 | Guy, Peacock, Rodgers, Rogers |
| | 2 | 09.12.50 | **Wrexham** (3N) | H | W | 2-1 | Rogers, Williams |
| | 3 | 06.01.51 | **Blackburn Rovers** (D2) | H | W | 2-1 | Rodgers 2 |
| | 4 | 27.01.51 | **Brighton** (3S) | H | W | 1-0 | Clark (p) |
| | 5 | 10.02.51 | **Birmingham City** (D2) | A | L | 0-2 | |
| 1951-52 (3S) | 1 | 24.11.51 | **Brighton** (3S) | A | W | 2-1 | Atyeo 2 |
| | 2 | 15.12.51 | **Colchester Utd** (3S) | A | L | 1-2 | Rodgers |
| 1952-53 (3S) | 1 | 22.11.52 | **Coventry City** (3S) | A | L | 0-2 | |
| 1953-54 (3S) | 1 | 21.11.53 | **Torquay Utd** (3S) | A | W | 3-1 | Micklewright 2, Atyeo |
| | 2 | 12.12.53 | **Rhyl** (CC) | A | W | 3-0 | Atyeo, Micklewright, Williams |
| | 3 | 09.01.54 | **Rotherham Utd** (D2) | H | L | 1-3 | Atyeo |
| 1954-55 (3S) | 1 | 20.11.54 | **Southend Utd** (3S) | H | L | 1-2 | Rodgers |
| 1955-56 (D2) | 3 | 07.01.56 | **Everton** (D1) | A | L | 1-3 | Atyeo |
| 1956-57 (D2) | 3 | 05.01.57 | **Rotherham Utd** (D2) | H | W | 4-1 | Atyeo 2, Curtis, Hinshelwood |
| | 4 | 26.01.57 | **Rhyl** (CC) | H | W | 3-0 | Atyeo 2, Etheridge |
| | 5 | 16.02.57 | **Aston Villa** (D1) | A | L | 1-2 | Atyeo |
| 1957-58 (D2) | 3 | 04.01.58 | **Accrington Stanley** (3N) | A | D | 2-2 | Curtis, Hinshelwood |
| | 3r | 07.01.58 | **Accrington Stanley** | H | W | 3-1 | Atyeo 2, Curtis |
| | 4 | 25.01.58 | **Notts County** (D2) | A | W | 2-1 | Etheridge, Hinshelwood |
| | 5 | 15.02.58 | **Bristol Rovers** (D2) | H | L | 3-4 | Burden, Etheridge, Watkins |
| 1958-59 (D2) | 3 | 19.01.59 | **Doncaster Rovers** (D3) | A | W | 2-0 | Tindill, Watkins |
| | 4 | 24.01.59 | **Blackpool** (D1) | H | D | 1-1 | Tindill |
| | 4r | 28.01.59 | **Blackpool** | A | L | 0-1 | |
| 1959-60 (D2) | 3 | 09.01.60 | **Charlton Athletic** (D2) | H | L | 2-3 | Atyeo, Cavanagh |
| 1960-61 (D3) | 1 | 05.11.60 | **Chichester C** (Sussex CL) | H | W | 11-0 | Atyeo 5, Adrian Williams 3, Tait, R Williams, og |
| | 2 | 26.11.60 | **King's Lynn** (SL) | A | D | 2-2 | Atyeo, Rogers |
| | 2r | 29.11.60 | **King's Lynn** | H | W | 3-0 | Rogers 2, Atyeo |
| | 3 | 07.01.61 | **Plymouth Argyle** (D2) | A | W | 1-0 | R Williams |
| | 4 | 28.01.61 | **Leicester City** (D1) | A | - | 0-0ab | |
| | | | *abandoned at half-time – waterlogged pitch* | | | | |
| | 4 | 31.01.61 | **Leicester City** | A | L | 1-5 | Norman og |
| 1961-62 (D3) | 1 | 04.11.61 | **Hereford Utd** (SL) | H | D | 1-1 | Tait |
| | 1r | 08.11.61 | **Hereford Utd** | A | W | 5-2 | Atyeo 2, Etheridge, Tait, R Williams |
| | 2 | 25.11.61 | **Dartford** (SL) | H | W | 8-2 | Tait 3, Derrick 2, Atyeo, Connor, Rogers |
| | 3 | 06.01.62 | **Walsall** (D2) | H | D | 0-0 | |
| | 3r | 09.01.62 | **Walsall** | A | L | 1-4 | Derrick |
| 1962-63 (D3) | 1 | 03.11.62 | **Wellington Town** (SL) | H | W | 4-2 | Atyeo 2, Derrick, Etheridge (p) |
| | 2 | 24.11.62 | **Wimbledon** (IL) | H | W | 2-1 | Clark 2 |
| | 3 | 16.01.63 | **Aston Villa** (D1) | H | D | 1-1 | Clark |
| | 3r | 07.03.63 | **Aston Villa** | A | L | 2-3 | Etheridge, R Williams |
| 1963-64 (D3) | 1 | 16.11.63 | **Corby Town** (SL) | A | W | 3-1 | Clark, Low, Williams |
| | 2 | 07.12.63 | **Exeter City** (D4) | A | W | 2-0 | Atyeo 2 |
| | 3 | 04.01.64 | **Doncaster Rovers** (D4) | A | D | 2-2 | Atyeo, Clark |
| | 3r | 07.01.64 | **Doncaster Rovers** | H | W | 2-0 | Atyeo, Hooper (p) |
| | 4 | 25.01.64 | **Sunderland** (D2) | A | L | 1-6 | Hooper |
| 1964-65 (D3) | 1 | 14.11.64 | **Brighton** (D4) | H | W | 1-0 | Savino |
| | 2 | 05.12.64 | **Bournemouth** (D3) | A | W | 3-0 | Sharpe 2, Clarke |
| | 3 | 09.01.65 | **Sheffield Utd** (D1) | H | D | 1-1 | Ford (p) |
| | 3r | 11.01.65 | **Sheffield Utd** | A | L | 0-3 | |
| 1965-66 (D2) | 3 | 22.01.66 | **Birmingham City** (D2) | A | L | 2-3 | Bush, Low |
| 1966-67 (D2) | 3 | 28.01.67 | **Halifax Town** (D4) | A | D | 1-1 | Peters |
| | 3r | 31.01.67 | **Halifax Town** | H | W | 4-1 | Crowe 2, Down, Peters |
| | 4 | 18.02.67 | **Southampton** (D1) | H | W | 1-0 | Bush |
| | 5 | 11.03.67 | **Tottenham Hotspur** (D1) | A | L | 0-2 | |

| | | | | | | | | |
|---|---|---|---|---|---|---|---|---|
| 1967-68 | (D2) | 3 | 27.01.68 | **Bristol Rovers** (D3) | H | D | 0-0 | |
| | | 3r | 30.01.68 | **Bristol Rovers** | A | W | 2-1 | Crowe, Galley |
| | | 4 | 17.02.68 | **Middlesbrough** (D2) | A | D | 1-1 | Garland |
| | | 4r | 20.02.68 | **Middlesbrough** | H | W | 2-1 | Connor, Galley |
| | | 5 | 09.03.68 | **Leeds Utd** (D1) | A | L | 0-2 | |
| 1968-69 | (D2) | 3 | 04.01.69 | **West Ham Utd** (D1) | A | L | 2-3 | Galley, Skirton |
| 1969-70 | (D2) | 3 | 03.01.70 | **Chester** (D4) | A | L | 1-2 | Skirton |
| 1970-71 | (D2) | 3 | 11.01.71 | **Southampton** (D1) | A | L | 0-3 | |
| 1971-72 | (D2) | 3 | 15.01.72 | **Preston North End** (D2) | A | L | 2-4 | Spiring, Wilson |
| 1972-73 | (D2) | 3 | 13.01.73 | **Portsmouth** (D2) | A | D | 1-1 | Gould |
| | | 3r | 16.01.73 | **Portsmouth** | H | W | 4-1 | Gould, Gow (p), Sweeney, Tainton |
| | | 4 | 03.02.73 | **Wolverhampton W** (D1) | A | L | 0-1 | |
| 1973-74 | (D2) | 3 | 05.01.74 | **Hull City** (D2) | H | D | 1-1 | Merrick |
| | | 3r | 08.01.74 | **Hull City** | A | W | 1-0 | Tainton |
| | | 4 | 26.01.74 | **Hereford Utd** (D3) | A | W | 1-0 | Merrick |
| | | 5 | 16.02.74 | **Leeds Utd** (D1) | H | D | 1-1 | Fear |
| | | 5r | 19.02.74 | **Leeds Utd** | A | W | 1-0 | Gillies |
| | | 6 | 09.03.74 | **Liverpool** (D1) | H | L | 0-1 | |
| 1974-75 | (D2) | 3 | 04.01.75 | **Sheffield Utd** (D1) | A | L | 0-2 | |
| 1975-76 | (D2) | 3 | 03.01.76 | **Coventry City** (D1) | A | L | 1-2 | Brolly |
| 1976-77 | (D1) | 3 | 08.01.77 | **Ipswich Town** (D1) | A | L | 1-4 | Fear |
| 1977-78 | (D1) | 3 | 07.01.78 | **Wrexham** (D3) | H | D | 4-4 | Mabbutt 2, Cormack, Ritchie |
| | | 3r | 09.01.78 | **Wrexham** | A | L | 0-3 | |
| 1978-79 | (D1) | 3 | 09.01.79 | **Bolton Wanderers** (D1) | H | W | 3-1 | Gow, Ritchie, Rodgers |
| | | 4 | 29.01.79 | **Crystal Palace** (D2) | A | L | 0-3 | |
| 1979-80 | (D1) | 3 | 05.01.80 | **Derby County** (D1) | H | W | 6-2 | Garland 2, Pritchard 2, Mann, Whitehead |
| | | 4 | 26.01.80 | **Ipswich Town** (D1) | H | L | 1-2 | Whitehead |
| 1980-81 | (D2) | 3 | 03.01.81 | **Derby County** (D2) | A | D | 0-0 | |
| | | 3r | 07.01.81 | **Derby County** | H | W | 2-0 | Mabbutt, Ritchie |
| | | 4 | 24.01.81 | **Carlisle Utd** (D3) | A | D | 1-1 | Mabbutt |
| | | 4r | 28.01.81 | **Carlisle Utd** | H | W | 5-0 | Mabbutt 2, Ritchie 2 (1p) Mann |
| | | 5 | 14.02.81 | **Nottingham Forest** (D1) | A | L | 1-2 | Mabbutt |
| 1981-82 | (D3) | 1 | 20.11.81 | **Torquay Utd** (D4) | H | D | 0-0 | |
| | | 1r | 26.11.81 | **Torquay Utd** | A | W | 2-1 | Mann 2 |
| | | 2 | 15.12.81 | **Northampton Town** (D4) | H | W | 3-0 | Harford 2, Tainton |
| | | 3 | 06.01.82 | **Peterborough Utd** (D4) | A | W | 1-0 | Chandler |
| | | 4 | 23.01.82 | **Aston Villa** (D1) | H | L | 0-1 | |
| 1982-83 | (D4) | 1 | 20.11.82 | **Orient** (D3) | A | L | 1-4 | Johnson |
| 1983-84 | (D4) | 1 | 19.11.83 | **Corinthian Casuals** (IL) *played at Dulwich Hamlet* | A | D | 0-0 | |
| | | 1r | 23.11.83 | **Corinthian Casuals** | H | W | 4-0 | Pritchard 3, Riley |
| | | 2 | 10.12.83 | **Bristol Rovers** (D3) | A | W | 2-1 | Hirst, Ritchie |
| | | 3 | 08.01.84 | **Notts County** (D1) | A | D | 2-2 | Crawford, Ritchie |
| | | 3r | 10.01.84 | **Notts County** | H | L | 0-2 | |
| 1984-85 | (D3) | 1 | 17.11.84 | **Fisher Athletic** (SL) | A | W | 1-0 | Riley |
| | | 2 | 08.12.84 | **Bristol Rovers** (D3) | H | L | 1-3 | Halliday |
| 1985-86 | (D3) | 1 | 17.11.85 | **Swindon Town** (D4) | A | D | 0-0 | |
| | | 1r | 20.11.85 | **Swindon Town** | H | W | 4-2 | Neville 3, Riley |
| | | 2 | 07.12.85 | **Exeter City** (D4) | H | L | 1-2 | Walsh (p) |
| 1986-87 | (D3) | 1 | 15.11.86 | **VS Rugby** (SL) | H | W | 3-1 | Hutchinson, Marshall, Walsh |
| | | 2 | 06.12.86 | **Bath City** (Conf) | H | D | 1-1 | Neville |
| | | 2r | 09.12.86 | **Bath City** *played at Ashton Gate* | A | W | 3-0 | Owen 2 (1p), Neville |
| | | 3 | 10.01.87 | **Plymouth Argyle** (D2) | H | D | 1-1 | Riley |
| | | 3r | 19.01.87 | **Plymouth Argyle** | A | L | 1-3aet | Marshall |
| 1987-88 | (D3) | 1 | 14.11.87 | **Aylesbury Utd** (SL) | H | W | 1-0 | Caldwell |
| | | 2 | 05.12.87 | **Torquay Utd** (D4) | H | L | 0-1 | |
| 1988-89 | (D3) | 1 | 19.11.88 | **Southend Utd** (D3) | H | W | 3-1 | Walsh, McGarvey, Shutt |
| | | 2 | 10.12.88 | **Aldershot** (D3) | A | D | 1-1 | Shutt |
| | | 2r | 13.12.88 | **Aldershot** | H | D | 0-0aet | |

| | | | | | | | |
|---|---|---|---|---|---|---|---|
| | 2 2r | 20.12.88 | **Aldershot** | A | D | 2-2aet | Shutt, Newman (p) |
| | 2 3r | 22.12.88 | **Aldershot** | H | W | 1-0 | Shutt |
| | 3 | 07.01.89 | **Hartlepool Utd** (D4) | A | L | 0-1 | |
| 1989-90 (D3) | 1 | 18.11.89 | **Barnet** (Conf) | H | W | 2-0 | Taylor, Turner |
| | 2 | 09.12.89 | **Fulham** (D3) | H | W | 2-1 | Taylor, Wimbleton (p) |
| | 3 | 06.01.90 | **Swindon Town** (D2) | H | W | 2-1 | Taylor, Newman |
| | 4 | 27.01.90 | **Chelsea** (D1) | H | W | 3-1 | Turner 2, Gavin |
| | 5 | 17.02.90 | **Cambridge Utd** (D4) | H | D | 0-0 | |
| | 5r | 21.02.90 | **Cambridge Utd** | A | D | 1-1aet | Taylor |
| | 5 2r | 27.02.90 | **Cambridge Utd** | A | L | 1-5 | Taylor |
| 1990-91 (D2) | 3 | 05.01.91 | **Norwich City** (D1) | A | L | 1-2 | Allison |
| 1991-92 (D2) | 3 | 04.01.92 | **Wimbledon** (D1) | H | D | 1-1 | Barton og |
| | 3r | 14.01.92 | **Wimbledon** | A | W | 1-0 | May |
| | 4 | 25.01.92 | **Leicester City** (D2) | A | W | 2-1 | Bent, Dziekanowski |
| | 5 | 15.02.92 | **Nottingham Forest** (D1) | A | L | 1-4 | Dziekanowski |
| 1992-93 (D1) | 3 | 19.01.93 | **Luton Town** (D1) | A | L | 0-2 | |
| 1993-94 (D1) | 3 | 08.01.94 | **Liverpool** (PL) | H | - | 1-1ab | W Allison |
| | | | *abandoned after 65 minutes – floodlight failure* | | | | |
| | 3 | 19.01.94 | **Liverpool** | H | D | 1-1 | W Allison |
| | 3r | 25.01.94 | **Liverpool** | A | W | 1-0 | Tinnion |
| | 4 | 09.02.94 | **Stockport County** (D2) | A | W | 4-0 | W Allison 3, Shail |
| | 5 | 19.02.94 | **Charlton Athletic** (D1) | H | D | 1-1 | Tinnion |
| | 5r | 02.03.94 | **Charlton Athletic** | A | L | 0-2 | |
| 1994-95 (D1) | 3 | 07.01.95 | **Stoke City** (D1) | H | D | 0-0 | |
| | 3r | 18.01.95 | **Stoke City** | A | W | 3-1aet | Bent, Baird, Tinnion |
| | 4 | 29.01.95 | **Everton** (PL) | H | L | 0-1 | |
| 1995-96 (D2) | 1 | 11.11.95 | **Bournemouth** (D2) | A | D | 0-0 | |
| | 1r | 21.11.95 | **Bournemouth** | H | L | 0-1 | |
| 1996-97 (D2) | 1 | 16.11.96 | **Swansea City** (D3) | A | D | 1-1 | M Kuhl |
| | 1r | 26.11.96 | **Swansea City** | H | W | 1-0 | Agostino |
| | 2 | 07.12.96 | **St Albans City** (IL) | H | W | 9-2 | Agostino 4, Hewlett 2, Goodridge, M Kuhl, Nugent |
| | 3 | 14.01.97 | **Chesterfield** (D2) | A | L | 0-2 | |
| 1997-98 (D2) | 1 | 15.11.97 | **Millwall** (D2) | H | W | 1-0 | Taylor |
| | 2 | 07.12.97 | **Bournemouth** (D2) | A | L | 1-3 | Cramb |
| 1998-99 (D1) | 3 | 02.01.99 | **Everton** (PL) | H | L | 0-2 | |
| 1999-00 (D2) | 1 | 30.10.99 | **Mansfield Town** (D3) | H | W | 3-2 | Tinnion 2, Murray |
| | 2 | 20.11.99 | **Bournemouth** (D2) | A | W | 2-0 | Murray 2 |
| | 3 | 11.12.99 | **Sheffield Wed** (PL) | A | L | 0-1 | |
| 2000-01 (D2) | 1 | 18.11.00 | **Chesterfield** (D3) | A | W | 1-0 | Thorpe |
| | 2 | 09.12.00 | **Kettering Town** (Conf) | H | W | 3-1 | Peacock, Clist, Thorpe |
| | 3 | 06.01.01 | **Huddersfield Town** (D1) | A | W | 2-0 | Clist, Beadle |
| | 4 | 27.01.01 | **Kingstonian** (Conf) | H | D | 1-1 | Thorpe |
| | 4r | 07.02.01 | **Kingstonian** | A | W | 1-0 | Murray |
| | 5 | 17.02.01 | **Leicester City** (PL) | A | L | 0-3 | |
| 2001-02 (D2) | 1 | 17.11.01 | **Leyton Orient** (D3) | H | L | 0-1 | |
| 2002-03 (D2) | 1 | 16.11.02 | **Heybridge Swifts** (IL) | A | W | 7-0 | Roberts 2, Tinnion (p), Murray 2, Lita 2 |
| | 2 | 08.12.02 | **Harrogate RA** (NCoE) | A | W | 3-1 | Walker og, Murray, Roberts |
| | 3 | 04.01.03 | **Leicester City** (D1) | A | L | 0-2 | |

## BRISTOL ROVERS

*Formed 1883. Best FA Cup performance: 6th round 1950-51, 1957-58. Record FA Cup win:15-1 v Weymouth, 3rd qualifying round, 17.11.1900; In Competition Proper: 6-0 v Merthyr Tydfil, 1st round, 14.11.1987; Record FA Cup defeat: 1-8 v Southampton, 5th qualifying round, 1897-98. In Competition Proper: 1-8 v QPR, 1st round, 27.11.1937*

| | |
|---|---|
| 1895-96 (WL) | P Warmley (H) 0-2 |
| 1896-97 (WL) | 1q Newbury T (A) 1-1; 1qr Newbury T (H) 2-1; 2q Bristol St George (H) 1-0; 3q RA Portsmouth, scratched |
| 1897-98 (BDL) | 1q Warmley (A) 0-0; 1qr Warmley (H) 6-2; 2q Bedminster (H) 3-2; 3q Eastleigh (H) 2-0; 4q Cowes (H) 6-2; 5q Southampton (A) 1-8 |
| 1898-99 (BDL) | 3q Reading (H) 0-1 |
| 1899-00 (SL) | 3q Eastleigh (H) 5-0; 4q Portsmouth (H) 1-1; 4qr Portsmouth (A) 0-4 |

| | | | | | | | | |
|---|---|---|---|---|---|---|---|---|
| 1900-01 | (SL) | | | 3q Weymouth (H) 15-1; 4q Swindon T (H) 5-1; 5q Luton T (A) 2-1 | | | | |
| | | 1 | 09.02.01 | **Reading** (SL) | A | L | 0-2 | |
| 1901-02 | (SL) | | | 3q Weymouth Whiteheads (H) 5-0; 4q Bristol C (H) 1-1aet; 4qr Bristol C (A) 3-2; 5q Swindon T (A) 1-0; Int Millwall A (A) 1-1; IntR Millwall A (H) 1-0 | | | | |
| | | 1 | 25.01.02 | **Middlesbrough** (D2) | A | D | 1-1 | Jones |
| | | 1r | 29.01.02 | **Middlesbrough** | H | W | 1-0 | Becton |
| | | 2 | 08.02.02 | **Stoke** (D1) | H | L | 0-1 | |
| 1902-03 | (SL) | | | Int Millwall A (H) 2-2; IntR Millwall A 0-0abandoned aet; IntR Millwall A 0-2 (at Villa Park) | | | | |
| 1903-04 | (SL) | | | Int Woolwich Arsenal (H) 1-1; IntR Woolwich Arsenal (A) 1-abandoned aet; Int 2r Woolwich Arsenal 0-1 (at White Hart Lane) | | | | |
| 1904-05 | (SL) | | | Int Brighton (A) 2-1 | | | | |
| | | 1 | 04.02.05 | **Bolton Wanderers** (D2) | A | D | 1-1 | Dunn |
| | | 1r | 08.02.05 | **Bolton Wanderers** | H | L | 0-3 | |
| 1905-06 | (SL) | 1 | 13.01.06 | **Sheffield Wed** (D1) | A | L | 0-1 | |
| 1906-07 | (SL) | 1 | 12.01.07 | **QPR** (SL) | H | D | 0-0 | |
| | | 1r | 14.01.07 | **QPR** | A | W | 1-0 | Clark |
| | | 2 | 02.02.07 | **Millwall Athletic** (SL) | H | W | 3-0 | Jarvie, Clark, Hutchinson |
| | | 3 | 23.02.07 | **Woolwich Arsenal** (D1) | H | L | 0-1 | |
| 1907-08 | (SL) | 1 | 11.01.08 | **Northampton Town** (SL) | A | W | 1-0 | Smith |
| | | 2 | 03.02.08 | **Chesterfield** (D2) | H | W | 2-0 | Clarke 2 |
| | | 3 | 22.02.08 | **Southampton** (SL) | A | L | 0-2 | |
| 1908-09 | (SL) | 1 | 16.01.09 | **Burnley** (D2) | H | L | 1-4 | Peplow |
| 1909-10 | (SL) | 1 | 15.01.10 | **Grimsby Town** (D2) | A | W | 2-0 | Peplow, Rodgers |
| | | 2 | 05.02.10 | **Barnsley** (D2) | A | L | 0-4 | |
| 1910-11 | (SL) | 1 | 14.01.11 | **Hull City** (D2) | H | D | 0-0 | |
| | | 1r | 19.01.11 | **Hull City** | A | L | 0-1aet | |
| 1911-12 | (SL) | 1 | 13.01.12 | **Portsmouth** (SL) | H | L | 1-2 | A Hughes |
| 1912-13 | (SL) | 1 | 11.01.13 | **Notts County** (D1) | H | W | 2-0 | Shervey, Roe |
| | | 2 | 03.02.13 | **Norwich City** (SL) | H | D | 1-1 | Brogan |
| | | 2r | 06.02.13 | **Norwich City** | A | D | 2-2aet | Peplow, Roe |
| | | 22r | 10.02.13 | **Norwich City** | | W | 1-0 | Shervey |
| | | | | *played at Stamford Bridge* | | | | |
| | | 3 | 22.02.13 | **Everton** (D1) | H | L | 0-4 | |
| 1913-14 | (SL) | 1 | 10.01.14 | **Preston North End** (D1) | A | L | 2-5 | Shervey 2 |
| 1914-15 | (SL) | | | 6q Bournemouth (H) 3-0 | | | | |
| | | 1 | 16.01.15 | **Southend Utd** (SL) | H | D | 0-0 | |
| | | 1r | 23.01.15 | **Southend Utd** | A | L | 0-3 | |
| 1919-20 | (SL) | | | 6q Northampton T (A) 2-2; 6qr Northampton T (H) 3-2 | | | | |
| | | 1 | 10.01.20 | **Tottenham Hotspur** (D2) | H | L | 1-4 | Crompton |
| 1920-21 | (D3) | | | 6q Worksop Town (H) 9-0 | | | | |
| | | 1 | 08.01.21 | **Tottenham Hotspur** (D1) | A | L | 2-6 | Walter, Norton |
| 1921-22 | (3S) | | | 5q Exeter C (H) 0-0; 5qr Exeter C (A) 2-0; 6q Swansea T (A) 0-2 | | | | |
| 1922-23 | (3S) | | | 5q Reading (A) 1-0; 6q Stalybridge Celtic (A) 0-0; 6qr Stalybridge Celtic (H) 1-2 | | | | |
| 1923-24 | (3S) | | | 5q Exeter C (A) 2-2; 5qr Exeter C (H) 0-1 | | | | |
| 1924-25 | (3S) | | | 5q Yeovil & Petters U (A) 4-2; 6q Weymouth (H) 0-0; 6qr Weymouth (A) 2-0 | | | | |
| | | 1 | 10.01.25 | **Bristol City** (3S) | H | L | 0-1 | |
| 1925-26 | (3S) | 1 | 28.11.25 | **Aberdare Athletic** (3S) | A | L | 1-4 | Lofthouse |
| 1926-27 | (3S) | 1 | 27.11.26 | **Torquay Utd** (SL) | A | D | 1-1 | Barrett |
| | | 1r | 01.12.26 | **Torquay Utd** | H | W | 1-0 | Williams |
| | | 2 | 11.12.26 | **Charlton Athletic** (3S) | H | W | 4-1 | Culley 2, Barrett, Evans |
| | | 3 | 08.01.27 | **Portsmouth** (D2) | H | D | 3-3 | Culley 2, Clennell |
| | | 3r | 12.01.27 | **Portsmouth** | A | L | 0-4 | |
| 1927-28 | (3S) | 1 | 26.11.27 | **Walsall** (3S) | H | W | 4-2 | Williams 2, Douglas, Culley |
| | | 2 | 10.12.27 | **Bournemouth** (3S) | A | L | 1-6 | Williams |
| 1928-29 | (3S) | 1 | 24.11.28 | **Wellingborough T** (UCL) | H | W | 2-1 | Rotherham (p), Murray |
| | | 2 | 08.12.28 | **Crystal Palace** (3S) | A | L | 1-3 | Phillips |
| 1929-30 | (3S) | 1 | 30.11.29 | **Nunhead** (IL) | A | W | 2-0 | Britton, Phillips |
| | | 2 | 14.12.29 | **Accrington Stanley** (3N) | H | W | 4-1 | Reay 2, Forbes, Phillips |
| | | 3 | 11.01.30 | **Clapton Orient** (3S) | A | L | 0-1 | |
| 1930-31 | (3S) | 1 | 29.11.30 | **Merthyr Town** (SL) | H | W | 4-1 | Attwood, Dix, Forbes, Hamilton |

| | | | | | | | |
|---|---|---|---|---|---|---|---|
| | 2 | 13.12.30 | **Stockport County** (3N) | H | W | 4-2 | Forbes 2, Ball, Dix |
| | 3 | 10.01.31 | **QPR** (3S) | H | W | 3-1 | Dennis 2 (2p), Attwood |
| | 4 | 24.01.31 | **Blackburn Rovers** (D1) | A | L | 1-5 | Dix |
| 1931-32 (3S) | 1 | 28.11.31 | **Gillingham** (3S) | H | W | 5-1 | Dix, Townrow, Oakton, Cook, Russell |
| | 2 | 12.12.31 | **Tranmere Rovers** (3N) | A | L | 0-2 | |
| 1932-33 (3S) | 1 | 26.11.32 | **Cardiff City** (3S) | A | D | 1-1 | Jackson |
| | 1r | 30.11.32 | **Cardiff City** | H | W | 4-1 | Eyres, McNestry, Jackson, Townrow |
| | 2 | 10.12.32 | **Gillingham** (3S) | H | D | 1-1 | Irving (p) |
| | 2r | 14.12.32 | **Gillingham** | A | W | 3-1 | Eyres, Jackson, McKay |
| | 3 | 14.01.33 | **Aldershot** (3S) | A | L | 0-1 | |
| 1933-34 (3S) | 1 | 25.11.33 | **Folkestone** (SL) | A | D | 0-0 | |
| | 1r | 29.11.33 | **Folkestone** | H | W | 3-1 | Taylor, McNestry, McKay |
| | 2 | 09.12.33 | **Accrington Stanley** (3N) | A | L | 0-1 | |
| 1934-35 (3S) | 1 | 24.11.34 | **Harwich & P** (ECL) | H | W | 3-0 | Smith, McNestry, Prout |
| | 2 | 08.12.34 | **Dartford** (SL) | A | W | 1-0 | McNestry (p) |
| | 3 | 12.01.35 | **Manchester Utd** (D2) | H | L | 1-3 | McNestry |
| 1935-36 (3S) | 1 | 30.11.35 | **Northampton Town** (3S) | A | D | 0-0 | |
| | 1r | 04.12.35 | **Northampton Town** | H | W | 3-1 | Prout 2, A Taylor |
| | 2 | 14.12.35 | **Oldham Athletic** (3N) | A | D | 1-1 | Houghton |
| | 2r | 18.12.35 | **Oldham Athletic** | H | W | 4-1 | A Taylor 3, Houghton |
| | 3 | 11.01.36 | **Arsenal** (D1) | H | L | 1-5 | Houghton |
| 1936-37 (3S) | 1 | 28.11.36 | **Corinthians** | A | W | 2-0 | Harris 2 |
| | 2 | 12.12.36 | **Southport** (3N) | H | W | 2-1 | Harris, McArthur |
| | 3 | 16.01.37 | **Leicester City** (D2) | H | L | 2-5 | Butterworth, McArthur |
| 1937-38 (3S) | 1 | 27.11.37 | **QPR** (3S) | H | L | 1-8 | Pendergast |
| 1938-39 (3S) | 1 | 26.11.38 | **Peterborough Utd** (ML) | H | W | 4-1 | Tolland 2, Curran, Spivey |
| | 2 | 10.12.38 | **Bournemouth** (3S) | H | L | 0-3 | |
| 1945-46 (3S) | 1 1L | 17.11.45 | **Swindon Town** (3S) | A | L | 0-1 | |
| | 1 2L | 24.11.45 | **Swindon Town** | H | W | 4-1 | Butterworth 2, Mills, Clarke |
| | 2 1L | 08.12.45 | **Bristol City** (3S) | A | L | 2-4 | Mills, Whitfield |
| | 2 2L | 15.12.45 | **Bristol City** | H | L | 0-2 | |
| 1946-47 (3S) | 1 | 30.11.46 | **Merthyr Tydfil** (SL) | A | L | 1-3 | Lambden |
| 1947-48 (3S) | 1 | 29.11.47 | **Leytonstone** (IL) | H | W | 3-2 | Baldie, Lambden, Morgan |
| | 2 | 13.12.47 | **New Brighton** (3N) | H | W | 4-0 | Morgan 2, McArthur, Lambden |
| | 3 | 10.01.48 | **Swansea Town** (3S) | H | W | 3-0 | Wookey, Lambden, Morgan |
| | 4 | 24.01.48 | **Fulham** (D2) | A | L | 2-5 | McArthur, Petherbridge |
| 1948-49 (3S) | 1 | 27.11.48 | **Walsall** (3S) | A | L | 1-2 | Lambden |
| 1949-50 (3S) | 1 | 26.11.49 | **Swindon Town** (3S) | A | L | 0-1 | |
| 1950-51 (3S) | 1 | 25.11.50 | **Llanelli** (SL) | H | D | 1-1 | Petherbridge |
| | 1r | 28.11.50 | **Llanelli** | A | D | 1-1aet | Bush |
| | 1 2r | 05.12.50 | **Llanelli** *played at Ninian Park* | | W | 3-1aet | Pitt, Petherbridge, Bradford |
| | 2 | 09.12.50 | **Gillingham** (3S) | H | D | 2-2 | Bush, Lambden |
| | 2r | 13.12.50 | **Gillingham** | A | D | 1-1aet | Gough |
| | 2 2r | 18.12.50 | **Gillingham** *played at White Hart Lane* | | W | 2-1 | Bradford, Warrem (p) |
| | 3 | 10.01.51 | **Aldershot** (3S) | H | W | 5-1 | Lambden 3, Roost, Petherbridge |
| | 4 | 27.01.51 | **Luton Town** (D2) | A | W | 2-1 | Lambden, Petherbridge |
| | 5 | 10.02.51 | **Hull City** (D2) | H | W | 3-0 | Lambden, Watling 2 |
| | 6 | 24.02.51 | **Newcastle Utd** (D1) | A | D | 0-0 | |
| | 6r | 28.02.51 | **Newcastle Utd** | H | L | 1-3 | Bradford |
| 1951-52 (3S) | 1 | 24.11.51 | **Kettering Town** (SL) | H | W | 3-0 | Lambden 2, Bradford |
| | 2 | 15.12.51 | **Weymouth** (SL) | H | W | 2-0 | Lambden, Petherbridge |
| | 3 | 12.01.52 | **Preston North End** (D1) | H | W | 2-0 | Lambden, Bradford |
| | 4 | 02.02.52 | **Southend Utd** (3S) | A | L | 1-2 | Bradford |
| 1952-53 (3S) | 1 | 22.11.52 | **Leyton Orient** (3S) | A | D | 1-1 | Bradford |
| | 1r | 24.11.52 | **Leyton Orient** | H | W | 1-0 | Roost |
| | 2 | 06.12.52 | **Peterborough Utd** (ML) | A | W | 1-0 | Lambden |
| | 3 | 10.01.53 | **Huddersfield Town** (D2) | A | L | 0-2 | |
| 1953-54 (D2) | 3 | 09.01.54 | **Blackburn Rovers** (D2) | H | L | 0-1 | |
| 1954-55 (D2) | 3 | 08.01.55 | **Portsmouth** (D1) | H | W | 2-1 | Bradford, Roost |

| | | | | | | | |
|---|---|---|---|---|---|---|---|
| | 4 | 29.01.55 | **Chelsea** (D1) | H | L | 1-3 | Pitt (p) |
| 1955-56 (D2) | 3 | 07.01.56 | **Manchester Utd** (D1) | H | W | 4-0 | Biggs 2, Meyer, Bradford |
| | 4 | 28.01.56 | **Doncaster Rovers** (D2) | H | D | 1-1 | Hooper (p) |
| | 4r | 31.01.56 | **Doncaster Rovers** | A | L | 0-1 | |
| 1956-57 (D2) | 3 | 05.01.57 | **Hull City** (3N) | A | W | 4-3 | Bradford 2, Ward, Biggs |
| | 4 | 26.01.57 | **Preston North End** (D1) | H | L | 1-4 | Hooper (p) |
| 1957-58 (D2) | 3 | 04.01.58 | **Mansfield Town** (3N) | H | W | 5-0 | Hooper 2, Biggs, Ward, Petherbridge |
| | 4 | 25.01.58 | **Burnley** (D1) | H | D | 2-2 | Hale, Shannon og |
| | 4r | 28.01.58 | **Burnley** | A | W | 3-2 | Sykes, Ward 2 |
| | 5 | 15.02.58 | **Bristol City** (D2) | A | W | 4-3 | Meyer, Sykes, Ward, Bradford |
| | 6 | 01.03.58 | **Fulham** (D2) | A | L | 1-3 | Bradford |
| 1958-59 (D2) | 3 | 10.01.59 | **Charlton Athletic** (D2) | H | L | 0-4 | |
| 1959-60 (D2) | 3 | 09.01.60 | **Doncaster Rovers** (D4) | H | D | 0-0 | |
| | 3r | 12.01.60 | **Doncaster Rovers** | A | W | 2-1 | Biggs, Ward |
| | 4 | 30.01.60 | **Preston North End** (D1) | H | D | 3-3 | Biggs 2, Smith og |
| | 4r | 02.02.60 | **Preston North End** | A | L | 1-5 | Hooper |
| 1960-61 (D2) | 3 | 07.01.61 | **Aston Villa** (D1) | H | D | 1-1 | Biggs |
| | 3r | 09.01.61 | **Aston Villa** | A | L | 0-4 | |
| 1961-62 (D2) | 3 | 08.01.62 | **Oldham Athletic** (D4) | H | D | 1-1 | Sykes |
| | 3r | 10.01.62 | **Oldham Athletic** | A | L | 0-2 | |
| 1962-63 (D3) | 1 | 03.11.62 | **Port Vale** (D3) | H | L | 0-2 | |
| 1963-64 (D3) | 1 | 16.11.63 | **Bournemouth** (D3) | A | W | 3-1 | Brown, Biggs (p), Stone |
| | 2 | 07.12.63 | **Coventry City** (D3) | A | W | 2-1 | Bradford, Jarman |
| | 3 | 04.01.64 | **Norwich City** (D2) | H | W | 2-1 | Jarman, Bradford |
| | 4 | 25.01.64 | **Manchester Utd** (D1) | A | L | 1-4 | Crerand og |
| 1964-65 (D3) | 1 | 14.11.64 | **Walsall** (D3) | A | W | 2-0 | Stone, R Jones |
| | 2 | 05.12.64 | **Weymouth** (SL) | H | W | 4-1 | Jarman 2, Hamilton, Munro |
| | 3 | 09.01.65 | **Stockport County** (D4) | H | D | 0-0 | |
| | 3r | 11.01.65 | **Stockport County** | A | L | 2-3 | R Mabbutt, R Jones |
| 1965-66 (D3) | 1 | 13.11.65 | **Reading** (D3) | A | L | 2-3 | Hillard, R Jones |
| 1966-67 (D3) | 1 | 26.11.66 | **Oxford City** (IL) | A | D | 2-2 | Davis (p), Lamb og |
| | 1r | 29.11.66 | **Oxford City** | H | W | 4-0 | Biggs 3, Ronaldson |
| | 2 | 07.01.67 | **Luton Town** (D4) | H | W | 3-2 | Williams, Jarman, Davis |
| | 3 | 28.01.67 | **Arsenal** (D1) | H | L | 0-3 | |
| 1967-68 (D3) | 1 | 09.12.67 | **Arnold Town** (ML) | A | W | 3-0 | W Jones, Jarman, Smith og |
| | 2 | 06.01.68 | **Wimbledon** (SL) | A | W | 4-0 | Biggs 2, W Jones, Ronaldson |
| | 3 | 27.01.68 | **Bristol City** (D2) | A | D | 0-0 | |
| | 3r | 30.01.68 | **Bristol City** | H | L | 1-2 | Taylor |
| 1968-69 (D3) | 1 | 16.11.68 | **Peterborough Utd** (D4) | H | W | 3-1 | Stanton, R Mabbutt, Graydon |
| | 2 | 07.12.68 | **Bournemouth** (D3) | A | D | 0-0 | |
| | 2r | 10.12.68 | **Bournemouth** | H | W | 1-0 | Graydon |
| | 3 | 04.01.69 | **Kettering Town** (SL) | H | D | 1-1 | Graydon |
| | 3r | 07.01.69 | **Kettering Town** | A | W | 2-1 | S Taylor, Gammon og |
| | 4 | 25.01.69 | **Bolton Wanderers** (D2) | A | W | 2-1 | W Jones 2 |
| | 5 | 12.02.69 | **Everton** (D1) | A | L | 0-1 | |
| 1969-70 (D3) | 1 | 15.11.69 | **Telford Utd** (SL) | A | W | 3-0 | R Jones, Graydon, Stubbs |
| | 2 | 06.12.69 | **Aldershot** (D4) | A | L | 1-3 | Stubbs |
| 1970-71 (D3) | 1 | 21.11.70 | **Fulham** (D3) | A | W | 2-1 | Gilbert 2 |
| | 2 | 12.12.70 | **Aldershot** (D4) | A | D | 1-1 | Jarman |
| | 2r | 15.12.70 | **Aldershot** | H | L | 1-3 | Stubbs |
| 1971-72 (D3) | 1 | 20.11.71 | **Telford Utd** (SL) | H | W | 3-0 | Bannister 2, Godfrey |
| | 2 | 11.12.71 | **Cambridge Utd** (D4) | H | W | 3-0 | Taylor, Bannister, Godfrey |
| | 3 | 15.01.72 | **Leeds Utd** (D1) | A | L | 1-4 | Allan |
| 1972-73 (D3) | 1 | 18.11.72 | **Hayes** (IL) | A | L | 0-1 | |
| 1973-74 (D3) | 1 | 24.11.73 | **Bideford** (SL) | A | W | 2-0 | Warboys, Bannister |
| | 2 | 15.12.73 | **Northampton Town** (D4) | A | W | 2-1 | Warboys, Fearnley |
| | 3 | 06.01.74 | **Nottingham Forest** | A | L | 3-4 | Prince, Dobson, Rudge |
| 1974-75 (D2) | 3 | 04.01.75 | **Blackburn Rovers** (D3) | A | W | 2-1 | Fearnley, Bannister |
| | 4 | 27.01.75 | **Derby County** (D1) | A | L | 0-2 | |
| 1975-76 (D2) | 3 | 01.01.76 | **Chelsea** (D2) | A | D | 1-1 | Warboys |
| | 3r | 03.01.76 | **Chelsea** | H | L | 0-1 | |

| | | | | | | | | |
|---|---|---|---|---|---|---|---|---|
| 1976-77 (D2) | 3 | 08.01.77 | **Nottingham Forest** (D2) | A | D | 1-1 | D Williams |
| | 3r | 11.01.77 | **Nottingham Forest** | H | D | 1-1aet | Warboys |
| | 32r | 18.01.77 | **Nottingham Forest** *played at Villa Park* | | L | 0-6 | |
| 1977-78 (D2) | 3 | 07.01.78 | **Sunderland** (D2) | A | W | 1-0 | Gould |
| | 4 | 28.01.78 | **Southampton** (D2) | H | W | 2-0 | Randall 2 |
| | 5 | 18.02.78 | **Ipswich Town** (D1) | H | D | 2-2 | Williams 2 |
| | 5r | 28.02.78 | **Ipswich Town** | A | L | 0-3 | |
| 1978-79 (D2) | 3 | 09.01.79 | **Swansea City** (D3) | A | W | 1-0 | White |
| | 4 | 05.02.79 | **Charlton Athletic** (D2) | H | W | 1-0 | White |
| | 5 | 26.02.79 | **Ipswich Town** (D1) | A | L | 1-6 | White |
| 1979-80 (D2) | 3 | 04.01.80 | **Aston Villa** (D1) | H | L | 1-2 | Barrowclough |
| 1980-81 (D2) | 3 | 03.01.81 | **Preston North End** (D2) | A | W | 4-3 | G Mabbutt, Barrowclough, Barrett, G Williams |
| | 4 | 24.01.81 | **Southampton** (D1) | A | L | 1-3 | G Williams |
| 1981-82 (D3) | 1 | 21.11.81 | **Fulham** (D3) | H | L | 1-2 | D Williams (p) |
| 1982-83 (D3) | 1 | 20.11.82 | **Wycombe W** (IL) | H | W | 1-0 | Stephens |
| | 2 | 11.12.82 | **Plymouth Argyle** (D3) | H | D | 2-2 | D Williams 2 |
| | 2r | 20.12.82 | **Plymouth Argyle** | A | L | 0-1 | |
| 1983-84 (D3) | 1 | 19.11.83 | **Barnet** (APL) | A | D | 0-0 | |
| | 1r | 22.11.83 | **Barnet** | H | W | 3-1 | Holloway, Barrett, Slatter |
| | 2 | 10.12.83 | **Bristol City** (D4) | H | L | 1-2 | Stephens |
| 1984-85 (D3) | 1 | 17.11.84 | **King's Lynn** (SL) | H | W | 2-1 | D Williams, Adams og |
| | 2 | 08.12.84 | **Bristol City** (D3) | A | W | 3-1 | O'Connor, Randall 2 |
| | 3 | 05.01.85 | **Ipswich Town** (D1) | H | L | 1-2 | Holloway |
| 1985-86 (D3) | 1 | 16.11.85 | **Brentford** (D3) | A | W | 3-1 | Penrice, White, Francis |
| | 2 | 07.12.85 | **Swansea City** (D3) | A | W | 2-1 | Morgan (p), White |
| | 3 | 04.01.86 | **Leicester City** (D1) | H | W | 3-1 | Stevenson, Morgan 2 |
| | 4 | 25.01.86 | **Luton Town** (D1) | A | L | 0-4 | |
| 1986-87 (D3) | 1 | 03.12.86 | **Brentford** (D3) | H | D | 0-0 | |
| | 1r | 06.12.86 | **Brentford** | A | L | 0-2 | |
| 1987-88 (D3) | 1 | 14.11.87 | **Merthyr Tydfil** (SL) | H | W | 6-0 | Penrice 3, White 2, Meacham |
| | 2 | 05.12.87 | **VS Rugby** (SL) | A | D | 1-1 | Meacham |
| | 2r | 17.12.87 | **VS Rugby** | H | W | 4-0 | Penrice, Alexander, White, Reece |
| | 3 | 09.01.88 | **Shrewsbury Town** (D2) | A | L | 1-2 | Penrice |
| 1988-89 (D3) | 1 | 20.11.88 | **Fisher Athletic** (Conf) | H | W | 3-0 | Jones, Penrice, Holloway (p) |
| | 2 | 10.12.88 | **Kettering Town** (Conf) | A | L | 1-2 | Reece |
| 1989-90 (D3) | 1 | 18.11.89 | **Reading** (D3) | H | D | 1-1 | Reece |
| | 1r | 21.11.89 | **Reading** | A | D | 1-1aet | Mehew |
| | 12r | 27.11.89 | **Reading** | H | L | 0-1 | |
| 1990-91 (D2) | 3 | 05.01.91 | **Crewe Alexandra** (D3) | H | L | 0-2 | |
| 1991-92 (D2) | 3 | 05.01.92 | **Plymouth Argyle** (D2) | H | W | 5-0 | Alexander, Saunders 4 |
| | 4 | 05.02.92 | **Liverpool** (D1) | H | D | 1-1 | Saunders |
| | 4r | 11.02.92 | **Liverpool** | A | L | 1-2 | Saunders |
| 1992-93 (D1) | 3 | 02.01.93 | **Aston Villa** (PL) | A | D | 1-1 | Browning |
| | 3r | 20.01.93 | **Aston Villa** | H | L | 0-3 | |
| 1993-94 (D2) | 1 | 14.11.93 | **Wycombe W** (D3) | H | L | 1-2 | Archer |
| 1994-95 (D2) | 1 | 12.11.94 | **Bath City** (Conf) | A | W | 5-0 | Miller 4, Stewart |
| | 2 | 03.12.94 | **Leyton Orient** (D2) | A | W | 2-0 | Stewart 2 |
| | 3 | 07.01.95 | **Luton Town** (D1) | A | D | 1-1 | Stewart |
| | 3r | 18.01.95 | **Luton Town** | H | L | 0-1 | |
| 1995-96 (D2) | 1 | 11.11.95 | **Hitchin Town** (IL) | A | L | 1-2 | Archer |
| 1996-97 (D2) | 1 | 16.11.96 | **Exeter City** (D3) | H | L | 1-2 | Parmenter |
| 1997-98 (D2) | 1 | 14.11.97 | **Gillingham** (D2) | H | D | 2-2 | Alsop, Holloway |
| | 1r | 25.11.97 | **Gillingham** | A | W | 2-0 | Hayles, Penrice |
| | 2 | 06.12.97 | **Wisbech Town** (SL) | A | W | 2-0 | Beadle, Hayles |
| | 3 | 03.01.98 | **Ipswich Town** (D1) | H | D | 1-1 | Beadle |
| | 3r | 13.01.98 | **Ipswich Town** | A | L | 0-1 | |
| 1998-99 (D2) | 1 | 14.11.98 | **Welling Utd** (Conf) | H | W | 3-0 | Roberts 3 |
| | 2 | 05.12.98 | **Exeter City** (D3) | A | D | 2-2 | Penrice, Cureton |
| | 2r | 15.12.98 | **Exeter City** | H | W | 5-0 | Zabek, Shore 2, Cureton, Roberts |

| | | | | | | | |
|---|---|---|---|---|---|---|---|
| | 3 | 02.01.99 | **Rotherham Utd** (D3) | A | W | 1-0 | Leoni |
| | 4 | 23.01.99 | **Leyton Orient** (D3) | H | W | 3-0 | Roberts 2, Lee |
| | 5 | 13.02.99 | **Barnsley** (D1) | A | L | 1-4 | Roberts |
| 1999-00 (D2) | 1 | 31.10.99 | **Preston North End** (D2) | H | L | 0-1 | |
| 2000-01 (D2) | 1 | 19.11.00 | **Cardiff City** (D3) | A | L | 1-5 | Jordan og |
| 2001-02 (D3) | 1 | 17.11.01 | **Aldershot Town** (IL) | A | D | 0-0 | |
| | 1r | 27.11.01 | **Aldershot Town** | H | W | 1-0 | Astafievs |
| | 2 | 08.12.01 | **Plymouth Argyle** (D3) | A | D | 1-1 | Walters |
| | 2r | 18.12.01 | **Plymouth Argyle** | H | W | 3-2 | Ommel, Hogg, Ellington |
| | 3 | 06.01.02 | **Derby County** (PL) | A | W | 3-1 | Ellington 3 |
| | 4 | 05.02.02 | **Gillingham** (D1) | A | L | 0-1 | |
| 2002-03 (D3) | 1 | 16.11.02 | **Runcorn** (NPL) | H | D | 0-0 | |
| | 1r | 26.11.02 | **Runcorn** | A | W | 3-1aet | Grazioli, Carlisle, Gilroy |
| | 2 | 07.12.02 | **Rochdale** (D3) | H | D | 1-1 | Allen |
| | 2r | 17.12.02 | **Rochdale** | A | L | 2-3 | Barrett, Tait |

## BROMLEY

*Formed 1892. First entered FA Cup: 1896-97. FA Amateur Cup winners: 1911, 1938; 1949. Members of the Isthmian League.*

| | | | | | | | |
|---|---|---|---|---|---|---|---|
| 1937-38 (AL) | 1 | 27.11.37 | **King's Lynn** (ECL) | A | W | 4-0 | Brown 2, Horsnall, Holbrook |
| | 2 | 11.12.37 | **Scarborough** (ML) | A | L | 1-4 | Brown |
| 1938-39 (AL) | 1 | 26.11.38 | **Apsley** (SPT) | H | W | 2-1 | Timorthy, Thomas |
| | 2 | 10.12.38 | **Lincoln City** (3N) | A | L | 1-8 | Reece |
| 1945-46 (AL) | 1 1L | 17.11.45 | **Slough Utd** (CRN) | H | - | 2-1ab | Scott, Coulsen |
| | | | *abandoned after 80 minutes – fog* | | | | |
| | 1 1L | 21.11.45 | **Slough Utd** | H | W | 6-1 | Scott 2, Viles, Ruddy, Crowther, Reece |
| | 1 2L | 24.11.45 | **Slough Utd** | A | L | 0-1 | |
| | 2 1L | 08.12.45 | **Watford** (3S) | H | L | 1-3 | Ruddy |
| | 2 2L | 15.12.45 | **Watford** | A | D | 1-1 | Coulson |
| 1947-48 (AL) | 1 | 29.11.47 | **Reading** (3S) | H | D | 3-3aet | Brown 2, Hopper |
| | 1r | 06.12.47 | **Reading** | A | L | 0-3 | |
| 1949-50 (AL) | 1 | 26.11.49 | **Watford** (3S) | H | L | 1-2 | J Jones |
| 1950-51 (AL) | 1 | 25.11.50 | **Aldershot** (3S) | A | D | 2-2 | G Brown 2 |
| | 1r | 29.11.50 | **Aldershot** | H | L | 0-1 | |
| 1951-52 (AL) | 1 | 24.11.51 | **Torquay Utd** (3S) | A | L | 2-3 | Dunmall, Jones |
| 1976-77 (IL) | 1 | 20.11.76 | **Swindon Town** (D3) | A | L | 0-7 | |
| 1996-97 (IL) | 1 | 16.11.96 | **Enfield** (IL) | H | L | 1-3 | Kane |

## BROMSGROVE ROVERS

*Formed 1885. First entered FA Cup: 1910-11. League club beaten: Northampton Town. Members of the Southern League.*

| | | | | | | | |
|---|---|---|---|---|---|---|---|
| 1947-48 (BC) | 1 | 29.11.47 | **Aldershot** (3S) | A | L | 1-2 | Cave |
| 1949-50 (BC) | 1 | 26.11.49 | **Hereford Utd** (SL) | A | L | 0-3 | |
| 1950-51 (BC) | 1 | 25.11.50 | **Hereford Utd** (SL) | H | L | 1-3 | Davenport |
| 1956-57 (BDL) | 1 | 17.11.56 | **Tooting & M** (IL) | A | L | 1-2 | Jakeman |
| 1986-87 (SL) | 1 | 15.11.86 | **Newport County** (D3) | H | L | 0-1 | |
| 1988-89 (SL) | 1 | 19.11.88 | **Welling Utd** (Conf) | A | L | 0-3 | |
| 1989-90 (SL) | 1 | 17.11.89 | **Basingstoke Town** (IL) | A | L | 0-3 | |
| 1991-92 (SL) | 1 | 16.11.91 | **Bournemouth** (D3) | A | L | 1-3 | O'Meara (p) |
| 1993-94 (Conf) | 1 | 13.11.93 | **Northampton Town** (D3) | A | W | 2-1 | Shilvock, Carter |
| | 2 | 04.12.93 | **Yeovil Town** (Conf) | A | W | 2-0 | Webb, Radburn |
| | 3 | 08.01.94 | **Barnsley** (D1) | H | L | 1-2 | Crisp |
| 1995-96 (Conf) | 1 | 11.11.95 | **Cinderford Town** (SL) | A | L | 1-2 | Skelding (p) |
| 1997-98 (SL) | 1 | 15.11.97 | **King's Lynn** (SL) | A | L | 0-1 | |

## BRONDESBURY

*Formed 1869. Played in north London. These were the only two FA Cup matches they played.*

| | | | | | | | |
|---|---|---|---|---|---|---|---|
| 1873-74 | 1 | 11.10.73 | **Royal Engineers** | A | L | 0-5 | |
| 1874-75 | 1 | 31.10.74 | **Oxford University** | A | L | 0-6 | |

## BRUSH SPORTS, LOUGHBOROUGH

*First entered the FA Cup: 1946-47. Became Loughborough United in 1960 and folded in 1963.*

| | | | | | | | | |
|---|---|---|---|---|---|---|---|---|
| 1946-47 | (N&D) | 1 | 30.11.46 | **Southend Utd** (3S) | H | L | 1-6 | Coleman |
| 1951-52 | (BDL) | 1 | 24.11.51 | **Weymouth** (SL) | H | L | 2-3 | A Naylor, Allen |

## BUCKINGHAM TOWN

*Formed 1883. First entered FA Cup: 1949-50. Members of the United Counties League.*

| | | | | | | | | |
|---|---|---|---|---|---|---|---|---|
| 1984-85 | (UCL) | 1 | 19.11.84 | **Orient** (D3) | H | L | 0-2 | |

## BURNLEY

*Formed 1882. Founder Member of Football League 1888. FA Cup Winnners: 1914. FA Cup runners-up: 1947, 1962. Record FA Cup win: 9-0 v Crystal Palace, 2nd round replay 10.02.1909; 9-0 v New Brighton, 4th round, 26.01.1957; 9-0 v Penrith, 1st round, 17.11.1984. Record FA Cup defeat: 0-11 v Darwen Old Wanderers 1st round, 17.10.1885*

| | | | | | | | | |
|---|---|---|---|---|---|---|---|---|
| 1885-86 | | 1 | 17.10.85 | **Darwen Old Wanderers** | A | L | 0-11 | |
| | | | | *Burnley fielded a reserve team* | | | | |
| 1886-87 | | 1 | 23.10.86 | **Astley Bridge** | A | D | 3-3 | Place Snr, 2 others |
| | | 1r | 30.10.86 | **Astley Bridge** | H | D | 2-2 | |
| | | | | *FA disqualified Burnley after protest* | | | | |
| 1887-88 | | 1 | 15.10.87 | **Darwen Old Wanderers** | H | W | 4-0 | Friel, McFettridge, 2 others |
| | | | | *FA ordered replay ordered after protest. Darwen Old Wanderers scratched* | | | | |
| | | 2 | 05.11.87 | **Accrington FC** | A | L | 2-3 | |
| 1888-89 | (D1) | 1 | 02.02.89 | **Old Westminsters** | H | W | 4-3 | Gallocher 2, Lang, W Brady |
| | | 2 | 16.02.89 | **WBA** (D1) | A | L | 1-5 | Gallocher |
| 1889-90 | (D1) | 1 | 18.01.90 | **Sheffield Utd** | A | L | 1-2 | Bury |
| 1890-91 | (D1) | 1 | 17.01.91 | **Crewe Alexandra** (FAll) | H | W | 4-2aet | Lambie, Oswald, McLardie, Hill |
| | | 2 | 31.01.91 | **Notts County** (D1) | A | L | 1-2 | McLardie |
| 1891-92 | (D1) | 1 | 16.01.92 | **Everton** (D1) | A | W | 4-2 | Hill 2, Nichol, AN Other |
| | | 2 | 30.01.92 | **Stoke** (D1) | H | L | 1-3 | Hill |
| 1892-93 | (D1) | 1 | 21.01.93 | **Small Heath** (D2) | H | W | 2-0 | McNab, Hill |
| | | 2 | 04.02.93 | **Sheffield Wed** (D1) | A | L | 0-1 | |
| 1893-94 | (D1) | 1 | 27.01.94 | **Notts County** (D2) | A | L | 0-1 | |
| 1894-95 | (D1) | 1 | 02.02.95 | **Newcastle Utd** (D2) | A | L | 1-2 | Bowes |
| 1895-96 | (D1) | 1 | 01.02.96 | **Woolwich Arsenal** (D2) | H | W | 6-1 | Place Jnr 2, Robertson 2, Nicol, Place Snr |
| | | 2 | 15.02.96 | **Stoke** (D1) | H | D | 1-1 | "scrimmage" |
| | | 2r | 20.02.96 | **Stoke** | A | L | 1-7 | Bowes |
| 1896-97 | (D1) | 1 | 30.01.97 | **Sunderland** (D1) | A | L | 0-1 | |
| 1897-98 | (D2) | 1 | 29.01.98 | **Woolwich Arsenal** (D2) | H | W | 3-1 | Taylor, Place Jnr, Ferguson |
| | | 2 | 12.02.98 | **Burslem PV** (ML) | H | W | 3-0 | Bowes, Beveridge, Ross |
| | | 3 | 26.02.98 | **Everton** (D1) | H | L | 1-3 | Place jnr |
| 1898-99 | (D1) | 1 | 28.01.99 | **Sheffield Utd** (D1) | H | D | 2-2 | Toman, Bowes |
| | | 1r | 02.02.99 | **Sheffield Utd** | A | L | 1-2 | Ross (p) |
| 1899-00 | (D1) | 1 | 27.01.00 | **Bury** (D1) | H | L | 0-1 | |
| 1900-01 | (D2) | 1 | 09.02.01 | **Newton Heath** (D2) | A | D | 0-0 | |
| | | 1r | 13.02.01 | **Newton Heath** | H | W | 7-1 | Morrison 2, Jenkinson 2, Mole, Bannister, Taylor |
| | | 2 | 23.02.01 | **Small Heath** (D2) | A | L | 0-1 | |
| 1901-02 | (D2) | | | Int Bishop Auckland (A) 3-2 | | | | |
| | | 1 | 25.01.02 | **Walsall** (ML) | A | L | 0-1 | |
| 1902-03 | (D2) | | | Int Reading (A) 0-1 | | | | |
| 1903-04 | (D2) | | | 3q Keswick (H) 8-0; 4q Darwen (A) 0-2 | | | | |
| 1904-05 | (D2) | | | Int Lincoln City (H) 1-1; Intr Lincoln City (A) 2-3 | | | | |
| 1905-06 | (D2) | 1 | 13.01.06 | **Tottenham Hotspur** (SL) | A | L | 0-2 | |
| 1906-07 | (D2) | 1 | 12.01.07 | **Aston Villa** (D1) | H | L | 1-3 | Whittaker |
| 1907-08 | (D2) | 1 | 11.01.08 | **Southampton** (SL) | A | L | 1-2 | Bell |
| 1908-09 | (D2) | 1 | 16.01.09 | **Bristol Rovers** (SL) | A | W | 4-1 | Ogden 3, R Smith |
| | | 2 | 06.02.09 | **Crystal Palace** (SL) | A | D | 0-0 | |
| | | 2r | 10.02.09 | **Crystal Palace** | H | W | 9-0 | R Smith 3, Abbott 2, Cretney 2, Smethams, og |
| | | 3 | 20.02.09 | **Tottenham Hotspur** (D2) | A | D | 0-0 | |

| | | | | | | | |
|---|---|---|---|---|---|---|---|
| | 3r | 24.02.09 | **Tottenham Hotspur** | H | W | 3-1 | Ogden, R Smith, Abbott |
| | 4 | 06.03.09 | **Manchester Utd** (D1) | H | - | 1-0ab | Ogden |
| | | | *abandoned after 72 minutes* | | | | |
| | 4 | 10.03.09 | **Manchester Utd** | H | L | 2-3 | Ogden 2 |
| 1909-10 (D2) | 1 | 15.01.10 | **Manchester Utd** (D1) | H | W | 2-0 | Green, Smethams |
| | 2 | 02.05.10 | **Swindon Town** (SL) | A | L | 0-2 | |
| 1910-11 (D2) | 1 | 14.01.11 | **Exeter City** (SL) | H | W | 2-0 | Morley, Mayson |
| | 2 | 04.02.11 | **Barnsley** (D2) | H | W | 2-0 | Morley, Green |
| | 3 | 25.02.11 | **Coventry City** (SL) | H | W | 5-0 | Green 2, Mayson 2, Watson, |
| | 4 | 11.03.11 | **Bradford City** (D1) | A | L | 0-1 | |
| 1911-12 (D2) | 1 | 13.01.12 | **Fulham** (D2) | A | L | 1-2 | Freeman |
| 1912-13 (D2) | 1 | 15.01.13 | **Leeds City** (D2) | A | W | 3-2 | Boyle (p), Lindley, Freeman |
| | 2 | 01.02.13 | **Gainsborough T** (ML) | H | W | 4-1 | Hodgson 2, Freeman, Boyle (p) |
| | 3 | 22.02.13 | **Middlesbrough** (D1) | H | W | 3-1 | Freeman 2, Hodgson |
| | 4 | 08.03.13 | **Blackburn Rovers** (D1) | A | W | 1-0 | Boyle (p) |
| | SF | 29.03.13 | **Sunderland** (D1) | | D | 0-0 | |
| | | | *played at Bramall Lane* | | | | |
| | SFr | 02.04.13 | **Sunderland** | | L | 2-3 | Freeman, Boyle |
| | | | *played at St Andrews* | | | | |
| 1913-14 (D1) | 1 | 10.01.14 | **South Shields** (Wear) | H | W | 3-1 | Lindley 2, Freeman |
| | 2 | 31.01.14 | **Derby County** (D1) | H | W | 3-2 | Hodgson 3 |
| | 3 | 21.02.14 | **Bolton Wanderers** (D1) | H | W | 3-0 | Freeman, Hodgson, Halley |
| | 4 | 07.03.14 | **Sunderland** (D1) | A | D | 0-0 | |
| | 4r | 11.03.14 | **Sunderland** | H | W | 2-1 | Lindley, Hodgson |
| | SF | 28.03.14 | **Sheffield Utd** (D1) | | D | 0-0 | |
| | | | *played at Old Trafford* | | | | |
| | SFr | 01.04.14 | **Sheffield Utd** | | W | 1-0 | Boyle |
| | | | *played at Goodison Park* | | | | |
| | F | 25.04.14 | **Liverpool** (D1) | | W | 1-0 | Freeman |
| | | | *played at Crystal Palace* | | | | |
| 1914-15 (D1) | 1 | 09.01.15 | **Huddersfield Town** (D2) | H | W | 3-1 | Freeman, Kelly, Thorpe |
| | 2 | 30.01.15 | **Southend Utd** (SL) | H | W | 6-0 | Freeman 2, Kelly, Watson, Boyle (p), Thorpe |
| | 3 | 20.02.15 | **Bolton Wanderers** (D1) | A | L | 1-2aet | Hodgson |
| 1919-20 (D1) | 1 | 10.01.20 | **Thornycrofts (Hants)** | A | D | 0-0 | |
| | | | *played at The Dell, Southampton* | | | | |
| | 1r | 13.01.20 | **Thornycrofts (Hants)** | H | W | 5-0 | Lindsay 3, Nesbitt, Cragg |
| | 2 | 31.01.20 | **Sunderland** (D1) | H | D | 1-1 | Kelly |
| | 2r | 04.02.20 | **Sunderland** | A | L | 0-2 | |
| 1920-21 (D1) | 1 | 08.01.21 | **Leicester City** (D2) | A | W | 7-3 | Anderson 5, Kelly, Cross |
| | 2 | 29.01.21 | **QPR** (D3) | H | W | 4-2 | Kelly 2, Anderson 2 |
| | 3 | 19.02.21 | **Hull City** (D2) | A | L | 0-3 | |
| 1921-22 (D1) | 1 | 07.01.22 | **Huddersfield Town** (D1) | H | D | 2-2 | Anderson, Mosscrop |
| | 1r | 11.01.22 | **Huddersfield Town** | A | L | 2-3 | Kelly, Boyle |
| 1922-23 (D1) | 1 | 13.01.23 | **Sunderland** (D1) | A | L | 1-3 | Anderson |
| 1923-24 (D1) | 1 | 12.01.24 | **South Shields** (D2) | H | W | 3-2 | Kelly 2, Cross |
| | 2 | 02.02.24 | **Fulham** (D2) | H | D | 0-0 | |
| | 2r | 07.02.24 | **Fulham** | A | W | 1-0 | Cross |
| | 3 | 23.02.24 | **Huddersfield Town** (D1) | H | W | 1-0 | Weaver |
| | 4 | 08.03.24 | **Swindon Town** (3S) | A | D | 1-1 | Weaver |
| | 4r | 12.03.24 | **Swindon Town** | H | W | 3-1 | Beel 2, Weaver |
| | SF | 29.03.24 | **Aston Villa** (D1) | | L | 0-3 | |
| | | | *played at Bramall Lane* | | | | |
| 1924-25 (D1) | 1 | 10.01.25 | **Everton** (D1) | A | L | 1-2 | Roberts |
| 1925-26 (D1) | 3 | 09.01.26 | **Cardiff City** (D1) | H | D | 2-2 | Beel 2 |
| | 3r | 13.01.26 | **Cardiff City** | A | L | 0-2 | |
| 1926-27 (D1) | 3 | 08.01.27 | **Grimsby Town** (D2) | H | W | 3-1 | Bruton, Beel, Page |
| | 4 | 29.01.27 | **Fulham** (D2) | A | W | 4-0 | Beel 2, Page, Bruton |
| | 5 | 19.02.27 | **Chelsea** (D2) | A | L | 1-2 | Cross |
| 1927-28 (D1) | 3 | 14.01.28 | **Aston Villa** (D1) | H | L | 0-2 | |
| 1928-29 (D1) | 3 | 12.01.29 | **Sheffield Utd** (D1) | H | W | 2-1 | Beel, Page |

| | | | | | | | | |
|---|---|---|---|---|---|---|---|---|
| | | 4 | 26.01.29 | **Swindon Town** (3S) | H | D | 3-3 | Devine, Page, McCluggage |
| | | 4r | 30.01.29 | **Swindon Town** | A | L | 2-3 | Beel, Devine |
| 1929-30 | (D1) | 3 | 11.01.30 | **Sheffield Wed** (D1) | A | L | 0-1 | |
| 1930-31 | (D2) | 3 | 10.01.31 | **Manchester City** (D1) | H | W | 3-0 | Prest, McCluggage, Jenkins |
| | | 4 | 24.01.31 | **Bradford Park A** (D2) | A | L | 0-2 | |
| 1931-32 | (D2) | 3 | 09.01.32 | **Derby County** (D1) | H | L | 0-4 | |
| 1932-33 | (D2) | 3 | 14.01.33 | **Swindon Town** (3S) | A | W | 2-1 | Harker, C Smith |
| | | 4 | 28.01.33 | **Sheffield Utd** (D1) | H | W | 3-1 | C Smith, Mee 2 |
| | | 5 | 18.02.33 | **Chesterfield** (D2) | A | W | 1-0 | Hancock |
| | | 6 | 04.03.33 | **Manchester City** (D1) | H | L | 0-1 | |
| 1933-34 | (D2) | 3 | 13.01.34 | **Bury** (D2) | H | D | 0-0 | |
| | | 3r | 17.01.34 | **Bury** | A | L | 2-3 | C Smith, Richmond |
| 1934-35 | (D2) | 3 | 12.01.35 | **Mansfield Town** (3N) | H | W | 4-2 | Hancock 2, G Brown, C Smith |
| | | 4 | 26.01.35 | **Luton Town** (3S) | H | W | 3-1 | G Brown, C Smith, Hancock |
| | | 5 | 16.02.35 | **Nottingham Forest** (D2) | A | D | 0-0 | |
| | | 5r | 19.02.35 | **Nottingham Forest** | H | W | 3-0 | Robinson, Hancock, G Brown |
| | | 6 | 06.03.35 | **Birmingham** (D1) | H | W | 3-2 | Hornby 2, Hancock |
| | | SF | 16.03.35 | **Sheffield Wed** (D1) | | L | 0-3 | |
| | | | | *played at Villa Park* | | | | |
| 1935-36 | (D2) | 3 | 11.01.36 | **Sheffield Utd** (D2) | H | D | 0-0 | |
| | | 3r | 16.01.36 | **Sheffield Utd** | A | L | 1-2 | Hancock |
| 1936-37 | (D2) | 3 | 16.01.37 | **Aston Villa** (D2) | A | W | 3-2 | Toll 2, Brocklebank |
| | | 4 | 30.01.37 | **Bury** (D2) | H | W | 4-1 | Stein, Toll, Brocklebank, Fletcher |
| | | 5 | 20.02.37 | **Arsenal** (D1) | H | L | 1-7 | Richardson |
| 1937-38 | (D2) | 3 | 08.01.38 | **Sheffield Wed** (D2) | A | D | 1-1 | Stein |
| | | 3r | 11.01.38 | **Sheffield Wed** | H | W | 3-1 | Brocklebank 2, Hornby |
| | | 4 | 22.01.38 | **Chesterfield** (D2) | A | L | 2-3 | Miller, Robson |
| 1938-39 | (D2) | 3 | 07.01.39 | **Notts County** (3S) | A | L | 1-3 | Brocklebank |
| 1945-46 | (D2) | 3 1L | 05.01.46 | **Stoke City** (D1) | A | L | 1-3 | Morris |
| | | 3 2L | 07.01.46 | **Stoke City** | H | W | 2-1 | Jackson, Kippax |
| 1946-47 | (D2) | 3 | 11.01.47 | **Aston Villa** (D1) | H | W | 5-1 | Morris 2, Harrison 2, Potts |
| | | 4 | 25.01.47 | **Coventry City** (D2) | H | W | 2-0 | Chew, Potts |
| | | 5 | 08.02.47 | **Luton Town** (D2) | A | D | 0-0 | |
| | | 5r | 11.02.47 | **Luton Town** | H | W | 3-0 | Harrison 3 |
| | | 6 | 01.03.47 | **Middlesbrough** (D1) | A | D | 1-1 | Morris |
| | | 6r | 04.03.47 | **Middlesbrough** | H | W | 1-0aet | Morris |
| | | SF | 29.03.47 | **Liverpool** (D1) | | D | 0-0aet | |
| | | | | *played at Ewood Park* | | | | |
| | | SFr | 12.04.47 | **Liverpool** (D1) | | W | 1-0 | Harrison |
| | | | | *played at Maine Road* | | | | |
| | | F | 26.04.47 | **Charlton Athletic** (D1) | | L | 0-1aet | |
| | | | | *played at Wembley Stadium* | | | | |
| 1947-48 | (D1) | 3 | 10.01.48 | **Swindon Town** (3S) | H | L | 0-2 | |
| 1948-49 | (D1) | 3 | 08.01.49 | **Charlton Athletic** (D1) | H | W | 2-1aet | McLaren, Clarke |
| | | 4 | 29.01.49 | **Rotherham Utd** (3N) | A | W | 1-0 | Spencer |
| | | 5 | 12.02.49 | **Brentford** (D2) | A | L | 2-4 | Attwell, Bray |
| 1949-50 | (D1) | 3 | 07.01.50 | **Notts County** (3S) | A | W | 4-1 | Spencer, Attwell, Potts, Wilson |
| | | 4 | 28.01.50 | **Port Vale** (3S) | H | W | 2-1 | Spencer, Hays |
| | | 5 | 11.02.50 | **Arsenal** (D1) | A | L | 0-2 | |
| 1950-51 | (D1) | 3 | 06.01.51 | **Aston Villa** (D1) | A | L | 0-2 | |
| 1951-52 | (D1) | 3 | 12.01.52 | **Hartlepools Utd** (3N) | H | W | 1-0 | Shanon |
| | | 4 | 02.02.52 | **Coventry City** (D2) | H | W | 2-0 | Holden, Elliott |
| | | 5 | 23.02.52 | **Liverpool** (D1) | H | W | 2-0 | Morris, Shannon |
| | | 6 | 08.03.52 | **Blackburn Rovers** (D2) | A | L | 1-3 | Chew |
| 1952-53 | (D1) | 3 | 10.01.53 | **Portsmouth** (D1) | A | D | 1-1 | Stephenson |
| | | 3r | 13.01.53 | **Portsmouth** | H | W | 3-1 | McIlroy, Shannon, Elliott |
| | | 4 | 31.01.53 | **Sunderland** (D1) | H | W | 2-0 | Holden 2 |
| | | 5 | 14.02.53 | **Arsenal** (D1) | H | L | 0-2 | |
| 1953-54 | (D1) | 3 | 09.01.54 | **Manchester Utd** (D1) | H | W | 5-3 | Shannon 2, Holden, McIlroy, Gray |
| | | 4 | 30.01.54 | **Newcastle Utd** (D1) | H | D | 1-1 | Pilkington |
| | | 4r | 03.02.54 | **Newcastle Utd** | A | L | 0-1 | |

| | | | | | | | | |
|---|---|---|---|---|---|---|---|---|
| 1954-55 | (D1) | 3 | 08.01.55 | **Sunderland** (D1) | A | L | 0-1 | |
| 1955-56 | (D1) | 3 | 07.01.56 | **Bury** (D2) | A | - | 2-2ab | McKay 2 |
| | | | | *abandoned after 65 minutes* | | | | |
| | | 3 | 10.01.56 | **Bury** | A | W | 1-0 | Gray |
| | | 4 | 28.01.56 | **Chelsea** (D1) | H | D | 1-1 | McKay |
| | | 4r | 01.02.56 | **Chelsea** | A | D | 1-1aet | Pilkington |
| | | 4 2r | 06.02.56 | **Chelsea** | | D | 2-2aet | McIlroy, McKay |
| | | | | *played at St Andrews* | | | | |
| | | 4 3r | 13.02.56 | **Chelsea** | | D | 0-0aet | |
| | | | | *played at Highbury* | | | | |
| | | 4 4r | 15.02.56 | **Chelsea** | | L | 0-2 | |
| | | | | *played at White Hart Lane* | | | | |
| 1956-57 | (D1) | 3 | 05.01.57 | **Chesterfield** (3N) | H | W | 7-0 | Lawson 4, Cheesebrough 2, Pilkington |
| | | 4 | 26.01.57 | **New Brighton** (LC) | H | W | 9-0 | McIlroy 3, Lawson 3, Newlands, Cheesebrough, Pilkington |
| | | 5 | 16.02.57 | **Huddersfield Town** (D2) | A | W | 2-1 | Lawson, Cheesebrough |
| | | 6 | 02.03.57 | **Aston Villa** (D1) | H | D | 1-1 | Aldis og |
| | | 6r | 06.03.57 | **Aston Villa** | A | L | 0-2 | |
| 1957-58 | (D1) | 3 | 04.01.58 | **Swansea Town** (D2) | H | W | 4-2 | McIlroy 2, Newlands, Cheesebrough |
| | | 4 | 25.01.58 | **Bristol Rovers** (D2) | A | D | 2-2 | Pointer, Connelly |
| | | 4r | 28.01.58 | **Bristol Rovers** | H | L | 2-3 | McIlroy, Pointer |
| 1958-59 | (D1) | 3 | 14.01.59 | **Stockport County** (D3) | A | W | 3-1 | Pointer 2, Pilkington |
| | | 4 | 28.01.59 | **Blackburn Rovers** (D1) | A | W | 2-1 | Robson, McIlroy |
| | | 5 | 14.02.59 | **Portsmouth** (D1) | H | W | 1-0 | Adamson |
| | | 6 | 28.02.59 | **Aston Villa** (D1) | A | D | 0-0 | |
| | | 6r | 03.03.59 | **Aston Villa** | H | L | 0-2 | |
| 1959-60 | (D1) | 3 | 09.01.60 | **Lincoln City** (D2) | A | D | 1-1 | Pointer |
| | | 3r | 12.01.60 | **Lincoln City** | H | W | 2-0 | McIlroy, Pilkington |
| | | 4 | 30.01.60 | **Swansea Town** (D2) | A | D | 0-0 | |
| | | 4r | 02.02.60 | **Swansea Town** | H | W | 2-1 | Robson 2 |
| | | 5 | 20.02.60 | **Bradford City** (D3) | A | D | 2-2 | Connelly 2 |
| | | 5r | 23.02.60 | **Bradford City** | H | W | 5-0 | Pointer 2, Robson 2, Connelly |
| | | 6 | 12.03.60 | **Blackburn Rovers** (D1) | H | D | 3-3 | Pointer, Pilkington, Connelly |
| | | 6r | 16.03.60 | **Blackburn Rovers** | A | L | 0-2 | |
| 1960-61 | (D1) | 3 | 07.01.61 | **Bournemouth** (D3) | H | W | 1-0 | Connelly |
| | | 4 | 28.01.61 | **Brighton** (D2) | A | D | 3-3 | Miller, Pointer, Robson |
| | | 4r | 31.01.61 | **Brighton** | H | W | 2-0 | Miller, Robson |
| | | 5 | 18.02.61 | **Swansea Town** (D2) | H | W | 4-0 | Robson 2, Pointer, Connelly |
| | | 6 | 04.03.61 | **Sheffield Wed** (D1) | A | D | 0-0 | |
| | | 6r | 07.03.61 | **Sheffield Wed** | H | W | 2-0 | McIlroy, Robson |
| | | SF | 18.03.61 | **Tottenham Hotspur** (D1) | | L | 0-3 | |
| | | | | *played at Villa Park* | | | | |
| 1961-62 | (D1) | 3 | 06.01.62 | **QPR** (D3) | H | W | 6-1 | Harris 2, Elder, Connelly, McIlroy, Ingham og |
| | | 4 | 30.01.62 | **Leyton Orient** (D2) | H | D | 1-1 | Harris |
| | | 4r | 06.02.62 | **Leyton Orient** | A | W | 1-0 | Miller |
| | | 5 | 17.02.62 | **Everton** (D1) | H | W | 3-1 | Miller, Connelly, Robson |
| | | 6 | 10.03.62 | **Sheffield Utd** (D1) | A | W | 1-0 | Pointer |
| | | SF | 31.03.62 | **Fulham** (D1) | | D | 1-1 | Connelly |
| | | | | *played at Villa Park* | | | | |
| | | SFr | 09.04.62 | **Fulham** | | W | 2-1 | Robson 2 |
| | | | | *played at Filbert Street* | | | | |
| | | F | 05.05.62 | **Tottenham Hotspur** (D1) | | L | 1-3 | Robson |
| | | | | *played at Wembley Stadium* | | | | |
| 1962-63 | (D1) | 3 | 16.01.63 | **Tottenham Hotspur** (D1) | A | W | 3-0 | Connelly, Lochhead, Harris |
| | | 4 | 26.01.63 | **Liverpool** (D1) | H | D | 1-1 | Connelly |
| | | 4r | 20.02.63 | **Liverpool** | A | L | 1-2aet | Elder |
| 1963-64 | (D1) | 3 | 04.01.64 | **Rotherham Utd** (D2) | H | D | 1-1 | Lochhead |
| | | 3r | 07.01.64 | **Rotherham Utd** | A | W | 3-2 | Lochhead, Connelly, Towers |
| | | 4 | 25.01.64 | **Newport County** (D4) | H | W | 2-1 | Morgan, Connelly |

| | | | | | | | | |
|---|---|---|---|---|---|---|---|---|
| | 5 | 15.02.64 | **Huddersfield Town** (D2) | H | W | 3-0 | Pointer, Lochhead, og |
| | 6 | 29.02.64 | **West Ham Utd** (D1) | A | L | 2-3 | Connelly, Pointer |
| 1964-65 (D1) | 3 | 09.01.65 | **Brentford** (D3) | H | D | 1-1 | Irvine |
| | 3r | 12.01.65 | **Brentford** | A | W | 2-0 | Irvine 2 |
| | 4 | 30.01.65 | **Reading** (D3) | A | D | 1-1 | Lochhead |
| | 4r | 02.02.65 | **Reading** | H | W | 1-0 | Lochhead |
| | 5 | 20.02.65 | **Manchester Utd** (D1) | A | L | 1-2 | Lochhead |
| 1965-66 (D1) | 3 | 22.01.66 | **Bournemouth** (D3) | A | D | 1-1 | Irvine |
| | 3r | 25.01.66 | **Bournemouth** | H | W | 7-0 | Lockhead 5, Irvine, Harris |
| | 4 | 12.02.66 | **Tottenham Hotspur** (D1) | A | L | 3-4 | Irvine 3 |
| 1966-67 (D1) | 3 | 28.01.67 | **Everton** (D1) | H | D | 0-0 | |
| | 3r | 31.01.67 | **Everton** | A | L | 1-2 | Irvine |
| 1967-68 (D1) | 3 | 27.01.68 | **West Ham Utd** (D1) | H | L | 1-3 | Casper |
| 1968-69 (D1) | 3 | 04.01.69 | **Derby County** (D2) | H | W | 3-1 | Casper 2, Blant |
| | 4 | 25.01.69 | **Liverpool** (D1) | A | L | 1-2 | Latcham |
| 1969-70 (D1) | 3 | 03.01.70 | **Wolverhampton W** (D1) | H | W | 3-0 | O'Neill, Dobson, Casper |
| | 4 | 24.01.70 | **Chelsea** (D1) | A | D | 2-2 | Dobson 2 |
| | 4r | 27.01.70 | **Chelsea** | H | L | 1-3aet | Coates |
| 1970-71 (D1) | 3 | 11.01.71 | **Oxford Utd** (D2) | A | L | 0-3 | |
| 1971-72 (D2) | 3 | 15.01.72 | **Huddersfield Town** (D1) | H | L | 0-1 | |
| 1972-73 (D2) | 3 | 13.01.73 | **Liverpool** (D1) | H | D | 0-0 | |
| | 3r | 16.01.73 | **Liverpool** | A | L | 0-3 | |
| 1973-74 (D1) | 3 | 05.01.74 | **Grimsby Town** (D3) | A | W | 2-0 | Newton, Hankin |
| | 4 | 26.01.74 | **Oldham Athletic** (D3) | A | W | 4-1 | Dobson 2, Fletcher, James |
| | 5 | 16.02.74 | **Aston Villa** (D2) | H | W | 1-0 | Fletcher |
| | 6 | 09.03.74 | **Wrexham** (D3) | H | W | 1-0 | Casper |
| | SF | 30.03.74 | **Newcastle Utd** (D1) *played at Hillsborough* | | L | 0-2 | |
| | 3/4 | 09.05.74 | **Leicester City** (D1) | A | W | 1-0 | Hankin |
| 1974-75 (D1) | 3 | 04.01.75 | **Wimbledon** (SL) | H | L | 0-1 | |
| 1975-76 (D1) | 3 | 03.01.76 | **Blackpool** (D2) | A | L | 0-1 | |
| 1976-77 (D2) | 3 | 08.01.77 | **Lincoln City** (D3) | H | D | 2-2 | Noble, Fletcher |
| | 3r | 12.01.77 | **Lincoln City** | A | W | 1-0 | Fletcher |
| | 4 | 29.01.77 | **Port Vale** (D3) | A | L | 1-2 | Flynn (p) |
| 1977-78 (D2) | 3 | 07.01.78 | **Fulham** (D2) | H | W | 1-0 | Fletcher |
| | 4 | 31.01.78 | **Chelsea** (D1) | A | L | 2-6 | Fletcher, Kindon |
| 1978-79 (D2) | 3 | 09.01.79 | **Birmingham City** (D1) | A | W | 2-0 | Morley, James |
| | 4 | 21.02.79 | **Sunderland** (D2) | H | D | 1-1 | Thompson |
| | 4r | 26.02.79 | **Sunderland** | A | W | 3-0 | Ingham, Fletcher, Kindon |
| | 5 | 28.02.79 | **Liverpool** (D1) | A | L | 0-3 | |
| 1979-80 (D2) | 3 | 05.01.80 | **Stoke City** (D1) | H | W | 1-0 | Dobson |
| | 4 | 26.01.80 | **Bury** (D3) | A | L | 0-1 | |
| 1980-81 (D3) | 1 | 22.11.80 | **Scarborough** (APL) | H | W | 1-0 | Hamilton |
| | 2 | 13.12.80 | **Port Vale** (D4) | H | D | 1-1 | Potts |
| | 2r | 16.12.80 | **Port Vale** | A | L | 0-2 | |
| 1981-82 (D3) | 1 | 21.11.81 | **Runcorn** (APL) | H | D | 0-0 | |
| | 1r | 24.11.81 | **Runcorn** | A | W | 2-1 | McGee 2 |
| | 2 | 02.01.82 | **Bury** (D4) | A | D | 1-1 | Taylor |
| | 2r | 04.01.82 | **Bury** | H | W | 2-1aet | Steven, Hamilton |
| | 3 | 18.01.82 | **Altrincham** (APL) | H | W | 6-1 | Hamilton 3, Taylor 2, Steven |
| | 4 | 23.01.82 | **Shrewsbury Town** (D2) | A | L | 0-1 | |
| 1982-83 (D2) | 3 | 08.01.83 | **Carlisle Utd** (D2) | A | D | 2-2 | Taylor, Wharton |
| | 3r | 11.01.83 | **Carlisle Utd** | H | W | 3-1 | Flynn, Stevens, Laws (p) |
| | 4 | 29.01.83 | **Swindon Town** (D4) | H | W | 3-1 | Hamilton 2, Steven |
| | 5 | 19.02.83 | **Crystal Palace** (D2) | A | D | 0-0 | |
| | 5r | 28.02.83 | **Crystal Palace** | H | W | 1-0 | Taylor (p) |
| | 6 | 12.03.83 | **Sheffield Wed** (D2) | H | D | 1-1 | Cassidy |
| | 6r | 15.03.83 | **Sheffield Wed** | A | L | 0-5 | |
| 1983-84 (D3) | 1 | 19.11.83 | **Hyde Utd** (NPL) *played at Turf Moor* | A | W | 2-0 | Reeves, Waldron |
| | 2 | 10.12.83 | **Chesterfield** (D4) | A | D | 2-2 | Dobson, Reeves |

| | | | | | | | | |
|---|---|---|---|---|---|---|---|---|
| | | 2r | 19.12.83 | **Chesterfield** | H | W | 3-2 | Hamilton 2, Reeves |
| | | 3 | 07.01.84 | **Oxford Utd** (D3) | H | D | 0-0 | |
| | | 3r | 11.01.84 | **Oxford Utd** | A | L | 1-2 | Hamilton |
| 1984-85 | (D3) | 1 | 17.11.84 | **Penrith** (NWC) | A | W | 9-0 | Hird 3(1p), Taylor 3, Powell 2, Grewcock |
| | | | | *played at Turf Moor* | | | | |
| | | 2 | 08.12.84 | **Halifax Town** (D4) | H | W | 3-1 | Hird, Devine, Biggins |
| | | 3 | 05.01.85 | **Wimbledon** (D2) | A | L | 1-3 | Devine |
| 1985-86 | (D4) | 1 | 16.11.85 | **Nuneaton B** (APL) | A | W | 3-2 | Devine 2, Malley |
| | | 2 | 07.12.85 | **Rotherham Utd** (D3) | A | L | 1-4 | Parker |
| 1986-87 | (D4) | 1 | 15.11.86 | **Telford Utd** (Conf) | A | L | 0-3 | |
| 1987-88 | (D4) | 1 | 14.11.87 | **Bolton Wanderers** (D4) | H | L | 0-1 | |
| 1988-89 | (D4) | 1 | 19.11.88 | **Chester City** (D3) | H | L | 0-2 | |
| 1989-90 | (D4) | 1 | 18.11.89 | **Stockport County** (D4) | H | D | 1-1 | White (p) |
| | | 1r | 22.11.89 | **Stockport County** | A | W | 2-1 | O'Connell, Futcher |
| | | 2 | 09.12.89 | **Scunthorpe Utd** (D4) | A | D | 2-2 | Deary, Mumby |
| | | 2r | 12.12.89 | **Scunthorpe Utd** | H | D | 1-1aet | Eli |
| | | 2 2r | 18.12.89 | **Scunthorpe Utd** | H | W | 5-0 | Eli 2, Futcher 2, Hardy |
| | | 3 | 06.01.90 | **Blackpool** (D3) | A | L | 0-1 | |
| 1990-91 | (D4) | 1 | 17.11.90 | **Stafford Rangers** (Conf) | A | W | 3-1 | Collymore og, White, Mumby |
| | | 2 | 12.12.90 | **Stoke City** (D3) | H | W | 2-0 | Francis, White |
| | | 3 | 06.01.91 | **Manchester City** (D1) | H | L | 0-1 | |
| 1991-92 | (D4) | 1 | 16.11.91 | **Doncaster Rovers** (D4) | H | D | 1-1 | Davis |
| | | 1r | 27.11.91 | **Doncaster Rovers** | A | W | 3-1 | Harper 2, Eli |
| | | 2 | 07.12.91 | **Rotherham Utd** (D4) | H | W | 2-0 | Conroy, Lancashire |
| | | 3 | 04.01.92 | **Derby County** (D2) | H | D | 2-2 | Harper, Eli |
| | | 3r | 14.01.92 | **Derby County** | A | - | 0-2 | |
| | | | | *abandoned after 76 minutes – fog* | | | | |
| | | 3r | 25.01.92 | **Derby County** | A | L | 0-2 | |
| 1992-93 | (D2) | 1 | 14.11.92 | **Scarborough** (D3) | H | W | 2-1 | Conroy, Curran og |
| | | 2 | 05.12.92 | **Shrewsbury Town** (D3) | H | D | 1-1 | Conroy |
| | | 2r | 15.12.92 | **Shrewsbury Town** | A | W | 2-1 | Pender, Conroy |
| | | 3 | 02.01.93 | **Sheffield Utd** (PL) | A | D | 2-2 | Heath 2 |
| | | 3r | 12.01.93 | **Sheffield Utd** | H | L | 2-4 | Heath, Monington |
| 1993-94 | (D2) | 1 | 13.11.93 | **York City** (D2) | H | D | 0-0 | |
| | | 1r | 30.11.93 | **York City** | A | W | 3-2 | Heath, Joyce, Eyres |
| | | 2 | 04.12.93 | **Rochdale** (D3) | H | W | 4-1 | Eyres 3, Ryan og |
| | | 3 | 08.01.94 | **Charlton Athletic** (D1) | A | L | 0-3 | |
| 1994-95 | (D1) | 1 | 12.11.94 | **Shrewsbury Town** (D2) | H | W | 2-1 | Heath, Deary |
| | | 2 | 04.12.94 | **Chester City** (D2) | A | W | 2-1 | Eyres (p), Heath |
| | | 3 | 07.01.95 | **Cambridge Utd** (D2) | A | W | 4-2 | Eyres (p), Robinson, Randall, Gayle |
| | | 4 | 28.01.95 | **Liverpool** (PL) | H | D | 0-0 | |
| | | 4r | 07.02.95 | **Liverpool** | A | L | 0-1 | |
| 1995-96 | (D2) | 1 | 10.11.95 | **Walsall** (D2) | H | L | 1-3 | Eyres |
| 1996-97 | (D2) | 1 | 16.11.96 | **Lincoln City** (D3) | H | W | 2-1 | Gleghorn, Matthew |
| | | 2 | 07.12.96 | **Walsall** (D2) | A | D | 1-1 | Eyres |
| | | 2r | 17.12.96 | **Walsall** | H | - | -0-1ab | |
| | | | | *abandoned at halftime – floodlight failure* | | | | |
| | | 2r | 23.12.96 | **Walsall** | H | D | 1-1aet | Barnes |
| | | | | *Burnley won 4-2 on penalties* | | | | |
| | | 3 | 04.01.97 | **Liverpool** (PL) | A | L | 0-1 | |
| 1997-98 | (D2) | 1 | 15.11.97 | **Rotherham Utd** (D3) | A | D | 3-3 | Cooke, Moore, Weller |
| | | 1r | 25.11.97 | **Rotherham Utd** | H | L | 0-3 | |
| 1998-99 | (D2) | 1 | 17.11.98 | **Darlington** (D3) | A | L | 2-3 | Payton 2(1p) |
| 1999-00 | (D2) | 1 | 31.10.99 | **Barnet** (D3) | A | W | 1-0 | Cook |
| | | 2 | 20.11.99 | **Rotherham Utd** (D3) | H | W | 2-0 | Cook, Mullin |
| | | 3 | 11.12.99 | **Derby County** (PL) | A | W | 1-0 | Cooke |
| | | 4 | 08.01.00 | **Coventry City** (PL) | A | L | 0-3 | |
| 2000-01 | (D1) | 3 | 06.01.01 | **Scunthorpe Utd** (D3) | H | D | 2-2 | Moore, Johnrose |
| | | 3r | 23.01.01 | **Scunthorpe Utd** | A | D | 1-1aet | Payton |
| | | | | *Scunthorpe Utd won 5-4 on penalties* | | | | |
| 2001-02 | (D1) | 3 | 05.01.02 | **Canvey Island** (IL) | H | W | 4-1 | I Moore, Little |

| | | | | | | | | |
|---|---|---|---|---|---|---|---|---|
| | | 4 | 27.01.02 | **Cheltenham Town** (D3) | A | L | 1-2 | A Moore |
| 2002-03 | (D1) | 3 | 04.01.03 | **Grimsby Town** (D1) | A | D | 2-2 | A Moore, Weller |
| | | 3r | 14.01.03 | **Grimsby Town** | H | W | 4-0 | I Moore 2, Little, Blake (p) |
| | | 4 | 25.01.03 | **Brentford** (D2) | A | W | 3-0 | Blake, Cook, Little |
| | | 5 | 16.02.03 | **Fulham** (PL) | A | D | 1-1 | A Moore |
| | | 5r | 26.02.03 | **Fulham** | H | W | 3-0 | Taylor, I Moore, Diallo |
| | | 6 | 09.03.03 | **Watford** (D1) | A | L | 0-2 | |

# BURSCOUGH

*Formed 1946. First entered FA Cup: 1946-47. FA Trophy winners: 2003. Members of the Northern Premier League.*

| | | | | | | | | |
|---|---|---|---|---|---|---|---|---|
| 1959-60 | (LC) | 1 | 14.11.59 | **Crewe Alexandra** (D4) | H | L | 1-3 | J Jones |
| 1977-78 | (CC) | 1 | 26.11.77 | **Blyth Spartans** (NL) | A | L | 0-1 | |
| 1979-80 | (CC) | 1 | 24.11.79 | **Sheffield Utd** (D3) | H | L | 0-3 | |
| | | | | *played at Bramall Lane* | | | | |
| 1980-81 | (CC) | 1 | 22.11.80 | **Altrincham** (APL) | H | L | 1-2 | Perry |

# BURTON ALBION

*Formed 1950. First entered FA Cup 1950-51. FA Trophy Runners-up: 1987. League clubs beaten: Halifax Town, Aldershot. Members of The Conference.*

| | | | | | | | | |
|---|---|---|---|---|---|---|---|---|
| 1955-56 | (BDL) | 1 | 19.11.55 | **Wycombe W** (IL) | A | W | 3-1 | Hughes, Bullock, Bowering |
| | | 2 | 10.12.55 | **Halifax Town** (3N) | A | D | 0-0 | |
| | | 2r | 14.12.55 | **Halifax Town** | H | W | 1-0 | Barker |
| | | 3 | 07.01.56 | **Charlton Athletic** (D1) | A | L | 0-7 | |
| 1956-57 | (BDL) | 1 | 17.11.56 | **Bournemouth** (3S) | A | L | 0-8 | |
| 1965-66 | (SL) | 1 | 13.11.65 | **Corby Town** (SL) | A | L | 3-6 | Aston, Round 2 |
| 1977-78 | (SL) | 1 | 26.11.77 | **Wrexham** (D3) | A | L | 0-2 | |
| 1979-80 | (NPL) | 1 | 24.11.79 | **Bury** (D3) | H | L | 0-2 | |
| 1980-81 | (NPL) | 1 | 22.11.80 | **Blyth Spartans** (NL) | A | L | 1-2 | Kent |
| 1983-84 | (NPL) | 1 | 19.11.83 | **Windsor & Eton** (IL) | H | L | 1-2 | Dolby |
| 1984-85 | (NPL) | 1 | 17.11.84 | **Staines Town** (IL) | H | W | 2-0 | Mell, Newton |
| | | 2 | 08.12.84 | **Aldershot** (D4) | A | W | 2-0 | Simmons, Mell |
| | | 3 | 05.01.85 | **Leicester City** (D1) | | L | 1-6 | Vaughan |
| | | | | *played at Baseball Ground, Derby. FA ordered match to be replayed behind closed doors after coin-throwing incident* | | | | |
| | | 3r | 16.01.85 | **Leicester City** (D1) | | L | 0-1 | |
| | | | | *played at Highfield Road, Coventry* | | | | |
| 1987-88 | (SL) | 1 | 14.11.87 | **York City** (D3) | A | D | 0-0 | |
| | | 1r | 18.11.87 | **York City** | H | L | 1-2 | Groves (p) |
| 1991-92 | (SL) | 4Q | 26.10.91 | **Colchester Utd** (Conf) | A | L | 0-5 | |
| 1995-96 | (SL) | 1 | 11.11.95 | **Bradford City** (D2) | A | L | 3-4 | Rhodes (p), Stride 2 |
| 1998-99 | (SL) | 1 | 14.11.98 | **Kingstonian** (Conf) | A | L | 0-1 | |
| 1999-00 | (SL) | 1 | 30.10.99 | **Rochdale** (D3) | H | D | 0-0 | |
| | | 1r | 09.11.99 | **Rochdale** | A | L | 0-3 | |
| 2000-01 | (SL) | 1 | 18.11.00 | **Kidderminster H** (D3) | A | D | 0-0 | |
| | | 1r | 28.11.00 | **Kidderminster H** | H | L | 2-4 | Blount, Wassall |
| 2002-03 | (Conf) | 1 | 16.11.02 | **Oldham Athletic** (D2) | A | D | 2-2 | Webster (p), Dudley |
| | | 1r | 27.11.02 | **Oldham Athletic** | H | D | 2-2aet | Moore 2 |
| | | | | *Oldham Athletic won 5-4 on penalties* | | | | |

# BURTON SWIFTS

*Formed 1870s as Burton Outward Star. Burton Swifts 1883. Merged with Burton Wanderers to form Burton United 1901.*

| | | | | | | | | |
|---|---|---|---|---|---|---|---|---|
| 1885-86 | | 1 | 31.10.85 | **Wednesbury Old Ath** | A | L | 1-5 | |
| 1886-87 | | 1 | 30.10.86 | **Crosswell's Brewery** | H | L | 0-1 | |
| 1887-88 | | 1 | 15.10.87 | **Birmingham Southfield** | H | W | 7-0 | |
| | | 2 | 05.11.87 | **Great Bridge Unity** | H | L | 2-5 | |
| 1888-89 | | | | 1q Leek (H) 1-3aet | | | | |
| 1889-90 | | | | 2q Great Bridge Unity (H) 5-3aet; 3q Walsall TS (H) 1-6 | | | | |
| 1890-91 | (TC) | | | 2q Sheffield U (H) 2-1 FA disqualified Burton for playing unregistered player | | | | |
| 1891-92 | (FAl) | | | 2q Walsall TS (A) 4-2; 3q Small Heath (A) 2-4 | | | | |
| 1892-93 | (D2) | | | P Singers FC, Coventry (H) 3-0; 1q Burslem PV (A) 2-0; 2q Leek (A) 3-0; 3q Walsall TS (A) 3-1; 4q Burton Wanderers (H) 3-2 | | | | |

| | | | | | | | | |
|---|---|---|---|---|---|---|---|---|
| | | 1 | 21.01.93 | **Preston North End** (D1) | A | L | 2-9 | Dewey, Emery |
| 1893-94 | (D2) | | | 1q Burslem PV (A) 4-3aet; 2q Brierley Hill Alliance (A) 1-3 | | | | |
| 1894-95 | (D2) | | | 2q Stourbridge (H) 3-2; 3q Burton Wanderers (A) 2-5 | | | | |
| 1895-96 | (D2) | | | 1q Wellington St G. (A) 6-1; 2q Burslem PV (A) 1-1; 2qr Burslem Port Vale (H) 1-0; 3q Singers FC, Coventry (A) 2-0; 4q Wrockwardine Wood (H) 3-1 | | | | |
| | | 1 | 01.02.96 | **Blackpool** (LL) | A | L | 1-4 | |
| 1896-97 | (D2) | | | 3q Wrockwardine Wood (H) 6-0; 4q Walsall (A) 1-1; 4qr Walsall (H) 1-0aet; 5q Burslem PV (A) 3-2 | | | | |
| | | 1 | 30.01.97 | **Liverpool** (D1) | A | L | 3-4 | Evans, Wyllie, AN Other |
| 1897-98 | (D2) | | | 3q Stourbridge (H) 0-2 | | | | |
| 1898-99 | (D2) | | | 2q Coalville T (H) 4-1; 3q Ilkeston T (H) 4-2; 4q Chesterfield (H) 1-0; 5q Heanor T (H) 0-0; 5qr Heanor T (A) 0-1 | | | | |
| 1899-00 | (D2) | | | 3q Kettering T (H) 8-2; 4q Leicester Fosse (A) 1-3 | | | | |
| 1900-01 | (D2) | | | 3q Newstead Byron (H) 2-2; 3qr Newstead Byron (A) 4-0; 4q Hinckley (A) 4-1; 5q Kettering T (H) 1-2 | | | | |

## BURTON TOWN

*Formed around 1900 as a junior club but became the senior club in Burton when Burton United folded in 1910. First entered the FA Cup: 1911-12 and competed until 1938-39 when they disbanded. League clubs beaten: Gateshead, York City*

| | | | | | | | | |
|---|---|---|---|---|---|---|---|---|
| 1931-32 | (BDL) | 1 | 28.11.31 | **Wigan Borough** (3N) | | | - | |
| | | | | *Wigan Borough had folded before the match. Burton Town walkover* | | | | |
| | | 2 | 12.12.31 | **Gateshead AFC** (3N) | H | W | 4-1 | Boswell 2, Causer, Reay |
| | | 3 | 09.01.32 | **Blackburn Rovers** (D1) | H | L | 0-4 | |
| 1934-35 | (BDL) | 1 | 24.11.34 | **York City** (3N) | H | L | 2-3 | Corbett, Mills |
| 1935-36 | (ML) | 1 | 30.11.35 | **York City** | A | W | 5-1 | Narol 2, McPhall, Bowater, Loftus |
| | | 2 | 14.12.35 | **Southend Utd** (3S) | A | L | 0-3 | |
| 1936-37 | (ML) | 1 | 28.11.36 | **Wigan Athletic** (CC) | H | W | 5-1 | Bridges 2, Hewitson 2, Jeavons |
| | | 2 | 12.12.36 | **Darlington** (3N) | H | L | 1-2 | Bridges |
| 1937-38 | (ML) | 1 | 27.11.37 | **Rotherham Utd** (3N) | H | D | 1-1 | Lowry |
| | | 1r | 29.11.37 | **Rotherham Utd** | A | L | 0-3 | |

## BURTON UNITED

*Formed 1901 by the amalgamation of Burton Swifts and Burton Wanderers. Disbanded 1910.*

| | | | | | | | | |
|---|---|---|---|---|---|---|---|---|
| 1901-02 | (D2) | | | 3q Whitwick White Cross (A) 3-0; 4q Northampton T (H) 0-0 abnd; 4q Northampton T (H) 0-0; 4qr Northampton T (A) 0-2 | | | | |
| 1902-03 | (D2) | | | 1q Sutton T walkover; 2q Newhall Red Rose walkover; 3q Northampton T (H) 2-0; 4q Kettering T (H) 3-1; 5q Wellingborough T (H) 5-1; Int Manchester U (H) 1-1; Int r Manchester U (A) 1-3 | | | | |
| 1903-04 | (D2) | | | 1q Gresley R (H) 2-0; 2q Hinckley T (H) 2-2; 2qr Hinckley T (A) 5-1; 3q Kettering T (H) 3-0; 4q Whitwick White Cross (A) 5-2; 5q Leicester Fosse (H) 1-1; 5qr Leicester Fosse (A) 2-2abandoned during extra time; 5qr Leicester Fosse 2-0 at Derby; Int Burslem PV (A) 0-3 | | | | |
| 1904-05 | (D2) | | | 3q Northampton T (H) 2-3 | | | | |
| 1905-06 | (D2) | | | 4q Accrington S (H) 3-0 | | | | |
| | | 1 | 13.01.06 | **Millwall Athletic** (SL) | A | L | 0-1 | |
| 1906-07 | (D2) | | | 5q Bishop Auckland (H) 6-0 | | | | |
| | | 1 | 12.01.07 | **New Brompton** (SL) | H | D | 0-0 | |
| | | 1r | 16.01.07 | **New Brompton** | A | - | 0-0ab | |
| | | | | *abandoned after 100 minutes* | | | | |
| | | 12r | 21.01.07 | **New Brompton** (SL) | | L | 0-2 | |
| | | | | *played at Craven Cottage* | | | | |

## BURTON WANDERERS

*Formed 1871. Merged with Burton Swifts to form Burton United 1901.*

| | | | | | | | | |
|---|---|---|---|---|---|---|---|---|
| 1885-86 | | 1 | 31.10.85 | **Small Heath Alliance** | A | L | 2-9 | |
| 1886-87 | | 1 | 30.10.86 | **WBA** | A | L | 0-5 | |
| 1887-88 | | 1 | 08.10.87 | **Aston Shakespeare** | A | W | 3-2 | |
| | | | | *FA ordered replay after protest. Burton Wanderers scratched.* | | | | |
| 1893-94 | (ML) | | | 1q Leek (H) 9-0; 2q Old Hill Wanderers (H) 5-0; 3q Hednesford T (H) 7-2; 4q Brierley Hill Alliance (H) 2-1 | | | | |
| | | 1 | 27.01.94 | **Stockport County** (TC) | A | W | 1-0 | Moore |
| | | 2 | 10.02.94 | **Notts County** (D2) | H | L | 1-2 | Adrian Capes |

| | | | | | | | | |
|---|---|---|---|---|---|---|---|---|
| 1894-95 | (D2) | | | 1q Walsal TS (H) 3-0; 2q Brierley Hill Alliance. (H) 3-1; 3q Burton Swifts (H) 5-2; 4q Old Hill Wanderers (H) 5-0 | | | | |
| | | 1 | 02.02.95 | **Blackburn Rovers** (D1) | H | L | 1-2 | Arthur Capes |
| 1895-96 | (D2) | 1 | 01.02.96 | **Sheffield Utd** (D1) | H | D | 1-1 | Brown |
| | | 1r | 06.02.96 | **Sheffield Utd** | A | L | 0-1 | |
| 1896-97 | (D2) | 1 | 30.01.97 | **Everton** (D1) | A | L | 2-5 | T Arkesden, AN Other |

# BURY

*Formed 1885. FA Cup winners: 1900, 1903. Their 6-0 victory over Derby County on April 18, 1903, remains the record victory in the FA Cup final. FA Cup record win: 12-1 v Stockton, 1st round replay, 02.02.1897. FA Cup record defeat: 0-6 v Leeds Utd, 3rd round, 22.01.1966.*

| | | | | | | | | |
|---|---|---|---|---|---|---|---|---|
| 1887-88 | | 1 | | **Blackburn Rovers** | | | - | |
| | | | | *Bury scratched. Blackburn Rovers walkover* | | | | |
| 1891-92 | (LL) | | | 1q Witton (H) 3-1; 2q Heywood Central (A) 2-1; 3q Blackpool (H) 5-5; 3qr Blackpool (A) 3-4 | | | | |
| 1892-93 | (LL) | | | 1q Southport (H) 9-0; 2q Stockport Co (H) 8-1; 3q Rossendale (A) 1-7 | | | | |
| 1893-94 | (LL) | | | 1q Nelson (A) 3-2aet; 2q Rossendale (A) 2-1; 3q Fleetwood R (H) 2-0; South Shore (A) 1-3aet | | | | |
| 1894-95 | (D2) | 1 | 02.02.95 | **Leicester Fosse** (D2) | H | W | 4-1 | Henderson 2, Lee, Plant |
| | | 2 | 16.02.95 | **Bolton Wanderers** (D1) | A | L | 0-1 | |
| 1895-96 | (D1) | 1 | 01.02.96 | **Small Heath** (D1) | A | W | 4-1 | Henderson, Millar 2, Barr |
| | | 2 | 15.02.96 | **Newcastle Utd** (D2) | A | W | 3-1 | Henderson, Millar, Plant |
| | | 3 | 29.02.96 | **Bolton Wanderers** (D1) | A | L | 0-2 | |
| 1896-97 | (D1) | 1 | 30.01.97 | **Stockton** (NL) | A | D | 0-0 | |
| | | 1r | 02.02.97 | **Stockton** | H | W | 12-1 | Millar 4, Wylie 3, Henderson 2, Hendry Ross, Wilson og |
| | | 2 | 13.02.97 | **Everton** (D1) | A | L | 0-3 | |
| 1897-98 | (D1) | 1 | 29.01.98 | **Stoke** (D1) | H | L | 1-2 | Plant |
| 1898-99 | (D1) | 1 | 28.01.99 | **Heanor Town** (ML) | A | W | 3-0 | Bennett, Sagar 2 |
| | | 2 | 11.02.99 | **WBA** (D1) | A | L | 1-2 | Pray |
| 1899-00 | (D1) | 1 | 27.01.00 | **Burnley** (D1) | A | W | 1-0 | Sagar |
| | | 2 | 10.02.00 | **Notts County** (D1) | A | D | 0-0 | |
| | | 2r | 14.02.00 | **Notts County** | H | W | 2-0 | Pray, Sagar |
| | | 3 | 24.02.00 | **Sheffield Utd** (D1) | A | D | 2-2 | McLuckie, Wood |
| | | 3r | 01.03.00 | **Sheffield Utd** | H | W | 2-0 | Plant, Richards |
| | | SF | 24.03.00 | **Nottingham Forest** (D1) | | D | 1-1 | Pray |
| | | | | *played at Victoria Ground, Stoke* | | | | |
| | | SFr | 29.03.00 | **Nottingham Forest** | | W | 3-2aet | McLuckie, Richards, Sagar |
| | | | | *played at Bramall Lane* | | | | |
| | | F | 21.04.00 | **Southampton** (SL) | | W | 4-0 | McLuckie 2, Wood, Plant |
| | | | | *played at Crystal Palace* | | | | |
| 1900-01 | (D1) | 1 | 09.02.01 | **Sheffield Wed** (D1) | A | W | 1-0 | Wood |
| | | 2 | 23.02.01 | **Tottenham Hotspur** (SL) | A | L | 1-2 | McLuckie |
| 1901-02 | (D1) | 1 | 25.01.02 | **WBA** (D2) | H | W | 5-1 | Sagar 3, Thorpe, Wood |
| | | 2 | 08.02.02 | **Walsall** (ML) | A | W | 5-0 | Sagar 2, Gray, Ross, Wood |
| | | 3 | 22.02.02 | **Southampton** (SL) | H | L | 2-3 | Ross, Sagar |
| 1902-03 | (D1) | 1 | 07.02.03 | **Wolverhampton W** (D1) | H | W | 1-0 | Richards |
| | | 2 | 21.02.03 | **Sheffield Utd** (D1) | A | W | 1-0 | Sagar |
| | | 3 | 07.03.03 | **Notts County** (D1) | H | W | 1-0 | Lindsay |
| | | SF | 21.03.03 | **Aston Villa** (D1) | | W | 3-0 | Richards, Sagar, Spencer og |
| | | | | *played at Goodison Park* | | | | |
| | | F | 18.04.03 | **Derby County** (D1) | | W | 6-0 | Ross, Sagar, Leeming 2, Wood, Plant |
| | | | | *played at Crystal Palace* | | | | |
| 1903-04 | (D1) | 1 | 06.02.04 | **Newcastle Utd** (D1) | H | W | 2-1 | Swann, Sagar |
| | | 2 | 20.02.04 | **Sheffield Utd** (D1) | H | L | 1-2 | Sagar |
| 1904-05 | (D1) | 1 | 04.02.05 | **Notts County** (D1) | H | W | 1-0 | Sagar |
| | | 2 | 18.02.05 | **Aston Villa** (D1) | A | L | 2-3 | Lindsay, Simpson |
| 1905-06 | (D1) | 1 | 13.01.06 | **Nottingham Forest** (D1) | H | D | 1-1 | Kilbourne |
| | | 1r | 17.01.06 | **Nottingham Forest** | A | L | 2-6 | Dow, Murphy |
| 1906-07 | (D1) | 1 | 12.01.07 | **Oxford City** (IL) | A | W | 3-0 | Bevan 2, Kay |
| | | 2 | 02.02.07 | **New Brompton** (SL) | H | W | 1-0 | Gildea |
| | | 3 | 23.02.07 | **Barnsley** (D2) | A | L | 0-1 | |

| | | | | | | | |
|---|---|---|---|---|---|---|---|
| 1907-08 (D1) | 1 | 11.01.08 | **Millwall Athletic** (SL) | H | W | 2-1 | Currie, Hibbert |
| | 2 | 01.02.08 | **Wolverhampton W** (D2) | A | L | 0-2 | |
| 1908-09 (D1) | 1 | 16.01.09 | **Kettering Town** (UCL) | H | W | 8-0 | Lindsay, Dewhurst, MacIntosh 3, |
| | | | | | | | Hibbert 2, Duffy |
| | 2 | 06.02.09 | **Bristol City** (D1) | A | D | 2-2 | Hibbert 2 |
| | 2r | 10.02.09 | **Bristol City** | H | L | 0-1 | |
| 1909-10 (D1) | 1 | 15.01.10 | **Glossop North End** (D2) | H | W | 2-1 | Dewhurst, Hibbert |
| | 2 | 05.02.10 | **Leicester Fosse** (D2) | A | L | 2-3 | Hibbert, Currie |
| 1910-11 (D1) | 1 | 14.01.11 | **Newcastle Utd** (D1) | A | L | 1-6 | Currie |
| 1911-12 (D1) | 1 | 13.01.12 | **Millwall Athletic** (SL) | H | W | 2-1 | Cannon, Duffy |
| | 2 | 03.02.12 | **Everton** (D1) | A | D | 1-1 | Kay |
| | 2r | 08.02.12 | **Everton** | A | L | 0-6 | |
| 1912-13 (D2) | 1 | 11.01.13 | **Southampton** (SL) | A | D | 1-1 | Peake |
| | 1r | 15.01.13 | **Southampton** | H | W | 2-1 | Peake 2 |
| | 2 | 01.02.13 | **Crystal Palace** (SL) | A | L | 0-2 | |
| 1913-14 (D2) | 1 | 10.01.14 | **Hull City** (D2) | A | D | 0-0 | |
| | 1r | 14.01.14 | **Hull City** | H | W | 2-1 | Peake 2 |
| | 2 | 31.01.14 | **Blackburn Rovers** (D1) | A | L | 0-2 | |
| 1914-15 (D2) | 1 | 09.01.15 | **Plymouth Argyle** (SL) | H | D | 1-1 | Lythgoe |
| | 1r | 16.01.15 | **Plymouth Argyle** | A | W | 2-1 | Peake, Connor |
| | 2 | 30.01.15 | **Bradford Park A** (D1) | H | L | 0-1 | |
| 1919-20 (D2) | 1 | 10.01.20 | **Stoke** (D2) | H | W | 2-0 | Lomes, Hird |
| | 2 | 31.01.20 | **West Ham Utd** (D2) | A | L | 0-6 | |
| 1920-21 (D2) | 1 | 08.01.21 | **Swansea Town** (D3) | A | L | 0-3 | |
| 1921-22 (D2) | 1 | 07.01.22 | **Bolton Wanderers** (D1) | A | L | 0-1 | |
| 1922-23 (D2) | 1 | 13.01.23 | **Luton Town** (3S) | H | W | 2-1 | McCrae, Bullock |
| | 2 | 03.02.23 | **Stoke** (D1) | H | W | 3-1 | Bullock, Aitken, Quinn |
| | 3 | 24.02.23 | **Southampton** (D2) | H | D | 0-0 | |
| | 3r | 28.02.23 | **Southampton** | A | L | 0-1 | |
| 1923-24 (D2) | 1 | 12.01.24 | **Derby County** (D2) | A | L | 1-2 | Ball |
| 1924-25 (D1) | 1 | 10.01.25 | **Sunderland** (D1) | H | L | 0-3 | |
| 1925-26 (D1) | 3 | 09.01.26 | **Rotherham Utd** (3N) | A | W | 3-2 | Porter, Ball, Matthews |
| | 4 | 30.01.26 | **Millwall** (3S) | H | D | 3-3 | Matthews, Bullock, Ball |
| | 4r | 04.02.26 | **Millwall** | A | L | 0-2 | |
| 1926-27 (D1) | 3 | 08.01.27 | **Swansea Town** (D2) | A | L | 1-4 | Amos |
| 1927-28 (D1) | 3 | 14.01.28 | **Charlton Athletic** (3S) | A | D | 1-1 | Ball |
| | 3r | 18.01.28 | **Charlton Athletic** | H | W | 4-3 | Amos, Vernon 2, Ball (p) |
| | 4 | 28.01.28 | **Manchester Utd** (D1) | H | D | 1-1 | Ball |
| | 4r | 01.02.28 | **Manchester Utd** | A | L | 0-1 | |
| 1928-29 (D1) | 3 | 12.01.29 | **Darlington** (3N) | A | W | 6-2 | Gale 2, Smith 2, Ball, Bullock |
| | 4 | 26.01.29 | **Manchester Utd** (D1) | A | W | 1-0 | Amos |
| | 5 | 16.02.29 | **Blackburn Rovers** (D1) | A | L | 0-1 | |
| 1929-30 (D2) | 3 | 11.01.30 | **Huddersfield Town** (D1) | H | D | 0-0 | |
| | 3r | 15.01.30 | **Huddersfield Town** | A | L | 1-3 | Amos |
| 1930-31 (D2) | 3 | 10.01.31 | **Torquay Utd** (3S) | H | D | 1-1 | Hope |
| | 3r | 14.01.31 | **Torquay Utd** | A | W | 2-1aet | Smith, Robbie |
| | 4 | 24.01.31 | **Exeter City** (3S) | H | L | 1-2 | Robbie |
| 1931-32 (D2) | 3 | 09.01.32 | **Swansea Town** (D2) | H | W | 2-1 | Lindsay 2 |
| | 4 | 23.01.32 | **Sheffield Utd** (D1) | H | W | 3-1 | Robbie, Lindsay, Amos |
| | 5 | 13.02.32 | **Stoke City** (D2) | H | W | 3-0 | Amos 2, Robbie |
| | 6 | 27.02.32 | **Manchester City** (D1) | H | L | 3-4 | Smith, Robbie, Amos |
| 1932-33 (D2) | 3 | 14.01.33 | **Nottingham Forest** (D2) | H | D | 2-2 | Amos, Vernon |
| | 3r | 18.01.33 | **Nottingham Forest** | A | W | 2-1 | Smith, Eagleston |
| | 4 | 28.01.33 | **Everton** (D1) | A | L | 1-3 | Vernon |
| 1933-34 (D2) | 3 | 13.01.34 | **Burnley** (D2) | A | D | 0-0 | |
| | 3r | 17.01.34 | **Burnley** | H | W | 3-2 | Vernon 2, Robbins |
| | 4 | 27.01.34 | **Swansea Town** (D2) | H | D | 1-1 | Robbie |
| | 4r | 01.02.34 | **Swansea Town** | A | L | 0-3 | |
| 1934-35 (D2) | 3 | 12.01.35 | **Bristol City** (3S) | A | D | 1-1 | Earl |
| | 3r | 16.01.35 | **Bristol City** | H | D | 2-2aet | Blyth, Robinson |
| | 32r | 21.01.35 | **Bristol City** | | L | 1-2 | Chalmers |
| | | | *played at Villa Park* | | | | |

| | | | | | | | | |
|---|---|---|---|---|---|---|---|---|
| 1935-36 | (D2) | 3 | 11.01.36 | **Darlington** (3N) | A | W | 3-2 | Jones, Chalmers 2 |
| | | 4 | 25.01.36 | **Leeds Utd** (D1) | A | - | 1-2ab | Buttery |
| | | | | *abandoned after 74 minutes – fog* | | | | |
| | | 4 | 28.01.36 | **Leeds Utd** | A | L | 2-3 | Matthews 2 |
| 1936-37 | (D2) | 3 | 16.01.37 | **QPR** (3S) | H | W | 1-0 | Graham |
| | | 4 | 30.01.37 | **Burnley** (D2) | A | L | 1-4 | Whitfield (p) |
| 1937-38 | (D2) | 3 | 08.01.38 | **Brighton** (3S) | H | W | 2-0 | Bargh, Davies |
| | | 4 | 22.01.38 | **Manchester City** (D1) | A | L | 1-3 | Acquroff |
| 1938-39 | (D2) | 3 | 07.01.39 | **Fulham** (D2) | A | L | 0-6 | |
| 1945-46 | (D2) | 3 1L | 05.01.46 | **Rochdale** (3N) | H | D | 3-3 | Halton 2, Davies |
| | | 3 2L | 08.01.46 | **Rochdale** | A | W | 4-2 | Tomkins, Jones, Moss, Davies |
| | | 4 1L | 26.01.46 | **Sunderland** (D1) | A | L | 1-3 | Davies, Roberts 3, Jones |
| | | 4 2L | 29.01.46 | **Sunderland** | H | W | 5-4aet | Davies, Roberts 3, Jones |
| 1946-47 | (D2) | 3 | 11.01.47 | **Southampton** (D2) | A | L | 1-5 | Halton (p) |
| 1947-48 | (D2) | 3 | 10.01.48 | **Leicester City** (D2) | A | L | 0-1 | |
| 1948-49 | (D2) | 3 | 08.01.49 | **Yeovil Town** (SL) | A | L | 1-3 | Massart |
| 1949-50 | (D2) | 3 | 07.01.50 | **Rotherham Utd** (3N) | H | W | 5-4 | Bardsley, Bellis, Whitworth 2, Massart |
| | | 4 | 28.01.50 | **Derby County** (D1) | H | D | 2-2 | Hazlett, Massart |
| | | 4r | 01.02.50 | **Derby County** | A | L | 2-5 | Bodie, Bellis |
| 1950-51 | (D2) | 3 | 06.01.51 | **Newcastle Utd** (D1) | A | L | 1-4 | W Griffiths (p) |
| 1951-52 | (D2) | 3 | 12.01.52 | **Rotherham Utd** (D2) | A | L | 1-2 | Bodie |
| 1952-53 | (D2) | 3 | 10.01.53 | **Grimsby Town** (3N) | A | W | 3-1 | Daniel, Fletcher, Imlach |
| | | 4 | 31.01.53 | **Arsenal** (D1) | A | L | 2-6 | Walton, Gleadall |
| 1953-54 | (D2) | 3 | 09.01.54 | **Chesterfield** (3N) | A | L | 0-2 | |
| 1954-55 | (D2) | 3 | 08.01.55 | **Stoke City** (D2) | H | D | 1-1aet | Daniel |
| | | 3r | 12.01.55 | **Stoke City** | A | - | 1-1ab | Daniel |
| | | | | *abandoned after 112 minutes – snowstorm* | | | | |
| | | 3 2r | 17.01.55 | **Stoke City** | | D | 3-3aet | Simm, Pearson, Tilley |
| | | | | *played at Goodison Park* | | | | |
| | | 3 3r | 19.01.55 | **Stoke City** | | D | 2-2aet | Kelly, Daniel |
| | | | | *played at Anfield* | | | | |
| | | 3 4r | 24.01.55 | **Stoke City** | | L | 2-3aet | Daniel 2 |
| | | | | *played at Old Trafford* | | | | |
| 1955-56 | (D2) | 3 | 07.01.56 | **Burnley** (D1) | H | - | 2-2ab | Neilson, Lawson |
| | | | | *abandoned after 65 minutes* | | | | |
| | | 3 | 10.01.56 | **Burnley** | H | L | 0-1 | |
| 1956-57 | (D2) | 3 | 05.01.57 | **Portsmouth** (D1) | H | L | 1-3 | Kelly |
| 1957-58 | (3N) | 1 | 16.11.57 | **Bishop Auckland** (NL) | A | D | 0-0 | |
| | | 1r | 19.11.57 | **Bishop Auckland** | H | W | 4-1 | Parker 2, Thursby og, Reid |
| | | 2 | 07.12.57 | **Scunthorpe Utd** (3N) | A | L | 0-2 | |
| 1958-59 | (D3) | 1 | 15.11.58 | **York City** (D4) | H | - | 0-0ab | |
| | | | | *abandoned after 60 minutes* | | | | |
| | | 1 | 18.11.58 | **York City** | H | W | 1-0 | Mercer |
| | | 2 | 06.12.58 | **Chester** (D4) | A | D | 1-1 | Parker |
| | | 2r | 09.12.58 | **Chester** | H | W | 2-1 | Watson, Lovie |
| | | 3 | 10.01.59 | **Arsenal** (D1) | H | L | 0-1 | |
| 1959-60 | (D3) | 1 | 14.11.59 | **Hartlepools Utd** (D4) | H | W | 5-0 | Hubbard, Holden, Watson, Jackson 2 |
| | | 2 | 05.12.59 | **Oldham Athletic** (D4) | H | W | 2-1 | Hubbard, Watson |
| | | 3 | 09.01.60 | **Bolton Wanderers** (D1) | H | D | 1-1 | Higgins og |
| | | 3r | 13.01.60 | **Bolton Wanderers** | A | L | 2-4aet | Calder, Watson |
| 1960-61 | (D3) | 1 | 05.11.60 | **Tranmere Rovers** (D3) | A | L | 0-1 | |
| 1961-62 | (D2) | 3 | 06.01.62 | **Sheffield Utd** (D1) | H | D | 0-0 | |
| | | 3r | 10.01.62 | **Sheffield Utd** | A | D | 2-2aet | Beaumont, Jones |
| | | 3 2r | 15.01.62 | **Sheffield Utd** | | L | 0-2 | |
| | | | | *played at Hillsborough* | | | | |
| 1962-63 | (D2) | 3 | 05.03.63 | **Birmingham City** (D1) | A | D | 3-3 | Griffin 2, Eastham |
| | | 3r | 07.03.63 | **Birmingham City** | H | W | 2-0 | Calder, Griffin |
| | | 4 | 13.03.63 | **Manchester City** (D1) | A | L | 0-1 | |
| 1963-64 | (D2) | 3 | 04.01.64 | **Yeovil Town** (SL) | A | W | 2-0 | Jones 2 |
| | | 4 | 25.01.64 | **Barnsley** (D3) | A | L | 1-2 | Bartley |
| 1964-65 | (D2) | 3 | 09.01.65 | **Crystal Palace** (D2) | A | L | 1-5 | Claxton |
| 1965-66 | (D2) | 3 | 22.01.66 | **Leeds Utd** (D1) | A | L | 0-6 | |

| | | | | | | | | |
|---|---|---|---|---|---|---|---|---|
| 1966-67 | (D2) | 3 | 28.01.67 | **Walsall** (D3) | H | W | 2-0 | Jones, Parry |
| | | 4 | 18.02.67 | **Swindon Town** (D3) | A | L | 1-2 | Lowes |
| 1967-68 | (D3) | 1 | 09.12.67 | **Hartlepools Utd** (D4) | A | W | 3-2 | Jones, Lindsay, Drysdale og |
| | | 2 | 06.01.68 | **Bradford City** (D4) | A | W | 3-2 | Owen, Collins, Farrell |
| | | 3 | 27.01.68 | **Orient** (D3) | A | L | 0-1 | |
| 1968-69 | (D2) | 3 | 04.01.69 | **Huddersfield Town** (D2) | H | L | 1-2 | Jones |
| 1969-70 | (D3) | 1 | 15.11.69 | **Mansfield Town** (D3) | H | D | 2-2 | Kerr 2 (1p) |
| | | 1r | 19.11.69 | **Mansfield Town** | A | L | 0-2 | |
| 1970-71 | (D3) | 1 | 21.11.70 | **Grimsby Town** (D4) | A | W | 1-0 | White |
| | | 2 | 12.12.70 | **Notts County** (D4) | H | D | 1-1 | Jones |
| | | 2r | 21.12.70 | **Notts County** | A | L | 0-3 | |
| 1971-72 | (D4) | 1 | 20.11.71 | **Lincoln City** (D4) | A | W | 2-1 | Jones 2 |
| | | 2 | 11.12.71 | **Workington** (D4) | A | W | 3-1 | McDermott, Murray, Jones |
| | | 3 | 15.01.72 | **Rotherham Utd** (D3) | H | D | 1-1 | Connelly |
| | | 3r | 19.01.72 | **Rotherham Utd** | A | L | 1-2 | Murray |
| 1972-73 | (D4) | 1 | 18.11.72 | **Doncaster Rovers** (D4) | A | L | 1-3 | Robson |
| 1973-74 | (D4) | 1 | 24.11.73 | **Tranmere Rovers** (D3) | A | L | 1-2 | Spence |
| 1974-75 | (D3) | 1 | 23.11.74 | **Southport** (D4) | H | W | 4-2 | Spence 2, Duffey 2 |
| | | 2 | 14.12.74 | **Grimsby Town** (D3) | A | D | 1-1 | Duffey |
| | | 2r | 17.12.74 | **Grimsby Town** | H | W | 2-1 | Spence, Duffey |
| | | 3 | 04.01.75 | **Millwall** (D2) | H | D | 2-2 | Hamstead, Williams |
| | | 3r | 07.01.75 | **Millwall** | A | D | 1-1aet | Thomson |
| | | 32r | 13.01.75 | **Millwall** | | W | 2-0 | Riley, Duffey |
| | | | | *played at The Hawthorns* | | | | |
| | | 4 | 25.01.75 | **Mansfield Town** (D4) | H | L | 1-2 | Hamstead |
| 1975-76 | (D3) | 1 | 22.11.75 | **Doncaster Rovers** (D4) | H | W | 4-3 | Riley, Hamstead, Rowland 2 |
| | | 2 | 13.12.75 | **Spennymoor Utd** (NL) | H | W | 3-0 | Kennedy, Buchan, Adams og |
| | | 3 | 03.01.76 | **Middlesbrough** (D1) | A | D | 0-0 | |
| | | 3r | 06.01.76 | **Middlesbrough** | H | W | 3-2 | McIlwraith, Hulme, Rowland |
| | | 4 | 24.01.76 | **Leicester City** (D1) | A | L | 0-1 | |
| 1976-77 | (D3) | 1 | 20.11.76 | **Workington** (D4) | H | W | 6-0 | Woolfall 2, Rowlands, Phillips, McIlwraith, Hatton |
| | | 2 | 14.12.76 | **Shrewsbury Town** (D3) | H | D | 0-0 | |
| | | 2r | 21.12.76 | **Shrewsbury Town** | A | L | 1-2 | Phillips |
| 1977-78 | (D3) | 1 | 26.11.77 | **Sheffield Wed** (D3) | A | L | 0-1 | |
| 1978-79 | (D3) | 1 | 25.11.78 | **Wigan Athletic** (D4) | A | D | 2-2 | Gregory, Brown og |
| | | 1r | 28.11.78 | **Wigan Athletic** | H | W | 4-1 | Gregory 2, Kennedy, Wilson (p) |
| | | 2 | 16.12.78 | **Blackpool** (D3) | H | W | 3-1 | Lugg, Gregory 2 |
| | | 3 | 09.01.79 | **Orient** (D2) | A | L | 2-3 | Gregory, Beamish |
| 1979-80 | (D3) | 1 | 24.11.79 | **Burton Albion** (NPL) | A | W | 2-0 | Madden, Hilton |
| | | 2 | 15.12.79 | **York City** (D4) | H | D | 0-0 | |
| | | 2r | 18.12.79 | **York City** | A | W | 2-0 | Hilton, Madden |
| | | 3 | 08.01.80 | **Rochdale** (D4) | A | D | 1-1 | Whitehead |
| | | 3r | 21.01.80 | **Rochdale** | H | W | 3-2 | Johnson 2, Wilson |
| | | 4 | 26.01.80 | **Burnley** (D2) | H | W | 1-0 | Whitehead |
| | | 5 | 16.02.80 | **Liverpool** (D1) | A | L | 0-2 | |
| 1980-81 | (D4) | 1 | 22.11.80 | **Darlington** (D4) | A | W | 2-0 | Jakub, Butler |
| | | 2 | 13.12.80 | **Lincoln City** (D4) | H | W | 2-0 | Hilton, Mullen |
| | | 3 | 03.01.81 | **Fulham** (D3) | H | D | 1-1 | Hilton |
| | | 3r | 06.01.81 | **Fulham** | A | D | 0-0aet | |
| | | 32r | 12.01.81 | **Fulham** | | L | 0-1 | |
| | | | | *played at The Hawthorns* | | | | |
| 1981-82 | (D4) | 1 | 21.11.81 | **Tranmere Rovers** (D4) | A | D | 1-1 | Madden |
| | | 1r | 24.11.81 | **Tranmere Rovers** | H | W | 3-1 | Madden 2, Johnson |
| | | 2 | 02.01.82 | **Burnley** (D3) | H | D | 1-1 | Madden |
| | | 2r | 04.01.82 | **Burnley** | A | L | 1-2aet | Johnson |
| 1982-83 | (D4) | 1 | 20.11.82 | **York City** (D4) | A | L | 1-3 | Hilton |
| 1983-84 | (D4) | 1 | 19.11.83 | **Boston Utd** (APL) | A | W | 3-0 | Entwistle 2, Madden |
| | | 2 | 10.12.83 | **Scunthorpe Utd** (D3) | A | L | 0-2 | |
| 1984-85 | (D4) | 1 | 17.11.84 | **Preston North End** (D3) | A | L | 3-4 | Entwistle, Madden, Ross |
| 1985-86 | (D3) | 1 | 16.11.85 | **Chester City** (D4) | H | W | 2-0 | Young, Kerr |

| | | | | | | | | |
|---|---|---|---|---|---|---|---|---|
| | | 2 | 07.12.85 | **Tranmere Rovers** (D4) | A | D | 1-1 | Madden |
| | | 2r | 10.12.85 | **Tranmere Rovers** | H | W | 2-1 | Valentine, Ross (p) |
| | | 3 | 13.01.86 | **Barnsley** (D2) | H | W | 2-0 | Owen, Jakub |
| | | 4 | 25.01.86 | **Reading** (D3) | A | D | 1-1 | Young |
| | | 4r | 28.01.86 | **Reading** | H | W | 3-0 | Madden 2, Dixon |
| | | 5 | 05.03.86 | **Watford** (D1) | A | D | 1-1 | Bramhall |
| | | 5r | 08.03.86 | **Watford** | H | L | 0-3 | |
| 1986-87 | (D3) | 1 | 15.11.86 | **Preston North End** (D4) | A | L | 1-5 | Flynn |
| 1987-88 | (D3) | 1 | 14.11.87 | **Scunthorpe Utd** (D4) | A | L | 1-3 | McIlroy |
| 1988-89 | (D3) | 1 | 19.11.88 | **Guisborough Town** (NL) | A | W | 1-0 | Parkinson |
| | | | | *played at Ayresome Park* | | | | |
| | | 2 | 10.12.88 | **Blackpool** (D3) | A | L | 0-3 | |
| 1989-90 | (D3) | 1 | 18.11.89 | **Rotherham Utd** (D3) | A | D | 0-0 | |
| | | 1r | 21.11.89 | **Rotherham Utd** | H | L | 1-2 | Bishop |
| 1990-91 | (D3) | 1 | 17.11.90 | **Chorley** (NPL) | A | L | 1-2 | Mauge |
| 1991-92 | (D3) | 1 | 16.11.91 | **Bradford City** (D3) | H | L | 0-1 | |
| 1992-93 | (D3) | 1 | 14.11.92 | **Witton Albion** (Conf) | H | W | 2-0 | Knill (p), Robinson (p) |
| | | 2 | 02.01.93 | **Wigan Athletic** (D2) | H | W | 1-0 | Mauge |
| | | 3 | 05.01.93 | **Manchester Utd** (PL) | A | L | 0-2 | |
| 1993-94 | (D3) | 1 | 13.11.93 | **Scarborough** (D3) | A | L | 0-1 | |
| 1994-95 | (D3) | 1 | 12.11.94 | **Bishop Auckland** (NPL) | A | D | 0-0 | |
| | | 1r | 22.11.94 | **Bishop Auckland** | H | D | 1-1aet | Paskin |
| | | | | *Bury won 4-2 on penalties* | | | | |
| | | 2 | 03.12.94 | **Crewe Alexandra** (D2) | A | W | 2-1 | Johnrose, Rigby |
| | | 3 | 07.01.95 | **Tranmere Rovers** (D1) | H | D | 2-2 | Lucketti, Stanislaus |
| | | 3r | 18.01.95 | **Tranmere Rovers** | A | L | 0-3 | |
| 1995-96 | (D3) | 1 | 11.11.95 | **Blyth Spartans** (NPL) | H | L | 0-2 | |
| 1996-97 | (D2) | 1 | 16.11.96 | **Chesterfield** (D2) | A | L | 0-1 | |
| 1997-98 | (D1) | 3 | 03.01.98 | **Sheffield Utd** (D1) | A | D | 1-1 | Andy Gray |
| | | 3r | 13.01.98 | **Sheffield Utd** | H | L | 1-2 | Andy Gray |
| 1998-99 | (D1) | 3 | 02.01.99 | **Stockport County** (D1) | H | L | 0-3 | |
| 1999-00 | (D2) | 1 | 30.10.99 | **Tamworth** (SL) | A | D | 2-2 | Bullock, Liitlejohn |
| | | 1r | 09.11.99 | **Tamworth** | H | W | 2-1aet | Billy, James |
| | | 2 | 20.11.99 | **Cardiff City** (D2) | H | D | 0-0 | |
| | | 2r | 30.11.99 | **Cardiff City** | A | L | 0-1 | |
| 2000-01 | (D2) | 1 | 18.11.00 | **Northwich V** (Conf) | H | D | 1-1 | Daws |
| | | 1r | 28.11.00 | **Northwich V** | A | L | 0-1 | |
| 2001-02 | (D2) | 1 | 17.11.01 | **Lincoln City** (D3) | A | D | 1-1 | Seddon |
| | | 1r | 27.11.01 | **Lincoln City** | H | D | 1-1aet | Singh |
| | | | | *Lincoln City won 3-2 on penalties* | | | | |
| 2002-03 | (D3) | 1 | 16.11.02 | **Plymouth Argyle** (D2) | H | L | 0-3 | |

## BURY TOWN

*Formed 1872. First entered FA Cup 1899-1900 as Bury St Edmunds. Members of the Eastern Counties League.*

| | | | | | | | | |
|---|---|---|---|---|---|---|---|---|
| 1968-69 | (Met) | 1 | 16.11.68 | **Bournemouth** (D3) | H | D | 0-0 | |
| | | 1r | 20.11.68 | **Bournemouth** | A | L | 0-3 | |

## BUXTON

*Formed 1877. First entered FA Cup: 1891-92. Members of the Northern Counties East League.*

| | | | | | | | | |
|---|---|---|---|---|---|---|---|---|
| 1951-52 | (CC) | 1 | 24.11.51 | **Rawmarsh Welfare** (SAL) | A | W | 4-1 | Machin 3, Crossley |
| | | 2 | 15.12.51 | **Aldershot** (3S) | H | W | 4-3 | Carter, Tomlinson, Machent, White |
| | | 3 | 12.01.52 | **Doncaster Rovers** (D2) | A | L | 0-2 | |
| 1958-59 | (CC) | 1 | 15.11.58 | **Crook Town** (NL) | H | W | 4-1 | Calderbank 2, Duggins 2 |
| | | 2 | 06.12.58 | **Accrington Stanley** (D3) | A | L | 1-6 | Duggins |
| 1962-63 | (CC) | 1 | 03.11.62 | **Barrow** (D4) | H | D | 2-2 | Farmer, Robinson og |
| | | 1r | 05.11.62 | **Barrow** | A | L | 1-3 | Riley |

## CAERNARFON TOWN

*Formed 1876 as Caernarfon Athletic. First entered FA Cup: 1929-30 as Caernarfon Athletic. League clubs beaten: Darlington, Stockport County, York City. Members of the League of Wales.*

| | | | | | | | | |
|---|---|---|---|---|---|---|---|---|
| 1929-30 | (Welsh) | 1 | 30.11.29 | **Darlington** (3N) | H | W | 4-2 | Smith 2, Taylor, Sutton |
| | | 2 | 14.12.29 | **Bournemouth** (3S) | H | D | 1-1 | Smith |
| | | 2r | 18.12.29 | **Bournemouth** | A | L | 2-5 | Smith, Murray |

| | | | | | | | | |
|---|---|---|---|---|---|---|---|---|
| 1986-87 | (NPL) | 1 | 15.11.86 | **Stockport County** (D4) | H | W | 1-0 | Salmon |
| | | 2 | 06.12.86 | **York City** (D3) | H | D | 0-0 | |
| | | 2r | 09.12.86 | **York City** | A | W | 2-1 | Salmon, Craven |
| | | 3 | 10.01.87 | **Barnsley** (D2) | H | D | 0-0 | |
| | | 3r | 26.01.87 | **Barnsley** | A | L | 0-1 | |

# CAERNARFON WANDERERS

*Formed 1885. Home ground was Bryn Sciont and the players used the Eagles Hotel as changing rooms.*

| | | | | | | | |
|---|---|---|---|---|---|---|---|
| 1886-87 | 1 | 30.10.86 | **Stoke** | A | L | 1-10 | |

# CAIUS COLLEGE, CAMBRIDGE

*Caius twice entered the FA Cup after Cambridge University had decided not to compete any further, but they scratched both times.*

| | | | | |
|---|---|---|---|---|
| 1880-81 | 1 | | Nottingham Forest | - |
| | | | *Caius College scratched. Nottingham Forest walkover* | |
| 1881-82 | 1 | | Dreadnought FC | - |
| | | | *Caius College scratched. Dreadnought walkover* | |

# CAMBERLEY TOWN

*Formed: 1896 as Camberley & Yorktown. Camberley FC 1946-47. Camberley Town from 1947. First entered FA Cup as Camberley & Yorktown: 1913-14. Members of the Isthmian League.*

| | | | | | | | | |
|---|---|---|---|---|---|---|---|---|
| 1998-99 | (IL) | 1 | 14.11.98 | **Brentford** (D3) | A | L | 0-5 | |

# CAMBRIDGE CITY

*Formed 1908 as Cambridge Town. 1951 Cambridge City. First entered FA Cup as Cambridge Town 1913-14. Members of the Southern League.*

**as Cambridge Town**

| | | | | | | | | |
|---|---|---|---|---|---|---|---|---|
| 1946-47 | (SPT) | 1 | 30.11.46 | **Swindon Town** (3S) | A | L | 1-4 | Wood |
| 1948-49 | (SPT) | 1 | 27.11.48 | **Walthamstow A** (IL) | A | L | 2-3 | Chapman, Ferguson |

**as Cambridge City**

| | | | | | | | | |
|---|---|---|---|---|---|---|---|---|
| 1966-67 | (SL) | 1 | 26.11.66 | **Ashford Town** (SL) | A | L | 1-4 | McVittie |
| 1993-94 | (SL) | 1 | 14.11.93 | **Hereford Utd** (D3) | H | L | 0-1 | |
| 1999-00 | (SL) | 1 | 30.10.99 | **Wigan Athletic** (D2) | H | L | 0-2 | |
| 2001-02 | (SL) | 1 | 17.11.01 | **Exeter City** (D3) | H | L | 0-3 | |

# CAMBRIDGE UNITED

*Formed 1919 as Abbey United. 1951 Cambridge United. First entered FA Cup: 1926-27; Best FA Cup Performances: 6th round, 1990, 1991; Record FA Cup record win: 10-0 v Potton Utd, 4th qualifying round, 04.10.1969. Record FA Cup defeat: (as Abbey Utd) 0-8 v Cambridge Town, 1st qualifying round, 1945-46; 0-8 v Wisbech Town, preliminary round replay 1949-50; In Competition Proper: 1-5 v AFC Bournemouth, 1st round, 18.11.1972; League club beaten as a Non-League club: Newport County.*

| | | | | | | | | |
|---|---|---|---|---|---|---|---|---|
| 1953-54 | (ECL) | 1 | 21.11.53 | **Newport County** (3S) | H | D | 2-2 | Stevens, Crowe |
| | | 1r | 26.11.53 | **Newport County** | A | W | 2-1 | Saward, Stevens |
| | | 2 | 12.12.53 | **Bradford Park A** (3N) | H | L | 1-2 | Whittaker (p) |
| 1954-55 | (ECL) | 1 | 20.11.54 | **Torquay Utd** (3S) | A | L | 0-4 | |
| 1962-62 | (SL) | 1 | 03.11.62 | **Bedford Town** (SL) | A | L | 1-2 | Howell |
| 1963-64 | (SL) | 1 | 16.11.63 | **Chelmsford City** (SL) | H | L | 0-1 | |
| 1964-65 | (SL) | 1 | 14.11.64 | **Barnet** (AL) | A | L | 1-2 | Day |
| 1970-71 | (D4) | 1 | 21.11.70 | **Enfield** (IL) | A | W | 1-0 | Hollett |
| | | 2 | 12.12.70 | **Colchester Utd** (D4) | A | L | 0-3 | |
| 1971-72 | (D4) | 1 | 20.11.71 | **Weymouth** (SL) | H | W | 2-1 | Collins, Hollett |
| | | 2 | 11.12.71 | **Bristol Rovers** (D3) | A | L | 0-3 | |
| 1972-73 | (D4) | 1 | 18.11.72 | **Bournemouth** (D3) | A | L | 1-5 | Collins |
| 1973-74 | (D3) | 1 | 24.11.73 | **Gillingham** (D4) | H | W | 3-2 | Simmons 3 |
| | | 2 | 15.12.73 | **Aldershot** (D3) | A | W | 2-1 | Simmons 2 |
| | | 3 | 06.01.74 | **Oldham Athletic** (D3) | H | D | 2-2 | Wood og, Eades |
| | | 3r | 08.01.74 | **Oldham Athletic** | A | D | 3-3aet | Ferguson, Simmons, Watson |
| | | 3 2r | 14.01.74 | **Oldham Athletic** | | L | 1-2 | Simmons |
| | | | | *played at City Ground, Nottingham* | | | | |
| 1974-75 | (D4) | 1 | 23.11.74 | **Hitchin Town** (IL) | A | D | 0-0 | |
| | | 1r | 26.11.74 | **Hitchin Town** | H | W | 3-0 | Cassidy 2, Shinton |
| | | 2 | 14.12.74 | **Hereford Utd** (D3) | H | W | 2-0 | Watson 2 |
| | | 3 | 04.01.75 | **Mansfield Town** (D4) | A | L | 0-1 | |

| | | | | | | | |
|---|---|---|---|---|---|---|---|
| 1975-76 (D3) | 1 | 22.11.75 | **Leatherhead** (IL) | A | L | 0-2 | |
| 1976-77 (D4) | 1 | 20.11.76 | **Colchester Utd** (D4) | H | D | 1-1 | Fallon |
| | 1r | 24.11.76 | **Colchester Utd** | A | L | 0-2 | |
| 1977-78 (D3) | 1 | 26.11.77 | **Lowestoft Town** (ECL) | A | W | 2-0 | Biley 2 |
| | 2 | 17.12.77 | **Plymouth Argyle** (D3) | A | L | 0-1 | |
| 1978-79 (D2) | 3 | 06.01.79 | **Shrewsbury Town** (D3) | A | L | 1-3 | Biley |
| 1979-80 (D2) | 3 | 05.01.80 | **Chesham Utd** (IL) | A | W | 2-0 | Gibbins, Reilly |
| | 4 | 26.01.80 | **Aston Villa** (D1) | H | D | 1-1 | Turner |
| | 4r | 30.01.80 | **Aston Villa** | A | L | 1-4 | Spriggs |
| 1980-81 (D2) | 3 | 03.01.81 | **Norwich City** (D1) | A | L | 0-1 | |
| 1981-82 (D2) | 3 | 02.01.82 | **Doncaster Rovers** (D3) | A | L | 1-2 | Taylor |
| 1982-83 (D2) | 3 | 08.01.83 | **Weymouth** (APL) | H | W | 1-0 | Reilly |
| | 4 | 29.01.83 | **Barnsley** (D2) | H | W | 1-0 | Mayo |
| | 5 | 19.02.83 | **Sheffield Wed** (D2) | H | L | 1-2 | Turner |
| 1983-84 (D2) | 3 | 07.01.84 | **Derby County** (D2) | H | L | 0-3 | |
| 1984-85 (D3) | 1 | 17.11.84 | **Peterborough Utd** (D4) | H | L | 0-2 | |
| 1985-86 (D4) | 1 | 16.11.85 | **Dagenham** (APL) | A | L | 1-2 | Crown |
| 1986-87 (D4) | 1 | 15.11.86 | **Exeter City** (D4) | A | D | 1-1 | Crown |
| | 1r | 19.11.86 | **Exeter City** | H | W | 2-0 | Dowman, Biley |
| | 2 | 07.12.86 | **Maidstone Utd** (Conf) | A | L | 0-1 | |
| 1987-88 (D4) | 1 | 14.11.87 | **Farnborough T** (IL) | H | W | 2-1 | Beattie, Benjamin |
| | 2 | 05.12.87 | **Yeovil Town** (IL) | H | L | 0-1 | |
| 1988-89 (D4) | 1 | 19.11.88 | **Woking** (IL) | A | W | 4-1 | Reilly 2, Croft 2 |
| | 2 | 10.12.88 | **Bognor Regis Town** (IL) | A | W | 1-0 | Chapple |
| | 3 | 07.01.89 | **Plymouth Argyle** (D2) | A | L | 0-2 | |
| 1989-90 (D4) | 1 | 18.11.89 | **Aldershot** (D4) | A | W | 1-0 | Taylor |
| | 2 | 09.12.89 | **Woking** (IL) | H | W | 3-1 | Cheetham, Leadbitter, Taylor |
| | 3 | 06.01.90 | **Darlington** (Conf) | H | D | 0-0 | |
| | 3r | 09.01.90 | **Darlington** | A | W | 3-1 | Taylor, Philpott, Dublin |
| | 4 | 27.01.90 | **Millwall** (D1) | A | D | 1-1 | Taylor |
| | 4r | 30.01.90 | **Millwall** | H | W | 1-0aet | Thompson og |
| | 5 | 17.02.90 | **Bristol City** (D3) | A | D | 0-0 | |
| | 5r | 21.02.90 | **Bristol City** | H | D | 1-1aet | Dublin |
| | 5 2r | 27.02.90 | **Bristol City** | H | W | 5-1 | Leadbitter, Philpott, Dublin 2, Taylor |
| | 6 | 10.03.90 | **Crystal Palace** (D1) | H | L | 0-1 | |
| 1990-91 (D3) | 1 | 17.11.90 | **Exeter City** (D3) | A | W | 2-1 | Taylor 2 |
| | 2 | 07.12.90 | **Fulham** (D3) | A | D | 0-0 | |
| | 2r | 11.12.90 | **Fulham** | H | W | 2-1 | Kimble (p), Dublin |
| | 3 | 05.01.91 | **Wolverhampton W** (D2) | A | W | 1-0 | Leadbitter |
| | 4 | 26.01.91 | **Middlesbrough** (D2) | H | W | 2-0 | Taylor 2 |
| | 5 | 16.02.91 | **Sheffield Wed** (D2) | H | W | 4-0 | Dublin 2, Philpott, Taylor |
| | 6 | 09.03.91 | **Arsenal** (D1) | A | L | 1-2 | Dublin |
| 1991-92 (D2) | 3 | 04.01.92 | **Coventry City** (D1) | A | D | 1-1 | Dublin |
| | 3r | 14.01.92 | **Coventry City** | H | W | 1-0 | Hurst og |
| | 4 | 25.01.92 | **Swindon Town** (D2) | H | L | 0-3 | |
| 1992-93 (D1) | 3 | 13.01.93 | **Sheffield Wed** (PL) | H | L | 1-2 | Heathcote |
| 1993-94 (D2) | 1 | 13.11.93 | **Reading** (D2) | H | D | 0-0 | |
| | 1r | 24.11.93 | **Reading** | A | W | 2-1 | Nyamah, Heathcote |
| | 2 | 04.12.93 | **Wycombe W** (D3) | A | L | 0-1 | |
| 1994-95 (D2) | 1 | 12.11.94 | **Brentford** (D2) | H | D | 2-2 | Lillis, Butler |
| | 1r | 22.11.94 | **Brentford** | A | W | 2-1 | Lillis, Butler (p) |
| | 2 | 03.12.94 | **Peterborough Utd** (D2) | A | W | 2-0 | Barrick, Hay |
| | 3 | 07.01.95 | **Burnley** (D1) | H | L | 2-4 | Butler 2(1p) |
| 1995-96 (D3) | 1 | 11.11.95 | **Swindon Town** (D2) | A | L | 1-4 | Butler |
| 1996-97 (D3) | 1 | 16.11.96 | **Welling Utd** (Conf) | H | W | 3-0 | Beall, Kyd, Barnwell-Edinboro |
| | 2 | 07.12.96 | **Woking** (Conf) | H | L | 0-2 | |
| 1997-98 (D3) | 1 | 15.11.97 | **Plymouth Argyle** (D2) | A | D | 0-0 | |
| | 1r | 25.11.97 | **Plymouth Argyle** | H | W | 3-2aet | Beall, T Benjamin, Wilson (p) |
| | 2 | 06.12.97 | **Stevenage B** (Conf) | H | D | 1-1 | Butler |
| | 2r | 15.12.97 | **Stevenage B** | A | L | 1-2 | Butler |
| 1998-99 (D3) | 1 | 14.11.98 | **Telford Utd** (Conf) | A | W | 2-0 | T Benjamin, Butler |

| | | | | | | | |
|---|---|---|---|---|---|---|---|
| | 2 | 05.12.98 | **Macclesfield T** (D2) | A | L | 1-4 | Campbell |
| 1999-00 (D2) | 1 | 30.10.99 | **Gateshead** (NPL) | H | W | 1-0 | Taylor |
| | 2 | 20.11.99 | **Bamber Bridge** (NPL) | H | W | 1-0 | Butler (p) |
| | 3 | 10.12.99 | **Crystal Palace** (D1) | H | W | 2-0 | T Benjamin, Wanless |
| | 4 | 08.01.00 | **Wrexham** (D2) | A | W | 2-1 | T Benjamin, Butler |
| | 5 | 29.01.00 | **Bolton Wanderers** (D1) | H | L | 1-3 | T Benjamin |
| 2000-01 (D2) | 1 | 18.11.00 | **Rochdale** (D3) | H | W | 2-1 | Axeldal, Hansen |
| | 2 | 09.12.00 | **Morecambe** (Conf) | A | L | 1-2 | Youngs |
| 2001-02 (D3) | 1 | 17.11.01 | **Notts County** (D2) | H | D | 1-1 | Tudor |
| | 1r | 27.11.01 | **Notts County** | A | L | 0-2 | |
| 2002-03 (D3) | 1 | 16.11.02 | **Scarborough** (Conf) | A | D | 0-0 | |
| | 1r | 26.11.02 | **Scarborough** | H | W | 2-1aet | Wanless, Hotte og |
| | 2 | 07.12.02 | **Northampton Town** (D2) | H | D | 2-2 | Tann 2 |
| | 2r | 17.12.02 | **Northampton Town** | A | W | 1-0 | O Riza |
| | 3 | 04.01.03 | **Millwall** (D1) | H | D | 1-1 | Youngs |
| | 3r | 14.01.03 | **Millwall** | A | L | 2-3 | Kitson, Youngs |

# CAMBRIDGE UNIVERSITY

*Forms of football had been played at Cambridge University for many years before 'The Cambridge Rules', the first codified laws of the game were drafted in 1848. There might have been a 'varsity' FA Cup final in 1877 when both Oxford and Cambridge reached the semi-finals. Oxford were given a bye to the final, but Cambridge lost to Wanderers in their semi and the chance was gone. Entered FA Cup: 1873-74 – 1879-80.*

| | | | | | | | |
|---|---|---|---|---|---|---|---|
| 1873-74 | 1 | 25.10.73 | **South Norwood** | H | W | 1-0 | Hurrell |
| | 2 | 15.11.73 | **Clapham Rovers** | A | D | 1-1 | |
| | 2r | 29.11.73 | **Clapham Rovers** | H | D | 1-1 | Mitford |
| | 2 2r | 20.12.73 | **Clapham Rovers** | H | L | 1-4 | Roberts |
| 1874-75 | 1 | 14.11.74 | **Crystal Palace (1861)** | A | D | 0-0 | |
| | 1r | 21.11.74 | **Crystal Palace (1861)** | H | W | 2-1 | Simpson, AN Other |
| | 2 | 05.12.74 | **Royal Engineers** | H | L | 0-5 | |
| 1875-76 | 1 | | Civil Service | | | - | |
| | | | *Civil Service scratched. Cambridge walkover* | | | | |
| | 2 | 11.12.75 | **Reigate Priory** | A | W | 8-0 | Cole 4, Roffey 2, Sparham, Steel |
| | 3 | 31.01.76 | **Oxford University** | H | L | 0-4 | |
| 1876-77 | 1 | | High Wycombe | | | - | |
| | | | *High Wycombe scratched. Cambridge walkover* | | | | |
| | 2 | 16.12.76 | **Clapham Rovers** | H | W | 2-1 | Hughes, AN Other |
| | 3 | 03.02.77 | **Rochester** | H | W | 4-0 | Hughes 2, Prior, Widnell |
| | 4 | 17.02.77 | **Royal Engineers** | H | W | 1-0 | Hargreaves |
| | SF | 20.03.77 | **Wanderers** | | L | 0-1 | |
| | | | *played at Kennington Oval* | | | | |
| 1877-78 | 1 | 02.11.77 | **Southall Park** | H | W | 3-1 | Churchill 2, A Lyttleton |
| | 2 | 08.12.77 | **Maidenhead** | H | W | 4-2aet | Jarvis, Steel, Styan, Wild |
| | 3 | 02.02.78 | **Old Harrovians** | A | D | 2-2 | Hill, Styan |
| | 3r | 09.02.78 | **Old Harrovians** | H | D | 2-2aet | Steel, Styan |
| | 3 2r | 16.02.78 | **Old Harrovians** | | L | 0-2 | |
| 1878-79 | 1 | 09.11.78 | **Herts Rangers** | H | W | 2-0 | Harvey, Wild |
| | 2 | 04.12.78 | **South Norwood** | H | W | 3-0 | Jarvis, Martin, Wild |
| | 3 | 02.02.79 | **Clapham Rovers** | A | L | 0-1aet | |
| 1879-80 | 1 | 13.11.79 | **Royal Engineers** | A | L | 0-2 | |

# CANNON FC

| | | | | | | | |
|---|---|---|---|---|---|---|---|
| 1886-87 | 1 | | Old Foresters | | | - | |
| | | | *Cannon scratched. Old Foresters walkover* | | | | |

# CANTERBURY CITY

*Formed 1947. First entered FA Cup: 1948-49.*

| | | | | | | | |
|---|---|---|---|---|---|---|---|
| 1964-65 (SL) | 1 | 14.11.64 | **Torquay Utd** (D4) | H | L | 0-6 | |
| 1968-69 (SL) | 1 | 16.11.68 | **Swindon Town** (D3) | A | L | 0-1 | |

# CANVEY ISLAND

*Formed 1926. First entered FA Cup: 1969-70. FA Trophy winners: 2001. League clubs beaten: Port Vale, Wigan Athletic, Northampton Town. Members of the Isthmian League.*

| | | | | | | | |
|---|---|---|---|---|---|---|---|
| 1995-96 (IL) | 1 | 12.11.95 | **Brighton** (D2) | H | D | 2-2 | Porter, Brett |
| | 1r | 21.11.95 | **Brighton** | A | L | 1-4 | Pennyfather |
| 2000-01 (IL) | 1 | 19.11.00 | **Port Vale** (D2) | H | D | 4-4 | Smith, Tilson (p), Jones, Vaughan |
| | 1r | 28.11.00 | **Port Vale** | A | W | 2-1aet | Gregory, Vaughan |
| | 2 | 10.12.00 | **Southend Utd** (D3) | H | L | 1-2 | Vaughan |
| | | | *played at Southend* | | | | |
| 2001-02 (IL) | 1 | 17.11.01 | **Wigan Athletic** (D2) | A | W | 1-0 | Gregory |
| | 2 | 09.12.01 | **Northampton Town** (D2) | H | W | 1-0 | Gregory |
| | 3 | 05.01.02 | **Burnley** (D1) | A | L | 1-4 | Boylan |

# CARDIFF CITY

*Formed 1899 as Riverside FC. Cardiff City 1908. First entered FA Cup 1910-11. FA Cup winners: 1927 (Only occasion the FA Cup has been won by a club from outside England). FA Cup runners-up: 1925. Welsh FA Cup winners: 22 times. Record FA Cup win: 8-0 v Enfield, 28.11.1931. Record FA Cup defeat: 1-6 v Aston Villa, 3rd round,.12.01.1929*

| | | | | | | | |
|---|---|---|---|---|---|---|---|
| 1910-11 (SL) | | | 1q Merthyr Town (H) 0-1 | | | | |
| 1911-12 (SL) | | | P Cardiff Corinthians (H) 3-0; 1q Mardy (H) 2-0; 2q Merthyr Town (A) 1-1; 2qr Merthyr Town (H) 1-2 | | | | |
| 1912-13 (SL) | | | 1q Merthyr Town (A) 5-1; 2q Pontypridd (H) 2-1; 3q Llanelli (A) 4-1; 4q Exeter (H) 5-1; 5q Southend U (H) 0-3 | | | | |
| 1913-14 (SL) | | | 4q Swansea Town (A) 0-2 | | | | |
| 1914-15 (SL) | 1 | 09.01.15 | **Bristol City** (D2) | A | L | 0-2 | |
| 1919-20 (SL) | 1 | 10.01. | **Oldham Athletic** (D1) | H | W | 2-0 | West, J Evans |
| | 2 | 31.01. | **Wolverhampton W** (D2) | A | W | 2-1 | Smith, Beare |
| | 3 | 21.02. | **Bristol City** (D2) | A | L | 1-2 | Beare |
| 1920-21 (D2) | 1 | 08.01.21 | **Sunderland** (D1) | A | W | 1-0 | Beare |
| | 2 | 29.01.21 | **Brighton** (D3) | A | D | 0-0 | |
| | 2r | 02.02.21 | **Brighton** | H | W | 1-0 | Cashmore |
| | 3 | 19.02.21 | **Southampton** (D3) | A | W | 1-0 | Gill |
| | 4 | 05.03.21 | **Chelsea** (D1) | H | W | 1-0 | Cashmore |
| | SF | 19.03.21 | **Wolverhampton W** (D2) | | D | 0-0 | |
| | | | *played at Anfield* | | | | |
| | SFr | 23.03.21 | **Wolverhampton W** | | L | 1-3 | Keenor (p) |
| | | | *played at Old Trafford* | | | | |
| 1921-22 (D1) | 1 | 07.01.22 | **Manchester Utd** (D1) | A | W | 4-1 | L Davies, Nash, Clennell |
| | 2 | 28.01.22 | **Southampton** (3S) | A | D | 1-1 | Gill |
| | 2r | 01.02.22 | **Southampton** | H | W | 2-0 | Gill, Clennell |
| | 3 | 18.02.22 | **Nottingham Forest** (D2) | H | W | 4-1 | L Davies 2, Gill, Clennell |
| | 4 | 04.03.22 | **Tottenham Hotspur** (D1) | H | D | 1-1 | L Davies |
| | 4r | 09.03.22 | **Tottenham Hotspur** | A | L | 1-2 | Gill |
| 1922-23 (D1) | 1 | 13.01.23 | **Watford** (3S) | H | D | 1-1 | J Evans |
| | 1r | 17.01.23 | **Watford** | A | D | 2-2 | L Davies, Clennell |
| | 1 2r | 22.01.23 | **Watford** | | W | 2-1 | L Davies, H Evans |
| | | | *played at Villa Park* | | | | |
| | 2 | 03.02.23 | **Leicester City** (D2) | A | W | 1-0 | L Davies |
| | 3 | 24.02.23 | **Tottenham Hotspur** (D1) | H | L | 2-3 | J Evans (p), Gill |
| 1923-24 (D1) | 1 | 12.01.24 | **Gillingham** (3S) | H | D | 0-0 | |
| | 1r | 16.01.24 | **Gillingham** | A | W | 2-0 | Gill, L Davies |
| | 2 | 02.02.24 | **Arsenal** (D1) | H | W | 1-0 | Gill |
| | 3 | 23.02.24 | **Bristol City** (D2) | H | W | 3-0 | Gill 2, Clennell |
| | 4 | 08.03.24 | **Manchester City** (D1) | A | D | 0-0 | |
| | 4r | 12.03.24 | **Manchester City** | H | L | 0-1aet | |
| 1924-25 (D1) | 1 | 10.01.25 | **Darlington** (3N) | H | D | 0-0 | |
| | 1r | 14.01.25 | **Darlington** | A | D | 0-0aet | |
| | 1 2r | 19.01.25 | **Darlington** | | W | 2-0 | L Davies, W Davies |
| | | | *played at Anfield* | | | | |
| | 2 | 31.01.25 | **Fulham** (D2) | H | W | 1-0 | L Davies |
| | 3 | 21.02.25 | **Notts County** (D1) | A | W | 2-0 | Nicholson, Gill |
| | 4 | 07.03.25 | **Leicester City** (D2) | H | W | 2-1 | Beadles, W Davies |

| | | | | | | | |
|---|---|---|---|---|---|---|---|
| | SF | 28.03.25 | **Blackburn Rovers** (D1) | | W | 3-1 | Nicholson, Gill, Beadles |
| | | | *played at Meadow Lane, Nottingham* | | | | |
| | F | 25.04.25 | **Sheffield Utd** (D1) | | L | 0-1 | |
| | | | *played at Wembley Stadium* | | | | |
| 1925-26 (D1) | 3 | 09.01.26 | **Burnley** (D1) | A | D | 2-2 | Cassidy, L Davies |
| | 3r | 13.01.26 | **Burnley** | H | W | 2-0 | Ferguson 2 |
| | 4 | 30.01.26 | **Newcastle Utd** (D1) | H | L | 0-2 | |
| 1926-27 (D1) | 3 | 08.01.27 | **Aston Villa** (D1) | H | W | 2-1 | L Davies, Curtis |
| | 4 | 29.01.27 | **Darlington** (D2) | A | W | 2-0 | McLachlan, Ferguson |
| | 5 | 19.02.27 | **Bolton Wanderers** (D1) | A | W | 3-0 | Ferguson (p), L Davies |
| | 6 | 05.03.27 | **Chelsea** (D2) | A | D | 0-0 | |
| | 6r | 09.03.27 | **Chelsea** | H | W | 3-2 | Irving, L Davies, Ferguson (p) |
| | SF | 26.03.27 | **Reading** (D2) | | W | 3-0 | Ferguson 2, Wake |
| | | | *played at Molineux* | | | | |
| | F | 23.04.27 | **Arsenal** (D1) | | W | 1-0 | Ferguson |
| | | | *played at Wembley Stadium* | | | | |
| 1927-28 (D1) | 3 | 14.01.28 | **Southampton** (D2) | H | W | 2-1 | Ferguson, L Davies |
| | 4 | 28.01.28 | **Liverpool** (D1) | H | W | 2-1 | McLachlan, Nelson |
| | 5 | 18.02.28 | **Nottingham Forest** (D2) | A | L | 1-2 | Ferguson |
| 1928-29 (D1) | 3 | 12.01.29 | **Aston Villa** (D1) | A | L | 1-6 | Hardy |
| 1929-30 (D2) | 3 | 11.01.30 | **Liverpool** (D1) | A | W | 2-1 | L Davies 2 |
| | 4 | 25.01.30 | **Sunderland** (D1) | A | L | 1-2 | L Davies |
| 1930-31 (D2) | 3 | 10.01.31 | **Brentford** (3S) | A | D | 2-2 | Jones, Valentine |
| | 3r | 14.01.31 | **Brentford** | H | L | 1-2 | Robbins |
| 1931-32 (3S) | 1 | 28.11.31 | **Enfield** (AL) | H | W | 8-0 | Keating 3, O'Neill 2, Emmerson 2, Harris |
| | 2 | 12.12.31 | **Clapton Orient** (3S) | H | W | 4-0 | McCambridge, Keating, Emmerson, Broadbent og |
| | 3 | 09.01.32 | **Bradford Park A** (D2) | A | L | 0-2 | |
| 1932-33 (3S) | 1 | 26.11.32 | **Bristol Rovers** (3S) | H | D | 1-1 | Harris |
| | 1r | 30.11.32 | **Bristol Rovers** | A | L | 1-4 | McCambridge |
| 1933-34 (3S) | 1 | 25.11.33 | **Aldershot** (3S) | H | D | 0-0 | |
| | 1r | 29.11.33 | **Aldershot** | A | L | 1-3 | Hill |
| 1934-35 (3S) | 1 | 24.11.34 | **Reading** (3S) | H | L | 1-2 | W Lewis |
| 1935-36 (3S) | 1 | 30.11.35 | **Dartford** (SL) | H | L | 0-3 | |
| 1936-37 (3S) | 1 | 28.11.36 | **Southall** (AL) | H | W | 3-1 | Walton, Talbot, Pugh |
| | 2 | 12.12.36 | **Swindon Town** (3S) | H | W | 2-1 | Granville, Prescot |
| | 3 | 16.01.37 | **Grimsby Town** (D1) | H | L | 1-3 | Melaniphy |
| 1937-38 (3S) | 1 | 27.11.37 | **Northampton Town** (3S) | A | W | 2-1 | Collins 2 |
| | 2 | 11.12.37 | **Bristol City** (3S) | H | D | 1-1 | Turner |
| | 2r | 15.12.37 | **Bristol City** | A | W | 2-0 | Collins 2 |
| | 3 | 08.01.38 | **Charlton Athletic** (D1) | A | L | 0-5 | |
| 1938-39 (3S) | 1 | 26.11.38 | **Cheltenham Town** (SL) | A | D | 1-1 | Prescott |
| | 1r | 30.11.38 | **Cheltenham Town** | H | W | 1-0 | Prescott |
| | 2 | 10.12.38 | **Crewe Alexandra** (3N) | H | W | 1-0 | Talbot |
| | 3 | 07.01.39 | **Charlton Athletic** (D1) | H | W | 1-0 | Walton |
| | 4 | 21.01.39 | **Newcastle Utd** (D2) | H | D | 0-0 | |
| | 4r | 25.01.39 | **Newcastle Utd** | A | L | 1-4 | Pugh |
| 1945-46 (3S) | 3 1L | 05.01.46 | **WBA** (D2) | H | D | 1-1 | Allen |
| | 3 2L | 09.01.46 | **WBA** | A | L | 0-4 | |
| 1946-47 (3S) | 3 | 11.01.47 | **Brentford** (D1) | A | L | 0-1 | |
| 1947-48 (D2) | 3 | 10.01.48 | **Sheffield Wed** (D2) | H | L | 1-2aet | Rees |
| 1948-49 (D2) | 3 | 08.01.49 | **Oldham Athletic** (3N) | A | W | 3-2 | Hollyman 2, Allen |
| | 4 | 29.01.49 | **Aston Villa** (D1) | A | W | 2-1 | Hollyman, Rees |
| | 5 | 12.02.49 | **Derby County** (D1) | A | L | 1-2 | Stevenson |
| 1949-50 (D2) | 3 | 07.01.50 | **WBA** (D1) | H | D | 2-2 | E Evans, G Williams |
| | 3r | 11.01.50 | **WBA** | A | W | 1-0 | Edwards |
| | 4 | 28.01.50 | **Charlton Athletic** (D1) | A | D | 1-1 | E Evans |
| | 4r | 01.02.50 | **Charlton Athletic** | H | W | 2-0 | E Evans 2 |
| | 5 | 11.02.50 | **Leeds Utd** (D2) | A | L | 1-3 | Sherwood (p) |
| 1950-51 (D2) | 3 | 06.01.51 | **West Ham Utd** (D2) | A | L | 1-2 | Grant |
| 1951-52 (D2) | 3 | 12.01.52 | **Swindon Town** (3S) | H | D | 1-1 | Grant |

| | | | | | | | | |
|---|---|---|---|---|---|---|---|---|
| | | 3r | 16.01.52 | **Swindon Town** | A | L | 0-1aet | |
| 1952-53 | (D1) | 3 | 10.01.53 | **Halifax Town** (3N) | A | L | 1-3 | W Baker |
| 1953-54 | (D1) | 3 | 09.01.54 | **Peterborough Utd** (ML) | H | W | 3-1 | Ford 2, Northcott |
| | | 4 | 30.01.54 | **Port Vale** (D3) | H | L | 0-2 | |
| 1954-55 | (D1) | 3 | 08.01.55 | **Arsenal** (D1) | A | L | 0-1 | |
| 1955-56 | (D1) | 3 | 07.01.56 | **Leeds Utd** (D2) | A | W | 2-1 | Hitchens, McSeveney |
| | | 4 | 28.01.56 | **West Ham Utd** (D2) | A | L | 1-2 | Ford |
| 1956-57 | (D1) | 3 | 05.01.57 | **Leeds Utd** (D1) | A | W | 2-1 | Stockin, McSeveney |
| | | 4 | 26.01.57 | **Barnsley** (D2) | H | L | 0-1 | |
| 1957-58 | (D2) | 3 | 04.01.58 | **Leeds Utd** (D1) | A | W | 2-1 | Harrington, Nugent |
| | | 4 | 25.01.58 | **Leyton Orient** (D2) | H | W | 4-1 | Bishop og, Walsh, Bonson 2 |
| | | 5 | 15.02.58 | **Blackburn Rovers** (D2) | H | D | 0-0 | |
| | | 5r | 20.02.58 | **Blackburn Rovers** | A | L | 1-2 | Hewitt |
| 1958-59 | (D2) | 3 | 10.01.59 | **Plymouth Argyle** (D3) | A | W | 3-0 | Hewitt (p), Reyolds, Bonson |
| | | 4 | 24.01.59 | **Norwich City** (D3) | A | L | 2-3 | Hewitt, Bonson |
| 1959-60 | (D2) | 3 | 09.01.60 | **Port Vale** (D3) | H | L | 0-2 | |
| 1960-61 | (D1) | 3 | 07.01.61 | **Manchester City** (D1) | H | D | 1-1 | Tapscott |
| | | 3r | 11.01.61 | **Manchester City** | A | D | 0-0aet | |
| | | 3 2r | 16.01.61 | **Manchester City** | | L | 0-2aet | |
| | | | | *played at Highbury* | | | | |
| 1961-62 | (D1) | 3 | 10.01.62 | **Middlesbrough** (D2) | A | L | 0-1 | |
| 1962-63 | (D2) | 3 | 18.02.63 | **Charlton Athletic** (D2) | A | L | 0-1 | |
| 1963-64 | (D2) | 3 | 04.01.64 | **Leeds Utd** (D2) | H | L | 0-1 | |
| 1964-65 | (D2) | 3 | 09.01.65 | **Charlton Athletic** (D2) | H | L | 1-2 | Tapscott |
| 1965-66 | (D2) | 3 | 26.01.66 | **Port Vale** (D4) | H | W | 2-1 | King, Hole |
| | | 4 | 12.02.66 | **Southport** (D4) | A | L | 0-2 | |
| 1966-67 | (D2) | 3 | 28.01.67 | **Barnsley** (D4) | A | D | 1-1 | Bird |
| | | 3r | 31.01.67 | **Barnsley** | H | W | 2-1 | Johnston (p), King |
| | | 4 | 18.02.67 | **Manchester City** (D1) | H | D | 1-1 | Williams |
| | | 4r | 22.02.67 | **Manchester City** | A | L | 1-3 | Johnston (p) |
| 1967-68 | (D2) | 3 | 27.01.68 | **Stoke City** (D1) | A | L | 1-4 | Jones |
| 1968-69 | (D2) | 3 | 04.01.69 | **Arsenal** (D1) | H | D | 0-0 | |
| | | 3r | 07.01.69 | **Arsenal** | A | L | 0-2 | |
| 1969-70 | (D2) | 3 | 03.01.70 | **York City** (D4) | A | D | 1-1 | Swallow og |
| | | 3r | 12.01.70 | **York City** | H | D | 1-1aet | Toshack |
| | | 3 2r | 15.01.70 | **York City** | | L | 1-3aet | King |
| | | | | *played at St Andrews* | | | | |
| 1970-71 | (D2) | 3 | 02.01.71 | **Brighton** (D3) | H | W | 1-0 | King |
| | | 4 | 23.01.71 | **Brentford** (D4) | H | L | 0-2 | |
| 1971-72 | (D2) | 3 | 15.01.72 | **Sheffield Utd** (D1) | A | W | 3-1 | Murray, Woodruff, Carver |
| | | 4 | 09.02.72 | **Sunderland** (D2) | H | D | 1-1 | King |
| | | 4r | 14.02.72 | **Sunderland** | A | D | 1-1aet | Clark |
| | | 4 2r | 16.02.72 | **Sunderland** | | W | 3-1 | Clark, Woodruff, Kellock |
| | | | | *played at Maine Road* | | | | |
| | | 5 | 26.02.72 | **Leeds Utd** (D1) | H | L | 0-2 | |
| 1972-73 | (D2) | 3 | 13.01.73 | **Scunthorpe Utd** (D3) | A | W | 3-2 | Kellock, McCulloch, Phillips |
| | | 4 | 03.02.73 | **Bolton Wanderers** (D3) | A | D | 2-2 | Kellock, Phillips |
| | | 4r | 07.02.73 | **Bolton Wanderers** | H | D | 1-1aet | McCulloch |
| | | 4 2r | 12.02.73 | **Bolton Wanderers** | | L | 0-1 | |
| | | | | *played at The Hawthorns* | | | | |
| 1973-74 | (D2) | 3 | 05.01.74 | **Birmingham City** (D1) | A | L | 2-5 | Impey, McCulloch |
| 1974-75 | (D2) | 3 | 04.01.75 | **Leeds Utd** (D1) | A | L | 1-4 | Showers |
| 1975-76 | (D3) | 1 | 22.11.75 | **Exeter City** (D4) | H | W | 6-2 | Alston 3, Reece 2, Evans |
| | | 2 | 13.12.75 | **Wycombe W** (IL) | H | W | 1-0 | Evans |
| | | 3 | 03.01.76 | **Orient** (D2) | A | W | 1-0 | Alston |
| | | 4 | 24.01.76 | **Southend Utd** (D3) | A | L | 1-2 | Evans |
| 1976-77 | (D2) | 3 | 08.01.77 | **Tottenham Hotspur** (D1) | H | W | 1-0 | Sayer |
| | | 4 | 29.01.77 | **Wrexham** (D3) | H | W | 3-2 | Giles, Sayer, Buchanan |
| | | 5 | 26.02.77 | **Everton** (D1) | H | L | 1-2 | Evans |
| 1977-78 | (D2) | 3 | 07.01.78 | **Ipswich Town** (D1) | H | L | 0-2 | |
| 1978-79 | (D2) | 3 | 09.01.79 | **Swindon Town** (D3) | A | L | 0-3 | |
| 1979-80 | (D2) | 3 | 05.01.80 | **Arsenal** (D1) | H | D | 0-0 | |

| | | | | | | | | |
|---|---|---|---|---|---|---|---|---|
| | | 3r | 08.01.80 | **Arsenal** | A | L | 1-2 | Buchanan |
| 1980-81 | (D2) | 3 | 03.01.81 | **Leicester City** (D1) | A | L | 0-3 | |
| 1981-82 | (D2) | 3 | 02.01.82 | **Manchester City** (D1) | A | L | 1-3 | Maddy |
| 1982-83 | (D3) | 1 | 20.11.82 | **Wokingham Town** (IL) | A | D | 1-1 | Tong |
| | | 1r | 23.11.82 | **Wokingham Town** | H | W | 3-0 | Jones, Hemmerman, Ingram |
| | | 2 | 11.12.82 | **Weymouth** (APL) | H | L | 2-3 | Gibbibns, Hemmerman |
| 1983-84 | (D2) | 3 | 07.01.84 | **Ipswich Town** (D1) | H | L | 0-3 | |
| 1984-85 | (D2) | 3 | 21.01.85 | **Gillingham** (D3) | A | L | 1-2 | Withey |
| 1985-86 | (D3) | 1 | 16.11.85 | **Exeter City** (D4) | A | L | 1-2 | Stevenson |
| 1986-87 | (D4) | 1 | 15.11.86 | **Ton Pentre** (Welsh) | A | W | 4-1 | Marustik 2, Wimbleton, Wheeler |
| | | 2 | 09.12.86 | **Brentford** (D3) | H | W | 2-0 | Wimbleton, Bartlett |
| | | 3 | 10.01.87 | **Millwall** (D2) | A | D | 0-0 | |
| | | 3r | 20.01.87 | **Millwall** | H | D | 2-2aet | Vaughan, Marustik |
| | | 3 2r | 26.01.87 | **Millwall** | H | W | 1-0 | Pike |
| | | 4 | 31.01.87 | **Stoke City** (D2) | A | L | 1-2 | Wimbleton |
| 1987-88 | (D4) | 1 | 14.11.87 | **Peterborough Utd** (D4) | A | L | 1-2 | Bartlett |
| 1988-89 | (D3) | 1 | 19.11.88 | **Hereford Utd** (D4) | H | W | 3-0 | Bartlett, Tupling, Gilligan |
| | | 2 | 11.12.88 | **Enfield** (Conf) | A | W | 4-1 | Wimbleton (p), Lynex, Gilligan 2 |
| | | 3 | 07.01.89 | **Hull City** (D2) | H | L | 1-2 | Gilligan |
| 1989-90 | (D3) | 1 | 18.11.89 | **Halesowen Town** (SL) | H | W | 1-0 | Pike |
| | | 2 | 09.12.89 | **Gloucester City** (SL) | H | D | 2-2 | Scott 2 |
| | | 2r | 12.12.89 | **Gloucester City** | A | W | 1-0 | Scott |
| | | 3 | 06.01.90 | **QPR** (D1) | H | D | 0-0 | |
| | | 3r | 10.01.90 | **QPR** | A | L | 0-2 | |
| 1990-91 | (D4) | 1 | 17.11.90 | **Hayes** (IL) | H | D | 0-0 | |
| | | 1r | 21.11.90 | **Hayes** | A | L | 0-1 | |
| | | | | *played at Griffin Park* | | | | |
| 1991-92 | (D4) | 1 | 16.11.91 | **Swansea City** (D3) | A | L | 1-2 | Pike |
| 1992-93 | (D3) | 1 | 14.11.92 | **Bath City** (Conf) | H | L | 2-3 | Millar, Blake |
| 1993-94 | (D2) | 1 | 13.11.93 | **Enfield** (IL) | A | D | 0-0 | |
| | | 1r | 30.11.93 | **Enfield** | H | W | 1-0 | Blake |
| | | 2 | 04.12.93 | **Brentford** (D2) | A | W | 3-1 | Westley og, Stant, Bird |
| | | 3 | 08.01.94 | **Middlesbrough** (D1) | H | D | 2-2 | Stant, Thompson |
| | | 3r | 19.01.94 | **Middlesbrough** | A | W | 2-1aet | Stant, Blake |
| | | 4 | 29.01.94 | **Manchester City** (PL) | H | W | 1-0 | Blake |
| | | 5 | 20.02.94 | **Luton Town** (D1) | H | L | 1-2 | Stant |
| 1994-95 | (D2) | 1 | 12.11.94 | **Enfield** (IL) | A | L | 0-1 | |
| 1995-96 | (D3) | 1 | 11.11.95 | **Rushden & D** (SL) | A | W | 3-1 | Dale 2, Jarman |
| | | 2 | 02.12.95 | **Swindon Town** (D2) | A | L | 0-2 | |
| 1996-97 | (D3) | 1 | 16.11.96 | **Hendon** (IL) | H | W | 2-0 | White, Middleton |
| | | 2 | 07.12.96 | **Gillingham** (D2) | H | L | 0-2 | |
| 1997-98 | (D3) | 1 | 15.11.97 | **Slough Town** (Conf) | A | D | 1-1 | O'Sullivan |
| | | 1r | 25.11.97 | **Slough Town** | H | W | 3-2aet | Dale, Saville, White |
| | | 2 | 06.12.97 | **Hendon** (IL) | H | W | 3-1 | Dale 2, Saville |
| | | 3 | 03.01.98 | **Oldham Athletic** (D2) | H | W | 1-0 | Fowler |
| | | 4 | 24.01.98 | **Reading** (D1) | H | D | 1-1 | Nugent |
| | | 4r | 03.02.98 | **Reading** | A | D | 1-1aet | Dale |
| | | | | *Reading won 4-3 on penalties* | | | | |
| 1998-99 | (D3) | 1 | 14.11.98 | **Chester City** (D3) | H | W | 6-0 | Fowler 2, Middleton, Williams 2, M Delaney |
| | | 2 | 05.12.98 | **Hednesford Town** (Conf) | H | W | 3-1 | Middleton, Fowler, Williams |
| | | 3 | 02.01.99 | **Yeovil Town** (Conf) | H | D | 1-1 | Nugent |
| | | 3r | 12.01.99 | **Yeovil Town** | A | W | 2-1aet | Eckhardt, Nugent |
| | | 4 | 27.01.99 | **Sheffield Utd** (D1) | A | L | 1-4 | Nugent |
| 1999-00 | (D2) | 1 | 30.10.99 | **Leyton Orient** (D3) | A | D | 1-1 | Nugent (p) |
| | | 1r | 09.11.99 | **Leyton Orient** | H | W | 3-1 | Brazier, Perrett, Nugent |
| | | 2 | 20.11.99 | **Bury** (D2) | A | D | 0-0 | |
| | | 2r | 30.11.99 | **Bury** | H | W | 1-0 | Ford |
| | | 3 | 21.12.99 | **Bolton Wanderers** (D1) | A | L | 0-1 | |
| 2000-01 | (D3) | 1 | 19.11.00 | **Bristol Rovers** (D2) | H | W | 5-1 | Earnshaw 3, Evans, Fortune-West |
| | | 2 | 09.12.00 | **Cheltenham Town** (D3) | H | W | 3-1 | Earnshaw 3(1p), Evans |

| | | | | | | | | |
|---|---|---|---|---|---|---|---|---|
| | | 3 | 06.01.01 | **Crewe Alexandra** (D1) | H | D | 1-1 | Young |
| | | 3r | 16.01.01 | **Crewe Alexandra** | A | L | 1-2 | Earnshaw |
| 2001-02 | (D2) | 1 | 17.11.01 | **Tiverton Town** (SL) | A | W | 3-1 | Brayson, Hamilton, Earnshaw |
| | | | | *played at Ninian Park* | | | | |
| | | 2 | 08.12.01 | **Port Vale** (D2) | H | W | 3-0 | Earnshaw, Gordon, Fortune-West |
| | | 3 | 06.01.02 | **Leeds Utd** (PL) | H | W | 2-1 | Kavanagh, Young |
| | | 4 | 27.01.02 | **Tranmere Rovers** (D2) | A | L | 1-3 | Kavanagh (p) |
| 2002-03 | (D2) | 1 | 16.11.02 | **Tranmere Rovers** (D2) | A | D | 2-2 | Collins, Kavanagh |
| | | 1r | 26.11.02 | **Tranmere Rovers** | H | W | 2-1 | Campbell, Collins |
| | | 2 | 07.12.02 | **Margate** (Conf) | A | W | 3-0 | Thorne, Boland, Fortune-West |
| | | 3 | 04.01.03 | **Coventry City** (D1) | H | D | 2-2 | Earnshaw, Campbell |
| | | 3r | 15.01.03 | **Coventry City** | A | L | 0-3 | |

# CARLISLE UNITED

*Formed 1903 by the merger of Carlisle Red Rose and Shaddongate United. First entered FA Cup: 1904-05. Best FA Cup performance: 6th round, 1975. Record FA Cup win: 9-1 v Windermere, 2nd qualifying round, 1907-8; 8-0 v Arlecdon Red Rose, 2nd qualifying round, 1921-22. In Competition Proper: 6-0 v Shepshed Dynamo, 1st round, 16.11.1996. Record FA Cup defeat: five defeats by five goal margins.*

| | | | | | | | | |
|---|---|---|---|---|---|---|---|---|
| 1904-05 | | | | 1q Workington (H) 2-2; 1qr Workington (A) 1-3 | | | | |
| 1905-06 | (LC) | | | 1q Red Rose (H) 3-0; 2q Barrow (A) 2-4 | | | | |
| 1906-07 | (NEL) | | | 2q Wigtown Harriers (H) 3-1; 3q Barrow (A) 2-1; 4q Southport Central (H) 0-4 | | | | |
| 1907-08 | (LC) | | | P Carlisle City (H) 1-0; 1q Lancaster Town (A) 4-1; 2q Windermere (H) 9-1; 3q Workington (A) 3-2; 4q Darlington (H) 7-0; 5q Southend U (H) 4-0 | | | | |
| | | 1 | 11.01.08 | **Brentford** (SL) | H | D | 2-2 | Powell 2 |
| | | 1r | 15.01.08 | **Brentford** | A | W | 3-1aet | McAteer, Robinson 2 |
| | | 2 | 01.02.08 | **Grimsby Town** (D2) | A | L | 2-6 | McAteer, Maher |
| 1908-09 | (NEL) | | | 5q Coventry City (A) 1-1; 5qr Coventry City (H) 1-1; 5q 2r Coventry City 3-1 (at Hyde Road, Manchester) | | | | |
| | | 1 | 16.01.09 | **Fulham** (D2) | A | L | 1-4 | Sanderson |
| 1909-10 | (LC) | | | 4q Tonge (H) 1-0; 5q Mexborough Town (A) 0-0; 5qr Mexborough Town (H) 4-0 | | | | |
| | | 1 | 15.01.10 | **West Ham Utd** (SL) | A | D | 1-1 | Carter |
| | | 1r | 20.01.10 | **West Ham Utd** | A | L | 0-5 | |
| 1910-11 | (NEL) | | | 4q Newburn (H) 3-0; 5q Crewe Alexandra (A) 1-1; 5qr Crewe Alexandra (H) 3-4 | | | | |
| 1911-12 | (NEL) | | | 4q Accrington Stanley (A) 0-3 | | | | |
| 1912-13 | (NEL) | | | 4q Barrow (A) 1-4 | | | | |
| 1913-14 | (NEL) | | | 1q Lancaster Town (A) 0-0; 1qr Lancaster Town (H) 4-2; 2q Frizington (H) 2-1; 3q Lowca (H) 7-1; 4q Southport Central (H) 2-1; 5q Glossop NE (A) 1-4 | | | | |
| 1914-15 | (NEL) | | | 1q Barrow St Mary's (H) 4-1; 2q Lancaster Town (H) 3-1; 3q Frizington (A) 1-3 | | | | |
| 1919-20 | (NEL) | | | 1q Wigton Harriers (H) 8-1; 2q Cleator Moor Celtic (H) 6-1; 3q Frizington (H) 3-1; 4q Barrow (A) 0-0; 4qr Barrow (H) 1-0; 5q South Liverpool (A) 1-3 | | | | |
| 1920-21 | (NEL) | | | 1q Frizington (H) 3-1; 2q Barrow (A) 1-1; 2qr Barrow (H) 1-0aet *FA disqualified Carlisle and awarded tie to Barrow after protest* | | | | |
| 1921-22 | (NEL) | | | P Vickerstown (H) 5-0; 1q Penrith (H) 6-1; 2q Arlecdon Red Rose (H) 8-0; 3q Cleator Moor Celtic (H) 2-0; 4q Stalybridge Celtic (H) 0-0; 4qr Stalybridge Celtic (A) 2-3 | | | | |
| 1922-23 | (NEL) | | | 4q Fleetwood (H) 7-1; 5q Felling Colliery (H) 6-0; 6q Aberdare Athletic (A) 0-0; 6qr Aberdare Athletic (H) 1-2 | | | | |
| 1923-24 | (NEL) | | | 4q Barrow (A) 2-1; 5q Ashington (A) 0-2 | | | | |
| 1924-25 | (NEL) | | | 1q Workington (A) 2-1; 2q Cleator Moor Celtic (H) 5-1; 3q Egremont (A) 6-2; 4q Bishop Auckland (H) 0-1 | | | | |
| 1925-26 | (NEL) | | | 4q Workington (H) 3-1 | | | | |
| | | 1 | 28.11.25 | **Chilton Col Rec A** (NAll) | H | L | 0-2 | |
| 1926-27 | (NEL) | | | 4q Whitehaven A (H) 7-1 | | | | |
| | | 1 | 27.11.26 | **Hartlepools Utd** (3N) | H | W | 6-2 | Sinclair, A Pigg, Ward, Hamilton, Graham 2 |
| | | 2 | 11.12.26 | **Bedlington Utd** (NEL) | H | W | 4-0 | Smiles 2, A Pigg 2 |
| | | 3 | 08.01.27 | **Wolverhampton W** (D2) | H | L | 0-2 | |
| 1927-28 | (NEL) | | | 4q Lancaster Town (A) 2-0 | | | | |
| | | 1 | 26.11.27 | **Doncaster Rovers** (3N) | H | W | 2-1 | Ward, McConnell |
| | | 2 | 10.12.27 | **Wrexham** (3N) | A | L | 0-1 | |
| 1928-29 | (3N) | 1 | 24.11.28 | **Wrexham** | A | W | 1-0 | Ward |
| | | 2 | 10.12.28 | **Lincoln City** (3N) | H | L | 0-1 | |

| | | | | | | | | |
|---|---|---|---|---|---|---|---|---|
| 1929-30 | (3N) | 1 | 30.11.29 | **Halifax Town** (3N) | H | W | 2-0 | McConnell, McLeod |
| | | 2 | 14.12.29 | **Crewe Alexandra** (3N) | H | W | 4-2 | Hutchinson 2, Watson, Cape |
| | | 3 | 11.01.30 | **Everton** (D1) | H | L | 2-4 | McConnell, Watson |
| 1930-31 | (3N) | 1 | 29.11.30 | **New Brighton** (3N) | H | W | 3-1 | Maskill, McConnell 2 |
| | | 2 | 13.12.30 | **Tunbridge Wells R** (KL) | H | W | 4-2 | Hutchinson 2, McConnell 2 |
| | | 3 | 10.01.31 | **Bolton Wanderers** (D1) | A | L | 0-1 | |
| 1931-32 | (3N) | 1 | 28.11.31 | **Yorkshire Amateurs** (YL) | A | W | 3-1 | Richmond, McConnell, Sharpe |
| | | 2 | 12.12.31 | **Darlington** (3N) | H | L | 0-2 | |
| 1932-33 | (3N) | 1 | 26.11.32 | **Denaby Utd** (ML) | H | W | 1-0 | Slinger |
| | | 2 | 10.12.32 | **Hull City** (3N) | H | D | 1-1 | Felton |
| | | 2r | 15.12.32 | **Hull City** | A | L | 1-2aet | Felton |
| 1933-34 | (3N) | 1 | 25.11.33 | **Wrexham** (3N) | H | W | 2-1 | Stevenson, Slinger |
| | | 2 | 09.12.33 | **Cheltenham Town** (BC) | H | L | 1-2 | Slinger |
| 1934-35 | (3N) | 1 | 24.11.34 | **Wigan Athletic** (CC) | H | L | 1-6 | Ranson |
| 1935-36 | (3N) | 1 | 30.11.35 | **Tranmere Rovers** (3N) | A | L | 0-3 | |
| 1936-37 | (3N) | 1 | 28.11.36 | **Stockport County** (3N) | H | W | 2-1 | Mantle, McArdle |
| | | 2 | 12.12.36 | **Clapton Orient** (3S) | H | W | 4-1 | McArdle 2, James, O'Grady |
| | | 3 | 16.01.37 | **Swansea Town** (D2) | A | L | 0-1 | |
| 1937-38 | (3N) | 1 | 27.11.37 | **Tranmere Rovers** (3N) | A | L | 1-2 | Leach |
| 1938-39 | (3N) | 1 | 26.11.38 | **Walsall** (3S) | A | L | 1-4 | Hammill |
| 1945-46 | (3N) | 1 1L | 17.11.45 | **North Shields** (NEL) | H | W | 5-1 | Adamson, Hamilton 2, Clarke, Cape |
| | | 1 2L | 24.11.45 | **North Shields** (NEL) | A | W | 3-2 | Hamilton, Douglas, Clarke |
| | | 2 1L | 08.12.45 | **Barrow** (3N) | A | L | 2-4 | Cape 2 |
| | | 2 2L | 15.12.45 | **Barrow** | H | L | 3-4 | Adamson, Clarke, Dellow |
| 1946-47 | (3N) | 1 | 30.11.46 | **Runcorn** (CC) | H | W | 4-0 | Dougal, Iceton 2, Broadis |
| | | 2 | 14.12.46 | **South Liverpool** (CC) | A | W | 3-2 | Iceton 2, Moir |
| | | 3 | 11.01.47 | **Sheffield Utd** (D1) | A | L | 0-3 | |
| 1947-48 | (3N) | 1 | 29.11.47 | **Barrow** (3N) | A | L | 2-3 | Broadis, Lindsay |
| 1948-49 | (3N) | 1 | 27.11.48 | **New Brighton** (3N) | A | L | 0-1 | |
| 1949-50 | (3N) | 1 | 26.11.49 | **Lincoln City** (3N) | H | W | 1-0 | Dick |
| | | 2 | 10.12.49 | **Swindon Town** (3S) | H | W | 2-0 | Lindsay 2 |
| | | 3 | 07.01.50 | **Leeds Utd** (D2) | H | L | 2-5 | Lindsay, Dick |
| 1950-51 | (3N) | 1 | 25.11.50 | **Barrow** (3N) | H | W | 2-1 | McCue, Turner |
| | | 2 | 09.12.50 | **Southport** (3N) | A | W | 3-1 | Lindsay, Turner 2 |
| | | 3 | 06.01.51 | **Arsenal** (D1) | A | D | 0-0 | |
| | | 3r | 11.01.51 | **Arsenal** | H | L | 1-4 | McCue |
| 1951-52 | (3N) | 1 | 24.11.51 | **Bradford City** (3N) | A | L | 1-6 | Brown |
| 1952-53 | (3N) | 1 | 22.11.52 | **Scunthorpe Utd** (3N) | A | L | 0-1 | |
| 1953-54 | (3N) | 1 | 21.11.53 | **Southport** (3N) | A | L | 0-1 | |
| 1954-55 | (3N) | 1 | 20.11.54 | **Stockport County** (3N) | A | W | 1-0 | Bond |
| | | 2 | 11.12.54 | **Watford** (3S) | H | D | 2-2 | Whitehouse, Ashman |
| | | 2r | 15.12.54 | **Watford** | A | L | 1-4 | Ashman |
| 1955-56 | (3N) | 1 | 19.11.55 | **Darlington** (3N) | A | D | 0-0 | |
| | | 1r | 22.11.55 | **Darlington** | H | D | 0-0aet | |
| | | 1 2r | 28.11.55 | **Darlington** | | L | 1-3 | Kinloch |
| | | | | *played at St James' Park* | | | | |
| 1956-57 | (3N) | 1 | 17.11.56 | **Billingham S** (NL) | H | W | 6-1 | Garvie 3, Ackerman 2, Broadis |
| | | 2 | 08.12.56 | **Darlington** (3N) | H | W | 2-1 | Ackerman 2 |
| | | 3 | 05.01.57 | **Birmingham City** (D1) | H | D | 0-0 | Ackerman 3 |
| | | 3r | 09.01.57 | **Birmingham City** | A | L | 0-4 | |
| 1957-58 | (3N) | 1 | 16.11.57 | **Rhyl** (CC) | H | W | 5-1 | Ackerman (p), Bond 2, Broadis 2 |
| | | 2 | 07.12.57 | **Accrington Stanley** (3N) | H | D | 1-1 | Ackerman |
| | | 2r | 11.12.57 | **Accrington Stanley** | A | L | 2-3 | Johnston, Ackerman |
| 1958-59 | (D4) | 1 | 15.11.58 | **Heanor Town** (CA) | A | W | 5-1 | Ackerman 2, Mooney, Fletcher 2 |
| | | 2 | 06.12.58 | **Chesterfield** (D3) | H | D | 0-0 | |
| | | 2r | 09.12.58 | **Chesterfield** | A | L | 0-1 | |
| 1959-60 | (D4) | 1 | 14.11.59 | **Rochdale** (D4) | A | D | 2-2 | McGill, Walker |
| | | 1r | 17.11.59 | **Rochdale** | H | L | 1-3aet | Devlin |
| 1960-61 | (D4) | 1 | 05.11.60 | **Chester** (D4) | A | W | 1-0 | Bevan |
| | | 2 | 26.11.60 | **Port Vale** (D3) | A | L | 1-2 | Walker |
| 1961-62 | (D4) | 1 | 04.11.61 | **Darlington** (D4) | A | W | 4-0 | Whitelaw 2, Brayton, Walker |

| | | | | | | | |
|---|---|---|---|---|---|---|---|
| | 2 | 25.11.61 | **Barnsley** (D3) | A | W | 2-1 | Walker, Taylor |
| | 3 | 08.01.62 | **Wolverhampton W** (D1) | A | L | 1-3 | R Thompson |
| 1962-63 (D3) | 1 | 03.11.62 | **Hartlepools Utd** (D4) | H | W | 2-1 | Thompon og, Brayton |
| | 2 | 24.11.62 | **Blyth Spartans** (NEL) | A | W | 2-0 | Walker, Brayton |
| | 3 | 29.01.63 | **Gravesend & N** (SL) | H | L | 0-1 | |
| 1963-64 (D4) | 1 | 16.11.63 | **York City** (D4) | A | W | 5-2 | Livingstone, McIlmoyle, Kirkup, Davies (p), Taylor |
| | 2 | 07.12.63 | **Gateshead AFC** (NRL) | H | W | 4-3 | McIlmoyle 3, Taylor |
| | 3 | 04.01.64 | **QPR** (D3) | H | W | 2-0 | Livingstone, McIlmoyle |
| | 4 | 25.01.64 | **Bedford Town** (SL) | A | W | 3-0 | Kirkup, Livingstone, Davies (p) |
| | 5 | 15.02.64 | **Preston North End** (D2) | A | L | 0-1 | |
| 1964-65 (D3) | 1 | 14.11.64 | **Crook Town** (NL) | A | L | 0-1 | |
| 1965-66 (D2) | 3 | 22.01.66 | **Crystal Palace** (D2) | H | W | 3-0 | McConnell, Welsh, Wilson |
| | 4 | 12.02.66 | **Shrewsbury Town** (D3) | A | D | 0-0 | |
| | 4r | 15.02.66 | **Shrewsbury Town** | H | D | 1-1aet | Dolbie og |
| | 4 2r | 21.02.66 | **Shrewsbury Town** *played at Deepdale, Preston* | | L | 3-4aet | Balderstone, Wilson, Carlin |
| 1966-67 (D2) | 3 | 28.01.67 | **Blackburn Rovers** (D2) | A | W | 2-1 | Wilson, Carlin |
| | 4 | 18.02.67 | **Ipswich Town** (D2) | A | L | 0-2 | |
| 1967-68 (D2) | 3 | 27.01.68 | **Newcastle Utd** (D1) | A | W | 1-0 | Murray |
| | 4 | 17.02.68 | **Everton** (D1) | H | L | 0-2 | |
| 1968-69 (D2) | 3 | 04.01.69 | **Chelsea** (D1) | A | L | 0-2 | |
| 1969-70 (D2) | 3 | 03.01.70 | **Nottingham Forest** (D1) | A | D | 0-0 | |
| | 3r | 06.01.70 | **Nottingham Forest** | H | W | 2-1 | Murray, McVitie |
| | 4 | 24.01.70 | **Aldershot** (D4) | H | D | 2-2 | Hatton, Balderstone |
| | 4r | 28.01.70 | **Aldershot** | A | W | 4-1 | Murray, McVitie, Caldwell, Barton |
| | 5 | 07.02.70 | **Middlesbrough** (D2) | H | L | 1-2 | Winstanley |
| 1970-71 (D2) | 3 | 11.01.71 | **Southend Utd** (D4) | A | W | 3-0 | Owen, Hatton 2 |
| | 4 | 23.01.71 | **Tottenham Hotspur** (D1) | H | L | 2-3 | Martin, Owen |
| 1971-72 (D2) | 3 | 15.01.72 | **Tottenham Hotspur** (D1) | A | D | 1-1 | Bowles |
| | 3r | 18.01.72 | **Tottenham Hotspur** | H | L | 1-3 | Martin |
| 1972-73 (D2) | 3 | 13.01.73 | **Huddersfield Town** (D2) | H | D | 2-2 | Gorman, Laidlaw |
| | 3r | 16.01.73 | **Huddersfield Town** | A | W | 1-0 | Dolan og |
| | 4 | 03.02.73 | **Sheffield Utd** (D1) | H | W | 2-1 | Martin, Delgado |
| | 5 | 24.02.73 | **Arsenal** (D1) | H | L | 1-2 | Martin |
| 1973-74 (D2) | 3 | 05.01.74 | **Sunderland** (D2) | H | D | 0-0 | |
| | 3r | 09.01.74 | **Sunderland** | A | W | 1-0 | Martin |
| | 4 | 26.01.74 | **Liverpool** (D1) | A | D | 0-0 | |
| | 4r | 29.01.74 | **Liverpool** | H | L | 0-2 | |
| 1974-75 (D1) | 3 | 04.01.75 | **Preston North End** (D3) | A | W | 1-0 | Laidlaw |
| | 4 | 25.01.75 | **WBA** (D2) | H | W | 3-2 | Clarke, Laidlaw, Owen |
| | 5 | 15.02.75 | **Mansfield Town** (D4) | A | W | 1-0 | Owen |
| | 6 | 08.03.75 | **Fulham** (D2) | H | L | 0-1 | |
| 1975-76 (D2) | 3 | 03.01.76 | **WBA** (D2) | A | L | 1-3 | Wile og |
| 1976-77 (D2) | 3 | 08.01.77 | **Matlock Town** (NPL) | H | W | 5-1 | Rafferty 2, McVitie, Clarke, Bonnyman |
| | 4 | 29.01.77 | **Liverpool** (D1) | A | L | 0-3 | |
| 1977-78 (D3) | 1 | 26.11.77 | **Stafford Rangers** (NPL) | H | W | 2-0 | Rafferty 2 |
| | 2 | 17.12.77 | **Chester** (D3) | H | W | 3-1 | Rafferty 2, McVitie |
| | 3 | 07.01.78 | **Manchester Utd** (D1) | H | D | 1-1 | McDonald |
| | 3r | 11.01.78 | **Manchester Utd** | A | L | 2-4 | Tait, Rafferty |
| 1978-79 (D3) | 1 | 25.11.78 | **Halifax Town** (D4) | H | W | 1-0 | Lumby |
| | 2 | 16.12.78 | **Hull City** (D3) | H | W | 3-0 | Lumby, McCartney (p), Kemp |
| | 3 | 10.01.79 | **Ipswich Town** (D1) | A | L | 2-3 | Tait, Kemp |
| 1979-80 (D3) | 1 | 24.11.79 | **Hull City** (D3) | H | D | 3-3 | Bonnyman (p), Ludlam, Bannon |
| | 1r | 28.11.79 | **Hull City** | A | W | 2-0 | Winstanley, Bonnyman |
| | 2 | 15.12.79 | **Sheffield Wed** (D3) | H | W | 3-0 | Staniforth, Beardsley, Ludlum |
| | 3 | 05.01.80 | **Bradford City** (D4) | H | W | 3-2 | Bonnyman (p), Ludlum, Hoolickin |
| | 4 | 26.01.80 | **Wrexham** (D2) | H | D | 0-0 | |
| | 4r | 29.01.80 | **Wrexham** | A | L | 1-3 | Bonnyman |
| 1980-81 (D3) | 1 | 22.11.80 | **Workington** (NPL) | A | D | 0-0 | |
| | 1r | 01.12.80 | **Workington** | H | W | 4-1 | Brown 2, Beardsley 2 |

| | | | | | | | | |
|---|---|---|---|---|---|---|---|---|
| | 2 | 13.12.80 | **Walsall** (D3) | H | W | 3-0 | Brown, Beardsley 2 |
| | 3 | 03.01.81 | **Mansfield Town** (D4) | A | D | 2-2 | Bannon, Bird og |
| | 3r | 06.01.81 | **Mansfield Town** | H | W | 2-1 | Beardsley, MacDonald |
| | 4 | 24.01.81 | **Bristol City** (D2) | H | D | 1-1 | Coady |
| | 4r | 28.01.81 | **Bristol City** | A | L | 0-5 | |
| 1981-82 (D3) | 1 | 21.11.81 | **Darlington** (D4) | A | D | 2-2 | Staniforth, Robson |
| | 1r | 24.11.81 | **Darlington** | H | W | 3-1 | Robson, Beardsley, Bannon |
| | 2 | 02.01.82 | **Bishop Auckland** (NL) | H | - | 0-0ab | |
| | | | *abandoned after 69 minutes – waterlogged pitch* | | | | |
| | 2 | 09.01.82 | **Bishop Auckland** | H | W | 1-0 | Lee |
| | | | *played at Workington* | | | | |
| | 3 | 23.01.82 | **Huddersfield Town** (D3) | H | L | 2-3 | Bannon, Robson |
| 1982-83 (D2) | 3 | 08.01.83 | **Burnley** (D2) | H | D | 2-2 | Bannon, Poskett |
| | 3r | 11.01.83 | **Burnley** | A | L | 1-3 | Poskett |
| 1983-84 (D2) | 3 | 07.01.84 | **Swindon Town** (D4) | H | D | 1-1 | Ashurst |
| | 3r | 10.01.84 | **Swindon Town** | A | L | 1-3 | Shoulder (p) |
| 1984-85 (D2) | 3 | 05.01.85 | **Dagenham** (APL) | H | W | 1-0 | Poskett |
| | 4 | 26.01.85 | **Leicester City** (D1) | A | L | 0-1 | |
| 1985-86 (D2) | 3 | 13.01.86 | **QPR** (D1) | H | W | 1-0 | Cooke |
| | 4 | 25.01.86 | **Peterborough Utd** (D4) | A | L | 0-1 | |
| 1986-87 (D3) | 1 | 15.11.86 | **Notts County** (D3) | A | D | 1-1 | Bishop |
| | 1r | 18.11.86 | **Notts County** | H | L | 0-3 | |
| 1987-88 (D4) | 1 | 14.11.87 | **Macclesfield T** (Conf) | A | L | 2-4 | Hetherington, Fulbrook |
| 1988-89 (D4) | 1 | 19.11.88 | **Telford Utd** (Conf) | A | D | 1-1 | Walsh |
| | 1r | 22.11.88 | **Telford Utd** | H | W | 4-1 | Saddington, Fitzpatrick, Gorman (p), Halpin |
| | 2 | 10.12.88 | **Scarborough** (D4) | A | W | 1-0 | Richards og |
| | 3 | 07.01.89 | **Liverpool** (D1) | H | L | 0-3 | |
| 1989-90 (D4) | 1 | 18.11.89 | **Wrexham** (D4) | H | W | 3-0 | Sendall, Proudlock 2 |
| | 2 | 09.12.89 | **Wigan Athletic** (D3) | A | L | 0-2 | |
| 1990-91 (D4) | 1 | 17.11.90 | **Wigan Athletic** | A | L | 0-5 | |
| 1991-92 (D4) | 1 | 16.11.91 | **Crewe Alexandra** (D4) | H | D | 1-1 | Watson |
| | 1r | 26.11.91 | **Crewe Alexandra** | A | L | 3-5aet | Barnsley (2p), Fyfe |
| 1992-93 (D3) | 1 | 14.11.92 | **Wigan Athletic** (D2) | A | L | 1-3 | Arnold |
| 1993-94 (D3) | 1 | 13.11.93 | **Knowsley Utd** (NPL) | A | W | 4-1 | Arnold 2, Davey, Reeves |
| | | | *played at Goodison Park* | | | | |
| | 2 | 04.12.93 | **Stalybridge Celtic** (Conf) | H | W | 3-1 | Edmondson, Gallimore, Arnold |
| | 3 | 08.01.94 | **Sunderland** (D1) | A | D | 1-1 | Edmondson |
| | 3r | 18.01.94 | **Sunderland** | H | L | 0-1aet | |
| 1994-95 (D3) | 1 | 13.11.94 | **Guiseley** (NPL) | A | W | 4-1 | Reeves 2, Conway, Mountfield |
| | | | *played at Valley Parade, Bradford* | | | | |
| | 2 | 04.12.94 | **Darlington** (D3) | H | W | 2-0 | Conway, Currie |
| | 3 | 07.01.95 | **Sunderland** (D1) | A | D | 1-1 | Davey |
| | 3r | 17.01.95 | **Sunderland** | H | L | 1-3 | Walling |
| 1995-96 (D2) | 1 | 11.11.95 | **Preston North End** (D3) | H | L | 1-2 | Reeves |
| 1996-97 (D3) | 1 | 16.11.96 | **Shepshed Dynamo** (SL) | H | W | 6-0 | Davidson og, Corbett og, Peacock, Conway, O Archdeacon (p), McAlindon |
| | 2 | 07.12.96 | **Darlington** (D3) | H | W | 1-0 | Edmondson |
| | 3 | 14.01.97 | **Tranmere Rovers** (D1) | H | W | 1-0 | O Archdeacon |
| | 4 | 25.01.97 | **Sheffield Wed** (PL) | H | L | 0-2 | |
| 1997-98 (D2) | 1 | 15.11.97 | **Wigan Athletic** (D2) | H | L | 0-1 | |
| 1998-99 (D3) | 1 | 14.11.98 | **Hartlepool Utd** (D3) | A | L | 1-2 | Stevens |
| 1999-00 (D3) | 1 | 30.10.99 | **Ilkeston Town** (SL) | A | L | 1-2 | Harries |
| 2000-01 (D3) | 1 | 18.11.00 | **Woking** (Conf) | H | W | 5-1 | Stevens 4, Dobie |
| | 2 | 09.12.00 | **Kidderminster H** (D3) | A | W | 2-0 | Connelly, Dobie |
| | 3 | 06.01.01 | **Arsenal** (PL) | H | L | 0-1 | |
| 2001-02 (D3) | 1 | 17.11.01 | **Barnet** (Conf) | A | D | 0-0 | |
| | 1r | 27.11.01 | **Barnet** | H | W | 1-0 | Soley |
| | 2 | 08.12.01 | **Tranmere Rovers** (D2) | A | L | 1-6 | Foran |
| 2002-03 (D3) | 1 | 16.11.02 | **Lincoln City** (D3) | H | W | 2-1 | Foran, Farrell |
| | 2 | 07.12.02 | **Scunthorpe Utd** (D3) | A | D | 0-0 | |
| | 2r | 23.12.02 | **Scunthorpe Utd** | H | L | 0-1 | |

## CARSHALTON ATHLETIC

*Formed 1905. First entered FA Cup: 1922-23. Ernie Taylor, who played in three cup finals for Newcastle United (1951), Blackpool (1953) and Manchester United (1958) started his career at Carshalton. Members of the Isthmian League.*

| | | | | | | | | |
|---|---|---|---|---|---|---|---|---|
| 1969-70 | (AL) | 1 | 15.11.69 | **Hendon** (IL) | A | L | 3-5 | Burnham 2, Cadman |
| 1982-83 | (IL) | 1 | 20.11.82 | **Barnet** (APL) | H | W | 4-0 | Dark, Lewington 2, Tuite |
| | | 2 | 11.12.82 | **Torquay Utd** (D4) | A | L | 1-4 | Lewington |
| 1987-88 | (IL) | 1 | 23.11.87 | **Welling Utd** (Conf) | A | L | 2-3 | Kane, Riley |
| 1993-94 | (IL) | 1 | 13.11.93 | **Barnet** (D2) | A | L | 1-2 | Annon |
| 1997-98 | (IL) | 1 | 15.11.97 | **Stevenage B** (Conf) | H | D | 0-0 | |
| | | 1r | 24.11.97 | **Stevenage B** | A | L | 0-5 | |

## CASTLEFORD TOWN

*Formed 1896. First entered FA Cup: 1906-07. Folded 1936. Their one appearance in the Competition Proper in 1919-20 came after eight wins (and one draw) through the qualifying rounds, accounting for future Football League team Halifax Town along the way.*

| | | | | | | | | |
|---|---|---|---|---|---|---|---|---|
| 1919-20 | (ML) | 1 | 10.01. | **Hednesford T** (WMRL) | H | W | 2-0 | Howson, Gedney |
| | | 2 | 31.01. | **Bradford Park A** (D1) | A | L | 2-3 | Howson, Dyer |

## CASUALS

*Formed 1883. Played their early matches on Wandsworth Common near the Surrey Arms pub. One of the great amateur clubs of the pre-World War Two era. Merged with the Corinthians in 1939 to form Corinthian Casuals. FA Amateur Cup winners: 1936; Runners-up 1894 See also Corinthian Casuals.*

| | | | | | | | | |
|---|---|---|---|---|---|---|---|---|
| 1884-85 | | 1 | 08.11.84 | **South Reading** | A | L | 1-4 | |
| 1885-86 | | 1 | 31.10.85 | **Swifts** | A | L | 1-7 | |
| 1886-87 | | 1 | 23.10.86 | **Dulwich** | H | L | 2-4 | |
| 1887-88 | | 1 | | Millwall Rovers | | | - | |
| | | | | *Casuals scratched. Millwall Rovers walkover.* | | | | |
| 1890-91 | | 1 | 17.01.91 | **Aston Villa** (D1) | A | L | 1-13 | A G Topham |
| 1891-92 | | 1 | 16.01.92 | **Stoke** (D1) | A | L | 0-3 | |
| 1892-93 | | 1 | 21.01.93 | **Nottingham Forest** (FAll) | A | L | 0-4 | |

## CHARLTON ATHLETIC

*Formed 1905. First entered FA Cup: 1914-15. FA Cup winners: 1947. FA Cup runners-up 1946. Record FA Cup win: 7-0 v Burton Albion, 3rd round, 07.01.1956; Record FA Cup defeat: 0-6 v Wrexham, 3rd round, 05.01.1980*

| | | | | | | | | |
|---|---|---|---|---|---|---|---|---|
| 1914-15 | (SSL) | | | 1q Dartford (A) 0-0; 1qr Dartford (A) 1-2 | | | | |
| 1919-20 | (KL) | | | P Sittingbourne (A) 2-7 | | | | |
| 1920-21 | (SL) | | | P Catford Southend (H) 6-0; 1q Margate (A) 0-0; 1qr Margate (H) 3-1; 2q Maidstone (H) 1-1; 2qr Maidstone (A) 0-2 | | | | |
| 1921-22 | (3S) | | | did not enter | | | | |
| 1922-23 | (3S) | | | 5q Northampton T (H) 2-0; 6q Darlington (H) 2-1 | | | | |
| | | 1 | 13.01.23 | **Manchester City** (D1) | A | W | 2-1 | Goodman, Whalley |
| | | 2 | 03.02.23 | **Preston North End** (D1) | H | W | 2-0 | Goodman, S Smith |
| | | 3 | 24.02.23 | **WBA** (D1) | H | W | 1-0 | Goodman |
| | | 4 | 10.03.23 | **Bolton Wanderers** (D1) | H | L | 0-1 | |
| 1923-24 | (3S) | 1 | 12.01.24 | **Accrington Stanley** (3N) | A | D | 0-0 | |
| | | 1r | 16.01.24 | **Accrington Stanley** | H | W | 1-0 | Hannaford |
| | | 2 | 02.02.24 | **Wolverhampton W** (3N) | H | D | 0-0 | |
| | | 2r | 07.02.24 | **Wolverhampton W** | A | L | 0-1 | |
| 1924-25 | (3S) | | | 5q Dulwich Hamlet (H) 4-0; 6q QPR (A) 1-1; 6qr QPR (H) 1-2 | | | | |
| 1925-26 | (3S) | 1 | 28.11.25 | **Windsor & Eton** (AL) | H | W | 4-2 | Millard 3, McCrorie |
| | | 2 | 12.12.25 | **QPR** (3S) | A | D | 1-1 | Pigg og |
| | | 2r | 17.12.25 | **QPR** | H | W | 1-0 | McGinn |
| | | 3 | 09.01.26 | **Huddersfield Town** (D1) | H | L | 0-1 | |
| 1926-27 | (3S) | 1 | 27.11.26 | **Woking** (IL) | A | W | 3-1 | J Rankin, Cairns, Tricker |
| | | 2 | 11.12.26 | **Bristol Rovers** (3S) | A | L | 1-4 | J Rankin |
| 1927-28 | (3S) | 1 | 26.11.27 | **Merthyr Town** (3S) | A | D | 0-0 | |
| | | 1r | 30.11.27 | **Merthyr Town** | H | W | 2-1 | Sherlaw, J Horton |
| | | 2 | 10.12.27 | **Kettering Town** (SL) | H | D | 1-1 | J Horton |
| | | 2r | 15.12.27 | **Kettering Town** | A | W | 2-1 | Biswell 2 |
| | | 3 | 14.01.28 | **Bury** (D1) | H | D | 1-1 | Biswell |
| | | 3r | 18.01.28 | **Bury** | A | L | 3-4 | W Welsh 2, Biswell |

| | | | | | | | | |
|---|---|---|---|---|---|---|---|---|
| 1928-29 | (3S) | 1 | 24.11.28 | **Peterborough & F** (SL) | A | W | 2-0 | Whitlow 2 |
| | | 2 | 08.12.28 | **Northfleet Utd** (SL) | A | W | 5-1 | Astley 2, Rowe og, Whitlow 2 |
| | | 3 | 12.01.29 | **Portsmouth** (D1) | A | L | 1-2 | J Rankin |
| 1929-30 | (D2) | 3 | 11.01.30 | **QPR** (3S) | H | D | 1-1 | Astley |
| | | 3r | 16.01.30 | **QPR** | A | W | 3-0 | Lennox, J Horton, Astley |
| | | 4 | 25.01.30 | **Middlesbrough** (D1) | A | D | 1-1 | Pugsley |
| | | 4r | 29.01.30 | **Middlesbrough** | H | D | 1-1 | Lennox |
| | | 4 2r | 03.02.30 | **Middlesbrough** | | L | 0-1aet | |
| | | | | *played at Maine Road* | | | | |
| 1930-31 | (D2) | 3 | 10.01.31 | **WBA** (D2) | A | D | 2-2 | Wyper, Astley |
| | | 3r | 14.01.31 | **WBA** | H | D | 1-1aet | Astley |
| | | 3 2r | 19.01.31 | **WBA** | | L | 1-3 | Lennox |
| | | | | *played at Villa Park* | | | | |
| 1931-32 | (D2) | 3 | 09.01.32 | **West Ham Utd** (D1) | H | L | 1-2 | J Horton |
| 1932-33 | (D2) | 3 | 14.01.33 | **Bolton Wanderers** (D1) | H | L | 1-5 | G Robinson |
| 1933-34 | (3S) | 1 | 25.11.33 | **Bath City** (SL) | A | D | 0-0 | |
| | | 1r | 29.11.33 | **Bath City** | H | W | 3-1 | Pearce, Hobbis, JT Smith |
| | | 2 | 09.12.33 | **Gillingham** (3S) | H | W | 1-0 | Pearce |
| | | 3 | 13.01.34 | **Port Vale** (D2) | H | W | 2-0 | Pearce, Hobbis |
| | | 4 | 27.01.34 | **Birmingham** (D1) | A | L | 0-1 | |
| 1934-35 | (3S) | 1 | 24.11.34 | **Exeter City** (3S) | H | D | 2-2 | Wilkinson, R Allen |
| | | 1r | 28.11.34 | **Exeter City** | A | L | 2-5 | Wilkinson, R Allen |
| 1935-36 | (D2) | 3 | 11.01.36 | **Clapton Orient** (3S) | A | L | 0-3 | |
| 1936-37 | (D1) | 3 | 16.01.37 | **Coventry City** (D2) | A | L | 0-2 | |
| 1937-38 | (D1) | 3 | 08.01.38 | **Cardiff City** (3S) | H | W | 5-0 | G Robinson, Bassett og, Boulter, Owens 2 |
| | | 4 | 22.01.38 | **Leeds Utd** (D1) | H | W | 2-1 | G Tadman 2 |
| | | 5 | 12.02.38 | **Aston Villa** (D2) | H | D | 1-1 | G Robinson |
| | | 5r | 16.02.38 | **Aston Villa** | A | D | 2-2 | R Brown 2 |
| | | 5 2r | 21.02.38 | **Aston Villa** | | L | 1-4 | G Tadman |
| | | | | *played at Highbury* | | | | |
| 1938-39 | (D1) | 3 | 07.01.39 | **Cardiff City** (3S) | A | L | 0-1 | |
| 1945-46 | (D1) | 3 1L | 05.01.46 | **Fulham** (D2) | H | W | 3-1 | Duffy, Fell, D Welsh |
| | | 3 2L | 07.01.46 | **Fulham** | A | L | 1-2 | M Tadman |
| | | 4 1L | 26.01.46 | **Wolverhampton W** (D1) | H | W | 5-2 | Duffy 2, A Turner, G Robinson, Fell |
| | | 4 2L | 30.01.46 | **Wolverhampton W** | A | D | 1-1 | Morris og |
| | | 5 1L | 09.02.46 | **Preston North End** (D1) | A | D | 1-1 | A Turner |
| | | 5 2L | 13.02.46 | **Preston North End** | H | W | 6-0 | Duffy 3, A Turner 2, Fell |
| | | 6 1L | 02.03.46 | **Brentford** (D1) | H | W | 6-3 | Brown, Duffy, A Turner 2, D Welsh 2 |
| | | 6 2L | 09.03.46 | **Brentford** | A | W | 3-1 | Duffy, D Welsh, A Turner |
| | | SF | 23.03.46 | **Bolton Wanderers** (D1) | | W | 2-0 | Duffy 2 |
| | | | | *played at Villa Park* | | | | |
| | | F | 27.04.46 | **Derby County** (D1) | | L | 1-4aet | H Turner |
| | | | | *played at Wembley Stadium* | | | | |
| 1946-47 | (D1) | 3 | 11.01.47 | **Rochdale** (3N) | H | W | 3-1 | Lancelotte, Duffy 2 |
| | | 4 | 25.01.47 | **WBA** (D2) | A | W | 2-1 | Duffy, W Robinson |
| | | 5 | 08.02.47 | **Blackburn Rovers** (D1) | H | W | 1-0 | Dawson |
| | | 6 | 01.03.47 | **Preston North End** (D1) | H | W | 2-1 | Duffy, Hurst |
| | | SF | 29.03.47 | **Newcastle Utd** (D2) | | W | 4-0 | D Welsh 2, Dawson, Hurst |
| | | | | *played at Elland Road* | | | | |
| | | F | 26.04.47 | **Burnley** (D2) | | W | 1-0aet | Duffy |
| | | | | *played at Wembley Stadium* | | | | |
| 1947-48 | (D1) | 3 | 10.01.48 | **Newcastle Utd** (D2) | H | W | 2-1 | W Robinson, Revell |
| | | 4 | 24.01.48 | **Stockport County** (3N) | H | W | 3-0 | Revell (p), C Vaughan, Staniforth og |
| | | 5 | 07.02.48 | **Manchester Utd** (D1) | A | L | 0-2 | |
| | | | | *played at Leeds Road, Huddersfield* | | | | |
| 1948-49 | (D1) | 3 | 08.01.49 | **Burnley** (D1) | A | L | 1-2aet | O'Linn |
| 1949-50 | (D1) | 3 | 07.01.50 | **Fulham** (D1) | H | D | 2-2 | Hurst 2 |
| | | 3r | 11.01.50 | **Fulham** | A | W | 2-1 | D'Arcy, C Vaughan |
| | | 4 | 28.01.50 | **Cardiff City** (D2) | H | D | 1-1 | C Vaughan |
| | | 4r | 01.02.50 | **Cardiff City** | A | L | 0-2 | |

| | | | | | | | | |
|---|---|---|---|---|---|---|---|---|
| 1950-51 (D1) | 3 | 06.01.51 | **Blackpool** (D1) | H | D | 2-2 | Revell (p), P Croker |
| | 3r | 10.01.51 | **Blackpool** | A | L | 0-3 | |
| 1951-52 (D1) | 3 | 12.01.52 | **Luton Town** (D2) | A | L | 0-1 | |
| 1952-53 (D1) | 3 | 10.01.53 | **Hull City** (D2) | A | L | 1-3 | Leary |
| 1953-54 (D1) | 3 | 09.01.54 | **Portsmouth** (D1) | A | D | 3-3 | Leary, Ayre 2 |
| | 3r | 14.01.54 | **Portsmouth** | H | L | 2-3aet | Leary, Kiernan |
| 1954-55 (D1) | 3 | 08.01.55 | **Rochdale** (3N) | A | W | 3-1 | Kiernan, Hammond, Hurst |
| | 4 | 29.01.55 | **WBA** (D1) | A | W | 4-2 | E Firmani (p), Ayre 3 |
| | 5 | 19.02.55 | **Wolverhampton W** (D1) | A | L | 1-4 | Hewie |
| 1955-56 (D1) | 3 | 07.01.56 | **Burton Albion** (BDL) | H | W | 7-0 | Kiernan 2, Gauld, Leary 3, Hurst |
| | 4 | 28.01.56 | **Swindon Town** (3S) | H | W | 2-1 | Hunt og, C Hammond |
| | 5 | 18.02.56 | **Arsenal** (D1) | H | L | 0-2 | |
| 1956-57 (D1) | 3 | 05.01.57 | **Middlesbrough** (D2) | A | D | 1-1 | JJ Ryan |
| | 3r | 10.01.57 | **Middlesbrough** | H | L | 2-3 | Leary, Barnard og |
| 1957-58 (D2) | 3 | 04.01.58 | **Huddersfield Town** (D2) | A | D | 2-2 | Summers, JJ Ryan |
| | 3r | 08.01.58 | **Huddersfield Town** | H | W | 1-0 | JJ Ryan |
| | 4 | 25.01.58 | **Fulham** (D2) | A | D | 1-1 | JJ Ryan |
| | 4r | 29.01.58 | **Fulham** | H | L | 0-2 | |
| 1958-59 (D2) | 3 | 10.01.59 | **Bristol Rovers** (D2) | A | W | 4-0 | Lawrie 2, R White, Summers |
| | 4 | 24.01.59 | **Everton** (D1) | H | D | 2-2 | Summers, Lawrie |
| | 4r | 28.01.59 | **Everton** | A | L | 1-4aet | Lawrie |
| 1959-60 (D2) | 3 | 09.01.60 | **Bristol City** (D2) | A | W | 3-2 | Lawrie 3 |
| | 4 | 30.01.60 | **Wolverhampton W** (D1) | A | L | 1-2 | Summers |
| 1960-61 (D2) | 3 | 07.01.61 | **Tottenham Hotspur** (D1) | A | L | 2-3 | Leary, Lawrie |
| 1961-62 (D2) | 3 | 06.01.62 | **Scunthorpe Utd** (D2) | H | W | 1-0 | Kinsey |
| | 4 | 27.01.62 | **Derby County** (D2) | H | W | 2-1 | Matthews, Kinsey |
| | 5 | 17.02.62 | **Aston Villa** (D1) | A | L | 1-2 | Kinsey |
| 1962-63 (D2) | 3 | 18.02.63 | **Cardiff City** (D2) | H | W | 1-0 | Glover |
| | 4 | 06.03.63 | **Chelsea** (D2) | H | L | 0-3 | |
| 1963-64 (D2) | 3 | 04.01.64 | **West Ham Utd** (D1) | A | L | 0-2 | |
| 1964-65 (D2) | 3 | 09.01.65 | **Cardiff City** (D2) | A | W | 2-1 | Haydock, M Bailey |
| | 4 | 30.01.65 | **Middlesbrough** (D2) | H | D | 1-1 | Kenning |
| | 4r | 01.02.65 | **Middlesbrough** | A | L | 1-2 | Matthews |
| 1965-66 (D2) | 3 | 22.01.66 | **Preston North End** (D2) | H | L | 2-3 | Singleton og, Tocknell |
| 1966-67 (D2) | 3 | 28.01.67 | **Sheffield Utd** (D1) | H | L | 0-1 | |
| 1967-68 (D2) | 3 | 27.01.68 | **Coventry City** (D1) | A | L | 0-3 | |
| 1968-69 (D2) | 3 | 04.01.69 | **Crystal Palace** (D2) | H | D | 0-0 | |
| | 3r | 08.01.69 | **Crystal Palace** | A | W | 2-0 | Treacy 2 |
| | 4 | 25.01.69 | **Arsenal** (D1) | A | L | 0-2 | |
| 1969-70 (D2) | 3 | 03.01.70 | **Aston Villa** (D2) | A | D | 1-1 | Treacy |
| | 3r | 12.01.70 | **Aston Villa** | H | W | 1-0 | Gregory |
| | 4 | 24.01.70 | **QPR** (D2) | H | L | 2-3 | Riddick, Gregory |
| 1970-71 (D2) | 3 | 02.01.71 | **Hull City** (D2) | A | L | 0-3 | |
| 1971-72 (D2) | 3 | 15.01.72 | **Tranmere Rovers** (D3) | H | D | 0-0 | |
| | 3r | 17.01.72 | **Tranmere Rovers** | A | L | 2-4 | Treacy 2 |
| 1972-73 (D3) | 1 | 18.11.72 | **Tonbridge** (SL) | A | W | 5-0 | Flanagan, Horsfield, Peacock 2, Gilchrist og |
| | 2 | 12.12.72 | **Walsall** (D3) | A | W | 2-1 | P Davies, Horsfield |
| | 3 | 13.01.73 | **Bolton Wanderers** (D3) | H | D | 1-1 | Curtis (p) |
| | 3r | 17.01.73 | **Bolton Wanderers** | A | L | 0-4 | |
| 1973-74 (D3) | 1 | 24.11.73 | **Bournemouth** (D3) | A | L | 0-1 | |
| 1974-75 (D3) | 1 | 23.11.74 | **Chelmsford City** (SL) | A | W | 1-0 | Horsfield |
| | 2 | 14.12.74 | **Peterborough Utd** (D3) | A | L | 0-3 | |
| 1975-76 (D2) | 3 | 03.01.76 | **Sheffield Wed** (D3) | H | W | 2-1 | Peacock, Warman |
| | 4 | 24.01.76 | **Portsmouth** (D2) | H | D | 1-1 | R Curtis (p) |
| | 4r | 27.01.76 | **Portsmouth** | A | W | 3-0 | Powell, Flanagan, Hope |
| | 5 | 14.02.76 | **Wolverhampton W** (D1) | A | L | 0-3 | |
| 1976-77 (D2) | 3 | 08.01.77 | **Blackburn Rovers** (D2) | H | D | 1-1 | Burman |
| | 3r | 12.01.77 | **Blackburn Rovers** | A | L | 0-2 | |
| 1977-78 (D2) | 3 | 07.01.78 | **Notts County** (D2) | H | L | 0-2 | |
| 1978-79 (D2) | 3 | 09.01.79 | **Maidstone Utd** (SL) | H | D | 1-1 | Flanagan |

| | | | | | | | |
|---|---|---|---|---|---|---|---|
| | 3r | 15.01.79 | **Maidstone Utd** | A | W | 2-1 | D Campbell, Robinson |
| | 4 | 05.02.79 | **Bristol Rovers** (D2) | A | L | 0-1 | |
| 1979-80 (D2) | 3 | 05.01.80 | **Wrexham** (D2) | A | L | 0-6 | |
| 1980-81 (D3) | 1 | 22.11.80 | **Harlow Town** (IL) | A | W | 2-0 | Robinson, Hales |
| | 2 | 13.12.80 | **Bournemouth** (D4) | H | W | 2-1 | P Walsh, Hales |
| | 3 | 03.01.81 | **Plymouth Argyle** (D3) | A | W | 2-1 | Powell, Hales |
| | 4 | 24.01.81 | **Fulham** (D3) | A | W | 2-1 | Shaw, Hales |
| | 5 | 14.02.81 | **Ipswich Town** (D1) | A | L | 0-2 | |
| 1981-82 (D2) | 3 | 02.01.82 | **Orient** (D2) | A | L | 0-1 | |
| 1982-83 (D2) | 3 | 08.01.83 | **Ipswich Town** (D1) | A | L | 2-3 | Robinson, Hales |
| 1983-84 (D2) | 3 | 07.01.84 | **Colchester Utd** (D4) | A | W | 1-0 | Phillips og |
| | 4 | 28.01.84 | **Watford** (D1) | H | L | 0-2 | |
| 1984-85 (D2) | 3 | 05.01.85 | **Tottenham Hotspur** (D1) | A | D | 1-1 | Aizlewood |
| | 3r | 23.01.85 | **Tottenham Hotspur** | H | L | 1-2 | Moore (p) |
| 1985-86 (D2) | 3 | 05.01.86 | **West Ham Utd** (D1) | H | L | 0-1 | |
| 1986-87 (D1) | 3 | 10.01.87 | **Walsall** (D3) | H | L | 1-2 | Stuart |
| 1987-88 (D1) | 3 | 09.01.88 | **West Ham Utd** (D1) | A | L | 0-2 | |
| 1988-89 (D1) | 3 | 07.01.89 | **Oldham Athletic** (D2) | H | W | 2-1 | Crooks, Williams |
| | 4 | 28.01.89 | **Kettering Town** (Conf) | H | W | 2-1 | Williams, Lee |
| | 5 | 18.02.89 | **West Ham Utd** (D1) | H | L | 0-1 | |
| 1989-90 (D1) | 3 | 07.01.90 | **Bradford City** (D2) | H | D | 1-1 | Jones |
| | 3r | 10.01.90 | **Bradford City** | A | W | 3-0 | Lee, Williams, Jones |
| | 4 | 27.01.90 | **WBA** (D2) | A | L | 0-1 | |
| 1990-91 (D2) | 3 | 05.01.91 | **Everton** (D1) | H | L | 1-2 | Dyer |
| 1991-92 (D2) | 3 | 05.01.92 | **Barnet** (D4) | H | W | 3-1 | Gatting, Leaburn, Grant |
| | 4 | 26.01.92 | **Sheffield Utd** (D1) | H | D | 0-0 | |
| | 4r | 05.02.92 | **Sheffield Utd** | A | L | 1-3 | Gatting |
| 1992-93 (D1) | 3 | 02.01.93 | **Leeds Utd** (PL) | A | D | 1-1 | Nelson |
| | 3r | 13.01.93 | **Leeds Utd** | H | L | 1-3 | Pitcher (p) |
| 1993-94 (D1) | 3 | 08.01.94 | **Burnley** (D2) | H | W | 3-0 | Pardew, Leaburn, Grant |
| | 4 | 29.01.94 | **Blackburn Rovers** (PL) | H | D | 0-0 | |
| | 4r | 08.02.94 | **Blackburn Rovers** | A | W | 1-0 | Pitcher |
| | 5 | 19.02.94 | **Bristol City** (D1) | A | D | 1-1 | Robson |
| | 5r | 02.03.94 | **Bristol City** | H | W | 2-0 | Pitcher (p), Grant |
| | 6 | 12.03.94 | **Manchester Utd** (PL) | A | L | 1-3 | Leaburn |
| 1994-95 (D1) | 3 | 07.01.95 | **Chelsea** (PL) | A | L | 0-3 | |
| 1995-96 (D1) | 3 | 06.01.96 | **Sheffield Wed** (PL) | H | W | 2-0 | Grant, Mortimore (p) |
| | 4 | 07.02.96 | **Brentford** (D2) | H | W | 3-2 | Robinson, Bowyer, Whyte |
| | 5 | 28.02.96 | **Liverpool** (PL) | A | L | 1-2 | Grant |
| 1996-97 (D1) | 3 | 05.01.97 | **Newcastle Utd** (PL) | H | D | 1-1 | Kinsella |
| | 3r | 15.01.97 | **Newcastle Utd** | A | L | 1-2aet | Robson |
| 1997-98 (D1) | 3 | 03.01.98 | **Nottingham Forest** (D1) | H | W | 4-1 | Robinson, Brown, Leaburn, Mendonca |
| | 4 | 24.01.98 | **Wolverhampton W** (D1) | H | D | 1-1 | Jones |
| | 4r | 03.02.98 | **Wolverhampton W** | A | L | 0-3 | |
| 1998-99 (PL) | 3 | 02.01.99 | **Blackburn Rovers** (PL) | A | L | 0-2 | |
| 1999-00 (D1) | 3 | 11.12.99 | **Swindon Town** (D1) | H | W | 2-1 | Kinsella 2 |
| | 4 | 08.01.00 | **QPR** (D1) | H | W | 1-0 | MacDonald |
| | 5 | 29.01.00 | **Coventry City** (PL) | A | W | 3-2 | Robinson, Newton, Hunt |
| | 6 | 19.02.00 | **Bolton Wanderers** (D1) | A | L | 0-1 | |
| 2000-01 (PL) | 3 | 06.01.01 | **Dagenham & Red** (Conf) | H | D | 1-1 | Salako |
| | 3r | 27.01.01 | **Dagenham & Red** | A | W | 1-0aet | Newton |
| | 4 | 07.02.01 | **Tottenham Hotspur** (PL) | H | L | 2-4 | Powell, Svensson |
| 2001-02 (PL) | 3 | 05.01.02 | **Blackpool** (D2) | H | W | 2-1 | Stuart (p), Euell |
| | 4 | 26.01.02 | **Walsall** (D1) | H | L | 1-2 | Stuart |
| 2002-03 (PL) | 3 | 04.01.03 | **Exeter City** (D3) | H | W | 3-1 | Johansson 2, Euell (p) |
| | 4 | 26.01.03 | **Fulham** (PL) | A | L | 0-3 | |

## CHATHAM

*Formed 1882. First entered FA Cup: 1882-83. Played their early matches at Great Lines in Chatham, a venue also used by the Royal Engineers. Reached FA Cup quarter-finals in 1889. Now known as Chatham Town. Members of the Southern League.*

| | | | | | | | |
|---|---|---|---|---|---|---|---|
| 1882-83 | 1 | | bye | | | | |
| | 2 | 02.12.82 | **Hendon (1874)** | A | L | 1-2 | |
| 1883-84 | 1 | 03.11.83 | **Old Westminsters** | A | L | 0-3 | |
| 1884-85 | 1 | | Windsor Home Park | | | - | |
| | | | *Windsor Home Park scratched. Chatham walkover* | | | | |
| | 2 | 06.12.84 | **Hendon (1874)** | H | W | 1-0 | Collins |
| | 3 | 03.01.85 | **Hanover Utd** | A | W | 2-0 | |
| | 4 | 24.01.85 | **Lower Darwen** | H | W | 1-0 | McLeod |
| | 5 | 07.02.85 | **Old Carthusians** | H | L | 0-3 | |
| 1885-86 | 1 | 31.10.85 | **Old Carthusians** | H | L | 0-2 | |
| 1886-87 | 1 | | Bournemouth Rovers | | | - | |
| | | | *Bournemouth Rovers scratched. Chatham walkover* | | | | |
| | 2 | 20.11.86 | **Hotspur FC** | H | W | 1-0 | |
| | 3 | 11.12.86 | **Old Foresters** | H | L | 1-4 | |
| 1887-88 | 1 | 15.10.87 | **Luton Town** | H | W | 5-1 | Mcleod 3, C Hibbard 2 |
| | 2 | 05.11.87 | **Royal Engineers** | H | W | 3-1 | |
| | 3 | 26.11.87 | **Crusaders** | A | L | 0-4 | |
| 1888-89 | 1 | 02.02.89 | **South Shore** | H | W | 2-1aet | Hobart, Conquer |
| | 2 | 16.02.89 | **Nottingham Forest** | H | D | 1-1aet | Hibbard |
| | 2r | 23.02.89 | **Nottingham Forest** | A | D | 2-2aet | Hibbard 2 |
| | 2 2r | 28.02.89 | **Nottingham Forest** | | W | 3-2 | Bathurst, Hibbard, Prall |
| | | | *played at Kenningtron Oval* | | | | |
| | 3 | 02.03.89 | **WBA** (D1) | H | L | 1-10 | Bryan |
| 1913-14 (KL) | 1 | 10.01.14 | **Sunderland** (D1) | A | L | 0-9 | |
| 1925-26 (KL) | 1 | 28.11.25 | **Sittingbourne** (KL) | H | L | 0-3 | |
| 1926-27 (KL) | 1 | 27.11.26 | **St Albans City** (IL) | H | W | 3-1 | Anderson og, Potter 2 |
| | 2 | 11.12.26 | **Norwich City** (3S) | A | L | 0-5 | |
| 1927-28 (SL) | 1 | 26.11.27 | **Kettering Town** (SL) | A | L | 0-2 | |
| 1928-29 (SL) | 1 | 24.11.28 | **Norwich City** (3S) | A | L | 1-6 | Brookes |

## CHELMSFORD

*Formed 1878. Amateur-based club who first competed in the FA Cup in 1902-03. A separate club from Chelmsford City which replaced them in 1938.*

| | | | | | | | |
|---|---|---|---|---|---|---|---|
| 1931-32 (Lon) | 1 | 28.11.31 | **Aldershot** (SL) | A | L | 0-7 | |

## CHELMSFORD CITY

*Formed 1938. First entered FA Cup: 1938-39. 1970 Merged with Brentwood Town although the FA refused to ratify the formal amalgamation of the two clubs. League clubs beaten: Darlington, Southampton, Oxford United. Members of the Southern League.*

| | | | | | | | |
|---|---|---|---|---|---|---|---|
| 1938-39 (SL) | 1 | 26.11.38 | **Kidderminster H** (BDL) | H | W | 4-0 | Wood, Palethorpe 3 |
| | 2 | 10.12.38 | **Darlington** (3N) | H | W | 3-1 | Coulter, Palethorpe, Landolla |
| | 3 | 07.01.39 | **Southampton** (D2) | H | W | 4-1 | Carnaby og, Coulter 2, Wright |
| | 4 | 21.01.39 | **Birmingham** (D1) | A | L | 0-6 | |
| 1945-46 (SL) | 1 1L | 17.11.45 | **Northampton Town** (3S) | A | L | 1-5 | Foreman |
| | 1 2L | 24.11.45 | **Northampton Town** | H | L | 0-5 | |
| 1948-49 (SL) | 1 | 27.11.48 | **Weymouth** (WL) | A | L | 1-2 | McClelland |
| 1949-50 (SL) | 1 | 26.11.49 | **Leytonstone** (IL) | A | W | 2-1 | McCormack, Gowers |
| | 2 | 10.12.49 | **Ipswich Town** (3S) | H | D | 1-1 | Hurst |
| | 2r | 14.12.49 | **Ipswich Town** | A | L | 0-1aet | |
| 1950-51 (SL) | 1 | 25.11.50 | **Tonbridge** (SL) | H | D | 2-2 | Plunkett 2 |
| | 1r | 29.11.50 | **Tonbridge** | A | W | 1-0aet | Plunkett |
| | 2 | 09.12.50 | **Mansfield Town** (3N) | H | L | 1-4 | Dicker |
| 1954-55 (SL) | 1 | 20.11.54 | **Aldershot** (3S) | A | L | 1-3 | Boxshall |
| 1958-59 (SL) | 1 | 15.11.58 | **Worcester City** (SL) | H | D | 0-0 | |
| | 1r | 20.11.58 | **Worcester City** | A | L | 1-3 | Smith |
| 1959-60 (SL) | 1 | 14.11.59 | **Crystal Palace** (D4) | A | L | 1-5 | Phillips |
| 1960-61 (SL) | 1 | 05.11.60 | **Port Vale** (D3) | H | L | 2-3 | Barnard 2 |
| 1961-62 (SL) | 1 | 04.11.61 | **King's Lynn** (SL) | H | L | 1-2 | Hatshell |
| 1962-63 (SL) | 1 | 03.11.62 | **Shrewsbury Town** (D3) | H | L | 2-6 | Nicholas, Hatshell |
| 1963-64 (SL) | 1 | 16.11.63 | **Cambridge Utd** (SL) | A | W | 1-0 | Nicholas |
| | 2 | 07.12.63 | **Bedford Town** (SL) | H | L | 0-1 | |
| 1964-65 (SL) | 1 | 14.11.64 | **Notts County** (D4) | A | L | 0-2 | |

| | | | | | | | | |
|---|---|---|---|---|---|---|---|---|
| 1966-67 | (SL) | 1 | 26.11.66 | **Brentford** (D4) | A | L | 0-1 | |
| 1967-68 | (SL) | 1 | 09.12.67 | **Oxford Utd** (D3) | H | D | 3-3 | Butcher 2, Pulley |
| | | 1r | 13.12.67 | **Oxford Utd** | A | D | 3-3aet | Butcher, Shreeves (p), Pulley |
| | | 1 2r | 18.12.67 | **Oxford Utd** *played at Griffin Park* | | W | 1-0 | Cassidy |
| | | 2 | 06.01.68 | **Colchester Utd** (D3) | A | L | 0-2 | |
| 1968-69 | (SL) | 1 | 16.11.68 | **Grantham Town** (ML) | A | L | 1-2 | Coughlin (p) |
| 1969-70 | (SL) | 1 | 15.11.69 | **Hereford Utd** (SL) | H | L | 1-2 | Andrews (p) |
| 1970-71 | (SL) | 1 | 21.11.70 | **Crawley Town** (SL) | A | D | 1-1 | Ferry |
| | | 1r | 23.11.70 | **Crawley Town** | H | W | 6-1 | Butcher 3, Price, Thornley, Stevenson (p) |
| | | 2 | 12.12.70 | **Torquay Utd** (D3) | H | L | 0-1 | |
| 1972-73 | (SL) | 1 | 18.11.72 | **Hillingdon Borough** (SL) | H | W | 2-0 | Woolcott 2 |
| | | 2 | 09.12.72 | **Telford Utd** (SL) | H | W | 5-0 | Woolcott 3, Peterson, Lewis |
| | | 3 | 13.01.73 | **Ipswich Town** (D1) | H | L | 1-3 | Woolcott |
| 1973-74 | (SL) | 1 | 24.11.73 | **Watford** (D3) | A | L | 0-1 | |
| 1974-75 | (SL) | 1 | 23.11.74 | **Charlton Athletic** (D3) | H | L | 0-1 | |
| 1983-84 | (SL) | 1 | 19.11.83 | **Wycombe W** (IL) | H | D | 0-0 | |
| | | 1r | 22.11.83 | **Wycombe W** | A | W | 2-1 | Bishop, Anderson |
| | | 2 | 10.12.83 | **Gillingham** (D3) | A | L | 1-6 | Bishop (p) |
| 1985-86 | (SL) | 1 | 16.11.85 | **Weymouth** (APL) | H | W | 1-0 | Poutney |
| | | 2 | 07.12.85 | **Wycombe W** (APL) | A | L | 0-2 | |
| 1986-87 | (SL) | 1 | 15.11.86 | **Woking** (IL) | A | D | 1-1 | Wilkins |
| | | 1r | 17.11.86 | **Woking** | H | W | 2-1 | Cowley, Dennehy |
| | | 2 | 06.12.86 | **Gillingham** (D3) | A | L | 0-2 | |
| 1987-88 | (SL) | 1 | 14.11.87 | **Bath City** (Conf) | H | L | 1-2 | Wilkins |
| 1990-91 | (SL) | 1 | 17.11.90 | **Barnet** (Conf) | A | D | 2-2 | Jarvis, Baptiste |
| | | 1r | 21.11.90 | **Barnet** | H | L | 0-2 | |
| 1994-95 | (SL) | 1 | 12.11.94 | **Wycombe W** (D2) | A | L | 0-4 | |
| 1999-00 | (SL) | 1 | 30.10.99 | **Oldham Athletic** (D2) | A | L | 0-4 | |

## CHELSEA

*Formed 1905. Elected to the Football League (Division 2) the same year. FA Cup winners: 1970, 1997, 2000. FA Cup runners-up: 1915, 1967, 1994, 2002. FA Cup record win: 9-1 v Worksop, 1st round, 31.01.1908; FA Cup Record Defeat: 0-6 v Sheffield Wed, 2nd round replay 05.02.1913; 1-7 v Crystal Palace, 3rd qualifying round, 16.01.1906 – the only occasion in FA Cup history when a Non-League club (Crystal Palace were in the Southern League at the time) has scored seven goals against a League club.*

| | | | | | | | | |
|---|---|---|---|---|---|---|---|---|
| 1905-06 | (D2) | | | 1q 1st Grenadiers (H) 6-1; 2q Southern Utd (A) 1-0; 3q Crystal Palace (A) 1-7 | | | | |
| 1906-07 | (D2) | 1 | 12.01.07 | **Lincoln City** (D2) | A | D | 2-2 | Kirwan, Whitehouse |
| | | 1r | 16.01.07 | **Lincoln City** | H | L | 0-1aet | |
| 1907-08 | (D1) | 1 | 11.01.08 | **Worksop Town** (ML) | H | W | 9-1 | Hilsdon 6, Windridge 2, Bridgeman |
| | | 2 | 01.02.08 | **Manchester Utd** (D1) | A | L | 0-1 | |
| 1908-09 | (D1) | 1 | 16.01.09 | **Hull City** (D2) | A | D | 1-1 | Hilsdon |
| | | 1r | 20.01.09 | **Hull City** | H | W | 1-0 | Warren |
| | | 2 | 06.02.09 | **Blackburn Rovers** (D1) | A | L | 1-2 | Hilsdon |
| 1909-10 | (D1) | 1 | 15.01.10 | **Hull City** (D2) | H | W | 2-1 | Brawn, Williams |
| | | 2 | 05.02.10 | **Tottenham Hotspur** (D1) | H | L | 0-1 | |
| 1910-11 | (D2) | 1 | 14.01.11 | **Leyton FC** (SL) | H | D | 0-0 | |
| | | 1r | 19.01.11 | **Leyton FC** | A | W | 2-0 | Downing, Hilsdon |
| | | 2 | 04.02.11 | **Chesterfield** (ML) | A | W | 4-1 | Woodward 2, Whittingham 2 |
| | | 3 | 25.02.11 | **Wolverhampton W** (D2) | A | W | 2-0 | Freeman, Woodward |
| | | 4 | 13.03.11 | **Swindon Town** (SL) | H | W | 3-1 | Whittingham 2, Bridgeman |
| | | SF | 25.03.11 | **Newcastle Utd** (D1) *played at St Andrews* | | L | 0-3 | |
| 1911-12 | (D2) | 1 | 13.01.12 | **Sheffield Utd** (D1) | H | W | 1-0 | Dodd |
| | | 2 | 03.02.12 | **Bradford City** (D1) | A | L | 0-2 | |
| 1912-13 | (D1) | 1 | 11.01.13 | **Southend Utd** (SL) | H | W | 5-2 | Whittingham 4, Woodward (p) |
| | | 2 | 01.02.13 | **Sheffield Wed** (D1) | H | D | 1-1 | Whittingham |
| | | 2r | 05.02.13 | **Sheffield Wed** | A | L | 0-6 | |
| 1913-14 | (D1) | 1 | 10.01.14 | **Millwall Athletic** (SL) | A | D | 0-0 | |
| | | 1r | 14.01.14 | **Millwall Athletic** | H | L | 0-1 | |
| 1914-15 | (D1) | 1 | 09.01.15 | **Swindon Town** (SL) | H | D | 1-1 | Thomson |

| | | | | | | | |
|---|---|---|---|---|---|---|---|
| | 1r | 16.01.15 | **Swindon Town** | A | W | 5-2aet | Thomson 3, Ford, McNeill |
| | | | *played at Stamford Bridge* | | | | |
| | 2 | 30.01.15 | **Arsenal** (D2) | H | W | 1-0 | Halse |
| | 3 | 20.02.15 | **Manchester City** (D1) | A | W | 1-0 | Thomson |
| | 4 | 06.03.15 | **Newcastle Utd** (D1) | H | D | 1-1aet | Thomson |
| | 4r | 13.03.15 | **Newcastle Utd** | A | W | 1-0aet | Ford |
| | SF | 27.03.15 | **Everton** (D1) | | W | 2-0 | Croal, Halse |
| | | | *played at Villa Park* | | | | |
| | F | 24.04.15 | **Sheffield Utd** (D1) | | L | 0-3 | |
| | | | *played at Old Trafford* | | | | |
| 1919-20 (D1) | 1 | 10.01.20 | **Bolton Wanderers** (D1) | A | W | 1-0 | Croal |
| | 2 | 31.01.20 | **Swindon Town** (SL) | H | W | 4-0 | McNeill 2, Cock, Ford |
| | 3 | 21.02.20 | **Leicester City** (D2) | H | W | 3-0 | Browning, Cock, Ford |
| | 4 | 06.03.20 | **Bradford Park A** (D1) | H | W | 4-1 | Sharp 2, Wilding, Logan |
| | SF | 27.03.20 | **Aston Villa** (D1) | | L | 1-3 | Croal |
| | | | *played at Bramall Lane* | | | | |
| 1920-21 (D1) | 1 | 08.01.21 | **Reading** (D3) | A | D | 0-0 | |
| | 1r | 12.01.21 | **Reading** | H | D | 2-2aet | Cock, Croal |
| | 1 2r | 16.01.21 | **Reading** | H | W | 3-1 | Wilding, Ferris, Sharp |
| | 2 | 29.01.21 | **Swindon Town** (D3) | A | W | 2-0 | Cock 2 |
| | 3 | 19.02.21 | **Plymouth Argyle** (D3) | A | D | 0-0 | |
| | 3r | 24.02.21 | **Plymouth Argyle** | H | D | 0-0aet | |
| | 3 2r | 28.02.21 | **Plymouth Argyle** | | W | 2-1 | Croal, McNeill |
| | | | *played at Ashton Gate* | | | | |
| | 4 | 05.03.21 | **Cardiff City** (D2) | A | L | 0-1 | |
| 1921-22 (D1) | 1 | 07.01.22 | **WBA** (D1) | A | L | 2-4 | Bell, Ford |
| 1922-23 (D1) | 1 | 13.01.23 | **Rotherham County** (D2) | H | W | 1-0 | Armstrong |
| | 2 | 03.02.23 | **Southampton** (D2) | H | D | 0-0 | |
| | 2r | 07.02.23 | **Southampton** | A | L | 0-1 | |
| 1923-24 (D1) | 1 | 12.01.24 | **Southampton** (D2) | H | D | 1-1 | Wilson |
| | 1r | 16.01.24 | **Southampton** | A | L | 0-2 | |
| 1924-25 (D2) | 1 | 10.01.25 | **Birmingham** (D1) | A | L | 0-2 | |
| 1925-26 (D2) | 3 | 09.01.26 | **Plymouth Argyle** (D3) | A | W | 2-1 | Turnbull, McNeill |
| | 4 | 30.01.26 | **Crystal Palace** (D3) | A | L | 1-2 | Thain |
| 1926-27 (D2) | 3 | 08.01.27 | **Luton Town** (D3) | H | W | 4-0 | Thain 2, Turnbull 2 |
| | 4 | 29.01.27 | **Accrington Stanley** (3N) | H | W | 7-2 | Turnbull 3, Thain 2, Wilson 2 |
| | 5 | 19.02.27 | **Burnley** (D1) | H | W | 2-1 | Wilding, Thain |
| | 6 | 05.03.27 | **Cardiff City** (D1) | H | D | 0-0 | |
| | 6r | 09.03.27 | **Cardiff City** | A | L | 2-3 | Priestley, Turnbull |
| 1927-28 (D2) | 3 | 14.01.28 | **Wolverhampton W** (D2) | A | L | 1-2 | Brown |
| 1928-29 (D2) | 3 | 12.01.29 | **Everton** (D1) | H | W | 2-0 | Thompson, Miller |
| | 4 | 27.01.29 | **Birmingham** (D1) | H | W | 1-0 | Miller |
| | 5 | 16.02.29 | **Portsmouth** (D1) | H | D | 1-1 | Law |
| | 5r | 20.02.29 | **Portsmouth** | A | L | 0-1 | |
| 1929-30 (D2) | 3 | 11.01.30 | **Arsenal** (D1) | A | L | 0-2 | |
| 1930-31 (D1) | 3 | 10.01.31 | **West Ham Utd** (D1) | A | W | 3-1 | Jackson 2, Wade og |
| | 4 | 24.01.31 | **Arsenal** (D1) | H | W | 2-1 | Bishop, Mills |
| | 5 | 14.02.31 | **Blackburn Rovers** (D1) | H | W | 3-0 | Cheyne, Mills, Law (p) |
| | 6 | 28.02.31 | **Birmingham** (D1) | A | D | 2-2 | Jackson, Crawford |
| | 6r | 04.03.31 | **Birmingham** | H | L | 0-3 | |
| 1931-32 (D1) | 3 | 09.01.32 | **Tranmere Rovers** (3N) | A | D | 2-2 | Gallacher 2 |
| | 3r | 13.01.32 | **Tranmere Rovers** | H | W | 5-3 | Law, Jackson, Pearson, Mills, Gallacher |
| | 4 | 23.01.32 | **West Ham Utd** (D1) | H | W | 3-1 | Mills 2, Gallacher |
| | 5 | 13.02.32 | **Sheffield Wed** (D1) | A | D | 1-1 | Law |
| | 5r | 17.02.32 | **Sheffield Wed** | H | W | 2-0 | Mills, Miller |
| | 6 | 27.02.32 | **Liverpool** (D1) | A | W | 2-0 | Gallacher, Pearson |
| | SF | 12.03.32 | **Newcastle Utd** (D1) | | L | 1-2 | Gallacher |
| | | | *played at Leeds Road, Huddersfield* | | | | |
| 1932-33 (D1) | 3 | 14.01.33 | **Brighton** (3S) | A | L | 1-2 | Barber |
| 1933-34 (D1) | 3 | 13.01.34 | **WBA** (D1) | H | D | 1-1 | Gregg |

| | | | | | | | |
|---|---|---|---|---|---|---|---|
| | 3r | 17.01.34 | **WBA** | A | W | 1-0 | Gallacher |
| | 4 | 27.01.34 | **Nottingham Forest** (D2) | H | D | 1-1 | Priestley |
| | 4r | 31.01.34 | **Nottingham Forest** | A | W | 3-0 | Gallacher 2, Gibson |
| | 5 | 17.02.34 | **Stoke City** (D1) | A | L | 1-3 | Oakton |
| 1934-35 (D1) | 3 | 12.01.35 | **Luton Town** (3S) | H | D | 1-1 | Argue |
| | 3r | 16.01.35 | **Luton Town** | A | L | 0-2 | |
| 1935-36 (D1) | 3 | 11.01.36 | **Norwich City** (D2) | A | D | 1-1 | Mitchell |
| | 3r | 15.01.36 | **Norwich City** | H | W | 3-1 | Bambrick 3 |
| | 4 | 25.01.36 | **Plymouth Argyle** (D2) | H | W | 4-1 | Bambrick 2, Burgess, Barraclough |
| | 5 | 19.02.36 | **Fulham** (D2) | H | D | 0-0 | |
| | 5r | 24.02.36 | **Fulham** | A | L | 2-3 | Barraclough 2 |
| 1936-37 (D1) | 3 | 16.01.37 | **Leeds Utd** (D1) | H | W | 4-0 | Spencer 2, Mills, Argue |
| | 4 | 30.01.37 | **Millwall** (3S) | A | L | 0-3 | |
| 1937-38 (D1) | 3 | 08.01.38 | **Everton** (D1) | H | L | 0-1 | |
| 1938-39 (D1) | 3 | 07.01.39 | **Arsenal** (D1) | H | W | 2-1 | Argue 2 |
| | 4 | 21.01.39 | **Fulham** (D2) | H | W | 3-0 | Payne, Hanson, Argue |
| | 5 | 11.02.39 | **Sheffield Wed** (D2) | H | D | 1-1 | Burgess |
| | 5r | 13.02.39 | **Sheffield Wed** | A | D | 0-0aet | |
| | 5 2r | 20.02.39 | **Sheffield Wed** *played at Highbury* | | W | 3-1 | Burgess 2, Payne |
| | 6 | 04.03.39 | **Grimsby Town** (D1) | H | L | 0-1 | |
| 1945-46 (D1) | 3 1L | 05.01.46 | **Leicester City** (D2) | H | D | 1-1 | Lawton |
| | 3 2L | 10.01.46 | **Leicester City** | A | W | 2-0 | Williams, Goulden |
| | 4 1L | 26.01.46 | **West Ham Utd** (D2) | H | W | 2-0 | Spencer, Machin |
| | 4 2L | 30.01.46 | **West Ham Utd** | A | L | 0-1 | |
| | 5 1L | 09.02.46 | **Aston Villa** (D1) | H | L | 0-1 | |
| | 5 2L | 12.02.46 | **Aston Villa** | A | L | 0-1 | |
| 1946-47 (D1) | 3 | 11 1 1947 | **Arsenal** (D1) | H | D | 1-1 | Walker |
| | 3r | 15.01.47 | **Arsenal** | A | D | 1-1 | Lawton |
| | 3 2r | 20.01.47 | **Arsenal** *played at White Hart Lane* | | W | 2-0 | Lawton 2 |
| | 4 | 25.01.47 | **Derby County** (D1) | H | D | 2-2 | Williams, Lawton |
| | 4r | 29.01.47 | **Derby County** | A | L | 0-1aet | |
| 1947-48 (D1) | 3 | 10.01.48 | **Barrow** (3N) | H | W | 5-0 | Armstrong 2, Gordon, Campbell, Bowie |
| | 4 | 24.01.48 | **Manchester City** (D1) | A | L | 0-2aet | |
| 1948-49 (D1) | 3 | 08.01.49 | **Bristol City** (3S) | A | W | 3-1 | Bentley 2, Jones |
| | 4 | 29.01.49 | **Everton** (D1) | H | W | 2-0 | Bowie, Williams |
| | 5 | 12.02.49 | **WBA** (D2) | A | L | 0-3 | |
| 1949-50 (D1) | 3 | 07.01.50 | **Brentford** (D2) | A | W | 1-0 | Bowie |
| | 4 | 28.01.50 | **Newcastle Utd** (D1) | H | W | 3-0 | Billington 2, Campbell |
| | 5 | 11.02.50 | **Chesterfield** (D2) | A | D | 1-1 | Bowie |
| | 5r | 15.02.50 | **Chesterfield** | H | W | 3-0 | Bentley 2, Billington |
| | 6 | 04.03.50 | **Manchester Utd** (D1) | H | W | 2-0 | Campbell, Bentley |
| | SF | 18.03.50 | **Arsenal** (D1) *played at White Hart Lane* | | D | 2-2 | Bentley 2 |
| | SFr | 22.03.50 | **Arsenal** *played at White Hart Lane* | | L | 0-1aet | |
| 1950-51 (D1) | 3 | 09.01.51 | **Rochdale** (3N) | A | W | 3-2 | Bentley 2, Billington |
| | 4 | 27.01.51 | **Exeter City** (3S) | A | D | 1-1 | Williams |
| | 4r | 31.01.51 | **Exeter City** | H | W | 2-0 | Smith 2 |
| | 5 | 10.02.51 | **Fulham** (D1) | H | D | 1-1 | Bentley |
| | 5r | 14.02.51 | **Fulham** | A | L | 0-3 | |
| 1951-52 (D1) | 3 | 12.01.52 | **Chester** (3N) | H | D | 2-2 | Armstrong, Gray |
| | 3r | 16.01.52 | **Chester** | A | W | 3-2aet | Smith, Bentley, Lee og |
| | 4 | 02.02.52 | **Tranmere Rovers** (3N) | H | W | 4-0 | Bentley 2, Armstrong, Jones |
| | 5 | 23.02.52 | **Leeds Utd** (D2) | A | D | 1-1 | Smith |
| | 5r | 27.02.52 | **Leeds Utd** | H | D | 1-1aet | D'Arcy |
| | 5 2r | 03.03.52 | **Leeds Utd** *played at Villa Park* | | W | 5-1 | Smith 3, Gray, Bentley |
| | 6 | 08.03.52 | **Sheffield Utd** (D2) | A | W | 1-0 | Bentley |

| | | | | | | | |
|---|---|---|---|---|---|---|---|
| | SFr | 07.04.52 | **Arsenal**<br>*played at White Hart Lane* | | L | 0-3 | |
| 1952-53 (D1) | 3 | 10.01.53 | **Derby County** (D1) | A | D | 4-4 | Bentley, McNichol, Parsons, Armstrong |
| | 3r | 14.01.53 | **Derby County** | H | W | 1-0aet | Parsons |
| | 4 | 31.01.53 | **WBA** (D1) | H | D | 1-1 | Bentley |
| | 4r | 04.02.53 | **WBA** | A | D | 0-0aet | |
| | 4 2r | 09.02.53 | **WBA**<br>*played at Villa Park* | | D | 1-1aet | Bentley |
| | 4 3r | 11.02.53 | **WBA**<br>*played at Highbury* | | W | 4-0 | Bentley 2, Campbell, Parsons |
| | 5 | 14.02.53 | **Birmingham City** (D2) | H | L | 0-4 | |
| 1953-54 (D1) | 3 | 09.01.54 | **WBA** (D1) | A | L | 0-1 | |
| 1954-55 (D1) | 3 | 08.01.55 | **Walsall** (3S) | H | W | 2-0 | O'Connell, Stubbs |
| | 4 | 29.01.55 | **Bristol Rovers** (D2) | A | W | 3-1 | Parsons, Bluntstone, McNicholl |
| | 5 | 19.02.55 | **Notts County** (D2) | A | L | 0-1 | |
| 1955-56 (D1) | 3 | 07.01.56 | **Hartlepools Utd** (3N) | A | W | 1-0 | Moore og |
| | 4 | 28.01.56 | **Burnley** (D1) | A | D | 1-1 | Parsons |
| | 4r | 01.02.56 | **Burnley** | H | D | 1-1aet | Bluntstone |
| | 4 2r | 06.02.56 | **Burnley**<br>*played at St Andrews* | | D | 2-2aet | P Sillett, Bentley |
| | 4 3r | 13.02.56 | **Burnley**<br>*played at Highbury* | | D | 0-0aet | |
| | 4 4r | 15.02.56 | **Burnley**<br>*played at White Hart Lane* | | W | 2-0 | Lewis, Tindall |
| | 5 | 18.02.56 | **Everton** (D1) | A | L | 0-1 | |
| 1956-57 (D1) | 3 | 05.01.57 | **Leyton Orient** (D2) | A | W | 2-0 | Brabrook, McNicholl |
| | 4 | 26.01.57 | **Tottenham Hotspur** (D1) | A | L | 0-4 | |
| 1957-58 (D1) | 3 | 04.01.58 | **Doncaster Rovers** (D2) | A | W | 2-0 | McNicholl 2 |
| | 4 | 25.01.58 | **Darlington** (3N) | H | D | 3-3 | McNicholl, Tindall, Lewis |
| | 4r | 29.01.58 | **Darlington** | A | L | 1-4 | McNicholl |
| 1958-59 (D1) | 3 | 19.01.59 | **Newcastle Utd** (D1) | A | W | 4-1 | Gibbs, Greaves, Mortimer, Cliss |
| | 4 | 24.01.59 | **Aston Villa** (D1) | H | L | 1-2 | Greaves |
| 1959-60 (D1) | 3 | 09.01.60 | **Bradford Park A** (D4) | H | W | 5-1 | Brabrook 2, Greaves, Livesey, Bluntstone |
| | 4 | 30.01.60 | **Aston Villa** (D2) | H | L | 1-2 | P Sillett (p) |
| 1960-61 (D1) | 3 | 07.01.61 | **Crewe Alexandra** (D4) | H | L | 1-2 | Bluntstone |
| 1961-62 (D1) | 3 | 06.01.62 | **Liverpool** (D2) | A | L | 3-4 | Tamblng 2, Bridges |
| 1962-63 (D2) | 3 | 05.01.63 | **Tranmere Rovers** (D4) | A | D | 2-2 | Tambling, Bridges |
| | 3r | 30.01.63 | **Tranmere Rovers** | H | W | 3-1 | Venables, Bridges, Moore |
| | 4 | 06.03.63 | **Charlton Athletic** (D2) | A | W | 3-0 | Mulholland, Murray, Tambling |
| | 5 | 16.03.63 | **Manchester Utd** (D1) | A | L | 1-2 | Sorrell |
| 1963-64 (D1) | 3 | 04.01.64 | **Tottenham Hotspur** (D1) | A | D | 1-1 | Murray |
| | 3r | 08.01.64 | **Tottenham Hotspur** | H | W | 2-0 | Murray, Tambling |
| | 4 | 25.01.64 | **Huddersfield Town** (D2) | H | L | 1-2 | Tambling |
| 1964-65 (D1) | 3 | 09.01.65 | **Northampton Town** (D2) | H | W | 4-1 | Bridges 2, Tambling, Foley og |
| | 4 | 30.01.65 | **West Ham Utd** (D1) | A | W | 1-0 | Tambling |
| | 5 | 20.02.65 | **Tottenham Hotspur** (D1) | H | W | 1-0 | Bridges |
| | 6 | 06.03.65 | **Peterborough Utd** (D3) | H | W | 5-1 | Tambling 2, Bridges, Hollins, Murray |
| | SF | 27.03.65 | **Liverpool** (D1)<br>*played at Villa Park* | | L | 0-2 | |
| 1965-66 (D1) | 3 | 22.01.66 | **Liverpool** | A | W | 2-1 | Tambling, Osgood |
| | 4 | 12.02.66 | **Leeds Utd** (D1) | H | W | 1-0 | Tambling |
| | 5 | 05.03.66 | **Shrewsbury Town** (D3) | H | W | 3-2 | Bridges 2, Graham |
| | 6 | 26.03.66 | **Hull City** (D3) | H | D | 2-2 | Graham, Tambling |
| | 6r | 31.03.66 | **Hull City** | A | W | 3-1 | Tambling 2, Graham |
| | SF | 23.04.66 | **Sheffield Wed** (D1)<br>*played at Villa Park* | | L | 0-2 | |
| 1966-67 (D1) | 3 | 28.01.67 | **Huddersfield Town** (D2) | A | W | 2-1 | Houseman, Tambling |
| | 4 | 18.02.67 | **Brighton** (D3) | A | D | 1-1 | Tambling |
| | 4r | 22.02.67 | **Brighton** | H | W | 4-0 | Tambling 2, Young, Baldwin |

| | | | | | | | |
|---|---|---|---|---|---|---|---|
| | 5 | 11.03.67 | **Sheffield Utd** (D1) | H | W | 2-0 | Tambling, Hateley |
| | 6 | 08.04.67 | **Sheffield Wed** (D1) | H | W | 1-0 | Baldwin |
| | SF | 29.04.67 | **Leeds Utd** (D1) | | W | 1-0 | Hateley |
| | | | *played at Villa Park* | | | | |
| | F | 20.05.67 | **Tottenham Hotspur** (D1) | | L | 1-2 | Tambling |
| | | | *played at Wembley Stadium* | | | | |
| 1967-68 (D1) | 3 | 27.01.68 | **Ipswich Town** (D2) | H | W | 3-0 | Birchenall 2, Tambling |
| | 4 | 17.02.68 | **Norwich City** (D2) | H | W | 1-0 | Cooke |
| | 5 | 09.03.68 | **Sheffield Wed** (D1) | A | D | 2-2 | Tambling, Baldwin |
| | 5r | 12.03.68 | **Sheffield Wed** | H | W | 2-0 | Tambling, Osgood |
| | 6 | 30.03.68 | **Birmingham City** (D2) | A | L | 0-1 | |
| 1968-69 (D1) | 3 | 04.01.69 | **Carlisle Utd** (D2) | H | W | 2-0 | Osgood, Tambling |
| | 4 | 25.01.69 | **Preston North End** (D2) | A | D | 0-0 | |
| | 4r | 29.01.69 | **Preston North End** | H | - | 2-0ab | Hutchinson, Birchenall |
| | | | *abandoned after 72 minutes – floodlight failure* | | | | |
| | 4r | 03.02.69 | **Preston North End** | H | W | 2-1 | Webb, Cooke |
| | 5 | 12.02.69 | **Stoke City** (D1) | H | W | 3-2 | Osgood 2, Birchenall |
| | 6 | 01.03.69 | **WBA** (D1) | H | L | 1-2 | Webb |
| 1969-70 (D1) | 3 | 03.01.70 | **Birmingham City** (D2) | H | W | 3-0 | Hutchinson 2, Osgood |
| | 4 | 24.01.70 | **Burnley** (D1) | H | D | 2-2 | Hollins, Osgood |
| | 4r | 27.01.70 | **Burnley** | A | W | 3-1aet | Houseman 2, Baldwin |
| | 5 | 07.02.70 | **Crystal Palace** (D1) | A | W | 4-1 | Osgood, Dempsey, Hutchinson, Houseman |
| | 6 | 21.02.70 | **QPR** (D2) | A | W | 4-2 | Osgood 3, Webb |
| | SF | 14.03.70 | **Watford** (D2) | | W | 5-1 | Webb, Osgood, Houseman 2, Hutchinson |
| | | | *played at White Hart Lane* | | | | |
| | F | 11.04.70 | **Leeds Utd** (D1) | | D | 2-2aet | Houseman, Hutchinson |
| | | | *played at Wembley Stadium* | | | | |
| | Fr | 29.04.70 | **Leeds Utd** | | W | 2-1aet | Osgood, Webb |
| | | | *played at Old Trafford* | | | | |
| 1970-71 (D1) | 3 | 02.01.71 | **Crystal Palace** (D1) | A | D | 2-2 | Osgood, Baldwin |
| | 3r | 06.01.71 | **Crystal Palace** | H | W | 2-0 | Baldwin, Houseman |
| | 4 | 23.01.71 | **Manchester City** (D1) | H | L | 0-3 | |
| 1971-72 (D1) | 3 | 15.01.72 | **Blackpool** (D2) | A | W | 1-0 | Dempsey |
| | 4 | 05.02.72 | **Bolton Wanderers** (D3) | H | W | 3-0 | Cooke, Houseman, Hollins (p) |
| | 5 | 26.02.72 | **Orient** (D2) | A | L | 2-3 | Webb, Osgood |
| 1972-73 (D1) | 3 | 13.01.73 | **Brighton** (D2) | A | W | 2-0 | Osgood 2 |
| | 4 | 03.02.73 | **Ipswich Town** (D1) | H | W | 2-0 | Garner 2 |
| | 5 | 24.02.73 | **Sheffield Wed** (D2) | A | W | 2-1 | Osgood, Garner |
| | 6 | 17.03.73 | **Arsenal** (D1) | H | D | 2-2 | Hollins, Osgood |
| | 6r | 20.03.73 | **Arsenal** | A | L | 1-2 | Houseman |
| 1973-74 (D1) | 3 | 05.01.74 | **QPR** (D1) | H | D | 0-0 | |
| | 3r | 15.01.74 | **QPR** | A | L | 0-1 | |
| 1974-75 (D1) | 3 | 04.01.75 | **Sheffield Wed** (D2) | H | W | 3-2 | Droy 2, Garland |
| | 4 | 25.01.75 | **Birmingham City** (D1) | H | L | 0-1 | |
| 1975-76 (D2) | 3 | 01.01.76 | **Bristol Rovers** (D2) | H | D | 1-1 | Garner |
| | 3r | 03.01.76 | **Bristol Rovers** | A | W | 1-0 | Swain |
| | 4 | 24.01.76 | **York City** (D2) | A | W | 2-0 | Garner, Hutchinson |
| | 5 | 14.02.76 | **Crystal Palace** (D3) | H | L | 2-3 | R Wilkins, Wicks |
| 1976-77 (D2) | 3 | 08.01.77 | **Southampton** (D2) | A | D | 1-1 | Locke |
| | 3r | 12.01.77 | **Southampton** | H | L | 0-3aet | |
| 1977-78 (D1) | 3 | 07.01.78 | **Liverpool** (D1) | H | W | 4-2 | Walker 2, Finniestone, Langley |
| | 4 | 31.01.78 | **Burnley** (D2) | H | W | 6-2 | Droy, Wicks, Swain (p), Walker, Langley, R Wilkins |
| | 5 | 18.02.78 | **Orient** (D2) | A | D | 0-0 | |
| | 5r | 27.02.78 | **Orient** | H | L | 1-2 | Roffey og |
| 1978-79 (D1) | 3 | 15.01.79 | **Manchester Utd** (D1) | A | L | 0-3 | |
| 1979-80 (D2) | 3 | 14.01.80 | **Wigan Athletic** (D4) | H | L | 0-1 | |
| 1980-81 (D2) | 3 | 03.01.81 | **Southampton** (D1) | A | L | 1-3 | Lee |
| 1981-82 (D2) | 3 | 18.01.82 | **Hull City** (D4) | H | D | 0-0 | |

| | | | | | | | | |
|---|---|---|---|---|---|---|---|---|
| | | 3r | 21.01.82 | **Hull City** | A | W | 2-0 | Bumstead, Mayes |
| | | 4 | 23.01.82 | **Wrexham** (D2) | H | D | 0-0 | |
| | | 4r | 26.01.82 | **Wrexham** | A | D | 1-1aet | Mayes |
| | | 4 2r | 01.02.82 | **Wrexham** | A | W | 2-1 | Droy, Mayes |
| | | 5 | 13.02.82 | **Liverpool** (D1) | H | W | 2-0 | Rhoades-Brown, Lee |
| | | 6 | 06.03.82 | **Tottenham Hotspur** (D1) | H | L | 2-3 | Mayes, Fillery |
| 1982-83 | (D2) | 3 | 08.01.83 | **Huddersfield Town** (D3) | A | D | 1-1 | Mayes |
| | | 3r | 12.01.83 | **Huddersfield Town** | H | W | 2-0 | Bumstead, Fillery |
| | | 4 | 29.01.83 | **Derby County** (D2) | A | L | 1-2 | Fillery |
| 1983-84 | (D2) | 3 | 07.01.84 | **Blackburn Rovers** (D2) | A | L | 0-1 | |
| 1984-85 | (D1) | 3 | 05.01.85 | **Wigan Athletic** (D3) | H | D | 2-2 | Nevin, Speedie |
| | | 3r | 26.01.85 | **Wigan Athletic** | A | W | 5-0 | Dixon 4 (1p), Speedie |
| | | 4 | 04.02.85 | **Millwall** (D3) | H | L | 2-3 | Spackman, Canoville |
| 1985-86 | (D1) | 3 | 04.01.86 | **Shrewsbury Town** (D2) | A | W | 1-0 | Speedie |
| | | 4 | 26.01.86 | **Liverpool** (D1) | H | L | 1-2 | Speedie |
| 1986-87 | (D1) | 3 | 10.01.87 | **Aston Villa** (D1) | A | D | 2-2 | Bumstead, Speedie |
| | | 3r | 21.01.87 | **Aston Villa** | H | W | 2-1aet | Durie, Hazard (p) |
| | | 4 | 01.02.87 | **Watford** (D1) | A | L | 0-1 | |
| 1987-88 | (D1) | 3 | 09.01.88 | **Derby County** (D1) | A | W | 3-1 | McAllister, Dixon, Wegerle |
| | | 4 | 30.01.88 | **Manchester Utd** (D1) | A | L | 0-2 | |
| 1988-89 | (D2) | 3 | 07.01.89 | **Barnsley** (D2) | A | L | 0-4 | |
| 1989-90 | (D1) | 3 | 06.01.90 | **Crewe Alexandra** (D3) | H | D | 1-1 | Clarke |
| | | 3r | 10.01.90 | **Crewe Alexandra** | A | W | 2-0 | Dixon 2 |
| | | 4 | 27.01.90 | **Bristol City** (D3) | A | L | 1-3 | K Wilson |
| 1990-91 | (D1) | 3 | 05.01.91 | **Oxford Utd** (D2) | H | L | 1-3 | Dixon |
| 1991-92 | (D1) | 3 | 04.01.92 | **Hull City** (D3) | A | W | 2-0 | Jones, Wise |
| | | 4 | 26.01.92 | **Everton** (D1) | H | W | 1-0 | Allen |
| | | 5 | 15.02.92 | **Sheffield Utd** (D1) | H | W | 1-0 | Stuart |
| | | 6 | 09.03.92 | **Sunderland** (D2) | H | D | 1-1 | Allen |
| | | 6r | 18.03.92 | **Sunderland** | A | L | 1-2 | Wise |
| 1992-93 | (PL) | 3 | 13.01.93 | **Middlesbrough** (PL) | A | L | 1-2 | Mohan og |
| 1993-94 | (PL) | 3 | 08.01.94 | **Barnet** (D2) | A | D | 0-0 | |
| | | | | *played at Stamford Bridge* | | | | |
| | | 3r | 19.01.94 | **Barnet** | H | W | 4-0 | Burley, Peacock, Stein, Shipperley |
| | | 4 | 29.01.94 | **Sheffield Wed** (PL) | H | D | 1-1 | Peacock |
| | | 4r | 09.02.94 | **Sheffield Wed** | A | W | 3-1aet | Spencer, Peacock, Burley |
| | | 5 | 19.02.94 | **Oxford Utd** (D1) | A | W | 2-1 | Spencer, Burley |
| | | 6 | 13.03.94 | **Wolverhampton W** (D1) | H | W | 1-0 | Peacock |
| | | SF | 09.04.94 | **Luton Town** (D1) | | W | 2-0 | Peacock 2 |
| | | | | *played at Wembley Stadium* | | | | |
| | | F | 14.05.94 | **Manchester Utd** (PL) | | L | 0-4 | |
| | | | | *played at Wembley Stadium* | | | | |
| 1994-95 | (PL) | 3 | 07.01.95 | **Charlton Athletic** (D1) | H | W | 3-0 | Peacock, Sinclair, Spencer |
| | | 4 | 28.01.95 | **Millwall** (D1) | A | D | 0-0 | |
| | | 4r | 08.02.95 | **Millwall** | H | D | 1-1aet | Stein |
| | | | | *Millwall won 5-4 on penalties* | | | | |
| 1995-96 | (PL) | 3 | 07.01.96 | **Newcastle Utd** (PL) | H | D | 1-1 | Hughes |
| | | 3r | 17.01.96 | **Newcastle Utd** | A | D | 2-2aet | Wise (p), Gullit |
| | | | | *Chelsea won 4-2 on penalties* | | | | |
| | | 4 | 29.01.96 | **QPR** (PL) | A | W | 2-1 | Peacock, Furlong |
| | | 5 | 21.02.96 | **Grimsby Town** (D1) | A | D | 0-0 | |
| | | 5r | 28.02.96 | **Grimsby Town** | H | W | 4-1 | Duberry, Hughes, Spencer, Peacock |
| | | 6 | 09.03.96 | **Wimbledon** (PL) | H | D | 2-2 | S Hughes, Gullit |
| | | 6r | 20.03.96 | **Wimbledon** | A | W | 3-1 | Petrescu, Duberry, Hughes |
| | | SF | 31.03.96 | **Manchester Utd** (PL) | | L | 1-2 | Gullit |
| | | | | *played at Villa Park* | | | | |
| 1996-97 | (PL) | 3 | 04.01.97 | **WBA** (D1) | H | W | 3-0 | Wise, Burley, Zola |
| | | 4 | 26.01.97 | **Liverpool** (PL) | H | W | 4-2 | Hughes, Zola, Vialli 2 |
| | | 5 | 16.02.97 | **Leicester City** (PL) | A | D | 2-2 | Di Matteo, Hughes |
| | | 5r | 26.02.97 | **Leicester City** | H | W | 1-0aet | Lebouef (p) |
| | | 6 | 09.03.97 | **Portsmouth** (D1) | A | W | 4-1 | Hughes, Wise 2, Zola |

| | | | | | | | |
|---|---|---|---|---|---|---|---|
| | SF | 13.04.97 | **Wimbledon** (PL) *played at Highbury* | | W | 3-0 | Petrescu, Duberry, Hughes |
| | F | 17.05.97 | **Middlesbrough** (PL) *played at Wembley Stadium* | | W | 2-0 | Di Matteo, Newton |
| 1997-98 (PL) | 3 | 04.01.98 | **Manchester Utd** (PL) | H | L | 3-5 | Le Saux, Vialli 2 |
| 1998-99 (PL) | 3 | 02.01.99 | **Oldham Athletic** (D2) | A | W | 2-0 | Vialli 2 |
| | 4 | 25.01.99 | **Oxford Utd** (D1) | A | D | 1-1 | Lebouef (p) |
| | 4r | 03.02.99 | **Oxford Utd** | H | W | 4-2 | Wise, Zola, Forsell 2 |
| | 5 | 13.02.99 | **Sheffield Wed** (PL) | A | W | 1-0 | Di Matteo |
| | 6 | 07.03.99 | **Manchester Utd** (PL) | A | D | 0-0 | |
| | 6r | 10.03.99 | **Manchester Utd** | H | L | 0-2 | |
| 1999-00 (PL) | 3 | 11.12.99 | **Hull City** (D3) | A | W | 6-1 | Poyet 3, Sutton, Di Matteo, Edwards og |
| | 4 | 19.01.00 | **Nottingham Forest** (D1) | H | W | 2-0 | Lebouef, Wise |
| | 5 | 30.01.00 | **Leicester City** (PL) | H | W | 2-1 | Poyet, Weah |
| | 6 | 20.02.00 | **Gillingham** (D2) | H | W | 5-0 | Flo, Terry, Weah, Zola (p), Morris |
| | SF | 09.04.00 | **Newcastle Utd** (PL) *played at Wembley Stadium* | | W | 2-1 | Poyet 2 |
| | F | 20.05.00 | **Aston Villa** (PL) *played at Wembley Stadium* | | W | 1-0 | Di Matteo |
| 2000-01 (PL) | 3 | 06.01.01 | **Peterborough Utd** (D2) | H | W | 5-0 | Zola 2, Hasselbaink, Gudjohnsen, Poyet |
| | 4 | 28.01.01 | **Gillingham** (D1) | A | W | 4-2 | Gudjohnsen 2, Gronkjaer 2 |
| | 5 | 18.02.01 | **Arsenal** (PL) | A | L | 1-3 | Hasselbaink |
| 2001-02 (PL) | 3 | 05.01.02 | **Norwich City** (D1) | A | D | 0-0 | |
| | 3r | 15.01.02 | **Norwich City** | H | W | 4-0 | Stanic, Lampard, Zola, Forsell |
| | 4 | 26.01.02 | **West Ham Utd** (PL) | H | D | 1-1 | Hasselbaink |
| | 4r | 06.02.02 | **West Ham Utd** | A | W | 3-2 | Hasselbaink, Forsell, Terry |
| | 5 | 17.02.02 | **Preston North End** (D1) | H | W | 3-1 | Gudjohnsen, Hasselbaink, Forsell |
| | 6 | 10.03.02 | **Tottenham Hotspur** (PL) | A | W | 4-0 | Gallas, Gudjohnsen 2, Le Saux |
| | SF | 14.04.02 | **Fulham** (PL) *played at Villa Park* | | W | 1-0 | Terry |
| | F | 04.05.02 | **Arsenal** (PL) *played at Millennium Stadium, Cardiff* | | L | 0-2 | |
| 2002-03 (PL) | 3 | 04.01.03 | **Middlesbrough** (PL) | H | W | 1-0 | Stanic |
| | 4 | 26.01.03 | **Shrewsbury Town** (D3) | A | W | 4-0 | Zola 2, Cole, Morris |
| | 5 | 16.02.03 | **Stoke City** (D1) | A | W | 2-0 | Hasselbaink, Gronkjaer |
| | 6 | 08.03.03 | **Arsenal** (PL) | A | D | 2-2 | Terry, Lampard |
| | 6r | 25.03.03 | **Arsenal** | H | L | 1-3 | Terry |

## CHELTENHAM TOWN

*Formed 1892. First entered FA Cup: 1914-15. FA Trophy winners: 1998; League club beaten as a Non-League club: Carlisle United. Promoted to the Football League 1999.*

| | | | | | | | |
|---|---|---|---|---|---|---|---|
| 1933-34 (BC) | 1 | 25.11.33 | **Barnet** (AL) | H | W | 5-1 | Payne 2, Knight 2, Yarwood |
| | 2 | 09.12.33 | **Carlisle Utd** (3N) | A | W | 2-1 | Smith, Bradley og |
| | 3 | 13.01.34 | **Blackpool** (D2) | H | L | 1-3 | Payne |
| 1935-36 (SL) | 1 | 30.11.35 | **Brighton** (3S) | A | D | 0-0 | |
| | 1r | 04.12.35 | **Brighton** | H | L | 0-6 | |
| 1937-38 (SL) | 1 | 27.11.37 | **Watford** (3S) | A | L | 0-3 | |
| 1938-39 (SL) | 1 | 26.11.38 | **Cardiff City** (3S) | H | D | 1-1 | Prior |
| | 1r | 30.11.38 | **Cardiff City** | A | L | 0-1 | |
| 1945-46 (SL) | 1 1L | 17.11.45 | **Bath City** (SL) | A | L | 2-3 | Edwards, Goring |
| | 1 2L | 24.11.45 | **Bath City** | H | L | 0-2 | |
| 1946-47 (SL) | 1 | 30.11.46 | **Aldershot** (3S) | A | L | 2-4 | Crowe 2 |
| 1947-48 (SL) | 1 | 29.11.47 | **Street** (WL) | H | W | 5-0 | Crowe, Goring 3, Tadman |
| | 2 | 13.12.47 | **Hull City** (3N) | A | L | 2-4 | Green, Goring |
| 1950-51 (SL) | 1 | 25.11.50 | **Reading** (3S) | A | L | 1-3 | Crowe |
| 1956-57 (SL) | 1 | 17.11.56 | **Reading** | H | L | 1-2 | McAllister |
| 1959-60 (SL) | 1 | 14.11.59 | **Watford** (D4) | H | D | 0-0 | |
| | 1r | 17.11.59 | **Watford** | A | L | 0-3 | |
| 1962-63 (SL) | 1 | 03.11.62 | **Enfield** (AL) | H | L | 3-6 | Palmer, Mitchinson, McCool |
| 1968-69 (SL) | 1 | 16.11.68 | **Watford** (D3) | H | L | 0-4 | |
| 1969-70 (SL) | 1 | 15.11.69 | **Oxford City** (IL) | H | L | 0-2 | |

| | | | | | | | | |
|---|---|---|---|---|---|---|---|---|
| 1970-71 | (SL) | 1 | 21.11.70 | **Brighton** (D3) | A | L | 0-4 | |
| 1974-75 | (SL) | 1 | 23.11.74 | **Wycombe W** (IL) | A | L | 1-3 | Lewis (p) |
| 1987-88 | (Conf) | 1 | 14.11.87 | **Wolverhampton W** (D4) | A | L | 1-5 | Angell |
| 1990-91 | (Conf) | 1 | 17.11.90 | **Birmingham City** (D3) | A | L | 0-1 | |
| 1992-93 | (SL) | 1 | 14.11.92 | **St Albans City** (IL) | A | W | 2-1 | Willetts (p), Purdie . |
| | | 2 | 05.12.92 | **Bournemouth** (D2) | H | D | 1-1 | Warren |
| | | 2r | 16.12.92 | **Bournemouth** | A | L | 0-3 | |
| 1996-97 | (SL) | 1 | 16.11.96 | **Peterborough Utd** (D2) | A | D | 0-0 | |
| | | 1r | 27.11.96 | **Peterborough Utd** | H | L | 1-3aet | Smith (p) |
| 1997-98 | (Conf) | 1 | 15.11.97 | **Tiverton Town** (WL) | H | W | 2-1 | Eaton, Walker |
| | | 2 | 06.12.97 | **Borehamwood** (IL) | H | D | 1-1 | Howells |
| | | 2r | 16.12.97 | **Borehamwood** | A | W | 2-0 | Bloomer, Smith |
| | | 3 | 13.01.98 | **Reading** (D1) | H | D | 1-1 | Watkins (p) |
| | | 3r | 20.01.98 | **Reading** | A | L | 1-2 | Walker |
| 1998-99 | (Conf) | 1 | 14.11.98 | **Lincoln City** (D2) | H | L | 0-1 | |
| 1999-00 | (D3) | 1 | 30.10.99 | **Gillingham** (D2) | H | D | 1-1 | Brough |
| | | 1r | 09.11.99 | **Gillingham** | A | L | 2-3 | Milton, Howarth |
| 2000-01 | (D3) | 1 | 18.11.00 | **Shrewsbury Town** (D3) | H | W | 4-1 | Howells, Grayson 2, Alsop |
| | | 2 | 09.12.00 | **Cardiff City** (D3) | A | L | 1-3 | Milton |
| 2001-02 | (D3) | 1 | 17.11.01 | **Kettering Town** (SL) | A | W | 6-1 | Naylor 2, Alsop 2, Howells, Devaney |
| | | 2 | 08.12.01 | **Hinckley Utd** (SL) | A | W | 2-0 | Naylor, Alsop |
| | | 3 | 06.01.02 | **Oldham Athletic** (D2) | H | W | 2-1 | Naylor 2 |
| | | 4 | 27.01.02 | **Burnley** (D1) | H | W | 2-1 | Milton, Alsop |
| | | 5 | 16.02.02 | **WBA** (D1) | A | L | 0-1 | |
| 2002-03 | (D2) | 1 | 16.11.02 | **Yeovil Town** (Conf) | A | W | 2-0 | Alsop, Devaney |
| | | 2 | 07.12.02 | **Oldham Athletic** (D2) | A | W | 2-1 | Yates, Brayson |
| | | 3 | 04.01.03 | **Sheffield Utd** (D1) | A | L | 0-4 | |

## CHESHAM

*Competed in the FA Cup from 1885-86 – 1897-98.*

| | | | | | | | |
|---|---|---|---|---|---|---|---|
| 1885-86 | 1 | 31.10.85 | **Luton Wanderers** | A | L | 2-3 | Ayres, Culverhouse |
| 1887-88 | 1 | 15.10.87 | **Watford Rovers** | H | W | 4-2 | |
| | | | *FA ordered replay after protest* | | | | |
| | 1r | 22.10.87 | **Watford Rovers** | H | L | 1-3 | |

## CHESHAM GENERALS

*Berks and Bucks Senior Cup winners 1901.*

| | | | | | | |
|---|---|---|---|---|---|---|
| 1886-87 | 1 | 30.10.86 | **Lyndhurst FC** | H | W | 4-2 |
| | 2 | 20.11.86 | **Old Etonians** | H | L | 1-7 |

## CHESHAM UNITED

*Formed 1886. FA Amateur Cup runners-up 1968. Some sources give a later founding date of 1919. Members of the Isthmian League,*

| | | | | | | | | |
|---|---|---|---|---|---|---|---|---|
| 1966-67 | (AL) | 1 | 26.11.66 | **Enfield** (IL) | A | L | 0-6 | |
| 1968-69 | (AL) | 1 | 16.11.68 | **Colchester Utd** (D4) | A | L | 0-5 | |
| 1976-77 | (IL) | 1 | 20.11.76 | **Brentford** (D4) | A | L | 0-2 | |
| 1979-80 | (IL) | 1 | 24.11.79 | **Minehead** (SL) | A | W | 2-1 | Woolfrey, Dodd |
| | | 2 | 19.12.79 | **Merthyr Tydfil** (SL) | H | D | 1-1 | Woolfrey |
| | | 2r | 22.12.79 | **Merthyr Tydfil** | A | W | 3-1 | Rosser og, Horastead, Watt |
| | | 3 | 05.01.80 | **Cambridge Utd** (D2) | H | L | 0-2 | |
| 1982-83 | (IL) | 1 | 20.11.82 | **Yeovil Town** (APL) | H | L | 0-1 | |
| 1994-95 | (IL) | 1 | 12.11.94 | **Bashley** (SL) | H | L | 0-1 | |

# CHESTER CITY

*Formed 1884 and played as Chester until changing to Chester City 99 years later. Best FA Cup performance: 5th round, 1977, 1980; FA Cup record win: 10-1 v Lostock Gralam, preliminary round, 1927-28. In Competition Proper: 6-1 v Darlington, 1st round, 25.11.1933; 5-0 v Crewe Alexandra, 1st round, 14.11.1964; 5-0 v Runcorn, 1st round replay, 28.11.1978; FA Cup Record Defeat: 0-7 v Blackburn Rovers, 2nd round, 31.01.1891; Welsh FA Cup winners: 1908, 1933, 1947. Ian Rush, who scored more FA Cup goals (44) in the 20th century than any other player including a record five in FA Cup finals, scored the first four of those goals at the start of his career with Chester. Members of The Conference.*

| | | | | | | | |
|---|---|---|---|---|---|---|---|
| 1886-87 | 1 | | bye | | | | |
| 1886-87 | 2 | 20.11.86 | **Goldenhill** | H | W | 1-0 | Turner |
| | | | *FA disqualified Chester following protest, Goldenhill re-instated* | | | | |
| 1887-88 | 1 | 15.10.87 | **Davenham** | H | L | 2-3 | Higginson, AN Other |
| 1888-89 | | | 1q Macclesfield (H) 2-2, Chester awarded tie; 2q Over Wanderers (H) 5-1; 3q Llangollen (H) 5-1; 4q Wreham (H) 2-3 | | | | |
| 1889-90 | | | 1q Over Wanderers (H) 2-0; 2q Burslem PV (H) 1-0; 3q Chester St Oswalds (A) 3-0; 4q Crewe Alexandra (H) 2-1 | | | | |
| 1889-90 | 1 | 18.01.90 | **Lincoln City** (ML) | A | L | 0-2 | |
| 1890-91 (TC) | | | 1q Chester St Oswalds (A) 6-0; 2q Northwich V (H) 2 -0; 3q Nantwich; T (A) 5-4; 4q Cliftonville (H) walkover | | | | |
| 1890-91 (TC) | 1 | 17.01.91 | **Lincoln City** (ML) | H | W | 1-0 | Roberts |
| | 2 | 31.01.91 | **Blackburn Rovers** (D1) | A | L | 0-7 | |
| 1891-92 (TC) | | | 2q Wrexham (H) 2-4 | | | | |
| 1892-93 (TC) | | | 1q Stanley (A) 4-1; 2q Prescot (H) 2-1; 3q Liverpool Caledonians (A) 2-3 | | | | |
| 1893-94 (TC) | | | 2q Macclesfield (A) 1-6 | | | | |
| 1894-95 (TC) | | | 1q Macclesfield (H) 1-2 | | | | |
| 1895-96 (TC) | | | 1q Port Sunlight (A) 5-1; 2q Middleton (H) 0-3 | | | | |
| 1896-97 (TC) | | | 1q Middleton (A) 2-3 | | | | |
| 1897-98 (TC) | | | 1q Stockport Co (A) 0-2 | | | | |
| 1898-99 (TC) | | | 1q Wrexham (A) 2-3 | | | | |
| 1899-00 (TC) | | | did not enter | | | | |
| 1900-01 (TC) | | | did not enter | | | | |
| 1901-02 (TC) | | | 1q Birkenhead (A) 1-1; 1qr Birkenhead (H) 5-4. FA awarded tie to Birkenhead after protest | | | | |
| 1902-03 (TC) | | | did not enter | | | | |
| 1903-04 (TC) | | | did not enter | | | | |
| 1904-05 (TC) | | | did not enter | | | | |
| 1905-06 (TC) | | | 1q Northern Nomads (H) 2-0; 2q Chirk (A) 0-2 | | | | |
| 1906-07 (TC) | | | did not enter | | | | |
| 1907-08 (TC) | | | 1q Tranmere R (H) 0-4 | | | | |
| 1908-09 (TC) | | | 1q Druids (H) 4-1; 2q Wellington T (H) 3-1; 3q Wrexham (H) 1-3 | | | | |
| 1909-10 (TC) | | | P Tranmere R (A) 0-6 | | | | |
| 1910-11 (LC) | | | P Druids (A) 3-1; 1q Wrexham (H) 3-0; 2q New Brighton Tower (A) 3-1; 3q Witton Albion (H) 7-1; 4q Crewe Alexandra (A) 3-4 | | | | |
| 1911-12 (LC) | | | 1q Shrewsbury T (H) 6-1; 2q Northern Nomads (H) 4-0; 3q Wrexham (A) 4-1; 4q Stockport Co (H) 1-4 | | | | |
| 1912-13 (LC) | | | P Wrexham (A) 0-2 | | | | |
| 1913-14 (LC) | | | P Nantwich T (A) 5-3; 1q Tranmere R (H) 2-1; 2q Port Vale ( H) 2-5 | | | | |
| 1914-15 (LC) | | | 1q Ormskirk (H) 2-0; 2q Tranmere R (A) 1-5 | | | | |
| 1919-20 (CC) | | | 1q Ormskirk (H) 2-0; 2q Tranmere R (A) 1-5; 1q Nantwich T | | | | |
| 1920-21 (CC) | | | did not enter | | | | |
| 1921-22 (CC) | | | P Machynlleth (H) 7-0; 1q Lostock Gralam (H) 2-0; 2q Harrowby bye 3q Northwich V (A) 3-3; 3qr Northwich V (H) W; 4q Crewe Alexandra (A) 1-1; 4qr Crewe Alex (H) 1-2 | | | | |
| 1922-23 (CC) | | | P New Brighton (A) 2-4 | | | | |
| 1923-24 (CC) | | | P Ellesmere Port C (H) 1-0; 1q Lostock Gralam (H) 5-1; 2q Ellesmere Port T (A) 1-2 | | | | |
| 1924-25 (CC) | | | P Witton Albion (A) 0-2 | | | | |
| 1925-26 (CC) | | | P Llandudno (A) 0-0; Pr Llandudno (H) W; 1q Sandbach (H) 2 -0; 2q Witton Albion (H) 2-2; 2qr Witton Albion (H) W; 3q Mold (H) 2-2; 3qr Mold (A) 0-5 | | | | |
| 1926-27 (CC) | | | P Llandudno (A) 0-2 | | | | |
| 1927-28 (CC) | | | P Lostock Gralam (H) 10-1; 1q Winsford U (H) 4-0; 2q Bangor C (A) 0-1 | | | | |
| 1928-29 (CC) | | | P Northwich V (A) 1-3 | | | | |

| | | | | | | | | |
|---|---|---|---|---|---|---|---|---|
| 1929-30 | (CC) | | | did not enter | | | | |
| 1930-31 | (CC) | | | did not enter | | | | |
| 1931-32 | (3N) | 1 | 28.11.31 | **Hartlepools Utd** (3N) | H | W | 4-1 | Hedley 2, Valentine, Bennett |
| | | 2 | 12.12.31 | **Darwen** (LC) | A | L | 1-2 | Murray og |
| 1932-33 | (3N) | 1 | 26.11.32 | **Rotherham Utd** (3N) | H | W | 4-0 | Mantle, Wyper 3 |
| | | 2 | 10.12.32 | **Yeovil & Petters Utd** (SL) | H | W | 2-1 | Cresswell, Hedley |
| | | 3 | 14.01.33 | **Fulham** (D2) | H | W | 5-0 | Mercer, Hedley 4 |
| | | 4 | 28.01.33 | **Halifax Town** (3N) | H | D | 0-0 | |
| | | 4r | 02.02.33 | **Halifax Town** | A | L | 2-3 | Mantle 2 |
| 1933-34 | (3N) | 1 | 25.11.33 | **Darlington** (3N) | H | W | 6-1 | Mantle 2, Armes 3, Cresswell |
| | | 2 | 09.12.33 | **Southend Utd** (3S) | A | L | 1-2 | Cresswell |
| 1934-35 | (3N) | 1 | 24.11.34 | **Dinnington Ath** (SAL) | H | W | 3-1 | Whittam, Kelly, Wallbanks |
| | | 2 | 08.12.34 | **Clapton Orient** (3S) | A | W | 3-1 | Cresswell, Kelly, Wallbanks |
| | | 3 | 12.01.35 | **Nottingham Forest** (D2) | H | L | 0-4 | |
| 1935-36 | (3N) | 1 | 30.11.35 | **Gateshead AFC** (3N) | H | W | 1-0 | Cresswell |
| | | 2 | 14.12.35 | **Reading** (3S) | H | D | 3-3 | Cresswell 2, Wrightson |
| | | 2r | 18.12.35 | **Reading** | A | L | 0-3 | |
| 1936-37 | (3N) | 3 | 16.01.37 | **Doncaster Rovers** (D2) | H | W | 4-0 | Gale, Alderson, Sargeant, Wrightson |
| | | 4 | 30.01.37 | **Coventry City** (D2) | A | L | 0-2 | |
| 1937-38 | (3N) | 3 | 08.01.38 | **Leeds Utd** (D1) | A | L | 1-3 | Gale |
| 1938-39 | (3N) | 1 | 26.11.38 | **Bradford City** (3N) | H | W | 3-1 | Horsman, Hinsley og, Pendergast |
| | | 2 | 10.12.38 | **Hull City** (3N) | H | D | 2-2 | Horsman, Gregg |
| | | 2r | 15.12.38 | **Hull City** | A | W | 1-0 | Horsman |
| | | 3 | 07.01.39 | **Coventry City** (D2) | H | W | 1-0 | Pendergast |
| | | 4 | 21.01.39 | **Sheffield Wed** (D2) | A | D | 1-1 | Sanders |
| | | 4r | 25.01.39 | **Sheffield Wed** | H | D | 1-1aet | Hanford og |
| | | 4 2r | 30.01.39 | **Sheffield Wed** | | L | 0-2 | |
| | | | | *played at Maine Road* | | | | |
| 1945-46 | (3N) | 3 1L | 05.01.46 | **Liverpool** (D1) | H | L | 0-2 | |
| | | 3 2L | 09.01.46 | **Liverpool** | A | L | 1-2 | Astbury |
| 1946-47 | (3N) | 3 | 11.01.47 | **Plymouth Argyle** (D2) | H | W | 2-0 | Astbury, Burden |
| | | 4 | 25.01.47 | **Stoke City** (D1) | H | D | 0-0 | |
| | | 4r | 29.01.47 | **Stoke City** | A | L | 2-3 | Hamilton, Yates |
| 1947-48 | (3N) | 1 | 29.11.47 | **Bishop Auckland** (NL) | H | W | 3-1 | Yates, Burden 2 |
| | | 2 | 13.12.47 | **Tranmere Rovers** (3N) | A | W | 1-0 | Burden |
| | | 3 | 10.01.48 | **Crystal Palace** (3S) | A | W | 1-0 | Burden |
| | | 4 | 24.01.48 | **Blackpool** (D1) | A | L | 0-4 | |
| 1948-49 | (3N) | 1 | 27.11.48 | **Hartlepools Utd** (3N) | A | W | 3-1 | Williamson, Harrigan, Forsyth |
| | | 2 | 11.12.48 | **Aldershot** (3S) | A | L | 0-1 | |
| 1949-50 | (3N) | 1 | 26.11.49 | **Goole Town** (ML) | H | W | 4-1 | Jackson 3, Burgess |
| | | 2 | 10.12.49 | **Exeter City** (3S) | A | L | 0-2 | |
| 1950-51 | (3N) | 1 | 25.11.50 | **Bradford Park A** (3N) | H | L | 1-2 | Coffin |
| 1951-52 | (3N) | 1 | 24.11.51 | **Accrington Stanley** (3N) | A | W | 2-1 | Fletcher, Kirkpatrick |
| | | 2 | 15.12.51 | **Leyton FC** (AL) | H | W | 5-2 | Dixon og, Moremont 2, Astbury, Jones |
| | | 3 | 12.01.52 | **Chelsea** (D1) | A | D | 2-2 | Coffin, Greenwood og |
| | | 3r | 16.01.52 | **Chelsea** | H | L | 2-3aet | Willemse og, Coffin |
| 1952-53 | (3N) | 1 | 22.11.52 | **Hartlepools Utd** (3N) | H | L | 0-1 | |
| 1953-54 | (3N) | 1 | 21.11.53 | **Stockport County** (3N) | A | L | 2-4 | Windle, Molyneux |
| 1954-55 | (3N) | 1 | 20.11.54 | **Gateshead AFC** (3N) | A | L | 0-6 | |
| 1955-56 | (3N) | 1 | 19.11.55 | **Chesterfield** (3N) | A | L | 0-1 | |
| 1956-57 | (3N) | 1 | 17.11.56 | **Barrow** (3N) | H | D | 0-0 | |
| | | 1r | 22.11.56 | **Barrow** | A | L | 1-3 | Turner |
| 1957-58 | (3N) | 1 | 16.11.57 | **Gateshead AFC** (3N) | H | W | 4-3 | Jepson, Mason, Pearson, Foulkes |
| | | 2 | 07.12.57 | **Bradford City** (3N) | H | D | 3-3 | Jepson 3 |
| | | 2r | 11.12.57 | **Bradford City** | A | L | 1-3 | Jepson |
| 1958-59 | (D4) | 1 | 15.11.58 | **Boston Utd** (SL) | H | W | 3-2 | Bullock, Boston, Pearson |
| | | 2 | 06.12.58 | **Bury** (D3) | H | D | 1-1 | Webster |
| | | 2r | 09.12.58 | **Bury** | A | L | 1-2 | Hunt |
| 1959-60 | (D4) | 1 | 14.11.59 | **Tranmere Rovers** (D3) | A | W | 1-0 | Kelly |
| | | 2 | 05.12.59 | **Mansfield Town** (D3) | A | L | 0-2 | |
| 1960-61 | (D4) | 1 | 05.11.60 | **Carlisle Utd** (D4) | H | L | 0-1 | |

| | | | | | | | |
|---|---|---|---|---|---|---|---|
| 1961-62 (D4) | 1 | 04.11.61 | **Ashington** (Nco) | H | W | 4-1 | Davies 2, Morris, Jones |
| | 2 | 25.11.61 | **Morecambe** (LC) | H | L | 0-1 | |
| 1962-63 (D4) | 1 | 03.11.62 | **Tranmere Rovers** (D4) | H | L | 0-2 | |
| 1963-64 (D4) | 1 | 16.11.63 | **Blyth Spartans** (NEL) | H | W | 3-2 | Lee 2, Morris |
| | 2 | 07.12.63 | **Barrow** (D4) | H | L | 0-2 | |
| 1964-65 (D4) | 1 | 14.11.64 | **Crewe Alexandra** (D4) | H | W | 5-0 | Talbot 3, Metcalf 2 (1p) |
| | 2 | 05.12.64 | **Barnsley** (D3) | A | W | 5-2 | Metcalf 3 (1p), Humes, Morris |
| | 3 | 09.01.65 | **Manchester Utd** (D1) | A | L | 1-2 | |
| 1965-66 (D4) | 1 | 13.11.65 | **Chesterfield** (D4) | A | W | 2-0 | Metcalf, Humes |
| | 2 | 04.12.65 | **Wigan Athletic** (CC) | H | W | 2-1 | Morris, Humes |
| | 3 | 22.01.66 | **Newcastle Utd** (D1) | H | L | 1-3 | Morris |
| 1966-67 (D4) | 1 | 26.11.66 | **Middlesbrough** (D3) | H | L | 2-5 | Metcalf, Morris |
| 1967-68 (D4) | 1 | 09.12.67 | **Port Vale** (D4) | A | W | 2-1 | Metcalf, Hancox |
| | 2 | 06.01.68 | **Chesterfield** (D4) | H | L | 0-1 | |
| 1968-69 (D4) | 1 | 16.11.68 | **Bradford City** (D4) | A | W | 2-1 | Dearden, Talbot |
| | 2 | 07.12.68 | **Lincoln City** (D4) | H | D | 1-1 | Dearden |
| | 2r | 11.12.68 | **Lincoln City** | A | L | 1-2 | Jones |
| 1969-70 (D4) | 1 | 15.11.69 | **Halifax Town** (D3) | A | D | 3-3 | Tarbuck 2, Dearden |
| | 1r | 19.11.69 | **Halifax Town** | H | W | 1-0 | Dearden |
| | 2 | 06.12.69 | **Doncaster Rovers** (D3) | H | D | 1-1 | Tarbuck |
| | 2r | 09.12.69 | **Doncaster Rovers** | A | W | 2-0 | Webber, Dearden |
| | 3 | 03.01.70 | **Bristol City** (D2) | H | W | 2-1 | Webber 2 |
| | 4 | 24.01.70 | **Swindon Town** (D2) | A | L | 2-4 | Cheetham, Lang |
| 1970-71 (D4) | 1 | 21.11.70 | **Preston North End** (D3) | A | D | 1-1 | Tarbuck |
| | 1r | 23.11.70 | **Preston North End** | H | W | 1-0 | Loyden |
| | 2 | 12.12.70 | **Crewe Alexandra** (D4) | H | W | 1-0 | Turner |
| | 3 | 02.01.71 | **Derby County** (D1) | H | L | 1-2 | Webber |
| 1971-72 (D4) | 1 | 20.11.71 | **Mansfield Town** (D3) | H | D | 1-1 | McHale |
| | 1r | 22.11.71 | **Mansfield Town** | A | L | 3-4 | Loyden, Kennedy, Draper |
| 1972-73 (D4) | 1 | 18.11.72 | **Bolton Wanderers** (D3) | A | D | 1-1 | Hollis |
| | 1r | 22.11.72 | **Bolton Wanderers** | H | L | 0-1 | |
| 1973-74 (D4) | 1 | 24.11.73 | **Telford Utd** (SL) | H | W | 1-0 | Grummett |
| | 2 | 15.12.73 | **Huddersfield Town** (D3) | H | W | 3-2 | Owens, James, Draper |
| | 3 | 05.01.74 | **Aston Villa** (D2) | A | L | 1-3 | James |
| 1974-75 (D4) | 1 | 23.11.74 | **Rotherham Utd** (D4) | A | L | 0-1 | |
| 1975-76 (D3) | 1 | 22.11.75 | **Darlington** (D4) | A | D | 0-0 | |
| | 1r | 26.11.75 | **Darlington** | H | W | 2-0 | Moore, Redfern |
| | 2 | 13.12.75 | **Shrewsbury Town** (D3) | A | L | 1-3 | Edwards |
| 1976-77 (D3) | 1 | 20.11.76 | **Hartlepool** (D4) | H | W | 1-0 | Edwards |
| | 2 | 11.12.76 | **Grimsby Town** (D3) | A | W | 1-0 | Howat |
| | 3 | 08.01.77 | **Southend Utd** (D4) | A | W | 4-0 | Howat, I Edwards 3 |
| | 4 | 29.01.77 | **Luton Town** (D2) | H | W | 1-0 | I Edwards |
| | 5 | 26.02.77 | **Wolverhampton W** (D2) | A | L | 0-1 | |
| 1977-78 (D3) | 1 | 26.11.77 | **Darlington** (D4) | H | W | 4-1 | Crossley 3, Kearney |
| | 2 | 17.12.77 | **Carlisle Utd** (D3) | A | L | 1-3 | Crossley |
| 1978-79 (D3) | 1 | 25.11.78 | **Runcorn** (NPL) | H | D | 1-1 | Phillips |
| | 1r | 28.11.78 | **Runcorn** | A | W | 5-0 | Mellor 2, Jones, Phillips, Howat |
| | 2 | 16.12.78 | **Darlington** (D4) | A | L | 1-2 | Mellor |
| 1979-80 (D3) | 1 | 24.11.79 | **Workington** (NPL) | H | W | 5-1 | Henderson 2, Sutcliffe, Jones, Rush |
| | 2 | 18.12.79 | **Barnsley** (D3) | H | W | 1-0 | Raynor (p) |
| | 3 | 05.01.80 | **Newcastle Utd** (D2) | A | W | 2-0 | Henderson, Rush |
| | 4 | 26.01.80 | **Millwall** (D3) | H | W | 2-0 | Storton, Rush |
| | 5 | 16.02.80 | **Ipswich Town** (D1) | A | L | 1-2 | Jones |
| 1980-81 (D3) | 1 | 22.11.80 | **Barnsley** (D3) | H | L | 1-2 | Birch |
| 1981-82 (D3) | 1 | 21.11.81 | **Penrith** (NL) | A | L | 0-1 | |
| 1982-83 (D4) | 1 | 20.11.82 | **Northwich V** (APL) | H | D | 1-1 | Lane |
| | 1r | 22.11.82 | **Northwich V** | A | L | 1-3aet | Williams |
| **as Chester City** | | | | | | | |
| 1983-84 (D4) | 1 | 19.11.83 | **Chesterfield** (D4) | H | L | 1-2 | Holden |
| 1984-85 (D4) | 1 | 17.11.84 | **Darlington** (D4) | A | L | 2-3 | Fox, Holden |
| 1985-86 (D4) | 1 | 16.11.85 | **Bury** (D3) | A | L | 0-2 | |

| | | | | | | | | |
|---|---|---|---|---|---|---|---|---|
| 1986-87 (D3) | 1 | 15.11.86 | **Rotherham Utd** (D3) | H | D | 1-1 | | Bennett (p) |
| | 1r | 18.11.86 | **Rotherham Utd** | A | D | 1-1 | aet | Kelly |
| | 1 2r | 24.11.86 | **Rotherham Utd** | H | W | 1-0 | | Croft |
| | 2 | 06.12.86 | **Doncaster Rovers** (D3) | H | W | 3-1 | | Bennett (p), Graham, Houghton |
| | 3 | 10.01.87 | **Wrexham** (D4) | A | W | 2-1 | | Bennett 2 |
| | 4 | 31.01.87 | **Sheffield Wed** (D1) | H | D | 1-1 | | Kelly |
| | 4r | 04.02.87 | **Sheffield Wed** | A | L | 1-3 | | Bennett |
| 1987-88 (D3) | 1 | 14.11.87 | **Runcorn** (Conf) | H | L | 0-1 | | |
| 1988-89 (D3) | 1 | 19.11.88 | **Burnley** (D4) | A | W | 2-0 | | Dale, Benjamin |
| | 2 | 10.12.88 | **Huddersfield Town** (D3) | A | L | 0-1 | | |
| 1989-90 (D3) | 1 | 18.11.89 | **Macclesfield T** (Conf) | A | D | 1-1 | | Painter |
| | 1r | 21.11.89 | **Macclesfield T** | H | W | 3-2 | | Abel (p), Butler, Croft |
| | 2 | 09.12.89 | **Blackpool** (D3) | A | L | 0-3 | | |
| 1990-91 (D3) | 1 | 17.11.90 | **Doncaster Rovers** (D4) | H | D | 2-2 | | Bennett, Dale |
| | 1r | 20.11.90 | **Doncaster Rovers** | A | W | 2-1 | aet | Dale, Painter |
| | 2 | 12.12.90 | **Leek Town** (NPL) | A | D | 1-1 | | Dale |
| | 2r | 17.12.90 | **Leek Town** | H | W | 4-0 | | Bertschin, Dale, Abel (p), Painter |
| | 3 | 05.01.91 | **Bournemouth** (D3) | H | L | 2-3 | | Croft 2 |
| 1991-92 (D3) | 1 | 16.11.91 | **Guiseley** (NPL) | H | W | 1-0 | | Barrow |
| | 2 | 07.12.91 | **Crewe Alexandra** (D4) | A | L | 0-2 | | |
| 1992-93 (D2) | 1 | 14.11.92 | **Altrincham** (Conf) | H | D | 1-1 | | Ryan |
| | 1r | 25.11.92 | **Altrincham** | A | L | 0-2 | | |
| 1993-94 (D3) | 1 | 13.11.93 | **Bradford City** (D2) | A | D | 0-0 | | |
| | 1r | 30.11.93 | **Bradford City** | H | W | 1-0 | | Lightfoot |
| | 2 | 04.12.93 | **Hull City** (D2) | H | W | 2-0 | | Preece, Leonard |
| | 3 | 08.01.94 | **Plymouth Argyle** (D2) | A | L | 0-1 | | |
| 1994-95 (D2) | 1 | 12.11.94 | **Witton Albion** (NPL) | H | W | 2-0 | | Page, Alsford |
| | 2 | 04.12.94 | **Burnley** (D1) | H | L | 1-2 | | Milner |
| 1995-96 (D3) | 1 | 11.11.95 | **Blackpool** (D2) | A | L | 1-2 | | Milner |
| 1996-97 (D3) | 1 | 16.11.96 | **Stalybridge Celtic** (Conf) | H | W | 3-0 | | Rimmer 2, Milner |
| | 2 | 07.12.96 | **Boston Utd** (NPL) | H | W | 1-0 | | Milner |
| | 3 | 04.01.97 | **Middlesbrough** (PL) | A | L | 0-6 | | |
| 1997-98 (D3) | 1 | 15.11.97 | **Winsford Utd** (NPL) | H | W | 2-1 | | Richardson, Priest |
| | 2 | 05.12.97 | **Wrexham** (D2) | H | L | 0-2 | | |
| 1998-99 (D3) | 1 | 14.11.98 | **Cardiff City** (D3) | A | L | 0-6 | | |
| 1999-00 (D3) | 1 | 30.10.99 | **Whyteleafe** (IL) | A | D | 0-0 | | |
| | 1r | 09.11.99 | **Whyteleafe** | H | W | 3-1 | | Cross 2, Beckett |
| | 2 | 20.11.99 | **Stalybridge Celtic** (NPL) | A | W | 2-1 | | Cross, Bennett |
| | 3 | 12.12.99 | **Manchester City** (D1) | H | L | 1-4 | | Richardson |
| 2000-01 (Conf) | 1 | 18.11.00 | **Plymouth Argyle** (D3) | H | D | 1-1 | | I Wright |
| | 1r | 28.11.00 | **Plymouth Argyle** | A | W | 2-1 | aet | Whitehall, Ruscoe |
| | 2 | 09.12.00 | **Oxford Utd** (D2) | H | W | 3-2 | | P Beesley, Whitehall 2 |
| | 3 | 06.01.01 | **Blackburn Rovers** (D1) | A | L | 0-2 | | |
| 2002-03 (Conf) | 1 | 16.11.02 | **Colchester Utd** (D2) | A | W | 1-0 | | Tate |
| | 2 | 07.12.02 | **Morecambe** (Conf) | A | L | 2-3 | | Bolland, Clare |

## CHESTER ST OSWALDS

*One of many amateur clubs that played in and around the Chester area in the 1880s.*

| | | | | | | |
|---|---|---|---|---|---|---|
| 1887-88 | 1 | 15.10.87 | **Chirk** | A | L | 1-4 |

## CHESTERFIELD

*Formed 1866, the fourth oldest League club after Stoke, Notts County and Nottingham Forest. Originally known as Chesterfield Municipal. 1919-1922 Chesterfield Town. 1922-present Chesterfield. Best FA Cup performance: 5th round, 1933, 1938, 1950 Record FA Cup win: 8-0 vs Swadlicote, 3rd qualifying round, 1900 Record FA Cup defeat: 1-8 vs West Ham, 1st round, 1st round,.10.01.1914; 0-7 vs Burnley*

**as Chesterfield Municipal**

1892-93 — 1q Gainsborough T (A) 2-4 abandoned; 1q Gainsborough T (A) 0-4

1893-94 — 1q Matlock T (A) 3-0; 2q Derby Junction (H) 4-0; 3q Heanor T (A) 1-3

1894-95 — 1q Clay Cross Town (H) 3-0; 2q Matlock T (H) 3-1; 3q Buxton (H) 4-0; 4q Long Eaton Rangers (A) 1-1; 4qr Long Eaton R (H) 3-0

| | | | | | | |
|---|---|---|---|---|---|---|
| | 1 | 02.02.95 | **Middlesbrough** (NL) | A | L | 0-4 |

| | | | | | | | | |
|---|---|---|---|---|---|---|---|---|
| 1895-96 | | | | 1q Eckington Works (H) 1-0; 2q Long Eaton Rangers (H) 2-1; 3q Heanor T (H) 3-0; 4q Ilkeston (H) 2-1 | | | | |
| 1895-96 | | 1 | 01.02.96 | **Newcastle Utd** (D2) | H | L | 0-4 | |
| 1896-97 | (ML) | | | 3q Swadlicote (H) 1-1; 3qr Swadlicote (A) 5-1; 4q Heanor T (H) 0-2 | | | | |
| 1897-98 | (ML) | | | 3q Long Eaton Rangers (A) 2-3 | | | | |
| 1898-99 | (ML) | | | 3q Swadlicote (H) 8-0; 4q Burton Swifts (A) 0-1 | | | | |
| 1899-00 | (D2) | | | 1q Ilkeston T (A) 2-1; 2q Stapleford T (H) 5-2; 3q Heanor T (H) 6-1; 4q Hunslet (H) 6-0; 5q Grimsby T (A) 2-3 | | | | |
| 1900-01 | (D2) | | | 3q Hunslet (H) 8-3; 4q Newark (A) 5-0; 5q Barnsley (A) 5-1; Int Walsall (H) 3-0 | | | | |
| 1900-01 | (D2) | 1 | 09.02.01 | **Kettering Town** (SL) | A | D | 1-1 | Munday |
| | | 1r | 13.02.01 | **Kettering Town** | H | L | 1-2aet | Gooing |
| 1901-02 | (D2) | | | Int Reading (A) 0-2 | | | | |
| 1902-03 | (D2) | | | 3q Newark (H) 6-0; 4q Barnsley (A) 2-3 | | | | |
| 1903-04 | (D2) | | | 3q Lincoln C (A) 2-0; 4q Bradford C (H) 2-1; 5q Gainsborough T (H) 0-2 | | | | |
| 1904-05 | (D2) | | | 6q Stockport Co (H) 2-0; Int Portsmouth (H) 0-0; Int R Portsmouth (A) 0-2 | | | | |
| 1905-06 | (D2) | 1 | 13.01.06 | **Clapton Orient** (D2) | A | D | 0-0 | |
| | | 1r | 17.01.06 | **Clapton Orient** | H | W | 3-0 | Dyal, Marples (p), Munday |
| | | 2 | 03.02.06 | **Everton** (D1) | A | L | 0-3 | |
| 1906-07 | (D2) | 1 | 12.01.07 | **Derby County** (D1) | A | D | 1-1 | Banner |
| | | 1r | 16.01.07 | **Derby County** | H | - | 1-2 | Marples |
| | | | | *abandoned after 114 minutes – bad light* | | | | |
| | | 1r | 21.01.07 | **Derby County** (D1) | | L | 0-4 | |
| | | | | *played at Trent Bridge, Nottingham* | | | | |
| 1907-08 | (D2) | | | 5q St Helens R (A) 4-1 | | | | |
| 1907-08 | (D2) | 1 | 11.01.08 | **Stockton** (NL) | H | W | 4-0 | Logan, Sprott, Munday, Marples (p) |
| | | 2 | 03.02.08 | **Bristol Rovers** (SL) | A | L | 0-2 | |
| 1908-09 | (D2) | | | 5q Rotherham T (H) 3-0 | | | | |
| 1908-09 | (D2) | 1 | 16.01.09 | **Glossop North End** (D2) | H | L | 0-2 | |
| 1909-10 | (ML) | | | 4q Cradley Heath St Lukes (H) 2-1; 5q Crewe Alex (H) 5-2 | | | | |
| 1909-10 | (ML) | 1 | 15.01.10 | **Fulham** (D2) | H | D | 0-0 | |
| | | 1r | 19.01.10 | **Fulham** | A | L | 1-2 | Bovill |
| 1910-11 | (ML) | | | 4q Desborough Town (A) 6-1; 5q Rotherham T (A) 2-1 | | | | |
| 1910-11 | (ML) | 1 | 14.01.11 | **Bolton Wanderers** (D2) | A | W | 2-0 | EJ Revill 2 |
| | | 2 | 04.02.11 | **Chelsea** (D2) | H | L | 1-4 | EJ Revill |
| 1911-12 | (ML) | | | 4q Ripley Town Athletic (A) 1-2 | | | | |
| 1912-13 | (ML) | | | 4q Sutton Town (H) 2-1; 5q Watford (H) 3-1 | | | | |
| 1912-13 | (ML) | 1 | 18.01.13 | **Nottingham Forest** (D2) | H | L | 1-4 | Donald |
| 1913-14 | (ML) | | | 4q Shirebrook (A) 1-1; 4qr Shirebrook (H) 2-0; 5q North Shields (A) 1-1; 5qr North Shields (H) 8-2 | | | | |
| 1913-14 | (ML) | 1 | 10.01.14 | **West Ham Utd** (SL) | A | L | 1-8 | Edgerton |
| 1914-15 | (ML) | | | 4q Rotherham T (A) 4-2; 5q Gainsborough T (A) 0-0; 5qr Gainsborough T (H) 3-1; 6q Goole T (A) 0-2 | | | | |
| **as Chesterfield Town** | | | | | | | | |
| 1919-20 | (ML) | | | P Clay Cross Town (H) 4-0; 1q Ilkeston U (H) 2-1; 2q South Normanton Col (H) 5-0 | | | | |
| 1920-21 | (ML) | | | P Dronfield Woodhouse (H) 11-1; 1q Clay Cross T (H) 2-1; 2q Ilkeston U (A) 0-0; 2qr Ilkeston U (H) 1-0; 3q Staveley T (A) 0-2 | | | | |
| 1921-22 | (3N) | | | 4q Irthlingborough T (H) 3-0; 5q Walsall (A) 0-2 | | | | |
| **as Chesterfield** | | | | | | | | |
| 1922-23 | (3N) | | | 4q Lincoln C (H) 2-0; 5q Higham Ferrers T (H) 4-4; 5qr Higham Ferrers T (A) 1-0; 6q Worksop T (A) 0-1 | | | | |
| 1923-24 | (3N) | | | 5q Worksop T (A) 2-0; 6q Grimsby T (H) 0-0; 6qr Grimsby T (A) 0-2 | | | | |
| 1924-25 | (3N) | | | 5q Grimsby T (A) 2-1; 6q Accrington Stanley (A) 0-1 | | | | |
| 1925-26 | (3N) | 1 | 28.11.25 | **Wath Athletic** (ML) | A | W | 5-0 | Cookson 2 (1p), Fisher, Roseboom, Whitfield |
| | | 2 | 12.12.25 | **Worksop Town** (ML) | A | W | 2-1 | Whitfield, Hopkinson |
| | | 3 | 09.01.26 | **Clapton Orient** (D2) | H | L | 0-1 | |
| 1926-27 | (3N) | 1 | 27.11.26 | **Mexborough T Ath** (ML) | H | - | 0-0ab | |
| | | | | *abandoned at half-time – fog* | | | | |
| | | 1 | 01.12.26 | **Mexborough T Ath** (ML) | H | W | 2-1 | Roseboom, Cookson |
| | | 2 | 11.12.26 | **Doncaster Rovers** (3N) | A | W | 1-0 | Cookson |
| | | 3 | 08.01.27 | **Fulham** (D2) | A | L | 3-4 | Roseboom 2, Ralphs |

| | | | | | | | |
|---|---|---|---|---|---|---|---|
| 1927-28 (3N) | 1 | 26.11.27 | **Darlington** (3N) | A | L | 1-4 | Roseboom |
| 1928-29 (3N) | 1 | 24.11.28 | **Rochdale** (3N) | H | W | 3-2 | Sam Taylor, Roseboom (p), Neale |
| | 2 | 08.12.28 | **Gainsborough T** (ML) | A | W | 3-2 | Roseboom, Yarwood, JW Lee |
| | 3 | 12.01.29 | **Huddersfield Town** (D1) | H | L | 1-7 | Wadsworth og |
| 1929-30 (3N) | 1 | 30.11.29 | **Southport** (3N) | A | D | 0-0 | |
| | 1r | 04.12.29 | **Southport** | H | W | 3-2 | JW Lee, Sam Taylor, Little og |
| | 2 | 14.12.29 | **Port Vale** (3N) | H | W | 2-0 | Sam Taylor, Bullock |
| | 3 | 11.01.30 | **Middlesbrough** (D1) | H | D | 1-1 | Sam Taylor |
| | 3r | 15.01.30 | **Middlesbrough** | A | L | 3-4 | JW Lee 2, S J Tayor |
| 1930-31 (3N) | 1 | 29.11.30 | **Notts County** (3S) | H | L | 1-2 | Pynegar |
| 1931-32 (D2) | 3 | 09.01.32 | **Nottingham Forest** (D2) | H | W | 5-2 | Abel 2, Ruddy 2, JW Lee |
| | 4 | 23.01.32 | **Liverpool** (D1) | H | L | 2-4 | Ruddy, Abel |
| 1932-33 (D2) | 3 | 14.01.33 | **Sheffield Wed** (D1) | A | D | 2-2 | Lee, Cook |
| | 3r | 18.01.33 | **Sheffield Wed** | H | W | 4-2 | Cook, Abel, Lee, Bacon |
| | 4 | 28.01.33 | **Darlington** (3N) | A | W | 2-0 | Austin, Lee |
| | 5 | 18.02.33 | **Burnley** (D2) | H | L | 0-1 | |
| 1933-34 (3N) | 3 | 13.01.34 | **Aston Villa** (D1) | H | D | 2-2 | Hughes, Cook |
| | 3r | 17.01.34 | **Aston Villa** | A | L | 0-2 | |
| 1934-35 (3N) | 3 | 12.01.35 | **Swindon Town** (3S) | A | L | 1-2 | Dawson |
| 1935-36 (3N) | 1 | 30.11.35 | **Southport** (3N) | H | W | 3-0 | Spence 2 (1p), Harvey |
| | 2 | 14.12.35 | **Walsall** (3N) | H | D | 0-0 | |
| | 2r | 19.12.35 | **Walsall** | A | L | 1-2 | Hamilton |
| 1936-37 (D2) | 3 | 16.01.37 | **Arsenal** (D1) | H | L | 1-5 | Sliman (p) |
| 1937-38 (D2) | 3 | 08.01.38 | **Bradford City** (3N) | A | D | 1-1 | Clifton |
| | 3r | 12.01.38 | **Bradford City** | H | D | 1-1aet | Spence |
| | 3 2r | 17.01.38 | **Bradford City** | | W | 2-0 | Ponting, Clifton |
| | | | *played at Bramall Lane* | | | | |
| | 4 | 22.01.38 | **Burnley** (D2) | H | W | 3-2 | Ponting (2), Spence |
| | 5 | 12.02.38 | **Tottenham Hotspur** (D2) | H | D | 2-2 | Clifton, Sliman |
| | 5r | 16.02.38 | **Tottenham Hotspur** | A | L | 1-2 | Ponting |
| 1938-39 (D2) | 3 | 07.01.39 | **Southend Utd** (3N) | H | - | 1-1ab | Spedding |
| | | | *abandoned after 73 minutes – fog* | | | | |
| | 3 | 11.01.39 | **Southend Utd** (3N) | H | D | 1-1 | Lyon |
| | 3r | 16.01.39 | **Southend Utd** | A | L | 3-4aet | Lyon, Hughes, Milburn (p) |
| 1945-46 (D2) | 3 1L | 05.01.46 | **York City** (3N) | H | D | 1-1 | Roberts |
| | 3 2L | 09.01.46 | **York City** | A | L | 2-3aet | Dooley, Roberts |
| 1946-47 (D2) | 3 | 11.01.47 | **Sunderland** (D1) | H | W | 2-1 | Ottewell, Milligan |
| | 4 | 25.01.47 | **Middlesbrough** (D1) | A | L | 1-2 | Swinscoe |
| 1947-48 (D2) | 3 | 10.01.48 | **Derby County** (D1) | A | L | 0-2 | |
| 1948-49 (D2) | 3 | 08.01.49 | **Wolverhampton W** (D1) | A | L | 0-6 | |
| 1949-50 (D2) | 3 | 07.01.50 | **Yeovil Town** (SL) | H | W | 3-1 | Costello 2, Thompson |
| | 4 | 28.01.50 | **Middlesbrough** (D1) | H | W | 3-2 | Dale, Merron, Costello |
| | 5 | 11.02.50 | **Chelsea** (D1) | H | D | 1-1 | Thompson |
| | 5r | 15.02.50 | **Chelsea** | A | L | 0-3 | |
| 1950-51 (D2) | 3 | 06.01.51 | **Brighton** (3S) | A | L | 1-2 | Booker |
| 1951-52 (3N) | 1 | 24.11.51 | **Barrow** (3N) | A | W | 2-0 | Wislon, Marron |
| | 2 | 15.12.51 | **Norwich City** (3S) | A | L | 1-3 | Marron |
| 1952-53 (3N) | 1 | 22.11.52 | **Workington** (3N) | H | W | 1-0 | Westcott |
| | 2 | 06.12.52 | **Shrewsbury Town** (3S) | A | D | 0-0 | |
| | 2r | 10.12.52 | **Shrewsbury Town** | H | L | 2-4 | Smith, Westcott |
| 1953-54 (3N) | 1 | 21.11.53 | **Gainsborough T** (ML) | A | W | 4-1 | Marsden 2, Edwards, Hatton |
| | 2 | 12.12.53 | **Southend Utd** (3S) | A | W | 2-1 | Smith, Keating |
| | 3 | 09.01.54 | **Bury** (D2) | H | W | 2-0 | Marsden 2 |
| | 4 | 30.01.54 | **Sheffield Wed** (D1) | A | D | 0-0 | |
| | 4r | 03.02.54 | **Sheffield Wed** | H | L | 2-4 | Marsden, Whiteside |
| 1954-55 (3N) | 1 | 20.11.54 | **Hartlepools Utd** (3N) | A | L | 0-1 | |
| 1955-56 (3N) | 1 | 19.11.55 | **Chester** (3N) | H | W | 1-0 | Sowden |
| | 2 | 10.12.55 | **Hartlepools Utd** (3N) | H | L | 1-2 | Smith |
| 1956-57 (3N) | 1 | 17.11.56 | **S Shields (1936)** (NEL) | A | D | 2-2 | Burrell, Smith |
| | 1r | 21.11.56 | **S Shields (1936)** | H | W | 4-0 | Cunliffe, Smallwood, Capel (p), Sowden |

| | | | | | | | | |
|---|---|---|---|---|---|---|---|---|
| | | 2 | 08.12.56 | **Barrow** (3N) | H | W | 4-1 | Capel (p), Smallwood, Sowden, Blakey |
| | | 3 | 05.01.57 | **Burnley** (D1) | A | L | 0-7 | |
| 1957-58 | (3N) | 1 | 16.11.57 | **York City** (3N) | A | L | 0-1 | |
| 1958-59 | (D3) | 1 | 15.11.58 | **Rhyl** (CC) | H | W | 3-0 | Hutchinson, Frear, Steele |
| | | 2 | 06.12.58 | **Carlisle Utd** (D4) | A | D | 0-0 | |
| | | 2r | 09.12.58 | **Carlisle Utd** | H | W | 1-0 | Frear |
| | | 3 | 10.01.59 | **Colchester Utd** (D3) | A | L | 0-2 | |
| 1959-60 | (D3) | 1 | 14.11.59 | **S Shields (1936)** (ML) | A | L | 1-2 | Lewis |
| 1960-61 | (D3) | 1 | 05.11.60 | **Doncaster Rovers** (D4) | H | D | 3-3 | Foley, Smallwood 2 |
| | | 1r | 09.11.60 | **Doncaster Rovers** | A | W | 1-0 | Foley |
| | | 2 | 26.11.60 | **Oldham Athletic** (D4) | H | D | 4-4 | Havenhand 2, Maddison, Foley |
| | | 2r | 29.11.60 | **Oldham Athletic** | A | W | 3-0 | Rackstraw 2, Gilbert |
| | | 3 | 07.01.61 | **Blackburn Rovers** (D1) | H | D | 0-0 | |
| | | 3r | 11.01.61 | **Blackburn Rovers** | A | L | 0-3 | |
| 1961-62 | (D4) | 1 | 04.11.61 | **Doncaster Rovers** (D4) | A | W | 4-0 | Kerry, Lovie, Rackstraw, Lunn |
| | | 2 | 25.11.61 | **Oldham Athletic** (D4) | H | D | 2-2 | Broadhurst, Rackstraw |
| | | 2r | 29.11.61 | **Oldham Athletic** | A | L | 2-4aet | Lovie, Lunn |
| 1962-63 | (D4) | 1 | 03.11.62 | **Stockport County** (D4) | H | W | 4-1 | Frear, Poole 2, Meredith |
| | | 2 | 24.11.62 | **Barnsley** (D3) | A | L | 1-2 | Poole |
| 1963-64 | (D4) | 1 | 16.11.63 | **Crook Town** (NL) | A | W | 2-1 | McQuarrie, J Beresford |
| | | 2 | 07.12.63 | **Netherfield** (LC) | A | D | 1-1 | Scott |
| | | 2r | 11.12.63 | **Netherfield** | H | W | 4-1 | Clarke (p), McQuarrie, Rackstraw, Holt og |
| | | 3 | 04.01.64 | **Oxford Utd** (D4) | A | L | 0-1 | |
| 1964-65 | (D4) | 1 | 14.11.64 | **S Shields (1936)** (NRL) | H | W | 2-0 | Stringfellow, Commons |
| | | 2 | 05.12.64 | **York City** (D4) | H | W | 2-1 | Stringfellow, Moor og |
| | | 3 | 09.01.65 | **Peterborough Utd** (D3) | H | L | 0-3 | |
| 1965-66 | (D4) | 1 | 13.11.65 | **Chester** (D4) | H | L | 0-2 | |
| 1966-67 | (D4) | 1 | 26.11.66 | **Wrexham** (D4) | A | L | 2-3 | Randall, Stark |
| 1967-68 | (D4) | 1 | 09.12.67 | **Barnsley** (D4) | H | W | 2-0 | Hollett, Wilson |
| | | 2 | 06.01.68 | **Chester** (D4) | A | W | 1-0 | Wilson |
| | | 3 | 27.01.68 | **Blackpool** (D2) | A | L | 1-2 | Hollett |
| 1968-69 | (D4) | 1 | 16.11.68 | **Skelmersdale Utd** (CC) | H | W | 2-0 | Moss, Randall |
| | | 2 | 07.12.68 | **Wrexham** (D4) | H | W | 2-1 | Moss 2 |
| | | 3 | 04.01.69 | **Portsmouth** (D2) | A | L | 0-3 | |
| 1969-70 | (D4) | 1 | 15.11.69 | **Tranmere Rovers** (D3) | A | L | 0-3 | |
| 1970-71 | (D3) | 1 | 21.11.70 | **Halifax Town** (D3) | H | W | 2-0 | Moss 2 |
| | | 2 | 12.12.70 | **Workington** (D4) | H | D | 0-0 | |
| | | 2r | 16.12.70 | **Workington** | A | L | 2-3 | Fenoughty, Moss |
| 1971-72 | (D3) | 1 | 20.11.71 | **Oldham Athletic** (D3) | H | W | 3-0 | Randall 2, Moss |
| | | 2 | 11.12.71 | **Barnsley** (D3) | A | D | 0-0 | |
| | | 2r | 15.12.71 | **Barnsley** | H | W | 1-0 | Moss |
| | | 3 | 15.01.72 | **Stoke City** (D1) | A | L | 1-2 | Randall |
| 1972-73 | (D3) | 1 | 18.11.72 | **Rhyl** (CC) | H | W | 4-2 | Ferris, McHale (p) Downes, Bell |
| | | 2 | 09.12.72 | **Grimsby Town** (D3) | A | D | 2-2 | Downes, Ferris |
| | | 2r | 13.12.72 | **Grimsby Town** | H | L | 0-1 | |
| 1973-74 | (D3) | 1 | 24.11.73 | **Barnsley** (D4) | H | D | 0-0 | |
| | | 1r | 28.11.73 | **Barnsley** | A | L | 1-2 | Large |
| 1974-75 | (D3) | 1 | 23.11.74 | **Boston Utd** (NPL) | H | W | 3-1 | Shanahan, Moss 2 |
| | | 2 | 14.12.74 | **Doncaster Rovers** (D4) | H | W | 1-0 | Moss |
| | | 3 | 04.01.75 | **Sunderland** (D2) | A | L | 0-2 | |
| 1975-76 | (D3) | 1 | 22.11.75 | **Bradford City** (D4) | A | L | 0-1 | |
| 1976-77 | (D3) | 1 | 20.11.76 | **Scunthorpe Utd** (D4) | A | W | 2-1 | McEwan, Jones |
| | | 2 | 11.12.76 | **Walsall** (D3) | H | D | 1-1 | Darling |
| | | 2r | 14.12.76 | **Walsall** | A | D | 0-0aet | |
| | | 2 2r | 21.12.76 | **Walsall** | | L | 0-1 | |
| | | | | *played at the Baseball Ground, Derby* | | | | |
| 1977-78 | (D3) | 1 | 26.11.77 | **Halifax Town** (D4) | H | W | 1-0 | Fern |
| | | 2 | 17.12.77 | **Blyth Spartans** (NL) | A | L | 0-1 | |
| 1978-79 | (D3) | 1 | 25.11.78 | **Darlington** (D4) | A | D | 1-1 | Flavell |

| | | | | | | | |
|---|---|---|---|---|---|---|---|
| | 1r | 06.12.78 | **Darlington** | H | L | 0-1 | |
| 1979-80 (D3) | 1 | 24.11.79 | **Grimsby Town** (D3) | A | D | 1-1 | Walker |
| | 1r | 27.11.79 | **Grimsby Town** | H | L | 2-3 | Green, Salmons |
| 1980-81 (D3) | 1 | 22.11.80 | **Wigan Athletic** (D4) | A | D | 2-2 | Wilson, Green |
| | 1r | 25.11.80 | **Wigan Athletic** | H | W | 2-0 | Salmons, Tartt |
| | 2 | 13.12.80 | **Sheffield Utd** (D3) | A | D | 1-1 | Birch (p) |
| | 2r | 16.12.80 | **Sheffield Utd** | H | W | 1-0 | Simpson |
| | 3 | 03.01.81 | **Peterborough Utd** (D4) | A | D | 1-1 | Crawford |
| | 3r | 06.01.81 | **Peterborough Utd** | H | L | 1-2 | Hunter |
| 1981-82 (D3) | 1 | 21.11.81 | **Preston North End** (D3) | H | W | 4-1 | Bonnyman 2, Henderson, Walker |
| | 2 | 12.12.81 | **Huddersfield Town** (D3) | H | L | 0-1 | |
| 1982-83 (D3) | 1 | 20.11.82 | **Peterborough Utd** (D4) | H | D | 2-2 | Walker 2 |
| | 1r | 24.11.82 | **Peterborough Utd** | A | L | 1-2 | Walker |
| 1983-84 (D4) | 1 | 19.11.83 | **Chester City** (D4) | A | W | 2-1 | Newton 2 |
| | 2 | 10.12.83 | **Burnley** (D3) | H | D | 2-2 | Birch (p), Newton |
| | 2r | 19.12.83 | **Burnley** | A | L | 2-3 | Bellamy, Birch (p) |
| 1984-85 (D4) | 1 | 17.11.84 | **Whitby Town** (NL) | A | W | 3-1 | Kendal, Brown, Newton |
| | 2 | 08.12.84 | **Walsall** (D3) | A | L | 0-1 | |
| 1985-86 (D3) | 1 | 16.11.85 | **Tranmere Rovers** (D4) | A | D | 2-2 | Batty, Henderson |
| | 1r | 19.11.85 | **Tranmere Rovers** | H | L | 0-1 | |
| 1986-87 (D3) | 1 | 15.11.86 | **Walsall** (D3) | A | L | 0-2 | |
| 1987-88 (D3) | 1 | 15.11.87 | **Notts County** (D3) | A | D | 3-3 | Travis 2, Waller |
| | 1r | 17.11.87 | **Notts County** | H | L | 0-1 | |
| 1988-89 (D3) | 1 | 19.11.88 | **Bolton Wanderers** (D3) | A | D | 0-0 | |
| | 1r | 28.11.88 | **Bolton Wanderers** | H | L | 2-3 | Morris 2 |
| 1989-90 (D4) | 1 | 18.11.89 | **Shrewsbury Town** (D3) | A | W | 3-2 | Waller, Gunn (p), Plummer |
| | 2 | 09.12.89 | **Huddersfield Town** (D3) | H | L | 0-2 | |
| 1990-91 (D4) | 1 | 17.11.90 | **Spennymoor Utd** (NCE) | H | W | 3-2 | Caldwell, Potts og, Barnes |
| | 2 | 11.12.90 | **Bolton Wanderers** (D3) | H | L | 3-4 | Morris, Cooke, Caldwell |
| 1991-92 (D4) | 1 | 16.11.91 | **Darlington** (D3) | A | L | 1-2 | Cooke |
| 1992-93 (D3) | 1 | 14.11.92 | **Macclesfield T** (Conf) | A | D | 0-0 | |
| | 1r | 25.11.92 | **Macclesfield T** | H | D | 2-2aet | Turnbull, Williams (p) |
| | | | *Macclesfield won 3-2 on penalties* | | | | |
| 1993-94 (D3) | 1 | 13.11.93 | **Rochdale** (D3) | H | L | 0-1 | |
| 1994-95 (D3) | 1 | 12.11.94 | **Scarborough** (D3) | H | D | 0-0 | |
| | 1r | 22.11.94 | **Scarborough** | A | L | 0-2 | |
| 1995-96 (D2) | 1 | 11.11.95 | **Scarborough** (D3) | A | W | 2-0 | Lormor 2 |
| | 2 | 02.12.95 | **Wrexham** (D2) | A | L | 2-3 | Davies 2 |
| 1996-97 (D2) | 1 | 16.11.96 | **Bury** (D2) | H | W | 1-0 | Williams |
| | 2 | 07.12.96 | **Scarborough** (D3) | H | W | 2-0 | Davies, Lormor |
| | 3 | 14.01.97 | **Bristol City** (D2) | H | W | 2-0 | Howard 2 |
| | 4 | 04.02.97 | **Bolton Wanderers** (D1) | A | W | 3-2 | Davies 3 |
| | 5 | 15.02.97 | **Nottingham Forest** (PL) | H | W | 1-0 | Curtis (p) |
| | 6 | 09.03.97 | **Wrexham** (D2) | H | W | 1-0 | Beaumont |
| | SF | 13.04.97 | **Middlesbrough** (PL) | | D | 3-3aet | Morris, Dyche (p), Hewitt |
| | | | *played at Old Trafford* | | | | |
| | SFr | 22.04.97 | **Middlesbrough** | | L | 0-3 | |
| | | | *played at Hillsborough* | | | | |
| 1997-98 (D2) | 1 | 15.11.97 | **Northwich V** (Conf) | H | W | 1-0 | Reeves |
| | 2 | 06.12.97 | **Grimsby Town** (D2) | A | D | 2-2 | Willis, Breckin |
| | 2r | 16.12.97 | **Grimsby Town** | H | L | 0-2 | |
| 1998-99 (D2) | 1 | 14.11.98 | **Wycombe W** (D2) | A | L | 0-1 | |
| 1999-00 (D2) | 1 | 30.10.99 | **Enfield** (IL) | H | L | 1-2 | Lomas |
| 2000-01 (D3) | 1 | 18.11.00 | **Bristol City** (D2) | H | L | 0-1 | |
| 2001-02 (D2) | 1 | 17.11.01 | **Stalybridge Celtic** (Conf) | A | W | 3-0 | Beckett, Scott og, D'Auria |
| | 2 | 08.12.01 | **Southend Utd** (D3) | H | D | 1-1 | Beckett |
| | 2r | 18.12.01 | **Southend Utd** | H | L | 0-2 | |
| 2002-03 (D3) | 1 | 16.11.02 | **Morecambe** (Conf) | H | L | 1-2 | Davies |

## CHESTERFIELD SPITAL

*Entered FA Cup: 1882-83 – 1884-85. Chesterfield-based amateur club.*

| | | | | | | | |
|---|---|---|---|---|---|---|---|
| 1882-83 | 1 | 04.11.82 | **Wednesbury Old Ath** | H | L | 1-7 | Bishop |

| | | | | | | | |
|---|---|---|---|---|---|---|---|
| 1883-84 | 1 | 10.11.83 | **Rotherham Town** | H | D | 1-1 | |
| | 1r | 17.11.83 | **Rotherham Town** | A | L | 2-7 | |
| 1884-85 | 1 | | bye | | | | |
| | 2 | 06.12.84 | **Sheffield FC** | A | L | 1-4 | Booker |

## CHICHESTER CITY

*Formed 1873 as Chichester FC. First entered FA Cup: 1927-28. Chichester City 1948-2000. Changed their name to Chichester City United when they merged with Portfield (formed 1896) in 2000. Members of the Sussex County League.*

| | | | | | | | |
|---|---|---|---|---|---|---|---|
| 1960-61 (SCL) | 1 | 05.11.60 | **Bristol City** (D3) | A | L | 0-11 | |

## CHILTON COLLIERY RECREATION ATHLETIC

*Formed 1919. Competed in the FA Cup: 1923-1939. Disbanded late 1940s. League club beaten: Rochdale.*

| | | | | | | | |
|---|---|---|---|---|---|---|---|
| 1925-26 (NAll) | 1 | 28.11.25 | **Carlisle Utd** (NEL) | A | W | 2-0 | Shephard, Scutt |
| | 2 | 12.12.25 | **Rochdale** (3N) | H | D | 1-1 | Catterick |
| | 2r | 17.12.25 | **Rochdale** | A | W | 2-1 | Martin, Thomson |
| | 3 | 09.01.26 | **South Shields** (D2) | A | L | 0-3 | |
| 1926-27 (NEL) | 1 | 27.11.26 | **Annfield Plain** (NEL) | A | W | 4-2 | Bowman 4 |
| | 2 | 11.12.26 | **Accrington Stanley** (3N) | H | L | 0-3 | |

## CHIPPENHAM TOWN

*Formed 1873. First entered FA Cup: 1897-98. FA Vase runners-up: 2000. Members of the Southern League.*

| | | | | | | | |
|---|---|---|---|---|---|---|---|
| 1951-52 (WL) | 1 | 24.11.51 | **Leyton FC** (AL) | A | L | 0-3 | |

## CHIRK

*Formed 1877. Competed in the FA Cup: 1884-85-1924-25. Welsh Cup Winners: 1887, 1888, 1890, 1892, 1894.*

| | | | | | | | |
|---|---|---|---|---|---|---|---|
| 1884-85 | 1 | 25.10.84 | **Davenham** | H | W | 4-2 | |
| | 2 | 29.11.84 | **Wrexham Olympic** | H | W | 4-1 | Griffiths, Povey, 2 others |
| | 3 | 10.01.85 | **Druids** | A | L | 1-4 | Povey |
| 1885-86 | 1 | 31.10.85 | **Burslem PV** | A | L | 0-3 | |
| 1886-87 | 1 | 23.10.86 | **Hartford St Johns** | H | W | 8-1 | |
| | 2 | 13.11.86 | **Northwich V** | A | D | 0-0 | |
| | 2r | 20.11.86 | **Northwich V** | H | W | 3-0 | Owen 2, Williams |
| | 3 | | Goldenhill | | | - | |
| | | | *Goldenhill scratched. Chirk walkover* | | | | |
| | 4 | | bye | | | | |
| | 5 | 22.01.87 | **Darwen** | H | L | 1-2 | W Owen |
| 1887-88 | 1 | 15.10.87 | **Chester St Oswalds** | H | W | 4-1 | |
| | 2 | 05.11.87 | **Shrewsbury Town** | H | W | 10-2 | G Griffiths 3, W Owen 4, Rogers, Williams, og |
| | 3 | 19.11.87 | **Davenham** | A | D | 2-2 | |
| | 3r | 26.11.87 | **Davenham** | H | W | 6-1 | |
| | 4 | | bye | | | | |
| | 5 | 31.12.87 | **Derby Junction** | H | L | 0-1 | |

## CHORLEY

*Formed 1883. First entered FA Cup: 1893-94. League clubs beaten: Accrington Stanley, Wolverhampton W, Bury. Members of the Northern Premier League.*

| | | | | | | | |
|---|---|---|---|---|---|---|---|
| 1899-00 (LL) | 1 | 27.01.00 | **Notts County** (D1) | A | L | 0-6 | |
| 1938-39 (LC) | 1 | 26.11.38 | **Horden CW** (NEL) | A | D | 1-1 | Ward |
| | 1r | 30.11.38 | **Horden CW** | H | L | 1-2 | Wright |
| 1945-46 (LC) | 1 1L | 17.11.45 | **Accrington Stanley** (3N) | H | W | 2-1 | Haworth, Harrison |
| | 1 2L | 24.11.45 | **Accrington Stanley** | A | L | 0-2 | |
| 1963-64 (LC) | 1 | 16.11.63 | **Rochdale** (D4) | A | L | 1-2 | Wroth |
| 1978-79 (CC) | 1 | 25.11.78 | **Scarborough** (NPL) | H | L | 0-1 | |
| 1985-86 (NPL) | 1 | 16.11.85 | **Altrincham** (APL) | H | L | 0-2 | |
| 1986-87 (NPL) | 1 | 15.11.86 | **Wolverhampton W** (D4) | H | D | 1-1 | Moss |
| | | | *played at Burnden Park* | | | | |
| | 1r | 18.11.86 | **Wolverhampton W** | A | D | 1-1aet | Moss |
| | 1 2r | 24.11.86 | **Wolverhampton W** | | W | 3-0 | Cooper 2, Edwards |
| | | | *played at Burnden Park* | | | | |
| | 2 | 06.12.86 | **Preston North End** (D4) | H | D | 0-0 | |
| | | | *played at Ewood Park* | | | | |

| | | | | | | | |
|---|---|---|---|---|---|---|---|
| | 2r | 09.12.86 | **Preston North End** | A | L | 0-5 | |
| 1987-88 (NPL) | 1 | 14.11.87 | **Hartlepool Utd** (D4) | H | L | 0-2 | |
| 1990-91 (NPL) | 1 | 17.11.90 | **Bury** (D3) | H | W | 2-1 | Aspinall, Moss |
| | 2 | 11.12.90 | **Shrewsbury Town** (D3) | A | L | 0-1 | |

## CHURCH FC

*Formed 1874. Competed in the FA Cup 1882-83 – 1887-88. Played at Spring Hill, Accrington.*

| | | | | | | | |
|---|---|---|---|---|---|---|---|
| 1882-83 | 1 | 02.09.82 | **Clitheroe** | H | W | 5-0 | Illingworth 2, Smith 3 |
| | 2 | | bye | | | | |
| | 3 | 06.01.83 | **Darwen** | H | D | 2-2 | Crawford, AN Other |
| | 3r | 20.01.83 | **Darwen** | A | W | 2-0 | |
| | 4 | 03.02.83 | **Blackburn Olympic** | A | L | 0-2 | |
| 1883-84 | 1 | 27.10.83 | **Darwen** | A | D | 2-2 | Gregson 2 |
| | 1r | 03.11.83 | **Darwen** | H | L | 0-1 | |
| 1884-85 | 1 | 18.10.84 | **Hurst** | H | W | 3-2 | |
| | 2 | 06.12.84 | **South Shore** | A | W | 3-2 | |
| | 3 | 03.01.85 | **Southport** | H | W | 10-0 | |
| | 4 | 17.01.85 | **Darwen** | H | W | 3-0 | Holden 2, AN Other |
| | 5 | | bye | | | | |
| | 6 | 14.02.85 | **Old Carthusians** | H | L | 0-1 | |
| 1885-86 | 1 | 31.10.85 | **Blackburn Olympic** | A | W | 3-1 | |
| | 2 | | Third Lanark | | | - | |
| | | | *Third Lanark scratched. Church walkover* | | | | |
| | 3 | 12.12.85 | **Rossendale FC** | H | W | 5-1 | |
| | 4 | | bye | | | | |
| | 5 | 16.01.86 | **Swifts** | H | L | 2-6 | Beresford, AN other |
| 1886-87 | 1 | 30.10.86 | **Rawtenstall** | H | D | 1-1 | |
| | 1r | 13.11.86 | **Rawtenstall** | A | W | 7-1 | |
| | 2 | 20.11.86 | **Glasgow Rangers** | A | L | 1-2 | Beresford |
| 1887-88 | 1 | | Cliftonville | | | - | |
| | | | *Cliftonville scratched. Church walkover* | | | | |
| | 2 | 05.11.87 | **Darwen** | A | L | 0-2 | |

## CINDERFORD TOWN

*Formed 1922. First entered FA Cup: 1948-49. Members of the Southern League.*

| | | | | | | | |
|---|---|---|---|---|---|---|---|
| 1995-96 (SL) | 1 | 11.11.95 | **Bromsgrove R** (Conf) | H | W | 2-1 | Price, Hill |
| | 2 | 02.12.95 | **Gravesend & N** (SL) | H | D | 1-1 | Thomas |
| | 2r | 14.12.95 | **Gravesend & N** (SL) | A | L | 0-3 | |

## CIVIL SERVICE

*Formed 1870. One of the 15 original entrants in the FA Cup in the 1871-72 season, their match against Barnes on November 11, 1871 was on the first ever day of FA Cup competition. Their early games were played at Richmond Athletic Ground and the Civil Service entered a team in the FA Cup on and off until the FA Cup's centenary season in 1971-72.*

| | | | | | | |
|---|---|---|---|---|---|---|
| 1871-72 | 1 | 11.11.71 | **Barnes** | A | L | 0-2 |
| 1872-73 | 1 | 26.10.72 | **Royal Engineers** | A | L | 0-3 |
| 1873-74 | 1 | | Maidenhead | | | - |
| | | | *Civil Service scratched. Maidenhead walkover* | | | |
| 1874-75 | 1 | | Harrow Chequers | | | - |
| | | | *Harrow Chequers scratched. Civil Service walkover* | | | |
| | 2 | 14.11.74 | **Shropshire Wanderers** | A | L | 0-1 |
| 1875-76 | 1 | | Cambridge University | | | - |
| | | | *Civil Service scratched. Cambridge walkover* | | | |

## CLACTON TOWN

*Formed 1892. First entered the FA Cup: 1919-20. Members of the Eastern Counties League.*

| | | | | | | | |
|---|---|---|---|---|---|---|---|
| 1960-61 (SL) | 1 | 05.11.60 | **Southend Utd** (D3) | H | L | 1-3 | Clark |

## CLAPHAM ROVERS

*Formed 1869. One of the 15 original entrants in the 1871-72 season, their match against Upton Park on November 11, 1871 was on the first-ever day of FA Cup competition. FA Cup winners: 1880; FA Cup runners-up: 1879. James Prinsep, who played for Clapham in the 1879 final, is, at 17 years 245 days, the youngest-ever FA Cup finalist. Played most of their home matches on Clapham Common, Tooting Bec Common and Wandsworth Common.*

| | | | | | | | |
|---|---|---|---|---|---|---|---|
| 1871-72 | 1 | 11.11.71 | **Upton Park** | A | W | 3-0 | Kenrick 2, Thompson |
| | 2 | 16.12.71 | **Wanderers** | H | L | 1-3 | |
| 1872-73 | 1 | | Hitchin Town | | | - | |
| | | | *Hitchin scratched. Clapham walkover* | | | | |
| | 2 | 23.11.72 | **Oxford University** | H | L | 0-3 | |
| 1873-74 | 1 | | Amateur Athletic Club (AAC) | H | | | - |
| | | | *AAC scratched. Clapham Rovers walkover* | | | | |
| | 2 | 15.11.73 | **Cambridge University** | H | D | 1-1 | |
| | 2r | 29.11.73 | **Cambridge University** | A | D | 1-1 | Kenrick |
| | 2 2r | 20.12.73 | **Cambridge University** | A | W | 4-1 | E Field 2, Kenrick, St Quintin |
| | 3 | 17.01.74 | **Sheffield FC** | H | W | 2-1 | Buchanan, Holden |
| | | | *played at Peterborough* | | | | |
| | SF | 28.02.74 | **Oxford University** | | L | 0-1 | |
| | | | *played at Kennington Oval* | | | | |
| 1874-75 | 1 | 07.11.74 | **Panthers** | H | W | 3-0 | |
| | 2 | 05.12.74 | **Pilgrims** | H | W | 2-0 | Bevington, Field |
| | 3 | 30.01.75 | **Royal Engineers** | A | L | 2-3 | Bevington, AN Other |
| 1875-76 | 1 | | Hitchin Town | | | - | |
| | | | *Hitchin scratched. Clapham walkover* | | | | |
| | 2 | 18.12.75 | **Leyton FC** | H | W | 12-0 | Geaves 3, Hunter 2, Bevington, 2ogs, Birkett, Buchanan, Smith, Stanley |
| | 3 | 29.01.76 | **Old Etonians** | A | L | 0-1 | |
| 1876-77 | 1 | 11.11.76 | **Reigate Priory** | H | W | 5-0 | Birkett, Buchanan, Cazenove, Hunter, Taylor |
| | 2 | 16.12.76 | **Cambridge University** | A | L | 1-2 | Fox |
| 1877-78 | 1 | 27.10.77 | **Grantham Town** | A | W | 2-0 | Mackern, W Taylor |
| | 2 | 22.12.77 | **Swifts** | H | W | 4-0 | Buchanan 2, Holden, Sedgwick |
| | 3 | 02.02.78 | **Oxford University** | A | L | 2-3 | Birkett, Rawson |
| 1878-79 | 1 | | Finchley | | | - | |
| | | | *Finchley scratched. Clapham walkover* | | | | |
| | 2 | 07.12.78 | **Forest School** | H | W | 10-1 | Payne 2, Scott 2, Smith 2, Stanley 2, Giles, Growse |
| | 3 | 02.02.79 | **Cambridge University** | H | W | 1-0aet | Growse |
| | 4 | 08.03.79 | **Swifts** | H | W | 8-1 | Bailey 2, Scott 2, Rawson, Stanley, og, 1 other |
| | SF | | bye | | | | |
| | F | 29.03.79 | **Old Etonians** | | L | 0-1 | |
| | | | *played at Kennington Oval* | | | | |
| 1879-80 | 1 | 08.11.79 | **Romford (1876)** | H | W | 7-0 | |
| | 2 | 20.12.79 | **South Norwood** | A | W | 4-1 | Stanley 2, Lloyd-Jones, Sparks |
| | 3 | 17.01.80 | **Pilgrims** | H | W | 7-0 | Sparks 3, Barry 2, Lloyd-Jones, Stanley |
| | 4 | 14.02.80 | **Hendon (1874)** | H | W | 2-0 | LLoyd-Jones 2 |
| | 5 | 21.02.80 | **Old Etonians** | H | W | 1-0 | LLoyd-Jones |
| | SF | | bye | | | | |
| | F | 10.04.80 | **Oxford University** | | W | 1-0 | Lloyd-Jones |
| | | | *played at Kennington Oval* | | | | |
| 1880-81 | 1 | 13.11.80 | **Finchley** | H | W | 15-0 | |
| | 2 | | bye | | | | |
| | 3 | 08.01.81 | **Swifts** | H | W | 2-1 | Ram, Wollaston |
| | 4 | 12.02.81 | **Upton Park** | A | W | 5-4 | Ram 2, Barry 2, Sparks |
| | 5 | 19.03.81 | **Old Carthusians** | A | L | 1-3aet | Lloyd-Jones |
| 1881-82 | 1 | 05.11.81 | **Old Etonians** | A | D | 2-2 | Payne, Taylor |
| | 1r | 19.11.81 | **Old Etonians** | H | L | 0-1 | |
| 1882-83 | 1 | 04.11.82 | **Kildare FC** | H | W | 3-0 | Pawson 2, og |
| | 2 | 02.12.82 | **Hanover Utd** | H | W | 7-1 | Ram 3, Coles, Holden-White, Howard-Maclean, Lloyd-Jones |
| | 3 | 06.01.83 | **Windsor Home Park** | A | W | 3-0 | Ram 2, Howard-Maclean |
| | 4 | | bye | | | | |
| | 5 | 20.02.83 | **Old Carthusians** | A | L | 3-5 | Pawson 2, Lloyd-Jones |
| 1883-84 | 1 | | Kildare FC | | | - | |
| | | | *Kildare scratched. Clapham walkover* | | | | |

| | | | | | | | |
|---|---|---|---|---|---|---|---|
| | 2 | 01.12.83 | **Rochester** | H | W | 7-0 | Kerr 4, Poulton 3 |
| | 3 | 22.12.83 | **Swifts** | H | L | 1-2 | Oxley |
| 1884-85 | 1 | 08.11.84 | **Hendon (1874)** | H | D | 3-3 | |
| | 1r | 22.11.84 | **Hendon (1874)** | A | L | 0-6 | |
| 1885-86 | 1 | 31.10.85 | **1st Surrey Rifles** | H | W | 12-0 | |
| | 2 | | bye | | | | |
| | 3 | 02.01.86 | **South Reading** | | | - | |
| | | | *FA disqualified Clapham Rovers. South Reading advanced* | | | | |
| 1886-87 | 1 | 30.10.86 | **Old Brightonians** | H | L | 0-6 | |

## CLAPTON

*Formed 1878. Have played at their famous Old Spotted Dog Ground at Forest Gate, East London since their formation. First entered FA Cup: 1883-84. FA Amateur Cup Winners: 1907, 1909, 1915, 1924. runners-up: 1905. League club defeated: Norwich City. Members of the Isthmian League.*

| | | | | | | | |
|---|---|---|---|---|---|---|---|
| 1884-85 | 1 | 01.11.84 | **Romford (1876)** | A | L | 2-3 | Davies, Jackson |
| 1885-86 | 1 | 24.10.85 | **Hendon (1874)** | A | W | 4-0 | |
| | 2 | 21.11.85 | **South Reading** | H | D | 1-1 | |
| | | | *FA disqualified Clapton after protest. South Reading advanced* | | | | |
| 1886-87 | 1 | 23.10.86 | **Crusaders** | H | L | 0-5 | |
| 1887-88 | 1 | 15.10.87 | **Old Westminsters** | A | L | 1-4 | |
| 1889-90 | 1 | 18.01.90 | **Small Heath** (FAll) | A | L | 1-3 | Burns |
| 1890-91 | 1 | 17.01.91 | **Nottingham Forest** (FAll) | H | L | 0-14 | |
| | | | *played at Upton Park* | | | | |
| 1925-26 (IL) | 1 | 28.11.25 | **Norwich City** (3S) | H | W | 3-1 | Massey 2, McNeill |
| | 2 | 12.12.25 | **Ilford** (IL) | H | W | 1-0 | Munden |
| | 3 | 09.01.26 | **Swindon Town** (3S) | H | L | 2-3 | Munden, Massey |
| | | | *played at Upton Park* | | | | |
| 1926-27 (IL) | 1 | 27.11.26 | **Brentford** (3S) | H | D | 1-1 | Morgan |
| | 1r | 01.12.26 | **Brentford** | A | L | 3-7 | Osborn 2, Massey |
| 1927-28 (IL) | 1 | 30.11.27 | **Luton Town** (3S) | A | L | 0-9 | |
| 1957-58 (IL) | 1 | 16.11.57 | **QPR** (3S) | H | D | 1-1 | Bennett |
| | 1r | 18.11.57 | **QPR** | A | L | 1-3 | Brewster |

## CLARENCE

*Formed 1876. Played at Battersea Park, London and these were the only two FA Cup matches they played.*

| | | | | | | | |
|---|---|---|---|---|---|---|---|
| 1879-80 | 1 | 01.11.79 | **Pilgrims** | A | L | 2-3 | T Stone, Wilsmshurst |
| 1880-81 | 1 | 30.10.80 | **Marlow** | A | L | 0-6 | |

## CLEATOR MOOR CELTIC

*Formed 1908. Entered FA Cup: 1919-20-1991-92. Still active at senior level in Cumberland and the North West.*

| | | | | | | | |
|---|---|---|---|---|---|---|---|
| 1950-51 (WCL) | 1 | 25.11.50 | **Tranmere Rovers** (3N) | H | L | 0-5 | |
| | | | *played at Workington* | | | | |

## CLEETHORPES TOWN

*Entered FA Cup: 1886-87 – 1930-31.*

| | | | | | | | |
|---|---|---|---|---|---|---|---|
| 1886-87 | 1 | 30.10.86 | **Mellors Ltd** | H | W | 2-1 | |
| | 2 | 20.11.86 | **Lockwood Bros** | H | L | 1-4 | |
| 1887-88 | 1 | 15.10.87 | **Grimsby Town** | H | L | 0-4 | |

## CLIFTONVILLE

*Formed 1879. One of the three clubs from Northern Ireland to take part in the Competition Proper. Northern Ireland FA Cup winners: 8 times; runners-up: 9 times. Members of the Irish League.*

| | | | | | | | |
|---|---|---|---|---|---|---|---|
| 1886-87 | 1 | 09.10.86 | **Blackburn Park Road** | A | D | 2-2 | Dobbin, Turner |
| | 1r | 23.10.86 | **Blackburn Park Road** | H | W | 7-2 | |
| | 2 | 13.11.86 | **Great Lever** | A | W | 3-1 | |
| | 3 | 04.12.86 | **Partick Thistle** | H | L | 0-11 | |
| 1887-88 | 1 | | Church FC | | | - | |
| | | | *Cliftonville scratched. Church walkover* | | | | |

## CLITHEROE

*Formed 1877. Played these early FA Cup matches at the Waterloo Field and at Church Meadow, Clitheroe. First entered FA Cup: 1882-83. FA Vase runners-up: 1996. Members of the North West Counties League.*

| | | | | | | | |
|---|---|---|---|---|---|---|---|
| 1882-83 | 1 | 02.09.82 | **Church FC** | A | L | 0-5 | |

| | | | | | | | |
|---|---|---|---|---|---|---|---|
| 1883-84 | 1 | 10.11.83 | **South Shore** | H | D | 3-3 | |
| | 1r | 24.11.83 | **South Shore** | A | L | 2-3 | Bell, AN Other |
| 1884-85 | 1 | | Witton | | | - | |
| | | | *Clitheroe scratched. Witton walkover* | | | | |
| 1885-86 | 1 | 24.10.85 | **Blackburn Rovers** | H | L | 0-2 | |

## CLITHEROE LOW MOOR

*Formed 1879. Played at Deek Field, Clitheroe.*

| | | | | | | | |
|---|---|---|---|---|---|---|---|
| 1883-84 | 1 | 27.10.83 | **Blackburn Park Road** | A | L | 0-6 | |
| 1884-85 | 1 | | Blackburn Park Road | | | - | |
| | | | *Blackburn Park Road scratched. Clitheroe Low Moor walkover* | | | | |
| | 2 | 22.11.84 | **Southport** | A | L | 1-3 | |
| 1885-86 | 1 | 24.10.85 | **Rossendale FC** | A | L | 2-6 | |

## CLYDESDALE

*Entered the FA Cup once and scratched without playing a game.*

| | | | | | | | |
|---|---|---|---|---|---|---|---|
| 1875-76 | 1 | | South Norwood | | | - | |
| | | | *Clydesdale scratched. South Norwood walkover* | | | | |

## COLCHESTER UNITED

*Formed 1937. First entered FA Cup: 1938-39. Best FA Cup performance: 6th round, 1970-71. Record FA Cup win: 7-1 v Yeovil Town, 3rd round,.11.12 1958; 7-1 v Woodford Town, 4th qualifying round 1950-51. Record FA Cup defeat: 0-5 v Reading, 1st round, 30.11.1946; 0-5 vs Blackpool, 5th round, 07.02.1948; 0-5 v Everton, 6th round, 06.03.1971. FA Trophy winners: 1992. League clubs beaten as a Non-League club: Wrexham, Huddersfield Town, Bradford Park Avenue, Reading.*

| | | | | | | | |
|---|---|---|---|---|---|---|---|
| 1938-39 (SL) | 1 | 26.11.38 | **Folkestone** (SL) | A | L | 1-2 | Leslie |
| 1945-46 (SL) | | | 4q Wisbech T (A) L 0-5 | | | | |
| 1946-47 (SL) | 1 | 30.11.46 | **Reading** (3S) | A | L | 0-5 | |
| 1947-48 (SL) | 1 | 29.11.47 | **Banbury Spencer** (BC) | H | W | 2-1 | Brown, Curry |
| | 2 | 13.12.47 | **Wrexham** (3N) | H | W | 1-0 | Curry |
| | 3 | 10.01.48 | **Huddersfield Town** (D1) | H | W | 1-0 | Curry |
| | 4 | 24.01.48 | **Bradford Park A** (D2) | H | W | 3-2 | Curry 2, Cutting |
| | 5 | 07.02.48 | **Blackpool** (D1) | A | L | 0-5 | |
| 1948-49 (SL) | 1 | 27.11.48 | **Reading** (3S) | H | - | 1-1ab | Curry |
| | | | *abandoned after 35 minutes – fog* | | | | |
| | 1 | 04.12.48 | **Reading** (3S) | H | L | 2-4 | Cater 2 |
| 1949-50 (SL) | | | 4q Wealdstone (A) 0-1 | | | | |
| 1950-51 (3S) | | | 4q Woodford T (A) 7-1 | | | | |
| | 1 | 25.11.50 | **Bournemouth** (3S) | A | L | 0-1 | |
| 1951-52 (3S) | 1 | 24.11.51 | **Port Vale** (3S) | H | W | 3-1 | Keeble, Scott, Elder |
| | 2 | 15.12.51 | **Bristol City** (3S) | H | W | 2-1 | Scott, Davidson |
| | 3 | 12.01.52 | **Barnsley** (D2) | A | L | 0-3 | |
| 1952-53 (3S) | 1 | 22.11.52 | **Weymouth** (SL) | A | D | 1-1 | Targett og |
| | 1r | 27.11.52 | **Weymouth** | H | W | 4-0 | Targett og, McKim, Edwards 2 |
| | 2 | 06.12.52 | **Llanelli** (SL) | H | W | 3-2 | Barlow, Church, McCurley |
| | 3 | 10.01.53 | **Rotherham Utd** (D2) | A | D | 2-2 | McCurley 2 |
| | 3r | 15.01.53 | **Rotherham Utd** | H | L | 0-2 | |
| 1953-54 (3S) | 1 | 21.11.53 | **Millwall** (3S) | H | D | 1-1 | McCurley |
| | 1r | 23.11.53 | **Millwall** | A | L | 0-4 | |
| 1954-55 (3S) | 1 | 20.11.54 | **Reading** (3S) | A | D | 3-3 | Birch, Grice, McKim |
| | 1r | 25.11.54 | **Reading** | H | L | 1-2 | Elder |
| 1955-56 (3S) | 1 | 19.11.55 | **Torquay Utd** (3S) | A | L | 0-2 | |
| 1956-57 (3S) | 1 | 17.11.56 | **Southend Utd** (3S) | H | L | 1-4 | McCurley |
| 1957-58 (3S) | 1 | 16.11.57 | **Wisbech Town** (ML) | A | L | 0-1 | |
| 1958-59 (D3) | 1 | 15.11.58 | **Bath City** (SL) | H | W | 2-0 | Plant, Langman |
| | 2 | 06.12.58 | **Yeovil Town** (SL) | H | D | 1-1 | Plant |
| | 2r | 11.12.58 | **Yeovil Town** | A | W | 7-1 | Langman 4, Williams, McLeod 2 |
| | 3 | 10.01.59 | **Chesterfield** (D3) | H | W | 2-0 | Evans, Langman |
| | 4 | 24.01.59 | **Arsenal** (D1) | H | D | 2-2 | Langman, J Evans |
| | 4r | 28.01.59 | **Arsenal** | A | L | 0-4 | |
| 1959-60 (D3) | 1 | 14.11.59 | **QPR** (D3) | H | L | 2-3 | McCurley, Wright |
| 1960-61 (D3) | 1 | 05.11.60 | **Maidenhead** (CRN) | H | W | 5-0 | Bobby Hunt 2, Langman 2, Williams |

| | | | | | | | | |
|---|---|---|---|---|---|---|---|---|
| | | 2 | 26.11.60 | **Aldershot** (D4) | A | L | 1-3 | Hill |
| 1961-62 | (D4) | 1 | 04.11.61 | **Peterborough Utd** (D3) | A | D | 3-3 | Abrey, Wright, Bobby Hunt |
| | | 1r | 06.11.61 | **Peterborough Utd** | H | D | 2-2aet | King, Bobby Hunt |
| | | 1r | 13.11.61 | **Peterborough Utd** | | L | 0-3 | |
| | | | | *played at Carrow Road* | | | | |
| 1962-63 | (D3) | 1 | 03.11.62 | **Wimbledon** (IL) | A | L | 1-2 | King |
| 1963-64 | (D3) | 1 | 16.11.63 | **Brighton** (D4) | A | W | 1-0 | Bobby Hunt |
| | | 2 | 07.12.63 | **QPR** (D3) | H | L | 0-1 | |
| 1964-65 | (D3) | 1 | 14.11.64 | **Bideford** (WL) | H | D | 3-3 | Salisbury, Longbottom, Trevis |
| | | 1r | 18.11.64 | **Bideford** | A | W | 2-1 | Connolly, Stark |
| | | 2 | 05.12.64 | **Torquay Utd** (D4) | A | L | 0-2 | |
| 1965-66 | (D4) | 1 | 13.11.65 | **QPR** (D3) | H | D | 3-3 | Blackwood 2, Hall |
| | | 1r | 17.11.65 | **QPR** | A | L | 0-4 | |
| 1966-67 | (D3) | 1 | 26.11.66 | **Gainsborough T** (ML) | A | W | 1-0 | Hall |
| | | 2 | 07.01.67 | **Peterborough Utd** (D3) | H | L | 0-3 | |
| 1967-68 | (D3) | 1 | 12.12.67 | **Torquay Utd** (D3) | A | D | 1-1 | Barlow |
| | | 1r | 18.12.67 | **Torquay Utd** | H | W | 2-1 | Trevis 2 |
| | | 2 | 06.01.68 | **Chelmsford City** (SL) | H | W | 2-0 | McKechnie, Stratton |
| | | 3 | 27.01.68 | **WBA** (D1) | H | D | 1-1 | Stratton |
| | | 3r | 31.01.68 | **WBA** | A | L | 0-4 | |
| 1968-69 | (D4) | 1 | 16.11.68 | **Chesham Utd** (AL) | H | W | 5-0 | Light 2, Hall 2, Price |
| | | 2 | 07.12.68 | **Exeter City** (D4) | H | L | 0-1 | |
| 1969-70 | (D4) | 1 | 15.11.69 | **Newport County** (D4) | A | L | 1-2 | Ferguson |
| 1970-71 | (D4) | 1 | 21.11.70 | **Ringmer** (SCL) | H | W | 3-0 | Crawford 3 |
| | | 2 | 12.12.70 | **Cambridge Utd** (D4) | H | W | 3-0 | Jones, Garvey, Gilchrist |
| | | 3 | 05.01.71 | **Barnet** (SL) | A | W | 1-0 | McMahon |
| | | 4 | 23.01.71 | **Rochdale** (D3) | A | D | 3-3 | Crawford 2, Lewis |
| | | 4r | 25.01.71 | **Rochdale** | H | W | 5-0 | Lewis, Simmons, Parry og, Crawford, Mahon |
| | | 5 | 13.02.71 | **Leeds Utd** (D1) | H | W | 3-2 | Crawford 2, Simmons |
| | | 6 | 06.03.71 | **Everton** (D1) | A | L | 0-5 | |
| 1971-72 | (D4) | 1 | 20.11.71 | **Shrewsbury Town** (D3) | H | L | 1-4 | Hall |
| 1972-73 | (D4) | 1 | 18.11.72 | **Bognor Regis Town** (SL) | H | W | 6-0 | Simmons 3, Morgan, Hall, Foley |
| | | 2 | 09.12.72 | **Bournemouth** (D3) | A | D | 0-0 | |
| | | 2r | 11.12.72 | **Bournemouth** | H | L | 0-2 | |
| 1973-74 | (D4) | 1 | 24.11.73 | **Peterborough Utd** (D4) | H | L | 2-3 | Mahon, Harford |
| 1974-75 | (D3) | 1 | 23.11.74 | **Watford** (D3) | A | W | 1-0 | Froggatt |
| | | 2 | 14.12.74 | **Leatherhead** (IL) | A | L | 0-1 | |
| 1975-76 | (D3) | 1 | 22.11.75 | **Dover** (SL) | H | D | 3-3 | Leslie, Dominey, Smith |
| | | 1r | 26.11.75 | **Dover** | A | L | 1-4aet | Packer (p) |
| 1976-77 | (D4) | 1 | 20.11.76 | **Cambridge Utd** (D4) | A | D | 1-1 | Packer (p) |
| | | 1r | 24.11.76 | **Cambridge Utd** | H | W | 2-0 | Garwood, Leslie |
| | | 2 | 11.12.76 | **Brentford** | H | - | 0-0ab | |
| | | | | *abandoned after 62 minutes – icebound pitch* | | | | |
| | | 2 | 20.12.76 | **Brentford** (D4) | H | W | 3-2 | Allinson, Froggat, Packer (p) |
| | | 3 | 08.01.77 | **Kettering Town** (SL) | A | W | 3-2 | Froggatt, Garwood 2 |
| | | 4 | 29.01.77 | **Derby County** (D1) | H | D | 1-1 | Garwood |
| | | 4r | 02.02.77 | **Derby County** | A | L | 0-1 | |
| 1977-78 | (D3) | 1 | 26.11.77 | **Bournemouth** (D4) | H | D | 1-1 | Gough |
| | | 1r | 29.11.77 | **Bournemouth** | A | D | 0-0aet | |
| | | 1 2r | 05.12.77 | **Bournemouth** | A | W | 4-1 | Dowman, Garwood 3 |
| | | 2 | 17.12.77 | **Watford** (D4) | A | L | 0-2 | |
| 1978-79 | (D3) | 1 | 25.11.78 | **Oxford Utd** (D3) | H | W | 4-2 | Gough 3, Foley |
| | | 2 | 16.12.78 | **Leatherhead** (IL) | A | D | 1-1 | Gough |
| | | 2r | 18.12.78 | **Leatherhead** | H | W | 4-0 | Lee, Gough, Dowman 2 |
| | | 3 | 09.01.79 | **Darlington** (D4) | A | W | 1-0 | Hodge |
| | | 4 | 30.01.79 | **Newport County** (D4) | A | D | 0-0 | |
| | | 4r | 05.02.79 | **Newport County** | H | W | 1-0 | Gough |
| | | 5 | 20.02.79 | **Manchester Utd** (D1) | H | L | 0-1 | |
| 1979-80 | (D3) | 1 | 24.11.79 | **Plymouth Argyle** (D3) | H | D | 1-1 | Rowles |
| | | 1r | 27.11.79 | **Plymouth Argyle** | A | W | 1-0aet | Allinson |

| | | | | | | | | |
|---|---|---|---|---|---|---|---|---|
| | | 2 | 15.12.79 | **Bournemouth** (D4) | H | W | 1-0 | Rowles |
| | | 3 | 05.01.80 | **Reading** (D3) | A | L | 0-2 | |
| 1980-81 | (D3) | 1 | 22.11.80 | **Portsmouth** (D3) | H | W | 3-0 | Lee, Allinson, Bremner |
| | | 2 | 13.12.80 | **Yeovil Town** (APL) | H | D | 1-1 | Wignall |
| | | 2r | 17.12.80 | **Yeovil Town** | A | W | 2-0 | Lee, Bremner |
| | | 3 | 03.01.81 | **Watford** (D2) | H | L | 0-1 | |
| 1981-82 | (D4) | 1 | 21.11.81 | **Newport County** (D3) | H | W | 2-0 | Leslie, Adcock |
| | | 2 | 16.12.81 | **Brentford** (D3) | A | D | 1-1 | Allinson |
| | | 2r | 30.12.81 | **Brentford** | H | W | 1-0 | McNichol og |
| | | 3 | 04.01.82 | **Newcastle Utd** (D2) | A | D | 1-1 | Wignall |
| | | 3r | 18.01.82 | **Newcastle Utd** | H | L | 3-4aet | Cook, Allinson 2 (2ps) |
| 1982-83 | (D4) | 1 | 20.11.82 | **Torquay Utd** (D4) | H | L | 0-2 | |
| 1983-84 | (D4) | 1 | 19.11.83 | **Torquay Utd** (D4) | A | W | 2-1 | Bowen 2 |
| | | 2 | 10.12.83 | **Wealdstone** (APL) | H | W | 4-0 | Bowen 3, Houston |
| | | 3 | 07.01.84 | **Charlton Athletic** (D2) | H | L | 0-1 | |
| 1984-85 | (D4) | 1 | 17.11.84 | **Southend Utd** (D4) | A | D | 2-2 | Irving, Houston |
| | | 1r | 21.11.84 | **Southend Utd** | H | W | 3-2aet | Adcock, Pennyfather og, Groves |
| | | 2 | 08.12.84 | **Gillingham** (D3) | H | L | 0-5 | |
| 1985-86 | (D4) | 1 | 16.11.85 | **Wycombe W** (APL) | A | L | 0-2 | |
| 1986-87 | (D4) | 1 | 15.11.86 | **Bishop's Stortford** (IL) | A | D | 1-1 | T English |
| | | 1r | 18.11.86 | **Bishop's Stortford** | H | W | 2-0 | T English, Adcock |
| | | 2 | 06.12.86 | **Aldershot** (D4) | A | L | 2-3 | T English, Grenfell |
| 1987-88 | (D4) | 1 | 14.11.87 | **Tamworth** (WMRL) | H | W | 3-0 | Wilkins, Tempest, Chatterton (p) |
| | | 2 | 05.12.87 | **Hereford Utd** (D4) | H | W | 3-2 | Chatterton, Wilkns, Hill |
| | | 3 | 11.01.88 | **Plymouth Argyle** (D2) | A | L | 0-2 | |
| 1988-89 | (D4) | 1 | 19.11.88 | **Fulham** (D3) | A | W | 1-0 | Walsh |
| | | 2 | 10.12.88 | **Swansea City** (D3) | H | D | 2-2 | Hedman, Wilkins |
| | | 2r | 13.12.88 | **Swansea City** | A | W | 3-1 | Hedman, Walsh, Wilkins |
| | | 3 | 07.01.89 | **Shrewsbury Town** (D2) | A | W | 3-0 | Walsh, Pratley og, Allinson |
| | | 4 | 28.01.89 | **Sheffield Utd** (D3) | A | D | 3-3 | Hicks, Hill, Hetzke |
| | | 4r | 31.01.89 | **Sheffield Utd** | H | L | 0-2 | |
| 1989-90 | (D4) | 1 | 18.11.89 | **Brentford** (D3) | A | W | 1-0 | Bennett |
| | | 2 | 09.12.89 | **Birmingham City** (D3) | H | L | 0-2 | |
| 1990-91 | (Conf) | 1 | 17.11.90 | **Reading** (D3) | H | W | 2-1 | Atkins (p), Marmon |
| | | 2 | 12.12.90 | **Leyton Orient** (D3) | H | D | 0-0 | |
| | | 2r | 17.12.90 | **Leyton Orient** | A | L | 1-4 | Masters |
| 1991-92 | (Conf) | 4Q | 26.10.91 | **Burton Albion** (SL) | H | W | 5-0 | McDonough (p), McGavin 2, Restarick, Kinsella |
| | | 1 | 16.11.91 | **Exeter City** (D3) | H | D | 0-0 | |
| | | 1r | 26.11.91 | **Exeter City** | A | D | 0-0aet | |
| | | | | *Exeter won 4-2 on penalties* | | | | |
| 1992-93 | (D3) | 1 | 14.11.92 | **Slough Town** (Conf) | H | W | 4-0 | Sorrell, Bennett 2, Ball |
| | | 2 | 05.12.92 | **Gillingham** (D3) | A | D | 1-1 | McGavin |
| | | 2r | 16.12.92 | **Gillingham** | H | L | 2-3 | Ball 2 |
| 1993-94 | (D3) | 1 | 13.11.93 | **Sutton Utd** (IL) | H | L | 3-4 | McGavin, S Brown, English |
| 1994-95 | (D3) | 1 | 12.11.94 | **Yeading** (IL) | A | D | 2-2 | Kinsella, Abrahams |
| | | 1r | 22.11.94 | **Yeading** | H | W | 7-1 | Abrahams 2, Whitton 2, S Brown 2, Kinsella |
| | | 2 | 03.12.94 | **Exeter City** (D3) | A | W | 2-1 | Whitton, English |
| | | 3 | 07.01.95 | **Wimbledon** (D1) | A | L | 0-1 | |
| 1995-96 | (D3) | 1 | 11.11.95 | **Gravesend & N** (SL) | A | L | 0-2 | |
| 1996-97 | (D3) | 1 | 16.11.96 | **Wycombe W** (D2) | H | L | 1-2 | Wilkins |
| 1997-98 | (D3) | 1 | 15.11.97 | **Brentford** (D2) | A | D | 2-2 | Sale, D Gregory |
| | | 1r | 25.11.97 | **Brentford** | H | D | 0-0aet | |
| | | | | *Colchester Utd won 4-2 on penalties* | | | | |
| | | 2 | 06.12.97 | **Hereford Utd** (Conf) | H | D | 1-1 | D Gregory |
| | | 2r | 16.12.97 | **Hereford Utd** | A | D | 1-1aet | Forbes |
| | | | | *Hereford Utd won 5-4 on penalties* | | | | |
| 1998-99 | (D2) | 1 | 14.11.98 | **Bedlington Terriers** (NL) | A | L | 1-4 | Adcock |
| 1999-00 | (D2) | 1 | 30.10.99 | **Swansea City** (D3) | A | L | 1-2 | Lua-Lua |
| 2000-01 | (D2) | 1 | 18.11.00 | **Yeovil Town** (Conf) | A | L | 1-5 | Duguid |

| | | | | | | | | |
|---|---|---|---|---|---|---|---|---|
| 2001-02 | (D2) | 1 | 17.11.01 | **York City** (D3) | H | D | 0-0 | |
| | | 1r | 27.11.01 | **York City** | A | D | 2-2aet | McGleish, Duguid |
| | | | | *York City won 3-2 on penalties* | | | | |
| 2002-03 | (D2) | 1 | 16.11.02 | **Chester City** (Conf) | H | L | 0-1 | |

## COLWYN BAY

*Formed 1885. First entered FA Cup: 1927-28. League club beaten: none in the FA Cup but Wrexham in the Welsh Cup. Members of the Northern Premier League.*

| | | | | | | | | |
|---|---|---|---|---|---|---|---|---|
| 1987-88 | (NWC) | 1 | 14.11.87 | **Northwich V** (Conf) | A | L | 0-1 | |
| 1995-96 | (NPL) | 1 | 11.11.95 | **Spennymoor Utd** (NPL) | A | W | 1-0 | Nicholas |
| | | 2 | 02.12.95 | **Blackpool** (D2) | A | L | 0-2 | |
| 1996-97 | (NPL) | 1 | 16.11.96 | **Wrexham** (D2) | H | D | 1-1 | G Roberts |
| | | 1r | 26.11.96 | **Wrexham** | A | L | 0-2 | |
| 1997-98 | (NPL) | 1 | 16.11.97 | **Notts County** (D3) | A | L | 0-2 | |

## CONGLETON TOWN

*Formed 1901. First entered FA Cup: 1905-06. Members of the North West Counties League.*

| | | | | | | | | |
|---|---|---|---|---|---|---|---|---|
| 1989-90 | (NPL) | 1 | 18.11.89 | **Crewe Alexandra** (D3) | A | L | 0-2 | |

## CONSETT

*Formed 1899. First entered FA Cup: 1927-28. Members of the Northern League.*

| | | | | | | | | |
|---|---|---|---|---|---|---|---|---|
| 1958-59 | (ML) | 1 | 15.11.58 | **Doncaster Rovers** (D3) | A | L | 0-5 | |
| 1996-97 | (NL) | 1 | 16.11.96 | **Mansfield Town** (D3) | A | L | 0-4 | |

## CORBY TOWN

*Formed 1948. Developed out of the Stewartds & Lloyds works club (formed 1935). First entered FA Cup: 1949-50. League club beaten: Luton Town. Members of the Southern League.*

| | | | | | | | | |
|---|---|---|---|---|---|---|---|---|
| 1954-55 | (ML) | 1 | 20.11.54 | **Watford** (3S) | H | L | 0-2 | |
| 1963-64 | (SL) | 1 | 16.11.63 | **Bristol City** (D3) | H | L | 1-3 | Crawley |
| 1964-65 | (SL) | 1 | 14.11.64 | **Hartlepools Utd** (D4) | H | L | 1-3 | Wright |
| 1965-66 | (SL) | 1 | 13.11.65 | **Burton Albion** (SL) | H | W | 6-3 | Goodall 2, Riley, Haazs, Garden 2 (1p) |
| | | 2 | 04.12.65 | **Luton Town** (D4) | H | D | 2-2 | Jagger, Goodall |
| | | 2r | 07.12.65 | **Luton Town** | A | W | 1-0 | Goodall |
| | | 3 | 22.01.66 | **Plymouth Argyle** (D2) | A | L | 0-6 | |
| 1967-68 | (SL) | 1 | 09.12.67 | **Boston Utd** (WMRL) | H | L | 0-3 | |

## CORINTHIAN CASUALS

*Formed 1939 by the merger of the famous Casuals and Corinthians clubs. First entered FA Cup as Corinthian Casuals: 1963-64. FA Amateur Cup runners-up: 1956. FA Cup Final commentator Martin Tyler is among their former players. Members of the Isthmian League.*

| | | | | | | | | |
|---|---|---|---|---|---|---|---|---|
| 1965-66 | (IL) | 1 | 13.11.65 | **Watford** (D3) | H | L | 1-5 | Phillips |
| 1983-84 | (IL) | 1 | 19.11.83 | **Bristol City** (D4) | H | D | 0-0 | |
| | | | | *played at Dulwich Hamlet* | | | | |
| | | 1r | 23.11.83 | **Bristol City** | A | L | 0-4 | |

## CORINTHIANS

*The Corinthians hold a unique place in the English game. During their heyday they were the top amateur side in the country, but they did not play in a League or in any competitve matches. They were formed in 1882 and would probably have won the FA Cup if their own rules had not barred them from taking part in competitive matches. They finally entered the cup in 1922 and were exempted from the early rounds until 1933. They merged with the Casuals in 1939.*

| | | | | | | | | |
|---|---|---|---|---|---|---|---|---|
| 1922-23 | | 1 | 13.01.23 | **Brighton** (3S) | A | D | 1-1 | Creek |
| | | 1r | 17.01.23 | **Brighton** | H | D | 1-1aet | Howell |
| | | | | *played at Crystal Palace* | | | | |
| | | 1 2r | 22.01.23 | **Brighton** | | L | 0-1 | |
| | | | | *played at Stamford Bridge* | | | | |
| 1923-24 | | 1 | 12.01.24 | **Blackburn Rovers** (D1) | H | W | 1-0 | Doggart |
| | | | | *played at Crystal Palace* | | | | |
| | | 2 | 02.02.24 | **WBA** (D1) | A | L | 0-5 | |
| 1924-25 | | 1 | 10.01.25 | **Sheffield Utd** (D1) | A | L | 0-5 | |
| 1925-26 | | 3 | 09.01.26 | **Manchester City** (D1) | H | D | 3-3 | Creek 2, Hegan |
| | | 3r | 13.01.26 | **Manchester City** | A | L | 0-4 | |
| 1926-27 | | 3 | 08.01.27 | **Walsall** (3N) | A | W | 4-0 | Ashton 2, Creek, Hegan |

| | | | | | | | |
|---|---|---|---|---|---|---|---|
| | 4 | 29.01.27 | **Newcastle Utd** (D1) | H | L | 1-3 | Ashton |
| | | | *played at Crystal Palace* | | | | |
| 1927-28 | 3 | 14.01.28 | **New Brighton** (3N) | A | L | 1-2 | Hartley |
| 1928-29 | 3 | 12.01.29 | **Norwich City** (3S) | A | W | 5-0 | Ashton 3, Doggart, Stone |
| | 4 | 26.01.29 | **West Ham Utd** (D1) | A | L | 0-3 | |
| 1929-30 | 3 | 11.01.30 | **Millwall** (D2) | H | D | 2-2 | Robins, Ashton |
| | 3r | 15.01.30 | **Millwall** | A | D | 1-1aet | Robins |
| | 3 2r | 20.01.30 | **Millwall** | | L | 1-5 | Doggart |
| | | | *played at Stamford Bridge* | | | | |
| 1930-31 | 3 | 10.01.31 | **Port Vale** (D2) | H | L | 1-3 | Doggart |
| 1931-32 | 3 | 09.01.32 | **Sheffield Utd** (D1) | A | L | 1-2 | Fabian |
| 1932-33 | 3 | 14.01.33 | **West Ham Utd** (D2) | H | L | 0-2 | |
| 1934-35 | 1 | 24.11.34 | **Watford** (3S) | A | L | 0-2 | |
| 1935-36 | 1 | 30.11.35 | **Reading** (3S) | A | L | 3-8 | Charlton 2, Whewell (p) |
| 1936-37 | 1 | 28.11.36 | **Bristol Rovers** (3S) | H | L | 0-2 | |
| 1937-38 | 1 | 27.11.37 | **Southend Utd** (3S) | H | L | 0-2 | |
| | | | *played at White City* | | | | |
| 1938-39 | 1 | 26.11.38 | **Southend Utd** (3N) | A | L | 0-3 | |

# COVENTRY CITY

*Formed 1883 as Singers FC. Coventry City 1898. FA Cup winners: 1987. Record FA Cup win: 7-0 v Scunthorpe United, 1st round, 24.11.1934; 7-0 v Macclesfield T, 3rd round, 02.01.1999; Record FA Cup defeat: 2-11 v Berwick Rangers (Worcester), 3rd qualifying round 1901-02.*

| | | | | | | | |
|---|---|---|---|---|---|---|---|
| **as Singers FC** | | | | | | | |
| 1892-93 | | | P Burton Swifts (A) 0-3 | | | | |
| 1893-94 | | | 1q Redditch (H) 1-4 | | | | |
| 1894-95 | | | did not enter | | | | |
| 1895-96 (BDL) | | | 1q Hereford Thistle (H) 6-1; 2q Kidderminster H (A) 0-0; 2qr Kidderminster H (H) 2-1; 3q Burton Swifts (H) 0-2 | | | | |
| 1896-97 (BDL) | | | 2q Stourbridge (A) 2-4 | | | | |
| 1897-98 (BDL) | | | 1q Wrockwardine Wood (A) 0-1 | | | | |
| **as Coventry City** | | | | | | | |
| 1898-99 (BDL) | | | 1q Hereford T (H) 0-0; 1qr Hereford T (A) 0-1 | | | | |
| 1899-00 (BDL) | | | 1q Stourbridge (A) 0-5 | | | | |
| 1900-01 (BDL) | | | 3q Oswestry U scratched; | | | | |
| 1901-02 (BDL) | | | 3q Berwick Rangers (Worcester) (A) 2-11 | | | | |
| 1902-03 (BDL) | | | 3q Aberaman (H) 3-1; 4q Stafford R (H) 5-2; 5q Kidderminster H (H) 2-2; 5qr Kidderminster H (A) 2-4 | | | | |
| 1903-04 (BDL) | | | 3q Walsall (H) 2-4 | | | | |
| 1904-05 (BDL) | | | 1q Halesowen (H) 2-2; 1qr Halesowen (H) 3-2; 2q Walsall (H) 2-0; 3q Stafford R (A) 2-3 | | | | |
| 1905-06 (BDL) | | | 1q Worcester C (H) 0-3 | | | | |
| 1906-07 (BDL) | | | did not enter | | | | |
| 1907-08 (BDL) | | | 1q Brierly Hill Alliance (A) 6-2; 2q Darlaston (H) 7-1; 3q Bilston (A) 2-1ab; 3q Bilston (H) 2-1; 4q Worcester C (H) 2-0; 5q Oswestry U (A) 2-2; 5qr Oswestry U (H) 2-0; 6q Bishop Auckland (H) 7-1 | | | | |
| | 1 | 11.01.08 | **Crystal Palace** (SL) | H | L | 2-4 | Warren, Lewis |
| 1908-09 (SL) | | | 5q Carlisle U (H) 1-1; 5qr Carlisle U (A) 1-1aet; 5q 2r Carlisle U 1-3 at Hyde Road, Manchester | | | | |
| 1909-10 (SL) | | | 4q Wrexham (H) 3-0; 5q Kettering T (A) 5-0 | | | | |
| | 1 | 15.01.10 | **Preston North End** (D1) | A | W | 2-1 | Hendren, Buckle |
| | 2 | 05.02.10 | **Portsmouth** (SL) | A | W | 1-0 | Chaplin |
| | 3 | 19.02.10 | **Nottingham Forest** (D1) | H | W | 3-1 | Warren 2, Smith |
| | 4 | 05.03.10 | **Everton** (D1) | H | L | 0-2 | |
| 1910-11 (SL) | 1 | 14.01.11 | **Sheffield Wed** (D1) | A | W | 2-1 | Smith, Buckle |
| | 2 | 04.02.11 | **Brighton** (SL) | A | D | 0-0 | |
| | 2r | 09.02.11 | **Brighton** | H | W | 2-0 | Parkes, Tickle |
| | 3 | 25.02.11 | **Burnley** (D2) | A | L | 0-5 | |
| 1911-12 (SL) | 1 | 13.01.12 | **Southampton** (SL) | A | W | 2-0 | Turnbull, Parkes |
| | 2 | 03.02.12 | **Manchester Utd** (D1) | H | L | 1-5 | Jones |
| 1912-13 (SL) | 1 | 11.01.13 | **Manchester Utd** | A | D | 1-1 | Mitchell |
| | 1r | 16.01.13 | **Manchester Utd** | H | L | 1-2 | Parkes |

| | | | | | | | | |
|---|---|---|---|---|---|---|---|---|
| 1913-14 | (SL) | | | 4q Port Vale (A) 1-3 | | | | |
| 1914-15 | (SL) | | | 6q GlossopNorth End (A) 1-3 | | | | |
| 1919-20 | (D2) | 1 | 10.01.20 | **Luton Town** (SL) | A | D | 2-2 | Walker, Jones |
| | | 1r | 16.01.20 | **Luton Town** | H | L | 0-1 | |
| 1920-21 | (D2) | | | 6q Rochdale (H) 1-1; 6qr Rochdale (A) 1-2 | | | | |
| 1921-22 | (D2) | | | 5q Rotherham Co (A) 1-1; 5qr Rotherham Co (H) 1-0; 6q Southport (A) 0-1 | | | | |
| 1922-23 | (D2) | | | 5q New Brighton (A) 0-3 | | | | |
| 1923-24 | (D2) | | | 5q Tranmere R (H) 2-2; 5qr Tranmere R (A) 2-3 | | | | |
| 1924-25 | (D2) | | | 5q Walsall (A) 2-1; 6q Nelson (A) 1-0 | | | | |
| | | 1 | 10.01.25 | **Notts County** (D1) | H | L | 0-2 | |
| 1925-26 | (3N) | 1 | 28.11.25 | **Worksop Town** (ML) | A | L | 0-1 | |
| 1926-27 | (3S) | 1 | 27.11.26 | **Kettering Town** (SL) | A | W | 3-2 | Dunne, Herbert 2 |
| | | 2 | 11.12.26 | **Lincoln City** (3N) | H | D | 1-1 | J Ramage |
| | | 2r | 15.12.26 | **Lincoln City** | A | L | 1-2 | Gaffney |
| 1927-28 | (3S) | 1 | 26.11.27 | **Bournemouth** (3S) | H | D | 2-2 | Bird, P Ramage |
| | | 1r | 30.11.27 | **Bournemouth** | A | L | 0-2 | |
| 1928-29 | (3S) | 1 | 24.11.28 | **Fulham** (3S) | H | L | 1-4 | Starsmore |
| 1929-30 | (3S) | 1 | 30.11.29 | **Norwich City** (3S) | A | D | 3-3 | Loughlin 2, Richards |
| | | 1r | 05.12.29 | **Norwich City** | H | W | 2-0 | Loughlin, Widdowson |
| | | 2 | 14.12.29 | **Bath City** (SL) | H | W | 7-1 | Loughlin 2, Lake 2, Widdowson, Pick, Dinsdale |
| | | 3 | 11.01.30 | **Sunderland** (D1) | H | L | 1-2 | Loughlin |
| 1930-31 | (3S) | 1 | 29.11.30 | **Northampton Town** (3S) | A | W | 2-1 | Lake, Bowden |
| | | 2 | 13.12.30 | **Exeter City** (3S) | A | D | 1-1 | Phillips |
| | | 2r | 18.12.30 | **Exeter City** | H | L | 1-2 | Bowden |
| 1931-32 | (3S) | 1 | 28.11.31 | **Clapton Orient** (3S) | H | D | 2-2 | Bourton, Lake |
| | | 1r | 03.12.31 | **Clapton Orient** | A | L | 0-2 | |
| 1932-33 | (3S) | 1 | 26.11.32 | **Guildford City** (SL) | A | W | 2-1 | Bourton, Woolhouse |
| | | 2 | 10.12.32 | **Reading** (3S) | A | D | 2-2 | Bourton, Lake |
| | | 2r | 15.12.32 | **Reading** | H | D | 3-3 | Bourton, Lake, Davison |
| | | 2 2r | 19.12.32 | **Reading** | | L | 0-1 | |
| | | | | *played at Stamford Bridge* | | | | |
| 1933-34 | (3S) | 1 | 25.11.33 | **Crewe Alexandra** (3N) | H | W | 3-0 | Baker 2, Lauderdale |
| | | 2 | 09.12.33 | **Rotherham Utd** (3N) | A | L | 1-2 | Lake |
| 1934-35 | (3S) | 1 | 24.11.34 | **Scunthorpe Utd** (ML) | H | W | 7-0 | Birtley 2, Lauderdale 2, Bourton, Jones, Liddle |
| | | 2 | 08.12.34 | **Hartlepools Utd** (3N) | A | W | 4-0 | Bourton 2, Jones, Birtley |
| | | 3 | 12.01.35 | **Birmingham** (D1) | A | L | 1-5 | Jones |
| 1935-36 | (3S) | 1 | 30.11.35 | **Scunthorpe Utd** (ML) | H | D | 1-1 | Lake |
| | | 1r | 09.12.35 | **Scunthorpe Utd** | A | L | 2-4 | Bourton 2 |
| 1936-37 | (D2) | 3 | 16.01.37 | **Charlton Athletic** (D1) | H | W | 2-0 | Lake 2 |
| | | 4 | 30.01.37 | **Chester** (3N) | H | W | 2-0 | Mason 2 (1p) |
| | | 5 | 20.02.37 | **WBA** (D1) | H | L | 2-3 | Jones, Brown |
| 1937-38 | (D2) | 3 | 08.01.38 | **York City** (3N) | A | L | 2-3 | Brown 2 |
| 1938-39 | (D2) | 3 | 07.01.39 | **Chester** (3N) | A | L | 0-1 | |
| 1945-46 | (D2) | 3 1L | 05.01.46 | **Aston Villa** (D1) | H | W | 2-1 | Barratt, Simpson |
| | | 3 2L | 08.01.46 | **Aston Villa** | A | L | 0-2 | |
| 1946-47 | (D2) | 3 | 11.01.47 | **Newport County** (D2) | H | W | 5-2 | Lowrie 3, Roberts, Ashall |
| | | 4 | 25.01.47 | **Burnley** (D2) | A | L | 0-2 | |
| 1947-48 | (D2) | 3 | 10.01.48 | **Walsall** (3S) | H | W | 2-1 | Warner 2 |
| | | 4 | 24.01.48 | **Luton Town** (D2) | A | L | 2-3 | Lockhart (p), Dearson |
| 1948-49 | (D2) | 3 | 08.01.49 | **Torquay Utd** (3S) | A | L | 0-1 | |
| 1949-50 | (D2) | 3 | 07.01.50 | **Bolton Wanderers** (D1) | H | L | 1-2 | Alderton |
| 1950-51 | (D2) | 3 | 06.01.51 | **Sunderland** (D1) | A | L | 0-2 | |
| 1951-52 | (D2) | 3 | 12.01.52 | **Leicester City** (D2) | A | D | 1-1 | Allen |
| | | 3r | 14.01.52 | **Leicester City** | H | W | 4-1 | Roberts, Chisholm, Lockhart 2 |
| | | 4 | 02.02.52 | **Burnley** (D1) | A | L | 0-2 | |
| 1952-53 | (3S) | 1 | 22.11.52 | **Bristol City** (3S) | H | W | 2-0 | Brown, P Hill |
| | | 2 | 06.12.52 | **Bishop Auckland** (NL) | A | W | 4-1 | Dorman, Waldock, Johnson, Marshall |
| | | 3 | 10.01.53 | **Plymouth Argyle** (D2) | A | L | 1-4 | Warner |
| 1953-54 | (3S) | 1 | 21.11.53 | **Brighton** (3S) | A | L | 1-5 | Dorman |

| | | | | | | | | |
|---|---|---|---|---|---|---|---|---|
| 1954-55 | (3S) | 1 | 20.11.54 | **Northampton Town** (3S) | A | W | 1-0 | Kirk |
| | | 2 | 11.12.54 | **Scunthorpe Utd** (3N) | H | W | 4-0 | Harvey, Lee, Capel 2 |
| | | 3 | 08.01.55 | **Huddersfield Town** (D1) | A | D | 3-3 | Lee, Capel 2 |
| | | 3r | 13.01.55 | **Huddersfield Town** | H | L | 1-2aet | Moore |
| 1955-56 | (3S) | 1 | 19.11.55 | **Exeter City** (3S) | H | L | 0-1 | |
| 1956-57 | (3S) | 1 | 17.11.56 | **Swindon Town** (3S) | A | L | 1-2 | McPherson |
| 1957-58 | (3S) | 1 | 16.11.57 | **Walthamstow A** (IL) | H | W | 1-0 | McPherson |
| | | 2 | 07.12.57 | **Aldershot** (3S) | A | L | 1-4 | P Hill |
| 1958-59 | (D4) | 1 | 15.11.58 | **Weymouth** (SL) | A | W | 5-2 | P Hill 2, Straw 2, Boxley |
| | | 2 | 06.12.58 | **Plymouth Argyle** (D3) | H | L | 1-3 | Straw |
| 1959-60 | (D3) | 1 | 14.11.59 | **Southampton** (D3) | H | D | 1-1 | Straw |
| | | 1r | 18.11.59 | **Southampton** | A | L | 1-5 | Daley |
| 1960-61 | (D3) | 1 | 05.11.60 | **Worcester City** (SL) | A | W | 4-1 | Farmer 2, Myerscough 2 |
| | | 2 | 26.11.60 | **QPR** (D3) | A | W | 2-1 | Straw, Cockell og |
| | | 3 | 07.01.61 | **Liverpool** (D2) | A | L | 2-3 | Straw, Myerscough |
| 1961-62 | (D3) | 1 | 04.11.61 | **Gillingham** (D4) | H | W | 2-0 | Hewitt, Satchwell |
| | | 2 | 25.11.61 | **King's Lynn** (SL) | H | L | 1-2 | Hindle og |
| 1962-63 | (D3) | 1 | 03.11.62 | **Bournemouth** (D3) | H | W | 1-0 | Whitehouse |
| | | 2 | 24.11.62 | **Millwall** (D3) | A | D | 0-0 | |
| | | 2r | 27.11.62 | **Millwall** | H | W | 2-1 | Barr, Whitehouse |
| | | 3 | 07.03.63 | **Lincoln City** (D4) | A | W | 5-1 | Jackson og, Whitehouse, Bly, Barr, Farmer |
| | | 4 | 13.03.63 | **Portsmouth** (D2) | A | D | 1-1 | Hale |
| | | 4r | 16.03.63 | **Portsmouth** | H | D | 2-2aet | Whitehouse 2 |
| | | 4 2r | 19.03.63 | **Portsmouth** *played at White Hart Lane* | | W | 2-1 | Bly, Whitehouse |
| | | 5 | 25.03.63 | **Sunderland** (D2) | H | W | 2-1 | Bruck, Curtis |
| | | 6 | 30.03.63 | **Manchester Utd** (D1) | H | L | 1-3 | Bly |
| 1963-64 | (D3) | 1 | 16.11.63 | **Trowbridge Town** (SL) | A | W | 6-1 | Hudson 3, Rees, Kearns, Prosser og |
| | | 2 | 07.12.63 | **Bristol Rovers** (D3) | H | L | 1-2 | Hale |
| 1964-65 | (D2) | 3 | 09.01.65 | **Aston Villa** (D1) | A | L | 0-3 | |
| 1965-66 | (D2) | 3 | 22.01.66 | **Swindon Town** (D3) | A | W | 2-1 | Rees, Trollope og |
| | | 4 | 12.02.66 | **Crewe Alexandra** (D4) | A | D | 1-1 | Rees |
| | | 4r | 14.02.66 | **Crewe Alexandra** | H | W | 4-1 | Hudson 2, Farmer (p), Mitten |
| | | 5 | 03.03.66 | **Everton** (D1) | A | L | 0-3 | |
| 1966-67 | (D2) | 3 | 28.01.67 | **Newcastle Utd** (D1) | H | L | 3-4 | Gibson, Rees, McNamee (og) |
| 1967-68 | (D1) | 3 | 27.01.68 | **Charlton Athletic** (D2) | H | W | 3-0 | Baker, Hannigan, Carr |
| | | 4 | 17.02.68 | **Tranmere Rovers** (D3) | H | D | 1-1 | Rees |
| | | 4r | 21.02.68 | **Tranmere Rovers** | A | L | 0-2 | |
| 1968-69 | (D1) | 3 | 04.01.69 | **Blackpool** (D2) | H | W | 3-1 | Machin, Curtis, Shepherd |
| | | 4 | 25.01.69 | **Everton** (D1) | A | L | 0-2 | |
| 1969-70 | (D1) | 3 | 07.01.70 | **Liverpool** (D1) | H | D | 1-1 | Martin |
| | | 3r | 12.01.70 | **Liverpool** | A | L | 0-3 | |
| 1970-71 | (D1) | 3 | 11.01.71 | **Rochdale** (D3) | A | L | 1-2 | Hunt |
| 1971-72 | (D1) | 3 | 15.01.72 | **WBA** (D1) | A | W | 2-1 | Rafferty, Chilton |
| | | 4 | 05.02.72 | **Hull City** (D2) | H | L | 0-1 | |
| 1972-73 | (D1) | 3 | 13.01.73 | **Orient** (D2) | A | W | 4-1 | Alderson 2, Carr, Hutchison |
| | | 4 | 03.02.73 | **Grimsby Town** (D3) | H | W | 1-0 | Coop (p) |
| | | 5 | 24.02.73 | **Hull City** (D2) | H | W | 3-0 | Alderson, Stein |
| | | 6 | 17.03.73 | **Wolverhampton W** (D1) | A | L | 0-2 | |
| 1973-74 | (D1) | 3 | 05.01.74 | **Sheffield Wed** (D2) | A | D | 0-0 | |
| | | 3r | 08.01.74 | **Sheffield Wed** | H | W | 3-1 | Cross, Hutchison, Coop (p) |
| | | 4 | 27.01.74 | **Derby County** (D1) | H | D | 0-0 | |
| | | 4r | 30.01.74 | **Derby County** | A | W | 1-0aet | Cross |
| | | 5 | 16.02.74 | **QPR** (D1) | H | D | 0-0 | |
| | | 5r | 19.02.74 | **QPR** | A | L | 2-3 | Cross 2 |
| 1974-75 | (D1) | 3 | 04.01.75 | **Norwich City** (D2) | H | W | 2-0 | Alderson, LLoyd |
| | | 4 | 25.01.75 | **Arsenal** (D1) | H | D | 1-1 | Alderson |
| | | 4r | 29.01.75 | **Arsenal** | A | L | 0-3 | |
| 1975-76 | (D1) | 3 | 03.01.76 | **Bristol City** (D2) | H | W | 2-1 | Cross, Merrick og |
| | | 4 | 24.01.76 | **Newcastle Utd** (D1) | H | D | 1-1 | Murphy |

| | | | | | | | |
|---|---|---|---|---|---|---|---|
| | 4r | 28.01.76 | **Newcastle Utd** | A | L | 0-5 | |
| 1976-77 (D1) | 3 | 08.01.77 | **Millwall** (D2) | H | W | 1-0 | McDonald |
| | 4 | 29.01.77 | **Arsenal** (D1) | A | L | 1-3 | Hutchison |
| 1977-78 (D1) | 3 | 07.01.78 | **Middlesbrough** (D1) | A | L | 0-3 | |
| 1978-79 (D1) | 3 | 09.01.79 | **WBA** (D1) | H | D | 2-2 | Blair, Green |
| | 3r | 15.01.79 | **WBA** | A | L | 0-4 | |
| 1979-80 (D1) | 3 | 05.01.80 | **Oldham Athletic** (D2) | A | W | 1-0 | Hutchison |
| | 4 | 26.01.80 | **Blackburn Rovers** (D3) | A | L | 0-1 | |
| 1980-81 (D1) | 3 | 03.01.81 | **Leeds Utd** (D1) | A | D | 1-1 | Thomas |
| | 3r | 06.01.81 | **Leeds Utd** | H | W | 1-0 | Thompson |
| | 4 | 24.01.81 | **Birmingham City** (D1) | H | W | 3-2 | Daly 2 (1p), Blair |
| | 5 | 14.02.81 | **Tottenham Hotspur** (D1) | A | L | 1-3 | English |
| 1981-82 (D1) | 3 | 02.01.82 | **Sheffield Wed** (D2) | H | W | 3-1 | Hunt 2, Hateley |
| | 4 | 23.01.82 | **Manchester City** (D1) | A | W | 3-1 | Hunt, Hateley, Bodak |
| | 5 | 13.02.82 | **Oxford Utd** (D3) | H | W | 4-0 | Thompson 2, Hateley 2 |
| | 6 | 06.03.82 | **WBA** (D1) | A | L | 0-2 | |
| 1982-83 (D1) | 3 | 08.01.83 | **Worcester City** (APL) | H | W | 3-1 | Whitton 2 (1p), Hateley |
| | 4 | 29.01.83 | **Norwich City** (D1) | H | D | 2-2 | Roberts, Thompson |
| | 4r | 02.02.83 | **Norwich City** | A | L | 1-2aet | Hateley |
| 1983-84 (D1) | 3 | 07.01.84 | **Wolverhampton W** (D1) | H | D | 1-1 | Withey |
| | 3r | 10.01.84 | **Wolverhampton W** | A | D | 1-1aet | Pike |
| | 3 2r | 16.01.84 | **Wolverhampton W** | H | W | 3-0 | Withey 2, Hunt |
| | 4 | 30.01.84 | **Sheffield Wed** (D2) | A | L | 2-3 | Gibson 2 |
| 1984-85 (D1) | 3 | 05.01.85 | **Manchester City** (D2) | H | W | 2-1 | Gibson 2 |
| | 4 | 26.01.85 | **Manchester Utd** (D1) | A | L | 1-2 | Gibson |
| 1985-86 (D1) | 3 | 04.01.86 | **Watford** (D1) | H | L | 1-3 | Kilcline |
| 1986-87 (D1) | 3 | 10.01.87 | **Bolton Wanderers** (D3) | H | W | 3-0 | Downs, Regis, Bennett |
| | 4 | 31.01.87 | **Manchester Utd** (D1) | A | W | 1-0 | Houchen |
| | 5 | 21.02.87 | **Stoke City** (D2) | A | W | 1-0 | Gynn |
| | 6 | 14.03.87 | **Sheffield Wed** (D1) | A | W | 3-1 | Regis, Houchen 2 |
| | SF | 12.04.87 | **Leeds Utd** (D2) | | W | 3-2aet | Gynn, Houchen, Bennett |
| | | | *played at Hillsborough* | | | | |
| | F | 16.05.87 | **Tottenham Hotspur** (D1) | | W | 3-2aet | Bennett, Houchen, Mabbutt og |
| | | | *played at Wembley Stadium* | | | | |
| 1987-88 (D1) | 3 | 09.01.88 | **Torquay Utd** (D4) | H | W | 2-0 | Kilcline (p), Regis |
| | 4 | 30.01.88 | **Watford** (D1) | H | L | 0-1 | |
| 1988-89 (D1) | 3 | 07.01.89 | **Sutton Utd** (Conf) | A | L | 1-2 | Phillips |
| 1989-90 (D1) | 3 | 06.01.90 | **Northampton Town** (D3) | A | L | 0-1 | |
| 1990-91 (D1) | 3 | 05.01.91 | **Wigan Athletic** (D3) | H | D | 1-1 | Gynn |
| | 3r | 09.01.91 | **Wigan Athletic** | A | W | 1-0 | Gynn |
| | 4 | 26.01.91 | **Southampton** (D1) | H | D | 1-1 | Kilcline |
| | 4r | 29.01.91 | **Southampton** | A | L | 0-2 | |
| 1991-92 (D1) | 3 | 04.01.92 | **Cambridge Utd** (D2) | H | D | 1-1 | Borrows (p) |
| | 3r | 14.01.92 | **Cambridge Utd** | A | L | 0-1 | |
| 1992-93 (PL) | 3 | 13.01.93 | **Norwich City** (PL) | A | L | 0-1 | |
| 1993-94 (PL) | 3 | 08.01.94 | **Newcastle Utd** (PL) | A | L | 0-2 | |
| 1994-95 (PL) | 3 | 07.01.95 | **WBA** (D1) | H | D | 1-1 | Wegerle (p) |
| | 3r | 18.01.95 | **WBA** | A | W | 2-1 | Dublin, Ndlovu |
| | 4 | 28.01.95 | **Norwich City** (PL) | H | D | 0-0 | |
| | 4r | 08.02.95 | **Norwich City** | A | L | 1-3aet | Ndlovu |
| 1995-96 (PL) | 3 | 06.01.96 | **Plymouth Argyle** (D3) | A | W | 3-1 | Pickering, Salako, Telfer |
| | 4 | 07.02.96 | **Manchester City** (PL) | H | D | 2-2 | Whelan, Dublin |
| | 4r | 14.02.96 | **Manchester City** | A | L | 1-2 | Dublin |
| 1996-97 (PL) | 3 | 25.01.97 | **Woking** (Conf) | H | D | 1-1 | Jess |
| | 3r | 04.02.97 | **Woking** | A | W | 2-1 | Whelan, Foster og |
| | 4 | 15.02.97 | **Blackburn Rovers** (PL) | A | W | 2-1 | Jess, Huckerby |
| | 5 | 26.02.97 | **Derby County** (PL) | A | L | 2-3 | Huckerby, Whelan |
| 1997-98 (PL) | 3 | 03.01.98 | **Liverpool** (PL) | A | W | 3-1 | Huckerby, Dublin, Telfer |
| | 4 | 24.01.98 | **Derby County** (PL) | H | W | 2-0 | Dublin 2 |
| | 5 | 14.02.98 | **Aston Villa** (PL) | A | W | 1-0 | Moldovan |
| | 6 | 07.03.98 | **Sheffield Utd** (D1) | H | D | 1-1 | Dublin (p) |

| | | | | | | | | |
|---|---|---|---|---|---|---|---|---|
| | | 6r | 17.03.98 | **Sheffield Utd** | A | D | 1-1aet | Telfer |
| | | | | *Sheffield Utd won 3-1 on penalties* | | | | |
| 1998-99 | (PL) | 3 | 02.01.99 | **Macclesfield T** (D2) | H | W | 7-0 | Huckerby 3, Froggatt, Whelan, Payne og, Boateng |
| | | 4 | 23.01.99 | **Leicester City** (PL) | A | W | 3-0 | Whelan, Telfer, Froggatt |
| | | 5 | 13.02.99 | **Everton** (PL) | A | L | 1-2 | McAllister |
| 1999-00 | (PL) | 3 | 11.12.99 | **Norwich City** (D1) | A | W | 3-1 | Whelan, Roussel, Eustace |
| | | 4 | 08.01.00 | **Burnley** (D2) | H | W | 3-0 | Chippo 2, Whelan |
| | | 5 | 29.01.00 | **Charlton Athletic** (D1) | H | L | 2-3 | Roussel 2 |
| 2000-01 | (PL) | 3 | 06.01.01 | **Swindon Town** (D2) | A | W | 2-0 | Bellamy, Hadji |
| | | 4 | 27.01.01 | **Manchester City** (PL) | A | L | 0-1 | |
| 2001-02 | (D1) | 3 | 16.01.02 | **Tottenham Hotspur** (PL) | H | L | 0-2 | |
| 2002-03 | (D1) | 3 | 04.01.03 | **Cardiff City** (D2) | A | D | 2-2 | Mills, McAllister |
| | | 3r | 15.01.03 | **Cardiff City** | H | W | 3-0 | Fowler, Holdsworth, Bothroyd |
| | | 4 | 25.01.03 | **Rochdale** (D3) | A | L | 0-2 | |

## COVENTRY SPORTING

*Formed 1946. First entered FA Cup 1949-50 under their original name of Coventry Amateurs. Folded 1989. League club beaten: Tranmere Rovers*

| | | | | | | | | |
|---|---|---|---|---|---|---|---|---|
| 1975-76 | (WMRL) | 1 | 22.11.75 | **Tranmere Rovers** (D4) | H | W | 2-0 | Gallagher 2 |
| | | | | *played at Highfield Road* | | | | |
| | | 2 | 13.12.75 | **Peterborough Utd** (D3) | H | L | 0-4 | |
| | | | | *played at Highfield Road* | | | | |

## COWLAIRS

*Formed 1876. One of the seven Scottish clubs to compete in the FA Cup. Based at Springburn, Glasgow. Folded 1896.*

| | | | | | | | | |
|---|---|---|---|---|---|---|---|---|
| 1886-87 | | 1 | 23.10.86 | **Darwen Old Wanderers** | A | W | 4-1 | |
| | | 2 | 20.11.86 | **Rossendale FC** | A | W | 10-2 | Clelland 4, Bishop 2, og, 3 others |
| | | 3 | 04.12.86 | **Glasgow Rangers** | A | L | 2-3 | |

## CRAWLEY TOWN

*Formed 1896. Folded and reformed in 1938, merging with Crawley Rangers and Crawley Athletic. First entered FA Cup: 1958-59. League club beaten: Northampton Town. Members of the Southern League.*

| | | | | | | | | |
|---|---|---|---|---|---|---|---|---|
| 1970-71 | (SL) | 1 | 21.11.70 | **Chelmsford City** (SL) | H | D | 1-1 | Basey |
| | | 1r | 23.11.70 | **Chelmsford City** | A | L | 1-6 | Griffiths |
| 1971-72 | (SL) | 1 | 20.11.71 | **Exeter City** (D4) | H | D | 0-0 | |
| | | 1r | 24.11.71 | **Exeter City** | A | L | 0-2 | |
| 1991-92 | (SL) | 1 | 16.11.91 | **Northampton Town** (D3) | H | W | 4-2 | Cant, Hulme, Whittington 2 |
| | | 2 | 07.12.91 | **Hayes** (IL) | A | W | 2-0 | Hulme 2 |
| | | 3 | 04.01.92 | **Brighton** (D2) | A | L | 0-5 | |
| 1993-94 | (SL) | 1 | 13.11.93 | **Metropolitan Police** (IL) | A | W | 2-0 | Whittington, Van Sittart |
| | | 2 | 04.12.93 | **Barnet** (D2) | H | L | 1-2 | Ford |
| 1994-95 | (SL) | 1 | 12.11.94 | **Exeter City** (D3) | A | L | 0-1 | |
| 2002-03 | (SL) | 1 | 16.11.02 | **Tiverton Town** (SL) | A | D | 1-1 | McDonnell |
| | | 1r | 26.11.02 | **Tiverton Town** | H | W | 3-2 | McDonnell 2, Bagnall |
| | | 2 | 07.12.02 | **Dagenham & Red** (Conf) | H | L | 1-2 | McDonnell |

## CRESWELL COLLIERY

*Entered FA Cup 1921-1954. On September 26, 1950 a fire at Creswell Colliery in Derbyshire claimed more than 80 lives in one of Britain's worst mining disasters. Memories of the tragedy were still fresh when the Colliery's football team made it to the First Round of the FA Cup four years later.*

| | | | | | | | | |
|---|---|---|---|---|---|---|---|---|
| 1954-55 | (CA) | 1 | 20.11.54 | **Accrington Stanley** (3N) | A | L | 1-7 | Atkin |

## CREWE ALEXANDRA

*Formed 1877. FA Cup best performance: Semi-final 1888. Record FA Cup win: 9-0 v Northwich V, 3rd qualifying round, 1889-90. In Competition Proper: 5-0 v Druids, 1st round, 15.10.1887. Record FA Cup defeat: 2-13 v Tottenham Hotspur, 4th round replay, 03.02.1960*

| | | | | | | | | |
|---|---|---|---|---|---|---|---|---|
| 1883-84 | | 1 | 06.10.83 | **Queen's Park, Glasgow** | H | L | 0-10 | |
| 1884-85 | | 1 | 08.11.84 | **Oswestry Town** | H | W | 2-1 | Watkins 2 |
| | | 2 | 06.12.84 | **Queen's Park, Glasgow** | A | L | 1-2 | Taylor |
| | | | | *FA ordered result to stand after match was abandoned in the 48th minute following a torrential storm* | | | | |
| 1885-86 | | 1 | 31.10.85 | **Stoke** | A | D | 2-2 | Snelson, AN Other |

| | | | | | | | | |
|---|---|---|---|---|---|---|---|---|
| | | 1r | 07.11.85 | **Stoke** | H | W | 1-0aet | "scrimmage" |
| | | 2 | 21.11.85 | **Oswestry Town** | A | D | 1-1 | Payne |
| | | | | *Oswestry scratched before the replay* | | | | |
| | | 3 | 12.12.85 | **Davenham** | A | L | 1-2 | Cross |
| 1886-87 | | 1 | 23.10.86 | **Wrexham Olympic** | A | W | 4-1 | Pearson 2, Payne, Price |
| | | 2 | 20.11.86 | **Stoke** | H | W | 6-4aet | Payne 3, Nelson 2, Ellis |
| | | 3 | | bye | | | | |
| | | 4 | 29.01.87 | **Leek** | H | L | 0-1 | |
| 1887-88 | | 1 | 15.10.87 | **Druids** | H | W | 5-0 | Osborne, Payne, Price, others 2 |
| | | 2 | 05.11.87 | **Northwich V** | A | W | 1-0 | Price |
| | | 3 | | bye | | | | |
| | | 4 | 10.12.87 | **Swifts** | H | D | 2-2 | Payne, Price |
| | | 4r | 17.12.87 | **Swifts** | H | L | 2-3 | Tinsley 2 |
| | | | | *FA ordered match to be replayed after protests about the size of the goals* | | | | |
| | | 4 2r | 31.12.87 | **Swifts** | | W | 2-1 | Pearson, Price |
| | | | | *played at Derby Cricket Ground* | | | | |
| | | 5 | 07.01.88 | **Derby County** | H | W | 1-0 | Pearson |
| | | 6 | 28.01.88 | **Middlesbrough** | A | W | 2-0 | Ellis, Price |
| | | SF | 18.02.88 | **Preston North End** | | L | 0-4 | |
| | | | | *played at Anfield* | | | | |
| 1888-89 | | 1 | 02.02.89 | **Halliwell** | A | D | 2-2aet | E Payne 2 |
| | | 1r | 09.02.89 | **Halliwell** | H | L | 1-5 | A Payne |
| 1889-90 | (FAll) | | | 3q Northwich V (H) 9-0; 4q Chester (A) 1-2 | | | | |
| 1890-91 | (FAll) | 1 | 17.01.91 | **Burnley** (D1) | A | L | 2-4aet | Lewis 2 |
| 1891-92 | (FAll) | | | 3q Wrexham (H) 3-1; 4q Northwich V (H) 1-2 FA ordered match to be replayed; 4qr Northwich V (H) 6-2 | | | | |
| | | 1 | 16.01.92 | **Wolverhampton W** (D1) | A | D | 2-2aet | |
| | | 1r | 23.01.92 | **Wolverhampton W** | H | L | 1-4 | Pearson |
| 1892-93 | (D2) | | | 1q Stourbridge (A) 0-1 | | | | |
| 1893-94 | (D2) | | | 2q Northwich V (A) 1-0; 3q Macclesfield (H) 3-2; 4q Stockport Co (A) 0-0 aet; 4qr Stockport Co (H) 1-2 | | | | |
| 1894-95 | (D2) | | | 1q Newtown (A) 3-1; 2q Fairfield (H) 3-6 | | | | |
| 1895-96 | (D2) | | | P Tranmere R (H) 2-1; 1q Stalybridge Rovers (H) 3-1; 2q Wrexham (A) 3-3aet; 2qr Wrexham (H) 5-2; 3q Middleton (A) 4-0; 4q Fairfield (A) 2-2; 4qr Fairfield (H) 4-3 | | | | |
| | | 1 | 01.02.96 | **Bolton Wanderers** (D1) | H | L | 0-4 | |
| 1896-97 | (TC) | | | 3q Buckley (H) 3-1 abnd; 3q Buckley (H) 1-0; 4q Fairfield (A) 0-4 | | | | |
| 1897-98 | (TC) | | | 3q Wrexham (H) 4-1; 4q New Brighton Tower (H) 1-1; 4qr New Brighton T (A) 1-4 | | | | |
| 1898-99 | (LL) | | | 3q South Liverpool (H) 4-1; 4q Glossop North End (A) 0-1 | | | | |
| 1899-00 | (LL) | | | 3q Wigan Co (H) 3-1; 4q Port Vale (H) 2-2; 4qr Port Vale (A) 1-3 | | | | |
| 1900-01 | (LL) | | | 3q Stalybridge Rovers (H) 3-0; 4q Stockport Co (A) 3-1; 5q Nantwich T (H) 5-1; Int Kettering (A) 0-1 | | | | |
| 1901-02 | (BDL) | | | 3q Stalybridge Rovers (A) 2-0; 4q Stockport Co (A) 0-1 abnd; 4qr Stockport Co (A) 2-3 | | | | |
| 1902-03 | (BDL) | | | 3q Glossop North End (H) 0-3 | | | | |
| 1903-04 | (BDL) | | | 3q Burslem PV (H) 0-0; 3qr Burslem PV (A) 1-2 | | | | |
| 1904-05 | (BDL) | | | 3q Wrexham (H) 0-3 | | | | |
| 1905-06 | (BDL) | | | 4q Darwen (H) 2-0 | | | | |
| | | 1 | 13.01.06 | **Barnsley** (D2) | H | D | 1-1 | Goldie |
| | | 1r | 18.01.06 | **Barnsley** | A | L | 0-4 | |
| 1906-07 | (BDL) | | | 5q Paulton R (A) 1-0 | | | | |
| | | 1 | 12.01.07 | **Accrington Stanley** (LC) | H | D | 1-1 | Cope |
| | | 1r | 16.01.07 | **Accrington Stanley** | A | L | 0-1 | |
| 1907-08 | (BDL) | | | 5q Rotherham T (H) 1-1; Rotherham T (A) 1-2 | | | | |
| 1908-09 | (BDL) | | | 5q Workington (A) 1-4 | | | | |
| 1909-10 | (BDL) | | | 4q Lincoln C (H) 2-1; 5q Chesterfield (A) 2-5 | | | | |
| 1910-11 | (BDL) | | | 4q Chester (H) 4-3; 5q Carlisle U (H) 1-1; 5qr Carlisle U (A) 4-3 | | | | |
| | | 1 | 14.01.11 | **Bristol City** (D1) | A | W | 3-0 | Mason, King, Chapple |
| | | 2 | 04.02.11 | **Grimsby Town** (ML) | H | L | 1-5 | Chapple |
| 1911-12 | (CL) | | | 4q Darlaston (A) 5-0; 5q Merthyr Town (H) 4-0 | | | | |
| | | 1 | 13.01.12 | **Blackpool** (D2) | H | D | 1-1 | Fiske og |

| | | | | | | | | |
|---|---|---|---|---|---|---|---|---|
| | | 1r | 17.01.12 | **Blackpool** | A | - | 1-2ab | Millward |
| | | | | *abandoned after 61 minutes – blizzard* | | | | |
| | | 1r | 22.01.12 | **Blackpool** | A | D | 2-2aet | Jukes, Smith |
| | | 1 2r | 25.01.12 | **Blackpool** | | L | 1-2 | Smith |
| | | | | *played at Maine Road* | | | | |
| 1912-13 | (CL) | | | 4q Walsall (A) 1-2 | | | | |
| 1913-14 | (CL) | | | 4q Dudley (H) 2-1; 5q Gainsborough T (A) 0-2 | | | | |
| 1914-15 | (CL) | | | 4q Port Vale (H) 1-1; 4qr Port Vale (A) 2-5 | | | | |
| 1919-20 | (CL) | | | 3q South Liverpool (H) 1-3 | | | | |
| 1920-21 | (CL) | | | 4q Eccles U (A) 0-2 | | | | |
| 1921-22 | (3N) | | | 4q Chester (H) 1-1; 4qr Chester (A) 2-1; 5q Wrexham (A) 0-5 | | | | |
| 1922-23 | (3N) | | | 4q New Brighton (A) 1-1; 4qr New Brighton (H) 0-1 | | | | |
| 1923-24 | (3N) | | | 5q Stockport Co (A) 0-1 | | | | |
| 1924-25 | (3N) | | | 4q Tranmere R (A) 1-1; 4qr Tranmere R (H) 0-2 | | | | |
| 1925-26 | (3N) | 1 | 28.11.25 | **Tranmere Rovers** (3N) | A | D | 0-0 | |
| | | 1r | 02.12.25 | **Tranmere Rovers** | H | W | 2-1aet | Jones, Mackay |
| | | 2 | 12.12.25 | **Wigan Borough** (3N) | H | D | 2-2 | Lovat, Jones |
| | | 2r | 16.12.25 | **Wigan Borough** | A | L | 1-2 | Lovatt |
| 1926-27 | (3N) | 1 | 01.12.26 | **Northern Nomads** | H | W | 4-1 | Jackson og, Kay 2, Brown |
| | | 2 | 11.12.26 | **Wigan Borough** (3N) | H | W | 4-1 | Morris, Cotton 2, Brown |
| | | 3 | 08.01.27 | **Barnsley** (D2) | A | L | 1-6 | Brown |
| 1927-28 | (3N) | 1 | 26.11.27 | **Ashington** (3N) | H | D | 2-2 | Richardson og, Wareham |
| | | 1r | 30.11.27 | **Ashington** | A | W | 2-0 | Ralphs, Ireland |
| | | 2 | 10.12.27 | **Stockport County** (3N) | H | W | 2-0 | Own, Kay |
| | | 3 | 14.01.28 | **London Cal** (IL) | A | W | 3-2 | Owen 2, Shaw |
| | | | | *played at Stamford Bridge* | | | | |
| | | 4 | 28.01.28 | **Aston Villa** (D1) | A | L | 0-3 | |
| 1928-29 | (3N) | 1 | 24.11.28 | **Gainsborough T** (ML) | A | L | 1-3 | Pither |
| 1929-30 | (3N) | 1 | 30.11.29 | **Nelson FC** (3N) | A | W | 3-0 | Owen, Green, Gorringe |
| | | 2 | 14.12.29 | **Carlisle Utd** (3N) | A | L | 2-4 | Scullion, Gorringe |
| 1930-31 | (3N) | 1 | 29.11.30 | **Jarrow** (NEL) | H | W | 1-0 | French |
| | | 2 | 13.12.30 | **QPR** (3S) | A | L | 2-4 | French, Rouse |
| 1931-32 | (3N) | 1 | 28.11.31 | **Gainsborough T** (ML) | H | D | 2-2 | Swindells, Deacon |
| | | 1r | 02.12.31 | **Gainsborough T** | A | L | 0-1 | |
| 1932-33 | (3N) | 1 | 26.11.32 | **Crook Town** (NEL) | H | W | 4-0 | Swindells 2, Deacon 2 |
| | | 2 | 10.12.32 | **Darlington** (3N) | H | L | 0-2 | |
| 1933-34 | (3N) | 1 | 25.11.33 | **Coventry City** (3S) | A | L | 0-3 | |
| 1934-35 | (3N) | 1 | 24.11.34 | **Walsall** (3N) | H | L | 1-2 | Mustard |
| 1935-36 | (3N) | 1 | 30.11.35 | **Boston Utd** (ML) | H | W | 4-2 | Wood, Swindells, Waring 2 |
| | | 2 | 14.12.35 | **Gillingham** (3S) | H | W | 2-1 | Black, Waring |
| | | 3 | 11.01.36 | **Sheffield Wed** (D1) | H | D | 1-1 | Rigby |
| | | 3r | 15.01.36 | **Sheffield Wed** | A | L | 1-3 | Swindells |
| 1936-37 | (3N) | 1 | 28.11.36 | **Rochdale** (3N) | H | W | 5-1 | Dyer 2, Nicol 2, Swindells |
| | | 2 | 12.12.36 | **Hartlepools Utd** (3N) | H | D | 1-1 | Dyer |
| | | 2r | 16.12.36 | **Hartlepools Utd** | A | W | 2-1 | Waring, Swindells |
| | | 3 | 16.01.37 | **Plymouth Argyle** (D2) | H | L | 0-2 | |
| 1937-38 | (3N) | 1 | 27.11.37 | **Barrow** (3N) | A | W | 1-0 | Essex |
| | | 2 | 11.12.37 | **New Brighton** (3N) | H | - | 1-0ab | Foster |
| | | | | *abandoned after 84 minutes* | | | | |
| | | 2 | 15.12.37 | **New Brighton** | H | D | 2-2 | Cobourne, Foster |
| | | 2r | 20.12.37 | **New Brighton** | A | L | 1-4 | Blake |
| 1938-39 | (3N) | 1 | 26.11.38 | **Oldham Athletic** (3N) | A | D | 2-2 | Foster, Gilchrist |
| | | 1r | 30.11.38 | **Oldham Athletic** | H | W | 1-0 | Johnson |
| | | 2 | 10.12.38 | **Cardiff City** (3S) | A | L | 0-1 | |
| 1945-46 | (3N) | 1 1L | 17.11.45 | **Wrexham** (3N) | H | W | 4-2 | Haywood, Boothway 2, Shaw |
| | | 1 2L | 24.11.45 | **Wrexham** | A | L | 0-3 | |
| 1946-47 | (3N) | 1 | 30.11.46 | **Rotherham Utd** (3N) | A | L | 0-2 | |
| 1947-48 | (3N) | 1 | 29.11.47 | **S Shields (1936)** (NEL) | H | W | 4-1 | Ferris, Finan, Harrigan, Taylor |
| | | 2 | 13.12.47 | **Workington** (NEL) | A | W | 2-1 | Meaney, Harrigan |
| | | 3 | 10.01.48 | **Sheffield Utd** (D1) | H | W | 3-1 | Finan 2, Jones |
| | | 4 | 24.01.48 | **Derby County** (D1) | H | L | 0-3 | |

| | | | | | | | |
|---|---|---|---|---|---|---|---|
| 1948-49 (3N) | 1 | 27.11.48 | **Billingham S** (NL) | H | W | 5-0 | Basford 4, Meaney |
| | 2 | 11.12.48 | **Millwall** (3S) | H | W | 3-2 | McCormick, Mitcheson 2 |
| | 3 | 08.01.49 | **Sunderland** (D1) | H | L | 0-2 | |
| 1949-50 (3N) | 1 | 26.11.49 | **Darlington** (3N) | A | D | 2-2 | Phillips 2 |
| | 1r | 30.11.49 | **Darlington** | H | W | 1-0aet | Mitcheson |
| | 2 | 10.12.49 | **Oldham Athletic** (3N) | H | D | 1-1 | Mullard |
| | 2r | 13.12.49 | **Oldham Athletic** | A | D | 0-0aet | |
| | 2 2r | 19.12.49 | **Oldham Athletic** | | L | 0-3 | |
| | | | *played at Maine Road* | | | | |
| 1950-51 (3N) | 1 | 25.11.50 | **North Shields** (NEL) | H | W | 4-0 | McGuigan 2, Travis, Basford |
| | 2 | 09.12.50 | **Plymouth Argyle** (3S) | H | D | 2-2 | Meaney, Travis |
| | 2r | 13.12.50 | **Plymouth Argyle** | A | L | 0-3 | |
| 1951-52 (3N) | 1 | 24.11.51 | **Lincoln City** (3N) | H | L | 2-4 | Smith 2 |
| 1952-53 (3N) | 1 | 22.11.52 | **Gateshead AFC** (3N) | A | L | 0-2 | |
| 1953-54 (3N) | 1 | 21.11.53 | **Bradford City** (3N) | H | D | 0-0 | |
| | 1r | 25.11.53 | **Bradford City** | A | W | 1-0 | Chapman |
| | 2 | 02.12.53 | **Walsall** (3S) | A | L | 0-3 | |
| 1954-55 (3N) | 1 | 20.11.54 | **Oldham Athletic** (3N) | A | L | 0-1 | |
| 1955-56 (3N) | 1 | 19.11.55 | **Barrow** (3N) | A | D | 0-0 | |
| | 1r | 23.11.55 | **Barrow** | H | L | 2-3aet | Rolfe, Samuels |
| 1956-57 (3N) | 1 | 17.11.56 | **Wrexham** (3N) | H | D | 2-2 | Connor, Williams |
| | 1r | 20.11.56 | **Wrexham** | A | L | 1-2 | Connor |
| 1957-58 (3N) | 1 | 16.11.57 | **Hull City** (3N) | A | L | 1-2 | Whiston |
| 1958-59 (D4) | 1 | 15.11.58 | **S Shields (1936)** (ML) | H | D | 2-2 | Colbridge, Llewellyn |
| | 1r | 19.11.58 | **S Shields (1936)** | A | L | 0-5 | |
| 1959-60 (D4) | 1 | 14.11.59 | **Burscough** (LC) | A | W | 3-1 | Keery (p), Riley, Llewellyn |
| | 2 | 05.12.59 | **Stockport County** (D4) | A | D | 0-0 | |
| | 2r | 09.12.59 | **Stockport County** | H | W | 2-0 | Wheatley 2 |
| | 3 | 09.01.60 | **Workington** (D4) | H | W | 2-0 | LLewellyn |
| | 4 | 30.01.60 | **Tottenham Hotspur** (D1) | H | D | 2-2 | M Jones, Llewellyn |
| | 4r | 03.02.60 | **Tottenham Hotspur** | A | L | 2-13 | Coleman, Llewellyn |
| 1960-61 (D4) | 1 | 05.11.60 | **Rochdale** (D4) | H | D | 1-1 | Coleman |
| | 1r | 08.11.60 | **Rochdale** | A | W | 2-1 | Riley, Stark |
| | 2 | 29.11.60 | **Halifax Town** (D3) | A | D | 2-2 | Stark, Jones |
| | 2r | 05.12.60 | **Halifax Town** | H | W | 3-0 | Foster 2, Wheatley |
| | 3 | 07.01.61 | **Chelsea** (D1) | A | W | 2-1 | Stark, Wheatley |
| | 4 | 28.01.61 | **Tottenham Hotspur** (D1) | A | L | 1-5 | Tighe |
| 1961-62 (D4) | 1 | 04.11.61 | **Lincoln City** (D3) | H | W | 2-0 | Lord, Riley |
| | 2 | 25.11.61 | **Port Vale** (D3) | H | D | 1-1 | McGill |
| | 2r | 27.11.61 | **Port Vale** | A | L | 0-3 | |
| 1962-63 (D4) | 1 | 03.11.62 | **Scarborough** (NEL) | H | D | 1-1 | Tighe |
| | 1r | 07.11.62 | **Scarborough** | A | W | 3-2aet | Lord, Wheatley, Haydock |
| | 2 | 24.11.62 | **York City** (D4) | A | L | 1-2 | Lord |
| 1963-64 (D3) | 1 | 16.11.63 | **Hull City** (D3) | A | D | 2-2 | Wheatley. Ewing |
| | 1r | 20.11.63 | **Hull City** | H | L | 0-3 | |
| 1964-65 (D4) | 1 | 14.11.64 | **Chester** (D4) | A | L | 0-5 | |
| 1965-66 (D4) | 1 | 13.11.65 | **Scunthorpe Utd** (D3) | H | W | 3-0 | King, Kane, Wheatley (p) |
| | 2 | 04.12.65 | **S Shields (1936)** (NRL) | H | W | 3-1 | Gowans, Bradshaw, Kane |
| | 3 | 22.01.66 | **Folkestone** (SL) | A | W | 5-1 | Sandiford, Barmes, Gowans 2,King |
| | 4 | 12.02.66 | **Coventry City** (D2) | H | D | 1-1 | Curtis og |
| | 4r | 14.02.66 | **Coventry City** | A | L | 1-4 | Sandiford (p) |
| 1966-67 (D4) | 1 | 26.11.66 | **Grimsby Town** (D3) | H | D | 1-1 | Regan |
| | 1r | 30.11.66 | **Grimsby Town** | A | W | 1-0 | Gowans |
| | 2 | 07.01.67 | **Darlington** (D3) | H | W | 2-1 | Barnes, Mahoney |
| | 3 | 28.01.67 | **Bolton Wanderers** (D2) | A | L | 0-1 | |
| 1967-68 (D4) | 1 | 13.12.67 | **Halifax Town** (D4) | A | L | 2-3 | Tarbuck, Archer |
| 1968-69 (D3) | 1 | 16.11.68 | **Altrincham** (NPL) | A | W | 1-0 | Emerson |
| | 2 | 07.12.68 | **Halifax Town** (D4) | A | D | 1-1 | Hollett |
| | 2r | 11.12.68 | **Halifax Town** | H | L | 1-3 | Hollett |
| 1969-70 (D4) | 1 | 15.11.69 | **Doncaster Rovers** (D3) | A | D | 1-1 | Turner |
| | 1r | 19.11.69 | **Doncaster Rovers** | H | L | 0-1 | |

| | | | | | | | | |
|---|---|---|---|---|---|---|---|---|
| 1970-71 | (D4) | 1 | 21.11.70 | **Doncaster Rovers** (D3) | H | D | 0-0 | |
| | | 1r | 24.11.70 | **Doncaster Rovers** | A | W | 3-1 | Bowles, Tewley, Morrissey |
| | | 2 | 12.12.70 | **Chester** (D4) | A | L | 0-1 | |
| 1971-72 | (D4) | 1 | 20.11.71 | **Blyth Spartans** (NL) | H | L | 0-1 | |
| 1972-73 | (D4) | 1 | 18.11.72 | **Stafford Rangers** (NPL) | H | W | 1-0 | Bradshaw |
| | | 2 | 09.12.72 | **Blackburn Rovers** (D3) | A | W | 1-0 | Manning |
| | | 3 | 13.01.73 | **Luton Town** (D2) | A | L | 0-2 | |
| 1973-74 | (D4) | 1 | 24.11.73 | **Scarborough** (NPL) | H | D | 0-0 | |
| | | 1r | 28.11.73 | **Scarborough** | A | L | 1-2 | Nicholls |
| 1974-75 | (D4) | 1 | 23.11.74 | **Gateshead Utd** (NPL) | H | D | 2-2 | Reed, Wain |
| | | 1r | 25.11.74 | **Gateshead Utd** | A | L | 0-1aet | |
| 1975-76 | (D4) | 1 | 22.11.75 | **Rotherham Utd** (D3) | A | L | 1-2 | Bevan |
| 1976-77 | (D4) | 1 | 20.11.76 | **Preston North End** (D3) | H | D | 1-1 | Lugg |
| | | 1r | 23.11.76 | **Preston North End** | A | D | 2-2aet | D Davies 2 |
| | | 1 2r | 29.11.76 | **Preston North End** | | L | 0-3 | |
| | | | | *played at at Anfield* | | | | |
| 1977-78 | (D4) | 1 | 26.11.77 | **Bradford City** (D3) | A | W | 1-0 | D Davies |
| | | 2 | 17.12.77 | **Scarborough** (NPL) | H | D | 0-0 | |
| | | 2r | 21.12.77 | **Scarborough** | A | L | 0-2 | |
| 1978-79 | (D4) | 1 | 25.11.78 | **Nuneaton B** (SL) | A | W | 2-0 | Coyne, Bowles |
| | | 2 | 16.12.78 | **Hartlepool Utd** (D4) | H | L | 0-1 | |
| 1979-80 | (D4) | 1 | 24.11.79 | **Altrincham** (APL) | A | L | 0-3 | |
| 1980-81 | (D4) | 1 | 22.11.80 | **Mossley** (NPL) | A | L | 0-1 | |
| 1981-82 | (D4) | 1 | 21.11.81 | **Willenhall Town** (WMRL) | A | W | 1-0 | Scott |
| | | 2 | 02.01.82 | **Scunthorpe Utd** (D4) | H | L | 1-3 | Haslegrave |
| 1982-83 | (D4) | 1 | 20.11.82 | **Boston Utd** (APL) | A | L | 1-3 | Palios |
| 1983-84 | (D4) | 1 | 19.11.83 | **Rochdale** (D4) | A | L | 0-1 | |
| 1984-85 | (D4) | 1 | 17.11.84 | **Northwich V** (APL) | A | L | 1-3 | King |
| 1985-86 | (D4) | 1 | 16.11.85 | **Derby County** (D3) | A | L | 1-5 | Micklewhite og |
| 1986-87 | (D4) | 1 | 15.11.86 | **York City** (D3) | A | L | 1-3 | Platt |
| 1987-88 | (D4) | 1 | 14.11.87 | **Lincoln City** (Conf) | A | L | 1-2 | Macowat |
| 1988-89 | (D4) | 1 | 19.11.88 | **Stafford Rangers** (Conf) | A | D | 2-2 | Fishenden, Cronin |
| | | 1r | 22.11.88 | **Stafford Rangers** | H | W | 3-2 | Murphy 2, Fishenden |
| | | 2 | 10.12.88 | **Runcorn** (Conf) | A | W | 3-0 | Gardiner, Fishenden, R Edwards |
| | | 3 | 07.01.89 | **Aston Villa** (D1) | H | L | 2-3 | Gardiner, Keown og |
| 1989-90 | (D3) | 1 | 18.11.89 | **Congleton Town** (NPL) | H | W | 2-0 | Cutler, Sussex |
| | | 2 | 09.12.89 | **Bishop Auckland** (NPL) | H | D | 1-1 | Murphy (p) |
| | | 2r | 13.12.89 | **Bishop Auckland** | A | W | 2-0 | Sussex 2 |
| | | 3 | 06.01.90 | **Chelsea** (D1) | A | D | 1-1 | Walters |
| | | 3r | 10.01.90 | **Chelsea** | H | L | 0-2 | |
| 1990-91 | (D3) | 1 | 17.11.90 | **Lincoln City** (D4) | A | W | 4-1 | Callaghan, Gardiner, McKearney, Ward |
| | | 2 | 12.12.90 | **Atherstone Utd** (SL) | H | W | 1-0 | Sussex |
| | | 3 | 05.01.91 | **Bristol Rovers** (D2) | A | W | 2-0 | Carr, Hignett |
| | | 4 | 26.01.91 | **Rotherham Utd** (D3) | H | W | 1-0 | Hignett |
| | | 5 | 16.02.91 | **West Ham Utd** (D2) | A | L | 0-1 | |
| 1991-92 | (D4) | 1 | 16.11.91 | **Carlisle Utd** (D4) | A | D | 1-1 | Hignett |
| | | 1r | 26.11.91 | **Carlisle Utd** | H | W | 5-3aet | Walters, Naylor 2, Gardiner, Barnsley og |
| | | 2 | 07.12.91 | **Chester City** (D3) | H | W | 2-0 | Hignett, Naylor |
| | | 3 | 06.01.92 | **Liverpool** (D1) | H | L | 0-4 | |
| 1992-93 | (D3) | 1 | 14.11.92 | **Wrexham** (D3) | H | W | 6-1 | Hignett 4, McKearney 2 |
| | | 2 | 05.12.92 | **Accrington Stanley** (NPL) | A | W | 6-1 | Carr, Naylor 2, Whalley 2, Clarkson |
| | | | | *played at Ewood Park* | | | | |
| | | 3 | 12.01.93 | **Marine** (NPL) | H | W | 3-1 | McKearney, Edwards, Clarkson |
| | | 4 | 23.01.93 | **Blackburn Rovers** (PL) | H | L | 0-3 | |
| 1993-94 | (D3) | 1 | 13.11.93 | **Darlington** (D3) | H | W | 4-2 | Edwards, Rowbotham, Gardiner, S Smith (p) |
| | | 2 | 04.12.93 | **Macclesfield T** (Conf) | H | W | 2-1 | Lennon, Whalley |
| | | 3 | 08.01.94 | **Leeds Utd** (PL) | A | L | 1-3 | Naylor |

| | | | | | | | | |
|---|---|---|---|---|---|---|---|---|
| 1994-95 | (D2) | 1 | 12.11.94 | **Gresley Rovers** (SL) | H | W | 7-1 | Ward 3, Rowbotham 2, S Smith, Garvey |
| | | 2 | 03.12.94 | **Bury** (D3) | H | L | 1-2 | Ward |
| 1995-96 | (D2) | 1 | 22.11.95 | **Altrincham** (Conf) | A | W | 2-0 | Adebola, Unsworth |
| | | 2 | 02.12.95 | **Mansfield Town** (D3) | H | W | 2-0 | Edwards, Rivers |
| | | 3 | 06.01.96 | **WBA** (D1) | H | W | 4-3 | Adebola, Rivers, Booty, Murphy |
| | | 4 | 07.02.96 | **Southampton** (PL) | A | D | 1-1 | Rivers |
| | | 4r | 13.02.96 | **Southampton** | H | L | 2-3 | Edwards, Westwood |
| 1996-97 | (D2) | 1 | 16.11.96 | **Kidderminster H** (Conf) | H | W | 4-1 | Macauley, Murphy 2, Lightfoot |
| | | 2 | 07.12.96 | **Hull City** (D3) | A | W | 5-1 | Garvey, Murphy, Adebola, S Smith, Brien og |
| | | 3 | 14.01.97 | **Wimbledon** (PL) | H | D | 1-1 | Westwood |
| | | 3r | 24.01.97 | **Wimbledon** | A | L | 0-2 | |
| 1997-98 | (D1) | 3 | 03.01.98 | **Birmingham City** (D1) | H | L | 1-2 | Rivers |
| 1998-99 | (D1) | 3 | 02.01.99 | **Oxford Utd** (D1) | H | L | 1-3 | T Johnson |
| 1999-00 | (D1) | 3 | 11.12.99 | **Bradford City** (PL) | H | L | 1-2 | Little |
| 2000-01 | (D1) | 3 | 06.01.01 | **Cardiff City** (D3) | A | D | 1-1 | Bowen og |
| | | 3r | 16.01.01 | **Cardiff City** | H | W | 2-1 | S Smith (p), Rivers |
| | | 4 | 27.01.01 | **Stockport County** (D1) | H | L | 0-1 | |
| 2001-02 | (D1) | 3 | 15.01.02 | **Sheffield Wed** (D1) | H | W | 2-1 | Rix, Foster |
| | | 4 | 26.01.02 | **Rotherham Utd** (D1) | A | W | 4-2 | Ashton 2, Thomas, Vaughan |
| | | 5 | 17.02.02 | **Everton** (PL) | A | D | 0-0 | |
| | | 5r | 26.02.02 | **Everton** | H | L | 1-2 | Ashton |
| 2002-03 | (D2) | 1 | 16.11.02 | **Port Vale** (D2) | A | W | 1-0 | Ashton |
| | | 2 | 07.12.02 | **Mansfield Town** (D2) | H | W | 3-0 | Rix, Brammer (p), Ashton |
| | | 3 | 04.01.03 | **Bournemouth** (D2) | A | D | 0-0 | |
| | | 3r | 14.01.03 | **Bournemouth** | H | D | 2-2aet | Jones, Sodje |
| | | | | *Bournemouth won 3-1 on penalties* | | | | |

# CROOK TOWN

*Formed 1889. Reformed 1943. First entered FA Cup: 1897-98. FA Amateur Cup winners: 1901, 1954, 1959, 1962, 1964. League clubs beaten: Stockport County, Carlisle United. Members of the Northern League.*

| | | | | | | | | |
|---|---|---|---|---|---|---|---|---|
| 1926-27 | (NL) | 1 | 27.11.26 | **Workington** (NEL) | A | W | 2-1 | Richardson, Colman |
| | | 2 | 11.12.26 | **Southport** (3N) | A | L | 0-2 | |
| 1927-28 | (NL) | 1 | 26.11.27 | **Rochdale** (3N) | A | L | 2-8 | Mitchell, Duffy |
| 1931-32 | (NEL) | 1 | 28.11.31 | **Stockport County** (3N) | H | W | 3-1 | Ferguson, Cook 2 |
| | | 2 | 12.12.31 | **Aldershot** (SL) | A | D | 1-1 | Studdick |
| | | 2r | 16.12.31 | **Aldershot** | H | W | 1-0 | Cook |
| | | 3 | 09.01.32 | **Leicester City** (D1) | H | L | 0-7 | |
| | | | | *played at Filbert Street* | | | | |
| 1932-33 | (NEL) | 1 | 26.11.32 | **Crewe Alexandra** (3N) | A | L | 0-4 | |
| 1954-55 | (NL) | 1 | 20.11.54 | **Stanley Utd** (NL) | H | W | 5-3 | Harrison 2, Armstrong, Taylor, McMillan |
| | | 2 | 11.12.54 | **Brentford** (3S) | A | L | 1-4 | Appleby |
| 1955-56 | (NL) | 1 | 19.11.55 | **Derby County** (3N) | H | D | 2-2 | McMillan, Harrison |
| | | 1r | 23.11.55 | **Derby County** | A | L | 1-5 | Harrison |
| 1957-58 | (NL) | 1 | 16.11.57 | **Workington** (3N) | A | L | 1-8 | Coates |
| 1958-59 | (NL) | 1 | 15.11.58 | **Buxton** (CC) | A | L | 1-4 | Eley |
| 1959-60 | (NL) | 1 | 14.11.59 | **Matlock Town** (CA) | H | D | 2-2 | O'Connell, McMillan |
| | | 1r | 19.11.59 | **Matlock Town** | A | W | 1-0 | Keating |
| | | 2 | 05.12.59 | **York City** (D3) | H | L | 0-1 | |
| 1962-63 | (NL) | 1 | 03.11.62 | **Hull City** (D3) | A | L | 4-5 | Cocking 2, Bowron, Garbutt |
| 1963-64 | (NL) | 1 | 16.11.63 | **Chesterfield** (D4) | H | L | 1-2 | Weir |
| 1964-65 | (NL) | 1 | 14.11.64 | **Carlisle Utd** (D3) | H | W | 1-0 | Brown |
| | | 2 | 02.12.64 | **Oldham Athletic** (D3) | H | L | 0-1 | |
| 1965-66 | (NL) | 1 | 13.11.65 | **Gateshead AFC** (NRL) | A | L | 2-4 | Brown 2 |
| 1976-77 | (NL) | 1 | 20.11.76 | **Nuneaton B** (SL) | H | L | 1-4 | White |

# CROSSWELL'S BREWERY

*The working men from Crosswell's Brewery in Oldbury never entered the FA Cup again after losing 14-0 to Wolverhampton W in 1886, one of only two 14-0 scorelines in the Competition Proper. The other was Nottingham Forest's 14-0 win over Clapton on 17.01.1891.*

| | | | | | | | | |
|---|---|---|---|---|---|---|---|---|
| 1886-87 | | 1 | 30.10.86 | **Burton Swifts** | A | W | 1-0 | |
| | | 2 | 13.11.86 | **Wolverhampton W** | A | L | 0-14 | |

## CROYDON

*Formed 1953 as Croydon Amateurs. Croydon 1974. First entered FA Cup: 1966-67. No relation to earlier Croydon FC which first competed in the FA Cup in 1903-04 but never reached the Competition Proper. Members of the Isthmian League.*

| | | | | | | | |
|---|---|---|---|---|---|---|---|
| 1979-80 (IL) | 1 | 24.11.79 | **Wycombe W** (IL) | A | W | 3-0 | R Ward, Constable, A Ward |
| | 2 | 15.12.79 | **Millwall** (D3) | H | D | 1-1 | R Ward |
| | | | *played at Selhurst Park* | | | | |
| | 2r | 18.12.79 | **Millwall** | A | L | 2-3aet | Constable 2 (1p) |

## CROYDON COMMON

*Formed 1897. Turned professional 1907. Folded 1917. Within those bare facts is the story of one of the truly 'lost' clubs of the London football scene. The only club in the first division of the Southern League not to survive World War One. Played their Southern League matches at The Nest, the home of Crystal Palace from 1918-24. The Nest was situated opposite Selhurst Station, is now the site of the railway company's Selhurst Depot and is passed unknowingly by thousands of fans on their way to watch Crystal Palace on match days.*

| | | | | | | | |
|---|---|---|---|---|---|---|---|
| 1908-09 (SL) | | | q Bradord Park Avenue (D2) A 2-1 | | | | |
| | 1 | 16.01.09 | **Woolwich Arsenal** (D1) | H | D | 1-1 | MacDonald |
| | 1r | 20.01.09 | **Woolwich Arsenal** | A | L | 0-2 | |
| 1910-11 (SL) | 1 | 14.01.11 | **Grimsby Town** (ML) | A | L | 0-3 | |
| | | | *FA ordered match to be replayed after protests* | | | | |
| | 1r | 26.01.11 | **Grimsby Town** | A | L | 1-8 | Wardlow |
| 1911-12 (SL) | 1 | 13.01.12 | **Leicester Fosse** (D2) | H | D | 2-2 | Yenson, Wood |
| | 1r | 22.01.12 | **Leicester Fosse** | A | L | 1-6 | Yenson |
| 1912-13 (SL) | 1 | 11.01.13 | **Woolwich Arsenal** (D1) | H | D | 0-0 | |
| | 1r | 15.01.13 | **Woolwich Arsenal** | A | L | 1-2 | Newton |
| 1914-15 (SL) | 1 | 09.01.15 | **Oldham Athletic** (D1) | H | L | 0-3 | |

## CRUSADERS

*Formed 1877, Entered FA Cup: 1886-87 until 1892-93. One of the founding member clubs of the FA on October 26, 1863. Played their early matches at Essex County Cricket ground at Leyton. London Charity Cup winners: 1892, 1893.*

| | | | | | | | |
|---|---|---|---|---|---|---|---|
| 1886-87 | 1 | 23.10.86 | **Clapton** | A | W | 5-0 | |
| | 2 | 13.11.86 | **Old Carthusians** | A | L | 2-4 | |
| 1887-88 | 1 | 15.10.87 | **Lyndhurst FC** | H | W | 9-0 | |
| | 2 | 29.10.87 | **Old Wykehamists** | A | W | 3-2 | |
| | 3 | 26.11.87 | **Chatham** | H | W | 4-0 | |
| | 4 | 07.12.87 | **Sheffield Wed** | H | L | 0-1 | |
| 1890-91 | 1 | 24.01.91 | **B'ham St Georges** (FAll) | H | L | 0-2 | |
| 1891-92 | 1 | 16.01.92 | **Accrington FC** (D1) | H | L | 1-4 | Connell |

## CRYSTAL PALACE

*Formed 1905 and not connected with the amateur Crystal Palace club which played in the FA Cup from 1871-75. FA Cup runners-up: 1990. FA Cup record win: 7-0 v Clapton, 1st qualifying round 1905-06. In Competition Proper: 7-0 v Luton Town, 3rd round, 16.01.1929. Record FA Cup defeat: 0-9 v Burnley, 2nd round replay,10.02.1909. 4-11 v Manchester City, 5th round, 20.02.1926. When Crystal Palace, then of the Southern League, defeated Chelsea, then of Division Two 7-1 in a third qualifying round tie on November 18, 1905, they became the only Non-League club ever to score seven goals against a League club in FA Cup history.*

| | | | | | | | |
|---|---|---|---|---|---|---|---|
| 1905-06 (SL) | | | 1q Clapham (H) 7-0; 2q Grenadier Guards (A) 3-0; 3q Chelsea (H) 7-1; 4q Luton T (H) 1-0 | | | | |
| | 1 | 13.01.06 | **Blackpool** (D2) | A | D | 1-1 | Harker |
| | 1r | 17.01.06 | **Blackpool** | H | D | 1-1aet | Birnie |
| | 1 2r | 22.01.06 | **Blackpool** | | L | 0-1 | |
| | | | *played at Villa Park* | | | | |
| 1906-07 (SL) | | | 5q Rotherham Co (H) 4-0 | | | | |
| | 1 | 12.01.07 | **Newcastle Utd** (D1) | A | W | 1-0 | Astley |
| | 2 | 02.02.07 | **Fulham** (SL) | A | D | 0-0 | |
| | 2r | 06.02.07 | **Fulham** | H | W | 1-0 | Woodger |
| | 3 | 23.02.07 | **Brentford** (SL) | H | D | 1-1 | Harker |
| | 3r | 27.02.07 | **Brentford** | A | W | 1-0 | Roberts |
| | 4 | 09.03.07 | **Everton** (D1) | H | D | 1-1 | Astley |
| | 4r | 13.03.07 | **Everton** | A | L | 0-4 | |
| 1907-08 (SL) | 1 | 11.01.08 | **Coventry City** (BDL) | A | W | 4-2 | Woodger 2, Roberts, Davies |

| | | | | | | | |
|---|---|---|---|---|---|---|---|
| | 2 | 01.02.08 | **Plymouth Argyle** (SL) | A | W | 3-2 | Swann, Roberts, Smith |
| | 3 | 22.02.08 | **Grimsby Town** (D2) | A | L | 0-1 | |
| 1908-09 (SL) | 1 | 16.01.09 | **Wolverhampton W** (D2) | A | D | 2-2 | Bauchop 2 |
| | 1r | 21.01.09 | **Wolverhampton W** | H | W | 4-2aet | Garratt, Lawrence, Bauchop, Needham |
| | 2 | 06.02.09 | **Burnley** (D2) | H | D | 0-0 | |
| | 2r | 10.02.09 | **Burnley** | A | L | 0-9 | |
| 1909-10 (SL) | 1 | 15.01.10 | **Swindon Town** (SL) | H | L | 1-3 | Payne |
| 1910-11 (SL) | 1 | 14.01.11 | **Everton** (D1) | H | L | 0-4 | |
| 1911-12 (SL) | 1 | 13.01.12 | **Brentford** (SL) | A | D | 0-0 | |
| | 1r | 17.01.12 | **Brentford** | H | W | 4-0 | Smith, Hewitt, Hanger, Harker |
| | 2 | 03.02.12 | **Sunderland** (D1) | H | D | 0-0 | |
| | 2r | 07.02.12 | **Sunderland** | A | L | 0-1aet | |
| 1912-13 (SL) | 1 | 11.01.13 | **Glossop North End** (D2) | H | W | 2-0 | Smith, Williams |
| | 2 | 01.02.13 | **Bury** (D2) | H | W | 2-0 | Smith, Davies |
| | 3 | 22.02.13 | **Aston Villa** (D1) | A | L | 0-5 | |
| 1913-14 (SL) | 1 | 10.01.14 | **Norwich City** (SL) | H | W | 2-1 | Hewitt, Smith |
| | 2 | 31.01.14 | **West Ham Utd** (SL) | A | L | 0-2 | |
| 1914-15 (SL) | 1 | 09.01.15 | **Birmingham** (D2) | A | D | 2-2 | Davies, Middleton |
| | 1r | 16.01.15 | **Birmingham** *played at St Andrews* | H | L | 0-3 | |
| 1919-20 (SL) | 1 | 10.01.20 | **Newcastle Utd** (D1) | A | L | 0-2 | |
| 1920-21 (D3) | 1 | 08.01.21 | **Manchester City** (D1) | H | W | 2-0 | Menlove, Bateman |
| | 2 | 29.01.21 | **Hull City** (D2) | H | L | 0-2 | |
| 1921-22 (D2) | 1 | 07.01.22 | **Everton** (D1) | A | W | 6-0 | Conner 2, Menlove 2, Whibley, Wood |
| | 2 | 28.01.22 | **Millwall Athletic** (3S) | H | D | 0-0 | |
| | 2r | 01.02.22 | **Millwall Athletic** | A | L | 0-2 | |
| 1922-23 (D2) | 1 | 13.01.23 | **QPR** (3S) | A | L | 0-1 | |
| 1923-24 (D2) | 1 | 12.01.24 | **Tottenham Hotspur** (D1) | H | W | 2-0 | Morgan 2 |
| | 2 | 02.02.24 | **Notts County** (D1) | H | D | 0-0 | |
| | 2r | 06.02.24 | **Notts County** | A | D | 0-0aet | |
| | 2 2r | 11.02.24 | **Notts County** *played at Villa Park* | | D | 0-0aet | |
| | 2 3r | 18.02.24 | **Notts County** *played at Villa Park* | | W | 2-1 | Hoddinott, Hand |
| | 3 | 23.02.24 | **Swindon Town** (3S) | H | L | 1-2 | Whitworth |
| 1924-25 (D2) | 1 | 10.01.25 | **South Shields** (D2) | H | W | 2-1 | Blakemore, Whitworth |
| | 2 | 31.01.25 | **Hull City** (D2) | A | L | 2-3 | Hoddinott, Groves |
| 1925-26 (D3) | 3 | 09.01.26 | **Northampton Town** (3S) | A | D | 3-3 | Cherrett 2, Blakemore |
| | 3r | 13.01.26 | **Northampton Town** | H | W | 2-1 | Cherrett 2 |
| | 4 | 30.01.26 | **Chelsea** (D2) | H | W | 2-1 | Cherrett, Hawkins |
| | 5 | 20.02.26 | **Manchester City** (D1) | A | L | 4-11 | Cherrett 2, Clarke, McCracken |
| 1926-27 (3S) | 1 | 27.11.26 | **Norwich City** (3S) | H | D | 0-0 | |
| | 1r | 02.12.26 | **Norwich City** | A | L | 0-1 | |
| 1927-28 (3S) | 1 | 26.11.27 | **Dartford** (SL) | A | W | 3-1 | Hopkins 2, Smith |
| | 2 | 10.12.27 | **Swindon Town** (3S) | A | D | 0-0 | |
| | 2r | 14.12.27 | **Swindon Town** | H | L | 1-2 | Hopkins |
| 1928-29 (3S) | 1 | 24.11.28 | **Kettering Town** (SL) | H | W | 2-0 | Butler, Clarke |
| | 2 | 08.12.28 | **Bristol Rovers** (3S) | H | W | 3-1 | Harry, Charlton, Havelock |
| | 3 | 12.01.29 | **Luton Town** (3S) | A | D | 0-0 | |
| | 3r | 16.01.29 | **Luton Town** | H | W | 7-0 | Havelock 3, Wilde, Griffith, Butler, Hamilton |
| | 4 | 26.01.29 | **Millwall** (D2) | A | D | 0-0 | |
| | 4r | 30.01.29 | **Millwall** | H | W | 5-3 | Butler 3, Griffiths, Harry |
| | 5 | 16.02.29 | **Huddersfield Town** (D1) | A | L | 2-5 | Griffiths, Charlton (p) |
| 1929-30 (3S) | 3 | 11.01.30 | **Leeds Utd** (D1) | A | L | 1-8 | Simpson |
| 1930-31 (3S) | 1 | 29.11.30 | **Taunton T (1927)** (WL) | H | W | 6-0 | Simpson 3, Clarke, Greener, Butler |
| | 2 | 13.12.30 | **Newark Town** (ML) | H | W | 6-0 | Simpson 4, Butler, Clarke |
| | 3 | 10.01.31 | **Reading** (D2) | H | D | 1-1 | Butler |
| | 3r | 14.01.31 | **Reading** | A | D | 1-1aet | Clarke |
| | 3 2r | 19.01.31 | **Reading** *played at Stamford Bridge* | | W | 2-0 | Clarke, Simpson |

| | | | | | | | | |
|---|---|---|---|---|---|---|---|---|
| | | 4 | 24.01.31 | **Everton** (D2) | H | L | 0-6 | |
| 1931-32 | (3S) | 1 | 28.11.31 | **Reading** (3S) | A | W | 1-0 | Clarke |
| | | 2 | 12.12.31 | **Bath City** (SL) | A | L | 1-2 | Simpson |
| 1932-33 | (3S) | 1 | 26.11.32 | **Brighton** (3S) | H | L | 1-2 | Simpson |
| 1933-34 | (3S) | 1 | 25.11.33 | **Norwich City** (3S) | H | W | 3-0 | Roberts, Manders, Turner |
| | | 2 | 09.12.33 | **Stockport County** (3N) | A | W | 2-1 | Simpson, Manders |
| | | 3 | 13.01.34 | **Aldershot** (3S) | H | W | 1-0 | Manders |
| | | 4 | 27.01.34 | **Arsenal** (D1) | A | L | 0-7 | |
| 1934-35 | (3S) | 1 | 24.11.34 | **Yeovil & Petters Utd** (SL) | A | L | 0-3 | |
| 1935-36 | (3S) | 1 | 30.11.35 | **Bristol City** (3S) | A | W | 1-0 | Dawes |
| | | 2 | 14.12.35 | **Margate** (SL) | A | L | 1-3 | Blackman |
| 1936-37 | (3S) | 1 | 28.11.36 | **Southend Utd** (3S) | H | D | 1-1 | Birtley |
| | | 1r | 02.12.36 | **Southend Utd** | A | L | 0-2 | |
| 1937-38 | (3S) | 1 | 27.11.37 | **Kettering Town** (UCL) | H | D | 2-2 | Gillespie, Davies |
| | | 1r | 02.12.37 | **Kettering Town** | A | W | 4-0 | Pritchard 2, Blackman, Waldron |
| | | 2 | 11.12.37 | **Accrington Stanley** (3N) | A | W | 1-0 | Owens |
| | | 3 | 08.01.38 | **Liverpool** (D1) | H | D | 0-0 | |
| | | 3r | 12.01.38 | **Liverpool** | A | L | 1-3aet | Waldron |
| 1938-39 | (3S) | 1 | 26.11.38 | **QPR** (3S) | H | D | 1-1 | Blackman |
| | | 1r | 28.11.38 | **QPR** | A | L | 0-3 | |
| 1945-46 | (3S) | 3 1L | 05.01.46 | **QPR** (3S) | A | D | 0-0 | |
| | | 3 2L | 09.01.46 | **QPR** | H | - | 0-0ab | |
| | | | | *abandoned after 117 minutes* | | | | |
| | | 3 2L | 16.01.46 | **QPR** | | L | 0-1 | |
| | | | | *played at Craven Cottage* | | | | |
| 1946-47 | (3S) | 3 | 11.01.47 | **Newcastle Utd** (D2) | A | L | 2-6 | Naylor 2 |
| 1947-48 | (3S) | 1 | 29.11.47 | **Port Vale** (3S) | H | W | 2-1 | Farrington, Clough |
| | | 2 | 13.12.47 | **Bristol City** (3S) | A | W | 1-0aet | Robson |
| | | 3 | 10.01.48 | **Chester** (3N) | H | L | 0-1 | |
| 1948-49 | (3S) | 1 | 27.11.48 | **Bristol City** (3S) | H | L | 0-1aet | |
| 1949-50 | (3S) | 1 | 26.11.49 | **Newport County** (3S) | A | L | 0-3 | |
| 1950-51 | (3S) | 1 | 25.11.50 | **Millwall** (3S) | H | - | 0-0ab | |
| | | | | *abandoned after 34 minutes – fog* | | | | |
| | | 1 | 29.11.50 | **Millwall** | H | L | 1-4 | Kelly |
| 1951-52 | (3S) | 1 | 24.11.51 | **Gillingham** (3S) | H | L | 0-1 | |
| 1952-53 | (3S) | 1 | 22.11.52 | **Reading** (3S) | H | D | 1-1 | Rainford |
| | | 1r | 26.11.52 | **Reading** | A | W | 3-1 | Fell 2, Rainford |
| | | 2 | 06.12.52 | **Finchley** (AL) | A | - | 1-3ab | Burgess |
| | | | | *abandoned after 61 minutes – fog* | | | | |
| | | 2 | 10.12.52 | **Finchley** | A | L | 1-3 | Thomas |
| 1953-54 | (3S) | 1 | 21.11.53 | **Great Yarmouth T** (ECL) | A | L | 0-1 | |
| 1954-55 | (3S) | 1 | 20.11.54 | **Swindon Town** (3S) | A | W | 2-0 | Hanlon, Randall |
| | | 2 | 11.12.54 | **Bishop Auckland** (NL) | H | L | 2-4 | Choules, Thomas |
| 1955-56 | (3S) | 1 | 19.11.55 | **Southampton** (3S) | H | D | 0-0 | |
| | | 1r | 23.11.55 | **Southampton** | A | L | 0-2 | |
| 1956-57 | (3S) | 1 | 17.11.56 | **Walthamstow A** (IL) | H | W | 2-0 | Murray, Cooper |
| | | 2 | 08.12.56 | **Brentford** (3S) | A | D | 1-1 | Pierce |
| | | 2r | 12.12.56 | **Brentford** | H | W | 3-2aet | Pierce 3 |
| | | 3 | 05.01.57 | **Millwall** (3S) | A | L | 0-2 | |
| 1957-58 | (3S) | 1 | 16.11.57 | **Margate** (KL) | A | W | 3-2 | Deakin 3 |
| | | 2 | 12.12.57 | **Southampton** (3S) | H | W | 1-0 | Berry |
| | | 3 | 04.01.58 | **Ipswich Town** (D2) | H | L | 0-1 | |
| 1958-59 | (D4) | 1 | 15.11.58 | **Ashford Town** (KL) | A | W | 1-0 | Collins |
| | | 2 | 06.12.58 | **Shrewsbury Town** (D4) | H | D | 2-2 | Deakin 2 |
| | | 2r | 11.12.58 | **Shrewsbury Town** | A | D | 2-2aet | Byrne 2 |
| | | 2 2r | 15.12.58 | **Shrewsbury Town** | | W | 4-1 | Collins, Byrne, Deakin |
| | | | | *played at Molineux* | | | | |
| | | 3 | 10.01.59 | **Sheffield Utd** (D2) | A | L | 0-2 | |
| 1959-60 | (D4) | 1 | 14.11.59 | **Chelmsford City** (SL) | H | W | 5-1 | Byrne 3, Woan, Sexton |
| | | 2 | 05.12.59 | **Margate** (SL) | A | D | 0-0 | |
| | | 2r | 09.12.59 | **Margate** | H | W | 3-0 | Roche 2, Woan |

| | | | | | | | | |
|---|---|---|---|---|---|---|---|---|
| | | 3 | 09.01.60 | **Scunthorpe Utd** (D2) | A | L | 0-1 | |
| 1960-61 | (D4) | 1 | 05.11.60 | **Hitchin Town** (AL) | H | W | 6-2 | Gavin 2, Uphill 2, Byrne, Heckman |
| | | 2 | 26.11.60 | **Watford** (D3) | H | D | 0-0 | |
| | | 2r | 29.11.60 | **Watford** | A | L | 0-1 | |
| 1961-62 | (D3) | 1 | 04.11.61 | **Portsmouth** (D3) | H | W | 3-0 | Heckman 2, Byrne |
| | | 2 | 25.11.61 | **Bridgwater Town** (WL) | A | W | 3-0 | Heckman 2, Smillie |
| | | 3 | 06.01.62 | **Aston Villa** (D1) | A | L | 3-4 | Byrne 2, Uphill |
| 1962-63 | (D3) | 1 | 03.11.62 | **Hereford Utd** (SL) | H | W | 2-0 | Wood, Werge |
| | | 2 | 24.11.62 | **Mansfield Town** (D4) | H | D | 2-2 | Burridge, Allen (p) |
| | | 2r | 26.11.62 | **Mansfield Town** | A | L | 2-7 | Summersby, Phillips og |
| 1963-64 | (D3) | 1 | 16.11.63 | **Harwich & P** (ECL) | H | W | 8-2 | Holton 3, Allen 2, Burridge, Sewell, Howe |
| | | 2 | 07.12.63 | **Yeovil Town** (SL) | A | L | 1-3 | Wood |
| 1964-65 | (D2) | 3 | 09.01.65 | **Bury** (D2) | H | W | 5-1 | Holton 3, Burnside, Wood |
| | | 4 | 30.01.65 | **Southampton** (D2) | A | W | 2-1 | Holton, Smith |
| | | 5 | 20.02.65 | **Nottingham Forest** (D1) | H | W | 3-1 | Burnside, Burridge, Holton |
| | | 6 | 10.03.65 | **Leeds Utd** (D1) | H | L | 0-3 | |
| 1965-66 | (D2) | 3 | 22.01.66 | **Carlisle Utd** (D2) | A | L | 0-3 | |
| 1966-67 | (D2) | 3 | 28.01.67 | **Leeds Utd** (D1) | A | L | 0-3 | |
| 1967-68 | (D2) | 3 | 27.01.68 | **Walsall** (D3) | A | D | 1-1 | White |
| | | 3r | 31.01.68 | **Walsall** | H | L | 1-2 | Byrne |
| 1968-69 | (D2) | 3 | 04.01.69 | **Charlton Athletic** (D2) | A | D | 0-0 | |
| | | 3r | 08.01.69 | **Charlton Athletic** | H | L | 0-2 | |
| 1969-70 | (D1) | 3 | 03.01.70 | **Walsall** (D3) | H | W | 2-0 | Gregg og, Blyth |
| | | 4 | 24.01.70 | **Tottenham Hotspur** (D1) | A | D | 0-0 | |
| | | 4r | 28.01.70 | **Tottenham Hotspur** | H | W | 1-0 | Queen |
| | | 5 | 07.02.70 | **Chelsea** (D1) | H | L | 1-4 | Hoy |
| 1970-71 | (D1) | 3 | 02.01.71 | **Chelsea** (D1) | H | D | 2-2 | McCormick, Birchenall |
| | | 3r | 06.01.71 | **Chelsea** | A | L | 0-2 | |
| 1971-72 | (D1) | 3 | 15.01.72 | **Everton** (D1) | H | D | 2-2 | Wallace 2 |
| | | 3r | 18.01.72 | **Everton** | A | L | 2-3 | Tambling 2 |
| 1972-73 | (D1) | 3 | 13.01.73 | **Southampton** (D1) | H | W | 2-0 | Rogers, Cooke |
| | | 4 | 03.02.73 | **Sheffield Wed** (D2) | A | D | 1-1 | Craven |
| | | 4r | 06.02.73 | **Sheffield Wed** | H | D | 1-1aet | Phillip |
| | | 4 2r | 19.02.73 | **Sheffield Wed** *played at Villa Park* | | L | 2-3 | Payne, Rogers |
| 1973-74 | (D2) | 3 | 05.01.74 | **Wrexham** (D3) | H | L | 0-2 | |
| 1974-75 | (D3) | 1 | 27.11.74 | **Tooting & M** (IL) | A | W | 2-1 | P Hinshelwood, Whittle |
| | | 2 | 14.12.74 | **Plymouth Argyle** (D3) | A | L | 1-2 | Swindlehurst |
| 1975-76 | (D3) | 1 | 22.11.75 | **Walton & H** (IL) | H | W | 1-0 | Kemp |
| | | 2 | 13.12.75 | **Millwall** (D3) | A | D | 1-1 | Swindlehurst |
| | | 2r | 16.12.75 | **Millwall** | H | W | 2-1 | Kemp, Taylor (p) |
| | | 3 | 03.01.76 | **Scarborough** (NPL) | A | W | 2-1 | Taylor, Evans |
| | | 4 | 24.01.76 | **Leeds Utd** (D1) | A | W | 1-0 | Swindlehurst |
| | | 5 | 14.02.76 | **Chelsea** (D2) | A | W | 3-2 | Taylor 2, Chatterton |
| | | 6 | 06.03.76 | **Sunderland** (D2) | A | W | 1-0 | Whittle |
| | | SF | 03.04.76 | **Southampton** (D2) *played at Stamford Bridge* | | L | 0-2 | |
| 1976-77 | (D3) | 1 | 20.11.76 | **Brighton** (D3) | A | D | 2-2 | Evans, Harcouk |
| | | 1r | 23.11.76 | **Brighton** | H | D | 1-1aet | Harkouk |
| | | 1 2r | 06.12.76 | **Brighton** *played at Stamford Bridge* | | W | 1-0 | Holder |
| | | 2 | 11.12.76 | **Enfield** (IL) | H | W | 4-0 | Swindlehurst 2, Silkman, P Hinshelwood |
| | | 3 | 08.01.77 | **Liverpool** (D1) | A | D | 0-0 | |
| | | 3r | 11.01.77 | **Liverpool** | H | L | 2-3 | P Hinshelwood, Graham |
| 1977-78 | (D2) | 3 | 07.01.78 | **Hartlepool Utd** (D4) | A | L | 1-2 | Chatterton |
| 1978-79 | (D2) | 3 | 09.01.79 | **Middlesbrough** (D1) | A | D | 1-1 | Walsh |
| | | 3r | 15.01.79 | **Middlesbrough** | H | W | 1-0 | Sansom |
| | | 4 | 29.01.79 | **Bristol City** (D1) | H | W | 3-0 | Nicholas, Fenwick, Kember |
| | | 5 | 26.02.79 | **Wolverhampton W** (D1) | H | L | 0-1 | |

| | | | | | | | | |
|---|---|---|---|---|---|---|---|---|
| 1979-80 | (D1) | 3 | 05.01.80 | **Swansea City** (D3) | A | D | 2-2 | Kember, Walsh |
| | | 3r | 08.01.80 | **Swansea City** | H | D | 3-3aet | Hinshelwood, Fenwick, Hilaire |
| | | 3 2r | 14.01.80 | **Swansea City** | | L | 1-2 | Boyle |
| | | | | *played at Ninian Park* | | | | |
| 1980-81 | (D1) | 3 | 03.01.81 | **Manchester City** (D1) | A | L | 0-4 | |
| 1981-82 | (D2) | 3 | 02.01.82 | **Enfield** (APL) | A | W | 3-2 | Hilaire 2, Price |
| | | 4 | 23.01.82 | **Bolton Wanderers** (D2) | H | W | 1-0 | Cannon (p) |
| | | 5 | 13.02.82 | **Orient** (D2) | H | D | 0-0 | |
| | | 5r | 16.02.82 | **Orient** | A | W | 1-0 | Smillie |
| | | 6 | 06.03.82 | **QPR** (D2) | A | L | 0-1 | |
| 1982-83 | (D2) | 3 | 08.01.83 | **York City** (D4) | H | W | 2-1 | Lovell, Langley |
| | | 4 | 29.01.83 | **Birmingham City** (D1) | H | W | 1-0 | Edwards |
| | | 5 | 19.02.83 | **Burnley** (D2) | H | D | 0-0 | |
| | | 5r | 28.02.83 | **Burnley** | A | L | 0-1 | |
| 1983-84 | (D2) | 3 | 07.01.84 | **Leicester City** (D1) | H | W | 1-0 | Gilbert |
| | | 4 | 28.01.84 | **West Ham Utd** (D1) | H | D | 1-1 | McCulloch |
| | | 4r | 31.01.84 | **West Ham Utd** | A | L | 0-2 | |
| 1984-85 | (D2) | 3 | 05.01.85 | **Millwall** (D3) | A | D | 1-1 | Mahoney |
| | | 3r | 23.01.85 | **Millwall** | H | L | 1-2 | Aylott |
| 1985-86 | (D2) | 3 | 06.01.86 | **Luton Town** (D1) | H | L | 1-2 | Taylor |
| 1986-87 | (D2) | 3 | 11.01.87 | **Nottingham Forest** (D1) | H | W | 1-0 | Irvine |
| | | 4 | 31.01.87 | **Tottenham Hotspur** (D1) | A | L | 0-4 | |
| 1987-88 | (D2) | 3 | 09.01.88 | **Newcastle Utd** (D1) | A | L | 0-1 | |
| 1988-89 | (D2) | 3 | 07.01.89 | **Stoke City** (D2) | A | L | 0-1 | |
| 1989-90 | (D1) | 3 | 06.01.90 | **Portsmouth** (D2) | H | W | 2-1 | Thomas, Gray (p) |
| | | 4 | 27.01.90 | **Huddersfield Town** (D3) | H | W | 4-0 | Bright 2, Hopkins, Salako |
| | | 5 | 17.02.90 | **Rochdale** (D4) | H | W | 1-0 | Barber |
| | | 6 | 10.03.90 | **Cambridge Utd** (D4) | A | W | 1-0 | Thomas |
| | | SF | 08.04.90 | **Liverpool** (D1) | | W | 4-3aet | Bright, O'Reilly, Gray, Pardew |
| | | | | *played at Villa Park* | | | | |
| | | F | 12.05.90 | **Manchester Utd** (D1) | | D | 3-3aet | Wright 2, O'Reilly |
| | | | | *played at Wembley Stadium* | | | | |
| | | Fr | 17.05.90 | **Manchester Utd** | | L | 0-1 | |
| | | | | *played at Wembley Stadium* | | | | |
| 1990-91 | (D1) | 3 | 06.01.91 | **Nottingham Forest** (D1) | H | D | 0-0 | |
| | | 3r | 21.01.91 | **Nottingham Forest** | A | D | 2-2aet | Wright, Salako |
| | | 3 2r | 28.01.91 | **Nottingham Forest** | A | L | 0-3 | |
| 1991-92 | (D1) | 3 | 04.01.92 | **Leicester City** (D2) | A | L | 0-1 | |
| 1992-93 | (PL) | 3 | 02.01.93 | **Hartlepool Utd** (D2) | A | L | 0-1 | |
| 1993-94 | (PL) | 3 | 08.01.94 | **Wolverhampton W** (D1) | A | L | 0-1 | |
| 1994-95 | (PL) | 3 | 08.01.95 | **Lincoln City** (D3) | H | W | 5-1 | Coleman, Armstrong, Gordon (p), Salako 2 |
| | | 4 | 28.01.95 | **Nottingham Forest** (PL) | A | W | 2-1 | Armstrong, Dowie |
| | | 5 | 18.02.95 | **Watford** (D1) | A | D | 0-0 | |
| | | 5r | 01.03.95 | **Watford** | H | W | 1-0aet | Ndah |
| | | 6 | 11.03.95 | **Wolverhampton W** (D1) | H | D | 1-1 | Dowie |
| | | 6r | 22.03.95 | **Wolverhampton W** | A | W | 4-1 | Armstrong 2, Dowie, Pitcher |
| | | SF | 09.04.95 | **Manchester Utd** (PL) | | D | 2-2aet | Dowie, Armstrong |
| | | | | *played at Villa Park* | | | | |
| | | SFr | 12.04.95 | **Manchester Utd** | | L | 0-2 | |
| | | | | *played at Villa Park* | | | | |
| 1995-96 | (D1) | 3 | 06.01.96 | **Port Vale** (D1) | H | D | 0-0 | |
| | | 3r | 16.01.96 | **Port Vale** | A | L | 3-4aet | Taylor, Cox, Dyer |
| 1996-97 | (D1) | 3 | 14.01.97 | **Leeds Utd** (PL) | H | D | 2-2 | Dyer (p), Veart |
| | | 3r | 25.01.97 | **Leeds Utd** | A | L | 0-1 | |
| 1997-98 | (PL) | 3 | 03.01.98 | **Scunthorpe Utd** (D3) | H | W | 2-0 | Emblen 2 |
| | | 4 | 24.01.98 | **Leicester City** (PL) | H | W | 3-0 | Dyer 3 |
| | | 5 | 15.02.98 | **Arsenal** (PL) | A | D | 0-0 | |
| | | 5r | 25.02.98 | **Arsenal** | H | L | 1-2 | Dyer |
| 1998-99 | (D1) | 3 | 02.01.99 | **Newcastle Utd** (PL) | A | L | 1-2 | Bradbury |
| 1999-00 | (D1) | 3 | 10.12.99 | **Cambridge Utd** (D2) | A | L | 0-2 | |
| 2000-01 | (D1) | 3 | 06.01.01 | **Sunderland** (PL) | A | D | 0-0 | |

| | | | | | | | |
|---|---|---|---|---|---|---|---|
| | 3r | 17.01.01 | **Sunderland** | H | L | 2-4aet | Morrison, Thompson |
| 2001-02 (D1) | 3 | 05.01.02 | **Newcastle Utd** (PL) | A | L | 0-2 | |
| 2002-03 (D1) | 3 | 04.01.03 | **Blackpool** (D2) | A | W | 2-1 | Black 2 |
| | 4 | 26.01.03 | **Liverpool** (PL) | H | D | 0-0 | |
| | 4r | 05.02.03 | **Liverpool** | A | W | 2-0 | Gray, Henchoz og |
| | 5 | 16.02.03 | **Leeds Utd** (PL) | H | L | 1-2 | Gray |

# CRYSTAL PALACE (1861)

*Formed 1861. One of the founding member clubs of the FA on October 26, 1863 and one of the 15 original entrants in the FA Cup in the 1871-72 season, their match against Hitchin on November 11, 1871 was the first ever 0-0 draw in competitive soccer history. Under the bizarre rules governing that competition, the match was not replayed and both teams went through to the second round. This amateur Crystal Palace club has no connection with the modern-day club. It last entered the FA Cup in 1875-76, long before the modern Crystal Palace was formed in 1905. Curiously, it could be argued that perhaps there was indeed a replay of that 1871 match after all. Hitchin played the modern Crystal Palace 79 years later – and lost 6-2.*

| | | | | | | | |
|---|---|---|---|---|---|---|---|
| 1871-72 | 1 | 11.11.71 | **Hitchin Town** | H | D | 0-0 | |
| | | | *Both teams qualified for second round* | | | | |
| | 2 | 16.12.71 | **Maidenhead** | H | W | 3-0 | Bouch, Chenery, LLoyd |
| | 3 | 20.01.72 | **Wanderers** | A | D | 0-0 | |
| | | | *Both teams qualified for semifinals* | | | | |
| | SF | 17.02.72 | **Royal Engineers** | | D | 0-0 | |
| | | | *played at Kennington Oval* | | | | |
| | SFr | 09.03.72 | **Royal Engineers** | | L | 0-3 | |
| | | | *played at Kennington Oval* | | | | |
| 1872-73 | 1 | 26.10.72 | **Oxford University** | A | L | 2-3 | Armitage, Soden |
| 1873-74 | 1 | 09.10.73 | **Swifts** | A | L | 0-1 | |
| 1874-75 | 1 | 14.11.74 | **Cambridge University** | H | D | 0-0 | |
| | 1r | 21.11.74 | **Cambridge University** | A | L | 1-2 | Fleet |
| 1875-76 | 1 | 06.11.75 | **105th Regiment** | A | D | 0-0 | |
| | 1r | 20.11.75 | **105th Regiment** | H | W | 3-0 | EP Barlow, Neame, CP Smith |
| | 2 | 11.12.75 | **Wanderers** | A | L | 0-3 | |

# DAGENHAM

*Formed 1949. First entered FA Cup: 1951-52. FA Amateur Cup runners-up: 1970, 1971. FA Trophy winners: 1980. Runners-up: 1977. Merged with Redbridge Forest to form Dagenham and Redbridge 1992. See also Ilford, Leytonstone and Walthamstow Ave. Redbridge Forest never qualified for the Competition Proper. League clubs beaten: Cambridge United, Swindon Town, Peterborough United*

| | | | | | | | |
|---|---|---|---|---|---|---|---|
| 1967-68 (AL) | 1 | 09.12.67 | **Tonbridge** (SL) | H | W | 1-0 | Greene |
| | 2 | 06.01.68 | **Reading** (D3) | A | D | 1-1 | Morris |
| | 2r | 15.01.68 | **Reading** | H | L | 0-1 | |
| 1969-70 (AL) | 1 | 15.11.69 | **Sutton Utd** (IL) | H | L | 0-1 | |
| 1970-71 (AL) | 1 | 21.11.70 | **Margate** (SL) | H | W | 2-0 | Dear, Smith |
| | 2 | 12.12.70 | **Southend Utd** (D4) | A | L | 0-1 | |
| 1971-72 (AL) | 1 | 20.11.71 | **Walsall** (D3) | A | L | 1-4 | Moore |
| 1973-74 (IL) | 1 | 24.11.73 | **Aldershot** (D3) | H | L | 0-4 | |
| 1977-78 (IL) | 1 | 26.11.77 | **Walsall** (D3) | A | L | 0-1 | |
| 1978-79 (IL) | 1 | 25.11.78 | **Watford** (D3) | A | L | 0-3 | |
| 1980-81 (IL) | 1 | 22.11.80 | **Gillingham** (D3) | A | L | 1-2 | Kidd |
| 1981-82 (APL) | 1 | 21.11.81 | **Yeovil Town** (APL) | H | D | 2-2 | Burton 2 |
| | 1r | 25.11.81 | **Yeovil Town** | A | W | 1-0aet | Stewart |
| | 2 | 30.12.81 | **Millwall** (D3) | H | L | 1-2 | Stein |
| 1982-83 (APL) | 1 | 20.11.82 | **Gillingham** (D3) | A | L | 0-1 | |
| 1983-84 (APL) | 1 | 19.11.83 | **Brentford** (D3) | H | D | 2-2 | Dunwell, Smith |
| | 1r | 22.11.83 | **Brentford** | A | L | 1-2 | Rhoden |
| 1984-85 (APL) | 1 | 19.11.84 | **Swindon Town** (D4) | H | D | 0-0 | |
| | 1r | 26.11.84 | **Swindon Town** | A | W | 2-1aet | Campbell, Whitton |
| | 2 | 08.12.84 | **Peterborough Utd** (D4) | H | W | 1-0 | Dunwell |
| | 3 | 05.01.85 | **Carlisle Utd** (D2) | A | L | 0-1 | |
| 1985-86 (APL) | 1 | 16.11.85 | **Cambridge Utd** (D4) | H | W | 2-1 | Sullivan, Scott |
| | 2 | 07.12.85 | **Bournemouth** (D3) | A | L | 1-4 | Cox |
| 1987-88 (Conf) | 1 | 14.11.87 | **Maidstone Utd** (Conf) | H | L | 0-2 | |
| 1988-89 (IL) | 1 | 19.11.88 | **Sutton Utd** (Conf) | H | L | 0-4 | |

## DAGENHAM & REDBRIDGE

*Formed 1992 by the merger of Dagenham (1949) and Redbridge Forest (1988). In effect this completed the transformation process started in 1979 which involved four of the leading senior Non-League and semi-professional clubs from the east London area effectively merging into one club over a 13-year period. Ilford (1881) and Leytonstone (1886) merged in 1979 to form Leytonstone-Ilford. That club and Walthamstow Ave (1900) merged in 1988 to form Redbridge Forest. Redbridge Forest merged with Dagenham to form the present club in 1992. FA Trophy runners-up: 1997. League clubs beaten: Lincoln City, Exeter City, Plymouth Argyle. Members of The Conference.*

| | | | | | | | | |
|---|---|---|---|---|---|---|---|---|
| 1992-93 | (Conf) | 1 | 14.11.92 | **Leyton Orient** (D2) | H | L | 4-5 | Broom, Conner, Butterworth, Cavell |
| 1996-97 | (IL) | 1 | 16.11.96 | **Ashford Town** (SL) | A | D | 2-2 | Stimson, Creaser |
| | | 1r | 25.11.96 | **Ashford Town** | H | D | 1-1aet | Rogers |
| | | | | *Ashford won 4-3 on penalties* | | | | |
| 1997-98 | (IL) | 1 | 15.11.97 | **Farnborough T** (Conf) | A | W | 1-0 | Stimson |
| | | 2 | 06.12.97 | **Peterborough Utd** (D3) | A | L | 2-3 | Cobb, Shipp |
| 2000-01 | (Conf) | 1 | 18.11.00 | **Hayes** (Conf) | H | W | 3-1 | Keen, Watts og, Jones |
| | | 2 | 09.12.00 | **Lincoln City** (D3) | A | W | 1-0 | Janney |
| | | 3 | 06.01.01 | **Charlton Athletic** (PL) | A | D | 1-1 | McDougald |
| | | 3r | 27.01.01 | **Charlton Athletic** | H | L | 0-1aet | |
| 2001-02 | (Conf) | 1 | 17.11.01 | **Southport** (Conf) | H | W | 1-0 | Stein (p) |
| | | 2 | 08.12.01 | **Exeter City** (D3) | A | D | 0-0 | |
| | | 2r | 19.12.01 | **Exeter City** | H | W | 3-0 | Janney, McDougald, Charlerey |
| | | 3 | 05.01.02 | **Ipswich Town** (PL) | H | L | 1-4 | McDougald |
| 2002-03 | (Conf) | 1 | 16.11.02 | **Havant & W** (SL) | H | W | 3-2 | McDougald, Shipp 2 |
| | | 2 | 07.12.02 | **Crawley Town** (SL) | A | W | 2-1 | McDougald, Janney |
| | | 3 | 04.01.03 | **Plymouth Argyle** (D2) | A | D | 2-2 | Terry, McDougald |
| | | 3r | 14.01.03 | **Plymouth Argyle** | H | W | 2-0 | Shipp, McDougald |
| | | 4 | 25.01.03 | **Norwich City** (D1) | A | L | 0-1 | |

## DAGENHAM TOWN

*Formed 1929 from Lombardians FC, members of the London Midweek League. First entered FA Cup: 1929-30. A separate club from Dagenham FC. Folded 1940.*

| | | | | | | | | |
|---|---|---|---|---|---|---|---|---|
| 1929-30 | (Lon) | 1 | 30.11.29 | **Barry Town** (SL) | A | D | 0-0 | |
| | | 1r | 04.12.29 | **Barry Town** | H | L | 0-1 | |
| | | | | *played at Upton Park* | | | | |

## DARLINGTON

*Formed 1883. Best FA Cup performance: 5th round, 1958. FA Cup record win: 13-1 v Scarborough, 2nd qualifying round, 1891-92. In Competition Proper: 7-2 v Evenwood Town, 1st round, 17.11.1956. FA Cup Record Defeat: 0-8 v Grimsby Town, 2nd round, 21.11.1885.*

| | | | | | | | | |
|---|---|---|---|---|---|---|---|---|
| 1885-86 | | 1 | | bye | | | | |
| | | 2 | 21.11.85 | **Grimsby Town** | A | L | 0-8 | |
| 1886-87 | | 1 | 30.10.86 | **Horncastle** | A | L | 0-2 | |
| 1887-88 | | 1 | 15.10.87 | **Gateshead Association** | A | W | 3-0 | Brooks, H Hope, Stabler |
| | | 2 | 05.11.87 | **Elswick Rangers** | H | W | 4-3aet | Rogers, 3 others |
| | | 3 | 26.11.87 | **Shankhouse** | H | L | 0-2 | |
| 1888-89 | | | | 1q Birtley (A) 0-2aet | | | | |
| 1889-90 | (NL) | | | 1q Darlington St Augustines (A) 0-5 | | | | |
| 1890-91 | (NL) | | | 2q Darlington West End, walkover; 3q Middlesbrough (A) 0-2; 4q Middlesbrough Iron (A) 0-6; FA ordered replay after protest 4qr Middlesbrough Iron (A) 0-3 | | | | |
| 1891-92 | (NL) | | | 1q Port Clarence (H) 3-0; 2q Scarborough (H) 13-1; 3q Leeds Albion, walkover; 4q Middlesbrough Iron (H) 0-3 | | | | |
| 1892-93 | (NL) | | | 1q Scarborough walkover; 2q Darlington St Augustines (H) 5-1; 3q Hurworth, walkover; 4q Stockton (H) 1-5 | | | | |
| 1893-94 | (NL) | | | 1q Willington A (A) 0-1 | | | | |
| 1894-95 | (NL) | | | 1q Darlington St Augustines (H) 7-0; 2q Stockton (H) 2-0; 3q Middlesbrough (H) 0-1 | | | | |
| 1895-96 | (NL) | | | P Tow Law T (A) 1-3 | | | | |
| 1896-97 | (NL) | | | 3q Blyth S (H) 7-1; 4q Stockton (H) 1-3 | | | | |
| 1897-98 | (NL) | | | 3q Stockton (A) 0-3 | | | | |
| 1898-99 | (NL) | | | 3q Bishop Auckland (A) 1-4 | | | | |
| 1899-00 | (NL) | | | P Tow Law T (H) 2-0; 1q Crook T (A) 1-1; 1qr Crook T (H) 2-3 | | | | |
| 1900-01 | (NL) | | | P Tow Law T (H) 3-0; 1q Darlington St Augustines (A) 1-1; 1qr Darlington St Augustines (H) 4-1; 2q Bishop Auckland (A) 0-3 | | | | |

| | | | | | | | |
|---|---|---|---|---|---|---|---|
| 1901-02 (NL) | | | P Leadgate Park (A) 0-3 | | | | |
| 1902-03 (NL) | | | P Leadgate Park (A) 5-0; 1q Tow Law T (A) 1-1; 1qr Tow Law T (H) 1-2 | | | | |
| 1903-04 (NL) | | | 1q Darlington St Augustines (H) 7-3; 2q Bishop Auckland (H) 5-2; 3q Sunderland Royal (A) 2-4 | | | | |
| 1904-05 (NL) | | | 3q Morpeth Harriers (A) 6-0; 4q Bishop Auckland (A) 1-3 | | | | |
| 1905-06 (NL) | | | 4q Bradford C (H) 0-4 | | | | |
| 1906-07 (NL) | | | P Elton Albion (H) 2-1; 1q South Bank (A) 0-6 | | | | |
| 1907-08 (NL) | | | 1q South Bank (H) 2-0; 2q Darlington St Augustines (A) 2-0; 3q Skinnigrove U (H) 6-0; 4q Carlisle U (A) 0-7 | | | | |
| 1908-09 (NEL) | | | 1q Scarborough (H) 3-2; 2q West Hartlepool Expansion (H) 4-0; 3q South Bank (A) 0-1 | | | | |
| 1909-10 (NEL) | | | P Horden Athletic (A) 1-1; Pr Horden Athletic (H) 2-0; 1q West Hartlepool Expansion (H) 2-1; 2q Hartlepools U (H) 1-0; 3q South Bank (A) 2-3 | | | | |
| 1910-11 (NEL) | | | 1q Hartlepools U (H) 1-1; 1qr Hartlepools U (A) 1-0; 2q Wingate Albion (H) 1-1; 2qr Wingate Albion (H) 3-3; 2q 2r Wingate Albion (H) 2-1; 3q Bishop Auckland (H) 2-0; 4q Shildon (H) 5-3; 5q Blackwell Colliery (A) 6-1 | | | | |
| | 1 | 14.01.11 | **Sheffield Utd** (D1) | A | W | 1-0 | Fraser |
| | 2 | 04.02.11 | **Bradford Park A** (D2) | H | W | 2-1 | Curnock, Dodds |
| | 3 | 25.02.11 | **Swindon Town** (SL) | H | L | 0-3 | |
| 1911-12 (NEL) | | | 4q Shildon (H) 6-0; 5q North Shields (A) 2-1 | | | | |
| | 1 | 13.01.12 | **Brighton** (SL) | H | W | 2-1 | Donnelly, Fraser |
| | 2 | 03.02.12 | **Northampton Town** (SL) | H | D | 1-1 | Donnelly |
| | 2r | 08.02.12 | **Northampton Town** | A | L | 0-2 | |
| 1912-13 (NEL) | | | 4q North Shields (H) 0-0; 4qr North Shields (A) 4-0; 5q Rochdale (A) 1-1; 5qr Rochdale (H) 0-1 | | | | |
| 1913-14 (NEL) | | | 4q Stockton (H) 4-1; 5q Port Vale (A) 2-2; 5qr Port Vale (H) 1-2 abnd; 5qr Port Vale 1-2 (at Sheffield) | | | | |
| 1914-15 (NEL) | | | 4q South Bank (A) 4-0; 5q Sunderland Rovers (A) 1-1; 5qr Sunderland R (H) 3-0; 6q London Caledonians (A) 1-0 | | | | |
| | 1 | 09.01.15 | **Bradford City** (D1) | H | L | 0-1 | |
| 1919-20 (NEL) | | | 4q South Bank (H) 4-2; 5q Bishop Auckland (H) 9-2; 6q Norwich C (H) 5-0 | | | | |
| | 1 | 14.01.20 | **Sheffield Wed** (D1) | H | D | 0-0 | |
| | 1r | 19.01.20 | **Sheffield Wed** | A | W | 2-0 | Stevens, Healey |
| | 2 | 31.01.20 | **Birmingham** (D2) | A | L | 0-4 | |
| 1920-21 (NEL) | | | 6q Blyth Spartans (H) 4-0 | | | | |
| | 1 | 08.01.21 | **Blackpool** (D2) | H | D | 2-2 | Healey 2 |
| | 1r | 12.01.21 | **Blackpool** | A | L | 1-2 | Travis |
| 1921-22 (3N) | | | 5q Durham C (A) 2-0; 6q Merthyr Town (A) 0-0; 6qr Merthyr Town (H) 1-0 | | | | |
| | 1 | 07.01.22 | **Manchester City** (D1) | A | L | 1-3 | Healey |
| 1922-23 (3N) | | | 5q Bishop Auckland (A) 2-1; 6q Charlton Athletic (A) 1-2 | | | | |
| 1923-24 (3N) | | | 5q Leadgate Park (A) 1-1; 5qr Leadgate Park (H) 1-0; 6q Southport (H) 3-0 | | | | |
| | 1 | 12.01.24 | **Wolverhampton W** (3N) | A | L | 1-3 | Hooper |
| 1924-25 (3N) | | | 5q Durham C (H) 3-1; 6q Reading (A) 1-0 | | | | |
| | 1 | 10.01.25 | **Cardiff City** (D1) | A | D | 0-0 | |
| | 1r | 14.01.25 | **Cardiff City** | H | D | 0-0aet | |
| | 1 2r | 19.01.25 | **Cardiff City** | | L | 0-2 | |
| | | | *played at Anfield* | | | | |
| 1925-26 (D2) | 1 | 28.11.25 | **Horden CW** (Wear) | A | W | 3-2 | Brown 2, Jackson |
| | 2 | 12.12.25 | **New Brighton** (3N) | A | L | 0-2 | |
| 1926-27 (D2) | 3 | 08.01.27 | **Rhyl** (Welsh) | H | W | 2-1 | Little, Ruddy |
| | 4 | 29.01.27 | **Cardiff City** (D1) | H | L | 0-2 | |
| 1927-28 (3N) | 1 | 26.11.27 | **Chesterfield** (3N) | H | W | 4-1 | Ruddy 3, Lees |
| | 2 | 10.12.27 | **Rochdale** (3N) | H | W | 2-1 | Ruddy 2 |
| | 3 | 14.01.28 | **Liverpool** (D1) | A | L | 0-1 | |
| 1928-29 (3N) | 1 | 24.11.28 | **New Brighton** (3N) | H | W | 3-0 | Cochrane, Lees 2 |
| | 2 | 08.12.28 | **Scarborough** (ML) | A | D | 2-2 | Lowe 2 |
| | 2r | 12.12.28 | **Scarborough** | H | W | 2-1 | Eden, Dickson |
| | 3 | 12.01.29 | **Bury** (D1) | H | L | 2-6 | Eden 2 |
| 1929-30 (3N) | 1 | 30.11.29 | **Caernarfon T** (Welsh) | A | L | 2-4 | Wellock 2 |
| 1930-31 (3N) | 1 | 29.11.30 | **Southport** (3N) | A | L | 2-4 | Halliday, Vine |
| 1931-32 (3N) | 1 | 28.11.31 | **Walsall** (3N) | H | W | 1-0 | Wellock |
| | 2 | 12.12.31 | **Carlisle Utd** (3N) | A | W | 2-0 | Hurst, Grieve |

| | | | | | | | | | |
|---|---|---|---|---|---|---|---|---|---|
| | | 3 | 09.01.32 | **Northampton Town** (3S) | H | D | 1-1 | Mitchell |
| | | 3r | 14.01.32 | **Northampton Town** | A | L | 0-2 | |
| 1932-33 | (3N) | 1 | 26.11.32 | **Boston Utd** (ML) | H | W | 1-0 | Waugh |
| | | 2 | 10.12.32 | **Crewe Alexandra** (3N) | A | W | 2-0 | Hurst, Johnson |
| | | 3 | 14.01.33 | **QPR** (3S) | H | W | 2-0 | Hurst, Johnson |
| | | 4 | 28.01.33 | **Chesterfield** (D2) | H | L | 0-2 | |
| 1933-34 | (3N) | 1 | 25.11.33 | **Chester** (3N) | A | L | 1-6 | Alderson |
| 1934-35 | (3N) | 1 | 24.11.34 | **Gateshead AFC** (3N) | A | W | 4-1 | Best 2, Edgar, Middleton |
| | | 2 | 08.12.34 | **Stockport County** (3N) | A | L | 2-3 | Eden, Best |
| 1935-36 | (3N) | 1 | 30.11.35 | **Accrington Stanley** (3N) | H | W | 4-2 | Anderson, Best, Towers, Reed |
| | | 2 | 14.12.35 | **Stalybridge Celtic** (CC) | A | W | 1-0 | Best |
| | | 3 | 11.01.36 | **Bury** (D2) | H | L | 2-3 | Reed, Alderson |
| 1936-37 | (3N) | 1 | 28.11.36 | **Halifax Town** (3N) | A | W | 2-1 | Stanger, Towers |
| | | 2 | 12.12.36 | **Burton Town** (ML) | A | W | 2-1 | Brattisford, Brown |
| | | 3 | 16.01.37 | **Dartford** (SL) | A | W | 1-0 | Lowery |
| | | 4 | 30.01.37 | **WBA** (D1) | A | L | 2-3 | Brattisford 2 |
| 1937-38 | (3N) | 1 | 27.11.37 | **Scarborough** (ML) | H | L | 0-2 | |
| 1938-39 | (3N) | 1 | 26.11.38 | **Stalybridge Celtic** (CC) | H | W | 4-0 | Feeney 3, Birley |
| | | 2 | 10.12.38 | **Chelmsford City** (SL) | A | L | 1-3 | Alderson |
| 1945-46 | (3N) | 1 1L | 17.11.45 | **Stockton** (NEL) | H | W | 2-0 | Clarke 2 |
| | | 1 2L | 24.11.45 | **Stockton** | A | W | 4-1 | Harrison 2, Towers, Sykes |
| | | 2 1L | 08.12.45 | **Gateshead AFC** (3N) | H | L | 2-4 | Towers, Varty |
| | | 2 2L | 15.12.45 | **Gateshead AFC** | A | W | 2-1 | Harrison 2 |
| 1946-47 | (3N) | 1 | 30.11.46 | **Gainsborough T** (ML) | A | W | 2-1 | Clarke 2 |
| | | 2 | 14.12.46 | **Hull City** (3N) | H | L | 1-2 | Stubbs |
| 1947-48 | (3N) | 1 | 29.11.47 | **Hartlepools Utd** (3N) | A | L | 0-1 | |
| 1948-49 | (3N) | 1 | 27.11.48 | **Tranmere Rovers** (3N) | A | W | 3-1 | Bower 2, Quinn |
| | | 2 | 11.12.48 | **Leyton Orient** (3S) | H | W | 1-0 | Milner |
| | | 3 | 08.01.49 | **Rotherham Utd** (3N) | A | L | 2-4 | Ward 2 |
| 1949-50 | (3N) | 1 | 26.11.49 | **Crewe Alexandra** (3N) | H | D | 2-2 | Brown 2 |
| | | 1r | 30.11.49 | **Crewe Alexandra** | A | L | 0-1aet | |
| 1950-51 | (3N) | 1 | 25.11.50 | **Rotherham Utd** (3N) | H | L | 2-7 | Murray, Steel |
| 1951-52 | (3N) | 1 | 24.11.51 | **Grimsby Town** (3N) | A | L | 0-4 | |
| 1952-53 | (3N) | 1 | 22.11.52 | **Grimsby Town** | H | L | 2-3 | Murray, Davison |
| 1953-54 | (3N) | 1 | 21.11.53 | **Port Vale** (D3) | H | L | 1-3 | Robson |
| 1954-55 | (3N) | 1 | 20.11.54 | **Barrow** (3N) | A | D | 1-1 | Davies |
| | | 1r | 24.11.54 | **Barrow** | H | W | 2-1 | Davis, Spuhler |
| | | 2 | 11.12.54 | **Walthamstow Ave** (IL) | A | W | 3-0 | Spuhler, Dunlop Furphy |
| | | 3 | 08.01.55 | **Hartlepools Utd** (3N) | A | D | 1-1 | Houlahan |
| | | 3r | 12.01.55 | **Hartlepools Utd** | H | D | 2-2aet | Walsh, Houlahan |
| | | 3 2r | 17.01.55 | **Hartlepools Utd** *played at Ayresome Park* | | L | 0-2 | |
| 1955-56 | (3N) | 1 | 19.11.55 | **Carlisle Utd** (3N) | H | D | 0-0 | |
| | | 1r | 22.11.55 | **Carlisle Utd** | A | D | 0-0aet | |
| | | 1 2r | 28.11.55 | **Carlisle Utd** *played at St James' Park* | | W | 3-1 | Rutherford, Bell, Furphy |
| | | 2 | 10.12.55 | **Accrington Stanley** (3N) | H | L | 0-1 | |
| 1956-57 | (3N) | 1 | 17.11.56 | **Evenwood Town** (NL) | H | W | 7-2 | Bell, Morton 3, Forster, Tulip 2 |
| | | 2 | 08.12.56 | **Carlisle Utd** (3N) | A | L | 1-2 | Davis |
| 1957-58 | (3N) | 1 | 16.11.57 | **Rochdale** (3N) | A | W | 2-0 | Harbertson 2 |
| | | 2 | 07.12.57 | **Boston Utd** (ML) | H | W | 5-3 | Harbertson 2 (1p), Carr 3 |
| | | 3 | 04.01.58 | **Norwich City** (3S) | A | W | 2-1 | Harbetson, Moran |
| | | 4 | 25.01.58 | **Chelsea** (D1) | A | D | 3-3 | Harbertson, Carr, Morton |
| | | 4r | 29.01.58 | **Chelsea** | H | W | 4-1 | Harbertson, Carr, Moran 2 |
| | | 5 | 15.02.58 | **Wolverhampton W** (D1) | A | L | 1-6 | Bell |
| 1958-59 | (D4) | 1 | 15.11.58 | **Wrexham** (D3) | A | W | 2-1 | McGrath 2 |
| | | 2 | 06.12.58 | **Halifax Town** (D3) | A | D | 1-1 | McGrath |
| | | 2r | 10.12.58 | **Halifax Town** | H | W | 3-0 | Morton, Carr, Bell |
| | | 3 | 10.01.59 | **Accrington Stanley** (D3) | A | L | 0-3 | |
| 1959-60 | (D4) | 1 | 14.11.59 | **Prescot Cables** (LC) | H | W | 4-0 | Fletcher og, Redfearn, Poole, Morton |
| | | 2 | 05.12.59 | **Doncaster Rovers** (D4) | A | L | 2-3 | Milner, Carr |

| | | | | | | | | |
|---|---|---|---|---|---|---|---|---|
| 1960-61 | (D4) | 1 | 05.11.60 | **Grimsby Town** (D3) | H | W | 2-0 | Robson 2 |
| | | 2 | 26.11.60 | **Hull City** (D3) | H | D | 1-1 | Baxter |
| | | 2r | 28.11.60 | **Hull City** | A | D | 1-1aet | Baxter |
| | | 2 2r | 05.12.60 | **Hull City** | | - | 1-1ab | Rayment |
| | | | | *played at Elland Road – match abandoned after 90 minutes – ground unplayable* | | | | |
| | | 2 3r | 12.12.60 | **Hull City** | | D | 0-0aet | |
| | | | | *played at Belle Vue, Doncaster* | | | | |
| | | 2 4r | 15.12.60 | **Hull City** | | L | 0-3 | |
| | | | | *played at Ayresome Park* | | | | |
| 1961-62 | (D4) | 1 | 04.11.61 | **Carlisle Utd** (D4) | H | L | 0-4 | |
| 1962-63 | (D4) | 1 | 03.11.62 | **Lincoln City** (D4) | A | D | 1-1 | Lawton |
| | | 1r | 07.11.62 | **Lincoln City** | H | L | 1-2 | Lawton |
| 1963-64 | (D4) | 1 | 16.11.63 | **Gateshead AFC** (NRL) | H | L | 1-4 | Lawton |
| 1964-65 | (D4) | 1 | 14.11.64 | **Scunthorpe Utd** (D3) | A | W | 2-1 | Lawton, Burlison |
| | | 2 | 05.12.64 | **Hartlepools Utd** (D4) | A | D | 0-0 | |
| | | 2r | 09.12.64 | **Hartlepools Utd** | H | W | 4-1 | Lawton 2, Maltby 2 (1p) |
| | | 3 | 09.01.65 | **Arsenal** (D1) | H | L | 0-2 | |
| 1965-66 | (D4) | 1 | 13.11.65 | **Bradford City** (D4) | H | W | 3-2 | Cummings, Greener, Conlon |
| | | 2 | 04.12.65 | **Oldham Athletic** (D3) | H | L | 0-1 | |
| 1966-67 | (D3) | 1 | 26.11.66 | **Stockport County** (D4) | H | D | 0-0 | |
| | | 1r | 29.11.66 | **Stockport County** | A | D | 1-1aet | Hellawell |
| | | 1 2r | 05.12.66 | **Stockport County** | | W | 4-2 | Conlon 2, Fidler, Hellawell |
| | | | | *played at Elland Road* | | | | |
| | | 2 | 07.01.67 | **Crewe Alexandra** (D4) | A | L | 1-2 | Ratcliffe |
| 1967-68 | (D4) | 1 | 13.12.67 | **Shrewsbury Town** (D3) | A | L | 0-3 | |
| 1968-69 | (D4) | 1 | 16.11.68 | **Grimsby Town** (D4) | H | W | 2-0 | Hale, Robson |
| | | 2 | 07.12.68 | **Barnsley** (D3) | H | D | 0-0 | |
| | | 2r | 10.12.68 | **Barnsley** | A | L | 0-1aet | |
| 1969-70 | (D4) | 1 | 15.11.69 | **Barnsley** (D3) | H | D | 0-0 | |
| | | 1r | 18.11.69 | **Barnsley** | A | L | 0-2 | |
| 1970-71 | (D4) | 1 | 21.11.70 | **Bangor City** (NPL) | H | W | 5-1 | Graham, Hale, Gauden 2, Harding |
| | | 2 | 12.12.70 | **Rochdale** (D3) | H | L | 0-2 | |
| 1971-72 | (D4) | 1 | 20.11.71 | **Barrow** (D4) | A | W | 2-0 | Peddelty, Sproates |
| | | 2 | 11.12.71 | **Port Vale** (D3) | A | L | 0-1 | |
| 1972-73 | (D4) | 1 | 18.11.72 | **Wrexham** (D3) | H | D | 1-1 | Sinclair |
| | | 1r | 22.11.72 | **Wrexham** | A | L | 0-5 | |
| 1973-74 | (D4) | 1 | 24.11.73 | **Scunthorpe Utd** (D4) | A | L | 0-1 | |
| 1974-75 | (D4) | 1 | 23.11.74 | **Workington** (D4) | H | W | 1-0 | Sinclair |
| | | 2 | 14.12.74 | **Blackburn Rovers** (D3) | A | L | 0-1 | |
| 1975-76 | (D4) | 1 | 22.11.75 | **Chester** (D3) | H | D | 0-0 | |
| | | 1r | 26.11.75 | **Chester** | A | L | 0-2 | |
| 1976-77 | (D4) | 1 | 20.11.76 | **Scarborough** (NPL) | A | D | 0-0 | |
| | | 1r | 22.11.76 | **Scarborough** | H | W | 4-1 | Rowles 3, Seal |
| | | 2 | 15.12.76 | **Sheffield Wed** (D3) | H | W | 1-0 | Ferguson |
| | | 3 | 08.01.77 | **Orient** (D2) | H | D | 2-2 | Seal 2 |
| | | 3r | 11.01.77 | **Orient** | A | D | 0-0aet | |
| | | 3 2r | 17.01.77 | **Orient** | | L | 0-3 | |
| | | | | *played at White Hart Lane* | | | | |
| 1977-78 | (D4) | 1 | 26.11.77 | **Chester** (D3) | A | L | 1-4 | Craig |
| 1978-79 | (D4) | 1 | 25.11.78 | **Chesterfield** (D3) | H | D | 1-1 | Ferguson |
| | | 1r | 06.12.78 | **Chesterfield** | A | W | 1-0 | Ferguson |
| | | 2 | 16.12.78 | **Chester** (D3) | H | W | 2-1 | Craig, Ferguson |
| | | 3 | 09.01.79 | **Colchester Utd** (D3) | H | L | 0-1 | |
| 1979-80 | (D4) | 1 | 24.11.79 | **Huddersfield Town** (D4) | H | D | 1-1 | Stalker |
| | | 1r | 27.11.79 | **Huddersfield Town** | A | W | 1-0 | Stalker |
| | | 2 | 15.12.79 | **Bradford City** (D4) | H | L | 0-1 | |
| 1980-81 | (D4) | 1 | 22.11.80 | **Bury** (D4) | H | L | 0-2 | |
| 1981-82 | (D4) | 1 | 21.11.81 | **Carlisle Utd** (D3) | H | D | 2-2 | Speedie, Walsh |
| | | 1r | 24.11.81 | **Carlisle Utd** | A | L | 1-3 | Smith |
| 1982-83 | (D4) | 1 | 20.11.82 | **Scunthorpe Utd** (D4) | H | L | 0-1 | |
| 1983-84 | (D4) | 1 | 19.11.83 | **Mossley** (NPL) | H | W | 5-0 | Barton, Walsh 3, McLean |
| | | 2 | 10.12.83 | **Altrincham** (APL) | H | D | 0-0 | |

| | | | | | | | | |
|---|---|---|---|---|---|---|---|---|
| | | 2r | 14.12.83 | **Altrincham** | A | W | 2-0 | Todd, Walsh |
| | | 3 | 07.01.84 | **Maidstone Utd** (APL) | H | W | 4-1 | Davies, Walsh, Cartwright, McLean |
| | | 4 | 28.01.84 | **Plymouth Argyle** (D3) | A | L | 1-2 | Todd |
| 1984-85 | (D4) | 1 | 17.11.84 | **Chester City** (D4) | H | W | 3-2 | Airey 2, MacDonald |
| | | 2 | 08.12.84 | **Frickley Athletic** (APL) | H | W | 1-0 | LLoyd |
| | | 3 | 05.01.85 | **Middlesbrough** (D2) | A | D | 0-0 | |
| | | 3r | 08.01.85 | **Middlesbrough** | H | W | 2-1 | MacDonald, LLoyd |
| | | 4 | 29.01.85 | **Telford Utd** (APL) | H | D | 1-1 | Forster |
| | | 4r | 04.02.85 | **Telford Utd** | A | L | 0-3 | |
| 1985-86 | (D3) | 1 | 16.11.85 | **Rochdale** (D4) | A | L | 1-2 | Hicks og |
| 1986-87 | (D3) | 1 | 16.11.86 | **Mansfield Town** (D3) | H | W | 2-1 | Ward, Graham og |
| | | 2 | 06.12.86 | **Wigan Athletic** (D3) | H | L | 0-5 | |
| 1987-88 | (D4) | 1 | 14.11.87 | **Sunderland** (D3) | A | L | 0-2 | |
| 1988-89 | (D4) | 1 | 19.11.88 | **Notts County** (D3) | H | L | 1-2 | Leonard og |
| 1989-90 | (Conf) | 4Q | 28.10.89 | **Runcorn** (Conf) | H | W | 4-2 | Borthwick, Corner (p), McJannet, Stephens |
| | | 1 | 18.11.89 | **Northwich Vic** (Conf) | H | W | 6-2 | Cork, McJannet, Corner 2, Toman, Anderson |
| | | 2 | 09.12.89 | **Halifax Town** (D4) | H | W | 3-0 | Coverdale, McJannet,Borthwick |
| | | 3 | 06.01.90 | **Cambridge Utd** (D4) | A | D | 0-0 | |
| | | 3r | 09.01.90 | **Cambridge Utd** | H | L | 1-3 | McJannet |
| 1990-91 | (D4) | 1 | 17.11.90 | **York City** (D4) | H | D | 1-1 | Gill |
| | | 1r | 19.11.90 | **York City** | A | L | 0-1 | |
| 1991-92 | (D3) | 1 | 16.11.91 | **Chesterfield** (D4) | H | W | 2-1 | Ellison (p), Smith |
| | | 2 | 17.12.91 | **Hartlepool Utd** (D3) | H | L | 1-2 | Toman |
| 1992-93 | (D3) | 1 | 14.11.92 | **Hull City** (D2) | H | L | 1-2 | Dobie |
| 1993-94 | (D3) | 1 | 13.11.93 | **Crewe Alexandra** (D3) | A | L | 2-4 | Ellison, Painter |
| 1994-95 | (D3) | 1 | 12.11.94 | **Hyde Utd** (NPL) | A | W | 3-1 | Slaven, Warboys 2 |
| | | 2 | 04.12.94 | **Carlisle Utd** (D3) | A | L | 0-2 | |
| 1995-96 | (D3) | 1 | 11.11.95 | **Hartlepool Utd** (D3) | A | W | 4-2 | Brumwell, Gaughan, Bannister, Painter |
| | | 2 | 02.12.95 | **Rochdale** (D3) | A | D | 2-2 | Shaw, Olsson |
| | | 2r | 12.12.95 | **Rochdale** | H | L | 0-1 | |
| 1996-97 | (D3) | 1 | 16.11.96 | **Runcorn** (NPL) | A | W | 4-1 | Naylor, Shaw, Crosby, Brumwell |
| | | 2 | 07.12.96 | **Carlisle Utd** (D3) | A | L | 0-1 | |
| 1997-98 | (D3) | 1 | 15.11.97 | **Solihull Borough** (SL) | H | D | 1-1 | Naylor |
| | | 1r | 26.11.97 | **Solihull Borough** | A | D | 3-3aet | Atkinson (p), Robinson, Dorner |
| | | | | *Darlington won 4-2 on penalties* | | | | |
| | | 2 | 06.12.97 | **Hednesford Town** (Conf) | A | W | 1-0 | Roberts (p) |
| | | 3 | 14.01.98 | **Wolverhampton W** (D1) | H | L | 0-4 | |
| 1998-99 | (D3) | 1 | 17.11.98 | **Burnley** (D2) | H | W | 3-2 | Atkinson, Dorner, Barnard |
| | | 2 | 04.12.98 | **Manchester City** (D2) | H | D | 1-1 | Bennett |
| | | 2r | 15.12.98 | **Manchester City** | A | L | 0-1aet | |
| 1999-00 | (D3) | 1 | 30.10.99 | **Southport** (Conf) | H | W | 2-1 | Tutill, Gabbiadini (p) |
| | | 2 | 20.11.99 | **Gillingham** (D2) | A | L | 1-3 | Duffield |
| | | | | *Darlington were re-instated in Round Three following a 'Lucky Loser' draw to fill the place left by Manchester United who did not enter the competition because of their involvement in the FIFA Club World Championship in Brazil* | | | | |
| | | 3 | 11.12.99 | **Aston Villa** (PL) | A | L | 1-2 | Heckingbottom |
| 2000-01 | (D3) | 1 | 18.11.00 | **AFC Sudbury** (ECL) | H | W | 6-1 | Naylor 3, Hodgson 2, Kyle |
| | | 2 | 09.12.00 | **Luton Town** (D2) | H | D | 0-0 | |
| | | 2r | 19.12.00 | **Luton Town** | A | L | 0-2 | |
| 2001-02 | (D3) | 1 | 17.11.01 | **Kidderminster H** (D3) | A | W | 1-0 | Campbell |
| | | 2 | 08.12.01 | **Altrincham** (NPL) | A | W | 2-1 | Chillingworth, Wainwright |
| | | 3 | 15.01.02 | **Peterborough Utd** (D2) | H | D | 2-2 | Wainwright, Conlon |
| | | 3r | 21.01.02 | **Peterborough Utd** | A | L | 0-2 | |
| 2002-03 | (D3) | 1 | 16.11.02 | **Wrexham** (D3) | A | W | 2-0 | Conlon, Liddle |
| | | 2 | 07.12.02 | **Stevenage B** (Conf) | H | W | 4-1 | Hodgson, Offiong 2, Conlon |
| | | 3 | 04.01.03 | **Farnborough T** (Conf) | H | L | 2-3 | Nicholls, Clark |

# DARTFORD

*Formed 1888. First entered FA Cup: 1895-96. FA Trophy runners-up: 1974. League clubs beaten: Cardiff City, Exeter City, Aldershot. Members of the Southern League.*

| | | | | | | | | |
|---|---|---|---|---|---|---|---|---|
| 1927-28 | (SL) | 1 | 26.11.27 | **Crystal Palace** (3S) | H | L | 1-3 | Thomson |
| 1932-33 | (SL) | 1 | 26.11.32 | **Yeovil & Petters Utd** (SL) | H | D | 0-0 | |
| | | 1r | 01.12.32 | **Yeovil & Petters Utd** | A | L | 2-4 | Hunt 2 |
| 1933-34 | (SL) | 1 | 25.11.33 | **Northfleet Utd** (KL) | A | W | 2-0 | Phillips, Haley |
| | | 2 | 09.12.33 | **Swindon Town** (3S) | A | L | 0-1 | |
| 1934-35 | (SL) | 1 | 24.11.34 | **Bedford Town** (UCL) | A | W | 3-2 | Meads 2, Starsmore |
| | | 2 | 08.12.34 | **Bristol Rovers** (3S) | H | L | 0-1 | |
| 1935-36 | (SL) | 1 | 30.11.35 | **Cardiff City** (3S) | A | W | 3-0 | Harron, Mercer, Meads |
| | | 2 | 14.12.35 | **Gainsborough T** (ML) | H | W | 4-0 | Dell 3, Meads |
| | | 3 | 11.01.36 | **Derby County** (D1) | A | L | 2-3 | Dell, Harron |
| 1936-37 | (SL) | 1 | 28.11.36 | **Peterborough Utd** (ML) | H | W | 3-0 | Gardiner, Meads 2 |
| | | 2 | 12.12.36 | **Shildon** (NL) | A | W | 3-0 | Meads, Moseley 2 |
| | | 3 | 16.01.37 | **Darlington** (3N) | H | L | 0-1 | |
| 1937-38 | (SL) | 1 | 27.11.37 | **Bournemouth** (3S) | A | D | 0-0 | |
| | | 1r | 01.12.37 | **Bournemouth** | H | L | 0-6 | |
| 1947-48 | (SL) | 1 | 29.11.47 | **Bristol City** (3S) | H | D | 0-0aet | |
| | | 1r | 06.12.47 | **Bristol City** | A | L | 2-9 | Gibbons 2 |
| 1948-49 | (SL) | 1 | 27.11.48 | **Leyton Orient** (3S) | H | L | 2-3 | Viles 2 |
| 1950-51 | (SL) | 1 | 25.11.50 | **Guildford City** (SL) | A | W | 5-1 | Jefferies, Kelly 2, Butler, Shallcross |
| | | 2 | 09.12.50 | **Reading** (3S) | A | L | 0-4 | |
| 1961-62 | (SL) | 1 | 04.11.61 | **Exeter City** (D4) | A | D | 3-3 | Taylor 2, White |
| | | 1r | 08.11.61 | **Exeter City** | H | W | 2-1 | Fletcher, Taylor |
| | | 2 | 25.11.61 | **Bristol City** (D3) | A | L | 2-8 | Fletcher, Pacey |
| 1962-63 | (SL) | 1 | 03.11.62 | **Yeovil Town** (SL) | A | L | 2-3 | Ripley, Pacey |
| 1964-65 | (SL) | 1 | 14.11.64 | **Aldershot** (D4) | H | D | 1-1 | Sitford |
| | | 1r | 17.11.64 | **Aldershot** | A | L | 0-1 | |
| 1965-66 | (SL) | 1 | 13.11.65 | **Barnet** (SL) | A | W | 2-0 | Stepney, Dennis |
| | | 2 | 04.12.65 | **Port Vale** (D4) | A | L | 0-1 | |
| 1968-69 | (SL) | 1 | 16.11.68 | **Aldershot** (D4) | H | W | 3-1 | Sitford, Burns (p), Ripley |
| | | 2 | 07.12.68 | **Kettering Town** (SL) | A | L | 0-5 | |
| 1974-75 | (SL) | 1 | 23.11.74 | **Plymouth Argyle** (D3) | H | L | 2-3 | Henderson 2 |
| 1975-76 | (SL) | 1 | 22.11.75 | **Bishop's Stortford** (IL) | H | L | 1-4 | Reeves |
| 1976-77 | (SL) | 1 | 20.11.76 | **Tooting & M** (IL) | A | L | 2-4 | Greenhalgh, Brown |
| 1978-79 | (SL) | 1 | 25.11.78 | **AP Leamington** (SL) | H | L | 1-2 | Jones |
| 1982-83 | (SL) | 1 | 20.11.82 | **Worthing** (IL) | A | L | 1-2 | Lazarus |
| 1983-84 | (SL) | 1 | 19.11.83 | **Millwall** (D3) | A | L | 1-2 | Simmonds (p) |
| 1984-85 | (APL) | 1 | 17.11.84 | **Metropolitan Police** (IL) | A | W | 3-0 | Burman, Cowley, Borg |
| | | 2 | 08.12.84 | **Bournemouth** (D3) | H | D | 1-1 | Robinson |
| | | 2r | 11.12.84 | **Bournemouth** | A | L | 1-4 | Dingwall |
| 1985-86 | (APL) | 1 | 16.11.85 | **Bournemouth** (D3) | A | D | 0-0 | |
| | | 1r | 19.11.85 | **Bournemouth** | H | L | 0-2 | |
| 1986-87 | (SL) | 1 | 15.11.86 | **Enfield** (Conf) | H | D | 1-1 | Robinson |
| | | 1r | 18.11.86 | **Enfield** | A | L | 0-3 | |
| 1988-89 | (SL) | 1 | 19.11.88 | **Kettering Town** (Conf) | A | L | 1-2 | Taylor (p) |
| 1989-90 | (SL) | 1 | 18.11.89 | **Exeter City** (D4) | H | D | 1-1 | Hessenthaler |
| | | 1r | 22.11.89 | **Exeter City** | A | L | 1-4 | Johnson |

# DARWEN

*Formed 1870. Reformed 1899. FA Cup best performance: Semi-finals 1881. Members of Football League 1891-99. League club beaten after leaving the Football League: Chester. Members of the North West Counties League.*

| | | | | | | | | |
|---|---|---|---|---|---|---|---|---|
| 1877-78 | | 1 | 07.11.77 | **Manchester FC** | H | W | 3-0 | Lewis, 2 others |
| | | 2 | 29.12.77 | **Sheffield FC** | A | L | 0-1 | |
| 1878-79 | | 1 | | **Birch, Manchester** | | | - | |
| | | | | *Birch scratched. Darwen walkover* | | | | |
| | | 2 | 07.12.78 | **Eagley** | H | D | 0-0 | |
| | | 2r | 21.12.78 | **Eagley** | A | W | 4-1 | Love 2, Gledhill, Marshall |
| | | 3 | 30.01.79 | **Remnants** | A | W | 3-2 | Love 2, Bury |
| | | 4 | 13.02.79 | **Old Etonians** | A | D | 5-5 | Love, og, 3 others |
| | | | | *played at Kennington Oval* | | | | |

| | | | | | | | | |
|---|---|---|---|---|---|---|---|---|
| | | 4r | 08.03.79 | **Old Etonians** | A | D | 2-2aet | Clerke, Whitfield |
| | | | | *played at Kennington Oval* | | | | |
| | | 4 2r | 15.03.79 | **Old Etonians** | A | L | 2-6 | Marshall, F Suter |
| | | | | *played at Kennington Oval* | | | | |
| 1879-80 | | 1 | 25.10.79 | **Eagley** | A | W | 1-0 | Rostron |
| | | 2 | 06.12.79 | **Blackburn Rovers** | A | L | 1-3 | E Suter |
| 1880-81 | | 1 | 13.11.80 | **Brigg Town** | H | W | 8-0 | Rostron 3, Marshall, Moorhouse, 3 others |
| | | 2 | 18.12.80 | **Sheffield FC** | A | W | 5-1 | Bury 2, Rostron, 2 others |
| | | *3* | | bye | | | | |
| | | 4 | 05.02.81 | **Sheffield Wed** | H | W | 5-2 | Bury 3, Rostron 2 |
| | | 5 | 05.03.81 | **Romford** (1876) | H | W | 15-0 | Kirkham 3, Marshall 3, Mellor 3, Rostron 3, Bury, 2 others |
| | | SF | 26.03.81 | **Old Carthusians** | | L | 1-4 | Marshall |
| | | | | *played at Kennington Oval* | | | | |
| 1881-82 | | 1 | 29.10.81 | **Blackburn Olympic** | H | W | 3-1 | Bury, Rostron, Towers |
| | | 2 | 26.11.81 | **Accrington FC** | H | W | 3-1 | Rostron 2, Marshall |
| | | 3 | 17.12.81 | **Turton** | H | W | 4-1 | Kirkham, Marshall, Rostron, Towers |
| | | 4 | 30.01.82 | **Blackburn Rovers** | A | L | 1-5 | own goal |
| 1882-83 | | 1 | 21.10.82 | **Blackburn Park Road** | H | W | 4-1 | |
| | | 2 | 02.12.82 | **Blackburn Rovers** | H | W | 1-0 | Mellor |
| | | 3 | 06.01.83 | **Church FC** | A | D | 2-2 | Ashton, Marshall |
| | | 3r | 20.01.83 | **Church FC** | H | L | 0-2 | |
| 1883-84 | | 1 | 27.10.83 | **Church FC** | H | D | 2-2 | |
| | | 1r | 03.11.83 | **Church FC** | A | W | 1-0 | |
| | | 2 | 01.12.83 | **Blackburn Olympic** | H | L | 1-2aet | |
| 1884-85 | | 1 | 11.10.84 | **Bradshaw** | H | W | 11-0 | Kenyon 2, Owers, 8 others |
| | | 2 | 22.11.84 | **Fishwick Ramblers** | A | W | 2-0 | Kenyon, Walsh |
| | | *3* | | bye | | | | |
| | | 4 | 17.01.85 | **Church FC** | A | L | 0-3 | |
| 1885-86 | | 1 | 31.10.85 | **Derby Junction** | H | D | 2-2 | |
| | | 1r | 07.11.85 | **Derby Junction** | H | W | 4-0 | |
| | | 2 | 21.11.85 | **Small Heath Alliance** | A | L | 1-3 | |
| 1886-87 | | 1 | 30.10.86 | **Heart of Midlothian** | H | W | 7-1 | Nightingale 4, Broughton, Rostron, Slater |
| | | 2 | | Astley Bridge | | | - | |
| | | | | *Astley Bridge scratched. Darwen walkover* | | | | |
| | | 3 | 11.12.86 | **Bolton Wanderers** | H | W | 4-3 | Rostron, 3 others |
| | | *4* | | bye | | | | |
| | | 5 | 22.01.87 | **Chirk** | A | W | 2-1 | Rostron 2 |
| | | 6 | 12.02.87 | **Aston Villa** | A | L | 2-3 | Rostron, Slater |
| 1887-88 | | 1 | 15.10.87 | **Rawtenstall** | A | W | 3-1 | |
| | | 2 | 05.11.87 | **Church FC** | H | W | 2-0 | |
| | | 3 | 26.11.87 | **Witton** | H | D | 1-1 | Shorrock |
| | | 3r | 03.12.87 | **Witton** | | W | 2-0 | Dimmock, Shorrock |
| | | | | *played at Blackburn* | | | | |
| | | 4 | 17.12.87 | **Notts Rangers** | H | W | 2-1 | Smith 2, Shorrock |
| | | 5 | 07.01.88 | **Blackburn Rovers** | H | L | 0-3 | |
| 1890-91 | (FAll) | 1 | 17.01.91 | **Kidderminster FC** (BDL) | H | W | 3-1 | Marsden 2, Atkins og |
| | | | | *FA ordered replay after protest* | | | | |
| | | 1r | 24.01.91 | **Kidderminster FC** (BDL) | H | W | 13-0 | Nightingale 2, Entwistle 2, Marsden, Owen, J Smith, R Smith, 5 others |
| | | 2 | 31.01.91 | **Sunderland** (D1) | H | L | 0-2 | |
| 1891-92 | (D1) | 1 | 16.01.92 | **Bootle** (FAll) | A | W | 2-0 | Alexander, Wade |
| | | 2 | 30.01.92 | **Aston Villa** (D1) | A | L | 0-2 | |
| 1892-93 | (D2) | 1 | 21.01.93 | **Aston Villa** (D1) | H | W | 5-4 | Entwistle 3, McAvoy, Sutherland |
| | | 2 | 03.02.93 | **Grimsby Town** (D2) | H | W | 2-0 | Sutherland, Wade |
| | | 3 | 18.02.93 | **Wolverhampton W** (D1) | A | L | 0-5 | |
| 1893-94 | (D1) | 1 | 27.01.94 | **Derby County** (D1) | A | L | 0-2 | |
| 1894-95 | (D2) | 1 | 02.02.95 | **Wolverhampton W** (D1) | H | D | 0-0 | |
| | | 1r | 06.02.95 | **Wolverhampton W** | A | L | 0-2 | |

| | | | | | | | | |
|---|---|---|---|---|---|---|---|---|
| 1895-96 | (D2) | 1 | 01.02.96 | **Grimsby Town** (D2) | H | L | 0-2 | |
| 1896-97 | (D2) | | | 3q Blackpool H 1-0abnd; 3q Blackpool (H) 1-2 | | | | |
| 1897-98 | (D2) | | | 3q Blackpool (H) 3-2; 4q Chorley (H) 2-2; 4qr Chorley (A) 0-0; 4q2r Chorley 2-1 at Blackburn; 5q Wigan Co (H) 1-1; 5qr Wigan Co (A) 0-4 | | | | |
| 1898-99 | (D2) | | | 3q Wigan Co (H) 1-5 | | | | |
| 1931-32 | (LC) | 1 | 28.11.31 | **Peterborough & F** (SL) | H | W | 4-1 | Dale 2, Crompton, Quigley |
| | | 2 | 12.12.31 | **Chester** (3N) | H | W | 2-1 | Preedy 2 |
| | | 3 | 09.01.32 | **Arsenal** (D1) | A | L | 1-11 | Dale |
| 1932-33 | (LC) | 1 | 26.11.32 | **Halifax Town** (3N) | A | L | 0-2 | |
| 1933-34 | (LC) | 1 | 25.11.33 | **Gateshead AFC** (3N) | A | L | 2-5 | Preedy, Cooper |
| 1934-35 | (LC) | 1 | 24.11.34 | **Boston Utd** (ML) | H | L | 1-2 | Reid |
| 1935-36 | (LC) | 1 | 30.11.35 | **Scarborough** (ML) | A | L | 0-2 | |

## DARWEN OLD WANDERERS

*Formed 1879. Entered FA Cup: 1884-85 – 1887-88.*

| | | | | | | | |
|---|---|---|---|---|---|---|---|
| 1884-85 | 1 | 11.10.84 | **Higher Walton** | A | D | 1-1 | |
| | 1r | 08.11.84 | **Higher Walton** | H | W | 4-1 | |
| | 2 | 29.11.84 | **Bolton Association** | H | W | 7-2 | |
| | 3 | 20.12.84 | **Lower Darwen** | A | L | 2-4 | |
| 1885-86 | 1 | 17.10.85 | **Burnley** | H | W | 11-0 | |
| | | | *Burnley fielded a reserve team* | | | | |
| | 2 | 21.11.85 | **Accrington FC** | H | W | 2-1 | |
| | 3 | 05.12.85 | **Blackburn Rovers** | A | L | 1-6 | |
| 1886-87 | 1 | 23.10.86 | **Cowlairs** | H | L | 1-4 | |
| 1887-88 | 1 | 15.10.87 | **Burnley** | A | L | 0-4 | |
| | | | *FA ordered replay ordered after protest. Darwen Old Wanderers scratched* | | | | |

## DARWEN RAMBLERS

*Formed 1878. played at the Hill House Ground, Darwen. Entered FA Cup: 1882-83 – 1884-85*

| | | | | | | | |
|---|---|---|---|---|---|---|---|
| 1882-83 | 1 | 14.10.82 | **South Shore** | H | W | 5-2 | |
| | 2 | 02.12.82 | **Haslingden** | H | W | 3-2 | |
| | 3 | 16.12.82 | **Blackburn Olympic** | A | L | 0-8 | |
| 1883-84 | 1 | 13.10.83 | **Blackburn Olympic** | A | L | 1-5 | T Kenyon |
| 1884-85 | 1 | 01.11.84 | **Fishwick Ramblers** | H | L | 1-2 | |

## DAVENHAM

*Formed 1879. Played home matches in the grounds of Davenham School, Northwich. Welsh FA Cup runners-up: 1887.*

| | | | | | | | |
|---|---|---|---|---|---|---|---|
| 1883-84 | 1 | 10.11.83 | **Macclesfield T** | H | W | 2-0 | |
| | 2 | 24.11.83 | **Northwich Vic** | A | L | 1-5 | Earlham |
| 1884-85 | 1 | 25.10.84 | **Chirk** | A | L | 2-4 | |
| 1885-86 | 1 | 31.10.85 | **Goldenhill** | H | W | 2-1 | |
| | 2 | 21.11.85 | **Macclesfield T** | H | W | 8-1 | |
| | 3 | 12.12.85 | **Crewe Alexandra** | H | W | 2-1 | |
| | *4* | | bye | | | | |
| | 5 | 16.01.86 | **Small Heath Alliance** | H | L | 1-2 | Brooks |
| 1886-87 | 1 | 30.10.86 | **Burslem PV** | H | D | 1-1aet | |
| | 1r | 13.11.86 | **Burslem PV** | A | L | 0-3 | |
| 1887-88 | 1 | 15.10.87 | **Chester** | A | W | 3-2 | Stringer, 2 others |
| | 2 | 05.11.87 | **Wrexham Olympic** | A | W | 2-1 | Rowbottom, AN other |
| | 3 | 19.11.87 | **Chirk** | H | D | 2-2 | |
| | 3r | 26.11.87 | **Chirk** | A | L | 1-6 | |

## DENABY UNITED

*Formed 1895. First entered FA Cup: 1899-1900.*

| | | | | | | | | |
|---|---|---|---|---|---|---|---|---|
| 1927-28 | (ML) | 1 | 26.11.27 | **Southport** (3N) | H | L | 2-3 | Kelly 2 |
| 1932-33 | (ML) | 1 | 26.11.32 | **Carlisle Utd** (3N) | A | L | 0-1 | |
| 1958-59 | (ML) | 1 | 15.11.58 | **Oldham Athletic** (D4) | H | L | 0-2 | |

## DENTON

*Formed 1880. played at Chapel Green, Denton, Manchester.*

| | | | | | | | |
|---|---|---|---|---|---|---|---|
| 1887-88 | 1 | | South Shore | | | - | |
| | | | *Denton scratched. South Shore walkover* | | | | |

# DERBY COUNTY

*Formed 1884. Founder Members of the Football League 1888. FA Cup winners: 1946; Runners-up: 1898, 1899, 1903; Record FA Cup win: 8-1 v Barnsley St Peters, 1st round, 30.01.1897; Record FA Cup defeat: 2-11 v Everton, 1st round, 18.01.1890. They were also on the receiving end of the biggest defeat in an FA Cup final when they lost 0-6 to Bury on 18.04.1903.*

| | | | | | | | | |
|---|---|---|---|---|---|---|---|---|
| 1884-85 | | 1 | 08.11.84 | **Walsall Town** | H | L | 0-7 | |
| 1885-86 | | 1 | 31.10.85 | **Birmingham St G** | H | W | 3-0 | Smith, Spilsbury, Evans |
| | | 2 | 14.11.85 | **Aston Villa** | H | W | 2-0 | Smith, Evans |
| | | 3 | 12.12.85 | **Small Heath Alliance** | A | L | 2-4 | Evans 2 |
| 1886-87 | | 1 | 30.10.86 | **Aston Unity** | A | W | 4-1 | Evans 2, L Cooper, Knox |
| | | 2 | 20.11.86 | **Birmingham St G** | H | L | 1-2 | Bakewell |
| 1887-88 | | 1 | 15.10.87 | **Staveley** | A | W | 2-1 | Monks 2 |
| | | 2 | 05.11.87 | **Ecclesfield** | H | W | 6-0 | Spilsbury 3, Williamson, Bakewell, Needham |
| | | 3 | 26.11.87 | **Owlerton** | H | W | 6-2 | Spilsbury 3, Needham 2, Nash |
| | | 4 | | bye | | | | |
| | | 5 | 07.01.88 | **Crewe Alexandra** | A | L | 0-1 | |
| 1888-89 | (D1) | 1 | 02.02.89 | **Derby Junction** | H | W | 1-0 | Higgins |
| | | 2 | 16.02.89 | **Aston Villa** (D1) | A | L | 3-5 | Cooper 2, L Plackett |
| 1889-90 | (D1) | 1 | 18.01.90 | **Everton** (D1) | H | L | 2-11 | J Goodall 2 |
| 1890-91 | (D1) | 1 | 17.01.91 | **Royal Arsenal** | A | W | 2-1 | Cooper, McMillan |
| | | 2 | 31.01.91 | **Sheffield Wed** (FAll) | H | L | 2-3 | Bakewell, J Goodall |
| 1891-92 | (D1) | 1 | 16.01.92 | **Blackburn Rovers** (D1) | A | L | 1-4 | Storer |
| 1892-93 | (D1) | 1 | 21.01.93 | **Sheffield Wed** (D1) | A | L | 2-3aet | J Goodall, Bloomer |
| | | | | *FA ordered match to be replayed because of protests* | | | | |
| | | 1 | 30.01.93 | **Sheffield Wed** (D1) | H | W | 1-0 | J Goodall |
| | | | | *FA ordered match to be replayed a second time because of various protests* | | | | |
| | | 1 | 02.02.93 | **Sheffield Wed** (D1) | A | L | 2-4 | J Goodall, Little |
| 1893-94 | (D1) | 1 | 27.01.94 | **Darwen** (D1) | H | W | 2-0 | J Goodall, McMillan |
| | | 2 | 10.02.94 | **Leicester Fosse** (ML) | A | D | 0-0 | |
| | | 2r | 17.02.94 | **Leicester Fosse** | H | W | 3-0 | Allan, McMillan, Francis |
| | | 3 | 24.02.94 | **Blackburn Rovers** (D1) | H | L | 1-4 | McMillan |
| 1894-95 | (D1) | 1 | 02.02.95 | **Aston Villa** (D1) | A | L | 1-2 | J Goodall |
| 1895-96 | (D1) | 1 | 01.02.96 | **Aston Villa** | H | W | 4-2 | Bloomer 2, Miller 2 |
| | | 2 | 15.02.96 | **Newton Heath** (D2) | A | D | 1-1 | Bloomer |
| | | 2r | 19.02.96 | **Newton Heath** | H | W | 5-1 | Miller 3, Bloomer, McQueen |
| | | 3 | 29.02.96 | **WBA** (D1) | H | W | 1-0 | A Goodall |
| | | SF | 21.03.96 | **Wolverhampton W** (D1) | | L | 1-2 | Bloomer |
| | | | | *played at Perry Barr, Birmingham* | | | | |
| 1896-97 | (D1) | 1 | 30.01.97 | **Barnsley** (ML) | H | W | 8-1 | Bloomer 3, Fisher 2, J Goodall, A Goodall, McQueen |
| | | 2 | 13.02.97 | **Bolton Wanderers** (D1) | H | W | 4-1 | Bloomer 3, Fisher |
| | | 3 | 27.02.97 | **Newton Heath** (D2) | H | W | 2-0 | Bloomer, McQueen |
| | | SF | 20.03.97 | **Everton** (D1) | | L | 2-3 | A Goodall, J Goodall |
| | | | | *played at Victoria Ground, Stoke* | | | | |
| 1897-98 | (D1) | 1 | 29.01.98 | **Aston Villa** (D1) | H | W | 1-0 | McQueen |
| | | 2 | 12.02.98 | **Wolverhampton W** (D1) | A | W | 1-0 | Leonard |
| | | 3 | 25.02.98 | **Liverpool** (D1) | H | D | 1-1 | Stevenson |
| | | 3r | 02.03.98 | **Liverpool** | A | W | 5-1 | Boag 3, Bloomer 2 |
| | | SF | 19.03.98 | **Everton** (D1) | | W | 3-1 | Bloomer 2, J Goodall |
| | | | | *played at Molineux* | | | | |
| | | F | 16.04.98 | **Nottingham Forest** (D1) | | L | 1-3 | Bloomer |
| | | | | *played at Crystal Palace* | | | | |
| 1898-99 | (D1) | 1 | 28.01.99 | **Woolwich Arsenal** (D2) | A | W | 6-0 | Bloomer 2, Boag 2, MacDonald, Allen |
| | | 2 | 11.02.99 | **Wolverhampton W** (D1) | H | W | 2-1 | Allen, MacDonald |
| | | 3 | 25.02.99 | **Southampton** (SL) | A | W | 2-1 | Bloomer, MacDonald |
| | | SF | 18.03.99 | **Stoke** (D1) | | W | 3-1 | Bloomer 3 |
| | | | | *played at Molineux* | | | | |
| | | F | 15.04.99 | **Sheffield Utd** (D1) | | L | 1-4 | Boag |
| | | | | *played at Crystal Palace* | | | | |
| 1899-00 | (D1) | 1 | 27.01.00 | **Sunderland** (D1) | H | D | 2-2 | A Goodall (p), Boag |

| | | | | | | | | |
|---|---|---|---|---|---|---|---|---|
| | | 1r | 31.01.00 | **Sunderland** | A | L | 0-3 | |
| 1900-01 | (D1) | 1 | 09.02.01 | **Bolton Wanderers** (D1) | A | L | 0-1 | |
| 1901-02 | (D1) | 1 | 01.02.02 | **Blackburn Rovers** (D1) | A | W | 2-0 | Warren 2 |
| | | 2 | 08.02.02 | **Lincoln City** (D2) | A | W | 3-1 | Warren 3 |
| | | 3 | 22.02.02 | **Portsmouth** (SL) | A | D | 0-0 | |
| | | 3r | 27.02.02 | **Portsmouth** | H | W | 6-3 | Bloomer 3, Warren 2, Boag |
| | | SF | 15.03.02 | **Sheffield Utd** (D1) | | D | 1-1 | Warren |
| | | | | *played at The Hawthorns* | | | | |
| | | SFr | 20.03.02 | **Sheffield Utd** (D1) | | D | 1-1aet | Wombwell |
| | | | | *played at Molineux* | | | | |
| | | SF 2r | 27.03.02 | **Sheffield Utd** (D1) | | L | 0-1 | |
| | | | | *played at City Ground, Nottingham* | | | | |
| 1902-03 | (D1) | 1 | 07.02.03 | **Small Heath** (D2) | H | W | 2-1 | Boag, Warrington |
| | | 2 | 21.02.03 | **Blackburn Rovers** (D1) | H | W | 2-0 | Bloomer, Warrington |
| | | 3 | 07.03.03 | **Stoke** (D1) | H | W | 3-0 | Warren, Davis, Warrington |
| | | SF | 21.03.03 | **Millwall Athletic** (SL) | | W | 3-0 | Warren, Boag, Richards |
| | | | | *played at Villa Park* | | | | |
| | | F | 18.04.03 | **Bury** (D1) | | L | 0-6 | |
| | | | | *played at Crystal Palace* | | | | |
| 1903-04 | (D1) | 1 | 06.02.04 | **Portsmouth** (SL) | A | W | 5-2 | Bloomer 2, Warren, Richards, Davis |
| | | 2 | 20.02.04 | **Wolverhampton W** (D1) | H | D | 2-2 | Warren 2 |
| | | 2r | 24.02.04 | **Wolverhampton W** | A | D | 2-2aet | Bloomer, Richards |
| | | 2 2r | 29.02.04 | **Wolverhampton W** | | W | 1-0 | Bloomer |
| | | | | *played at Villa Park* | | | | |
| | | 3 | 05.03.04 | **Blackburn Rovers** (D1) | H | W | 2-1 | Warrington, Bloomer |
| | | SF | 19.03.04 | **Bolton Wanderers** (D2) | | L | 0-1 | |
| | | | | *played at Molineux* | | | | |
| 1904-05 | (D1) | 1 | 04.02.05 | **Preston North End** (D1) | H | L | 0-2 | |
| 1905-06 | (D1) | 1 | 13.01.06 | **Kettering Town** (UCL) | H | W | 4-0 | J Davis, Hall, Warren (p), Fletcher |
| | | 2 | 03.02.06 | **Newcastle Utd** (D1) | H | D | 0-0 | |
| | | 2r | 07.02.06 | **Newcastle Utd** | A | L | 1-2 | Orr og |
| 1906-07 | (D1) | 1 | 12.01.07 | **Chesterfield** (D2) | H | D | 1-1 | Ransford |
| | | 1r | 16.01.07 | **Chesterfield** | A | - | 2-1ab | Long, Ransford |
| | | | | *abandoned after 114 minutes – bad light* | | | | |
| | | 1r | 21.01.07 | **Chesterfield** | | W | 4-0 | Long, A Wood, Bentley, Morris |
| | | | | *played at Trent Bridge, Nottingham* | | | | |
| | | 2 | 02.02.07 | **Lincoln City** (D2) | H | W | 1-0 | Bentley |
| | | 3 | 23.02.07 | **WBA** (D2) | A | L | 0-2 | |
| 1907-08 | (D2) | 1 | 11.01.08 | **Liverpool** (D1) | A | L | 2-4 | Bentley (p), Bevan |
| 1908-09 | (D2) | 1 | 16.01.09 | **Northampton Town** (SL) | A | D | 1-1 | Bentley |
| | | 1r | 20.01.09 | **Northampton Town** | H | W | 4-2 | Bentley 2, Davis, Thompson |
| | | 2 | 06.02.09 | **Leicester Fosse** (D1) | A | W | 2-0 | Bentley (p), Trueman |
| | | 3 | 20.02.09 | **Plymouth Argyle** (SL) | H | W | 1-0 | Bentley |
| | | 4 | 06.03.09 | **Nottingham Forest** (D1) | H | W | 3-0 | Bentley 3 |
| | | SF | 27.03.09 | **Bristol City** (D1) | | D | 1-1 | Garry |
| | | | | *played at Stamford Bridge* | | | | |
| | | SFr | 31.03.09 | **Bristol City** | | L | 1-2 | Davis |
| | | | | *played at St Andrews* | | | | |
| 1909-10 | (D2) | 1 | 15.01.10 | **Millwall Athletic** (SL) | H | W | 5-0 | Hall 2, Bentley, Davis, Barnes |
| | | 2 | 05.02.10 | **Aston Villa** (D1) | A | L | 1-6 | Bauchop |
| 1910-11 | (D2) | 1 | 14.01.11 | **Plymouth Argyle** (SL) | H | W | 2-1 | Bloomer, Barnes |
| | | 2 | 04.02.11 | **WBA** (D2) | H | W | 2-0 | Bauchop, Bloomer |
| | | 3 | 25.02.11 | **Everton** (D1) | H | W | 5-0 | Bloomer 2 (1p), Bentley, Barnes, Bauchop |
| | | 4 | 13.03.11 | **Newcastle Utd** (D1) | A | L | 0-4 | |
| 1911-12 | (D2) | 1 | 13.01.12 | **Newcastle Utd** | H | W | 3-0 | Bauchop, Richards, Leonard |
| | | 2 | 03.02.12 | **Blackburn Rovers** (D1) | H | L | 1-2 | Bloomer (p) |
| 1912-13 | (D1) | 1 | 15.01.13 | **Aston Villa** (D1) | H | L | 1-3 | Bloomer |
| 1913-14 | (D1) | 1 | 10.01.14 | **Northampton Town** (SL) | H | W | 1-0 | Moore |
| | | 2 | 31.01.14 | **Burnley** (D1) | A | L | 2-3 | Barnes, Waugh |
| 1914-15 | (D1) | 1 | 09.01.15 | **Leeds City** (D2) | H | L | 1-2 | Fordham |

| | | | | | | | | |
|---|---|---|---|---|---|---|---|---|
| 1919-20 | (D1) | 1 | 10.01.20 | **Blackpool** (D2) | A | D | 0-0 | |
| | | 1r | 14.01.20 | **Blackpool** | H | L | 1-4 | Burton |
| 1920-21 | (D1) | 1 | 08.01.21 | **Middlesbrough** (D1) | H | W | 2-0 | Murray, Burton |
| | | 2 | 29.01.21 | **Wolverhampton W** (D2) | H | D | 1-1 | Thornewell |
| | | 2r | 03.02.21 | **Wolverhampton W** | A | L | 0-1 | |
| 1921-22 | (D2) | 1 | 07.01.22 | **Aston Villa** (D1) | A | L | 1-6 | Moore |
| 1922-23 | (D2) | 1 | 13.01.23 | **Blackpool** (D2) | H | W | 2-0 | Moore, Lyons |
| | | 2 | 03.02.23 | **Bristol City** (3S) | A | W | 3-0 | Moore 2, Lyons (p) |
| | | 3 | 24.02.23 | **Sheffield Wed** (D2) | H | W | 1-0 | Moore |
| | | 4 | 10.03.23 | **Tottenham Hotspur** (D1) | A | W | 1-0 | Galloway |
| | | SF | 24.03.23 | **West Ham Utd** (D2) | | L | 2-5 | Moore, Henderson og |
| | | | | *played at Stamford Bridge* | | | | |
| 1923-24 | (D2) | 1 | 12.01.24 | **Bury** (D2) | H | W | 2-1 | Murphy, Whitehouse |
| | | 2 | 02.02.24 | **Newcastle Utd** (D1) | H | D | 2-2 | Storer 2 |
| | | 2r | 06.02.24 | **Newcastle Utd** | A | D | 2-2aet | Galloway, Mooney og |
| | | 2 2r | 11.02.24 | **Newcastle Utd** | | D | 2-2aet | Galloway, Thornewell |
| | | | | *played at Burnden Park* | | | | |
| | | 2 3r | 13.02.24 | **Newcastle Utd** | | L | 3-5 | Galloway 2, Storer |
| | | | | *played at St James' Park* | | | | |
| 1924-25 | (D2) | 1 | 10.01.25 | **Bradford City** (D2) | H | L | 0-1 | |
| 1925-26 | (D2) | 3 | 09.01.26 | **Portsmouth** (D2) | H | D | 0-0 | |
| | | 3r | 13.01.26 | **Portsmouth** | A | D | 1-1aet | Bedford |
| | | 3 2r | 18.01.26 | **Portsmouth** | | W | 2-0 | Thornewell, Bromage |
| | | | | *played at Filbert Street* | | | | |
| | | 4 | 30.01.26 | **Southend Utd** (3S) | A | L | 1-4 | Murphy |
| 1926-27 | (D1) | 3 | 08.01.27 | **Bradford City** (D2) | A | W | 6-2 | Bedford 4, Whitehouse, Murphy |
| | | 4 | 29.01.27 | **Millwall** (3S) | H | L | 0-2 | |
| 1927-28 | (D1) | 3 | 14.01.28 | **Millwall** | A | W | 2-1 | Stephenson, Bedford |
| | | 4 | 28.01.28 | **Nottingham Forest** (D2) | H | D | 0-0 | |
| | | 4r | 01.02.28 | **Nottingham Forest** | A | L | 0-2 | |
| 1928-29 | (D1) | 3 | 12.01.29 | **Notts County** (D2) | H | W | 4-3 | Bedford 2, Whitehouse 2 |
| | | 4 | 26.01.29 | **Blackburn Rovers** (D1) | A | D | 1-1 | Bedford |
| | | 4r | 30.01.29 | **Blackburn Rovers** | H | L | 0-3 | |
| 1929-30 | (D1) | 3 | 11.01.30 | **Bristol City** (D2) | H | W | 5-1 | Stephenson 2, Barclay 2, Bedford |
| | | 4 | 25.01.30 | **Bradford Park A** (D2) | H | D | 1-1 | Barclay |
| | | 4r | 29.01.30 | **Bradford Park A** | A | L | 1-2 | Ramage |
| 1930-31 | (D1) | 3 | 10.01.31 | **Exeter City** (3S) | A | L | 2-3 | Bowers 2 |
| 1931-32 | (D1) | 3 | 09.01.32 | **Burnley** (D2) | A | W | 4-0 | Neal 2, Alderman, Crooks |
| | | 4 | 23.01.32 | **Blackburn Rovers** (D1) | H | W | 3-2 | Ramage 2, Bowers |
| | | 5 | 13.02.32 | **Manchester City** (D1) | A | L | 0-3 | |
| 1932-33 | (D1) | 3 | 14.01.33 | **Wolverhampton W** (D1) | A | W | 6-3 | Bowers 3, Duncan 2, Crooks |
| | | 4 | 28.01.33 | **Southend Utd** (3S) | A | W | 3-2 | Bowers 2, Fabian |
| | | 5 | 18.02.33 | **Aldershot** (3S) | H | W | 2-0 | Bowers 2 |
| | | 6 | 04.03.33 | **Sunderland** (D1) | H | D | 4-4 | Duncan 2, Ramage, Bowers |
| | | 6r | 08.03.33 | **Sunderland** | A | W | 1-0 | Ramage |
| | | SF | 18.03.33 | **Manchester City** (D1) | | L | 2-3 | Fabian, Crooks |
| | | | | *played at Leeds Road, Huddersfield* | | | | |
| 1933-34 | (D1) | 3 | 13.01.34 | **Bristol City** (3S) | A | D | 1-1 | Nicholas |
| | | 3r | 17.01.34 | **Bristol City** | H | W | 1-0 | Bowers |
| | | 4 | 27.01.34 | **Wolverhampton W** (D1) | H | W | 3-0 | Bowers 2, Crooks |
| | | 5 | 17.02.34 | **Arsenal** (D1) | A | L | 0-1 | |
| 1934-35 | (D1) | 3 | 12.01.35 | **York City** (3N) | A | W | 1-0 | Crooks |
| | | 4 | 26.01.35 | **Swansea Town** (D2) | H | W | 3-0 | Duncan, Groves, Gallacher |
| | | 5 | 16.02.35 | **Everton** (D1) | A | L | 1-3 | Crooks |
| 1935-36 | (D1) | 3 | 11.01.36 | **Dartford** (SL) | H | W | 3-2 | Gallacher, Crooks, Napier |
| | | 4 | 25.01.36 | **Nottingham Forest** (D2) | H | W | 2-0 | Halford, Bowers |
| | | 5 | 15.02.36 | **Bradford City** (D2) | A | W | 1-0 | Bowers |
| | | 6 | 29.02.36 | **Fulham** (D2) | A | L | 0-3 | |
| 1936-37 | (D1) | 3 | 16.01.37 | **Bradford Park A** (D2) | A | W | 4-0 | Napier, Astley, Duncan, Stockill |
| | | 4 | 30.01.37 | **Brentford** (D1) | H | W | 3-0 | Astley 3 |
| | | 5 | 20.02.37 | **Millwall** (3S) | A | L | 1-2 | Keen |

| | | | | | | | | |
|---|---|---|---|---|---|---|---|---|
| 1937-38 | (D1) | 3 | 08.01.38 | **Stoke City** (D1) | H | L | 1-2 | Nicholas (p) |
| 1938-39 | (D1) | 3 | 07.01.39 | **Everton** (D1) | H | L | 0-1 | |
| 1945-46 | (D1) | 3 1L | 05.01.46 | **Luton Town** (D2) | A | W | 6-0 | Stamps 4, Crooks, Carter |
| | | 3 2L | 09.01.46 | **Luton Town** | H | W | 3-0 | Carter 2, Morrison |
| | | 4 1L | 26.01.46 | **WBA** (D2) | H | W | 1-0 | Doherty |
| | | 4 2L | 30.01.46 | **WBA** | A | W | 3-1 | Carter, Stamps (p), Harrison |
| | | 5 1L | 09.02.46 | **Brighton** (3S) | A | W | 4-1 | Doherty 2 (1p), Carter 2 |
| | | 5 2L | 13.02.46 | **Brighton** | H | W | 6-0 | Carter 3, Doherty 2, Crooks |
| | | 6 1L | 02.03.46 | **Aston Villa** (D1) | A | W | 4-3 | Doherty 2, Carter, Crooks |
| | | 6 2L | 09.03.46 | **Aston Villa** | H | D | 1-1 | Carter |
| | | SF | 23.03.46 | **Birmingham City** (D2) *played at Hillsborough* | | D | 1-1 | Carter |
| | | SFr | 27.03.46 | **Birmingham City** *played at Maine Road* | | W | 4-0aet | Doherty 2, Stamps 2 |
| | | F | 27.04.46 | **Charlton Athletic** (D1) *played at Wembley Stadium* | | W | 4-1aet | Stamps 2, Doherty, Turner og |
| 1946-47 | (D1) | 3 | 11.01.47 | **Bournemouth** (3S) | A | W | 2-0 | Ward, Carter |
| | | 4 | 25.01.47 | **Chelsea** (D1) | A | D | 2-2 | Stamps, Carter |
| | | 4r | 29.01.47 | **Chelsea** | H | W | 1-0aet | Stamps |
| | | 5 | 08.02.47 | **Liverpool** (D1) | A | L | 0-1 | |
| 1947-48 | (D1) | 3 | 10.01.48 | **Chesterfield** (D2) | H | W | 2-0 | Stamps, Harrison |
| | | 4 | 24.01.48 | **Crewe Alexandra** (3N) | A | W | 3-0 | Steel 2, Harrison |
| | | 5 | 07.02.48 | **Middlesbrough** (D1) | A | W | 2-1 | Harrison, Stamps |
| | | 6 | 28.02.48 | **QPR** (3S) | A | D | 1-1aet | Steel |
| | | 6r | 06.03.48 | **QPR** | H | W | 5-0 | Stamps 2, Carter 2, Steel |
| | | SF | 13.03.48 | **Manchester Utd** (D1) *played at Hillsborough* | | L | 1-3 | Steel |
| 1948-49 | (D1) | 3 | 08.01.49 | **Southport** (3N) | H | W | 4-1 | Harrison 2, Powell 2 |
| | | 4 | 29.01.49 | **Arsenal** (D1) | H | W | 1-0 | Steel |
| | | 5 | 12.02.49 | **Cardiff City** (D2) | H | W | 2-1 | Taft, Harrison |
| | | 6 | 26.02.49 | **Portsmouth** (D1) | A | L | 1-2 | Stamps |
| 1949-50 | (D1) | 3 | 07.01.50 | **Manchester City** (D1) | A | W | 5-3 | Stamps 3 (1p), Steel, Powell |
| | | 4 | 28.01.50 | **Bury** (D2) | A | D | 2-2 | Powell, Stamps |
| | | 4r | 01.02.50 | **Bury** | H | W | 5-2 | Stamps 3, Morris, Powell |
| | | 5 | 11.02.50 | **Northampton Town** (3S) | H | W | 4-2 | McLaren 2, Morris, Powell |
| | | 6 | 04.03.50 | **Everton** (D1) | H | L | 1-2 | Powell |
| 1950-51 | (D1) | 3 | 06.01.51 | **WBA** (D1) | H | D | 2-2 | Stamps 2 |
| | | 3r | 10.01.51 | **WBA** | A | W | 1-0 | Stamps |
| | | 4 | 27.01.51 | **Birmingham City** (D2) | H | L | 1-3 | Lee |
| 1951-52 | (D1) | 3 | 12.01.52 | **Middlesbrough** (D1) | A | D | 2-2 | Morris, Nielson |
| | | 3r | 16.01.52 | **Middlesbrough** | H | L | 0-2 | |
| 1952-53 | (D1) | 3 | 10.01.53 | **Chelsea** (D1) | H | D | 4-4 | Lee, Parry, McLachlan, McLaren |
| | | 3r | 14.01.53 | **Chelsea** | A | L | 0-1aet | |
| 1953-54 | (D2) | 3 | 09.01.54 | **Preston North End** (D1) | H | L | 0-2 | |
| 1954-55 | (D2) | 3 | 08.01.55 | **Manchester City** (D1) | H | L | 1-3 | Pye |
| 1955-56 | (3N) | 1 | 19.11.55 | **Crook Town** (NL) | A | D | 2-2 | Straw, Parry |
| | | 1r | 23.11.55 | **Crook Town** | H | W | 5-1 | Straw 2, Parry 2, Pye |
| | | 2 | 10.12.55 | **Boston Utd** (ML) | H | L | 1-6 | Pye (p) |
| 1956-57 | (3N) | 1 | 17.11.56 | **Bradford City** (3N) | H | W | 2-1 | Woodhead, Powell |
| | | 2 | 08.12.56 | **New Brighton** (LC) | H | L | 1-3 | Ryan |
| 1957-58 | (D2) | 3 | 04.01.58 | **Middlesbrough** (D2) | A | L | 0-5 | |
| 1958-59 | (D2) | 3 | 10.01.59 | **Preston North End** (D1) | H | D | 2-2 | Parry, Darwin |
| | | 3r | 19.01.59 | **Preston North End** | A | L | 2-4 | Cargill 2 (1p) |
| 1959-60 | (D2) | 3 | 09.01.60 | **Manchester Utd** (D1) | H | L | 2-4 | Thompson, Barrowcliffe (p) |
| 1960-61 | (D2) | 3 | 07.01.61 | **Brighton** (D2) | A | L | 1-3 | Thompson |
| 1961-62 | (D2) | 3 | 06.01.62 | **Leeds Utd** (D2) | A | D | 2-2 | Curry, Swallow |
| | | 3r | 10.01.62 | **Leeds Utd** | H | W | 3-1 | Curry 2, Bell og |
| | | 4 | 27.01.62 | **Charlton Athletic** (D2) | A | L | 1-2 | Curry |
| 1962-63 | (D2) | 3 | 04.02.63 | **Peterborough Utd** (D3) | H | W | 2-0 | Hutchinson 2 |
| | | 4 | 04.03.63 | **Leyton Orient** (D1) | A | L | 0-3 | |
| 1963-64 | (D2) | 3 | 04.01.64 | **Liverpool** (D1) | A | L | 0-5 | |

| | | | | | | | | |
|---|---|---|---|---|---|---|---|---|
| 1964-65 | (D2) | 3 | 09.01.65 | **Plymouth Argyle** (D2) | A | L | 2-4 | Durban, Hopkinson |
| 1965-66 | (D2) | 3 | 22.01.66 | **Manchester Utd** (D1) | H | L | 2-5 | Richardson (p), Upton |
| 1966-67 | (D2) | 3 | 28.01.67 | **Norwich City** (D2) | A | L | 0-3 | |
| 1967-68 | (D2) | 3 | 27.01.68 | **Leeds Utd** (D1) | A | L | 0-2 | |
| 1968-69 | (D2) | 3 | 04.01.69 | **Burnley** (D1) | A | L | 1-3 | Durban |
| 1969-70 | (D1) | 3 | 03.01.70 | **Preston North End** (D2) | A | D | 1-1 | Durban |
| | | 3r | 07.01.70 | **Preston North End** | H | W | 4-1 | Hector 2, Durban 2 |
| | | 4 | 24.01.70 | **Sheffield Utd** (D2) | H | W | 3-0 | O'Hare 2, Durban |
| | | 5 | 07.02.70 | **QPR** (D2) | A | L | 0-1 | |
| 1970-71 | (D1) | 3 | 02.01.71 | **Chester** (D4) | A | W | 2-1 | Wignall, Gemmill |
| | | 4 | 23.01.71 | **Wolverhampton W** (D1) | H | W | 2-1 | Hinton (p), O'Hare |
| | | 5 | 13.02.71 | **Everton** (D1) | A | L | 0-1 | |
| 1971-72 | (D1) | 3 | 15.01.72 | **Shrewsbury Town** (D3) | H | W | 2-0 | Hector 2 |
| | | 4 | 05.02.72 | **Notts County** (D3) | H | W | 6-0 | Durban 3, Robson, Hector, Hinton (p) |
| | | 5 | 26.02.72 | **Arsenal** (D1) | H | D | 2-2 | Durban, Hinton (p) |
| | | 5r | 29.02.72 | **Arsenal** | A | D | 0-0aet | |
| | | 5 2r | 13.03.72 | **Arsenal** | | L | 0-1 | |
| | | | | *played at Filbert Street* | | | | |
| 1972-73 | (D1) | 3 | 13.01.73 | **Peterborough Utd** (D4) | A | W | 1-0 | Davies |
| | | 4 | 03.02.73 | **Tottenham Hotspur** (D1) | H | D | 1-1 | Davies |
| | | 4r | 07.02.73 | **Tottenham Hotspur** | A | W | 5-3aet | Davies 3, Hector 2 |
| | | 5 | 24.02.73 | **QPR** (D2) | H | W | 4-2 | Hector 3, Davies |
| | | 6 | 17.03.73 | **Leeds Utd** (D1) | H | L | 0-1 | |
| 1973-74 | (D1) | 3 | 05.01.74 | **Boston Utd** (NPL) | H | D | 0-0 | |
| | | 3r | 09.01.74 | **Boston Utd** | A | W | 6-1 | Gemmill 3 (1p), Bourne 2, Nash |
| | | 4 | 27.01.74 | **Coventry City** (D1) | A | D | 0-0 | |
| | | 4r | 30.01.74 | **Coventry City** | H | L | 0-1aet | |
| 1974-75 | (D1) | 3 | 04.01.75 | **Orient** (D2) | A | D | 2-2 | Todd 2 |
| | | 3r | 08.01.75 | **Orient** | H | W | 2-1 | Lee, Rioch |
| | | 4 | 27.01.75 | **Bristol Rovers** (D2) | H | W | 2-0 | Hector, Rioch (p) |
| | | 5 | 18.02.75 | **Leeds Utd** (D1) | H | L | 0-1 | |
| 1975-76 | (D1) | 3 | 03.01.76 | **Everton** (D1) | H | W | 2-1 | George 2 |
| | | 4 | 24.01.76 | **Liverpool** (D1) | H | W | 1-0 | Davies |
| | | 5 | 14.02.76 | **Southend Utd** (D3) | H | W | 1-0 | Rioch |
| | | 6 | 06.03.76 | **Newcastle Utd** (D1) | H | W | 4-2 | Rioch 2, Newton, George |
| | | SF | 03.04.76 | **Manchester Utd** (D1) | | L | 0-2 | |
| | | | | *played at Hillsborough* | | | | |
| 1976-77 | (D1) | 3 | 08.01.77 | **Blackpool** (D2) | A | D | 0-0 | |
| | | 3r | 19.01.77 | **Blackpool** | H | W | 3-2 | Hales, James, George |
| | | 4 | 29.01.77 | **Colchester Utd** (D4) | A | D | 1-1 | Hales |
| | | 4r | 02.02.77 | **Colchester Utd** | H | W | 1-0 | James |
| | | 5 | 26.02.77 | **Blackburn Rovers** (D2) | H | W | 3-1 | George 2 (1p), Hector |
| | | 6 | 19.03.77 | **Everton** (D1) | A | L | 0-2 | |
| 1977-78 | (D1) | 3 | 07.01.78 | **Southend Utd** (D4) | H | W | 3-2 | Masson, Ryan, Young og |
| | | 4 | 01.02.78 | **Birmingham City** (D1) | H | W | 2-1 | Daly, Masson |
| | | 5 | 22.02.78 | **WBA** (D1) | H | L | 2-3 | Rioch 2 |
| 1978-79 | (D1) | 3 | 16.01.79 | **Preston North End** (D2) | A | L | 0-3 | |
| 1979-80 | (D1) | 3 | 05.01.80 | **Bristol City** (D1) | A | L | 2-6 | Davies, Daly |
| 1980-81 | (D2) | 3 | 03.01.81 | **Bristol City** (D2) | H | D | 0-0 | |
| | | 3r | 07.01.81 | **Bristol City** | A | L | 0-2 | |
| 1981-82 | (D2) | 3 | 02.01.82 | **Bolton Wanderers** (D2) | A | L | 1-3 | B Powell |
| 1982-83 | (D2) | 3 | 08.01.83 | **Nottingham Forest** (D1) | H | W | 2-0 | Gemmill, Hill |
| | | 4 | 29.01.83 | **Chelsea** (D2) | H | W | 2-1 | Wilson 2 |
| | | 5 | 19.02.83 | **Manchester Utd** (D1) | H | L | 0-1 | |
| 1983-84 | (D2) | 3 | 07.01.84 | **Cambridge Utd** (D2) | A | W | 3-0 | Wilson, Plummer, McAlle |
| | | 4 | 01.02.84 | **Telford Utd** (APL) | H | W | 3-2 | Davison 3 |
| | | 5 | 18.02.84 | **Norwich City** (D1) | H | W | 2-1 | Gemmill (p), Davison |
| | | 6 | 10.03.84 | **Plymouth Argyle** (D3) | A | D | 0-0 | |
| | | 6r | 14.03.84 | **Plymouth Argyle** | H | L | 0-1 | |
| 1984-85 | (D3) | 1 | 17.11.84 | **Hartlepool Utd** (D4) | A | L | 1-2 | Buckley (p) |
| 1985-86 | (D3) | 1 | 16.11.85 | **Crewe Alexandra** (D4) | H | W | 5-1 | Davison 2, Christie 2, Chandler (p) |
| | | 2 | 09.12.85 | **Telford Utd** (APL) | H | W | 6-1 | Chandler 3, Micklewhite 2, Gregory |

| | | | | | | | | |
|---|---|---|---|---|---|---|---|---|
| | | 3 | 04.01.86 | **Gillingham** (D3) | A | D | 1-1 | Garner |
| | | 3r | 13.01.86 | **Gillingham** | H | W | 3-1aet | Micklewhite, Garner, Christie |
| | | 4 | 25.01.86 | **Sheffield Utd** (D2) | A | W | 1-0 | Hindmarch |
| | | 5 | 26.02.86 | **Sheffield Wed** (D1) | H | D | 1-1 | Davison |
| | | 5r | 05.03.86 | **Sheffield Wed** | A | L | 0-2 | |
| 1986-87 | (D2) | 3 | 26.01.87 | **Sheffield Wed** (D1) | A | L | 0-1 | |
| 1987-88 | (D1) | 3 | 09.01.88 | **Chelsea** (D1) | H | L | 1-3 | Penney |
| 1988-89 | (D1) | 3 | 07.01.89 | **Southampton** (D1) | H | D | 1-1 | Hebberd |
| | | 3r | 10.01.89 | **Southampton** | A | W | 2-1aet | McMinn, Callaghan |
| | | 4 | 28.01.89 | **Watford** (D2) | A | L | 1-2 | Micklewhite |
| 1989-90 | (D1) | 3 | 07.01.90 | **Port Vale** (D2) | A | D | 1-1 | Hebberd |
| | | 3r | 10.01.90 | **Port Vale** | H | L | 2-3 | Ramage, Francis |
| 1990-91 | (D1) | 3 | 05.01.91 | **Newcastle Utd** (D2) | A | L | 0-2 | |
| 1991-92 | (D2) | 3 | 04.01.92 | **Burnley** (D4) | A | D | 2-2 | Chalk, Comyn |
| | | 3r | 14.01.92 | **Burnley** | H | - | 2-0ab | Gee, Patterson |
| | | | | *abandoned after 76 minutes – fog* | | | | |
| | | 3r | 25.01.92 | **Burnley** (D4) | H | W | 2-0 | P Williams, Ormondroyd |
| | | 4 | 05.02.92 | **Aston Villa** (D1) | H | L | 3-4 | Gee 2, P Williams |
| 1992-93 | (D1) | 3 | 02.01.93 | **Stockport County** (D2) | H | W | 2-1 | Short, Miller og |
| | | 4 | 23.01.93 | **Luton Town** (D1) | A | W | 5-1 | Short, Pembridge 3, Gabbiadini |
| | | 5 | 13.02.93 | **Bolton Wanderers** (D2) | H | W | 3-1 | Short 2, Williams |
| | | 6 | 08.03.93 | **Sheffield Wed** (PL) | H | D | 3-3 | Nicholson, Gabiadini, Kitson |
| | | 6r | 17.03.93 | **Sheffield Wed** | A | L | 0-1 | |
| 1993-94 | (D1) | 3 | 08.01.94 | **Oldham Athletic** (PL) | A | L | 1-2 | Johnson |
| 1994-95 | (D1) | 3 | 07.01.95 | **Everton** (PL) | A | L | 0-1 | |
| 1995-96 | (D1) | 3 | 07.01.96 | **Leeds Utd** (PL) | H | L | 2-4 | Gabbiadini, Simpson |
| 1996-97 | (PL) | 3 | 14.01.97 | **Gillingham** (D2) | A | - | 0-0ab | |
| | | | | *abandoned after 66 minutes – frozen pitch* | | | | |
| | | 3 | 21.01.97 | **Gillingham** | A | W | 2-0 | Willems, Van der Laan |
| | | 4 | 25.01.97 | **Aston Villa** (PL) | H | W | 3-1 | Van der Laan, Sturridge,Williams |
| | | 5 | 26.02.97 | **Coventry City** (PL) | H | W | 3-2 | Ward, Van der Laan, D Sturridge |
| | | 6 | 08.03.97 | **Middlesbrough** (PL) | H | L | 0-2 | |
| 1997-98 | (PL) | 3 | 03.01.98 | **Southampton** (PL) | H | W | 2-0 | Baiano, C Powell |
| | | 4 | 24.01.98 | **Coventry City** (PL) | A | L | 0-2 | |
| 1998-99 | (PL) | 3 | 02.01.99 | **Plymouth Argyle** (D3) | A | W | 3-0 | Burton 2, Eranio (p) |
| | | 4 | 23.01.99 | **Swansea City** (D3) | A | W | 1-0 | Harper |
| | | 5 | 13.02.99 | **Huddersfield Town** (D1) | A | D | 2-2 | Burton, Dorigo |
| | | 5r | 24.02.99 | **Huddersfield Town** | H | W | 3-1 | Dorigo, Baiano 2 |
| | | 6 | 06.03.99 | **Arsenal** (PL) | A | L | 0-1 | |
| 1999-00 | (PL) | 3 | 11.12.99 | **Burnley** (D2) | H | L | 0-1 | |
| 2000-01 | (PL) | 3 | 06.01.01 | **WBA** (D1) | H | W | 3-2 | Christie 2, Eranio |
| | | 4 | 27.01.01 | **Blackburn Rovers** (D1) | A | D | 0-0 | |
| | | 4r | 07.02.01 | **Blackburn Rovers** | H | L | 2-5 | Riggott, Eranio |
| 2001-02 | (PL) | 3 | 06.01.02 | **Bristol Rovers** (D3) | H | L | 1-3 | Ravanelli |
| 2002-03 | (D1) | 3 | 04.01.03 | **Brentford** (D2) | A | L | 0-1 | |

## DERBY JUNCTION

*Originally entered as Junction Street School, Derby. Reached FA Cup semi-finals, 1888. Entered FA Cup: 1884-85 – 1895-96.*

| | | | | | | | |
|---|---|---|---|---|---|---|---|
| 1884-85 | 1 | 25.10.84 | **WBA** | H | L | 1-7 | Malpass |
| 1885-86 | 1 | 31.10.85 | **Darwen** | A | D | 2-2 | |
| | 1r | 07.11.85 | **Darwen** | A | L | 0-4 | |
| 1886-87 | 1 | 30.10.86 | **Wellington St Georges** | A | W | 1-0 | |
| | 2 | 20.11.86 | **WBA** | A | L | 1-2 | Peach |
| 1887-88 | 1 | 15.10.87 | **Derby St Lukes** | H | W | 3-2 | |
| | 2 | 05.11.87 | **Rotherham Town** | H | W | 3-2 | Radford 2, S Smith |
| | 3 | 19.11.87 | **Lockwood Bros** | H | W | 2-1 | |
| | *4* | | bye | | | | |
| | 5 | 31.12.87 | **Chirk** | A | W | 1-0 | S Smith |
| | 6 | 28.01.88 | **Blackburn Rovers** | H | W | 2-1 | Hopkins, AN Other |
| | SF | 18.02.88 | **WBA** | | L | 0-3 | |
| | | | *played at Victoria Ground, Stoke* | | | | |
| 1888-89 | 1 | 02.02.89 | **Derby County** (D1) | A | L | 0-1 | |

## DERBY MIDLAND

*Formed 1881. Played on fields by the Midland Station. Entered FA Cup: 1883-84 – 1890-91.*

| | | | | | | | | |
|---|---|---|---|---|---|---|---|---|
| *1883-84* | | *1* | | bye | | | | |
| | | 2 | 01.12.83 | **Birmingham Excelsior** | A | D | 1-1 | |
| | | 2r | 15.12.83 | **Birmingham Excelsior** | H | W | 2-1 | Ward, G Wignall |
| | | 3 | 29.12.83 | **Wednesbury Town** | A | L | 0-1 | |
| 1884-85 | | 1 | 08.11.84 | **Wednesbury Old Ath** | H | L | 1-2 | |
| 1885-86 | | 1 | 31.10.85 | **Birmingham Excelsior** | H | W | 2-1 | |
| | | 2 | 14.11.85 | **Walsall Swifts** | H | L | 1-3 | |
| 1886-87 | | 1 | 30.10.86 | **Birmingham Excelsior** | A | D | 3-3 | |
| | | 1r | 13.11.86 | **Birmingham Excelsior** | H | W | 2-1 | |
| | | 2 | 20.11.86 | **Aston Villa** | A | L | 1-6 | Ward |
| 1887-88 | | 1 | 15.10.87 | **Ecclesfield** | A | L | 1-4 | |
| 1889-90 | (ML) | 1 | 18.01.90 | **Nottingham Forest** (FAll) | H | W | 3-0 | Daft, Garden, Mills |
| | | 2 | 01.02.90 | **Bootle** (FAll) | A | L | 1-2 | Garden |

## DERBY ST LUKES

*Formed 1870. played at Peet Street, off the New Uttoxeter Road, Derby. Entered FA Cup: 1884-85 – 1890-91.*

| | | | | | | | |
|---|---|---|---|---|---|---|---|
| 1884-85 | 1 | 08.11.84 | **Wolverhampton W** | A | D | 0-0 | |
| | 1r | 22.11.84 | **Wolverhampton W** | H | W | 4-2aet | |
| | 2 | 06.12.84 | **Walsall Swifts** | H | L | 0-1 | |
| 1885-86 | 1 | 31.10.85 | **Wolverhampton W** | A | L | 0-7 | |
| 1886-87 | 1 | 30.10.86 | **Walsall Town** | H | D | 3-3 | Hawkesworth 2, Wild |
| | 1r | 13.11.86 | **Walsall Town** | A | L | 1-6 | |
| 1887-88 | 1 | 15.10.87 | **Derby Junction** | A | L | 2-3 | |

## DERBY TOWN

*Entered the FA Cup once in 1881-82 and this was the only match they played.*

| | | | | | | | |
|---|---|---|---|---|---|---|---|
| 1881-82 | 1 | 17.10.81 | **Small Heath Alliance** | A | L | 1-4 | Shaw |

## DERBYSHIRE FC

| | | | | | | | |
|---|---|---|---|---|---|---|---|
| 1880-81 | 1 | 04.11.80 | **Notts County** | A | D | 4-4 | Evans 2, Taylor, AN Other |
| | 1r | 27.11.80 | **Notts County** | H | L | 2-4 | Shaw, AN Other |

## DESBOROUGH TOWN

*Formed 1896. First entered FA Cup: 1899-1900. Members of the United Counties League.*

| | | | | | | | |
|---|---|---|---|---|---|---|---|
| 1926-27 | (UCL) | 1 | 27.11.26 | **Doncaster Rovers** (3N) | A | - | 0-0ab |
| | | | | *abandoned after 80 mins – fog* | | | |
| | | 1 | 02.12.26 | **Doncaster Rovers** | A | L | 0-3 |

## DINNINGTON ATHLETIC

*Entered FA Cup: 1920-21 – 1948-49.*

| | | | | | | | | |
|---|---|---|---|---|---|---|---|---|
| 1934-35 | (SAL) | 1 | 24.11.34 | **Chester** (3N) | A | L | 1-3 | Fearnley |

## DISTILLERY, BELFAST

*Formed 1879. Winners of the Irish FA Cup 12 times, runners-up eight times. One of three Irish teams to play in the Competition Proper. Now known as Lisburn Distillery. Members of the Irish League.*

| | | | | | | | |
|---|---|---|---|---|---|---|---|
| 1887-88 | 1 | 08.10.87 | **Blackburn Park Road** | A | L | 1-2 | McManus |
| | | | *FA disqualified Park Road after a protest, Distillery re-instated* | | | | |
| | 2 | 05.11.87 | **Witton** | H | L | 2-4 | McManus, Stewart |
| 1889-90 | 1 | 18.01.90 | **Bolton Wanderers** (D1) | A | L | 2-10 | Reynolds, og |

## DONCASTER ROVERS

*Formed 1879. FA Cup best performance: 5th round, 1952, 1954, 1955, 1956. Record FA Cup win: 8-1 v Parkgate Utd, 3rd qualifying round, 1898-99; In Competition Proper: 7-0 v Blyth Spartans, 1st round, 27.11.1937; Record FA Cup defeat: 1-9 v Rotherham Town, 1st qualifying round, 1888-89; In Competition Proper: 0-8 v Everton, 4th round, 21.01.1939. Members of The Conference 1998-2003: Non-League clubs beaten: Southend United. Promoted to Football League 2003.*

| | | |
|---|---|---|
| 1888-89 | | 1q Rotherham T (H) 1-9 |
| 1889-90 | (MA) | 1q Rotherham T (A) 0-2 |
| 1890-91 | (MA) | 2q Kilnhurst (H) 4-5 |
| 1891-92 | (ML) | 1q Lincoln C (A) 1-3 |
| 1892-93 | (ML) | 1q Mansfield T (H) 2-0; 2q Grimsby T (H) 1-1aet; 2qr Grimsby T (H) 1-2 |

| | | | | | | | | |
|---|---|---|---|---|---|---|---|---|
| 1893-94 | (ML) | | | 2q Grantham R (H) 1-2 | | | | |
| 1894-95 | (ML) | | | 1q Mexborough (H) 1-2 | | | | |
| 1895-96 | (ML) | | | 1q Mexborough (A) 1-1; 1qr Mexborough (H) 4-1; 2q Rotherham T (H) 0-7 | | | | |
| 1896-97 | (ML) | | | 3q Sheffield Club (A) 1-3 | | | | |
| 1897-98 | (ML) | | | 3q Sheffield Club (A) 4-0; 4q Mexborough (A) 0-0; 4qr Mexborough (H) 1-1; 4qr 2r Mexborough 1-1 abnd (at Bramall Lane); 4q 3r Mexborough 1-2 (at Barnsley) | | | | |
| 1898-99 | (ML) | | | 2q Wath-on-Dearne (H) 6-1; 3q Parkgate U (H) 8-1; 4q Barnsley (H) 1-2 | | | | |
| 1899-00 | (ML) | | | 1q Gainsborough T (A) 4-1; 2q Newark (H) 3-1; 3q Grimsby T (A) 1-3 | | | | |
| 1900-01 | (ML) | | | P Rotherham T (H) 6-1; 1q Attercliffe (A) 2-0; 2q Worksop T (A) 0-0; 2qr Worksop T (H) 2-1; 3q Barnsley (A) 1-2 | | | | |
| 1901-02 | (D2) | | | 3q Royston U (A) 3-1; 4q Lincoln C (A) 0-1 | | | | |
| 1902-03 | (D2) | | | 3q Gainsborough T (A) 0-1 | | | | |
| 1903-04 | (ML) | | | 3q Belper T (H) 2-0; 4q Gainsborough T (H) 0-1 | | | | |
| 1904-05 | (D2) | | | 3q Mexborough T (H) 0-0; 3qr Mexborough T (A) 1-3 | | | | |
| 1905-06 | (ML) | | | 1q Denaby U (A) 2-4 | | | | |
| 1906-07 | (ML) | | | P Morley (A) 4-1; 1q Denaby U (A) 0-0; 1qr Denaby U (H) 2-2; 1q 2r Denaby U 1-3 | | | | |
| 1907-08 | (ML) | | | 1q Goole T (H) 1-1; 1qr Goole T (A) 1-2 | | | | |
| 1908-09 | (ML) | | | 1q Castleford T (H) 1-1; 1qr Castleford T (A) 1-4 | | | | |
| 1909-10 | (ML) | | | 4q Mexborough T (H) 0-0; 4qr Mexborough T (A) 1-2 | | | | |
| 1910-11 | (ML) | | | P Hull Day St OB (H) 7-0; 1q Grimsby Rovers (H) 5-4; 2q Mexborough T (H) 1-0; 3q Denaby U (A) 1-2 | | | | |
| 1911-12 | (ML) | | | 1q Castleford T (A) 0-1 | | | | |
| 1912-13 | (ML) | | | P Denaby U (A) 2-1; 1q Castleford T (A) 0-2 | | | | |
| 1913-14 | (ML) | | | P Goole T (A) 1-2 | | | | |
| 1914-15 | (ML) | | | P Grimsby Haycroft R (A) 3-0; 1q Cleethorpes (H) 3-1; 2q Scunthorpe U (A) 0-1 | | | | |
| 1919-20 | (ML) | | | did not enter | | | | |
| 1920-21 | (ML) | | | ExP Atlas & NW (H) 6-0; P Wombwell (H) 0-1 | | | | |
| 1921-22 | (ML) | | | ExP Rotherham T (H) 2-0; P Wombwell (A) 0-1 | | | | |
| 1922-23 | (ML) | | | 1q Denaby U (A) 0-0; 1qr Denaby U (H) 4-1; 2q Mexborough T (A) 0-0; 2qr Mexborough T (H) 2-1; 3q Wath A (H) 0-0; 3qr Wath A (A) 1-2 | | | | |
| 1923-24 | (3N) | | | P Fryston Colliery (H) scratched | | | | |
| 1924-25 | (3N) | | | 4q Mansfield T (H) 3-2; 5q Rotherham Co (A) 3-2; 6q Southport (H) 1-0 | | | | |
| | | 1 | 10.01.25 | **Norwich City** (3S) | H | L | 1-2 | Campbell |
| 1925-26 | (3N) | 1 | 28.11.25 | **Wellington Town** (BDL) | H | W | 2-0 | H Keetley, Hargreaves |
| | | 2 | 12.12.25 | **Rotherham Utd** (3N) | H | L | 0-2 | |
| 1926-27 | (3N) | 1 | 27.11.26 | **Desborough Town** (UCL) | H | - | 0-0ab | |
| | | | | *abandoned after 80 mins – fog* | | | | |
| | | 1 | 02.12.26 | **Desborough Town** (UCL) | H | W | 3-0 | F Keetley 2, T Keetley |
| | | 2 | 11.12.26 | **Chesterfield** (3N) | H | L | 0-1 | |
| 1927-28 | (3N) | 1 | 26.11.27 | **Carlisle Utd** (NEL) | A | L | 1-2 | Jepson (p) |
| 1928-29 | (3N) | 1 | 24.11.28 | **Bradford City** (3N) | A | L | 1-4 | T Keetley |
| 1929-30 | (3N) | 1 | 30.11.29 | **Shildon** (NEL) | H | D | 0-0 | |
| | | 1r | 04.12.29 | **Shildon** | A | D | 1-1aet | Robisnon |
| | | 1 2r | 09.12.29 | **Shildon** | | W | 3-0 | Paterson 2, R Smith |
| | | | | *played at Bootham Crescent, York* | | | | |
| | | 2 | 14.12.29 | **New Brighton** (3N) | H | W | 1-0 | Whitelaw |
| | | 3 | 11.01.30 | **Stoke City** (D2) | H | - | 2-3ab | Batt, Bowman |
| | | | | *abandoned after 68 minutes – snowstorm* | | | | |
| | | 3 | 16.01.30 | **Stoke City** | H | W | 1-0 | Whitelaw |
| | | 4 | 25.01.30 | **Millwall** (D2) | A | L | 0-4 | |
| 1930-31 | (3N) | 1 | 29.11.30 | **Rochdale** (3N) | A | W | 2-1 | Bott, Smith |
| | | 2 | 13.12.30 | **Notts County** (3S) | H | L | 0-1 | |
| 1931-32 | (3N) | 1 | 28.11.31 | **Barrow** (3N) | A | D | 3-3 | Flowers, Gladwin, Bowman |
| | | 1r | 03.12.31 | **Barrow** | H | D | 1-1aet | Smith |
| | | 1 2r | 07.12.31 | **Barrow** | | D | 1-1aet | Bowman |
| | | | | *played at Maine Road* | | | | |
| | | 1 3r | 09.12.31 | **Barrow** | | W | 1-0aet | Gladwin |
| | | | | *played at Elland Road* | | | | |
| | | 2 | 12.12.31 | **Brighton** (3S) | A | L | 0-5 | |
| 1932-33 | (3N) | 1 | 26.11.32 | **Gainsborough T** (ML) | H | W | 4-1 | Beresford, Atherton, Beynon 2 |

| | | | | | | | | |
|---|---|---|---|---|---|---|---|---|
| | | 2 | 10.12.32 | **Northampton Town** (3S) | A | W | 1-0 | Atherton |
| | | 3 | 14.01.33 | **Halifax Town** (3N) | H | L | 0-3 | |
| 1933-34 | (3N) | 1 | 25.11.33 | **Barrow** (3N) | A | L | 2-4 | Waterston, Smith |
| 1934-35 | (3N) | 1 | 24.11.34 | **Barrow** | H | L | 0-2 | |
| 1935-36 | (D2) | 3 | 11.01.36 | **Nottingham Forest** (D2) | H | L | 1-2 | Turner |
| 1936-37 | (D2) | 3 | 16.01.37 | **Chester** (3N) | A | L | 0-4 | |
| 1937-38 | (3N) | 1 | 27.11.37 | **Blyth Spartans** (NEL) | H | W | 7-0 | Morgan 2, Burton, Killourghy 4. |
| | | 2 | 11.12.37 | **Guildford City** (SL) | H | W | 4-0 | Burton, Dutton, Malam, Killourghy |
| | | 3 | 08.01.38 | **Sheffield Utd** (D2) | H | L | 0-2 | |
| 1938-39 | (3N) | 1 | 26.11.38 | **New Brighton** (3N) | H | W | 4-2 | Leyfield, Little, Dell 2 |
| | | 2 | 10.12.38 | **Gainsborough T** (ML) | A | W | 1-0 | Dell |
| | | 3 | 10.01.39 | **Southport** (3N) | A | D | 1-1 | Potts |
| | | 3r | 12.01.39 | **Southport** | H | W | 2-1 | Dell, Malam |
| | | 4 | 21.01.39 | **Everton** (D1) | A | L | 0-8 | |
| 1945-46 | (3N) | 1 1L | 17.11.45 | **Rotherham Utd** (3N) | H | L | 0-1 | |
| | | 1 2L | 24.11.45 | **Rotherham Utd** | A | L | 1-2 | Todd |
| 1946-47 | (3N) | 1 | 30.11.46 | **Accrington Stanley** (3N) | H | D | 2-2 | Thompson, Dodd |
| | | 1r | 04.12.46 | **Accrington Stanley** | A | W | 5-0 | Kirkcaldie 3, Todd, Jordan |
| | | 2 | 14.12.46 | **Oldham Athletic** (3N) | H | W | 2-1 | Jordan, Maddison |
| | | 3 | 11.01.47 | **Portsmouth** (D1) | H | L | 2-3 | Kirkaldie, Todd |
| 1947-48 | (D2) | 3 | 10.01.48 | **Fulham** (D2) | A | L | 0-2 | |
| 1948-49 | (3N) | 1 | 04.12.48 | **Bradford City** (3N) | A | L | 3-4 | Calverley, Antonio, Reeve |
| 1949-50 | (3N) | 1 | 26.11.49 | **New Brighton** (3N) | H | W | 5-1 | Calverley, Tindill 2, Todd, Doherty |
| | | 2 | 10.12.49 | **Mansfield Town** (3N) | H | W | 1-0 | Todd |
| | | 3 | 07.01.50 | **Reading** (3S) | A | W | 3-2 | Todd 2, Doherty |
| | | 4 | 28.01.50 | **Blackpool** (D1) | A | L | 1-2 | Doherty |
| 1950-51 | (D2) | 3 | 06.01.51 | **Rotherham Utd** (3N) | A | L | 1-2 | Miller (p) |
| 1951-52 | (D2) | 3 | 12.01.52 | **Buxton** (CC) | H | W | 2-0 | Harrison 2 |
| | | 4 | 06.02.52 | **Middlesbrough** (D1) | A | W | 4-1 | Lawlor 2, Harrison, Tindill |
| | | 5 | 23.02.52 | **Portsmouth** (D1) | A | L | 0-4 | |
| 1952-53 | (D2) | 3 | 10.01.53 | **Arsenal** (D1) | A | L | 0-4 | |
| 1953-54 | (D2) | 3 | 09.01.54 | **Sunderland** (D1) | A | W | 2-0 | McMorran 2 |
| | | 4 | 30.01.54 | **Plymouth Argyle** (D2) | A | W | 2-0 | Tindill 2 |
| | | 5 | 20.02.54 | **Leyton Orient** (3S) | A | L | 1-3 | McMorran |
| 1954-55 | (D2) | 3 | 08.01.55 | **Watford** (3S) | A | W | 2-1 | Tindill 2 |
| | | 4 | 29.01.55 | **Aston Villa** (D1) | H | D | 0-0 | |
| | | 4r | 02.02.55 | **Aston Villa** | A | D | 2-2aet | Tindill, Mooney |
| | | 4 2r | 07.02.55 | **Aston Villa** | | D | 1-1aet | Jeffrey |
| | | | | *played at Maine Road* | | | | |
| | | 4 3r | 14.02.55 | **Aston Villa** | | - | 0-0ab | |
| | | | | *played at Hillsborough – abandoned after 90 minutes – bad light* | | | | |
| | | 4 4r | 15.02.55 | **Aston Villa** | | W | 3-1 | Jeffrey 2, G Walker |
| | | | | *played at The Hawthorns* | | | | |
| | | 5 | 19.02.55 | **Birmingham City** (D2) | A | L | 1-2 | Mooney |
| 1955-56 | (D2) | 3 | 07.01.56 | **Nottingham Forest** (D2) | H | W | 3-0 | McMorran 2, A Jeffrey |
| | | 4 | 28.01.56 | **Bristol Rovers** (D2) | A | D | 1-1 | McMorran |
| | | 4r | 31.01.56 | **Bristol Rovers** | H | W | 1-0 | Tindill |
| | | 5 | 18.02.56 | **Tottenham Hotspur** (D1) | H | L | 0-2 | |
| 1956-57 | (D2) | 3 | 05.01.57 | **WBA** (D1) | H | D | 1-1 | Cavanagh |
| | | 3r | 09.01.57 | **WBA** | A | L | 0-2 | |
| 1957-58 | (D2) | 3 | 04.01.58 | **Chelsea** (D1) | H | L | 0-2 | |
| 1958-59 | (D3) | 1 | 15.11.58 | **Consett** (ML) | H | W | 5-0 | Sharp, Mooney 2, Reeson, Stephens |
| | | 2 | 06.12.58 | **Tranmere Rovers** (3N) | A | W | 2-1 | Reeson, Callan |
| | | 3 | 19.01.59 | **Bristol City** (D2) | H | L | 0-2 | |
| 1959-60 | (D4) | 1 | 14.11.59 | **Gainsborough T** (ML) | H | D | 3-3 | Walker 2, Chappell |
| | | 1r | 18.11.59 | **Gainsborough T** | A | W | 1-0 | Walker |
| | | 2 | 05.12.59 | **Darlington** (D4) | H | W | 3-2 | Sharp 2, Chappell |
| | | 3 | 09.01.60 | **Bristol Rovers** (D2) | A | D | 0-0 | |
| | | 3r | 12.01.60 | **Bristol Rovers** | H | L | 1-2 | Broadbent |
| 1960-61 | (D4) | 1 | 05.11.60 | **Chesterfield** (D3) | A | D | 3-3 | Curtis 2 (2p), Swallow |
| | | 1r | 09.11.60 | **Chesterfield** | H | L | 0-1 | |

| | | | | | | | | | |
|---|---|---|---|---|---|---|---|---|---|
| 1961-62 | (D4) | 1 | 04.11.61 | **Chesterfield** (D4) | H | L | 0-4 | |
| 1962-63 | (D4) | 1 | 03.11.62 | **S Shields (1936)** (NEL) | A | D | 0-0 | |
| | | 1r | 08.11.62 | **S Shields (1936)** | H | W | 2-1 | Booth, Billings |
| | | 2 | 24.11.62 | **Tranmere Rovers** (D4) | H | L | 1-4 | Booth |
| 1963-64 | (D4) | 1 | 16.11.63 | **Tranmere Rovers** | H | W | 3-0 | Robinson, Nibloe, Ripley |
| | | 2 | 07.12.63 | **Notts County** (D3) | H | D | 1-1 | Booth |
| | | 2r | 10.12.63 | **Notts County** | A | W | 2-1 | Broadbent (p), Hale |
| | | 3 | 04.01.64 | **Bristol City** (D3) | H | D | 2-2 | Taylor, Ripley |
| | | 3r | 07.01.64 | **Bristol City** | A | L | 0-2 | |
| 1964-65 | (D4) | 1 | 14.11.64 | **Bradford Park A** (D4) | A | W | 3-2 | Ricketts, Jeffrey 2 |
| | | 2 | 05.12.64 | **Scarborough** (ML) | H | D | 0-0 | |
| | | 2r | 09.12.64 | **Scarborough** | A | W | 2-1 | Hale (p), Robinson |
| | | 3 | 09.01.65 | **Huddersfield Town** (D2) | H | L | 0-1 | |
| 1965-66 | (D4) | 1 | 13.11.65 | **Wigan Athletic** (CC) | H | D | 2-2 | Ricketts, Kelly |
| | | 1r | 17.11.65 | **Wigan Athletic** | A | L | 1-3 | Ogden |
| 1966-67 | (D3) | 1 | 26.11.66 | **Halifax Town** (D4) | A | D | 2-2 | Gilfillan, Ogden |
| | | 1r | 29.11.66 | **Halifax Town** | H | L | 1-3aet | Ogden |
| 1967-68 | (D4) | 1 | 09.12.67 | **York City** (D4) | A | W | 1-0 | Jeffrey |
| | | 2 | 06.01.68 | **Workington** (D4) | H | D | 1-1 | Gilfillan |
| | | 2r | 10.01.68 | **Workington** | A | W | 2-1aet | Watson, Webber |
| | | 3 | 27.01.68 | **Swansea Town** (D4) | H | L | 0-2 | |
| 1968-69 | (D4) | 1 | 16.11.68 | **Notts County** (D4) | H | W | 1-0 | Jeffrey |
| | | 2 | 07.12.68 | **Southport** (D3) | H | W | 2-1 | Regan 2 |
| | | 3 | 04.01.69 | **Liverpool** (D1) | A | L | 0-2 | |
| 1969-70 | (D3) | 1 | 15.11.69 | **Crewe Alexandra** (D4) | H | D | 1-1 | Sheffield |
| | | 1r | 19.11.69 | **Crewe Alexandra** | A | W | 1-0 | Robertson |
| | | 2 | 06.12.69 | **Chester** (D4) | A | D | 1-1 | Johnson |
| | | 2r | 09.12.69 | **Chester** | H | L | 0-2 | |
| 1970-71 | (D3) | 1 | 21.11.70 | **Crewe Alexandra** (D4) | A | D | 0-0 | |
| | | 1r | 24.11.70 | **Crewe Alexandra** | H | L | 1-3 | Watson |
| 1971-72 | (D4) | 1 | 20.11.71 | **Stockport County** (D4) | H | L | 1-2 | Uzelac |
| 1972-73 | (D4) | 1 | 18.11.72 | **Bury** (D4) | H | W | 3-1 | Kitchen, Elwiss, Rabjohn |
| | | 2 | 09.12.72 | **Scarborough** (NPL) | A | W | 2-1 | Kitchen, Elwiss |
| | | 3 | 13.01.73 | **Reading** (D4) | A | L | 0-2 | |
| 1973-74 | (D4) | 1 | 24.11.73 | **Lincoln City** (D4) | H | W | 1-0 | Murray (p) |
| | | 2 | 15.12.73 | **Tranmere Rovers** (D3) | H | W | 3-0 | Kitchen, Woods, Elwiss |
| | | 3 | 05.01.74 | **Liverpool** (D1) | A | D | 2-2 | Kitchen, O'Callaghan |
| | | 3r | 08.01.74 | **Liverpool** | H | L | 0-2 | |
| 1974-75 | (D4) | 1 | 23.11.74 | **Oswestry Town** (CC) | A | W | 3-1 | O'Callaghan, Kitchen 2 |
| | | 2 | 14.12.74 | **Chesterfield** (D3) | A | L | 0-1 | |
| 1975-76 | (D4) | 1 | 22.11.75 | **Bury** (D3) | A | L | 3-4 | Uzelac 2 |
| 1976-77 | (D4) | 1 | 20.11.76 | **Shrewsbury Town** (D3) | H | D | 2-2 | Kitchen 2 |
| | | 1r | 23.11.76 | **Shrewsbury Town** | A | L | 3-4 | Miller, Kitchen, Reed |
| 1977-78 | (D4) | 1 | 26.11.77 | **Shrewsbury Town** (D3) | H | L | 0-1 | |
| 1978-79 | (D4) | 1 | 25.11.78 | **Huddersfield Town** (D4) | H | W | 2-1 | Lewis, Laidlaw |
| | | 2 | 16.12.78 | **Shrewsbury Town** (D3) | H | L | 0-3 | |
| 1979-80 | (D4) | 1 | 23.11.79 | **Port Vale** (D4) | A | W | 3-1 | Lewis, Pugh, Nimmo |
| | | 2 | 15.12.79 | **Mansfield Town** (D3) | H | L | 1-2 | Nimmo |
| 1980-81 | (D4) | 1 | 22.11.80 | **Sutton Coldfield T** (WMRL) | A | W | 2-0 | Dowd, Lally |
| | | 2 | 13.12.80 | **Blackpool** (D3) | H | W | 2-1 | Little, Mell |
| | | 3 | 03.01.81 | **Hull City** (D3) | A | L | 0-1 | |
| 1981-82 | (D3) | 1 | 21.11.81 | **Mansfield Town** (D4) | A | W | 1-0 | Douglas |
| | | 2 | 12.12.81 | **Penrith** (NL) | H | W | 3-0 | Warboys 2, Little |
| | | 3 | 02.01.82 | **Cambridge Utd** (D2) | H | W | 2-1 | Reilly og, Warboys |
| | | 4 | 23.01.82 | **Norwich City** (D2) | A | L | 1-2 | Dawson |
| 1982-83 | (D3) | 1 | 20.11.82 | **Workington** (NPL) | A | W | 2-1 | Owen, Austin |
| | | 2 | 11.12.82 | **Peterborough Utd** (D4) | A | L | 2-5 | I Snodin, Mell |
| 1983-84 | (D4) | 1 | 19.11.83 | **Mansfield Town** (D4) | A | L | 0-3 | |
| 1984-85 | (D3) | 1 | 17.11.84 | **Rochdale** (D4) | A | W | 2-1 | Philliben, G Snodin |
| | | 2 | 08.12.84 | **Altrincham** (APL) | A | W | 3-1 | Harle, Douglas 2 |
| | | 3 | 05.01.85 | **QPR** (D1) | H | W | 1-0 | Harle |

| | | | | | | | | |
|---|---|---|---|---|---|---|---|---|
| | | 4 | 26.01.85 | **Everton** (D1) | A | L | 0-2 | |
| 1985-86 | (D3) | 1 | 16.11.85 | **Wigan Athletic** (D3) | A | L | 1-4 | Douglas |
| 1986-87 | (D3) | 1 | 15.11.86 | **Whitby Town** (NL) | A | D | 2-2 | Russell, Deane |
| | | 1r | 18.11.86 | **Whitby Town** | H | W | 3-2 | Woods, Stead, Redfearn (p) |
| | | 2 | 06.12.86 | **Chester City** (D3) | A | L | 1-3 | Woods |
| 1987-88 | (D3) | 1 | 14.11.87 | **Rotherham Utd** (D3) | H | D | 1-1 | Holmes |
| | | 1r | 17.11.87 | **Rotherham Utd** | A | L | 0-2 | |
| 1988-89 | (D4) | 1 | 19.11.88 | **Brandon Utd** (NL) | H | D | 0-0 | |
| | | 1r | 22.11.88 | **Brandon Utd** | A | W | 2-1 | Dobson 2 |
| | | | | *played at Doncaster* | | | | |
| | | 2 | 11.12.88 | **Sheffield Utd** (D3) | H | L | 1-3 | Daly |
| 1989-90 | (D4) | 1 | 18.11.89 | **Notts County** (D3) | H | W | 1-0 | Noteman |
| | | 2 | 09.12.89 | **Grimsby Town** (D4) | A | L | 0-1 | |
| 1990-91 | (D4) | 1 | 17.11.90 | **Chester City** (D3) | A | D | 2-2 | Gormley, Rankine |
| | | 1r | 20.11.90 | **Chester City** | H | L | 1-2aet | Noteman |
| 1991-92 | (D4) | 1 | 16.11.91 | **Burnley** (D4) | A | D | 1-1 | Rankine |
| | | 1r | 27.11.91 | **Burnley** | H | L | 1-3 | Whitehurst |
| 1992-93 | (D3) | 1 | 14.11.92 | **Hartlepool Utd** (D2) | H | L | 1-2 | Quinlan |
| 1993-94 | (D3) | 1 | 13.11.93 | **Shrewsbury Town** (D3) | A | D | 1-1 | Williamson |
| | | 1r | 01.12.93 | **Shrewsbury Town** | H | L | 1-2aet | Williamson |
| 1994-95 | (D3) | 1 | 12.11.94 | **Huddersfield Town** (D2) | H | L | 1-4 | Jones |
| 1995-96 | (D3) | 1 | 11.11.95 | **Mansfield Town** (D3) | A | L | 2-4 | Jones (p), Carmichael |
| 1996-97 | (D3) | 1 | 16.11.96 | **Stockport County** (D2) | A | L | 1-2 | Cramb |
| 1997-98 | (D3) | 1 | 15.11.97 | **Preston North End** (D2) | A | L | 2-3 | Mike, Hammond |
| 1998-99 | (Conf) | 1 | 14.11.98 | **Southend Utd** (D3) | A | W | 1-0 | Penney |
| | | 1 | 05.12.98 | **Rushden & D** (Conf) | H | D | 0-0 | |
| | | 1r | 15.12.98 | **Rushden & D** | A | L | 2-4 | Sutherland, Maamria |
| 1999-00 | (Conf) | 1 | 30.10.99 | **Halifax Town** (D3) | H | L | 0-2 | |
| 2001-02 | (Conf) | 1 | 17.11.01 | **Scunthorpe Utd** (D3) | H | L | 2-3 | Tierney, Watson |
| 2002-03 | (Conf) | 1 | 16.11.02 | **Bournemouth** (D2) | A | L | 1-2 | Gill |

## DONINGTON GRAMMAR SCHOOL, SPALDING

*Formed 1870. One of the 15 original entrants in the FA Cup in the 1871-72 season. Scratched without playing a match and never entered again. To mark the 100th anniversary of the match that never took place, a team from Donington School did make the journey to Glasgow to play Queen's Park. They lost.*

| | | | | | |
|---|---|---|---|---|---|
| 1871-72 | 1 | | Queen's Park, Glasgow | - | |
| | | | *Clubs could not arrange a date so both advanced to second round* | | |
| | 2 | | Queen's Park, Glasgow | - | |
| | | | *Donington School scratched. Queen's Park walkover* | | |

## DORCHESTER TOWN

*Formed 1880. First entered FA Cup: 1948-49. Members of the Southern League.*

| | | | | | | | | |
|---|---|---|---|---|---|---|---|---|
| 1954-55 | (WL) | 1 | 20.11.54 | **Bedford Town** (SL) | H | W | 2-0 | Dobson, Spink |
| | | 2 | 11.12.54 | **York City** (3N) | H | L | 2-5 | Curtis, Gale |
| 1955-56 | (WL) | 1 | 19.11.55 | **Norwich City** (3S) | A | L | 0-4 | |
| 1956-57 | (WL) | 1 | 17.11.56 | **QPR** (3S) | A | L | 0-4 | |
| 1957-58 | (WL) | 1 | 16.11.57 | **Wycombe W** (IL) | H | W | 3-2 | Stroud (p), Cheney 2 |
| | | 2 | 07.12.57 | **Plymouth Argyle** (3S) | A | L | 2-5 | Barker, Stroud (p) |
| 1959-60 | (WL) | 1 | 14.11.59 | **Port Vale** (D3) | H | L | 1-2 | Gillett |
| 1981-82 | (SL) | 1 | 21.11.81 | **Minehead** (SL) | H | D | 3-3 | Miller, Steele 2 |
| | | 1r | 23.11.81 | **Minehead** | A | W | 4-0 | Senior 3, Chutter |
| | | 2 | 12.12.81 | **Bournemouth** (D4) | H | D | 1-1 | Thorne |
| | | 2r | 15.12.81 | **Bournemouth** | A | L | 1-2aet | Steele |
| 1989-90 | (SL) | 1 | 18.11.89 | **Gloucester City** (SL) | A | L | 0-1 | |
| 1995-96 | (SL) | 1 | 11.11.95 | **Oxford Utd** (D2) | A | L | 1-9 | Killick (p) |
| 2000-01 | (SL) | 1 | 18.11.00 | **Wigan Athletic** (D2) | A | L | 1-3 | Holmes |

## DORKING

*Formed 1880. First entered FA Cup: 1906-07. Their record attendace of 4,500 was set for two FA Cup matches: v Folkestone Town, 1st qualifying round, 1955 and for the 1st round match v Plymouth Argyle in 1992. Members of the Isthmian League.*

| | | | | | | | | |
|---|---|---|---|---|---|---|---|---|
| 1992-93 | (IL) | 1 | 14.11.92 | **Plymouth Argyle** (D2) | H | L | 2-3 | Grainger, Lunn |

## DOVER

*Originally formed 1891 as Dover FC but various linked clubs have folded and been reformed through the years. Original Dover FC folded 1910. Dover United formed 1920, folded 1933. Dover FC reformed 1934, wound-up 1983. Reformed as Dover Athletic in 1983. Originally entered FA Cup: 1894-95. League club beaten: Colchester United. Members of the Southern League.*

| | | | | | | | | |
|---|---|---|---|---|---|---|---|---|
| 1960-61 (SL) | 1 | 05.11.60 | **Peterborough Utd** (D4) | H | L | 1-4 | Taylor |
| 1971-72 (SL) | 1 | 20.11.71 | **Guildford City** (SL) | A | D | 0-0 | |
| | 1r | 24.11.71 | **Guildford City** | H | L | 0-2 | |
| 1975-76 (SL) | 1 | 22.11.75 | **Colchester Utd** (D3) | A | D | 3-3 | Coupland, Waite, Rogers |
| | 1r | 26.11.75 | **Colchester Utd** | H | W | 4-1aet | Hamshare, Coxhill (p), Coupland 2 |
| | 2 | 13.12.75 | **Southend Utd** (D3) | A | L | 1-4 | Housden |
| 1981-82 (SL) | 1 | 21.11.81 | **Oxford Utd** (D3) | H | L | 0-2 | |
| 2002-03 (SL) | 1 | 16.11.02 | **Oxford Utd** | H | L | 0-1 | |

## DREADNOUGHT FC

*Formed 1875. played at West Ham Park, east London. Entered FA Cup: 1880-81 – 1883-84.*

| | | | | | | | |
|---|---|---|---|---|---|---|---|
| 1880-81 | 1 | 13.11.80 | **Rochester** | A | W | 2-1 | Wyllie, AN Other |
| | 2 | 11.12.80 | **Old Carthusians** | A | L | 1-5 | Wyllie |
| 1881-82 | 1 | | Caius College, Cambridge | | | - | |
| | | | *Caius College scratched. Dreadnought walkover* | | | | |
| | 2 | | bye | | | | |
| | 3 | 17.12.81 | **Marlow** | H | L | 1-2 | |
| 1882-83 | 1 | 21.10.82 | **South Reading** | A | L | 1-2 | Pettigrew |
| | | | *FA ordered replay after protest* | | | | |
| | 1r | 04.11.82 | **South Reading** | H | L | 1-2 | |
| 1883-84 | 1 | 10.11.83 | **Old Foresters** | A | L | 1-2 | Fabian |

## DROYLESDEN

*Formed 1892. First entered FA Cup: 1931-32. League club beaten: Rochdale. Members of the Northern Premier League.*

| | | | | | | | |
|---|---|---|---|---|---|---|---|
| 1976-77 (CC) | 1 | 20.11.76 | **Grimsby Town** (D3) | H | D | 0-0 | |
| | 1r | 23.11.76 | **Grimsby Town** | A | L | 3-5 | Haughton, Williams, Seddon |
| 1978-79 (CC) | 1 | 25.11.78 | **Rochdale** (D4) | A | W | 1-0 | Taylor |
| | 2 | 16.12.78 | **Altrincham** (NPL) | H | L | 0-2 | |

## DRUIDS

*Formed 1874. The first Welsh club to compete in the FA Cup. Originally played at Plas Madoc Park, Ruabon. Welsh FA Cup winners eight times. Folded 1918. The present day Druids United were founded in 1930.*

| | | | | | | | |
|---|---|---|---|---|---|---|---|
| 1876-77 | 1 | | Shropshire Wanderers | | | - | |
| | | | *Druids scratched. Shropshire Wanderers walkover* | | | | |
| 1877-78 | 1 | 12.11.77 | **Shropshire Wanderers** | H | W | 1-0 | |
| | 2 | | Queen's Park, Glasgow | | | - | |
| | | | *Queen's Park scratched. Druids walkover* | | | | |
| | 3 | 30.01.78 | **Royal Engineers** | A | L | 0-8 | |
| 1882-83 | 1 | 04.11.82 | **Oswestry Town** | H | D | 1-1 | |
| | 1r | 18.11.82 | **Oswestry Town** | A | W | 2-0 | WP Owen, AN Other |
| | 2 | 09.12.82 | **Northwich Vic** | H | W | 5-0 | |
| | 3 | 06.01.83 | **Bolton Wanderers** | H | D | 0-0 | |
| | 3r | 22.01.83 | **Bolton Wanderers** | A | D | 1-1aet | Vaughan |
| | 3 2r | 29.01.83 | **Bolton Wanderers** | | W | 1-0 | Doughty |
| | | | *played at Wrexham Racecourse* | | | | |
| | 4 | 10.02.83 | **Eagley** | H | W | 2-1aet | Vaughan, AN Other |
| | 5 | 24.02.83 | **Blackburn Olympic** | A | L | 1-4 | |
| 1883-84 | 1 | 10.11.83 | **Northwich Vic** | H | L | 0-1 | |
| 1884-85 | 1 | 08.11.84 | **Liverpool Ramblers** | H | W | 6-1 | Doughty, 5 others |
| | 2 | 20.12.84 | **Newtown** | A | D | 1-1 | |
| | 2r | 27.12.84 | **Newtown** | H | W | 6-0 | |
| | 3 | 10.01.85 | **Chirk** | H | W | 4-1 | Powell 2, Doughty, AN Other |
| | 4 | 24.01.85 | **WBA** | A | L | 0-1 | |
| 1885-86 | 1 | 31.10.85 | **Stafford Rangers** | A | W | 4-1 | |
| | 2 | 21.11.85 | **Burslem PV** | H | D | 2-2aet | Green, AN Other |
| | 2r | 28.11.85 | **Burslem PV** | A | L | 1-5 | |

| | | | | | | | | |
|---|---|---|---|---|---|---|---|---|
| 1886-87 | 1 | 23.10.86 | **Leek** | A | L | 1-2 | |
| 1887-88 | 1 | 15.10.87 | **Crewe Alexandra** | A | L | 0-5 | |

## DUDLEY TOWN

*Formed 1893. First entered FA Cup: 1899-1900. Duncan Edwards, who played for Manchester United in the 1957 Cup Final and lost his life in the Munich Air Crash nine months later, was born in Dudley. Members of the West Midlands League.*

| | | | | | | | |
|---|---|---|---|---|---|---|---|
| 1976-77 (WMRL) | 1 | 20.11.76 | **York City** (D3) | H | D | 1-1 | Walker |
| | 1r | 23.11.76 | **York City** | A | L | 1-4 | Molyneux (p) |

## DULWICH

*Entered FA Cup 1884-85 – 1887-88*

| | | | | | | | |
|---|---|---|---|---|---|---|---|
| 1884-85 | 1 | 08.11.84 | **Pilgrims** | H | W | 3-2 | |
| | 2 | 06.12.84 | **Romford** (1876) | A | L | 0-3 | |
| 1885-86 | 1 | 31.10.85 | **South Reading** | H | L | 1-2 | |
| 1886-87 | 1 | 23.10.86 | **Casuals** | A | W | 4-2 | |
| | 2 | 20.11.86 | **Maidenhead** | A | W | 3-2 | |
| | 3 | 11.12.86 | **Marlow** | A | L | 0-2 | |
| 1887-88 | 1 | 15.10.87 | **Reading** | A | W | 2-0 | Quint 2 |
| | | | *FA ordered replay after protests. Reading scratched. Dulwich walkover* | | | | |
| | 2 | 05.11.87 | **Hotspur FC** | H | W | 2-1 | |
| | 3 | 26.11.87 | **Swifts** | H | L | 1-3 | |

## DULWICH HAMLET

*Formed 1893. First entered FA Cup: 1919-20. FA Amateur Cup winners: 1920, 1932, 1934, 1937. The most famous FA Cup match involving Dulwich was their 8-7 win over St Albans City in a fourth qualifying round replay in November 1922 when Wilfred (Billy) Minter scored all seven goals for St Albans and still finished on the losing side. Members of the Isthmian League,*

| | | | | | | | |
|---|---|---|---|---|---|---|---|
| 1925-26 (IL) | 1 | 28.11.25 | **Southend Utd** (3S) | A | L | 1-5 | Nicol |
| 1926-27 (IL) | 1 | 27.11.26 | **Southend Utd** | H | L | 1-4 | Robbins |
| 1927-28 (IL) | 1 | 26.11.27 | **Ilford** (IL) | A | L | 0-4 | |
| 1928-29 (IL) | 1 | 24.11.28 | **Merthyr Town** (3S) | A | L | 2-4 | Holland, Kall |
| 1929-30 (IL) | 1 | 30.11.29 | **Plymouth Argyle** (3S) | H | L | 0-3 | |
| 1930-31 (IL) | 1 | 29.11.30 | **Newport County** (3S) | H | D | 2-2 | Smith, Hugo |
| | 1 | 04.12.30 | **Newport County** | A | L | 1-4 | Morrish |
| 1932-33 (IL) | 1 | 26.11.32 | **Swindon Town** (3S) | A | L | 1-4 | Smith |
| 1933-34 (IL) | 1 | 25.11.33 | **Newport County** (3S) | H | D | 2-2 | Ede, Miller |
| | 1r | 30.11.33 | **Newport County** | A | L | 2-6 | Jordan og, Levy |
| 1934-35 (IL) | 1 | 24.11.34 | **Torquay Utd** (3S) | H | L | 1-2 | Court |
| 1935-36 (IL) | 1 | 30.11.35 | **Torquay Utd** | H | L | 2-3 | Ready, Murray (p) |
| 1936-37 (IL) | 1 | 28.11.36 | **Swindon Town** (3S) | A | L | 0-6 | |
| 1937-38 (IL) | 1 | 27.11.37 | **Aldershot** (3S) | H | L | 1-2 | Morrish |
| 1948-49 (IL) | 1 | 27.11.48 | **Northampton Town** (3S) | A | L | 1-2 | Davies |
| 1998-99 (IL) | 1 | 14.11.98 | **Southport** (Conf) | H | L | 0-1 | |

## DUNSTABLE TOWN

*Originally formed 1895. First entered FA Cup: 1950-51. Folded 1976. Reformed 1998 claiming roots and records back to 1895 club. Members of the South Midlands League.*

| | | | | | | | |
|---|---|---|---|---|---|---|---|
| 1956-57 (HEL) | 1 | 17.11.56 | **Margate** (KL) | A | L | 1-3 | Grandham |

## DURHAM CITY

*Formed 1918. First entered FA Cup: 1919-20. Members of the Football League: 1921-1928. Disbanded 1938. Reformed 1949. Durham forgot to claim exemption from the early qualifying rounds in 1923-24 and failed to make it through to the Competition Proper. Members of the Northern League.*

| | | | | | | | |
|---|---|---|---|---|---|---|---|
| 1921-22 (3N) | | | 5q Darlington (H) 0-2 | | | | |
| 1922-23 (3N) | | | 4q West Stanley (H) 2-1; 5q Hartlepools U (H) 0-1 | | | | |
| 1923-24 (3N) | | | P West Stanley (H) 2-2; Pr West Stanley (A) 1-1; P 2r West Stanley (A) 1-0; 1q Dipton U (A) 0-1 | | | | |
| 1924-25 (3N) | | | 4q Blyth Spartans (H) 3-1; 5q Darlington (A) 1-3 | | | | |
| 1925-26 (3N) | 1 | 02.12.25 | **Ashington** (3N) | H | W | 4-1 | Stephenson 2, Johnson, Dent |
| | 2 | 12.12.25 | **Southport** (3N) | H | L | 0-3 | |
| 1926-27 (3N) | | | did not enter | | | | |
| 1927-28 (3N) | 1 | 26.11.27 | **Wrexham** (3N) | H | D | 1-1 | Stokes |

| | | | | | | | | |
|---|---|---|---|---|---|---|---|---|
| | 1r | 30.11.27 | **Wrexham** | A | L | 0-4 | |
| 1955-56 (NL) | 1 | 19.11.55 | **Bishop Auckland** (NL) | A | L | 1-3 | Smith |
| 1957-58 (NL) | 1 | 16.11.57 | **Spalding Utd** (ECL) | H | W | 3-1 | Armstrong, Ayre, Johnstone |
| | 2 | 07.12.57 | **Tranmere Rovers** (3N) | H | L | 0-3 | |

## EAGLEY

*Formed 1875. Entered FA Cup: 1878-79 – 1885-86. Played at Eagley Fields, Bolton.*

| | | | | | | | |
|---|---|---|---|---|---|---|---|
| 1878-79 | 1 | | bye | | | | |
| | 2 | 07.12.78 | **Darwen** | A | D | 0-0 | |
| | 2r | 21.12.78 | **Darwen** | H | L | 1-4 | Sarples |
| 1879-80 | 1 | 25.10.79 | **Darwen** | H | L | 0-1 | |
| 1880-81 | 1 | 30.10.80 | **Astley Bridge** | A | L | 0-4 | |
| 1881-82 | 1 | 22.10.81 | **Bolton Wanderers** | A | D | 5-5 | |
| | 1r | 12.11.81 | **Bolton Wanderers** | H | L | 0-1 | |
| 1882-83 | 1 | 04.11.82 | **Bolton Olympic** | A | W | 7-4 | Eagley 2, Hardiker, Whittam, Derham, Burgess, R Hall |
| | 2 | 02.12.82 | **Halliwell** | H | W | 3-1 | Corless 2, AN Other |
| | 3 | | bye | | | | |
| | 4 | 10.02.83 | **Druids** | A | L | 1-2aet | |
| 1883-84 | 1 | 13.10.83 | **Halliwell** | A | W | 5-2 | |
| | 2 | | bye | | | | |
| | 3 | 29.12.83 | **Preston North End** | A | L | 1-9 | |
| 1885-86 | 1 | 17.10.85 | **Bolton Wanderers** | A | L | 0-6 | |

## EASINGTON COLLIERY WELFARE

*Formed 1913. First entered FA Cup: 1931-32. On May 29, 1951, 83 men were killed as a result of an explosion and fire at Easington Colliery. As with the Creswell Colliery disaster, memories of the tragedy were still fresh when the colliery team made it through to the Competition Proper four years later. Members of the Northern League.*

| | | | | | | |
|---|---|---|---|---|---|---|
| 1955-56 (Wear) | 1 | 19.11.55 | **Tranmere Rovers** (3N) | H | L | 0-2 |

## EAST SHEEN

*Formed 1873. Played at Sheen Common. This was the only FA Cup match they played.*

| | | | | | | |
|---|---|---|---|---|---|---|
| 1887-88 | 1 | 15.10.87 | **Old St Marks** | A | L | 2-7 |

## EASTWOOD TOWN

*Formed 1953. First entered FA Cup: 1968-69. No relation to an earlier Eastwood Town that played in the FA Cup in the 1890s. Members of the Northern Premier League.*

| | | | | | | | |
|---|---|---|---|---|---|---|---|
| 1999-00 (NPL) | 1 | 30.10.99 | **Exeter City** (D3) | A | L | 1-2 | Smith |

## ECCLES UNITED

*Formed 1908 as Eccles Borough. Eccles United 1915. Entered FA Cup: 1919-20 – 1925-26*

| | | | | | | | |
|---|---|---|---|---|---|---|---|
| 1920-21 (LC) | 1 | 08.01.21 | **Southend Utd** (D3) | A | L | 1-5 | Schofield |

## ECCLESFIELD

*Formed 1873. Played at Fareham's Croft, Ecclesfield, Yorkshire. Entered FA Cup: 1887-88 – 1890-91. In 1892-93 they were founder members of the Sheffield League.*

| | | | | | | |
|---|---|---|---|---|---|---|
| 1887-88 | 1 | 15.10.87 | **Derby Midland** | H | W | 4-1 |
| | 2 | 05.11.87 | **Derby County** | A | L | 0-6 |

## ECKINGTON WORKS

*Entered FA Cup: 1885-86 – 1926-27. Eckington Works were also founder members of the Sheffield League.*

| | | | | | | |
|---|---|---|---|---|---|---|
| 1885-86 | 1 | 19.10.85 | **Sheffield Heeley** | A | L | 1-2 |
| 1887-88 | 1 | 15.10.87 | **Owlerton** | A | L | 1-2 |

## ELLESMERE PORT TOWN

*Entered FA Cup: 1921-22 – 1974-75. Joe Mercer, Arsenal skipper when they won the FA Cup in 1950 and Manchester City's victorious FA Cup winning manager in 1969, was born in Ellesmere Port and played for the club early in his career. Also born in the town was Stan Cullis, captain and later manager of Wolves, who was twice winner of the FA Cup when a manager.*

| | | | | | | |
|---|---|---|---|---|---|---|
| 1971-72 (NPL) | 1 | 20.11.71 | **Boston Utd** (NPL) | H | L | 0-3 |

## ELSWICK RANGERS

| | | | | | | |
|---|---|---|---|---|---|---|
| 1887-88 | 1 | 15.10.87 | **Bishop Auckland** (CL) | H | D | 3-3aet |

| | | | | | | | | |
|---|---|---|---|---|---|---|---|---|
| | | 1r | 22.10.87 | **Bishop Auckland** | A | W | 2-0 | |
| | | 2 | 05.11.87 | **Darlington** | A | L | 3-4aet | McCallum, McDonald, Nugent |

## ELY CITY

*Formed: 1885. First entered FA Cup: 1954-55. Members of the Eastern Counties League.*

| | | | | | | | | |
|---|---|---|---|---|---|---|---|---|
| 1956-57 | (PDL) | 1 | 17.11.56 | **Torquay Utd** (3S) | H | L | 2-6 | Oliver, King |

## EMLEY

*Formed 1903. First entered FA Cup: 1971-72. FA Vase runners-up: 1988. Changed name to Wakefield & Emley 2002. League club beaten (on penalties): Lincoln City. Members of the Northern Premier League.*

| | | | | | | | | |
|---|---|---|---|---|---|---|---|---|
| 1991-92 | (NPL) | 1 | 17.11.91 | **Bolton Wanderers** (D3) | H | L | 0-3 | |
| | | | | *played at Leeds Road, Huddersfield* | | | | |
| 1997-98 | (NPL) | 1 | 15.11.97 | **Morecambe** (Conf) | A | D | 1-1 | Banks (p) |
| | | 1r | 25.11.97 | **Morecambe** | H | D | 3-3aet | Hurst 2, Marshall |
| | | | | *Emley won 3-1 on penalties* | | | | |
| | | 2 | 06.12.97 | **Lincoln City** (D3) | A | D | 2-2 | Hurst, Graham |
| | | 2r | 17.12.97 | **Lincoln City** | H | D | 3-3aet | Graham, Nicholson 2(1p) |
| | | | | *Emley won 4-3 on penalties* | | | | |
| | | 3 | 03.01.98 | **West Ham Utd** (PL) | A | L | 1-2 | David |
| 1998-99 | (NPL) | 1 | 15.11.98 | **Rotherham Utd** (D3) | H | D | 1-1 | Bambrook |
| | | | | *played at Oakwell, Barnsley* | | | | |
| | | 1r | 24.11.98 | **Rotherham Utd** (D3) | A | L | 1-3 | Bambrook |

## ENDERBY TOWN

*Formed 1900. First entered FA Cup: 1972-73. Changed name to Leicester United 1981. Folded 1997.*

| | | | | | | | | |
|---|---|---|---|---|---|---|---|---|
| 1977-78 | (SL) | 1 | 26.11.77 | **AP Leamington** (SL) | A | L | 1-6 | Cooper |

## ENFIELD

*Formed 1893. First entered FA Cup: 1896-97 FA Trophy Winners: 1982, 1988; FA Amateur Cup winners: 1967, 1970; Runners-up: 1964, 1972; League clubs beaten: Aldershot, Exeter City, Cardiff City, Chesterfield, Hereford United, Leyton Orient, Northampton Town, Port Vale, Torquay United, Wimbledon (2). Members of the Isthmian League.*

| | | | | | | | | |
|---|---|---|---|---|---|---|---|---|
| 1931-32 | (AL) | 1 | 28.11.31 | **Cardiff City** (3S) | A | L | 0-8 | |
| 1937-38 | (AL) | 1 | 27.11.37 | **Bristol City** (3S) | A | L | 0-3 | |
| 1959-60 | (AL) | 1 | 14.11.59 | **Headington Utd** (SL) | H | W | 4-3 | Thomas, McDonnell (p), Long, Lawrence |
| | | 2 | 05.12.59 | **Bournemouth** (D3) | H | L | 1-5 | McDonnell |
| 1962-63 | (AL) | 1 | 03.11.62 | **Cheltenham Town** (SL) | A | W | 6-3 | Thomas 2, Lawrence, Quail, Terry (p), Bloomfield |
| | | 2 | 24.11.62 | **Peterborough Utd** (D3) | A | L | 0-1 | |
| 1963-64 | (IL) | 1 | 16.11.63 | **Reading** (D3) | A | D | 2-2 | Thomas, Broomfield |
| | | 1r | 19.11.63 | **Reading** | H | L | 2-4aet | Thomas, Day |
| 1964-65 | (IL) | 1 | 14.11.64 | **Romford** (SL) | A | D | 0-0 | |
| | | 1r | 17.11.64 | **Romford** | H | D | 0-0aet | |
| | | 1 2r | 23.11.64 | **Romford** | | W | 4-2 | Day, Thomas 2, Howard |
| | | | | *played at Highbury* | | | | |
| | | 2 | 05.12.64 | **Barnet** (AL) | H | D | 4-4 | Kingsland, Day 2 (2ps), Thomas |
| | | 2r | 08.12.64 | **Barnet** | A | L | 0-3 | |
| 1966-67 | (IL) | 1 | 26.11.66 | **Chesham Utd** (AL) | H | W | 6-0 | Connell 3, Churchill (p), Adams, Reid |
| | | 2 | 07.01.67 | **Watford** (D3) | H | L | 2-4 | Williams og, Churchill |
| 1967-68 | (IL) | 1 | 18.12.67 | **Swansea Town** (D4) | A | L | 0-2 | |
| 1969-70 | (IL) | 1 | 15.11.69 | **Brighton** (D3) | A | L | 1-2 | Day (p) |
| 1970-71 | (IL) | 1 | 21.11.70 | **Cambridge Utd** (D4) | H | L | 0-1 | |
| 1971-72 | (IL) | 1 | 20.11.71 | **Maidenhead** (IL) | H | W | 2-0 | Turley, Hill |
| | | 2 | 11.12.71 | **Peterborough Utd** (D4) | A | L | 0-4 | |
| 1972-73 | (IL) | 1 | 18.11.72 | **Bishop's Stortford** (IL) | H | D | 1-1 | Brooks |
| | | 1r | 21.11.72 | **Bishop's Stortford** | A | L | 0-1 | |
| 1976-77 | (IL) | 1 | 20.11.76 | **Harwich & Park** (IL) | H | D | 0-0 | |
| | | 1r | 23.11.76 | **Harwich & Park** | A | W | 3-0 | Searle, Wilson, Reeve |
| | | 2 | 11.12.76 | **Crystal Palace** (D3) | A | L | 0-4 | |
| 1977-78 | (IL) | 1 | 26.11.77 | **Wimbledon** (D4) | H | W | 3-0 | Knapman, Bass, O'Sullivan |
| | | 2 | 17.12.77 | **Northampton Town** (D4) | A | W | 2-0 | Searle 2 |

| | | | | | | | | |
|---|---|---|---|---|---|---|---|---|
| | | 3 | 07.01.78 | **Blyth Spartans** (NL) | A | L | 0-1 | |
| 1978-79 | (IL) | 1 | 25.11.78 | **Wealdstone** (SL) | A | W | 5-0 | O'Sullivan, Searle, King 2, Wright |
| | | 2 | 16.12.78 | **Swindon Town** (D3) | A | L | 0-3 | |
| 1979-80 | (IL) | 1 | 24.11.79 | **Yeovil Town** (APL) | H | L | 0-1 | |
| 1980-81 | (IL) | 1 | 22.11.80 | **Wembley** (IL) | H | W | 3-0 | Holmes, Wade, Jennings |
| | | 2 | 13.12.80 | **Hereford Utd** (D4) | H | W | 2-0 | Burton 2 |
| | | 3 | 03.01.81 | **Port Vale** (D4) | A | D | 1-1 | Bishop |
| | | 3r | 06.01.81 | **Port Vale** | H | W | 3-0 | Bishop, King, Howell |
| | | 4 | 24.01.81 | **Barnsley** (D3) | A | D | 1-1 | Burton |
| | | 4r | 28.01.81 | **Barnsley**<br>*played at White Hart Lane* | H | L | 0-3 | |
| 1981-82 | (APL) | 1 | 21.11.81 | **Hastings Utd** (SL) | H | W | 2-0 | Oliver, Ashford |
| | | 2 | 15.12.81 | **Wimbledon** (D3) | H | W | 4-1 | Turner, Ironton, Oliver, Waite |
| | | 3 | 02.01.82 | **Crystal Palace** (D2) | H | L | 2-3 | Ironton, Oliver |
| 1982-83 | (APL) | 1 | 20.11.82 | **Newport County** (D3) | H | D | 0-0 | |
| | | 1r | 23.11.82 | **Newport County** | A | L | 2-4 | Taylor, Turner (p) |
| 1983-84 | (APL) | 1 | 19.11.83 | **Wealdstone** (APL) | A | D | 1-1 | Flint |
| | | 1r | 22.11.83 | **Wealdstone** | H | D | 2-2aet | Holmes 2 |
| | | 1 2r | 28.11.83 | **Wealdstone** | A | L | 0-2 | |
| 1984-85 | (APL) | 1 | 17.11.84 | **Exeter City** (D4) | A | D | 2-2 | Cox (p), Ashford |
| | | 1r | 20.11.84 | **Exeter City** | H | W | 3-0 | Ironton, Taylor 2 |
| | | 2 | 08.12.84 | **Millwall** (D3) | A | L | 0-1 | |
| 1985-86 | (APL) | 1 | 16.11.85 | **Bognor Regis Town** (IL) | H | L | 0-2 | |
| 1986-87 | (Conf) | 1 | 15.11.86 | **Dartford** (SL) | A | D | 1-1 | Duffield (p) |
| | | 1r | 18.11.86 | **Dartford** | H | W | 3-0 | Duffield (p), King, Keen |
| | | 2 | 06.12.86 | **Swindon Town** (D3) | A | L | 0-3 | |
| 1988-89 | (Conf) | 1 | 19.11.88 | **Leyton Orient** (D4) | H | D | 1-1 | Furlong |
| | | 1r | 23.11.88 | **Leyton Orient** | A | D | 2-2aet | Lewis, Howell |
| | | 1 2r | 28.11.88 | **Leyton Orient** | A | W | 1-0 | Lewis |
| | | 2 | 11.12.88 | **Cardiff City** (D3) | H | L | 1-4 | Bate |
| 1991-92 | (IL) | 1 | 16.11.91 | **Aldershot** (D4) | A | W | 1-0 | Brush |
| | | 2 | 07.12.91 | **Barnet** (D4) | H | L | 1-4 | Robinson |
| 1993-94 | (IL) | 1 | 13.11.93 | **Cardiff City** (D2) | H | D | 0-0 | |
| | | 1r | 30.11.93 | **Cardiff City** | A | L | 0-1 | |
| 1994-95 | (IL) | 1 | 12.11.94 | **Cardiff City** (D2) | H | W | 1-0 | Abbott |
| | | 2 | 03.12.94 | **Torquay Utd** (D3) | H | D | 1-1 | Abbott |
| | | 2r | 13.12.94 | **Torquay Utd** | A | W | 1-0 | Kerr |
| | | 3 | 07.01.95 | **Leicester City** (PL) | A | L | 0-2 | |
| 1995-96 | (IL) | 1 | 11.11.95 | **Newport (IOW)** (SL) | A | D | 1-1 | Abbott |
| | | 1r | 21.11.95 | **Newport (IOW)** | H | W | 2-1 | Abbott 2(1p) |
| | | 2 | 02.12.95 | **Woking** (Conf) | H | D | 1-1 | Gentle |
| | | 2r | 12.12.95 | **Woking** | A | L | 1-2 | Abbott |
| 1996-97 | (IL) | 1 | 16.11.96 | **Bromley** (IL) | A | W | 3-1 | West 3 |
| | | 2 | 07.12.96 | **Peterborough Utd** (D2) | H | D | 1-1 | Marshall |
| | | 2r | 17.12.96 | **Peterborough Utd** | A | L | 1-4 | St Hilaire |
| 1998-99 | (IL) | 1 | 14.11.98 | **York City** (D2) | H | D | 2-2 | Dunwell, Richardson |
| | | 1r | 24.11.98 | **York City** | A | L | 1-2 | Dunwell |
| 1999-00 | (IL) | 1 | 30.10.99 | **Chesterfield** (D2) | A | W | 2-1 | Bunn, Brown |
| | | 2 | 20.11.99 | **Preston North End** (D2) | A | D | 0-0 | |
| | | 2r | 30.11.99 | **Preston North End**<br>*played at Clarence Park, St Albans* | H | L | 0-3 | |

# EPSOM AND EWELL TOWN

*Formed 1917. First entered FA Cup: 1925-26. FA Vase runners-up: 1975. Played in 1933 as Epsom Town. Members of the Isthmian League.*

| | | | | | | | | |
|---|---|---|---|---|---|---|---|---|
| 1933-34 | (Lon) | 1 | 25.11.33 | **Clapton Orient** (3S) | A | L | 2-4 | Marlow, Graves |

# ESHER LEOPOLD

*Entered the FA Cup in 1881-82, playing this match only.*

| | | | | | | | | |
|---|---|---|---|---|---|---|---|---|
| 1881-82 | | 1 | 05.11.81 | **Old Carthusians** | A | L | 0-5 | |

# ETONIAN RAMBLERS

*Eton-based Victorian amateurs who played these two FA Cup matches only.*

| | | | | | | | |
|---|---|---|---|---|---|---|---|
| 1882-83 | 1 | 21.10.82 | **Romford (1876)** | H | W | 6-2 | |
| | 2 | 02.12.82 | **Old Carthusians** | A | L | 0-7 | |

# EVENWOOD TOWN

*Formed 1890. First entered FA Cup: 1929-30. Members of the Northern League.*

| | | | | | | | |
|---|---|---|---|---|---|---|---|
| 1956-57 (NL) | 1 | 17.11.56 | **Darlington** (3N) | A | L | 2-7 | Chisen, Calbrook |

# EVERTON

*Formed 1878. Founder Members of the Football League 1888. FA Cup winners: (5 times) 1906, 1933, 1966, 1984, 1995. FA Cup runners-up (7 times) 1893, 1897, 1907, 1968, 1985, 1986, 1989; Hold joint-record (with Arsenal) of 23 semi-final appearances. FA Cup record win: 11-2 v Derby Co, 1st round, 18.01.1890; FA Cup Record defeat: 0-6 v Crystal Palace, 1st round, 07.01.1922.*

| | | | | | | | |
|---|---|---|---|---|---|---|---|
| 1886-87 | 1 | 30.10.86 | **Glasgow Rangers** | H | L | 0-1 | |
| 1887-88 | 1 | 15.10.87 | **Bolton Wanderers** | A | L | 0-1 | |
| | | | *FA ordered replay after Bolton player declared ineligible* | | | | |
| | 1r | 29.10.87 | **Bolton Wanderers** | H | D | 2-2 | Farmer, Watson |
| | 1 2r | 12.11.87 | **Bolton Wanderers** | A | D | 1-1 | Farmer |
| | 1 3r | 19.11.87 | **Bolton Wanderers** | H | W | 2-1 | Goodie, Watson |
| | | | *FA disqualified Everton for ineligible players. Bolton re-instated* | | | | |
| | 2 | 26.11.87 | **Preston North End** | A | L | 0-6 | |
| | | | *FA declared match void. Everton were disqualified. Bolton, who lost to Everton in the previous round, were re-instated* | | | | |
| 1888-89 (D1) | | | Everton withdrew after being drawn to play Ulster away in 1st qualifying round | | | | |
| 1889-90 (D1) | 1 | 18.01.90 | **Derby County** (D1) | A | W | 11-2 | Brady 3, Geary 3, Milward 3, Doyle, Kirkwood |
| | 2 | 03.02.90 | **Stoke** (D1) | A | L | 2-4 | Geary, Milward |
| 1890-91 (D1) | 1 | 17.01.91 | **Sunderland** (D1) | A | L | 0-1 | |
| 1891-92 (D1) | 1 | 16.01.92 | **Burnley** (D1) | H | L | 2-4 | Chadwick, Robertson |
| 1892-93 (D1) | 1 | 21.01.93 | **WBA** (D1) | H | W | 4-1 | Geary 2, Latta, Maxwell |
| | 2 | 04.02.93 | **Nottingham Forest** (FAll) | H | W | 4-2 | Milward 2, E Chadwick, Geary |
| | 3 | 18.02.93 | **Sheffield Wed** (D1) | H | W | 3-0 | E Chadwick, Geary, Maxwell |
| | SF | 04.03.93 | **Preston North End** (D1) | | D | 2-2 | E Chadwick, Gordon |
| | | | *played at Bramall Lane* | | | | |
| | SFr | 16.03.93 | **Preston North End** | | D | 0-0aet | |
| | | | *played at Ewood Park* | | | | |
| | SF 2r | 20.03.93 | **Preston North End** | | W | 2-1 | Gordon, Maxwell |
| | | | *played at Trent Bridge, Nottingham* | | | | |
| | F | 25.03.93 | **Wolverhampton W** (D1) | | L | 0-1 | |
| | | | *played at Fallowfield, Manchester* | | | | |
| 1893-94 (D1) | 1 | 27.01.94 | **Stoke** (D1) | A | L | 0-1 | |
| 1894-95 (D1) | 1 | 02.02.95 | **Southport** (LL) | A | W | 3-0 | Bell 3 |
| | 2 | 16.02.95 | **Blackburn Rovers** (D1) | H | D | 1-1 | Chadwick |
| | 2r | 20.02.95 | **Blackburn Rovers** | A | W | 3-2 | Chadwick 2, Hartley |
| | 3 | 02.03.95 | **Sheffield Wed** (D1) | A | L | 0-2 | |
| 1895-96 (D1) | 1 | 01.02.96 | **Nottingham Forest** (D1) | A | W | 2-0 | Chadwick, Milward |
| | 2 | 15.02.96 | **Sheffield Utd** (D1) | H | W | 3-0 | Bell, Cameron, Milward |
| | 3 | 29.02.96 | **Sheffield Wed** (D1) | A | L | 0-4 | |
| 1896-97 (D1) | 1 | 30.01.97 | **Burton Wanderers** (D2) | H | W | 5-2 | Bell, Chadwick, Holt, Milward, og |
| | 2 | 13.02.97 | **Bury** (D1) | H | W | 3-0 | Taylor 2, Milward |
| | 3 | 27.02.97 | **Blackburn Rovers** (D1) | H | W | 2-0 | Hartley 2 |
| | SF | 20.03.97 | **Derby County** (D1) | | W | 3-2 | Chadwick, Hartley, Milward |
| | | | *played at Victoria Ground, Stoke* | | | | |
| | F | 10.04.97 | **Aston Villa** (D1) | | L | 2-3 | Bell, Boyle |
| | | | *played at Crystal Palace* | | | | |
| 1897-98 (D1) | 1 | 29.01.98 | **Blackburn Rovers** (D1) | H | W | 1-0 | Williams |
| | 2 | 12.02.98 | **Stoke** (D1) | A | D | 0-0 | |
| | 2r | 17.02.98 | **Stoke** | H | W | 5-1 | L Bell 2, Cameron, Chadwick, Taylor |
| | 3 | 26.02.98 | **Burnley** (D2) | A | W | 3-1 | Taylor 2, L Bell |
| | SF | 19.03.98 | **Derby County** (D1) | | L | 1-3 | Chadwick |
| | | | *played at Molineux* | | | | |

| | | | | | | | | |
|---|---|---|---|---|---|---|---|---|
| 1898-99 | (D1) | 1 | 28.01.99 | **Jarrow** (NAll) | H | W | 3-1 | Chadwick, Proudfoot, Taylor |
| | | 2 | 11.02.99 | **Nottingham Forest** (D1) | H | L | 0-1 | |
| 1899-00 | (D1) | 1 | 27.01.00 | **Southampton** (SL) | A | L | 0-3 | |
| 1900-01 | (D1) | 1 | 09.02.01 | **Southampton** | A | W | 3-1 | Settle, Taylor, Turner |
| | | 2 | 23.02.01 | **Sheffield Utd** (D1) | A | L | 0-2 | |
| 1901-02 | (D1) | 1 | 25.01.02 | **Liverpool** (D1) | A | D | 2-2 | J Sharp, Young |
| | | 1r | 30.01.02 | **Liverpool** | H | L | 0-2 | |
| 1902-03 | (D1) | 1 | 07.02.03 | **Portsmouth** (SL) | H | W | 5-0 | Bell 2, Abbott, Bearley, Sharp |
| | | 2 | 21.02.03 | **Manchester Utd** (D2) | H | W | 3-1 | Abbott, Booth, Taylor |
| | | 3 | 07.03.03 | **Millwall Athletic** (SL) | A | L | 0-1 | |
| 1903-04 | (D1) | 1 | 06.02.04 | **Tottenham Hotspur** (SL) | H | L | 1-2 | Taylor |
| 1904-05 | (D1) | 1 | 04.02.05 | **Liverpool** (D1) | A | D | 1-1 | Makepeace |
| | | 1r | 08.02.05 | **Liverpool** | H | W | 2-1 | Hardman, McDermott |
| | | 2 | 18.02.05 | **Stoke** (D1) | A | W | 4-0 | McDermott 2, Makepeace, Settle |
| | | 3 | 04.03.05 | **Southampton** (SL) | H | W | 4-0 | Settle 3, McDermott |
| | | SF | 25.03.05 | **Aston Villa** (D1) | | D | 1-1 | Sharp |
| | | | | *played at Victoria Ground, Stoke* | | | | |
| | | SFr | 29.03.05 | **Aston Villa** | | L | 1-2 | Sharp |
| | | | | *played at Trent Bridge, Nottingham* | | | | |
| 1905-06 | (D1) | 1 | 13.01.06 | **WBA** (D2) | H | W | 3-1 | Hardman, Makepeace, Sharp |
| | | 2 | 03.02.06 | **Chesterfield** (D2) | H | W | 3-0 | Settle, Taylor, Young |
| | | 3 | 24.02.06 | **Bradford City** (D2) | H | W | 1-0 | Makepeace |
| | | 4 | 10.03.06 | **Sheffield Wed** (D1) | H | W | 4-3 | Bolton, Booth Sharp, Taylor |
| | | SF | 31.03.06 | **Liverpool** (D1) | | W | 2-0 | Abbott, Hardman |
| | | | | *played at Villa Park* | | | | |
| | | F | 21.04.06 | **Newcastle Utd** (D1) | | W | 1-0 | Young |
| | | | | *played at Crystal Palace* | | | | |
| 1906-07 | (D1) | 1 | 12.01.07 | **Sheffield Utd** (D1) | H | W | 1-0 | Johnson og |
| | | 2 | 02.02.07 | **West Ham Utd** (SL) | A | W | 2-1 | Settle, Sharp |
| | | 3 | 23.02.07 | **Bolton Wanderers** (D1) | H | D | 0-0 | |
| | | 3r | 27.02.07 | **Bolton Wanderers** | A | W | 3-0 | Abbot, Settle, Taylor |
| | | 4 | 09.03.07 | **Crystal Palace** (SL) | A | D | 1-1 | Taylor |
| | | 4r | 13.03.07 | **Crystal Palace** | H | W | 4-0 | Settle 2, Hardman, Young |
| | | SF | 23.03.07 | **WBA** (D2) | | W | 2-1 | Sharp, G Wilson |
| | | | | *played at Burnden Park* | | | | |
| | | F | 20.04.07 | **Sheffield Wed** (D1) | | L | 1-2 | Sharp |
| | | | | *played at Crystal Palace* | | | | |
| 1907-08 | (D1) | 1 | 11.01.08 | **Tottenham Hotspur** (SL) | H | W | 1-0 | Young |
| | | 2 | 01.02.08 | **Oldham Athletic** (D2) | A | D | 0-0 | |
| | | 2r | 05.02.08 | **Oldham Athletic** | H | W | 6-1 | Bolton 4, Abbot, Young |
| | | 3 | 22.02.08 | **Bolton Wanderers** (D1) | A | D | 3-3 | Settle 2, Bolton |
| | | 3r | 26.02.08 | **Bolton Wanderers** | H | W | 3-1aet | Young 2, Settle |
| | | 4 | 07.03.08 | **Southampton** (SL) | H | D | 0-0 | |
| | | 4r | 11.03.08 | **Southampton** | A | L | 2-3 | Bolton, Young |
| 1908-09 | (D1) | 1 | 16.01.09 | **Barnsley** (D2) | H | W | 3-1 | Coleman, Sharp, White |
| | | 2 | 06.02.09 | **Manchester Utd** (D1) | A | L | 0-1 | |
| 1909-10 | (D1) | 1 | 15.01.10 | **Middlesbrough** (D1) | A | D | 1-1 | White |
| | | 1r | 19.01.10 | **Middlesbrough** | H | W | 5-3 | Freeman, Makepeace, Taylor, White, Young |
| | | 2 | 05.02.10 | **Woolwich Arsenal** (D1) | H | W | 5-0 | Sharp 2, Barlow, Freeman, Young |
| | | 3 | 19.02.10 | **Sunderland** (D1) | H | W | 2-0 | Makepeace, Young |
| | | 4 | 05.03.10 | **Coventry City** (SL) | A | W | 2-0 | Freeman 2 |
| | | SF | 26.03.10 | **Barnsley** (D2) | | D | 0-0 | |
| | | | | *played at Elland Road* | | | | |
| | | SFr | 31.03.10 | **Barnsley** (D2) | | L | 0-3 | |
| | | | | *played at Old Trafford* | | | | |
| 1910-11 | (D1) | 1 | 14.01.11 | **Crystal Palace** (SL) | A | W | 4-0 | Gourlay, Magner, A Young, R Young |
| | | 2 | 04.02.11 | **Liverpool** (D1) | H | W | 2-1 | A Young 2 |
| | | 3 | 25.02.11 | **Derby County** (D2) | A | L | 0-5 | |
| 1911-12 | (D1) | 1 | 13.01.12 | **Clapton Orient** (D2) | A | W | 2-1 | Beare, Browell |
| | | 2 | 03.02.12 | **Bury** (D1) | H | D | 1-1 | Maconnachie |

| | | | | | | | |
|---|---|---|---|---|---|---|---|
| | 2r | 08.02.12 | **Bury** (D1) | H | W | 6-0 | Browell 4, Davidson, Jefferis |
| | 3 | 24.02.12 | **Oldham Athletic** (D1) | A | W | 2-0 | Browell 2 |
| | 4 | 09.03.12 | **Swindon Town** (SL) | A | L | 1-2 | Makepeace |
| 1912-13 (D1) | 1 | 11.01.13 | **Stockport County** (D2) | H | - | 1-1ab | T Browell |
| | | | *abandoned after 48 minutes* | | | | |
| | 1 | 15.01.13 | **Stockport County** | H | W | 5-1 | T Browell 3, Bradshaw, Wareing |
| | 2 | 01.02.13 | **Brighton** (SL) | A | D | 0-0 | |
| | 2r | 05.02.13 | **Brighton** | H | W | 1-0 | Jefferis |
| | 3 | 22.02.13 | **Bristol Rovers** (SL) | A | W | 4-0 | T Browell, Fleetwood, Harris, Jefferis |
| | 4 | 08.03.13 | **Oldham Athletic** (D1) | H | L | 0-1 | |
| 1913-14 (D1) | 1 | 10.01.14 | **Glossop North End** (D2) | A | L | 1-2 | Bradshaw |
| 1914-15 (D1) | 1 | 09.01.15 | **Barnsley** (D2) | H | W | 3-0 | Galt 2, Parker |
| | 2 | 30.01.15 | **Bristol City** (D2) | H | W | 4-0 | Clennell, Kirsopp, Parker, Wareing |
| | 3 | 20.02.15 | **QPR** (SL) | A | W | 2-1 | Clennell, Millington og |
| | | | *played at Stamford Bridge* | | | | |
| | 4 | 06.03.15 | **Bradford City** (D1) | A | W | 2-0 | Chedgzoy, Clennell |
| | SF | 27.03.15 | **Chelsea** (D1) | | L | 0-2 | |
| | | | *played at Villa Park* | | | | |
| 1919-20 (D1) | 1 | 10.01.20 | **Birmingham** (D2) | A | L | 0-2 | |
| 1920-21 (D1) | 1 | 08.01.21 | **Stockport County** (D2) | H | W | 1-0 | Brewster og |
| | 2 | 29.01.21 | **Sheffield Wed** (D2) | H | D | 1-1 | Parker |
| | 2r | 03.02.21 | **Sheffield Wed** | A | W | 1-0 | Crossley |
| | 3 | 19.02.21 | **Newcastle Utd** (D1) | H | W | 3-0 | Crossley 2, Davies |
| | 4 | 05.03.21 | **Wolverhampton W** (D2) | H | L | 0-1 | |
| 1921-22 (D1) | 1 | 07.01.22 | **Crystal Palace** (D2) | H | L | 0-6 | |
| 1922-23 (D1) | 1 | 13.01.23 | **Bradford Park A** (3N) | H | D | 1-1 | Chedgzoy |
| | 1r | 17.01.23 | **Bradford Park A** | A | L | 0-1 | |
| 1923-24 (D1) | 1 | 12.01.24 | **Preston North End** (D1) | H | W | 3-1 | Chadwick, Chedgzoy, Cock |
| | 2 | 02.02.24 | **Brighton** (3S) | A | L | 2-5 | Chadwick, Cock |
| 1924-25 (D1) | 1 | 10.01.25 | **Burnley** (D1) | H | W | 2-1 | Chadwick 2 |
| | 2 | 31.01.25 | **Sunderland** (D1) | A | D | 0-0 | |
| | 2r | 04.02.25 | **Sunderland** | H | W | 2-1 | Chadwick, Irvine |
| | 3 | 21.02.25 | **Sheffield Utd** (D1) | A | L | 0-1 | |
| 1925-26 (D1) | 3 | 09.01.26 | **Fulham** (D2) | H | D | 1-1 | Dean |
| | 3r | 14.01.26 | **Fulham** | A | L | 0-1 | |
| 1926-27 (D1) | 3 | 08.01.27 | **Poole Town** (SL) | H | W | 3-1 | Dean, Irvine, Troop |
| | 4 | 22.01.27 | **Hull City** (D2) | A | D | 1-1 | Virr |
| | 4r | 02.02.27 | **Hull City** | H | D | 2-2aet | Dean, Troop |
| | 4 2r | 07.02.27 | **Hull City** | | L | 2-3aet | Dean, Dominy |
| | | | *played at Villa Park* | | | | |
| 1927-28 (D1) | 3 | 14.01.28 | **Preston North End** (D2) | A | W | 3-0 | Dean, Irvine, Ward og |
| | 4 | 28.01.28 | **Arsenal** (D1) | A | L | 3-4 | Dean 2, Troop |
| 1928-29 (D1) | 3 | 12.01.29 | **Chelsea** (D2) | A | L | 0-2 | |
| 1929-30 (D1) | 3 | 11.01.30 | **Carlisle Utd** (3N) | A | W | 4-2 | Critchley 2, Dean 2 |
| | 4 | 25.01.30 | **Blackburn Rovers** (D1) | A | L | 1-4 | Martin |
| 1930-31 (D2) | 3 | 10.01.31 | **Plymouth Argyle** (D2) | A | W | 2-0 | Dunn, Stein |
| | 4 | 24.01.31 | **Crystal Palace** (3S) | A | W | 6-0 | Dean 4, Johnson, og |
| | 5 | 14.02.31 | **Grimsby Town** (D1) | H | W | 5-3 | Johnson 2, Stein 2, Dean |
| | 6 | 28.02.31 | **Southport** (3N) | H | W | 9-1 | Dean 4, Critchley 2, Dunn 2, Johnson |
| | SF | 14.03.31 | **WBA** (D2) | | L | 0-1 | |
| | | | *played at Old Trafford* | | | | |
| 1931-32 (D1) | 3 | 09.01.32 | **Liverpool** (D1) | H | L | 1-2 | Dean |
| 1932-33 (D1) | 3 | 14.01.33 | **Leicester City** (D1) | A | W | 3-2 | Dean, Dunn, Stein |
| | 4 | 28.01.33 | **Bury** (D2) | H | W | 3-1 | Johnson 2, Dean |
| | 5 | 18.02.33 | **Leeds Utd** (D1) | H | W | 2-0 | Dean, Stein |
| | 6 | 03.03.33 | **Luton Town** (3S) | H | W | 6-0 | Johnson 2, Stein 2, Dean, Dunn |
| | SF | 18.03.33 | **West Ham Utd** (D2) | | W | 2-1 | Critchley, Dunn |
| | | | *played at Molineux* | | | | |
| | F | 29.04.33 | **Manchester City** (D1) | | W | 3-0 | Dean, Dunn, Stein |
| | | | *played at Wembley Stadium* | | | | |
| 1933-34 (D1) | 3 | 13.01.34 | **Tottenham Hotspur** (D1) | A | L | 0-3 | |

| | | | | | | | |
|---|---|---|---|---|---|---|---|
| 1934-35 (D1) | 3 | 12.01.35 | **Grimsby Town** (D1) | H | W | 6-3 | Geldard 3, Stevenson 2, Cunliffe |
| | 4 | 26.01.35 | **Sunderland** (D1) | A | D | 1-1 | Cunliffe |
| | 4r | 30.01.35 | **Sunderland** | H | W | 6-4aet | Coulter 3, Geldard 2, Stevenson |
| | 5 | 16.02.35 | **Derby County** (D1) | H | W | 3-1 | Coulter 2, Dean |
| | 6 | 02.03.35 | **Bolton Wanderers** (D2) | H | L | 1-2 | Coulter |
| 1935-36 (D1) | 3 | 11.01.36 | **Preston North End** (D1) | H | L | 1-3 | Geldard |
| 1936-37 (D1) | 3 | 16.01.37 | **Bournemouth** (3S) | H | W | 5-0 | Gillick 2, Stevenson 2, Cunliffe |
| | 4 | 30.01.37 | **Sheffield Wed** (D1) | H | W | 3-0 | Britton, Coulter, Dean |
| | 5 | 20.02.37 | **Tottenham Hotspur** (D2) | H | D | 1-1 | Coulter |
| | 5r | 22.02.37 | **Tottenham Hotspur** | A | L | 3-4 | Dean 2, Lawton |
| 1937-38 (D1) | 3 | 08.01.38 | **Chelsea** (D1) | A | W | 1-0 | Stevenson |
| | 4 | 22.01.38 | **Sunderland** (D1) | H | L | 0-1 | |
| 1938-39 (D1) | 3 | 07.01.39 | **Derby County** (D1) | A | W | 1-0 | Boyes |
| | 4 | 21.01.39 | **Doncaster Rovers** (3N) | H | W | 8-0 | Lawton 4, Boyes 2, Gillick, Stevenson |
| | 5 | 11.02.39 | **Birmingham** (D1) | A | D | 2-2 | Boyes, Stevenson |
| | 5r | 15.02.39 | **Birmingham** | H | W | 2-1 | Cook, Gillick |
| | 6 | 04.03.39 | **Wolverhampton W** (D1) | A | L | 0-2 | |
| 1945-46 (D1) | 3 1L | 05.01.46 | **Preston North End** (D1) | A | L | 1-2 | Catterick |
| | 3 2L | 09.01.46 | **Preston North End** | H | D | 2-2aet | Elliott, Mercer |
| 1946-47 (D1) | 3 | 11.01.47 | **Southend Utd** (3S) | H | W | 4-2 | Fielding, Jones, McIlhatton, Wainwright |
| | 4 | 25.01.47 | **Sheffield Wed** (D2) | A | L | 1-2 | Wainwright |
| 1947-48 (D1) | 3 | 10.01.48 | **Grimsby Town** (D1) | A | W | 4-1 | Wainwright 2, Dodds, Farrell |
| | 4 | 24.01.48 | **Wolverhampton W** (D1) | A | D | 1-1aet | Catterick |
| | 4r | 31.01.48 | **Wolverhampton W** | H | W | 3-2aet | Fielding 2, Grant |
| | 5 | 07.02.48 | **Fulham** (D2) | A | D | 1-1aet | Eglington |
| | 5r | 14.02.48 | **Fulham** | H | L | 0-1 | |
| 1948-49 (D1) | 3 | 08.01.49 | **Manchester City** (D1) | H | W | 1-0 | Higgins |
| | 4 | 29.01.49 | **Chelsea** (D1) | A | L | 0-2 | |
| 1949-50 (D1) | 3 | 07.01.50 | **QPR** (D2) | A | W | 2-0 | Buckle, Catterick |
| | 4 | 28.01.50 | **West Ham Utd** (D2) | A | W | 2-1 | Catterick 2 |
| | 5 | 11.02.50 | **Tottenham Hotspur** (D2) | H | W | 1-0 | Wainwright |
| | 6 | 04.03.50 | **Derby County** (D1) | A | W | 2-1 | Buckle, Wainwright |
| | SF | 25.03.50 | **Liverpool** (D1) *played at Maine Road* | | L | 0-2 | |
| 1950-51 (D1) | 3 | 06.01.51 | **Hull City** (D2) | A | L | 0-2 | |
| 1951-52 (D2) | 3 | 12.01.52 | **Leyton Orient** (3S) | A | D | 0-0 | |
| | 3r | 16.01.52 | **Leyton Orient** | H | L | 1-3 | Parker |
| 1952-53 (D2) | 3 | 10.01.53 | **Ipswich Town** (3S) | H | W | 3-2 | Hickson 2, Fielding |
| | 4 | 31.01.53 | **Nottingham Forest** (D2) | H | W | 4-1 | Parker 2, Clinton, Eglington |
| | 5 | 14.02.53 | **Manchester Utd** (D1) | H | W | 2-1 | Eglington, Hickson |
| | 6 | 28.02.53 | **Aston Villa** (D1) | A | W | 1-0 | Hickson |
| | SF | 21.03.53 | **Bolton Wanderers** (D1) *played at Maine Road* | | L | 3-4 | Parker 2, Farrall |
| 1953-54 (D2) | 3 | 09.01.54 | **Notts County** (D2) | H | W | 2-1 | Eglington, Hickson |
| | 4 | 30.01.54 | **Swansea Town** (D2) | H | W | 3-0 | Parker 2, Hickson |
| | 5 | 20.02.54 | **Sheffield Wed** (D1) | A | L | 1-3 | Hickson |
| 1954-55 (D1) | 3 | 08.01.55 | **Southend Utd** (3S) | H | W | 3-1 | Fielding, Hickson, Potts |
| | 4 | 29.01.55 | **Liverpool** (D2) | H | L | 0-4 | |
| 1955-56 (D1) | 3 | 07.01.56 | **Bristol City** (D2) | H | W | 3-1 | Eglington, J Harris, Wainwright |
| | 4 | 28.01.56 | **Port Vale** (D2) | A | W | 3-2 | Eglington, B Harris, Wainwright |
| | 5 | 18.02.56 | **Chelsea** (D1) | H | W | 1-0 | Farrall |
| | 6 | 03.03.56 | **Manchester City** (D1) | A | L | 1-2 | J Harris |
| 1956-57 (D1) | 3 | 05.01.57 | **Blackburn Rovers** (D2) | H | W | 1-0 | J Harris |
| | 4 | 26.01.57 | **West Ham Utd** (D2) | H | W | 2-1 | Farrall, Gauld |
| | 5 | 16.02.57 | **Manchester Utd** (D1) | A | L | 0-1 | |
| 1957-58 (D1) | 3 | 04.01.58 | **Sunderland** (D1) | A | D | 2-2 | Hickson 2 |
| | 3r | 08.01.58 | **Sunderland** | H | W | 3-1 | Keeley 2, Hickson |
| | 4 | 29.01.58 | **Blackburn Rovers** (D2) | H | L | 1-2 | J Harris |
| 1958-59 (D1) | 3 | 10.01.59 | **Sunderland** (D2) | H | W | 4-0 | Hickson 2, J Harris, Thomas |
| | 4 | 24.01.59 | **Charlton Athletic** (D2) | A | D | 2-2 | Collins, Thomas |

| | | | | | | | | |
|---|---|---|---|---|---|---|---|---|
| | | 4r | 28.01.59 | **Charlton Athletic** | H | W | 4-1aet | Collins 2, Hickson 2 |
| | | 5 | 14.02.59 | **Aston Villa** (D1) | H | L | 1-4 | Hickson |
| 1959-60 | (D1) | 3 | 09.01.60 | **Bradford City** (D3) | A | L | 0-3 | |
| 1960-61 | (D1) | 3 | 07.01.61 | **Sheffield Utd** (D2) | H | L | 0-1 | |
| 1961-62 | (D1) | 3 | 06.01.62 | **King's Lynn** (SL) | H | W | 4-0 | Bingham, Collins, Fell, Vernon |
| | | 4 | 27.01.62 | **Manchester City** (D1) | H | W | 2-0 | Lill, Vernon |
| | | 5 | 17.02.62 | **Burnley** (D1) | A | L | 1-3 | Collins |
| 1962-63 | (D1) | 3 | 15.01.63 | **Barnsley** (D3) | A | W | 3-0 | Harris, Stevens, Vernon |
| | | 4 | 29.01.63 | **Swindon Town** (D3) | A | W | 5-1 | Vernon 2, Bingham, Gabriel, Morrissey |
| | | 5 | 16.03.63 | **West Ham Utd** (D1) | A | L | 0-1 | |
| 1963-64 | (D1) | 3 | 04.01.64 | **Hull City** (D3) | A | D | 1-1 | Scott |
| | | 3r | 07.01.64 | **Hull City** | H | W | 2-1 | Harris, Scott |
| | | 4 | 25.01.64 | **Leeds Utd** (D2) | A | D | 1-1 | Vernon |
| | | 4r | 28.01.64 | **Leeds Utd** | H | W | 2-0 | Gabriel, Vernon |
| | | 5 | 15.02.64 | **Sunderland** (D2) | A | L | 1-3 | Harris |
| 1964-65 | (D1) | 3 | 09.01.65 | **Sheffield Wed** (D1) | H | D | 2-2 | Burgin og, Pickering |
| | | 3r | 13.01.65 | **Sheffield Wed** | A | W | 3-0 | Harvey, Pickering, Temple |
| | | 4 | 30.01.65 | **Leeds Utd** (D1) | A | D | 1-1 | Pickering |
| | | 4r | 02.02.65 | **Leeds Utd** | H | L | 1-2 | Pickering |
| 1965-66 | (D1) | 3 | 22.01.66 | **Sunderland** (D1) | H | W | 3-0 | Pickering, Temple, Young |
| | | 4 | 12.02.66 | **Bedford Town** (SL) | A | W | 3-0 | Temple 2, Pickering |
| | | 5 | 03.03.66 | **Coventry City** (D2) | H | W | 3-0 | Pickering, Temple, Young |
| | | 6 | 26.03.66 | **Manchester City** (D2) | A | D | 0-0 | |
| | | 6r | 29.03.66 | **Manchester City** | H | D | 0-0aet | |
| | | 6 2r | 05.04.66 | **Manchester City** *played at Molineux* | | W | 2-0 | Pickering, Temple |
| | | SF | 23.04.66 | **Manchester Utd** (D1) *played at Burnden Park* | | W | 1-0 | Harvey |
| | | F | 14.05.66 | **Sheffield Wed** (D1) *played at Wembley Stadium* | | W | 3-2 | Trebilcock 2, Temple |
| 1966-67 | (D1) | 3 | 28.01.67 | **Burnley** (D1) | A | D | 0-0 | |
| | | 3r | 31.01.67 | **Burnley** | H | W | 2-1 | Young 2 |
| | | 4 | 18.02.67 | **Wolverhampton W** (D2) | A | D | 1-1 | Ball |
| | | 4r | 21.02.67 | **Wolverhampton W** | H | W | 3-1 | Husband 2, Temple |
| | | 5 | 11.03.67 | **Liverpool** (D1) | H | W | 1-0 | Ball |
| | | 6 | 08.04.67 | **Nottingham Forest** (D1) | A | L | 2-3 | Husband 2 |
| 1967-68 | (D1) | 4 | 17.02.68 | **Carlisle Utd** (D2) | A | W | 2-0 | Husband, Royle |
| | | 5 | 09.03.68 | **Tranmere Rovers** (D3) | H | W | 2-0 | Morrissey, Royle |
| | | 6 | 30.03.68 | **Leicester City** (D1) | A | W | 3-1 | Husband 2, Kendall |
| | | SF | 27.04.68 | **Leeds Utd** (D1) *played at Old Trafford* | | W | 1-0 | Morrissey |
| | | F | 18.05.68 | **WBA** (D1) *played at Wembley Stadium* | | L | 0-1aet | |
| 1968-69 | (D1) | 3 | 04.01.69 | **Ipswich Town** (D1) | H | W | 2-1 | Hurst, Royle |
| | | 4 | 25.01.69 | **Coventry City** (D1) | H | W | 2-0 | Hurst, Royle |
| | | 5 | 12.02.69 | **Bristol Rovers** (D3) | H | W | 1-0 | Royle |
| | | 6 | 01.03.69 | **Manchester Utd** (D1) | A | W | 1-0 | Royle |
| | | SF | 22.03.69 | **Manchester City** (D1) *played at Villa Park* | | L | 0-1 | |
| 1969-70 | (D1) | 3 | 03.01.70 | **Sheffield Utd** (D2) | A | L | 1-2 | Ball |
| 1970-71 | (D1) | 3 | 02.01.71 | **Blackburn Rovers** (D2) | H | W | 2-0 | Husband 2 |
| | | 4 | 23.01.71 | **Middlesbrough** (D2) | H | W | 3-0 | Harvey, H Newton, Royle |
| | | 5 | 13.02.71 | **Derby County** (D1) | H | W | 1-0 | Johnson |
| | | 6 | 06.03.71 | **Colchester Utd** (D4) | H | W | 5-0 | Kendall 2, Ball, Husband, Royle |
| | | SF | 27.03.71 | **Liverpool** (D1) *played at Old Trafford* | | L | 1-2 | Ball |
| | | 3/4 | 07.05.71 | **Stoke City** (D1) *played at Selhurst Park* | | L | 2-3 | Whittle, Ball |
| 1971-72 | (D1) | 3 | 15.01.72 | **Crystal Palace** (D1) | A | D | 2-2 | Harvey, Whittle |
| | | 3r | 18.01.72 | **Crystal Palace** | H | W | 3-2 | Hurst, Kenyon, Scott |

| | | | | | | | |
|---|---|---|---|---|---|---|---|
| | 4 | 05.02.72 | **Walsall** (D3) | H | W | 2-1 | Johnson, Whittle |
| | 5 | 26.02.72 | **Tottenham Hotspur** (D1) | H | L | 0-2 | |
| 1972-73 (D1) | 3 | 13.01.73 | **Aston Villa** (D2) | H | W | 3-2 | Belfitt, Buckley, Harper |
| | 4 | 03.02.73 | **Millwall** (D2) | H | L | 0-2 | |
| 1973-74 (D1) | 3 | 05.01.74 | **Blackburn Rovers** (D3) | H | W | 3-0 | Clements, Harper, Hurst |
| | 4 | 27.01.74 | **WBA** (D2) | H | D | 0-0 | |
| | 4r | 30.01.74 | **WBA** | A | L | 0-1 | |
| 1974-75 (D1) | 3 | 04.01.75 | **Altrincham** (NPL) | H | D | 1-1 | Clements |
| | 3r | 07.01.75 | **Altrincham** *played at Old Trafford* | | W | 2-0 | Latchford, Lyons |
| | 4 | 25.01.75 | **Plymouth Argyle** (D3) | A | W | 3-1 | Lyons 2, Pearson |
| | 5 | 15.02.75 | **Fulham** (D2) | H | L | 1-2 | Kenyon |
| 1975-76 (D1) | 3 | 03.01.76 | **Derby County** (D1) | A | L | 1-2 | G Jones |
| 1976-77 (D1) | 3 | 08.01.77 | **Stoke City** (D1) | H | W | 2-0 | Lyons, McKenzie |
| | 4 | 29.01.77 | **Swindon Town** (D3) | A | D | 2-2 | Latchford, Mckenzie |
| | 4r | 01.02.77 | **Swindon Town** | H | W | 2-1 | Dobson, Jones |
| | 5 | 26.02.77 | **Cardiff City** (D2) | A | W | 2-1 | Latchford, McKenzie |
| | 6 | 19.03.77 | **Derby County** (D1) | H | W | 2-0 | Latchford, Pearson |
| | SF | 23.04.77 | **Liverpool** (D1) *played at Maine Road* | | D | 2-2 | McKenzie, Rioch |
| | SFr | 27.04.77 | **Liverpool** *played at Maine Road* | | L | 0-3 | |
| 1977-78 (D1) | 3 | 07.01.78 | **Aston Villa** (D1) | H | W | 4-1 | King, Latchford, McKenzie, Ross |
| | 4 | 28.01.78 | **Middlesbrough** (D1) | A | L | 2-3 | Lyons, Telfer |
| 1978-79 (D1) | 3 | 10.01.79 | **Sunderland** (D2) | A | L | 1-2 | Dobson |
| 1979-80 (D1) | 3 | 05.01.80 | **Aldershot** (D4) | H | W | 4-1 | Hartford, Kidd, King, Latchford |
| | 4 | 26.01.80 | **Wigan Athletic** (D4) | H | W | 3-0 | Kidd, Latchford, McBride |
| | 5 | 16.02.80 | **Wrexham** (D2) | H | W | 5-2 | Eastoe 2, Latchford, Megson, Ross |
| | 6 | 08.03.80 | **Ipswich Town** (D1) | H | W | 2-1 | Kidd, Latchford |
| | SF | 12.04.80 | **West Ham Utd** (D2) *played at Villa Park* | | D | 1-1 | Kidd |
| | SFr | 16.04.80 | **West Ham Utd** *played at Elland Road* | | L | 1-2 | Latchford |
| 1980-81 (D1) | 3 | 03.01.81 | **Arsenal** (D1) | H | W | 2-0 | Sansom og, Lyons |
| | 4 | 24.01.81 | **Liverpool** (D1) | H | W | 2-1 | Eastoe, Varadi |
| | 5 | 14.02.81 | **Southampton** (D1) | A | D | 0-0 | |
| | 5r | 17.02.81 | **Southampton** | H | W | 1-0aet | O'Keefe |
| | 6 | 07.03.81 | **Manchester City** (D1) | H | D | 2-2 | Eastoe, Ross |
| | 6r | 11.03.81 | **Manchester City** | A | L | 1-3 | Eastoe |
| 1981-82 (D1) | 3 | 02.01.82 | **West Ham Utd** (D1) | A | L | 1-2 | Eastoe |
| 1982-83 (D1) | 3 | 08.01.83 | **Newport County** (D3) | A | D | 1-1 | Sheedy |
| | 3r | 11.01.83 | **Newport County** | H | W | 2-1 | King, Sharp |
| | 4 | 30.01.83 | **Shrewsbury Town** (D2) | H | W | 2-1 | Heath, Sheedy |
| | 5 | 19.02.83 | **Tottenham Hotspur** (D1) | H | W | 2-0 | King, Sharp |
| | 6 | 12.03.83 | **Manchester Utd** (D1) | A | L | 0-1 | |
| 1983-84 (D1) | 3 | 07.01.84 | **Stoke City** (D1) | A | W | 2-0 | Gray, Irvine |
| | 4 | 28.01.84 | **Gillingham** (D3) | H | D | 0-0 | |
| | 4r | 31.01.84 | **Gillingham** | A | D | 0-0aet | |
| | 4 2r | 06.02.84 | **Gillingham** | A | W | 3-0 | Sheedy 2, Heath |
| | 5 | 18.02.84 | **Shrewsbury Town** (D2) | H | W | 3-0 | Irvine, Reid, Griffin og |
| | 6 | 10.03.84 | **Notts County** (D1) | A | W | 2-1 | Gray, Richardson |
| | SF | 14.04.84 | **Southampton** (D1) *played at Highbury* | | W | 1-0aet | Heath |
| | F | 19.05.84 | **Watford** (D1) *played at Wembley Stadium* | | W | 2-0 | Gray, Sharp |
| 1984-85 (D1) | 3 | 04.01.85 | **Leeds Utd** (D2) | A | W | 2-0 | Sharp (p), Sheedy |
| | 4 | 26.01.85 | **Doncaster Rovers** (D3) | H | W | 2-0 | Steven, Stevens |
| | 5 | 16.02.85 | **Telford Utd** (APL) | H | W | 3-0 | Reid, Sheedy, Steven |
| | 6 | 09.03.85 | **Ipswich Town** (D1) | H | D | 2-2 | Mountfield, Sheedy |
| | 6r | 13.03.85 | **Ipswich Town** | A | W | 1-0 | Sharp |
| | SF | 13.04.85 | **Luton Town** (D1) *played at Villa Park* | | W | 2-1aet | Mountfield, Sheedy |

| | | | | | | | |
|---|---|---|---|---|---|---|---|
| | F | 18.05.85 | **Manchester Utd** (D1) | | L | 0-1aet | |
| | | | *played at Wembley Stadium* | | | | |
| 1985-86 (D1) | 3 | 05.01.86 | **Exeter City** (D4) | H | W | 1-0 | Stevens |
| | 4 | 25.01.86 | **Blackburn Rovers** (D2) | H | W | 3-1 | Lineker 2, Van den Hauwe |
| | 5 | 04.03.86 | **Tottenham Hotspur** (D1) | A | W | 2-1 | Heath, Lineker |
| | 6 | 08.03.86 | **Luton Town** (D1) | A | D | 2-2 | Donaghy og, Heath |
| | 6r | 12.03.86 | **Luton Town** | H | W | 1-0 | Lineker |
| | SF | 05.04.86 | **Sheffield Wed** (D1) | | W | 2-1aet | Harper, Sharp |
| | | | *played at Villa Park* | | | | |
| | F | 10.05.86 | **Liverpool** (D1) | | L | 1-3 | Lineker |
| | | | *played at Wembley Stadium* | | | | |
| 1986-87 (D1) | 3 | 10.01.87 | **Southampton** (D1) | H | W | 2-1 | Sharp 2 |
| | 4 | 31.01.87 | **Bradford City** (D2) | A | W | 1-0 | Snodin |
| | 5 | 22.02.87 | **Wimbledon** (D1) | A | L | 1-3 | Wilkinson |
| 1987-88 (D1) | 3 | 09.01.88 | **Sheffield Wed** (D1) | A | D | 1-1 | Reid |
| | 3r | 13.01.88 | **Sheffield Wed** | H | D | 1-1aet | Sharp |
| | 3 2r | 25.01.88 | **Sheffield Wed** | H | D | 1-1aet | Steven |
| | 3 3r | 27.01.88 | **Sheffield Wed** | A | W | 5-0 | Sharp 3, Heath, Snodin |
| | 4 | 30.01.88 | **Middlesbrough** (D2) | H | D | 1-1 | Sharp |
| | 4r | 03.02.88 | **Middlesbrough** | A | D | 2-2aet | Steven, Watson |
| | 4 2r | 09.02.88 | **Middlesbrough** | H | W | 2-1 | Sharp, Mowbray og |
| | 5 | 21.02.88 | **Liverpool** (D1) | H | L | 0-1 | |
| 1988-89 (D1) | 3 | 07.01.89 | **WBA** (D2) | A | D | 1-1 | Sheedy (p) |
| | 3r | 11.01.89 | **WBA** | H | W | 1-0 | Sheedy |
| | 4 | 28.01.89 | **Plymouth Argyle** (D2) | A | D | 1-1 | Sheedy (p) |
| | 4r | 31.01.89 | **Plymouth Argyle** | H | W | 4-0 | Sharp 2, Nevin, Sheedy |
| | 5 | 19.02.89 | **Barnsley** (D2) | A | W | 1-0 | Sharp |
| | 6 | 19.03.89 | **Wimbledon** (D1) | H | W | 1-0 | McCall |
| | SF | 15.04.89 | **Norwich City** (D1) | | W | 1-0 | Nevin |
| | | | *played at Villa Park* | | | | |
| | F | 20.05.89 | **Liverpool** (D1) | | L | 2-3aet | McCall 2 |
| | | | *played at Wembley Stadium* | | | | |
| 1989-90 (D1) | 3 | 06.01.90 | **Middlesbrough** (D2) | A | D | 0-0 | |
| | 3r | 10.01.90 | **Middlesbrough** | H | D | 1-1aet | Sheedy |
| | 3 2r | 17.01.90 | **Middlesbrough** | H | W | 1-0 | Whiteside |
| | 4 | 28.01.90 | **Sheffield Wed** (D1) | A | W | 2-1 | Whiteside 2 |
| | 5 | 17.02.90 | **Oldham Athletic** (D2) | A | D | 2-2 | Sharp, Cottee |
| | 5r | 21.02.90 | **Oldham Athletic** | H | D | 1-1aet | Sheedy |
| | 5 2r | 10.03.90 | **Oldham Athletic** | A | L | 1-2aet | Cottee |
| 1990-91 (D1) | 3 | 05.01.91 | **Charlton Athletic** (D2) | A | W | 2-1 | Ebbrell 2 |
| | 4 | 27.01.91 | **Woking** (IL) | H | W | 1-0 | Sheedy |
| | | | *played at Goodison Park* | | | | |
| | 5 | 17.02.91 | **Liverpool** (D1) | A | D | 0-0 | |
| | 5r | 20.02.91 | **Liverpool** | H | D | 4-4aet | Sharp 2, Cottee 2 |
| | 5 2r | 27.02.91 | **Liverpool** | H | W | 1-0 | Watson |
| | 6 | 11.03.91 | **West Ham Utd** (D2) | A | L | 1-2 | Watson |
| 1991-92 (D1) | 3 | 04.01.92 | **Southend Utd** (D2) | H | W | 1-0 | Beardsley |
| | 4 | 26.01.92 | **Chelsea** (D1) | A | L | 0-1 | |
| 1992-93 (PL) | 3 | 02.01.93 | **Wimbledon** (PL) | A | D | 0-0 | |
| | 3r | 12.01.93 | **Wimbledon** | H | L | 1-2 | Watson |
| 1993-94 (PL) | 3 | 08.01.94 | **Bolton Wanderers** (D1) | A | D | 1-1 | Rideout |
| | 3r | 19.01.94 | **Bolton Wanderers** | H | L | 2-3aet | Barlow 2 |
| 1994-95 (PL) | 3 | 07.01.95 | **Derby County** (D1) | H | W | 1-0 | Hinchcliffe |
| | 4 | 29.01.95 | **Bristol City** (D1) | A | W | 1-0 | Jackson |
| | 5 | 18.02.95 | **Norwich City** (PL) | H | W | 5-0 | Limpar, Parkinson, Rideout, Ferguson, Stuart |
| | 6 | 12.03.95 | **Newcastle Utd** (PL) | H | W | 1-0 | Watson |
| | SF | 09.04.95 | **Tottenham Hotspur** (PL) | | W | 4-1 | Jackson, Stuart, Amokachi 2 |
| | | | *played at Elland Road* | | | | |
| | F | 20.05.95 | **Manchester Utd** (PL) | | W | 1-0 | Rideout |
| | | | *played at Wembley Stadium* | | | | |
| 1995-96 (PL) | 3 | 07.01.96 | **Stockport County** (D2) | H | D | 2-2 | Ablett, Stuart |

| | | | | | | | | |
|---|---|---|---|---|---|---|---|---|
| | | 3r | 17.01.96 | **Stockport County** | A | W | 3-2 | Ferguson, Stuart, Ebbrell |
| | | 4 | 27.01.96 | **Port Vale** (D1) | H | D | 2-2 | Amokachi, Ferguson |
| | | 4r | 14.02.96 | **Port Vale** | A | L | 1-2 | Stuart |
| 1996-97 | (PL) | 3 | 05.01.97 | **Swindon Town** (D1) | H | W | 3-0 | Kanchelskis (p), Barmby, Ferguson |
| | | 4 | 25.01.97 | **Bradford City** (D1) | H | L | 2-3 | O'Brien og, Speed |
| 1997-98 | (PL) | 3 | 04.01.98 | **Newcastle Utd** (PL) | H | L | 0-1 | |
| 1998-99 | (PL) | 3 | 02.01.99 | **Bristol City** (D1) | A | W | 2-0 | Bakayoko 2 |
| | | 4 | 23.01.99 | **Ipswich Town** (D1) | H | W | 1-0 | Barmby |
| | | 5 | 13.02.99 | **Coventry City** (PL) | H | W | 2-1 | Jeffers, Oster |
| | | 6 | 07.03.99 | **Newcastle Utd** (PL) | A | L | 1-4 | Unsworth |
| 1999-00 | (PL) | 3 | 11.12.99 | **Exeter City** (D3) | A | D | 0-0 | |
| | | 3r | 21.12.99 | **Exeter City** | H | W | 1-0 | Barmby |
| | | 4 | 08.01.00 | **Birmingham City** (D1) | H | W | 2-0 | Unsworth 2(2p) |
| | | 5 | 29.01.00 | **Preston North End** (D2) | H | W | 2-0 | Unsworth, Moore |
| | | 6 | 20.02.00 | **Aston Villa** (PL) | H | L | 1-2 | Moore |
| 2000-01 | (PL) | 3 | 06.01.01 | **Watford** (D1) | A | W | 2-1 | Hughes, Watson |
| | | 4 | 27.01.01 | **Tranmere Rovers** (D1) | H | L | 0-3 | |
| 2001-02 | (PL) | 3 | 05.01.02 | **Stoke City** (D2) | A | W | 1-0 | Stubbs |
| | | 4 | 26.01.02 | **Leyton Orient** (D3) | H | W | 4-1 | McGhee og, Ferguson, Campbell 2 |
| | | 5 | 17.02.02 | **Crewe Alexandra** (D1) | H | D | 0-0 | |
| | | 5r | 26.02.02 | **Crewe Alexandra** | A | W | 2-1 | Radzinski, Campbell |
| | | 6 | 10.03.02 | **Middlesbrough** (PL) | A | L | 0-3 | |
| 2002-03 | (PL) | 3 | 04.01.03 | **Shrewsbury Town** (D3) | A | L | 1-2 | Alexandersson |

# EXETER CITY

*Formed 1904. Best performance in the FA Cup: 6th round, 1931, 1981; Record FA Cup win: 14-0 v Weymouth, 1st qualifying round, 1908-09. In Competition Proper: 9-1 v Aberdare Athletic, 1st round, 26.11.1927; Record FA Cup defeat: 2-6 v Cardiff City, 1st round, 22.11.1975. Relegated to The Conference 2003.*

| | | | | | | | | |
|---|---|---|---|---|---|---|---|---|
| 1908-09 | (SL) | | | 1q Weymouth (H) 14-0; 2q Longfleet St Mary 1-1 at Poole; 2qr Longfleet St Mary (H) 10-1; 3q Whiteheads Weymouth (H) 4-0; 4q Kingswood R 2-0 (at Bristol); 5q Barnet A, (A) 3-0 | | | | |
| | | 1 | 16.01.09 | **Wrexham** (BDL) | A | D | 1-1 | Watson |
| | | 1r | 20.01.09 | **Wrexham** | H | W | 2-1 | Chadwick (p), McGuigan |
| | | 2 | 06.02.09 | **Plymouth Argyle** (SL) | A | L | 0-2 | |
| 1909-10 | (SL) | | | 4q Nunhead (H) 7-1; 5q Stoke (A) 0-0; 5qr Stoke (H) 1-1; 5q 2r Stoke 1-2 (at Craven Cottage) | | | | |
| 1910-11 | (SL) | | | 4q Reading (A) 1-1; 4qr Reading (H) 1-0 after abandoned match; 5q Nelson (A) 4-3 | | | | |
| | | 1 | 14.01.11 | **Burnley** (D2) | A | L | 0-2 | |
| 1911-12 | (SL) | | | 4q Merthyr Town (H) 1-1; 4qr Merthyr T (A) 0-0aet; 4q 2r Merthyr T 0-2 at Ashton Gate | | | | |
| 1912-13 | (SL) | | | 4q Cardiff C (A) 1-5 | | | | |
| 1913-14 | (SL) | 1 | 10.01.14 | **Portsmouth** (SL) | A | W | 4-0 | Holt 2, Marshall 2 |
| | | 2 | 31.01.14 | **Aston Villa** (D1) | H | L | 1-2 | McCann |
| 1914-15 | (SL) | 1 | 09.01.15 | **Aston Villa** (D1) | A | L | 0-2 | |
| 1919-20 | (SL) | | | 6q Newport County (A) 0-1 | | | | |
| 1920-21 | (D3) | 1 | 08.01.21 | **Watford** (D3) | A | L | 0-3 | |
| 1921-22 | (3S) | | | 5q Bristol R (A) 0-0; 5qr Bristol R (H) 0-2 | | | | |
| 1922-23 | (3S) | | | 4q Bournemouth (H) 0-0; 4qr Bournemouth (A) 3-1; 5q Bath C (H) 1-2 | | | | |
| 1923-24 | (3S) | | | 4q Newport Co (A) 2-0; 5q Bristol R (H) 2-2; 5qr Bristol R (A) 1-0; 6q Sittingbourne (A) 2-0 | | | | |
| | | 1 | 12.01.24 | **Grimsby Town** (3N) | H | W | 1-0 | Davis |
| | | 2 | 02.02.24 | **Watford** (3S) | H | D | 0-0 | |
| | | 2r | 07.02.24 | **Watford** | A | L | 0-1 | |
| 1924-25 | (3S) | | | 5q Newport Co (H) 1-1; 5qr Newport Co (A) 3-3aet; 5q 2r Newport Co 1-0 (at Ashton Gate); 6q Barnet (H) 3-0 | | | | |
| | | 1 | 10.01.25 | **Southampton** (D2) | A | - | 0-5ab | |
| | | | | *abandoned after 80 minutes – fog* | | | | |
| | | 1 | 14.01.25 | **Southampton** | A | L | 1-3 | Kirk |
| 1925-26 | (3S) | 1 | 28.11.25 | **Swansea Town** (D2) | H | L | 1-3 | Compton |
| 1926-27 | (3S) | 1 | 27.11.26 | **Aberdare Athletic** (3S) | H | W | 3-0 | Compton 2, Purcell |
| | | 2 | 11.12.26 | **Northampton Town** (3S) | H | W | 1-0 | McDevitt |
| | | 3 | 08.01.27 | **Accrington Stanley** (3N) | H | L | 0-2 | |

| | | | | | | | | |
|---|---|---|---|---|---|---|---|---|
| 1927-28 | (3S) | 1 | 26.11.27 | **Aberdare Athletic** (SL) | H | W | 9-1 | Dent 4, Vaughan 2, Purcell 2, Compton |
| | | 2 | 10.12.27 | **Ilford** (IL) | H | W | 5-3 | Dent 2, Purcell 2, McDevitt |
| | | 3 | 14.01.28 | **Rotherham Utd** (3N) | A | D | 3-3 | Vaughan, Mason, Jackson og |
| | | 3r | 18.01.28 | **Rotherham Utd** | H | W | 3-1 | Vaughan 2, Purcell |
| | | 4 | 28.01.28 | **Blackburn Rovers** (D1) | H | D | 2-2 | Gee (p), Mason |
| | | 4r | 02.02.28 | **Blackburn Rovers** | A | L | 1-3aet | Compton |
| 1928-29 | (3S) | 1 | 24.11.28 | **Barking** (AL) | H | W | 6-0 | Purcell, Doncaster, Clarke, Death, Cameron, Vango og |
| | | 2 | 08.12.28 | **Torquay Utd** (3S) | A | W | 1-0 | Purcell |
| | | 3 | 12.01.29 | **Leeds Utd** (D1) | H | D | 2-2 | Doncaster, Purcell |
| | | 3r | 16.01.29 | **Leeds Utd** | A | L | 1-5 | Doncaster |
| 1929-30 | (3S) | 1 | 30.11.29 | **Walsall** (3S) | A | L | 0-1 | |
| 1930-31 | (3S) | 1 | 29.11.30 | **Northfleet Utd** (SL) | A | W | 3-0 | Houghton, Purcellm, Maitland og |
| | | 2 | 13.12.30 | **Coventry City** (3S) | H | D | 1-1 | Varco |
| | | 2r | 18.12.30 | **Coventry City** | A | W | 2-1 | Varco, Doncaster |
| | | 3 | 10.01.31 | **Derby County** (D1) | H | W | 3-2 | Varco, Armfield, Houghton |
| | | 4 | 24.01.31 | **Bury** (D2) | A | W | 2-1 | Varco, Houghton |
| | | 5 | 14.02.31 | **Leeds Utd** (D1) | H | W | 3-1 | Armfield 2, Purcell |
| | | 6 | 28.02.31 | **Sunderland** (D1) | A | D | 1-1 | Houghton |
| | | 6r | 04.03.31 | **Sunderland** | H | L | 2-4 | Varco, Purcell |
| 1931-32 | (3S) | 3 | 09.01.32 | **Grimsby Town** (D1) | A | L | 1-4 | Woodward |
| 1932-33 | (3S) | 1 | 26.11.32 | **Southend Utd** (3S) | A | D | 1-1 | Whitlow |
| | | 1r | 30.11.32 | **Southend Utd** | H | L | 0-1 | |
| 1933-34 | (3S) | 1 | 25.11.33 | **Northampton Town** (3S) | A | L | 0-2 | |
| 1934-35 | (3S) | 1 | 24.11.34 | **Charlton Athletic** (3S) | A | D | 2-2 | Hurst 2 |
| | | 1r | 28.11.34 | **Charlton Athletic** | H | W | 5-2 | T Scott 2, Hurst, Wrightson, J Scott |
| | | 2 | 08.12.34 | **Yeovil & Petters Utd** (SL) | A | L | 1-4 | Angus |
| 1935-36 | (3S) | 1 | 30.11.35 | **Gillingham** (3S) | H | L | 0-4 | |
| 1936-37 | (3S) | 1 | 28.11.36 | **Folkestone** (SL) | H | W | 3-0 | Keane 2, Williams |
| | | 2 | 12.12.36 | **Walthamstow Ave** (AL) | A | - | 1-1ab | Clarke (p) |
| | | | | *abandoned after 65 minutes – fog* | | | | |
| | | 2 | 17.12.36 | **Walthamstow Ave** | A | W | 3-2 | Williams 2, Keane |
| | | 3 | 16.01.37 | **Oldham Athletic** (3N) | H | W | 3-0 | Williams 2, Smith |
| | | 4 | 30.01.37 | **Leicester City** (D2) | H | W | 3-1 | Williams 2, Bussey |
| | | 5 | 20.02.37 | **Preston North End** (D1) | A | L | 3-5 | Owen 2, F Smith |
| 1937-38 | (3S) | 1 | 27.11.37 | **Folkestone** (SL) | H | W | 1-0 | Pope |
| | | 2 | 11.12.37 | **Hull City** (3N) | H | L | 1-2 | Liddle |
| 1938-39 | (3S) | 1 | 26.11.38 | **Torquay Utd** (3S) | A | L | 1-3 | Riley |
| 1945-46 | (3S) | 1 1L | 17.11.45 | **Trowbridge Town** (WL) | A | W | 3-1 | Challis, Walker, Ebdon |
| | | 1 2L | 24.11.45 | **Trowbridge Town** | H | W | 7-2 | Walker 4, Challis, Tickell, Atack og |
| | | 2 1L | 08.12.45 | **Newport County** (D2) | A | L | 1-5 | Gallagher |
| | | 2 2L | 15.12.45 | **Newport County** | H | L | 1-3 | Crawshaw |
| 1946-47 | (3S) | 1 | 30.11.46 | **Bournemouth** (3S) | A | L | 2-4 | Regan, Hydes |
| 1947-48 | (3S) | 1 | 29.11.47 | **Northampton Town** (3S) | H | D | 1-1aet | Bartholomew |
| | | 1r | 06.12.47 | **Northampton Town** | A | L | 0-2 | |
| 1948-49 | (3S) | 1 | 04.12.48 | **Barnet** (AL) | A | W | 6-2 | Smith 4, Bartholomew, Dymond |
| | | 2 | 11.12.48 | **Hereford Utd** (SL) | H | W | 2-1 | Dymond 2 |
| | | 3 | 03.01.49 | **Grimsby Town** (D2) | A | L | 1-2 | Regan |
| 1949-50 | (3S) | 1 | 26.11.49 | **Millwall** (3S) | A | W | 5-3 | Smart 3, Regan, Smith |
| | | 2 | 10.12.49 | **Chester** (3N) | H | W | 2-0 | Regan 2 (1p) |
| | | 3 | 07.01.50 | **Nuneaton B** (BC) | H | W | 3-0 | Greenwood, Regan, Fallon |
| | | 4 | 28.01.50 | **Liverpool** (D1) | A | L | 1-3 | Smart |
| 1950-51 | (3S) | 1 | 25.11.50 | **Glastonbury** (WL) | A | W | 2-1 | Smith, Mackay |
| | | 2 | 09.12.50 | **Swindon Town** (3S) | H | W | 3-0 | Smith, Fallon, Mackay |
| | | 3 | 06.01.51 | **Grimsby Town** (D2) | A | D | 3-3 | Mackay 2, McClelland |
| | | 3r | 10.01.51 | **Grimsby Town** | H | W | 4-2 | McClelland 2, Smith 2 |
| | | 4 | 27.01.51 | **Chelsea** (D1) | H | D | 1-1 | Regan |
| | | 4r | 31.01.51 | **Chelsea** | A | L | 0-2 | |
| 1951-52 | (3S) | 1 | 24.11.51 | **King's Lynn** (ECL) | A | W | 3-1 | McClelland 2, Smart |
| | | 2 | 15.12.51 | **Ipswich Town** (3S) | A | L | 0-4 | |

| | | | | | | | | |
|---|---|---|---|---|---|---|---|---|
| 1952-53 | (3S) | 1 | 22.11.52 | **Port Vale** (3N) | A | L | 1-2 | Murphy |
| 1953-54 | (3S) | 1 | 21.11.53 | **Hereford Utd** (SL) | H | D | 1-1 | Samuels |
| | | 1r | 26.11.53 | **Hereford Utd** | A | L | 0-2 | |
| 1954-55 | (3S) | 1 | 20.11.54 | **Millwall** (3S) | A | L | 2-3 | Murphy, Mackay |
| 1955-56 | (3S) | 1 | 19.11.55 | **Coventry City** (3S) | A | W | 1-0 | Rees |
| | | 2 | 10.12.55 | **Hendon** (AL) | H | W | 6-2 | Rees 2, Iggleden 2, Simpson, Murphy |
| | | 3 | 07.01.56 | **Stoke City** (D2) | H | D | 0-0 | |
| | | 3r | 09.01.56 | **Stoke City** | A | L | 0-3 | |
| 1956-57 | (3S) | 1 | 17.11.56 | **Plymouth Argyle** (3S) | H | L | 0-2 | |
| 1957-58 | (3S) | 1 | 16.11.57 | **Bath City** (SL) | A | L | 1-2 | Calland |
| 1958-59 | (D4) | 1 | 15.11.58 | **Brentford** (D3) | A | L | 2-3 | Calland, Mitchell (p) |
| 1959-60 | (D4) | 1 | 14.11.59 | **Barnstaple Town** (WL) | H | W | 4-0 | Rees 2, Wilkinson, Stiffle |
| | | 2 | 05.12.59 | **Brentford** (D3) | H | W | 3-1 | Dale, Rees, Stiffle |
| | | 3 | 09.01.60 | **Luton Town** (D1) | H | L | 1-2 | Daniel og |
| 1960-61 | (D4) | 1 | 05.11.60 | **Bournemouth** (D3) | H | D | 1-1 | Bond |
| | | 1r | 09.11.60 | **Bournemouth** | A | L | 1-3 | Bond |
| 1961-62 | (D4) | 1 | 04.11.61 | **Dartford** (SL) | H | D | 3-3 | McMillan 2, Mabey og |
| | | 1r | 08.11.61 | **Dartford** | A | L | 1-2 | Carter |
| 1962-63 | (D4) | 1 | 03.11.62 | **Gravesend & N** (SL) | A | L | 2-3 | Carter 2 |
| 1963-64 | (D4) | 1 | 16.11.63 | **Shrewsbury Town** (D3) | H | W | 2-1 | Curtis, Anderson |
| | | 2 | 07.12.63 | **Bristol City** (D3) | H | L | 0-2 | |
| 1964-65 | (D3) | 1 | 14.11.64 | **Hayes** (AL) | H | W | 1-0 | Ley |
| | | 2 | 05.12.64 | **Shrewsbury Town** (D3) | H | L | 1-2 | Mitchell |
| 1965-66 | (D3) | 1 | 13.11.65 | **Bedford Town** (SL) | H | L | 1-2 | Curtis |
| 1966-67 | (D4) | 1 | 26.11.66 | **Luton Town** (D4) | H | D | 1-1 | Keeley |
| | | 1r | 01.12.66 | **Luton Town** | A | L | 0-2 | |
| 1967-68 | (D4) | 1 | 09.12.67 | **Nuneaton B** (SL) | A | D | 0-0 | |
| | | 1r | 13.12.67 | **Nuneaton B** | H | D | 0-0aet | |
| | | 1 2r | 18.12.67 | **Nuneaton B** | | W | 1-0 | Banks |
| | | | | *played at Ashton Gate* | | | | |
| | | 2 | 06.01.68 | **Walsall** (D3) | H | L | 1-3 | Blain (p) |
| 1968-69 | (D4) | 1 | 16.11.68 | **Newport County** (D4) | H | D | 0-0 | |
| | | 1r | 18.11.68 | **Newport County** | A | W | 3-1 | Balson, Williams og, Wood og |
| | | 2 | 07.12.68 | **Colchester Utd** (D4) | A | W | 1-0 | Banks |
| | | 3 | 04.01.69 | **Manchester Utd** (D1) | H | L | 1-3 | Banks |
| 1969-70 | (D4) | 1 | 15.11.69 | **Fulham** (D3) | H | W | 2-0 | Corr, Banks |
| | | 2 | 06.12.69 | **Northampton Town** (D4) | A | D | 1-1 | Wingate |
| | | 2r | 10.12.69 | **Northampton Town** | H | D | 0-0aet | |
| | | 2 2r | 15.12.69 | **Northampton Town** | | L | 1-2 | Mitten (p) |
| | | | | *played at County Ground, Swindon* | | | | |
| 1970-71 | (D4) | 1 | 21.11.70 | **Swansea City** (D3) | A | L | 1-4 | Wingate |
| 1971-72 | (D4) | 1 | 20.11.71 | **Crawley Town** (SL) | A | D | 0-0 | |
| | | 1r | 24.11.71 | **Crawley Town** | H | W | 2-0 | Binney, Rowan |
| | | 2 | 11.12.71 | **Swansea City** (D3) | A | D | 0-0 | |
| | | 2r | 15.12.71 | **Swansea City** | H | L | 0-1 | |
| 1972-73 | (D4) | 1 | 18.11.72 | **Walton & H** (IL) | A | L | 1-2 | Stacey |
| 1973-74 | (D4) | 1 | 24.11.73 | **Alvechurch** (WMRL) | H | L | 0-1 | |
| 1974-75 | (D4) | 1 | 23.11.74 | **Newport County** (D4) | H | L | 1-2 | Hodge |
| 1975-76 | (D4) | 1 | 22.11.75 | **Cardiff City** (D3) | A | L | 2-6 | Beer, Bowker |
| 1976-77 | (D4) | 1 | 20.11.76 | **Southend Utd** (D4) | H | D | 1-1 | Hatch |
| | | 1r | 22.11.76 | **Southend Utd** | A | L | 1-2aet | Kellow |
| 1977-78 | (D3) | 1 | 26.11.77 | **Newport County** (D4) | A | D | 1-1 | Bowker |
| | | 1r | 30.11.77 | **Newport County** | H | W | 4-2 | Roberts, Hatch, Kellow, Templeman |
| | | 2 | 17.12.77 | **Minehead** (SL) | A | W | 3-0 | Randell 2, Kellow |
| | | 3 | 07.01.78 | **Wolverhampton W** (D1) | H | D | 2-2 | Roberts, Holman |
| | | 3r | 10.01.78 | **Wolverhampton W** | A | L | 1-3 | Kellow |
| 1978-79 | (D3) | 1 | 25.11.78 | **Brentford** (D3) | H | W | 1-0 | Forbes |
| | | 2 | 16.12.78 | **Maidstone Utd** (SL) | A | L | 0-1 | |
| 1979-80 | (D3) | 1 | 24.11.79 | **Aldershot** (D4) | A | L | 1-4 | Neville |
| 1980-81 | (D3) | 1 | 22.11.80 | **Leatherhead** (IL) | H | W | 5-0 | Kellow 2, Pearson, L Roberts, Hinshelwood (og) |

| | | | | | | | | |
|---|---|---|---|---|---|---|---|---|
| | | 2 | 13.12.80 | **Millwall** (D3) | A | W | 1-0 | P Rogers |
| | | 3 | 03.01.81 | **Maidstone Utd** (APL) | A | W | 4-2 | Pullar 2, Kellow, P Rogers |
| | | 4 | 24.01.81 | **Leicester City** (D1) | A | D | 1-1 | Pullar |
| | | 4r | 28.01.81 | **Leicester City** | H | W | 3-1 | Kellow 3 (1p) |
| | | 5 | 14.02.81 | **Newcastle Utd** (D2) | A | D | 1-1 | L Roberts |
| | | 5r | 18.02.81 | **Newcastle Utd** | H | W | 4-0 | Hatch, Pearson, P Roberts, M Rogers |
| | | 6 | 07.03.81 | **Tottenham Hotspur** (D1) | A | L | 0-2 | |
| 1981-82 | (D3) | 1 | 21.11.81 | **Brentford** (D3) | A | L | 0-2 | |
| 1982-83 | (D3) | 1 | 20.11.82 | **Plymouth Argyle** (D3) | A | L | 0-2 | |
| 1983-84 | (D3) | 1 | 19.11.83 | **Maidstone Utd** (APL) | H | D | 1-1 | O'Connor |
| | | 1r | 23.11.83 | **Maidstone Utd** | A | L | 1-2 | Neville |
| 1984-85 | (D4) | 1 | 17.11.84 | **Enfield** (APL) | H | D | 2-2 | Neville, Sims |
| | | 1r | 20.11.84 | **Enfield** | A | L | 0-3 | |
| 1985-86 | (D4) | 1 | 16.11.85 | **Cardiff City** (D3) | H | W | 2-1 | Gale 2 |
| | | 2 | 07.12.85 | **Bristol City** (D3) | A | W | 2-1 | Kellow, Crawford |
| | | 3 | 05.01.86 | **Everton** (D1) | A | L | 0-1 | |
| 1986-87 | (D4) | 1 | 15.11.86 | **Cambridge Utd** (D4) | H | D | 1-1 | Viney |
| | | 1r | 19.11.86 | **Cambridge Utd** | A | L | 0-2 | |
| 1987-88 | (D4) | 1 | 14.11.87 | **Leyton Orient** (D4) | A | L | 0-2 | |
| 1988-89 | (D4) | 1 | 19.11.88 | **Bognor Regis Town** (IL) | A | L | 1-2 | Rowbotham |
| 1989-90 | (D4) | 1 | 18.11.89 | **Dartford** (SL) | A | D | 1-1 | Rowbotham (p) |
| | | 1r | 22.11.89 | **Dartford** | H | W | 4-1 | Bailey, Batty, Harrower, Neville |
| | | 2 | 09.12.89 | **Maidstone Utd** (D4) | A | D | 1-1 | Cooper |
| | | 2r | 13.12.89 | **Maidstone Utd** | H | W | 3-2 | Rowbotham 2, McDermott |
| | | 3 | 06.01.90 | **Norwich City** (D1) | H | D | 1-1 | Rowbotham |
| | | 3r | 10.01.90 | **Norwich City** | A | L | 0-2 | |
| 1990-91 | (D3) | 1 | 17.11.90 | **Cambridge Utd** (D3) | H | L | 1-2 | Neville |
| 1991-92 | (D3) | 1 | 16.11.91 | **Colchester Utd** (Conf) | A | D | 0-0 | |
| | | 1r | 26.11.91 | **Colchester Utd** | H | D | 0-0aet | |
| | | | | *Exeter won 4-2 on penalties* | | | | |
| | | 2 | 07.12.91 | **Swansea City** (D3) | H | D | 0-0 | |
| | | 2r | 17.12.91 | **Swansea City** | A | W | 2-1 | Brown, Marshall |
| | | 3 | 04.01.92 | **Portsmouth** (D2) | H | L | 1-2 | Moran |
| 1992-93 | (D2) | 1 | 14.11.92 | **Kidderminster H** (Conf) | H | W | 1-0 | Moran |
| | | 2 | 05.12.92 | **Swansea City** (D2) | H | - | 1-2ab | Dolan |
| | | | | *abandoned after 86 minutes – floodlight failure* | | | | |
| | | 2 | 15.12.92 | **Swansea City** (D2) | H | L | 2-5 | Moran, Cook |
| 1993-94 | (D2) | 1 | 13.11.93 | **Farnborough T** (SL) | A | W | 3-1 | Worthington, Jepson, Ross |
| | | 2 | 04.12.93 | **Leyton Orient** (D2) | A | D | 1-1 | Bailey |
| | | 2r | 14.12.93 | **Leyton Orient** | H | D | 2-2aet | Storer, Harris |
| | | | | *Exeter won 5-4 on penalties* | | | | |
| | | 3 | 08.01.94 | **Aston Villa** (PL) | H | L | 0-1 | |
| 1994-95 | (D3) | 1 | 12.11.94 | **Crawley Town** (SL) | H | W | 1-0 | Cecere |
| | | 2 | 03.12.94 | **Colchester Utd** (D3) | H | L | 1-2 | Morgan |
| 1995-96 | (D3) | 1 | 11.11.95 | **Peterborough Utd** (D2) | H | L | 0-1 | |
| 1996-97 | (D3) | 1 | 16.11.96 | **Bristol Rovers** (D2) | A | W | 2-1 | Rowbotham, Flack |
| | | 2 | 06.12.96 | **Plymouth Argyle** (D2) | A | L | 1-4 | Sharpe |
| 1997-98 | (D3) | 1 | 15.11.97 | **Northampton Town** (D2) | H | D | 1-1 | Rowbotham |
| | | 1r | 25.11.97 | **Northampton Town** | A | L | 1-3 | Clark |
| 1998-99 | (D3) | 1 | 14.11.98 | **Tamworth** (SL) | A | D | 2-2 | Gittens, Richardson |
| | | 1r | 24.11.98 | **Tamworth** | H | W | 4-1 | Rowe og, Rowbotham 2, Flack |
| | | 2 | 05.12.98 | **Bristol Rovers** (D2) | H | D | 2-2 | Flack, Gardner |
| | | 2r | 15.12.98 | **Bristol Rovers** | A | L | 0-5 | |
| 1999-00 | (D3) | 1 | 30.10.99 | **Eastwood Town** (NPL) | H | W | 2-1 | Flack, Gale |
| | | 2 | 20.11.99 | **Aldershot Town** (IL) | H | W | 2-0 | Alexander, Flack |
| | | 3 | 11.12.99 | **Everton** (PL) | H | D | 0-0 | |
| | | 3r | 21.12.99 | **Everton** | A | L | 0-1 | |
| 2000-01 | (D3) | 1 | 18.11.00 | **Walsall** (D2) | A | L | 0-4 | |
| 2001-02 | (D3) | 1 | 17.11.01 | **Cambridge City** (SL) | A | W | 3-0 | Curran, Tomlinson, Roscoe |
| | | 2 | 08.12.01 | **Dagenham & Red** (Conf) | H | D | 0-0 | |
| | | 2r | 19.12.01 | **Dagenham & Red** | A | L | 0-3 | |

| | | | | | | | | |
|---|---|---|---|---|---|---|---|---|
| 2002-03 | (D3) | 1 | 17.11.02 | **Forest Green R** (Conf) | A | D | 0-0 | |
| | | 1r | 26.11.02 | **Forest Green R** | H | W | 2-1 | Sheldon, Lock |
| | | 2 | 07.12.02 | **Rushden & D** (D3) | H | W | 3-1 | McConnell, Walker (p), Moor |
| | | 3 | 04.01.03 | **Charlton Athletic** (PL) | A | L | 1-3 | Gaia |

## FAIRFIELD

*Entered FA Cup 1891-92 – 1908-09. Manchester-based, Lancashire League champions 1895, failed to complete their fixtures just three years later.*

| | | | | | | | | |
|---|---|---|---|---|---|---|---|---|
| 1894-95 | (LL) | 1 | 02.02.95 | **Sunderland** (D1) | A | L | 1-11 | Allen |

## FALMOUTH TOWN

*Formed 1949. First entered FA Cup: 1961-62. Members of the South Western League.*

| | | | | | | | | |
|---|---|---|---|---|---|---|---|---|
| 1962-63 | (SWL) | 1 | 03.11.62 | **Oxford Utd** (D4) | H | L | 1-2 | Penny |
| 1967-68 | (SWL) | 1 | 12.12.67 | **Peterborough Utd** (D3) | A | L | 2-5 | Gray 2 |
| 1969-70 | (SWL) | 1 | 15.11.69 | **Peterborough Utd** (D4) | H | L | 1-4 | Ewings |

## FAREHAM TOWN

*Formed: 1947 by the amalgamation of three local sides with 19th-century roots. First entered FA Cup: 1954-55. Members of the Wessex League.*

| | | | | | | | | |
|---|---|---|---|---|---|---|---|---|
| 1979-80 | (SL) | 1 | 24.11.79 | **Merthyr Tydfil** (SL) | H | L | 2-3 | Atkins, Warren |
| 1985-86 | (SL) | 1 | 16.11.85 | **Maidstone Utd** (APL) | H | L | 0-3 | |
| 1986-87 | (SL) | 1 | 15.11.86 | **Bournemouth** (D3) | A | L | 2-7 | Wilkes 2 |
| 1988-89 | (SL) | 1 | 19.11.88 | **Torquay Utd** (D4) | A | D | 2-2 | Maddock, Carroll |
| | | 1r | 23.11.88 | **Torquay Utd** | H | L | 2-3 | Carroll, Maddock |

## FARNBOROUGH TOWN

*Formed 1967. First entered FA Cup:1972-73. League clubs beaten: Torquay United, Darlington. Members of The Conference.*

| | | | | | | | | |
|---|---|---|---|---|---|---|---|---|
| 1980-81 | (IL) | 1 | 22.11.80 | **Yeovil Town** (APL) | A | L | 1-2 | Parkin (p) |
| 1983-84 | (IL) | 1 | 19.11.83 | **Barking** (IL) | A | L | 1-2 | Bromme |
| 1984-85 | (IL) | 1 | 17.11.84 | **Hereford Utd** (D4) | A | L | 0-3 | |
| 1985-86 | (IL) | 1 | 16.11.85 | **Bath City** (APL) | H | L | 0-4 | |
| 1986-87 | (IL) | 1 | 15.11.86 | **Swindon Town** (D3) | A | L | 0-4 | |
| 1987-88 | (IL) | 1 | 14.11.87 | **Cambridge Utd** (D4) | A | L | 1-2 | Bailey |
| 1989-90 | (Conf) | 1 | 18.11.89 | **Hereford Utd** (D4) | H | L | 0-1 | |
| 1990-91 | (SL) | 1 | 17.11.90 | **Fulham** (D3) | A | L | 1-2 | Horton |
| 1991-92 | (Conf) | 1 | 16.11.91 | **Halesowen T** (SL) | A | D | 2-2 | Hobson, Broome |
| | | 1r | 26.11.91 | **Halesowen T** | H | W | 4-0 | Read 3, Coombs (p) |
| | | 2 | 07.12.91 | **Torquay Utd** (D3) | A | D | 1-1 | Read |
| | | 2r | 17.12.91 | **Torquay Utd** | H | W | 4-3 | Coney, Read, Doherty, Broome |
| | | 3 | 04.01.92 | **West Ham Utd** (D1) *played at Upton Park* | H | D | 1-1 | Coney (p) |
| | | 3r | 14.01.92 | **West Ham Utd** (D1) | A | L | 0-1 | |
| 1993-94 | (SL) | 1 | 13.11.93 | **Exeter City** (D2) | H | L | 1-3 | Jones |
| 1995-96 | (Conf) | 1 | 11.11.95 | **Brentford** (D2) | A | D | 1-1 | Senior |
| | | 1r | 22.11.95 | **Brentford** | H | L | 0-4 | |
| 1996-97 | (Conf) | 1 | 16.11.96 | **Barnet** (D3) | H | D | 2-2 | Wingfield, Booth |
| | | 1r | 26.11.96 | **Barnet** | A | L | 0-1 | |
| 1997-98 | (Conf) | 1 | 15.11.97 | **Dagenham & Red** (IL) | H | L | 0-1 | |
| 2001-02 | (Conf) | 1 | 17.11.01 | **Halifax Town** (D3) | A | L | 1-2 | Piper |
| 2002-03 | (Conf) | 1 | 16.11.02 | **Harrogate Town** (NPL) | H | W | 5-1 | Baptiste 2, Taggart, Charlerey, Piper |
| | | 2 | 07.12.02 | **Southport** (Conf) | A | W | 3-0 | Piper, Carroll, Green |
| | | 3 | 04.01.03 | **Darlington** (D3) | A | W | 3-2 | Baptiste, Carroll 2 |
| | | 4 | 25.01.03 | **Arsenal** (PL) *played at Highbury* | H | L | 1-5 | Baptiste |

## FARNHAM UNITED BREWERIES

*Entered FA Cup: 1921-22 – 1927-28.*

| | | | | | | | | |
|---|---|---|---|---|---|---|---|---|
| 1925-26 | (SSL) | 1 | 28.11.25 | **Swindon Town** (3S) | H | L | 1-10 | Bicknell |

## FARNINGHAM

*Formed 1872. Home ground was in Kent, a mile from Farningham Road Station near the Lion Hotel. Never played another FA Cup match after losing 16-0 to Wanderers which remained the record victory in the competition until Preston beat Hyde 26-0 in 1887.*

| | | | | | | | | |
|---|---|---|---|---|---|---|---|---|
| 1873-74 | | 1 | | Trojans | | | - | |
| | | | | *Farningham scratched. Trojans walkover* | | | | |
| 1874-75 | | 1 | 10.10.74 | **Wanderers** | A | L | 0-16 | |

## FARSLEY CELTIC

*Formed 1908. First entered FA Cup: 1928-29. Members of the Northern Premier League.*

| | | | | | | | | |
|---|---|---|---|---|---|---|---|---|
| 1974-75 | (YL) | 1 | 23.11.74 | **Tranmere Rovers** (D3) | H | L | 0-2 | |
| | | | | *played at Elland Road* | | | | |

## FERRYHILL ATHLETIC

*Formed 1921. First entered FA Cup: 1922-23.*

| | | | | | | | | |
|---|---|---|---|---|---|---|---|---|
| 1935-36 | (NL) | 1 | 30.11.35 | **Oldham Athletic** (3N) | A | L | 1-6 | Booth |
| 1953-54 | (NL) | 1 | 21.11.53 | **Workington** (3N) | A | L | 0-3 | |

## FINCHLEY

*Formed 1874. First entered FA Cup: 1878-79. Merged with Wingate FC to form Wingate & Finchley 1992. League club beaten: Crystal Palace. Members of the Isthmian League.*

| | | | | | | | | |
|---|---|---|---|---|---|---|---|---|
| 1878-79 | | 1 | | Clapham Rovers | | | - | |
| | | | | *Finchley scratched. Clapham walkover* | | | | |
| 1879-80 | | 1 | 08.11.79 | **Old Harrovians** | H | L | 1-2 | |
| 1880-81 | | 1 | 13.11.80 | **Clapham Rovers** | A | L | 0-15 | |
| 1881-82 | | 1 | 29.10.81 | **Acton** | A | D | 0-0 | |
| | | 1r | 12.11.81 | **Acton** | H | L | 0-4 | |
| 1946-47 | (AL) | 1 | 30.11.46 | **Port Vale** (3S) | A | L | 0-5 | |
| 1952-53 | (AL) | 1 | 22.11.52 | **Kidderminster H** (SL) | A | W | 1-0 | Ault |
| | | 2 | 06.12.52 | **Crystal Palace** (3S) | H | - | 3-1ab | Robb 2, Nottage |
| | | | | *abandoned after 61 minutes – fog* | | | | |
| | | 2 | 10.12.52 | **Crystal Palace** | H | W | 3-1 | Robb, Duke, Nottage |
| | | 3 | 10.01.53 | **Shrewsbury Town** (3S) | A | L | 0-2 | |
| 1953-54 | (AL) | 1 | 21.11.53 | **Southend Utd** (3S) | H | L | 1-3 | Walton |

## FISHER ATHLETIC

*Formed 1908 by the John Fisher Catholic Society in south-east London. Reformed 1966. Briefly known as Fisher'93 from 1993-96. Members of the Southern League.*

| | | | | | | | | |
|---|---|---|---|---|---|---|---|---|
| 1984-85 | (SL) | 1 | 17.11.84 | **Bristol City** (D3) | H | L | 0-1 | |
| 1988-89 | (Conf) | 1 | 20.11.88 | **Bristol Rovers** (D3) | A | L | 0-3 | |

## FISHWICK RAMBLERS

*Formed 1871. Played at The Brow, Fishwick, Preston. Entered FA Cup for just two seasons.*

| | | | | | | | | |
|---|---|---|---|---|---|---|---|---|
| 1884-85 | | 1 | 01.11.84 | **Darwen Ramblers** | A | W | 2-1 | |
| | | 2 | 22.11.84 | **Darwen** | H | L | 0-2 | |
| 1885-86 | | 1 | 31.10.85 | **Halliwell** | A | L | 1-2 | |

## FLEETWOOD RANGERS

*Entered FA Cup: 1886-1898. Founder members of the Lancashire League 1889.*

| | | | | | | | | |
|---|---|---|---|---|---|---|---|---|
| 1886-87 | | 1 | 30.10.86 | **Newton Heath** | 1 H | D | 2-2 | Wright, Fisher |
| | | | | *Fleetwood awarded tie as Newton Heath refused to play extra time* | | | | |
| | | 2 | 20.11.86 | **Partick Thistle** | A | L | 0-7 | |
| 1887-88 | | 1 | 15.10.87 | **West Manchester** | H | W | 4-1 | |
| | | 2 | 05.11.87 | **Higher Walton** | H | L | 1-3 | |

## FLEETWOOD TOWN

*First entered FA Cup: 1909. Reformed as Fleetwood Town, 1977. FA Vase runners-up: 1985. Disbanded 1996. Reformed 1997.*

**as Fleetwood**

| | | | | | | | | |
|---|---|---|---|---|---|---|---|---|
| 1949-50 | (LC) | 1 | 26.11.49 | **Bradford City** (3N) | A | L | 0-9 | |
| 1965-66 | (LC) | 1 | 13.11.65 | **Rochdale** (D4) | H | D | 2-2 | Robinson, Strachan |
| | | 1r | 17.11.65 | **Rochdale** | A | L | 0-5 | |

**as Fleetwood Town**

| | | | | | | | | |
|---|---|---|---|---|---|---|---|---|
| 1980-81 | (CC) | 1 | 22.11.80 | **Blackpool** (D3) | A | L | 0-4 | |
| 1990-91 | (NPL) | 1 | 17.11.90 | **Atherstone Utd** (SL) | A | L | 1-3 | Madden |

## FOLKESTONE

*Formed 1884. First entered FA Cup: 1890-91. Folded 1990. League clubs beaten: Norwich City, Newport County, Gillingham.*

| | | | | | | | | |
|---|---|---|---|---|---|---|---|---|
| 1925-26 | (SL) | 1 | 28.11.25 | **Luton Town** (3S) | A | L | 0-3 | |
| 1929-30 | (SL) | 1 | 30.11.29 | **Clapton Orient** (3S) | A | D | 0-0 | |
| | | 1r | 04.12.29 | **Clapton Orient** | H | D | 2-2aet | Brookes, Clamp |
| | | 1 2r | 09.12.29 | **Clapton Orient** (3S) *played at Highbury* | | L | 1-4 | Clamp |
| 1930-31 | (SL) | 1 | 29.11.30 | **Sittingbourne** (KL) | H | W | 5-3 | Brookes 2, Vinall, Middleton, Weall |
| | | 2 | 13.12.30 | **Gateshead AFC** (3N) | A | L | 2-3 | Saunders, Brooks |
| 1931-32 | (SL) | 1 | 28.11.31 | **Brighton** (3S) | H | L | 2-5 | Woodward,Cook |
| 1932-33 | (SL) | 1 | 26.11.32 | **Norwich City** (3S) | H | W | 1-0 | Richards |
| | | 2 | 10.12.32 | **Newport County** (3S) | H | W | 2-1 | J Havelock 2 |
| | | 3 | 14.01.33 | **Huddersfield Town** (D1) | A | L | 0-2 | |
| 1933-34 | (SL) | 1 | 25.11.33 | **Bristol Rovers** (3S) | H | D | 0-0 | |
| | | 1r | 29.11.33 | **Bristol Rovers** | A | L | 1-3 | Havelock |
| 1934-35 | (SL) | 1 | 24.11.34 | **Brighton** (3S) | A | L | 1-3 | Richardson |
| 1935-36 | (SL) | 1 | 30.11.35 | **Romford** (AL) | A | D | 3-3 | Godling 2, Woodward |
| | | 1r | 04.12.35 | **Romford** | H | W | 2-1aet | Murray, Woodward |
| | | 2 | 14.12.35 | **Clapton Orient** (3S) | H | L | 1-2 | Hobson |
| 1936-37 | (SL) | 1 | 28.11.36 | **Exeter City** (3S) | A | L | 0-3 | |
| 1937-38 | (SL) | 1 | 27.11.37 | **Exeter City** | A | L | 0-1 | |
| 1938-39 | (SL) | 1 | 26.11.38 | **Colchester Utd** (SL) | H | W | 2-1 | Birch og, Ashley |
| | | 2 | 10.12.38 | **Yeovil & Petters Utd** (SL) | H | D | 1-1 | Baker |
| | | 2r | 15.12.38 | **Yeovil & Petters Utd** | A | L | 0-1 | |
| 1951-52 | (KL) | 1 | 24.11.51 | **Barnstaple Town** (WL) | A | D | 2-2 | Day, Hassell |
| | | 1r | 28.11.51 | **Barnstaple Town** | H | W | 5-2 | Day 3, Wiltshire, Himsworth |
| | | 2 | 15.12.51 | **Stockton** (NEL) | A | L | 1-2 | Himsworth |
| 1963-64 | (SL) | 1 | 16.11.63 | **Oxford Utd** (D4) | A | L | 0-2 | |
| 1965-66 | (SL) | 1 | 13.11.65 | **Gillingham** (D3) | A | W | 2-1 | Catleugh, Biggs |
| | | 2 | 04.12.65 | **Wimbledon** (SL) | A | W | 1-0 | Churms |
| | | 3 | 22.01.66 | **Crewe Alexandra** (D4) | H | L | 1-5 | Legate |
| 1966-67 | (SL) | 1 | 26.11.66 | **Swansea Town** (D3) | H | D | 2-2 | Catleugh, Ireland |
| | | 1r | 29.11.66 | **Swansea Town** | A | L | 2-7 | Ballagher, Biggs |

**as Folkestone & Shepway**

| | | | | | | | | |
|---|---|---|---|---|---|---|---|---|
| 1977-78 | (SL) | 1 | 26.11.77 | **Brentford** (D4) | A | L | 0-2 | |
| 1982-83 | (SL) | 1 | 20.11.82 | **Oxford Utd** (D3) | A | L | 2-5 | N Fusco (p), Plews |

## FORD UNITED

*Formed 1934. First entered FA Cup as Ford Sports: 1935-36. Amalgamated with Briggs Sports in 1958 to form Ford United. Members of the Isthmian League.*

| | | | | | | | |
|---|---|---|---|---|---|---|---|
| 1998-99 | (IL) | 1 | 14.11.98 | **Preston North End** (D2) | A | L | 0-3 |

## FOREST GREEN ROVERS

*Formed 1890. First entered FA Cup: 1977-78. FA Trophy runners-up: 1999, 2001. FA Vase winners: 1982. Known as Stroud FC 1989-92. Based in Nailsworth, Gloucestershire. Members of The Conference.*

| | | | | | | | | |
|---|---|---|---|---|---|---|---|---|
| 1999-00 | (Conf) | 1 | 30.10.99 | **Guiseley** (NPL) | H | W | 6-0 | L Hunt 3, McGregor, Drysdale, Sykes |
| | | 2 | 21.11.99 | **Torquay Utd** (D3) | H | L | 0-3 | |
| 2000-01 | (Conf) | 1 | 18.11.00 | **Morecambe** (Conf) | H | L | 0-3 | |
| 2001-02 | (Conf) | 1 | 17.11.01 | **Macclesfield T** (D3) | A | D | 2-2 | Meechan, Cooper (p) |
| | | 1r | 28.11.01 | **Macclesfield T** *Macclesfield T won 11-10 on penalties* | H | D | 1-1aet | Cooper |
| 2002-03 | (Conf) | 1 | 17.11.02 | **Exeter City** (D3) | H | D | 0-0 | |
| | | 1r | 26.11.02 | **Exeter City** | A | L | 1-2 | Richardson |

## FOREST SCHOOL

*Formed in late 1850s – probably 1859. One of the founding member clubs of the FA on October 26, 1863. Their ground was at Forest School at Snaresbrook, Epping Forest. This school team were the forerunners of the famous Wanderers.*

| | | | | | | | | |
|---|---|---|---|---|---|---|---|---|
| 1875-76 | | 1 | 30.10.75 | **Oxford University** | A | L | 0-6 | |
| 1876-77 | | 1 | 04.11.76 | **Gresham** | H | W | 4-1 | Crawley 2, Fairclough, Knowles |
| | | 2 | 29.11.76 | **Marlow** | A | L | 0-1 | |
| 1877-78 | | 1 | 07.11.77 | **1st Surrey Rifles** | A | L | 0-1 | |
| 1878-79 | | 1 | 02.11.78 | **Rochester** | H | W | 7-2 | |
| | | 2 | 07.12.78 | **Clapham Rovers** | A | L | 1-10 | Shaw |

# FORMBY

*Formed 1919. First entered FA Cup: 1937-38. Members of the North West Counties League.*

| | | | | | | | | |
|---|---|---|---|---|---|---|---|---|
| 1973-74 | (CC) | 1 | 24.11.73 | **Oldham Athletic** (D3) | H | L | 0-2 | |

# FRICKLEY ATHLETIC

*Formed 1910. First entered FA Cup 1910-11 as Frickley Colliery. Changed name to Frickley Athletic 1974. League club beaten: Harlepool. Members of the Northern Premier League.*

**as Frickley Colliery**

| | | | | | | | | |
|---|---|---|---|---|---|---|---|---|
| 1936-37 | (ML) | 1 | 28.11.36 | **Southport** (3N) | H | L | 0-2 | |
| 1957-58 | (ML) | 1 | 16.11.57 | **South Shields (1936)** (NEL) | A | L | 2-3 | Lambert, Hargreaves |
| 1963-64 | (CC) | 1 | 16.11.63 | **Notts County** (D3) | A | L | 1-2 | Cartwright |
| 1971-72 | (ML) | 1 | 20.11.71 | **Rotherham Utd** (D3) | H | D | 2-2 | Moran, Holland |
| | | 1r | 23.11.71 | **Rotherham Utd** | A | L | 0-4 | |
| 1973-74 | (ML) | 1 | 24.11.73 | **Halifax Town** (D3) | A | L | 1-6 | Morgan |

**as Frickley Athletic**

| | | | | | | | | |
|---|---|---|---|---|---|---|---|---|
| 1983-84 | (APL) | 1 | 19.11.83 | **Altrincham** (APL) | H | L | 0-1 | |
| 1984-85 | (APL) | 1 | 17.11.84 | **Stalybridge Celtic** (NWC) | H | W | 2-1 | Hooley (p), Reed |
| | | 2 | 08.12.84 | **Darlington** (D4) | A | L | 0-1 | |
| 1985-86 | (APL) | 1 | 16.11.85 | **Halesowen T** (WMRL) | H | D | 1-1 | Bishop |
| | | 1r | 18.11.85 | **Halesowen T** | A | W | 3-1 | Bishop, Wilson, Wilcox (p) |
| | | 2 | 07.12.85 | **Hartlepool Utd** (D4) | A | W | 1-0 | Wilson |
| | | 3 | 04.01.86 | **Rotherham Utd** (D3) | H | L | 1-3 | Bishop |
| 1986-87 | (Conf) | 1 | 15.11.86 | **Altrincham** (Conf) | H | D | 0-0 | |
| | | 1r | 18.11.86 | **Altrincham** | A | L | 0-4 | |
| 1988-89 | (NPL) | 1 | 19.11.88 | **Northwich Vic** (Conf) | H | L | 0-2 | |
| 2000-01 | (NPL) | 1 | 18.11.00 | **Northampton Town** (D2) | A | L | 0-4 | |

# FROME TOWN

*Formed 1904. First entered FA Cup: 1906-07. Members of the Western League.*

| | | | | | | | | |
|---|---|---|---|---|---|---|---|---|
| 1954-55 | (WL) | 1 | 20.11.54 | **Leyton Orient** (3S) | H | L | 0-3 | |

# FULHAM

*Formed 1879. FA Cup runners-up: 1975. Record FA Cup win: 7-0 v Swansea City, 1st round, 11.11 1995. Record FA Cup defeat: 0-7 v QPR, 3rd qualifying round, 1900-01. In Competition Proper: 0-6 v Newcastle Utd, semi-final, 28.03.1908 – this also stands as a record score in any FA Cup semi-final.*

| | | | | | | | | |
|---|---|---|---|---|---|---|---|---|
| 1896-97 | (LL) | | | 2q Swanscombe (A) 0-5 | | | | |
| 1897-98 | (LL) | | | did not enter | | | | |
| 1898-99 | (SL) | | | did not enter | | | | |
| 1899-00 | (SL) | | | 1q QPR (A) 0-3 | | | | |
| 1900-01 | (SL) | | | 3q QPR (A) 0-7 | | | | |
| 1901-02 | (SL) | | | P Chiswick (A) 3-2; 1q Crouch End Vampires (A) 2-4 | | | | |
| 1902-03 | (SL) | | | P Civil Service (H) 2-0; 1q Crouch End Vampires (H) 4-0; 2q Willesden T (H) 0-0; 2qr Willesden T (H) 5-0; 3q Watford (A) 1-1; 3qr Watford (H) 3-0; 4q Luton Am. (H) 4-1; 5q Luton T (A) 1-5 | | | | |
| 1903-04 | (SL) | | | 1q Hampstead (H) 3-0; 2q Crouch End Vampires (A) 5-0; 3q Civil Service (H) 3-3; 3qr Civil Service (A) 3-0; 4q QPR (A) 1-1; 4qr QPR (H) 3-1; 5q West Norwood (H) 4-0; 6q Luton T (H) 3-1; Int West Ham (A) 1-0 | | | | |
| | | 1 | 06.02.04 | **Woolwich Arsenal** (D2) | A | L | 0-1 | |
| 1904-05 | (SL) | | | 6q Luton T (H) 4-0; Int Manchester U (A) 2-2; Int r Manchester U (H) 0-0; Int 2r Manchester U 1-0 (at Villa Park) | | | | |
| | | 1 | 04.02.05 | **Reading** (SL) | H | D | 0-0 | |
| | | 1r | 08.02.05 | **Reading** | A | D | 0-0aet | |
| | | 1 2r | 13.02.05 | **Reading** *played at White Hart Lane* | | W | 1-0aet | Fraser |

| | | | | | | | |
|---|---|---|---|---|---|---|---|
| | 2 | 18.02.05 | **Nottingham Forest** (D1) | H | W | 1-0 | Wardrope |
| | 3 | 04.03.05 | **Aston Villa** (D1) | A | L | 0-5 | |
| 1905-06 (SL) | 1 | 13.01.06 | **QPR** (SL) | H | W | 1-0 | Collins |
| | 2 | 03.02.06 | **Nottingham Forest** (D1) | H | L | 1-3 | Fraser |
| 1906-07 (SL) | 1 | 12.01.07 | **Stockport County** (D2) | H | D | 0-0 | |
| | 1r | 16.01.07 | **Stockport County** | H | W | 2-1 | Freeman, Threlfall |
| | 2 | 02.02.07 | **Crystal Palace** (SL) | H | D | 0-0 | |
| | 2r | 06.02.07 | **Crystal Palace** | A | L | 0-1 | |
| 1907-08 (D2) | 1 | 11.01.08 | **Luton Town** (SL) | A | W | 8-3 | Dalrymple 2, Harrison 2, Millington 2, Morrison, Ross |
| | 2 | 01.02.08 | **Norwich City** (SL) | H | W | 2-0 | Millington, Threlfall |
| | 3 | 22.02.08 | **Manchester City** (D1) | A | D | 1-1 | Harrison |
| | 3r | 26.02.08 | **Manchester City** | H | W | 3-1 | Ross, Harrison, Dalrymle |
| | 4 | 07.03.08 | **Manchester Utd** (D1) | H | W | 2-1 | Harrison 2 |
| | SF | 28.03.08 | **Newcastle Utd** (D1) *played at Anfield* | | L | 0-6 | |
| 1908-09 (D2) | 1 | 16.01.09 | **Carlisle Utd** (NEL) | H | W | 4-1 | Freeman 2, Millington, Collins |
| | 2 | 06.02.09 | **Tottenham Hotspur** (D2) | A | L | 0-1 | |
| 1909-10 (D2) | 1 | 15.01.10 | **Chesterfield** (ML) | A | D | 0-0 | |
| | 1r | 19.01.10 | **Chesterfield** | H | W | 2-1 | Dalrymple, Harrison |
| | 2 | 05.02.10 | **Newcastle Utd** (D1) | A | L | 0-4 | |
| 1910-11 (D2) | 2 | 14.01.11 | **WBA** (D2) | A | L | 1-4 | Mouncher |
| 1911-12 (D2) | 1 | 13.01.12 | **Burnley** (D2) | H | W | 2-1 | Coleman, Brown |
| | 2 | 03.02.12 | **Liverpool** (D1) | H | W | 3-0 | Coleman 2, Pearce |
| | 3 | 24.02.12 | **Northampton Town** (SL) | H | W | 2-1 | Brown 2 |
| | 4 | 09.03.12 | **WBA** (D1) | A | L | 0-3 | |
| 1912-13 (D2) | 1 | 11.01.13 | **Hull City** (D2) | H | L | 0-2 | |
| 1913-14 (D2) | 1 | 10.01.14 | **Manchester City** (D1) | A | L | 0-3 | |
| 1914-15 (D2) | 1 | 09.01.15 | **South Shields** (NEL) | A | W | 2-1 | Taylor, Walker |
| | 2 | 21.01.15 | **Southampton** (SL) | H | L | 2-3aet | Taylor, Pearce |
| 1919-20 (D2) | 1 | 10.01.20 | **Swindon Town** (SL) | H | L | 1-2 | Hoare |
| 1920-21 (D2) | 1 | 08.01.21 | **Blackburn Rovers** (D1) | A | D | 1-1 | Cock |
| | 1r | 13.01.21 | **Blackburn Rovers** | H | W | 1-0 | McDonald |
| | 2 | 29.01.21 | **Lincoln City** (ML) | A | D | 0-0 | |
| | 2r | 07.02.21 | **Lincoln City** | H | W | 1-0 | Morris |
| | 3 | 19.02.21 | **Wolverhampton W** (D2) | H | L | 0-1 | |
| 1921-22 (D2) | 1 | 07.01.22 | **Plymouth Argyle** (3S) | A | D | 1-1 | Travers |
| | 1r | 11.01.22 | **Plymouth Argyle** | H | W | 1-0 | Shea |
| | 2 | 28.01.22 | **Leicester City** (D2) | A | L | 0-2 | |
| 1922-23 (D2) | 1 | 13.01.23 | **Leicester City** | A | L | 0-3 | |
| 1923-24 (D2) | 1 | 12.01.24 | **Llanelli** (SL) | H | W | 2-0 | Edmonds 2 |
| | 2 | 02.02.24 | **Burnley** (D1) | A | D | 0-0 | |
| | 2r | 07.02.24 | **Burnley** | H | L | 0-1 | |
| 1924-25 (D2) | 1 | 10.01.25 | **Swindon Town** (3S) | A | W | 2-1 | Edmonds, Richards |
| | 2 | 31.01.25 | **Cardiff City** (D1) | A | L | 0-1 | |
| 1925-26 (D2) | 3 | 09.01.26 | **Everton** (D1) | A | D | 1-1 | Craig |
| | 3r | 14.01.26 | **Everton** | H | W | 1-0 | White |
| | 4 | 30.01.26 | **Liverpool** (D1) | H | W | 3-1 | Pape 2, Penn |
| | 5 | 20.02.26 | **Notts County** (D1) | A | W | 1-0 | Prouse |
| | 6 | 06.03.26 | **Manchester Utd** (D1) | H | L | 1-2 | Pape |
| 1926-27 (D2) | 3 | 08.01.27 | **Chesterfield** (3N) | H | W | 4-3 | Tonner 2, Pape, Craig |
| | 4 | 29.01.27 | **Burnley** (D1) | H | L | 0-4 | |
| 1927-28 (D2) | 3 | 14.01.28 | **Southport** (3N) | A | L | 0-3 | |
| 1928-29 (3S) | 1 | 24.11.28 | **Coventry City** (3S) | A | W | 4-1 | Temple 2, Price, Penn |
| | 2 | 08.12.28 | **Luton Town** (3S) | H | D | 0-0 | |
| | 2r | 13.12.28 | **Luton Town** | A | L | 1-4 | Temple |
| 1929-30 (3S) | 1 | 30.11.29 | **Thames** (SL) | H | W | 4-0 | Barrett 2, Penn, Avey |
| | 2 | 14.12.29 | **Leyton FC** (AL) | A | W | 4-1 | Penn 2, Barrett, Hammond |
| | 3 | 11.01.30 | **Bournemouth** (3S) | H | D | 1-1 | Penn |
| | 3r | 15.01.30 | **Bournemouth** | A | W | 2-0 | Haley, Barrett |
| | 4 | 25.01.30 | **Nottingham Forest** (D2) | A | L | 1-2 | Haley |

| | | | | | | | | |
|---|---|---|---|---|---|---|---|---|
| 1930-31 | (3S) | 1 | 30.11.30 | **Wimbledon** (IL) | H | D | 1-1 | Price |
| | | 1r | 03.12.30 | **Wimbledon** | A | W | 6-0 | Penn 2, Gibbons 2, Watkins, Hammond |
| | | 2 | 13.12.30 | **Halifax Town** (3N) | H | W | 4-0 | Haley 2, Watkins, Hammond |
| | | 3 | 10.01.31 | **Portsmouth** (D1) | H | L | 0-2 | |
| 1931-32 | (3S) | 1 | 28.11.31 | **Guildford City** (SL) | H | W | 2-0 | Hammond 2 |
| | | 2 | 12.12.31 | **Yeovil & Petters Utd** (SL) | H | D | 0-0 | |
| | | 2r | 17.12.31 | **Yeovil & Petters Utd** | A | W | 5-2 | Newton 3, Price, Richards |
| | | 3 | 09.01.32 | **Watford** (3S) | A | D | 1-1 | Newton |
| | | 3r | 14.01.32 | **Watford** | H | L | 0-3 | |
| 1932-33 | (D2) | 3 | 14.01.33 | **Chester** (3N) | A | L | 0-5 | |
| 1933-34 | (D2) | 3 | 13.01.34 | **Liverpool** (D1) | A | D | 1-1 | Lambert |
| | | 3r | 17.01.34 | **Liverpool** | H | L | 2-3aet | Hammond, Arnold |
| 1934-35 | (D2) | 3 | 12.01.35 | **Sunderland** (D1) | A | L | 2-3 | Finch, Arnold |
| 1935-36 | (D2) | 3 | 11.01.36 | **Brighton** (3S) | H | W | 2-1 | Worsley, Hammond |
| | | 4 | 25.01.36 | **Blackpool** (D2) | H | W | 5-2 | Perry 4, Hammond |
| | | 5 | 19.02.36 | **Chelsea** (D1) | A | D | 0-0 | |
| | | 5r | 24.02.36 | **Chelsea** | H | W | 3-2 | Smith, Hammond, Arnold |
| | | 6 | 29.02.36 | **Derby County** (D1) | H | W | 3-0 | Arnold, Barrett, Smith |
| | | SF | 21.03.36 | **Sheffield Utd** (D2) *played at Molineux* | | L | 1-2 | Arnold |
| 1936-37 | (D2) | 3 | 16.01.37 | **Millwall** (3S) | A | L | 0-2 | |
| 1937-38 | (D2) | 3 | 08.01.38 | **Brentford** (D1) | A | L | 1-3 | O'Callaghan |
| 1938-39 | (D2) | 3 | 07.01.39 | **Bury** (D2) | H | W | 6-0 | Rooke 6 |
| | | 4 | 21.01.39 | **Chelsea** (D1) | A | L | 0-3 | |
| 1945-46 | (D2) | 3 1L | 05.01.46 | **Charlton Athletic** (D1) | A | L | 1-3 | Rampling |
| | | 3 2L | 07.01.46 | **Charlton Athletic** | H | W | 2-1 | Rooke 2 |
| 1946-47 | (D2) | 3 | 11.01.47 | **Birmingham City** (D2) | H | L | 1-2 | Watson |
| 1947-48 | (D2) | 3 | 10.01.48 | **Doncaster Rovers** (D2) | H | W | 2-0 | Ayres, Stevens |
| | | 4 | 24.01.48 | **Bristol Rovers** (3S) | H | W | 5-2 | Stevens 3, Ayres 2 |
| | | 5 | 07.02.48 | **Everton** (D1) | H | D | 1-1aet | Quested |
| | | 5r | 14.02.48 | **Everton** | A | W | 1-0 | R Thomas |
| | | 6 | 28.02.48 | **Blackpool** (D1) | H | L | 0-2 | |
| 1948-49 | (D2) | 3 | 08.01.49 | **Walsall** (3S) | H | L | 0-1aet | |
| 1949-50 | (D1) | 3 | 07.01.50 | **Charlton Athletic** (D1) | A | D | 2-2 | R Thomas, Freeman |
| | | 3r | 11.01.50 | **Charlton Athletic** | H | L | 1-2 | McDonald |
| 1950-51 | (D1) | 3 | 06.01.51 | **Sheffield Wed** (D1) | H | W | 1-0 | Brennan |
| | | 4 | 27.01.51 | **Millwall** (3S) | A | W | 1-0 | Campbell |
| | | 5 | 10.02.51 | **Chelsea** (D1) | A | D | 1-1 | Campbell |
| | | 5r | 14.02.51 | **Chelsea** | H | W | 3-0 | Brennan 2, Stevens |
| | | 6 | 24.02.51 | **Blackpool** (D1) | A | L | 0-1 | |
| 1951-52 | (D1) | 3 | 12.01.52 | **Birmingham City** (D2) | H | L | 0-1 | |
| 1952-53 | (D2) | 3 | 14.01.53 | **Bolton Wanderers** (D1) | A | L | 1-3 | Mitten |
| 1953-54 | (D2) | 3 | 09.01.54 | **Grimsby Town** (3N) | A | D | 5-5 | Taylor 3, Stevens, Hill |
| | | 3r | 13.01.54 | **Grimsby Town** *abandoned at half-time – ground waterlogged* | H | - | 0-0ab | |
| | | 3r | 18.01.54 | **Grimsby Town** | H | W | 3-1 | Haynes 2, Taylor |
| | | 4 | 30.01.54 | **Leyton Orient** (3S) | A | L | 1-2 | Robson |
| 1954-55 | (D2) | 3 | 08.01.55 | **Preston North End** (D1) | H | L | 2-3 | Haynes, Stevens |
| 1955-56 | (D2) | 3 | 07.01.56 | **Notts County** (D2) | A | W | 1-0 | Haynes |
| | | 4 | 28.01.56 | **Newcastle Utd** (D1) | H | L | 4-5 | Chamberlain 3, Hill |
| 1956-57 | (D2) | 3 | 05.01.57 | **Ipswich Town** (3S) | A | W | 3-2 | Stevens 2, Dwight |
| | | 4 | 26.01.57 | **Blackpool** (D1) | A | L | 2-6 | Lowe, Bentley |
| 1957-58 | (D2) | 3 | 04.01.58 | **Yeovil Town** (SL) | H | W | 4-0 | Hill 2, Key, Doherty |
| | | 4 | 25.01.58 | **Charlton Athletic** (D2) | H | D | 1-1 | Hill |
| | | 4r | 29.01.58 | **Charlton Athletic** | A | W | 2-0 | Bentley, Stevens |
| | | 5 | 15.02.58 | **West Ham Utd** (D2) | A | W | 3-2 | Dwight, Hill, Haynes |
| | | 6 | 01.03.58 | **Bristol Rovers** (D2) | H | W | 3-1 | Stevens 2, Hill |
| | | SF | 22.03.58 | **Manchester Utd** (D1) *played at Villa Park* | | D | 2-2 | Stevens, Hill |
| | | SFr | 26.03.58 | **Manchester Utd** *played at Highbury* | | L | 3-5 | Dwight, Stevens, Chamberlain |

| | | | | | | | | |
|---|---|---|---|---|---|---|---|---|
| 1958-59 | (D2) | 3 | 10.01.59 | **Peterborough Utd** (ML) | H | D | 0-0 | |
| | | 3r | 24.01.59 | **Peterborough Utd** | A | W | 1-0 | Johnson |
| | | 4 | 28.01.59 | **Birmingham City** (D1) | A | D | 1-1 | Hill |
| | | 4r | 04.02.59 | **Birmingham City** | H | L | 2-3 | Leggat, Hill |
| 1959-60 | (D1) | 3 | 09.01.60 | **Hull City** (D2) | H | W | 5-0 | Leggat 2, Chamberlain Cook, Hill |
| | | 4 | 30.01.60 | **Leicester City** (D1) | A | L | 1-2 | Cunningham og |
| 1960-61 | (D1) | 3 | 07.01.61 | **Newcastle Utd** (D1) | A | L | 0-5 | |
| 1961-62 | (D1) | 3 | 06.01.62 | **Hartlepools Utd** (D4) | H | W | 3-1 | Cook 2, Key |
| | | 4 | 27.01.62 | **Walsall** (D2) | H | D | 2-2 | Cook, Henderson |
| | | 4r | 30.01.62 | **Walsall** | A | W | 2-0 | Lowe, Metchick |
| | | 5 | 17.02.62 | **Port Vale** (D3) | H | W | 1-0 | Langley |
| | | 6 | 10.03.62 | **Blackburn Rovers** (D1) | H | D | 2-2 | Woods og, Haynes |
| | | 6r | 14.03.62 | **Blackburn Rovers** | A | W | 1-0 | Cook |
| | | SF | 31.03.62 | **Burnley** (D1) | | D | 1-1 | Leggat |
| | | | | *played at Villa Park* | | | | |
| | | SFr | 09.04.62 | **Burnley** | | L | 1-2 | Langley |
| | | | | *played at Filbert Street* | | | | |
| 1962-63 | (D1) | 3 | 04.02.63 | **West Ham Utd** (D1) | A | D | 0-0 | |
| | | 3r | 20.02.63 | **West Ham Utd** | H | L | 1-2 | Robson |
| 1963-64 | (D1) | 3 | 04.01.64 | **Luton Town** (D3) | H | W | 4-1 | Mullery, Leggat, Cook, Howfield |
| | | 4 | 25.01.64 | **Blackburn Rovers** (D1) | A | L | 0-2 | |
| 1964-65 | (D1) | 3 | 09.01.65 | **Millwall** (D4) | H | D | 3-3 | Stratton 2, Key |
| | | 3r | 11.01.65 | **Millwall** | A | L | 0-2 | |
| 1965-66 | (D1) | 3 | 22.01.66 | **Sheffield Utd** (D1) | A | L | 1-3 | Dempsey |
| 1966-67 | (D1) | 3 | 28.01.67 | **Bradford Park A** (D4) | A | W | 3-1 | Clarke 2, Haynes |
| | | 4 | 18.02.67 | **Sheffield Utd** (D1) | H | D | 1-1 | Clarke |
| | | 4r | 01.03.67 | **Sheffield Utd** | A | L | 1-3 | Callaghan |
| 1967-68 | (D1) | 3 | 27.01.68 | **Macclesfield T** (CC) | H | W | 4-2 | Clarke 2, Gilroy, Haynes |
| | | 4 | 17.02.68 | **Portsmouth** (D2) | H | D | 0-0 | |
| | | 4r | 21.02.68 | **Portsmouth** | A | L | 0-1 | |
| 1968-69 | (D2) | 3 | 04.01.69 | **Sunderland** (D1) | A | W | 4-1 | Mullen 2, Brown, Haynes |
| | | 4 | 25.01.69 | **WBA** (D1) | H | L | 1-2 | Brown |
| 1969-70 | (D3) | 1 | 15.11.69 | **Exeter City** (D4) | A | L | 0-2 | |
| 1970-71 | (D3) | 1 | 21.11.70 | **Bristol Rovers** (D3) | H | L | 1-2 | Johnston |
| 1971-72 | (D2) | 3 | 15.01.72 | **QPR** (D2) | A | D | 1-1 | John Conway |
| | | 3r | 18.01.72 | **QPR** | H | W | 2-1 | Cross 2 |
| | | 4 | 05.02.72 | **Huddersfield Town** (D1) | A | L | 0-3 | |
| 1972-73 | (D2) | 3 | 13.01.73 | **Sheffield Wed** (D2) | A | L | 0-2 | |
| 1973-74 | (D2) | 3 | 05.01.74 | **Preston North End** (D2) | H | W | 1-0 | John Conway |
| | | 4 | 26.01.74 | **Leicester City** (D1) | H | D | 1-1 | Mullery |
| | | 4r | 30.01.74 | **Leicester City** | A | L | 1-2aet | Barret |
| 1974-75 | (D2) | 3 | 04.01.75 | **Hull City** (D2) | H | D | 1-1 | Jim Conway |
| | | 3r | 07.01.75 | **Hull City** | A | D | 2-2aet | Busby 2 |
| | | 3 2r | 13.01.75 | **Hull City** | | W | 1-0 | Slough |
| | | | | *played at Filbert Street* | | | | |
| | | 4 | 28.01.75 | **Nottingham Forest** (D2) | H | D | 0-0 | |
| | | 4r | 03.02.75 | **Nottingham Forest** | A | D | 1-1aet | Dowie |
| | | 4 2r | 05.02.75 | **Nottingham Forest** | H | D | 1-1aet | Slough |
| | | 4 3r | 10.02.75 | **Nottingham Forest** | A | W | 2-1 | Busby 2 |
| | | 5 | 15.02.75 | **Everton** (D1) | A | W | 2-1 | Busby 2 |
| | | 6 | 08.03.75 | **Carlisle Utd** (D1) | A | W | 1-0 | Barrett |
| | | SF | 05.04.75 | **Birmingham City** (D1) | | D | 1-1 | Mitchell |
| | | | | *played at Hillsborough* | | | | |
| | | SFr | 09.04.75 | **Birmingham City** | | W | 1-0aet | Mitchell |
| | | | | *played at Maine Road* | | | | |
| | | F | 03.05.75 | **West Ham Utd** (D1) | | L | 0-2 | |
| | | | | *played at Wembley Stadium* | | | | |
| 1975-76 | (D2) | 3 | 03.01.76 | **Huddersfield Town** (D4) | H | L | 2-3 | Jim Conway |
| 1976-77 | (D2) | 3 | 08.01.77 | **Swindon Town** (D3) | H | D | 3-3 | Marsh, Howe, Barrett |
| | | 3r | 11.01.77 | **Swindon Town** | A | L | 0-5 | |
| 1977-78 | (D2) | 3 | 07.01.78 | **Burnley** (D2) | A | L | 0-1 | |

| | | | | | | | | |
|---|---|---|---|---|---|---|---|---|
| 1978-79 | (D2) | 3 | 06.01.79 | **QPR** (D1) | H | W | 2-0 | Margerrison, Davies |
| | | 4 | 31.01.79 | **Manchester Utd** (D1) | H | D | 1-1 | Margerrison |
| | | 4r | 12.02.79 | **Manchester Utd** | A | L | 0-1 | |
| 1979-80 | (D2) | 3 | 05.01.80 | **Blackburn Rovers** (D3) | A | D | 1-1 | Money |
| | | 3r | 15.01.80 | **Blackburn Rovers** | H | L | 0-1 | |
| 1980-81 | (D3) | 1 | 22.11.80 | **Reading** (D3) | A | W | 2-1 | Davies, Mahoney |
| | | 2 | 13.12.80 | **Brentford** (D3) | H | W | 1-0 | Greenaway |
| | | 3 | 03.01.81 | **Bury** (D4) | A | D | 1-1 | Mahoney |
| | | 3r | 06.01.81 | **Bury** | H | D | 0-0aet | |
| | | 3 2r | 12.01.81 | **Bury** | | W | 1-0 | Davies |
| | | | | *played at The Hawthorns* | | | | |
| | | 4 | 24.01.81 | **Charlton Athletic** (D3) | H | L | 1-2 | Davies |
| 1981-82 | (D3) | 1 | 21.11.81 | **Bristol Rovers** (D3) | A | W | 2-1 | Coney 2 |
| | | 2 | 02.01.82 | **Hereford Utd** (D4) | A | L | 0-1 | |
| 1982-83 | (D2) | 3 | 08.01.83 | **Oldham Athletic** (D2) | A | W | 2-0 | Coney, Houghton |
| | | 4 | 29.01.83 | **Watford** (D1) | A | D | 1-1 | Coney |
| | | 4r | 01.02.83 | **Watford** | H | L | 1-2 | Lewington |
| 1983-84 | (D2) | 3 | 07.01.84 | **Tottenham Hotspur** (D1) | H | D | 0-0 | |
| | | 3r | 11.01.84 | **Tottenham Hotspur** | A | L | 0-2 | |
| 1984-85 | (D2) | 3 | 05.01.85 | **Sheffield Wed** (D1) | H | L | 2-3 | Houghton 2 |
| 1985-86 | (D2) | 3 | 13.01.86 | **Sheffield Utd** (D2) | A | L | 0-2 | |
| 1986-87 | (D3) | 1 | 15.11.86 | **Hereford Utd** (D4) | A | D | 3-3 | Barnett, Marshall, Coney |
| | | 1r | 24.11.86 | **Hereford Utd** | H | W | 4-0 | Davies 2, Marshall, Coney |
| | | 2 | 06.12.86 | **Newport County** (D3) | H | W | 2-0 | Oakes, Davies |
| | | 3 | 10.01.87 | **Swindon Town** (D3) | H | L | 0-1 | |
| 1987-88 | (D3) | 1 | 14.11.87 | **Gillingham** (D3) | A | L | 1-2 | Rosenior |
| 1988-89 | (D3) | 1 | 19.11.88 | **Colchester Utd** (D4) | H | L | 0-1 | |
| 1989-90 | (D3) | 1 | 19.11.89 | **Bath City** (SL) | A | D | 2-2 | Peters, Walker |
| | | 1r | 22.11.89 | **Bath City** | H | W | 2-1 | Marshall, Watson |
| | | 2 | 09.12.89 | **Bristol City** (D3) | A | L | 1-2 | Scott |
| 1990-91 | (D3) | 1 | 17.11.90 | **Farnborough T** (SL) | H | W | 2-1 | Pike, Brazil (p) |
| | | 2 | 07.12.90 | **Cambridge Utd** (D3) | H | D | 0-0 | |
| | | 2r | 11.12.90 | **Cambridge Utd** | A | L | 1-2 | Davies |
| 1991-92 | (D3) | 1 | 15.11.91 | **Hayes** (IL) | H | L | 0-2 | |
| 1992-93 | (D2) | 1 | 14.11.92 | **Northampton Town** (D3) | A | L | 1-3 | Farrell |
| 1993-94 | (D2) | 1 | 14.11.93 | **Yeovil Town** (Conf) | A | L | 0-1 | |
| 1994-95 | (D3) | 1 | 12.11.94 | **Ashford Town** (SL) | A | D | 2-2 | Adams 2(2p) |
| | | 1r | 22.11.94 | **Ashford Town** | H | W | 5-3aet | Adams 2, Morgan, Blake, Cork |
| | | 2 | 03.12.94 | **Gillingham** (D3) | A | D | 1-1 | Hamill |
| | | 2r | 13.12.94 | **Gillingham** | H | L | 1-2aet | Hamill |
| 1995-96 | (D3) | 1 | 11.11.95 | **Swansea City** (D2) | H | W | 7-0 | Conroy 3, Jupp, Cusack, Brooker, Thomas |
| | | 2 | 02.12.95 | **Brighton** (D2) | H | D | 0-0 | |
| | | 2r | 14.12.95 | **Brighton** | A | D | 0-0aet | |
| | | | | *Fulham won 4-1 on penalties* | | | | |
| | | 3 | 06.01.96 | **Shrewsbury Town** (D2) | H | D | 1-1 | Angus |
| | | 3r | 16.01.96 | **Shrewsbury Town** | A | L | 1-2 | Hamill |
| 1996-97 | (D3) | 1 | 16.11.96 | **Plymouth Argyle** (D2) | A | L | 0-5 | |
| 1997-98 | (D2) | 1 | 16.11.97 | **Margate** (SL) | A | W | 2-1 | Carpenter, Scott |
| | | 2 | 06.12.97 | **Southend Utd** (D2) | H | W | 1-0 | Blake (p) |
| | | 3 | 05.01.98 | **Tottenham Hotspur** (PL) | A | L | 1-3 | Smith |
| 1998-99 | (D2) | 1 | 15.11.98 | **Leigh RMI** (NPL) | H | D | 1-1 | Lehmann |
| | | 1r | 24.11.98 | **Leigh RMI** | A | W | 2-0 | Peschisolido 2(1p) |
| | | 2 | 05.12.98 | **Hartlepool Utd** (D3) | H | W | 4-2 | Horsfield 2, Di Lella og, Morgan |
| | | 3 | 02.01.99 | **Southampton** (PL) | A | D | 1-1 | Hayward |
| | | 3r | 13.01.99 | **Southampton** | H | W | 1-0 | Hayles |
| | | 4 | 23.01.99 | **Aston Villa** (PL) | A | W | 2-0 | Morgan, Hayward |
| | | 5 | 14.02.99 | **Manchester Utd** (PL) | A | L | 0-1 | |
| 1999-00 | (D1) | 3 | 11.12.99 | **Luton Town** (D2) | H | D | 2-2 | Horsfield, Davis |
| | | 3r | 21.12.99 | **Luton Town** | A | W | 3-0 | Hayles 2, Hayward |
| | | 4 | 08.01.00 | **Wimbledon** (PL) | H | W | 3-0 | Collins 2, Finnan |

| | | | | | | | |
|---|---|---|---|---|---|---|---|
| | 5 | 29.01.00 | **Tranmere Rovers** (D1) | H | L | 1-2 | Coleman |
| 2000-01 (D1) | 3 | 06.01.01 | **Manchester Utd** (PL) | H | L | 1-2 | Fernandes |
| 2001-02 (PL) | 3 | 08.01.02 | **Wycombe W** (D2) | A | D | 2-2 | Legwinski, Marlet |
| | 3r | 15.01.02 | **Wycombe W** | H | W | 1-0 | Hayles |
| | 4 | 26.01.02 | **York City** (D3) | A | W | 2-0 | Malbranque, Marlet |
| | 5 | 16.02.02 | **Walsall** (D1) | A | W | 2-1 | Bennett og, Hayles |
| | 6 | 10.03.02 | **WBA** (D1) | A | W | 1-0 | Marlet |
| | SF | 14.04.02 | **Chelsea** (PL) | | L | 0-1 | |
| | | | *played at Villa Park* | | | | |
| 2002-03 (PL) | 3 | 05.01.03 | **Birmingham City** (PL) | H | W | 3-1 | Sava, Goldbaek, Saha |
| | 4 | 26.01.03 | **Charlton Athletic** (PL) | H | W | 3-0 | Malbranque 3(2p) |
| | 5 | 16.02.03 | **Burnley** (D1) | H | D | 1-1 | Malbranque |
| | 5r | 26.02.03 | **Burnley** | A | L | 0-3 | |

## FURNESS VALE ROVERS

| | | | | | | | |
|---|---|---|---|---|---|---|---|
| 1886-87 | 1 | 30.10.86 | **Northwich Vic** | A | L | 0-10 | |

## GAINSBOROUGH TRINITY

*Formed 1873. First entered FA Cup: 1885. Members of the Football League 1896-1912. 1st round reached: 34 times. League clubs beaten as a Non-League club: Crewe Alexandra (2), Port Vale, Gateshead, Mansfield Town. Members of the Northern Premier League.*

| | | | | | | | |
|---|---|---|---|---|---|---|---|
| 1885-86 | 1 | 24.10.85 | **Grantham Town** | H | W | 4-1 | |
| | 2 | 21.11.85 | **Middlesbrough** | A | L | 1-2 | Eason |
| 1886-87 | 1 | 30.10.86 | **South Bank** | A | W | 4-0 | |
| | 2 | 20.11.86 | **Newcastle West End** | A | W | 6-2 | |
| | 3 | 11.12.86 | **Lincoln City** | H | D | 2-2aet | Booth, Vamplen |
| | 3r | 24.01.87 | **Lincoln City** | | L | 0-1 | |
| | | | *played at Bramall Lane* | | | | |
| 1887-88 | 1 | 15.10.87 | **Boston Utd** | H | W | 9-0 | |
| | 2 | 05.11.87 | **Lincoln City** | A | L | 1-2 | Robinson |
| 1896-97 (D2) | | | 3q Lincoln City (A) 0-1 | | | | |
| 1897-98 (D2) | | | 3q Park Gate (H) 5-0; 4q Lincoln C (H) 5-1; 5q Mexborough T (A) 1-0 | | | | |
| | 1 | 29.01.98 | **Long Eaton Rangers** (ML) | A | W | 1-0 | Scott |
| | 2 | 12.02.98 | **Nottingham Forest** (D1) | A | L | 0-4 | |
| 1898-99 (D2) | | | 3q Barnsley (H) 2-2; 3qr Barnsley (A) 0-4 | | | | |
| 1899-00 (D2) | | | 1q Doncaster Rovers (H) 1-4 | | | | |
| 1900-01 (D2) | | | 3q Lincoln City (A) 0-0; 3qr Lincoln City (H) 0-0 abandoned in extra time; 3q 2r Lincoln City 1-3 (at Bramall Lane) | | | | |
| 1901-02 (D2) | | | 3q Barnsley (A) 0-1 | | | | |
| 1902-03 (D2) | | | 3q Doncaaster Rovers (H) 1-0; 4q Rotherham Town (H) 3-0; 5q Barnsley (A) 2-3 | | | | |
| 1903-04 (D2) | | | 3q Mexborough T (A) 2-0; 4q Doncaster R (A) 1-0; 5q Chesterfield T (A) 2-0; Int Reading (A) 0-1 | | | | |
| 1904-05 (D2) | | | 3q Ilkeston Utd (H) 4-1; 4q Grimethorpe U (H) 5-1; 5q Mexborough T (A) 1-1; 5qr Mexborough T (H) 7-0; 6q Green Waves (A) 3-1; Int Grimsby Town (A) 0-2 Int Grimsby Town (A) 0-2 | | | | |
| 1905-06 (D2) | | | 4q Weymouth (H) 2-1 | | | | |
| | 1 | 13.01.06 | **Burslem PV** (D2) | A | W | 3-0 | Langham, Morley, Foxall |
| | 2 | 03.02.06 | **Sunderland** (D1) | A | D | 1-1 | Dixon |
| | 2r | 07.02.06 | **Sunderland** | H | L | 0-3 | |
| | | | *played at Roker Park* | | | | |
| 1906-07 (D2) | 1 | 12.01.07 | **Luton Town** (SL) | H | D | 0-0 | |
| | 1r | 16.01.07 | **Luton Town** | A | L | 1-2 | Foxall |
| 1907-08 (D2) | 1 | 11.01.08 | **Watford** (SL) | H | W | 1-0 | Brawn |
| | 2 | 01.02.08 | **Stoke** (D2) | A | D | 1-1 | Murphy |
| | 2r | 05.02.08 | **Stoke** | H | D | 2-2aet | Taylor, Murphy |
| | 2 2r | 10.02.08 | **Stoke** | | L | 1-3 | Kitchen |
| | | | *played at City Ground, Nottingham* | | | | |
| 1908-09 (D2) | | | 5q Northern Nomads (H) 4-0 | | | | |
| | 1 | 16.01.09 | **Brentford** (SL) | A | L | 0-2 | |
| 1909-10 (D2) | 1 | 15.01.10 | **Southend Utd** (SL) | H | D | 1-1 | Splevins |
| | 1r | 19.01.10 | **Southend Utd** | A | L | 0-1 | |

| | | | | | | | | |
|---|---|---|---|---|---|---|---|---|
| 1910-11 | (D2) | | | 4q Ilkeston U (A) 0-0; 4qr Ilkeston U (H) 0-0aet; 4q 2r Ilkeston U 5-0 (at Bramall Lane); 5q Shrewsbury Town (H) 4-0 | | | | |
| | | 1 | 14.01.11 | **Liverpool** (D1) | A | L | 2-3 | Pattinson, Coulbeck |
| 1911-12 | (D2) | | | 4q Rotherham County (H) 1-0; 5q Tunbridge Wells R (H) 1-1; 5qr Tunbridge Wells R (A) 1-0 | | | | |
| | | 1 | 03.01.12 | **West Ham Utd** (SL) | A | L | 1-2 | Bullivant |
| 1912-13 | (ML) | 1 | 11.01.13 | **South Shields** (NEL) | A | - | 0-1ab | |
| | | | | *abandoned at half-time* | | | | |
| | | 1 | 18.01.13 | **South Shields** | A | W | 1-0 | Parker |
| | | 2 | 01.02.13 | **Burnley** (D2) | A | L | 1-4 | Ibbotson |
| 1913-14 | (ML) | 1 | 10.01.14 | **Leeds City** (D2) | A | L | 2-4 | Ibbotson 2 |
| 1927-28 | (ML) | 1 | 26.11.27 | **Stockton** (NL) | H | W | 6-0 | Smith 2, Shaw 3, Bennett |
| | | 2 | 10.12.27 | **Lincoln City** (3N) | H | L | 0-2 | |
| 1928-29 | (ML) | 1 | 24.11.28 | **Crewe Alexandra** (3N) | H | W | 3-1 | Morris 2, Keating |
| | | 2 | 08.12.28 | **Chesterfield** (3N) | H | L | 2-3 | Smith, Keating |
| 1929-30 | (ML) | 1 | 30.11.29 | **Port Vale** (3N) | H | D | 0-0 | |
| | | 1r | 04.12.29 | **Port Vale** | A | L | 0-5 | |
| 1930-31 | (ML) | 1 | 29.11.30 | **Scunthorpe Utd** (ML) | H | W | 1-0 | Hancock |
| | | 2 | 13.12.30 | **Southport** (3N) | H | L | 0-4 | |
| 1931-32 | (ML) | 1 | 28.11.31 | **Crewe Alexandra** (3N) | A | D | 2-2 | Mills, Robinson |
| | | 1r | 02.12.31 | **Crewe Alexandra** | H | W | 1-0 | Green |
| | | 2 | 12.12.31 | **Watford** (3S) | H | L | 2-5 | O'Brien og, Robinson |
| 1932-33 | (ML) | 1 | 26.11.32 | **Doncaster Rovers** (3N) | A | L | 1-4 | Halliday |
| 1933-34 | (ML) | 1 | 25.11.33 | **Altrincham** (CC) | H | W | 1-0 | Green |
| | | 2 | 09.12.33 | **Aldershot** (3S) | H | L | 0-2 | |
| 1935-36 | (ML) | 1 | 30.11.35 | **Blyth Spartans** (NEL) | H | W | 3-1 | Evers, Kirk, Taylor |
| | | 2 | 14.12.35 | **Dartford** (SL) | A | L | 0-4 | |
| 1937-38 | (ML) | 1 | 27.11.37 | **Port Vale** (3N) | A | D | 1-1 | Bratley |
| | | 1r | 01.12.37 | **Port Vale** | H | W | 2-1aet | Hall, Kirk |
| | | 2 | 11.12.37 | **Yeovil & Petters Utd** (SL) | A | L | 1-2 | Ranshaw |
| 1938-39 | (ML) | 1 | 26.11.38 | **Gateshead AFC** (3N) | H | W | 2-1 | Green, Hall |
| | | 2 | 10.12.38 | **Doncaster Rovers** (3N) | H | L | 0-1 | |
| 1945-46 | (ML) | 1 1L | 17.11.45 | **Mansfield Town** (3S) | A | L | 0-3 | |
| | | 1 2L | 24.11.45 | **Mansfield Town** | H | W | 4-2aet | Sampson, Curry, Curtis, Bratley |
| 1946-47 | (ML) | 1 | 30.11.46 | **Darlington** (3N) | H | L | 1-2 | North |
| 1948-49 | (ML) | 1 | 27.11.48 | **Witton Albion** (CC) | H | W | 1-0 | Moseley |
| | | 2 | 11.12.48 | **Walsall** (3S) | A | L | 3-4 | Churm, Vaux (p), Bates |
| 1950-51 | (ML) | 1 | 25.11.50 | **Plymouth Argyle** (3S) | H | L | 0-3 | |
| 1951-52 | (ML) | 1 | 24.11.51 | **Witton Albion** (CC) | A | L | 1-2 | Robinson |
| 1952-53 | (ML) | 1 | 22.11.52 | **Netherfield** (LC) | H | D | 1-1 | Morley |
| | | 1r | 27.11.52 | **Netherfield** | A | W | 3-0 | Hughes, Churm, Morley |
| | | 2 | 06.12.52 | **Newport County** (3S) | A | L | 1-2 | Robinson |
| 1953-54 | (ML) | 1 | 21.11.53 | **Chesterfield** (3N) | H | L | 1-4 | Churm |
| 1959-60 | (ML) | 1 | 14.11.59 | **Doncaster Rovers** (D4) | A | D | 3-3 | Purvis, Simpson, Haydon |
| | | 1r | 18.11.59 | **Doncaster Rovers** | H | L | 0-1 | |
| 1966-67 | (ML) | 1 | 26.11.66 | **Colchester Utd** (D3) | H | L | 0-1 | |
| 1983-84 | (NPL) | 1 | 19.11.83 | **Blackpool** (D4) | H | L | 0-2 | |
| 1997-98 | (NPL) | 1 | 15.11.97 | **Lincoln City** (D3) | A | D | 1-1 | Morrow |
| | | 1r | 25.11.97 | **Lincoln City** | H | L | 2-3 | Maxwell, Price |
| | | | | *played at Sincil Bank* | | | | |

## GATESHEAD

*Formed 1976. See under Gateshead AFC for a potted history of senior football in the Gateshead and South Shields areas. First entered FA Cup: 1978-79. Members of the Northern Premier League.*

| | | | | | | | | |
|---|---|---|---|---|---|---|---|---|
| 1980-81 | (NPL) | 1 | 22.11.80 | **Lincoln City** (D4) | A | L | 0-1 | |
| 1992-93 | (Conf) | 1 | 14.11.92 | **Accrington Stanley** (NPL) | A | L | 2-3 | Lamb, Bell |
| 1999-00 | (NPL) | 1 | 30.10.99 | **Cambridge Utd** (D2) | A | L | 0-1 | |
| 2000-01 | (NPL) | 1 | 18.11.00 | **Halifax Town** (D3) | A | W | 2-0 | Hall, Dalton |
| | | 2 | 09.12.00 | **Swindon Town** (D2) | A | L | 0-5 | |

# GATESHEAD AFC

*The history of football in the Gateshead and South Shields areas is probably the most complex concerning senior English clubs. Indeed, until Wimbledon moved from London to Milton Keynes in 2003, the club that played in the Football League from 1919-1960 was the only one that had moved home from one town to another while retaining unbroken League membership. Besides that club, there have been four other Gateshead clubs and at least three other South Shields clubs all playing senior football. The records listed here are of the South Shields/Gateshead ex-Football League club which survived until 1973. See under 'South Shields' for the record of the club formed in 1936. This club changed its name to Gateshead United in 1974 and folded in 1977. The records for 'Gateshead FC' are for the club formed in 1976.*

| | | | | | | | | |
|---|---|---|---|---|---|---|---|---|
| 1930-31 | (3N) | 1 | 29.11.30 | **Tranmere Rovers** (3N) | A | D | 4-4 | McNaughton 2, Barkas 2 |
| | | 1r | 03.12.30 | **Tranmere Rovers** | H | W | 3-2 | Chalton, Barkas 2 |
| | | 2 | 13.12.30 | **Folkestone** (SL) | H | W | 3-2 | Barkas, Charlton, McNaughton |
| | | 3 | 10.01.31 | **Sheffield Wed** (D1) | H | L | 2-6 | Kennedy, Charlton |
| 1931-32 | (3N) | 1 | 28.11.31 | **Wrexham** (3N) | H | W | 3-2 | Meek 2, Kennedy |
| | | 2 | 12.12.31 | **Burton Town** (BDL) | A | L | 1-4 | Welsh |
| 1932-33 | (3N) | 1 | 26.11.32 | **Barrow** (3N) | A | W | 1-0 | Charlton |
| | | 2 | 10.12.32 | **Margate** (KL) | H | W | 5-2 | Kennedy 3, Ransom 2 |
| | | 3 | 14.01.33 | **Manchester City** (D1) | H | D | 1-1 | Kennedy |
| | | 3r | 18.01.33 | **Manchester City** | A | L | 0-9 | |
| 1933-34 | (3N) | 1 | 25.11.33 | **Darwen** (LC) | H | W | 5-2 | Leek 2, Atkin, Temple, McDermott |
| | | 2 | 09.12.33 | **North Shields** (NEL) | H | W | 1-0 | Wesley |
| | | 3 | 13.01.34 | **Workington** (NEL) | A | L | 1-4 | McDermott |
| 1934-35 | (3N) | 1 | 24.11.34 | **Darlington** (3N) | H | L | 1-4 | Hamilton |
| 1935-36 | (3N) | 1 | 30.11.35 | **Chester** (3N) | A | L | 0-1 | |
| 1936-37 | (3N) | 1 | 28.11.36 | **Notts County** (3S) | H | W | 2-0 | Reed, Mathieson |
| | | 2 | 12.12.36 | **Millwall** (3S) | A | L | 0-7 | |
| 1937-38 | (3N) | 1 | 27.11.37 | **Walsall** (3S) | A | L | 0-4 | |
| 1938-39 | (3N) | 1 | 26.11.38 | **Gainsborough T** (ML) | A | L | 1-2 | Miller |
| 1945-46 | (3N) | 1 1L | 17.11.45 | **Hartlepools Utd** (3N) | A | W | 2-1 | Cairns 2 |
| | | 1 2L | 24.11.45 | **Hartlepools Utd** | H | W | 6-2 | McCormack 3, Cairns 2, Howden |
| | | 2 1L | 08.12.45 | **Darlington** (3N) | A | W | 4-2 | Rutherford, J Callender, Cairns, McCormack |
| | | 2 2L | 15.12.45 | **Darlington** (3N) | H | L | 1-2 | McCormack |
| | | 3 1L | 05.01.46 | **Rotherham Utd** (3N) | A | D | 2-2 | Atkinson, Thompson |
| | | 3 2L | 09.01.46 | **Rotherham Utd** | H | L | 0-2 | |
| 1946-47 | (3N) | 1 | 30.11.46 | **Bradford City** (3N) | H | W | 3-1 | Small 2, McCormack |
| | | 2 | 14.12.46 | **Lancaster City** (LC) | H | W | 4-0 | Gallon, T Callender, McCormack, Small |
| | | 3 | 11.01.47 | **Manchester City** (D2) | A | L | 0-3 | |
| 1947-48 | (3N) | 1 | 29.11.47 | **Bradford City** (3N) | H | L | 1-3 | Small |
| 1948-49 | (3N) | 1 | 27.11.48 | **Netherfield** (LC) | H | W | 3-0 | J Callender (p), Small, Atkinson |
| | | 2 | 11.12.48 | **Scarborough** (ML) | H | W | 3-0 | T Callender (p), Ingham, Robinson |
| | | 3 | 08.01.49 | **Aldershot** (3S) | H | W | 3-1 | Kendall 2, Wilbert |
| | | 4 | 29.01.49 | **WBA** (D2) | H | L | 1-3aet | J Callender |
| 1949-50 | (3N) | 1 | 26.11.49 | **York City** (3N) | H | W | 3-1 | Marley 2, Campbell |
| | | 2 | 10.12.49 | **Newport County** (3S) | A | D | 1-1 | Winters |
| | | 2r | 14.12.49 | **Newport County** | H | L | 1-2aet | J. Callender |
| 1950-51 | (3N) | 3 | 06.01.51 | **Sheffield Utd** (D2) | A | L | 0-1 | |
| 1951-52 | (3N) | 1 | 24.11.51 | **Stockport County** (3N) | A | D | 2-2aet | T Callender, Buchan |
| | | 1r | 28.11.51 | **Stockport County** | H | D | 1-1aet | Campbell |
| | | 1 2r | 03.12.51 | **Stockport County** *played at Hillsborough* | | W | 2-1 | Thompson 2 |
| | | 2 | 15.12.51 | **Guildford City** (SL) | H | W | 2-0 | Ingham, Winters |
| | | 3 | 12.01.52 | **Ipswich Town** (3S) | A | D | 2-2 | Wilbert, Ingham |
| | | 3r | 16.01.52 | **Ipswich Town** | H | D | 3-3aet | J Callender, Buchan, Johnson |
| | | 3 2r | 21.01.52 | **Ipswich Town** *played at Bramall Lane* | | W | 2-1aet | Ingham 2 |
| | | 4 | 06.02.52 | **WBA** (D1) *played at St James' Park* | H | L | 0-2 | |
| 1952-53 | (3N) | 1 | 22.11.52 | **Crewe Alexandra** (3N) | H | W | 2-0 | Smith, Price |
| | | 2 | 06.12.52 | **Bradford Park A** (3N) | A | W | 2-1 | Ingham 2 |
| | | 3 | 10.01.53 | **Liverpool** (D1) | H | W | 1-0 | Winters |

| | | | | | | | | |
|---|---|---|---|---|---|---|---|---|
| | | 4 | 31.01.53 | **Hull City** (D2) | A | W | 2-1 | Ingham, Phillips og |
| | | 5 | 14.02.53 | **Plymouth Argyle** (D2) | A | W | 1-0 | Winters |
| | | 6 | 28.02.53 | **Bolton Wanderers** (D1) | H | L | 0-1 | |
| 1953-54 | (3N) | 1 | 21.11.53 | **Tranmere Rovers** (3N) | H | L | 1-2 | Smith |
| 1954-55 | (3N) | 1 | 20.11.54 | **Chester** (3N) | H | W | 6-0 | Campbell, Ingham, Anderson 2, Smith, Oliver |
| | | 2 | 11.12.54 | **Barnsley** (3N) | H | D | 3-3 | Ingham 2, Campbell |
| | | 2r | 16.12.54 | **Barnsley** | A | W | 1-0 | Smith |
| | | 3 | 08.01.55 | **Tottenham Hotspur** (D1) | H | L | 0-2 | |
| 1955-56 | (3N) | 1 | 19.11.55 | **Hartlepools Utd** (3N) | A | L | 0-3 | |
| 1956-57 | (3N) | 1 | 17.11.56 | **Hull City** (3N) | A | L | 0-4 | |
| 1957-58 | (3N) | 1 | 16.11.57 | **Chester** (3N) | A | L | 3-4 | Baldridge, Ingham, J Callender |
| 1958-59 | (D4) | 1 | 15.11.58 | **Bradford Park A** (D4) | H | L | 1-4 | Johnstone |
| 1959-60 | (D4) | 1 | 14.11.59 | **Halifax Town** (D3) | H | L | 3-4 | A Trewick 2, Armstrong |
| 1960-61 | (NCo) | 1 | 05.11.60 | **Barnsley** (D3) | H | D | 0-0 | |
| | | 1r | 09.11.60 | **Barnsley** | A | L | 0-2 | |
| 1961-62 | (NRL) | 1 | 04.11.61 | **Tranmere Rovers** (D4) | A | W | 3-2 | Lydon, McCullough, McGugan og |
| | | 2 | 25.11.61 | **Workington** (D4) | H | L | 0-2 | |
| 1962-63 | (NRL) | 1 | 03.11.62 | **Wigan Athletic** (CC) | H | W | 2-1 | Steele, Burridge |
| | | 2 | 24.11.62 | **Bradford City** (D4) | A | L | 2-3 | Steele, McKenna |
| 1963-64 | (NRL) | 1 | 16.11.63 | **Darlington** (D4) | A | W | 4-1 | Lindsay 2, Steele 2 |
| | | 2 | 07.12.63 | **Carlisle Utd** (D4) | A | L | 3-4 | Lindsay 2, McKenna |
| 1965-66 | (NRL) | 1 | 13.11.65 | **Crook Town** (NL) | H | W | 4-2 | Steele, McKenna, Mitchell (p), Rayment |
| | | 2 | 08.12.65 | **Hull City** (D3) | H | L | 0-4 | |

## GATESHEAD ASSOCIATION

*This Gateshead club was formed in 1883 and originally played at Bensham.*

| | | | | | | | | |
|---|---|---|---|---|---|---|---|---|
| 1887-88 | | 1 | 15.10.87 | **Darlington** | H | L | 0-3 | |

## GATESHEAD UNITED

**See South Shields (1936)**

| | | | | | | | | |
|---|---|---|---|---|---|---|---|---|
| 1974-75 | (NPL) | 1 | 23.11.74 | **Crewe Alexandra** (D4) | A | D | 2-2 | N Smith, Wilson |
| | | 1r | 25.11.74 | **Crewe Alexandra** | H | W | 1-0aet | Mutrie |
| | | 2 | 14.12.74 | **Altrincham** (NPL) | A | L | 0-3 | |
| 1975-76 | (NPL) | 1 | 22.11.75 | **Grimsby Town** (D3) | A | W | 3-1 | Common, Mutrie, Thompson |
| | | 2 | 13.12.75 | **Rochdale** (D4) | H | D | 1-1 | Guthrie |
| | | 2r | 16.12.75 | **Rochdale** | A | L | 1-3 | Morrison |
| 1976-77 | (NPL) | 1 | 20.11.76 | **Wrexham** (D3) | A | L | 0-6 | |

## GILLINGHAM

*Formed 1893 as New Brompton. Gillingham 1912. FA Cup best performance: 5th round, 1970. FA Cup record win: 10-1 v Gorleston, 1st round, 16.11.1957; FA Cup Record defeat: 1-6 v Stoke City, 3rd round, 14.01.1928.*

**as New Brompton**

| | | | |
|---|---|---|---|
| 1893-94 | | | 1q Ilford (A) 3-6 |
| 1894-95 | | | 2q Chatham Town (H) 2-0; 3q Millwall Athletic ( H) 0-2 |
| 1895-96 | (SL) | | 1q Millwall Athletic (H) 0-1 |
| 1896-97 | (SL) | | 1q Faversham (H) 6-1; 2q Gravesend (A) 4-1; 3q Northfleet Utd (A) 1-3 |
| 1897-98 | (SL) | | 1q Northfleet Utd (A) 3-1; 2q Eastbourne Swifts (H) 2-0; 3q Grays Utd (H) 6-2; 4q Chatham T (H) 1-0; 5q Woolwich Arsenal (A) 2-4 |
| 1898-99 | (SL) | | 3q Grays Utd (H) 3-0; 4q Sheppey Utd (H) 2-1; 5q Gravesend Utd (A) 1-1; 5qr Gravesend U (H) 2-0 |
| | | 1 28.01.99 | **Southampton** (SL) H L 0-1 |
| 1899-00 | (SL) | | 3q Woolwich Arsenal (A) 1-1; 3qr Woolwich Arsenal (H) 0-0 aet; 3q 2r W Arsenal 2-2 aet (at Millwall); 3q 3r W Arsenal 1-1aet (at White Hart Lane) 1-1; 3q 4r W Arsenal 1-0 aet (at Gravesend); 4q Thames Ironworks (H) 0-0; 4qr Thames Ironworks (A) 0-2 |
| 1900-01 | (SL) | | 3q Grays Utd (A) 2-0; 4q West Ham Utd (H) 1-1; 4qr West Ham Utd i(A) 1-4 |
| 1901-02 | (SL) | | 3q Ilford (H) 6-1; 4q Clapton (A) 2-2; 4qr Clapton (H) 2-0; 5q Grays Utd (H) 1-0; Int Walsall (A) 0-2 |
| 1902-03 | (SL) | | 3q Clapton (H) 2-0; 4q Maidstone Utd (A) 3-0; 5q Ilford (H) 4-1; Int Glossop North End (A) 1-2 |
| 1903-04 | (SL) | | Int Bristol City (H) 1-1; IntR Bristol City (A) 2-5 |
| 1904-05 | (SL) | | 3q Clapton (A) 6-2; 4q Brighton (H) 0-1 |

| | | | | | | | |
|---|---|---|---|---|---|---|---|
| 1905-06 (SL) | 1 | 13.01.06 | **Northampton Town** (SL) | H | W | 2-1 | Beadsworth, Marriott |
| | 2 | 03.02.06 | **Southampton** (SL) | H | D | 0-0 | |
| | 2r | 07.02.06 | **Southampton** | A | L | 0-1 | |
| 1906-07 (SL) | 1 | 12.01.07 | **Burton Utd** (D2) | A | D | 0-0 | |
| | 1r | 16.01.07 | **Burton Utd** | H | - | 0-0ab | |
| | | | *abandoned after 100 minutes* | | | | |
| | 1 2r | 21.01.07 | **Burton Utd** | | W | 2-0 | Hartley 2 |
| | | | *played at Craven Cottage* | | | | |
| | 2 | 02.02.07 | **Bury** (D1) | A | L | 0-1 | |
| 1907-08 (SL) | 5q Shepherds Bush (H) 6-0 | | | | | | |
| | 1 | 11.01.08 | **Sunderland** (D1) | H | W | 3-1 | McGibbon 3 |
| | 2 | 01.02.08 | **Manchester City** (D1) | A | D | 1-1 | McGibbon |
| | 2r | 05.02.08 | **Manchester City** | H | L | 1-2 | McGibbon |
| 1908-09 (SL) | | | 5q Hastings Utd (A) 2-2; 5qr Hastings Utd (H) 1-2 | | | | |
| 1909-10 (SL) | | | 4q Oxford City (H) 9-1; 5q Rotherham Town (A) 1-0 | | | | |
| | 1 | 15.01.10 | **Leyton FC** (SL) | A | D | 0-0 | |
| | 1r | 19.01.10 | **Leyton FC** | H | D | 2-2aet | Court, Pickett |
| | 1 2r | 24.01.10 | **Leyton FC** | | L | 0-1 | |
| | | | *played at White Hart Lane* | | | | |
| 1910-11 (SL) | | | 4q Aldershot Royal Engineers (A) 2-2; 4qr Aldershot Royal Engineers (H) 7-0; 5q Catford Southend (H) 4-1 | | | | |
| | 1 | 14.01.11 | **Bradford City** (D1) | H | L | 0-1 | |
| 1911-12 (SL) | | | 4q Croydon Common (H) 2-0 abandoned 4qr Croydon Common (H) 1-2 | | | | |
| **as Gillingham** | | | | | | | |
| 1912-13 (SL) | | | 4q Leyton walkover; 5q Spennymoor U (A) 1-1; 5qr Spennymoor U (H) 3-0 | | | | |
| | 1 | 11.01.13 | **Barnsley** (D2) | H | D | 0-0 | |
| | 1r | 16.01.13 | **Barnsley** | A | L | 1-3 | Goffin |
| 1913-14 (SL) | | | 4q Nunhead (H) 2-0; 5q Watford (H) 1-0 | | | | |
| | 1 | 10.01.14 | **Blackpool** (D2) | H | W | 1-0 | Leslie |
| | 2 | 31.01.14 | **Liverpool** (D1) | A | L | 0-2 | |
| 1914-15 (SL) | 1 | 09.01.15 | **Rochdale** (CL) | A | L | 0-2 | |
| 1919-20 (SL) | | | 6q Swansea T (A) 1-1; 6qr Swansea T (H) 1-1 6q 2r Swansea T (at Ninian Park) 0-0; 6q 3r Swansea T (at Stamford Bridge) 3-1 | | | | |
| | 1 | 10.01.20 | **West Stanley** (NEL) | A | L | 1-3 | Reid |
| 1920-21 (D3) | | | 4q Maidstone U (H) 1-0; 5q Dulwich Hamlet (H) 2-1; 6q Northampton T (A) 1-3 | | | | |
| 1921-22 (3S) | | | 5q Northfleet U (A) 0-0; 5qr Northfleet U (H) 3-1; 6q St Albans C (H) 3-1 | | | | |
| | 1 | 07.01.22 | **Oldham Athletic** (D1) | H | L | 1-3 | Howard |
| 1922-23 (3S) | | | 5q London Caledonians (A) 2-1; 6q Blyth Spartans (H) 1-4 | | | | |
| 1923-24 (3S) | | | 5q Nunhead (A) 6-0; 6q Tranmere R (H) 1-0 | | | | |
| | 1 | 12.01.24 | **Cardiff City** (D1) | A | D | 0-0 | |
| | 1r | 16.01.24 | **Cardiff City** | H | L | 0-2 | |
| 1924-25 (3S) | | | 5q Kettering T (A) 1-1; 5qr Kettering T (H) 6-2; 6q Barrow (A) 1-1; 6qr Barrow (H) 0-0; 6q 2r Barrow 1-1 (at Molineux) 6q 3r Barrow 1-1 (at Highbury); 6q 4r Barrow 1-2 (at Millwall) | | | | |
| 1925-26 (3S) | 1 | 28.11.25 | **Southall** (AL) | A | W | 6-0 | McKee, Adams og, Marshall, Brown, Berry, Rutherford |
| | 2 | 12.12.25 | **Southend Utd** (3S) | A | L | 0-1 | |
| 1926-27 (3S) | 1 | 27.11.26 | **Barking** (AL) | A | D | 0-0 | |
| | 1r | 01.12.26 | **Barking** | H | W | 2-0 | Marshall, Brown |
| | 2 | 11.12.26 | **Brentford** (3S) | H | D | 1-1 | Amos |
| | 2r | 15.12.26 | **Brentford** | A | L | 0-1 | |
| 1927-28 (3S) | 1 | 26.11.27 | **Plymouth Argyle** (3S) | H | W | 2-1 | Boswell, Meston |
| | 2 | 10.12.27 | **Southend Utd** (3S) | H | W | 2-0 | Wilcox 2 |
| | 3 | 14.01.28 | **Stoke City** (D2) | A | L | 1-6 | Wilcox |
| 1928-29 (3S) | 1 | 24.11.28 | **Torquay Utd** (3S) | H | D | 0-0 | |
| | 1r | 28.11.28 | **Torquay Utd** | A | L | 1-5 | Poxton (p) |
| 1929-30 (3S) | 1 | 30.11.29 | **Margate** (KL) | H | L | 0-2 | |
| 1930-31 (3S) | 1 | 29.11.30 | **Guildford City** (SL) | H | W | 7-2 | Loasby 3, Cheesmur, Death 2, Beacham |
| | 2 | 13.12.30 | **Aldershot Town** (SL) | H | L | 1-3 | Death |
| 1931-32 (3S) | 1 | 28.11.31 | **Bristol Rovers** (3S) | A | L | 1-5 | Bethall |

| | | | | | | | | |
|---|---|---|---|---|---|---|---|---|
| 1932-33 | (3S) | 1 | 26.11.32 | **Wycombe W** (IL) | H | D | 1-1 | Liddle |
| | | 1r | 30.11.32 | **Wycombe W** | A | W | 4-2 | Cox og, Cropper, Nicol 2 |
| | | 2 | 10.12.32 | **Bristol Rovers** (3S) | A | D | 1-1 | Nicol |
| | | 2r | 14.12.32 | **Bristol Rovers** | H | L | 1-3 | Purcell |
| 1933-34 | (3S) | 1 | 25.11.33 | **Oxford City** (IL) | A | W | 5-1 | Scott, Mills, Liddle, Purcell, Nicol |
| | | 2 | 09.12.33 | **Charlton Athletic** (3S) | A | L | 0-1 | |
| 1934-35 | (3S) | 1 | 24.11.34 | **Bristol City** (3S) | A | L | 0-2 | |
| 1935-36 | (3S) | 1 | 30.11.35 | **Exeter City** (3S) | A | W | 4-0 | Tadman, Baldwin 3 |
| | | 2 | 14.12.35 | **Crewe Alexandra** (3N) | A | L | 1-2 | Baldwin |
| 1936-37 | (3S) | 1 | 28.11.36 | **Ryde Sports** (HL) | A | W | 5-1 | Wilson, Fowler 2, Watson 2 |
| | | 2 | 12.12.36 | **Wrexham** (3N) | A | L | 0-2 | |
| 1937-38 | (3S) | 1 | 27.11.37 | **Swindon Town** (3S) | H | L | 3-4 | Watson 3 |
| 1938-39 | (SL) | | | 4q Tunbridge Wells Rangers (H) 2-4 | | | | |
| 1945-46 | (SL) | | | 4q Sutton U (H) 3-9 | | | | |
| 1946-47 | (SL) | | | 4q Guildford C (A) 2-1 | | | | |
| | | 1 | 30.11.46 | **Gravesend & N** (SL) | H | W | 4-1 | Russell 2, Briggs, Warsap |
| | | 2 | 14.12.46 | **Bristol City** (3S) | A | W | 2-1 | Wilson, Russell |
| | | 3 | 11.01.47 | **Swansea Town** (D2) | A | L | 1-4 | Wilson |
| 1947-48 | (SL) | | | 4q Barnet (H) 3-1aet | | | | |
| | | 1 | 29.11.47 | **Leyton Orient** (3S) | H | W | 1-0 | Akers |
| | | 2 | 13.12.47 | **Rochdale** (3N) | A | D | 1-1aet | Russell |
| | | 2r | 20.12.47 | **Rochdale** | H | W | 3-0 | Forrester, Wilson, Briggs |
| | | 3 | 10.01.48 | **QPR** (3S) | H | D | 1-1aet | Russell |
| | | 3r | 17.01.48 | **QPR** | A | L | 1-3 | Warsap |
| 1948-49 | (SL) | | | 4q Romford (A) 1-2aet | | | | |
| 1949-50 | (SL) | | | 4q Guildford C (A) 3-2 | | | | |
| | | 1 | 26.11.49 | **Hastings Utd** (SL) | A | W | 3-1 | Collins, Russell, W Burtenshaw |
| | | 2 | 10.12.49 | **Yeovil Town** (SL) | A | L | 1-3 | Russell (p) |
| 1950-51 | (3S) | 1 | 25.11.50 | **Linby Colliery** (CA) | A | W | 4-1 | Thomas, C Burtenshaw, W Burtenshaw, Jenkins |
| | | 2 | 09.12.50 | **Bristol Rovers** (3S) | A | D | 2-2 | Thomas, Carr |
| | | 2r | 13.12.50 | **Bristol Rovers** | H | D | 1-1aet | Carr |
| | | 2 2r | 18.12.50 | **Bristol Rovers** | | L | 1-2 | Lewis |
| | | | | *played at White Hart Lane* | | | | |
| 1951-52 | (3S) | 1 | 24.11.51 | **Crystal Palace** (3S) | A | W | 1-0 | Thomas |
| | | 2 | 15.12.51 | **Rochdale** (3N) | H | L | 0-3 | |
| 1952-53 | (3S) | 1 | 22.11.52 | **Wellington Town** (CC) | A | D | 1-1 | Forrester |
| | | 1r | 26.11.52 | **Wellington Town** | H | W | 3-0 | Scarth, Forrester, Long |
| | | 2 | 06.12.52 | **Stockport County** (3N) | A | L | 1-3 | Thomas |
| 1953-54 | (3S) | 1 | 21.11.53 | **Walthamstow Ave** (IL) | A | L | 0-1 | |
| 1954-55 | (3S) | 1 | 20.11.54 | **Newport County** (3S) | H | W | 2-0 | Morgan, Miller |
| | | 2 | 11.12.54 | **Reading** (3S) | H | D | 1-1 | Durkin |
| | | 2r | 13.12.54 | **Reading** | A | L | 3-5 | Sowden, Morgan, Marks |
| 1955-56 | (3S) | 1 | 19.11.55 | **Shrewsbury Town** (3S) | H | D | 1-1 | Millar |
| | | 1r | 24.11.55 | **Shrewsbury Town** | A | L | 1-4aet | Millar |
| 1956-57 | (3S) | 1 | 17.11.56 | **Yiewsley** (CRN) | A | D | 2-2 | Rigg, Morgan |
| | | 1r | 20.11.56 | **Yiewsley** | H | W | 2-0 | Morgan, Pollock |
| | | 2 | 08.12.56 | **Newport County** (3S) | H | L | 1-2 | Crossan |
| 1957-58 | (3S) | 1 | 16.11.57 | **Gorleston** (ECL) | H | W | 10-1 | Saunders 5, Clark 2, Fletcher 2, Morgan |
| | | 2 | 07.12.57 | **Millwall** (3S) | A | D | 1-1 | Fletcher |
| | | 2r | 11.12.57 | **Millwall** | H | W | 6-1 | Payne 2, Fletcher 2, Saunders, Hutton |
| | | 3 | 04.01.58 | **Nottingham Forest** (D1) | A | L | 0-2 | |
| 1958-59 | (D4) | 1 | 15.11.58 | **Plymouth Argyle** (D3) | A | D | 2-2 | Patrick, Edgar |
| | | 1r | 19.11.58 | **Plymouth Argyle** | H | L | 1-4 | Terry |
| 1959-60 | (D4) | 1 | 14.11.59 | **Bedford Town** (SL) | A | W | 4-0 | Albury, Terry 2, Pulley |
| | | 2 | 05.12.59 | **Torquay Utd** (D4) | H | D | 2-2 | Albury 2 (1p) |
| | | 2r | 09.12.59 | **Torquay Utd** | A | W | 2-1 | Terry, Hanaway |
| | | 3 | 09.01.60 | **Swansea Town** (D2) | H | L | 1-4 | Griffith og |
| 1960-61 | (D4) | 1 | 05.11.60 | **Ashford Town** (SL) | A | W | 2-1 | Hughes, Shepherd |

| | | | | | | | |
|---|---|---|---|---|---|---|---|
| | 2 | 26.11.60 | **Southend Utd** (D3) | H | W | 3-2 | Terry, Shepherd 2 |
| | 3 | 07.01.61 | **Leyton Orient** (D2) | H | L | 2-6 | Terry, Hughes (p) |
| 1961-62 (D4) | 1 | 04.11.61 | **Coventry City** (D3) | A | L | 0-2 | |
| 1962-63 (D4) | 1 | 03.11.62 | **Andover** (SL) | A | W | 1-0 | Godfrey |
| | 2 | 24.11.62 | **Bedford Town** (SL) | H | W | 3-0 | Farrall 2, Gibbs |
| | 3 | 27.02.63 | **Port Vale** (D3) | H | L | 2-4 | Gibbs, Francis |
| 1963-64 (D4) | 1 | 16.11.63 | **QPR** (D3) | A | L | 1-4 | Arnott |
| 1964-65 (D3) | 1 | 14.11.64 | **Guildford City** (SL) | A | D | 2-2 | Riggs, Gibbs |
| | 1r | 18.11.64 | **Guildford City** | H | W | 1-0 | Gibbs |
| | 2 | 05.12.64 | **Luton Town** (D3) | A | L | 0-1 | |
| 1965-66 (D3) | 1 | 13.11.65 | **Folkestone** (SL) | H | L | 1-2 | R Taylor |
| 1966-67 (D3) | 1 | 26.11.66 | **Tamworth** (WMRL) | H | W | 4-1 | Rackstraw (p), Yeo 2, Gibbs |
| | 2 | 07.01.67 | **Walsall** (D3) | A | L | 1-3 | Gibbs |
| 1967-68 (D3) | 1 | 18.12.67 | **Newport County** (D4) | A | L | 0-3 | |
| 1968-69 (D3) | 1 | 16.11.68 | **Orient** (D3) | A | D | 1-1 | Smillie |
| | 1r | 20.11.68 | **Orient** | H | W | 2-1 | Riddick 2 |
| | 2 | 07.12.68 | **Luton Town** (D3) | A | L | 1-3 | Yeo (p) |
| 1969-70 (D3) | 1 | 15.11.69 | **Southend Utd** (D4) | A | D | 0-0 | |
| | 1r | 19.11.69 | **Southend Utd** | H | W | 2-1 | Yeo 2 |
| | 2 | 06.12.69 | **Tamworth** (WMRL) | H | W | 6-0 | Pound, Bailey 3, Green, Smillie |
| | 3 | 03.01.70 | **Newport County** (D4) | H | W | 1-0 | Machin |
| | 4 | 24.01.70 | **Peterborough Utd** (D4) | H | W | 5-1 | Green 2, Yeo 2, Ronaldson |
| | 5 | 07.02.70 | **Watford** (D2) | A | L | 1-2 | Yeo |
| 1970-71 (D3) | 1 | 21.11.70 | **Brentford** (D4) | A | L | 1-2 | Green |
| 1971-72 (D4) | 1 | 20.11.71 | **Plymouth Argyle** (D3) | H | W | 3-2 | Galvin, Wilks, Yeo |
| | 2 | 11.12.71 | **Romford** (SL) | A | W | 1-0 | Wilks |
| | 3 | 15.01.72 | **Swansea City** (D3) | A | L | 0-1 | |
| 1972-73 (D4) | 1 | 18.11.72 | **Reading** (D4) | H | L | 1-2 | Tydeman |
| 1973-74 (D4) | 1 | 24.11.73 | **Cambridge Utd** (D3) | A | L | 2-3 | Richardson, Tydeman |
| 1974-75 (D3) | 1 | 26.11.74 | **Hereford Utd** (D3) | A | L | 0-1 | |
| 1975-76 (D3) | 1 | 22.11.75 | **Weymouth** (SL) | A | W | 2-0 | Richardson 2 |
| | 2 | 13.12.75 | **Brighton** (D3) | H | L | 0-1 | |
| 1976-77 (D3) | 1 | 20.11.76 | **Watford** (D4) | H | L | 0-1 | |
| 1977-78 (D3) | 1 | 26.11.77 | **Weymouth** (SL) | H | D | 1-1 | Westwood |
| | 1r | 30.11.77 | **Weymouth** | A | W | 1-0 | Shipperley |
| | 2 | 17.12.77 | **Peterborough Utd** (D3) | H | D | 1-1 | Nicholl |
| | 2r | 20.12.77 | **Peterborough Utd** | A | L | 0-2 | |
| 1978-79 (D3) | 1 | 25.11.78 | **Reading** (D4) | A | D | 0-0 | |
| | 1r | 28.11.78 | **Reading** | H | L | 1-2aet | Westwood |
| 1979-80 (D3) | 1 | 24.11.79 | **Wimbledon** (D3) | H | D | 0-0 | |
| | 1r | 27.11.79 | **Wimbledon** | A | L | 2-4 | Price |
| 1980-81 (D3) | 1 | 22.11.80 | **Dagenham** (IL) | H | W | 2-1 | Price, Ford |
| | 2 | 13.12.80 | **Maidstone Utd** (APL) | H | D | 0-0 | |
| | 2r | 16.12.80 | **Maidstone Utd** | A | D | 0-0aet | |
| | 2 2r | 22.12.80 | **Maidstone Utd** | H | L | 0-2 | |
| 1981-82 (D3) | 1 | 21.11.81 | **Plymouth Argyle** (D3) | A | D | 0-0 | |
| | 1r | 24.11.81 | **Plymouth Argyle** | H | W | 1-0 | Bowman |
| | 2 | 15.12.81 | **Barking** (IL) | H | D | 1-1 | White (p) |
| | 2r | 02.01.82 | **Barking** *played at Gillingham* | | W | 3-1aet | Bruce, Price, Powell |
| | 3 | 05.01.82 | **Oldham Athletic** (D2) | H | W | 2-1 | Kemp, White (p) |
| | 4 | 23.01.82 | **WBA** (D1) | H | L | 0-1 | |
| 1982-83 (D3) | 1 | 20.11.82 | **Dagenham** (APL) | H | W | 1-0 | Cascarino |
| | 2 | 11.12.82 | **Northampton Town** (D4) | H | D | 1-1 | Johnson |
| | 2r | 14.12.82 | **Northampton Town** | A | L | 2-3 | Weatherley 2 |
| 1983-84 (D3) | 1 | 19.11.83 | **AP Leamington** (SL) | A | W | 1-0 | Handford |
| | 2 | 10.12.83 | **Chelmsford City** (SL) | H | W | 6-1 | Shaw, Weatherly 2, Sage, Mehmet, Leslie |
| | 3 | 07.01.84 | **Brentford** (D3) | H | W | 5-3 | Cochrane, Musker, Weaterley, Leslie, Cascarino |
| | 4 | 28.01.84 | **Everton** (D1) | A | D | 0-0 | |

| | | | | | | | |
|---|---|---|---|---|---|---|---|
| | 4r | 31.01.84 | **Everton** | H | D | 0-0aet | |
| | 4 2r | 06.02.84 | **Everton** | H | L | 0-3 | |
| 1984-85 (D3) | 1 | 17.11.84 | **Windsor & Eton** (IL) | H | W | 2-1 | Mehmet, Cascarino |
| | 2 | 08.12.84 | **Colchester Utd** (D4) | A | W | 5-0 | Robinson, Shearer 3, Cascarino |
| | 3 | 21.01.85 | **Cardiff City** (D2) | H | W | 2-1 | Robinson, Leslie |
| | 4 | 26.01.85 | **Ipswich Town** (D1) | A | L | 2-3 | Leslie, Sage |
| 1985-86 (D3) | 1 | 16.11.85 | **Northampton Town** (D4) | H | W | 3-0 | Mundee og, Mehmet, Cochrane |
| | 2 | 07.12.85 | **Bognor Regis Town** (IL) | H | W | 6-1 | Cascarino 2, Robinson, Shearer, Cochrane, Hales |
| | 3 | 04.01.86 | **Derby County** (D3) | H | D | 1-1 | Robinson |
| | 3r | 13.01.86 | **Derby County** | A | L | 1-3aet | Robinson |
| 1986-87 (D3) | 1 | 15.11.86 | **Kettering Town** (Conf) | A | W | 3-0 | Robinson, Hinnigan, Kellock og |
| | 2 | 06.12.86 | **Chelmsford City** (SL) | H | W | 2-0 | Cascarino 2 |
| | 3 | 19.01.87 | **Wigan Athletic** (D3) | A | L | 1-2 | Greenall (p) |
| 1987-88 (D3) | 1 | 14.11.87 | **Fulham** (D3) | H | W | 2-1 | Lillis, Pritchard |
| | 2 | 05.12.87 | **Walsall** (D3) | H | W | 2-1 | Lovell, Elsey |
| | 3 | 09.01.88 | **Birmingham City** (D2) | H | L | 0-3 | |
| 1988-89 (D3) | 1 | 19.11.88 | **Peterborough Utd** (D4) | H | D | 3-3 | Lovell, Quow, Smith |
| | 1r | 23.11.88 | **Peterborough Utd** | A | L | 0-1aet | |
| 1989-90 (D4) | 1 | 18.11.89 | **Welling Utd** (Conf) | H | D | 0-0 | |
| | 1r | 22.11.89 | **Welling Utd** | A | L | 0-1 | |
| 1990-91 (D4) | 1 | 17.11.90 | **Bournemouth** (D3) | A | L | 1-2 | Crown |
| 1991-92 (D3) | 1 | 18.11.91 | **Brentford** (D3) | A | D | 3-3 | Walker 2, Smith |
| | 1r | 26.11.91 | **Brentford** | H | L | 1-3 | Walker |
| 1992-93 (D3) | 1 | 14.11.92 | **Kettering Town** (Conf) | H | W | 3-2 | Clark, Crown, Forster |
| | 2 | 05.12.92 | **Colchester Utd** (D3) | H | D | 1-1 | Crown |
| | 2r | 16.12.92 | **Colchester Utd** | A | W | 3-2 | Forster, Arnott, Henry (p) |
| | 3 | 02.01.93 | **Huddersfield Town** (D2) | H | D | 0-0 | |
| | 3r | 13.01.93 | **Huddersfield Town** | A | L | 1-2 | Green (p) |
| 1993-94 (D3) | 1 | 13.11.93 | **Yeading** (IL) | A | D | 0-0 | |
| | | | *played at Hayes FC* | | | | |
| | 1r | 30.11.93 | **Yeading** | H | W | 3-1 | Smith, Micklewhite, Baker |
| | 2 | 04.12.93 | **Plymouth Argyle** (D2) | A | L | 0-2 | |
| 1994-95 (D3) | 1 | 11.11.94 | **Heybridge Swifts** (IL) | A | W | 2-0 | Reinelt, Pike |
| | | | *played at Layer Road, Colchester* | | | | |
| | 2 | 03.12.94 | **Fulham** (D3) | H | D | 1-1 | Pike |
| | 2r | 13.12.94 | **Fulham** | A | W | 2-1aet | Pike, Reinelt |
| | 3 | 07.01.95 | **Sheffield Wed** (PL) | H | L | 1-2 | Pike (p) |
| 1995-96 (D3) | 1 | 13.11.95 | **Wycombe W** (D2) | A | D | 1-1 | Bailey |
| | 1r | 21.11.95 | **Wycombe W** | H | W | 1-0 | Howard og |
| | 2 | 02.12.95 | **Hitchin Town** (IL) | H | W | 3-0 | Fortune-West 2, Ratcliffe |
| | 3 | 06.01.96 | **Reading** (D1) | A | L | 1-3 | Martin |
| 1996-97 (D2) | 1 | 16.11.96 | **Hereford Utd** (D3) | H | W | 1-0 | Butler |
| | 2 | 07.12.96 | **Cardiff City** (D3) | A | W | 2-0 | Onuora, Hessenthaler |
| | 3 | 14.01.97 | **Derby County** (PL) | H | - | 0-0ab | |
| | | | *abandoned after 66 minutes – frozen pitch* | | | | |
| | 3 | 21.01.97 | **Derby County** | H | L | 0-2 | |
| 1997-98 (D2) | 1 | 14.11.97 | **Bristol Rovers** (D2) | A | D | 2-2 | Onuora, Akinbiyi |
| | 1r | 25.11.97 | **Bristol Rovers** | H | L | 0-2 | |
| 1998-99 (D2) | 1 | 14.11.98 | **Oldham Athletic** (D2) | A | L | 0-2 | |
| 1999-00 (D2) | 1 | 30.10.99 | **Cheltenham Town** (D3) | A | D | 1-1 | Southall |
| | 1r | 09.11.99 | **Cheltenham Town** | H | W | 3-2 | Thomson, Pennock, McGlinchey |
| | 2 | 20.11.99 | **Darlington** (D3) | H | W | 3-1 | Butters, Taylor 2 |
| | | | *Darlington were re-instated in Round Three following a 'Lucky Loser' draw to fill the place left by Manchester United who did not enter the competition because of their involvement in the FIFA Club World Championship in Brazil* | | | | |
| | 3 | 11.12.99 | **Walsall** (D1) | A | D | 1-1 | Southall |
| | 3r | 08.01.00 | **Walsall** | H | W | 2-1aet | Barras og, Thomson |
| | 4 | 11.01.00 | **Bradford City** (PL) | H | W | 3-1 | Thomson, Ashby, Hodge |
| | 5 | 29.01.00 | **Sheffield Wed** (PL) | H | W | 3-1 | D Saunders, Thomson, Southall |
| | 6 | 20.02.00 | **Chelsea** (PL) | A | L | 0-5 | |
| 2000-01 (D1) | 3 | 06.01.01 | **Bournemouth** (D2) | A | W | 3-2 | Hope, Hessenthaler, Shaw |

| | | | | | | | |
|---|---|---|---|---|---|---|---|
| | 4 | 28.01.01 | **Chelsea** (PL) | H | L | 2-4 | Shaw, Onuora |
| 2001-02 (D1) | 3 | 05.01.02 | **Wolverhampton W** (D1) | A | W | 1-0 | Shaw |
| | 4 | 05.02.02 | **Bristol Rovers** (D3) | H | W | 1-0 | Jones og |
| | 5 | 16.02.02 | **Arsenal** (PL) | A | L | 2-5 | King, Gooden |
| 2002-03 (D1) | 3 | 07.01.03 | **Sheffield Wed** (D1) | H | W | 4-1 | King 2(1p), Ipoua, Hope |
| | 4 | 25.01.03 | **Leeds Utd** (PL) | H | D | 1-1 | Sidibe |
| | 4r | 04.02.03 | **Leeds Utd** | A | L | 1-2 | Ipoua |

## GITANOS FC

*Formed 1864. Played their home matches in Battersea Park and around south London.*

| | | | | | | | |
|---|---|---|---|---|---|---|---|
| 1873-74 | 1 | 28.10.73 | **Uxbridge** | A | L | 0-3 | |

## GLASGOW RANGERS

*Formed 1873. One of the seven Scottish clubs that played in the Competition Proper in the 1880s. Reached the semi-finals in their only season in the competition in 1886-87. Scottish FA Cup winners 31 times.*

| | | | | | | | |
|---|---|---|---|---|---|---|---|
| 1885-86 | 1 | | Rawtenstall<br>*Rangers scratched. Rawtenstall walkover* | | | - | |
| 1886-87 | 1 | 30.10.86 | **Everton** | A | W | 1-0 | Heggie |
| | 2 | 20.11.86 | **Church FC** | H | W | 2-1 | Lawrie AN Other |
| | 3 | 04.12.86 | **Cowlairs** | H | W | 3-2 | Fisher, Lawrie, Peacock |
| | 4 | | bye | | | | |
| | 5 | 29.01.87 | **Lincoln City** | H | W | 3-0 | Fraser, Lindsay, Peacock |
| | 6 | 19.02.87 | **Old Westminsters** | H | W | 5-1 | Lafferty, Lawrie, 3 others |
| | SF | 05.03.87 | **Aston Villa**<br>*played at Nantwich Road, Crewe* | | L | 1-3 | Lafferty |

## GLASTONBURY

*Formed 1890. First entered FA Cup: 1902-03.*

| | | | | | | | |
|---|---|---|---|---|---|---|---|
| 1950-51 (WL) | 1 | 25.11.50 | **Exeter City** (3S) | H | L | 1-2 | Thomas |

## GLOSSOP NORTH END

*Formed 1886. First entered FA Cup: 1895. Reformed 1919, 1945 and 1992. Glossop North End 1886-1898. Glossop FC 1898-1992. Glossop North End since 1992. Members of the Football League 1899-1915. Members of the North West Counties League.*

| | | | | | | | |
|---|---|---|---|---|---|---|---|
| 1896-97 (ML) | 1 | 30.01.97 | **Stoke** (D1) | A | L | 2-5 | McFarlane, Platt |
| 1897-98 (ML) | | | 3q Aberystwyth (A) 0-1 | | | | |
| 1898-99 (D2) | | | 3q New Brighton Tower (H) 4-2; 4q Crewe Alexandra (H) 1-0; 5q Stockport County (A) 2-0 | | | | |
| | 1 | 28.01.99 | **Newcastle Utd** (D1) | H | L | 0-1 | |
| 1899-00 (D1) | | | 3q Stockport County (H) 2-2; 3qr Stockport County (A) 0-3 | | | | |
| 1900-01 (D2) | | | Int Stoke (A) 0-1 | | | | |
| 1901-02 (D2) | | | 3q St Helens Town (H) 5-2; 4q Nantwich Town (A) 3-1; 5q Stockport County (H) 2-0; Int Leicester Fosse (A) 1-0 | | | | |
| | 1 | 25.01.02 | **Nottingham Forest** (D1) | H | L | 1-3 | Goddard |
| 1902-03 (D2) | | | 3q Crewe Alexandra (A) 3-0; 4q Wrexham (H) 4-0; 5q St Helens Town (H) 5-0; Int New Brompton (H) 2-1 | | | | |
| | 1 | 07.02.03 | **Stoke** (D1) | H | L | 2-3 | Badenoch, Burgess |
| 1903-04 (D2) | | | 2q Heywood scratched | | | | |
| 1904-05 (D2) | | | 3q Nantwich Town (A) 2-1; 4q Stockport County (H) 1-1; 4qr Stockport County (A) 0-0; 4q 2r Stockport County (H) 0-0; 4q 3r Stockport County (A) 0-1 | | | | |
| 1905-06 (D2) | | | 4q Brighton (H) 0-1 | | | | |
| 1906-07 (D2) | | | 5q Newhall Swifts (A) 2-1 | | | | |
| | 1 | 12.01.07 | **Brentford** (SL) | A | L | 1-2 | McKie |
| 1907-08 (D2) | | | 5q West Stanley (A) 3-0 | | | | |
| | 1 | 11.01.08 | **Manchester City** (D1) | H | D | 0-0 | |
| | 1r | 15.01.08 | **Manchester City** | A | L | 0-6 | |
| 1908-09 (D2) | 1 | 16.01.09 | **Chesterfield** (D2) | A | W | 2-0 | Raine, Stapley |
| | 2 | 06.02.09 | **Stockport County** (D2) | A | D | 1-1 | Robertson |
| | 2r | 09.02.09 | **Stockport County** | H | W | 1-0aet | Greechan |
| | 3 | 20.02.09 | **Sheffield Wed** (D1) | A | W | 1-0 | Greechan |
| | 4 | 06.03.09 | **Bristol City** (D1) | H | D | 0-0 | |
| | 4r | 10.03.09 | **Bristol City** | A | L | 0-1 | |

| | | | | | | | | | |
|---|---|---|---|---|---|---|---|---|---|
| 1909-10 | (D2) | 1 | 15.01.10 | **Bury** (D1) | A | L | 1-2 | Hoare |
| 1910-11 | (D2) | 1 | 14.01.11 | **Middlesbrough** (D1) | A | L | 0-1 | |
| 1911-12 | (D2) | 1 | 13.01.12 | **Leeds City** (D2) | A | L | 0-1 | |
| 1912-13 | (D2) | | | 4q Ripley (H) 2-0; 5q Southall (H) 11-1 | | | | |
| | | 1 | 11.01.13 | **Crystal Palace** (SL) | A | L | 0-2 | |
| 1913-14 | (D2) | | | 4q Hinckley Utd (H) 5-1; 5q Carlisle Utd (H) 4-1 | | | | |
| | | 1 | 10.01.14 | **Everton** (D1) | H | W | 2-1 | Montgomery, Barnett |
| | | 2 | 31.01.14 | **Preston North End** (D1) | H | L | 0-1 | |
| 1914-15 | (D2) | | | 6q Coventry City (H) 3-1 | | | | |
| | | 1 | 09.01.15 | **QPR** (SL) | A | L | 1-2 | Toward |

# GLOUCESTER CITY

*Formed 1889. First entered FA Cup: 1928-29. Members of the Southern League.*

| | | | | | | | | |
|---|---|---|---|---|---|---|---|---|
| 1948-49 | (SL) | 1 | 27.11.48 | **Mansfield Town** (3N) | A | L | 0-4 | |
| 1949-50 | (SL) | 1 | 26.11.49 | **Norwich City** (3S) | H | L | 2-3 | Hunt 2 |
| 1950-51 | (SL) | 1 | 25.11.50 | **Bristol City** (3S) | A | L | 0-4 | |
| 1989-90 | (SL) | 1 | 18.11.89 | **Dorchester Town** (SL) | H | W | 1-0 | Talboys |
| | | 2 | 09.12.89 | **Cardiff City** (D3) | A | D | 2-2 | Talboys, Townsend |
| | | 2r | 12.12.89 | **Cardiff City** | H | L | 0-1 | |

# GOLDENHILL

*Staffordshire-based amateur club which played in the FA Cup for three seasons in the 1880s*

| | | | | | | | | |
|---|---|---|---|---|---|---|---|---|
| 1884-85 | | 1 | 18.10.84 | **Wrexham Olympic** | A | L | 0-1 | |
| 1885-86 | | 1 | 31.10.85 | **Davenham** | A | L | 1-2 | |
| 1886-87 | | 1 | 30.10.86 | **Macclesfield T** | H | W | 4-2 | |
| | | | | *FA ordered replay after protest* | | | | |
| | | 1r | 13.11.86 | **Macclesfield T** | A | W | 3-2 | |
| | | 2 | 20.11.86 | **Chester** | A | L | 0-1 | |
| | | | | *FA disqualified Chester following protest, Goldenhill re-instated* | | | | |
| | | 3 | | Chirk | | | - | |
| | | | | *Goldenhill scratched. Chirk walkover* | | | | |

# GOOLE TOWN

*Formed 1900. First entered FA Cup: 1906-07. League club beaten: Workington. Members of the Northern Counties East League.*

| | | | | | | | | |
|---|---|---|---|---|---|---|---|---|
| 1914-15 | | 1 | 09.01.15 | **Middlesbrough** (D1) | A | L | 3-9 | Morley, Spavin, Ford |
| 1949-50 | (ML) | 1 | 26.11.49 | **Chester** (3N) | A | L | 1-4 | Cutts |
| 1951-52 | (ML) | 1 | 24.11.51 | **Tranmere Rovers** (3N) | A | L | 2-4 | Kimber, Coop |
| 1955-56 | (ML) | 1 | 19.11.55 | **Halifax Town** (3N) | H | L | 1-2 | Steadman |
| 1956-57 | (ML) | 1 | 17.11.56 | **Wigan Athletic** (LC) | A | W | 2-1 | Handley 2 |
| | | 2 | 08.12.56 | **Workington** (3N) | H | D | 2-2 | Handley, Iggleden |
| | | 2r | 12.12.56 | **Workington** | A | W | 1-0 | Handley |
| | | 3 | 05.01.57 | **Nottingham Forest** (D2) | A | L | 0-6 | |
| 1957-58 | (ML) | 1 | 16.11.57 | **Scunthorpe Utd** (3N) | A | L | 1-2 | Johnson (p) |
| 1967-68 | (ML) | 1 | 09.12.67 | **Spennymoor Utd** (NL) | H | D | 0-0 | |
| | | 1r | 13.12.67 | **Spennymoor Utd** | A | L | 1-3 | Wagstaffe |
| 1968-69 | (NPL) | 1 | 16.11.68 | **Barrow** (D3) | H | L | 1-3 | Thompson |
| 1976-77 | (NPL) | 1 | 20.11.76 | **Barrow** (NPL) | A | W | 2-0 | Whiteley, Taylor |
| | | 2 | 11.12.76 | **Wrexham** (D3) | A | D | 1-1 | Kelly |
| | | 2r | 14.12.76 | **Wrexham** | H | L | 0-1 | |
| 1977-78 | (NPL) | 1 | 26.11.77 | **Spennymoor Utd** (NL) | A | L | 1-3 | Thompson |
| 1984-85 | (NPL) | 1 | 17.11.84 | **Halifax Town** (D4) | A | L | 0-2 | |

# GORLESTON

*Formed 1884. First entered FA Cup: 1909-10. Members of the Eastern Counties League.*

| | | | | | | | | |
|---|---|---|---|---|---|---|---|---|
| 1951-52 | (ECL) | 1 | 24.11.51 | **Leyton Orient** (3S) | A | D | 2-2 | Hunter, Chapman |
| | | 1r | 29.11.51 | **Leyton Orient** | H | D | 0-0aet | |
| | | 1 2r | 03.12.51 | **Leyton Orient** | | L | 4-5 | Hunter 2, Chapman, Guy |
| | | | | *played at Highbury* | | | | |
| 1957-58 | (ECL) | 1 | 16.11.57 | **Gillingham** (3S) | A | L | 1-10 | Sells |

## GRANTHAM TOWN

*Formed 1874. First entered FA Cup: 1876-77. League clubs beaten: Stockport County, Rochdale. Members of the Southern League.*

| | | | | | | | | |
|---|---|---|---|---|---|---|---|---|
| 1877-78 | | 1 | 27.10.77 | **Clapham Rovers** | H | L | 0-2 | |
| 1878-79 | | 1 | 28.10.78 | **Sheffield FC** | A | D | 1-1 | Hutchinson |
| | | 1r | 16.11.78 | **Sheffield FC** | H | L | 1-2 | Britten |
| 1880-81 | | 1 | 11.11.80 | **Birmingham Calthorpe** | A | W | 2-1 | Frith, Howard |
| | | 2 | 11.12.80 | **Stafford Road** | H | D | 1-1 | O'Dowds |
| | | 2r | 16.12.80 | **Stafford Road** | A | L | 1-7 | Maule |
| 1881-82 | | 1 | 05.11.81 | **Brigg Town** | H | W | 6-0 | |
| | | 2 | 28.11.81 | **Staveley** | A | L | 1-3 | |
| 1882-83 | | 1 | | Phoenix Bessemer | | | - | |
| | | | | *Grantham scratched. Phoenix Bessemer walkover* | | | | |
| 1883-84 | | 1 | 10.11.83 | **Spilsby** | H | W | 3-2 | Curtis, Bell, Lee |
| | | 2 | 26.11.83 | **Grimsby Town** | H | W | 4-0 | T Bryan, Bell, Curtis, AN Other |
| | | 3 | 15.12.83 | **Notts County** | H | L | 0-4 | |
| 1884-85 | | 1 | 25.10.84 | **Grimsby Town** | H | D | 1-1 | |
| | | 1r | 08.11.84 | **Grimsby Town** | A | L | 0-1 | |
| 1885-86 | | 1 | 24.10.85 | **Gainsborough T** | A | L | 1-4 | |
| 1886-87 | | 1 | 23.10.86 | **Lincoln Lindum** | A | W | 1-0 | |
| | | 2 | 20.11.86 | **Redcar** | H | W | 3-2 | |
| | | 3 | 09.12.86 | **Horncastle** | A | L | 0-2 | |
| 1887-88 | | 1 | 15.10.87 | **Lincoln Lindum** | H | W | 4-0 | |
| | | 2 | 05.11.87 | **Notts Rangers** | A | L | 0-4 | |
| 1928-29 | (ML) | 1 | 24.11.28 | **Rhyl** (Welsh) | H | W | 1-0 | Spaven |
| | | 2 | 08.12.28 | **Wigan Borough** (3N) | A | L | 1-2 | Spaven |
| 1935-36 | (ML) | 1 | 30.11.35 | **Notts County** (3S) | H | L | 0-2 | |
| 1945-46 | (ML) | 1 1L | 17.11.45 | **Kettering Town** (UCL) | A | W | 5-1 | Searby,Ashton, Ranshaw 2, Wood |
| | | 1 2L | 24.11.45 | **Kettering Town** | H | D | 2-2 | Russell, Ranshaw |
| | | 2 1L | 08.12.45 | **Mansfield Town** (3S) | H | L | 1-2 | Searby |
| | | 2 2L | 15.12.45 | **Mansfield Town** | A | L | 1-2 | Searby |
| 1947-48 | (ML) | 1 | 29.11.47 | **Stockton** (NEL) | A | L | 1-2 | Searby |
| 1949-50 | (ML) | 1 | 26.11.49 | **Wrexham** (3N) | A | L | 1-4 | McCartney |
| 1961-62 | (ML) | 1 | 04.11.61 | **Brierley Hill All** (BDL) | A | L | 0-3 | |
| 1965-66 | (ML) | 1 | 13.11.65 | **Hendon** (IL) | H | W | 4-1 | Alexander 4 |
| | | 2 | 04.12.65 | **Swindon Town** (D3) | H | L | 1-6 | Alexander |
| 1966-67 | (ML) | 1 | 26.11.66 | **Wimbledon** (SL) | H | W | 2-1 | Martin og, South |
| | | 2 | 07.01.67 | **Oldham Athletic** (D3) | H | L | 0-4 | |
| 1967-68 | (ML) | 1 | 09.12.67 | **Altrincham** (CC) | H | L | 0-3 | |
| 1968-69 | (ML) | 1 | 16.11.68 | **Chelmsford City** (SL) | H | W | 2-1 | Tomlinson, Bly |
| | | 2 | 07.12.68 | **Swindon Town** (D3) | H | L | 0-2 | |
| 1969-70 | (ML) | 1 | 15.11.69 | **Oldham Athletic** (D4) | A | L | 1-3 | Benskin |
| 1970-71 | (ML) | 1 | 21.11.70 | **Stockport County** (D4) | H | W | 2-1 | Tomlinson, Norris |
| | | 2 | 12.12.70 | **Rotherham Utd** (D3) | H | L | 1-4 | Nixon |
| 1972-73 | (SL) | 1 | 18.11.72 | **Bradford City** (D4) | A | L | 0-3 | |
| 1973-74 | (SL) | 1 | 24.11.73 | **Hillingdon Borough** (SL) | A | W | 4-0 | Norris 2, Benskin, Horobin |
| | | 2 | 15.12.73 | **Rochdale** (D3) | H | D | 1-1 | Benskin |
| | | 2r | 18.12.73 | **Rochdale** | A | W | 5-3aet | Chambers 3, Norris, Horobin |
| | | 3 | 05.01.74 | **Middlesbrough** (D2) | H | L | 0-2 | |
| 1975-76 | (SL) | 1 | 22.11.75 | **Port Vale** (D3) | H | D | 2-2 | Benskin, Norris |
| | | 1r | 24.11.75 | **Port Vale** | A | L | 1-4 | Norris |

## GRAVESEND & NORTHFLEET

*Formed 1946 by the merger of Gravesend United (formed 1893) and Northfleet United (formed 1890). First entered FA Cup as Gravesend & Northfleet 1946-47. League clubs beaten: Exeter City, Carlisle United, Colchester United. See also Northfleet United. Members of The Conference.*

| | | | | | | | | |
|---|---|---|---|---|---|---|---|---|
| 1946-47 | (SL) | 1 | 30.11.46 | **Gillingham** (SL) | A | L | 1-4 | Crowe |
| 1949-50 | (SL) | 1 | 26.11.49 | **Torquay Utd** (3S) | H | L | 1-3 | Viles |
| 1962-63 | (SL) | 1 | 03.11.62 | **Exeter City** (D4) | H | W | 3-2 | Williams 2, McNichol |
| | | 2 | 24.11.62 | **Wycombe W** (IL) | H | W | 3-1 | Cameron, Skingley 2 |
| | | 3 | 29.01.63 | **Carlisle Utd** (D3) | A | W | 1-0 | Sitford |

| | | | | | | | | |
|---|---|---|---|---|---|---|---|---|
| | | 4 | 12.02.63 | **Sunderland** (D2) | H | D | 1-1 | Skingley |
| | | 4r | 18.02.63 | **Sunderland** | A | L | 2-5 | McNicol, Sitford |
| 1963-64 | (SL) | 1 | 16.11.63 | **Tooting & M** (IL) | A | W | 2-1 | Wilkins, Easton (p) |
| | | 2 | 07.12.63 | **Brentford** (D3) | A | L | 0-1 | |
| 1964-65 | (SL) | 1 | 14.11.64 | **Bournemouth** (D3) | A | L | 0-7 | |
| 1965-66 | (SL) | 1 | 13.11.65 | **Wimbledon** (SL) | A | L | 1-4 | Chamberlain |
| 1978-79 | (SL) | 1 | 25.11.78 | **Wimbledon** (D4) | H | D | 0-0 | |
| | | 1r | 28.11.78 | **Wimbledon** | A | L | 0-1 | |
| 1979-80 | (APL) | 1 | 24.11.79 | **Torquay Utd** (D4) | H | L | 0-1 | |
| 1980-81 | (APL) | 1 | 22.11.80 | **St Albans City** (IL) | H | L | 1-2 | Stonebridge |
| 1993-94 | (SL) | 1 | 13.11.93 | **Leyton Orient** (D2) | A | L | 1-2 | Portway |
| 1995-96 | (SL) | 1 | 11.11.95 | **Colchester Utd** (D3) | H | W | 2-0 | Jackson, Mortley |
| | | 2 | 02.12.95 | **Cinderford Town** (SL) | A | D | 1-1 | Blewden |
| | | 2r | 14.12.95 | **Cinderford Town** | H | W | 3-0 | Best, Munday, Powell |
| | | 3 | 06.01.96 | **Aston Villa** (PL) | H | L | 0-3 | |
| | | | | *played at Villa Park* | | | | |
| 2000-01 | (IL) | 1 | 08.12.00 | **Notts County** (D2) | H | L | 1-2 | Jackson |
| 2001-02 | (IL) | 1 | 17.11.01 | **Huddersfield Town** (D2) | A | L | 1-2 | Clarke og |

## GRAYS ATHLETIC

*Formed 1890. First entered FA Cup: 1911-12. Members of the Isthmian League.*

| | | | | | | | | |
|---|---|---|---|---|---|---|---|---|
| 1952-53 | (CRN) | 1 | 22.11.52 | **Llanelli** (SL) | H | L | 0-5 | |
| 1988-89 | (IL) | 1 | 19.11.88 | **Bath City** (SL) | A | L | 0-2 | |
| 2000-01 | (IL) | 1 | 18.11.00 | **Reading** (D2) | A | L | 0-4 | |
| 2001-02 | (IL) | 1 | 17.11.01 | **Hinckley Utd** (SL) | H | L | 1-2 | Lock |

## GREAT BRIDGE UNITY

*Formed 1879. Played at Horseley Heath, Horseley, Tipton.*

| | | | | | | | | |
|---|---|---|---|---|---|---|---|---|
| 1887-88 | | 1 | 15.10.87 | **Stafford Road** | A | L | 1-2 | |
| | | FA ordered replay after protest | | | | | | |
| | | 1r | 22.10.87 | **Stafford Road** | H | D | 1-1 | |
| | | | | *Stafford Road scratched before second replay. Great Bridge walkover* | | | | |
| | | 2 | 05.11.87 | **Burton Swifts** | A | W | 5-2 | |
| | | 3 | 26.11.87 | **Birmingham Excelsior** | H | W | 2-1 | |
| | | 4 | 17.12.87 | **Bootle** | H | L | 1-2 | |

## GREAT HARWOOD

*Formed 1877. First entered FA Cup: 1900. Reformed 1965. Members of the North West Counties League.*

| | | | | | | | | |
|---|---|---|---|---|---|---|---|---|
| 1970-71 | (NPL) | 1 | 24.11.70 | **Rotherham Utd** (D3) | H | L | 2-6 | Beardall, Vernon |

## GREAT LEVER

*Formed 1877. Played in the Woodside area of Bolton. Albert Shepherd, the first player to score a penalty in the FA Cup final (for Newcastle in the 1910 replay) was born in Great Lever.*

| | | | | | | | | |
|---|---|---|---|---|---|---|---|---|
| 1882-83 | | 1 | 21.10.82 | **Halliwell** | A | L | 2-3 | |
| 1883-84 | | 1 | 20.10.83 | **Astley Bridge** | H | W | 4-1 | Hardman, Howarth, Rostron, AN Other |
| | | 2 | 01.12.83 | **Preston North End** | A | L | 1-4 | |
| 1885-86 | | 1 | | Preston North End | | | - | |
| | | | | *Great Lever scratched. Preston walkover* | | | | |
| 1886-87 | | 1 | 16.10.86 | **Bootle** | A | W | 4-2 | |
| | | 2 | 13.11.86 | **Cliftonville** | H | L | 1-3 | |

## GREAT YARMOUTH TOWN

*Formed 1897. First entered FA Cup: 1900-01. League club beaten: Crystal Palace. Members of the Eastern Counties League.*

| | | | | | | | | |
|---|---|---|---|---|---|---|---|---|
| 1947-48 | (ECL) | 1 | 29.11.47 | **Shrewsbury Town** (ML) | H | L | 1-4 | Daynes |
| 1952-53 | (ECL) | 1 | 22.11.52 | **Guildford City** (SL) | A | D | 2-2 | Plunkett, Keaveney |
| | | 1r | 27.11.52 | **Guildford City** | H | W | 1-0 | Horsfall og |
| | | 2 | 06.12.52 | **Wrexham** (3N) | H | L | 1-2 | Cutting |
| 1953-54 | (ECL) | 1 | 21.11.53 | **Crystal Palace** (3S) | H | W | 1-0 | Rackham |
| | | 2 | 12.12.53 | **Barrow** (3N) | A | L | 2-5 | Plunkett 2 |

## GRESHAM

*Formed 1874. Played at South Hackney Common, now part of Hackney Downs. Used the Bedford Hotel in Victoria Park Road as their changing rooms.*

| | | | | | | | |
|---|---|---|---|---|---|---|---|
| 1876-77 | 1 | 04.11.76 | **Forest School** | A | L | 1-4 | |
| 1879-80 | 1 | 01.11.79 | **Kildare FC** | H | W | 3-0 | Cullen 2, Jeffrey |
| | 2 | 20.12.79 | **Grey Friars** | A | L | 0-9 | |

## GRESLEY ROVERS

*Formed 1882. First entered FA Cup: 1895-96. FA Vase runners-up: 1991. Members of the Southern League.*

| | | | | | | | |
|---|---|---|---|---|---|---|---|
| 1930-31 (BC) | 1 | 29.11.30 | **York City** (3N) | A | L | 1-3 | Warren |
| 1994-95 (SL) | 1 | 12.11.94 | **Crewe Alexandra** (D2) | A | L | 1-7 | Devaney |
| 1998-99 (SL) | 1 | 14.11.98 | **Walsall** (D2) | A | L | 0-1 | |

## GRETNA

*Formed 1946. Became the first Scottish club to play in the Competition Proper for 105 years in 1991. Competed in the Northern League at the time. Joined the Scottish League in 2001-02.*

| | | | | | | | |
|---|---|---|---|---|---|---|---|
| 1991-92 (NL) | 1 | 16.11.91 | **Rochdale** (D4) | H | D | 0-0 | |
| | 1r | 27.11.91 | **Rochdale** | A | L | 1-3 | Carruthers |
| 1993-94 (NPL) | 1 | 13.11.93 | **Bolton Wanderers** (D1) | H | L | 2-3 | Townsley, Dobie |

## GREY FRIARS

*Formed 1876. Played at The Greyhound fields, Dulwich, south London. Used The Greyhound pub as their changing rooms.*

| | | | | | | | |
|---|---|---|---|---|---|---|---|
| 1878-79 | 1 | 09.11.78 | **Marlow** | H | W | 2-1 | |
| | 2 | 07.12.78 | **Minerva** | H | L | 0-3 | |
| 1879-80 | 1 | 08.11.79 | **Hanover Utd** | H | W | 2-1 | |
| | 2 | 20.12.79 | **Gresham** | H | W | 9-0 | Broadhurst, Green 2, Stransham, Sharp, Kirkpatrick, og 2, AN Other |
| | 3 | | bye | | | | |
| | 4 | 18.02.80 | **Royal Engineers** | A | L | 0-1 | |
| 1880-81 | 1 | 13.11.80 | **Windsor Home Park** | H | D | 0-0 | |
| | 1r | 20.11.80 | **Windsor Home Park** | A | W | 3-1 | |
| | 2 | 11.12.80 | **Maidenhead** | H | W | 1-0 | Thompson |
| | 3 | | bye | | | | |
| | 4 | 19.02.81 | **Old Etonians** | A | L | 0-4 | |

## GRIMSBY DISTRICT

*Formed 1878. Played at Cleethorpes Road, Grimsby. A separate club from Grimsby Town*

| | | | | | | | |
|---|---|---|---|---|---|---|---|
| 1884-85 | 1 | | Middlesbrough | | | - | |
| | | | *Grimsby District scratched. Middlesbrough walkover* | | | | |
| 1885-86 | 1 | 17.10.85 | **Lincoln Lindum** | A | L | 0-4 | |

## GRIMSBY TOWN

*Formed 1878. FA Cup best performance: Semi-finals, 1936 and 1939. FA Cup record win: 10-0 v Boston Town, 2nd qualifying round, 1891. In Competition Proper: 8-0 v Darlington, 2nd round, 21.11.1885. FA Cup Record defeat: 1-9 v Phoenix Bessemer, 2nd round, 25.11.1882*

| | | | | | | | |
|---|---|---|---|---|---|---|---|
| 1882-83 | 1 | | Queen's Park, Glasgow | | | - | |
| | | | *Queen's Park scratched. Grimsby Town walkover* | | | | |
| | 2 | 25.11.82 | **Phoenix Bessemer** | H | L | 1-9 | Monument |
| 1883-84 | 1 | 03.11.83 | **Hull Town** | A | W | 3-1 | |
| | 2 | 26.11.83 | **Grantham Town** | A | L | 0-4 | |
| 1884-85 | 1 | 25.10.84 | **Grantham Town** | A | D | 1-1 | Mundahl |
| | 1r | 08.11.84 | **Grantham Town** | H | W | 1-0 | Garnham |
| | 2 | 06.12.84 | **Redcar** | H | W | 3-1 | Garnham 2, Raynes |
| | 3 | 03.01.85 | **Lincoln City** | H | W | 1-0 | Mundahl |
| | 4 | 24.01.85 | **Old Carthusians** | A | L | 0-3 | |
| 1885-86 | 1 | 31.10.85 | **Lincoln City** | A | W | 2-0 | Sharman, Monument |
| | 2 | 21.11.85 | **Darlington** | H | W | 8-0 | Monument 4, Seal 3, Atkinson |
| | 3 | 19.12.85 | **Middlesbrough** | A | L | 1-2 | Monument |
| 1886-87 | 1 | 30.10.86 | **Sheffield Heeley** | A | W | 4-1 | Pearson 3, Chapman |
| | 2 | 13.11.86 | **Nottingham Forest** | A | D | 2-2 | Garnham, Caborn og |
| | 2r | 20.11.86 | **Nottingham Forest** | H | L | 0-1 | |

| | | | | | | | |
|---|---|---|---|---|---|---|---|
| 1887-88 | 1 | 15.10.87 | **Cleethorpes Town** | A | W | 4-0 | Lundie, Smith, Lee, Atkinson og |
| | 2 | | bye | | | | |
| | 3 | 26.11.87 | **Lincoln City** | H | W | 2-0 | Lundie, Lee |
| | 4 | 17.12.87 | **Old Foresters** | A | L | 2-4 | Atkinson, Lee |
| 1888-89 (TC) | | | 1q Lincoln City (H) 1-1aet; 1qr Lincoln City (A) 1-1aet; 1q 2r Lincoln City 3-1 at Bramall Lane; 2q Newark (A) 4-4; 2qr Newark (H) 9-0; 3q Cleethorpes T (H) 5-0 | | | | |
| | 1 | 15.12.88 | **Sunderland Albion** (FAll) | H | W | 3-1 | McBeth 2, J. Taylor |
| | 2 | 16.02.89 | **Preston North End** (D1) | H | L | 0-2 | |
| 1889-90 (FAll) | 1 | 18.01.90 | **Newcastle West End** (NL) | A | W | 2-1 | McBeth, Black |
| | 2 | 01.02.90 | **Blackburn Rovers** (D1) | A | L | 0-3 | |
| 1890-91 (FAll) | | | 1q Ecclesfield (A) 2-8 | | | | |
| 1891-92 (FAll) | | | 1q Long Eaton Rangers (H) 2-1; 2q Boston Town (H) 10-0; 3q Sheffield Utd (H) 1-2 | | | | |
| 1892-93 (D2) | | | 1q Attercliffe (A) 2-0; 2q Doncaster Rovers (H) 1-1; 2qr Doncaster Rovers (A) 2-1; 3q Gainsborough T (H) 1-0; 4q Lincoln City (H) 5-0 | | | | |
| | 1 | 21.01.93 | **Stockton** (NL) | H | W | 5-0 | Mullen 2, Higgins, Ackroyd, og |
| | 2 | 03.02.93 | **Darwen** (D2) | A | L | 0-2 | |
| 1893-94 (D2) | | | 1q Kilnhurst (H) 5-1; 2q Lincoln City (A) 5-2; 3q Grantham R (A) 6-2; 4q Gainsborough T (H) 6-1 | | | | |
| | 1 | 27.01.94 | **Liverpool** (D2) | A | L | 0-3 | |
| 1894-95 (D2) | | | 1q Lincoln City (A) 3-0; 2q Attercliffe (H) 2-2; 2qr Attercliffe (H) 8-0; 3q Worksop Town (H) 0-1 | | | | |
| 1895-96 (D2) | | | 1q Staveley (A) 5-0; 2q Kilnhurst (A) 4-1; 3q Lincoln C (A) 4-2; 4q Rotherham T (H) 4-0 | | | | |
| | 1 | 01.02.96 | **Darwen** (D2) | A | W | 2-0 | Graham, Pratt |
| | 2 | 15.02.96 | **WBA** (D1) | H | D | 1-1 | Gray |
| | 2r | 20.02.96 | **WBA** | A | L | 0-3 | |
| 1896-97 (D2) | 1 | 30.01.97 | **Bolton Wanderers** (D1) | H | D | 0-0 | |
| | 1r | 08.02.97 | **Bolton Wanderers** | A | D | 3-3aet | Rogers, Bell, McCairns |
| | 1 2r | 11.02.97 | **Bolton Wanderers** *played at Bramall Lane* | | L | 2-3 | Fletcher, og |
| 1897-98 (D2) | 1 | 29.01.98 | **Nottingham Forest** (D1) | A | L | 0-4 | |
| 1898-99 (D2) | | | 3q Mexborough (H) 5-0; 4q Lincoln City (H) 2-1; 5q Barnsley (A) 0-0; 5qr Barnsley (H) 2-1 | | | | |
| | 1 | 28.01.99 | **Preston North End** (D1) | A | L | 0-7 | |
| 1899-00 (D2) | | | 3q Doncaster Rovers (H) 3-1; 4q Barnsley (H) 3-2; 5q Chesterfield (H) 3-2 | | | | |
| | 1 | 27.01.00 | **Nottingham Forest** (D1) | A | L | 0-3 | |
| 1900-01 (D2) | | | Int Middlesbrough (H) 0-1 | | | | |
| 1901-02 (D1) | 1 | 25.01.02 | **Portsmouth** (SL) | H | D | 1-1 | Appleyard |
| | 1r | 29.01.02 | **Portsmouth** | A | L | 0-2 | |
| 1902-03 (D1) | 1 | 07.02.03 | **Newcastle Utd** (D1) | H | W | 2-1 | Fletcher, Ronaldson |
| | 2 | 21.02.03 | **Notts County** (D1) | H | L | 0-2 | |
| 1903-04 (D2) | Int | 12.12.03 | **Barnsley** (D2) | H | W | 2-0 | Hodginson, Wilkinson |
| | 1 | 06.02.04 | **Preston North End** (D2) | A | L | 0-1 | |
| 1904-05 (D2) | Int | 14.01.05 | **Gainsborough T** (D2) | H | W | 2-0 | Reynolds, Baker |
| | 1 | 04.02.05 | **Stoke** (D1) | A | L | 0-2 | |
| 1905-06 (D2) | 1 | 13.01.06 | **Newcastle Utd** (D1) | A | L | 0-6 | |
| 1906-07 (D2) | 1 | 12.01.07 | **Woolwich Arsenal** (D1) | | D | 1-1 | Hooper |
| | 1r | 16.01.07 | **Woolwich Arsenal** | A | L | 0-3 | |
| 1907-08 (D2) | 1 | 11.01.08 | **Bristol City** (D1) | A | D | 0-0 | |
| | 1r | 15.01.08 | **Bristol City** | H | W | 2-1 | Lee, Blanthorne |
| | 2 | 01.02.08 | **Carlisle Utd** (LC) | H | W | 6-2 | Blanthorne 5, Kilbourne |
| | 3 | 22.02.08 | **Crystal Palace** (SL) | H | W | 1-0 | Blanthorne |
| | 4 | 07.03.08 | **Newcastle Utd** (D1) | A | L | 1-5 | Kilbourne |
| 1908-09 (D2) | 1 | 16.01.09 | **Stockport County** (D2) *abandoned after 75 minutes – fog* | H | - | 0-2ab | |
| | 1 | 20.01.09 | **Stockport County** | H | L | 0-2 | |
| 1909-10 (D2) | 1 | 15.01.10 | **Bristol Rovers** (SL) | H | L | 0-2 | |
| 1910-11 (ML) | 1 | 14.01.11 | **Croydon Common** (SL) *FA ordered match to be replayed after protests* | H | W | 3-0 | Leonard 3 |
| | 1r | 26.01.11 | **Croydon Common** (SL) | H | W | 8-1 | Leonard 3, Hubbard 2, Worth 2, Springthorpe |
| | 2 | 04.02.11 | **Crewe Alexandra** (BDL) | A | W | 5-1 | Hubbard 2, Gordon, Springthorpe, Leonard (p) |

| | | | | | | | |
|---|---|---|---|---|---|---|---|
| | 3 | 25.02.11 | **Bradford City** (D1) | A | L | 0-1 | |
| 1911-12 (D2) | | | 4q Lincoln City (A) 2-3 | | | | |
| 1912-13 (D2) | 1 | 16.01.13 | **Sheffield Wed** (D1) | A | L | 1-5 | Rippon |
| 1913-14 (D2) | 1 | 10.01.14 | **WBA** (D1) | A | L | 0-2 | |
| 1914-15 (D2) | 1 | 09.01.15 | **Northampton Town** (SL) | H | L | 0-3 | |
| 1919-20 (D2) | 1 | 10.01.20 | **Bristol City** (D2) | H | L | 1-2 | Thompson |
| 1920-21 (D3) | | | 6q Kettering Town (A) 4-2 | | | | |
| | 1 | 08.01.21 | **Norwich City** (D3) | H | W | 1-0 | Smith (p) |
| | 2 | 29.01.21 | **Southampton** (D3) | H | L | 1-3 | Storer |
| 1921-22 (3N) | | | 5q Kettering Town (H) 1-1; 5qr Kettering Town (A) 2-0; 6q Tufnell Park (H) 1-1; 6qr Tufnell Park (A) 2-1 | | | | |
| | 1 | 07.01.22 | **Notts County** (D2) | H | D | 1-1 | Carmichael |
| | 1r | 12.01.22 | **Notts County** | A | L | 0-3 | |
| 1922-23 (3N) | | | 5q Worksop Town (H) 0-2 | | | | |
| 1923-24 (3N) | | | 5q Hinckley (A) 3-0; 6q Chesterfield (A) 0-0; 6qr Chesterfield (H) 2-0 | | | | |
| | 1 | 12.01.24 | **Exeter City** (3S) | A | L | 0-1 | |
| 1924-25 (3N) | | | 5q Chesterfield (H) 1-2 | | | | |
| 1925-26 (3N) | 1 | 28.11.25 | **Walsall** (3N) | A | W | 1-0 | McKenna |
| | 2 | 12.12.25 | **Kettering Town** (SL) | A | D | 1-1 | Carmichael |
| | 2r | 15.12.25 | **Kettering Town** | H | W | 3-1 | Devan, Carmichael, McKenna |
| | 3 | 09.01.26 | **Birmingham** (D1) | A | L | 0-2 | |
| 1926-27 (D2) | 1 | 27.11.26 | **Halifax Town** (3N) | H | W | 3-2 | Pugsley (p), McKenna, Marshall |
| | 2 | 11.12.26 | **York City** (ML) | H | W | 2-1 | Bestall, Robson |
| | 3 | 08.01.27 | **Burnley** (D1) | A | L | 1-3 | Hardy |
| 1927-28 (D2) | 3 | 14.01.28 | **Reading** (D2) | A | L | 0-4 | |
| 1928-29 (D2) | 3 | 12.01.29 | **WBA** (D2) | H | D | 1-1 | Cooper |
| | 3r | 16.01.29 | **WBA** | A | L | 0-2 | |
| 1929-30 (D1) | 3 | 11.01.30 | **Brighton** (3S) | A | D | 1-1 | Prior |
| | 3r | 14.01.30 | **Brighton** | H | L | 0-1 | |
| 1930-31 (D1) | 3 | 10.01.31 | **Scarborough** (ML) | A | W | 2-1 | Prior, Bestall |
| | 4 | 24.01.31 | **Manchester Utd** (D1) | H | W | 1-0 | Marshall |
| | 5 | 14.02.31 | **Everton** (D2) | A | L | 3-5 | Bestall, Coleman, Marshall |
| 1931-32 (D1) | 3 | 09.01.32 | **Exeter City** (3S) | H | W | 4-1 | Glover 4 |
| | 4 | 23.01.32 | **Birmingham** (D1) | H | W | 2-1 | Bestall 2 |
| | 5 | 13.02.32 | **Liverpool** (D1) | A | L | 0-1 | |
| 1932-33 (D2) | 3 | 14.01.33 | **Portsmouth** (D1) | H | W | 3-2 | Glover 2, Dyson |
| | 4 | 28.01.33 | **Bolton Wanderers** (D1) | A | L | 1-2 | Craven |
| 1933-34 (D2) | 3 | 13.01.34 | **Clapton Orient** (3S) | H | W | 1-0 | Glover |
| | 4 | 27.01.34 | **Portsmouth** (D1) | A | L | 0-2 | |
| 1934-35 (D1) | 3 | 12.01.35 | **Everton** (D1) | A | L | 3-6 | Glover 2, Craven |
| 1935-36 (D1) | 3 | 04.01.36 | **Hartlepools Utd** (3N) | A | D | 0-0 | |
| | 3r | 11.01.36 | **Hartlepools Utd** | H | W | 4-1 | Glover 2, Buck, Bestall |
| | 4 | 25.01.36 | **Port Vale** (D2) | A | W | 4-0 | Baldry 2, Bestall, Craven |
| | 5 | 15.02.36 | **Manchester City** (D1) | H | W | 3-2 | Lewis 2, Glover |
| | 6 | 29.02.36 | **Middlesbrough** (D1) | H | W | 3-1 | Glover, Craven, Smailes |
| | SF | 21.03.36 | **Arsenal** (D1) *played at Leeds Road, Huddersfield* | | L | 0-1 | |
| 1936-37 (D1) | 3 | 16.01.37 | **Cardiff City** (3S) | A | W | 3-1 | Glover, Craven, Lewis |
| | 4 | 30.01.37 | **Walsall** (3S) | H | W | 5-1 | Glover 3, Lewis, Buck |
| | 5 | 20.02.37 | **Wolverhampton W** (D1) | H | D | 1-1 | Craven |
| | 5r | 24.02.37 | **Wolverhampton W** | A | L | 2-6 | Craven, Lewis |
| 1937-38 (D1) | 3 | 08.01.38 | **Swindon Town** (3S) | H | D | 1-1 | Tomlinson |
| | 3r | 12.01.38 | **Swindon Town** | A | L | 1-2aet | Tomlinson |
| 1938-39 (D1) | 3 | 10.01.39 | **Tranmere Rovers** (D2) | H | W | 6-0 | Howe 2, Beattie 2, Vincent (p), Lewis |
| | 4 | 21.01.39 | **Millwall** (D2) | A | D | 2-2 | Howe 2 |
| | 4r | 24.01.39 | **Millwall** | H | W | 3-2 | Boyd, Howe, Jones |
| | 5 | 11.02.39 | **Sheffield Utd** (D2) | A | D | 0-0 | |
| | 5r | 14.02.39 | **Sheffield Utd** | H | W | 1-0 | Howe |
| | 6 | 04.03.39 | **Chelsea** (D1) | A | W | 1-0 | Crack |
| | SF | 25.03.39 | **Wolverhampton W** (D1) *played at Old Trafford* | | L | 0-5 | |

| | | | | | | | | |
|---|---|---|---|---|---|---|---|---|
| 1945-46 | (D1) | 3 1L | 05.01.46 | **Sunderland** (D1) | H | L | 1-3 | Rodi |
| | | 3 2L | 09.01.46 | **Sunderland** | A | L | 1-2 | Moore |
| 1946-47 | (D1) | 3 | 11.01.47 | **Reading** (3S) | A | D | 2-2 | Cairns 2 |
| | | 3r | 14.01.47 | **Reading** | H | W | 3-1 | Cairns 2, Keeble |
| | | 4 | 25.01.47 | **Liverpool** (D1) | A | L | 0-2 | |
| 1947-48 | (D1) | 3 | 10.01.48 | **Everton** (D1) | H | L | 1-4 | Whitfield |
| 1948-49 | (D2) | 3 | 03.01.49 | **Exeter City** (3S) | H | W | 2-1 | Whitfield, Cairns |
| | | 4 | 29.01.49 | **Hull City** (3N) | H | L | 2-3 | Forrest, Biggs |
| 1949-50 | (D2) | 3 | 07.01.50 | **Luton Town** (D2) | A | W | 4-3 | Briggs 4 |
| | | 4 | 28.01.50 | **Portsmouth** (D1) | A | L | 0-5 | |
| 1950-51 | (D2) | 3 | 06.01.51 | **Exeter City** (3S) | H | D | 3-3 | Scotson, Bloomer, Mackenzie |
| | | 3r | 10.01.51 | **Exeter City** | A | L | 2-4 | Squires, Bloomer |
| 1951-52 | (3N) | 1 | 24.11.51 | **Darlington** (3N) | H | W | 4-0 | Cairns 3, Bloomer |
| | | 2 | 15.12.51 | **Lincoln City** (3N) | A | L | 1-3 | Cairns |
| 1952-53 | (3N) | 1 | 22.11.52 | **Darlington** (3N) | A | W | 3-2 | Johnston, Millar, Rayner |
| | | 2 | 06.12.52 | **Bath City** (SL) | H | W | 1-0 | Johnston |
| | | 3 | 10.01.53 | **Bury** (D2) | H | L | 1-3 | McCue |
| 1953-54 | (3N) | 1 | 21.11.53 | **Rochdale** (3N) | H | W | 2-0 | Smith, Maddison |
| | | 2 | 12.12.53 | **Witton Albion** (CC) | A | D | 1-1 | Rayner |
| | | 2r | 15.12.53 | **Witton Albion** | H | W | 6-1 | Rayner 3, Bloomer, Wright, Maddison |
| | | 3 | 09.01.54 | **Fulham** (D2) | H | D | 5-5 | Bloomer 3, Scotson, Brice og |
| | | 3r | 13.01.54 | **Fulham** | A | - | 0-0ab | |
| | | | | *abandoned at half-time – ground waterlogged* | | | | |
| | | 3r | 18.01.54 | **Fulham** | A | L | 1-3 | Stroud |
| 1954-55 | (3N) | 1 | 20.11.54 | **Halifax Town** (3N) | H | W | 2-1 | Hughes, Maddison |
| | | 2 | 11.12.54 | **Southampton** (3S) | H | W | 4-1 | Harbertson 2, Harrison 2 |
| | | 3 | 08.01.55 | **Wolverhampton W** (D1) | H | L | 2-5 | Harrison, Stokes |
| 1955-56 | (3N) | 1 | 19.11.55 | **Netherfield** (LC) | A | W | 5-1 | Crosbie 2, Reeson 2, Evans |
| | | 2 | 10.12.55 | **Southport** (3N) | A | D | 0-0 | |
| | | 2r | 14.12.55 | **Southport** | H | W | 3-2 | Priestley, Crosbie (p), Reeson |
| | | 3 | 07.01.56 | **Portsmouth** (D1) | A | L | 1-3 | Maddison |
| 1956-57 | (D2) | 3 | 05.01.57 | **West Ham Utd** (D2) | A | L | 3-5 | Conner, Priestley, Rafferty |
| 1957-58 | (D2) | 3 | 04.01.58 | **Sheffield Utd** (D2) | A | L | 1-5 | Evans |
| 1958-59 | (D2) | 3 | 10.01.59 | **Manchester City** (D1) | H | D | 2-2 | Cullen, Stockin |
| | | 3r | 24.01.59 | **Manchester City** | A | W | 2-1 | Cockerill 2 |
| | | 4 | 28.01.59 | **Nottingham Forest** (D1) | A | L | 1-4 | Scott |
| 1959-60 | (D3) | 1 | 14.11.59 | **Rhyl** (CC) | A | W | 2-1 | Reynolds og, Mills og |
| | | 2 | 05.12.59 | **Wrexham** (D3) | H | L | 2-3 | Rafferty, Hunt |
| 1960-61 | (D3) | 1 | 05.11.60 | **Darlington** (D4) | A | L | 0-2 | |
| 1961-62 | (D3) | 1 | 04.11.61 | **Mansfield Town** (D4) | A | L | 2-3 | Portwood, Rafferty |
| 1962-63 | (D2) | 3 | 07.01.63 | **Leicester City** (D1) | H | L | 1-3 | Scott (p) |
| 1963-64 | (D2) | 3 | 04.01.64 | **Blackburn Rovers** (D1) | A | L | 0-4 | |
| 1964-65 | (D3) | 1 | 14.11.64 | **Barrow** (D4) | A | D | 1-1 | Barratt |
| | | 1r | 17.11.64 | **Barrow** | H | D | 2-2aet | Cockerill (p), Foster |
| | | 1 2r | 23.11.64 | **Barrow** | | W | 2-0 | Pennington, Tees |
| | | | | *played at Old Trafford* | | | | |
| | | 2 | 05.12.64 | **Stockport County** | A | - | 0-0ab | |
| | | | | *abandoned after 50 minutes – fog* | | | | |
| | | 2 | 07.12.64 | **Stockport County** (D4) | A | L | 0-1 | |
| 1965-66 | (D3) | 1 | 13.11.65 | **Barrow** (D4) | A | W | 2-1 | Tees, Foster |
| | | 2 | 04.12.65 | **Barnsley** (D4) | A | D | 1-1 | Green (p) |
| | | 2r | 08.12.65 | **Barnsley** | H | W | 2-0aet | Tees 2 |
| | | 3 | 22.01.66 | **Portsmouth** (D2) | H | D | 0-0 | |
| | | 3r | 26.01.66 | **Portsmouth** | A | W | 3-1 | Green 2, Tees |
| | | 4 | 12.02.66 | **Manchester City** (D2) | A | L | 0-2 | |
| 1966-67 | (D3) | 1 | 26.11.66 | **Crewe Alexandra** (D4) | A | D | 1-1 | Tees |
| | | 1r | 30.11.66 | **Crewe Alexandra** | H | L | 0-1 | |
| 1967-68 | (D3) | 1 | 09.12.67 | **Bradford Park A** (D4) | H | D | 1-1 | Ross (p) |
| | | 1r | 11.12.67 | **Bradford Park A** | A | L | 1-4 | Worthington |
| 1968-69 | (D4) | 1 | 16.11.68 | **Darlington** (D4) | A | L | 0-2 | |
| 1969-70 | (D4) | 1 | 15.11.69 | **Bradford City** (D3) | A | L | 1-2 | Boylen |

| | | | | | | | | |
|---|---|---|---|---|---|---|---|---|
| 1970-71 | (D4) | 1 | 21.11.70 | **Bury** (D3) | H | L | 0-1 | |
| 1971-72 | (D4) | 1 | 20.11.71 | **York City** (D3) | A | L | 2-4 | Thomson 2 (2ps) |
| 1972-73 | (D3) | 1 | 18.11.72 | **Wigan Athletic** (NPL) | H | W | 2-1 | Brace, Boylen |
| | | 2 | 09.12.72 | **Chesterfield** (D3) | H | D | 2-2 | Hickman, Gauden |
| | | 2r | 13.12.72 | **Chesterfield** | A | W | 1-0 | Brace |
| | | 3 | 13.01.73 | **Preston North End** (D2) | H | D | 0-0 | |
| | | 3r | 15.01.73 | **Preston North End** | A | W | 1-0 | Gauden |
| | | 4 | 03.02.73 | **Coventry City** (D1) | A | L | 0-1 | |
| 1973-74 | (D3) | 1 | 24.11.73 | **Runcorn** (NPL) | A | W | 1-0 | Barton |
| | | 2 | 15.12.73 | **Blyth Spartans** (NL) | H | D | 1-1 | Hickman |
| | | 2r | 18.12.73 | **Blyth Spartans** | A | W | 2-0 | Hickman, Hubbard |
| | | 3 | 05.01.74 | **Burnley** (D1) | H | L | 0-2 | |
| 1974-75 | (D3) | 1 | 23.11.74 | **Huddersfield Town** (D3) | H | W | 1-0 | Hutt og |
| | | 2 | 14.12.74 | **Bury** (D3) | H | D | 1-1 | Barton |
| | | 2r | 17.12.74 | **Bury** | A | L | 1-2 | Lewis |
| 1975-76 | (D3) | 1 | 22.11.75 | **Gateshead Utd** (NPL) | H | L | 1-3 | Booth |
| 1976-77 | (D3) | 1 | 20.11.76 | **Droylesden** (CC) | A | D | 0-0 | |
| | | 1r | 23.11.76 | **Droylesden** | H | W | 5-3 | Partridge 2 (1p), Gray, Lewis, Wigg |
| | | 2 | 11.12.76 | **Chester** (D3) | H | L | 0-1 | |
| 1977-78 | (D4) | 1 | 26.11.77 | **Workington** (NPL) | A | W | 2-0 | Waters, Liddell |
| | | 2 | 17.12.77 | **Barnsley** (D4) | H | W | 2-0 | Donovan 2 |
| | | 3 | 07.01.78 | **Southampton** (D2) | H | D | 0-0 | |
| | | 3r | 10.01.78 | **Southampton** | A | D | 0-0aet | |
| | | 3 2r | 17.01.78 | **Southampton** | | L | 1-4 | Waters |
| | | | | *played at Filbert Street* | | | | |
| 1978-79 | (D4) | 1 | 25.11.78 | **Hartlepool Utd** (D4) | A | L | 0-1 | |
| 1979-80 | (D3) | 1 | 24.11.79 | **Chesterfield** (D3) | H | D | 1-1 | Waters |
| | | 1r | 27.11.79 | **Chesterfield** | A | W | 3-2 | K Moore, Drinkell |
| | | 2 | 15.12.79 | **Sheffield Utd** (D3) | H | W | 2-0 | Waters, Crombie |
| | | 3 | 05.01.80 | **Liverpool** (D1) | A | L | 0-5 | |
| 1980-81 | (D2) | 3 | 03.01.81 | **WBA** (D1) | A | L | 0-3 | |
| 1981-82 | (D2) | 3 | 05.01.82 | **Millwall** (D3) | A | W | 6-1 | Drinkell 2, Cumming 2, Whymark, Brolly |
| | | 4 | 23.01.82 | **Newcastle Utd** (D2) | A | W | 2-1 | Kilmore, Drinkell |
| | | 5 | 13.02.82 | **QPR** (D2) | A | L | 1-3 | K Moore |
| 1982-83 | (D2) | 3 | 08.01.83 | **Scunthorpe Utd** (D4) | A | D | 0-0 | |
| | | 3r | 11.01.83 | **Scunthorpe Utd** | H | W | 2-0 | Waters (p), Ford |
| | | 4 | 29.01.83 | **Ipswich Town** (D1) | A | L | 0-2 | |
| 1983-84 | (D2) | 3 | 07.01.84 | **Portsmouth** (D2) | A | L | 1-2 | Drinkell |
| 1984-85 | (D2) | 3 | 05.01.85 | **Notts County** (D2) | A | D | 2-2 | Ford, Lund |
| | | 3r | 08.01.85 | **Notts County** | H | W | 4-2 | Lund 3, Wilkinson |
| | | 4 | 26.01.85 | **Watford** (D1) | H | L | 1-3 | Foley |
| 1985-86 | (D2) | 3 | 04.01.86 | **Arsenal** (D1) | H | L | 3-4 | Lund, Lyons, Peake (p) |
| 1986-87 | (D2) | 3 | 10.01.87 | **Stoke City** (D2) | H | D | 1-1 | Walsh |
| | | 3r | 26.01.87 | **Stoke City** | A | D | 1-1aet | K Moore |
| | | 3 2r | 28.01.87 | **Stoke City** | A | L | 0-6 | |
| 1987-88 | (D3) | 1 | 14.11.87 | **Scarborough** (D4) | A | W | 2-1 | McGarvey, North |
| | | 2 | 05.12.87 | **Halifax Town** (D4) | H | D | 0-0 | |
| | | 2r | 08.12.87 | **Halifax Town** | A | L | 0-2 | |
| 1988-89 | (D4) | 1 | 19.11.88 | **Wolverhampton W** (D3) | H | W | 1-0 | Cockerill |
| | | 2 | 10.12.88 | **Rotherham Utd** (D4) | H | W | 3-2 | North, Cunnington, Russell og |
| | | 3 | 07.01.89 | **Middlesbrough** (D1) | A | W | 2-1 | North 2 |
| | | 4 | 28.01.89 | **Reading** (D3) | H | D | 1-1 | North |
| | | 4r | 01.02.89 | **Reading** | A | W | 2-1 | Cunnington, Jobling |
| | | 5 | 18.02.89 | **Wimbledon** (D1) | A | L | 1-3 | Alexander |
| 1989-90 | (D4) | 1 | 18.11.89 | **York City** (D4) | A | W | 2-1 | Hargreaves 2 |
| | | 2 | 09.12.89 | **Doncaster Rovers** (D4) | H | W | 1-0 | Cockerill |
| | | 3 | 06.01.90 | **Huddersfield Town** (D3) | A | L | 1-3 | Gilbert |
| 1990-91 | (D3) | 1 | 17.11.90 | **Blackpool** (D4) | A | L | 0-2 | |
| 1991-92 | (D2) | 1 | 16.11.91 | **Blackpool** | A | L | 1-2 | Cunnington |
| 1992-93 | (D1) | 3 | 02.01.93 | **Brentford** (D1) | A | W | 2-0 | Mendonca, Dobbin |
| | | 4 | 02.02.93 | **Swansea City** (D2) | A | D | 0-0 | |

| | | | | | | | | |
|---|---|---|---|---|---|---|---|---|
| | | 4r | 09.02.93 | **Swansea City** | H | W | 2-0 | Mendonca, Gilbert |
| | | 5 | 13.02.93 | **Ipswich Town** (PL) | A | L | 0-4 | |
| 1993-94 | (D1) | 3 | 08.01.94 | **Wigan Athletic** (D3) | H | W | 1-0 | Croft |
| | | 4 | 29.01.94 | **Aston Villa** (PL) | H | L | 1-2 | Groves |
| 1994-95 | (D1) | 3 | 07.01.95 | **Norwich City** (PL) | H | L | 0-1 | |
| 1995-96 | (D1) | 3 | 06.01.96 | **Luton Town** (D1) | H | W | 7-1 | Forrester 2, Livingstone 2, Bonetti, Southall, Woods |
| | | 4 | 07.02.96 | **West Ham Utd** (PL) | A | D | 1-1 | Laws |
| | | 4r | 14.02.96 | **West Ham Utd** | H | W | 3-0 | Childs, Woods, Forrester |
| | | 5 | 21.02.96 | **Chelsea** (PL) | H | D | 0-0 | |
| | | 5r | 28.02.96 | **Chelsea** | A | L | 1-4 | Groves |
| 1996-97 | (D1) | 3 | 04.01.97 | **Sheffield Wed** (PL) | A | L | 1-7 | Oster |
| 1997-98 | (D2) | 1 | 15.11.97 | **Shrewsbury Town** (D3) | A | D | 1-1 | Southall |
| | | 1r | 25.11.97 | **Shrewsbury Town** | H | W | 4-0 | Nogan, Herbert og, Lester, Jobling |
| | | 2 | 06.12.97 | **Chesterfield** (D2) | H | D | 2-2 | Rodger, Nogan |
| | | 2r | 16.12.97 | **Chesterfield** | A | W | 2-0 | Lester, Groves |
| | | 3 | 03.01.98 | **Norwich City** (D1) | H | W | 3-0 | McDermott, Woods, Donovan |
| | | 4 | 24.01.98 | **Leeds Utd** (PL) | A | L | 0-2 | |
| 1998-99 | (D1) | 3 | 02.01.99 | **Bradford City** (D1) | A | L | 1-2 | McDermott |
| 1999-00 | (D1) | 3 | 11.12.99 | **Stockport County** (D1) | H | W | 3-2 | Livingstone 2, Allen |
| | | 4 | 08.01.00 | **Bolton Wanderers** (D1) | H | L | 0-2 | |
| 2000-01 | (D1) | 3 | 06.01.01 | **Wycombe W** (D2) | A | D | 1-1 | Nielsen |
| | | 3r | 16.01.01 | **Wycombe W** | H | L | 1-3 | Jeffrey |
| 2001-02 | (D1) | 3 | 05.01.02 | **York City** (D3) | H | D | 0-0 | |
| | | 3r | 15.01.02 | **York City** | A | L | 0-1 | |
| 2002-03 | (D1) | 3 | 04.01.03 | **Burnley** (D1) | H | D | 2-2 | Cooke (p), Mansaram |
| | | 3r | 14.01.03 | **Burnley** | A | L | 0-4 | |

## GUILDFORD CITY

*Formed 1921 as Guildford United. Guildford City 1927. First entered FA Cup: 1921-22. Merged with Dorking in 1974 to become Guildford and Dorking United. Folded December 9, 1976 – their Southern League record for the season was expunged. League clubs beaten: QPR, Reading, Brentford.*

| | | | | | | | | |
|---|---|---|---|---|---|---|---|---|
| 1928-29 | (SL) | 1 | 24.11.28 | **QPR** (3S) | H | W | 4-2 | Hetherington 2, J Smith, S Smith |
| | | 2 | 08.12.28 | **Bournemouth** (3S) | H | L | 1-5 | J Smith |
| 1930-31 | (SL) | 1 | 29.11.30 | **Gillingham** (3S) | A | L | 2-7 | Coundon, William |
| 1931-32 | (SL) | 1 | 28.11.31 | **Fulham** (3S) | A | L | 0-2 | |
| 1932-33 | (SL) | 1 | 26.11.32 | **Coventry City** (3S) | H | L | 1-2 | Burke |
| 1934-35 | (SL) | 1 | 24.11.34 | **Bath City** (SL) | H | L | 1-2 | Thom |
| 1937-38 | (SL) | 1 | 27.11.37 | **Reading** (3S) | H | W | 1-0 | J Brown |
| | | 2 | 11.12.37 | **Doncaster Rovers** (3N) | A | L | 0-4 | |
| 1938-39 | (SL) | 1 | 26.11.38 | **Aldershot** (3S) | A | D | 1-1 | J Brown |
| | | 1r | 30.11.38 | **Aldershot** | H | L | 3-4 | R Brown 2, J Brown |
| 1947-48 | (SL) | 1 | 29.11.47 | **Bournemouth** (3S) | A | L | 0-2 | |
| 1950-51 | (SL) | 1 | 25.11.50 | **Dartford** (SL) | H | L | 1-5 | Passmore |
| 1951-52 | (SL) | 1 | 24.11.51 | **Hereford Utd** (SL) | H | W | 4-1 | Baynham 2, Langley, Passmore |
| | | 2 | 15.12.51 | **Gateshead AFC** (3N) | A | L | 0-2 | |
| 1952-53 | (SL) | 1 | 22.11.52 | **Great Yarmouth T** (ECL) | H | D | 2-2 | Perkins, Sutherland |
| | | 1r | 27.11.52 | **Great Yarmouth T** | A | L | 0-1 | |
| 1953-54 | (SL) | 1 | 21.11.53 | **Hastings Utd** (SL) | A | L | 0-1 | |
| 1956-57 | (SL) | 1 | 17.11.56 | **Brentford** (3S) | A | L | 0-3 | |
| 1957-58 | (SL) | 1 | 16.11.57 | **Yeovil Town** (SL) | H | D | 2-2 | Edwards, Devine |
| | | 1r | 21.11.57 | **Yeovil Town** | A | L | 0-1 | |
| 1958-59 | (SL) | 1 | 15.11.58 | **Hereford Utd** (SL) | H | L | 1-2 | Clarke |
| 1964-65 | (SL) | 1 | 14.11.64 | **Gillingham** (D3) | H | D | 2-2 | Stevens, Porter |
| | | 1r | 18.11.64 | **Gillingham** | A | L | 0-1 | |
| 1965-66 | (SL) | 1 | 13.11.65 | **Wycombe W** (IL) | H | D | 2-2 | Massey, Vafiadis |
| | | 1r | 17.11.65 | **Wycombe W** | A | W | 1-0 | |
| | | 2 | 04.12.65 | **QPR** (D3) | A | L | 0-3 | |
| 1967-68 | (SL) | 1 | 09.12.67 | **Brentford** (D4) | A | - | 2-1ab | Brown, Burge |
| | | | | *abandoned after 53 minutes – snow* | | | | |
| | | 1 | 14.12.67 | **Brentford** (D4) | A | D | 2-2 | Brown 2 |
| | | 1r | 18.12.67 | **Brentford** | H | W | 2-1 | Hudson, Brown |

| | | | | | | | | |
|---|---|---|---|---|---|---|---|---|
| | | 2 | 06.01.68 | **Newport County** (D4) | H | L | 0-1 | |
| 1971-72 | (SL) | 1 | 20.11.71 | **Dover** (SL) | H | D | 0-0 | |
| | | 1r | 24.11.71 | **Dover** | A | W | 2-0 | Malley, Burge |
| | | 2 | 11.12.71 | **Shrewsbury Town** (D3) | A | L | 1-2 | Dyson |
| 1972-73 | (SL) | 1 | 18.11.72 | **Watford** (D3) | A | L | 2-4 | Tyler, Burns |
| 1973-74 | (SL) | 1 | 24.11.73 | **Hitchin Town** (IL) | A | D | 1-1 | Westburgh |
| | | 1r | 28.11.73 | **Hitchin Town** | H | L | 1-4 | Burge |

## GUISBOROUGH TOWN

*Formed 1973. FA Vase runners-up: 1980. Members of the Northern League.*

| | | | | | | | | |
|---|---|---|---|---|---|---|---|---|
| 1988-89 | (NL) | 1 | 19.11.88 | **Bury** (D3) *played at Ayresome Park* | H | L | 0-1 | |

## GUISELEY

*Formed 1909. First entered FA Cup: 1929-30. FA Vase winners: 1991; Runners-up: 1992. Members of the Northern Premier League.*

| | | | | | | | | |
|---|---|---|---|---|---|---|---|---|
| 1991-92 | (NPL) | 1 | 16.11.91 | **Chester City** (D3) | A | L | 0-1 | |
| 1994-95 | (NPL) | 1 | 13.11.94 | **Carlisle Utd** (D3) *played at Valley Parade, Bradford* | H | L | 1-4 | Brockie |
| 1999-00 | (NPL) | 1 | 30.10.99 | **Forest Green R** (Conf) | A | L | 0-6 | |
| 2002-03 | (NPL) | 1 | 16.11.02 | **Luton Town** (D2) | A | L | 0-4 | |

## HALESOWEN TOWN

*Formed 1873. First entered FA Cup: 1898-99. FA Vase winners: 1985, 1986. Runners-up: 1983. Members of the Southern League.*

| | | | | | | | | |
|---|---|---|---|---|---|---|---|---|
| 1955-56 | (BDL) | 1 | 19.11.55 | **Hendon** (AL) | H | L | 2-4 | Dugmore (p), Basterfield |
| 1985-86 | (WMRL) | 1 | 16.11.85 | **Frickley Athletic** (APL) | A | D | 1-1 | P Joinson |
| | | 1r | 18.11.85 | **Frickley Athletic** | H | L | 1-3 | Sherwood (p) |
| 1986-87 | (SL) | 1 | 15.11.86 | **Southend United** (D4) | A | L | 1-4 | Moss |
| 1987-88 | (SL) | 1 | 14.11.87 | **Kidderminster H** (Conf) | H | D | 2-2 | L Joinson, Moss |
| | | 1r | 16.11.87 | **Kidderminster H** | A | L | 0-4 | |
| 1988-89 | (SL) | 1 | 19.11.88 | **Brentford** (D3) | A | L | 0-2 | |
| 1989-90 | (SL) | 1 | 18.11.89 | **Cardiff City** (D3) | A | L | 0-1 | |
| 1990-91 | (SL) | 1 | 17.11.90 | **Tranmere Rovers** (D3) | H | L | 1-2 | Flynn |
| 1991-92 | (SL) | 1 | 16.11.91 | **Farnborough T** (Conf) | H | D | 2-2 | Flynn, Hazelwood |
| | | 1r | 26.11.91 | **Farnborough T** | A | L | 0-4 | |

## HALIFAX TOWN

*Formed 1911. First entered FA Cup: 1912-13. FA Cup best performance: 5th round, 1933, 1953; Record FA Cup win: 12-0 v West Vale Ramblers, 1st qualifying round, 1913-14; In Competition Proper: 7-0 v Bishop Auckland, 2nd round replay, 10.01.1967; Record FA Cup defeat: 0-5 v Wrexham, 1st round, 29.11.47. Members of The Conference.*

| | | | | | | | | |
|---|---|---|---|---|---|---|---|---|
| 1912-13 | (ML) | | | P Horsforth (A) 4-2; 1q Hebden Bridge (A) 3-2; 2q Knaresborough (H) 6-2; 3qS Kirkby Colliery (H) 6-4; 4q Nelson (H) 3-3; 4qr Nelson (A) 3-2; 5q Walsall (A) 0-0; 5q r Walsall (H) 1-0 | | | | |
| | | 1 | 11.01.13 | **QPR** (SL) | A | L | 2-4 | Roscoe, Pentland |
| 1913-14 | (ML) | | | 1q West Vale Ramblers (H) 12-0; 2q Rothwell (A) 1-1; 2q r Rothwell (H) 6-0; 3q Mirfield (H) 2-0; 4q Rotherham Co (A) 1-1; 4qr Rotherham Co (H) 5-2; 5q Norwich C (A) 0-2 | | | | |
| 1914-15 | (ML) | | | P Castleford Town (A) 1-2 | | | | |
| 1919-20 | (ML) | | | 1q Apperley Bridge (H) 7-0; 2q Castleford Town (A) 0-3 | | | | |
| 1920-21 | (ML) | | | ExP Rowntrees (H) 5-3; P Liversedge (H) 3-1; 1q Allerton Bywater (H) 4-1; 2q Harrogate (H) 1-0; 3q Calverley (A) 4-2; 4q Castleford Town (A) 1-3 | | | | |
| 1921-22 | (3N) | | | did not enter | | | | |
| 1922-23 | (3N) | | | 4q Rotherham Town (H) 6-1; 5q Accrington Stanley (A) 1-1; 5q r Accrington Stanley (H) 1-0; 6q Mansfield Town (A) 2-0 | | | | |
| | | 1 | 13.01.23 | **South Shields** (D2) | A | L | 1-3 | Price |
| 1923-24 | (3N) | | | 5q Peterborough & Fletton (A) 1-0; 6q Rotherham Co (H) 1-0 | | | | |
| | | 1 | 12.01.24 | **Northampton Town** (3N) | A | D | 1-1 | Dixon |
| | | 1r | 16.01.24 | **Northampton Town** | H | D | 1-1aet | Dixon |
| | | 1 2r | 21.01.24 | **Northampton Town** *played at Bramall Lane* | | W | 4-2 | Dixon, Wilde, Moore, Whalley |
| | | 2 | 02.02.24 | **Manchester City** (D1) | A | D | 2-2 | Moore, E Hall |
| | | 2r | 06.02.24 | **Manchester City** | A | D | 0-0aet | |

| | | | | | | | | |
|---|---|---|---|---|---|---|---|---|
| | | 2 2r | 11.02.24 | **Manchester City** | | L | 0-3 | |
| | | | | *played at Old Trafford* | | | | |
| 1924-25 | (3N) | | | 5q Rochdale (H) 0-1 | | | | |
| 1925-26 | (3N) | 1 | 28.11.25 | **Rotherham United** (3N) | | L | 0-3 | |
| 1926-27 | (3N) | 1 | 27.11.26 | **Grimsby Town** (D2) | A | L | 2-3 | McCafferty, Dixon |
| 1927-28 | (3N) | 1 | 26.11.27 | **Hartlepools Utd** (3N) | H | W | 3-0 | Proctor, Seabrook, Coleman |
| | | 2 | 10.12.27 | **Tranmere Rovers** (3N) | A | L | 1-3 | Seabrook |
| 1928-29 | (3N) | 1 | 24.11.28 | **Stockport County** (3N) | A | L | 0-1 | |
| 1929-30 | (3N) | 1 | 30.11.29 | **Carlisle Utd** (3N) | A | L | 0-2 | |
| 1930-31 | (3N) | 1 | 29.11.30 | **Mansfield Town** (ML) | A | D | 2-2 | Cooper, Pape |
| | | 1r | 03.12.30 | **Mansfield Town** | H | W | 2-1 | Cooper, Pape |
| | | 2 | 13.12.30 | **Fulham** (3S) | A | L | 0-4 | |
| 1931-32 | (3N) | 1 | 28.11.31 | **Newark Town** (ML) | A | D | 1-1 | Mays |
| | | 1r | 02.12.31 | **Newark Town** | H | W | 2-1 | Crawford, Mays |
| | | 2 | 12.12.31 | **Accrington Stanley** (3N) | H | W | 3-0 | McFarlane, Mays, Betteridge |
| | | 3 | 09.01.32 | **Bournemouth** (3S) | H | L | 1-3 | Betteridge |
| 1932-33 | (3N) | 1 | 26.11.32 | **Darwen** (LC) | H | W | 2-0 | Wellock 2 |
| | | 2 | 10.12.32 | **Workington** (NEL) | H | W | 2-1 | Davies, Wilson og |
| | | 3 | 14.01.33 | **Doncaster Rovers** (3N) | A | W | 3-0 | Chambers 2, Brown |
| | | 4 | 28.01.33 | **Chester** (3N) | A | D | 0-0 | Wellock 2, Davies |
| | | 4r | 02.02.33 | **Chester** | H | W | 3-2 | Wellock 2, Davies |
| | | 5 | 18.02.33 | **Luton Town** (3S) | H | L | 0-2 | |
| 1933-34 | (3N) | 1 | 25.11.33 | **Barnsley** (3N) | H | W | 3-2 | Brown, Ferguson, Chambers |
| | | 2 | 09.12.33 | **Hartlepools Utd** (3N) | H | D | 1-1 | Brown |
| | | 2r | 13.12.33 | **Hartlepools Utd** | A | W | 2-1aet | Brown, Cooke |
| | | 3 | 13.01.34 | **Bolton Wanderers** (D2) | A | L | 1-3 | Tunstall |
| 1934-35 | (3N) | 1 | 24.11.34 | **Hartlepools Utd** (3N) | H | D | 1-1 | Atherton |
| | | 1r | 28.11.34 | **Hartlepools Utd** (3N) | A | L | 0-2 | |
| 1935-36 | (3N) | 1 | 30.11.35 | **Rochdale** (3N) | H | W | 4-0 | Barkas 2, Betteridge 2 |
| | | 2 | 14.12.35 | **Hartlepools Utd** (3N) | H | D | 1-1 | Valentine |
| | | 2r | 18.12.35 | **Hartlepools Utd** | A | D | 0-0aet | |
| | | 2 2r | 23.12.35 | **Hartlepools Utd** | | L | 1-4aet | Cook |
| | | | | *played at St James' Park* | | | | |
| 1936-37 | (3N) | 1 | 28.11.36 | **Darlington** (3N) | H | L | 1-2 | Valentine |
| 1937-38 | (3N) | 1 | 27.11.37 | **York City** (3N) | A | D | 1-1 | Barkas |
| | | 1r | 01.12.37 | **York City** | H | L | 0-1 | |
| 1938-39 | (3N) | 1 | 26.11.38 | **Rochdale** (3N) | H | W | 7-3 | Widdowfield 4, Wood 2, Jackson |
| | | 2 | 10.12.38 | **Mansfield Town** (3S) | H | D | 1-1 | Griffiths |
| | | 2r | 14.12.38 | **Mansfield Town** | A | D | 3-3aet | Griffiths, Widdowfield, Wood |
| | | 2 2r | 19.12.38 | **Mansfield Town** | | D | 0-0aet | |
| | | | | *played at Belle Vue, Doncaster* | | | | |
| | | 2 3r | 21.12.38 | **Mansfield Town** | | W | 2-1aet | Widdowfield, Bungay og |
| | | | | *played at Old Trafford* | | | | |
| | | 3 | 07.01.39 | **Birmingham** (D1) | A | L | 0-2 | |
| 1945-46 | (3N) | 1 1L | 17.11.45 | **York City** (3N) | H | W | 1-0 | Gordon |
| | | 1 2L | 24.11.45 | **York City** | A | L | 2-4 | Barkas 2 |
| 1946-47 | (3N) | 1 | 30.11.46 | **Barrow** (3N) | A | D | 0-0 | |
| | | 1r | 04.12.46 | **Barrow** | H | W | 1-0aet | Waters |
| | | 2 | 14.12.46 | **Stockport County** (3N) | H | D | 1-1 | Waters |
| | | 2r | 18.12.46 | **Stockport County** | A | L | 1-2 | Massey |
| 1947-48 | (3N) | 1 | 29.11.47 | **Wrexham** (3N) | A | L | 0-5 | |
| 1948-49 | (3N) | 1 | 04.12.48 | **Scunthorpe Utd** (ML) | H | D | 0-0aet | |
| | | 1r | 06.12.48 | **Scunthorpe Utd** | A | L | 0-1 | |
| 1949-50 | (3N) | 1 | 26.11.49 | **Tranmere Rovers** (3N) | A | L | 1-2 | Hindle |
| 1950-51 | (3N) | 1 | 25.11.50 | **Ashington** (NEL) | H | L | 2-3 | Glaister, Core |
| 1951-52 | (3N) | 1 | 24.11.51 | **Wrexham** (3N) | A | L | 0-3 | |
| 1952-53 | (3N) | 1 | 22.11.52 | **Ashton Utd** (LC) | H | D | 1-1 | Holt |
| | | 1r | 25.11.52 | **Ashton Utd** | A | W | 2-1 | Lorenson, Moncrieff |
| | | 2 | 06.12.52 | **Southport** (3N) | H | W | 4-2 | Moncrieff 2, Hampson, Holt |
| | | 3 | 10.01.53 | **Cardiff City** (D1) | H | W | 3-1 | Priestley, Murphy, Moncrieff |
| | | 4 | 31.01.53 | **Stoke City** (D1) | H | W | 1-0 | Priestley |
| | | 5 | 14.02.53 | **Tottenham Hotspur** (D1) | H | L | 0-3 | |

| | | | | | | | | |
|---|---|---|---|---|---|---|---|---|
| 1953-54 | (3N) | 1 | 21.11.53 | **Rhyl** (CC) | H | D | 0-0 | |
| | | 1r | 26.11.53 | **Rhyl** | A | L | 3-4aet | Murphy, Priestley, Haddington |
| 1954-55 | (3N) | 1 | 20.11.54 | **Grimsby Town** (3N) | A | L | 1-2 | Watkinson |
| 1955-56 | (3N) | 1 | 19.11.55 | **Goole Town** (ML) | A | W | 2-1 | Lonsdale, Watson |
| | | 2 | 10.12.55 | **Burton Albion** (BDL) | H | D | 0-0 | |
| | | 2r | 14.12.55 | **Burton Albion** | A | L | 0-1 | |
| 1956-57 | (3N) | 1 | 17.11.56 | **Oldham Athletic** (3N) | H | L | 2-3 | Hutchinson, Smith |
| 1957-58 | (3N) | 1 | 16.11.57 | **Mansfield Town** (3N) | A | L | 0-2 | |
| 1958-59 | (D3) | 1 | 15.11.58 | **Southport** (D4) | A | W | 2-0 | Tilley, South |
| | | 2 | 06.12.58 | **Darlington** (D4) | H | D | 1-1 | Harrison |
| | | 2r | 10.12.58 | **Darlington** | A | L | 0-3 | |
| 1959-60 | (D3) | 1 | 14.11.59 | **Gateshead AFC** (D4) | A | W | 4-3 | Tilley 2, Roscoe, Smith |
| | | 2 | 05.12.59 | **Workington** (D4) | A | L | 0-1 | |
| 1960-61 | (D3) | 1 | 05.11.60 | **Hartlepools Utd** (D4) | H | W | 5-1 | Large, Whitelaw, Priestley, Sinclair, Blackburn |
| | | 2 | 29.11.60 | **Crewe Alexandra** (D4) | H | D | 2-2 | Large, Sinclair |
| | | 2r | 05.12.60 | **Crewe Alexandra** | A | L | 0-3 | |
| 1961-62 | (D3) | 1 | 04.11.61 | **Rochdale** (D4) | A | L | 0-2 | |
| 1962-63 | (D3) | 1 | 03.11.62 | **Bradford Park A** (D3) | H | W | 1-0 | Redfearn |
| | | 2 | 24.11.62 | **Lincoln City** (D4) | A | L | 0-1 | |
| 1963-64 | (D4) | 1 | 16.11.63 | **Workington** (D4) | A | L | 1-4 | Granger |
| 1964-65 | (D4) | 1 | 14.11.64 | **South Liverpool** (LC) | H | D | 2-2 | South, Westlake |
| | | 1r | 18.11.64 | **South Liverpool** | A | L | 2-4 | Frear, Westlake |
| 1965-66 | (D4) | 1 | 13.11.65 | **Southport** (D4) | A | L | 0-2 | |
| 1966-67 | (D4) | 1 | 26.11.66 | **Doncaster Rovers** (D3) | H | D | 2-2 | Hutchinson 2 |
| | | 1r | 29.11.66 | **Doncaster Rovers** | A | W | 3-1aet | Parks, McCarthy, Atkins |
| | | 2 | 07.01.67 | **Bishop Auckland** (NL) | A | D | 0-0 | |
| | | 2r | 10.01.67 | **Bishop Auckland** | H | W | 7-0 | Hutchinson 2, Taylor 2, Parks 2, Atkins |
| | | 3 | 28.01.67 | **Bristol City** (D2) | H | D | 1-1 | Parks |
| | | 3r | 31.01.67 | **Bristol City** | A | L | 1-4 | Hutchinson |
| 1967-68 | (D4) | 1 | 13.12.67 | **Crewe Alexandra** (D4) | H | W | 3-2 | Ryden 2, Wallace |
| | | 2 | 06.01.68 | **Scunthorpe Utd** (D3) | H | W | 1-0 | Russell |
| | | 3 | 27.01.68 | **Birmingham City** (D2) | H | L | 2-4 | Holt, Ryden |
| 1968-69 | (D4) | 1 | 16.11.68 | **Bilston Town** (WMRL) | A | W | 3-1 | Massie, Lawther, Flower |
| | | 2 | 07.12.68 | **Crewe Alexandra** (D3) | H | D | 1-1 | Wallace |
| | | 2r | 11.12.68 | **Crewe Alexandra** | A | W | 3-1 | Shawcross 2, Massie |
| | | 3 | 04.01.69 | **Swansea Town** (D4) | A | W | 1-0 | Massie |
| | | 4 | 25.01.69 | **Stoke City** (D1) | A | D | 1-1 | Massie |
| | | 4r | 28.01.69 | **Stoke City** | H | L | 0-3 | |
| 1969-70 | (D3) | 1 | 15.11.69 | **Chester** (D4) | H | D | 3-3 | Atkins, Lawther, Hill |
| | | 1r | 19.11.69 | **Chester** | A | L | 0-1 | |
| 1970-71 | (D3) | 1 | 21.11.70 | **Chesterfield** (D3) | A | L | 0-2 | |
| 1971-72 | (D3) | 1 | 20.11.71 | **Wigan Athletic** (NPL) | A | L | 1-2 | Burgin |
| 1972-73 | (D3) | 1 | 18.11.72 | **Barnsley** (D4) | A | D | 1-1 | Shanahan |
| | | 1r | 21.11.72 | **Barnsley** | H | W | 2-1 | Robertson, Kemp |
| | | 2 | 09.12.72 | **Scunthorpe Utd** (D3) | A | L | 2-3 | Robertson 2 |
| 1973-74 | (D3) | 1 | 24.11.73 | **Frickley Colliery** (ML) | H | W | 6-1 | Gwyther 3, Ford, Hale (p), Rhodes |
| | | 2 | 15.12.73 | **Oldham Athletic** (D3) | H | L | 0-1 | |
| 1974-75 | (D3) | 1 | 23.11.74 | **Barnsley** (D4) | A | W | 2-1 | Jones 2 |
| | | 2 | 14.12.74 | **Stafford Rangers** (NPL) | A | L | 1-2 | Gwyther |
| 1975-76 | (D3) | 1 | 22.11.75 | **Altrincham** (NPL) | H | W | 3-1 | McHale 2 (1p), Rhodes |
| | | 2 | 13.12.75 | **Stafford Rangers** (NPL) | A | W | 3-1 | McHale (p), Downes, Gwyther |
| | | 3 | 03.01.76 | **Ipswich Town** (D1) | A | L | 1-3 | McHale (p) |
| 1976-77 | (D4) | 1 | 20.11.76 | **Stafford Rangers** (NPL) | A | D | 0-0 | |
| | | 1r | 23.11.76 | **Stafford Rangers** | H | W | 1-0 | Phelan |
| | | 2 | 14.12.76 | **Preston North End** (D3) | H | W | 1-0 | Lawson |
| | | 3 | 08.01.77 | **Luton Town** (D2) | H | L | 0-1 | |
| 1977-78 | (D4) | 1 | 26.11.77 | **Chesterfield** (D3) | A | L | 0-1 | |
| 1978-79 | (D4) | 1 | 25.11.78 | **Carlisle Utd** (D3) | A | L | 0-1 | |
| 1979-80 | (D4) | 1 | 24.11.79 | **Scarborough** (APL) | H | W | 2-0 | Burke, Stafford |

| | | | | | | | | | |
|---|---|---|---|---|---|---|---|---|---|
| | | 2 | 15.12.79 | **Walsall** (D4) | A | D | 1-1 | Kennedy |
| | | 2r | 18.12.79 | **Walsall** | H | D | 1-1aet | Harris |
| | | 2 2r | 24.12.79 | **Walsall** | H | W | 2-0aet | Burke, Smith |
| | | 3 | 05.01.80 | **Manchester City** (D1) | H | W | 1-0 | Hendrie |
| | | 4 | 26.01.80 | **Bolton Wanderers** (D1) | A | L | 0-2 | |
| 1980-81 | (D4) | 1 | 22.11.80 | **Hull City** (D3) | A | L | 1-2 | Firth |
| 1981-82 | (D4) | 1 | 21.11.81 | **Peterborough Utd** (D4) | H | L | 0-3 | |
| 1982-83 | (D4) | 1 | 20.11.82 | **North Shields** (NL) | H | L | 0-1 | |
| 1983-84 | (D4) | 1 | 19.11.83 | **Whitby Town** (NL) | H | L | 2-3 | Ward, Evans |
| 1984-85 | (D4) | 1 | 17.11.84 | **Goole Town** (NPL) | H | W | 2-0 | Gallagher, Cook |
| | | 2 | 08.12.84 | **Burnley** (D3) | A | L | 1-3 | Gallagher |
| 1985-86 | (D4) | 1 | 16.11.85 | **Scunthorpe Utd** (D4) | H | L | 1-3 | Kendall |
| 1986-87 | (D4) | 1 | 15.11.86 | **Bolton Wanderers** (D3) | H | D | 1-1 | Longhurst |
| | | 1r | 18.11.86 | **Bolton Wanderers** | A | D | 1-1aet | Brown |
| | | 1 2r | 24.11.86 | **Bolton Wanderers** | H | L | 1-3 | Galloway |
| 1987-88 | (D4) | 1 | 14.11.87 | **Billingham S** (NL) | A | W | 4-2 | Black 2, Robinson, N Mattews |
| | | | | *played at Victoria Ground, Hartlepool* | | | | |
| | | 2 | 05.12.87 | **Grimsby Town** (D3) | A | D | 0-0 | |
| | | 2r | 08.12.87 | **Grimsby Town** | H | W | 2-0 | M Mathews, Thornber |
| | | 3 | 09.01.88 | **Nottingham Forest** (D1) | H | L | 0-4 | |
| 1988-89 | (D4) | 1 | 19.11.88 | **York City** (D4) | H | W | 1-0 | McPhllips |
| | | 2 | 10.12.88 | **Altrincham** (Conf) | A | W | 3-0 | W Barr, Allison 2 |
| | | 3 | 07.01.89 | **Kettering Town** (Conf) | A | D | 1-1 | Watson |
| | | 3r | 10.01.89 | **Kettering Town** | H | L | 2-3 | Bramhall, W Barr |
| 1989-90 | (D4) | 1 | 18.11.89 | **Stafford Rangers** (Conf) | A | W | 3-2 | Fleming, Horner 2 |
| | | 2 | 09.12.89 | **Darlington** (Conf) | A | L | 0-3 | |
| 1990-91 | (D4) | 1 | 17.11.90 | **Wrexham** (D4) | H | W | 3-2 | Norris, Graham. Juryeff |
| | | 2 | 11.12.90 | **Rotherham Utd** (D3) | A | D | 1-1 | Juryeff |
| | | 2r | 17.12.90 | **Rotherham Utd** | H | L | 1-2 | Norris |
| 1991-92 | (D4) | 1 | 16.11.91 | **Witton Albion** (Conf) | A | D | 1-1 | Hildesley |
| | | 1r | 27.11.91 | **Witton Albion** | H | L | 1-2aet | Richardson |
| 1992-93 | (D3) | 1 | 14.11.92 | **Marine** (NPL) | A | L | 1-4 | German |
| 1993-94 | (Conf) | 1 | 14.11.93 | **WBA** (D1) | H | W | 2-1 | Peake, D Saunders |
| | | 2 | 04.12.93 | **Stockport County** (D2) | A | L | 1-5 | Barr (p) |
| 1994-95 | (Conf) | 1 | 12.11.94 | **Runcorn** (Conf) | H | D | 1-1 | Kiwomya |
| | | 1r | 21.11.94 | **Runcorn** | A | W | 3-1aet | Lancaster 2, Lambert |
| | | 2 | 03.12.94 | **Mansfield Town** (D3) | H | D | 0-0 | |
| | | 2r | 13.12.94 | **Mansfield Town** | A | L | 1-2 | Lancaster |
| 1998-99 | (D3) | 1 | 13.11.98 | **Manchester City** (D2) | A | L | 0-3 | |
| 1999-00 | (D3) | 1 | 30.10.99 | **Doncaster Rovers** (Conf) | A | W | 2-0 | Tate, Paterson |
| | | 2 | 20.11.99 | **Reading** (D2) | A | D | 1-1 | Mitchell |
| | | 2r | 30.11.99 | **Reading** | H | L | 0-1 | |
| 2000-01 | (D3) | 1 | 18.11.00 | **Gateshead** (NPL) | H | L | 0-2 | |
| 2001-02 | (D3) | 1 | 17.11.01 | **Farnborough T** (Conf) | H | W | 2-1 | Middleton, Wood |
| | | 2 | 08.12.01 | **Stoke City** (D2) | H | D | 1-1 | Harsley |
| | | 2r | 12.12.01 | **Stoke City** | A | L | 0-3 | |

## HALLIWELL

*Formed 1877. Played at an open field near the Crofter's Arms, Halliwell, Bolton.*
*Entered FA Cup: 1882-83 – 1892-93.*

| | | | | | | | | |
|---|---|---|---|---|---|---|---|---|
| 1882-83 | 1 | 21.10.82 | **Great Lever** | H | W | 3-2 | Bell, Harper, Rhodes |
| | 2 | 02.12.82 | **Eagley** | A | L | 1-3 | Harper |
| 1883-84 | 1 | 13.10.83 | **Eagley** | H | L | 2-5 | |
| 1884-85 | 1 | 11.10.84 | **Lower Darwen** | A | L | 1-4 | |
| 1885-86 | 1 | 31.10.85 | **Fishwick Ramblers** | H | W | 2-1 | |
| | 2 | | Hurst | | | - | |
| | | | *Hurst scratched. Halliwell walkover* | | | | |
| | 3 | 19.12.85 | **South Shore** | H | L | 1-6 | |
| 1886-87 | 1 | | Blackburn Rovers | | | - | |
| | | | *Halliwell scratched. Blackburn Rovers walkover.* | | | | |
| 1887-88 | 1 | 15.10.87 | **Liverpool Stanley** | A | W | 5-1 | |
| | 2 | 05.11.87 | **Astley Bridge** | A | W | 4-0 | |

| | | | | | | | |
|---|---|---|---|---|---|---|---|
| | 3 | 03.12.87 | **Preston North End** | A | L | 0-4 | |
| 1888-89 | 1 | 02.02.89 | **Crewe Alexandra** | H | D | 2-2aet | Hewitson 2 |
| | 1r | 09.02.89 | **Crewe Alexandra** | A | W | 5-1 | McGuiness 2, Edge, Cross 2 |
| | 2 | 16.02.89 | **Birmingham St Georges** | H | L | 2-3 | Hay, Edge |
| 1890-91 | 1 | 17.01.91 | **Sheffield Wed** (FAll) | A | L | 0-12 | |

## HAMPSTEAD HEATHENS

*Formed 1869. One of the 15 original entrants in the 1871-72 season but did not enter the competition again. A junior club of the same name still plays in north London.*

| | | | | | | | |
|---|---|---|---|---|---|---|---|
| 1871-72 | 1 | | bye | | | | |
| | 2 | 23.12.71 | **Barnes** | A | D | 1-1 | Barker |
| | 2r | 06.01.72 | **Barnes** | H | W | 1-0 | Leach |
| | 3 | 27.01.72 | **Royal Engineers** | A | L | 0-3 | |

## HAMPTON & RICHMOND BOROUGH

*Formed 1920. First entered FA Cup: 1966-67. Members of the Isthmian League.*

| | | | | | | | |
|---|---|---|---|---|---|---|---|
| 2000-01 (IL) | 1 | 18.11.00 | **Barnet** (D3) | A | L | 1-2 | Maskell |

## HANOVER UNITED

*Formed 1873. Played at The Limes, in Barnes, south west London. The first club believed to have used the name 'United' in its title.*

| | | | | | | |
|---|---|---|---|---|---|---|
| 1879-80 | 1 | 08.11.79 | **Grey Friars** | A | L | 1-2 |
| 1880-81 | 1 | 06.11.80 | **West End** | A | L | 0-1 |
| 1881-82 | 1 | | bye | | | |
| | 2 | 26.11.81 | **Upton Park** | H | L | 1-3 |
| 1882-83 | 1 | 04.11.82 | **Mosquitoes** | H | W | 1-0 |
| | 2 | 02.12.82 | **Clapham Rovers** | A | L | 1-7 |
| 1883-84 | 1 | 03.11.83 | **Brentwood** | H | L | 1-6 |
| 1884-85 | 1 | 08.11.84 | **Reading Minster** | H | W | 1-0 |
| | 2 | 29.11.84 | **Old Foresters** | H | W | 2-1 |
| | 3 | 03.01.85 | **Chatham** | H | L | 0-2 |
| 1885-86 | 1 | 31.10.85 | **Romford (1876)** | H | D | 1-1 |
| | 1r | 07.11.85 | **Romford (1876)** | A | L | 0-3 |
| 1886-87 | 1 | 30.10.86 | **Old Wykehamists** | A | L | 0-3 |
| 1887-88 | 1 | 15.10.87 | **Old Carthusians** | A | L | 0-5 |

## HARLOW TOWN

*Formed 1879. First entered FA Cup: 1937-38. League clubs beaten: Southend United, Leicester City. Members of the Isthmian League.*

| | | | | | | | |
|---|---|---|---|---|---|---|---|
| 1979-80 (IL) | 1 | 24.11.79 | **Leytonstone-Ilford** (IL) | H | W | 2-1 | Twigg, Fairclough |
| | 2 | 15.12.79 | **Southend Utd** (D3) | A | D | 1-1 | Prosser |
| | 2r | 18.12.79 | **Southend Utd** | H | W | 1-0 | Mann |
| | 3 | 05.01.80 | **Leicester City** (D2) | A | D | 1-1 | Prosser |
| | 3r | 08.01.80 | **Leicester City** | H | W | 1-0 | Mackenzie |
| | 4 | 26.01.80 | **Watford** (D2) | A | L | 3-4 | Prosser, Mackenzie 2 |
| 1980-81 (IL) | 1 | 22.11.80 | **Charlton Athletic** (D3) | H | L | 0-2 | |
| 1981-82 (IL) | 1 | 21.11.81 | **Barnet** (APL) | H | D | 0-0 | |
| | 1r | 24.11.81 | **Barnet** | A | L | 0-1 | |
| 1991-92 (IL) | 1 | 16.11.91 | **Peterborough Utd** (D3) | A | L | 0-7 | |

## HARROGATE RAILWAY ATHLETIC

*Formed 1935. First entered FA Cup: 1954-55. Reached the First Round for the first time in 2002-03, as did their neighbours Harrogate Town. Members of the Northern Counties East League.*

| | | | | | | | |
|---|---|---|---|---|---|---|---|
| 2002-03 (NCoE) | 1 | 16.11.02 | **Slough Town** (IL) | A | W | 2-1 | Smith, Davey |
| | 2 | 08.12.02 | **Bristol City** (D2) | H | L | 1-3 | Davey |

## HARROGATE TOWN

*Formed 1919. First entered FA Cup: 1950-51, and coincidentally reached the First Round for the first time in 2002-03 along with neighbours Harrogate Railway Athletic. Members of the Northern Premier League.*

| | | | | | | | |
|---|---|---|---|---|---|---|---|
| 2002-03 (NPL) | 1 | 16.11.02 | **Farnborough T** (Conf) | A | L | 1-5 | Hunter |

## HARROW BOROUGH

*Formed 1933 as Roxonian FC. Harrow Town 1938. Harrow Borough 1966. First entered FA Cup in the 1939-40 season, abandoned after the Extra-Preliminary round, played on September 2, 1939, the day before World War Two was declared. For the record, Harrow lost 3-0 at home to Finchley. Members of the Isthmian League.*

| | | | | | | | |
|---|---|---|---|---|---|---|---|
| 1983-84 (IL) | 1 | 19.11.83 | **Yeovil Town** (APL) | A | W | 1-0 | Duck |
| | 2 | 10.12.83 | **Newport County** (D3) | H | L | 1-3 | Pearce |
| 2000-01 (IL) | 1 | 18.11.00 | **Wycombe W** (D2) | A | L | 0-3 | |

## HARROW CHEQUERS

*Formed 1865. One of the original entrants in the 1871-72 FA Cup but did not play a game in that competition or any other. Used the Kennington Oval for their home matches, but never managed to fulfil an FA Cup tie there. However the name of this obscure Victorian outfit has lived on in FA Cup folklore as Morton Peto Betts, the scorer of the first FA Cup final goal for Wanderers in 1872 used the pseudonym 'AH Chequer' (A Harrow Chequer) when he played for Wanderers in the final. Betts, a member of the cup's founding committee, was registered to play for Harrow in that competition before his team scratched, and, strictly speaking, should not have been allowed to appear for Wanderers in the later stages. He also played Test cricket once for England in 1877 and made a few appearances for Middlesex and Kent. All in his own name.*

| | | | |
|---|---|---|---|
| 1871-72 | 1 | Wanderers | - |
| | | *Harrow Chequers scratched. Wanderers walkover* | |
| 1874-75 | 1 | Civil Service | - |
| | | *Harrow Chequers scratched. Civil Service walkover* | |
| 1875-76 | 1 | Leyton FC | - |
| | | *Harrow Chequers scratched. Leyton FC walkover* | |

## HARTFORD ST JOHNS

*Formed 1876. Played at Hartford, near Northwich, Chesire. Entered the FA Cup: 1883-84 – 1888-89.*

| | | | | | | |
|---|---|---|---|---|---|---|
| 1883-84 | 1 | 10.11.83 | **Oswestry Town** | A | L | 0-7 |
| 1884-85 | 1 | 08.11.84 | **Macclesfield T** | A | L | 0-9 |
| 1885-86 | 1 | 24.10.85 | **Newtown** | H | L | 1-3 |
| 1886-87 | 1 | 23.10.86 | **Chirk** | A | L | 1-8 |

## HARTLEPOOL UNITED

*Formed 1908. First entered FA Cup: 1908-09. Hartlepools United, 1908-1968. Hartlepool 1968-1977; Hartlepool United 1977-present. FA Cup best performance: 4th round, 1955, 1978, 1989, 1993; Record FA Cup win: 10-1 v St Peters Albion, 4th qualifying round, 1923-24. Billy Smith scored seven of the 10 goals – five of them in the first half. In Competition Proper: 6-0 v North Shields, 1st round, 30.11.1946; Record FA Cup defeat: 0-6 v Manchester City, 3rd round, 03.01.1976; 0-6 v Port Vale, 1st round, 12.11.1994.*

**as Hartlepools Utd**

| | | | | | | | |
|---|---|---|---|---|---|---|---|
| 1908-09 (NEL) | | | 1q West Hartlepool (H) 2-1; 2q South Bank (A) 2-2; 2q r South Bank (H) 0-2 | | | | |
| 1909-10 (NEL) | | | 1q Wingate A (H) 6-3; 2q Darlington (H) 0-1 | | | | |
| 1910-11 (NEL) | | | P Horden A (H) 5-0; 1q Darlington (A) 1-1; 1qr Darlington (H) 0-1 | | | | |
| 1911-12 (NEL) | | | 4q North Shields A (A) 1-2 | | | | |
| 1912-13 (NEL) | | | 1q Houghton R (H) 3-1; 2q Wingate A (H) 4-1; 3q Sunderland R (H) 2-1; 4q Castleford Town (H) 1-0; 5q Gainsborough T (A) 0-4 | | | | |
| 1913-14 (NEL) | | | P Sunderland R (H) 0-0; Pr Sunderland R (A) 2-1; 1q Annfield Plain (H) 6-1; 2q Birtley (H) 4-0; 3q Horden A (H) 4-0; 4q Gateshead (H) 0-1 | | | | |
| 1914-15 (NEL) | | | 4q Bishop Auckland (H) 6-2; 5q Rochdale (A) 0-2 | | | | |
| 1919-20 (NEL) | | | 4q Bishop Auckland (A) 0-1 | | | | |
| 1920-21 (NEL) | | | P South Bank East End (H) 7-0; 1q Haverton Hill (A) 2-2; 1qr Haverton Hill (H) 0-0aet; 1q 2r Haverton Hill 1-0 at Ayresome Pk; 2q Scarborough T (A) 4-1; 3q Loftus A (H) 2-1; 4q Houghton R (H) 3-0; 5q Bishop Auckland (H) 1-1; 5q r Bishop Auckland (A) 5-0; 6q Swansea T (A) 0-3 | | | | |
| 1921-22 (3N) | | | 5q Stalybridge C (A) 0-2 | | | | |
| 1922-23 (3N) | | | 5q Durham C (A) 1-0; 6q Wrexham (A) 0-1 | | | | |
| 1923-24 (3N) | | | 4q St Peters Albion (H) 10-1; 5q Shildon (H) 3-1; 6q Ashington (A) 1-2 | | | | |
| 1924-25 (3N) | | | 4q Ashington (H) 0-0; 4qr Ashington (A) 0-2 Ashington disqualified – ineligible player; Hartlepools Utd re-instated; 5q Bishop Auckland (H) 2-0; 6q St Albans C (H) 4-0 | | | | |
| | 1 | 10.01.25 | **Newcastle Utd** (D1) | A | L | 1-4 | S Hardy |
| 1925-26 (3N) | 1 | 28.11.25 | **Blyth Spartans** (NEL) | A | D | 2-2 | S Hardy, Best |
| | 1r | 02.12.25 | **Blyth Spartans** | H | D | 1-1aet | C Hardy |
| | 1 2r | 07.12.25 | **Blyth Spartans** | | D | 1-1aet | Hunter |
| | | | *played at St James' Park* | | | | |

| | | | | | | | | |
|---|---|---|---|---|---|---|---|---|
| | | 1 3r | 09.12.25 | **Blyth Spartans** (NEL) | | L | 1-2 | Wensley |
| | | | | *played at Roker Park* | | | | |
| 1926-27 | (3N) | 1 | 27.11.26 | **Carlisle Utd** (NEL) | A | L | 2-6 | W Robinson, Craig |
| 1927-28 | (3N) | 1 | 26.11.27 | **Halifax Town** (3N) | A | L | 0-3 | |
| 1928-29 | (3N) | 1 | 24.11.28 | **Spennymoor Utd** (NEL) | A | L | 2-5 | T Mordue, Duncan og |
| 1929-30 | (3N) | 1 | 30.11.29 | **Scunthorpe Utd** (ML) | A | L | 0-1 | |
| 1930-31 | (3N) | 1 | 29.11.30 | **Stockport County** (3N) | H | L | 2-3 | Dickinson, Waller |
| 1931-32 | (3N) | 1 | 28.11.31 | **Chester** (3N) | A | L | 1-4 | Wigham |
| 1932-33 | (3N) | 1 | 26.11.32 | **Marine** (LCC) | A | W | 5-2 | Wigham 2, Thornton, Hewett, Dixon |
| | | 2 | 10.12.32 | **Walsall** (3N) | A | L | 1-2 | Thornton |
| 1933-34 | (3N) | 1 | 25.11.33 | **York City** (3N) | A | W | 3-2 | Hewitt, Redwell, Wigham |
| | | 2 | 09.12.33 | **Halifax Town** (3N) | A | D | 1-1 | Hardy |
| | | 2r | 13.12.33 | **Halifax Town** | H | L | 1-2aet | Pedwell |
| 1934-35 | (3N) | 1 | 24.11.34 | **Halifax Town** (3N) | A | D | 1-1 | Bonass |
| | | 1r | 28.11.34 | **Halifax Town** | H | W | 2-0 | Bonass, Lindsay |
| | | 2 | 08.12.34 | **Coventry City** (3S) | H | L | 0-4 | |
| 1935-36 | (3N) | 1 | 30.11.35 | **Mansfield Town** (3N) | A | W | 3-2 | Bonass, Robertson, Procter (p) |
| | | 2 | 14.12.35 | **Halifax Town** (3N) | A | D | 1-1 | Robertson |
| | | 2r | 18.12.35 | **Halifax Town** | H | D | 0-0aet | |
| | | 2 2r | 23.12.35 | **Halifax Town** | | W | 4-1aet | Wigham 3, Robertson |
| | | | | *played at St James' Park* | | | | |
| | | 3 | 04.01.36 | **Grimsby Town** (D1) | H | D | 0-0 | |
| | | 3r | 11.01.36 | **Grimsby Town** | A | L | 1-4 | Bonas |
| 1936-37 | (3N) | 1 | 28.11.36 | **Rotherham Utd** (3N) | A | D | 4-4 | Proctor (p), English, Self, Park |
| | | 1r | 02.12.36 | **Rotherham Utd** | H | W | 2-0 | Self, Scott |
| | | 2 | 12.12.36 | **Crewe Alexandra** (3N) | A | D | 1-1 | English |
| | | 2r | 16.12.36 | **Crewe Alexandra** | H | L | 1-2 | Self |
| 1937-38 | (3N) | 1 | 27.11.37 | **Southport** (3N) | H | W | 3-1 | Scott, English, Embleton |
| | | 2 | 11.12.37 | **Tranmere Rovers** (3N) | A | L | 1-3 | Hamilton og |
| 1938-39 | (3N) | 1 | 26.11.38 | **Accrington Stanley** (3N) | H | W | 2-1 | Woods, Self |
| | | 2 | 10.12.38 | **QPR** (3S) | H | L | 0-2 | |
| 1945-46 | (3N) | 1 1L | 17.11.45 | **Gateshead AFC** (3N) | H | L | 1-2 | McMahon |
| | | 1 2L | 24.11.45 | **Gateshead AFC** | A | L | 2-6 | Holland, McMahon |
| 1946-47 | (3N) | 1 | 30.11.46 | **North Shields** (NEL) | H | W | 6-0 | Sloan 4, Scott 2 |
| | | 2 | 14.12.46 | **Rochdale** (3N) | A | L | 1-6 | McMahon |
| 1947-48 | (3N) | 1 | 29.11.47 | **Darlington** (3N) | H | W | 1-0 | Isaac |
| | | 2 | 13.12.47 | **Brighton** (3S) | H | D | 1-1aet | Isaac |
| | | 2r | 20.12.47 | **Brighton** | A | L | 1-2 | Harden |
| 1948-49 | (3N) | 1 | 27.11.48 | **Chester** (3N) | H | L | 1-3 | Price |
| 1949-50 | (3N) | 1 | 26.11.49 | **Accrington Stanley** (3N) | A | W | 1-0 | Owens |
| | | 2 | 10.12.49 | **Norwich City** (3S) | H | D | 1-1 | Clarke |
| | | 2r | 15.12.49 | **Norwich City** | A | L | 1-5 | Harden |
| 1950-51 | (3N) | 1 | 25.11.50 | **Worcester City** (SL) | A | W | 4-1 | Burnett, Wildon, McGuigan 2 |
| | | 2 | 09.12.50 | **Oldham Athletic** (3N) | H | L | 1-2 | Stamper |
| 1951-52 | (3N) | 1 | 24.11.51 | **Rhyl** (CC) | H | W | 2-0 | Elder, Harden |
| | | 2 | 15.12.51 | **Watford** (3S) | A | W | 2-1 | McClure, Burnett |
| | | 3 | 12.01.52 | **Burnley** (D1) | A | L | 0-1 | |
| 1952-53 | (3N) | 1 | 22.11.52 | **Chester** (3N) | A | W | 1-0 | McClure |
| | | 2 | 06.12.52 | **Tranmere Rovers** (3N) | A | L | 1-2 | Elder |
| 1953-54 | (3N) | 1 | 21.11.53 | **Mansfield Town** (3N) | H | D | 1-1 | Willetts |
| | | 1r | 25.11.53 | **Mansfield Town** | A | W | 3-0 | Wildon, Richardson, W Linacre |
| | | 2 | 12.12.53 | **Northampton Town** (3S) | A | D | 1-1 | Harden |
| | | 2r | 16.12.53 | **Northampton Town** | H | W | 1-0aet | W Linacre |
| | | 3 | 09.01.54 | **Stoke City** (D2) | A | L | 2-6 | Richardson 2 |
| 1954-55 | (3N) | 1 | 20.11.54 | **Chesterfield** (3N) | H | W | 1-0 | Richardson |
| | | 2 | 11.12.54 | **Aldershot** (3S) | H | W | 4-0 | McGuigan 2, Richardson, Willetts |
| | | 3 | 08.01.55 | **Darlington** (3N) | H | D | 1-1 | Harden |
| | | 3r | 12.01.55 | **Darlington** | A | D | 2-2aet | Richardson 2 |
| | | 3 2r | 17.01.55 | **Darlington** | | W | 2-0 | Richardson, Newton |
| | | | | *played at Ayresome Park* | | | | |
| | | 4 | 29.01.55 | **Nottingham Forest** (D2) | H | D | 1-1 | Newton |
| | | 4r | 02.02.55 | **Nottingham Forest** | A | L | 1-2aet | Stamper |

| | | | | | | | |
|---|---|---|---|---|---|---|---|
| 1955-56 (3N) | 1 | 19.11.55 | **Gateshead AFC** (3N) | H | W | 3-0 | Luke 2, Lumley |
| | 2 | 10.12.55 | **Chesterfield** (3N) | A | W | 2-1 | Luke 2 |
| | 3 | 07.01.56 | **Chelsea** (D1) | H | L | 0-1 | |
| 1956-57 (3N) | 1 | 17.11.56 | **Selby Town** (YL) | H | W | 3-1 | Luke, Stamper, Robinson |
| | 2 | 08.12.56 | **Blyth Spartans** (NEL) | A | W | 1-0 | Johnson |
| | 3 | 05.01.57 | **Manchester Utd** (D1) | H | L | 3-4 | Stamper, Johnson, Newton |
| 1957-58 (3N) | 1 | 16.11.57 | **Prescot Cables** (LC) | H | W | 5-0 | Newton, P Thompson 4 |
| | 2 | 07.12.57 | **Stockport County** (3N) | A | L | 1-2 | Johnson |
| 1958-59 (D4) | 1 | 15.11.58 | **Rochdale** (D3) | H | D | 1-1 | Luke |
| | 1r | 19.11.58 | **Rochdale** | A | D | 3-3aet | Luke 2, Johnson |
| | 1 2r | 27.11.58 | **Rochdale** | | W | 2-1aet | Smith, Johnson |
| | | | *played at Old Trafford* | | | | |
| | 2 | 06.12.58 | **Barrow** (D4) | A | L | 0-2 | |
| 1959-60 (D4) | 1 | 14.11.59 | **Bury** (D3) | A | L | 0-5 | |
| 1960-61 (D4) | 1 | 05.11.60 | **Halifax Town** (D3) | A | L | 1-5 | Cooper |
| 1961-62 (D4) | 1 | 04.11.61 | **Blyth Spartans** (NCo) | H | W | 5-1 | Folland 3, Johnson, Parkes |
| | 2 | 25.11.61 | **Accrington Stanley** (D4) | H | W | 2-1 | Folland, McLean |
| | 3 | 06.01.62 | **Fulham** (D1) | A | L | 1-3 | Burlison |
| 1962-63 (D4) | 1 | 03.11.62 | **Carlisle Utd** (D3) | A | L | 1-2 | McConnell og |
| 1963-64 (D4) | 1 | 16.11.63 | **Lincoln City** (D4) | H | L | 0-1 | |
| 1964-65 (D4) | 1 | 14.11.64 | **Corby Town** (SL) | A | W | 3-1 | Entwistle 2, Fogarty (p) |
| | 2 | 05.12.64 | **Darlington** (D4) | H | D | 0-0 | |
| | 2r | 09.12.64 | **Darlington** | A | L | 1-4 | Fogarty |
| 1965-66 (D4) | 1 | 13.11.65 | **Workington** (D3) | H | W | 3-1 | McPheat 2, Brass |
| | 2 | 04.12.65 | **Wrexham** (D4) | H | W | 2-0 | Wright, Mulvaney |
| | 3 | 24.01.66 | **Huddersfield Town** (D2) | A | L | 1-3 | Thompson |
| 1966-67 (D4) | 1 | 26.11.66 | **Shrewsbury Town** (D3) | A | L | 2-5 | Phythian, Fogarty |
| 1967-68 (D4) | 1 | 09.12.67 | **Bury** (D3) | H | L | 2-3 | Bell, Wright |
| **as Hartlepool** | | | | | | | |
| 1968-69 (D3) | 1 | 16.11.68 | **Rotherham Utd** (D3) | H | D | 1-1 | Young |
| | 1r | 19.11.68 | **Rotherham Utd** | A | L | 0-3 | |
| 1969-70 (D4) | 1 | 15.11.69 | **North Shields** (NL) | H | W | 3-0 | Bell 2, Kirk |
| | 2 | 06.12.69 | **Wrexham** (D4) | H | L | 0-1 | |
| 1970-71 (D4) | 1 | 21.11.70 | **Rhyl** (CC) | A | L | 0-1 | |
| 1971-72 (D4) | 1 | 20.11.71 | **Scarborough** (NPL) | H | W | 6-1 | Ellis, Young 2, Warnock, Veart 2 |
| | 2 | 11.12.71 | **Boston Utd** (NPL) | A | L | 1-2 | Veart |
| 1972-73 (D4) | 1 | 18.11.72 | **Scunthorpe Utd** (D3) | H | D | 0-0 | |
| | 1r | 21.11.72 | **Scunthorpe Utd** | A | D | 0-0aet | |
| | 1 2r | 27.11.72 | **Scunthorpe Utd** | | L | 1-2aet | Veart |
| | | | *played at Roker Park* | | | | |
| 1973-74 (D4) | 1 | 24.11.73 | **Altrincham** (NPL) | A | L | 0-2 | |
| 1974-75 (D4) | 1 | 23.11.74 | **Bradford City** (D4) | H | W | 1-0 | Honour |
| | 2 | 14.12.74 | **Lincoln City** (D4) | H | D | 0-0 | |
| | 2r | 17.12.74 | **Lincoln City** | A | L | 0-1 | |
| 1975-76 (D4) | 1 | 22.11.75 | **Stockport County** (D4) | H | W | 3-0 | D Smith, McMahon, Potter |
| | 2 | 13.12.75 | **Marine** (CC) | A | D | 1-1 | Scaife |
| | 2r | 15.12.75 | **Marine** | H | W | 6-3 | Moore 3, Johnson (p), Rowlands, Scaife |
| | 3 | 03.01.76 | **Manchester City** (D1) | A | L | 0-6 | |
| 1976-77 (D4) | 1 | 20.11.76 | **Chester** (D3) | A | L | 0-1 | |
| **as Hartlepool Utd** | | | | | | | |
| 1977-78 (D4) | 1 | 26.11.77 | **Tranmere Rovers** (D3) | A | D | 1-1 | T Smith |
| | 1r | 29.11.77 | **Tranmere Rovers** | H | W | 3-1 | Newton, Ayre, Bielby |
| | 2 | 17.12.77 | **Runcorn** (NPL) | H | W | 4-2 | Bielby, Newton 2, Poskett (p) |
| | 3 | 07.01.78 | **Crystal Palace** (D2) | H | W | 2-1 | Newton 2 |
| | 4 | 28.01.78 | **Ipswich Town** (D1) | A | L | 1-4 | Downing |
| 1978-79 (D4) | 1 | 25.11.78 | **Grimsby Town** (D4) | H | W | 1-0 | Goldthorpe |
| | 2 | 16.12.78 | **Crewe Alexandra** (D4) | A | W | 1-0 | Crumplin |
| | 3 | 18.01.79 | **Leeds Utd** (D1) | H | L | 2-6 | Newton 2 (2ps) |
| 1979-80 (D4) | 1 | 24.11.79 | **Barnsley** (D3) | A | L | 2-5 | J Linacre, Newton |
| 1980-81 (D4) | 1 | 22.11.80 | **Scunthorpe Utd** (D4) | A | L | 1-3 | Hampton |

| | | | | | | | |
|---|---|---|---|---|---|---|---|
| 1981-82 (D4) | 1 | 21.11.81 | **Wigan Athletic** (D4) | A | D | 2-2 | P Linacre, Newton |
| | 1r | 25.11.81 | **Wigan Athletic** | H | W | 1-0 | Newton |
| | 2 | 04.01.82 | **Hull City** (D4) | A | L | 0-2 | |
| 1982-83 (D4) | 1 | 20.11.83 | **Lincoln City** (D3) | H | W | 3-0 | P Linacre 2, Hogan |
| | 2 | 11.12.82 | **York City** (D4) | H | D | 1-1 | Dobson |
| | 2r | 14.12.82 | **York City** | A | L | 0-4 | |
| 1983-84 (D4) | 1 | 19.11.83 | **Rotherham Utd** (D3) | A | D | 0-0 | |
| | 1r | 23.11.83 | **Rotherham Utd** | H | L | 0-1aet | |
| 1984-85 (D4) | 1 | 17.11.84 | **Derby County** (D3) | H | W | 2-1 | Taylor, Dixon |
| | 2 | 08.12.84 | **York City** (D3) | H | L | 0-2 | |
| 1985-86 (D4) | 1 | 16.11.85 | **Macclesfield T** (NPL) | A | W | 2-1 | Shoulder 2 |
| | 2 | 07.12.85 | **Frickley Athletic** (APL) | H | L | 0-1 | |
| 1986-87 (D4) | 1 | 15.11.86 | **Wrexham** (D4) | A | L | 1-2 | Hogan |
| 1987-88 (D4) | 1 | 14.11.87 | **Chorley** (NPL) | A | W | 2-0 | Gibb, Baker |
| | 2 | 05.12.87 | **York City** (D3) | A | D | 1-1 | Baker |
| | 2r | 09.12.87 | **York City** | H | W | 3-1 | Baker, Toman 2 |
| | 3 | 09.01.88 | **Luton Town** (D1) | H | L | 1-2 | Toman |
| 1988-89 (D4) | 1 | 19.11.88 | **Wigan Athletic** (D3) | H | W | 2-0 | Smith, Borthwick |
| | 2 | 10.12.88 | **Notts County** (D3) | H | W | 1-0 | Allon |
| | 3 | 07.01.89 | **Bristol City** (D3) | H | W | 1-0 | Baker (p) |
| | 4 | 28.01.89 | **Bournemouth** (D2) | H | D | 1-1 | Honour |
| | 4r | 31.01.89 | **Bournemouth** | A | L | 2-5 | Allon, Toman |
| 1989-90 (D4) | 1 | 18.11.89 | **Huddersfield Town** (D3) | H | L | 0-2 | |
| 1990-91 (D4) | 1 | 17.11.90 | **Runcorn** (Conf) | A | W | 3-0 | Allon 3 |
| | 2 | 08.12.90 | **Wigan Athletic** (D3) | A | L | 0-2 | |
| 1991-92 (D3) | 1 | 16.11.91 | **Shrewsbury Town** (D3) | H | W | 3-2 | Tinkler, Johnson, Baker (p) |
| | 2 | 17.12.91 | **Darlington** (D3) | A | W | 2-1 | Dalton, Honour |
| | 3 | 04.01.92 | **Ipswich Town** (D2) | A | D | 1-1 | Baker |
| | 3r | 15.01.92 | **Ipswich Town** | H | L | 0-2 | |
| 1992-93 (D2) | 1 | 14.11.92 | **Doncaster Rovers** (D3) | A | W | 2-1 | Johnrose, Saville (p) |
| | 2 | 06.12.92 | **Southport** (NPL) | H | W | 4-0 | Peverall, Saville 3 |
| | 3 | 02.01.93 | **Crystal Palace** (PL) | H | W | 1-0 | Saville (p) |
| | 4 | 23.01.93 | **Sheffield Utd** (PL) | A | L | 0-1 | |
| 1993-94 (D2) | 1 | 13.11.93 | **Macclesfield T** (Conf) | A | L | 0-2 | |
| 1994-95 (D3) | 1 | 12.11.94 | **Port Vale** (D1) | A | L | 0-6 | |
| 1995-96 (D3) | 1 | 11.11.95 | **Darlington** (D3) | H | L | 2-4 | Sloan, Halliday |
| 1996-97 (D3) | 1 | 16.11.96 | **York City** (D2) | H | D | 0-0 | |
| | 1r | 26.11.96 | **York City** | A | L | 0-3 | |
| 1997-98 (D3) | 1 | 15.11.97 | **Macclesfield T** (D3) | H | L | 2-4 | Breech, Pedersen |
| 1998-99 (D3) | 1 | 14.11.98 | **Carlisle Utd** (D3) | H | W | 2-1 | Howard, Miller |
| | 2 | 05.12.98 | **Fulham** (D2) | A | L | 2-4 | Midgley, Howard |
| 1999-00 (D3) | 1 | 31.10.99 | **Millwall** (D2) | H | W | 1-0 | Jones |
| | 2 | 21.11.99 | **Hereford Utd** (Conf) | A | L | 0-1 | |
| 2000-01 (D3) | 1 | 18.11.00 | **Scunthorpe Utd** (D3) | A | L | 1-3 | Midgley |
| 2001-02 (D3) | 1 | 17.11.01 | **Swindon Town** (D2) | A | L | 1-3 | Clarke |
| 2002-03 (D3) | 1 | 16.11.02 | **Southend Utd** (D3) | A | D | 1-1 | Barron |
| | 1r | 26.11.02 | **Southend Utd** | H | L | 1-2 | Richardson |

## HARWICH & PARKESTON

*Formed 1875. First entered FA Cup: 1898-99. FA Amateur Cup runners-up: 1899, 1953. Members of the Eastern Counties League.*

| | | | | | | | |
|---|---|---|---|---|---|---|---|
| 1934-35 (ECL) | 1 | 24.11.34 | **Bristol Rovers** (3S) | A | L | 0-3 | |
| 1936-37 (ECL) | 1 | 28.11.36 | **Bournemouth** (3S) | A | L | 1-5 | W Ceasar |
| 1953-54 (ECL) | 1 | 21.11.53 | **Headington Utd** (SL) | H | L | 2-3 | McDonagh, Pearson |
| 1961-62 (ECL) | 1 | 04.11.61 | **Torquay Utd** (D3) | A | L | 1-5 | Sanderson |
| 1963-64 (ECL) | 1 | 16.11.63 | **Crystal Palace** (D3) | A | L | 2-8 | Stevens 2 |
| 1976-77 (IL) | 1 | 20.11.76 | **Enfield** (IL) | A | D | 0-0 | |
| | 1r | 23.11.76 | **Enfield** | H | L | 0-3 | |

## HASLINGDEN

*Formed 1876. Played at Rye Hill, Haslingden, Lancashire.*

| | | | | | | | |
|---|---|---|---|---|---|---|---|
| 1882-83 | 1 | | bye | | | | |
| | 2 | 02.12.82 | **Darwen Ramblers** | A | L | 2-3 | |

## HASTINGS & ST LEONARDS

*Formed 1898 as St Leonards United. Hastings and St Leonards 1906. Hastings Town 1980. First entered FA Cup: 1901-02. A separate club from Hastings United (see below), but now known as Hastings United themselves. Members of the Southern League.*

| | | | | | | | | |
|---|---|---|---|---|---|---|---|---|
| 1906-07 | (SL) | 1 | 12.01.07 | **Norwich City** (SL) | A | L | 1-3 | Beney |
| 1907-08 | (SL) | 1 | 11.01.08 | **Portsmouth** (SL) | H | L | 0-1 | |
| 1908-09 | (SL) | 1 | 16.01.09 | **Blackpool** (D2) | A | L | 0-2 | |

## HASTINGS UNITED

*Formed 1948. First entered FA Cup: 1949-50. Folded with debts of £92,000 in 1985. League club beaten: Swindon Town. Later reformed and now members of the Southern League. The 'new' Hastings United now claims its starting date as that of the old Hastings & St Leonards club.*

| | | | | | | | | |
|---|---|---|---|---|---|---|---|---|
| 1949-50 | (SL) | 1 | 26.11.49 | **Gillingham** (SL) | H | L | 1-3 | Moore |
| 1953-54 | (SL) | 1 | 21.11.53 | **Guildford City** (SL) | H | W | 1-0 | Hillman |
| | | 2 | 12.12.53 | **Swindon Town** (3S) | H | W | 4-1 | Hunt og, Huckstepp, Asher, Hillman |
| | | 3 | 09.01.54 | **Norwich City** (3S) | H | D | 3-3 | Parks 2, Girling |
| | | 3r | 13.01.54 | **Norwich City** (3S) | A | L | 0-3 | |
| 1954-55 | (SL) | 1 | 20.11.54 | **Hounslow Town** (CRN) | A | W | 4-2 | Burgess 2, Parks, Asher |
| | | 2 | 11.12.54 | **Selby Town** (YL) | A | W | 2-0 | Girling, Asher |
| | | 3 | 08.01.55 | **Sheffield Wed** (D1) | A | L | 1-2 | Asher |
| 1955-56 | (SL) | 1 | 19.11.55 | **Southall** (AL) | H | W | 6-1 | Burgess 2, Parks 2, Asher 2 (1p) |
| | | 2 | 10.12.55 | **Northampton Town** (3S) | A | L | 1-4 | Asher |
| 1956-57 | (SL) | 1 | 17.11.56 | **Ipswich Town** (3S) | A | L | 0-4 | |
| 1959-60 | (SL) | 1 | 14.11.59 | **Notts County** (D4) | H | L | 1-2 | McCorkindale |
| 1960-61 | (SL) | 1 | 05.11.60 | **Northampton Town** (D4) | A | L | 1-2 | Smith |
| 1981-82 | (SL) | 1 | 21.11.81 | **Enfield** (APL) | A | L | 0-2 | |
| 2002-03 | (SL) | 1 | 16.11.02 | **Stevenage B** (Conf) | A | L | 0-1 | |

## HAVANT & WATERLOOVILLE

*Formed 1998 by the merger of Havant Town and Waterlooville, two clubs with roots stretching back more than 100 years. The merged club first entered the FA Cup in 1998-99. Members of the Southern League. See also Waterlooville.*

| | | | | | | | | |
|---|---|---|---|---|---|---|---|---|
| 2000-01 | (SL) | 1 | 18.11.00 | **Southport** (Conf) | H | L | 1-2 | Wood |
| 2002-03 | (SL) | 1 | 16.11.02 | **Dagenham & Red** (Conf) | A | L | 2-3 | Haughton 2 |

## HAWKS

*Southern-based amateurs who played these three FA Cup matches before swooping off into the mists of time.*

| | | | | | | | | |
|---|---|---|---|---|---|---|---|---|
| 1877-78 | | 1 | 03.11.77 | **Minerva** | H | W | 5-2 | JR Fox, J Hamilton, Pitman, Ram, Rumball |
| | | 2 | 22.12.77 | **Remnants** | A | L | 0-2 | |
| 1878-79 | | 1 | 09.11.78 | **Swifts** | A | L | 1-2 | Ram |

## HAYES

*Formed 1909 as Botwell Mission. Hayes 1930. First entered FA Cup as Hayes: 1930-31. FA Amateur Cup runners-up: 1931. League clubs beaten: Bristol Rovers, Cardiff City, Fulham. Members of the Isthmian League.*

| | | | | | | | | |
|---|---|---|---|---|---|---|---|---|
| 1931-32 | (AL) | 1 | 28.11.31 | **Yeovil & Petters Utd** (SL) | A | L | 1-3 | Caesar |
| 1933-34 | (AL) | 1 | 25.11.33 | **Bournemouth** (3S) | A | L | 0-3 | |
| 1938-39 | (AL) | 1 | 26.11.38 | **Clapton Orient** (3S) | A | L | 1-3 | Ward |
| 1946-47 | (AL) | 1 | 30.11.46 | **Bristol City** (3S) | A | L | 3-9 | Dowse, Crout, Nolan |
| 1964-65 | (AL) | 1 | 14.11.64 | **Exeter City** (D3) | A | L | 0-1 | |
| 1972-73 | (IL) | 1 | 18.11.72 | **Bristol Rovers** (D3) | H | W | 1-0 | Hatt |
| | | 2 | 09.12.72 | **Reading** (D4) | A | D | 0-0 | |
| | | 2r | 11.12.72 | **Reading** | H | L | 0-1 | |
| 1973-74 | (IL) | 1 | 24.11.73 | **Boston Utd** (NPL) | A | D | 0-0 | |
| | | 1r | 28.11.73 | **Boston Utd** | H | L | 1-2aet | Hutchinson |
| 1987-88 | (IL) | 1 | 14.11.87 | **Swansea City** (D4) | H | L | 0-1 | |
| 1988-89 | (IL) | 1 | 19.11.88 | **Aldershot** (D3) | A | L | 0-1 | |
| 1989-90 | (IL) | 1 | 18.11.89 | **Peterborough Utd** (D4) | A | D | 1-1 | Barrowcliffe |
| | | 1r | 21.11.89 | **Peterborough Utd** | H | L | 0-1 | |
| 1990-91 | (IL) | 1 | 17.11.90 | **Cardiff City** (D4) | A | D | 0-0 | |
| | | 1r | 21.11.90 | **Cardiff City** *played at Griffin Park* | H | W | 1-0 | Clarke |

| | | | | | | | | |
|---|---|---|---|---|---|---|---|---|
| | | 2 | 08.12.90 | **Bournemouth** (D3) | A | L | 0-1 | |
| 1991-92 | (IL) | 1 | 15.11.91 | **Fulham** (D3) | A | W | 2-0 | Day, Stephen |
| | | 2 | 07.12.91 | **Crawley Town** (SL) | H | L | 0-2 | |
| 1992-93 | (IL) | 1 | 14.11.92 | **Brighton** (D2) | A | L | 0-2 | |
| 1995-96 | (IL) | 1 | 11.11.95 | **Northampton Town** (D3) | A | L | 0-1 | |
| 1996-97 | (Conf) | 1 | 16.11.96 | **Stevenage Boro** (Conf) | A | D | 2-2 | Williams, Haynes |
| | | 1r | 26.11.96 | **Stevenage Boro** | H | L | 0-2 | |
| 1997-98 | (Conf) | 1 | 15.11.97 | **Borehamwood** (IL) | H | L | 0-1 | |
| 1998-99 | (Conf) | 1 | 14.11.98 | **Mansfield Town** (D3) | A | L | 1-2 | Flynn |
| 1999-00 | (Conf) | 1 | 30.10.99 | **Runcorn** (NPL) | H | W | 2-1 | Bunce, Charles (p) |
| | | 2 | 20.11.99 | **Hull City** (D3) | H | D | 2-2 | Charles 2(1p) |
| | | 2r | 30.11.99 | **Hull City** | A | L | 2-3aet | Gallen, Charles |
| 2000-01 | (Conf) | 1 | 18.11.00 | **Dagenham & Red** (Conf) | A | L | 1-3 | Boylan |
| 2001-02 | (Conf) | 1 | 16.11.01 | **Wycombe W** (D2) | H | L | 3-4 | K Warner, Clark (p), D Warner |

## HEANOR TOWN

*Formed 1883. First entered FA Cup: 1889-90. Members of the Central Midlands League.*

| | | | | | | | | |
|---|---|---|---|---|---|---|---|---|
| 1891-92 | | 1 | 16.01.92 | **Aston Villa** (D1) | A | L | 1-4 | Shepherd |
| 1893-94 | | 1 | 27.01.94 | **Nottingham Forest** (D1) | A | L | 0-1aet | |
| 1896-97 | (ML) | 1 | 30.01.97 | **Soton St Marys** (SL) | A | D | 1-1 | McCallum |
| | | 1r | 03.02.97 | **Soton St Marys** | H | L | 0-1 | |
| 1898-99 | (ML) | 1 | 28.01.99 | **Bury** (D1) | H | L | 0-3 | |
| 1958-59 | (CA) | 1 | 15.11.58 | **Carlisle Utd** (D4) | H | L | 1-5 | Johnston |
| 1963-64 | (ML) | 1 | 16.11.63 | **Bradford Park A** (D4) | A | L | 1-3 | Fidler |

## HEART OF MIDLOTHIAN

*Formed 1874. Competed in FA Cup: 1885-86 – 1886-87. Scottish FA Cup winners 5 times. One of the seven Scottish clubs that played in the FA Cup in the 1880s.*

| | | | | | | | | |
|---|---|---|---|---|---|---|---|---|
| 1885-86 | | 1 | | Padiham | - | | | |
| | | | | *Hearts scratched. Padiham walkover* | | | | |
| 1886-87 | | 1 | 30.10.86 | **Darwen** | A | L | 1-7 | McKay |

## HEDNESFORD TOWN

*Formed 1880. First entered FA Cup: 1890-91. Welsh FA Cup runners-up: 1992. League clubs beaten: Blackpool, York City, Hull City, Barnet. Members of the Southern League.*

| | | | | | | | | |
|---|---|---|---|---|---|---|---|---|
| 1919-20 | (BDL) | 1 | 10.01.20 | **Castleford Town** (ML) | A | L | 0-2 | |
| 1996-97 | (Conf) | 1 | 16.11.96 | **Southport** (Conf) | H | W | 2-1 | Russell, O'Connor |
| | | 2 | 07.12.96 | **Blackpool** (D2) | A | W | 1-0 | O'Connor |
| | | 3 | 13.01.97 | **York City** (D2) | H | W | 1-0 | Russell (p) |
| | | 4 | 25.01.97 | **Middlesbrough** (PL) | H | L | 2-3 | O'Connor 2 |
| | | | | *played at Riverside Stadium* | | | | |
| 1997-98 | (Conf) | 1 | 15.11.97 | **Hull City** (D3) | A | W | 2-0 | Norbury (p), O'Connor |
| | | 2 | 06.12.97 | **Darlington** (D3) | H | L | 0-1 | |
| 1998-99 | (Conf) | 1 | 14.11.98 | **Barnet** (D3) | H | W | 3-1 | Davis, Kimmins, Carty |
| | | 2 | 05.12.98 | **Cardiff City** (D3) | A | L | 1-3 | Carty |
| 1999-00 | (Conf) | 1 | 30.10.99 | **Aldershot Town** (IL) | A | D | 1-1 | Robinson |
| | | 1r | 08.11.99 | **Aldershot Town** | H | L | 1-2 | Lake |
| 2000-01 | (Conf) | 1 | 18.11.00 | **Oldham Athletic** (D2) | H | L | 2-4 | Pointon, Davis |

## HENDON

*Formed 1908 as Hampstead Town. Golders Green 1933-46. Hendon 1946. No connection with the earlier Hendon club who competed in the FA Cup in the 19th century. First entered FA Cup: 1925-26. FA Amateur Cup winners: 1960, 1965, 1972. Runners-up: 1955, 1966. Denis and Leslie Compton, who played for Arsenal in the 1950 FA Cup final both started their careers at Hendon. League clubs beaten: Reading, Leyton Orient. Members of the Isthmian League.*

**as Golders Green**

| | | | | | | | | |
|---|---|---|---|---|---|---|---|---|
| 1934-35 | (AL) | 1 | 24.11.34 | **Southend Utd** (3S) | A | L | 1-10 | Drinkwater |

**as Hendon**

| | | | | | | | | |
|---|---|---|---|---|---|---|---|---|
| 1952-53 | (AL) | 1 | 22.11.52 | **Northampton Town** (3S) | H | D | 0-0 | |
| | | 1r | 27.11.52 | **Northampton Town** | A | L | 0-2 | |
| 1955-56 | (AL) | 1 | 19.11.55 | **Halesowen Town** (BDL) | A | W | 4-2 | Matthews, Rawlings, Spector, Edwards |

| | | | | | | | |
|---|---|---|---|---|---|---|---|
| | 2 | 10.12.55 | **Exeter City** (3S) | A | L | 2-6 | Spector, Avis |
| 1960-61 (AL) | 1 | 05.11.60 | **Oxford Utd** (SL) | H | D | 2-2 | Spector, Figg |
| | 1r | 09.11.60 | **Oxford Utd** | A | L | 2-3 | Quail, Howard |
| 1964-65 (IL) | 1 | 14.11.64 | **Port Vale** (D3) | A | L | 1-2 | Hyde |
| 1965-66 (IL) | 1 | 13.11.65 | **Grantham Town** (ML) | A | L | 1-4 | Hyde |
| 1966-67 (IL) | 1 | 26.11.66 | **Reading** (D3) | H | L | 1-3 | Ashworth |
| 1969-70 (IL) | 1 | 15.11.69 | **Carshalton Athletic** (AL) | H | W | 5-3 | Baker 2, Collett 2, Anderson |
| | 2 | 06.12.69 | **Brentwood Town** (SL) | H | L | 0-2 | |
| 1970-71 (IL) | 1 | 21.11.70 | **Aldershot** (D4) | H | L | 0-2 | |
| 1972-73 (IL) | 1 | 18.11.72 | **Plymouth Argyle** (D3) | A | L | 0-1 | |
| 1973-74 (IL) | 1 | 24.11.73 | **Leytonstone** (IL) | H | W | 3-0 | Somers 2, Baker |
| | 2 | 15.12.73 | **Merthyr Tydfil** (SL) | A | W | 3-0 | Baker, Phillips, Somers |
| | 3 | 05.01.74 | **Newcastle Utd** (D1) | A | D | 1-1 | Haider |
| | 3r | 09.01.74 | **Newcastle Utd** | H | L | 0-4 | |
| | | | *played at Vicarage Road* | | | | |
| 1975-76 (IL) | 1 | 22.11.75 | **Reading** (D4) | H | W | 1-0 | Phillips |
| | 2 | 13.12.75 | **Swindon Town** (D3) | H | L | 0-1 | |
| 1977-78 (IL) | 1 | 26.11.77 | **Watford** (D4) | A | L | 0-2 | |
| 1981-82 (IL) | 1 | 21.11.81 | **Wycombe W** (IL) | H | D | 1-1 | Bennett |
| | 1r | 24.11.81 | **Wycombe W** | A | L | 0-2 | |
| 1988-89 (IL) | 1 | 19.11.88 | **Reading** (D3) | A | L | 2-4 | Keen, Dowie |
| 1996-97 (IL) | 1 | 16.11.96 | **Cardiff City** (D3) | A | L | 0-2 | |
| 1997-98 (IL) | 1 | 15.11.97 | **Leyton Orient** (D3) | H | D | 2-2 | Simpson 2 |
| | 1r | 25.11.97 | **Leyton Orient** | A | W | 1-0 | Lewis |
| | 2 | 06.12.97 | **Cardiff City** (D3) | A | L | 1-3 | Bashir |
| 1998-99 (IL) | 1 | 15.11.98 | **Notts County** (D2) | H | D | 0-0 | |
| | 1r | 01.12.98 | **Notts County** | A | L | 0-3 | |
| 1999-00 (IL) | 1 | 30.10.99 | **Bath City** (SL) | A | W | 2-0 | Gentle, Guentchev |
| | 2 | 20.11.99 | **Blackpool** (D2) | A | L | 0-2 | |

# HENDON (1874)

*Formed 1874. The original Hendon club played on open ground in Brent Street on land long ago re-developed first as the Rose and Crown pub which was demolished in 1970. A shopping precinct is now at the site.*

| | | | | | | | |
|---|---|---|---|---|---|---|---|
| 1877-78 | 1 | 03.11.77 | **Marlow** | A | L | 0-2 | |
| 1878-79 | 1 | 09.11.78 | **Reading** | A | L | 0-1 | |
| 1879-80 | 1 | 08.11.79 | **Old Foresters** | H | D | 1-1 | Williams |
| | 1r | 15.11.79 | **Old Foresters** | A | D | 2-2 | Buck, AN Other |
| | 1 2r | 22.11.79 | **Old Foresters** | H | W | 3-1 | Buck, HO Ince, Morice |
| | 2 | 20.12.79 | **Mosquitoes** | H | W | 7-1 | HO Ince 3, Morice, J Powell, R Powell, og |
| | 3 | | bye | | | | |
| | 4 | 14.02.80 | **Clapham Rovers** | A | L | 0-2 | |
| 1880-81 | 1 | 06.11.80 | **St Peters Institute** | A | W | 8-1 | |
| | 2 | 04.12.80 | **Old Etonians** | H | L | 0-2 | |
| 1881-82 | 1 | 29.10.81 | **Reading** | A | L | 0-5 | |
| 1882-83 | 1 | 04.11.82 | **West End** | A | W | 3-1 | |
| | 2 | 02.12.82 | **Chatham** | H | W | 2-1 | |
| | 3 | 06.01.83 | **South Reading** | H | W | 11-1 | Clarkson 3, A Redford 3, Coutts 2, Morton, Perry, 1 other |
| | 4 | 27.01.83 | **Marlow** | A | W | 3-0 | |
| | 5 | 03.02.83 | **Old Etonians** | H | L | 2-4 | |
| 1883-84 | 1 | 10.11.83 | **Old Etonians** | H | W | 3-2 | KP Wilson, AN Other 2 |
| | 2 | 01.12.83 | **Old Westminsters** | A | L | 1-2 | |
| 1884-85 | 1 | 08.11.84 | **Clapham Rovers** | A | D | 3-3 | |
| | 1r | 22.11.84 | **Clapham Rovers** | H | W | 6-0 | |
| | 2 | 06.12.84 | **Chatham** | A | L | 0-1 | |
| 1885-86 | 1 | 24.10.85 | **Clapton** | H | L | 0-4 | |
| 1886-87 | 1 | 30.10.86 | **London Caledonians** | H | L | 1-2 | |
| 1887-88 | 1 | 15.10.87 | **Old Harrovians** | H | L | 2-4 | |

# HENLEY FC

*Formed 1871. First entered FA Cup: 1879-80. Henley Town from 1913-14. Members of the Hellenic League.*

| | | | | | | | |
|---|---|---|---|---|---|---|---|
| 1879-80 | 1 | | Reading | | | - | |
| | | | *Reading scratched. Henley walkover* | | | | |
| | 2 | 29.11.79 | **Maidenhead** | H | L | 1-3 | Cooper |
| 1880-81 | 1 | 13.11.80 | **Weybridge Swallows** | A | L | 1-3 | |
| 1881-82 | 1 | 16.10.81 | **Maidenhead** | H | L | 0-2 | |
| 1884-85 | 1 | | bye | | | | |
| | 2 | 06.12.84 | **Old Westminsters** | A | L | 0-7 | |

# HEREFORD UNITED

*Formed 1924. First entered FA Cup: 1924-25. Members of the Football League: 1972-1997. Record FA Cup win: 11-0 v Thynnes Athletic, preliminary round, 1947-48. In Competition Proper: 6-1 v QPR, 2nd round, 07.12.57. Record FA Cup defeat: 2-7 v Arsenal, 3rd round replay, 22.01.1985. Welsh FA Cup winners 1990. League clubs beaten as a Non-League club: Exeter City, Aldershot, QPR, Millwall, Northampton Town (2), Newcastle United, Brighton, York City, Hartlepool United, Wrexham. Members of The Conference.*

| | | | | | | | |
|---|---|---|---|---|---|---|---|
| 1932-33 (BDL) | 1 | 26.11.32 | **Accrington Stanley** (3N) | A | L | 1-2 | Hann |
| 1948-49 (SL) | 1 | 27.11.48 | **Kidderminster H** (SL) | A | W | 3-0 | Hogben, C Thompson, Duggan |
| | 2 | 11.12.48 | **Exeter City** (3S) | A | L | 1-2 | Thompson |
| 1949-50 (SL) | 1 | 26.11.49 | **Bromsgrove Rovers** (BC) | H | W | 3-0 | Thompson, Clifford, Dymond |
| | 2 | 10.12.49 | **Weymouth** (SL) | A | L | 1-2 | Clifford |
| 1950-51 (SL) | 1 | 25.11.50 | **Bromsgrove Rovers** (BC) | A | W | 3-1 | Bowen, Duggan, Best |
| | 2 | 09.12.50 | **Newport County** (3S) | H | L | 0-3 | |
| 1951-52 (SL) | 1 | 24.11.51 | **Guildford City** (SL) | A | L | 1-4 | Allum |
| 1952-53 (SL) | 1 | 22.11.52 | **Leyton FC** (AL) | A | D | 0-0 | |
| | 1r | 27.11.52 | **Leyton FC** | H | W | 3-2 | Coulson 2, Bowen |
| | 2 | 06.12.52 | **Scunthorpe Utd** (3N) | H | D | 0-0 | |
| | 2r | 11.12.52 | **Scunthorpe Utd** | A | L | 1-2 | Thompson |
| 1953-54 (SL) | 1 | 21.11.53 | **Exeter City** (3S) | A | D | 1-1 | O'Hara |
| | 1r | 26.11.53 | **Exeter City** | H | W | 2-0 | O'Hara 2 |
| | 2 | 12.12.53 | **Wigan Athletic** (LC) | A | L | 1-4 | T Lewis |
| 1955-56 (SL) | 1 | 19.11.55 | **Swindon Town** (3S) | A | L | 0-4 | |
| 1956-57 (SL) | 1 | 17.11.56 | **Aldershot** (3S) | H | W | 3-2 | Bowen, Mulgrew, Williams |
| | 2 | 08.12.56 | **Southend Utd** (3S) | H | L | 2-3 | Bowen 2 |
| 1957-58 (SL) | 1 | 16.11.57 | **Newport (IOW)** (HL) | A | W | 3-0 | Beech, Williams 2 |
| | 2 | 07.12.57 | **QPR** (3S) | H | W | 6-1 | Horton 2 (2p), Beech, Clayton, Williams, Bowen |
| | 3 | 04.01.58 | **Sheffield Wed** (D1) | H | L | 0-3 | |
| 1958-59 (SL) | 1 | 15.11.58 | **Guildford City** (SL) | A | W | 2-1 | Morris, Hardiman |
| | 2 | 06.12.58 | **Newport County** (D3) | H | L | 0-2 | |
| 1959-60 (SL) | 1 | 14.11.59 | **Newport County** | A | L | 2-4 | Hardiman, Beech |
| 1960-61 (SL) | 1 | 05.11.60 | **Bridgwater Town** (WL) | A | L | 0-3 | |
| 1961-62 (SL) | 1 | 04.11.61 | **Bristol City** (D3) | A | D | 1-1 | Biggs |
| | 1r | 08.11.61 | **Bristol City** | H | L | 2-5 | Daniel, Smith |
| 1962-63 (SL) | 1 | 03.11.62 | **Crystal Palace** (D3) | A | L | 0-2 | |
| 1963-64 (SL) | 1 | 16.11.63 | **Newport County** (D4) | H | D | 1-1 | Dixon |
| | 1r | 18.11.63 | **Newport County** | A | L | 0-4 | |
| 1964-65 (SL) | 1 | 14.11.64 | **Oldham Athletic** (D3) | A | L | 0-4 | |
| 1965-66 (SL) | 1 | 13.11.65 | **Leytonstone** (IL) | A | W | 1-0 | Punter |
| | 2 | 04.12.65 | **Millwall** (D3) | H | W | 1-0 | Fogg |
| | 3 | 22.01.66 | **Bedford Town** (SL) | A | L | 1-2 | Fogg |
| 1966-67 (SL) | 1 | 26.11.66 | **Peterborough Utd** (D3) | A | L | 1-4 | Holliday |
| 1967-68 (SL) | 1 | 13.12.67 | **Barnet** (SL) | H | W | 3-2 | Cocker, Derrick, Timms |
| | 2 | 06.01.68 | **Watford** (D3) | A | L | 0-3 | |
| 1968-69 (SL) | 1 | 16.11.68 | **Torquay Utd** (D3) | H | D | 0-0 | |
| | 1r | 20.11.68 | **Torquay Utd** | A | L | 2-4 | Charles, Scarrott |
| 1969-70 (SL) | 1 | 15.11.69 | **Chelmsford City** (SL) | A | W | 2-1 | Tyler, Lewis |
| | 2 | 06.12.69 | **Newport County** (D4) | A | L | 1-2 | Punter |
| 1970-71 (SL) | 1 | 21.11.70 | **Northampton Town** (D4) | H | D | 2-2 | Jones, Owen |
| | 1r | 24.11.70 | **Northampton Town** | A | W | 2-1 | Meadows, Owen |
| | 2 | 12.12.70 | **Brighton** (D3) | H | L | 1-2 | Charles |
| 1971-72 (SL) | 1 | 20.11.71 | **King's Lynn** (SL) | A | D | 0-0 | |

| | | | | | | | | |
|---|---|---|---|---|---|---|---|---|
| | | 1r | 24.11.71 | **King's Lynn** | H | W | 1-0 | Gough |
| | | 2 | 11.12.71 | **Northampton Town** (D4) | H | D | 0-0 | |
| | | 2r | 14.12.71 | **Northampton Town** | A | D | 2-2aet | Tyler, Owen |
| | | 2 2r | 20.12.71 | **Northampton Town** *played at The Hawthorns* | | W | 2-1aet | Mallender, Tyler |
| | | 3 | 24.01.72 | **Newcastle Utd** (D1) | A | D | 2-2 | Addison, Owen |
| | | 3r | 05.02.72 | **Newcastle Utd** | H | W | 2-1aet | Radford, George |
| | | 4 | 09.02.72 | **West Ham Utd** (D1) | H | D | 0-0 | |
| | | 4r | 14.02.72 | **West Ham Utd** | A | L | 1-3 | Meadows |
| 1972-73 | (D4) | 1 | 18.11.72 | **Torquay Utd** (D4) | A | L | 0-3 | |
| 1973-74 | (D3) | 1 | 24.11.73 | **Torquay Utd** | H | W | 3-1 | Evans, Hinch, Owen |
| | | 2 | 15.12.73 | **Walton & H** (IL) | H | W | 3-0 | Hinch, Tyler, Jones |
| | | 3 | 05.01.74 | **West Ham Utd** (D1) | A | D | 1-1 | Redrobe |
| | | 3r | 09.01.74 | **West Ham Utd** | H | W | 2-1 | Naylor (p), Jones |
| | | 4 | 26.01.74 | **Bristol City** (D2) | H | L | 0-1 | |
| 1974-75 | (D3) | 1 | 26.11.74 | **Gillingham** (D3) | H | W | 1-0 | Tucker |
| | | 2 | 14.12.74 | **Cambridge Utd** (D4) | A | L | 0-2 | |
| 1975-76 | (D3) | 1 | 22.11.75 | **Torquay Utd** (D4) | H | W | 2-0 | Carter, Tucker |
| | | 2 | 13.12.75 | **Bournemouth** (D4) | A | D | 2-2 | McNeil, Tyler |
| | | 2r | 17.12.75 | **Bournemouth** | H | W | 2-0 | Layton, McNeil |
| | | 3 | 03.01.76 | **York City** (D2) | A | L | 1-2 | Layton |
| 1976-77 | (D2) | 3 | 08.01.77 | **Reading** (D3) | H | W | 1-0 | Briley |
| | | 4 | 29.01.77 | **Middlesbrough** (D1) | A | L | 0-4 | |
| 1977-78 | (D3) | 1 | 26.11.77 | **Wealdstone** (SL) | A | D | 0-0 | |
| | | 1r | 29.11.77 | **Wealdstone** | H | L | 2-3 | Sheedy, Davey |
| 1978-79 | (D4) | 1 | 25.11.78 | **Newport County** (D4) | H | L | 0-1 | |
| 1979-80 | (D4) | 1 | 24.11.79 | **Northampton Town** (D4) | H | W | 1-0 | Layton |
| | | 2 | 15.12.79 | **Aldershot** (D4) | H | L | 1-2 | McGrellis |
| 1980-81 | (D4) | 1 | 22.11.80 | **Southend Utd** (D4) | A | W | 1-0 | Jones |
| | | 2 | 13.12.80 | **Enfield** (IL) | A | L | 0-2 | |
| 1981-82 | (D4) | 1 | 21.11.81 | **Southend Utd** (D3) | H | W | 3-1 | Harvey, Laidlaw, Phillips |
| | | 2 | 02.01.82 | **Fulham** (D3) | H | W | 1-0 | Laidlaw |
| | | 3 | 06.01.82 | **Scunthorpe Utd** (D4) | A | D | 1-1 | Showers |
| | | 3r | 20.01.82 | **Scunthorpe Utd** | H | W | 4-1 | Showers, Harvey, Overson, Phillips |
| | | 4 | 23.01.82 | **Leicester City** (D2) | H | L | 0-1 | |
| 1982-83 | (D4) | 1 | 20.11.82 | **Portsmouth** (D3) | A | L | 1-4 | Showers |
| 1983-84 | (D4) | 1 | 19.11.83 | **Reading** (D4) | A | L | 0-2 | |
| 1984-85 | (D4) | 1 | 17.11.84 | **Farnborough T** (IL) | H | W | 3-0 | Kearns 2, Phillips |
| | | 2 | 08.12.84 | **Plymouth Argyle** (D3) | A | D | 0-0 | |
| | | 2r | 12.12.84 | **Plymouth Argyle** | H | W | 2-0 | Kearns, Phillips |
| | | 3 | 05.01.85 | **Arsenal** (D1) | H | D | 1-1 | Price |
| | | 3r | 22.01.85 | **Arsenal** | A | L | 2-7 | Kearns, Pejic |
| 1985-86 | (D4) | 1 | 16.11.85 | **Yeovil Town** (IL) | A | W | 4-2 | Carter 3, Kearns |
| | | 2 | 07.12.85 | **Reading** (D3) | A | L | 0-2 | |
| 1986-87 | (D4) | 1 | 15.11.86 | **Fulham** (D3) | H | D | 3-3 | Kearns, Wells, Spooner |
| | | 1r | 24.11.86 | **Fulham** | A | L | 0-4 | |
| 1987-88 | (D4) | 1 | 14.11.87 | **Barnet** (Conf) | A | W | 1-0 | Stant |
| | | 2 | 05.12.87 | **Colchester Utd** (D4) | A | L | 2-3 | Stant, Phillips |
| 1988-89 | (D4) | 1 | 19.11.88 | **Cardiff City** (D3) | A | L | 0-3 | |
| 1989-90 | (D4) | 1 | 18.11.89 | **Farnborough T** (Conf) | A | W | 1-0 | Peacock |
| | | 2 | 09.12.89 | **Merthyr Tydfil** (Conf) | H | W | 3-2 | Robinson, MA Jones, Tester |
| | | 3 | 06.01.90 | **Walsall** (D3) | H | W | 2-1 | M Jones (p), Pejic |
| | | 4 | 28.01.90 | **Manchester Utd** (D1) | H | L | 0-1 | |
| 1990-91 | (D4) | 1 | 17.11.90 | **Peterborough Utd** (D4) | H | D | 1-1 | Narbett |
| | | 1r | 20.11.90 | **Peterborough Utd** | A | L | 1-2 | Pejic |
| 1991-92 | (D4) | 1 | 16.11.91 | **Atherstone Utd** (SL) | A | D | 0-0 | |
| | | 1r | 26.11.91 | **Atherstone Utd** | H | W | 3-0 | Lowndes, Brain 2 |
| | | 2 | 07.12.91 | **Aylesbury Utd** (IL) | A | W | 3-2 | Fry, Heritage, Brain |
| | | 3 | 04.01.92 | **Woking** (IL) | A | D | 0-0 | |
| | | 3r | 14.01.92 | **Woking** | H | W | 2-1aet | Narbett, Brain |
| | | 4 | 26.01.92 | **Nottingham Forest** (D1) | A | L | 0-2 | |

| | | | | | | | | |
|---|---|---|---|---|---|---|---|---|
| 1992-93 | (D3) | 1 | 14.11.92 | **Sutton Utd** (IL) | A | W | 2-1 | Pickard, Barton og |
| | | 2 | 05.12.92 | **Yeovil Town** (Conf) | A | D | 0-0 | |
| | | 2r | 15.12.92 | **Yeovil Town** | H | L | 1-2 | Pickard |
| 1993-94 | (D3) | 1 | 14.11.93 | **Cambridge City** (SL) | A | W | 1-0 | Pike |
| | | 2 | 05.12.93 | **Bath City** (Conf) | A | L | 1-2 | Hall |
| 1994-95 | (D3) | 1 | 12.11.94 | **Hitchin Town** (IL) | H | D | 2-2 | Lyne 2 |
| | | 1r | 22.11.94 | **Hitchin Town** | A | L | 2-4 | White, Pick |
| 1995-96 | (D3) | 1 | 11.11.95 | **Stevenage Boro** (Conf) | H | W | 2-1 | White, Cross |
| | | 2 | 02.12.95 | **Sutton Utd** (IL) | H | W | 2-0 | White 2 |
| | | 3 | 06.01.96 | **Tottenham Hotspur** (PL) | H | D | 1-1 | Brough |
| | | 3r | 17.01.96 | **Tottenham Hotspur** | A | L | 1-5 | Stoker |
| 1996-97 | (D3) | 1 | 16.11.96 | **Gillingham** (D2) | A | L | 0-1 | |
| 1997-98 | (Conf) | 1 | 15.11.97 | **Brighton** (D3) | H | W | 2-1 | Grayson 2(1p) |
| | | 2 | 06.12.97 | **Colchester Utd** (D3) | A | D | 1-1 | Grayson |
| | | 2r | 16.12.97 | **Colchester Utd** | H | D | 1-1aet | Grayson |
| | | | | *Hereford Utd won 5-4 on penalties* | | | | |
| | | 3 | 13.01.98 | **Tranmere Rovers** (D1) | H | L | 0-3 | |
| 1999-00 | (Conf) | 1 | 30.10.99 | **York City** (D3) | H | W | 1-0 | D May |
| | | 2 | 21.11.99 | **Hartlepool Utd** (D3) | H | W | 1-0 | Elms |
| | | 3 | 11.12.99 | **Leicester City** (PL) | H | D | 0-0 | |
| | | 3r | 22.12.99 | **Leicester City** | A | L | 1-2aet | Fewings |
| 2001-02 | (Conf) | 1 | 18.11.01 | **Wrexham** (D2) | H | W | 1-0 | I Wright |
| | | 2 | 08.12.01 | **Swindon Town** (D2) | A | L | 2-3 | G Williams, I Wright |
| 2002-03 | (Conf) | 1 | 16.11.02 | **Wigan Athletic** (D2) | H | L | 0-1 | |

## HERTS RANGERS

*Formed about 1865, the premier club in Hertfordshire for a number of years and one of the forerunners of the modern Watford. Originally played in Langley Road, Watford, near the present-day Watford Junction Station. Entered FA Cup 1875-76 – 1881-82.*

| | | | | | | | |
|---|---|---|---|---|---|---|---|
| 1875-76 | 1 | 06.11.75 | **Rochester** | H | W | 4-0 | Day 2, Gilbert, Sparks |
| | 2 | 18.12.75 | **Oxford University** | A | L | 2-8 | Gilbert, AN Other |
| 1876-77 | 1 | 04.11.76 | **Marlow** | H | L | 1-2 | |
| 1877-78 | 1 | 03.11.77 | **Oxford University** | A | L | 2-5 | |
| 1878-79 | 1 | 09.11.78 | **Cambridge University** | A | L | 0-2 | |
| 1879-80 | 1 | 15.11.79 | **Minerva** | H | W | 2-1 | Hill 2 |
| | 2 | | Pilgrims | | | - | |
| | | | *Herts Rangers scratched. Pilgrims walkover* | | | | |
| 1880-81 | 1 | 06.11.80 | **Barnes** | H | W | 6-0 | |
| | 2 | | bye | | | | |
| | 3 | 05.02.81 | **Old Etonians** | H | L | 0-3 | |
| 1881-82 | 1 | 05.11.81 | **Swifts** | A | L | 0-4 | |

## HEYBRIDGE SWIFTS

*Formed 1880. First entered FA Cup: 1981-82. Members of the Isthmian League.*

| | | | | | | | |
|---|---|---|---|---|---|---|---|
| 1994-95 | (IL) | 1 | 11.11.94 | **Gillingham** (D3) | H | L | 0-2 |
| | | | | *played at Layer Road, Colchester* | | | |
| 1997-98 | (IL) | 1 | 15.11.97 | **Bournemouth** (D2) | A | L | 0-3 |
| 2002-03 | (IL) | 1 | 16.11.02 | **Bristol City** (D2) | H | L | 0-7 |

## HEYWOOD CENTRAL

*Formed 1887. Played at the Phoenix Pleasure Ground, near the Britannia Hotel, Heywood. Entered FA Cup: 1887-88 – 1894-95 but this was the only match they played in the Competition Proper.*

| | | | | | | |
|---|---|---|---|---|---|---|
| 1887-88 | 1 | 15.10.87 | **Higher Walton** | A | L | 1-8 |

## HIGH WYCOMBE

*Formed around 1870. A separate club from the later Wycombe Wanderers club formed in 1877. Entered FA Cup: 1873-74 – 1877-78. It is understood the founders of Wycombe Wanderers took their name after Wanderers visited the town and thrashed High Wycombe 9-0 in the last match the old club played in the competition.*

| | | | | | | |
|---|---|---|---|---|---|---|
| 1873-74 | 1 | | Old Etonians | | | - |
| | | | *Old Etonians scratched. High Wycombe walkover* | | | |
| | 2 | 22.11.73 | **Maidenhead** | A | L | 0-1 |
| 1874-75 | 1 | 31.10.74 | **Woodford Wells** | A | L | 0-1 |
| 1875-76 | 1 | 10.11.75 | **Royal Engineers** | A | L | 0-15 |

| | | | | | | | | |
|---|---|---|---|---|---|---|---|---|
| 1876-77 | | 1 | | Cambridge University | | | - | |
| | | | | *High Wycombe scratched. Cambridge walkover* | | | | |
| 1877-78 | | 1 | 27.10.77 | **Wood Grange** | H | W | 4-0 | Grange 2, Wellicombe, AN Other |
| | | 2 | 15.12.77 | **Wanderers** | H | L | 0-9 | |

# HIGHBURY UNION

*Formed 1873. Entered FA Cup: 1876-77 – 1882-83. North London-based amateurs who played at Highbury Place open space, less than half-a-mile from where Arsenal later moved from Woolwich.*

| | | | | | | | | |
|---|---|---|---|---|---|---|---|---|
| 1876-77 | | 1 | 04.11.76 | **Rochester** | A | L | 0-5 | |
| 1877-78 | | 1 | | Royal Engineers | | | - | |
| | | | | *Highbury scratched. Royal Engineers walkover* | | | | |
| 1881-82 | | 1 | 05.11.81 | **Hotspur FC** | A | L | 0-1 | |
| 1882-83 | | 1 | 04.11.82 | **Swifts** | A | L | 1-4 | |

# HIGHER WALTON

*Formed 1882. Played at the Higher Walton ground, near the Greyhound Hotel.*
*Entered FA Cup: 1884-85 – 1893-94.*

| | | | | | | | | |
|---|---|---|---|---|---|---|---|---|
| 1884-85 | | 1 | 11.10.84 | **Darwen Old Wanderers** | H | D | 1-1 | |
| | | 1r | 08.11.84 | **Darwen Old Wanderers** | A | L | 1-4 | |
| 1885-86 | | 1 | 17.10.85 | **South Shore** | H | L | 3-4 | |
| 1886-87 | | 1 | 16.10.86 | **Third Lanark** | A | L | 0-5 | |
| 1887-88 | | 1 | 15.10.87 | **Heywood Central** | H | W | 8-1 | |
| | | 2 | 05.11.87 | **Fleetwood Rangers** | A | W | 3-1 | |
| | | 3 | 26.11.87 | **Bootle** | H | L | 1-6 | |

# HILLINGDON BOROUGH

*Formed 1872 as Yiewsley FC. Hillingdon Borough 1964. Hillingdon 1983. Folded mid-1980s. Reformed 1990 as Hillingdon Borough. First entered FA Cup 1908-09. FA Trophy runners-up: 1971. Jackie Milburn, the legendary Newcastle United centre-forward who played in three FA Cup Finals in the 1950s was player-coach from 1961-63. League clubs beaten: Luton Town, Torquay United. Members of the South Midlands League.*

**as Yiewsley**

| | | | | | | | | |
|---|---|---|---|---|---|---|---|---|
| 1956-57 | (CRN) | 1 | 17.11.56 | **Gillingham** (3S) | H | D | 2-2 | Moore 2 |
| | | 1r | 20.11.56 | **Gillingham** | A | L | 0-2 | |

**as Hillingdon Borough**

| | | | | | | | | |
|---|---|---|---|---|---|---|---|---|
| 1969-70 | (SL) | 1 | 15.11.69 | **Wimbledon** (SL) | H | W | 2-0 | Carter, Vafiadis |
| | | 2 | 06.12.69 | **Luton Town** (D3) | H | W | 2-1 | Reeve, Townend |
| | | 3 | 06.01.70 | **Sutton Utd** (IL) | H | D | 0-0 | |
| | | 3r | 12.01.70 | **Sutton Utd** | A | L | 1-4 | Terry |
| 1971-72 | (SL) | 1 | 20.11.71 | **Brighton** (D3) | A | L | 1-7 | Bishop |
| 1972-73 | (SL) | 1 | 18.11.72 | **Chelmsford City** (SL) | A | L | 0-2 | |
| 1973-74 | (SL) | 1 | 24.11.73 | **Grantham Town** (SL) | H | L | 0-4 | |
| 1976-77 | (SL) | 1 | 20.11.76 | **Torquay Utd** (D4) | A | W | 2-1 | Metchick, Smith |
| | | 2 | 11.12.76 | **Watford** (D4) | H | L | 2-3 | Basey, Ryan |
| 1978-79 | (SL) | 1 | 25.11.78 | **Swansea City** (D3) | A | L | 1-4 | Williams |

# HINCKLEY ATHLETIC

*Formed 1879. First entered FA Cup: 1895-96. Hinckley Athletic merged with Hinckley Town (previously known as Westfield Rovers from 1958-66) to form Hinckley United 1997.*

| | | | | | | | | |
|---|---|---|---|---|---|---|---|---|
| 1954-55 | (WMRL) | 1 | 20.11.54 | **Newport (IOW)** (HL) | H | W | 4-3 | Grant, Burnett, Taulbutt og, Perry |
| | | 2 | 11.12.54 | **Rochdale** (3N) | A | L | 1-2 | Perry |
| 1962-63 | (SL) | 1 | 03.11.62 | **Sittingbourne** (SL) | H | W | 3-0 | S Round 2, Lockton |
| | | 2 | 24.11.62 | **QPR** (D3) | A | L | 2-7 | Asron, S Round |

# HINCKLEY UNITED

*Formed 1997 by the merger of Hinckley Athletic and Hinckley Town (see above). Members of the Southern League.*

| | | | | | | | | |
|---|---|---|---|---|---|---|---|---|
| 2001-02 | (SL) | 1 | 17.11.01 | **Grays Athletic** (IL) | A | W | 2-1 | Hunter, Lenton |
| | | 2 | 08.12.01 | **Cheltenham Town** (D3) | H | L | 0-2 | |

# HITCHIN TOWN

*Formed 1861. One of the 15 original entrants in the FA Cup in the 1871-72 season, their match against Crystal Palace on November 11, 1871 was the first-ever 0-0 draw in competitive soccer history. Under the bizarre rules governing that competition, the match was not replayed and both teams went through to the second round. It could be argued that there was a belated replay of that 1871 match after all. Hitchin played the modern Crystal*

*Palace 79 years later – and lost 6-2. Renamed Hitchin Town 1906. Reformed 1928. League clubs beaten: Hereford United, Bristol Rovers. Members of the Isthmian League.*

| | | | | | | | | |
|---|---|---|---|---|---|---|---|---|
| 1871-72 | | 1 | 11.11.71 | **Crystal Palace (1861)** | A | D | 0-0 | |
| | | | | *Both teams qualified for second round* | | | | |
| | | 2 | 10.01.72 | **Royal Engineers** | H | L | 0-5 | |
| 1872-73 | | 1 | | Clapham Rovers | | | - | |
| | | | | *Hitchin scratched. Clapham walkover* | | | | |
| 1874-75 | | 1 | 14.11.74 | **Maidenhead** | H | L | 0-1 | |
| 1875-76 | | 1 | | Clapham Rovers | | | - | |
| | | | | *Hitchin scratched. Clapham walkover* | | | | |
| 1887-88 | | 1 | 08.10.87 | **Old Wykehamists** | H | L | 2-5 | |
| 1953-54 | (AL) | 1 | 21.11.53 | **Peterborough Utd** (ML) | H | L | 1-3 | Hammond |
| 1958-59 | (AL) | 1 | 15.11.58 | **Millwall** (D4) | H | D | 1-1 | Hammond |
| | | 1r | 17.11.58 | **Millwall** | A | L | 1-2 | |
| 1960-61 | (AL) | 1 | 05.11.60 | **Crystal Palace** (D4) | A | L | 2-6 | Waldock, Randall |
| 1973-74 | (IL) | 1 | 24.11.73 | **Guildford City** (SL) | H | D | 1-1 | Kettleborough |
| | | 1r | 28.11.73 | **Guildford City** | A | W | 4-1 | Kettleborough 2, Martin, Giggle |
| | | 2 | 15.12.73 | **Boston Utd** (NPL) | A | L | 0-1 | |
| 1974-75 | (IL) | 1 | 23.11.74 | **Cambridge Utd** (D4) | H | D | 0-0 | |
| | | 1r | 26.11.74 | **Cambridge Utd** | A | L | 0-3 | |
| 1976-77 | (IL) | 1 | 20.11.76 | **Weymouth** (SL) | A | D | 1-1 | Watson |
| | | 1r | 23.11.76 | **Weymouth** | H | D | 2-2aet | Martin, Giggle |
| | | 1 2r | 29.11.76 | **Weymouth** | | D | 3-3aet | Watson 2, Mulkern |
| | | | | *played at Aldershot* | | | | |
| | | 1 3r | 02.12.76 | **Weymouth** (SL) | | W | 3-1 | Bunker, Watson 2 |
| | | | | *played at Salisbury* | | | | |
| | | 2 | 11.12.76 | **Swindon Town** (D3) | H | D | 1-1 | Bunker |
| | | 2r | 21.12.76 | **Swindon Town** | A | L | 1-3aet | Bunker |
| 1978-79 | (IL) | 1 | 25.11.78 | **Bournemouth** (D4) | A | L | 1-2 | Taylor |
| 1994-95 | (IL) | 1 | 12.11.94 | **Hereford Utd** (D3) | A | D | 2-2 | Marshall 2 |
| | | 1r | 22.11.94 | **Hereford Utd** | H | W | 4-2 | Bone, Williams, Wilson, Marshall |
| | | 2 | 03.12.94 | **Wycombe W** (D2) | H | L | 0-5 | |
| 1995-96 | (IL) | 1 | 11.11.95 | **Bristol Rovers** (D2) | H | W | 2-1 | Conroy, Burns |
| | | 2 | 02.12.95 | **Gillingham** (D3) | A | L | 0-3 | |

## HODDESDON TOWN

*Formed 1879. First entered FA Cup: 1884-85 and did not enter again until 1931-32. FA Vase winners: 1975 (first winners). Members of the South Midlands League.*

| | | | | | | | | |
|---|---|---|---|---|---|---|---|---|
| 1884-85 | | 1 | 01.11.84 | **Old Foresters** | A | L | 0-8 | |

## HOLBEACH UNITED

*Formed 1929. First entered FA Cup: 1938-39. Members of the United Counties League.*

| | | | | | | | | |
|---|---|---|---|---|---|---|---|---|
| 1982-83 | (UCL) | 1 | 20.11.82 | **Wrexham** (D3) | H | L | 0-4 | |
| | | | | *played at London Road, Peterborough* | | | | |

## HORDEN COLLIERY WELFARE

*Formed 1908 as Horden Athletic. Horden Colliery Welfare 1928. Reformed 1980. First entered FA Cup:1909-10. Based in Peterlee, County Durham. Members of the Northern League*

| | | | | | | | | |
|---|---|---|---|---|---|---|---|---|
| 1925-26 | (Wear) | 1 | 28.11.25 | **Darlington** (D2) | H | L | 2-3 | Temple 2 |
| 1938-39 | (NEL) | 1 | 26.11.38 | **Chorley** (LC) | H | D | 1-1 | Armes |
| | | 1r | 30.11.38 | **Chorley** | A | W | 2-1 | Armes 2 |
| | | 2 | 10.12.38 | **Newport County** (3S) | H | L | 2-3 | Low og, Dunmore |
| 1948-49 | (NEL) | 1 | 27.11.48 | **Southport** (3N) | A | L | 1-2 | W Hayward |
| 1952-53 | (NEL) | 1 | 22.11.52 | **Accrington Stanley** (3N) | H | L | 1-2 | Ivey |
| 1953-54 | (NEL) | 1 | 21.11.53 | **Wrexham** (3N) | H | L | 0-1 | |
| 1954-55 | (NEL) | 1 | 20.11.54 | **Scunthorpe Utd** (3N) | H | L | 0-1 | |
| 1981-82 | (NL) | 1 | 21.11.81 | **Blackpool** (D4) | H | L | 0-1 | |
| | | | | *played at Victoria Ground, Hartlepool* | | | | |

## HORNCASTLE

*Formed 1879. Played at The Wong Ground. Entered FA Cup: 1885-86 – 1888-89.*

| | | | | | | | | |
|---|---|---|---|---|---|---|---|---|
| 1885-86 | | 1 | | Middlesbrough | | | - | |
| | | | | *Horncastle scratched. Middlesbrough walkover* | | | | |

| | | | | | | | |
|---|---|---|---|---|---|---|---|
| 1886-87 | 1 | 30.10.86 | **Darlington** | H | W | 2-0 | Allen, J Turner |
| | 2 | | bye | | | | |
| | 3 | 09.12.86 | **Grantham Town** | H | W | 2-0 | |
| | 4 | | bye | | | | |
| | 5 | 05.02.87 | **Aston Villa** | A | L | 0-5 | |
| 1887-88 | 1 | 15.10.87 | **Lincoln City** | A | L | 1-4 | |

## HORNCHURCH

*Formed 1878. No connection with the modern Hornchurch FC (1923) which plays in the Isthmian League. This Hornchurch club entered the FA Cup twice and decided enough was enough after the 9-0 spanking from Marlow.*

| | | | | | | | |
|---|---|---|---|---|---|---|---|
| 1882-83 | 1 | 28.10.82 | **Marlow** | A | L | 0-2 | |
| 1883-84 | 1 | 10.11.83 | **Marlow** | H | L | 0-9 | |

## HORSHAM

*Formed 1885. First entered FA Cup: 1903-04. Members of the Isthmian League.*

| | | | | | | | |
|---|---|---|---|---|---|---|---|
| 1947-48 (SCL) | 1 | 29.11.47 | **Notts County** (3S) | A | L | 1-9 | Smallwood |
| 1966-67 (AL) | 1 | 26.11.66 | **Swindon Town** (D3) | H | L | 0-3 | |

## HORWICH RMI

*Formed 1896. Entered FA Cup: 1914-15 – 1994-95. Changed name to Leigh RMI 1995. See Leigh RMI.*

| | | | | | | | |
|---|---|---|---|---|---|---|---|
| 1928-29 (LC) | 1 | 24.11.28 | **Scarborough** (ML) | H | L | 1-2 | Keetley |
| 1982-83 (NWC) | 1 | 20.11.82 | **Blackpool** (D4) | A | L | 0-3 | |

## HOTSPUR FC

*Formed 1878. Ironically in the light of the subsequent development of football in north London, they played most of their matches in the Highbury area. How close they were to calling themselves Highbury Hotspur we shall never know. No connection with the modern day Tottenham Hotspur (formed in 1882). Entered FA Cup: 1879-80 – 1887-88.*

| | | | | | | | |
|---|---|---|---|---|---|---|---|
| 1879-80 | 1 | 08.11.79 | **Argonauts** | H | D | 1-1 | Winter |
| | 1r | 15.11.79 | **Argonauts** | A | W | 1-0 | Cherry |
| | 2 | 06.12.79 | **West End** | A | L | 0-1 | |
| 1880-81 | 1 | 13.11.80 | **Reading** | A | L | 1-5 | Maugham |
| 1881-82 | 1 | 05.11.81 | **Highbury Union** | H | W | 1-0 | |
| | 2 | 26.11.81 | **Reading Abbey** | A | W | 4-1 | |
| | 3 | 17.12.81 | **Reading Minster** | H | D | 0-0 | |
| | 3r | 26.12.81 | **Reading Minster** | A | W | 2-0 | |
| | 4 | 21.01.82 | **Upton Park** | A | L | 0-5 | |
| 1882-83 | 1 | 04.11.82 | **Rochester** | A | L | 0-2 | |
| 1884-85 | 1 | 08.11.84 | **Uxbridge** | A | W | 3-1 | |
| | 2 | 06.12.84 | **Old Wykehamists** | H | L | 1-2 | Whittaker |
| 1885-86 | 1 | 31.10.85 | **Old Westminsters** | A | L | 1-3 | |
| 1886-87 | 1 | 23.10.86 | **Luton Town** | A | W | 3-1 | Johnson, C Sutton, J Sutton |
| | 2 | 20.11.86 | **Chatham** | A | L | 0-1 | |
| 1887-88 | 1 | | bye | | | | |
| | 2 | 05.11.87 | **Dulwich** | A | L | 1-2 | |

## HOUNSLOW TOWN

*Formed 1884. First entered FA Cup: 1883-84. FA Amateur Cup runners-up: 1962. Merged with Feltham FC 1991 to become Feltham & Hounslow Borough.*

| | | | | | | | |
|---|---|---|---|---|---|---|---|
| 1954-55 (CRN) | 1 | 20.11.54 | **Hastings Utd** (SL) | H | L | 2-4 | Page 2 |
| 1962-63 (AL) | 1 | 03.11.62 | **Mansfield Town** (D4) | H | D | 3-3 | Walsh, Somers, Bigmore |
| | 1r | 05.11.62 | **Mansfield Town** | A | L | 2-9 | Creasey (p), Black |

## HUCKNALL ST JOHNS

*Entered FA Cup: 1893-94 – 1898-99.*

| | | | | | | | |
|---|---|---|---|---|---|---|---|
| 1897-98 | 1 | 29.01.98 | **Liverpool** (D1) | A | L | 0-2 | |

## HUDDERSFIELD TOWN

*Formed 1908. FA Cup winners: 1922. Runners-up: 1920, 1928, 1930, 1938. Record FA Cup win: 11-0 v Heckmondwike, preliminary round, 1909-10; In Competition Proper: 7-0 v Lincoln United, 1st round, 16.11.1991. Record FA Cup defeat: 0-6 v Sunderland, 3rd round, 07.01.1950*

1909-10 (ML) P Heckmondwike (A) 11-0; 1q Mirfield (H) 6-0; 2q Rothwell White Rose (H) 7-0; 3q South Kirkby Coll (H) 5-2; 4q Rotherham Town (H) 2-2; 4qr Rotherham T (A) 1-2

| | | | | | | | |
|---|---|---|---|---|---|---|---|
| 1910-11 (D2) | | | 1q Horsforth (H) 6-0; 2q Mirfield (H) 2-0; 3q South Kirkby Colliery (A) 5-1; 4q Lincoln City (H) 1-1; 4qr Lincoln City (A) 0-1 | | | | |
| 1911-12 (D2) | 1 | 13.01.12 | **Manchester Utd** (D1) | A | L | 1-3 | Macauley |
| 1912-13 (D2) | 1 | 15.01.13 | **Sheffield Utd** (D1) | H | W | 3-1 | Elliott 2, Mann |
| | 2 | 01.02.13 | **Swindon Town** (SL) | H | L | 1-2 | Macauley |
| 1913-14 (D2) | 1 | 10.01.14 | **London Cal** (IL) | H | W | 3-0 | Islip 2, Armour |
| | 2 | 31.01.14 | **Birmingham** (D2) | A | L | 0-1 | |
| 1914-15 (D2) | 1 | 09.01.15 | **Burnley** (D1) | A | L | 1-3 | Fayers |
| 1919-20 (D2) | 1 | 10.01.20 | **Brentford** (SL) | H | W | 5-1 | Taylor 2, Smith, Swann, Shields |
| | 2 | 31.01.20 | **Newcastle Utd** (D1) | A | W | 1-0 | Mann |
| | 3 | 21.02.2200 | **Plymouth Argyle** (SL) | H | W | 3-1 | Taylor, Slade, Swann |
| | 4 | 06.0320. | **Liverpool** (D1) | H | W | 2-1 | Swann, Taylor |
| | SF | 27.0320. | **Bristol City** (D2) | | W | 2-1 | Taylor 2 |
| | | | *played at Stamford Bridge* | | | | |
| | F | 24.0420. | **Aston Villa** (D1) | | L | 0-1aet | |
| | | | *played at Stamford Bridge* | | | | |
| 1920-21 (D1) | 1 | 08.01.21 | **Brentford** (D3) | A | W | 2-1 | Islip, Wright |
| | 2 | 29.01.21 | **Bradford Park A** (D1) | A | W | 1-0 | Mann |
| | 3 | 19.02.21 | **Aston Villa** (D1) | A | L | 0-2 | |
| 1921-22 (D1) | 1 | 07.01.22 | **Burnley** (D1) | A | D | 2-2 | Islip, Watson |
| | 1r | 11.01.22 | **Burnley** | H | W | 3-2 | Stephenson 2, Mann |
| | 2 | 28.01.22 | **Brighton** (3S) | A | D | 0-0 | |
| | 2r | 01.02.22 | **Brighton** | H | W | 2-0 | Stephenson, Richardson |
| | 3 | 18.02.22 | **Blackburn Rovers** (D1) | A | D | 1-1 | Mann |
| | 3r | 22.02.22 | **Blackburn Rovers** | H | W | 5-0 | Islip 2, WH Smith 2, Mann |
| | 4 | 04.03.22 | **Millwall Athletic** (3S) | H | W | 3-0 | Stephenson 2, Islip |
| | SF | 25.03.22 | **Notts County** (D2) | | W | 3-1 | Mann, WH Smith, Stephenson |
| | | | *played at Turf Moor* | | | | |
| | F | 29.04.22 | **Preston North End** (D1) | | W | 1-0 | Smith (p) |
| | | | *played at Stamford Bridge* | | | | |
| 1922-23 (D1) | 1 | 13.01.23 | **Birmingham** (D1) | H | W | 2-1 | Stephenson, C Wilson |
| | 2 | 03.02.23 | **Millwall Athletic** (3S) | A | D | 0-0 | |
| | 2r | 07.02.23 | **Millwall Athletic** | H | W | 3-0 | C Wilson 2, Richardson |
| | 3 | 24.02.23 | **Bolton Wanderers** (D1) | H | D | 1-1 | Islip |
| | 3r | 28.02.23 | **Bolton Wanderers** | A | L | 0-1 | |
| 1923-24 (D1) | 1 | 12.01.24 | **Birmingham** (D1) | H | W | 1-0 | Johnstone |
| | 2 | 02.02.24 | **Manchester Utd** (D2) | A | W | 3-0 | C Wilson 2, Stephenson |
| | 3 | 23.02.24 | **Burnley** (D1) | A | L | 0-1 | |
| 1924-25 (D1) | 1 | 10.01.25 | **Bolton Wanderers** (D1) | A | L | 0-3 | |
| 1925-26 (D1) | 3 | 09.01.26 | **Charlton Athletic** (3S) | A | W | 1-0 | Goodall (p) |
| | 4 | 30.01.26 | **Manchester City** (D1) | A | L | 0-4 | |
| 1926-27 (D1) | 3 | 08.01.27 | **Millwall** (3S) | A | L | 1-3 | Brown |
| 1927-28 (D1) | 3 | 14.01.28 | **Lincoln City** (3N) | H | W | 4-2 | Brown, WH Smith, Goodall (p), Steele |
| | 4 | 28.01.28 | **West Ham Utd** (D1) | H | W | 2-1 | Brown, Jackson |
| | 5 | 18.02.28 | **Middlesbrough** (D1) | H | W | 4-0 | Steele, Brown, Jackson, WH Smith |
| | 6 | 03.03.28 | **Tottenham Hotspur** (D1) | H | W | 6-1 | Brown 4, WH Smith 2 |
| | SF | 24.03.28 | **Sheffield Utd** (D1) | | D | 2-2aet | Jackson, Brown |
| | | | *played at Old Trafford* | | | | |
| | SFr | 26.03.28 | **Sheffield Utd** | | D | 0-0aet | |
| | | | *played at Goodison Park* | | | | |
| | SF 2r | 02.04.28 | **Sheffield Utd** | | W | 1-0 | Jackson |
| | | | *played at Maine Road* | | | | |
| | F | 21.04.28 | **Blackburn Rovers** (D1) | | L | 1-3 | Jackson |
| | | | *played at Wembley Stadium* | | | | |
| 1928-29 (D1) | 3 | 12.01.29 | **Chesterfield** (3N) | A | W | 7-1 | Brown 4, Cumming 2, Jackson |
| | 4 | 26.01.29 | **Leeds Utd** (D1) | H | W | 3-0 | Jackson 2, Smith |
| | 5 | 16.02.29 | **Crystal Palace** (3S) | H | W | 5-2 | Brown 3, Smith, Kelly |
| | 6 | 02.03.29 | **WBA** (D2) | A | D | 1-1 | Brown |
| | 6r | 06.03.29 | **WBA** | H | W | 2-1 | Jackson, Kelly |
| | SF | 23.03.29 | **Bolton Wanderers** (D1) | | L | 1-3 | Jackson |
| | | | *played at Anfield* | | | | |

| | | | | | | | | |
|---|---|---|---|---|---|---|---|---|
| 1929-30 | (D1) | 3 | 11.01.30 | **Bury** (D2) | A | D | 0-0 | |
| | | 3r | 15.01.30 | **Bury** | H | W | 3-1 | Jackson 3 |
| | | 4 | 25.01.30 | **Sheffield Utd** (D1) | H | W | 2-1 | Jackson 2 |
| | | 5 | 15.02.30 | **Bradford City** (D2) | H | W | 2-1 | R Kelly, Jackson |
| | | 6 | 01.03.30 | **Aston Villa** (D1) | A | W | 2-1 | Smith, Jackson |
| | | SF | 22.03.30 | **Sheffield Wed** (D1) | | W | 2-1 | Jackson 2 |
| | | | | *played at Old Trafford* | | | | |
| | | F | 26.04.30 | **Arsenal** (D1) | | L | 0-2 | |
| | | | | *played at Wembley Stadium* | | | | |
| 1930-31 | (D1) | 3 | 10.01.31 | **Leeds Utd** (D1) | A | L | 0-2 | |
| 1931-32 | (D1) | 3 | 09.01.32 | **Oldham Athletic** (D2) | A | D | 1-1 | Mangnall |
| | | 3r | 13.01.32 | **Oldham Athletic** | H | W | 6-0 | Mangnall 4, McLean, Luke |
| | | 4 | 23.01.32 | **QPR** (3S) | H | W | 5-0 | Mangnall 2, Luke 2, Campbell |
| | | 5 | 13.02.32 | **Preston North End** (D2) | H | W | 4-0 | Mangnall 2, Luke,Ward og |
| | | 6 | 27.02.32 | **Arsenal** (D1) | H | L | 0-1 | |
| 1932-33 | (D1) | 3 | 14.01.33 | **Folkestone** (SL) | H | W | 2-0 | Luke, Willingham |
| | | 4 | 28.01.33 | **Blackpool** (D1) | A | L | 0-2 | |
| 1933-34 | (D1) | 3 | 13.01.34 | **Plymouth Argyle** (D2) | A | D | 1-1 | McLean |
| | | 3r | 17.01.34 | **Plymouth Argyle** | H | W | 6-2 | Mangnall 3, Luke Bott, Mclean |
| | | 4 | 27.01.34 | **Northampton Town** (3S) | H | L | 0-2 | |
| 1934-35 | (D1) | 3 | 12.01.35 | **Portsmouth** (D1) | A | D | 1-1 | Lythgoe |
| | | 3r | 16.01.35 | **Portsmouth** | H | L | 2-3 | Lythgoe, Lang |
| 1935-36 | (D1) | 3 | 11.01.36 | **Aston Villa** (D1) | A | W | 1-0 | Luke |
| | | 4 | 25.01.36 | **Tottenham Hotspur** (D2) | A | L | 0-1 | |
| 1936-37 | (D1) | 3 | 16.01.37 | **Brentford** (D1) | A | L | 0-5 | |
| 1937-38 | (D1) | 3 | 08.01.38 | **Hull City** (3N) | H | W | 3-1 | Lythgoe 2, Beasley |
| | | 4 | 22.01.38 | **Notts County** (3S) | H | W | 1-0 | Beattie |
| | | 5 | 12.02.38 | **Liverpool** (D1) | A | W | 1-0 | Barclay |
| | | 6 | 05.03.38 | **York City** (3N) | A | D | 0-0 | |
| | | 6r | 09.03.38 | **York City** | H | W | 2-1 | E Watson, Chivers |
| | | SF | 26.03.38 | **Sunderland** (D1) | | W | 3-1 | Beasley, Barclay, McFadyen |
| | | | | *played at Ewood Park* | | | | |
| | | F | 30.04.38 | **Preston North End** (D1) | | L | 0-1aet | |
| | | | | *played at Wembley Stadium* | | | | |
| 1938-39 | (D1) | 3 | 11.01.39 | **Nottingham Forest** (D2) | H | D | 0-0 | |
| | | 3r | 16.01.39 | **Nottingham Forest** | A | W | 3-0 | Isaac 2, Price |
| | | 4 | 21.01.39 | **Leeds Utd** (D1) | A | W | 4-2 | Price 3, Barclay |
| | | 5 | 11.02.39 | **Walsall** (3S) | H | W | 3-0 | Price 2, McCall |
| | | 6 | 04.03.39 | **Blackburn Rovers** (D2) | H | D | 1-1 | Price |
| | | 6r | 09.03.39 | **Blackburn Rovers** | A | W | 2-1 | Mahon, Beasley |
| | | SF | 25.03.39 | **Portsmouth** (D1) | | L | 1-2 | Barclay |
| | | | | *played at Highbury* | | | | |
| 1945-46 | (D1) | 3 1L | 05.01.46 | **Sheffield Utd** (D1) | H | D | 1-1 | Price |
| | | 3 2L | 07.01.46 | **Sheffield Utd** | A | L | 0-2 | |
| 1946-47 | (D1) | 3 | 11.01.47 | **Barnsley** (D2) | H | L | 3-4 | Doherty 2, Bateman |
| 1947-48 | (D1) | 3 | 10.01.48 | **Colchester Utd** (SL) | A | L | 0-1 | |
| 1948-49 | (D1) | 3 | 08.01.49 | **QPR** (D2) | A | D | 0-0aet | |
| | | 3r | 15.01.49 | **QPR** | H | W | 5-0 | Glazzard 2, Nightingale, McKenna, Bateman |
| | | 4 | 29.01.49 | **Newport County** (3S) | A | D | 3-3aet | Glazzard 2, Doherty |
| | | 4r | 05.02.49 | **Newport County** | H | L | 1-3 | Metcalfe |
| 1949-50 | (D1) | 3 | 07.01.50 | **Sunderland** (D1) | A | L | 0-6 | |
| 1950-51 | (D1) | 3 | 06.01.51 | **Tottenham Hotspur** (D1) | H | W | 2-0 | Taylor, Glazzard |
| | | 4 | 27.01.51 | **Preston North End** (D2) | A | W | 2-0 | Metcalfe (p), Taylor |
| | | 5 | 10.02.51 | **Wolverhampton W** (D1) | A | L | 0-2 | |
| 1951-52 | (D1) | 3 | 12.01.52 | **Tranmere Rovers** (3N) | H | L | 1-2 | Metcalfe (p) |
| 1952-53 | (D2) | 3 | 10.01.53 | **Bristol Rovers** (3S) | H | W | 2-0 | Glazzard, Watson |
| | | 4 | 31.01.53 | **Blackpool** (D1) | A | L | 0-1 | |
| 1953-54 | (D1) | 3 | 09.01.54 | **West Ham Utd** (D2) | A | L | 0-4 | |
| 1954-55 | (D1) | 3 | 08.01.55 | **Coventry City** (3S) | H | D | 3-3 | Glazzard 2, Watson |
| | | 3r | 13.01.55 | **Coventry City** | A | W | 2-1aet | Glazzard, Watson |
| | | 4 | 29.01.55 | **Torquay Utd** (3S) | A | W | 1-0 | Glazzard |

| | | | | | | | | |
|---|---|---|---|---|---|---|---|---|
| | | 5 | 19.02.55 | **Liverpool** (D2) | A | W | 2-0 | Glazzard, Hobson |
| | | 6 | 12.03.55 | **Newcastle Utd** (D1) | H | D | 1-1 | Glazzard |
| | | 6r | 16.03.55 | **Newcastle Utd** | A | L | 0-2aet | |
| 1955-56 | (D1) | 3 | 07.01.56 | **Bolton Wanderers** (D1) | A | - | 0-0ab | |
| | | | | *abandoned after 47 minutes* | | | | |
| | | 3 | 11.01.56 | **Bolton Wanderers** | A | L | 0-3 | |
| 1956-57 | (D2) | 3 | 05.01.57 | **Sheffield Utd** (D2) | H | D | 0-0 | |
| | | 3r | 07.01.57 | **Sheffield Utd** | A | D | 1-1aet | Simpson |
| | | 3 2r | 14.01.57 | **Sheffield Utd** | | W | 2-1 | Quested, Hickson |
| | | | | *played at Maine Road* | | | | |
| | | 4 | 26.01.57 | **Peterborough Utd** (ML) | H | W | 3-1 | Law, Hickson, Simpson |
| | | 5 | 16.02.57 | **Burnley** (D1) | H | L | 1-2 | Hickson |
| 1957-58 | (D2) | 3 | 04.01.58 | **Charlton Athletic** (D2) | H | D | 2-2 | Law, Massie |
| | | 3r | 08.01.58 | **Charlton Athletic** | A | L | 0-1 | |
| 1958-59 | (D2) | 3 | 10.01.59 | **Ipswich Town** (D2) | A | L | 0-1 | |
| 1959-60 | (D2) | 3 | 09.01.60 | **West Ham Utd** (D1) | H | D | 1-1 | Law |
| | | 3r | 13.01.60 | **West Ham Utd** | A | W | 5-1 | Massie 2, Connor 2, McGarry |
| | | 4 | 30.01.60 | **Luton Town** (D1) | H | L | 0-1 | |
| 1960-61 | (D2) | 3 | 07.01.61 | **Wolverhampton W** (D1) | A | D | 1-1 | Stokes |
| | | 3r | 11.01.61 | **Wolverhampton W** | H | W | 2-1 | Stokes, O'Grady |
| | | 4 | 01.02.61 | **Barnsley** (D3) | H | D | 1-1 | Coddington (p) |
| | | 4r | 06.02.61 | **Barnsley** | A | L | 0-1 | |
| 1961-62 | (D2) | 3 | 09.01.62 | **Rotherham Utd** (D2) | H | W | 4-3 | McHale 2, Massie, Kerray |
| | | 4 | 27.01.62 | **Aston Villa** (D1) | A | L | 1-2 | McHale |
| 1962-63 | (D2) | 3 | 04.03.63 | **Manchester Utd** (D1) | A | L | 0-5 | |
| 1963-64 | (D2) | 3 | 04.01.64 | **Plymouth Argyle** (D2) | A | W | 1-0 | McHale |
| | | 4 | 25.01.64 | **Chelsea** (D1) | A | W | 2-1 | McHale, White |
| | | 5 | 15.02.64 | **Burnley** (D1) | A | L | 0-3 | |
| 1964-65 | (D2) | 3 | 09.01.65 | **Doncaster Rovers** (D4) | A | W | 1-0 | Massie |
| | | 4 | 30.01.65 | **Swansea Town** (D2) | A | L | 0-1 | |
| 1965-66 | (D2) | 3 | 24.01.66 | **Hartlepools Utd** (D4) | H | W | 3-1 | Quigley 2, Leighton |
| | | 4 | 12.02.66 | **Plymouth Argyle** (D2) | A | W | 2-0 | Smith, Massie |
| | | 5 | 05.03.66 | **Sheffield Wed** (D1) | H | L | 1-2 | Smith |
| 1966-67 | (D2) | 3 | 28.01.67 | **Chelsea** (D1) | H | L | 1-2 | Leighton |
| 1967-68 | (D2) | 3 | 27.01.68 | **Tranmere Rovers** (D3) | A | L | 1-2 | Worthington |
| 1968-69 | (D2) | 3 | 04.01.69 | **Bury** (D2) | A | W | 2-1 | Hill, Nicholson |
| | | 4 | 25.01.69 | **West Ham Utd** (D1) | H | L | 0-2 | |
| 1969-70 | (D2) | 3 | 03.01.70 | **Aldershot** (D4) | H | D | 1-1 | Smith |
| | | 3r | 12.01.70 | **Aldershot** | A | L | 1-3 | Worthington |
| 1970-71 | (D1) | 3 | 02.01.71 | **Birmingham City** (D2) | H | D | 1-1 | Hoy |
| | | 3r | 05.01.71 | **Birmingham City** | A | W | 2-0 | Krzywicki, Worthington |
| | | 4 | 23.01.71 | **Stoke City** (D1) | A | D | 3-3 | Worthington, Chapman, Mahoney |
| | | 4r | 26.01.71 | **Stoke City** | H | D | 0-0aet | |
| | | 4 2r | 08.02.71 | **Stoke City** | | L | 0-1 | |
| | | | | *played at Old Trafford* | | | | |
| 1971-72 | (D1) | 3 | 15.01.72 | **Burnley** (D2) | A | W | 1-0 | Clarke |
| | | 4 | 05.02.72 | **Fulham** (D2) | H | W | 3-0 | J Lawson 2, Chapman |
| | | 5 | 26.02.72 | **West Ham Utd** (D1) | H | W | 4-2 | J Lawson, Dolan, D Smith, Worthington |
| | | 6 | 18.03.72 | **Birmingham City** (D2) | A | L | 1-3 | Cherry |
| 1972-73 | (D2) | 3 | 13.01.73 | **Carlisle Utd** (D2) | A | D | 2-2 | Fairclough 2 |
| | | 3r | 16.01.73 | **Carlisle Utd** | H | L | 0-1 | |
| 1973-74 | (D3) | 1 | 24.11.73 | **Wigan Athletic** (NPL) | H | W | 2-0 | Newton 2 |
| | | 2 | 15.12.73 | **Chester** (D4) | A | L | 2-3 | Saunders, Gowling |
| 1974-75 | (D3) | 1 | 23.11.74 | **Grimsby Town** (D3) | A | L | 0-1 | |
| 1975-76 | (D4) | 1 | 22.11.75 | **Walsall** (D3) | A | W | 1-0 | Belfitt |
| | | 2 | 13.12.75 | **Port Vale** (D3) | H | W | 2-1 | Belfitt, Baines |
| | | 3 | 03.01.76 | **Fulham** (D2) | A | W | 3-2 | Gray 2, Lawson |
| | | 4 | 24.01.76 | **Bolton Wanderers** (D2) | H | L | 0-1 | |
| 1976-77 | (D4) | 1 | 20.11.76 | **Mansfield Town** (D3) | H | D | 0-0 | |
| | | 1r | 22.11.76 | **Mansfield Town** | A | L | 1-2 | Sidebottom |

| | | | | | | | | |
|---|---|---|---|---|---|---|---|---|
| 1977-78 | (D4) | 1 | 26.11.77 | **Barnsley** (D4) | A | L | 0-1 | |
| 1978-79 | (D4) | 1 | 25.11.78 | **Doncaster Rovers** (D4) | A | L | 1-2 | Fletcher |
| 1979-80 | (D4) | 1 | 24.11.79 | **Darlington** (D4) | A | D | 1-1 | Hart |
| | | 1r | 27.11.79 | **Darlington** | H | L | 0-1 | |
| 1980-81 | (D3) | 1 | 22.11.80 | **Northwich V** (APL) | A | D | 1-1 | Stanton |
| | | 1r | 25.11.80 | **Northwich V** | H | W | 6-0 | Santon 2, Robins 2, Hanvey, Laverick |
| | | 2 | 13.12.80 | **Tranmere Rovers** (D4) | A | W | 3-0 | Robins 2, Stanton |
| | | 3 | 03.01.81 | **Shrewsbury Town** (D2) | H | L | 0-3 | |
| 1981-82 | (D3) | 1 | 21.11.81 | **Workington** (NPL) | A | D | 1-1 | Brown |
| | | 1r | 24.11.81 | **Workington** | H | W | 5-0 | Laverick 2, Robins, Lillis, Brown |
| | | 2 | 12.12.81 | **Chesterfield** (D3) | A | W | 1-0 | Cowling |
| | | 3 | 23.01.82 | **Carlisle Utd** (D3) | A | W | 3-2 | Fletcher 3 |
| | | 4 | 26.01.82 | **Orient** (D2) | H | D | 1-1 | Austin |
| | | 4r | 01.02.82 | **Orient** | A | L | 0-2 | |
| 1982-83 | (D3) | 1 | 20.11.82 | **Mossley** (NPL) | H | W | 1-0 | Brown |
| | | 2 | 11.12.82 | **Altrincham** (APL) | A | W | 1-0 | Stanton |
| | | 3 | 08.01.83 | **Chelsea** (D2) | H | D | 1-1 | Stanton |
| | | 3r | 12.01.83 | **Chelsea** | A | L | 0-2 | |
| 1983-84 | (D2) | 3 | 07.01.84 | **QPR** (D1) | H | W | 2-1 | Lillis, Stonehouse |
| | | 4 | 01.02.84 | **Notts County** (D1) | H | L | 1-2 | Stonehouse |
| 1984-85 | (D2) | 3 | 05.01.85 | **Wolverhampton W** (D2) | A | D | 1-1 | Tempest |
| | | 3r | 23.01.85 | **Wolverhampton W** | H | W | 3-1 | Lillis 2 (1p), Pugh |
| | | 4 | 26.01.85 | **Luton Town** (D1) | A | L | 0-2 | |
| 1985-86 | (D2) | 3 | 04.01.86 | **Reading** (D3) | H | D | 0-0 | |
| | | 3r | 13.01.86 | **Reading** | A | L | 1-2aet | Cowling |
| 1986-87 | (D2) | 3 | 10.01.87 | **Norwich City** (D1) | A | D | 1-1 | Shearer |
| | | 3r | 21.01.87 | **Norwich City** | H | L | 2-4 | Brown (p), Cork |
| 1987-88 | (D2) | 3 | 09.01.88 | **Manchester City** (D2) | H | D | 2-2 | Shearer 2 |
| | | 3r | 12.01.88 | **Manchester City** | A | D | 0-0aet | |
| | | 3 2r | 25.01.88 | **Manchester City** | H | L | 0-3 | |
| 1988-89 | (D3) | 1 | 19.11.88 | **Rochdale** (D4) | H | D | 1-1 | May |
| | | 1r | 28.11.88 | **Rochdale** | A | W | 4-3 | Withe, O'Shaughnessy og, Maskell, Bent |
| | | 2 | 10.12.88 | **Chester City** (D3) | H | W | 1-0 | O'Regan |
| | | 3 | 07.01.89 | **Sheffield Utd** (D3) | H | L | 0-1 | |
| 1989-90 | (D3) | 1 | 18.11.89 | **Hartlepool Utd** (D4) | A | W | 2-0 | Cecere 2 (2 p) |
| | | 2 | 09.12.89 | **Chesterfield** (D4) | A | W | 2-0 | Cecere (p), Maskell |
| | | 3 | 06.01.90 | **Grimsby Town** (D4) | H | W | 3-1 | Smith, Maskell, Lever og |
| | | 4 | 27.01.90 | **Crystal Palace** (D1) | A | L | 0-4 | |
| 1990-91 | (D3) | 1 | 18.11.90 | **Altrincham** (Conf) | A | W | 2-1 | Onuora, Roberts |
| | | 2 | 10.12.90 | **Blackpool** (D4) | H | L | 0-2 | |
| 1991-92 | (D3) | 1 | 16.11.91 | **Lincoln Utd** (CML) | H | W | 7-0 | O'Regan, Donovan 2, Stapleton, Roberts 2, Onuora |
| | | 2 | 07.12.91 | **Rochdale** (D4) | A | W | 2-1 | Roberts, Onuora |
| | | 3 | 04.01.92 | **Millwall** (D2) | H | L | 0-4 | |
| 1992-93 | (D2) | 1 | 14.11.92 | **Scunthorpe Utd** (D3) | A | D | 0-0 | |
| | | 1r | 25.11.92 | **Scunthorpe Utd** | H | W | 2-1aet | Barnett 2 |
| | | 2 | 06.12.92 | **Bradford City** (D2) | A | W | 2-0 | Dunn, O'Regan (p) |
| | | 3 | 02.01.93 | **Gillingham** (D3) | A | D | 0-0 | |
| | | 3r | 13.01.93 | **Gillingham** | H | W | 2-1 | Robinson, Dunn |
| | | 4 | 23.01.93 | **Southend Utd** (D1) | H | L | 1-2 | Mitchell |
| 1993-94 | (D2) | 1 | 13.11.93 | **Telford Utd** (Conf) | A | D | 1-1 | Rowe |
| | | 1r | 23.11.93 | **Telford Utd** | H | W | 1-0 | Jackson |
| | | 2 | 03.12.93 | **Port Vale** (D2) | A | L | 0-1 | |
| 1994-95 | (D2) | 1 | 12.11.94 | **Doncaster Rovers** (D3) | A | W | 4-1 | Bullock, Booth, Jepson, D Dunn |
| | | 2 | 03.12.94 | **Lincoln City** (D3) | A | L | 0-1 | |
| 1995-96 | (D1) | 3 | 06.01.96 | **Blackpool** (D2) | H | W | 2-1 | Jepson 2(1p) |
| | | 4 | 06.02.96 | **Peterborough Utd** (D2) | H | W | 2-0 | Bullock, Booth |
| | | 5 | 17.02.96 | **Wimbledon** (PL) | H | D | 2-2 | Rowe, Cowan |
| | | 5r | 28.02.96 | **Wimbledon** | A | L | 1-3 | Booth |
| 1996-97 | (D1) | 3 | 04.01.97 | **QPR** (D1) | A | D | 1-1 | Crosby |

| | | | | | | | | |
|---|---|---|---|---|---|---|---|---|
| | | 3r | 14.01.97 | **QPR** | H | L | 1-2 | Edwards |
| 1997-98 | (D1) | 3 | 13.01.98 | **Bournemouth** (D2) | A | W | 1-0 | Stewart |
| | | 4 | 24.01.98 | **Wimbledon** (PL) | H | L | 0-1 | |
| 1998-99 | (D1) | 3 | 02.01.99 | **QPR** (D1) | A | W | 1-0 | Allison |
| | | 4 | 23.01.99 | **Wrexham** (D2) | A | D | 1-1 | Allison |
| | | 4r | 03.02.99 | **Wrexham** | H | W | 2-1 | Stewart, Thornley |
| | | 5 | 13.02.99 | **Derby County** (PL) | H | D | 2-2 | Beech, Stewart |
| | | 5r | 24.02.99 | **Derby County** | A | L | 1-3 | Beech |
| 1999-00 | (D1) | 3 | 12.12.99 | **Liverpool** (PL) | H | L | 0-2 | |
| 2000-01 | (D1) | 3 | 06.01.01 | **Bristol City** (D2) | H | L | 0-2 | |
| 2001-02 | (D2) | 1 | 17.11.01 | **Gravesend & N** (IL) | H | W | 2-1 | Moses, Knight |
| | | 2 | 08.12.01 | **Mansfield Town** (D3) | A | L | 0-4 | |
| 2002-03 | (D2) | 1 | 16.11.02 | **Swindon Town** (D2) | A | L | 0-1 | |

# HULL CITY

*Formed 1904. First entered FA Cup: 1904-05. Best FA Cup Performance: Semi-finals, 1930. Record FA Cup win: 8-1 v Grimethorpe Utd, 1st qualifying round, 7.10.05; In Competition Proper: 8-2 v Stalybridge Celtic, 1st round, 26.11.32; Record FA Cup defeat: 0-5 v Fulham, 3rd round, 09.01.1960; 1-6 v Chelsea, 3rd round, 11.12.1999*

| | | | | | | | | |
|---|---|---|---|---|---|---|---|---|
| 1904-05 | | | | P Stockton (A) 3-3; Pr Stockton (A) 1-4 | | | | |
| 1905-06 | (D2) | | | 1q Grimethorpe U (H) 8-1; 2q Denaby U (A) 2-0; 3q Leeds City (H) 1-1; 3q r Leeds City (A) 2-1; 4q Oldham A (H) 2-1 | | | | |
| | | 1 | 13.01.06 | **Reading** (SL) | H | L | 0-1 | |
| 1906-07 | (D2) | 1 | 12.01.07 | **Tottenham Hotspur** (SL) | A | D | 0-0 | |
| | | 1r | 17.01.07 | **Tottenham Hotspur** | H | - | 0-0ab | |
| | | | | *abandoned after 100 minutes – bad light* | | | | |
| | | 1r | 21.01.07 | **Tottenham Hotspur** (SL) | A | L | 0-1 | |
| 1907-08 | (D2) | 1 | 11.01.08 | **Woolwich Arsenal** (D1) | A | D | 0-0 | |
| | | 1r | 16.01.08 | **Woolwich Arsenal** | H | W | 4-1 | Shaw 2, Temple, Jack Smith |
| | | 2 | 01.02.08 | **Aston Villa** (D1) | A | L | 0-3 | |
| 1908-09 | (D2) | 1 | 16.01.09 | **Chelsea** (D1) | H | D | 1-1 | Temple |
| | | 1r | 20.01.09 | **Chelsea** | A | L | 0-1 | |
| 1909-10 | (D2) | 1 | 15.01.10 | **Chelsea** (D1) | A | L | 1-2 | Temple |
| 1910-11 | (D2) | 1 | 14.01.11 | **Bristol Rovers** (SL) | A | D | 0-0 | |
| | | 1r | 19.01.11 | **Bristol Rovers** | H | W | 1-0aet | McQuillan |
| | | 2 | 04.02.11 | **Oldham Athletic** (D1) | H | W | 1-0 | Temple |
| | | 3 | 25.02.11 | **Newcastle Utd** (D1) | A | L | 2-3 | Joe Smith 2 |
| 1911-12 | (D2) | 1 | 13.01.12 | **Oldham Athletic** (D1) | A | D | 1-1 | Best |
| | | 1r | 16.01.12 | **Oldham Athletic** | H | L | 0-1 | |
| 1912-13 | (D2) | 1 | 11.01.13 | **Fulham** (D2) | A | W | 2-0 | Fazackerley, Stevens |
| | | 2 | 01.02.13 | **Newcastle Utd** (D1) | H | D | 0-0 | |
| | | 2r | 05.02.13 | **Newcastle Utd** | A | L | 0-3 | |
| 1913-14 | (D2) | 1 | 10.01.14 | **Bury** (D2) | H | D | 0-0 | |
| | | 1r | 14.01.14 | **Bury** (D2) | A | L | 1-2 | Lee |
| 1914-15 | (D2) | 1 | 09.01.15 | **WBA** (D1) | H | W | 1-0 | Stevens |
| | | 2 | 30.01.15 | **Northampton Town** (SL) | H | W | 2-1 | Stevens 2 |
| | | 3 | 20.02.15 | **Southampton** (SL) | A | D | 2-2aet | Cameron, Lee |
| | | 3r | 27.02.15 | **Southampton** | H | W | 4-0 | Stevens 2, Cameron, Lee |
| | | 4 | 06.03.15 | **Bolton Wanderers** (D1) | A | L | 2-4 | Deacey, Stevens |
| 1919-20 | (D2) | 1 | 14.01.20 | **Sunderland** (D1) | A | L | 2-6 | Stevens |
| 1920-21 | (D2) | 1 | 08.01.21 | **Bath City** (SL) | H | W | 3-0 | Wilson, Sergeaunt, Crawford |
| | | 2 | 29.01.21 | **Crystal Palace** (D3) | A | W | 2-0 | Wilson, Crawford |
| | | 3 | 19.02.21 | **Burnley** (D1) | H | W | 3-0 | Brandon 2, Wilson |
| | | 4 | 05.03.21 | **Preston North End** (D1) | H | D | 0-0 | |
| | | 4r | 10.03.21 | **Preston North End** | A | L | 0-1 | |
| 1921-22 | (D2) | 1 | 07.01.22 | **Middlesbrough** (D1) | H | W | 5-0 | Coverdale 2, Mills, Bleakley, Crawford |
| | | 2 | 28.01.22 | **Nottingham Forest** (D2) | A | L | 0-3 | |
| 1922-23 | (D2) | 1 | 13.01.23 | **West Ham Utd** (D2) | H | L | 2-3 | Crawford, Mills |
| 1923-24 | (D2) | 1 | 12.01.24 | **Bolton Wanderers** (D1) | H | D | 2-2 | Martin, Mills |
| | | 2 | 16.01.24 | **Bolton Wanderers** | A | L | 0-4 | |
| 1924-25 | (D2) | 1 | 10.01.25 | **Wolverhampton W** (D1) | H | D | 1-1 | Mills |
| | | 1r | 15.01.25 | **Wolverhampton W** | A | W | 1-0aet | Mills |

| | | | | | | | | |
|---|---|---|---|---|---|---|---|---|
| | | 2 | 31.01.25 | **Crystal Palace** (D2) | H | W | 3-2 | Mills 2, Bleakley |
| | | 3 | 21.02.25 | **Leicester City** (D2) | H | D | 1-1 | O'Brien |
| | | 3r | 26.02.25 | **Leicester City** | A | L | 1-3 | Hamilton |
| 1925-26 | (D2) | 3 | 09.01.26 | **Aston Villa** (D1) | H | L | 0-3 | |
| 1926-27 | (D2) | 3 | 08.01.27 | **WBA** (D1) | H | W | 2-1 | Cowan, Scott |
| | | 4 | 22.01.27 | **Everton** (D1) | H | D | 1-1 | Martin |
| | | 4r | 02.02.27 | **Everton** | A | D | 2-2aet | Guyan, Scott |
| | | 4 2r | 07.02.27 | **Everton** | | W | 3-2aet | Whitworth, Guyan, Scott |
| | | | | *played at Villa Park* | | | | |
| | | 5 | 19.02.27 | **Wolverhampton W** (D2) | A | L | 0-1 | |
| 1927-28 | (D2) | 3 | 14.01.28 | **Leicester City** (D1) | H | L | 0-1 | |
| 1928-29 | (D2) | 3 | 12.01.29 | **Bradford Park A** (D2) | H | D | 1-1 | McDonald |
| | | 3r | 16.01.29 | **Bradford Park A** | A | L | 1-3 | McDonald |
| 1929-30 | (D2) | 3 | 11.01.30 | **Plymouth Argyle** (3S) | A | W | 4-3 | Alexander 3, Duncan |
| | | 4 | 25.01.30 | **Blackpool** (D2) | H | W | 3-1 | Alexander, Starling, Mills |
| | | 5 | 15.02.30 | **Manchester City** (D1) | A | W | 2-1 | Taylor, Mills |
| | | 6 | 01.03.30 | **Newcastle Utd** (D1) | A | D | 1-1 | Alexander |
| | | 6r | 06.03.30 | **Newcastle Utd** | H | W | 1-0 | Howieson |
| | | SF | 22.03.30 | **Arsenal** (D1) | | D | 2-2 | Howieson, Duncan |
| | | | | *played at Elland Road* | | | | |
| | | SFr | 26.03.30 | **Arsenal** | | L | 0-1 | |
| | | | | *played at Villa Park* | | | | |
| 1930-31 | (3N) | 3 | 10.01.31 | **Blackpool** (D1) | H | L | 1-2 | D Duncan |
| 1931-32 | (3N) | 1 | 28.11.31 | **Mansfield Town** (3S) | H | W | 4-1 | Wainscoat 2, Speed, Munnings |
| | | 2 | 12.12.31 | **New Brighton** (3N) | A | W | 4-0 | Speed 2, Wainscoat, Munnings |
| | | 3 | 09.01.32 | **Stoke City** (D2) | A | L | 0-3 | |
| 1932-33 | (3N) | 1 | 26.11.32 | **Stalybridge Celtic** (CC) | A | W | 8-2 | Wainscoat 4, McNaughton, Forward, Sargeant, Hill |
| | | 2 | 10.12.32 | **Carlisle Utd** (3N) | A | D | 1-1 | Sargeant |
| | | 2r | 15.12.32 | **Carlisle Utd** | H | W | 2-1aet | Wainscoat, Forward |
| | | 3 | 14.01.33 | **Sunderland** (D1) | H | L | 0-2 | |
| 1933-34 | (D2) | 3 | 13.01.34 | **Brentford** (D2) | H | W | 1-0 | Hubbard |
| | | 4 | 27.01.34 | **Manchester City** (D1) | H | D | 2-2 | Hill, Dale og |
| | | 4r | 31.01.34 | **Manchester City** | A | L | 1-4 | McNaughton |
| 1934-35 | (D2) | 3 | 12.01.35 | **Newcastle Utd** (D2) | H | L | 1-5 | Charlton |
| 1935-36 | (D2) | 3 | 11.01.36 | **WBA** (D1) | A | L | 0-2 | |
| 1936-37 | (3N) | 1 | 28.11.36 | **York City** (3N) | A | L | 2-5 | Mayson, Hubbard |
| 1937-38 | (3N) | 1 | 27.11.37 | **Scunthorpe Utd** (ML) | H | W | 4-0 | MacNeill 2, Pears 2 |
| | | 2 | 11.12.37 | **Exeter City** (3S) | A | W | 2-1 | Hubbard, Fryer |
| | | 3 | 08.01.38 | **Huddersfield Town** (D1) | A | L | 1-3 | Pears |
| 1938-39 | (3N) | 1 | 26.11.38 | **Rotherham Utd** (3N) | H | W | 4-1 | Hubbard 2, Cunliffe, Davies |
| | | 2 | 10.12.38 | **Chester** (3N) | A | D | 2-2 | Davies 2 |
| | | 2r | 15.12.38 | **Chester** | H | L | 0-1 | |
| 1945-46 | (3N) | | | did not enter | | | | |
| 1946-47 | (3N) | 1 | 30.11.46 | **New Brighton** (3N) | H | D | 0-0 | |
| | | 1r | 04.12.46 | **New Brighton** | A | W | 2-1aet | Lester, Chadwick |
| | | 2 | 14.12.46 | **Darlington** (3N) | A | W | 2-1 | Lester, Peach |
| | | 3 | 11.01.47 | **Blackburn Rovers** (D1) | A | D | 1-1 | Cook |
| | | 3r | 16.01.47 | **Blackburn Rovers** | H | L | 0-3 | |
| 1947-48 | (3N) | 1 | 29.11.47 | **Southport** (3N) | H | D | 1-1aet | Gallacher |
| | | 1r | 06.12.47 | **Southport** | A | W | 3-2 | Richardson, Reagan, McGorrighan |
| | | 2 | 13.12.47 | **Cheltenham Town** (SL) | H | W | 4-2 | Richardson 3, Reagan |
| | | 3 | 10.01.48 | **Middlesbrough** (D1) | H | L | 1-3 | Murphy |
| 1948-49 | (3N) | 1 | 27.11.48 | **Accrington Stanley** (3N) | H | W | 3-1 | Carter 2, Jensen |
| | | 2 | 11.12.48 | **Reading** (3S) | H | D | 0-0aet | |
| | | 2r | 18.12.48 | **Reading** | A | W | 2-1 | Moore 2 |
| | | 3 | 08.01.49 | **Blackburn Rovers** (D2) | H | W | 2-1aet | Moore, Buchan |
| | | 4 | 29.01.49 | **Grimsby Town** (D2) | A | W | 3-2 | Moore 2, Carter |
| | | 5 | 12.02.49 | **Stoke City** (D1) | A | W | 2-0 | Moore, Greenhalgh |
| | | 6 | 26.02.49 | **Manchester Utd** (D1) | H | L | 0-1 | |
| 1949-50 | (D2) | 3 | 07.01.50 | **Southport** (3N) | A | D | 0-0 | |

| | | | | | | | |
|---|---|---|---|---|---|---|---|
| | | 3r | 12.01.50 | **Southport** | H | W 5-0 | Moore, Revie, Harrison, Burbanks, Greenhalgh |
| | | 4 | 28.01.50 | **Stockport County** (3N) | A | D 0-0 | |
| | | 4r | 02.02.50 | **Stockport County** | H | L 0-2 | |
| 1950-51 | (D2) | 3 | 06.01.51 | **Everton** (D1) | H | W 2-0 | Carter, Gerrie |
| | | 4 | 27.01.51 | **Rotherham Utd** (3N) | H | W 2-0 | Carter, Harrison |
| | | 5 | 10.02.51 | **Bristol Rovers** (3S) | A | L 0-3 | |
| 1951-52 | (D2) | 3 | 12.01.52 | **Manchester Utd** (D1) | A | W 2-0 | Harrison, Gerrie |
| | | 4 | 02.02.52 | **Blackburn Rovers** (D2) | A | L 0-2 | |
| 1952-53 | (D2) | 3 | 10.01.53 | **Charlton Athletic** (D1) | H | W 3-1 | Horton, Jensen, Harris |
| | | 4 | 31.01.53 | **Gateshead AFC** (3N) | H | L 1-2 | Gerrie |
| 1953-54 | (D2) | 3 | 09.01.54 | **Brentford** (D2) | A | D 0-0 | |
| | | 3r | 14.01.54 | **Brentford** | H | D 2-2aet | Horton, Crosbie |
| | | 3 2r | 18.01.54 | **Brentford** *played at Belle Vue, Doncaster* | | W 5-2 | Horton 2, Crosbie 2, Ackerman |
| | | 4 | 30.01.54 | **Blackburn Rovers** (D2) | A | D 2-2 | Crosbie, K Harrison |
| | | 4r | 04.02.54 | **Blackburn Rovers** | H | W 2-1 | Ackerman, Bulless |
| | | 5 | 20.02.54 | **Tottenham Hotspur** (D1) | H | D 1-1 | Jensen |
| | | 5r | 24.02.54 | **Tottenham Hotspur** | A | L 0-2 | |
| 1954-55 | (D2) | 3 | 08.01.55 | **Birmingham City** (D2) | H | L 0-2 | |
| 1955-56 | (D2) | 3 | 07.01.56 | **Aston Villa** (D1) | A | D 1-1 | Clarke |
| | | 3r | 12.01.56 | **Aston Villa** | H | L 1-2 | Atkinson |
| 1956-57 | (3N) | 1 | 17.11.56 | **Gateshead AFC** (3N) | H | W 4-0 | Mortensen 2, Bradbury, Cripsey |
| | | 2 | 08.12.56 | **York City** (3N) | H | W 2-1 | Bulless 2 |
| | | 3 | 05.01.57 | **Bristol Rovers** (D2) | H | L 3-4 | Clarke 2, Stephens |
| 1957-58 | (3N) | 1 | 16.11.57 | **Crewe Alexandra** (3N) | H | W 2-1 | Bradbury, Clarke |
| | | 2 | 07.12.57 | **Port Vale** (3S) | A | D 2-2 | Bradbury, Davidson |
| | | 2r | 09.12.57 | **Port Vale** | H | W 4-3aet | Bradbury 2, Cleary og, Carberry og |
| | | 3 | 04.01.58 | **Barnsley** (D2) | H | D 1-1 | Bradbury |
| | | 3r | 08.01.58 | **Barnsley** | A | W 2-0 | Clarke, Bulless |
| | | 4 | 29.01.58 | **Sheffield Wed** (D1) | A | L 3-4 | Bradbury, Bulless, Stephens |
| 1958-59 | (D3) | 1 | 15.11.58 | **Stockport County** (D3) | H | L 0-1 | |
| 1959-60 | (D2) | 3 | 09.01.60 | **Fulham** (D1) | A | L 0-5 | |
| 1960-61 | (D3) | 1 | 05.11.60 | **Sutton Town** (CA) | H | W 3-0 | Sewell, Price, Gubbins |
| | | 2 | 26.11.60 | **Darlington** (D4) | A | D 1-1 | Price |
| | | 2r | 28.11.60 | **Darlington** | H | D 1-1aet | Chilton |
| | | 2 2r | 05.12.60 | **Darlington** *played at Elland Road. Match abandoned after 90 minutes – ground unplayable* | | - 1-1ab | Price |
| | | 2 3r | 12.12.60 | **Darlington** *played at Belle Vue, Doncaster* | | D 0-0aet | |
| | | 2 4r | 15.12.60 | **Darlington** *played at Ayresome Park* | | W 3-0 | Clarke, Gubbins, King |
| | | 3 | 07.01.61 | **Bolton Wanderers** (D1) | H | L 0-1 | |
| 1961-62 | (D3) | 1 | 04.11.61 | **Rhyl** (CC) | H | W 5-0 | Chilton 2, McSeveney, Henderson, McMillan |
| | | 2 | 25.11.61 | **Bradford City** (D4) | H | L 0-2 | |
| 1962-63 | (D3) | 1 | 03.11.62 | **Crook Town** (NL) | H | W 5-4 | McSeveney 2, Henderson 2, Chilton |
| | | 2 | 24.11.62 | **Workington** (D4) | H | W 2-0 | McSeveney 2 |
| | | 3 | 11.02.63 | **Leyton Orient** (D1) | A | D 1-1 | Chilton |
| | | 3r | 19.02.63 | **Leyton Orient** | H | L 0-2aet | |
| 1963-64 | (D3) | 1 | 16.11.63 | **Crewe Alexandra** (D3) | H | D 2-2 | Chilton, Shaw |
| | | 1r | 20.11.63 | **Crewe Alexandra** | A | W 3-0 | Wilkinson 2, Henderson |
| | | 2 | 07.12.63 | **Wrexham** (D3) | A | W 2-0 | Chilton, Henderson |
| | | 3 | 04.01.64 | **Everton** (D1) | H | D 1-1 | Wilkinson |
| | | 3r | 07.01.64 | **Everton** | A | L 1-2 | McSeveney |
| 1964-65 | (D3) | 1 | 14.11.64 | **Kidderminster H** (WMRL) | A | W 4-1 | Wilkinson 2, McSeveney, Heath |
| | | 2 | 05.12.64 | **Lincoln City** (D4) | H | D 1-1 | Summers |
| | | 2r | 09.12.64 | **Lincoln City** | A | L 1-3 | McSeveney |
| 1965-66 | (D3) | 1 | 13.11.65 | **Bradford Park A** (D4) | A | W 3-2 | Houghton, Chilton, I Butler |
| | | 2 | 08.12.65 | **Gateshead AFC** (NRL) | A | W 4-0 | Henderson, Wagstaff, Houghton, I Butler |

| | | | | | | | | |
|---|---|---|---|---|---|---|---|---|
| | | 3 | 22.01.66 | **Southampton** (D2) | H | W | 1-0 | Houghton |
| | | 4 | 12.02.66 | **Nottingham Forest** (D1) | H | W | 2-0 | Heath 2 |
| | | 5 | 05.03.66 | **Southport** (D4) | H | W | 2-0 | Chilton 2 |
| | | 6 | 26.03.66 | **Chelsea** (D1) | A | D | 2-2 | Wagstaff 2 |
| | | 6r | 31.03.66 | **Chelsea** | H | L | 1-3 | Simpkin |
| 1966-67 | (D2) | 3 | 28.01.67 | **Portsmouth** (D2) | H | D | 1-1 | Houghton |
| | | 3r | 01.02.67 | **Portsmouth** | A | D | 2-2aet | Houghton, Chilton |
| | | 3 2r | 06.02.67 | **Portsmouth** | | L | 1-3 | Chilton |
| | | | | *played at Highfield Road, Coventry* | | | | |
| 1967-68 | (D2) | 3 | 27.01.68 | **Middlesbrough** (D2) | A | D | 1-1 | Chilton |
| | | 3r | 31.01.68 | **Middlesbrough** | H | D | 2-2aet | Wagstaff 2 |
| | | 3 2r | 07.02.68 | **Middlesbrough** | | L | 0-1 | |
| | | | | *played at Bootham Crescent, York* | | | | |
| 1968-69 | (D2) | 3 | 04.01.69 | **Wolverhampton W** (D1) | H | L | 1-3 | Chilton |
| 1969-70 | (D2) | 3 | 03.01.70 | **Manchester City** (D1) | H | L | 0-1 | |
| 1970-71 | (D2) | 3 | 02.01.71 | **Charlton Athletic** (D2) | H | W | 3-0 | Wagstaff, Houghton, I Butler |
| | | 4 | 23.01.71 | **Blackpool** (D1) | H | W | 2-0 | Wagstaff, Chilton |
| | | 5 | 13.02.71 | **Brentford** (D4) | H | W | 2-1 | Houghton, Chilton |
| | | 6 | 06.03.71 | **Stoke City** (D1) | H | L | 2-3 | Wagstaff 2 |
| 1971-72 | (D2) | 3 | 15.01.72 | **Norwich City** (D2) | A | W | 3-0 | Wagstaff, Butler, McGill |
| | | 4 | 05.02.72 | **Coventry City** (D1) | A | W | 1-0 | Wagstaff |
| | | 5 | 26.02.72 | **Stoke City** (D1) | A | L | 1-4 | Wagstaff |
| 1972-73 | (D2) | 3 | 13.01.73 | **Stockport County** (D4) | A | D | 0-0 | |
| | | 3r | 23.01.73 | **Stockport County** | H | W | 2-0aet | Wagstaff, Houghton |
| | | 4 | 03.02.73 | **West Ham Utd** (D1) | H | W | 1-0 | Houghton |
| | | 5 | 24.02.73 | **Coventry City** (D1) | A | L | 0-3 | |
| 1973-74 | (D2) | 3 | 05.01.74 | **Bristol City** (D2) | A | D | 1-1 | Galvin |
| | | 3r | 08.01.74 | **Bristol City** | H | L | 0-1 | |
| 1974-75 | (D2) | 3 | 04.01.75 | **Fulham** (D2) | A | D | 1-1 | Wagstaff |
| | | 3r | 07.01.75 | **Fulham** | H | D | 2-2aet | Fletcher, Croft |
| | | 3 2r | 13.01.75 | **Fulham** | | L | 0-1 | |
| | | | | *played at Filbert Street* | | | | |
| 1975-76 | (D2) | 3 | 03.01.76 | **Plymouth Argyle** (D2) | H | D | 1-1 | Grimes |
| | | 3r | 06.01.76 | **Plymouth Argyle** | A | W | 4-1 | Wood 2, Hawley, Sutton og |
| | | 4 | 02.02.76 | **Sunderland** (D2) | A | L | 0-1 | |
| 1976-77 | (D2) | 3 | 08.01.77 | **Port Vale** (D3) | H | D | 1-1 | Nisbet |
| | | 3r | 10.01.77 | **Port Vale** | A | L | 1-3aet | Hemmerman |
| 1977-78 | (D2) | 3 | 07.01.78 | **Leicester City** (D1) | H | L | 0-1 | |
| 1978-79 | (D3) | 1 | 25.11.78 | **Stafford Rangers** (NPL) | H | W | 2-1 | Seargeant og, Edwards |
| | | 2 | 16.12.78 | **Carlisle Utd** (D3) | A | L | 0-3 | |
| 1979-80 | (D3) | 1 | 24.11.79 | **Carlisle Utd** (D3) | A | D | 3-3 | Hugh, Tait, G Roberts |
| | | 1r | 28.11.79 | **Carlisle Utd** | H | L | 0-2 | |
| 1980-81 | (D3) | 1 | 22.11.80 | **Halifax Town** (D4) | H | W | 2-1 | Edwards 2 |
| | | 2 | 13.12.80 | **Blyth Spartans** (NL) | H | D | 1-1 | Edwards |
| | | 2r | 16.12.80 | **Blyth Spartans** | A | D | 2-2aet | Edwards, Norrie |
| | | 2 2r | 22.12.80 | **Blyth Spartans** | H | W | 2-1aet | Norrie, Croft |
| | | | | *played at Elland Road* | | | | |
| | | 3 | 03.01.81 | **Doncaster Rovers** (D4) | H | W | 1-0 | Deacy |
| | | 4 | 24.01.81 | **Tottenham Hotspur** (D1) | A | L | 0-2 | |
| 1981-82 | (D4) | 1 | 21.11.81 | **Rochdale** (D4) | A | D | 2-2 | Whitehurst, McClaren |
| | | 1r | 24.11.81 | **Rochdale** | H | D | 2-2aet | Whitehurst, Swann |
| | | 1 2r | 30.11.81 | **Rochdale** | | W | 1-0aet | McClaren |
| | | | | *played at Elland Road* | | | | |
| | | 2 | 04.01.82 | **Hartlepool Utd** (D4) | H | W | 2-0 | Marwood, Mutrie |
| | | 3 | 18.01.82 | **Chelsea** (D2) | A | D | 0-0 | |
| | | 3r | 21.01.82 | **Chelsea** | H | L | 0-2 | |
| 1982-83 | (D4) | 1 | 20.11.82 | **Sheffield Utd** (D3) | H | D | 1-1 | Kenworthy og |
| | | 1r | 23.11.82 | **Sheffield Utd** | A | L | 0-2 | |
| 1983-84 | (D3) | 1 | 19.11.83 | **Penrith** (NWC) | A | W | 2-0 | Whitehurst, G Roberts |
| | | 2 | 10.12.83 | **Rotherham Utd** (D3) | A | L | 1-2 | Flounders |
| 1984-85 | (D3) | 1 | 17.11.84 | **Bolton Wanderers** (D3) | H | W | 2-1 | Massey, Flounders |

| | | | | | | | |
|---|---|---|---|---|---|---|---|
| | 2 | 08.12.84 | **Tranmere Rovers** (D4) | A | W | 3-0 | Ring, McLaren, Skipper |
| | 3 | 05.01.85 | **Brighton** (D2) | A | L | 0-1 | |
| 1985-86 (D2) | 3 | 04.01.86 | **Plymouth Argyle** (D3) | H | D | 2-2 | Flounders 2 |
| | 3r | 07.01.86 | **Plymouth Argyle** | A | W | 1-0 | Roberts |
| | 4 | 25.01.86 | **Brighton** (D2) | H | L | 2-3 | Roberts, McEwan |
| 1986-87 (D2) | 3 | 31.01.87 | **Shrewsbury Town** (D2) | A | W | 2-1 | Bunn, Saville |
| | 4 | 03.02.87 | **Swansea City** (D4) | A | W | 1-0 | Jobson |
| | 5 | 21.02.87 | **Wigan Athletic** (D3) | A | L | 0-3 | |
| 1987-88 (D2) | 3 | 09.01.88 | **Watford** (D1) | A | D | 1-1 | Roberts |
| | 3r | 12.01.88 | **Watford** | H | D | 2-2aet | Williams, Dyer |
| | 3 2r | 18.01.88 | **Watford** | A | L | 0-1 | |
| 1988-89 (D2) | 3 | 07.01.89 | **Cardiff City** (D3) | A | W | 2-1 | Brown, Edwards |
| | 4 | 28.01.89 | **Bradford City** (D2) | A | W | 2-1 | Whitehurst, Edwards |
| | 5 | 18.02.89 | **Liverpool** (D1) | H | L | 2-3 | Whitehurst, Edwards |
| 1989-90 (D2) | 3 | 06.01.90 | **Newcastle Utd** (D1) | H | L | 0-1 | |
| 1990-91 (D2) | 3 | 05.01.91 | **Notts County** (D2) | H | L | 2-5 | Buckley, McParland |
| 1991-92 (D3) | 1 | 16.11.91 | **Morecambe** (NPL) | A | W | 1-0 | Wilcox |
| | 2 | 07.12.91 | **Blackpool** (D4) | A | W | 1-0 | Hunter |
| | 3 | 04.01.92 | **Chelsea** (D1) | H | L | 0-2 | |
| 1992-93 (D2) | 1 | 14.11.92 | **Darlington** (D3) | A | W | 2-1 | Atkinson, Norton |
| | 2 | 05.12.92 | **Rotherham Utd** (D2) | A | L | 0-1 | |
| 1993-94 (D2) | 1 | 13.11.93 | **Runcorn** (Conf) | A | - | 1-0ab | Atkinson |
| | | | *Match abandoned after 29 minutes for safety reasons following the collapse of a wall* | | | | |
| | 1 | 23.11.93 | **Runcorn** | A | W | 2-0 | Brown, Hargreaves |
| | | | *played at Witton Albion* | | | | |
| | 2 | 04.12.93 | **Chester City** (D3) | A | L | 0-2 | |
| 1994-95 (D2) | 1 | 12.11.94 | **Lincoln City** (D3) | H | L | 0-1 | |
| 1995-96 (D2) | 1 | 11.11.95 | **Wrexham** (D2) | H | D | 0-0 | |
| | 1r | 21.11.95 | **Wrexham** | A | D | 0-0aet | |
| | | | *Wrexham won 3-1 on penalties* | | | | |
| 1996-97 (D3) | 1 | 17.11.96 | **Whitby Town** (NL) | A | D | 0-0 | |
| | 1r | 26.11.96 | **Whitby Town** | H | W | 8-4aet | Darby 6, Peacock, Mann |
| | 2 | 07.12.96 | **Crewe Alexandra** (D2) | H | L | 1-5 | Joyce |
| 1997-98 (D3) | 1 | 15.11.97 | **Hednesford Town** (Conf) | H | L | 0-2 | |
| 1998-99 (D3) | 1 | 14.11.98 | **Salisbury City** (SL) | A | W | 2-0 | Rioch, McGinty |
| | 2 | 05.12.98 | **Luton Town** (D2) | A | W | 2-1 | Morley, Dewhurst |
| | 3 | 02.01.99 | **Aston Villa** (PL) | A | L | 0-3 | |
| 1999-00 (D3) | 1 | 30.10.99 | **Macclesfield T** (D3) | A | D | 0-0 | |
| | 1r | 09.11.99 | **Macclesfield T** | H | W | 4-0 | Eyre 2, Greaves, Brown |
| | 2 | 20.11.99 | **Hayes** (Conf) | A | D | 2-2 | Roddis og, Edwards |
| | 2r | 30.11.99 | **Hayes** | H | W | 3-2aet | Brown, Edwards, Wood |
| | 3 | 11.12.99 | **Chelsea** (PL) | H | L | 1-6 | Brown |
| 2000-01 (D3) | 1 | 18.11.00 | **Kettering Town** (Conf) | A | D | 0-0 | |
| | 1r | 28.11.00 | **Kettering Town** | H | L | 0-1 | |
| 2001-02 (D3) | 1 | 17.11.01 | **Northwich V** (Conf) | A | W | 5-2 | Johnsson, Matthews, Dudfield, Alexander, Barnard og |
| | 2 | 08.12.01 | **Oldham Athletic** (D2) | H | L | 2-3 | Dudfield, Alexander |
| 2002-03 (D3) | 1 | 16.11.02 | **Macclesfield T** (D3) | H | L | 0-3 | |

## HULL TOWN

*Formed 1879. Played on open space at Argyll Street, near the Nag's Head Inn. Entered FA Cup for two seasons only.*

| | | | | | | | |
|---|---|---|---|---|---|---|---|
| 1883-84 | 1 | 03.11.83 | **Grimsby Town** | H | L | 1-3 | Percy |
| 1884-85 | 1 | 01.11.84 | **Lincoln City** | H | L | 1-5 | |

## HUNGERFORD TOWN

*Formed 1886. First entered FA Cup: 1973-74. Members of the Isthmian League.*

| | | | | | | | |
|---|---|---|---|---|---|---|---|
| 1979-80 (IL) | 1 | 24.11.79 | **Slough Town** (IL) | A | L | 1-3 | Farr |

# HURST

**See Ashton United**

| | | | | | | | | |
|---|---|---|---|---|---|---|---|---|
| 1883-84 | | 1 | 20.10.83 | **Turton** | H | W | 3-0 | |
| | | 2 | 01.12.83 | **Irwell Springs** | H | W | 3-2 | |
| | | | | *FA ordered replay after protest, but Hurst scratched* | | | | |
| 1884-85 | | 1 | 18.10.84 | **Church FC** | A | L | 2-3 | |
| 1885-86 | | 1 | 31.10.85 | **Bradshaw** | H | W | 3-1 | |
| | | 2 | | Halliwell | | | - | |
| | | | | *Hurst scratched. Halliwell walkover* | | | | |
| 1887-88 | | 1 | 15.10.87 | **Astley Bridge** | H | W | 5-3 | |
| | | | | *FA disqualified Hurst after protest* | | | | |

# HYDE UNITED

*Formed 1885 as Hyde FC. Reformed 1919 as Hyde United. Hyde FC gained an everlasting place in English soccer history when they lost 26-0 to Preston North End on October 15, 1887 – the biggest ever winning margin in FA Cup history. Members of the Northern Premier League.*

**as Hyde FC**

| | | | | | | | | |
|---|---|---|---|---|---|---|---|---|
| 1887-88 | | 1 | 15.10.87 | **Preston North End** | A | L | 0-26 | |

**as Hyde Utd**

| | | | | | | | | |
|---|---|---|---|---|---|---|---|---|
| 1954-55 | (CC) | 1 | 20.11.54 | **Workington** (3N) | A | L | 1-5 | Hilton |
| 1983-84 | (NPL) | 1 | 19.11.83 | **Burnley** (D3) | H | L | 0-2 | |
| | | | | *played at Turf Moor* | | | | |
| 1994-95 | (NPL) | 1 | 12.11.94 | **Darlington** (D3) | H | L | 1-3 | Kimmins |

# ILFORD

*Formed 1881. First entered FA Cup: 1890-91. FA Amateur Cup winners: 1929, 1930. Runners-up: 1936, 1958, 1974. Merged with Leytonstone to form Leytonstone-Ilford 1979, but lost their identity when Leytonstone-Ilford merged with Walthamstow Ave in 1988 to form Redbridge Forest. However, a separate Ilford FC was reconstituted in 1987, claiming 1881 as their original formation date. Now play in the Essex Senior League. See also Leytonstone-Ilford.*

| | | | | | | | | |
|---|---|---|---|---|---|---|---|---|
| 1925-26 | (IL) | 1 | 28.11.25 | **London Cal** (IL) | A | W | 2-1 | V F Welch, Adey |
| | | 2 | 12.12.25 | **Clapton** (IL) | A | L | 0-1 | |
| 1927-28 | (IL) | 1 | 26.11.27 | **Dulwich Hamlet** (IL) | H | W | 4-0 | Drane 2, Dellow 2 |
| | | 2 | 10.12.27 | **Exeter City** (3S) | A | L | 3-5 | Drane, Holmes 2 |
| 1928-29 | (IL) | 1 | 24.11.28 | **Northfleet Utd** (SL) | A | L | 2-5 | Craymer, Drane |
| 1929-30 | (IL) | 1 | 30.11.29 | **Watford** (3S) | H | L | 0-3 | |
| 1930-31 | (IL) | 1 | 29.11.30 | **Brentford** (3S) | H | L | 1-6 | Peploe |
| 1932-33 | (IL) | 1 | 26.11.32 | **Newport County** (3S) | A | L | 2-4 | Drane, Charlton og |
| 1933-34 | (IL) | 1 | 25.11.33 | **Swindon Town** (3S) | H | L | 2-4 | Halerow, Hellard |
| 1936-37 | (IL) | 1 | 28.11.36 | **Reading** (3S) | H | L | 2-4 | Watts, Hellard |
| 1958-59 | (IL) | 1 | 15.11.58 | **Norwich City** (D3) | A | L | 1-3 | Winch |
| 1974-75 | (IL) | 1 | 23.11.74 | **Romford** (SL) | A | W | 2-0 | Butterfield, Turley |
| | | 2 | 14.12.74 | **Southend Utd** (D3) | H | L | 0-2 | |

# ILKESTON TOWN

*Formed 1894. First entered FA Cup: 1894-95. League club beaten: Carlisle United. Members of the Southern League.*

| | | | | | | | | |
|---|---|---|---|---|---|---|---|---|
| 1951-52 | (ML) | 1 | 24.11.51 | **Rochdale** (3N) | H | L | 0-2 | |
| 1956-57 | (ML) | 1 | 17.11.56 | **Blyth Spartans** (NEL) | H | L | 1-5 | Marsh |
| 1997-98 | (SL) | 1 | 15.11.97 | **Boston Utd** (NPL) | H | W | 2-1 | Carmichael 2 |
| | | 2 | 06.12.97 | **Scunthorpe Utd** (D3) | A | D | 1-1 | Robinson |
| | | 2r | 17.12.97 | **Scunthorpe Utd** | H | L | 1-2 | Moore |
| 1999-00 | (SL) | 1 | 30.10.99 | **Carlisle Utd** (D3) | H | W | 2-1 | Moore, Raynor |
| | | 2 | 20.11.99 | **Rushden & D** (Conf) | H | D | 1-1 | Eshelby |
| | | 2r | 30.11.99 | **Rushden & D** | A | L | 0-3 | |
| 2000-01 | (SL) | 1 | 18.11.00 | **Swindon Town** (D2) | A | L | 1-4 | Cox |

# IPSWICH TOWN

*Formed 1878. First entered FA Cup: 1890-91. FA Cupwinners: 1978. Record FA Cup win: 11-0 v Cromer, 3rd qualifying round, 31.10.36. In Competition Proper: 7-0 v Street, 1st round, 26.11.38; Record FA Cup defeat: 1-7 v Southampton, 3rd round, 02.02.1974.*

1890-91 1q Reading (H) 2-0; 2q Norwich Thorpe (A) 4-0; 3q Huntington Co (H) 5-2; 4q 93rd Highlanders (H) 1-4

| | | | | | | | |
|---|---|---|---|---|---|---|---|
| 1891-92 | | | 1q Old Westminsters (A) 0-5 | | | | |
| 1892-93 | | | 1q Old Wykehamists (H) 4-0; 2q Old Westminsters (A) 1-4 | | | | |
| 1893-94 – 1929-30 | | | did not enter | | | | |
| 1930-31 (SAL) | | | ExP Harwich & P (H) 5-0; P Leiston Works (H) 5-2; 1q Severalls A (H) 6-1; 2q Crittalls A (H) 2-3 | | | | |
| 1931-32 (SAL) | | | P Leiston Works (A) 2-3 | | | | |
| 1932-33 (SAL) | | | ExP Kirkley (H) 0-0; ExPr Kirkley (A) 3-2; P Cambridge T (A) 2-2; Pr Cambridge T (H) 1-2 | | | | |
| 1933-34 (SAL) | | | ExP Gorleston (A) 2-3 | | | | |
| 1934-35 (SAL) | | | P Norwich St Barnabas (H) 3-2; 1q Norwich YMCA (H) 1-1; 1qr Norwich YMCA (H) 4-2; 2q Frost A (H) 2-0; 3q Gorleston (A) 0-2 | | | | |
| 1935-36 (ECL) | | | 1q Yarmouth T (H) 0-0; 1qr Yarmouth T (A) 1-4 | | | | |
| 1936-37 (SL) | | | P Eastern Co. U. (H) 7-0; 1q Stowmarket (H) 8-0; 2q Lowestoft T (A) 1-1; 2q r Lowestoft T (H) 7-1; 3q Cromer (H) 11-0; 4q Cambridge T (H) 2-1 | | | | |
| | 1 | 28.11.36 | **Watford** (3S) | H | W | 2-1 | Bruce, Carter |
| | 2 | 12.12.36 | **Spennymoor Utd** (NEL) | H | L | 1-2 | Carter |
| 1937-38 (SL) | | | 4q Hoffmann A (A) 3-0 | | | | |
| | 1 | 27.11.37 | **Yeovil & Petters Utd** (SL) | A | L | 1-2 | Astill |
| 1938-39 (3S) | 1 | 26.11.38 | **Street** (WL) | H | W | 7-0 | Chadwick 4, Davies 2, Fletcher |
| | 2 | 10.12.38 | **Torquay Utd** (3S) | H | W | 4-1 | Little 2, Jones, Chadwick |
| | 3 | 07.01.39 | **Aston Villa** (D1) | A | D | 1-1 | Hutcheson |
| | 3r | 11.01.39 | **Aston Villa** | H | L | 1-2 | Jones |
| 1945-46 (3S) | 1 1L | 17.11.45 | **Wisbech Town** (UCL) | A | W | 3-0 | Little 2, Fletcher |
| | 1 2L | 24.11.45 | **Wisbech Town** | H | W | 5-0 | Parker 3, Price 2 |
| | 2 1L | 08.12.45 | **QPR** (3S) | A | L | 0-4 | |
| | 2 2L | 15.12.45 | **QPR** | H | L | 0-2 | |
| 1946-47 (3S) | 1 | 30.11.46 | **Torquay Utd** (3S) | H | W | 2-0 | T Parker, S Parker |
| | 2 | 14.12.46 | **Walsall** (3S) | A | D | 0-0 | |
| | 2r | 18.12.46 | **Walsall** | H | L | 0-1 | |
| 1947-48 (3S) | 1 | 29.11.47 | **Swindon Town** (3S) | A | L | 2-4 | T Parker, S Parker |
| 1948-49 (3S) | 1 | 27.11.48 | **Aldershot** (3S) | H | - | 1-0ab | Dempsey |
| | | | *abandoned after 63 minutes – fog* | | | | |
| | 1 | 04.12.48 | **Aldershot** (3S) | H | L | 0-3 | |
| 1949-50 (3S) | 1 | 26.11.49 | **Brighton** (3S) | H | W | 2-1 | Baird, Brown |
| | 2 | 10.12.49 | **Chelmsford City** (SL) | A | D | 1-1 | Brown |
| | 2r | 14.12.49 | **Chelmsford City** | H | W | 1-0aet | S Parker |
| | 3 | 07.01.50 | **West Ham Utd** (D2) | A | L | 1-5 | S Parker |
| 1950-51 (3S) | 1 | 25.11.50 | **Leyton Orient** (3S) | A | W | 2-1 | T Parker, Jennings |
| | 2 | 09.12.50 | **Brighton** (3S) | A | L | 0-2 | |
| 1951-52 (3S) | 1 | 29.11.51 | **Merthyr Tydfil** (SL) | A | D | 2-2aet | McCrory, Garneys |
| | 1r | 05.12.51 | **Merthyr Tydfil** | H | W | 1-0 | Roberts |
| | 2 | 15.12.51 | **Exeter City** (3S) | H | W | 4-0 | Garneys 2, Driver, Dobson |
| | 3 | 12.01.52 | **Gateshead AFC** (3N) | H | D | 2-2 | Garneys, Myles |
| | 3r | 16.01.52 | **Gateshead AFC** | A | D | 3-3aet | Dobson 2, Roberts |
| | 3 2r | 21.01.52 | **Gateshead AFC** | | L | 1-2aet | Garneys |
| | | | *played at Bramall Lane* | | | | |
| 1952-53 (3S) | 1 | 22.11.52 | **Bournemouth** (3S) | H | D | 2-2 | Elsworthy, Garneys |
| | 1r | 26.11.52 | **Bournemouth** | A | D | 2-2aet | Elsworthy, Garneys |
| | 1 2r | 01.12.52 | **Bournemouth** | | W | 3-2 | Garneys 2, Gaynor |
| | | | *played at Highbury* | | | | |
| | 2 | 06.12.52 | **Bradford City** (3N) | A | D | 1-1 | Elsworthy |
| | 2r | 10.12.52 | **Bradford City** | H | W | 5-1 | Brown 2, Elsworthy 2, Garneys |
| | 3 | 10.01.53 | **Everton** (D2) | A | L | 2-3 | Brown, Garneys |
| 1953-54 (3S) | 1 | 21.11.53 | **Reading** (3S) | H | W | 4-1 | Garneys 2, Elsworthy, Crowe |
| | 2 | 12.12.53 | **Walthamstow Ave** (IL) | H | D | 2-2 | Myles, Brown |
| | 2r | 16.12.53 | **Walthamstow Ave** | A | W | 1-0 | Crowe |
| | 3 | 09.01.54 | **Oldham Athletic** (D2) | H | D | 3-3 | Myles, Reed, Garneys |
| | 3r | 12.01.54 | **Oldham Athletic** | A | W | 1-0 | Garneys |
| | 4 | 30.01.54 | **Birmingham City** (D2) | H | W | 1-0 | Reed |
| | 5 | 20.02.54 | **Preston North End** (D1) | A | L | 1-6 | Garneys |
| 1954-55 (D2) | 3 | 08.01.55 | **Bishop Auckland** (NL) | H | D | 2-2 | Reed, Garneys |

| | | | | | | | | |
|---|---|---|---|---|---|---|---|---|
| | | 3r | 12.01.55 | **Bishop Auckland** | A | L | 0-3 | |
| 1955-56 | (3S) | 1 | 19.11.55 | **Peterborough Utd** (ML) | A | L | 1-3 | T Parker |
| 1956-57 | (3S) | 1 | 17.11.56 | **Hastings Utd** (SL) | H | W | 4-0 | Phillips 2, Leadbetter, Garneys |
| | | 2 | 08.12.56 | **Watford** (3S) | A | W | 3-1 | Phillips 2, Garneys |
| | | 3 | 05.01.57 | **Fulham** (D2) | H | L | 2-3 | Phillips, Garneys |
| 1957-58 | (D2) | 3 | 04.01.58 | **Crystal Palace** (3S) | A | W | 1-0 | McLuckie |
| | | 4 | 25.01.58 | **Manchester Utd** (D1) | A | L | 0-2 | |
| 1958-59 | (D2) | 3 | 10.01.59 | **Huddersfield Town** (D2) | H | W | 1-0 | Crawford |
| | | 4 | 24.01.59 | **Stoke City** (D2) | A | W | 1-0 | Rees |
| | | 5 | 14.02.59 | **Luton Town** (D1) | H | L | 2-5 | Rees 2 |
| 1959-60 | (D2) | 3 | 09.01.60 | **Peterborough Utd** (ML) | H | L | 2-3 | Phillips, Millward |
| 1960-61 | (D2) | 3 | 07.01.61 | **Southampton** (D2) | A | L | 1-7 | Page og |
| 1961-62 | (D1) | 3 | 06.01.62 | **Luton Town** (D2) | H | D | 1-1 | Phillips |
| | | 3r | 10.01.62 | **Luton Town** | A | D | 1-1aet | Elsworthy |
| | | 3 2r | 15.01.62 | **Luton Town** | | W | 5-1 | Stephenson 2, Phillips 2, Moran |
| | | | | *played at Highbury* | | | | |
| | | 4 | 27.01.62 | **Norwich City** (D2) | A | D | 1-1 | Leadbetter |
| | | 4r | 30.01.62 | **Norwich City** | H | L | 1-2 | Crawford |
| 1962-63 | (D1) | 3 | 09.01.63 | **Mansfield Town** (D4) | A | W | 3-2 | Leadbetter 3 |
| | | 4 | 30.01.63 | **Leicester City** (D1) | A | L | 1-3 | Blackwood |
| 1963-64 | (D1) | 3 | 04.01.64 | **Oldham Athletic** (D3) | H | W | 6-3 | Baker 3, Hegan 2, Broadfoot |
| | | 4 | 25.01.64 | **Stoke City** (D1) | H | D | 1-1 | Baxter |
| | | 4r | 29.01.64 | **Stoke City** | A | L | 0-1 | |
| 1964-65 | (D2) | 3 | 09.01.65 | **Swindon Town** (D2) | A | W | 2-1 | Brogan 2 |
| | | 4 | 30.01.65 | **Tottenham Hotspur** (D1) | A | L | 0-5 | |
| 1965-66 | (D2) | 3 | 22.01.66 | **Southport** (D4) | A | D | 0-0 | |
| | | 3r | 25.01.66 | **Southport** | H | L | 2-3 | Baker, Brogan |
| 1966-67 | (D2) | 3 | 28.01.67 | **Shrewsbury Town** (D3) | H | W | 4-1 | Hegan, Crawford, Brogan, Harper |
| | | 4 | 18.02.67 | **Carlisle Utd** (D2) | H | W | 2-0 | Brogan, Crawford |
| | | 5 | 11.03.67 | **Manchester City** (D1) | H | D | 1-1 | Crawford |
| | | 5r | 14.03.67 | **Manchester City** | A | L | 0-3 | |
| 1967-68 | (D2) | 3 | 27.01.68 | **Chelsea** (D1) | A | L | 0-3 | |
| 1968-69 | (D1) | 3 | 04.01.69 | **Everton** (D1) | A | L | 1-2 | O'Rourke |
| 1969-70 | (D1) | 3 | 03.01.70 | **Manchester Utd** (D1) | H | L | 0-1 | |
| 1970-71 | (D1) | 3 | 11.01.71 | **Newcastle Utd** (D1) | A | D | 1-1 | Mills |
| | | 3r | 13.01.71 | **Newcastle Utd** | H | W | 2-1 | Viljoen, Hill |
| | | 4 | 23.01.71 | **WBA** (D1) | A | D | 1-1 | Clarke |
| | | 4r | 26.01.71 | **WBA** | H | W | 3-0 | Viljoen, Clarke, Robertson |
| | | 5 | 13.02.71 | **Stoke City** (D1) | A | D | 0-0 | |
| | | 5r | 16.02.71 | **Stoke City** | H | L | 0-1 | |
| 1971-72 | (D1) | 3 | 15.01.72 | **Peterborough Utd** (D4) | A | W | 2-0 | Hill, Viljoen |
| | | 4 | 05.02.72 | **Birmingham City** (D2) | A | L | 0-1 | |
| 1972-73 | (D1) | 3 | 13.01.73 | **Chelmsford City** (SL) | A | W | 3-1 | Hamilton, Harper, Johnson |
| | | 4 | 03.02.73 | **Chelsea** (D1) | A | L | 0-2 | |
| 1973-74 | (D1) | 3 | 05.01.74 | **Sheffield Utd** (D1) | H | W | 3-2 | Beattie 2, Hamilton |
| | | 4 | 26.01.74 | **Manchester Utd** (D1) | A | W | 1-0 | Beattie |
| | | 5 | 16.02.74 | **Liverpool** (D1) | A | L | 0-2 | |
| 1974-75 | (D1) | 3 | 04.01.75 | **Wolverhampton W** (D1) | A | W | 2-1 | Viljoen, Johnson |
| | | 4 | 25.01.75 | **Liverpool** (D1) | H | W | 1-0 | Mills |
| | | 5 | 15.02.75 | **Aston Villa** (D2) | H | W | 3-2 | Hamilton 2, Johnson |
| | | 6 | 08.03.75 | **Leeds Utd** (D1) | H | D | 0-0 | |
| | | 6r | 11.03.75 | **Leeds Utd** | A | D | 1-1aet | Johnson |
| | | 6 2r | 25.03.75 | **Leeds Utd** | | D | 0-0aet | |
| | | | | *played at Filbert Street* | | | | |
| | | 6 3r | 27.03.75 | **Leeds Utd** | | W | 3-2 | Whymark, Woods, Hamilton |
| | | | | *played at Filbert Street* | | | | |
| | | SF | 05.04.75 | **West Ham Utd** (D1) | | D | 0-0 | |
| | | | | *played at Villa Park* | | | | |
| | | SFr | 09.04.75 | **West Ham Utd** | | L | 1-2 | Jennings og |
| | | | | *played at Stamford Bridge* | | | | |
| 1975-76 | (D1) | 3 | 03.01.76 | **Halifax Town** (D3) | H | W | 3-1 | Lambert 3 |

| | | | | | | | |
|---|---|---|---|---|---|---|---|
| | 4 | 24.01.76 | **Wolverhampton W** (D1) | H | D | 0-0 | |
| | 4r | 27.01.76 | **Wolverhampton W** | A | L | 0-1 | |
| 1976-77 (D1) | 3 | 08.01.77 | **Bristol City** (D1) | H | W | 4-1 | Mariner 2, Gates, Whymark |
| | 4 | 29.01.77 | **Wolverhampton W** (D2) | H | D | 2-2 | Mariner, Burley |
| | 4r | 02.02.77 | **Wolverhampton W** | A | L | 0-1 | |
| 1977-78 (D1) | 3 | 07.01.78 | **Cardiff City** (D2) | A | W | 2-0 | Mariner |
| | 4 | 28.01.78 | **Hartlepool Utd** (D4) | H | W | 4-1 | Viljoen 2, Mariner, Talbot |
| | 5 | 18.02.78 | **Bristol Rovers** (D2) | A | D | 2-2 | Turner 2 |
| | 5r | 28.02.78 | **Bristol Rovers** | H | W | 3-0 | Mills, Mariner, Woods |
| | 6 | 11.03.78 | **Millwall** (D2) | A | W | 6-1 | Mariner 3, Burley, Talbot, Wark |
| | SF | 08.04.78 | **WBA** (D1) | | W | 3-1 | Talbot, Mills, Wark |
| | | | *played at Highbury* | | | | |
| | F | 06.05.78 | **Arsenal** (D1) | | W | 1-0 | Osborne |
| | | | *played at Wembley Stadium* | | | | |
| 1978-79 (D1) | 3 | 10.01.79 | **Carlisle Utd** (D3) | H | W | 3-2 | Wark, Muhren, Beattie |
| | 4 | 27.01.79 | **Orient** (D2) | H | D | 0-0 | |
| | 4r | 30.01.79 | **Orient** | A | W | 2-0 | Mariner 2 |
| | 5 | 26.02.79 | **Bristol Rovers** (D2) | H | W | 6-1 | Brazil 2, Mills, Mariner, Muhren, Geddis |
| | 6 | 10.03.79 | **Liverpool** (D1) | H | L | 0-1 | |
| 1979-80 (D1) | 3 | 05.01.80 | **Preston North End** (D2) | A | W | 3-0 | Mariner 2, Brazil |
| | 4 | 26.01.80 | **Bristol City** (D1) | A | W | 2-1 | Wark, Mariner |
| | 5 | 16.02.80 | **Chester** (D3) | H | W | 2-1 | Wark, Burley |
| | 6 | 08.03.80 | **Everton** (D1) | A | L | 1-2 | Beattie |
| 1980-81 (D1) | 3 | 03.01.81 | **Aston Villa** (D1) | A | W | 1-0 | Mariner |
| | 4 | 24.01.81 | **Shrewsbury Town** (D2) | H | D | 0-0 | |
| | 4r | 27.01.81 | **Shrewsbury Town** | A | W | 3-0 | Gates 2, Wark |
| | 5 | 14.02.81 | **Charlton Athletic** (D3) | H | W | 2-0 | Wark, Mariner |
| | 6 | 07.03.81 | **Nottingham Forest** (D1) | A | D | 3-3 | Mariner, Anderson og, Thyssen |
| | 6r | 10.03.81 | **Nottingham Forest** | H | W | 1-0 | Muhren |
| | SF | 11.04.81 | **Manchester City** (D1) | | L | 0-1aet | |
| | | | *played at Villa Park* | | | | |
| 1981-82 (D1) | 3 | 02.01.82 | **Birmingham City** (D1) | A | W | 3-2 | Brazil 2, Wark |
| | 4 | 23.01.82 | **Luton Town** (D2) | A | W | 3-0 | Gates 2, Brazil |
| | 5 | 13.02.82 | **Shrewsbury Town** (D2) | A | L | 1-2 | D'Avray |
| 1982-83 (D1) | 3 | 08.01.83 | **Charlton Athletic** (D2) | H | W | 3-2 | Wark 2, Thijssen |
| | 4 | 29.01.83 | **Grimsby Town** (D2) | H | W | 2-0 | Osman, McCall |
| | 5 | 19.02.83 | **Norwich City** (D1) | A | L | 0-1 | |
| 1983-84 (D1) | 3 | 07.01.84 | **Cardiff City** (D2) | A | W | 3-0 | Gates 3 |
| | 4 | 28.01.84 | **Shrewsbury Town** (D2) | A | L | 0-2 | |
| 1984-85 (D1) | 3 | 05.01.85 | **Bristol Rovers** (D3) | A | W | 2-1 | Dozzell, Brennan |
| | 4 | 26.01.85 | **Gillingham** (D3) | H | W | 3-2 | Wilson, Sage og, Dozzell |
| | 5 | 04.03.85 | **Sheffield Wed** (D1) | H | W | 3-2 | Zondervan, Burley, Sunderland |
| | 6 | 09.03.85 | **Everton** (D1) | A | D | 2-2 | Wilson, Zondervan |
| | 6r | 13.03.85 | **Everton** | H | L | 0-1 | |
| 1985-86 (D1) | 3 | 04.01.86 | **Bradford City** (D2) | H | D | 4-4 | Evans, Wilson, Brennan, D'Avray |
| | 3r | 13.01.86 | **Bradford City** | A | W | 1-0 | Brennan |
| | | | *played at Elland Road* | | | | |
| | 4 | 25.01.86 | **West Ham Utd** (D1) | A | D | 0-0 | |
| | 4r | 04.02.86 | **West Ham Utd** | H | D | 1-1aet | Dozzell |
| | 4 2r | 06.02.86 | **West Ham Utd** | H | L | 0-1aet | |
| 1986-87 (D2) | 3 | 10.01.87 | **Birmingham City** (D2) | H | L | 0-1 | |
| 1987-88 (D2) | 3 | 10.01.88 | **Manchester Utd** (D1) | H | L | 1-2 | Humes |
| 1988-89 (D2) | 3 | 07.01.89 | **Nottingham Forest** (D1) | A | L | 0-3 | |
| 1989-90 (D2) | 3 | 06.01.90 | **Leeds Utd** (D2) | A | W | 1-0 | Dozzell |
| | 4 | 27.01.90 | **Barnsley** (D2) | A | L | 0-2 | |
| 1990-91 (D2) | 3 | 05.01.91 | **Southampton** (D1) | A | L | 2-3 | Dozzell 2 |
| 1991-92 (D2) | 3 | 04.01.92 | **Hartlepool Utd** (D3) | H | D | 1-1 | Dozzell |
| | 3r | 15.01.92 | **Hartlepool Utd** | A | W | 2-0 | Dozzell, Milton |
| | 4 | 05.02.92 | **Bournemouth** (D3) | H | W | 3-0 | Dozzell, Whitton, Kiwomya |
| | 5 | 16.02.92 | **Liverpool** (D1) | H | D | 0-0 | |

| | | | | | | | | |
|---|---|---|---|---|---|---|---|---|
| | | 5r | 26.02.92 | **Liverpool** | A | L | 2-3aet | Johnson, Dozzell |
| 1992-93 | (PL) | 3 | 12.01.93 | **Plymouth Argyle** (D2) | H | W | 3-1 | Thompson, Dozzell, Whitton (p) |
| | | 4 | 23.01.93 | **Tranmere Rovers** (D1) | A | W | 2-1 | Dozzell, Guentchev |
| | | 5 | 13.02.93 | **Grimsby Town** (D1) | H | W | 4-0 | Guentchev 3, Wark |
| | | 6 | 06.03.93 | **Arsenal** (PL) | H | L | 2-4 | Kiwomya, Guentchev |
| 1993-94 | (PL) | 3 | 08.01.94 | **Swindon Town** (PL) | A | D | 1-1 | Marshall |
| | | 3r | 18.01.94 | **Swindon Town** | H | W | 2-1aet | Stockwell, Marshall |
| | | 4 | 29.01.94 | **Tottenham Hotspur** (PL) | H | W | 3-0 | Marshall, T Johnson, Thompson |
| | | 5 | 19.02.94 | **Wolverhampton W** (D1) | A | D | 1-1 | Wark |
| | | 5r | 02.03.94 | **Wolverhampton W** | H | L | 1-2 | Palmer |
| 1994-95 | (PL) | 3 | 07.01.95 | **Wrexham** (D2) | A | L | 1-2 | Linighan |
| 1995-96 | (D1) | 3 | 06.01.96 | **Blackburn Rovers** (PL) | H | D | 0-0 | |
| | | 3r | 16.01.96 | **Blackburn Rovers** | A | W | 1-0aet | Mason |
| | | 4 | 13.02.96 | **Walsall** (D2) | H | W | 1-0 | Mason |
| | | 5 | 17.02.96 | **Aston Villa** (PL) | H | L | 1-3 | Mason |
| 1996-97 | (D1) | 3 | 04.01.97 | **Nottingham Forest** (PL) | A | L | 0-3 | |
| 1997-98 | (D1) | 3 | 03.01.98 | **Bristol Rovers** (D2) | A | D | 1-1 | Stockwell |
| | | 3r | 13.01.98 | **Bristol Rovers** | H | W | 1-0 | T Johnson |
| | | 4 | 24.01.98 | **Sheffield Utd** (D1) | H | D | 1-1 | T Johnson |
| | | 4r | 03.02.98 | **Sheffield Utd** | A | L | 0-1 | |
| 1998-99 | (D1) | 3 | 02.01.99 | **Tranmere Rovers** (D1) | A | W | 1-0 | McGreal og |
| | | 4 | 23.01.99 | **Everton** (PL) | A | L | 0-1 | |
| 1999-00 | (D1) | 3 | 13.12.99 | **Southampton** (PL) | H | L | 0-1 | |
| 2000-01 | (PL) | 3 | 06.01.01 | **Morecambe** (Conf) | A | W | 3-0 | Stewart, Armstrong, Wright |
| | | 4 | 27.01.01 | **Sunderland** (PL) | A | L | 0-1 | |
| 2001-02 | (PL) | 3 | 05.01.02 | **Dagenham & Red** (Conf) | A | W | 4-1 | Peralta 2, Magilton, Stewart |
| | | 4 | 27.01.02 | **Manchester City** (D1) | H | L | 1-4 | M Bent |
| 2002-03 | (D1) | 3 | 04.01.03 | **Morecambe** (Conf) | H | W | 4-0 | Clapham, D Bent 2, Ambrose |
| | | 4 | 25.01.03 | **Sheffield Utd** (D1) | A | L | 3-4 | Miller (p), D Bent, Gaardsoe |

## IRTHLINGBOROUGH TOWN

*Entered FA Cup 1902-03 – 1927-28. No connection with later Irthlingborough Diamonds who subsequently merged with Rushden Town to form Rushden & Diamonds.*

| | | | | | | | | |
|---|---|---|---|---|---|---|---|---|
| 1906-07 | (UCL) | 1 | 12.01.07 | **Burslem PV** (D2) | H | L | 1-7 | Barker |

## IRWELL SPRINGS

*Formed 1879. Entered FA Cup: 1882-83 – 1888-89. Based in Bacup, and played at the Broad Clough, near The Roebuck Inn.*

| | | | | | | | | |
|---|---|---|---|---|---|---|---|---|
| 1882-83 | | 1 | 28.10.82 | **Lower Darwen** | A | L | 2-5 | Banham, Pickles |
| 1883-84 | | 1 | 17.11.83 | **Rossendale FC** | A | L | 2-6 | |
| | | | | *FA disqualified Rossendale for professionalism, Irwell Springs re-instated* | | | | |
| | | 2 | 01.12.83 | **Hurst** | A | L | 2-3 | |
| | | | | *FA ordered replay after protest, but Hurst scratched* | | | | |
| | | 3 | 29.12.83 | **Bolton Wanderers** | A | L | 1-8 | |

## JARDINES FC

*Formed 1874. A Nottingham-based works team from Jardines Limited who had an enclosed pitch at Sherwood Forest. Entered FA Cup: 1887-88 – 1890-91.*

| | | | | | | | | |
|---|---|---|---|---|---|---|---|---|
| 1887-88 | | 1 | 15.10.87 | **Notts Rangers** | A | L | 1-10 | |

## JARROW

*First entered FA Cup: 1895-96 and took part until 1949-50. Alf Common, who became the first player to be transferred for £1,000 when he moved from Sunderland to Middlesbrough in February 1905, had a spell at Jarrow early in his career.*

| | | | | | | | | |
|---|---|---|---|---|---|---|---|---|
| 1898-99 | (NAll) | 1 | 28.01.99 | **Everton** (D1) | A | L | 1-3 | McDonald |
| 1899-00 | (NAll) | 1 | 27.01.00 | **Millwall Athletic** (SL) | H | L | 0-2 | |
| 1930-31 | (NEL) | 1 | 29.11.30 | **Crewe Alexandra** (3N) | A | L | 0-1 | |

## KELLS UNITED

*First entered FA Cup: 1931-32. Kells were a mining works club team from Whitehaven.*

| | | | | | | | | |
|---|---|---|---|---|---|---|---|---|
| 1935-36 | (Cumb) | 1 | 30.11.35 | **Stalybridge Celtic** (CC) | A | L | 0-4 | |

# KETTERING TOWN

*Formed 1880. First entered FA Cup: 1888-89. FA Trophy runners-up: 1979, 2000. League clubs beaten: Loughborough, Leicester Fosse, Chesterfield, Swindon Town, Millwall, Swansea City, Oxford United, Bristol Rovers, Halifax, Maidstone United, Hull City. Relegated from The Conference to the Isthmian League 2003.*

| | | | | | | | | |
|---|---|---|---|---|---|---|---|---|
| 1895-96 | (ML) | 1 | 01.02.96 | **Newton Heath** (D2) | A | L | 1-2 | Pell |
| 1896-97 | (ML) | 1 | 30.01.97 | **Newton Heath** (D2) | A | L | 1-5 | Dixon |
| 1898-99 | (ML) | | | 4q Loughborough (D2) (H) 2-1; 5q Leicester Fosse (D2) (H) 1-1; 5q r Leicester Fosse (A) 2-1 | | | | |
| | | 1 | 28.01.99 | **Notts County** (D1) | A | L | 0-2 | |
| 1900-01 | (SL) | 1 | 09.02.01 | **Chesterfield** (D2) | H | D | 1-1 | McMain |
| | | 1r | 13.02.01 | **Chesterfield** | A | W | 2-1aet | Webb 2 |
| | | 2 | 23.02.01 | **Middlesbrough** (D2) | A | L | 0-5 | |
| 1905-06 | (UCL) | 1 | 13.01.06 | **Derby County** (D1) | A | L | 0-4 | |
| 1908-09 | (UCL) | 1 | 16.01.09 | **Bury** (D1) | A | L | 0-8 | |
| 1925-26 | (SL) | 1 | 28.11.25 | **Worcester City** (BDL) | A | D | 0-0 | |
| | | 1r | 03.12.25 | **Worcester City** | H | D | 0-0aet | |
| | | 1 2r | 07.12.25 | **Worcester City** *played at St Andrews* | | W | 2-0 | Alison Starsmore |
| | | 2 | 12.12.25 | **Grimsby Town** (3N) | H | D | 1-1 | Allison |
| | | 2r | 15.12.25 | **Grimsby Town** | A | L | 1-3 | Cairns |
| 1926-27 | (SL) | 1 | 27.11.26 | **Coventry City** (3S) | H | L | 2-3 | Chalmers, Butler |
| 1927-28 | (SL) | 1 | 26.11.27 | **Chatham** (SL) | H | W | 2-0 | Simpson, Starsmore |
| | | 2 | 10.12.27 | **Charlton Athletic** (3S) | A | D | 1-1 | Alison |
| | | 2r | 15.12.27 | **Charlton Athletic** | H | L | 1-2 | Charlesworth |
| 1928-29 | (SL) | 1 | 24.11.28 | **Crystal Palace** (3S) | A | L | 0-2 | |
| 1929-30 | (SL) | 1 | 30.11.29 | **Newport County** (3S) | A | L | 2-3 | Houston, Duncan |
| 1933-34 | (UCL) | 1 | 25.11.33 | **QPR** (3S) | A | L | 0-6 | |
| 1937-38 | (UCL) | 1 | 27.11.37 | **Crystal Palace** (3S) | A | D | 2-2 | Carr, Potter |
| | | 1r | 02.12.37 | **Crystal Palace** | H | L | 0-4 | |
| 1945-46 | (UCL) | 1 1L | 17.11.45 | **Grantham Town** (ML) | H | L | 1-5 | Smith |
| | | 1 2L | 24.11.45 | **Grantham Town** | A | D | 2-2 | Smith, Malloy |
| 1951-52 | (SL) | 1 | 24.11.51 | **Bristol Rovers** (3S) | A | L | 0-3 | |
| 1953-54 | (SL) | 1 | 21.11.53 | **Leyton Orient** (3S) | A | L | 0-3 | |
| 1954-55 | (SL) | 1 | 20.11.54 | **Bishop Auckland** (NL) | A | L | 1-5 | Lane |
| 1958-59 | (SL) | 1 | 15.11.58 | **Peterborough Utd** (ML) | A | D | 2-2 | Toseland, Draper |
| | | 1r | 20.11.58 | **Peterborough Utd** | H | L | 2-3aet | Draper, Burrows |
| 1959-60 | (SL) | 1 | 14.11.59 | **Margate** (SL) | H | D | 1-1 | Burrows |
| | | 1r | 19.11.59 | **Margate** | A | L | 2-3 | Toseland 2 |
| 1960-61 | (SL) | 1 | 05.11.60 | **Wycombe W** (IL) | A | W | 2-1 | Morrow, Walden |
| | | 2 | 26.11.60 | **Reading** (D3) | A | L | 2-4 | Walden, Morrow |
| 1961-62 | (SL) | 1 | 04.11.61 | **Swindon Town** (D3) | A | D | 2-2 | Golding, Curran (p) |
| | | 1r | 08.11.61 | **Swindon Town** | H | W | 3-0 | Curran 2 (1p), Ritchie |
| | | 2 | 25.11.61 | **Northampton Town** (D3) | A | L | 0-3 | |
| 1963-64 | (SL) | 1 | 16.11.63 | **Millwall** (D3) | H | D | 1-1 | Snowdon og |
| | | 1r | 25.11.63 | **Millwall** | A | W | 3-2 | Armour 2, Daldy |
| | | 2 | 07.12.63 | **Oxford Utd** (D4) | A | L | 1-2 | Curran |
| 1964-65 | (SL) | 1 | 14.11.64 | **Millwall** (D4) | A | L | 0-2 | |
| 1968-69 | (SL) | 1 | 16.11.68 | **Waterlooville** (SL) | A | W | 2-1 | Gully, Daldy |
| | | 2 | 07.12.68 | **Dartford** (SL) | H | W | 5-0 | Lillis og, Gully, Daldy, Smith, Walden |
| | | 3 | 04.01.69 | **Bristol Rovers** (D3) | A | D | 1-1 | Reed |
| | | 3r | 07.01.69 | **Bristol Rovers** | H | L | 1-2 | Daldy |
| 1969-70 | (SL) | 1 | 15.11.69 | **Swansea Town** (D4) | H | L | 0-2 | |
| 1971-72 | (SL) | 1 | 20.11.71 | **Barnet** (SL) | H | L | 2-4 | King og, Jacques |
| 1972-73 | (SL) | 1 | 18.11.72 | **Walsall** (D3) | A | D | 3-3 | Clayton 2, Pawley |
| | | 1r | 22.11.72 | **Walsall** | H | L | 1-2 | Pawley |
| 1974-75 | (SL) | 1 | 26.11.74 | **Swansea City** (D4) | A | D | 1-1 | Atkinson |
| | | 1r | 02.12.74 | **Swansea City** | H | W | 3-1 | Pawley, Ashby (p), Clayton |
| | | 2 | 14.12.74 | **Wimbledon** (SL) | A | L | 0-2 | |
| 1976-77 | (SL) | 1 | 20.11.76 | **Oxford Utd** (D3) | H | D | 1-1 | Merrick |
| | | 1r | 23.11.76 | **Oxford Utd** | A | W | 1-0 | Dougan |
| | | 2 | 11.12.76 | **Tooting & M** (IL) | H | W | 1-0 | Clayton |

| | | | | | | | | |
|---|---|---|---|---|---|---|---|---|
| | | 3 | 08.01.77 | **Colchester Utd** (D4) | H | L | 2-3 | Clayton, Kellock |
| 1977-78 | (SL) | 1 | 26.11.77 | **Tilbury** (IL) | A | W | 1-0 | Phipps |
| | | | | *FA declared match void as Kettering fielded ineligible player* | | | | |
| | | 1 | 05.12.77 | **Tilbury** | A | D | 2-2 | Kellock, Phipps |
| | | 1r | 07.12.77 | **Tilbury** | H | L | 2-3 | Kellock, Phipps |
| 1979-80 | (APL) | 1 | 24.11.79 | **Reading** (D3) | A | L | 2-4 | Phipps 2 |
| 1980-81 | (APL) | 1 | 22.11.80 | **Maidstone Utd** (APL) | H | D | 1-1 | Guy |
| | | 1r | 26.11.80 | **Maidstone Utd** | A | D | 0-0aet | |
| | | 1 2r | 01.12.80 | **Maidstone Utd** | A | L | 1-3 | Middleton |
| 1981-82 | (APL) | 1 | 21.11.81 | **Boston Utd** (APL) | A | W | 1-0 | Atkins |
| | | 2 | 02.01.82 | **Blackpool** (D4) | H | L | 0-3 | |
| 1982-83 | (APL) | 1 | 20.11.82 | **Walsall** (D3) | A | L | 0-3 | |
| 1983-84 | (APL) | 1 | 19.11.83 | **Swindon Town** (D4) | H | L | 0-7 | |
| 1984-85 | (APL) | 1 | 17.11.84 | **Bournemouth** (D3) | H | D | 0-0 | |
| | | 1r | 20.11.84 | **Bournemouth** | A | L | 2-3 | Alexander, Jeffrey |
| 1986-87 | (Conf) | 1 | 15.11.86 | **Gillingham** (D3) | H | L | 0-3 | |
| 1988-89 | (Conf) | 1 | 19.11.88 | **Dartford** (SL) | H | W | 2-1 | Lewis, Griffith |
| | | 2 | 10.12.88 | **Bristol Rovers** (D3) | H | W | 2-1 | Cooke 2 |
| | | 3 | 07.01.89 | **Halifax Town** (D4) | H | D | 1-1 | Griffith |
| | | 3r | 10.01.89 | **Halifax Town** | A | W | 3-2 | Lewis, Cooke 2 |
| | | 4 | 28.01.89 | **Charlton Athletic** (D1) | A | L | 1-2 | Cooke |
| 1989-90 | (Conf) | 1 | 18.11.89 | **Northampton Town** (D3) | H | L | 0-1 | |
| 1991-92 | (Conf) | 1 | 16.11.91 | **Wycombe W** (Conf) | H | D | 1-1 | Christie |
| | | 1r | 27.11.91 | **Wycombe W** | A | W | 2-0 | Brown, Graham |
| | | 2 | 07.12.91 | **Maidstone Utd** (D4) | A | W | 2-1 | Brown, Oxbrow og |
| | | 3 | 04.01.92 | **Blackburn Rovers** (D2) | A | L | 1-4 | Brown |
| 1992-93 | (Conf) | 1 | 14.11.92 | **Gillingham** (D3) | A | L | 2-3 | Brown, Hill (p) |
| 1993-94 | (Conf) | 1 | 13.11.93 | **Kidderminster H** (Conf) | A | L | 0-3 | |
| 1994-95 | (Conf) | 1 | 13.11.94 | **Plymouth Argyle** (D2) | H | L | 0-1 | |
| 1999-00 | (Conf) | 1 | 30.10.99 | **Wrexham** (D2) | A | D | 1-1 | Brown |
| | | 1r | 10.11.99 | **Wrexham** | H | L | 0-2 | |
| 2000-01 | (Conf) | 1 | 18.11.00 | **Hull City** (D3) | H | D | 0-0 | |
| | | 1r | 28.11.00 | **Hull City** | A | W | 1-0 | Fisher |
| | | 2 | 09.12.00 | **Bristol City** (D2) | A | L | 1-3 | Collins |
| 2001-02 | (SL) | 1 | 17.11.01 | **Cheltenham Town** (D3) | H | L | 1-6 | Norman |

## KIDDERMINSTER HARRIERS

*Formed 1886. First entered FA Cup: 1890-91. FA Trophy winners: 1991; Runners-up 1995. Welsh FA Cup runners-up: 1986, 1989. League clubs beaten as a Non-League club: Birmingham City, Preston North End. Promoted to the Football League: 2000.*

**as Kidderminster FC**

| | | | | | | | | |
|---|---|---|---|---|---|---|---|---|
| 1890-91 | (BDL) | 1 | 17.01.91 | **Darwen** (Fall) | A | L | 1-3 | Smith |
| | | | | *FA ordered replay after protest* | | | | |
| | | 1r | 24.01.91 | **Darwen** | A | L | 0-13 | |

**as Kidderminster Harriers**

| | | | | | | | | |
|---|---|---|---|---|---|---|---|---|
| 1906-07 | (BDL) | 1 | 17.01.07 | **Oldham Athletic** (LC) | A | L | 0-5 | |
| 1935-36 | (BDL) | 1 | 30.11.35 | **Bishop Auckland** (NL) | H | W | 4-1 | Boswell 3, Salters |
| | | 2 | 14.12.35 | **Workington** (NEL) | A | L | 1-5 | Boswell |
| 1937-38 | (BDL) | 1 | 27.11.37 | **Newport County** (3S) | H | D | 2-2 | Salters, Buck |
| | | 1r | 02.12.37 | **Newport County** | A | L | 1-4 | Birch |
| 1938-39 | (BDL) | 1 | 26.11.38 | **Chelmsford City** (SL) | A | L | 0-4 | |
| 1948-49 | (SL) | 1 | 27.11.48 | **Hereford Utd** (SL) | H | L | 0-3 | |
| 1952-53 | (SL) | 1 | 22.11.52 | **Finchley** (AL) | H | L | 0-1 | |
| 1964-65 | (WMRL) | 1 | 14.11.64 | **Hull City** (D3) | H | L | 1-4 | Gosling |
| 1965-66 | (WMRL) | 1 | 13.11.65 | **Peterborough Utd** (D3) | A | L | 1-2 | Gilbert |
| 1967-68 | (WMRL) | 1 | 09.12.67 | **Walthamstow Ave** (IL) | A | L | 1-2 | P Wassall (p) |
| 1968-69 | (WMRL) | 1 | 16.11.68 | **Brighton** (D3) | A | D | 2-2 | P Wassall, B Wassall |
| | | 1r | 20.11.68 | **Brighton** | H | L | 0-1 | |
| 1979-80 | (SL) | 1 | 24.11.79 | **Blackburn Rovers** (D3) | H | L | 0-2 | |
| 1980-81 | (SL) | 1 | 22.11.80 | **Millwall** (D3) | H | D | 1-1 | Wright |
| | | 1r | 25.11.80 | **Millwall** | A | L | 0-1 | |
| 1987-88 | (Conf) | 1 | 14.11.87 | **Halesowen Town** (SL) | A | D | 2-2 | Hazelwood, Woodhall |

| | | | | | | | | |
|---|---|---|---|---|---|---|---|---|
| | | 1r | 16.11.87 | **Halesowen Town** | H | W | 4-0 | Tuohy 2, Davies, R Jones |
| | | 2 | 05.12.87 | **Maidstone Utd** (Conf) | A | D | 1-1 | Davies |
| | | 2r | 07.12.87 | **Maidstone Utd** | H | D | 2-2aet | Tuohy, Casey |
| | | 2 2r | 14.12.87 | **Maidstone Utd** | H | D | 0-0aet | |
| | | 2 3r | 16.12.87 | **Maidstone Utd** | A | L | 1-2 | Casey |
| 1989-90 | (Conf) | 1 | 18.11.89 | **Swansea City** (D3) | H | L | 2-3 | Forsyth, Bancroft |
| 1990-91 | (Conf) | 1 | 17.11.90 | **Woking** (IL) | A | D | 0-0 | |
| | | 1r | 21.11.90 | **Woking** | H | D | 1-1aet | Davies |
| | | 1 2r | 26.11.90 | **Woking** (IL) | H | L | 1-2 | Lilwall |
| 1991-92 | (Conf) | 1 | 16.11.91 | **Aylesbury Utd** (IL) | H | L | 0-1 | |
| 1992-93 | (Conf) | 1 | 14.11.92 | **Exeter City** (D2) | A | L | 0-1 | |
| 1993-94 | (Conf) | 1 | 13.11.93 | **Kettering Town** (Conf) | H | W | 3-0 | Brindley, Forsyth (p), Davies |
| | | 2 | 04.12.93 | **Woking** (Conf) | H | W | 1-0 | Forsyth (p) |
| | | 3 | 08.01.94 | **Birmingham City** (D1) | A | W | 2-1 | Cartwright, Purdie |
| | | 4 | 29.01.94 | **Preston North End** (D3) | H | W | 1-0 | Humphreys |
| | | 5 | 19.02.94 | **West Ham Utd** (PL) | H | L | 0-1 | |
| 1994-95 | (Conf) | 1 | 12.11.94 | **Torquay Utd** (D3) | H | D | 1-1 | Humphreys |
| | | 1r | 23.11.94 | **Torquay Utd** | A | L | 0-1 | |
| 1995-96 | (Conf) | 1 | 11.11.95 | **Sutton Utd** (IL) | H | D | 2-2 | Hughes, Webb (p) |
| | | 1r | 21.11.95 | **Sutton Utd** | A | D | 1-1aet | Casey |
| | | | | *Sutton Utd won 3-2 on penalties* | | | | |
| 1996-97 | (Conf) | 1 | 16.11.96 | **Crewe Alexandra** (D2) | A | L | 1-4 | Yates |
| 1998-99 | (Conf) | 1 | 14.11.98 | **Plymouth Argyle** (D3) | A | D | 0-0 | |
| | | 1r | 24.11.98 | **Plymouth Argyle** | H | - | 0-0ab | |
| | | | | *abandoned at half-time – fog* | | | | |
| | | 1r | 01.12.98 | **Plymouth Argyle** | H | D | 0-0aet | |
| | | | | *Plymouth won 5-4 on penalties* | | | | |
| 2000-01 | (D3) | 1 | 18.11.00 | **Burton Albion** (SL) | H | D | 0-0 | |
| | | 1r | 28.11.00 | **Burton Albion** | A | W | 4-2 | Hadley 2, Bogie, Bird |
| | | 2 | 09.12.00 | **Carlisle Utd** (D3) | H | L | 0-2 | |
| 2001-02 | (D3) | 1 | 17.11.01 | **Darlington** (D3) | H | L | 0-1 | |
| 2002-03 | (D3) | 1 | 16.11.02 | **Rushden & D** (D3) | H | D | 2-2 | Setchell og, Broughton |
| | | 1r | 26.11.02 | **Rushden & D** | A | L | 1-2 | Broughton |

## KILDARE FC

*Formed 1877. Played at Kensal Green in north west London, using a pub called the Mason's Circus as their changing rooms.*

| | | | | | | | |
|---|---|---|---|---|---|---|---|
| 1879-80 | 1 | 01.11.79 | **Gresham** | A | L | 0-3 | |
| 1880-81 | 1 | 13.11.80 | **Acton** | A | D | 1-1 | |
| | 1r | 20.11.80 | **Acton** | H | L | 0-5 | |
| 1881-82 | 1 | 05.11.81 | **Royal Engineers** | A | L | 0-6 | |
| 1882-83 | 1 | 04.11.82 | **Clapham Rovers** | A | L | 0-3 | |
| 1883-84 | 1 | | Clapham Rovers | | | - | |
| | | | *Kildare scratched. Clapham walkover* | | | | |

## KING'S LYNN

*Formed 1879. First entered FA Cup: 1900-01; FA Amateur Cup runners-up: 1901. League clubs beaten: Aldershot, Coventry City. Members of the Southern League.*

| | | | | | | | | |
|---|---|---|---|---|---|---|---|---|
| 1905-06 | (N&S) | 1 | 13.01.06 | **Aston Villa** (D1) | A | L | 0-11 | |
| 1937-38 | (ECL) | 1 | 27.11.37 | **Bromley** (AL) | H | L | 0-4 | |
| 1949-50 | (ECL) | 1 | 26.11.49 | **Nuneaton B** (BC) | A | L | 1-2 | Everitt |
| 1951-52 | (ECL) | 1 | 24.11.51 | **Exeter City** (3S) | H | L | 1-3 | Whitelumb |
| 1958-59 | (SL) | 1 | 15.11.58 | **Merthyr Tydfil** (SL) | H | W | 2-1 | Neilson, Dixon |
| | | 2 | 06.12.58 | **Brentford** (D3) | A | L | 1-3 | Dixon |
| 1959-60 | (SL) | 1 | 14.11.59 | **Aldershot** (D4) | H | W | 3-1 | Dixon 2, Luke |
| | | 2 | 05.12.59 | **Reading** (D3) | A | L | 2-4 | Luke, Dixon |
| 1960-61 | (SL) | 1 | 05.11.60 | **Loughborough Utd** (CA) | A | D | 0-0 | |
| | | 1r | 09.11.60 | **Loughborough Utd** | H | W | 3-0 | Sewell, Sharp, Dixon |
| | | 2 | 26.11.60 | **Bristol City** (D3) | H | D | 2-2 | Sewell, Dunn |
| | | 2r | 29.11.60 | **Bristol City** | A | L | 0-3 | |
| 1961-62 | (SL) | 1 | 04.11.61 | **Chelmsford City** (SL) | A | W | 2-1 | Bacon, Wright |
| | | 2 | 25.11.61 | **Coventry City** (D3) | A | W | 2-1 | Johnson, Wright |

| | | | | | | | | |
|---|---|---|---|---|---|---|---|---|
| | | 3 | 06.01.62 | **Everton** (D1) | A | L | 0-4 | |
| 1962-63 | (SL) | 1 | 03.11.62 | **Boston Utd** (ML) | A | W | 2-1 | Coates 2 |
| | | 2 | 24.11.62 | **Oxford Utd** (D4) | H | L | 1-2 | Wright |
| 1964-65 | (SL) | 1 | 14.11.64 | **Shrewsbury Town** (D3) | H | L | 0-1 | |
| 1968-69 | (SL) | 1 | 16.11.68 | **Southend Utd** (D4) | A | L | 0-9 | |
| 1971-72 | (SL) | 1 | 20.11.71 | **Hereford Utd** (SL) | H | D | 0-0 | |
| | | 1r | 24.11.71 | **Hereford Utd** | A | L | 0-1 | |
| 1973-74 | (SL) | 1 | 24.11.73 | **Wimbledon** (SL) | H | W | 1-0 | Elliott |
| | | 2 | 15.12.73 | **Alvechurch** (WMRL) | A | L | 1-6 | Lindsay |
| 1984-85 | (SL) | 1 | 17.11.84 | **Bristol Rovers** (D3) | A | L | 1-2 | Adams |
| 1997-98 | (SL) | 1 | 15.11.97 | **Bromsgrove Rovers** (SL) | H | W | 1-0 | Hudson |
| | | 2 | 06.12.97 | **Rotherham Utd** (D3) | A | L | 0-6 | |

# KINGSTONIAN

*Formed 1885. First entered FA Cup: 1919-20. FA Trophy winners: 1999, 2000. FA Amateur Cup winners: 1933. Runners-up: 1960. Their 0-9 defeat to Nunhead in 1926 is the joint-highest defeat suffered by one Non-League against another since the competition was re-organised in 1925. See also the records of Bath City and Nunhead. League clubs beaten: Brighton, Brentford, Southend United. Members of the Isthmian league.*

| | | | | | | | | |
|---|---|---|---|---|---|---|---|---|
| 1926-27 | (AL) | 1 | 27.11.26 | **Nunhead** (IL) | A | L | 0-9 | |
| 1930-31 | (IL) | 1 | 29.11.30 | **Tunbridge Wells R** (KL) | A | L | 0-3 | |
| 1932-33 | (IL) | 1 | 26.11.32 | **Luton Town** (3S) | A | D | 2-2 | Gibson, Birks |
| | | 1r | 30.11.32 | **Luton Town** | H | L | 2-3 | Birks, Gibson |
| 1933-34 | (IL) | 1 | 25.11.33 | **Bristol City** (3S) | H | L | 1-7 | Whitehead |
| 1992-93 | (IL) | 1 | 14.11.92 | **Peterborough Utd** (D1) | H | D | 1-1 | Russell |
| | | 1r | 25.11.92 | **Peterborough Utd** | A | L | 1-9 | Finch |
| | | | | *FA ordered match to be replayed behind closed doors after Kingstonian goalkeeper was hit by coins and injured* | | | | |
| | | 1r | 04.12.92 | **Peterborough Utd** | A | L | 0-1 | |
| | | | | *Played at Peterborough behind closed doors* | | | | |
| 1994-95 | (IL) | 1 | 12.11.94 | **Brighton** (D2) | H | W | 2-1 | J Ndah 2 |
| | | 2 | 03.12.94 | **Aylesbury Utd** (IL) | H | L | 1-4 | Akuamoah (p) |
| 1995-96 | (IL) | 1 | 11.11.95 | **Wisbech Town** (ECL) | H | W | 5-1 | Wingfield 2, Riley, Warden, Akuamoah |
| | | 2 | 03.12.95 | **Plymouth Argyle** (D3) | H | L | 1-2 | Warden |
| 1998-99 | (Conf) | 1 | 14.11.98 | **Burton Albion** (SL) | H | W | 1-0 | Holligan |
| | | 2 | 06.12.98 | **Leyton Orient** (D3) | H | D | 0-0 | |
| | | 2r | 15.12.98 | **Leyton Orient** | A | L | 1-2 | Holligan |
| 1999-00 | (Conf) | 1 | 30.10.99 | **Luton Town** (D2) | A | L | 2-4 | Crossley, Leworthy |
| 2000-01 | (Conf) | 1 | 18.11.00 | **Brentford** (D2) | A | W | 3-1 | D Pitcher, Winston 2 |
| | | 2 | 09.12.00 | **Southport** (Conf) | A | W | 2-1 | Harris, D Pitcher |
| | | 3 | 06.01.01 | **Southend Utd** (D3) | A | W | 1-0 | Akuamoah |
| | | 4 | 27.01.01 | **Bristol City** (D2) | A | D | 1-1 | Wingfield |
| | | 4r | 07.02.01 | **Bristol City** | H | L | 0-1 | |

# KIRKBY TOWN

*Formed 1962. First entered FA Cup: 1966-67. Disbanded and reformed twice before changing their name to Knowsley United in 1988.*

| | | | | | | | | |
|---|---|---|---|---|---|---|---|---|
| 1969-70 | (LC) | 1 | 15.11.69 | **Bangor City** (NPL) | A | L | 0-6 | |

# KNOWSLEY UNITED

*Formed 1988 as Knowsley United after earlier incarnation as Kirkby Town. Folded 1997.*

| | | | | | | | | |
|---|---|---|---|---|---|---|---|---|
| 1993-94 | (NPL) | 1 | 13.11.93 | **Carlisle Utd** (D3) | H | L | 1-4 | Joyce og |
| | | | | *played at Goodison Park* | | | | |

# LANCASTER CITY

*Formed 1902 as Lancaster Town. Lancaster City 1938. First entered FA Cup: 1906-07. League clubs beaten: Barrow, Stockport County, Members of the Northern Premier League.*

**as Lancaster Town**

| | | | | | | | | |
|---|---|---|---|---|---|---|---|---|
| 1921-22 | (LC) | | | 4q Barrow (3N) A 2-2; 4qr Barrow (H) 1-0; 5q Stockport County (3n) H 2-0; 6q Northampton Town (3S) A 0-1 | | | | |
| 1928-29 | (LC) | 1 | 24.11.28 | **Lincoln City** (3N) | H | L | 1-3 | Grass |
| 1929-30 | (LC) | 1 | 30.11.29 | **New Brighton** (3N) | A | L | 1-4 | Longworth |

| | | | | | | | | |
|---|---|---|---|---|---|---|---|---|
| 1930-31 | (LC) | 1 | 29.11.30 | **Accrington Stanley** (3N) | A | L | 1-3 | Pilkington |
| 1931-32 | (LC) | 1 | 28.11.31 | **Blyth Spartans** (NEL) | H | L | 0-3 | |
| 1933-34 | (LC) | 1 | 25.11.33 | **Stockport County** (3N) | H | L | 0-1 | |
| 1937-38 | (LC) | 1 | 27.11.37 | **Accrington Stanley** (3N) | A | D | 1-1 | Lewitt |
| | | 1r | 01.12.37 | **Accrington Stanley** | H | D | 1-1 | Clarke |
| | | 1 2r | 06.12.37 | **Accrington Stanley** | | L | 0-4 | |
| | | | | *played at Deepdale, Preston* | | | | |

**as Lancaster City**

| | | | | | | | | |
|---|---|---|---|---|---|---|---|---|
| 1938-39 | (LC) | 1 | 26.11.38 | **Scunthorpe Utd** (ML) | A | L | 2-4 | Heaton, O'Connor |
| 1946-47 | (LC) | 1 | 30.11.46 | **Spennymoor Utd** (NEL) | H | W | 1-0 | Downham |
| | | 2 | 14.12.46 | **Gateshead AFC** (3N) | A | L | 0-4 | |
| 1947-48 | (LC) | 1 | 29.11.47 | **Oldham Athletic** (3N) | A | L | 0-6 | |
| 1972-73 | (NPL) | 1 | 18.11.72 | **Boston Utd** (NPL) | A | W | 2-1 | Donegan, Cullingford |
| | | 2 | 09.12.72 | **Notts County** (D3) | A | L | 1-2 | Whitbread |
| 1998-99 | (NPL) | 1 | 14.11.98 | **Northampton Town** (D2) | A | L | 1-2 | Thomson |
| 2001-02 | (NPL) | 1 | 17.11.01 | **Altrincham** (NPL) | A | D | 1-1 | Whittaker |
| | | 1r | 27.11.01 | **Altrincham** | H | L | 1-4aet | Mayers |

# LANCING OLD BOYS

*Team formed by the Old Boys of Lancing School who competed in the FA Cup from 1885-86 until 1888-89 when they were eliminated in the second qualifying round after a first qualifying round win over Millwall Athletic.*

| | | | | | | | | |
|---|---|---|---|---|---|---|---|---|
| 1885-86 | | 1 | 31.10.85 | **Barnes** | A | W | 7-1 | |
| | | 2 | 14.11.85 | **Brentwood** | A | L | 1-6 | |
| 1887-88 | | 1 | 08.10.87 | **Old Etonians** | A | L | 2-4 | |

# LEATHERHEAD

*Formed 1946 by the amalgamation of Leatherhead United and Leatherhead Rose. First entered FA Cup: 1948-49. FA Trophy runners-up: 1974. League clubs beaten: Colchester United, Brighton, Cambridge United, Northampton Town. Members of the Isthmian league.*

| | | | | | | | | |
|---|---|---|---|---|---|---|---|---|
| 1974-75 | (IL) | 1 | 23.11.74 | **Bishop's Stortford** (IL) | A | D | 0-0 | |
| | | 1r | 26.11.74 | **Bishop's Stortford** | H | W | 2-0 | Layers, Doyle |
| | | 2 | 14.12.74 | **Colchester Utd** (D3) | H | W | 1-0 | Doyle |
| | | 3 | 04.01.75 | **Brighton** (D3) | A | W | 1-0 | Kelly |
| | | 4 | 25.01.75 | **Leicester City** (D1) | H | L | 2-3 | McGillicuddy, Kelly |
| | | | | *played at Filbert Street* | | | | |
| 1975-76 | (IL) | 1 | 22.11.75 | **Cambridge Utd** (D3) | H | W | 2-0 | Batson og, Doyle |
| | | 2 | 13.12.75 | **Tooting & M** (IL) | H | D | 0-0 | |
| | | 2r | 16.12.75 | **Tooting & M** | A | - | 1-1ab | Cooper |
| | | | | *abandoned after 57 minutes – icy pitch* | | | | |
| | | 2r | 22.12.75 | **Tooting & M** (IL) | A | L | 1-2aet | Reid |
| 1976-77 | (IL) | 1 | 20.11.76 | **Northampton Town** (D3) | H | W | 2-0 | Doyle 2 |
| | | 2 | 14.12.76 | **Wimbledon** (SL) | H | L | 1-3 | Reid |
| 1977-78 | (IL) | 1 | 26.11.77 | **Swansea City** (D4) | H | D | 0-0 | |
| | | 1r | 29.11.77 | **Swansea City** | A | L | 1-2 | Baker |
| 1978-79 | (IL) | 1 | 25.11.78 | **Merthyr Tydfil** (SL) | H | W | 2-1 | Baker, Camp |
| | | 2 | 16.12.78 | **Colchester Utd** (D3) | H | D | 1-1 | Kelly |
| | | 2r | 18.12.78 | **Colchester Utd** | A | L | 0-4 | |
| 1980-81 | (IL) | 1 | 22.11.80 | **Exeter City** (D3) | A | L | 0-5 | |

# LEEDS CITY

*Formed 1904. First entered FA Cup: 1904-05. Wound-up by the FA in October 1919 following allegations of illegal payments and bonuses to players. Herbert Chapman, who went on to enjoy fame with Huddersfield Town and Arsenal, was manager at the time.*

| | | | | | | | | |
|---|---|---|---|---|---|---|---|---|
| 1904-05 | (WYL) | | | 1q Rockingham Colliery (A) 1-3 | | | | |
| 1905-06 | (D2) | | | 1q Morley (H) 11-0; 2q Mexborough (H) 1-1; 2qr Mexborough (A) 1-1; 2q 2r Mexborough (H) 3-1; 3q Hull City (A) 1-1; 3qr Hull City (H) 1-2 | | | | |
| 1906-07 | (D2) | 1 | 12.01.07 | **Bristol City** (D1) | A | L | 1-4 | McLeod |
| 1907-08 | (D2) | 1 | 11.01.08 | **Oldham Athletic** (D2) | A | L | 1-2 | Parnell |
| 1908-09 | (D2) | 1 | 16.01.09 | **Oldham Athletic** | A | D | 1-1 | McLeod |
| | | 1r | 20.01.09 | **Oldham Athletic** | H | W | 2-0 | McLeod (p), Guy |
| | | 2 | 06.02.09 | **West Ham Utd** (SL) | H | D | 1-1 | Burnett |
| | | 2r | 11.02.09 | **West Ham Utd** | A | L | 1-2aet | Bowman |
| 1909-10 | (D2) | 1 | 15.01.10 | **Sunderland** (D1) | A | L | 0-1 | |

| | | | | | | | | |
|---|---|---|---|---|---|---|---|---|
| 1910-11 | (D2) | 1 | 14.01.11 | **Brighton** (SL) | H | L | 1-3 | Roberts |
| 1911-12 | (D2) | 1 | 13.01.12 | **Glossop North End** (D2) | H | W | 1-0 | Roberts |
| | | 2 | 03.02.12 | **WBA** (D1) | H | L | 0-1 | |
| 1912-13 | (D2) | 1 | 15.01.13 | **Burnley** (D2) | H | L | 2-3 | McLeod, Foley |
| 1913-14 | (D2) | 1 | 10.01.14 | **Gainsborough T** (ML) | H | W | 4-2 | Jackson 2, Law, McLeod |
| | | 2 | 31.01.14 | **WBA** (D1) | H | L | 0-2 | |
| 1914-15 | (D2) | 1 | 09.01.15 | **Derby County** (D1) | A | W | 2-1 | McLeod, Sharpe |
| | | 2 | 30.01.15 | **QPR** (SL) | A | L | 0-1 | |

# LEEDS UNITED

*Formed 1919 following FA's closure of Leeds City. Spent inaugural season in the Midland League. First entered FA Cup: 1920-21. FA Cup winners: 1972. FA Cup runners-up: 1965, 1970, 1973. Record FA Cup win: 8-1 v Crystal Palace, 3rd round,11.01.1930; Record FA Cup defeat: 2-7 v Middlesbrough, 3rd round, 2nd leg, 09.01.1946.*

| | | | | | | | | |
|---|---|---|---|---|---|---|---|---|
| 1919-20 | (ML) | | | did not enter | | | | |
| 1920-21 | (D2) | | | 1q Boothtown (H) 5-2; 2q Leeds Steelworks (H) 7-0. Leeds withdrew | | | | |
| 1921-22 | (D2) | 1 | 07.01.22 | **Swindon Town** (3S) | A | L | 1-2 | Swann |
| 1922-23 | (D2) | 1 | 13.01.23 | **Portsmouth** (3S) | A | D | 0-0 | |
| | | 1r | 17.01.23 | **Portsmouth** | H | W | 3-1 | Whipp, Armitage, Swann |
| | | 2 | 03.02.23 | **Bolton Wanderers** (D1) | A | L | 1-3 | Swan |
| 1923-24 | (D2) | 1 | 12.01.24 | **Stoke** (D2) | H | W | 1-0 | Whipp |
| | | 2 | 02.02.24 | **West Ham Utd** (D1) | A | D | 1-1 | Coates |
| | | 2r | 06.02.24 | **West Ham Utd** | H | W | 1-0 | Whipp |
| | | 3 | 23.02.24 | **Aston Villa** (D1) | A | L | 0-3 | |
| 1924-25 | (D1) | 1 | 10.01.25 | **Liverpool** (D1) | A | L | 0-3 | |
| 1925-26 | (D1) | 3 | 09.01.26 | **Middlesbrough** (D2) | A | L | 1-5 | Armand (p) |
| 1926-27 | (D1) | 3 | 08.01.27 | **Sunderland** (D1) | H | W | 3-2 | Jennings 2 (1p), Duggan |
| | | 4 | 29.01.27 | **Bolton Wanderers** (D1) | H | D | 0-0 | |
| | | 4r | 02.02.27 | **Bolton Wanderers** | A | L | 0-3 | |
| 1927-28 | (D2) | 3 | 14.01.28 | **Manchester City** (D2) | A | L | 0-1 | |
| 1928-29 | (D1) | 3 | 12.01.29 | **Exeter City** (3S) | A | D | 2-2 | Keetley, Menzies |
| | | 3r | 16.01.29 | **Exeter City** | H | W | 5-1 | Waisncoat, Reed, Cochrane, Keetley, Lowton og |
| | | 4 | 26.01.29 | **Huddersfield Town** (D1) | A | L | 0-3 | |
| 1929-30 | (D1) | 3 | 11.01.30 | **Crystal Palace** (3S) | H | W | 8-1 | Wainscoat 3, Jennnigs 2, White 2, Turnbull |
| | | 4 | 25.01.30 | **West Ham Utd** (D1) | A | L | 1-4 | Jennings |
| 1930-31 | (D1) | 3 | 10.01.31 | **Huddersfield Town** (D1) | H | W | 2-0 | Hydes, Furness |
| | | 4 | 24.01.31 | **Newcastle Utd** (D1) | H | W | 4-1 | Wainscoat 2, Furness, Mitchell |
| | | 5 | 14.02.31 | **Exeter City** (3S) | A | L | 1-3 | Mitchell |
| 1931-32 | (D2) | 3 | 09.01.32 | **QPR** (3S) | A | L | 1-3 | J Milburn (p) |
| 1932-33 | (D1) | 3 | 14.01.33 | **Newcastle Utd** (D1) | A | W | 3-0 | Hydes 3 |
| | | 4 | 28.01.33 | **Tranmere Rovers** (3N) | A | D | 0-0 | |
| | | 4r | 01.02.33 | **Tranmere Rovers** | H | W | 4-0 | J Milburn (p), Mahon, Cochrane, Hydes |
| | | 5 | 18.02.33 | **Everton** (D1) | A | L | 0-2 | |
| 1933-34 | (D1) | 3 | 13.01.34 | **Preston North End** (D2) | H | L | 0-1 | |
| 1934-35 | (D1) | 3 | 12.01.35 | **Bradford Park A** (D2) | H | W | 4-1 | Hydes 2, Furness, Mahon |
| | | 4 | 26.01.35 | **Norwich City** (D2) | A | D | 3-3 | Mahon, Duggan, Cochrane |
| | | 4r | 30.01.35 | **Norwich City** | H | L | 1-2 | Hydes |
| 1935-36 | (D1) | 3 | 11.01.36 | **Wolverhampton W** (D1) | A | D | 1-1 | McDougall |
| | | 3r | 15.01.36 | **Wolverhampton W** | H | W | 3-1 | J Kelly, Cochrane, Duggan |
| | | 4 | 25.01.36 | **Bury** | H | - | 2-1ab | Furness, Kelly |
| | | | | *abandoned after 74 minutes – fog* | | | | |
| | | 4 | 28.01.36 | **Bury** (D2) | H | W | 3-2 | Brown 2, Duggan |
| | | 5 | 15.02.36 | **Sheffield Utd** (D2) | A | L | 1-3 | Furness |
| 1936-37 | (D1) | 3 | 16.01.37 | **Chelsea** (D1) | A | L | 0-4 | |
| 1937-38 | (D1) | 3 | 08.01.38 | **Chester** (3N) | H | W | 3-1 | Buckley 2, Armes |
| | | 4 | 22.01.38 | **Charlton Athletic** (D1) | A | L | 1-2 | Hodgson |
| 1938-39 | (D1) | 3 | 17.01.39 | **Bournemouth** (3S) | H | W | 3-1 | Stephenson, Hargreaves, Cochrane |
| | | 4 | 21.01.39 | **Huddersfield Town** (D1) | H | L | 2-4 | Hodgson, Cochrane |
| 1945-46 | (D1) | 3 1L | 05.01.46 | **Middlesbrough** (D1) | H | D | 4-4 | Henry, Ainsley, Hardwick og, Short |
| | | 3 2L | 09.01.46 | **Middlesbrough** | A | L | 2-7 | Grainger, Ainsley |

| | | | | | | | | |
|---|---|---|---|---|---|---|---|---|
| 1946-47 | (D1) | 3 | 11.01.47 | **WBA** (D2) | A | L | 1-2 | Ainsley |
| 1947-48 | (D2) | 3 | 10.01.48 | **Blackpool** (D1) | A | L | 0-4 | |
| 1948-49 | (D2) | 3 | 08.01.49 | **Newport County** (3S) | H | L | 1-3 | Browning |
| 1949-50 | (D2) | 3 | 07.01.50 | **Carlisle Utd** (3N) | A | W | 5-2 | Browning, Dudley 2, Williams, Cochrane |
| | | 4 | 28.01.50 | **Bolton Wanderers** (D1) | H | D | 1-1 | Williams |
| | | 4r | 01.02.50 | **Bolton Wanderers** | A | W | 3-2aet | Dudley 2, Browning |
| | | 5 | 11.02.50 | **Cardiff City** (D2) | H | W | 3-1 | Williams, Cochrane, Iggleden |
| | | 6 | 04.03.50 | **Arsenal** (D1) | A | L | 0-1 | |
| 1950-51 | (D2) | 3 | 06.01.51 | **Middlesbrough** (D1) | H | W | 1-0 | Browning |
| | | 4 | 27.01.51 | **Manchester Utd** (D1) | A | L | 0-4 | |
| 1951-52 | (D2) | 3 | 12.01.52 | **Rochdale** (3N) | A | W | 2-0 | Kirk 2 |
| | | 4 | 02.02.52 | **Bradford Park A** (3N) | H | W | 2-0 | Milburn, Iggleden |
| | | 5 | 23.02.52 | **Chelsea** (D1) | H | D | 1-1 | Milburn |
| | | 5r | 27.02.52 | **Chelsea** | A | D | 1-1aet | Kirk |
| | | 5 2r | 03.03.52 | **Chelsea** *played at Villa Park* | | L | 1-5 | Mills |
| 1952-53 | (D2) | 3 | 10.01.53 | **Brentford** (D2) | A | L | 1-2 | Charles |
| 1953-54 | (D2) | 3 | 09.01.54 | **Tottenham Hotspur** (D1) | H | D | 3-3 | Iggleden, Charles, Ramsey og |
| | | 3r | 13.01.54 | **Tottenham Hotspur** | A | L | 0-1 | |
| 1954-55 | (D2) | 3 | 08.01.55 | **Torquay Utd** (3S) | H | D | 2-2 | Kerfoot, Charles |
| | | 3r | 12.01.55 | **Torquay Utd** | A | L | 0-4 | |
| 1955-56 | (D2) | 3 | 07.01.56 | **Cardiff City** (D1) | H | L | 1-2 | Brook |
| 1956-57 | (D1) | 3 | 05.01.57 | **Cardiff City** (D1) | H | L | 1-2 | Charles |
| 1957-58 | (D1) | 3 | 04.01.58 | **Cardiff City** (D1) | H | L | 1-2 | Forrest |
| 1958-59 | (D1) | 3 | 10.01.59 | **Luton Town** (D1) | A | L | 1-5 | Shackleton |
| 1959-60 | (D1) | 3 | 09.01.60 | **Aston Villa** (D2) | A | L | 1-2 | McCole |
| 1960-61 | (D2) | 3 | 07.01.61 | **Sheffield Wed** (D1) | A | L | 0-2 | |
| 1961-62 | (D2) | 3 | 06.01.62 | **Derby County** (D2) | H | D | 2-2 | Peyton, Charlton |
| | | 3r | 10.01.62 | **Derby County** | A | L | 1-3 | McAdams |
| 1962-63 | (D2) | 3 | 06.03.63 | **Stoke City** (D2) | H | W | 3-1 | Charlton, Reaney, Hair |
| | | 4 | 16.03.63 | **Middlesbrough** (D2) | A | W | 2-0 | Storrie, Johanneson |
| | | 5 | 19.03.63 | **Nottingham Forest** (D1) | A | L | 0-3 | |
| 1963-64 | (D2) | 3 | 04.01.64 | **Cardiff City** (D2) | A | W | 1-0 | Bremner |
| | | 4 | 25.01.64 | **Everton** (D1) | H | D | 1-1 | Lawson |
| | | 4r | 28.01.64 | **Everton** | A | L | 0-2 | |
| 1964-65 | (D1) | 3 | 09.01.65 | **Southport** (D4) | H | W | 3-0 | Greenhoff, Johanneson, Johnson |
| | | 4 | 30.01.65 | **Everton** (D1) | H | D | 1-1 | Storrie |
| | | 4r | 02.02.65 | **Everton** | A | W | 2-1 | Charlton, Weston |
| | | 5 | 20.02.65 | **Shrewsbury Town** (D3) | H | W | 2-0 | Giles, Johanneson |
| | | 6 | 10.03.65 | **Crystal Palace** (D2) | A | W | 3-0 | Peacock 2, Storrie |
| | | SF | 27.03.65 | **Manchester Utd** (D1) *played at Hillsborough* | | D | 0-0aet | |
| | | SFr | 31.03.65 | **Manchester Utd** *played at City Ground, Nottingham* | | W | 1-0 | Bremner |
| | | F | 01.05.65 | **Liverpool** (D1) *played at Wembley Stadium* | | L | 1-2aet | Bremner |
| 1965-66 | (D1) | 3 | 22.01.66 | **Bury** (D2) | H | W | 6-0 | Lorimer 3, Reaney, Greenhoff, Giles |
| | | 4 | 12.02.66 | **Chelsea** (D1) | A | L | 0-1 | |
| 1966-67 | (D1) | 3 | 28.01.67 | **Crystal Palace** (D2) | H | W | 3-0 | O'Grady, Bell, Johanneson |
| | | 4 | 18.02.67 | **WBA** (D1) | H | W | 5-0 | Lorimer 2, Madeley, Belfitt 2 |
| | | 5 | 11.03.67 | **Sunderland** (D1) | A | D | 1-1 | Charlton |
| | | 5r | 15.03.67 | **Sunderland** | H | D | 1-1aet | Giles |
| | | 5 2r | 20.03.67 | **Sunderland** *played at Boothferry Park* | | W | 2-1 | Belfitt, Giles (p) |
| | | 6 | 08.04.67 | **Manchester City** (D1) | H | W | 1-0 | Charlton |
| | | SF | 29.04.67 | **Chelsea** (D1) *played at Villa Park* | | L | 0-1 | |
| 1967-68 | (D1) | 3 | 27.01.68 | **Derby County** (D2) | H | W | 2-0 | Charlton, Lorimer |
| | | 4 | 17.02.68 | **Nottingham Forest** (D1) | H | W | 2-1 | Jones, Giles |
| | | 5 | 09.03.68 | **Bristol City** (D2) | H | W | 2-0 | Jones, Lorimer |
| | | 6 | 30.03.68 | **Sheffield Utd** (D1) | H | W | 1-0 | Madeley |

| | | | | | | | |
|---|---|---|---|---|---|---|---|
| | SF | 27.04.68 | **Everton** (D1)<br>*played at Old Trafford* | | L | 0-1 | |
| 1968-69 (D1) | 3 | 04.01.69 | **Sheffield Wed** (D1) | A | D | 1-1 | Lorimer (p) |
| | 3r | 08.01.69 | **Sheffield Wed** | H | L | 1-3 | Johanneson |
| 1969-70 (D1) | 3 | 03.01.70 | **Swansea Town** (D4) | H | W | 2-1 | Giles, Jones |
| | 4 | 24.01.70 | **Sutton Utd** (IL) | A | W | 6-0 | Clarke 4, Lorimer 2 |
| | 5 | 07.02.70 | **Mansfield Town** (D3) | H | W | 2-0 | Giles, Clarke |
| | 6 | 21.02.70 | **Swindon Town** (D2) | A | W | 2-0 | Clarke 2 |
| | SF | 14.03.70 | **Manchester Utd** (D1)<br>*played at Hillsborough* | | D | 0-0 | |
| | SFr | 23.03.70 | **Manchester Utd**<br>*played at Villa Park* | | D | 0-0aet | |
| | SF 2r | 26.03.70 | **Manchester Utd**<br>*played at Burnden Park* | | W | 1-0 | Bremner |
| | F | 11.04.70 | **Chelsea** (D1)<br>*played at Wembley Stadium* | | D | 2-2aet | Charlton, Jones |
| | Fr | 29.04.70 | **Chelsea**<br>*played at Old Trafford* | | L | 1-2aet | Jones |
| 1970-71 (D1) | 3 | 11.01.71 | **Rotherham Utd** (D3) | A | D | 0-0 | |
| | 3r | 18.01.71 | **Rotherham Utd** | H | W | 3-2 | Lorimer 2, Giles |
| | 4 | 23.01.71 | **Swindon Town** (D2) | H | W | 4-0 | Jones 3, Clarke |
| | 5 | 13.02.71 | **Colchester Utd** (D4) | A | L | 2-3 | Hunter, Giles |
| 1971-72 (D1) | 3 | 15.01.72 | **Bristol Rovers** (D3) | H | W | 4-1 | Giles 2 (1p), Lorimer 2 |
| | 4 | 05.02.72 | **Liverpool** (D1) | A | D | 0-0 | |
| | 4r | 09.02.72 | **Liverpool** | H | W | 2-0 | Clarke 2 |
| | 5 | 26.02.72 | **Cardiff City** (D2) | A | W | 2-0 | Giles 2 |
| | 6 | 18.03.72 | **Tottenham Hotspur** (D1) | H | W | 2-1 | Clarke, Charlton |
| | SF | 15.04.72 | **Birmingham City** (D2)<br>*played at Hillsborough* | | W | 3-0 | Jones 2, Lorimer |
| | F | 06.05.72 | **Arsenal** (D1)<br>*played at Wembley Stadium* | | W | 1-0 | Clarke |
| 1972-73 (D1) | 3 | 13.01.73 | **Norwich City** (D1) | A | D | 1-1 | Lorimer |
| | 3r | 17.01.73 | **Norwich City** | H | D | 1-1aet | Giles |
| | 3 2r | 29.01.73 | **Norwich City**<br>*played at Villa Park* | | W | 5-0 | Clarke 3, Jones, Lorimer |
| | 4 | 03.02.73 | **Plymouth Argyle** (D3) | H | W | 2-1 | Clarke, Bates |
| | 5 | 24.02.73 | **WBA** (D1) | H | W | 2-0 | Clarke 2 |
| | 6 | 17.03.73 | **Derby County** (D1) | A | W | 1-0 | Lorimer |
| | SF | 07.04.73 | **Wolverhampton W** (D1)<br>*played at Maine Road* | | W | 1-0 | Bremner |
| | F | 05.05.73 | **Sunderland** (D2)<br>*played at Wembley Stadium* | | L | 0-1 | |
| 1973-74 (D1) | 3 | 05.01.74 | **Wolverhampton W** (D1) | A | D | 1-1 | Lorimer (p) |
| | 3r | 09.01.74 | **Wolverhampton W** | H | W | 1-0 | Jones |
| | 4 | 26.01.74 | **Peterborough Utd** (D4) | A | W | 4-1 | Lorimer, Jordan 2, Yorath |
| | 5 | 16.02.74 | **Bristol City** (D2) | A | D | 1-1 | Bremner |
| | 5r | 19.02.74 | **Bristol City** | H | L | 0-1 | |
| 1974-75 (D1) | 3 | 04.01.75 | **Cardiff City** (D2) | H | W | 4-1 | E Gray, Clarke 2, McKenzie |
| | 4 | 25.01.75 | **Wimbledon** (SL) | H | D | 0-0 | |
| | 4r | 10.02.75 | **Wimbledon**<br>*played at Selhurst Park* | A | W | 1-0 | Bassett og |
| | 5 | 18.02.75 | **Derby County** (D1) | A | W | 1-0 | Nish og |
| | 6 | 08.03.75 | **Ipswich Town** (D1) | A | D | 0-0 | |
| | 6r | 11.03.75 | **Ipswich Town** | H | D | 1-1aet | McKenzie |
| | 6 2r | 25.03.75 | **Ipswich Town**<br>*played at Filbert Street* | | D | 0-0aet | |
| | 6 3r | 27.03.75 | **Ipswich Town**<br>*played at Filbert Street* | | L | 2-3 | Clarke, Giles |
| 1975-76 (D1) | 3 | 03.01.76 | **Notts County** (D2) | A | W | 1-0 | Clarke |
| | 4 | 24.01.76 | **Crystal Palace** (D3) | H | L | 0-1 | |
| 1976-77 (D1) | 3 | 08.01.77 | **Norwich City** (D1) | H | W | 5-2 | Clarke, Reaney, Jordan, McQueen, Hampton |

| | | | | | | | |
|---|---|---|---|---|---|---|---|
| | 4 | 29.01.77 | **Birmingham City** (D1) | A | W | 2-1 | Jordan, Clarke |
| | 5 | 26.02.77 | **Manchester City** (D1) | H | W | 1-0 | Cherry |
| | 6 | 19.03.77 | **Wolverhampton W** (D2) | A | W | 1-0 | E Gray |
| | SF | 23.04.77 | **Manchester Utd** (D1) *played at Hillsborough* | | L | 1-2 | Clarke (p) |
| 1977-78 (D1) | 3 | 07.01.78 | **Manchester City** (D1) | H | L | 1-2 | F Gray |
| 1978-79 (D1) | 3 | 18.01.79 | **Hartlepool Utd** (D4) | A | W | 6-2 | E Gray 2, Hart, Graham, Harris, F Gray |
| | 4 | 26.02.79 | **WBA** (D1) *played at The Hawthorns* | H | D | 3-3 | F Gray, Graham, Harris |
| | 4r | 01.03.79 | **WBA** (D1) | A | L | 0-2aet | |
| 1979-80 (D1) | 3 | 05.01.80 | **Nottingham Forest** (D1) | H | L | 1-4 | Lloyd og |
| 1980-81 (D1) | 3 | 03.01.81 | **Coventry City** (D1) | H | D | 1-1 | Hird (p) |
| | 3r | 06.01.81 | **Coventry City** | A | L | 0-1 | |
| 1981-82 (D1) | 3 | 02.01.82 | **Wolverhampton W** (D1) | A | W | 3-1 | Hamson, Hird, E Gray |
| | 4 | 23.01.82 | **Tottenham Hotspur** (D1) | A | L | 0-1 | |
| 1982-83 (D2) | 3 | 08.01.83 | **Preston North End** (D3) | H | W | 3-0 | Sheridan, Connor, Graham |
| | 4 | 29.01.83 | **Arsenal** (D1) | A | D | 1-1 | Nicholas og |
| | 4r | 02.02.83 | **Arsenal** | H | D | 1-1aet | Butterworth |
| | 4 2r | 09.02.83 | **Arsenal** | A | L | 1-2 | Connor |
| 1983-84 (D2) | 3 | 07.01.84 | **Scunthorpe Utd** (D3) | H | D | 1-1 | Wright |
| | 3r | 10.01.84 | **Scunthorpe Utd** | A | D | 1-1aet | Wright |
| | 3 2r | 16.01.84 | **Scunthorpe Utd** | A | L | 2-4 | Wright, Ritchie |
| 1984-85 (D2) | 3 | 04.01.85 | **Everton** (D1) | H | L | 0-2 | |
| 1985-86 (D2) | 3 | 04.01.86 | **Peterborough Utd** (D4) | A | L | 0-1 | |
| 1986-87 (D2) | 3 | 11.01.87 | **Telford Utd** (Conf) *played at The Hawthorns* | A | W | 2-1 | Baird 2 |
| | 4 | 03.02.87 | **Swindon Town** (D3) | A | W | 2-1 | Quinn og, Baird |
| | 5 | 21.02.87 | **QPR** (D1) | H | W | 2-1 | Baird, Ormsby |
| | 6 | 15.03.87 | **Wigan Athletic** (D3) | A | W | 2-0 | Stiles, Adams |
| | SF | 12.04.87 | **Coventry City** (D1) *played at Hillsborough* | | L | 2-3aet | Rennie, Edwards |
| 1987-88 (D2) | 3 | 09.01.88 | **Aston Villa** (D2) | H | L | 1-2 | Davidson |
| 1988-89 (D2) | 3 | 07.01.89 | **Brighton** (D2) | A | W | 2-1 | Baird 2 |
| | 4 | 28.01.89 | **Nottingham Forest** (D1) | A | L | 0-2 | |
| 1989-90 (D2) | 3 | 06.01.90 | **Ipswich Town** (D2) | H | L | 0-1 | |
| 1990-91 (D1) | 3 | 06.01.91 | **Barnsley** (D2) | A | D | 1-1 | Sterland |
| | 3r | 09.01.91 | **Barnsley** | H | W | 4-0 | Smith og, Chapman, McAllister, Strachan (p) |
| | 4 | 27.01.91 | **Arsenal** (D1) | A | D | 0-0 | |
| | 4r | 30.01.91 | **Arsenal** | H | D | 1-1aet | Chapman |
| | 4 2r | 13.02.91 | **Arsenal** | A | D | 0-0aet | |
| | 4 3r | 16.02.91 | **Arsenal** | H | L | 1-2 | Chapman |
| 1991-92 (D1) | 3 | 15.01.92 | **Manchester Utd** (D1) | H | L | 0-1 | |
| 1992-93 (PL) | 3 | 02.01.93 | **Charlton Athletic** (D1) | H | D | 1-1 | Speed |
| | 3r | 13.01.93 | **Charlton Athletic** | A | W | 3-1 | Speed, Garland og, McAllister |
| | 4 | 25.01.93 | **Arsenal** (PL) | A | D | 2-2 | Speed, Chapman |
| | 4r | 03.02.93 | **Arsenal** | H | L | 2-3aet | Shutt, McAllister |
| 1993-94 (PL) | 3 | 08.01.94 | **Crewe Alexandra** (D3) | H | W | 3-1 | Deane, Forrester 2 |
| | 4 | 29.01.94 | **Oxford Utd** (D1) | A | D | 2-2 | Speed, Wetherall |
| | 4r | 09.02.94 | **Oxford Utd** | H | L | 2-3aet | Strachan, White |
| 1994-95 (PL) | 3 | 07.01.95 | **Walsall** (D3) | A | D | 1-1 | Wetherall |
| | 3r | 17.01.95 | **Walsall** | H | W | 5-2aet | Deane, Wetherall, Masinga 3 |
| | 4 | 28.01.95 | **Oldham Athletic** (D1) | H | W | 3-2 | White, Palmer, Massinga |
| | 5 | 19.02.95 | **Manchester Utd** (PL) | A | L | 1-3 | Yeboah |
| 1995-96 (PL) | 3 | 07.01.96 | **Derby County** (D1) | A | W | 4-2 | Deane, McAllister, Speed, Yeboah |
| | 4 | 14.02.96 | **Bolton Wanderers** (PL) | A | W | 1-0 | Wallace |
| | 5 | 21.02.96 | **Port Vale** (D1) | H | D | 0-0 | |
| | 5r | 28.02.96 | **Port Vale** | A | W | 2-1 | McAllister 2 |
| | 6 | 10.03.96 | **Liverpool** (PL) | H | D | 0-0 | |
| | 6r | 20.03.96 | **Liverpool** | A | L | 0-3 | |
| 1996-97 (PL) | 3 | 14.01.97 | **Crystal Palace** (D1) | A | D | 2-2 | Deane, Andersen og |

| | | | | | | | |
|---|---|---|---|---|---|---|---|
| | 3r | 25.01.97 | **Crystal Palace** | H | W | 1-0 | Wallace |
| | 4 | 04.02.97 | **Arsenal** (PL) | A | W | 1-0 | Wallace |
| | 5 | 15.02.97 | **Portsmouth** (D1) | H | L | 2-3 | Bowyer 2 |
| 1997-98 (PL) | 3 | 03.01.98 | **Oxford Utd** (D1) | H | W | 4-0 | Radebe, Hasselbaink (p), Kewell 2 |
| | 4 | 24.01.98 | **Grimsby Town** (D2) | H | W | 2-0 | Molenaar, Hasselbaink |
| | 5 | 14.02.98 | **Birmingham City** (D1) | H | W | 3-2 | Wallace, Hasselbaink 2 |
| | 6 | 07.03.98 | **Wolverhampton W** (D1) | H | L | 0-1 | |
| 1998-99 (PL) | 3 | 02.01.99 | **Rushden & D** (Conf) | A | D | 0-0 | |
| | 3r | 13.01.99 | **Rushden & D** | H | W | 3-1 | Smith 2, Hasselbaink |
| | 4 | 23.01.99 | **Portsmouth** (D1) | A | W | 5-1 | Wetherall, Harte, Kewell, Ribeiro, Wijnhardt |
| | 5 | 13.02.99 | **Tottenham Hotspur** (PL) | H | D | 1-1 | Harte |
| | 5r | 24.02.99 | **Tottenham Hotspur** | A | L | 0-2 | |
| 1999-00 (PL) | 3 | 12.12.99 | **Port Vale** (D1) | H | W | 2-0 | Bakke 2 |
| | 4 | 09.01.00 | **Manchester City** (D1) | A | W | 5-2 | Bakke, Smith, Kewell 2, Bowyer |
| | 5 | 30.01.00 | **Aston Villa** (PL) | A | L | 2-3 | Harte, Bakke |
| 2000-01 (PL) | 3 | 06.01.01 | **Barnsley** (D1) | H | W | 1-0 | Viduka |
| | 4 | 27.01.01 | **Liverpool** (PL) | H | L | 0-2 | |
| 2001-02 (PL) | 3 | 06.01.02 | **Cardiff City** (D2) | A | L | 1-2 | Viduka |
| 2002-03 (PL) | 3 | 04.01.03 | **Scunthorpe Utd** (D3) | A | W | 2-0 | Viduka (p), Bakke |
| | 4 | 25.01.03 | **Gillingham** (D1) | A | D | 1-1 | Smith |
| | 4r | 04.02.03 | **Gillingham** | H | W | 2-1 | Viduka, Bakke |
| | 5 | 16.02.03 | **Crystal Palace** (D1) | A | W | 2-1 | Kelly, Kewell |
| | 6 | 09.03.03 | **Sheffield Utd** (D1) | A | L | 0-1 | |

## LEEK FC

*Entered FA Cup: 1884-85 – 1893-94. No direct link with modern-day Leek Town.*

| | | | | | | | |
|---|---|---|---|---|---|---|---|
| 1884-85 | 1 | 08.11.84 | **Northwich V** | H | W | 4-3 | |
| | 2 | 06.12.84 | **Macclesfield T** | A | W | 5-1 | |
| | 3 | 03.01.85 | **Queen's Park, Glasgow** | H | L | 2-3 | |
| 1885-86 | 1 | 31.10.85 | **Wrexham Olympic** | H | W | 6-3 | |
| | 2 | | Newtown<br>*Newtown scratched. Leek walkover* | | | - | |
| | 3 | | Burslem PV<br>*Leek scratched. Burslem PV walkover* | | | - | |
| 1886-87 | 1 | 23.10.86 | **Druids** | H | W | 2-1 | |
| | 2 | 20.11.86 | **Oswestry Town** | H | W | 4-2 | |
| | 3 | 11.12.86 | **Burslem PV** | H | D | 2-2 | Rider, AN Other |
| | 3r | 20.01.87 | **Burslem PV** | A | W | 3-1 | Allen, Stonehewer, Vickerstaffe |
| | 4 | 29.01.87 | **Crewe Alexandra** | A | W | 1-0 | Allen |
| | 5 | 05.02.87 | **Old Carthusians** | H | L | 0-2 | |
| 1887-88 | 1 | 15.10.87 | **Northwich V** | H | D | 2-2 | |
| | 1r | 22.10.87 | **Northwich V** | A | L | 2-4 | |

## LEEK TOWN

*Formed 1946. First entered FA Cup: 1956-57. FA Trophy runners-up: 1990. League club beaten: Scarborough. Members of the Northern Premier League.*

| | | | | | | | |
|---|---|---|---|---|---|---|---|
| 1990-91 (NPL) | 1 | 17.11.90 | **Scarborough** (D4) | A | W | 2-0 | Sommerville, Sutton |
| | 2 | 12.12.90 | **Chester City** (D3) | H | D | 1-1 | Griffiths |
| | 2r | 17.12.90 | **Chester City** | A | L | 0-4 | |
| 1993-94 (NPL) | 1 | 12.11.93 | **Wigan Athletic** (D3) | H | D | 2-2 | D Sutton 2 |
| | 1r | 30.11.93 | **Wigan Athletic** | A | L | 0-3 | |

## LEICESTER CITY

*Formed 1884 as Leicester Fosse. 1919 Leicester City. FA Cup runners-up: 1949, 1961, 1963, 1969. They are the only club to have played in as many as four finals and lost them all. FA Cup record win: 13-0 v Notts Olympic, 1st qualifying round, 13.10.1894; In Competition Proper: 7-0 v Crook Town, 3rd round, 09.01.1932. FA Cup record defeat: 3-7 v Burnley, 1st round, 08.01.1921 and six other four goal defeats.*

**as Leicester Fosse**

| | |
|---|---|
| 1890-91 | 1q Burton W (H) 0-4 |
| 1891-92 (ML) | 1q Small Heath (H) 2-6 |

| | | | | | | | | |
|---|---|---|---|---|---|---|---|---|
| 1892-93 | (ML) | | | 1q Rushden (H) 7-0; 2q Notts Olympic (A) 3-3aet; 2qr Notts Olympic (H) 7-0; 3q Buxton (H) 1-2 | | | | |
| 1893-94 | (ML) | | | 2q Mansfield Town (H) 1-0; 3q Mansfield Greenhalgh (H) 5-0; 4q Loughborough (A) 1-0 | | | | |
| | | 1 | 27.01.94 | **South Shore** (LL) | H | W | 2-1 | Hill, Brown |
| | | 2 | 10.02.94 | **Derby County** (D1) | H | D | 0-0 | |
| | | 2r | 17.02.94 | **Derby County** | A | L | 0-3 | |
| 1894-95 | (D2) | | | 1q Notts Olympic (H) 13-0; 2q Kimberley (H) 7-2; 3q Rushden (A) 3-2; 4q Loughborough (H) 1-1; 4qr Loughborough (A) 2-2aet; 4q 2r Loughborough (H) 3-0 | | | | |
| | | 1 | 02.02.95 | **Bury** (D2) | A | L | 1-4 | McArthur |
| 1895-96 | (D2) | | | 1q Hinckley Town (H) 4-0; 2q Hucknall St Johns (H) 3-1; 3q Kimberley (A) 3-1; 4q Kettering Town (H) 1-2 | | | | |
| 1896-97 | (D2) | | | 3q Bulwell U (H) 3-1; 4q Wellingborough Town (A) 3-2; 5q Kettering Town (A) 1-2 | | | | |
| 1897-98 | (D2) | 1 | 29.01.98 | **Southampton** (SL) | A | L | 1-2 | McLeod |
| 1898-99 | (D2) | | | 3q Kimberley (H) 9-0; 4q Rushden (H) 2-1; 5q Kettering Town (A) 1-1; 5qr Kettering Town (H) 1-2 | | | | |
| 1899-00 | (D2) | | | 3q Wellingborough T (H) 3-1; 4q Burton Swifts (H) 3-1; 5q Hucknall Portland (H) 6-1 | | | | |
| | | 1 | 27.01.00 | **Sheffield Utd** (D1) | A | L | 0-1 | |
| 1900-01 | (D2) | 1 | 09.02.01 | **Nottingham Forest** (D1) | A | L | 1-5 | Kyle |
| 1901-02 | (D2) | | | Int Glossop North End (H) 0-1 | | | | |
| 1902-03 | (D2) | | | 3q IrthlingboroughTown (A) 1-0; 4q Wellingborough Town (A) 1-4 | | | | |
| 1903-04 | (D2) | | | 3q Market Harborough (H) 10-0; 4q Wellingborough Town (A) 2-1; 5q Burton Utd (A) 1-1; 5qr Burton Utd (H) 2-2 – abandoned during extra time; 5q 2r Burton Utd 0-2 at Baseball Ground | | | | |
| 1904-05 | (D2) | | | 3q Linby Church (H) 10-1; 4q Gresley R (H) 5-0; 5q Northampton Town (A) 2-2; 5qr Northampton Town (H) 2-0; 6qr Southall (A) 4-0; Int WBA (A) 5-2 | | | | |
| | | 1 | 04.02.05 | **Aston Villa** (D1) | A | L | 1-5 | Mounteney (p) |
| 1905-06 | (D2) | 1 | 13.01.06 | **Liverpool** (D1) | A | L | 1-2 | Moody |
| 1906-07 | (D2) | 1 | 12.01.07 | **Sunderland** (D1) | A | L | 1-4 | Bannister |
| 1907-08 | (D2) | 1 | 11.01.08 | **Blackburn Rovers** (D1) | H | W | 2-0 | Humphreys, Pollock (p) |
| | | 2 | 01.02.08 | **Portsmouth** (SL) | A | L | 0-1 | |
| 1908-09 | (D1) | 1 | 16.01.09 | **Watford** (SL) | A | D | 1-1 | Shinton |
| | | 1r | 20.01.09 | **Watford** | H | W | 3-1 | Donnelly, Walker, RF Turner |
| | | 2 | 06.02.09 | **Derby County** (D2) | H | L | 0-2 | |
| 1909-10 | (D2) | 1 | 15.01.10 | **Birmingham** (D2) | A | W | 4-1 | Hubbard 2, Shinton 2 |
| | | 2 | 05.02.10 | **Bury** (D1) | H | W | 3-2 | Threlfall 2, Owen |
| | | 3 | 19.02.10 | **Leyton FC** (SL) | A | W | 1-0 | Threlfall |
| | | 4 | 05.03.10 | **Newcastle Utd** (D1) | A | L | 0-3 | |
| 1910-11 | (D2) | 1 | 14.01.11 | **Southampton** (SL) | H | W | 3-1 | Walker, Osborn, Threlfall |
| | | 2 | 04.02.11 | **Middlesbrough** (D1) | A | D | 0-0 | |
| | | 2r | 09.02.11 | **Middlesbrough** | H | L | 1-2 | Currie (p) |
| 1911-12 | (D2) | 1 | 13.01.12 | **Croydon Common** (SL) | A | D | 2-2 | Mills, Humphreys |
| | | 1r | 22.01.12 | **Croydon Common** | H | W | 6-1 | Hubbard, Osborn, Humphreys 2, Hanger, og |
| | | 2 | 03.02.12 | **Barnsley** (D2) | A | L | 0-1 | |
| 1912-13 | (D2) | 1 | 11.01.13 | **Norwich City** (SL) | H | - | 0-0ab | |
| | | | | *abandoned after 65 minutes – snowstorm* | | | | |
| | | 1 | 16.01.13 | **Norwich City** (SL) | H | L | 1-4 | Proctor |
| 1913-14 | (D2) | 1 | 10.01.14 | **Tottenham Hotspur** (D1) | H | D | 5-5 | Stoodley 3, Mortimer, Currie |
| | | 1r | 15.01.14 | **Tottenham Hotspur** | A | L | 0-2 | |
| **as Leicester City** | | | | | | | | |
| 1919-20 | (D2) | 1 | 10.01.20 | **Newport County** (SL) | A | D | 0-0 | |
| | | 1r | 15.01.20 | **Newport County** | H | W | 2-0 | Walker, Paterson |
| | | 2 | 31.01.20 | **Manchester City** (D1) | H | W | 3-0 | Douglas, Walker, T Smith |
| | | 3 | 21.02.20 | **Chelsea** (D1) | A | L | 0-3 | |
| 1920-21 | (D2) | 1 | 08.01.21 | **Burnley** (D1) | H | L | 3-7 | Smith, J Roxburgh, Paterson |
| 1921-22 | (D2) | 1 | 07.01.22 | **Clapton Orient** (D2) | H | W | 2-0 | Pynegar (p), Trotter |
| | | 2 | 28.01.22 | **Fulham** (D2) | H | W | 2-0 | Graham, Paterson |
| | | 3 | 18.02.22 | **Arsenal** (D1) | A | L | 0-3 | |
| 1922-23 | (D2) | 1 | 13.01.23 | **Fulham** (D2) | H | W | 3-0 | J Duncan 2, Smith, Graham |
| | | 2 | 03.02.23 | **Cardiff City** (D1) | H | L | 0-1 | |
| 1923-24 | (D2) | 1 | 12.01.24 | **Sheffield Wed** (D2) | A | L | 1-4 | Barrett (p) |

| | | | | | | | | |
|---|---|---|---|---|---|---|---|---|
| 1924-25 | (D2) | 1 | 10.01.25 | **Stoke** (D2) | H | W | 3-0 | Duncan 2, Chandler |
| | | 2 | 31.01.25 | **Newcastle Utd** (D1) | A | D | 2-2 | Chandler 2 |
| | | 2r | 05.02.25 | **Newcastle Utd** | H | W | 1-0 | Carr |
| | | 3 | 21.02.25 | **Hull City** (D2) | A | D | 1-1 | Duncan |
| | | 3r | 26.02.25 | **Hull City** | H | W | 3-1 | Chandler 3 |
| | | 4 | 07.03.25 | **Cardiff City** (D1) | A | L | 1-2 | Duncan |
| 1925-26 | (D1) | 3 | 09.01.26 | **Notts County** (D1) | A | L | 0-2 | |
| 1926-27 | (D1) | 3 | 08.01.27 | **Middlesbrough** (D2) | A | L | 3-5 | Duncan, Hine, Chandler |
| 1927-28 | (D1) | 3 | 14.01.28 | **Hull City** (D2) | A | W | 1-0 | Barry |
| | | 4 | 28.01.28 | **Reading** (D2) | A | W | 1-0 | Adcock |
| | | 5 | 18.02.28 | **Tottenham Hotspur** (D1) | H | L | 0-3 | |
| 1928-29 | (D1) | 3 | 12.01.29 | **Lincoln City** (3N) | A | W | 1-0 | Lochhead |
| | | 4 | 26.01.29 | **Swansea Town** (D2) | H | W | 1-0 | Lochhead |
| | | 5 | 16.02.29 | **Bolton Wanderers** (D1) | H | L | 1-2 | Lochhead |
| 1929-30 | (D1) | 3 | 11.01.30 | **Sheffield Utd** (D1) | A | L | 1-2 | Hine |
| 1930-31 | (D1) | 3 | 10.01.31 | **Brighton** (3S) | H | L | 1-2 | Lochhead |
| 1931-32 | (D1) | 3 | 09.01.32 | **Crook Town** (NEL) *played at Filbert Street* | A | W | 7-0 | Hine 5, Langford, Chandler |
| | | 4 | 23.01.32 | **Port Vale** (D2) | A | W | 2-1 | Hine, Chandler |
| | | 5 | 13.02.32 | **Newcastle Utd** (D1) | A | L | 1-3 | Lochhead |
| 1932-33 | (D1) | 3 | 14.01.33 | **Everton** (D1) | H | L | 2-3 | Campbell 2 |
| 1933-34 | (D1) | 3 | 13.01.34 | **Lincoln City** (D2) | H | W | 3-0 | Maw, Lochhead, Paterson |
| | | 4 | 27.01.34 | **Millwall** (D2) | A | W | 6-3 | Smith, Chandler 2, Maw, Liddle, Lochhead |
| | | 5 | 17.02.34 | **Birmingham** (D1) | A | W | 2-1 | Chandler 2 |
| | | 6 | 03.03.34 | **Preston North End** (D2) | A | W | 1-0 | Chandler |
| | | SF | 17.03.34 | **Portsmouth** (D1) *played at St Andrews* | | L | 1-4 | Lochhead |
| 1934-35 | (D1) | 3 | 12.01.35 | **Blackpool** (D2) | H | W | 2-1 | Maw, Ritchie |
| | | 4 | 26.01.35 | **Arsenal** (D1) | H | L | 0-1 | |
| 1935-36 | (D2) | 3 | 11.01.36 | **Brentford** (D1) | H | W | 1-0 | Maw |
| | | 4 | 25.01.36 | **Watford** (3S) | H | W | 6-3 | Maw 2, Dewis, Liddle 3 |
| | | 5 | 15.02.36 | **Middlesbrough** (D1) | A | L | 1-2 | McNally |
| 1936-37 | (D2) | 3 | 16.01.37 | **Bristol Rovers** (3S) | A | W | 5-2 | Bowers 2, Carroll, O'Callaghan, Stubbs |
| | | 4 | 30.01.37 | **Exeter City** (3S) | A | L | 1-3 | Liddle |
| 1937-38 | (D1) | 3 | 08.01.38 | **Mansfield Town** (3S) | A | W | 2-1 | Liddle, Bowers |
| | | 4 | 22.01.38 | **Preston North End** (D1) | A | L | 0-2 | |
| 1938-39 | (D1) | 3 | 07.01.39 | **Stoke City** (D1) | H | D | 1-1 | Dewis |
| | | 3r | 11.01.39 | **Stoke City** | A | W | 2-1 | Dewis, Liddle |
| | | 4 | 21.01.39 | **Wolverhampton W** (D1) | A | L | 1-5 | Bowers |
| 1945-46 | (D2) | 3 1L | 05.01.46 | **Chelsea** (D1) | A | D | 1-1 | Adam |
| | | 3 2L | 10.01.46 | **Chelsea** | H | L | 0-2 | |
| 1946-47 | (D2) | 3 | 11.01.47 | **West Ham Utd** (D2) | A | W | 2-1 | Adam, Dewis |
| | | 4 | 25.01.47 | **Brentford** (D1) | A | D | 0-0 | |
| | | 4r | 30.01.47 | **Brentford** | H | D | 0-0aet | |
| | | 4 2r | 03.02.47 | **Brentford** *played at Villa Park* | | W | 4-1 | Griffiths, A Smith 2, Dewis |
| | | 5 | 08.02.47 | **Newcastle Utd** (D2) | A | D | 1-1 | Dewis |
| | | 5r | 20.02.47 | **Newcastle Utd** | H | L | 1-2 | S Smith (p) |
| 1947-48 | (D2) | 3 | 10.01.48 | **Bury** (D2) | H | W | 1-0 | Lee |
| | | 4 | 24.01.48 | **Sheffield Wed** (D2) | H | W | 2-1 | W Harrison, Haines |
| | | 5 | 07.02.48 | **Tottenham Hotspur** (D2) | A | L | 2-5 | W Harrison, Lee |
| 1948-49 | (D2) | 3 | 08.01.49 | **Birmingham City** (D1) | A | D | 1-1aet | Revie (p) |
| | | 3r | 15.01.49 | **Birmingham City** | H | D | 1-1aet | Griffiths |
| | | 3 2r | 17.01.49 | **Birmingham City** | A | W | 2-1 | J Harrison, Revie |
| | | 4 | 29.01.49 | **Preston North End** (D1) | H | W | 2-0 | Lee (p), Griffiths |
| | | 5 | 12.02.49 | **Luton Town** (D2) | A | D | 5-5aet | Lee 4, Griffiths |
| | | 5r | 19.02.49 | **Luton Town** | H | W | 5-3 | Lee 2 (1p), Griffiths 2, Chisholm |
| | | 6 | 26.02.49 | **Brentford** (D2) | A | W | 2-0 | Lee, Griffiths |
| | | SF | 26.03.49 | **Portsmouth** (D1) *played at Highbury* | | W | 3-1 | Revie 2, Chisholm |

| | | | | | | | |
|---|---|---|---|---|---|---|---|
| | F | 30.04.49 | **Wolverhampton W** (D1) | | L | 1-3 | Griffiths |
| | | | *played at Wembley Stadium* | | | | |
| 1949-50 (D2) | 3 | 07.01.50 | **Sheffield Utd** (D2) | A | L | 1-3 | Adam |
| 1950-51 (D2) | 3 | 06.01.51 | **Preston North End** (D2) | H | L | 0-3 | |
| 1951-52 (D2) | 3 | 12.01.52 | **Coventry City** (D2) | H | D | 1-1 | Griffiths |
| | 3r | 14.01.52 | **Coventry City** | A | L | 1-4 | Dryburgh |
| 1952-53 (D2) | 3 | 10.01.53 | **Notts County** (D2) | H | L | 2-4 | Rowley 2 (1p) |
| 1953-54 (D2) | 3 | 09.01.54 | **Middlesbrough** (D1) | A | D | 0-0 | |
| | 3r | 14.01.54 | **Middlesbrough** | H | W | 3-2 | Rowley 3 |
| | 4 | 30.01.54 | **Stoke City** (D2) | A | D | 0-0 | |
| | 4r | 02.02.54 | **Stoke City** | H | W | 3-1 | Morris, Small 2 |
| | 5 | 20.02.54 | **Norwich City** (3S) | A | W | 2-1 | Rowley (p), Small |
| | 6 | 13.03.54 | **Preston North End** (D1) | H | D | 1-1 | Jackson |
| | 6r | 17.03.54 | **Preston North End** | A | D | 2-2aet | Small, Rowley |
| | 6 2r | 22.03.54 | **Preston North End** | | L | 1-3 | Rowley |
| | | | *played at Hillsborough* | | | | |
| 1954-55 (D1) | 3 | 08.01.55 | **Rotherham Utd** (D2) | A | L | 0-1 | |
| 1955-56 (D2) | 3 | 11.01.56 | **Luton Town** (D1) | A | W | 4-0 | Gardiner, Rowley 3 |
| | 4 | 28.01.56 | **Stoke City** (D2) | H | D | 3-3 | Rowley 2 (1p), Griffiths |
| | 4r | 30.01.56 | **Stoke City** | A | L | 1-2 | Rowley |
| 1956-57 (D2) | 3 | 05.01.57 | **Tottenham Hotspur** (D1) | A | L | 0-2 | |
| 1957-58 (D1) | 3 | 04.01.58 | **Tottenham Hotspur** (D1) | A | L | 0-4 | |
| 1958-59 (D1) | 3 | 10.01.59 | **Lincoln City** (D2) | H | D | 1-1 | Kelly |
| | 3r | 14.01.59 | **Lincoln City** | A | W | 2-0 | Kelly, Hines |
| | 4 | 24.01.59 | **Luton Town** (D1) | H | D | 1-1 | McNeill |
| | 4r | 28.01.59 | **Luton Town** | A | L | 1-4 | Leek |
| 1959-60 (D1) | 3 | 09.01.60 | **Wrexham** (D3) | A | W | 2-1 | Cheesebrough, Leek |
| | 4 | 30.01.60 | **Fulham** (D1) | H | W | 2-1 | McDonald, Wills |
| | 5 | 20.02.60 | **WBA** (D1) | H | W | 2-1 | Walsh, Cheesebrough |
| | 6 | 12.03.60 | **Wolverhampton W** (D1) | H | L | 1-2 | McDonald |
| 1960-61 (D1) | 3 | 07.01.61 | **Oxford Utd** (SL) | H | W | 3-1 | Walsh Leek, Riley |
| | 4 | 28.01.61 | **Bristol City** (D3) | H | - | 0-0ab | |
| | | | *abandoned at half-time – waterlogged pitch* | | | | |
| | 4 | 31.01.61 | **Bristol City** | H | W | 5-1 | Wills, Leek 2, Walsh 2 |
| | 5 | 18.02.61 | **Birmingham City** (D1) | A | D | 1-1 | Riley |
| | 5r | 22.02.61 | **Birmingham City** | H | W | 2-1 | Leek 2 |
| | 6 | 04.03.61 | **Barnsley** (D3) | H | D | 0-0 | |
| | 6r | 08.03.61 | **Barnsley** | A | W | 2-1aet | Riley, Leek |
| | SF | 18.03.61 | **Sheffield Utd** (D2) | | D | 0-0 | |
| | | | *played at Elland Road* | | | | |
| | SFr | 23.03.61 | **Sheffield Utd** | | D | 0-0aet | |
| | | | *played at the City Ground, Nottingham* | | | | |
| | SF 2r | 27.03.61 | **Sheffield Utd** | | W | 2-0aet | Walsh, Leek |
| | | | *played at St Andrews* | | | | |
| | F | 06.05.61 | **Tottenham Hotspur** (D1) | | L | 0-2 | |
| | | | *played at Wembley Stadium* | | | | |
| 1961-62 (D1) | 3 | 10.01.62 | **Stoke City** (D2) | H | D | 1-1 | Riley |
| | 3r | 15.01.62 | **Stoke City** | A | L | 2-5 | Riley (p), Keyworth |
| 1962-63 (D1) | 3 | 07.01.63 | **Grimsby Town** (D2) | A | W | 3-1 | Gibson 2, Keyworth |
| | 4 | 30.01.63 | **Ipswich Town** (D1) | H | W | 3-1 | Cross, Keyworth 2 |
| | 5 | 16.03.63 | **Leyton Orient** (D1) | A | W | 1-0 | Keyworth |
| | 6 | 30.03.63 | **Norwich City** (D2) | A | W | 2-0 | Stringfellow, Gibson |
| | SF | 27.04.63 | **Liverpool** (D1) | | W | 1-0 | Stringfellow |
| | | | *played at Hillsborough* | | | | |
| | F | 25.05.63 | **Manchester Utd** (D1) | | L | 1-3 | Keyworth |
| | | | *played at Wembley Stadium* | | | | |
| 1963-64 (D1) | 3 | 04.01.64 | **Leyton Orient** (D2) | H | L | 2-3 | Cross, Keyworth |
| 1964-65 (D1) | 3 | 09.01.65 | **Blackburn Rovers** (D1) | H | D | 2-2 | Stringfellow, Roberts |
| | 3r | 14.01.65 | **Blackburn Rovers** | A | W | 2-1 | Roberts, Cross |
| | 4 | 30.01.65 | **Plymouth Argyle** (D2) | H | W | 5-0 | Stringfellow, Goodfellow 2, Gibson, Roberts |

| | | | | | | | |
|---|---|---|---|---|---|---|---|
| | 5 | 20.02.65 | **Middlesbrough** (D2) | A | W | 3-0 | Cross 2, Gibson |
| | 6 | 06.03.65 | **Liverpool** (D1) | H | D | 0-0 | |
| | 6r | 10.03.65 | **Liverpool** | A | L | 0-1 | |
| 1965-66 (D1) | 3 | 22.01.66 | **Aston Villa** (D1) | A | W | 2-1 | Dougan, Stringfellow |
| | 4 | 12.02.66 | **Birmingham City** (D2) | A | W | 2-1 | Sinclair, Goodfellow |
| | 5 | 05.03.66 | **Manchester City** (D2) | A | D | 2-2 | Sinclair, Stringfellow |
| | 5r | 09.03.66 | **Manchester City** | H | L | 0-1 | |
| 1966-67 (D1) | 3 | 28.01.67 | **Manchester City** (D1) | A | L | 1-2 | Sweenie |
| 1967-68 (D1) | 3 | 27.01.68 | **Barrow** (D3) | A | W | 2-1 | Sjoberg, Arrowsmith og |
| | 4 | 17.02.68 | **Manchester City** (D1) | A | D | 0-0 | |
| | 4r | 19.02.68 | **Manchester City** | H | W | 4-3 | Fern, Large 2, Nish |
| | 5 | 09.03.68 | **Rotherham Utd** (D2) | A | D | 1-1 | Nish (p) |
| | 5r | 13.03.68 | **Rotherham Utd** | H | W | 2-0aet | Large, Stringfellow |
| | 6 | 30.03.68 | **Everton** (D1) | H | L | 1-3 | Nish |
| 1968-69 (D1) | 3 | 04.01.69 | **Barnsley** (D3) | A | D | 1-1 | Glover |
| | 3r | 08.01.69 | **Barnsley** | H | W | 2-1 | Fern, Glover |
| | 4 | 25.01.69 | **Millwall** (D2) | A | W | 1-0 | Glover |
| | 5 | 01.03.69 | **Liverpool** (D1) | H | D | 0-0 | |
| | 5r | 03.03.69 | **Liverpool** | A | W | 1-0 | Lochhead |
| | 6 | 08.03.69 | **Mansfield Town** (D3) | A | W | 1-0 | Fern |
| | SF | 29.03.69 | **WBA** (D1) | | W | 1-0 | Clarke |
| | | | *played at Hillsborough* | | | | |
| | F | 26.04.69 | **Manchester City** (D1) | | L | 0-1 | |
| | | | *played at Wembley Stadium* | | | | |
| 1969-70 (D2) | 3 | 03.01.70 | **Sunderland** (D1) | H | W | 1-0 | Roberts |
| | 4 | 24.01.70 | **Southampton** (D1) | A | D | 1-1 | Farrington |
| | 4r | 28.01.70 | **Southampton** | H | W | 4-2aet | Lochhead 2, Farrington, Nish (p) |
| | 5 | 07.02.70 | **Liverpool** (D1) | A | D | 0-0 | |
| | 5r | 11.02.70 | **Liverpool** | H | L | 0-2 | |
| 1970-71 (D2) | 3 | 02.01.71 | **Notts County** (D4) | H | W | 2-0 | Brown, Partridge |
| | 4 | 25.01.71 | **Torquay Utd** (D3) | H | W | 3-0 | Glover, Partridge, Cross |
| | 5 | 13.02.71 | **Oxford Utd** (D2) | H | D | 1-1 | Partridge |
| | 5r | 17.02.71 | **Oxford Utd** | A | W | 3-1aet | Brown, Fern 2 |
| | 6 | 06.03.71 | **Arsenal** (D1) | H | D | 0-0 | |
| | 6r | 15.03.71 | **Arsenal** | A | L | 0-1 | |
| 1971-72 (D1) | 3 | 15.01.72 | **Wolverhampton W** (D1) | A | D | 1-1 | Farrington |
| | 3r | 19.01.72 | **Wolverhampton W** | H | W | 2-0 | Farrington, Glover |
| | 4 | 05.02.72 | **Orient** (D2) | H | L | 0-2 | |
| 1972-73 (D1) | 3 | 13.01.73 | **Arsenal** (D1) | A | D | 2-2 | Worthington, Farrington |
| | 3r | 17.01.73 | **Arsenal** | H | L | 1-2 | Farrington |
| 1973-74 (D1) | 3 | 05.01.74 | **Tottenham Hotspur** (D1) | H | W | 1-0 | Earle |
| | 4 | 26.01.74 | **Fulham** (D2) | A | D | 1-1 | Glover |
| | 4r | 30.01.74 | **Fulham** | H | W | 2-1aet | Glover, Worthington |
| | 5 | 16.02.74 | **Luton Town** (D2) | A | W | 4-0 | Earle 2, Worthington, Weller |
| | 6 | 09.03.74 | **QPR** (D1) | A | W | 2-0 | Waters 2 |
| | SF | 30.03.74 | **Liverpool** (D1) | | D | 0-0 | |
| | | | *played at Old Trafford* | | | | |
| | SFr | 03.04.74 | **Liverpool** | | L | 1-3 | Glover |
| | | | *played at Villa Park* | | | | |
| | 3/4 | 09.05.74 | **Burnley** (D1) | H | L | 0-1 | |
| 1974-75 (D1) | 3 | 04.01.75 | **Oxford Utd** (D2) | H | W | 3-1 | Earle 2, Worthington |
| | 4 | 25.01.75 | **Leatherhead** (IL) | A | W | 3-2 | Sammels, Earle, Weller |
| | | | *played at Filbert Street* | | | | |
| | 5 | 15.02.75 | **Arsenal** (D1) | A | D | 0-0 | |
| | 5r | 19.02.75 | **Arsenal** | H | D | 1-1aet | Birchenall |
| | 5 2r | 24.02.75 | **Arsenal** | H | L | 0-1aet | |
| 1975-76 (D1) | 3 | 03.01.76 | **Sheffield Utd** (D1) | H | W | 3-0 | Garland 3 |
| | 4 | 24.01.76 | **Bury** (D3) | H | W | 1-0 | Lee |
| | 5 | 14.02.76 | **Manchester Utd** (D1) | H | L | 1-2 | Lee |
| 1976-77 (D1) | 3 | 08.01.77 | **Aston Villa** (D1) | H | L | 0-1 | |
| 1977-78 (D1) | 3 | 07.01.78 | **Hull City** (D2) | A | W | 1-0 | Armstrong |
| | 4 | 28.01.78 | **Walsall** (D3) | A | L | 0-1 | |

| | | | | | | | | |
|---|---|---|---|---|---|---|---|---|
| 1978-79 (D2) | 3 | 06.01.79 | **Norwich City** (D1) | H | W | 3-0 | May, Weller, Henderson |
| | 4 | 26.02.79 | **Oldham Athletic** (D2) | A | L | 1-3 | Henderson |
| 1979-80 (D2) | 3 | 05.01.80 | **Harlow Town** (IL) | H | D | 1-1 | Henderson |
| | 3r | 08.01.80 | **Harlow Town** | A | L | 0-1 | |
| 1980-81 (D1) | 3 | 03.01.81 | **Cardiff City** (D2) | H | W | 3-0 | Lineker, Buchanan, Melrose |
| | 4 | 24.01.81 | **Exeter City** (D3) | H | D | 1-1 | Henderson |
| | 4r | 28.01.81 | **Exeter City** | A | L | 1-3 | Melrose |
| 1981-82 (D2) | 3 | 02.01.82 | **Southampton** (D1) | H | W | 3-1 | Young 2, Lineker |
| | 4 | 23.01.82 | **Hereford Utd** (D4) | A | W | 1-0 | May |
| | 5 | 13.02.82 | **Watford** (D2) | H | W | 2-0 | O'Neill, Terry og |
| | 6 | 06.03.82 | **Shrewsbury Town** (D2) | H | W | 5-2 | May, Melrose 2, Lineker, Cross og |
| | SF | 03.04.82 | **Tottenham Hotspur** (D1) | | L | 0-2 | |
| | | | *played at Villa Park* | | | | |
| 1982-83 (D2) | 3 | 08.01.83 | **Notts County** (D1) | H | L | 2-3 | A Smith, Wilson |
| 1983-84 (D1) | 3 | 07.01.84 | **Crystal Palace** (D2) | A | L | 0-1 | |
| 1984-85 (D1) | 3 | 05.01.85 | **Burton Albion** (NPL) | | W | 6-1 | Lineker 3, A Smith 2, Lynex |
| | | | *played at Baseball Ground, Derby. FA ordered match to be replayed behind closed doors after coin-throwing incident* | | | | |
| | 3r | 16.01.85 | **Burton Albion** (NPL) | | W | 1-0 | Ramsey |
| | | | *played at Highfield Road, Coventry* | | | | |
| | 4 | 26.01.85 | **Carlisle Utd** (D2) | H | W | 1-0 | B Smith |
| | 5 | 19.02.85 | **Millwall** (D3) | A | L | 0-2 | |
| 1985-86 (D1) | 3 | 04.01.86 | **Bristol Rovers** (D3) | A | L | 1-3 | McAllister (p) |
| 1986-87 (D1) | 3 | 10.01.87 | **QPR** (D1) | A | L | 2-5 | A Smith, McAllister (p) |
| 1987-88 (D2) | 3 | 09.01.88 | **Oxford Utd** (D1) | A | L | 0-2 | |
| 1988-89 (D2) | 3 | 07.01.89 | **Manchester City** (D2) | A | L | 0-1 | |
| 1989-90 (D2) | 3 | 06.01.90 | **Barnsley** (D2) | H | L | 1-2 | Paris |
| 1990-91 (D2) | 3 | 05.01.91 | **Millwall** (D2) | A | L | 1-2 | James |
| 1991-92 (D2) | 3 | 04.01.92 | **Crystal Palace** (D1) | H | W | 1-0 | R Smith |
| | 4 | 25.01.92 | **Bristol City** (D2) | H | L | 1-2 | Kitson |
| 1992-93 (D1) | 3 | 13.01.93 | **Barnsley** (D1) | H | D | 2-2 | Thompson (p), Oldfield |
| | 3r | 20.01.93 | **Barnsley** | A | D | 1-1aet | Joachim |
| | | | *Barnsley won 5-4 on penalties* | | | | |
| 1993-94 (D1) | 3 | 08.01.94 | **Manchester City** (PL) | A | L | 1-4 | Oldfield |
| 1994-95 (PL) | 3 | 07.01.95 | **Enfield** (IL) | H | W | 2-0 | Oldfield, Roberts |
| | 4 | 28.01.95 | **Portsmouth** (D1) | A | W | 1-0 | Roberts |
| | 5 | 18.02.95 | **Wolverhampton W** (D1) | A | L | 0-1 | |
| 1995-96 (D1) | 3 | 06.01.96 | **Manchester City** (PL) | H | D | 0-0 | |
| | 3r | 17.01.96 | **Manchester City** | A | L | 0-5 | |
| 1996-97 (PL) | 3 | 15.01.97 | **Southend Utd** (D1) | H | W | 2-0 | Claridge, Marshall |
| | 4 | 25.01.97 | **Norwich City** (D1) | H | W | 2-1 | Marshall, Parker (p) |
| | 5 | 16.02.97 | **Chelsea** (PL) | H | D | 2-2 | Walsh, Newton og |
| | 5r | 26.02.97 | **Chelsea** | A | L | 0-1aet | |
| 1997-98 (PL) | 3 | 03.01.98 | **Northampton Town** (D2) | H | W | 4-0 | Marshall, Parker (p), Savage, Cottee |
| | 4 | 24.01.98 | **Crystal Palace** (PL) | A | L | 0-3 | |
| 1998-99 (PL) | 3 | 02.01.99 | **Birmingham City** (D1) | H | W | 4-2 | Sinclair, Ullathorne, Cottee, Guppy |
| | 4 | 23.01.99 | **Coventry City** (PL) | H | L | 0-3 | |
| 1999-00 (PL) | 3 | 11.12.99 | **Hereford Utd** (Conf) | A | D | 0-0 | |
| | 3r | 22.12.99 | **Hereford Utd** | H | W | 2-1aet | Elliott, Izzet |
| | 4 | 09.01.00 | **Arsenal** (PL) | A | D | 0-0 | |
| | 4r | 19.01.00 | **Arsenal** | H | D | 0-0aet | |
| | | | *Leicester City won 6-5 on penalties* | | | | |
| | 5 | 30.01.00 | **Chelsea** (PL) | A | L | 1-2 | Elliott |
| 2000-01 (PL) | 3 | 06.01.01 | **York City** (D3) | H | W | 3-0 | Rowett, Izzet (p), Cresswell |
| | 4 | 27.01.01 | **Aston Villa** (PL) | A | W | 2-1 | Akinbiyi, Gunnlaugsson |
| | 5 | 17.02.01 | **Bristol City** (D2) | H | W | 3-0 | Sturridge, Hill og, Izzet (p) |
| | 6 | 10.03.01 | **Wycombe W** (D2) | H | L | 1-2 | Izzet |
| 2001-02 (PL) | 3 | 05.01.02 | **Mansfield Town** (D3) | H | W | 2-1 | Scowcroft 2 |
| | 4 | 26.01.02 | **WBA** (D1) | A | L | 0-1 | |
| 2002-03 (D1) | 3 | 04.01.03 | **Bristol City** (D2) | H | W | 2-0 | Elliott, Dickov |
| | 4 | 25.01.03 | **Wolverhampton W** (D1) | A | L | 1-4 | Dickov (p) |

# LEIGH RMI

*Formed 1896 as Horwich RMI. Changed name to Leigh RMI 1995. See also Horwich RMI. Members of The Conference.*

| | | | | | | | | |
|---|---|---|---|---|---|---|---|---|
| 1998-99 | (NPL) | 1 | 15.11.98 | **Fulham** (D2) | A | D | 1-1 | Whealing |
| | | 1r | 24.11.98 | **Fulham** | H | L | 0-2 | |
| 2000-01 | (Conf) | 1 | 19.11.00 | **Millwall** (D2) *played at New Den* | H | L | 0-3 | |

# LEWES

*Formed 1885. First entered FA Cup: 1912-13. Members of the Isthmian League.*

| | | | | | | | | |
|---|---|---|---|---|---|---|---|---|
| 2001-02 | (IL) | 1 | 18.11.01 | **Stoke City** (D2) *played at Britania Stadium, Stoke* | H | L | 0-2 | |

# LEYTON FC

*Formed 1868. Disbanded 1880. Reformed 1889 as Matlock Swifts. Re-adopted Leyton name 1894. Merged with Wingate FC in 1975 to form Leyton-Wingate. Merged 1992 with Walthamstow Pennant to become Leyton Pennant. First entered FA Cup: 1874-75. FA Amateur Cup winners: 1927, 1928. Runners-up: 1929, 1934, 1937, 1952. League clubs beaten: Stockport County, Merthyr Town. Members of the Isthmian League.*

| | | | | | | | | |
|---|---|---|---|---|---|---|---|---|
| 1874-75 | | 1 | 14.11.74 | **Southall Park** | A | D | 0-0 | |
| | | 1r | 28.11.74 | **Southall Park** | H | L | 0-5 | |
| 1875-76 | | 1 | | Harrow Chequers *Harrow Chequers scratched. Leyton FC walkover* | | | - | |
| | | 2 | 18.12.75 | **Clapham Rovers** | A | L | 0-12 | |
| 1876-77 | | 1 | 28.10.76 | **Upton Park** | A | L | 0-7 | |
| 1877-78 | | 1 | 07.11.77 | **Swifts** | A | L | 2-3 | Rawson 2 |
| 1878-79 | | 1 | | South Norwood *Leyton FC scratched. South Norwood walkover* | | | - | |
| 1909-10 | (SL) | 1 | 15.01.10 | **New Brompton** (SL) | H | D | 0-0 | |
| | | 1r | 19.01.10 | **New Brompton** | A | D | 2-2aet | Ryder, Robertson |
| | | 1 2r | 24.01.10 | **New Brompton** *played at White Hart Lane* | | W | 1-0 | Shanks |
| | | 2 | 05.02.10 | **Stockport County** (D2) | A | W | 2-0 | Ryder, Robertson |
| | | 3 | 19.02.10 | **Leicester Fosse** (D2) | H | L | 0-1 | |
| 1910-11 | (SL) | 1 | 14.01.11 | **Chelsea** (D2) | A | D | 0-0 | |
| | | 1r | 19.01.11 | **Chelsea** | H | L | 0-2 | |
| 1911-12 | (SL) | 1 | 13.01.12 | **Liverpool** (D1) | A | L | 0-1 | |
| 1925-26 | (Lon) | 1 | 28.11.25 | **St Albans City** (IL) | H | W | 1-0 | Hall |
| | | 2 | 12.12.25 | **Reading** (3S) | A | L | 0-6 | |
| 1927-28 | (AL) | 1 | 26.11.27 | **Northampton Town** (3S) | A | L | 0-8 | |
| 1928-29 | (AL) | 1 | 24.11.28 | **Watford** (3S) | H | L | 0-2 | |
| 1929-30 | (AL) | 1 | 30.11.29 | **Merthyr Town** (3S) | H | W | 4-1 | G Collins 2, Margetts, Keeble |
| | | 2 | 14.12.29 | **Fulham** (3S) | H | L | 1-4 | GD Collins |
| 1934-35 | (AL) | 1 | 24.11.34 | **Wimbledon** (IL) | A | D | 1-1 | Lloyd |
| | | 1r | 29.11.34 | **Wimbledon** | H | L | 0-1 | |
| 1951-52 | (AL) | 1 | 24.11.51 | **Chippenham Town** (WL) | H | W | 3-0 | Goddard 2, Casey |
| | | 2 | 15.12.51 | **Chester** (3N) | A | L | 2-5 | Fitch, Hasley |
| 1952-53 | (AL) | 1 | 22.11.52 | **Hereford Utd** (SL) | H | D | 0-0 | |
| | | 1r | 27.11.52 | **Hereford Utd** | A | L | 2-3 | Goddard, Bessex |
| 1955-56 | (AL) | 1 | 19.11.55 | **Bedford Town** (SL) | A | L | 0-3 | |

# LEYTON ORIENT

*Formed 1881. First entered FA Cup: 1904-05. Clapton Orient 1881-1946. Leyton Orient 1946-1967. Orient 1967-1987. Leyton Orient from 1987. FA Cup best performance: Semi-finals 1978. Record FA Cup win: 7-1 v Lovells Athletic, 1st round, 19.11.1955. Record FA Cup defeat: 0-8 v Aston Villa, 4th round, 30.01.1929.*

**as Clapton Orient**

| | | | | | | | | |
|---|---|---|---|---|---|---|---|---|
| 1904-05 | (SL) | | | P Enfield (H) 4-1; 1q Cheshunt (A) 0-0; 1q Cheshunt (H) 4-1; 2q Leytonstone (H) 1-1; 2qr Leytonstone (A) 5-2; 3q New Brompton (H) 2-6 | | | | |
| 1905-06 | (D2) | | | Felstead (A) 1-1; 1qr Felstead (H) 5-1; 2q Barking (H) 3-1; 3q Leyton (A) 3-1; 4q Clapton (A) 2-0 | | | | |
| | | 1 | 13.01.06 | **Chesterfield** (D2) | H | D | 0-0 | |
| | | 1r | 17.01.06 | **Chesterfield** | A | L | 0-3 | |
| 1906-07 | (D2) | | | did not enter | | | | |

| | | | | | | | | |
|---|---|---|---|---|---|---|---|---|
| 1907-08 | (D2) | | | 1q Custom House (H) 3-0; 2q Romford (A) 6-3; 3q Old Newportians (H) 5-2; 4q Southend Utd (H) 1-1; 4qr Southend Utd (A) 1-3 | | | | |
| 1908-09 | (D2) | 1 | 16.01.09 | **Newcastle Utd** (D1) | A | L | 0-5 | |
| 1909-10 | (D2) | 1 | 15.01.10 | **WBA** (D2) | A | L | 0-2 | |
| 1910-11 | (D2) | 1 | 14.01.11 | **Woolwich Arsenal** (D1) | H | - | 0-1ab | |
| | | | | *abandoned afer 55 minutes* | | | | |
| | | 1 | 16.01.11 | **Woolwich Arsenal** | H | L | 1-2 | Goffin |
| 1911-12 | (D2) | 1 | 13.01.12 | **Everton** (D1) | H | L | 1-2 | Bevan |
| 1912-13 | (D2) | 1 | 11.01.13 | **Sunderland** (D1) | A | L | 0-6 | |
| 1913-14 | (D2) | 1 | 10.01.14 | **Nottingham Forest** (D2) | H | D | 2-2 | McFadden, Jonas |
| | | 1r | 14.01.14 | **Nottingham Forest** | A | W | 1-0 | McFadden |
| | | 2 | 31.01.14 | **Brighton** (SL) | A | L | 1-3 | Scott |
| 1914-15 | (D2) | 1 | 09.01.15 | **Millwall Athletic** (SL) | A | L | 1-2 | Jonas (p) |
| 1919-20 | (D2) | 1 | 10.01.20 | **Manchester City** (D1) | A | L | 1-4 | J Tonner |
| 1920-21 | (D2) | | | 6q Port Vale (H) 1-0 | | | | |
| | | 1 | 08.01.21 | **Bradford Park A** (D1) | A | L | 0-1 | |
| 1921-22 | (D2) | 1 | 07.01.22 | **Leicester City** (D2) | A | L | 0-2 | |
| 1922-23 | (D2) | 1 | 13.01.23 | **Millwall Athletic** (3S) | H | L | 0-2 | |
| 1923-24 | (D2) | 1 | 12.01.24 | **Swansea Town** (3S) | A | D | 1-1 | Williams |
| | | 1r | 17.01.24 | **Swansea Town** | H | D | 1-1aet | Rennox |
| | | 1 2r | 21.01.24 | **Swansea Town** | | L | 1-2 | Williams (p) |
| | | | | *played at White Hart Lane* | | | | |
| 1924-25 | (D2) | 1 | 10.01.25 | **Nottingham Forest** (D1) | A | L | 0-1 | |
| 1925-26 | (D2) | 3 | 09.01.26 | **Chesterfield** (3N) | A | W | 1-0 | J Tonner |
| | | 4 | 30.01.26 | **Middlesbrough** (D2) | H | W | 4-2 | J Tonner 2, Henderson, Cock |
| | | 5 | 20.02.26 | **Newcastle Utd** (D1) | H | W | 2-0 | Galbraith, Cock |
| | | 6 | 06.03.26 | **Manchester City** (D1) | H | L | 1-6 | Cock |
| 1926-27 | (D2) | 3 | 08.01.27 | **Port Vale** (D2) | H | D | 1-1 | Dennison |
| | | 3r | 12.01.27 | **Port Vale** | A | L | 1-5 | Dennison |
| 1927-28 | (D2) | 3 | 14.01.28 | **Swindon Town** (3S) | A | L | 1-2 | Whipp |
| 1928-29 | (D2) | 3 | 12.01.29 | **Southampton** (D2) | A | D | 0-0 | |
| | | 3r | 17.01.29 | **Southampton** | H | W | 2-1 | Dennison, Corkindale |
| | | 4 | 26.01.29 | **Aston Villa** (D1) | A | D | 0-0 | |
| | | 4r | 30.01.29 | **Aston Villa** | H | L | 0-8 | |
| 1929-30 | (3S) | 1 | 30.11.29 | **Folkestone** (SL) | H | D | 0-0 | |
| | | 1r | 04.12.29 | **Folkestone** | A | D | 2-2aet | Mills, Campbell |
| | | 1 2r | 09.12.29 | **Folkestone** | | W | 4-1 | Eastman, Vanner, Campbell, Grimsdell |
| | | | | *played at Highbury* | | | | |
| | | 2 | 14.01.30 | **Northfleet Utd** (SL) | H | W | 2-0 | Grimsdell, Mills |
| | | 3 | 11.01.30 | **Bristol Rovers** (3S) | H | W | 1-0 | Lyons (p) |
| | | 4 | 25.01.30 | **Newcastle Utd** (D1) | A | L | 1-3 | Mills |
| 1930-31 | (3S) | 1 | 29.11.30 | **Luton Town** (3S) | A | D | 2-2 | Tricker, McGinnile og |
| | | 1r | 04.12.30 | **Luton Town** | H | L | 2-4 | Tricker, Cropper |
| | | | | *played at Highbury* | | | | |
| 1931-32 | (3S) | 1 | 28.11.31 | **Coventry City** (3S) | A | D | 2-2 | Fletcher, Sanders |
| | | 1r | 03.12.31 | **Coventry City** | H | W | 2-0 | Tricker, Fletcher |
| | | 2 | 12.12.31 | **Cardiff City** (3S) | A | L | 0-4 | |
| 1932-33 | (3S) | 1 | 26.11.32 | **Aldershot** (3S) | H | L | 0-1 | |
| 1933-34 | (3S) | 1 | 25.11.33 | **Epsom and Ewell T** (Lon) | H | W | 4-2 | Morris 2, Rigby (p), Taylor |
| | | 2 | 09.12.33 | **Walsall** (3N) | A | D | 0-0 | |
| | | 2r | 14.12.33 | **Walsall** | H | W | 2-0 | Morris, Taylor |
| | | 3 | 13.01.34 | **Grimsby Town** (D2) | A | L | 0-1 | |
| 1934-35 | (3S) | 1 | 24.11.34 | **Ashford Town** (KL) | A | W | 4-1 | Halliday 2, Mayson, Ware |
| | | 2 | 08.12.34 | **Chester** (3N) | H | L | 1-3 | Halliday |
| 1935-36 | (3S) | 1 | 30.11.35 | **Aldershot** (3S) | H | D | 0-0 | |
| | | 1r | 04.12.35 | **Aldershot** | A | W | 1-0 | Crawford |
| | | 2 | 14.12.35 | **Folkestone** (SL) | A | W | 2-1 | McAleer, Crawford |
| | | 3 | 11.01.36 | **Charlton Athletic** (D2) | H | W | 3-0 | H Taylor, Foster |
| | | 4 | 25.01.36 | **Middlesbrough** (D1) | A | L | 0-3 | |
| 1936-37 | (3S) | 1 | 28.11.36 | **Torquay Utd** (3S) | H | W | 2-1 | H Smith, Crawford |
| | | 2 | 12.12.36 | **Carlisle Utd** (3N) | A | L | 1-4 | Crawford |

| | | | | | | | | |
|---|---|---|---|---|---|---|---|---|
| 1937-38 | (3S) | 1 | 27.11.37 | **Torquay Utd** (3S) | A | W | 2-1 | Tully, Graham |
| | | 2 | 11.12.37 | **York City** (3N) | H | D | 2-2 | Lane, H Smith |
| | | 2r | 15.12.37 | **York City** | A | L | 0-1 | |
| 1938-39 | (3S) | 1 | 26.11.38 | **Hayes** (AL) | H | W | 3-1 | H Smith, Williams, Crawford |
| | | 2 | 10.12.38 | **Walsall** (3S) | A | L | 2-4 | Crawford, Williams |
| 1945-46 | (3S) | 1 1L | 17.11.45 | **Newport (IOW)** (HL) | H | W | 2-1 | Gore, Parr (p) |
| | | 1 2L | 24.11.45 | **Newport (IOW)** | A | L | 0-2 | |
| **as Leyton Orient** | | | | | | | | |
| 1946-47 | (3S) | 1 | 30.11.46 | **Notts County** (3S) | H | L | 1-2 | Hunt |
| 1947-48 | (3S) | 1 | 29.11.47 | **Gillingham** (SL) | A | L | 0-1 | |
| 1948-49 | (3S) | 1 | 27.11.48 | **Dartford** (SL) | A | W | 3-2 | Connelly, Deverall, McGreachy, |
| | | 2 | 11.12.48 | **Darlington** (3N) | A | L | 0-1 | |
| 1949-50 | (3S) | 1 | 26.11.49 | **Southend Utd** (3S) | H | L | 0-2 | |
| 1950-51 | (3S) | 1 | 25.11.50 | **Ipswich Town** (3S) | H | L | 1-2 | Rees |
| 1951-52 | (3S) | 1 | 24.11.51 | **Gorleston** (ECL) | H | D | 2-2 | Banner (p), Blatchford |
| | | 1r | 29.11.51 | **Gorleston** | A | D | 0-0aet | |
| | | 1 2r | 03.12.51 | **Gorleston** *played at Highbury* | | W | 5-4 | Pacey 3, Brown 2 |
| | | 2 | 15.12.51 | **Wrexham** (3N) | A | D | 1-1 | Pacey |
| | | 2r | 19.12.51 | **Wrexham** | H | W | 3-2 | Rees 3 |
| | | 3 | 12.01.52 | **Everton** (D2) | H | D | 0-0 | |
| | | 3r | 16.01.52 | **Everton** | A | W | 3-1 | Harris, Pacey 2 |
| | | 4 | 02.02.52 | **Birmingham City** (D2) | A | W | 1-0 | Harris |
| | | 5 | 23.02.52 | **Arsenal** (D1) | H | L | 0-3 | |
| 1952-53 | (3S) | 1 | 22.11.52 | **Bristol Rovers** (3S) | H | D | 1-1 | Pacey |
| | | 1r | 24.11.52 | **Bristol Rovers** | A | L | 0-1 | |
| 1953-54 | (3S) | 1 | 21.11.53 | **Kettering Town** (SL) | H | W | 3-0 | Poulton 2, Facey |
| | | 2 | 12.12.53 | **Weymouth** (SL) | H | W | 4-0 | Rees 2, Mogan, Pacey |
| | | 3 | 09.01.54 | **Tranmere Rovers** (3N) | A | D | 2-2 | Rees, Facey (p) |
| | | 3r | 14.01.54 | **Tranmere Rovers** | H | W | 4-1 | Pacey 3, rees |
| | | 4 | 30.01.54 | **Fulham** (D2) | H | W | 2-1 | Poulton, Davies |
| | | 5 | 20.02.54 | **Doncaster Rovers** (D2) | H | W | 3-1 | Morgan, Pacey, Burgess |
| | | 6 | 13.03.54 | **Port Vale** (D3) | H | L | 0-1 | |
| 1954-55 | (3S) | 1 | 20.11.54 | **Frome Town** (WL) | A | W | 3-0 | Facey, Groves, Fitz og |
| | | 2 | 11.12.54 | **Workington** (3N) | H | L | 0-1 | |
| 1955-56 | (3S) | 1 | 19.11.55 | **Lovell's Athletic** (SL) | H | W | 7-1 | Heckman 5, Facey, Hartburn |
| | | 2 | 10.12.55 | **Brentford** (3S) | H | W | 4-1 | Heckman, Facey, Hartburn, Burgess |
| | | 3 | 07.01.56 | **Plymouth Argyle** (D2) | H | W | 1-0 | Hartburn |
| | | 4 | 28.01.56 | **Birmingham City** (D1) | H | L | 0-4 | |
| 1956-57 | (D2) | 3 | 05.01.57 | **Chelsea** (D1) | H | L | 0-2 | |
| 1957-58 | (D2) | 3 | 04.01.58 | **Reading** (3S) | H | W | 1-0 | Johnston |
| | | 4 | 25.01.58 | **Cardiff City** (D2) | A | L | 1-4 | Julians |
| 1958-59 | (D2) | 3 | 10.01.59 | **Blackburn Rovers** (D1) | A | L | 2-4 | Lewis 2 |
| 1959-60 | (D2) | 3 | 09.01.60 | **Liverpool** (D2) | A | L | 1-2 | Foster |
| 1960-61 | (D2) | 3 | 07.01.61 | **Gillingham** (D4) | A | W | 6-2 | Elwood 2, Lewis 2 (2p), Johnston, McDonald |
| | | 4 | 28.01.61 | **Southampton** (D2) | A | W | 1-0 | Gibbs |
| | | 5 | 18.02.61 | **Sheffield Wed** (D1) | H | L | 0-2 | |
| 1961-62 | (D2) | 3 | 06.01.62 | **Brentford** (D3) | A | D | 1-1 | Foster |
| | | 3r | 08.01.62 | **Brentford** | H | W | 2-1 | Foster, Elwood |
| | | 4 | 30.01.62 | **Burnley** (D1) | A | D | 1-1 | Foster |
| | | 4r | 06.02.62 | **Burnley** | H | L | 0-1 | |
| 1962-63 | (D1) | 3 | 11.02.63 | **Hull City** (D3) | H | D | 1-1 | Musgrove |
| | | 3r | 19.02.63 | **Hull City** | A | W | 2-0aet | Musgrove, Gibbs |
| | | 4 | 04.03.63 | **Derby County** (D2) | H | W | 3-0 | Dunmore, Elwood, Deeley |
| | | 5 | 16.03.63 | **Leicester City** (D1) | H | L | 0-1 | |
| 1963-64 | (D2) | 3 | 04.01.64 | **Leicester City** | A | W | 3-2 | Musgrove 2, King og |
| | | 4 | 25.01.64 | **West Ham Utd** (D1) | H | D | 1-1 | Deeley |
| | | 4r | 29.01.64 | **West Ham Utd** | A | L | 0-3 | |
| 1964-65 | (D2) | 3 | 09.01.65 | **Southampton** (D2) | A | L | 1-3 | Dunmore |
| 1965-66 | (D2) | 3 | 22.01.66 | **Norwich City** (D2) | H | L | 1-3 | Price |
| 1966-67 | (D3) | 1 | 26.11.66 | **Lowestoft Town** (ECL) | H | W | 2-1 | Whitehouse, Metchick |

| | | | | | | | |
|---|---|---|---|---|---|---|---|
| | 2 | 07.01.67 | **Brentford** (D4) | H | D | 0-0 | |
| | 2r | 10.01.67 | **Brentford** | A | L | 1-3 | Metchick |
| **as Orient** | | | | | | | |
| 1967-68 (D3) | 1 | 09.12.67 | **Weymouth** (SL) | A | W | 2-0 | Halom 2 |
| | 2 | 06.01.68 | **Boston Utd** (WMRL) | A | D | 1-1 | Simpson |
| | 2r | 15.01.68 | **Boston Utd** | H | W | 2-1 | Mancini, Halom |
| | 3 | 27.01.68 | **Bury** (D3) | H | W | 1-0 | Massey |
| | 4 | 17.02.68 | **Birmingham City** (D2) | A | L | 0-3 | |
| 1968-69 (D3) | 1 | 16.11.68 | **Gillingham** (D3) | H | D | 1-1 | Bloomfield |
| | 1r | 20.11.68 | **Gillingham** | A | L | 1-2 | Slater |
| 1969-70 (D3) | 1 | 15.11.69 | **Walsall** (D3) | A | D | 0-0 | |
| | 1r | 17.11.69 | **Walsall** | H | L | 0-2 | |
| 1970-71 (D2) | 3 | 11.01.71 | **Sunderland** (D2) | A | W | 3-0 | Fairbrother, Dyson, Lazarus |
| | 4 | 23.01.71 | **Nottingham Forest** (D1) | A | D | 1-1 | Dyson |
| | 4r | 25.01.71 | **Nottingham Forest** | H | - | 0-0ab | |
| | | | *abandoned at half-time – ground unplayable* | | | | |
| | 4r | 01.02.71 | **Nottingham Forest** | H | L | 0-1 | |
| 1971-72 (D2) | 3 | 15.01.72 | **Wrexham** (D3) | H | W | 3-0 | Dyson (p), Fairbrother, Bowyer |
| | 4 | 05.02.72 | **Leicester City** (D1) | A | W | 2-0 | Bowyer, Allen |
| | 5 | 26.02.72 | **Chelsea** (D1) | H | W | 3-2 | Hoadley, Bullock, Fairbrother |
| | 6 | 18.03.72 | **Arsenal** (D1) | H | L | 0-1 | |
| 1972-73 (D2) | 3 | 13.01.73 | **Coventry City** (D1) | H | L | 1-4 | Arber (p) |
| 1973-74 (D2) | 3 | 05.01.74 | **Bournemouth** (D3) | H | W | 2-1 | Fairbrother 2 |
| | 4 | 27.01.74 | **Portsmouth** (D2) | A | D | 0-0 | |
| | 4r | 29.01.74 | **Portsmouth** | H | D | 1-1aet | Fairbrother |
| | 4 2r | 05.02.74 | **Portsmouth** | | L | 0-2 | |
| | | | *played at Selhurst Park* | | | | |
| 1974-75 (D2) | 3 | 04.01.75 | **Derby County** (D1) | H | D | 2-2 | Possee, Queen |
| | 3r | 08.01.75 | **Derby County** | A | L | 1-2 | Fairbrother |
| 1975-76 (D2) | 3 | 03.01.76 | **Cardiff City** (D3) | H | L | 0-1 | |
| 1976-77 (D2) | 3 | 08.01.77 | **Darlington** (D4) | A | D | 2-2 | Possee, Hoadley |
| | 3r | 11.01.77 | **Darlington** | H | D | 0-0aet | |
| | 3 2r | 17.01.77 | **Darlington** | | W | 3-0 | Whittle 2, Roffey |
| | | | *played at White Hart Lane* | | | | |
| | 4 | 29.01.77 | **Blackburn Rovers** (D2) | A | L | 0-3 | |
| 1977-78 (D2) | 3 | 06.01.78 | **Norwich City** (D1) | H | D | 1-1 | Kitchen |
| | 3r | 16.01.78 | **Norwich City** | A | W | 1-0 | Kitchen |
| | 4 | 28.01.78 | **Blackburn Rovers** (D2) | H | W | 3-1 | Kitchen 2, Mayo |
| | 5 | 18.02.78 | **Chelsea** (D1) | H | D | 0-0 | |
| | 5r | 27.02.78 | **Chelsea** | A | W | 2-1 | Kitchen 2 |
| | 6 | 11.03.78 | **Middlesbrough** (D1) | A | D | 0-0 | |
| | 6r | 14.03.78 | **Middlesbrough** | H | W | 2-1 | Kitchen, Mayo |
| | SF | 08.04.78 | **Arsenal** (D1) | | L | 0-3 | |
| | | | *played at Stamford Bridge* | | | | |
| 1978-79 (D2) | 3 | 09.01.79 | **Bury** (D3) | H | W | 3-2 | Kitchen 2, Chiedozie |
| | 4 | 27.01.79 | **Ipswich Town** (D1) | A | D | 0-0 | |
| | 4r | 30.01.79 | **Ipswich Town** | H | L | 0-2 | |
| 1979-80 (D2) | 3 | 05.01.80 | **Altrincham** (APL) | A | D | 1-1 | Jennings |
| | 3r | 09.01.80 | **Altrincham** | H | W | 2-1 | Mayo, Jennings |
| | 4 | 26.01.80 | **West Ham Utd** (D2) | H | L | 2-3 | Taylor (p), Chiedozie |
| 1980-81 (D2) | 3 | 03.01.81 | **Luton Town** (D2) | H | L | 1-3 | Jennings |
| 1981-82 (D2) | 3 | 02.01.82 | **Charlton Athletic** (D2) | H | W | 1-0 | Moores |
| | 4 | 26.01.82 | **Huddersfield Town** (D3) | A | D | 1-1 | Moores |
| | 4r | 01.02.82 | **Huddersfield Town** | H | W | 2-0 | Foster, Moores |
| | 5 | 13.02.82 | **Crystal Palace** (D2) | A | D | 0-0 | |
| | 5r | 16.02.82 | **Crystal Palace** | H | L | 0-1 | |
| 1982-83 (D3) | 1 | 20.11.82 | **Bristol City** (D4) | H | W | 4-1 | Foster, Godfery 2, Sussex |
| | 2 | 11.12.82 | **Newport County** (D3) | A | L | 0-1 | |
| 1983-84 (D3) | 1 | 19.11.83 | **Wimbledon** (D3) | A | L | 1-2 | Smith og |
| 1984-85 (D3) | 1 | 19.11.84 | **Buckingham Town** (UCL) | A | W | 2-0 | Cornwell (p), McNeil |
| | 2 | 08.12.84 | **Torquay Utd** (D4) | H | W | 3-0 | Godfery, Jones, Foster |
| | 3 | 05.01.85 | **WBA** (D1) | H | W | 2-1 | Silkman, Cadette |

| | | | | | | | | |
|---|---|---|---|---|---|---|---|---|
| | | 4 | 26.01.85 | **Southampton** (D1) | H | L | 0-2 | |
| 1985-86 | (D4) | 1 | 16.11.85 | **VS Rugby** (SL) | A | D | 2-2 | Brooks 2 (1p), |
| | | 1r | 19.11.85 | **VS Rugby** | H | W | 4-1 | Jones, Castle, Juryeff, Brooks |
| | | 2 | 07.12.85 | **Slough Town** (IL) | H | D | 2-2 | Cornwell, Juryeff |
| | | 2r | 10.12.85 | **Slough Town** | A | W | 3-2 | Juryeff, Godfery, Shinners |
| | | 3 | 06.01.86 | **Oldham Athletic** (D2) | A | W | 2-1 | Shinners, Foster |
| | | 4 | 25.01.86 | **Sheffield Wed** (D1) | A | L | 0-5 | |
| 1986-87 | (D4) | 1 | 15.11.86 | **Woodford Town** (SL) | A | W | 1-0 | Foster |
| | | 2 | 06.12.86 | **Bournemouth** (D3) | A | W | 1-0 | Harvey |
| | | 3 | 10.01.87 | **West Ham Utd** (D1) | H | D | 1-1 | Castle (p) |
| | | 3r | 31.01.87 | **West Ham Utd** | A | L | 1-4 | Brooks |
| **as Leyton Orient** | | | | | | | | |
| 1987-88 | (D4) | 1 | 14.11.87 | **Exeter City** (D4) | H | W | 2-0 | Godfery, Hull |
| | | 2 | 05.12.87 | **Swansea City** (D4) | H | W | 2-0 | Shinners, Comfort |
| | | 3 | 09.01.88 | **Stockport County** (D4) | A | W | 2-1 | Juryeff, Shinners |
| | | 4 | 30.01.88 | **Nottingham Forest** (D1) | H | L | 1-2 | Juryeff |
| 1988-89 | (D4) | 1 | 19.11.88 | **Enfield** (Conf) | A | D | 1-1 | Ward |
| | | 1r | 23.11.88 | **Enfield** | H | D | 2-2aet | Juryeff 2 |
| | | 1 2r | 28.11.88 | **Enfield** | H | L | 0-1 | |
| 1989-90 | (D3) | 1 | 17.11.89 | **Birmingham City** (D3) | H | L | 0-1 | |
| 1990-91 | (D3) | 1 | 17.11.90 | **Southend Utd** (D3) | H | W | 3-2 | Castle 2, Nugent |
| | | 2 | 12.12.90 | **Colchester Utd** (Conf) | A | D | 0-0 | |
| | | 2r | 17.12.90 | **Colchester Utd** | H | W | 4-1 | Carter, Howard, Pike, Castle |
| | | 3 | 05.01.91 | **Swindon Town** (D2) | H | D | 1-1 | Pike |
| | | 3r | 14.01.91 | **Swindon Town** | A | - | 1-1ab | Dickenson |
| | | | | *abandoned after 54 minutes – frozen pitch* | | | | |
| | | 3r | 21.01.91 | **Swindon Town** (D2) | A | L | 0-1 | |
| 1991-92 | (D3) | 1 | 16.11.91 | **Welling Utd** (Conf) | H | W | 2-1 | Howard, Cooper |
| | | 2 | 09.12.91 | **WBA** (D3) | H | W | 2-1 | Berry 2 |
| | | 3 | 04.01.92 | **Oldham Athletic** (D1) | A | D | 1-1 | Day |
| | | 3r | 15.01.92 | **Oldham Athletic** | H | W | 4-2aet | Harvey, Nugent 2, Castle (p) |
| | | 4 | 25.01.92 | **Portsmouth** (D2) | A | L | 0-2 | |
| 1992-93 | (D2) | 1 | 14.11.92 | **Dagenham & Red** (Conf) | A | W | 5-4 | Howard, Whitbread, Cooper 2, Jones |
| | | 2 | 05.12.92 | **Reading** (D2) | A | L | 0-3 | |
| 1993-94 | (D2) | 1 | 13.11.93 | **Gravesend & N** (SL) | H | W | 2-1 | Lakin, Hackett |
| | | 2 | 04.12.93 | **Exeter City** (D2) | H | D | 1-1 | Cooper |
| | | 2r | 14.12.93 | **Exeter City** | A | D | 2-2aet | Carter, Hackett |
| | | | | *Exeter won 5-4 on penalties* | | | | |
| 1994-95 | (D2) | 1 | 12.11.94 | **Tiverton Town** (WL) | A | W | 3-1 | Gray, Carter, West |
| | | 2 | 03.12.94 | **Bristol Rovers** (D2) | H | L | 0-2 | |
| 1995-96 | (D3) | 1 | 11.11.95 | **Torquay Utd** (D3) | A | L | 0-1 | |
| 1996-97 | (D3) | 1 | 16.11.96 | **Merthyr Tydfil** (SL) | H | W | 2-1 | Winston, West |
| | | 2 | 07.12.96 | **Stevenage B** (Conf) | H | L | 1-2 | Channing |
| 1997-98 | (D3) | 1 | 15.11.97 | **Hendon** (IL) | A | D | 2-2 | Harris, Smith |
| | | 1r | 25.11.97 | **Hendon** | H | L | 0-1 | |
| 1998-99 | (D3) | 1 | 14.11.98 | **Brighton** (D3) | H | W | 4-2 | Richards 3, Walschaerts |
| | | 2 | 06.12.98 | **Kingstonian** (Conf) | A | D | 0-0 | |
| | | 2r | 15.12.98 | **Kingstonian** | H | W | 2-1 | Walschaerts, Simba |
| | | 3 | 02.01.99 | **Southport** (Conf) | A | W | 2-0 | Smith (p), Griffiths |
| | | 4 | 23.01.99 | **Bristol Rovers** (D2) | A | L | 0-3 | |
| 1999-00 | (D3) | 1 | 30.10.99 | **Cardiff City** (D2) | H | D | 1-1 | Ampadu |
| | | 1r | 09.11.99 | **Cardiff City** | A | L | 1-3 | Smith |
| 2000-01 | (D3) | 1 | 18.11.00 | **Barrow** (NPL) | A | W | 2-0 | Griffiths, Watts |
| | | 2 | 09.12.00 | **Northwich V** (Conf) | A | D | 3-3 | Griffiths 2, Tate |
| | | 2r | 20.12.00 | **Northwich V** | H | W | 3-2aet | Griffiths, Simpson og, R Houghton |
| | | 3 | 06.01.01 | **Tottenham Hotspur** (PL) | H | L | 0-1 | |
| 2001-02 | (D3) | 1 | 17.11.01 | **Bristol City** (D2) | A | W | 1-0 | Watts |
| | | 2 | 08.12.01 | **Lincoln City** (D3) | H | W | 2-1 | Ibehre, Watts |
| | | 3 | 05.01.02 | **Portsmouth** (D1) | A | W | 4-1 | Smith, Watts, Gray, M Christie |
| | | 4 | 26.01.02 | **Everton** (PL) | A | L | 1-4 | Canham |
| 2002-03 | (D3) | 1 | 16.11.02 | **Margate** (Conf) | H | D | 1-1 | Martin |
| | | 1r | 26.11.02 | **Margate** (Conf) | A | L | 0-1 | |

## LEYTON-WINGATE

*Leyton (1869) and Wingate (1948) merged in 1975 before going their separate ways in 1992.*

| | | | | | | | |
|---|---|---|---|---|---|---|---|
| 1985-86 (IL) | 1 | 16.11.85 | **Swansea City** (D3) | A | L | 0-2 | |

## LEYTONSTONE

*Formed 1886. First entered FA Cup: 1896-97. FA Amateur Cup winners: 1947, 1948, 1968. Merged with Ilford to form Leytonstone-Ilford in 1979 and subsequently lost their identity in 1989 when a second merger with Walthamstow Ave created Redbridge Forest. That club then merged with Dagenham in 1992 to create the present day Dagenham & Redbridge. League clubs beaten: Watford, Shrewsbury Town.*

| | | | | | | | |
|---|---|---|---|---|---|---|---|
| 1946-47 (IL) | 1 | 30.11.46 | **Walsall** (3S) | H | L | 1-6 | Banham |
| 1947-48 (IL) | 1 | 29.11.47 | **Bristol Rovers** (3S) | A | L | 2-3 | Bunce, Groves |
| 1948-49 (IL) | 1 | 27.11.48 | **Watford** (3S) | H | - | 1-1ab | Noble |
| | | | *abandoned after 63 minutes – fog* | | | | |
| | 1 | 04.12.48 | **Watford** | H | W | 2-1 | Smith, Joseph |
| | 2 | 11.12.48 | **Newport County** (3S) | H | L | 3-4aet | Noble 2, Kavanagh |
| 1949-50 (IL) | 1 | 26.11.49 | **Chelmsford City** (SL) | H | L | 1-2 | Noble |
| 1951-52 (IL) | 1 | 24.11.51 | **Shrewsbury Town** (3S) | H | W | 2-0 | Joseph, Noble |
| | 2 | 15.12.51 | **Newport County** (3S) | H | D | 2-2 | Noble 2 |
| | 2r | 20.12.51 | **Newport County** | A | L | 0-3 | |
| 1952-53 (IL) | 1 | 22.11.52 | **Watford** (3S) | H | L | 0-2 | |
| 1965-66 (IL) | 1 | 13.11.65 | **Hereford Utd** (SL) | H | L | 0-1 | |
| 1967-68 (IL) | 1 | 09.12.67 | **Walsall** (D3) | H | L | 0-1 | |
| 1968-69 (IL) | 1 | 16.11.68 | **Walsall** | H | L | 0-1 | |
| 1973-74 (IL) | 1 | 24.11.73 | **Hendon** (IL) | A | L | 0-3 | |

## LEYTONSTONE-ILFORD

*Leytonstone and Ilford amalgamated in 1979. See also Leytonstone (above) and Ilford.*

| | | | | | | | |
|---|---|---|---|---|---|---|---|
| 1979-80 (IL) | 1 | 24.11.79 | **Harlow Town** (IL) | A | L | 1-2 | Powell |
| 1981-82 (IL) | 1 | 21.11.81 | **Aldershot** (D4) | A | L | 0-2 | |

## LINBY COLLIERY

*Formed 1892. Entered FA Cup: 1949-50 – 1956-57. Colliery closed 1987 and although Linby no longer enter the FA Cup they still play in the Notts Alliance League as Linby Colliery Welfare.*

| | | | | | | | |
|---|---|---|---|---|---|---|---|
| 1950-51 (CA) | 1 | 25.11.50 | **Gillingham** (3S) | H | L | 1-4 | Dulson |

## LINCOLN ALBION

*Formed 1882. Played at West Common, near the Vine Inn, and this was the only FA Cup match they played.*

| | | | | | | | |
|---|---|---|---|---|---|---|---|
| 1887-88 | 1 | 15.10.87 | **Basford Rovers** | A | L | 2-3 | |

## LINCOLN CITY

*Formed 1883. FA Cup best performance: (last 16): 1887, 1890, 1902. Record FA Cup win: 13-0 v Peterborough FC, 1st qualifying round, 1895-96. In Competition Proper: 8-1 v Bromley, 2nd round,.10.12.1938. Record FA Cup defeat: 0-5 v Grimsby Town, 4th qualifying round, 1892-93. In Competition Proper: 0-5 v Stoke, 1st round, 11.01.07.*

| | | | | | | | |
|---|---|---|---|---|---|---|---|
| 1884-85 | 1 | 01.11.84 | **Hull Town** | A | W | 5-1 | Fox 2, C Newsum, H Newsum, AN Other |
| | 2 | | bye | | | | |
| | 3 | 03.01.85 | **Grimsby Town** | A | L | 0-1 | |
| 1885-86 | 1 | 31.10.85 | **Grimsby Town** | H | L | 0-2 | |
| 1886-87 | 1 | | bye | | | | |
| | 2 | 20.11.86 | **Middlesbrough** | A | D | 1-1 | Slater |
| | 2r | 27.11.86 | **Middlesbrough** | H | W | 2-0 | Gregson, Simpson |
| | 3 | 11.12.86 | **Gainsborough T** | A | D | 2-2aet | Gregson, AN Other |
| | 3r | 24.01.87 | **Gainsborough T** | H | W | 1-0 | |
| | | | *played at Bramall Lane* | | | | |
| | 5 | 29.01.87 | **Glasgow Rangers** | A | L | 0-3 | |
| 1887-88 | 1 | 15.10.87 | **Horncastle** | H | W | 4-1 | |
| | 2 | 05.11.87 | **Gainsborough T** | H | W | 2-1 | |
| | 3 | 26.11.87 | **Grimsby Town** | A | L | 0-2 | |
| 1888-89 | | | 1q Grimsby Town (A) 1-1aet; 1qr Grimsby Town (H) 1-1aet; 1q 2r Grimsby Town 1-3 (at Bramall Lane) | | | | |
| 1889-90 (ML) | | | 2q Notts Olympic (H) 2-1; 3q Notts Rangers (A) 7-2; 4q Gainsborough T (H) 5-3 | | | | |
| | 1 | 18.01.90 | **Chester** | H | W | 2-0 | Mckay, Duckworth |

| | | | | | | | | |
|---|---|---|---|---|---|---|---|---|
| | | 2 | 01.02.90 | **Preston North End** (D1) | A | L | 0-4 | |
| 1890-91 | (ML) | | | 1q Gainsborough T (A) 3-1; 2q Boston (H) 9-0; 3q Ecclesfield (H) 3-0; 4q Staveley (H) 4-1 | | | | |
| | | 1 | 17.01.91 | **Chester** (TC) | A | L | 0-1 | |
| 1891-92 | (ML) | | | 1q Doncaster Rovers (H) 3-1; 2q Sheffield Utd (A) 1-4 | | | | |
| 1892-93 | (D2) | | | 1q Newark (H) 3-1 abandoned; 1q Newark (A) 4-3 2q Hednesford Town (A) 3-0; 3q Rotherham Town (H) 2-0; 4q Grimsby Town (A) 0-5 | | | | |
| 1893-94 | (D2) | | | 1q Sheffield Club (A) 2-0; 2q Grimsby Town (H) 2-5 | | | | |
| 1894-95 | (D2) | | | 1q Grimsby Town (H) 0-3 | | | | |
| 1895-96 | (D2) | | | 1q Peterborough Club (A) 13-0; 2q Worksop Town (A) 3-0; 3q Grimsby Town (H) 2-4 | | | | |
| 1896-97 | (D2) | | | 3q Gainsborough T (H) 1-0; 4q Worksop Town (A) 3-3; 4qr Worksop Town (H) 8-0; 5q Barnsley (H) 1-2 | | | | |
| 1897-98 | (D2) | | | 3q Attercliffe (H) 5-0; 4q Gainsborough T (A) 1-5 | | | | |
| 1898-99 | (D2) | | | 3q Attercliffe (H) 5-0; 4q Grimsby Town (A) 1-2 | | | | |
| 1899-00 | (D2) | | | 3q Barnsley (A) 0-1 | | | | |
| 1900-01 | (D2) | | | 3q Gainsborough T (H) 0-0; 3qr Gainsborough T (A) 1-1 abandoned; 3qr Gainsborough T 3-1 at Bramall Lane; 4q Barnsley (A) 0-1 | | | | |
| 1901-02 | (D2) | | | 3q Worksop Town(A) 4-0; 4q Doncaster Rovers (H) 1-0; 5q Barnsley (A) 0-0; 5qr Barnsley (H) 3-1; Int Newton Heath (A) 2-1 | | | | |
| | | 1 | 25.01.02 | **Oxford City** (n/af) | A | D | 0-0 | |
| | | 1r | 29.01.02 | **Oxford City** | H | W | 4-0 | McInnes 2, O'Donnell, AN Other |
| | | 2 | 08.02.02 | **Derby County** (D1) | H | L | 1-3 | McInnes |
| 1902-03 | (D2) | | | Int West Ham Utd (H) 2-0 | | | | |
| | | 1 | 07.02.03 | **Barnsley** (D2) | A | L | 0-2 | |
| 1903-04 | (D2) | | | 3q Chesterfield (H) 0-2 | | | | |
| 1904-05 | (D2) | | | 6q Watford (A) 1-1; 6qr Watford (H) 2-1; Int Burnley (A) 1-1; Int R Burnley (H) 3-2 | | | | |
| | | 1 | 04.02.05 | **Manchester City** (D1) | H | L | 1-2 | D. O'Donnell |
| 1905-06 | (D2) | 1 | 13.01.06 | **Stockport County** (D2) | H | W | 4-2 | Watson, Martin 2, F Simpson |
| | | 2 | 03.02.06 | **Brentford** (SL) | A | L | 0-3 | |
| 1906-07 | (D2) | 1 | 12.01.07 | **Chelsea** (D2) | H | D | 2-2 | E Dixon, W Watson |
| | | 1r | 16.01.07 | **Chelsea** | A | W | 1-0aet | Mackin |
| | | 2 | 02.02.07 | **Derby County** (D1) | A | L | 0-1 | |
| 1907-08 | (D2) | 1 | 11.01.08 | **Stoke** (D2) | A | L | 0-5 | |
| 1908-09 | (ML) | | | 5q Stockton (H) 1-0 | | | | |
| | | 1 | 16.01.09 | **Liverpool** (D1) | A | L | 1-5 | Morris |
| 1909-10 | (D2) | | | 4q Crewe Alexandra (A) 1-2 | | | | |
| 1910-11 | (D2) | | | 4q Huddersfield Town (A) 1-1; 4qr Huddersfield Town (H) 1-0l 5q Stoke (A) 0-4 | | | | |
| 1911-12 | (CL) | | | 4q Grimsby Town (H) 3-2; 5q Crook Town (A) 3-2; | | | | |
| | | 1 | 13.01.12 | **Stockport County** (D2) | H | W | 2-0 | McCubbin, Batty |
| | | 2 | 03.02.12 | **Wolverhampton W** (D2) | A | L | 1-2 | Brindley |
| 1912-13 | (D2) | | | 4q Rotherham County (A) 3-1; 5q South Shields (A) 0-1 | | | | |
| 1913-14 | (D2) | 1 | 10.01.14 | **Plymouth Argyle** (SL) | A | L | 1-4 | Barrell |
| 1914-15 | (D2) | | | 6q Rotherham County (H) 6-0 | | | | |
| | | 1 | 09.01.15 | **Brighton** (SL) | A | L | 1-2 | Egerton |
| 1919-20 | (D2) | 1 | 14.01.20 | **Middlesbrough** (D1) | A | L | 1-4 | Ball |
| 1920-21 | (ML) | | | 6q Bromley (H) 5-0 | | | | |
| | | 1 | 08.01.21 | **Millwall Athletic** (D3) | A | W | 3-0 | Rippon 2, Bretnall |
| | | 2 | 29.01.21 | **Fulham** (D2) | H | D | 0-0 | |
| | | 2r | 07.02.21 | **Fulham** | A | L | 0-1 | |
| 1921-22 | (3N) | | | 5q Northampton Town (H) 1-2 | | | | |
| 1922-23 | (3N) | | | 4q Chesterfield (A) 0-2 | | | | |
| 1923-24 | (3N) | | | 4q Denaby Utd (A) 2-1; 5q Northampton Town (A) 1-5 | | | | |
| 1924-25 | (3N) | | | 4q Rossington Main (H) 3-0; 5q Alfreton Town (A) 0-1 | | | | |
| 1925-26 | (3N) | 1 | 28.11.25 | **Bradford Park A** (3N) | A | D | 2-2 | Havelock, Merritt |
| | | 1r | 02.12.25 | **Bradford Park A** | H | D | 1-1aet | McGraham |
| | | 1 2r | 07.12.25 | **Bradford Park A** *played at Bramall Lane* | | L | 1-2 | Hooper |
| 1926-27 | (3N) | 1 | 27.11.26 | **Rotherham Utd** (3N) | H | W | 2-0 | Pringle, Andrews |
| | | 2 | 11.12.26 | **Coventry City** (3S) | A | D | 1-1 | Andrews |
| | | 2r | 15.12.26 | **Coventry City** | H | W | 2-1 | Dinsdale, Bosberry |
| | | 3 | 08.01.27 | **Preston North End** (D2) | H | L | 2-4 | Dinsdale 2 |

| | | | | | | | | |
|---|---|---|---|---|---|---|---|---|
| 1927-28 | (3N) | 1 | 26.11.27 | **Accrington Stanley** (3N) | A | W | 5-2 | Dinsdale 2, Pringle, Andrews, Bosberry |
| | | 2 | 10.12.27 | **Gainsborough T** (ML) | A | W | 2-0 | Bosberry 2 |
| | | 3 | 14.01.28 | **Huddersfield Town** (D1) | A | L | 2-4 | Pringle, Dinsdale |
| 1928-29 | (3N) | 1 | 24.11.28 | **Lancaster Town** (LC) | A | W | 3-1 | Dinsdale 2, Pringle |
| | | 2 | 10.12.28 | **Carlisle Utd** (3N) | A | W | 1-0 | Roberts |
| | | 3 | 12.01.29 | **Leicester City** (D1) | H | L | 0-1 | |
| 1929-30 | (3N) | 1 | 30.11.29 | **Wigan Borough** (3N) | H | W | 3-1 | Maidment 2, Thursby |
| | | 2 | 14.12.29 | **QPR** (3S) | A | L | 1-2 | Maidment |
| 1930-31 | (3N) | 1 | 29.11.30 | **Barrow** (3N) | H | W | 8-3 | Dinsdale 4, Cartwright, Lax 2, Kitching |
| | | 2 | 13.12.30 | **Scarborough** (ML) | A | L | 4-6 | Cartwright, Lax, Dinsdale 2 |
| 1931-32 | (3N) | 1 | 28.11.31 | **Manchester Central** (CC) | A | W | 3-0 | Riley 3 |
| | | 2 | 12.12.31 | **Luton Town** (3S) | H | D | 2-2 | Hall 2 |
| | | 2r | 16.12.31 | **Luton Town** | A | L | 1-4 | Hall |
| 1932-33 | (D2) | 3 | 14.01.33 | **Blackburn Rovers** (D1) | H | L | 1-5 | Horne |
| 1933-34 | (D2) | 3 | 13.01.34 | **Leicester City** (D1) | A | L | 0-3 | |
| 1934-35 | (3N) | 1 | 24.11.34 | **Shildon** (NL) | A | D | 2-2 | Wilkinson 2 |
| | | 1r | 28.11.34 | **Shildon** | H | W | 4-0 | Burke, Read 3 |
| | | 2 | 08.12.34 | **Swindon Town** (3S) | A | L | 3-4 | Read, Campbell, Iverson |
| 1935-36 | (3N) | 1 | 30.11.35 | **Walsall** (3N) | A | L | 0-2 | |
| 1936-37 | (3N) | 1 | 28.11.36 | **New Brighton** (3N) | H | D | 1-1 | Towler |
| | | 1r | 02.12.36 | **New Brighton** | A | W | 3-2 | Towler, Campbell, Horne |
| | | 2 | 12.12.36 | **Oldham Athletic** (3N) | H | L | 2-3 | Towler 2 |
| 1937-38 | (3N) | 1 | 27.11.37 | **Rochdale** (3N) | A | D | 1-1 | Deacon |
| | | 1r | 01.12.37 | **Rochdale** | H | W | 2-0 | Whyte, Campbell |
| | | 2 | 11.12.37 | **Mansfield Town** (3S) | A | - | 2-1ab | Whyte, Towler |
| | | | | *abandoned after 62 minutes* | | | | |
| | | 2 | 15.12.37 | **Mansfield Town** | A | L | 1-2 | Campbell |
| 1938-39 | (3N) | 1 | 26.11.38 | **Barrow** (3N) | H | W | 4-1 | Wilson, Hancock, Deacon, Ponting |
| | | 2 | 10.12.38 | **Bromley** (AL) | H | W | 8-1 | Clare 2, Ponting 3, Wilson, Deacon, White |
| | | 3 | 07.01.39 | **Portsmouth** (D1) | A | L | 0-4 | |
| 1945-46 | (3N) | 1 1L | 17.11.45 | **Yorkshire Amateurs** (YL) | A | L | 0-1 | |
| | | 1 2L | 24.11.45 | **Yorkshire Amateurs** | H | W | 5-1 | Cheetham 2, Marlow, Wroe, Farman og |
| | | 2 1L | 08.12.45 | **Rotherham Utd** (3N) | A | L | 1-2 | Marlow |
| | | 2 2L | 15.12.45 | **Rotherham Utd** | H | D | 1-1 | Marlow |
| 1946-47 | (3N) | 1 | 30.11.46 | **Stockton** (NL) | A | W | 4-2 | Cheetham, Hutchinson, Davies, Marlow |
| | | 2 | 14.12.46 | **Wrexham** (3N) | H | D | 1-1 | Marlow |
| | | 2r | 18.12.46 | **Wrexham** | A | D | 3-3aet | Cheetham 2, Hutchinson |
| | | 2 2r | 23.12.46 | **Wrexham** | | W | 2-1 | Marlow, Cheetham |
| | | | | *played at Maine Road* | | | | |
| | | 3 | 11.01.47 | **Nottingham Forest** (D2) | H | L | 0-1 | |
| 1947-48 | (3N) | 1 | 29.11.47 | **Workington** (NEL) | H | L | 0-2 | |
| 1948-49 | (D2) | 3 | 08.01.49 | **WBA** (D2) | H | L | 0-1 | |
| 1949-50 | (3N) | 1 | 26.11.49 | **Carlisle Utd** (3N) | A | L | 0-1 | |
| 1950-51 | (3N) | 1 | 25.11.50 | **Southport** (3N) | H | D | 1-1 | Graver |
| | | 1r | 28.11.50 | **Southport** | A | L | 2-3 | Troops, Windle |
| 1951-52 | (3N) | 1 | 24.11.51 | **Crewe Alexandra** (3N) | A | W | 4-2 | Garvie, Graver, Whittle, Young |
| | | 2 | 15.12.51 | **Grimsby Town** (3N) | H | W | 3-1 | Graver 2, Galbraith og |
| | | 3 | 12.01.52 | **Portsmouth** (D1) | A | L | 0-4 | |
| 1952-53 | (D2) | 3 | 10.01.53 | **Southampton** (D2) | H | D | 1-1 | Birch |
| | | 3r | 14.01.53 | **Southampton** | A | L | 1-2 | Finch |
| 1953-54 | (D2) | 3 | 09.01.54 | **Walsall** (3S) | H | D | 1-1 | Graver |
| | | 3r | 14.01.54 | **Walsall** | A | D | 1-1aet | Finch |
| | | 3 2r | 18.01.54 | **Walsall** | | W | 2-1 | Whittle, Green (og) |
| | | | | *played at City Ground, Nottingham* | | | | |
| | | 4 | 30.01.54 | **Preston North End** (D1) | H | L | 0-2 | |
| 1954-55 | (D2) | 3 | 08.01.55 | **Liverpool** (D2) | H | D | 1-1 | Munro |

| | | | | | | | | |
|---|---|---|---|---|---|---|---|---|
| | | 3r | 12.01.55 | **Liverpool** | A | L | 0-1aet | |
| 1955-56 | (D2) | 3 | 07.01.56 | **Southend Utd** (3S) | H | L | 2-3 | Bannan, Troops |
| 1956-57 | (D2) | 3 | 05.01.57 | **Peterborough Utd** (ML) | A | D | 2-2 | Watson, Troops |
| | | 3r | 09.01.57 | **Peterborough Utd** | H | L | 4-5aet | Bannan 2 (1p), Neal, Northcott |
| 1957-58 | (D2) | 3 | 04.01.58 | **Wolverhampton W** (D1) | H | L | 0-1 | |
| 1958-59 | (D2) | 3 | 10.01.59 | **Leicester City** (D1) | A | D | 1-1 | McClelland |
| | | 3r | 14.01.59 | **Leicester City** | H | L | 0-2 | |
| 1959-60 | (D2) | 3 | 09.01.60 | **Burnley** (D1) | H | D | 1-1 | Herbertson |
| | | 3r | 12.01.60 | **Burnley** | A | L | 0-2 | |
| 1960-61 | (D2) | 3 | 07.01.61 | **WBA** (D1) | H | W | 3-1 | Graver, Linnecor, McClelland |
| | | 4 | 28.01.61 | **Sheffield Utd** (D2) | A | L | 1-3 | Graver |
| 1961-62 | (D3) | 1 | 04.11.61 | **Crewe Alexandra** (D4) | A | L | 0-2 | |
| 1962-63 | (D4) | 1 | 03.11.62 | **Darlington** (D4) | H | D | 1-1 | Scanlon |
| | | 1r | 07.11.62 | **Darlington** | A | W | 2-1 | Campbell 2 |
| | | 2 | 24.11.62 | **Halifax Town** (D3) | H | W | 1-0 | Campbell |
| | | 3 | 07.03.63 | **Coventry City** (D3) | H | L | 1-5 | Punter |
| 1963-64 | (D4) | 1 | 16.11.63 | **Hartlepools Utd** (D4) | A | W | 1-0 | Holmes |
| | | 2 | 07.12.63 | **Southport** (D4) | H | W | 2-0 | Morton, Wilkinson |
| | | 3 | 04.01.64 | **Sheffield Utd** (D1) | H | L | 0-4 | |
| 1964-65 | (D4) | 1 | 14.11.64 | **Tranmere Rovers** (D4) | A | D | 0-0 | |
| | | 1r | 18.11.64 | **Tranmere Rovers** | H | W | 1-0 | Hawksby |
| | | 2 | 05.12.64 | **Hull City** (D3) | A | D | 1-1 | Houghton |
| | | 2r | 09.12.64 | **Hull City** | H | W | 3-1 | Houghton, Fencott, Milner |
| | | 3 | 09.01.65 | **Rotherham Utd** (D2) | A | L | 1-5 | Houghton |
| 1965-66 | (D4) | 1 | 13.11.65 | **Barnsley** (D4) | H | L | 1-3 | Ellis |
| 1966-67 | (D4) | 1 | 26.11.66 | **Scunthorpe Utd** (D3) | H | L | 3-4 | Chapman, Bonson, Grummett |
| 1967-68 | (D4) | 1 | 09.12.67 | **Southport** (D3) | A | L | 1-3 | Cobb |
| 1968-69 | (D4) | 1 | 16.11.68 | **Macclesfield T** (CC) | A | W | 3-1 | Kearns, Smith, Thom |
| | | 2 | 07.12.68 | **Chester** (D4) | A | D | 1-1 | Corner |
| | | 2r | 11.12.68 | **Chester** | H | W | 2-1 | Kearns, Smith |
| | | 3 | 04.01.69 | **Birmingham City** (D2) | A | L | 1-2 | Smith |
| 1969-70 | (D4) | 1 | 15.11.69 | **Southport** (D3) | H | W | 2-0 | Smith, Fletcher |
| | | 2 | 06.12.69 | **Bradford City** (D3) | A | L | 0-3 | |
| 1970-71 | (D4) | 1 | 21.11.70 | **Barrow** (D4) | H | W | 2-1 | Svarc, Smith |
| | | 2 | 12.12.70 | **Bradford City** (D3) | H | D | 2-2 | Trevis, Svarc |
| | | 2r | 16.12.70 | **Bradford City** | A | D | 2-2aet | Fletcher, Svarc |
| | | 2 2r | 21.12.70 | **Bradford City** | | W | 4-1 | Freeman 2, Svarc, W Taylor |
| | | | | *played at Belle Vue, Doncaster* | | | | |
| | | 3 | 02.01.71 | **Torquay Utd** (D3) | A | L | 3-4 | Freeman 2, Hubbard |
| 1971-72 | (D4) | 1 | 20.11.71 | **Bury** (D4) | H | L | 1-2 | Gilliver |
| 1972-73 | (D4) | 1 | 18.11.72 | **Blackburn Rovers** (D3) | H | D | 2-2 | Freeman, Bradley |
| | | 1r | 27.11.72 | **Blackburn Rovers** | A | L | 1-4 | Smith |
| 1973-74 | (D4) | 1 | 24.11.73 | **Doncaster Rovers** (D4) | A | L | 0-1 | |
| 1974-75 | (D4) | 1 | 23.11.74 | **Port Vale** (D3) | A | D | 2-2 | Dulson og, Krzywicki |
| | | 1r | 27.11.74 | **Port Vale** | H | W | 2-0 | Graham, Harding |
| | | 2 | 14.12.74 | **Hartlepool** (D4) | A | D | 0-0 | |
| | | 2r | 17.12.74 | **Hartlepool** | H | W | 1-0 | Cooper |
| | | 3 | 04.01.75 | **Swindon Town** (D3) | A | L | 0-2 | |
| 1975-76 | (D4) | 1 | 22.11.75 | **Boston Utd** (NPL) | A | W | 1-0 | Freeman |
| | | 2 | 13.12.75 | **Mansfield Town** (D3) | A | W | 2-1 | Branfoot, Freeman |
| | | 3 | 03.01.76 | **Aldershot** (D3) | A | W | 2-1 | Ward, Ellis (p) |
| | | 4 | 24.01.76 | **WBA** (D2) | A | L | 2-4 | Ellis (p), Fleming |
| 1976-77 | (D3) | 1 | 20.11.76 | **Morecambe** (NPL) | H | W | 1-0 | Freeman |
| | | 2 | 11.12.76 | **Nuneaton B** (SL) | H | W | 6-0 | Ellis 2 (2ps), Harding, Ward, Graham 2 |
| | | 3 | 08.01.77 | **Burnley** (D2) | A | D | 2-2 | Ward, Harding |
| | | 3r | 12.01.77 | **Burnley** | H | L | 0-1 | |
| 1977-78 | (D3) | 1 | 26.11.77 | **Preston North End** (D3) | A | L | 2-3 | Harding, Wigginton (p) |
| 1978-79 | (D3) | 1 | 25.11.78 | **Blackpool** (D3) | A | L | 1-2 | Ward |
| 1979-80 | (D4) | 1 | 24.11.79 | **Sheffield Wed** (D3) | A | L | 0-3 | |
| 1980-81 | (D4) | 1 | 22.11.80 | **Gateshead** (NPL) | H | W | 1-0 | Turner |
| | | 2 | 13.12.80 | **Bury** (D4) | A | L | 0-2 | |
| 1981-82 | (D3) | 1 | 21.11.81 | **Port Vale** (D4) | H | D | 2-2 | S Thompson, Cammack |

| | | | | | | | | |
|---|---|---|---|---|---|---|---|---|
| | | 1r | 30.11.81 | **Port Vale** | A | D | 0-0aet | |
| | | 1 2r | 02.12.81 | **Port Vale** | A | L | 0-2 | |
| 1982-83 | (D3) | 1 | 20.11.83 | **Hartlepool Utd** (D4) | A | L | 0-3 | |
| 1983-84 | (D3) | 1 | 19.11.83 | **Port Vale** (D3) | A | W | 2-1 | Jack, Shipley |
| | | 2 | 10.12.83 | **Sheffield Utd** (D3) | H | D | 0-0 | |
| | | 2r | 19.12.83 | **Sheffield Utd** | A | L | 0-1 | |
| 1984-85 | (D3) | 1 | 17.11.84 | **Telford Utd** (APL) | H | D | 1-1 | Redfearn |
| | | 1r | 20.11.84 | **Telford Utd** | A | L | 1-2 | Walker |
| 1985-86 | (D3) | 1 | 16.11.85 | **Blackpool** (D3) | H | L | 0-1 | |
| 1986-87 | (D4) | 1 | 15.11.86 | **Wigan Athletic** (D3) | A | L | 1-3 | Lund |
| 1987-88 | (Conf) | | | 4q Brigg Town (NCoE) (H) 4-1 | | | | |
| | | 1 | 14.11.87 | **Crewe Alexandra** (D4) | H | W | 2-1 | McGinley, Cumming |
| | | 2 | 05.12.87 | **Mansfield Town** (D3) | A | L | 3-4 | Smith, Brown, Clarke |
| 1988-89 | (D4) | 1 | 19.11.88 | **Altrincham** (Conf) | A | L | 2-3 | Davis, Sertori |
| 1989-90 | (D4) | 1 | 18.11.89 | **Billingham Syn** (NL) | H | W | 1-0 | Nicholson |
| | | 2 | 09.12.89 | **Rochdale** (D4) | A | L | 0-3 | |
| 1990-91 | (D4) | 1 | 17.11.90 | **Crewe Alexandra** (D3) | H | L | 1-4 | Lormor |
| 1991-92 | (D4) | 1 | 16.11.91 | **Stockport County** (D3) | A | L | 1-3 | Lee |
| 1992-93 | (D3) | 1 | 14.11.92 | **Stafford Rangers** (Conf) | H | D | 0-0 | |
| | | 1r | 25.11.92 | **Stafford Rangers** | A | L | 1-2 | Costello |
| 1993-94 | (D3) | 1 | 13.11.93 | **Witton Albion** (Conf) | A | W | 2-0 | West, Lormor |
| | | 2 | 04.12.93 | **Bolton Wanderers** (D1) | H | L | 1-3 | D Johnson |
| 1994-95 | (D3) | 1 | 12.11.94 | **Hull City** (D2) | A | W | 1-0 | Bannister |
| | | 2 | 03.12.94 | **Huddersfield Town** (D2) | H | W | 1-0 | D Johnson |
| | | 3 | 08.01.95 | **Crystal Palace** (PL) | A | L | 1-5 | Greenall |
| 1995-96 | (D3) | 1 | 11.11.95 | **Stockport County** (D2) | A | L | 0-5 | |
| 1996-97 | (D3) | 1 | 16.11.96 | **Burnley** (D2) | A | L | 1-2 | Bos |
| 1997-98 | (D3) | 1 | 15.11.97 | **Gainsborough T** (NPL) | H | D | 1-1 | Walling |
| | | 1r | 25.11.97 | **Gainsborough T** | A | W | 3-2 | Walling 2, Whitney |
| | | | | *played at Sincil Bank* | | | | |
| | | 2 | 06.12.97 | **Emley** (NPL) | H | D | 2-2 | Fleming 2 |
| | | 2r | 17.12.97 | **Emley** | A | D | 3-3aet | Whitney, Alcide, Hone |
| | | | | *Emley won 4-3 on penalties* | | | | |
| 1998-99 | (D2) | 1 | 14.11.98 | **Cheltenham Town** (Conf) | A | W | 1-0 | Thorpe |
| | | 2 | 05.12.98 | **Stevenage B** (Conf) | H | W | 4-1 | Battersby, Alcide, Finnigan, Holmes |
| | | 3 | 02.01.99 | **Sunderland** (D1) | H | L | 0-1 | |
| 1999-00 | (D3) | 1 | 30.10.99 | **Welling Utd** (Conf) | H | W | 1-0 | Smith |
| | | 2 | 19.11.99 | **Luton Town** (D2) | A | D | 2-2 | Gordon, D Barnett |
| | | 2r | 30.11.99 | **Luton Town** | H | L | 0-1 | |
| 2000-01 | (D3) | 1 | 18.11.00 | **Bracknell Town** (IL) | H | W | 4-0 | Gain, Peacock, Bere og, Gordon |
| | | 2 | 09.12.00 | **Dagenham & Red** (Conf) | H | L | 0-1 | |
| 2001-02 | (D3) | 1 | 17.11.01 | **Bury** (D2) | H | D | 1-1 | Holmes |
| | | 1r | 27.11.01 | **Bury** | A | D | 1-1aet | Cameron |
| | | | | *Lincoln City won 3-2 on penalties* | | | | |
| | | 2 | 08.12.01 | **Leyton Orient** (D3) | A | L | 1-2 | Hamilton |
| 2002-03 | (D3) | 1 | 16.11.02 | **Carlisle Utd** (D3) | A | L | 1-2 | Futcher |

## LINCOLN LINDUM

*Formed 1868. Played at Wragby Road field, Lincoln. Entered the FA Cup for these three seasons in the 1880s.*

| | | | | | | |
|---|---|---|---|---|---|---|
| 1885-86 | 1 | 17.10.85 | **Grimsby District** | H | W | 4-0 |
| | 2 | 21.11.85 | **Redcar** | A | L | 0-2 |
| 1886-87 | 1 | 23.10.86 | **Grantham Town** | H | L | 0-1 |
| 1887-88 | 1 | 15.10.87 | **Grantham Town** | A | L | 0-4 |

## LINCOLN RAMBLERS

*Formed 1878. Played at the Cowpaddle Ground, Lincoln. This was the only FA Cup match they played.*

| | | | | | | |
|---|---|---|---|---|---|---|
| 1887-88 | 1 | 15.10.87 | **Notts County** | A | L | 0-9 |

# LINCOLN UNITED

*Formed 1938 as Lincoln Amateurs. Lincoln United 1954. First entered FA Cup: 1970-71 Members of the Northern Premier League.*

| | | | | | | | | |
|---|---|---|---|---|---|---|---|---|
| 1991-92 | (CML) | 1 | 16.11.91 | **Huddersfield Town** (D3) | A | L | 0-7 | |
| 1997-98 | (NPL) | 1 | 15.11.97 | **Walsall** (D2) | A | L | 0-2 | |

# LINFIELD ATHLETIC

*Formed 1886. One of the three clubs from Northern Ireland to take part in the Competition Proper, recording a solid 4-0 win over Bolton Wanderers in a qualifying round in 1888-89, the first season of the Football League. Played for two seasons but failed to get past the qualifiers in 1889-90. Played in the FA Cup as Linfield Athletic. Irish FA Cup winners 36 times. Members of the Irish League.*

| | | | | | | | | |
|---|---|---|---|---|---|---|---|---|
| 1888-89 | | | | 2q Ulster (A) 7-1; 3q Bolton Wanderers (H) 4-0; 4q Cliftonville (A) 3-3; 4qr Cliftonville (H) 3-3; 4q2r Cliftonville (H) 7-0 | | | | |
| | | 1 | 02.02.89 | **Nottingham Forest** | A | D | 2-2 | Pedan 2 |
| | | | | *Linfield scratched before replay took place. Nottingham Forest walkover* | | | | |

# LITTLEHAMPTON TOWN

*Formed 1894. First entered FA Cup: 1912-13. Record gate 4,000 v Northampton Town, 1st round, November 1990. Members of the Sussex County League.*

| | | | | | | | | |
|---|---|---|---|---|---|---|---|---|
| 1990-91 | (SCL) | 1 | 17.11.90 | **Northampton Town** (D4) | H | L | 0-4 | |

# LIVERPOOL

*Formed 1892. FA Cup and League double 1986. FA Cup winners: 1965, 1974, 1986, 1989, 1992, 2001. FA Cup runners-up: 1914, 1950, 1971, 1977, 1988, 1996. FA Cup record win: 9-0 v Newtown, 2nd qualifying round, 29.10.1892. In Competition Proper: 8-0 v Swansea City, 3rd round replay, 09.01.90. Record FA Cup defeat: 0-5 v Bolton Wanderers, 4th round, 1st leg, 26.01.1946.*

| | | | | | | | | |
|---|---|---|---|---|---|---|---|---|
| 1892-93 | (LL) | | | 1q Nantwich (A) 4-0aet; 2q Newtown (H) 9-0; 3q Northwich V (A) 1-2 | | | | |
| 1893-94 | (D2) | 1 | 27.01.94 | **Grimsby Town** (D2) | H | W | 3-0 | Bradshaw 2, McQue |
| | | 2 | 10.02.94 | **Preston North End** (D1) | H | W | 3-2 | Henderson 2, McVean |
| | | 3 | 24.02.94 | **Bolton Wanderers** (D1) | A | L | 0-3 | |
| 1894-95 | (D1) | 1 | 02.02.95 | **Barnsley** | A | W | 2-1aet | McLean, Ross |
| | | | | *FA ordered replay after protest* | | | | |
| | | 1r | 11.02.95 | **Barnsley** | H | W | 4-0 | Bradshaw, Drummond, McVean, McQueen |
| | | 2 | 16.02.95 | **Nottingham Forest** (D1) | H | L | 0-2 | |
| 1895-96 | (D2) | 1 | 01.02.96 | **Millwall Athletic** (SL) | H | W | 4-1 | Ross, Becton, Allan, Bradshaw |
| | | 2 | 15.02.96 | **Wolverhampton W** (D1) | A | L | 0-2 | |
| 1896-97 | (D1) | 1 | 30.01.97 | **Burton Swifts** (D2) | H | W | 4-3 | Hannah, Allan, Cleghorn, Ross |
| | | 2 | 13.02.97 | **WBA** (D1) | A | W | 2-1 | McVean, Neill |
| | | 3 | 27.02.97 | **Nottingham Forest** (D1) | H | D | 1-1 | Becton |
| | | 3r | 03.03.97 | **Nottingham Forest** | A | W | 1-0 | Allan |
| | | SF | 20.03.97 | **Aston Villa** (D1) | | L | 0-3 | |
| | | | | *played at Bramall Lane* | | | | |
| 1897-98 | (D1) | 1 | 29.01.98 | **Hucknall St Johns** | H | W | 2-0 | Becton, McQue |
| | | 2 | 12.02.98 | **Newton Heath** (D2) | A | D | 0-0 | |
| | | 2r | 16.02.98 | **Newton Heath** | H | W | 2-1 | Wilkie, Cunliffe |
| | | 3 | 25.02.98 | **Derby County** (D1) | A | D | 1-1 | Bradshaw |
| | | 3r | 02.03.98 | **Derby County** | H | L | 1-5 | Becton |
| 1898-99 | (D1) | 1 | 28.01.99 | **Blackburn Rovers** (D1) | H | W | 2-0 | Cox, Allan |
| | | 2 | 11.02.99 | **Newcastle Utd** (D1) | H | W | 3-1 | Morgan, Raisbeck, Higgins og |
| | | 3 | 25.02.99 | **WBA** (D1) | A | W | 2-0 | Morgan, Robertson |
| | | SF | 18.03.99 | **Sheffield Utd** (D1) | | D | 2-2 | Allan, Morgan |
| | | | | *played at City Ground, Nottingham* | | | | |
| | | SFr | 23.03.99 | **Sheffield Utd** | | D | 4-4aet | Walker, Allan, Cox, Boyle og |
| | | | | *played at Burnden Park, Bolton* | | | | |
| | | SF2r | 27.03.99 | **Sheffield Utd** | | - | 1-0ab | Allan |
| | | | | *played at Fallowfield, Manchester – abandoned at half-time due to crowd trouble and darkness* | | | | |
| | | SF3r | 30.03.99 | **Sheffield Utd** | | L | 0-1 | |
| | | | | *played at the Baseball Ground, Derby* | | | | |
| 1899-00 | (D1) | 1 | 27.01.00 | **Stoke** (D1) | A | D | 0-0 | |
| | | 1r | 01.02.00 | **Stoke** | H | W | 1-0 | Hunter |

| | | | | | | | |
|---|---|---|---|---|---|---|---|
| | 2 | 17.02.00 | **WBA** (D1) | H | D | 1-1 | Cox |
| | 2r | 21.02.00 | **WBA** | A | L | 1-2 | Robertson |
| 1900-01 (D1) | 1 | 09.02.01 | **Notts County** (D1) | A | L | 0-2 | |
| 1901-02 (D1) | 1 | 25.01.02 | **Everton** (D1) | H | D | 2-2 | T Robertson (p), Hunter |
| | 1r | 30.01.02 | **Everton** | A | W | 2-0 | Raisbeck, Hunter |
| | 2 | 08.02.02 | **Southampton** (SL) | A | L | 1-4 | Fleming |
| 1902-03 (D1) | 1 | 07.02.03 | **Manchester Utd** (D2) | A | L | 1-2 | Raybould |
| 1903-04 (D1) | 1 | 06.02.04 | **Blackburn Rovers** (D1) | A | L | 1-3 | Raybould |
| 1904-05 (D1) | 1 | 04.02.05 | **Everton** (D1) | H | D | 1-1 | Parkinson |
| | 1r | 08.02.05 | **Everton** | A | L | 1-2 | Goddard |
| | 2 | 03.02.06 | **Barnsley** (D2) | H | W | 1-0 | West |
| 1905-06 (D1) | 1 | 13.01.06 | **Leicester Fosse** (D2) | H | W | 2-1 | Raybould, Goddard |
| | 2 | 03.02.06 | **Barnsley** (D2) | H | W | 1-0 | West |
| | 3 | 24.02.06 | **Brentford** (SL) | H | W | 2-0 | Hewitt, Goddard |
| | 4 | 10.03.06 | **Southampton** (SL) | H | W | 3-0 | Raybould 3 |
| | SF | 31.03.06 | **Everton** (D1) | | L | 0-2 | |
| | | | *played at Villa Park* | | | | |
| 1906-07 (D1) | 1 | 12.01.07 | **Birmingham** (D1) | H | W | 2-1 | Raybould 2 |
| | 2 | 02.02.07 | **Oldham Athletic** (LC) | A | W | 1-0 | McPherson |
| | 3 | 23.02.07 | **Bradford City** (D2) | H | W | 1-0 | Cox |
| | 4 | 09.03.07 | **Sheffield Wed** (D1) | A | L | 0-1 | |
| 1907-08 (D1) | 1 | 11.01.08 | **Derby County** (D2) | H | W | 4-2 | Cox, Gorman, Bradley, Parkinson |
| | 2 | 01.02.08 | **Brighton** (SL) | H | D | 1-1 | Cox |
| | 2r | 05.02.08 | **Brighton** | A | W | 3-0 | Bradley 2, Cox |
| | 3 | 22.02.08 | **Newcastle Utd** (D1) | A | L | 1-3 | Saul |
| 1908-09 (D1) | 1 | 16.01.09 | **Lincoln City** (ML) | H | W | 5-1 | Orr 3, Hewitt, Parkinson |
| | 2 | 06.02.09 | **Norwich City** (SL) | H | L | 2-3 | Cox, Robinson |
| 1909-10 (D1) | 1 | 15.01.10 | **Bristol City** (D1) | A | L | 0-2 | |
| 1910-11 (D1) | 1 | 14.01.11 | **Gainsborough T** (D2) | H | W | 3-2 | Bowyer 2, Goddard |
| | 2 | 04.02.11 | **Everton** (D1) | A | L | 1-2 | Parkinson |
| 1911-12 (D1) | 1 | 13.01.12 | **Leyton FC** (SL) | H | W | 1-0 | Parkinson |
| | 2 | 03.02.12 | **Fulham** (D2) | A | L | 0-3 | |
| 1912-13 (D1) | 1 | 15.01.13 | **Bristol City** (D2) | H | W | 3-0 | Goddard (p), Peake, Lacey |
| | 2 | 01.02.13 | **Woolwich Arsenal** (D1) | A | W | 4-1 | Metcalfe 3, Lacey |
| | 3 | 22.02.13 | **Newcastle Utd** (D1) | H | D | 1-1 | Lacey |
| | 3r | 26.02.13 | **Newcastle Utd** | A | L | 0-1 | |
| 1913-14 (D1) | 1 | 10.01.14 | **Barnsley** (D2) | H | D | 1-1 | Lacey |
| | 1r | 15.01.14 | **Barnsley** | A | W | 1-0 | Lacey |
| | 2 | 31.01.14 | **Gillingham** (SL) | H | W | 2-0 | Lacey, Ferguson |
| | 3 | 21.01.14 | **West Ham Utd** (SL) | A | D | 1-1 | Miller |
| | 3r | 25.01.14 | **West Ham Utd** | H | W | 5-1 | Lacey 2, Miller 2, Metcalfe |
| | 4 | 07.03.14 | **QPR** (SL) | H | W | 2-1 | Sheldon, Miller |
| | SF | 28.03.14 | **Aston Villa** (D1) | | W | 2-0 | Nicholl 2 |
| | | | *played at White Hart Lane* | | | | |
| | F | 25.04.14 | **Burnley** (D1) | | L | 0-1 | |
| | | | *played at Crystal Palace* | | | | |
| 1914-15 (D1) | 1 | 09.01.15 | **Stockport County** (D2) | H | W | 3-0 | Pagnam 2, Metcalfe |
| | 2 | 30.01.15 | **Sheffield Utd** (D1) | A | L | 0-1 | |
| 1919-20 (D1) | 1 | 10.01.20 | **South Shields** (D2) | A | D | 1-1 | Lewis |
| | 1r | 14.01.20 | **South Shields** | H | W | 2-0 | Lewis, Sheldon |
| | 2 | 31.01.20 | **Luton Town** (SL) | A | W | 2-0 | Lacey 2 |
| | 3 | 21.02.20 | **Birmingham** (D2) | H | W | 2-0 | Sheldon, T Miller |
| | 4 | 06.03.20 | **Huddersfield Town** (D2) | A | L | 1-2 | T Miller |
| 1920-21 (D1) | 1 | 08.01.21 | **Manchester Utd** (D1) | H | D | 1-1 | Chambers |
| | 1r | 12.01.21 | **Manchester Utd** | A | W | 2-1 | Lacey, Chambers |
| | 2 | 29.01.21 | **Newcastle Utd** (D1) | A | L | 0-1 | |
| 1921-22 (D1) | 1 | 07.01.22 | **Sunderland** (D1) | A | D | 1-1 | Forshaw |
| | 1r | 11.01.22 | **Sunderland** | H | W | 5-0 | Forshaw 2, Chambers 2, W Wadsworth |
| | 2 | 28.01.22 | **WBA** (D1) | H | L | 0-1 | |
| 1922-23 (D1) | 1 | 13.01.23 | **Arsenal** (D1) | H | D | 0-0 | |

| | | | | | | | | |
|---|---|---|---|---|---|---|---|---|
| | | 1r | 17.01.23 | **Arsenal** | A | W | 4-1 | Chambers 2, Johnson, McKinley (p) |
| | | 2 | 03.02.23 | **Wolverhampton W** (D2) | A | W | 2-0 | Johnson, Forshaw |
| | | 3 | 24.02.23 | **Sheffield Utd** (D1) | H | L | 1-2 | Chambers |
| 1923-24 | (D1) | 1 | 12.01.24 | **Bradford City** (D2) | H | W | 2-1 | Chambers 2 |
| | | 3 | 23.02.24 | **Southampton** (D2) | A | D | 0-0 | |
| | | 3 | 02.02.24 | **Bolton Wanderers** (D1) | A | W | 4-1 | Walsh 3, Chambers |
| | | 3r | 27.02.24 | **Southampton** (D2) | H | W | 2-0 | Chambers, Forshaw |
| | | 4 | 08.03.24 | **Newcastle Utd** (D1) | A | L | 0-1 | |
| 1924-25 | (D1) | 1 | 10.01.25 | **Leeds Utd** (D1) | H | W | 3-0 | Shone 2, Hopkin |
| | | 2 | 31.01.25 | **Bristol City** (3S) | A | W | 1-0 | Rawlings |
| | | 3 | 21.02.25 | **Birmingham** (D1) | H | W | 2-1 | Rawlings, Shone |
| | | 4 | 07.03.25 | **Southampton** (D2) | A | L | 0-1 | |
| 1925-26 | (D1) | 3 | 09.01.26 | **Southampton** (D2) | A | D | 0-0 | |
| | | 3r | 13.01.26 | **Southampton** | H | W | 1-0 | Forshaw |
| | | 4 | 30.01.26 | **Fulham** (D2) | A | L | 1-3 | Forshaw |
| 1926-27 | (D1) | 3 | 08.01.27 | **Bournemouth** (3S) | A | D | 1-1 | Hodgson |
| | | 3r | 12.01.27 | **Bournemouth** | H | W | 4-1 | Chambers 3, Hopkin |
| | | 4 | 29.01.27 | **Southport** (3N) | H | W | 3-1 | Hodgson, Chambers, Edmed |
| | | 5 | 19.02.27 | **Arsenal** (D1) | A | L | 0-2 | |
| 1927-28 | (D1) | 3 | 14.01.28 | **Darlington** (3N) | H | W | 1-0 | Chambers |
| | | 4 | 28.01.28 | **Cardiff City** (D1) | A | L | 1-2 | Edmed (p) |
| 1928-29 | (D1) | 3 | 12.01.29 | **Bristol City** (D2) | A | W | 2-0 | Salisbury, Hodgson |
| | | 4 | 26.01.29 | **Bolton Wanderers** (D1) | H | D | 0-0 | |
| | | 4r | 30.01.29 | **Bolton Wanderers** | A | L | 2-5aet | Lindsay, Hodgson |
| 1929-30 | (D1) | 3 | 11.01.30 | **Cardiff City** (D2) | H | L | 1-2 | McPherson |
| 1930-31 | (D1) | 3 | 10.01.31 | **Birmingham** (D1) | H | L | 0-2 | |
| 1931-32 | (D1) | 3 | 09.01.32 | **Everton** (D1) | A | W | 2-1 | Gunson, Hodgson |
| | | 4 | 23.01.32 | **Chesterfield** (D2) | A | W | 4-2 | Barton 4 |
| | | 5 | 13.02.32 | **Grimsby Town** (D1) | H | W | 1-0 | Gunson |
| | | 6 | 27.02.32 | **Chelsea** (D1) | H | L | 0-2 | |
| 1932-33 | (D1) | 3 | 14.01.33 | **WBA** (D1) | A | L | 0-2 | |
| 1933-34 | (D1) | 3 | 13.01.34 | **Fulham** (D2) | H | D | 1-1 | Hodgson |
| | | 3r | 17.01.34 | **Fulham** | A | W | 3-2aet | Hanson, Bradshaw, Roberts |
| | | 4 | 27.01.34 | **Tranmere Rovers** (3N) | H | W | 3-1 | English 2, Nieuwenhuys |
| | | 5 | 17.02.34 | **Bolton Wanderers** (D2) | H | L | 0-3 | |
| 1934-35 | (D1) | 3 | 12.01.35 | **Yeovil & Petters Utd** (SL) | A | W | 6-2 | Roberts 2, Hodgson 2, Nieuwenhuys, Wright |
| | | 4 | 26.01.35 | **Blackburn Rovers** (D1) | A | L | 0-1 | |
| 1935-36 | (D1) | 3 | 11.01.36 | **Swansea Town** (D2) | H | W | 1-0 | Wright |
| | | 4 | 25.01.36 | **Arsenal** (D1) | H | L | 0-2 | |
| 1936-37 | (D1) | 3 | 16.01.37 | **Norwich City** (D2) | A | L | 0-3 | |
| 1937-38 | (D1) | 3 | 08.01.38 | **Crystal Palace** (3S) | A | D | 0-0 | |
| | | 3r | 12.01.38 | **Crystal Palace** | H | W | 3-1aet | Shafto, Fagan (p),Collins og |
| | | 4 | 22.01.38 | **Sheffield Utd** (D2) | A | D | 1-1 | Hanson |
| | | 4r | 26.01.38 | **Sheffield Utd** | H | W | 1-0 | Johnson og |
| | | 5 | 12.02.38 | **Huddersfield Town** (D1) | H | L | 0-1 | |
| 1938-39 | (D1) | 3 | 07.01.39 | **Luton Town** (D2) | H | W | 3-0 | Balmer 2, Paterson |
| | | 4 | 21.01.39 | **Stockport County** (3N) | H | W | 5-1 | Nieuwenhuys 2, Balmer 2, Eastham |
| | | 5 | 11.02.39 | **Wolverhampton W** (D1) | A | L | 1-4 | Fagan (p) |
| 1945-46 | (D1) | 3 1L | 05.01.46 | **Chester** (3N) | A | W | 2-0 | Liddell, Fagan |
| | | 3 2L | 09.01.46 | **Chester** | H | W | 2-1 | Fagan 2 |
| | | 4 1L | 26.01.46 | **Bolton Wanderers** (D1) | A | L | 0-5 | |
| | | 4 2L | 30.01.46 | **Bolton Wanderers** | H | W | 2-0 | Balmer, Nieuwenhuys |
| 1946-47 | (D1) | 3 | 11.01.47 | **Walsall** (3S) | A | W | 5-2 | Balmer 2, Liddell, Done, Foulkes og |
| | | 4 | 25.01.47 | **Grimsby Town** (D1) | H | W | 2-0 | Stubbins, Done |
| | | 5 | 08.02.47 | **Derby County** (D1) | H | W | 1-0 | Balmer |
| | | 6 | 01.03.47 | **Birmingham City** (D2) | H | W | 4-1 | Stubbins 3, Balmer |
| | | SF | 29.03.47 | **Burnley** (D2) *played at Ewood Park* | | D | 0-0aet | |
| | | SFr | 12.04.47 | **Burnley** *played at Maine Road* | | L | 0-1 | |

| | | | | | | | | |
|---|---|---|---|---|---|---|---|---|
| 1947-48 (D1) | 3 | 10.01.48 | **Nottingham Forest** (D2) | H | W | 4-1 | Stubbins 2, Liddell, Priday |
| | 4 | 24.01.48 | **Manchester Utd** (D1) | A | L | 0-3 | |
| | | | *played at Goodison Park* | | | | |
| 1948-49 (D1) | 3 | 08.01.49 | **Nottingham Forest** (D2) | A | D | 2-2aet | Fagan, Paisley |
| | 3r | 15.01.49 | **Nottingham Forest** | H | W | 4-0 | Balmer 2, Stubbins, Payne |
| | 4 | 29.01.49 | **Notts County** (3S) | H | W | 1-0 | Liddell |
| | 5 | 12.02.49 | **Wolverhampton W** (D1) | A | L | 1-3 | Done |
| 1949-50 (D1) | 3 | 07.01.50 | **Blackburn Rovers** (D2) | A | D | 0-0 | |
| | 3r | 11.01.50 | **Blackburn Rovers** | H | W | 2-1 | Payne, Fagan |
| | 4 | 28.01.50 | **Exeter City** (3S) | H | W | 3-1 | Barron, Fagan, Payne |
| | 5 | 11.02.50 | **Stockport County** (3N) | A | W | 2-1 | Fagan, Stubbins |
| | 6 | 04.03.50 | **Blackpool** (D1) | H | W | 2-1 | Fagan, Liddell |
| | SF | 25.03.50 | **Everton** (D1) | | W | 2-0 | Paisley, Liddell |
| | | | *played at Maine Road* | | | | |
| | F | 29.04.50 | **Arsenal** (D1) | | L | 0-2 | |
| | | | *played at Wembley Stadium* | | | | |
| 1950-51 (D1) | 3 | 06.01.51 | **Norwich City** (3S) | A | L | 1-3 | Balmer |
| 1951-52 (D1) | 3 | 12.01.52 | **Workington** (3N) | H | W | 1-0 | Payne |
| | 4 | 02.02.52 | **Wolverhampton W** (D1) | H | W | 2-1 | Paisley, Done |
| | 5 | 23.02.52 | **Burnley** (D1) | A | L | 0-2 | |
| 1952-53 (D1) | 3 | 10.01.53 | **Gateshead AFC** (3N) | A | L | 0-1 | |
| 1953-54 (D1) | 3 | 09.01.54 | **Bolton Wanderers** (D1) | A | L | 0-1 | |
| 1954-55 (D2) | 3 | 08.01.55 | **Lincoln City** (D2) | A | D | 1-1 | Evans |
| | 3r | 12.01.55 | **Lincoln City** | H | W | 1-0aet | Evans |
| | 4 | 29.01.55 | **Everton** (D1) | A | W | 4-0 | Evans 2, Liddell, A'Court |
| | 5 | 19.02.55 | **Huddersfield Town** (D1) | H | L | 0-2 | |
| 1955-56 (D2) | 3 | 07.01.56 | **Accrington Stanley** (3N) | H | W | 2-0 | Liddell 2 |
| | 4 | 28.01.56 | **Scunthorpe Utd** (3N) | H | D | 3-3 | Liddell 2, Payne |
| | 4r | 06.02.56 | **Scunthorpe Utd** | A | W | 2-1aet | Liddell, Arnell |
| | 5 | 18.02.56 | **Manchester City** (D1) | A | D | 0-0 | |
| | 5r | 22.02.56 | **Manchester City** | H | L | 1-2 | Arnell |
| 1956-57 (D2) | 3 | 05.01.57 | **Southend Utd** (3S) | A | L | 1-2 | Wheeler |
| 1957-58 (D2) | 3 | 04.01.58 | **Southend Utd** (3S) | H | D | 1-1 | Smith og |
| | 3r | 08.01.58 | **Southend Utd** | A | W | 3-2 | Molyneux, White, Rowley |
| | 4 | 25.01.58 | **Northampton Town** (3S) | H | W | 3-1 | Liddell, Bimpson, Collins og |
| | 5 | 15.02.58 | **Scunthorpe Utd** (3N) | A | W | 1-0 | Murdoch |
| | 6 | 01.03.58 | **Blackburn Rovers** (D2) | A | L | 1-2 | Murdoch |
| 1958-59 (D2) | 3 | 15.01.59 | **Worcester City** (SL) | A | L | 1-2 | Twentyman (p) |
| 1959-60 (D2) | 3 | 09.01.60 | **Leyton Orient** (D2) | H | W | 2-1 | Hunt 2 |
| | 4 | 30.01.60 | **Manchester Utd** (D1) | H | L | 1-3 | Wheeler |
| 1960-61 (D2) | 3 | 07.01.61 | **Coventry City** (D3) | H | W | 3-2 | Hunt, Lewis, Harrower |
| | 4 | 28.01.61 | **Sunderland** (D2) | H | L | 0-2 | |
| 1961-62 (D2) | 3 | 06.01.62 | **Chelsea** (D1) | H | W | 4-3 | St John 2, Hunt, A'Court |
| | 4 | 27.01.62 | **Oldham Athletic** (D4) | A | W | 2-1 | St John 2 |
| | 5 | 17.02.62 | **Preston North End** (D2) | H | D | 0-0 | |
| | 5r | 20.02.62 | **Preston North End** | A | D | 0-0aet | |
| | 5 2r | 26.02.62 | **Preston North End** | | L | 0-1 | |
| | | | *played at Old Trafford* | | | | |
| 1962-63 (D1) | 3 | 09.01.63 | **Wrexham** (D3) | A | W | 3-0 | Hunt, Lewis, Melia |
| | 4 | 26.01.63 | **Burnley** (D1) | A | D | 1-1 | Lewis |
| | 4r | 20.02.63 | **Burnley** | H | W | 2-1aet | St John, Moran (p) |
| | 5 | 16.03.63 | **Arsenal** (D1) | A | W | 2-1 | Melia, Moran (p) |
| | 6 | 30.03.63 | **West Ham Utd** (D1) | H | W | 1-0 | Hunt |
| | SF | 27.04.63 | **Leicester City** (D1) | | L | 0-1 | |
| | | | *played at Hillsborough* | | | | |
| 1963-64 (D1) | 3 | 04.01.64 | **Derby County** (D2) | H | W | 5-0 | Arrowsmith 4, Hunt |
| | 4 | 25.01.64 | **Port Vale** (D3) | H | D | 0-0 | |
| | 4r | 27.01.64 | **Port Vale** | A | W | 2-1aet | Hunt, Thompson |
| | 5 | 15.02.64 | **Arsenal** (D1) | A | W | 1-0 | St John |
| | 6 | 29.02.64 | **Swansea Town** (D2) | H | L | 1-2 | Thompson |
| 1964-65 (D1) | 3 | 09.01.65 | **WBA** (D1) | A | W | 2-1 | Hunt, St John |
| | 4 | 30.01.65 | **Stockport County** (D4) | H | D | 1-1 | Milne |

| | | | | | | | |
|---|---|---|---|---|---|---|---|
| | 4r | 03.02.65 | **Stockport County** | A | W | 2-0 | Hunt 2 |
| | 5 | 20.02.65 | **Bolton Wanderers** (D2) | A | W | 1-0 | Callaghan |
| | 6 | 06.03.65 | **Leicester City** (D1) | A | D | 0-0 | |
| | 6r | 10.03.65 | **Leicester City** | H | W | 1-0 | Hunt |
| | SF | 27.03.65 | **Chelsea** (D1) | | W | 2-0 | Thompson, Stevenson (p) |
| | | | *played at Villa Park* | | | | |
| | F | 01.05.65 | **Leeds Utd** (D1) | | W | 2-1aet | Hunt, St John |
| | | | *played at Wembley Stadium* | | | | |
| 1965-66 (D1) | 3 | 22.01.66 | **Chelsea** (D1) | H | L | 1-2 | Hunt |
| 1966-67 (D1) | 3 | 28.01.67 | **Watford** (D3) | A | D | 0-0 | |
| | 3r | 01.02.67 | **Watford** | H | W | 3-1 | St John, Hunt, Lawler |
| | 4 | 18.02.67 | **Aston Villa** (D1) | H | W | 1-0 | St John |
| | 5 | 11.03.67 | **Everton** (D1) | A | L | 0-1 | |
| 1967-68 (D1) | 3 | 27.01.68 | **Bournemouth** (D3) | A | D | 0-0 | |
| | 3r | 30.01.68 | **Bournemouth** | H | W | 4-1 | Hateley, Thompson, Hunt, Lawler |
| | 4 | 17.02.68 | **Walsall** (D3) | A | D | 0-0 | |
| | 4r | 19.02.68 | **Walsall** | H | W | 5-2 | Hateley 4, Strong |
| | 5 | 09.03.68 | **Tottenham Hotspur** (D1) | A | D | 1-1 | Hateley |
| | 5r | 12.03.68 | **Tottenham Hotspur** | H | W | 2-1 | Hunt, Smith (p) |
| | 6 | 30.03.68 | **WBA** (D1) | A | D | 0-0 | |
| | 6r | 08.04.68 | **WBA** | H | D | 1-1aet | Hateley |
| | 6 2r | 18.04.68 | **WBA** | | L | 1-2 | Hateley |
| | | | *played at Maine Road* | | | | |
| 1968-69 (D1) | 3 | 04.01.69 | **Doncaster Rovers** (D4) | H | W | 2-0 | Hunt, Callaghan |
| | 4 | 25.01.69 | **Burnley** (D1) | H | W | 2-1 | Smith (p), Hughes |
| | 5 | 01.03.69 | **Leicester City** (D1) | A | D | 0-0 | |
| | 5r | 03.03.69 | **Leicester City** | H | L | 0-1 | |
| 1969-70 (D1) | 3 | 07.01.70 | **Coventry City** (D1) | A | D | 1-1 | Graham |
| | 3r | 12.01.70 | **Coventry City** | H | W | 3-0 | Ross, Thompson, Graham |
| | 4 | 24.01.70 | **Wrexham** (D4) | H | W | 3-1 | Graham 2, St John |
| | 5 | 07.02.70 | **Leicester City** (D2) | H | D | 0-0 | |
| | 5r | 11.02.70 | **Leicester City** | A | W | 2-0 | Evans 2 |
| | 6 | 21.02.70 | **Watford** (D2) | A | L | 0-1 | |
| 1970-71 (D1) | 3 | 02.01.71 | **Aldershot** (D4) | H | W | 1-0 | McLaughlin |
| | 4 | 23.01.71 | **Swansea City** (D3) | H | W | 3-0 | Toshack, St John, Lawler |
| | 5 | 13.02.71 | **Southampton** (D1) | H | W | 1-0 | Lawler |
| | 6 | 06.03.71 | **Tottenham Hotspur** (D1) | H | D | 0-0 | |
| | 6r | 16.03.71 | **Tottenham Hotspur** | A | W | 1-0 | Heighway |
| | SF | 27.03.71 | **Everton** (D1) | | W | 2-1 | Evans, Hall |
| | | | *played at Old Trafford* | | | | |
| | F | 08.05.71 | **Arsenal** (D1) | | L | 1-2aet | Heighway |
| | | | *played at Wembley Stadium* | | | | |
| 1971-72 (D1) | 3 | 15.01.72 | **Oxford Utd** (D2) | A | W | 3-0 | Keegan 2, Lindsay |
| | 4 | 05.02.72 | **Leeds Utd** (D1) | H | D | 0-0 | |
| | 4r | 09.02.72 | **Leeds Utd** | A | L | 0-2 | |
| 1972-73 (D1) | 3 | 13.01.73 | **Burnley** (D2) | A | D | 0-0 | |
| | 3r | 16.01.73 | **Burnley** | H | W | 3-0 | Toshack 2, Cormack |
| | 4 | 03.02.73 | **Manchester City** (D1) | H | D | 0-0 | |
| | 4r | 07.02.73 | **Manchester City** | A | L | 0-2 | |
| 1973-74 (D1) | 3 | 05.01.74 | **Doncaster Rovers** (D4) | H | D | 2-2 | Keegan 2 |
| | 3r | 08.01.74 | **Doncaster Rovers** | A | W | 2-0 | Heighway, Cormack |
| | 4 | 26.01.74 | **Carlisle Utd** (D2) | H | D | 0-0 | |
| | 4r | 29.01.74 | **Carlisle Utd** | A | W | 2-0 | Boersma, Toshack |
| | 5 | 16.02.74 | **Ipswich Town** (D1) | H | W | 2-0 | Hall, Keegan |
| | 6 | 09.03.74 | **Bristol City** (D2) | A | W | 1-0 | Toshack |
| | SF | 30.03.74 | **Leicester City** (D1) | | D | 0-0 | |
| | | | *played at Old Trafford* | | | | |
| | SFr | 03.04.74 | **Leicester City** | | W | 3-1 | Hall, Keegan, Toshack |
| | | | *played at Villa Park* | | | | |
| | F | 04.05.74 | **Newcastle Utd** (D1) | | W | 3-0 | Keegan 2, Heighway |
| | | | *played at Wembley Stadium* | | | | |

| | | | | | | | |
|---|---|---|---|---|---|---|---|
| 1974-75 (D1) | 3 | 04.01.75 | **Stoke City** (D1) | H | W | 2-0 | Heighway, Keegan |
| | 4 | 25.01.75 | **Ipswich Town** (D1) | A | L | 0-1 | |
| 1975-76 (D1) | 3 | 03.01.76 | **West Ham Utd** (D1) | A | W | 2-0 | Keegan, Toshack |
| | 4 | 24.01.76 | **Derby County** (D1) | A | L | 0-1 | |
| 1976-77 (D1) | 3 | 08.01.77 | **Crystal Palace** (D3) | H | D | 0-0 | |
| | 3r | 11.01.77 | **Crystal Palace** | A | W | 3-2 | Heighway 2, Keegan |
| | 4 | 29.01.77 | **Carlisle Utd** (D2) | H | W | 3-0 | Keegan, Toshack, Heighway |
| | 5 | 26.02.77 | **Oldham Athletic** (D2) | H | W | 3-1 | Keegan, Case, Neal (p) |
| | 6 | 19.03.77 | **Middlesbrough** (D1) | H | W | 2-0 | Fairclough, Keegan |
| | SF | 23.04.77 | **Everton** (D1) | | D | 2-2 | McDermott, Case |
| | | | *played at Maine Road* | | | | |
| | SFr | 27.04.77 | **Everton** | | W | 3-0 | Neal (p), Case, R Kennedy |
| | | | *played at Maine Road* | | | | |
| | F | 21.05.77 | **Manchester Utd** (D1) | | L | 1-2 | Case |
| | | | *played at Wembley Stadium* | | | | |
| 1977-78 (D1) | 3 | 07.01.78 | **Chelsea** (D1) | A | L | 2-4 | Johnson, Dalglish |
| 1978-79 (D1) | 3 | 10.01.79 | **Southend Utd** (D3) | A | D | 0-0 | |
| | 3r | 17.01.79 | **Southend Utd** | H | W | 3-0 | Case, Dalglish, R Kennedy |
| | 4 | 30.01.79 | **Blackburn Rovers** (D2) | H | W | 1-0 | Dalglish |
| | 5 | 28.02.79 | **Burnley** (D2) | H | W | 3-0 | Johnson 2, Souness |
| | 6 | 10.03.79 | **Ipswich Town** (D1) | A | W | 1-0 | Dalglish |
| | SF | 31.03.79 | **Manchester Utd** (D1) | | D | 2-2 | Dalglish, Hanson |
| | | | *played at Maine Road* | | | | |
| | SFr | 04.04.79 | **Manchester Utd** | | L | 0-1 | |
| | | | *played at Goodison Park* | | | | |
| 1979-80 (D1) | 3 | 05.01.80 | **Grimsby Town** (D3) | H | W | 5-0 | Johnson 3, Souness, Case |
| | 4 | 26.01.80 | **Nottingham Forest** (D1) | A | W | 2-0 | Dalglish, McDermott (p) |
| | 5 | 16.02.80 | **Bury** (D3) | H | W | 2-0 | Fairclough 2 |
| | 6 | 08.03.80 | **Tottenham Hotspur** (D1) | A | W | 1-0 | McDermott |
| | SF | 12.04.80 | **Arsenal** (D1) | | D | 0-0 | |
| | | | *played at Hillsborough* | | | | |
| | SFr | 16.04.80 | **Arsenal** | | D | 1-1aet | Fairclough |
| | | | *played at Villa Park* | | | | |
| | SF 2r | 28.04.80 | **Arsenal** | | D | 1-1aet | Dalglish |
| | | | *played at Villa Park* | | | | |
| | SF 3r | 01.05.80 | **Arsenal** | | L | 0-1 | |
| | | | *played at Highfield Road, Coventry* | | | | |
| 1980-81 (D1) | 3 | 03.01.81 | **Altrincham** (APL) | H | W | 4-1 | Dalglish 2, McDermott, R Kennedy |
| | 4 | 24.01.81 | **Everton** (D1) | A | L | 1-2 | Case |
| 1981-82 (D1) | 3 | 02.01.82 | **Swansea City** (D1) | A | W | 4-0 | Rush 2, Hansen, Lawrenson |
| | 4 | 23.01.82 | **Sunderland** (D1) | A | W | 3-0 | Dalglish 2, Rush |
| | 5 | 13.02.82 | **Chelsea** (D2) | A | L | 0-2 | |
| 1982-83 (D1) | 3 | 08.01.83 | **Blackburn Rovers** (D2) | A | W | 2-1 | Hodgson, Rush |
| | 4 | 29.01.83 | **Stoke City** (D1) | H | W | 2-0 | Dalglish, Rush |
| | 5 | 20.02.83 | **Brighton** (D1) | H | L | 1-2 | Johnson |
| 1983-84 (D1) | 3 | 06.01.84 | **Newcastle Utd** (D2) | H | W | 4-0 | Rush 2, Johnson, Robinson |
| | 4 | 29.01.84 | **Brighton** (D2) | A | L | 0-2 | |
| 1984-85 (D1) | 3 | 05.01.85 | **Aston Villa** (D1) | H | W | 3-0 | Rush 2, Wark |
| | 4 | 27.01.85 | **Tottenham Hotspur** (D1) | H | W | 1-0 | Rush |
| | 5 | 16.02.85 | **York City** (D3) | A | D | 1-1 | Rush |
| | 5r | 20.02.85 | **York City** | H | W | 7-0 | Wark 3, Whelan 2, Neal, Walsh |
| | 6 | 10.03.85 | **Barnsley** (D2) | A | W | 4-0 | Rush 3, Whelan |
| | SF | 13.04.85 | **Manchester Utd** (D1) | | D | 2-2aet | Whelan, Walsh |
| | | | *played at Goodison Park* | | | | |
| | SFr | 17.04.85 | **Manchester Utd** | | L | 1-2 | McGrath og |
| | | | *played at Maine Road* | | | | |
| 1985-86 (D1) | 3 | 04.01.86 | **Norwich City** (D2) | H | W | 5-0 | McDonald, Walsh, McMahon, Whelan, Wark |
| | 4 | 26.01.86 | **Chelsea** (D1) | A | W | 2-1 | Rush, Lawrenson |
| | 5 | 15.02.86 | **York City** (D3) | A | D | 1-1 | Molby (p) |
| | 5r | 18.02.86 | **York City** | H | W | 3-1aet | Wark, Molby, Dalglish |
| | 6 | 11.03.86 | **Watford** (D1) | H | D | 0-0 | |

| | | | | | | | |
|---|---|---|---|---|---|---|---|
| | 6r | 17.03.86 | **Watford** | A | W | 2-1aet | Molby (p), Rush |
| | SF | 05.04.86 | **Southampton** (D1) | | W | 2-0aet | Rush 2 |
| | | | *played at White Hart Lane* | | | | |
| | F | 10.05.86 | **Everton** (D1) | | W | 3-1 | Rush 2, Johnson |
| | | | *played at Wembley Stadium* | | | | |
| 1986-87 (D1) | 3 | 11.01.87 | **Luton Town** (D1) | A | D | 0-0 | |
| | 3r | 26.01.87 | **Luton Town** | H | D | 0-0aet | |
| | 3 2r | 28.01.87 | **Luton Town** | A | L | 0-3 | |
| 1987-88 (D1) | 3 | 09.01.88 | **Stoke City** (D2) | A | D | 0-0 | |
| | 3r | 12.01.88 | **Stoke City** | H | W | 1-0 | Beardsley |
| | 4 | 31.01.88 | **Aston Villa** (D2) | A | W | 2-0 | Barnes, Beardsley |
| | 5 | 21.02.88 | **Everton** (D1) | A | W | 1-0 | Houghton |
| | 6 | 13.03.88 | **Manchester City** (D2) | A | W | 4-0 | Houghton, Beardsley (p), Johnson, Barnes |
| | SF | 09.04.88 | **Nottingham Forest** (D1) | | W | 2-1 | Aldridge 2 (1p) |
| | | | *played at Hillsborough* | | | | |
| | F | 14.05.88 | **Wimbledon** (D1) | | L | 0-1 | |
| | | | *played at Wembley Stadium* | | | | |
| 1988-89 (D1) | 3 | 07.01.89 | **Carlisle Utd** (D4) | A | W | 3-0 | McMahon 2, Barnes |
| | 4 | 29.01.89 | **Millwall** (D1) | A | W | 2-0 | Aldridge, Rush |
| | 5 | 18.02.89 | **Hull City** (D2) | A | W | 3-2 | Aldridge 2, Barnes |
| | 6 | 18.03.89 | **Brentford** (D3) | H | W | 4-0 | Beardsley 2, McMahon, Barnes |
| | SF | 15.04.89 | **Nottingham Forest** (D1) | | - | 0-0ab | |
| | | | *Played at Hillsborough.The Hillsborough Disaster. Abandoned after six minutes as the scale of the disaster unfolded. Ninety-six Liverpool fans died as a result of the tragedy.* | | | | |
| | SF | 07.05.89 | **Nottingham Forest** | | W | 3-1 | Aldridge 2, Laws og |
| | | | *played at Old Trafford* | | | | |
| | F | 20.05.89 | **Everton** (D1) | | W | 3-2aet | Rush 2, Aldridge |
| | | | *played at Wembley Stadium* | | | | |
| 1989-90 (D1) | 3 | 06.01.90 | **Swansea City** (D3) | A | D | 0-0 | |
| | 3r | 09.01.90 | **Swansea City** | H | W | 8-0 | Rush 3, Barnes 2, Whelan, Beardsley, Nichol |
| | 4 | 28.01.90 | **Norwich City** (D1) | A | D | 0-0 | |
| | 4r | 31.01.90 | **Norwich City** | H | W | 3-1 | Nichol, Barnes, Beardlsey |
| | 5 | 17.02.90 | **Southampton** (D1) | H | W | 3-0 | Rush, Beardlsey, Nichol |
| | 6 | 11.03.90 | **QPR** (D1) | A | D | 2-2 | Barnes, Rush |
| | 6r | 14.03.90 | **QPR** | H | W | 1-0 | Beardsley |
| | SF | 08.04.90 | **Crystal Palace** (D1) | | L | 3-4aet | Rush, McMahon, Barnes |
| | | | *played at Villa Park* | | | | |
| 1990-91 (D1) | 3 | 05.01.91 | **Blackburn Rovers** (D2) | A | D | 1-1 | Atkins og |
| | 3r | 08.01.91 | **Blackburn Rovers** | H | W | 3-0 | Houghton, Rush, Staunton |
| | 4 | 26.01.91 | **Brighton** (D2) | H | D | 2-2 | Rush 2 |
| | 4r | 30.01.91 | **Brighton** | A | W | 3-2aet | McMahon 2, Rush |
| | 5 | 17.02.91 | **Everton** (D1) | H | D | 0-0 | |
| | 5r | 20.02.91 | **Everton** | A | D | 4-4aet | Beardsley 2, Rush, Barnes |
| | 5 2r | 27.02.91 | **Everton** | A | L | 0-1 | |
| 1991-92 (D1) | 3 | 06.01.92 | **Crewe Alexandra** (D4) | A | W | 4-0 | McManaman, Barnes 3 (1p) |
| | 4 | 05.02.92 | **Bristol Rovers** (D2) | A | D | 1-1 | Saunders |
| | 4r | 11.02.92 | **Bristol Rovers** | H | W | 2-1 | McManaman, Saunders |
| | 5 | 16.02.92 | **Ipswich Town** (D2) | A | D | 0-0 | |
| | 5r | 26.02.92 | **Ipswich Town** | H | W | 3-2aet | Houghton, Molby, McManaman |
| | 6 | 08.03.92 | **Aston Villa** (D1) | H | W | 1-0 | Thomas |
| | SF | 05.04.92 | **Portsmouth** (D2) | | D | 1-1aet | Whelan |
| | | | *played at Highbury* | | | | |
| | SFr | 13.04.92 | **Portsmouth** | | D | 0-0aet | |
| | | | *played at Villa Park – Liverpool won 3-1 on penalties* | | | | |
| | F | 09.05.92 | **Sunderland** (D2) | | W | 2-0 | Thomas, Rush |
| | | | *played at Wembley Stadium* | | | | |
| 1992-93 (PL) | 3 | 03.01.93 | **Bolton Wanderers** (D2) | A | D | 2-2 | Winstanley og, Rush |
| | 3r | 15.01.93 | **Bolton Wanderers** | H | L | 0-2 | |

| | | | | | | | |
|---|---|---|---|---|---|---|---|
| 1993-94 (PL) | 3 | 08.01.94 | **Bristol City** (D1) | A | - | 1-1ab | Rush |
| | | | *abandoned after 65 minutes – floodlight failure* | | | | |
| | 3 | 19.01.94 | **Bristol City** | A | D | 1-1 | Rush |
| | 3r | 25.01.94 | **Bristol City** | H | L | 0-1 | |
| 1994-95 (PL) | 3 | 07.01.95 | **Birmingham City** (D2) | A | D | 0-0 | |
| | 3r | 18.01.95 | **Birmingham City** | H | D | 1-1aet | Redknapp |
| | | | *Liverpool won 2-0 on penalties* | | | | |
| | 4 | 28.01.95 | **Burnley** (D1) | A | D | 0-0 | |
| | 4r | 07.02.95 | **Burnley** | H | W | 1-0 | Barnes |
| | 5 | 19.02.95 | **Wimbledon** (PL) | H | D | 1-1 | Fowler |
| | 5r | 28.02.95 | **Wimbledon** | A | W | 2-0 | Barnes, Rush |
| | 6 | 11.03.95 | **Tottenham Hotspur** (PL) | H | L | 1-2 | Fowler |
| 1995-96 (PL) | 3 | 06.01.96 | **Rochdale** (D3) | H | W | 7-0 | Collymore 3, Fowler, Valentine og, Rush, McAteer |
| | 4 | 18.02.96 | **Shrewsbury Town** (D2) | A | W | 4-0 | Collymore, Walton og, Fowler, McAteer |
| | 5 | 28.02.96 | **Charlton Athletic** (D1) | H | W | 2-1 | Fowler, Collymore |
| | 6 | 10.03.96 | **Leeds Utd** (PL) | A | D | 0-0 | |
| | 6r | 20.03.96 | **Leeds Utd** | H | W | 3-0 | McManaman 2, Fowler |
| | SF | 31.03.96 | **Aston Villa** (PL) | | W | 3-0 | Fowler 2, McAteer |
| | | | *played at Old Trafford* | | | | |
| | F | 11.05.96 | **Manchester Utd** (PL) | | L | 0-1 | |
| | | | *played at Wembley Stadium* | | | | |
| 1996-97 (PL) | 3 | 04.01.97 | **Burnley** (D2) | H | W | 1-0 | Collymore |
| | 4 | 26.01.97 | **Chelsea** (PL) | A | L | 2-4 | Fowler, Collymore |
| 1997-98 (PL) | 3 | 03.01.98 | **Coventry City** (PL) | H | L | 1-3 | Redknapp |
| 1998-99 (PL) | 3 | 03.01.99 | **Port Vale** (D1) | A | W | 3-0 | Owen (p), Ince, Fowler |
| | 4 | 24.01.99 | **Manchester Utd** (PL) | A | L | 1-2 | Owen |
| 1999-00 (PL) | 3 | 12.12.99 | **Huddersfield Town** (D1) | A | W | 2-0 | Camara, Matteo |
| | 4 | 10.01.00 | **Blackburn Rovers** (D1) | H | L | 0-1 | |
| 2000-01 (PL) | 3 | 06.01.01 | **Rotherham Utd** (D2) | H | W | 3-0 | Heskey 2, Hamann |
| | 4 | 27.01.01 | **Leeds Utd** (PL) | A | W | 2-0 | Barmby, Heskey |
| | 5 | 18.02.01 | **Manchester City** (PL) | H | W | 4-2 | Litmanen (p), Heskey, Smicer (p), Babbel |
| | 6 | 11.03.01 | **Tranmere Rovers** (D1) | A | W | 4-2 | Murphy, Owen, Gerrard, Fowler |
| | SF | 08.04.01 | **Wycombe W** (D2) | | W | 2-1 | Heskey, Fowler |
| | | | *played at Villa Park* | | | | |
| | F | 12.05.01 | **Arsenal** (PL) | | W | 2-1 | Owen 2 |
| | | | *played at the Millennium Stadium, Cardiff* | | | | |
| 2001-02 (PL) | 3 | 05.01.02 | **Birmingham City** (D1) | H | W | 3-0 | Owen 2, Anelka |
| | 4 | 27.01.02 | **Arsenal** (PL) | A | L | 0-1 | |
| 2002-03 (PL) | 3 | 05.01.03 | **Manchester City** (PL) | A | W | 1-0 | Murphy (p) |
| | 4 | 26.01.03 | **Crystal Palace** (D1) | A | D | 0-0 | |
| | 4r | 05.02.03 | **Crystal Palace** (D1) | H | L | 0-2 | |

## LIVERPOOL RAMBLERS

*Formed 1862. The present-day Liverpool Ramblers Cricket Club claims links going back to the formation of the original football club.*

| | | | | | | |
|---|---|---|---|---|---|---|
| 1882-83 | 1 | 21.10.82 | **Southport** | H | D | 1-1 |
| | 1r | 04.11.82 | **Southport** | A | W | 4-0 |
| | 2 | 02.12.82 | **Bolton Wanderers** | A | L | 0-3 |
| | 2 | 30.11.82 | **Bolton Wanderers** | A | L | 0-3 |
| 1883-84 | 1 | | Wrexham Olympic | | | - |
| | | | *Liverpool Ramblers scratched. Wrexham Olympic walkover* | | | |
| 1884-85 | 1 | 08.11.84 | **Druids** | A | L | 1-6 |

## LIVERPOOL STANLEY

*Formed 1882. Entered FA Cup: 1887-88 – 1895-96. Home ground was in Kirkdale.*

| | | | | | | |
|---|---|---|---|---|---|---|
| 1887-88 | 1 | 15.10.87 | **Halliwell** | H | L | 1-5 |

# LLANELLI

*Formed 1896. Entered FA Cup: 1911-12 – 1987-88. Welsh FA Cup runners-up: 1914. League clubs beaten: Merthyr Town, Southend United. Members of the League of Wales.*

| | | | | | | | | |
|---|---|---|---|---|---|---|---|---|
| 1923-24 | (SL) | | | 5q Merthyr Town (3S) 3-1; 6q Southend Utd (3S) 2-1 | | | | |
| | | 1 | 12.01.24 | **Fulham** (D2) | A | L | 0-2 | |
| 1950-51 | (SL) | 1 | 25.11.50 | **Bristol Rovers** (3S) | A | D | 1-1 | McInnes |
| | | 1r | 28.11.50 | **Bristol Rovers** | H | D | 1-1aet | Wallace |
| | | 1 2r | 05.12.50 | **Bristol Rovers** | | L | 1-3aet | Massie |
| | | | | *played at Ninian Park* | | | | |
| 1952-53 | (SL) | 1 | 22.11.52 | **Grays Athletic** (CRN) | A | W | 5-0 | Comley, Ross, Love, Neilson, Morris |
| | | 2 | 06.12.52 | **Colchester Utd** (3S) | A | L | 2-3 | Morris, Neilson |
| 1953-54 | (SL) | 1 | 21.11.53 | **Northampton Town** (3S) | A | L | 0-3 | |

# LLANGOLLEN

| | | | | | | | | |
|---|---|---|---|---|---|---|---|---|
| 1887-88 | | 1 | 08.10.87 | **Oswestry Town** | H | W | 7-3 | |
| | | | | *FA ordered replay after protest* | | | | |
| | | 1r | 22.10.87 | **Oswestry Town** | H | L | 0-2 | |

# LLOYDS FC (SITTINGBOURNE)

*Entered FA Cup 1932-33 – 1948-49. The works team of the Lloyds paper factory in Sittingbourne, Kent.*

| | | | | | | | | |
|---|---|---|---|---|---|---|---|---|
| 1932-33 | (KL) | 1 | 26.11.32 | **Northampton Town** (3S) | A | L | 1-8 | Mantle |

# LOCKWOOD BROS (SHEFFIELD)

*Formed 1870. Works team from the Lockwood Brothers factory that played in the Heeley district. Entered FA Cup: 1881-82 – 1887-88.*

| | | | | | | | | |
|---|---|---|---|---|---|---|---|---|
| 1881-82 | | 1 | 17.10.81 | **Sheffield Heeley** | A | L | 1-5 | Beard |
| 1882-83 | | 1 | 04.11.82 | **Macclesfield T** | H | W | 4-3 | West, others 3 |
| | | 2 | 02.12.82 | **Sheffield Wed** | A | L | 0-6 | |
| 1883-84 | | 1 | 10.11.83 | **Sheffield FC** | H | W | 4-1 | |
| | | 2 | 01.12.83 | **Rotherham Town** | H | W | 3-1 | |
| | | 3 | 29.12.83 | **Staveley** | A | L | 0-1 | |
| 1884-85 | | 1 | 08.11.84 | **Sheffield FC** | H | L | 0-3 | |
| 1885-86 | | 1 | 31.10.85 | **Notts Rangers** | H | D | 2-2 | |
| | | 1r | 07.11.85 | **Notts Rangers** | A | L | 0-4 | |
| 1886-87 | | 1 | 30.10.86 | **Long Eaton Rangers** | H | W | 1-0 | |
| | | 2 | 20.11.86 | **Cleethorpes Town** | A | W | 4-1 | |
| | | 3 | 11.12.86 | **Nottingham Forest** | H | W | 2-1 | |
| | | 4 | | bye | | | | |
| | | 5 | 29.01.87 | **WBA** | H | L | 0-1aet | |
| | | | | *FA ordered replay following protests* | | | | |
| | | 5r | 12.02.87 | **WBA** | | L | 1-2 | |
| | | | | *played at Derby Cricket Ground* | | | | |
| 1887-88 | | 1 | 15.10.87 | **Sheffield FC** | A | W | 3-1 | |
| | | 2 | | bye | | | | |
| | | 3 | 19.11.87 | **Derby Junction** | A | L | 1-2 | |

# LONDON CALEDONIANS

*Formed 1886 at Anderton's Hotel in Fleet Street. FA Amateur Cup winners: 1923; Entered FA Cup: 1886-87 – 1938-39. Originally based at Dulwich, later played at Tufnell Park. Disbanded during World War Two.*

| | | | | | | | | |
|---|---|---|---|---|---|---|---|---|
| 1886-87 | | 1 | 30.10.86 | **Hendon (1874)** | A | W | 2-1 | |
| | | 2 | 20.11.86 | **Old Wykehamists** | A | W | 1-0 | |
| | | 3 | | Old Carthusians | | | - | |
| | | | | *London Caledonians scratched. Old Carthusians walkover* | | | | |
| 1887-88 | | 1 | 15.10.87 | **Old Foresters** | H | L | 1-6 | |
| 1912-13 | (IL) | 1 | 18.01.13 | **Wolverhampton W** (D2) | A | L | 1-3 | How |
| 1913-14 | (IL) | 1 | 10.01.14 | **Huddersfield Town** (D2) | A | L | 0-3 | |
| 1925-26 | (IL) | 1 | 28.11.25 | **Ilford** (IL) | H | L | 1-2 | Allen og |
| 1926-27 | (IL) | 1 | 27.11.26 | **Luton Town** (D3) | A | L | 2-4 | Noble, May |
| 1927-28 | (IL) | 1 | 26.11.27 | **Northfleet Utd** (SL) | A | W | 1-0 | McGeorge |
| | | 2 | 10.12.27 | **Bath City** (SL) | H | W | 1-0 | Conridge |
| | | 3 | 14.01.28 | **Crewe Alexandra** (3N) | H | L | 2-3 | Noble, Hamilton |
| | | | | *played at Stamford Bridge* | | | | |

## LONDON OLYMPIC

| | | | | | | | | |
|---|---|---|---|---|---|---|---|---|
| 1882-83 | | 1 | 04.11.82 | **United Hospital** | A | L | 0-3 | |

## LONDON PAPER MILLS (DARTFORD)

*Entered FA Cup: 1933-34 – 1938-39. Team continued until the factory closed in 1965.*

| | | | | | | | | |
|---|---|---|---|---|---|---|---|---|
| 1933-34 | (KL) | 1 | 25.11.33 | **Southend Utd** (3S) | H | L | 0-1 | |

## LONG EATON RANGERS

*Formed 1882. Played at The Recreation Ground, Long Eaton. Entered FA Cup: 1883-84 – 1898-99.*

| | | | | | | | | |
|---|---|---|---|---|---|---|---|---|
| 1883-84 | | 1 | 27.10.83 | **Wolverhampton W** | A | L | 1-4 | |
| 1884-85 | | 1 | 08.11.84 | **Sheffield Wed** | A | L | 0-1 | |
| 1885-86 | | 1 | 31.10.85 | **Sheffield Wed** | H | W | 2-0 | Hexter, Winfield |
| | | 2 | 21.11.85 | **Staveley** | H | L | 1-4 | |
| 1886-87 | | 1 | 30.10.86 | **Lockwood Bros** | A | L | 0-1 | |
| 1887-88 | | 1 | 15.10.87 | **Park Grange** | H | W | 6-3 | |
| | | 2 | 05.11.87 | **Sheffield Wed** | H | L | 1-2aet | Plackett |
| 1888-89 | | 1 | 02.02.89 | **Birmingham St G** | A | L | 2-3 | Lowe, Locker |
| 1890-91 | (ML) | 1 | 17.01.91 | **Wolverhampton W** (D1) | H | L | 1-2aet | J Start |
| 1897-98 | (ML) | 1 | 29.01.98 | **Gainsborough T** (D2) | H | L | 0-1 | |

## LOUGHBOROUGH

*Formed 1886. Member of the Football League 1895-1900 but never played in the Competition Proper as a League team. Folded June 1900.*

| | | | | | | | | |
|---|---|---|---|---|---|---|---|---|
| 1892-93 | (ML) | 1 | 21.01.93 | **Northwich V** (D2) | H | L | 1-2 | Carnelly |
| 1895-96 | (D2) | | | 1q Bulwell U (H) 5-2; 2q Newstead (A) 0-0; 2qr Newstead (H) 1-0; 3q Kettering Town (A) 1-2 | | | | |
| 1896-97 | (D2) | | | 3q Mansfield (A) 1-2 | | | | |
| 1897-98 | (D2) | | | 3q Bulwell U (A) 0-3 | | | | |
| 1898-99 | (D2) | | | 1q Mansfield (H) 4-0; 2q Rothwell TS (H) 7-0; 3q Wellingborough (H) 0-0; 3qr Wellingborough (A) 3-1; 4q Kettering Town (A) 1-2 | | | | |
| 1899-00 | (D2) | | | 3q Hinckley Town(H) 1-2 | | | | |

## LOUGHBOROUGH UNITED

*Formed around 1914 as Brush Works, the works team of the Brush Electrical Engineering Company who later played as Loughborough Brush Works. Became Brush Sports 1939. Loughborough Utd 1960. Entered FA Cup as Loughborough Utd 1960-61 – 1972-73. Folded 1973.*

| | | | | | | | | |
|---|---|---|---|---|---|---|---|---|
| 1960-61 | (CA) | 1 | 05.11.60 | **King's Lynn** (SL) | H | D | 0-0 | |
| | | 1r | 09.11.60 | **King's Lynn** | A | L | 0-3 | |
| 1963-64 | (ML) | 1 | 16.11.63 | **Netherfield** (LC) | A | L | 1-6 | Broadhurst |

## LOVELL'S ATHLETIC

*Formed 1918. Entered FA Cup: 1921-22 – 1968-69. Welsh FA Cup winners: 1948. Based in Newport, Wales, they were the works team of the Lovell's toffee-making company. League club beaten: Bournemouth. Folded 1969.*

| | | | | | | | | |
|---|---|---|---|---|---|---|---|---|
| 1945-46 | (Welsh) | 1 1L | 17.11.45 | **Bournemouth** (3S) | H | W | 4-1 | Clarke 2, Williams 2 |
| | | 1 2L | 24.11.45 | **Bournemouth** | A | L | 2-3 | Holland 2 |
| | | 2 1L | 08.12.45 | **Bath City** (SL) | H | W | 2-1 | Morgan, Williams |
| | | 2 2L | 15.12.45 | **Bath City** | A | W | 5-2 | Williams, Hardwick 2, Morgan, Holland |
| | | 3 1L | 05.01.46 | **Wolverhampton W** (D1) | H | L | 2-4 | Morgan, Hardwick |
| | | 3 2L | 09.01.46 | **Wolverhampton W** | A | L | 1-8 | Prangley |
| 1955-56 | (SL) | 1 | 19.11.55 | **Leyton Orient** (3S) | A | L | 1-7 | Ridsdale |

## LOWER DARWEN

| | | | | | | | | |
|---|---|---|---|---|---|---|---|---|
| 1882-83 | | 1 | 28.10.82 | **Irwell Springs** | H | W | 5-2 | RT Duckworth 4, Brindle |
| | | 2 | 09.12.82 | **Blackburn Olympic** | A | L | 1-8 | Marsden |
| 1883-84 | | 1 | 31.10.83 | **Padiham** | A | L | 1-3 | |
| 1884-85 | | 1 | 11.10.84 | **Halliwell** | H | W | 4-1 | |
| | | 2 | | bye | | | | |
| | | 3 | 20.12.84 | **Darwen Old Wanderers** | H | W | 4-2 | |
| | | 4 | 24.01.85 | **Chatham** | A | L | 0-1 | |
| 1885-86 | | 1 | 31.10.85 | **Oswaldtwistle Rovers** | A | L | 1-3 | |

# LOWESTOFT TOWN

*Formed 1890. FA Amateur Cup runners-up: 1900. First entered FA Cup: 1898-99. Members of the Eastern Counties League.*

| | | | | | | | | |
|---|---|---|---|---|---|---|---|---|
| 1926-27 | (N&S) | 1 | 27.11.26 | **Watford** (3S) | A | L | 1-10 | Hook |
| 1938-39 | (ECL) | 1 | 26.11.38 | **Swindon Town** (3S) | A | L | 0-6 | |
| 1966-67 | (ECL) | 1 | 26.11.66 | **Leyton Orient** (D3) | A | L | 1-2 | Cassidy |
| 1967-68 | (ECL) | 1 | 09.12.67 | **Watford** (D3) | H | L | 0-1 | |
| 1977-78 | (ECL) | 1 | 26.11.77 | **Cambridge Utd** (D3) | H | L | 0-2 | |

# LUTON TOWN

*Formed 1885 by the amalgamation of Luton Wanderers and Excelsior FC. First entered FA Cup: 1885-86. FA Cup runners-up: 1959. Record FA Cup win: 15-0 v Great Yarmouth Town, 4th qualifying round, 21.11.1914. In Competition Proper: 9-0 v Clapton FC, 1st round replay, 30.11.1927. Record FA Cup defeat: 0-7 v 93rd Highland Regiment, 1st qualifying round, 04.10.1890. In Competition Proper: 0-7 v Crystal Palace, 1st round, 16.01.29.*

| | | | | | | | | |
|---|---|---|---|---|---|---|---|---|
| 1885-86 | | 1 | 31.10.85 | **Marlow** | A | L | 0-3 | |
| 1886-87 | | 1 | 23.10.86 | **Hotspur FC** | H | L | 1-3 | Ellingham |
| 1887-88 | | 1 | 15.10.87 | **Chatham** | A | L | 1-5 | Deacon |
| 1888-89 | | | | 1q Reading (H) 4-0; 2q Chesham (A) 3-3; 2qr Chesham (H) 10-2; 3q Old Brightonians (A) 1-3 | | | | |
| 1889-90 | | | | 2q Maidenhead (A) 2-1; 3q Old St Pauls (A) 0-4 | | | | |
| 1890-91 | | | | 1q 93rd Highland Regiment (A) 0-7 | | | | |
| 1891-92 | | | | 1q Swindon (H) 3-1; 2q Windsor Phoenix (H) 3-0; 3q Bedminster (A) 4-1; 4q Clifton (A) 3-0 | | | | |
| | | 1 | 16.01.92 | **Middlesbrough** (NL) | H | L | 0-3 | |
| 1892-93 | | | | 1q Old St Marks (H) 4-0; 2q Old Etonians (H) 4-2; 3q Merton Polytechnic (A) 2-4 | | | | |
| 1893-94 | | | | 2q Old Westminsters (A) 1-0; 3q Norwich CEYMS (H) 5-1; 4q Sherwood Foresters (H) 2-1 | | | | |
| | | 1 | 27.01.94 | **Middlesbrough Iron** (D2) | A | L | 1-2 | Dimmock |
| 1894-95 | (SL) | | | 1q City Ramblers (H) 8-2; 2q St Albans (A) 6-1; 3q Ilford (A) 2-0; 4q Tottenham H (A) 2-2; 4qr Tottenham H (H) 4-0 | | | | |
| | | 1 | 02.02.95 | **Preston North End** (D1) | H | L | 0-2 | |
| 1895-96 | (SL) | | | 1q Tottenham H (H) 1-2 | | | | |
| 1896-97 | (D2) | | | 3q 1st Scots Guards (H) 7-0; 4q Marlow (A) 5-0; 5q Tottenham H (H) 3-0 | | | | |
| | | 1 | 30.01.97 | **WBA** (D1) | H | L | 0-1 | |
| 1897-88 | (D2) | | | 4q Tottenham H (A) 4-3; 5q Clapton (A) 2-0 | | | | |
| | | 1 | 29.01.98 | **Bolton Wanderers** (D1) | H | L | 0-1 | |
| 1897-98 | (D2) | 1 | 29.01.98 | **Bolton Wanderers** (D1) | H | L | 0-1 | |
| 1898-99 | (D2) | | | 3q Watford (H) 2-2; 3qr Watford (A) 1-0; 4q Shepherds Bush (H) 4-3; 5q Tottenham H (A) 1-1; 5qr Tottenham H (H) 1-1; 5q2r Tottenham 0-2 (at Tufnell Park) | | | | |
| 1899-00 | (D2) | | | 3q Lowestoft (A) 2-0; 4q Watford (H) 3-2; 5q QPR (H) 1-1; 5qr QPR (A) 1-4 | | | | |
| 1900-01 | (SL) | | | 3q Kings Lynn (A) 4-1; 4q Civil Service (H) 9-1; 5q QPR (H) 3-0; Int Bristol R (H) 0-2 | | | | |
| 1901-02 | (SL) | | | 1q Aspley Guise (H) 13-1; 2q Bedford Queens (H) 4-2; 3q Lowestoft (A) 2-1; 4q Watford (A) 2-1; 5q QPR (H) 2-0; Int. W Arsenal (A) 1-1; IntR W Arsenal (H) 0-2 | | | | |
| 1902-03 | (SL) | | | 3q QPR (A) 3-0; 4q Lowestoft (H) 5-1; 5q Fulham (H) 6-1; Int. Kidderminster (H) 3-0 | | | | |
| | | 1 | 07.02.03 | **Millwall Athletic** (SL) | A | L | 0-3 | |
| 1903-04 | (SL) | | | 3q Hitchin (A) 2-1; 4q Watford (H) 4-1; 5q Fulham (A) 1-3 | | | | |
| 1904-05 | (SL) | | | 6q Fulham (A) 0-4 | | | | |
| 1905-06 | (SL) | | | 4q Crystal Palace (A) 0-1 | | | | |
| 1906-07 | (SL) | 1 | 12.01.07 | **Gainsborough T** (D2) | A | D | 0-0 | |
| | | 1r | 16.01.07 | **Gainsborough T** | H | W | 2-1 | Warner, Brown |
| | | 2 | 02.02.07 | **Sunderland** (D1) | H | D | 0-0 | |
| | | 2r | 06.02.07 | **Sunderland** | A | L | 0-1 | |
| 1907-08 | (SL) | 1 | 11.01.08 | **Fulham** (D2) | H | L | 3-8 | Rigate, Rankin, Moody |
| 1908-09 | (SL) | | | 5q Southend (H) 1-1; 5qr Southend (A) 4-2 | | | | |
| | | 1 | 16.01.09 | **Millwall Athletic** (SL) | H | L | 1-2 | Menzies |
| 1909-10 | (SL) | | | 4q Brentford (A) 1-2 | | | | |
| 1910-11 | (SL) | | | 4q Cambridge C (H) 9-1; 5q Rochdale (H) 1-1; 5qr Rochdale (A) 3-2 | | | | |
| | | 1 | 14.01.11 | **Northampton Town** (SL) | A | L | 1-5 | Moody |
| 1911-12 | (SL) | 1 | 13.01.12 | **Notts County** (D1) | H | L | 2-4 | Streeton, Moody |
| 1912-13 | (SL) | | | 4q Tunbridge Wells R (H) 3-0; 5q Croydon Common (A) 0-2 | | | | |
| 1913-14 | (SL) | | | 4q Croydon Common (H) 3-0; 5q South Shields (H) 0-0; 5qr South Shields (A) 0-2 | | | | |

| | | | | | | | |
|---|---|---|---|---|---|---|---|
| 1914-15 (SL) | | | 4q Gt Yarmouth (H) 15-0; 5q Oxford C (A) 1-0; 6q Bromley (H) 5-1 | | | | |
| | 1 | 09.01.15 | **Southampton** (SL) | A | L | 0-3 | |
| 1919-20 (SL) | | | 6q Brighton (A) 1-0 | | | | |
| | 1 | 10.01.20 | **Coventry City** (D2) | H | D | 2-2 | Parker, Dodd |
| | 1r | 16.01.20 | **Coventry City** | A | W | 1-0 | Hoar |
| | 2 | 31.01.20 | **Liverpool** (D1) | H | L | 0-2 | |
| 1920-21 (3S) | | | 6q Rotherham Co (A) 3-1 | | | | |
| | 1 | 08.01.21 | **Birmingham** (D2) | H | W | 2-1 | Simms, Bookman |
| | 2 | 29.01.21 | **South Shields** (D2) | A | W | 4-0 | Higginbotham, Butcher 2, Simms |
| | 3 | 19.02.21 | **Preston North End** (D1) | H | L | 2-3 | Higginbotham 2 |
| 1921-22 (3S) | 1 | 07.01.22 | **Portsmouth** (3S) | A | D | 1-1 | Bassett |
| | 1r | 11.01.22 | **Portsmouth** | H | W | 2-1 | Higginbotham, Hoar |
| | 2 | 28.01.22 | **Aston Villa** (D1) | A | L | 0-1 | |
| 1922-23 (3S) | 1 | 13.01.23 | **Bury** (D2) | A | L | 1-2 | Tirrell (p) |
| 1923-24 (3S) | 1 | 12.01.24 | **Arsenal** (D1) | A | L | 1-4 | Green |
| 1924-25 (3S) | 1 | 10.01.25 | **WBA** (D1) | A | L | 0-4 | |
| 1925-26 (3S) | 1 | 28.11.25 | **Folkestone** (SL) | H | W | 3-0 | Reid, Littlewood, Shankly |
| | 2 | 12.12.25 | **Aberdare Athletic** (3S) | A | L | 0-1 | |
| 1926-27 (D3) | 1 | 27.11.26 | **London Cal** (IL) | H | W | 4-2 | Reid 2, Clark, Pointon |
| | 2 | 11.12.26 | **Northfleet Utd** (KL) | H | W | 6-2 | Woods 3, Reid 2, Rennie |
| | 3 | 08.01.27 | **Chelsea** (D2) | A | L | 0-4 | |
| 1927-28 (3S) | 1 | 30.11.27 | **Clapton** (IL) | H | W | 9-0 | Dennis 2, Woods, Yardley 4, Reid 2 |
| | 2 | 10.12.27 | **Norwich City** (3S) | H | W | 6-0 | Reid 3, Woods, Yardley, Dennis |
| | 3 | 14.01.28 | **Bolton Wanderers** (D1) | A | L | 1-2 | Reid |
| 1928-29 (3S) | 1 | 24.11.28 | **Southend Utd** (3S) | H | W | 5-1 | Rennie 4, Bedford |
| | 2 | 08.12.28 | **Fulham** (3S) | A | D | 0-0 | |
| | 2r | 13.12.28 | **Fulham** | H | W | 4-1 | Yardley 2, Rennie, Bedford |
| | 3 | 12.01.29 | **Crystal Palace** (3S) | H | D | 0-0 | |
| | 3r | 16.01.29 | **Crystal Palace** | A | L | 0-7 | |
| 1929-30 (3S) | 1 | 30.11.29 | **QPR** (3S) | H | L | 2-3 | Yardley 2 |
| 1930-31 (3S) | 1 | 29.11.30 | **Clapton Orient** (3S) | H | D | 2-2 | Rennie, Bryce |
| | 1r | 04.12.30 | **Clapton Orient** *played at Highbury* | A | W | 4-2 | McNestry, Rennie 2, Armstrong |
| | 2 | 13.12.30 | **Watford** (3S) | A | L | 1-3 | Yardley |
| 1931-32 (3S) | 1 | 28.11.31 | **Swindon Town** (3S) | A | W | 5-0 | McNestry, Rennie 2, Yardley 2 |
| | 2 | 12.12.31 | **Lincoln City** (3N) | A | D | 2-2 | Yardley 2 |
| | 2r | 16.12.31 | **Lincoln City** | H | W | 4-1 | Tait 2, Yardley, Slicer |
| | 3 | 09.01.32 | **Wolverhampton W** (D2) | H | L | 1-2 | Yardley |
| 1932-33 (3S) | 1 | 26.11.32 | **Kingstonian** (IL) | H | D | 2-2 | Rennie, Tait |
| | 1r | 30.11.32 | **Kingstonian** | A | W | 3-2 | McGinnigle, Rennie, Tait |
| | 2 | 10.12.32 | **Stockport County** (3N) | A | W | 3-2 | Kean, Rennie, Tait |
| | 3 | 14.01.33 | **Barnsley** (3N) | A | D | 0-0 | |
| | 3r | 18.01.33 | **Barnsley** | H | W | 2-0 | Rennie 2 |
| | 4 | 28.01.33 | **Tottenham Hotspur** (D2) | H | W | 2-0 | Alderson, Tait |
| | 5 | 18.02.33 | **Halifax Town** (3N) | A | W | 2-0 | Nelson, Tait |
| | 6 | 03.03.33 | **Everton** (D1) | A | L | 0-6 | |
| 1933-34 (3S) | 3 | 13.01.34 | **Arsenal** (D1) | H | L | 0-1 | |
| 1934-35 (3S) | 3 | 12.01.35 | **Chelsea** (D1) | A | D | 1-1 | Bell |
| | 3r | 16.01.35 | **Chelsea** | H | W | 2-0 | Ball, Roberts |
| | 4 | 26.01.35 | **Burnley** (D2) | A | L | 1-3 | Stephenson |
| 1935-36 (3S) | 3 | 11.01.36 | **West Ham Utd** (D2) | A | D | 2-2 | Ball, Roberts |
| | 3r | 15.01.36 | **West Ham Utd** | H | W | 4-0 | Ball, Crompton, Roberts, Stephenson |
| | 4 | 25.01.36 | **Manchester City** (D1) | A | L | 1-2 | Martin |
| 1936-37 (3S) | 3 | 16.01.37 | **Blackpool** (D2) | H | D | 3-3 | Payne 2, Stephenson |
| | 3r | 20.01.37 | **Blackpool** | A | W | 2-1 | Sloan, Roberts |
| | 4 | 30.01.37 | **Sunderland** (D1) | H | D | 2-2 | Roberts 2 |
| | 4r | 03.02.37 | **Sunderland** | A | L | 1-3 | Payne |
| 1937-38 (D2) | 3 | 08.01.38 | **Scarborough** (ML) | A | D | 1-1 | Ferguson |
| | 3r | 12.01.38 | **Scarborough** | H | W | 5-1 | Vinall 2, Ferguson, Dawes, Stephenson |
| | 4 | 22.01.38 | **Swindon Town** (3S) | H | W | 2-1 | Ferguson, Stephenson |

| | | | | | | | |
|---|---|---|---|---|---|---|---|
| | 5 | 12.02.38 | **Manchester City** (D1) | H | L | 1-3 | Payne |
| 1938-39 (D2) | 3 | 07.01.39 | **Liverpool** (D1) | A | L | 0-3 | |
| 1945-46 (D2) | 3 1L | 05.01.46 | **Derby County** (D1) | H | L | 0-6 | |
| | 3 2L | 09.01.46 | **Derby County** | A | L | 0-3 | |
| 1946-47 (D2) | 3 | 11.01.47 | **Notts County** (3S) | H | W | 6-0 | Billington 5, Daniel |
| | 4 | 25.01.47 | **Swansea Town** (D2) | H | W | 2-0 | Daniel, Roberts og |
| | 5 | 08.02.47 | **Burnley** (D2) | H | D | 0-0 | |
| | 5r | 11.02.47 | **Burnley** | A | L | 0-3 | |
| 1947-48 (D2) | 3 | 10.01.48 | **Plymouth Argyle** (D2) | A | W | 4-2 | Brennan 2, Billington 2 |
| | 4 | 24.01.48 | **Coventry City** (D2) | H | W | 3-2 | Soo, Waugh, Ottewell |
| | 5 | 07.02.48 | **QPR** (3S) | A | L | 1-3 | Waugh |
| 1948-49 (D2) | 3 | 08.01.49 | **West Ham Utd** (D2) | H | W | 3-1 | Kiernan, Arnison, Watkins |
| | 4 | 29.01.49 | **Walsall** (3S) | H | W | 4-0 | Brennan 3, Watkins |
| | 5 | 12.02.49 | **Leicester City** (D2) | H | D | 5-5aet | Kiernan 2, Small, Brennan, Watkins |
| | 5r | 19.02.49 | **Leicester City** | A | L | 3-5 | Brennan 2, Arnison |
| 1949-50 (D2) | 3 | 07.01.50 | **Grimsby Town** (D2) | H | L | 3-4 | Kiernan, Waugh |
| 1950-51 (D2) | 3 | 06.01.51 | **Portsmouth** (D1) | H | W | 2-0 | Davie, Havenga |
| | 4 | 27.01.51 | **Bristol Rovers** (3S) | H | L | 1-2 | Watkins |
| 1951-52 (D2) | 3 | 12.01.52 | **Charlton Athletic** (D1) | H | W | 1-0 | Turner |
| | 4 | 02.02.52 | **Brentford** (D2) | H | D | 2-2 | Turner, Taylor |
| | 4r | 06.02.52 | **Brentford** | A | D | 0-0aet | |
| | 4 2r | 18.02.52 | **Brentford** *played at Highbury* | | W | 3-2aet | Taylor, Moore, Morton |
| | 5 | 23.02.52 | **Swindon Town** (3S) | H | W | 3-1 | Taylor 2, Davies |
| | 6 | 08.03.52 | **Arsenal** (D1) | H | L | 2-3 | Moore, Mitchell (p) |
| 1952-53 (D2) | 3 | 10.01.53 | **Blackburn Rovers** (D2) | H | W | 6-1 | Pye 3, Taylor 2, Moore |
| | 4 | 31.01.53 | **Manchester City** (D1) | A | D | 1-1 | Pye |
| | 4r | 04.02.53 | **Manchester City** | H | W | 5-1 | Turner 3, Mitchell, Little og |
| | 5 | 14.02.53 | **Bolton Wanderers** (D1) | H | L | 0-1 | |
| 1953-54 (D2) | 3 | 09.01.54 | **Blackpool** (D1) | A | D | 1-1 | Cummins |
| | 3r | 13.01.54 | **Blackpool** | H | D | 0-0aet | |
| | 3 2r | 18.01.54 | **Blackpool** *played at Villa Park* | | D | 1-1aet | Cummins |
| | 3 3r | 25.01.54 | **Blackpool** *played at Molineux* | | L | 0-2 | |
| 1954-55 (D2) | 3 | 08.01.55 | **Workington** (3N) | H | W | 5-0 | Turner 2, Cummins, Cullen 2 |
| | 4 | 29.01.55 | **Rotherham Utd** (D2) | A | W | 5-1 | Turner 3, Cummins, Cullen |
| | 5 | 19.02.55 | **Manchester City** (D1) | H | L | 0-2 | |
| 1955-56 (D1) | 3 | 11.01.56 | **Leicester City** (D2) | H | L | 0-4 | |
| 1956-57 (D1) | 3 | 05.01.57 | **Aston Villa** (D1) | H | D | 2-2 | Davies, Turner (p) |
| | 3r | 07.01.57 | **Aston Villa** | A | L | 0-2 | |
| 1957-58 (D1) | 3 | 04.01.58 | **Stockport County** (3N) | A | L | 0-3 | |
| 1958-59 (D1) | 3 | 10.01.59 | **Leeds Utd** (D1) | H | W | 5-1 | Bingham 2, Morton, Gregory 2 |
| | 4 | 24.01.59 | **Leicester City** (D1) | A | D | 1-1 | Bingham |
| | 4r | 28.01.59 | **Leicester City** | H | W | 4-1 | Brown 3, Gregory |
| | 5 | 14.02.59 | **Ipswich Town** (D2) | A | W | 5-2 | Pacey, Morton 2, Bingham, Gregory |
| | 6 | 28.02.59 | **Blackpool** (D1) | A | D | 1-1 | Bingham |
| | 6r | 04.03.59 | **Blackpool** | H | W | 1-0 | Brown |
| | SF | 14.03.59 | **Norwich City** (D3) *played at White Hart Lane* | | D | 1-1 | Brown |
| | SFr | 18.03.59 | **Norwich City** (D3) *played at St Andrews* | | W | 1-0 | Bingham |
| | F | 02.05.59 | **Nottingham Forest** (D1) *played at Wembley Stadium* | | L | 1-2 | Pacey |
| 1959-60 (D1) | 3 | 09.01.60 | **Exeter City** (D4) | A | W | 2-1 | Turner 2 |
| | 4 | 30.01.60 | **Huddersfield Town** (D2) | A | W | 1-0 | Gregory |
| | 5 | 20.02.60 | **Wolverhampton W** (D1) | H | L | 1-4 | Turner |
| 1960-61 (D2) | 3 | 07.01.61 | **Northampton Town** (D4) | H | W | 4-0 | Turner 2, Brown, Ashworth |
| | 4 | 28.01.61 | **Manchester City** (D1) *abandoned after 69 minutes – waterlogged pitch* | H | - | 2-6ab | Ashworth 2 |
| | 4 | 01.02.61 | **Manchester City** (D1) | H | W | 3-1 | Ashworth 2, Fleming |

| | | | | | | | | |
|---|---|---|---|---|---|---|---|---|
| | | 5 | 18.02.61 | **Barnsley** (D3) | A | L | 0-1 | |
| 1961-62 | (D2) | 3 | 06.01.62 | **Ipswich Town** (D1) | A | D | 1-1 | Chandler |
| | | 3r | 10.01.62 | **Ipswich Town** | H | D | 1-1aet | Pacey |
| | | 3 2r | 15.01.62 | **Ipswich Town** | | L | 1-5 | Ashworth |
| | | | | *played at Highbury* | | | | |
| 1962-63 | (D2) | 3 | 26.01.63 | **Swindon Town** (D3) | H | L | 0-2 | |
| 1963-64 | (D3) | 1 | 16.11.63 | **Bridgwater Town** (WL) | A | W | 3-0 | McKechnie 2, Turner |
| | | 2 | 07.12.63 | **Reading** (D3) | H | W | 2-1 | Fairchild, Turner |
| | | 3 | 04.01.64 | **Fulham** (D1) | A | L | 1-4 | Smith |
| 1964-65 | (D3) | 1 | 14.11.64 | **Southend Utd** (D3) | H | W | 1-0 | Bramwell |
| | | 2 | 05.12.64 | **Gillingham** (D3) | H | W | 1-0 | Riddick |
| | | 3 | 09.01.65 | **Sunderland** (D1) | H | L | 0-3 | |
| 1965-66 | (D4) | 1 | 13.11.65 | **Romford** (SL) | A | D | 1-1 | Harris og |
| | | 1r | 18.11.65 | **Romford** | H | W | 1-0 | O'Rourke |
| | | 2 | 04.12.65 | **Corby Town** (SL) | A | D | 2-2 | O'Rourke, Whittaker (p) |
| | | 2r | 07.12.65 | **Corby Town** | H | L | 0-1 | |
| 1966-67 | (D4) | 1 | 26.11.66 | **Exeter City** (D4) | A | D | 1-1 | Whittaker |
| | | 1r | 01.12.66 | **Exeter City** | H | W | 2-0 | Rioch, Pleat |
| | | 2 | 07.01.67 | **Bristol Rovers** (D3) | A | L | 2-3 | Kevan 2 |
| 1967-68 | (D4) | 1 | 09.12.67 | **Oxford City** (IL) | A | W | 2-1 | Rioch, Buxton |
| | | | | *played at Kenilworth Road* | | | | |
| | | 2 | 06.01.68 | **Swindon Town** (D3) | A | L | 2-3 | Allen, Whittaker (p) |
| 1968-69 | (D3) | 1 | 16.11.68 | **Ware** (AL) | H | W | 6-1 | Potter, Slough 2, Allen 3 |
| | | 2 | 07.12.68 | **Gillingham** (D3) | H | W | 3-1 | French, Harrison 2 |
| | | 3 | 04.01.69 | **Manchester City** (D1) | A | L | 0-1 | |
| 1969-70 | (D3) | 1 | 15.11.69 | **Bournemouth** (D3) | A | D | 1-1 | Collins |
| | | 1r | 18.11.69 | **Bournemouth** | H | W | 3-1 | Collins, Tees, MacDonald |
| | | 2 | 06.12.69 | **Hillingdon Borough** (SL) | A | L | 1-2 | Tees |
| 1970-71 | (D2) | 3 | 02.01.71 | **Nottingham Forest** (D1) | A | D | 1-1 | MacDonald |
| | | 3r | 11.01.71 | **Nottingham Forest** | H | L | 3-4 | MacDonald 3 |
| 1971-72 | (D2) | 3 | 15.01.72 | **West Ham Utd** (D1) | A | L | 1-2 | Givens |
| 1972-73 | (D2) | 3 | 13.01.73 | **Crewe Alexandra** (D4) | H | W | 2-0 | Jim Ryan, Butlin |
| | | 4 | 03.02.73 | **Newcastle Utd** (D1) | A | W | 2-0 | Aston 2 |
| | | 5 | 24.02.73 | **Bolton Wanderers** (D3) | A | W | 1-0 | Garner |
| | | 6 | 17.03.73 | **Sunderland** (D2) | A | L | 0-2 | |
| 1973-74 | (D2) | 3 | 05.01.74 | **Port Vale** (D3) | A | D | 1-1 | Jim Ryan |
| | | 3r | 09.01.74 | **Port Vale** | H | W | 4-2 | Aston, Anderson 2, Jim Ryan |
| | | 4 | 26.01.74 | **Bradford City** (D4) | H | W | 3-0 | Fretwell og, Butlin, Jim Ryan |
| | | 5 | 16.02.74 | **Leicester City** (D1) | H | L | 0-4 | |
| 1974-75 | (D1) | 3 | 04.01.75 | **Birmingham City** (D1) | H | L | 0-1 | |
| 1975-76 | (D2) | 3 | 03.01.76 | **Blackburn Rovers** (D2) | H | W | 2-0 | R Futcher, Chambers |
| | | 4 | 24.01.76 | **Norwich City** (D1) | A | L | 0-2 | |
| 1976-77 | (D2) | 3 | 08.01.77 | **Halifax Town** (D4) | A | W | 1-0 | Aston |
| | | 4 | 29.01.77 | **Chester** (D3) | A | L | 0-1 | |
| 1977-78 | (D2) | 3 | 07.01.78 | **Oldham Athletic** (D2) | H | D | 1-1 | Fuccillo |
| | | 3r | 10.01.78 | **Oldham Athletic** | A | W | 2-1 | Boersma 2 |
| | | 4 | 31.01.78 | **Millwall** (D2) | A | L | 0-4 | |
| 1978-79 | (D2) | 3 | 09.01.79 | **York City** (D4) | A | L | 0-2 | |
| 1979-80 | (D2) | 3 | 05.01.80 | **Swindon Town** (D3) | H | L | 0-2 | |
| 1980-81 | (D2) | 3 | 03.01.81 | **Orient** (D2) | A | W | 3-1 | Moss 2, Ingram |
| | | 4 | 24.01.81 | **Newcastle Utd** (D2) | A | L | 1-2 | Ingram |
| 1981-82 | (D2) | 3 | 02.01.82 | **Swindon Town** (D3) | H | W | 2-1 | Moss, Horton |
| | | 4 | 23.01.82 | **Ipswich Town** (D1) | H | L | 0-3 | |
| 1982-83 | (D1) | 3 | 08.01.83 | **Peterborough Utd** (D4) | H | W | 3-0 | Horton, Hill, Walsh |
| | | 4 | 29.01.83 | **Manchester Utd** (D1) | H | L | 0-2 | |
| 1983-84 | (D1) | 3 | 07.01.84 | **Watford** (D1) | H | D | 2-2 | Nwajiobi, B Stein |
| | | 3r | 10.01.84 | **Watford** | A | L | 3-4 | Donaghy, Walsh 2 |
| 1984-85 | (D1) | 3 | 05.01.85 | **Stoke City** (D1) | H | D | 1-1 | Foster |
| | | 3r | 09.01.85 | **Stoke City** | A | W | 3-2 | Hill, Harford, Donaghy |
| | | 4 | 26.01.85 | **Huddersfield Town** (D2) | H | W | 2-0 | Donaghy, B Stein |
| | | 5 | 04.03.85 | **Watford** (D1) | H | D | 0-0 | |

| | | | | | | | | |
|---|---|---|---|---|---|---|---|---|
| | | 5r | 06.03.85 | **Watford** | A | D | 2-2aet | Nwajiobi, Hill |
| | | 5 2r | 09.03.85 | **Watford** | H | W | 1-0 | Turner |
| | | 6 | 13.03.85 | **Millwall** (D3) | H | W | 1-0 | B Stein |
| | | SF | 13.04.85 | **Everton** (D1) | | L | 1-2aet | Hill |
| | | | | *played at Villa Park* | | | | |
| 1985-86 | (D1) | 3 | 06.01.86 | **Crystal Palace** (D2) | A | W | 2-1 | B Stein, Preece |
| | | 4 | 25.01.86 | **Bristol Rovers** (D3) | H | W | 4-0 | Hill, Harford, North, Parkin og |
| | | 5 | 15.02.86 | **Arsenal** (D1) | H | D | 2-2 | Hill, Harford |
| | | 5r | 03.03.86 | **Arsenal** | A | D | 0-0aet | |
| | | 5 2r | 05.03.86 | **Arsenal** | H | W | 3-0 | M Stein, Foster, O'Leary og |
| | | 6 | 08.03.86 | **Everton** (D1) | H | D | 2-2 | M Stein, Harford |
| | | 6r | 12.03.86 | **Everton** | A | L | 0-1 | |
| 1986-87 | (D1) | 3 | 11.01.87 | **Liverpool** (D1) | H | D | 0-0 | |
| | | 3r | 26.01.87 | **Liverpool** | A | D | 0-0aet | |
| | | 3 2r | 28.01.87 | **Liverpool** | H | W | 3-0 | B Stein, Harford, Newell |
| | | 4 | 31.01.87 | **QPR** (D1) | H | D | 1-1 | Harford |
| | | 4r | 04.02.87 | **QPR** | A | L | 1-2 | Harford |
| 1987-88 | (D1) | 3 | 09.01.88 | **Hartlepool Utd** (D4) | A | W | 2-1 | Weir, McDonough |
| | | 4 | 30.01.88 | **Southampton** (D1) | H | W | 2-1 | Allinson, B Stein |
| | | 5 | 20.02.88 | **QPR** (D1) | A | D | 1-1 | Harford |
| | | 5r | 24.02.88 | **QPR** | H | W | 1-0 | Neill og |
| | | 6 | 12.03.88 | **Portsmouth** (D1) | H | W | 3-1 | Wilson, M Stein, Harford |
| | | SF | 09.04.88 | **Wimbledon** (D1) | | L | 1-2 | Harford |
| | | | | *played at White Hart Lane* | | | | |
| 1988-89 | (D1) | 3 | 07.01.89 | **Millwall** (D1) | A | L | 2-3 | Black, Wilson (p) |
| 1989-90 | (D1) | 3 | 06.01.90 | **Brighton** (D2) | A | L | 1-4 | Wilson |
| 1990-91 | (D1) | 3 | 05.01.91 | **Sheffield Utd** (D1) | A | W | 3-1 | Farrell, Elstrup 2 |
| | | 4 | 26.01.91 | **West Ham Utd** (D2) | H | D | 1-1 | Black |
| | | 4r | 30.01.91 | **West Ham Utd** | A | L | 0-5 | |
| 1991-92 | (D1) | 3 | 04.01.92 | **Sheffield Utd** (D1) | A | L | 0-4 | |
| 1992-93 | (D1) | 3 | 19.01.93 | **Bristol City** (D1) | H | W | 2-0 | Gray Hughes |
| | | 4 | 23.01.93 | **Derby County** (D1) | H | L | 1-5 | Telfer |
| 1993-94 | (D1) | 3 | 08.01.94 | **Southend Utd** (D1) | H | W | 1-0 | Telfer |
| | | 4 | 29.01.94 | **Newcastle Utd** (PL) | A | D | 1-1 | Thorpe |
| | | 4r | 09.02.94 | **Newcastle Utd** | H | W | 2-0 | Hartson, Oakes |
| | | 5 | 20.02.94 | **Cardiff City** (D2) | A | W | 2-1 | Oakes, Preece |
| | | 6 | 14.03.94 | **West Ham Utd** (PL) | A | D | 0-0 | |
| | | 6r | 23.03.94 | **West Ham Utd** | H | W | 3-2 | Oakes 3 |
| | | SF | 09.04.94 | **Chelsea** (PL) | | L | 0-2 | |
| | | | | *played at Wembley Stadium* | | | | |
| 1994-95 | (D1) | 3 | 07.01.95 | **Bristol Rovers** (D2) | H | D | 1-1 | Hartson |
| | | 3r | 18.01.95 | **Bristol Rovers** | A | W | 1-0 | Marshall |
| | | 4 | 28.01.95 | **Southampton** (PL) | H | D | 1-1 | Biggins |
| | | 4r | 08.02.95 | **Southampton** | A | L | 0-6 | |
| 1995-96 | (D1) | 3 | 06.01.96 | **Grimsby Town** (D1) | A | L | 1-7 | Marshall |
| 1996-97 | (D2) | 1 | 16.11.96 | **Torquay Utd** (D3) | A | W | 1-0 | Hughes |
| | | 2 | 07.12.96 | **Borehamwood** (IL) | H | W | 2-1 | Marshall 2 |
| | | 3 | 21.01.97 | **Bolton Wanderers** (D1) | H | D | 1-1 | Johnson |
| | | 3r | 25.01.97 | **Bolton Wanderers** | A | L | 2-6 | Marshall, Thorpe |
| 1997-98 | (D2) | 1 | 15.11.97 | **Torquay Utd** (D3) | H | L | 0-1 | |
| 1998-99 | (D2) | 1 | 15.11.98 | **Borehamwood** (IL) | A | W | 3-2 | Gray 2, Davis |
| | | 2 | 05.12.98 | **Hull City** (D3) | H | L | 1-2 | Davis |
| 1999-00 | (D2) | 1 | 30.10.99 | **Kingstonian** (Conf) | H | W | 4-2 | Gray, George, Spring, Taylor |
| | | 2 | 19.11.99 | **Lincoln City** (D3) | H | D | 2-2 | Doherty 2 |
| | | 2r | 30.11.99 | **Lincoln City** | A | W | 1-0 | Douglas |
| | | 3 | 11.12.99 | **Fulham** (D1) | A | D | 2-2 | George, Spring |
| | | 3r | 21.12.99 | **Fulham** | H | L | 0-3 | |
| 2000-01 | (D2) | 1 | 17.11.00 | **Rushden & D** (Conf) | H | W | 1-0 | George |
| | | 2 | 09.12.00 | **Darlington** (D3) | A | D | 0-0 | |
| | | 2r | 19.12.00 | **Darlington** | H | W | 2-0 | Nogan, McLaren |
| | | 3 | 06.01.01 | **QPR** (D1) | H | D | 3-3 | Fotiadis, George, Douglas |
| | | 3r | 17.01.01 | **QPR** | A | L | 1-2aet | Mansell |

| | | | | | | | | | |
|---|---|---|---|---|---|---|---|---|---|
| 2001-02 | (D3) | 1 | 17.11.01 | **Southend Utd** (D3) | A | L | 2-3 | Forbes, Brkovic |
| 2002-03 | (D2) | 1 | 16.11.02 | **Guiseley** (NPL) | H | W | 4-0 | Spring, Thorpe, Brkovic 2 |
| | | 2 | 07.12.02 | **Wigan Athletic** (D2) | A | L | 0-3 | |

# LUTON WANDERERS

*Formed 1880. First entered FA Cup 1884-85. Played at Dallow Lane, near the Cricketer's Arms pub. Merged with Excelsior FC to form Luton Town in 1885 although some members kept the club going in their own right for another few seasons.*

| | | | | | | | | | |
|---|---|---|---|---|---|---|---|---|---|
| 1884-85 | | 1 | 08.11.84 | **Old Etonians** | H | L | 1-3 | Ellingham |
| 1885-86 | | 1 | 31.10.85 | **Chesham** | H | W | 3-2 | Ellingham, G Smith, AN Other |
| | | 2 | 21.11.85 | **Old Wykehamists** | A | L | 0-10 | |
| 1886-87 | | 1 | 23.10.86 | **Swifts** | A | L | 0-13 | |

# LYNDHURST FC

*Formed 1883. Entered FA Cup 1886-87 – 1889-90. Played at Denmark Hill, south London and changed at a pub called The Fox Under The Hill. Surrey Senior Cup winners 1888.*

| | | | | | | | | |
|---|---|---|---|---|---|---|---|---|
| 1886-87 | | 1 | 30.10.86 | **Chesham Generals** | A | L | 2-4 | |
| 1887-88 | | 1 | 15.10.87 | **Crusaders** | A | L | 0-9 | |

# LYTHAM FC

*Formed 1880. Entered FA Cup: 1922-23 – 1984-85. The club based in Lytham St Annes, the Lancashire coastal resort that for many years was the headquarters of the Football League, had very little success in the FA Cup and this match was their only appearance in the Competition Proper.*

| | | | | | | | | |
|---|---|---|---|---|---|---|---|---|
| 1925-26 | (LC) | 1 | 28.11.25 | **Oldham Athletic** (D2) | A | L | 1-10 | Leeming |

# MACCLESFIELD TOWN

*Formed 1874. First entered FA Cup: 1882-83. FA Trophy winners: 1970 (first winners); 1996. FA Trophy runners-up: 1989. Record FA Cup victory (In Competition proper): 9-0 v Hartford St Johns, 1st round, 08.11.1884; Record FA Cup defeat: 1-8 v Davenham, 2nd round, 21.11.1885; 0-7 v Walsall, 2nd round, 06.12.1997; 0-7 v Coventry City, 3rd round, 02.01.1999. FA Cup best performance: 3rd round (5 times): 1967-68; 1987-88; 1998-99; 2001-02; 2002-03. League clubs beaten as a Non-League club: Stockport County, Carlisle United, Rotherham United, Chesterfield, Hartlepool United.*

| | | | | | | | | |
|---|---|---|---|---|---|---|---|---|
| 1882-83 | | 1 | 04.11.82 | **Lockwood Bros** | A | L | 3-4 | Goldthorpe, Sadler 2 |
| 1883-84 | | 1 | 10.11.83 | **Davenham** | A | L | 0-2 | |
| 1884-85 | | 1 | 08.11.84 | **Hartford St Johns** | H | W | 9-0 | |
| | | 2 | 06.12.84 | **Leek** | H | L | 1-5 | |
| 1885-86 | | 1 | 31.10.85 | **Northwich V** | H | W | 4-1 | |
| | | 2 | 21.11.85 | **Davenham** | A | L | 1-8 | |
| 1886-87 | | 1 | 30.10.86 | **Goldenhill** | A | L | 2-4 | |
| | | | | *FA ordered replay after protest* | | | | |
| | | 1r | 13.11.86 | **Goldenhill** | H | L | 2-3 | |
| 1887-88 | | 1 | 15.10.87 | **Shrewsbury Town** | A | L | 1-3 | |
| 1960-61 | (CC) | 1 | 05.11.60 | **Southport** (D4) | A | L | 2-7 | |
| 1964-65 | (CC) | 1 | 14.11.64 | **Wrexham** (D4) | H | L | 1-2 | |
| 1967-68 | (CC) | 1 | 09.12.67 | **Stockport County** (D3) | A | D | 1-1 | Calder |
| | | 1r | 13.12.67 | **Stockport County** | H | W | 2-1 | Taberner, Fidler (p) |
| | | 2 | 06.01.68 | **Spennymoor Utd** (NL) | H | W | 2-0 | |
| | | 3 | 27.01.68 | **Fulham** (D1) | A | L | 2-4 | Taberner, Fidler |
| 1968-69 | (CC) | 1 | 16.11.68 | **Lincoln City** (D4) | H | L | 1-3 | Clay (p) |
| 1969-70 | (NPL) | 1 | 15.11.69 | **Scunthorpe Utd** (D4) | H | D | 1-1 | Lyon |
| | | 1r | 18.11.69 | **Scunthorpe Utd** | A | L | 2-4 | Young, Sievewright |
| 1970-71 | (NPL) | 1 | 21.11.70 | **Bradford City** (D3) | A | L | 2-3 | Fidler, Lyon |
| 1975-76 | (NPL) | 1 | 22.11.75 | **Sheffield Wed** (D3) | A | L | 1-3 | Eccleshare |
| 1982-83 | (NPL) | 1 | 20.11.82 | **Worcester City** (APL) | H | L | 1-5 | Long |
| 1983-84 | (NPL) | 1 | 19.11.83 | **York City** (D4) | H | D | 0-0 | |
| | | 1r | 22.11.83 | **York City** | A | L | 0-2 | |
| 1984-85 | (NPL) | 1 | 17.11.84 | **Port Vale** (D4) | H | L | 1-2 | White (p) |
| 1985-86 | (NPL) | 1 | 16.11.85 | **Hartlepool Utd** (D4) | H | L | 1-2 | Askey |
| 1987-88 | (Conf) | 1 | 14.11.87 | **Carlisle Utd** (D4) | H | W | 4-2 | Hardman, Askey, Tobin, Burr |
| | | 2 | 06.12.87 | **Rotherham Utd** (D3) | H | W | 4-0 | Burr 3, Grant |
| | | 3 | 10.01.88 | **Port Vale** (D3) | A | L | 0-1 | |
| 1989-90 | (Conf) | 1 | 18.11.89 | **Chester City** (D3) | H | D | 1-1 | Burr |
| | | 1r | 21.11.89 | **Chester City** | A | L | 2-3 | Burr 2 |

| | | | | | | | | |
|---|---|---|---|---|---|---|---|---|
| 1992-93 | (Conf) | 1 | 14.11.92 | **Chesterfield** (D3) | H | D | 0-0 | |
| | | 1r | 25.11.92 | **Chesterfield** | A | D | 2-2aet | Mitchell 2 |
| | | | | *Macclesfield Town won 3-2 on penalties* | | | | |
| | | 2 | 05.12.92 | **Stockport County** (D2) | H | L | 0-2 | |
| 1993-94 | (Conf) | 1 | 13.11.93 | **Hartlepool Utd** (D2) | H | W | 2-0 | Sorwel, MacDonald |
| | | 2 | 04.12.93 | **Crewe Alexandra** (D3) | A | L | 1-2 | Askey |
| 1996-97 | (Conf) | 1 | 16.11.96 | **Rochdale** (D3) | H | L | 0-2 | |
| 1997-98 | (D3) | 1 | 15.11.97 | **Hartlepool Utd** (D3) | A | W | 4-2 | Wood 2, Whittaker 2 |
| | | 2 | 06.12.97 | **Walsall** (D2) | H | L | 0-7 | |
| 1998-99 | (D2) | 1 | 14.11.98 | **Slough Town** (IL) | H | D | 2-2 | Tomlinson, Sodje |
| | | 1r | 24.11.98 | **Slough Town** | A | D | 1-1aet | Sedgemore |
| | | | | *Macclesfield Town won 9-8 on penalties* | | | | |
| | | 2 | 05.12.98 | **Cambridge Utd** (D3) | H | W | 4-1 | Askey, Tomlinson 3 |
| | | 3 | 02.01.99 | **Coventry City** (PL) | A | L | 0-7 | |
| 1999-00 | (D3) | 1 | 30.10.99 | **Hull City** (D3) | H | D | 0-0 | |
| | | 1r | 09.11.99 | **Hull City** | A | L | 0-4 | |
| 2000-01 | (D3) | 1 | 18.11.00 | **Oxford Utd** (D2) | H | L | 0-1 | |
| 2001-02 | (D3) | 1 | 17.11.01 | **Forest Green R** (Conf) | H | D | 2-2 | Lambert 2 |
| | | 1r | 28.11.01 | **Forest Green R** | A | D | 1-1aet | Keen |
| | | | | *Macclesfield Town won 11-10 on penalties* | | | | |
| | | 2 | 08.12.01 | **Swansea City** (D3) | H | W | 4-1 | Byrne 2, Glover 2 |
| | | 3 | 06.01.02 | **West Ham Utd** (PL) | H | L | 0-3 | |
| 2002-03 | (D3) | 1 | 16.11.02 | **Hull City** (D3) | A | W | 3-0 | Tipton, Lightbourne, Whittaker |
| | | 2 | 07.12.02 | **Vauxhall M (EP)** (NPL) | H | W | 2-0 | Lightbourne, Tipton |
| | | 3 | 04.01.03 | **Watford** (D1) | H | L | 0-2 | |

# MAIDENHEAD

*Formed 1869. One of the 15 original entrants in 1871-72, their match against Marlow on November 11, 1871 was on the first-ever day of competition. Have taken part every season, apart from 1876-77. Reached the last four of the FA Cup in 1873 – although under the strange rules of that competition, it was deemed to be the fourth round, and not the semi-finals! Did reach the quarter-finals in 1874, 1875 and 1876. Members of the Isthmian League.*

| | | | | | | | |
|---|---|---|---|---|---|---|---|
| 1871-72 | 1 | 11.11.71 | **Marlow** | H | W | 2-0 | Young 2 |
| | 2 | 16.12.71 | **Crystal Palace (1861)** | A | L | 0-3 | |
| 1872-73 | 1 | 26.10.72 | **Marlow** | H | W | 1-0 | Carter |
| | 2 | 23.11.72 | **1st Surrey Rifles** | H | W | 3-0 | Collings, Goulden, Hebbes |
| | 3 | 21.12.72 | **Windsor Home Park** | A | W | 1-0 | Hebbes |
| | 4 | 03.02.73 | **Oxford University** | A | L | 0-4 | |
| 1873-74 | 1 | | Civil Service | | | - | |
| | | | *Civil Service scratched. Maidenhead walkover.* | | | | |
| | 2 | 22.11.73 | **High Wycombe** | H | W | 1-0 | W Wild |
| | 3 | 10.12.73 | **Royal Engineers** | A | L | 0-7 | |
| 1874-75 | 1 | 14.11.74 | **Hitchin Town** | A | W | 1-0 | Nicholls |
| | 2 | 05.12.74 | **Reigate Priory** | H | W | 2-1 | Burnham 2 |
| | 3 | 23.01.75 | **Old Etonians** | A | L | 0-1 | |
| 1875-76 | 1 | 23.10.75 | **Ramblers** | H | W | 2-0 | Goulden, Price |
| | 2 | 14.11.75 | **Old Etonians** | A | L | 0-8 | |
| 1877-78 | 1 | 27.10.77 | **Reading Hornets** | H | W | 10-0 | F Price, others 9 |
| | 2 | 08.12.77 | **Cambridge University** | A | L | 2-4aet | Mackie 2 |
| 1878-79 | 1 | 19.10.78 | **Barnes** | A | D | 1-1 | Tilley |
| | 1r | 09.11.78 | **Barnes** | H | L | 0-4 | |
| 1879-80 | 1 | 25.10.79 | **Birmingham Calthorpe** | H | W | 3-1 | Bassett, Blackwell, Goldsmith |
| | 2 | 29.11.79 | **Henley FC** | A | W | 3-1 | Lovegrove 2, Harris |
| | 3 | | bye | | | | |
| | 4 | 14.02.80 | **Oxford University** | A | L | 0-1 | |
| 1880-81 | 1 | 13.11.80 | **Old Harrovians** | H | D | 0-0 | |
| | 1r | 20.11.80 | **Old Harrovians** | A | W | 1-0 | Goodchild |
| | 2 | 11.12.80 | **Grey Friars** | A | L | 0-1 | |
| 1881-82 | 1 | 16.10.81 | **Henley FC** | A | W | 2-0 | |
| | 2 | 03.12.81 | **Acton** | H | W | 2-1aet | Blackwell, Green |
| | 3 | | bye | | | | |
| | 4 | 14.01.82 | **Old Etonians** | A | L | 3-6 | Blackwell 2, Bailey |

| | | | | | | | | |
|---|---|---|---|---|---|---|---|---|
| 1882-83 | | 1 | 04.11.82 | **Old Westminsters** | A | L | 0-2 | |
| 1883-84 | | 1 | 10.11.83 | **West End** | H | L | 0-1 | |
| 1884-85 | | 1 | 08.11.84 | **Old Wykehamists** | H | L | 0-3 | |
| 1885-86 | | 1 | 31.10.85 | **Brentwood** | A | L | 0-3 | |
| 1886-87 | | 1 | 30.10.86 | **South Reading** | A | W | 2-0 | |
| | | 2 | 20.11.86 | **Dulwich** | H | L | 2-3 | |
| 1887-88 | | 1 | 15.10.87 | **Swifts** | A | L | 1-3 | |
| 1960-61 | (CRN) | 1 | 05.11.60 | **Colchester Utd** (D3) | A | L | 0-5 | |
| 1962-63 | (CRN) | 1 | 03.11.62 | **Wycombe W** (IL) | H | L | 0-3 | |
| 1963-64 | (AL) | 1 | 16.11.63 | **Bath City** (SL) | H | L | 0-2 | |
| 1971-72 | (IL) | 1 | 20.11.71 | **Enfield** (IL) | A | L | 0-2 | |

# MAIDSTONE UNITED

*Formed 1897. Entered FA Cup: 1897-98 – 1992-93. Members of the Football League: 1989-1992. Resigned from the Football League and went into liquidation August 1992. Reformed later that year and re-entered junior level football. Because they had already entered that season's competition they were still included in the draw for the First Round the following November, resulting in a bye for Swansea City. League clubs beaten as a Non-League club: Exeter City, Gillingham, Cambridge United. Members of the Kent League.*

| | | | | | | | | |
|---|---|---|---|---|---|---|---|---|
| 1974-75 | (SL) | 1 | 23.11.74 | **Nuneaton B** (SL) | A | D | 2-2 | Morton, McVeigh |
| | | 1r | 26.11.74 | **Nuneaton B** | H | W | 2-0 | Basey, Tough |
| | | 2 | 14.12.74 | **Swindon Town** (D3) | A | L | 1-3 | McLaughlin og |
| 1978-79 | (SL) | 1 | 25.11.78 | **Wycombe W** (IL) | H | W | 1-0 | Aitken |
| | | 2 | 16.12.78 | **Exeter City** (D3) | H | W | 1-0 | Hill |
| | | 3 | 09.01.79 | **Charlton Athletic** (D2) | A | D | 1-1 | Coupland |
| | | 3r | 15.01.79 | **Charlton Athletic** | H | L | 1-2 | Coupland |
| 1980-81 | (APL) | 1 | 22.11.80 | **Kettering Town** (APL) | A | D | 1-1 | Ovard |
| | | 1r | 26.11.80 | **Kettering Town** | H | D | 0-0aet | |
| | | 1 2r | 01.12.80 | **Kettering Town** | H | W | 3-1 | Woon 2, Newson (p) |
| | | 2 | 13.12.80 | **Gillingham** (D3) | A | D | 0-0 | |
| | | 2r | 16.12.80 | **Gillingham** | H | D | 0-0aet | |
| | | 2 2r | 22.12.80 | **Gillingham** | A | W | 2-0 | Newson, Ovard |
| | | 3 | 03.01.81 | **Exeter City** (D3) | H | L | 2-4 | Woon, Ovard |
| 1982-83 | (APL) | 1 | 20.11.82 | **Weymouth** (APL) | A | L | 3-4 | Hil, Bartley 2 |
| 1983-84 | (APL) | 1 | 19.11.83 | **Exeter City** (D3) | A | D | 1-1 | Newson |
| | | 1r | 23.11.83 | **Exeter City** | H | W | 2-1 | Lazarus, Dingwall |
| | | 2 | 10.12.83 | **Worcester City** (APL) | H | W | 3-2 | Moore, Bartley, Donn |
| | | 3 | 07.01.84 | **Darlington** (D4) | A | L | 1-4 | Lazarus |
| 1985-86 | (APL) | 1 | 16.11.85 | **Fareham Town** (SL) | A | W | 3-0 | Cugley 2, Barnes |
| | | 2 | 07.12.85 | **Plymouth Argyle** (D3) | A | L | 0-3 | |
| 1986-87 | (Conf) | 1 | 15.11.86 | **Welling Utd** (Conf) | A | D | 1-1 | Glover |
| | | 1r | 24.11.86 | **Welling Utd** | H | W | 4-1 | Torrance, Butler, Hatter, Galloway |
| | | 2 | 07.12.86 | **Cambridge Utd** (D4) | H | W | 1-0 | Galloway |
| | | 3 | 10.01.87 | **Watford** (D1) | A | L | 1-3 | Galloway |
| 1987-88 | (Conf) | 1 | 14.11.87 | **Dagenham** (Conf) | A | W | 2-0 | Butler (p), Harrison |
| | | 2 | 05.12.87 | **Kidderminster H** (Conf) | H | D | 1-1 | Rogers |
| | | 2r | 07.12.87 | **Kidderminster H** | A | D | 2-2aet | Doherty, Pamphlett |
| | | 2 2r | 14.12.87 | **Kidderminster H** | A | D | 0-0aet | |
| | | 2 3r | 16.12.87 | **Kidderminster H** | H | W | 2-1 | Butler 2 (1p) |
| | | 3 | 09.01.88 | **Sheffield Utd** (D2) | A | L | 0-1 | |
| 1988-89 | (Conf) | 1 | 19.11.88 | **Newport County** (Conf) | A | W | 2-1 | Hill, Gall |
| | | 2 | 10.12.88 | **Reading** (D3) | A | D | 1-1 | Sorrell |
| | | 2r | 14.12.88 | **Reading** | H | L | 1-2 | Gall |
| 1989-90 | (D4) | 1 | 18.11.89 | **Yeovil Town** (Conf) | H | W | 2-1 | Gall, Barton |
| | | 2 | 09.12.89 | **Exeter City** (D4) | H | D | 1-1 | Elsey |
| | | 2r | 13.12.89 | **Exeter City** | A | L | 2-3 | Butler, Gall |
| 1990-91 | (D4) | 1 | 17.11.90 | **Torquay Utd** (D4) | H | W | 4-1 | Butler 2, Osborne, Gall |
| | | 2 | 08.12.90 | **Aldershot** (D4) | A | L | 1-2 | Gall |
| 1991-92 | (D4) | 1 | 16.11.91 | **Sutton Utd** (IL) | H | W | 1-0 | Thompson |
| | | 2 | 07.12.91 | **Kettering Town** (Conf) | H | L | 1-2 | Henry |

# MANCHESTER CENTRAL

*Entered FA Cup: 1929-30 – 1931-32. Played at Belle Vue Stadium.*

| | | | | | | | | |
|---|---|---|---|---|---|---|---|---|
| 1929-30 | (LC) | 1 | 30.11.29 | **Mansfield Town** (ML) | A | W | 2-0 | Roberts, Pelan |
| | | 2 | 14.12.29 | **Wrexham** (3N) | H | L | 0-1 | |
| 1931-32 | (CC) | 1 | 28.11.31 | **Lincoln City** (3N) | H | L | 0-3 | |

# MANCHESTER CITY

*Formed 1887 as Ardwick FC. Manchester City 1894. FA Cup winners: 1904, 1934, 1956, 1969; Runners-up: 1926, 1933, 1955, 1981; FA Cup record win: (as Ardwick) 12-0 v Liverpool Stanley, 1st qualifying round, 04.10.1890. In Competition Proper: 10-1 v Swindon Town, 4th round, 29.01.1930; 9-0 v Gateshead AFC, 3rd round replay, 18.01.1933. FA Cup record defeat: 0-6 v Preston NE, 1st round, 30.01.1897; 2-8 v Bradford Park Avenue, 4th round, 2nd leg, 30.10.1946.*

**as Ardwick**

| | | | | | | | | |
|---|---|---|---|---|---|---|---|---|
| 1890-91 | | | | 1q Liverpool Stanley (H) 12-0; 2q Halliwell – scratched. Halliwell walkover | | | | |
| 1891-92 | (FAll) | | | 1q Newton Heath (A) 1-5 | | | | |
| 1892-93 | (D2) | | | 1q Fleetwood (A) 1-1; 1qr Fleetwood (H) 0-2 | | | | |
| 1893-94 | (D2) | | | 1q West Manchester (A) 0-3 | | | | |

**as Manchester City**

| | | | | | | | | |
|---|---|---|---|---|---|---|---|---|
| 1894-95 | (D2) | | | did not enter | | | | |
| 1896-97 | (D2) | 1 | 30.01.97 | **Preston North End** (D1) | | L | 0-6 | |
| 1897-98 | (D2) | 1 | 29.01.98 | **Wigan County** (LL) | | W | 1-0 | Gillespie |
| | | 2 | 12.02.98 | **Bolton Wanderers** (D1) | A | L | 0-1 | |
| 1898-99 | (D2) | 1 | 28.01.99 | **Small Heath** (D2) | A | L | 2-3 | Meredith, Gillespie |
| 1899-00 | (D1) | 1 | 27.01.00 | **Aston Villa** (D1) | H | D | 1-1 | Ross |
| | | 1r | 31.01.00 | **Aston Villa** | A | L | 0-3 | |
| 1900-01 | (D1) | 1 | 26.01.01 | **WBA** (D1) | A | L | 0-1 | |
| 1901-02 | (D1) | 1 | 25.01.02 | **Preston North End** (D2) | A | - | 1-1ab | Henderson |
| | | | | *abandoned in extra time* | | | | |
| | | 1 | 29.01.02 | **Preston North End** | H | D | 0-0aet | |
| | | 1r | 03.02.02 | **Preston North End** | A | W | 4-2aet | Smith 3, Morgan |
| | | 2 | 08.02.02 | **Nottingham Forest** (D1) | H | L | 0-2 | |
| 1902-03 | (D2) | 1 | 07.02.03 | **Preston North End** (D2) | A | L | 1-3 | Turnbull |
| 1903-04 | (D1) | 1 | 06.02.04 | **Sunderland** (D1) | H | W | 3-2 | Turnbull 2, Gillespie |
| | | 2 | 20.02.04 | **Woolwich Arsenal** (D2) | A | W | 2-0 | Turnbull, Booth |
| | | 3 | 05.03.04 | **Middlesbrough** (D1) | H | D | 0-0 | |
| | | 3r | 09.03.04 | **Middlesbrough** | A | W | 3-1 | Livingstone, Gillespie, Turnbull |
| | | SF | 19.03.04 | **Sheffield Wed** (D1) | | W | 3-0 | Meredith, Gillespie, Turnbull |
| | | | | *played at Goodison Park* | | | | |
| | | F | 23.04.04 | **Bolton Wanderers** (D2) | | W | 1-0 | Meredith |
| | | | | *played at Crystal Palace* | | | | |
| 1904-05 | (D1) | 1 | 04.02.05 | **Lincoln City** (D2) | A | W | 2-1 | Meredith, Turnbull |
| | | 2 | 18.02.05 | **Bolton Wanderers** (D2) | H | L | 1-2 | Gillespie |
| 1905-06 | (D1) | 1 | 13.01.06 | **Sheffield Utd** (D1) | A | L | 1-4 | Bannister |
| 1906-07 | (D1) | 1 | 12.01.07 | **Blackburn Rovers** (D1) | A | D | 2-2 | Dorsett, Thornley |
| | | 1r | 16.01.07 | **Blackburn Rovers** | H | L | 0-1 | |
| 1907-08 | (D1) | 1 | 11.01.08 | **Glossop North End** (D2) | A | D | 0-0 | |
| | | 1r | 15.01.08 | **Glossop North End** | H | W | 6-0 | Buchan, Wood, Dorsett, Grieve, Jones, Conlin |
| | | 2 | 01.02.08 | **New Brompton** (SL) | H | D | 1-1 | Jones |
| | | 2r | 05.02.08 | **New Brompton** | A | W | 2-1 | Buchan, Wood |
| | | 3 | 22.02.08 | **Fulham** (D2) | H | D | 1-1 | Blair |
| | | 3r | 26.02.08 | **Fulham** | A | L | 1-3 | Wood |
| 1908-09 | (D2) | 1 | 16.01.09 | **Tottenham Hotspur** (D2) | H | L | 3-4 | Holford 3 |
| 1909-10 | (D2) | 1 | 15.01.10 | **Workington** (NEL) | A | W | 2-1 | Wynn 2 |
| | | 2 | 05.02.10 | **Southampton** (SL) | A | W | 5-0 | Dorsett, Stewart, Jones, Conlin, Holford |
| | | 3 | 19.02.10 | **Aston Villa** (D1) | A | W | 2-1 | Stewart, Jones |
| | | 4 | 05.03.10 | **Swindon Town** (SL) | A | L | 0-2 | |
| 1910-11 | (D2) | 1 | 14.01.11 | **Stoke** (BDL) | A | W | 2-1 | J Smith, Jones |
| | | 2 | 04.02.11 | **Wolverhampton W** (D2) | A | L | 0-1 | |
| 1911-12 | (D1) | 1 | 13.01.12 | **Preston North End** (D1) | A | W | 1-0 | Wynn |

| | | | | | | | |
|---|---|---|---|---|---|---|---|
| | 2 | 03.02.12 | **Oldham Athletic** (D1) | H | L | 0-1 | |
| 1912-13 (D1) | 1 | 11.01.13 | **Birmingham** (D2) | H | W | 4-0 | Wynn 2, Hoad, Taylor |
| | 2 | 01.02.13 | **Sunderland** (D1) | H | - | 0-2ab | |
| | | | *abandoned after 60 minutes due to dangerous overcrowding in the ground* | | | | |
| | 2 | 05.02.13 | **Sunderland** | A | L | 0-2 | |
| 1913-14 (D1) | 1 | 10.01.14 | **Fulham** (D2) | H | W | 3-0 | Hindmarsh, Howard |
| | 2 | 31.01.14 | **Tottenham Hotspur** (D1) | H | W | 2-1 | Howard, Browell |
| | 3 | 21.02.14 | **Blackburn Rovers** (D1) | A | W | 2-1 | Howard, Cartwright |
| | 4 | 07.03.14 | **Sheffield Utd** (D1) | H | D | 0-0 | |
| | 4r | 12.03.14 | **Sheffield Utd** | A | D | 0-0 | |
| | 4 2r | 16.03.14 | **Sheffield Utd** | | L | 0-1 | |
| | | | *played at Villa Park* | | | | |
| 1914-15 (D1) | 1 | 09.01.15 | **Preston North End** (D2) | A | D | 0-0 | |
| | 1r | 16.01.15 | **Preston North End** | H | W | 3-0 | Barnes 2, Hughes |
| | 2 | 30.01.15 | **Aston Villa** (D1) | H | W | 1-0 | Cartwright |
| | 3 | 20.02.15 | **Chelsea** (D1) | H | L | 0-1 | |
| 1919-20 (D1) | 1 | 10.01.20 | **Clapton Orient** (D2) | H | W | 4-1 | Goodwin 2, Barnes, Murphy |
| | 2 | 31.01.20 | **Leicester City** (D2) | A | L | 0-3 | |
| 1920-21 (D1) | 1 | 08.01.21 | **Crystal Palace** (D3) | A | L | 0-2 | |
| 1921-22 (D1) | 1 | 07.01.22 | **Darlington** (3N) | H | W | 3-1 | Browell 3 |
| | 2 | 28.01.22 | **Bolton Wanderers** (D1) | A | W | 3-1 | Browell 2, Kelly |
| | 3 | 18.02.22 | **Tottenham Hotspur** (D1) | A | L | 1-2 | Kelly |
| 1922-23 (D1) | 1 | 13.01.23 | **Charlton Athletic** (3S) | H | L | 1-2 | Johnson |
| 1923-24 (D1) | 1 | 12.01.24 | **Nottingham Forest** (D1) | H | W | 2-0 | Roberts, Barnes |
| | 2 | 02.02.24 | **Halifax Town** (3N) | H | D | 2-2 | Hamill, Roberts |
| | 2r | 06.02.24 | **Halifax Town** | H | D | 0-0aet | |
| | 2 2r | 11.02.24 | **Halifax Town** | | W | 3-0 | Roberts 2, Browell |
| | | | *played at Old Trafford* | | | | |
| | 3 | 23.02.24 | **Brighton** (3S) | A | W | 5-1 | Browell 2, Meredith, Barnes, Sharp |
| | 4 | 08.03.24 | **Cardiff City** (D1) | H | D | 0-0 | |
| | 4r | 12.03.24 | **Cardiff City** | A | W | 1-0aet | Browell |
| | SF | 29.03.24 | **Newcastle Utd** (D1) | | L | 0-2 | |
| | | | *played at St Andrews* | | | | |
| 1924-25 (D1) | 1 | 10.01.25 | **Preston North End** (D1) | A | L | 1-4 | Roberts |
| 1925-26 (D1) | 3 | 09.01.26 | **Corinthians** | A | D | 3-3 | Cookson, Roberts, Hicks |
| | 3r | 13.01.26 | **Corinthians** | H | W | 4-0 | Austin 2, Johnson, Hicks |
| | 4 | 30.01.26 | **Huddersfield Town** (D1) | H | W | 4-0 | Hicks 2, Browell, Roberts |
| | 5 | 20.02.26 | **Crystal Palace** (D3) | H | W | 11-4 | Roberts 5, Browell 3, Austin, Johnson, Hicks |
| | 6 | 06.03.26 | **Clapton Orient** (D2) | A | W | 6-1 | Johnson 3, Hicks, Roberts, Browell |
| | SF | 27.03.26 | **Manchester Utd** (D1) | | W | 3-0 | Browell 2, Roberts |
| | | | *played at Bramall Lane* | | | | |
| | F | 24.04.26 | **Bolton Wanderers** (D1) | | L | 0-1 | |
| | | | *played at Wembley Stadium* | | | | |
| 1926-27 (D2) | 3 | 08.01.27 | **Birmingham** (D1) | A | L | 1-4 | Hicks |
| 1927-28 (D2) | 3 | 14.01.28 | **Leeds Utd** (D2) | H | W | 1-0 | Johnson |
| | 4 | 28.01.28 | **Sunderland** (D1) | A | W | 2-1 | Broadhurst, Hicks |
| | 5 | 18.02.28 | **Stoke City** (D2) | H | L | 0-1 | |
| 1928-29 (D1) | 3 | 12.01.29 | **Birmingham** (D1) | A | L | 1-3 | Austin |
| 1929-30 (D1) | 3 | 11.01.30 | **Tottenham Hotspur** (D2) | A | D | 2-2 | Toseland, Cowan |
| | 3r | 15.01.30 | **Tottenham Hotspur** | H | W | 4-1 | Busby 2, Toseland, Marshall |
| | 4 | 25.01.30 | **Swindon Town** (3S) | A | D | 1-1 | Cowan |
| | 4r | 29.01.30 | **Swindon Town** | H | W | 10-1 | Marshall 5, Tait 3, Johnson, Brook |
| | 5 | 15.02.30 | **Hull City** (D2) | H | L | 1-2 | Toseland |
| 1930-31 (D1) | 3 | 10.01.31 | **Burnley** (D2) | A | L | 0-3 | |
| 1931-32 (D1) | 3 | 09.01.32 | **Millwall** (D2) | A | W | 3-2 | Halliday 2, Toseland |
| | 4 | 23.01.32 | **Brentford** (3S) | H | W | 6-1 | Tilson 3, Brook 2, Halliday |
| | 5 | 13.02.32 | **Derby County** (D1) | H | W | 3-0 | Marshall 2, Brook |
| | 6 | 27.02.32 | **Bury** (D2) | A | W | 4-3 | Toseland 2, Halliday, Cowan |
| | SF | 12.03.32 | **Arsenal** (D1) | | L | 0-1 | |
| | | | *played at Villa Park* | | | | |

| | | | | | | | | |
|---|---|---|---|---|---|---|---|---|
| 1932-33 | (D1) | 3 | 14.01.33 | **Gateshead AFC** (3N) | A | D | 1-1 | Toseland |
| | | 3r | 18.01.33 | **Gateshead AFC** | H | W | 9-0 | Tilson 3, Cowan 2, Busby, Barrass, McMullen, Brook |
| | | 4 | 28.01.33 | **Walsall** (3N) | H | W | 2-0 | Brook 2 |
| | | 5 | 18.02.33 | **Bolton Wanderers** (D1) | A | W | 4-2 | Brook 3, Tilson |
| | | 6 | 04.03.33 | **Burnley** (D2) | A | W | 1-0 | Tilson |
| | | SF | 18.03.33 | **Derby County** (D1) *played at Leeds Road, Huddersfield* | | W | 3-2 | Toseland, Tilson, McMullen |
| | | F | 29.04.33 | **Everton** (D1) *played at Wembley Stadium* | | L | 0-3 | |
| 1933-34 | (D1) | 3 | 13.01.34 | **Blackburn Rovers** (D1) | H | W | 3-1 | Toseland 2, Brook |
| | | 4 | 27.01.34 | **Hull City** (D2) | A | D | 2-2 | Herd, Brook |
| | | 4r | 31.01.34 | **Hull City** | H | W | 4-1 | Tilson 2, Toseland, Marshall |
| | | 5 | 17.02.34 | **Sheffield Wed** (D1) | A | D | 2-2 | Herd 2 |
| | | 5r | 21.02.34 | **Sheffield Wed** | H | W | 2-0 | Marshall, Tilson |
| | | 6 | 03.03.34 | **Stoke City** (D1) | H | W | 1-0 | Brook |
| | | SF | 17.03.34 | **Aston Villa** (D1) *played at Leeds Road, Huddersfield* | | W | 6-1 | Tilson 4, Herd, Toseland |
| | | F | 28.04.34 | **Portsmouth** (D1) *played at Wembley Stadium* | | W | 2-1 | Tilson 2 |
| 1934-35 | (D1) | 3 | 12.01.35 | **Tottenham Hotspur** (D1) | A | L | 0-1 | |
| 1935-36 | (D1) | 3 | 11.01.36 | **Portsmouth** (D1) | H | W | 3-1 | Brook 3 |
| | | 4 | 25.01.36 | **Luton Town** (3S) | H | W | 2-1 | Herd, McLeod |
| | | 5 | 15.02.36 | **Grimsby Town** (D1) | A | L | 2-3 | McLeod, Tilson |
| 1936-37 | (D1) | 3 | 16.01.37 | **Wrexham** (3N) | A | W | 3-1 | Herd, Tilson, Brook |
| | | 4 | 30.01.37 | **Accrington Stanley** (3N) | H | W | 2-0 | Tilson, Doherty |
| | | 5 | 20.02.37 | **Bolton Wanderers** (D1) | A | W | 5-0 | Herd 2, Doherty, Brook, Tilson |
| | | 6 | 06.03.37 | **Millwall** (3S) | A | L | 0-2 | |
| 1937-38 | (D1) | 3 | 08.01.38 | **Millwall** (3S) | A | D | 2-2 | Herd 2 |
| | | 3r | 12.01.38 | **Millwall** | H | W | 3-1 | Herd, Heale, Brook |
| | | 4 | 22.01.38 | **Bury** (D2) | H | W | 3-1 | Toseland 2, Whitfield og |
| | | 5 | 12.02.38 | **Luton Town** (D2) | A | W | 3-1 | Doherty, Heale, Nelson og |
| | | 6 | 06.03.38 | **Aston Villa** (D2) | A | L | 2-3 | Doherty, Allen og |
| 1938-39 | (D2) | 3 | 12.01.39 | **Norwich City** (D2) | A | W | 5-0 | Herd 2, Milsom, Doherty |
| | | 4 | 21.01.39 | **Sheffield Utd** (D2) | A | L | 0-2 | |
| 1945-46 | (D2) | 3 1L | 05.01.46 | **Barrow** (3N) | H | W | 6-2 | Herd 3, Constantine 3 |
| | | 3 2L | 10.01.46 | **Barrow** | A | D | 2-2 | Dunkley, Hart |
| | | 4 1L | 26.01.46 | **Bradford Park A** (D2) | A | W | 3-1 | Smith 2, Herd |
| | | 4 2L | 30.01.46 | **Bradford Park A** | H | L | 2-8 | Constantine, Smith |
| 1946-47 | (D2) | 3 | 11.01.47 | **Gateshead AFC** (3N) | H | W | 3-0 | Jackson, Capel, Westwood |
| | | 4 | 25.01.47 | **Bolton Wanderers** (D1) | A | D | 3-3 | Black 2, Capel |
| | | 4r | 29.01.47 | **Bolton Wanderers** | H | W | 1-0 | Westwood |
| | | 5 | 08.02.47 | **Birmingham City** (D2) | A | L | 0-5 | |
| 1947-48 | (D1) | 3 | 10.01.48 | **Barnsley** (D2) | H | W | 2-1 | Smith, Black |
| | | 4 | 24.01.48 | **Chelsea** (D1) | H | W | 2-0aet | Linacre, Smith |
| | | 5 | 07.02.48 | **Preston North End** (D1) | H | L | 0-1 | |
| 1948-49 | (D1) | 3 | 08.01.49 | **Everton** (D1) | A | L | 0-1 | |
| 1949-50 | (D1) | 3 | 07.01.50 | **Derby County** (D1) | H | L | 3-5 | Black 2, Clarke |
| 1950-51 | (D2) | 3 | 06.01.51 | **Birmingham City** (D2) | A | L | 0-2 | |
| 1951-52 | (D1) | 3 | 12.01.52 | **Wolverhampton W** (D1) | H | D | 2-2 | Meadows, Revie |
| | | 3r | 16.01.52 | **Wolverhampton W** | A | L | 1-4 | Clarke |
| 1952-53 | (D1) | 3 | 10.01.53 | **Swindon Town** (3S) | H | W | 7-0 | Hart 4, Williams, Cunliffe, Broadis |
| | | 4 | 31.01.53 | **Luton Town** (D2) | H | D | 1-1 | Broadis |
| | | 4r | 04.02.53 | **Luton Town** | A | L | 1-5 | Spurdle |
| 1953-54 | (D1) | 3 | 09.01.54 | **Bradford Park A** (3N) | A | W | 5-2 | McAdams 3, Revie, Clarke |
| | | 4 | 30.01.54 | **Tottenham Hotspur** (D1) | H | L | 0-1 | |
| 1954-55 | (D1) | 3 | 08.01.55 | **Derby County** (D2) | A | W | 3-1 | Barnes, Hayes, Revie |
| | | 4 | 29.01.55 | **Manchester Utd** (D1) | H | W | 2-0 | Hayes, Revie |
| | | 5 | 19.02.55 | **Luton Town** (D2) | A | W | 2-0 | Clarke 2 |
| | | 6 | 12.03.55 | **Birmingham City** (D2) | A | W | 1-0 | Hart |

| | | | | | | | | |
|---|---|---|---|---|---|---|---|---|
| | | SF | 26.03.55 | **Sunderland** (D1) | | W | 1-0 | Clarke |
| | | | | *played at Villa Park* | | | | |
| | | F | 07.05.55 | **Newcastle Utd** (D1) | | L | 1-3 | Johnstone |
| | | | | *played at Wembley Stadium* | | | | |
| 1955-56 | (D1) | 3 | 07.01.56 | **Blackpool** (D1) | H | - | 1-1ab | Dyson |
| | | | | *abandoned after 56 minutes – fog* | | | | |
| | | 3 | 11.01.56 | **Blackpool** | H | W | 2-1 | Johnstone, Dyson |
| | | 4 | 28.01.56 | **Southend Utd** (3S) | A | W | 1-0 | Hayes |
| | | 5 | 18.02.56 | **Liverpool** (D2) | H | D | 0-0 | |
| | | 5r | 22.02.56 | **Liverpool** | A | W | 2-1 | Hayes, Dyson |
| | | 6 | 03.03.56 | **Everton** (D1) | H | W | 2-1 | Hayes, Johnstone |
| | | SF | 17.03.56 | **Tottenham Hotspur** (D1) | | W | 1-0 | Johnstone |
| | | | | *played at Villa Park* | | | | |
| | | F | 05.05.56 | **Birmingham City** (D1) | | W | 3-1 | Johnstone, Hayes, Dyson |
| | | | | *played at Wembley Stadium* | | | | |
| 1956-57 | (D1) | 3 | 05.01.57 | **Newcastle Utd** (D1) | A | D | 1-1 | Johnstone |
| | | 3r | 09.01.57 | **Newcastle Utd** | H | L | 4-5aet | Stokoe og, Johnstone 2, Fagan |
| 1957-58 | (D1) | 3 | 04.01.58 | **WBA** (D1) | A | L | 1-5 | Hayes |
| 1958-59 | (D1) | 3 | 10.01.59 | **Grimsby Town** (D2) | A | D | 2-2 | Barlow, Hayes |
| | | 3r | 24.01.59 | **Grimsby Town** | H | L | 1-2 | Johnstone |
| 1959-60 | (D1) | 3 | 09.01.60 | **Southampton** (D3) | H | L | 1-5 | Barlow |
| 1960-61 | (D1) | 3 | 07.01.61 | **Cardiff City** (D1) | A | D | 1-1 | Harrington og |
| | | 3r | 11.01.61 | **Cardiff City** | H | D | 0-0aet | |
| | | 3 2r | 16.01.61 | **Cardiff City** | | W | 2-0aet | Law, Hayes |
| | | | | *played at Highbury* | | | | |
| | | 4 | 28.01.61 | **Luton Town** (D2) | A | - | 6-2ab | Law 6 |
| | | | | *abandoned after 69 minutes – waterlogged pitch* | | | | |
| | | 4 | 01.02.61 | **Luton Town** | A | L | 1-3 | Law |
| 1961-62 | (D1) | 3 | 06.01.62 | **Notts County** (D3) | A | W | 1-0 | Young |
| | | 4 | 27.01.62 | **Everton** (D1) | A | L | 0-2 | |
| 1962-63 | (D1) | 3 | 06.03.63 | **Walsall** (D2) | A | W | 1-0 | Harley |
| | | 4 | 13.03.63 | **Bury** (D2) | H | W | 1-0 | Harley |
| | | 5 | 16.03.63 | **Norwich City** (D2) | H | L | 1-2 | Oakes |
| 1963-64 | (D2) | 3 | 04.01.64 | **Swindon Town** (D2) | A | L | 1-2 | Oakes |
| 1964-65 | (D2) | 3 | 09.01.65 | **Shrewsbury Town** (D3) | H | D | 1-1 | Kevan |
| | | 3r | 13.01.65 | **Shrewsbury Town** | A | L | 1-3 | Gray |
| 1965-66 | (D2) | 3 | 22.01.66 | **Blackpool** (D1) | A | D | 1-1 | Crossan |
| | | 3r | 24.01.66 | **Blackpool** | H | W | 3-1 | Summerbee, Doyle, Crossan |
| | | 4 | 12.02.66 | **Grimsby Town** (D3) | H | W | 2-0 | Cockerill og, Summerbee |
| | | 5 | 05.03.66 | **Leicester City** (D1) | H | D | 2-2 | Young 2 |
| | | 5r | 09.03.66 | **Leicester City** | A | W | 1-0 | Young |
| | | 6 | 26.03.66 | **Everton** (D1) | H | D | 0-0 | |
| | | 6r | 29.03.66 | **Everton** | A | D | 0-0aet | |
| | | 6 2r | 05.04.66 | **Everton** | | L | 0-2 | |
| | | | | *played at Molineux* | | | | |
| 1966-67 | (D1) | 3 | 28.01.67 | **Leicester City** (D1) | H | W | 2-1 | Pardoe, Doyle Pardoe |
| | | 4 | 18.02.67 | **Cardiff City** (D2) | A | D | 1-1 | Coldrick og |
| | | 4r | 22.02.67 | **Cardiff City** | H | W | 3-1 | Bell, Young, Crossan |
| | | 5 | 11.03.67 | **Ipswich Town** (D2) | A | D | 1-1 | Young |
| | | 5r | 14.03.67 | **Ipswich Town** | H | W | 3-0 | Summerbee 2, McNeill og |
| | | 6 | 08.04.67 | **Leeds Utd** (D1) | A | L | 0-1 | |
| 1967-68 | (D1) | 3 | 27.01.68 | **Reading** (D3) | H | D | 0-0 | |
| | | 3r | 31.01.68 | **Reading** | A | W | 7-0 | Summerbee 3, Young, Coleman, Heslop, Bell |
| | | 4 | 17.02.68 | **Leicester City** (D1) | H | D | 0-0 | |
| | | 4r | 19.02.68 | **Leicester City** | A | L | 3-4 | Summerbee, Bell, Lee |
| 1968-69 | (D1) | 3 | 04.01.69 | **Luton Town** (D3) | H | W | 1-0 | Lee |
| | | 4 | 25.01.69 | **Newcastle Utd** (D1) | A | D | 0-0 | |
| | | 4r | 29.01.69 | **Newcastle Utd** | H | W | 2-0 | Owen, Young |
| | | 5 | 24.02.69 | **Blackburn Rovers** (D2) | A | W | 4-1 | Lee 2, Coleman 2 |
| | | 6 | 01.03.69 | **Tottenham Hotspur** (D1) | H | W | 1-0 | Lee |

| | | | | | | | | |
|---|---|---|---|---|---|---|---|---|
| | | SF | 22.03.69 | **Everton** (D1)<br>*played at Villa Park* | | W | 1-0 | Booth |
| | | F | 26.04.69 | **Leicester City** (D1)<br>*played at Wembley Stadium* | | W | 1-0 | Young |
| 1969-70 | (D1) | 3 | 03.01.70 | **Hull City** (D2) | A | W | 1-0 | Young |
| | | 4 | 24.01.70 | **Manchester Utd** (D1) | A | L | 0-3 | |
| 1970-71 | (D1) | 3 | 02.01.71 | **Wigan Athletic** (NPL) | H | W | 1-0 | Bell |
| | | 4 | 23.01.71 | **Chelsea** (D1) | A | W | 3-0 | Bell 2, Bowyer |
| | | 5 | 17.02.71 | **Arsenal** (D1) | H | L | 1-2 | Bell |
| 1971-72 | (D1) | 3 | 15.01.72 | **Middlesbrough** (D2) | H | D | 1-1 | Lee |
| | | 3r | 18.01.72 | **Middlesbrough** | A | L | 0-1 | |
| 1972-73 | (D1) | 3 | 13.01.73 | **Stoke City** (D1) | H | W | 3-2 | Summerbee, Bell, Marsh |
| | | 4 | 03.02.73 | **Liverpool** (D1) | A | D | 0-0 | |
| | | 4r | 07.02.73 | **Liverpool** | H | W | 2-0 | Bell, Booth |
| | | 5 | 24.02.73 | **Sunderland** (D2) | H | D | 2-2 | Towers, Montgomery og |
| | | 5r | 27.02.73 | **Sunderland** | A | L | 1-3 | Lee |
| 1973-74 | (D1) | 3 | 05.01.74 | **Oxford Utd** (D2) | A | W | 5-2 | Law 2, Summerbee 2, Marsh |
| | | 4 | 27.01.74 | **Nottingham Forest** (D2) | A | L | 1-4 | Carrodus |
| 1974-75 | (D1) | 3 | 04.01.75 | **Newcastle Utd** (D1) | H | L | 0-2 | |
| 1975-76 | (D1) | 3 | 03.01.76 | **Hartlepool** (D4) | H | W | 6-0 | Tueart 2, Booth 2, Hartford, Oakes |
| | | 4 | 28.01.76 | **Stoke City** (D1) | A | L | 0-1 | |
| 1976-77 | (D1) | 3 | 08.01.77 | **WBA** (D1) | H | D | 1-1 | Kidd |
| | | 3r | 11.01.77 | **WBA** | A | W | 1-0 | Royle |
| | | 4 | 29.01.77 | **Newcastle Utd** (D1) | A | W | 3-1 | D Craig og, Royle, Owen |
| | | 5 | 26.02.77 | **Leeds Utd** (D1) | A | L | 0-1 | |
| 1977-78 | (D1) | 3 | 07.01.78 | **Leeds Utd** | A | W | 2-1 | Barnes, Tueart |
| | | 4 | 31.01.78 | **Nottingham Forest** (D1) | A | L | 1-2 | Kidd |
| 1978-79 | (D1) | 3 | 15.01.79 | **Rotherham Utd** (D3) | H | D | 0-0 | |
| | | 3r | 17.01.79 | **Rotherham Utd** | A | W | 4-2 | Kidd 2, Barnes, Owen |
| | | 4 | 27.01.79 | **Shrewsbury Town** (D3) | A | L | 0-2 | |
| 1979-80 | (D1) | 3 | 05.01.80 | **Halifax Town** (D4) | A | L | 0-1 | |
| 1980-81 | (D1) | 3 | 03.01.81 | **Crystal Palace** (D1) | H | W | 4-0 | Reeves 2, Power, Boyer |
| | | 4 | 24.01.81 | **Norwich City** (D1) | H | W | 6-0 | McDonald, Reeves, Mackenzie, Power, Gow, Bennett |
| | | 5 | 14.02.81 | **Peterborough Utd** (D4) | A | W | 1-0 | Booth |
| | | 6 | 07.03.81 | **Everton** (D1) | A | D | 2-2 | Power, Gow |
| | | 6r | 11.03.81 | **Everton** | H | W | 3-1 | McDonald 2, Power |
| | | SF | 11.04.81 | **Ipswich Town** (D1)<br>*played at Villa Park* | | W | 1-0aet | Power |
| | | F | 09.05.81 | **Tottenham Hotspur** (D1)<br>*played at Wembley Stadium* | | D | 1-1aet | Hutchison |
| | | Fr | 14.05.81 | **Tottenham Hotspur**<br>*played at Wembley Stadium* | | L | 2-3 | Mackenzie, Reeves (p) |
| 1981-82 | (D1) | 3 | 02.01.82 | **Cardiff City** (D2) | H | W | 3-1 | Francis 2, McDonald |
| | | 4 | 23.01.82 | **Coventry City** (D1) | H | L | 1-3 | Bond |
| 1982-83 | (D1) | 3 | 08.01.83 | **Sunderland** (D1) | A | D | 0-0 | |
| | | 3r | 12.01.83 | **Sunderland** | H | W | 2-1 | Cross, Hartford |
| | | 4 | 29.01.83 | **Brighton** (D1) | A | L | 0-4 | |
| 1983-84 | (D2) | 3 | 07.01.84 | **Blackpool** (D4) | A | L | 1-2 | Hetzke og |
| 1984-85 | (D2) | 3 | 05.01.85 | **Coventry City** (D1) | A | L | 1-2 | Power |
| 1985-86 | (D1) | 3 | 04.01.86 | **Walsall** (D3) | A | W | 3-1 | Simpson 2, Davies |
| | | 4 | 25.01.86 | **Watford** (D1) | H | D | 1-1 | Davies |
| | | 4r | 03.02.86 | **Watford** | A | D | 0-0aet | |
| | | 4 2r | 06.02.86 | **Watford** | H | L | 1-3 | Kinsey |
| 1986-87 | (D1) | 3 | 10.01.87 | **Manchester Utd** (D1) | A | L | 0-1 | |
| 1987-88 | (D2) | 3 | 09.01.88 | **Huddersfield Town** (D2) | A | D | 2-2 | Brightwell, Gidman |
| | | 3r | 12.01.88 | **Huddersfield Town** | H | D | 0-0aet | |
| | | 3 2r | 25.01.88 | **Huddersfield Town** | A | W | 3-0 | Hinchcliffe, White, Varadi |
| | | 4 | 30.01.88 | **Blackpool** (D3) | A | D | 1-1 | Lake |
| | | 4r | 03.02.88 | **Blackpool** | H | W | 2-1 | Stewart, Simpson |
| | | 5 | 20.02.88 | **Plymouth Argyle** (D2) | H | W | 3-1 | Scott, Simpson, Moulden |

| | | | | | | | | |
|---|---|---|---|---|---|---|---|---|
| | | 6 | 13.03.88 | **Liverpool** (D1) | H | L | 0-4 | |
| 1988-89 | (D2) | 3 | 07.01.89 | **Leicester City** (D2) | H | W | 1-0 | McNab (p) |
| | | 4 | 28.01.89 | **Brentford** (D3) | A | L | 1-3 | Gleghorn |
| 1989-90 | (D1) | 3 | 06.01.90 | **Millwall** (D1) | H | D | 0-0 | |
| | | 3r | 09.01.90 | **Millwall** | A | D | 1-1aet | Hendry |
| | | 3 2r | 15.01.90 | **Millwall** | A | L | 1-3 | Lake |
| 1990-91 | (D1) | 3 | 06.01.91 | **Burnley** (D4) | A | W | 1-0 | Hendry |
| | | 4 | 26.01.91 | **Port Vale** (D2) | A | W | 2-1 | Quinn, Allen |
| | | 5 | 16.02.91 | **Notts County** (D2) | A | L | 0-1 | |
| 1991-92 | (D1) | 3 | 04.01.92 | **Middlesbrough** (D2) | A | L | 1-2 | Reid |
| 1992-93 | (PL) | 3 | 02.01.93 | **Reading** (D2) | H | D | 1-1 | Sheron |
| | | 3r | 13.01.93 | **Reading** | A | W | 4-0 | Sheron, Holden, Flitcroft, Quinn |
| | | 4 | 23.01.93 | **QPR** (PL) | A | W | 2-1 | White, Vonk |
| | | 5 | 13.02.93 | **Barnsley** (D1) | H | W | 2-0 | White 2 |
| | | 6 | 07.03.93 | **Tottenham Hotspur** (PL) | H | L | 2-4 | Sheron, Phelan |
| 1993-94 | (PL) | 3 | 08.01.94 | **Leicester City** (D1) | H | W | 4-1 | Ingebritsen 3, Kerraghan |
| | | 4 | 29.01.94 | **Cardiff City** (D2) | A | L | 0-1 | |
| 1994-95 | (PL) | 3 | 08.01.95 | **Notts County** (D1) | A | D | 2-2 | Beagrie, D Brightwell |
| | | 3r | 18.01.95 | **Notts County** | H | W | 5-2 | Rosler 4, Gaudino |
| | | 4 | 28.01.95 | **Aston Villa** (PL) | H | W | 1-0 | Walsh |
| | | 5 | 19.02.95 | **Newcastle Utd** (PL) | A | L | 1-3 | Rosler |
| 1995-96 | (PL) | 3 | 06.01.96 | **Leicester City** (D1) | A | D | 0-0 | |
| | | 3r | 17.01.96 | **Leicester City** | H | W | 5-0 | Rosler, Kinkladze, Quinn, Lomas, Creaney |
| | | 4 | 07.02.96 | **Coventry City** (PL) | A | D | 2-2 | Busst og, G Flitcroft |
| | | 4r | 14.02.96 | **Coventry City** | H | W | 2-1 | Clough, Quinn |
| | | 5 | 18.02.96 | **Manchester Utd** (PL) | A | L | 1-2 | Rosler |
| 1996-97 | (D1) | 3 | 25.01.97 | **Brentford** (D2) | A | W | 1-0 | Summerbee |
| | | 4 | 05.02.97 | **Watford** (D2) | H | W | 3-1 | Heaney, Summerbee, Rosler |
| | | 5 | 15.02.97 | **Middlesbrough** (PL) | H | L | 0-1 | |
| 1997-98 | (D1) | 3 | 03.01.98 | **Bradford City** (D1) | H | W | 2-0 | Rosler, Brown |
| | | 4 | 25.01.98 | **West Ham Utd** (PL) | H | L | 1-2 | Kinkladze |
| 1998-99 | (D2) | 1 | 13.11.98 | **Halifax Town** (D3) | H | W | 3-0 | Russell 2, Goater |
| | | 2 | 04.12.98 | **Darlington** (D3) | A | D | 1-1 | Dickov |
| | | 2r | 15.12.98 | **Darlington** | H | W | 1-0aet | Brown |
| | | 3 | 02.01.99 | **Wimbledon** (PL) | A | L | 0-1 | |
| 1999-00 | (D1) | 3 | 12.12.99 | **Chester City** (D3) | A | W | 4-1 | Goater 2, Bishop, Doughty og |
| | | 4 | 09.01.00 | **Leeds Utd** (PL) | H | L | 2-5 | Goater, Bishop |
| 2000-01 | (PL) | 3 | 06.01.01 | **Birmingham City** (D1) | H | W | 3-2 | Morrison, Huckerby, Goater (p) |
| | | 4 | 27.01.01 | **Coventry City** (PL) | H | W | 1-0 | Goater |
| | | 5 | 18.02.01 | **Liverpool** (PL) | A | L | 2-4 | Kanchelskis, Goater |
| 2001-02 | (D1) | 3 | 05.01.02 | **Swindon Town** (D2) | H | W | 2-0 | Wanchope, Horlock |
| | | 4 | 27.01.02 | **Ipswich Town** (PL) | A | W | 4-1 | Berkovic, Goater 2, Huckerby |
| | | 5 | 17.02.02 | **Newcastle Utd** (PL) | A | L | 0-1 | |
| 2002-03 | (PL) | 3 | 05.01.03 | **Liverpool** (PL) | H | L | 0-1 | |

# MANCHESTER FC

*Formed 1866. Played at Whalley Range, Manchester, the venue for the FA Cup semi-finals in 1882 and 1883. No connection with either Manchester City or Manchester United.*

| | | | | | | | |
|---|---|---|---|---|---|---|---|
| 1877-78 | 1 | 07.11.77 | **Darwen** | A | L | 0-3 | |
| 1883-84 | 1 | 10.11.83 | **Stoke** | A | W | 2-1 | Colhurst, Bassett |
| | 2 | 01.12.83 | **Queen's Park, Glasgow** | A | L | 0-15 | |

# MANCHESTER UNITED

*Formed 1878 as Newton Heath. Manchester United 1902. FA Cup and League double 1993-94, 1995-96, 1998-99 when they also became the first English club to win the treble of the FA Cup, League Championship and European Cup in the same season. FA Cup winners (10 times, the current record): 1909, 1948, 1963, 1977, 1983, 1985, 1990, 1994, 1996, 1999. Runners-up: 1957, 1958, 1976, 1979, 1995. Record FA Cup win: 8-0 v Yeovil Town, 5th round, 12.02.1949. Record FA Cup defeat: 1-7 v Burnley, 1st round replay, 13.02.1901; 0-6 v Sheffield Wednesday, 2nd round, 20.02.1904. In 1999-2000 United failed to enter the competition because of their obligation to take part in the inaugural FIFA Club World Championship in Brazil.*

**as Newton Heath**

| | | | | | | | | |
|---|---|---|---|---|---|---|---|---|
| 1886-87 | | 1 | 30.10.86 | **Fleetwood Rangers** | A | D | 2-2 | Doughty 2 |
| | | | | *Fleetwood awarded tie as Newton Heath refused to play extra time* | | | | |
| 1887-88 | | 1 | | did not enter | | | | |
| 1888-89 | | 1 | | did not enter | | | | |
| 1889-90 | (FAll) | 1 | 18.01.90 | **Preston North End** (D1) | A | L | 1-6 | Craig |
| 1890-91 | (FAll) | | | 1q Higher Walton (H) 2-0; 2q Bootle Reserves (A) 0-1 | | | | |
| 1891-92 | (FAll) | | | 1q Ardwick (H) 5-1; 2q Heywood (H) walkover; 3q South Shore (A) 2-0; 4q Blackpool (H) 3-4 | | | | |
| 1892-93 | (D1) | 1 | 21.01.93 | **Blackburn Rovers** (D1) | A | L | 0-4 | |
| 1893-94 | (D1) | 1 | 27.01.94 | **Middlesbrough** (D2) | H | W | 4-0 | Donaldson 2, Farman, Peden |
| | | 2 | 10.02.94 | **Blackburn Rovers** (D1) | H | D | 0-0 | |
| | | 2r | 17.02.94 | **Blackburn Rovers** | A | L | 1-5 | Donaldson |
| 1894-95 | (D2) | 1 | 02.02.95 | **Stoke** (D1) | H | L | 2-3 | Smith, Peters |
| 1895-96 | (D2) | 1 | 01.02.96 | **Kettering Town** (ML) | H | W | 2-1 | Donaldson, Smith |
| | | 2 | 15.02.96 | **Derby County** (D1) | H | D | 1-1 | Kennedy |
| | | 2r | 19.02.96 | **Derby County** | A | L | 1-5 | Donaldson |
| 1896-97 | (D2) | | | 1q West Manchester (H) 7-0; 2q Nelson (H) 3-0; 3q Blackpool (H) 2-2; 3qr Blackpool (A) 2-1 | | | | |
| | | 1 | 30.01.97 | **Kettering Town** (ML) | H | W | 5-1 | Cassidy 3, Donaldson 2 |
| | | 2 | 13.02.97 | **Soton St Marys** (SL) | A | D | 1-1 | Donaldson |
| | | 2r | 17.02.97 | **Soton St Marys** | H | W | 3-1 | Bryant 2, Cassidy |
| | | 3 | 27.02.97 | **Derby County** (D1) | A | L | 0-2 | |
| 1897-98 | (D2) | 1 | 29.01.98 | **Walsall** (D2) | H | W | 1-0 | own goal |
| | | 2 | 12.02.98 | **Liverpool** (D1) | H | D | 0-0 | |
| | | 2r | 16.02.98 | **Liverpool** | A | L | 1-2 | Collinson |
| 1898-99 | (D2) | 1 | 28.01.99 | **Tottenham Hotspur** (SL) | A | D | 1-1 | Cassidy |
| | | 1r | 01.02.99 | **Tottenham Hotspur** | H | L | 3-5 | Bryant 3 |
| 1899-00 | (D2) | | | 1q South Shore (A) 1-3 | | | | |
| 1900-01 | (D2) | | | Int Portsmouth (H) 3-0 | | | | |
| | | 1 | 09.02.01 | **Burnley** (D2) | H | D | 0-0 | |
| | | 1r | 13.02.01 | **Burnley** | A | L | 1-7 | Schofield |
| 1901-02 | (D2) | | | Int Lincoln City (H) 1-2 | | | | |

**as Manchester Utd**

| | | | | | | | | |
|---|---|---|---|---|---|---|---|---|
| 1902-03 | (D2) | | | 3q Accrington Stanley (H) 7-0; 4q Oswaldtwistle (H) 3-2; 5q Southport Central (H) 4-1; Int Burton Utd (H) 1-1; Int r Burton Utd (H) 3-1 | | | | |
| | | 1 | 07.02.03 | **Liverpool** (D1) | H | W | 2-1 | Peddie 2 |
| | | 2 | 21.02.03 | **Everton** (D1) | A | L | 1-3 | Griffiths |
| 1903-04 | (D2) | | | Int Small Heath (H) 1-1; Int r Small Heath (A) 1-1aet; Int 2r Small Heath 1-1aet; (at Bramall Lane); Int 3r Small Heath 3-1 (at Hyde Road, Manchester) | | | | |
| | | 1 | 06.02.04 | **Notts County** (D1) | A | D | 3-3 | Downie, Schofield, Arkesden |
| | | 1r | 10.02.04 | **Notts County** | H | W | 2-1 | Morrison, Pegg |
| | | 2 | 20.02.04 | **Sheffield Wed** (D1) | A | L | 0-6 | |
| 1904-05 | (D2) | | | Int Fulham (H) 2-2; Int r Fulham (A) 0-0; Int 2r Fulham 0-1 (at Villa Park) | | | | |
| 1905-06 | (D2) | 1 | 13.01.06 | **Staple Hill** (WL) | H | W | 7-2 | Beddow 3, Picken 2, Allen, Williams |
| | | 2 | 03.02.06 | **Norwich City** (SL) | H | W | 3-0 | Downie, Peddie, Sagar |
| | | 3 | 24.02.06 | **Aston Villa** (D1) | H | W | 5-1 | Picken 3, Sagar 2 |
| | | 4 | 10.03.06 | **Woolwich Arsenal** (D1) | H | L | 2-3 | Peddie, Sagar |
| 1906-07 | (D1) | 1 | 12.01.07 | **Portsmouth** (SL) | A | D | 2-2 | Picken, Wall |
| | | 1r | 16.01.07 | **Portsmouth** | H | L | 1-2 | Wall |
| 1907-08 | (D1) | 1 | 11.01.08 | **Blackpool** (D2) | H | W | 3-1 | Wall 2, Bannister |
| | | 2 | 01.02.08 | **Chelsea** (D1) | H | W | 1-0 | Sandy Turnbull |
| | | 3 | 22.02.08 | **Aston Villa** (D1) | A | W | 2-0 | Sandy Turnbull, Wall |
| | | 4 | 07.03.08 | **Fulham** (D2) | A | L | 1-2 | J Turnbull |
| 1908-09 | (D1) | 1 | 16.01.09 | **Brighton** (SL) | H | W | 1-0 | Halse |
| | | 2 | 06.02.09 | **Everton** (D1) | H | W | 1-0 | Halse |
| | | 3 | 20.02.09 | **Blackburn Rovers** (D1) | H | W | 6-1 | Sandy Turnbull 3, J Turnbull 3 |
| | | 4 | 06.03.09 | **Burnley** (D2) | A | - | 0-1ab | |
| | | | | *abandoned after 72 minutes* | | | | |
| | | 4 | 10.03.09 | **Burnley** (D2) | A | W | 3-2 | J Turnbull 2, Halse |
| | | SF | 27.03.09 | **Newcastle Utd** (D1) | | W | 1-0 | Halse |
| | | | | *played at Bramall Lane* | | | | |

| | | | | | | | | |
|---|---|---|---|---|---|---|---|---|
| | | F | 24.04.09 | **Bristol City** (D1) *played at Crystal Palace* | | W | 1-0 | Sandy Turnbull |
| 1909-10 | (D1) | 1 | 15.01.10 | **Burnley** (D2) | A | L | 0-2 | |
| 1910-11 | (D1) | 1 | 14.01.11 | **Blackpool** (D2) | H | W | 2-1 | Picken, West |
| | | 2 | 04.02.11 | **Aston Villa** (D1) | H | W | 2-1 | Halse, Wall |
| | | 3 | 25.02.11 | **West Ham Utd** (SL) | A | L | 1-2 | Sandy Turnbull |
| 1911-12 | (D1) | 1 | 13.01.12 | **Huddersfield Town** (D2) | H | W | 3-1 | West 2, Halse |
| | | 2 | 03.02.12 | **Coventry City** (SL) | A | W | 5-1 | Halse 2, West, Sandy Turnbull, Wall |
| | | 3 | 24.02.12 | **Reading** (SL) | A | D | 1-1 | West |
| | | 3r | 29.02.12 | **Reading** | H | W | 3-0 | Sandy Turnbull 2, Halse |
| | | 4 | 09.03.12 | **Blackburn Rovers** (D1) | H | D | 1-1 | Walmsley og |
| | | 4r | 14.03.12 | **Blackburn Rovers** | A | L | 2-4aet | West 2 |
| 1912-13 | (D1) | 1 | 11.01.13 | **Coventry City** (SL) | H | D | 1-1 | Wall |
| | | 1r | 16.01.13 | **Coventry City** | A | W | 2-1 | Anderson, Roberts |
| | | 2 | 01.02.13 | **Plymouth Argyle** (SL) | A | W | 2-0 | Anderson, Wall |
| | | 3 | 22.02.13 | **Oldham Athletic** (D1) | A | D | 0-0 | |
| | | 3r | 26.02.13 | **Oldham Athletic** | H | L | 1-2 | West |
| 1913-14 | (D1) | 1 | 10.01.14 | **Swindon Town** (SL) | A | L | 0-1 | |
| 1914-15 | (D1) | 1 | 09.01.15 | **Sheffield Wed** (D1) | A | L | 0-1 | |
| 1919-20 | (D1) | 1 | 10.01.20 | **Port Vale** (D2) | A | W | 1-0 | Toms |
| | | 2 | 31.01.20 | **Aston Villa** (D1) | H | L | 1-2 | Woodcock |
| 1920-21 | (D1) | 1 | 08.01.21 | **Liverpool** (D1) | A | D | 1-1 | Miller |
| | | 1r | 12.01.21 | **Liverpool** | H | L | 1-2 | Partridge |
| 1921-22 | (D1) | 1 | 07.01.22 | **Cardiff City** (D1) | H | L | 1-4 | Sapsford |
| 1922-23 | (D2) | 1 | 13.01.23 | **Bradford City** (D2) | A | D | 1-1 | Partridge |
| | | 1r | 17.01.23 | **Bradford City** | H | W | 2-0 | Barber, Goldthorpe |
| | | 2 | 03.02.23 | **Tottenham Hotspur** (D1) | A | L | 0-4 | |
| 1923-24 | (D2) | 1 | 12.01.24 | **Plymouth Argyle** (3S) | H | W | 1-0 | McPherson |
| | | 2 | 02.02.24 | **Huddersfield Town** (D1) | H | L | 0-3 | |
| 1924-25 | (D2) | 1 | 10.01.25 | **Sheffield Wed** (D2) | A | L | 0-2 | |
| 1925-26 | (D1) | 3 | 09.01.26 | **Port Vale** (D2) | A | W | 3-2 | Spence 2, McPherson |
| | | 4 | 30.01.26 | **Tottenham Hotspur** (D1) | A | D | 2-2 | Spence, Thomas |
| | | 4r | 03.02.26 | **Tottenham Hotspur** | H | W | 2-0 | Spence, Rennox |
| | | 5 | 20.02.26 | **Sunderland** (D1) | A | D | 3-3 | Smith 2, McPherson |
| | | 5r | 24.02.26 | **Sunderland** | H | W | 2-1 | Smith, McPherson |
| | | 6 | 06.03.26 | **Fulham** (D2) | A | W | 2-1 | Smith, McPherson |
| | | SF | 27.03.26 | **Manchester City** (D1) *played at Bramall Lane* | | L | 0-3 | |
| 1926-27 | (D1) | 3 | 08.01.27 | **Reading** (D2) | A | D | 1-1 | Bennion |
| | | 3r | 12.01.27 | **Reading** | H | D | 2-2aet | Spence, Sweeney |
| | | 3 2r | 17.01.27 | **Reading** *played at Villa Park* | | L | 1-2 | McPherson |
| 1927-28 | (D1) | 3 | 14.01.28 | **Brentford** (3S) | H | W | 7-1 | Hanson 4, Spence, McPherson, Johnston |
| | | 4 | 28.01.28 | **Bury** (D1) | A | D | 1-1 | Johnston |
| | | 4r | 01.02.28 | **Bury** | H | W | 1-0 | Spence |
| | | 5 | 18.02.28 | **Birmingham** (D1) | H | W | 1-0 | Johnston |
| | | 6 | 03.03.28 | **Blackburn Rovers** (D1) | A | L | 0-2 | |
| 1928-29 | (D1) | 3 | 12.01.29 | **Port Vale** (D2) | A | W | 3-0 | Spence, Hanson, Taylor |
| | | 4 | 26.01.29 | **Bury** (D1) | H | L | 0-1 | |
| 1929-30 | (D1) | 3 | 11.01.30 | **Swindon Town** (3S) | H | L | 0-2 | |
| 1930-31 | (D1) | 3 | 10.01.31 | **Stoke City** (D2) | A | D | 3-3 | Reid 3 |
| | | 3r | 14.01.31 | **Stoke City** | H | D | 0-0aet | |
| | | 3 2r | 19.01.31 | **Stoke City** *played at Anfield* | | W | 4-2 | Hopkinson 2, Spence, Gallimore |
| | | 4 | 24.01.31 | **Grimsby Town** (D1) | A | L | 0-1 | |
| 1931-32 | (D1) | 3 | 09.01.32 | **Plymouth Argyle** (D2) | A | L | 1-4 | Reid |
| 1932-33 | (D2) | 3 | 14.01.33 | **Middlesbrough** (D1) | H | L | 1-4 | Spence |
| 1933-34 | (D2) | 3 | 13.01.34 | **Portsmouth** (D1) | H | D | 1-1 | McLenahan |
| | | 3r | 17.01.34 | **Portsmouth** | A | L | 1-4 | Ball |
| 1934-35 | (D2) | 3 | 12.01.35 | **Bristol Rovers** (3S) | A | W | 3-1 | Bamford 2, Mutch |

| | | | | | | | | |
|---|---|---|---|---|---|---|---|---|
| | | 4 | 26.01.35 | **Nottingham Forest** (D2) | A | D | 0-0 | |
| | | 4r | 30.01.35 | **Nottingham Forest** | H | L | 0-3 | |
| 1935-36 | (D2) | 3 | 11.01.36 | **Reading** (3S) | A | W | 3-1 | Mutch 2, Manley |
| | | 4 | 25.01.36 | **Stoke City** (D1) | A | D | 0-0 | |
| | | 4r | 29.01.36 | **Stoke City** | H | L | 0-2 | |
| 1936-37 | (D1) | 3 | 16.01.37 | **Reading** (3S) | H | W | 1-0 | Bamford |
| | | 4 | 30.01.37 | **Arsenal** (D1) | A | L | 0-5 | |
| 1937-38 | (D2) | 3 | 08.01.38 | **Yeovil & Petters Utd** (SL) | H | W | 3-0 | Baird, Bamford, Pearson |
| | | 4 | 22.01.38 | **Barnsley** (D2) | A | D | 2-2 | Baird, Carey |
| | | 4r | 26.01.38 | **Barnsley** | H | W | 1-0 | Baird |
| | | 5 | 12.02.38 | **Brentford** (D1) | A | L | 0-2 | |
| 1938-39 | (D1) | 3 | 07.01.39 | **WBA** (D2) | A | D | 0-0 | |
| | | 3r | 11.01.39 | **WBA** | H | L | 1-5 | Redwood |
| 1945-46 | (D1) | 3 1L | 05.01.46 | **Accrington Stanley** (3N) | A | D | 2-2 | Smith, Wrigglesworth |
| | | 3 2L | 09.01.46 | **Accrington Stanley** | H | W | 5-1 | Rowley 2, Bainbridge, Wrigglesworth, Briggs og |
| | | | | *played at Maine Road* | | | | |
| | | 4 1L | 26.01.46 | **Preston North End** (D1) | H | W | 1-0 | Hanlon |
| | | | | *played at Maine Road* | | | | |
| | | 4 2L | 30.01.46 | **Preston North End** | A | L | 1-3 | Hanlon |
| 1946-47 | (D1) | 3 | 11.01.47 | **Bradford Park A** (D2) | A | W | 3-0 | Rowley 2, Buckle |
| | | 4 | 25.01.47 | **Nottingham Forest** (D2) | H | L | 0-2 | |
| | | | | *played at Maine Road* | | | | |
| 1947-48 | (D1) | 3 | 10.01.48 | **Aston Villa** (D1) | A | W | 6-4 | Pearson 2, Morris 2, Delaney, Rowley |
| | | 4 | 24.01.48 | **Liverpool** (D1) | H | W | 3-0 | Morris, Rowley, Mitten |
| | | | | *played at Goodison Park* | | | | |
| | | 5 | 07.02.48 | **Charlton Athletic** (D1) | H | W | 2-0 | Warner, Mitten |
| | | | | *played at Leeds Road, Huddersfield* | | | | |
| | | 6 | 28.02.48 | **Preston North End** (D1) | H | W | 4-1 | Pearson 2, Rowley, Mitten |
| | | | | *played at Maine Road* | | | | |
| | | SF | 13.03.48 | **Derby County** (D1) | | W | 3-1 | Pearson 3 |
| | | | | *played at Hillsborough* | | | | |
| | | F | 24.04.48 | **Blackpool** (D1) | | W | 4-2 | Rowley 2, Pearson, Anderson |
| | | | | *played at Wembley Stadium* | | | | |
| 1948-49 | (D1) | 3 | 08.01.49 | **Bournemouth** (3S) | H | W | 6-0 | Burke 2, Rowley 2, Pearson, Mitten |
| | | 4 | 29.01.49 | **Bradford Park A** (D2) | H | D | 1-1aet | Mitten |
| | | | | *played at Maine Road* | | | | |
| | | 4r | 05.02.49 | **Bradford Park A** | A | D | 1-1aet | Mitten |
| | | 4 2r | 07.02.49 | **Bradford Park A** | H | W | 5-0aet | Burke 2, Rowley 2, Pearson |
| | | | | *played at Maine Road* | | | | |
| | | 5 | 12.02.49 | **Yeovil Town** (SL) | H | W | 8-0 | Rowley 5, Burke 2, Mitten |
| | | | | *played at Maine Road* | | | | |
| | | 6 | 26.02.49 | **Hull City** (3N) | A | W | 1-0 | Pearson |
| | | SF | 26.03.49 | **Wolverhampton W** (D1) | | D | 1-1aet | Mitten |
| | | | | *played at Hillsborough* | | | | |
| | | SFr | 02.04.49 | **Wolverhampton W** | | L | 0-1 | |
| | | | | *played at Goodison Park* | | | | |
| 1949-50 | (D1) | 3 | 07.01.50 | **Weymouth** (SL) | H | W | 4-0 | Rowley 2, Pearson, Delaney |
| | | 4 | 28.01.50 | **Watford** (3S) | A | W | 1-0 | Rowley |
| | | 5 | 11.02.50 | **Portsmouth** (D1) | H | D | 3-3 | Mitten 2, Pearson |
| | | 5r | 15.02.50 | **Portsmouth** | A | W | 3-1 | Delaney, Downie, Mitten |
| | | 6 | 04.03.50 | **Chelsea** (D1) | A | L | 0-2 | |
| 1950-51 | (D1) | 3 | 06.01.51 | **Oldham Athletic** (3N) | H | W | 4-1 | Pearson, Aston, Birch, Whyte og |
| | | 4 | 27.01.51 | **Leeds Utd** (D2) | H | W | 4-0 | Pearson 3, Rowley |
| | | 5 | 10.02.51 | **Arsenal** (D1) | H | W | 1-0 | Pearson |
| | | 6 | 24.02.51 | **Birmingham City** (D2) | A | L | 0-1 | |
| 1951-52 | (D1) | 3 | 12.01.52 | **Hull City** (D2) | H | L | 0-2 | |
| 1952-53 | (D1) | 3 | 10.01.53 | **Millwall** (3S) | A | W | 1-0 | Pearson |
| | | 4 | 31.01.53 | **Walthamstow Ave** (AL) | H | D | 1-1 | Lewis |
| | | 4r | 05.02.53 | **Walthamstow Ave** | A | W | 5-2 | Rowley 2, Byrne, Lewis, Pearson |
| | | | | *played at Highbury* | | | | |

| | | | | | | | |
|---|---|---|---|---|---|---|---|
| | 5 | 14.02.53 | **Everton** (D2) | A | L | 1-2 | Rowley |
| 1953-54 (D1) | 3 | 09.01.54 | **Burnley** (D1) | A | L | 3-5 | Blanchflower, Taylor, Viollet |
| 1954-55 (D1) | 3 | 08.01.55 | **Reading** (3S) | A | D | 1-1 | Webster |
| | 3r | 12.01.55 | **Reading** | H | W | 4-1 | Webster 2, Viollet, Rowley |
| | 4 | 29.01.55 | **Manchester City** (D1) | A | L | 0-2 | |
| 1955-56 (D1) | 3 | 07.01.56 | **Bristol Rovers** (D2) | A | L | 0-4 | |
| 1956-57 (D1) | 3 | 05.01.57 | **Hartlepools Utd** (3N) | A | W | 4-3 | Whelan 2, Berry, Taylor |
| | 4 | 26.01.57 | **Wrexham** (3N) | A | W | 5-0 | Whelan 2, Taylor 2, Byrne |
| | 5 | 16.02.57 | **Everton** (D1) | H | W | 1-0 | Edwards |
| | 6 | 02.03.57 | **Bournemouth** (3S) | A | W | 2-1 | Berry 2 |
| | SF | 23.03.57 | **Birmingham City** (D1) | | W | 2-0 | Berry, Charlton |
| | | | *played at Hillsborough* | | | | |
| | F | 04.05.57 | **Aston Villa** (D1) | | L | 1-2 | Taylor |
| | | | *played at Wembley Stadium* | | | | |
| 1957-58 (D1) | 3 | 04.01.58 | **Workington** (3N) | A | W | 3-1 | Viollet 3 |
| | 4 | 25.01.58 | **Ipswich Town** (D2) | H | W | 2-0 | Charlton 2 |
| | 5 | 19.02.58 | **Sheffield Wed** (D1) | H | W | 3-0 | Brennan 2, Dawson |
| | 6 | 01.03.58 | **WBA** (D1) | A | D | 2-2 | E Taylor, Dawson |
| | 6r | 05.03.58 | **WBA** | H | W | 1-0 | Webster |
| | SF | 22.03.58 | **Fulham** (D2) | | D | 2-2 | Charlton 2 |
| | | | *played at Villa Park* | | | | |
| | SFr | 26.03.58 | **Fulham** | | W | 5-3 | Dawson 3, Charlton, Brennan |
| | | | *played at Highbury* | | | | |
| | F | 03.05.58 | **Bolton Wanderers** (D1) | | L | 0-2 | |
| | | | *played at Wembley Stadium* | | | | |
| 1958-59 (D1) | 3 | 10.01.59 | **Norwich City** (D3) | A | L | 0-3 | |
| 1959-60 (D1) | 3 | 09.01.60 | **Derby County** (D2) | A | W | 4-2 | Goodwin, Charlton, Scanlon, Barrowcliffe og |
| | 4 | 30.01.60 | **Liverpool** (D2) | A | W | 3-1 | Charlton 2, Bradley |
| | 5 | 20.02.60 | **Sheffield Wed** (D1) | A | L | 0-1 | |
| 1960-61 (D1) | 3 | 07.01.61 | **Middlesbrough** (D2) | H | W | 3-0 | Dawson 2, Cantwell |
| | 4 | 28.01.61 | **Sheffield Wed** (D1) | A | D | 1-1 | Cantwell |
| | 4r | 01.02.61 | **Sheffield Wed** | H | L | 2-7 | Dawson, Pearson |
| 1961-62 (D1) | 3 | 06.01.62 | **Bolton Wanderers** (D1) | H | W | 2-1 | Nicholson, Herd |
| | 4 | 31.01.62 | **Arsenal** (D1) | H | W | 1-0 | Setters |
| | 5 | 17.02.62 | **Sheffield Wed** (D1) | H | D | 0-0 | |
| | 5r | 21.02.62 | **Sheffield Wed** | A | W | 2-0 | Charlon, Giles |
| | 6 | 10.03.62 | **Preston North End** (D2) | A | D | 0-0 | |
| | 6r | 14.03.62 | **Preston North End** | H | W | 2-1 | Herd, Charlton |
| | SF | 31.03.62 | **Tottenham Hotspur** (D1) | | L | 1-3 | Herd |
| | | | *played at Hillsborough* | | | | |
| 1962-63 (D1) | 3 | 04.03.63 | **Huddersfield Town** (D2) | H | W | 5-0 | Law 3, Giles, Quixall |
| | 4 | 11.03.63 | **Aston Villa** (D1) | H | W | 1-0 | Quixall |
| | 5 | 16.03.63 | **Chelsea** (D2) | H | W | 2-1 | Quixall, Law |
| | 6 | 30.03.63 | **Coventry City** (D3) | A | W | 3-1 | Charlton 2, Quixall |
| | SF | 27.04.63 | **Southampton** (D2) | | W | 1-0 | Law |
| | | | *played at Villa Park* | | | | |
| | F | 25.05.63 | **Leicester City** (D1) | | W | 3-1 | Herd 2, Law |
| | | | *played at Wembley Stadium* | | | | |
| 1963-64 (D1) | 3 | 04.01.64 | **Southampton** (D2) | A | W | 3-2 | Crerand, Moore, Herd |
| | 4 | 25.01.64 | **Bristol Rovers** (D3) | H | W | 4-1 | Law 3, Herd |
| | 5 | 15.02.64 | **Barnsley** (D3) | A | W | 4-0 | Law 2, Best, Herd |
| | 6 | 29.02.64 | **Sunderland** (D2) | H | D | 3-3 | Charlton, Best, Hurley og |
| | 6r | 04.03.64 | **Sunderland** | A | D | 2-2aet | Charlton, Law |
| | 6 2r | 09.03.64 | **Sunderland** | | W | 5-1 | Law 3, Chisnall, Herd |
| | | | *played at Leeds Road, Huddersfield* | | | | |
| | SF | 14.03.64 | **West Ham Utd** (D1) | | L | 1-3 | Law |
| | | | *played at Hillsborough* | | | | |
| 1964-65 (D1) | 3 | 09.01.65 | **Chester** (D4) | H | W | 2-1 | Kinsey, Best |
| | 4 | 30.01.65 | **Stoke City** (D1) | A | D | 0-0 | |
| | 4r | 03.02.65 | **Stoke City** | H | W | 1-0 | Herd |
| | 5 | 20.02.65 | **Burnley** (D1) | H | W | 2-1 | Crerand, Law |

| | | | | | | | |
|---|---|---|---|---|---|---|---|
| | 6 | 10.03.65 | **Wolverhampton W** (D1) | A | W | 5-3 | Law 2, Crerand, Herd, Best |
| | SF | 27.03.65 | **Leeds Utd** (D1) | | D | 0-0aet | |
| | | | *played at Hillsborough* | | | | |
| | SFr | 31.03.65 | **Leeds Utd** | | L | 0-1 | |
| | | | *played at the City Ground, Nottingham* | | | | |
| 1965-66 (D1) | 3 | 22.01.66 | **Derby County** (D2) | A | W | 5-2 | Best 2, Law 2, Herd |
| | 4 | 12.02.66 | **Rotherham Utd** (D3) | H | D | 0-0 | |
| | 4r | 15.02.66 | **Rotherham Utd** | A | W | 1-0aet | Connelly |
| | 5 | 05.03.66 | **Wolverhampton W** (D2) | A | W | 4-2 | Law 2, Herd, Best |
| | 6 | 26.03.66 | **Preston North End** (D2) | A | D | 1-1 | Herd |
| | 6r | 30.03.66 | **Preston North End** | H | W | 3-1 | Law 2, Connelly |
| | SF | 23.04.66 | **Everton** (D1) | | L | 0-1 | |
| | | | *played at Burnden Park* | | | | |
| 1966-67 (D1) | 3 | 28.01.67 | **Stoke City** (D1) | H | W | 2-0 | Law, Herd |
| | 4 | 18.02.67 | **Norwich City** (D2) | H | L | 1-2 | Law |
| 1967-68 (D1) | 3 | 27.01.68 | **Tottenham Hotspur** (D1) | H | D | 2-2 | Best, Charlton |
| | 3r | 31.01.68 | **Tottenham Hotspur** | A | L | 0-1aet | |
| 1968-69 (D1) | 3 | 04.01.69 | **Exeter City** (D4) | A | W | 3-1 | Fitzpatrick, Newman og, Kidd |
| | 4 | 25.01.69 | **Watford** (D3) | H | D | 1-1 | Law |
| | 4r | 03.02.69 | **Watford** | A | W | 2-0 | Law 2 |
| | 5 | 11.02.69 | **Birmingham City** (D2) | A | D | 2-2 | Law, Best |
| | 5r | 24.02.69 | **Birmingham City** | H | W | 6-2 | Law 3, Kidd, Morgan, Crerand |
| | 6 | 01.03.69 | **Everton** (D1) | H | L | 0-1 | |
| 1969-70 (D1) | 3 | 03.01.70 | **Ipswich Town** (D1) | A | W | 1-0 | McNeil og |
| | 4 | 24.01.70 | **Manchester City** (D1) | H | W | 3-0 | Kidd 2, Morgan |
| | 5 | 07.02.70 | **Northampton Town** (D4) | A | W | 8-2 | Best 6, Kidd 2 |
| | 6 | 21.02.70 | **Middlesbrough** (D2) | A | D | 1-1 | Sartori |
| | 6r | 25.02.70 | **Middlesbrough** | H | W | 2-1 | Charlton, Morgan |
| | SF | 14.03.70 | **Leeds Utd** (D1) | | D | 0-0 | |
| | | | *played at Hillsborough* | | | | |
| | SFr | 23.03.70 | **Leeds Utd** | | D | 0-0aet | |
| | | | *played at Villa Park* | | | | |
| | SF 2r | 26.03.70 | **Leeds Utd** | | L | 0-1 | |
| | | | *played at Burnden Park* | | | | |
| | 3/4 | 10.04.70 | **Watford** (D2) | | W | 2-0 | Kidd 2 |
| | | | *played at Highbury* | | | | |
| 1970-71 (D1) | 3 | 02.01.71 | **Middlesbrough** (D2) | H | D | 0-0 | |
| | 3r | 05.01.71 | **Middlesbrough** | A | L | 1-2 | Best |
| 1971-72 (D1) | 3 | 15.01.72 | **Southampton** (D1) | A | D | 1-1 | Charlton |
| | 3r | 19.01.72 | **Southampton** | H | W | 4-1aet | Best 2, Sadler, Aston |
| | 4 | 05.02.72 | **Preston North End** (D2) | A | W | 2-0 | Gowling 2 |
| | 5 | 26.02.72 | **Middlesbrough** (D2) | H | D | 0-0 | |
| | 5r | 29.02.72 | **Middlesbrough** | A | W | 3-0 | Morgan, Charlton, Best |
| | 6 | 18.03.72 | **Stoke City** (D1) | H | D | 1-1 | Best |
| | 6r | 22.03.72 | **Stoke City** | A | L | 1-2aet | Best |
| 1972-73 (D1) | 3 | 13.01.73 | **Wolverhampton W** (D1) | A | L | 0-1 | |
| 1973-74 (D1) | 3 | 05.01.74 | **Plymouth Argyle** (D3) | H | W | 1-0 | Macari |
| | 4 | 26.01.74 | **Ipswich Town** (D1) | H | L | 0-1 | |
| 1974-75 (D2) | 3 | 04.01.75 | **Walsall** (D3) | H | D | 0-0 | |
| | 3r | 07.01.75 | **Walsall** | A | L | 2-3aet | McIlroy, Daly |
| 1975-76 (D1) | 3 | 03.01.76 | **Oxford Utd** (D2) | H | W | 2-1 | Daly 2 |
| | 4 | 24.01.76 | **Peterborough Utd** (D3) | H | W | 3-1 | Forsyth, McIlroy, Hill |
| | 5 | 14.02.76 | **Leicester City** (D1) | A | W | 2-1 | Daly, Macari |
| | 6 | 06.03.76 | **Wolverhampton W** (D1) | H | D | 1-1 | Daly |
| | 6r | 09.03.76 | **Wolverhampton W** | A | W | 3-2aet | B Greenhoff, McIlroy, Pearson |
| | SF | 03.04.76 | **Derby County** (D1) | | W | 2-0 | Hill 2 |
| | | | *played at Hillsborough* | | | | |
| | F | 01.05.76 | **Southampton** (D2) | | L | 0-1 | |
| | | | *played at Wembley Stadium* | | | | |
| 1976-77 (D1) | 3 | 08.01.77 | **Walsall** (D3) | H | W | 1-0 | Hill |
| | 4 | 29.01.77 | **QPR** (D1) | H | W | 1-0 | Macari |

| | | | | | | | |
|---|---|---|---|---|---|---|---|
| | 5 | 26.02.77 | **Southampton** (D2) | A | D | 2-2 | Macari, Hill |
| | 5r | 08.03.77 | **Southampton** | H | W | 2-1 | J Greenhoff 2 |
| | 6 | 19.03.77 | **Aston Villa** (D1) | H | W | 2-1 | Houston, Macari |
| | SF | 23.04.77 | **Leeds Utd** (D1) *played at Hillsborough* | | W | 2-1 | Coppell, J Greenhoff |
| | F | 21.05.77 | **Liverpool** (D1) *played at Wembley Stadium* | | W | 2-1 | Pearson, J Greenhoff |
| 1977-78 (D1) | 3 | 07.01.78 | **Carlisle Utd** (D3) | A | D | 1-1 | Macari |
| | 3r | 11.01.78 | **Carlisle Utd** | H | W | 4-2 | Pearson 2, Macari 2 |
| | 4 | 28.01.78 | **WBA** (D1) | H | D | 1-1 | Coppell |
| | 4r | 01.02.78 | **WBA** | A | L | 2-3aet | Pearson, Hill |
| 1978-79 (D1) | 3 | 15.01.79 | **Chelsea** (D1) | H | W | 3-0 | Coppell, J Greenhoff, Grimes |
| | 4 | 31.01.79 | **Fulham** (D2) | A | D | 1-1 | J Greenhoff |
| | 4r | 12.02.79 | **Fulham** | H | W | 1-0 | J Greenhoff |
| | 5 | 20.02.79 | **Colchester Utd** (D3) | A | W | 1-0 | J Greenhoff |
| | 6 | 10.03.79 | **Tottenham Hotspur** (D1) | A | D | 1-1 | Thomas |
| | 6r | 14.03.79 | **Tottenham Hotspur** | H | W | 2-0 | McIlroy, Jordan |
| | SF | 31.03.79 | **Liverpool** (D1) *played at Maine Road* | | D | 2-2 | Jordan, B Greenhoff |
| | SFr | 04.04.79 | **Liverpool** *played at Goodison Park* | | W | 1-0 | J Greenhoff |
| | F | 12.05.79 | **Arsenal** (D1) *played at Wembley Stadium* | | L | 2-3 | McQueen, McIlroy |
| 1979-80 (D1) | 3 | 05.01.80 | **Tottenham Hotspur** (D1) | A | D | 1-1 | McIlroy |
| | 3r | 09.01.80 | **Tottenham Hotspur** | H | L | 0-1aet | |
| 1980-81 (D1) | 3 | 03.01.81 | **Brighton** (D1) | H | D | 2-2 | Duxbury, Thomas |
| | 3r | 07.01.81 | **Brighton** | A | W | 2-0 | Nicholl, Birtles |
| | 4 | 24.01.81 | **Nottingham Forest** (D1) | A | L | 0-1 | |
| 1981-82 (D1) | 3 | 02.01.82 | **Watford** (D2) | A | L | 0-1 | |
| 1982-83 (D1) | 3 | 08.01.83 | **West Ham Utd** (D2) | H | W | 2-0 | Coppell, Stapleton |
| | 4 | 29.01.83 | **Luton Town** (D1) | A | W | 2-0 | Moses, Moran |
| | 5 | 19.02.83 | **Derby County** (D2) | A | W | 1-0 | Whiteside |
| | 6 | 12.03.83 | **Everton** (D1) | H | W | 1-0 | Stapleton |
| | SF | 16.04.83 | **Arsenal** (D1) *played at Villa Park* | | W | 2-1 | Robson, Whiteside |
| | F | 21.05.83 | **Brighton** (D1) *played at Wembley Stadium* | | D | 2-2aet | Stapleton, Wilkins |
| | Fr | 26.05.83 | **Brighton** *played at Wembley Stadium* | | W | 4-0 | Robson 2, Whiteside, Muhren (p) |
| 1983-84 (D1) | 3 | 07.01.84 | **Bournemouth** (D3) | A | L | 0-2 | |
| 1984-85 (D1) | 3 | 05.01.85 | **Bournemouth** | A | W | 3-0 | Strachan, McQueen, Stapleton |
| | 4 | 26.01.85 | **Coventry City** (D1) | H | W | 2-1 | Hughes, McGrath |
| | 5 | 15.02.85 | **Blackburn Rovers** (D2) | A | W | 2-0 | Strachan, McGrath |
| | 6 | 09.03.85 | **West Ham Utd** (D1) | H | W | 4-2 | Hughes, Whiteside 3 |
| | SF | 13.04.85 | **Liverpool** (D1) *played at Goodison Park* | | D | 2-2aet | Robson, Stapleton |
| | SFr | 17.04.85 | **Liverpool** *played at Maine Road* | | W | 2-1 | Robson, Hughes |
| | F | 18.05.85 | **Everton** (D1) *played at Wembley Stadium* | | W | 1-0aet | Whiteside |
| 1985-86 (D1) | 3 | 09.01.86 | **Rochdale** (D4) | H | W | 2-0 | Stapleton, Hughes |
| | 4 | 25.01.86 | **Sunderland** (D2) | A | D | 0-0 | |
| | 4r | 29.01.86 | **Sunderland** | H | W | 3-0 | Olsen 2 (1p), Whiteside |
| | 5 | 05.03.86 | **West Ham Utd** (D1) | A | D | 1-1 | Stapleton |
| | 5r | 09.03.86 | **West Ham Utd** | H | L | 0-2 | |
| 1986-87 (D1) | 3 | 10.01.87 | **Manchester City** (D1) | H | W | 1-0 | Whiteside |
| | 4 | 31.01.87 | **Coventry City** (D1) | H | L | 0-1 | |
| 1987-88 (D1) | 3 | 10.01.88 | **Ipswich Town** (D2) | A | W | 2-1 | D'Avray og, Anderson |
| | 4 | 30.01.88 | **Chelsea** (D1) | H | W | 2-0 | Whiteside, McClair |
| | 5 | 20.02.88 | **Arsenal** (D1) | A | L | 1-2 | McClair |
| 1988-89 (D1) | 3 | 07.01.89 | **QPR** (D1) | H | D | 0-0 | |

| | | | | | | | |
|---|---|---|---|---|---|---|---|
| | 3r | 11.01.89 | **QPR** | A | D | 2-2aet | Gill, Graham |
| | 3 2r | 23.01.89 | **QPR** | H | W | 3-0 | McClair 2 (1p), Robson |
| | 4 | 28.01.89 | **Oxford Utd** (D2) | H | W | 4-0 | Hughes, Bruce, J Phillips og, Robson |
| | 5 | 18.02.89 | **Bournemouth** (D2) | A | D | 1-1 | Hughes |
| | 5r | 22.02.89 | **Bournemouth** | H | W | 1-0 | McClair |
| | 6 | 18.03.89 | **Nottingham Forest** (D1) | H | L | 0-1 | |
| 1989-90 (D1) | 3 | 07.01.90 | **Nottingham Forest** (D1 | A | W | 1-0 | Robins |
| | 4 | 28.01.90 | **Hereford Utd** (D4) | A | W | 1-0 | Blackmore |
| | 5 | 18.02.90 | **Newcastle Utd** (D1) | A | W | 3-2 | Robins, Wallace, McClair |
| | 6 | 11.03.90 | **Sheffield Utd** (D2) | A | W | 1-0 | McClair |
| | SF | 08.04.90 | **Oldham Athletic** (D2) | | D | 3-3aet | Robson, Webb, Wallace |
| | | | *played at Maine Road* | | | | |
| | SFr | 11.04.90 | **Oldham Athletic** | | W | 2-1aet | McClair, Robins |
| | | | *played at Maine Road* | | | | |
| | F | 12.05.90 | **Crystal Palace** (D1) | | D | 3-3aet | Hughes 2, Robson |
| | | | *played at Wembley Stadium* | | | | |
| | Fr | 17.05.90 | **Crystal Palace** | | W | 1-0 | Martin |
| | | | *played at Wembley Stadium* | | | | |
| 1990-91 (D1) | 3 | 05.01.91 | **QPR** (D1) | H | W | 2-1 | Hughes, McClair |
| | 4 | 26.01.91 | **Bolton Wanderers** (D3) | H | W | 1-0 | Hughes |
| | 5 | 18.02.91 | **Norwich City** (D1) | A | L | 1-2 | McClair |
| 1991-92 (D1) | 3 | 15.01.92 | **Leeds Utd** (D1) | A | W | 1-0 | Hughes |
| | 4 | 27.01.92 | **Southampton** (D1) | A | D | 0-0 | |
| | 4r | 05.02.92 | **Southampton** | H | D | 2-2aet | Kanchelskis, McClair |
| | | | *Southampton won 4-2 on penalties* | | | | |
| 1992-93 (PL) | 3 | 05.01.93 | **Bury** (D3) | H | W | 2-0 | Phelan, Gillespie |
| | 4 | 23.01.93 | **Brighton** (D2) | H | W | 1-0 | Giggs |
| | 5 | 14.02.93 | **Sheffield Utd** (PL) | A | L | 1-2 | Giggs |
| 1993-94 (PL) | 3 | 09.01.94 | **Sheffield Utd** | A | W | 1-0 | Hughes |
| | 4 | 30.01.94 | **Norwich City** (PL) | A | W | 2-0 | Keane, Cantona |
| | 5 | 20.02.94 | **Wimbledon** (PL) | A | W | 3-0 | Cantona, Ince, D Irwin |
| | 6 | 12.03.94 | **Charlton Athletic** (D1) | H | W | 3-1 | Hughes, Kanchelskis 2 |
| | SF | 10.04.94 | **Oldham Athletic** | | D | 1-1aet | Hughes |
| | | | *played at Wembley Stadium* | | | | |
| | SFr | 13.04.94 | **Oldham Athletic** | | W | 4-1 | Irwin, Kanchelskis, Robson, Giggs |
| | | | *played at Maine Road* | | | | |
| | F | 14.05.94 | **Chelsea** (PL) | | W | 4-0 | Cantona 2(2p), Hughes, McClair |
| | | | *played at Wembley Stadium* | | | | |
| 1994-95 (PL) | 3 | 09.01.95 | **Sheffield Utd** (D1) | A | W | 2-0 | Hughes, Cantona |
| | 4 | 28.01.95 | **Wrexham** (D2) | H | W | 5-2 | Irwin 2 (1p), Giggs, McClair, Humes og |
| | 5 | 19.02.95 | **Leeds Utd** (PL) | H | W | 3-1 | Bruce, McClair, Hughes |
| | 6 | 12.03.95 | **QPR** (PL) | H | W | 2-0 | Irwin, Sharpe |
| | SF | 09.04.95 | **Crystal Palace** (PL) | | D | 2-2aet | Irwin, Pallister |
| | | | *played at Villa Park* | | | | |
| | SFr | 12.04.95 | **Crystal Palace** | | W | 2-0 | Bruce, Pallister |
| | | | *played at Villa Park* | | | | |
| | F | 20.05.95 | **Everton** (PL) | | L | 0-1 | |
| | | | *played at Wembley Stadium* | | | | |
| 1995-96 (PL) | 3 | 06.01.96 | **Sunderland** (D1) | H | D | 2-2 | Butt, Cantona |
| | 3r | 16.01.96 | **Sunderland** | A | W | 2-1 | Scholes, Cole |
| | 4 | 27.01.96 | **Reading** (D1) | A | W | 3-0 | Giggs, Parker, Cantona |
| | 5 | 18.02.96 | **Manchester City** (PL) | H | W | 2-1 | Cantona (p), Sharpe |
| | 6 | 11.03.96 | **Southampton** (PL) | H | W | 2-0 | Cantona, Sharpe |
| | SF | 31.03.96 | **Chelsea** (PL) | | W | 2-1 | Cole, Beckham |
| | | | *played at Villa Park* | | | | |
| | F | 11.05.96 | **Liverpool** (PL) | | W | 1-0 | Cantona |
| | | | *played at Wembley Stadium* | | | | |
| 1996-97 (PL) | 3 | 05.01.97 | **Tottenham Hotspur** (PL) | H | W | 2-0 | Scholes, Beckham |
| | 4 | 25.01.97 | **Wimbledon** (PL) | H | D | 1-1 | Scholes |
| | 4r | 04.02.97 | **Wimbledon** | A | L | 0-1 | |
| 1997-98 (PL) | 3 | 04.01.98 | **Chelsea** (PL) | A | W | 5-3 | Beckham 2, Cole 2, Sheringham |

| | | | | | | | |
|---|---|---|---|---|---|---|---|
| | 4 | 24.01.98 | **Walsall** (D2) | H | W | 5-1 | Cole 2, Solskjaer 2, Johnsen |
| | 5 | 15.02.98 | **Barnsley** (PL) | H | D | 1-1 | Sheringham |
| | 5r | 25.02.98 | **Barnsley** | A | L | 2-3 | Sheringham, Cole |
| 1998-99 (PL) | 3 | 03.01.99 | **Middlesbrough** (PL) | H | W | 3-1 | Cole, Irwin (p), Giggs |
| | 4 | 24.01.99 | **Liverpool** (PL) | H | W | 2-1 | Yorke, Solskjaer |
| | 5 | 14.02.99 | **Fulham** (D2) | H | W | 1-0 | Cole |
| | 6 | 07.03.99 | **Chelsea** (PL) | H | D | 0-0 | |
| | 6r | 10.03.99 | **Chelsea** | A | W | 2-0 | Yorke 2 |
| | SF | 11.04.99 | **Arsenal** (PL)<br>*played at Villa Park* | | D | 0-0aet | |
| | SFr | 14.04.99 | **Arsenal**<br>*played at Villa Park* | | W | 2-1aet | Beckham, Giggs |
| | F | 22.05.99 | **Newcastle Utd** (PL)<br>*played at Wembley Stadium* | | W | 2-0 | Sheringham, Scholes |
| 1999-00 (PL) | | | *Did not enter due to commitment to take part in inaugural FIFA Club World Championship in Brazil in January 2000* | | | | |
| 2000-01 (PL) | 3 | 06.01.01 | **Fulham** (D1) | A | W | 2-1 | Solskjaer, Sheringham |
| | 4 | 28.01.01 | **West Ham Utd** (PL) | H | L | 0-1 | |
| 2001-02 (PL) | 3 | 06.01.02 | **Aston Villa** (PL) | A | W | 3-2 | Solskjaer, Van Nistelrooy 2 |
| | 4 | 26.01.02 | **Middlesbrough** (PL) | A | L | 0-2 | |
| 2002-03 (PL) | 3 | 04.01.03 | **Portsmouth** (D1) | H | W | 4-1 | Van Nistelrooy 2(2p), Beckham, Scholes |
| | 4 | 26.01.03 | **West Ham Utd** (PL) | H | W | 6-0 | Giggs 2, Van Nistelrooy 2, P Neville, Solskjaer |
| | 5 | 15.02.03 | **Arsenal** (PL) | H | L | 0-2 | |

## MANSFIELD TOWN

*Formed 1910. An earlier Mansfield Town played in the FA Cup in the 1890s, but they were a separate club. First entered FA Cup: 1910-11. Best FA Cup performance: 6th round, 1969. FA Cup record win: 10-1 v Highgate (Rotherham) 4th qualifying round, 1930-31. In Competition Proper: 8-0 v Scarborough, 1st round, 22.11.1952. Record FA Cup defeat: 0-8 v Worksop Town, 5th qualifying round replay, 1920-21. In Competition Proper: 0-5 v Sheffield Wed, 3rd round, 2nd leg, 09.01.1946; 0-5 v Bristol Rovers, 3rd round, 04.01.1958.*

| | | | | | | | |
|---|---|---|---|---|---|---|---|
| 1910-11 (CA) | | | P Market Harborough (A) 5-0; 1q Loughborough Cen. (H) 3-0; 2q Basford U (H) 2-2; 2qr Basford U (A) 3-1; 3q Hinckley U (A) 2-1; 4q Blackwell Colliery (H) 0-1 | | | | |
| 1911-12 (CA) | | | 1q Hinckley U (A) 0-1 | | | | |
| 1912-13 (CA) | | | P Notts Rangers (H) 5-0; 1q Netherfield Rangers (A) 3-2; 2q Loughborough Cen. (H) 5-2; 3q Sutton T (A) 1-3 | | | | |
| 1913-14 (CA) | | | P Mapperley (H) 3-1; 1q Netherfield R (H) 2-2; 1qr Netherfield R (A) 4-0; 2q Hinckley U (H) 1-3 | | | | |
| 1914-15 (CA) | | | P Sutton T (A) 0-5 | | | | |
| 1919-20 (CA) | | | P Shirebrook (A) 1-3 | | | | |
| 1920-21 (CA) | | | P Sutton Junction (H) 8-1; 1q Hucknall Byron (H) 2-1; 2q Grantham T (A) 3-1; 3q Boots Athletic (H) 3-0; 4q Scunthorpe U (A) 1-0; 5q Worksop T (A) 2-2; 5qr Worksop T (H) 0-8 | | | | |
| 1921-22 (CA) | | | P Mansfield Colliery (H) 8-0; 1q Stanton Hill (H) 6-0; 2q Grantham T (H) 2-0; 3q Welbeck Colliery (A) 2-1; 4q Gainsborough T (A) 2-1; 5q Darlaston (H) 2-0 6q Walsall (H) 1-1; 6qr Walsall (A) 0-4 | | | | |
| 1922-23 (CA) | | | P Langwith A (H) 2-1; 1q Shirebrook (H) 3-1; 2q Sutton Junction (H) 3-0; 3q Sutton T (H) 4-1; 4q Coalville Swifts (A) 2-0; 5q Wath Ath (H) 1-0; 6q Halifax T (H) 0-2 | | | | |
| 1923-24 (CA) | | | 1q Shirebrook (H) 1-1; 1qr Shirebrook (A) 2-4 | | | | |
| 1924-25 (CA) | | | P Sneinton (H) 6-1; 1q Whitwell Colliery (H) 7-0; 2q Sutton Junction (H) 3-0; 3q Grantham T (H) 1-0; 4q Doncaster R (A) 2-3 | | | | |
| 1925-26 (ML) | | | 4q Gainsborough T (H) 2-0 | | | | |
| | 1 | 28.11.25 | **Boston Utd** (ML) | A | L | 2-5 | Hart, Heathcote |
| 1926-27 (ML) | | | 4q Burton T (H) 2-1 | | | | |
| | 1 | 27.11.26 | **Wellington Town** (BDL) | A | W | 2-1 | Stamforth, Laycock |
| | 2 | 11.12.26 | **Walsall** (3N) | A | L | 0-2 | |
| 1927-28 (ML) | | | 4q Gainsborough T (A) 0-5 | | | | |
| 1928-29 (ML) | | | 4q Ardsley Ath (A) 2-2; 4qr Ardsley A (H) 2-0 | | | | |
| | 1 | 24.11.28 | **Shirebrook** (ML) | A | W | 4-2 | Morris 2, Staniforth, Kerry |
| | 2 | 08.12.28 | **Barrow** (3N) | A | W | 2-1 | Morris 2 |

| | | | | | | | | |
|---|---|---|---|---|---|---|---|---|
| | | 3 | 12.01.29 | **Wolverhampton W** (D2) | A | W | 1-0 | McLachlan |
| | | 4 | 26.01.29 | **Arsenal** (D1) | A | L | 0-2 | |
| 1929-30 | (ML) | 1 | 30.11.29 | **Manchester Central** (LC) | H | L | 0-2 | |
| 1930-31 | (ML) | | | 4q Highgate (H) 10-1 | | | | |
| | | 1 | 29.11.30 | **Halifax Town** (3N) | H | D | 2-2 | Devlin, Chambers |
| | | 1r | 03.12.30 | **Halifax Town** | A | L | 1-2 | Murphy |
| 1931-32 | (3S) | 1 | 28.11.31 | **Hull City** (3N) | A | L | 1-4 | Death |
| 1932-33 | (3N) | 1 | 26.11.32 | **Walsall** (3N) | A | L | 1-4 | Johnson |
| 1933-34 | (3N) | 1 | 25.11.33 | **New Brighton** (3N) | A | D | 0-0 | |
| | | 1r | 29.11.33 | **New Brighton** | H | L | 3-4 | Raynor, Johnson 2 |
| 1934-35 | (3N) | 1 | 24.11.34 | **Accrington Stanley** (3N) | H | W | 6-1 | Hunt 2, Atkinson, Dellow, Johnson 2 |
| | | 2 | 08.12.34 | **Tranmere Rovers** (3N) | H | W | 4-2 | Dellow, Johnson 2, Hunt |
| | | 3 | 12.01.35 | **Burnley** (D2) | A | L | 2-4 | Hunt, Johnson |
| 1935-36 | (3N) | 1 | 30.11.35 | **Hartlepools Utd** (3N) | H | L | 2-3 | Harston, Atkinson |
| 1936-37 | (3N) | 1 | 28.11.36 | **Barrow** (3N) | A | W | 6-0 | Magnall 4 (1p), Thorogood, Thomas |
| | | 2 | 12.12.36 | **Bournemouth** (3S) | H | L | 0-3 | |
| 1937-38 | (3S) | 1 | 27.11.37 | **Wellington Town** (BDL) | A | W | 2-1 | O'Connor, Bangay |
| | | 2 | 11.12.37 | **Lincoln City** | H | - | 1-2ab | Holmes |
| | | | | *abandoned after 62 minutes* | | | | |
| | | 2 | 15.12.37 | **Lincoln City** (3N) | H | W | 2-1 | Holmes, Crawshaw |
| | | 3 | 08.01.38 | **Leicester City** (D1) | H | L | 1-2 | Johnston |
| 1938-39 | (3S) | 1 | 26.11.38 | **Workington** (NEL) | A | D | 1-1 | Somerfield |
| | | 1r | 30.11.38 | **Workington** | | W | 2-1 | Somerfield, Dutton |
| | | 2 | 10.12.38 | **Halifax Town** (3N) | A | D | 1-1 | Somerfield |
| | | 2r | 14.12.38 | **Halifax Town** | H | D | 3-3aet | Dutton, Bell, Wilson |
| | | 2 2r | 19.12.38 | **Halifax Town** | | D | 0-0aet | |
| | | | | *played at Belle Vue, Doncaster* | | | | |
| | | 2 3r | 21.12.38 | **Halifax Town** | | L | 1-2aet | Somerfield |
| | | | | *played at Old Trafford* | | | | |
| 1945-46 | (3S) | 1 1L | 17.11.45 | **Gainsborough T** (ML) | H | W | 3-0 | Harkin, Wombwell 2 |
| | | 1 2L | 24.11.45 | **Gainsborough T** | A | L | 2-4aet | Poole, Wombwell |
| | | 2 1L | 08.12.45 | **Grantham Town** (ML) | A | W | 2-1 | Thorpe, Wombwell |
| | | 2 2L | 15.12.45 | **Grantham Town** | H | W | 2-1 | Hogg, Wombwell |
| | | 3 1L | 05.01.46 | **Sheffield Wed** (D2) | H | D | 0-0 | |
| | | 3 2L | 09.01.46 | **Sheffield Wed** | A | L | 0-5 | |
| 1946-47 | (3S) | 1 | 30.11.46 | **Northampton Town** (3S) | A | L | 0-2 | |
| 1947-48 | (3N) | 1 | 29.11.47 | **Wimbledon** (IL) | A | W | 1-0 | Cooling |
| | | 2 | 13.12.47 | **Oldham Athletic** (3N) | A | W | 1-0 | Cooling |
| | | 3 | 10.01.48 | **Stoke City** (D1) | H | L | 2-4 | Oscroft, Butt (p) |
| 1948-49 | (3N) | 1 | 27.11.48 | **Gloucester City** (SL) | H | W | 4-0 | Mercer 3, Oscroft |
| | | 2 | 11.12.48 | **Northampton Town** (3S) | H | W | 2-1aet | Mercer, Oscroft |
| | | 3 | 08.01.49 | **Preston North End** (D1) | A | L | 1-2 | Oscroft |
| 1949-50 | (3N) | 1 | 26.11.49 | **Walsall** (3S) | H | W | 4-1 | Antonio, Coole (2), Steele |
| | | 2 | 10.12.49 | **Doncaster Rovers** (3N) | A | L | 0-1 | |
| 1950-51 | (3N) | 1 | 25.11.50 | **Walthamstow Ave** (IL) | H | W | 1-0 | Steele |
| | | 2 | 09.12.50 | **Chelmsford City** (SL) | A | W | 4-1 | Coole, Donaldson 2, Barks |
| | | 3 | 06.01.51 | **Swansea Town** (D2) | H | W | 2-0 | Steele 2 |
| | | 4 | 27.01.51 | **Sheffield Utd** (D2) | A | D | 0-0 | |
| | | 4r | 31.01.51 | **Sheffield Utd** | H | W | 2-1aet | Steele, Ottewell |
| | | 5 | 10.02.51 | **Blackpool** (D1) | A | L | 0-2 | |
| 1951-52 | (3N) | 1 | 24.11.51 | **Stockton** (NEL) | A | D | 1-1 | Lewis |
| | | 1r | 28.11.51 | **Stockton** | H | L | 0-2 | |
| 1952-53 | (3N) | 1 | 22.11.52 | **Scarborough** (ML) | A | W | 8-0 | Watson, Marron 2, Adam 2, Fox 3 |
| | | 2 | 06.12.52 | **Accrington Stanley** (3N) | A | W | 2-0 | Fox, Adam |
| | | 3 | 10.01.53 | **Nottingham Forest** (D2) | H | L | 0-1 | |
| 1953-54 | (3N) | 1 | 21.11.53 | **Hartlepools Utd** (3N) | A | D | 1-1 | S Watson |
| | | 1r | 25.11.53 | **Hartlepools Utd** | H | L | 0-3 | |
| 1954-55 | (3N) | 1 | 20.11.54 | **Bradford City** (3N) | A | L | 1-3 | Adam |
| 1955-56 | (3N) | 1 | 19.11.55 | **Stockport County** (3N) | H | W | 2-0 | Watkin, Jepson |
| | | 2 | 10.12.55 | **York City** (3N) | A | L | 1-2 | Darwin |
| 1956-57 | (3N) | 1 | 17.11.56 | **Workington** (3N) | H | D | 1-1 | Murray |

| | | | | | | | | |
|---|---|---|---|---|---|---|---|---|
| | | 1r | 20.11.56 | **Workington** | A | L | 1-2 | Jepson |
| 1957-58 | (3N) | 1 | 16.11.57 | **Halifax Town** (3N) | H | W | 2-0 | Chapman, Mitten (p) |
| | | 2 | 07.12.57 | **Wigan Athletic** (LC) | A | D | 1-1 | Chapman |
| | | 2r | 11.12.57 | **Wigan Athletic** | H | W | 3-1 | Mitten, Morris 2 |
| | | 3 | 04.01.58 | **Bristol Rovers** (D2) | A | L | 0-5 | |
| 1958-59 | (D3) | 1 | 15.11.58 | **Bradford City** (D3) | H | L | 3-4 | B Thomas, Uphill 2 |
| 1959-60 | (D3) | 1 | 14.11.59 | **Accrington Stanley** (D3) | A | W | 2-1 | Nugent, Humble |
| | | 2 | 05.12.59 | **Chester** (D4) | H | W | 2-0 | Fitzsimmons, Jones |
| | | 3 | 09.01.60 | **Blackpool** (D1) | A | L | 0-3 | |
| 1960-61 | (D4) | 1 | 05.11.60 | **Blyth Spartans** (NCo) | H | W | 3-1 | Fitzsimmons, Coates, Wragg |
| | | 2 | 30.11.60 | **Accrington Stanley** (D4) | A | L | 0-3 | |
| 1961-62 | (D4) | 1 | 04.11.61 | **Grimsby Town** (D3) | H | W | 3-2 | Wagstaff, Hall 2 |
| | | 2 | 25.11.61 | **Southport** (D4) | A | L | 2-4 | Stringfellow, Shaw |
| 1962-63 | (D4) | 1 | 03.11.62 | **Hounslow Town** (AL) | A | D | 3-3 | Hollett 2, Wagstaff |
| | | 1r | 05.11.62 | **Hounslow Town** | H | W | 9-2 | Chapman 3, Hollett 3, Weir, Wagstaff, Askey |
| | | 2 | 24.11.62 | **Crystal Palace** (D3) | A | D | 2-2 | Wagstaff 2 |
| | | 2r | 26.11.62 | **Crystal Palace** | H | W | 7-2 | Wagstaff 3, Long og, Askey, R Chapman 2 |
| | | 3 | 09.01.63 | **Ipswich Town** (D1) | H | L | 2-3 | Hall, Askey |
| 1963-64 | (D3) | 1 | 20.11.63 | **Oldham Athletic** (D3) | A | L | 2-3 | R Chapman, Hall |
| 1964-65 | (D3) | 1 | 14.11.64 | **Oxford Utd** (D4) | A | W | 1-0 | Hall |
| | | 2 | 05.12.64 | **Newport County** (D4) | A | L | 0-3 | |
| 1965-66 | (D3) | 1 | 13.11.65 | **Oldham Athletic** (D3) | H | L | 1-3 | MacReady |
| 1966-67 | (D3) | 1 | 26.11.66 | **Bangor City** (CC) | H | W | 4-1 | Mitchinson, Brace, Curry 2 |
| | | 2 | 07.01.67 | **Scunthorpe Utd** (D3) | H | W | 2-1 | Mitchinson, Brace |
| | | 3 | 28.01.67 | **Middlesbrough** (D3) | H | W | 2-0 | Brace, Curry |
| | | 4 | 18.02.67 | **Sheffield Wed** (D1) | A | L | 0-4 | |
| 1967-68 | (D3) | 1 | 09.01.67 | **Tow Law Town** (NL) | A | - | 0-0ab | |
| | | | | *abandoned at half-time – blizzard* | | | | |
| | | 1 | 13.01.67 | **Tow Law Town** | A | L | 1-5 | Melling |
| 1968-69 | (D3) | 1 | 16.11.68 | **Tow Law Town** (NL) | H | W | 4-1 | Ledger 2, Sharkey, Keeley |
| | | 2 | 07.12.68 | **Rotherham Utd** (D3) | A | D | 2-2 | Sharkey, Keeley |
| | | 2r | 09.12.68 | **Rotherham Utd** | H | W | 1-0 | Ledger |
| | | 3 | 04.01.69 | **Sheffield Utd** (D2) | H | W | 2-1 | Roberts 2 |
| | | 4 | 25.01.69 | **Southend Utd** (D4) | H | W | 2-1 | Sharkey, Roberts |
| | | 5 | 26.02.69 | **West Ham Utd** (D1) | H | W | 3-0 | Roberts, Keeley, Sharkey |
| | | 6 | 08.03.69 | **Leicester City** (D1) | H | L | 0-1 | |
| 1969-70 | (D3) | 1 | 15.11.69 | **Bury** (D3) | A | D | 2-2 | Keeley, Stenson |
| | | 1r | 19.11.69 | **Bury** | H | W | 2-0 | Bates, Patridge |
| | | 2 | 06.12.69 | **Shrewsbury Town** (D3) | A | W | 2-1 | Keeley, Roberts |
| | | 3 | 03.01.70 | **Barnsley** (D3) | H | W | 3-2 | Walter, Patridge, Goodfellow (p) |
| | | 4 | 24.01.70 | **Blackpool** (D2) | A | W | 2-0 | D Jones 2 |
| | | 5 | 07.02.70 | **Leeds Utd** (D1) | A | L | 0-2 | |
| 1970-71 | (D3) | 1 | 21.11.70 | **Wrexham** (D3) | H | W | 2-0 | Stenson, D Roberts |
| | | 2 | 12.12.70 | **Scunthorpe Utd** (D4) | A | L | 0-3 | |
| 1971-72 | (D3) | 1 | 20.11.71 | **Chester** (D4) | A | D | 1-1 | Bingham |
| | | 1r | 22.11.71 | **Chester** | H | W | 4-3 | Bingham, Fairbrother, Thompson, Roberts (p) |
| | | 2 | 11.12.71 | **Tranmere Rovers** (D3) | H | D | 2-2 | Thompson, Fairbrother |
| | | 2r | 15.12.71 | **Tranmere Rovers** | A | L | 2-4 | Fairbrother 2 |
| 1972-73 | (D4) | 1 | 18.11.72 | **York City** (D4) | A | L | 1-2 | Fairbrother |
| 1973-74 | (D4) | 1 | 24.11.73 | **York City** (D3) | A | D | 0-0 | |
| | | 1r | 10.12.73 | **York City** | H | W | 5-3 | Thompson, C Foster, Walker, McCaffrey, Eccles |
| | | 2 | 15.12.73 | **Scunthorpe Utd** (D4) | H | D | 1-1 | Eccles |
| | | 2r | 18.12.73 | **Scunthorpe Utd** | A | L | 0-1 | |
| 1974-75 | (D4) | 1 | 23.11.74 | **Wrexham** (D3) | H | W | 3-1 | Eccles 2, McCaffrey |
| | | 2 | 14.12.74 | **Wigan Athletic** (NPL) | A | D | 1-1 | Eccles |
| | | 2r | 16.12.74 | **Wigan Athletic** | H | W | 3-1 | Hodgson, O'Connor 2 |
| | | 3 | 04.01.75 | **Cambridge Utd** (D4) | H | W | 1-0 | Clarke |
| | | 4 | 25.01.75 | **Bury** (D3) | A | W | 2-1 | McCaffrey, Clarke |

| | | | | | | | | |
|---|---|---|---|---|---|---|---|---|
| | | 5 | 15.02.75 | **Carlisle Utd** (D1) | H | L | 0-1 | |
| 1975-76 | (D3) | 1 | 22.11.75 | **Wrexham** (D3) | H | D | 1-1 | Eccles |
| | | 1r | 24.11.75 | **Wrexham** | A | D | 1-1aet | Eccles |
| | | 1 2r | 08.12.75 | **Wrexham** | | W | 2-1 | Laverick, May og |
| | | | | *played at Villa Park* | | | | |
| | | 2 | 13.12.75 | **Lincoln City** (D4) | H | L | 1-2 | McDonald |
| 1976-77 | (D3) | 1 | 20.11.76 | **Huddersfield Town** (D4) | A | D | 0-0 | |
| | | 1r | 22.11.76 | **Huddersfield Town** | H | W | 2-1 | Randall, Eccles |
| | | 2 | 15.12.76 | **Matlock Town** (NPL) | H | L | 2-5 | Matthews, C Foster |
| 1977-78 | (D2) | 3 | 07.01.78 | **Plymouth Argyle** (D3) | H | W | 1-0 | Miller |
| | | 4 | 06.02.78 | **Bolton Wanderers** (D2) | A | L | 0-1 | |
| 1978-79 | (D3) | 1 | 25.11.78 | **Shrewsbury Town** (D3) | H | L | 0-2 | |
| 1979-80 | (D3) | 1 | 24.11.79 | **Blyth Spartans** (NL) | A | W | 2-0 | McClelland, Allen |
| | | 2 | 15.12.79 | **Doncaster Rovers** (D4) | A | W | 2-1 | Curtis, Austin |
| | | 3 | 05.01.80 | **Brighton** (D1) | H | L | 0-2 | |
| 1980-81 | (D4) | 1 | 22.11.80 | **Rochdale** (D4) | H | W | 3-1 | Parkinson 2 (2ps), Caldwell |
| | | 2 | 13.12.80 | **Mossley** (NPL) | A | W | 3-1 | Allen (p), Thomson, Caldwell |
| | | 3 | 03.01.81 | **Carlisle Utd** (D3) | H | D | 2-2 | Bird, Parkinson |
| | | 3r | 06.01.81 | **Carlisle Utd** | A | L | 1-2 | Pollard |
| 1981-82 | (D4) | 1 | 21.11.81 | **Doncaster Rovers** (D3) | H | L | 0-1 | |
| 1982-83 | (D4) | 1 | 20.11.82 | **Stockport County** (D4) | H | W | 3-2 | Bell, Dungworth 2 |
| | | 2 | 11.12.82 | **Bradford City** (D3) | H | D | 1-1 | Dungworth (p) |
| | | 2r | 15.12.82 | **Bradford City** | A | L | 2-3 | Dungworth, Bell |
| 1983-84 | (D4) | 1 | 19.11.83 | **Doncaster Rovers** (D4) | H | W | 3-0 | Caldwell, Calderwood,Barrowclough |
| | | 2 | 10.12.83 | **Bolton Wanderers** (D3) | A | L | 0-2 | |
| 1984-85 | (D4) | 1 | 17.11.84 | **Rotherham Utd** (D3) | H | W | 2-1 | Caldwell, Lowery |
| | | 2 | 08.12.84 | **Bradford City** (D3) | A | L | 1-2 | Barrowclough |
| 1985-86 | (D4) | 1 | 16.11.85 | **Port Vale** (D4) | H | D | 1-1 | Chamberlain |
| | | 1r | 18.11.85 | **Port Vale** | A | L | 0-1 | |
| 1986-87 | (D3) | 1 | 16.11.86 | **Darlington** (D3) | A | L | 1-2 | Foster |
| 1987-88 | (D3) | 1 | 14.11.87 | **Preston North End** (D3) | A | D | 1-1 | Stringfellow |
| | | 1r | 17.11.87 | **Preston North End** | H | W | 4-2 | Cassells 2, Charles (p), Kent |
| | | 2 | 05.12.87 | **Lincoln City** (Conf) | H | W | 4-3 | Lowery, Foster, Cassells, Kent |
| | | 3 | 09.01.88 | **Bath City** (Conf) | H | W | 4-0 | Ryan, Withey (og), Charles 2 |
| | | 4 | 30.01.88 | **Wimbledon** (D1) | H | L | 1-2 | Kent |
| 1988-89 | (D3) | 1 | 19.11.88 | **Sheffield Utd** (D3) | H | D | 1-1 | Kent |
| | | 1r | 22.11.88 | **Sheffield Utd** | A | L | 1-2 | Kearney |
| 1989-90 | (D3) | 1 | 19.11.89 | **Wigan Athletic** (D3) | A | L | 0-2 | |
| 1990-91 | (D3) | 1 | 17.11.90 | **Preston North End** (D3) | A | W | 1-0 | Kearney |
| | | 2 | 17.12.90 | **York City** (D4) | H | W | 2-1 | Charles, Wilkinson |
| | | 3 | 05.01.91 | **Sheffield Wed** (D2) | H | L | 0-2 | |
| 1991-92 | (D4) | 1 | 16.11.91 | **Preston North End** (D3) | H | - | 1-1ab | Wilkinson |
| | | | | *abandoned after 32 minutes – fog* | | | | |
| | | 1 | 27.11.91 | **Preston North End** | H | L | 0-1 | |
| 1992-93 | (D2) | 1 | 14.11.92 | **Shrewsbury Town** (D3) | A | L | 1-3 | Fairclough |
| 1993-94 | (D3) | 1 | 13.11.93 | **Preston North End** (D3) | H | L | 1-2 | Wilkinson |
| 1994-95 | (D3) | 1 | 22.11.94 | **Northwich V** (Conf) | H | W | 3-1 | Hadley, Holland 2 |
| | | 2 | 03.12.94 | **Halifax Town** (Conf) | A | D | 0-0 | |
| | | 2r | 13.12.94 | **Halifax Town** | H | W | 2-1 | Aspinall, Holland |
| | | 3 | 07.01.95 | **Wolverhampton W** (D1) | H | L | 2-3 | Donaldson, Ireland |
| 1995-96 | (D3) | 1 | 11.11.95 | **Doncaster Rovers** (D3) | H | W | 4-2 | Harper, Sherlock, Parkin, Doolan |
| | | 2 | 02.12.95 | **Crewe Alexandra** (D2) | A | L | 0-2 | |
| 1996-97 | (D3) | 1 | 16.11.96 | **Consett** (NL) | H | W | 4-0 | Ford, Eustace, Doolan, Wood |
| | | 2 | 07.12.96 | **Stockport County** (D2) | H | L | 0-3 | |
| 1997-98 | (D3) | 1 | 15.11.97 | **Oldham Athletic** (D2) | A | D | 1-1 | Whitehall |
| | | 1r | 25.11.97 | **Oldham Athletic** | H | L | 0-1 | |
| 1998-99 | (D3) | 1 | 14.11.98 | **Hayes** (Conf) | H | W | 2-1 | Clarke, Lormor |
| | | 2 | 05.12.98 | **Southport** (Conf) | H | L | 1-2 | Lormor |
| 1999-00 | (D3) | 1 | 30.10.99 | **Bristol City** (D2) | A | L | 2-3 | Lormor (p), Blake |
| 2000-01 | (D3) | 1 | 18.11.00 | **Peterborough Utd** (D2) | H | D | 1-1 | Greenacre (p) |
| | | 1r | 28.11.00 | **Peterborough Utd** | A | L | 0-4 | |

| | | | | | | | |
|---|---|---|---|---|---|---|---|
| 2001-02 (D3) | 1 | 17.11.01 | **Oxford Utd** (D3) | H | W | 1-0 | Greenacre |
| | 2 | 08.12.01 | **Huddersfield Town** (D2) | H | W | 4-0 | Greenacre 3, Corden |
| | 3 | 05.01.02 | **Leicester City** (PL) | A | L | 1-2 | Greenacre |
| 2002-03 (D2) | 1 | 16.11.02 | **Team Bath** (WL) | A | W | 4-2 | Lawrence 2, Tisdale og, Christie |
| | 2 | 07.12.02 | **Crewe Alexandra** (D2) | A | L | 0-3 | |

## MARCH TOWN UNITED

*Formed 1885. First entered FA Cup: 1950-51. Members of the Eastern Counties League.*

| | | | | | | | |
|---|---|---|---|---|---|---|---|
| 1955-56 (ECL) | 1 | 19.11.55 | **Brentford** (3S) | A | L | 0-4 | |
| 1978-79 (ECL) | 1 | 25.11.78 | **Swindon Town** (D3) | A | L | 0-2 | |

## MARGATE

*Formed 1896. Folded 1928. Reformed 1929. First entered FA Cup: 1913-14. Known as Thanet United 1981 before reverting to Margae in 1989. League clubs beaten: Gillingham, QPR, Crystal Palace, Bournemouth, Swansea City, Leyton Orient. Members of The Conference.*

| | | | | | | | |
|---|---|---|---|---|---|---|---|
| 1929-30 (KL) | 1 | 30.11.29 | **Gillingham** (3S) | A | W | 2-0 | Adams, Kitto |
| | 2 | 14.12.29 | **Northampton Town** (3S) | A | L | 0-6 | |
| 1932-33 (KL) | 1 | 26.11.32 | **Ryde Sports** (HL) | H | W | 5-0 | Harris, Mays, Hughes, Moran, Mayn |
| | 2 | 10.12.32 | **Gateshead AFC** (3N) | A | L | 2-5 | Harris, Mays |
| 1933-34 (SL) | 1 | 25.11.33 | **Torquay Utd** (3S) | A | D | 1-1 | Mays |
| | 1r | 30.11.33 | **Torquay Utd** | H | L | 0-2 | |
| 1935-36 (SL) | 1 | 30.11.35 | **QPR** (3S) | H | W | 3-1 | Clare, Robbie, Lambert |
| | 2 | 14.12.35 | **Crystal Palace** (3S) | H | W | 3-1 | Evans 3 |
| | 3 | 11.01.36 | **Blackpool** (D2) | A | L | 1-3 | Clare |
| 1955-56 (KL) | 1 | 19.11.55 | **Walsall** (3S) | H | D | 2-2 | Kelly 2 |
| | 1r | 24.11.55 | **Walsall** | A | L | 1-6 | Phillips |
| 1956-57 (KL) | 1 | 17.11.56 | **Dunstable Town** (HEL) | H | W | 3-1 | Bennett, Marsh, Roche |
| | 2 | 08.12.56 | **Millwall** (3S) | A | L | 0-4 | |
| 1957-58 (KL) | 1 | 16.11.57 | **Crystal Palace** (3S) | H | L | 2-3 | Bostock, Kearns |
| 1958-59 (KL) | 1 | 15.11.58 | **Headington Utd** (SL) | A | L | 2-3 | Yeomans 2 |
| 1959-60 (SL) | 1 | 14.11.59 | **Kettering Town** (SL) | A | D | 1-1 | Kearns |
| | 1r | 19.11.59 | **Kettering Town** | H | W | 3-2 | Kearns 3 |
| | 2 | 05.12.59 | **Crystal Palace** (D4) | H | D | 0-0 | |
| | 2r | 09.12.59 | **Crystal Palace** | A | L | 0-3 | |
| 1961-62 (SL) | 1 | 04.11.61 | **Bournemouth** (D3) | A | W | 3-0 | Roche, Blackburn, Fraser |
| | 2 | 25.11.61 | **Notts County** (D3) | H | D | 1-1 | Barnett |
| | 2r | 30.11.61 | **Notts County** | A | L | 1-3 | Blackburn |
| 1962-63 (SL) | 1 | 03.11.62 | **Millwall** (D3) | A | L | 1-3 | Jeans |
| 1963-64 (SL) | 1 | 16.11.63 | **Brentford** (D3) | A | D | 2-2 | Roche, Blackburn |
| | 1r | 20.11.63 | **Brentford** | H | L | 0-2 | |
| 1967-68 (SL) | 1 | 13.12.67 | **Yeovil Town** (SL) | A | W | 3-1 | Amato 2, Fahy |
| | 2 | 06.01.68 | **Peterborough Utd** (D3) | H | L | 0-4 | |
| 1968-69 (SL) | 1 | 16.11.68 | **Northampton Town** (D3) | A | L | 1-3 | Houston |
| 1969-70 (SL) | 1 | 15.11.69 | **Aldershot** (D4) | H | L | 2-7 | Ray, Houston |
| 1970-71 (SL) | 1 | 21.11.70 | **Dagenham** (AL) | A | L | 0-2 | |
| 1971-72 (SL) | 1 | 20.11.71 | **Bournemouth** (D3) | A | L | 0-11 | |
| 1972-73 (SL) | 1 | 18.11.72 | **Swansea City** (D3) | H | W | 1-0 | Jones |
| | 2 | 09.12.72 | **Walton & Hersham** (IL) | A | W | 1-0 | Brown |
| | 3 | 13.01.73 | **Tottenham Hotspur** (D1) | H | L | 0-6 | |
| 1997-98 (SL) | 1 | 16.11.97 | **Fulham** (D2) | H | L | 1-2 | Munday (p) |
| 2002-03 (Conf) | 1 | 16.11.02 | **Leyton Orient** (D3) | A | D | 1-1 | Keister |
| | 1r | 26.11.02 | **Leyton Orient** | H | W | 1-0 | Keister (p) |
| | 2 | 07.12.02 | **Cardiff City** (D2) | H | L | 0-3 | |

## MARINE

*Formed 1894 as Waterloo Melville. Marine 1903. Based in Crosby, Liverpool. First entered FA Cup: 1920-21. FA Amateur Cup runners-up: 1932. League clubs beaten: Barnsley, Halifax Town. Members of the Northern Premier League.*

| | | | | | | | |
|---|---|---|---|---|---|---|---|
| 1932-33 (LCC) | 1 | 26.11.32 | **Hartlepools Utd** (3N) | H | L | 2-5 | Constantine, Jones |
| 1945-46 (LCC) | 1 1L | 17.11.45 | **Stalybridge Celtic** (CC) | H | W | 4-0 | Fenton 2, Jackson, Bretton |
| | 1 2L | 24.11.45 | **Stalybridge Celtic** | A | D | 3-3 | Bretton, Fenton, Jolliffe |
| | 2 1L | 08.12.45 | **Port Vale** (3S) | A | L | 1-3 | Peacock |

| | | | | | | | | |
|---|---|---|---|---|---|---|---|---|
| | | 2 2L | 15.12.45 | **Port Vale** | H | D | 1-1 | Hanson |
| 1946-47 | (LC) | 1 | 30.11.46 | **Wrexham** (3N) | A | L | 0-5 | |
| 1947-48 | (LC) | 1 | 29.11.47 | **New Brighton** (3N) | A | L | 0-4 | |
| 1974-75 | (CC) | 1 | 23.11.74 | **Rochdale** (D4) | A | D | 0-0 | |
| | | 1r | 27.11.74 | **Rochdale** | H | L | 1-2aet | Woosey |
| 1975-76 | (CC) | 1 | 22.11.75 | **Barnsley** (D4) | H | W | 3-1 | Burke og, Glover 2 |
| | | 2 | 13.12.75 | **Hartlepool** (D4) | H | D | 1-1 | Shergold |
| | | 2r | 15.12.75 | **Hartlepool** | A | L | 3-6 | Edwards, P Smith (p), Shergold |
| 1989-90 | (NPL) | 1 | 17.11.89 | **Rochdale** (D4) | H | L | 0-1 | |
| | | | | *played at Anfield* | | | | |
| 1992-93 | (NPL) | 1 | 14.11.92 | **Halifax Town** (D3) | H | W | 4-1 | Ward, Gautrey, Rowland, Camden |
| | | 2 | 05.12.92 | **Stafford Rangers** (Conf) | H | W | 3-2 | Murray, Gautrey |
| | | 3 | 12.01.93 | **Crewe Alexandra** (D3) | A | L | 1-3 | Johnson |
| 1993-94 | (NPL) | 1 | 13.11.93 | **Stalybridge Celtic** (Conf) | A | D | 1-1 | Rowlands |
| | | 1r | 29.11.93 | **Stalybridge Celtic** | H | D | 4-4aet | Camden 2, Murray, Doherty (p) |
| | | | | *Stalybridge Celtic won 4-2 on penalties* | | | | |
| 1995-96 | (NPL) | 1 | 11.11.95 | **Shrewsbury Town** (D2) | A | L | 2-11 | Penman, Rowlands |

## MARLOW

*Formed 1870 as Great Marlow. One of the 15 original entrants in the FA Cup in the 1871-72 season, their match against local rivals Maidenhead on November 11, 1871 was on the first day of FA Cup competition. Have entered every FA Cup since then, apart from the 1910-11 season. League club beaten: Oxford United. Members of the Isthmian League.*

| | | | | | | | |
|---|---|---|---|---|---|---|---|
| 1871-72 | 1 | 11.11.71 | **Maidenhead** | A | L | 0-2 | |
| 1872-73 | 1 | 26.10.72 | **Maidenhead** | A | L | 0-1 | |
| 1873-74 | 1 | 09.10.73 | **Pilgrims** | A | L | 0-1 | |
| 1874-75 | 1 | 07.11.74 | **Royal Engineers** | A | L | 0-3 | |
| 1875-76 | 1 | 03.11.75 | **Swifts** | A | L | 0-2 | |
| 1876-77 | 1 | 04.11.76 | **Herts Rangers** | A | W | 2-1 | |
| | 2 | 29.11.76 | **Forest School** | H | W | 1-0 | Cox |
| | 3 | 24.01.77 | **Upton Park** | A | D | 2-2 | Price, Vardy |
| | 3r | 27.01.77 | **Upton Park** | A | L | 0-1 | |
| 1877-78 | 1 | 03.11.77 | **Hendon (1874)** | H | W | 2-0 | Flint 2 |
| | 2 | 15.12.77 | **Barnes** | A | L | 1-3 | |
| 1878-79 | 1 | 09.11.78 | **Grey Friars** | A | L | 1-2 | |
| 1879-80 | 1 | 06.11.79 | **Oxford University** | A | D | 1-1 | Flint |
| | 1r | 10.11.79 | **Oxford University** | H | L | 0-1 | |
| 1880-81 | 1 | 30.10.80 | **Clarence** | H | W | 6-0 | RA Lunnon 3, Shaw 2, Flint |
| | 2 | 11.12.80 | **West End** | H | W | 4-0 | J Flint, R A Lunnon, R H Lunnon, Milward |
| | 4 | 19.02.81 | **Romford (1876)** | A | L | 1-2 | R H Lunnon |
| 1881-82 | 1 | 17.10.81 | **Brentwood** | H | W | 3-1 | G Flint 2, RH Lunnon |
| | 2 | 30.11.81 | **St Bart's Hospital** | H | W | 2-0 | R A Lunnon, R H. Lunnon |
| | 3 | 17.12.81 | **Dreadnought FC** | A | W | 2-1 | Shaw |
| | 4 | | Reading | | | - | |
| | | | *Reading scratched. Marlow walkover* | | | | |
| | 5 | 14.02.82 | **Old Foresters** | A | D | 0-0 | Shaw |
| | 5r | 18.02.82 | **Old Foresters** | H | W | 1-0 | |
| | SF | 04.03.82 | **Old Etonians** | | L | 0-5 | |
| | | | *played at Kennington Oval* | | | | |
| 1882-83 | 1 | 28.10.82 | **Hornchurch** | H | W | 2-0 | |
| | 2 | | Reading Minster | | | - | |
| | | | *Reading Minster scratched. Marlow walkover* | | | | |
| | 3 | | bye | | | | |
| | 4 | 27.01.83 | **Hendon (1874)** | H | L | 0-3 | |
| 1883-84 | 1 | 10.11.83 | **Hornchurch** | A | W | 9-0 | R A. Lunnon 5, Shaw 2, Walker 2 |
| | 2 | 01.12.83 | **Swifts** | A | L | 0-2 | |
| 1884-85 | 1 | 08.11.84 | **Royal Engineers** | H | W | 10-1 | R H Lunnon 2, Walker 2, R A Lunnon, Bailey, 4 others |
| | 2 | 06.12.84 | **Old Carthusians** | A | L | 3-5 | R A Lunnon, Pigg, Speller |
| 1885-86 | 1 | 31.10.85 | **Luton Town** | H | W | 3-0 | H Walker 2, og |
| | 2 | 21.11.85 | **Old Etonians** | H | W | 6-1 | |

| | | | | | | | |
|---|---|---|---|---|---|---|---|
| | 3 | | Old Wykehamists | | | - | |
| | | | *Marlow scratched. Old Wykehamists walkover* | | | | |
| 1886-87 | 1 | 23.10.86 | **Rochester** | A | W | 2-0 | |
| | 2 | 20.11.86 | **Upton Park** | H | W | 4-0 | |
| | 3 | 11.12.86 | **Dulwich** | H | W | 2-0 | |
| | 4 | | bye | | | | |
| | 5 | 29.01.87 | **Notts County** | A | L | 2-5 | |
| 1887-88 | 1 | 08.10.87 | **South Reading** | H | W | 4-1 | |
| | 2 | 05.11.87 | **Old Foresters** | H | L | 2-3aet | |
| 1892-93 | 1 | 21.01.93 | **Middlesbrough Iron** (NL) | H | L | 1-3 | Shaw |
| 1991-92 (IL) | 1 | 16.11.91 | **WBA** (D3) | A | L | 0-6 | |
| 1992-93 (IL) | 1 | 14.11.92 | **Salisbury City** (SL) | H | D | 3-3 | Lay, Watkins, Glasgow |
| | 1r | 05.12.92 | **Salisbury City** | A | D | 2-2aet | Hannigan, Glasgow |
| | | | *Marlow won 4-3 on penalties* | | | | |
| | 2 | 09.12.92 | **VS Rugby** (SL) | A | D | 0-0 | |
| | 2r | 15.12.92 | **VS Rugby** | H | W | 2-0 | Bushay, Watkins |
| | 3 | 02.01.93 | **Tottenham Hotspur** (PL) | H | L | 1-5 | Lay |
| | | | *played at White Hart Lane* | | | | |
| 1993-94 (IL) | 1 | 13.11.93 | **Plymouth Argyle** (D2) | H | L | 0-2 | |
| 1994-95 (IL) | 1 | 13.11.94 | **Oxford Utd** (D2) | H | W | 2-0 | Ceasar 2 |
| | 2 | 04.12.94 | **Woking** (Conf) | H | W | 2-1 | R Evans, C Evans |
| | 3 | 07.01.95 | **Swindon Town** (D1) | A | L | 0-2 | |

## MATLOCK TOWN

*Formed 1885. First entered FA Cup: 1885-86. FA Trophy winners: 1975. League club beaten: Mansfield Town. Members of the Northern Premier League.*

| | | | | | | | |
|---|---|---|---|---|---|---|---|
| 1885-86 | 1 | 17.10.85 | **Stafford Road** | A | L | 0-7 | |
| 1886-87 | 1 | 30.10.86 | **Wolverhampton W** | A | L | 0-6 | |
| 1887-88 | 1 | 15.10.87 | **Rotherham Town** | H | L | 2-3 | Turner og, AN Other |
| 1959-60 (CA) | 1 | 14.11.59 | **Crook Town** (NL) | A | D | 2-2 | Lambert (p), Boot |
| | 1r | 19.11.59 | **Crook Town** | H | L | 0-1 | |
| 1974-75 (NPL) | 1 | 23.11.74 | **Blackburn Rovers** (D3) | H | L | 1-4 | Stuart |
| 1975-76 (NPL) | 1 | 22.11.75 | **Wigan Athletic** (NPL) | A | L | 1-4 | N Fenoughty |
| 1976-77 (NPL) | 1 | 20.11.76 | **Wigan Athletic** | H | W | 2-0 | T Fenoughty, N Fenoughty |
| | 2 | 15.12.76 | **Mansfield Town** (D3) | A | W | 5-2 | Goodwin, N Fenoughty 2 (1p), Oxley, Scott |
| | 3 | 08.01.77 | **Carlisle Utd** (D2) | A | L | 1-5 | Oxley |
| 1989-90 (NPL) | 1 | 17.11.89 | **Scunthorpe Utd** (D4) | A | L | 1-4 | Walker |

## MELLORS LIMITED (NOTTINGHAM)

*Formed 1883. Entered FA Cup: 1885-86 – 1888-89. Works team that played at Arkwright Street, Nottingham.*

| | | | | | | | |
|---|---|---|---|---|---|---|---|
| 1885-86 | 1 | 31.10.85 | **Nottingham Forest** | A | L | 2-6 | Rouse, AN Other |
| 1886-87 | 1 | 30.10.86 | **Cleethorpes Town** | A | L | 1-2 | |
| 1887-88 | 1 | 15.10.87 | **Notts Olympic** | A | W | 6-3aet | |
| | | | *FA ordered replay after protest* | | | | |
| | 1r | 22.10.87 | **Notts Olympic** | A | W | 2-1 | |
| | 2 | 05.11.87 | **Nottingham Forest** | A | L | 0-2 | |

## MERTHYR TOWN

*Formed 1908. Entered FA Cup: 1910-11 – 1934-35. Members of the Football League: 1922-1930. Folded 1934. See also Merthyr Tydfil.*

| | | | | | | | |
|---|---|---|---|---|---|---|---|
| 1913-14 (SL) | 1 | 10.01.14 | **Swansea Town** (SL) | A | L | 0-2 | |
| 1914-15 (SL) | 1 | 09.01.15 | **Arsenal** (D2) | A | L | 0-3 | |
| 1922-23 (3S) | | | 5q Swansea Town (3S) H 0-0; 5qr Swansea Town (A) 1-0; 6q Brentford (3S) A 1-0 | | | | |
| | 1 | 13.01.23 | **Wolverhampton W** (D2) | H | L | 0-1 | |
| 1923-24 (3S) | | | 5q Llanelli (A) 1-3 | | | | |
| 1924-25 (3S) | | | 5q Weymouth (A) 2-3 | | | | |
| 1925-26 (3S) | 1 | 28.11.25 | **Bournemouth** (3S) | A | L | 0-3 | |
| 1926-27 (3S) | 1 | 27.11.26 | **Bristol City** (3S) | H | L | 0-2 | |
| 1927-28 (3S) | 1 | 26.11.27 | **Charlton Athletic** (3S) | H | D | 0-0 | |
| | 1r | 30.11.27 | **Charlton Athletic** | A | L | 1-2 | Jones |
| 1928-29 (3S) | 1 | 24.11.28 | **Dulwich Hamlet** (IL) | H | W | 4-2 | Borland, Jones, Mercer, Brown |

| | | | | | | | | |
|---|---|---|---|---|---|---|---|---|
| | | 2 | 08.12.28 | **Watford** (3S) | A | L | 0-2 | |
| 1929-30 | (3S) | 1 | 30.11.29 | **Leyton FC** (AL) | A | L | 1-4 | Woodward |
| 1930-31 | (SL) | 1 | 29.11.30 | **Bristol Rovers** (3S) | A | L | 1-4 | Williams |
| 1932-33 | (SL) | 1 | 26.11.32 | **QPR** (3S) | H | D | 1-1 | Murphy |
| | | 1r | 01.12.32 | **QPR** | A | L | 1-5 | Williams |

## MERTHYR TYDFIL

*Formed 1945. Played at Peenydarren Park, vacated when Merthyr Town folded in 1934. First entered FA Cup: 1946-47. Welsh FA Cup winners: 1949, 1951, 1987. League club beaten: Bristol Rovers. Members of the Southern League.*

| | | | | | | | | |
|---|---|---|---|---|---|---|---|---|
| 1946-47 | (SL) | 1 | 30.11.46 | **Bristol Rovers** (3S) | H | W | 3-1 | Hullett 2, Crisp |
| | | 2 | 14.12.46 | **Reading** (3S) | H | L | 1-3 | Hallett |
| 1947-48 | (SL) | 1 | 29.11.47 | **Norwich City** (3S) | A | L | 0-3 | |
| 1951-52 | (SL) | 1 | 29.11.51 | **Ipswich Town** (3S) | H | D | 2-2aet | Squires, Phillips |
| | | 1r | 05.12.51 | **Ipswich Town** | A | L | 0-1 | |
| 1954-55 | (SL) | 1 | 20.11.54 | **Wellington Town** (CC) | H | D | 1-1 | Reynolds |
| | | 1r | 24.11.54 | **Wellington Town** | A | W | 6-1 | Reynolds 3, Driscoll, Jarman 2 |
| | | 2 | 11.12.54 | **Bradford City** (3N) | A | L | 1-7 | Jarman |
| 1958-59 | (SL) | 1 | 15.11.58 | **King's Lynn** (SL) | A | L | 1-2 | Watkins |
| 1965-66 | (SL) | 1 | 13.11.65 | **Swindon Town** (D3) | A | L | 1-5 | Jenkins |
| 1973-74 | (SL) | 1 | 24.11.73 | **Weymouth** (SL) | A | W | 1-0 | Bryant |
| | | 2 | 15.12.73 | **Hendon** (IL) | H | L | 0-3 | |
| 1978-79 | (SL) | 1 | 25.11.78 | **Leatherhead** (IL) | A | L | 1-2 | Pratt |
| 1979-80 | (SL) | 1 | 24.11.79 | **Fareham Town** (SL) | A | W | 3-2 | Pratt 3 |
| | | 2 | 19.12.79 | **Chesham Utd** (IL) | A | D | 1-1 | Docherty |
| | | 2r | 22.12.79 | **Chesham Utd** | H | L | 1-3 | Elliott |
| 1987-88 | (SL) | 1 | 14.11.87 | **Bristol Rovers** (D3) | A | L | 0-6 | |
| 1988-89 | (SL) | 1 | 19.11.88 | **Yeovil Town** (SL) | A | L | 2-3 | Rogers, Webley |
| 1989-90 | (Conf) | 1 | 18.11.89 | **Redditch Utd** (SL) | A | W | 3-1 | Thompson 2, Rodgers |
| | | 2 | 09.12.89 | **Hereford Utd** (D4) | A | L | 2-3 | Webley 2 |
| 1990-91 | (Conf) | 1 | 17.11.90 | **Sutton Utd** (Conf) | H | D | 1-1 | Sanderson |
| | | 1r | 21.11.90 | **Sutton Utd** | A | W | 1-0 | Webley |
| | | 2 | 08.12.90 | **Woking** (IL) | A | L | 1-5 | Haig |
| 1992-93 | (Conf) | 1 | 14.11.92 | **Wycombe W** (Conf) | A | L | 1-3 | Rogers |
| 1996-97 | (SL) | 1 | 16.11.96 | **Leyton Orient** (D3) | A | L | 1-2 | Evans |
| 1999-00 | (SL) | 1 | 02.11.99 | **Stalybridge Celtic** (NPL) | H | D | 2-2 | Mitchell 2 |
| | | 1r | 09.11.99 | **Stalybridge Celtic** | A | L | 1-3 | Lima |

## METROPOLITAN POLICE

*Formed 1919. First entered FA Cup: 1924-25. Home ground is at Imber Court, East Molesey, Surrey. Members of the Isthmian League.*

| | | | | | | | |
|---|---|---|---|---|---|---|---|
| 1931-32 | (SPT) | 1 | 28.11.31 | **Northampton Town** (3S) | A | L | 0-9 |
| 1984-85 | (IL) | 1 | 17.11.84 | **Dartford** (APL) | H | L | 0-3 |
| 1993-94 | (IL) | 1 | 13.11.93 | **Crawley Town** (SL) | H | L | 0-2 |

## MEXBOROUGH TOWN ATHLETIC

*Formed 1890. Entered FA Cup: 1903-04 – 1982-83.*

| | | | | | | | | |
|---|---|---|---|---|---|---|---|---|
| 1885-86 | | 1 | 31.10.85 | **Staveley** | A | D | 1-1 | |
| | | | | *Mexborough scratched before replay took place. Staveley walkover* | | | | |
| 1926-27 | (ML) | 1 | 27.11.26 | **Chesterfield** (3N) | A | - | 0-0ab | |
| | | | | *abandoned at half-time – fog* | | | | |
| | | 1 | 01.12.26 | **Chesterfield** (3N) | A | L | 1-2 | Dent |

## MIDDLESBROUGH

*Formed 1876. FA Cup runners-up: 1997. FA Amateur Cup winners: 1895, 1898. FA Cup record win: 11-0 v Scarborough, 1st qualifying round, 1890-91. In Competition Proper: 9-3 v Goole Town, 1st round, 09.01.1915. FA Cup record defeat: 1-8 v Hebburn Argyle, 3rd qualifying round, 1896-97; In Competition Proper: 1-6 v Sheffield Wed, 2nd round, 16.01.1895; 1-6 v Southampton, 3rd round, 24.02.1906; 1-6 v Wolverhampton W, 3rd round, 16.01.1937.*

| | | | | | | | | |
|---|---|---|---|---|---|---|---|---|
| 1883-84 | | 1 | 10.11.83 | **Staveley** | H | L | 1-4 | Pringle |
| 1884-85 | | 1 | | Grimsby District | | | - | |
| | | | | *Grimsby District scratched. Middlesbrough walkover* | | | | |

| | | | | | | | |
|---|---|---|---|---|---|---|---|
| | 2 | 06.12.84 | **Newark FC** | H | W | 4-1 | Borrie, Hardwick, Pringle 2 |
| | 3 | | bye | | | | |
| | 4 | 24.01.85 | **Old Etonians** | A | L | 2-5 | Borrie, Pringle |
| 1885-86 | 1 | | Horncastle | | | - | |
| | | | *Horncastle scratched. Middlesbrough walkover* | | | | |
| | 2 | 21.11.85 | **Gainsborough T** | H | W | 2-1 | Thompson, Wilson |
| | 3 | 19.12.85 | **Grimsby Town** | H | W | 2-1 | Pickstock, Borrie |
| | 4 | | bye | | | | |
| | 5 | 23.01.86 | **Redcar** | A | L | 1-2 | Pickstock |
| 1886-87 | 1 | 23.10.86 | **Bishop Auckland Cl** | A | W | 1-0 | Dennis |
| | 2 | 20.11.86 | **Lincoln City** | H | D | 1-1 | Borrie |
| | 2r | 27.11.86 | **Lincoln City** | A | L | 0-2 | |
| 1887-88 | 1 | 15.10.87 | **Whitburn** | H | W | 4-0 | Borrie, 3 others |
| | 2 | 05.11.87 | **South Bank** | H | W | 4-1 | Borrie 2, EJ Wilson, Dennis |
| | 3 | 26.11.87 | **Sunderland** | H | D | 2-2 | McCrie, Dennis |
| | 3r | 03.12.87 | **Sunderland** | A | L | 2-4 | Cochrane, AN Other |
| | | | *FA disqualified Sunderland for professionalism and re-instated Middlesbrough* | | | | |
| | 4 | | bye | | | | |
| | 5 | 07.01.88 | **Old Foresters** | H | W | 4-0 | Borrie, Dennis, Fox, EJ Wilson |
| | | | *FA ordered replay after protest but Old Foresters scratched rather than travel back to Middlesbrough. Middlesbrough walkover* | | | | |
| | 6 | 28.01.88 | **Crewe Alexandra** | H | L | 0-2 | |
| 1888-89 | | | 1q Ecclesfield (H) 0-1 | | | | |
| 1889-90 (NL) | | | 1q South Bank (H) 3-4 | | | | |
| 1890-91 (NL) | | | 1q Scarborough (H) 11-0; 2q Darlington St Augustines (A) 4-1; 3q Darlington (H) 2-0. FA disqualified Middlesbrough for fielding an unregistered player | | | | |
| 1891-92 (NL) | 1 | 16.01.92 | **Luton Town** | A | W | 3-0 | Bell, Bache, own goal |
| | 2 | 30.01.92 | **Preston North End** (D1) | H | L | 1-2 | |
| 1892-93 (NL) | 1 | 21.01.93 | **Newcastle Utd** (NL) | A | W | 3-2 | Black, Blyth, McKnight |
| | 2 | 04.02.93 | **Wolverhampton W** (D1) | A | L | 1-2aet | Black |
| 1893-94 (D2) | | | 1q Leadgate Exiles (A) 4-2; 2q Gateshead NER (H) 2-1; 3q Tow Law (H) 3-0; 4q Willington (A) 4-1 | | | | |
| | 1 | 27.01.94 | **Newton Heath** (D1) | A | L | 0-4 | |
| 1894-95 (NL) | | | 1q Willington (H) 2-1; 2q Howden R (H) 4-1; 3q Darlington (A) 1-0; 4q Bishop Auckland (H) 3-1 | | | | |
| | 1 | 02.02.95 | **Chesterfield Municipal** | H | W | 4-0 | Davidson 2, Rogers, Mullen |
| | 2 | 16.02.95 | **Sheffield Wed** (D1) | A | L | 1-6 | Nelmes |
| 1895-96 (NL) | | | 1q Jarrow (A) 3-0; 2q Newcastle U (A) 1-4 | | | | |
| 1896-97 (ML) | | | 3q Hebburn Arg. (A) 1-8 | | | | |
| 1897-98 (NL) | | | 1q South Bank (A) 3-2; 2q Rendel (A) 1-0; 3q Bishop Auckland (H) 3-1; 4q Hebburn Arg. (H) 2-0; 5q Newcastle U (H) 0-2 | | | | |
| 1898-99 (NL) | | | 3q Hebburn Argyle (H) 0-1 | | | | |
| 1899-00 (D2) | | | 1q Jarrow (H) 1-2 | | | | |
| 1900-01 (D2) | | | 1q Willington A (H) 3-3; 1qr Willington A (A) 0-0; 1q 2r Willington A (H) 8-0; Int Grimsby Town (A) 1-0 ; 2q Jarrow (H) 3-0; 3q Bishop Auckland (H) 4-0 | | | | |
| | 1 | 09.02.01 | **Newcastle Utd** (D1) | H | W | 3-1 | A Robertson, McCowie, Wardrope |
| | 2 | 23.02.01 | **Kettering Town** (SL) | H | W | 5-0 | A Robertson 3, McCowie, Wilkie |
| | 3 | 23.03.01 | **WBA** (D1) | H | L | 0-1 | |
| 1901-02 (D2) | 1 | 25.01.02 | **Bristol Rovers** (SL) | H | D | 1-1 | Cassidy |
| | 1r | 29.01.02 | **Bristol Rovers** | A | L | 0-1 | |
| 1902-03 (D1) | 1 | 13.12.02 | **Bristol City** (D2) | A | L | 1-3 | A Robertson |
| 1903-04 (D1) | 1 | 06.02.04 | **Millwall Athletic** (SL) | A | W | 2-0 | A Brown 2 |
| | 2 | 20.02.04 | **Preston North End** (D2) | A | W | 3-0 | A Brown 2, Atherton |
| | 3 | 05.03.04 | **Manchester City** (D1) | A | D | 0-0 | |
| | 3r | 09.03.04 | **Manchester City** | H | L | 1-3 | A Brown |
| 1904-05 (D1) | 1 | 04.02.05 | **Tottenham Hotspur** (SL) | H | D | 1-1 | Astley |
| | 1r | 09.02.05 | **Tottenham Hotspur** | A | L | 0-1 | |
| 1905-06 (D1) | 1 | 13.01.06 | **Bolton Wanderers** (D1) | H | W | 3-0 | Common, Hewitt, Thackeray |
| | 2 | 03.02.06 | **Brighton** (SL) | A | D | 1-1 | Hewitt |
| | 2r | 07.02.06 | **Brighton** | H | D | 1-1aet | Common |
| | 2 2r | 12.02.06 | **Brighton** | | W | 3-1 | Common 3 |
| | | | *played at Bramall Lane* | | | | |

| | | | | | | | | |
|---|---|---|---|---|---|---|---|---|
| | | 3 | 24.02.06 | **Southampton** (SL) | A | L | 1-6 | RH Walker |
| 1906-07 | (D1) | 1 | 12.01.07 | **Northampton Town** (SL) | H | W | 4-2 | Bloomer 2, Common, Brawn |
| | | 2 | 02.02.07 | **Brentford** (SL) | A | L | 0-1 | |
| 1907-08 | (D1) | 1 | 11.01.08 | **Notts County** (D1) | A | L | 0-2 | |
| 1908-09 | (D1) | 1 | 16.01.09 | **Preston North End** (D1) | A | L | 0-1 | |
| 1909-10 | (D1) | 1 | 15.01.10 | **Everton** (D1) | H | D | 1-1 | Thackeray |
| | | 1r | 19.01.10 | **Everton** | A | L | 3-5 | Common, Cail, Bloomer |
| 1910-11 | (D1) | 1 | 14.01.11 | **Glossop North End** (D2) | H | W | 1-0 | Cail |
| | | 2 | 04.02.11 | **Leicester Fosse** (D2) | H | D | 0-0 | |
| | | 2r | 09.02.11 | **Leicester Fosse** | A | W | 2-1 | Cail, Dixon |
| | | 3 | 25.02.11 | **Blackburn Rovers** (D1) | H | L | 0-3 | |
| 1911-12 | (D1) | 1 | 13.01.12 | **Sheffield Wed** (D1) | H | D | 0-0 | |
| | | 1r | 25.01.12 | **Sheffield Wed** | A | W | 2-1 | James, Windridge |
| | | 2 | 03.02.12 | **West Ham Utd** (SL) | H | D | 1-1 | Elliott |
| | | 2r | 08.02.12 | **West Ham Utd** | A | L | 1-2 | Elliott |
| 1912-13 | (D1) | 1 | 11.01.13 | **Millwall Athletic** (SL) | A | D | 0-0 | |
| | | 1r | 15.01.13 | **Millwall Athletic** | H | W | 4-1 | J Carr 3 (1p), Elliott |
| | | 2 | 01.02.13 | **QPR** (SL) | H | W | 3-2 | Elliott 2, Eyre |
| | | 3 | 22.02.13 | **Burnley** (D2) | A | L | 1-3 | Eyre |
| 1913-14 | (D1) | 1 | 10.01.14 | **Blackburn Rovers** (D1) | A | L | 0-3 | |
| 1914-15 | (D1) | 1 | 09.01.15 | **Goole Town** | H | W | 9-3 | J Carr 3, Elliott 3, Tinsley 3 |
| | | 2 | 30.01.15 | **Bradford City** (D1) | A | L | 0-1 | |
| 1919-20 | (D1) | 1 | 14.01.20 | **Lincoln City** (D2) | H | W | 4-1 | Elliott 3, W Carr |
| | | 2 | 31.01.20 | **Notts County** (D1) | A | L | 0-1 | |
| 1920-21 | (D1) | 1 | 08.01.21 | **Derby County** (D1) | A | L | 0-2 | |
| 1921-22 | (D1) | 1 | 07.01.22 | **Hull City** (D2) | A | L | 0-5 | |
| 1922-23 | (D1) | 1 | 13.01.23 | **Oldham Athletic** (D1) | A | W | 1-0 | Birrell |
| | | 2 | 03.02.23 | **Sheffield Utd** (D1) | H | D | 1-1 | AN Wilson (p) |
| | | 2r | 08.02.23 | **Sheffield Utd** | A | L | 0-3 | |
| 1923-24 | (D1) | 1 | 12.01.24 | **Watford** (3S) | H | L | 0-1 | |
| 1924-25 | (D2) | 1 | 10.01.25 | **Bradford Park A** (3N) | A | L | 0-1 | |
| 1925-26 | (D2) | 3 | 09.01.26 | **Leeds Utd** (D1) | H | W | 5-1 | McClelland 5 |
| | | 4 | 30.01.26 | **Clapton Orient** (D2) | A | L | 2-4 | McClelland, Birrell |
| 1926-27 | (D2) | 3 | 08.01.27 | **Leicester City** (D1) | H | W | 5-3 | Birrell 2, O Williams, Pease, Camsell |
| | | 4 | 29.01.27 | **Preston North End** (D2) | A | W | 3-0 | Camsell 3 |
| | | 5 | 19.02.27 | **Millwall** (3S) | A | L | 2-3 | O Williams, Pease |
| 1927-28 | (D1) | 3 | 14.01.28 | **South Shields** (D2) | H | W | 3-0 | Peacock 2, Camsell |
| | | 4 | 28.01.28 | **Southport** (3N) | A | W | 3-0 | Camsell 3 |
| | | 5 | 18.02.28 | **Huddersfield Town** (D1) | A | L | 0-4 | |
| 1928-29 | (D2) | 3 | 12.01.29 | **Walsall** (3S) | A | D | 1-1 | Camsell |
| | | 3r | 21.01.29 | **Walsall** | H | W | 5-1 | Camsell 2, Pease 2, Williams |
| | | 4 | 26.01.29 | **WBA** (D2) | A | L | 0-1 | |
| 1929-30 | (D1) | 3 | 11.01.30 | **Chesterfield** (3N) | A | D | 1-1 | Bruce (p) |
| | | 3r | 15.01.30 | **Chesterfield** | H | W | 4-3 | Camsell 2, Bruce 2 |
| | | 4 | 25.01.30 | **Charlton Athletic** (D2) | H | D | 1-1 | Muttitt |
| | | 4r | 29.01.30 | **Charlton Athletic** | A | D | 1-1 | Bruce |
| | | 4 2r | 03.02.30 | **Charlton Athletic** <br>*played at Maine Road* | | W | 1-0aet | McKay |
| | | 5 | 15.02.30 | **Arsenal** (D1) | H | L | 0-2 | |
| 1930-31 | (D1) | 3 | 14.01.31 | **Bradford City** (D2) | H | D | 1-1 | Warren |
| | | 3r | 19.01.31 | **Bradford City** | A | L | 1-2 | Barkas og |
| 1931-32 | (D1) | 3 | 09.01.32 | **Portsmouth** (D1) | H | D | 1-1 | Bruce |
| | | 3r | 13.01.32 | **Portsmouth** | A | L | 0-3 | |
| 1932-33 | (D1) | 3 | 14.01.33 | **Manchester Utd** (D2) | A | W | 4-1 | Bruce 2, JJ Williams, Blackmore |
| | | 4 | 28.01.33 | **Stoke City** (D2) | H | W | 4-1 | Blackmore 2, Camsell, Baxter |
| | | 5 | 18.02.33 | **Birmingham** (D1) | H | D | 0-0 | |
| | | 5r | 22.02.33 | **Birmingham** | A | L | 0-3 | |
| 1933-34 | (D1) | 3 | 13.01.34 | **Sunderland** (D1) | A | D | 1-1 | Camsell |
| | | 3r | 17.01.34 | **Sunderland** | H | L | 1-2 | Ferguson |
| 1934-35 | (D1) | 3 | 12.01.35 | **Blackburn Rovers** (D1) | H | D | 1-1 | JJ Williams |
| | | 3r | 17.01.35 | **Blackburn Rovers** | A | L | 0-1 | |

| | | | | | | | | |
|---|---|---|---|---|---|---|---|---|
| 1935-36 | (D1) | 3 | 11.01.36 | **Southampton** (D2) | H | W | 1-0 | Cunliffe |
| | | 4 | 25.01.36 | **Clapton Orient** (3S) | H | W | 3-0 | Camsell 2, Cunliffe |
| | | 5 | 15.02.36 | **Leicester City** (D2) | H | W | 2-1 | Camsell, Forrest |
| | | 6 | 29.02.36 | **Grimsby Town** (D1) | A | L | 1-3 | Camsel |
| 1936-37 | (D1) | 3 | 16.01.37 | **Wolverhampton W** (D1) | A | L | 1-6 | Birkett |
| 1937-38 | (D1) | 3 | 08.01.38 | **Stockport County** (3N) | H | W | 2-0 | Fenton 2 (1p) |
| | | 4 | 22.01.38 | **Nottingham Forest** (D2) | A | W | 3-1 | Mannion, Camsell, Milne |
| | | 5 | 12.02.38 | **York City** (3N) | A | L | 0-1 | |
| 1938-39 | (D1) | 3 | 07.01.39 | **Bolton Wanderers** (D1) | H | D | 0-0 | |
| | | 3r | 11.01.39 | **Bolton Wanderers** | A | D | 0-0aet | |
| | | 3 2r | 16.01.39 | **Bolton Wanderers** | | W | 1-0 | Fenton |
| | | | | *played at Elland Road* | | | | |
| | | 4 | 21.01.39 | **Sunderland** (D1) | H | L | 0-2 | |
| 1945-46 | (D1) | 3 1L | 05.01.46 | **Leeds Utd** (D1) | A | D | 4-4 | Dews 2, Fenton, Murphy |
| | | 3 2L | 09.01.46 | **Leeds Utd** | H | W | 7-2 | Fenton 3, Gordon, Hardwick (p), Spuhler, Douglas |
| | | 4 1L | 26.01.46 | **Blackpool** (D1) | A | L | 2-3 | Suart og, Spuhler |
| | | 4 2L | 30.01.46 | **Blackpool** | H | W | 3-2 | Fenton 2, Spuhler |
| | | 4r | 04.02.46 | **Blackpool** | | W | 1-0aet | Hardwick (p) |
| | | | | *played at Elland Road* | | | | |
| | | 5 1L | 09.02.46 | **Bolton Wanderers** (D1) | A | L | 0-1 | |
| | | 5 2L | 13.02.46 | **Bolton Wanderers** | H | D | 1-1 | Fenton |
| 1946-47 | (D1) | 3 | 11.01.47 | **QPR** (3S) | A | D | 1-1 | Fenton |
| | | 3r | 15.01.47 | **QPR** | H | W | 3-1 | Fenton 2, Mannion |
| | | 4 | 25.01.47 | **Chesterfield** (D2) | H | W | 2-1 | Spuhler 2 |
| | | 5 | 08.02.47 | **Nottingham Forest** (D2) | A | D | 2-2 | Mannion, Spuhler |
| | | 5r | 12.02.47 | **Nottingham Forest** | H | W | 6-2 | Mannion 3 (1p), Fenton 2, Spuhler |
| | | 6 | 01.03.47 | **Burnley** (D2) | H | D | 1-1 | Walker |
| | | 6r | 04.03.47 | **Burnley** | A | L | 0-1aet | |
| 1947-48 | (D1) | 3 | 10.01.48 | **Hull City** (3N) | A | W | 3-1 | Dobbie 2, Mannion |
| | | 4 | 24.01.48 | **Brentford** (D2) | A | W | 2-1 | Spuhler, McCormack |
| | | 5 | 07.02.48 | **Derby County** (D1) | H | L | 1-2 | Spuhler |
| 1948-49 | (D1) | 3 | 08.01.49 | **Brentford** (D2) | A | L | 2-3aet | Walker, Spuhler |
| 1949-50 | (D1) | 3 | 07.01.50 | **Aston Villa** (D1) | A | D | 2-2 | Linacre, McKennan |
| | | 3r | 11.01.50 | **Aston Villa** | H | D | 0-0aet | |
| | | 3 2r | 16.01.50 | **Aston Villa** | | W | 3-0 | McCrae 2, Mannion |
| | | | | *played at Elland Road* | | | | |
| | | 4 | 28.01.50 | **Chesterfield** (D2) | A | L | 2-3 | Walker, Spuhler |
| 1950-51 | (D1) | 3 | 06.01.51 | **Leeds Utd** (D2) | A | L | 0-1 | |
| 1951-52 | (D1) | 3 | 12.01.52 | **Derby County** (D1) | H | D | 2-2 | Mannion 2 |
| | | 3r | 16.01.52 | **Derby County** | A | W | 2-0 | Delapenha 2 |
| | | 4 | 06.02.52 | **Doncaster Rovers** (D2) | H | L | 1-4 | Bell |
| 1952-53 | (D1) | 3 | 10.01.53 | **Aston Villa** (D1) | A | L | 1-3 | Fitzsimons |
| 1953-54 | (D1) | 3 | 09.01.54 | **Leicester City** (D2) | H | D | 0-0 | |
| | | 3r | 14.01.54 | **Leicester City** | A | L | 2-3 | Spuhler, Mannion |
| 1954-55 | (D2) | 3 | 08.01.55 | **Notts County** (D2) | H | L | 1-4 | Wayman |
| 1955-56 | (D2) | 3 | 07.01.56 | **Bradford Park A** (3N) | A | W | 4-0 | Scott 2, Delapenha, Wayman |
| | | 4 | 28.01.56 | **Tottenham Hotspur** (D1) | A | L | 1-3 | Scott |
| 1956-57 | (D2) | 3 | 05.01.57 | **Charlton Athletic** (D1) | H | D | 1-1 | Scott |
| | | 3r | 10.01.57 | **Charlton Athletic** | A | W | 3-2 | Day, Clough, Fitzsimons |
| | | 4 | 26.01.57 | **Aston Villa** (D1) | H | L | 2-3 | Clough, Harris |
| 1957-58 | (D2) | 3 | 04.01.58 | **Derby County** (D2) | H | W | 5-0 | Peacock 2, Day, Holliday, Clough |
| | | 4 | 25.01.58 | **Stoke City** (D2) | A | L | 1-3 | Clough |
| 1958-59 | (D2) | 3 | 24.01.59 | **Birmingham City** (D1) | H | L | 0-1 | |
| 1959-60 | (D2) | 3 | 09.01.60 | **Sheffield Wed** (D1) | A | L | 1-2 | Clough |
| 1960-61 | (D2) | 3 | 07.01.61 | **Manchester Utd** (D1) | A | L | 0-3 | |
| 1961-62 | (D2) | 3 | 10.01.62 | **Cardiff City** (D1) | H | W | 1-0 | Peacock |
| | | 4 | 27.01.62 | **Shrewsbury Town** (D3) | A | D | 2-2 | Peacock 2 |
| | | 4r | 31.01.62 | **Shrewsbury Town** | H | W | 5-1 | Holliday 2, Harris, Peacock, Kaye |
| | | 5 | 17.02.62 | **Blackburn Rovers** (D1) | A | L | 1-2 | Burbeck |
| 1962-63 | (D2) | 3 | 05.03.63 | **Blackburn Rovers** (D1) | A | D | 1-1 | Orritt |
| | | 3r | 11.03.63 | **Blackburn Rovers** | H | W | 3-1 | Peacock 2, Kaye (p) |

| | | | | | | | |
|---|---|---|---|---|---|---|---|
| | 4 | 16.03.63 | **Leeds Utd** (D2) | H | L | 0-2 | |
| 1963-64 (D2) | 3 | 04.01.64 | **Brentford** (D3) | A | L | 1-2 | Kaye |
| 1964-65 (D2) | 3 | 09.01.65 | **Oldham Athletic** (D3) | H | W | 6-2 | Irvine 3, Horsfield 2, Kaye |
| | 4 | 30.01.65 | **Charlton Athletic** (D2) | A | D | 1-1 | Nurse |
| | 4r | 01.02.65 | **Charlton Athletic** | H | W | 2-1 | Gibson, Masson |
| | 5 | 20.02.65 | **Leicester City** (D1) | H | L | 0-3 | |
| 1965-66 (D2) | 3 | 22.01.66 | **Tottenham Hotspur** (D1) | A | L | 0-4 | |
| 1966-67 (D3) | 1 | 26.11.66 | **Chester** (D4) | A | W | 5-2 | O'Rourke 3, Downing, Hickton |
| | 2 | 07.01.67 | **York City** (D4) | H | D | 1-1 | Hickton |
| | 2r | 11.01.67 | **York City** | A | D | 0-0aet | |
| | 2 2r | 16.01.67 | **York City** | | W | 4-1 | Lawson, Lugg, Horsfield, Jackson og |
| | | | *played at St James' Park* | | | | |
| | 3 | 28.01.67 | **Mansfield Town** (D3) | A | L | 0-2 | |
| 1967-68 (D2) | 3 | 27.01.68 | **Hull City** (D2) | H | D | 1-1 | Crossan |
| | 3r | 31.01.68 | **Hull City** | A | D | 2-2aet | Horsfield |
| | 3 2r | 07.02.68 | **Hull City** | | W | 1-0 | Downing |
| | | | *played at Bootham Crescent, York* | | | | |
| | 4 | 17.02.68 | **Bristol City** (D2) | H | D | 1-1 | Parr og |
| | 4r | 20.02.68 | **Bristol City** | A | L | 1-2 | Hickton |
| 1968-69 (D2) | 3 | 04.01.69 | **Millwall** (D2) | H | D | 1-1 | Allen |
| | 3r | 06.01.69 | **Millwall** | A | L | 0-1 | |
| 1969-70 (D2) | 3 | 03.01.70 | **West Ham Utd** (D1) | H | W | 2-1 | McIlmoyle, Downing |
| | 4 | 24.01.70 | **York City** (D4) | H | W | 4-1 | McMordie, G Smith, Hickton (p), Laidlaw |
| | 5 | 07.02.70 | **Carlisle Utd** (D2) | A | W | 2-1 | Hickton, Downing |
| | 6 | 21.02.70 | **Manchester Utd** (D1) | H | D | 1-1 | Hickton |
| | 6r | 25.02.70 | **Manchester Utd** | A | L | 1-2 | Hickton |
| 1970-71 (D2) | 3 | 02.01.71 | **Manchester Utd** (D1) | A | D | 0-0 | |
| | 3r | 05.01.71 | **Manchester Utd** | H | W | 2-1 | McIlmoyle, Downing |
| | 4 | 23.01.71 | **Everton** (D1) | A | L | 0-3 | |
| 1971-72 (D2) | 3 | 15.01.72 | **Manchester City** (D1) | A | D | 1-1 | Mills |
| | 3r | 18.01.72 | **Manchester City** | H | W | 1-0 | Hickton |
| | 4 | 05.02.72 | **Millwall** (D2) | A | D | 2-2 | Hickton, Downing |
| | 4r | 08.02.72 | **Millwall** | H | W | 2-1 | Downing, Hickton (p) |
| | 5 | 26.02.72 | **Manchester Utd** (D1) | A | D | 0-0 | |
| | 5r | 29.02.72 | **Manchester Utd** | H | L | 0-3 | |
| 1972-73 (D2) | 3 | 13.01.73 | **Plymouth Argyle** (D3) | A | L | 0-1 | |
| 1973-74 (D2) | 3 | 05.01.74 | **Grantham Town** (SL) | A | W | 2-0 | Mills, Armstrong |
| | 4 | 26.01.74 | **Wrexham** (D3) | A | L | 0-1 | |
| 1974-75 (D1) | 3 | 04.01.75 | **Wycombe W** (IL) | A | D | 0-0 | |
| | 3r | 07.01.75 | **Wycombe W** | H | W | 1-0 | Armstrong (p) |
| | 4 | 25.01.75 | **Sunderland** (D2) | H | W | 3-1 | Hickton 2 (2p), Murdoch |
| | 5 | 15.02.75 | **Peterborough Utd** (D3) | A | D | 1-1 | Mills |
| | 5r | 18.02.75 | **Peterborough Utd** | H | W | 2-0 | Foggon |
| | 6 | 08.03.75 | **Birmingham City** (D1) | A | L | 0-1 | |
| 1975-76 (D1) | 3 | 03.01.76 | **Bury** (D3) | H | D | 0-0 | |
| | 3r | 06.01.76 | **Bury** | A | L | 2-3 | Brine, Hickton (p) |
| 1976-77 (D1) | 3 | 08.01.77 | **Wimbledon** (SL) | A | D | 0-0 | |
| | 3r | 11.01.77 | **Wimbledon** | H | W | 1-0 | Armsrong (p) |
| | 4 | 29.01.77 | **Hereford Utd** (D2) | H | W | 4-0 | Armstrong 2 (1p), Souness, Willey |
| | 5 | 26.02.77 | **Arsenal** (D1) | H | W | 4-1 | Mills 3, Armstrong |
| | 6 | 19.03.77 | **Liverpool** (D1) | A | L | 0-2 | |
| 1977-78 (D1) | 3 | 07.01.78 | **Coventry City** (D1) | H | W | 3-0 | Mills 2, McAndrew |
| | 4 | 28.01.78 | **Everton** (D1) | H | W | 3-2 | Mills 2, Mahoney |
| | 5 | 27.02.78 | **Bolton Wanderers** (D2) | H | W | 2-0 | Ashcroft, Cummins |
| | 6 | 11.03.78 | **Orient** (D2) | H | D | 0-0 | |
| | 6r | 14.03.78 | **Orient** | A | L | 1-2 | Armstrong |
| 1978-79 (D1) | 3 | 09.01.79 | **Crystal Palace** (D2) | H | D | 1-1 | Ashcroft |
| | 3r | 15.01.79 | **Crystal Palace** | A | L | 0-1 | |
| 1979-80 (D1) | 3 | 09.01.80 | **Portsmouth** (D4) | A | D | 1-1 | Cochrane |
| | 3r | 14.01.80 | **Portsmouth** | H | W | 3-0 | Cochrane, Johnson, Armstrong |

| | | | | | | | | |
|---|---|---|---|---|---|---|---|---|
| | | 4 | 26.01.80 | **Birmingham City** (D2) | A | L | 1-2 | Hodgson |
| 1980-81 | (D1) | 3 | 03.01.81 | **Swansea City** (D2) | A | W | 5-0 | Hodgson 2, Ashcroft, Angus, Cochrane |
| | | 4 | 24.01.81 | **WBA** (D1) | H | W | 1-0 | Bailey |
| | | 5 | 14.02.81 | **Barnsley** (D3) | H | W | 2-1 | Proctor, Jankovic |
| | | 6 | 07.03.81 | **Wolverhampton W** (D1) | H | D | 1-1 | Cochrane |
| | | 6r | 10.03.81 | **Wolverhampton W** | A | L | 1-3aet | Hodgson |
| 1981-82 | (D1) | 3 | 02.01.82 | **QPR** (D2) | A | D | 1-1 | Thomson |
| | | 3r | 18.01.82 | **QPR** | H | L | 2-3 | Otto, Thomson |
| 1982-83 | (D2) | 3 | 08.01.83 | **Bishop's Stortford** (IL) | H | D | 2-2 | S Bell 2 |
| | | 3r | 11.01.83 | **Bishop's Stortford** | A | W | 2-1 | Shearer 2 |
| | | 4 | 29.01.83 | **Notts County** (D1) | H | W | 2-0 | Hankin, Beattie (p) |
| | | 5 | 19.02.83 | **Arsenal** (D1) | H | D | 1-1 | Otto |
| | | 5r | 28.02.83 | **Arsenal** | A | L | 2-3 | Shearer 2 |
| 1983-84 | (D2) | 3 | 07.01.84 | **Arsenal** (D1) | H | W | 3-2 | Macdonald, Sugrue, Baxter |
| | | 4 | 31.01.84 | **Bournemouth** (D3) | H | W | 2-0 | Sugrue 2 |
| | | 5 | 18.02.84 | **Notts County** (D1) | A | L | 0-1 | |
| 1984-85 | (D2) | 3 | 05.01.85 | **Darlington** (D4) | H | D | 0-0 | |
| | | 3r | 08.01.85 | **Darlington** | A | L | 1-2 | McAndrew |
| 1985-86 | (D2) | 3 | 13.01.86 | **Southampton** (D1) | H | L | 1-3 | O'Riordan |
| 1986-87 | (D3) | 1 | 15.11.86 | **Blackpool** (D3) | H | W | 3-0 | Slaven 3 |
| | | 2 | 07.12.86 | **Notts County** (D3) | A | W | 1-0 | Hamilton |
| | | 3 | 10.01.87 | **Preston North End** (D4) | H | L | 0-1 | |
| 1987-88 | (D2) | 3 | 09.01.88 | **Sutton Utd** (Conf) | A | D | 1-1 | Pallister |
| | | 3r | 12.01.88 | **Sutton Utd** | H | W | 1-0aet | Kerr |
| | | 4 | 30.01.88 | **Everton** (D1) | A | D | 1-1 | Kerr |
| | | 4r | 03.02.88 | **Everton** | H | D | 2-2aet | Mowbray, Kernaghan |
| | | 4 2r | 09.02.88 | **Everton** | A | L | 1-2 | Ripley |
| 1988-89 | (D1) | 3 | 07.01.89 | **Grimsby Town** (D4) | H | L | 1-2 | Slaven |
| 1989-90 | (D2) | 3 | 06.01.90 | **Everton** (D1) | H | D | 0-0 | |
| | | 3r | 10.01.90 | **Everton** | A | D | 1-1aet | Parkinson |
| | | 3 2r | 17.01.90 | **Everton** | A | L | 0-1 | |
| 1990-91 | (D2) | 3 | 05.01.91 | **Plymouth Argyle** (D2) | H | D | 0-0 | |
| | | 3r | 14.01.91 | **Plymouth Argyle** | A | W | 2-1 | Baird, Kerr |
| | | 4 | 26.01.91 | **Cambridge Utd** (D3) | A | L | 0-2 | |
| 1991-92 | (D2) | 3 | 04.01.92 | **Manchester City** (D1) | H | W | 2-1 | Kernaghan, Wilkinson |
| | | 4 | 04.02.92 | **Sheffield Wed** (D1) | A | W | 2-1 | Hendrie, Wilkinson |
| | | 5 | 15.02.92 | **Portsmouth** (D2) | A | D | 1-1 | Kernaghan |
| | | 5r | 26.02.92 | **Portsmouth** | H | L | 2-4 | Wilkinson 2 |
| 1992-93 | (PL) | 3 | 13.01.93 | **Chelsea** (PL) | H | W | 2-1 | Wright, Falconer |
| | | 4 | 23.01.93 | **Nottingham Forest** (PL) | A | D | 1-1 | Falconer |
| | | 4r | 03.02.93 | **Nottingham Forest** | H | L | 0-3 | |
| 1993-94 | (D1) | 3 | 08.01.94 | **Cardiff City** (D2) | A | D | 2-2 | Wilkinson, Moore |
| | | 3r | 19.01.94 | **Cardiff City** | H | L | 1-2aet | Kavanagh |
| 1994-95 | (D1) | 3 | 07.01.95 | **Swansea City** (D2) | A | D | 1-1 | Moore |
| | | 3r | 17.01.95 | **Swansea City** | H | L | 1-2 | Hendrie |
| 1995-96 | (PL) | 3 | 06.01.96 | **Notts County** (D2) | A | W | 2-1 | Pollock, Barmby |
| | | 4 | 07.02.96 | **Wimbledon** (PL) | H | D | 0-0 | |
| | | 4r | 13.02.96 | **Wimbledon** | A | L | 0-1 | |
| 1996-97 | (PL) | 3 | 04.01.97 | **Chester City** (D3) | H | W | 6-0 | Ravanelli 2, Hignett, Cox, Beck, Stamp |
| | | 4 | 25.01.97 | **Hednesford Town** (Conf) *played at Riverside Stadium* | A | W | 3-2 | Lambert og, Fjortoft, Ravanelli |
| | | 5 | 15.02.97 | **Manchester City** (D1) | A | W | 1-0 | Juninho |
| | | 6 | 08.03.97 | **Derby County** (PL) | A | W | 2-0 | Juninho, Ravanelli |
| | | SF | 13.04.97 | **Chesterfield** (D2) *played at Old Trafford* | | D | 3-3aet | Ravanelli, Hignett (p), Festa |
| | | SFr | 22.04.97 | **Chesterfield** *played at Hillsborough* | | W | 3-0 | Beck, Ravanelli, Emerson |
| | | F | 17.05.97 | **Chelsea** (PL) *played at Wembley Stadium* | | L | 0-2 | |

| | | | | | | | | |
|---|---|---|---|---|---|---|---|---|
| 1997-98 (D1) | 1 | 03.01.98 | **QPR** (D1) | A | D | 2-2 | Hignett, Mustoe |
| | 1r | 13.01.98 | **QPR** | H | W | 2-0 | Campbell, Mustoe |
| | 4 | 24.01.98 | **Arsenal** (PL) | H | L | 1-2 | Merson |
| 1998-99 (PL) | 3 | 03.01.99 | **Manchester Utd** (PL) | A | L | 1-3 | Townsend |
| 1999-00 (PL) | 3 | 11.12.99 | **Wrexham** (D2) | A | L | 1-2 | Deane |
| 2000-01 (PL) | 3 | 08.01.01 | **Bradford City** (PL) | A | W | 1-0 | Ricard |
| | 4 | 06.02.01 | **Wimbledon** (PL) | H | D | 0-0 | |
| | 4r | 13.02.01 | **Wimbledon** | A | L | 1-3aet | Ricard |
| 2001-02 (PL) | 3 | 08.01.02 | **Wimbledon** (D1) | A | D | 0-0 | |
| | 3r | 15.01.02 | **Wimbledon** | H | W | 2-0 | Whelan, Cunningham og |
| | 4 | 26.01.02 | **Manchester Utd** (PL) | H | W | 2-0 | Whelan, Campbell |
| | 5 | 16.02.02 | **Blackburn Rovers** (PL) | H | W | 1-0 | Ehiogu |
| | 6 | 10.03.02 | **Everton** (PL) | H | W | 3-0 | Whelan, Nemeth, Ince |
| | SF | 14.04.02 | **Arsenal** (PL) | | L | 0-1 | |
| | | | *played at Old Trafford* | | | | |
| 2002-03 (PL) | 3 | 04.01.03 | **Chelsea** (PL) | A | L | 0-1 | |

## MIDDLESBROUGH IRONOPOLIS

*Forrmed 1889. Entered FA Cup: 1890-91 – 1994-95. FA Cup quarter-finalists 1892-93. Played in maroon shirts with light green stripes. Members of the Football League: 1893-94. Folded 1894.*

| | | | | | | | |
|---|---|---|---|---|---|---|---|
| 1890-91 (NL) | 1 | 17.01.91 | **Blackburn Rovers** (D1) | H | L | 1-2aet | McReddie |
| | | | *FA ordered replay after protest* | | | | |
| | 1r | 24.01.91 | **Blackburn Rovers** | H | L | 0-3 | |
| 1891-92 (NL) | 1 | 16.01.92 | **Preston North End** (D1) | A | - | 2-2ab | Hughes, McNair |
| | | | *abandoned – bad weather and frosty pitch* | | | | |
| | 1 | 23.01.92 | **Preston North End** | A | L | 0-6 | |
| 1892-93 (NL) | 1 | 21.01.93 | **Marlow** | A | W | 3-1 | Hill, McArthur, Seymour |
| | 2 | 04.02.93 | **Notts County** (D1) | H | W | 3-2 | Hill, Hughes, McArthur |
| | 3 | 18.02.93 | **Preston North End** (D1) | A | D | 2-2 | Hill, McArthur |
| | 3r | 25.02.93 | **Preston North End** | H | L | 0-7 | |
| 1893-94 (D2) | 1 | 27.01.94 | **Luton Town** | H | W | 2-1 | Hunt, Adams |
| | 2 | 10.02.94 | **Nottingham Forest** (D1) | H | L | 0-2 | |

## MILLWALL

*Formed 1885 as Millwall Rovers. Millwall Athletic 1894. Millwall 1925. Best FA Cup performance: Semi-finals 1900, 1903, 1937. Their first two semi-final appearances were as a Southern League club. In 1937 they became the first club from the old Third Division to reach the semi-finals. Record FA Cup win: 7-0 v Clapton FC, 3rd qualifying round, 1899-1900. In Competition Proper: 7-0 v Gateshead AFC, 2nd round, 12.12.1936. Record FA Cup defeat: 1-9 v Aston Villa, 4th round, 2nd leg, 09.01.1946.*

**as Millwall Rovers**

| | | | | | | | |
|---|---|---|---|---|---|---|---|
| 1887-88 | 1 | | Casuals | | - | | |
| | | | *Casuals scratched. Millwall Rovers walkover.* | | | | |
| | 2 | 05.11.87 | **Old Westminsters** | A | L | 1-8 | |
| 1888-89 | | | 1q Lancing Old Boys (A) 0-4 | | | | |
| 1889-90 | | | 1q Schorne College (H) 0-4 | | | | |
| 1890-91 | | | 1q Ilford (H) 2-3 | | | | |
| 1891-92 | | | 1q Rochester (A) 2-1 aet; 2q 1st Highland Light Infantry (H) 3-4 | | | | |
| 1892-93 | | | 1q Folkestone (H) 6-1; 2q West Kent Regiment (H) 2-0; 3q Woolwich Arsenal (A) 2-3 | | | | |

**as Millwall Athletic**

| | | | | | | | |
|---|---|---|---|---|---|---|---|
| 1893-94 | | | 1q bye; 2q Ilford (A) 3-1; 3q Woolwich Arsenal (A) 0-2 | | | | |
| 1894-95 (SL) | | | 1q Folkestone (H) 5-0; 2q Royal Engineers Taining Battalion (A) 4-1; 3q New Brompton (A) 2-0; 4q Royal Ordnance (A) 3-0 | | | | |
| | 1 | 02.02.95 | **Sheffield Utd** (D1) | A | L | 1-3 | Geddes |
| 1895-96 (SL) | | | 1q New Brompton (A) 1-0; 2q Folkestone (H) 5-0; 3q Sheppy Utd (H) 4-0; 4q Royal Ordnance (A) 2-1 | | | | |
| | 1 | 01.02.96 | **Liverpool** (D2) | A | L | 1-4 | Geddes |
| 1896-97 (SL) | | | 3q Sheppey Utd (A) 3-3; 3q Sheppey Utd (H) 3-1; 4q Northfleet Utd (H) 6-1; 5q Woolwich Arsenal (H) 4-2 | | | | |
| | 1 | 30.01.97 | **Wolverhampton W** (D1) | H | L | 1-2 | McKenzie |
| 1897-98 (SL) | | | 3q Sheppey Utd (H) 5-1 FA ordered match to be replayed following protests; 3q Sheppey Utd (A) 0-5 | | | | |
| 1898-99 (SL) | | | 3q Brighton Utd (H) 3-0; 4q Gravesend Utd (A) 1-3 | | | | |

| | | | | | | | |
|---|---|---|---|---|---|---|---|
| 1899-00 (SL) | | | 3q Clapton (H) 7-0; 4q Chatham Town (H) 3-0; 5q West Ham Utd (A) 2-1 | | | | |
| | 1 | 27.01.00 | **Jarrow** (NAll) | A | W | 2-0 | Banks, Brearley |
| | 2 | 17.02.00 | **QPR** (SL) | A | W | 2-0 | Gettins 2 |
| | 3 | 24.02.00 | **Aston Villa** (D1) | H | D | 1-1 | Nicol |
| | 3r | 28.02.00 | **Aston Villa** | A | D | 0-0aet | |
| | 3 2r | 05.03.00 | **Aston Villa** | | W | 2-1 | Banks, Gettins |
| | | | *played at Elm Park, Reading* | | | | |
| | SF | 24.03.00 | **Southampton** (SL) | | D | 0-0 | |
| | | | *played at Crystal Palace* | | | | |
| | SFr | 28.03.00 | **Southampton** | | L | 0-3 | |
| | | | *played at Elm Park, Reading* | | | | |
| 1900-01 (SL) | 1 | 26.01.01 | **Aston Villa** (D1) | A | L | 0-5 | |
| 1901-02 (SL) | | | Int Bristol Rovers (H) 1-1; Int r Bristol Rovers (A) 0-1 | | | | |
| 1902-03 (SL) | | | Int Bristol Rovers (A) 2-2; Int r Bristol Rovers (H) 0-0abandoned aet; Int 2r Bristol Rovers (at Villa Park) 2-0 | | | | |
| | 1 | 07.02.03 | **Luton Town** (SL) | H | W | 3-0 | Hulse, Jones, Watkins |
| | 2 | 21.02.03 | **Preston North End** (D2) | H | W | 4-1 | Gettins, Jones, Moran, Derbyshire og |
| | 3 | 07.03.03 | **Everton** (D1) | H | W | 1-0 | Watkins |
| | SF | 21.03.03 | **Derby County** (D1) | | L | 0-3 | |
| | | | *played at Villa Park* | | | | |
| 1903-04 (SL) | 1 | 06.02.04 | **Middlesbrough** (D1) | H | L | 0-2 | |
| 1904-05 (SL) | | | Int Bradford City (A) 4-1 | | | | |
| | 1 | 04.02.05 | **Southampton** (SL) | A | L | 1-3 | Benson og |
| 1905-06 (SL) | 1 | 13.01.06 | **Burton Utd** (D2) | H | W | 1-0 | Heaton |
| | 2 | 03.02.06 | **Sheffield Wed** (D1) | A | D | 1-1 | Hunter |
| | 2r | 08.02.06 | **Sheffield Wed** | H | L | 0-3 | |
| 1906-07 (SL) | 1 | 12.01.07 | **Plymouth Argyle** (SL) | H | W | 2-0 | Dean, Milsom |
| | 2 | 02.02.07 | **Bristol Rovers** (SL) | A | L | 0-3 | |
| 1907-08 (SL) | 1 | 11.01.08 | **Bury** (D1) | A | L | 1-2 | Jones |
| 1908-09 (SL) | 1 | 16.01.09 | **Luton Town** (SL) | A | W | 2-1 | Dean, Tellum |
| | 2 | 06.02.09 | **Woolwich Arsenal** (D1) | A | D | 1-1 | Twigg |
| | 2r | 10.02.09 | **Woolwich Arsenal** | H | W | 1-0 | Jones |
| | 3 | 20.02.09 | **Nottingham Forest** (D1) | A | L | 1-3 | Shand |
| 1909-10 (SL) | 1 | 15.01.10 | **Derby County** (D2) | A | L | 0-5 | |
| 1910-11 (SL) | 1 | 14.01.11 | **Tottenham Hotspur** (D1) | A | L | 1-2 | Martin |
| 1911-12 (SL) | 1 | 13.01.12 | **Bury** (D1) | A | L | 1-2 | Davis |
| 1912-13 (SL) | 1 | 11.01.13 | **Middlesbrough** (D1) | H | D | 0-0 | |
| | 1r | 15.01.13 | **Middlesbrough** | A | L | 1-4 | Wilson |
| 1913-14 (SL) | 1 | 10.01.14 | **Chelsea** (D1) | H | D | 0-0 | |
| | 1r | 14.01.14 | **Chelsea** | A | W | 1-0 | Davis |
| | 2 | 31.01.14 | **Bradford City** (D1) | H | W | 1-0 | Davis |
| | 3 | 21.02.14 | **Sheffield Utd** (D1) | H | L | 0-4 | |
| 1914-15 (SL) | 1 | 09.01.15 | **Clapton Orient** (D2) | H | W | 2-1 | Moody 2 |
| | 2 | 30.01.15 | **Bolton Wanderers** (D1) | A | D | 0-0 | |
| | 2r | 06.02.15 | **Bolton Wanderers** | H | D | 2-2aet | Davis, Moody |
| | 2 2r | 13.02.15 | **Bolton Wanderers** | A | L | 1-4 | Davis |
| 1919-20 (SL) | 1 | 10.01.20 | **Notts County** (D1) | A | L | 0-2 | |
| 1920-21 (D3) | 1 | 08.01.21 | **Lincoln City** (ML) | H | L | 0-3 | |
| 1921-22 (3S) | 1 | 07.01.22 | **Ashington** (3N) | H | W | 4-2 | Taylor, Moule, Keen 2 |
| | 2 | 28.01.22 | **Crystal Palace** (D2) | A | D | 0-0 | |
| | 2r | 01.02.22 | **Crystal Palace** | H | W | 2-0 | Moule, Dorsett |
| | 3 | 18.02.22 | **Swansea Town** (3S) | H | W | 4-0 | Keen 4 |
| | 4 | 04.03.22 | **Huddersfield Town** (D1) | A | L | 0-3 | |
| 1922-23 (3S) | 1 | 13.01.23 | **Clapton Orient** (D2) | A | W | 2-0 | Hannaford 2 |
| | 2 | 03.02.23 | **Huddersfield Town** (D1) | H | D | 0-0 | |
| | 2r | 07.02.23 | **Huddersfield Town** | A | L | 0-3 | |
| 1923-24 (3S) | 1 | 12.01.24 | **WBA** (D1) | H | L | 0-1 | |
| 1924-25 (3S) | 1 | 10.01.25 | **Barnsley** (D2) | H | D | 0-0 | |
| | 1r | 15.01.25 | **Barnsley** | A | L | 1-2 | Lincoln |
| **as Millwall** | | | | | | | |
| 1925-26 (3S) | 3 | 09.01.26 | **Oldham Athletic** (D2) | H | D | 1-1 | Chance |

| | | | | | | | | |
|---|---|---|---|---|---|---|---|---|
| | | 3r | 12.01.26 | **Oldham Athletic** | A | W | 1-0 | Parker |
| | | 4 | 30.01.26 | **Bury** (D1) | A | D | 3-3 | Amos 2 (2ps), Parker |
| | | 4r | 04.02.26 | **Bury** | H | W | 2-0 | Parker, Moule |
| | | 5 | 20.02.26 | **Swansea Town** (D2) | H | L | 0-1 | |
| 1926-27 | (3S) | 3 | 08.01.27 | **Huddersfield Town** (D1) | H | W | 3-1 | Phillips, Gomm, Black |
| | | 4 | 29.01.27 | **Derby County** (D1) | A | W | 2-0 | Parker, Phillips (p) |
| | | 5 | 19.02.27 | **Middlesbrough** (D2) | H | W | 3-2 | Gomm, Black, Chance |
| | | 6 | 05.03.27 | **Southampton** (D2) | H | D | 0-0 | |
| | | 6r | 09.03.27 | **Southampton** | A | L | 0-2 | |
| 1927-28 | (3S) | 3 | 14.01.28 | **Derby County** (D1) | H | L | 1-2 | Cock |
| 1928-29 | (D2) | 3 | 12.01.29 | **Northampton Town** (3S) | H | D | 1-1 | Phillips (p) |
| | | 3r | 17.01.29 | **Northampton Town** | A | D | 2-2aet | Cock, Readman |
| | | 3 2r | 21.01.29 | **Northampton Town** | | W | 2-0 | Landells, Cock |
| | | | | *played at Highbury* | | | | |
| | | 4 | 26.01.29 | **Crystal Palace** (3S) | H | D | 0-0 | |
| | | 4r | 30.01.29 | **Crystal Palace** | A | L | 3-5 | Cock, Landells, Black |
| 1929-30 | (D2) | 3 | 11.01.30 | **Corinthians** | A | D | 2-2 | Forsyth, Phillips |
| | | 3r | 15.01.30 | **Corinthians** | H | D | 1-1aet | Poxton |
| | | 3 2r | 20.01.30 | **Corinthians** | | W | 5-1 | Forsyth, Corkindale 2, Cock 2 |
| | | | | *played at Stamford Bridge* | | | | |
| | | 4 | 25.01.30 | **Doncaster Rovers** (3N) | H | W | 4-0 | Hawkins 2, Corkindale, Wadsworth |
| | | 5 | 15.02.30 | **West Ham Utd** (D1) | A | L | 1-4 | Wadsworth |
| 1930-31 | (D2) | 3 | 10.01.31 | **Southport** (3N) | A | L | 1-3 | Poxton |
| 1931-32 | (D2) | 3 | 09.01.32 | **Manchester City** (D1) | H | L | 2-3 | Smith, Poxton |
| 1932-33 | (D2) | 3 | 14.01.33 | **Reading** (3S) | H | - | 2-0ab | Poxton (p), Bloxham |
| | | | | *abandoned after 75 minutes- fog* | | | | |
| | | 3 | 18.01.33 | **Reading** | H | D | 1-1 | Poxton |
| | | 3r | 23.01.33 | **Reading** | A | W | 2-0 | Bloxham, Bond |
| | | 4 | 28.01.33 | **Aldershot** (3S) | A | L | 0-1 | |
| 1933-34 | (D2) | 3 | 13.01.34 | **Accrington Stanley** (3N) | H | W | 3-0 | Yardley 2, Phillips |
| | | 4 | 27.01.34 | **Leicester City** (D1) | H | L | 3-6 | Phillips, Yardley 2 |
| 1934-35 | (3S) | 3 | 12.01.35 | **Wigan Athletic** (CC) | A | W | 4-1 | Yardley 2, Thorogood, Alexander |
| | | 4 | 26.01.35 | **Reading** (3S) | A | L | 0-1 | |
| 1935-36 | (3S) | 3 | 11.01.36 | **Stoke City** (D1) | H | D | 0-0 | |
| | | 3r | 15.01.36 | **Stoke City** | A | L | 0-4 | |
| 1936-37 | (3S) | 1 | 28.11.36 | **Aldershot** (3S) | A | W | 6-1 | Mangnall 4 (1p), Thorogood, Thomas |
| | | 2 | 12.12.36 | **Gateshead AFC** (3N) | H | W | 7-0 | Mangnall, Thorogood, McCartney 2, Burditt 2, Thomas (p) |
| | | 3 | 16.01.37 | **Fulham** (D2) | H | W | 2-0 | Burditt, Mangnall |
| | | 4 | 30.01.37 | **Chelsea** (D1) | H | W | 3-0 | Burditt 2, Thorogood |
| | | 5 | 20.02.37 | **Derby County** (D1) | H | W | 2-1 | Mangnall, McCartney |
| | | 6 | 06.03.37 | **Manchester City** (D1) | H | W | 2-0 | Mangnall 2 |
| | | SF | 10.04.37 | **Sunderland** (D1) | | L | 1-2 | Mangnall |
| | | | | *played at Leeds Road, Huddersfield* | | | | |
| 1937-38 | (3S) | 3 | 08.01.38 | **Manchester City** (D1) | H | D | 2-2 | JR Smith, Walsh |
| | | 3r | 12.01.38 | **Manchester City** | A | L | 1-3 | Burditt |
| 1938-39 | (D2) | 3 | 11.01.39 | **York City** (3N) | A | W | 5-0 | McLeod 4, Rawlings |
| | | 4 | 21.01.39 | **Grimsby Town** (D1) | H | D | 2-2 | McLeod 2 |
| | | 4r | 24.01.39 | **Grimsby Town** | A | L | 2-3 | Richardson, McLeod |
| 1945-46 | (D2) | 3 1L | 05.01.46 | **Northampton Town** (3S) | A | D | 2-2 | JR Smith, Ridley |
| | | 3 2L | 07.01.46 | **Northampton Town** | H | W | 3-0 | Smalley og, Phillips, JR Smith |
| | | 4 1L | 26.01.46 | **Aston Villa** (D1) | H | L | 2-4 | Jinks 2 |
| | | 4 2L | 28.01.46 | **Aston Villa** | A | L | 1-9 | JR Smith |
| 1946-47 | (D2) | 3 | 11.01.47 | **Port Vale** (3S) | H | L | 0-3 | |
| 1947-48 | (D2) | 3 | 10.01.48 | **Preston North End** (D1) | H | L | 1-2 | Mansfield |
| 1948-49 | (3S) | 1 | 27.11.48 | **Tooting & M** (AL) | H | W | 1-0 | McMillen |
| | | 2 | 11.12.48 | **Crewe Alexandra** (3N) | A | L | 2-3 | Constantine 2 |
| 1949-50 | (3S) | 1 | 26.11.49 | **Exeter City** (3S) | H | L | 3-5 | Constantine, Brolly |
| 1950-51 | (3S) | 1 | 25.11.50 | **Crystal Palace** (3S) | A | - | 0-0ab | |
| | | | | *abandoned after 34 minutes – fog* | | | | |
| | | 1 | 29.11.50 | **Crystal Palace** | A | W | 4-1 | Johnson, Morgan, Constantine, Neary |

| | | | | | | | | |
|---|---|---|---|---|---|---|---|---|
| | | 2 | 09.12.50 | **Bradford Park A** (3N) | H | D | 1-1 | Neary |
| | | 2r | 13.12.50 | **Bradford Park A** | A | W | 1-0 | Morgan |
| | | 3 | 06.01.51 | **QPR** (D2) | A | W | 4-3 | Neary 2, Johnson, Constantine |
| | | 4 | 27.01.51 | **Fulham** (D1) | H | L | 0-1 | |
| 1951-52 | (3S) | 1 | 24.11.51 | **Plymouth Argyle** (3S) | H | W | 1-0 | White |
| | | 2 | 15.12.51 | **Scunthorpe Utd** (3N) | H | D | 0-0 | |
| | | 2r | 20.12.51 | **Scunthorpe Utd** | A | L | 0-3 | |
| 1952-53 | (3S) | 1 | 22.11.52 | **Aldershot** (3S) | A | D | 0-0 | |
| | | 1r | 27.11.52 | **Aldershot** | H | W | 7-1 | Neary, Monkhouse 3, Shepherd 3 |
| | | 2 | 06.12.52 | **Barrow** (3N) | A | D | 2-2 | Stobbart, Neary |
| | | 2r | 10.12.52 | **Barrow** | H | W | 4-1 | Stobbart, Shepherd 3 |
| | | 3 | 10.01.53 | **Manchester Utd** (D1) | H | L | 0-1 | |
| 1953-54 | (3S) | 1 | 21.11.53 | **Colchester Utd** (3S) | A | D | 1-1 | Stobbart |
| | | 1r | 23.11.53 | **Colchester Utd** | H | W | 4-0 | Stobbart 2, Hazlett, Neary |
| | | 2 | 12.12.53 | **Headington Utd** (SL) | H | D | 3-3 | Shepherd, Neary, Short |
| | | 2r | 17.12.53 | **Headington Utd** | A | L | 0-1 | |
| 1954-55 | (3S) | 1 | 20.11.54 | **Exeter City** (3S) | H | W | 3-2 | Pacey 2, Jardine |
| | | 2 | 11.12.54 | **Accrington Stanley** (3N) | H | W | 3-2 | Prior, Ramscar, Pacey |
| | | 3 | 08.01.55 | **Bolton Wanderers** (D1) | A | L | 1-3 | Smith |
| 1955-56 | (3S) | 1 | 19.11.55 | **Northampton Town** (3S) | A | L | 1-4 | Pacey |
| 1956-57 | (3S) | 1 | 17.11.56 | **Brighton** (3S) | A | D | 1-1 | Shepherd |
| | | 1r | 19.11.56 | **Brighton** | H | W | 3-1 | Shepherd, Anslow 2 (2ps) |
| | | 2 | 08.12.56 | **Margate** (KL) | H | W | 4-0 | Shepherd 3, Rawson |
| | | 3 | 05.01.57 | **Crystal Palace** (3S) | H | W | 2-0 | Anslow, Shepherd |
| | | 4 | 26.01.57 | **Newcastle Utd** (D1) | H | W | 2-1 | Anslow 2 |
| | | 5 | 16.02.57 | **Birmingham City** (D1) | H | L | 1-4 | Shepherd |
| 1957-58 | (3S) | 1 | 16.11.57 | **Brentford** (3S) | H | W | 1-0 | Morrison |
| | | 2 | 07.12.57 | **Gillingham** (3S) | H | D | 1-1 | Shepherd |
| | | 2r | 11.12.57 | **Gillingham** | A | L | 1-6 | Summersby |
| 1958-59 | (D4) | 1 | 15.11.58 | **Hitchin Town** (AL) | A | D | 1-1 | Summersby |
| | | 1r | 17.11.58 | **Hitchin Town** | H | W | 2-1 | Heckman, Hutton |
| | | 2 | 06.12.58 | **Worcester City** (SL) | A | L | 2-5 | Roche, Moyse |
| 1959-60 | (D4) | 1 | 14.11.59 | **Bath City** (SL) | A | L | 1-3 | Wilson |
| 1960-61 | (D4) | 1 | 05.11.60 | **Reading** (D3) | A | L | 2-6 | Burridge 2 |
| 1961-62 | (D4) | 1 | 04.11.61 | **Northampton Town** (D3) | A | L | 0-2 | |
| 1962-63 | (D3) | 1 | 03.11.62 | **Margate** (SL) | H | W | 3-1 | Terry, Jones, Haverty |
| | | 2 | 24.11.62 | **Coventry City** (D3) | H | D | 0-0 | |
| | | 2r | 27.11.62 | **Coventry City** | A | L | 1-2 | Jones (p) |
| 1963-64 | (D3) | 1 | 16.11.63 | **Kettering Town** (SL) | A | D | 1-1 | McLaughlin |
| | | 1r | 25.11.63 | **Kettering Town** | H | L | 2-3 | Obeney, Fraser |
| 1964-65 | (D4) | 1 | 14.11.64 | **Kettering Town** (SL) | H | W | 2-0 | Rowan 2 |
| | | 2 | 05.12.64 | **Port Vale** (D3) | H | W | 4-0 | Julians, Nicholson og, Whitehouse 2 |
| | | 3 | 09.01.65 | **Fulham** (D1) | A | D | 3-3 | Curran, Whitehouse 2 |
| | | 3r | 11.01.65 | **Fulham** | H | W | 2-0 | Harper, Rowan |
| | | 4 | 30.01.65 | **Shrewsbury Town** (D3) | H | L | 1-2 | John |
| 1965-66 | (D3) | 1 | 13.11.65 | **Wealdstone** (IL) | H | W | 3-1 | Brown, Jacks, Rowan |
| | | 2 | 04.12.65 | **Hereford Utd** (SL) | A | L | 0-1 | |
| 1966-67 | (D2) | 3 | 28.01.67 | **Tottenham Hotspur** (D1) | H | D | 0-0 | |
| | | 3r | 01.02.67 | **Tottenham Hotspur** | A | L | 0-1 | |
| 1967-68 | (D2) | 3 | 27.01.68 | **Aston Villa** (D2) | A | L | 0-3 | |
| 1968-69 | (D2) | 3 | 04.01.69 | **Middlesbrough** (D2) | A | D | 1-1 | Possee |
| | | 3r | 06.01.69 | **Middlesbrough** | H | W | 1-0 | Howell |
| | | 4 | 25.01.69 | **Leicester City** (D1) | H | L | 0-1 | |
| 1969-70 | (D2) | 3 | 03.01.70 | **Scunthorpe Utd** (D4) | A | L | 1-2 | Bolland |
| 1970-71 | (D2) | 3 | 02.01.71 | **Stoke City** (D1) | A | L | 1-2 | Possee |
| 1971-72 | (D2) | 3 | 15.01.72 | **Nottingham Forest** (D1) | H | W | 3-1 | Bolland (p), Smethurst, Possee |
| | | 4 | 05.02.72 | **Middlesbrough** (D2) | H | D | 2-2 | Smethurst, Possee |
| | | 4r | 08.02.72 | **Middlesbrough** | A | L | 1-2 | Burnett |
| 1972-73 | (D2) | 3 | 13.01.73 | **Newport County** (D4) | H | W | 3-0 | Burnett, Smethurst, Wood |
| | | 4 | 03.02.73 | **Everton** (D1) | A | W | 2-0 | Cripps, Wood |
| | | 5 | 24.02.73 | **Wolverhampton W** (D1) | A | L | 0-1 | |
| 1973-74 | (D2) | 3 | 05.01.74 | **Scunthorpe Utd** (D4) | H | D | 1-1 | Wood |

| | | | | | | | |
|---|---|---|---|---|---|---|---|
| | 3r | 08.01.74 | **Scunthorpe Utd** | A | L | 0-1 | |
| 1974-75 (D2) | 3 | 04.01.75 | **Bury** (D3) | A | D | 2-2 | Bolland (p), Hill |
| | 3r | 07.01.75 | **Bury** | H | D | 1-1aet | Summerhill |
| | 3 2r | 13.01.75 | **Bury** | | L | 0-2 | |
| | | | *played at The Hawthorns* | | | | |
| 1975-76 (D3) | 1 | 22.11.75 | **Yeovil Town** (SL) | A | D | 1-1 | Kitchener |
| | 1r | 25.11.75 | **Yeovil Town** | H | D | 2-2aet | Salvage, Welsh |
| | 1 2r | 03.12.75 | **Yeovil Town** | | W | 1-0 | Hart |
| | | | *played at Recreation Ground, Aldershot* | | | | |
| | 2 | 13.12.75 | **Crystal Palace** (D3) | H | D | 1-1 | Summerhill |
| | 2r | 16.12.75 | **Crystal Palace** | A | L | 1-2 | Moore |
| 1976-77 (D2) | 3 | 08.01.77 | **Coventry City** (D1) | A | L | 0-1 | |
| 1977-78 (D2) | 3 | 07.01.78 | **Rotherham Utd** (D3) | A | D | 1-1 | Kitchener |
| | 3r | 09.01.78 | **Rotherham Utd** | H | W | 2-0 | Lee 2 |
| | 4 | 31.01.78 | **Luton Town** (D2) | H | W | 4-0 | Pearson 3, Seasman |
| | 5 | 18.02.78 | **Notts County** (D2) | H | W | 2-1 | Chambers (p), Walker |
| | 6 | 11.03.78 | **Ipswich Town** (D1) | H | L | 1-6 | Mehmet |
| 1978-79 (D2) | 3 | 10.01.79 | **Blackburn Rovers** (D2) | H | L | 1-2 | Walker |
| 1979-80 (D3) | 1 | 24.11.79 | **Salisbury City** (SL) | A | W | 2-1 | Mitchell, Donaldson |
| | | | *played at The Dell, Southampton* | | | | |
| | 2 | 15.12.79 | **Croydon** (IL) | A | D | 1-1 | Chatterton |
| | | | *played at Selhurst Park* | | | | |
| | 2r | 18.12.79 | **Croydon** | H | W | 3-2aet | O'Callaghan, Towner (p), Mitchell |
| | 3 | 05.01.80 | **Shrewsbury Town** (D2) | H | W | 5-1 | McKenna, Tagg, Lyons 3 |
| | 4 | 26.01.80 | **Chester** (D3) | A | L | 0-2 | |
| 1980-81 (D3) | 1 | 22.11.80 | **Kidderminster H** (SL) | A | D | 1-1 | Williams og |
| | 1r | 25.11.80 | **Kidderminster H** | H | W | 1-0 | Chatterton |
| | 2 | 13.12.80 | **Exeter City** (D3) | H | L | 0-1 | |
| 1981-82 (D3) | 1 | 21.11.81 | **Portsmouth** (D3) | A | D | 1-1 | Chatterton (p) |
| | 1r | 25.11.81 | **Portsmouth** | H | W | 3-2aet | Allardyce, Chatterton, Hayes |
| | 2 | 30.12.81 | **Dagenham** (APL) | A | W | 2-1 | Allardyce, Chatterton |
| | 3 | 05.01.82 | **Grimsby Town** (D2) | H | L | 1-6 | Neal |
| 1982-83 (D3) | 1 | 20.11.82 | **Slough Town** (IL) | A | L | 0-1 | |
| 1983-84 (D3) | 1 | 19.11.83 | **Dartford** (SL) | H | W | 2-1 | Massey, Cusack |
| | 2 | 10.12.83 | **Swindon Town** (D4) | H | L | 2-3 | Lovell (p), Martin |
| 1984-85 (D3) | 1 | 17.11.84 | **Weymouth** (APL) | A | W | 3-0 | Lovell (p), Bremner, Otulakowski |
| | 2 | 08.12.84 | **Enfield** (APL) | H | W | 1-0 | Neal |
| | 3 | 05.01.85 | **Crystal Palace** (D2) | H | D | 1-1 | Neal |
| | 3r | 23.01.85 | **Crystal Palace** | A | W | 2-1 | Briley, Lovell |
| | 4 | 04.02.85 | **Chelsea** (D1) | A | W | 3-2 | Lovell 2 (1p), John Fashanu |
| | 5 | 19.02.85 | **Leicester City** (D1) | H | W | 2-0 | McLeary, John Fashanu |
| | 6 | 13.03.85 | **Luton Town** (D1) | A | L | 0-1 | |
| 1985-86 (D2) | 3 | 04.01.86 | **Wimbledon** (D2) | H | W | 3-1 | Lovell, John Fashanu, Walker |
| | 4 | 25.01.86 | **Aston Villa** (D1) | A | D | 1-1 | McLeary |
| | 4r | 29.01.86 | **Aston Villa** | H | W | 1-0 | John Fashanu |
| | 5 | 15.02.86 | **Southampton** (D1) | A | D | 0-0 | |
| | 5r | 03.02.86 | **Southampton** | H | L | 0-1 | |
| 1986-87 (D2) | 3 | 10.01.87 | **Cardiff City** (D4) | H | D | 0-0 | |
| | 3r | 20.01.87 | **Cardiff City** | A | D | 2-2aet | Leslie, Morgan |
| | 3 2r | 26.01.87 | **Cardiff City** | A | L | 0-1 | |
| 1987-88 (D2) | 3 | 09.01.88 | **Arsenal** (D1) | A | L | 0-2 | |
| 1988-89 (D1) | 3 | 07.01.89 | **Luton Town** (D1) | H | W | 3-2 | Cascarino, Carter, Sheringham |
| | 4 | 29.01.89 | **Liverpool** (D1) | H | L | 0-2 | |
| 1989-90 (D1) | 3 | 06.01.90 | **Manchester City** (D1) | A | D | 0-0 | |
| | 3r | 09.01.90 | **Manchester City** | H | D | 1-1aet | Carter |
| | 3 2r | 15.01.90 | **Manchester City** | H | W | 3-1 | Goddard, Sheringham 2 |
| | 4 | 27.01.90 | **Cambridge Utd** (D4) | H | D | 1-1 | Cascarino |
| | 4r | 30.01.90 | **Cambridge Utd** | A | L | 0-1aet | |
| 1990-91 (D2) | 3 | 05.01.91 | **Leicester City** (D2) | H | W | 2-1 | Sheringham, Stephenson |
| | 4 | 26.01.91 | **Sheffield Wed** (D2) | H | D | 4-4 | Stephenson, Rae 2, Sheringham |
| | 4r | 30.01.91 | **Sheffield Wed** | A | L | 0-2 | |

| | | | | | | | | |
|---|---|---|---|---|---|---|---|---|
| 1991-92 | (D2) | 3 | 04.01.92 | **Huddersfield Town** (D3) | A | W | 4-0 | Thompson, Verveer, Rae 2 |
| | | 4 | 05.02.92 | **Norwich City** (D1) | A | L | 1-2 | Kerr |
| 1992-93 | (D1) | 3 | 13.01.93 | **Southend Utd** (D1) | A | L | 0-1 | |
| 1993-94 | (D1) | 3 | 09.01.94 | **Arsenal** (PL) | H | L | 0-1 | |
| 1994-95 | (D1) | 3 | 07.01.95 | **Arsenal** (PL) | H | D | 0-0 | |
| | | 3r | 18.01.95 | **Arsenal** | A | W | 2-0 | Beard, Kennedy |
| | | 4 | 28.01.95 | **Chelsea** (PL) | H | D | 0-0 | |
| | | 4r | 08.02.95 | **Chelsea** | A | D | 1-1aet | Savage |
| | | | | *Millwall won 5-4 on penalties* | | | | |
| | | 5 | 18.02.95 | **QPR** (PL) | H | L | 0-1 | |
| 1995-96 | (D1) | 3 | 06.01.96 | **Oxford Utd** (D2) | H | D | 3-3 | Rae 2, Malkin |
| | | 3r | 16.01.96 | **Oxford Utd** | A | L | 0-1 | |
| 1996-97 | (Conf) | 1 | 15.11.96 | **Woking** (Conf) | A | D | 2-2 | Savage, Crawford |
| | | 1r | 26.11.96 | **Woking** | H | L | 0-1 | |
| 1997-98 | (D2) | 1 | 15.11.97 | **Bristol City** (D2) | A | L | 0-1 | |
| 1998-99 | (D2) | 1 | 13.11.98 | **Swansea City** (D3) | A | L | 0-3 | |
| 1999-00 | (D2) | 1 | 31.10.99 | **Hartlepool Utd** (D3) | A | L | 0-1 | |
| 2000-01 | (D2) | 1 | 19.11.00 | **Leigh RMI** (Conf) | A | W | 3-0 | Harris (p), Bircham, Moody |
| | | | | *played at the New Den* | | | | |
| | | 2 | 10.12.00 | **Wycombe W** (D2) | H | D | 0-0 | |
| | | 2r | 19.12.00 | **Wycombe W** | A | L | 1-2 | Dolan |
| 2001-02 | (D1) | 3 | 05.01.02 | **Scunthorpe Utd** (D3) | H | W | 2-1 | Sadlier 2 |
| | | 4 | 26.01.02 | **Blackburn Rovers** (PL) | H | L | 0-1 | |
| 2002-03 | (D1) | 3 | 04.01.03 | **Cambridge Utd** (D3) | A | D | 1-1 | Claridge |
| | | 3r | 14.01.03 | **Cambridge Utd** | H | W | 3-2 | Claridge (p), Robinson, Ifill |
| | | 4 | 25.01.03 | **Southampton** (PL) | A | D | 1-1 | Claridge |
| | | 4r | 05.02.03 | **Southampton** | H | L | 1-2aet | Reid |

## MINEHEAD

*Formed 1889. First entered FA Cup: 1912-13. League club beaten: Swansea City. Members of the Western League.*

| | | | | | | | | |
|---|---|---|---|---|---|---|---|---|
| 1970-71 | (WL) | 1 | 21.11.70 | **Shrewsbury Town** (D3) | H | L | 1-2 | Bryant |
| 1976-77 | (SL) | 1 | 20.11.76 | **Swansea City** (D4) | A | W | 1-0 | Leitch |
| | | 2 | 11.12.76 | **Portsmouth** (D3) | A | L | 1-2 | Leitch |
| 1977-78 | (SL) | 1 | 26.11.77 | **Wycombe W** (IL) | H | W | 2-0 | Brown, Leitch |
| | | 2 | 17.12.77 | **Exeter City** (D3) | H | L | 0-3 | |
| 1979-80 | (SL) | 1 | 24.11.79 | **Chesham Utd** (IL) | H | L | 1-2 | Brown |
| 1980-81 | (SL) | 1 | 22.11.80 | **Barnet** (APL) | A | D | 2-2 | Chick, Brown |
| | | 1r | 25.11.80 | **Barnet** | H | L | 1-2 | Druce |
| 1981-82 | (SL) | 1 | 21.11.81 | **Dorchester Town** (SL) | A | D | 3-3 | Guscott, Hodgson, Darke |
| | | 1r | 23.11.81 | **Dorchester Town** | H | L | 0-4 | |

## MINERVA

*Entered the FA Cup for these three seasons only.*

| | | | | | | | | |
|---|---|---|---|---|---|---|---|---|
| 1877-78 | | 1 | 03.11.77 | **Hawks** | A | L | 2-5 | Clegg, Duthie |
| 1878-79 | | 1 | | 105th Regiment | | | - | |
| | | | | *105th Regiment scratched. Minerva walkover* | | | | |
| | | 2 | 07.12.78 | **Grey Friars** | A | W | 3-0 | Bain, Hearn, Turner |
| | | 3 | 11.01.79 | **Old Etonians** | A | L | 2-5 | Thompson, Ware |
| 1879-80 | | 1 | 15.11.79 | **Herts Rangers** | A | L | 1-2 | Fabian |

## MOLD FC

*Formed 1874. Entered FA Cup: 1925-26 – 1926-27.*

| | | | | | | | | |
|---|---|---|---|---|---|---|---|---|
| 1925-26 | (Welsh) | 1 | 28.11.25 | **Southport** (3N) | A | L | 0-1 | |

## MOLESEY

*Formed 1952. First entered FA Cup: 1968-69. Based in West Molesey, Surrey. Members of the Isthmian League.*

| | | | | | | | | |
|---|---|---|---|---|---|---|---|---|
| 1993-94 | (IL) | 1 | 13.11.93 | **Bath City** (Conf) | H | L | 0-4 | |

## MOOR GREEN

*Formed 1906. First entered FA Cup: 1934-35. Members of the Southern League.*

| | | | | | | | | |
|---|---|---|---|---|---|---|---|---|
| 1979-80 | (MC) | 1 | 24.11.79 | **Stafford Rangers** (APL) | A | L | 2-3 | Howell, Clamp (p) |
| 2002-03 | (SL) | 1 | 16.11.02 | **Barrow** (NPL) | A | L | 0-2 | |

## MORECAMBE

*Formed 1920. First entered FA Cup: 1920-21. FA Trophy winners: 1974. League clubs beaten: Chester, Cambridge United, Chesterfield. Members of The Conference.*

| | | | | | | | | |
|---|---|---|---|---|---|---|---|---|
| 1936-37 | (LC) | 1 | 28.11.36 | **South Liverpool** (LC) | A | L | 0-1 | |
| 1956-57 | (LC) | 1 | 17.11.56 | **Accrington Stanley** (3N) | A | L | 1-4 | Horton |
| 1958-59 | (LC) | 1 | 15.11.58 | **Blyth Spartans** (ML) | H | L | 1-2 | Borrowdale |
| 1961-62 | (LC) | 1 | 04.11.61 | **S Shields (1936)** (NCO) | H | W | 2-1 | Shields og, Whitehead |
| | | 2 | 25.11.61 | **Chester** (D4) | A | W | 1-0 | Howarth |
| | | 3 | 06.01.62 | **Weymouth** (SL) | H | L | 0-1 | |
| 1962-63 | (LC) | 1 | 03.11.62 | **Blyth Spartans** (NEL) | A | L | 1-2 | Whitehead |
| 1966-67 | (LC) | 1 | 26.11.66 | **York City** (D4) | A | D | 0-0 | |
| | | 1r | 05.12.66 | **York City** | H | D | 1-1aet | Lear |
| | | 1 2r | 08.12.66 | **York City** | | L | 0-1 | |
| | | | | *played at Maine Road* | | | | |
| 1968-69 | (NPL) | 1 | 16.11.68 | **Bangor City** (NPL) | A | W | 3-2 | Wroth, Porter, Lancaster (p) |
| | | 2 | 07.12.68 | **York City** (D4) | A | L | 0-2 | |
| 1974-75 | (NPL) | 1 | 23.11.74 | **Bishop Auckland** (NL) | A | L | 0-5 | |
| 1975-76 | (NPL) | 1 | 22.11.75 | **Scarborough** (NPL) | A | L | 0-2 | |
| 1976-77 | (NPL) | 1 | 20.11.76 | **Lincoln City** (D3) | A | L | 0-1 | |
| 1978-79 | (NPL) | 1 | 25.11.78 | **Stockport County** (D4) | A | L | 1-5 | Towers |
| 1979-80 | (NPL) | 1 | 24.11.79 | **Rotherham Utd** (D3) | H | D | 1-1 | McLachlan (p) |
| | | 1r | 27.11.79 | **Rotherham Utd** | A | L | 0-2 | |
| 1985-86 | (NPL) | 1 | 16.11.85 | **York City** (D3) | A | D | 0-0 | |
| | | 1r | 19.11.85 | **York City** | H | L | 0-2 | |
| | | | | *played at Maine Road* | | | | |
| 1991-92 | (NPL) | 1 | 16.11.91 | **Hull City** (D3) | H | L | 0-1 | |
| 1996-97 | (Conf) | 1 | 16.11.96 | **Boston Utd** (NPL) | A | L | 0-3 | |
| 1997-98 | (Conf) | 1 | 15.11.97 | **Emley** (NPL) | H | D | 1-1 | Bignall |
| | | 1r | 25.11.97 | **Emley** | A | D | 3-3aet | Mayers, Takano, Monk |
| | | | | *Emley won 3-1 on penalties* | | | | |
| 1999-00 | (Conf) | 1 | 30.10.99 | **Oxford Utd** (D2) | A | L | 2-3 | Wright, Jackson |
| 2000-01 | (Conf) | 1 | 18.11.00 | **Forest Green R** (Conf) | A | W | 3-0 | Hatswell og, Norman, Thompson |
| | | 2 | 09.12.00 | **Cambridge Utd** (D2) | H | W | 2-1 | Hardicker, Quayle |
| | | 3 | 06.01.01 | **Ipswich Town** (PL) | H | L | 0-3 | |
| 2001-02 | (Conf) | 1 | 17.11.01 | **Brentford** (D2) | A | L | 0-1 | |
| 2002-03 | (Conf) | 1 | 16.11.02 | **Chesterfield** (D3) | A | W | 2-1 | Elam, Thompson |
| | | 2 | 07.12.02 | **Chester City** (Conf) | H | W | 3-2 | Bentley 2, Rigoglioso |
| | | 3 | 04.01.03 | **Ipswich Town** (D1) | A | L | 0-4 | |

## MORPETH HARRIERS

*Northumberland-based amateurs. Entered FA Cup: 1887-88 – 1908-09.*

| | | | | | | | |
|---|---|---|---|---|---|---|---|
| 1887-88 | 1 | 15.10.87 | **Sunderland** | A | L | 2-4 | |
| | | | *FA ordered replay after protest* | | | | |
| | 1r | 22.10.87 | **Sunderland** | H | L | 2-3 | Crackett, Waterson |

## MORTON RANGERS

*A London-based amateur club who entered the FA Cup once. No connection with Scottish League club Morton.*

| | | | | | | |
|---|---|---|---|---|---|---|
| 1881-82 | 1 | 05.11.81 | **Old Foresters** | A | L | 0-3 |

## MOSQUITOES

*Formed 1870. Played at the Greyhound Field, Dulwich and used the Greyhound pub as their changing rooms. Entered the FA Cup: 1879-80 – 1883-84.*

| | | | | | | | |
|---|---|---|---|---|---|---|---|
| 1879-80 | 1 | 01.11.79 | **St Peters Institute** | H | W | 3-1 | Davey 2, Borman |
| | 2 | 20.12.79 | **Hendon (1874)** | A | L | 1-7 | Ginger |
| 1880-81 | 1 | 13.11.80 | **Upton Park** | A | L | 1-8 | |
| 1881-82 | 1 | 05.11.81 | **Pilgrims** | H | D | 1-1 | A Cornford |
| | 1r | 12.11.81 | **Pilgrims** | A | L | 0-5 | |
| 1882-83 | 1 | 04.11.82 | **Hanover Utd** | A | L | 0-1 | |
| 1883-84 | 1 | 10.11.83 | **Pilgrims** | H | W | 3-2 | J Cornford, others 2 |
| | 2 | 01.12.83 | **Romford (1876)** | A | L | 1-3 | Soulby |

# MOSSLEY

*Formed 1903. First entered FA Cup: 1948-49. FA Trophy runners-up: 1980. League club beaten: Crewe Alexandra. Members of the North West Counties League.*

| | | | | | | | | |
|---|---|---|---|---|---|---|---|---|
| 1949-50 | (CC) | 1 | 26.11.49 | **Witton Albion** (CC) | A | W | 1-0 | Moss |
| | | 2 | 10.12.49 | **Nuneaton B** (BC) | A | D | 0-0 | |
| | | 2r | 17.12.49 | **Nuneaton B** | H | L | 0-3 | |
| 1969-70 | (CC) | 1 | 15.11.69 | **Stockport County** (D3) | A | D | 1-1 | Batty |
| | | 1r | 18.11.69 | **Stockport County** | H | L | 0-1 | |
| 1977-78 | (NPL) | 1 | 26.11.77 | **Rotherham Utd** (D3) | A | L | 0-3 | |
| 1979-80 | (NPL) | 1 | 24.11.79 | **York City** (D4) | A | L | 2-5 | Smith 2 |
| 1980-81 | (NPL) | 1 | 22.11.80 | **Crewe Alexandra** (D4) | H | W | 1-0 | Mobley |
| | | 2 | 13.12.80 | **Mansfield Town** (D4) | H | L | 1-3 | Skeete |
| 1981-82 | (NPL) | 1 | 21.11.81 | **Stockport County** (D4) | A | L | 1-3 | Moore |
| 1982-83 | (NPL) | 1 | 20.11.82 | **Huddersfield Town** (D3) | A | L | 0-1 | |
| 1983-84 | (NPL) | 1 | 19.11.83 | **Darlington** (D4) | A | L | 0-5 | |

# NELSON FC

*Formed 1881. First entered FA Cup: 1893-94. Members of the Football League: 1921-1931. Members of the North West Counties League.*

| | | | | | | | | |
|---|---|---|---|---|---|---|---|---|
| 1921-22 | (3N) | | | 4q Accrington Stanley (H) 1-0; 5q Rochdale (H) 3-2; 6q Worksop Town (A) 1-2 | | | | |
| 1922-23 | (3N) | | | 4q Rochdale (H) 1-0; 5q Stalybridge Celtic (A) 0-1 | | | | |
| 1923-24 | (D2) | | | 5q Wigan Borough (A) 1-1; 5qr Wigan Borough (H) 0-1 | | | | |
| 1924-25 | (3N) | | | 5q Winsford Utd (H) 4-1; 6q Coventry City (H) 0-1 | | | | |
| 1925-26 | (3N) | 1 | 02.12.25 | **Wigan Borough** (3N) | A | L | 0-3 | |
| 1926-27 | (3N) | 1 | 27.11.26 | **Stockport County** (3N) | H | W | 4-1 | Hampson 2, Sharp, Stevenson |
| | | 2 | 11.12.26 | **Ashington** (3N) | A | L | 1-2 | Stevenson |
| 1927-28 | (3N) | 1 | 26.11.27 | **Bradford Park A** (3N) | H | L | 0-3 | |
| 1928-29 | (3N) | | | did not compete – failed to enter competion by deadline | | | | |
| 1929-30 | (3N) | 1 | 30.11.29 | **Crewe Alexandra** (3N) | H | L | 0-3 | |
| 1930-31 | (3N) | 1 | 29.11.30 | **Workington** (NEL) | H | W | 4-0 | Raisbeck 3, Hawes |
| | | 2 | 13.12.30 | **York City** (3N) | H | D | 1-1 | Allam |
| | | 2r | 17.12.30 | **York City** | A | - | 0-2ab | |
| | | | | *abandoned because of fog* | | | | |
| | | 2r | 18.12.30 | **York City** | A | L | 2-3 | H Robinson, Raisbeck |
| 1932-33 | (LC) | 1 | 26.11.32 | **Southport** (3N) | A | D | 3-3 | J Howarth, Chadwick, Garbutt |
| | | 1r | 29.11.32 | **Southport** | H | L | 0-4 | |
| 1950-51 | (LC) | 1 | 25.11.50 | **Witton Albion** (CC) | A | W | 2-1 | Burns, Cowell |
| | | 2 | 09.12.50 | **Port Vale** (3S) | A | L | 2-3 | Ward. Coates |
| 1951-52 | (LC) | 1 | 24.11.51 | **Oldham Athletic** (3N) | H | L | 0-4 | |
| 1953-54 | (LC) | 1 | 21.11.53 | **Witton Albion** (CC) | A | L | 1-4 | Wolstanholme |

# NETHERFIELD

*Formed 1920. First entered FA Cup: 1925-26. Re-named Netherfield Kendal 1996. Kendal Town 2000. Members of the Northern Premier League.*

| | | | | | | | | |
|---|---|---|---|---|---|---|---|---|
| 1945-46 | (LC) | 1 1L | 17.11.45 | **Barrow** (3N) | A | L | 0-1 | |
| | | 1 2L | 24.11.45 | **Barrow** | H | D | 2-2 | Hickton, Carswell |
| 1948-49 | (LC) | 1 | 27.11.48 | **Gateshead AFC** (3N) | A | L | 0-3 | |
| 1949-50 | (LC) | 1 | 26.11.49 | **North Shields** (NEL) | H | W | 4-3 | Offord, Reed, Ashworth, Ferguson |
| | | 2 | 10.12.49 | **Watford** (3S) | A | L | 0-6 | |
| 1952-53 | (LC) | 1 | 22.11.52 | **Gainsborough T** (ML) | A | D | 1-1 | Rooke |
| | | 1r | 27.11.52 | **Gainsborough T** | H | L | 0-3 | |
| 1954-55 | (LC) | 1 | 20.11.54 | **Wrexham** (3N) | H | D | 3-3 | Ferguson, Parker og, Rooke |
| | | 1r | 24.11.54 | **Wrexham** | A | L | 0-4 | |
| 1955-56 | (LC) | 1 | 19.11.55 | **Grimsby Town** (3N) | H | L | 1-5 | Hayes |
| 1963-64 | (LC) | 1 | 16.11.63 | **Loughborough Utd** (ML) | H | W | 6-1 | Brownlee 4, Hodgson, Lambert |
| | | 2 | 07.12.63 | **Chesterfield** (D4) | H | D | 1-1 | Brownlee |
| | | 2r | 11.12.63 | **Chesterfield** | A | L | 1-4 | Lambert |
| 1964-65 | (LC) | 1 | 14.11.64 | **Barnsley** (D3) | H | L | 1-3 | Hodgson |

# NEW BRIGHTON

*Formed 1921. First entered FA Cup: 1922-23. Members of the Football League: 1923-1951. Folded 1983. League clubs beaten as a Non-League club: Crewe Alexandra, Coventry City, Stockport County, Derby County, Torquay United.*

| | | | | | | | | |
|---|---|---|---|---|---|---|---|---|
| 1922-23 | (LC) | | | 4q Crewe Alexandra (3N) (H) 1-1; 4qr Crewe Alexandra (A) 1-0; 5q Coventry City (D2) (H) 3-0 | | | | |
| | | 1 | 13.01.23 | **Sheffield Wed** (D2) | A | L | 0-3 | |
| 1923-24 | (3N) | | | 4q Southport (A) 1-1; 4qr Southport (H) 0-1 | | | | |
| 1924-25 | (3N) | | | 5q Accrington Stanley (H) 0-0; 5qr Accrington Stanley (A) 2- 3 | | | | |
| 1925-26 | (3N) | 1 | 28.11.25 | **Barrow** (3N) | H | W | 2-0 | Dunne, Whitter |
| | | 2 | 12.12.25 | **Darlington** (D2) | H | W | 2-0 | Kelly 2 |
| | | 3 | 09.01.26 | **Sheffield Wed** (D2) | H | W | 2-1 | Gee, Broad |
| | | 4 | 30.01.26 | **Notts County** (D1) | A | L | 0-2 | |
| 1926-27 | (3N) | 1 | 27.11.26 | **Wrexham** (3N) | A | D | 1-1 | Williams |
| | | 1r | 01.12.26 | **Wrexham** | | D | 2-2 | Whitter, Worrall |
| | | 1 2r | 06.12.26 | **Wrexham** | | L | 1-3 | Hawksworth |
| | | | | *played at Anfield* | | | | |
| 1927-28 | (3N) | 1 | 26.11.27 | **Shildon** (NEL) | A | W | 3-1 | Whitter, Harley 2 |
| | | 2 | 10.12.27 | **Rhyl** (Welsh) | H | W | 7-2 | Lewis, Dixon og, Harley 4, Reid |
| | | 3 | 14.01.28 | **Corinthians** | H | W | 2-1 | Whitter 2 |
| | | 4 | 28.01.28 | **Port Vale** (D2) | A | L | 0-3 | |
| 1928-29 | (3N) | 1 | 24.11.28 | **Darlington** (3N) | A | L | 0-3 | |
| 1929-30 | (3N) | 1 | 30.11.29 | **Lancaster Town** (LC) | H | W | 4-1 | Taylor 2, Johnson, Roscoe |
| | | 2 | 14.12.29 | **Doncaster Rovers** (3N) | A | L | 0-1 | |
| 1930-31 | (3N) | 1 | 29.11.30 | **Carlisle Utd** (3N) | A | L | 1-3 | Pither |
| 1931-32 | (3N) | 1 | 28.11.31 | **York City** (3N) | H | W | 3-1 | Johnson og, Stevens 2 |
| | | 2 | 12.12.31 | **Hull City** (3N) | H | L | 0-4 | |
| 1932-33 | (3N) | 1 | 26.11.32 | **Tranmere Rovers** (3N) | A | L | 0-3 | |
| 1933-34 | (3N) | 1 | 25.11.33 | **Mansfield Town** (3N) | H | D | 0-0 | |
| | | 1r | 29.11.33 | **Mansfield Town** | A | W | 4-3 | Barley 3, Page |
| | | 2 | 09.12.33 | **QPR** (3S) | A | D | 1-1 | Barley |
| | | 2r | 13.12.33 | **QPR** | H | L | 0-4 | |
| 1934-35 | (3N) | 1 | 24.11.34 | **Southport** (3N) | A | D | 1-1 | L Carr |
| | | 1r | 28.11.34 | **Southport** | H | D | 1-1aet | Allen |
| | | 1 2r | 03.12.34 | **Southport** | | W | 2-1 | Kenyon, Butler |
| | | | | *played at Goodison Park* | | | | |
| | | 2 | 08.12.34 | **York City** (3N) | A | L | 0-1 | |
| 1935-36 | (3N) | 1 | 30.11.35 | **Workington** (NEL) | H | L | 1-3 | Lawrence |
| 1936-37 | (3N) | 1 | 28.11.36 | **Lincoln City** (3N) | A | D | 1-1 | Griffiths |
| | | 1r | 02.12.36 | **Lincoln City** | H | L | 2-3 | Mustard, Watters |
| 1937-38 | (3N) | 1 | 27.11.37 | **Workington** (NEL) | H | W | 5-0 | Montogmery 4, Mustard |
| | | 2 | 11.12.37 | **Crewe Alexandra** (3N) | A | - | 0-1ab | |
| | | | | *abandoned after 84 minutes* | | | | |
| | | 2 | 15.12.37 | **Crewe Alexandra** | A | D | 2-2 | Wright, Montgomery |
| | | 2r | 20.12.37 | **Crewe Alexandra** | H | W | 4-1 | Ainsworth, Smith, Gilchrist og, Montgomery |
| | | 3 | 08.01.38 | **Plymouth Argyle** (D2) | H | W | 1-0 | Mustard |
| | | 4 | 22.01.38 | **Tottenham Hotspur** (D2) | H | D | 0-0 | |
| | | 4r | 26.01.38 | **Tottenham Hotspur** | A | L | 2-5 | Hitchins og, Bulloch |
| 1938-39 | (3N) | 1 | 26.11.38 | **Doncaster Rovers** (3N) | A | L | 2-4 | Stamps, Allmark |
| 1945-46 | (3N) | | | did not enter | | | | |
| 1946-47 | (3N) | 1 | 30.11.46 | **Hull City** (3N) | A | D | 0-0 | |
| | | 1r | 04.12.46 | **Hull City** | H | L | 1-2aet | Wells |
| 1947-48 | (3N) | 1 | 29.11.47 | **Marine** (LC) | H | W | 4-0 | McGeachie, Ainsworth, Hope, Pendergast |
| | | 2 | 13.12.47 | **Bristol Rovers** (3S) | A | L | 0-4 | |
| 1948-49 | (3N) | 1 | 27.11.48 | **Carlisle Utd** (3N) | H | W | 1-0 | Lyon |
| | | 2 | 11.12.48 | **Bradford City** (3N) | A | D | 0-0 | |
| | | 2r | 18.12.48 | **Bradford City** | H | W | 1-0 | Lyon |
| | | 3 | 08.01.49 | **Sheffield Utd** (D1) | A | L | 2-5 | Carter, Latham og |
| 1949-50 | (3N) | 1 | 26.11.49 | **Doncaster Rovers** (3N) | A | L | 1-5 | Carter |
| 1950-51 | (3N) | 1 | 25.11.50 | **Port Vale** (3S) | A | L | 2-3 | Carter 2 |

| | | | | | | | | |
|---|---|---|---|---|---|---|---|---|
| 1956-57 (LC) | 1 | 17.11.56 | **Stockport County** (3N) | H | D | 3-3 | Vincent 2, Windle |
| | 1r | 20.11.56 | **Stockport County** | A | W | 3-2 | Burgess, Vincent, Windle |
| | 2 | 08.12.56 | **Derby County** (3N) | A | W | 3-1 | Lewis, Burgess, Vincent |
| | 3 | 05.01.57 | **Torquay Utd** (3S) | H | W | 2-1 | Windle 2 |
| | 4 | 26.01.57 | **Burnley** (D1) | A | L | 0-9 | |

# NEW BRIGHTON TOWER

*Formed 1897. Entered FA Cup: 1897-98 – 1901-02. Members of the Football League: 1898-1901. This club folded in August 1901 and was a separate club from New Brighton FC.*

| | | | | | | | |
|---|---|---|---|---|---|---|---|
| 1897-98 (LL) | 1 | 29.01.98 | **WBA** (D1) | A | L | 0-2 | |
| 1898-99 (D2) | | | 3q Glossop North End (A) 2-4 | | | | |
| 1899-00 (D2) | | | P Birkenhead (H) 5-0; 1q Wirral Railways (H) 7-1; 2q South Liverpool (A) 2-3 | | | | |
| 1900-01 (D2) | | | Int Port Vale (A) 3-1 | | | | |
| | 1 | 09.02.01 | **Wolverhampton W** (D1) | A | L | 1-5 | Hulse |

# NEW CRUSADERS

*Formed 1905. Entered FA Cup: 1905-06 – 1914-15. Based in Sidcup, Kent. Six brothers from the Farnfield family played in the match against Plymouth – and three of them scored. London Senior Cup winners 1906. Middlesex Senior Cup winners 1907.*

| | | | | | | | |
|---|---|---|---|---|---|---|---|
| 1905-06 | 1 | 13.01.06 | **Plymouth Argyle** (SL) | H | L | 3-6 | G Farnfield, H Farnfield, B Farnfield |

# NEWARK FC

*Entered FA Cup: 1884-85 – 1907-08.*

| | | | | | | | |
|---|---|---|---|---|---|---|---|
| 1884-85 | 1 | 08.11.84 | **Spilsby** | H | W | 7-3 | |
| | 2 | 06.12.84 | **Middlesbrough** | A | L | 1-4 | Huskinson |
| 1885-86 | 1 | 31.10.85 | **Sheffield FC** | H | L | 0-3 | |

# NEWARK TOWN

*Entered FA Cup: 1927-28 – 1937-38. Folded mid-1980s.*

| | | | | | | | |
|---|---|---|---|---|---|---|---|
| 1929-30 (ML) | 1 | 30.11.29 | **Barrow** (3N) | A | L | 0-1 | |
| 1930-31 (ML) | 1 | 29.11.30 | **Rotherham Utd** (3N) | H | W | 2-1 | Speed 2 |
| | 2 | 13.12.30 | **Crystal Palace** (3S) | A | L | 0-6 | |
| 1931-32 (ML) | 1 | 28.11.31 | **Halifax Town** (3N) | H | D | 1-1 | Hill |
| | 1r | 02.12.31 | **Halifax Town** | A | L | 1-2 | Hill |
| 1933-34 (ML) | 1 | 25.11.33 | **Tranmere Rovers** (3N) | A | L | 0-7 | |

# NEWCASTLE EAST END

*Formed 1882 after Stanley FC and Rosewood FC amalgamated. East End played at the Heaton Junction ground, Chillingham Road and transferred to St James' Park when they took over the liabilities of Newcastle West End in 1892. East End are regarded as the principal forerunners of Newcastle Utd. Entered FA Cup as Newcastle East End: 1887-88 – 1891-92.*

| | | | | | | | |
|---|---|---|---|---|---|---|---|
| 1887-88 | 1 | 15.10.87 | **South Bank** | A | L | 2-3aet | W Muir 2 |
| 1888-89 | | | 1q Port Clarence (H) 3-1; 2q Stockton (H) 2-1; 3q Sunderland (A) 0-2aet | | | | |
| 1889-90 (NL) | | | 1q Shankhouse Black Watch (H) 4-0; 2q Darlington St Augustine's (A) 1-2 | | | | |
| 1890-91 (NL) | | | 2q Bishop Auckland (A) 2-1; 3q Shankhouse Black Watch (H) 5-0; 4q Sunderland Albion (H) 2-2; 4qr Sunderland Albion (H) 0-2 | | | | |
| 1891-92 (NL) | | | 1q Tow Law Town (A) 5-1; 2q Newcastle West End (A) 3-0; 3q Shankhouse Black Watch (H) 3-2; 4q Bishop Auckland (H) 7-0 | | | | |
| | 1 | 16.01.92 | **Nottingham Forest** (FAll) | A | L | 1-2 | Brown og |

# NEWCASTLE TOWN

*Formed 1964. Based at Newcastle-under-Lyne, Staffordshire. First entered FA Cup: 1991-92. Members of the North West Counties League.*

| | | | | | | | |
|---|---|---|---|---|---|---|---|
| 1996-97 (NWC) | 1 | 17.11.96 | **Notts County** (D2) | H | L | 0-2 | |
| | | | *played at Victoria Ground, Stoke* | | | | |

# NEWCASTLE UNITED

*Formed 1892 by the merger of Newcastle West End and Newcastle East End. FA Cup winners: 1910, 1924, 1932, 1951, 1952, 1955. Runners-up: 1905, 1906, 1908, 1911, 1974, 1998, 1999. Record FA Cup win: 9-0 v Southport, 4th round, 01.02.1932; Record FA Cup defeat: 1-7 v Aston Villa, 2nd round, 16.02.1895.*

| | | | | | | | |
|---|---|---|---|---|---|---|---|
| 1892-93 (NL) | 1 | 21.01.93 | **Middlesbrough** (NL) | H | L | 2-3 | Reay, Thompson |
| 1893-94 (D2) | 1 | 27.01.94 | **Sheffield Utd** (D1) | H | W | 2-0 | Wallace 2 |
| | 2 | 10.02.94 | **Bolton Wanderers** (D1) | H | L | 1-2 | Crate |
| 1894-95 (D2) | 1 | 02.02.95 | **Burnley** (D1) | H | W | 2-1 | Rendell 2 |

| | | | | | | | | |
|---|---|---|---|---|---|---|---|---|
| | | 2 | 16.02.95 | **Aston Villa** (D1) | A | L | 1-7 | Thompson |
| 1895-96 | (D2) | | | P Leadgate Exiles (A) walkover; 1q W Hartlepool NER (A) 8-0; 2q Middlesbrough (H) 4-1; 3q Rendel (H) 5-0; 4q Tow Law Town (H) 4-0 | | | | |
| | | 1 | 01.02.96 | **Chesterfield** | A | W | 4-0 | Wardrope 2, Aitken, Thompson |
| | | 2 | 15.02.96 | **Bury** (D1) | H | L | 1-3 | Thompson |
| 1896-97 | (D2) | 1 | 30.01.97 | **Aston Villa** (D1) | A | L | 0-5 | |
| 1897-98 | (D2) | | | 3q Willington Athletic (H) 6-0; 4q Stockton (A) 4-1; 5q Middlesbrough (A) 2-0 | | | | |
| | | 1 | 29.01.98 | **Preston North End** (D1) | A | W | 2-1 | Peddie 2 |
| | | 2 | 12.02.98 | **Southampton** (SL) | A | L | 0-1 | |
| 1898-99 | (D1) | 1 | 28.01.99 | **Glossop North End** (D2) | A | W | 1-0 | Peddie |
| | | 2 | 11.02.99 | **Liverpool** (D1) | A | L | 1-3 | Peddie |
| 1899-00 | (D1) | 1 | 27.01.00 | **Reading** (SL) | H | W | 2-1 | Stevenson, Rogers |
| | | 2 | 10.02.00 | **Southampton** (SL) | A | - | 0-0ab | |
| | | | | *abandoned after 50 minutes – bad light* | | | | |
| | | 2 | 17.02.00 | **Southampton** (SL) | A | L | 1-4 | Peddie |
| 1900-01 | (D1) | 1 | 09.02.01 | **Middlesbrough** (D2) | A | L | 1-3 | Aitken |
| 1901-02 | (D1) | 1 | 25.01.02 | **Woolwich Arsenal** (D2) | A | W | 2-0 | Veitch, A Gardner |
| | | 2 | 12.02.02 | **Sunderland** (D1) | H | W | 1-0 | Orr |
| | | 3 | 22.02.02 | **Sheffield Utd** (D1) | H | D | 1-1 | Stewart |
| | | 3r | 27.02.02 | **Sheffield Utd** | A | L | 1-2 | McColl |
| 1902-03 | (D1) | 1 | 07.02.03 | **Grimsby Town** (D1) | A | L | 1-2 | McColl |
| 1903-04 | (D1) | 1 | 06.02.04 | **Bury** (D1) | A | L | 1-2 | Templeton |
| 1904-05 | (D1) | 1 | 04.02.05 | **Plymouth Argyle** (SL) | H | D | 1-1 | Gosnell |
| | | 1r | 08.02.05 | **Plymouth Argyle** | A | D | 1-1aet | Gosnell |
| | | 1 2r | 13.02.05 | **Plymouth Argyle** | | W | 2-0 | Orr 2 (1p) |
| | | | | *played at Plumstead* | | | | |
| | | 2 | 18.02.05 | **Tottenham Hotspur** (SL) | A | D | 1-1 | Howie |
| | | 2r | 22.02.05 | **Tottenham Hotspur** | H | W | 4-0 | Orr 2, Appleyard, Howie |
| | | 3 | 04.03.05 | **Bolton Wanderers** (D2) | A | W | 2-0 | Appleyard, Howie |
| | | SF | 25.03.05 | **Sheffield Wed** (D1) | | W | 1-0 | Howie |
| | | | | *played at Hyde Road, Manchester* | | | | |
| | | F | 15.04.05 | **Aston Villa** (D1) | | L | 0-2 | |
| | | | | *played at Crystal Palace* | | | | |
| 1905-06 | (D1) | 1 | 13.01.06 | **Grimsby Town** (D2) | H | W | 6-0 | Orr 2, Gosnell, Appleyard 2, J Rutherford |
| | | 2 | 03.02.06 | **Derby County** (D1) | A | D | 0-0 | |
| | | 2r | 07.02.06 | **Derby County** | H | W | 2-1 | Appleyard, J Rutherford |
| | | 3 | 24.02.06 | **Blackpool** (D2) | H | W | 5-0 | Orr 2, Appleyard, Gardner, og |
| | | 4 | 10.03.06 | **Birmingham** (D1) | A | D | 2-2 | Veitch 2 (1p) |
| | | 4r | 14.03.06 | **Birmingham** | H | W | 3-0 | Appleyard 2, Howie |
| | | SF | 31.03.06 | **Woolwich Arsenal** (D1) | | W | 2-0 | Veitch, Howie |
| | | | | *played at the Victoria Ground, Stoke* | | | | |
| | | F | 21.04.06 | **Everton** (D1) | | L | 0-1 | |
| | | | | *played at Crystal Palace* | | | | |
| 1906-07 | (D1) | 1 | 12.01.07 | **Crystal Palace** (SL) | H | L | 0-1 | |
| 1907-08 | (D1) | 1 | 11.01.08 | **Nottingham Forest** (D1) | H | W | 2-0 | Appleyard, Rutherford |
| | | 2 | 01.02.08 | **West Ham Utd** (SL) | H | W | 2-0 | Appleyard 2 |
| | | 3 | 22.02.08 | **Liverpool** (D1) | H | W | 3-1 | Speedie, Appleyard, Rutherford |
| | | 4 | 07.03.08 | **Grimsby Town** (D2) | H | W | 5-1 | Appleyard 3, Gardner, Vincett og |
| | | SF | 28.03.08 | **Fulham** (D2) | | W | 6-0 | Appleyard, Gardner, Howie 2, Rutherford 2 |
| | | | | *played at Anfield* | | | | |
| | | F | 25.04.08 | **Wolverhampton W** (D2) | | L | 1-3 | Howie |
| | | | | *played at Crystal Palace* | | | | |
| 1908-09 | (D1) | 1 | 16.01.09 | **Clapton Orient** (D2) | H | W | 5-0 | Anderson, Shepherd, Wilson 3 |
| | | 2 | 06.02.09 | **Blackpool** (D2) | H | W | 2-1 | Howie, Rutherford |
| | | 3 | 20.02.09 | **West Ham Utd** (SL) | A | D | 0-0 | |
| | | 3r | 24.02.09 | **West Ham Utd** | H | W | 2-1 | Anderson, Shepherd (p) |
| | | 4 | 06.03.09 | **Sunderland** (D1) | H | D | 2-2 | Rutherford, Wilson |
| | | 4r | 10.03.09 | **Sunderland** | A | W | 3-0 | Shepherd 2, Wilson |
| | | SF | 27.03.09 | **Manchester Utd** (D1) | | L | 0-1 | |
| | | | | *played at Bramall Lane* | | | | |

| | | | | | | | |
|---|---|---|---|---|---|---|---|
| 1909-10 (D1) | 1 | 15.01.10 | **Stoke** (BDL) | A | D | 1-1 | Howie |
| | 1r | 19.01.10 | **Stoke** | H | W | 2-1 | Higgins, Howie |
| | 2 | 05.02.10 | **Fulham** (D2) | H | W | 4-0 | Higgins 2, Rutherford, McCracken (p) |
| | 3 | 19.02.10 | **Blackburn Rovers** (D1) | H | W | 3-1 | Higgins, Howie, Rutherford |
| | 4 | 05.03.10 | **Leicester Fosse** (D2) | H | W | 3-0 | Wilson, Shepherd, Howie |
| | SF | 26.03.10 | **Swindon Town** (SL) *played at White Hart Lane* | | W | 2-0 | Stewart, Rutherford |
| | F | 23.04.10 | **Barnsley** (D2) *played at Crystal Palace* | | D | 1-1 | Rutherford |
| | Fr | 28.04.10 | **Barnsley** *played at Goodison Park* | | W | 2-0 | Shepherd 2 (1p) |
| 1910-11 (D1) | 1 | 14.01.11 | **Bury** (D1) | H | W | 6-1 | Shepherd 3, Stewart, Duncan, McWilliam |
| | 2 | 04.02.11 | **Northampton Town** (SL) | H | D | 1-1 | Higgins |
| | 2r | 08.02.11 | **Northampton Town** *played at St James' Park* | A | W | 1-0 | Shepherd (p) |
| | 3 | 25.02.11 | **Hull City** (D2) | H | W | 3-2 | Shepherd 2, Veitch |
| | 4 | 13.03.11 | **Derby County** (D2) | H | W | 4-0 | Shepherd, Stewart, Rutherford, Willis |
| | SF | 25.03.11 | **Chelsea** (D2) *played at St Andrews* | | W | 3-0 | Wilson, Shepherd, Stewart |
| | F | 22.04.11 | **Bradford City** (D1) *played at Crystal Palace* | | D | 0-0 | |
| | Fr | 26.04.11 | **Bradford City** *played at Old Trafford* | | L | 0-1 | |
| 1911-12 (D1) | 1 | 13.01.12 | **Derby County** (D2) | A | L | 0-3 | |
| 1912-13 (D1) | 1 | 11.01.13 | **Bradford City** (D1) *abandoned at half-time – gale* | H | - | 0-0ab | G Wilson |
| | 1 | 16.01.13 | **Bradford City** | H | W | 1-0 | G Wilson |
| | 2 | 01.02.13 | **Hull City** (D2) | A | D | 0-0 | |
| | 2r | 05.02.13 | **Hull City** | H | W | 3-0 | Hibbert, Rutherford, Hudspeth (p) |
| | 3 | 22.02.13 | **Liverpool** (D1) | A | D | 1-1 | Shepherd |
| | 3r | 26.02.13 | **Liverpool** | H | W | 1-0 | Hudspeth (p) |
| | 4 | 08.03.13 | **Sunderland** (D1) | A | D | 0-0 | |
| | 4r | 12.03.13 | **Sunderland** | H | D | 2-2aet | McTavish, Veitch |
| | 4 2r | 17.03.13 | **Sunderland** | H | L | 0-3 | |
| 1913-14 (D1) | 1 | 10.01.14 | **Sheffield Utd** (D1) | H | L | 0-5 | |
| 1914-15 (D1) | 1 | 09.01.15 | **West Ham Utd** (SL) | A | D | 2-2 | Goodwill 2 |
| | 1r | 16.01.15 | **West Ham Utd** | H | W | 3-2 | Pailor 2, Hibbert |
| | 2 | 30.01.15 | **Swansea Town** (SL) | H | D | 1-1aet | McCracken (p) |
| | 2r | 06.02.15 | **Swansea Town** | A | W | 2-0 | King, Pailor |
| | 3 | 20.02.15 | **Sheffield Wed** (D1) | A | W | 2-1 | King, Hibbert |
| | 4 | 06.03.15 | **Chelsea** (D1) | A | D | 1-1aet | Goodwill |
| | 4r | 13.03.15 | **Chelsea** | H | L | 0-1aet | |
| 1919-20 (D1) | 1 | 10.01.20 | **Crystal Palace** (SL) | H | W | 2-0 | Dixon, Hall |
| | 2 | 31.01.20 | **Huddersfield Town** (D2) | H | L | 0-1 | |
| 1920-21 (D1) | 1 | 08.01.21 | **Nottingham Forest** (D2) | H | D | 1-1 | Harris |
| | 1r | 12.01.21 | **Nottingham Forest** | H | W | 2-0 | Seymour, Harris |
| | 2 | 29.01.21 | **Liverpool** (D1) | H | W | 1-0 | Harris |
| | 3 | 19.02.21 | **Everton** (D1) | A | L | 0-3 | |
| 1921-22 (D1) | 1 | 07.01.22 | **Newport County** (3S) | H | W | 6-0 | McDonald 2, Harris, Dixon 2, Mooney |
| | 2 | 28.01.22 | **Preston North End** (D1) | A | L | 1-3 | Seymour |
| 1922-23 (D1) | 1 | 13.01.23 | **Southampton** (D2) | H | D | 0-0 | |
| | 1r | 17.01.23 | **Southampton** | A | L | 1-3 | Harris |
| 1923-24 (D1) | 1 | 12.01.24 | **Portsmouth** (3S) | A | W | 4-2 | Seymour, Harris, J Low, Gibson |
| | 2 | 02.02.24 | **Derby County** (D2) | A | D | 2-2 | McDonald 2 |
| | 2r | 06.02.24 | **Derby County** | H | D | 2-2aet | Harris, Cowan |
| | 2 2r | 11.02.24 | **Derby County** *played at Burnden Park* | | D | 2-2aet | Seymour, Hudspeth (p) |
| | 2 3r | 13.02.24 | **Derby County** *played at St James' Park* | | W | 5-3 | Seymour, Harris 3, Cowan |
| | 3 | 23.02.24 | **Watford** (3S) | A | W | 1-0 | Seymour |

| | | | | | | | | |
|---|---|---|---|---|---|---|---|---|
| | | 4 | 08.03.24 | **Liverpool** (D1) | H | W | 1-0 | McDonald |
| | | SF | 29.03.24 | **Manchester City** (D1) | | W | 2-0 | Harris 2 |
| | | | | *played at St Andrews* | | | | |
| | | F | 26.04.24 | **Aston Villa** (D1) | | W | 2-0 | Harris, Seymour |
| | | | | *played at Wembley Stadium* | | | | |
| 1924-25 | (D1) | 1 | 10.01.25 | **Hartlepools Utd** (3N) | H | W | 4-1 | Cowan, Harris, McDonald, McKenzie |
| | | 2 | 31.01.25 | **Leicester City** (D2) | H | D | 2-2 | McDonald (p), Cowan |
| | | 2r | 05.02.25 | **Leicester City** | A | L | 0-1 | |
| 1925-26 | (D1) | 3 | 09.01.26 | **Aberdare Athletic** (3S) | H | W | 4-1 | Cowan, Gallacher 2, Gibson |
| | | 4 | 30.01.26 | **Cardiff City** (D1) | A | W | 2-0 | Seymour 2 |
| | | 5 | 20.02.26 | **Clapton Orient** (D2) | A | L | 0-2 | |
| 1926-27 | (D1) | 3 | 08.01.27 | **Notts County** (D2) | H | W | 8-1 | Gallacher 3, McDonald 3, Seymour, Urwin |
| | | 4 | 29.01.27 | **Corinthians** | A | W | 3-1 | McDonald 2, McKay |
| | | | | *played at Crystal Palace* | | | | |
| | | 5 | 19.02.27 | **Southampton** (D2) | A | L | 1-2 | McDonald (p) |
| 1927-28 | (D1) | 3 | 14.01.28 | **Blackburn Rovers** (D1) | A | L | 1-4 | Seymour |
| 1928-29 | (D1) | 3 | 12.01.29 | **Swindon Town** (3S) | A | L | 0-2 | |
| 1929-30 | (D1) | 3 | 11.01.30 | **York City** (3N) | H | D | 1-1 | Gallacher |
| | | 3r | 15.01.30 | **York City** | A | W | 2-1 | Gallacher, Hutchinson |
| | | 4 | 25.01.30 | **Clapton Orient** (3S) | H | W | 3-1 | JR Richardson 3 |
| | | 5 | 15.02.30 | **Brighton** (3S) | H | W | 3-0 | Gallacher 3 |
| | | 6 | 01.03.30 | **Hull City** (D2) | H | D | 1-1 | Lang |
| | | 6r | 06.03.30 | **Hull City** | A | L | 0-1 | |
| 1930-31 | (D1) | 3 | 10.01.31 | **Nottingham Forest** (D2) | H | W | 4-0 | Bedford, Hutchinson 3 |
| | | 4 | 24.01.31 | **Leeds Utd** (D1) | A | L | 1-4 | Hutchinson (p) |
| 1931-32 | (D1) | 3 | 09.01.32 | **Blackpool** (D1) | A | D | 1-1 | Lang |
| | | 3r | 13.01.32 | **Blackpool** | H | W | 1-0 | Boyd |
| | | 4 | 23.01.32 | **Southport** (3N) | H | D | 1-1 | Boyd |
| | | 4r | 26.01.32 | **Southport** | A | D | 1-1aet | Boyd |
| | | 4 2r | 01.02.32 | **Southport** | | W | 9-0 | Lang, McMenemy, Cape 2, Weaver, Boyd, JR Richardson 3 |
| | | | | *played at Hillsborough* | | | | |
| | | 5 | 13.02.32 | **Leicester City** (D1) | H | W | 3-1 | Allen, Lang, Weaver |
| | | 6 | 27.02.32 | **Watford** (3S) | H | W | 5-0 | Allen 3, Boyd, JR Richardson |
| | | SF | 12.03.32 | **Chelsea** (D1) | | W | 2-1 | Allen, Lang |
| | | | | *played at Leeds Road, Huddersfield* | | | | |
| | | F | 23.04.32 | **Arsenal** (D1) | | W | 2-1 | Allen 2 |
| | | | | *played at Wembley Stadium* | | | | |
| 1932-33 | (D1) | 3 | 14.01.33 | **Leeds Utd** (D1) | H | L | 0-3 | |
| 1933-34 | (D1) | 3 | 13.01.34 | **Wolverhampton W** (D1) | A | L | 0-1 | |
| 1934-35 | (D2) | 3 | 12.01.35 | **Hull City** (D2) | A | W | 5-1 | Bott 2, Cairns, Pearson, Quantick og |
| | | 4 | 26.01.35 | **Tottenham Hotspur** (D1) | A | L | 0-2 | |
| 1935-36 | (D2) | 3 | 11.01.36 | **Walsall** (3N) | A | W | 2-0 | Connelly, J Smith |
| | | 4 | 25.01.36 | **Sheffield Wed** (D1) | A | D | 1-1 | Pearson |
| | | 4r | 29.01.36 | **Sheffield Wed** | H | W | 3-1 | Bott 2, J Smith |
| | | 5 | 15.02.36 | **Arsenal** (D1) | H | D | 3-3 | Pearson, J Smith 2 |
| | | 5r | 19.02.36 | **Arsenal** | A | L | 0-3 | |
| 1936-37 | (D2) | 3 | 16.01.37 | **Preston North End** (D1) | A | L | 0-2 | |
| 1937-38 | (D2) | 3 | 08.01.38 | **WBA** (D1) | A | L | 0-1 | |
| 1938-39 | (D2) | 3 | 07.01.39 | **Brentford** (D1) | A | W | 2-0 | Clifton, Mooney |
| | | 4 | 21.01.39 | **Cardiff City** (3S) | A | D | 0-0 | |
| | | 4r | 25.01.39 | **Cardiff City** | H | W | 4-1 | Clifton, Gordon, Mooney, Park |
| | | 5 | 11.02.39 | **Preston North End** (D1) | H | L | 1-2 | Cairns |
| 1945-46 | (D2) | 3 1L | 05.01.46 | **Barnsley** (D2) | H | W | 4-2 | Milburn 2, Hair, Stubbins |
| | | 3 2L | 09.01.46 | **Barnsley** | A | L | 0-3 | |
| 1946-47 | (D2) | 3 | 11.01.47 | **Crystal Palace** (3S) | H | W | 6-2 | Bentley, Pearson, Shackleton 2, Stobbart, Wayman |
| | | 4 | 25.01.47 | **Southampton** (D2) | H | W | 3-1 | Wayman 3 |
| | | 5 | 08.02.47 | **Leicester City** (D2) | H | D | 1-1 | Shackleton |
| | | 5r | 20.02.47 | **Leicester City** | A | W | 2-1 | Bentley, Pearson |

| | | | | | | | |
|---|---|---|---|---|---|---|---|
| | 6 | 01.03.47 | **Sheffield Utd** (D1) | A | W | 2-0 | Bentley (p), Milburn |
| | SF | 29.03.47 | **Charlton Athletic** (D1) | | L | 0-4 | |
| | | | *played at Elland Road* | | | | |
| 1947-48 (D2) | 3 | 10.01.48 | **Charlton Athletic** | A | L | 1-2 | Pearson |
| 1948-49 (D1) | 3 | 08.01.49 | **Bradford Park A** (D2) | H | L | 0-2 | |
| 1949-50 (D1) | 3 | 07.01.50 | **Oldham Athletic** (3N) | A | W | 7-2 | Milburn 3, Mitchell, Walker 2, Houghton |
| | 4 | 28.01.50 | **Chelsea** (D1) | A | L | 0-3 | |
| 1950-51 (D1) | 3 | 06.01.51 | **Bury** (D2) | H | W | 4-1 | Milburn, G Robledo, Taylor, Walker |
| | 4 | 27.01.51 | **Bolton Wanderers** (D1) | H | W | 3-2 | Milburn 2, Mitchell |
| | 5 | 10.02.51 | **Stoke City** (D1) | A | W | 4-2 | Milburn, Mitchell, G Robledo 2 |
| | 6 | 24.02.51 | **Bristol Rovers** (3S) | H | D | 0-0 | |
| | 6r | 28.02.51 | **Bristol Rovers** | A | W | 3-1 | Crowe, Milburn, Taylor |
| | SF | 10.03.51 | **Wolverhampton W** (D1) | | D | 0-0aet | |
| | | | *played at Hillsborough* | | | | |
| | SFr | 14.03.51 | **Wolverhampton W** | | W | 2-1 | Milburn, Mitchell |
| | | | *played at Leeds Road, Huddersfield* | | | | |
| | F | 28.04.51 | **Blackpool** (D1) | | W | 2-0 | Milburn 2 |
| | | | *played at Wembley Stadium* | | | | |
| 1951-52 (D1) | 3 | 12.01.52 | **Aston Villa** (D1) | H | W | 4-2 | Foulkes, Mitchell 2, G Robledo |
| | 4 | 02.02.52 | **Tottenham Hotspur** (D1) | A | W | 3-0 | Mitchell, G Robledo 2 |
| | 5 | 23.02.52 | **Swansea Town** (D2) | A | W | 1-0 | Mitchell |
| | 6 | 08.03.52 | **Portsmouth** (D1) | A | W | 4-2 | Milburn 3, G Robledo |
| | SF | 29.03.52 | **Blackburn Rovers** (D2) | | D | 0-0aet | |
| | | | *played at Hillsborough* | | | | |
| | SFr | 02.04.52 | **Blackburn Rovers** | | W | 2-1 | Mitchell (p), G Robledo |
| | | | *played at Elland Road* | | | | |
| | F | 03.05.52 | **Arsenal** (D1) | | W | 1-0 | G Robledo |
| | | | *played at Wembley Stadium* | | | | |
| 1952-53 (D1) | 3 | 10.01.53 | **Swansea Town** (D2) | H | - | 0-0ab | |
| | | | *abandoned after eight minutes – fog* | | | | |
| | 3 | 14.01.53 | **Swansea Town** | H | W | 3-0 | Davies, Keeble, Mitchell |
| | 4 | 31.01.53 | **Rotherham Utd** (D2) | H | L | 1-3 | Keeble |
| 1953-54 (D1) | 3 | 09.01.54 | **Wigan Athletic** (LC) | H | D | 2-2 | Broadis, Milburn |
| | 3r | 13.01.54 | **Wigan Athletic** | A | W | 3-2 | Broadis, Keeble, White |
| | 4 | 30.01.54 | **Burnley** (D1) | A | D | 1-1 | Broadis |
| | 4r | 03.02.54 | **Burnley** | H | W | 1-0 | Mitchell (p) |
| | 5 | 20.02.54 | **WBA** (D1) | A | L | 2-3 | Milburn, Mitchell |
| 1954-55 (D1) | 3 | 08.01.55 | **Plymouth Argyle** (D2) | A | W | 1-0 | Keeble |
| | 4 | 29.01.55 | **Brentford** (3S) | H | W | 3-2 | Curry, Hannah, R Mitchell |
| | 5 | 19.02.55 | **Nottingham Forest** (D2) | A | D | 1-1 | Milburn |
| | 5r | 28.02.55 | **Nottingham Forest** | H | D | 2-2aet | Keeble, R Mitchell |
| | 5 2r | 02.03.55 | **Nottingham Forest** | H | W | 2-1aet | Monkhouse 2 |
| | 6 | 12.03.55 | **Huddersfield Town** (D1) | A | D | 1-1 | White |
| | 6r | 16.03.55 | **Huddersfield Town** | H | W | 2-0aet | Keeble, R Mitchell |
| | SF | 26.03.55 | **York City** (3N) | | D | 1-1 | Keeble |
| | | | *played at Hillsborough* | | | | |
| | SFr | 30.03.55 | **York City** | | W | 2-0 | Keeble, White |
| | | | *played at Roker Park* | | | | |
| | F | 07.05.55 | **Manchester City** (D1) | | W | 3-1 | Milburn, R Mitchell, Hannah |
| | | | *played at Wembley Stadium* | | | | |
| 1955-56 (D1) | 3 | 07.01.56 | **Sheffield Wed** (D2) | A | W | 3-1 | Curry, Keeble, Milburn |
| | 4 | 28.01.56 | **Fulham** (D2) | A | W | 5-4 | Casey, Keeble 2, Milburn, Stokoe |
| | 5 | 18.02.56 | **Stoke City** (D2) | H | W | 2-1 | Curry, Mitchell |
| | 6 | 03.03.56 | **Sunderland** (D1) | H | L | 0-2 | |
| 1956-57 (D1) | 3 | 05.01.57 | **Manchester City** (D1) | H | D | 1-1 | White |
| | 3r | 09.01.57 | **Manchester City** | A | W | 5-4aet | Curry, Tait, White 2, Casey (p) |
| | 4 | 26.01.57 | **Millwall** (3S) | A | L | 1-2 | Tait |
| 1957-58 (D1) | 3 | 04.01.58 | **Plymouth Argyle** (3S) | A | W | 6-1 | Eastham 2, R Mitchell, White 3 |
| | 4 | 25.01.58 | **Scunthorpe Utd** (3N) | H | L | 1-3 | Paterson |
| 1958-59 (D1) | 3 | 19.01.59 | **Chelsea** (D1) | H | L | 1-4 | Eastham |

| | | | | | | | | |
|---|---|---|---|---|---|---|---|---|
| 1959-60 | (D1) | 3 | 09.01.60 | **Wolverhampton W** (D1) | H | D | 2-2 | Allchurch, Eastham |
| | | 3r | 13.01.60 | **Wolverhampton W** | A | L | 2-4 | Eastham, White |
| 1960-61 | (D1) | 3 | 07.01.61 | **Fulham** (D1) | H | W | 5-0 | Allchurch, Neale 3, Woods |
| | | 4 | 01.02.61 | **Stockport County** (D4) | H | W | 4-0 | Allchurch, White, Woods 2 |
| | | 5 | 18.02.61 | **Stoke City** (D2) | H | W | 3-1 | Scanlon, Allchurch, McKinney (p) |
| | | 6 | 04.03.61 | **Sheffield Utd** (D2) | H | L | 1-3 | McGuigan |
| 1961-62 | (D2) | 3 | 06.01.62 | **Peterborough Utd** (D3) | H | L | 0-1 | |
| 1962-63 | (D2) | 3 | 07.03.63 | **Bradford City** (D4) | A | W | 6-1 | McGarry 2, Thomas, Hilley, Hughes 2 |
| | | 4 | 13.03.63 | **Norwich City** (D2) | A | L | 0-5 | |
| 1963-64 | (D2) | 3 | 04.01.64 | **Bedford Town** (SL) | H | L | 1-2 | Anderson |
| 1964-65 | (D2) | 3 | 09.01.65 | **Swansea Town** (D2) | A | L | 0-1 | |
| 1965-66 | (D1) | 3 | 22.01.66 | **Chester** (D4) | A | W | 3-1 | Robson, McGarry, Craig |
| | | 4 | 12.02.66 | **Sheffield Wed** (D1) | H | L | 1-2 | Suddick |
| 1966-67 | (D1) | 3 | 28.01.67 | **Coventry City** (D2) | A | W | 4-3 | Davies 3, B Robson |
| | | 4 | 18.02.67 | **Nottingham Forest** (D1) | A | L | 0-3 | |
| 1967-68 | (D1) | 3 | 27.01.68 | **Carlisle Utd** (D2) | H | L | 0-1 | |
| 1968-69 | (D1) | 3 | 04.01.69 | **Reading** (D3) | H | W | 4-0 | Craig, Dyson, B Robson, Scott |
| | | 4 | 25.01.69 | **Manchester City** (D1) | H | D | 0-0 | |
| | | 4r | 29.01.69 | **Manchester City** | A | L | 0-2 | |
| 1969-70 | (D1) | 3 | 03.01.70 | **Southampton** (D1) | A | L | 0-3 | |
| 1970-71 | (D1) | 3 | 11.01.71 | **Ipswich Town** (D1) | H | D | 1-1 | Mitchell |
| | | 3r | 13.01.71 | **Ipswich Town** | A | L | 1-2 | Robson |
| 1971-72 | (D1) | 3 | 24.01.72 | **Hereford Utd** (SL) | H | D | 2-2 | Tudor, Macdonald |
| | | 3r | 05.02.72 | **Hereford Utd** | A | L | 1-2aet | Macdonald |
| 1972-73 | (D1) | 3 | 13.01.73 | **Bournemouth** (D3) | H | W | 2-0 | Macdonald, Cave og |
| | | 4 | 03.02.73 | **Luton Town** (D2) | H | L | 0-2 | |
| 1973-74 | (D1) | 3 | 05.01.74 | **Hendon** (IL) | H | D | 1-1 | Howard |
| | | 3r | 09.01.74 | **Hendon** | A | W | 4-0 | Hibbitt, Tudor, Macdonald, McDermott (p) |
| | | | | *played at Vicarage Road* | | | | |
| | | 4 | 26.01.74 | **Scunthorpe Utd** (D4) | H | D | 1-1 | McDermott |
| | | 4r | 30.01.74 | **Scunthorpe Utd** | A | W | 3-0 | Macdonald 2, Barrowclough |
| | | 5 | 16.02.74 | **WBA** (D2) | A | W | 3-0 | Tudor, Macdonald, Barrowclough |
| | | 6 | 09.03.74 | **Nottingham Forest** (D2) | H | W | 4-3 | Tudor, Moncur, McDermott (p), DJ Craig |
| | | | | *FA ordered replay after pitch invasion when Forest were leading 3-1* | | | | |
| | | 6r | 18.03.74 | **Nottingham Forest** | | D | 0-0 | |
| | | | | *played at Goodison Park* | | | | |
| | | 6 2r | 21.03.74 | **Nottingham Forest** | | W | 1-0 | Macdonald |
| | | | | *played at Goodison Park* | | | | |
| | | SF | 30.03.74 | **Burnley** (D1) | | W | 2-0 | Macdonald 2 |
| | | | | *played at Hillsborough* | | | | |
| | | F | 04.05.74 | **Liverpool** (D1) | | L | 0-3 | |
| | | | | *played at Wembley Stadium* | | | | |
| 1974-75 | (D1) | 3 | 04.01.75 | **Manchester City** (D1) | A | W | 2-0 | Burns, Nulty |
| | | 4 | 25.01.75 | **Walsall** (D3) | A | L | 0-1 | |
| 1975-76 | (D1) | 3 | 03.01.76 | **QPR** (D1) | A | D | 0-0 | |
| | | 3r | 07.01.76 | **QPR** | H | W | 2-1 | T Craig (p), Gowling |
| | | 4 | 24.01.76 | **Coventry City** (D1) | A | D | 1-1 | Gowling |
| | | 4r | 28.01.76 | **Coventry City** | H | W | 5-0 | Gowling, Macdonald 2, Cassidy, Burns |
| | | 5 | 14.02.76 | **Bolton Wanderers** (D2) | A | D | 3-3 | Gowling, Macdonald 2 |
| | | 5r | 18.02.76 | **Bolton Wanderers** | H | D | 0-0aet | |
| | | 5 2r | 23.02.76 | **Bolton Wanderers** | | W | 2-1 | Gowling, Burns |
| | | | | *played at Elland Road* | | | | |
| | | 6 | 06.03.76 | **Derby County** (D1) | A | L | 2-4 | Gowling 2 |
| 1976-77 | (D1) | 3 | 08.01.77 | **Sheffield Utd** (D2) | A | D | 0-0 | |
| | | 3r | 24.01.77 | **Sheffield Utd** | H | W | 3-1 | T Craig, Burns, McCaffery |
| | | 4 | 29.01.77 | **Manchester City** (D1) | H | L | 1-3 | Gowling |
| 1977-78 | (D1) | 3 | 07.01.78 | **Peterborough Utd** (D3) | A | D | 1-1 | Hudson |
| | | 3r | 11.01.78 | **Peterborough Utd** | H | W | 2-0 | T Craig (p), Blackhall |

| | | | | | | | |
|---|---|---|---|---|---|---|---|
| | 4 | 28.01.78 | **Wrexham** (D3) | H | D | 2-2 | Bird, Blackhall |
| | 4r | 06.02.78 | **Wrexham** | A | L | 1-4 | Burns |
| 1978-79 (D2) | 3 | 16.01.79 | **Torquay Utd** (D4) | H | W | 3-1 | Robinson, Withe, Nattrass (p) |
| | 4 | 27.01.79 | **Wolverhampton W** (D1) | H | D | 1-1 | Withe |
| | 4r | 22.02.79 | **Wolverhampton W** | A | L | 0-1 | |
| 1979-80 (D2) | 3 | 05.01.80 | **Chester** (D3) | H | L | 0-2 | |
| 1980-81 (D2) | 3 | 03.01.81 | **Sheffield Wed** (D2) | H | W | 2-1 | Waddle 2 |
| | 4 | 24.01.81 | **Luton Town** (D2) | H | W | 2-1 | Clarke, Martin |
| | 5 | 14.02.81 | **Exeter City** (D3) | H | D | 1-1 | Shoulder |
| | 5r | 18.02.81 | **Exeter City** | A | L | 0-4 | |
| 1981-82 (D2) | 3 | 04.01.82 | **Colchester Utd** (D4) | H | D | 1-1 | Varadi |
| | 3r | 18.01.82 | **Colchester Utd** | A | W | 4-3aet | Waddle, Varadi, Saunders, Brownlie |
| | 4 | 23.01.82 | **Grimsby Town** (D2) | H | L | 1-2 | K Moore og |
| 1982-83 (D2) | 3 | 08.01.83 | **Brighton** (D1) | A | D | 1-1 | McDermott |
| | 3r | 12.01.83 | **Brighton** | H | L | 0-1 | |
| 1983-84 (D2) | 3 | 06.01.84 | **Liverpool** (D1) | A | L | 0-4 | |
| 1984-85 (D1) | 3 | 06.01.85 | **Nottingham Forest** (D1) | A | D | 1-1 | Megson |
| | 3r | 09.01.85 | **Nottingham Forest** | H | L | 1-3aet | Waddle |
| 1985-86 (D1) | 3 | 04.01.86 | **Brighton** (D2) | H | L | 0-2 | |
| 1986-87 (D1) | 3 | 21.01.87 | **Northampton Town** (D4) | H | W | 2-1 | A Thomas, Goddard |
| | 4 | 31.01.87 | **Preston North End** (D4) | H | W | 2-0 | Roeder, Goddard |
| | 5 | 21.02.87 | **Tottenham Hotspur** (D1) | A | L | 0-1 | |
| 1987-88 (D1) | 3 | 09.01.88 | **Crystal Palace** (D2) | H | W | 1-0 | Gascoigne |
| | 4 | 30.01.88 | **Swindon Town** (D2) | H | W | 5-0 | D Jackson, Goddard, Gascoigne 2 (1p), O'Neill |
| | 5 | 20.02.88 | **Wimbledon** (D1) | H | L | 1-3 | McDonald |
| 1988-89 (D1) | 3 | 07.01.89 | **Watford** (D2) | H | D | 0-0 | |
| | 3r | 10.01.89 | **Watford** | A | D | 2-2aet | Brock, Mirandinha (p) |
| | 3 2r | 16.01.89 | **Watford** | H | D | 0-0aet | |
| | 3 3r | 18.01.89 | **Watford** | A | L | 0-1aet | |
| 1989-90 (D1) | 3 | 06.01.90 | **Hull City** (D2) | A | W | 1-0 | O'Brien |
| | 4 | 27.01.90 | **Reading** (D3) | A | D | 3-3 | McGhee 2, Quinn |
| | 4r | 31.01.90 | **Reading** | H | W | 4-1 | McGhee 2, Quinn, Robinson |
| | 5 | 18.02.90 | **Manchester Utd** (D1) | H | L | 2-3 | McGhee (p), Scott |
| 1990-91 (D2) | 3 | 05.01.91 | **Derby County** (D1) | H | W | 2-0 | Quinn, Stimson |
| | 4 | 13.02.91 | **Nottingham Forest** (D1) | H | D | 2-2 | Quinn, McGhee |
| | 4r | 18.02.91 | **Nottingham Forest** | A | L | 0-3 | |
| 1991-92 (D2) | 3 | 04.01.92 | **Bournemouth** (D3) | A | D | 0-0 | |
| | 3r | 14.01.92 | **Bournemouth** | H | - | 0-0 | |
| | | | *abandoned after 17 minutes – fog* | | | | |
| | 3r | 22.01.92 | **Bournemouth** | H | D | 2-2 | Peacock, Hunt |
| | | | *Bournemouth won 4-3 on penalties* | | | | |
| 1992-93 (D1) | 3 | 02.01.93 | **Port Vale** (D2) | H | W | 4-0 | Peacock 2, Lee, Sheedy |
| | 4 | 23.01.93 | **Rotherham Utd** (D2) | A | D | 1-1 | Lee |
| | 4r | 03.02.93 | **Rotherham Utd** | H | W | 2-0 | Kelly, Clark |
| | 5 | 13.02.93 | **Blackburn Rovers** (PL) | A | L | 0-1 | |
| 1993-94 (PL) | 3 | 08.01.94 | **Coventry City** (PL) | H | W | 2-0 | Cole, Beardsley |
| | 4 | 29.01.94 | **Luton Town** (D1) | H | D | 1-1 | Beardsley (p) |
| | 4r | 09.02.94 | **Luton Town** | A | L | 0-2 | |
| 1994-95 (PL) | 3 | 08.01.95 | **Blackburn Rovers** (PL) | H | D | 1-1 | Lee |
| | 3r | 18.01.95 | **Blackburn Rovers** | A | W | 2-1 | Hottiger, Clark |
| | 4 | 28.01.95 | **Swansea City** (D2) | H | W | 3-0 | Kitson 3 |
| | 5 | 19.02.95 | **Manchester City** (PL) | H | W | 3-1 | Gillespie 2, Beresford |
| | 6 | 12.03.95 | **Everton** (PL) | A | L | 0-1 | |
| 1995-96 (PL) | 3 | 07.01.96 | **Chelsea** (PL) | A | D | 1-1 | Ferdinand |
| | 3r | 17.01.96 | **Chelsea** | H | D | 2-2aet | Albert, Beardsley (p) |
| | | | *Chelsea won 4-2 on penalties* | | | | |
| 1996-97 (PL) | 3 | 05.01.97 | **Charlton Athletic** (D1) | A | D | 1-1 | Lee |
| | 3r | 15.01.97 | **Charlton Athletic** | H | W | 2-1aet | Clark, Shearer |
| | 4 | 26.01.97 | **Nottingham Forest** (PL) | H | L | 1-2 | Ferdinand |
| 1997-98 (PL) | 3 | 04.01.98 | **Everton** (PL) | A | W | 1-0 | Rush |

| | | | | | | | |
|---|---|---|---|---|---|---|---|
| | 4 | 25.01.98 | **Stevenage B** (Conf) | A | D | 1-1 | Shearer |
| | 4r | 04.02.98 | **Stevenage B** | H | W | 2-1 | Shearer 2 |
| | 5 | 14.02.98 | **Tranmere Rovers** (D1) | H | W | 1-0 | Shearer |
| | 6 | 08.03.98 | **Barnsley** (PL) | H | W | 3-1 | Ketsbaia, Speed, Batty |
| | SF | 05.04.98 | **Sheffield Utd** (D1) | | W | 1-0 | Shearer |
| | | | *played at Old Trafford* | | | | |
| | F | 16.05.98 | **Arsenal** (PL) | | L | 0-2 | |
| | | | *played at Wembley Stadium* | | | | |
| 1998-99 (PL) | 3 | 02.01.99 | **Crystal Palace** (D1) | H | W | 2-1 | Speed, Shearer |
| | 4 | 23.01.99 | **Bradford City** (D1) | H | W | 3-0 | Hamann, Shearer, Ketsbaia |
| | 5 | 14.02.99 | **Blackburn Rovers** (PL) | H | D | 0-0 | |
| | 5r | 24.02.99 | **Blackburn Rovers** | A | W | 1-0 | Saha |
| | 6 | 07.03.99 | **Everton** (PL) | H | W | 4-1 | Ketsbaia 2, Georgidis, Shearer |
| | SF | 11.04.99 | **Tottenham Hotspur** (PL) | | W | 2-0aet | Shearer 2 (1p) |
| | | | *played at Old Trafford* | | | | |
| | F | 22.05.99 | **Manchester Utd** (PL) | | L | 0-2 | |
| | | | *played at Wembley Stadium* | | | | |
| 1999-00 (PL) | 3 | 12.12.99 | **Tottenham Hotspur** (PL) | A | D | 1-1 | Speed |
| | 3r | 22.12.99 | **Tottenham Hotspur** | H | W | 6-1 | Shearer 2 (1p), Speed, Dabizas, Ferguson, Dyer |
| | 4 | 08.01.00 | **Sheffield Utd** (D1) | H | W | 4-1 | Shearer, Dabizas, Ferguson, Gallacher |
| | 5 | 31.01.00 | **Blackburn Rovers** (D1) | A | W | 2-1 | Shearer 2 |
| | 6 | 20.02.00 | **Tranmere Rovers** (D1) | A | W | 3-2 | Speed, Domi, Ferguson |
| | SF | 09.04.00 | **Chelsea** (PL) | | L | 1-2 | Lee |
| | | | *played at Wembley Stadium* | | | | |
| 2000-01 (PL) | 3 | 06.01.01 | **Aston Villa** (PL) | H | D | 1-1 | Solano |
| | 3r | 17.01.01 | **Aston Villa** | A | L | 0-1 | |
| 2001-02 (PL) | 3 | 05.01.02 | **Crystal Palace** (D1) | H | W | 2-0 | Shearer, Acuna |
| | 4 | 27.01.02 | **Peterborough Utd** (D2) | A | W | 4-2 | O'Brien, McClen, Shearer (p), Hughes |
| | 5 | 17.02.02 | **Manchester City** (D1) | H | W | 1-0 | Solano |
| | 6 | 09.03.02 | **Arsenal** (PL) | H | D | 1-1 | Robert |
| | 6r | 23.03.02 | **Arsenal** | A | L | 0-3 | |
| 2002-03 (PL) | 3 | 05.01.03 | **Wolverhampton W** (D1) | A | L | 2-3 | Jenas, Shearer (p) |

## NEWCASTLE WEST END

*Formed 1882. Their ground was on the site subsequently developed as St James' Park. Heavily in debt in 1892, they amalgamated with Newcastle East End to form Newcastle United. Entered FA Cup: 1886-87 – 1891-92.*

| | | | | | | | |
|---|---|---|---|---|---|---|---|
| 1886-87 | 1 | 30.10.86 | **Sunderland** | A | L | 1-2aet | Campbell |
| | | | *FA declared match void after protest from West End and ordered a replay* | | | | |
| | 1r | 13.11.86 | **Sunderland** | H | W | 1-0 | Angus |
| | 2 | 20.11.86 | **Gainsborough T** | H | L | 2-6 | Aitken, Dobson |
| 1887-88 | 1 | 15.10.87 | **Redcar** | H | W | 5-1 | Angus 2, Barker, McDonald, Nicholson |
| | 2 | 05.11.87 | **Sunderland** | A | L | 1-3aet | McColl |
| 1888-89 | | | 1q Bishop Auckland (H) 7-2; 2q Sunderland Albion (H) 3-5. FA declared match void and ordered a replay. 2qr Sunderland Albion (H) 1-2aet | | | | |
| 1889-90 (NL) | | | 1q Port Clarence (H) 9-1; 2q Birtley (A) 2-1; 3q South Bank (H) 5-2; 4q Stockton (A) 1-0 | | | | |
| | 1 | 18.01.90 | **Grimsby Town** (FAll) | H | L | 1-2 | McColl |
| 1890-91 (NL) | | | 1q Elswick Rangers (A) 5-2; 2q Southwick (H) 8-1; 3q Sunderland Albion (H) 0-3 | | | | |
| 1891-92 (NL) | | | 2q Newcastle East End (H) 0-3 | | | | |

## NEWPORT (IOW)

*Formed 1888. First entered FA Cup: 1929-30. League club beaten: Clapton Orient. Members of the Southern League.*

| | | | | | | | |
|---|---|---|---|---|---|---|---|
| 1935-36 (HL) | 1 | 30.11.35 | **Yeovil & Petters Utd** (SL) | A | W | 1-0 | Gardiner |
| | 2 | 14.12.35 | **Southall** (AL) | A | L | 0-8 | |
| 1945-46 (HL) | 1 1L | 17.11.45 | **Clapton Orient** (3S) | A | L | 1-2 | Rose |
| | 1 2L | 24.11.45 | **Clapton Orient** | H | W | 2-0 | Rose, Merritt |
| | 2 1L | 08.12.45 | **Aldershot** (3S) | A | L | 0-7 | |
| | 2 2L | 15.12.45 | **Aldershot** | H | L | 0-5 | |
| 1952-53 (HL) | 1 | 22.11.52 | **Swindon Town** (3S) | A | L | 0-5 | |

| | | | | | | | | |
|---|---|---|---|---|---|---|---|---|
| 1953-54 | (HL) | 1 | 21.11.53 | **Swindon Town** | A | L | 1-2 | Gilfillan |
| 1954-55 | (HL) | 1 | 20.11.54 | **Hinckley Ath** (WMRL) | A | L | 3-4 | Slade, Gilfillan 2 |
| 1956-57 | (HL) | 1 | 17.11.56 | **Watford** (3S) | H | L | 0-6 | |
| 1957-58 | (HL) | 1 | 16.11.57 | **Hereford Utd** (SL) | H | L | 0-3 | |
| 1958-59 | (HL) | 1 | 15.11.58 | **Shrewsbury Town** (D4) | H | D | 0-0 | |
| | | 1r | 20.11.58 | **Shrewsbury Town** | A | L | 0-5 | |
| 1994-95 | (SL) | 1 | 12.11.94 | **Aylesbury Utd** (IL) | H | L | 2-3 | Soares 2 |
| 1995-96 | (SL) | 1 | 11.11.95 | **Enfield** (IL) | H | D | 1-1 | Fearon |
| | | 1r | 21.11.95 | **Enfield** | A | L | 1-2 | Leader |

## NEWPORT COUNTY

*Formed 1912. Members of the Football League 1921-1931 then 1932-1988. Spent the 1931-32 season in the Southern League after failing to gain re-election to Division Three South in May 1931. Welsh FA Cup winners: 1980. Runners-up: 1963, 1987. First entered FA Cup: 1913-14. FA Cup best performance: 5th round, 1949. Since leaving the Football League, the club have had an eventful few years. The original club were wound up on February 27, 1989 with debts of £126,000, and were expelled from The Conference for failing to fulfil their fixtures. The club were re-formed as Newport AFC playing at junior level in 1989 in the English pyramid system rather than becoming involved with Welsh league football. They gradually worked their way back up the Non-League pyramid. The name Newport County was re-adopted in 1999. Members of the Southern League.*

| | | | | | | | | |
|---|---|---|---|---|---|---|---|---|
| 1919-20 | (SL) | 1 | 10.01.20 | **Leicester City** (D2) | H | D | 0-0 | |
| | | 1r | 15.01.20 | **Leicester City** | A | L | 0-2 | |
| 1920-21 | (D3) | | | 4q Merthr Tydfil (H) 0-0; 4qr Merthyr Tydfil (H) 0-4 | | | | |
| 1921-22 | (3S) | | | 5q Bath City (H) 2-0; 6q Wrexham (A) 0-0; 6qr Wrexham (H) 3-0 | | | | |
| | | 1 | 07.01.22 | **Newcastle Utd** (D1) | A | L | 0-6 | |
| 1922-23 | (3S) | | | 5q Aberdare Athletic (A) 1-1; 5qr Aberdare Athletic (H) 1-1aet; 5q 2r Aberdare Athletic (at Ninian Park) 1-2 | | | | |
| 1923-24 | (3S) | | | 4q Exeter City (H) 0-2 | | | | |
| 1924-25 | (3S) | | | 4q Aberdare Athletic (A) 0-0; 4qr Aberdare Athletic (H) 3-0; 5q Exeter City (A) 1-1; 5qr Exeter City (H) 3-3aet; 5q 2r Exeter City (Ashton Gate) 0-1 | | | | |
| 1925-26 | (3S) | 1 | 28.11.25 | **Weymouth** (SL) | A | W | 1-0 | Taylor |
| | | 2 | 12.12.25 | **Northampton Town** (3S) | A | L | 1-3 | Drinnan |
| 1926-27 | (3S) | 1 | 27.11.26 | **Poole Town** (SL) | A | L | 0-1 | |
| 1927-28 | (3S) | 1 | 26.11.27 | **Swindon Town** (3S) | H | L | 0-1 | |
| 1928-29 | (3S) | 1 | 24.11.28 | **Woking** (IL) | H | W | 7-0 | Young 3, Pugh 2, Reid, Gittens |
| | | 2 | 08.12.28 | **Norwich City** (3S) | A | L | 0-6 | |
| 1929-30 | (3S) | 1 | 30.11.29 | **Kettering Town** (SL) | H | W | 3-2 | Morris, Thomas, Martin |
| | | 2 | 14.12.29 | **Walsall** (3S) | H | L | 2-3 | Martin, Morris |
| 1930-31 | (3S) | 1 | 29.11.30 | **Dulwich Hamlet** (IL) | A | D | 2-2 | Pearce 2 |
| | | 1 | 04.12.30 | **Dulwich Hamlet** | H | W | 4-1 | Pearce, Brown, Davies, Bagley |
| | | 2 | 13.12.30 | **Walsall** (3S) | A | L | 0-4 | |
| 1931-32 | (SL) | | | did not enter | | | | |
| 1932-33 | (3S) | 1 | 26.11.32 | **Ilford** (IL) | H | W | 4-2 | Reed, Weale, Green 2 |
| | | 2 | 10.12.32 | **Folkestone** (SL) | A | L | 1-2 | Weale |
| 1933-34 | (3S) | 1 | 25.11.33 | **Dulwich Hamlet** (IL) | A | D | 2-2 | Burgess, Higgins |
| | | 1r | 30.11.33 | **Dulwich Hamlet** | H | W | 6-2 | Burgess 2, Taylor 2, Reynolds, Thomas |
| | | 2 | 09.12.33 | **Workington** (NEL) | A | L | 1-3 | Higgins |
| 1934-35 | (3S) | 1 | 24.11.34 | **Swindon Town** (3S) | A | L | 0-4 | |
| 1935-36 | (3S) | 1 | 30.11.35 | **Southend Utd** (3S) | H | L | 0-1 | |
| 1936-37 | (3S) | 1 | 28.11.36 | **Bristol City** (3S) | H | W | 3-0 | Duggan, Sullivan, Chadwick |
| | | 2 | 12.12.36 | **Reading** (3S) | A | L | 2-7 | Duggan 2 |
| 1937-38 | (3S) | 1 | 27.11.37 | **Kidderminster H** (BDL) | A | D | 2-2 | Webb, Derrick |
| | | 1r | 02.12.37 | **Kidderminster H** | H | W | 4-1 | Brinton 3, Duggan |
| | | 2 | 11.12.37 | **Bournemouth** (3S) | H | W | 2-1 | Duggan, Derrick |
| | | 3 | 08.01.38 | **Bradford Park A** (D2) | A | L | 4-7 | Duggan, Derrick, W Owen, Hickman |
| 1938-39 | (3S) | 1 | 26.11.38 | **Reading** (3S) | A | D | 3-3 | Hydes 2, Derrick |
| | | 1r | 05.12.38 | **Reading** | H | W | 3-1 | Wood 2, Hydes |
| | | 2 | 10.12.38 | **Horden CW** (NEL) | A | W | 3-2 | Wood 2, Hickman |
| | | 3 | 07.01.39 | **Walsall** (3S) | H | L | 0-2 | |
| 1945-46 | (D2) | 1 1L | 17.11.45 | **Torquay Utd** (3S) | A | W | 1-0 | Derrick |
| | | 1 2L | 24.11.45 | **Torquay Utd** | H | D | 1-1 | Derrick |
| | | 2 1L | 08.12.45 | **Exeter City** (3S) | H | W | 5-1 | Wookey, Derrick 2, Brinton, Carr |

| | | | | | | | | |
|---|---|---|---|---|---|---|---|---|
| | | 2 2L | 15.12.45 | **Exeter City** | A | W | 3-1 | Hydes 2, Wilkins |
| | | 3 1L | 05.01.46 | **Southampton** (D2) | A | L | 3-4 | Granville, Derrick, Wookey |
| | | 3 2L | 10.01.46 | **Southampton** | H | L | 1-2 | Owen |
| 1946-47 | (D2) | 3 | 11.01.47 | **Coventry City** (D2) | A | L | 2-5 | Batty, Haywood |
| 1947-48 | (3S) | 1 | 29.11.47 | **Southend Utd** (3S) | H | W | 3-2 | Roffi, Allen, Lewis |
| | | 2 | 13.12.47 | **Reading** (3S) | A | L | 0-3 | |
| 1948-49 | (3S) | 1 | 27.11.48 | **Brighton** (3S) | H | W | 3-1 | Parker, Comley 2 |
| | | 2 | 11.12.48 | **Leytonstone** (IL) | A | W | 4-3aet | Harper, Carr 2, Comley |
| | | 3 | 08.01.49 | **Leeds Utd** (D2) | A | W | 3-1 | Roffi, Carr, Comley |
| | | 4 | 29.01.49 | **Huddersfield Town** (D1) | H | D | 3-3aet | Comley, Williams, Carr |
| | | 4r | 05.02.49 | **Huddersfield Town** | A | W | 3-1 | Carr 2, Parker |
| | | 5 | 12.02.49 | **Portsmouth** (D1) | A | L | 2-3aet | Harper, Carr |
| 1949-50 | (3S) | 1 | 26.11.49 | **Crystal Palace** (3S) | H | W | 3-0 | Comley, Payne, Griffiths |
| | | 2 | 10.12.49 | **Gateshead AFC** (3N) | H | D | 1-1 | Harper |
| | | 2r | 14.12.49 | **Gateshead AFC** | A | W | 2-1aet | Parker, Harper |
| | | 3 | 07.01.50 | **Port Vale** (3S) | H | L | 1-2 | Comley |
| 1950-51 | (3S) | 1 | 25.11.50 | **Walsall** (3S) | H | W | 4-2 | Parker 2, Shergold, Haywood |
| | | 2 | 09.12.50 | **Hereford Utd** (SL) | A | W | 3-0 | Shergold, Moore 2 |
| | | 3 | 06.01.51 | **Reading** (3S) | H | W | 3-2 | Shergold, Birch, Parker |
| | | 4 | 27.01.51 | **Norwich City** (3S) | H | L | 0-2 | |
| 1951-52 | (3S) | 1 | 24.11.51 | **Barry Town** (SL) | H | W | 4-0 | Moore 3, Beattie |
| | | 2 | 15.12.51 | **Leytonstone** (IL) | A | D | 2-2 | Birch, Beattie |
| | | 2r | 20.12.51 | **Leytonstone** | H | W | 3-0 | Moore 2, Beattie |
| | | 3 | 12.01.52 | **Sheffield Utd** (D2) | A | L | 0-2 | |
| 1952-53 | (3S) | 1 | 22.11.52 | **Walsall** (3S) | H | W | 2-1 | Moore, Beattie |
| | | 2 | 06.12.52 | **Gainsborough T** (ML) | H | W | 2-1 | Beattie, Parker |
| | | 3 | 10.01.53 | **Sheffield Utd** (D2) | H | L | 1-4 | Moore |
| 1953-54 | (3S) | 1 | 21.11.53 | **Cambridge Utd** (ECL) | A | D | 2-2 | Thomas, Birch |
| | | 1r | 26.11.53 | **Cambridge Utd** | H | L | 1-2 | Parker |
| 1954-55 | (3S) | 1 | 20.11.54 | **Gillingham** (3S) | A | L | 0-2 | |
| 1955-56 | (3S) | 1 | 19.11.55 | **Brighton** (3S) | A | L | 1-8 | Johnstone |
| 1956-57 | (3S) | 1 | 17.11.56 | **Walsall** (3S) | A | W | 1-0 | Terry |
| | | 2 | 08.12.56 | **Gillingham** (3S) | A | W | 2-1 | Terry, Brown |
| | | 3 | 05.01.57 | **Southampton** (3S) | H | D | 3-3 | Hudson, Harris 2 |
| | | 3r | 09.01.57 | **Southampton** | A | W | 1-0 | Harris |
| | | 4 | 26.01.57 | **Arsenal** (D1) | H | L | 0-2 | |
| 1957-58 | (3S) | 1 | 16.11.57 | **Northampton Town** (3S) | A | L | 0-3 | |
| 1958-59 | (D3) | 1 | 15.11.58 | **Wisbech Town** (SL) | A | D | 2-2 | Graham, McPherson |
| | | 1r | 17.11.58 | **Wisbech Town** | H | W | 4-1aet | McSeveney 2, McPherson, Graham |
| | | 2 | 06.12.58 | **Hereford Utd** (SL) | A | W | 2-0 | Graham, McPherson |
| | | 3 | 10.01.59 | **Torquay Utd** (D4) | H | D | 0-0 | |
| | | 3r | 14.01.59 | **Torquay Utd** | A | W | 1-0 | McPherson |
| | | 4 | 24.01.59 | **Tottenham Hotspur** (D1) | A | L | 1-4 | Hollyman |
| 1959-60 | (D3) | 1 | 14.11.59 | **Hereford Utd** (SL) | H | W | 4-2 | Meyer, McPherson, McSeveney, Dixon |
| | | 2 | 05.12.59 | **Salisbury City** (WL) | A | W | 1-0 | Meyer |
| | | 3 | 09.01.60 | **Tottenham Hotspur** (D1) | H | L | 0-4 | |
| 1960-61 | (D3) | 1 | 05.11.60 | **Shrewsbury Town** (D3) | A | L | 1-4 | McSeveney |
| 1961-62 | (D3) | 1 | 04.11.61 | **Reading** (D3) | A | D | 1-1 | W Herritty |
| | | 1r | 06.11.61 | **Reading** | H | W | 1-0 | W Herritty |
| | | 2 | 25.11.61 | **Weymouth** (SL) | A | L | 0-1 | |
| 1962-63 | (D4) | 1 | 03.11.62 | **QPR** (D3) | A | L | 2-3 | W Herritty, Bonson |
| 1963-64 | (D4) | 1 | 16.11.63 | **Hereford Utd** (SL) | A | D | 1-1 | Hunt |
| | | 1r | 18.11.63 | **Hereford Utd** | H | W | 4-0 | Hunt 3, Webster |
| | | 2 | 07.12.63 | **Watford** (D3) | H | W | 2-0 | Smith 2 |
| | | 3 | 04.01.64 | **Sheffield Wed** (D1) | H | W | 3-2 | Bonson 2, Hunt |
| | | 4 | 25.01.64 | **Burnley** (D1) | A | L | 1-2 | Sheffield |
| 1964-65 | (D4) | 1 | 14.11.64 | **Spalding Utd** (ML) | H | W | 5-3 | Frowen, Morgan, Swindells 2, Reece |
| | | 2 | 05.12.64 | **Mansfield Town** (D3) | H | W | 3-0 | Sheffield 2 (1p), Smith |
| | | 3 | 09.01.65 | **Reading** (D3) | A | D | 2-2 | Swindells, Reece |
| | | 3r | 11.01.65 | **Reading** | H | L | 0-1 | |

| | | | | | | | | | |
|---|---|---|---|---|---|---|---|---|---|
| 1965-66 | (D4) | 1 | 13.11.65 | **Bath City** (SL) | A | L | 0-2 | |
| 1966-67 | (D4) | 1 | 26.11.66 | **Brighton** (D3) | H | L | 1-2 | Thomas |
| 1967-68 | (D4) | 1 | 18.12.67 | **Gillingham** (D3) | H | W | 3-0 | A Williams, Hill, King (p) |
| | | 2 | 06.01.68 | **Guildford City** (SL) | A | W | 1-0 | Buck |
| | | 3 | 27.01.68 | **Southampton** (D1) | A | D | 1-1 | King (p) |
| | | 3r | 30.01.68 | **Southampton** | H | L | 2-3 | A Williams, Hill |
| 1968-69 | (D4) | 1 | 16.11.68 | **Exeter City** (D4) | A | D | 0-0 | |
| | | 1r | 18.11.68 | **Exeter City** | H | L | 1-3 | Buck |
| 1969-70 | (D4) | 1 | 15.11.69 | **Colchester Utd** (D4) | H | W | 2-1 | White, Thomas |
| | | 2 | 06.12.69 | **Hereford Utd** (SL) | H | W | 2-1 | Thomas, Wood |
| | | 3 | 03.01.70 | **Gillingham** (D3) | A | L | 0-1 | |
| 1970-71 | (D4) | 1 | 21.11.70 | **Barnet** (SL) | A | L | 1-6 | Jones |
| 1971-72 | (D4) | 1 | 20.11.71 | **Notts County** (D3) | A | L | 0-6 | |
| 1972-73 | (D4) | 1 | 18.11.72 | **Alton Town** (HL) | H | W | 5-1 | Harris 2, White, Brown, R Jones (p) |
| | | 2 | 09.12.72 | **Torquay Utd** (D4) | A | W | 1-0 | Brown |
| | | 3 | 13.01.73 | **Millwall** (D2) | A | L | 0-3 | |
| 1973-74 | (D4) | 1 | 24.11.73 | **Wycombe W** (IL) | A | L | 1-3 | Hooper |
| 1974-75 | (D4) | 1 | 23.11.74 | **Exeter City** (D4) | A | W | 2-1 | White, Giles og |
| | | 2 | 14.12.74 | **Walsall** (D3) | H | L | 1-3 | Jones |
| 1975-76 | (D4) | 1 | 22.11.75 | **Swindon Town** (D3) | H | D | 2-2 | Godfrey, Parsons |
| | | 1r | 25.11.75 | **Swindon Town** | A | L | 0-3 | |
| 1976-77 | (D4) | 1 | 20.11.76 | **Bournemouth** (D4) | A | D | 0-0 | |
| | | 1r | 23.11.76 | **Bournemouth** | H | W | 3-0 | Parsons 2, Woods |
| | | 2 | 11.12.76 | **Southend Utd** (D4) | A | L | 0-3 | |
| 1977-78 | (D4) | 1 | 26.11.77 | **Exeter City** (D3) | H | D | 1-1 | Goddard |
| | | 1r | 30.11.77 | **Exeter City** | A | L | 2-4 | Clark, Goddard |
| 1978-79 | (D4) | 1 | 25.11.78 | **Hereford Utd** (D4) | A | W | 1-0 | Goddard (p) |
| | | 2 | 16.12.78 | **Worcester City** (SL) | H | D | 0-0 | |
| | | 2r | 18.12.78 | **Worcester City** | A | W | 2-1 | Pemberton og, Goddard |
| | | 3 | 09.01.79 | **West Ham Utd** (D2) | H | W | 2-1 | Goddard, Woods |
| | | 4 | 30.01.79 | **Colchester Utd** (D3) | H | D | 0-0 | |
| | | 4r | 05.02.79 | **Colchester Utd** | A | L | 0-1 | |
| 1979-80 | (D4) | 1 | 24.11.79 | **Portsmouth** (D4) | A | L | 0-1 | |
| 1980-81 | (D3) | 1 | 22.11.80 | **Plymouth Argyle** (D3) | A | L | 0-2 | |
| 1981-82 | (D3) | 1 | 21.11.81 | **Colchester Utd** (D4) | A | L | 0-2 | |
| 1982-83 | (D3) | 1 | 20.11.82 | **Enfield** (APL) | A | D | 0-0 | |
| | | 1r | 23.11.82 | **Enfield** | H | W | 4-2 | Tynan 3 (1p), Aldridge |
| | | 2 | 11.12.82 | **Orient** (D3) | H | W | 1-0 | Tynan (p) |
| | | 3 | 08.01.83 | **Everton** (D1) | H | D | 1-1 | Gwyther |
| | | 3r | 11.01.83 | **Everton** | A | L | 1-2 | Aldridge |
| 1983-84 | (D3) | 1 | 20.11.83 | **Poole Town** (SL) | A | D | 0-0 | |
| | | 1r | 22.11.83 | **Poole Town** | H | W | 3-1 | Oakes, Aldridge, Lewis |
| | | 2 | 10.12.83 | **Harrow Borough** (IL) | A | W | 3-1 | Aldridge 2, Chamberlain |
| | | 3 | 07.01.84 | **Plymouth Argyle** (D3) | A | D | 2-2 | Aldridge 2 |
| | | 3r | 10.01.84 | **Plymouth Argyle** | H | L | 0-1 | |
| 1984-85 | (D3) | 1 | 17.11.84 | **Aldershot** (D4) | H | D | 1-1 | Pulis |
| | | 1r | 20.11.84 | **Aldershot** | A | L | 0-4 | |
| 1985-86 | (D3) | 1 | 16.11.85 | **Southend Utd** (D4) | A | W | 1-0 | Mardenborough |
| | | 2 | 07.12.85 | **Torquay Utd** (D4) | H | D | 1-1 | Berry |
| | | 2r | 10.12.85 | **Torquay Utd** | A | W | 3-2aet | Boyle, Jones, James |
| | | 3 | 04.01.86 | **Sunderland** (D2) | A | L | 0-2 | |
| 1986-87 | (D3) | 1 | 15.11.86 | **Bromsgrove R** (SL) | A | W | 1-0 | Vinter |
| | | 2 | 06.12.86 | **Fulham** (D3) | A | L | 0-2 | |
| 1987-88 | (D4) | 1 | 14.11.87 | **Northampton Town** (D3) | A | L | 1-2 | Holtham |
| 1988-89 | (Conf) | 1 | 19.11.88 | **Maidstone Utd** (Conf) | H | L | 1-2 | Sugrue |
| 2001-02 | (SL) | 1 | 17.11.01 | **Blackpool** (D2) | A | D | 2-2 | Hughes og, Clark |
| | | 1r | 28.11.01 | **Blackpool** | H | L | 1-4aet | Rose |

## NEWTOWN

*Formed in 1875, Originally known as Newton White Stars FC. First entered FA Cup: 1884-85. Welsh FA Cup winners: 1879, 1895. Runners-up: 1881, 1886, 1888, 1897. Based in Newtown, Powys. Members of the League of Wales.*

| | | | | | | | | |
|---|---|---|---|---|---|---|---|---|
| 1884-85 | | 1 | | Stafford Rangers | | | - | |
| | | | | *Stafford Rangers scratched. Newtown walkover* | | | | |
| | | 2 | 20.12.84 | **Druids** | H | D | 1-1 | |
| | | 2r | 27.12.84 | **Druids** | A | L | 0-6 | |
| 1885-86 | | 1 | 24.10.85 | **Hartford St Johns** | A | W | 3-1 | |
| | | 2 | | Leek | | | - | |
| | | | | *Newtown scratched. Leek walkover* | | | | |

## NORTH SHIELDS

*Formed 1898 as North Shields Athletic. Reformed as North Shields 1928. First entered FA Cup: 1905-06. FA Amateur Cup winners: 1969. The last northern club to win the trophy. Folded, then reformed 1992. League club beaten: Halifax Town. Members of the Wearside League.*

| | | | | | | | | |
|---|---|---|---|---|---|---|---|---|
| 1933-34 | (NEL) | 1 | 25.11.33 | **Scarborough** (ML) | H | W | 3-0 | Dryden, Cole, Forster |
| | | 2 | 09.12.33 | **Gateshead AFC** (3N) | A | L | 0-1 | |
| 1938-39 | (NEL) | 1 | 26.11.38 | **Stockport County** (3N) | H | L | 1-4 | Coyde |
| 1945-46 | (NEL) | 1 1L | 17.11.45 | **Carlisle Utd** (3N) | A | L | 1-5 | Jamieson |
| | | 1 2L | 24.11.45 | **Carlisle Utd** | H | L | 2-3 | McLean, Jamieson |
| 1946-47 | (NEL) | 1 | 30.11.46 | **Hartlepools Utd** (3N) | A | L | 0-6 | |
| 1949-50 | (NEL) | 1 | 26.11.49 | **Netherfield** (LC) | A | L | 3-4 | Cooper, Pyle, McGarry |
| 1950-51 | (NEL) | 1 | 25.11.50 | **Crewe Alexandra** (3N) | A | L | 0-4 | |
| 1952-53 | (NEL) | 1 | 22.11.52 | **Stockport County** (3N) | H | L | 3-6 | Wood, McKenna, Robson |
| 1962-63 | (NEL) | 1 | 03.11.62 | **Workington** (D4) | H | D | 2-2 | Trewick, Doyle |
| | | 1r | 08.11.62 | **Workington** | A | L | 2-7 | Thompson, Prior |
| 1969-70 | (NL) | 1 | 15.11.69 | **Hartlepool** (D4) | A | L | 0-3 | |
| 1982-83 | (NL) | 1 | 20.11.82 | **Halifax Town** (D4) | A | W | 1-0 | McCaffery |
| | | 2 | 11.12.82 | **Walsall** (D3) | H | L | 0-3 | |

## NORTHAMPTON TOWN

*Formed 1897. First entered FA Cup: 1898-99. FA Cup best performance: 5th round, 1934, 1950, 1970. Record FA Cup win: 10-0 v Sutton Town, 5th qualifying round, 1907-08. In Competition Proper: 9-0 v Met Police, 1st round, 28.11.1931. Record FA Cup defeat: 2-8 v Manchester Utd, 5th round, 07.02.1970.*

| | | | | | | | | |
|---|---|---|---|---|---|---|---|---|
| 1898-99 | (ML) | | | 1q Hinckley Town (A) 2-1; 2q Wellingborough Town (A) 2-0 FA ordered match to be replayed after protest; 2qr Wellingborough Town (A) 1-6 | | | | |
| 1899-00 | (ML) | | | 1q Wellingborough Town (H) 1-2 | | | | |
| 1900-01 | (ML) | | | 3q Hinckley Town (A) 0-2 | | | | |
| 1901-02 | (SL) | | | 3q Gresley Rovers (A) 2-0; 4q Burton Utd (A) 0-0 abandoned; 4q Burton Utd (A) 0-0; 4qr Burton Utd (H) 2-0; 5q Kettering T (A) 2-2; 5qr Kettering T (H) 2-0; Int Darwen (H) 4-1 | | | | |
| | | 1 | 25.01.02 | **Sheffield Utd** (D1) | H | L | 0-2 | |
| 1902-03 | (SL) | | | 3q Burton Utd (A) 0-2 | | | | |
| 1903-04 | (SL) | | | 3q Wellingborough Town (A) 0-2 | | | | |
| 1904-05 | (SL) | | | 3q Burton Utd (A) 3-2; 4q Kettering Town (A) 3-0; 5q Leicester Fosse (H) 2-2; 5qr Leicester Fosse (A) 0-2 | | | | |
| 1905-06 | (SL) | | | 4q West Stanley (A) 1-1; 4qr West Stanley (H) 3-0 | | | | |
| | | 1 | 13.01.06 | **New Brompton** (SL) | | L | 1-2 | Springthorpe |
| 1906-07 | (SL) | | | 5q Southport Central (H) 2-1 | | | | |
| | | 1 | 12.01.07 | **Middlesbrough** (D1) | A | L | 2-4 | Dunkerley, Watkins |
| 1907-08 | (SL) | | | 5q Sutton Town (H) 10-0 | | | | |
| | | 1 | 11.01.08 | **Bristol Rovers** (SL) | H | L | 0-1 | |
| 1908-09 | (SL) | 1 | 16.01.09 | **Derby County** (D2) | H | D | 1-1 | McDiarmid |
| | | 1r | 20.01.09 | **Derby County** | A | L | 2-4 | McCartney, Lewis |
| 1909-10 | (SL) | 1 | 15.01.10 | **Sheffield Wed** (D1) | H | D | 0-0 | |
| | | 1r | 20.01.10 | **Sheffield Wed** | A | W | 1-0 | Walker |
| | | 2 | 05.02.10 | **Nottingham Forest** (D1) | H | D | 0-0 | |
| | | 2r | 09.02.10 | **Nottingham Forest** | A | L | 0-1 | |
| 1910-11 | (SL) | 1 | 14.01.11 | **Luton Town** (SL) | H | W | 5-1 | Bradshaw 2, Lessons 2, Lewis |
| | | 2 | 04.02.11 | **Newcastle Utd** (D1) | A | D | 1-1 | Bradshaw |

| | | | | | | | |
|---|---|---|---|---|---|---|---|
| | 2r | 08.02.11 | **Newcastle Utd** | H | L | 0-1 | |
| | | | *played at St James' Park* | | | | |
| 1911-12 (SL) | 1 | 13.01.12 | **Bristol City** (D2) | H | W | 1-0 | Lewis |
| | 2 | 03.02.12 | **Darlington** (NEL) | A | D | 1-1 | King |
| | 2r | 08.02.12 | **Darlington** | H | W | 2-0 | King, Lessons |
| | 3 | 24.02.12 | **Fulham** (D2) | A | L | 1-2 | Lewis |
| 1912-13 (SL) | 1 | 18.01.13 | **Blackburn Rovers** (D1) | A | L | 2-7 | Walden, Suttie og |
| 1913-14 (SL) | 1 | 10.01.14 | **Derby County** (D1) | A | L | 0-1 | |
| 1914-15 (SL) | 1 | 09.01.15 | **Grimsby Town** (D2) | A | W | 3-0 | Smith, Lockett, Freeman |
| | 2 | 30.01.15 | **Hull City** (D2) | A | L | 1-2 | Freeman |
| 1919-20 (SL) | | | 6q Bristol Rovers (H) 2-2; 6qr Bristol Rovers (A) 2-3 | | | | |
| 1920-21 (D3) | | | 6q Gillingham (H) 3-1 | | | | |
| | 1 | 08.01.21 | **Southampton** (D3) | H | D | 0-0 | |
| | 1r | 11.01.21 | **Southampton** | A | L | 1-4 | Lockett |
| 1921-22 (3S) | | | 5q Lincoln City (A) 2-1; 6q Lancaster Town (H) 1-0 | | | | |
| | 1 | 07.01.22 | **Reading** (3S) | H | W | 3-0 | Lockett 3 |
| | 2 | 28.01.22 | **Stoke** (D2) | H | D | 2-2 | Hewisson, Lockett |
| | 2r | 02.02.22 | **Stoke** | A | L | 0-3 | |
| 1922-23 (3S) | | | 5q Charlton Athletic (A) 0-2 | | | | |
| 1923-24 (3N) | | | 5q Lincoln City (H) 5-1; 6q Wigan Borough (A) 6-0 | | | | |
| | 1 | 12.01.24 | **Halifax Town** (3N) | H | D | 1-1 | Lockett |
| | 1r | 16.01.24 | **Halifax Town** | A | D | 1-1aet | Wood |
| | 1 2r | 21.01.24 | **Halifax Town** | | L | 2-4 | Wood, Lockett |
| | | | *played at Bramall Lane* | | | | |
| 1924-25 (3S) | 1 | 10.01.25 | **Tottenham Hotspur** (D1) | A | L | 0-3 | |
| 1925-26 (3S) | 1 | 28.11.25 | **Barnsley** (D2) | H | W | 3-1 | George 2, Robinson |
| | 2 | 12.12.25 | **Newport County** (3S) | H | W | 3-1 | Robinson 3 |
| | 3 | 09.01.26 | **Crystal Palace** (D3) | H | D | 3-3 | Robinson 2, Lockett |
| | 3r | 13.01.26 | **Crystal Palace** | A | L | 1-2 | Pease |
| 1926-27 (3S) | 1 | 27.11.26 | **Boston Utd** (ML) | A | D | 1-1 | Gunnell |
| | 1r | 02.12.26 | **Boston Utd** | H | W | 2-1 | Hoten, Watson |
| | 2 | 11.12.26 | **Exeter City** (3S) | A | L | 0-1 | |
| 1927-28 (3S) | 1 | 26.11.27 | **Leyton FC** (AL) | H | W | 8-0 | Whitehurst 4, Clennell 3, Martin |
| | 2 | 10.12.27 | **Brighton** (3S) | H | W | 1-0 | Daly |
| | 3 | 14.01.28 | **Sunderland** (D1) | A | D | 3-3 | Daly, Cowen, Wells |
| | 3r | 19.01.28 | **Sunderland** | H | L | 0-3 | |
| 1928-29 (3S) | 3 | 12.01.29 | **Millwall** (D2) | A | D | 1-1 | Weston |
| | 3r | 17.01.29 | **Millwall** | H | D | 2-2aet | Hoten 2 |
| | 3 2r | 21.01.29 | **Millwall** | | L | 0-2 | |
| | | | *played at Highbury* | | | | |
| 1929-30 (3S) | 1 | 30.11.29 | **Aldershot Town** (SL) | A | W | 1-0 | Weston |
| | 2 | 14.12.29 | **Margate** (KL) | H | W | 6-0 | Sissons, Hoten 3, Bowen 2 |
| | 3 | 11.01.30 | **Blackburn Rovers** (D1) | A | L | 1-4 | Wells |
| 1930-31 (3S) | 1 | 29.11.30 | **Coventry City** (3S) | H | L | 1-2 | Bowen |
| 1931-32 (3S) | 1 | 28.11.31 | **Met Police** (SPT) | H | W | 9-0 | Dawes 3, Riches, Bowen 2, Woodcock og,Wells 2 |
| | 2 | 12.12.31 | **Southend Utd** (3S) | H | W | 3-0 | Dawes, Bowen, Lovett |
| | 3 | 09.01.32 | **Darlington** (3N) | A | D | 1-1 | Lovett |
| | 3r | 14.01.32 | **Darlington** | H | W | 2-0 | Lovett, Dawes |
| | 4 | 23.01.32 | **Bradford Park A** (D2) | A | L | 2-4 | Wells, Lovett |
| 1932-33 (3S) | 1 | 26.11.32 | **Lloyds FC** (KL) | H | W | 8-1 | A Dawes 5, Mcfarlane, Wells, Dowsey |
| | 2 | 10.12.32 | **Doncaster Rovers** (3N) | H | L | 0-1 | |
| 1933-34 (3S) | 1 | 25.11.33 | **Exeter City** (3S) | H | W | 2-0 | Wells, Dowsey |
| | 2 | 09.12.33 | **Torquay Utd** (3S) | H | W | 3-0 | A Dawes 2, Boyle |
| | 3 | 13.01.34 | **Southampton** (D2) | A | D | 1-1 | Wells |
| | 3r | 17.01.34 | **Southampton** | H | W | 1-0 | Henson |
| | 4 | 27.01.34 | **Huddersfield Town** (D1) | A | W | 2-0 | Boyle, Wells |
| | 5 | 17.02.34 | **Preston North End** (D2) | A | L | 0-4 | |
| 1934-35 (3S) | 1 | 24.11.34 | **Barry Town** (SL) | A | W | 1-0 | Cochrane |
| | 2 | 08.12.34 | **Workington** (NEL) | H | D | 0-0 | |
| | 2r | 13.12.34 | **Workington** | A | W | 1-0 | Hobbs |

| | | | | | | | | |
|---|---|---|---|---|---|---|---|---|
| | | 3 | 12.01.35 | **Bolton Wanderers** (D2) | H | L | 0-2 | |
| 1935-36 | (3S) | 1 | 30.11.35 | **Bristol Rovers** (3S) | H | D | 0-0 | |
| | | 1r | 04.12.35 | **Bristol Rovers** | A | L | 1-3 | Deacon |
| 1936-37 | (3S) | 1 | 28.11.36 | **Walthamstow Ave** (AL) | A | L | 1-6 | Hewitt |
| 1937-38 | (3S) | 1 | 27.11.37 | **Cardiff City** (3S) | H | L | 1-2 | Tolland |
| 1938-39 | (3S) | 1 | 26.11.38 | **Watford** (3S) | A | L | 1-4 | Tilson |
| 1945-46 | (3S) | 1 1L | 17.11.45 | **Chelmsford City** (SL) | H | W | 5-1 | Roberts, Hughes 2, Morrall 2 |
| | | 1 2L | 24.11.45 | **Chelmsford City** | A | W | 5-0 | Roberts, Morrall 2, Fowler, Smith |
| | | 2 1L | 08.12.45 | **Notts County** (3S) | H | W | 3-1 | Morrall 2, Blunt |
| | | 2 2L | 15.12.45 | **Notts County** | A | L | 0-1 | |
| | | 3 1L | 05.01.46 | **Millwall** (D2) | H | D | 2-2 | Hughes, Black |
| | | 3 2L | 07.01.46 | **Millwall** | A | L | 0-3 | |
| 1946-47 | (3S) | 1 | 30.11.46 | **Mansfield Town** (3S) | H | W | 2-0 | Garrett, Blunt |
| | | 2 | 14.12.46 | **Peterborough Utd** (ML) | A | D | 1-1 | Garrett |
| | | 2r | 19.12.46 | **Peterborough Utd** | H | D | 1-1aet | Garrett |
| | | 2 2r | 23.12.46 | **Peterborough Utd** | | W | 8-1 | Garrett 4, Roberts 2, Morrell 2 |
| | | | | *played at Highfield Road, Coventry* | | | | |
| | | 3 | 11.01.47 | **Preston North End** (D1) | H | L | 1-2 | Roberts |
| 1947-48 | (3S) | 1 | 29.11.47 | **Exeter City** (3S) | A | D | 1-1aet | Roberts |
| | | 1r | 06.12.47 | **Exeter City** | H | W | 2-0 | Briscoe, Jenkins |
| | | 2 | 13.12.47 | **Torquay Utd** (3S) | H | D | 1-1aet | Heaslegrave |
| | | 2r | 20.12.47 | **Torquay Utd** | A | L | 0-2 | |
| 1948-49 | (3S) | 1 | 27.11.48 | **Dulwich Hamlet** (IL) | H | W | 2-1 | W Smith, D Smith |
| | | 2 | 11.12.48 | **Mansfield Town** (3N) | A | L | 1-2aet | English |
| 1949-50 | (3S) | 1 | 26.11.49 | **Walthamstow Ave** (IL) | H | W | 4-1 | Mitchell 2, Dixon, McCulloch |
| | | 2 | 10.12.49 | **Torquay Utd** (3S) | H | W | 4-2 | Mitchell 3 (1p), Dixon |
| | | 3 | 07.01.50 | **Southampton** (D2) | H | D | 1-1 | McCulloch |
| | | 3r | 11.01.50 | **Southampton** | A | W | 3-2 | Dixon, Hughes, Candlin |
| | | 4 | 28.01.50 | **Bournemouth** (3S) | A | D | 1-1 | Mitchell |
| | | 4r | 02.02.50 | **Bournemouth** | H | W | 2-1 | English, McCullough |
| | | 5 | 11.02.50 | **Derby County** (D1) | A | L | 2-4 | Dixon 2 |
| 1950-51 | (3S) | 3 | 06.01.51 | **Barnsley** (D2) | H | W | 3-1 | Murphy, Mitchell 2 (1p) |
| | | 4 | 27.01.51 | **Arsenal** (D1) | A | L | 2-3 | English 2 |
| 1951-52 | (3S) | 1 | 24.11.51 | **Norwich City** (3S) | A | L | 2-3 | Payne, Ramscar |
| 1952-53 | (3S) | 1 | 22.11.52 | **Hendon** (AL) | A | D | 0-0 | |
| | | 1r | 27.11.52 | **Hendon** | H | W | 2-0 | Ramscar, Fowler |
| | | 2 | 06.12.52 | **Swindon Town** (3S) | A | L | 0-2 | |
| 1953-54 | (3S) | 1 | 21.11.53 | **Llanelli** (SL) | H | W | 3-0 | Ramscar, Fowler, Cross |
| | | 2 | 12.12.53 | **Hartlepools Utd** (3N) | H | D | 1-1 | Ramscar |
| | | 2r | 16.12.53 | **Hartlepools Utd** | A | L | 0-1aet | |
| 1954-55 | (3S) | 1 | 20.11.54 | **Coventry City** (3S) | H | L | 0-1 | |
| 1955-56 | (3S) | 1 | 19.11.55 | **Millwall** (3S) | H | W | 4-1 | English 3, Hurley og |
| | | 2 | 10.12.55 | **Hastings Utd** (SL) | H | W | 4-1 | Draper 2, E Smith, English |
| | | 3 | 07.01.56 | **Blackburn Rovers** (D2) | H | L | 1-2 | English |
| 1956-57 | (3S) | 1 | 17.11.56 | **Southampton** (3S) | A | L | 0-2 | |
| 1957-58 | (3S) | 1 | 16.11.57 | **Newport County** (3S) | H | W | 3-0 | Gale, N Robinson, Mills |
| | | 2 | 07.12.57 | **Bournemouth** (3S) | H | W | 4-1 | Woan, Fowler, Hughes og, Norris og |
| | | 3 | 04.01.58 | **Arsenal** (D1) | H | W | 3-1 | Tebbutt, Leek, Hawkings |
| | | 4 | 25.01.58 | **Liverpool** (D2) | A | L | 1-3 | Hawkings |
| 1958-59 | (D4) | 1 | 15.11.58 | **Wycombe W** (IL) | H | W | 2-0 | Kirkup, Fowler |
| | | 2 | 06.12.58 | **Tooting & M** (IL) | A | L | 1-2 | Kirkup |
| 1959-60 | (D4) | 1 | 14.11.59 | **Torquay Utd** (D4) | A | L | 1-7 | Kane |
| 1960-61 | (D4) | 1 | 05.11.60 | **Hastings Utd** (SL) | H | W | 2-1 | Wilson, Brown |
| | | 2 | 26.11.60 | **Romford** (SL) | A | W | 5-1 | Brown 2, Leck 3 |
| | | 3 | 07.01.61 | **Luton Town** (D2) | A | L | 0-4 | |
| 1961-62 | (D3) | 1 | 04.11.61 | **Millwall** (D4) | H | W | 2-0 | Lines, Terry |
| | | 2 | 25.11.61 | **Kettering Town** (SL) | H | W | 3-0 | Holton 3 |
| | | 3 | 06.01.62 | **Port Vale** (D3) | A | L | 1-3 | Moran |
| 1962-63 | (D3) | 1 | 03.11.62 | **Torquay Utd** (D4) | H | L | 1-2 | Everitt |
| 1963-64 | (D2) | 3 | 04.01.64 | **Sunderland** (D2) | A | L | 0-2 | |
| 1964-65 | (D2) | 3 | 09.01.65 | **Chelsea** (D1) | A | L | 1-4 | Foley (p) |

| | | | | | | | | |
|---|---|---|---|---|---|---|---|---|
| 1965-66 | (D1) | 3 | 22.01.66 | **Nottingham Forest** (D1) | H | L | 1-2 | Brown |
| 1966-67 | (D2) | 3 | 28.01.67 | **WBA** (D1) | H | L | 1-3 | Foley (p) |
| 1967-68 | (D3) | 1 | 09.12.67 | **Bournemouth** (D3) | A | L | 0-2 | |
| 1968-69 | (D3) | 1 | 16.11.68 | **Margate** (SL) | H | W | 3-1 | Fairbrother, Roberts 2 |
| | | 2 | 07.12.68 | **Brighton** (D3) | A | W | 2-1 | Townsend, Hatton |
| | | 3 | 04.01.69 | **Bolton Wanderers** (D2) | A | L | 1-2 | Knox |
| 1969-70 | (D4) | 1 | 15.11.69 | **Weymouth** (SL) | H | D | 0-0 | |
| | | 1r | 19.11.69 | **Weymouth** | A | W | 3-1 | Fairbrother, Rankmore 2 (1p) |
| | | 2 | 06.12.69 | **Exeter City** (D4) | H | D | 1-1 | Neal |
| | | 2r | 10.12.69 | **Exeter City** | A | D | 0-0aet | |
| | | 2 2r | 15.12.69 | **Exeter City** | | W | 2-1 | Large, McNeill |
| | | | | *played at the County Ground, Swindon* | | | | |
| | | 3 | 12.01.70 | **Brentwood Town** (SL) | A | W | 1-0 | Fairbrother |
| | | 4 | 24.01.70 | **Tranmere Rovers** (D3) | A | D | 0-0 | |
| | | 4r | 27.01.70 | **Tranmere Rovers** | H | W | 2-1 | Felton, Rankmore |
| | | 5 | 07.02.70 | **Manchester Utd** (D1) | H | L | 2-8 | McNeil, Large |
| 1970-71 | (D4) | 1 | 21.11.70 | **Hereford Utd** (SL) | A | D | 2-2 | Fairbrother, McNeil |
| | | 1r | 24.11.70 | **Hereford Utd** | H | L | 1-2 | Rankmore |
| 1971-72 | (D4) | 1 | 20.11.71 | **Basingstoke Town** (SL) | A | W | 5-1 | Buchanan 2, McNeil 2, Large |
| | | 2 | 11.12.71 | **Hereford Utd** (SL) | A | D | 0-0 | |
| | | 2r | 14.12.71 | **Hereford Utd** | H | D | 2-2aet | Large, Hawkins |
| | | 2 2r | 20.12.71 | **Hereford Utd** | | L | 1-2aet | Large |
| | | | | *played at The Hawthorns* | | | | |
| 1972-73 | (D4) | 1 | 18.11.72 | **Peterborough Utd** (D4) | A | L | 0-1 | |
| 1973-74 | (D4) | 1 | 24.11.73 | **Banbury Utd** (SL) | A | D | 0-0 | |
| | | 1r | 29.11.73 | **Banbury Utd** | H | W | 3-2 | Best, Robertson, Felton |
| | | 2 | 15.12.73 | **Bristol Rovers** (D3) | H | L | 1-2 | Buchanan |
| 1974-75 | (D4) | 1 | 23.11.74 | **Torquay Utd** (D4) | A | W | 1-0 | Gregory |
| | | 2 | 14.12.74 | **Rotherham Utd** (D4) | A | L | 1-2 | Stratford |
| 1975-76 | (D4) | 1 | 22.11.75 | **Brentford** (D4) | A | L | 0-2 | |
| 1976-77 | (D3) | 1 | 20.11.76 | **Leatherhead** (IL) | A | L | 0-2 | |
| 1977-78 | (D4) | 1 | 26.11.77 | **Tooting & M** (IL) | A | W | 2-1 | Christie, Martin |
| | | 2 | 17.12.77 | **Enfield** (IL) | H | L | 0-2 | |
| 1978-79 | (D4) | 1 | 25.11.78 | **Portsmouth** (D4) | A | L | 0-2 | |
| 1979-80 | (D4) | 1 | 24.11.79 | **Hereford Utd** (D4) | A | L | 0-1 | |
| 1980-81 | (D4) | 1 | 22.11.80 | **Peterborough Utd** (D4) | H | L | 1-4 | Phillips |
| 1981-82 | (D4) | 1 | 21.11.81 | **Weymouth** (APL) | A | D | 0-0 | |
| | | 1r | 24.11.81 | **Weymouth** | H | W | 6-2 | Gage 2, Sandy, Carlton, Phillips, Mahoney |
| | | 2 | 15.12.81 | **Bristol City** (D3) | A | L | 0-3 | |
| 1982-83 | (D4) | 1 | 20.11.82 | **Wimbledon** (D4) | H | D | 2-2 | Burrows, Denyer |
| | | 1r | 23.11.82 | **Wimbledon** | A | W | 2-0 | Coffill 2 |
| | | 2 | 11.12.82 | **Gillingham** (D3) | A | D | 1-1 | Saxby |
| | | 2r | 14.12.82 | **Gillingham** | H | W | 3-2 | Belfon 2, Massey |
| | | 3 | 08.01.83 | **Aston Villa** (D1) | H | L | 0-1 | |
| 1983-84 | (D4) | 1 | 19.11.83 | **Waterlooville** (SL) | H | D | 1-1 | Gage |
| | | 1r | 23.11.83 | **Waterlooville** | A | D | 1-1aet | Austin |
| | | 1 2r | 28.11.83 | **Waterlooville** | H | W | 2-0 | O'Neill (p), Mundee |
| | | 2 | 10.12.83 | **Telford Utd** (APL) | H | D | 1-1 | Austin |
| | | 2r | 14.12.83 | **Telford Utd** | A | L | 2-3 | Muir, Jeffrey |
| 1984-85 | (D4) | 1 | 17.11.84 | **VS Rugby** (SL) | H | D | 2-2 | Lee, Train |
| | | 1r | 21.11.84 | **VS Rugby** | A | W | 1-0 | Gage |
| | | 2 | 08.12.84 | **Brentford** (D3) | A | D | 2-2 | Lee, Train |
| | | 2r | 11.12.84 | **Brentford** | H | - | 0-0ab | |
| | | | | *abandoned after 26 minutes – fog* | | | | |
| | | 2r | 17.12.84 | **Brentford** | H | L | 0-2 | |
| 1985-86 | (D4) | 1 | 16.11.85 | **Gillingham** (D3) | A | L | 0-3 | |
| 1986-87 | (D4) | 1 | 16.11.86 | **Peterborough Utd** (D4) | H | W | 3-0 | McGoldrick, Gilbert (p), Benjamin |
| | | 2 | 05.12.86 | **Southend Utd** (D4) | A | D | 4-4 | Donald, Hill 2, Benjamin |
| | | 2r | 10.12.86 | **Southend Utd** | H | W | 3-2 | Benjamin, Gilbert 2 (2ps) |
| | | 3 | 21.01.87 | **Newcastle Utd** (D1) | A | L | 1-2 | Hill |

| | | | | | | | | |
|---|---|---|---|---|---|---|---|---|
| 1987-88 | (D3) | 1 | 14.11.87 | **Newport County** (D4) | H | W | 2-1 | Chard, Morley |
| | | 2 | 05.12.87 | **Brighton** (D3) | H | L | 1-2 | Morley |
| 1988-89 | (D3) | 1 | 19.11.88 | **Swansea City** (D3) | A | L | 1-3 | Berry |
| 1989-90 | (D3) | 1 | 18.11.89 | **Kettering Town** (Conf) | A | W | 1-0 | Thomas |
| | | 2 | 09.12.89 | **Aylesbury Utd** (IL) | H | D | 0-0 | |
| | | 2r | 13.12.89 | **Aylesbury Utd** | A | W | 1-0aet | Barnes |
| | | 3 | 06.01.90 | **Coventry City** (D1) | H | W | 1-0 | Berry |
| | | 4 | 27.01.90 | **Rochdale** (D4) | A | L | 0-3 | |
| 1990-91 | (D4) | 1 | 17.11.90 | **Littlehampton T** (SCL) | A | W | 4-0 | Barnes 2, Campbell, Beavon |
| | | 2 | 08.12.90 | **Barnet** (Conf) | A | D | 0-0 | |
| | | 2r | 12.12.90 | **Barnet** | H | L | 0-1 | |
| 1991-92 | (D3) | 1 | 16.11.91 | **Crawley Town** (SL) | A | L | 2-4 | Chard, Adcock |
| 1992-93 | (D3) | 1 | 14.11.92 | **Fulham** (D2) | H | W | 3-1 | Wilkin, Brown, Terry |
| | | 2 | 06.12.92 | **Bath City** (Conf) | A | D | 2-2 | Brown, Chard |
| | | 2r | 15.12.92 | **Bath City** | H | W | 3-0 | McParland, Wilkin, Bell |
| | | 3 | 12.01.93 | **Rotherham Utd** (D2) | H | L | 0-1 | |
| 1993-94 | (D3) | 1 | 13.11.93 | **Bromsgrove R** (Conf) | H | L | 1-2 | Aldridge |
| 1994-95 | (D3) | 1 | 12.11.94 | **Peterborough Utd** (D2) | A | L | 0-4 | |
| 1995-96 | (D3) | 1 | 11.11.95 | **Hayes** (IL) | H | W | 1-0 | Warburton |
| | | 2 | 02.12.95 | **Oxford Utd** (D2) | A | L | 0-2 | |
| 1996-97 | (D3) | 1 | 17.11.96 | **Watford** (D2) | H | L | 0-1 | |
| 1997-98 | (D2) | 1 | 15.11.97 | **Exeter City** (D3) | A | D | 1-1 | Hunter |
| | | 1r | 25.11.97 | **Exeter City** | H | W | 3-1 | Hunter, Heggs |
| | | 2 | 06.12.97 | **Basingstoke Town** (IL) | H | D | 1-1 | Seal |
| | | 2r | 16.12.97 | **Basingstoke Town** | A | D | 0-0aet | |
| | | | | *Northampton won 4-3 on penalties* | | | | |
| | | 3 | 03.01.98 | **Leicester City** (PL) | A | L | 0-4 | |
| 1998-99 | (D2) | 1 | 14.11.98 | **Lancaster City** (NPL) | H | W | 2-1 | Thompson og, Sampson |
| | | 2 | 05.12.98 | **Yeovil Town** (Conf) | A | L | 0-2 | |
| 1999-00 | (D3) | 1 | 30.10.99 | **Shrewsbury Town** (D3) | A | L | 1-2 | Hendon |
| 2000-01 | (D2) | 1 | 18.11.00 | **Frickley Athletic** (NPL) | H | W | 4-0 | Forrester 2, Frain, Hunt |
| | | 2 | 09.12.00 | **Rotherham Utd** (D2) | A | L | 0-1 | |
| 2001-02 | (D2) | | 17.11.01 | **Torquay Utd** (D3) | A | W | 2-1 | Gabbiadini 2 |
| | | 2 | 09.12.01 | **Canvey Island** (IL) | A | L | 0-1 | |
| 2002-03 | (D2) | 1 | 16.11.02 | **Boston Utd** (D3) | H | W | 3-2 | Harstey, Gabbiadini, Asamoah |
| | | 2 | 07.12.02 | **Cambridge Utd** (D3) | A | D | 2-2 | Stamp, Hargreaves |
| | | 2r | 17.12.02 | **Cambridge Utd** | H | L | 0-1 | |

## NORTHERN NOMADS

*Formed 1900 and in the early days of the 20th century were mainly a touring side, once beating a combined Austrian-Hungarian International XI. Reformed 1952. FA Amateur Cup winners:1926; Runners-up: 1914. Entered FA Cup: 1905-06 – 1937-38. Disbanded 1985.*

| | | | | | | | | |
|---|---|---|---|---|---|---|---|---|
| 1926-27 | | 1 | 01.12.26 | **Crewe Alexandra** (3N) | A | L | 1-4 | Randle |

## NORTHFLEET UNITED

*Formed 1890. Entered FA Cup: 1985-96 – 1936-37. Merged with Gravesend 1946 to become Gravesend & Northfleet FC. See also Gravesend & Northfleet.*

| | | | | | | | | |
|---|---|---|---|---|---|---|---|---|
| 1925-26 | (KL) | 1 | 28.11.25 | **QPR** (3S) | H | D | 2-2 | Pilcher 2 |
| | | 1r | 03.12.25 | **QPR** | A | L | 0-2 | |
| 1926-27 | (KL) | 1 | 27.11.26 | **Sittingbourne** (KL) | A | W | 3-1 | Sanders 3 |
| | | 2 | 11.12.26 | **Luton Town** (D3) | A | L | 2-6 | Bell 2 |
| 1927-28 | (SL) | 1 | 26.11.27 | **London Cal** (IL) | H | L | 0-1 | |
| 1928-29 | (SL) | 1 | 24.11.28 | **Ilford** (IL) | H | W | 5-2 | Bell 2, Sanders, Johnson 2 |
| | | 2 | 08.12.28 | **Charlton Athletic** (3S) | H | L | 1-5 | Johnson |
| 1929-30 | (SL) | 1 | 30.11.29 | **Wimbledon** (IL) | A | W | 4-1 | Bell 2, Hopper, Howe |
| | | 2 | 14.01.30 | **Clapton Orient** (3S) | A | L | 0-2 | |
| 1930-31 | (SL) | 1 | 29.11.30 | **Exeter City** (3S) | H | L | 0-3 | |
| 1931-32 | (KL) | 1 | 28.11.31 | **Bournemouth** (3S) | A | D | 1-1 | Sparke |
| | | 1r | 02.12.31 | **Bournemouth** | H | L | 0-1 | |
| 1933-34 | (KL) | 1 | 25.11.33 | **Dartford** (SL) | H | L | 0-2 | |

# NORTHWICH VICTORIA

*Formed 1873. First entered FA Cup: 1882-83. FA Trophy winners: 1984. Runners-up: 1983, 1996. Members of the Football League: 1892-1894. FA Cup quarter-finalists 1883-84. Billy Meredith, who played in FA Cup finals for both Manchester City (1904) and Manchester United (1909) also played for Northwich Victoria. League clubs beaten as a Non-League club: Rochdale, Peterborough United, Watford, Chester, Crewe Alexandra, Bury. Members of The Conference.*

| | | | | | | | | |
|---|---|---|---|---|---|---|---|---|
| 1882-83 | | 1 | 28.10.82 | **Astley Bridge** | H | W | 3-2 | Plant 3 |
| | | 2 | 09.12.82 | **Druids** | A | L | 0-5 | |
| 1883-84 | | 1 | 10.11.83 | **Druids** | A | W | 1-0 | |
| | | 2 | 24.11.83 | **Davenham** | H | W | 5-1 | Malham 3, Brook, Hankey |
| | | 3 | | bye | | | | |
| | | 4 | 19.01.84 | **Brentwood** | H | W | 3-0 | Atherton, Plant, Rhodes |
| | | 5 | 09.02.84 | **Blackburn Olympic** | A | L | 1-9 | Rhodes |
| 1884-85 | | 1 | 08.11.84 | **Leek** | A | L | 3-4 | |
| 1885-86 | | 1 | 31.10.85 | **Macclesfield T** | A | L | 1-4 | |
| 1886-87 | | 1 | 30.10.86 | **Furness Vale Rovers** | H | W | 10-0 | |
| | | 2 | 13.11.86 | **Chirk** | H | D | 0-0 | |
| | | 2r | 20.11.86 | **Chirk** | A | L | 0-3 | |
| 1887-88 | | 1 | 15.10.87 | **Leek** | A | D | 2-2 | |
| | | 1r | 22.10.87 | **Leek** | H | W | 4-2 | |
| | | 2 | 05.11.87 | **Crewe Alexandra** | H | L | 0-1 | |
| 1892-93 | (D2) | 1 | 21.01.93 | **Loughborough** (ML) | A | W | 2-1 | Bradshaw, Drinkwater |
| | | 2 | 04.02.93 | **Blackburn Rovers** (D1) | A | L | 1-4 | Hargreaves |
| 1893-94 | (D2) | | | 1q bye 2q Crewe Alexandra (H) 0-1 | | | | |
| 1955-56 | (CC) | 1 | 19.11.55 | **Boston Utd** (ML) | A | L | 2-3 | Adams 2 |
| 1961-62 | (CC) | 1 | 04.11.61 | **Southport** (D4) | A | L | 0-1 | |
| 1976-77 | (NPL) | 1 | 20.11.76 | **Rochdale** (D4) | A | D | 1-1 | Nieman |
| | | 1r | 22.11.76 | **Rochdale** | H | D | 0-0aet | |
| | | 1 2r | 29.11.76 | **Rochdale** | | W | 2-1 | Smith, Collier |
| | | | | *played at Maine Road* | | | | |
| | | 2 | 11.12.76 | **Peterborough Utd** (D3) | H | - | 0-1ab | |
| | | | | *abandoned after 20 minutes – fog* | | | | |
| | | 2 | 14.12.76 | **Peterborough Utd** (D3) | H | W | 4-0 | Smith 2, Wain (p), Swede |
| | | 3 | 08.01.77 | **Watford** (D4) | H | W | 3-2 | Swede, Wain (p), Corrigan |
| | | 4 | 29.01.77 | **Oldham Athletic** (D2) | | L | 1-3 | Collie |
| | | | | *played at Maine Road* | | | | |
| 1979-80 | (NPL) | 1 | 24.11.79 | **Nuneaton B** (APL) | A | D | 3-3 | Stromek, Smith 2 (1p) |
| | | 1r | 26.11.79 | **Nuneaton B** | H | W | 3-0 | Nieman, Collier, Smith |
| | | 2 | 24.12.79 | **Wigan Athletic** (D4) | H | - | 0-3ab | |
| | | | | *abandoned after 65 minutes – fog* | | | | |
| | | 2 | 05.01.80 | **Wigan Athletic** | H | D | 2-2 | Smith (p), Mayman |
| | | 2r | 07.01.80 | **Wigan Athletic** | A | L | 0-1 | |
| 1980-81 | (APL) | 1 | 22.11.80 | **Huddersfield Town** (D3) | H | D | 1-1 | Denham |
| | | 1r | 25.11.80 | **Huddersfield Town** | A | L | 0-6 | |
| 1982-83 | (APL) | 1 | 20.11.82 | **Chester** (D4) | A | D | 1-1 | Wilson |
| | | 1r | 22.11.82 | **Chester** | H | W | 3-1aet | Chesters, Ward 2 |
| | | 2 | 11.12.82 | **Scunthorpe Utd** (D4) | A | L | 1-2 | Chesters |
| 1983-84 | (APL) | 1 | 19.11.83 | **Bangor City** (APL) | H | D | 1-1 | Reid |
| | | 1r | 22.11.83 | **Bangor City** | A | L | 0-1 | |
| 1984-85 | (APL) | 1 | 17.11.84 | **Crewe Alexandra** (D4) | H | W | 3-1 | Forshaw, Reid, Craven |
| | | 2 | 08.12.84 | **Wigan Athletic** (D3) | A | L | 1-2 | Power |
| 1987-88 | (Conf) | 1 | 14.11.87 | **Colwyn Bay** (NWC) | H | W | 1-0 | Sayer (p) |
| | | 2 | 06.12.87 | **Blackpool** (D3) | H | L | 0-2 | |
| 1988-89 | (Conf) | 1 | 19.11.88 | **Frickley Athletic** (NPL) | A | W | 2-0 | O'Connor, Howey og |
| | | 2 | 10.12.88 | **Tranmere Rovers** (D4) | H | L | 1-2 | O'Connor |
| 1989-90 | (Conf) | 1 | 18.11.89 | **Darlington** (Conf) | A | L | 2-6 | Hanchard, Callaghan |
| 1994-95 | (Conf) | 1 | 22.11.94 | **Mansfield Town** (D3) | A | L | 1-3 | Oghani |
| 1995-96 | (Conf) | 1 | 11.11.95 | **Scunthorpe Utd** (D3) | H | L | 1-3 | Cooke |
| 1996-97 | (Conf) | 1 | 16.11.96 | **Walsall** (D2) | H | D | 2-2 | Cooke 2 |
| | | 1r | 26.11.96 | **Walsall** | A | L | 1-3 | Tait |
| 1997-98 | (Conf) | 1 | 15.11.97 | **Chesterfield** (D2) | A | L | 0-1 | |

| | | | | | | | | |
|---|---|---|---|---|---|---|---|---|
| 2000-01 | (Conf) | 1 | 18.11.00 | **Bury** (D2) | A | D | 1-1 | Fletcher |
| | | 1r | 28.11.00 | **Bury** | H | W | 1-0 | Mike |
| | | 2 | 09.12.00 | **Leyton Orient** (D3) | H | D | 3-3 | Fletcher 2, Mike |
| | | 2r | 20.12.00 | **Leyton Orient** | A | L | 2-3aet | Cooke, Mike |
| 2001-02 | (Conf) | 1 | 17.11.01 | **Hull City** (D3) | H | L | 2-5 | Blundell, Mike |
| 2002-03 | (Conf) | 1 | 16.11.02 | **Scunthorpe Utd** (D3) | H | L | 0-3 | |

# NORWICH CITY

*Formed 1902. First entered FA Cup: 1902-03. FA Cup best performance: Semi-finals 1959 (as a Third Division club), 1989, 1992. Record FA Cup win: 8-0 v Sutton Utd, 4th round, 28.01.1989. Record FA Cup defeat: 0-6 v Luton Town, 2nd round,.10.12.1927; 0-6 v Manchester United, 4th round, 24.01.1981.*

| | | | | | | | | |
|---|---|---|---|---|---|---|---|---|
| 1902-03 | (NSL) | | | P Lowestoft Town (A) 0-5 | | | | |
| 1903-04 | (NSL) | | | P Lowestoft Town (H) 4-1; 1q Great Yarmouth Town (A) 2-1; 2q Harwich & Parkeston (A) 4-2; 3q West Norwood (H) 1-1; 3qr West Norwood scratched | | | | |
| 1904-05 | (NSL) | | | 3q Grays Utd (H) 0-0; 3qr Grays Utd (A) 2-3; | | | | |
| 1905-06 | (SL) | | | 4q Sheppey Utd (A) 2-0 | | | | |
| | | 1 | 13.01.06 | **Tunbridge Wells R** (SL) | H | D | 1-1 | Bowman |
| | | 1r | 17.01.06 | **Tunbridge Wells R** (SL) | A | W | 5-0 | Ross 3, Graham 2 |
| | | 2 | 03.02.06 | **Manchester Utd** (D2) | A | L | 0-3 | |
| 1906-07 | (SL) | 1 | 12.01.07 | **Hastings & St L** (SL) | H | W | 3-1 | Ross 2, Archer |
| | | 2 | 02.02.07 | **WBA** (D2) | A | L | 0-1 | |
| 1907-08 | (SL) | 1 | 11.01.08 | **Sheffield Wed** (D1) | H | W | 2-0 | Beauchop, Allsopp |
| | | 2 | 01.02.08 | **Fulham** (D2) | A | L | 0-2 | |
| 1908-09 | (SL) | 1 | 16.01.09 | **Reading** (SL) | | D | 0-0 | |
| | | | | *played at Stamford Bridge* | | | | |
| | | 1r | 20.01.09 | **Reading** | A | D | 1-1aet | Allsopp |
| | | 1 2r | 25.01.09 | **Reading** | | W | 3-2aet | Tomlinson, Flanagan, Allsopp |
| | | | | *played at Villa Park* | | | | |
| | | 2 | 06.02.09 | **Liverpool** (D1) | A | W | 3-2 | Tomlinson, Smith, Allsopp |
| | | 3 | 20.02.09 | **Bristol City** (D1) | A | L | 0-2 | |
| 1909-10 | (SL) | 1 | 15.01.10 | **QPR** (SL) | H | D | 0-0 | |
| | | 1r | 19.01.10 | **QPR** | A | L | 0-3 | |
| 1910-11 | (SL) | 1 | 14.01.11 | **Sunderland** (D1) | H | W | 3-1 | Hampson 2, Whiteside |
| | | 2 | 04.02.11 | **Bradford City** (D1) | A | L | 1-2 | Ingham |
| 1911-12 | (SL) | 1 | 13.01.12 | **Blackburn Rovers** (D1) | A | L | 1-4 | Birchall |
| 1912-13 | (SL) | 1 | 11.01.13 | **Leicester Fosse** | A | - | 0-0ab | |
| | | | | *abandoned after 65 minutes – snowstorm* | | | | |
| | | 1 | 16.01.13 | **Leicester Fosse** (D2) | A | W | 4-1 | Osborne, Hughes, Woodlands, Wolstenholme |
| | | 2 | 03.02.13 | **Bristol Rovers** (SL) | A | D | 1-1 | Woods |
| | | 2r | 06.02.13 | **Bristol Rovers** | H | D | 2-2aet | Woods, Sutcliffe |
| | | 2 2r | 10.02.13 | **Bristol Rovers** | | L | 0-1 | |
| | | | | *played at Stamford Bridge* | | | | |
| 1913-14 | (SL) | | | 4q Walthamstow Grange (H) 6-0; 5q Halifax Town (H) 2-0 | | | | |
| | | 1 | 10.01.14 | **Crystal Palace** (SL) | A | L | 1-2 | McDonald |
| 1914-15 | (SL) | 1 | 09.01.15 | **Nottingham Forest** (D2) | A | W | 4-1 | Ritchie, Potter, Wilson, Taylor |
| | | 2 | 30.01.15 | **Tottenham Hotspur** (D1) | H | W | 3-2 | Wilson 2, Taylor |
| | | 3 | 20.02.15 | **Bradford City** (D1) | A | D | 1-1aet | Potter |
| | | 3r | 27.02.15 | **Bradford City** | H | D | 0-0aet | |
| | | 3 2r | 03.03.15 | **Bradford City** | | L | 0-2 | |
| | | | | *played at Sincil Bank, Lincoln* | | | | |
| 1919-20 | (SL) | | | 6q Darlington (A) 0-5 | | | | |
| 1920-21 | (D3) | 1 | 08.01.21 | **Grimsby Town** (D3) | A | L | 0-1 | |
| 1921-22 | (D3) | | | 5q Metrogas London (A) 2-1; 6q Oxford City (A) 1-1; 6qr Oxford City (H) 3-0 | | | | |
| | | 1 | 07.01.22 | **Barnsley** (D2) | A | D | 1-1 | Woodhouse |
| | | 1r | 11.01.22 | **Barnsley** | H | L | 1-2 | Austin |
| 1922-23 | (3S) | | | 5q Southend Utd (A) 2-2; 5qr Southend Utd (H) 2-1; 6q Ilford (H) 5-1 | | | | |
| | | 1 | 13.01.23 | **Bolton Wanderers** (D1) | H | L | 0-2 | |
| 1923-24 | (3S) | | | 5q Folkestone Town (A) 3-2; 6q Stockport County (H) 2-0 | | | | |
| | | 1 | 12.01.24 | **Bristol City** (D2) | H | L | 0-1 | |
| 1924-25 | (3S) | | | 5q Folkestone Town (H) 2-0; 6q Rochdale (H) 1-0 | | | | |
| | | 1 | 10.01.25 | **Doncaster Rovers** (3N) | A | W | 2-1 | Banks 2 |

| | | | | | | | |
|---|---|---|---|---|---|---|---|
| | 2 | 31.01.25 | **Notts County** (D1) | A | L | 0-4 | |
| 1925-26 (3S) | 1 | 28.11.25 | **Clapton** (IL) | A | L | 1-3 | Jackson |
| 1926-27 (3S) | 1 | 27.11.26 | **Crystal Palace** (3S) | A | D | 0-0 | |
| | 1r | 02.12.26 | **Crystal Palace** | H | W | 1-0 | Jackson |
| | 2 | 11.12.26 | **Chatham** (KL) | H | W | 5-0 | Cropper 2, Jackson 2, McWhirr |
| | 3 | 08.01.27 | **Southampton** (D2) | A | L | 0-3 | |
| 1927-28 (3S) | 1 | 26.11.27 | **Poole Town** (SL) | A | D | 1-1 | Robinson |
| | 1r | 01.12.27 | **Poole Town** | H | W | 5-0 | Varco 3, Robinson, Moule |
| | 2 | 10.12.27 | **Luton Town** (3S) | A | L | 0-6 | |
| 1928-29 (3S) | 1 | 24.11.28 | **Chatham** (SL) | H | W | 6-1 | Varco 2, Hannah, Porter, Hooper, Rowden og |
| | 2 | 08.12.28 | **Newport County** (3S) | H | W | 6-0 | Varco 4, Hannah, Slicer |
| | 3 | 12.01.29 | **Corinthians** | H | L | 0-5 | |
| 1929-30 (3S) | 1 | 30.11.29 | **Coventry City** (3S) | H | D | 3-3 | Varco, Slicer, Greenwell |
| | 1r | 05.12.29 | **Coventry City** | A | L | 0-2 | |
| 1930-31 (3S) | 1 | 29.11.30 | **Swindon Town** (3S) | H | W | 2-0 | Peed 2 |
| | 2 | 13.12.30 | **Brentford** (3S) | A | L | 0-1 | |
| 1931-32 (3S) | 1 | 28.11.31 | **Wimbledon** (IL) | A | W | 3-1 | Thompson, Burditt, Murphy |
| | 2 | 12.12.31 | **Brentford** (3S) | A | L | 1-4 | Burditt |
| 1932-33 (3S) | 1 | 26.11.32 | **Folkestone** (SL) | A | L | 0-1 | |
| 1933-34 (3S) | 1 | 25.11.33 | **Crystal Palace** (3S) | A | L | 0-3 | |
| 1934-35 (D2) | 3 | 12.01.35 | **Bath City** (SL) | H | W | 2-0 | Vinall, Kirchen |
| | 4 | 26.01.35 | **Leeds Utd** (D1) | H | D | 3-3 | Kirchen 2, Vinall |
| | 4r | 30.01.35 | **Leeds Utd** | A | W | 2-1 | Burditt, Vinall |
| | 5 | 16.02.35 | **Sheffield Wed** (D1) | H | L | 0-1 | |
| 1935-36 (D2) | 3 | 11.01.36 | **Chelsea** (D1) | H | D | 1-1 | Manders |
| | 3r | 15.01.36 | **Chelsea** | A | L | 1-3 | Warnes |
| 1936-37 (D2) | 3 | 16.01.37 | **Liverpool** (D1) | H | W | 3-0 | Vinall, Scott |
| | 4 | 30.01.37 | **Bolton Wanderers** (D1) | A | D | 1-1 | O'Reilly |
| | 4r | 04.02.37 | **Bolton Wanderers** | H | L | 1-2aet | Manders |
| 1937-38 (D2) | 3 | 08.01.38 | **Aston Villa** (D2) | H | L | 2-3 | Coleman, Manders |
| 1938-39 (D2) | 3 | 12.01.39 | **Manchester City** (D2) | H | L | 0-5 | |
| 1945-46 (3S) | 3 1L | 05.01.46 | **Brighton** (3S) | H | L | 1-2 | Graham |
| | 3 2L | 09.01.46 | **Brighton** | A | L | 1-4 | Ware |
| 1946-47 (3S) | 1 | 30.11.46 | **Brighton** (3S) | H | W | 7-2 | Eyre 5, Robinson, Johnson |
| | 2 | 14.12.46 | **QPR** (3S) | H | D | 4-4 | Eyre 2, Johnson, Jones |
| | 2r | 18.12.46 | **QPR** | A | L | 0-2 | |
| 1947-48 (3S) | 1 | 29.11.47 | **Merthyr Tydfil** (SL) | H | W | 3-0 | Dutton, Kinsey, Eyre |
| | 2 | 13.12.47 | **Walsall** (3S) | H | D | 2-2aet | Hold, Kinsey |
| | 2r | 20.12.47 | **Walsall** | A | L | 2-3 | Hold, Kinsey |
| 1948-49 (3S) | 1 | 27.11.48 | **Wellington Town** (CC) | H | W | 1-0 | Ashman |
| | 2 | 11.12.48 | **Torquay Utd** (3S) | A | L | 1-3 | Kinsey |
| 1949-50 (3S) | 1 | 26.11.49 | **Gloucester City** (SL) | A | W | 3-2 | Kinsey, Jones, Ryder |
| | 2 | 10.12.49 | **Hartlepools Utd** (3N) | A | D | 1-1 | Pickwick |
| | 2r | 15.12.49 | **Hartlepools Utd** | H | W | 5-1 | Ryder 3, Kinsey, Eyre |
| | 3 | 07.01.50 | **Portsmouth** (D1) | A | D | 1-1 | Kinsey |
| | 3r | 12.01.50 | **Portsmouth** | H | L | 0-2 | |
| 1950-51 (3S) | 1 | 25.11.50 | **Watford** (3S) | H | W | 2-0 | Eyre, Hollis |
| | 2 | 09.12.50 | **Rhyl** (CC) | A | W | 1-0 | Kinsey |
| | 3 | 06.01.51 | **Liverpool** (D1) | H | W | 3-1 | Docherty 2, Eyre |
| | 4 | 27.01.51 | **Newport County** (3S) | A | W | 2-0 | Docherty, Dutton |
| | 5 | 10.02.51 | **Sunderland** (D1) | A | L | 1-3 | Gavin |
| 1951-52 (3S) | 1 | 24.11.51 | **Northampton Town** (3S) | H | W | 3-2 | Ackerman, Hollis, Kinsey |
| | 2 | 15.12.51 | **Chesterfield** (3N) | H | W | 3-1 | Hollis, Ackerman, Gavin |
| | 3 | 12.01.52 | **Arsenal** (D1) | H | L | 0-5 | |
| 1952-53 (3S) | 1 | 22.11.52 | **Tonbridge** (SL) | A | D | 2-2 | Ackerman 2 |
| | 1r | 27.11.52 | **Tonbridge** | H | W | 1-0 | Summers |
| | 2 | 06.12.52 | **Brighton** (3S) | A | L | 0-2 | |
| 1953-54 (3S) | 1 | 21.11.53 | **Yeovil Town** (SL) | A | W | 2-0 | Summers 2 |
| | 2 | 12.12.53 | **Barnsley** (3N) | H | W | 2-1 | Johnston 2 |
| | 3 | 09.01.54 | **Hastings Utd** (SL) | A | D | 3-3 | Brennan, Hansell, Gavin |
| | 3r | 13.01.54 | **Hastings Utd** | H | W | 3-0 | Hansell 2, Johnston |

| | | | | | | | | |
|---|---|---|---|---|---|---|---|---|
| | | 4 | 30.01.54 | **Arsenal** (D1) | A | W | 2-1 | Johnston 2 |
| | | 5 | 20.02.54 | **Leicester City** (D2) | H | L | 1-2 | Brennan |
| 1954-55 | (3S) | 1 | 20.11.54 | **Headington Utd** (SL) | H | W | 4-2 | Keans 3, Pickwick |
| | | 2 | 11.12.54 | **Brighton** (3S) | H | D | 0-0 | |
| | | 2r | 15.12.54 | **Brighton** | A | L | 1-5 | Woan |
| 1955-56 | (3S) | 1 | 19.11.55 | **Dorchester Town** (WL) | H | W | 4-0 | Gordon 2, Hunt, Gavin |
| | | 2 | 10.12.55 | **Brighton** (3S) | A | W | 2-1 | Hunt, Gavin |
| | | 3 | 07.01.56 | **Sunderland** (D1) | A | L | 2-4 | McCrohan, Gordon |
| 1956-57 | (3S) | 1 | 17.11.56 | **Bedford Town** (SL) | A | L | 2-4 | Hunt, Coxon |
| 1957-58 | (3S) | 1 | 16.11.57 | **Redhill** (AL) | H | W | 6-1 | Milne 2, Gavin 2, Coxon, Hunt |
| | | 2 | 07.12.57 | **Brighton** (3S) | H | D | 1-1 | Gavin |
| | | 2r | 11.12.57 | **Brighton** | A | W | 2-1 | Gavin, Hunt |
| | | 3 | 04.01.58 | **Darlington** (3N) | H | L | 1-2 | Gavin |
| 1958-59 | (D3) | 1 | 15.11.58 | **Ilford** (IL) | H | W | 3-1 | Brennan 2, Hill |
| | | 2 | 06.12.58 | **Swindon Town** (D3) | A | D | 1-1 | Hill |
| | | 2r | 11.12.58 | **Swindon Town** | H | W | 1-0 | Crossan |
| | | 3 | 10.01.59 | **Manchester Utd** (D1) | H | W | 3-0 | Bly 2, Crossan |
| | | 4 | 24.01.59 | **Cardiff City** (D2) | H | W | 3-2 | Bly 2, Crossan |
| | | 5 | 14.02.59 | **Tottenham Hotspur** (D1) | A | D | 1-1 | Allcock |
| | | 5r | 18.02.59 | **Tottenham Hotspur** | H | W | 1-0 | Bly |
| | | 6 | 28.02.59 | **Sheffield Utd** (D2) | A | D | 1-1 | Crossan |
| | | 6r | 04.03.59 | **Sheffield Utd** | H | W | 3-2 | Bly 2, Brennan |
| | | SF | 14.03.59 | **Luton Town** (D1) | | D | 1-1 | Brennan |
| | | | | *played at White Hart Lane* | | | | |
| | | SFr | 18.03.59 | **Luton Town** | | L | 0-1 | |
| | | | | *played at St Andrews* | | | | |
| 1959-60 | (D3) | 1 | 14.11.59 | **Reading** (D3) | H | D | 1-1 | Moran |
| | | 1r | 18.11.59 | **Reading** | A | L | 1-2 | Crowe |
| 1960-61 | (D2) | 3 | 07.01.61 | **York City** (D4) | A | D | 0-0 | |
| | | 3r | 11.01.61 | **York City** | H | W | 1-0 | Crowe |
| | | 4 | 28.01.61 | **Scunthorpe Utd** (D2) | A | W | 4-1 | Punton, Hill, Larkin, McCrohon |
| | | 5 | 18.02.61 | **Sunderland** (D2) | H | L | 0-1 | |
| 1961-62 | (D2) | 3 | 10.01.62 | **Wrexham** (D4) | H | W | 3-1 | Allcock, Whitehouse, Lythgoe |
| | | 4 | 27.01.62 | **Ipswich Town** (D1) | H | D | 1-1 | Allcock |
| | | 4r | 30.01.62 | **Ipswich Town** | A | W | 2-1 | Allcock 2 |
| | | 5 | 17.02.62 | **Sheffield Utd** (D1) | A | L | 1-3 | Hill |
| 1962-63 | (D2) | 3 | 04.03.63 | **Blackpool** (D1) | H | D | 1-1 | Bryceland |
| | | 3r | 06.03.63 | **Blackpool** | A | W | 3-1aet | Hill, Punton, Mannion |
| | | 4 | 13.03.63 | **Newcastle Utd** (D2) | H | W | 5-0 | Allcock 4, Mullett |
| | | 5 | 16.03.63 | **Manchester City** (D1) | A | W | 2-1 | Allcock 2 |
| | | 6 | 30.03.63 | **Leicester City** (D1) | H | L | 0-2 | |
| 1963-64 | (D2) | 3 | 04.01.64 | **Bristol Rovers** (D3) | A | L | 1-2 | Davies |
| 1964-65 | (D2) | 3 | 09.01.65 | **Nottingham Forest** (D1) | A | L | 0-1 | |
| 1965-66 | (D2) | 3 | 22.01.66 | **Leyton Orient** (D2) | A | W | 3-1 | Anderson, Heath, Webb og |
| | | 4 | 12.02.66 | **Walsall** (D3) | H | W | 3-2 | Heath, Allcock, Mullett |
| | | 5 | 05.03.66 | **Blackburn Rovers** (D1) | H | D | 2-2 | Davies 2 |
| | | 5r | 09.03.66 | **Blackburn Rovers** | A | L | 2-3 | Davies, Bryceland |
| 1966-67 | (D2) | 3 | 28.01.67 | **Derby County** (D2) | H | W | 3-0 | Kenning 2, Anderson |
| | | 4 | 18.02.67 | **Manchester Utd** (D1) | A | W | 2-1 | Heath, Bolland |
| | | 5 | 11.03.67 | **Sheffield Wed** (D1) | H | L | 1-3 | Bryceland |
| 1967-68 | (D2) | 3 | 27.01.68 | **Sunderland** (D1) | H | D | 1-1 | Curran |
| | | 3r | 31.01.68 | **Sunderland** | A | W | 1-0 | Manning |
| | | 4 | 17.02.68 | **Chelsea** (D1) | A | L | 0-1 | |
| 1968-69 | (D2) | 3 | 04.01.69 | **WBA** (D1) | A | L | 0-3 | |
| 1969-70 | (D2) | 3 | 03.01.70 | **Wrexham** (D4) | H | L | 1-2 | Howard |
| 1970-71 | (D2) | 3 | 02.01.71 | **Wolverhampton W** (D1) | A | L | 1-5 | Foggo |
| 1971-72 | (D2) | 3 | 15.01.72 | **Hull City** (D2) | H | L | 0-3 | |
| 1972-73 | (D1) | 3 | 13.01.73 | **Leeds Utd** (D1) | H | D | 1-1 | Cross |
| | | 3r | 17.01.73 | **Leeds Utd** | A | D | 1-1aet | Cross |
| | | 3 2r | 29.01.73 | **Leeds Utd** | | L | 0-5 | |
| | | | | *played at Villa Park* | | | | |

| | | | | | | | | |
|---|---|---|---|---|---|---|---|---|
| 1973-74 | (D1) | 3 | 05.01.74 | **Arsenal** (D1) | H | L | 0-1 | |
| 1974-75 | (D2) | 3 | 04.01.75 | **Coventry City** (D1) | A | L | 0-2 | |
| 1975-76 | (D1) | 3 | 03.01.76 | **Rochdale** (D4) | H | D | 1-1 | MacDougall |
| | | 3r | 06.01.76 | **Rochdale** | A | D | 0-0aet | |
| | | 3 2r | 13.01.76 | **Rochdale** | H | W | 2-1 | MacDougall, Suggett |
| | | 4 | 24.01.76 | **Luton Town** (D2) | H | W | 2-0 | Peters, Jones |
| | | 5 | 23.02.76 | **Bradford City** (D4) | H | L | 1-2 | Peters |
| 1976-77 | (D1) | 3 | 08.01.77 | **Leeds Utd** (D1) | A | L | 2-5 | Suggett, Peters |
| 1977-78 | (D1) | 3 | 06.01.78 | **Orient** (D2) | A | D | 1-1 | Gibbins |
| | | 3r | 16.01.78 | **Orient** | H | L | 0-1 | |
| 1978-79 | (D1) | 3 | 06.01.79 | **Leicester City** (D2) | A | L | 0-3 | |
| 1979-80 | (D1) | 3 | 05.01.80 | **Yeovil Town** (APL) | A | W | 3-0 | Robson, Justin Fashanu, Paddon |
| | | 4 | 26.01.80 | **Wolverhampton W** (D1) | A | D | 1-1 | Bond |
| | | 4r | 30.01.80 | **Wolverhampton W** | H | L | 2-3 | Mendham, Bond |
| 1980-81 | (D1) | 3 | 03.01.81 | **Cambridge Utd** (D2) | H | W | 1-0 | Downs |
| | | 4 | 24.01.81 | **Manchester City** (D1) | A | L | 0-6 | |
| 1981-82 | (D2) | 3 | 02.01.82 | **Stoke City** (D1) | A | W | 1-0 | Jack |
| | | 4 | 23.01.82 | **Doncaster Rovers** (D3) | H | W | 2-1 | Jack, Watson |
| | | 5 | 13.02.82 | **WBA** (D1) | A | L | 0-1 | |
| 1982-83 | (D1) | 3 | 08.01.83 | **Swansea City** (D1) | H | W | 2-1 | Bertschin |
| | | 4 | 29.01.83 | **Coventry City** (D1) | A | D | 2-2 | Hareide, Barham |
| | | 4r | 02.02.83 | **Coventry City** | H | W | 2-1aet | Bertschin, Roberts og |
| | | 5 | 19.02.83 | **Ipswich Town** (D1) | H | W | 1-0 | Bertschin |
| | | 6 | 12.03.83 | **Brighton** (D1) | A | L | 0-1 | |
| 1983-84 | (D1) | 3 | 07.01.84 | **Aston Villa** (D1) | A | D | 1-1 | Deehan |
| | | 3r | 11.01.84 | **Aston Villa** | H | W | 3-0 | Channon, Mendham, Bertschin |
| | | 4 | 28.01.84 | **Tottenham Hotspur** (D1) | A | D | 0-0 | |
| | | 4r | 01.02.84 | **Tottenham Hotspur** | H | W | 2-1 | Van Wyck, Channon |
| | | 5 | 18.02.84 | **Derby County** (D2) | A | L | 1-2 | Deehan |
| 1984-85 | (D1) | 3 | 05.01.85 | **Birmingham City** (D2) | A | D | 0-0 | |
| | | 3r | 23.01.85 | **Birmingham City** | H | D | 1-1aet | Haylock |
| | | 3 2r | 26.01.85 | **Birmingham City** | A | D | 1-1aet | Mendham |
| | | 3 3r | 28.01.85 | **Birmingham City** | H | W | 1-0 | Bruce |
| | | 4 | 04.02.85 | **West Ham Utd** (D1) | A | L | 1-2 | Donowa |
| 1985-86 | (D2) | 3 | 04.01.86 | **Liverpool** (D1) | A | L | 0-5 | |
| 1986-87 | (D1) | 3 | 10.01.87 | **Huddersfield Town** (D2) | H | D | 1-1 | Drinkell |
| | | 3r | 21.01.87 | **Huddersfield Town** | A | W | 4-2 | Phelan, Rosario, Drinkell, Gordon |
| | | 4 | 31.01.87 | **Wigan Athletic** (D3) | A | L | 0-1 | |
| 1987-88 | (D1) | 3 | 09.01.88 | **Swindon Town** (D2) | A | D | 0-0 | |
| | | 3r | 13.01.88 | **Swindon Town** | H | L | 0-2 | |
| 1988-89 | (D1) | 3 | 08.01.89 | **Port Vale** (D3) | A | W | 3-1 | Townsend 2, Fleck |
| | | 4 | 28.01.89 | **Sutton Utd** (Conf) | H | W | 8-0 | Allen 4, Fleck 3, Putney |
| | | 5 | 18.02.89 | **Sheffield Utd** (D3) | H | W | 3-2 | Allen (p), Gordon, Thompson og |
| | | 6 | 18.03.89 | **West Ham Utd** (D1) | A | D | 0-0 | |
| | | 6r | 22.03.89 | **West Ham Utd** | H | W | 3-1 | Allen 2, Gordon |
| | | SF | 15.04.89 | **Everton** (D1) | | L | 0-1 | |
| | | | | *played at Villa Park* | | | | |
| 1989-90 | (D1) | 3 | 06.01.90 | **Exeter City** (D4) | A | D | 1-1 | Fleck |
| | | 3r | 10.01.90 | **Exeter City** | H | W | 2-0 | Rosario, Gordon |
| | | 4 | 28.01.90 | **Liverpool** (D1) | H | D | 0-0 | |
| | | 4r | 31.01.90 | **Liverpool** | A | L | 1-3 | Fleck |
| 1990-91 | (D1) | 3 | 05.01.91 | **Bristol City** (D2) | H | W | 2-1 | Rosario, Fleck |
| | | 4 | 26.01.91 | **Swindon Town** (D2) | H | W | 3-1 | Gordon, Mortensen, Fleck |
| | | 5 | 18.02.91 | **Manchester Utd** (D1) | H | W | 2-1 | Fleck, Gordon |
| | | 6 | 09.03.91 | **Nottingham Forest** (D1) | H | L | 0-1 | |
| 1991-92 | (D1) | 3 | 04.01.92 | **Barnsley** (D2) | H | W | 1-0 | Fleck (p) |
| | | 4 | 05.02.92 | **Millwall** (D2) | H | W | 2-1 | Bowen, Fleck |
| | | 5 | 15.02.92 | **Notts County** (D1) | H | W | 3-0 | Sutton 2, Phillips |
| | | 6 | 07.03.92 | **Southampton** (D1) | A | D | 0-0 | |
| | | 6r | 18.03.92 | **Southampton** | H | W | 2-1aet | Newman, Sutton |
| | | SF | 05.04.92 | **Sunderland** (D2) | | L | 0-1 | |
| | | | | *played at Hillsborough* | | | | |

| | | | | | | | | |
|---|---|---|---|---|---|---|---|---|
| 1992-93 | (PL) | 3 | 13.01.93 | **Coventry City** (PL) | H | W | 1-0 | Beckford |
| | | 4 | 24.01.93 | **Tottenham Hotspur** (PL) | H | L | 0-2 | |
| 1993-94 | (PL) | 3 | 08.01.94 | **Wycombe W** (D3) | A | W | 2-0 | Sutton 2 |
| | | 4 | 30.01.94 | **Manchester Utd** (PL) | H | L | 0-2 | |
| 1994-95 | (PL) | 3 | 07.01.95 | **Grimsby Town** (D1) | A | W | 1-0 | Crook |
| | | 4 | 28.01.95 | **Coventry City** (PL) | A | D | 0-0 | |
| | | 4r | 08.02.95 | **Coventry City** | H | W | 3-1aet | Sheron 2, Eadie |
| | | 5 | 18.02.95 | **Everton** (PL) | A | L | 0-5 | |
| 1995-96 | (D1) | 3 | 06.01.96 | **Brentford** (D2) | H | L | 1-2 | Newsome |
| 1996-97 | (D1) | 3 | 04.01.97 | **Sheffield Utd** (D1) | H | W | 1-0 | Polston |
| | | 4 | 25.01.97 | **Leicester City** (PL) | A | L | 1-2 | Adams (p) |
| 1997-98 | (D1) | 3 | 03.01.98 | **Grimsby Town** (D2) | A | L | 0-3 | |
| 1998-99 | (D1) | 3 | 03.01.99 | **Sheffield Wed** (PL) | A | L | 1-4 | Roberts |
| 1999-00 | (D1) | 3 | 11.12.99 | **Coventry City** (PL) | H | L | 1-3 | Llewellyn |
| 2000-01 | (D1) | 3 | 06.01.01 | **Sheffield Wed** (D1) | A | L | 1-2 | Roberts |
| 2001-02 | (D1) | 3 | 05.01.02 | **Chelsea** (PL) | H | D | 0-0 | |
| | | 3r | 15.01.02 | **Chelsea** | A | L | 0-4 | |
| 2002-03 | (D1) | 3 | 14.01.03 | **Brighton** (D1) | H | W | 3-1 | Mulryne 2, McVeigh |
| | | 4 | 25.01.03 | **Dagenham & Red** (Conf) | H | W | 1-0 | Abbey |
| | | 5 | 15.02.03 | **Southampton** (PL) | A | L | 0-2 | |

## NOTTINGHAM FOREST

*Formed 1865, one of the four oldest clubs in the country. FA Cup winners: 1898, 1959. Runners-up: 1991. Record FA Cup win: 14-0 v Clapton, 1st round, 17.01.1891; Record FA Cup defeat: 0-5 v Southampton, 6th round, 2nd replay, 08.04.1963.*

| | | | | | | | |
|---|---|---|---|---|---|---|---|
| 1878-79 | 1 | 16.11.78 | **Notts County** | A | W | 3-1aet | Turner, Goodyer, Smith |
| | 2 | 21.12.78 | **Sheffield FC** | H | W | 2-0 | Smith, Moss og |
| | 3 | 18.01.79 | **Old Harrovians** | A | W | 2-0 | Widdowson, Welch og |
| | 4 | 25.02.79 | **Oxford University** | H | W | 2-1 | Goodyer, Smith |
| | SF | 22.03.79 | **Old Etonians** | | L | 1-2 | Bishop |
| | | | *played at Kennington Oval* | | | | |
| 1879-80 | 1 | 08.11.79 | **Notts County** | H | W | 4-0 | Widdowson 2, Smith 2 |
| | 2 | 13.12.79 | **Turton** | A | W | 6-0 | Turner, Earp, Widdowson 2, Smith 2 |
| | 3 | 31.01.80 | **Blackburn Rovers** | H | W | 6-0 | Goodyer 2, Widdowson 2, Smith, Turner |
| | 4 | 19.02.80 | **Sheffield FC** | H | D | 2-2 | Smith, Widdowson |
| | | | *FA awarded the tie to Forest after Sheffield refused to play extra time* | | | | |
| | 5 | | bye | | | | |
| | SF | 27.03.80 | **Oxford University** | | L | 0-1 | |
| | | | *played at Kennington Oval* | | | | |
| 1880-81 | 1 | | Caius College, Cambridge | | | - | |
| | | | *Caius College scratched. Nottingham Forest walkover* | | | | |
| | 2 | 04.12.80 | **Aston Villa** | H | L | 1-2 | Widdowson |
| 1881-82 | 1 | 05.11.81 | **Aston Villa** | A | L | 1-4 | Laws og |
| 1882-83 | 1 | | Brigg Britannia | | | - | |
| | | | *Brigg Britannia scratched. Nottingham Forest walkover* | | | | |
| | 2 | 02.12.82 | **Sheffield Heeley** | H | W | 7-2 | Widdowson 4, Parr, Earp, Fletcher |
| | 3 | 06.01.83 | **Sheffield Wed** | H | D | 2-2 | Widdowson, Ledger og |
| | 3r | 13.01.83 | **Sheffield Wed** | A | L | 2-3 | Parr, Earp |
| 1883-84 | 1 | | Redcar | | | - | |
| | | | *Redcar scratched. Nottingham Forest walkover* | | | | |
| | 2 | 01.12.83 | **Notts County** | A | L | 0-3 | |
| 1884-85 | 1 | 08.11.84 | **Rotherham Town** | H | W | 5-0 | Unwin, Widdowson 3, Fox |
| | 2 | 06.12.84 | **Sheffield Heeley** | H | W | 4-2 | Billyeald, Fox 3 |
| | 3 | 03.01.85 | **Sheffield Wed** | A | W | 2-1 | Lindley, Widdowson |
| | 4 | 24.01.85 | **Swifts** | A | W | 1-0 | Widdowson |
| | 5 | | bye | | | | |
| | 6 | 21.02.85 | **Old Etonians** | A | W | 2-0 | |
| | SF | 14.03.85 | **Queen's Park, Glasgow** | | D | 1-1 | Danks |
| | | | *played at Derby Cricket Ground* | | | | |
| | SFr | 28.03.85 | **Queen's Park, Glasgow** | | L | 0-3 | |
| | | | *played at Merchiston Castle School, Edinburgh* | | | | |

| | | | | | | | | |
|---|---|---|---|---|---|---|---|---|
| 1885-86 | | 1 | 31.10.85 | **Mellors Ltd** | H | W | 6-2 | Tutin 4, Fox, Danks |
| | | 2 | 21.11.85 | **Notts Olympic** | H | W | 4-1 | Unwin 2, Leighton, Norman |
| | | 3 | 12.12.85 | **Staveley** | A | L | 1-2 | Lindley |
| 1886-87 | | 1 | 30.10.86 | **Notts Olympic** | H | W | 3-0 | Unwin, Danks, Leighton |
| | | 2 | 13.11.86 | **Grimsby Town** | H | D | 2-2 | Leighton 2 |
| | | 2r | 20.11.86 | **Grimsby Town** | A | W | 1-0 | Tutin |
| | | 3 | 11.12.86 | **Lockwood Bros** | A | L | 1-2 | Norman |
| 1887-88 | | 1 | 15.10.87 | **Notts Swifts** | H | W | 2-1 | G Tutin, Norman |
| | | 2 | 05.11.87 | **Mellors Ltd** | H | W | 2-0 | Leighton 2 |
| | | 3 | 26.11.87 | **Notts County** | H | W | 2-1 | Lindley, Burton |
| | | 4 | 17.12.87 | **Old Etonians** | H | W | 6-0 | Fox 2, Danks 2, Norman, Lindley |
| | | 5 | 07.01.88 | **Sheffield Wed** | H | L | 2-4 | Lindley, Burton |
| 1888-89 | | 1 | 02.02.89 | **Linfield Athletic** | H | D | 2-2 | Norman, Burton |
| | | | | *Linfield scratched before replay took place. Nottingham Forest walkover* | | | | |
| | | 2 | 16.02.89 | **Chatham** | A | D | 1-1aet | Lindley |
| | | 2r | 23.02.89 | **Chatham** | H | D | 2-2aet | Tolley, Lindley |
| | | 2 2r | 28.02.89 | **Chatham** | | L | 2-3 | H Pike, Lindley |
| | | | | *played at Kenningtron Oval* | | | | |
| 1889-90 | (FAll) | 1 | 18.01.90 | **Derby Midland** (ML) | A | L | 0-3 | |
| 1890-91 | (FAll) | 1 | 17.01.91 | **Clapton** | A | W | 14-0 | Higgins 5, Lindley 4, McCallum 2, W Smith 2, Shaw |
| | | | | *played at Upton Park* | | | | |
| | | 2 | 31.01.91 | **Sunderland Albion** (FAll) | A | D | 1-1 | W Smith |
| | | 2r | 07.02.91 | **Sunderland Albion** | H | D | 3-3aet | Higgins 3 |
| | | 2 2r | 11.02.91 | **Sunderland Albion** | | W | 5-0 | W Smith, Higgins 2, Shaw, Lindley |
| | | | | *played at Bramall Lane* | | | | |
| | | 3 | 14.02.91 | **Sunderland** (D1) | A | L | 0-4 | |
| 1891-92 | (FAll) | 1 | 16.01.92 | **Newcastle East End** (NL) | H | W | 2-1 | Higgins 2 |
| | | 2 | 30.01.92 | **Sunderland Albion** (FAll) | A | W | 1-0 | Higgins |
| | | 3 | 13.02.92 | **Preston North End** (D1) | H | W | 2-0 | Higgins, W Smith |
| | | SF | 27.02.92 | **WBA** (D1) | | D | 1-1 | Lindley |
| | | | | *played at Molineux* | | | | |
| | | SFr | 05.03.92 | **WBA** (D1) | | D | 0-0 | |
| | | | | *played at Molineux* | | | | |
| | | SF 2r | 09.03.92 | **WBA** (D1) | | L | 2-6 | Higgins 2 |
| | | | | *played at the Racecourse Ground, Derby* | | | | |
| 1892-93 | (FAll) | 1 | 21.01.93 | **Casuals** | H | W | 4-0 | Shaw, McInnes, Pike, Higgins |
| | | 2 | 04.02.93 | **Everton** (D1) | A | L | 2-4 | Pike, Shaw |
| 1893-94 | (D1) | 1 | 27.01.94 | **Heanor Town** | H | W | 1-0aet | Brodie |
| | | 2 | 10.02.94 | **Middlesbrough Iron** (D2) | A | W | 2-0 | Brodie, Higgins |
| | | 3 | 24.02.94 | **Notts County** (D2) | H | D | 1-1 | McInnes |
| | | 3r | 03.03.94 | **Notts County** | A | L | 1-4 | McInnes |
| 1894-95 | (D1) | 1 | 02.02.95 | **Soton St Marys** (SL) | A | W | 4-1 | Pike, Rose 2, Carnelly |
| | | 2 | 16.02.95 | **Liverpool** (D1) | A | W | 2-0 | Stewart, McInnes |
| | | 3 | 02.03.95 | **Aston Villa** (D1) | A | L | 1-6 | Stewart, McInnes |
| 1895-96 | (D1) | 1 | 01.02.96 | **Everton** (D1) | H | L | 0-2 | |
| 1896-97 | (D1) | 1 | 30.01.97 | **Sheffield Wed** (D1) | A | W | 1-0 | Arthur Capes |
| | | 2 | 13.02.97 | **Sunderland** (D1) | A | W | 3-1 | FR Foreman 2, McInnes |
| | | 3 | 27.02.97 | **Liverpool** (D1) | A | D | 1-1 | McInnes |
| | | 3r | 03.03.97 | **Liverpool** | H | L | 0-1 | |
| 1897-98 | (D1) | 1 | 29.01.98 | **Grimsby Town** (D2) | H | W | 4-0 | Richards, Capes 2, McInnes |
| | | 2 | 12.02.98 | **Gainsborough T** (D2) | H | W | 4-0 | Benbow, Richards 2, McInnes |
| | | 3 | 26.02.98 | **WBA** (D1) | A | W | 3-2 | F Foreman, Richards, Spouncer |
| | | SF | 19.03.98 | **Southampton** (SL) | | D | 1-1 | Benbow |
| | | | | *played at Bramall Lane* | | | | |
| | | SFr | 23.03.98 | **Southampton** | | W | 2-0 | McInnes, Richards |
| | | | | *played at Crystal Palace* | | | | |
| | | F | 16.04.98 | **Derby County** (D1) | | W | 3-1 | Capes 2, McPherson |
| | | | | *played at Crystal Palace* | | | | |
| 1898-99 | (D1) | 1 | 28.01.99 | **Aston Villa** (D1) | H | W | 2-1 | Capes, FR Foreman |
| | | 2 | 11.02.99 | **Everton** (D1) | A | W | 1-0 | FR Foreman |
| | | 3 | 25.02.99 | **Sheffield Utd** (D1) | H | L | 0-1 | |

| | | | | | | | |
|---|---|---|---|---|---|---|---|
| 1899-00 (D1) | 1 | 27.01.00 | **Grimsby Town** (D2) | H | W | 3-0 | Calvey, Morris 2 |
| | 2 | 10.02.00 | **Sunderland** (D1) | H | W | 3-0 | Beveridge 2, Morris |
| | 3 | 24.02.00 | **Preston North End** (D1) | A | D | 0-0 | |
| | 3r | 28.02.00 | **Preston North End** | H | W | 1-0 | Capes |
| | SF | 24.03.00 | **Bury** (D1) | | D | 1-1 | Capes |
| | | | *played at the Victoria Ground, Stoke* | | | | |
| | SFr | 29.03.00 | **Bury** | | L | 2-3aet | Capes, Calvey |
| | | | *played at Bramall Lane* | | | | |
| 1900-01 (D1) | 1 | 09.02.01 | **Leicester Fosse** (D2) | H | W | 5-1 | Calvey 3, Morris, FR Foreman |
| | 2 | 23.02.01 | **Aston Villa** (D1) | A | D | 0-0 | |
| | 2r | 27.02.01 | **Aston Villa** | H | L | 1-3aet | Spouncer |
| 1901-02 (D1) | 1 | 25.01.02 | **Glossop North End** (D2) | A | W | 3-1 | Morris 2, F Foreman |
| | 2 | 08.02.02 | **Manchester City** (D1) | A | W | 2-0 | Calvey, F Foreman |
| | 3 | 22.02.02 | **Stoke** (D1) | H | W | 2-0 | F Foreman 2 |
| | SF | 15.03.02 | **Southampton** (SL) | | L | 1-3 | Calvey |
| | | | *played at White Hart Lane* | | | | |
| 1902-03 (D1) | 1 | 07.02.03 | **Reading** (SL) | A | D | 0-0 | |
| | 1r | 11.02.03 | **Reading** | H | W | 6-3aet | Calvey 2, Morris 2, Iremonger, FR Foreman |
| | 2 | 21.02.03 | **Stoke** (D1) | H | D | 0-0 | |
| | 2r | 26.02.03 | **Stoke** | A | L | 0-2 | |
| 1903-04 (D1) | 1 | 06.02.04 | **WBA** (D1) | A | D | 1-1 | Shearman |
| | 1r | 13.02.04 | **WBA** | H | W | 3-1 | Morris, Shearman, Spouncer |
| | 2 | 20.02.04 | **Blackburn Rovers** (D1) | A | L | 1-3 | Morris |
| 1904-05 (D1) | 1 | 04.02.05 | **Sheffield Utd** (D1) | H | W | 2-0 | Morris, Shearman |
| | 2 | 18.02.05 | **Fulham** (SL) | A | L | 0-1 | |
| 1905-06 (D1) | 1 | 13.01.06 | **Bury** (D1) | A | D | 1-1 | Morris |
| | 1r | 17.01.06 | **Bury** | H | W | 6-2 | Craggs, Holmes, Shearman 3, West |
| | 2 | 03.02.06 | **Fulham** (SL) | A | W | 3-1 | Morris 2, West |
| | 3 | 24.02.06 | **Sheffield Wed** (D1) | A | L | 1-4 | Spouncer |
| 1906-07 (D2) | 1 | 12.01.07 | **Barnsley** (D2) | H | D | 1-1 | Morris |
| | 1r | 17.01.07 | **Barnsley** | A | L | 1-2 | Hughes |
| 1907-08 (D1) | 1 | 11.01.08 | **Newcastle Utd** (D1) | A | L | 0-2 | |
| 1908-09 (D1) | 1 | 16.01.09 | **Aston Villa** (D1) | H | W | 2-0 | Spouncer, Hooper |
| | 2 | 06.02.09 | **Brentford** (SL) | H | W | 1-0 | West |
| | 3 | 20.02.09 | **Millwall Athletic** (SL) | H | W | 3-1 | West 2 (1p), Hooper |
| | 4 | 06.03.09 | **Derby County** (D2) | A | L | 0-3 | |
| 1909-10 (D1) | 1 | 15.01.10 | **Sheffield Utd** (D1) | H | W | 3-2 | West 2, Armstrong |
| | 2 | 05.02.10 | **Northampton Town** (SL) | A | D | 0-0 | |
| | 2r | 09.02.10 | **Northampton Town** | H | W | 1-0 | Marrison |
| | 3 | 19.02.10 | **Coventry City** (SL) | A | L | 1-3 | Morris |
| 1910-11 (D1) | 1 | 14.01.11 | **West Ham Utd** (SL) | A | L | 1-2 | Morris |
| 1911-12 (D2) | 1 | 13.01.12 | **Bradford Park A** (D2) | H | L | 0-1 | |
| 1912-13 (D2) | 1 | 18.01.13 | **Chesterfield** (ML) | A | W | 4-1 | Gibson 3, Morris |
| | 2 | 01.02.13 | **Oldham Athletic** (D1) | A | L | 1-5 | Derrick |
| 1913-14 (D2) | 1 | 10.01.14 | **Clapton Orient** (D2) | A | D | 2-2 | McKnight, Bell |
| | 1r | 14.01.14 | **Clapton Orient** | H | L | 0-1 | |
| 1914-15 (D2) | 1 | 09.01.15 | **Norwich City** (SL) | H | L | 1-4 | Neve |
| 1919-20 (D2) | 1 | 10.01.20 | **Bradford Park A** (D1) | A | L | 0-3 | |
| 1920-21 (D2) | 1 | 08.01.21 | **Newcastle Utd** (D1) | A | D | 1-1 | Bedford |
| | 1r | 12.01.21 | **Newcastle Utd** | A | L | 0-2 | |
| 1921-22 (D2) | 1 | 07.01.22 | **Bristol City** (D2) | A | D | 0-0 | |
| | 1r | 11.01.22 | **Bristol City** | H | W | 3-1 | Spaven 2, R Parker |
| | 2 | 28.01.22 | **Hull City** (D2) | H | W | 3-0 | Dennis, Spaven 2 |
| | 3 | 18.02.22 | **Cardiff City** (D1) | A | L | 1-4 | Burton |
| 1922-23 (D1) | 1 | 13.01.23 | **Sheffield Utd** (D1) | H | D | 0-0 | |
| | 1r | 18.01.23 | **Sheffield Utd** | A | D | 0-0aet | |
| | 1 2r | 22.01.23 | **Sheffield Utd** | | D | 1-1aet | Green |
| | | | *played at Meadow Lane, Nottingham* | | | | |
| | 1 3r | 25.01.23 | **Sheffield Utd** | | L | 0-1 | |
| | | | *played at Hillsborough* | | | | |

| | | | | | | | | | |
|---|---|---|---|---|---|---|---|---|---|
| 1923-24 | (D1) | 1 | 12.01.24 | **Manchester City** (D1) | A | L | 0-2 | |
| 1924-25 | (D1) | 1 | 10.01.25 | **Clapton Orient** (D2) | H | W | 1-0 | Walker |
| | | 2 | 31.01.25 | **West Ham Utd** (D1) | H | L | 0-2 | |
| 1925-26 | (D2) | 3 | 09.01.26 | **Bradford City** (D2) | H | W | 1-0 | Gibson |
| | | 4 | 30.01.26 | **Swindon Town** (3S) | H | W | 2-0 | Walker 2 |
| | | 5 | 20.02.26 | **Southend Utd** (3S) | A | W | 1-0 | Walker |
| | | 6 | 06.03.26 | **Bolton Wanderers** (D1) | H | D | 2-2 | Stocks, Burton |
| | | 6r | 10.03.26 | **Bolton Wanderers** | A | D | 0-0aet | |
| | | 6 2r | 15.03.26 | **Bolton Wanderers** | | L | 0-1 | |
| | | | | *played at Old Trafford* | | | | |
| 1926-27 | (D2) | 3 | 08.01.27 | **Ashington** (3N) | A | W | 2-0 | Burton, Stocks |
| | | 4 | 29.01.27 | **Wolverhampton W** (D2) | A | L | 0-2 | |
| 1927-28 | (D2) | 3 | 14.01.28 | **Tranmere Rovers** (3N) | H | W | 1-0 | Wadsworth |
| | | 4 | 28.01.28 | **Derby County** (D1) | A | D | 0-0 | |
| | | 4r | 01.02.28 | **Derby County** | H | W | 2-0 | Gibson, Stocks |
| | | 5 | 18.02.28 | **Cardiff City** (D1) | H | W | 2-1 | Thompson (p), Stocks |
| | | 6 | 03.03.28 | **Sheffield Utd** (D1) | A | L | 0-3 | |
| 1928-29 | (D2) | 3 | 12.01.29 | **Swansea Town** (D2) | H | L | 1-2 | Jennings |
| 1929-30 | (D2) | 3 | 11.01.30 | **Rotherham Utd** (3N) | A | W | 5-0 | Dent 3, Loftus, Scott |
| | | 4 | 25.01.30 | **Fulham** (3S) | H | W | 2-1 | Loftus 2 |
| | | 5 | 15.02.30 | **Sunderland** (D1) | A | D | 2-2 | Dickinson 2 |
| | | 5r | 19.02.30 | **Sunderland** | H | W | 3-1 | Loftus, Scott, Burton |
| | | 6 | 01.03.30 | **Sheffield Wed** (D1) | H | D | 2-2 | Loftus, Dickinson |
| | | 6r | 08.03.30 | **Sheffield Wed** | A | L | 1-3 | Burton |
| 1930-31 | (D2) | 3 | 10.01.31 | **Newcastle Utd** (D1) | A | L | 0-4 | |
| 1931-32 | (D2) | 3 | 09.01.32 | **Chesterfield** (D2) | A | L | 2-5 | Simpson, Dickinson (p) |
| 1932-33 | (D2) | 3 | 14.01.33 | **Bury** (D2) | A | D | 2-2 | Dickinson, J Graham |
| | | 3r | 18.01.33 | **Bury** | H | L | 1-2 | Simpson |
| 1933-34 | (D2) | 3 | 13.01.34 | **QPR** (3S) | H | W | 4-0 | Peacock 3, Simpson |
| | | 4 | 27.01.34 | **Chelsea** (D1) | A | D | 1-1 | Peacock |
| | | 4r | 31.01.34 | **Chelsea** | H | L | 0-3 | |
| 1934-35 | (D2) | 3 | 12.01.35 | **Chester** (3N) | A | W | 4-0 | Race 2, Dennison, Masters |
| | | 4 | 26.01.35 | **Manchester Utd** (D2) | H | D | 0-0 | |
| | | 4r | 30.01.35 | **Manchester Utd** | A | W | 3-0 | Mawson, Masters, Race |
| | | 5 | 16.02.35 | **Burnley** (D2) | H | D | 0-0 | |
| | | 5r | 19.02.35 | **Burnley** | A | L | 0-3 | |
| 1935-36 | (D2) | 3 | 11.01.36 | **Doncaster Rovers** (D2) | A | W | 2-1 | Race, Peacock |
| | | 4 | 25.01.36 | **Derby County** (D1) | A | L | 0-2 | |
| 1936-37 | (D2) | 3 | 16.01.37 | **Sheffield Utd** (D2) | H | L | 2-4 | Martin 2 |
| 1937-38 | (D2) | 3 | 08.01.38 | **Southampton** (D2) | H | W | 3-1 | Martin 2, McNaughton |
| | | 4 | 22.01.38 | **Middlesbrough** (D1) | H | L | 1-3 | Martin |
| 1938-39 | (D2) | 3 | 11.01.39 | **Huddersfield Town** (D1) | A | D | 0-0 | |
| | | 3r | 16.01.39 | **Huddersfield Town** | H | L | 0-3 | |
| 1945-46 | (D2) | 3 1L | 05.01.46 | **Watford** (3S) | H | D | 1-1 | Allen |
| | | 3 2L | 09.01.46 | **Watford** | A | D | 1-1aet | Barks |
| | | 3r | 16.01.46 | **Watford** | | L | 0-1aet | |
| | | | | *played at White Hart Lane* | | | | |
| 1946-47 | (D2) | 3 | 11.01.47 | **Lincoln City** (3N) | A | W | 1-0 | Rawson |
| | | 4 | 25.01.47 | **Manchester Utd** (D1) | A | W | 2-0 | Barks, Lyman |
| | | | | *played at Maine Road* | | | | |
| | | 5 | 08.02.47 | **Middlesbrough** (D1) | H | D | 2-2 | Scott, Mannion og |
| | | 5r | 12.02.47 | **Middlesbrough** | A | L | 2-6 | Barks, Edwards |
| 1947-48 | (D2) | 3 | 10.01.48 | **Liverpool** (D1) | A | L | 1-4 | Wilkins |
| 1948-49 | (D2) | 3 | 08.01.49 | **Liverpool** | H | D | 2-2aet | Jones og, Scott |
| | | 3r | 15.01.49 | **Liverpool** | A | L | 0-4 | |
| 1949-50 | (3S) | 1 | 26.11.49 | **Bristol City** (3S) | H | W | 1-0 | Kaile |
| | | 2 | 10.12.49 | **Stockport County** (3N) | H | L | 0-2 | |
| 1950-51 | (3S) | 1 | 24.11.50 | **Torquay Utd** (3S) | H | W | 6-1 | Johnson 3, Collindridge 2, Scott |
| | | 2 | 09.12.50 | **Rotherham Utd** (3N) | A | L | 1-3 | Capel |
| 1951-52 | (D2) | 3 | 12.01.52 | **Blackburn Rovers** (D2) | H | D | 2-2 | Capel, Scott |
| | | 3r | 16.01.52 | **Blackburn Rovers** | A | L | 0-2 | |

| | | | | | | | | |
|---|---|---|---|---|---|---|---|---|
| 1952-53 | (D2) | 3 | 10.01.53 | **Mansfield Town** (3N) | A | W | 1-0 | Ardron |
| | | 4 | 31.01.53 | **Everton** (D2) | A | L | 1-4 | Capel |
| 1953-54 | (D2) | 3 | 09.01.54 | **Plymouth Argyle** (D2) | A | L | 0-2 | |
| 1954-55 | (D2) | 3 | 08.01.55 | **Sheffield Utd** (D1) | A | W | 3-1 | Scott, Barrett, Burkitt |
| | | 4 | 29.01.55 | **Hartlepools Utd** (3N) | A | D | 1-1 | Scott |
| | | 4r | 02.02.55 | **Hartlepools Utd** | H | W | 2-1aet | Kelly (p), Wilson |
| | | 5 | 19.02.55 | **Newcastle Utd** (D1) | H | D | 1-1 | Small |
| | | 5r | 28.02.55 | **Newcastle Utd** | A | D | 2-2aet | Barrett, Scott |
| | | 5 2r | 02.03.55 | **Newcastle Utd** | A | L | 1-2aet | Wilson |
| 1955-56 | (D2) | 3 | 07.01.56 | **Doncaster Rovers** (D2) | A | L | 0-3 | |
| 1956-57 | (D2) | 3 | 05.01.57 | **Goole Town** (ML) | H | W | 6-0 | Barrett 3, Wilson, Baily, Higham |
| | | 4 | 26.01.57 | **Portsmouth** (D1) | A | W | 3-1 | Baily 2, Imlach |
| | | 5 | 16.02.57 | **Barnsley** (D2) | A | W | 2-1 | Wilson, Imlach |
| | | 6 | 02.03.57 | **Birmingham City** (D1) | A | D | 0-0 | |
| | | 6r | 07.03.57 | **Birmingham City** | H | L | 0-1 | |
| 1957-58 | (D1) | 3 | 04.01.58 | **Gillingham** (3S) | H | W | 2-0 | Imlach, Quigley |
| | | 4 | 25.01.58 | **WBA** (D1) | A | D | 3-3 | Wilson 2 (1p), Imlach |
| | | 4r | 28.01.58 | **WBA** | H | L | 1-5 | Wilson |
| 1958-59 | (D1) | 3 | 10.01.59 | **Tooting & M** (IL) | A | D | 2-2 | Murphy og, Gray (p) |
| | | 3r | 24.01.59 | **Tooting & M** | H | W | 3-0 | Dwight, Wilson, Imlach |
| | | 4 | 28.01.59 | **Grimsby Town** (D2) | H | W | 4-1 | Gray 2 (1p), Whitefoot, Wilson |
| | | 5 | 14.02.59 | **Birmingham City** (D1) | A | D | 1-1 | Wilson |
| | | 5r | 18.02.59 | **Birmingham City** | H | D | 1-1aet | Dwight |
| | | 5 2r | 23.02.59 | **Birmingham City** *played at Filbert Street* | | W | 5-0 | Dwight 3, Gray 2 (1p) |
| | | 6 | 28.02.59 | **Bolton Wanderers** (D1) | H | W | 2-1 | Wilson 2 |
| | | SF | 14.03.59 | **Aston Villa** (D1) *played at Hillsborough* | | W | 1-0 | Quigley |
| | | F | 02.05.59 | **Luton Town** (D1) *played at Wembley Stadium* | | W | 2-1 | Dwight, Wilson |
| 1959-60 | (D1) | 3 | 09.01.60 | **Reading** (D3) | H | W | 1-0 | Iley |
| | | 4 | 30.01.60 | **Sheffield Utd** (D2) | A | L | 0-3 | |
| 1960-61 | (D1) | 3 | 07.01.61 | **Birmingham City** (D1) | H | L | 0-2 | |
| 1961-62 | (D1) | 3 | 06.01.62 | **Workington** (D4) | A | W | 2-1 | Booth, Julians |
| | | 4 | 27.01.62 | **Sheffield Wed** (D1) | H | L | 0-2 | |
| 1962-63 | (D1) | 3 | 29.01.63 | **Wolverhampton W** (D1) | H | W | 4-3 | Addison, Quigley, Hockey Le Flem |
| | | 4 | 06.03.63 | **WBA** (D1) | A | D | 0-0 | |
| | | 4r | 11.03.63 | **WBA** | H | W | 2-1aet | Addison (p), Cram og |
| | | 5 | 19.03.63 | **Leeds Utd** (D2) | H | W | 3-0 | Addison, Quigley, Hockey |
| | | 6 | 30.03.63 | **Southampton** (D2) | H | D | 1-1 | McKinlay |
| | | 6r | 03.04.63 | **Southampton** | A | D | 3-3aet | Addison, Vowden 2 |
| | | 6 2r | 08.04.63 | **Southampton** *played at White Hart Lane* | | L | 0-5 | |
| 1963-64 | (D1) | 3 | 04.01.64 | **Preston North End** (D2) | H | D | 0-0 | |
| | | 3r | 13.01.64 | **Preston North End** | A | L | 0-1aet | |
| 1964-65 | (D1) | 3 | 09.01.65 | **Norwich City** (D2) | H | W | 1-0 | Addison |
| | | 4 | 30.01.65 | **Sunderland** (D1) | A | W | 3-1 | Addison, Wignall, Crowe |
| | | 5 | 20.02.65 | **Crystal Palace** (D2) | A | L | 1-3 | Wignall |
| 1965-66 | (D1) | 3 | 22.01.66 | **Northampton Town** (D1) | A | W | 2-1 | Wignall, Crowe |
| | | 4 | 12.02.66 | **Hull City** (D3) | A | L | 0-2 | |
| 1966-67 | (D1) | 3 | 28.01.67 | **Plymouth Argyle** (D2) | H | W | 2-1 | Baker, Wignall |
| | | 4 | 18.02.67 | **Newcastle Utd** (D1) | H | W | 3-0 | Barnwell, Baker, Storey-Moore |
| | | 5 | 11.03.67 | **Swindon Town** (D3) | H | D | 0-0 | |
| | | 5r | 14.03.67 | **Swindon Town** | A | D | 1-1aet | Hindley |
| | | 5 2r | 20.03.67 | **Swindon Town** *played at Villa Park* | | W | 3-0 | Lyons, Baker, Barnwell |
| | | 6 | 08.04.67 | **Everton** (D1) | H | W | 3-2 | Storey-Moore 3 |
| | | SF | 29.04.67 | **Tottenham Hotspur** (D1) *played at Hillsborough* | | L | 1-2 | Hennessey |
| 1967-68 | (D1) | 3 | 07.01.68 | **Bolton Wanderers** (D2) | H | W | 4-2 | Hilley, Baker, Wignall, Winfield |
| | | 4 | 17.02.68 | **Leeds Utd** (D1) | A | L | 1-2 | Baker |

| | | | | | | | | |
|---|---|---|---|---|---|---|---|---|
| 1968-69 | (D1) | 3 | 04.01.69 | **Preston North End** (D2) | A | L | 0-3 | |
| 1969-70 | (D1) | 3 | 03.01.70 | **Carlisle Utd** (D2) | H | D | 0-0 | |
| | | 3r | 06.01.70 | **Carlisle Utd** | A | L | 1-2 | McCaffrey |
| 1970-71 | (D1) | 3 | 02.01.71 | **Luton Town** (D2) | H | D | 1-1 | McIntosh |
| | | 3r | 11.01.71 | **Luton Town** | A | W | 4-3 | Cormack, Collier, Lyons, Rees |
| | | 4 | 23.01.71 | **Orient** (D2) | H | D | 1-1 | Storey-Moore (p) |
| | | 4r | 25.01.71 | **Orient** | A | - | 0-0ab | |
| | | | | *abandoned at half-time – ground unplayable* | | | | |
| | | 4r | 01.02.71 | **Orient** (D2) | A | W | 1-0 | Collier |
| | | 5 | 13.02.71 | **Tottenham Hotspur** (D1) | A | L | 1-2 | Storey-Moore (p) |
| 1971-72 | (D1) | 3 | 15.01.72 | **Millwall** (D2) | A | L | 1-3 | Richardson |
| 1972-73 | (D2) | 3 | 13.01.73 | **WBA** (D1) | A | D | 1-1 | Galley |
| | | 3r | 16.01.73 | **WBA** | H | - | 1-1ab | Lyons |
| | | | | *abandoned after 80 minutes – fog* | | | | |
| | | 3r | 22.01.73 | **WBA** | H | D | 0-0aet | |
| | | 3 2r | 29.01.73 | **WBA** | | L | 1-3 | Galley |
| | | | | *played at Filbert Street* | | | | |
| 1973-74 | (D2) | 3 | 06.01.74 | **Bristol Rovers** (D3) | H | W | 4-3 | Martin 2, Lyall (p), Chapman |
| | | 4 | 27.01.74 | **Manchester City** (D1) | H | W | 4-1 | Bowyer 2, McKenzie, Lyall |
| | | 5 | 17.02.74 | **Portsmouth** (D2) | H | W | 1-0 | McKenzie (p) |
| | | 6 | 09.03.74 | **Newcastle Utd** (D1) | A | L | 3-4 | Bowyer, O'Kane, Lyall |
| | | | | *FA ordered replay after pitch invasion when Forest were leading 3-1* | | | | |
| | | 6r | 18.03.74 | **Newcastle Utd** (D1) | | D | 0-0 | |
| | | | | *played at Goodison Park* | | | | |
| | | 6 2r | 21.03.74 | **Newcastle Utd** | | L | 0-1 | |
| | | | | *played at Goodison Park* | | | | |
| 1974-75 | (D2) | 3 | 04.01.75 | **Tottenham Hotspur** (D1) | H | D | 1-1 | Jones |
| | | 3r | 08.01.75 | **Tottenham Hotspur** | A | W | 1-0 | Martin |
| | | 4 | 28.01.75 | **Fulham** (D2) | A | D | 0-0 | |
| | | 4r | 03.02.75 | **Fulham** | H | D | 1-1aet | Martin |
| | | 4 2r | 05.02.75 | **Fulham** | A | D | 1-1aet | Robertson |
| | | 4 3r | 10.02.75 | **Fulham** | H | L | 1-2 | Chapman |
| 1975-76 | (D2) | 3 | 01.01.76 | **Peterborough Utd** (D3) | H | D | 0-0 | |
| | | 3r | 07.01.76 | **Peterborough Utd** | A | L | 0-1 | |
| 1976-77 | (D2) | 3 | 08.01.77 | **Bristol Rovers** (D2) | H | D | 1-1 | Robertson (p) |
| | | 3r | 11.01.77 | **Bristol Rovers** | A | D | 1-1aet | Woodcock |
| | | 3 2r | 18.01.77 | **Bristol Rovers** | | W | 6-0 | Woodcock 2, Bowyer, Withe, Anderson, O'Hare |
| | | | | *played at Villa Park* | | | | |
| | | 4 | 29.01.77 | **Southampton** (D2) | H | D | 3-3 | Robertson 2 (1p), Woodcock |
| | | 4r | 01.02.77 | **Southampton** | A | L | 1-2 | Woodcock |
| 1977-78 | (D1) | 3 | 07.01.78 | **Swindon Town** (D3) | H | W | 4-1 | Woodcock 2, Withe, Robertson |
| | | 4 | 31.01.78 | **Manchester City** (D1) | H | W | 2-1 | Robertson, Withe |
| | | 5 | 18.02.78 | **QPR** (D1) | A | D | 1-1 | O'Neill |
| | | 5r | 27.02.78 | **QPR** | H | D | 1-1aet | Robertson (p) |
| | | 5 2r | 02.03.78 | **QPR** | H | W | 3-1 | O'Neill, Woodcock 2 |
| | | 6 | 11.03.78 | **WBA** (D1) | A | L | 0-2 | |
| 1978-79 | (D1) | 3 | 10.01.79 | **Aston Villa** (D1) | H | W | 2-0 | Needham, Woodcock |
| | | 4 | 27.01.79 | **York City** (D4) | H | W | 3-1 | LLoyd, McGovern, O'Neill |
| | | 5 | 26.02.79 | **Arsenal** (D1) | H | L | 0-1 | |
| 1979-80 | (D1) | 3 | 05.01.80 | **Leeds Utd** (D1) | A | W | 4-1 | Gray, Birtles, Bowyer, Robertson |
| | | 4 | 26.01.80 | **Liverpool** (D1) | H | L | 0-2 | |
| 1980-81 | (D1) | 3 | 03.01.81 | **Bolton Wanderers** (D2) | H | D | 3-3 | Francis 2, Ponte |
| | | 3r | 06.01.81 | **Bolton Wanderers** | A | W | 1-0aet | Francis |
| | | 4 | 24.01.81 | **Manchester Utd** (D1) | H | W | 1-0 | Francis |
| | | 5 | 14.02.81 | **Bristol City** (D2) | H | W | 2-1 | Wallace, Robertson (p) |
| | | 6 | 07.03.81 | **Ipswich Town** (D1) | H | D | 3-3 | Francis, Walsh, Robertson (p) |
| | | 6r | 10.03.81 | **Ipswich Town** | A | L | 0-1 | |
| 1981-82 | (D1) | 3 | 02.01.82 | **Wrexham** (D2) | H | L | 1-3 | Proctor |
| 1982-83 | (D1) | 3 | 08.01.83 | **Derby County** (D2) | A | L | 0-2 | |
| 1983-84 | (D1) | 3 | 07.01.84 | **Southampton** (D1) | H | L | 1-2 | Hart |

| | | | | | | | | |
|---|---|---|---|---|---|---|---|---|
| 1984-85 | (D1) | 3 | 06.01.85 | **Newcastle Utd** (D1) | H | D | 1-1 | Bowyer |
| | | 3r | 09.01.85 | **Newcastle Utd** | A | W | 3-1aet | Davenport (p), Bowyer, Christie |
| | | 4 | 26.01.85 | **Wimbledon** (D2) | H | D | 0-0 | |
| | | 4r | 30.01.85 | **Wimbledon** | A | L | 0-1 | |
| 1985-86 | (D1) | 3 | 04.01.86 | **Blackburn Rovers** (D2) | H | D | 1-1 | Birtles |
| | | 3r | 13.01.86 | **Blackburn Rovers** | A | L | 2-3 | Walsh, Birtles |
| 1986-87 | (D1) | 3 | 11.01.87 | **Crystal Palace** (D2) | A | L | 0-1 | |
| 1987-88 | (D1) | 3 | 09.01.88 | **Halifax Town** (D4) | A | W | 4-0 | Wilson, Pearce, Plummer, Wilkinson |
| | | 4 | 30.01.88 | **Leyton Orient** (D4) | A | W | 2-1 | Glover, Plummer |
| | | 5 | 20.02.88 | **Birmingham City** (D2) | A | W | 1-0 | Crosby |
| | | 6 | 12.03.88 | **Arsenal** (D1) | A | W | 2-1 | Wilkinson, Rice |
| | | SF | 09.04.88 | **Liverpool** (D1) | | L | 1-2 | Clough |
| | | | | *played at Hillsborough* | | | | |
| 1988-89 | (D1) | 3 | 07.01.89 | **Ipswich Town** (D2) | H | W | 3-0 | Yallop og, Gaynor, Chapman |
| | | 4 | 28.01.89 | **Leeds Utd** (D2) | H | W | 2-0 | Chapman, Parker |
| | | 5 | 19.02.89 | **Watford** (D2) | A | W | 3-0 | Webb, Chapman, Laws |
| | | 6 | 18.03.89 | **Manchester Utd** (D1) | A | W | 1-0 | Parker |
| | | SF | 15.04.89 | **Liverpool** (D1) | | - | 0-0ab | |
| | | | | *Played at Hillsborough – The Hillsborough Disaster. Abandoned after six minutes as the scale of the disaster unfolded. Ninety-six Liverpool fans died as a result of the tragedy.* | | | | |
| | | SF | 07.05.89 | **Liverpool** | | L | 1-3 | Webb |
| | | | | *played at Old Trafford* | | | | |
| 1989-90 | (D1) | 3 | 07.01.90 | **Manchester Utd** (D1) | H | L | 0-1 | |
| 1990-91 | (D1) | 3 | 06.01.91 | **Crystal Palace** (D1) | A | D | 0-0 | |
| | | 3r | 21.01.91 | **Crystal Palace** | H | D | 2-2aet | Wilson, Pearce |
| | | 3 2r | 28.01.91 | **Crystal Palace** | H | W | 3-0 | Parker 2, Crosby |
| | | 4 | 13.02.91 | **Newcastle Utd** (D2) | A | D | 2-2 | Pearce, Clough |
| | | 4r | 18.02.91 | **Newcastle Utd** | H | W | 3-0 | Clough, Hodge, Parker |
| | | 5 | 25.02.91 | **Southampton** (D1) | A | D | 1-1 | Hodge |
| | | 5r | 04.03.91 | **Southampton** | H | W | 3-1 | Jemson 3 (1p) |
| | | 6 | 09.03.91 | **Norwich City** (D1) | A | W | 1-0 | Keane |
| | | SF | 14.04.91 | **West Ham Utd** (D2) | | W | 4-0 | Crosby, Keane, Pearce, Charles |
| | | | | *played at Villa Park* | | | | |
| | | F | 18.05.91 | **Tottenham Hotspur** (D1) | | L | 1-2aet | Pearce |
| | | | | *played at Wembley Stadium* | | | | |
| 1991-92 | (D1) | 3 | 04.01.92 | **Wolverhampton W** (D2) | H | W | 1-0 | Clough |
| | | 4 | 26.01.92 | **Hereford Utd** (D4) | H | W | 2-0 | Pearce, Sheringham |
| | | 5 | 15.02.92 | **Bristol City** (D2) | H | W | 4-1 | Llewellyn og, Clough, Pearce, Sheringham |
| | | 6 | 07.03.92 | **Portsmouth** (D2) | A | L | 0-1 | |
| 1992-93 | (PL) | 3 | 03.01.93 | **Southampton** (PL) | H | W | 2-1 | Keane, Webb |
| | | 4 | 23.01.93 | **Middlesbrough** (PL) | H | D | 1-1 | Webb |
| | | 4r | 03.02.93 | **Middlesbrough** | A | W | 3-0 | Bannister, Clough, Wilson |
| | | 5 | 13.02.93 | **Arsenal** (PL) | A | L | 0-2 | |
| 1993-94 | (D1) | 3 | 08.01.94 | **Sheffield Wed** (PL) | A | D | 1-1 | Cooper |
| | | 3r | 19.01.94 | **Sheffield Wed** | H | L | 0-2 | |
| 1994-95 | (PL) | 3 | 07.01.95 | **Plymouth Argyle** (D2) | H | W | 2-0 | Collymore, Gemmill |
| | | 4 | 28.01.95 | **Crystal Palace** (PL) | H | L | 1-2 | Bohinen |
| 1995-96 | (PL) | 3 | 06.01.96 | **Stoke City** (D1) | A | D | 1-1 | Pearce |
| | | 3r | 17.01.96 | **Stoke City** | H | W | 2-0 | Campbell, Pearce (p) |
| | | 4 | 07.02.96 | **Oxford Utd** (D2) | H | D | 1-1 | Campbell |
| | | 4r | 13.02.96 | **Oxford Utd** | A | W | 3-0 | Campbell, Woan (p), Silenzi |
| | | 5 | 19.02.96 | **Tottenham Hotspur** (PL) | H | - | 0-0ab | |
| | | | | *abandoned after 15 minutes – blizzard* | | | | |
| | | 5 | 28.02.96 | **Tottenham Hotspur** | H | D | 2-2 | Woan 2 |
| | | 5r | 09.03.96 | **Tottenham Hotspur** | A | D | 1-1aet | Roy |
| | | | | *Nottingham Forest won 3-1 on penalties* | | | | |
| | | 6 | 13.03.96 | **Aston Villa** (PL) | H | L | 0-1 | |
| 1996-97 | (PL) | 3 | 04.01.97 | **Ipswich Town** (D1) | H | W | 3-0 | Saunders 2, Allen |
| | | 4 | 26.01.97 | **Newcastle Utd** (PL) | A | W | 2-1 | Woan 2 |
| | | 5 | 15.02.97 | **Chesterfield** (D2) | A | L | 0-1 | |

| | | | | | | | |
|---|---|---|---|---|---|---|---|
| 1997-98 (D1) | 3 | 03.01.98 | **Charlton Athletic** (D1) | A | L | 1-4 | Van Hooijdonk |
| 1998-99 (PL) | 3 | 02.01.99 | **Portsmouth** (D1) | H | L | 0-1 | |
| 1999-00 (D1) | 3 | 10.12.99 | **Oxford Utd** (D2) | H | D | 1-1 | Freedman |
| | 3r | 08.01.00 | **Oxford Utd** | A | W | 3-1 | Bart-Williams 2 (1p), Rogers |
| | 4 | 19.01.00 | **Chelsea** (PL) | A | L | 0-2 | |
| 2000-01 (D1) | 3 | 06.01.01 | **Wolverhampton W** (D1) | H | L | 0-1 | |
| 2001-02 (D1) | 3 | 05.01.02 | **Sheffield Utd** (D1) | A | L | 0-1 | |
| 2002-03 (D1) | 3 | 04.01.03 | **West Ham Utd** (PL) | A | L | 2-3 | Harewood, Reid |

# NOTTS COUNTY

*Formed 1862, the oldest club in the Football League. FA Cup winners: 1894. Runners-up: 1891. Record FA Cup win: 15-0 v Thornhill Utd (later Rotherham Town), 1st round, 24.10.1885; Record FA Cup defeat: 1-8 v Newcastle United, 3rd round, 08.01.1927. Henry 'Harry' Cursham is the all-time record FA Cup goalscorer with 49 goals for Notts County between 1877 and 1889. He scored 48 in the Competition Proper and one in the qualifying competition against Staveley in 1888-89.*

| | | | | | | | |
|---|---|---|---|---|---|---|---|
| 1877-78 | 1 | 03.11.77 | **Sheffield FC** | H | D | 1-1 | HA Cursham |
| | 1r | 01.12.77 | **Sheffield FC** | A | L | 0-3 | |
| 1878-79 | 1 | 16.11.78 | **Nottingham Forest** | H | L | 1-3aet | Owen |
| 1879-80 | 1 | 08.11.79 | **Nottingham Forest** | A | L | 0-4 | |
| 1880-81 | 1 | 04.11.80 | **Derbyshire FC** | H | D | 4-4 | AW Curhsam, HA Cursham 2, AN Other |
| | 1r | 27.11.80 | **Derbyshire FC** | A | W | 4-2 | HA Cursham 2, Greenhalgh, Morse |
| | 2 | | bye | | | | |
| | 3 | 12.02.81 | **Aston Villa** | H | L | 1-3 | CL Cursham |
| 1881-82 | 1 | | Birmingham Calthorpe | | | - | |
| | | | *Birmingham Calthorpe scratched. Notts County walkover.* | | | | |
| | 2 | 24.11.81 | **Wednesbury Strollers** | H | W | 5-2 | HA Cursham 2, AW Cursham 2, Knowles og |
| | | | *FA ordered replay after protest* | | | | |
| | 2r | 10.12.81 | **Wednesbury Strollers** | | W | 11-1 | HA Cursham 6, CL Cursham, CF Dobson, AW Cursham 2, Bausor |
| | | | *played at Derby Cricket Ground* | | | | |
| | 3 | 31.12.81 | **Aston Villa** | A | D | 2-2aet | Bausor 2 |
| | 3r | 07.01.82 | **Aston Villa** | H | D | 2-2aet | Chapman, AW Cursham |
| | 3 2r | 14.01.82 | **Aston Villa** | A | L | 1-4 | HA Cursham |
| 1882-83 | 1 | 04.11.82 | **Sheffield FC** | H | W | 6-1 | AW Curhsam 3, HA Cursham 2, Smith |
| | 2 | | bye | | | | |
| | 3 | 27.12.82 | **Phoenix Bessemer** | H | W | 4-1 | Gunn 2, AW Cursham, HA Cursham |
| | 4 | 12.02.83 | **Sheffield Wed** | A | W | 4-1 | AW Cursham 2, HA Cursham, Smith |
| | 5 | 03.03.83 | **Aston Villa** | H | W | 4-3 | HA Cursham 3, Gunn |
| | SF | 17.03.83 | **Old Etonians** | | L | 1-2 | HA Cursham |
| | | | *played at Kennington Oval* | | | | |
| 1883-84 | 1 | 10.11.83 | **Sheffield Heeley** | H | W | 3-1 | HA Cursham 3 |
| | 2 | 01.12.83 | **Nottingham Forest** | H | W | 3-0 | Dixon, AW Cursham, CF Dobson |
| | 3 | 15.12.83 | **Grantham Town** | A | W | 4-0 | HA Cursham 2, AW Cursham, Macrae |
| | 4 | 19.01.84 | **Bolton Wanderers** | H | D | 2-2aet | AW Cursham, Macrae |
| | 4r | 02.02.84 | **Bolton Wanderers** | A | W | 2-1 | CF Dobson 2 |
| | 5 | 09.02.84 | **Swifts** | H | D | 1-1aet | HA Cursham |
| | 5r | 14.02.84 | **Swifts** | A | W | 1-0 | HA Cursham |
| | SF | 01.03.84 | **Blackburn Rovers** | | L | 0-1 | |
| | | | *played at Aston Lower Grounds, Birmingham* | | | | |
| 1884-85 | 1 | 08.11.84 | **Notts Olympic** | H | W | 2-0 | Dixon, Emmitt |
| | 2 | 06.12.84 | **Staveley** | A | W | 2-0 | Gunn, HA Cursham |
| | 3 | 03.01.85 | **Sheffield FC** | H | W | 5-0 | HA Cursham, CF Dobson, Gunn, Jackson, Marshall |
| | 4 | 24.01.85 | **Walsall Swifts** | A | W | 4-0 | Jackson 2, Brown, Gunn |
| | 5 | | bye | | | | |
| | 6 | 21.02.85 | **Queen's Park, Glasgow** | H | D | 2-2 | HA Cursham, Gunn |
| | 6r | 28.02.85 | **Queen's Park, Glasgow** | | L | 1-2 | Jackson |
| | | | *played at Derby Cricket Ground* | | | | |

| | | | | | | | | |
|---|---|---|---|---|---|---|---|---|
| 1885-86 | | 1 | 24.10.85 | **Rotherham Town** | H | W | 15-0 | HA Cursham 4, Jackson 3, Daft 2, A Moore 2, CF Dobson, Emmitt, Gunn, RJ Brown og |
| | | 2 | 21.11.85 | **Sheffield FC** | H | W | 8-0 | Gunn 3, Jackson 3, HA Cursham, Daft |
| | | 3 | 12.12.85 | **Notts Rangers** | H | W | 3-0 | HA Cursham 3 |
| | | 4 | | bye | | | | |
| | | 5 | 23.01.86 | **South Shore** | A | L | 1-2 | Emmitt |
| 1886-87 | | 1 | 30.10.86 | **Basford Rovers** | H | W | 13-0 | Burton 5, Daft 5, HA Cursham, Jackson, Slater og |
| | | 2 | 13.11.86 | **Notts Rangers** | H | D | 3-3 | Burton, HA Cursham, Jackson |
| | | 2r | 20.11.86 | **Notts Rangers** | A | W | 5-0 | HA Cursham 3, Burton, Jackson |
| | | 3 | 11.12.86 | **Staveley** | A | W | 3-0 | HA Cursham, Jackson, Emmitt |
| | | 4 | | bye | | | | |
| | | 5 | 29.01.87 | **Marlow** | H | W | 5-2 | HA Cursham 3, Jackson, Speller og |
| | | 6 | 19.02.87 | **WBA** | H | L | 1-2 | HA Cursham |
| 1887-88 | | 1 | 15.10.87 | **Lincoln Ramblers** | H | W | 9-0 | Daft 3, Moore 3, Jackson 2, Gunn |
| | | 2 | | Basford Rovers | | | - | |
| | | | | *Basford Rovers scratched. Notts County walkover.* | | | | |
| | | 3 | 26.11.87 | **Nottingham Forest** | A | L | 1-2 | Gunn |
| 1888-89 | (D1) | | | 1q Eckington (H) 4-1; 2q Beeston St Johns (H) 4-2; 3q Derby Midland (H) 2-1; 4q Staveley (A) 3-1 | | | | |
| | | 1 | 02.02.89 | **Old Brightonians** | H | W | 2-0 | C Shelton, Moore |
| | | 2 | 16.02.89 | **Sheffield Wed** | A | L | 2-3 | A Shelton, Snook |
| 1889-90 | (D1) | 1 | 18.01.90 | **Birmingham St G** (FAll) | A | D | 4-4 | John Oswald 2, Daft, McInnes |
| | | 1r | 25.01.90 | **Birmingham St G** | H | W | 6-2 | May 2, McInnes 2, Daft, John Oswald |
| | | 2 | 01.02.90 | **Aston Villa** (D1) | H | W | 4-1 | May 3, James Oswald |
| | | 3 | 15.02.90 | **Sheffield Wed** (FAll) | A | L | 0-5 | |
| | | | | *FA ordered replay after protest* | | | | |
| | | 3r | 22.02.90 | **Sheffield Wed** | H | W | 3-2 | Daft, John Oswald, W Smith |
| | | | | *FA ordered second replay after protest* | | | | |
| | | 3 2r | 03.03.90 | **Sheffield Wed** | | L | 1-2 | McInnes |
| | | | | *played at Derby Racecourse Ground* | | | | |
| 1890-91 | (D1) | 1 | 17.01.91 | **Sheffield Utd** (ML) | A | W | 9-1 | McGregor 4, Oswald 2, Daft, Locker, McInnes |
| | | 2 | 31.01.91 | **Burnley** (D1) | H | W | 2-1 | Daft 2 |
| | | 3 | 14.02.91 | **Stoke** (FAll) | H | W | 1-0 | Locker |
| | | SF | 28.02.91 | **Sunderland** (D1) | | D | 3-3 | McGregor,McInnes, Oswald |
| | | | | *played at Bramall Lane* | | | | |
| | | SFr | 11.03.91 | **Sunderland** | | W | 2-0 | Oswald 2 |
| | | | | *played at Bramall Lane* | | | | |
| | | F | 21.03.91 | **Blackburn Rovers** (D1) | | L | 1-3 | Oswald |
| | | | | *played at Kennington Oval* | | | | |
| 1891-92 | (D1) | 1 | 16.01.92 | **Sunderland** (D1) | A | L | 0-3 | |
| | | | | *FA ordered replay after protest about dangerous, icy pitch* | | | | |
| | | 1r | 23.01.92 | **Sunderland** | A | L | 0-4 | |
| 1892-93 | (D1) | 1 | 21.01.93 | **Shankhouse** | H | W | 4-0 | McInnes 2, Oswald 2 |
| | | 2 | 04.02.93 | **Middlesbrough Iron** (NL) | A | L | 2-3 | Burke, Walkerdine |
| 1893-94 | (D2) | 1 | 27.01.94 | **Burnley** (D1) | H | W | 1-0 | Logan |
| | | 2 | 10.02.94 | **Burton Wanderers** (ML) | A | W | 2-1 | Donnelly, Logan |
| | | 3 | 24.02.94 | **Nottingham Forest** (D1) | A | D | 1-1 | Bruce |
| | | 3r | 03.03.94 | **Nottingham Forest** | H | W | 4-1 | Bruce 2, Donnelly, Logan |
| | | SF | 10.03.94 | **Blackburn Rovers** (D1) | | W | 1-0 | Daft |
| | | | | *played at Bramall Lane* | | | | |
| | | F | 31.03.94 | **Bolton Wanderers** (D1) | | W | 4-1 | Logan 3, Watson |
| | | | | *played at Goodison Park* | | | | |
| 1894-95 | (D2) | 1 | 02.02.95 | **Sheffield Wed** (D1) | A | L | 1-5 | Allsopp |
| 1895-96 | (D1) | 1 | 01.02.96 | **Wolverhampton W** (D1) | A | D | 2-2 | Bull 2 |
| | | 1r | 05.02.96 | **Wolverhampton W** | H | L | 3-4 | Allan, Allsopp, Bull |
| 1896-97 | (D2) | 1 | 30.01.97 | **Small Heath** (D2) | A | W | 2-1 | Allan, Boucher |
| | | 2 | 13.02.97 | **Aston Villa** (D1) | A | L | 1-2 | Murphy |
| 1897-98 | (D1) | 1 | 29.01.98 | **Wolverhampton W** (D1) | H | L | 0-1 | |

| | | | | | | | | |
|---|---|---|---|---|---|---|---|---|
| 1898-99 | (D1) | 1 | 28.01.99 | **Kettering Town** (ML) | H | W | 2-0 | Maconnachie, Fletcher |
| | | 2 | 11.02.99 | **Southampton** (SL) | H | L | 0-1 | |
| 1899-00 | (D1) | 1 | 27.01.00 | **Chorley** (LL) | H | W | 6-0 | Ball, Bull, Chalmers, Goss, Macconachie, McMain |
| | | 2 | 10.02.00 | **Bury** (D1) | H | D | 0-0 | |
| | | 2r | 14.02.00 | **Bury** | A | L | 0-2 | |
| 1900-01 | (D1) | 1 | 09.02.01 | **Liverpool** (D1) | H | W | 2-0 | Morris 2 |
| | | 2 | 23.02.01 | **Wolverhampton W** (D1) | H | L | 2-3 | Morris, Warner |
| 1901-02 | (D1) | 1 | 25.01.02 | **Reading** (SL) | H | L | 1-2 | Lewis |
| 1902-03 | (D1) | 1 | 07.02.03 | **Southampton** (SL) | H | D | 0-0 | |
| | | 1r | 11.02.03 | **Southampton** | A | D | 2-2 | Gee 2 |
| | | 1 2r | 16.02.03 | **Southampton** | | W | 2-1aet | Green, Humphreys |
| | | | | *played at St Andrews* | | | | |
| | | 2 | 21.02.03 | **Grimsby Town** (D1) | A | W | 2-0 | Green, Humphreys |
| | | 3 | 07.03.03 | **Bury** (D1) | A | L | 0-1 | |
| 1903-04 | (D1) | 1 | 06.02.04 | **Manchester Utd** (D2) | H | D | 3-3 | Ross, Humphreys, Bonthron og |
| | | 1r | 10.02.04 | **Manchester Utd** | A | L | 1-2 | Green |
| 1904-05 | (D1) | 1 | 04.02.05 | **Bury** (D1) | A | L | 0-1 | |
| 1905-06 | (D1) | 1 | 13.01.06 | **Sunderland** (D1) | A | L | 0-1 | |
| 1906-07 | (D1) | 1 | 12.01.07 | **Preston North End** (D1) | H | W | 1-0 | Matthews |
| | | 2 | 02.02.07 | **Burslem PV** (D2) | A | D | 2-2 | Matthews, Humphreys |
| | | 2r | 06.02.07 | **Burslem PV** | H | W | 5-0 | Emberton, Matthews 2, Humphreys, Jones |
| | | 3 | 23.02.07 | **Tottenham Hotspur** (SL) | H | W | 4-0 | Dean 2, Matthews, Humphreys |
| | | 4 | 09.03.07 | **WBA** (D2) | A | L | 1-3 | Jones |
| 1907-08 | (D1) | 1 | 11.01.08 | **Middlesbrough** (D1) | H | W | 2-0 | Jones 2 |
| | | 2 | 01.02.08 | **Bolton Wanderers** (D1) | H | D | 1-1 | Matthews |
| | | 2r | 05.02.08 | **Bolton Wanderers** | A | L | 1-2aet | Tarplin |
| 1908-09 | (D1) | 1 | 16.01.09 | **Blackburn Rovers** (D1) | H | L | 0-1 | |
| 1909-10 | (D1) | 1 | 15.01.10 | **Bradford City** (D1) | A | L | 2-4 | Jones 2 |
| 1910-11 | (D1) | 1 | 14.01.11 | **Swindon Town** (SL) | A | L | 1-3 | Dean |
| 1911-12 | (D1) | 1 | 13.01.12 | **Luton Town** (SL) | A | W | 4-2 | Matthews, Cantrell, Richards, Waterall |
| | | 2 | 03.02.12 | **Swindon Town** (SL) | A | L | 0-2 | |
| 1912-13 | (D1) | 1 | 11.01.13 | **Bristol Rovers** (SL) | A | L | 0-2 | |
| 1913-14 | (D2) | 1 | 10.01.14 | **Sheffield Wed** (D1) | A | L | 2-3 | Flint, Peart |
| 1914-15 | (D1) | 1 | 09.01.15 | **Bolton Wanderers** (D1) | A | L | 1-2 | Richards |
| 1919-20 | (D1) | 1 | 10.01.20 | **Millwall Athletic** (SL) | H | W | 2-0 | Hill, McLeod |
| | | 2 | 31.01.20 | **Middlesbrough** (D1) | H | W | 1-0 | Cook |
| | | 3 | 23.02.20 | **Bradford Park A** (D1) | H | L | 3-4 | Gibson, McLeod, Henshall |
| 1920-21 | (D2) | 1 | 08.01.21 | **WBA** (D1) | H | W | 3-0 | Took, Stevens 2 |
| | | 2 | 29.01.21 | **Aston Villa** (D1) | H | D | 0-0 | |
| | | 2r | 02.02.21 | **Aston Villa** | A | L | 0-1 | |
| 1921-22 | (D2) | 1 | 07.01.22 | **Grimsby Town** (3N) | A | D | 1-1 | Hill |
| | | 1r | 12.01.22 | **Grimsby Town** | H | W | 3-0 | Cook, Hill, Henshall |
| | | 2 | 28.01.22 | **Bradford City** (D1) | A | D | 1-1 | Widdowson |
| | | 2r | 01.02.22 | **Bradford City** | H | D | 0-0aet | |
| | | 2 3r | 06.02.22 | **Bradford City** | | W | 1-0 | Widdowson |
| | | | | *played at Bramall Lane* | | | | |
| | | 3 | 18.02.22 | **WBA** (D1) | A | D | 1-1 | Widdowson |
| | | 3r | 22.02.22 | **WBA** | H | W | 2-0 | Cook, Hill |
| | | 4 | 04.03.22 | **Aston Villa** (D1) | H | D | 2-2 | Chipperfield 2 |
| | | 4r | 08.03.22 | **Aston Villa** | A | W | 4-3 | Cook, Widdowson, Hill, Chipperfield |
| | | SF | 25.03.22 | **Huddersfield Town** (D1) | | L | 1-3 | Hill |
| | | | | *played at Turf Moor* | | | | |
| 1922-23 | (D2) | 1 | 13.01.23 | **Plymouth Argyle** (3S) | A | D | 0-0 | |
| | | 1r | 17.01.23 | **Plymouth Argyle** | H | L | 0-1 | |
| 1923-24 | (D1) | 1 | 12.01.24 | **QPR** (3S) | A | W | 2-1 | Pape, Price |
| | | 2 | 02.02.24 | **Crystal Palace** (D2) | A | D | 0-0 | |
| | | 2r | 06.02.24 | **Crystal Palace** | H | D | 0-0aet | |
| | | 2 2r | 11.02.24 | **Crystal Palace** | | D | 0-0aet | |
| | | | | *played at Villa Park* | | | | |

| | | | | | | | |
|---|---|---|---|---|---|---|---|
| | 2 3r | 18.02.24 | **Crystal Palace**<br>*played at Villa Park* | | L | 1-2 | Widdowson |
| 1924-25 (D1) | 1 | 10.01.25 | **Coventry City** (D2) | A | W | 2-0 | Cock, Davis |
| | 2 | 31.01.25 | **Norwich City** (3S) | H | W | 4-0 | Davis 2, Cook, Barry |
| | 3 | 21.02.25 | **Cardiff City** (D1) | H | L | 0-2 | |
| 1925-26 (D1) | 3 | 09.01.26 | **Leicester City** (D1) | H | W | 2-0 | Widdowson, Taylor |
| | 4 | 30.01.26 | **New Brighton** (3N) | H | W | 2-0 | Harris 2 |
| | 5 | 20.02.26 | **Fulham** (D2) | H | L | 0-1 | |
| 1926-27 (D2) | 3 | 08.01.27 | **Newcastle Utd** (D1) | A | L | 1-8 | Widdowson |
| 1927-28 (D2) | 3 | 14.01.28 | **Sheffield Utd** (D1) | H | L | 2-3 | Taylor, Mills |
| 1928-29 (D2) | 3 | 12.01.29 | **Derby County** (D1) | A | L | 3-4 | Andrews 2, Haden |
| 1929-30 (D2) | 3 | 11.01.30 | **West Ham Utd** (D1) | A | L | 0-4 | |
| 1930-31 (3S) | 1 | 29.11.30 | **Chesterfield** (3N) | A | W | 2-1 | Fenner, Taylor |
| | 2 | 13.12.30 | **Doncaster Rovers** (3N) | A | W | 1-0 | Bowman og |
| | 3 | 10.01.31 | **Swansea Town** (D2) | H | W | 3-1 | Andrews 2, Keetley |
| | 4 | 24.01.31 | **Sheffield Utd** (D1) | A | L | 1-4 | Keetley |
| 1931-32 (D2) | 3 | 09.01.32 | **Bristol City** (D2) | H | D | 2-2 | Keetley 2 |
| | 3r | 13.01.32 | **Bristol City** | A | L | 2-3 | Hall, Andrews |
| 1932-33 (D2) | 3 | 14.01.33 | **Tranmere Rovers** (3N) | A | L | 1-2 | Corkhill |
| 1933-34 (D2) | 3 | 13.01.34 | **Swansea Town** (D2) | A | L | 0-1 | |
| 1934-35 (D2) | 3 | 12.01.35 | **Wolverhampton W** (D1) | A | L | 0-4 | |
| 1935-36 (3S) | 1 | 30.11.35 | **Grantham Town** (ML) | A | W | 2-0 | Green, Fallon |
| | 2 | 14.12.35 | **Torquay Utd** (3S) | H | W | 3-0 | Rickard, Fallon, R Hunt og |
| | 3 | 11.01.36 | **Tranmere Rovers** (3N) | H | D | 0-0 | |
| | 3r | 15.01.36 | **Tranmere Rovers** | A | L | 3-4 | Chandler, Richards, Steele |
| 1936-37 (3S) | 1 | 28.11.36 | **Gateshead AFC** (3N) | A | L | 0-2 | |
| 1937-38 (3S) | 3 | 08.01.38 | **Aldershot** (3S) | A | W | 3-1 | Rickard, Chalmers, Gallagher |
| | 4 | 22.01.38 | **Huddersfield Town** (D1) | A | L | 0-1 | |
| 1938-39 (3S) | 3 | 07.01.39 | **Burnley** (D2) | H | W | 3-1 | Cooper 2, Clayton |
| | 4 | 21.01.39 | **Walsall** (3S) | H | D | 0-0 | |
| | 4r | 26.01.39 | **Walsall** | A | L | 0-4 | |
| 1945-46 (3S) | 1 1L | 17.11.45 | **Bradford City** (3N) | H | D | 2-2 | I McPherson, Hubbard |
| | 1 2L | 24.11.45 | **Bradford City** | A | W | 2-1 | I McPherson, Parker |
| | 2 1L | 08.12.45 | **Northampton Town** (3S) | A | L | 1-3 | I McPherson |
| | 2 2L | 15.12.45 | **Northampton Town** | H | W | 1-0 | Martin |
| 1946-47 (3S) | 1 | 30.11.46 | **Leyton Orient** (3S) | A | W | 2-1 | Cumner, Jayes |
| | 2 | 14.12.46 | **Swindon Town** (3S) | H | W | 2-1 | Sewell, Fallon |
| | 3 | 11.01.47 | **Luton Town** (D2) | A | L | 0-6 | |
| 1947-48 (3S) | 1 | 29.11.47 | **Horsham** (SCL) | H | W | 9-1 | Lawton 3, Sewell 3, Marsh 2, Freeman |
| | 2 | 13.12.47 | **Stockton** (NEL) | H | D | 1-1aet | Sewell |
| | 2r | 20.12.47 | **Stockton**<br>*played at Ayresome Park* | | W | 4-1 | Lawton 3, Cumner |
| | 3 | 10.01.48 | **Birmingham City** (D2) | A | W | 2-0 | Corkhill, Marsh |
| | 4 | 24.01.48 | **Swindon Town** (3S) | A | L | 0-1 | |
| 1948-49 (3S) | 1 | 27.11.48 | **Port Vale** (3S) | H | W | 2-1 | Lawton 2 |
| | 2 | 11.12.48 | **Barrow** (3N) | H | W | 3-2 | Lawton, Johnston 2 |
| | 3 | 08.01.49 | **Plymouth Argyle** (D2) | A | W | 1-0aet | Sewell |
| | 4 | 29.01.49 | **Liverpool** (D1) | A | L | 0-1 | |
| 1949-50 (3S) | 1 | 26.11.49 | **Tilbury** (Lon) | H | W | 4-0 | Lawton, Sewell, Broome 2 |
| | 2 | 10.12.49 | **Rochdale** (3N) | A | W | 2-1 | Johnston, Lawton |
| | 3 | 07.01.50 | **Burnley** (D1) | H | L | 1-4 | Johnston |
| 1950-51 (D2) | 3 | 06.01.51 | **Southampton** (D2) | H | L | 3-4 | Broome, Leuty, Simpson |
| 1951-52 (D2) | 3 | 12.01.52 | **Stockton** (NEL) | H | W | 4-0 | Broome 2, McCormack, Lawton |
| | 4 | 02.02.52 | **Portsmouth** (D1) | H | L | 1-2 | Lawton |
| 1952-53 (D2) | 3 | 10.01.53 | **Leicester City** (D2) | A | W | 4-2 | Crookes, Broome, McPherson 2 |
| | 4 | 31.01.53 | **Bolton Wanderers** (D1) | A | D | 1-1 | K McPherson |
| | 4r | 05.02.53 | **Bolton Wanderers** | H | D | 2-2aet | Jackson, K McPherson |
| | 4 2r | 09.02.53 | **Bolton Wanderers**<br>*played at Hillsborough* | | L | 0-1 | |
| 1953-54 (D2) | 3 | 09.01.54 | **Everton** (D2) | A | L | 1-2 | Wylie |
| 1954-55 (D2) | 3 | 08.01.55 | **Middlesbrough** (D2) | A | W | 4-1 | Broadbent, Wylie 2, Wills |

| | | | | | | | | |
|---|---|---|---|---|---|---|---|---|
| | | 4 | 29.01.55 | **Sheffield Wed** (D1) | A | D | 1-1 | Conwell og |
| | | 4r | 03.02.55 | **Sheffield Wed** | H | W | 1-0aet | Jackson |
| | | 5 | 19.02.55 | **Chelsea** (D1) | H | W | 1-0 | Broadbent |
| | | 6 | 12.03.55 | **York City** (3N) | H | L | 0-1 | |
| 1955-56 | (D2) | 3 | 07.01.56 | **Fulham** (D2) | H | L | 0-1 | |
| 1956-57 | (D2) | 3 | 05.01.57 | **Rhyl** (CC) | H | L | 1-3 | P Bircumshaw |
| 1957-58 | (D2) | 3 | 04.01.58 | **Tranmere Rovers** (3N) | H | W | 2-0 | Tucker (p), Jackson |
| | | 4 | 25.01.58 | **Bristol City** (D2) | H | L | 1-2 | Pritchard |
| 1958-59 | (D3) | 1 | 15.11.58 | **Barrow** (D4) | H | L | 1-2 | P Bircumshaw |
| 1959-60 | (D4) | 1 | 14.11.59 | **Hastings Utd** (SL) | A | W | 2-1 | P Bircumshaw 2 |
| | | 2 | 05.12.59 | **Bath City** (SL) | H | L | 0-1 | |
| 1960-61 | (D3) | 1 | 05.11.60 | **Aldershot** (D4) | A | L | 0-2 | |
| 1961-62 | (D3) | 1 | 04.11.61 | **Yeovil Town** (SL) | H | W | 4-2 | Withers 2, Hateley, P Bircumshaw |
| | | 2 | 25.11.61 | **Margate** (SL) | A | D | 1-1 | Loxley |
| | | 2r | 30.11.61 | **Margate** | H | W | 3-1 | P Bircumshaw 2, Hateley |
| | | 3 | 06.01.62 | **Manchester City** (D1) | H | L | 0-1 | |
| 1962-63 | (D3) | 1 | 03.11.62 | **Peterborough Utd** (D3) | H | L | 0-3 | |
| 1963-64 | (D3) | 1 | 16.11.63 | **Frickley Colliery** (CC) | H | W | 2-1 | Astle, Tait |
| | | 2 | 07.12.63 | **Doncaster Rovers** (D4) | A | D | 1-1 | Bly |
| | | 2r | 10.12.63 | **Doncaster Rovers** | H | L | 1-2 | Tait |
| 1964-65 | (D4) | 1 | 14.11.64 | **Chelmsford City** (SL) | H | W | 2-0 | Raynor, Cavanagh |
| | | 2 | 05.12.64 | **Brentford** (D3) | A | L | 0-4 | |
| 1965-66 | (D4) | 1 | 13.11.65 | **Southend Utd** (D3) | A | L | 1-3 | Sheridan |
| 1966-67 | (D4) | 1 | 26.11.66 | **Oldham Athletic** (D3) | A | L | 1-3 | Marshall |
| 1967-68 | (D4) | 1 | 09.12.67 | **Runcorn** (CC) | A | L | 0-1 | |
| 1968-69 | (D4) | 1 | 16.11.68 | **Doncaster Rovers** (D4) | A | L | 0-1 | |
| 1969-70 | (D4) | 1 | 15.11.69 | **Rotherham Utd** (D3) | H | L | 0-3 | |
| 1970-71 | (D4) | 1 | 21.11.70 | **Port Vale** (D3) | H | W | 1-0 | Crickmore (p) |
| | | 2 | 12.12.70 | **Bury** (D3) | A | D | 1-1 | Nixon |
| | | 2r | 21.12.70 | **Bury** | H | W | 3-0 | Hateley, Crickmore, Needham |
| | | 3 | 02.01.71 | **Leicester City** (D2) | A | L | 0-2 | |
| 1971-72 | (D3) | 1 | 20.11.71 | **Newport County** (D4) | H | W | 6-0 | Hateley, Cozens, Bradd, Nixon, Stubbs, Carlin |
| | | 2 | 11.12.71 | **S Shields (1936)** (NPL) | A | W | 3-1 | Masson, Cozens, Bradd |
| | | 3 | 15.01.72 | **Watford** (D2) | A | W | 4-1 | Nixon, Cozens 2, Masson |
| | | 4 | 05.02.72 | **Derby County** (D1) | A | L | 0-6 | |
| 1972-73 | (D3) | 1 | 18.11.72 | **Altrincham** (NPL) | A | W | 1-0 | Randall (p) |
| | | 2 | 09.12.72 | **Lancaster City** (NPL) | H | W | 2-1 | Randall (p), Bradd |
| | | 3 | 13.01.73 | **Sunderland** (D2) | H | D | 1-1 | Bradd |
| | | 3r | 16.01.73 | **Sunderland** | A | L | 0-2 | |
| 1973-74 | (D2) | 3 | 05.01.74 | **WBA** (D2) | A | L | 0-4 | |
| 1974-75 | (D2) | 3 | 03.01.75 | **Portsmouth** (D2) | H | W | 3-1 | Needham, Randall 2 |
| | | 4 | 24.01.75 | **QPR** (D1) | A | L | 0-3 | |
| 1975-76 | (D2) | 3 | 03.01.76 | **Leeds Utd** (D1) | H | L | 0-1 | |
| 1976-77 | (D2) | 3 | 08.01.77 | **Arsenal** (D1) | H | L | 0-1 | |
| 1977-78 | (D2) | 3 | 07.01.78 | **Charlton Athletic** (D2) | A | W | 2-0 | Vintner 2 |
| | | 4 | 31.01.78 | **Brighton** (D2) | A | W | 2-1 | Vintner 2 |
| | | 5 | 18.02.78 | **Millwall** (D2) | A | L | 1-2 | Chapman |
| 1978-79 | (D2) | 3 | 09.01.79 | **Reading** (D4) | H | W | 4-2 | Vintner, Hooks, Mann, Masson |
| | | 4 | 27.01.79 | **Arsenal** (D1) | A | L | 0-2 | |
| 1979-80 | (D2) | 3 | 05.01.80 | **Wolverhampton W** (D1) | H | L | 1-3 | Hunt |
| 1980-81 | (D2) | 3 | 03.01.81 | **Blackburn Rovers** (D2) | H | W | 2-1 | Manns, Christie |
| | | 4 | 24.01.81 | **Peterborough Utd** (D4) | H | L | 0-1 | |
| 1981-82 | (D1) | 3 | 05.01.82 | **Aston Villa** (D1) | H | L | 0-6 | |
| 1982-83 | (D1) | 3 | 08.01.83 | **Leicester City** (D2) | A | W | 3-2 | Justin Fashanu 2, McCulloch |
| | | 4 | 29.01.83 | **Middlesbrough** (D2) | A | L | 0-2 | |
| 1983-84 | (D1) | 3 | 08.01.84 | **Bristol City** (D4) | H | D | 2-2 | Christie 2 (1p) |
| | | 3r | 10.01.84 | **Bristol City** | A | W | 2-0 | Kilcline, McCulloch |
| | | 4 | 01.02.84 | **Huddersfield Town** (D2) | A | W | 2-1 | Kilcline, Harkouk |
| | | 5 | 18.02.84 | **Middlesbrough** (D2) | H | W | 1-0 | Chiedozie |
| | | 6 | 10.03.84 | **Everton** (D1) | H | L | 1-2 | Chiedozie |

| | | | | | | | | |
|---|---|---|---|---|---|---|---|---|
| 1984-85 | (D2) | 3 | 05.01.85 | **Grimsby Town** (D2) | H | D | 2-2 | McParland 2 |
| | | 3r | 08.01.85 | **Grimsby Town** | A | L | 2-4 | Harkouk, Wilkinson og |
| 1985-86 | (D3) | 1 | 17.11.85 | **Scarborough** (APL) | H | W | 6-1 | Hunt, Harkouk 3, Young, McParland |
| | | 2 | 07.12.85 | **Wrexham** (D4) | H | D | 2-2 | Waitt 2 |
| | | 2r | 10.12.85 | **Wrexham** | A | W | 3-0 | Clarke, Waitt, McParland |
| | | 3 | 13.01.86 | **Stoke City** (D2) | A | W | 2-0 | Waitt, McParland |
| | | 4 | 25.01.86 | **Tottenham Hotspur** (D1) | H | D | 1-1 | McParland |
| | | 4r | 29.01.86 | **Tottenham Hotspur** | A | L | 0-5 | |
| 1986-87 | (D3) | 1 | 15.11.86 | **Carlisle Utd** (D3) | H | D | 1-1 | Davis |
| | | 1r | 18.11.86 | **Carlisle Utd** | A | W | 3-0 | Young, McParland 2 |
| | | 2 | 07.12.86 | **Middlesbrough** (D3) | H | L | 0-1 | |
| 1987-88 | (D3) | 1 | 15.11.87 | **Chesterfield** (D3) | H | D | 3-3 | Kevan, McParland, Birtles |
| | | 1r | 17.11.87 | **Chesterfield** | A | W | 1-0 | Pike (p) |
| | | 2 | 05.12.87 | **Port Vale** (D3) | A | L | 0-2 | |
| 1988-89 | (D3) | 1 | 19.11.88 | **Darlington** (D4) | A | W | 2-1 | Thorpe, Pike |
| | | 2 | 10.12.88 | **Hartlepool Utd** (D4) | A | L | 0-1 | |
| 1989-90 | (D3) | 1 | 18.11.89 | **Doncaster Rovers** (D4) | A | L | 0-1 | |
| 1990-91 | (D2) | 3 | 05.01.91 | **Hull City** (D2) | A | W | 5-2 | Buckley og, Turner, O'Riordan, Bartlett, Lund |
| | | 4 | 26.01.91 | **Oldham Athletic** (D2) | H | W | 2-0 | Turner, Craig Short |
| | | 5 | 16.02.91 | **Manchester City** (D1) | H | W | 1-0 | Lund |
| | | 6 | 10.03.91 | **Tottenham Hotspur** (D1) | A | L | 1-2 | O'Riordan |
| 1991-92 | (D1) | 3 | 05.01.92 | **Wigan Athletic** (D3) | H | W | 2-0 | T Johnson, Turner |
| | | 4 | 04.02.92 | **Blackburn Rovers** (D2) | H | W | 2-1 | Lund, Draper |
| | | 5 | 15.02.92 | **Norwich City** (D1) | A | L | 0-3 | |
| 1992-93 | (D1) | 3 | 12.01.93 | **Sunderland** (D1) | H | L | 0-2 | |
| 1993-94 | (D1) | 3 | 08.01.94 | **Sutton Utd** (IL) | H | W | 3-2 | M Draper, Agana, Devlin |
| | | 4 | 29.01.94 | **West Ham Utd** (PL) | H | D | 1-1 | Lund |
| | | 4r | 09.02.94 | **West Ham Utd** | A | L | 0-1aet | |
| 1994-95 | (D1) | 3 | 08.01.95 | **Manchester City** (PL) | H | D | 2-2 | Matthews, White |
| | | 3r | 18.01.95 | **Manchester City** | A | L | 2-5 | McSwegan, Matthews |
| 1995-96 | (D2) | 1 | 12.11.95 | **York City** (D2) | A | W | 1-0 | Legg |
| | | 2 | 02.12.95 | **Telford Utd** (Conf) | A | W | 2-0 | Gallagher, Legg |
| | | 3 | 06.01.96 | **Middlesbrough** (PL) | H | L | 1-2 | Rogers |
| 1996-97 | (D2) | 1 | 17.11.96 | **Newcastle Town** (NWC) | A | W | 2-0 | Kennedy, Robinson |
| | | | | *played at the Victoria Ground, Stoke* | | | | |
| | | 2 | 07.12.96 | **Rochdale** (D3) | H | W | 3-1 | Jones, Arkins, Agana |
| | | 3 | 14.01.97 | **Aston Villa** (PL) | H | D | 0-0 | |
| | | 3r | 22.01.97 | **Aston Villa** | A | L | 0-3 | |
| 1997-98 | (D3) | 1 | 16.11.97 | **Colwyn Bay** (NPL) | H | W | 2-0 | Hogg, Richardson |
| | | 2 | 06.12.97 | **Preston North End** (D2) | A | D | 2-2 | Finnan, Derry |
| | | 2r | 16.12.97 | **Preston North End** | H | L | 1-2aet | Farrell |
| 1998-99 | (D2) | 1 | 15.11.98 | **Hendon** (IL) | A | D | 0-0 | |
| | | 1r | 01.12.98 | **Hendon** | H | W | 3-0 | Owers, Jones 2 |
| | | 2 | 05.12.98 | **Wigan Athletic** (D2) | H | D | 1-1 | Jones |
| | | 2r | 15.12.98 | **Wigan Athletic** | A | D | 0-0aet | |
| | | | | *Notts County won 4-2 on penalties* | | | | |
| | | 3 | 02.01.99 | **Sheffield Utd** (D1) | A | D | 1-1 | Jones |
| | | 3r | 23.01.99 | **Sheffield Utd** | H | L | 3-4aet | Jones 2, Murray |
| 1999-00 | (D2) | 1 | 30.10.99 | **Bournemouth** (D2) | H | D | 1-1 | Rapley |
| | | 1r | 09.11.99 | **Bournemouth** | A | L | 2-4 | Redmile, Tierney |
| 2000-01 | (D2) | 1 | 08.12.00 | **Gravesend & N** (IL) | A | W | 2-1 | Stallard, Hughes |
| | | 2 | 12.12.00 | **Wigan Athletic** (D2) | A | D | 1-1 | Stallard |
| | | 2r | 19.12.00 | **Wigan Athletic** | H | W | 2-1aet | Liburd 2 |
| | | 3 | 06.01.01 | **Wimbledon** (PL) | A | D | 2-2 | Hughes, Stallard |
| | | 3r | 27.01.01 | **Wimbledon** | H | L | 0-1aet | |
| 2001-02 | (D2) | 1 | 17.11.01 | **Cambridge Utd** (D3) | A | D | 1-1 | Allsopp |
| | | 1r | 27.11.01 | **Cambridge Utd** | H | W | 2-0 | Allsopp, Owers |
| | | 2 | 08.12.01 | **Wycombe W** (D2) | A | L | 0-3 | |
| 2002-03 | (D2) | 1 | 16.11.02 | **Southport** (Conf) | A | L | 2-4 | Allsopp 2 |

## NOTTS OLYMPIC

*Formed 1884. Entered FA Cup: 1894-95 – 1895-96. Played at Churchville Fields. In 1892-93 were founder members of the Midland Alliance.*

| | | | | | | | |
|---|---|---|---|---|---|---|---|
| 1884-85 | 1 | 08.11.84 | **Notts County** | A | L | 0-2 | |
| 1885-86 | 1 | 31.10.85 | **Notts Wanderers** | H | D | 2-2 | |
| | 1r | 07.11.85 | **Notts Wanderers** | A | W | 4-1 | |
| | 2 | 21.11.85 | **Nottingham Forest** | A | L | 1-4 | |
| 1886-87 | 1 | 30.10.86 | **Nottingham Forest** | A | L | 0-3 | |
| 1887-88 | 1 | 15.10.87 | **Mellors Ltd** | H | L | 3-6aet | |
| | | | *FA ordered replay after protest* | | | | |
| | 1r | 22.10.87 | **Mellors Ltd** | H | L | 1-2 | |

## NOTTS RANGERS

*Formed 1868. Entered FA Cup: 1884-85 – 1914-15. Played at an enclosure near Nottingham Castle. In 1889-90 were founder members of the Midland League.*

| | | | | | | | |
|---|---|---|---|---|---|---|---|
| 1884-85 | 1 | 08.11.84 | **Staveley** | A | L | 1-4 | H Shelton |
| 1885-86 | 1 | 31.10.85 | **Lockwood Bros** | A | D | 2-2 | |
| | 1r | 07.11.85 | **Lockwood Bros** | H | W | 4-0 | |
| | 2 | 21.11.85 | **Sheffield Heeley** | A | W | 6-1 | Hodder 3, Stokes 2, Saddler |
| | 3 | 12.12.85 | **Notts County** | A | L | 0-3 | |
| 1886-87 | 1 | 30.10.86 | **Sheffield FC** | A | W | 3-0 | Hodder 2, Geary |
| | 2 | 13.11.86 | **Notts County** | A | D | 3-3 | Archer, Hodder, May |
| | 2r | 20.11.86 | **Notts County** | H | L | 0-5 | |
| 1887-88 | 1 | 15.10.87 | **Jardines FC** | H | W | 10-1 | |
| | 2 | 05.11.87 | **Grantham Town** | H | W | 4-0 | |
| | 3 | | bye | | | | |
| | 4 | 17.12.87 | **Darwen** | A | L | 1-2 | Partington |
| 1888-89 | 1 | 02.02.89 | **Sheffield Wed** | H | D | 1-1 | James |
| | 1r | 09.02.89 | **Sheffield Wed** | A | L | 0-3 | |

## NOTTS SWIFTS

| | | | | | | | |
|---|---|---|---|---|---|---|---|
| 1887-88 | 1 | 15.10.87 | **Nottingham Forest** | A | L | 1-2 | Daft |

## NOTTS WANDERERS

| | | | | | | |
|---|---|---|---|---|---|---|
| 1884-85 | 1 | 08.11.84 | **Sheffield Heeley** | A | L | 0-1 |
| 1885-86 | 1 | 31.10.85 | **Notts Olympic** | A | D | 2-2 |
| | 1r | 07.11.85 | **Notts Olympic** | H | L | 1-4 |

## NUNEATON BOROUGH

*Formed 1937. First entered FA Cup: 1945-46. League clubs beaten: Watford, Swansea (2), Oxford United, Stoke City. Members of The Conference.*

| | | | | | | | |
|---|---|---|---|---|---|---|---|
| 1949-50 (BC) | 1 | 26.11.49 | **King's Lynn** (ECL) | H | W | 2-1 | Plant 2 |
| | 2 | 10.12.49 | **Mossley** (CC) | H | D | 0-0 | |
| | 2r | 17.12.49 | **Mossley** | A | W | 3-0 | Black 2, Plant |
| | 3 | 07.01.50 | **Exeter City** (3S) | A | L | 0-3 | |
| 1953-54 (BDL) | 1 | 21.11.53 | **Watford** (3S) | H | W | 3-0 | Wright 2, Jessop |
| | 2 | 12.12.53 | **QPR** (3S) | A | D | 1-1 | Davies |
| | 2r | 17.12.53 | **QPR** | H | L | 1-2 | Morrow |
| 1954-55 (BDL) | 1 | 20.11.54 | **Brentford** (3S) | A | L | 1-2 | Jessop |
| 1966-67 (SL) | 1 | 26.11.66 | **Wealdstone** (IL) | A | W | 2-0 | Richards, Cutler |
| | 2 | 07.01.67 | **Swansea Town** (D3) | H | W | 2-0 | Crawley, Coughlin og |
| | 3 | 28.01.67 | **Rotherham Utd** (D2) | H | D | 1-1 | Cutler |
| | 3r | 31.01.67 | **Rotherham Utd** | A | L | 0-1 | |
| 1967-68 (SL) | 1 | 09.12.67 | **Exeter City** (D4) | H | D | 0-0 | |
| | 1r | 13.12.67 | **Exeter City** | A | D | 0-0aet | |
| | 1 2r | 18.12.67 | **Exeter City** | | L | 0-1 | |
| | | | *played at Ashton Gate, Bristol* | | | | |
| 1971-72 (SL) | 1 | 20.11.71 | **Torquay Utd** (D3) | A | L | 0-1 | |
| 1972-73 (SL) | 1 | 18.11.72 | **Telford Utd** (SL) | A | L | 2-3 | Gill, Harris |
| 1974-75 (SL) | 1 | 23.11.74 | **Maidstone Utd** (SL) | H | D | 2-2 | Briscoe, Lewis |
| | 1r | 26.11.74 | **Maidstone Utd** | A | L | 0-2 | |
| 1975-76 (SL) | 1 | 22.11.75 | **Wimbledon** (SL) | H | L | 0-1 | |
| 1976-77 (SL) | 1 | 20.11.76 | **Crook Town** (NL) | A | W | 4-1 | Jones 2, Briscoe, White og |

| | | | | | | | | |
|---|---|---|---|---|---|---|---|---|
| | | 2 | 11.12.76 | **Lincoln City** (D3) | A | L | 0-6 | |
| 1977-78 | (SL) | 1 | 26.11.77 | **Oxford Utd** (D3) | H | W | 2-0 | Lang, Phillips (p) |
| | | 2 | 17.12.77 | **Tilbury** (IL) | H | L | 1-2 | Vincent |
| 1978-79 | (SL) | 1 | 25.11.78 | **Crewe Alexandra** (D4) | H | L | 0-2 | |
| 1979-80 | (APL) | 1 | 24.11.79 | **Northwich V** (NPL) | H | D | 3-3 | Pugh 3 |
| | | 1r | 26.11.79 | **Northwich V** | A | L | 0-3 | |
| 1981-82 | (SL) | 1 | 21.11.81 | **Bishop Auckland** (NL) | A | L | 1-4 | Jones |
| 1984-85 | (APL) | 1 | 17.11.84 | **Scunthorpe Utd** (D4) | H | D | 1-1 | Hill |
| | | 1r | 20.11.84 | **Scunthorpe Utd** | A | L | 1-2aet | Culpin |
| 1985-86 | (APL) | 1 | 16.11.85 | **Burnley** (D4) | H | L | 2-3 | Bennyworth, Murphy |
| 1986-87 | (APL) | 1 | 15.11.86 | **Rochdale** (D4) | H | L | 0-3 | |
| 1992-93 | (SL) | 1 | 14.11.92 | **Woking** (Conf) | A | L | 2-3 | Bullock, Culpin |
| 1993-94 | (SL) | 1 | 13.11.93 | **Swansea City** (D2) | A | D | 1-1 | Shearer |
| | | 1r | 23.11.93 | **Swansea City** | H | W | 2-1aet | Simpson 2 |
| | | 2 | 04.12.93 | **Bournemouth** (D2) | A | D | 1-1 | Green |
| | | 2r | 15.12.93 | **Bournemouth** | H | L | 0-1 | |
| 1995-96 | (SL) | 1 | 11.11.95 | **Barrow** (NPL) | A | L | 1-2 | Simpson |
| 2000-01 | (Conf) | 1 | 18.11.00 | **Stoke City** (D2) | A | D | 0-0 | |
| | | 1r | 21.11.00 | **Stoke City** | H | W | 1-0 | McGregor |
| | | 2 | 09.12.00 | **Bournemouth** (D2) | A | L | 0-3 | |

## NUNHEAD

*Formed 1890. Entered FA Cup: 1905-06 – 1918-19. Folded 1942. They have a curious claim to FA Cup fame. Their 9-0 win over Kingstonian is the joint-highest victory by one Non-League side over another since the competition was re-organised in 1925. They share the record with Bath City – who equalled it when they beat Nunhead 9-0 in 1931.*

| | | | | | | | | |
|---|---|---|---|---|---|---|---|---|
| 1926-27 | (IL) | 1 | 27.11.26 | **Kingstonian** (AL) | H | W | 9-0 | Daniels 3, Hill 2, Sanders 2, Booker, Colwell |
| | | 2 | 11.12.26 | **Poole Town** (SL) | H | L | 1-2 | Colwell |
| 1929-30 | (IL) | 1 | 30.11.29 | **Bristol Rovers** (3S) | H | L | 0-2 | |
| 1931-32 | (IL) | 1 | 28.11.31 | **Bath City** (SL) | A | L | 0-9 | |
| 1935-36 | (IL) | 1 | 30.11.35 | **Watford** (3S) | H | L | 2-4 | Read, Aislatt |

## OLD BRIGHTONIANS

*Formed 1871. One of a number of clubs based around the Dulwich area that used The Greyhound pub as their base.*

| | | | | | | | |
|---|---|---|---|---|---|---|---|
| 1884-85 | 1 | 08.11.84 | **Swifts** | A | L | 0-3 | |
| 1885-86 | 1 | 31.10.85 | **Acton** | H | W | 2-1 | |
| | 2 | 21.11.85 | **Old Westminsters** | A | L | 0-3 | |
| 1886-87 | 1 | 30.10.86 | **Clapham Rovers** | A | W | 6-0 | |
| | 2 | 16.11.86 | **Old Westminsters** | H | D | 1-1 | |
| | 2r | 20.11.86 | **Old Westminsters** | A | L | 0-3 | |
| 1887-88 | 1 | 08.10.87 | **Swindon Town** | H | W | 1-0 | N Leete |
| | 2 | 05.11.87 | **Old Harrovians** | A | W | 4-0 | |
| | 3 | 24.11.87 | **Old Carthusians** | A | L | 0-5 | |
| 1888-89 | 1 | 02.02.89 | **Notts County** (D1) | A | L | 0-2 | |

## OLD CARTHUSIANS

*Formed 1875. Entered FA Cup: 1879-80 – 1891-92. FA Cup winners: 1881. FA Amateur Cup winners: 1894 (first winners), 1897. Runners-up: 1895. Old Carthusians and Wimbledon are the only clubs to have won both the FA Cup and the FA Amateur Cup.*

| | | | | | | | |
|---|---|---|---|---|---|---|---|
| 1879-80 | 1 | 08.11.79 | **Acton** | A | W | 4-0 | |
| | 2 | 10.01.80 | **Wanderers** | A | L | 0-1 | |
| 1880-81 | 1 | 23.10.80 | **Saffron Walden** | H | W | 7-0 | Parry 4, Growse, Richards, AN Other |
| | 2 | 11.12.80 | **Dreadnought FC** | H | W | 5-1 | Jenner 3, Richards 2 |
| | 3 | | bye | | | | |
| | 4 | 19.02.81 | **Royal Engineers** | H | W | 2-0 | Wynyard, Price |
| | 5 | 19.03.81 | **Clapham Rovers** | H | W | 3-1aet | Page 2, Parry |
| | SF | 26.03.81 | **Darwen** *played at Kennington Oval* | | W | 4-1 | Hansell, Todd, Vincent, Wynyard |
| | F | 09.04.81 | **Old Etonians** *played at Kennington Oval* | | W | 3-0 | Wynyard, Parry, Todd |
| 1881-82 | 1 | 05.11.81 | **Esher Leopold** | H | W | 5-0 | |
| | 2 | 03.12.81 | **Barnes** | H | W | 7-1 | Page 2, Parry 2, Wynyard 2, Richards |
| | 3 | 20.12.81 | **Royal Engineers** | H | L | 0-2 | |

| | | | | | | | |
|---|---|---|---|---|---|---|---|
| 1882-83 | 1 | 21.10.82 | **Pilgrims** | H | W | 6-0 | Parry 3, Last, Page, Wilson |
| | 2 | 02.12.82 | **Etonian Ramblers** | H | W | 7-0 | |
| | 3 | 16.12.82 | **Old Westminsters** | H | W | 3-2 | Page 2, Parry |
| | 4 | 25.01.83 | **Royal Engineers** | H | W | 6-2 | Parry 3, Cobbold 2, Page |
| | 5 | 20.02.83 | **Clapham Rovers** | H | W | 5-3 | Cobbold, Last, Page, Richards, AN Other |
| | SF | 17.03.83 | **Blackburn Olympic** *played at Whalley Range, Manchester* | | L | 0-4 | |
| 1883-84 | 1 | 10.11.83 | **Reading Minster** | A | W | 10-1 | Parry 5, Last 2, Escombe, King-Harman, AN Other 1 |
| | 2 | 24.11.83 | **Old Foresters** | H | L | 2-7 | Cobbold, Hansell |
| 1884-85 | 1 | 08.11.84 | **Acton** | A | W | 7-1 | |
| | 2 | 06.12.84 | **Marlow** | H | W | 5-3 | Cobbold 2, Last, Smith, AN Other |
| | 3 | | bye | | | | |
| | 4 | 24.01.85 | **Grimsby Town** | H | W | 3-0 | Cobbold, Parry, own goal |
| | 5 | 07.02.85 | **Chatham** | A | W | 3-0 | Barmby 2, Hansell |
| | 6 | 14.02.85 | **Church FC** | A | W | 1-0 | Parry |
| | SF | 07.03.85 | **Blackburn Rovers** *played at Trent Bridge, Nottingham* | | L | 1-5 | Barmby |
| 1885-86 | 1 | 31.10.85 | **Chatham** | A | W | 2-0 | |
| | 2 | 21.11.85 | **Upton Park** | H | W | 6-0 | |
| | 3 | | bye | | | | |
| | 4 | | bye | | | | |
| | 5 | 23.01.86 | **WBA** | A | L | 0-1 | |
| 1886-87 | 1 | 23.10.86 | **Reading** | H | W | 2-1 | Escombe, Smith |
| | 2 | 13.11.86 | **Crusaders** | H | W | 4-2 | |
| | 3 | | London Caledonians *London Caledonians scratched – Old Carthusians walkover* | | | - | |
| | 4 | | bye | | | | |
| | 5 | 05.02.87 | **Leek** | A | W | 2-0 | |
| | 6 | 02.03.87 | **Preston North End** | H | L | 1-2aet | Cobbold |
| 1887-88 | 1 | 15.10.87 | **Hanover Utd** | H | W | 5-0 | Price 3, Waddington, White |
| | 2 | 05.11.87 | **Watford Rovers** | A | W | 3-1 | Price 3 |
| | 3 | 24.11.87 | **Old Brightonians** | H | W | 5-0 | Parry 2, Currey, Escombe, Price |
| | 4 | | bye | | | | |
| | 5 | 07.01.88 | **Bootle** | H | W | 2-0 | Cobbold 2 |
| | 6 | 28.01.88 | **WBA** | A | L | 2-4 | Price 2 |
| 1888-89 | 1 | 02.02.89 | **Wolverhampton W** (D1) | A | L | 3-4 | Currey 2, Leman |
| 1889-90 | 1 | 18.01.90 | **Wolverhampton W** | A | L | 0-2 | |

# OLD ETONIANS

*Formed 1865. Entered FA Cup: 1873-74 – 1892-93. FA Cup winners: 1879, 1882. Runners-up: 1876, 1881, 1883.*

| | | | | | | | |
|---|---|---|---|---|---|---|---|
| 1873-74 | 1 | | High Wycombe *Old Etonians scratched High Wycombe walkover* | | | - | |
| 1874-75 | 1 | 05.11.74 | **Swifts** | A | D | 0-0 | |
| | 1r | 14.11.74 | **Swifts** | H | D | 1-1 | Bonsor |
| | 1 2r | 26.11.74 | **Swifts** | H | W | 3-0 | |
| | 2 | | bye | | | | |
| | 3 | 23.01.75 | **Maidenhead** | H | W | 1-0 | |
| | SF | 27.02.75 | **Shropshire Wanderers** *played at Kennington Oval* | | W | 1-0 | Bonsor |
| | F | 13.03.75 | **Royal Engineers** *played at Kennington Oval* | | D | 1-1 | Bonsor |
| | Fr | 16.03.75 | **Royal Engineers** *played at Kennington Oval* | | L | 0-2 | |
| 1875-76 | 1 | 09.11.75 | **Pilgrims** | H | W | 4-1 | Bonsor, A Lyttleton, Patton, Wilson |
| | 2 | 14.11.75 | **Maidenhead** | H | W | 8-0 | Patton 3, Thompson 2, Courthorpe, Griffith, og |
| | 3 | 29.01.76 | **Clapham Rovers** | H | W | 1-0 | Bonsor |
| | SF | 19.02.76 | **Oxford University** *played at Kennington Oval* | | W | 1-0 | Sturgis |
| | F | 11.03.76 | **Wanderers** *played at Kennington Oval* | | D | 1-1 | Bonsor |

| | | | | | | | |
|---|---|---|---|---|---|---|---|
| | Fr | 18.03.76 | **Wanderers** | | L | 0-3 | |
| | | | *played at Kennington Oval* | | | | |
| 1876-77 | 1 | | Barnes | | | - | |
| | | | *Barnes walkover Old Etonians scratched* | | | | |
| 1877-78 | | | did not enter | | | | |
| 1878-79 | 1 | 09.11.78 | **Wanderers** | A | W | 7-2 | Calvert, Goodhart, Lyttleton, Novelli 2, Sedwick, og |
| | 2 | 18.12.78 | **Reading** | A | W | 1-0 | |
| | 3 | 11.01.79 | **Minerva** | H | W | 5-2 | Sturgis 3, Goodhart 2 |
| | 4 | 13.02.79 | **Darwen** | H | D | 5-5 | Goodhart 3, Christian, Whitfield |
| | | | *played at Kennington Oval* | | | | |
| | 4r | 08.03.79 | **Darwen** | H | D | 2-2aet | Clerke, Whitfield |
| | | | *played at Kennington Oval* | | | | |
| | 4 2r | 15.03.79 | **Darwen** | H | W | 6-2 | Goodhart 2, Sedgwick 2, Clerke, Whitfield |
| | | | *played at Kennington Oval* | | | | |
| | SF | 22.03.79 | **Nottingham Forest** | | W | 2-1 | Whitfield, Clerke |
| | | | *played at Kennington Oval* | | | | |
| | F | 29.03.79 | **Clapham Rovers** | | W | 1-0 | Clerke |
| | | | *played at Kennington Oval* | | | | |
| 1879-80 | 1 | | Barnes | | | - | |
| | | | *Old Etonians walkover. Barnes scratched* | | | | |
| | 2 | | bye | | | | |
| | 3 | 24.01.80 | **Wanderers** | H | W | 3-1 | Goodhart 2, Sedgwick |
| | 4 | 07.02.80 | **West End** | H | W | 5-1 | Goodhart 3, Kinnaird 2 |
| | 5 | 21.02.80 | **Clapham Rovers** | A | L | 0-1 | |
| 1880-81 | 1 | 06.11.80 | **Brentwood** | A | W | 10-0 | Goodhart 3, Whitfield 2, others 5 |
| | 2 | 04.12.80 | **Hendon (1874)** | A | W | 2-0 | Novelli, Whitfield |
| | 3 | 05.02.81 | **Herts Rangers** | A | W | 3-0 | Anderson, Chevallier, Macauley |
| | 4 | 19.02.81 | **Grey Friars** | H | W | 4-0 | |
| | 5 | 19.03.81 | **Stafford Road** | A | W | 2-1 | Anderson, AN Other |
| | SF | | bye | | | | |
| | F | 09.04.81 | **Old Carthusians** | | L | 0-3 | |
| | | | *played at Kennington Oval* | | | | |
| 1881-82 | 1 | 05.11.81 | **Clapham Rovers** | H | D | 2-2 | Goodhart, MacAuley |
| | 1r | 19.11.81 | **Clapham Rovers** | A | W | 1-0 | |
| | 2 | | bye | | | | |
| | 3 | 17.12.81 | **Swifts** | H | W | 3-0 | Dunn 2, MacAuley |
| | 4 | 14.01.82 | **Maidenhead** | H | W | 6-3 | Chitty 2, Anderson, MacAuley, Foley, AN Other |
| | 5 | | bye | | | | |
| | SF | 04.03.82 | **Marlow** | | W | 5-0 | Goodhart 3, Dunn, MacAuley |
| | | | *played at Kennington Oval* | | | | |
| | F | 25.03.82 | **Blackburn Rovers** | | W | 1-0 | Anderson |
| | | | *played at Kennington Oval* | | | | |
| 1882-83 | 1 | 04.11.82 | **Old Foresters** | H | D | 1-1 | Anderson |
| | 1r | 18.11.82 | **Old Foresters** | H | W | 3-1 | Anderson, Dunn, Goodhart |
| | 2 | 02.12.82 | **Brentwood** | H | W | 2-1 | Anderson, Whitfield |
| | 3 | 16.12.82 | **Rochester** | H | W | 7-0 | |
| | 4 | 24.01.83 | **Swifts** | H | W | 2-0 | Goodhart 2 |
| | 5 | 03.02.83 | **Hendon (1874)** | A | W | 4-2 | |
| | SF | 17.03.83 | **Notts County** | | W | 2-1 | MacAuley, Anderson |
| | | | *played at Kennington Oval* | | | | |
| | F | 31.03.83 | **Blackburn Olympic** | | L | 1-2aet | Goodhart |
| | | | *played at Kennington Oval* | | | | |
| 1883-84 | 1 | 10.11.83 | **Hendon (1874)** | A | L | 2-3 | |
| 1884-85 | 1 | 08.11.84 | **Luton Wanderers** | A | W | 3-1 | Chevallier 2, Whitfield |
| | 2 | 06.12.84 | **Brentwood** | A | D | 2-2 | Bury, Goodhart |
| | 2r | 20.12.84 | **Brentwood** | H | W | 6-1 | Chevallier 2, Dunn, French, Goodhart, og |
| | 3 | | bye | | | | |
| | 4 | 24.01.85 | **Middlesbrough** | H | W | 5-2 | Goodhart 3, Chevallier, Marchant |
| | 6 | 21.02.85 | **Nottingham Forest** | H | L | 0-2 | |

| | | | | | | | |
|---|---|---|---|---|---|---|---|
| 1885-86 | 1 | | Bournemouth Rovers | | | - | |
| | | | *Bournemouth Rovers scratched. Old Etonians walkover* | | | | |
| | 2 | 21.11.85 | **Marlow** | A | L | 1-6 | |
| 1886-87 | 1 | 30.10.86 | **Royal Engineers** | H | W | 1-0 | |
| | 2 | 20.11.86 | **Chesham Generals** | A | W | 7-1 | |
| | 3 | 11.12.86 | **Old Westminsters** | A | L | 0-3 | |
| 1887-88 | 1 | 08.10.87 | **Lancing Old Boys** | H | W | 4-2 | |
| | 2 | 05.11.87 | **Old St Marks** | H | W | 3-2 | |
| | 3 | 26.11.87 | **Old Westminsters** | H | W | 7-2 | |
| | 4 | 17.12.87 | **Nottingham Forest** | A | L | 0-6 | |

# OLD FORESTERS

*Formed 1876. Entered FA Cup: 1877-78 – 1888-89. Based at Snaresbrook, Essex. Essex Senior Cup winners 1885, 1886, 1887. London Senior Cup winners 1885, 1894.*

| | | | | | | | |
|---|---|---|---|---|---|---|---|
| 1877-78 | 1 | | Old Wykehamists | | | - | |
| | | | *Old Wykehamists scratched. Old Foresters walkover* | | | | |
| | 2 | 15.12.77 | **Oxford University** | A | L | 0-1 | |
| 1878-79 | 1 | 09.11.78 | **Royal Engineers** | A | L | 0-3 | |
| 1879-80 | 1 | 08.11.79 | **Hendon (1874)** | A | D | 1-1 | |
| | 1r | 15.11.79 | **Hendon (1874)** | H | D | 2-2 | Day, J Guy |
| | 1 2r | 22.11.79 | **Hendon (1874)** | A | L | 1-3 | |
| 1880-81 | 1 | 06.11.80 | **Swifts** | A | D | 1-1 | |
| | 1r | 20.11.80 | **Swifts** | H | L | 1-2 | Woolley |
| 1881-82 | 1 | 05.11.81 | **Morton Rangers** | H | W | 3-0 | |
| | 2 | 03.12.81 | **Pilgrims** | H | W | 3-1 | |
| | 3 | | bye | | | | |
| | 4 | 21.01.82 | **Royal Engineers** | H | W | 2-1 | Burrows, Matthews |
| | 5 | 14.02.82 | **Marlow** | H | D | 0-0 | |
| | 5r | 18.02.82 | **Marlow** | A | L | 0-1 | |
| 1882-83 | 1 | 04.11.82 | **Old Etonians** | A | D | 1-1 | Fairclough |
| | 1r | 18.11.82 | **Old Etonians** | A | L | 1-3 | Knowles |
| 1883-84 | 1 | 10.11.83 | **Dreadnought FC** | H | W | 2-1 | J Guy, Horner |
| | 2 | 24.11.83 | **Old Carthusians** | A | W | 7-2 | Horner 3, R Guy, others 3 |
| | 3 | | bye | | | | |
| | 4 | 19.01.84 | **Swifts** | A | L | 1-2 | Fairclough |
| 1884-85 | 1 | 01.11.84 | **Hoddesdon Town** | H | W | 8-0 | |
| | 2 | 29.11.84 | **Hanover Utd** | A | L | 1-2 | |
| 1885-86 | 1 | 31.10.85 | **Royal Engineers** | A | W | 5-1 | |
| | 2 | 21.11.85 | **Old Harrovians** | A | L | 1-2 | |
| 1886-87 | 1 | | Cannon FC | | | - | |
| | | | *Cannon scratched. Old Foresters walkover* | | | | |
| | 2 | | bye | | | | |
| | 3 | 11.12.86 | **Chatham** | A | W | 4-1 | |
| | 4 | 15.01.87 | **Swifts** | A | W | 2-0 | Horner, Newbery |
| | 5 | 29.01.87 | **Preston North End** | H | L | 0-3 | |
| 1887-88 | 1 | 15.10.87 | **London Caledonians** | A | W | 6-1 | |
| | 2 | 05.11.87 | **Marlow** | A | W | 3-2aet | |
| | 3 | | bye | | | | |
| | 4 | 17.12.87 | **Grimsby Town** | H | W | 4-2 | H Guy 2, R Guy, Johnson |
| | 5 | 07.01.88 | **Middlesbrough** | A | L | 0-4 | |
| | | | *FA ordered replay after protest but Old Foresters scratched rather than travel back to Middlesbrough. Middlesbrough walkover* | | | | |

# OLD HARROVIANS

*Formed 1872. Entered FA Cup: 1876-77 – 1892-93. FA Cup semi-finalists 1878.*

| | | | | | | | |
|---|---|---|---|---|---|---|---|
| 1876-77 | 1 | 04.11.76 | **Royal Engineers** | A | L | 1-2 | H Longman |
| 1877-78 | 1 | 07.11.77 | **105th Regiment** | A | W | 2-0 | Bevington, Betts |
| | 2 | 22.12.77 | **1st Surrey Rifles** | H | W | 6-0 | Bevington 2, Prior 2, Colbeck, Hadow |
| | 3 | 02.02.78 | **Cambridge University** | H | D | 2-2 | Bevington, Greaves |
| | 3r | 09.02.78 | **Cambridge University** | A | D | 2-2aet | Colbeck, Harvey |
| | 3 2r | 16.02.78 | **Cambridge University** | | W | 2-0 | Lowis, Prior |

| | | | | | | | |
|---|---|---|---|---|---|---|---|
| | 4 | 09.03.78 | **Upton Park** | H | W | 3-1 | Betts 2, Colbeck |
| | SF | 16.03.78 | **Royal Engineers** | | L | 1-2 | Prior |
| | | | *played at Kennington Oval* | | | | |
| 1878-79 | 1 | 02.11.78 | **Southall Park** | H | W | 8-0 | Howell 2, Lowis 2, Prior 2, Colbeck, Davidson |
| | 2 | 21.12.78 | **Panthers** | H | W | 3-0 | Prior 2, AN Other |
| | 3 | 18.01.79 | **Nottingham Forest** | H | L | 0-2 | |
| 1879-80 | 1 | 08.11.79 | **Finchley** | A | W | 2-1 | |
| | 2 | | bye | | | | |
| | 3 | 04.02.80 | **Royal Engineers** | A | L | 0-2 | |
| 1880-81 | 1 | 13.11.80 | **Maidenhead** | A | D | 0-0 | |
| | 1r | 20.11.80 | **Maidenhead** | H | L | 0-1 | |
| 1881-82 | 1 | 05.11.81 | **Olympic FC** | H | W | 4-2 | |
| | 2 | 03.12.81 | **Swifts** | A | L | 1-7 | Gray |
| 1885-86 | 1 | | St James's | | | - | |
| | | | *St James's scratched. Old Harrovians walkover* | | | | |
| | 2 | 21.11.85 | **Old Foresters** | H | W | 2-1 | |
| | 3 | | Swifts | | | - | |
| | | | *FA disqualifed Old Harrovians. Swifts walkover* | | | | |
| 1886-87 | 1 | 30.10.86 | **Old Westminsters** | H | L | 0-4 | |
| 1887-88 | 1 | 15.10.87 | **Hendon (1874)** | A | W | 4-2 | |
| | 2 | 05.11.87 | **Old Brightonians** | H | L | 0-4 | |

## OLD PHILBERDIANS

*Based in Maidenhead Entered the FA Cup once but never played a match Joint-winners of the Berks and Bucks Senior Cup with Swifts 1879-80.*

| | | | | | | | |
|---|---|---|---|---|---|---|---|
| 1880-81 | 1 | | Pilgrims | | | - | |
| | | | *Old Philberdians scratched – Pilgrims walkover* | | | | |

## OLD SALOPIANS

*Entered the FA Cup once but never played a match.*

| | | | | | | | |
|---|---|---|---|---|---|---|---|
| 1876-77 | 1 | | Oxford University | | | - | |
| | | | *Old Salopians scratched – Oxford University walkover* | | | | |

## OLD ST MARKS

*Formed 1885. Entered FA Cup: 1887-88 – 1892-93. Based in south west London and used The Limes ground at Barnes as their home pitch.*

| | | | | | | | |
|---|---|---|---|---|---|---|---|
| 1887-88 | 1 | 15.10.87 | **East Sheen** | H | W | 7-2 | |
| | 2 | 05.11.87 | **Old Etonians** | A | L | 2-3 | |

## OLD WESTMINSTERS

*Formed 1870 and played in and around the London area. Entered FA Cup: 1882-83 – 1893-94. FA Cup quarter-finalists 1884, 1886, 1887. London Senior Cup winners 1887 (joint with Casuals), 1888, 1890, 1892, 1893.*

| | | | | | | | |
|---|---|---|---|---|---|---|---|
| 1882-83 | 1 | 04.11.82 | **Maidenhead** | H | W | 2-0 | Allington, Bury |
| | 2 | | bye | | | | |
| | 3 | 16.12.82 | **Old Carthusians** | A | L | 2-3 | Bury, Sandwith |
| 1883-84 | 1 | 03.11.83 | **Chatham** | H | W | 3-0 | Allington 2, Jenner |
| | 2 | 01.12.83 | **Hendon (1874)** | H | W | 2-1 | Bain, Burridge |
| | 3 | | bye | | | | |
| | 4 | 19.01.84 | **Wednesbury Town** | H | W | 5-0 | Patrick 3, Burridge 2 |
| | 5 | 09.02.84 | **Queen's Park, Glasgow** | H | L | 0-1 | |
| 1884-85 | 1 | 01.11.84 | **Bournemouth Rovers** | H | W | 6-0 | Hurst 3, A Heath, Scoones, og |
| | 2 | 06.12.84 | **Henley FC** | H | W | 7-0 | Bain 2, Hurst 2, Bailey, Janson, C Heath |
| | 3 | 03.01.85 | **Swifts** | A | D | 1-1 | Bain |
| | 3r | 14.01.85 | **Swifts** | H | D | 2-2 | C Heath, Hurst |
| | 3 2r | 21.01.85 | **Swifts** | A | L | 1-2 | C Heath |
| 1885-86 | 1 | 31.10.85 | **Hotspur FC** | H | W | 3-1 | |
| | 2 | 21.11.85 | **Old Brightonians** | H | W | 3-0 | |
| | 3 | 12.12.85 | **Romford (1876)** | H | W | 5-1 | |
| | 4 | | bye | | | | |
| | 5 | 01.02.86 | **Bolton Wanderers** | | | - | |
| | | | *FA disqualified Bolton for professionalism – Old Westminsters advanced* | | | | |

| | | | | | | | |
|---|---|---|---|---|---|---|---|
| | 6 | 13.02.86 | **WBA** | A | L | 0-6 | |
| 1886-87 | 1 | 30.10.86 | **Old Harrovians** | A | W | 4-0 | |
| | 2 | 16.11.86 | **Old Brightonians** | A | D | 1-1 | |
| | 2r | 20.11.86 | **Old Brightonians** | H | W | 3-0 | |
| | 3 | 11.12.86 | **Old Etonians** | H | W | 3-0 | |
| | 4 | | bye | | | | |
| | 5 | 29.01.87 | **Partick Thistle** | H | W | 1-0 | Bain |
| | 6 | 19.02.87 | **Glasgow Rangers** | A | L | 1-5 | Janson |
| 1887-88 | 1 | 15.10.87 | **Clapton** | H | W | 4-1 | |
| | 2 | 05.11.87 | **Millwall Rovers** | H | W | 8-1 | |
| | 3 | 26.11.87 | **Old Etonians** | A | L | 2-7 | |
| 1888-89 | 1 | 02.02.89 | **Burnley** (D1) | A | L | 3-4 | Bedford, Phillimore, AN Other |
| 1889-90 | 1 | 18.01.90 | **Stoke** (D1) | A | L | 0-3 | |
| 1890-91 | 1 | | WBA (D1) | | | - | |
| | | | *Old Westminsters scratched. WBA walkover* | | | | |
| 1891-92 | 1 | 16.01.92 | **WBA** (D1) | H | L | 2-3 | Sandilands, McCulloch og |

## OLD WYKEHAMISTS

*Formed 1876. Entered FA Cup: 1876-77 – 1892-93. Home ground was originally in West Drayton, Middlesex.*

| | | | | | | | |
|---|---|---|---|---|---|---|---|
| 1876-77 | 1 | | Southall Park | | | - | |
| | | | *Old Wykehamists scratched. Southall Park walkover* | | | | |
| 1877-78 | 1 | | Old Foresters | | | - | |
| | | | *Old Wykehamists scratched. Old Foresters walkover* | | | | |
| 1883-84 | 1 | 10.11.83 | **Upton Rangers** | A | W | 7-0 | |
| | 2 | 01.12.83 | **Windsor Home Park** | A | W | 1-0 | Chitty |
| | 3 | | bye | | | | |
| | 4 | 19.01.84 | **Blackburn Olympic** | A | L | 0-6 | |
| 1884-85 | 1 | 08.11.84 | **Maidenhead** | A | W | 3-0 | Blackburn, Fort, AN Other |
| | 2 | 06.12.84 | **Hotspur FC** | A | W | 2-1 | Fort, Ingram |
| | 3 | 03.01.85 | **Upton Park** | H | W | 2-1 | |
| | 4 | 17.01.85 | **Queen's Park, Glasgow** | A | L | 0-7 | |
| 1885-86 | 1 | 31.10.85 | **Uxbridge** | H | W | 5-0 | |
| | 2 | 21.11.85 | **Luton Wanderers** | H | W | 10-0 | |
| | 3 | | Marlow | | | - | |
| | | | *Marlow scratched. Old Wykehamists walkover* | | | | |
| 1886-87 | 1 | 30.10.86 | **Hanover Utd** | H | W | 3-0 | |
| | 2 | 20.11.86 | **London Caledonians** | H | L | 0-1 | |
| 1887-88 | 1 | 08.10.87 | **Hitchin Town** | A | W | 5-2 | |
| | 2 | 29.10.87 | **Crusaders** | H | L | 2-3 | |

## OLDBURY TOWN

*Entered FA Cup: 1887-88 – 1890-91. In 1889 were founder members of the Birmingham & District League.*

| | | | | | | | |
|---|---|---|---|---|---|---|---|
| 1887-88 | 1 | 15.10.87 | **Aston Villa** | H | L | 0-4 | |

## OLDHAM ATHLETIC

*Formed 1875 as Pine Villa. Oldham Athletic 1899. First entered FA Cup: 1905-06; FA Cup best performance: semi-finals 1913, 1990, 1994. Record FA Cup win: 10-1 v Lytham, 1st round, 28.11.1925; Record FA Cup defeat: 0-6 v Huddersfield Town, 3rd round, 13.01.1932; 0-6 v Tottenham Hotspur, 3rd round, 14.01.1933. Oldham suffered these two defeats in successive ties.*

| | | | | | | | |
|---|---|---|---|---|---|---|---|
| 1905-06 (LC) | | | 1q Ashton Town (H) 2-1; 2q Fairfield (H) 8-0; 3q Stalybridge Rovers (H) 1-1; 3qr Stalybridge Rovers (A) 3-1; 4q Hull City (A) 1-2 | | | | |
| 1906-07 (LC) | | | 1q Hyde (H) 5-0; 2q Newton Heath (H) 4-1; 3q Buxton (A) 3-1; 4q Atherton Church (A) 1-1; 4qr Atherton Church (H) 4-1; 5q South Bank (H) 9-1 | | | | |
| | 1 | 17.01.07 | **Kidderminster H** (BDL) | H | W | 5-0 | Hancock 2, D Walders, Shadbolt, Brunton |
| | 2 | 02.02.07 | **Liverpool** (D1) | H | L | 0-1 | |
| 1907-08 (D2) | | | Int Darwen (H) 8-1 | | | | |
| | 1 | 11.01.08 | **Leeds City** (D2) | H | W | 2-1 | Whaites, Newton |
| | 2 | 01.02.08 | **Everton** (D1) | H | D | 0-0 | |
| | 2r | 05.02.08 | **Everton** | A | L | 1-6 | Whaites |
| 1908-09 (D2) | 1 | 16.01.09 | **Leeds City** (D2) | H | D | 1-1 | Hamilton |
| | 1r | 20.01.09 | **Leeds City** | A | L | 0-2 | |
| 1909-10 (D2) | 1 | 15.01.10 | **Aston Villa** (D1) | H | L | 1-2 | Toward |

| | | | | | | | | | |
|---|---|---|---|---|---|---|---|---|---|
| 1910-11 | (D1) | 1 | 14.01.11 | **Birmingham** (D2) | A | D | 1-1 | Toward |
| | | 1r | 17.01.11 | **Birmingham** | H | W | 2-0 | Wilson, Woodger |
| | | 2 | 04.02.11 | **Hull City** (D2) | A | L | 0-1 | |
| 1911-12 | (D1) | 1 | 13.01.12 | **Hull City** (D2) | H | D | 1-1 | Wilson |
| | | 1r | 16.01.12 | **Hull City** | A | W | 1-0 | Woodger |
| | | 2 | 03.02.12 | **Manchester City** (D1) | A | W | 1-0 | Woodger |
| | | 3 | 24.02.12 | **Everton** (D1) | H | L | 0-2 | |
| 1912-13 | (D1) | 1 | 11.01.13 | **Bolton Wanderers** (D1) | H | W | 2-0 | Tummon 2 |
| | | 2 | 01.02.13 | **Nottingham Forest** (D2) | H | W | 5-1 | Kemp 2, Walters, Tummon, Woodger |
| | | 3 | 22.02.13 | **Manchester Utd** (D1) | H | D | 0-0 | |
| | | 3r | 26.02.13 | **Manchester Utd** | A | W | 2-1 | Gee, Toward |
| | | 4 | 08.03.13 | **Everton** (D1) | A | W | 1-0 | Gee |
| | | SF | 29.03.13 | **Aston Villa** (D1) | | L | 0-1 | |
| | | | | *played at Ewood Park* | | | | |
| 1913-14 | (D1) | 1 | 10.01.14 | **Brighton** (SL) | H | D | 1-1 | Donnachie |
| | | 1r | 14.01.14 | **Brighton** | A | L | 0-1aet | |
| 1914-15 | (D1) | 1 | 09.01.15 | **Croydon Common** (SL) | A | W | 3-0 | Wilson, Tummon, Kemp |
| | | 2 | 30.01.15 | **Rochdale** (CL) | H | W | 3-0 | Kemp, Gee, Donachie |
| | | 3 | 20.02.15 | **Birmingham** (D2) | A | W | 3-2 | Kemp, Cashmore, Pilkington |
| | | 4 | 06.03.15 | **Sheffield Utd** (D1) | H | D | 0-0 | |
| | | 4r | 13.03.15 | **Sheffield Utd** | A | L | 0-3 | |
| 1919-20 | (D1) | 1 | 10.01.20 | **Cardiff City** (SL) | A | L | 0-2 | |
| 1920-21 | (D1) | 1 | 08.01.21 | **Brighton** (D3) | A | L | 1-4 | JH Marshall |
| 1921-22 | (D1) | 1 | 07.01.22 | **Gillingham** (3S) | A | W | 3-1 | F Broadbent 2, W Taylor |
| | | 2 | 28.01.22 | **Barnsley** (D2) | A | L | 1-3 | F Broadbent |
| 1922-23 | (D1) | 1 | 13.01.23 | **Middlesbrough** (D1) | H | L | 0-1 | |
| 1923-24 | (D2) | 1 | 12.01.24 | **Sunderland** (D1) | H | W | 2-1 | JE Blair, Staniforth |
| | | 2 | 02.02.24 | **Swindon Town** (3S) | A | L | 0-2 | |
| 1924-25 | (D2) | 1 | 10.01.25 | **Blackburn Rovers** (D1) | A | L | 0-1 | |
| 1925-26 | (D2) | 1 | 28.11.25 | **Lytham FC** (LC) | H | W | 10-1 | Barnes 3, Ormston 2, Pynegar 2, Watson 2, Naylor |
| | | 2 | 12.12.25 | **Stockton** (NL) | A | W | 6-4 | Watson 4, Pynegar, Wynne (p) |
| | | 3 | 09.01.26 | **Millwall** (3S) | A | D | 1-1 | Douglas |
| | | 3r | 12.01.26 | **Millwall** | H | L | 0-1 | |
| 1926-27 | (D2) | 3 | 08.01.27 | **Brentford** (3S) | H | - | 2-1ab | Pynegar, Watson |
| | | | | *abandoned after 73 minutes – fog* | | | | |
| | | 3 | 10.01.27 | **Brentford** (3S) | H | L | 2-4 | Pynegar, Barnes |
| 1927-28 | (D2) | 3 | 14.01.28 | **Blackpool** (D2) | A | W | 4-1 | Watson 2, Stanton, King |
| | | 4 | 28.01.28 | **Tottenham Hotspur** (D1) | A | L | 0-3 | |
| 1928-29 | (D2) | 3 | 12.01.29 | **Bolton Wanderers** (D1) | A | L | 0-2 | |
| 1929-30 | (D2) | 3 | 11.01.30 | **Wolverhampton W** (D2) | H | W | 1-0 | Goodier |
| | | 4 | 25.01.30 | **Sheffield Wed** (D1) | H | L | 3-4 | Littlewood 2, Adlam |
| 1930-31 | (D2) | 3 | 10.01.31 | **Watford** (3S) | H | L | 1-3 | Fitton |
| 1931-32 | (D2) | 3 | 09.01.32 | **Huddersfield Town** (D1) | H | D | 1-1 | Ivill |
| | | 3r | 13.01.32 | **Huddersfield Town** | A | L | 0-6 | |
| 1932-33 | (D2) | 3 | 14.01.33 | **Tottenham Hotspur** (D2) | H | L | 0-6 | |
| 1933-34 | (D2) | 3 | 13.01.34 | **Reading** (3S) | A | W | 2-1 | Rowley, Bailey |
| | | 4 | 27.01.34 | **Sheffield Wed** (D1) | H | D | 1-1 | Reid |
| | | 4r | 31.01.34 | **Sheffield Wed** | A | L | 1-6 | Bailey |
| 1934-35 | (D2) | 3 | 12.01.35 | **Sheffield Wed** (D1) | A | L | 1-3 | Walsh |
| 1935-36 | (3N) | 1 | 30.11.35 | **Ferryhill Athletic** (NL) | H | W | 6-1 | Davis 2, Brunskill, Agar, Walsh, Buckley |
| | | 2 | 14.12.35 | **Bristol Rovers** (3S) | H | D | 1-1 | Walsh |
| | | 2r | 18.12.35 | **Bristol Rovers** | A | L | 1-4 | Robson |
| 1936-37 | (3N) | 1 | 28.11.36 | **Tranmere Rovers** (3N) | H | W | 1-0 | Davis |
| | | 2 | 12.12.36 | **Lincoln City** (3N) | A | W | 3-2 | McCormick 2, Davis |
| | | 3 | 16.01.37 | **Exeter City** (3S) | A | L | 0-3 | |
| 1937-38 | (3N) | 1 | 27.11.37 | **Wrexham** (3N) | A | L | 1-2 | Hilton (p) |
| 1938-39 | (3N) | 1 | 26.11.38 | **Crewe Alexandra** (3N) | H | D | 2-2 | Ferrier, Blackshaw |
| | | 1r | 30.11.38 | **Crewe Alexandra** | A | L | 0-1 | |
| 1945-46 | (3N) | 1 1L | 17.11.45 | **Southport** (3N) | A | W | 2-1 | Chapman 2 |

| | | | | | | | |
|---|---|---|---|---|---|---|---|
| | 1 2L | 24.11.45 | **Southport** | H | W | 3-1 | Lawton, West, Standring |
| | 2 1L | 08.12.45 | **Accrington Stanley** (3N) | H | W | 2-1 | West, Standring |
| | 2 2L | 15.12.45 | **Accrington Stanley** | A | L | 1-3 | Ferrier |
| 1946-47 (3N) | 1 | 30.11.46 | **Tranmere Rovers** (3N) | H | W | 1-0 | Tomlinson |
| | 2 | 14.12.46 | **Doncaster Rovers** (3N) | A | L | 1-2 | Bowden |
| 1947-48 (3N) | 1 | 29.11.47 | **Lancaster City** (LC) | H | W | 6-0 | Haddington 2, Horton, Gemmell, Wilson, Brierley |
| | 2 | 13.12.47 | **Mansfield Town** (3N) | H | L | 0-1 | |
| 1948-49 (3N) | 1 | 27.11.48 | **Wrexham** (3N) | A | W | 3-0 | Stock, Gemmell, Jessop |
| | 2 | 11.12.48 | **Walthamstow Ave** (IL) | A | D | 2-2aet | Tomlinson, Gemmell |
| | 2r | 18.12.48 | **Walthamstow Ave** | H | W | 3-1 | Haddington 2, Gemmell |
| | 3 | 08.01.49 | **Cardiff City** (D2) | H | L | 2-3 | Gemmell, Haddington |
| 1949-50 (3N) | 1 | 26.11.49 | **Stockton** (NEL) | H | W | 4-0 | Haddington 2, Spurdle, Gemmell |
| | 2 | 10.12.49 | **Crewe Alexandra** (3N) | A | D | 1-1 | Jessop |
| | 2r | 13.12.49 | **Crewe Alexandra** | H | D | 0-0aet | |
| | 2 2r | 19.12.49 | **Crewe Alexandra** *played at Maine Road* | | W | 3-0 | Haddington 2 (1p), Spurdle |
| | 3 | 07.01.50 | **Newcastle Utd** (D1) | H | L | 2-7 | Spurdle, Haddington |
| 1950-51 (3N) | 1 | 25.11.50 | **Bradford City** (3N) | A | D | 2-2 | Gemmell 2 (1p) |
| | 1r | 28.11.50 | **Bradford City** | H | W | 2-1 | Goodfellow, Munro |
| | 2 | 09.12.50 | **Hartlepools Utd** (3N) | A | W | 2-1 | Ormond, Newton og |
| | 3 | 06.01.51 | **Manchester Utd** (D1) | A | L | 1-4 | Smith |
| 1951-52 (3N) | 1 | 24.11.51 | **Nelson FC** (LC) | A | W | 4-0 | McKennan 3, Gemmell |
| | 2 | 15.12.51 | **Southend Utd** (3S) | A | L | 0-5 | |
| 1952-53 (3N) | 1 | 22.11.52 | **Boston Utd** (ML) | A | W | 2-1 | Clarke, McKennan |
| | 2 | 06.12.52 | **Port Vale** (3N) | A | W | 3-0 | Gemmell 2, Ormond |
| | 3 | 10.01.53 | **Birmingham City** (D2) | H | L | 1-3 | McKennan |
| 1953-54 (D2) | 3 | 09.01.54 | **Ipswich Town** (3S) | A | D | 3-3 | McIlvenny 2, Clarke |
| | 3r | 12.01.54 | **Ipswich Town** | H | L | 0-1 | |
| 1954-55 (3N) | 1 | 20.11.54 | **Crewe Alexandra** (3N) | H | W | 1-0 | McShane |
| | 2 | 11.12.54 | **Bournemouth** (3S) | A | L | 0-1 | |
| 1955-56 (3N) | 1 | 19.11.55 | **Bradford City** (3N) | A | L | 1-3 | Scrine |
| 1956-57 (3N) | 1 | 17.11.56 | **Halifax Town** (3N) | A | W | 3-2 | Neale 2, Pearson |
| | 2 | 08.12.56 | **Accrington Stanley** (3N) | A | L | 1-2 | Neale |
| 1957-58 (3N) | 1 | 16.11.57 | **Bradford Park A** (3N) | H | W | 2-0 | Fawley, Duffy |
| | 2 | 07.12.57 | **Workington** (3N) | H | L | 1-5 | Murray |
| 1958-59 (D4) | 1 | 15.11.58 | **Denaby Utd** (ML) | A | W | 2-0 | Thompson 2 |
| | 2 | 06.12.58 | **S Shields (1936)** (ML) | H | W | 2-0 | Bourne, Phoenix |
| | 3 | 10.01.59 | **Stoke City** (D2) | A | L | 1-5 | Duffy |
| 1959-60 (D4) | 1 | 14.11.59 | **Shildon** (NL) | A | D | 1-1 | Spurdle |
| | 1r | 17.11.59 | **Shildon** | H | W | 3-0 | McGill, Bazley, Walters |
| | 2 | 05.12.59 | **Bury** (D3) | A | L | 1-2 | Phoenix |
| 1960-61 (D4) | 1 | 05.11.60 | **Rhyl** (CC) | A | W | 1-0 | Lister |
| | 2 | 26.11.60 | **Chesterfield** (D3) | A | D | 4-4 | Lister 2, Phoenix, Johnstone |
| | 2r | 29.11.60 | **Chesterfield** | H | L | 0-3 | |
| 1961-62 (D4) | 1 | 04.11.61 | **Shildon** (NL) | H | W | 5-2 | Lister 3, Jarvis, Johnstone (p) |
| | 2 | 25.11.61 | **Chesterfield** (D4) | A | D | 2-2 | Lister, Colquhoun |
| | 2r | 29.11.61 | **Chesterfield** | H | W | 4-2aet | Colquhoun 2, Johnstone (p), Powell og |
| | 3 | 08.01.62 | **Bristol Rovers** (D2) | A | D | 1-1 | Phoenix |
| | 3r | 10.01.62 | **Bristol Rovers** | H | W | 2-0 | Colquhoun 2 |
| | 4 | 27.01.62 | **Liverpool** (D2) | H | L | 1-2 | Colquhoun |
| 1962-63 (D4) | 1 | 03.11.62 | **Bradford City** (D4) | H | L | 2-5 | Frizzell, Whitaker |
| 1963-64 (D3) | 1 | 20.11.63 | **Mansfield Town** (D3) | H | W | 3-2 | Ledger, Colquhoun, Whitaker |
| | 2 | 07.12.63 | **Bradford Park A** (D4) | H | W | 2-0 | Bowie, Scoular og |
| | 3 | 04.01.64 | **Ipswich Town** (D1) | A | L | 3-6 | Lister 2, Bowie |
| 1964-65 (D3) | 1 | 14.11.64 | **Hereford Utd** (SL) | H | W | 4-0 | Colquhoun 3, Lister |
| | 2 | 02.12.64 | **Crook Town** (NL) | A | W | 1-0 | Bartley |
| | 3 | 09.01.65 | **Middlesbrough** (D2) | A | L | 2-6 | Williams, Martin (p) |
| 1965-66 (D3) | 1 | 13.11.65 | **Mansfield Town** (D3) | A | W | 3-1 | Holden 2, Jackson |
| | 2 | 04.12.65 | **Darlington** (D4) | A | W | 1-0 | Dearden |
| | 3 | 22.01.66 | **West Ham Utd** (D1) | H | D | 2-2 | Blore 2 |
| | 3r | 24.01.66 | **West Ham Utd** | A | L | 1-2 | Pennington |

| | | | | | | | | |
|---|---|---|---|---|---|---|---|---|
| 1966-67 | (D3) | 1 | 26.11.66 | **Notts County** (D4) | H | W | 3-1 | Asprey, Large, Collins |
| | | 2 | 07.01.67 | **Grantham Town** (ML) | A | W | 4-0 | Collins 2, Wood, Bebbington |
| | | 3 | 28.01.67 | **Wolverhampton W** (D2) | H | D | 2-2 | Bebbington 2 |
| | | 3r | 01.02.67 | **Wolverhampton W** | A | L | 1-4 | Bebbington |
| 1967-68 | (D3) | 1 | 09.12.67 | **Barrow** (D3) | A | L | 0-2 | |
| 1968-69 | (D3) | 1 | 16.11.68 | **Wrexham** (D4) | A | L | 2-4 | Bebbington, Chapman |
| 1969-70 | (D4) | 1 | 15.11.69 | **Grantham Town** (ML) | H | W | 3-1 | Wood, Colquhoun, Bingham (p) |
| | | 2 | 06.12.69 | **S Shields (1936)** (NPL) | A | D | 0-0 | |
| | | 2r | 09.12.69 | **S Shields (1936)** | H | L | 1-2 | Bebbington |
| 1970-71 | (D4) | 1 | 21.11.70 | **Rochdale** (D3) | A | L | 0-2 | |
| 1971-72 | (D3) | 1 | 20.11.71 | **Chesterfield** (D3) | A | L | 0-3 | |
| 1972-73 | (D3) | 1 | 18.11.72 | **Scarborough** (NPL) | H | D | 1-1 | Shaw |
| | | 1r | 22.11.72 | **Scarborough** | A | L | 1-2 | Collins |
| 1973-74 | (D3) | 1 | 24.11.73 | **Formby** (CC) | A | W | 2-0 | Jones 2 |
| | | 2 | 15.12.73 | **Halifax Town** (D3) | A | W | 1-0 | McVitie |
| | | 3 | 06.01.74 | **Cambridge Utd** (D3) | A | D | 2-2 | Lochead, Edwards |
| | | 3r | 08.01.74 | **Cambridge Utd** | H | D | 3-3aet | Robins 2, McVitie |
| | | 3 2r | 14.01.74 | **Cambridge Utd** | | W | 2-1 | Jones, Garwood |
| | | | | *played at the City Ground, Nottingham* | | | | |
| | | 4 | 26.01.74 | **Burnley** (D1) | H | L | 1-4 | Whittle (p) |
| 1974-75 | (D2) | 3 | 04.01.75 | **Aston Villa** (D2) | H | L | 0-3 | |
| 1975-76 | (D2) | 3 | 03.01.76 | **Sunderland** (D2) | A | L | 0-2 | |
| 1976-77 | (D2) | 3 | 08.01.77 | **Plymouth Argyle** (D2) | H | W | 3-0 | Whittle, Robins, Halom |
| | | 4 | 29.01.77 | **Northwich V** (NPL) | | W | 3-1 | Halom 2, Valentine |
| | | | | *played at Maine Road* | | | | |
| | | 5 | 26.02.77 | **Liverpool** (D1) | A | L | 1-3 | Shaw |
| 1977-78 | (D2) | 3 | 07.01.78 | **Luton Town** (D2) | A | D | 1-1 | Taylor |
| | | 3r | 10.01.78 | **Luton Town** | H | L | 1-2 | Young |
| 1978-79 | (D2) | 3 | 06.01.79 | **Stoke City** (D2) | A | - | 0-2ab | |
| | | | | *abandoned at half-time* | | | | |
| | | 3 | 17.01.79 | **Stoke City** | A | W | 1-0 | Wood |
| | | 4 | 26.02.79 | **Leicester City** (D2) | H | W | 3-1 | Young 3 |
| | | 5 | 28.02.79 | **Tottenham Hotspur** (D1) | A | L | 0-1 | |
| 1979-80 | (D2) | 3 | 05.01.80 | **Coventry City** (D1) | H | L | 0-1 | |
| 1980-81 | (D2) | 3 | 03.01.81 | **Wimbledon** (D4) | A | D | 0-0 | |
| | | 3r | 06.01.81 | **Wimbledon** | H | L | 0-1 | |
| 1981-82 | (D2) | 3 | 05.01.82 | **Gillingham** (D3) | A | L | 1-2 | Heaton (p) |
| 1982-83 | (D2) | 3 | 08.01.83 | **Fulham** (D2) | H | L | 0-2 | |
| 1983-84 | (D2) | 3 | 07.01.84 | **Shrewsbury Town** (D2) | A | L | 0-3 | |
| 1984-85 | (D2) | 3 | 05.01.85 | **Brentford** (D3) | H | W | 2-1 | Quinn, Harrison |
| | | 4 | 26.01.85 | **Sheffield Wed** (D1) | A | L | 1-5 | Bowden |
| 1985-86 | (D2) | 3 | 06.01.86 | **Orient** (D4) | H | L | 1-2 | Palmer |
| 1986-87 | (D2) | 3 | 10.01.87 | **Bradford City** (D2) | H | D | 1-1 | McGuire |
| | | 3r | 19.01.87 | **Bradford City** | A | L | 1-5 | Wright |
| 1987-88 | (D2) | 3 | 09.01.88 | **Tottenham Hotspur** (D1) | H | L | 2-4 | Wright, Cecere |
| 1988-89 | (D2) | 3 | 07.01.89 | **Charlton Athletic** (D1) | A | L | 1-2 | Milligan |
| 1989-90 | (D2) | 3 | 06.01.90 | **Birmingham City** (D3) | A | D | 1-1 | Bunn |
| | | 3r | 10.01.90 | **Birmingham City** | H | W | 1-0 | R Holden |
| | | 4 | 27.01.90 | **Brighton** (D2) | H | W | 2-1 | McGarvey, Ritchie |
| | | 5 | 17.02.90 | **Everton** (D1) | H | D | 2-2 | Ritchie (p), Palmer |
| | | 5r | 21.02.90 | **Everton** | A | D | 1-1aet | Marshall |
| | | 5 2r | 10.03.90 | **Everton** | H | W | 2-1aet | Palmer, Marshall (p) |
| | | 6 | 14.03.90 | **Aston Villa** (D1) | H | W | 3-0 | R Holden, Price og, Redfearn |
| | | SF | 08.04.90 | **Manchester Utd** (D1) | | D | 3-3aet | Barrett Marshall, Palmer |
| | | | | *played at Maine Road* | | | | |
| | | SFr | 11.04.90 | **Manchester Utd** (D1) | | L | 1-2aet | Ritchie |
| | | | | *played at Maine Road* | | | | |
| 1990-91 | (D2) | 3 | 05.01.91 | **Brentford** (D3) | H | W | 3-1 | Redfearn 2 (2ps), Adams |
| | | 4 | 26.01.91 | **Notts County** (D2) | A | L | 0-2 | |
| 1991-92 | (D1) | 3 | 04.01.92 | **Leyton Orient** (D3) | H | D | 1-1 | Sharp |
| | | 3r | 15.01.92 | **Leyton Orient** | A | L | 2-4aet | Adams, Palmer |

| | | | | | | | | |
|---|---|---|---|---|---|---|---|---|
| 1992-93 | (PL) | 3 | 02.01.93 | **Tranmere Rovers** (D1) | H | D | 2-2 | Olney Bernard |
| | | 3r | 12.01.93 | **Tranmere Rovers** | A | L | 0-3 | |
| 1993-94 | (PL) | 3 | 08.01.94 | **Derby County** (D1) | H | W | 2-1 | Beckford, Holden |
| | | 4 | 29.01.94 | **Stoke City** (D1) | H | D | 0-0 | |
| | | 4r | 09.02.94 | **Stoke City** | A | W | 1-0 | Beckford |
| | | 5 | 19.02.94 | **Barnsley** (D1) | H | W | 1-0 | Ritchie |
| | | 6 | 12.03.94 | **Bolton Wanderers** (D1) | A | W | 1-0 | Beckford |
| | | SF | 10.04.94 | **Manchester Utd** (PL) | | D | 1-1aet | Pointon |
| | | | | *played at Wembley Stadium* | | | | |
| | | SFr | 13.04.94 | **Manchester Utd** | | L | 1-4 | Pointon |
| | | | | *played at Maine Road* | | | | |
| 1994-95 | (D1) | 3 | 07.01.95 | **Reading** (D1) | A | W | 3-1 | Sharpe, Richardson, Halle |
| | | 4 | 28.01.95 | **Leeds Utd** (PL) | A | L | 2-3 | Halle, Palmer og |
| 1995-96 | (D1) | 3 | 06.01.96 | **Barnsley** (D1) | A | D | 0-0 | |
| | | 3r | 23.01.96 | **Barnsley** | H | W | 2-1 | Beckford 2 (1p) |
| | | 4 | 12.02.96 | **Swindon Town** (D2) | A | L | 0-1 | |
| 1996-97 | (D1) | 3 | 14.01.97 | **Barnsley** (D1) | A | L | 0-2 | |
| 1997-98 | (D2) | 1 | 15.11.97 | **Mansfield Town** (D3) | H | D | 1-1 | McCarthy |
| | | 1r | 25.11.97 | **Mansfield Town** | A | W | 1-0 | Serrant |
| | | 2 | 06.12.97 | **Blackpool** (D2) | H | W | 2-1 | Graham, Barrlow |
| | | 3 | 03.01.98 | **Cardiff City** (D3) | A | L | 0-1 | |
| 1998-99 | (D2) | 1 | 14.11.98 | **Gillingham** (D2) | H | W | 2-0 | Salt, S McNiven |
| | | 2 | 05.12.98 | **Brentford** (D3) | H | D | 1-1 | McGinlay (p) |
| | | 2r | 15.12.98 | **Brentford** | A | D | 2-2aet | McGinlay, Duxbury |
| | | | | *Oldham Athletic won 4-2 on penalties* | | | | |
| | | 3 | 02.01.99 | **Chelsea** (PL) | H | L | 0-2 | |
| 1999-00 | (D2) | 1 | 30.10.99 | **Chelmsford City** (SL) | H | W | 4-0 | Dudley, Sheridan, Duxbury, Whitehall |
| | | 1 | 20.11.99 | **Swansea City** (D3) | H | W | 1-0 | Whitehall |
| | | 3 | 11.12.99 | **Preston North End** (D2) | A | L | 1-2 | Adams |
| 2000-01 | (D2) | 1 | 18.11.00 | **Hednesford Town** (Conf) | A | W | 4-2 | Duxbury, Dudley, Corazzin, Tipton |
| | | 2 | 09.12.00 | **Peterborough Utd** (D2) | A | D | 1-1 | Dudley |
| | | 2r | 19.12.00 | **Peterborough Utd** | H | L | 0-1 | |
| 2001-02 | (D2) | 1 | 17.11.01 | **Barrow** (NPL) | H | D | 1-1 | Duxbury |
| | | 1r | 27.11.01 | **Barrow** | A | W | 1-0 | Eyres |
| | | 2 | 08.12.01 | **Hull City** (D3) | A | W | 3-2 | J Sheridan, Eyres, Duxbury |
| | | 3 | 06.01.02 | **Cheltenham Town** (D3) | A | L | 1-2 | Eyres |
| 2002-03 | (D2) | 1 | 16.11.02 | **Burton Albion** (Conf) | H | D | 2-2 | Low, Hall |
| | | 1r | 27.11.02 | **Burton Albion** | A | D | 2-2aet | Wijnhard, Eyres |
| | | | | *Oldham Athletic won 5-4 on penalties* | | | | |
| | | 2 | 07.12.02 | **Cheltenham Town** (D2) | H | L | 1-2 | Haining |

## OLYMPIC FC

*Formed 1869. Entered the FA Cup: 1881-82 and then from 1899-1900 – 1903-04. Originally played in the Upton Park area, but there are no links with the modern-day West Ham.*

| | | | | | | | |
|---|---|---|---|---|---|---|---|
| 1881-82 | 1 | 05.11.81 | **Old Harrovians** | A | L | 2-4 | |

## OSWALDTWISTLE ROVERS

*Formed 1877. Entered FA Cup: 1884-85 – 1909-10. In 1889-90 were founder members of the Lancashire League.*

| | | | | | | | |
|---|---|---|---|---|---|---|---|
| 1884-85 | 1 | 11.10.84 | **Blackburn Olympic** | A | L | 0-12 | |
| 1885-86 | 1 | 31.10.85 | **Lower Darwen** | H | W | 3-1 | |
| | 2 | 21.11.85 | **Blackburn Rovers** | A | L | 0-1 | |
| 1886-87 | 1 | 23.10.86 | **Witton** | H | L | 2-3 | |
| 1887-88 | 1 | 15.10.87 | **Witton** | H | L | 3-4 | |

## OSWESTRY TOWN

*Formed 1860, Entered FA Cup: 1882-83 – 1986-87. Folded 1988. Reformed 1994. Members of the League of Wales.*

| | | | | | | | |
|---|---|---|---|---|---|---|---|
| 1882-83 | 1 | 04.11.82 | **Druids** | A | D | 1-1 | |
| | 1r | 18.11.82 | **Druids** | H | L | 0-2 | |
| 1883-84 | 1 | 10.11.83 | **Hartford St Johns** | H | W | 7-0 | |
| | 2 | 01.12.83 | **Wrexham Olympic** | A | W | 4-3 | Roberts 3, Shaw |

| | | | | | | | | |
|---|---|---|---|---|---|---|---|---|
| | | 3 | 29.12.83 | **Queen's Park, Glasgow** | H | L | 1-7 | Foulkes |
| 1884-85 | | 1 | 08.11.84 | **Crewe Alexandra** | A | L | 1-2 | |
| 1885-86 | | 1 | 24.10.85 | **Bollington** | A | W | 5-0 | |
| | | 2 | 21.11.85 | **Crewe Alexandra** | H | D | 1-1 | Bryan |
| | | | | *Oswestry scratched before the replay* | | | | |
| 1886-87 | | 1 | 30.10.86 | **Bollington** | A | W | 8-2 | |
| | | 2 | 20.11.86 | **Leek** | A | L | 2-4 | |
| 1887-88 | | 1 | 08.10.87 | **Llangollen** | A | L | 3-7 | |
| | | | | *FA ordered replay after protest* | | | | |
| | | 1r | 22.10.87 | **Llangollen** | A | W | 2-0 | |
| | | 3 | 26.11.87 | **Stoke** | A | L | 0-3 | |
| 1927-28 | (BDL) | 1 | 26.11.27 | **Stockport County** (3N) | A | L | 2-5 | W Jones, R Jones |
| 1957-58 | (BDL) | 1 | 16.11.57 | **Bournemouth** (3S) | H | L | 1-5 | Thomas |
| 1959-60 | (CC) | 1 | 14.11.59 | **Southend Utd** (D3) | A | L | 0-6 | |
| 1974-75 | (CC) | 1 | 23.11.74 | **Doncaster Rovers** (D4) | H | L | 1-3 | Price |

## OVER WANDERERS

*Formed 1883. Became Winsford United 1899. Entered FA Cup as Over Wanderers: 1887-88 – 1890-91. See Winsford United.*

| | | | | | | | |
|---|---|---|---|---|---|---|---|
| 1887-88 | 1 | 15.10.87 | **Wellington St Georges** | H | W | 3-1 | |
| | 2 | 05.11.87 | **Stoke** | H | L | 0-2 | |

## OWLERTON

*Formed 1869. Entered FA Cup: 1887-88 – 1890-91. Played at Owlerton Fields, Sheffield. No direct links to either Sheffield United or Sheffield Wed, although Wednesday are based in Hillsborough, near the Owlerton district of Sheffield.*

| | | | | | | | |
|---|---|---|---|---|---|---|---|
| 1887-88 | 1 | 15.10.87 | **Eckington Works** | H | W | 2-1 | |
| | 2 | 05.11.87 | **Sheffield Heeley** | H | W | 1-0 | |
| | 3 | 26.11.87 | **Derby County** | A | L | 2-6 | Judge, AN Other |

## OXFORD CITY

*Formed 1882. First entered FA Cup: 1895-96. FA Amateur Cup winners: 1906. Runners-up: 1903, 1913. FA Vase runners-up: 1995. Oxford City set an FA Cup record with Alvechurch in 1971-72 when their fourth qualifying round tie needed six attempts before Alvechurch won 1-0. League club beaten: New Brighton Tower (walkover) 1901-02. Members of the Isthmian League.*

| | | | | | | | | |
|---|---|---|---|---|---|---|---|---|
| 1901-02 | (n/af) | Int | | New Brighton Tower (D2) walkover | | | | |
| | | 1 | 25.01.02 | **Lincoln City** (D2) | H | D | 0-0 | |
| | | 1r | 29.01.02 | **Lincoln City** | A | L | 0-4 | |
| 1906-07 | (IL) | 1 | 12.01.07 | **Bury** (D1) | H | L | 0-3 | |
| 1933-34 | (IL) | 1 | 25.11.33 | **Gillingham** (3S) | H | L | 1-5 | James |
| 1966-67 | (IL) | 1 | 26.11.66 | **Bristol Rovers** (D3) | H | D | 2-2 | Woodley, Bradbury |
| | | 1r | 29.11.66 | **Bristol Rovers** | A | L | 0-4 | |
| 1967-68 | (IL) | 1 | 09.12.67 | **Luton Town** (D4) | H | L | 1-2 | Woodley |
| | | | | *played at Kenilworth Road* | | | | |
| 1968-69 | (IL) | 1 | 16.11.68 | **Swansea Town** (D4) | H | L | 2-3 | Pentecost, Woodley |
| 1969-70 | (IL) | 1 | 15.11.69 | **Cheltenham Town** (SL) | A | W | 2-0 | Oram, Woodley |
| | | 2 | 06.12.69 | **Swansea Town** (D4) | H | L | 1-5 | Woodley |
| 1970-71 | (IL) | 1 | 21.11.70 | **Bournemouth** (D4) | H | D | 1-1 | Marcham |
| | | 1r | 23.11.70 | **Bournemouth** | A | L | 1-8 | Holifield |
| 1999-00 | (IL) | 1 | 30.10.99 | **Wycombe W** (D2) | A | D | 1-1 | Pierson |
| | | 1r | 09.11.99 | **Wycombe W** | H | - | 1-1ab | Strong |
| | | | | *abandoned – fire broke out at the end of 90 minutes before the penalty shoot-out started* | | | | |
| | | 1 2r | 16.11.99 | **Wycombe W** (D2) | H | L | 0-1 | |
| | | | | *played at the Manor Ground, Oxford* | | | | |

## OXFORD UNITED

*Formed 1893 as Headington United. Oxford United 1960. Elected to Football League 1962. First Entered FA Cup: 1931-32. FA Cup best performance: Quarter-finals 1962 (as a Fourth Division club), 1982. Record FA Cup win: 9-1 v Dorchester Town, 1st round, 11.11.1995. Record FA Cup defeat: 1-8 v Banbury Spencer, Extra-preliminary round, 1945-46. In Competition Proper: 1-5 v Arsenal, 3rd round, 30.01.1963.*

| | | | | | | | |
|---|---|---|---|---|---|---|---|
| **as Headington United** | | | | | | | |
| 1953-54 (SL) | 1 | 21.11.53 | **Harwich & P** (ECL) | A | W | 3-2 | Steel, Duncan, Craig (p) |
| | 2 | 12.12.53 | **Millwall** (3S) | A | D | 3-3 | Peart, Steel, Maskel |
| | 2r | 17.12.53 | **Millwall** | H | W | 1-0 | K Smith |
| | 3 | 09.01.54 | **Stockport County** (3N) | A | D | 0-0 | |
| | 3r | 14.01.54 | **Stockport County** | H | W | 1-0 | Peart |
| | 4 | 30.01.54 | **Bolton Wanderers** (D1) | H | L | 2-4 | Peart, Smith |
| 1954-55 (SL) | 1 | 20.11.54 | **Norwich City** (3S) | A | L | 2-4 | Yates, K Smith |
| 1958-59 (SL) | 1 | 15.11.58 | **Margate** (KL) | H | W | 3-2 | Jackson, Rees, Dickson |
| | 2 | 06.12.58 | **Peterborough Utd** (ML) | A | L | 2-4 | Rees 2 |
| 1959-60 (SL) | 1 | 14.11.59 | **Enfield** (AL) | A | L | 3-4 | Rivers, Mathers, Denial (p) |
| **as Oxford United** | | | | | | | |
| 1960-61 (SL) | 1 | 05.11.60 | **Hendon** (AL) | A | D | 2-2 | Luke, Jones |
| | 1r | 09.11.60 | **Hendon** | H | W | 3-2 | Jones, McIntosh, Love |
| | 2 | 26.11.60 | **Bridgwater Town** (WL) | H | W | 2-1 | Dickson, Kyle |
| | 3 | 07.01.61 | **Leicester City** (D1) | A | L | 1-3 | Jones |
| 1961-62 (SL) | 1 | 04.11.61 | **Brentford** (D3) | A | L | 0-3 | |
| 1962-63 (D4) | 1 | 03.11.62 | **Falmouth Town** (SWL) | A | W | 2-1 | G Atkinson, Houghton |
| | 2 | 24.11.62 | **King's Lynn** (SL) | A | W | 2-1 | Jones, Houghton |
| | 3 | 30.01.63 | **Arsenal** (D1) | A | L | 1-5 | Jones |
| 1963-64 (D4) | 1 | 16.11.63 | **Folkestone** (SL) | H | W | 2-0 | Longbottom, Peplow og |
| | 2 | 07.12.63 | **Kettering Town** (SL) | H | W | 2-1 | Longbottom, Calder |
| | 3 | 04.01.64 | **Chesterfield** (D4) | H | W | 1-0 | Willey |
| | 4 | 25.01.64 | **Brentford** (D3) | H | D | 2-2 | Calder, Willey |
| | 4r | 28.01.64 | **Brentford** | A | W | 2-1 | Calder 2 |
| | 5 | 15.02.64 | **Blackburn Rovers** (D1) | H | W | 3-1 | Jones 2, Calder |
| | 6 | 29.02.64 | **Preston North End** (D2) | H | L | 1-2 | Jones |
| 1964-65 (D4) | 1 | 14.11.64 | **Mansfield Town** (D3) | H | L | 0-1 | |
| 1965-66 (D3) | 1 | 13.11.65 | **Port Vale** (D4) | H | D | 2-2 | Spelman (p), Calder |
| | 1r | 15.11.65 | **Port Vale** | A | L | 2-3 | Poole og, Calder |
| 1966-67 (D3) | 1 | 26.11.66 | **Yeovil Town** (SL) | A | W | 3-1 | G Atkinson, Harrington, Kerr |
| | 2 | 11.01.67 | **Bedford Town** (SL) | H | D | 1-1 | G Atkinson |
| | 2r | 16.01.67 | **Bedford Town** | A | L | 0-1 | |
| 1967-68 (D3) | 1 | 09.12.67 | **Chelmsford City** (SL) | A | D | 3-3 | Wilson og, Shuker, Clark |
| | 1r | 13.12.67 | **Chelmsford City** | H | D | 3-3aet | Skeen, Bullock, G Atkinson |
| | 1 2r | 18.12.67 | **Chelmsford City** *played at Griffin Park* | | L | 0-1 | |
| 1968-69 (D2) | 3 | 04.01.69 | **Southampton** (D1) | H | D | 1-1 | Sloan |
| | 3r | 08.01.69 | **Southampton** | A | L | 0-2 | |
| 1969-70 (D2) | 3 | 03.01.70 | **Stoke City** (D1) | H | D | 0-0 | |
| | 3r | 07.01.70 | **Stoke City** | A | L | 2-3 | G Atkinson, Skeen |
| 1970-71 (D2) | 3 | 11.01.71 | **Burnley** (D1) | H | W | 3-0 | Skeen, G Atkinson, Cassidy |
| | 4 | 23.01.71 | **Watford** (D2) | H | D | 1-1 | Skeen |
| | 4r | 27.01.71 | **Watford** | A | W | 2-1 | Skeen, C Clarke |
| | 5 | 13.02.71 | **Leicester City** (D2) | A | D | 1-1 | Lucas |
| | 5r | 17.02.71 | **Leicester City** | H | L | 1-3aet | R Atkinson |
| 1971-72 (D2) | 3 | 15.01.72 | **Liverpool** (D1) | H | L | 0-3 | |
| 1972-73 (D2) | 3 | 13.01.73 | **York City** (D4) | A | W | 1-0 | Gough |
| | 4 | 03.02.73 | **QPR** (D2) | H | L | 0-2 | |
| 1973-74 (D2) | 3 | 05.01.74 | **Manchester City** (D1) | H | L | 2-5 | Curran (p), G Atkinson |
| 1974-75 (D2) | 3 | 04.01.75 | **Leicester City** (D1) | A | L | 1-3 | D Clarke |
| 1975-76 (D2) | 3 | 03.01.76 | **Manchester Utd** (D1) | A | L | 1-2 | D Clarke |
| 1976-77 (D3) | 1 | 20.11.76 | **Kettering Town** (SL) | A | D | 1-1 | Foley |
| | 1r | 23.11.76 | **Kettering Town** | H | L | 0-1 | |
| 1977-78 (D3) | 1 | 26.11.77 | **Nuneaton B** (SL) | A | L | 0-2 | |
| 1978-79 (D3) | 1 | 25.11.78 | **Colchester Utd** (D3) | A | L | 2-4 | Foley, Seacole |
| 1979-80 (D3) | 1 | 24.11.79 | **Barking** (IL) | A | L | 0-1 | |
| 1980-81 (D3) | 1 | 22.11.80 | **Aldershot** (D4) | H | W | 1-0 | Foley |
| | 2 | 13.12.80 | **Plymouth Argyle** (D3) | A | L | 0-3 | |
| 1981-82 (D3) | 1 | 21.11.81 | **Dover** (SL) | A | W | 2-0 | Smithers, Thomas |
| | 2 | 15.12.81 | **Aldershot** (D4) | A | D | 2-2 | Cassells 2 |

| | | | | | | | |
|---|---|---|---|---|---|---|---|
| | 2r | 30.12.81 | **Aldershot** | H | W | 4-2 | Cassells 3, Thomas |
| | 3 | 02.01.82 | **Bournemouth** (D4) | A | W | 2-0 | Cassells, Thomas |
| | 4 | 23.01.82 | **Brighton** (D1) | A | W | 3-0 | Cassells, Foley 2 |
| | 5 | 13.02.82 | **Coventry City** (D1) | A | L | 0-4 | |
| 1982-83 (D3) | 1 | 20.11.82 | **Folkestone & S** (SL) | H | W | 5-2 | Foley 2, Shotton, Fogg (p), Vinter |
| | 2 | 11.12.82 | **Worthing** (IL) | H | W | 4-0 | Hebberd, Foley, Vinter 2 |
| | 3 | 08.01.83 | **Torquay Utd** (D4) | H | D | 1-1 | Foley |
| | 3r | 12.01.83 | **Torquay Utd** | A | L | 1-2 | Fogg (p) |
| 1983-84 (D3) | 1 | 19.11.83 | **Peterborough Utd** (D4) | H | W | 2-0 | Biggins, Mcdonald |
| | 2 | 10.12.83 | **Reading** (D4) | A | D | 1-1 | Biggins |
| | 2r | 14.12.83 | **Reading** | H | W | 3-0 | Brock, Vinter, Mcdonald |
| | 3 | 07.01.84 | **Burnley** (D3) | A | D | 0-0 | |
| | 3r | 11.01.84 | **Burnley** | H | W | 2-1 | Lawrence, Scott og |
| | 4 | 28.01.84 | **Blackpool** (D4) | H | W | 2-1 | Macdonad 2 (2p) |
| | 5 | 18.02.84 | **Sheffield Wed** (D2) | H | L | 0-3 | |
| 1984-85 (D2) | 3 | 05.01.85 | **Shrewsbury Town** (D2) | A | W | 2-0 | McDermott, Aldridge |
| | 4 | 30.01.85 | **Blackburn Rovers** (D2) | H | L | 0-1 | |
| 1985-86 (D1) | 3 | 04.01.86 | **Tottenham Hotspur** (D1) | H | D | 1-1 | Slatter |
| | 3r | 08.01.86 | **Tottenham Hotspur** | A | L | 1-2aet | Aldridge |
| 1986-87 (D1) | 3 | 10.01.87 | **Aldershot** (D4) | A | L | 0-3 | |
| 1987-88 (D1) | 3 | 09.01.88 | **Leicester City** (D2) | H | W | 2-0 | Foyle, Saunders |
| | 4 | 30.01.88 | **Bradford City** (D2) | A | L | 2-4 | Rhoades-Brown, Saunders (p) |
| 1988-89 (D2) | 3 | 07.01.89 | **Sunderland** (D2) | A | D | 1-1 | Hill |
| | 3r | 11.01.89 | **Sunderland** | H | W | 2-0 | Hill 2 |
| | 4 | 28.01.89 | **Manchester Utd** (D1) | A | L | 0-4 | |
| 1989-90 (D2) | 3 | 06.01.90 | **Plymouth Argyle** (D2) | A | W | 1-0 | Simpson |
| | 4 | 27.01.90 | **Southampton** (D1) | A | L | 0-1 | |
| 1990-91 (D2) | 3 | 05.01.91 | **Chelsea** (D1) | A | W | 3-1 | Nogan, Durnin, Magilton |
| | 4 | 26.01.91 | **Tottenham Hotspur** (D1) | A | L | 2-4 | Foyle 2 |
| 1991-92 (D2) | 3 | 04.01.92 | **Tranmere Rovers** (D2) | H | W | 3-1 | Beauchamp, Magilton (p), Vickers og |
| | 4 | 05.02.92 | **Sunderland** (D2) | H | L | 2-3 | Simpson, Penney |
| 1992-93 (D1) | 3 | 02.01.93 | **Swansea City** (D2) | A | D | 1-1 | Cusack |
| | 3r | 12.01.93 | **Swansea City** | H | D | 2-2aet | Magilton, Beauchamp |
| | | | *Swansea City won 5-4 on penalties* | | | | |
| 1993-94 (D1) | 3 | 08.01.94 | **Tranmere Rovers** (D1) | H | W | 2-0 | Elliott, Byrne |
| | 4 | 29.01.94 | **Leeds Utd** (PL) | H | D | 2-2 | Dyer, Elliott |
| | 4r | 09.02.94 | **Leeds Utd** | A | W | 3-2aet | Byrne, Allen, Magilton |
| | 5 | 19.02.94 | **Chelsea** (PL) | H | L | 1-2 | Beauchamp |
| 1994-95 (D2) | 1 | 13.11.94 | **Marlow** (IL) | A | L | 0-2 | |
| 1995-96 (D2) | 1 | 11.11.95 | **Dorchester Town** (SL) | H | W | 9-1 | Moody 3, Wood 2, M Ford, R Ford, Rush, Beauchamp |
| | 2 | 02.12.95 | **Northampton Town** (D3) | H | W | 2-0 | Massey, Moody |
| | 3 | 06.01.96 | **Millwall** (D1) | A | D | 3-3 | Massey, Moody, R Ford |
| | 3r | 16.01.96 | **Millwall** | H | W | 1-0 | Massey |
| | 4 | 07.02.96 | **Nottingham Forest** (PL) | A | D | 1-1 | Massey |
| | 4r | 13.02.96 | **Nottingham Forest** | H | L | 0-3 | |
| 1996-97 (D1) | 3 | 21.01.97 | **Watford** (D2) | A | L | 0-2 | |
| 1997-98 (D1) | 3 | 03.01.98 | **Leeds Utd** (PL) | A | L | 0-4 | |
| 1998-99 (D1) | 3 | 02.01.99 | **Crewe Alexandra** (D1) | A | W | 3-1 | Windass, Murphy 2 |
| | 4 | 25.01.99 | **Chelsea** (PL) | H | D | 1-1 | Windass |
| | 4r | 03.02.99 | **Chelsea** | A | L | 2-4 | Gilchrist, Windass (p) |
| 1999-00 (D2) | 1 | 30.10.99 | **Morecambe** (Conf) | H | W | 3-2 | Lilley, Powell, Abbey |
| | 2 | 20.11.99 | **Shrewsbury Town** (D3) | A | D | 2-2 | Murphy, Folland |
| | 2r | 30.11.99 | **Shrewsbury Town** | H | W | 2-1aet | Murphy 2 |
| | 3 | 10.12.99 | **Nottingham Forest** (D1) | A | D | 1-1 | Powell |
| | 3r | 08.01.00 | **Nottingham Forest** | H | L | 1-3 | Powell |
| 2000-01 (D2) | 1 | 18.11.00 | **Macclesfield Town** (D3) | A | W | 1-0 | Gray |
| | 2 | 09.12.00 | **Chester City** (Conf) | A | L | 2-3 | Gray, Murphy |
| 2001-02 (D3) | 1 | 17.11.01 | **Mansfield Town** (D3) | A | L | 0-1 | |
| 2002-03 (D3) | 1 | 16.11.02 | **Dover** (SL) | A | W | 1-0 | Oldfield |
| | 2 | 07.12.02 | **Swindon Town** (D2) | H | W | 1-0 | Louis |
| | 3 | 04.01.03 | **Arsenal** (PL) | A | L | 0-2 | |

# OXFORD UNIVERSITY

*Formed 1860s. Entered FA Cup: 1872-73 – 1879-80. FA Cup winners: 1874. Runners-up: 1873, 1877, 1880. Were the last student team to take part in the Competition Proper for 122 years until Team Bath reached the first round of the FA Cup in 2002-03.*

| | | | | | | | |
|---|---|---|---|---|---|---|---|
| 1872-73 | 1 | 26.10.72 | **Crystal Palace (1861)** | H | W | 3-2 | Dixon, Longman, Summer |
| | 2 | 23.11.72 | **Clapham Rovers** | A | W | 3-0 | Dixon, AK Smith, Ottaway |
| | 3 | 09.12.72 | **Royal Engineers** | H | W | 1-0 | AK Smith |
| | 4 | 03.02.73 | **Maidenhead** | H | W | 4-0 | Dixon, Ottaway, W Paton, Vidal |
| | SF | | Queen's Park, Glasgow | | | - | |
| | | | *Queen's Park scratched. Oxford University walkover* | | | | |
| | F | 23.03.73 | **Wanderers** | | L | 0-2 | |
| | | | *played at Lillie Bridge* | | | | |
| 1873-74 | 1 | 29.10.73 | **Upton Park** | H | W | 4-0 | Hughes, Ottaway, W Paton, Vidal |
| | 2 | 22.11.73 | **Barnes** | H | W | 2-0 | |
| | 3 | 06.12.73 | **Wanderers** | A | D | 1-1 | |
| | 3r | 31.01.74 | **Wanderers** | H | W | 1-0 | Hughes |
| | SF | 28.02.74 | **Clapham Rovers** | | W | 1-0 | Vidal |
| | | | *played at Kennington Oval* | | | | |
| | F | 14.03.74 | **Royal Engineers** | | W | 2-0 | Mackarness, Patton |
| | | | *played at Kennington Oval* | | | | |
| 1874-75 | 1 | 31.10.74 | **Brondesbury** | H | W | 6-0 | Parry 3, Hughes 2, Cripps |
| | 2 | | Windsor Home Park | | | - | |
| | | | *Windsor Home Park scratched. Oxford University walkover* | | | | |
| | 3 | 30.01.75 | **Wanderers** | A | W | 2-1 | Otter, Simpson |
| | SF | 27.02.75 | **Royal Engineers** | | D | 1-1 | Bain |
| | | | *played at Kennington Oval* | | | | |
| | SFr | 05.03.75 | **Royal Engineers** | | L | 0-1aet | |
| | | | *played at Kennington Oval* | | | | |
| 1875-76 | 1 | 30.10.75 | **Forest School** | H | W | 6-0 | Bain 2, Otter, Parry, Simpson, og |
| | 2 | 18.12.75 | **Herts Rangers** | H | W | 8-2 | Simpson 2, Bain, Parry, 4 others |
| | 3 | 31.01.76 | **Cambridge University** | A | W | 4-0 | Bain, Parry, 2 ogs |
| | SF | 19.02.76 | **Old Etonians** | | L | 0-1 | |
| | | | *played at Kennington Oval* | | | | |
| 1876-77 | 1 | | Old Salopians | | | - | |
| | | | *Old Salopians scratched. Oxford University walkover* | | | | |
| | 2 | 14.12.76 | **105th Regiment** | H | W | 6-1 | Hills 2, Vidal 2, Bain, Todd |
| | 3 | | Queen's Park, Glasgow | | | - | |
| | | | *Queen's Park scratched. Oxford University walkover* | | | | |
| | 4 | 24.02.77 | **Upton Park** | H | D | 0-0 | |
| | 4r | 10.03.77 | **Upton Park** | A | W | 1-0 | Bain |
| | SF | | bye | | | | |
| | F | 24.03.77 | **Wanderers** | | L | 1-2aet | Waddington |
| | | | *played at Kennington Oval* | | | | |
| 1877-78 | 1 | 03.11.77 | **Herts Rangers** | H | W | 5-2 | |
| | 2 | 15.12.77 | **Old Foresters** | H | W | 1-0 | own goal |
| | 3 | 02.02.78 | **Clapham Rovers** | H | W | 3-2 | Heygate, Otter, Parry |
| | 4 | 15.02.78 | **Royal Engineers** | A | D | 3-3 | |
| | 4r | 27.02.78 | **Royal Engineers** | H | D | 2-2aet | Otter 2 |
| | 4 2r | 12.03.78 | **Royal Engineers** | A | L | 2-4 | Crowdy, AN Other |
| 1878-79 | 1 | 02.11.78 | **Wednesbury Strollers** | H | W | 7-0 | |
| | 2 | 07.12.78 | **Royal Engineers** | H | W | 4-0 | Childs 2, Mulholland, Page |
| | 3 | 02.02.79 | **Barnes** | H | W | 2-1 | Blaine, AN Other |
| | 4 | 25.02.79 | **Nottingham Forest** | A | L | 1-2 | Blaine |
| 1879-80 | 1 | 06.11.79 | **Marlow** | H | D | 1-1 | Aston |
| | 1r | 10.11.79 | **Marlow** | A | W | 1-0 | |
| | 2 | 19.01.80 | **Birmingham Club** | H | W | 6-0 | |
| | 3 | | Aston Villa | | | - | |
| | | | *Aston Villa scratched. Oxford University walkover* | | | | |
| | 4 | 14.02.80 | **Maidenhead** | H | W | 1-0 | |
| | 5 | 05.03.80 | **Royal Engineers** | H | D | 1-1aet | Lubbock |
| | 5r | 15.03.80 | **Royal Engineers** | A | W | 1-0 | Childs |

| | | | | | | | |
|---|---|---|---|---|---|---|---|
| | SF | 27.03.80 | **Nottingham Forest**<br>*played at Kennington Oval* | | W | 1-0 | Childs |
| | F | 10.04.80 | **Clapham Rovers**<br>*played at Kennington Oval* | | L | 0-1 | |

## PADIHAM

*Formed 1878. Entered FA Cup: 1883-84 – 1914-15. Played these early FA Cup matches at Albert Mill, Padiham. Members of the North West Counties League.*

| | | | | | | | |
|---|---|---|---|---|---|---|---|
| 1883-84 | 1 | 31.10.83 | **Lower Darwen** | H | W | 3-1 | |
| | 2 | | bye | | | | |
| | 3 | 24.12.83 | **Blackburn Rovers** | A | L | 0-3 | |
| 1885-86 | 1 | | Heart of Midlothian<br>*Hearts scratched. Padiham walkover* | | | - | |
| | 2 | 21.11.85 | **Rossendale FC** | A | L | 1-9 | |

## PANTHERS

*Entered FA Cup: 1874-75 – 1879-80.*

| | | | | | | | |
|---|---|---|---|---|---|---|---|
| 1874-75 | 1 | 07.11.74 | **Clapham Rovers** | A | L | 0-3 | |
| 1875-76 | 1 | 06.11.75 | **Woodford Wells** | H | W | 1-0 | |
| | 2 | | Royal Engineers<br>*Panthers scratched. Royal Engineers walkover* | | | - | |
| 1876-77 | 1 | 08.11.76 | **Wood Grange** | H | W | 3-0 | E Farquharson, AN Other 2 |
| | 2 | 09.12.76 | **Pilgrims** | A | L | 0-1 | |
| 1877-78 | 1 | 07.11.77 | **Wanderers** | A | L | 1-9 | E Farquharson |
| 1878-79 | 1 | | Runnymede<br>*Runnymede scratched. Panthers walkover* | | | - | |
| | 2 | 21.12.78 | **Old Harrovians** | A | L | 0-3 | |
| 1879-80 | 1 | | Birmingham Club<br>*Panthers scratched. Birmingham walkover* | | | - | |

## PARK GRANGE

*Entered FA Cup for two seasons in 1887-88 and 1888-89, playing this match in the Competition Proper.*

| | | | | | | | |
|---|---|---|---|---|---|---|---|
| 1887-88 | 1 | 15.10.87 | **Long Eaton Rangers** | A | L | 3-6 | |

## PARTICK THISTLE

*Formed 1876. Entered FA Cup: 1885-86 and 1886-87. One of the seven Scottish clubs that took part in the FA Cup in the 1880s, reaching the last 16 in 1887. Scottish FA Cup winners: 1921. Runners-up: 1930.*

| | | | | | | | |
|---|---|---|---|---|---|---|---|
| 1885-86 | 1 | 31.10.85 | **Queen's Park, Glasgow** | A | L | 1-5 | |
| 1886-87 | 1 | 23.10.86 | **Blackburn Olympic** | A | W | 3-1 | Paul 2, Johnstone |
| | 2 | 20.11.86 | **Fleetwood Rangers** | H | W | 7-0 | J Marshall, R Marshall, Paul, 4 others |
| | 3 | 04.12.86 | **Cliftonville** | A | W | 11-0 | Paul 4, Suter 2, Marshall, Johnstone, 3 others |
| | 4 | | bye | | | | |
| | 5 | 29.01.87 | **Old Westminsters** | A | L | 0-1 | |

## PENRITH

*Formed 1894. First entered FA Cup: 1906-07. League club beaten: Chester. Members of the Northern League.*

| | | | | | | | |
|---|---|---|---|---|---|---|---|
| 1981-82 (NL) | 1 | 21.11.81 | **Chester** (D3) | H | W | 1-0 | Fell |
| | 2 | 12.12.81 | **Doncaster Rovers** (D3) | A | L | 0-3 | |
| 1983-84 (NWC) | 1 | 19.11.83 | **Hull City** (D3) | H | L | 0-2 | |
| 1984-85 (NWC) | 1 | 17.11.84 | **Burnley** (D3)<br>*played at Turf Moor* | H | L | 0-9 | |

## PETERBOROUGH & FLETTON UNITED

*Formed 1923 when Peterborough City amalgamated with Fletton United. Entered FA Cup: 1924-25 – 1931-32. The FA suspended the club for financial irregularities and it disbanded on August 6, 1932. Peterborough United was formed 18 months later and the two are separate entities.*

| | | | | | | | |
|---|---|---|---|---|---|---|---|
| 1927-28 (SL) | 1 | 30.11.27 | **Botwell Mission** (SPT) | A | W | 4-3 | Bruton 2, McNaughton, Baker |
| | 2 | 10.12.27 | **Aldershot Town** (SL) | H | W | 2-1 | McNaughton, Bruton |
| | 3 | 14.01.28 | **Birmingham** (D1) | A | L | 3-4 | Bruton 2, McGuigan |
| 1928-29 (SL) | 1 | 24.11.28 | **Charlton Athletic** (3S) | H | L | 0-2 | |
| 1929-30 (SL) | 1 | 30.11.29 | **Brighton** (3S) | A | L | 0-4 | |
| 1930-31 (SL) | 1 | 29.11.30 | **Aldershot Town** (SL) | A | L | 1-4 | Hoyland |
| 1931-32 (SL) | 1 | 28.11.31 | **Darwen** (LC) | A | L | 1-4 | Willis |

# PETERBOROUGH UNITED

*Formed 1934 following the demise of Peterborough & Fletton United. First entered FA Cup: 1935-36. FA Cup best performance: Quarter-finals 1965. Record FA Cup win: 9-1 v Rushden Town, 1st qualifying round, 1945-46. In Competition Proper: 7-0 v Harlow Town, 1st round, 16.11.1991. Their 9-1 win over Kingstonian in November 1992 was declared void by the FA following a coin-throwing incident. Record FA Cup defeat: 1-8 v Northampton Town, 2nd round replay, 18.12.1946.*

| | | | | | | | | |
|---|---|---|---|---|---|---|---|---|
| 1936-37 | (ML) | 1 | 28.11.36 | **Dartford** (SL) | A | L | 0-3 | |
| 1938-39 | (ML) | 1 | 26.11.38 | **Bristol Rovers** (3S) | A | L | 1-4 | Fielding |
| 1946-47 | (ML) | 1 | 30.11.46 | **Yeovil Town** (SL) | A | D | 2-2 | Rudkin, Bayliss |
| | | 1r | 05.12.46 | **Yeovil Town** | H | W | 1-0 | Rudkin |
| | | 2 | 14.12.46 | **Northampton Town** (3S) | H | D | 1-1 | Bramham |
| | | 2r | 19.12.46 | **Northampton Town** | A | D | 1-1aet | Padgett |
| | | 2 2r | 23.12.46 | **Northampton Town** | | L | 1-8 | Brooksbanks |
| | | | | *played at Highfield Road, Coventry* | | | | |
| 1948-49 | (ML) | 1 | 27.11.48 | **Torquay Utd** (3S) | H | L | 0-1 | |
| 1952-53 | (ML) | 1 | 22.11.52 | **Torquay Utd** | H | W | 2-1 | Sloan, Martin |
| | | 2 | 06.12.52 | **Bristol Rovers** (3S) | H | L | 0-1 | |
| 1953-54 | (ML) | 1 | 21.11.53 | **Hitchin Town** (AL) | A | W | 3-1 | Campbell, Taft 2 |
| | | 2 | 12.12.53 | **Aldershot** (3S) | H | W | 2-1 | Martin, Taft |
| | | 3 | 09.01.54 | **Cardiff City** (D1) | A | L | 1-3 | Martin |
| 1955-56 | (ML) | 1 | 19.11.55 | **Ipswich Town** (3S) | H | W | 3-1 | Emery 2, Hair |
| | | 2 | 10.12.55 | **Swindon Town** (3S) | A | D | 1-1 | Emery |
| | | 2r | 15.12.55 | **Swindon Town** | H | L | 1-2aet | Emery |
| 1956-57 | (ML) | 1 | 17.11.56 | **Yeovil Town** (SL) | A | W | 3-1 | Emery 2, Hails |
| | | 2 | 08.12.56 | **Bradford Park A** (3N) | H | W | 3-0 | Emery, Hails, Donaldson |
| | | 3 | 05.01.57 | **Lincoln City** (D2) | H | D | 2-2 | Emery 2 |
| | | 3r | 09.01.57 | **Lincoln City** | A | W | 5-4aet | Emery, Donaldson 3, Smith |
| | | 4 | 26.01.57 | **Huddersfield Town** (D2) | A | L | 1-3 | Shaw |
| 1957-58 | (ML) | 1 | 16.11.57 | **Torquay Utd** (3S) | H | D | 3-3 | Emery, Donaldson 2 |
| | | 1r | 20.11.57 | **Torquay Utd** | A | L | 0-1 | |
| 1958-59 | (ML) | 1 | 15.11.58 | **Kettering Town** (SL) | H | D | 2-2 | Emery, Hails |
| | | 1r | 20.11.58 | **Kettering Town** | A | W | 3-2aet | Emery, Hails, Reynolds og |
| | | 2 | 06.12.58 | **Headington Utd** (SL) | H | W | 4-2 | Emery 2, Hails, Rayner |
| | | 3 | 10.01.59 | **Fulham** (D2) | A | D | 0-0 | |
| | | 3r | 24.01.59 | **Fulham** | H | L | 0-1 | |
| 1959-60 | (ML) | 1 | 14.11.59 | **Shrewsbury Town** (D3) | H | W | 4-3 | Emery 2, Rayner, Smith |
| | | 2 | 05.12.59 | **Walsall** (D4) | A | W | 3-2 | Rayner, Smith, McNamee |
| | | 3 | 09.01.60 | **Ipswich Town** (D2) | A | W | 3-2 | Emery 2, Raynor |
| | | 4 | 30.01.60 | **Sheffield Wed** (D1) | A | L | 0-2 | |
| 1960-61 | (D4) | 1 | 05.11.60 | **Dover** (SL) | A | W | 4-1 | Emery 2, Bly, Ripley |
| | | 2 | 26.11.60 | **Torquay Utd** (D3) | A | W | 3-1 | McNamee 2, Bly |
| | | 3 | 07.01.61 | **Portsmouth** (D2) | A | W | 2-1 | Ripley, Hails |
| | | 4 | 28.01.61 | **Aston Villa** (D1) | H | D | 1-1 | Hails |
| | | 4r | 01.02.61 | **Aston Villa** | A | L | 1-2 | McNamee |
| 1961-62 | (D3) | 1 | 04.11.61 | **Colchester Utd** (D4) | H | D | 3-3 | McNamee, Bly, Hudson |
| | | 1r | 06.11.61 | **Colchester Utd** | A | D | 2-2aet | Emery, Bly |
| | | 1r | 13.11.61 | **Colchester Utd** | | W | 3-0 | Hudson 3 |
| | | | | *played at Carrow Road* | | | | |
| | | 2 | 25.11.61 | **Torquay Utd** (D3) | A | W | 4-1 | Hudson 2, Hails, Bly |
| | | 3 | 06.01.62 | **Newcastle Utd** (D2) | A | W | 1-0 | Bly |
| | | 4 | 27.01.62 | **Sheffield Utd** (D1) | H | L | 1-3 | Hudson |
| 1962-63 | (D3) | 1 | 03.11.62 | **Notts County** (D3) | A | W | 3-0 | Hudson 2, McNamee |
| | | 2 | 24.11.62 | **Enfield** (AL) | H | W | 1-0 | Hudson |
| | | 3 | 04.02.63 | **Derby County** (D2) | A | L | 0-2 | |
| 1963-64 | (D3) | 1 | 16.11.63 | **Watford** (D3) | H | D | 1-1 | Bell og |
| | | 1r | 19.11.63 | **Watford** | A | L | 1-2aet | Senior |
| 1964-65 | (D3) | 1 | 14.11.64 | **Salisbury City** (WL) | H | W | 5-1 | Dougan 3, Deakin, Crowe |
| | | 2 | 05.12.64 | **QPR** (D3) | A | D | 3-3 | Barnes, Deakin (p), McNamee |
| | | 2r | 09.12.64 | **QPR** | H | W | 2-1aet | Deakin 2 |
| | | 3 | 09.01.65 | **Chesterfield** (D4) | A | W | 3-0 | Dougan 3 |
| | | 4 | 30.01.65 | **Arsenal** (D1) | H | W | 2-1 | Dougan, McNamee |

| | | | | | | | |
|---|---|---|---|---|---|---|---|
| | 5 | 20.02.65 | **Swansea Town** (D2) | H | D | 0-0 | |
| | 5r | 24.02.65 | **Swansea Town** | A | W | 2-0 | Deakin 2 (1p) |
| | 6 | 06.03.65 | **Chelsea** (D1) | A | L | 1-5 | Crowe |
| 1965-66 (D3) | 1 | 13.11.65 | **Kidderminster H** (WMRL) | H | W | 2-1 | Deakin 2 |
| | 2 | 04.12.65 | **Shrewsbury Town** (D3) | A | L | 2-3 | Deakin, Birks |
| 1966-67 (D3) | 1 | 26.11.66 | **Hereford Utd** (SL) | H | W | 4-1 | Fairbrother, Byrne, Conmy, Griffiths og |
| | 2 | 07.01.67 | **Colchester Utd** (D3) | A | W | 3-0 | Watson 2, Fairbrother |
| | 3 | 28.01.67 | **Bedford Town** (SL) | A | W | 6-2 | Watson 3, Conmy, Orr, Fairbrother |
| | 4 | 18.02.67 | **Sunderland** (D1) | A | L | 1-7 | Watson |
| 1967-68 (D3) | 1 | 12.12.67 | **Falmouth Town** (SWL) | H | W | 5-2 | Fairbrother 3, Brace, Byrne |
| | 2 | 06.01.68 | **Margate** (SL) | A | W | 4-0 | Brace, Thompson, Deakin, Conmy |
| | 3 | 27.01.68 | **Portsmouth** (D2) | H | L | 0-1 | |
| 1968-69 (D4) | 1 | 16.11.68 | **Bristol Rovers** (D3) | A | L | 1-3 | Downes |
| 1969-70 (D4) | 1 | 15.11.69 | **Falmouth Town** (SWL) | A | W | 4-1 | Hall 2, Robson, Price |
| | 2 | 06.12.69 | **Plymouth Argyle** (D3) | H | W | 2-0 | Conmy, Price |
| | 3 | 03.01.70 | **Rotherham Utd** (D3) | A | W | 1-0 | Hall |
| | 4 | 24.01.70 | **Gillingham** (D3) | A | L | 1-5 | Price |
| 1970-71 (D4) | 1 | 21.11.70 | **Wimbledon** (SL) | H | W | 3-1 | Garwood, Hall, Moss |
| | 2 | 12.12.70 | **Wigan Athletic** (NPL) | A | L | 1-2 | Moss |
| 1971-72 (D4) | 1 | 20.11.71 | **Redditch Utd** (WMRL) | A | D | 1-1 | Price |
| | 1r | 22.11.71 | **Redditch Utd** | H | W | 6-0 | Price, Hall 2, Barker 2, Robson |
| | 2 | 11.12.71 | **Enfield** (IL) | H | W | 4-0 | Price 2, Hall 2 |
| | 3 | 15.01.72 | **Ipswich Town** (D1) | H | L | 0-2 | |
| 1972-73 (D4) | 1 | 18.11.72 | **Northampton Town** (D4) | H | W | 1-0 | Hall |
| | 2 | 09.12.72 | **Bishop's Stortford** (IL) | A | D | 2-2 | Cozens, Robson |
| | 2r | 11.12.72 | **Bishop's Stortford** | H | W | 3-1 | Robson, Hall, Heath |
| | 3 | 13.01.73 | **Derby County** (D1) | H | L | 0-1 | |
| 1973-74 (D4) | 1 | 24.11.73 | **Colchester Utd** (D4) | A | W | 3-2 | Cozens 2, Murray |
| | 2 | 15.12.73 | **Wycombe W** (IL) | A | W | 3-1 | Cozens 2, Hall |
| | 3 | 05.01.74 | **Southend Utd** (D3) | H | W | 3-1 | Cozens, Hill, Robson |
| | 4 | 26.01.74 | **Leeds Utd** (D1) | H | L | 1-4 | Cozens |
| 1974-75 (D3) | 1 | 23.11.74 | **Weymouth** (SL) | H | D | 0-0 | |
| | 1r | 04.12.74 | **Weymouth** | A | D | 3-3aet | Turner, Gregory, Llewelyn |
| | 12r | 09.12.74 | **Weymouth** | H | W | 3-0 | Turner, Gregory 2 |
| | 2 | 14.12.74 | **Charlton Athletic** (D3) | H | W | 3-0 | Murray, Gregory, Nixon |
| | 3 | 04.01.75 | **Tranmere Rovers** (D3) | H | W | 1-0 | Bradley |
| | 4 | 24.01.75 | **Stafford Rangers** (NPL) | | W | 2-1 | Nixon, Gregory |
| | | | *played at the the Victoria Ground, Stoke* | | | | |
| | 5 | 15.02.75 | **Middlesbrough** (D1) | H | D | 1-1 | Nixon |
| | 5r | 18.02.75 | **Middlesbrough** | A | L | 0-2 | |
| 1975-76 (D3) | 1 | 22.11.75 | **Winsford Utd** (CC) | H | W | 4-1 | Nixon, Gregory, Turner, Cozens |
| | 2 | 13.12.75 | **Coventry Sporting** (WMRL) | A | W | 4-0 | Gregory, Hughes, Jones, D Jones og |
| | | | *played at Highfield Road* | | | | |
| | 3 | 01.01.76 | **Nottingham Forest** (D2) | A | D | 0-0 | |
| | 3r | 07.01.76 | **Nottingham Forest** | H | W | 1-0 | Nixon |
| | 4 | 24.01.76 | **Manchester Utd** (D1) | A | L | 1-3 | Cozens |
| 1976-77 (D3) | 1 | 20.11.76 | **Tranmere Rovers** (D3) | A | W | 4-0 | Carmichael, Moss, Cozens, Robson |
| | 2 | 11.12.76 | **Northwich V** (NPL) | A | - | 1-0ab | Nixon |
| | | | *abandoned after 20 minutes – fog* | | | | |
| | 2 | 14.12.76 | **Northwich V** (NPL) | A | L | 0-4 | |
| 1977-78 (D3) | 1 | 26.11.77 | **Barnet** (SL) | A | W | 2-1 | Slough, Robson |
| | 2 | 17.12.77 | **Gillingham** (D3) | A | D | 1-1 | Slough |
| | 2r | 20.12.77 | **Gillingham** | H | W | 2-0 | Sargent, Carmichael |
| | 3 | 07.01.78 | **Newcastle Utd** (D1) | H | D | 1-1 | Sargent |
| | 3r | 11.01.78 | **Newcastle Utd** | A | L | 0-2 | |
| 1978-79 (D3) | 1 | 25.11.78 | **Southend Utd** (D3) | A | L | 2-3 | Butlin, Anderson |
| 1979-80 (D4) | 1 | 24.11.79 | **Bournemouth** (D4) | H | L | 1-2 | Kellock |
| 1980-81 (D4) | 1 | 22.11.80 | **Northampton Town** (D4) | A | W | 4-1 | Robson 2, Slack, Quow |
| | 2 | 13.12.80 | **Barnet** (APL) | A | W | 1-0 | Robson |
| | 3 | 03.01.81 | **Chesterfield** (D3) | H | D | 1-1 | Cooke |
| | 3r | 06.01.81 | **Chesterfield** | A | W | 2-1 | Cooke 2 |
| | 4 | 24.01.81 | **Notts County** (D2) | A | W | 1-0 | Cooke |

| | | | | | | | |
|---|---|---|---|---|---|---|---|
| | 5 | 14.02.81 | **Manchester City** (D1) | H | L | 0-1 | |
| 1981-82 (D4) | 1 | 21.11.81 | **Halifax Town** (D4) | A | W | 3-0 | Cooke 2, Syrett |
| | 2 | 02.01.82 | **Walsall** (D3) | H | W | 2-1 | Cooke, Chard |
| | 3 | 06.01.82 | **Bristol City** (D3) | H | L | 0-1 | |
| 1982-83 (D4) | 1 | 20.11.82 | **Chesterfield** (D3) | A | D | 2-2 | Gynn, Clarke |
| | 1r | 24.11.82 | **Chesterfield** | H | W | 2-1 | Gynn, Cooke |
| | 2 | 11.12.82 | **Doncaster Rovers** (D3) | H | W | 5-2 | Gynn, Cooke 2, Clarke, Quow |
| | 3 | 08.01.83 | **Luton Town** (D1) | A | L | 0-3 | |
| 1983-84 (D4) | 1 | 19.11.83 | **Oxford Utd** (D3) | A | L | 0-2 | |
| 1984-85 (D4) | 1 | 17.11.84 | **Cambridge Utd** (D3) | A | W | 2-0 | Kelly 2 |
| | 2 | 08.12.84 | **Dagenham** (APL) | A | L | 0-1 | |
| 1985-86 (D4) | 1 | 16.11.85 | **Bishop's Stortford** (IL) | A | D | 2-2 | Worrell, Hull og |
| | 1r | 20.11.85 | **Bishop's Stortford** | H | W | 3-1 | Kowalski, Gallagher, Cassidy |
| | 2 | 07.12.85 | **Bath City** (APL) | H | W | 1-0 | Gallagher |
| | 3 | 04.01.86 | **Leeds Utd** (D2) | H | W | 1-0 | Shepherd |
| | 4 | 25.01.86 | **Carlisle Utd** (D2) | H | W | 1-0 | Shepherd |
| | 5 | 15.02.86 | **Brighton** (D2) | H | D | 2-2 | Shepherd, Kelly |
| | 5r | 03.03.86 | **Brighton** | A | L | 0-1 | |
| 1986-87 (D4) | 1 | 16.11.86 | **Northampton Town** (D4) | A | L | 0-3 | |
| 1987-88 (D4) | 1 | 14.11.87 | **Cardiff City** (D4) | H | W | 2-1 | Goodall 2 |
| | 2 | 05.12.87 | **Sutton Utd** (Conf) | H | L | 1-3 | Lawrence |
| 1988-89 (D4) | 1 | 19.11.88 | **Gillingham** (D3) | A | D | 3-3 | Longhurst 3 |
| | 1r | 23.11.88 | **Gillingham** | H | W | 1-0aet | Haines og |
| | 2 | 10.12.88 | **Brentford** (D3) | H | D | 0-0 | |
| | 2r | 14.12.88 | **Brentford** | A | L | 2-3 | Halsall, Cusack |
| 1989-90 (D4) | 1 | 18.11.89 | **Hayes** (IL) | H | D | 1-1 | Sterling |
| | 1r | 21.11.89 | **Hayes** | A | W | 1-0 | Robinson |
| | 2 | 09.12.89 | **Swansea City** (D3) | A | L | 1-3 | Andrews |
| 1990-91 (D4) | 1 | 17.11.90 | **Hereford Utd** (D4) | A | D | 1-1 | Riley |
| | 1r | 20.11.90 | **Hereford Utd** | H | W | 2-1 | Sterling, Riley |
| | 2 | 12.12.90 | **Wycombe W** (Conf) | A | D | 1-1 | Culpin |
| | 2r | 17.12.90 | **Wycombe W** | H | W | 2-0 | Halsall, Culpin |
| | 3 | 05.01.91 | **Port Vale** (D2) | A | L | 1-2 | Halsall |
| 1991-92 (D3) | 1 | 16.11.91 | **Harlow Town** (IL) | H | W | 7-0 | Cooper 2 (1p), Riley, Sterling, Halsall, Charlery, Culpin |
| | 2 | 07.12.91 | **Reading** (D3) | H | D | 0-0 | |
| | 2r | 17.12.91 | **Reading** | A | L | 0-1 | |
| 1992-93 (D1) | 1 | 14.11.92 | **Kingstonian** (IL) | A | D | 1-1 | Adcock |
| | 1r | 25.11.92 | **Kingstonian** | H | W | 9-1 | Philliskirk 5, Adcock 2, Cooper, Harlow og |
| | | | *FA ordered match to be replayed behind closed doors after Kingstonian goalkeeper was hit by coins and injured* | | | | |
| | 1r | 04.12.92 | **Kingstonian** (IL) | H | W | 1-0 | Sterling |
| | | | *played at Peterborough behind closed dooors* | | | | |
| | 2 | 09.12.92 | **Plymouth Argyle** (D2) | A | L | 2-3 | Philliskirk, Sterling |
| 1993-94 (D1) | 3 | 08.01.94 | **Tottenham Hotspur** (PL) | H | D | 1-1 | Brisett |
| | 3r | 19.01.94 | **Tottenham Hotspur** | A | D | 1-1aet | K Charlerey |
| | | | *Tottenham Hotspur won 5-4 on penalties* | | | | |
| 1994-95 (D2) | 1 | 12.11.94 | **Northampton Town** (D3) | H | W | 4-0 | K Charlerey 2 (1p), Willems, T Henry |
| | 2 | 03.12.94 | **Cambridge Utd** (D2) | H | L | 0-2 | |
| 1995-96 (D2) | 1 | 11.11.95 | **Exeter City** (D3) | A | W | 1-0 | Le Bihan |
| | 2 | 02.12.95 | **Bognor Regis Town** (IL) | H | W | 4-0 | Farrell 3, Ebdon |
| | 3 | 06.01.96 | **Wrexham** (D2) | H | W | 1-0 | Le Bihan |
| | 4 | 06.02.96 | **Huddersfield Town** (D1) | A | L | 0-2 | |
| 1996-97 (D2) | 1 | 16.11.96 | **Cheltenham Town** (SL) | H | D | 0-0 | |
| | 1r | 27.11.96 | **Cheltenham Town** | A | W | 3-1aet | K Charlerey 2, Grazioli |
| | 2 | 07.12.96 | **Enfield** (IL) | A | D | 1-1 | K Charlerey |
| | 2r | 17.12.96 | **Enfield** | H | W | 4-1 | R Houghton, K Charlerey, Carruthers 2 |
| | 3 | 04.01.97 | **Plymouth Argyle** (D2) | A | W | 1-0 | K Charlerey |
| | 4 | 04.02.97 | **Wrexham** (D2) | H | L | 2-4 | K Charlerey, Griffiths |
| 1997-98 (D3) | 1 | 14.11.97 | **Swansea City** (D3) | A | W | 4-1 | Quinn, Castle 2, Carruthers |
| | 2 | 06.12.97 | **Dagenham & Red** (IL) | H | W | 3-2 | Carruthers, Quinn 2 |

| | | | | | | | |
|---|---|---|---|---|---|---|---|
| | 3 | 13.01.98 | **Walsall** (D2) | H | L | 0-2 | |
| 1998-99 (D3) | 1 | 14.11.98 | **Wrexham** (D2) | A | L | 0-1 | |
| 1999-00 (D3) | 1 | 30.10.99 | **Brighton** (D3) | H | D | 1-1 | Clarke |
| | 1r | 09.11.99 | **Brighton** | A | L | 0-3 | |
| 2000-01 (D2) | 1 | 18.11.00 | **Mansfield Town** (D3) | A | D | 1-1 | Farrell |
| | 1r | 28.11.00 | **Mansfield Town** | H | W | 4-0 | Oldfield, Edwards, Clarke, Shields |
| | 2 | 09.12.00 | **Oldham Athletic** (D2) | H | D | 1-1 | Lee |
| | 2r | 19.12.00 | **Oldham Athletic** | A | W | 1-0 | Forsyth |
| | 3 | 06.01.01 | **Chelsea** (PL) | A | L | 0-5 | |
| 2001-02 (D2) | 1 | 17.11.01 | **Bedford Town** (IL) | A | D | 0-0 | |
| | 1r | 27.11.01 | **Bedford Town** | H | W | 2-1 | A Clarke, Fenn |
| | 2 | 08.12.01 | **Bournemouth** (D2) | H | W | 1-0 | Danielsson |
| | 3 | 15.01.02 | **Darlington** (D3) | A | D | 2-2 | Farrell, Bullard (p) |
| | 3r | 21.01.02 | **Darlington** | H | W | 2-0 | McKenzie, A Clarke |
| | 4 | 27.01.02 | **Newcastle Utd** (PL) | H | L | 2-4 | O'Brien og, Farrell |
| 2002-03 (D2) | 1 | 16.11.02 | **Rochdale** (D3) | A | L | 2-3 | Fenn, Clarke |

## PHOENIX BESSEMER

*Formed 1876. Entered the FA Cup once in 1882-83. Played at Clifton Lane, Rotherham.*

| | | | | | | | |
|---|---|---|---|---|---|---|---|
| 1882-83 | 1 | | Grantham Town | | | - | |
| | | | *Grantham scratched. Phoenix Bessemer walkover* | | | | |
| | 2 | 25.11.82 | **Grimsby Town** | A | W | 9-1 | Marples 2, D Willey 2, F Thomas 2, Emmett 2, AN Other |
| | 3 | 27.12.82 | **Notts County** | A | L | 1-4 | Douglas |

## PILGRIMS

*Formed 1870 as Clapton Pilgrims. Entered FA Cup: 1873-74 – 1884-85. Played in and around Walthamstow and Hackney Downs in east London.*

| | | | | | | | |
|---|---|---|---|---|---|---|---|
| 1873-74 | 1 | 09.10.73 | **Marlow** | H | W | 1-0 | Foley |
| | 2 | 22.11.73 | **Sheffield FC** | A | L | 0-1 | |
| 1874-75 | 1 | 10.10.74 | **South Norwood** | H | W | 3-1 | Good 2, AN Other |
| | 2 | 05.12.74 | **Clapham Rovers** | A | L | 0-2 | |
| 1875-76 | 1 | 09.11.75 | **Old Etonians** | A | L | 1-4 | T Letchford |
| 1876-77 | 1 | 14.10.76 | **Ramblers** | H | W | 4-1 | Detmar, Elmslie, T Letchford, Lloyd |
| | 2 | 09.12.76 | **Panthers** | H | W | 1-0 | Baker |
| | 3 | 20.01.77 | **Wanderers** | A | L | 0-3 | |
| 1877-78 | 1 | 03.11.77 | **Ramblers** | H | D | 0-0 | |
| | 1r | 09.11.77 | **Ramblers** | H | W | 1-0 | Redwood |
| | 2 | 08.12.77 | **Royal Engineers** | A | L | 0-6 | |
| 1878-79 | 1 | 09.11.78 | **Brentwood** | A | W | 3-1 | Mott 2, Grieve |
| | 2 | 21.12.78 | **Remnants** | A | L | 2-6 | Grieve, Wohlgemuth |
| 1879-80 | 1 | 01.11.79 | **Clarence** | H | W | 3-2 | Ramsey 2, F Last, Mott, Poland |
| | 2 | | Herts Rangers | | | - | |
| | | | *Herts Rangers scratched. Pilgrims walkover* | | | | |
| | 3 | 17.01.80 | **Clapham Rovers** | A | L | 0-7 | |
| 1880-81 | 1 | | Old Philberdians | | | - | |
| | | | *Old Philberdians scratched. Pilgrims walkover* | | | | |
| | 2 | 09.12.80 | **Royal Engineers** | A | L | 0-1 | |
| 1881-82 | 1 | 05.11.81 | **Mosquitoes** | A | D | 1-1 | Scott |
| | 1r | 12.11.81 | **Mosquitoes** | H | W | 5-0 | |
| | 2 | 03.12.81 | **Old Foresters** | A | L | 1-3 | |
| 1882-83 | 1 | 21.10.82 | **Old Carthusians** | A | L | 0-6 | |
| 1883-84 | 1 | 10.11.83 | **Mosquitoes** | A | L | 2-3 | |
| 1884-85 | 1 | 08.11.84 | **Dulwich** | A | L | 2-3 | |

## PLYMOUTH ARGYLE

*Formed 1886 as the Argyle Athletic Club. Plymouth Argyle 1903. FA Cup best performance: semi-finals 1984 (as a Third Division club). Record FA Cup win: 7-0 v Whiteheads, 1st qualifying round 1903-04. In Competition Proper: 6-0 v Corby Town, 3rd round, 22.01.1966. Record FA Cup defeat: 1-7 v Tottenham Hotspur, 1st round replay, 19.01.1910.*

| | | | | | | | |
|---|---|---|---|---|---|---|---|
| 1903-04 (SL) | | | 1q Whiteheads (H) 7-0; 2q Freemantle (H) 5-1; 3q Swindon Town (H) 2-0; Int Brentford (A) 1-1; Int r Brentford (H) 4-1 | | | | |
| | 1 | 06.02.04 | **Sheffield Wed** (D1) | H | D | 2-2 | Dalrymple, Peddie |
| | 1r | 10.02.04 | **Sheffield Wed** | A | L | 0-2 | |

| | | | | | | | | |
|---|---|---|---|---|---|---|---|---|
| 1904-05 | (SL) | | | Int Barnsley (H) 2-0 | | | | |
| | | 1 | 04.02.05 | **Newcastle Utd** (D1) | A | D | 1-1 | Dalrymple |
| | | 1r | 08.02.05 | **Newcastle Utd** | H | D | 1-1aet | McLuckie |
| | | 1 2r | 13.02.05 | **Newcastle Utd** | | L | 0-2 | |
| | | | | *played at Plumstead* | | | | |
| 1905-06 | (SL) | 1 | 13.01.06 | **New Crusaders** | A | W | 6-3 | Wilcox 3, Banks, Briercliffe, Saul |
| | | 2 | 03.02.06 | **Aston Villa** (D1) | A | D | 0-0 | |
| | | 2r | 07.02.06 | **Aston Villa** | H | L | 1-5 | Buck |
| 1906-07 | (SL) | 1 | 12.01.07 | **Millwall Athletic** (SL) | A | L | 0-2 | |
| 1907-08 | (SL) | 1 | 11.01.08 | **Barnsley** (D2) | H | W | 1-0 | Leonard |
| | | 2 | 01.02.08 | **Crystal Palace** (SL) | H | L | 2-3 | Ingham, Morris |
| 1908-09 | (SL) | 1 | 16.01.09 | **Swindon Town** (SL) | H | W | 1-0 | Hindmarsh |
| | | 2 | 06.02.09 | **Exeter City** (SL) | H | W | 2-0 | Hindmarsh, Leavey |
| | | 3 | 20.02.09 | **Derby County** (D2) | A | L | 0-1 | |
| 1909-10 | (SL) | 1 | 15.01.10 | **Tottenham Hotspur** (D1) | H | D | 1-1 | Griffiths |
| | | 1r | 19.01.10 | **Tottenham Hotspur** | A | L | 1-7 | Burch |
| 1910-11 | (SL) | 1 | 14.01.11 | **Derby County** (D2) | A | L | 1-2 | Dixon |
| 1911-12 | (SL) | 1 | 13.01.12 | **Sunderland** (D1) | A | L | 1-3 | Burch |
| 1912-13 | (SL) | 1 | 11.01.13 | **Preston North End** (D2) | H | W | 2-0 | McCormick, Bell |
| | | 2 | 01.02.13 | **Manchester Utd** (D1) | H | L | 0-2 | |
| 1913-14 | (SL) | 1 | 10.01.14 | **Lincoln City** (D2) | H | W | 4-1 | Raymond 2, Burch, Butler |
| | | 2 | 31.01.14 | **Sunderland** (D1) | A | L | 1-2 | Bowler |
| 1914-15 | (SL) | 1 | 09.01.15 | **Bury** (D2) | A | D | 1-1 | Bowler |
| | | 1r | 16.01.15 | **Bury** | H | L | 1-2 | Raymond |
| 1919-20 | (SL) | 1 | 10.01.20 | **Reading** (SL) | H | W | 2-0 | Jack 2 |
| | | 2 | 31.01.20 | **Barnsley** (D2) | H | W | 4-1 | Jack 2, Bowler 2 |
| | | 3 | 21.02.20 | **Huddersfield Town** (D2) | A | L | 1-3 | Jack |
| 1920-21 | (D3) | 1 | 08.01.21 | **Rochdale** (CL) | H | W | 2-0 | Sheffield, Russell |
| | | 2 | 29.01.21 | **Swansea Town** (D3) | A | W | 2-1 | Bowler, Toms |
| | | 3 | 19.02.21 | **Chelsea** (D1) | H | D | 0-0 | |
| | | 3r | 24.02.21 | **Chelsea** | A | D | 0-0aet | |
| | | 3 2r | 28.02.21 | **Chelsea** | | L | 1-2 | Toms |
| | | | | *played at Ashton Gate* | | | | |
| 1921-22 | (3S) | 1 | 07.01.22 | **Fulham** (D2) | H | D | 1-1 | Baker |
| | | 1r | 11.01.22 | **Fulham** | A | L | 0-1 | |
| 1922-23 | (3S) | 1 | 13.01.23 | **Notts County** (D2) | H | D | 0-0 | |
| | | 1r | 17.01.23 | **Notts County** | A | W | 1-0 | Gallogley |
| | | 2 | 03.02.23 | **Bradford Park A** (3N) | H | W | 4-1 | Richardson 4 |
| | | 3 | 24.02.23 | **West Ham Utd** (D2) | A | L | 0-2 | |
| 1923-24 | (3S) | 1 | 12.01.24 | **Manchester Utd** (D2) | A | L | 0-1 | |
| 1924-25 | (3S) | 1 | 10.01.25 | **Swansea Town** (3S) | A | L | 0-3 | |
| 1925-26 | (D3) | 3 | 09.01.26 | **Chelsea** (D2) | H | L | 1-2 | Cock |
| 1926-27 | (3S) | 3 | 08.01.27 | **South Shields** (D2) | A | L | 1-3 | Cock |
| 1927-28 | (3S) | 1 | 26.11.27 | **Gillingham** (3S) | A | L | 1-2 | Matthews |
| 1928-29 | (3S) | 1 | 04.11.28 | **Yeovil & Petters Utd** (SL) | H | W | 4-1 | Bowden 2, Leslie, Matthews |
| | | 2 | 08.12.28 | **Brentford** (3S) | A | W | 1-0 | Forbes |
| | | 3 | 12.01.29 | **Blackpool** (D2) | H | W | 3-0 | Black 3 |
| | | 4 | 26.01.29 | **Bradford Park A** (D2) | H | L | 0-1 | |
| 1929-30 | (3S) | 1 | 30.11.29 | **Dulwich Hamlet** (IL) | A | W | 3-0 | Bowden 2, Black 2 |
| | | 2 | 14.12.29 | **Watford** (3S) | A | D | 1-1 | Bland |
| | | 2r | 18.12.29 | **Watford** | H | W | 3-0 | Vidler 3 |
| | | 3 | 11.01.30 | **Hull City** (D2) | H | L | 3-4 | Vidler, Leslie, Black |
| 1930-31 | (D2) | 3 | 10.01.31 | **Everton** (D2) | H | L | 0-2 | |
| 1931-32 | (D2) | 3 | 09.01.32 | **Manchester Utd** (D1) | H | W | 4-1 | Grozier 2, Vidler, Pullen |
| | | 4 | 23.01.32 | **Arsenal** (D1) | A | L | 2-4 | Vidler, Leslie |
| 1932-33 | (D2) | 3 | 14.01.33 | **Bradford Park A** (D2) | A | L | 1-5 | Leslie |
| 1933-34 | (D2) | 3 | 13.01.34 | **Huddersfield Town** (D1) | H | D | 1-1 | Cookson |
| | | 3r | 17.01.34 | **Huddersfield Town** | A | L | 2-6 | Briggs |
| 1934-35 | (D2) | 3 | 12.01.35 | **Brentford** (D2) | A | W | 1-0 | S Black |
| | | 4 | 26.01.35 | **Bolton Wanderers** (D2) | H | L | 1-4 | Briggs |
| 1935-36 | (D2) | 3 | 11.01.36 | **Stockport County** (3N) | A | W | 3-2 | S Black, Eggleston, Sloan |

| | | | | | | | | |
|---|---|---|---|---|---|---|---|---|
| | | 4 | 25.01.36 | **Chelsea** (D1) | A | L | 1-4 | Vidler |
| 1936-37 | (D2) | 3 | 16.01.37 | **Crewe Alexandra** (3N) | A | W | 2-0 | Vidler, McNeill |
| | | 4 | 30.01.37 | **Tottenham Hotspur** (D2) | A | L | 0-1 | |
| 1937-38 | (D2) | 3 | 08.01.38 | **New Brighton** (3N) | A | L | 0-1 | |
| 1938-39 | (D2) | 3 | 07.01.39 | **Sunderland** (D1) | A | L | 0-3 | |
| 1945-46 | (D2) | 3 1L | 05.01.46 | **Aldershot** (3S) | A | L | 0-2 | |
| | | 3 2L | 09.01.46 | **Aldershot** | H | L | 0-1 | |
| 1946-47 | (D2) | 3 | 11.01.47 | **Chester** (3N) | A | L | 0-2 | |
| 1947-48 | (D2) | 3 | 10.01.48 | **Luton Town** (D2) | H | L | 2-4 | Dews, Thomas |
| 1948-49 | (D2) | 3 | 08.01.49 | **Notts County** (3S) | H | L | 0-1aet | |
| 1949-50 | (D2) | 3 | 07.01.50 | **Wolverhampton W** (D1) | H | D | 1-1 | Williams |
| | | 3r | 11.01.50 | **Wolverhampton W** | A | L | 0-3 | |
| 1950-51 | (3S) | 1 | 25.11.50 | **Gainsborough T** (ML) | A | W | 3-0 | Tadman 3 |
| | | 2 | 09.12.50 | **Crewe Alexandra** (3N) | A | D | 2-2 | Govan, Strauss |
| | | 2r | 13.12.50 | **Crewe Alexandra** | H | W | 3-0 | Dews 2, Strauss |
| | | 3 | 06.01.51 | **Wolverhampton W** (D1) | H | L | 1-2 | Dews |
| 1951-52 | (3S) | 1 | 24.11.51 | **Millwall** (3S) | A | L | 0-1 | |
| 1952-53 | (D2) | 3 | 10.01.53 | **Coventry City** (3S) | H | W | 4-1 | Dews, Smith, Astall, Govan |
| | | 4 | 31.01.53 | **Barnsley** (D2) | H | W | 1-0 | Govan |
| | | 5 | 14.02.53 | **Gateshead AFC** (3N) | H | L | 0-1 | |
| 1953-54 | (D2) | 3 | 09.01.54 | **Nottingham Forest** (D2) | H | W | 2-0 | McJarrow, Tadman |
| | | 4 | 30.01.54 | **Doncaster Rovers** (D2) | H | L | 0-2 | |
| 1954-55 | (D2) | 3 | 08.01.55 | **Newcastle Utd** (D1) | H | L | 0-1 | |
| 1955-56 | (D2) | 3 | 07.01.56 | **Leyton Orient** (3S) | A | L | 0-1 | |
| 1956-57 | (3S) | 1 | 17.11.56 | **Exeter City** (3S) | A | W | 2-0 | N Langman, Rowley |
| | | 2 | 08.12.56 | **Torquay Utd** (3S) | A | L | 0-1 | |
| 1957-58 | (3S) | 1 | 16.11.57 | **Watford** (3S) | H | W | 6-2 | Barnes 2, Carter 2, Anderson, Gauld |
| | | 2 | 07.12.57 | **Dorchester Town** (WL) | H | W | 5-2 | Carter 3, Penk, Gauld |
| | | 3 | 04.01.58 | **Newcastle Utd** (D1) | H | L | 1-6 | Carter |
| 1958-59 | (D3) | 1 | 15.11.58 | **Gillingham** (D4) | H | D | 2-2 | Carter, Anderson |
| | | 1r | 19.11.58 | **Gillingham** | A | W | 4-1 | Meyer 3, Gauld |
| | | 2 | 06.12.58 | **Coventry City** (D4) | A | W | 3-1 | Carter 2, Baker |
| | | 3 | 10.01.59 | **Cardiff City** (D2) | H | L | 0-3 | |
| 1959-60 | (D2) | 3 | 09.01.60 | **WBA** (D1) | A | L | 2-3 | Anderson, Penk |
| 1960-61 | (D2) | 3 | 07.01.61 | **Bristol City** (D3) | H | L | 0-1 | |
| 1961-62 | (D2) | 3 | 06.01.62 | **West Ham Utd** (D1) | H | W | 3-0 | Carter, JS Williams, Maloy |
| | | 4 | 27.01.62 | **Tottenham Hotspur** (D1) | H | L | 1-5 | Anderson |
| 1962-63 | (D2) | 3 | 05.01.63 | **WBA** (D1) | H | L | 1-5 | McAnearney |
| 1963-64 | (D2) | 3 | 04.01.64 | **Huddersfield Town** (D2) | H | L | 0-1 | |
| 1964-65 | (D2) | 3 | 09.01.65 | **Derby County** (D2) | H | W | 4-2 | Jones 2, Jennings, Trebilcock |
| | | 4 | 30.01.65 | **Leicester City** (D1) | A | L | 0-5 | |
| 1965-66 | (D2) | 3 | 22.01.66 | **Corby Town** (SL) | H | W | 6-0 | Bickle 3, Piper, Jackson, Jones |
| | | 4 | 12.02.66 | **Huddersfield Town** (D2) | H | L | 0-2 | |
| 1966-67 | (D2) | 3 | 28.01.67 | **Nottingham Forest** (D1) | A | L | 1-2 | Bloomfield |
| 1967-68 | (D2) | 3 | 27.01.68 | **Sheffield Wed** (D1) | A | L | 0-3 | |
| 1968-69 | (D3) | 1 | 16.11.68 | **Reading** (D3) | A | L | 0-1 | |
| 1969-70 | (D3) | 1 | 15.11.69 | **Brentford** (D4) | A | D | 0-0 | |
| | | 1r | 19.11.69 | **Brentford** | H | W | 2-0 | Burnside, Davey |
| | | 2 | 06.12.69 | **Peterborough Utd** (D4) | A | L | 0-2 | |
| 1970-71 | (D3) | 1 | 21.11.70 | **Walsall** (D3) | A | L | 0-3 | |
| 1971-72 | (D3) | 1 | 20.11.71 | **Gillingham** (D4) | A | L | 2-3 | Reed 2 |
| 1972-73 | (D3) | 1 | 18.11.72 | **Hendon** (IL) | H | W | 1-0 | Hague |
| | | 2 | 09.12.72 | **Yeovil Town** (SL) | A | W | 2-0 | Dowling, Welsh |
| | | 3 | 13.01.73 | **Middlesbrough** (D2) | H | W | 1-0 | Hinch |
| | | 4 | 03.02.73 | **Leeds Utd** (D1) | A | L | 1-2 | Rickard |
| 1973-74 | (D3) | 1 | 24.11.73 | **Brentford** (D4) | H | W | 2-1 | Houston og, Mariner |
| | | 2 | 15.12.73 | **Walsall** (D3) | H | W | 1-0 | Mariner |
| | | 3 | 05.01.74 | **Manchester Utd** (D1) | A | L | 0-1 | |
| 1974-75 | (D3) | 1 | 23.11.74 | **Dartford** (SL) | A | W | 3-2 | Randall 2, Mariner |
| | | 2 | 14.12.74 | **Crystal Palace** (D3) | H | W | 2-1 | Green, Rafferty |
| | | 3 | 04.01.75 | **Blackpool** (D2) | H | W | 2-0 | Rafferty 2 |
| | | 4 | 25.01.75 | **Everton** (D1) | H | L | 1-3 | Vassallo |

| | | | | | | | | |
|---|---|---|---|---|---|---|---|---|
| 1975-76 | (D2) | 3 | 03.01.76 | **Hull City** (D2) | A | D | 1-1 | Rafferty |
| | | 3r | 06.01.76 | **Hull City** | H | L | 1-4 | Green |
| 1976-77 | (D2) | 3 | 08.01.77 | **Oldham Athletic** (D2) | A | L | 0-3 | |
| 1977-78 | (D3) | 1 | 26.11.77 | **Bath City** (SL) | A | D | 0-0 | |
| | | 1r | 29.11.77 | **Bath City** | H | W | 2-0 | Taylor 2 |
| | | 2 | 17.12.77 | **Cambridge Utd** (D3) | H | W | 1-0 | Johnson |
| | | 3 | 07.01.78 | **Mansfield Town** (D2) | A | L | 0-1 | |
| 1978-79 | (D3) | 1 | 25.11.78 | **Worcester City** (SL) | A | L | 0-2 | |
| 1979-80 | (D3) | 1 | 24.11.79 | **Colchester Utd** (D3) | A | D | 1-1 | Hodges |
| | | 1r | 27.11.79 | **Colchester Utd** | H | L | 0-1aet | |
| 1980-81 | (D3) | 1 | 22.11.80 | **Newport County** (D3) | H | W | 2-0 | Kemp, Murphy |
| | | 2 | 13.12.80 | **Oxford Utd** (D3) | H | W | 3-0 | Sims, Kemp, Murphy |
| | | 3 | 03.01.81 | **Charlton Athletic** (D3) | H | L | 1-2 | Kemp |
| 1981-82 | (D3) | 1 | 21.11.81 | **Gillingham** (D3) | H | D | 0-0 | |
| | | 1r | 24.11.81 | **Gillingham** | A | L | 0-1 | |
| 1982-83 | (D3) | 1 | 20.11.82 | **Exeter City** (D3) | H | W | 2-0 | Hodges, Sims |
| | | 2 | 11.12.82 | **Bristol Rovers** (D3) | A | D | 2-2 | Rogers, Sims |
| | | 2r | 20.12.82 | **Bristol Rovers** | H | W | 1-0 | McCartney |
| | | 3 | 08.01.83 | **Watford** (D1) | A | L | 0-2 | |
| 1983-84 | (D3) | 1 | 19.11.83 | **Southend Utd** (D3) | A | D | 0-0 | |
| | | 1r | 22.11.83 | **Southend Utd** | H | W | 2-0aet | Stead og, Tynan |
| | | 2 | 10.12.83 | **Barking** (IL) | H | W | 2-1 | Rowe, Smith |
| | | 3 | 07.01.84 | **Newport County** (D3) | H | D | 2-2 | Hodges, Tynan |
| | | 3r | 10.01.84 | **Newport County** | A | W | 1-0 | Rogers |
| | | 4 | 28.01.84 | **Darlington** (D4) | H | W | 2-1 | Uzzell, Staniforth |
| | | 5 | 18.02.84 | **WBA** (D1) | A | W | 1-0 | Tynan |
| | | 6 | 10.03.84 | **Derby County** (D2) | H | D | 0-0 | |
| | | 6r | 14.03.84 | **Derby County** | A | W | 1-0 | Rogers |
| | | SF | 14.04.84 | **Watford** (D1) | | L | 0-1 | |
| | | | | *played at Villa Park* | | | | |
| 1984-85 | (D3) | 1 | 17.11.84 | **Barnet** (APL) | H | W | 3-0 | Goodyear, Tynan, Staniforth |
| | | 2 | 08.12.84 | **Hereford Utd** (D4) | H | D | 0-0 | |
| | | 2r | 12.12.84 | **Hereford Utd** | A | L | 0-2 | |
| 1985-86 | (D3) | 1 | 16.11.85 | **Aldershot** (D4) | H | W | 1-0 | Coughlin |
| | | 2 | 07.12.85 | **Maidstone Utd** (APL) | H | W | 3-0 | L Cooper, Nelson, Summerfield |
| | | 3 | 04.01.86 | **Hull City** (D2) | A | D | 2-2 | Clayton, L Cooper |
| | | 3r | 07.01.86 | **Hull City** | H | L | 0-1 | |
| 1986-87 | (D2) | 3 | 10.01.87 | **Bristol City** (D3) | A | D | 1-1 | Summerfield |
| | | 3r | 19.01.87 | **Bristol City** | H | W | 3-1aet | Summerfield, Nelson, Tynan |
| | | 4 | 31.01.87 | **Arsenal** (D1) | A | L | 1-6 | Rowbotham |
| 1987-88 | (D2) | 3 | 11.01.88 | **Colchester Utd** (D4) | H | W | 2-0 | S Cooper, Matthews |
| | | 4 | 30.01.88 | **Shrewsbury Town** (D2) | H | W | 1-0 | Evans |
| | | 5 | 20.02.88 | **Manchester City** (D2) | A | L | 1-3 | Hodges |
| 1988-89 | (D2) | 3 | 07.01.89 | **Cambridge Utd** (D4) | H | W | 2-0 | Tynan, Summerfield |
| | | 4 | 28.01.89 | **Everton** (D1) | H | D | 1-1 | McCarthy |
| | | 4r | 31.01.89 | **Everton** | A | L | 0-4 | |
| 1989-90 | (D2) | 3 | 06.01.90 | **Oxford Utd** (D2) | H | L | 0-1 | |
| 1990-91 | (D2) | 3 | 05.01.91 | **Middlesbrough** (D2) | A | D | 0-0 | |
| | | 3r | 14.01.91 | **Middlesbrough** | H | L | 1-2 | Marker (p) |
| 1991-92 | (D2) | 3 | 05.01.92 | **Bristol Rovers** (D2) | A | L | 0-5 | |
| 1992-93 | (D2) | 1 | 14.11.92 | **Dorking** (IL) | A | W | 3-2 | Dalton 2, Marshall |
| | | 2 | 09.12.92 | **Peterborough Utd** (D1) | H | W | 3-2 | Marshall 2, Castle |
| | | 3 | 12.01.93 | **Ipswich Town** (PL) | A | L | 1-3 | Castle |
| 1993-94 | (D2) | 1 | 13.11.93 | **Marlow** (IL) | A | W | 2-0 | Dalton 2 |
| | | 2 | 04.12.93 | **Gillingham** (D3) | H | W | 2-0 | Nugent 2 |
| | | 3 | 08.01.94 | **Chester City** (D3) | H | W | 1-0 | Nugent |
| | | 4 | 29.01.94 | **Barnsley** (D1) | H | D | 2-2 | Marshall, Dalton |
| | | 4r | 09.02.94 | **Barnsley** | A | L | 0-1 | |
| 1994-95 | (D2) | 1 | 13.11.94 | **Kettering Town** (Conf) | A | W | 1-0 | Skinner |
| | | 2 | 03.12.94 | **Bournemouth** (D2) | H | W | 2-1 | Ross 2 |
| | | 3 | 07.01.95 | **Nottingham Forest** (PL) | A | L | 0-2 | |

| | | | | | | | |
|---|---|---|---|---|---|---|---|
| 1995-96 (D3) | 1 | 11.11.95 | **Slough Town** (Conf) | A | W | 2-0 | Harvey og, Heathcote |
| | 2 | 03.12.95 | **Kingstonian** (IL) | A | W | 2-1 | Leadbitter, Littlejohn |
| | 3 | 06.01.96 | **Coventry City** (PL) | H | L | 1-3 | Baird |
| 1996-97 (D2) | 1 | 16.11.96 | **Fulham** (D3) | H | W | 5-0 | Mauge, Evans 2 (1p), Littlejohn, Corazzin |
| | 2 | 06.12.96 | **Exeter City** (D3) | H | W | 4-1 | Evans, Mauge, Billy, Littlejohn |
| | 3 | 04.01.97 | **Peterborough Utd** (D2) | H | L | 0-1 | |
| 1997-98 (D2) | 1 | 15.11.97 | **Cambridge Utd** (D3) | H | D | 0-0 | |
| | 1r | 25.11.97 | **Cambridge Utd** | A | L | 2-3aet | Mauge, Jean |
| 1998-99 (D3) | 1 | 14.11.98 | **Kidderminster H** (Conf) | H | D | 0-0 | |
| | 1r | 24.11.98 | **Kidderminster H** | A | - | 0-0ab | |
| | | | *abandoned at half-time – fog* | | | | |
| | 1r | 01.12.98 | **Kidderminster H** (Conf) | A | D | 0-0aet | |
| | | | *Plymouth won 5-4 on penalties* | | | | |
| | 2 | 05.12.98 | **Wycombe W** (D2) | A | D | 1-1 | McCarthy og |
| | 2r | 15.12.98 | **Wycombe W** | H | W | 3-2 | Wotton (p), Heathcote, Sweeney |
| | 3 | 02.01.99 | **Derby County** (PL) | H | L | 0-3 | |
| 1999-00 (D3) | 1 | 30.10.99 | **Brentford** (D2) | A | D | 2-2 | Stonebridge, McGregor |
| | 1r | 09.11.99 | **Brentford** | H | W | 2-1aet | McGregor 2 |
| | 2 | 20.11.99 | **Brighton** (D3) | H | D | 0-0 | |
| | 2r | 30.11.99 | **Brighton** | A | W | 2-1 | Bastow, Hargreaves |
| | 3 | 11.12.99 | **Reading** (D2) | A | D | 1-1 | McIntyre |
| | 3r | 21.12.99 | **Reading** | H | W | 1-0 | Heathcote |
| | 4 | 08.01.00 | **Preston North End** (D2) | H | L | 0-3 | |
| 2000-01 (D3) | 1 | 18.11.00 | **Chester City** (Conf) | A | D | 1-1 | Peake |
| | 1r | 28.11.00 | **Chester City** | H | L | 1-2aet | McGregor |
| 2001-02 (D3) | 1 | 17.11.01 | **Whitby Town** (NPL) | A | D | 1-1 | Phillips |
| | 1r | 27.11.01 | **Whitby Town** | H | W | 3-2 | Bent, Stonebridge, Phillips |
| | 2 | 08.12.01 | **Bristol Rovers** (D3) | H | D | 1-1 | Wotton |
| | 2r | 18.12.01 | **Bristol Rovers** | A | L | 2-3 | Friio 2 |
| 2002-03 (D2) | 1 | 16.11.02 | **Bury** (D3) | A | W | 3-0 | Evans, Nelson og, Wotton |
| | 2 | 07.12.02 | **Stockport County** (D2) | A | W | 3-0 | Stonebridge, Friio, Wotton (p) |
| | 3 | 04.01.03 | **Dagenham & Red** (Conf) | H | D | 2-2 | Stonebridge, Wotton (p) |
| | 3r | 14.01.03 | **Dagenham & Red** | A | L | 0-2 | |

# POOLE TOWN

*Formed 1880. Entered FA Cup: 1891-92 – 1995-96. League club beaten: Newport County. Folded 1996. Reformed and now members of the Hampshire League.*

| | | | | | | | |
|---|---|---|---|---|---|---|---|
| 1926-27 (SL) | 1 | 27.11.26 | **Newport County** (3S) | H | W | 1-0 | Daws |
| | 2 | 11.12.26 | **Nunhead** (IL) | A | W | 2-1 | Daws 2 |
| | 3 | 08.01.27 | **Everton** (D1) | A | L | 1-3 | Batten |
| 1927-28 (SL) | 1 | 26.11.27 | **Norwich City** (3S) | H | D | 1-1 | Rhodes |
| | 1r | 01.12.27 | **Norwich City** | A | L | 0-5 | |
| 1928-29 (SL) | 1 | 24.11.28 | **Bournemouth** (3S) | H | L | 1-4 | Harris |
| 1946-47 (WL) | 1 | 30.11.46 | **QPR** (3S) | A | D | 2-2 | Langley, Ames (p) |
| | 1r | 04.12.46 | **QPR** | H | L | 0-6 | |
| 1962-63 (SL) | 1 | 03.11.62 | **Watford** (D3) | A | D | 2-2 | Bellett, Osmond |
| | 1r | 06.11.62 | **Watford** | H | L | 1-2 | Pring (p) |
| 1966-67 (SL) | 1 | 26.11.66 | **QPR** (D3) | A | L | 2-3 | Saunders, France |
| 1983-84 (SL) | 1 | 20.11.83 | **Newport County** (D3) | H | D | 0-0 | |
| | 1r | 22.11.83 | **Newport County** | A | L | 1-3 | Allen |

# PORT VALE

*Formed 1876 as Burslem Port Vale. Port Vale 1912. First entered FA Cup: 1885-86. FA Cup best performance: semi-finals 1954 (as a Third Division club). Record FA Cup win: 7-1 v Irthlingborough Town, 1st round, 12.01.1907. Record FA Cup defeat: 0-7 v Small Heath Alliance, 5th qualifying round, 1898-99. Record FA Cup defeat: 0-6 v Aston Villa, 4th round, 27.01.1990.*

**as Burslem Port Vale**

| | | | | | | | |
|---|---|---|---|---|---|---|---|
| 1885-86 | 1 | 31.10.85 | **Chirk** | H | W | 3-0 | |
| | 2 | 21.11.85 | **Druids** | A | D | 2-2aet | Reynolds, Simpson |
| | 2r | 28.11.85 | **Druids** | H | W | 5-1 | Reynolds 2, Smith 2, Simpson |
| | 3 | | Leek | | | - | |
| | | | *Leek scratched. Burslem Port Vale walkover* | | | | |

| | | | | | | | |
|---|---|---|---|---|---|---|---|
| | 4 | | bye | | | | |
| | 5 | 16.01.86 | **Brentwood** | H | D | 1-1 | Reynolds |
| | 5r | 13.02.86 | **Brentwood** | A | D | 3-3aet | Smith, 2 others |
| | *Port Vale scratched before second replay took place* | | | | | | |
| 1886-87 | 1 | 30.10.86 | **Davenham** | A | D | 1-1aet | |
| | 1r | 13.11.86 | **Davenham** | H | W | 3-0 | |
| | 2 | | bye | | | | |
| | 3 | 11.12.86 | **Leek** | A | D | 2-2 | |
| | 3r | 20.01.87 | **Leek** | H | L | 1-3 | |
| 1887-88 | 1 | 15.10.87 | **Stoke** | A | L | 0-1 | |
| 1888-89 | | | 2q Small Heath Alliance (A) 2-3 | | | | |
| 1889-90 | | | 2q Chester (A) 0-1 | | | | |
| 1890-91 | | | 1q Warwick County (A) 3-1; 2q Walsall Town Swifts (H) 2-3 | | | | |
| 1891-92 | | | 1q Burton Wanderers (H) 2-4 | | | | |
| 1892-93 (D2) | | | 1q Burton Swifts (H) 0-2 | | | | |
| 1893-94 (D2) | | | 1q Burton Swifts (H) 3-4aet | | | | |
| 1894-95 (D2) | | | 1q Stourbridge (A) 3-5 | | | | |
| 1895-96 (D2) | | | 1q Hereford Thistle walkover; 2q Burton Swifts (H) 1-1; 2qr Burton Swifts (A) 0-1 | | | | |
| 1896-97 (ML) | | | 3q Hereford walkover; 4q Stourbridge (A) 3-1; 5q Burton Swifts (H) 2-3 | | | | |
| 1897-98 (ML) | | | 3q Small Heath Alliance (H) 2-1; 4q Kidderminster H walkover; 5q Burton Wanderers (H) 2-1 | | | | |
| | 1 | 29.01.98 | **Sheffield Utd** (D1) | A | D | 1-1 | McDonald |
| | 1r | 02.02.98 | **Sheffield Utd** (D1) | H | W | 2-1aet | R Evans, Boullemier |
| | 2 | 12.02.98 | **Burnley** (D2) | A | L | 0-3 | |
| 1898-99 (D2) | | | 3q Wellington Town (H) 5-0; 4q Burton Wanderers (H) 3-0; 5q Small Heath Alliance (A) 0-7 | | | | |
| 1899-00 (D2) | | | 3q Nantwich Town (H) 2-0; 4q Crewe Alexandra (A) 2-2; 4qr Crewe Alexandra (H) 3-1; 5q Stalybridge Rovers (H) 0-1 | | | | |
| 1900-01 (D2) | | | Int New Brighton Tower (H) 1-3 | | | | |
| 1901-02 (D2) | | | 3q Wellington Town (H) 6-0; 4q Wrexham (A) 1-2 abandoned; 4q Wrexham (A) 0-0; 4qr Wrexham (H) 3-1; 5q Walsall (H) 1-2 | | | | |
| 1902-03 (D2) | | | 3q Stalybridge Rovers (H) 3-1; 4q St Helens Recreation (A) 1-2 | | | | |
| 1903-04 (D2) | | | 3q Crewe Alexandra (A) 0-0; 3qr Crewe Alexandra (H) 2-1; 4q Stockport County (A) 0-0; 4qr Stockport Co (H) 6-0; 5q Nantwich Town (A) 1-0; Int Burton Utd (H) 3-0 | | | | |
| | 1 | 06.02.04 | **Southampton** (SL) | A | L | 0-3 | |
| 1904-05 (D2) | | | 6q Barnsley (A) 0-0; 6qr Barnsley (H) 1-2 | | | | |
| 1905-06 (D2) | | | 4q Oxford City (A) 1-0 | | | | |
| | 1 | 13.01.06 | **Gainsborough T** (D2) | H | L | 0-3 | |
| 1906-07 (D2) | | | 5q Swindon Town (A) 2-1 | | | | |
| | 1 | 12.01.07 | **Irthlingborough T** (UCL) | A | W | 7-1 | Coxon 3, Dodds 2, Mountford 2 |
| | 2 | 02.02.07 | **Notts County** (D1) | H | D | 2-2 | Beats, Mountford |
| | 2r | 06.02.07 | **Notts County** | A | L | 0-5 | |
| 1907-08 (D2) | | | did not enter | | | | |
| 1908-09 (D2) | | | did not enter | | | | |
| 1909-10 (D2) | | | did not enter | | | | |
| 1910-11 (D2) | | | did not enter | | | | |
| 1911-12 (D2) | | | did not enter | | | | |
| **as Port Vale** | | | | | | | |
| 1912-13 (D2) | | | P New Brighton Tower (H) 7-0; 1q Northern Nomads (H) 4-1; 2q Harrowby (A) 2-0; 3q Northwich V (A) 1-3 | | | | |
| 1913-14 (CL) | | | P Harrowby (H) 3-1; 1q Northern Nomads (H) 5-0; 2q Chester (A) 5-2; 3q South Liverpool (H) 5-0; 4q Coventry City (H) 3-1; 5q Darlington (H) 2-2; 5qr Darlington (A) 2-1 abandoned; 5q 2r Darlington 1-0 (at Bramall Lane) | | | | |
| | 1 | 10.01.14 | **Bolton Wanderers** (D1) | A | L | 0-3 | |
| 1914-15 (CL) | | | 4q Crewe Alexandra (A) 1-1; 4qr Crewe Alex (H) 5-2; 5q Swansea Town (A) 0-1 | | | | |
| 1919-20 (D2) | | | 6q Loughborough Corinthians (H) 4-0 | | | | |
| | 1 | 10.01.20 | **Manchester Utd** (D1) | H | L | 0-1 | |
| 1920-21 (D2) | | | 6q Clapton Orient (A) 0-1 | | | | |
| 1921-22 (D2) | 1 | 07.01.22 | **Stoke** (D2) | H | L | 2-4 | Brough 2 |
| 1922-23 (D2) | | | 5q Wrexham (H) 0-2 | | | | |
| 1923-24 (D2) | | | 5q Wrexham (A) 1-5 | | | | |

| | | | | | | | | |
|---|---|---|---|---|---|---|---|---|
| 1924-25 | (D2) | | | 5q Boston Town (H) 6-1; 6q Alfreton Town (A) 8-2 | | | | |
| | | 1 | 10.01.25 | **Aston Villa** (D1) | A | L | 2-7 | Kirkham 2 |
| 1925-26 | (D2) | 3 | 09.01.26 | **Manchester Utd** (D1) | H | L | 2-3 | Maddock, Page |
| 1926-27 | (D2) | 3 | 08.01.27 | **Clapton Orient** (D2) | A | D | 1-1 | Simms |
| | | 3r | 12.01.27 | **Clapton Orient** | H | W | 5-1 | Kirkham 2, Page, Simms, Strange |
| | | 4 | 29.01.27 | **Arsenal** (D1) | H | D | 2-2 | Parker og, Kirkham |
| | | 4r | 02.02.27 | **Arsenal** | A | L | 0-1 | |
| 1927-28 | (D2) | 3 | 14.01.28 | **Barnsley** (D2) | H | W | 3-0 | Simms, Page, Maddock |
| | | 4 | 28.01.28 | **New Brighton** (3N) | H | W | 3-0 | Page, Kirkham, Anstiss |
| | | 5 | 18.02.28 | **Blackburn Rovers** (D1) | A | L | 1-2 | Anstiss |
| 1928-29 | (D2) | 3 | 12.01.29 | **Manchester Utd** (D1) | H | L | 0-3 | |
| 1929-30 | (3N) | 1 | 30.11.29 | **Gainsborough T** (ML) | A | D | 0-0 | |
| | | 1r | 04.12.29 | **Gainsborough T** | H | W | 5-0 | Jennings 2, Anstiss 2, Pynegar |
| | | 2 | 14.12.29 | **Chesterfield** (3N) | A | L | 0-2 | |
| 1930-31 | (D2) | 3 | 10.01.31 | **Corinthians** | A | W | 3-1 | Roberts, Anstiss, Jennings |
| | | 4 | 24.01.31 | **Birmingham** (D1) | A | L | 0-2 | |
| 1931-32 | (D2) | 3 | 09.01.32 | **Brighton** (3S) | A | W | 2-1 | Nolan 2 |
| | | 4 | 23.01.32 | **Leicester City** (D1) | H | L | 1-2 | Nolan |
| 1932-33 | (D2) | 3 | 14.01.33 | **Blackpool** (D1) | A | L | 1-2 | Mills |
| 1933-34 | (D2) | 3 | 13.01.34 | **Charlton Athletic** (3S) | A | L | 0-2 | |
| 1934-35 | (D2) | 3 | 12.01.35 | **WBA** (D1) | A | L | 1-2 | Morton |
| 1935-36 | (D2) | 3 | 11.01.36 | **Sunderland** (D1) | A | D | 2-2 | Stabb, Caldwell |
| | | 3r | 13.01.36 | **Sunderland** | H | W | 2-0 | Stabb, Rhodes |
| | | 4 | 25.01.36 | **Grimsby Town** (D1) | H | L | 0-4 | |
| 1936-37 | (3N) | 3 | 16.01.37 | **Sheffield Wed** (D1) | A | L | 0-2 | |
| 1937-38 | (3N) | 1 | 27.11.37 | **Gainsborough T** (ML) | H | D | 1-1 | Roberts |
| | | 1r | 01.12.37 | **Gainsborough T** | A | L | 1-2aet | Roberts |
| 1938-39 | (3S) | 1 | 26.11.38 | **Wrexham** (3N) | A | W | 2-1 | Roberts 2 |
| | | 2 | 10.12.38 | **Southend Utd** (3N) | H | L | 0-1 | |
| 1945-46 | (3S) | 1 1L | 17.11.45 | **Wellington Town** (CC) | H | W | 4-0 | McDowall 2, Pointon, Glennoe og |
| | | 1 2L | 24.11.45 | **Wellington Town** | A | W | 2-0 | McDowall, Bellis |
| | | 2 1L | 08.12.45 | **Marine** (LCC) | H | W | 3-1 | Allen 2, Gregory |
| | | 2 2L | 15.12.45 | **Marine** | A | D | 1-1 | Gregory |
| | | 3 1L | 05.01.46 | **Bradford Park A** (D2) | A | L | 1-2 | Bellis |
| | | 3 2L | 07.01.46 | **Bradford Park A** | H | D | 1-1 | Bellis |
| 1946-47 | (3S) | 1 | 30.11.46 | **Finchley** (AL) | H | W | 5-0 | M Jones, Pointon, Bellis 2, Wooton |
| | | 2 | 14.12.46 | **Watford** (3S) | A | D | 1-1 | M.Jones |
| | | 2r | 17.12.46 | **Watford** (3S) | H | W | 2-1 | M.Jones, Wooton |
| | | 3 | 11.01.47 | **Millwall** (D2) | A | W | 3-0 | Triner, Pointon 2 |
| | | 4 | 25.02.47 | **Blackburn Rovers** (D1) | A | L | 0-2 | |
| 1947-48 | (3S) | 1 | 29.11.47 | **Crystal Palace** (3S) | A | L | 1-2 | Smith |
| 1948-49 | (3S) | 1 | 27.11.48 | **Notts County** (3S) | A | L | 1-2 | Martin (p) |
| 1949-50 | (3S) | 1 | 26.11.49 | **Wealdstone** (AL) | H | W | 1-0 | Pinchbeck |
| | | 2 | 10.12.49 | **Tranmere Rovers** (3N) | H | W | 1-0 | Pinchbeck |
| | | 3 | 07.01.50 | **Newport County** (3S) | A | W | 2-1 | Allen 2 |
| | | 4 | 28.01.50 | **Burnley** (D1) | A | L | 1-2 | Martin |
| 1950-51 | (3S) | 1 | 25.11.50 | **New Brighton** (3N) | H | W | 3-2 | Aveyard 2, Pinchbeck |
| | | 2 | 09.12.50 | **Nelson FC** (LC) | H | W | 3-2 | Pinchbeck, Aveyard, Hulligan |
| | | 3 | 06.01.51 | **Stoke City** (D1) | A | D | 2-2 | Bennett, Pinchbeck |
| | | 3r | 08.01.51 | **Stoke City** | H | L | 0-1 | |
| 1951-52 | (3S) | 1 | 24.11.51 | **Colchester Utd** (3S) | A | L | 1-3 | Pinchbeck |
| 1952-53 | (3N) | 1 | 22.11.52 | **Exeter City** (3S) | H | W | 2-1 | Mullard, Griffiths |
| | | 2 | 06.12.52 | **Oldham Athletic** (3N) | H | L | 0-3 | |
| 1953-54 | (D3) | 1 | 21.11.53 | **Darlington** (3N) | A | W | 3-1 | Leake, Hayward, Cunliffe |
| | | 2 | 12.12.53 | **Southport** (3N) | A | D | 1-1 | Hayward |
| | | 2r | 14.12.53 | **Southport** | H | W | 2-0 | Hayward, Askey |
| | | 3 | 09.01.54 | **QPR** (3S) | A | W | 1-0 | Leake |
| | | 4 | 30.01.54 | **Cardiff City** (D1) | A | W | 2-0 | Leake, Griffiths |
| | | 5 | 20.02.54 | **Blackpool** (D1) | H | W | 2-0 | Leake 2 |
| | | 6 | 13.03.54 | **Leyton Orient** (3S) | A | W | 1-0 | Leake |
| | | SF | 27.03.54 | **WBA** (D1) | | L | 1-2 | Leake |
| | | | | *played at Villa Park* | | | | |

| | | | | | | | |
|---|---|---|---|---|---|---|---|
| 1954-55 (D2) | 3 | 08.01.55 | **West Ham Utd** (D2) | A | D | 2-2 | Cunliffe, Smith |
| | 3r | 10.01.55 | **West Ham Utd** | H | W | 3-1 | Cunliffe, Leake, Smith |
| | 4 | 29.01.55 | **Tottenham Hotspur** (D1) | A | L | 2-4 | Griffiths 2 |
| 1955-56 (D2) | 3 | 07.01.56 | **Walsall** (3S) | A | W | 1-0 | Stephenson |
| | 4 | 28.01.56 | **Everton** (D1) | H | L | 2-3 | Stephenson, Sproson |
| 1956-57 (D2) | 3 | 05.01.57 | **Barnsley** (D2) | A | D | 3-3 | Stephenson, Poole 2 |
| | 3r | 07.01.57 | **Barnsley** | H | L | 0-1 | |
| 1957-58 (3S) | 1 | 16.11.57 | **Shrewsbury Town** (3S) | H | W | 2-1 | Wilkinson 2 |
| | 2 | 07.12.57 | **Hull City** (3N) | H | D | 2-2 | Poole, Askey |
| | 2r | 09.12.57 | **Hull City** | A | L | 3-4aet | Poole, Steele, Sproson |
| 1958-59 (D4) | 1 | 15.11.58 | **Torquay Utd** (D4) | A | L | 0-1 | |
| 1959-60 (D3) | 1 | 14.11.59 | **Dorchester Town** (WL) | A | W | 2-1 | Poole, Barnett |
| | 2 | 05.12.59 | **QPR** (D3) | A | D | 3-3 | Portwood, Leake, Raine |
| | 2r | 07.12.59 | **QPR** | H | W | 2-1 | Barnett 2 |
| | 3 | 09.01.60 | **Cardiff City** (D2) | A | W | 2-0 | Steele, Portwood |
| | 4 | 30.01.60 | **Scunthorpe Utd** (D2) | A | W | 1-0 | Portwood |
| | 5 | 20.02.60 | **Aston Villa** (D2) | H | L | 1-2 | Jackson (p) |
| 1960-61 (D3) | 1 | 05.11.60 | **Chelmsford City** (SL) | A | W | 3-2 | Portwood 2, Jackson |
| | 2 | 26.11.60 | **Carlisle Utd** (D4) | H | W | 2-1 | Jackson, Fidler |
| | 3 | 07.01.61 | **Swansea Town** (D2) | A | L | 0-3 | |
| 1961-62 (D3) | 1 | 04.11.61 | **Bradford Park A** (D3) | A | W | 1-0 | Jackson |
| | 2 | 25.11.61 | **Crewe Alexandra** (D4) | A | D | 1-1 | Longbottom |
| | 2r | 27.11.61 | **Crewe Alexandra** | H | W | 3-0 | Longbottom 2, Llewellyn |
| | 3 | 06.01.62 | **Northampton Town** (D3) | H | W | 3-1 | Llewelleyn 3 |
| | 4 | 27.01.62 | **Sunderland** (D2) | A | D | 0-0 | |
| | 4r | 31.01.62 | **Sunderland** | H | W | 3-1 | Jackson, Poole, Longbottom |
| | 5 | 17.02.62 | **Fulham** (D1) | A | L | 0-1 | |
| 1962-63 (D3) | 1 | 03.11.62 | **Bristol Rovers** (D3) | A | W | 2-0 | Llewelleyn 2 |
| | 2 | 24.11.62 | **Aldershot** (D4) | H | W | 2-0 | Llewelleyn, Edwards (p) |
| | 3 | 27.02.63 | **Gillingham** (D4) | A | W | 4-2 | Steele, Edwards, Ford, Grainger (p) |
| | 4 | 13.03.63 | **Sheffield Utd** (D1) | H | L | 1-2 | Grainger |
| 1963-64 (D3) | 1 | 16.11.63 | **Bradford City** (D4) | A | W | 2-1 | Whalley, Richards |
| | 2 | 07.12.63 | **Workington** (D4) | H | W | 2-1 | Steele, Bingham |
| | 3 | 04.01.64 | **Birmingham City** (D1) | A | W | 2-1 | Sproson, Mudie |
| | 4 | 25.01.64 | **Liverpool** (D1) | A | D | 0-0 | |
| | 4r | 27.01.64 | **Liverpool** (D1) | H | L | 1-2aet | Cheeseborough |
| 1964-65 (D3) | 1 | 14.11.64 | **Hendon** (IL) | H | W | 2-1 | Smith, Mitchell |
| | 2 | 05.12.64 | **Millwall** (D4) | A | L | 0-4 | |
| 1965-66 (D4) | 1 | 13.11.65 | **Oxford Utd** (D3) | A | D | 2-2 | Sproson, Cumming |
| | 1r | 15.11.65 | **Oxford Utd** | H | W | 3-2 | Taylor, Mudie, Hill |
| | 2 | 04.12.65 | **Dartford** (SL) | H | W | 1-0 | Hill |
| | 3 | 26.01.66 | **Cardiff City** (D2) | A | L | 1-2 | Rowland |
| 1966-67 (D4) | 1 | 26.11.66 | **Bradford City** (D4) | A | W | 2-1 | Ritchie, Lawson |
| | 2 | 07.01.67 | **Barnsley** (D4) | A | D | 1-1 | Hill |
| | 2r | 16.01.67 | **Barnsley** | H | L | 0-3 | |
| 1967-68 (D4) | 1 | 09.12.67 | **Chester** (D4) | H | L | 1-2 | Goodfellow |
| 1968-69 (D4) | 1 | 16.11.68 | **Shrewsbury Town** (D3) | A | D | 1-1 | Gough |
| | 1r | 18.11.68 | **Shrewsbury Town** | H | W | 3-1 | Gough, Morris, Mahon |
| | 2 | 07.12.68 | **Workington** (D4) | H | D | 0-0 | |
| | 2r | 11.12.68 | **Workington** | A | W | 2-1 | Chapman, Jones |
| | 3 | 04.01.69 | **Watford** (D3) | A | L | 0-2 | |
| 1969-70 (D4) | 1 | 15.11.69 | **Wigan Athletic** (NPL) | A | D | 1-1 | James |
| | 1r | 18.11.69 | **Wigan Athletic** | H | D | 2-2aet | McLaren, Sproson |
| | 1 2r | 24.11.69 | **Wigan Athletic** | | W | 1-0aet | James |
| | | | *played at Old Trafford* | | | | |
| | 2 | 06.12.69 | **Tranmere Rovers** (D3) | H | D | 2-2 | James, Green |
| | 2r | 08.12.69 | **Tranmere Rovers** | A | L | 1-3 | Magee |
| 1970-71 (D3) | 1 | 21.11.70 | **Notts County** (D4) | A | L | 0-1 | |
| 1971-72 (D3) | 1 | 20.11.71 | **Blackburn Rovers** (D3) | A | D | 1-1 | Horton |
| | 1r | 22.11.71 | **Blackburn Rovers** | H | W | 3-1 | Horton 2 (1p), Morgan |
| | 2 | 11.12.71 | **Darlington** (D4) | H | W | 1-0 | Morgan |

| | | | | | | | | |
|---|---|---|---|---|---|---|---|---|
| | | 3 | 15.01.72 | **Birmingham City** (D2) | A | L | 0-3 | |
| 1972-73 | (D3) | 1 | 18.11.72 | **Southport** (D4) | H | W | 2-1 | James, Horton |
| | | 2 | 09.12.72 | **Wrexham** (D3) | H | W | 1-0 | Brodie |
| | | 3 | 13.01.73 | **West Ham Utd** (D1) | H | L | 0-1 | |
| 1973-74 | (D3) | 1 | 24.11.73 | **Stockport County** (D4) | A | W | 1-0 | Summerscales |
| | | 2 | 15.12.73 | **Scarborough** (NPL) | H | W | 2-1 | Harris, Woodward |
| | | 3 | 05.01.74 | **Luton Town** (D2) | H | D | 1-1 | Harris |
| | | 3r | 09.01.74 | **Luton Town** | A | L | 2-4 | Mountford, Woodward |
| 1974-75 | (D3) | 1 | 23.11.74 | **Lincoln City** (D4) | H | D | 2-2 | Bailey, Mountford |
| | | 1r | 27.11.74 | **Lincoln City** | A | L | 0-2 | |
| 1975-76 | (D3) | 1 | 22.11.75 | **Grantham Town** (SL) | A | D | 2-2 | Brownbill 2 |
| | | 1r | 24.11.75 | **Grantham Town** | H | W | 4-1 | Cullerton, Brownbill 2, Tartt |
| | | 2 | 13.12.75 | **Huddersfield Town** (D4) | A | L | 1-2 | Brownbill |
| 1976-77 | (D3) | 1 | 20.11.76 | **Southport** (D4) | A | W | 2-1 | Rogers 2 |
| | | 2 | 11.12.76 | **Barnsley** (D4) | H | W | 3-0 | Williams, Griffiths, Beamish |
| | | 3 | 08.01.77 | **Hull City** (D2) | A | D | 1-1 | Beamish |
| | | 3r | 10.01.77 | **Hull City** | H | W | 3-1aet | Beamish 2, Kennerley |
| | | 4 | 29.01.77 | **Burnley** (D2) | H | W | 2-1 | Tartt, Brownbill |
| | | 5 | 26.02.77 | **Aston Villa** (D1) | A | L | 0-3 | |
| 1977-78 | (D3) | 1 | 26.11.77 | **Arnold Town** (ML) | A | D | 0-0 | |
| | | 1r | 28.11.77 | **Arnold Town** | H | W | 5-2 | Bailey, Beamish, Ridley, Sutcliffe 2 |
| | | 2 | 17.12.77 | **Walsall** (D3) | A | D | 1-1 | Beamish |
| | | 2r | 19.12.77 | **Walsall** | H | L | 1-3 | Beamish |
| 1978-79 | (D4) | 1 | 25.11.78 | **Bradford City** (D4) | A | L | 0-1 | |
| 1979-80 | (D4) | 1 | 23.11.79 | **Doncaster Rovers** (D4) | H | L | 1-3 | Beech |
| 1980-81 | (D4) | 1 | 22.11.80 | **Bradford City** (D4) | H | W | 4-2 | Bennett (p), N.Chamberlain 2, Beech |
| | | 2 | 13.12.80 | **Burnley** (D3) | A | D | 1-1 | Miller |
| | | 2r | 16.12.80 | **Burnley** | H | W | 2-0 | Farrell, M.Chamberlain |
| | | 3 | 03.01.81 | **Enfield** (IL) | H | D | 1-1 | Beech |
| | | 3r | 06.01.81 | **Enfield** | A | L | 0-3 | |
| 1981-82 | (D4) | 1 | 21.11.81 | **Lincoln City** (D3) | A | D | 2-2 | N Chamberlain, M Chamberlain |
| | | 1r | 30.11.81 | **Lincoln City** | H | D | 0-0aet | |
| | | 1 2r | 02.12.81 | **Lincoln City** | H | W | 2-0 | Armstrong, N Chamberlain |
| | | 2 | 02.01.82 | **Stockport County** (D4) | H | W | 4-1 | Moss 2, N Chamberlain 2 |
| | | 3 | 05.01.82 | **Shrewsbury Town** (D2) | A | L | 0-1 | |
| 1982-83 | (D4) | 1 | 20.11.82 | **Bradford City** (D3) | H | L | 0-1 | |
| 1983-84 | (D3) | 1 | 19.11.83 | **Lincoln City** (D3) | H | L | 1-2 | Bright |
| 1984-85 | (D4) | 1 | 17.11.84 | **Macclesfield T** (NPL) | A | W | 2-1 | Brown, Earle |
| | | 2 | 07.12.84 | **Scunthorpe Utd** (D4) | H | W | 4-1 | Brown, O'Keefe (p), Bromage, I Griffiths |
| | | 3 | 05.01.85 | **West Ham Utd** (D1) | A | L | 1-4 | Griffiths |
| 1985-86 | (D4) | 1 | 16.11.85 | **Mansfield Town** (D4) | A | D | 1-1 | Earle |
| | | 1r | 18.11.85 | **Mansfield Town** | H | W | 1-0 | Maguire (p) |
| | | 2 | 08.12.85 | **Walsall** (D3) | H | D | 0-0 | |
| | | 2r | 10.12.85 | **Walsall** | A | L | 1-2 | Brown |
| 1986-87 | (D3) | 1 | 15.11.86 | **Stafford Rangers** (Conf) | H | W | 1-0 | Earle |
| | | 2 | 06.12.86 | **Walsall** (D3) | A | L | 0-5 | |
| 1987-88 | (D3) | 1 | 14.11.87 | **Tranmere Rovers** (D4) | A | D | 2-2 | |
| | | 1r | 16.11.87 | **Tranmere Rovers** | H | W | 3-1 | O'Kelly, Hamson, Riley |
| | | 2 | 05.12.87 | **Notts County** (D3) | H | W | 2-0 | Beckford, Sproson |
| | | 3 | 10.01.88 | **Macclesfield T** (Conf) | H | W | 1-0 | Finney |
| | | 4 | 30.01.88 | **Tottenham Hotspur** (D1) | H | W | 2-1 | Walker, Sproson |
| | | 5 | 20.02.88 | **Watford** (D1) | H | D | 0-0 | |
| | | 5r | 23.02.88 | **Watford** | A | L | 0-2 | |
| 1988-89 | (D3) | 1 | 19.11.88 | **Southport** (NPL) | A | W | 2-0 | Sproson, Riley |
| | | 2 | 10.12.88 | **Bolton Wanderers** (D3) | A | W | 2-1 | Futcher, Earle |
| | | 3 | 08.01.89 | **Norwich City** (D1) | H | L | 1-3 | Webb |
| 1989-90 | (D2) | 3 | 07.01.90 | **Derby County** (D1) | H | D | 1-1 | Beckford |
| | | 3r | 10.01.90 | **Derby County** | A | W | 3-2 | Hindmarch og, Walker, Cross |
| | | 4 | 27.01.90 | **Aston Villa** (D1) | A | L | 0-6 | |
| 1990-91 | (D2) | 3 | 05.01.91 | **Peterborough Utd** (D4) | H | W | 2-1 | Walker (p), Beckford |

| | | | | | | | |
|---|---|---|---|---|---|---|---|
| | 4 | 26.01.91 | **Manchester City** (D1) | H | L | 1-2 | Beckford |
| 1991-92 (D2) | 3 | 04.01.92 | **Sunderland** (D2) | A | L | 0-3 | |
| 1992-93 (D2) | 1 | 16.11.92 | **Stoke City** (D2) | A | D | 0-0 | |
| | 1r | 24.11.92 | **Stoke City** | H | W | 3-1 | Foyle 2, Porter |
| | 2 | 05.12.92 | **Altrincham** (Conf) | A | W | 4-1 | Swan, Foyle, Taylor, Van der Laan |
| | 3 | 02.01.93 | **Newcastle Utd** (D1) | A | L | 0-4 | |
| 1993-94 (D2) | 1 | 13.11.93 | **Blackpool** (D2) | H | W | 2-0 | Kerr, Foyle |
| | 2 | 03.12.93 | **Huddersfield Town** (D2) | H | W | 1-0 | Tankard |
| | 3 | 08.01.94 | **Southampton** (PL) | A | D | 1-1 | Porter |
| | 3r | 18.01.94 | **Southampton** | H | W | 1-0 | Slaven |
| | 4 | 29.01.94 | **Wolverhampton W** (D1) | H | L | 0-2 | |
| 1994-95 (D1) | 1 | 12.11.94 | **Hartlepool Utd** (D3) | H | W | 6-0 | Foyle 3, Griffiths, Allon, D Glover |
| | 2 | 03.12.94 | **Scarborough** (D3) | A | L | 0-1 | |
| 1995-96 (D1) | 3 | 06.01.96 | **Crystal Palace** (D1) | A | D | 0-0 | |
| | 3r | 16.01.96 | **Crystal Palace** | H | W | 4-3aet | Walker 2, Porter (p), Foyle |
| | 4 | 27.01.96 | **Everton** (PL) | A | D | 2-2 | Foyle, Bogie |
| | 4r | 14.02.96 | **Everton** | H | W | 2-1 | Bogie, McCarthy |
| | 5 | 21.02.96 | **Leeds Utd** (PL) | A | D | 0-0 | |
| | 5r | 28.02.96 | **Leeds Utd** | H | L | 1-2 | Naylor |
| 1996-97 (D1) | 3 | 04.01.97 | **Blackburn Rovers** (PL) | A | L | 0-1 | |
| 1997-98 (D1) | | 03.01.98 | **Arsenal** (PL) | A | D | 0-0 | |
| | 3r | 14.01.98 | **Arsenal** | H | D | 1-1aet | Corden |
| | | | *Arsenal won 4-3 on penalties* | | | | |
| 1998-99 (D1) | 3 | 03.01.99 | **Liverpool** (PL) | H | L | 0-3 | |
| 1999-00 (D1) | 3 | 12.12.99 | **Leeds Utd** | Pl | A | L | 0-2 |
| 2000-01 (D2) | 1 | 19.11.00 | **Canvey Island** (IL) | A | D | 4-4 | Minton 2, Brammer, Bridge-Wilkinson |
| | 1r | 28.11.00 | **Canvey Island** | H | L | 1-2aet | Naylor |
| 2001-02 (D2) | 1 | 17.11.01 | **Aylesbury Utd** (IL) | H | W | 3-0 | Burgess, Cummins, Brooker |
| | 2 | 08.12.01 | **Cardiff City** (D2) | A | L | 0-3 | |
| 2002-03 (D2) | 1 | 16.11.02 | **Crewe Alexandra** (D2) | H | L | 0-1 | |

## PORTSMOUTH

*Formed 1898. First entered FA Cup: 1899-00. FA Cup winners: 1939. Runners-up: 1929, 1934. Record FA Cup win: 10-0 v Ryde, 1st qualifying round, 30.09.1899. In Competition Proper: 7-0 v Stockport County, 3rd round, 08.01.1949. Record FA Cup defeat: 0-5 v Blackburn Rovers, 1st round, second replay, 05.02.1900; 0-5 v Everton, 1st round, 07.02.1903; 0-5 v Tottenham Hotspur, 3rd round, 16.01.1937.*

| | | | | | | | |
|---|---|---|---|---|---|---|---|
| 1899-00 (SL) | | | 1q Ryde (H) 10-0; 2q Cowes (H) 3-2; 3q Swindon Town (H) 2-1; 4q Bristol Rovers (A) 1-1; 4qr Bristol Rovers (H) 4-0; 5q Bedminster (A) 2-1 | | | | |
| | 1 | 27.01.00 | **Blackburn Rovers** (D1) | H | D | 0-0 | |
| | 1r | 01.02.00 | **Blackburn Rovers** | A | D | 1-1aet | Cunliffe |
| | 1 2r | 05.02.00 | **Blackburn Rovers** | | L | 0-5 | |
| | | | *played at Villa Park* | | | | |
| 1900-01 (SL) | | | Int Newton Heath (A) 0-3 | | | | |
| 1901-02 (SL) | | | Int Small Heath (H) 2-1 | | | | |
| | 1 | 25.01.02 | **Grimsby Town** (D1) | A | D | 1-1 | Cunliffe |
| | 1r | 29.01.02 | **Grimsby Town** | H | W | 2-0 | Bedingfield, Chadwick |
| | 2 | 08.02.02 | **Reading** (SL) | A | W | 1-0 | Bedingfield |
| | 3 | 22.02.02 | **Derby County** (D1) | H | D | 0-0 | |
| | 3r | 27.02.02 | **Derby County** | A | L | 3-6 | Chadwick, Cunliffe, Smith |
| 1902-03 (SL) | 1 | 07.02.03 | **Everton** (D1) | A | L | 0-5 | |
| 1903-04 (SL) | 1 | 06.02.04 | **Derby County** (D1) | H | L | 2-5 | Whelton 2 |
| 1904-05 (SL) | | | Int Chesterfield (H) 0-0; Int R Chesterfield (H) 2-0 | | | | |
| | 1 | 04.02.05 | **Small Heath** (D1) | A | W | 2-0 | Lee, S.Smith |
| | 2 | 18.02.05 | **Sheffield Wed** (D1) | A | L | 1-2 | Cunliffe |
| 1905-06 (SL) | 1 | 13.01.06 | **Southampton** (SL) | A | L | 1-5 | Kirby |
| 1906-07 (SL) | 1 | 12.01.07 | **Manchester Utd** (D1) | H | D | 2-2 | Hunter, Bainbridge |
| | 1r | 16.01.07 | **Manchester Utd** | A | W | 2-1 | Kirby, Hunter |
| | 2 | 02.02.07 | **Barnsley** (D2) | A | L | 0-1 | |
| 1907-08 (SL) | 1 | 11.01.08 | **Hastings & St L** (SL) | A | W | 1-0 | Bellamy |
| | 2 | 01.02.08 | **Leicester Fosse** (D2) | H | W | 1-0 | McDonald |
| | 3 | 22.02.08 | **Stoke** (D2) | H | L | 0-1 | |
| 1908-09 (SL) | 1 | 16.01.09 | **Birmingham** (D2) | A | W | 5-2 | Reid 4, McMahon |

| | | | | | | | | |
|---|---|---|---|---|---|---|---|---|
| | | 2 | 06.02.09 | **Sheffield Wed** (D1) | H | D | 2-2 | Dix, Kirby |
| | | 2r | 11.02.09 | **Sheffield Wed** | A | L | 0-3 | |
| 1909-10 | (SL) | 1 | 15.01.10 | **Shrewsbury Town** (BDL) | H | W | 3-0 | Long, Bowman 2 |
| | | 2 | 05.02.10 | **Coventry City** (SL) | H | L | 0-1 | |
| 1910-11 | (SL) | 1 | 14.01.11 | **Aston Villa** (D1) | H | L | 1-4 | Long |
| 1911-12 | (SL) | 1 | 13.01.12 | **Bristol Rovers** (SL) | A | W | 2-1 | Louch, Jones |
| | | 2 | 03.02.12 | **Bradford Park A** (D2) | A | L | 0-2 | |
| 1912-13 | (SL) | 1 | 15.01.13 | **Brighton** (SL) | H | L | 1-2 | Mounteney |
| 1913-14 | (SL) | 1 | 10.01.14 | **Exeter City** (SL) | H | L | 0-4 | |
| 1914-15 | (SL) | 1 | 09.01.15 | **Bradford Park A** (D1) | A | L | 0-1 | |
| 1919-20 | (SL) | 1 | 10.01.20 | **Bradford City** | A | - | 2-2ab | Turner, Stringfellow |
| | | | | *abandoned after 63 minutes – waterlogged pitch* | | | | |
| | | 1 | 17.01.20 | **Bradford City** (D1) | A | L | 0-2 | |
| 1920-21 | (D3) | 1 | 08.01.21 | **South Shields** (D2) | A | L | 0-3 | |
| 1921-22 | (3S) | 1 | 07.01.22 | **Luton Town** (3S) | H | D | 1-1 | Stringfellow |
| | | 1r | 11.01.22 | **Luton Town** | A | L | 1-2 | Stringfellow |
| 1922-23 | (3S) | 1 | 13.01.23 | **Leeds Utd** (D2) | H | D | 0-0 | |
| | | 1r | 17.01.23 | **Leeds Utd** | A | L | 1-3 | Meikle |
| 1923-24 | (3S) | | | 5q London Caledonians (A) 5-1; 6q Brentford (A) 1-1; 6qr Brentford 1-0aet | | | | |
| | | 1 | 12.01.24 | **Newcastle Utd** (D1) | H | L | 2-4 | Mackie, Haines |
| 1924-25 | (D2) | 1 | 10.01.25 | **Accrington Stanley** (3N) | A | W | 5-2 | Haines 2, J Martin, Meikle, Mackie |
| | | 2 | 31.01.25 | **Blackburn Rovers** (D1) | A | D | 0-0 | |
| | | 2r | 04.02.25 | **Blackburn Rovers** | H | D | 0-0aet | |
| | | 2 2r | 09.02.25 | **Blackburn Rovers** | | L | 0-1 | |
| | | | | *played at Highbury* | | | | |
| 1925-26 | (D2) | 3 | 09.01.26 | **Derby County** (D2) | A | D | 0-0 | |
| | | 3r | 13.01.26 | **Derby County** | H | D | 1-1aet | Mackie |
| | | 3 2r | 18.01.26 | **Derby County** | | L | 0-2 | |
| | | | | *played at Filbert Street* | | | | |
| 1926-27 | (D2) | 3 | 08.01.27 | **Bristol Rovers** (3S) | A | D | 3-3 | Mackie, Goodwin, Haines |
| | | 3r | 12.01.27 | **Bristol Rovers** | H | W | 4-0 | Watson, Mackie, Haines, McGolgan |
| | | 4 | 29.01.27 | **Reading** (D2) | A | L | 1-3 | Haines |
| 1927-28 | (D1) | 3 | 14.01.28 | **West Ham Utd** (D1) | H | L | 0-2 | |
| 1928-29 | (D1) | 3 | 12.01.29 | **Charlton Athletic** (3S) | H | W | 2-1 | McNeil, Smith |
| | | 4 | 26.01.29 | **Bradford City** (3N) | H | W | 2-0 | Irvine, McNeil |
| | | 5 | 16.02.29 | **Chelsea** (D2) | A | D | 1-1 | Weddle |
| | | 5r | 20.02.29 | **Chelsea** | H | W | 1-0 | Weddle |
| | | 6 | 02.03.29 | **West Ham Utd** (D1) | H | W | 3-2 | Smith, Cook, Weddle |
| | | SF | 23.03.29 | **Aston Villa** (D1) | | W | 1-0 | Smith (p) |
| | | | | *played at Highbury* | | | | |
| | | F | 27.04.29 | **Bolton Wanderers** (D1) | | L | 0-2 | |
| | | | | *played at Wembley Stadium* | | | | |
| 1929-30 | (D1) | 3 | 11.01.30 | **Preston North End** (D2) | H | W | 2-0 | Smith, Forward |
| | | 4 | 25.01.30 | **Brighton** (3S) | H | L | 0-1 | |
| 1930-31 | (D1) | 3 | 10.01.31 | **Fulham** (3S) | A | W | 2-0 | Forward, Easson |
| | | 4 | 24.01.31 | **Brentford** (3S) | A | W | 1-0 | Smith |
| | | 5 | 14.02.31 | **WBA** (D2) | H | L | 0-1 | |
| 1931-32 | (D1) | 3 | 09.01.32 | **Middlesbrough** (D1) | A | D | 1-1 | Weddle |
| | | 3r | 13.01.32 | **Middlesbrough** | H | W | 3-0 | Easson 2, Worrall |
| | | 4 | 23.01.32 | **Aston Villa** (D1) | H | D | 1-1 | Thackeray |
| | | 4r | 27.01.32 | **Aston Villa** | A | W | 1-0 | Easson |
| | | 5 | 13.02.32 | **Arsenal** (D1) | H | L | 0-2 | |
| 1932-33 | (D1) | 3 | 14.01.33 | **Grimsby Town** (D2) | A | L | 2-3 | J Smith, McCarthy |
| 1933-34 | (D1) | 3 | 13.01.34 | **Manchester Utd** (D2) | A | D | 1-1 | Bagley |
| | | 3r | 17.01.34 | **Manchester Utd** | H | W | 4-1 | Weddle 2, McCarthy, JJ Smith |
| | | 4 | 27.01.34 | **Grimsby Town** (D2) | H | W | 2-0 | Weddle, J Smith |
| | | 5 | 17.02.34 | **Swansea Town** (D2) | A | W | 1-0 | Worrall |
| | | 6 | 03.03.34 | **Bolton Wanderers** (D2) | A | W | 3-0 | Weddle, Rutherford 2 |
| | | SF | 17.03.34 | **Leicester City** (D1) | | W | 4-1 | Weddle 3, Rutherford |
| | | | | *played at St Andrews* | | | | |
| | | F | 28.04.34 | **Manchester City** (D1) | | L | 1-2 | Rutherford |
| | | | | *played at Wembley Stadium* | | | | |

| | | | | | | | | |
|---|---|---|---|---|---|---|---|---|
| 1934-35 | (D1) | 3 | 12.01.35 | **Huddersfield Town** (D1) | H | D | 1-1 | Worrall |
| | | 3r | 16.01.35 | **Huddersfield Town** | A | W | 3-2 | Weddle 2, Easson |
| | | 4 | 26.01.35 | **Bristol City** (3S) | H | D | 0-0 | |
| | | 4r | 30.01.35 | **Bristol City** | A | L | 0-2 | |
| 1935-36 | (D1) | 3 | 11.01.36 | **Manchester City** (D1) | A | L | 1-3 | Worrall |
| 1936-37 | (D1) | 3 | 16.01.37 | **Tottenham Hotspur** (D2) | H | L | 0-5 | |
| 1937-38 | (D1) | 3 | 08.01.38 | **Tranmere Rovers** (3N) | A | W | 2-1 | Beattie, Groves |
| | | 4 | 22.01.38 | **Brentford** (D1) | A | L | 1-2 | Parker |
| 1938-39 | (D1) | 3 | 07.01.39 | **Lincoln City** (3N) | H | W | 4-0 | Anderson 2, Parker, Worrall |
| | | 4 | 21.01.39 | **WBA** (D2) | H | W | 2-0 | Anderson 2 |
| | | 5 | 11.02.39 | **West Ham Utd** (D2) | H | W | 2-0 | Parker, Worrall |
| | | 6 | 04.03.39 | **Preston North End** (D1) | H | W | 1-0 | Anderson |
| | | SF | 25.03.39 | **Huddersfield Town** (D1) | | W | 2-1 | Barlow, Anderson |
| | | | | *played at Highbury* | | | | |
| | | F | 29.04.39 | **Wolverhampton W** (D1) | | W | 4-1 | Barlow 2, Anderson, Parker |
| | | | | *played at Wembley Stadium* | | | | |
| 1945-46 | (D2) | 3 1L | 05.01.46 | **Birmingham City** (D2) | A | L | 0-1 | |
| | | 3 2L | 09.01.46 | **Birmingham City** | H | D | 0-0 | |
| 1946-47 | (D1) | 3 | 11.01.47 | **Doncaster Rovers** (3N) | A | W | 3-2 | Froggatt 2, Evans |
| | | 4 | 25.01.47 | **Birmingham City** (D2) | A | L | 0-1 | |
| 1947-48 | (D1) | 3 | 10.01.48 | **Brighton** (3S) | H | W | 4-1 | Wharton, Reid, Clarke, Harris |
| | | 4 | 24.01.48 | **Preston North End** (D1) | H | L | 1-3 | Williams og |
| 1948-49 | (D1) | 3 | 08.01.49 | **Stockport County** (3N) | H | W | 7-0 | Phillips 2, Harris 3, Clarke 2 |
| | | 4 | 29.01.49 | **Sheffield Wed** (D2) | H | W | 2-1 | Harris, Phillips |
| | | 5 | 12.02.49 | **Newport County** (3S) | H | W | 3-2aet | Phillips 2, Froggatt |
| | | 6 | 26.02.49 | **Derby County** (D1) | H | W | 2-1 | Clarke 2 |
| | | SF | 26.03.49 | **Leicester City** (D2) | | L | 1-3 | Harris |
| | | | | *played at Highbury* | | | | |
| 1949-50 | (D1) | 3 | 07.01.50 | **Norwich City** (3S) | H | D | 1-1 | Delapenha |
| | | 3r | 12.01.50 | **Norwich City** | A | W | 2-0 | Reid 2 (1p) |
| | | 4 | 28.01.50 | **Grimsby Town** (D2) | H | W | 5-0 | Froggatt 2, Clarke 2, Phillips |
| | | 5 | 11.02.50 | **Manchester Utd** (D1) | A | D | 3-3 | Clarke, Parker, Ferrier |
| | | 5r | 15.02.50 | **Manchester Utd** | H | L | 1-3 | Harris |
| 1950-51 | (D1) | 3 | 06.01.51 | **Luton Town** (D2) | A | L | 0-2 | |
| 1951-52 | (D1) | 3 | 12.01.52 | **Lincoln City** (3N) | H | W | 4-0 | Clarke, Gaillard 2, Mundy |
| | | 4 | 02.02.52 | **Notts County** (D2) | A | W | 2-1 | Gaillard, Mundy |
| | | 5 | 23.02.52 | **Doncaster Rovers** (D2) | H | W | 4-0 | Harris, Phillips, Gaillard, Rouse og |
| | | 6 | 08.03.52 | **Newcastle Utd** (D1) | H | L | 2-4 | Gaillard, Reid |
| 1952-53 | (D1) | 3 | 10.01.53 | **Burnley** (D1) | H | D | 1-1 | Gordon |
| | | 3r | 13.01.53 | **Burnley** | A | L | 1-3 | Gaillard |
| 1953-54 | (D1) | 3 | 09.01.54 | **Charlton Athletic** (D1) | H | D | 3-3 | Vaughan 2, Gordon |
| | | 3r | 14.01.54 | **Charlton Athletic** | A | W | 3-2aet | Harris 2, Barnard |
| | | 4 | 30.01.54 | **Scunthorpe Utd** (3N) | A | D | 1-1 | Harris |
| | | 4r | 03.02.54 | **Scunthorpe Utd** | H | D | 2-2aet | Henderson 2 |
| | | 4 2r | 08.02.54 | **Scunthorpe Utd** | | W | 4-0 | Froggatt 2, Harris, Henderson |
| | | | | *played at Highbury* | | | | |
| | | 5 | 20.02.54 | **Bolton Wanderers** (D1) | A | D | 0-0 | |
| | | 5r | 24.02.54 | **Bolton Wanderers** | H | L | 1-2 | Gordon |
| 1954-55 | (D1) | 3 | 08.01.55 | **Bristol Rovers** (D2) | A | L | 1-2 | Gordon |
| 1955-56 | (D1) | 3 | 07.01.56 | **Grimsby Town** (3N) | H | W | 3-1 | Mansell, Dickinson, Harris |
| | | 4 | 28.01.56 | **WBA** (D1) | A | L | 0-2 | |
| 1956-57 | (D1) | 3 | 05.01.57 | **Bury** (D2) | A | W | 3-1 | Harris 2, McClellan |
| | | 4 | 26.01.57 | **Nottingham Forest** (D2) | H | L | 1-3 | Weddle |
| 1957-58 | (D1) | 3 | 04.01.58 | **Aldershot** (3S) | H | W | 5-1 | Gordon 2, Newman 2, Barnard |
| | | 4 | 25.01.58 | **Wolverhampton W** (D1) | A | L | 1-5 | Crawford |
| 1958-59 | (D1) | 3 | 10.01.59 | **Swansea Town** (D2) | H | W | 3-1 | Saunders, Newman, Hughes og |
| | | 4 | 24.01.59 | **Accrington Stanley** (D3) | A | D | 0-0 | |
| | | 4r | 28.01.59 | **Accrington Stanley** | H | W | 4-1 | Newman, Weddle, Saunders 2 |
| | | 5 | 14.02.59 | **Burnley** (D1) | A | L | 0-1 | |
| 1959-60 | (D2) | 3 | 09.01.60 | **Sheffield Utd** (D2) | A | L | 0-3 | |
| 1960-61 | (D2) | 3 | 07.01.61 | **Peterborough Utd** (D4) | H | L | 1-2 | Wilson |

| | | | | | | | | |
|---|---|---|---|---|---|---|---|---|
| 1961-62 | (D3) | 1 | 04.11.61 | **Crystal Palace** (D3) | A | L | 0-3 | |
| 1962-63 | (D2) | 3 | 26.01.63 | **Scunthorpe Utd** (D2) | H | D | 1-1 | Gordon |
| | | 3r | 07.03.63 | **Scunthorpe Utd** | A | W | 2-1 | Saunders 2 |
| | | 4 | 13.03.63 | **Coventry City** (D3) | H | D | 1-1 | Saunders |
| | | 4r | 16.03.63 | **Coventry City** | A | D | 2-2aet | McCann, Saunders |
| | | 4 2r | 19.03.63 | **Coventry City** | | L | 1-2 | Saunders |
| | | | | *played at White Hart Lane* | | | | |
| 1963-64 | (D2) | 3 | 04.01.64 | **Stoke City** (D1) | A | L | 1-4 | Saunders (p) |
| 1964-65 | (D2) | 3 | 09.01.65 | **Wolverhampton W** (D1) | H | D | 0-0 | |
| | | 3r | 12.01.65 | **Wolverhampton W** | A | L | 2-3 | McClelland, Hiron |
| 1965-66 | (D2) | 3 | 22.01.66 | **Grimsby Town** (D3) | A | D | 0-0 | |
| | | 3r | 26.01.66 | **Grimsby Town** | H | L | 1-3 | Portwood |
| 1966-67 | (D2) | 3 | 28.01.67 | **Hull City** (D2) | A | D | 1-1 | McCann |
| | | 3r | 01.02.67 | **Hull City** | H | D | 2-2aet | Edwards, Pack |
| | | 3 2r | 06.02.67 | **Hull City** | | W | 3-1 | McCann 2 (1p), Edwards |
| | | | | *played at Highfield Road, Coventry* | | | | |
| | | 4 | 18.02.67 | **Tottenham Hotspur** (D1) | A | L | 1-3 | Tindall |
| 1967-68 | (D2) | 3 | 27.01.68 | **Peterborough Utd** (D3) | A | W | 1-0 | Hiron |
| | | 4 | 17.02.68 | **Fulham** (D1) | A | D | 0-0 | |
| | | 4r | 21.02.68 | **Fulham** | H | W | 1-0 | Trebilcock |
| | | 5 | 09.03.68 | **WBA** (D1) | H | L | 1-2 | Hiron |
| 1968-69 | (D2) | 3 | 04.01.69 | **Chesterfield** (D4) | H | W | 3-0 | Jennings 2, McCann |
| | | 4 | 25.01.69 | **Blackburn Rovers** (D2) | A | L | 0-4 | |
| 1969-70 | (D2) | 3 | 03.01.70 | **Tranmere Rovers** (D3) | H | L | 1-2 | Jennings |
| 1970-71 | (D2) | 3 | 02.01.71 | **Sheffield Utd** (D2) | H | W | 2-0 | Hiron, Trebilcock |
| | | 4 | 23.01.71 | **Arsenal** (D1) | H | D | 1-1 | Trebilcock |
| | | 4r | 01.02.71 | **Arsenal** | A | L | 2-3 | Piper, Ley |
| 1971-72 | (D2) | 3 | 15.01.72 | **Boston Utd** (NPL) | A | W | 1-0 | Jennings |
| | | 4 | 05.02.72 | **Swansea City** (D3) | H | W | 2-0 | Williams og, Trebilcock |
| | | 5 | 26.02.72 | **Birmingham City** (D2) | A | L | 1-3 | Reynolds |
| 1972-73 | (D2) | 3 | 13.01.73 | **Bristol City** (D2) | H | D | 1-1 | Piper |
| | | 3r | 16.01.73 | **Bristol City** | A | L | 1-4 | Hiron |
| 1973-74 | (D2) | 3 | 05.01.74 | **Swindon Town** (D2) | A | D | 3-3 | Davies, Went, Kellard (p) |
| | | 3r | 09.01.74 | **Swindon Town** | H | W | 1-0 | Kellard |
| | | 4 | 27.01.74 | **Orient** (D2) | H | D | 0-0 | |
| | | 4r | 29.01.74 | **Orient** | A | D | 1-1aet | Mellows |
| | | 4 2r | 05.02.74 | **Orient** | | W | 2-0 | Kellard, Davies |
| | | | | *played at Selhurst Park* | | | | |
| | | 5 | 17.02.74 | **Nottingham Forest** (D2) | A | L | 0-1 | |
| 1974-75 | (D2) | 3 | 03.01.75 | **Notts County** (D2) | A | L | 1-3 | Marinello |
| 1975-76 | (D2) | 3 | 03.01.76 | **Birmingham City** (D1) | H | D | 1-1 | Eames |
| | | 3r | 06.01.76 | **Birmingham City** | A | W | 1-0 | McGuinness |
| | | 4 | 24.01.76 | **Charlton Athletic** (D2) | A | D | 1-1 | Piper |
| | | 4r | 27.01.76 | **Charlton Athletic** | H | L | 0-3 | |
| 1976-77 | (D3) | 1 | 20.11.76 | **Aldershot** (D4) | A | D | 1-1 | Mellows |
| | | 1r | 23.11.76 | **Aldershot** | H | W | 2-1 | Green, Foster |
| | | 2 | 11.12.76 | **Minehead** (SL) | H | W | 2-1 | Kemp, Kamara |
| | | 3 | 08.01.77 | **Birmingham City** (D1) | A | L | 0-1 | |
| 1977-78 | (D3) | 1 | 26.11.77 | **Bideford** (WL) | H | W | 3-1 | Stokes, Pullar, Mellows |
| | | 2 | 17.12.77 | **Swansea City** (D4) | H | D | 2-2 | Kemp 2 |
| | | 2r | 20.12.77 | **Swansea City** | A | L | 1-2 | Foster |
| 1978-79 | (D4) | 1 | 25.11.78 | **Northampton Town** (D4) | H | W | 2-0 | Hemmerman 2 |
| | | 2 | 16.12.78 | **Reading** (D4) | H | L | 0-1 | |
| 1979-80 | (D4) | 1 | 24.11.79 | **Newport County** (D4) | H | W | 1-0 | Brisley |
| | | 2 | 18.12.79 | **Wimbledon** (D3) | A | D | 0-0 | |
| | | 2r | 24.12.79 | **Wimbledon** | H | D | 3-3aet | Gregory, Laidlaw, Bryant |
| | | 2 2r | 05.01.80 | **Wimbledon** | A | W | 1-0 | Hemmerman |
| | | 3 | 09.01.80 | **Middlesbrough** (D1) | H | D | 1-1 | Brisley |
| | | 3r | 14.01.80 | **Middlesbrough** | A | L | 0-3 | |
| 1980-81 | (D3) | 1 | 22.11.80 | **Colchester Utd** (D3) | A | L | 0-3 | |
| 1981-82 | (D3) | 1 | 21.11.81 | **Millwall** (D3) | H | D | 1-1 | Hemmerman |

| | | | | | | | | |
|---|---|---|---|---|---|---|---|---|
| | | 1r | 25.11.81 | **Millwall** | A | L | 2-3aet | Tait, Hemmerman |
| 1982-83 | (D3) | 1 | 20.11.82 | **Hereford Utd** (D4) | H | W | 4-1 | Biley 2, Rafferty 2 |
| | | 2 | 11.12.82 | **Aldershot** (D4) | H | L | 1-3 | Webb |
| 1983-84 | (D2) | 3 | 07.01.84 | **Grimsby Town** (D2) | H | W | 2-1 | Hateley, Morgan |
| | | 4 | 28.01.84 | **Southampton** (D1) | H | L | 0-1 | |
| 1984-85 | (D2) | 3 | 04.01.85 | **Blackburn Rovers** (D2) | H | D | 0-0 | |
| | | 3r | 26.01.85 | **Blackburn Rovers** | A | L | 1-2 | Kennedy |
| 1985-86 | (D2) | 3 | 04.01.86 | **Aston Villa** (D1) | H | D | 2-2 | Blake, Dillon |
| | | 3r | 13.01.86 | **Aston Villa** | A | L | 2-3aet | Stanley 2 (1p) |
| 1986-87 | (D2) | 3 | 10.01.87 | **Blackburn Rovers** (D2) | H | W | 2-0 | Quinn 2 |
| | | 4 | 31.01.87 | **Wimbledon** (D1) | A | L | 0-4 | |
| 1987-88 | (D1) | 3 | 09.01.88 | **Blackburn Rovers** (D2) | A | W | 2-1 | Quinn, Dillon |
| | | 4 | 01.02.88 | **Sheffield Utd** (D2) | H | W | 2-1 | Dillon, Quinn |
| | | 5 | 20.02.88 | **Bradford City** (D2) | H | W | 3-0 | Blake, Quinn, Connor |
| | | 6 | 12.03.88 | **Luton Town** (D1) | A | L | 1-3 | Quinn |
| 1988-89 | (D2) | 3 | 07.01.89 | **Swindon Town** (D2) | H | D | 1-1 | Quinn |
| | | 3r | 10.01.89 | **Swindon Town** | A | L | 0-2 | |
| 1989-90 | (D2) | 3 | 06.01.90 | **Crystal Palace** (D1) | A | L | 1-2 | Whittingham |
| 1990-91 | (D2) | 3 | 05.01.91 | **Barnet** (Conf) | A | W | 5-0 | Aspinall, Whittingham 3, Clarke |
| | | 4 | 26.01.91 | **Bournemouth** (D3) | H | W | 5-1 | Clarke, Whittingham 4 |
| | | 5 | 16.02.91 | **Tottenham Hotspur** (D1) | H | L | 1-2 | Chamberlain |
| 1991-92 | (D2) | 3 | 04.01.92 | **Exeter City** (D3) | A | W | 2-1 | Whittingham, Aspinall |
| | | 4 | 25.01.92 | **Leyton Orient** (D3) | H | W | 2-0 | Anderton 2 |
| | | 5 | 15.02.92 | **Middlesbrough** (D2) | H | D | 1-1 | Whittingham |
| | | 5r | 26.02.92 | **Middlesbrough** | A | W | 4-2 | Clarke 2, Anderton 2 |
| | | 6 | 07.03.92 | **Nottingham Forest** (D1) | H | W | 1-0 | McLoughlin |
| | | SF | 05.04.92 | **Liverpool** (D1) | | D | 1-1aet | Anderton |
| | | | | *played at Highbury* | | | | |
| | | SFr | 13.04.92 | **Liverpool** | | D | 0-0aet | |
| | | | | *played at Villa Park – Liverpool won 3-1 on penalties* | | | | |
| 1992-93 | (D1) | 3 | 02.01.93 | **Brighton** (D2) | A | L | 0-1 | |
| 1993-94 | (D1) | 3 | 08.01.94 | **Blackburn Rovers** (PL) | A | D | 3-3 | McLoughlin 3 |
| | | 3r | 19.01.94 | **Blackburn Rovers** | H | L | 1-3 | McLoughlin |
| 1994-95 | (D1) | 3 | 07.01.95 | **Bolton Wanderers** (D1) | H | W | 3-1 | Creaney, Radosavljevic 2 |
| | | 4 | 28.01.95 | **Leicester City** (PL) | H | L | 0-1 | |
| 1995-96 | (D1) | 3 | 07.01.96 | **Southampton** (PL) | A | L | 0-3 | |
| 1996-97 | (D1) | 3 | 04.01.97 | **Wolverhampton W** (D1) | A | W | 2-1 | McLoughlin, Hall |
| | | 4 | 25.01.97 | **Reading** (D1) | H | W | 3-0 | Hall, Bradbury, Hillier |
| | | 5 | 15.02.97 | **Leeds Utd** (PL) | A | W | 3-2 | McLoughlin, Svensson, Bradbury |
| | | 6 | 09.03.97 | **Chelsea** (PL) | H | L | 1-4 | Burton |
| 1997-98 | (D1) | 3 | 03.01.98 | **Aston Villa** (PL) | H | D | 2-2 | Foster 2 |
| | | 3r | 14.01.98 | **Aston Villa** | A | L | 0-1 | |
| 1998-99 | (D1) | 3 | 02.01.99 | **Nottingham Forest** (PL) | A | W | 1-0 | Claridge |
| | | 4 | 23.01.99 | **Leeds Utd** (PL) | H | L | 1-5 | Nightingale |
| 1999-00 | (D1) | 3 | 11.12.99 | **Sunderland** (D1) | A | L | 0-1 | |
| 2000-01 | (D1) | 3 | 06.01.01 | **Tranmere Rovers** (D1) | H | L | 1-2 | Bradbury |
| 2001-02 | (D1) | 3 | 05.01.02 | **Leyton Orient** (D3) | H | L | 1-4 | Smith og |
| 2002-03 | (D1) | 3 | 04.01.03 | **Manchester Utd** (PL) | A | L | 1-4 | Stone |

## PRESCOT CABLES

*Formed 1884. First entered FA Cup: 1891-92. Members of the North West Counties League.*

| | | | | | | | |
|---|---|---|---|---|---|---|---|
| 1957-58 | (LC) | 1 | 16.11.57 | **Hartlepools Utd** (3N) | A | L | 0-5 |
| 1959-60 | (LC) | 1 | 14.11.59 | **Darlington** (D4) | A | L | 0-4 |

## PRESTON NORTH END

*Formed 1881. Founder Members of the Football League 1888 and the first Football League champions 1888-89 when they also won the double, winning the championship without losing a match and winning the FA Cup without conceding a goal. FA Cup winners: 1889, 1938. Runners-up: 1888, 1922, 1937, 1954, 1964. FA Cup record win: 26-0 v Hyde, 1st round, 15.10.1887 – the biggest winning margin in FA Cup history. FA Cup Record defeat: 0-6 v Charlton Athletic, 5th round, second leg, 13.02.1946. James Ross also holds the individual scoring record of 19 goals in one season in the FA Cup. He actually scored 20 in his record-breaking season of 1887-88, but 'lost' one goal when Preston's second round match against Everton was declared void.*

| | | | | | | | |
|---|---|---|---|---|---|---|---|
| 1883-84 | 1 | | bye | | | | |
| | 2 | 01.12.83 | **Great Lever** | H | W | 4-1 | Belger 2, Drummond, AN Other |
| | 3 | 29.12.83 | **Eagley** | H | W | 9-1 | Dewhurst 4, Russell 2, Belger, Drummond, Gordon |
| | 4 | 19.01.84 | **Upton Park** | H | D | 1-1 | Smalley |
| | | | *FA disqualified Preston for professionalism. Upton Park advanced* | | | | |
| 1884-85 | | | | did not enter | | | |
| 1885-86 | 1 | | Great Lever | | | - | |
| | | | *Great Lever scratched. Preston walkover* | | | | |
| | 2 | 18.11.85 | **Astley Bridge** | H | W | 11-3 | |
| | 3 | 12.12.85 | **Bolton Wanderers** | A | W | 3-2 | Dempsey, Dewhurst, AN Other |
| | | | *FA disqualified Preston for professionalism. Bolton re-instated* | | | | |
| 1886-87 | 1 | 30.10.86 | **Queen's Park, Glasgow** | A | W | 3-0 | Gordon, others 2 |
| | 2 | 13.11.86 | **Witton** | H | W | 6-0 | Dewhurst 4, Thomson 2 |
| | 3 | 22.01.87 | **Renton** | A | W | 2-0 | Gordon, JD Ross |
| | 4 | | bye | | | | |
| | 5 | 29.01.87 | **Old Foresters** | A | W | 3-0 | Thomson 2, own goal |
| | 6 | 02.03.87 | **Old Carthusians** | A | W | 2-1aet | Graham, Gordon |
| | SF | 05.03.87 | **WBA** | | L | 1-3 | Thomson |
| | | | *played at Trent Bridge* | | | | |
| 1887-88 | 1 | 15.10.87 | **Hyde FC** | H | W | 26-0 | JD Ross 8, Gordon 5, Thomson 5, Drummond 3, Dewhurst 2, Goodall, Russell, NJ Ross |
| | 2 | 10.12.87 | **Bolton Wanderers** | H | W | 9-1 | JD Ross 6, Dewhurst, Goodall, Gordon |
| | 2 | 26.11.87 | **Everton** | H | W | 6-0 | Goodall 2, Dewhurst, Drummond, Gordon, JD Ross |
| | | | *FA declared match void. Everton were disqualified. Bolton, who lost to Everton in the previous round, were reinstated.* | | | | |
| | 3 | 03.12.87 | **Halliwell** | H | W | 4-0 | JD Ross 2, Dewhurst, Goodall |
| | 4 | | bye | | | | |
| | 5 | 07.01.88 | **Aston Villa** | A | W | 3-1 | JD Ross, Goodall 2 |
| | 6 | 30.01.88 | **Sheffield Wed** | A | W | 3-1 | JD Ross, Thomson 2 |
| | SF | 18.02.88 | **Crewe Alexandra** | | W | 4-0 | JD Ross, Goodall 3 |
| | | | *played at Anfield* | | | | |
| | F | 24.03.88 | **WBA** | | L | 1-2 | Dewhurst |
| | | | *played at Kennington Oval* | | | | |
| 1888-89 (D1) | 1 | 02.02.89 | **Bootle** | A | W | 3-0 | Goodall, Gordon, Thomson |
| | 2 | 16.02.89 | **Grimsby Town** (TC) | A | W | 2-0 | Goodall, Gordon |
| | 3 | 02.03.89 | **Birmingham St G** | H | W | 2-0 | Holmes, Thomson |
| | SF | 16.03.89 | **WBA** (D1) | | W | 1-0 | Russell |
| | | | *played at Bramall Lane* | | | | |
| | F | 30.03.89 | **Wolverhampton W** (D1) | | W | 3-0 | Dewhurst, JD Ross, Thomson |
| | | | *played at Kennington Oval* | | | | |
| 1889-90 (D1) | 1 | 18.01.90 | **Newton Heath** (Fall) | H | W | 6-1 | Drummond 4, JD Ross, NJ Ross |
| | 2 | 01.02.90 | **Lincoln City** (ML) | H | W | 4-0 | Gillespie 2, JD Ross, NJ Ross |
| | 3 | 15.02.90 | **Bolton Wanderers** (D1) | H | L | 2-3 | Pauls, Thomson |
| 1890-91 (D1) | 1 | 17.01.91 | **Stoke** (Fall) | A | L | 0-3 | |
| 1891-92 (D1) | 1 | 16.01.92 | **Middlesbrough Iron** (NL) | H | - | 2-2ab | Becton, Towie |
| | | | *abandoned – bad weather and frosty pitch* | | | | |
| | 1 | 23.01.92 | **Middlesbrough Iron** | H | W | 6-0 | JD Ross, Sharp, Becton, Stewart, Towie |
| | 2 | 30.01.92 | **Middlesbrough** (NL) | A | W | 2-1 | Gallacher, JD Ross |
| | 3 | 13.02.92 | **Nottingham Forest** (FAll) | A | L | 0-2 | |
| 1892-93 (D1) | 1 | 21.01.93 | **Burton Swifts** (D2) | H | W | 9-2 | JD Ross 4, Beckton 3, Drummond, Gordon |
| | 2 | 04.02.93 | **Accrington FC** (D1) | A | W | 4-1 | Becton 3, Cowan |
| | 3 | 18.02.93 | **Middlesbrough Iron** (NL) | H | D | 2-2 | Gordon, Russell |
| | 3r | 25.02.93 | **Middlesbrough Iron** | A | W | 7-0 | Becton 3, Cowan, JD Ross, Russell 2 |
| | SF | 04.03.93 | **Everton** (D1) | | D | 2-2 | Cowan, Gordon |
| | | | *played at Bramall Lane* | | | | |

| | | | | | | | | |
|---|---|---|---|---|---|---|---|---|
| | | SFr | 16.03.93 | **Everton** (D1) | | D | 0-0aet | |
| | | | | *played at Ewood Park* | | | | |
| | | SF2r | 20.03.93 | **Everton** | | L | 1-2 | Gordon |
| | | | | *played at Trent Bridge, Nottingham* | | | | |
| 1893-94 | (D1) | 1 | 27.01.94 | **Reading** | H | W | 18-0 | Becton 6, JD Ross 6, Cowan 5, Sanders |
| | | 2 | 10.02.94 | **Liverpool** (D2) | A | L | 2-3 | Becton 2 |
| 1894-95 | (D1) | 1 | 02.02.95 | **Luton Town** (SL) | A | W | 2-0 | Henderson, Sanders |
| | | 2 | 16.02.95 | **Sunderland** (D1) | A | L | 0-2 | |
| 1895-96 | (D1) | 1 | 01.02.96 | **Sunderland** | A | L | 1-4 | Cunningham |
| 1896-97 | (D1) | 1 | 30.01.97 | **Manchester City** (D2) | | W | 6-0 | Boyd 2, Henderson 2, Orr, Stevenson |
| | | 2 | 13.02.97 | **Stoke** (D1) | H | W | 2-1 | Smith, Stevenson |
| | | 3 | 27.02.97 | **Aston Villa** (D1) | H | D | 1-1 | Stevenson |
| | | 3r | 03.03.97 | **Aston Villa** | A | D | 0-0 | |
| | | 3 2r | 10.03.97 | **Aston Villa** | | L | 2-3 | Blyth 2 |
| | | | | *played at Bramall Lane* | | | | |
| 1897-98 | (D1) | 1 | 29.01.98 | **Newcastle Utd** (D2) | H | L | 1-2 | own goal |
| 1898-99 | (D1) | 1 | 28.01.99 | **Grimsby Town** (D2) | H | W | 7-0 | Pratt 4, Brown 2, Chalmers |
| | | 2 | 11.02.99 | **Sheffield Utd** (D1) | H | D | 2-2 | Brown, Halsall |
| | | 2r | 16.02.99 | **Sheffield Utd** | A | L | 1-2 | Brown |
| 1899-00 | (D1) | 1 | 27.01.00 | **Tottenham Hotspur** (SL) | H | W | 1-0 | Stevenson |
| | | 2 | 17.02.00 | **Blackburn Rovers** (D1) | H | W | 1-0 | Henderson |
| | | 3 | 24.02.00 | **Nottingham Forest** (D1) | H | D | 0-0 | |
| | | 3r | 28.02.00 | **Nottingham Forest** | A | L | 0-1 | |
| 1900-01 | (D1) | 1 | 09.02.01 | **Tottenham Hotspur** (SL) | A | D | 1-1 | McMahon |
| | | 1r | 13.02.01 | **Tottenham Hotspur** | H | L | 2-4 | Becton, Pratt |
| 1901-02 | (D2) | 1 | 25.01.02 | **Manchester City** (D1) | H | - | 1-1ab | Rogers |
| | | | | *abandoned in extra time* | | | | |
| | | 1 | 29.01.02 | **Manchester City** | A | D | 0-0aet | |
| | | 1r | 03.02.02 | **Manchester City** | H | L | 2-4aet | Pratt, Wilcox |
| 1902-03 | (D2) | | | Int Bishop Auckland (A) 3-1 | | | | |
| | | 1 | 07.02.03 | **Manchester City** (D2) | H | W | 3-1 | Hunter, Pearson, Smith |
| | | 2 | 21.02.03 | **Millwall Athletic** (SL) | A | L | 1-4 | Pearson |
| 1903-04 | (D2) | | | Int Darwen (H) 2-1 | | | | |
| | | 1 | 06.02.04 | **Grimsby Town** (D2) | H | W | 1-0 | Wilcox |
| | | 2 | 20.02.04 | **Middlesbrough** (D1) | H | L | 0-3 | |
| 1904-05 | (D1) | 1 | 04.02.05 | **Derby County** (D1) | A | W | 2-0 | Bond, Bell |
| | | 2 | 18.02.05 | **Bristol City** (D2) | A | D | 0-0 | |
| | | 2r | 23.02.05 | **Bristol City** | H | W | 1-0 | Bourne |
| | | 3 | 04.03.05 | **Sheffield Wed** (D1) | H | D | 1-1 | Bond |
| | | 3r | 09.03.05 | **Sheffield Wed** | A | L | 0-3 | |
| 1905-06 | (D1) | 1 | 13.01.06 | **Birmingham** (D1) | A | L | 0-1 | |
| 1906-07 | (D1) | 1 | 12.01.07 | **Notts County** (D1) | A | L | 0-1 | |
| 1907-08 | (D1) | 1 | 11.01.08 | **Brighton** (SL) | A | D | 1-1 | Winchester |
| | | 1r | 16.01.08 | **Brighton** | H | - | 1-2ab | Bond |
| | | | | *abandoned after 112 minutes – fog* | | | | |
| | | 1r | 20.01.08 | **Brighton** | | L | 0-1 | |
| | | | | *played at Stamford Bridge* | | | | |
| 1908-09 | (D1) | 1 | 16.01.09 | **Middlesbrough** (D1) | H | W | 1-0 | Lyon |
| | | 2 | 06.02.09 | **Sunderland** (D1) | H | L | 1-2 | Dawson |
| 1909-10 | (D1) | 1 | 15.01.10 | **Coventry City** (SL) | H | L | 1-2 | McLean |
| 1910-11 | (D1) | 1 | 14.01.11 | **Brentford** (SL) | A | W | 1-0 | Rodway |
| | | 2 | 04.02.11 | **West Ham Utd** (SL) | A | L | 0-3 | |
| 1911-12 | (D1) | 1 | 13.01.12 | **Manchester City** (D1) | H | L | 0-1 | |
| 1912-13 | (D2) | 1 | 11.01.13 | **Plymouth Argyle** (SL) | A | L | 0-2 | |
| 1913-14 | (D1) | 1 | 10.01.14 | **Bristol Rovers** (SL) | H | W | 5-2 | Osborne 3, Barlow, Marshall |
| | | 2 | 31.01.14 | **Glossop North End** (D2) | A | W | 1-0 | Osborne |
| | | 3 | 21.02.14 | **Sunderland** (D1) | A | L | 0-2 | |
| 1914-15 | (D2) | 1 | 09.01.15 | **Manchester City** (D1) | H | D | 0-0 | |
| | | 1r | 16.01.15 | **Manchester City** | A | L | 0-3 | |
| 1919-20 | (D1) | 1 | 10.01.20 | **Stockport County** (D2) | H | W | 3-1 | Bainbridge, Woodhouse, Roberts |

| | | | | | | | |
|---|---|---|---|---|---|---|---|
| | 2 | 31.01.20 | **Blackpool** (D2) | H | W | 2-1 | Roberts 2 |
| | 3 | 21.02.20 | **Bradford City** (D1) | H | L | 0-3 | |
| 1920-21 (D1) | 1 | 08.01.21 | **Bolton Wanderers** (D1) | H | W | 2-0 | Rawlings, Roberts |
| | 2 | 29.01.21 | **Watford** (D3) | H | W | 4-1 | Roberts 3, Woodhouse |
| | 3 | 19.02.21 | **Luton Town** (3S) | A | W | 3-2 | Roberts 3 |
| | 4 | 05.03.21 | **Hull City** (D2) | A | D | 0-0 | |
| | 4r | 10.03.21 | **Hull City** | H | W | 1-0 | Jefferies |
| | SF | 19.03.21 | **Tottenham Hotspur** (D1) *played at Hillsborough* | | L | 1-2 | Clay og |
| 1921-22 (D1) | 1 | 07.01.22 | **Wolverhampton W** (D2) | H | W | 3-0 | Roberts 2, Jefferies |
| | 2 | 28.01.22 | **Newcastle Utd** (D1) | H | W | 3-1 | Rawlings, Roberts, Woodhouse |
| | 3 | 18.02.22 | **Barnsley** (D2) | A | D | 1-1 | Rawlings |
| | 3r | 22.02.22 | **Barnsley** | H | W | 3-0 | Roberts, Woodhouse 2 |
| | 4 | 04.03.22 | **Arsenal** (D1) | A | D | 1-1 | Jefferies |
| | 4r | 08.03.22 | **Arsenal** | H | W | 2-1aet | Roberts 2 |
| | SF | 25.03.22 | **Tottenham Hotspur** (D1) *played at Hillsborough* | | W | 2-1aet | Rawlings, Roberts |
| | F | 29.04.22 | **Huddersfield Town** (D1) *played at Stamford Bridge* | | L | 0-1 | |
| 1922-23 (D1) | 1 | 13.01.23 | **Aberdare Athletic** (3S) | A | W | 3-1 | Rawlings, Roberts, Woodhouse |
| | 2 | 03.02.23 | **Charlton Athletic** (3S) | A | L | 0-2 | |
| 1923-24 (D1) | 1 | 12.01.24 | **Everton** (D1) | A | L | 1-3 | Rawlings |
| 1924-25 (D1) | 1 | 10.01.25 | **Manchester City** (PL) | H | W | 4-1 | Woodhouse 3, Paterson |
| | 2 | 31.01.25 | **WBA** (D1) | A | L | 0-2 | |
| 1925-26 (D2) | 3 | 09.01.26 | **Blackburn Rovers** (D1) | A | D | 1-1 | Jackson |
| | 3r | 14.01.26 | **Blackburn Rovers** | H | L | 1-4 | Jackson |
| 1926-27 (D2) | 3 | 08.01.27 | **Lincoln City** (3N) | A | W | 4-2 | Roberts 4 |
| | 4 | 29.01.27 | **Middlesbrough** (D2) | H | L | 0-3 | |
| 1927-28 (D2) | 3 | 14.01.28 | **Everton** (D1) | H | L | 0-3 | |
| 1928-29 (D2) | 3 | 12.01.29 | **Watford** (3S) | A | L | 0-1 | |
| 1929-30 (D2) | 3 | 11.01.30 | **Portsmouth** (D1) | A | L | 0-2 | |
| 1930-31 (D2) | 3 | 10.01.31 | **Tottenham Hotspur** (D2) | A | L | 1-3 | Tremelling |
| 1931-32 (D2) | 3 | 09.01.32 | **Bolton Wanderers** (D1) | H | D | 0-0 | |
| | 3r | 13.01.32 | **Bolton Wanderers** | A | W | 5-2 | Crawford, Finney og, Harper, Wagstaffe og, Birch |
| | 4 | 23.01.32 | **Wolverhampton W** (D2) | H | W | 2-0 | Rowley, Harper |
| | 5 | 13.02.32 | **Huddersfield Town** (D1) | A | L | 0-4 | |
| 1932-33 (D2) | 3 | 14.01.33 | **Birmingham** (D1) | A | L | 1-2 | Rowley |
| 1933-34 (D2) | 3 | 13.01.34 | **Leeds Utd** (D1) | A | W | 1-0 | Kelly |
| | 4 | 27.01.34 | **Workington** (NEL) | A | W | 2-1 | Kelly, Fitton |
| | 5 | 17.02.34 | **Northampton Town** (3S) | H | W | 4-0 | McGuire og, Palethorpe 3 |
| | 6 | 03.03.34 | **Leicester City** (D1) | H | L | 0-1 | |
| 1934-35 (D1) | 3 | 12.01.35 | **Barnsley** (D2) | H | D | 0-0 | |
| | 3r | 16.01.35 | **Barnsley** | A | W | 1-0 | Maxwell |
| | 4 | 26.01.35 | **Swindon Town** (3S) | A | W | 2-0 | Hetherington, Friar |
| | 5 | 16.02.35 | **Bristol City** (3S) | A | D | 0-0 | |
| | 5r | 25.02.35 | **Bristol City** | H | W | 5-0 | Maxwell 2, Hughes og, Fitton, Dougall |
| | 6 | 02.03.35 | **WBA** (D1) | A | L | 0-1 | |
| 1935-36 (D1) | 3 | 11.01.36 | **Everton** (D1) | A | W | 3-1 | Maxwell 2, F O'Donnell |
| | 4 | 25.01.36 | **Sheffield Utd** (D2) | H | D | 0-0 | |
| | 4r | 30.01.36 | **Sheffield Utd** | A | L | 0-2 | |
| 1936-37 (D1) | 3 | 16.01.37 | **Newcastle Utd** (D2) | H | W | 2-0 | Beresford, F O'Donnell |
| | 4 | 30.01.37 | **Stoke City** (D1) | H | W | 5-1 | Turner og, Dougall, F O'Donnell 3 |
| | 5 | 20.02.37 | **Exeter City** (3S) | H | W | 5-3 | F O'Donnell 3, H O'Donnell, Beresford |
| | 6 | 06.03.37 | **Tottenham Hotspur** (D2) | A | W | 3-1 | H O'Donnell, F O'Donnell, Dougall |
| | SF | 10.04.37 | **WBA** (D1) *played at Highbury* | | W | 4-1 | F O'Donnell 2, Dougall 2 |
| | F | 01.05.37 | **Sunderland** (D1) *played at Wembley Stadium* | | L | 1-3 | F O'Donnell |

| | | | | | | | | |
|---|---|---|---|---|---|---|---|---|
| 1937-38 | (D1) | 3 | 08.01.38 | **West Ham Utd** (D2) | H | W | 3-0 | Mutch 3 |
| | | 4 | 22.01.38 | **Leicester City** (D1) | H | W | 2-0 | Mutch, H O'Donnell |
| | | 5 | 12.02.38 | **Arsenal** (D1) | A | W | 1-0 | Dougall |
| | | 6 | 05.03.38 | **Brentford** (D1) | A | W | 3-0 | R Beattie 2, ? O'Donnell |
| | | SF | 26.03.38 | **Aston Villa** (D2) *played at Bramall Lane* | | W | 2-1 | H O'Donnell, Mutch |
| | | F | 30.04.38 | **Huddersfield Town** (D1) *played at Wembley Stadium* | | W | 1-0aet | Mutch (p) |
| 1938-39 | (D1) | 3 | 07.01.39 | **Runcorn** (CC) | A | W | 4-2 | Milne 2, Mutch, Beattie |
| | | 4 | 21.01.39 | **Aston Villa** (D1) | H | W | 2-0 | White 2 |
| | | 5 | 11.02.39 | **Newcastle Utd** (D2) | A | W | 2-1 | R Beattie, Mutch |
| | | 6 | 04.03.39 | **Portsmouth** (D1) | A | L | 0-1 | |
| 1945-46 | (D1) | 3 1L | 05.01.46 | **Everton** (D1) | H | W | 2-1 | Humphreys og, Livesey |
| | | 3 2L | 09.01.46 | **Everton** | A | D | 2-2aet | McIntosh, Shankly |
| | | 4 1L | 26.01.46 | **Manchester Utd** (D1) *played at Maine Road* | A | L | 0-1 | Shankly, Livesey, McIntosh |
| | | 4 2L | 30.01.46 | **Manchester Utd** | H | W | 3-1 | Shankly, Livesey, McIntosh |
| | | 5 1L | 09.02.46 | **Charlton Athletic** (D1) | H | D | 1-1 | Wharton |
| | | 5 2L | 13.02.46 | **Charlton Athletic** | A | L | 0-6 | |
| 1946-47 | (D1) | 3 | 11.01.47 | **Northampton Town** (3S) | A | W | 2-1 | McIntosh, McLaren |
| | | 4 | 25.01.47 | **Barnsley** (D2) | H | W | 6-0 | Finney 2, R.Beattie, McIntosh 2, Hamilton |
| | | 5 | 20.02.47 | **Sheffield Wed** (D2) | A | W | 2-0 | McIntosh, Wilson |
| | | 6 | 01.03.47 | **Charlton Athletic** (D1) | A | L | 1-2 | McIntosh |
| 1947-48 | (D1) | 3 | 10.01.48 | **Millwall** (D2) | A | W | 2-1 | Anders, McLaren |
| | | 4 | 24.01.48 | **Portsmouth** (D1) | A | W | 3-1 | McIntosh, Finney, Shankly |
| | | 5 | 07.02.48 | **Manchester City** (D1) | A | W | 1-0 | McIntosh |
| | | 6 | 28.02.48 | **Manchester Utd** *played at Maine Road* | A | L | 1-4 | McIntosh |
| 1948-49 | (D1) | 3 | 08.01.49 | **Mansfield Town** (3N) | H | W | 2-1 | Finney 2 |
| | | 4 | 29.01.49 | **Leicester City** (D2) | A | L | 0-2 | |
| 1949-50 | (D2) | 3 | 07.01.50 | **Watford** (3S) | A | D | 2-2 | Brown, Finney |
| | | 3r | 11.01.50 | **Watford** | H | L | 0-1 | |
| 1950-51 | (D2) | 3 | 06.01.51 | **Leicester City** (D2) | A | W | 3-0 | Wayman 2, Horton |
| | | 4 | 27.01.51 | **Huddersfield Town** (D1) | H | L | 0-2 | |
| 1951-52 | (D1) | 3 | 12.01.52 | **Bristol Rovers** (3S) | A | L | 0-2 | |
| 1952-53 | (D1) | 3 | 10.01.53 | **Wolverhampton W** (D1) | H | W | 5-2 | Finney, Wayman 3, Lewis |
| | | 4 | 31.01.53 | **Tottenham Hotspur** (D1) | H | D | 2-2 | Finney, Lewis |
| | | 4r | 04.02.53 | **Tottenham Hotspur** | A | L | 0-1 | |
| 1953-54 | (D1) | 3 | 09.01.54 | **Derby County** (D2) | A | W | 2-0 | Finney, Wayman |
| | | 4 | 30.01.54 | **Lincoln City** (D2) | A | W | 2-0 | Baxter, Wayman |
| | | 5 | 20.02.54 | **Ipswich Town** (3S) | H | W | 6-1 | Morrison, Wayman 2, Baxter 2, Finney |
| | | 6 | 13.03.54 | **Leicester City** (D2) | A | D | 1-1 | Morrison |
| | | 6r | 17.03.54 | **Leicester City** | H | D | 2-2aet | Wayman, Morrison |
| | | 6 2r | 22.03.54 | **Leicester City** *played at Hillsborough* | | W | 3-1 | Baxter, Foster, Finney |
| | | SF | 27.03.54 | **Sheffield Wed** (D1) *played at Maine Road* | | W | 2-0 | Wayman, Baxter |
| | | F | 01.05.54 | **WBA** (D1) *played at Wembley Stadium* | | L | 2-3 | Morrison, Wayman |
| 1954-55 | (D1) | 3 | 08.01.55 | **Fulham** (D2) | A | W | 3-2 | Hatsell 2, Finney |
| | | 4 | 29.01.55 | **Sunderland** (D1) | H | D | 3-3 | Finney, Morrison, Foster |
| | | 4r | 02.02.55 | **Sunderland** | A | L | 0-2 | |
| 1955-56 | (D1) | 3 | 07.01.56 | **West Ham Utd** (D2) | A | L | 2-5 | T.Thompson, Finney |
| 1956-57 | (D1) | 3 | 05.01.57 | **Sheffield Wed** (D1) | H | D | 0-0 | |
| | | 3r | 09.01.57 | **Sheffield Wed** | A | D | 2-2aet | Taylor, Finney |
| | | 3 2r | 14.01.57 | **Sheffield Wed** *played at Goodison Park* | | W | 5-1 | Taylor, O'Farrell, Baxter, Thompson 2 |
| | | 4 | 26.01.57 | **Bristol Rovers** (D2) | A | W | 4-1 | Finney 2, Dagger, Taylor |
| | | 5 | 16.02.57 | **Arsenal** (D1) | H | D | 3-3 | Finney 2, Thompson |

| | | | | | | | | |
|---|---|---|---|---|---|---|---|---|
| | | 5r | 19.02.57 | **Arsenal** | A | L | 1-2 | Dagger |
| 1957-58 | (D1) | 3 | 04.01.58 | **Bolton Wanderers** (D1) | H | L | 0-3 | |
| 1958-59 | (D1) | 3 | 10.01.59 | **Derby County** (D2) | A | D | 2-2 | Farrall, Hatsell |
| | | 3r | 19.01.59 | **Derby County** | H | W | 4-2 | Thompson, Farrall, Mayers, Smith |
| | | 4 | 24.01.59 | **Bradford City** (D3) | H | W | 3-2 | Farrall, O'Farrell, Hatsell |
| | | 5 | 14.02.59 | **Bolton Wanderers** (D1) | A | D | 2-2 | Campbell, Thompson (p) |
| | | 5r | 18.02.59 | **Bolton Wanderers** | H | D | 1-1aet | Smith |
| | | 5 2r | 23.02.59 | **Bolton Wanderers** | | L | 0-1 | |
| | | | | *played at Ewood Park* | | | | |
| 1959-60 | (D1) | 3 | 09.01.60 | **Stoke City** (D2) | A | D | 1-1 | Sneddon |
| | | 3r | 12.01.60 | **Stoke City** | H | W | 3-1 | Finney, Thompson, Mayers |
| | | 4 | 30.01.60 | **Bristol Rovers** (D2) | A | D | 3-3 | Sneddon, Finney, Taylor |
| | | 4r | 02.02.60 | **Bristol Rovers** | H | W | 5-1 | Finney 2, Thompson, Taylor 2 |
| | | 5 | 20.02.60 | **Brighton** (D2) | H | W | 2-1 | Taylor, Sneddon |
| | | 6 | 12.03.60 | **Aston Villa** (D2) | A | L | 0-2 | |
| 1960-61 | (D1) | 3 | 07.01.61 | **Accrington Stanley** (D4) | H | D | 1-1 | T Thompson |
| | | 3r | 09.01.61 | **Accrington Stanley** | A | W | 4-0 | T Thompson, P Thompson, Sneddon, Mayers |
| | | 4 | 28.01.61 | **Swansea Town** (D2) | A | L | 1-2 | Alston |
| 1961-62 | (D2) | 3 | 06.01.62 | **Watford** (D3) | H | W | 3-2 | Biggs, Smith, Dawson |
| | | 4 | 27.01.62 | **Weymouth** (SL) | H | - | 0-0ab | |
| | | | | *abandoned after 14 minutes – fog* | | | | |
| | | 4 | 29.01.62 | **Weymouth** (SL) | H | W | 2-0 | Dawson, Thompson |
| | | 5 | 17.02.62 | **Liverpool** (D2) | A | D | 0-0 | |
| | | 5r | 20.02.62 | **Liverpool** | H | D | 0-0aet | |
| | | 5 2r | 26.02.62 | **Liverpool** | | W | 1-0 | Thompson |
| | | | | *played at Old Trafford* | | | | |
| | | 6 | 10.03.62 | **Manchester Utd** (D1) | H | D | 0-0 | |
| | | 6r | 14.03.62 | **Manchester Utd** | A | L | 1-2 | Spavin |
| 1962-63 | (D2) | 3 | 05.01.63 | **Sunderland** (D2) | H | L | 1-4 | Holden |
| 1963-64 | (D2) | 3 | 04.01.64 | **Nottingham Forest** (D1) | A | D | 0-0 | |
| | | 3r | 13.01.64 | **Nottingham Forest** | H | W | 1-0aet | Kendall |
| | | 4 | 25.01.64 | **Bolton Wanderers** (D1) | A | D | 2-2 | Dawson 2 |
| | | 4r | 27.01.64 | **Bolton Wanderers** | H | W | 2-1 | Dawson, Lawton |
| | | 5 | 15.02.64 | **Carlisle Utd** (D4) | H | W | 1-0 | Spavin |
| | | 6 | 29.02.64 | **Oxford Utd** (D4) | A | W | 2-1 | Dawson, Godfrey |
| | | SF | 14.03.64 | **Swansea Town** (D2) | | W | 2-1 | Dawson, Singleton |
| | | | | *played at Villa Park* | | | | |
| | | F | 02.05.64 | **West Ham Utd** (D1) | | L | 2-3 | Holden, Dawson |
| | | | | *played at Wembley Stadium* | | | | |
| 1964-65 | (D2) | 3 | 09.01.65 | **Barnet** (AL) | A | W | 3-2 | Kendall, Godfrey, Casey og |
| | | 4 | 30.01.65 | **Bolton Wanderers** (D2) | H | L | 1-2 | Dawson |
| 1965-66 | (D2) | 3 | 22.01.66 | **Charlton Athletic** (D2) | A | W | 3-2 | Hannigan 2, Lee |
| | | 4 | 12.02.66 | **Bolton Wanderers** (D2) | A | D | 1-1 | Dawson |
| | | 4r | 14.02.66 | **Bolton Wanderers** | H | W | 3-2 | Godfrey 2 (2ps), Dawson |
| | | 5 | 05.03.66 | **Tottenham Hotspur** (D1) | H | W | 2-1 | Dawson, Hannigan |
| | | 6 | 26.03.66 | **Manchester Utd** (D1) | H | D | 1-1 | Dawson |
| | | 6r | 30.03.66 | **Manchester Utd** | A | L | 1-3 | Singleton |
| 1966-67 | (D2) | 3 | 28.01.67 | **Aston Villa** (D1) | H | L | 0-1 | |
| 1967-68 | (D2) | 3 | 27.01.68 | **QPR** (D2) | A | W | 3-1 | Charnley 2, Gemmell |
| | | 4 | 17.02.68 | **Tottenham Hotspur** (D1) | A | L | 1-3 | Charnley |
| 1968-69 | (D2) | 3 | 04.01.69 | **Nottingham Forest** (D1) | H | W | 3-0 | Irvine 2 (1p), Temple |
| | | 4 | 25.01.69 | **Chelsea** (D1) | H | D | 0-0 | |
| | | 4r | 29.01.69 | **Chelsea** | A | - | 0-2ab | |
| | | | | *abandoned after 72 minutes – floodlight failure* | | | | |
| | | 4r | 03.02.69 | **Chelsea** | A | L | 1-2 | Ingram |
| 1969-70 | (D2) | 3 | 03.01.70 | **Derby County** (D1) | H | D | 1-1 | Lyall |
| | | 3r | 07.01.70 | **Derby County** | A | L | 1-4 | Hawkins |
| 1970-71 | (D3) | 1 | 21.11.70 | **Chester** (D4) | H | D | 1-1 | Heppolette |
| | | 1r | 23.11.70 | **Chester** | A | L | 0-1 | |
| 1971-72 | (D2) | 3 | 15.01.72 | **Bristol City** (D2) | H | W | 4-2 | Clark 2, Lyall, Ingram |

| | | | | | | | | |
|---|---|---|---|---|---|---|---|---|
| | | 4 | 05.02.72 | **Manchester Utd** (D1) | H | L | 0-2 | |
| 1972-73 | (D2) | 3 | 13.01.73 | **Grimsby Town** (D3) | A | D | 0-0 | |
| | | 3r | 15.01.73 | **Grimsby Town** | H | L | 0-1 | |
| 1973-74 | (D2) | 3 | 05.01.74 | **Fulham** (D2) | A | L | 0-1 | |
| 1974-75 | (D3) | 1 | 23.11.74 | **Blyth Spartans** (NL) | A | D | 1-1 | Holden |
| | | 1r | 26.11.74 | **Blyth Spartans** | H | W | 5-1 | Holden 4, Elwiss |
| | | 2 | 14.12.74 | **Bishop Auckland** (NL) | A | W | 2-0 | Charlton, Morley |
| | | 3 | 04.01.75 | **Carlisle Utd** (D1) | H | L | 0-1 | |
| 1975-76 | (D3) | 1 | 22.11.75 | **Scunthorpe Utd** (D4) | H | W | 2-1 | Morley (p), Elwiss |
| | | 2 | 13.12.75 | **Scarborough** (NPL) | A | L | 2-3 | Smith 2 |
| 1976-77 | (D3) | 1 | 20.11.76 | **Crewe Alexandra** (D4) | A | D | 1-1 | Coleman |
| | | 1r | 23.11.76 | **Crewe Alexandra** | H | D | 2-2aet | D.Davies 2 |
| | | 1 2r | 29.11.76 | **Crewe Alexandra** | | W | 3-0 | Sadler, Brown, Elwiss |
| | | | | *played at at Anfield* | | | | |
| | | 2 | 14.12.76 | **Halifax Town** (D4) | A | L | 0-1 | |
| 1977-78 | (D3) | 1 | 26.11.77 | **Lincoln City** (D3) | H | W | 3-2 | Elwiss 2, Bruce |
| | | 2 | 17.12.77 | **Wrexham** (D3) | H | L | 0-2 | |
| 1978-79 | (D2) | 3 | 16.01.79 | **Derby County** (D1) | H | W | 3-0 | Bruce 2, Burns |
| | | 4 | 12.02.79 | **Southampton** (D1) | H | L | 0-1 | |
| 1979-80 | (D2) | 3 | 05.01.80 | **Ipswich Town** (D1) | H | L | 0-3 | |
| 1980-81 | (D2) | 3 | 03.01.81 | **Bristol Rovers** (D2) | H | L | 3-4 | Houston, Bruce, McGee |
| 1981-82 | (D3) | 1 | 21.11.81 | **Chesterfield** (D3) | A | L | 1-4 | Doyle |
| 1982-83 | (D3) | 1 | 20.11.82 | **Shepshed C** (NCoE) | H | W | 5-1 | Elliott 2, Kelly, Coleman, McAteer |
| | | 2 | 11.12.82 | **Blackpool** (D4) | H | W | 2-1 | Coleman, O'Riordan |
| | | 3 | 08.01.83 | **Leeds Utd** (D2) | A | L | 0-3 | |
| 1983-84 | (D3) | 1 | 19.11.83 | **Scunthorpe Utd** (D3) | A | L | 0-1 | |
| 1984-85 | (D3) | 1 | 17.11.84 | **Bury** (D4) | H | W | 4-3 | Gray, Johnson 2, Naughton |
| | | 2 | 08.12.84 | **Telford Utd** (APL) | H | L | 1-4 | Hunter |
| 1985-86 | (D4) | 1 | 16.11.85 | **Walsall** (D3) | A | L | 3-7 | Thomas, Brazil, Martin |
| 1986-87 | (D4) | 1 | 15.11.86 | **Bury** (D3) | H | W | 5-1 | Thomas 3 (1p), Jones, Williams |
| | | 2 | 06.12.86 | **Chorley** (NPL) | A | D | 0-0 | |
| | | | | *played at Ewood Park* | | | | |
| | | 2r | 09.12.86 | **Chorley** | H | W | 5-0 | Thomas 3 (1p), Williams, Brazil |
| | | 3 | 10.01.87 | **Middlesbrough** (D3) | A | W | 1-0 | Hildersley |
| | | 4 | 31.01.87 | **Newcastle Utd** (D1) | A | L | 0-2 | |
| 1987-88 | (D3) | 1 | 14.11.87 | **Mansfield Town** (D3) | H | D | 1-1 | Atkins |
| | | 1r | 17.11.87 | **Mansfield Town** | A | L | 2-4 | Brazil, Jemson |
| 1988-89 | (D3) | 1 | 19.11.88 | **Tranmere Rovers** (D4) | H | D | 1-1 | Atkins |
| | | 1r | 22.11.88 | **Tranmere Rovers** | A | L | 0-3 | |
| 1989-90 | (D3) | 1 | 18.11.89 | **Tranmere Rovers** (D3) | H | W | 1-0 | Joyce |
| | | 2 | 09.12.89 | **Whitley Bay** (NPL) | A | L | 0-2 | |
| 1990-91 | (D3) | 1 | 17.11.90 | **Mansfield Town** (D3) | H | L | 0-1 | |
| 1991-92 | (D3) | 1 | 16.11.91 | **Mansfield Town** | A | - | 1-1ab | Shaw |
| | | | | *abandoned after 32 minutes – fog* | | | | |
| | | 1 | 27.11.91 | **Mansfield Town** | A | W | 1-0 | Thomas |
| | | 2 | 07.12.91 | **Witton Albion** (Conf) | H | W | 5-1 | Shaw, Swann, Senior, Flynn, Greenwood |
| | | 3 | 04.01.92 | **Sheffield Wed** (D1) | H | L | 0-2 | |
| 1992-93 | (D2) | 1 | 14.11.92 | **Bradford City** (D2) | A | D | 1-1 | Fowler |
| | | 1r | 25.11.92 | **Bradford City** | H | L | 4-5 | Graham, Ellis, Davidson, Callaghan |
| 1993-94 | (D3) | 1 | 13.11.93 | **Mansfield Town** (D3) | A | W | 2-1 | Ellis 2 (1p) |
| | | 2 | 04.12.93 | **Shrewsbury Town** (D3) | A | W | 1-0 | Raynor |
| | | 3 | 08.01.94 | **Bournemouth** (D2) | H | W | 2-1 | Moyes, Conroy |
| | | 4 | 29.01.94 | **Kidderminster H** (Conf) | A | L | 0-1 | |
| 1994-95 | (D3) | 1 | 14.11.94 | **Blackpool** (D2) | A | W | 1-0 | Conroy |
| | | 2 | 03.12.94 | **Walsall** (D3) | H | D | 1-1 | Smart |
| | | 2r | 13.12.94 | **Walsall** | A | L | 0-4 | |
| 1995-96 | (D3) | 1 | 11.11.95 | **Carlisle Utd** (D2) | A | W | 2-1 | Cartwright, J.Wilcox |
| | | 2 | 02.12.95 | **Bradford City** (D2) | A | L | 1-2 | Wilkinson |
| 1996-97 | (D2) | 1 | 16.11.96 | **Altrincham** (Conf) | H | W | 4-1 | Reeves 3, Ashcroft |
| | | 2 | 07.12.96 | **York City** (D2) | H | L | 2-3 | Ashcroft 2 (1p) |

| | | | | | | | | |
|---|---|---|---|---|---|---|---|---|
| 1997-98 (D2) | 1 | 15.11.97 | **Doncaster Rovers** (D3) | H | W | 3-2 | Gregan 2, Eyres |
| | 2 | 06.12.97 | **Notts County** (D3) | H | D | 2-2 | Parkinson, Ashcroft |
| | 2r | 16.12.97 | **Notts County** | A | W | 2-1aet | Moyes, Eyres |
| | 3 | 03.01.98 | **Stockport County** (D1) | H | L | 1-2 | Ashcroft (p) |
| 1998-99 (D2) | 1 | 14.11.98 | **Ford Utd** (IL) | H | W | 3-0 | Rankine, Harris, Derby |
| | 2 | 05.12.98 | **Walsall** (D2) | H | W | 2-0 | Nogan, McKenna |
| | 3 | 04.01.99 | **Arsenal** (PL) | H | L | 2-4 | Nogan 2 |
| 1999-00 (D2) | 1 | 31.10.99 | **Bristol Rovers** (D2) | A | W | 1-0 | McKenna |
| | 2 | 20.11.99 | **Enfield** (IL) | H | D | 0-0 | |
| | 2r | 30.11.99 | **Enfield** | A | W | 3-0 | Eyres, Alexander (p), Gunnlaughsson |
| | | | *played at Clarence Park, St Albans* | | | | |
| | 3 | 11.12.99 | **Oldham Athletic** (D2) | H | W | 2-1 | Macken, Alexander (p) |
| | 4 | 08.01.00 | **Plymouth Argyle** (D3) | A | W | 3-0 | O'Sullivan og, Alexander (p), Beswetherick og |
| | 5 | 29.01.00 | **Everton** (PL) | A | L | 0-2 | |
| 2000-01 (D1) | 3 | 06.01.01 | **Stockport County** (D1) | H | L | 0-1 | |
| 2001-02 (D1) | 3 | 15.01.02 | **Brighton** (D2) | A | W | 2-0 | Skora, Macken |
| | 4 | 26.01.02 | **Sheffield Utd** (D1) | H | W | 2-1 | Cresswell, Alexander (p) |
| | 5 | 17.02.02 | **Chelsea** (PL) | A | L | 1-3 | Cresswell |
| 2002-03 (D1) | 3 | 04.01.03 | **Rochdale** (D3) | H | L | 1-2 | Anderson |

## PRESTON ZINGARI

| | | | | | | | |
|---|---|---|---|---|---|---|---|
| 1884-85 | 1 | | Bolton Wanderers | | | - | |
| | | | *Match not played, both teams withdrew* | | | | |

## QUEEN'S PARK, GLASGOW

*Formed 1867. One of the 15 original entrants in the FA Cup in the 1871-72 season, although the only match they played was a 0-0 draw in the semi-final against Wanderers before scratching. One of the seven Scottish clubs that took part in the FA Cup in the 1870s and 1880s, they entered from 1871-72 – 1886-87. FA Cup runners-up: 1884, 1885. Scottish FA Cup winners: 10 times. In 1884 they were runners-up in the English FA Cup final and winners of the Scottish Cup final.*

| | | | | | | | |
|---|---|---|---|---|---|---|---|
| 1871-72 | 1 | | Donington GS, Spalding | | | - | |
| | | | *teams could not arrange a date so both advanced to second round* | | | | |
| | 2 | | Donington GS, Spalding | | | - | |
| | | | *Donington School scratched. Queen's Park walkover* | | | | |
| | 3 | | bye | | | | |
| | SF | 05.03.72 | **Wanderers** | | D | 0-0 | |
| | | | *played at Kennington Oval Queen's Park scratched before the replay. Wanderers gained walkover into the Cup Final .* | | | | |
| 1872-73 | | | Exempt until semi-final because of travel difficulties | | | | |
| | SF | | Oxford University | | | - | |
| | | | *Queen's Park scratched. Oxford University walkover* | | | | |
| 1876-77 | 1 | | bye | | | | |
| | 3 | | Oxford University | | | - | |
| | | | *Queen's Park scratched. Oxford University walkover* | | | | |
| 1877-78 | 1 | | bye | | | | |
| | 2 | | Druids | | | - | |
| | | | *Queen's Park scratched. Druids walkover* | | | | |
| 1879-80 | 1 | | Sheffield FC | | | - | |
| | | | *Queen's Park scratched. Sheffield FC walkover* | | | | |
| 1880-81 | 1 | | Sheffield Wed | | | - | |
| | | | *Queen's Park scratched. Sheffield Wed walkover* | | | | |
| 1881-82 | 1 | | Accrington FC | | | - | |
| | | | *Queen's Park scratched. Accrington FC walkover* | | | | |
| 1882-83 | 1 | | Grimsby Town | | | - | |
| | | | *Queen's Park scratched. Grimsby Town walkover* | | | | |
| 1883-84 | 1 | 06.10.83 | **Crewe Alexandra** | A | W | 10-0 | Fraser 3, Christie 2, Anderson 2, Smither 2, Harrower |
| | 2 | 01.12.83 | **Manchester FC** | H | W | 15-0 | Anderson 4, Harrower 3, Smith 3, Fraser 2, Allan, Christie, AN Other |
| | 3 | 29.12.83 | **Oswestry Town** | A | W | 7-1 | Anderson 2, Allan, Christie, Smith, others 2 |
| | 4 | 19.01.84 | **Aston Villa** | H | W | 6-1 | Anderson 3, Campbell, Harrower, Smith |

| | | | | | | | |
|---|---|---|---|---|---|---|---|
| | 5 | 09.02.84 | **Old Westminsters** | A | W | 1-0 | Allan |
| | SF | 01.03.84 | **Blackburn Olympic** | | W | 4-1 | Smith 3, Watt |
| | | | *played at Trent Bridge, Nottingham* | | | | |
| | F | 29.03.84 | **Blackburn Rovers** | | L | 1-2 | Christie |
| | | | *played at Kennington Oval* | | | | |
| 1884-85 | 1 | | Stoke | | | - | |
| | | | *Stoke scratched. Queen's Park walkover* | | | | |
| | 2 | 06.12.84 | **Crewe Alexandra** | H | W | 2-1 | Allan, Christie |
| | | | *FA ordered result to stand after match was abandoned in the 48th minute following a torrential storm* | | | | |
| | 3 | 03.01.85 | **Leek** | A | W | 3-2 | |
| | 4 | 17.01.85 | **Old Wykehamists** | H | W | 7-0 | Anderson 2, Watt 2, Christie 2, Allan |
| | 5 | | bye | | | | |
| | 6 | 21.02.85 | **Notts County** | A | D | 2-2 | Christie 2 |
| | 6r | 28.02.85 | **Notts County** | | W | 2-1 | Arnott, Sellar |
| | | | *played at Derby Cricket Ground* | | | | |
| | SF | 14.03.85 | **Nottingham Forest** | | D | 1-1 | |
| | | | *played at Derby Cricket Ground* | | | | |
| | SFr | 28.03.85 | **Nottingham Forest** | | W | 3-0 | Sellar 2, Widdowson og |
| | | | *played at Merchiston Castle School, Edinburgh* | | | | |
| | F | 04.04.85 | **Blackburn Rovers** | | L | 0-2 | |
| | | | *played at Kennington Oval* | | | | |
| 1885-86 | 1 | 31.10.85 | **Partick Thistle** | H | W | 5-1 | |
| | 2 | | South Shore | | | - | |
| | | | *Queen's Park scratched. South Shore walkover* | | | | |
| 1886-87 | 1 | 30.10.86 | **Preston North End** | H | L | 0-3 | |

# QUEENS PARK RANGERS

*Formed 1885 as St Jude's Institute. Queens Park Rangers 1898. FA Cup runners-up: 1982. Record FA Cup win: 8-1 v Bristol Rovers, 1st round, 27.11.1937. Record FA Cup defeat: 0-6 v Arsenal, 4th round, 27.01.2001.*

**As St Jude's Institute**

| | | | | | | | |
|---|---|---|---|---|---|---|---|
| 1895-96 | | | 1q Old St Stephens (H) 1-1; 1qr Old St Stephens (A) 0-1 | | | | |
| 1896-97 (Lon) | | | 1q Marlow (H) 1-3 | | | | |
| 1897-98 | | | P Windsor & Eton (H) 3-0; 1q Wolverton LNWR (A) 2-1; 2q Chesham Generals (H) 4-0; 3q Clapton (A) 0-1 | | | | |

**As Queens Park Rangers**

| | | | | | | | |
|---|---|---|---|---|---|---|---|
| 1898-99 | | | P Richmond Association (A) 0-3 | | | | |
| 1899-00 (SL) | | | P London Welsh (A) 4-2; 1q Fulham (H) 3-0; 2q West Hampstead (H) 5-0; 3q Wandsworth (H) 7-1; 4q Civil Service (H) 3-0; 5q Luton Town (A) 1-1; 5qr Luton Town (H) 4-1 | | | | |
| | 1 | 27.01.00 | **Wolverhampton W** (D1) | H | D | 1-1 | Haywood |
| | 1r | 31.01.00 | **Wolverhampton W** | A | W | 1-0aet | Bedingfield |
| | 2 | 17.02.00 | **Millwall Athletic** (SL) | H | L | 0-2 | |
| 1900-01 (SL) | | | 3q Fulham (H) 7-0; 4q Watford (A) 1-1; 4qr Watford (H) 4-1; 5q Luton Town (A) 0-3 | | | | |
| 1901-02 (SL) | | | 3q Crouch End Vampires (H) 2-0; 4q West Norwood (H) 4-0; 5q Luton Town (A) 0-2 | | | | |
| 1902-03 (SL) | | | 3q Luton Town (H) 0-3 | | | | |
| 1903-04 (SL) | | | 3q Fulham (H) 1-1; 3qr Fulham (A) 1-3 | | | | |
| 1904-05 (SL) | | | 6q Brentford (H) 1-2 | | | | |
| 1905-06 (SL) | 1 | 13.01.06 | **Fulham** (SL) | A | L | 0-1 | |
| 1906-07 (SL) | 1 | 12.01.07 | **Bristol Rovers** (SL) | A | D | 0-0 | |
| | 1r | 14.01.07 | **Bristol Rovers** | H | L | 0-1 | |
| 1907-08 (SL) | 1 | 11.01.08 | **Reading** (SL) | H | W | 1-0 | Barnes |
| | 2 | 01.02.08 | **Swindon Town** (SL) | A | L | 1-2 | Walker |
| 1908-09 (SL) | 1 | 16.01.09 | **West Ham Utd** (SL) | H | D | 0-0 | |
| | 1r | 20.01.09 | **West Ham Utd** | A | L | 0-1 | |
| 1909-10 (SL) | 1 | 15.01.10 | **Norwich City** (SL) | A | D | 0-0 | |
| | 1r | 19.01.10 | **Norwich City** | H | W | 3-0 | Steer, McNaught, Whyman |
| | 2 | 05.02.10 | **Southend Utd** (SL) | A | D | 0-0 | |
| | 2r | 09.02.10 | **Southend Utd** | H | W | 3-2 | Steer 2, Travers |
| | 3 | 19.02.10 | **West Ham Utd** (SL) | H | D | 1-1 | Steer |
| | 3r | 24.02.10 | **West Ham Utd** | A | W | 1-0aet | Steer |
| | 4 | 05.03.10 | **Barnsley** (D2) | A | L | 0-1 | |
| 1910-11 (SL) | 1 | 14.01.11 | **Bradford Park A** (D2) | A | L | 3-5 | Steer, McKie 2 |

| | | | | | | | | |
|---|---|---|---|---|---|---|---|---|
| 1911-12 | (SL) | 1 | 13.01.12 | **Bradford City** (D1) | H | D | 0-0 | |
| | | 1r | 18.01.12 | **Bradford City** | A | L | 0-4 | |
| 1912-13 | (SL) | 1 | 11.01.13 | **Halifax Town** (ML) | H | W | 4-2 | Owens, Birch, Whyman, Revill |
| | | 2 | 01.02.13 | **Middlesbrough** (D1) | A | L | 2-3 | Birch 2 |
| 1913-14 | (SL) | 1 | 10.01.14 | **Bristol City** (D2) | H | D | 2-2 | Birch, Miller |
| | | 1r | 14.01.14 | **Bristol City** | A | W | 2-0aet | Birch, Gregory |
| | | 2 | 31.01.14 | **Swansea Town** (SL) | A | W | 2-1 | Birch 2 |
| | | 3 | 21.02.14 | **Birmingham** (D2) | A | W | 2-1 | Miller, Gregory |
| | | 4 | 07.03.14 | **Liverpool** (D1) | A | L | 1-2 | Mitchell (p) |
| 1914-15 | (SL) | 1 | 09.01.15 | **Glossop North End** (D2) | H | W | 2-1 | Miller, Birch |
| | | 2 | 30.01.15 | **Leeds City** (D2) | H | W | 1-0 | Simons |
| | | 3 | 20.02.15 | **Everton** (D1) | H | L | 1-2 | Birch |
| | | | | *played at Stamford Bridge* | | | | |
| 1919-20 | (SL) | 1 | 10.01.20 | **Aston Villa** (D1) | A | L | 1-2 | Birch |
| 1920-21 | (D3) | 1 | 08.01.21 | **Arsenal** (D1) | H | W | 2-0 | Chandler, O'Brien |
| | | 2 | 29.01.21 | **Burnley** (D1) | A | L | 2-4 | Smith, Birch |
| 1921-22 | (3S) | 1 | 07.01.22 | **Arsenal** (D1) | A | D | 0-0 | |
| | | 1r | 11.01.22 | **Arsenal** | H | L | 1-2 | Smith |
| 1922-23 | (3S) | 1 | 13.01.23 | **Crystal Palace** (D2) | H | W | 1-0 | Gregory |
| | | 2 | 03.02.23 | **Wigan Borough** (3N) | A | W | 4-2 | Parker 2, Chandler, Birch |
| | | 3 | 24.02.23 | **South Shields** (D2) | H | W | 3-0 | Gregory, Parker 2 |
| | | 4 | 10.03.23 | **Sheffield Utd** (D1) | H | L | 0-1 | |
| 1923-24 | (3S) | 1 | 12.01.24 | **Notts County** (D1) | H | L | 1-2 | Davis |
| 1924-25 | (3S) | | | 5q Clapton (H) 4-4; 5qr Clapton (A) 2-0; 6q Charlton Athletic (H) 1-1; 6qr Charlton Athletic (A) 2-1 | | | | |
| | | 1 | 10.01.25 | **Stockport County** (D2) | H | L | 1-3 | Myers |
| 1925-26 | (3S) | 1 | 28.11.25 | **Northfleet Utd** (KL) | A | D | 2-2 | Birch 2 |
| | | 1r | 03.12.25 | **Northfleet Utd** | H | W | 2-0 | Birch 2 |
| | | 2 | 12.12.25 | **Charlton Athletic** (3S) | H | D | 1-1 | Hirst |
| | | 2r | 17.12.25 | **Charlton Athletic** | A | L | 0-1 | |
| 1926-27 | (3S) | | | *QPR failed to enter by the FA deadline and did not compete in the 1926-27 season* | | | | |
| 1927-28 | (3S) | 1 | 26.11.27 | **Aldershot Town** (SL) | A | - | 1-0ab | Neil |
| | | | | *abandoned because of fog* | | | | |
| | | 1 | 30.11.27 | **Aldershot Town** | A | L | 1-2 | Johnson |
| 1928-29 | (3S) | 1 | 24.11.28 | **Guildford City** (SL) | A | L | 2-4 | Goddard, Burns |
| 1929-30 | (3S) | 1 | 30.11.29 | **Luton Town** (3S) | A | W | 3-2 | Goddard, Cowan, Pierce (p) |
| | | 2 | 14.12.29 | **Lincoln City** (3N) | H | W | 2-1 | Burns 2 |
| | | 3 | 11.01.30 | **Charlton Athletic** (D2) | A | D | 1-1 | Goddard |
| | | 3r | 16.01.30 | **Charlton Athletic** | H | L | 0-3 | |
| 1930-31 | (3S) | 1 | 29.11.30 | **Thames** (3S) | H | W | 5-0 | Burns 2, Goddard 2 (1p), Rounce |
| | | 2 | 13.12.30 | **Crewe Alexandra** (3N) | H | W | 4-2 | Goddard 2, Howe, Rounce |
| | | 3 | 10.01.31 | **Bristol Rovers** (3S) | A | L | 1-3 | Coward |
| 1931-32 | (3S) | 1 | 28.11.31 | **Barnet** (AL) | A | W | 7-3 | Goddard 2, Coward 2, Cribb 3 |
| | | 2 | 12.12.31 | **Scunthorpe Utd** (ML) | A | W | 4-1 | Rounce 3, Cribb |
| | | 3 | 09.01.32 | **Leeds Utd** (D2) | H | W | 3-1 | Cribb 2, Rounce |
| | | 4 | 23.01.32 | **Huddersfield Town** (D1) | A | L | 0-5 | |
| 1932-33 | (3S) | 1 | 26.11.32 | **Merthyr Town** (SL) | A | D | 1-1 | Rounce |
| | | 1r | 01.12.32 | **Merthyr Town** | H | W | 5-1 | Goddard 3, Marcroft, Rounce |
| | | 2 | 10.12.32 | **Torquay Utd** (3S) | A | D | 1-1 | Rounce |
| | | 2r | 15.12.32 | **Torquay Utd** | H | W | 3-1 | Rounce 3 |
| | | 3 | 14.01.33 | **Darlington** (3N) | A | L | 0-2 | |
| 1933-34 | (3S) | 1 | 25.11.33 | **Kettering Town** (UCL) | H | W | 6-0 | Brown, Emmerson 2, Blackman 2, Allen |
| | | 2 | 09.12.33 | **New Brighton** (3N) | H | D | 1-1 | Blackman |
| | | 2r | 13.12.33 | **New Brighton** | A | W | 4-0 | Blackman 4 |
| | | 3 | 13.01.34 | **Nottingham Forest** (D2) | A | L | 0-4 | |
| 1934-35 | (3S) | 1 | 24.11.34 | **Walthamstow Ave** (AL) | H | W | 2-0 | Emmerson, Devine |
| | | 2 | 08.12.34 | **Brighton** (3S) | H | L | 1-2 | Crawford |
| 1935-36 | (3S) | 1 | 30.11.35 | **Margate** (SL) | A | L | 1-3 | Cheetham |
| 1936-37 | (3S) | 1 | 28.11.36 | **Brighton** (3S) | H | W | 5-1 | Cheetham, Fitzgerald 3 (1p) McMahon |

| | | | | | | | | |
|---|---|---|---|---|---|---|---|---|
| | | 2 | 12.12.36 | **South Liverpool** (LC) | A | W | 1-0 | Fitzgerald |
| | | 3 | 16.01.37 | **Bury** (D2) | A | L | 0-1 | |
| 1937-38 | (3S) | 1 | 27.11.37 | **Bristol Rovers** (3S) | A | W | 8-1 | Fitzgerald 3, Cheetham 3, Bott 2 |
| | | 2 | 11.12.37 | **Swindon Town** (3S) | A | L | 1-2 | Cape |
| 1938-39 | (3S) | 1 | 26.11.38 | **Crystal Palace** (3S) | A | D | 1-1 | Cheetham |
| | | 1r | 28.11.38 | **Crystal Palace** | H | W | 3-0 | Cheetham 2, Bott (p) |
| | | 2 | 10.12.38 | **Hartlepools Utd** (3N) | A | W | 2-0 | McCarthy, Cheetham |
| | | 3 | 07.01.39 | **West Ham Utd** (D2) | H | L | 1-2 | Cheetham |
| 1945-46 | (3S) | 1 1L | 17.11.45 | **Barnet** (AL) | A | W | 6-2 | Heathcote, Mallett 2, Neary 3 |
| | | 1 2L | 24.11.45 | **Barnet** | H | W | 2-1 | Swinfen, Neary |
| | | 2 1L | 08.12.45 | **Ipswich Town** (3S) | H | W | 4-0 | Neary, Stock, Addinall 2 |
| | | 2 2L | 15.12.45 | **Ipswich Town** | A | W | 2-0 | Daniels, Addinall |
| | | 3 1L | 05.01.46 | **Crystal Palace** (3S) | H | D | 0-0 | |
| | | 3 2L | 09.01.46 | **Crystal Palace** | A | - | 0-0aet | |
| | | | | *abandoned after 117 minutes* | | | | |
| | | 3 2L | 16.01.46 | **Crystal Palace** | | W | 1-0 | Addinall |
| | | | | *played at Craven Cottage* | | | | |
| | | 4 1L | 26.01.46 | **Southampton** (D2) | A | W | 1-0 | Addinall |
| | | 4 2L | 30.01.46 | **Southampton** | H | W | 4-3 | Addinall 3, Stock |
| | | 5 1L | 09.02.46 | **Brentford** (D1) | H | L | 1-3 | Pattison |
| | | 5 2L | 14.02.46 | **Brentford** | A | D | 0-0 | |
| 1946-47 | (3S) | 1 | 30.11.46 | **Poole Town** (WL) | H | D | 2-2 | Pattison, Hatton |
| | | 1r | 04.12.46 | **Poole Town** | A | W | 6-0 | Mallett 2, Hatton, Harris, Pattison 2 |
| | | 2 | 14.12.46 | **Norwich City** (3S) | A | D | 4-4 | Mills 2, Pattison, McEwan |
| | | 2r | 18.12.46 | **Norwich City** | H | W | 2-0 | Hatton, Mills |
| | | 3 | 11.01.47 | **Middlesbrough** (D1) | H | D | 1-1 | Pattison |
| | | 3r | 15.01.47 | **Middlesbrough** | A | L | 1-3 | Boxshall |
| 1947-48 | (3S) | 3 | 10.01.48 | **Gillingham** (SL) | A | D | 1-1aet | Boxshall |
| | | 3r | 17.01.48 | **Gillingham** | H | W | 3-1 | Hartburn, Hatton, McEwan |
| | | 4 | 24.01.48 | **Stoke City** (D1) | H | W | 3-0 | Hatton 2, Ramscar |
| | | 5 | 07.02.48 | **Luton Town** (D2) | H | W | 3-1 | Hatton, Boxshall, McEwan |
| | | 6 | 28.02.48 | **Derby County** (D1) | H | D | 1-1aet | Hartburn |
| | | 6r | 06.03.48 | **Derby County** | A | L | 0-5 | |
| 1948-49 | (D2) | 3 | 08.01.49 | **Huddersfield Town** (D1) | H | D | 0-0aet | |
| | | 3r | 15.01.49 | **Huddersfield Town** | A | L | 0-5 | |
| 1949-50 | (D2) | 3 | 07.01.50 | **Everton** (D1) | H | L | 0-2 | |
| 1950-51 | (D2) | 3 | 06.01.51 | **Millwall** (3S) | H | L | 3-4 | Parkinson 2, Addinall |
| 1951-52 | (D2) | 3 | 12.01.52 | **Brentford** (D2) | A | L | 1-3 | Shepherd |
| 1952-53 | (3S) | 1 | 22.11.52 | **Shrewsbury Town** (3S) | H | D | 2-2 | Cameron 2 |
| | | 1r | 27.11.52 | **Shrewsbury Town** | A | D | 2-2aet | Addinall, Smith |
| | | 1 2r | 01.12.52 | **Shrewsbury Town** | | L | 1-4 | Smith |
| | | | | *played at Villa Park* | | | | |
| 1953-54 | (3S) | 1 | 21.11.53 | **Shrewsbury Town** (3S) | H | W | 2-0 | Hurrell 2 |
| | | 2 | 12.12.53 | **Nuneaton B** (BDL) | H | D | 1-1 | Tomkys |
| | | 2r | 17.12.53 | **Nuneaton B** | A | W | 2-1 | Petchey, Shepherd |
| | | 3 | 09.01.54 | **Port Vale** (D3) | H | L | 0-1 | |
| 1954-55 | (3S) | 1 | 20.11.54 | **Walthamstow Ave** (IL) | H | D | 2-2 | Fidler, Smith |
| | | 1r | 25.11.54 | **Walthamstow Ave** | A | D | 2-2aet | Fidler, Tomkeys |
| | | 1 2r | 29.11.54 | **Walthamstow Ave** | | L | 0-4 | |
| | | | | *played at Highbury* | | | | |
| 1955-56 | (3S) | 1 | 19.11.55 | **Southend Utd** (3S) | A | L | 0-2 | |
| 1956-57 | (3S) | 1 | 17.11.56 | **Dorchester Town** (WL) | H | W | 4-0 | Hellawell, Balogun, Locke, Cameron |
| | | 2 | 08.12.56 | **Tooting & M** (IL) | A | W | 2-0 | Balogun, Longbottom |
| | | 3 | 05.01.57 | **Sunderland** (D1) | A | L | 0-4 | |
| 1957-58 | (3S) | 1 | 16.11.57 | **Clapton** (IL) | A | D | 1-1 | Dawson |
| | | 1r | 18.11.57 | **Clapton** | H | W | 3-1 | Locke, Walsh og, Longbottom |
| | | 2 | 07.12.57 | **Hereford Utd** (SL) | A | L | 1-6 | E.Smith |
| 1958-59 | (D3) | 1 | 15.11.58 | **Walsall** (D4) | A | W | 1-0 | Dawson |
| | | 2 | 06.12.58 | **Southampton** (D2) | H | L | 0-1 | |
| 1959-60 | (D3) | 1 | 14.11.59 | **Colchester Utd** (D3) | A | W | 3-2 | Petchey, Bedford, Angell |
| | | 2 | 05.12.59 | **Port Vale** (D3) | H | D | 3-3 | Longbottom 2, Bedford |

| | | | | | | | | |
|---|---|---|---|---|---|---|---|---|
| | | 2r | 07.12.59 | **Port Vale** | A | L | 1-2 | Andrews |
| 1960-61 | (D3) | 1 | 05.11.60 | **Walthamstow Ave** (IL) | H | W | 3-2 | Bedford 3 |
| | | 2 | 26.11.60 | **Coventry City** (D3) | H | L | 1-2 | Longbottom |
| 1961-62 | (D3) | 1 | 04.11.61 | **Barry Town** (SL) | A | D | 1-1 | McLellan og |
| | | 1r | 06.11.61 | **Barry Town** | H | W | 7-0 | Evans 2, Collins 2, Bedford 3 |
| | | 2 | 25.11.61 | **Ashford Town** (SL) | A | W | 3-0 | McClelland, Evans, Collins |
| | | 3 | 06.01.62 | **Burnley** (D1) | A | L | 1-6 | Evans |
| 1962-63 | (D3) | 1 | 03.11.62 | **Newport County** (D4) | H | W | 3-2 | Barber 2, Large |
| | | 2 | 24.11.62 | **Hinckley Athletic** (SL) | H | W | 7-2 | Bedford 3, McClelland, Collins, Lazarus, Large |
| | | 3 | 26.01.63 | **Swansea Town** (D2) | A | L | 0-2 | |
| 1963-64 | (D3) | 1 | 16.11.63 | **Gillingham** (D4) | H | W | 4-1 | Leary, Malcolm, Graham, Bedford |
| | | 2 | 07.12.63 | **Colchester Utd** (D3) | A | W | 1-0 | Leary |
| | | 3 | 04.01.64 | **Carlisle Utd** (D4) | A | L | 0-2 | |
| 1964-65 | (D3) | 1 | 14.11.64 | **Bath City** (SL) | H | W | 2-0 | Collins, Leary |
| | | 2 | 05.12.64 | **Peterborough Utd** (D3) | H | D | 3-3 | R Brady, Keen (p), Bedford |
| | | 2r | 09.12.64 | **Peterborough Utd** | A | L | 1-2aet | McAdams |
| 1965-66 | (D3) | 1 | 13.11.65 | **Colchester Utd** (D4) | A | D | 3-3 | Collins, L Allen, Sanderson |
| | | 1r | 17.11.65 | **Colchester Utd** | H | W | 4-0 | L Allen 2, R Morgan, Sanderson |
| | | 2 | 04.12.65 | **Guildford City** (SL) | H | W | 3-0 | Hunt og, Sibley, Lazarus |
| | | 3 | 22.01.66 | **Shrewsbury Town** (D3) | H | D | 0-0 | |
| | | 3r | 26.01.66 | **Shrewsbury Town** | H | L | 0-1 | |
| 1966-67 | (D3) | 1 | 26.11.66 | **Poole Town** (SL) | H | W | 3-2 | Marsh 3 |
| | | 2 | 07.01.67 | **Bournemouth** (D3) | H | W | 2-0 | Langley (p), Lazarus |
| | | 3 | 28.01.67 | **Sheffield Wed** (D1) | A | L | 0-3 | |
| 1967-68 | (D2) | 3 | 27.01.68 | **Preston North End** (D2) | H | L | 1-3 | Keen |
| 1968-69 | (D1) | 3 | 04.01.69 | **Aston Villa** (D2) | A | L | 1-2 | I Morgan |
| 1969-70 | (D2) | 3 | 03.01.70 | **S Shields (1936)** (NPL) | H | W | 4-1 | Marsh 2, Clarke, Ferguson |
| | | 4 | 24.01.70 | **Charlton Athletic** (D2) | A | W | 3-2 | Marsh 2, Clarke |
| | | 5 | 07.02.70 | **Derby County** (D1) | H | W | 1-0 | Mackay og |
| | | 6 | 21.02.70 | **Chelsea** (D1) | H | L | 2-4 | Venables (p), Bridges |
| 1970-71 | (D2) | 3 | 02.01.71 | **Swindon Town** (D2) | H | L | 1-2 | Marsh (p) |
| 1971-72 | (D2) | 3 | 15.01.72 | **Fulham** (D2) | H | D | 1-1 | Mancini |
| | | 3r | 18.01.72 | **Fulham** | A | L | 1-2 | Clement |
| 1972-73 | (D2) | 3 | 13.01.73 | **Barnet** (SL) | H | D | 0-0 | |
| | | 3r | 16.01.73 | **Barnet** | A | W | 3-0 | Leach, Bowles, Mancini |
| | | 4 | 03.02.73 | **Oxford Utd** (D2) | A | W | 2-0 | Clement, Givens |
| | | 5 | 24.02.73 | **Derby County** (D1) | A | L | 2-4 | Leach, Givens |
| 1973-74 | (D1) | 3 | 05.01.74 | **Chelsea** (D1) | A | D | 0-0 | |
| | | 3r | 15.01.74 | **Chelsea** | H | W | 1-0 | Bowles |
| | | 4 | 26.01.74 | **Birmingham City** (D1) | H | W | 2-0 | Leach, Givens |
| | | 5 | 16.02.74 | **Coventry City** (D1) | A | D | 0-0 | |
| | | 5r | 19.02.74 | **Coventry City** | H | W | 3-2 | Givens, Thomas, Bowles |
| | | 6 | 09.03.74 | **Leicester City** (D1) | H | L | 0-2 | |
| 1974-75 | (D1) | 3 | 04.01.75 | **Southend Utd** (D3) | A | D | 2-2 | Gillard, Francis |
| | | 3r | 07.01.75 | **Southend Utd** | H | W | 2-0 | Givens 2 |
| | | 4 | 24.01.75 | **Notts County** (D2) | H | W | 3-0 | Thomas, Bowles (p), Givens |
| | | 5 | 15.02.75 | **West Ham Utd** (D1) | A | L | 1-2 | Clement |
| 1975-76 | (D1) | 3 | 03.01.76 | **Newcastle Utd** (D1) | H | D | 0-0 | |
| | | 3r | 07.01.76 | **Newcastle Utd** | A | L | 1-2 | Masson |
| 1976-77 | (D1) | 3 | 08.01.77 | **Shrewsbury Town** (D3) | H | W | 2-1 | Bowles, Givens |
| | | 4 | 29.01.77 | **Manchester Utd** (D1) | A | L | 0-1 | |
| 1977-78 | (D1) | 3 | 07.01.78 | **Wealdstone** (SL) | H | W | 4-0 | Givens, James, Bowles (p), Howe |
| | | 4 | 28.01.78 | **West Ham Utd** (D1) | A | D | 1-1 | Howe |
| | | 4r | 31.01.78 | **West Ham Utd** | H | W | 6-1 | Busby 2, Givens, Hollins, Bowles (p), James |
| | | 5 | 18.02.78 | **Nottingham Forest** (D1) | H | D | 1-1 | Busby |
| | | 5r | 27.02.78 | **Nottingham Forest** | A | D | 1-1aet | Shanks |
| | | 5 2r | 02.03.78 | **Nottingham Forest** | A | L | 1-3 | Bowles |
| 1978-79 | (D1) | 3 | 06.01.79 | **Fulham** (D2) | A | L | 0-2 | |
| 1979-80 | (D2) | 3 | 05.01.80 | **Watford** (D2) | H | L | 1-2 | Hazell |

| | | | | | | | | |
|---|---|---|---|---|---|---|---|---|
| 1980-81 | (D2) | 3 | 03.01.81 | **Tottenham Hotspur** (D1) | H | D | 0-0 | |
| | | 3r | 07.01.81 | **Tottenham Hotspur** | A | L | 1-3 | Stainrod |
| 1981-82 | (D2) | 3 | 02.01.82 | **Middlesbrough** (D1) | H | D | 1-1 | Stainrod |
| | | 3r | 18.01.82 | **Middlesbrough** | A | W | 3-2 | Stainrod 2, Neill |
| | | 4 | 23.01.82 | **Blackpool** (D4) | A | D | 0-0 | |
| | | 4r | 26.01.82 | **Blackpool** | H | W | 5-1 | C Allen 4, Stainrod (p) |
| | | 5 | 13.02.82 | **Grimsby Town** (D2) | H | W | 3-1 | Stainrod, C Allen, Howe |
| | | 6 | 06.03.82 | **Crystal Palace** (D2) | H | W | 1-0 | C Allen |
| | | SF | 03.04.82 | **WBA** (D1) | | W | 1-0 | C Allen |
| | | | | *played at Highbury* | | | | |
| | | F | 22.05.82 | **Tottenham Hotspur** (D1) | | D | 1-1 | Fenwick |
| | | | | *played at Wembley Stadium* | | | | |
| | | Fr | 27.05.82 | **Tottenham Hotspur** | | L | 0-1 | |
| | | | | *played at Wembley Stadium* | | | | |
| 1982-83 | (D2) | 3 | 08.01.83 | **WBA** (D1) | A | L | 2-3 | Fenwick (p), Micklewhite |
| 1983-84 | (D1) | 3 | 07.01.84 | **Huddersfield Town** (D2) | A | L | 1-2 | Gregory |
| 1984-85 | (D1) | 3 | 05.01.85 | **Doncaster Rovers** (D3) | A | L | 0-1 | |
| 1985-86 | (D1) | 3 | 13.01.86 | **Carlisle Utd** (D2) | A | L | 0-1 | |
| 1986-87 | (D1) | 3 | 10.01.87 | **Leicester City** (D1) | H | W | 5-2 | Fenwick 2 (1p), Lee, James, Byrne |
| | | 4 | 31.01.87 | **Luton Town** (D1) | A | D | 1-1 | Fenwick (p) |
| | | 4r | 04.02.87 | **Luton Town** | H | W | 2-1 | Fenwick, Byrne |
| | | 5 | 21.02.87 | **Leeds Utd** (D2) | A | L | 1-2 | Rennie og |
| 1987-88 | (D1) | 3 | 09.01.88 | **Yeovil Town** (IL) | A | W | 3-0 | Falco 2, Brock |
| | | 4 | 30.01.88 | **West Ham Utd** (D1) | H | W | 3-1 | Pizanti, Bannister, M Allen |
| | | 5 | 20.02.88 | **Luton Town** (D1) | H | D | 1-1 | Neill |
| | | 5r | 24.02.88 | **Luton Town** | A | L | 0-1 | |
| 1988-89 | (D1) | 3 | 07.01.89 | **Manchester Utd** (D1) | A | D | 0-0 | |
| | | 3r | 11.01.89 | **Manchester Utd** | H | D | 2-2aet | Stein, McDonald |
| | | 3 2r | 23.01.89 | **Manchester Utd** | A | L | 0-3 | |
| 1989-90 | (D1) | 3 | 06.01.90 | **Cardiff City** (D3) | A | D | 0-0 | |
| | | 3r | 10.01.90 | **Cardiff City** | H | W | 2-0 | Wilkins, Wegerle |
| | | 4 | 27.01.90 | **Arsenal** (D1) | A | D | 0-0 | |
| | | 4r | 31.01.90 | **Arsenal** | H | W | 2-0 | Sansom, Sinton |
| | | 5 | 18.02.90 | **Blackpool** (D3) | A | D | 2-2 | Clarke 2 |
| | | 5r | 21.02.90 | **Blackpool** | H | D | 0-0aet | |
| | | 5 2r | 26.02.90 | **Blackpool** | H | W | 3-0 | Sinton, Sansom, Barker |
| | | 6 | 11.03.90 | **Liverpool** (D1) | H | D | 2-2 | Wilkins, Barker |
| | | 6r | 14.03.90 | **Liverpool** | A | L | 0-1 | |
| 1990-91 | (D1) | 3 | 05.01.91 | **Manchester Utd** (D1) | A | L | 1-2 | Maddix |
| 1991-92 | (D1) | 3 | 04.01.92 | **Southampton** (D1) | A | L | 0-2 | |
| 1992-93 | (PL) | 3 | 02.01.93 | **Swindon Town** (D1) | H | W | 3-0 | Ferdinand 2, Penrice |
| | | 4 | 23.01.93 | **Manchester City** (PL) | H | L | 1-2 | Holloway |
| 1993-94 | (PL) | 3 | 08.01.94 | **Stockport County** (D2) | A | L | 1-2 | Barker |
| 1994-95 | (PL) | 3 | 07.01.95 | **Aylesbury Utd** (IL) | A | W | 4-0 | Maddix, Ferdinand, Gallen, Meaker |
| | | 4 | 28.01.95 | **West Ham Utd** (PL) | H | W | 1-0 | Impey |
| | | 5 | 18.02.95 | **Millwall** (D1) | A | W | 1-0 | Wilson (p) |
| | | 6 | 12.03.95 | **Manchester Utd** (PL) | A | L | 0-2 | |
| 1995-96 | (PL) | 3 | 06.01.96 | **Tranmere Rovers** (D1) | A | W | 2-0 | Quashie, Sinclair |
| | | 4 | 29.01.96 | **Chelsea** (PL) | H | L | 1-2 | Quashie |
| 1996-97 | (D1) | 3 | 04.01.97 | **Huddersfield Town** (D1) | H | D | 1-1 | Hateley |
| | | 3r | 14.01.97 | **Huddersfield Town** | A | W | 2-1 | Peacock, McDonald |
| | | 4 | 25.01.97 | **Barnsley** (D1) | H | W | 3-2 | Peacock, Spencer, Sinclair |
| | | 5 | 15.02.97 | **Wimbledon** (PL) | A | L | 1-2 | Hateley |
| 1997-98 | (D1) | 1 | 03.01.98 | **Middlesbrough** (D1) | H | D | 2-2 | Spencer, Galllen |
| | | 1r | 13.01.98 | **Middlesbrough** | A | L | 0-2 | |
| 1998-99 | (D1) | 3 | 02.01.99 | **Huddersfield Town** (D1) | H | L | 0-1 | |
| 1999-00 | (D1) | 3 | 11.12.99 | **Torquay Utd** (D3) | H | D | 1-1 | Wardley |
| | | 3r | 21.12.99 | **Torquay Utd** | A | W | 3-2 | Wardley 2, Kiwomya |
| | | 4 | 08.01.00 | **Charlton Athletic** (D1) | A | L | 0-1 | |
| 2000-01 | (D1) | 3 | 06.01.01 | **Luton Town** (D2) | A | D | 3-3 | Crouch 2, Peacock (p) |
| | | 3r | 17.01.01 | **Luton Town** | H | W | 2-1aet | Kiwomya 2 |

| | | | | | | | |
|---|---|---|---|---|---|---|---|
| | 4 | 27.01.01 | **Arsenal** (PL) | H | L | 0-6 | |
| 2001-02 (D2) | 1 | 18.11.01 | **Swansea City** (D3) | A | L | 0-4 | |
| 2002-03 (D2) | 1 | 16.11.02 | **Vauxhall M (E P)** (NPL) | A | D | 0-0 | |
| | | | *played at Deva Stadium, Chester* | | | | |
| | 1r | 26.11.02 | **Vauxhall M (E P)** | H | D | 1-1aet | Thomson |
| | | | *Vauxhall Motors won 4-3 on penalties* | | | | |

## RADCLIFFE BOROUGH

*Formed 1949. First entered FA Cup: 1971-72. Members of the Northern Premier League.*

| | | | | | | | |
|---|---|---|---|---|---|---|---|
| 2000-01 (NPL) | 1 | 19.11.00 | **York City** (D3) | H | L | 1-4 | Handy |
| | | | *played at Gigg Lane, Bury* | | | | |

## RAMBLERS

*Formed 1874. Entered FA Cup 1875-76 – 1878-79. Played their home matches at Woolwich Common and used the Perseverance Hotel as their headquarters.*

| | | | | | | | |
|---|---|---|---|---|---|---|---|
| 1875-76 | 1 | 23.10.75 | **Maidenhead** | A | L | 0-2 | |
| 1876-77 | 1 | 14.10.76 | **Pilgrims** | A | L | 1-4 | Sang |
| 1877-78 | 1 | 03.11.77 | **Pilgrims** | A | D | 0-0 | |
| | 1r | 09.11.77 | **Pilgrims** | A | L | 0-1 | |
| 1878-79 | 1 | 02.11.78 | **Romford (1876)** | A | L | 1-3 | Andrews |

## RAMSGATE ATHLETIC

*Formed 1945. First entered FA Cup: 1945-46. Voluntarilly liquidated and renamed Ramsgate 1976. Members of the Kent League.*

| | | | | | | | |
|---|---|---|---|---|---|---|---|
| 1955-56 (KL) | 1 | 19.11.55 | **Watford** (3S) | A | L | 3-5 | Davies, McCulloch, Durkin |

## RANGERS FC, LONDON

*Formed 1876. Entered FA Cup: 1880-81 and 1881-82. played at Clapham Common and used the Invitation pub in Auckland Road as their changing rooms.*

| | | | | | | | |
|---|---|---|---|---|---|---|---|
| 1880-81 | 1 | | Wanderers | | | - | |
| | | | *Wanderers scratched. Rangers FC walkover* | | | | |
| | 2 | | bye | | | | |
| | 3 | 09.02.81 | **Royal Engineers** | | L | 0-6 | |
| 1881-82 | 1 | | Romford (1876) | | | - | |
| | | | *Rangers FC scratched. Romford (1876) walkover* | | | | |

## RAWMARSH WELFARE

*Entered FA Cup: 1930-31 – 1973-74. Played at the Hill 60 Ground in Peashill Street, Rawmarsh, near Rotherham.*

| | | | | | | | |
|---|---|---|---|---|---|---|---|
| 1951-52 (SAL) | 1 | 24.11.51 | **Buxton** (CC) | H | L | 1-4 | Swales |

## RAWTENSTALL

*Formed 1879. Entered FA Cup: 1884-85 – 1888-89. Played at Burnley Road, Rawtenstall, Lancashire, near the White Lion pub. Spent three seasons in the Lancashire Combination in the 1890s and were once disqualified from the FA Cup for professionalism.*

| | | | | | | | |
|---|---|---|---|---|---|---|---|
| 1884-85 | 1 | | South Shore | | | - | |
| | | | *Rawtenstall scratched. South Shore walkover* | | | | |
| 1885-86 | 1 | | Glasgow Rangers | | | - | |
| | | | *Rangers scratched. Rawtenstall walkover* | | | | |
| | 2 | 21.11.85 | **Bolton Wanderers** | H | D | 3-3 | |
| | | | *FA disqualified Rawtenstall for professionalism, Bolton advanced* | | | | |
| 1886-87 | 1 | 30.10.86 | **Church FC** | A | D | 1-1 | |
| | 1r | 13.11.86 | **Church FC** | H | L | 1-7 | |
| 1887-88 | 1 | 15.10.87 | **Darwen** | H | L | 1-3 | |

## READING

*Formed 1871. Later absorbed Reading Hornets (1877) and Earley (1889). FA Cup best performance: semi-finals 1927. Record FA Cup win: 11-0 v Chesham Generals, 4th qualifying round, 1900-01; In Competition Proper: 6-0 v Leyton FC, 2nd round, 12.12.1925. Record FA Cup defeat: 0-18 v Preston North End, 1st round, 27.01.1894.*

| | | | | | | | |
|---|---|---|---|---|---|---|---|
| 1877-78 | 1 | 07.11.77 | **South Norwood** | H | W | 2-0 | Field, H Wilson og |
| | 2 | 08.12.77 | **Upton Park** | A | L | 0-1 | |
| 1878-79 | 1 | 09.11.78 | **Hendon (1874)** | H | W | 1-0 | Holbrook |
| | 2 | 18.12.78 | **Old Etonians** | H | L | 0-1 | |

| | | | | | | | | |
|---|---|---|---|---|---|---|---|---|
| 1879-80 | | 1 | | Henley FC | | | - | |
| | | | | *Reading scratched. Henley walkover* | | | | |
| 1880-81 | | 1 | 13.11.80 | **Hotspur FC** | H | W | 5-1 | C Field, Fuller, Holbrook, Turner, Silence |
| | | 2 | 18.12.80 | **Swifts** | H | L | 0-1 | |
| 1881-82 | | 1 | 29.10.81 | **Hendon (1874)** | H | W | 5-0 | Thompson 2, C Field, Franklin, Turner |
| | | 2 | 26.11.81 | **West End** | H | D | 1-1 | Field |
| | | | | *FA disqualified West End, Reading advanced* | | | | |
| | | 3 | | bye | | | | |
| | | 4 | | Marlow | | | - | |
| | | | | *Reading scratched. Marlow walkover* | | | | |
| 1882-83 | | 1 | | bye | | | | |
| | | 2 | 29.11.82 | **Royal Engineers** | A | L | 0-8 | |
| 1883-84 | | 1 | 10.11.83 | **South Reading** | H | D | 2-2 | Lushington, Turner |
| | | 1r | 17.11.83 | **South Reading** | A | W | 4-0 | C Field 2, Beacon, AN Other |
| | | 2 | 01.12.83 | **West End** | H | W | 1-0 | C Field |
| | | 3 | 22.12.83 | **Upton Park** | H | L | 1-6 | |
| 1884-85 | | 1 | 08.11.84 | **Rochester** | H | W | 2-0 | Egerton, E Field |
| | | 2 | 06.12.84 | **Upton Park** | A | L | 1-3 | Thompson |
| 1885-86 | | 1 | 31.10.85 | **Rochester** | A | L | 1-6 | |
| 1886-87 | | 1 | 23.10.86 | **Old Carthusians** | A | L | 1-2 | Murdoch |
| 1887-88 | | 1 | 15.10.87 | **Dulwich** | H | L | 0-2 | |
| | | | | *FA ordered replay after protests. Reading scratched. Dulwich walkover* | | | | |
| 1888-89 | | | | 1q Luton Town (A) 0-4 | | | | |
| 1889-90 | | | | 1q Old St Pauls (H) 3-4aet | | | | |
| 1890-91 | | | | 1q Ipswich Town (A) 0-2 | | | | |
| 1891-92 | | | | 1q Newbury Town (H) 2-1; 2q Southampton St Mary's (A) 0-7, Southampton disqualified by FA, Reading re-instated; 3q Clifton (A) 2-8 | | | | |
| 1892-93 | | | | 1q Clifton (H) 6-1; 2q Uxbridge (A) 3-2; 3q Swindon Town (A) 1-2 | | | | |
| 1893-94 | | | | 1q Warmley (H) 3-0; 2q Newbury Town (A) 2-1; 3q Southampton St Marys (H) 2-1; 4q Swindon Town (A) 2-0 | | | | |
| | | 1 | 27.01.94 | **Preston North End** (D1) | A | L | 0-18 | |
| 1894-95 | (SL) | | | 1q Clifton (A) 7-3; 2q Southampton St Marys (A) 2-5 | | | | |
| 1895-96 | (SL) | | | 1q Bristol St Georges (H) 7-2; 2q Eastleigh (H) 2-1; 3q Southampton St Marys (A) 0-3 | | | | |
| 1896-97 | (SL) | | | 3q Bedminster (A) 5-0; 4q Southampton St Marys (H) 1-4 | | | | |
| 1897-98 | (SL) | | | 3q Swindon Town (H) 0-0; 4q Swindon Town (A) 2-3 | | | | |
| 1898-99 | (SL) | | | 3q Bristol Rovers (A) 1-0; 4q Warmley (H) 1-1; 4qr Warmley (H) 3-0; 5q Bristol City (A) 2-3 | | | | |
| 1899-00 | (SL) | | | 3q Wycombe W (A) 8-0; 4q Marlow (H) 2-1; 5q Chesham T (H) 7-1 | | | | |
| | | 1 | 27.01.00 | **Newcastle Utd** (D1) | A | L | 1-2 | Barlow |
| 1900-01 | (SL) | | | 3q Oxford City (A) 4-0; 4q Chesham Generals (H) 11-0; 5q Richmond Association (H) 2-0; Int Bristol City (H) 1-1; Int r Bristol City (A) 0-0aet; Int 2r Bristol City 2-1 at Swindon | | | | |
| | | 1 | 09.02.01 | **Bristol Rovers** (SL) | H | W | 2-0 | Barnes, Pegg |
| | | 2 | 23.02.01 | **Bolton Wanderers** (D1) | A | W | 1-0 | A.Sharp |
| | | 3 | 23.03.01 | **Tottenham Hotspur** (SL) | H | D | 1-1 | Evans |
| | | 3r | 28.03.01 | **Tottenham Hotspur** | A | L | 0-3 | |
| 1901-02 | (SL) | | | Int Chesterfield (H) 2-1 | | | | |
| | | 1 | 25.01.02 | **Notts County** (D1) | A | W | 2-1 | Allison, Davidson |
| | | 2 | 08.02.02 | **Portsmouth** (SL) | H | L | 0-1 | |
| 1902-03 | (SL) | | | Int Burnley (H) 1-0 | | | | |
| | | 1 | 07.02.03 | **Nottingham Forest** (D1) | H | D | 0-0 | |
| | | 1r | 11.02.03 | **Nottingham Forest** | A | L | 3-6aet | Craggs 2, Lyon |
| 1903-04 | (SL) | | | Int Gainsborough Tinity (H) 1-0 | | | | |
| | | 1 | 06.02.04 | **Bolton Wanderers** (D2) | H | D | 1-1 | Bevan |
| | | 1r | 10.02.04 | **Bolton Wanderers** | | L | 2-3 | Bevan 2 |
| 1904-05 | (SL) | | | Int Brentford (A) 1-1; Int r Brentford (H) 2-0 | | | | |
| | | 1 | 04.02.05 | **Fulham** (SL) | A | D | 0-0 | |
| | | 1r | 08.02.05 | **Fulham** | H | D | 0-0aet | |
| | | 1 2r | 13.02.05 | **Fulham** | | L | 0-1aet | |
| | | | | *played at White Hart Lane* | | | | |

| | | | | | | | | |
|---|---|---|---|---|---|---|---|---|
| 1905-06 | (SL) | 1 | 13.01.06 | **Hull City** (D2) | A | W | 1-0 | McCafferty |
| | | 2 | 03.02.06 | **Tottenham Hotspur** (SL) | A | L | 2-3 | McCafferty 2 |
| 1906-07 | (SL) | 1 | 12.01.07 | **Bradford City** (D2) | A | L | 0-2 | |
| 1907-08 | (SL) | 1 | 11.01.08 | **QPR** (SL) | A | L | 0-1 | |
| 1908-09 | (SL) | 1 | 16.01.09 | **Norwich City** (SL) | | D | 0-0 | |
| | | | | *played at Stamford Bridge* | | | | |
| | | 1r | 20.01.09 | **Norwich City** | H | D | 1-1aet | Huggins |
| | | 1 2r | 25.01.09 | **Norwich City** | | L | 2-3aet | Wheatcroft 2 |
| | | | | *played at Villa Park* | | | | |
| 1909-10 | (SL) | 1 | 15.01.10 | **Wolverhampton W** (D2) | A | L | 0-5 | |
| 1910-11 | (SL) | | | 4q Exeter City (H) 1-1; 4qr Exeter City (A) 0-1 | | | | |
| 1911-12 | (SL) | | | 4q Southall (H) 7-1; 5q Castleford Town (A) 2-1 | | | | |
| | | 1 | 13.01.12 | **Southport** (CL) | A | W | 2-0 | Lee, Andrews |
| | | 2 | 03.02.12 | **Aston Villa** (D1) | A | D | 1-1 | Bailey |
| | | 2r | 07.02.12 | **Aston Villa** | H | W | 1-0 | Foster |
| | | 3 | 24.02.12 | **Manchester Utd** (D1) | H | D | 1-1 | Bradley |
| | | 3r | 29.02.12 | **Manchester Utd** | A | L | 0-3 | |
| 1912-13 | (SL) | 1 | 11.01.13 | **Stoke** (SL) | A | - | 2-1ab | Burton 2 |
| | | | | *abandoned after 25 minutes* | | | | |
| | | 1r | 16.01.13 | **Stoke** | A | D | 2-2 | Foster, Pinfield |
| | | 1 2r | 22.01.13 | **Stoke** | H | W | 3-0 | Morris, Burton, Pinfield |
| | | 2 | 01.02.13 | **Tottenham Hotspur** (D1) | H | W | 1-0 | Pinfield |
| | | 3 | 22.02.13 | **Blackburn Rovers** (D1) | H | L | 1-2 | Bailey |
| 1913-14 | (SL) | 1 | 10.01.14 | **Bradford Park A** (D2) | A | L | 1-5 | Foster |
| 1914-15 | (SL) | 1 | 09.01.15 | **Wolverhampton W** (D2) | H | L | 0-1 | |
| 1919-20 | (SL) | 1 | 10.01.20 | **Plymouth Argyle** (SL) | A | L | 0-2 | |
| 1920-21 | (D3) | 1 | 08.01.21 | **Chelsea** (D1) | H | D | 0-0 | |
| | | 1r | 12.01.21 | **Chelsea** | A | D | 2-2aet | Mavin, Broskon |
| | | 1 2r | 16.01.21 | **Chelsea** | A | L | 1-3 | Bailey |
| 1921-22 | (3S) | 1 | 07.01.22 | **Northampton Town** (3S) | A | L | 0-3 | |
| 1922-23 | (3S) | | | 5q Bristol Rovers (H) 0-1 | | | | |
| 1923-24 | (3S) | | | 5q Aberdare Athletic (A) 0-1 | | | | |
| 1924-25 | (3S) | | | 4q Erith & Belvedere (A) 2-0; 5q Southend Utd (H) 2-1; 6q Darlington (H) 0-1 | | | | |
| 1925-26 | (3S) | 1 | 28.11.25 | **Torquay Utd** (SL) | A | D | 1-1 | Messer |
| | | 1r | 02.12.25 | **Torquay Utd** | H | D | 1-1aet | Davey |
| | | 1 2r | 07.12.25 | **Torquay Utd** | | W | 2-0 | Braithwaite, Davey |
| | | | | *played at Ashton Gate* | | | | |
| | | 2 | 12.12.25 | **Leyton FC** (Lon) | H | W | 6-0 | Robson 2, Davey, Smith, Braithwaite 2 |
| | | 3 | 09.01.26 | **Bournemouth** (3S) | A | L | 0-2 | |
| 1926-27 | (D2) | 1 | 27.11.26 | **Weymouth** (SL) | H | D | 4-4 | Richardson 2, Johnstone 2 |
| | | 1r | 01.12.26 | **Weymouth** | H | W | 5-0 | Johnstone 3, Porter, Robson |
| | | 2 | 11.12.26 | **Southend Utd** (3S) | H | W | 3-2 | Braithwaite 2, Richardson |
| | | 3 | 08.01.27 | **Manchester Utd** (D1) | H | D | 1-1 | Richardson |
| | | 3r | 12.01.27 | **Manchester Utd** | A | D | 2-2aet | Richardson 2 |
| | | 3 2r | 17.01.27 | **Manchester Utd** | | W | 2-1 | Richhardson (p), Johnstone |
| | | | | *played at Villa Park* | | | | |
| | | 4 | 29.01.27 | **Portsmouth** (D2) | H | W | 3-1 | Richardson, Macdonald, Johnstone |
| | | 5 | 19.02.27 | **Brentford** (3S) | H | W | 1-0 | Richardson |
| | | 6 | 05.03.27 | **Swansea Town** (D2) | A | W | 3-1 | Johnstone 2, McDonald |
| | | SF | 26.03.27 | **Cardiff City** (D1) | | L | 0-3 | |
| | | | | *played at Molineux* | | | | |
| 1927-28 | (D2) | 3 | 14.01.28 | **Grimsby Town** (D2) | H | W | 4-0 | Richardson 2, Batten, McDonald |
| | | 4 | 28.01.28 | **Leicester City** (D1) | H | L | 0-1 | |
| 1928-29 | (D2) | 3 | 12.01.29 | **Tottenham Hotspur** (D2) | H | W | 2-0 | Johnstone 2 |
| | | 4 | 26.01.29 | **Sheffield Wed** (D1) | H | W | 1-0 | Johnstone |
| | | 5 | 16.02.29 | **Aston Villa** (D1) | H | L | 1-3 | Oswald |
| 1929-30 | (D2) | 3 | 11.01.30 | **Aston Villa** | A | L | 1-5 | Douglas |
| 1930-31 | (D2) | 3 | 10.01.31 | **Crystal Palace** (3S) | A | D | 1-1 | Bacon |
| | | 3r | 14.01.31 | **Crystal Palace** | H | D | 1-1aet | Gilhesby |
| | | 3 2r | 19.01.31 | **Crystal Palace** | | L | 0-2 | |
| | | | | *played at Stamford Bridge* | | | | |

| | | | | | | | |
|---|---|---|---|---|---|---|---|
| 1931-32 (3S) | 1 | 28.11.31 | **Crystal Palace** (3S) | H | L | 0-1 | |
| 1932-33 (3S) | 1 | 26.11.32 | **Brentford** (3S) | H | W | 3-2 | Oxberry, McPherson, Ritchie |
| | 2 | 10.12.32 | **Coventry City** (3S) | H | D | 2-2 | Bacon, McPherson |
| | 2r | 15.12.32 | **Coventry City** | A | D | 3-3 | Liddle 2, McPherson |
| | 2 2r | 19.12.32 | **Coventry City** | | W | 1-0 | Oxberry |
| | | | *played at Stamford Bridge* | | | | |
| | 3 | 14.01.33 | **Millwall** (D2) | A | - | 0-2ab | |
| | | | *abandoned after 75 minutes- fog* | | | | |
| | 3 | 18.01.33 | **Millwall** | A | D | 1-1 | Pipe og |
| | 3r | 23.01.33 | **Millwall** | H | L | 0-2 | |
| 1933-34 (3S) | 1 | 25.11.33 | **Watford** (3S) | A | W | 3-0 | McGough 2, Newton |
| | 2 | 09.12.33 | **Sutton Town** (DSL) | A | W | 2-1 | Newton, Oxberry |
| | 3 | 13.01.34 | **Oldham Athletic** (D2) | H | L | 1-2 | Hayhurst |
| 1934-35 (3S) | 1 | 24.11.34 | **Cardiff City** (3S) | A | W | 2-1 | Tait 2 |
| | 2 | 08.12.34 | **Wrexham** (3N) | H | W | 3-0 | Butler 2, Tait |
| | 3 | 12.01.35 | **Aldershot** (3S) | A | D | 0-0 | |
| | 3r | 16.01.35 | **Aldershot** | H | W | 3-1 | Tait 2, Butler |
| | 4 | 26.01.35 | **Millwall** (3S) | H | W | 1-0 | Tait |
| | 5 | 16.02.35 | **Arsenal** (D1) | H | L | 0-1 | |
| 1935-36 (3S) | 1 | 30.11.35 | **Corinthians** | H | W | 8-3 | Tait 2, Fielding 2, Liddle 3, McGough |
| | 2 | 14.12.35 | **Chester** (3N) | A | D | 3-3 | Tait, Liddle, Hayhurst |
| | 2r | 18.12.35 | **Chester** | H | W | 3-0 | Tait, Paterson, Fielding |
| | 3 | 11.01.36 | **Manchester Utd** (D2) | H | L | 1-3 | Pateman |
| 1936-37 (3S) | 1 | 28.11.36 | **Ilford** (IL) | A | W | 4-2 | Gregory, Tait, Fielding, Wright |
| | 2 | 12.12.36 | **Newport County** (3S) | H | W | 7-2 | Fielding, Watkin 4, Tait, Paterson |
| | 3 | 16.01.37 | **Manchester Utd** (D1) | A | L | 0-1 | |
| 1937-38 (3S) | 1 | 27.11.37 | **Guildford City** (SL) | A | L | 0-1 | |
| 1938-39 (3S) | 1 | 26.11.38 | **Newport County** (3S) | H | D | 3-3 | McPhee, Tait, Gledden |
| | 1r | 05.12.38 | **Newport County** | A | L | 1-3 | Tait |
| 1945-46 (3S) | 1 1L | 17.11.45 | **Aldershot** (3S) | H | W | 3-1 | Edelston, Summerfield, Layton |
| | 1 2L | 24.11.45 | **Aldershot** | A | L | 3-7 | McPhee 2, Summerfield |
| 1946-47 (3S) | 1 | 30.11.46 | **Colchester Utd** (SL) | H | W | 5-0 | Edelston 2, McPhee, Chitty, Barney |
| | 2 | 14.12.46 | **Merthyr Tydfil** (SL) | A | W | 3-1 | Deverall, Barnes, Edelston |
| | 3 | 11.01.47 | **Grimsby Town** (D1) | H | D | 2-2 | McPhee, Henley |
| | 3r | 14.01.47 | **Grimsby Town** | A | L | 1-3 | Edelston |
| 1947-48 (3S) | 1 | 29.11.47 | **Bromley** (AL) | A | D | 3-3aet | Green, Goldenberg, Birchston |
| | 1r | 06.12.47 | **Bromley** | H | W | 3-0 | Dix, Fisher, McPhee |
| | 2 | 13.12.47 | **Newport County** (3S) | H | W | 3-0 | Edelston 2, McPhee |
| | 3 | 10.01.48 | **WBA** (D2) | A | L | 0-2 | |
| 1948-49 (3S) | 1 | 27.11.48 | **Colchester Utd** (SL) | A | - | 1-1ab | McPhee |
| | | | *abandoned after 35 minutes – fog* | | | | |
| | 1 | 04.12.48 | **Colchester Utd** (SL) | A | W | 4-2 | Edelston 2, McPhee, Dix |
| | 2 | 11.12.48 | **Hull City** (3N) | A | D | 0-0aet | |
| | 2r | 18.12.48 | **Hull City** | H | L | 1-2 | McPhee |
| 1949-50 (3S) | 3 | 07.01.50 | **Doncaster Rovers** (3N) | H | L | 2-3 | Blackman 2 |
| 1950-51 (3S) | 1 | 25.11.50 | **Cheltenham Town** (SL) | H | W | 3-1 | Bainbridge, Blackman 2 |
| | 2 | 09.12.50 | **Dartford** (SL) | H | W | 4-0 | Henry, Edelston, Blackman, Bainbridge |
| | 3 | 06.01.51 | **Newport County** (3S) | A | L | 2-3 | Blackman 2 |
| 1951-52 (3S) | 1 | 24.11.51 | **Walsall** (3S) | H | W | 1-0 | Blackman |
| | 2 | 15.12.51 | **Southport** (3N) | H | D | 1-1 | Henley |
| | 2r | 19.12.51 | **Southport** | A | D | 1-1aet | Brice |
| | 2 2r | 01.01.52 | **Southport** | | W | 2-0 | Henley, Hacking og |
| | | | *played at Villa Park* | | | | |
| | 3 | 12.01.52 | **Swansea Town** (D2) | H | L | 0-3 | |
| 1952-53 (3S) | 1 | 22.11.52 | **Crystal Palace** (3S) | A | D | 1-1 | McLean |
| | 1r | 26.11.52 | **Crystal Palace** | H | L | 1-3 | Brooks |
| 1953-54 (3S) | 1 | 21.11.53 | **Ipswich Town** (3S) | A | L | 1-4 | Blackman |
| 1954-55 (3S) | 1 | 20.11.54 | **Colchester Utd** (3S) | H | D | 3-3 | Wheeler, Uphill, Hill og |
| | 1r | 25.11.54 | **Colchester Utd** | A | W | 2-1 | Uphill, Mansell |
| | 2 | 11.12.54 | **Gillingham** (3S) | A | D | 1-1 | Wheeler |

| | | | | | | | |
|---|---|---|---|---|---|---|---|
| | 2r | 13.12.54 | **Gillingham** | H | W | 5-3 | Wheeler 2, Uphill 2, Chung |
| | 3 | 08.01.55 | **Manchester Utd** (D1) | H | D | 1-1 | Chilton og |
| | 3r | 12.01.55 | **Manchester Utd** | A | L | 1-4 | Uphill |
| 1955-56 (3S) | 1 | 19.11.55 | **Bournemouth** (3S) | H | W | 1-0 | Anderton |
| | 2 | 10.12.55 | **Aldershot** (3S) | H | D | 2-2 | Dixon, Cross |
| | 2r | 14.12.55 | **Aldershot** | A | L | 0-3aet | |
| 1956-57 (3S) | 1 | 17.11.56 | **Cheltenham Town** (SL) | A | W | 2-1 | Dixon 2 |
| | 2 | 08.12.56 | **Bedford Town** (SL) | H | W | 1-0 | Campbell |
| | 3 | 05.01.57 | **Wrexham** (3N) | A | D | 1-1 | Wheeler |
| | 3r | 09.01.57 | **Wrexham** | H | L | 1-2 | Dixon |
| 1957-58 (3S) | 1 | 16.11.57 | **Swindon Town** (3S) | H | W | 1-0 | Dixon |
| | 2 | 07.12.57 | **Wisbech Town** (ML) | H | W | 2-1 | Whitehouse, Dixon |
| | 3 | 04.01.58 | **Leyton Orient** (D2) | A | L | 0-1 | |
| 1958-59 (D3) | 1 | 15.11.58 | **Watford** (D4) | A | D | 1-1 | Wheeler |
| | 1r | 19.11.58 | **Watford** | H | L | 0-2 | |
| 1959-60 (D3) | 1 | 14.11.59 | **Norwich City** (D3) | A | D | 1-1 | Wheeler |
| | 1r | 18.11.59 | **Norwich City** | H | W | 2-1 | Wheeler, Reeves |
| | 2 | 05.12.59 | **King's Lynn** (SL) | H | W | 4-2 | Ayre 2, Reeves (p), Wheeler |
| | 3 | 09.01.60 | **Nottingham Forest** (D1) | A | L | 0-1 | |
| 1960-61 (D3) | 1 | 05.11.60 | **Millwall** (D4) | H | W | 6-2 | McIlvenny, Wheeler 3, Lacey, Evans |
| | 2 | 26.11.60 | **Kettering Town** (SL) | H | W | 4-2 | Lacey 3, McIlvenny |
| | 3 | 07.01.61 | **Barnsley** (D3) | H | D | 1-1 | Whitehouse |
| | 3r | 11.01.61 | **Barnsley** | A | L | 1-3 | Whitehouse |
| 1961-62 (D3) | 1 | 04.11.61 | **Newport County** (D3) | H | D | 1-1 | D Webb |
| | 1r | 06.11.61 | **Newport County** | A | L | 0-1 | |
| 1962-63 (D3) | 1 | 03.11.62 | **Swindon Town** (D3) | A | L | 2-4 | Wheeler, Walker (p) |
| 1963-64 (D3) | 1 | 16.11.63 | **Enfield** (IL) | H | D | 2-2 | Allen, Wheeler |
| | 1r | 19.11.63 | **Enfield** | A | W | 4-2aet | Wheeler, D Webb 2, Tindall |
| | 2 | 07.12.63 | **Luton Town** (D3) | A | L | 1-2 | D Webb |
| 1964-65 (D3) | 1 | 14.11.64 | **Watford** (D3) | H | W | 3-1 | Walker (p), Norton, D Webb |
| | 2 | 05.12.64 | **Aldershot** (D4) | A | W | 3-1 | Terry 2, D Webb |
| | 3 | 09.01.65 | **Newport County** (D4) | H | D | 2-2 | Spiers, D Webb |
| | 3r | 11.01.65 | **Newport County** | A | W | 1-0 | Shreeves |
| | 4 | 30.01.65 | **Burnley** (D1) | H | D | 1-1 | Kerr |
| | 4r | 02.02.65 | **Burnley** | A | L | 0-1 | |
| 1965-66 (D3) | 1 | 13.11.65 | **Bristol Rovers** (D3) | H | W | 3-2 | Terry, Allen 2 |
| | 2 | 04.12.65 | **Brentford** (D3) | H | W | 5-0 | Allen, Webb 2, Terry, Evans |
| | 3 | 22.01.66 | **Sheffield Wed** (D1) | H | L | 2-3 | Thornhill, Evans |
| 1966-67 (D3) | 1 | 26.11.66 | **Hendon** (IL) | A | W | 3-1 | Harris, Thornhill 2 |
| | 2 | 16.01.67 | **Aldershot** (D4) | A | L | 0-1 | |
| 1967-68 (D3) | 1 | 13.12.67 | **Aldershot** | H | W | 6-2 | Silvester 2, Allen 2, Collins, Harris |
| | 2 | 06.01.68 | **Dagenham** (AL) | H | D | 1-1 | Harris |
| | 2r | 15.01.68 | **Dagenham** | A | W | 1-0 | Sainty |
| | 3 | 27.01.68 | **Manchester City** (D1) | A | D | 0-0 | |
| | 3r | 31.01.68 | **Manchester City** | H | L | 0-7 | |
| 1968-69 (D3) | 1 | 16.11.68 | **Plymouth Argyle** (D3) | H | W | 1-0 | Henderson |
| | 2 | 07.12.68 | **Torquay Utd** (D3) | H | D | 0-0 | |
| | 2r | 11.12.68 | **Torquay Utd** | A | W | 2-1 | Harris, Silvester |
| | 3 | 04.01.69 | **Newcastle Utd** (D1) | A | L | 0-4 | |
| 1969-70 (D3) | 1 | 15.11.69 | **Brentwood Town** (SL) | A | L | 0-1 | |
| 1970-71 (D3) | 1 | 21.11.70 | **Bishop's Stortford** (AL) | H | W | 6-1 | Habbin 3, Bell 2, Cumming |
| | 2 | 12.12.70 | **Shrewsbury Town** (D3) | A | D | 2-2 | Cumming, Williams |
| | 2r | 21.12.70 | **Shrewsbury Town** | H | W | 1-0 | Habbin |
| | 3 | 06.01.71 | **Watford** (D2) | A | L | 0-5 | |
| 1971-72 (D4) | 1 | 20.11.71 | **Bridgwater Town** (WL) | A | W | 3-0 | Prescott og, Flannigan, Cumming |
| | 2 | 11.12.71 | **Aldershot** (D4) | H | W | 1-0 | Harman |
| | 3 | 15.01.72 | **Blyth Spartans** (NL) | A | D | 2-2 | B Wagstaff, Cumming (p) |
| | 3r | 19.01.72 | **Blyth Spartans** | H | W | 6-1 | Harman 3, Cumming, B Wagstaff, Habbin |
| | 4 | 05.02.72 | **Arsenal** (D1) | H | L | 1-2 | Wagstaff |
| 1972-73 (D4) | 1 | 18.11.72 | **Gillingham** (D4) | A | W | 2-1 | Habbin, Dixon |

| | | | | | | | |
|---|---|---|---|---|---|---|---|
| | 2 | 09.12.72 | **Hayes** (IL) | H | D | 0-0 | |
| | 2r | 11.12.72 | **Hayes** | A | W | 1-0 | Chappell |
| | 3 | 13.01.73 | **Doncaster Rovers** (D4) | H | W | 2-0 | Chappell, Cummings |
| | 4 | 03.02.73 | **Sunderland** (D2) | A | D | 1-1 | Chappell |
| | 4r | 07.02.73 | **Sunderland** | H | L | 1-3 | Cumming (p) |
| 1973-74 (D4) | 1 | 24.11.73 | **Slough Town** (IL) | H | W | 3-0 | Bromley, Hetzke, Chappell |
| | 2 | 15.12.73 | **Southend Utd** (D3) | A | L | 0-2 | |
| 1974-75 (D4) | 1 | 23.11.74 | **Swindon Town** (D3) | A | L | 0-4 | |
| 1975-76 (D4) | 1 | 22.11.75 | **Hendon** (IL) | A | L | 0-1 | |
| 1976-77 (D3) | 1 | 20.11.76 | **Wealdstone** (SL) | H | W | 1-0 | Murray |
| | 2 | 11.12.76 | **Wycombe W** (IL) | A | W | 2-1 | Friday 2 |
| | 3 | 08.01.77 | **Hereford Utd** (D2) | A | L | 0-1 | |
| 1977-78 (D4) | 1 | 26.11.77 | **Aldershot** (D4) | H | W | 3-1 | Earles 2, Kearns |
| | 2 | 17.12.77 | **Wealdstone** (SL) | A | L | 1-2 | Earles |
| 1978-79 (D4) | 1 | 25.11.78 | **Gillingham** (D3) | H | D | 0-0 | |
| | 1r | 28.11.78 | **Gillingham** | A | W | 2-1aet | Lewis, Kearney |
| | 2 | 16.12.78 | **Portsmouth** (D4) | A | W | 1-0 | Alexander |
| | 3 | 09.01.79 | **Notts County** (D2) | A | L | 2-4 | Kearney 2 |
| 1979-80 (D3) | 1 | 24.11.79 | **Kettering Town** (APL) | H | W | 4-2 | Kearney 2, Heale, Kearns |
| | 2 | 15.12.79 | **Barking** (IL) | H | W | 3-1 | Bowman (p), SAnchez, Heale |
| | 3 | 05.01.80 | **Colchester Utd** (D3) | H | W | 2-0 | Earles, Heale |
| | 4 | 26.01.80 | **Swansea City** (D3) | A | L | 1-4 | Kearney |
| 1980-81 (D3) | 1 | 22.11.80 | **Fulham** (D3) | H | L | 1-2 | Earles |
| 1981-82 (D3) | 1 | 21.11.81 | **Bournemouth** (D4) | A | L | 0-1 | |
| 1982-83 (D3) | 1 | 20.11.82 | **Bishop's Stortford** (IL) | H | L | 1-2 | Earles |
| 1983-84 (D4) | 1 | 19.11.83 | **Hereford Utd** (D4) | H | W | 2-0 | Senior, Horrix |
| | 2 | 10.12.83 | **Oxford Utd** (D3) | H | D | 1-1 | Price |
| | 2r | 14.12.83 | **Oxford Utd** | A | L | 0-3 | |
| 1984-85 (D3) | 1 | 17.11.84 | **Barry Town** (Welsh) | A | W | 2-1 | Beavon, Senior |
| | 2 | 08.12.84 | **Bognor Regis Town** (IL) | H | W | 6-2 | Juryeff 2, Beavon, Senior 2, White |
| | 3 | 05.01.85 | **Barnsley** (D2) | A | L | 3-4 | Horrix (p), Senior, Crown |
| 1985-86 (D3) | 1 | 16.11.85 | **Wealdstone** (APL) | H | W | 1-0 | Horrix (p) |
| | 2 | 07.12.85 | **Hereford Utd** (D4) | H | W | 2-0 | Senior, Horrix |
| | 3 | 04.01.86 | **Huddersfield Town** (D2) | A | D | 0-0 | |
| | 3r | 13.01.86 | **Huddersfield Town** | H | W | 2-1aet | Senior 2 |
| | 4 | 25.01.86 | **Bury** (D3) | H | D | 1-1 | Senior |
| | 4r | 28.01.86 | **Bury** | A | L | 0-3 | |
| 1986-87 (D2) | 3 | 10.01.87 | **Arsenal** (D1) | H | L | 1-3 | Senior |
| 1987-88 (D2) | 3 | 09.01.88 | **Southampton** (D1) | H | L | 0-1 | |
| 1988-89 (D3) | 1 | 19.11.88 | **Hendon** (IL) | H | W | 4-2 | L Taylor 2, Elsey, Senior |
| | 2 | 10.12.88 | **Maidstone Utd** (Conf) | H | D | 1-1 | Senior |
| | 2r | 14.12.88 | **Maidstone Utd** | A | W | 2-1 | Gernon, Senior |
| | 3 | 07.01.89 | **Tranmere Rovers** (D4) | A | D | 1-1 | Elsey |
| | 3r | 11.01.89 | **Tranmere Rovers** | H | W | 2-1 | Senior, Franklin |
| | 4 | 28.01.89 | **Grimsby Town** (D4) | A | D | 1-1 | Saunders og |
| | 4r | 01.02.89 | **Grimsby Town** | H | L | 1-2 | Moran |
| 1989-90 (D3) | 1 | 18.11.89 | **Bristol Rovers** (D3) | A | D | 1-1 | Conroy |
| | 1r | 21.11.89 | **Bristol Rovers** | H | D | 1-1aet | Senior |
| | 1 2r | 27.11.89 | **Bristol Rovers** | A | W | 1-0 | Senior |
| | 2 | 09.12.89 | **Welling Utd** (Conf) | H | D | 0-0 | |
| | 2r | 13.12.89 | **Welling Utd** | A | D | 1-1aet | Beavon (p) |
| | 2 2r | 19.12.89 | **Welling Utd** | H | D | 0-0aet | |
| | 2 3r | 22.12.89 | **Welling Utd** | A | W | 2-1 | Moran 2 |
| | 3 | 06.01.90 | **Sunderland** (D2) | H | W | 2-1 | Jones 2 |
| | 4 | 27.01.90 | **Newcastle Utd** (D1) | H | D | 3-3 | Jones, Senior, Gilkes |
| | 4r | 31.01.90 | **Newcastle Utd** | A | L | 1-4 | Senior |
| 1990-91 (D3) | 1 | 17.11.90 | **Colchester Utd** (Conf) | A | L | 1-2 | Hicks |
| 1991-92 (D3) | 1 | 16.11.91 | **Slough Town** (Conf) | A | D | 3-3 | Williams, Gooding, Taylor |
| | 1r | 27.11.91 | **Slough Town** | H | W | 2-1 | Williams, Lovell |
| | 2 | 07.12.91 | **Peterborough Utd** (D3) | A | D | 0-0 | |
| | 2r | 17.12.91 | **Peterborough Utd** | H | W | 1-0 | Lovell |

| | | | | | | | | |
|---|---|---|---|---|---|---|---|---|
| | | 3 | 04.01.92 | **Bolton Wanderers** (D3) | A | L | 0-2 | |
| 1992-93 | (D2) | 1 | 15.11.92 | **Birmingham City** (D1) | H | W | 1-0 | Quinn |
| | | 2 | 05.12.92 | **Leyton Orient** (D2) | H | W | 3-0 | Quinn 2 (1p), Parkinson |
| | | 3 | 02.01.93 | **Manchester City** (PL) | A | D | 1-1 | Taylor |
| | | 3r | 13.01.93 | **Manchester City** | H | L | 0-4 | |
| 1993-94 | (D2) | 1 | 13.11.93 | **Cambridge Utd** (D2) | A | D | 0-0 | |
| | | 1r | 24.11.93 | **Cambridge Utd** | H | L | 1-2 | Gooding |
| 1994-95 | (D1) | 3 | 07.01.95 | **Oldham Athletic** (D1) | H | L | 1-3 | Taylor |
| 1995-96 | (D1) | 3 | 06.01.96 | **Gillingham** (D3) | H | W | 3-1 | Morley, Quinn 2 |
| | | 4 | 27.01.96 | **Manchester Utd** (PL) | H | L | 0-3 | |
| 1996-97 | (D1) | 3 | 04.01.97 | **Southampton** (PL) | H | W | 3-1 | Lambert, Caskey, Morley (p) |
| | | 4 | 25.01.97 | **Portsmouth** (D1) | A | L | 0-3 | |
| 1997-98 | (D1) | 3 | 13.01.98 | **Cheltenham Town** (Conf) | A | D | 1-1 | Morley |
| | | 3r | 20.01.98 | **Cheltenham Town** | H | W | 2-1 | Morley, Booty |
| | | 4 | 24.01.98 | **Cardiff City** (D3) | A | D | 1-1 | Asaba |
| | | 4r | 03.02.98 | **Cardiff City** | H | D | 1-1aet | Morley |
| | | | | *Reading won 4-3 on penalties* | | | | |
| | | 5 | 13.02.98 | **Sheffield Utd** (D1) | A | L | 0-1 | |
| 1998-99 | (D2) | 1 | 14.11.98 | **Stoke City** (D2) | H | L | 0-1 | |
| 1999-00 | (D2) | 1 | 30.10.99 | **Yeovil Town** (Conf) | H | W | 4-2 | Bernal, Caskey (p), Hunter, M Williams |
| | | 2 | 20.11.99 | **Halifax Town** (D3) | H | D | 1-1 | Caskey (p) |
| | | 2r | 30.11.99 | **Halifax Town** | A | W | 1-0 | Caskey (p) |
| | | 3 | 11.12.99 | **Plymouth Argyle** (D3) | H | D | 1-1 | McIntyre |
| | | 3r | 21.12.99 | **Plymouth Argyle** | A | L | 0-1 | |
| 2000-01 | (D2) | 1 | 18.11.00 | **Grays Athletic** (IL) | H | W | 4-0 | Hodges, Cureton, Butler, Jones |
| | | 2 | 09.12.00 | **York City** (D3) | A | D | 2-2 | Newman, Butler |
| | | 2r | 19.12.00 | **York City** | H | L | 1-3 | Caskey |
| 2001-02 | (D2) | 1 | 17.11.01 | **Welling Utd** (SL) | H | W | 1-0 | Cureton |
| | | 2 | 08.12.01 | **York City** (D3) | A | L | 0-2 | |
| 2002-03 | (D1) | 3 | 04.01.03 | **Walsall** (D1) | A | D | 0-0 | |
| | | 3r | 14.01.03 | **Walsall** | H | D | 1-1aet | Aranalde og |
| | | | | *Walsall won 4-1 on penalties* | | | | |

## READING ABBEY

*Formed 1875. Entered FA Cup: 1880-81 and 1881-82. Played at King's Meadows, Reading.*

| | | | | | | | |
|---|---|---|---|---|---|---|---|
| 1880-81 | 1 | 13.11.80 | **St Albans (1877)** | H | W | 1-0 | |
| | 2 | 11.12.80 | **Acton** | H | W | 2-1 | |
| | 3 | 12.02.81 | **Romford (1876)** | A | L | 0-2 | |
| 1881-82 | 1 | 22.10.81 | **Woodford Bridge** | A | D | 1-1 | Vaisley |
| | 1r | 12.11.81 | **Woodford Bridge** | H | W | 2-1 | |
| | 2 | 26.11.81 | **Hotspur FC** | H | L | 1-4 | |

## READING HORNETS

*Formed early 1870s and merged with Reading 1877. Entered FA Cup: 1876-77 and 1877-78.*

| | | | | | | |
|---|---|---|---|---|---|---|
| 1876-77 | 1 | 04.11.76 | **Swifts** | A | L | 0-2 |
| 1877-78 | 1 | 27.10.77 | **Maidenhead** | A | L | 0-10 |

## READING MINSTER

| | | | | | | |
|---|---|---|---|---|---|---|
| 1880-81 | 1 | 13.11.80 | **Romford (1876)** | A | D | 1-1 |
| | | | *Reading Minster scratched before replay. Romford walkover* | | | |
| 1881-82 | 1 | 22.10.81 | **Windsor Home Park** | A | W | 1-0 |
| | 2 | 03.12.81 | **Romford (1876)** | H | W | 3-1 |
| | 3 | 17.12.81 | **Hotspur FC** | A | D | 0-0 |
| | 3r | 26.12.81 | **Hotspur FC** | H | L | 0-2 |
| 1882-83 | 1 | | Remnants | | | - |
| | | | *Remnants scratched. Reading Minster walkover* | | | |
| | 2 | | Marlow | | | - |
| | | | *Reading Minster scratched. Marlow walkover* | | | |
| 1883-84 | 1 | 10.11.83 | **Old Carthusians** | H | L | 1-10 |
| 1884-85 | 1 | 08.11.84 | **Hanover Utd** | A | L | 0-1 |

# REDCAR

*Entered FA Cup: 1883-84 – 1888-89. Reformed 1913. Entered FA Cup again: 1913-14 – 1921-22 when the club disbanded.*

| | | | | | | | |
|---|---|---|---|---|---|---|---|
| 1883-84 | 1 | | Nottingham Forest | | | - | |
| | | | *Redcar scratched. Nottingham Forest walkover* | | | | |
| 1884-85 | 1 | 08.11.84 | **Sunderland** | H | W | 3-1 | Bulman, Harrison, Agar |
| | 2 | 06.12.84 | **Grimsby Town** | A | L | 1-3 | Hikesley |
| 1885-86 | 1 | 24.10.85 | **Sunderland** | H | W | 3-0 | Bulman, Hikesley, Tufts |
| | 2 | 21.11.85 | **Lincoln Lindum** | H | W | 2-0 | |
| | 3 | | bye | | | | |
| | 4 | | bye | | | | |
| | 5 | 23.01.86 | **Middlesbrough** | H | W | 2-1 | Simpson, Hikesley |
| | 6 | 13.02.86 | **Small Heath Alliance** | A | L | 0-2 | |
| 1886-87 | 1 | 30.10.86 | **Tyne Association** | H | W | 4-0 | |
| | 2 | 20.11.86 | **Grantham Town** | A | L | 2-3 | |
| 1887-88 | 1 | 15.10.87 | **Newcastle West End** | A | L | 1-5 | Pearson |

# REDDITCH UNITED

*Formed 1891 as Redditch Town. First entered FA Cup: 1893-94. Members of the Southern League.*

| | | | | | | | |
|---|---|---|---|---|---|---|---|
| 1971-72 (WMRL) | 1 | 20.11.71 | **Peterborough Utd** (D4) | H | D | 1-1 | Howell |
| | 1r | 22.11.71 | **Peterborough Utd** | A | L | 0-6 | |
| 1989-90 (SL) | 1 | 18.11.89 | **Merthyr Tydfil** (Conf) | H | L | 1-3 | Campbell |

# REDHILL

*Formed 1894. First entered FA Cup: 1897-98. Members of the Sussex County League.*

| | | | | | | | |
|---|---|---|---|---|---|---|---|
| 1957-58 (AL) | 1 | 16.11.57 | **Norwich City** (3S) | A | L | 1-6 | Hills |

# REIGATE PRIORY

*One of the 15 original entrants in the FA Cup in the 1871-72 season. However, they scratched after being drawn against the Royal Engineers in the first round. Entered the FA Cup until 1876-77. After a gap of 51 years a Reigate Priory team re-entered the FA Cup from 1927-28 – 1929-30 losing in the early preliminary rounds. Surrey Senior Cup winners six times.*

| | | | | | | | |
|---|---|---|---|---|---|---|---|
| 1871-72 | 1 | | Royal Engineers | | | - | |
| | | | *Reigate Priory scratched. Royal Engineers walkover* | | | | |
| 1872-73 | 1 | 26.10.72 | **Windsor Home Park** | A | L | 2-4 | Clutton 2 |
| 1873-74 | 1 | 11.10.73 | **Woodford Wells** | A | L | 2-3 | Pawle, AN Other |
| 1874-75 | 1 | | bye | | | | |
| | 2 | 05.12.74 | **Maidenhead** | A | L | 1-2 | W Laker |
| 1875-76 | 1 | 30.10.75 | **Barnes** | H | W | 1-0 | |
| | 2 | 11.12.75 | **Cambridge University** | H | L | 0-8 | |
| 1876-77 | 1 | 11.11.76 | **Clapham Rovers** | A | L | 0-5 | |

# REMNANTS

*Entered FA Cup: 1877-78 – 1882-83.*

| | | | | | | | |
|---|---|---|---|---|---|---|---|
| 1877-78 | 1 | 07.11.77 | **St Stephen's** | H | W | 4-0 | |
| | 2 | 22.12.77 | **Hawks** | H | W | 2-0 | Keyser, AN Other |
| | 3 | 19.01.78 | **Upton Park** | A | L | 0-3 | |
| 1878-79 | 1 | | Unity FC | | | - | |
| | | | *Unity FC scratched. Remnants walkover* | | | | |
| | 2 | 21.12.78 | **Pilgrims** | H | W | 6-2 | Parry 4, E Hawtrey, Keyser |
| | 3 | 30.01.79 | **Darwen** | H | L | 2-3 | E Hawtrey 2 |
| 1879-80 | 1 | 15.11.79 | **Upton Park** | H | D | 1-1 | Cuppage |
| | 1r | 25.11.79 | **Upton Park** | A | L | 2-5 | E Hawtrey, Cuppage |
| 1880-81 | 1 | 13.11.80 | **Royal Engineers** | A | D | 0-0 | |
| | 1r | 20.11.80 | **Royal Engineers** | H | L | 0-1 | |
| 1881-82 | 1 | 29.10.81 | **West End** | A | L | 2-3 | Deare, Hughes |
| 1882-83 | 1 | | Reading Minster | | | - | |
| | | | *Remnants scratched. Reading Minster walkover* | | | | |

# RENTON

*Formed 1873. Entered FA Cup: 1886-87. Played at Tontine Park, Renton. One of the seven Scottish clubs that played in the FA Cup in the 1880s. Their victory over Blackburn Rovers in December 1886 ended Blackburn's record unbeaten run of 23 matches. Scottish FA Cup winners: 1885, 1888. Runners-up: 1875, 1886, 1895.*

| | | | | | | | | |
|---|---|---|---|---|---|---|---|---|
| 1886-87 | | 1 | 30.10.86 | **Accrington FC** | H | W | 1-0 | Campbell |
| | | 2 | 20.11.86 | **Blackburn Rovers** | H | D | 2-2aet | Campbell, AN Other |
| | | 2r | 04.12.86 | **Blackburn Rovers** | A | W | 2-0 | Barbour, McNee |
| | | 3 | 22.01.87 | **Preston North End** | H | L | 0-2 | |

# RHYL

*Formed 1870 as Rhyl Skull & Crossbones. First entered FA Cup: 1923-24. Welsh FA Cup winners: 1952, 1953. Runners-up: 1930, 1937, 1993. Welsh Amateur Cup winners: 1973. League clubs beaten: Stoke City, Wrexham, Wigan Borough, Halifax Town, Notts County, Hartlepool, Barnsley. Members of the League of Wales.*

| | | | | | | | | |
|---|---|---|---|---|---|---|---|---|
| 1926-27 | (Welsh) | 1 | 27.11.26 | **Stoke City** (3N) | H | D | 1-1 | Hoddinott |
| | | 1r | 02.12.26 | **Stoke City** | | D | 1-1aet | Lewis |
| | | 1 2r | 06.12.26 | **Stoke City** | | W | 2-1 | Murray, Groves |
| | | | | *played at Old Trafford* | | | | |
| | | 2 | 11.12.26 | **Wrexham** (3N) | H | W | 3-1 | Groves 2, Broad |
| | | 3 | 08.01.27 | **Darlington** (D2) | A | L | 1-2 | Hoddinott |
| 1927-28 | (Welsh) | 1 | 26.11.27 | **Wigan Borough** (3N) | H | W | 4-3 | Murray 2, Wood, Miller |
| | | 2 | 10.12.27 | **New Brighton** (3N) | A | L | 2-7 | Lindsay 2 (1p) |
| 1928-29 | (Welsh) | 1 | 24.11.28 | **Grantham Town** (ML) | A | L | 0-1 | |
| 1930-31 | (NWC) | 1 | 29.11.30 | **Scarborough** (ML) | A | L | 0-6 | |
| 1948-49 | (CC) | 1 | 04.12.48 | **Scarborough** | H | L | 0-2 | |
| 1949-50 | (CC) | 1 | 26.11.49 | **Rochdale** (3N) | H | L | 0-3 | |
| 1950-51 | (CC) | 1 | 25.11.50 | **Scarborough** (ML) | A | W | 2-1 | Brown, McMinn |
| | | 2 | 09.12.50 | **Norwich City** (3S) | H | L | 0-1 | |
| 1951-52 | (CC) | 1 | 24.11.51 | **Hartlepools Utd** (3N) | A | L | 0-2 | |
| 1952-53 | (CC) | 1 | 22.11.52 | **Bradford City** (3N) | A | L | 0-4 | |
| 1953-54 | (CC) | 1 | 21.11.53 | **Halifax Town** (3N) | A | D | 0-0 | |
| | | 1r | 26.11.53 | **Halifax Town** | H | W | 4-3aet | Valentine 2, Stafford, Hanlon |
| | | 2 | 12.12.53 | **Bristol City** (3S) | H | L | 0-3 | |
| 1954-55 | (CC) | 1 | 20.11.54 | **Selby Town** (YL) | A | L | 1-2 | Hitchen |
| 1955-56 | (CC) | 1 | 19.11.55 | **Bradford Park A** (3N) | H | L | 0-3 | |
| 1956-57 | (CC) | 1 | 17.11.56 | **Scarborough** (ML) | H | W | 3-2 | Hughes, Russell 2 |
| | | 2 | 08.12.56 | **Bishop Auckland** (NL) | H | W | 3-1 | H Williams, Donaldson, Hughes |
| | | 3 | 05.01.57 | **Notts County** (D2) | A | W | 3-1 | H Williams, Hughes, Meakin |
| | | 4 | 26.01.57 | **Bristol City** (D2) | A | L | 0-3 | |
| 1957-58 | (CC) | 1 | 16.11.57 | **Carlisle Utd** (3N) | A | L | 1-5 | C Williams |
| 1958-59 | (CC) | 1 | 15.11.58 | **Chesterfield** (D3) | A | L | 0-3 | |
| 1959-60 | (CC) | 1 | 14.11.59 | **Grimsby Town** (D3) | H | L | 1-2 | Bullock |
| 1960-61 | (CC) | 1 | 05.11.60 | **Oldham Athletic** (D4) | H | L | 0-1 | |
| 1961-62 | (CC) | 1 | 04.11.61 | **Hull City** (D3) | A | L | 0-5 | |
| 1962-63 | (CC) | 1 | 03.11.62 | **Barnsley** (D3) | A | L | 0-4 | |
| 1970-71 | (CC) | 1 | 21.11.70 | **Hartlepool** (D4) | H | W | 1-0 | Metcalf |
| | | 2 | 12.12.70 | **Barnsley** (D3) | H | D | 0-0 | |
| | | 2r | 15.12.70 | **Barnsley** | A | D | 1-1aet | Metcalf |
| | | 2 2r | 21.12.70 | **Barnsley** | A | W | 2-0 | E Davies, L Davies |
| | | 3 | 02.01.71 | **Swansea City** (D3) | A | L | 1-6 | L Davies |
| 1972-73 | (CC) | 1 | 18.11.72 | **Chesterfield** (D3) | A | L | 2-4 | Evans, L Davies |

# RINGMER

*Formed 1906. First entered FA Cup: 1970-71. Members of the Sussex County League.*

| | | | | | | | |
|---|---|---|---|---|---|---|---|
| 1970-71 | (SCL) | 1 | 21.11.70 | **Colchester Utd** (D4) | A | L | 0-3 |

# ROCHDALE

*Rochdale AFC was first formed in 1896 and the original club survived until January 1, 1901. Later in 1901 Rochdale Town were formed, but they folded in 1903. There was no club in existence between 1903 and 1907 when the present club was formed, playing in the FA Cup for the first time in the 1908-09 season.*

**as Rochdale AFC**

| | |
|---|---|
| 1897-98 | 1q Bay Moss Exchange (A) 5-3; 2q Horwich (H) 1-1; 2qr Horwich (A) 2-6 |
| 1898-99 | 2q Middleton (A) 2-3 |
| 1899-00 | 1q Middleton (A) 0-2 |
| 1900-01 | 1q Rossendale Utd (H) 1-0; 2q Freetown (A) 3-0; 3q Workington scratched |

**as Rochdale Town**

| | |
|---|---|
| 1901-02 | did not enter |
| 1902-03 | did not enter |

**as Rochdale**

| | | | | | | | |
|---|---|---|---|---|---|---|---|
| 1908-09 (LC) | | | 1q Accrington Stanley (H) 3-5 | | | | |
| 1909-10 (LC) | | | 1q Haslingden (A) 1-3 | | | | |
| 1910-11 (LC) | | | P Earlestown (H) 2-1; 1q St Helens Town(A) 2-1; 2q Heywood Utd (A) 4-3; 3q St Helens Recreation (H) 1-0; 4q Stockport County (H) 0-0; 4qr Stockport County (A) 0-0; 4q 2r Stockport County (at Oldham) 1-0; 5q Luton Town (H) 1-1; 5qr Luton Town (A) 2-3 | | | | |
| 1911-12 (LC) | | | 4q Barrow (A) 0-1 | | | | |
| 1912-13 (CL) | | | 1q Macclesfield (A) 5-3; 2q Newton Heath Athletic (A) 5-0; 3q Stalybridge Celtic (H) 2-1; 4q Accrington Stanley (H) 6-1; 5q Darlington (H) 1-1; 5qr Darlington (A) 1-0 | | | | |
| | 1 | 11.01.13 | **Swindon Town** (SL) | H | L | 0-2 | |
| 1913-14 (CL) | | | 4q Barrow (A) 0-3 | | | | |
| 1914-15 (CL) | | | 4q Stalybridge Celtic (H) 3-2; 5q Hartlepool Utd (H) 2-0; 6q Watford (H) 2-0 | | | | |
| | 1 | 09.01.15 | **Gillingham** (SL) | H | W | 2-0 | Walker, Hawksworth |
| | 2 | 30.01.15 | **Oldham Athletic** (D1) | A | L | 0-3 | |
| 1919-20 (CL) | | | 4q Monks Hall (H) 1-0; 5q Stalybridge Celtic (H) 1-0; 6q South Liverpool (A) 2-1 | | | | |
| | 1 | 10.01.20 | **Arsenal** (D1) | A | L | 2-4 | Mallalieu 2 |
| 1920-21 (CL) | | | 4q Fleetwood (H) 1-0; 5q Tranmere Rovers (H) 1-0; 6q Coventry City (A) 1-1; 6qr Coventry City (H) 2-1 | | | | |
| | 1 | 08.01.21 | **Plymouth Argyle** (D3) | A | L | 0-2 | |
| 1921-22 (3N) | | | 5q Nelson (A) 2-3 | | | | |
| 1922-23 (3N) | | | 4q Nelson (H) 0-1 | | | | |
| 1923-24 (3N) | | | 4q Skelmersdale Utd (H) 4-0; 5q Accrington Stanley (A) 0-1 | | | | |
| 1924-25 (3N) | | | 5q Halifax Town (A) 1-0; 6q Norwich City (A) 0-1 | | | | |
| 1925-26 (3N) | 1 | 28.11.25 | **West Stanley** (NEL) | H | - | 1-1ab | Hughes |
| | | | *abandoned at half-time – ground unplayable* | | | | |
| | 1r | 01.12.25 | **West Stanley** (NEL) | H | W | 4-0 | Hughes 2, Martin (p), Ferguson |
| | 2 | 12.12.25 | **Chilton Coll** (NAll) | A | D | 1-1 | Ferguson |
| | 2r | 17.12.25 | **Chilton Coll** | H | L | 1-2 | Parkes |
| 1926-27 (3N) | 1 | 27.11.26 | **Accrington Stanley** (3N) | A | L | 3-4 | Whitehurst 2, Bertram |
| 1927-28 (3N) | 1 | 26.11.27 | **Crook Town** (NL) | H | W | 8-2 | Whitehurst 4, Clenmell 3, Martin |
| | 2 | 10.12.27 | **Darlington** (3N) | A | L | 1-2 | Bertram |
| 1928-29 (3N) | 1 | 24.11.28 | **Chesterfield** (3N) | A | L | 2-3 | Martin, Milsom |
| 1929-30 (3N) | 1 | 30.11.29 | **Accrington Stanley** (3N) | A | L | 1-3 | Milsom |
| 1930-31 (3N) | 1 | 29.11.30 | **Doncaster Rovers** (3N) | H | L | 1-2 | Cowan |
| 1931-32 (3N) | 1 | 28.11.31 | **Scunthorpe Utd** (ML) | A | L | 1-2 | Murray |
| 1932-33 (3N) | 1 | 26.11.32 | **Stockport County** (3N) | H | L | 0-2 | |
| 1933-34 (3N) | 1 | 25.11.33 | **Sutton Town** (DSL) | A | L | 1-2 | Rigby |
| 1934-35 (3N) | 1 | 24.11.34 | **Wrexham** (3N) | A | L | 1-4 | Smith |
| 1935-36 (3N) | 1 | 30.11.35 | **Halifax Town** (3N) | A | L | 0-4 | |
| 1936-37 (3N) | 1 | 28.11.36 | **Crewe Alexandra** (3N) | A | L | 1-5 | Hunt |
| 1937-38 (3N) | 1 | 27.11.37 | **Lincoln City** (3N) | H | D | 1-1 | Hunt |
| | 1r | 01.12.37 | **Lincoln City** | A | L | 0-2 | |
| 1938-39 (3N) | 1 | 26.11.38 | **Halifax Town** (3N) | A | L | 3-7 | Wynn, Duff, Goodier |
| 1945-46 (3N) | 1 1L | 17.11.45 | **Stockport County** (3N) | A | W | 2-1 | Brindle, Woods |
| | 1 2L | 24.11.45 | **Stockport County** | H | D | 1-1 | Hargreaves |
| | 2 1L | 08.12.45 | **Tranmere Rovers** (3N) | A | L | 1-3 | Cunliffe |
| | 2 2L | 15.12.45 | **Tranmere Rovers** | H | W | 3-0 | Hargreaves 2, Makin |
| | 3 1L | 05.01.46 | **Bury** (D2) | A | D | 3-3 | Cunliffe 2, Reynolds |
| | 3 2L | 08.01.46 | **Bury** | H | L | 2-4 | Hargreaves 2 (1p) |
| 1946-47 (3N) | 1 | 30.11.46 | **Bishop Auckland** (NL) | H | W | 6-1 | Woods, Hargreaves 2, Birch, Barkas, Carruthers |
| | 2 | 14.12.46 | **Hartlepools Utd** (3N) | H | W | 6-1 | Woods 3, Carruthers 2, Cunliffe |
| | 3 | 11.01.47 | **Charlton Athletic** (D1) | A | L | 1-3 | Woods |
| 1947-48 (3N) | 1 | 29.11.47 | **York City** (3N) | A | W | 1-0 | Birch (p) |
| | 2 | 13.12.47 | **Gillingham** (SL) | H | D | 1-1aet | O'Donnell |
| | 2r | 20.12.47 | **Gillingham** | A | L | 0-3 | |
| 1948-49 (3N) | 1 | 27.11.48 | **Barrow** (3N) | H | D | 1-1aet | Middlebrough |
| | | | *played at Boundary Park, Oldham* | | | | |
| | 1r | 04.12.48 | **Barrow** | A | L | 0-2 | |
| 1949-50 (3N) | 1 | 26.11.49 | **Rhyl** (CC) | A | W | 3-0 | Arthur, Connor 2 |
| | 2 | 10.12.49 | **Notts County** (3S) | H | L | 1-2 | Brown |

| | | | | | | | | |
|---|---|---|---|---|---|---|---|---|
| 1950-51 | (3N) | 1 | 25.11.50 | **Willington** (NL) | H | W | 3-1 | Whitehouse 2 (1p), Middlebrough |
| | | 2 | 09.12.50 | **Ashington** (NEL) | A | W | 2-1 | Livesey, Steen |
| | | 3 | 09.01.51 | **Chelsea** (D1) | H | L | 2-3 | Connor, Arthur |
| 1951-52 | (3N) | 1 | 24.11.51 | **Ilkeston Town** (ML) | A | W | 2-0 | Betts 2 |
| | | 2 | 15.12.51 | **Gillingham** (3S) | A | W | 3-0 | Tomlinson 2, Arthur |
| | | 3 | 12.01.52 | **Leeds Utd** (D2) | H | L | 0-2 | |
| 1952-53 | (3N) | 1 | 22.11.52 | **Bradford Park A** (3N) | A | L | 1-2 | J Lynn (p) |
| 1953-54 | (3N) | 1 | 21.11.53 | **Grimsby Town** (3N) | A | L | 0-2 | |
| 1954-55 | (3N) | 1 | 20.11.54 | **Tranmere Rovers** (3N) | A | D | 3-3 | Mitcheson, Anders, Gemmill |
| | | 1r | 23.11.54 | **Tranmere Rovers** | H | W | 1-0 | Gemmil |
| | | 2 | 11.12.54 | **Hinckley Athletic** (WMRL) | H | W | 2-1 | Kendall, Anders |
| | | 3 | 08.01.55 | **Charlton Athletic** (D1) | H | L | 1-3 | Haines |
| 1955-56 | (3N) | 1 | 19.11.55 | **York City** (3N) | H | L | 0-1 | |
| 1956-57 | (3N) | 1 | 17.11.56 | **Scunthorpe Utd** (3N) | A | L | 0-1 | |
| 1957-58 | (3N) | 1 | 16.11.57 | **Darlington** (3N) | H | L | 0-2 | |
| 1958-59 | (D3) | 1 | 15.11.58 | **Hartlepools Utd** (D4) | A | D | 1-1 | Wainwright |
| | | 1r | 19.11.58 | **Hartlepools Utd** | H | D | 3-3aet | Finney, Wainwright, Spencer |
| | | 1 2r | 27.11.58 | **Hartlepools Utd** *played at Old Trafford* | | L | 1-2aet | Wainwright |
| 1959-60 | (D4) | 1 | 14.11.59 | **Carlisle Utd** (D4) | H | D | 2-2 | Cairns, Collins |
| | | 1r | 17.11.59 | **Carlisle Utd** | A | W | 3-1aet | Brown, Barnes, Cairns |
| | | 2 | 05.12.59 | **Bradford City** (D3) | H | D | 1-1 | Spencer |
| | | 2r | 09.12.59 | **Bradford City** | A | L | 1-2 | Anderson |
| 1960-61 | (D4) | 1 | 05.11.60 | **Crewe Alexandra** (D4) | A | D | 1-1 | Pollitt |
| | | 1r | 08.11.60 | **Crewe Alexandra** | H | L | 1-2 | Cairns |
| 1961-62 | (D4) | 1 | 04.11.61 | **Halifax Town** (D3) | H | W | 2-0 | Milburn (p), Hepton |
| | | 2 | 25.11.61 | **Wrexham** (D4) | H | L | 1-2 | Cairns |
| 1962-63 | (D4) | 1 | 03.11.62 | **York City** (D4) | A | D | 0-0 | |
| | | 1r | 06.11.62 | **York City** | H | L | 1-2 | Phoenix |
| 1963-64 | (D4) | 1 | 16.11.63 | **Chorley** (LC) | H | W | 2-1 | Watson, Richardson |
| | | 2 | 07.12.63 | **Barnsley** (D3) | A | L | 1-3 | Richardson |
| 1964-65 | (D4) | 1 | 14.11.64 | **Workington** (D3) | A | L | 0-2 | |
| 1965-66 | (D4) | 1 | 13.11.65 | **Fleetwood** (LC) | A | D | 2-2 | Lister, Sievwright |
| | | 1r | 17.11.65 | **Fleetwood** | H | W | 5-0 | Jenkins 3, Calloway, Lister |
| | | 2 | 08.12.65 | **Altrincham** (CC) | H | L | 1-3 | Jenkins |
| 1966-67 | (D4) | 1 | 26.11.66 | **Barrow** (D4) | H | L | 1-3 | Storf |
| 1967-68 | (D4) | 1 | 09.12.67 | **Tranmere Rovers** (D3) | A | L | 1-5 | Fletcher |
| 1968-69 | (D4) | 1 | 09.11.68 | **Barnsley** (D3) | A | D | 0-0 | |
| | | 1r | 18.11.68 | **Barnsley** | H | L | 0-1 | |
| 1969-70 | (D3) | 1 | 15.11.69 | **Workington** (D4) | A | L | 1-2 | Whitehead |
| 1970-71 | (D3) | 1 | 21.11.70 | **Oldham Athletic** (D4) | H | W | 2-0 | Arrowsmith 2 |
| | | 2 | 12.12.70 | **Darlington** (D4) | A | W | 2-0 | Cross, Downes |
| | | 3 | 11.01.71 | **Coventry City** (D1) | H | W | 2-1 | Cross, Butler |
| | | 4 | 23.01.71 | **Colchester Utd** (D4) | H | D | 3-3 | Buck 2, Ashworth |
| | | 4r | 25.01.71 | **Colchester Utd** | A | L | 0-5 | |
| 1971-72 | (D3) | 1 | 20.11.71 | **Barnsley** (D3) | H | L | 1-3 | Arrowsmith |
| 1972-73 | (D3) | 1 | 18.11.72 | **Bangor City** (NPL) | H | L | 1-2 | Jenkins (p) |
| 1973-74 | (D3) | 1 | 24.11.73 | **S Shields (1936)** (NPL) | H | W | 2-0 | Marsh, Brogden |
| | | 2 | 15.12.73 | **Grantham Town** (SL) | A | D | 1-1 | Brogden |
| | | 2r | 18.12.73 | **Grantham Town** | H | L | 3-5aet | Taylor, Hanvey, Downes |
| 1974-75 | (D4) | 1 | 23.11.74 | **Marine** (CC) | H | D | 0-0 | |
| | | 1r | 27.11.74 | **Marine** | A | W | 2-1aet | Carrick, Young |
| | | 2 | 14.12.74 | **Tranmere Rovers** (D3) | H | D | 1-1 | Brears |
| | | 2r | 16.12.74 | **Tranmere Rovers** | A | L | 0-1 | |
| 1975-76 | (D4) | 1 | 22.11.75 | **Workington** (D4) | A | D | 1-1 | Ferguson |
| | | 1r | 25.11.75 | **Workington** | H | W | 2-1aet | Mounthead, Whelan |
| | | 2 | 13.12.75 | **Gateshead Utd** (NPL) | A | D | 1-1 | Albeson og |
| | | 2r | 16.12.75 | **Gateshead Utd** | H | W | 3-1 | Mountford, Morrison og, Tobin |
| | | 3 | 03.01.76 | **Norwich City** (D1) | A | D | 1-1 | Mullington |
| | | 3r | 06.01.76 | **Norwich City** | H | D | 0-0aet | |
| | | 3 2r | 13.01.76 | **Norwich City** | A | L | 1-2 | Mountford |
| 1976-77 | (D4) | 1 | 20.11.76 | **Northwich V** (NPL) | H | D | 1-1 | Helliwell |

| | | | | | | | |
|---|---|---|---|---|---|---|---|
| | 1r | 22.11.76 | **Northwich V** | A | D | 0-0aet | |
| | 1 2r | 29.11.76 | **Northwich V** | | L | 1-2 | Tarbuck |
| | | | *played at Maine Road* | | | | |
| 1977-78 (D4) | 1 | 26.11.77 | **Scarborough** (NPL) | A | L | 2-4 | Owen 2 |
| 1978-79 (D4) | 1 | 25.11.78 | **Droylesden** (CC) | H | L | 0-1 | |
| 1979-80 (D4) | 1 | 24.11.79 | **Scunthorpe Utd** (D4) | H | W | 2-1 | Hart, Jones |
| | 2 | 15.12.79 | **Tranmere Rovers** (D4) | A | D | 2-2 | Hilditch 2 |
| | 2r | 18.12.79 | **Tranmere Rovers** | H | W | 2-1 | Hilditch, Hart |
| | 3 | 08.01.80 | **Bury** (D3) | H | D | 1-1 | O'Coughlin |
| | 3r | 21.01.80 | **Bury** | A | L | 2-3 | Scaife 2 |
| 1980-81 (D4) | 1 | 22.11.80 | **Mansfield Town** (D4) | A | L | 1-3 | Jones (p) |
| 1981-82 (D4) | 1 | 21.11.81 | **Hull City** (D4) | H | D | 2-2 | Dolan, Esser |
| | 1r | 24.11.81 | **Hull City** | A | D | 2-2aet | Burke, Esser |
| | 1 2r | 30.11.81 | **Hull City** | | L | 0-1aet | |
| | | | *played at Elland Road* | | | | |
| 1982-83 (D4) | 1 | 20.11.82 | **Altrincham** (APL) | A | L | 1-2 | Wellings (p) |
| 1983-84 (D4) | 1 | 19.11.83 | **Crewe Alexandra** (D4) | H | W | 1-0 | Farrell |
| | 2 | 13.12.83 | **York City** (D4) | A | W | 2-0 | Johnson 2 |
| | 3 | 07.01.84 | **Telford Utd** (APL) | H | L | 1-4 | Allatt |
| 1984-85 (D4) | 1 | 17.11.84 | **Doncaster Rovers** (D3) | H | L | 1-2 | Russell og |
| 1985-86 (D4) | 1 | 16.11.85 | **Darlington** (D3) | H | W | 2-1 | Taylor 2 |
| | 2 | 07.12.85 | **Scunthorpe Utd** (D4) | A | D | 2-2 | Taylor 2 (1p) |
| | 2r | 10.12.85 | **Scunthorpe Utd** | H | W | 2-1 | Taylor, Moore |
| | 3 | 09.01.86 | **Manchester Utd** (D1) | A | L | 0-2 | |
| 1986-87 (D4) | 1 | 15.11.86 | **Nuneaton B** (APL) | A | W | 3-0 | Wakenshaw, Mills, Johnson |
| | 2 | 06.12.86 | **Wrexham** (D4) | H | L | 1-4 | Wakenshaw |
| 1987-88 (D4) | 1 | 14.11.87 | **Wrexham** | H | L | 0-2 | |
| 1988-89 (D4) | 1 | 19.11.88 | **Huddersfield Town** (D3) | A | D | 1-1 | Edmonds |
| | 1r | 28.11.88 | **Huddersfield Town** | H | L | 3-4 | Beaumont, Reid, Frain |
| 1989-90 (D4) | 1 | 17.11.89 | **Marine** (NPL) | A | W | 1-0 | Stonehouse |
| | | | *played at Anfield* | | | | |
| | 2 | 09.12.89 | **Lincoln City** (D4) | H | W | 3-0 | Ward, Johnson, O'Shaughnessy |
| | 3 | 06.01.90 | **Whitley Bay** (NPL) | H | W | 1-0 | Johnson |
| | 4 | 27.01.90 | **Northampton Town** (D3) | H | W | 3-0 | O'Shaughnessy, Dawson, Goodison (p) |
| | 5 | 17.02.90 | **Crystal Palace** (D1) | A | L | 0-1 | |
| 1990-91 (D4) | 1 | 17.11.90 | **Scunthorpe Utd** (D4) | H | D | 1-1 | Costello |
| | 1r | 20.11.90 | **Scunthorpe Utd** | A | L | 1-2aet | Costello |
| 1991-92 (D4) | 1 | 16.11.91 | **Gretna** (NL) | A | D | 0-0 | |
| | 1r | 27.11.91 | **Gretna** | H | W | 3-1 | Bowden, Milner, Flounders |
| | 2 | 07.12.91 | **Huddersfield Town** (D3) | H | L | 1-2 | Halpin |
| 1992-93 (D3) | 1 | 14.11.92 | **Blackpool** (D2) | A | D | 1-1 | Whitehall |
| | 1r | 25.11.92 | **Blackpool** | H | W | 1-0aet | Reid |
| | 2 | 05.12.92 | **Bolton Wanderers** (D2) | A | L | 0-4 | |
| 1993-94 (D3) | 1 | 13.11.93 | **Chesterfield** (D3) | A | W | 1-0 | Stuart (p) |
| | 2 | 04.12.93 | **Burnley** (D2) | A | L | 1-4 | Whitehall (p) |
| 1994-95 (D3) | 1 | 12.11.94 | **Walsall** (D3) | A | L | 0-3 | |
| 1995-96 (D3) | 1 | 11.11.95 | **Rotherham Utd** (D2) | H | W | 5-3 | Moulden 2, Whitehall (p), Peake 2 |
| | 2 | 02.12.95 | **Darlington** (D3) | H | D | 2-2 | Deary 2 |
| | 2r | 12.12.95 | **Darlington** | A | W | 1-0 | Martin |
| | 3 | 06.01.96 | **Liverpool** (PL) | A | L | 0-7 | |
| 1996-97 (D3) | 1 | 16.11.96 | **Macclesfield T** (Conf) | A | W | 2-0 | Deary, T Johnson |
| | 2 | 07.12.96 | **Notts County** (D2) | A | L | 1-3 | Thackeray |
| 1997-98 (D3) | 1 | 15.11.97 | **Wrexham** (D2) | H | L | 0-2 | |
| 1998-99 (D3) | 1 | 14.11.98 | **Scarborough** (D3) | A | D | 1-1 | Bryson |
| | 1r | 24.11.98 | **Scarborough** | H | W | 2-0 | Mornington, Bryson |
| | 2 | 05.12.98 | **Rotherham Utd** (D3) | H | D | 0-0 | |
| | 2r | 15.12.98 | **Rotherham Utd** | A | L | 0-4 | |
| 1999-00 (D3) | 1 | 30.10.99 | **Burton Albion** (SL) | A | D | 0-0 | |
| | 1r | 09.11.99 | **Burton Albion** | H | W | 3-0 | Platt, Peake, Dowe |
| | 2 | 20.11.99 | **Wrexham** (D2) | A | L | 1-2 | Atkinson |
| 2000-01 (D3) | 1 | 18.11.00 | **Cambridge Utd** (D2) | A | L | 1-2 | Platt |
| 2001-02 (D3) | 1 | 17.11.01 | **Tamworth** (SL) | A | D | 1-1 | Doughty |

| | | | | | | | |
|---|---|---|---|---|---|---|---|
| | 1r | 27.11.01 | **Tamworth** | H | W | 1-0 | Oliver |
| | 2 | 08.12.01 | **Blackpool** (D2) | A | L | 0-2 | |
| 2002-03 (D3) | 1 | 16.11.02 | **Peterborough Utd** (D2) | H | W | 3-2 | Connor, Platt, Beach |
| | 2 | 07.12.02 | **Bristol Rovers** (D3) | A | D | 1-1 | Platt |
| | 2r | 17.12.02 | **Bristol Rovers** | H | W | 3-2 | Platt, Connor, McCourt |
| | 3 | 04.01.03 | **Preston North End** (D1) | A | W | 2-1 | McEvilly, Simpson |
| | 4 | 25.01.03 | **Coventry City** (D1) | H | W | 2-0 | Connor, Griffiths |
| | 5 | 16.02.03 | **Wolverhampton W** (D1) | A | L | 1-3 | Melaugh |

# ROCHESTER

*Formed 1866. Entered FA Cup: 1875-76 – 1892-93. Played at The Borstal Grounds, near the Kings's Head pub, Rochester.*

| | | | | | | | |
|---|---|---|---|---|---|---|---|
| 1875-76 | 1 | 06.11.75 | **Herts Rangers** | A | L | 0-4 | |
| 1876-77 | 1 | 04.11.76 | **Highbury Union** | H | W | 5-0 | G Blackett, Gramshaw, Prall, Ramage, og |
| | 2 | 16.12.76 | **Swifts** | H | W | 1-0 | J Blackett |
| | 3 | 03.02.77 | **Cambridge University** | A | L | 0-4 | |
| 1877-78 | 1 | 07.11.77 | **Upton Park** | A | L | 0-3 | |
| 1878-79 | 1 | 02.11.78 | **Forest School** | A | L | 2-7 | |
| 1879-80 | 1 | 15.11.79 | **Wanderers** | H | L | 0-6 | |
| 1880-81 | 1 | 13.11.80 | **Dreadnought FC** | H | L | 1-2 | A Henry |
| 1881-82 | 1 | 05.11.81 | **Barnes** | A | L | 1-3 | |
| 1882-83 | 1 | 04.11.82 | **Hotspur FC** | H | W | 2-0 | S Henry, Jones |
| | 2 | | bye | | | | |
| | 3 | 16.12.82 | **Old Etonians** | A | L | 0-7 | |
| 1883-84 | 1 | 03.11.83 | **Uxbridge** | H | W | 2-1 | |
| | 2 | 01.12.83 | **Clapham Rovers** | A | L | 0-7 | |
| 1884-85 | 1 | 08.11.84 | **Reading** | A | L | 0-2 | |
| 1885-86 | 1 | 31.10.85 | **Reading** | H | W | 6-1 | Mallinson 4, Mitchell, H Prall |
| | 2 | 21.11.85 | **Swifts** | A | L | 1-5 | |
| 1886-87 | 1 | 23.10.86 | **Marlow** | H | L | 0-2 | |
| 1887-88 | 1 | 15.10.87 | **Royal Engineers** | A | W | 3-0 | |
| | | | *FA ordered match to be replayed after protest but Rochester scratched.* | | | | |

# ROMFORD

*Formed 1929. Entered FA Cup: 1929-30 – 1977-78. FA Amateur Cup winners: 1949 (the first winners at Wembley Stadium). Disbanded 1977. Following the demise of this club the third senior Romford club was formed in 1992. Members of the Essex Senior League.*

| | | | | | | | |
|---|---|---|---|---|---|---|---|
| 1932-33 (AL) | 1 | 26.11.32 | **Bristol City** (3S) | A | L | 0-4 | |
| 1935-36 (AL) | 1 | 30.11.35 | **Folkestone** (SL) | H | D | 3-3 | Osborne 2, Patterson (p) |
| | 1r | 04.12.35 | **Folkestone** | A | L | 1-2aet | Thomas |
| 1945-46 (IL) | 1 1L | 17.11.45 | **Brighton** (3S) | A | L | 1-3 | Longton og |
| | 1 2L | 24.11.45 | **Brighton** | H | D | 1-1 | Bolton |
| 1948-49 (IL) | 1 | 27.11.48 | **Yeovil Town** (SL) | A | L | 0-4 | |
| 1949-50 (IL) | 1 | 26.11.49 | **Yeovil Town** | A | L | 1-4 | Jennings |
| 1960-61 (SL) | 1 | 05.11.60 | **Sutton Utd** (AL) | A | D | 2-2 | Beck og, Holmes |
| | 1r | 09.11.60 | **Sutton Utd** | H | W | 5-0 | Holmes 2, Hencher 2 (2ps), Sanders |
| | 2 | 26.11.60 | **Northampton Town** (D4) | H | L | 1-5 | Cappi |
| 1961-62 (SL) | 1 | 04.11.61 | **Walthamstow Ave** (IL) | A | W | 3-2 | Lloyd, Cappi, Allison (p) |
| | 2 | 25.11.61 | **Watford** (D3) | H | L | 1-3 | Evans (p) |
| 1964-65 (SL) | 1 | 14.11.64 | **Enfield** (IL) | H | D | 0-0 | |
| | 1r | 17.11.64 | **Enfield** | A | D | 0-0aet | |
| | 1 2r | 23.11.64 | **Enfield** | | L | 2-4 | Coates, Brown |
| | | | *played at Highbury* | | | | |
| 1965-66 (SL) | 1 | 13.11.65 | **Luton Town** (D4) | H | D | 1-1 | Barnett |
| | 1r | 18.11.65 | **Luton Town** | A | L | 0-1 | |
| 1967-68 (SL) | 1 | 09.12.67 | **Wimbledon** (SL) | A | L | 0-3 | |
| 1971-72 (SL) | 1 | 20.11.71 | **Witney Town** (HEL) | A | W | 3-0 | King 2, Chandler |
| | 2 | 11.12.71 | **Gillingham** (D4) | H | L | 0-1 | |
| 1974-75 (SL) | 1 | 23.11.74 | **Ilford** (IL) | H | L | 0-2 | |
| 1975-76 (SL) | 1 | 22.11.75 | **Tooting & M** (IL) | H | L | 0-1 | |

# ROMFORD (1876)

*Formed 1876. Entered FA Cup: 1878-79 – 1914-15. Played their early games at Great Mawneys fields, Romford. Disbanded during World War One.*

| | | | | | | | |
|---|---|---|---|---|---|---|---|
| 1878-79 | 1 | 02.11.78 | **Ramblers** | H | W | 3-1 | Barnes, Lyon, Thirlwell |
| | 2 | 21.12.78 | **Swifts** | A | L | 1-3 | Lyon |
| 1879-80 | 1 | 08.11.79 | **Clapham Rovers** | A | L | 0-7 | |
| 1880-81 | 1 | 13.11.80 | **Reading Minster** | H | D | 1-1 | |
| | | | *Reading Minster scratched before replay. Romford (1876) walkover* | | | | |
| | 2 | | bye | | | | |
| | 3 | 12.02.81 | **Reading Abbey** | H | W | 2-0 | Cornell, AN Other |
| | 4 | 19.02.81 | **Marlow** | H | W | 2-1 | Cornell 2 |
| | 5 | 05.03.81 | **Darwen** | A | L | 0-15 | |
| 1881-82 | 1 | | Rangers FC, London | | | - | |
| | | | *Rangers FC scratched. Romford (1876) walkover* | | | | |
| | 2 | 03.12.81 | **Reading Minster** | A | L | 1-3 | |
| 1882-83 | 1 | 21.10.82 | **Etonian Ramblers** | A | L | 2-6 | |
| 1883-84 | 1 | 03.11.83 | **Woodford Bridge** | H | W | 3-0 | JA Macfarlane, Earle, Oliver |
| | 2 | 01.12.83 | **Mosquitoes** | H | W | 3-1 | Cornell, Earle, Goadby |
| | 3 | 29.12.83 | **Brentwood** | H | L | 1-4 | Cornell |
| 1884-85 | 1 | 01.11.84 | **Clapton** | H | W | 3-2 | Clark, Goadby, Oliver |
| | 2 | 06.12.84 | **Dulwich** | H | W | 3-0 | Oliver 2, Wright |
| | 3 | | bye | | | | |
| | 4 | 19.01.85 | **Blackburn Rovers** | A | L | 0-8 | |
| 1885-86 | 1 | 31.10.85 | **Hanover Utd** | A | D | 1-1 | |
| | 1r | 07.11.85 | **Hanover Utd** | H | W | 3-0 | |
| | 2 | | bye | | | | |
| | 3 | 12.12.85 | **Old Westminsters** | A | L | 1-5 | |

# ROSSENDALE UNITED

*Formed 1877 as Rossendale FC. Reformed as Rossendale United 1898. First entered FA Cup: 1883-84. Members of the Northern Premier League.*

**as Rossendale FC**

| | | | | | | | |
|---|---|---|---|---|---|---|---|
| 1883-84 | 1 | 17.11.83 | **Irwell Springs** | H | W | 6-2 | |
| | | | *FA disqualified Rossendale for professionalism. Irwell Springs re-instated* | | | | |
| 1884-85 | 1 | 11.10.84 | **Blackburn Rovers** | A | L | 0-11 | |
| 1885-86 | 1 | 24.10.85 | **Clitheroe Low Moor** | H | W | 6-2 | |
| | 2 | 21.11.85 | **Padiham** | H | W | 9-1 | |
| | 3 | 12.12.85 | **Church FC** | A | L | 1-5 | |
| 1886-87 | 2 | 20.11.86 | **Cowlairs** | H | L | 2-10 | |
| 1887-88 | 1 | 15.10.87 | **Accrington FC** | A | L | 0-11 | |

**as Rossendale Utd**

| | | | | | | | |
|---|---|---|---|---|---|---|---|
| 1971-72 (CC) | 1 | 23.11.71 | **Altrincham** (NPL) | H | W | 1-0 | Wild (p) |
| | 2 | 11.12.71 | **Bolton Wanderers** (D3) | H | L | 1-4 | Clay |
| | | | *played at Gigg Lane, Bury* | | | | |
| 1975-76 (CC) | 1 | 22.11.75 | **Shrewsbury Town** (D3) | H | L | 0-1 | |

# ROTHERHAM COUNTY

*Formed 1877 as Thornhill United. Rotherham County 1905. Entered FA Cup: 1901-02 – 1924-25. Merged with Rotherham Town to form Rotherham United 1925.*

| | | | | | | |
|---|---|---|---|---|---|---|
| 1919-20 (D2) | | | 6q West Stanley (A) 0-1 | | | |
| 1920-21 (D2) | | | 6q Luton Town (H) 1-3 | | | |
| 1921-22 (D2) | | | 5q Coventry City (H) 1-1 5qr Coventry City (A) 0-1 | | | |
| 1922-23 (D2) | 1 | 13.01.23 | **Chelsea** (D1) | A | L | 0-1 |
| 1923-24 (3N) | | | 5q Scunthorpe Utd (A) 1-1; 5qr Scunthorpe Utd (H) 2-0; 6q Halifax Town (A) 0-1 | | | |
| 1924-25 (3N) | | | 5q Doncaster Rovers (H) 2-3 | | | |

# ROTHERHAM TOWN

*Formed 1870 as Rotherham. Added 'Town' in late 1880s. Entered FA Cup: 1883-84 – 1924-25. Members of the Football League 1893-96. Merged with Rotherham County to form Rotherham United 1925.*

| | | | | | | | |
|---|---|---|---|---|---|---|---|
| 1883-84 | 1 | 10.11.83 | **Chesterfield Spital** | A | D | 1-1 | |
| | 1r | 17.11.83 | **Chesterfield Spital** | H | W | 7-2 | Douglas 2, Musson 2, Lampard 2, Kelly |

| | | | | | | | | |
|---|---|---|---|---|---|---|---|---|
| | | 2 | 01.12.83 | **Lockwood Bros** | A | L | 1-3 | |
| 1884-85 | | 1 | 08.11.84 | **Nottingham Forest** | A | L | 0-5 | |
| 1885-86 | | 1 | 24.10.85 | **Notts County** | A | L | 0-15 | |
| 1886-87 | | | | | bye | | | |
| | | 2 | 20.11.86 | **Staveley** | A | L | 0-4 | |
| 1887-88 | | 1 | 15.10.87 | **Matlock Town** | A | W | 3-2 | McCormack 2,AN Other |
| | | 2 | 05.11.87 | **Derby Junction** | A | L | 2-3 | Medley, McCormack |
| 1888-89 | | | | 1q Doncaster Rovers (A) 9-1; 2q Owlerton (A) 1-2 | | | | |
| 1889-90 | (ML) | | | 1q Doncaster Rovers (H) 2-0; 2q Redcar (A) 8-1; 3q Rotherham Swifts (A) 0-0aet; 3qr Rotherham Swifts (H) 2-1; 4q Sheffield Utd (H) 2-2; 4qr Sheffield Utd (A) 1-2 | | | | |
| 1890-91 | (ML) | | | 1q Sheffield FC (A) 13-0; 2q Owlerton (A) 4-1; 3q Beeston (H) 6-1; Long Eaton Rangers (A) 1-2 | | | | |
| 1891-92 | (ML) | | | 1q Attercliffe (A) 2-1; 2q Kilnhurst (H) 5-1; 3q Gainsborough Tinity (A) 2-3 | | | | |
| 1892-93 | (ML) | | | 1q Grantham Rovers (H) 4-0; 2q Kilnhurst (A) 3-0; 3q Lincoln City (A) 0-2 | | | | |
| 1893-94 | (D2) | | | 1q Worksop Town (A) 2-3 | | | | |
| 1894-95 | (D2) | | | 1q Gainsborough Tinity (A) 1-5 | | | | |
| 1895-96 | (D2) | | | 1q Barnsley St Peters (H) 1-1; 1qr Barnsley St Peters (A) 7-3; 2q Doncaster Rovers (A) 7-0; 3q Gainsborough Tinity (A) 2-0; 4q Grimsby Town (A) 0-4 | | | | |
| 1907-08 | (ML) | 1 | 11.01.08 | **West Ham Utd** (SL) | A | L | 0-1 | |

# ROTHERHAM UNITED

*Formed 1925 when Rotherham County merged with Rotherham Town. FA Cup best performance: 5th round, 1953, 1968. Record FA Cup win: 6-0 v Spennymoor United, 2nd round, 17.12.1977; 6-0 v Wolverhampton Wanderers, 1st round, 16.11.1986; 6-0 v King's Lynn, 2nd round, 06.12.1997. Record FA Cup defeat: 0-6 v Brighton, 4th round, second replay, 08.02.1960.*

**as Thornhill Utd**

| | |
|---|---|
| 1901-02 | P Denaby (A) 2-2; Pr Denaby (H) 2-3 |
| 1902-03 | 1q Channing R walkover; 2q Rotherham Town (A) 1-3 |
| 1903-04 | P Sheffield FC (H) 2-0; 1q Mexborough West End (A) 0-3 |
| 1904-05 | ExP Rotherham Town (A) 1-0; P Mexborough (A) 0-1 |

**as Rotherham Utd**

| | | | | | | | | |
|---|---|---|---|---|---|---|---|---|
| 1925-26 | (3N) | 1 | 28.11.25 | **Halifax Town** (3N) | | W | 3-0 | Lee, Boulton, Chambers |
| | | 2 | 12.12.25 | **Doncaster Rovers** (3N) | A | W | 2-0 | Pickin, Lee |
| | | 3 | 09.01.26 | **Bury** (D1) | H | L | 2-3 | Hammerton, Emmett |
| 1926-27 | (3N) | 1 | 27.11.26 | **Lincoln City** (3N) | A | L | 0-2 | |
| 1927-28 | (3N) | 1 | 26.11.27 | **Spennymoor Utd** (NEL) | A | D | 1-1 | Nicholson |
| | | 1r | 01.12.27 | **Spennymoor Utd** | H | W | 4-2 | Lievesley 2 Phillips, Hall |
| | | 2 | 10.12.27 | **Bradford City** (3N) | A | W | 3-2 | Clayton 2, Lievesley |
| | | 3 | 14.01.28 | **Exeter City** (3S) | H | D | 3-3 | Scott 2, Hemmingway |
| | | 3r | 18.01.28 | **Exeter City** | A | L | 1-3 | Scott |
| 1928-29 | (3N) | 1 | 24.11.28 | **Tranmere Rovers** (3N) | A | L | 1-2 | Orr |
| 1929-30 | (3N) | 1 | 30.11.29 | **Ashington** (NEL) | H | W | 3-0 | Davies 2, Sellars |
| | | 2 | 14.12.29 | **Scunthorpe Utd** (ML) | A | D | 3-3 | Davies 2, Cooke og |
| | | 2r | 19.12.29 | **Scunthorpe Utd** | H | W | 5-4 | Sellars 2, Lievesley 2, Orr |
| | | 3 | 11.01.30 | **Nottingham Forest** (D2) | H | L | 0-5 | |
| 1930-31 | (3N) | 1 | 29.11.30 | **Newark Town** (ML) | A | L | 1-2 | Murden |
| 1931-32 | (3N) | 1 | 28.11.31 | **Accrington Stanley** (3N) | H | D | 0-0 | |
| | | 1r | 02.12.31 | **Accrington Stanley** | A | L | 0-5 | |
| 1932-33 | (3N) | 1 | 26.11.32 | **Chester** (3N) | A | L | 0-4 | |
| 1933-34 | (3N) | 1 | 25.11.33 | **South Bank St P** (TSL) | H | W | 3-2 | Raynor, Hicks 2 |
| | | 2 | 09.12.33 | **Coventry City** (3S) | H | W | 2-1 | Raynor, McConnell |
| | | 3 | 13.01.34 | **Sheffield Wed** (D1) | H | L | 0-3 | |
| 1934-35 | (3N) | 1 | 24.11.34 | **Spennymoor Utd** (NEL) | H | W | 2-0 | Dickinson, Briggs |
| | | 2 | 08.12.34 | **Bristol City** (3S) | H | L | 1-2 | Fenoughty |
| 1935-36 | (3N) | 1 | 30.11.35 | **Wigan Athletic** (CC) | A | W | 2-1 | Dickinson, Bastow |
| | | 2 | 14.12.35 | **Watford** (3S) | H | D | 1-1 | Dickinson |
| | | 2r | 18.12.35 | **Watford** | A | L | 0-1 | |
| 1936-37 | (3N) | 1 | 28.11.36 | **Hartlepools Utd** (3N) | H | D | 4-4 | Pedwell 2, Brown 2 |
| | | 1r | 02.12.36 | **Hartlepools Utd** | A | L | 0-2 | |
| 1937-38 | (3N) | 1 | 27.11.37 | **Burton Town** (ML) | A | D | 1-1 | Smith |
| | | 1r | 29.11.37 | **Burton Town** | H | W | 3-0 | Bramham 2, Hawkins |

| | | | | | | | |
|---|---|---|---|---|---|---|---|
| | 2 | 11.12.37 | **Aldershot** (3S) | H | L | 1-3 | Hanson |
| 1938-39 (3N) | 1 | 26.11.38 | **Hull City** (3N) | A | L | 1-4 | Bramham |
| 1945-46 (3N) | 1 1L | 17.11.45 | **Doncaster Rovers** (3N) | A | W | 1-0 | Ardron |
| | 1 2L | 24.11.45 | **Doncaster Rovers** | H | W | 2-1 | Kearney, Nightingale |
| | 2 1L | 08.12.45 | **Lincoln City** (3N) | H | W | 2-1 | Nightingale, J Shaw |
| | 2 2L | 15.12.45 | **Lincoln City** | A | D | 1-1 | Ardron |
| | 3 1L | 05.01.46 | **Gateshead AFC** (3N) | H | D | 2-2 | J Shaw, Dawson |
| | 3 2L | 09.01.46 | **Gateshead AFC** | A | W | 2-0 | Kearney, Ardron |
| | 4 1L | 26.01.46 | **Barnsley** (D2) | A | L | 0-3 | |
| | 4 2L | 31.01.46 | **Barnsley** | H | W | 2-1 | Wilson og, R Shaw |
| 1946-47 (3N) | 1 | 30.11.46 | **Crewe Alexandra** (3N) | H | W | 2-0 | Wilson, Armitage |
| | 2 | 14.12.46 | **Scunthorpe Utd** (ML) | H | W | 4-1 | Ardron 2, Wilson, R.Shaw |
| | 3 | 11.01.47 | **Wolverhampton W** (D1) | A | L | 0-3 | |
| 1947-48 (3N) | 3 | 10.01.48 | **Brentford** (D2) | H | L | 0-3 | |
| 1948-49 (3N) | 3 | 08.01.49 | **Darlington** (3N) | H | W | 4-2 | Ardron 2, Grainger, Noble |
| | 4 | 29.01.49 | **Burnley** (D1) | H | L | 0-1 | |
| 1949-50 (3N) | 3 | 07.01.50 | **Bury** (D2) | A | L | 4-5 | Rudd, Bower, Noble, J Shaw |
| 1950-51 (3N) | 1 | 25.11.50 | **Darlington** (3N) | A | W | 7-2 | J Shaw 5, Williams, Guest |
| | 2 | 09.12.50 | **Nottingham Forest** (3S) | H | W | 3-1 | J Shaw 3 |
| | 3 | 06.01.51 | **Doncaster Rovers** (D2) | H | W | 2-1 | Williams, J Shaw |
| | 4 | 27.01.51 | **Hull City** (D2) | A | L | 0-2 | |
| 1951-52 (D2) | 3 | 12.01.52 | **Bury** (D2) | H | W | 2-1 | Guest, J Shaw |
| | 4 | 02.02.52 | **Swansea Town** (D2) | A | L | 0-3 | |
| 1952-53 (D2) | 3 | 10.01.53 | **Colchester Utd** (3S) | H | D | 2-2 | J Shaw 2 |
| | 3r | 15.01.53 | **Colchester Utd** | A | W | 2-0 | J Shaw, Rawson |
| | 4 | 31.01.53 | **Newcastle Utd** (D1) | A | W | 3-1 | Grainger 2, Rickett |
| | 5 | 14.02.53 | **Aston Villa** (D1) | H | L | 1-3 | J Shaw |
| 1953-54 (D2) | 3 | 09.01.54 | **Bristol City** (3S) | A | W | 3-1 | Grainger 3 |
| | 4 | 30.01.54 | **WBA** (D1) | A | L | 0-4 | |
| 1954-55 (D2) | 3 | 08.01.55 | **Leicester City** (D1) | H | W | 1-0 | Pell |
| | 4 | 29.01.55 | **Luton Town** (D2) | H | L | 1-5 | Guest |
| 1955-56 (D2) | 3 | 07.01.56 | **Scunthorpe Utd** (3N) | H | D | 1-1 | Grainger |
| | 3r | 12.01.56 | **Scunthorpe Utd** | A | L | 2-4 | Farmer, Grainger |
| 1956-57 (D2) | 3 | 05.01.57 | **Bristol City** (D2) | A | L | 1-4 | Stephenson |
| 1957-58 (D2) | 3 | 04.01.58 | **Blackburn Rovers** (D2) | H | L | 1-4 | Stephens |
| 1958-59 (D2) | 3 | 10.01.59 | **Aston Villa** (D1) | A | L | 1-2 | Sawyer |
| 1959-60 (D2) | 3 | 09.01.60 | **Arsenal** (D1) | H | D | 2-2 | Sawyer, Myerscough (p) |
| | 3r | 13.01.60 | **Arsenal** | A | D | 1-1aet | Webster |
| | 3 2r | 18.01.60 | **Arsenal** *played at Hillsborough* | | W | 2-0 | Kettleborough, Sawyer |
| | 4 | 30.01.60 | **Brighton** (D2) | H | D | 1-1 | Kirkman |
| | 4r | 03.02.60 | **Brighton** | A | D | 1-1aet | Sawyer |
| | 4 2r | 08.02.60 | **Brighton** *played at Highbury* | | L | 0-6 | |
| 1960-61 (D2) | 3 | 07.01.61 | **Watford** (D3) | H | W | 1-0 | Houghton |
| | 4 | 28.01.61 | **Birmingham City** (D1) | A | L | 0-4 | |
| 1961-62 (D2) | 3 | 09.01.62 | **Huddersfield Town** (D2) | A | L | 3-4 | Houghton, Weston 2 |
| 1962-63 (D2) | 3 | 20.02.63 | **Watford** (D3) | A | L | 0-2 | |
| 1963-64 (D2) | 3 | 04.01.64 | **Burnley** (D1) | A | D | 1-1 | Casper |
| | 3r | 07.01.64 | **Burnley** | H | L | 2-3 | Lyons 2 |
| 1964-65 (D2) | 3 | 09.01.65 | **Lincoln City** (D4) | H | W | 5-1 | Madden, Bennett 2, Galley 2 |
| | 4 | 30.01.65 | **Wolverhampton W** (D1) | A | D | 2-2 | Bennett, Pring |
| | 4r | 02.02.65 | **Wolverhampton W** | H | L | 0-3 | |
| 1965-66 (D3) | 3 | 22.01.66 | **Southend Utd** (D3) | H | W | 3-2 | Wilcockson, Rabjohn, Bradbury og |
| | 4 | 12.02.66 | **Manchester Utd** (D1) | A | D | 0-0 | |
| | 4r | 15.02.66 | **Manchester Utd** | H | L | 0-1aet | |
| 1966-67 (D2) | 3 | 28.01.67 | **Nuneaton B** (SL) | A | D | 1-1 | Chambers |
| | 3r | 31.01.67 | **Nuneaton B** | H | W | 1-0 | Chappell |
| | 4 | 18.02.67 | **Birmingham City** (D2) | H | D | 0-0 | |
| | 4r | 21.02.67 | **Birmingham City** | A | L | 1-2 | Galley |
| 1967-68 (D2) | 3 | 27.01.68 | **Wolverhampton W** (D1) | H | W | 1-0 | Storrie |

| | | | | | | | |
|---|---|---|---|---|---|---|---|
| | 4 | 17.02.68 | **Aston Villa** (D2) | A | W | 1-0 | Storrie |
| | 5 | 09.03.68 | **Leicester City** (D1) | H | D | 1-1 | Downs |
| | 5r | 13.03.68 | **Leicester City** | A | L | 0-2aet | |
| 1968-69 (D3) | 1 | 16.11.68 | **Hartlepool** (D3) | A | D | 1-1 | Womble |
| | 1r | 19.11.68 | **Hartlepool** | H | W | 3-0 | G Watson 2, Storrie |
| | 2 | 07.12.68 | **Mansfield Town** (D3) | H | D | 2-2 | Gilliver 2 |
| | 2r | 09.12.68 | **Mansfield Town** | A | L | 0-1 | |
| 1969-70 (D3) | 1 | 15.11.69 | **Notts County** (D4) | A | W | 3-0 | Hague, Downes 2 |
| | 2 | 06.12.69 | **Workington** (D4) | H | W | 3-0 | Downes, Swift, Fantham |
| | 3 | 03.01.70 | **Peterborough Utd** (D4) | H | L | 0-1 | |
| 1970-71 (D3) | 1 | 24.11.70 | **Great Harwood** (NPL) | A | W | 6-2 | Watson 2, Fantham 2, Bentley, Mullen |
| | 2 | 12.12.70 | **Grantham Town** (ML) | A | W | 4-1 | Watson, Hague, Fantham 2 |
| | 3 | 11.01.71 | **Leeds Utd** (D1) | H | D | 0-0 | |
| | 3r | 18.01.71 | **Leeds Utd** | A | L | 2-3 | Womble, Bentley |
| 1971-72 (D3) | 1 | 20.11.71 | **Frickley Colliery** (ML) | A | D | 2-2 | Mullen, Bentley |
| | 1r | 23.11.71 | **Frickley Colliery** | H | W | 4-0 | Bentley, Gilbert 3 |
| | 2 | 11.12.71 | **York City** (D3) | H | D | 1-1 | Gilbert |
| | 2r | 13.12.71 | **York City** | A | W | 3-2aet | Ham 2, Womble |
| | 3 | 15.01.72 | **Bury** (D4) | A | D | 1-1 | Gilbert |
| | 3r | 19.01.72 | **Bury** | H | W | 2-1 | Swift, Gilbert (p) |
| | 4 | 05.02.72 | **Tottenham Hotspur** (D1) | A | L | 0-2 | |
| 1972-73 (D3) | 1 | 18.11.72 | **S Shields (1936)** (NPL) | H | W | 4-0 | Womble, Swift 2, Mielczarek |
| | 2 | 09.12.72 | **Stockport County** (D4) | H | L | 0-1 | |
| 1973-74 (D4) | 1 | 24.11.73 | **Southport** (D3) | H | W | 2-1 | Wigg, Phillips |
| | 2 | 15.12.73 | **Wrexham** (D3) | A | L | 0-3 | |
| 1974-75 (D4) | 1 | 23.11.74 | **Chester** (D4) | H | W | 1-0 | Delgado |
| | 2 | 14.12.74 | **Northampton Town** (D4) | H | W | 2-1 | Wigg 2 |
| | 3 | 04.01.75 | **Stafford Rangers** (NPL) | A | D | 0-0 | |
| | 3r | 07.01.75 | **Stafford Rangers** | H | L | 0-2 | |
| 1975-76 (D3) | 1 | 22.11.75 | **Crewe Alexandra** (D4) | H | W | 2-1 | Crawford, Stancliffe |
| | 2 | 13.12.75 | **Bradford City** (D4) | H | L | 0-3 | |
| 1976-77 (D3) | 1 | 20.11.76 | **Altrincham** (NPL) | H | W | 5-0 | Gwyther, Finney 2, Breckin, Crawford (p) |
| | 2 | 11.12.76 | **York City** (D3) | H | D | 0-0 | |
| | 2r | 14.12.76 | **York City** | A | D | 1-1aet | Crawford |
| | 2 2r | 21.12.76 | **York City** | H | W | 2-1aet | Crawford 2 (1p) |
| | 3 | 08.01.77 | **Wolverhampton W** (D2) | A | L | 2-3 | Crawford 2 (1p) |
| 1977-78 (D3) | 1 | 26.11.77 | **Mossley** (NPL) | H | W | 3-0 | Gwyther, Finney, Phillips |
| | 2 | 17.12.77 | **Spennymoor Utd** (NL) | H | W | 6-0 | Phillips 3, Crawford 2, Gwyther |
| | 3 | 07.01.78 | **Millwall** (D2) | H | D | 1-1 | Finney |
| | 3r | 09.01.78 | **Millwall** | A | L | 0-2 | |
| 1978-79 (D3) | 1 | 25.11.78 | **Workington** (NPL) | H | W | 3-0 | Gwyther 2, Breckin |
| | 2 | 16.12.78 | **Barnsley** (D4) | A | D | 1-1 | Crawford |
| | 2r | 09.01.79 | **Barnsley** | H | W | 2-1 | Gwyther, Phillips |
| | 3 | 15.01.79 | **Manchester City** (D1) | A | D | 0-0 | |
| | 3r | 17.01.79 | **Manchester City** | H | L | 2-4 | Breckin, Green |
| 1979-80 (D3) | 1 | 24.11.79 | **Morecambe** (NPL) | A | D | 1-1 | Finney |
| | 1r | 27.11.79 | **Morecambe** | H | W | 2-0 | Green, Stancliffe |
| | 2 | 15.12.79 | **Altrincham** (APL) | H | L | 0-2 | |
| 1980-81 (D3) | 1 | 22.11.80 | **Boston Utd** (APL) | A | W | 4-0 | Taylor, Moore 2, Carr |
| | 2 | 13.12.80 | **Barnsley** (D3) | H | L | 0-1 | |
| 1981-82 (D2) | 3 | 02.01.82 | **Sunderland** (D1) | H | D | 1-1 | Towner |
| | 3r | 18.01.82 | **Sunderland** | A | L | 0-1 | |
| 1982-83 (D2) | 3 | 08.01.83 | **Shrewsbury Town** (D2) | A | L | 1-2 | Seasman |
| 1983-84 (D3) | 1 | 19.11.83 | **Hartlepool Utd** (D4) | H | D | 0-0 | |
| | 1r | 23.11.83 | **Hartlepool Utd** | A | W | 1-0aet | Kilmore |
| | 2 | 10.12.83 | **Hull City** (D3) | H | W | 2-1 | Kllmore 2 |
| | 3 | 07.01.84 | **WBA** (D1) | H | D | 0-0 | |
| | 3r | 11.01.84 | **WBA** | A | L | 0-3 | |
| 1984-85 (D3) | 1 | 17.11.84 | **Mansfield Town** (D4) | A | L | 1-2 | Gooding |

| | | | | | | | |
|---|---|---|---|---|---|---|---|
| 1985-86 (D3) | 1 | 16.11.85 | **Wolverhampton W** (D3) | H | W | 6-0 | Tynan, Simmons, Gooding, Birch 2, Smith |
| | 2 | 07.12.85 | **Burnley** (D4) | H | W | 4-1 | Birch, Trusson 2, Tynan |
| | 3 | 04.01.86 | **Frickley Athletic** (APL) | A | W | 3-1 | Gooding, Pugh, Tynan |
| | 4 | 25.01.86 | **Arsenal** (D1) | A | L | 1-5 | Tynan |
| 1986-87 (D3) | 1 | 15.11.86 | **Chester City** (D3) | A | D | 1-1 | Gooding (p) |
| | 1r | 18.11.86 | **Chester City** | H | D | 1-1aet | Evans |
| | 1 2r | 24.11.86 | **Chester City** | A | L | 0-1 | |
| 1987-88 (D3) | 1 | 14.11.87 | **Doncaster Rovers** (D3) | A | D | 1-1 | Dungworth (p) |
| | 1r | 17.11.87 | **Doncaster Rovers** | H | W | 2-0 | Haycock 2 |
| | 2 | 06.12.87 | **Macclesfield T** (Conf) | A | L | 0-4 | |
| 1988-89 (D4) | 1 | 19.11.88 | **Barrow** (NPL) | H | W | 3-1 | Williamson (p), Gordon og, Green |
| | 2 | 10.12.88 | **Grimsby Town** (D4) | A | L | 2-3 | Grealish, Dempsey (p) |
| 1989-90 (D3) | 1 | 18.11.89 | **Bury** (D3) | H | D | 0-0 | |
| | 1r | 21.11.89 | **Bury** | A | W | 2-1 | Hazel, Evans |
| | 2 | 09.12.89 | **Walsall** (D3) | A | L | 0-1 | |
| 1990-91 (D3) | 1 | 17.11.90 | **Stockport County** (D4) | H | W | 1-0 | Dempsey |
| | 2 | 11.12.90 | **Halifax Town** (D4) | H | D | 1-1 | Goater |
| | 2r | 17.12.90 | **Halifax Town** | A | W | 2-1 | Evans, Johnson |
| | 3 | 05.01.91 | **Swansea City** (D3) | A | D | 0-0 | |
| | 3r | 21.01.91 | **Swansea City** | H | W | 4-0 | Dempsey, Mendonca 2, Goater |
| | 4 | 26.01.91 | **Crewe Alexandra** (D3) | A | L | 0-1 | |
| 1991-92 (D4) | 1 | 16.11.91 | **Scunthorpe Utd** (D4) | A | D | 1-1 | Cunningham |
| | 1r | 26.11.91 | **Scunthorpe Utd** | H | D | 3-3aet | Page 2, Goodwin |
| | | | *Rotherham won 7-6 on penalties* | | | | |
| | 2 | 07.12.91 | **Burnley** (D4) | A | L | 0-2 | |
| 1992-93 (D2) | 1 | 14.11.92 | **Walsall** (D3) | H | W | 4-0 | Goodwin 2, Cunningham, Howard |
| | 2 | 05.12.92 | **Hull City** (D2) | H | W | 1-0 | Cunningham |
| | 3 | 12.01.93 | **Northampton Town** (D3) | A | W | 1-0 | Howard |
| | 4 | 23.01.93 | **Newcastle Utd** (D1) | H | D | 1-1 | Johnson |
| | 4r | 03.02.93 | **Newcastle Utd** | A | L | 0-2 | |
| 1993-94 (D2) | 1 | 13.11.93 | **Stockport County** (D2) | H | L | 1-2 | Wilder (p) |
| 1994-95 (D2) | 1 | 12.11.94 | **York City** (D2) | A | D | 3-3 | Goater 2, Helliwell |
| | 1r | 22.11.94 | **York City** | H | W | 3-0 | Davison 2, Goater |
| | 2 | 03.12.94 | **Wrexham** (D2) | A | L | 2-5 | Davison, Hurst |
| 1995-96 (D2) | 1 | 11.11.95 | **Rochdale** (D3) | A | L | 3-5 | Goater 2 (1p), McGlashan |
| 1996-97 (D2) | 1 | 16.11.96 | **Scunthorpe Utd** (D3) | A | L | 1-4 | McGlashan |
| 1997-98 (D3) | 1 | 15.11.97 | **Burnley** (D2) | H | D | 3-3 | Roscoe 2, Knill |
| | 1r | 25.11.97 | **Burnley** | A | W | 3-0 | White, Berry, Gardner |
| | 2 | 06.12.97 | **King's Lynn** (SL) | H | W | 6-0 | Glover, Richardson, Garner, Druce, Berry, Hudson |
| | 3 | 03.01.98 | **Sunderland** (D1) | H | L | 1-5 | Garner |
| 1998-99 (D3) | 1 | 15.11.98 | **Emley** (NPL) | A | D | 1-1 | Hudson |
| | | | *played at Oakwell, Barnsley* | | | | |
| | 1r | 24.11.98 | **Emley** | H | W | 3-1 | Glover, Hurst, Garner |
| | 2 | 05.12.98 | **Rochdale** (D3) | A | D | 0-0 | |
| | 2r | 15.12.98 | **Rochdale** | H | W | 4-0 | Garner, Berry, Glover, R Scott |
| | 3 | 02.01.99 | **Bristol Rovers** (D2) | H | L | 0-1 | |
| 1999-00 (D3) | 1 | 30.10.99 | **Worthing** (IL) | H | W | 3-0 | Thompson, Garner, Martindale (p) |
| | 2 | 20.11.99 | **Burnley** (D2) | A | L | 0-2 | |
| 2000-01 (D2) | 1 | 18.11.00 | **Wrexham** (D2) | A | W | 1-0 | Lee |
| | 2 | 09.12.00 | **Northampton Town** (D2) | H | W | 1-0 | Hughes og |
| | 3 | 06.01.01 | **Liverpool** (PL) | A | L | 0-3 | |
| 2001-02 (D1) | 3 | 16.01.02 | **Southampton** (PL) | H | W | 2-1 | Barker, Mullin |
| | 4 | 26.01.02 | **Crewe Alexandra** (D1) | H | L | 2-4 | Mullin, Warne |
| 2002-03 (D1) | 3 | 04.01.03 | **Wimbledon** (D1) | H | L | 0-3 | |

## ROYAL ENGINEERS

*Formed 1867. One of the 15 original entrants in the FA Cup in the 1871-72 season. They were runners-up in the first FA Cup final in 1872 when they lost to the Wanderers. FA Cup winners: 1875; Runners-up: 1872, 1874, 1878. They played their home matches at Great Lines, Chatham. Entered the FA Cup until the 1888-89 season when they lost in the first qualifying round.*

| | | | | | | | |
|---|---|---|---|---|---|---|---|
| 1871-72 | 1 | | Reigate Priory | | | - | |
| | | | *Reigate Priory scratched. Royal Engineers walkover* | | | | |
| | 2 | 10.01.72 | **Hitchin Town** | A | W | 5-0 | |
| | 3 | 27.01.72 | **Hampstead Heathens** | H | W | 3-0 | |
| | SF | 17.02.72 | **Crystal Palace (1861)** | | D | 0-0 | |
| | | | *played at Kennington Oval* | | | | |
| | SFr | 09.03.72 | **Crystal Palace (1861)** | | W | 3-0 | Renny-Tailyour 2, Mitchell |
| | | | *played at Kennington Oval* | | | | |
| | F | 16.03.72 | **Wanderers** | | L | 0-1 | |
| | | | *played at Kennington Oval* | | | | |
| 1872-73 | 1 | 26.10.72 | **Civil Service** | H | W | 3-0 | |
| | 2 | | bye | | | | |
| | 3 | 09.12.72 | **Oxford University** | A | L | 0-1 | |
| 1873-74 | 1 | 11.10.73 | **Brondesbury** | H | W | 5-0 | Addison, 4 others |
| | 2 | 26.11.73 | **Uxbridge** | H | W | 2-1 | |
| | 3 | 10.12.73 | **Maidenhead** | H | W | 7-0 | |
| | SF | 28.01.74 | **Swifts** | | W | 2-0 | Renny-Tailyour 2 |
| | | | *played at Kennington Oval* | | | | |
| | F | 14.03.74 | **Oxford University** | | L | 0-2 | |
| | | | *played at Kennington Oval* | | | | |
| 1874-75 | 1 | 07.11.74 | **Marlow** | H | W | 3-0 | von Donop, others 2 |
| | 2 | 05.12.74 | **Cambridge University** | A | W | 5-0 | Mulholland, Rawson, Stafford, others 2 |
| | 3 | 30.01.75 | **Clapham Rovers** | H | W | 3-2 | Mein, Stafford, AN Other |
| | SF | 27.02.75 | **Oxford University** | | D | 1-1 | Renny-Tailyour |
| | | | *played at Kennington Oval* | | | | |
| | SFr | 05.03.75 | **Oxford University** | | W | 1-0aet | Renny-Tailyour |
| | | | *played at Kennington Oval* | | | | |
| | F | 13.03.75 | **Old Etonians** | | D | 1-1 | Renny-Tailyour |
| | | | *played at Kennington Oval* | | | | |
| | Fr | 16.03.75 | **Old Etonians** | | W | 2-0 | Renny-Tailyour, Stafford |
| | | | *played at Kennington Oval* | | | | |
| 1875-76 | 1 | 10.11.75 | **High Wycombe** | H | W | 15-0 | Middlemiss 5, Rawson 5, Blackburn 2, von Donop 2, Tower |
| | 2 | | Panthers | | | - | |
| | | | *Panthers scratched. Royal Engineers walkover* | | | | |
| | 3 | 29.01.76 | **Swifts** | H | L | 1-3 | Rawson |
| 1876-77 | 1 | 04.11.76 | **Old Harrovians** | H | W | 2-1 | Rawson, AN Other |
| | 2 | 09.12.76 | **Shropshire Wanderers** | H | W | 3-0 | Hedley, others 2 |
| | 3 | 20.01.77 | **Sheffield FC** | H | W | 1-0 | Rawson |
| | 4 | 17.02.77 | **Cambridge University** | A | L | 0-1 | |
| 1877-78 | 1 | | Highbury Union | | | - | |
| | | | *Highbury scratched. Royal Engineers walkover* | | | | |
| | 2 | 08.12.77 | **Pilgrims** | H | W | 6-0 | Hedley 3, others 3 |
| | 3 | 30.01.78 | **Druids** | H | W | 8-0 | Hedley 3, Tower 2, Haynes, Lindsay, AN Other |
| | 4 | 15.02.78 | **Oxford University** | H | D | 3-3 | |
| | 4r | 27.02.78 | **Oxford University** | A | D | 2-2aet | Bond, Haynes |
| | 4 2r | 12.03.78 | **Oxford University** | H | W | 4-2 | Barnet, Bond, Ruck, AN Other |
| | SF | 16.03.78 | **Old Harrovians** | | W | 2-1 | Barnet, Mayne |
| | | | *played at Kennington Oval* | | | | |
| | F | 23.03.78 | **Wanderers** | | L | 1-3 | "scored from a rush" |
| | | | *played at Kennington Oval* | | | | |
| 1878-79 | 1 | 09.11.78 | **Old Foresters** | H | W | 3-0 | |
| | 2 | 07.12.78 | **Oxford University** | A | L | 0-4 | |
| 1879-80 | 1 | | bye | | | | |
| | 1 | 13.11.79 | **Cambridge University** | H | W | 2-0 | |
| | 2 | 23.12.79 | **Upton Park** | H | W | 4-1 | Learoyd 2, Paterson, AN Other |
| | 3 | 04.02.80 | **Old Harrovians** | H | W | 2-0 | |
| | 4 | 18.02.80 | **Grey Friars** | H | W | 1-0 | Tanner |
| | 5 | 05.03.80 | **Oxford University** | A | D | 1-1aet | Massey |
| | 5r | 15.03.80 | **Oxford University** | H | L | 0-1 | |

| | | | | | | | |
|---|---|---|---|---|---|---|---|
| 1880-81 | 1 | | bye | | | | |
| | 1 | 13.11.80 | **Remnants** | H | D | 0-0 | |
| | 1r | 20.11.80 | **Remnants** | A | W | 1-0 | |
| | 2 | 09.12.80 | **Pilgrims** | H | W | 1-0 | Massey |
| | 3 | 09.02.81 | **Rangers FC, London** | | W | 6-0 | |
| | 4 | 19.02.81 | **Old Carthusians** | A | L | 0-2 | |
| 1881-82 | 1 | 05.11.81 | **Kildare FC** | H | W | 6-0 | |
| | 2 | | bye | | | | |
| | 3 | 20.12.81 | **Old Carthusians** | A | W | 2-0 | Williams, own goal |
| | 4 | 21.01.82 | **Old Foresters** | A | L | 1-2 | Kincaid |
| 1882-83 | 1 | 21.10.82 | **Woodford Bridge** | H | W | 3-1 | Newman, Petrie, Stafford |
| | 2 | 29.11.82 | **Reading** | H | W | 8-0 | Kincaid 3, Godby 2, Ruck, Stafford, AN Other |
| | 3 | | bye | | | | |
| | 4 | 25.01.83 | **Old Carthusians** | A | L | 2-6 | Kincaid, Lindsay |
| 1883-84 | 1 | 10.11.83 | **Windsor Home Park** | A | L | 3-5 | Kincaid 2, Wingfield-Stratford |
| 1884-85 | 1 | 08.11.84 | **Marlow** | A | L | 1-10 | Stafford |
| 1885-86 | 1 | 31.10.85 | **Old Foresters** | H | L | 1-5 | |
| 1886-87 | 1 | 30.10.86 | **Old Etonians** | A | L | 0-1 | |
| 1887-88 | 1 | 15.10.87 | **Rochester** | H | L | 0-3 | |
| | | | *FA ordered match to be replayed after protest but Rochester scratched* | | | | |
| | 2 | 05.11.87 | **Chatham** | A | L | 1-3 | |

# RUNCORN

*Formed 1918. First entered FA Cup: 1919-20. FA Trophy runners-up: 1986, 1993, 1994. Renamed Runcorn FC Halton 2002. League clubs beaten: Aldershot, Notts County, Southport, Chester City, Wrexham. Members of the Northern Premier League.*

| | | | | | | | | |
|---|---|---|---|---|---|---|---|---|
| 1938-39 | (CC) | 1 | 26.11.38 | **Wellington Town** (CC) | H | W | 3-0 | Searth, Fitton, Mayson |
| | | 2 | 10.12.38 | **Aldershot** (3S) | H | W | 3-1 | Long, Mayson, Fitton |
| | | 3 | 07.01.39 | **Preston North End** (D1) | H | L | 2-4 | Mayson, Houghton |
| 1946-47 | (CC) | 1 | 30.11.46 | **Carlisle Utd** (3N) | A | L | 0-4 | |
| 1947-48 | (CC) | 1 | 29.11.47 | **Scunthorpe Utd** (ML) | H | W | 4-2 | Malam, Bailey, Coogan 2 |
| | | 2 | 13.12.47 | **Barrow** (3N) | H | L | 0-1 | |
| 1948-49 | (CC) | 1 | 27.11.48 | **York City** (3N) | A | L | 1-2 | JS Brown |
| 1967-68 | (CC) | 1 | 09.12.67 | **Notts County** (D4) | H | W | 1-0 | Ryan |
| | | 2 | 06.01.68 | **Southport** (D3) | A | L | 2-4 | Ryan 2 |
| 1973-74 | (NPL) | 1 | 24.11.73 | **Grimsby Town** (D3) | H | L | 0-1 | |
| 1977-78 | (NPL) | 1 | 26.11.77 | **Southport** (D4) | A | D | 2-2 | Whitbread, Lyon |
| | | 1r | 28.11.77 | **Southport** | H | W | 1-0 | Whitbread |
| | | 2 | 17.12.77 | **Hartlepool Utd** (D4) | A | L | 2-4 | Spencer, Wiggett og |
| 1978-79 | (NPL) | 1 | 25.11.78 | **Chester** (D3) | A | D | 1-1 | Keynon |
| | | 1r | 28.11.78 | **Chester** | H | L | 0-5 | |
| 1981-82 | (APL) | 1 | 21.11.81 | **Burnley** (D3) | A | D | 0-0 | |
| | | 1r | 24.11.81 | **Burnley** | H | L | 1-2 | Seddon |
| 1985-86 | (Conf) | 1 | 16.11.85 | **Boston Utd** (Conf) | H | D | 2-2 | Smith 2 |
| | | 1r | 20.11.85 | **Boston Utd** | A | D | 1-1aet | Carter |
| | | 1 2r | 25.11.85 | **Boston Utd** | H | W | 4-1 | Mather, Carter 2, S Crompton |
| | | 2 | 07.12.85 | **Wigan Athletic** (D3) | H | D | 1-1 | Mather |
| | | 2r | 10.12.85 | **Wigan Athletic** | A | L | 0-4 | |
| 1986-87 | (Conf) | 1 | 15.11.86 | **Boston Utd** (Conf) | H | D | 1-1 | Carter |
| | | 1r | 19.11.86 | **Boston Utd** | A | W | 2-1aet | Carter (p), Rowlands |
| | | 2 | 06.12.86 | **Scunthorpe Utd** (D4) | A | L | 0-1 | |
| 1987-88 | (Conf) | 1 | 14.11.87 | **Chester City** (D3) | A | W | 1-0 | Carter |
| | | 2 | 05.12.87 | **Stockport County** (D4) | H | L | 0-1 | |
| 1988-89 | (Conf) | 1 | 19.11.88 | **Wrexham** (D4) | H | D | 2-2 | Page, Anderson |
| | | 1r | 22.11.88 | **Wrexham** | A | W | 3-2 | Reid, Pugh, Rodwell |
| | | 2 | 10.12.88 | **Crewe Alexandra** (D4) | H | L | 0-3 | |
| 1989-90 | (Conf) | 4Q | 28.10.89 | **Darlington** (Conf) | A | L | 2-4 | |
| 1990-91 | (Conf) | 1 | 17.11.90 | **Hartlepool Utd** (D4) | H | L | 0-3 | |
| 1991-92 | (Conf) | 1 | 16.11.91 | **Tranmere Rovers** (D2) | A | L | 0-3 | |
| 1993-94 | (Conf) | 1 | 13.11.93 | **Hull City** (D2) | H | - | 0-1ab | |
| | | | | *abandoned after 29 minutes for safety reasons following the collapse of a wall* | | | | |

| | | | | | | | | |
|---|---|---|---|---|---|---|---|---|
| | | 1 | 23.11.93 | **Hull City** (D2) | H | L | 0-2 | |
| | | | | *played at Witton Albion* | | | | |
| 1994-95 | (Conf) | 1 | 12.11.94 | **Halifax Town** (Conf) | A | D | 1-1 | Thomas (p) |
| | | 1r | 21.11.94 | **Halifax Town** | H | L | 1-3aet | Pugh |
| 1995-96 | (Conf) | 1 | 11.11.95 | **Wigan Athletic** (D3) | H | D | 1-1 | Bignall |
| | | 1r | 21.11.95 | **Wigan Athletic** | A | L | 2-4 | Ruffer, Smith (p) |
| 1996-97 | (NPL) | 1 | 16.11.96 | **Darlington** (D3) | H | L | 1-4 | Heavey |
| 1998-99 | (NPL) | 1 | 14.11.98 | **Stevenage Boro** (Conf) | H | D | 1-1 | McNally |
| | | 1r | 23.11.98 | **Stevenage Boro** | A | L | 0-2 | |
| 1999-00 | (NPL) | 1 | 30.10.99 | **Hayes** (Conf) | A | L | 1-2 | McDonald |
| 2002-03 | (NPL) | 1 | 16.11.02 | **Bristol Rovers** (D3) | A | D | 0-0 | |
| | | 1r | 26.11.02 | **Bristol Rovers** | H | L | 1-3aet | Barrett og |

## RUNNYMEDE

*Entered the FA Cup once in the 1878-79 season but never played a match in the competition.*

| | | | | | | | | |
|---|---|---|---|---|---|---|---|---|
| 1878-79 | | 1 | | Panthers | | | - | |
| | | | | *Runnymede scratched. Panthers walkover* | | | | |

## RUSHDEN & DIAMONDS

*Formed 1992 by the amalgamation of Rushden Town (formed 1919) and Irthlingborough Diamonds (formed 1946). First entered FA Cup: 1992-93. Promoted to Football League 2001.*

| | | | | | | | | |
|---|---|---|---|---|---|---|---|---|
| 1995-96 | (SL) | 1 | 11.11.95 | **Cardiff City** (D3) | H | L | 1-3 | Hannigan |
| 1996-97 | (Conf) | 1 | 16.11.96 | **Borehamwood** (IL) | A | D | 1-1 | Hackett |
| | | 1r | 26.11.96 | **Borehamwood** | H | L | 2-3 | Wilkin, Collins |
| 1998-99 | (Conf) | 1 | 14.11.98 | **Shrewsbury Town** (D3) | H | W | 1-0 | Underwood |
| | | 1 | 05.12.98 | **Doncaster Rovers** (Conf) | A | D | 0-0 | |
| | | 1r | 15.12.98 | **Doncaster Rovers** | H | W | 4-2 | Hamsher (p), West 2, Brady |
| | | 3 | 02.01.99 | **Leeds Utd** (PL) | H | D | 0-0 | |
| | | 3r | 13.01.99 | **Leeds Utd** | A | L | 1-3 | Heggs |
| 1999-00 | (Conf) | 1 | 29.10.99 | **Scunthorpe Utd** (D2) | H | W | 2-0 | Warburton, Hamsher (p) |
| | | 2 | 20.11.99 | **Ilkeston Town** (SL) | A | D | 1-1 | De Souza |
| | | 2r | 30.11.99 | **Ilkeston Town** | H | W | 3-0 | Wooding, Town, Collins |
| | | 3 | 12.12.99 | **Sheffield Utd** (D1) | A | D | 1-1 | Brady |
| | | 3r | 21.12.99 | **Sheffield Utd** | H | D | 1-1aet | Warburton |
| | | | | *Sheffield Utd won 6-5 on penalties* | | | | |
| 2000-01 | (Conf) | 1 | 17.11.00 | **Luton Town** (D2) | A | L | 0-1 | |
| 2001-02 | (D3) | 1 | 17.11.01 | **Worcester City** (SL) | A | W | 1-0 | Hanlon |
| | | 2 | 08.12.01 | **Brighton** (D2) | A | L | 1-2 | Hanlon (p) |
| 2002-03 | (D3) | 1 | 16.11.02 | **Kidderminster H** (D3) | A | D | 2-2 | Duffy 2 |
| | | 1r | 26.11.02 | **Kidderminster H** | H | W | 2-1 | Duffy, Wardley |
| | | 2 | 07.12.02 | **Exeter City** (D3) | A | L | 1-3 | Lowe |

## RYDE SPORTS

*Formed 1888. Entered FA Cup: 1898-99 – 1996-97.*

| | | | | | | | |
|---|---|---|---|---|---|---|---|
| 1932-33 | (HL) | 1 | 26.11.32 | **Margate** (KL) | A | L | 0-5 |
| 1936-37 | (HL) | 1 | 28.11.36 | **Gillingham** (3S) | H | L | 1-5 |

## RYHOPE COLLIERY WELFARE

*Formed 1898 as Ryhope Villa. First entered FA Cup: 1912-13. Renamed Ryhope Community Association 1993.*

| | | | | | | | |
|---|---|---|---|---|---|---|---|
| 1967-68 | (Wear) | 1 | 09.12.67 | **Workington** (D4) | H | L | 0-1 |

## SAFFRON WALDEN

*Formed 1872. First entered FA Cup: 1876-77. Members of the Essex Senior League.*

| | | | | | | | |
|---|---|---|---|---|---|---|---|
| 1876-77 | | 1 | | Wanderers | | | - |
| | | | | *Saffron Walden scratched. Wanderers walkover* | | | |
| 1878-79 | | 1 | 30.10.78 | **Upton Park** | A | L | 0-5 |
| 1880-81 | | 1 | 23.10.80 | **Old Carthusians** | A | L | 0-7 |

## SALISBURY CITY

*Formed 1947. First entered FA Cup: 1947-48. Known as Salisbury 1947-1992. Members of the Southern League.*

| | | | | | | | | |
|---|---|---|---|---|---|---|---|---|
| 1955-56 | (WL) | 1 | 19.11.55 | **Weymouth** (SL) | A | L | 2-3 | Oakley, Prentice |
| 1959-60 | (WL) | 1 | 14.11.59 | **Barnet** (AL) | H | W | 1-0 | Onslow |
| | | 2 | 05.12.59 | **Newport County** (D3) | H | L | 0-1 | |

| | | | | | | | | | |
|---|---|---|---|---|---|---|---|---|---|
| 1964-65 | (WL) | 1 | 14.11.64 | **Peterborough Utd** (D3) | A | L | 1-5 | Stocks |
| 1967-68 | (WL) | 1 | 12.12.67 | **Swindon Town** (D3) | A | L | 0-4 | |
| 1979-80 | (SL) | 1 | 24.11.79 | **Millwall** (D3) | H | L | 1-2 | Hibbs |
| | | | | *played at The Dell, Southampton* | | | | |
| 1992-93 | (SL) | 1 | 14.11.92 | **Marlow** (IL) | A | D | 3-3 | Loveridge, Sanders, Fletcher |
| | | 1r | 05.12.92 | **Marlow** | H | D | 2-2aet | Chalk, Sanders |
| | | | | *Marlow won 4-3 on penalties* | | | | |
| 1998-99 | (SL) | 1 | 14.11.98 | **Hull City** (D3) | H | L | 0-2 | |

# SAXONS

*Entered the FA Cup just once in 1876-77, losing the only match they ever played.*

| | | | | | | | | |
|---|---|---|---|---|---|---|---|---|
| 1876-77 | | 1 | 04.11.76 | **South Norwood** | A | L | 1-4 | Sharpe |

# SCARBOROUGH

*Formed 1879. First entered FA Cup: 1887-88. Best FA Cup performance: 3rd round, 1931, 1938, 1976, 1978, 1995. FA Trophy winners: 1973, 1976, 1977. Runners-up: 1975. Members of the Football League: 1987-1998. League clubs beaten (as a Non-League club): Lincoln City, York City, Darlington, Bradford City, Oldham Athletic, Crewe Alexandra (2), Preston North End, Rochdale. Members of The Conference.*

| | | | | | | | | |
|---|---|---|---|---|---|---|---|---|
| 1887-88 | | 1 | 15.10.87 | **Shankhouse** | H | L | 3-5 | |
| 1928-29 | (ML) | 1 | 24.11.28 | **Horwich RMI** (LC) | A | W | 2-1 | Wainwright, Glayson |
| | | 2 | 08.12.28 | **Darlington** (3N) | H | D | 2-2 | Glayson, Wainwright |
| | | 2r | 12.12.28 | **Darlington** | A | L | 1-2 | Glayson |
| 1930-31 | (ML) | 1 | 29.11.30 | **Rhyl** (NWC) | H | W | 6-0 | Rand 2, Hill, Palfreman 2, Small |
| | | 2 | 13.12.30 | **Lincoln City** (3N) | H | W | 6-4 | Palfreman, Hickman 2, Rand 2, Hill |
| | | 3 | 10.01.31 | **Grimsby Town** (D1) | H | L | 1-2 | Palfreman |
| 1932-33 | (ML) | 1 | 26.11.32 | **York City** (3N) | A | W | 3-1 | Jenkinson, Swann, Halfort |
| | | 2 | 10.12.32 | **Southend Utd** (3S) | A | L | 1-4 | Wraith |
| 1933-34 | (ML) | 1 | 25.11.33 | **North Shields** (NEL) | A | L | 0-3 | |
| 1935-36 | (ML) | 1 | 30.11.35 | **Darwen** (LC) | H | W | 2-0 | Boyle, Smithson |
| | | 2 | 14.12.35 | **Brighton** (3S) | H | D | 1-1 | Smithson |
| | | 2r | 18.12.35 | **Brighton** | A | L | 0-3 | |
| 1937-38 | (ML) | 1 | 27.11.37 | **Darlington** (3N) | A | W | 2-0 | Nicol, Beckett |
| | | 2 | 11.12.37 | **Bromley** (AL) | H | W | 4-1 | Agar, Beckett, Nicol 2 |
| | | 3 | 08.01.38 | **Luton Town** (D2) | H | D | 1-1 | Barty |
| | | 3r | 12.01.38 | **Luton Town** | A | L | 1-5 | Burke |
| 1938-39 | (ML) | 1 | 26.11.38 | **Southport** (3N) | H | D | 0-0 | |
| | | 1r | 29.11.38 | **Southport** | A | L | 3-5 | Lister, Rivers, Hardy |
| 1948-49 | (ML) | 1 | 04.12.48 | **Rhyl** (CC) | A | W | 2-0 | Langford 2 |
| | | 2 | 11.12.48 | **Gateshead AFC** (3N) | A | L | 0-3 | |
| 1950-51 | (ML) | 1 | 25.11.50 | **Rhyl** (CC) | H | L | 1-2 | Cooling |
| 1952-53 | (ML) | 1 | 22.11.52 | **Mansfield Town** (3N) | H | L | 0-8 | |
| 1953-54 | (ML) | 1 | 21.11.53 | **Wigan Athletic** (LC) | A | L | 0-4 | |
| 1954-55 | (ML) | 1 | 20.11.54 | **York City** (3N) | A | L | 2-3 | Barber, Pickard |
| 1955-56 | (ML) | 1 | 19.11.55 | **Workington** (3N) | A | L | 2-4 | Michell, Parkinson (p) |
| 1956-57 | (ML) | 1 | 17.11.56 | **Rhyl** (CC) | A | L | 2-3 | Parkinson, Bowman |
| 1957-58 | (ML) | 1 | 16.11.57 | **Bradford City** (3N) | A | L | 0-6 | |
| 1959-60 | (ML) | 1 | 14.11.59 | **Bradford Park A** (D4) | A | L | 1-6 | Whittle |
| 1960-61 | (NCo) | 1 | 05.11.60 | **Bradford City** (D3) | A | D | 0-0 | |
| | | 1r | 09.11.60 | **Bradford City** | H | L | 1-3aet | Franks |
| 1962-63 | (NEL) | 1 | 03.11.62 | **Crewe Alexandra** (D4) | A | D | 1-1 | Franks |
| | | 1r | 07.11.62 | **Crewe Alexandra** | H | L | 2-3aet | Whyke, G Smith |
| 1964-65 | (ML) | 1 | 14.11.64 | **Bradford City** (D4) | H | W | 1-0 | Edgar |
| | | 2 | 05.12.64 | **Doncaster Rovers** (D4) | A | D | 0-0 | |
| | | 2r | 09.12.64 | **Doncaster Rovers** | H | L | 1-2 | Cade |
| 1965-66 | (ML) | 1 | 13.11.65 | **Altrincham** (CC) | A | L | 0-6 | |
| 1970-71 | (NPL) | 1 | 21.11.70 | **Workington** (D4) | H | L | 2-3 | Siddle, Barmby (p) |
| 1971-72 | (NPL) | 1 | 20.11.71 | **Hartlepool** (D4) | A | L | 1-6 | Lee |
| 1972-73 | (NPL) | 1 | 18.11.72 | **Oldham Athletic** (D3) | A | D | 1-1 | Barmby |
| | | 1r | 22.11.72 | **Oldham Athletic** | H | W | 2-1 | Franks, Donaghue |
| | | 2 | 09.12.72 | **Doncaster Rovers** (D4) | H | L | 1-2 | Appleton |
| 1973-74 | (NPL) | 1 | 24.11.73 | **Crewe Alexandra** (D4) | A | D | 0-0 | |
| | | 1r | 28.11.73 | **Crewe Alexandra** | H | W | 2-1 | Donaghue (p), Dunn |

| | | | | | | | | |
|---|---|---|---|---|---|---|---|---|
| | | 2 | 15.12.73 | **Port Vale** (D3) | A | L | 1-2 | Lee |
| 1975-76 | (NPL) | 1 | 22.11.75 | **Morecambe** (NPL) | H | W | 2-0 | Hewitt, Marshall |
| | | 2 | 13.12.75 | **Preston North End** (D3) | H | W | 3-2 | Dunn, Woodall, Marshall |
| | | 3 | 03.01.76 | **Crystal Palace** (D3) | H | L | 1-2 | Abbey |
| 1976-77 | (NPL) | 1 | 20.11.76 | **Darlington** (D4) | H | D | 0-0 | |
| | | 1r | 22.11.76 | **Darlington** | A | L | 1-4 | Barney |
| 1977-78 | (NPL) | 1 | 26.11.77 | **Rochdale** (D4) | H | W | 4-2 | HA Dunn, D Smith 3 |
| | | 2 | 17.12.77 | **Crewe Alexandra** (D4) | A | D | 0-0 | |
| | | 2r | 21.12.77 | **Crewe Alexandra** | H | W | 2-0 | Woodall, Donoghue |
| | | 3 | 07.01.78 | **Brighton** (D2) | A | L | 0-3 | |
| 1978-79 | (NPL) | 1 | 25.11.78 | **Chorley** (CC) | A | W | 1-0 | HA Dunn |
| | | 2 | 16.12.78 | **York City** (D4) | A | L | 0-3 | |
| 1979-80 | (APL) | 1 | 24.11.79 | **Halifax Town** (D4) | A | L | 0-2 | |
| 1980-81 | (APL) | 1 | 22.11.80 | **Burnley** (D3) | A | L | 0-1 | |
| 1982-83 | (APL) | 1 | 20.11.82 | **Tranmere Rovers** (D4) | A | L | 2-4 | Hamson 2 |
| 1985-86 | (APL) | 1 | 17.11.85 | **Notts County** (D3) | A | L | 1-6 | Burke (p) |
| 1987-88 | (D4) | 1 | 14.11.87 | **Grimsby Town** (D3) | H | L | 1-2 | Graham |
| 1988-89 | (D4) | 1 | 19.11.88 | **Stockport County** (D4) | H | W | 2-1 | Brook, Cook (p) |
| | | 2 | 10.12.88 | **Carlisle Utd** (D4) | H | L | 0-1 | |
| 1989-90 | (D4) | 1 | 18.11.89 | **Whitley Bay** (NPL) | H | L | 0-1 | |
| 1990-91 | (D4) | 1 | 17.11.90 | **Leek Town** (NPL) | H | L | 0-2 | |
| 1991-92 | (D4) | 1 | 16.11.91 | **Wigan Athletic** (D3) | H | L | 0-2 | |
| 1992-93 | (D3) | 1 | 14.11.92 | **Burnley** (D2) | A | L | 1-2 | Mockler |
| 1993-94 | (D3) | 1 | 13.11.93 | **Bury** (D3) | H | W | 1-0 | Young |
| | | 2 | 04.12.93 | **Wigan Athletic** (D3) | A | L | 0-1 | |
| 1994-95 | (D3) | 1 | 12.11.94 | **Chesterfield** (D3) | A | D | 0-0 | |
| | | 1r | 22.11.94 | **Chesterfield** | H | W | 2-0 | Toman, White |
| | | 2 | 03.12.94 | **Port Vale** (D1) | H | W | 1-0 | Swann |
| | | 3 | 07.01.95 | **Watford** (D1) | H | D | 0-0 | |
| | | 3r | 17.01.95 | **Watford** | A | L | 0-2 | |
| 1995-96 | (D3) | 1 | 11.11.95 | **Chesterfield** (D2) | H | L | 0-2 | |
| 1996-97 | (D3) | 1 | 16.11.96 | **Shrewsbury Town** (D2) | A | D | 1-1 | Ritchie |
| | | 1r | 26.11.96 | **Shrewsbury Town** | H | W | 1-0 | Kay |
| | | 2 | 07.12.96 | **Chesterfield** (D2) | A | L | 0-2 | |
| 1997-98 | (D3) | 1 | 15.11.97 | **Scunthorpe Utd** (D3) | A | L | 1-2 | Robinson |
| 1998-99 | (D3) | 1 | 14.11.98 | **Rochdale** (D3) | H | D | 1-1 | Williams |
| | | 1r | 24.11.98 | **Rochdale** | A | L | 0-2 | |
| 2002-03 | (Conf) | 1 | 16.11.02 | **Cambridge Utd** (D3) | H | D | 0-0 | |
| | | 1r | 26.11.02 | **Cambridge Utd** | A | L | 1-2aet | Jordan |

## SCUNTHORPE UNITED

*Formed 1899. First entered FA Cup 1912-13. FA Cup best performance: 5th round, 1958, 1970; Record FA Cup win: 10-0 v Hull Holderness, 1st qualifying round, 1922-23 and 10-0 v Hull Holderness, preliminary round 1926-27. In Competition Proper: 9-0 v Boston Utd, 1st round, 21.11.1953. Record FA Cup defeat: 0-7 v Coventry City, 1st round, 24.11.1934.*

| | | |
|---|---|---|
| 1912-13 | (ML) | P Brodsworth Colliery (A) 3-2; 1q Goole Town (H) 2-1; 2q York City (H) 2-2; 2qr York City (A) 4-5 |
| 1913-14 | (ML) | P Mexborough Town (A) 2-2; Pr Mexborough Town(H) 3-0; 1q York City (A) 1-2 |
| 1914-15 | (ML) | P Hull School Old Boys (H) 5-1; 1q Grimsby Rovers (A) 4-0; 2q Doncaster Rovers (H) 1-0; 3q Goole Town (H) 1-1; 3qr Goole Town (A) 1-5 |
| 1919-20 | (ML) | P Goole Town (H) 7-0; 1q Brodsworth Colliery (H) 2-1; 2q Cleethorpes T (H) 0-1 |
| 1920-21 | (ML) | P Hull Brunswick (H) 6-0; 1q Bentley Colliery (H) 3-0; 2q Grimsby Charltons (A) 4-1; 3q Brodsworth Colliery (H) 1-1; 3qr Brodsworth Colliery (A) 0-0aet; 3q 2r Brodsworth Colliery 3-1 at Bramall Lane; 4q Mansfield Town (A) 0-1 |
| 1921-22 | (ML) | P Retford (A) 2-1; 1q Hull Holderness (H) 10-0; 2q Brodsworth Colliery (H) 4-1; 3q Gainsborough T (A) 0-2 |
| 1922-23 | (ML) | 1q Grimsby Charltons (H) 3-0; 2q Gainsborough T (A) 2-1; 3q Boston Town (A) 1-0; 4q Worksop Town (A) 2-4 |
| 1923-24 | (ML) | P Grimsby Rovers (H) 5-1; 1q Cleethorpes Town(H) 5-0; 2q Gainsborough T (H) 2-0; 3q Boston Town (H) 2-0; 4q Rotherham Town (H) 0-0; 4qr Rotherham Town (A) 1-0; 5q Rotherham County (H) 1-1; 5qr Rotherham County (A) 0-2 |
| 1924-25 | (ML) | P Barton Town (H) 2-1; 1q Boston Town (H) 0-0; 1qr Boston Town (A) 0-3 |

| | | | | | | | |
|---|---|---|---|---|---|---|---|
| 1925-26 (ML) | | | P Cleethorpes Town (A) 4-0; 1q Grimsby Haycroft (H) 5-1; 2q Gainsborough Tr (H) 2-2; 2qr Gainsborough T (A) 0-1 | | | | |
| 1926-27 (ML) | | | P Hull Holderness (H) 10-0; 1q Grimsby Haycroft (H) 7-2; 2q Selby Olympia (A) 0-0; 2qr Selby Oly (H) 1-0; 3q Gainsborough T (A) 3-3; 3qr Gainsborough T (H) 1-0; 4q Kettering Town (H) 1-2 | | | | |
| 1927-28 (ML) | | | P Cleethorpes Town (H) 5-2; 1q Gainsborough T (A) 0-3 | | | | |
| 1928-29 (ML) | | | P Barton Town (A) 3-2; 1q Spalding (A) 3-0; 2q Cleethorpes Town(H) 4-3; 3q Boston Town (A) 1-0; 4q Grantham (A) 1-2 | | | | |
| 1929-30 (ML) | | | P Selby Town (A) 3-1; 1q Selby Olympia (H) 1-0; 2q Goole Town (H) 2-1; 3q Broughton (H) 7-0; 4q South Kirby (A) 6-1 | | | | |
| | 1 | 30.11.29 | **Hartlepools Utd** (3N) | H | W | 1-0 | Smalley |
| | 2 | 14.12.29 | **Rotherham Utd** (3N) | H | D | 3-3 | Smalley, Calladine 2 |
| | 2r | 19.12.29 | **Rotherham Utd** | A | L | 4-5 | Beynon 2, Smalley, Calladine |
| 1930-31 (ML) | | | 4q Worcester City (H) 3-0 | | | | |
| | 1 | 29.11.30 | **Gainsborough T** (ML) | A | L | 0-1 | |
| 1931-32 (ML) | | | 4q Sutton Junction (H) 7-1 | | | | |
| | 1 | 28.11.31 | **Rochdale** (3N) | H | W | 2-1 | Hubbard, Methven |
| | 2 | 12.12.31 | **QPR** (3S) | H | L | 1-4 | Baynam (p) |
| 1932-33 (ML) | | | 4q Burton Town (H) 4-1 | | | | |
| | 1 | 26.11.32 | **Workington** (NEL) | A | L | 1-5 | Tucker |
| 1933-34 (ML) | | | 1q Selby Town (H) 4-1; 2q Humber Utd (H) 5-0; 3q Louth (H) 4-1; 4q Heanor Town (H) 4-2 | | | | |
| | 1 | 25.11.33 | **Accrington Stanley** (3N) | H | D | 1-1 | Sumpter |
| | 1r | 29.11.33 | **Accrington Stanley** | A | L | 0-3 | |
| 1934-35 (ML) | | | 4q Kettering Town (H) 2-2; 4qr Kettering Town (A) 3-1 | | | | |
| | 1 | 24.11.34 | **Coventry City** (3S) | A | L | 0-7 | |
| 1935-36 (ML) | | | 4q Denaby Utd (H) 4-1 | | | | |
| | 1 | 30.11.35 | **Coventry City** | A | D | 1-1 | Snaith |
| | 1r | 09.12.35 | **Coventry City** | H | W | 4-2 | Davies, Roberts, Lewis, Kilsby |
| | 2 | 14.12.35 | **Tranmere Rovers** (3N) | A | L | 2-6 | Lewis, Allen |
| 1936-37 (ML) | | | 4q Gainsborough T (A) 1-0 | | | | |
| | 1 | 28.11.36 | **Walsall** (3S) | A | L | 0-3 | |
| 1937-38 (ML) | | | 4q Grantham (H) 4-2 | | | | |
| | 1 | 27.11.37 | **Hull City** (3N) | A | L | 0-4 | |
| 1938-39 (ML) | | | 1q Barton Town (H) 9-1; 2q Appleby-Frodingham (H) 4-1; 3q Lysaghts Sports (H) 11-3; 4q Boston Town (H) 2-1 | | | | |
| | 1 | 26.11.38 | **Lancaster City** (LC) | H | W | 4-2 | Johnson, Nightingale, Fleetwood 2 |
| | 2 | 10.12.38 | **Watford** (3S) | H | L | 1-2 | Jones |
| 1945-46 (ML) | | | 3q Lysaghts Sports (H) 4-1; 4q Yorkshire Amateurs (H) 1-2 | | | | |
| 1946-47 (ML) | | | P Norton Woodseats (H) 5-2; 1q Harworth Colliery (H) 5-2; 2q Rawmarsh (A) 3-0; 3q Wombwell (A) 5-2; 4q Boston Town (H) 4-1 | | | | |
| | 1 | 04.12.46 | **York City** (3N) | A | W | 1-0 | Marriott |
| | 2 | 14.12.46 | **Rotherham Utd** (3N) | A | L | 1-4 | Bowers |
| 1947-48 (ML) | | | P Sheffield FC (H) 5-1; 1q Rawmarsh (H) 8-0; 2q Denaby Utd (H) 1-0; 3q Norton Woodseats (H) 2-1; 4q Gainsborough T (H) 4-2 | | | | |
| | 1 | 29.11.47 | **Runcorn** (CC) | A | L | 2-4 | Bowers, Rowney |
| 1948-49 (ML) | | | 4q Selby Town (H) 2-1 | | | | |
| | 1 | 04.12.48 | **Halifax Town** (3N) | A | D | 0-0aet | |
| | 1r | 06.12.48 | **Halifax Town** | H | W | 1-0 | Barker |
| | 2 | 11.12.48 | **Stockport County** (3N) | H | L | 0-1 | |
| 1949-50 (ML) | | | 4q Goole Town (H) 0-0; 4qr Goole Town (A) 1-3 | | | | |
| 1950-51 (3N) | | | 4q Hereford Utd (A) 0-1 | | | | |
| 1951-52 (3N) | 1 | 24.11.51 | **Billingham Syn** (NL) | H | W | 5-0 | Powell 2, Wallace 2, Hubbard |
| | 2 | 15.12.51 | **Millwall** (3S) | A | D | 0-0 | |
| | 2r | 20.12.51 | **Millwall** | H | W | 3-0 | Powell 2, Rudd |
| | 3 | 12.01.52 | **Tottenham Hotspur** (D1) | H | L | 0-3 | |
| 1952-53 (3N) | 1 | 22.11.52 | **Carlisle Utd** (3N) | H | W | 1-0 | Whitfield |
| | 2 | 06.12.52 | **Hereford Utd** (SL) | A | D | 0-0 | |
| | 2r | 11.12.52 | **Hereford Utd** | H | W | 2-1 | Haigh, Whitfield |
| | 3 | 10.01.53 | **Sunderland** (D1) | A | D | 1-1 | McGill |

| | | | | | | | | | |
|---|---|---|---|---|---|---|---|---|---|
| | | 3r | 15.01.53 | **Sunderland** | H | L | 1-2 | Daley |
| 1953-54 | (3N) | 1 | 21.11.53 | **Boston Utd** (ML) | H | W | 9-0 | Jones 2, Haigh 3, Whitfield 2, Gregory, Mosby |
| | | 2 | 12.12.53 | **Bournemouth** (3S) | H | W | 1-0 | Brown |
| | | 3 | 09.01.54 | **Wrexham** (3N) | A | D | 3-3 | Bushby 2, Mosby |
| | | 3r | 14.01.54 | **Wrexham** | H | W | 3-1 | Gregory, Brownsword, Whitfield |
| | | 4 | 30.01.54 | **Portsmouth** (D1) | H | D | 1-1 | Jones |
| | | 4r | 03.02.54 | **Portsmouth** | A | D | 2-2aet | Jones 2 |
| | | 4 2r | 08.02.54 | **Portsmouth** *played at Highbury* | | L | 0-4 | |
| 1954-55 | (3N) | 1 | 20.11.54 | **Horden Coll Wel** (NEL) | A | W | 1-0 | McGill |
| | | 2 | 11.12.54 | **Coventry City** (3S) | A | L | 0-4 | |
| 1955-56 | (3N) | 1 | 19.11.55 | **Shildon** (NL) | H | W | 3-0 | Davies, Brown, Gregory |
| | | 2 | 10.12.55 | **Bishop Auckland** (NL) | A | D | 0-0 | |
| | | 2r | 15.12.55 | **Bishop Auckland** | H | W | 2-0 | Davies, Hubbard |
| | | 3 | 07.01.56 | **Rotherham Utd** (D2) | A | D | 1-1 | Brown |
| | | 3r | 12.01.56 | **Rotherham Utd** | H | W | 4-2 | Brown 3, Davies |
| | | 4 | 28.01.56 | **Liverpool** (D2) | A | D | 3-3 | Gregory, Davies 2 |
| | | 4r | 06.02.56 | **Liverpool** | H | L | 1-2aet | Davies |
| 1956-57 | (3N) | 1 | 17.11.56 | **Rochdale** (3N) | H | W | 1-0 | Brown |
| | | 2 | 08.12.56 | **Wrexham** (3N) | H | D | 0-0 | |
| | | 2r | 12.12.56 | **Wrexham** | A | L | 2-6aet | Gregory 2 |
| 1957-58 | (3N) | 1 | 16.11.57 | **Goole Town** (ML) | H | W | 2-1 | Fletcher, Davies |
| | | 2 | 07.12.57 | **Bury** (3N) | H | W | 2-0 | Waldock, Jones |
| | | 3 | 04.01.58 | **Bradford City** (3N) | H | W | 1-0 | Haigh |
| | | 4 | 25.01.58 | **Newcastle Utd** (D1) | A | W | 3-1 | Haigh, Davies 2 |
| | | 5 | 15.02.58 | **Liverpool** (D2) | H | L | 0-1 | |
| 1958-59 | (D2) | 3 | 10.01.59 | **Bolton Wanderers** (D1) | H | L | 0-2 | |
| 1959-60 | (D2) | 3 | 09.01.60 | **Crystal Palace** (D4) | H | W | 1-0 | Middleton |
| | | 4 | 30.01.60 | **Port Vale** (D3) | H | L | 0-1 | |
| 1960-61 | (D2) | 3 | 07.01.61 | **Blackpool** (D1) | H | W | 6-2 | Bonson 3, Thomas 3 |
| | | 4 | 28.01.61 | **Norwich City** (D2) | H | L | 1-4 | Bakes |
| 1961-62 | (D2) | 3 | 06.01.62 | **Charlton Athletic** (D2) | A | L | 0-1 | |
| 1962-63 | (D2) | 3 | 26.01.63 | **Portsmouth** (D2) | A | D | 1-1 | Godfrey |
| | | 3r | 07.03.63 | **Portsmouth** | H | L | 1-2 | McGuigan |
| 1963-64 | (D2) | 3 | 04.01.64 | **Barnsley** (D3) | H | D | 2-2 | Wilson, Lawther |
| | | 3r | 07.01.64 | **Barnsley** | A | L | 2-3aet | Brownsword 2 |
| 1964-65 | (D3) | 1 | 14.11.64 | **Darlington** (D4) | H | L | 1-2 | Greener og |
| 1965-66 | (D3) | 1 | 13.11.65 | **Crewe Alexandra** (D4) | A | L | 0-3 | |
| 1966-67 | (D3) | 1 | 26.11.66 | **Lincoln City** (D4) | A | W | 4-3 | Smith, Burrows, Barton, Mahy |
| | | 2 | 07.01.67 | **Mansfield Town** (D3) | A | L | 1-2 | Foxon |
| 1967-68 | (D3) | 1 | 09.12.67 | **Skelmersdale Utd** (LC) | H | W | 2-0 | Colquhoun, Barton (p) |
| | | 2 | 06.01.68 | **Halifax Town** (D4) | A | L | 0-1 | |
| 1968-69 | (D4) | 1 | 16.11.68 | **Workington** (D4) | A | L | 0-2 | |
| 1969-70 | (D4) | 1 | 15.11.69 | **Macclesfield T** (NPL) | A | D | 1-1 | Heath |
| | | 1r | 18.11.69 | **Macclesfield T** | H | W | 4-2 | Keegan 2, Rusling, Cassidy |
| | | 2 | 06.12.69 | **Stockport County** (D3) | A | D | 0-0 | |
| | | 2r | 09.12.69 | **Stockport County** | H | W | 4-0 | Cassidy, Kerr 2, Keegan |
| | | 3 | 03.01.70 | **Millwall** (D2) | H | W | 2-1 | Deere. Heath |
| | | 4 | 24.01.70 | **Sheffield Wed** (D1) | A | W | 2-1 | Barker, Cassidy |
| | | 5 | 07.02.70 | **Swindon Town** (D2) | A | L | 1-3 | Cassidy |
| 1970-71 | (D4) | 1 | 21.11.70 | **Tranmere Rovers** (D3) | A | D | 1-1 | Woolmer |
| | | 1r | 24.11.70 | **Tranmere Rovers** | H | D | 0-0aet | |
| | | 1 2r | 30.11.70 | **Tranmere Rovers** *played at Goodison Park* | | W | 1-0aet | Rusling |
| | | 2 | 12.12.70 | **Mansfield Town** (D3) | H | W | 3-0 | Rusling 2, Kirk |
| | | 3 | 02.01.71 | **WBA** (D1) | A | D | 0-0 | |
| | | 3r | 11.01.71 | **WBA** | H | L | 1-3 | Deere |
| 1971-72 | (D4) | 1 | 20.11.71 | **S Shields (1936)** (NPL) | A | D | 3-3 | Deere, Kerr 2 |
| | | 1r | 24.11.71 | **S Shields (1936)** | H | L | 2-3 | Fletcher, Kirk |
| 1972-73 | (D3) | 1 | 18.11.72 | **Hartlepool** (D4) | A | D | 0-0 | |

| | | | | | | | |
|---|---|---|---|---|---|---|---|
| | 1r | 21.11.72 | **Hartlepool** | H | D | 0-0aet | |
| | 2 2r | 27.11.72 | **Hartlepool** | | W | 2-1aet | Dawes og, Deere |
| | | | *played at Roker Park* | | | | |
| | 2 | 09.12.72 | **Halifax Town** (D3) | H | W | 3-2 | Heath, Fletcher, Wellbourne |
| | 3 | 13.01.73 | **Cardiff City** (D2) | H | L | 2-3 | Wellbourne, Kirk |
| 1973-74 (D4) | 1 | 24.11.73 | **Darlington** (D4) | H | W | 1-0 | Houghton |
| | 2 | 15.12.73 | **Mansfield Town** (D4) | A | D | 1-1 | Houghton |
| | 2r | 18.12.73 | **Mansfield Town** | H | W | 1-0 | Warnock |
| | 3 | 05.01.74 | **Millwall** (D2) | A | D | 1-1 | Collier |
| | 3r | 08.01.74 | **Millwall** | H | W | 1-0 | Pilling |
| | 4 | 26.01.74 | **Newcastle Utd** (D1) | A | D | 1-1 | Keeley |
| | 4r | 30.01.74 | **Newcastle Utd** | H | L | 0-3 | |
| 1974-75 (D4) | 1 | 23.11.74 | **Altrincham** (NPL) | H | D | 1-1 | Keeley |
| | 1r | 25.11.74 | **Altrincham** | A | L | 1-3 | Collier |
| 1975-76 (D4) | 1 | 22.11.75 | **Preston North End** (D3) | A | L | 1-2 | Green |
| 1976-77 (D4) | 1 | 20.11.76 | **Chesterfield** (D3) | H | L | 1-2 | Keeley |
| 1977-78 (D4) | 1 | 26.11.77 | **Stockport County** (D4) | A | L | 0-3 | |
| 1978-79 (D4) | 1 | 25.11.78 | **Sheffield Wed** (D3) | H | D | 1-1 | Pilling |
| | 1r | 28.11.78 | **Sheffield Wed** | A | L | 0-1 | |
| 1979-80 (D4) | 1 | 24.11.79 | **Rochdale** (D4) | A | L | 1-2 | Pilling |
| 1980-81 (D4) | 1 | 22.11.80 | **Hartlepool Utd** (D4) | H | W | 3-1 | Grimes, Green, Partridge (p) |
| | 2 | 13.12.80 | **Altrincham** (APL) | H | D | 0-0 | |
| | 2r | 15.12.80 | **Altrincham** | A | L | 0-1 | |
| 1981-82 (D4) | 1 | 21.11.81 | **Bradford City** (D4) | H | W | 1-0 | Cowling |
| | 2 | 02.01.82 | **Crewe Alexandra** (D4) | A | W | 3-1 | Cowling, Telfer, Dall |
| | 3 | 06.01.82 | **Hereford Utd** (D4) | H | D | 1-1 | Stewart |
| | 3r | 20.01.82 | **Hereford Utd** | A | L | 1-4 | Grimes |
| 1982-83 (D4) | 1 | 20.11.82 | **Darlington** (D4) | A | W | 1-0 | Cammack |
| | 2 | 11.12.82 | **Northwich V** (APL) | H | W | 2-1 | Cowling, O'Berg |
| | 3 | 08.01.83 | **Grimsby Town** (D2) | H | D | 0-0 | |
| | 3r | 11.01.83 | **Grimsby Town** | A | L | 0-2 | |
| 1983-84 (D3) | 1 | 19.11.83 | **Preston North End** (D3) | H | W | 1-0 | Cammack (p) |
| | 2 | 10.12.83 | **Bury** (D4) | H | W | 2-0 | Pashley og, Cammack |
| | 3 | 07.01.84 | **Leeds Utd** (D2) | A | D | 1-1 | Cammack |
| | 3r | 10.01.84 | **Leeds Utd** | H | D | 1-1aet | Dey |
| | 3 2r | 16.01.84 | **Leeds Utd** | H | W | 4-2 | Brolly, Cammack, Lester, Graham |
| | 4 | 01.02.84 | **WBA** (D1) | A | L | 0-1 | |
| 1984-85 (D4) | 1 | 17.11.84 | **Nuneaton B** (APL) | A | D | 1-1 | Dixey og |
| | 1r | 20.11.84 | **Nuneaton B** | H | W | 2-1aet | Lester, Cammack |
| | 2 | 07.12.84 | **Port Vale** (D4) | A | L | 1-4 | Ridley og |
| 1985-86 (D4) | 1 | 16.11.85 | **Halifax Town** (D4) | A | W | 3-1 | Hill, Broddle, Lister |
| | 2 | 07.12.85 | **Rochdale** (D4) | H | D | 2-2 | Graham, Hill |
| | 2r | 10.12.85 | **Rochdale** | A | L | 1-2 | Broddle |
| 1986-87 (D4) | 1 | 15.11.86 | **Southport** (NPL) | H | W | 2-0 | Hill, Broddle |
| | 2 | 06.12.86 | **Runcorn** (Conf) | H | W | 1-0 | Broddle |
| | 3 | 10.01.87 | **Tottenham Hotspur** (D1) | A | L | 2-3 | Johnson, DeMange |
| 1987-88 (D4) | 1 | 14.11.87 | **Bury** (D3) | H | W | 3-1 | Russell 3 (1p) |
| | 2 | 05.12.87 | **Sunderland** (D3) | H | W | 2-1 | Taylor, Harle |
| | 3 | 09.01.88 | **Blackpool** (D3) | H | D | 0-0 | |
| | 3r | 12.01.88 | **Blackpool** | A | L | 0-1 | |
| 1988-89 (D4) | 1 | 19.11.88 | **Blackpool** | A | L | 1-2 | Harle (p) |
| 1989-90 (D4) | 1 | 17.11.89 | **Matlock Town** (NPL) | H | W | 4-1 | Lillis 3, Hodkinson |
| | 2 | 09.12.89 | **Burnley** (D4) | H | D | 2-2 | Taylor 2 |
| | 2r | 12.12.89 | **Burnley** | A | D | 1-1aet | Daws |
| | 2 2r | 18.12.89 | **Burnley** | A | L | 0-5 | |
| 1990-91 (D4) | 1 | 17.11.90 | **Rochdale** (D4) | A | D | 1-1 | Hicks |
| | 1r | 20.11.90 | **Rochdale** | H | W | 2-1aet | Flounders, Lillis |
| | 2 | 08.12.90 | **Tranmere Rovers** (D3) | H | W | 3-2 | Ward, Lillis, Flounders |
| | 3 | 05.01.91 | **Brighton** (D2) | A | L | 2-3 | Flounders (p), Bramhall |
| 1991-92 (D4) | 1 | 16.11.91 | **Rotherham Utd** (D4) | H | D | 1-1 | Helliwell |
| | 1r | 26.11.91 | **Rotherham Utd** | A | D | 3-3aet | Helliwell, Dawes, White |
| | | | *Rotherham Utd won 7-6 on penalties* | | | | |

| | | | | | | | | |
|---|---|---|---|---|---|---|---|---|
| 1992-93 | (D3) | 1 | 14.11.92 | **Huddersfield Town** (D2) | H | D | 0-0 | |
| | | 1r | 25.11.92 | **Huddersfield Town** | A | L | 1-2aet | Buckley |
| 1993-94 | (D3) | 1 | 14.11.93 | **Accrington Stanley** (NPL) | A | W | 3-2 | Toman, Goodacre 2 |
| | | 2 | 04.12.93 | **Walsall** (D3) | A | D | 1-1 | Carmichael |
| | | 2r | 14.12.93 | **Walsall** | H | D | 0-0aet | |
| | | | | *Scunthorpe Utd won 7-6 on penalties* | | | | |
| | | 3 | 08.01.94 | **Wimbledon** (PL) | A | L | 0-3 | |
| 1994-95 | (D3) | 1 | 12.11.94 | **Bradford City** (D2) | A | D | 1-1 | Hope |
| | | 1r | 22.11.94 | **Bradford City** | H | W | 3-2aet | Carmichael, Alexander, Thompstone |
| | | 2 | 02.12.94 | **Birmingham City** (D2) | A | D | 0-0 | |
| | | 2r | 14.12.94 | **Birmingham City** | H | L | 1-2 | Bullimore |
| 1995-96 | (D3) | 1 | 11.11.95 | **Northwich V** (Conf) | A | W | 3-1 | Ford, McFarlane 2 |
| | | 2 | 02.12.95 | **Shrewsbury Town** (D2) | H | D | 1-1 | Eyre |
| | | 2r | 12.12.95 | **Shrewsbury Town** | A | L | 1-2 | Patterson |
| 1996-97 | (D3) | 1 | 16.11.96 | **Rotherham Utd** (D2) | H | W | 4-1 | Baker 2, D'Auria, Clarkson |
| | | 2 | 07.12.96 | **Wrexham** (D2) | A | D | 2-2 | Baker 2 (1p) |
| | | 2r | 17.12.96 | **Wrexham** | H | L | 2-3aet | Baker, Clarkson |
| 1997-98 | (D3) | 1 | 15.11.97 | **Scarborough** (D3) | H | W | 2-1 | J.Wilcox, Calvo-Garcia |
| | | 2 | 06.12.97 | **Ilkeston Town** (SL) | H | D | 1-1 | Forrester |
| | | 2r | 17.12.97 | **Ilkeston Town** | A | W | 2-1 | Forrester, J.Wilcox |
| | | 3 | 03.01.98 | **Crystal Palace** (PL) | A | L | 0-2 | |
| 1998-99 | (D3) | 1 | 14.11.98 | **Woking** (Conf) | A | W | 1-0 | Forrester |
| | | 2 | 05.12.98 | **Bedlington Terriers** (NL) | H | W | 2-0 | Eyre (p), Forrester |
| | | 3 | 02.01.99 | **Wrexham** (D2) | A | L | 3-4 | Housham, Eyre, Harsley |
| 1999-00 | (D2) | 1 | 29.10.99 | **Rushden & D** (Conf) | A | L | 0-2 | |
| 2000-01 | (D3) | 1 | 18.11.00 | **Hartlepool Utd** (D3) | H | W | 3-1 | Ipoua 3 |
| | | 2 | 09.12.00 | **Brighton** (D3) | H | W | 2-1 | Torpey, Sheldon |
| | | 3 | 06.01.01 | **Burnley** (D1) | A | D | 2-2 | Hodges, Ipoua |
| | | 3r | 23.01.01 | **Burnley** | H | D | 1-1aet | Dawson |
| | | | | *Scunthorpe Utd won 5-4 on penalties* | | | | |
| | | 4 | 28.01.01 | **Bolton Wanderers** (D1) | A | L | 1-5 | Calvo-Garcia |
| 2001-02 | (D3) | 1 | 17.11.01 | **Doncaster Rovers** (Conf) | A | W | 3-2 | Hodges, Carruthers, Calvo-Garcia |
| | | 2 | 08.12.01 | **Brentford** (D2) | H | W | 3-2 | Carruthers 2, Calvo-Garcia |
| | | 3 | 05.01.02 | **Millwall** (D1) | A | L | 1-2 | McCombe |
| 2002-03 | (D3) | 1 | 16.11.02 | **Northwich V** (Conf) | A | W | 3-0 | Torpey 3 (1p) |
| | | 2 | 07.12.02 | **Carlisle Utd** (D3) | H | D | 0-0 | |
| | | 2r | 23.12.02 | **Carlisle Utd** | A | W | 1-0 | Carruthers |
| | | 3 | 04.01.03 | **Leeds Utd** (PL) | H | L | 0-2 | |

## SELBY TOWN

*Formed 1918. First entered FA Cup: 1921-22. Members of the Northern Counties East League.*

| | | | | | | | | |
|---|---|---|---|---|---|---|---|---|
| 1952-53 | (YL) | 1 | 22.11.52 | **Bishop Auckland** (NL) | H | L | 1-5 | Benn |
| 1953-54 | (YL) | 1 | 21.11.53 | **Bradford Park A** (3N) | H | L | 0-2 | |
| 1954-55 | (YL) | 1 | 20.11.54 | **Rhyl** (CC) | H | W | 2-1 | Campbell, Deyes |
| | | 2 | 11.12.54 | **Hastings Utd** (SL) | H | L | 0-2 | |
| 1956-57 | (YL) | 1 | 17.11.56 | **Hartlepools Utd** (3N) | A | L | 1-3 | Clark |

## SHANKHOUSE

*An amateur side from a Northumberland mining village. First entered FA Cup: 1887-88 and played for two seasons. Their fourth round tie against Aston Villa in December 1887 produced the first £100 gate receipts in Northumberland.*

| | | | | | | | |
|---|---|---|---|---|---|---|---|
| 1887-88 | 1 | 15.10.87 | **Scarborough** | A | W | 5-3 | |
| | 2 | | bye | | | | |
| | 3 | 26.11.87 | **Darlington** | A | W | 2-0 | Matthews, Meltcalfe |
| | 4 | 17.12.87 | **Aston Villa** | H | L | 0-9 | |
| 1892-93 | 1 | 21.01.93 | **Notts County** (D1) | A | L | 0-4 | |

## SHEFFIELD FC

*Formed October 24, 1857 and recognised as the oldest football club in the world. Hugely influential in the early days of the game, Sheffield FC is still in existence. Members of the Northern Counties East League. First entered FA Cup: 1873-74. FA Amateur Cup winners: 1904. FA Vase Runners-up: 1977.*

| | | | | | | | |
|---|---|---|---|---|---|---|---|
| 1873-74 | 1 | 30.10.73 | **Shropshire W** | H | D | 0-0 | |

| | | | | | | | |
|---|---|---|---|---|---|---|---|
| | 1r | 17.11.73 | **Shropshire W** | A | D | 0-0 | |
| | | | *The only FA Cup match to be decided on the toss of a coin. Sheffield called correctly and advanced* | | | | |
| | 2 | 22.11.73 | **Pilgrims** | H | W | 1-0 | Sorby |
| | 3 | 17.01.74 | **Clapham Rovers** | A | L | 1-2 | Kirke-Smith |
| | | | *played at Peterborough* | | | | |
| 1874-75 | 1 | | Shropshire W | | | - | |
| | | | *Sheffield FC scratched. Shropshire W walkover* | | | | |
| 1875-76 | 1 | | Shropshire W | | | - | |
| | | | *Shropshire W scratched. Sheffield FC walkover* | | | | |
| | 2 | | Upton Park | | | - | |
| | | | *Upton Park scratched. Sheffield FC walkover* | | | | |
| | 3 | 29.01.76 | **Wanderers** | A | L | 0-2 | |
| 1876-77 | 1 | | Trojans | | | - | |
| | | | *Trojans scratched. Sheffield FC walkover* | | | | |
| | 2 | 02.12.76 | **South Norwood** | A | W | 7-0 | Owen 5, AW Cursham, Matthews |
| | 3 | 20.01.77 | **Royal Engineers** | A | L | 0-1 | |
| 1877-78 | 1 | 03.11.77 | **Notts County** | A | D | 1-1 | AW Cursham |
| | 1r | 01.12.77 | **Notts County** | H | W | 3-0 | AW Cursham 2, Matthews |
| | 2 | 29.12.77 | **Darwen** | H | W | 1-0 | Matthews |
| | 3 | | bye | | | | |
| | 4 | 16.02.78 | **Wanderers** | A | L | 0-3 | |
| 1878-79 | 1 | 28.10.78 | **Grantham Town** | H | D | 1-1 | Sorby |
| | 1r | 16.11.78 | **Grantham Town** | A | W | 2-1 | J Barber 2, J Willey |
| | 2 | 21.12.78 | **Nottingham Forest** | A | L | 0-2 | |
| 1879-80 | 1 | | Queen's Park, Glasgow | | | - | |
| | | | *Queen's Park scratched. Sheffield FC walkover* | | | | |
| | 2 | 15.12.79 | **Sheffield Providence** | H | D | 3-3 | Matthews, Moss, AN Other |
| | 2r | 29.12.79 | **Sheffield Providence** | H | W | 3-0 | AW Cursham, Matthews, Sorby |
| | 3 | | bye | | | | |
| | 4 | 19.02.80 | **Nottingham Forest** | A | D | 2-2 | H Barber, AN Other |
| | | | *FA awarded the tie to Forest after Sheffield refused to play extra time* | | | | |
| 1880-81 | 1 | 30.10.80 | **Blackburn Olympic** | H | W | 4-3 | E Barber, H Barber, Sorby, og, AN Other |
| | 2 | 18.12.80 | **Darwen** | H | L | 1-5 | H Barber |
| 1881-82 | 1 | 05.11.81 | **Brigg Britannia** | H | W | 8-0 | Marsden 3, E Barber, Beardshaw, J Bradbury, others 2 |
| | 2 | 26.11.81 | **Sheffield Heeley** | H | L | 0-4 | |
| 1882-83 | 1 | 04.11.82 | **Notts County** | A | L | 1-6 | |
| 1883-84 | 1 | 10.11.83 | **Lockwood Bros** | A | L | 1-4 | |
| 1884-85 | 1 | 08.11.84 | **Lockwood Bros** | A | W | 3-0 | J Barber, Liddall, Twining |
| | 2 | 06.12.84 | **Chesterfield Spital** | H | W | 4-1 | Davy 3, E Barber |
| | 3 | 03.01.85 | **Notts County** | A | L | 0-5 | |
| 1885-86 | 1 | 31.10.85 | **Newark FC** | A | W | 3-0 | |
| | 2 | 21.11.85 | **Notts County** | A | L | 0-8 | |
| 1886-87 | 1 | 30.10.86 | **Notts Rangers** | H | L | 0-3 | |
| 1887-88 | 1 | 15.10.87 | **Lockwood Bros** | H | L | 1-3 | |

## SHEFFIELD HEELEY

*Formed 1860. Entered FA Cup: 1881-82 – 1891-92. Played at Meersbrooke Park, Heeley, Sheffield near the Red Lion pub.*

| | | | | | | | |
|---|---|---|---|---|---|---|---|
| 1881-82 | 1 | 17.10.81 | **Lockwood Bros** | H | W | 5-1 | Whitham 2, Ibbotson, Martin, Wild |
| | 2 | 26.11.81 | **Sheffield FC** | A | W | 4-0 | |
| | 3 | | bye | | | | |
| | 4 | 21.01.82 | **Sheffield Wed** | A | L | 1-3 | |
| 1882-83 | 1 | | bye | | | | |
| | 2 | 02.12.82 | **Nottingham Forest** | A | L | 2-7 | |
| 1883-84 | 1 | 10.11.83 | **Notts County** | A | L | 1-3 | Marsden |
| 1884-85 | 1 | 08.11.84 | **Notts Wanderers** | H | W | 1-0 | Stokes |
| | 2 | 06.12.84 | **Nottingham Forest** | A | L | 2-4 | Sayer |
| 1885-86 | 1 | 19.10.85 | **Eckington Works** | H | W | 2-1 | |
| | 2 | 21.11.85 | **Notts Rangers** | H | L | 1-6 | |

| | | | | | | | |
|---|---|---|---|---|---|---|---|
| 1886-87 | 1 | 30.10.86 | **Grimsby Town** | H | L | 1-4 | Jackson |
| 1887-88 | 1 | 15.10.87 | **Attercliffe** | H | W | 9-0 | |
| | 2 | 05.11.87 | **Owlerton** | A | L | 0-1 | |
| 1888-89 | 1 | 02.02.89 | **Walsall Town Swifts** | A | L | 1-5 | A Jackson |

## SHEFFIELD PROVIDENCE

*Formed 1871. Entered FA Cup: 1879-80 – 1881-82. Played at Hyde Park, Sheffield.*

| | | | | | | | |
|---|---|---|---|---|---|---|---|
| 1879-80 | 1 | | bye | | | | |
| | 2 | 15.12.79 | **Sheffield FC** | A | D | 3-3 | Brownhill, own goal, AN Other |
| | 2r | 29.12.79 | **Sheffield FC** | A | L | 0-3 | |
| 1880-81 | 1 | 30.10.80 | **Blackburn Rovers** | A | L | 2-6 | Hobson, A Woodcock |
| 1881-82 | 1 | 05.11.81 | **Sheffield Wed** | A | L | 0-2 | |

## SHEFFIELD UNITED

*Formed 1889. FA Cup winners: 1899, 1902, 1915, 1925. Runners-up: 1901, 1936. Record FA Cup Victory: 6-1 v Scarborough, 1st qualifying round, 1889-90; 6-1 v Loughborough, 4th qualifying round, 1890-91. In Competition Proper: 5-0 v Corinthians, 1st round, 10.1.1925; 5-0 v Newcastle Utd, 1st round, 10.1.1914; 5-0 v Barrow, 3rd round, 7.1.1956. Record FA Cup defeat: 0-13 v Bolton Wanderers, 2nd round, 1.2.1890*

| | | | | | | | | |
|---|---|---|---|---|---|---|---|---|
| 1889-90 | | | | 1q Scarborough (A) 6-1; 2q Sheffield Heeley (A) 1-0; 3q Sheffield FC (H) 3-0; 4q Rotherham Town (A) 2-2; 4qr Rotherham Town (H) 2-1 | | | | |
| | | 1 | 18.01.90 | **Burnley** (D1) | H | W | 2-1 | Robertson, T.Wilson |
| | | 2 | 01.02.90 | **Bolton Wanderers** (D1) | A | L | 0-13 | |
| 1890-91 | (ML) | | | 1q Derby Junction (A) 1-0; 2q Burton Swifts (A) 1-2; FA disqualified Burton for playing an unregistered player. Sheffield Utd re-instated. 3q Matlock (H) 3-0; 4q Loughborough (A) 6-1 | | | | |
| | | 1 | 17.01.91 | **Notts County** (D1) | H | L | 1-9 | Calder |
| 1891-92 | (NL) | | | 2q Lincoln City (H) 4-1; 3q Grimsby Town (A) 2-1; 4q Gainsborough T (A) 1-0 | | | | |
| | | 1 | 16.01.92 | **Blackpool** (LL) | A | W | 3-0 | Wallace 2 Scott |
| | | 2 | 30.01.92 | **Wolverhampton W** (D1) | A | L | 1-3 | Dobson |
| 1892-93 | (D2) | 1 | 21.01.93 | **Blackpool** (LL) | A | W | 3-1 | Needham 2, Hammond |
| | | 2 | 04.02.93 | **Sunderland** (D1) | H | L | 1-3 | Watson |
| 1893-94 | (D1) | 1 | 27.01.94 | **Newcastle Utd** (D2) | A | L | 0-2 | |
| 1894-95 | (D1) | 1 | 02.02.95 | **Millwall Athletic** (SL) | H | W | 3-1 | Davies, R Hill, Hammond |
| | | 2 | 16.02.95 | **WBA** (D1) | H | D | 1-1 | Davies |
| | | 2r | 20.02.95 | **WBA** | A | L | 1-2 | Watson |
| 1895-96 | (D1) | 1 | 01.02.96 | **Burton Wanderers** (D2) | A | D | 1-1 | Needham |
| | | 1r | 06.02.96 | **Burton Wanderers** | H | W | 1-0 | Needham |
| | | 2 | 15.02.96 | **Everton** (D1) | A | L | 0-3 | |
| 1896-97 | (D1) | 1 | 30.01.97 | **Blackburn Rovers** (D1) | A | L | 1-2 | Walls |
| 1897-98 | (D1) | 1 | 29.01.98 | **Burslem Port Vale** (ML) | H | D | 1-1 | Needham (p) |
| | | 1r | 02.02.98 | **Burslem Port Vale** | A | L | 1-2aet | Thickett |
| 1898-99 | (D1) | 1 | 28.01.99 | **Burnley** (D1) | A | D | 2-2 | Beer 2 |
| | | 1r | 02.02.99 | **Burnley** | H | W | 2-1 | Bennett, Morren |
| | | 2 | 11.02.99 | **Preston North End** (D1) | A | D | 2-2 | Bennett, Hedley |
| | | 2r | 16.02.99 | **Preston North End** | H | W | 2-1 | Needham 2 (1p) |
| | | 3 | 25.02.99 | **Nottingham Forest** (D1) | A | W | 1-0 | Priest |
| | | SF | 18.03.99 | **Liverpool** (D1) | | D | 2-2 | Hedley, Needham |
| | | | | *played at City Ground, Nottingham* | | | | |
| | | SFr | 23.03.99 | **Liverpool** | | D | 4-4aet | Priest 2, Beer, Bennett |
| | | | | *played at Burnden Park, Bolton* | | | | |
| | | SF 2r | 27.03.99 | **Liverpool** | | - | 0-1ab | |
| | | | | *played at Fallowfield, Manchester – abandoned at half-time due to crowd trouble and darkness* | | | | |
| | | SF 3r | 30.03.99 | **Liverpool** | | W | 1-0 | Priest |
| | | | | *played at Baseball Ground, Derby* | | | | |
| | | F | 15.04.99 | **Derby County** (D1) | | W | 4-1 | Bennett, Beer, Almond, Priest |
| | | | | *played at Crystal Palace* | | | | |
| 1899-00 | (D1) | 1 | 27.01.00 | **Leicester Fosse** (D2) | H | W | 1-0 | Bennett |
| | | 2 | 10.02.00 | **Sheffield Wed** (D2) | H | D | 0-0 | |
| | | 2r | 17.02.00 | **Sheffield Wed** | H | D | 1-1 | Almond |
| | | 2 2r | 19.02.00 | **Sheffield Wed** | A | W | 2-0 | Beer, Needham (p) |
| | | 3 | 24.02.00 | **Bury** (D1) | H | D | 2-2 | Priest, Needham (p) |

| | | | | | | | |
|---|---|---|---|---|---|---|---|
| | 3r | 01.03.00 | **Bury** | A | L | 0-2 | |
| 1900-01 (D1) | 1 | 09.02.01 | **Sunderland** (D1) | A | W | 2-1 | Lipsham, Priest |
| | 2 | 23.02.01 | **Everton** (D1) | H | W | 2-0 | Bennett 2 |
| | 3 | 23.03.01 | **Wolverhampton W** (D1) | A | W | 4-0 | Priest, Hedley, Bennett, Barker og |
| | SF | 06.04.01 | **Aston Villa** (D1)<br>*played at City Ground, Nottingham* | | D | 2-2 | Lipsham, Priest |
| | SFr | 11.04.01 | **Aston Villa**<br>*played at Baseball Ground, Derby* | | W | 3-0 | Priest 2, Bennett |
| | F | 20.04.01 | **Tottenham Hotspur** (SL)<br>*played at Crystal Palace* | | D | 2-2 | Priest, Bennett |
| | Fr | 27.04.01 | **Tottenham Hotspur**<br>*played at Burnden Park, Bolton* | | L | 1-3 | Priest |
| 1901-02 (D1) | 1 | 25.01.02 | **Northampton Town** (SL) | A | W | 2-0 | Bennett, Common |
| | 2 | 08.02.02 | **Bolton Wanderers** (D1) | H | W | 2-1 | Bennett, Priest |
| | 3 | 22.02.02 | **Newcastle Utd** (D1) | A | D | 1-1 | Priest |
| | 3r | 27.02.02 | **Newcastle Utd** | H | W | 2-1 | Needham, Common |
| | SF | 15.03.02 | **Derby County** (D1)<br>*played at The Hawthorns* | | D | 1-1 | Hedley |
| | SFr | 20.03.02 | **Derby County**<br>*played at Molineux* | | D | 1-1aet | Priest |
| | SF 2r | 27.03.02 | **Derby County**<br>*played at City Ground, Nottingham* | | W | 1-0 | Priest |
| | F | 19.04.02 | **Southampton** (SL)<br>*played at Crystal Palace* | | D | 1-1 | Common |
| | Fr | 28.04.02 | **Southampton**<br>*played at Crystal Palace* | | W | 2-1 | Hedley, Barnes |
| 1902-03 (D1) | 1 | 07.02.03 | **Woolwich Arsenal** (D2) | A | W | 3-1 | Hedley, E Needham, Priest |
| | 2 | 21.02.03 | **Bury** (D1) | H | L | 0-1 | |
| 1903-04 (D1) | 1 | 06.02.04 | **Bristol City** (D2) | A | W | 3-1 | Brown, Priest, Johnson |
| | 2 | 20.02.04 | **Bury** (D1) | A | W | 2-1 | Parker, Bennett |
| | 3 | 05.03.04 | **Bolton Wanderers** (D2) | H | L | 0-2 | |
| 1904-05 (D1) | 1 | 04.02.05 | **Nottingham Forest** (D1) | A | L | 0-2 | |
| 1905-06 (D1) | 1 | 13.01.06 | **Manchester City** (D1) | H | W | 4-1 | Brown 3, Lipsham |
| | 2 | 03.02.06 | **Blackpool** (D2) | H | L | 1-2 | Lipsham |
| 1906-07 (D1) | 1 | 12.01.07 | **Everton** (D1) | A | L | 0-1 | |
| 1907-08 (D1) | 1 | 11.01.08 | **Swindon Town** (SL) | A | D | 0-0 | |
| | 1r | 16.01.08 | **Swindon Town** | H | L | 2-3aet | Brown, Lipsham |
| 1908-09 (D1) | 1 | 16.01.09 | **Sunderland** (D1) | H | L | 2-3 | Batty, Hardinge |
| 1909-10 (D1) | 1 | 15.01.10 | **Nottingham Forest** (D1) | A | L | 2-3 | Benson, Walton |
| 1910-11 (D1) | 1 | 14.01.11 | **Darlington** (NEL) | H | L | 0-1 | |
| 1911-12 (D1) | 1 | 13.01.12 | **Chelsea** (D2) | A | L | 0-1 | |
| 1912-13 (D1) | 1 | 15.01.13 | **Huddersfield Town** (D2) | A | L | 1-3 | Gillespie |
| 1913-14 (D1) | 1 | 10.01.14 | **Newcastle Utd** (D1) | A | W | 5-0 | Simmons 2, Kitchen, Gillespie, Revill |
| | 2 | 31.01.14 | **Bradford Park A** (D2) | H | W | 3-1 | Utley 2, Simmons |
| | 3 | 21.02.14 | **Millwall Athletic** (SL) | A | W | 4-0 | Utley 2, Kitchen (p), Gillespie |
| | 4 | 07.03.14 | **Manchester City** (D1) | A | D | 0-0 | |
| | 4r | 12.03.14 | **Manchester City** | H | D | 0-0 | |
| | 4 2r | 16.03.14 | **Manchester City**<br>*played at Villa Park* | | W | 1-0 | Simmons |
| | SF | 28.03.14 | **Burnley** (D1)<br>*played at Old Trafford* | | D | 0-0 | |
| | SFr | 01.04.14 | **Burnley**<br>*played at Goodison Park* | | L | 0-1 | |
| 1914-15 (D1) | 1 | 09.01.15 | **Blackpool** (D2) | A | W | 2-1 | Masterman 2 |
| | 2 | 30.01.15 | **Liverpool** (D1) | H | W | 1-0 | Kitchen |
| | 3 | 20.02.15 | **Bradford Park A** (D1) | H | W | 1-0aet | Kitchen |
| | 4 | 06.03.15 | **Oldham Athletic** (D1) | A | D | 0-0 | |
| | 4r | 13.03.15 | **Oldham Athletic** | H | W | 3-0 | Kitchen 2, Fazakerley |
| | SF | 27.03.15 | **Bolton Wanderers** (D1)<br>*played at Ewood Park* | | W | 2-1 | Simmons, Utley |
| | F | 24.04.15 | **Chelsea** (D1)<br>*played at Old Trafford* | | W | 3-0 | Simmons, Masterman, Kitchen |

| | | | | | | | | |
|---|---|---|---|---|---|---|---|---|
| 1919-20 | (D1) | 1 | 10.01.20 | **Southend Utd** (SL) | H | W | 3-0 | Fazackerley 2, Milton |
| | | 2 | 31.01.20 | **Bradford City** (D1) | A | L | 1-2 | Johnson |
| 1920-21 | (D1) | 1 | 08.01.21 | **Swindon Town** (D3) | A | L | 0-1 | |
| 1921-22 | (D1) | 1 | 07.01.22 | **Brighton** (3S) | A | L | 0-1 | |
| 1922-23 | (D1) | 1 | 13.01.23 | **Nottingham Forest** (D1) | A | D | 0-0 | |
| | | 1r | 18.01.23 | **Nottingham Forest** | H | D | 0-0aet | |
| | | 1 2r | 22.01.23 | **Nottingham Forest** | | D | 1-1aet | Johnson |
| | | | | *played at Meadow Lane, Nottingham* | | | | |
| | | 1 3r | 25.01.23 | **Nottingham Forest** | | W | 1-0 | Gillespie |
| | | | | *played at Hillsborough* | | | | |
| | | 2 | 03.02.23 | **Middlesbrough** (D1) | A | D | 1-1 | Sampy |
| | | 2r | 08.02.23 | **Middlesbrough** | H | W | 3-0 | Johnson, Gillespie, Sampy |
| | | 3 | 24.02.23 | **Liverpool** (D1) | A | W | 2-1 | Gillespie, Waugh |
| | | 4 | 10.03.23 | **QPR** (3S) | A | W | 1-0 | Sampy |
| | | SF | 24.03.23 | **Bolton Wanderers** (D1) | | L | 0-1 | |
| | | | | *played at Old Trafford* | | | | |
| 1923-24 | (D1) | 1 | 12.01.24 | **Blackpool** (D2) | A | L | 0-1 | |
| 1924-25 | (D1) | 1 | 10.01.25 | **Corinthians** | H | W | 5-0 | Johnson 4, Boyle |
| | | 2 | 31.01.25 | **Sheffield Wed** (D2) | H | W | 3-2 | Sampy 2, Green |
| | | 3 | 21.02.25 | **Everton** (D1) | H | W | 1-0 | Tunstall |
| | | 4 | 07.03.25 | **WBA** (D1) | H | W | 2-0 | Johnson, Tunstall |
| | | SF | 28.03.25 | **Southampton** (D2) | | W | 2-0 | Tunstall, Parker og |
| | | | | *played at Stamford Bridge* | | | | |
| | | F | 25.04.25 | **Cardiff City** (D1) | | W | 1-0 | Tunstall |
| | | | | *played at Wembley Stadium* | | | | |
| 1925-26 | (D1) | 3 | 09.01.26 | **Stockport County** (D2) | H | W | 2-0 | Gillespie, Boyle |
| | | 4 | 30.01.26 | **Sunderland** (D1) | H | L | 1-2 | Johnson |
| 1926-27 | (D1) | 3 | 08.01.27 | **Arsenal** (D1) | H | L | 2-3 | Johnson, D Mercer |
| 1927-28 | (D1) | 3 | 14.01.28 | **Notts County** (D2) | A | W | 3-2 | Johnson 2, Tunstall |
| | | 4 | 28.01.28 | **Wolverhampton W** (D2) | H | W | 3-1 | Johnson 2, Partridge |
| | | 5 | 18.02.28 | **Sheffield Wed** (D1) | A | D | 1-1 | Partridge |
| | | 5r | 22.02.28 | **Sheffield Wed** | H | W | 4-1 | Johnson 3, Partridge (p) |
| | | 6 | 03.03.28 | **Nottingham Forest** (D2) | H | W | 3-0 | Johnson, Gillespie, Partridge |
| | | SF | 24.03.28 | **Huddersfield Town** (D1) | | D | 2-2aet | Johnson 2 |
| | | | | *played at Old Trafford* | | | | |
| | | SFr | 26.03.28 | **Huddersfield Town** | | D | 0-0aet | |
| | | | | *played at Goodison Park* | | | | |
| | | SF 2r | 02.04.28 | **Huddersfield Town** | | L | 0-1 | |
| | | | | *played at Maine Road* | | | | |
| 1928-29 | (D1) | 3 | 12.01.29 | **Burnley** (D1) | A | L | 1-2 | Gillespie |
| 1929-30 | (D1) | 3 | 11.01.30 | **Leicester City** (D1) | H | W | 2-1 | S Gibson, Dunne |
| | | 4 | 25.01.30 | **Huddersfield Town** (D1) | A | L | 1-2 | Dunne |
| 1930-31 | (D1) | 3 | 10.01.31 | **York City** (3N) | H | D | 1-1 | S Gibson |
| | | 3r | 14.01.31 | **York City** | A | W | 2-0 | S Gibson, Dunne |
| | | 4 | 24.01.31 | **Notts County** (3S) | H | W | 4-1 | Dunne 3, S Gibson |
| | | 5 | 14.02.31 | **Sunderland** (D1) | A | L | 1-2 | Dunne |
| 1931-32 | (D1) | 3 | 09.01.32 | **Corinthians** | H | W | 2-1 | Dunne 2 |
| | | 4 | 23.01.32 | **Bury** (D2) | A | L | 1-3 | Pickering |
| 1932-33 | (D1) | 3 | 14.01.33 | **Swansea Town** (D2) | A | W | 3-2 | Dunne 2, Oswald |
| | | 4 | 28.01.33 | **Burnley** (D2) | A | L | 1-3 | Holmes |
| 1933-34 | (D1) | 3 | 13.01.34 | **Birmingham** (D1) | A | L | 1-2 | Boyd |
| 1934-35 | (D2) | 3 | 12.01.35 | **Southend Utd** (3S) | A | W | 4-0 | Pickering, Barton, Barclay, Pears |
| | | 4 | 26.01.35 | **WBA** (D1) | A | L | 1-7 | Pickering |
| 1935-36 | (D2) | 3 | 11.01.36 | **Burnley** (D2) | A | D | 0-0 | |
| | | 3r | 16.01.36 | **Burnley** | H | W | 2-1 | Barton, Barclay |
| | | 4 | 25.01.36 | **Preston North End** (D1) | A | D | 0-0 | |
| | | 4r | 30.01.36 | **Preston North End** | H | W | 2-0 | Dodds, Barton |
| | | 5 | 15.02.36 | **Leeds Utd** (D1) | H | W | 3-1 | Pickering 2, Dodds |
| | | 6 | 29.02.36 | **Tottenham Hotspur** (D2) | H | W | 3-1 | Dodds 2, Barclay |
| | | SF | 21.03.36 | **Fulham** (D2) | | W | 2-1 | Pickering, Bird |
| | | | | *played at Molineux* | | | | |

| | | | | | | | |
|---|---|---|---|---|---|---|---|
| | F | 25.04.36 | **Arsenal** (D1)<br>*played at Wembley Stadium* | | L | 0-1 | |
| 1936-37 (D2) | 3 | 16.01.37 | **Nottingham Forest** (D2) | A | W | 4-2 | Dodds 2, Ashton, Pickering |
| | 4 | 30.01.37 | **Wolverhampton W** (D1) | A | D | 2-2 | Barton, Dodds |
| | 4r | 04.02.37 | **Wolverhampton W** | H | L | 1-2 | Dodds |
| 1937-38 (D2) | 3 | 08.01.38 | **Doncaster Rovers** (3N) | A | W | 2-0 | Barton, Pickering |
| | 4 | 22.01.38 | **Liverpool** (D1) | H | D | 1-1 | Dodds |
| | 4r | 26.01.38 | **Liverpool** | A | L | 0-1 | |
| 1938-39 (D2) | 3 | 07.01.39 | **Blackpool** (D1) | A | W | 2-1 | Hagan, Hooper |
| | 4 | 21.01.39 | **Manchester City** (D2) | H | W | 2-0 | Pickering, Dodds |
| | 5 | 11.02.39 | **Grimsby Town** (D1) | H | D | 0-0 | |
| | 5r | 14.02.39 | **Grimsby Town** | A | L | 0-1 | |
| 1945-46 (D1) | 3 1L | 05.01.46 | **Huddersfield Town** (D1) | A | D | 1-1 | Jones |
| | 3 2L | 07.01.46 | **Huddersfield Town** | H | W | 2-0 | Collindridge, Brook |
| | 4 1L | 26.01.46 | **Stoke City** (D1) | A | L | 0-2 | |
| | 4 2L | 28.01.46 | **Stoke City** | H | W | 3-2 | Collindridge 3 |
| 1946-47 (D1) | 3 | 11.01.47 | **Carlisle Utd** (3N) | H | W | 3-0 | Nightingale, Hagan, Brook |
| | 4 | 25.01.47 | **Wolverhampton W** (D1) | A | D | 0-0 | |
| | 4r | 29.01.47 | **Wolverhampton W** | H | W | 2-0 | Brook, Nightingale |
| | 5 | 08.02.47 | **Stoke City** (D1) | A | W | 1-0 | Brook |
| | 6 | 01.03.47 | **Newcastle Utd** (D2) | H | L | 0-2 | |
| 1947-48 (D1) | 3 | 10.01.48 | **Crewe Alexandra** (3N) | A | L | 1-3 | Collindridge |
| 1948-49 (D1) | 3 | 08.01.49 | **New Brighton** (3N) | H | W | 5-2 | Jones 3, Hagan, Warhurst |
| | 4 | 29.01.49 | **Wolverhampton W** (D1) | H | L | 0-3 | |
| 1949-50 (D2) | 3 | 07.01.50 | **Leicester City** (D2) | H | W | 3-1 | Thompson, Collindridge, Brook |
| | 4 | 28.01.50 | **Wolverhampton W** (D1) | A | D | 0-0 | |
| | 4r | 31.01.50 | **Wolverhampton W** | H | L | 3-4 | Brook 3 (1p) |
| 1950-51 (D2) | 3 | 06.01.51 | **Gateshead AFC** (3N) | H | W | 1-0 | Hagan |
| | 4 | 27.01.51 | **Mansfield Town** (3N) | H | D | 0-0 | |
| | 4r | 31.01.51 | **Mansfield Town** | A | L | 1-2aet | Thompson |
| 1951-52 (D2) | 3 | 12.01.52 | **Newport County** (3S) | H | W | 2-0 | Brook, Ringstead |
| | 4 | 02.02.52 | **West Ham Utd** (D2) | A | D | 0-0 | |
| | 4r | 06.02.52 | **West Ham Utd** | H | W | 4-2 | Hawksworth 2, Ringstead, Browning |
| | 5 | 23.02.52 | **Southend Utd** (3S) | A | W | 2-1 | Ringstead, Browning |
| | 6 | 08.03.52 | **Chelsea** (D1) | H | L | 0-1 | |
| 1952-53 (D2) | 3 | 10.01.53 | **Newport County** (3S) | A | W | 4-1 | Bottom 2, Browning, Ringstead |
| | 4 | 31.01.53 | **Birmingham City** (D2) | H | D | 1-1 | Hagan |
| | 4r | 04.02.53 | **Birmingham City** | A | L | 1-3 | Bannister og |
| 1953-54 (D1) | 3 | 09.01.54 | **Sheffield Wed** (D1) | A | D | 1-1 | Toner |
| | 3r | 13.01.54 | **Sheffield Wed** | H | L | 1-3 | Hawksworth |
| 1954-55 (D1) | 3 | 08.01.55 | **Nottingham Forest** (D2) | H | L | 1-3 | Ringstead |
| 1955-56 (D1) | 3 | 07.01.56 | **Barrow** (3N) | H | W | 5-0 | Hoyland 2, Hawksworth, Grainger, Wragg |
| | 4 | 28.01.56 | **Bolton Wanderers** (D1) | A | W | 2-1 | Wragg 2 (1p) |
| | 5 | 18.02.56 | **Sunderland** (D1) | H | D | 0-0 | |
| | 5r | 22.02.56 | **Sunderland** | A | L | 0-1 | |
| 1956-57 (D2) | 3 | 05.01.57 | **Huddersfield Town** (D2) | A | D | 0-0 | |
| | 3r | 07.01.57 | **Huddersfield Town** | H | D | 1-1aet | Spencer |
| | 3 2r | 14.01.57 | **Huddersfield Town**<br>*played at Maine Road* | | L | 1-2 | Johnson |
| 1957-58 (D2) | 3 | 04.01.58 | **Grimsby Town** (D2) | H | W | 5-1 | Lewis 2, Summers, Hawksworth, Howitt |
| | 4 | 25.01.58 | **Tottenham Hotspur** (D1) | A | W | 3-0 | Pace, Russell, Hawksworth |
| | 5 | 15.02.58 | **WBA** (D1) | H | D | 1-1 | Lewis |
| | 5r | 19.02.58 | **WBA** | A | L | 1-4 | Dudley og |
| 1958-59 (D2) | 3 | 10.01.59 | **Crystal Palace** (D4) | H | W | 2-0 | Russell 2 |
| | 4 | 24.01.59 | **Worcester City** (SL) | A | W | 2-0 | Lewis, Simpson |
| | 5 | 14.02.59 | **Arsenal** (D1) | A | D | 2-2 | Simpson, Pace |
| | 5r | 18.02.59 | **Arsenal** | H | W | 3-0 | Russell, Pace, Lewis |
| | 6 | 28.02.59 | **Norwich City** (D3) | H | D | 1-1 | Russell |
| | 6r | 04.03.59 | **Norwich City** | A | L | 2-3 | Pace, Summers |

| | | | | | | | |
|---|---|---|---|---|---|---|---|
| | 6r | 04.03.59 | **Norwich City** | A | L | 2-3 | Pace, Summers |
| 1959-60 (D2) | 3 | 09.01.60 | **Portsmouth** (D2) | H | W | 3-0 | Pace 2, Lewis |
| | 4 | 30.01.60 | **Nottingham Forest** (D1) | H | W | 3-0 | Pace 3 |
| | 5 | 20.02.60 | **Watford** (D4) | H | W | 3-2 | Pace 3 |
| | 6 | 12.03.60 | **Sheffield Wed** (D1) | H | L | 0-2 | |
| 1960-61 (D2) | 3 | 07.01.61 | **Everton** (D1) | A | W | 1-0 | Russell |
| | 4 | 28.01.61 | **Lincoln City** (D2) | H | W | 3-1 | Russell 2, Mason |
| | 5 | 18.02.61 | **Blackburn Rovers** (D1) | H | W | 2-1 | Russell, Hodgson |
| | 6 | 04.03.61 | **Newcastle Utd** (D1) | A | W | 3-1 | Russell 3 |
| | SF | 18.03.61 | **Leicester City** (D1)<br>*played at Elland Road* | | D | 0-0 | |
| | SFr | 23.03.61 | **Leicester City**<br>*played at City Ground, Nottingham* | | D | 0-0aet | |
| | SF 2r | 27.03.61 | **Leicester City**<br>*played at St Andrews* | | L | 0-2aet | |
| 1961-62 (D1) | 3 | 06.01.62 | **Bury** (D2) | A | D | 0-0 | |
| | 3r | 10.01.62 | **Bury** | H | D | 2-2aet | Pace, Allchurch |
| | 3 2r | 15.01.62 | **Bury**<br>*played at Hillsborough* | | W | 2-0 | Pace 2 |
| | 4 | 27.01.62 | **Peterborough Utd** (D3) | A | W | 3-1 | Russell 2, Pace |
| | 5 | 17.02.62 | **Norwich City** (D2) | H | W | 3-1 | Kettlebrough, Russell, Pace |
| | 6 | 10.03.62 | **Burnley** (D1) | H | L | 0-1 | |
| 1962-63 (D1) | 3 | 06.03.63 | **Bolton Wanderers** (D1) | H | W | 3-1 | Kettlebrough 2, Summers |
| | 4 | 13.03.63 | **Port Vale** (D3) | A | W | 2-1 | Allchurch (p), Pace |
| | 5 | 16.03.63 | **Southampton** (D2) | A | L | 0-1 | |
| 1963-64 (D1) | 3 | 04.01.64 | **Lincoln City** (D4) | A | W | 4-0 | Jones 2, Wagstaff, Hartle |
| | 4 | 25.01.64 | **Swansea Town** (D2) | H | D | 1-1 | Jones |
| | 4r | 28.01.64 | **Swansea Town** | A | L | 0-4 | |
| 1964-65 (D1) | 3 | 09.01.65 | **Bristol City** (D3) | A | D | 1-1 | Jones |
| | 3r | 11.01.65 | **Bristol City** | H | W | 3-0 | Jones 2, Woodward |
| | 4 | 30.01.65 | **Aston Villa** (D1) | H | L | 0-2 | |
| 1965-66 (D1) | 3 | 22.01.66 | **Fulham** (D1) | H | W | 3-1 | Birchenall 2, Woodward |
| | 4 | 12.02.66 | **Wolverhampton W** (D2) | A | L | 0-3 | |
| 1966-67 (D1) | 3 | 28.01.67 | **Charlton Athletic** (D2) | A | W | 1-0 | Jones |
| | 4 | 18.02.67 | **Fulham** (D1) | A | D | 1-1 | Jones |
| | 4r | 01.03.67 | **Fulham** | H | W | 3-1 | Punton 2, Jones |
| | 5 | 11.03.67 | **Chelsea** (D1) | A | L | 0-2 | |
| 1967-68 (D1) | 3 | 27.01.68 | **Watford** (D3) | A | W | 1-0 | Hill |
| | 4 | 17.02.68 | **Blackpool** (D2) | H | W | 2-1 | Woodward, Addison |
| | 5 | 09.03.68 | **West Ham Utd** (D1) | A | W | 2-1 | Cliff 2 |
| | 6 | 30.03.68 | **Leeds Utd** (D1) | A | L | 0-1 | |
| 1968-69 (D2) | 3 | 04.01.69 | **Mansfield Town** (D3) | A | L | 1-2 | Tudor |
| 1969-70 (D2) | 3 | 03.01.70 | **Everton** (D1) | H | W | 2-1 | Reece, Addison |
| | 4 | 24.01.70 | **Derby County** (D1) | A | L | 0-3 | |
| 1970-71 (D2) | 3 | 02.01.71 | **Portsmouth** (D2) | A | L | 0-2 | |
| 1971-72 (D1) | 3 | 15.01.72 | **Cardiff City** (D2) | H | L | 1-3 | Mackenzie |
| 1972-73 (D1) | 3 | 13.01.73 | **Watford** (D3) | A | W | 1-0 | Eddy |
| | 4 | 03.02.73 | **Carlisle Utd** (D2) | A | L | 1-2 | Dearden |
| 1973-74 (D1) | 3 | 05.01.74 | **Ipswich Town** (D1) | A | L | 2-3 | Salmons, Currie |
| 1974-75 (D1) | 3 | 04.01.75 | **Bristol City** (D2) | H | W | 2-0 | Dearden, Currie |
| | 4 | 25.01.75 | **Aston Villa** (D2) | A | L | 1-4 | Field |
| 1975-76 (D1) | 3 | 03.01.76 | **Leicester City** (D1) | A | L | 0-3 | |
| 1976-77 (D2) | 3 | 08.01.77 | **Newcastle Utd** (D1) | H | D | 0-0 | |
| | 3r | 24.01.77 | **Newcastle Utd** | A | L | 1-3 | Garner |
| 1977-78 (D2) | 3 | 07.01.78 | **Arsenal** (D1) | H | L | 0-5 | |
| 1978-79 (D2) | 3 | 09.01.79 | **Aldershot** (D4) | H | D | 0-0 | |
| | 3r | 15.01.79 | **Aldershot** | A | L | 0-1 | |
| 1979-80 (D3) | 1 | 24.11.79 | **Burscough** (CC)<br>*played at Bramall Lane* | A | W | 3-0 | MacPhail, Speight, Matthews |
| | 2 | 15.12.79 | **Grimsby Town** (D3) | A | L | 0-2 | |
| 1980-81 (D3) | 1 | 22.11.80 | **Stockport County** (D4) | A | D | 0-0 | |

| | | | | | | | | |
|---|---|---|---|---|---|---|---|---|
| | | 1r | 25.11.80 | **Stockport County** | H | W | 3-2aet | Charles, Kenworthy, Sherlock og |
| | | 2 | 13.12.80 | **Chesterfield** (D3) | H | D | 1-1 | Hatton |
| | | 2r | 16.12.80 | **Chesterfield** | A | L | 0-1 | |
| 1981-82 | (D4) | 1 | 21.11.81 | **Altrincham** (APL) | H | D | 2-2 | Edwards, Hatton |
| | | 1r | 23.11.81 | **Altrincham** | A | L | 0-3 | |
| 1982-83 | (D3) | 1 | 20.11.82 | **Hull City** (D4) | A | D | 1-1 | Edwards |
| | | 1r | 23.11.82 | **Hull City** | H | W | 2-0 | Morris, Edwards |
| | | 3 | 08.01.83 | **Stoke City** (D1) | H | D | 0-0 | |
| | | 3r | 12.01.83 | **Stoke City** | A | L | 2-3 | Edwards, Morris (p) |
| 1983-84 | (D3) | 1 | 19.11.83 | **Wrexham** (D4) | A | W | 5-1 | Edwards 4, Arnott |
| | | 2 | 10.12.83 | **Lincoln City** (D3) | A | D | 0-0 | |
| | | 2r | 19.12.83 | **Lincoln City** | H | W | 1-0 | Stancliffe |
| | | 3 | 06.01.84 | **Birmingham City** (D1) | H | D | 1-1 | Brazil |
| | | 3r | 10.01.84 | **Birmingham City** | A | L | 0-2 | |
| 1984-85 | (D2) | 3 | 05.01.85 | **Watford** (D1) | A | L | 0-5 | |
| 1985-86 | (D2) | 3 | 13.01.86 | **Fulham** (D2) | H | W | 2-0 | Morris 2 |
| | | 4 | 25.01.86 | **Derby County** (D3) | H | L | 0-1 | |
| 1986-87 | (D2) | 3 | 10.01.87 | **Brighton** (D2) | H | D | 0-0 | |
| | | 3r | 21.01.87 | **Brighton** | A | W | 2-1 | Foley, Withe |
| | | 4 | 09.02.87 | **West Ham Utd** (D1) | A | L | 0-4 | |
| 1987-88 | (D2) | 3 | 09.01.88 | **Maidstone Utd** (Conf) | H | W | 1-0 | Dempsey |
| | | 4 | 01.02.88 | **Portsmouth** (D1) | A | L | 1-2 | Philliskirk |
| 1988-89 | (D3) | 1 | 19.11.88 | **Mansfield Town** (D3) | A | D | 1-1 | Deane |
| | | 1r | 22.11.88 | **Mansfield Town** | H | W | 2-1 | Bryson, Kenworthy og |
| | | 2 | 11.12.88 | **Doncaster Rovers** (D4) | A | W | 3-1 | Stancliffe, Duffield, Agana |
| | | 3 | 07.01.89 | **Huddersfield Town** (D3) | A | W | 1-0 | Agana |
| | | 4 | 28.01.89 | **Colchester Utd** (D4) | H | D | 3-3 | Todd, Deane, Bryson |
| | | 4r | 31.01.89 | **Colchester Utd** | A | W | 2-0 | Deane 2 |
| | | 5 | 18.02.89 | **Norwich City** (D1) | A | L | 2-3 | Deane, Agana |
| 1989-90 | (D2) | 3 | 06.01.90 | **Bournemouth** (D2) | H | W | 2-0 | Bryson, Agana |
| | | 4 | 27.01.90 | **Watford** (D2) | H | D | 1-1 | Ashby og |
| | | 4r | 30.01.90 | **Watford** | A | W | 2-1 | Deane, Stancliffe |
| | | 5 | 18.02.90 | **Barnsley** (D2) | H | D | 2-2 | Bradshaw, Bryson |
| | | 5r | 21.02.90 | **Barnsley** | A | D | 0-0aet | |
| | | 5 2r | 05.03.90 | **Barnsley** | A | W | 1-0aet | Agana (p) |
| | | 6 | 11.03.90 | **Manchester Utd** (D1) | H | L | 0-1 | |
| 1990-91 | (D1) | 3 | 05.01.91 | **Luton Town** (D1) | H | L | 1-3 | Bradshaw |
| 1991-92 | (D1) | 3 | 04.01.92 | **Luton Town** | H | W | 4-0 | Hodges, Deane, Lake, Whitehouse |
| | | 4 | 26.01.92 | **Charlton Athletic** (D2) | A | D | 0-0 | |
| | | 4r | 05.02.92 | **Charlton Athletic** | H | W | 3-1 | Deane, Gayle, Bradshaw |
| | | 5 | 15.02.92 | **Chelsea** (D1) | A | L | 0-1 | |
| 1992-93 | (PL) | 3 | 02.01.93 | **Burnley** (D2) | H | D | 2-2 | Hodges, Beesley |
| | | 3r | 12.01.93 | **Burnley** | A | W | 4-2 | Deane 3, Littlejohn |
| | | 4 | 23.01.93 | **Hartlepool Utd** (D2) | H | W | 1-0 | Cork |
| | | 5 | 14.02.93 | **Manchester Utd** (PL) | H | W | 2-1 | Hoyland, Hodges |
| | | 6 | 06.03.93 | **Blackburn Rovers** (PL) | A | D | 0-0 | |
| | | 6r | 16.03.93 | **Blackburn Rovers** | H | D | 2-2aet | Ward 2 |
| | | | | *Sheffield Utd won 5-3 on penalties* | | | | |
| | | SF | 03.04.93 | **Sheffield Wed** (PL) | | L | 1-2aet | Cork |
| | | | | *played at Wembley Stadium* | | | | |
| 1993-94 | (PL) | 3 | 09.01.94 | **Manchester Utd** (PL) | H | L | 0-1 | |
| 1994-95 | (D1) | 3 | 09.01.95 | **Manchester Utd** | H | L | 0-2 | |
| 1995-96 | (D1) | 3 | 06.01.96 | **Arsenal** (PL) | A | D | 1-1 | Whitehouse |
| | | 3r | 17.01.96 | **Arsenal** | H | W | 1-0 | Veart |
| | | 4 | 28.01.96 | **Aston Villa** (PL) | H | L | 0-1 | |
| 1996-97 | (D1) | 3 | 04.01.97 | **Norwich City** (D1) | A | L | 0-1 | |
| 1997-98 | (D1) | 3 | 03.01.98 | **Bury** (D1) | H | D | 1-1 | Fjortoft |
| | | 3r | 13.01.98 | **Bury** | A | W | 2-1 | Saunders, Fjortoft |
| | | 4 | 24.01.98 | **Ipswich Town** (D1) | A | D | 1-1 | Saunders |
| | | 4r | 03.02.98 | **Ipswich Town** | H | W | 1-0 | Hutchison (p) |
| | | 5 | 13.02.98 | **Reading** (D1) | H | W | 1-0 | Sandford |
| | | 6 | 07.03.98 | **Coventry City** (PL) | A | D | 1-1 | Marcelo |

| | | | | | | | |
|---|---|---|---|---|---|---|---|
| | 6r | 17.03.98 | **Coventry City** | H | D | 1-1aet | Holdsworth |
| | | | *Sheffield Utd won 3-1 on penalties* | | | | |
| | SF | 05.04.98 | **Newcastle Utd** (PL) | | L | 0-1 | |
| | | | *played at Old Trafford* | | | | |
| 1998-99 (D1) | 3 | 02.01.99 | **Notts County** (D2) | H | D | 1-1 | Marcelo |
| | 3r | 23.01.99 | **Notts County** | A | W | 4-3aet | Borbokis, Holdsworth, Marcelo 2 |
| | 4 | 27.01.99 | **Cardiff City** (D3) | H | W | 4-1 | Devlin, Holdsworth, Morris, Stuart |
| | 5 | 13.02.99 | **Arsenal** (PL) | A | L | 1-2 | Marcelo |
| | | | *result declared void* | | | | |
| | 5 | 23.02.99 | **Arsenal** (PL) | A | L | 1-2 | Morris |
| 1999-00 (D1) | 3 | 12.12.99 | **Rushden & D** (Conf) | H | D | 1-1 | Bent |
| | 3r | 21.12.99 | **Rushden & D** | A | D | 1-1aet | Derry |
| | | | *Sheffield Utd won 6-5 on penalties* | | | | |
| | 4 | 08.01.00 | **Newcastle Utd** (PL) | A | L | 1-4 | Smith |
| 2000-01 (D1) | 3 | 06.01.01 | **Southampton** (PL) | A | L | 0-1 | |
| 2001-02 (D1) | 3 | 05.01.02 | **Nottingham Forest** (D1) | H | W | 1-0 | Brown |
| | 4 | 26.01.02 | **Preston North End** (D1) | A | L | 1-2 | Ndlovu |
| 2002-03 (D1) | 3 | 04.01.03 | **Cheltenham Town** (D2) | H | W | 4-0 | Murphy, McGovern, Kabba 2 |
| | 4 | 25.01.03 | **Ipswich Town** (D1) | H | W | 4-3 | Brown, Jagielka, Peschisolido |
| | 5 | 15.02.03 | **Walsall** (D1) | H | W | 2-0 | Mooney, Ndlovu |
| | 6 | 09.03.03 | **Leeds Utd** (PL) | H | W | 1-0 | Kabba |
| | SF | 13.04.03 | **Arsenal** (PL) | | L | 0-1 | |
| | | | *played at Old Trafford* | | | | |

# SHEFFIELD WEDNESDAY

*Formed 1867. FA Cup winners 1896, 1907, 1935; Runners-up 1890, 1966, 1993. Record FA Cup win: 12-0 v Halliwell, 1st round, 17.1.1891; Record FA Cup defeat: 0-5 v Wolverhampton W 3rd round, 02.03.1889; 1-6 v Blackburn Rovers, FA Cup Final, 29.03.1890; 0-5 v Everton, 3rd round replay, 27.01.1988.*

| | | | | | | | |
|---|---|---|---|---|---|---|---|
| 1880-81 | 1 | | Queen's Park, Glasgow | | - | | |
| | | | *Queen's Park scratched. Sheffield Wed walkover* | | | | |
| | 2 | 18.12.80 | **Blackburn Rovers** | H | W | 4-0 | Gregory 3, Winterbottom |
| | 3 | 08.01.81 | **Turton** | A | W | 2-0 | Gregory, Rhodes |
| | 4 | 05.02.81 | **Darwen** | A | L | 2-5 | Gregory 2 |
| 1881-82 | 1 | 05.11.81 | **Sheffield Providence** | H | W | 2-0 | Cawley, Anthony |
| | 2 | | bye | | | | |
| | 3 | 28.12.81 | **Staveley** | H | D | 2-2 | Rhodes, Cawley |
| | 3r | 07.01.81 | **Staveley** | A | D | 0-0 | |
| | 3 2r | 09.01.81 | **Staveley** | A | W | 5-1 | Rhodes 4, Cawley |
| | 4 | 21.01.82 | **Sheffield Heeley** | H | W | 3-1 | Rhodes, Cawley, Mosforth |
| | 5 | 07.02.82 | **Upton Park** | H | W | 6-0 | Cawley 3, Mosforth 2, Rhodes |
| | SF | 06.03.82 | **Blackburn Rovers** | | D | 0-0 | |
| | | | *played at St John's Rugby Ground, Huddersfield* | | | | |
| | SFr | 15.03.82 | **Blackburn Rovers** | | L | 1-5 | Suter og |
| | | | *played at Whalley Range, Manchester* | | | | |
| 1882-83 | 1 | 04.11.82 | **Spilsby** | H | W | 12-2 | Gregory 5, Cawley 3, Newbould 3, Anthony |
| | 2 | 02.12.82 | **Lockwood Bros** | H | W | 6-0 | Gregory 2, Anthony, Newbould, Mosforth, Cawley |
| | 3 | 06.01.83 | **Nottingham Forest** | A | D | 2-2 | Gregory, Harrison |
| | 3r | 13.01.83 | **Nottingham Forest** | H | W | 3-2 | Harrison 2, Mosforth |
| | 4 | 12.02.83 | **Notts County** | H | L | 1-4 | Bentley |
| 1883-84 | 1 | | bye | | | | |
| | 2 | 01.12.83 | **Staveley** | A | L | 1-3 | Winterbottom |
| 1884-85 | 1 | 08.11.84 | **Long Eaton Rangers** | H | W | 1-0 | Cawley |
| | 2 | | bye | | | | |
| | 3 | 03.01.85 | **Nottingham Forest** | H | L | 1-2 | Sayer |
| 1885-86 | 1 | 31.10.85 | **Long Eaton Rangers** | A | L | 0-2 | |
| 1886-87 | | | did not enter | | | | |
| 1887-88 | 1 | 15.10.87 | **Belper Town** | A | W | 3-2 | Cawley 2, Waller |
| | 2 | 05.11.87 | **Long Eaton Rangers** | A | W | 2-1aet | Mosforth, Waller |
| | 3 | | bye | | | | |
| | 4 | 07.12.87 | **Crusaders** | A | W | 1-0 | Hiller |

| | | | | | | | | |
|---|---|---|---|---|---|---|---|---|
| | | 5 | 07.01.88 | **Nottingham Forest** | A | W | 4-2 | Ingram 3, Winterbottom |
| | | 6 | 30.01.88 | **Preston North End** | H | L | 1-3 | Ingram |
| 1888-89 | | 1 | 02.02.89 | **Notts Rangers** | A | D | 1-1 | Thompson |
| | | 1r | 09.02.89 | **Notts Rangers** | H | W | 3-0 | Dungworth 2, Cawley |
| | | 2 | 16.02.89 | **Notts County** (D1) | H | W | 3-2 | Ingram, Cawley, Winterbottom |
| | | 3 | 02.03.89 | **Wolverhampton W** (D1) | A | L | 0-3 | |
| 1889-90 | (FAll) | 1 | 20.01.90 | **Swifts** | H | W | 6-1 | Cawley 2, Mumford 2, Bennett 2 |
| | | 2 | 01.02.90 | **Accrington FC** (D1) | H | W | 2-1 | Cawley, Winterbottom |
| | | 3 | 15.02.90 | **Notts County** (D1) | H | W | 5-0 | Cawley 2, Ingram, Mumford, og |
| | | | | *FA ordered replay after protest* | | | | |
| | | 3r | 22.02.90 | **Notts County** (D1) | A | L | 2-3 | Ingram, Brayshaw |
| | | | | *FA ordered second replay after protest* | | | | |
| | | 3 2r | 03.03.90 | **Notts County** (D1) | | W | 2-1 | Cawley 2 |
| | | | | *played at Derby Racecourse Ground* | | | | |
| | | SF | 08.03.90 | **Bolton Wanderers** (D1) | | W | 2-1 | Mumford 2 |
| | | | | *played at Perry Barr, Birmingham* | | | | |
| | | F | 29.03.90 | **Blackburn Rovers** (D1) | | L | 1-6 | Bennett |
| | | | | *played at Kennington Oval* | | | | |
| 1890-91 | (FAll) | 1 | 17.01.91 | **Halliwell** | H | W | 12-0 | Woolhouse 5, Cawley 2, R Brandon 2, H Brandon, Ingram, Mumford |
| | | 2 | 31.01.91 | **Derby County** (D1) | A | W | 3-2 | Hodder, H Brandon, Winterbottom |
| | | 3 | 14.02.91 | **WBA** (D1) | H | L | 0-2 | |
| 1891-92 | (FAll) | 1 | 16.01.92 | **Bolton Wanderers** (D1) | H | W | 2-1 | |
| | | | | *FA ordered replay following protests over ground conditions* | | | | |
| | | 1r | 23.01.92 | **Bolton Wanderers** | H | W | 4-1 | Spiksley 2, Brown, Richardson |
| | | 2 | 30.01.92 | **Small Heath** (FAll) | H | W | 2-0 | Richardson, Thompson |
| | | 3 | 13.02.92 | **WBA** (D1) | H | L | 1-2 | Richardson |
| 1892-93 | (D1) | 1 | 21.01.93 | **Derby County** (D1) | H | W | 3-2aet | Spiksley 3 |
| | | | | *FA ordered match to be replayed because of protests* | | | | |
| | | 1 | 30.01.93 | **Derby County** | A | L | 0-1 | |
| | | | | *FA ordered match to be replayed a second time because of various protests* | | | | |
| | | 1 | 02.02.93 | **Derby County** | H | W | 4-2 | Betts, Spiksley, Woolhouse, Chalmers |
| | | 2 | 04.02.93 | **Burnley** (D1) | H | W | 1-0 | Spiksley |
| | | 3 | 18.02.93 | **Everton** (D1) | A | L | 0-3 | |
| 1893-94 | (D1) | 1 | 27.01.94 | **Woolwich Arsenal** (D2) | A | W | 2-1 | Spiksley 2 |
| | | 2 | 10.02.94 | **Stoke** (D1) | H | W | 1-0 | Woolhouse |
| | | 3 | 24.02.94 | **Aston Villa** (D1) | H | W | 3-2aet | Spiksley 2, Woolhouse |
| | | SF | 10.03.94 | **Bolton Wanderers** (D1) | | L | 1-2 | Woolhouse |
| | | | | *played at Fallowfield, Manchester* | | | | |
| 1894-95 | (D1) | 1 | 02.02.95 | **Notts County** (D2) | H | W | 5-1 | Brash 2, Davis, Spiksley, Ferrier |
| | | 2 | 16.02.95 | **Middlesbrough** (NL) | H | W | 6-1 | Davis 3, Spiksley 2, Brady |
| | | 3 | 02.03.95 | **Everton** (D1) | H | W | 2-0 | Brady, Ferrier |
| | | SF | 16.03.95 | **WBA** (D1) | | L | 0-2 | |
| | | | | *played at Derby Cricket Ground* | | | | |
| 1895-96 | (D1) | 1 | 01.02.96 | **Southampton St M** (SL) | A | W | 3-2 | Brady 2, Davis |
| | | 2 | 15.02.96 | **Sunderland** (D1) | H | W | 2-1 | Bell, Spiksley |
| | | 3 | 29.02.96 | **Everton** (D1) | H | W | 4-0 | Bell 2, Brash 2 |
| | | SF | 21.03.96 | **Bolton Wanderers** (D1) | | D | 1-1 | Brash |
| | | | | *played at Goodison Park* | | | | |
| | | SFr | 28.03.96 | **Bolton Wanderers** | | W | 3-1 | Crawshaw, Davis, Spiksley |
| | | | | *played at Town Ground, Nottingham* | | | | |
| | | F | 18.04.96 | **Wolverhampton W** (D1) | | W | 2-1 | Spiksley 2 |
| | | | | *played at Crystal Palace* | | | | |
| 1896-97 | (D1) | 1 | 30.01.97 | **Nottingham Forest** (D1) | H | L | 0-1 | |
| 1897-98 | (D1) | 1 | 29.01.98 | **Sunderland** (D1) | A | W | 1-0 | Kaye |
| | | 2 | 12.02.98 | **WBA** (D1) | A | L | 0-1 | |
| 1898-99 | (D1) | 1 | 28.01.99 | **Stoke** (D1) | H | D | 2-2 | Earp, Crawshaw |
| | | 1r | 02.02.99 | **Stoke** | A | L | 0-2 | |
| 1899-00 | (D2) | 1 | 27.01.00 | **Bolton Wanderers** (D2) | H | W | 1-0 | Wright |
| | | 2 | 10.02.00 | **Sheffield Utd** (D1) | A | D | 0-0 | |
| | | 2r | 17.02.00 | **Sheffield Utd** | A | D | 1-1 | Brash |

| | | | | | | | | |
|---|---|---|---|---|---|---|---|---|
| | | 2 2r | 19.02.00 | **Sheffield Utd** | H | L | 0-2 | |
| 1900-01 | (D1) | 1 | 09.02.01 | **Bury** (D1) | H | L | 0-1 | |
| 1901-02 | (D1) | 1 | 25.01.02 | **Sunderland** (D1) | A | L | 0-1 | |
| 1902-03 | (D1) | 1 | 07.02.03 | **Blackburn Rovers** (D1) | H | D | 0-0 | |
| | | 1r | 12.02.03 | **Blackburn Rovers** | A | L | 0-1 | |
| 1903-04 | (D1) | 1 | 06.02.04 | **Plymouth Argyle** (SL) | A | D | 2-2 | Wilson 2 |
| | | 1r | 10.02.04 | **Plymouth Argyle** | H | W | 2-0 | Davis, Chapman (p) |
| | | 2 | 20.02.04 | **Manchester Utd** (D2) | H | W | 6-0 | VS Simpson 3, Davis 2, G Simpson |
| | | 3 | 05.03.04 | **Tottenham Hotspur** (SL) | A | D | 1-1 | Davis |
| | | 3r | 09.03.04 | **Tottenham Hotspur** | H | W | 2-0 | Davis, Chapman |
| | | SF | 19.03.04 | **Manchester City** (D1) | | L | 0-3 | |
| | | | | *played at Goodison Park* | | | | |
| 1904-05 | (D1) | 1 | 04.02.05 | **Blackburn Rovers** (D1) | A | W | 2-1 | Chapman, Hemmingfield |
| | | 2 | 18.02.05 | **Portsmouth** (SL) | H | W | 2-1 | Stewart, Davis |
| | | 3 | 04.03.05 | **Preston North End** (D1) | A | D | 1-1 | Wilson |
| | | 3r | 09.03.05 | **Preston North End** | H | W | 3-0 | G Simpson, Wilson, Stewart |
| | | SF | 25.03.05 | **Newcastle Utd** (D1) | | L | 0-1 | |
| | | | | *played at Hyde Road, Manchester* | | | | |
| 1905-06 | (D1) | 1 | 13.01.06 | **Bristol Rovers** (SL) | H | W | 1-0 | G Simpson |
| | | 2 | 03.02.06 | **Millwall Athletic** (SL) | H | D | 1-1 | Stewart |
| | | 2r | 08.02.06 | **Millwall Athletic** | A | W | 3-0 | G Simpson, Chapman, Davis (p) |
| | | 3 | 24.02.06 | **Nottingham Forest** (D1) | H | W | 4-1 | Wilson, G Simpson, Chapman, Stewart |
| | | 4 | 10.03.06 | **Everton** (D1) | A | L | 3-4 | Wilson, Bartlett, Davis (p) |
| 1906-07 | (D1) | 1 | 12.01.07 | **Wolverhampton W** (D2) | H | W | 3-2 | Stewart, G Simpson, Tummon |
| | | 2 | 02.02.07 | **Southampton** (SL) | A | D | 1-1 | Wilson |
| | | 2r | 07.02.07 | **Southampton** | H | W | 3-1 | Wilson, Stewart, Chapman |
| | | 3 | 23.02.07 | **Sunderland** (D1) | H | D | 0-0 | |
| | | 3r | 27.02.07 | **Sunderland** | A | W | 1-0 | G Simpson |
| | | 4 | 09.03.07 | **Liverpool** (D1) | H | W | 1-0 | Chapman |
| | | SF | 23.03.07 | **Woolwich Arsenal** (D1) | | W | 3-1 | Wilson 2, Stewart |
| | | | | *played at St Andrews* | | | | |
| | | F | 20.04.07 | **Everton** (D1) | | W | 2-1 | Stewart, G.Simpson |
| | | | | *played at Crystal Palace* | | | | |
| 1907-08 | (D1) | 1 | 11.01.08 | **Norwich City** (SL) | A | L | 0-2 | |
| 1908-09 | (D1) | 1 | 16.01.09 | **Stoke** (BDL) | H | W | 5-0 | Wilson 2, Bradshaw 2, Chapman |
| | | 2 | 06.02.09 | **Portsmouth** (SL) | A | D | 2-2 | Tummon 2 |
| | | 2r | 11.02.09 | **Portsmouth** | H | W | 3-0 | Brittleton, Rollinson, Wilson |
| | | 3 | 20.02.09 | **Glossop North End** (D2) | H | L | 0-1 | |
| 1909-10 | (D1) | 1 | 15.01.10 | **Northampton Town** (SL) | A | D | 0-0 | |
| | | 1r | 20.01.10 | **Northampton Town** | H | L | 0-1 | |
| 1910-11 | (D1) | 1 | 14.01.11 | **Coventry City** (SL) | H | L | 1-2 | Wilson |
| 1911-12 | (D1) | 1 | 13.01.12 | **Middlesbrough** (D1) | A | D | 0-0 | |
| | | 1r | 25.01.12 | **Middlesbrough** | H | L | 1-2 | McLean |
| 1912-13 | (D1) | 1 | 16.01.13 | **Grimsby Town** (D2) | H | W | 5-1 | McLean 4, Brittleton |
| | | 2 | 01.02.13 | **Chelsea** (D1) | A | D | 1-1 | McLean |
| | | 2r | 05.02.13 | **Chelsea** | H | W | 6-0 | McLean 3, Wilson 2, Kirkman |
| | | 3 | 22.02.13 | **Bradford Park A** (D2) | A | L | 1-2 | Kirkman |
| 1913-14 | (D1) | 1 | 10.01.14 | **Notts County** (D2) | H | W | 3-2 | JD Burkinshaw, L Burkinshaw, Brittleton |
| | | 2 | 31.01.14 | **Wolverhampton W** (D2) | A | D | 1-1 | McLean |
| | | 2r | 04.02.14 | **Wolverhampton W** | H | W | 1-0 | Kirkman |
| | | 3 | 24.02.14 | **Brighton** (SL) | H | W | 3-0 | McLean, Gill, JD Burkinshaw |
| | | 4 | 07.03.14 | **Aston Villa** (D1) | H | L | 0-1 | |
| 1914-15 | (D1) | 1 | 09.01.15 | **Manchester Utd** (D1) | H | W | 1-0 | Wilson |
| | | 2 | 30.01.15 | **Wolverhampton W** (D2) | H | W | 2-0 | Robertson, Glennon |
| | | 3 | 20.02.15 | **Newcastle Utd** (D1) | H | L | 1-2 | McLean |
| 1919-20 | (D1) | 1 | 14.01.20 | **Darlington** (NEL) | A | D | 0-0 | |
| | | 1r | 19.01.20 | **Darlington** | H | L | 0-2 | |
| 1920-21 | (D2) | 1 | 08.01.21 | **West Ham Utd** (D2) | H | W | 1-0 | Price |
| | | 2 | 29.01.21 | **Everton** (D1) | A | D | 1-1 | Taylor |

| | | | | | | | |
|---|---|---|---|---|---|---|---|
| | 2r | 03.02.21 | **Everton** | H | L | 0-1 | |
| 1921-22 (D2) | 1 | 07.01.22 | **Bradford Park A** (D2) | A | L | 0-1 | |
| 1922-23 (D2) | 1 | 13.01.23 | **New Brighton** (LC) | H | W | 3-0 | Binks 2, Smailes |
| | 2 | 03.02.23 | **Barnsley** (D2) | H | W | 2-1 | Smailes, Binks |
| | 3 | 24.02.23 | **Derby County** (D2) | A | L | 0-1 | |
| 1923-24 (D2) | 1 | 12.01.24 | **Leicester City** (D2) | H | W | 4-1 | Taylor 2, Binks (p), Petrie |
| | 2 | 02.02.24 | **Bristol City** (D2) | H | D | 1-1 | Harron |
| | 2r | 06.02.24 | **Bristol City** | A | L | 0-2 | |
| 1924-25 (D2) | 1 | 10.01.25 | **Manchester Utd** (D2) | H | W | 2-0 | Hill 2 |
| | 2 | 31.01.25 | **Sheffield Utd** (D1) | A | L | 2-3 | Trotter 2 |
| 1925-26 (D2) | 3 | 09.01.26 | **New Brighton** (3N) | A | L | 1-2 | Trotter |
| 1926-27 (D1) | 3 | 08.01.27 | **Brighton** (3S) | H | W | 2-0 | Hill, Trottter |
| | 4 | 29.01.27 | **South Shields** (D2) | H | D | 1-1 | Trotter |
| | 4r | 02.02.27 | **South Shields** | A | L | 0-1 | |
| 1927-28 (D1) | 3 | 14.01.28 | **Bournemouth** (3S) | H | W | 3-0 | Harper 2, Seed |
| | 4 | 28.01.28 | **Swindon Town** (3S) | A | W | 2-1 | Seed, Harper |
| | 5 | 18.02.28 | **Sheffield Utd** (D1) | H | D | 1-1 | Wilkinson |
| | 5r | 22.02.28 | **Sheffield Utd** | A | L | 1-4 | Hooper |
| 1928-29 (D1) | 3 | 12.01.29 | **Wigan Borough** (3N) | A | W | 3-1 | Allen 2, Hooper |
| | 4 | 26.01.29 | **Reading** (D2) | A | L | 0-1 | |
| 1929-30 (D1) | 3 | 11.01.30 | **Burnley** (D1) | H | W | 1-0 | Allen |
| | 4 | 25.01.30 | **Oldham Athletic** (D2) | A | W | 4-3 | Allen 2, Hooper, Seed |
| | 5 | 15.02.30 | **Bradford Park A** (D2) | H | W | 5-1 | Seed, Rimmer, Allen, Hooper, Bentley og |
| | 6 | 01.03.30 | **Nottingham Forest** (D2) | A | D | 2-2 | Allen, Rimmer |
| | 6r | 08.03.30 | **Nottingham Forest** | H | W | 3-1 | Seed, Allen, Burgess |
| | SF | 22.03.30 | **Huddersfield Town** (D1) *played at Old Trafford* | | L | 1-2 | Hooper |
| 1930-31 (D1) | 3 | 10.01.31 | **Gateshead AFC** (3N) | A | W | 6-2 | Rimmer 2, Hooper, Burgess, Allen, Ball |
| | 4 | 24.01.31 | **Barnsley** (D2) | A | L | 1-2 | Ball |
| 1931-32 (D1) | 3 | 09.01.32 | **Tottenham Hotspur** (D2) | A | D | 2-2 | Burgess, Rimmer |
| | 3r | 13.01.32 | **Tottenham Hotspur** | H | W | 3-1 | Millership, Rimmer, Stephenson |
| | 4 | 23.01.32 | **Bournemouth** (3S) | H | W | 7-0 | Millership 4, Burgess 3 |
| | 5 | 13.02.32 | **Chelsea** (D1) | H | D | 1-1 | Stephenson |
| | 5r | 17.02.32 | **Chelsea** | A | L | 0-2 | |
| 1932-33 (D1) | 3 | 14.01.33 | **Chesterfield** (D2) | H | D | 2-2 | Ball 2 |
| | 3r | 18.01.33 | **Chesterfield** | A | L | 2-4 | Millership, Stephenson |
| 1933-34 (D1) | 3 | 13.01.34 | **Rotherham Utd** (3N) | A | W | 3-0 | Dewar, Leach, Hooper |
| | 4 | 27.01.34 | **Oldham Athletic** (D2) | A | D | 1-1 | Hooper |
| | 4r | 31.01.34 | **Oldham Athletic** | H | W | 6-1 | Dewar 3, Hooper, Rimmer, Burgess |
| | 5 | 17.02.34 | **Manchester City** (D1) | H | D | 2-2 | Rimmer, Dewar |
| | 5r | 21.02.34 | **Manchester City** | A | L | 0-2 | |
| 1934-35 (D1) | 3 | 12.01.35 | **Oldham Athletic** (D2) | H | W | 3-1 | Palethorpe, Rimmer, Surtees |
| | 4 | 26.01.35 | **Wolverhampton W** (D1) | A | W | 2-1 | Palethorpe, Rimmer |
| | 5 | 16.02.35 | **Norwich City** (D2) | A | W | 1-0 | Rimmer |
| | 6 | 02.03.35 | **Arsenal** (D1) | H | W | 2-1 | Hooper, Rimmer |
| | SF | 16.03.35 | **Burnley** (D2) *played at Villa Park* | | W | 3-0 | Rimmer 2, Palethorpe |
| | F | 27.04.35 | **WBA** (D1) *played at Wembley Stadium* | | W | 4-2 | Rimmer 2, Palethorpe, Hooper |
| 1935-36 (D1) | 3 | 11.01.36 | **Crewe Alexandra** (3N) | A | D | 1-1 | Surtees |
| | 3r | 15.01.36 | **Crewe Alexandra** | H | W | 3-1 | Dewar, Rimmer, Surtees |
| | 4 | 25.01.36 | **Newcastle Utd** (D2) | H | D | 1-1 | Dewar |
| | 4r | 29.01.36 | **Newcastle Utd** | A | L | 1-3 | Rimmer |
| 1936-37 (D1) | 3 | 16.01.37 | **Port Vale** (3N) | H | W | 2-0 | Robinson, Drury |
| | 4 | 30.01.37 | **Everton** (D1) | A | L | 0-3 | |
| 1937-38 (D2) | 3 | 08.01.38 | **Burnley** (D2) | H | D | 1-1 | Millership |
| | 3r | 11.01.38 | **Burnley** | A | L | 1-3 | Drury |
| 1938-39 (D2) | 3 | 07.01.39 | **Yeovil & Petters Utd** (SL) | H | D | 1-1 | Robinson |
| | 3r | 12.01.39 | **Yeovil & Petters Utd** | A | W | 2-1 | Lewis, Napier |

| | | | | | | | | |
|---|---|---|---|---|---|---|---|---|
| | | 4 | 21.01.39 | **Chester** (3N) | H | D | 1-1 | Millership |
| | | 4r | 25.01.39 | **Chester** | A | D | 1-1aet | Robinson |
| | | 4 2r | 30.01.39 | **Chester** | | W | 2-0 | Robinson, Hunt |
| | | | | *played at Maine Road* | | | | |
| | | 5 | 11.02.39 | **Chelsea** (D1) | A | D | 1-1 | Robinson |
| | | 5r | 13.02.39 | **Chelsea** | H | D | 0-0aet | |
| | | 5 2r | 20.02.39 | **Chelsea** | | L | 1-3 | Fallon |
| | | | | *played at Highbury* | | | | |
| 1945-46 | (D2) | 3 1L | 05.01.46 | **Mansfield Town** (3S) | A | D | 0-0 | |
| | | 3 2L | 09.01.46 | **Mansfield Town** | H | W | 5-0 | J Thompson, Ward, Tomlinson, Aveyard, Froggatt |
| | | 4 1L | 26.01.46 | **York City** (3N) | H | W | 5-1 | Driver 2, J Thompson, Aveyard, Froggatt |
| | | 4 2L | 30.01.46 | **York City** | A | W | 6-1 | Tomlinson 3, Driver, J Thompson, Froggatt |
| | | 5 1L | 09.02.46 | **Stoke City** (D1) | A | L | 0-2 | |
| | | 5 2L | 11.02.46 | **Stoke City** | H | D | 0-0 | |
| 1946-47 | (D2) | 3 | 11.01.47 | **Blackpool** (D1) | H | W | 4-1 | Froggatt 2, Fox, Hunt |
| | | 4 | 25.01.47 | **Everton** (D1) | H | W | 2-1 | Froggatt, Tomlinson |
| | | 5 | 20.02.47 | **Preston North End** (D1) | H | L | 0-2 | |
| 1947-48 | (D2) | 3 | 10.01.48 | **Cardiff City** (D2) | A | W | 2-1aet | Lowes, Quigley (p) |
| | | 4 | 24.01.48 | **Leicester City** (D2) | A | L | 1-2 | Lowes |
| 1948-49 | (D2) | 3 | 08.01.49 | **Southampton** (D2) | H | W | 2-1 | Dailey, Quigley |
| | | 4 | 29.01.49 | **Portsmouth** (D1) | A | L | 1-2 | Quigley |
| 1949-50 | (D2) | 3 | 07.01.50 | **Arsenal** (D1) | A | L | 0-1 | |
| 1950-51 | (D1) | 3 | 06.01.51 | **Fulham** (D1) | A | L | 0-1 | |
| 1951-52 | (D2) | 3 | 12.01.52 | **Bradford Park A** (3N) | A | L | 1-2 | Dooley |
| 1952-53 | (D1) | 3 | 10.01.53 | **Blackpool** (D1) | H | L | 1-2 | Sewell |
| 1953-54 | (D1) | 3 | 09.01.54 | **Sheffield Utd** (D1) | H | D | 1-1 | Shaw |
| | | 3r | 13.01.54 | **Sheffield Utd** | A | W | 3-1 | Finney, Davies, Sewell |
| | | 4 | 30.01.54 | **Chesterfield** (3N) | H | D | 0-0 | |
| | | 4r | 03.02.54 | **Chesterfield** | A | W | 4-2 | Shaw 2, Sewell, Woodhead |
| | | 5 | 20.02.54 | **Everton** (D2) | H | W | 3-1 | Shaw, Sewell, Woodhead |
| | | 6 | 13.03.54 | **Bolton Wanderers** (D1) | H | D | 1-1 | Woodhead |
| | | 6r | 17.03.54 | **Bolton Wanderers** | A | W | 2-0 | Sewell, Shaw |
| | | SF | 27.03.54 | **Preston North End** (D1) | | L | 0-2 | |
| | | | | *played at Maine Road* | | | | |
| 1954-55 | (D1) | 3 | 08.01.55 | **Hastings Utd** (SL) | H | W | 2-1 | Shaw, Greensmith |
| | | 4 | 29.01.55 | **Notts County** (D2) | H | D | 1-1 | Watson |
| | | 4r | 03.02.55 | **Notts County** | A | L | 0-1aet | |
| 1955-56 | (D2) | 3 | 07.01.56 | **Newcastle Utd** (D1) | H | L | 1-3 | Gibson |
| 1956-57 | (D1) | 3 | 05.01.57 | **Preston North End** (D1) | A | D | 0-0 | |
| | | 3r | 09.01.57 | **Preston North End** | H | D | 2-2aet | Quixall, Shiner |
| | | 3 2r | 14.01.57 | **Preston North End** | | L | 1-5 | Quixall |
| | | | | *played at Goodison Park* | | | | |
| 1957-58 | (D1) | 3 | 04.01.58 | **Hereford Utd** (SL) | A | W | 3-0 | Froggatt 2, Shiner |
| | | 4 | 29.01.58 | **Hull City** (3N) | H | W | 4-3 | Froggatt, Shiner, Wilkinson, Davison og |
| | | 5 | 19.02.58 | **Manchester Utd** (D1) | A | L | 0-3 | |
| 1958-59 | (D2) | 3 | 19.01.59 | **WBA** (D1) | H | L | 0-2 | |
| 1959-60 | (D1) | 3 | 09.01.60 | **Middlesbrough** (D2) | H | W | 2-1 | Ellis, McAnearney (p) |
| | | 4 | 30.01.60 | **Peterborough Utd** (ML) | H | W | 2-0 | Craig 2 |
| | | 5 | 20.02.60 | **Manchester Utd** (D1) | H | W | 1-0 | McAnearney (p) |
| | | 6 | 12.03.60 | **Sheffield Utd** (D2) | A | W | 2-0 | Wilkinson 2 |
| | | SF | 26.03.60 | **Blackburn Rovers** (D1) | | L | 1-2 | Fantham |
| | | | | *played at Maine Road* | | | | |
| 1960-61 | (D1) | 3 | 07.01.61 | **Leeds Utd** (D2) | H | W | 2-0 | Quinn, Ellis |
| | | 4 | 28.01.61 | **Manchester Utd** (D1) | H | D | 1-1 | Wilkinson |
| | | 4r | 01.02.61 | **Manchester Utd** | A | W | 7-2 | Ellis 3, Fantham 2, Finney 2 |
| | | 5 | 18.02.61 | **Leyton Orient** (D2) | A | W | 2-0 | Fantham, Ellis |
| | | 6 | 04.03.61 | **Burnley** (D1) | H | D | 0-0 | |
| | | 6r | 07.03.61 | **Burnley** | A | L | 0-2 | |

| | | | | | | | | |
|---|---|---|---|---|---|---|---|---|
| 1961-62 | (D1) | 3 | 09.01.62 | **Swansea Town** (D2) | H | W | 1-0 | Finney |
| | | 4 | 27.01.62 | **Nottingham Forest** (D1) | A | W | 2-0 | Craig, Ellis |
| | | 5 | 17.02.62 | **Manchester Utd** (D1) | A | D | 0-0 | |
| | | 5r | 21.02.62 | **Manchester Utd** | H | L | 0-2 | |
| 1962-63 | (D1) | 3 | 21.02.63 | **Shrewsbury Town** (D3) | A | D | 1-1 | Layne |
| | | 3r | 07.03.63 | **Shrewsbury Town** | H | W | 2-1aet | Finney, Fantham |
| | | 4 | 12.03.63 | **Arsenal** (D1) | A | L | 0-2 | |
| 1963-64 | (D1) | 3 | 04.01.64 | **Newport County** (D4) | A | L | 2-3 | Holliday, Finney |
| 1964-65 | (D1) | 3 | 09.01.65 | **Everton** (D1) | A | D | 2-2 | Fantham, Quinn |
| | | 3r | 13.01.65 | **Everton** | H | L | 0-3 | |
| 1965-66 | (D1) | 3 | 22.01.66 | **Reading** (D3) | A | W | 3-2 | Fantham 2, McCalliog |
| | | 4 | 12.02.66 | **Newcastle Utd** (D1) | A | W | 2-1 | Dobson, Mcgrath og |
| | | 5 | 05.03.66 | **Huddersfield Town** (D2) | A | W | 2-1 | Ford, Usher |
| | | 6 | 26.03.66 | **Blackburn Rovers** (D1) | A | W | 2-1 | Ford 2 |
| | | SF | 23.04.66 | **Chelsea** (D1) | | W | 2-0 | Pugh, McCalliog |
| | | | | *played at Villa Park* | | | | |
| | | F | 14.05.66 | **Everton** (D1) | | L | 2-3 | McCalliog, Ford |
| | | | | *played at Wembley Stadium* | | | | |
| 1966-67 | (D1) | 3 | 28.01.67 | **QPR** (D3) | H | W | 3-0 | Ritchie 3 |
| | | 4 | 18.02.67 | **Mansfield Town** (D3) | H | W | 4-0 | Ritchie 2 Fantham, McCalliog |
| | | 5 | 11.03.67 | **Norwich City** (D2) | A | W | 3-1 | Quinn, Ford, Fantham |
| | | 6 | 08.04.67 | **Chelsea** (D1) | A | L | 0-1 | |
| 1967-68 | (D1) | 3 | 27.01.68 | **Plymouth Argyle** (D2) | H | W | 3-0 | Whitham, Fantham, Ritchie (p) |
| | | 4 | 17.02.68 | **Swindon Town** (D3) | H | W | 2-1 | Smith, Ritchie |
| | | 5 | 09.03.68 | **Chelsea** (D1) | H | D | 2-2 | Ritchie, Megson |
| | | 5r | 12.03.68 | **Chelsea** | A | L | 0-2 | |
| 1968-69 | (D1) | 3 | 04.01.69 | **Leeds Utd** (D1) | H | D | 1-1 | Ritchie |
| | | 3r | 08.01.69 | **Leeds Utd** | A | W | 3-1 | Woodall 2, Ritchie |
| | | 4 | 25.01.69 | **Birmingham City** (D2) | H | D | 0-0 | McCalliog, Young |
| | | 4r | 28.01.69 | **Birmingham City** | A | L | 1-2 | Young |
| 1969-70 | (D1) | 3 | 03.01.70 | **WBA** (D1) | H | W | 2-1 | Whitham 2 |
| | | 4 | 24.01.70 | **Scunthorpe Utd** (D4) | H | L | 1-2 | Whitham |
| 1970-71 | (D2) | 3 | 02.01.71 | **Tottenham Hotspur** (D1) | A | L | 1-4 | Sunley |
| 1971-72 | (D2) | 3 | 15.01.72 | **Sunderland** (D2) | A | L | 0-3 | |
| 1972-73 | (D2) | 3 | 13.01.73 | **Fulham** (D2) | H | W | 2-0 | Prendergast, Joicey |
| | | 4 | 03.02.73 | **Crystal Palace** (D1) | H | D | 1-1 | Craig (p) |
| | | 4r | 06.02.73 | **Crystal Palace** | A | D | 1-1aet | Sunley |
| | | 4 2r | 19.02.73 | **Crystal Palace** | | W | 3-2 | Joicey 3 |
| | | | | *played at Villa Park* | | | | |
| | | 5 | 24.02.73 | **Chelsea** (D1) | H | L | 1-2 | Coyle |
| 1973-74 | (D2) | 3 | 05.01.74 | **Coventry City** (D1) | H | D | 0-0 | |
| | | 3r | 08.01.74 | **Coventry City** | A | L | 1-3 | Sunley |
| 1974-75 | (D2) | 3 | 04.01.75 | **Chelsea** (D1) | A | L | 2-3 | Thompson (p) Shaw |
| 1975-76 | (D3) | 1 | 22.11.75 | **Macclesfield T** (NPL) | H | W | 3-1 | Prendergast, Knighton, Proudlove |
| | | 2 | 13.12.75 | **Wigan Athletic** (NPL) | H | W | 2-0 | Sunley, Nimmo |
| | | 3 | 03.01.76 | **Charlton Athletic** (D2) | A | L | 1-2 | Sunley |
| 1976-77 | (D3) | 1 | 20.11.76 | **Stockport County** (D4) | H | W | 2-0 | Tynan, Wylde |
| | | 2 | 15.12.76 | **Darlington** (D4) | A | L | 0-1 | |
| 1977-78 | (D3) | 1 | 26.11.77 | **Bury** (D3) | H | W | 1-0 | Hope |
| | | 2 | 17.12.77 | **Wigan Athletic** (NPL) | A | L | 0-1 | |
| 1978-79 | (D3) | 1 | 25.11.78 | **Scunthorpe Utd** (D4) | A | D | 1-1 | Nimmo |
| | | 1r | 28.11.78 | **Scunthorpe Utd** | H | W | 1-0 | Nimmo |
| | | 2 | 16.12.78 | **Tranmere Rovers** (D3) | A | D | 1-1 | Leman |
| | | 2r | 19.12.78 | **Tranmere Rovers** | H | W | 4-0 | Wylde 2, Lowey, Hornsby (p) |
| | | 3 | 06.01.79 | **Arsenal** (D1) | H | D | 1-1 | Johnson |
| | | 3r | 09.01.79 | **Arsenal** | A | D | 1-1aet | Wylde |
| | | 3 2r | 15.01.79 | **Arsenal** | | D | 2-2aet | Hornsby 2 (1p) |
| | | | | *played at Filbert Street* | | | | |
| | | 3 3r | 17.01.79 | **Arsenal** | | D | 3-3aet | Rushbury, Lowey, Hornsby (p) |
| | | | | *played at Filbert Street* | | | | |

| | | | | | | | | |
|---|---|---|---|---|---|---|---|---|
| | | 3 4r | 22.01.79 | **Arsenal** *played at Filbert Street* | | L | 0-2 | |
| 1979-80 | (D3) | 1 | 24.11.79 | **Lincoln City** (D4) | H | W | 3-0 | Smith (p), McCulloch, King |
| | | 2 | 15.12.79 | **Carlisle Utd** (D3) | A | L | 0-3 | |
| 1980-81 | (D2) | 3 | 03.01.81 | **Newcastle Utd** (D2) | A | L | 1-2 | Pearson |
| 1981-82 | (D2) | 3 | 02.01.82 | **Coventry City** (D1) | A | L | 1-3 | McCulloch |
| 1982-83 | (D2) | 3 | 08.01.83 | **Southend Utd** (D3) | A | D | 0-0 | |
| | | 3r | 11.01.83 | **Southend Utd** | H | D | 2-2aet | Smith, Megson |
| | | 3 2r | 24.01.83 | **Southend Utd** | H | W | 2-1 | Taylor 2 |
| | | 4 | 29.01.83 | **Torquay Utd** (D4) | A | W | 3-2 | Sterland, Lyons, Megson |
| | | 5 | 19.02.83 | **Cambridge Utd** (D2) | A | W | 2-1 | Megson 2 |
| | | 6 | 12.03.83 | **Burnley** (D2) | A | D | 1-1 | Bannister |
| | | 6r | 15.03.83 | **Burnley** | H | W | 5-0 | Shelton 2, McCulloch 2, Megson (p) |
| | | SF | 16.04.83 | **Brighton** (D1) *played at Highbury* | | L | 1-2 | Mirocevic |
| 1983-84 | (D2) | 3 | 07.01.84 | **Barnsley** (D2) | H | W | 1-0 | Pearson |
| | | 4 | 30.01.84 | **Coventry City** (D1) | H | W | 3-2 | Sterland (p), Bannister, Shirtliff |
| | | 5 | 18.02.84 | **Oxford Utd** (D3) | A | W | 3-0 | Bannister 2, Varadi |
| | | 6 | 11.03.84 | **Southampton** (D1) | H | D | 0-0 | |
| | | 6r | 20.03.84 | **Southampton** | A | L | 1-5 | Shirtliff |
| 1984-85 | (D1) | 3 | 05.01.85 | **Fulham** (D2) | A | W | 3-2 | Chapman 2, Sterland |
| | | 4 | 26.01.85 | **Oldham Athletic** (D2) | H | W | 5-1 | Varadi 3, Chapman, Marwood |
| | | 5 | 04.03.85 | **Ipswich Town** (D1) | A | L | 2-3 | Lyons, Varadi |
| 1985-86 | (D1) | 3 | 13.01.86 | **WBA** (D1) | H | D | 2-2 | Sterland, Smith |
| | | 3r | 16.01.86 | **WBA** | A | W | 3-2 | Marwood, Chapman, Chamberlain |
| | | 4 | 25.01.86 | **Orient** (D4) | H | W | 5-0 | Sterland, Marwood, Blair, Thompson, Chapman |
| | | 5 | 26.02.86 | **Derby County** (D3) | A | D | 1-1 | Christie og |
| | | 5r | 05.03.86 | **Derby County** | H | W | 2-0 | Shutt 2 |
| | | 5 2r | 12.03.86 | **West Ham Utd** (D1) | H | W | 2-1 | Worthington, Shutt |
| | | SF | 05.04.86 | **Everton** (D1) *played at Villa Park* | | L | 1-2aet | Shutt |
| 1986-87 | (D1) | 3 | 26.01.87 | **Derby County** (D2) | H | W | 1-0 | Bradshaw |
| | | 4 | 31.01.87 | **Chester City** (D3) | A | D | 1-1 | Chapman |
| | | 4r | 04.02.87 | **Chester City** | H | W | 3-1 | Chapman, Bradshaw, Abel og |
| | | 5 | 21.02.87 | **West Ham Utd** (D1) | H | D | 1-1 | Shelton |
| | | 5r | 25.02.87 | **West Ham Utd** | A | W | 2-0 | Chapman, Bradshaw |
| | | 6 | 14.03.87 | **Coventry City** (D1) | H | L | 1-3 | Megson |
| 1987-88 | (D1) | 3 | 09.01.88 | **Everton** (D1) | H | D | 1-1 | West |
| | | 3r | 13.01.88 | **Everton** | A | D | 1-1aet | Chapman |
| | | 3 2r | 25.01.88 | **Everton** | A | D | 1-1aet | Chapman |
| | | 3 3r | 27.01.88 | **Everton** | H | L | 0-5 | |
| 1988-89 | (D1) | 3 | 07.01.89 | **Torquay Utd** (D4) | H | W | 5-1 | Jonsson, Hodgson, Varadi 2, Proctor |
| | | 4 | 28.01.89 | **Blackburn Rovers** (D2) | A | L | 1-2 | Hirst |
| 1989-90 | (D1) | 3 | 06.01.90 | **Wolverhampton W** (D2) | A | W | 2-1 | Shirtliff, Atkinson |
| | | 4 | 28.01.90 | **Everton** (D1) | H | L | 1-2 | Hirst |
| 1990-91 | (D2) | 3 | 05.01.91 | **Mansfield Town** (D3) | A | W | 2-0 | Shirtliff, Sheridan (p) |
| | | 4 | 26.01.91 | **Millwall** (D2) | A | D | 4-4 | Hirst, Francis, Pearson, Palmer |
| | | 4r | 30.01.91 | **Millwall** | H | W | 2-0 | Anderson, Hirst |
| | | 5 | 16.02.91 | **Cambridge Utd** (D3) | A | L | 0-4 | |
| 1991-92 | (D1) | 3 | 04.01.92 | **Preston North End** (D3) | A | W | 2-0 | Sheridan, Bart-Williams |
| | | 4 | 04.02.92 | **Middlesbrough** (D2) | H | L | 1-2 | Hirst |
| 1992-93 | (PL) | 3 | 13.01.93 | **Cambridge Utd** (D1) | A | W | 2-1 | Harkes, Bright |
| | | 4 | 24.01.93 | **Sunderland** (D1) | H | W | 1-0 | Bright |
| | | 5 | 13.02.93 | **Southend Utd** (D1) | H | W | 2-0 | Warhurst 2 |
| | | 6 | 08.03.93 | **Derby County** (D1) | A | D | 3-3 | Warhurst 2, Sheridan (p) |
| | | 6r | 17.03.93 | **Derby County** | H | W | 1-0 | Warhurst |
| | | SF | 03.04.93 | **Sheffield Utd** (PL) *played at Wembley Stadium* | | W | 2-1aet | Waddle, Bright |
| | | F | 15.05.93 | **Arsenal** (PL) *played at Wembley Stadium* | | D | 1-1aet | Waddle |

| | | | | | | | | |
|---|---|---|---|---|---|---|---|---|
| | | Fr | 20.05.93 | **Arsenal** | | L | 1-2aet | Hirst |
| | | | | *played at Wembley Stadium* | | | | |
| 1993-94 | (PL) | 3 | 08.01.94 | **Nottingham Forest** (D1) | H | D | 1-1 | Bright |
| | | 3r | 19.01.94 | **Nottingham Forest** | A | W | 2-0 | Pearce, Bart-Williams |
| | | 4 | 29.01.94 | **Chelsea** (PL) | A | D | 1-1 | Hyde |
| | | 4r | 09.02.94 | **Chelsea** | H | L | 1-3aet | Bright |
| 1994-95 | (PL) | 3 | 07.01.95 | **Gillingham** (D3) | A | W | 2-1 | Waddle, Bright |
| | | 4 | 30.01.95 | **Wolverhampton W** (D1) | H | D | 0-0 | |
| | | 4r | 08.02.95 | **Wolverhampton W** | A | D | 1-1aet | Bright |
| | | | | *Wolverhampton W won 4-3 on penalties* | | | | |
| 1995-96 | (PL) | 3 | 06.01.96 | **Charlton Athletic** (D1) | A | L | 0-2 | |
| 1996-97 | (PL) | 3 | 04.01.97 | **Grimsby Town** (D1) | H | W | 7-1 | Humphreys 2, Booth 2, Hyde, Pembridge, Fickling og |
| | | 4 | 25.01.97 | **Carlisle Utd** (D3) | A | W | 2-0 | Whittingham, Booth |
| | | 5 | 16.02.97 | **Bradford City** (D1) | A | W | 1-0 | Humphreys |
| | | 6 | 09.03.97 | **Wimbledon** (PL) | H | L | 0-2 | |
| 1997-98 | (PL) | 3 | 03.01.98 | **Watford** (D2) | A | D | 1-1 | Alexandersson |
| | | 3r | 14.01.98 | **Watford** | H | D | 0-0aet | |
| | | | | *Sheffield Wed won 5-3 on penalties* | | | | |
| | | 4 | 26.01.98 | **Blackburn Rovers** (PL) | H | L | 0-3 | |
| 1998-99 | (PL) | 3 | 03.01.99 | **Norwich City** (D1) | H | W | 4-1 | Humphreys 2, Rudi, Stefanovic |
| | | 4 | 23.01.99 | **Stockport County** (D1) | H | W | 2-0 | Emerson, Carbone |
| | | 5 | 13.02.99 | **Chelsea** (PL) | H | L | 0-1 | |
| 1999-00 | (PL) | 3 | 11.12.99 | **Bristol City** (D2) | H | W | 1-0 | Booth |
| | | 4 | 08.01.00 | **Wolverhampton W** (D1) | H | D | 1-1 | Alexandersson |
| | | 4r | 18.01.00 | **Wolverhampton W** | A | D | 0-0aet | |
| | | | | *Sheffield Wed won 4-3 on penalties* | | | | |
| | | 5 | 29.01.00 | **Gillingham** (D2) | A | L | 1-3 | Sibon |
| 2000-01 | (D1) | 3 | 06.01.01 | **Norwich City** (D1) | H | W | 2-1 | Hamshaw, Sibon |
| | | 4 | 27.01.01 | **Southampton** (PL) | A | L | 1-3 | Booth |
| 2001-02 | (D1) | 3 | 15.01.02 | **Crewe Alexandra** (D1) | A | L | 1-2 | Hamshaw |
| 2002-03 | (D1) | 3 | 07.01.03 | **Gillingham** (D1) | A | L | 1-4 | Sibon |

## SHEPSHED DYNAMO

*Formed 1890 as Shepshed. First entered FA Cup: 1897-98. Shepshed Albion 1891-1975. Shepshed Charterhouse 1975-1991. Shepshed Albion 1991-94. Reformed as Shepshed Dynamo 1994. Based in Leicestershire. Members of the Southern League.*

**as Shepshed Charterhouse**

| | | | | | | | | |
|---|---|---|---|---|---|---|---|---|
| 1982-83 | (NCoE) | 1 | 20.11.82 | **Preston North End** (D3) | A | L | 1-5 | Jenas |

**as Shepshed Dynamo**

| | | | | | | | | |
|---|---|---|---|---|---|---|---|---|
| 1996-97 | (SL) | 1 | 16.11.96 | **Carlisle Utd** (D3) | A | L | 0-6 | |

## SHILDON

*Formed 1890. First entered FA Cup: 1903-04. Members of the Northern League.*

| | | | | | | | | |
|---|---|---|---|---|---|---|---|---|
| 1927-28 | (NEL) | 1 | 26.11.27 | **New Brighton** (3N) | H | L | 1-3 | Brown |
| 1929-30 | (NEL) | 1 | 30.11.29 | **Doncaster Rovers** (3N) | A | D | 0-0 | |
| | | 1r | 04.12.29 | **Doncaster Rovers** | H | D | 1-1aet | Trotter |
| | | 1 2r | 09.12.29 | **Doncaster Rovers** | | L | 0-3 | |
| | | | | *played at Bootham Crescent, York* | | | | |
| 1934-35 | (NL) | 1 | 24.11.34 | **Lincoln City** (3N) | H | D | 2-2 | Oliver 2 |
| | | 1r | 28.11.34 | **Lincoln City** | A | L | 0-4 | |
| 1936-37 | (NL) | 1 | 28.11.36 | **Stalybridge Celtic** (CC) | H | W | 4-2 | Downing, Charlton 3 |
| | | 2 | 12.12.36 | **Dartford** (SL) | H | L | 0-3 | |
| 1955-56 | (NL) | 1 | 19.11.55 | **Scunthorpe Utd** (3N) | A | L | 0-3 | |
| 1959-60 | (NL) | 1 | 14.11.59 | **Oldham Athletic** (D4) | H | D | 1-1 | Bell |
| | | 1r | 17.11.59 | **Oldham Athletic** | A | L | 0-3 | |
| 1961-62 | (NL) | 1 | 04.11.61 | **Oldham Athletic** (D4) | A | L | 2-5 | Sinclair, Armstrong |

## SHIREBROOK

*Formed 1912. Entered FA Cup: 1912-13 – 1952-53. Nottinghamshire based mining works club. Disbanded 1939, Reformed late 1940s. Disbanded 1954.*

| | | | | | | | | |
|---|---|---|---|---|---|---|---|---|
| 1927-28 | (ML) | 1 | 26.11.27 | **Tranmere Rovers** (3N) | H | L | 1-3 | Miller |
| 1928-29 | (ML) | 1 | 24.11.28 | **Mansfield Town** (ML) | H | L | 2-4 | Bramley, Parker |

# SHREWSBURY TOWN

*Formed 1886. FA Cup best performance: 6th round, 1979, 1982. Record FA Cup win: 12-0 v Cannock Town, Extra-preliminary round, 07.09.1929. In Competition Proper: 11-2 v Marine, 1st round, 11.11.1995; Record FA Cup defeat: 2-10 v Chirk, 2nd round, 05.11.1887. Welsh FA Cup winners: 1891, 1938, 1977, 1979, 1984, 1985. Runners-up: 1931, 1948, 1980. Relegated from Football League to The Conference 2003.*

| | | | | | | | | |
|---|---|---|---|---|---|---|---|---|
| 1887-88 | | 1 | 15.10.87 | **Macclesfield T** | H | W | 3-1 | Pearson 3 |
| | | 2 | 05.11.87 | **Chirk** | A | L | 2-10 | Watkins, AN Other |
| 1903-04 | (BDL) | | | Int Stockton (A) 1-2 | | | | |
| 1909-10 | (BDL) | 1 | 15.01.10 | **Portsmouth** (SL) | A | L | 0-3 | |
| 1914-15 | (BDL) | | | 6q Nottingham Forest (A) 1-6 | | | | |
| 1945-46 | (ML) | 1 1L | 17.11.45 | **Walsall** (3S) | H | W | 5-0 | Maund 3, Bailey, Nicholls |
| | | 1 2L | 24.11.45 | **Walsall** | A | L | 1-4 | Nicholls |
| | | 2 1L | 08.12.45 | **Wrexham** (3N) | H | L | 0-1 | |
| | | 2 2L | 15.12.45 | **Wrexham** | A | D | 1-1 | Jones |
| 1947-48 | (ML) | 1 | 29.11.47 | **Great Yarmouth T** (ECL) | A | W | 4-1 | Davies 2, Mulvaney 2 |
| | | 2 | 13.12.47 | **Stockport County** (3N) | A | - | 1-1ab | Davie |
| | | | | *abandoned after 110 minutes – fog* | | | | |
| | | 2 | 20.12.47 | **Stockport County** | A | D | 2-2aet | Sheen, Argue |
| | | 2r | 22.12.47 | **Stockport County** | | L | 2-3 | Phillips, Butler |
| | | | | *played at Maine Road* | | | | |
| 1950-51 | (3N) | | | Withdrew, rather than play in the qualifying rounds following their election to the Football League | | | | |
| 1951-52 | (3S) | 1 | 24.11.51 | **Leytonstone** (IL) | A | L | 0-2 | |
| 1952-53 | (3S) | 1 | 22.11.52 | **QPR** (3S) | A | D | 2-2 | Brown, Butler |
| | | 1r | 27.11.52 | **QPR** | H | D | 2-2aet | Jackson, Reagan |
| | | 1 2r | 01.12.52 | **QPR** | | W | 4-1 | Brown, Jackson, Butler, Fisher |
| | | | | *played at Villa Park* | | | | |
| | | 2 | 06.12.52 | **Chesterfield** (3N) | H | D | 0-0 | |
| | | 2r | 10.12.52 | **Chesterfield** | A | W | 4-2 | Brown 2, Fisher, Reagan |
| | | 3 | 10.01.53 | **Finchley** (AL) | H | W | 2-0 | Roberts 2 |
| | | 4 | 31.01.53 | **Southampton** (D2) | H | L | 1-4 | Jackson |
| 1953-54 | (3S) | 1 | 21.11.53 | **QPR** (3S) | A | L | 0-2 | |
| 1954-55 | (3S) | 1 | 20.11.54 | **Walsall** (3S) | A | L | 2-5 | Brennan, O'Donnell |
| 1955-56 | (3S) | 1 | 19.11.55 | **Gillingham** (3S) | A | D | 1-1 | Russell |
| | | 1r | 24.11.55 | **Gillingham** | H | W | 4-1aet | McCue 2, Price, Arnott |
| | | 2 | 10.12.55 | **Torquay Utd** (3S) | H | D | 0-0 | |
| | | 2r | 14.12.55 | **Torquay Utd** | A | L | 1-5 | O'Donnell |
| 1956-57 | (3S) | 1 | 17.11.56 | **Weymouth** (SL) | A | L | 0-1 | |
| 1957-58 | (3S) | 1 | 16.11.57 | **Port Vale** (3S) | A | L | 1-2 | Smith |
| 1958-59 | (D4) | 1 | 15.11.58 | **Newport (IOW)** (HL) | A | D | 0-0 | |
| | | 1r | 20.11.58 | **Newport (IOW)** | H | W | 5-0 | Russell 2, Edgley, Walter, Whitaker |
| | | 2 | 06.12.58 | **Crystal Palace** (D4) | A | D | 2-2 | Russell 2 |
| | | 2r | 11.12.58 | **Crystal Palace** | H | D | 2-2aet | Skeech (p), Rowley |
| | | 2 2r | 15.12.58 | **Crystal Palace** | | L | 1-4 | Russell |
| | | | | *played at Molineux* | | | | |
| 1959-60 | (D3) | 1 | 14.11.59 | **Peterborough Utd** (ML) | A | L | 3-4 | Starkey 2, Rowley |
| 1960-61 | (D3) | 1 | 05.11.60 | **Newport County** (D3) | H | W | 4-1 | McLaughlin 2, Riggs og, Rowley |
| | | 2 | 26.11.60 | **Swindon Town** (D3) | A | W | 1-0 | Rowley |
| | | 3 | 07.01.61 | **Aldershot** (D4) | A | D | 1-1 | Starkey |
| | | 3r | 11.01.61 | **Aldershot** | H | D | 2-2aet | McLaughlin, Starkey |
| | | 3 2r | 16.01.61 | **Aldershot** | | L | 0-2 | |
| | | | | *played at Villa Park* | | | | |
| 1961-62 | (D3) | 1 | 04.11.61 | **Banbury Spencer** (BDL) | H | W | 7-1 | McLaughlin 2, Kenning 2, Rowley 2, Starkey |
| | | 2 | 25.11.61 | **Brierley Hill All** (BDL) | H | W | 3-0 | Hines 2, McLaughlin |
| | | 3 | 09.01.62 | **Southport** (D4) | A | W | 3-1 | Rowley, Hines, McLaughlin |
| | | 4 | 27.01.62 | **Middlesbrough** (D2) | H | D | 2-2 | Rowley, Kenning |
| | | 4r | 31.01.62 | **Middlesbrough** | A | L | 1-5 | Rowley |
| 1962-63 | (D3) | 1 | 03.11.62 | **Chelmsford City** (SL) | A | W | 6-2 | Rowley, McLaughlin 4, Clarke |
| | | 2 | 24.11.62 | **Torquay Utd** (D4) | H | W | 2-1 | Middleton 2 |
| | | 3 | 21.02.63 | **Sheffield Wed** (D1) | H | D | 1-1 | Harley |

| | | | | | | | | |
|---|---|---|---|---|---|---|---|---|
| | | 3r | 07.03.63 | **Sheffield Wed** | A | L | 1-2aet | Rowley |
| 1963-64 | (D3) | 1 | 16.11.63 | **Exeter City** (D4) | A | L | 1-2 | Middleton |
| 1964-65 | (D3) | 1 | 14.11.64 | **King's Lynn** (SL) | A | W | 1-0 | Regan |
| | | 2 | 05.12.64 | **Exeter City** (D3) | A | W | 2-1 | Regan 2 |
| | | 3 | 09.01.65 | **Manchester City** (D2) | A | D | 1-1 | Ross |
| | | 3r | 13.01.65 | **Manchester City** | H | W | 3-1 | Dolby, Meredith, Regan |
| | | 4 | 30.01.65 | **Millwall** (D4) | A | W | 2-1 | Boardman, Meredith |
| | | 5 | 20.02.65 | **Leeds Utd** (D1) | A | L | 0-2 | |
| 1965-66 | (D3) | 1 | 13.11.65 | **Torquay Utd** (D4) | H | W | 2-1 | Clarke 2, Broadbent |
| | | 2 | 04.12.65 | **Peterborough Utd** (D3) | H | W | 3-2 | Meredith 2 (1p), Clarke |
| | | 3 | 22.01.66 | **QPR** (D3) | A | D | 0-0 | |
| | | 3r | 26.01.66 | **QPR** | A | W | 1-0 | Meredith |
| | | 4 | 12.02.66 | **Carlisle Utd** (D2) | H | D | 0-0 | |
| | | 4r | 15.02.66 | **Carlisle Utd** | A | D | 1-1aet | Ross |
| | | 4 2r | 21.02.66 | **Carlisle Utd** | | W | 4-3aet | Broadie, Broadbent, Clarke, Boardman |
| | | | | *played at Deepdale, Preston* | | | | |
| | | 5 | 05.03.66 | **Chelsea** (D1) | A | L | 2-3 | Broadbent, Clarke |
| 1966-67 | (D3) | 1 | 26.11.66 | **Hartlepools Utd** (D4) | H | W | 5-2 | Clarke, Manning 2, Turner 2 |
| | | 2 | 07.01.67 | **Wrexham** (D4) | H | W | 5-1 | Boardman 3, Meredith, Manning |
| | | 3 | 28.01.67 | **Ipswich Town** (D2) | A | L | 1-4 | Meredith |
| 1967-68 | (D3) | 1 | 13.12.67 | **Darlington** (D4) | H | W | 3-0 | Clarke 2, Boardman |
| | | 2 | 15.01.68 | **Tow Law Town** (NL) | A | D | 1-1 | Clarke |
| | | 2r | 18.01.68 | **Tow Law Town** | H | W | 6-2 | Brodie 3, Boardman, Dolby (p), McLaughlin |
| | | 3 | 27.01.68 | **Arsenal** (D1) | H | D | 1-1 | Dolby |
| | | 3r | 30.01.68 | **Arsenal** | A | L | 0-2 | |
| 1968-69 | (D3) | 1 | 16.11.68 | **Port Vale** (D4) | H | D | 1-1 | Wood |
| | | 1r | 18.11.68 | **Port Vale** | A | L | 1-3 | Wood |
| 1969-70 | (D3) | 1 | 15.11.69 | **Yeovil Town** (SL) | A | W | 3-2 | McLaughlin, Jones og, R Moir |
| | | 2 | 06.12.69 | **Mansfield Town** (D3) | H | L | 1-2 | R Moir |
| 1970-71 | (D3) | 1 | 21.11.70 | **Minehead** (WL) | A | W | 2-1 | R Moir, Andrews |
| | | 2 | 12.12.70 | **Reading** (D3) | H | D | 2-2 | Andrews, Clapham (p) |
| | | 2r | 21.12.70 | **Reading** | A | L | 0-1 | |
| 1971-72 | (D3) | 1 | 20.11.71 | **Colchester Utd** (D4) | A | W | 4-1 | Andrews 3, Wood |
| | | 2 | 11.12.71 | **Guildford City** (SL) | H | W | 2-1 | Wood, R Moir |
| | | 3 | 15.01.72 | **Derby County** (D1) | A | L | 0-2 | |
| 1972-73 | (D3) | 1 | 18.11.72 | **Spennymoor Utd** (NL) | A | D | 1-1 | Dolby |
| | | 1r | 21.11.72 | **Spennymoor Utd** | H | W | 3-1 | R Moir, Andrews 2 |
| | | 2 | 09.12.72 | **Bolton Wanderers** (D3) | A | L | 0-3 | |
| 1973-74 | (D3) | 1 | 24.11.73 | **Wrexham** (D3) | A | D | 1-1 | Marlowe |
| | | 1r | 27.11.73 | **Wrexham** | H | L | 0-1 | |
| 1974-75 | (D4) | 1 | 23.11.74 | **Wigan Athletic** (NPL) | H | D | 1-1 | Kearney |
| | | 1r | 25.11.74 | **Wigan Athletic** | A | L | 1-2 | Haywood |
| 1975-76 | (D3) | 1 | 22.11.75 | **Rossendale Utd** (CC) | A | W | 1-0 | Bates |
| | | 2 | 13.12.75 | **Chester** (D3) | H | W | 3-1 | Bates 2, Durban |
| | | 3 | 03.01.76 | **Bradford City** (D4) | H | L | 1-2 | Kearney |
| 1976-77 | (D3) | 1 | 20.11.76 | **Doncaster Rovers** (D4) | A | D | 2-2 | Atkins, Maguire |
| | | 1r | 23.11.76 | **Doncaster Rovers** | H | W | 4-3 | Maguire 3, Bates |
| | | 2 | 14.12.76 | **Bury** (D3) | A | D | 0-0 | |
| | | 2r | 21.12.76 | **Bury** | H | W | 2-1 | Irvine, Turner |
| | | 3 | 08.01.77 | **QPR** (D1) | A | L | 1-2 | Bates |
| 1977-78 | (D3) | 1 | 26.11.77 | **Doncaster Rovers** (D4) | A | W | 1-0 | Nixon |
| | | 2 | 17.12.77 | **Stockport County** (D4) | H | D | 1-1 | Maguire |
| | | 2r | 19.12.77 | **Stockport County** | A | W | 2-1 | Maguire, Lindsay |
| | | 3 | 07.01.78 | **Blackburn Rovers** (D2) | A | L | 1-2 | Hornsby |
| 1978-79 | (D3) | 1 | 25.11.78 | **Mansfield Town** (D3) | A | W | 2-0 | Atkins, Biggins |
| | | 2 | 16.12.78 | **Doncaster Rovers** (D4) | A | W | 3-0 | Chapman, Maguire 2 |
| | | 3 | 06.01.79 | **Cambridge Utd** (D2) | H | W | 3-1 | Maguire, Turner, Chapman |
| | | 4 | 27.01.79 | **Manchester City** (D1) | H | W | 2-0 | Maguire, Chapman |
| | | 5 | 20.02.79 | **Aldershot** (D4) | A | D | 2-2 | Maguire, Tong |

| | | | | | | | | |
|---|---|---|---|---|---|---|---|---|
| | 5r | 26.02.79 | **Aldershot** | H | W | 3-1aet | Biggins 2, Leonard |
| | 6 | 10.03.79 | **Wolverhampton W** (D1) | A | D | 1-1 | Atkins (p) |
| | 6r | 13.03.79 | **Wolverhampton W** | H | L | 1-3 | Keay |
| 1979-80 (D2) | 3 | 05.01.80 | **Millwall** (D3) | A | L | 1-5 | Maguire |
| 1980-81 (D2) | 3 | 03.01.81 | **Huddersfield Town** (D3) | A | W | 3-0 | Topping og, Cross, Bates |
| | 4 | 24.01.81 | **Ipswich Town** (D1) | A | D | 0-0 | |
| | 4r | 27.01.81 | **Ipswich Town** | H | L | 0-3 | |
| 1981-82 (D2) | 3 | 05.01.82 | **Port Vale** (D4) | H | W | 1-0 | Bates |
| | 4 | 23.01.82 | **Burnley** (D3) | H | W | 1-0 | Bates |
| | 5 | 13.02.82 | **Ipswich Town** (D1) | H | W | 2-1 | Cross, King |
| | 6 | 06.03.82 | **Leicester City** (D2) | A | L | 2-5 | Bates, Keay |
| 1982-83 (D2) | 3 | 08.01.83 | **Rotherham Utd** (D2) | H | W | 2-1 | Brown 2 |
| | 4 | 30.01.83 | **Everton** (D1) | A | L | 1-2 | Cross |
| 1983-84 (D2) | 3 | 07.01.84 | **Oldham Athletic** (D2) | H | W | 3-0 | Stevens, MacLaren (p), Robinson |
| | 4 | 28.01.84 | **Ipswich Town** (D1) | H | W | 2-0 | Hackett, Robinson |
| | 5 | 18.02.84 | **Everton** (D1) | A | L | 0-3 | |
| 1984-85 (D2) | 3 | 05.01.85 | **Oxford Utd** (D2) | H | L | 0-2 | |
| 1985-86 (D2) | 3 | 04.01.86 | **Chelsea** (D1) | H | L | 0-1 | |
| 1986-87 (D2) | 3 | 31.01.87 | **Hull City** (D2) | H | L | 1-2 | Waller |
| 1987-88 (D2) | 3 | 09.01.88 | **Bristol Rovers** (D3) | H | W | 2-1 | Moyes, B Williams |
| | 4 | 30.01.88 | **Plymouth Argyle** (D2) | A | L | 0-1 | |
| 1988-89 (D2) | 3 | 07.01.89 | **Colchester Utd** (D4) | H | L | 0-3 | |
| 1989-90 (D3) | 1 | 18.11.89 | **Chesterfield** (D4) | H | L | 2-3 | McGinlay 2 (2ps) |
| 1990-91 (D3) | 1 | 17.11.90 | **Bradford City** (D3) | A | D | 0-0 | |
| | 1r | 21.11.90 | **Bradford City** | H | W | 2-1 | Shaw 2 |
| | 2 | 11.12.90 | **Chorley** (NPL) | H | W | 1-0 | Spink |
| | 3 | 05.01.91 | **Watford** (D2) | H | W | 4-1 | Brown, Kelly (p), Shaw 2 |
| | 4 | 26.01.91 | **Wimbledon** (D1) | H | W | 1-0 | Shaw |
| | 5 | 27.02.91 | **Arsenal** (D1) | H | L | 0-1 | |
| 1991-92 (D3) | 1 | 16.11.91 | **Hartlepool Utd** (D3) | A | L | 2-3 | Lyne, Smith |
| 1992-93 (D3) | 1 | 14.11.92 | **Mansfield Town** (D2) | H | W | 3-1 | Summerfield, Lyne, Williams |
| | 2 | 05.12.92 | **Burnley** (D2) | A | D | 1-1 | Griffiths |
| | 2r | 15.12.92 | **Burnley** | H | L | 1-2 | Griffiths |
| 1993-94 (D3) | 1 | 13.11.93 | **Doncaster Rovers** (D3) | H | D | 1-1 | Gallen |
| | 1r | 01.12.93 | **Doncaster Rovers** | A | W | 2-1aet | Spink, Walton |
| | 2 | 04.12.93 | **Preston North End** (D3) | H | L | 0-1 | |
| 1994-95 (D2) | 1 | 12.11.94 | **Burnley** (D1) | A | L | 1-2 | Spink |
| 1995-96 (D2) | 1 | 11.11.95 | **Marine** (NPL) | H | W | 11-2 | Spink 3, Whiston 2, Proctor og, Withe, Scott, Evans, Stevens, Dempsey |
| | 2 | 02.12.95 | **Scunthorpe Utd** (D3) | A | D | 1-1 | Scott |
| | 2r | 12.12.95 | **Scunthorpe Utd** | H | W | 2-1 | Scott, Rowbotham (p) |
| | 3 | 06.01.96 | **Fulham** (D3) | A | D | 1-1 | Evans |
| | 3r | 16.01.96 | **Fulham** | H | W | 2-1 | Anthrobus, Dempsey |
| | 4 | 18.02.96 | **Liverpool** (PL) | H | L | 0-4 | |
| 1996-97 (D2) | 1 | 16.11.96 | **Scarborough** (D3) | H | D | 1-1 | Stevens |
| | 1r | 26.11.96 | **Scarborough** | A | L | 0-1 | |
| 1997-98 (D3) | 1 | 15.11.97 | **Grimsby Town** (D2) | H | D | 1-1 | Herbert |
| | 1r | 25.11.97 | **Grimsby Town** | A | L | 0-4 | |
| 1998-99 (D3) | 1 | 14.11.98 | **Rushden & D** (Conf) | A | L | 0-1 | |
| 1999-00 (D3) | 1 | 30.10.99 | **Northampton Town** (D3) | H | W | 2-1 | Kerrigan, Wilding |
| | 2 | 20.11.99 | **Oxford Utd** (D2) | H | D | 2-2 | Kerrigan 2 |
| | 2r | 30.11.99 | **Oxford Utd** | A | L | 1-2aet | Jagielka |
| 2000-01 (D3) | 1 | 18.11.00 | **Cheltenham Town** (D3) | A | L | 1-4 | Freestone |
| 2001-02 (D3) | 1 | 17.11.01 | **Brighton** (D2) | A | L | 0-1 | |
| 2002-03 (D3) | 1 | 16.11.02 | **Stafford Rangers** (SL) | H | W | 4-0 | Jemson, Wilding 2, Tolley |
| | 2 | 07.12.02 | **Barrow** (NPL) | H | W | 3-1 | Van Blerk, Jemson 2 |
| | 3 | 04.01.03 | **Everton** (PL) | H | W | 2-1 | Jemson 2 |
| | 4 | 26.01.03 | **Chelsea** (PL) | H | L | 0-4 | |

## SHROPSHIRE WANDERERS

*Entered FA Cup: 1873-74 – 1877-78. FA Cup semi-finalists 1875. Acquired a footnote in FA Cup folklore as their match against Sheffield FC on November 17, 1873 is the only one ever to be decided on the toss of a coin.*

| | | | | | | | |
|---|---|---|---|---|---|---|---|
| 1873-74 | 1 | 30.10.73 | **Sheffield FC** | A | D | 0-0 | |
| | 1r | 17.11.73 | **Sheffield FC** | H | D | 0-0 | |
| | | | *The only FA Cup match to be decided on the toss of a coin. Sheffield called correctly and advanced.* | | | | |
| 1874-75 | 1 | | Sheffield FC | | | - | |
| | | | *Sheffield FC scratched. Shropshire W walkover* | | | | |
| | 2 | 14.11.74 | **Civil Service** | H | W | 1-0 | |
| | 3 | 23.01.75 | **Woodford Wells** | H | D | 1-1aet | Fletcher |
| | 3r | 06.02.75 | **Woodford Wells** | A | W | 2-0 | Randall, Fraser |
| | SF | 27.02.75 | **Old Etonians** | | L | 0-1 | |
| | | | *played at Kennington Oval* | | | | |
| 1875-76 | 1 | | Sheffield FC | | | - | |
| | | | *Shropshire W scratched. Sheffield FC walkover* | | | | |
| 1876-77 | 1 | | Druids | | | - | |
| | | | *Druids scratched. Shropshire W walkover* | | | | |
| | 2 | 09.12.76 | **Royal Engineers** | A | L | 0-3 | |
| 1877-78 | 1 | 12.11.77 | **Druids** | A | L | 0-1 | |

## SITTINGBOURNE

*Formed 1881 as Sittingbourne United. Sittingbourne 1886. First entered FA Cup: 1893-94. Members of the Southern League.*

| | | | | | | | |
|---|---|---|---|---|---|---|---|
| 1925-26 (KL) | 1 | 28.11.25 | **Chatham** (KL) | A | W | 3-0 | Waterall, Dowell, Thompson |
| | 2 | 12.12.25 | **Swindon Town** (3S) | A | L | 0-7 | |
| 1926-27 (KL) | 1 | 27.11.26 | **Northfleet Utd** (KL) | H | L | 1-3 | McEly |
| 1928-29 (SL) | 1 | 24.11.28 | **Southall** (AL) | H | W | 2-1 | H Wiles 2 |
| | 2 | 08.12.28 | **Walsall** (3S) | A | L | 1-2 | H Wiles |
| 1930-31 (KL) | 1 | 29.11.30 | **Folkestone** (SL) | A | L | 3-5 | Handley 2, Dickie |
| 1962-63 (SL) | 1 | 03.11.62 | **Hinckley Athletic** (SL) | A | L | 0-3 | |

## SKEGNESS TOWN

*Formed 1947. Entered FA Cup: 1949-50 – 1985-86.*

| | | | | | | | |
|---|---|---|---|---|---|---|---|
| 1955-56 (Lincs) | 1 | 19.11.55 | **Worksop Town** (ML) | H | L | 0-4 | |

## SKELMERSDALE UNITED

*Formed 1882. First entered FA Cup: 1905-06. FA Amateur Cup winners: 1971. Runners-up: 1967. Members of the North West Counties League.*

| | | | | | | | |
|---|---|---|---|---|---|---|---|
| 1967-68 (LC) | 1 | 09.12.67 | **Scunthorpe Utd** (D3) | A | L | 0-2 | |
| 1968-69 (CC) | 1 | 16.11.68 | **Chesterfield** (D4) | A | L | 0-2 | |
| 1971-72 (NPL) | 1 | 20.11.71 | **Tranmere Rovers** (D3) | H | L | 0-4 | |

## SLOUGH TOWN

*Formed 1890. First entered FA Cup: 1945-46 as Slough United. Slough Town 1948. League club beaten: Millwall. Members of the Isthmian League.*

| | | | | | | | |
|---|---|---|---|---|---|---|---|
| **as Slough Utd** | | | | | | | |
| 1945-46 (CRN) | 1 1L | 17.11.45 | **Bromley** (AL) | A | - | 1-2ab | Clarke |
| | | | *abandoned after 80 minutes – fog* | | | | |
| | 1 1L | 21.11.45 | **Bromley** | A | L | 1-6 | Clarke |
| | 1 2L | 24.11.45 | **Bromley** | H | W | 1-0 | Brown |
| **as Slough Town** | | | | | | | |
| 1970-71 (AL) | 1 | 21.11.70 | **Wycombe W** (IL) | A | D | 1-1 | Hobbis |
| | 1r | 24.11.70 | **Wycombe W** | H | W | 1-0 | Adams (p) |
| | 2 | 12.12.70 | **Barnet** (SL) | H | L | 0-1 | |
| 1973-74 (IL) | 1 | 24.11.73 | **Reading** (D4) | A | L | 0-3 | |
| 1974-75 (IL) | 1 | 23.11.74 | **Brentford** (D4) | H | L | 1-4 | Chatterton |
| 1979-80 (IL) | 1 | 24.11.79 | **Hungerford Town** (IL) | H | W | 3-1 | Turl, Feely, Russell |
| | 2 | 15.12.79 | **Yeovil Town** (APL) | A | L | 0-1 | |
| 1982-83 (IL) | 1 | 20.11.82 | **Millwall** (D3) | H | W | 1-0 | Attrell |
| | 2 | 11.12.82 | **Bishop's Stortford** (IL) | H | L | 1-4 | Evans |
| 1985-86 (IL) | 1 | 16.11.85 | **Aylesbury Utd** (SL) | H | D | 2-2 | Dodds, White |

| | | | | | | | | |
|---|---|---|---|---|---|---|---|---|
| | | 1r | 19.11.85 | **Aylesbury Utd** *played at Tring* | A | W | 5-2 | Woodley, White, Kiely, Dodds 2 |
| | | 2 | 07.12.85 | **Orient** (D4) | A | D | 2-2 | Dodds, Wilson |
| | | 2r | 10.12.85 | **Orient** | H | L | 2-3 | White, Harris (p) |
| 1986-87 | (IL) | 1 | 15.11.86 | **Bognor Regis Town** (IL) | H | D | 1-1 | White |
| | | 1r | 17.11.86 | **Bognor Regis Town** | A | W | 1-0 | Bateman |
| | | 2 | 06.12.86 | **Swansea City** (D4) | A | L | 0-3 | |
| 1989-90 | (IL) | 1 | 18.11.89 | **Woking** (IL) | H | L | 1-2 | Langley |
| 1991-92 | (Conf) | 1 | 16.11.91 | **Reading** (D3) | H | D | 3-3 | Pluckrose, Fielder, McKinnon |
| | | 1r | 27.11.91 | **Reading** | A | L | 1-2 | Joseph |
| 1992-93 | (Conf) | 1 | 14.11.92 | **Colchester Utd** (D3) | A | L | 0-4 | |
| 1993-94 | (Conf) | 1 | 13.11.93 | **Torquay Utd** (D3) | H | L | 1-2 | Scott |
| 1994-95 | (IL) | 1 | 12.11.94 | **Birmingham City** (D2) *played at St Andrews* | H | L | 0-4 | |
| 1995-96 | (Conf) | 1 | 11.11.95 | **Plymouth Argyle** (D3) | H | L | 0-2 | |
| 1997-98 | (Conf) | 1 | 15.11.97 | **Cardiff City** (D3) | H | D | 1-1 | Bolt |
| | | 1r | 25.11.97 | **Cardiff City** | A | L | 2-3aet | Owusu, Angus |
| 1998-99 | (IL) | 1 | 14.11.98 | **Macclesfield T** (D2) | A | D | 2-2 | Pierson, Deaner |
| | | 1r | 24.11.98 | **Macclesfield T** *Macclesfield T won 9-8 on penalties* | H | D | 1-1aet | Hughes |
| 2002-03 | (IL) | 1 | 16.11.02 | **Harrogate RA** (NCoE) | H | L | 1-2 | B Bubb |

## SOLIHULL BOROUGH

*Formed 1953 as Lincoln FC at the Lincoln Road Cafe, Acocks Green, Solihull. Solihull Borough 1970. First entered FA Cup: 1990-91. Members of the Southern League.*

| | | | | | | | | |
|---|---|---|---|---|---|---|---|---|
| 1992-93 | (SL) | 1 | 14.11.92 | **VS Rugby** (SL) | H | D | 2-2 | Canning, Carter |
| | | 1r | 25.11.92 | **VS Rugby** | A | L | 1-2aet | Canning (p) |
| 1997-98 | (SL) | 1 | 15.11.97 | **Darlington** (D3) | A | D | 1-1 | Cross |
| | | 1r | 26.11.97 | **Darlington** *Darlington won 4-2 on penalties* | H | D | 3-3aet | Dowling 2, Cross |

## SOUTH BANK

*Formed 1868. Entered FA Cup: 1886-87 – 1992-93. Were based in Middlesbrough. FA Amateur Cup winners: 1913. Runners-up: 1910, 1922.*

| | | | | | | | | |
|---|---|---|---|---|---|---|---|---|
| 1886-87 | | 1 | 30.10.86 | **Gainsborough T** | H | L | 0-4 | |
| 1887-88 | | 1 | 15.10.87 | **Newcastle East End** | H | W | 3-2aet | Knox, Jones, Beattie |
| | | 2 | 05.11.87 | **Middlesbrough** | A | L | 1-4 | Duck |
| 1925-26 | (NL) | 1 | 03.12.25 | **Stockton** (NL) | H | L | 1-4 | Muffitt |

## SOUTH BANK ST PETERS

*Entered FA Cup: 1932-33 – 1937-38. Arguably the most junior club to play in the Competition Proper since World War One, they were members of the Teesside League. Disbanded in the mid-1950s but a club of the same name reformed in the mid-1990s and plays local league football. Based in Middlesbrough.*

| | | | | | | | | |
|---|---|---|---|---|---|---|---|---|
| 1933-34 | (TSL) | 1 | 25.11.33 | **Rotherham Utd** (3N) | A | L | 2-3 | Sherrington, Calvert |

## SOUTH LIVERPOOL

*Formed 1894. First entered FA Cup: 1898-99. Welsh FA Cup winners: 1939. Folded 1992. Jimmy Case, who played for Liverpool in the 1977 FA Cup final and for Brighton in 1983, and John Aldridge, who played for Liverpool in the 1988 and 1989 FA Cup finals, both had spells at South Liverpool. League club beaten: Halifax.*

| | | | | | | | | |
|---|---|---|---|---|---|---|---|---|
| 1936-37 | (LC) | 1 | 28.11.36 | **Morecambe** (LC) | H | W | 1-0 | Roscoe |
| | | 2 | 12.12.36 | **QPR** (3S) | H | L | 0-1 | |
| 1937-38 | (LC) | 1 | 27.11.37 | **Wigan Athletic** (CC) | A | W | 4-1 | Houghton, Carr, G Jones 2 |
| | | 2 | 11.12.37 | **Brighton** (3S) | H | D | 1-1 | Roscoe |
| | | 2r | 15.12.37 | **Brighton** | A | L | 0-6 | |
| 1945-46 | (CC) | 1 1L | 17.11.45 | **Tranmere Rovers** (3N) | H | D | 1-1 | G Jones |
| | | 1 2L | 24.11.45 | **Tranmere Rovers** | A | L | 1-6 | G Jones |
| 1946-47 | (CC) | 1 | 30.11.46 | **Workington** (NEL) | H | W | 2-1 | Frost 2 |
| | | 2 | 14.12.46 | **Carlisle Utd** (3N) | H | L | 2-3 | Powell, Urmston |
| 1964-65 | (LC) | 1 | 14.11.64 | **Halifax Town** (D4) | A | D | 2-2 | Eales, Watson |
| | | 1r | 18.11.64 | **Halifax Town** | H | W | 4-2 | Watson 2, Saunders, Gorman |
| | | 2 | 05.12.64 | **Workington** (D3) | H | L | 0-2 | |
| 1965-66 | (LC) | 1 | 13.11.65 | **Wrexham** (D4) | A | L | 1-4 | Eales |

| | | | | | | | | |
|---|---|---|---|---|---|---|---|---|
| 1972-73 (NPL) | 1 | 18.11.72 | **Tranmere Rovers** (D3) | H | L | 0-2 | |
| 1985-86 (NPL) | 1 | 16.11.85 | **Whitby Town** (NL) | A | L | 0-1 | |

## SOUTH NORWOOD

*Formed 1871. Entered FA Cup: 1782-73 – 1879-80. Played at Portland Road, South Norwood, not far from where Selhurst Park was later built.*

| | | | | | | | |
|---|---|---|---|---|---|---|---|
| 1872-73 | 1 | 19.10.72 | **Barnes** | A | W | 1-0 | Walshe |
| | 2 | 23.11.72 | **Windsor Home Park** | H | W | 1-0 | White |
| | | | *FA ordered replay after match ended before 90 minutes were played* | | | | |
| | 2r | 07.12.72 | **Windsor Home Park** | A | L | 0-3 | |
| 1873-74 | 1 | 25.10.73 | **Cambridge University** | A | L | 0-1 | |
| 1874-75 | 1 | 10.10.74 | **Pilgrims** | A | L | 1-3 | |
| 1875-76 | 1 | | Clydesdale | | | - | |
| | | | *Clydesdale scratched. South Norwood walkover* | | | | |
| | 2 | 11.12.75 | **Swifts** | H | L | 0-5 | |
| 1876-77 | 1 | 04.11.76 | **Saxons** | H | W | 4-1 | Ram 2, White 2 |
| | 2 | 02.12.76 | **Sheffield FC** | H | L | 0-7 | |
| 1877-78 | 1 | 07.11.77 | **Reading** | A | L | 0-2 | |
| 1878-79 | 1 | | Leyton FC | | | - | |
| | | | *Leyton scratched. South Norwood walkover* | | | | |
| | 2 | 04.12.78 | **Cambridge University** | A | L | 0-3 | |
| 1879-80 | 1 | 01.11.79 | **Brentwood** | H | W | 4-2 | Knight 2, Hamilton, Robertson |
| | 2 | 20.12.79 | **Clapham Rovers** | H | L | 1-4 | |

## SOUTH READING

*Formed 1879. Entered FA Cup: 1882-83 – 1887-88. Played at Whitby Park Farm, Reading.*

| | | | | | | | |
|---|---|---|---|---|---|---|---|
| 1882-83 | 1 | 21.10.82 | **Dreadnought FC** | H | W | 2-1 | Callan 2 |
| | | | *FA ordered replay after protest* | | | | |
| | 1r | 04.11.82 | **Dreadnought FC** | A | W | 2-1 | |
| | 2 | | bye | | | | |
| | 3 | 06.01.83 | **Hendon (1874)** | A | L | 1-11 | |
| 1883-84 | 1 | 10.11.83 | **Reading** | A | D | 2-2 | |
| | 1r | 17.11.83 | **Reading** | H | L | 0-4 | |
| 1884-85 | 1 | 08.11.84 | **Casuals** | H | W | 4-1 | |
| | 2 | 06.12.84 | **Swifts** | A | L | 2-3 | |
| 1885-86 | 1 | 31.10.85 | **Dulwich** | A | W | 2-1 | |
| | 2 | 21.11.85 | **Clapton** | A | D | 1-1 | |
| | | | *FA disqualified Clapton after protest. South Reading advanced* | | | | |
| | 3 | 02.01.86 | **Clapham Rovers** | | | - | |
| | | | *FA disqualified Clapham Rovers. South Reading advanced* | | | | |
| | 4 | 02.01.86 | **Brentwood** | H | L | 0-3 | |
| 1886-87 | 1 | 30.10.86 | **Maidenhead** | H | L | 0-2 | |
| 1887-88 | 1 | 08.10.87 | **Marlow** | A | L | 1-4 | |

## SOUTH SHIELDS

*See under 'Gateshead AFC' for an explanation of the geneology of the various South Shields and Gateshead clubs which have appeared in the FA Cup over the last century.*

| | | | | | | | |
|---|---|---|---|---|---|---|---|
| 1912-13 (NEL) | 1 | 11.01.13 | **Gainsborough T** (ML) | H | - | 1-0ab | Hogg |
| | | | *abandoned at half-time* | | | | |
| | 1 | 18.01.13 | **Gainsborough T** | H | L | 0-1 | |
| 1913-14 (Wear) | 1 | 10.01.14 | **Burnley** (D1) | A | L | 1-3 | Keenlyside |
| 1914-15 (NEL) | 1 | 09.01.15 | **Fulham** (D2) | H | L | 1-2 | Whittingham |
| 1919-20 (D2) | 1 | 10.01. | **Liverpool** (D1) | H | D | 1-1 | Woods |
| | 1r | 14.01. | **Liverpool** | A | L | 0-2 | |
| 1920-21 (D2) | 1 | 08.01.21 | **Portsmouth** (D3) | H | W | 3-0 | Maitland, Hawes, Potts og |
| | 2 | 29.01.21 | **Luton Town** (3S) | H | L | 0-4 | |
| 1921-22 (D2) | 1 | 07.01.22 | **Southampton** (3S) | A | L | 1-3 | Greenwell |
| 1922-23 (D2) | 1 | 13.01.23 | **Halifax Town** (3N) | H | W | 3-1 | Oxberry, Keenlyside, Maitland |
| | 2 | 03.02.23 | **Blackburn Rovers** (D1) | H | D | 0-0 | |
| | 2r | 08.02.23 | **Blackburn Rovers** | A | W | 1-0 | Smith |
| | 3 | 24.02.23 | **QPR** (3S) | A | L | 0-3 | |
| 1923-24 (D2) | 1 | 12.01.24 | **Burnley** (D1) | A | L | 2-3 | Crown, Greenwell |

| | | | | | | | | |
|---|---|---|---|---|---|---|---|---|
| 1924-25 | (D2) | 1 | 10.01.25 | **Crystal Palace** (D2) | A | L | 1-2 | Smith |
| 1925-26 | (D2) | 3 | 09.01.26 | **Chilton Coll** (NAII) | H | W | 3-0 | Trotter, Wilson, Parker |
| | | 4 | 30.01.26 | **Birmingham** (D1) | H | W | 2-1 | Smith, Thirlaway |
| | | 5 | 20.02.26 | **Bolton Wanderers** (D1) | A | L | 0-3 | |
| 1926-27 | (D2) | 3 | 08.01.27 | **Plymouth Argyle** (3S) | H | W | 3-1 | Smith, Oxberry, Hunter |
| | | 4 | 29.01.27 | **Sheffield Wed** (D1) | A | D | 1-1 | Matthewson |
| | | 4r | 02.02.27 | **Sheffield Wed** | H | W | 1-0 | Smith |
| | | 5 | 19.02.27 | **Swansea Town** (D2) | H | D | 2-2 | Smith, Trotter |
| | | 5r | 24.02.27 | **Swansea Town** | A | L | 1-2 | Parker |
| 1927-28 | (D2) | 3 | 14.01.28 | **Middlesbrough** (D1) | A | L | 0-3 | |
| 1928-29 | (3N) | 1 | 24.11.28 | **Accrington Stanley** (3N) | A | L | 1-2 | Parker |
| 1929-30 | (3N) | 1 | 30.11.29 | **Wrexham** (3N) | H | L | 2-4 | Mustard, Maycock |

## SOUTH SHIELDS (1936)

*Formed 1936. Entered FA Cup: 1937-38 – 1973-74. Changed name to Gateshead United 1974. Folded 1977. League clubs beaten: Crewe Alexandra, Chesterfield, York City, Bradford Park Anue, Oldham Athletic, Scunthorpe Utd. See under 'Gateshead' for an explanation of the genealogy of the various South Shields and Gateshead clubs which have appeared in the FA Cup over the last century. See also Gateshead United.*

| | | | | | | | | |
|---|---|---|---|---|---|---|---|---|
| 1947-48 | (NEL) | 1 | 29.11.47 | **Crewe Alexandra** (3N) | A | L | 1-4 | Middlesmiss |
| 1956-57 | (NEL) | 1 | 17.11.56 | **Chesterfield** (3N) | H | D | 2-2 | Powell, Richardson |
| | | 1r | 21.11.56 | **Chesterfield** | A | L | 0-4 | |
| 1957-58 | (NEL) | 1 | 16.11.57 | **Frickley Colliery** (ML) | H | W | 3-2 | Powell, Evans, Monkhouse |
| | | 2 | 07.12.57 | **York City** (3N) | H | L | 1-3 | Monkhouse (p) |
| 1958-59 | (ML) | 1 | 15.11.58 | **Crewe Alexandra** (D4) | A | D | 2-2 | Crickett, Robson |
| | | 1r | 19.11.58 | **Crewe Alexandra** | H | W | 5-0 | Robson 2, Crickett 2, Monkhouse |
| | | 2 | 06.12.58 | **Oldham Athletic** (D4) | A | L | 0-2 | |
| 1959-60 | (ML) | 1 | 14.11.59 | **Chesterfield** (D3) | H | W | 2-1 | Powell, Robson |
| | | 2 | 05.12.59 | **Bradford Park A** (D4) | H | L | 1-5 | Garbutt |
| 1961-62 | (NCO) | 1 | 04.11.61 | **Morecambe** (LC) | A | L | 1-2 | Butler |
| 1962-63 | (NEL) | 1 | 03.11.62 | **Doncaster Rovers** (D4) | H | D | 0-0 | |
| | | 1r | 08.11.62 | **Doncaster Rovers** | A | L | 1-2 | Smith |
| 1964-65 | (NRL) | 1 | 14.11.64 | **Chesterfield** (D4) | A | L | 0-2 | |
| 1965-66 | (NRL) | 1 | 13.11.65 | **York City** (D3) | H | W | 3-1 | Donoghue, Todd, Smith |
| | | 2 | 04.12.65 | **Crewe Alexandra** (D4) | A | L | 1-3 | Smith |
| 1966-67 | (NRL) | 1 | 26.11.66 | **Workington** (D3) | H | L | 1-4 | Smith |
| 1968-69 | (NPL) | 1 | 16.11.68 | **York City** (D4) | H | L | 0-6 | |
| 1969-70 | (NPL) | 1 | 15.11.69 | **Bradford Park A** (D4) | H | W | 2-1 | Smith 2 |
| | | 2 | 06.12.69 | **Oldham Athletic** (D4) | H | D | 0-0 | |
| | | 2r | 09.12.69 | **Oldham Athletic)** | A | W | 2-1 | Potter, Smith |
| | | 3 | 03.01.70 | **QPR** (D2) | A | L | 1-4 | Smith (p) |
| 1970-71 | (NPL) | 1 | 21.11.70 | **Wigan Athletic** (NPL) | H | D | 1-1 | Bains |
| | | 1r | 23.11.70 | **Wigan Athletic** | A | L | 0-2 | |
| 1971-72 | (NPL) | 1 | 20.11.71 | **Scunthorpe Utd** (D4) | H | D | 3-3 | Leask, O'Donnell 2 |
| | | 1r | 24.11.71 | **Scunthorpe Utd** | A | W | 3-2 | O'Donnell, Morton, Bains |
| | | 2 | 11.12.71 | **Notts County** (D3) | H | L | 1-3 | Bains |
| 1972-73 | (NPL) | 1 | 18.11.72 | **Rotherham Utd** (D3) | A | L | 0-4 | |
| 1973-74 | (NPL) | 1 | 24.11.73 | **Rochdale** (D3) | A | L | 0-2 | |

## SOUTH SHORE

*Formed late 1870s. Entered FA Cup: 1882-83 – 1899-1900. Merged with Blackpool FC in December 1899.*

| | | | | | | | |
|---|---|---|---|---|---|---|---|
| 1882-83 | 1 | 14.10.82 | **Darwen Ramblers** | A | L | 2-5 | |
| 1883-84 | 1 | 10.11.83 | **Clitheroe** | A | D | 3-3 | |
| | 1r | 24.11.83 | **Clitheroe** | H | W | 3-2 | Eaton, Elston AN Other |
| | 2 | 01.12.83 | **Blackburn Rovers** | H | L | 0-7 | |
| 1884-85 | 1 | | Rawtenstall | | | - | |
| | | | *Rawtenstall scratched. South Shore walkover* | | | | |
| | 2 | 06.12.84 | **Church FC** | H | L | 2-3 | |
| 1885-86 | 1 | 17.10.85 | **Higher Walton** | A | W | 4-3 | |
| | 2 | | Queen's Park, Glasgow | | | - | |
| | | | *Queen's Park scratched. South Shore walkover* | | | | |
| | 3 | 19.12.85 | **Halliwell** | A | W | 6-1 | Robert Elston 2, Hall, Thackeray, others 2 |

| | | | | | | | |
|---|---|---|---|---|---|---|---|
| | 5 | 23.01.86 | **Notts County** | H | W | 2-1 | Richard Elston AN Other |
| | 6 | 13.02.86 | **Swifts** | H | L | 1-2 | Tattersall |
| 1886-87 | 1 | 30.10.86 | **Bolton Wanderers** | A | L | 3-5 | Watson, Walsh, Elston |
| 1887-88 | 1 | | Denton | | | - | |
| | | | *Denton scratched. South Shore walkover* | | | | |
| | 2 | 05.11.87 | **Bootle** | A | D | 1-1 | |
| | 2r | 12.11.87 | **Bootle** | H | L | 0-3 | |
| 1888-89 | 1 | 02.02.89 | **Chatham** | A | L | 1-2aet | Elston |
| 1889-90 | 1 | 18.01.90 | **Aston Villa** (D1) | H | L | 2-4 | Cookson 2 |
| 1893-94 (LL) | 1 | 27.01.94 | **Leicester Fosse** (ML) | A | L | 1-2 | S.Parkinson |
| 1898-99 (LL) | 1 | 28.01.99 | **WBA** (D1) | A | L | 0-8 | |

# SOUTHALL

*Formed 1871 as Southall Park, Southall 1901. First entered FA Cup: 1873-74. FA Amateur Cup runners-up: 1925. FA Vase Runners-up: 1986. League club beaten: Swindon Town. Members of the Combined Counties League.*

**as Southall Park**

| | | | | | | | |
|---|---|---|---|---|---|---|---|
| 1873-74 | 1 | | Wanderers | | | - | |
| | | | *Southall Park scratched. Wanderers walkover* | | | | |
| 1874-75 | 1 | 14.11.74 | **Leyton FC** | H | D | 0-0 | |
| | 1r | 28.11.74 | **Leyton FC** | A | W | 5-0 | |
| | 2 | 05.12.74 | **Woodford Wells** | A | L | 0-3 | |
| 1875-76 | 1 | 23.10.75 | **Upton Park** | A | L | 0-1 | |
| 1876-77 | 1 | | Old Wykehamists | | | - | |
| | | | *Old Wykehamists scratched. Southall Park walkover* | | | | |
| | 2 | 16.12.76 | **Wanderers** | A | L | 0-6 | |
| 1877-78 | 1 | 02.11.77 | **Cambridge University** | A | L | 1-3 | |
| 1878-79 | 1 | 02.11.78 | **Old Harrovians** | A | L | 0-8 | |

**as Southall**

| | | | | | | | |
|---|---|---|---|---|---|---|---|
| 1925-26 (AL) | 1 | 28.11.25 | **Gillingham** (3S) | H | L | 0-6 | |
| 1927-28 (AL) | 1 | 26.11.27 | **Bath City** (SL) | A | L | 0-2 | |
| 1928-29 (AL) | 1 | 24.11.28 | **Sittingbourne** (SL) | A | L | 1-2 | Yates |
| 1935-36 (AL) | 1 | 30.11.35 | **Swindon Town** (3S) | H | W | 3-1 | Leahy, Willshaw, Poxon |
| | 2 | 14.12.35 | **Newport (IOW)** (HL) | H | W | 8-0 | Willshaw 3, Graves 3, Foss, Ette |
| | 3 | 11.01.36 | **Watford** (3S) | H | L | 1-4 | Jones |
| 1936-37 (AL) | 1 | 28.11.36 | **Cardiff City** (3S) | A | L | 1-3 | Leahy |
| 1955-56 (AL) | 1 | 19.11.55 | **Hastings Utd** (SL) | A | L | 1-6 | Stevens |

# SOUTHAMPTON

*Formed 1885 as Southampton St Mary's. Southampton 1897. FA Cup winners: 1976; Runners-up: 1900, 1902, 2003. Southampton were in the Southern League when they appeared in the 1900 and 1902 FA Cup finals. Record FA Cup win: 14-0 v Newbury, 1st qualifying round, 13.10.1894. In Competition Proper: 7-1 v Ipswich Town, 3rd round, 07.01.1961; Record FA Cup defeat: 0-5 v Manchester City, 2nd round, 05.02.1910.*

**as Southampton St Marys**

| | | | | | | | |
|---|---|---|---|---|---|---|---|
| 1891-92 | | | 1q Warmley (A) 4-1; 2q Reading (H) 7-0. FA disqualified Southampton St Marys. Reading re-instated. | | | | |
| 1892-93 | | | 1q Newbury (H) 4-1; 2q Maidenhead (H) 0-4 | | | | |
| 1893-94 | | | 1q Uxbridge (H) 3-1; 2q Reading (A) 1-2 | | | | |
| 1894-95 (SL) | | | 1q Newbury (H) 14-0; 2q Reading (H) 5-2; 3q Marlow (H) 7-3; 4q Warmley (H) 5-1 | | | | |
| | 1 | 02.02.95 | **Nottingham Forest** (D1) | H | L | 1-4 | Ward |
| 1895-96 (SL) | | | 1q Freemantle (A) 5-1; 2q Marlow (H) 5-0; 3q Reading (H) 3- 0; 4q Uxbridge (H) 3-0 | | | | |
| | 1 | 01.02.96 | **Sheffield Wed** (D1) | H | L | 2-3 | Keay, Turner |
| 1896-97 (SL) | | | 3q Cowes (A) 6-0; 4q Reading (A) 4-1; 5q Swindon Town (H) 8-2 | | | | |
| | 1 | 30.01.97 | **Heanor Town** (ML) | H | D | 1-1 | Turner |
| | 1r | 03.02.97 | **Heanor Town** | A | W | 1-0 | Farrell |
| | 2 | 13.02.97 | **Newton Heath** (D2) | H | D | 1-1 | Turner |
| | 2r | 17.02.97 | **Newton Heath** | A | L | 1-3 | Buchanan |

**as Southampton**

| | | | | | | | |
|---|---|---|---|---|---|---|---|
| 1897-98 (SL) | | | 3q Bristol City (H) 2-0; 4q Swindon Town (A) 3-0; 5q Eastville Rovers (H) 8-1 | | | | |
| | 1 | 29.01.98 | **Leicester Fosse** (D2) | H | W | 2-1 | Meston, Buchanan |
| | 2 | 12.02.98 | **Newcastle Utd** (D2) | H | W | 1-0 | Buchanan |
| | 3 | 26.02.98 | **Bolton Wanderers** (D1) | A | D | 0-0 | |

| | | | | | | | |
|---|---|---|---|---|---|---|---|
| | 3r | 02.03.98 | **Bolton Wanderers** | H | W | 4-0 | Turner 2, Yates, Farrell |
| | SF | 19.03.98 | **Nottingham Forest** (D1) | | D | 1-1 | Haynes |
| | | | *played at Bramall Lane* | | | | |
| | SFr | 23.03.98 | **Nottingham Forest** (D1) | | L | 0-2 | |
| | | | *played at Crystal Palace* | | | | |
| 1898-99 (SL) | 1 | 28.01.99 | **New Brompton** (SL) | A | W | 1-0 | Hartley |
| | 2 | 11.02.99 | **Notts County** (D1) | A | W | 1-0 | Hartley |
| | 3 | 25.02.99 | **Derby County** (D1) | H | L | 1-2 | Nicol |
| 1899-00 (SL) | 1 | 27.01.00 | **Everton** (D1) | H | W | 3-0 | Milward 2, Turner |
| | 2 | 10.02.00 | **Newcastle Utd** (D1) | H | - | 0-0ab | |
| | | | *abandoned after 50 minutes – bad light* | | | | |
| | 2 | 17.02.00 | **Newcastle Utd** | H | W | 4-1 | McLeod 2, Yates, Turner |
| | 3 | 24.02.00 | **WBA** (D1) | H | W | 2-1 | Turner, McLeod |
| | SF | 24.03.00 | **Millwall Athletic** (SL) | | D | 0-0 | |
| | | | *played at Crystal Palace* | | | | |
| | SFr | 28.03.00 | **Millwall Athletic** | | W | 3-0 | Milward 2, Yates |
| | | | *played at Elm Park, Reading* | | | | |
| | F | 21.04.00 | **Bury** (D1) | | L | 0-4 | |
| | | | *played at Crystal Palace* | | | | |
| 1900-01 (SL) | 1 | 09.02.01 | **Everton** (D1) | H | L | 1-3 | Chadwick |
| 1901-02 (SL) | 1 | 25.01.02 | **Tottenham Hotspur** (SL) | A | D | 1-1 | Bowman |
| | 1r | 29.01.02 | **Tottenham Hotspur** | H | D | 2-2aet | Chadwick, J Turner |
| | 1 2r | 03.02.02 | **Tottenham Hotspur** | | W | 2-1 | A Turner, Brown |
| | | | *played at Elm Park, Reading* | | | | |
| | 2 | 08.02.02 | **Liverpool** (D1) | H | W | 4-1 | Chadwick 2, J Turner, Lee |
| | 3 | 22.02.02 | **Bury** (D1) | A | W | 3-2 | Wood, Chadwick, J Turner |
| | SF | 15.03.02 | **Nottingham Forest** (D1) | | W | 3-1 | Brown 2, Chadwick |
| | | | *played at White Hart Lane* | | | | |
| | F | 19.04.02 | **Sheffield Utd** (D1) | | D | 1-1 | Wood |
| | | | *played at Crystal Palace* | | | | |
| | Fr | 28.04.02 | **Sheffield Utd** | | L | 1-2 | Brown |
| | | | *played at Crystal Palace* | | | | |
| 1902-03 (SL) | 1 | 07.02.03 | **Notts County** (D1) | A | D | 0-0 | |
| | 1r | 11.02.03 | **Notts County** | H | D | 2-2 | J Turner, Bell |
| | 1 2r | 16.02.03 | **Notts County** | | L | 1-2aet | Barlow |
| | | | *played at St Andrews* | | | | |
| 1903-04 (SL) | 1 | 06.02.04 | **Burslem Port Vale** (D2) | H | W | 3-0 | J Turner, Wood, Fraser |
| | 2 | 20.02.04 | **Bolton Wanderers** (D2) | A | L | 1-4 | Mouncher |
| 1904-05 (SL) | 1 | 04.02.05 | **Millwall Athletic** (SL) | H | W | 3-1 | Bluff 2, Harrison |
| | 2 | 18.02.05 | **Wolverhampton W** (D1) | A | W | 3-2 | Harrison 2, Bluff |
| | 3 | 04.03.05 | **Everton** (D1) | A | L | 0-4 | |
| 1905-06 (SL) | 1 | 13.01.06 | **Portsmouth** (SL) | H | W | 5-1 | Brown 2, Tomlinson, Harrison, Hedley |
| | 2 | 03.02.06 | **New Brompton** (SL) | A | D | 0-0 | |
| | 2r | 07.02.06 | **New Brompton** | H | W | 1-0 | Hedley |
| | 3 | 24.02.06 | **Middlesbrough** (D1) | H | W | 6-1 | Hedley 2, Brown 2, Tomlinson, Harrison |
| | 4 | 10.03.06 | **Liverpool** (D1) | A | L | 0-3 | |
| 1906-07 (SL) | 1 | 12.01.07 | **Watford** (SL) | H | W | 2-1 | Hoskins, Mouncher |
| | 2 | 02.02.07 | **Sheffield Wed** (D1) | H | D | 1-1 | Hoskins |
| | 2r | 07.02.07 | **Sheffield Wed** | A | L | 1-3 | Hoskins |
| 1907-08 (SL) | 1 | 11.01.08 | **Burnley** (D2) | H | W | 2-1 | Bainbridge 2 |
| | 2 | 01.02.08 | **WBA** (D2) | H | W | 1-0 | Robertson |
| | 3 | 22.02.08 | **Bristol Rovers** (SL) | H | W | 2-0 | Bainbridge, Costello |
| | 4 | 07.03.08 | **Everton** (D1) | A | D | 0-0 | |
| | 4r | 11.03.08 | **Everton** | H | W | 3-2 | Costello 2, Bainbridge |
| | SF | 28.03.08 | **Wolverhampton W** (D2) | | L | 0-2 | |
| | | | *played at Stamford Bridge* | | | | |
| 1908-09 (SL) | 1 | 16.01.09 | **Bristol City** (D1) | A | D | 1-1 | Jordan |
| | 1r | 20.01.09 | **Bristol City** | H | L | 0-2 | |
| 1909-10 (SL) | 1 | 15.01.10 | **Brighton** (SL) | A | W | 1-0 | McGibbon |
| | 2 | 05.02.10 | **Manchester City** (D2) | H | L | 0-5 | |

| | | | | | | | |
|---|---|---|---|---|---|---|---|
| 1910-11 (SL) | 1 | 14.01.11 | **Leicester Fosse** (D2) | A | L | 1-3 | H Brown |
| 1911-12 (SL) | 1 | 13.01.12 | **Coventry City** (SL) | H | L | 0-2 | |
| 1912-13 (SL) | 1 | 11.01.13 | **Bury** (D2) | H | D | 1-1 | Andrews |
| | 1r | 15.01.13 | **Bury** | A | L | 1-2 | Turnbull |
| 1913-14 (SL) | 1 | 10.01.14 | **Wolverhampton W** (D2) | A | L | 0-3 | |
| 1914-15 (SL) | 1 | 09.01.15 | **Luton Town** (SL) | H | W | 3-0 | Andrews 2 (1p), Kimpton |
| | 2 | 21.01.15 | **Fulham** (D2) | A | W | 3-2aet | Jones, Andrews (p), Kimpton |
| | 3 | 20.02.15 | **Hull City** (D2) | H | D | 2-2aet | Andrews, Jones |
| | 3r | 27.02.15 | **Hull City** | A | L | 0-4 | |
| 1919-20 (SL) | 1 | 10.01.20 | **West Ham Utd** (D2) | H | D | 0-0 | |
| | 1r | 15.01.20 | **West Ham Utd** | A | L | 1-3 | Barratt |
| 1920-21 (D3) | 1 | 08.01.21 | **Northampton Town** (D3) | A | D | 0-0 | |
| | 1r | 11.01.21 | **Northampton Town** | H | W | 4-1 | Dominy 2, Rawlings 2 |
| | 2 | 29.01.21 | **Grimsby Town** (D3) | A | W | 3-1 | Dominy, Rawlings 2 |
| | 3 | 19.02.21 | **Cardiff City** (D2) | H | L | 0-1 | |
| 1921-22 (3S) | 1 | 07.01.22 | **South Shields** (D2) | H | W | 3-1 | Johnson, Rawlings, Dominy |
| | 2 | 28.01.22 | **Cardiff City** (D1) | H | D | 1-1 | Rawlings |
| | 2r | 01.02.22 | **Cardiff City** | A | L | 0-2 | |
| 1922-23 (D2) | 1 | 13.01.23 | **Newcastle Utd** (D1) | A | D | 0-0 | |
| | 1r | 17.01.23 | **Newcastle Utd** | H | W | 3-1 | Dominy 2, Rawlings |
| | 2 | 03.02.23 | **Chelsea** (D1) | A | D | 0-0 | |
| | 2r | 07.02.23 | **Chelsea** | H | W | 1-0 | Dominy |
| | 3 | 24.02.23 | **Bury** (D2) | A | D | 0-0 | |
| | 3r | 28.02.23 | **Bury** | H | W | 1-0 | Dominy |
| | 4 | 10.03.23 | **West Ham Utd** (D2) | H | D | 1-1 | Elkes |
| | 4r | 14.03.23 | **West Ham Utd** | A | D | 1-1aet | Rawlings |
| | 4 2r | 19.03.23 | **West Ham Utd** | | L | 0-1 | |
| | | | *played at Villa Park* | | | | |
| 1923-24 (D2) | 1 | 12.01.24 | **Chelsea** (D1) | A | D | 1-1 | Dominy |
| | 1r | 16.01.24 | **Chelsea** | H | W | 2-0 | Dominy, Rawlings |
| | 2 | 02.02.24 | **Blackpool** (D2) | H | W | 4-1 | Rawlings, Dominy, Price |
| | 3 | 23.02.24 | **Liverpool** (D1) | H | D | 0-0 | |
| | 3r | 27.02.24 | **Liverpool** | A | L | 0-2 | |
| 1924-25 (D2) | 1 | 10.01.25 | **Exeter City** (3S) | H | - | 5-0ab | Dominy 2, Price 2, Parker |
| | | | *abandoned after 80 minutes – fog* | | | | |
| | 1 | 14.01.25 | **Exeter City** | H | W | 3-1 | Dominy, Rawlings, Price |
| | 2 | 31.01.25 | **Brighton** (3S) | H | W | 1-0 | Parker (p) |
| | 3 | 21.02.25 | **Bradford City** (D2) | H | W | 2-0 | Dominy, Harkus |
| | 4 | 07.03.25 | **Liverpool** (D1) | H | W | 1-0 | Rawlings |
| | SF | 28.03.25 | **Sheffield Utd** (D1) | | L | 0-2 | |
| | | | *played at Stamford Bridge* | | | | |
| 1925-26 (D2) | 3 | 09.01.26 | **Liverpool** (D1) | H | D | 0-0 | |
| | 3r | 13.01.26 | **Liverpool** | A | L | 0-1 | |
| 1926-27 (D2) | 3 | 08.01.27 | **Norwich City** (3S) | H | W | 3-0 | Keeping, Rowley 2 |
| | 4 | 29.01.27 | **Birmingham** (D1) | H | W | 4-1 | Rowley, Rawlings 2, Harkus |
| | 5 | 19.02.27 | **Newcastle Utd** (D1) | H | W | 2-1 | Rowley 2 |
| | 6 | 05.03.27 | **Millwall** (3S) | A | D | 0-0 | |
| | 6r | 09.03.27 | **Millwall** | H | W | 2-0 | Rawlings 2 |
| | SF | 26.03.27 | **Arsenal** (D1) | | L | 1-2 | Rawlings |
| | | | *played at Stamford Bridge* | | | | |
| 1927-28 (D2) | 3 | 14.01.28 | **Cardiff City** (D1) | A | L | 1-2 | Rawlings |
| 1928-29 (D2) | 3 | 12.01.29 | **Clapton Orient** (D2) | H | D | 0-0 | |
| | 3r | 17.01.29 | **Clapton Orient** | A | L | 1-2 | Bradford |
| 1929-30 (D2) | 3 | 11.01.30 | **Bradford City** (D2) | A | L | 1-4 | Rowley |
| 1930-31 (D2) | 3 | 10.01.31 | **Sunderland** (D1) | A | L | 0-2 | |
| 1931-32 (D2) | 3 | 09.01.32 | **Sunderland** (D1) | A | D | 0-0 | |
| | 3r | 13.01.32 | **Sunderland** | H | L | 2-4 | Sillett, Keeping |
| 1932-33 (D2) | 3 | 14.01.33 | **Stoke City** (D2) | A | L | 0-1 | |
| 1933-34 (D2) | 3 | 13.01.34 | **Northampton Town** (3S) | H | D | 1-1 | Drake |
| | 3r | 17.01.34 | **Northampton Town** | A | L | 0-1 | |
| 1934-35 (D2) | 3 | 12.01.35 | **Walsall** (3N) | A | W | 2-1 | Fishlock 2 |

| | | | | | | | | |
|---|---|---|---|---|---|---|---|---|
| | | 4 | 26.01.35 | **Birmingham** (D1) | H | L | 0-3 | |
| 1935-36 | (D2) | 3 | 11.01.36 | **Middlesbrough** (D1) | A | L | 0-1 | |
| 1936-37 | (D2) | 3 | 16.01.37 | **Sunderland** (D1) | H | L | 2-3 | Holt, Summers |
| 1937-38 | (D2) | 3 | 08.01.38 | **Nottingham Forest** (D2) | A | L | 1-3 | Dunn |
| 1938-39 | (D2) | 3 | 07.01.39 | **Chelmsford City** (SL) | A | L | 1-4 | Tomlinson |
| 1945-46 | (D2) | 3 1L | 05.01.46 | **Newport County** (D2) | H | W | 4-3 | Bates, Bradley, McGibbon, Roper |
| | | 3 2L | 10.01.46 | **Newport County** | A | W | 2-1 | McGibbon, Veck |
| | | 4 1L | 26.01.46 | **QPR** (3S) | H | L | 0-1 | |
| | | 4 2L | 30.01.46 | **QPR** | A | L | 3-4 | Bradley, Bevis, Ellerington |
| 1946-47 | (D2) | 3 | 11.01.47 | **Bury** (D2) | H | W | 5-1 | Lewis 3, Bradley, Bevis |
| | | 4 | 25.01.47 | **Newcastle Utd** (D2) | A | L | 1-3 | Roper |
| 1947-48 | (D2) | 3 | 10.01.48 | **Sunderland** (D1) | H | W | 1-0 | Day |
| | | 4 | 24.01.48 | **Blackburn Rovers** (D1) | H | W | 3-2 | Day 2, Wayman |
| | | 5 | 07.02.48 | **Swindon Town** (3S) | H | W | 3-0 | Wayman, Curtis, Ithell og |
| | | 6 | 28.02.48 | **Tottenham Hotspur** (D2) | H | L | 0-1 | |
| 1948-49 | (D2) | 3 | 08.01.49 | **Sheffield Wed** (D2) | A | L | 1-2 | Grant |
| 1949-50 | (D2) | 3 | 07.01.50 | **Northampton Town** (3S) | A | D | 1-1 | Scott |
| | | 3r | 11.01.50 | **Northampton Town** | H | L | 2-3 | Wayman 2 |
| 1950-51 | (D2) | 3 | 06.01.51 | **Notts County** (D2) | A | W | 4-3 | Brown 2, Day 2 |
| | | 4 | 27.01.51 | **Sunderland** (D1) | A | L | 0-2 | |
| 1951-52 | (D2) | 3 | 12.01.52 | **Southend Utd** (3S) | A | L | 0-3 | |
| 1952-53 | (D2) | 3 | 10.01.53 | **Lincoln City** (D2) | A | D | 1-1 | Dudley |
| | | 3r | 14.01.53 | **Lincoln City** | H | W | 2-1 | Purves, Day |
| | | 4 | 31.01.53 | **Shrewsbury Town** (3S) | A | W | 4-1 | Hoskins 2, Walker, Day |
| | | 5 | 14.02.53 | **Blackpool** (D1) | A | D | 1-1 | Horton |
| | | 5r | 18.02.53 | **Blackpool** | H | L | 1-2 | Walker |
| 1953-54 | (3S) | 1 | 21.11.53 | **Bournemouth** (3S) | H | D | 1-1 | Day |
| | | 1r | 25.11.53 | **Bournemouth** | A | L | 1-3 | Purves |
| 1954-55 | (3S) | 1 | 20.11.54 | **Barnet** (AL) | A | W | 4-1 | Day 2, Mulgrew 2 |
| | | 2 | 11.12.54 | **Grimsby Town** (3N) | A | L | 1-4 | Walker |
| 1955-56 | (3S) | 1 | 19.11.55 | **Crystal Palace** (3S) | A | D | 0-0 | |
| | | 1r | 23.11.55 | **Crystal Palace** | H | W | 2-0 | Reeves, Day |
| | | 2 | 10.12.55 | **Walsall** (3S) | A | L | 1-2 | Flood |
| 1956-57 | (3S) | 1 | 17.11.56 | **Northampton Town** (3S) | H | W | 2-0 | Reeves, Mulgrew |
| | | 2 | 08.12.56 | **Weymouth** (SL) | H | W | 3-2 | Mulgrew 2, Reeves |
| | | 3 | 05.01.57 | **Newport County** (3S) | A | D | 3-3 | Walker, Shields, Wilkins |
| | | 3r | 09.01.57 | **Newport County** | H | L | 0-1 | |
| 1957-58 | (3S) | 1 | 16.11.57 | **Walton & H** (AL) | A | W | 6-1 | Reeves 4, Hoskins, Mulgrew |
| | | 2 | 12.12.57 | **Crystal Palace** (3S) | A | L | 0-1 | |
| 1958-59 | (D2) | 1 | 15.11.58 | **Woking** (IL) | H | W | 4-1 | Mulgrew 2, Livesey, Paine |
| | | 2 | 06.12.58 | **QPR** (D3) | A | W | 1-0 | Rutter og |
| | | 3 | 10.01.59 | **Blackpool** (D1) | H | L | 1-2 | Reeves |
| 1959-60 | (D3) | 1 | 14.11.59 | **Coventry City** (D3) | A | D | 1-1 | Reeves |
| | | 1r | 18.11.59 | **Coventry City** | H | W | 5-1 | Page, Simpson 2, O'Brien, Paine |
| | | 2 | 05.12.59 | **Southend Utd** (D3) | H | W | 3-0 | Paine 2, Reeves |
| | | 3 | 09.01.60 | **Manchester City** (D1) | A | W | 5-1 | Reeves 4, O'Brien |
| | | 4 | 30.01.60 | **Watford** (D4) | H | D | 2-2 | O'Brien 2 |
| | | 4r | 02.02.60 | **Watford** | A | L | 0-1 | |
| 1960-61 | (D2) | 3 | 07.01.61 | **Ipswich Town** (D2) | H | W | 7-1 | O'Brien 3, Mulgrew 2, Penk, Paine |
| | | 4 | 28.01.61 | **Leyton Orient** (D2) | H | L | 0-1 | |
| 1961-62 | (D2) | 3 | 06.01.62 | **Sunderland** (D2) | H | D | 2-2 | O'Brien 2 |
| | | 3r | 10.01.62 | **Sunderland** | A | L | 0-3 | |
| 1962-63 | (D2) | 3 | 13.02.63 | **York City** (D4) | H | W | 5-0 | Wimshurst, O'Brien 3, Burnside |
| | | 4 | 27.02.63 | **Watford** (D3) | H | W | 3-1 | O'Brien 2, Kirby |
| | | 5 | 16.03.63 | **Sheffield Utd** (D1) | H | W | 1-0 | Kirby |
| | | 6 | 30.03.63 | **Nottingham Forest** (D1) | A | D | 1-1 | Paine |
| | | 6r | 03.04.63 | **Nottingham Forest** | H | D | 3-3aet | Kirby 2, Burnside |
| | | 6 2r | 08.04.63 | **Nottingham Forest** *played at White Hart Lane* | | W | 5-0 | Burnside 2, O'Brien 2, Wimshurst |
| | | SF | 27.04.63 | **Manchester Utd** (D1) *played at Villa Park* | | L | 0-1 | |

| | | | | | | | | |
|---|---|---|---|---|---|---|---|---|
| 1963-64 (D2) | 3 | 04.01.64 | **Manchester Utd** (D1) | H | L | 2-3 | Chivers, Paine |
| 1964-65 (D2) | 3 | 09.01.65 | **Leyton Orient** (D2) | H | W | 3-1 | Chivers, O'Brien 2 |
| | 4 | 30.01.65 | **Crystal Palace** (D2) | H | L | 1-2 | O'Brien |
| 1965-66 (D2) | 3 | 22.01.66 | **Hull City** (D3) | A | L | 0-1 | |
| 1966-67 (D1) | 3 | 28.01.67 | **Barrow** (D4) | A | D | 2-2 | Chivers, Davies |
| | 3r | 01.02.67 | **Barrow** | H | W | 3-0 | Davies 2, Chivers |
| | 4 | 18.02.67 | **Bristol City** (D2) | A | L | 0-1 | |
| 1967-68 (D1) | 3 | 27.01.68 | **Newport County** (D4) | H | D | 1-1 | Saul |
| | 3r | 30.01.68 | **Newport County** | A | W | 3-2 | Saul, Sydenham, Channon |
| | 4 | 17.02.68 | **WBA** (D1) | A | D | 1-1 | Saul |
| | 4r | 21.02.68 | **WBA** | H | L | 2-3 | Saul, Fisher |
| 1968-69 (D1) | 3 | 04.01.69 | **Oxford Utd** (D2) | A | D | 1-1 | Davies |
| | 3r | 08.01.69 | **Oxford Utd** | H | W | 2-0 | Paine 2 |
| | 4 | 25.01.69 | **Aston Villa** (D2) | H | D | 2-2 | McGrath, Davies |
| | 4r | 29.01.69 | **Aston Villa** | A | L | 1-2 | Channon |
| 1969-70 (D1) | 3 | 03.01.70 | **Newcastle Utd** (D1) | H | W | 3-0 | Channon, Saul 2 |
| | 4 | 24.01.70 | **Leicester City** (D2) | H | D | 1-1 | Stokes |
| | 4r | 28.01.70 | **Leicester City** | A | L | 2-4aet | Paine, Channon |
| 1970-71 (D1) | 3 | 11.01.71 | **Bristol City** (D2) | H | W | 3-0 | O'Neil, Davies 2 |
| | 4 | 23.01.71 | **York City** (D4) | A | D | 3-3 | Gabriel, Channon, Davies |
| | 4r | 01.02.71 | **York City** | H | W | 3-2 | O'Neil, Kirkup, Davies |
| | 5 | 13.02.71 | **Liverpool** (D1) | A | L | 0-1 | |
| 1971-72 (D1) | 3 | 15.01.72 | **Manchester Utd** (D1) | H | D | 1-1 | Channon |
| | 3r | 19.01.72 | **Manchester Utd** | A | L | 1-4aet | Channon |
| 1972-73 (D1) | 3 | 13.01.73 | **Crystal Palace** (D1) | A | L | 0-2 | |
| 1973-74 (D1) | 3 | 05.01.74 | **Blackpool** (D2) | H | W | 2-1 | Paine, Bennett |
| | 4 | 26.01.74 | **Bolton Wanderers** (D2) | H | D | 3-3 | Fisher, Channon, Stokes |
| | 4r | 30.01.74 | **Bolton Wanderers** | A | W | 2-0aet | Stokes 2 |
| | 5 | 16.02.74 | **Wrexham** (D3) | H | L | 0-1 | |
| 1974-75 (D2) | 3 | 04.01.75 | **West Ham Utd** (D1) | H | L | 1-2 | Channon (p) |
| 1975-76 (D2) | 3 | 03.01.76 | **Aston Villa** (D1) | H | D | 1-1 | Fisher |
| | 3r | 07.01.76 | **Aston Villa** | A | W | 2-1aet | McCalliog 2 |
| | 4 | 24.01.76 | **Blackpool** (D2) | H | W | 3-1 | Channon 2, Stokes |
| | 5 | 14.02.76 | **WBA** (D2) | A | D | 1-1 | Stokes |
| | 5r | 17.02.76 | **WBA** | H | W | 4-0 | Channon 3 (1p), Gilchrist |
| | 6 | 06.03.76 | **Bradford City** (D4) | A | W | 1-0 | McCalliog |
| | SF | 03.04.76 | **Crystal Palace** (D3) | | W | 2-0 | Peach (p), Gilchrist |
| | | | *played at Stamford Bridge* | | | | |
| | F | 01.05.76 | **Manchester Utd** (D1) | | W | 1-0 | Stokes |
| | | | *played at Wembley Stadium* | | | | |
| 1976-77 (D2) | 3 | 08.01.77 | **Chelsea** (D2) | H | D | 1-1 | Channon |
| | 3r | 12.01.77 | **Chelsea** | A | W | 3-0aet | MacDougall, Channon, Peach |
| | 4 | 29.01.77 | **Nottingham Forest** (D2) | A | D | 3-3 | Ball, Channon, Osgood |
| | 4r | 01.02.77 | **Nottingham Forest** | H | W | 2-1 | Williams, MacDougall |
| | 5 | 26.02.77 | **Manchester Utd** (D1) | H | D | 2-2 | Peach (p), Holmes |
| | 5r | 08.03.77 | **Manchester Utd** | A | L | 1-2 | Peach |
| 1977-78 (D2) | 3 | 07.01.78 | **Grimsby Town** (D4) | A | D | 0-0 | |
| | 3r | 10.01.78 | **Grimsby Town** | H | D | 0-0aet | |
| | 3 2r | 17.01.78 | **Grimsby Town** | | W | 4-1 | Peach, Boyer, Holmes, MacDougall |
| | | | *played at Filbert Street* | | | | |
| | 4 | 28.01.78 | **Bristol Rovers** (D2) | A | L | 0-2 | |
| 1978-79 (D1) | 3 | 09.01.79 | **Wimbledon** (D4) | A | W | 2-0 | Boyer 2 |
| | 4 | 12.02.79 | **Preston North End** (D2) | A | W | 1-0 | Ball |
| | 5 | 10.03.79 | **WBA** (D1) | A | D | 1-1 | Boyer |
| | 5r | 12.03.79 | **WBA** | H | W | 2-1aet | Peach (p), Boyer |
| | 6 | 19.03.79 | **Arsenal** (D1) | H | D | 1-1 | Hayes |
| | 6r | 21.03.79 | **Arsenal** | A | L | 0-2 | |
| 1979-80 (D1) | 3 | 05.01.80 | **Birmingham City** (D2) | A | L | 1-2 | Channon (p) |
| 1980-81 (D1) | 3 | 03.01.81 | **Chelsea** (D2) | H | W | 3-1 | Baker, Moran, Keegan |
| | 4 | 24.01.81 | **Bristol Rovers** (D2) | H | W | 3-1 | Moran 2, Williams |
| | 5 | 14.02.81 | **Everton** (D1) | H | D | 0-0 | |

| | | | | | | | | |
|---|---|---|---|---|---|---|---|---|
| | | 5r | 17.02.81 | **Everton** | A | L | 0-1aet | |
| 1981-82 | (D1) | 3 | 02.01.82 | **Leicester City** (D2) | A | L | 1-3 | Keegan |
| 1982-83 | (D1) | 3 | 08.01.83 | **Tottenham Hotspur** (D1) | A | L | 0-1 | |
| 1983-84 | (D1) | 3 | 07.01.84 | **Nottingham Forest** (D1) | A | W | 2-1 | Moran 2 |
| | | 4 | 28.01.84 | **Portsmouth** (D2) | A | W | 1-0 | Moran |
| | | 5 | 18.02.84 | **Blackburn Rovers** (D2) | A | W | 1-0 | Armstrong |
| | | 6 | 11.03.84 | **Sheffield Wed** (D2) | A | D | 0-0 | |
| | | 6r | 20.03.84 | **Sheffield Wed** | H | W | 5-1 | Williams, Oliver og, Wright, Armstrong, Moran |
| | | SF | 14.04.84 | **Everton** (D1) *played at Highbury* | | L | 0-1aet | |
| 1984-85 | (D1) | 3 | 05.01.85 | **Sunderland** (D1) | H | W | 4-0 | Moran 2, Curtis, Jordan |
| | | 4 | 26.01.85 | **Orient** (D3) | A | W | 2-0 | Jordan, Moran |
| | | 5 | 04.03.85 | **Barnsley** (D2) | H | L | 1-2 | Moran |
| 1985-86 | (D1) | 3 | 13.01.86 | **Middlesbrough** (D2) | A | W | 3-1 | D Wallace 3 |
| | | 4 | 25.01.86 | **Wigan Athletic** (D3) | H | W | 3-0 | Armstrong 2, Cockerill |
| | | 5 | 15.02.86 | **Millwall** (D2) | H | D | 0-0 | |
| | | 5r | 03.02.86 | **Millwall** | A | W | 1-0 | D Wallace |
| | | 6 | 08.03.86 | **Brighton** (D2) | A | W | 2-0 | Cockerill, Moran |
| | | SF | 05.04.86 | **Liverpool** (D1) *played at White Hart Lane* | | L | 0-2aet | |
| 1986-87 | (D1) | 3 | 10.01.87 | **Everton** (D1) | A | L | 1-2 | Hobson |
| 1987-88 | (D1) | 3 | 09.01.88 | **Reading** (D2) | A | W | 1-0 | Le Tissier |
| | | 4 | 30.01.88 | **Luton Town** (D1) | A | L | 1-2 | Clarke |
| 1988-89 | (D1) | 3 | 07.01.89 | **Derby County** (D1) | A | D | 1-1 | Statham (p) |
| | | 3r | 10.01.89 | **Derby County** | H | L | 1-2aet | Forrest |
| 1989-90 | (D1) | 3 | 06.01.90 | **Tottenham Hotspur** (D1) | A | W | 3-1 | Le Tissier, Horne, Rod Wallace |
| | | 4 | 27.01.90 | **Oxford Utd** (D2) | H | W | 1-0 | Ruddock |
| | | 5 | 17.02.90 | **Liverpool** (D1) | A | L | 0-3 | |
| 1990-91 | (D1) | 3 | 05.01.91 | **Ipswich Town** (D2) | H | W | 3-2 | Shearer, Le Tissier 2 |
| | | 4 | 26.01.91 | **Coventry City** (D1) | A | D | 1-1 | Shearer (p) |
| | | 4r | 29.01.91 | **Coventry City** | H | W | 2-0 | Case, Rod Wallace |
| | | 5 | 25.02.91 | **Nottingham Forest** (D1) | H | D | 1-1 | Ruddock |
| | | 5r | 04.03.91 | **Nottingham Forest** | A | L | 1-3 | Rod Wallace |
| 1991-92 | (D1) | 3 | 04.01.92 | **QPR** (D1) | H | W | 2-0 | Wood, Le Tissier |
| | | 4 | 27.01.92 | **Manchester Utd** (D1) | H | D | 0-0 | |
| | | 4r | 05.02.92 | **Manchester Utd** *Southampton won 4-2 on penalties* | A | D | 2-2aet | Gray, Shearer |
| | | 5 | 16.02.92 | **Bolton Wanderers** (D3) | A | D | 2-2 | Hall 2 |
| | | 5r | 26.02.92 | **Bolton Wanderers** | H | W | 3-2aet | Shearer, Horne 2 |
| | | 6 | 07.03.92 | **Norwich City** (D1) | H | D | 0-0 | |
| | | 6r | 18.03.92 | **Norwich City** | A | L | 1-2aet | Ruddock |
| 1992-93 | (PL) | 3 | 03.01.93 | **Nottingham Forest** (PL) | A | L | 1-2 | Le Tissier |
| 1993-94 | (PL) | 3 | 08.01.94 | **Port Vale** (D2) | H | D | 1-1 | Dowie |
| | | 3r | 18.01.94 | **Port Vale** | A | L | 0-1 | |
| 1994-95 | (PL) | 3 | 07.01.95 | **Southend Utd** (D1) | H | W | 2-0 | Heaney, Le Tissier |
| | | 4 | 28.01.95 | **Luton Town** (D1) | A | D | 1-1 | Shipperley |
| | | 4r | 08.02.95 | **Luton Town** | H | W | 6-0 | Le Tissier 2 (1p), Magilton, Heaney, Monkou, Hughes |
| | | 5 | 18.02.95 | **Tottenham Hotspur** (PL) | A | D | 1-1 | Le Tissier (p) |
| | | 5r | 01.03.95 | **Tottenham Hotspur** | H | L | 2-6aet | Shipperley, Le Tissier (p) |
| 1995-96 | (PL) | 3 | 07.01.96 | **Portsmouth** (D1) | H | W | 3-0 | Magilton 2, Shipperley |
| | | 4 | 07.02.96 | **Crewe Alexandra** (D2) | H | D | 1-1 | Le Tissier |
| | | 4r | 13.02.96 | **Crewe Alexandra** | A | W | 3-2 | Shipperley, Hall, Dodd |
| | | 5 | 17.02.96 | **Swindon Town** (D2) | A | D | 1-1 | Watson |
| | | 5r | 28.02.96 | **Swindon Town** | H | W | 2-0 | Oakley, Shipperley |
| | | 6 | 11.03.96 | **Manchester Utd** (PL) | A | L | 0-2 | |
| 1996-97 | (PL) | 3 | 04.01.97 | **Reading** (D1) | A | L | 1-3 | Ostenstad |
| 1997-98 | (PL) | 3 | 03.01.98 | **Derby County** (PL) | A | L | 0-2 | |
| 1998-99 | (PL) | 3 | 02.01.99 | **Fulham** (D2) | H | D | 1-1 | Ostenstad |
| | | 3r | 13.01.99 | **Fulham** | A | L | 0-1 | |

| | | | | | | | | |
|---|---|---|---|---|---|---|---|---|
| 1999-00 | (PL) | 3 | 13.12.99 | **Ipswich Town** (D1) | A | W | 1-0 | Richards |
| | | 4 | 08.01.00 | **Aston Villa** (PL) | A | L | 0-1 | |
| 2000-01 | (PL) | 3 | 06.01.01 | **Sheffield Utd** (D1) | H | W | 1-0 | Dodd (p) |
| | | 4 | 27.01.01 | **Sheffield Wed** (D1) | H | W | 3-1 | Davies, Dodd (p), Beattie |
| | | 5 | 17.02.01 | **Tranmere Rovers** (D1) | H | D | 0-0 | |
| | | 5r | 20.02.01 | **Tranmere Rovers** | A | L | 3-4 | Kachloul, Tessem, Richards |
| 2001-02 | (PL) | 3 | 16.01.02 | **Rotherham Utd** (D1) | A | L | 1-2 | Pahars (p) |
| 2002-03 | (PL) | 3 | 04.01.03 | **Tottenham Hotspur** (PL) | H | W | 4-0 | M Svensson, Tessem, A Svensson, Beattie |
| | | 4 | 25.01.03 | **Millwall** (D1) | H | D | 1-1 | Davies |
| | | 4r | 05.02.03 | **Millwall** | A | W | 2-1aet | Oakley 2 |
| | | 5 | 15.02.03 | **Norwich City** (D1) | H | W | 2-0 | A Svensson, Tessem |
| | | 6 | 09.03.03 | **Wolverhampton W** (D1) | H | W | 2-0 | Marsden, Butler og |
| | | SF | 13.04.03 | **Watford** (D1) *played at Villa Park* | | W | 2-1 | Ormerod, Robinson og |
| | | F | 17.05.03 | **Arsenal** (PL) *played at the Millennium Stadium, Cardiff* | | L | 0-1 | |

# SOUTHEND UNITED

*Formed 1906. FA Cup best performance: 5th round: 1926, 1952, 1976, 1993. Old 3rd round (5th round equivalent) 1921. Record FA Cup win: 10-1 v Golders Green (later Hendon), 1st round, 24.11.1934; 10-1 v Brentwood Town, 2nd round, 07.12.1968. Record FA Cup defeat: 0-6 v Burnley, 2nd round, 30.01.1915*

| | | | | | | | | |
|---|---|---|---|---|---|---|---|---|
| 1907-08 | (SL) | | | P East Ham (H) 3-0; 1q Clapton (A) 1-0; 2q Ilford (H) 3-1; 3q Clapton O (A) 1-1; 3qr Clapton Orient (H) 3-1; 4q 4th Kings Rifles (H) 6-0; 5q Carlisle Utd (A) 0-4 | | | | |
| 1908-09 | (SL) | | | P London Caledonians (A) 4-0; 1q Leyton FC (A) 1-0; 2q Shoeburyness Garrison (H) 4-0; 3q Ilford (A) 3-1; 4q Cromer (H) 2-0; 5q Luton Town (A) 1-1; 5qr Luton Town (H) 2-4 | | | | |
| 1909-10 | (SL) | | | 4q Barnet Alston (H) 5-2; 5q Hastings Utd (H) 4-2 | | | | |
| | | 1 | 15.01.10 | **Gainsborough T** (D2) | A | D | 1-1 | King |
| | | 1r | 19.01.10 | **Gainsborough T** | H | W | 1-0 | King |
| | | 2 | 05.02.10 | **QPR** (SL) | H | D | 0-0 | |
| | | 2r | 09.02.10 | **QPR** | A | L | 2-3 | Sugden, Frost |
| 1910-11 | (SL) | | | 4q Enfield (A) 3-3; 4qr Enfield (H) 3-1; 5q Tunbridge Wells R (H) 1-0 | | | | |
| | | 1 | 14.01.11 | **Blackburn Rovers** (D1) | A | L | 1-5 | Curtis |
| 1911-12 | (SL) | | | 4q London Caldeonians (A) 3-1; 5q Brentford (H) 0-1 | | | | |
| 1912-13 | (SL) | | | 3q Custom House (A) 1-0; 4q Clapton (A) 2-1; 5q Cardiff City (A) 3-0 | | | | |
| | | 1 | 11.01.13 | **Chelsea** (D1) | A | L | 2-5 | Frost 2 |
| 1913-14 | (SL) | | | 4q Tunbridge Wells Rangers (H) 3-0; 5q Brentford (A) 1-1; 5qr Brentford (H) 2-0 | | | | |
| | | 1 | 10.01.14 | **Birmingham** (D2) | A | L | 1-2 | Wiseman |
| 1914-15 | (SL) | 1 | 16.01.15 | **Bristol Rovers** (SL) | A | D | 0-0 | |
| | | 1r | 23.01.15 | **Bristol Rovers** | H | W | 3-0 | Wiseman 2, Frost |
| | | 2 | 30.01.15 | **Burnley** (D1) | A | L | 0-6 | |
| 1919-20 | (SL) | | | 6q Watford (H) 1-0 | | | | |
| | | 1 | 10.01.20 | **Sheffield Utd** (D1) | A | L | 0-3 | |
| 1920-21 | (D3) | | | 6q Hednesford Town (H) 3-1 | | | | |
| | | 1 | 08.01.21 | **Eccles Utd** (LC) | H | W | 5-1 | Myers 2, Nuttall 2, Walters |
| | | 2 | 29.01.21 | **Blackpool** (D2) | H | W | 1-0 | Dorsett |
| | | 3 | 19.02.21 | **Tottenham Hotspur** (D1) | H | L | 1-4 | Nicholls |
| 1921-22 | (3S) | 1 | 07.01.22 | **Worksop Town** (ML) | A | W | 2-1 | Buddery, Kettle |
| | | 2 | 28.01.22 | **Swansea Town** (3S) | H | L | 0-1 | |
| 1922-23 | (3S) | | | 4q Sittingbourne (A) 0-0; 4qr Sittingbourne (H) 4-2; 5q Norwich City (H) 2-2; 5qr Norwich City (A) 1-2 | | | | |
| 1923-24 | (3S) | | | 4q Kings Lynn (H) 1-0; 5q Clapton (A) 3-1; 6q Llanelli (A) 1-2 | | | | |
| 1924-25 | (3S) | | | 4q London Caledonians (H) 3-3; 4qr London Cale (A) 4-1; 5q Reading (A) 1-2 | | | | |
| 1925-26 | (3S) | 1 | 28.11.25 | **Dulwich Hamlet** (IL) | H | W | 5-1 | Morris Shaw, Watkins, Blissett, og |
| | | 2 | 12.12.25 | **Gillingham** (3S) | H | W | 1-0 | Watkins |
| | | 3 | 09.01.26 | **Southport** (3N) | H | W | 5-2 | Smith, Shaw, Hick 2, Blissett |
| | | 4 | 30.01.26 | **Derby County** (D2) | H | W | 4-1 | Andrews, Graver, Hick 2 |
| | | 5 | 20.02.26 | **Nottingham Forest** (D2) | H | L | 0-1 | |
| 1926-27 | (3S) | 1 | 27.11.26 | **Dulwich Hamlet** (IL) | A | W | 4-1 | Donovan 3, Hick |
| | | 2 | 11.12.26 | **Reading** (D2) | A | L | 2-3 | Hick, Purdy |
| 1927-28 | (3S) | 1 | 26.11.27 | **Wellington Town** (BDL) | H | W | 1-0 | Hick |

| | | | | | | | | |
|---|---|---|---|---|---|---|---|---|
| | | 2 | 10.12.27 | **Gillingham** (3S) | A | L | 0-2 | |
| 1928-29 | (3S) | 1 | 24.11.28 | **Luton Town** (3S) | A | L | 1-5 | Shankly |
| 1929-30 | (3S) | 1 | 30.11.29 | **Brentford** (3S) | H | W | 1-0 | Barnett |
| | | 2 | 14.12.29 | **York City** (3N) | H | L | 1-4 | Turnbull |
| 1930-31 | (3S) | 1 | 29.11.30 | **Torquay Utd** (3S) | H | L | 0-1 | |
| 1931-32 | (3S) | 1 | 28.11.31 | **Torquay Utd** | A | W | 3-1 | Shankly 2, Fowler og |
| | | 2 | 12.12.31 | **Northampton Town** (3S) | A | L | 0-3 | |
| 1932-33 | (3S) | 1 | 26.11.32 | **Exeter City** | H | D | 1-1 | Morfitt |
| | | 1r | 30.11.32 | **Exeter City** (3S) | A | W | 1-0 | Morfitt |
| | | 2 | 10.12.32 | **Scarborough** (ML) | H | W | 4-1 | Morfitt 3, Robson |
| | | 3 | 14.01.33 | **Watford** (3S) | A | D | 1-1 | Clenshaw |
| | | 3r | 18.01.33 | **Watford** | H | W | 2-0 | Morfitt, Clenshaw |
| | | 4 | 28.01.33 | **Derby County** (D1) | H | L | 2-3 | Pike, Morfitt |
| 1933-34 | (3S) | 1 | 25.11.33 | **London Paper Mills** (KL) | A | W | 1-0 | Fryer |
| | | 2 | 09.12.33 | **Chester** (3N) | H | W | 2-1 | Stevens, Barnett |
| | | 3 | 13.01.34 | **Tranmere Rovers** (3N) | A | L | 0-3 | |
| 1934-35 | (3S) | 1 | 24.11.34 | **Golders Green** (AL) | H | W | 10-1 | Johnson 5, Cheesmur 2, Deacon, Carr, Lane |
| | | 2 | 08.12.34 | **Wimbledon** (IL) | A | W | 5-1 | Johnson, Cheesmur 3, Deacon |
| | | 3 | 12.01.35 | **Sheffield Utd** (D2) | H | L | 0-4 | |
| 1935-36 | (3S) | 1 | 30.11.35 | **Newport County** (3S) | A | W | 1-0 | Lane |
| | | 2 | 14.12.35 | **Burton Town** (ML) | H | W | 3-0 | Oswald 3, Bolan, Cheesmur |
| | | 3 | 11.01.36 | **Tottenham Hotspur** (D2) | A | D | 4-4 | Bolan 3, Lane |
| | | 3r | 15.01.36 | **Tottenham Hotspur** | H | L | 1-2 | Bolan |
| 1936-37 | (3S) | 1 | 28.11.36 | **Crystal Palace** (3S) | A | D | 1-1 | Dickinson |
| | | 1r | 02.12.36 | **Crystal Palace** | H | W | 2-0 | Bolan, Goddard |
| | | 2 | 12.12.36 | **York City** (3N) | H | D | 3-3 | Lane, Willshaw, Dickinson |
| | | 2r | 16.12.36 | **York City** | A | L | 1-2aet | Dickinson |
| 1937-38 | (3S) | 1 | 27.11.37 | **Corinthians** *played at White City* | A | W | 2-0 | Dickinson, Martin |
| | | 2 | 11.12.37 | **Walthamstow Ave** (AL) | A | W | 1-0 | Bolan |
| | | 3 | 08.01.38 | **Barnsley** (D2) | H | D | 2-2 | Martin, Dickinson |
| | | 3r | 12.01.38 | **Barnsley** | A | L | 1-3 | Bell |
| 1938-39 | (3N) | 1 | 26.11.38 | **Corinthians** | H | W | 3-0 | Smirke 3 |
| | | 2 | 10.12.38 | **Port Vale** (3S) | A | W | 1-0 | Trainer |
| | | 3 | 07.01.39 | **Chesterfield** (D2) *abandoned after 73 minutes – fog* | A | - | 1-1ab | Hague |
| | | 3 | 11.01.39 | **Chesterfield** | A | D | 1-1 | Bushby |
| | | 3r | 16.01.39 | **Chesterfield** | H | W | 4-3aet | Bell 2, Bushby, Bolan |
| | | 4 | 21.01.39 | **Blackburn Rovers** (D2) | A | L | 2-4 | Bushby, Bell |
| 1945-46 | (3S) | 1 1L | 17.11.45 | **Watford** (3S) | A | D | 1-1 | Smirke |
| | | 1 2L | 24.11.45 | **Watford** | H | L | 0-3 | |
| 1946-47 | (3S) | 1 | 30.11.46 | **Brush Sports** (N&D) | A | W | 6-1 | Sibley, Bennett 2, Smirk, Thompson 2 |
| | | 2 | 14.12.46 | **Barnet** (AL) | A | W | 9-2 | Lane 3, Thompson, Sibley 2, Bennett 2, Bunker og |
| | | 3 | 11.01.47 | **Everton** (D1) | A | L | 2-4 | Thompson, Bennett |
| 1947-48 | (3S) | 1 | 29.11.47 | **Newport County** (3S) | A | L | 2-3 | Bennett 2 |
| 1948-49 | (3S) | 1 | 04.12.48 | **Swansea Town** (3S) | H | L | 1-2aet | Dudley |
| 1949-50 | (3S) | 1 | 26.11.49 | **Leyton Orient** (3S) | A | W | 2-0 | Wakefield 2 |
| | | 2 | 10.12.49 | **Wrexham** (3N) | A | D | 2-2 | Wakefield 2 |
| | | 2r | 14.12.49 | **Wrexham** | H | W | 2-0 | Clough, Wakefield |
| | | 3 | 07.01.50 | **Blackpool** (D1) | A | L | 0-4 | |
| 1950-51 | (3S) | 1 | 29.11.50 | **Swindon Town** (3S) | H | L | 0-3 | |
| 1951-52 | (3S) | 1 | 24.11.51 | **Bournemouth** (3S) | H | W | 6-1 | Stubbs 2, Wakefield 2, Bird og, French |
| | | 2 | 15.12.51 | **Oldham Athletic** (3N) | H | W | 5-0 | Wakefield 3, Stubbs, Grant |
| | | 3 | 12.01.52 | **Southampton** (D2) | H | W | 3-0 | Sibley, Stubbs, French |
| | | 4 | 02.02.52 | **Bristol Rovers** (3S) | H | W | 2-1 | Stubbs, French |
| | | 5 | 23.02.52 | **Sheffield Utd** (D2) | H | L | 1-2 | Wakefield |
| 1952-53 | (3S) | 1 | 22.11.52 | **Bath City** (SL) | A | L | 1-3 | Thompson |
| 1953-54 | (3S) | 1 | 21.11.53 | **Finchley** (AL) | A | W | 3-1 | Sibley, McAlinden, O'Neil |

| | | | | | | | | |
|---|---|---|---|---|---|---|---|---|
| | | 2 | 12.12.53 | **Chesterfield** (3N) | H | L | 1-2 | Dicker |
| 1954-55 | (3S) | 1 | 20.11.54 | **Bristol City** (3S) | A | W | 2-1 | Hollis 2 |
| | | 2 | 11.12.54 | **Bradford Park A** (3N) | A | W | 3-2 | Hollis 3 |
| | | 3 | 08.01.55 | **Everton** (D1) | A | L | 1-3 | Baron |
| 1955-56 | (3S) | 1 | 19.11.55 | **QPR** (3S) | H | W | 2-0 | Barker, Hollis |
| | | 2 | 10.12.55 | **Weymouth** (SL) | A | W | 1-0 | Lockhart |
| | | 3 | 07.01.56 | **Lincoln City** (D2) | A | W | 3-2 | Hollis 2, McCrory |
| | | 4 | 28.01.56 | **Manchester City** (D1) | H | L | 0-1 | |
| 1956-57 | (3S) | 1 | 17.11.56 | **Colchester Utd** (3S) | A | W | 4-1 | Hollis, McCrory 3 |
| | | 2 | 08.12.56 | **Hereford Utd** (SL) | A | W | 3-2 | Thomson 2, McGuigan |
| | | 3 | 05.01.57 | **Liverpool** (D2) | H | W | 2-1 | Duthie, Thomson |
| | | 4 | 26.01.57 | **Birmingham City** (D1) | H | L | 1-6 | Hollis |
| 1957-58 | (3S) | 1 | 16.11.57 | **Trowbridge Town** (WL) | A | W | 2-0 | Hollis 2 |
| | | 2 | 07.12.57 | **Torquay Utd** (3S) | A | D | 1-1 | McCrory |
| | | 2r | 11.12.57 | **Torquay Utd** | H | W | 2-1 | Hollis, McCrory |
| | | 3 | 04.01.58 | **Liverpool** (D2) | A | D | 1-1 | McGuigan |
| | | 3r | 08.01.58 | **Liverpool** | H | L | 2-3 | Molyneux og, McCrory |
| 1958-59 | (D3) | 1 | 15.11.58 | **Yeovil Town** (SL) | H | D | 0-0 | |
| | | 1r | 20.11.58 | **Yeovil Town** | A | L | 0-1 | |
| 1959-60 | (D3) | 1 | 14.11.59 | **Oswestry Town** (CC) | H | W | 6-0 | McCrory, G Jones og, Hollis 2, Price, Kellard |
| | | 2 | 05.12.59 | **Southampton** (D3) | A | L | 0-3 | |
| 1960-61 | (D3) | 1 | 05.11.60 | **Clacton Town** (SL) | A | W | 3-1 | Corthine, Kellard, Houghton |
| | | 2 | 26.11.60 | **Gillingham** (D4) | A | L | 2-3 | Fryatt, Stenhouse |
| 1961-62 | (D3) | 1 | 04.11.61 | **Watford** (D3) | H | L | 0-2 | |
| 1962-63 | (D3) | 1 | 03.11.62 | **Brighton** (D3) | H | W | 2-1 | Jones 2 |
| | | 2 | 24.11.62 | **Watford** (D3) | H | L | 0-2 | |
| 1963-64 | (D3) | 1 | 16.11.63 | **Yeovil Town** (SL) | A | L | 0-1 | |
| 1964-65 | (D3) | 1 | 14.11.64 | **Luton Town** (D3) | A | L | 0-1 | |
| 1965-66 | (D3) | 1 | 13.11.65 | **Notts County** (D4) | H | W | 3-1 | Slack, McKinven, Bentley |
| | | 2 | 04.12.65 | **Watford** (D3) | H | W | 2-1 | Firmani 2 |
| | | 3 | 22.01.66 | **Rotherham Utd** (D3) | A | L | 2-3 | Banks, Bentley |
| 1966-67 | (D4) | 1 | 26.11.66 | **Watford** (D3) | A | L | 0-1 | |
| 1967-68 | (D4) | 1 | 13.12.67 | **Brighton** (D3) | A | L | 0-1 | |
| 1968-69 | (D4) | 1 | 16.11.68 | **King's Lynn** (SL) | H | W | 9-0 | Moore 3, Best 3, Chisnall 2, Haskins og |
| | | 2 | 07.12.68 | **Brentwood Town** (SL) | H | W | 10-1 | Best 5, Moore 4, McMillan |
| | | 3 | 04.01.69 | **Swindon Town** (D3) | A | W | 2-0 | Hamilton, Best |
| | | 4 | 25.01.69 | **Mansfield Town** (D3) | A | L | 1-2 | Best |
| 1969-70 | (D4) | 1 | 15.11.69 | **Gillingham** (D3) | H | D | 0-0 | |
| | | 1r | 19.11.69 | **Gillingham** | A | L | 1-2 | Best |
| 1970-71 | (D4) | 1 | 21.11.70 | **Weymouth** (SL) | H | W | 7-0 | Garner 4, Best 2, Lewis |
| | | 2 | 12.12.70 | **Dagenham** (AL) | H | W | 1-0 | Best |
| | | 3 | 11.01.71 | **Carlisle Utd** (D2) | H | L | 0-3 | |
| 1971-72 | (D4) | 1 | 20.11.71 | **Aston Villa** (D3) | H | W | 1-0 | Best |
| | | 2 | 11.12.71 | **Bournemouth** (D3) | A | L | 0-2 | |
| 1972-73 | (D3) | 1 | 18.11.72 | **Aldershot** (D4) | H | L | 0-2 | |
| 1973-74 | (D3) | 1 | 24.11.73 | **Borehamwood** (AL) | H | W | 3-0 | T Johnson, Albeson (p), Kierstenton og |
| | | 2 | 15.12.73 | **Reading** (D4) | H | W | 2-0 | Brace, T Johnson |
| | | 3 | 05.01.74 | **Peterborough Utd** (D4) | A | L | 1-3 | Moody |
| 1974-75 | (D3) | 1 | 23.11.74 | **AP Leamington** (SL) | A | W | 2-1 | Guthrie, Silvester |
| | | 2 | 14.12.74 | **Ilford** (IL) | A | W | 2-0 | Townsend, Guthrie |
| | | 3 | 04.01.75 | **QPR** (D1) | H | D | 2-2 | Guthrie, Brace |
| | | 3r | 07.01.75 | **QPR** | A | L | 0-2 | |
| 1975-76 | (D3) | 1 | 22.11.75 | **Swansea City** (D4) | H | W | 2-0 | Parker 2 |
| | | 2 | 13.12.75 | **Dover** (SL) | H | W | 4-1 | Parker, Silvester 2, Moody (p) |
| | | 3 | 03.01.76 | **Brighton** (D3) | H | W | 2-1 | Silvester, Brace |
| | | 4 | 24.01.76 | **Cardiff City** (D3) | H | W | 2-1 | Parker 2 |
| | | 5 | 14.02.76 | **Derby County** (D1) | A | L | 0-1 | |
| 1976-77 | (D4) | 1 | 20.11.76 | **Exeter City** (D4) | A | D | 1-1 | Pountney |
| | | 1r | 22.11.76 | **Exeter City** | H | W | 2-1aet | Parker, Hadley |
| | | 2 | 11.12.76 | **Newport County** (D4) | H | W | 3-0 | Hadley, Pountney, Parker |

| | | | | | | | | |
|---|---|---|---|---|---|---|---|---|
| | | 3 | 08.01.77 | **Chester** (D3) | H | L | 0-4 | |
| 1977-78 | (D4) | 1 | 26.11.77 | **Torquay Utd** (D4) | A | W | 2-1 | Parker, Fell |
| | | 2 | 17.12.77 | **AP Leamington** (SL) | A | D | 0-0 | |
| | | 2r | 19.12.77 | **AP Leamington** | H | W | 4-0 | Moody (p), Parker, Laverick, Morris |
| | | 3 | 07.01.78 | **Derby County** (D1) | A | L | 2-3 | Parker 2 |
| 1978-79 | (D3) | 1 | 25.11.78 | **Peterborough Utd** (D3) | H | W | 3-2 | Pountney, Carmichael og, Parker |
| | | 2 | 16.12.78 | **Watford** (D3) | A | D | 1-1 | Parker |
| | | 2r | 18.12.78 | **Watford** | H | W | 1-0 | Polycarpou |
| | | 3 | 10.01.79 | **Liverpool** (D1) | H | D | 0-0 | |
| | | 3r | 17.01.79 | **Liverpool** | A | L | 0-3 | |
| 1979-80 | (D3) | 1 | 24.11.79 | **Wealdstone** (SL) | A | W | 1-0 | Walker |
| | | 2 | 15.12.79 | **Harlow Town** (IL) | H | D | 1-1 | Parker |
| | | 2r | 18.12.79 | **Harlow Town** | A | L | 0-1 | |
| 1980-81 | (D4) | 1 | 22.11.80 | **Hereford Utd** (D4) | H | L | 0-1 | |
| 1981-82 | (D3) | 1 | 21.11.81 | **Hereford Utd** | A | L | 1-3 | Gray |
| 1982-83 | (D3) | 1 | 20.11.82 | **Bournemouth** (D3) | A | W | 2-0 | Spackman og, Morgan og |
| | | 2 | 11.12.82 | **Yeovil Town** (APL) | H | W | 3-0 | Phillips, Poutney 2 |
| | | 3 | 08.01.83 | **Sheffield Wed** (D2) | H | D | 0-0 | |
| | | 3r | 11.01.83 | **Sheffield Wed** | A | D | 2-2aet | Mercer, Poutney |
| | | 3 2r | 24.01.83 | **Sheffield Wed** | A | L | 1-2 | Cusack (p) |
| 1983-84 | (D3) | 1 | 19.11.83 | **Plymouth Argyle** (D3) | H | D | 0-0 | |
| | | 1r | 22.11.83 | **Plymouth Argyle** | A | L | 0-2aet | |
| 1984-85 | (D4) | 1 | 17.11.84 | **Colchester Utd** (D4) | H | D | 2-2 | Clark, Phillips (p) |
| | | 1r | 21.11.84 | **Colchester Utd** | A | L | 2-3aet | Shepherd, Phillips |
| 1985-86 | (D4) | 1 | 16.11.85 | **Newport County** (D3) | H | L | 0-1 | |
| 1986-87 | (D4) | 1 | 15.11.86 | **Halesowen Town** (SL) | H | W | 4-1 | Hall, McDonough 2, Cadette |
| | | 2 | 05.12.86 | **Northampton Town** (D4) | H | D | 4-4 | Cadette 3, McDonough |
| | | 2r | 10.12.86 | **Northampton Town** | A | L | 2-3 | Pennyfather, Cadette |
| 1987-88 | (D3) | 1 | 14.11.87 | **Walsall** (D3) | H | D | 0-0 | |
| | | 1r | 17.11.87 | **Walsall** | A | L | 1-2 | Hall (p) |
| 1988-89 | (D3) | 1 | 19.11.88 | **Bristol City** (D3) | A | L | 1-3 | Ling |
| 1989-90 | (D4) | 1 | 18.11.89 | **Aylesbury Utd** (IL) | A | L | 0-1 | |
| 1990-91 | (D3) | 1 | 17.11.90 | **Leyton Orient** (D3) | A | L | 2-3 | Angell 2 |
| 1991-92 | (D2) | 3 | 04.01.92 | **Everton** (D1) | A | L | 0-1 | |
| 1992-93 | (D1) | 3 | 13.01.93 | **Millwall** (D1) | H | W | 1-0 | Collymore |
| | | 4 | 23.01.93 | **Huddersfield Town** (D2) | A | W | 2-1 | Collymore 2 |
| | | 5 | 13.02.93 | **Sheffield Wed** (PL) | A | L | 0-2 | |
| 1993-94 | (D1) | 3 | 08.01.94 | **Luton Town** (D1) | A | L | 0-1 | |
| 1994-95 | (D1) | 3 | 07.01.95 | **Southampton** (PL) | A | L | 0-2 | |
| 1995-96 | (D1) | 3 | 06.01.96 | **West Ham Utd** (PL) | A | L | 0-2 | |
| 1996-97 | (D1) | 3 | 15.01.97 | **Leicester City** (PL) | A | L | 0-2 | |
| 1997-98 | (D2) | 1 | 15.11.97 | **Woking** (Conf) | A | W | 2-0 | Jones, Gridelet |
| | | 2 | 06.12.97 | **Fulham** (D2) | A | L | 0-1 | |
| 1998-99 | (D3) | 1 | 14.11.98 | **Doncaster Rovers** (Conf) | H | L | 0-1 | |
| 1999-00 | (D3) | 1 | 30.10.99 | **Torquay Utd** (D3) | A | L | 0-1 | |
| 2000-01 | (D3) | 1 | 18.11.00 | **Torquay Utd** | A | D | 1-1 | Williamson |
| | | 1r | 28.11.00 | **Torquay Utd** | H | W | 2-1aet | Williamson, Roget |
| | | 2 | 10.12.00 | **Canvey Island** (IL) *played at Southend* | A | W | 2-1 | Forbes, Abbey |
| | | 3 | 06.01.01 | **Kingstonian** (Conf) | H | L | 0-1 | |
| 2001-02 | (D3) | 1 | 17.11.01 | **Luton Town** (D3) | H | W | 3-2 | Rawle, Bramble 2 |
| | | 2 | 08.12.01 | **Chesterfield** (D2) | A | D | 1-1 | Bramble |
| | | 2r | 18.12.01 | **Chesterfield** | A | W | 2-0 | N Whelan, Belgrave |
| | | 3 | 08.01.02 | **Tranmere Rovers** (D2) | H | L | 1-3 | Belgrave |
| 2002-03 | (D3) | 1 | 16.11.02 | **Hartlepool Utd** (D3) | H | D | 1-1 | Lee og |
| | | 1r | 26.11.02 | **Hartlepool Utd** | A | W | 2-1 | Bramble, Cort |
| | | 2 | 07.12.02 | **Bournemouth** (D2) | H | D | 1-1 | Rawle |
| | | 2r | 17.12.02 | **Bournemouth** | A | L | 2-3 | Bramble, Rawle |

# SOUTHPORT

*Formed 1881 as Southport Central. Southport Wanderers 1894. Southport Central 1895. Southport Vulcan 1915. Southport 1919. First entered FA Cup: 1882-83. FA Cup best performance: Quarter-finals 1931. FA Trophy runners-up: 1998. Members of the Football League: 1921-1978. League teams beaten as a Non-League club: Mansfield Town, Notts County. Relegated from The Conference to the Northern Premier League 2003.*

| | | | | | | | |
|---|---|---|---|---|---|---|---|
| **As Southport Central** | | | | | | | |
| 1882-83 | 1 | 21.10.82 | **Liverpool Ramblers** | A | D | 1-1 | |
| | 1r | 04.11.82 | **Liverpool Ramblers** | H | L | 0-4 | |
| 1883-84 | 1 | 20.11.83 | **Blackburn Rovers** | A | L | 0-7 | |
| 1884-85 | 1 | 11.10.84 | **Accrington FC** | A | L | 0-3 | |
| | | | *Accrington disqualified for professionalism, Southport reinstated* | | | | |
| | 2 | 22.11.84 | **Clitheroe Low Moor** | H | W | 3-1 | Briggs, Mellor, og |
| | 3 | 03.01.85 | **Church FC** | A | L | 0-10 | |
| 1885-86 | 1 | 10.10.85 | **Astley Bridge** | A | L | 2-3 | |
| **As Southport Wanderers** | | | | | | | |
| 1894-95 (LL) | 1 | 02.02.95 | **Everton** (D1) | H | L | 0-3 | |
| **As Southport Central** | | | | | | | |
| 1911-12 (CL) | 1 | 13.01.12 | **Reading** (SL) | H | L | 0-2 | |
| **As Southport** | | | | | | | |
| 1921-22 (3N) | | | 5q Altrincham (H) 3-0; 6q Coventry City (D2) 1-0 | | | | |
| | 1 | 07.01.22 | **Blackburn Rovers** (D1) | A | D | 1-1 | Glover |
| | 1r | 12.01.22 | **Blackburn Rovers** (D1) | H | L | 0-2 | |
| 1922-23 (3N) | | | 5q Wigan Borough (H) 1-1; 5qr Wigan Borough (A) 1-3 | | | | |
| 1923-24 (3N) | | | 5q Workington (A) 2-1; 6q Darlington (A) 0-3 | | | | |
| 1924-25 (3N) | | | 5q Tranmere Rovers (H) 1-0; 6q Doncaster Rovers (A) 0-1 | | | | |
| 1925-26 (3N) | 1 | 28.11.25 | **Mold FC** (Welsh) | H | W | 1-0 | Sapsford |
| | 2 | 12.12.25 | **Durham City** (3N) | A | W | 3-0 | Oxley 2, Sapsford |
| | 3 | 09.01.26 | **Southend Utd** (3S) | A | L | 2-5 | Oxley, Sapsford |
| 1926-27 (3N) | 1 | 27.11.26 | **Tranmere Rovers** (3N) | H | D | 1-1 | Sapsford |
| | 1r | 02.12.26 | **Tranmere Rovers** | A | W | 2-1 | Beadles, Jones |
| | 2 | 11.12.26 | **Crook Town** (NL) | H | W | 2-0 | Bradley 2 |
| | 3 | 08.01.27 | **Blackburn Rovers** (D1) | H | W | 2-0 | White, Beadles |
| | 4 | 29.01.27 | **Liverpool** (D1) | A | L | 1-3 | White |
| 1927-28 (3N) | 1 | 26.11.27 | **Denaby Utd** (ML) | A | W | 3-2 | Marshall, Tait 2 |
| | 2 | 10.12.27 | **Bradford Park A** (3N) | A | W | 2-0 | Marshall, Tait |
| | 3 | 14.01.28 | **Fulham** (D2) | H | W | 3-0 | Horler og, Tait 2 |
| | 4 | 28.01.28 | **Middlesbrough** (D1) | H | L | 0-3 | |
| 1928-29 (3N) | 1 | 24.11.28 | **Annfield Plain** (NEL) | A | W | 4-1 | Beadles 2, Mundy, Sissons |
| | 2 | 10.12.28 | **Stockport County** (3N) | A | L | 0-3 | |
| 1929-30 (3N) | 1 | 30.11.29 | **Chesterfield** (3N) | H | D | 0-0 | |
| | 1r | 04.12.29 | **Chesterfield** | A | L | 2-3 | Allen, Cowen |
| 1930-31 (3N) | 1 | 29.11.30 | **Darlington** (3N) | H | W | 4-2 | McConnell 2, Waterston, Hills |
| | 2 | 13.12.30 | **Gainsborough T** (ML) | A | W | 4-0 | Cowen, Waterston 2, Hills |
| | 3 | 10.01.31 | **Millwall** (D2) | H | W | 3-1 | Hills, Cowen 2 |
| | 4 | 26.01.31 | **Blackpool** (D1) | H | W | 2-1 | Waterston 2 |
| | 5 | 14.02.31 | **Bradford Park A** (D2) | H | W | 1-0 | Cowen |
| | 6 | 28.02.31 | **Everton** (D2) | A | L | 1-9 | Waterston |
| 1931-32 (3N) | 3 | 09.01.32 | **Barnsley** (D2) | A | D | 0-0 | |
| | 3r | 12.01.32 | **Barnsley** | H | W | 4-1 | Waterston 2, Dobson, Bell |
| | 4 | 23.01.32 | **Newcastle Utd** (D1) | A | D | 1-1 | Cowen |
| | 4r | 26.01.32 | **Newcastle Utd** | H | D | 1-1aet | Cowen |
| | 4 2r | 01.02.32 | **Newcastle Utd** | | L | 0-9 | |
| | | | *played at Hillsborough* | | | | |
| 1932-33 (3N) | 1 | 26.11.32 | **Nelson FC** (LC) | H | D | 3-3 | Appleby 2, Dobson |
| | 1r | 29.11.32 | **Nelson FC** | A | W | 4-0 | Bell 3, Dobson |
| | 2 | 10.12.32 | **Swindon Town** (3S) | H | L | 1-2 | Appleby |
| 1933-34 (3N) | 1 | 25.11.33 | **Workington** (NEL) | A | L | 0-1 | |
| 1934-35 (3N) | 1 | 24.11.34 | **New Brighton** (3N) | H | D | 1-1 | Worswick |
| | 1r | 28.11.34 | **New Brighton** | A | D | 1-1aet | Pickering |
| | 1 2r | 03.12.34 | **New Brighton** | | L | 1-2 | Worswick |
| | | | *played at Goodison Park* | | | | |

| | | | | | | | | |
|---|---|---|---|---|---|---|---|---|
| 1935-36 | (3N) | 1 | 30.11.35 | **Chesterfield** (3N) | A | L | 0-3 | |
| 1936-37 | (3N) | 1 | 28.11.36 | **Frickley Colliery** (ML) | A | W | 2-0 | Patrick 2 |
| | | 2 | 12.12.36 | **Bristol Rovers** (3S) | A | L | 1-2 | McCarthy |
| 1937-38 | (3N) | 1 | 27.11.37 | **Hartlepools Utd** (3N) | A | L | 1-3 | Kitchin |
| 1938-39 | (3N) | 1 | 26.11.38 | **Scarborough** (ML) | A | D | 0-0 | |
| | | 1r | 29.11.38 | **Scarborough** | H | W | 5-3 | Patrick 3, Hawkins, A Scott |
| | | 2 | 10.12.38 | **Swindon Town** (3S) | H | W | 2-0 | Patrick 2 |
| | | 3 | 10.01.39 | **Doncaster Rovers** (3N) | H | D | 1-1 | Patrick |
| | | 3r | 12.01.39 | **Doncaster Rovers** | A | L | 1-2 | Stapleton |
| 1945-46 | (3N) | 1 1L | 17.11.45 | **Oldham Athletic** (3N) | H | L | 1-2 | Oakes |
| | | 1 2L | 24.11.45 | **Oldham Athletic** | A | L | 1-3 | Oakes |
| 1946-47 | (3N) | 1 | 30.11.46 | **Stockport County** (3N) | A | L | 0-2 | |
| 1947-48 | (3N) | 1 | 29.11.47 | **Hull City** (3N) | A | D | 1-1aet | Wyles |
| | | 1r | 06.12.47 | **Hull City** | H | L | 2-3 | Wyles 2 |
| 1948-49 | (3N) | 1 | 27.11.48 | **Horden Coll Wel** (NEL) | H | W | 2-1 | Owens, Wyles |
| | | 2 | 11.12.48 | **York City** (3N) | H | D | 2-2aet | Wyles, Banks |
| | | 2r | 18.12.48 | **York City** | A | W | 2-0 | Marriott, Wyles |
| | | 3 | 08.01.49 | **Derby County** (D1) | A | L | 1-4 | Marriott |
| 1949-50 | (3N) | 1 | 26.11.49 | **Barrow** (3N) | H | D | 1-1 | Dainty |
| | | 1r | 01.12.49 | **Barrow** | A | W | 1-0 | Marriott |
| | | 2 | 10.12.49 | **Bradford City** (3N) | H | W | 2-1 | Meadows 2 |
| | | 3 | 07.01.50 | **Hull City** (D2) | H | D | 0-0 | |
| | | 3r | 12.01.50 | **Hull City** | A | L | 0-5 | |
| 1950-51 | (3N) | 1 | 25.11.50 | **Lincoln City** (3N) | A | D | 1-1 | Meadows |
| | | 1r | 28.11.50 | **Lincoln City** | H | W | 3-2 | Ross, Meadows, Nuttall |
| | | 2 | 09.12.50 | **Carlisle Utd** (3N) | H | L | 1-3 | Ross (p) |
| 1951-52 | (3N) | 1 | 24.11.51 | **Bangor City** (CC) | A | D | 2-2 | Billingham, Livesey |
| | | 1r | 27.11.51 | **Bangor City** | H | W | 3-0 | Billingham, Nuttall, Livesey |
| | | 2 | 15.12.51 | **Reading** (3S) | A | D | 1-1 | Lindsay |
| | | 2r | 19.12.51 | **Reading** | H | D | 1-1aet | Lindsay |
| | | 2 2r | 01.01.52 | **Reading** *played at Villa Park* | | L | 0-2 | |
| 1952-53 | (3N) | 1 | 22.11.52 | **Bangor City** (CC) | H | W | 3-1 | Pennington, Nuttall 2 |
| | | 2 | 06.12.52 | **Halifax Town** (3N) | A | L | 2-4 | Hitchen, Nuttall |
| 1953-54 | (3N) | 1 | 21.11.53 | **Carlisle Utd** (3N) | H | W | 1-0 | Hitchen |
| | | 2 | 12.12.53 | **Port Vale** (D3) | H | D | 1-1 | Whitworth |
| | | 2r | 14.12.53 | **Port Vale** | A | L | 0-2 | |
| 1954-55 | (3N) | 1 | 20.11.54 | **Bradford Park A** (3N) | A | L | 0-2 | |
| 1955-56 | (3N) | 1 | 19.11.55 | **Ashton Utd** (LC) | H | W | 6-1 | Bromilow 5, Lawrenson |
| | | 2 | 10.12.55 | **Grimsby Town** (3N) | H | D | 0-0 | |
| | | 2r | 14.12.55 | **Grimsby Town** | A | L | 2-3 | Brownilow, Holmes |
| 1956-57 | (3N) | 1 | 17.11.56 | **York City** (3N) | H | D | 0-0 | |
| | | 1r | 20.11.56 | **York City** | A | L | 1-2 | Prescott |
| 1957-58 | (3N) | 1 | 16.11.57 | **Wigan Athletic** (LC) | H | L | 1-2 | W Phoenix |
| 1958-59 | (D4) | 1 | 15.11.58 | **Halifax Town** (D3) | H | L | 0-2 | |
| 1959-60 | (D4) | 1 | 14.11.59 | **Workington** (D4) | H | D | 2-2 | Harrison 2 (1p) |
| | | 1r | 18.11.59 | **Workington** | A | L | 0-3 | |
| 1960-61 | (D4) | 1 | 05.11.60 | **Macclesfield T** (CC) | H | W | 7-2 | Blore 3, Blain 2, Griffiths, Booth |
| | | 2 | 26.11.60 | **Bangor City** (CC) | A | D | 1-1 | Hannaway |
| | | 2r | 29.11.60 | **Bangor City** | H | W | 3-1 | E Jones, Blain, Blore |
| | | 3 | 07.01.61 | **Stockport County** (D4) | A | L | 1-3 | Blore |
| 1961-62 | (D4) | 1 | 04.11.61 | **Northwich V** (CC) | H | W | 1-0 | Blore |
| | | 2 | 25.11.61 | **Mansfield Town** (D4) | H | W | 4-2 | Blain 2, Blore, Fielding |
| | | 3 | 09.01.62 | **Shrewsbury Town** (D3) | H | L | 1-3 | Jones |
| 1962-63 | (D4) | 1 | 03.11.62 | **Wrexham** (D3) | H | D | 1-1 | Cooper |
| | | 1r | 07.11.62 | **Wrexham** | A | L | 2-3 | Blain, Fielding |
| 1963-64 | (D4) | 1 | 16.11.63 | **Walsall** (D3) | H | W | 2-1 | Spence, Latham |
| | | 2 | 07.12.63 | **Lincoln City** (D4) | A | L | 0-2 | |
| 1964-65 | (D4) | 1 | 14.11.64 | **Annfield Plain** (Wear) | A | W | 6-1 | S Taylor, Hobson og, Russell 2 (1p), Spence, Hepton |
| | | 2 | 05.12.64 | **Wrexham** (D4) | A | W | 3-2 | Russell (p), Spence |

| | | | | | | | | |
|---|---|---|---|---|---|---|---|---|
| | | 3 | 09.01.65 | **Leeds Utd** (D1) | A | L | 0-3 | |
| 1965-66 | (D4) | 1 | 13.11.65 | **Halifax Town** (D4) | H | W | 2-0 | Russell 2 |
| | | 2 | 04.12.65 | **Stockport County** (D4) | H | D | 3-3 | Smith 2, Spence |
| | | 2r | 13.12.65 | **Stockport County** | A | W | 2-0 | Barratt, Spence |
| | | 3 | 22.01.66 | **Ipswich Town** (D2) | H | D | 0-0 | |
| | | 3r | 25.01.66 | **Ipswich Town** | A | W | 3-2 | Spence 2, Alty |
| | | 4 | 12.02.66 | **Cardiff City** (D2) | H | W | 2-0 | Spence, Smith |
| | | 5 | 05.03.66 | **Hull City** (D3) | A | L | 0-2 | |
| 1966-67 | (D4) | 1 | 26.11.66 | **Barnsley** (D4) | A | L | 1-3 | Fryatt |
| 1967-68 | (D3) | 1 | 09.12.67 | **Lincoln City** (D4) | H | W | 3-1 | Redrobe 2, Andrews |
| | | 2 | 06.01.68 | **Runcorn** (CC) | H | W | 4-2 | Andrews 2, Harkin, Redrobe |
| 1968-69 | (D3) | 1 | 16.11.68 | **Tranmere Rovers** (D3) | A | W | 1-0 | Spence |
| | | 2 | 07.12.68 | **Doncaster Rovers** (D4) | A | L | 1-2 | Andrews |
| 1969-70 | (D3) | 1 | 15.11.69 | **Lincoln City** (D4) | A | L | 0-2 | |
| 1970-71 | (D4) | 1 | 21.11.70 | **Boston Utd** (NPL) | H | L | 0-2 | |
| 1971-72 | (D4) | 1 | 20.11.71 | **Workington** (D4) | H | L | 1-3 | Dunleavy |
| 1972-73 | (D4) | 1 | 18.11.72 | **Port Vale** (D3) | A | L | 1-2 | Provan |
| 1973-74 | (D3) | 1 | 24.11.73 | **Rotherham Utd** (D4) | A | L | 1-2 | Noble (p) |
| 1974-75 | (D4) | 1 | 23.11.74 | **Bury** (D3) | A | L | 2-4 | Sibbald (p), Russell |
| 1975-76 | (D4) | 1 | 22.11.75 | **Spennymoor Utd** (NL) | A | L | 1-4 | O'Neil |
| 1976-77 | (D4) | 1 | 20.11.76 | **Port Vale** (D3) | H | L | 1-2 | Wilson |
| 1977-78 | (D4) | 1 | 26.11.77 | **Runcorn** (NPL) | H | D | 2-2 | Brooks, O'Neil |
| | | 1r | 28.11.77 | **Runcorn** | A | L | 0-1 | |
| 1978-79 | (NPL) | 1 | 25.11.78 | **Altrincham** (NPL) | A | L | 3-4 | Nolan, Dewsnip, Whittle |
| 1986-87 | (NPL) | 1 | 15.11.86 | **Scunthorpe Utd** (D4) | A | L | 0-2 | |
| 1988-89 | (NPL) | 1 | 19.11.88 | **Port Vale** (D3) | H | L | 0-2 | |
| 1992-93 | (NPL) | 1 | 14.11.92 | **Blyth Spartans** (NL) | A | W | 2-1 | Haw, Withers |
| | | 2 | 06.12.92 | **Hartlepool Utd** (D2) | A | L | 0-4 | |
| 1994-95 | (Conf) | 1 | 12.11.94 | **Altrincham** (Conf) | A | L | 2-3 | Cunningham, McDonald |
| 1996-97 | (Conf) | 1 | 16.11.96 | **Hednesford Town** (Conf) | A | L | 1-2 | Collins og |
| 1997-98 | (Conf) | 1 | 15.11.97 | **York City** (D2) | H | L | 0-4 | |
| 1998-99 | (Conf) | 1 | 14.11.98 | **Dulwich Hamlet** (IL) | A | W | 1-0 | Houghton og |
| | | 2 | 05.12.98 | **Mansfield Town** (D3) | A | W | 2-1 | Gamble (p), Ross |
| | | 3 | 02.01.99 | **Leyton Orient** (D3) | H | L | 0-2 | |
| 1999-00 | (Conf) | 1 | 30.10.99 | **Darlington** (D3) | A | L | 1-2 | Bolland |
| 2000-01 | (Conf) | 1 | 18.11.00 | **Havant & W** (SL) | A | W | 2-1 | Stuart, Arnold |
| | | 2 | 09.12.00 | **Kingstonian** (Conf) | H | L | 1-2 | Maamria |
| 2001-02 | (Conf) | 1 | 17.11.01 | **Dagenham & Red** (Conf) | A | L | 0-1 | |
| 2002-03 | (Conf) | 1 | 16.11.02 | **Notts County** (D2) | H | W | 4-2 | Pickford 2, Thomson, Lane |
| | | 2 | 07.12.02 | **Farnborough T** (Conf) | H | L | 0-3 | |

## SOUTHWICK

*Formed 1882. First entered FA Cup: 1890-91. Members of the Sussex County League*

| | | | | | | | | |
|---|---|---|---|---|---|---|---|---|
| 1974-75 | (SCL) | 1 | 23.11.74 | **Bournemouth** (D3) | A | L | 0-5 | |

## SPALDING UNITED

*Formed 1921. First entered FA Cup: 1921-22. Members of the Southern League.*

| | | | | | | | | |
|---|---|---|---|---|---|---|---|---|
| 1957-58 | (ECL) | 1 | 16.11.57 | **Durham City** (NL) | A | L | 1-3 | Jefferies |
| 1964-65 | (ML) | 1 | 14.11.64 | **Newport County** (D4) | A | L | 3-5 | Fox, Vest, Price |

## SPENNYMOOR UNITED

*Formed 1904. First entered FA Cup: 1905-06. League clubs beaten: Hartlepools United, Southport. Members of the Northern Premier League.*

| | | | | | | | | |
|---|---|---|---|---|---|---|---|---|
| 1927-28 | (NEL) | 1 | 26.11.27 | **Rotherham Utd** (3N) | H | D | 1-1 | Benstead |
| | | 1r | 01.12.27 | **Rotherham Utd** | A | L | 2-4 | Benstead, Kipling |
| 1928-29 | (NEL) | 1 | 24.11.28 | **Hartlepools Utd** (3N) | H | W | 5-2 | Barkins 4, A. Middleton . |
| | | 2 | 08.12.28 | **Accrington Stanley** (3N) | A | L | 0-7 | |
| 1932-33 | (NEL) | 1 | 26.11.32 | **Wrexham** (3N) | A | L | 0-3 | |
| 1933-34 | (NEL) | 1 | 25.11.33 | **Walsall** (3N) | A | L | 0-4 | |
| 1934-35 | (NEL) | 1 | 24.11.34 | **Rotherham Utd** (3N) | A | L | 0-2 | |
| 1936-37 | (NEL) | 1 | 28.11.36 | **Boston Utd** (ML) | A | D | 1-1 | Hill |
| | | 1r | 02.12.36 | **Boston Utd** | H | W | 2-0 | Wyness, Hill |

| | | | | | | | | |
|---|---|---|---|---|---|---|---|---|
| | | 2 | 12.12.36 | **Ipswich Town** (SL) | A | W | 2-1 | Wyness, Hill |
| | | 3 | 16.01.37 | **WBA** (D1) | A | L | 1-7 | Hill |
| 1946-47 | (NEL) | 1 | 30.11.46 | **Lancaster City** (LC) | A | L | 0-1 | |
| 1953-54 | (NEL) | 1 | 21.11.53 | **Barrow** (3N) | H | L | 0-3 | |
| 1967-68 | (NL) | 1 | 09.12.67 | **Goole Town** (ML) | A | D | 0-0 | |
| | | 1r | 13.12.67 | **Goole Town** | H | W | 3-1 | Summerill 2, Knowles og |
| | | 2 | 06.01.68 | **Macclesfield T** (CC) | A | L | 0-2 | |
| 1969-70 | (NL) | 1 | 15.11.69 | **Wrexham** (D4) | H | L | 1-4 | White |
| 1972-73 | (NL) | 1 | 18.11.72 | **Shrewsbury Town** (D3) | H | D | 1-1 | Banks |
| | | 1r | 21.11.72 | **Shrewsbury Town** | A | L | 1-3 | Davies |
| 1975-76 | (NL) | 1 | 22.11.75 | **Southport** (D4) | H | W | 4-1 | Banks 2, Mulligan, Reilly |
| | | 2 | 13.12.75 | **Bury** (D3) | A | L | 0-3 | |
| 1977-78 | (NL) | 1 | 26.11.77 | **Goole Town** (NPL) | H | W | 3-1 | Davies 2 (1p), Mulligan |
| | | 2 | 17.12.77 | **Rotherham Utd** (D3) | A | L | 0-6 | |
| 1986-87 | (NL) | 1 | 15.11.86 | **Tranmere Rovers** (D4) | H | L | 2-3 | Fowler, Mohan |
| 1990-91 | (NCE) | 1 | 17.11.90 | **Chesterfield** (D4) | A | L | 2-3 | Peattie, Boagey |
| 1994-95 | (NPL) | 1 | 12.11.94 | **Wigan Athletic** (D3) | A | L | 0-4 | |
| 1995-96 | (NPL) | 1 | 11.11.95 | **Colwyn Bay** (NPL) | H | L | 0-1 | |

## SPILSBY

*Entered FA Cup: 1880-81 – 1921-22. Played at The Cricket Ground, Spilsby, Lincolnshire.*

| | | | | | | | |
|---|---|---|---|---|---|---|---|
| 1880-81 | 1 | 06.11.80 | **Stafford Road** | H | L | 0-7 | |
| 1881-82 | 1 | 29.10.81 | **Staveley** | A | L | 1-5 | |
| 1882-83 | 1 | 04.11.82 | **Sheffield Wed** | A | L | 2-12 | B Robinson, Barrett |
| 1883-84 | 1 | 10.11.83 | **Grantham Town** | A | L | 2-3 | B Robinson, AN Other |
| 1884-85 | 1 | 08.11.84 | **Newark FC** | A | L | 3-7 | |

## ST ALBANS (1877)

*Formed 1877. Entered FA Cup 1880-81 and 1881-82. Played at the Upton Ground, St Albans, near the Princess Anne pub. No connection with later St Albans City club formed in 1908.*

| | | | | | | |
|---|---|---|---|---|---|---|
| 1880-81 | 1 | 13.11.80 | **Reading Abbey** | A | L | 0-1 |
| 1881-82 | 1 | 22.10.81 | **Upton Park** | A | L | 0-3 |

## ST ALBANS CITY

*Formed 1908. First entered FA Cup: 1908-09. The most famous FA Cup match involving St Albans City was their 8-7 defeat by Dulwich Hamlet in a fourth qualifying round replay in November 1922 when Wilfred (Billy) Minter scored all seven goals for St Albans and still finished on the losing side.League club beaten: Brentford. Members of the Isthmian League.*

| | | | | | | | | |
|---|---|---|---|---|---|---|---|---|
| 1924-25 | (IL) | | | 5q Brentford (3S) (H) 5-3; 6q Hartlepools Utd (3N) (A) 0-4 | | | | |
| 1925-26 | (IL) | 1 | 28.11.25 | **Leyton FC** (Lon) | A | L | 0-1 | |
| 1926-27 | (IL) | 1 | 27.11.26 | **Chatham** (KL) | A | L | 1-3 | Bethell |
| 1968-69 | (IL) | 1 | 16.11.68 | **Wealdstone** (IL) | A | D | 1-1 | Childs (p) |
| | | 1r | 19.11.68 | **Wealdstone** | H | W | 1-0 | Neville |
| | | 2 | 07.12.68 | **Walsall** (D3) | H | D | 1-1 | Ratty |
| | | 2r | 10.12.68 | **Walsall** | A | L | 1-3 | Butterfield |
| 1980-81 | (IL) | 1 | 22.11.80 | **Gravesend & N** (APL) | A | W | 2-1 | Whitehead 2 (2ps) |
| | | 2 | 13.12.80 | **Torquay Utd** (D4) | H | D | 1-1 | Mayles |
| | | 2r | 17.12.80 | **Torquay Utd** | A | L | 1-4 | Whitehead (p) |
| 1992-93 | (IL) | 1 | 14.11.92 | **Cheltenham Town** (SL) | H | L | 1-2 | Duffield (p) |
| 1996-97 | (IL) | 1 | 16.11.96 | **Wisbech Town** (ECL) | A | W | 2-1 | Howell 2 |
| | | 2 | 07.12.96 | **Bristol City** (D2) | A | L | 2-9 | Clark, Daly |
| 1999-00 | (IL) | 1 | 30.10.99 | **Bamber Bridge** (NPL) | H | L | 0-2 | |
| 2002-03 | (IL) | 1 | 16.11.02 | **Stockport County** (D2) | A | L | 1-4 | D Browne |

## ST BART'S HOSPITAL

*Formed 1866. Entered FA Cup only once in 1881-82, but they brought to a close an era in the FA Cup. Drawn to play the five-time FA Cup winners Wanderers in the first round, Wanderers scratched and never entered the FA Cup again. St Bart's played their home games at Battersea Park, south London.*

| | | | | | | |
|---|---|---|---|---|---|---|
| 1881-82 | 1 | | Wanderers | - | | |
| | | | *Wanderers scratched. St Bart's walkover* | | | |
| | 2 | 30.11.81 | **Marlow** | A | L | 0-2 |

## ST JAMES'S

| | | | | | | | | |
|---|---|---|---|---|---|---|---|---|
| 1885-86 | | 1 | | Old Harrovians | | | - | |
| | | | | *St James's scratched. Old Harrovians walkover* | | | | |

## ST MARK'S

| | | | | | | | | |
|---|---|---|---|---|---|---|---|---|
| 1877-78 | | 1 | | Barnes | | | - | |
| | | | | *St Mark's scratched. Barnes walkover* | | | | |

## ST NEOTS TOWN

*Formed 1879. First entered FA Cup: 1957-58. Members of the United Counties League.*

| | | | | | | | | |
|---|---|---|---|---|---|---|---|---|
| 1966-67 | (Met) | 1 | 26.11.66 | **Walsall** (D3) | A | L | 0-2 | |

## ST PETER'S INSTITUTE

*Formed 1877. Originally played at Battersea Park in south London and continued until 1905 when they were absorbed by Staines.*

| | | | | | | | | |
|---|---|---|---|---|---|---|---|---|
| 1879-80 | | 1 | 01.11.79 | **Mosquitoes** | A | L | 1-3 | Daville |
| 1880-81 | | 1 | 06.11.80 | **Hendon (1874)** | H | L | 1-8 | |

## ST STEPHEN'S

| | | | | | | | | |
|---|---|---|---|---|---|---|---|---|
| 1877-78 | | 1 | 07.11.77 | **Remnants** | A | L | 0-4 | |

## STAFFORD RANGERS

*Formed 1876. First entered FA Cup: 1884-85. FA Trophy winners: 1972, 1979. Runners-up: 1976. League clubs beaten: Stockport County, Halifax Town, Rotherham United, Lincoln City. Members of the Southern League.*

| | | | | | | | | |
|---|---|---|---|---|---|---|---|---|
| 1884-85 | | 1 | | Newtown | | | - | |
| | | | | *Stafford Rangers scratched. Newtown walkover* | | | | |
| 1885-86 | | 1 | 31.10.85 | **Druids** | H | L | 1-4 | |
| 1972-73 | (NPL) | 1 | 18.11.72 | **Crewe Alexandra** (D4) | A | L | 0-1 | |
| 1974-75 | (NPL) | 1 | 23.11.74 | **Stockport County** (D4) | A | D | 0-0 | |
| | | 1r | 26.11.74 | **Stockport County** | H | W | 1-0 | Albeson og |
| | | 2 | 14.12.74 | **Halifax Town** (D3) | H | W | 2-1 | Cullerton, Sargeant |
| | | 3 | 04.01.75 | **Rotherham Utd** (D4) | H | D | 0-0 | |
| | | 3r | 07.01.75 | **Rotherham Utd** | A | W | 2-0 | Chapman, Cullerton |
| | | 4 | 24.01.75 | **Peterborough Utd** (D3) | | L | 1-2 | Cullerton |
| | | | | *played at the Victoria Ground, Stoke* | | | | |
| 1975-76 | (NPL) | 1 | 22.11.75 | **AP Leamington** (SL) | A | W | 3-2 | Jones 2, Hughes |
| | | 2 | 13.12.75 | **Halifax Town** (D3) | H | L | 1-3 | B Sedden |
| 1976-77 | (NPL) | 1 | 20.11.76 | **Halifax Town** | H | D | 0-0 | |
| | | 1r | 23.11.76 | **Halifax Town** | A | L | 0-1 | |
| 1977-78 | (NPL) | 1 | 26.11.77 | **Carlisle Utd** (D3) | A | L | 0-2 | |
| 1978-79 | (NPL) | 1 | 25.11.78 | **Hull City** (D3) | A | L | 1-2 | Wood |
| 1979-80 | (APL) | 1 | 24.11.79 | **Moor Green** (MC) | H | W | 3-2 | Seddon, Howell og, Chapman |
| | | 2 | 17.12.79 | **Blackburn Rovers** (D3) | A | L | 0-2 | |
| 1980-81 | (APL) | 1 | 22.11.80 | **Walsall** (D3) | A | L | 0-3 | |
| 1981-82 | (APL) | 1 | 21.11.81 | **York City** (D4) | H | L | 1-2 | Burr |
| 1986-87 | (Conf) | 1 | 15.11.86 | **Port Vale** (D3) | A | L | 0-1 | |
| 1988-89 | (Conf) | 1 | 19.11.88 | **Crewe Alexandra** (D4) | H | D | 2-2 | Camden 2 |
| | | 1r | 22.11.88 | **Crewe Alexandra** | A | L | 2-3 | Cavell, Thacker |
| 1989-90 | (Conf) | 1 | 18.11.89 | **Halifax Town** (D4) | H | L | 2-3 | Camden 2 (2ps) |
| 1990-91 | (Conf) | 1 | 17.11.90 | **Burnley** (D4) | H | L | 1-3 | Anastasi |
| 1992-93 | (Conf) | 1 | 14.11.92 | **Lincoln City** (D3) | A | D | 0-0 | |
| | | 1r | 25.11.92 | **Lincoln City** | H | W | 2-1 | Boughey, Bradshaw |
| | | 2 | 05.12.92 | **Marine** (NPL) | A | L | 2-3 | Berry (p), Palgrave |
| 2002-03 | (SL) | 1 | 16.11.02 | **Shrewsbury Town** (D3) | A | L | 0-4 | |

## STAFFORD ROAD

*Formed 1874. Entered FA Cup: 1879-80 – 1887-88. Played at the Stafford Road Railway Works recreation ground, Wolverhampton.*

| | | | | | | | | |
|---|---|---|---|---|---|---|---|---|
| 1879-80 | | 1 | 08.11.79 | **Wednesbury Strollers** | H | W | 2-0 | |
| | | 2 | 13.12.79 | **Aston Villa** | H | D | 1-1 | |
| | | 2r | 24.01.80 | **Aston Villa** | A | L | 1-3 | Crump |
| 1880-81 | | 1 | 06.11.80 | **Spilsby** | A | W | 7-0 | |
| | | 2 | 11.12.80 | **Grantham Town** | A | D | 1-1 | |

| | | | | | | | |
|---|---|---|---|---|---|---|---|
| | 2r | 16.12.80 | **Grantham Town** | H | W | 7-1 | |
| | 3 | | bye | | | | |
| | 4 | 19.02.81 | **Aston Villa** | A | W | 3-2 | Gowland 2, Crump |
| | 5 | 19.03.81 | **Old Etonians** | H | L | 1-2 | og |
| 1881-82 | 1 | 05.11.81 | **Wednesbury Strollers** | A | L | 1-3 | Gowland |
| 1882-83 | 1 | 04.11.82 | **Small Heath Alliance** | A | D | 3-3 | |
| | 1r | 18.11.82 | **Small Heath Alliance** | H | W | 6-2 | |
| | 2 | 02.12.82 | **Walsall Town** | A | L | 1-4 | Foster |
| 1883-84 | 1 | 10.11.83 | **Aston Unity** | H | W | 5-1 | |
| | 2 | 01.12.83 | **Aston Villa** | H | L | 1-5 | |
| 1884-85 | 1 | 08.11.84 | **Walsall Swifts** | H | D | 0-0 | |
| | 1r | 17.11.84 | **Walsall Swifts** | A | L | 1-2 | Thomas |
| 1885-86 | 1 | 17.10.85 | **Matlock Town** | H | W | 7-0 | |
| | 2 | 21.11.85 | **Wolverhampton W** | A | L | 2-4 | B Jones, AN Other |
| 1887-88 | 1 | 15.10.87 | **Great Bridge Unity** | H | W | 2-1 | |
| | | | *FA ordered replay after protest* | | | | |
| | 1r | 22.10.87 | **Great Bridge Unity** | A | D | 1-1 | |
| | | | *Stafford Road scratched before second replay. Great Bridge walkover* | | | | |

## STAINES TOWN

*Formed 1892. First entered FA Cup: 1904-05. Members of the Isthmian League.*

| | | | | | | | |
|---|---|---|---|---|---|---|---|
| 1984-85 (IL) | 1 | 17.11.84 | **Burton Albion** (NPL) | A | L | 0-2 | |

## STALYBRIDGE CELTIC

*Formed 1909. First entered FA Cup: 1912-13. Members of the Football League 1921-1923. Members of the Northern Premier League.*

| | | | | | | | |
|---|---|---|---|---|---|---|---|
| 1921-22 (3N) | | | 4q Carlisle Utd (A) 0-0; 4qr Carlisle Utd (H) 3-2; 5q Hartlepools Utd (H) 2-0; 6q Ashington (A) 0-1 | | | | |
| 1922-23 (3N) | | | 5q Nelson (H) 1-0; 6q Bristol Rovers (H) 0-0; 6qr Bristol Rovers (A) 2-1 | | | | |
| | 1 | 13.01.23 | **WBA** (D1) | A | D | 0-0 | |
| | 1r | 17.01.23 | **WBA** | H | L | 0-2 | |
| 1932-33 (CC) | 1 | 26.11.32 | **Hull City** (3N) | H | L | 2-8 | Hurst, Wright |
| 1934-35 (CC) | 1 | 24.11.34 | **Tranmere Rovers** (3N) | A | L | 1-3 | Slater |
| 1935-36 (CC) | 1 | 30.11.35 | **Kells Utd** (Cumb) | H | W | 4-0 | Cheetham 3, Jones |
| | 2 | 14.12.35 | **Darlington** (3N) | H | L | 0-1 | |
| 1936-37 (CC) | 1 | 28.11.36 | **Shildon** (NL) | A | L | 2-4 | Webster, Charles |
| 1938-39 (CC) | 1 | 26.11.38 | **Darlington** (3N) | A | L | 0-4 | |
| 1945-46 (CC) | 1 1L | 17.11.45 | **Marine** (LCC) | A | L | 0-4 | |
| | 1 2L | 24.11.45 | **Marine** | H | D | 3-3 | Webster 2, Egerton |
| 1947-48 (CC) | 1 | 29.11.47 | **Tranmere Rovers** (3N) | A | L | 0-2 | |
| 1984-85 (NWC) | 1 | 17.11.84 | **Frickley Athletic** (APL) | A | L | 1-2 | Stewart (p) |
| 1993-94 (Conf) | 1 | 13.11.93 | **Marine** (NPL) | H | D | 1-1 | Aspinall |
| | 1r | 29.11.93 | **Marine** | A | D | 4-4aet | Hill, Shaughnessy, Aspinall, Kirkham |
| | | | *Stalybridge Celtic won 4-2 on penalties* | | | | |
| | 2 | 04.12.93 | **Carlisle Utd** (D3) | A | L | 1-3 | Kirkham |
| 1996-97 (Conf) | 1 | 16.11.96 | **Chester City** (D3) | A | L | 0-3 | |
| 1999-00 (NPL) | 1 | 02.11.99 | **Merthyr Tydfil** (SL) | A | D | 2-2 | Parr, Sullivan |
| | 1r | 09.11.99 | **Merthyr Tydfil** | H | W | 3-1 | Bauress (p), Pickford, Sullivan |
| | 2 | 20.11.99 | **Chester City** (D3) | H | L | 1-2 | Scott |
| 2001-02 (Conf) | 1 | 17.11.01 | **Chesterfield** (D2) | H | L | 0-3 | |

## STALYBRIDGE ROVERS

*Entered FA Cup: 1894-95 – 1907-08.*

| | | | | | | | |
|---|---|---|---|---|---|---|---|
| 1899-00 (LL) | 1 | 27.01.00 | **Bristol City** (SL) | A | L | 1-2 | Green |

## STANLEY UNITED

*Formed 1890. Entered FA Cup: 1900-01 – 1974-75. Tommy Cummings, who played for Burnley in the 1962 FA Cup final, and Geoff Strong, who played for Liverpool in 1965, both had spells with Stanley United.*

| | | | | | | | |
|---|---|---|---|---|---|---|---|
| 1954-55 (NL) | 1 | 20.11.54 | **Crook Town** (NL) | A | L | 3-5 | Bell, Hepple 2 |

## STAPLE HILL

*Formed 1892. Entered FA Cup: 1895-96 – 1909-10.*

| | | | | | | | |
|---|---|---|---|---|---|---|---|
| 1905-06 (WL) | 1 | 13.01.06 | **Manchester Utd** (D2) | A | L | 2-7 | Tippett, G Williams |

# STAVELEY

*Formed 1875. Entered FA Cup: 1881-82 – 1895-96. Played at the Recreation Ground, Staveley, Chesterfield.*

| | | | | | | | |
|---|---|---|---|---|---|---|---|
| 1881-82 | 1 | 29.10.81 | **Spilsby** | H | W | 5-1 | Wallace 2, Beresford 2, Kenyon |
| | 2 | 28.11.81 | **Grantham Town** | H | W | 3-1 | |
| | 3 | 28.12.81 | **Sheffield Wed** | A | D | 2-2 | G Marples, H Marples |
| | 3r | 07.01.81 | **Sheffield Wed** | H | D | 0-0 | |
| | 3 2r | 09.01.81 | **Sheffield Wed** | H | L | 1-5 | H Marples |
| 1882-83 | 1 | 21.10.82 | **Walsall Town** | A | L | 1-4 | Mather |
| 1883-84 | 1 | 10.11.83 | **Middlesbrough** | A | W | 4-1 | Potter, 4 others |
| | 2 | 01.12.83 | **Sheffield Wed** | H | W | 3-1 | Crookes |
| | 3 | 29.12.83 | **Lockwood Bros** | H | W | 1-0 | Crookes |
| | 4 | 19.01.84 | **Blackburn Rovers** | A | L | 1-5 | H Marples |
| 1884-85 | 1 | 08.11.84 | **Notts Rangers** | H | W | 4-1 | |
| | 2 | 06.12.84 | **Notts County** | H | L | 0-2 | |
| 1885-86 | 1 | 31.10.85 | **Mexborough Town A** | H | D | 1-1 | |
| | | | *Mexborough scratched before replay took place. Staveley walkover* | | | | |
| | 2 | 21.11.85 | **Long Eaton Rangers** | A | W | 4-1 | |
| | 3 | 12.12.85 | **Nottingham Forest** | H | W | 2-1 | J Hay, Young |
| | 4 | | bye | | | | |
| | 4 | 23.01.86 | **Blackburn Rovers** | A | L | 1-7 | Needham |
| 1886-87 | 1 | 30.10.86 | **Attercliffe** | H | W | 7-0 | |
| | 2 | 20.11.86 | **Rotherham Town** | H | W | 4-0 | Marshall, Needham, Potter, Shaw |
| | 3 | 11.12.86 | **Notts County** | H | L | 0-3 | |
| 1887-88 | 1 | 15.10.87 | **Derby County** | H | L | 1-2 | Rollinson |

# STEVENAGE BOROUGH

*Formed 1976. First entered FA Cup: 1983-84. FA Trophy Runners-up 2002. League clubs beaten: Leyton Orient, Cambridge United, Swindon Town. Members of The Conference.*

| | | | | | | | |
|---|---|---|---|---|---|---|---|
| 1995-96 (Conf) | 1 | 11.11.95 | **Hereford Utd** (D3) | A | L | 1-2 | Crawshaw |
| 1996-97 (Conf) | 1 | 16.11.96 | **Hayes** (Conf) | H | D | 2-2 | Catlin, Hayles |
| | 1r | 26.11.96 | **Hayes** | A | W | 2-0 | Hayles 2 |
| | 2 | 07.12.96 | **Leyton Orient** (D3) | A | W | 2-1 | Brown, Catlin |
| | 3 | 04.01.97 | **Birmingham City** (D1) | H | L | 0-2 | |
| | | | *played at St Andrews* | | | | |
| 1997-98 (Conf) | 1 | 15.11.97 | **Carshalton Athletic** (IL) | A | D | 0-0 | |
| | 1r | 24.11.97 | **Carshalton Athletic** | H | W | 5-0 | Love 2, Perkins, Smith, Trott |
| | 2 | 06.12.97 | **Cambridge Utd** (D3) | A | D | 1-1 | Crawshaw (p) |
| | 2r | 15.12.97 | **Cambridge Utd** | H | W | 2-1 | Campbell og, Beevor |
| | 3 | 03.01.98 | **Swindon Town** (D1) | A | W | 2-1 | Soloman, Grazioli |
| | 4 | 25.01.98 | **Newcastle Utd** (PL) | H | D | 1-1 | Grazioli |
| | 4r | 04.02.98 | **Newcastle Utd** | A | L | 1-2 | Crawshaw |
| 1998-99 (Conf) | 1 | 14.11.98 | **Runcorn** (NPL) | A | D | 1-1 | Alford |
| | 1r | 23.11.98 | **Runcorn** | H | W | 2-0 | Love, Alford |
| | 2 | 05.12.98 | **Lincoln City** (D2) | A | L | 1-4 | Alford |
| 2002-03 (Conf) | 1 | 16.11.02 | **Hastings Utd** (SL) | H | W | 1-0 | Howell |
| | 2 | 07.12.02 | **Darlington** (D3) | A | L | 1-4 | Howell |

# STOCKPORT COUNTY

*Formed 1883. First entered FA Cup: 1892-93. FA Cup best performance: 5th round, 1935. 1950. Record FA Cup win: 6-0 v Barnton Rovers, 1st qualifying round, 1896-97. In Competition Proper: 6-2 v West Auckland Town, 1st round, 14.11.1959. Record FA Cup defeat: 1-8 v Bury, 2nd qualifying round, 1892-93. In Competition Proper: 0-7 v Portsmouth, 3rd round, 08.01.1949.*

| | | | | | | | |
|---|---|---|---|---|---|---|---|
| 1892-93 (TC) | | | 1q Halliwell (H) 4-0 FA ordered match be be replayed after protest 1q Halliwell (H) 4-2aet; 2q Bury (A) 1-8 | | | | |
| 1893-94 (TC) | | | 1q Bootle walkover; 2q Tranmere Rovers (H) 2-1; 3q Wrexham (H) 3-2; 4q Crewe Alexandra (H) 0-0aet; 4qr Crewe Alexandra (A) 2-1 | | | | |
| | 1 | 27.01.94 | **Burton Wanderers** (ML) | H | L | 0-1 | |
| 1894-95 (LL) | | | 1q Fairfield (H) 2-3 | | | | |
| 1895-96 (LL) | | | 1q Liverpool South End (H) 2-0; 2q Fairfield (A) 1-5 | | | | |
| 1896-97 (LL) | | | 1q Barnton R (H) 6-0; 2q Druids (A) 2-3 | | | | |
| 1897-98 (LL) | | | 1q Chester (H) 2-0; 2q Oswestry Town (H) 2-1; 3q Rock Ferry (H) 2-1; 4q Aberystwyth (H) 5-0; 5q New Brighton Tower (H) 0-1 | | | | |

| | | | | | | | | |
|---|---|---|---|---|---|---|---|---|
| 1898-99 | (LL) | | | 3q Ashton NE (A) 2-2; 3qr Ashton NE (H) 2-0; 4q Middleton (H) 3-0; 5q Glossop North End (H) 0-2 | | | | |
| 1899-00 | (LL) | | | 3q Glossop North (A) 2-2; 3qr Glossop North End (H) 3-0; 4q Stalybridge Rovers (A) 0-2 | | | | |
| 1900-01 | (D2) | | | 3q Wrexham (H) 6-2; 4q Crewe Alexandra (H) 1-3 | | | | |
| 1901-02 | (D2) | | | 3q Buxton (A) 2-0; 4q Crewe Alexandra (H) 3-2; 5q Glossop North End (A) 0-2 | | | | |
| 1902-03 | (D2) | | | 1q Stalybridge Rovers (H) 0-1 | | | | |
| 1903-04 | (D2) | | | 3q Heywood (H) 4-0; 4q Port Vale (H) 0-0; 4qr Port Vale (A) 0-6 | | | | |
| 1904-05 | (ML) | | | 3q Stalybridge Rovers (H) 2-0; 4q Glossop North End (A) 1-1; 4qr Glossop North (H) 0-0; 4q 2r Glossop North End (A) 0-0; 4q 3r Glossop North End (H) 1-0; 5q Wrexham (H) 4-0; 6q Chesterfield (A) 0-2 | | | | |
| 1905-06 | (D2) | | | 4q Walsall (A) 3-3; 4qr Walsall (H) 5-0 | | | | |
| | | 1 | 13.01.06 | **Lincoln City** (D2) | A | L | 2-4 | Schofield, Bardsley |
| 1906-07 | (D2) | 1 | 12.01.07 | **Fulham** (SL) | A | D | 0-0 | |
| | | 1r | 16.01.07 | **Fulham** | A | L | 1-2 | Pass |
| 1907-08 | (D2) | 1 | 11.01.08 | **Aston Villa** (D1) | A | L | 0-3 | |
| 1908-09 | (D2) | 1 | 16.01.09 | **Grimsby Town** (D2) | A | - | 2-0ab | Green, Whitehouse |
| | | | | *abandoned after 75 minutes – fog* | | | | |
| | | 1 | 20.01.09 | **Grimsby Town** | A | W | 2-0 | Whitehouse, Lomax |
| | | 2 | 06.02.09 | **Glossop North End** (D2) | H | D | 1-1 | Whitehouse |
| | | 2r | 09.02.09 | **Glossop North End** | A | L | 0-1aet | |
| 1909-10 | (D2) | 1 | 15.01.10 | **Bolton Wanderers** (D1) | H | W | 4-1 | Whitehouse 2, Newman, Greechan |
| | | 2 | 05.02.10 | **Leyton FC** (SL) | H | L | 0-2 | |
| 1910-11 | (D2) | | | 4q Rochdale (A) 0-0; 4qr Rochdale (H) 0-0; 4q 2r Rochdale 0-1 (at Oldham) | | | | |
| 1911-12 | (D2) | | | 4q Chester (A) 4-1; 5q Catford Southend (H) 4-0 | | | | |
| | | 1 | 13.01.12 | **Lincoln City (CL)** | A | L | 0-2 | |
| 1912-13 | (D2) | | | 4q Willenhall (A) 2-0; 5q Kings Lynn (A) 7-2 | | | | |
| | | 1 | 11.01.13 | **Everton** (D1) | A | - | 1-1ab | Tatersall |
| | | | | *abandoned after 48 minutes* | | | | |
| | | 1 | 15.01.13 | **Everton** | A | L | 1-5 | Maconnachie og |
| 1913-14 | (D2) | | | 4q Gainsborough T (A) 2-3 | | | | |
| 1914-15 | (D2) | 1 | 09.01.15 | **Liverpool** (D1) | A | L | 0-3 | |
| 1919-20 | (D2) | 1 | 10.01.20 | **Preston North End** (D1) | A | L | 1-3 | Rogers |
| 1920-21 | (D2) | 1 | 08.01.21 | **Everton** (D1) | A | L | 0-1 | |
| 1921-22 | (3N) | | | 5q Lancaster Town (A) 0-2 | | | | |
| 1922-23 | (D2) | | | 5q Barrow (A) 2-3 | | | | |
| 1923-24 | (D2) | | | 5q Crewe Alexandra (H) 1-0; 6q Norwich City (A) 0-2 | | | | |
| 1924-25 | (D2) | 1 | 10.01.25 | **QPR** (3S) | A | W | 3-1 | Waterall, Blood, Simms |
| | | 2 | 31.01.25 | **Birmingham** (D1) | A | L | 0-1 | |
| 1925-26 | (D2) | 3 | 09.01.26 | **Sheffield Utd** (D1) | A | L | 0-2 | |
| 1926-27 | (3N) | 1 | 27.11.26 | **Nelson FC** (3N) | A | L | 1-4 | Scutt |
| 1927-28 | (3N) | 1 | 26.11.27 | **Oswestry Town** (BDL) | H | W | 5-2 | J Smith 2 (1p), Scutt, Pearson, Duffus |
| | | 2 | 10.12.27 | **Crewe Alexandra** (3N) | A | L | 0-2 | |
| 1928-29 | (3N) | 1 | 24.11.28 | **Halifax Town** (3N) | H | W | 1-0 | Fielding |
| | | 2 | 10.12.28 | **Southport** (3N) | H | W | 3-0 | Newton 2, Burgem |
| | | 3 | 12.01.29 | **Bradford City** (3N) | A | L | 0-2 | |
| 1929-30 | (3N) | 1 | 30.11.29 | **Wellington Town** (BDL) | A | W | 4-1 | Newton 2, Gee, Tompkinson |
| | | 2 | 14.12.29 | **Barrow** (3N) | H | W | 4-0 | Lincoln 2, Boardman, Newton |
| | | 3 | 11.01.30 | **Blackpool** (D2) | A | L | 1-2 | Boardman |
| 1930-31 | (3N) | 1 | 29.11.30 | **Hartlepools Utd** (3N) | A | W | 3-2 | F Newton, Lincoln, Webster |
| | | 2 | 13.12.30 | **Bristol Rovers** (3S) | A | L | 2-4 | Lincoln, F Newton |
| 1931-32 | (3N) | 1 | 28.11.31 | **Crook Town** (NEL) | A | L | 1-3 | Smith |
| 1932-33 | (3N) | 1 | 26.11.32 | **Rochdale** (3N) | A | W | 2-0 | Taylor, Vincent |
| | | 2 | 10.12.32 | **Luton Town** (3S) | H | L | 2-3 | Taylor, Foulkes |
| 1933-34 | (3N) | 1 | 25.11.33 | **Lancaster Town** (LC) | A | W | 1-0 | Lythgoe |
| | | 2 | 09.12.33 | **Crystal Palace** (3S) | H | L | 1-2 | Vincent |
| 1934-35 | (3N) | 1 | 24.11.34 | **Blyth Spartans** (NEL) | A | D | 1-1 | Foulkes |
| | | 1r | 28.11.34 | **Blyth Spartans** | H | W | 4-1 | Stevenson 2, Unwin, Foulkes |
| | | 2 | 08.12.34 | **Darlington** (3N) | H | W | 3-2 | Green 2, Hill |
| | | 3 | 12.01.35 | **West Ham Utd** (D2) | A | D | 1-1 | Barrett og |
| | | 3r | 16.01.35 | **West Ham Utd** | H | W | 1-0 | Hill |

| | | | | | | | | |
|---|---|---|---|---|---|---|---|---|
| | | 4 | 26.01.35 | **Bradford City** (D2) | A | D | 0-0 | |
| | | 4r | 31.01.35 | **Bradford City** | H | W | 3-2aet | Hill 2, Green |
| | | 5 | 16.02.35 | **WBA** (D1) | H | L | 0-5 | |
| 1935-36 | (3N) | 3 | 11.01.36 | **Plymouth Argyle** (D2) | H | L | 2-3 | Rae og, McNaughton |
| 1936-37 | (3N) | 1 | 28.11.36 | **Carlisle Utd** (3N) | A | L | 1-2 | Still |
| 1937-38 | (3N) | 3 | 08.01.38 | **Middlesbrough** (D1) | A | L | 0-2 | |
| 1938-39 | (3N) | 1 | 26.11.38 | **North Shields** (NEL) | A | W | 4-1 | Bagley, Essex, Sargeant 2 |
| | | 2 | 10.12.38 | **Walthamstow Ave** (AL) | H | D | 0-0 | |
| | | 2r | 15.12.38 | **Walthamstow Ave** | A | W | 3-1 | Sargeant 3 |
| | | 3 | 07.01.39 | **Barnsley** (3N) | A | W | 2-1 | Essex, Sargeant |
| | | 4 | 21.01.39 | **Liverpool** (D1) | A | L | 1-5 | Reid |
| 1945-46 | (3N) | 1 1L | 17.11.45 | **Rochdale** (3N) | H | L | 1-2 | Shaw |
| | | 1 2L | 24.11.45 | **Rochdale** | A | D | 1-1 | Hyde |
| 1946-47 | (3N) | 1 | 30.11.46 | **Southport** (3N) | H | W | 2-0 | Brinton, Cocker |
| | | 2 | 14.12.46 | **Halifax Town** (3N) | A | D | 1-1 | Shaw |
| | | 2r | 18.12.46 | **Halifax Town** | H | W | 2-1 | Earl, McCulloch |
| | | 3 | 11.01.47 | **Bolton Wanderers** (D1) | A | L | 1-5 | Walker |
| 1947-48 | (3N) | 1 | 29.11.47 | **Accrington Stanley** (3N) | H | W | 3-1 | Stock 2, Morris |
| | | 2 | 13.12.47 | **Shrewsbury Town** (ML) | H | - | 1-1ab | Barkas |
| | | | | *abandoned after 110 minutes – fog* | | | | |
| | | 2 | 20.12.47 | **Shrewsbury Town** | H | D | 2-2aet | Shaw, Glaister |
| | | 2r | 22.12.47 | **Shrewsbury Town** | | W | 3-2 | glaister 2, McCulloch |
| | | | | *played at Maine Road* | | | | |
| | | 3 | 10.01.48 | **Torquay Utd** (3S) | H | W | 3-0 | Morris, Barkas 2 |
| | | 4 | 24.01.48 | **Charlton Athletic** (D1) | A | L | 0-3 | |
| 1948-49 | (3N) | 1 | 27.11.48 | **Workington** (NEL) | A | W | 3-0 | Herd 2, Glaister |
| | | 2 | 11.12.48 | **Scunthorpe Utd** (ML) | A | W | 1-0 | Glaister |
| | | 3 | 08.01.49 | **Portsmouth** (D1) | A | L | 0-7 | |
| 1949-50 | (3N) | 1 | 26.11.49 | **Billingham Syn** (NL) | H | W | 3-0 | McGuigan 2, Herd |
| | | 2 | 10.12.49 | **Nottingham Forest** (3S) | A | W | 2-0 | McGuigan, Herd |
| | | 3 | 07.01.50 | **Barnsley** (D2) | H | W | 4-2 | Cocker 2, Swinscoe, McGuigan |
| | | 4 | 28.01.50 | **Hull City** (D2) | H | D | 0-0 | |
| | | 4r | 02.02.50 | **Hull City** | A | W | 2-0 | Herd, Cocker |
| | | 5 | 11.02.50 | **Liverpool** (D1) | H | L | 1-2 | Herd |
| 1950-51 | (3N) | 3 | 06.01.51 | **Brentford** (D2) | H | W | 2-1 | Cocker, Dixon |
| | | 4 | 27.01.51 | **Blackpool** (D1) | A | L | 1-2 | Black |
| 1951-52 | (3N) | 1 | 24.11.51 | **Gateshead AFC** (3N) | H | D | 2-2aet | Oliver, Weigh |
| | | 1r | 28.11.51 | **Gateshead AFC** | A | D | 1-1aet | Weigh |
| | | 1 2r | 03.12.51 | **Gateshead AFC** | | L | 1-2 | Glover |
| | | | | *played at Hillsborough* | | | | |
| 1952-53 | (3N) | 1 | 22.11.52 | **North Shields** (NEL) | A | W | 6-3 | Bodie 2, Connor 3, Oliver |
| | | 2 | 06.12.52 | **Gillingham** (3S) | H | W | 3-1 | Oliver, Bodie, Connor |
| | | 3 | 10.01.53 | **Walthamstow Ave** (AL) | A | L | 1-2 | Moran |
| 1953-54 | (3N) | 1 | 21.11.53 | **Chester** (3N) | H | W | 4-2 | Clempson, Connor 3 |
| | | 2 | 12.12.53 | **Workington** (3N) | H | W | 2-1 | Connor, Cushin og |
| | | 3 | 09.01.54 | **Headington Utd** (SL) | H | D | 0-0 | |
| | | 3r | 14.01.54 | **Headington Utd** | A | L | 0-1 | |
| 1954-55 | (3N) | 1 | 20.11.54 | **Carlisle Utd** (3N) | H | L | 0-1 | |
| 1955-56 | (3N) | 1 | 19.11.55 | **Mansfield Town** (3N) | A | L | 0-2 | |
| 1956-57 | (3N) | 1 | 17.11.56 | **New Brighton** (LC) | A | D | 3-3 | Finney, Moran 2 |
| | | 1r | 20.11.56 | **New Brighton** | H | L | 2-3 | Finney, Daley |
| 1957-58 | (3N) | 1 | 16.11.57 | **Barrow** (3N) | H | W | 2-1 | Davock, Wilson |
| | | 2 | 07.12.57 | **Hartlepools Utd** (3N) | H | W | 2-1 | Davock, Sowden |
| | | 3 | 04.01.58 | **Luton Town** (D1) | H | W | 3-0 | Jackson, Holden 2 |
| | | 4 | 25.01.58 | **West Ham Utd** (D2) | A | L | 2-3 | Holden, Finney |
| 1958-59 | (D3) | 1 | 15.11.58 | **Hull City** (D3) | A | W | 1-0 | Jackson |
| | | 2 | 06.12.58 | **Blyth Spartans** (ML) | A | W | 4-3 | Wilson, Clarke, Clempson, Jackson |
| | | 3 | 14.01.59 | **Burnley** (D1) | H | L | 1-3 | Jackson |
| 1959-60 | (D4) | 1 | 14.11.59 | **West Auckland T** (NL) | A | W | 6-2 | Guy 2, Betts, Wilson, Davock, Ritchie |
| | | 2 | 05.12.59 | **Crewe Alexandra** (D4) | H | D | 0-0 | |
| | | 2r | 09.12.59 | **Crewe Alexandra** | A | L | 0-2 | |

| | | | | | | | | |
|---|---|---|---|---|---|---|---|---|
| 1960-61 | (D4) | 1 | 05.11.60 | **Workington** (D4) | H | W | 1-0 | Anderson |
| | | 2 | 26.11.60 | **Bishop Auckland** (NL) | H | W | 2-0 | Davock 2 |
| | | 3 | 07.01.61 | **Southport** (D4) | H | W | 3-1 | Anderson 2, Wilson |
| | | 4 | 01.02.61 | **Newcastle Utd** (D1) | A | L | 0-4 | |
| 1961-62 | (D4) | 1 | 04.11.61 | **Accrington Stanley** (D4) | H | L | 0-1 | |
| 1962-63 | (D4) | 1 | 03.11.62 | **Chesterfield** (D4) | A | L | 1-4 | Bentley |
| 1963-64 | (D4) | 1 | 16.11.63 | **Barnsley** (D3) | A | L | 0-1 | |
| 1964-65 | (D4) | 1 | 14.11.64 | **Wigan Athletic** (CC) | H | W | 2-1 | Eckershall (p), Nibloe |
| | | 2 | 05.12.64 | **Grimsby Town** | H | - | 0-0ab | |
| | | | | *abandoned after 50 minutes – fog* | | | | |
| | | 2 | 07.12.64 | **Grimsby Town** (D3) | H | W | 1-0 | Hodgkinson |
| | | 3 | 09.01.65 | **Bristol Rovers** (D3) | A | D | 0-0 | |
| | | 3r | 11.01.65 | **Bristol Rovers** | H | W | 3-2 | Hodgkinson, Beaumont, Sandford |
| | | 4 | 30.01.65 | **Liverpool** (D1) | A | D | 1-1 | White |
| | | 4r | 03.02.65 | **Liverpool** | H | L | 0-2 | |
| 1965-66 | (D4) | 1 | 13.11.65 | **Tranmere Rovers** (D4) | A | W | 1-0 | Price |
| | | 2 | 04.12.65 | **Southport** (D4) | A | D | 3-3 | Allen 2, Shawcross (p) |
| | | 2r | 13.12.65 | **Southport** | H | L | 0-2 | |
| 1966-67 | (D4) | 1 | 26.11.66 | **Darlington** (D3) | A | D | 0-0 | |
| | | 1r | 29.11.66 | **Darlington** | H | D | 1-1aet | Morrin |
| | | 1 2r | 05.12.66 | **Darlington** | | L | 2-4 | Greener og, Sykes |
| | | | | *played at Elland Road* | | | | |
| 1967-68 | (D3) | 1 | 09.12.67 | **Macclesfield T** (CC) | H | D | 1-1 | Atkins |
| | | 1r | 13.12.67 | **Macclesfield T** | A | L | 1-2 | Kevan |
| 1968-69 | (D3) | 1 | 16.11.68 | **Bradford Park A** (D4) | H | W | 3-0 | Atkins, Harley, Lowe (p) |
| | | 2 | 07.12.68 | **Barrow** (D3) | H | W | 2-0 | Young, Atkins |
| | | 3 | 04.01.69 | **Blackburn Rovers** (D2) | A | L | 0-2 | |
| 1969-70 | (D3) | 1 | 15.11.69 | **Mossley** (CC) | H | D | 1-1 | Collier |
| | | 1r | 18.11.69 | **Mossley** | A | W | 1-0 | Rowlands |
| | | 2 | 06.12.69 | **Scunthorpe Utd** (D4) | H | D | 0-0 | |
| | | 2r | 09.12.69 | **Scunthorpe Utd** | A | L | 0-4 | |
| 1970-71 | (D4) | 1 | 21.11.70 | **Grantham Town** (ML) | A | L | 1-2 | McMillan |
| 1971-72 | (D4) | 1 | 20.11.71 | **Doncaster Rovers** (D4) | A | W | 2-1 | McMillan, Lawther |
| | | 2 | 11.12.71 | **Blyth Spartans** (NL) | A | L | 0-1 | |
| 1972-73 | (D4) | 1 | 18.11.72 | **Workington** (D4) | H | W | 1-0 | Spratt (p) |
| | | 2 | 09.12.72 | **Rotherham Utd** (D3) | A | W | 1-0 | Davidson |
| | | 3 | 13.01.73 | **Hull City** (D2) | H | D | 0-0 | |
| | | 3r | 23.01.73 | **Hull City** | A | L | 0-2aet | |
| 1973-74 | (D4) | 1 | 24.11.73 | **Port Vale** (D3) | H | L | 0-1 | |
| 1974-75 | (D4) | 1 | 23.11.74 | **Stafford Rangers** (NPL) | H | D | 0-0 | |
| | | 1r | 26.11.74 | **Stafford Rangers** | A | L | 0-1 | |
| 1975-76 | (D4) | 1 | 22.11.75 | **Hartlepool** (D4) | A | L | 0-3 | |
| 1976-77 | (D4) | 1 | 20.11.76 | **Sheffield Wed** (D3) | A | L | 0-2 | |
| 1977-78 | (D4) | 1 | 26.11.77 | **Scunthorpe Utd** (D4) | H | W | 3-0 | Fletcher, Massey, Fogarty |
| | | 2 | 17.12.77 | **Shrewsbury Town** (D3) | A | D | 1-1 | Summerbee |
| | | 2r | 19.12.77 | **Shrewsbury Town** | H | L | 1-2 | Prudham |
| 1978-79 | (D4) | 1 | 25.11.78 | **Morecambe** (NPL) | H | W | 5-1 | Prudham, Bradd, Park 3 |
| | | 2 | 16.12.78 | **Bradford City** (D4) | H | W | 4-2 | Fogarty, Lee, Bradd, Park |
| | | 3 | 01.02.79 | **Wrexham** (D2) | A | L | 2-6 | Lee, Park |
| 1979-80 | (D4) | 1 | 24.11.79 | **Walsall** (D4) | A | L | 0-2 | |
| 1980-81 | (D4) | 1 | 22.11.80 | **Sheffield Utd** (D3) | H | D | 0-0 | |
| | | 1r | 25.11.80 | **Sheffield Utd** | A | L | 2-3aet | Coyle, Sunley |
| 1981-82 | (D4) | 1 | 21.11.81 | **Mossley** (NPL) | H | W | 3-1 | Williams 2, Park |
| | | 2 | 02.01.82 | **Port Vale** (D4) | A | L | 1-4 | Smith |
| 1982-83 | (D4) | 1 | 20.11.82 | **Mansfield Town** (D4) | A | L | 2-3 | Williams, Park |
| 1983-84 | (D4) | 1 | 19.11.83 | **Telford Utd** (APL) | A | L | 0-3 | |
| 1984-85 | (D4) | 1 | 17.11.84 | **Walsall** (D3) | H | L | 1-2 | Taylor |
| 1985-86 | (D4) | 1 | 16.11.85 | **Telford Utd** (APL) | H | L | 0-1 | |
| 1986-87 | (D4) | 1 | 15.11.86 | **Caernarfon Town** (NPL) | A | L | 0-1 | |
| 1987-88 | (D4) | 1 | 14.11.87 | **Telford Utd** (Conf) | A | D | 1-1 | Entwistle |
| | | 1r | 17.11.87 | **Telford Utd** | H | W | 2-0 | Colville, Hodkinson (p) |

| | | | | | | | | |
|---|---|---|---|---|---|---|---|---|
| | | 2 | 05.12.87 | **Runcorn** (Conf) | A | W | 1-0 | Colville |
| | | 3 | 09.01.88 | **Leyton Orient** (D4) | H | L | 1-2 | Colville |
| 1988-89 | (D4) | 1 | 19.11.88 | **Scarborough** (D4) | A | L | 1-2 | Colville |
| 1989-90 | (D4) | 1 | 18.11.89 | **Burnley** (D4) | A | D | 1-1 | Angell |
| | | 1r | 22.11.89 | **Burnley** | H | L | 1-2 | Edwards |
| 1990-91 | (D4) | 1 | 17.11.90 | **Rotherham Utd** (D3) | A | L | 0-1 | |
| 1991-92 | (D3) | 1 | 16.11.91 | **Lincoln City** (D4) | H | W | 3-1 | Gannon, Ward (og), Francis |
| | | 2 | 07.12.91 | **Wigan Athletic** (D3) | A | L | 0-2 | |
| 1992-93 | (D2) | 1 | 14.11.92 | **York City** (D3) | A | W | 3-1 | Francis 2, Todd |
| | | 2 | 05.12.92 | **Macclesfield T** (Conf) | A | W | 2-0 | Preece, B Williams |
| | | 3 | 02.01.93 | **Derby County** (D1) | A | L | 1-2 | McCourd |
| 1993-94 | (D2) | 1 | 13.11.93 | **Rotherham Utd** (D2) | A | W | 2-1 | Todd, Preece |
| | | 2 | 04.12.93 | **Halifax Town** (Conf) | H | W | 5-1 | Frain, Francis 2, Beaumont, Wallace |
| | | 3 | 08.01.94 | **QPR** (PL) | H | W | 2-1 | Francis, Preece |
| | | 4 | 09.02.94 | **Bristol City** (D1) | H | L | 0-4 | |
| 1994-95 | (D2) | 1 | 12.11.94 | **Wrexham** (D2) | A | L | 0-1 | |
| 1995-96 | (D2) | 1 | 11.11.95 | **Lincoln City** (D3) | H | W | 5-0 | Eckhardt 3, Barnett og, C Armstrong |
| | | 2 | 02.12.95 | **Blyth Spartans** (NPL) | H | W | 2-0 | Eckhardt, Raffell og |
| | | 3 | 07.01.96 | **Everton** (PL) | A | D | 2-2 | C Armstrong, Helliwell |
| | | 3r | 17.01.96 | **Everton** | H | L | 2-3 | Bound, Armstrong |
| 1996-97 | (D2) | 1 | 16.11.96 | **Doncaster Rovers** (D3) | H | W | 2-1 | Flynn, Mutch |
| | | 2 | 07.12.96 | **Mansfield Town** (D3) | A | W | 3-0 | Ford og, Durkan 2 |
| | | 3 | 15.01.97 | **Stoke City** (D1) | A | W | 2-0 | Durkan, Armstrong |
| | | 4 | 25.01.97 | **Birmingham City** (D1) | A | L | 1-3 | Angell |
| 1997-98 | (D1) | 3 | 03.01.98 | **Preston North End** (D2) | A | W | 2-1 | Angell 2 |
| | | 4 | 24.01.98 | **Birmingham City** (D1) | A | L | 1-2 | Armstrong |
| 1998-99 | (D1) | 3 | 02.01.99 | **Bury** (D1) | A | W | 3-0 | Angell, Lucketti og, Woodthorpe |
| | | 4 | 23.01.99 | **Sheffield Wed** (PL) | A | L | 0-2 | |
| 1999-00 | (D1) | 3 | 11.12.99 | **Grimsby Town** (D1) | A | L | 2-3 | Bailey, Moore |
| 2000-01 | (D1) | 3 | 06.01.01 | **Preston North End** (D1) | A | W | 1-0 | Fradin |
| | | 4 | 27.01.01 | **Crewe Alexandra** (D1) | A | W | 1-0 | Wiss |
| | | 5 | 17.02.01 | **Tottenham Hotspur** (PL) | A | L | 0-4 | |
| 2001-02 | (D1) | 3 | 16.01.02 | **Bolton Wanderers** (PL) | H | L | 1-4 | Daly (p) |
| 2002-03 | (D2) | 1 | 16.11.02 | **St Albans City** (IL) | H | W | 4-1 | Beckett, Fradin, Burgess 2 (1p) |
| | | 2 | 07.12.02 | **Plymouth Argyle** (D2) | H | L | 0-3 | |

# STOCKTON

*Formed 1882. First entered FA Cup: 1888-89. FA Amateur Cup winners: 1899, 1903, 1912. League club beaten: Mansfield Town. Folded 1975.*

| | | | | | | | | |
|---|---|---|---|---|---|---|---|---|
| 1892-93 | (NL) | 1 | 21.01.93 | **Grimsby Town** (D2) | A | L | 0-5 | |
| 1896-97 | (NL) | 1 | 30.01.97 | **Bury** (D1) | H | D | 0-0 | |
| | | 1r | 02.02.97 | **Bury** | A | L | 1-12 | Daniels |
| 1903-04 | (NL) | 1 | 06.02.04 | **Wolverhampton W** (D1) | H | L | 1-4 | Blake |
| 1907-08 | (NL) | 1 | 11.01.08 | **Chesterfield** (D2) | A | L | 0-4 | |
| 1925-26 | (NL) | 1 | 03.12.25 | **South Bank** (NL) | A | W | 4-1 | Harrison 2, Thompson, Longstaffe |
| | | 2 | 12.12.25 | **Oldham Athletic** (D2) | H | L | 4-6 | Thompson 2, Smith 2 |
| 1926-27 | (NL) | 1 | 27.11.26 | **Ashington** (3N) | H | L | 1-2 | Smith |
| 1927-28 | (NL) | 1 | 26.11.27 | **Gainsborough T** (ML) | A | L | 0-6 | |
| 1945-46 | (NEL) | 1 1L | 17.11.45 | **Darlington** (3N) | A | L | 0-2 | |
| | | 1 2L | 24.11.45 | **Darlington** | H | L | 1-4 | Middleton |
| 1946-47 | (NL) | 1 | 30.11.46 | **Lincoln City** (3N) | H | L | 2-4 | Glassey, Davie |
| 1947-48 | (NEL) | 1 | 29.11.47 | **Grantham Town** (ML) | H | W | 2-1 | Laidman 2 |
| | | 2 | 13.12.47 | **Notts County** (3S) | A | D | 1-1aet | Leicester |
| | | 2r | 20.12.47 | **Notts County** | | L | 1-4 | Pears |
| | | | | *played at Ayresome Park* | | | | |
| 1949-50 | (NEL) | 1 | 26.11.49 | **Oldham Athletic** (3N) | A | L | 0-4 | |
| 1951-52 | (NEL) | 1 | 24.11.51 | **Mansfield Town** (3N) | H | D | 1-1 | Clarke |
| | | 1r | 28.11.51 | **Mansfield Town** | A | W | 2-0 | Chadwick, Clarke |
| | | 2 | 15.12.51 | **Folkestone** (KL) | H | W | 2-1 | Liddle 2 |
| | | 3 | 12.01.52 | **Notts County** (D2) | A | L | 0-4 | |

# STOKE CITY

*Formed 1863 as Stoke. Founder Members of the Football League 1888. Stoke City 1925. FA Cup best performance: Semi-finals 1899, 1971, 1972. Record FA Cup win: 11-0 v Stourbridge, preliminary round, 1914-15. In Competition Proper: 7-1 v Burnley, 2nd round replay, 10.02.1896. Record FA Cup defeat: 0-8 v Wolverhampton Wanderers, 3rd round replay, 22.02.1890.*

**as Stoke**

| | | | | | | | | |
|---|---|---|---|---|---|---|---|---|
| 1883-84 | | 1 | 10.11.83 | **Manchester FC** | H | L | 1-2 | Johnson |
| 1884-85 | | 1 | | **Queen's Park, Glasgow** | | | - | |
| | | | | *Stoke scratched. Queen's Park walkover* | | | | |
| 1885-86 | | 1 | 31.10.85 | **Crewe Alexandra** | H | D | 2-2 | |
| | | 1r | 07.11.85 | **Crewe Alexandra** | A | L | 0-1aet | |
| 1886-87 | | 1 | 30.10.86 | **Caernarfon Wanderers** | H | W | 10-1 | |
| | | 2 | 20.11.86 | **Crewe Alexandra** | A | L | 4-6aet | Edge 2, Bennett, Conde og |
| 1887-88 | | 1 | 15.10.87 | **Burslem Port Vale** | H | W | 1-0 | Lawton |
| | | 2 | 05.11.87 | **Over Wanderers** | A | W | 2-0 | Owen, AN Other |
| | | 3 | 26.11.87 | **Oswestry Town** | H | W | 3-0 | |
| 1887-88 | | 4 | | bye | | | | |
| 1887-88 | | 5 | 07.01.88 | **WBA** | A | L | 1-4 | Owen |
| 1888-89 | (D1) | | | 1q Warwick County (H) 1-2 | | | | |
| 1889-90 | (D1) | 1 | 18.01.90 | **Old Westminsters** | H | W | 3-0 | Gee, Ramsey, Sayer |
| | | 2 | 03.02.90 | **Everton** (D1) | H | W | 4-2 | Edge 3, Dunn |
| | | 3 | 15.02.90 | **Wolverhampton W** (D1) | A | L | 0-4 | |
| | | | | *FA ordered match to be replayed after Stoke protested about the pitch* | | | | |
| | | 3 | 22.02.90 | **Wolverhampton W** | A | L | 0-8 | |
| 1890-91 | (FAll) | 1 | 17.01.91 | **Preston North End** (D1) | H | W | 3-0 | Balham, Coupar, Turner |
| | | 2 | 31.01.91 | **Aston Villa** (D1) | H | W | 3-0 | Balham 2, Coupar |
| | | 3 | 14.02.91 | **Notts County** (D1) | A | L | 0-1 | |
| 1891-92 | (D1) | 1 | 16.01.92 | **Casuals** | H | W | 3-0 | Dunn 2, Evans |
| | | 2 | 30.01.92 | **Burnley** (D1) | A | W | 3-1 | Schofield, Turner, 1 other |
| | | 3 | 13.02.92 | **Sunderland** (D1) | H | D | 2-2aet | Turner, Schofield |
| | | 3r | 20.02.92 | **Sunderland** | A | L | 0-4 | |
| 1892-93 | (D1) | 1 | 21.01.93 | **Accrington FC** (D1) | A | L | 1-2 | Brodie |
| 1893-94 | (D1) | 1 | 27.01.94 | **Everton** (D1) | H | W | 1-0 | Schofield |
| | | 2 | 10.02.94 | **Sheffield Wed** (D1) | A | L | 0-1 | |
| 1894-95 | (D1) | 1 | 02.02.95 | **Newton Heath** (D2) | A | W | 3-2 | Dickson 2, Robertson |
| | | 2 | 16.02.95 | **Wolverhampton W** (D1) | A | L | 0-2 | |
| 1895-96 | (D1) | 1 | 01.02.96 | **Tottenham Hotspur** (SL) | H | W | 5-0 | A Maxwell 2, W Maxwell 2, Dickson |
| | | 2 | 15.02.96 | **Burnley** (D1) | A | D | 1-1 | Johnson |
| | | 2r | 20.02.96 | **Burnley** | H | W | 7-1 | Hyslop 4, A Maxwell 3 |
| | | 3 | 29.02.96 | **Wolverhampton W** (D1) | A | L | 0-3 | |
| 1896-97 | (D1) | 1 | 30.01.97 | **Glossop North End** (ML) | H | W | 5-2 | W Maxwell 3, Hingerty 2 |
| | | 2 | 13.02.97 | **Preston North End** (D1) | A | L | 1-2 | W Maxwell |
| 1897-98 | (D1) | 1 | 29.01.98 | **Bury** (D1) | A | W | 2-1 | W Maxwell, Hill |
| | | 2 | 12.02.98 | **Everton** (D1) | H | D | 0-0 | |
| | | 2r | 17.02.98 | **Everton** | A | L | 1-5 | Hill |
| 1898-99 | (D1) | 1 | 28.01.99 | **Sheffield Wed** (D1) | A | D | 2-2 | Kennedy, own goal |
| | | 1r | 02.02.99 | **Sheffield Wed** | H | W | 2-0 | W Maxwell, Schofield |
| | | 2 | 11.02.99 | **Small Heath** (D2) | H | D | 2-2 | W Maxwell, Schofield |
| | | 2r | 15.02.99 | **Small Heath** | A | W | 2-1 | W Maxwell 2 |
| | | 3 | 25.02.99 | **Tottenham Hotspur** (SL) | H | W | 4-1 | Cain og, Kennedy, Turner, Johnson |
| | | SF | 18.03.99 | **Derby County** (D1) | | L | 1-3 | W Maxwell |
| | | | | *played at Molineux* | | | | |
| 1899-00 | (D1) | 1 | 27.01.00 | **Liverpool** (D1) | H | D | 0-0 | |
| | | 1r | 01.02.00 | **Liverpool** | A | L | 0-1 | |
| 1900-01 | (D1) | 1 | 09.02.01 | **Small Heath** (D2) | H | D | 1-1 | Watkins |
| | | 1r | 13.02.01 | **Small Heath** | A | L | 1-2aet | Benbow |
| 1901-02 | (D1) | 1 | 25.01.02 | **Aston Villa** (D1) | H | D | 2-2 | Holford, Johnson |
| | | 1r | 29.01.02 | **Aston Villa** | A | W | 2-1aet | Higginson, Johnson |
| | | 2 | 08.02.02 | **Bristol Rovers** (SL) | A | W | 1-0 | own goal |
| | | 3 | 22.02.02 | **Nottingham Forest** (D1) | A | L | 0-2 | |
| 1902-03 | (D1) | 1 | 07.02.03 | **Glossop North End** (D2) | A | W | 3-2 | Capes, Watkins, Whitehouse |

| | | | | | | | | |
|---|---|---|---|---|---|---|---|---|
| | | 2 | 21.02.03 | **Nottingham Forest** (D1) | A | D | 0-0 | |
| | | 2r | 26.02.03 | **Nottingham Forest** | H | W | 2-0 | Bradley, Higginson |
| | | 3 | 07.03.03 | **Derby County** (D1) | A | L | 0-3 | |
| 1903-04 | (D1) | 1 | 06.02.04 | **Aston Villa** (D1) | H | L | 2-3 | Baddeley, Higginson |
| 1904-05 | (D1) | 1 | 04.02.05 | **Grimsby Town** (D2) | H | W | 2-0 | Baddeley, Godley |
| | | 2 | 18.02.05 | **Everton** (D1) | H | L | 0-4 | |
| 1905-06 | (D1) | 1 | 13.01.06 | **Blackburn Rovers** (D1) | H | W | 1-0 | Sturgess |
| | | 2 | 03.02.06 | **Birmingham** (D1) | H | L | 0-1 | |
| 1906-07 | (D1) | 1 | 12.01.07 | **WBA** (D2) | A | D | 1-1 | Baddeley |
| | | 1r | 17.01.07 | **WBA** | H | D | 2-2aet | Fielding, Arrowsmith |
| | | 1 2r | 21.01.07 | **WBA** | | L | 0-2 | |
| | | | | *played at Villa Park* | | | | |
| 1907-08 | (D2) | 1 | 11.01.08 | **Lincoln City** (D2) | H | W | 5-0 | Brown, Holford, Gallimore 3 |
| | | 2 | 01.02.08 | **Gainsborough T** (D2) | H | D | 1-1 | Baddeley |
| | | 2r | 05.02.08 | **Gainsborough T** | A | D | 2-2aet | Baddeley, Brown |
| | | 2 2r | 10.02.08 | **Gainsborough T** | | W | 3-1 | Watkins, Brown, Holford |
| | | | | *played at City Ground, Nottingham* | | | | |
| | | 3 | 22.02.08 | **Portsmouth** (SL) | A | W | 1-0 | Holford |
| | | 4 | 07.03.08 | **Wolverhampton W** (D2) | H | L | 0-1 | |
| 1908-09 | (BDL) | 1 | 16.01.09 | **Sheffield Wed** (D1) | A | L | 0-5 | |
| 1909-10 | (BDL) | | | 4q Ilkeston Utd (H) 2-0; 5q Exeter City (H) 0-0; 5qr Exeter City (A) 1-1; 5q 2r Exeter City 2-1 at Craven Cottage | | | | |
| 1909-10 | (BDL) | 1 | 15.01.10 | **Newcastle Utd** (D1) | H | D | 1-1 | A Baddeley |
| | | 1r | 19.01.10 | **Newcastle Utd** | A | L | 1-2 | Griffiths |
| 1910-11 | (BDL) | | | 4q Worcester City (H) 7-0; 5q Lincoln City (H) 4-0 | | | | |
| 1910-11 | (BDL) | 1 | 14.01.11 | **Manchester City** (D2) | H | L | 1-2 | A Smith |
| 1911-12 | (SL) | | | 4q Walsall (A) 1-2 | | | | |
| 1912-13 | (SL) | 1 | 11.01.13 | **Reading** (SL) | H | - | 1-2ab | Herbert, Revill |
| | | | | *abandoned after 25 minutes* | | | | |
| | | 1r | 16.01.13 | **Reading** | H | D | 2-2 | Revill, A Smith |
| | | 1 2r | 22.01.13 | **Reading** | A | L | 0-3 | |
| 1913-14 | (SL) | | | 4q Shrewsbury Town (H) 2-0; 5q Barrow (H) 3-1 | | | | |
| 1913-14 | (SL) | 1 | 10.01.14 | **Aston Villa** (D1) | A | L | 0-4 | |
| 1914-15 | (SL) | | | P Stourbridge (H) 11-0; 1q Birmingham Corporation Tramways (A) 3-2; 2q Brierley Hill Alliance (H) 1-0; 3q Walsall (A) 0-1 | | | | |
| 1919-20 | (D2) | 1 | 10.01.20 | **Bury** (D2) | A | L | 0-2 | |
| 1920-21 | (D2) | 1 | 08.01.21 | **Wolverhampton W** (D2) | A | L | 2-3 | Burton, Watkins |
| 1921-22 | (D2) | 1 | 07.01.22 | **Port Vale** (D2) | A | W | 4-2 | Watkin 3, Tempest |
| | | 2 | 28.01.22 | **Northampton Town** (3S) | A | D | 2-2 | Watkin 2 |
| | | 2r | 02.02.22 | **Northampton Town** | H | W | 3-0 | J Broad 2, Tempest |
| | | 3 | 18.02.22 | **Aston Villa** (D1) | H | D | 0-0 | |
| | | 3r | 22.02.22 | **Aston Villa** | A | L | 0-4 | |
| 1922-23 | (D1) | 1 | 13.01.23 | **Blyth Spartans** (NEL) | A | W | 3-0 | J Broad 2, Nicholas |
| | | 2 | 03.02.23 | **Bury** (D2) | A | L | 1-3 | J Broad |
| 1923-24 | (D2) | 1 | 12.01.24 | **Leeds Utd** (D2) | A | L | 0-1 | |
| 1924-25 | (D2) | 1 | 10.01.25 | **Leicester City** (D2) | A | L | 0-3 | |
| 1925-26 | (D2) | 3 | 09.01.26 | **Wigan Borough** (3N) | A | W | 5-2 | Davies 2, R Johnson 3 |
| | | 4 | 30.01.26 | **Swansea Town** (D2) | A | L | 3-6 | Davies, Johnson, Bestwick |
| 1926-27 | (3N) | 1 | 27.11.26 | **Rhyl** (Welsh) | A | D | 1-1 | Wilson |
| | | 1r | 02.12.26 | **Rhyl** | | D | 1-1aet | Davies |
| | | 1 2r | 06.12.26 | **Rhyl** | | L | 1-2 | Davies |
| | | | | *played at Old Trafford* | | | | |
| 1927-28 | (D2) | 3 | 14.01.28 | **Gillingham** (3S) | H | W | 6-1 | Wilson 2, Williamson 2, Archibald, Bussey |
| | | 4 | 28.01.28 | **Bolton Wanderers** (D1) | H | W | 4-2 | Archibald, Davies, Wilson 2 |
| | | 5 | 18.02.28 | **Manchester City** (D2) | A | W | 1-0 | Wilson |
| | | 6 | 03.03.28 | **Arsenal** (D1) | A | L | 1-4 | Wilson |
| 1928-29 | (D2) | 3 | 12.01.29 | **Arsenal** | A | L | 1-2 | Bussey |
| 1929-30 | (D2) | 3 | 11.01.30 | **Doncaster Rovers** (3N) | A | - | 3-2ab | Williamson, Wilson, Bussey |
| | | | | *abandoned after 68 minutes – snowstorm* | | | | |
| | | 3 | 16.01.30 | **Doncaster Rovers** (3N) | A | L | 0-1 | |

| | | | | | | | | |
|---|---|---|---|---|---|---|---|---|
| 1930-31 | (D2) | 3 | 10.01.31 | **Manchester Utd** (D1) | H | D | 3-3 | Wilson, Sale 2 |
| | | 3r | 14.01.31 | **Manchester Utd** | A | D | 0-0aet | |
| | | 3 2r | 19.01.31 | **Manchester Utd** *played at Anfield* | | L | 2-4 | Archibald, Liddle |
| 1931-32 | (D2) | 3 | 09.01.32 | **Hull City** (3N) | H | W | 3-0 | Sellars, Bussey, Mawson, |
| | | 4 | 23.01.32 | **Sunderland** (D1) | A | D | 1-1 | Mawson |
| | | 4r | 28.01.32 | **Sunderland** | H | D | 1-1aet | Bussey |
| | | 4 2r | 01.02.32 | **Sunderland** *played at Maine Road* | | W | 2-1 | Mawson 2 |
| | | 5 | 13.02.32 | **Bury** (D2) | A | L | 0-3 | |
| 1932-33 | (D2) | 3 | 14.01.33 | **Southampton** (D2) | H | W | 1-0 | Davies |
| | | 4 | 28.01.33 | **Middlesbrough** (D1) | A | L | 1-4 | Liddle |
| 1933-34 | (D1) | 3 | 13.01.34 | **Bradford Park A** (D2) | H | W | 3-0 | Sale, Matthews, Soo |
| | | 4 | 27.01.34 | **Blackpool** (D2) | H | W | 3-0 | Matthews, Soo, Sale |
| | | 5 | 17.02.34 | **Chelsea** (D1) | H | W | 3-1 | Matthews 2, Johnson |
| | | 6 | 03.03.34 | **Manchester City** (D1) | A | L | 0-1 | |
| 1934-35 | (D1) | 3 | 12.01.35 | **Swansea Town** (D2) | A | L | 1-4 | Matthews |
| 1935-36 | (D1) | 3 | 11.01.36 | **Millwall** (3S) | A | D | 0-0 | |
| | | 3r | 15.01.36 | **Millwall** | H | W | 4-0 | Steele 3, Liddle |
| | | 4 | 25.01.36 | **Manchester Utd** (D2) | H | D | 0-0 | |
| | | 4r | 29.01.36 | **Manchester Utd** | A | W | 2-0 | Sale, Robson |
| | | 5 | 15.02.36 | **Barnsley** (D2) | A | L | 1-2 | Davies |
| 1936-37 | (D1) | 3 | 16.01.37 | **Birmingham** (D1) | H | W | 4-1 | Steele 3, Johnson |
| | | 4 | 30.01.37 | **Preston North End** (D1) | A | L | 1-5 | Johnson |
| 1937-38 | (D1) | 3 | 08.01.38 | **Derby County** (D1) | A | W | 2-1 | Baker, Bell og |
| | | 4 | 22.01.38 | **Bradford Park A** (D2) | A | D | 1-1 | Soo |
| | | 4r | 26.01.38 | **Bradford Park A** | H | L | 1-2 | Soo |
| 1938-39 | (D1) | 3 | 07.01.39 | **Leicester City** (D1) | A | D | 1-1 | Soo |
| | | 3r | 11.01.39 | **Leicester City** | H | L | 1-2 | Steele |
| 1945-46 | (D1) | 3 1L | 05.01.46 | **Burnley** (D2) | H | W | 3-1 | Steele 3 |
| | | 3 2L | 07.01.46 | **Burnley** | A | L | 1-2 | Antonio |
| | | 4 1L | 26.01.46 | **Sheffield Utd** (D1) | H | W | 2-0 | G Mountford, Steele |
| | | 4 2L | 28.01.46 | **Sheffield Utd** | A | L | 2-3 | Antonio, Steele |
| | | 5 1L | 09.02.46 | **Sheffield Wed** (D2) | H | W | 2-0 | Steele 2 |
| | | 5 2L | 11.02.46 | **Sheffield Wed** | A | D | 0-0 | |
| | | 6 1L | 02.03.46 | **Bolton Wanderers** (D1) | H | L | 0-2 | |
| | | 6 2L | 09.03.46 | **Bolton Wanderers** | A | D | 0-0 | |
| 1946-47 | (D1) | 3 | 11.01.47 | **Tottenham Hotspur** (D2) | A | D | 2-2 | Ludford og, F Mountford |
| | | 3r | 15.01.47 | **Tottenham Hotspur** | H | W | 1-0 | Matthews |
| | | 4 | 25.01.47 | **Chester** (3N) | A | D | 0-0 | |
| | | 4r | 29.01.47 | **Chester** | H | W | 3-2 | Steele 2, Ormston |
| | | 5 | 08.02.47 | **Sheffield Utd** (D1) | H | L | 0-1 | |
| 1947-48 | (D1) | 3 | 10.01.48 | **Mansfield Town** (3N) | A | W | 4-2 | Sellars, Kiernan, Steele 2 |
| | | 4 | 24.01.48 | **QPR** (3S) | A | L | 0-3 | |
| 1948-49 | (D1) | 3 | 08.01.49 | **Swindon Town** (3S) | A | W | 3-1 | G Mountford 2, Steele |
| | | 4 | 29.01.49 | **Blackpool** (D1) | H | D | 1-1aet | F Mountford (p) |
| | | 4r | 05.02.49 | **Blackpool** | A | W | 1-0 | G Mountford |
| | | 5 | 12.02.49 | **Hull City** (3N) | H | L | 0-2 | |
| 1949-50 | (D1) | 3 | 07.01.50 | **Tottenham Hotspur** (D2) | H | L | 0-1 | |
| 1950-51 | (D1) | 3 | 06.01.51 | **Port Vale** (3S) | H | D | 2-2 | Mullard 2 |
| | | 3r | 08.01.51 | **Port Vale** | A | W | 1-0 | Bowyer |
| | | 4 | 27.01.51 | **West Ham Utd** (D2) | H | W | 1-0 | Bowyer |
| | | 5 | 10.02.51 | **Newcastle Utd** (D1) | H | L | 2-4 | Bowyer, F Mountford |
| 1951-52 | (D1) | 3 | 12.01.52 | **Sunderland** (D1) | A | D | 0-0 | |
| | | 3r | 14.01.52 | **Sunderland** | H | W | 3-1 | McIntosh, Smyth, Malkin |
| | | 4 | 02.02.52 | **Swindon Town** (3S) | A | D | 1-1 | Smyth |
| | | 4r | 04.02.52 | **Swindon Town** | H | L | 0-1 | |
| 1952-53 | (D1) | 3 | 10.01.53 | **Wrexham** (3N) | H | W | 2-1 | Whiston, Finney |
| | | 4 | 31.01.53 | **Halifax Town** (3N) | A | L | 0-1 | |
| 1953-54 | (D2) | 3 | 09.01.54 | **Hartlepools Utd** (3N) | H | W | 6-2 | Bowyer 4, Hutton, King |
| | | 4 | 30.01.54 | **Leicester City** (D2) | H | D | 0-0 | |

| | | | | | | | |
|---|---|---|---|---|---|---|---|
| | 4r | 02.02.54 | **Leicester City** | A | L | 1-3 | Malkin |
| 1954-55 (D2) | 3 | 08.01.55 | **Bury** (D2) | A | D | 1-1aet | King |
| | 3r | 12.01.55 | **Bury** | H | - | 1-1ab | Ratcliffe |
| | | | *abandoned after 112 minutes – snowstorm* | | | | |
| | 3 2r | 17.01.55 | **Bury** | | D | 3-3aet | Bowyer 2, King |
| | | | *played at Goodison Park* | | | | |
| | 3 3r | 19.01.55 | **Bury** | | D | 2-2aet | King, Ratcliffe |
| | | | *played at Anfield* | | | | |
| | 3 4r | 24.01.55 | **Bury** | | W | 3-2aet | Thomson, Coleman 2 |
| | | | *played at Old Trafford* | | | | |
| | 4 | 29.01.55 | **Swansea Town** (D2) | A | L | 1-3 | Malkin |
| 1955-56 (D2) | 3 | 07.01.56 | **Exeter City** (3S) | A | D | 0-0 | |
| | 3r | 09.01.56 | **Exeter City** | H | W | 3-0 | Oscroft, Bowyer, Coleman |
| | 4 | 28.01.56 | **Leicester City** (D2) | A | D | 3-3 | Bowyer, Graver, King |
| | 4r | 30.01.56 | **Leicester City** | H | W | 2-1 | Oscroft, Graver |
| | 5 | 18.02.56 | **Newcastle Utd** (D1) | A | L | 1-2 | King |
| 1956-57 (D2) | 3 | 05.01.57 | **Arsenal** (D1) | A | L | 2-4 | Coleman, Oscroft |
| 1957-58 (D2) | 3 | 04.01.58 | **Aston Villa** (D1) | H | D | 1-1 | Kelly |
| | 3r | 08.01.58 | **Aston Villa** | A | D | 3-3aet | Coleman, Kelly, Oscroft |
| | 3 2r | 13.01.58 | **Aston Villa** | | W | 2-0 | Cairns (p), Coleman |
| | | | *played at Molineux* | | | | |
| | 4 | 25.01.58 | **Middlesbrough** (D2) | H | W | 3-1 | Wilshaw 3 |
| | 5 | 15.02.58 | **Bolton Wanderers** (D1) | A | L | 1-3 | Cairns (p) |
| 1958-59 (D2) | 3 | 10.01.59 | **Oldham Athletic** (D4) | H | W | 5-1 | Howitt, Asprey, Wilshaw 3 |
| | 4 | 24.01.59 | **Ipswich Town** (D2) | H | L | 0-1 | |
| 1959-60 (D2) | 3 | 09.01.60 | **Preston North End** (D1) | H | D | 1-1 | Howitt |
| | 3r | 12.01.60 | **Preston North End** | A | L | 1-3 | Bowyer |
| 1960-61 (D2) | 3 | 07.01.61 | **West Ham Utd** (D1) | A | D | 2-2 | Ratcluiffe, Andrew |
| | 3r | 11.01.61 | **West Ham Utd** | H | W | 1-0 | Wilshaw |
| | 4 | 28.01.61 | **Aldershot** (D4) | H | D | 0-0 | |
| | 4r | 01.02.61 | **Aldershot** | A | D | 0-0aet | |
| | 4 2r | 06.02.61 | **Aldershot** | | W | 3-0 | Wilshaw 2, Asprey |
| | | | *played at Molineux* | | | | |
| | 5 | 18.02.61 | **Newcastle Utd** (D1) | A | L | 1-3 | King |
| 1961-62 (D2) | 3 | 10.01.62 | **Leicester City** (D1) | A | D | 1-1 | Mudie |
| | 3r | 15.01.62 | **Leicester City** | H | W | 5-2 | Matthews, Allen, Bullock, Nibloe, Thompson |
| | 4 | 27.01.62 | **Blackburn Rovers** (D1) | H | L | 0-1 | |
| 1962-63 (D2) | 3 | 06.03.63 | **Leeds Utd** (D2) | A | L | 1-3 | Bebbington |
| 1963-64 (D1) | 3 | 04.01.64 | **Portsmouth** (D2) | H | W | 4-1 | Viollet 2, Ritchie 2 |
| | 4 | 25.01.64 | **Ipswich Town** | A | D | 1-1 | McIlroy |
| | 4r | 29.01.64 | **Ipswich Town** (D1) | H | W | 1-0 | McIlroy |
| | 5 | 15.02.64 | **Swansea Town** (D2) | H | D | 2-2 | Matthews, McIlroy |
| | 5r | 18.02.64 | **Swansea Town** | A | L | 0-2 | |
| 1964-65 (D1) | 3 | 11.01.65 | **Blackpool** (D1) | H | W | 4-1 | Ritchie 2, Viollet 2 |
| | 4 | 30.01.65 | **Manchester Utd** (D1) | H | D | 0-0 | |
| | 4r | 03.02.65 | **Manchester Utd** | A | L | 0-1 | |
| 1965-66 (D1) | 3 | 22.01.66 | **Walsall** (D3) | H | L | 0-2 | |
| 1966-67 (D1) | 3 | 28.01.67 | **Manchester Utd** (D1) | A | L | 0-2 | |
| 1967-68 (D1) | 3 | 27.01.68 | **Cardiff City** (D2) | H | W | 4-1 | Vernon, Stevenson, Burrows 2 |
| | 4 | 17.02.68 | **West Ham Utd** (D1) | H | L | 0-3 | |
| 1968-69 (D1) | 3 | 04.01.69 | **York City** (D4) | A | W | 2-0 | Burrows 2 |
| | 4 | 25.01.69 | **Halifax Town** (D4) | H | D | 1-1 | Dobing |
| | 4r | 28.01.69 | **Halifax Town** | A | W | 3-0 | Burrows, Conroy 2 |
| | 5 | 12.02.69 | **Chelsea** (D1) | A | L | 2-3 | Burrows, Dobing |
| 1969-70 (D1) | 3 | 03.01.70 | **Oxford Utd** (D2) | A | D | 0-0 | |
| | 3r | 07.01.70 | **Oxford Utd** | H | W | 3-2 | Stevenson, Richardson 2 |
| | 4 | 24.01.70 | **Watford** (D2) | A | L | 0-1 | |
| 1970-71 (D1) | 3 | 02.01.71 | **Millwall** | H | W | 2-1 | Ritchie, J Greenhoff |
| | 4 | 23.01.71 | **Huddersfield Town** (D1) | H | D | 3-3 | J Greenhoff, Conroy, Burrows |
| | 4r | 26.01.71 | **Huddersfield Town** | A | D | 0-0aet | |

| | | | | | | | |
|---|---|---|---|---|---|---|---|
| | 4 2r | 08.02.71 | **Huddersfield Town** | | W | 1-0 | J Greenhoff |
| | | | *played at Old Trafford* | | | | |
| | 5 | 13.02.71 | **Ipswich Town** (D1) | H | D | 0-0 | |
| | 5r | 16.02.71 | **Ipswich Town** | A | W | 1-0 | D Smith |
| | 6 | 06.03.71 | **Hull City** (D2) | A | W | 3-2 | Conroy, Ritchie 2 |
| | SF | 27.03.71 | **Arsenal** (D1) | | D | 2-2 | Smith, Ritchie |
| | | | *played at Hillsborough* | | | | |
| | SFr | 31.03.71 | **Arsenal** | | L | 0-2 | |
| | | | *played at Villa Park* | | | | |
| | 3/4 | 07.05.71 | **Everton** (D1) | | W | 3-2 | Ritchie 2, Bernard |
| | | | *played at Selhurst Park* | | | | |
| 1971-72 (D1) | 3 | 15.01.72 | **Chesterfield** (D3) | H | W | 2-1 | Conroy, Dobing |
| | 4 | 05.02.72 | **Tranmere Rovers** (D3) | A | D | 2-2 | Conroy, Ritchie |
| | 4r | 09.02.72 | **Tranmere Rovers** | H | W | 2-0 | Bernard, J. Greenhoff (p) |
| | 5 | 26.02.72 | **Hull City** (D2) | H | W | 4-1 | J Greenhoff 2, Conroy, Ritchie |
| | 6 | 18.03.72 | **Manchester Utd** (D1) | A | D | 1-1 | J Greenhoff |
| | 6r | 22.03.72 | **Manchester Utd** | H | W | 2-1aet | Smith, Conroy |
| | SF | 15.04.72 | **Arsenal** (D1) | | D | 1-1 | Simpson og |
| | | | *played at Villa Park* | | | | |
| | SFr | 19.04.72 | **Arsenal** | | L | 1-2 | J Greenhoff (p) |
| | | | *played at Goodison Park* | | | | |
| | 3/4 | 05.08.72 | **Birmingham City** (D2) | A | D | 0-0 | |
| | | | *played at St Andrews – Birmingham won 4-3 on penalties* | | | | |
| 1972-73 (D1) | 3 | 13.01.73 | **Manchester City** (D1) | A | L | 2-3 | J Greenhoff 2 |
| 1973-74 (D1) | 3 | 05.01.74 | **Bolton Wanderers** (D2) | A | L | 2-3 | Ritchie, Haslegrave (p) |
| 1974-75 (D1) | 3 | 04.01.75 | **Liverpool** (D1) | A | L | 0-2 | |
| 1975-76 (D1) | 3 | 03.01.76 | **Tottenham Hotspur** (D1) | A | D | 1-1 | Mahoney |
| | 3r | 24.01.76 | **Tottenham Hotspur** | H | W | 2-1 | Moores, Salmon (p) |
| | 4 | 28.01.76 | **Manchester City** (D1) | H | W | 1-0 | J Greenhoff |
| | 5 | 14.02.76 | **Sunderland** (D2) | H | D | 0-0 | |
| | 5r | 17.02.76 | **Sunderland** | A | L | 1-2 | Smith |
| 1976-77 (D1) | 3 | 08.01.77 | **Everton** (D1) | A | L | 0-2 | |
| 1977-78 (D2) | 3 | 07.01.78 | **Tilbury** (IL) | H | W | 4-0 | Cook 2, Gregory, Waddington |
| | 4 | 06.02.78 | **Blyth Spartans** (NL) | H | L | 2-3 | Busby, Crooks |
| 1978-79 (D2) | 3 | 06.01.79 | **Oldham Athletic** (D2) | H | - | 2-0ab | Irvine 2 |
| | | | *abandoned at half-time* | | | | |
| | 3 | 17.01.79 | **Oldham Athletic** | H | L | 0-1 | |
| 1979-80 (D1) | 3 | 05.01.80 | **Burnley** (D2) | A | L | 0-1 | |
| 1980-81 (D1) | 3 | 03.01.81 | **Wolverhampton W** (D1) | H | D | 2-2 | Chapman, Bracewell |
| | 3r | 06.01.81 | **Wolverhampton W** | A | L | 1-2 | Heath |
| 1981-82 (D1) | 3 | 02.01.82 | **Norwich City** (D2) | H | L | 0-1 | |
| 1982-83 (D1) | 3 | 08.01.83 | **Sheffield Utd** (D3) | A | D | 0-0 | |
| | 3r | 12.01.83 | **Sheffield Utd** | H | W | 3-2 | McAughtrie, Painter, Henderson og |
| | 4 | 29.01.83 | **Liverpool** (D1) | A | L | 0-2 | |
| 1983-84 (D1) | 3 | 07.01.84 | **Everton** (D1) | H | L | 0-2 | |
| 1984-85 (D1) | 3 | 05.01.85 | **Luton Town** (D1) | A | D | 1-1 | Painter |
| | 3r | 09.01.85 | **Luton Town** | H | L | 2-3 | Painter (p), M.Chamberlain |
| 1985-86 (D2) | 3 | 13.01.86 | **Notts County** (D3) | H | L | 0-2 | |
| 1986-87 (D2) | 3 | 10.01.87 | **Grimsby Town** (D2) | A | D | 1-1 | Saunders |
| | 3r | 26.01.87 | **Grimsby Town** | H | D | 1-1aet | Saunders |
| | 3 2r | 28.01.87 | **Grimsby Town** | H | W | 6-0 | Morgan 2, Talbot, Heath, Saunders 2 |
| | 4 | 31.01.87 | **Cardiff City** (D4) | H | W | 2-1 | Saunders, Heath |
| | 5 | 21.02.87 | **Coventry City** (D1) | H | L | 0-1 | |
| 1987-88 (D2) | 3 | 09.01.88 | **Liverpool** (D1) | H | D | 0-0 | |
| | 3r | 12.01.88 | **Liverpool** | A | L | 0-1 | |
| 1988-89 (D2) | 3 | 07.01.89 | **Crystal Palace** (D2) | H | W | 1-0 | Shaw |
| | 4 | 28.01.89 | **Barnsley** (D2) | H | D | 3-3 | Bamber, Berry, Beagrie |
| | 4r | 31.01.89 | **Barnsley** | A | L | 1-2 | Bamber |
| 1989-90 (D2) | 3 | 06.01.90 | **Arsenal** (D1) | H | L | 0-1 | |
| 1990-91 (D3) | 1 | 17.11.90 | **Telford Utd** (Conf) | A | D | 0-0 | |
| | 1r | 21.11.90 | **Telford Utd** | H | W | 1-0 | Sandford |

| | | | | | | | | |
|---|---|---|---|---|---|---|---|---|
| | | 2 | 12.12.90 | **Burnley** (D4) | A | L | 0-2 | |
| 1991-92 | (D3) | 1 | 16.11.91 | **Telford Utd** (Conf) | H | D | 0-0 | |
| | | 1r | 26.11.91 | **Telford Utd** | A | L | 1-2 | Beeston |
| 1992-93 | (D2) | 1 | 16.11.92 | **Port Vale** (D2) | H | D | 0-0 | |
| | | 1r | 24.11.92 | **Port Vale** | A | L | 1-3 | Sandford |
| 1993-94 | (D1) | 3 | 08.01.94 | **Bath City** (Conf) | H | D | 0-0 | |
| | | 3r | 18.01.94 | **Bath City** | A | W | 4-1 | Regis 2, Cranson, Oriygsson |
| | | 4 | 29.01.94 | **Oldham Athletic** (PL) | A | D | 0-0 | |
| | | 4r | 09.02.94 | **Oldham Athletic** | H | L | 0-1 | |
| 1994-95 | (D1) | 3 | 07.01.95 | **Bristol City** (D1) | A | D | 0-0 | |
| | | 3r | 18.01.95 | **Bristol City** | H | L | 1-3aet | Scott |
| 1995-96 | (D1) | 3 | 06.01.96 | **Nottingham Forest** (PL) | H | D | 1-1 | Sturridge |
| | | 3r | 17.01.96 | **Nottingham Forest** | A | L | 0-2 | |
| 1996-97 | (D1) | 3 | 15.01.97 | **Stockport County** (D2) | H | L | 0-2 | |
| 1997-98 | (D1) | 3 | 13.01.98 | **WBA** (D1) | A | L | 1-3 | Gabbiadini |
| 1998-99 | (D2) | 1 | 14.11.98 | **Reading** (D2) | A | W | 1-0 | Lightbourne |
| | | 2 | 05.12.98 | **Swansea City** (D3) | A | L | 0-1 | |
| 1999-00 | (D2) | 1 | 30.10.99 | **Blackpool** (D2) | A | L | 0-2 | |
| 2000-01 | (D2) | 1 | 18.11.00 | **Nuneaton B** (Conf) | H | D | 0-0 | |
| | | 1r | 21.11.00 | **Nuneaton B** | A | L | 0-1 | |
| 2001-02 | (D2) | 1 | 18.11.01 | **Lewes** (IL) | A | W | 2-0 | Handyside, Gunnarson |
| | | | | *played at Brittania Stadium, Stoke* | | | | |
| | | 2 | 08.12.01 | **Halifax Town** (D3) | A | D | 1-1 | Cooke |
| | | 2r | 12.12.01 | **Halifax Town** | H | W | 3-0 | Gudjonsson, Iwelumo, Gunnarson |
| | | 3 | 05.01.02 | **Everton** (PL) | H | L | 0-1 | |
| 2002-03 | (D1) | 3 | 04.01.03 | **Wigan Athletic** (D2) | H | W | 3-0 | Greenacre 2, Iwelumo |
| | | 4 | 26.01.03 | **Bournemouth** (D2) | H | W | 3-0 | Iwelumo 2 (1p), Hoekstra |
| | | 5 | 16.02.03 | **Chelsea** (PL) | H | L | 0-2 | |

## STREET

*Formed 1880. First entered FA Cup: 1899-1900. Members of the Western League.*

| | | | | | | | | |
|---|---|---|---|---|---|---|---|---|
| 1938-39 | (WL) | 1 | 26.11.38 | **Ipswich Town** (3S) | A | L | 0-7 | |
| 1947-48 | (WL) | 1 | 29.11.47 | **Cheltenham Town** (SL) | A | L | 0-5 | |

## SUNDERLAND

*Formed 1879. FA Cup winners: 1937, 1973. Runners-up: 1913, 1992; Record FA Cup win: 11-1 v Fairfield, 1st round, 02.02.1895. Record FA Cup defeat: 2-7 v Aston Villa, 4th round, 27.01.1934.*

| | | | | | | | | |
|---|---|---|---|---|---|---|---|---|
| 1884-85 | | 1 | 08.11.84 | **Redcar** | A | L | 1-3 | |
| 1885-86 | | 1 | 24.10.85 | **Redcar** | A | L | 0-3 | |
| 1886-87 | | 1 | 30.10.86 | **Newcastle West End** | H | W | 2-1aet | Lord 2 |
| | | | | *FA declared match void after protest from West End and ordered a replay* | | | | |
| | | 1r | 13.11.86 | **Newcastle West End** | A | L | 0-1 | |
| 1887-88 | | 1 | 15.10.87 | **Morpeth Harriers** | H | W | 4-2 | Monaghan 3, Smith |
| | | | | *FA ordered replay after protest* | | | | |
| | | 1r | 22.10.87 | **Morpeth Harriers** | A | W | 3-2 | Monaghan 2, Stewart |
| | | 2 | 05.11.87 | **Newcastle West End** | H | W | 3-1aet | Stewart 2, Halliday |
| | | 3 | 26.11.87 | **Middlesbrough** | A | D | 2-2 | Gloag 2 |
| | | 3r | 03.12.87 | **Middlesbrough** | H | W | 4-2 | Halliday, Monaghan, others 2 |
| | | | | *FA disqualified Sunderland for professionalism and re-instated Middlesbrough* | | | | |
| 1888-89 | (D1) | | | 2q Elswick R (H) 5-3; 3q Newcastle East End (H) 2-0aet; 4q Sunderland Albion scratched | | | | |
| 1889-90 | | 1 | 18.01.90 | **Blackburn Rovers** (D1) | A | L | 2-4aet | Hannah, Scott |
| 1890-91 | (D1) | 1 | 17.01.91 | **Everton** (D1) | H | W | 1-0 | Campbell |
| | | 2 | 31.01.91 | **Darwen** (FAll) | A | W | 2-0 | Scott, Hannah |
| | | 3 | 14.02.91 | **Nottingham Forest** (FAll) | H | W | 4-0 | Millar 2, Campbell 2 |
| | | SF | 28.02.91 | **Notts County** (D1) | | D | 3-3 | Smith, Harvey, Campbell |
| | | | | *played at Bramall Lane* | | | | |
| | | SFr | 11.03.91 | **Notts County** | | L | 0-2 | |
| | | | | *played at Bramall Lane* | | | | |
| 1891-92 | (D1) | 1 | 16.01.92 | **Notts County** (D1) | H | W | 3-0 | Millar, Campbell, J Hannah |
| | | | | *FA ordered replay after protest about dangerous, icy pitch* | | | | |
| | | 1r | 23.01.92 | **Notts County** | H | W | 4-0 | Campbell 2, Hannah, Smith |

| | | | | | | | |
|---|---|---|---|---|---|---|---|
| | 2 | 30.01.92 | **Accrington FC** (D1) | A | L | 0-1 | |
| | | | *FA declared match void after protests and ordered a replay* | | | | |
| | 2r | 06.02.92 | **Accrington FC** | A | W | 3-1 | Campbell 3 |
| | 3 | 13.02.92 | **Stoke** (D1) | A | D | 2-2aet | Campbell, Miller |
| | 3r | 20.02.92 | **Stoke** | H | W | 4-0 | Campbell, Miller, D Hannah, J Miller |
| | SF | 27.02.92 | **Aston Villa** (D1) | | L | 1-4 | Scott |
| | | | *played at Bramall Lane* | | | | |
| 1892-93 (D1) | 1 | 21.01.93 | **Royal Arsenal** | H | W | 6-0 | Millar 3, Campbell 2, D Hannah |
| | 2 | 04.02.93 | **Sheffield Utd** (D2) | A | W | 3-1 | Campbell, Gillespie, D Hannah |
| | 3 | 18.02.93 | **Blackburn Rovers** (D1) | A | L | 0-3 | |
| 1893-94 (D1) | 1 | 27.01.94 | **Accrington FC** (LL) | H | W | 3-0 | Gillespie, J Hannah, Wilson |
| | 2 | 10.02.94 | **Aston Villa** (D1) | H | D | 2-2aet | Gillespie, Wilson |
| | 2r | 21.02.94 | **Aston Villa** | A | L | 1-3 | J Hannah |
| 1894-95 (D1) | 1 | 02.02.95 | **Fairfield** (LL) | H | W | 11-1 | Millar 5, J Hannah 3, Gillespie, McCreadie,Scott |
| | 2 | 16.02.95 | **Preston North End** (D1) | H | W | 2-0 | Campbell 2 |
| | 3 | 02.03.95 | **Bolton Wanderers** (D1) | H | W | 2-1 | Wilson 2 |
| | SF | 16.03.95 | **Aston Villa** (D1) | A | L | 1-2 | J.Hannah |
| | | | *played at Ewood Park* | | | | |
| 1895-96 (D1) | 1 | 01.02.96 | **Preston North End** (D1) | H | W | 4-1 | Campbell 3, Millar |
| | 2 | 15.02.96 | **Sheffield Wed** (D1) | A | L | 1-2 | Millar |
| 1896-97 (D1) | 1 | 30.01.97 | **Burnley** (D1) | H | W | 1-0 | Morgan |
| | 2 | 13.02.97 | **Nottingham Forest** (D1) | H | L | 1-3 | Harvey |
| 1897-98 (D1) | 1 | 29.01.98 | **Sheffield Wed** (D1) | H | L | 0-1 | |
| 1898-99 (D1) | 1 | 28.01.99 | **Bristol City** (SL) | A | W | 4-2 | Leslie, Crawford, Fulton, Wilson |
| | 2 | 11.02.99 | **Tottenham Hotspur** (SL) | A | L | 1-2 | Fulton |
| 1899-00 (D1) | 1 | 27.01.00 | **Derby County** (D1) | A | D | 2-2 | Fulton, McLatchie |
| | 1r | 31.01.00 | **Derby County** | H | W | 3-0 | R Hogg 2, W Hogg |
| | 2 | 10.02.00 | **Nottingham Forest** (D1) | A | L | 0-3 | |
| 1900-01 (D1) | 1 | 09.02.01 | **Sheffield Utd** (D1) | H | L | 1-2 | McLatchie |
| 1901-02 (D1) | 1 | 25.01.02 | **Sheffield Wed** (D1) | H | W | 1-0 | Millar |
| | 2 | 12.02.02 | **Newcastle Utd** (D1) | A | L | 0-1 | |
| 1902-03 (D1) | 1 | 07.02.03 | **Aston Villa** (D1) | A | L | 1-4 | Bridgett |
| 1903-04 (D1) | 1 | 06.02.04 | **Manchester City** (D1) | A | L | 2-3 | Craggs, Buckle |
| 1904-05 (D1) | 1 | 04.02.05 | **Wolverhampton W** (D1) | H | D | 1-1 | Common |
| | 1r | 08.02.05 | **Wolverhampton W** | A | L | 0-1 | |
| 1905-06 (D1) | 1 | 13.01.06 | **Notts County** (D1) | H | W | 1-0 | Shaw |
| | 2 | 03.02.06 | **Gainsborough T** (D2) | H | D | 1-1 | Barrie |
| | 2r | 07.02.06 | **Gainsborough T** | A | W | 3-0 | Bridgett, Brown, Holley |
| | | | *played at Roker Park* | | | | |
| | 3 | 24.02.06 | **Woolwich Arsenal** (D1) | A | L | 0-5 | |
| 1906-07 (D1) | 1 | 12.01.07 | **Leicester Fosse** (D2) | H | W | 4-1 | Raine, McIntosh 2, Bridgett |
| | 2 | 02.02.07 | **Luton Town** (SL) | A | D | 0-0 | |
| | 2r | 06.02.07 | **Luton Town** | H | W | 1-0 | McIntosh |
| | 3 | 23.02.07 | **Sheffield Wed** (D1) | A | D | 0-0 | |
| | 3r | 27.02.07 | **Sheffield Wed** | H | L | 0-1 | |
| 1907-08 (D1) | 1 | 11.01.08 | **New Brompton** (SL) | A | L | 1-3 | Holley |
| 1908-09 (D1) | 1 | 16.01.09 | **Sheffield Utd** (D1) | A | W | 3-2 | Thomson, Hogg, Brown |
| | 2 | 06.02.09 | **Preston North End** (D1) | A | W | 2-1 | Low, Bridgett |
| | 3 | 20.02.09 | **Bradford City** (D1) | A | W | 1-0 | Holley |
| | 4 | 06.03.09 | **Newcastle Utd** (D1) | A | D | 2-2 | Brown, Mordue |
| | 4r | 10.03.09 | **Newcastle Utd** | H | L | 0-3 | |
| 1909-10 (D1) | 1 | 15.01.10 | **Leeds City** (D2) | H | W | 1-0 | Holley |
| | 2 | 05.02.10 | **Bradford Park A** (D2) | H | W | 3-1 | Low 2, Bridgett |
| | 3 | 19.02.10 | **Everton** (D1) | A | L | 0-2 | |
| 1910-11 (D1) | 1 | 14.01.11 | **Norwich City** (SL) | A | L | 1-3 | Bridgett |
| 1911-12 (D1) | 1 | 13.01.12 | **Plymouth Argyle** (SL) | H | W | 3-1 | Mordue 2, Bridgett |
| | 2 | 03.02.12 | **Crystal Palace** (SL) | A | D | 0-0 | |
| | 2r | 07.02.12 | **Crystal Palace** | H | W | 1-0aet | Low |
| | 3 | 24.02.12 | **WBA** (D1) | H | L | 1-2 | Bridgett |
| 1912-13 (D1) | 1 | 11.01.13 | **Clapton Orient** (D2) | H | W | 6-0 | Richardson 4, Holley, Martin |

| | | | | | | | |
|---|---|---|---|---|---|---|---|
| | 2 | 01.02.13 | **Manchester City** (D1) | A | - | 2-0ab | Buchan, Richardson |
| | | | *abandoned after 60 minutes due to dangerous overcrowding in the ground* | | | | |
| | 2 | 05.02.13 | **Manchester City** | H | W | 2-0 | Mordue, Holley |
| | 3 | 22.02.13 | **Swindon Town** (SL) | H | W | 4-2 | Gladwin, Buchan, Richardson 2 |
| | 4 | 08.03.13 | **Newcastle Utd** (D1) | H | D | 0-0 | |
| | 4r | 12.03.13 | **Newcastle Utd** | A | D | 2-2aet | Holley, Buchan |
| | 4 2r | 17.03.13 | **Newcastle Utd** | A | W | 3-0 | Holley, Buchan, Mordue |
| | SF | 29.03.13 | **Burnley** (D2) | | D | 0-0 | |
| | | | *played at Bramall Lane* | | | | |
| | SFr | 02.04.13 | **Burnley** | | W | 3-2 | Buchan, Mordue, Holley |
| | | | *played at St Andrews* | | | | |
| | F | 19.04.13 | **Aston Villa** (D1) | | L | 0-1 | |
| | | | *played at Crystal Palace* | | | | |
| 1913-14 (D1) | 1 | 10.01.14 | **Chatham** (KL) | H | W | 9-0 | Richardson 4, Best 2, Mordue, Buchan, Thomson |
| | 2 | 31.01.14 | **Plymouth Argyle** (SL) | H | W | 2-1 | Mordue, Conner |
| | 3 | 21.02.14 | **Preston North End** (D1) | H | W | 2-0 | Buchan, Conner |
| | 4 | 07.03.14 | **Burnley** (D1) | H | D | 0-0 | |
| | 4r | 11.03.14 | **Burnley** | A | L | 1-2 | Conner |
| 1914-15 (D1) | 1 | 09.01.15 | **Tottenham Hotspur** (D1) | A | L | 1-2 | Mordue |
| 1919-20 (D1) | 1 | 14.01.20 | **Hull City** (D2) | H | W | 6-2 | Buchan 3, Travers 2, Deacey og |
| | 2 | 31.01.20 | **Burnley** (D1) | A | D | 1-1 | Travers |
| | 2r | 04.02.20 | **Burnley** | H | W | 2-0 | Buchan, Poole |
| | 3 | 21.02.20 | **Aston Villa** (D1) | A | L | 0-1 | |
| 1920-21 (D1) | 1 | 08.01.21 | **Cardiff City** (D2) | H | L | 0-1 | |
| 1921-22 (D1) | 1 | 07.01.22 | **Liverpool** (D1) | H | D | 1-1 | Stannard |
| | 1r | 11.01.22 | **Liverpool** | A | L | 0-5 | |
| 1922-23 (D1) | 1 | 13.01.23 | **Burnley** (D1) | H | W | 3-1 | Paterson 3 |
| | 2 | 03.02.23 | **WBA** (D1) | A | L | 1-2 | Buchan |
| 1923-24 (D1) | 1 | 12.01.24 | **Oldham Athletic** (D2) | A | L | 1-2 | Buchan |
| 1924-25 (D1) | 1 | 10.01.25 | **Bury** (D1) | A | W | 3-0 | Clunes, Buchan, Rodgers |
| | 2 | 31.01.25 | **Everton** (D1) | H | D | 0-0 | |
| | 2r | 04.02.25 | **Everton** | A | L | 1-2 | Marshall |
| 1925-26 (D1) | 3 | 09.01.26 | **Boston Utd** (ML) | H | W | 8-1 | Kelly 3, Marshall 3, Halliday 2 |
| | 4 | 30.01.26 | **Sheffield Utd** (D1) | A | W | 2-1 | Prior, Kelly |
| | 5 | 20.02.26 | **Manchester Utd** (D1) | H | D | 3-3 | Marshall, Death 2 |
| | 5r | 24.02.26 | **Manchester Utd** | A | L | 1-2 | Halliday |
| 1926-27 (D1) | 3 | 08.01.27 | **Leeds Utd** (D1) | A | L | 2-3 | Marshall, Halliday |
| 1927-28 (D1) | 3 | 14.01.28 | **Northampton Town** (3S) | H | D | 3-3 | Wright, Hargreaves, Halliday |
| | 3r | 19.01.28 | **Northampton Town** | A | W | 3-0 | Halliday 2, Clunas (p) |
| | 4 | 28.01.28 | **Manchester City** (D2) | H | L | 1-2 | Halliday |
| 1928-29 (D1) | 3 | 12.01.29 | **West Ham Utd** (D1) | A | L | 0-1 | |
| 1929-30 (D1) | 3 | 11.01.30 | **Coventry City** (3S) | A | W | 2-1 | Gallacher, Gurney |
| | 4 | 25.01.30 | **Cardiff City** (D2) | H | W | 2-1 | Gurney, McLean |
| | 5 | 15.02.30 | **Nottingham Forest** (D2) | H | D | 2-2 | McLean, Gunson |
| | 5r | 19.02.30 | **Nottingham Forest** | A | L | 1-3 | Eden |
| 1930-31 (D1) | 3 | 10.01.31 | **Southampton** (D2) | H | W | 2-0 | Eden, Urwin |
| | 4 | 24.01.31 | **Bolton Wanderers** (D1) | A | D | 1-1 | Leonard |
| | 4r | 27.01.31 | **Bolton Wanderers** | H | W | 3-1 | Connor 2, Leonard |
| | 5 | 14.02.31 | **Sheffield Utd** (D1) | H | W | 2-1 | Connor, Gurney |
| | 6 | 28.02.31 | **Exeter City** (3S) | H | D | 1-1 | Connor |
| | 6r | 04.03.31 | **Exeter City** | A | W | 4-2 | Connor 2, Eden, Gurney |
| | SF | 14.03.31 | **Birmingham** (D1) | | L | 0-2 | |
| | | | *played at Elland Road* | | | | |
| 1931-32 (D1) | 3 | 09.01.32 | **Southampton** (D2) | H | D | 0-0 | |
| | 3r | 13.01.32 | **Southampton** | A | W | 4-2 | Vinall, Poulter 2, Shaw |
| | 4 | 23.01.32 | **Stoke City** (D2) | H | D | 1-1 | MacDougall |
| | 4r | 28.01.32 | **Stoke City** | A | D | 1-1aet | Gallacher |
| | 4 2r | 01.02.32 | **Stoke City** | | L | 1-2 | Gallacher |
| | | | *played at Maine Road* | | | | |
| 1932-33 (D1) | 3 | 14.01.33 | **Hull City** (3N) | A | W | 2-0 | Gurney, Connor |

| | | | | | | | |
|---|---|---|---|---|---|---|---|
| | 4 | 28.01.33 | **Aston Villa** (D1) | A | W | 3-0 | Gurney 3 |
| | 5 | 18.02.33 | **Blackpool** (D1) | H | W | 1-0 | Gurney |
| | 6 | 04.03.33 | **Derby County** (D1) | A | D | 4-4 | Gurney 2, Davis, Connor |
| | 6r | 08.03.33 | **Derby County** | H | L | 0-1 | |
| 1933-34 (D1) | 3 | 13.01.34 | **Middlesbrough** (D1) | H | D | 1-1 | Carter |
| | 3r | 17.01.34 | **Middlesbrough** | A | W | 2-1 | Vernon, Gurney |
| | 4 | 27.01.34 | **Aston Villa** (D1) | A | L | 2-7 | Carter, Hastings |
| 1934-35 (D1) | 3 | 12.01.35 | **Fulham** (D2) | H | W | 3-2 | Gurney 3 |
| | 4 | 26.01.35 | **Everton** (D1) | H | D | 1-1 | Carter |
| | 4r | 30.01.35 | **Everton** | A | L | 4-6aet | Davies, Connor 2, Gurney |
| 1935-36 (D1) | 3 | 11.01.36 | **Port Vale** (D2) | H | D | 2-2 | Connor, Gallacher |
| | 3r | 13.01.36 | **Port Vale** | A | L | 0-2 | |
| 1936-37 (D1) | 3 | 16.01.37 | **Southampton** (D2) | A | W | 3-2 | Gurney, Hornby, Gallacher |
| | 4 | 30.01.37 | **Luton Town** (3S) | A | D | 2-2 | Connor, Duns |
| | 4r | 03.02.37 | **Luton Town** | H | W | 3-1 | Duns, Connor, Carter |
| | 5 | 20.02.37 | **Swansea Town** (D2) | H | W | 3-0 | Gurney, Duns, Caldwell og |
| | 6 | 06.03.37 | **Wolverhampton W** (D1) | A | D | 1-1 | Duns |
| | 6r | 10.03.37 | **Wolverhampton W** | H | D | 2-2aet | Gurney, Duns |
| | 6 2r | 15.03.37 | **Wolverhampton W** *played at Hillsborough* | | W | 4-0 | Gurney, Carter, Gallacher |
| | SF | 10.04.37 | **Millwall** (3S) *played at Leeds Road, Huddersfield* | | W | 2-1 | Gurney, Gallacher |
| | F | 01.05.37 | **Preston North End** (D1) *played at Wembley Stadium* | | W | 3-1 | Gurney, Carter, Burbanks |
| 1937-38 (D1) | 3 | 08.01.38 | **Watford** (3S) | H | W | 1-0 | Duns |
| | 4 | 22.01.38 | **Everton** (D1) | A | W | 1-0 | Gurney |
| | 5 | 12.02.38 | **Bradford Park A** (D2) | H | W | 1-0 | Duns |
| | 6 | 05.03.38 | **Tottenham Hotspur** (D2) | A | W | 1-0 | Carter |
| | SF | 26.03.38 | **Huddersfield Town** (D1) *played at Ewood Park* | | L | 1-3 | Burbanks |
| 1938-39 (D1) | 3 | 07.01.39 | **Plymouth Argyle** (D2) | H | W | 3-0 | Clark og, Gorman, Carter |
| | 4 | 21.01.39 | **Middlesbrough** (D1) | A | W | 2-0 | Carter, Smeaton |
| | 5 | 11.02.39 | **Blackburn Rovers** (D2) | H | D | 1-1 | Hastings |
| | 5r | 16.02.39 | **Blackburn Rovers** | A | D | 0-0aet | |
| | 5 2r | 20.02.39 | **Blackburn Rovers** *played at Hillsborough* | | L | 0-1aet | |
| 1945-46 (D1) | 3 1L | 05.01.46 | **Grimsby Town** (D1) | A | W | 3-1 | White, Hastings 2 |
| | 3 2L | 09.01.46 | **Grimsby Town** | H | W | 2-1 | Whitelum, Hastings |
| | 4 1L | 26.01.46 | **Bury** (D2) | H | W | 3-1 | Brown 2, Duns |
| | 4 2L | 29.01.46 | **Bury** | A | L | 4-5aet | White, Walshaw, Brown, Burbanks |
| | 5 1L | 09.02.46 | **Birmingham City** (D2) | H | W | 1-0 | Duns |
| | 5 2L | 13.02.46 | **Birmingham City** | A | L | 1-3 | Brown |
| 1946-47 (D1) | 3 | 11.01.47 | **Chesterfield** (D2) | A | L | 1-2 | Robinson |
| 1947-48 (D1) | 3 | 10.01.48 | **Southampton** (D2) | A | L | 0-1 | |
| 1948-49 (D1) | 3 | 08.01.49 | **Crewe Alexandra** (3N) | A | W | 2-0 | Turnbull 2 |
| | 4 | 29.01.49 | **Yeovil Town** (SL) | A | L | 1-2aet | Robinson |
| 1949-50 (D1) | 3 | 07.01.50 | **Huddersfield Town** (D1) | H | W | 6-0 | Davis 2, Broadis 2, Shackleton 2 |
| | 4 | 28.01.50 | **Tottenham Hotspur** (D2) | A | L | 1-5 | Davis |
| 1950-51 (D1) | 3 | 06.01.51 | **Coventry City** (D2) | H | W | 2-0 | T.Wright, A.Wright |
| | 4 | 27.01.51 | **Southampton** (D2) | H | W | 2-0 | Davis 2 |
| | 5 | 10.02.51 | **Norwich City** (3S) | H | W | 3-1 | Davis, Watson, T.Wright |
| | 6 | 24.02.51 | **Wolverhampton W** (D1) | H | D | 1-1 | Davis |
| | 6r | 28.02.51 | **Wolverhampton W** | A | L | 1-3 | Ford |
| 1951-52 (D1) | 3 | 12.01.52 | **Stoke City** (D1) | H | D | 0-0 | |
| | 3r | 14.01.52 | **Stoke City** | A | L | 1-3 | McSeveney |
| 1952-53 (D1) | 3 | 10.01.53 | **Scunthorpe Utd** (3N) | H | D | 1-1 | Ford |
| | 3r | 15.01.53 | **Scunthorpe Utd** | A | W | 2-1 | T.Wright, Ford |
| | 4 | 31.01.53 | **Burnley** (D1) | A | L | 0-2 | |
| 1953-54 (D1) | 3 | 09.01.54 | **Doncaster Rovers** (D2) | H | L | 0-2 | |
| 1954-55 (D1) | 3 | 08.01.55 | **Burnley** (D1) | H | W | 1-0 | Elliott |
| | 4 | 29.01.55 | **Preston North End** (D1) | A | D | 3-3 | Purdon, Chisholm, Shackleton |
| | 4r | 02.02.55 | **Preston North End** | H | W | 2-0 | Chisholm |

| | | | | | | | |
|---|---|---|---|---|---|---|---|
| | 5 | 19.02.55 | **Swansea Town** (D2) | A | D | 2-2 | Chisholm 2 |
| | 5r | 23.02.55 | **Swansea Town** | H | W | 1-0 | Fleming |
| | 6 | 12.03.55 | **Wolverhampton W** (D1) | H | W | 2-0 | Purdon 2 |
| | SF | 26.03.55 | **Manchester City** (D1) | | L | 0-1 | |
| | | | *played at Villa Park* | | | | |
| 1955-56 (D1) | 3 | 07.01.56 | **Norwich City** (3S) | H | W | 4-2 | Fleming 3, Elliott |
| | 4 | 28.01.56 | **York City** (3N) | A | D | 0-0 | |
| | 4r | 01.02.56 | **York City** | H | W | 2-1 | Anderson, Fleming |
| | 5 | 18.02.56 | **Sheffield Utd** (D1) | A | D | 0-0 | |
| | 5r | 22.02.56 | **Sheffield Utd** | H | W | 1-0 | Daniel |
| | 6 | 03.03.56 | **Newcastle Utd** (D1) | A | W | 2-0 | Holden 2 |
| | SF | 17.03.56 | **Birmingham City** (D1) | | L | 0-3 | |
| | | | *played at Hillsborough* | | | | |
| 1956-57 (D1) | 3 | 05.01.57 | **QPR** (3S) | H | W | 4-0 | Elliott, Hannigan 2, Fleming |
| | 4 | 26.01.57 | **WBA** (D1) | A | L | 2-4 | Fleming, Bingham |
| 1957-58 (D1) | 3 | 04.01.58 | **Everton** (D1) | H | D | 2-2 | Bingham, Frogarty |
| | 3r | 08.01.58 | **Everton** | A | L | 1-3 | Fleming |
| 1958-59 (D2) | 3 | 10.01.59 | **Everton** | A | L | 0-4 | |
| 1959-60 (D2) | 3 | 09.01.60 | **Blackburn Rovers** (D1) | H | D | 1-1 | Lawther |
| | 3r | 13.01.60 | **Blackburn Rovers** | A | L | 1-4 | O'Neill |
| 1960-61 (D2) | 3 | 07.01.61 | **Arsenal** (D1) | H | W | 2-1 | Anderson 2 |
| | 4 | 28.01.61 | **Liverpool** (D2) | A | W | 2-0 | Hooper, Lawther |
| | 5 | 18.02.61 | **Norwich City** (D2) | A | W | 1-0 | Hurley |
| | 6 | 04.03.61 | **Tottenham Hotspur** (D1) | H | D | 1-1 | McPheat |
| | 6r | 08.03.61 | **Tottenham Hotspur** | A | L | 0-5 | |
| 1961-62 (D2) | 3 | 06.01.62 | **Southampton** (D2) | A | D | 2-2 | Anderson, Hooper (p) |
| | 3r | 10.01.62 | **Southampton** | H | W | 3-0 | McPheat, Herd 2 |
| | 4 | 27.01.62 | **Port Vale** (D3) | H | D | 0-0 | |
| | 4r | 31.01.62 | **Port Vale** | A | L | 1-3 | McPheat |
| 1962-63 (D2) | 3 | 05.01.63 | **Preston North End** (D2) | A | W | 4-1 | Sharkey 2, Fogarty, Davison |
| | 4 | 12.02.63 | **Gravesend & N** (SL) | A | D | 1-1 | Mulhall |
| | 4r | 18.02.63 | **Gravesend & N** | H | W | 5-2 | Finch og, Crossan 2, Fogarty, Sharkey |
| | 5 | 25.03.63 | **Coventry City** (D3) | A | L | 1-2 | Crossan |
| 1963-64 (D2) | 3 | 04.01.64 | **Northampton Town** (D2) | H | W | 2-0 | Usher, Crossan |
| | 4 | 25.01.64 | **Bristol City** (D3) | H | W | 6-1 | Herd 2, Hurley, Sharkey, Crossan 2 |
| | 5 | 15.02.64 | **Everton** (D1) | H | W | 3-1 | McNab, Hurley, Meagan og |
| | 6 | 29.02.64 | **Manchester Utd** (D1) | A | D | 3-3 | Mulhall, Crossan 2 (1p) |
| | 6r | 04.03.64 | **Manchester Utd** | H | D | 2-2aet | Sharkey, Setters og |
| | 6 2r | 09.03.64 | **Manchester Utd** | | L | 1-5 | Sharkey |
| | | | *played at Leeds Road, Huddersfield* | | | | |
| 1964-65 (D1) | 3 | 09.01.65 | **Luton Town** (D3) | A | W | 3-0 | Sharkey 2, Mulhall |
| | 4 | 30.01.65 | **Nottingham Forest** (D1) | H | L | 1-3 | Hood |
| 1965-66 (D1) | 3 | 22.01.66 | **Everton** (D1) | A | L | 0-3 | |
| 1966-67 (D1) | 3 | 28.01.67 | **Brentford** (D4) | H | W | 5-2 | Martin 2, Mulhall, Baxter (p), O'Hare |
| | 4 | 18.02.67 | **Peterborough Utd** (D3) | H | W | 7-1 | O'Hare, Martin 3, Kerr 2, Baxter (p) |
| | 5 | 11.03.67 | **Leeds Utd** (D1) | H | D | 1-1 | Martin |
| | 5r | 15.03.67 | **Leeds Utd** | A | D | 1-1aet | O'Hare |
| | 5 2r | 20.03.67 | **Leeds Utd** | | L | 1-2 | Gauden |
| | | | *played at Boothferry Park* | | | | |
| 1967-68 (D1) | 3 | 27.01.68 | **Norwich City** (D2) | A | D | 1-1 | Suggett |
| | 3r | 31.01.68 | **Norwich City** | H | L | 0-1 | |
| 1968-69 (D1) | 3 | 04.01.69 | **Fulham** (D2) | H | L | 1-4 | Kerr |
| 1969-70 (D1) | 3 | 03.01.70 | **Leicester City** (D2) | A | L | 0-1 | |
| 1970-71 (D2) | 3 | 11.01.71 | **Orient** (D2) | H | L | 0-3 | |
| 1971-72 (D2) | 3 | 15.01.72 | **Sheffield Wed** (D2) | H | W | 3-0 | Porterfield, Watson, Chambers |
| | 4 | 09.02.72 | **Cardiff City** (D2) | A | D | 1-1 | Chambers |
| | 4r | 14.02.72 | **Cardiff City** | H | D | 1-1aet | Kerr |
| | 4 2r | 16.02.72 | **Cardiff City** | | L | 1-3 | McGiven |
| | | | *played at Maine Road* | | | | |
| 1972-73 (D2) | 3 | 13.01.73 | **Notts County** (D3) | A | D | 1-1 | Watson |
| | 3r | 16.01.73 | **Notts County** | H | W | 2-0 | Watson, Tueart |

| | | | | | | | |
|---|---|---|---|---|---|---|---|
| | 4 | 03.02.73 | **Reading** (D4) | H | D | 1-1 | Tueart |
| | 4r | 07.02.73 | **Reading** | A | W | 3-1 | Watson, Tueart, Kerr |
| | 5 | 24.02.73 | **Manchester City** (D1) | A | D | 2-2 | Horswill, Hughes |
| | 5r | 27.02.73 | **Manchester City** | H | W | 3-1 | Halom, Hughes 2 |
| | 6 | 17.03.73 | **Luton Town** (D2) | H | W | 2-0 | Watson, Guthrie |
| | SF | 07.04.73 | **Arsenal** (D1) *played at Hillsborough* | | W | 2-1 | Halom, Hughes |
| | F | 05.05.73 | **Leeds Utd** (D1) *played at Wembley Stadium* | | W | 1-0 | Porterfield |
| 1973-74 (D2) | 3 | 05.01.74 | **Carlisle Utd** (D2) | A | D | 0-0 | |
| | 3r | 09.01.74 | **Carlisle Utd** | H | L | 0-1 | |
| 1974-75 (D2) | 3 | 04.01.75 | **Chesterfield** (D3) | H | W | 2-0 | Bolton, Robson |
| | 4 | 25.01.75 | **Middlesbrough** (D1) | A | L | 1-3 | Robson |
| 1975-76 (D2) | 3 | 03.01.76 | **Oldham Athletic** (D2) | H | W | 2-0 | Holden, Robson |
| | 4 | 02.02.76 | **Hull City** (D2) | H | W | 1-0 | Finney |
| | 5 | 14.02.76 | **Stoke City** (D1) | A | D | 0-0 | |
| | 5r | 17.02.76 | **Stoke City** | H | W | 2-1 | Holden, Robson |
| | 6 | 06.03.76 | **Crystal Palace** (D3) | H | L | 0-1 | |
| 1976-77 (D1) | 3 | 08.01.77 | **Wrexham** (D3) | H | D | 2-2 | Holton, Holden |
| | 3r | 12.01.77 | **Wrexham** | A | L | 0-1 | |
| 1977-78 (D2) | 3 | 07.01.78 | **Bristol Rovers** (D2) | H | L | 0-1 | |
| 1978-79 (D2) | 3 | 10.01.79 | **Everton** (D1) | H | W | 2-1 | Rowell (p), Lee |
| | 4 | 21.02.79 | **Burnley** (D2) | A | D | 1-1 | Entwhistle |
| | 4r | 26.02.79 | **Burnley** | H | L | 0-3 | |
| 1979-80 (D2) | 3 | 05.01.80 | **Bolton Wanderers** (D1) | H | L | 0-1 | |
| 1980-81 (D1) | 3 | 03.01.81 | **Birmingham City** (D1) | A | D | 1-1 | Chisholm |
| | 3r | 07.01.81 | **Birmingham City** | H | L | 1-2aet | Rowell |
| 1981-82 (D1) | 3 | 02.01.82 | **Rotherham Utd** (D2) | A | D | 1-1 | Rowell |
| | 3r | 18.01.82 | **Rotherham Utd** | H | W | 1-0 | Buckley |
| | 4 | 23.01.82 | **Liverpool** (D1) | H | L | 0-3 | |
| 1982-83 (D1) | 3 | 08.01.83 | **Manchester City** (D1) | H | D | 0-0 | |
| | 3r | 12.01.83 | **Manchester City** | A | L | 1-2 | Chisholm |
| 1983-84 (D1) | 3 | 07.01.84 | **Bolton Wanderers** (D3) | A | W | 3-0 | West, Chapman, Rowell |
| | 4 | 28.01.84 | **Birmingham City** (D1) | H | L | 1-2 | West |
| 1984-85 (D1) | 3 | 05.01.85 | **Southampton** (D1) | A | L | 0-4 | |
| 1985-86 (D2) | 3 | 04.01.86 | **Newport County** (D3) | H | W | 2-0 | Burley, Corner |
| | 4 | 25.01.86 | **Manchester Utd** (D1) | H | D | 0-0 | |
| | 4r | 29.01.86 | **Manchester Utd** | A | L | 0-3 | |
| 1986-87 (D2) | 3 | 10.01.87 | **Wimbledon** (D1) | A | L | 1-2 | Gates |
| 1987-88 (D3) | 1 | 14.11.87 | **Darlington** (D4) | H | W | 2-0 | Atkinson 2 |
| | 2 | 05.12.87 | **Scunthorpe Utd** (D4) | A | L | 1-2 | Gates |
| 1988-89 (D2) | 3 | 07.01.89 | **Oxford Utd** (D2) | H | D | 1-1 | Ord |
| | 3r | 11.01.89 | **Oxford Utd** | A | L | 0-2 | |
| 1989-90 (D2) | 3 | 06.01.90 | **Reading** (D3) | A | L | 1-2 | Armstrong |
| 1990-91 (D1) | 3 | 05.01.91 | **Arsenal** (D1) | A | L | 1-2 | O'Leary og |
| 1991-92 (D2) | 3 | 04.01.92 | **Port Vale** (D2) | H | W | 3-0 | Davenport, Byrne, Atkinson |
| | 4 | 05.02.92 | **Oxford Utd** (D2) | A | W | 3-2 | Byrne, Hardyman, Atkinson |
| | 5 | 15.02.92 | **West Ham Utd** (D1) | H | D | 1-1 | Byrne |
| | 5r | 26.02.92 | **West Ham Utd** | A | W | 3-2 | Byrne 2, Rush |
| | 6 | 09.03.92 | **Chelsea** (D1) | A | D | 1-1 | Byrne |
| | 6r | 18.03.92 | **Chelsea** | H | W | 2-1 | Davenport, Armstrong |
| | SF | 05.04.92 | **Norwich City** (D1) *played at Hillsborough* | | W | 1-0 | Byrne |
| | F | 09.05.92 | **Liverpool** (D1) *played at Wembley Stadium* | | L | 0-2 | |
| 1992-93 (D1) | 3 | 12.01.93 | **Notts County** (D1) | A | W | 2-0 | Cunnington, Goodman |
| | 4 | 24.01.93 | **Sheffield Wed** (PL) | A | L | 0-1 | |
| 1993-94 (D1) | 3 | 08.01.94 | **Carlisle Utd** (D3) | H | D | 1-1 | Ferguson |
| | 3r | 18.01.94 | **Carlisle Utd** | A | W | 1-0aet | Howey |
| | 4 | 29.01.94 | **Wimbledon** (PL) | A | L | 1-2 | Smith |
| 1994-95 (D1) | 3 | 07.01.95 | **Carlisle Utd** (D3) | H | D | 1-1 | Russell |

| | | | | | | | | |
|---|---|---|---|---|---|---|---|---|
| | | 3r | 17.01.95 | **Carlisle Utd** | A | W | 3-1 | C Armstrong 2, P Gray |
| | | 4 | 29.01.95 | **Tottenham Hotspur** (PL) | H | L | 1-4 | P Gray |
| 1995-96 | (D1) | 3 | 06.01.96 | **Manchester Utd** (PL) | A | D | 2-2 | Agnew, Russell |
| | | 3r | 16.01.96 | **Manchester Utd** | H | L | 1-2 | P Gray |
| 1996-97 | (PL) | 3 | 04.01.97 | **Arsenal** (PL) | A | D | 1-1 | P Gray |
| | | 3r | 15.01.97 | **Arsenal** | H | L | 0-2 | |
| 1997-98 | (D1) | 3 | 03.01.98 | **Rotherham Utd** (D3) | A | W | 5-1 | Phillips 4(1p), Quinn |
| | | 4 | 24.01.98 | **Tranmere Rovers** (D1) | A | L | 0-1 | |
| 1998-99 | (D1) | 3 | 02.01.99 | **Lincoln City** (D2) | A | W | 1-0 | McCann |
| | | 4 | 23.01.99 | **Blackburn Rovers** (PL) | A | L | 0-1 | |
| 1999-00 | (D1) | 3 | 11.12.99 | **Portsmouth** (D1) | H | W | 1-0 | McCann |
| | | 4 | 08.01.00 | **Tranmere Rovers** (D1) | A | L | 0-1 | |
| 2000-01 | (PL) | 3 | 06.01.01 | **Crystal Palace** (D1) | H | D | 0-0 | |
| | | 3r | 17.01.01 | **Crystal Palace** | A | W | 4-2aet | Quinn, Phillips 2, Kilbane |
| | | 4 | 27.01.01 | **Ipswich Town** (PL) | H | W | 1-0 | Dichio |
| | | 5 | 17.02.01 | **West Ham Utd** (PL) | H | L | 0-1 | |
| 2001-02 | (PL) | 3 | 05.01.02 | **WBA** (D1) | H | L | 1-2 | Phillips |
| 2002-03 | (PL) | 3 | 04.01.03 | **Bolton Wanderers** (PL) | A | D | 1-1 | Phillips |
| | | 3r | 14.01.03 | **Bolton Wanderers** | H | W | 2-0aet | Arca, Proctor |
| | | 4 | 25.01.03 | **Blackburn Rovers** (PL) | A | D | 3-3 | Stewart, Proctor, Phillips |
| | | 4r | 05.02.03 | **Blackburn Rovers** | H | D | 2-2aet | Phillips, McCann |
| | | | | *Sunderland won 3-0 on penalties* | | | | |
| | | 5 | 15.02.03 | **Watford** (D1) | H | L | 0-1 | |

## SUNDERLAND ALBION

*Formed 1888. Entered FA Cup: 1888-89 – 1891-92. A short-lived breakaway club from Sunderland FC. Folded 1892.*

| | | | | | | | | |
|---|---|---|---|---|---|---|---|---|
| 1888-89 | (FAll) | 1 | 15.12.88 | **Grimsby Town** (TC) | A | L | 1-3 | J Stewart |
| 1889-90 | (FAll) | 1 | 18.01.90 | **Bootle** (FAll) | A | W | 3-1 | Hannah, Weir, Sawers |
| | | | | *FA disqualified Sunderland Albion for ineligible players and awarded tie to Bootle* | | | | |
| 1890-91 | (FAll) | 1 | 17.01.91 | **93rd Highland Regiment** | H | W | 2-0 | Rae, Crozier |
| | | 2 | 31.01.91 | **Nottingham Forest** (FAll) | H | D | 1-1 | McClellan |
| | | 2r | 07.02.91 | **Nottingham Forest** | A | D | 3-3aet | Hannah, Smith, McClellan |
| | | 2 2r | 11.02.91 | **Nottingham Forest** | | L | 0-5 | |
| | | | | *played at Bramall Lane* | | | | |
| 1891-92 | (FAll) | 1 | 16.01.92 | **Birmingham St G's** (FAll) | H | L | 1-2 | Gillespie |
| | | | | *FA ordered replay, match only lasted one hour* | | | | |
| | | 1r | 23.01.92 | **Birmingham St G's** | H | W | 4-0 | Strachan 2, Gilespie, Mackie |
| | | 2 | 30.01.92 | **Nottingham Forest** (FAll) | H | L | 0-1 | |

## SUTTON COLDFIELD TOWN

*Formed 1879. First entered FA Cup: 1956-57. Members of the Southern League.*

| | | | | | | | | |
|---|---|---|---|---|---|---|---|---|
| 1980-81 | (WMRL) | 1 | 22.11.80 | **Doncaster Rovers** (D4) | H | L | 0-2 | |
| 1992-93 | (SL) | 1 | 14.11.92 | **Bolton Wanderers** (D2) | A | L | 1-2 | Gale |

## SUTTON JUNCTION

*Entered FA Cup: 1906-07 – 1933-44. Henry Martin, who played for Sunderland in the 1913 FA Cup final, started his career with Sutton Junction.*

| | | | | | | | | |
|---|---|---|---|---|---|---|---|---|
| 1911-12 | (CA) | 1 | 13.01.12 | **Swindon Town** (SL) | A | L | 0-5 | |

## SUTTON TOWN

*First entered FA Cup: 1892-93. Members of the Central Midlands League.*

| | | | | | | | | |
|---|---|---|---|---|---|---|---|---|
| 1933-34 | (DSL) | 1 | 25.11.33 | **Rochdale** (3N) | H | W | 2-1 | Newbold, Egan |
| | | 2 | 09.12.33 | **Reading** (3S) | H | L | 1-2 | Wright |
| 1960-61 | (CA) | 1 | 05.11.60 | **Hull City** (D3) | A | L | 0-3 | |

## SUTTON UNITED

*Formed 1898. First entered FA Cup: 1911-12. League clubs beaten: Aldershot, Peterborough United, Coventry City, Colchester United. Members of the Isthmian League*

| | | | | | | | | |
|---|---|---|---|---|---|---|---|---|
| 1945-46 | (AL) | 1 1L | 17.11.45 | **Walthamstow Ave** (IL) | H | L | 1-4 | Baughan |
| | | 1 2L | 24.11.45 | **Walthamstow Ave** | A | L | 2-7 | Scott, Hinshelwood |
| 1946-47 | (AL) | 1 | 30.11.46 | **Barnet** (AL) | A | L | 0-3 | |

| | | | | | | | | | |
|---|---|---|---|---|---|---|---|---|---|
| 1960-61 | (AL) | 1 | 05.11.60 | **Romford** (SL) | H | D | 2-2 | Hermitage, Green |
| | | 1r | 09.11.60 | **Romford** (SL) | A | L | 0-5 | |
| 1963-64 | (IL) | 1 | 16.11.63 | **Aldershot** (D4) | H | L | 0-4 | |
| 1966-67 | (IL) | 1 | 26.11.66 | **Bath City** (SL) | A | L | 0-1 | |
| 1969-70 | (IL) | 1 | 15.11.69 | **Dagenham** (AL) | A | W | 1-0 | Faulkner |
| | | 2 | 06.12.69 | **Barnet** (SL) | A | W | 2-0 | Howard, Drabwell |
| | | 3 | 06.01.70 | **Hillingdon Borough** (SL) | A | D | 0-0 | |
| | | 3r | 12.01.70 | **Hillingdon Borough** | H | W | 4-1 | Mellows, Howard, Bladon 2 |
| | | 4 | 24.01.70 | **Leeds Utd** (D1) | H | L | 0-6 | |
| 1975-76 | (IL) | 1 | 22.11.75 | **Bournemouth** (D4) | H | D | 1-1 | Kidd |
| | | 1r | 26.11.75 | **Bournemouth** | A | L | 0-1 | |
| 1981-82 | (IL) | 1 | 21.11.81 | **Bishop's Stortford** (IL) | A | D | 2-2 | Bradford og, Sunnucks |
| | | 1r | 24.11.81 | **Bishop's Stortford** | H | W | 2-1 | Rogers, J Rains |
| | | 2 | 15.12.81 | **Swindon Town** (D3) | A | L | 1-2 | Joyce |
| 1987-88 | (Conf) | 1 | 14.11.87 | **Aldershot** (D3) | H | W | 3-0 | McKinnon 2, Cornwell |
| | | 2 | 05.12.87 | **Peterborough Utd** (D4) | A | W | 3-1 | Lawrence og, Cornwell, Dennis |
| | | 3 | 09.01.88 | **Middlesbrough** (D2) | H | D | 1-1 | M Golley |
| | | 3r | 12.01.88 | **Middlesbrough** | A | L | 0-1aet | |
| 1988-89 | (Conf) | 1 | 19.11.88 | **Dagenham** (IL) | A | W | 4-0 | McKinnon 2, Dennis, Rogers |
| | | 2 | 10.12.88 | **Aylesbury Utd** (Conf) | A | W | 1-0 | Dennis |
| | | 3 | 07.01.89 | **Coventry City** (D1) | H | W | 2-1 | Rains., Hanlan |
| | | 4 | 28.01.89 | **Norwich City** (D1) | A | L | 0-8 | |
| 1989-90 | (Conf) | 1 | 18.11.89 | **Torquay Utd** (D4) | H | D | 1-1 | McKinnon |
| | | 1r | 22.11.89 | **Torquay Utd** | A | L | 0-4 | |
| 1990-91 | (Conf) | 1 | 17.11.90 | **Merthyr Tydfil** (Conf) | A | D | 1-1 | Gill |
| | | 1r | 21.11.90 | **Merthyr Tydfil** | H | L | 0-1 | |
| 1991-92 | (IL) | 1 | 16.11.91 | **Maidstone Utd** (D4) | A | L | 0-1 | |
| 1992-93 | (IL) | 1 | 14.11.92 | **Hereford Utd** (D3) | H | L | 1-2 | Quail |
| 1993-94 | (IL) | 1 | 13.11.93 | **Colchester Utd** (D3) | A | W | 4-3 | Quail, Smart, Newman, Morah |
| | | 2 | 04.12.93 | **Torquay Utd** (D3) | A | W | 1-0 | Jones |
| | | 3 | 08.01.94 | **Notts County** (D1) | A | L | 2-3 | Barrowcliffe, Smart |
| 1995-96 | (IL) | 1 | 11.11.95 | **Kidderminster H** (Conf) | A | D | 2-2 | Hynes, Vansittart |
| | | 1r | 21.11.95 | **Kidderminster H** | H | D | 1-1aet | Payne |
| | | | | *Sutton Utd won 3-2 on penalties* | | | | |
| | | 2 | 02.12.95 | **Hereford Utd** (D3) | A | L | 0-2 | |

## SWANSEA CITY

*Formed 1912 as Swansea Town. Swansea City 1970. FA Cup best performance: Semi-finals: 1926, 1964. Welsh FA Cup winners: 10 times. Runners-up: 8 times. Record FA Cup Victory: 8-1 v Caerleon Athletic, 1st qualifying round, 1913-14. In Competition Proper: 7-2 v Folkestone, 1st round replay, 29.11.1966. Record FA Cup defeat: 0-8 v Liverpool, 3rd round replay, 09.01.1990.*

**as Swansea Town**

| | | | | | | | | |
|---|---|---|---|---|---|---|---|---|
| 1913-14 | (SL) | | | P Port Talbot (H) 4-0; 1q Caerleon Athletic (H) 8-1; 2q Mid-Rhondda (H) 1-0; 3q Aberdare Athletic (H) 4-0; 4q Cardiff City (H) 2-0; 5q Willington (H) 3-0 | | | | |
| | | 1 | 10.01.14 | **Merthyr Town** (SL) | H | W | 2-0 | Weir, Ball |
| | | 2 | 31.01.14 | **QPR** (SL) | H | L | 1-2 | Greer |
| 1914-15 | (SL) | | | 4q Newport County (H) 1-0; 5q Port Vale (H) 1-0; 6q Leicester Fosse (H) 1-0 | | | | |
| | | 1 | 09.01.15 | **Blackburn Rovers** (D1) | H | W | 1-0 | Benyon |
| | | 2 | 30.01.15 | **Newcastle Utd** (D1) | A | D | 1-1aet | Lloyd |
| | | 2r | 06.02.15 | **Newcastle Utd** | H | L | 0-2 | |
| 1919-20 | (SL) | | | 6q Gillingham (H) 1-1; 6qr Gillingham (A) 1-1; 6q 2r Gillingham 0-0 at (Ninian Park); 6q 3r Gillingham 1-3 (at Stamford Bridge) | | | | |
| 1920-21 | (D3) | | | 6q Hartlepools United (H) 3-0 | | | | |
| | | 1 | 08.01.21 | **Bury** (D2) | H | W | 3-0 | Edmondson 2, Brown |
| | | 2 | 29.01.21 | **Plymouth Argyle** (D3) | H | L | 1-2 | Edmondson |
| 1921-22 | (3S) | | | 6q Bristol Rovers (H) 2-0 | | | | |
| | | 1 | 07.01.22 | **West Ham Utd** (D2) | H | D | 0-0 | |
| | | 1r | 11.01.22 | **West Ham Utd** | A | D | 1-1aet | Hole |
| | | 1 2r | 16.01.22 | **West Ham Utd** | | W | 1-0 | Spottiswoode |
| | | | | *played at Ashton Gate* | | | | |
| | | 2 | 28.01.22 | **Southend Utd** (3S) | A | W | 1-0 | Jones |
| | | 3 | 18.02.22 | **Millwall Athletic** (3S) | A | L | 0-4 | |

| | | | | | | | | | |
|---|---|---|---|---|---|---|---|---|---|
| 1922-23 | (3S) | | | 5q Merthyr Town (A) 0-0; 5qr Merthyr Town (H) 0-1 | | | | | |
| 1923-24 | (3S) | 1 | 12.01.24 | **Clapton Orient** (D2) | H | D | 1-1 | Smith |
| | | 1r | 17.01.24 | **Clapton Orient** | A | D | 1-1aet | Roulson |
| | | 1 2r | 21.01.24 | **Clapton Orient** | | W | 2-1 | Smith, S Tonner og |
| | | | | *played at White Hart Lane* | | | | |
| | | 2 | 02.02.24 | **Aston Villa** (D1) | H | L | 0-2 | |
| 1924-25 | (3S) | 1 | 10.01.25 | **Plymouth Argyle** (3S) | H | W | 3-0 | Thompson 2, Deacon |
| | | 2 | 31.01.25 | **Aston Villa** (D1) | H | L | 1-3 | Deacon |
| 1925-26 | (D2) | 1 | 28.11.25 | **Exeter City** (3S) | A | W | 3-1 | Thompson, Deacon, Pacey og |
| | | 2 | 12.12.25 | **Watford** (3S) | H | W | 3-2 | Nicholas, Fowler, Thompson |
| | | 3 | 09.01.26 | **Blackpool** (D2) | A | W | 2-0 | Fowler, Deacon |
| | | 4 | 30.01.26 | **Stoke City** (D2) | H | W | 6-3 | Fowler 4, Thompson, Hole |
| | | 5 | 20.02.26 | **Millwall** (3S) | A | W | 1-0 | Fowler |
| | | 6 | 06.03.26 | **Arsenal** (D1) | H | W | 2-1 | Thompson, Fowler |
| | | SF | 27.03.26 | **Bolton Wanderers** (D1) | | L | 0-3 | |
| | | | | *played at White Hart Lane* | | | | |
| 1926-27 | (D2) | 3 | 08.01.27 | **Bury** (D1) | H | W | 4-1 | Thompson 3, Deacon |
| | | 4 | 29.01.27 | **Barnsley** (D2) | A | W | 3-1 | Fowler 2, Hole |
| | | 5 | 19.02.27 | **South Shields** (D2) | A | D | 2-2 | Fowler, Deacon |
| | | 5r | 24.02.27 | **South Shields** | H | W | 2-1 | Deacon, Thompson |
| | | 6 | 05.03.27 | **Reading** (D2) | H | L | 1-3 | McPherson |
| 1927-28 | (D2) | 3 | 14.01.28 | **Wrexham** (3N) | A | L | 1-2 | Hole |
| 1928-29 | (D2) | 3 | 12.01.29 | **Nottingham Forest** (D2) | A | W | 2-1 | Graham og, Deacon |
| | | 4 | 26.01.29 | **Leicester City** (D1) | A | L | 0-1 | |
| 1929-30 | (D2) | 3 | 11.01.30 | **Walsall** (3S) | A | L | 0-2 | |
| 1930-31 | (D2) | 3 | 10.01.31 | **Notts County** (3S) | A | L | 1-3 | Martin |
| 1931-32 | (D2) | 3 | 09.01.32 | **Bury** (D2) | A | L | 1-2 | Gunn |
| 1932-33 | (D2) | 3 | 14.01.33 | **Sheffield Utd** (D1) | H | L | 2-3 | Martin 2 |
| 1933-34 | (D2) | 3 | 13.01.34 | **Notts County** (D2) | H | W | 1-0 | Martin |
| | | 4 | 27.01.34 | **Bury** (D2) | A | D | 1-1 | Matthews og |
| | | 4r | 01.02.34 | **Bury** | H | W | 3-0 | Davies 2, Hanford |
| | | 5 | 17.02.34 | **Portsmouth** (D1) | H | L | 0-1 | |
| 1934-35 | (D2) | 3 | 12.01.35 | **Stoke City** (D1) | H | W | 4-1 | Lowry 2, Blair, Bussey |
| | | 4 | 26.01.35 | **Derby County** (D1) | A | L | 0-3 | |
| 1935-36 | (D2) | 3 | 11.01.36 | **Liverpool** (D1) | A | L | 0-1 | |
| 1936-37 | (D2) | 3 | 16.01.37 | **Carlisle Utd** (3N) | H | W | 1-0 | Williams |
| | | 4 | 30.01.37 | **York City** (3N) | H | D | 0-0 | |
| | | 4r | 03.02.37 | **York City** | A | W | 3-1 | Henson 2, Williams |
| | | 5 | 20.02.37 | **Sunderland** (D1) | A | L | 0-3 | |
| 1937-38 | (D2) | 3 | 08.01.38 | **Wolverhampton W** (D1) | H | L | 0-4 | |
| 1938-39 | (D2) | 3 | 07.01.39 | **Blackburn Rovers** (D2) | A | L | 0-2 | |
| 1945-46 | (D2) | 3 1L | 05.01.46 | **Bristol City** (3S) | A | L | 1-5 | Ford |
| | | 3 2L | 10.01.46 | **Bristol City** | H | D | 2-2 | Ford 2 |
| 1946-47 | (D2) | 3 | 11.01.47 | **Gillingham** (SL) | H | W | 4-1 | McGrory, Payne, Squires, Jones |
| | | 4 | 25.01.47 | **Luton Town** (D2) | A | L | 0-2 | |
| 1947-48 | (3S) | 3 | 10.01.48 | **Bristol Rovers** (3S) | A | L | 0-3 | |
| 1948-49 | (3S) | 1 | 04.12.48 | **Southend Utd** (3S) | A | W | 2-1aet | Burns, O'Driscoll |
| | | 2 | 11.12.48 | **Bristol City** (3S) | A | L | 1-3 | O'Driscoll |
| 1949-50 | (D2) | 3 | 07.01.50 | **Birmingham City** (D1) | H | W | 3-0 | I Allchurch, Burns, Scrine |
| | | 4 | 28.01.50 | **Arsenal** (D1) | A | L | 1-2 | Scrine |
| 1950-51 | (D2) | 3 | 06.01.51 | **Mansfield Town** (3N) | A | L | 0-2 | |
| 1951-52 | (D2) | 3 | 12.01.52 | **Reading** (3S) | A | W | 3-0 | I Allchurch, Medwin, Bellis |
| | | 4 | 02.02.52 | **Rotherham Utd** (D2) | H | W | 3-0 | I Allchurch, Scrine, Williams |
| | | 5 | 23.02.52 | **Newcastle Utd** (D1) | H | L | 0-1 | |
| 1952-53 | (D2) | 3 | 10.01.53 | **Newcastle Utd** (D1) | A | - | 0-0ab | |
| | | | | *abandoned after eight minutes – fog* | | | | |
| | | 3 | 14.01.53 | **Newcastle Utd** | A | L | 0-3 | |
| 1953-54 | (D2) | 3 | 09.01.54 | **Barrow** (3N) | A | D | 2-2 | Thomas, Beech |
| | | 3r | 14.01.54 | **Barrow** | H | W | 4-2 | Kiley, Beech, I Allchurch 2 |
| | | 4 | 30.01.54 | **Everton** (D2) | A | L | 0-3 | |
| 1954-55 | (D2) | 3 | 08.01.55 | **Blackburn Rovers** (D2) | A | W | 2-0 | Medwin, Jones |
| | | 4 | 29.01.55 | **Stoke City** (D2) | H | W | 3-1 | Medwin, I Allchurch, Griffiths |

| | | | | | | | | |
|---|---|---|---|---|---|---|---|---|
| | | 5 | 19.02.55 | **Sunderland** (D1) | H | D | 2-2 | Charles, Medwin |
| | | 5r | 23.02.55 | **Sunderland** | A | L | 0-1 | |
| 1955-56 | (D2) | 3 | 07.01.56 | **York City** (3N) | H | L | 1-2 | Griffiths |
| 1956-57 | (D2) | 3 | 05.01.57 | **Wolverhampton W** (D1) | A | L | 3-5 | Palmer 2, I Allchurch |
| 1957-58 | (D2) | 3 | 04.01.58 | **Burnley** (D1) | A | L | 2-4 | Charles, Lewis |
| 1958-59 | (D2) | 3 | 10.01.59 | **Portsmouth** (D1) | A | L | 1-3 | Charles |
| 1959-60 | (D2) | 3 | 09.01.60 | **Gillingham** (D4) | A | W | 4-1 | B Jones, Hughes, Williams 2 |
| | | 4 | 30.01.60 | **Burnley** (D1) | H | D | 0-0 | |
| | | 4r | 02.02.60 | **Burnley** | A | L | 1-2 | Nurse |
| 1960-61 | (D2) | 3 | 07.01.61 | **Port Vale** (D3) | H | W | 3-0 | L Allchurch, Reynolds 2 |
| | | 4 | 28.01.61 | **Preston North End** (D1) | H | W | 2-1 | Reynolds, R.Davies |
| | | 5 | 18.02.61 | **Burnley** (D1) | A | L | 0-4 | |
| 1961-62 | (D2) | 3 | 09.01.62 | **Sheffield Wed** (D1) | A | L | 0-1 | |
| 1962-63 | (D2) | 3 | 26.01.63 | **QPR** (D3) | H | W | 2-0 | Thomas, Reynolds |
| | | 4 | 04.03.63 | **West Ham Utd** (D1) | A | L | 0-1 | |
| 1963-64 | (D2) | 3 | 04.01.64 | **Barrow** (D4) | H | W | 4-1 | B Evans, R Evans (p), Thomas, M Williams |
| | | 4 | 25.01.64 | **Sheffield Utd** (D1) | A | D | 1-1 | Thomas |
| | | 4r | 28.01.64 | **Sheffield Utd** | H | W | 4-0 | Draper 2, McLaughlin, Thomas |
| | | 5 | 15.02.64 | **Stoke City** (D1) | A | D | 2-2 | Todd 2 |
| | | 5r | 18.02.64 | **Stoke City** | H | W | 2-0 | McLaughlin, Todd |
| | | 6 | 29.02.64 | **Liverpool** (D1) | A | W | 2-1 | McLaughlin, Thomas |
| | | SF | 14.03.64 | **Preston North End** (D2) *played at Villa Park* | | L | 1-2 | McLaughlin |
| 1964-65 | (D2) | 3 | 09.01.65 | **Newcastle Utd** (D2) | H | W | 1-0 | McLaughlin |
| | | 4 | 30.01.65 | **Huddersfield Town** (D2) | H | W | 1-0 | Kirby |
| | | 5 | 20.02.65 | **Peterborough Utd** (D3) | A | D | 0-0 | |
| | | 5r | 24.02.65 | **Peterborough Utd** | H | L | 0-2 | |
| 1965-66 | (D3) | 1 | 13.11.65 | **Walsall** (D3) | A | L | 3-6 | Gregg og, Todd, McLaughlin |
| 1966-67 | (D3) | 1 | 26.11.66 | **Folkestone** (SL) | A | D | 2-2 | McLaughlin 2 |
| | | 1r | 29.11.66 | **Folkestone** | H | W | 7-2 | McLaughlin 3, Humphries 2, Evans, Patrick og |
| | | 2 | 07.01.67 | **Nuneaton B** (SL) | A | L | 0-2 | |
| 1967-68 | (D4) | 1 | 18.12.67 | **Enfield** (IL) | H | W | 2-0 | B Evans, Humphries |
| | | 2 | 06.01.68 | **Brighton** (D3) | H | W | 2-1 | Allchurch, Humphries |
| | | 3 | 27.01.68 | **Doncaster Rovers** (D4) | A | W | 2-0 | Todd, Williams |
| | | 4 | 17.02.68 | **Arsenal** (D1) | H | L | 0-1 | |
| 1968-69 | (D4) | 1 | 16.11.68 | **Oxford City** (IL) | A | W | 3-2 | Gwyther 2, Thomas (p) |
| | | 2 | 07.12.68 | **Weymouth** (SL) | A | D | 1-1 | Screen |
| | | 2r | 10.12.68 | **Weymouth** | H | W | 2-0 | Biggs, Thomas |
| | | 3 | 04.01.69 | **Halifax Town** (D4) | H | L | 0-1 | |
| 1969-70 | (D4) | 1 | 15.11.69 | **Kettering Town** (SL) | A | W | 2-0 | H Williams 2 |
| | | 2 | 06.12.69 | **Oxford City** (IL) | A | W | 5-1 | Gwyther 4, Evans |
| | | 3 | 03.01.70 | **Leeds Utd** (D1) | A | L | 1-2 | Gwyther |
| **as Swansea City** | | | | | | | | |
| 1970-71 | (D3) | 1 | 21.11.70 | **Exeter City** (D4) | H | W | 4-1 | Thomas 2, Evans, Gwyther |
| | | 2 | 12.12.70 | **Telford Utd** (SL) | H | W | 6-2 | Gwyther 3, Hole, L Allchurch, H Williams |
| | | 3 | 02.01.71 | **Rhyl** (CC) | H | W | 6-1 | Gwyther 3, Evans 2, Smart og |
| | | 4 | 23.01.71 | **Liverpool** (D1) | A | L | 0-3 | |
| 1971-72 | (D3) | 1 | 20.11.71 | **Brentford** (D4) | H | D | 1-1 | Davies |
| | | 1r | 22.11.71 | **Brentford** | A | W | 3-2 | A Williams, Gwyther, Thomas |
| | | 2 | 11.12.71 | **Exeter City** (D4) | H | D | 0-0 | |
| | | 2r | 15.12.71 | **Exeter City** | A | W | 1-0 | Holme |
| | | 3 | 15.01.72 | **Gillingham** (D4) | H | W | 1-0 | Gwyther |
| | | 4 | 05.02.72 | **Portsmouth** (D2) | A | L | 0-2 | |
| 1972-73 | (D3) | 1 | 18.11.72 | **Margate** (SL) | A | L | 0-1 | |
| 1973-74 | (D4) | 1 | 24.11.73 | **Walsall** (D3) | A | L | 0-1 | |
| 1974-75 | (D4) | 1 | 26.11.74 | **Kettering Town** (SL) | H | D | 1-1 | Lally |
| | | 1r | 02.12.74 | **Kettering Town** | A | L | 1-3 | W Evans |
| 1975-76 | (D4) | 1 | 22.11.75 | **Southend Utd** (D3) | A | L | 0-2 | |

| | | | | | | | | |
|---|---|---|---|---|---|---|---|---|
| 1976-77 | (D4) | 1 | 20.11.76 | **Minehead** (SL) | H | L | 0-1 | |
| 1977-78 | (D4) | 1 | 26.11.77 | **Leatherhead** (IL) | A | D | 0-0 | |
| | | 1r | 29.11.77 | **Leatherhead** | H | W | 2-1 | Charles, Curtis |
| | | 2 | 17.12.77 | **Portsmouth** (D3) | A | D | 2-2 | Curtis, K Moore |
| | | 2r | 20.12.77 | **Portsmouth** | H | W | 2-1 | Denyer og, G Moore |
| | | 3 | 07.01.78 | **Walsall** (D3) | A | L | 1-4 | R James |
| 1978-79 | (D3) | 1 | 25.11.78 | **Hillingdon Borough** (SL) | H | W | 4-1 | R James, Charles 2, Waddle |
| | | 2 | 16.12.78 | **Woking** (IL) | H | D | 2-2 | Curtis 2 |
| | | 2r | 19.12.78 | **Woking** | A | W | 5-3aet | Curtis 3, Toshack, R James |
| | | 3 | 09.01.79 | **Bristol Rovers** (D2) | H | L | 0-1 | |
| 1979-80 | (D3) | 3 | 05.01.80 | **Crystal Palace** (D1) | H | D | 2-2 | Toshack 2 |
| | | 3r | 08.01.80 | **Crystal Palace** | A | D | 3-3aet | Waddle, Giles, Toshack |
| | | 3 2r | 14.01.80 | **Crystal Palace** | | W | 2-1 | R James, Giles |
| | | | | *played at Ninian Park* | | | | |
| | | 4 | 26.01.80 | **Reading** (D3) | H | W | 4-1 | Giles 2, Waddle, James |
| | | 5 | 16.02.80 | **West Ham Utd** (D2) | A | L | 0-2 | |
| 1980-81 | (D2) | 3 | 03.01.81 | **Middlesbrough** (D1) | H | L | 0-5 | |
| 1981-82 | (D1) | 3 | 02.01.82 | **Liverpool** (D1) | H | L | 0-4 | |
| 1982-83 | (D1) | 3 | 08.01.83 | **Norwich City** (D1) | A | L | 1-2 | Gale |
| 1983-84 | (D2) | 3 | 07.01.84 | **Brighton** (D2) | A | L | 0-2 | |
| 1984-85 | (D3) | 1 | 17.11.84 | **Bognor Regis Town** (IL) | H | D | 1-1 | Richards |
| | | 1r | 21.11.84 | **Bognor Regis Town** | A | L | 1-3 | Marustik |
| 1985-86 | (D3) | 1 | 16.11.85 | **Leyton-Wingate** (IL) | H | W | 2-0 | Waddle, Williams |
| | | 2 | 07.12.85 | **Bristol Rovers** (D3) | H | L | 1-2 | Burrows |
| 1986-87 | (D4) | 1 | 15.11.86 | **Wealdstone** (Conf) | A | D | 1-1 | Williams |
| | | 1r | 20.11.86 | **Wealdstone** | H | - | 2-1ab | Love, McCarthy |
| | | | | *abandoned after 54 minutes – waterlogged pitch* | | | | |
| | | 1r | 24.11.86 | **Wealdstone** | H | W | 4-1 | Williams, Hough, McCarthy, Hutchison |
| | | 2 | 06.12.86 | **Slough Town** (IL) | H | W | 3-0 | Pascoe, McCarthy (p), Hutchison |
| | | 3 | 10.01.87 | **WBA** (D2) | H | W | 3-2 | McCarthy 2, Melville |
| | | 4 | 03.02.87 | **Hull City** (D2) | H | L | 0-1 | |
| 1987-88 | (D4) | 1 | 14.11.87 | **Hayes** (IL) | A | W | 1-0 | Pascoe |
| | | 2 | 05.12.87 | **Leyton Orient** (D4) | A | L | 0-2 | |
| 1988-89 | (D3) | 1 | 19.11.88 | **Northampton Town** (D3) | H | W | 3-1 | Melville, Hutchison, Wade |
| | | 2 | 10.12.88 | **Colchester Utd** (D4) | A | D | 2-2 | Coleman, Melville |
| | | 2r | 13.12.88 | **Colchester Utd** | H | L | 1-3 | Wade |
| 1989-90 | (D3) | 1 | 18.11.89 | **Kidderminster H** (Conf) | A | W | 3-2 | Melville 2, Davies |
| | | 2 | 09.12.89 | **Peterborough Utd** (D4) | H | W | 3-1 | Raynor (p), Chalmers 2 |
| | | 3 | 06.01.90 | **Liverpool** (D1) | H | D | 0-0 | |
| | | 3r | 09.01.90 | **Liverpool** | A | L | 0-8 | |
| 1990-91 | (D3) | 1 | 17.11.90 | **Welling Utd** (Conf) | H | W | 5-2 | Gilligan (p), Connor, Legg 2, Thornber |
| | | 2 | 08.12.90 | **Walsall** (D4) | H | W | 2-1 | Connor, Gilligan (p) |
| | | 3 | 05.01.91 | **Rotherham Utd** (D3) | H | D | 0-0 | |
| | | 3r | 21.01.91 | **Rotherham Utd** | A | L | 0-4 | |
| 1991-92 | (D3) | 1 | 16.11.91 | **Cardiff City** (D4) | H | W | 2-1 | Gilligan, Harris |
| | | 2 | 07.12.91 | **Exeter City** (D3) | A | D | 0-0 | |
| | | 2r | 17.12.91 | **Exeter City** | H | L | 1-2 | Walker |
| 1992-93 | (D2) | 1 | | bye | | | | |
| | | 2 | 05.12.92 | **Exeter City** (D2) | A | - | 2-1ab | Cornforth, Jenkins |
| | | | | *abandoned after 86 minutes – floodlight failure* | | | | |
| | | 2 | 15.12.92 | **Exeter City** | A | W | 5-2 | West, Legg, Wimbleton, Cullen, Bowen |
| | | 3 | 02.01.93 | **Oxford Utd** (D1) | H | D | 1-1 | West |
| | | 3r | 12.01.93 | **Oxford Utd** | A | D | 2-2aet | Cornforth, Legg |
| | | | | *Swansea City won 5-4 on penalties* | | | | |
| | | 4 | 02.02.93 | **Grimsby Town** (D1) | H | D | 0-0 | |
| | | 4r | 09.02.93 | **Grimsby Town** | A | L | 0-2 | |
| 1993-94 | (D2) | 1 | 13.11.93 | **Nuneaton B** (SL) | H | D | 1-1 | Torpey |
| | | 1r | 23.11.93 | **Nuneaton B** | A | L | 1-2aet | Torpey |
| 1994-95 | (D2) | 1 | 21.11.94 | **Walton & H** (IL) | A | W | 2-0 | Ford, Ampadu |

| | | | | | | | | |
|---|---|---|---|---|---|---|---|---|
| | | 2 | 04.12.94 | **Bashley** (SL) | A | W | 1-0 | Torpey |
| | | 3 | 07.01.95 | **Middlesbrough** (D1) | H | D | 1-1 | Ford |
| | | 3r | 17.01.95 | **Middlesbrough** | A | W | 2-1 | Torpey, Penney |
| | | 4 | 28.01.95 | **Newcastle Utd** (PL) | A | L | 0-3 | |
| 1995-96 | (D2) | 1 | 11.11.95 | **Fulham** (D3) | A | L | 0-7 | |
| 1996-97 | (D3) | 1 | 16.11.96 | **Bristol City** (D2) | H | D | 1-1 | Torpey |
| | | 1r | 26.11.96 | **Bristol City** | A | L | 0-1 | |
| 1997-98 | (D3) | 1 | 14.11.97 | **Peterborough Utd** (D3) | H | L | 1-4 | Appleby |
| 1998-99 | (D3) | 1 | 13.11.98 | **Millwall** (D2) | H | W | 3-0 | Price, Thomas, Alsop |
| | | 2 | 05.12.98 | **Stoke City** (D2) | H | W | 1-0 | Appleby |
| | | 3 | 02.01.99 | **West Ham Utd** (PL) | A | D | 1-1 | Smith |
| | | 3r | 13.01.99 | **West Ham Utd** | H | W | 1-0 | Thomas |
| | | 4 | 23.01.99 | **Derby County** (PL) | H | L | 0-1 | |
| 1999-00 | (D3) | 1 | 30.10.99 | **Colchester Utd** (D2) | H | W | 2-1 | Cusack, Watkin |
| | | 1 | 20.11.99 | **Oldham Athletic** (D2) | A | L | 0-1 | |
| 2000-01 | (D2) | 1 | 18.11.00 | **Bournemouth** (D2) | A | L | 0-2 | |
| 2001-02 | (D3) | 1 | 18.11.01 | **QPR** (D2) | H | W | 4-0 | Williams, Cusack, Sidibe, Watkin |
| | | 2 | 08.12.01 | **Macclesfield T** (D3) | A | L | 1-4 | Cusack |
| 2002-03 | (D3) | 1 | 26.11.02 | **York City** (D3) | A | L | 1-2 | Murphy |

## SWIFTS

*Formed 1868. One of the more successful amateur clubs in the early days of the competition. Semi-finalists: 1874, 1886. Based in Slough and played their early matches at a ground near The Dolphin pub in the town centre. Berks and Bucks Senior Cup winners 1882. Joint-holders with Old Philberdians 1880.*

| | | | | | | | |
|---|---|---|---|---|---|---|---|
| 1873-74 | 1 | 09.10.73 | **Crystal Palace (1861)** | H | W | 1-0 | Jeans |
| | 2 | 22.11.73 | **Woodford Wells** | H | W | 2-1 | EH Bambridge, Nicholls |
| | 3 | | bye | | | | |
| | SF | 28.01.74 | **Royal Engineers** | | L | 0-2 | |
| | | | *played at Kennington Oval* | | | | |
| 1874-75 | 1 | 05.11.74 | **Old Etonians** | H | D | 0-0 | |
| | 1r | 14.11.74 | **Old Etonians** | A | D | 1-1 | Joll |
| | 1 2r | 26.11.74 | **Old Etonians** | A | L | 0-3 | |
| 1875-76 | 1 | 03.11.75 | **Marlow** | H | W | 2-0 | Joll, Talbot |
| | 2 | 11.12.75 | **South Norwood** | A | W | 5-0 | W Bambridge, Post, Sale, Talbot, AN Other |
| | 3 | 29.01.76 | **Royal Engineers** | A | W | 3-1 | W Bambridge, Sale, Selwyn |
| | SF | 26.02.76 | **Wanderers** | | L | 1-2 | Sale |
| | | | *played at Kennington Oval* | | | | |
| 1876-77 | 1 | 04.11.76 | **Reading Hornets** | H | W | 2-0 | Joll, Rawson |
| | 2 | 16.12.76 | **Rochester** | A | L | 0-1 | |
| 1877-78 | 1 | 07.11.77 | **Leyton FC** | H | W | 3-2 | WS Bambridge 2, Short |
| | 2 | 22.12.77 | **Clapham Rovers** | A | L | 0-4 | |
| 1878-79 | 1 | 09.11.78 | **Hawks** | H | W | 2-1 | WS Bambridge, Turner |
| | 2 | 21.12.78 | **Romford (1876)** | H | W | 3-1 | EG Bambridge 2, Parry |
| | 3 | | bye | | | | |
| | 4 | 08.03.79 | **Clapham Rovers** | A | L | 1-8 | Bain |
| 1879-80 | 1 | | West End | | | - | |
| | | | *Swifts scratched. West End walkover* | | | | |
| 1880-81 | 1 | 06.11.80 | **Old Foresters** | H | D | 1-1 | |
| | 1r | 20.11.80 | **Old Foresters** | A | W | 2-1 | Parke, og |
| | 2 | 18.12.80 | **Reading** | A | W | 1-0 | |
| | 3 | 08.01.81 | **Clapham Rovers** | A | L | 1-2 | E Wild |
| 1881-82 | 1 | 05.11.81 | **Herts Rangers** | H | W | 4-0 | EC Bambridge 4 |
| | 2 | 03.12.81 | **Old Harrovians** | H | W | 7-1 | EC Bambridge 5, Bain, Keyser |
| | 3 | 17.12.81 | **Old Etonians** | A | L | 0-3 | |
| 1882-83 | 1 | 04.11.82 | **Highbury Union** | H | W | 4-1 | |
| | 2 | 30.11.82 | **Upton Park** | H | D | 2-2 | Parr, Thorpe |
| | 2r | 02.12.82 | **Upton Park** | A | W | 3-2 | Parr 3 |
| | 3 | | bye | | | | |
| | 4 | 24.01.83 | **Old Etonians** | A | L | 0-2 | |
| 1883-84 | 1 | | bye | | | | |
| | 2 | 01.12.83 | **Marlow** | H | W | 2-0 | EC Bambridge, Jessop |

| | | | | | | | |
|---|---|---|---|---|---|---|---|
| | 3 | 22.12.83 | **Clapham Rovers** | A | W | 2-1 | EC Bambridge, Davenport |
| | 4 | 19.01.84 | **Old Foresters** | H | W | 2-1 | EC Bambridge, Perkins |
| | 5 | 09.02.84 | **Notts County** | A | D | 1-1aet | AL Bambridge |
| | 5r | 14.02.84 | **Notts County** | H | L | 0-1 | |
| 1884-85 | 1 | 08.11.84 | **Old Brightonians** | H | W | 3-0 | |
| | 2 | 06.12.84 | **South Reading** | H | W | 3-2 | EC Bambridge 2, AN Other |
| | 3 | 03.01.85 | **Old Westminsters** | H | D | 1-1 | |
| | 3r | 14.01.85 | **Old Westminsters** | A | D | 2-2 | Pawson, og |
| | 3 2r | 21.01.85 | **Old Westminsters** | H | W | 2-1 | Brann, AN Other |
| | 4 | 24.01.85 | **Nottingham Forest** | H | L | 0-1 | |
| 1885-86 | 1 | 31.10.85 | **Casuals** | H | W | 7-1 | |
| | 2 | 21.11.85 | **Rochester** | H | W | 5-1 | Bryan 2, Playford 2, Miller |
| | 3 | | Old Harrovians | | | - | |
| | | | *FA disqualifed Old Harrovians, Swifts gained a walkover* | | | | |
| | 4 | | bye | | | | |
| | 5 | 16.01.86 | **Church FC** | A | W | 6-2 | EC Bambridge, Brann, Smith, 3 others |
| | 6 | 13.02.86 | **South Shore** | A | W | 2-1 | Brann, og |
| | SF | 13.03.86 | **Blackburn Rovers** | | L | 1-2 | EC Bambridge |
| | | | *played at Derby Cricket Ground* | | | | |
| 1886-87 | 1 | 23.10.86 | **Luton Wanderers** | H | W | 13-0 | |
| | 2 | 20.11.86 | **Swindon Town** | H | W | 7-1 | EC Bambridge 3, Challen 2, Playford 2 |
| | 3 | | bye | | | | |
| | 4 | 15.01.87 | **Old Foresters** | H | L | 0-2 | |
| 1887-88 | 1 | 15.10.87 | **Maidenhead** | H | W | 3-1 | |
| | 2 | | bye | | | | |
| | 3 | 26.11.87 | **Dulwich** | A | W | 3-1 | |
| | 4 | 10.12.87 | **Crewe Alexandra** | A | D | 2-2 | EC Bambridge, Challen |
| | 4r | 17.12.87 | **Crewe Alexandra** | A | W | 3-2 | Holden-White, Ingram, og |
| | | | *FA ordered match to be replayed after protests about the size of the goals* | | | | |
| | 4 2r | 31.12.87 | **Crewe Alexandra** | | L | 1-2 | EC Bambridge |
| | | | *played at Derby Cricket Ground* | | | | |
| 1888-89 | 1 | 02.02.89 | **Wrexham** | H | W | 3-1 | Wilson, Humphrey, Challen |
| | 2 | 16.02.89 | Blackburn Rovers (D1) | | | - | |
| | | | *Swifts scratched. Blackburn Rovers walkover* | | | | |
| 1889-90 | 4q | | Royal Arsenal (A) 5-1 | | | | |
| | 1 | 20.01.90 | **Sheffield Wed** (FAll) | A | L | 1-6 | Challen |

## SWINDON TOWN

*Formed 1881. FA Cup best performance: Semi-finals: 1910, 1912 (both times as a Southern League club. Swindon are the last Non-League club to reach the last four). FA Cup Record Win: 10-1 v Farnham United Breweries, 1st round, 28.11.1925. Record FA Cup defeat: 1-10 v Manchester City, 4th round replay, 25.01.1930*

| | | | | | | | |
|---|---|---|---|---|---|---|---|
| 1886-87 | 1 | 23.10.86 | **Watford Rovers** | A | W | 1-0 | R Jones |
| | 2 | 20.11.86 | **Swifts** | A | L | 1-7 | J Thomas |
| 1887-88 | 1 | 08.10.87 | **Old Brightonians** | A | L | 0-1 | |
| 1888-89 | | | 2q Marlow (H) 2-5 | | | | |
| 1889-90 | | | 1q Watford Rovers (A) 3-5 | | | | |
| 1890-91 | | | 1q Maidenhead (H) 9-0; 2q Marlow (H) 2-0; 3q 93rd Highland Regiment (A) 0-6 | | | | |
| 1891-92 | | | 1q Luton Town (A) 3-4 | | | | |
| 1892-93 | | | 1q Cowes (A) 2-1aet; 2q Warmley (H) 8-1; 3q Reading (H) 2-1; 4q Marlow (A) 0-1 | | | | |
| 1893-94 | | | 1q Maidenhead (H) 4-0; 2q Marlow (H) 1-0; 3q Weymouth (A) 4-0; 4q Reading (H) 0-2 | | | | |
| 1894-95 (SL) | | | 1q Bristol St Georges (H) 4-2; 2q Marlow (A) 2-4 | | | | |
| 1895-96 (SL) | | | 1q Trowbridge Town (A) 3-1; 2q Warmley (H) 2-1; 3q Uxbridge (A) 0-5 | | | | |
| 1896-97 (SL) | | | 3q Uxbridge (H) 3-2; 4q Royal Artillery (H) 4-1; 5q Southampton St Marys (A) 2-8 | | | | |
| 1897-98 (SL) | | | 3q Reading (A) 0-0; 3qr Reading (H) 3-2; 4q Southampton St Marys (H) 1-3 | | | | |
| 1898-99 (SL) | | | 3q Warmley (A) 0-1 | | | | |
| 1899-00 (SL) | | | 3q Portsmouth (A) 1-2 | | | | |
| 1900-01 (SL) | | | 3q Bristol East (H) 1-1; 3qr Bristol East (H) 5-0; 4q Staple Hill (H) 2-2; 4qr Staple Hill (H) 6-0; 5q Bristol Rovers (A) 1-5 | | | | |
| 1901-02 (SL) | | | 3q Yeovil Casuals (H) 4-0; 4q Weymouth (H) 2-1; 5q Bristol Rovers (H) 0-1 | | | | |
| 1902-03 (SL) | | | 2q Chippenham Town (H) 5-0; 3q Yeovil Casuals (A) 4-0; 4q Poole Town (H) | | | | |

| | | | | | | | | |
|---|---|---|---|---|---|---|---|---|
| | | | | 7-1; 5q Whiteheads Torpedo (A) 9-0; Int Barnsley (A) 0-4 | | | | |
| 1903-04 | (SL) | | | 3q Poole Town (H) 9-0; 4q Staple Hill (H) 5-0; 5q Plymouth Argyle (A) 0-2 | | | | |
| 1904-05 | (SL) | | | 3q Whiteheads Torpedo (H) 7-0; 4q Longfleet St Marys (H) 8-0; 5q Green Waves (A) 1-2 | | | | |
| 1905-06 | (SL) | | | 5q West Hampstead (H) 4-0 | | | | |
| | | 1 | 13.01.06 | **Brighton** (SL) | A | L | 0-3 | |
| 1906-07 | (SL) | | | 5q Burslem Port Vale (H) 1-2 | | | | |
| 1907-08 | (SL) | 1 | 11.01.08 | **Sheffield Utd** (D1) | H | D | 0-0 | |
| | | 1r | 16.01.08 | **Sheffield Utd** | A | W | 3-2aet | Warburton, Tout, Johnston |
| | | 2 | 01.02.08 | **QPR** (SL) | H | W | 2-1 | Johnston, Warburton |
| | | 3 | 22.02.08 | **Wolverhampton W** (D2) | A | L | 0-2 | |
| 1908-09 | (SL) | 1 | 16.01.09 | **Plymouth Argyle** (SL) | A | L | 0-1 | |
| 1909-10 | (SL) | 1 | 15.01.10 | **Crystal Palace** (SL) | A | W | 3-1 | Tout, Fleming, Bown |
| | | 2 | 02.05.10 | **Burnley** (D2) | H | W | 2-0 | Bown, Fleming |
| | | 3 | 19.02.10 | **Tottenham Hotspur** (D1) | H | W | 3-2 | Fleming 3 |
| | | 4 | 05.03.10 | **Manchester City** (D2) | H | W | 2-0 | Jefferson, Bown |
| | | SF | 26.03.10 | **Newcastle Utd** (D1) | | L | 0-2 | |
| | | | | *played at White Hart Lane* | | | | |
| 1910-11 | (SL) | 1 | 14.01.11 | **Notts County** (D1) | H | W | 3-1 | Bown 2, Fleming |
| | | 2 | 04.02.11 | **Woolwich Arsenal** (D1) | H | W | 1-0 | Jefferson |
| | | 3 | 25.02.11 | **Darlington** (NEL) | A | W | 3-0 | Bolland, Fleming, Jefferson |
| | | 4 | 13.03.11 | **Chelsea** (D2) | A | L | 1-3 | Bown |
| 1911-12 | (SL) | 1 | 13.01.12 | **Sutton Junction** (CA) | H | W | 5-0 | Fleming 4, Bown |
| | | 2 | 03.02.12 | **Notts County** (D1) | H | W | 2-0 | Jefferson, Wheatcroft |
| | | 3 | 24.02.12 | **West Ham Utd** (SL) | A | D | 1-1 | Fleming |
| | | 3r | 28.02.12 | **West Ham Utd** | H | W | 4-0 | Glover 2ogs, Jefferson, Wheatcroft |
| | | 4 | 09.03.12 | **Everton** (D1) | H | W | 2-1 | Jefferson, Bown |
| | | SF | 30.03.12 | **Barnsley** (D2) | | D | 0-0 | |
| | | | | *played at Stamford Bridge* | | | | |
| | | SFr | 03.04.12 | **Barnsley** | | L | 0-1 | |
| | | | | *played at Meadow Lane, Nottingham* | | | | |
| 1912-13 | (SL) | 1 | 11.01.13 | **Rochdale** (CL) | A | W | 2-0 | Bown, Jefferson |
| | | 2 | 01.02.13 | **Huddersfield Town** (D2) | A | W | 2-1 | Wheatcroft, Bown |
| | | 3 | 22.02.13 | **Sunderland** (D1) | A | L | 2-4 | Fleming, Wheatcroft |
| 1913-14 | (SL) | 1 | 10.01.14 | **Manchester Utd** (D1) | H | W | 1-0 | Fleming |
| | | 2 | 31.01.14 | **Bolton Wanderers** (D1) | A | L | 2-4 | Batty 2 |
| 1914-15 | (SL) | 1 | 09.01.15 | **Chelsea** (D1) | A | D | 1-1 | Denyer |
| | | 1r | 16.01.15 | **Chelsea** | H | L | 2-5aet | Wheatcroft Jefferson |
| | | | | *played at Stamford Bridge* | | | | |
| 1919-20 | (SL) | 1 | 10.01.20 | **Fulham** (D2) | A | W | 2-1 | Travers 2 |
| | | 2 | 31.01.20 | **Chelsea** (D1) | A | L | 0-4 | |
| 1920-21 | (D3) | 1 | 08.01.21 | **Sheffield Utd** (D1) | H | W | 1-0 | Fleming |
| | | 2 | 29.01.21 | **Chelsea** (D1) | H | L | 0-2 | |
| 1921-22 | (3S) | 1 | 07.01.22 | **Leeds Utd** (D2) | H | W | 2-1 | Fleming 2 |
| | | 2 | 28.01.22 | **Blackburn Rovers** (D1) | H | L | 0-1 | |
| 1922-23 | (3S) | 1 | 13.01.23 | **Barnsley** (D2) | H | D | 0-0 | |
| | | 1r | 18.01.23 | **Barnsley** | A | L | 0-2 | |
| 1923-24 | (3S) | 1 | 12.01.24 | **Bradford Park A** (3N) | H | W | 4-0 | Wareing, Crossley, Denyer, Johnson |
| | | 2 | 02.02.24 | **Oldham Athletic** (D2) | H | W | 2-0 | Denyer, Crossley |
| | | 3 | 23.02.24 | **Crystal Palace** (D2) | A | W | 2-1 | Wareing, Fleming |
| | | 4 | 08.03.24 | **Burnley** (D1) | H | D | 1-1 | Fleming |
| | | 4r | 12.03.24 | **Burnley** | A | L | 1-3 | Johnson |
| 1924-25 | (3S) | 1 | 10.01.25 | **Fulham** (D2) | H | L | 1-2 | Johnson |
| 1925-26 | (3S) | 1 | 28.11.25 | **Farnham UB** (SSL) | A | W | 10-1 | Richardson 4, Johnson 3, Denyer 2, Wall |
| | | 2 | 12.12.25 | **Sittingbourne** (KL) | H | W | 7-0 | Richardson 4, Davies 2, Denyer |
| | | 3 | 09.01.26 | **Clapton** (IL) | A | W | 3-2 | Richardson 2, Moore og |
| | | | | *played at Upton Park* | | | | |
| | | 4 | 30.01.26 | **Nottingham Forest** (D2) | A | L | 0-2 | |
| 1926-27 | (3S) | 1 | 27.11.26 | **Bournemouth** (3S) | A | D | 1-1 | Morris |
| | | 1r | 29.11.26 | **Bournemouth** | H | L | 3-4 | Thom, Wall 2 |

| | | | | | | | |
|---|---|---|---|---|---|---|---|
| 1927-28 (3S) | 1 | 26.11.27 | **Newport County** (3S) | A | W | 1-0 | Morris |
| | 2 | 10.12.27 | **Crystal Palace** (3S) | H | D | 0-0 | |
| | 2r | 14.12.27 | **Crystal Palace** | A | W | 2-1 | Morris 2 |
| | 3 | 14.01.28 | **Clapton Orient** (D2) | H | W | 2-1 | Morris 2 |
| | 4 | 28.01.28 | **Sheffield Wed** (D1) | H | L | 1-2 | Morris |
| 1928-29 (3S) | 3 | 12.01.29 | **Newcastle Utd** (D1) | H | W | 2-0 | Morris 2 |
| | 4 | 26.01.29 | **Burnley** (D1) | A | D | 3-3 | Morris 2, Denyer |
| | 4r | 30.01.29 | **Burnley** | H | W | 3-2 | Dickenson (p), Eddleston, Morris |
| | 5 | 16.02.29 | **Arsenal** (D1) | H | D | 0-0 | |
| | 5r | 20.02.29 | **Arsenal** | A | L | 0-1 | |
| 1929-30 (3S) | 3 | 11.01.30 | **Manchester Utd** (D1) | A | W | 2-0 | Eddleston, Roberts |
| | 4 | 25.01.30 | **Manchester City** (D1) | H | D | 1-1 | McCloy og |
| | 4r | 29.01.30 | **Manchester City** | A | L | 1-10 | Morris |
| 1930-31 (3S) | 1 | 29.11.30 | **Norwich City** (3S) | A | L | 0-2 | |
| 1931-32 (3S) | 1 | 28.11.31 | **Luton Town** (3S) | H | L | 0-5 | |
| 1932-33 (3S) | 1 | 26.11.32 | **Dulwich Hamlet** (IL) | H | W | 4-1 | Starsmore, Quinn 2, Brooks |
| | 2 | 10.12.32 | **Southport** (3N) | A | W | 2-1 | Little og, Morris |
| | 3 | 14.01.33 | **Burnley** (D2) | H | L | 1-2 | Munnings |
| 1933-34 (3S) | 1 | 25.11.33 | **Ilford** (IL) | A | W | 4-2 | Armstrong, Fisher, Timbrell, Flanagan |
| | 2 | 09.12.33 | **Dartford** (SL) | H | W | 1-0 | Armstrong (p) |
| | 3 | 13.01.34 | **Brighton** (3S) | A | L | 1-3 | Helsby |
| 1934-35 (3S) | 1 | 24.11.34 | **Newport County** (3S) | H | W | 4-0 | Fowler 3, Gunson |
| | 2 | 08.12.34 | **Lincoln City** (3N) | H | W | 4-3 | Fowler 2, Bowl, Gunson |
| | 3 | 12.01.35 | **Chesterfield** (3N) | H | W | 2-1 | Bowl, Fowler |
| | 4 | 26.01.35 | **Preston North End** (D1) | H | L | 0-2 | |
| 1935-36 (3S) | 1 | 30.11.35 | **Southall** (AL) | A | L | 1-3 | Bowl |
| 1936-37 (3S) | 1 | 28.11.36 | **Dulwich Hamlet** (IL) | H | W | 6-0 | Hetherington, Bradley 2, Cookson, E Jones, Fowler |
| | 2 | 12.12.36 | **Cardiff City** (3S) | A | L | 1-2 | Cookson |
| 1937-38 (3S) | 1 | 27.11.37 | **Gillingham** (3S) | A | W | 4-3 | Bradley 3 (2ps), E.Jones |
| | 2 | 11.12.37 | **QPR** (3S) | H | W | 2-1 | E Jones 2 |
| | 3 | 08.01.38 | **Grimsby Town** (D1) | A | D | 1-1 | E Jones |
| | 3r | 12.01.38 | **Grimsby Town** | H | W | 2-1aet | Morton, Fowler |
| | 4 | 22.01.38 | **Luton Town** (D2) | A | L | 1-2 | Morton |
| 1938-39 (3S) | 1 | 26.11.38 | **Lowestoft Town** (ECL) | H | W | 6-0 | Morton 3, Lucas 2, E Jones |
| | 2 | 10.12.38 | **Southport** (3N) | A | L | 0-2 | |
| 1945-46 (3S) | 1 1L | 17.11.45 | **Bristol Rovers** (3S) | H | W | 1-0 | Emery |
| | 1 2L | 24.11.45 | **Bristol Rovers** | A | L | 1-4 | Francis |
| 1946-47 (3S) | 1 | 30.11.46 | **Cambridge Town** (SPT) | H | W | 4-1 | Lucas 2, JW Stephens 2 (1p) |
| | 2 | 14.12.46 | **Notts County** (3S) | A | L | 1-2 | Paterson |
| 1947-48 (3S) | 1 | 29.11.47 | **Ipswich Town** (3S) | H | W | 4-2 | WM Jones 2, Bell og, Lucas |
| | 2 | 13.12.47 | **Aldershot** (3S) | A | D | 0-0aet | |
| | 2r | 20.12.47 | **Aldershot** | H | W | 2-0 | WM Jones 2 |
| | 3 | 10.01.48 | **Burnley** (D1) | A | W | 2-0 | Dryden, Owen |
| | 4 | 24.01.48 | **Notts County** (3S) | H | W | 1-0 | Lucas |
| | 5 | 07.02.48 | **Southampton** (D2) | A | L | 0-3 | |
| 1948-49 (3S) | 3 | 08.01.49 | **Stoke City** (D1) | H | L | 1-3 | Owen |
| 1949-50 (3S) | 1 | 26.11.49 | **Bristol Rovers** (3S) | H | W | 1-0 | Owen |
| | 2 | 10.12.49 | **Carlisle Utd** (3N) | A | L | 0-2 | |
| 1950-51 (3S) | 1 | 29.11.50 | **Southend Utd** (3S) | A | W | 3-0 | Bain, Simner, Onslow |
| | 2 | 09.12.50 | **Exeter City** (3S) | A | L | 0-3 | |
| 1951-52 (3S) | 1 | 24.11.51 | **Bedford Town** (SL) | H | W | 2-0 | Betteridge, Owen |
| | 2 | 15.12.51 | **Torquay Utd** (3S) | H | D | 3-3 | Owen 2, Millar |
| | 2r | 19.12.51 | **Torquay Utd** | A | D | 1-1aet | Betteridge |
| | 2 2r | 02.01.52 | **Torquay Utd** *played at Ashton Gate* | | W | 3-1 | Onslow, Bain, Owen |
| | 3 | 12.01.52 | **Cardiff City** (D2) | A | D | 1-1 | Owen |
| | 3r | 16.01.52 | **Cardiff City** | H | W | 1-0aet | Owen |
| | 4 | 02.02.52 | **Stoke City** (D1) | H | D | 1-1 | Bain |
| | 4r | 04.02.52 | **Stoke City** | A | W | 1-0 | Millar |
| | 5 | 23.02.52 | **Luton Town** (D2) | A | L | 1-3 | Betteridge |

| | | | | | | | | | |
|---|---|---|---|---|---|---|---|---|---|
| 1952-53 | (3S) | 1 | 22.11.52 | **Newport (IOW)** (HL) | H | W | 5-0 | Lunn, Owen 3, Millar |
| | | 2 | 06.12.52 | **Northampton Town** (3S) | H | W | 2-0 | Owen, Millar |
| | | 3 | 10.01.53 | **Manchester City** (D1) | A | L | 0-7 | |
| 1953-54 | (3S) | 1 | 21.11.53 | **Newport (IOW)** (HL) | H | W | 2-1 | Batchelor 2 |
| | | 2 | 12.12.53 | **Hastings Utd** (SL) | A | L | 1-4 | Sampson |
| 1954-55 | (3S) | 1 | 20.11.54 | **Crystal Palace** (3S) | H | L | 0-2 | |
| 1955-56 | (3S) | 1 | 19.11.55 | **Hereford Utd** (SL) | H | W | 4-0 | Micklewright 2, Gibson, Owen |
| | | 2 | 10.12.55 | **Peterborough Utd** (ML) | H | D | 1-1 | Owen |
| | | 2r | 15.12.55 | **Peterborough Utd** | A | W | 2-1aet | Micklewright, Cross |
| | | 3 | 07.01.56 | **Worksop Town** (ML) | H | W | 1-0 | Edwards |
| | | 4 | 28.01.56 | **Charlton Athletic** (D1) | A | L | 1-2 | Edwards |
| 1956-57 | (3S) | 1 | 17.11.56 | **Coventry City** (3S) | H | W | 2-1 | Edwards, Richards |
| | | 2 | 08.12.56 | **Bournemouth** (3S) | H | L | 0-1 | |
| 1957-58 | (3S) | 1 | 16.11.57 | **Reading** (3S) | A | L | 0-1 | |
| 1958-59 | (D3) | 1 | 15.11.58 | **Aldershot** (D4) | H | W | 5-0 | Edwards, Darcy 3, Kelly |
| | | 2 | 06.12.58 | **Norwich City** (D3) | H | D | 1-1 | Richards |
| | | 2r | 11.12.58 | **Norwich City** | A | L | 0-1 | |
| 1959-60 | (D3) | 1 | 14.11.59 | **Walsall** (D4) | H | L | 2-3 | Edwards, Darcy |
| 1960-61 | (D3) | 1 | 05.11.60 | **Bath City** (SL) | H | D | 2-2 | RP Hunt, Layne |
| | | 1r | 10.11.60 | **Bath City** | A | W | 6-4 | Layne 4, RP Hunt 2 |
| | | 2 | 26.11.60 | **Shrewsbury Town** (D3) | H | L | 0-1 | |
| 1961-62 | (D3) | 1 | 04.11.61 | **Kettering Town** (SL) | H | D | 2-2 | McPherson, RA Hunt |
| | | 1r | 08.11.61 | **Kettering Town** | A | L | 0-3 | |
| 1962-63 | (D3) | 1 | 03.11.62 | **Reading** (D3) | H | W | 4-2 | Smith, RP Hunt 2, Spiers og |
| | | 2 | 24.11.62 | **Yeovil Town** (SL) | A | W | 2-0 | RP Hunt, Jackson |
| | | 3 | 26.01.63 | **Luton Town** (D2) | A | W | 2-0 | Jackson 2 |
| | | 4 | 29.01.63 | **Everton** (D1) | H | L | 1-5 | Smith |
| 1963-64 | (D2) | 3 | 04.01.64 | **Manchester City** (D2) | H | W | 2-1 | Smart 2 |
| | | 4 | 25.01.64 | **Aldershot** (D4) | A | W | 2-1 | Rogers, Atkins |
| | | 5 | 15.02.64 | **West Ham Utd** (D1) | H | L | 1-3 | McPherson |
| 1964-65 | (D2) | 3 | 09.01.65 | **Ipswich Town** (D2) | H | L | 1-2 | Brown |
| 1965-66 | (D3) | 1 | 13.11.65 | **Merthyr Tydfil** (SL) | H | W | 5-1 | East 4, Smart |
| | | 2 | 04.12.65 | **Grantham Town** (ML) | A | W | 6-1 | Weaver, Nurse, Brown, Smart 2, East |
| | | 3 | 22.01.66 | **Coventry City** (D2) | H | L | 1-2 | Brown |
| 1966-67 | (D3) | 1 | 26.11.66 | **Horsham** (AL) | A | W | 3-0 | Rogers, Nurse, Brown |
| | | 2 | 10.01.67 | **Ashford Town** (SL) | H | W | 5-0 | Brown, Rogers 2 (1p), Walker, Penman |
| | | 3 | 28.01.67 | **West Ham Utd** (D1) | A | D | 3-3 | Rogers 2, Brown |
| | | 3r | 31.01.67 | **West Ham Utd** | H | W | 3-1 | Penman, Rogers, Skeen |
| | | 4 | 18.02.67 | **Bury** (D2) | H | W | 2-1 | Morgan, Rogers |
| | | 5 | 11.03.67 | **Nottingham Forest** (D1) | A | D | 0-0 | |
| | | 5r | 14.03.67 | **Nottingham Forest** | H | D | 1-1aet | Walker |
| | | 5 2r | 20.03.67 | **Nottingham Forest** *played at Villa Park* | | L | 0-3 | |
| 1967-68 | (D3) | 1 | 12.12.67 | **Salisbury City** (WL) | H | W | 4-0 | Penman, Terry 3 |
| | | 2 | 06.01.68 | **Luton Town** (D4) | H | W | 3-2 | Rogers 2 (1p), Heath |
| | | 3 | 27.01.68 | **Blackburn Rovers** (D2) | H | W | 1-0 | Nurse |
| | | 4 | 17.02.68 | **Sheffield Wed** (D1) | A | L | 1-2 | Smart |
| 1968-69 | (D3) | 1 | 16.11.68 | **Canterbury City** (SL) | H | W | 1-0 | Rogers (p) |
| | | 2 | 07.12.68 | **Grantham Town** (ML) | A | W | 2-0 | Jones, Smith |
| | | 3 | 04.01.69 | **Southend Utd** (D4) | H | L | 0-2 | |
| 1969-70 | (D2) | 3 | 03.01.70 | **Blackburn Rovers** (D2) | A | W | 4-0 | Smith, Horsfield, Rogers, Butler |
| | | 4 | 24.01.70 | **Chester** (D4) | H | W | 4-2 | Horsfield 2, Jones, Smart |
| | | 5 | 07.02.70 | **Scunthorpe Utd** (D4) | H | W | 3-1 | Noble, Horsfield, Trollope |
| | | 6 | 21.02.70 | **Leeds Utd** (D1) | H | L | 0-2 | |
| 1970-71 | (D2) | 3 | 02.01.71 | **QPR** (D2) | A | W | 2-1 | Horsfield, Noble |
| | | 4 | 23.01.71 | **Leeds Utd** (D1) | A | L | 0-4 | |
| 1971-72 | (D2) | 3 | 15.01.72 | **Arsenal** (D1) | H | L | 0-2 | |
| 1972-73 | (D2) | 3 | 13.01.73 | **Birmingham City** (D1) | H | W | 2-0 | Butler, Treacey (p) |
| | | 4 | 03.02.73 | **WBA** (D1) | A | L | 0-2 | |
| 1973-74 | (D2) | 3 | 05.01.74 | **Portsmouth** (D2) | H | D | 3-3 | Jenkins, Moss, Trollope |

| | | | | | | | |
|---|---|---|---|---|---|---|---|
| | 3r | 09.01.74 | **Portsmouth** | A | L | 0-1 | |
| 1974-75 (D3) | 1 | 23.11.74 | **Reading** (D4) | H | W | 4-0 | Anderson, Eastoe, Lenarduzzi og, Moss (p) |
| | 2 | 14.12.74 | **Maidstone Utd** (SL) | H | W | 3-1 | Prophett, Eastoe 2 |
| | 3 | 04.01.75 | **Lincoln City** (D4) | H | W | 2-0 | Eastoe, Moss |
| | 4 | 25.01.75 | **West Ham Utd** (D1) | A | D | 1-1 | Eastoe |
| | 4r | 28.01.75 | **West Ham Utd** | H | L | 1-2 | Anderson |
| 1975-76 (D3) | 1 | 22.11.75 | **Newport County** (D4) | A | D | 2-2 | Moss, Syrett |
| | 1r | 25.11.75 | **Newport County** | H | W | 3-0 | Love og, Trollope, Dixon |
| | 2 | 13.12.75 | **Hendon** (IL) | A | W | 1-0 | Moss (p) |
| | 3 | 03.01.76 | **Tooting & M** (IL) | H | D | 2-2 | Eastoe, Dixon |
| | 3r | 06.01.76 | **Tooting & M** | A | L | 1-2 | Green og |
| 1976-77 (D3) | 1 | 20.11.76 | **Bromley** (IL) | H | W | 7-0 | McHale, Syrett 2, Moss 2, Anderson 2 |
| | 2 | 11.12.76 | **Hitchin Town** (IL) | A | D | 1-1 | Dixon |
| | 2r | 21.12.76 | **Hitchin Town** | H | W | 3-1aet | Syrett, Moss 2 |
| | 3 | 08.01.77 | **Fulham** (D2) | A | D | 3-3 | Anderson, Moss, McHale |
| | 3r | 11.01.77 | **Fulham** | H | W | 5-0 | Anderson, Syrett 2, Moss 2 |
| | 4 | 29.01.77 | **Everton** (D1) | H | D | 2-2 | Syrett, Stroud |
| | 4r | 01.02.77 | **Everton** | A | L | 1-2 | Anderson |
| 1977-78 (D3) | 1 | 26.11.77 | **Borehamwood** (AL) | A | D | 0-0 | |
| | 1r | 29.11.77 | **Borehamwood** | H | W | 2-0 | Moss, McHale |
| | 2 | 17.12.77 | **Brentford** (D4) | H | W | 2-1 | Prophett, McHale |
| | 3 | 07.01.78 | **Nottingham Forest** (D1) | A | L | 1-4 | Moss |
| 1978-79 (D3) | 1 | 25.11.78 | **March Town Utd** (ECL) | H | W | 2-0 | Gilchrist, Bates |
| | 2 | 16.12.78 | **Enfield** (IL) | H | W | 3-0 | Bates, Carter, Gilchrist |
| | 3 | 09.01.79 | **Cardiff City** (D2) | H | W | 3-0 | McHale, Kamara 2 |
| | 4 | 30.01.79 | **Aldershot** (D4) | A | L | 1-2 | Rowland |
| 1979-80 (D3) | 1 | 24.11.79 | **Brentford** (D3) | H | W | 4-1 | Miller 2, Kamara, Carter |
| | 2 | 18.12.79 | **Torquay Utd** (D4) | A | D | 3-3 | Mayes, Tucker, Rowland |
| | 2r | 22.12.79 | **Torquay Utd** | H | W | 3-2 | Rowland, Mayes 2 |
| | 3 | 05.01.80 | **Luton Town** (D2) | A | W | 2-0 | Rowland, Williams |
| | 4 | 26.01.80 | **Tottenham Hotspur** (D1) | H | D | 0-0 | |
| | 4r | 30.01.80 | **Tottenham Hotspur** | A | L | 1-2 | McHale (p) |
| 1980-81 (D3) | 1 | 22.11.80 | **Weymouth** (APL) | H | W | 3-2 | Mayes, Lewis, Kamara |
| | 2 | 13.12.80 | **Wimbledon** (D4) | A | L | 0-2 | |
| 1981-82 (D3) | 1 | 21.11.81 | **Taunton Town** (WL) | H | W | 2-1 | Pritchard 2 |
| | 2 | 15.12.81 | **Sutton Utd** (IL) | H | W | 2-1 | Carter, Pritchard |
| | 3 | 02.01.82 | **Luton Town** (D2) | A | L | 1-2 | Emmanuel |
| 1982-83 (D4) | 1 | 20.11.82 | **Wealdstone** (APL) | H | W | 2-0 | Henry, Rideout |
| | 2 | 11.12.82 | **Brentford** (D3) | H | D | 2-2 | Lewis, Barnard |
| | 2r | 14.12.82 | **Brentford** | A | W | 3-1aet | Rowland, Pritchard, Batty |
| | 3 | 08.01.83 | **Aldershot** (D4) | H | W | 7-0 | Pritchard 3, Rowland 3, Batty |
| | 4 | 29.01.83 | **Burnley** (D2) | A | L | 1-3 | Pritchard |
| 1983-84 (D4) | 1 | 19.11.83 | **Kettering Town** (APL) | A | W | 7-0 | Gibson, Quinn 2, Rowland, Henry, Batty |
| | 2 | 10.12.83 | **Millwall** (D3) | A | W | 3-2 | Quinn 2, Batty |
| | 3 | 07.01.84 | **Carlisle Utd** (D2) | A | D | 1-1 | Rowland |
| | 3r | 10.01.84 | **Carlisle Utd** | H | W | 3-1 | Quinn, Batty, Rowland |
| | 4 | 28.01.84 | **Blackburn Rovers** (D2) | H | L | 1-2 | Quinn |
| 1984-85 (D4) | 1 | 19.11.84 | **Dagenham** (APL) | A | D | 0-0 | |
| | 1r | 26.11.84 | **Dagenham** | H | L | 1-2aet | Mayes |
| 1985-86 (D4) | 1 | 17.11.85 | **Bristol City** (D3) | H | D | 0-0 | |
| | 1r | 20.11.85 | **Bristol City** | A | L | 2-4 | Ramsey, Barnard |
| 1986-87 (D3) | 1 | 15.11.86 | **Farnborough T** (IL) | H | W | 4-0 | Coyne, Wade, Gilligan, Baker og |
| | 2 | 06.12.86 | **Enfield** (Conf) | H | W | 3-0 | Wade, Bamber, Jones |
| | 3 | 10.01.87 | **Fulham** (D3) | A | W | 1-0 | Bamber |
| | 4 | 03.02.87 | **Leeds Utd** (D2) | H | L | 1-2 | Bamber |
| 1987-88 (D2) | 3 | 09.01.88 | **Norwich City** (D1) | H | D | 0-0 | |
| | 3r | 13.01.88 | **Norwich City** | A | W | 2-0 | Bamber 2 |
| | 4 | 30.01.88 | **Newcastle Utd** (D1) | A | L | 0-5 | |
| 1988-89 (D2) | 3 | 07.01.89 | **Portsmouth** (D2) | A | D | 1-1 | Foley |

| | | | | | | | | |
|---|---|---|---|---|---|---|---|---|
| | | 3r | 10.01.89 | **Portsmouth** | H | W | 2-0 | Foley, Shearer |
| | | 4 | 28.01.89 | **West Ham Utd** (D1) | H | D | 0-0 | |
| | | 4r | 01.02.89 | **West Ham Utd** | A | L | 0-1 | |
| 1989-90 | (D2) | 3 | 06.01.90 | **Bristol City** (D3) | A | L | 1-2 | Shearer |
| 1990-91 | (D2) | 3 | 05.01.91 | **Leyton Orient** (D3) | A | D | 1-1 | Shearer |
| | | 3r | 14.01.91 | **Leyton Orient** | H | - | 1-1ab | Bodin |
| | | | | *abandoned after 54 minutes – frozen pitch* | | | | |
| | | 3r | 21.01.91 | **Leyton Orient** | H | W | 1-0 | White |
| | | 4 | 26.01.91 | **Norwich City** (D1) | A | L | 1-3 | White |
| 1991-92 | (D2) | 3 | 04.01.92 | **Watford** (D2) | H | W | 3-2 | Shearer 2, Mitchell |
| | | 4 | 25.01.92 | **Cambridge Utd** (D2) | A | W | 3-0 | Calderwood, Shearer 2 |
| | | 5 | 16.02.92 | **Aston Villa** (D1) | H | L | 1-2 | Mitchell |
| 1992-93 | (D1) | 3 | 02.01.93 | **QPR** (PL) | A | L | 0-3 | |
| 1993-94 | (PL) | 3 | 08.01.94 | **Ipswich Town** (PL) | H | D | 1-1 | Mutch |
| | | 3r | 18.01.94 | **Ipswich Town** | A | L | 1-2aet | Fjortoft |
| 1994-95 | (D1) | 3 | 07.01.95 | **Marlow** (IL) | H | W | 2-0 | Fjortoft, Nijholt |
| | | 4 | 28.01.95 | **Watford** (D1) | A | L | 0-1 | |
| 1995-96 | (D2) | 1 | 11.11.95 | **Cambridge Utd** (D3) | H | W | 4-1 | Horlock 2, Finney, Allen |
| | | 2 | 02.12.95 | **Cardiff City** (D3) | H | W | 2-0 | Allison, Finney |
| | | 3 | 06.01.96 | **Woking** (Conf) | H | W | 2-0 | Allison, Bodin |
| | | 4 | 12.02.96 | **Oldham Athletic** (D1) | H | W | 1-0 | Ling |
| | | 5 | 17.02.96 | **Southampton** (PL) | H | D | 1-1 | Horlock |
| | | 5r | 28.02.96 | **Southampton** | A | L | 0-2 | |
| 1996-97 | (D1) | 3 | 05.01.97 | **Everton** (PL) | A | L | 0-3 | |
| 1997-98 | (D1) | 3 | 03.01.98 | **Stevenage B** (Conf) | H | L | 1-2 | Walters |
| 1998-99 | (D1) | 3 | 02.01.99 | **Barnsley** (D1) | H | D | 0-0 | |
| | | 3r | 19.01.99 | **Barnsley** | A | L | 1-3 | Walters |
| 1999-00 | (D1) | 3 | 11.12.99 | **Charlton Athletic** (D1) | A | L | 1-2 | Gooden |
| 2000-01 | (D2) | 1 | 18.11.00 | **Ilkeston Town** (SL) | H | W | 4-1 | Willis, M Williams, Howe, Young |
| | | 2 | 09.12.00 | **Gateshead** (NPL) | H | W | 5-0 | O'Halloran 2, Cowe 2, Howe |
| | | 3 | 06.01.01 | **Coventry City** (PL) | H | L | 0-2 | |
| 2001-02 | (D2) | 1 | 17.11.01 | **Hartlepool Utd** (D3) | H | W | 3-1 | Ruddock (p), Invincible, Heywood |
| | | 2 | 08.12.01 | **Hereford Utd** (Conf) | H | W | 3-2 | Invincible, P Edwards, Howe |
| | | 3 | 05.01.02 | **Manchester City** (D1) | A | L | 0-2 | |
| 2002-03 | (D2) | 1 | 16.11.02 | **Huddersfield Town** (D2) | H | W | 1-0 | Gurney |
| | | 2 | 07.12.02 | **Oxford Utd** (D3) | A | L | 0-1 | |

## TAMWORTH

*Formed 1933. First entered FA Cup: 1934-35. FA Trophy runners-up: 2003. FA Vase winners: 1989. League club beaten: Torquay United. Members of The Conference.*

| | | | | | | | | |
|---|---|---|---|---|---|---|---|---|
| 1966-67 | (WMRL) | 1 | 26.11.66 | **Gillingham** (D3) | A | L | 1-4 | McCarthy |
| 1969-70 | (WMRL) | 1 | 15.11.69 | **Torquay Utd** (D3) | H | W | 2-1 | Holmes, Jessop |
| | | 2 | 06.12.69 | **Gillingham** (D3) | A | L | 0-6 | |
| 1970-71 | (WMRL) | 1 | 21.11.70 | **York City** (D4) | H | D | 0-0 | |
| | | 1r | 23.11.70 | **York City** | A | L | 0-5 | |
| 1987-88 | (WMRL) | 1 | 14.11.87 | **Colchester Utd** (D4) | A | L | 0-3 | |
| 1990-91 | (SL) | 1 | 17.11.90 | **Whitley Bay** (NPL) | H | L | 4-6 | Eccleston, Smith 2, Gordon |
| 1998-99 | (SL) | 1 | 14.11.98 | **Exeter City** (D3) | H | D | 2-2 | Shaw, Smith |
| | | 1r | 24.11.98 | **Exeter City** | A | L | 1-4 | Smith |
| 1999-00 | (SL) | 1 | 30.10.99 | **Bury** (D2) | H | D | 2-2 | Haughton, Hallam |
| | | 1r | 09.11.99 | **Bury** | A | L | 1-2aet | Haughton |
| 2001-02 | (SL) | 1 | 17.11.01 | **Rochdale** (D3) | H | D | 1-1 | Wilson |
| | | 1r | 27.11.01 | **Rochdale** | A | L | 0-1 | |

## TAUNTON TOWN

*Formed 1947. First entered FA Cup: 1970-71. FA Vase winners: 2001. Runners-up: 1994. Members of the Southern League.*

| | | | | | | | | |
|---|---|---|---|---|---|---|---|---|
| 1981-82 | (WL) | 1 | 21.11.81 | **Swindon Town** (D3) | A | L | 1-2 | Hains |

# TAUNTON TOWN (1927)

*Originally known as Taunton United, they changed their name to Taunton Town in 1927. Entered FA Cup: 1928-29 – 1933-34. No connection to modern-day Taunton Town formed in 1947.*

| | | | | | | | | | |
|---|---|---|---|---|---|---|---|---|---|
| 1930-31 | (WL) | 1 | 29.11.30 | **Crystal Palace** | (3S) | A | L | 0-6 | |

# TEAM BATH

*Formed 2000. First entered FA Cup: 2002-03. Bath University's football team became the first student team since Oxford University in 1880 to play in the Competition Proper when they reached the First Round in 2002. Completed a memorable 2002-03 season by finishing champions and gaining promotion from the Western League.*

| | | | | | | | | | |
|---|---|---|---|---|---|---|---|---|---|
| 2002-03 | (WL) | 1 | 16.11.02 | **Mansfield Town** | (D2) | H | L | 2-4 | Heiniger, Kamara-Taylor |

# TELFORD UNITED

*Formed 1876 as Wellington Town. Telford United 1970. First entered FA Cup (as Wellington Town): 1895-96. FA Trophy winners: 1971, 1983, 1989. Runners-up: 1970; 1988. Welsh FA Cup winners: 1902, 1906, 1940. Six men who played in FA Cup finals later managed or coached the club: Gordon Banks, Geoff Hurst, Alan Spavin, Ron Flowers, Johnny Hancocks and Gerry Daly. League clubs beaten: Wigan Athletic, Stockport County (2), Northampton Town, Rochdale, Lincoln City, Preston North End, Bradford City, Darlington, Burnley, Stoke City. In 1984-85 Telford beat four Football League clubs and reached the fifth round of the competition. Members of The Conference.*

**as Wellington Town**

| | | | | | | | | | |
|---|---|---|---|---|---|---|---|---|---|
| 1925-26 | (BDL) | 1 | 28.11.25 | **Doncaster Rovers** | (3N) | A | L | 0-2 | |
| 1926-27 | (BDL) | 1 | 27.11.26 | **Mansfield Town** | (ML) | H | L | 1-2 | Jones |
| 1927-28 | (BDL) | 1 | 26.11.27 | **Southend Utd** | (3S) | A | L | 0-1 | |
| 1929-30 | (BDL) | 1 | 30.11.29 | **Stockport County** | (3N) | H | L | 1-4 | Prowse |
| 1930-31 | (BDL) | 1 | 29.11.30 | **Wombwell Town** | (ML) | H | D | 0-0 | |
| | | 1r | 04.12.30 | **Wombwell Town** | | A | W | 3-0 | Capewell, Shirley, Lloyd |
| | | 2 | 13.12.30 | **Wrexham** | (3N) | H | L | 2-4 | Bromage, Shirley |
| 1936-37 | (BDL) | 1 | 28.11.36 | **Accrington Stanley** | (3N) | A | L | 1-3 | Sims |
| 1937-38 | (BDL) | 1 | 27.11.37 | **Mansfield Town** | (3S) | H | L | 1-2 | Griffiths |
| 1938-39 | (CC) | 1 | 26.11.38 | **Runcorn** | (CC) | A | L | 0-3 | |
| 1945-46 | (CC) | 1 1L | 17.11.45 | **Port Vale** | (3S) | A | L | 0-4 | |
| | | 1 2L | 24.11.45 | **Port Vale** | | H | L | 0-2 | |
| 1946-47 | (CC) | 1 | 30.11.46 | **Watford** | (3S) | H | D | 1-1 | Hopley |
| | | 1r | 04.12.46 | **Watford** | | A | L | 0-1 | |
| 1948-49 | (CC) | 1 | 27.11.48 | **Norwich City** | (3S) | A | L | 0-1 | |
| 1952-53 | (CC) | 1 | 22.11.52 | **Gillingham** | (3S) | H | D | 1-1 | Ford |
| | | 1r | 26.11.52 | **Gillingham** | | A | L | 0-3 | |
| 1953-54 | (CC) | 1 | 21.11.53 | **Aldershot** | (3S) | A | L | 3-5 | Skull, Davies, Turner |
| 1954-55 | (CC) | 1 | 20.11.54 | **Merthyr Tydfil** | (SL) | A | D | 1-1 | Windsor |
| | | 1r | 24.11.54 | **Merthyr Tydfil** | | H | L | 1-6 | Antonio (p) |
| 1962-63 | (SL) | 1 | 03.11.62 | **Bristol City** | (D3) | A | L | 2-4 | Russell, Rodgers |

**as Telford United**

| | | | | | | | | | |
|---|---|---|---|---|---|---|---|---|---|
| 1969-70 | (SL) | 1 | 15.11.69 | **Bristol Rovers** | (D3) | H | L | 0-3 | |
| 1970-71 | (SL) | 1 | 21.11.70 | **Walton & H** | (AL) | A | W | 5-2 | Owen, Harris, Jagger, Bentley, Fudge |
| | | 2 | 12.12.70 | **Swansea City** | (D3) | A | L | 2-6 | Fudge, Ray |
| 1971-72 | (SL) | 1 | 20.11.71 | **Bristol Rovers** | (D3) | A | L | 0-3 | |
| 1972-73 | (SL) | 1 | 18.11.72 | **Nuneaton B** | (SL) | H | W | 3-2 | Jones og, Fudge, Colton |
| | | 2 | 09.12.72 | **Chelmsford City** | (SL) | A | L | 0-5 | |
| 1973-74 | (SL) | 1 | 24.11.73 | **Chester** | (D4) | A | L | 0-1 | |
| 1982-83 | (APL) | 1 | 21.11.82 | **Wigan Athletic** | (D3) | A | D | 0-0 | |
| | | 1r | 23.11.82 | **Wigan Athletic** | | H | W | 2-1 | Walker, Neale |
| | | 2 | 11.12.82 | **Tranmere Rovers** | (D4) | H | D | 1-1 | Mather (p) |
| | | 2r | 14.12.82 | **Tranmere Rovers** | | A | L | 1-2 | Mather |
| 1983-84 | (APL) | 1 | 19.11.83 | **Stockport County** | (D4) | H | W | 3-0 | Mather 2, Barnett |
| | | 2 | 10.12.83 | **Northampton Town** | (D4) | A | D | 1-1 | Burrows og |
| | | 2r | 14.12.83 | **Northampton Town** | | H | W | 3-2 | Bailey, Williams, Mather (p) |
| | | 3 | 07.01.84 | **Rochdale** | (D4) | A | W | 4-1 | Edwards, Bailey, Hogan, Williams |
| | | 4 | 01.02.84 | **Derby County** | (D2) | A | L | 2-3 | Eaton, Bailey |
| 1984-85 | (APL) | 1 | 17.11.84 | **Lincoln City** | (D3) | A | D | 1-1 | Turner (p) |
| | | 1r | 20.11.84 | **Lincoln City** | | H | W | 2-1 | Williams 2 |

| | | | | | | | | |
|---|---|---|---|---|---|---|---|---|
| | | 2 | 08.12.84 | **Preston North End** (D3) | A | W | 4-1 | Turner, McKenna, Williams 2 |
| | | 3 | 05.01.85 | **Bradford City** (D3) | H | W | 2-1 | Williams, Hancock |
| | | 4 | 29.01.85 | **Darlington** (D4) | A | D | 1-1 | Williams |
| | | 4r | 04.02.85 | **Darlington** | H | W | 3-0 | Mather, Hogan, Alcock |
| | | 5 | 16.02.85 | **Everton** (D1) | A | L | 0-3 | |
| 1985-86 | (APL) | 1 | 16.11.85 | **Stockport County** (D4) | A | W | 1-0 | McGinty (p) |
| | | 2 | 09.12.85 | **Derby County** (D3) | A | L | 1-6 | McKenna |
| 1986-87 | (Conf) | 1 | 15.11.86 | **Burnley** (D4) | H | W | 3-0 | Morgan, McGinty (p), McKenna |
| | | 2 | 06.12.86 | **Altrincham** (Conf) | H | W | 1-0 | Williams |
| | | 3 | 11.01.87 | **Leeds Utd** (D2) | H | L | 1-2 | Williams |
| | | | | *played at The Hawthorns* | | | | |
| 1987-88 | (Conf) | 1 | 14.11.87 | **Stockport County** (D4) | H | D | 1-1 | Biggins |
| | | 1r | 17.11.87 | **Stockport County** | A | L | 0-2 | |
| 1988-89 | (Conf) | 1 | 19.11.88 | **Carlisle Utd** (D4) | H | D | 1-1 | Lloyd |
| | | 1r | 22.11.88 | **Carlisle Utd** | A | L | 1-4 | Hanchard |
| 1989-90 | (Conf) | 1 | 18.11.89 | **Walsall** (D3) | H | L | 0-3 | |
| 1990-91 | (Conf) | 1 | 17.11.90 | **Stoke City** (D3) | H | D | 0-0 | |
| | | 1r | 21.11.90 | **Stoke City** | A | L | 0-1 | |
| 1991-92 | (Conf) | 1 | 16.11.91 | **Stoke City** (D3) | A | D | 0-0 | |
| | | 1r | 26.11.91 | **Stoke City** | H | W | 2-1 | Benbow 2 |
| | | 2 | 07.12.91 | **Wrexham** (D4) | H | L | 0-1 | |
| 1993-94 | (Conf) | 1 | 13.11.93 | **Huddersfield Town** (D2) | H | D | 1-1 | Bignot |
| | | 1r | 23.11.93 | **Huddersfield Town** | A | L | 0-1 | |
| 1995-96 | (Conf) | 1 | 11.11.95 | **Witton Albion** (NPL) | H | W | 2-1 | Foster, Langford |
| | | 2 | 02.12.95 | **Notts County** (D2) | H | L | 0-2 | |
| 1998-99 | (Conf) | 1 | 14.11.98 | **Cambridge Utd** (D3) | H | L | 0-2 | |
| 2000-01 | (Conf) | 1 | 18.11.00 | **Blackpool** (D2) | A | L | 1-3 | Martindale |

## THAMES

*Formed 1928. Entered FA Cup: 1929-30 – 1931-32. Members of the Football League: 1930-32. Folded 1932. Short-lived London-based League club. Jimmy Dimmock, who scored the winning goal for Tottenham Hotspur in the 1921 FA Cup final, scored two of the three Thames' goals scored in the four FA Cup matches they played. Thames played at West Ham Stadium, Prince Regent's Lane, Custom House, which at one time had a capacity of 120,000. It was demolished in the early 1970s.*

| | | | | | | | | |
|---|---|---|---|---|---|---|---|---|
| 1929-30 | (SL) | 1 | 30.11.29 | **Fulham** (3S) | A | L | 0-4 | |
| 1930-31 | (3S) | 1 | 29.11.30 | **QPR** (3S) | A | L | 0-5 | |
| 1931-32 | (3S) | 1 | 28.11.31 | **Watford** (3S) | H | D | 2-2 | Dimmock, Lennox |
| | | 1r | 01.12.31 | **Watford** | A | L | 1-2 | Dimmock |

## THIRD LANARK

*Formed 1872. One of the seven Scottish clubs that took part in the FA Cup in the 1880s. Scottish FA Cup winners: 1889, 1905. Runners-up: 1876, 1878, 1906, 1936. Folded 1967.*

| | | | | | | | | |
|---|---|---|---|---|---|---|---|---|
| 1885-86 | | 1 | 17.10.85 | **Blackburn Park Road** | H | W | 4-2 | |
| | | 2 | | Church FC | | | - | |
| | | | | *Third Lanark scratched. Church walkover* | | | | |
| 1886-87 | | 1 | 16.10.86 | **Higher Walton** | H | W | 5-0 | Marshall 2, McIntyre, Park, Thompson |
| | | 2 | 13.11.86 | **Bolton Wanderers** | H | L | 2-3 | McIntyre, J Weir |

## THORNYCROFTS

*Works club based at Woolston, Hampshire. Entered FA Cup: 1919-20 – 1924-25. Folded 1926.*

| | | | | | | | | |
|---|---|---|---|---|---|---|---|---|
| 1919-20 | (HL) | 1 | 10.01. | **Burnley** (D1) | H | D | 0-0 | |
| | | | | *played at The Dell, Southampton* | | | | |
| | | 1r | 13.01. | **Burnley** | A | L | 0-5 | |

## TILBURY

*Formed 1900. First entered FA Cup: 1927-28. Members of the Isthmian League.*

| | | | | | | | | |
|---|---|---|---|---|---|---|---|---|
| 1949-50 | (Lon) | 1 | 26.11.49 | **Notts County** (3S) | A | L | 0-4 | |
| 1977-78 | (IL) | 1 | 26.11.77 | **Kettering Town** (SL) | H | L | 0-1 | |
| | | | | *FA declared match void as Kettering fielded ineligible player* | | | | |
| | | 1 | 05.12.77 | **Kettering Town** | H | D | 2-2 | Smith 2 |
| | | 1r | 07.12.77 | **Kettering Town** | A | W | 3-2 | Gray, C Wallace, Barnett |
| | | 2 | 17.12.77 | **Nuneaton B** (SL) | A | W | 2-1 | C Wallace, Gray |
| | | 3 | 07.01.78 | **Stoke City** (D2) | A | L | 0-4 | |

## TIVERTON TOWN

*Formed 1920. First entered FA Cup: 1933-34. FA Vase winners: 1998, 1999. Runners-up: 1993. Members of the Southern League.*

| | | | | | | | | |
|---|---|---|---|---|---|---|---|---|
| 1990-91 | (WL) | 1 | 17.11.90 | **Aldershot** (D4) | A | L | 2-6 | Jones, Durham |
| 1991-92 | (WL) | 1 | 16.11.91 | **Barnet** (D4) | A | L | 0-5 | |
| 1994-95 | (WL) | 1 | 12.11.94 | **Leyton Orient** (D2) | H | L | 1-3 | Smith |
| 1997-98 | (WL) | 1 | 15.11.97 | **Cheltenham Town** (Conf) | A | L | 1-2 | Saunders |
| 2001-02 | (SL) | 1 | 17.11.01 | **Cardiff City** (D2) | H | L | 1-3 | Nancekivell |
| | | | | *played at Ninian Park* | | | | |
| 2002-03 | (SL) | 1 | 16.11.02 | **Crawley Town** (SL) | H | D | 1-1 | Pears |
| | | 1r | 26.11.02 | **Crawley Town** | A | L | 2-3 | Pears 2 |

## TON PENTRE

*Reformed 1935. First entered FA Cup: 1909-10. Members of the Welsh League.*

| | | | | | | | | |
|---|---|---|---|---|---|---|---|---|
| 1986-87 | (Welsh) | 1 | 15.11.86 | **Cardiff City** (D4) | H | L | 1-4 | Bees |

## TONBRIDGE

*Formed 1948. First entered FA Cup: 1948-49. Members of the Southern League.*

| | | | | | | | | |
|---|---|---|---|---|---|---|---|---|
| 1950-51 | (SL) | 1 | 25.11.50 | **Chelmsford City** (SL) | A | D | 2-2 | Mills, Mulheron |
| | | 1r | 29.11.50 | **Chelmsford City** | H | L | 0-1aet | |
| 1951-52 | (SL) | 1 | 24.11.51 | **Aldershot** (3S) | H | D | 0-0 | |
| | | 1r | 28.11.51 | **Aldershot** | A | L | 2-3aet | Jordan, Suttle |
| 1952-53 | (SL) | 1 | 22.11.52 | **Norwich City** (3S) | H | D | 2-2 | Mulheron, Butler |
| | | 1r | 27.11.52 | **Norwich City** | A | L | 0-1 | |
| 1967-68 | (SL) | 1 | 09.12.67 | **Dagenham** (AL) | A | L | 0-1 | |
| 1972-73 | (SL) | 1 | 18.11.72 | **Charlton Athletic** (D3) | H | L | 0-5 | |

## TOOTING & MITCHAM UNITED

*Formed 1931 by the amalgamation of Tooting FC (formed 1887) and Mitcham FC (1912) . First entered FA Cup as Tooting & Mitcham: 1945-46. League clubs beaten: Bournemouth, Northampton Town, Swindon Town. Members of the Isthmian League.*

| | | | | | | | | |
|---|---|---|---|---|---|---|---|---|
| 1948-49 | (AL) | 1 | 27.11.48 | **Millwall** (3S) | A | L | 0-1 | |
| 1950-51 | (AL) | 1 | 25.11.50 | **Brighton** (3S) | H | L | 2-3 | Rhodes, Parker |
| 1956-57 | (IL) | 1 | 17.11.56 | **Bromsgrove R** (BDL) | H | W | 2-1 | Hasty, Bumpstead |
| | | 2 | 08.12.56 | **QPR** (3S) | H | L | 0-2 | |
| 1958-59 | (IL) | 1 | 15.11.58 | **Bournemouth** (D3) | H | W | 3-1 | Viney 2, Slade |
| | | 2 | 06.12.58 | **Northampton Town** (D4) | H | W | 2-1 | Viney, Hasty |
| | | 3 | 10.01.59 | **Nottingham Forest** (D1) | H | D | 2-2 | Grainger, Murphy |
| | | 3r | 24.01.59 | **Nottingham Forest** | A | L | 0-3 | |
| 1963-64 | (IL) | 1 | 16.11.63 | **Gravesend & N** (SL) | H | L | 1-2 | Browning |
| 1974-75 | (IL) | 1 | 27.11.74 | **Crystal Palace** (D3) | H | L | 1-2 | Grubb |
| 1975-76 | (IL) | 1 | 22.11.75 | **Romford** (SL) | A | W | 1-0 | Ives |
| | | 2 | 13.12.75 | **Leatherhead** (IL) | A | D | 0-0 | |
| | | 2r | 16.12.75 | **Leatherhead** | H | - | 1-1ab | Juneman (p) |
| | | | | *abandoned after 57 minutes – icy pitch* | | | | |
| | | 2r | 22.12.75 | **Leatherhead** | H | W | 2-1aet | Juneman (p), Howell |
| | | 3 | 03.01.76 | **Swindon Town** (D3) | A | D | 2-2 | Glover, Casey |
| | | 3r | 06.01.76 | **Swindon Town** | H | W | 2-1 | Juneman, Ives |
| | | 4 | 24.01.76 | **Bradford City** (D4) | A | L | 1-3 | Juneman |
| 1976-77 | (IL) | 1 | 20.11.76 | **Dartford** (SL) | H | W | 4-2 | Ives 2 (2p), Juneman, Glover |
| | | 2 | 11.12.76 | **Kettering Town** (SL) | A | L | 0-1 | |
| 1977-78 | (IL) | 1 | 26.11.77 | **Northampton Town** (D4) | H | L | 1-2 | Smith |

## TORQUAY UNITED

*Formed 1898 as Torquay Town. Merged with Babbacombe FC to become Torquay United in 1921. Neither Torquay Town or Babbacombe United reached the Competition Proper. FA Cup best performance: 4th round, 1949, 1955, 1971, 1983, 1990. Record FA Cup win: 7-1 v Northampton Town, 1st round, 14.11.1959; Record FA Cup defeat: 1-7 v Birmingham City, 3rd round, 07.01.1956.*

| | | |
|---|---|---|
| 1921-22 | (WL) | P Frome Town (H) 1-1; Pr Frome Town (A) 3-1; 1q Spencer Moulton (H) 5-2; 2q St Georges Sports (H) 6-0; 3q Hanham Athletic (H) 2-2; 3qr Hanham Athletic (A) 3-1; 4q Boscombe (H) 0-1 |
| 1922-23 | (SL) | P Clevedon (H) 3-0; 1q Welton Rovers(A) 2-3 |

| | | | | | | | | |
|---|---|---|---|---|---|---|---|---|
| 1923-24 | (SL) | | | ExP Taunton & Newton Utd (A) 3-0; P Green Waves (A) 3-0; 1q Coleford A (A) 6-0; 2q Trowbridge Town (H) 3-0; 3q Yeovil & Petters (A) 1-1; 3qr Yeovil & Petters (H) 2-1; 4q Aberdare Athletic (H) 0-0; 4qr Aberdare At (A) 0-4 | | | | |
| 1924-25 | (SL) | | | P Green Waves (H) 2-0; 1q Taunton & Newton Utd (H) 1-1; 1q Taunton & Newton Utd (A) 1-2 | | | | |
| 1925-26 | (SL) | | | 4q Yeovil & Petters (H) 3-1 | | | | |
| | | 1 | 28.11.25 | **Reading** (3S) | H | D | 1-1 | Valla |
| | | 1r | 02.12.25 | **Reading** | A | D | 1-1aet | Appleyard |
| | | 1 2r | 07.12.25 | **Reading** | | L | 0-2 | |
| | | | | *played at Ashton Gate* | | | | |
| 1926-27 | (SL) | 1 | 27.11.26 | **Bristol Rovers** (3S) | H | D | 1-1 | Bloxham |
| | | 1r | 01.12.26 | **Bristol Rovers** | A | L | 0-1 | |
| 1927-28 | (3S) | | | did not enter | | | | |
| 1928-29 | (3S) | 1 | 24.11.28 | **Gillingham** (3S) | A | D | 0-0 | |
| | | 1r | 28.11.28 | **Gillingham** | H | W | 5-1 | Gardiner 2, Waller, Kelly, Hemingway |
| | | 2 | 08.12.28 | **Exeter City** (3S) | H | L | 0-1 | |
| 1929-30 | (3S) | 1 | 30.11.29 | **Bournemouth** (3S) | A | L | 0-2 | |
| 1930-31 | (3S) | 1 | 29.11.30 | **Southend Utd** (3S) | A | W | 1-0 | Trotter |
| | | 2 | 13.12.30 | **Accrington Stanley** (3N) | A | W | 1-0 | Bell |
| | | 3 | 10.01.31 | **Bury** (D2) | A | D | 1-1 | Trotter |
| | | 3r | 14.01.31 | **Bury** | H | L | 1-2aet | Trotter |
| 1931-32 | (3S) | 1 | 28.11.31 | **Southend Utd** (3S) | H | L | 1-3 | Trotter |
| 1932-33 | (3S) | 1 | 26.11.32 | **Bournemouth** (3S) | H | D | 0-0 | |
| | | 1r | 30.11.32 | **Bournemouth** | A | D | 2-2aet | Bird,Tennant |
| | | 1 2r | 05.12.32 | **Bournemouth** | | W | 3-2 | Stabb, Birkett, Hutchinson |
| | | | | *played at Ashton Gate* | | | | |
| | | *2* | *10.12.32* | ***QPR*** *(3S)* | *H* | *D* | *1-1* | *Hutchinson* |
| | | 2r | 15.12.32 | **QPR** | A | L | 1-3 | Stabb |
| 1933-34 | (3S) | 1 | 25.11.33 | **Margate** (SL) | H | D | 1-1 | Kennedy |
| | | 1r | 30.11.33 | **Margate** | A | W | 2-0 | Walters, Stabb |
| | | 2 | 09.12.33 | **Northampton Town** (3S) | A | L | 0-3 | |
| 1934-35 | (3S) | 1 | 24.11.34 | **Dulwich Hamlet** (IL) | A | W | 2-1 | Prothero, Walters |
| | | 2 | 08.12.34 | **Wigan Athletic** (CC) | A | L | 2-3 | Morgan, Protheroe |
| 1935-36 | (3S) | 1 | 30.11.35 | **Dulwich Hamlet** (IL) | A | W | 3-2 | Daniels, Dodds, SW Hunt |
| | | 2 | 14.12.35 | **Notts County** (3S) | A | L | 0-3 | |
| 1936-37 | (3S) | 1 | 28.11.36 | **Clapton Orient** (3S) | A | L | 1-2 | Lievesly |
| 1937-38 | (3S) | 1 | 27.11.37 | **Clapton Orient** | H | L | 1-2 | Shelley |
| 1938-39 | (3S) | 1 | 26.11.38 | **Exeter City** (3S) | H | W | 3-1 | Brown, Allen, Rhodes |
| | | 2 | 10.12.38 | **Ipswich Town** (3S) | A | L | 1-4 | Allen |
| 1945-46 | (3S) | 1 1L | 17.11.45 | **Newport County** (D2) | H | L | 0-1 | |
| | | 1 2L | 24.11.45 | **Newport County** | A | D | 1-1 | Conley |
| 1946-47 | (3S) | 1 | 30.11.46 | **Ipswich Town** (3S) | A | L | 0-2 | |
| 1947-48 | (3S) | 1 | 29.11.47 | **Watford** (3S) | A | D | 1-1aet | Hill |
| | | 1r | 06.12.47 | **Watford** | H | W | 3-0 | Conley, Shaw, Hill |
| | | 2 | 13.12.47 | **Northampton Town** (3S) | A | D | 1-1aet | Hill |
| | | 2r | 20.12.47 | **Northampton Town** | H | W | 2-0 | Hill, Mercer |
| | | 3 | 10.01.48 | **Stockport County** (3N) | A | L | 0-3 | |
| 1948-49 | (3S) | 1 | 27.11.48 | **Peterborough Utd** (ML) | A | W | 1-0 | Lewis |
| | | 2 | 11.12.48 | **Norwich City** (3S) | H | W | 3-1 | Collins 2, Cameron |
| | | 3 | 08.01.49 | **Coventry City** (D2) | H | W | 1-0 | Cameron |
| | | 4 | 29.01.49 | **Brentford** (D2) | A | L | 0-1 | |
| 1949-50 | (3S) | 1 | 26.11.49 | **Gravesend & N** (SL) | A | W | 3-1 | Cameron, Whitfield, Lewis |
| | | 2 | 10.12.49 | **Northampton Town** (3S) | A | L | 2-4 | Cameron, Conley |
| 1950-51 | (3S) | 1 | 24.11.50 | **Nottingham Forest** (3S) | A | L | 1-6 | Collins |
| 1951-52 | (3S) | 1 | 24.11.51 | **Bromley** (AL) | H | W | 3-2 | Northcott, Shaw 2 |
| | | 2 | 15.12.51 | **Swindon Town** (3S) | A | D | 3-3 | Collins, Edds 2 |
| | | 2r | 19.12.51 | **Swindon Town** | H | D | 1-1aet | Collins |
| | | 2 2r | 02.01.52 | **Swindon Town** | | L | 1-3 | Northcott |
| | | | | *played at Ashton Gate* | | | | |
| 1952-53 | (3S) | 1 | 22.11.52 | **Peterborough Utd** (ML) | A | L | 1-2 | Edds |
| 1953-54 | (3S) | 1 | 21.11.53 | **Bristol City** (3S) | H | L | 1-3 | Collins |

| | | | | | | | |
|---|---|---|---|---|---|---|---|
| 1954-55 (3S) | 1 | 20.11.54 | **Cambridge Utd** (ECL) | H | W | 4-0 | Collins, Dobbie 2, Bond |
| | 2 | 11.12.54 | **Blyth Spartans** (NEL) | A | W | 3-1 | JT Smith 2, Webber |
| | 3 | 08.01.55 | **Leeds Utd** (D2) | A | D | 2-2 | JT Smith 2 |
| | 3r | 12.01.55 | **Leeds Utd** | H | W | 4-0 | Collins, Dobbie, Shaw, Mills |
| | 4 | 29.01.55 | **Huddersfield Town** (D1) | H | L | 0-1 | |
| 1955-56 (3S) | 1 | 19.11.55 | **Colchester Utd** (3S) | H | W | 2-0 | S Collins, JT Smith |
| | 2 | 10.12.55 | **Shrewsbury Town** (3S) | A | D | 0-0 | |
| | 2r | 14.12.55 | **Shrewsbury Town** | H | W | 5-1 | A Collins 2, JT Smith, R Collins, Shaw |
| | 3 | 07.01.56 | **Birmingham City** (D1) | H | L | 1-7 | Shaw |
| 1956-57 (3S) | 1 | 17.11.56 | **Ely City** (PDL) | A | W | 6-2 | R Collins 3, Shaw, Calland 2 |
| | 2 | 08.12.56 | **Plymouth Argyle** (3S) | H | W | 1-0 | R Collins |
| | 3 | 05.01.57 | **New Brighton** (LC) | A | L | 1-2 | R Collins |
| 1957-58 (3S) | 1 | 16.11.57 | **Peterborough Utd** (ML) | A | D | 3-3 | Pym 2, Johnson |
| | 1r | 20.11.57 | **Peterborough Utd** | H | W | 1-0 | Johnson |
| | 2 | 07.12.57 | **Southend Utd** (3S) | H | D | 1-1 | Bond |
| | 2r | 11.12.57 | **Southend Utd** | A | L | 1-2 | Northcott |
| 1958-59 (D4) | 1 | 15.11.58 | **Port Vale** (D4) | H | W | 1-0 | Mills |
| | 2 | 06.12.58 | **Watford** (D4) | H | W | 2-0 | T Northcott, Cox |
| | 3 | 10.01.59 | **Newport County** (D3) | A | D | 0-0 | |
| | 3r | 14.01.59 | **Newport County** | H | L | 0-1 | |
| 1959-60 (D4) | 1 | 14.11.59 | **Northampton Town** (D4) | H | W | 7-1 | Bond 3, Pym 3, T Northcott |
| | 2 | 05.12.59 | **Gillingham** (D4) | A | D | 2-2 | Cox, Bond |
| | 2r | 09.12.59 | **Gillingham** | H | L | 1-2 | Pym |
| 1960-61 (D3) | 1 | 05.11.60 | **Weymouth** (SL) | A | W | 3-1 | Pym, T Northcott 2 |
| | 2 | 26.11.60 | **Peterborough Utd** (D4) | H | L | 1-3 | Court |
| 1961-62 (D3) | 1 | 04.11.61 | **Harwich & P** (ECL) | H | W | 5-1 | Pym 2 (1p), T Northcott, Wilson og, Spencer |
| | 2 | 25.11.61 | **Peterborough Utd** (D3) | H | L | 1-4 | Bond |
| 1962-63 (D4) | 1 | 03.11.62 | **Northampton Town** (D3) | A | W | 2-1 | Handley 2 |
| | 2 | 24.11.62 | **Shrewsbury Town** (D3) | A | L | 1-2 | T Northcott |
| 1963-64 (D4) | 1 | 16.11.63 | **Barnet** (AL) | H | W | 6-2 | Hancock 2, T Northcott, Swindells (p), Stubbs, Adlington |
| | 2 | 07.12.63 | **Aldershot** (D4) | H | L | 2-3 | Pym, Jenkins |
| 1964-65 (D4) | 1 | 14.11.64 | **Canterbury City** (SL) | A | W | 6-0 | Cox 2, Stubbs 2, T Northcott 2 |
| | 2 | 05.12.64 | **Colchester Utd** (D3) | H | W | 2-0 | Northcott, Stubbs |
| | 3 | 09.01.65 | **Tottenham Hotspur** (D1) | H | D | 3-3 | Stubbs 3 |
| | 3r | 18.01.65 | **Tottenham Hotspur** | A | L | 1-5 | Stubbs |
| 1965-66 (D4) | 1 | 13.11.65 | **Shrewsbury Town** (D3) | A | L | 1-2 | Spratt |
| 1966-67 (D3) | 1 | 26.11.66 | **Aldershot** (D4) | A | L | 1-2 | Clarke |
| 1967-68 (D3) | 1 | 12.12.67 | **Colchester Utd** (D3) | H | D | 1-1 | Welsh |
| | 1r | 18.12.67 | **Colchester Utd** | A | L | 1-2 | Barnes |
| 1968-69 (D3) | 1 | 16.11.68 | **Hereford Utd** (SL) | A | D | 0-0 | |
| | 1r | 20.11.68 | **Hereford Utd** | H | W | 4-2 | Cave 2, Benson, Bond |
| | 2 | 07.12.68 | **Reading** (D3) | A | D | 0-0 | |
| | 2r | 11.12.68 | **Reading** | H | L | 1-2 | Stubbs |
| 1969-70 (D3) | 1 | 15.11.69 | **Tamworth** (WMRL) | A | L | 1-2 | Rudge |
| 1970-71 (D3) | 1 | 21.11.70 | **Aston Villa** (D3) | H | W | 3-1 | Kitchener, Bradley og, Edwards |
| | 2 | 12.12.70 | **Chelmsford City** (SL) | A | W | 1-0 | Rudge |
| | 3 | 02.01.71 | **Lincoln City** (D4) | H | W | 4-3 | Cave, Rudge (p), Barnard 2 |
| | 4 | 25.01.71 | **Leicester City** (D2) | A | L | 0-3 | |
| 1971-72 (D3) | 1 | 20.11.71 | **Nuneaton B** (SL) | H | W | 1-0 | Tearse |
| | 2 | 11.12.71 | **Barnet** (SL) | A | W | 4-1 | Welsh 3, Tearse |
| | 3 | 15.01.72 | **Bolton Wanderers** (D3) | A | L | 1-2 | Tearse |
| 1972-73 (D4) | 1 | 18.11.72 | **Hereford Utd** (D4) | H | W | 3-0 | Stocks, Harrison, Twitchin |
| | 2 | 09.12.72 | **Newport County** (D4) | H | L | 0-1 | |
| 1973-74 (D4) | 1 | 24.11.73 | **Hereford Utd** (D3) | A | L | 1-3 | Morrall |
| 1974-75 (D4) | 1 | 23.11.74 | **Northampton Town** (D4) | H | L | 0-1 | |
| 1975-76 (D4) | 1 | 22.11.75 | **Hereford Utd** (D3) | A | L | 0-2 | |
| 1976-77 (D4) | 1 | 20.11.76 | **Hillingdon Borough** (SL) | H | L | 1-2 | Brown |
| 1977-78 (D4) | 1 | 26.11.77 | **Southend Utd** (D4) | H | L | 1-2 | Brown |

| | | | | | | | | |
|---|---|---|---|---|---|---|---|---|
| 1978-79 (D4) | 1 | 25.11.78 | **Walsall** (D3) | A | W | 2-0 | Cooper, Wilson |
| | 2 | 16.12.78 | **AP Leamington** (SL) | A | W | 1-0 | Twitchin |
| | 3 | 16.01.79 | **Newcastle Utd** (D2) | A | L | 1-3 | Lawrence |
| 1979-80 (D4) | 1 | 24.11.79 | **Gravesend & N** (APL) | A | W | 1-0 | Cooper |
| | 2 | 18.12.79 | **Swindon Town** (D3) | H | D | 3-3 | Sermanni, Cooper, Lawrence |
| | 2r | 22.12.79 | **Swindon Town** | A | L | 2-3 | Tucker og, Murphy |
| 1980-81 (D4) | 1 | 22.11.80 | **Barton Rovers** (IL) | H | W | 2-0 | Weston, Cooper |
| | 2 | 13.12.80 | **St Albans City** (IL) | A | D | 1-1 | Fell |
| | 2r | 17.12.80 | **St Albans City** | H | W | 4-1 | Cooper, Fell 3 (2ps) |
| | 3 | 03.01.81 | **Barnsley** (D3) | A | L | 1-2 | Lawrence |
| 1981-82 (D4) | 1 | 20.11.81 | **Bristol City** (D3) | A | D | 0-0 | |
| | 1r | 26.11.81 | **Bristol City** | H | L | 1-2 | Lawrence |
| 1982-83 (D4) | 1 | 20.11.82 | **Colchester Utd** (D4) | A | W | 2-0 | Little, Cooper |
| | 2 | 11.12.82 | **Carshalton Athletic** (IL) | H | W | 4-1 | Anderson, Bishop 2, Wilson |
| | 3 | 08.01.83 | **Oxford Utd** (D3) | A | D | 1-1 | Gallagher |
| | 3r | 12.01.83 | **Oxford Utd** | H | W | 2-1 | Cooper, Gallagher |
| | 4 | 29.01.83 | **Sheffield Wed** (D2) | H | L | 2-3 | Hughes, Bishop |
| 1983-84 (D4) | 1 | 19.11.83 | **Colchester Utd** (D4) | H | L | 1-2 | Curle |
| 1984-85 (D4) | 1 | 17.11.84 | **Yeovil Town** (APL) | H | W | 2-0 | Laryea, Kelly |
| | 2 | 08.12.84 | **Orient** (D3) | A | L | 0-3 | |
| 1985-86 (D4) | 1 | 16.11.85 | **Windsor & Eton** (IL) | A | D | 1-1 | Durham |
| | 1r | 19.11.85 | **Windsor & Eton** | H | W | 3-0 | Walsh 2, Loram |
| | 2 | 07.12.85 | **Newport County** (D3) | A | D | 1-1 | Loram |
| | 2r | 10.12.85 | **Newport County** | H | L | 2-3aet | Walsh 2 |
| 1986-87 (D4) | 1 | 15.11.86 | **Aldershot** (D4) | A | L | 0-1 | |
| 1987-88 (D4) | 1 | 14.11.87 | **Bognor Regis Town** (IL) | A | W | 3-0 | Dobson, Pearce, Gardiner |
| | 2 | 05.12.87 | **Bristol City** (D3) | A | W | 1-0 | Caldwell |
| | 3 | 09.01.88 | **Coventry City** (D1) | A | L | 0-2 | |
| 1988-89 (D4) | 1 | 19.11.88 | **Fareham Town** (SL) | H | D | 2-2 | Joyce, Smith |
| | 1r | 23.11.88 | **Fareham Town** | A | W | 3-2 | McNichol, Smith, Loram |
| | 2 | 10.12.88 | **Yeovil Town** (SL) | A | D | 1-1 | Loram |
| | 2r | 14.12.88 | **Yeovil Town** | H | W | 1-0 | Thompson |
| | 3 | 07.01.89 | **Sheffield Wed** (D1) | A | L | 1-5 | Edwards |
| 1989-90 (D4) | 1 | 18.11.89 | **Sutton Utd** (Conf) | A | D | 1-1 | Uzzell |
| | 1r | 22.11.89 | **Sutton Utd** | H | W | 4-0 | Lloyd, Smith 2, Elliott |
| | 2 | 09.12.89 | **Basingstoke Town** (IL) | A | W | 3-2 | Elliott, Mottashed og, Loram |
| | 3 | 06.01.90 | **West Ham Utd** (D2) | H | W | 1-0 | Hirons |
| | 4 | 27.01.90 | **Blackpool** (D3) | A | L | 0-1 | |
| 1990-91 (D4) | 1 | 17.11.90 | **Maidstone Utd** (D4) | A | L | 1-4 | Tynan |
| 1991-92 (D3) | 1 | 16.11.91 | **Birmingham City** (D3) | H | W | 3-0 | Tynan, Hall 2 |
| | 2 | 07.12.91 | **Farnborough T** (Conf) | H | D | 1-1 | Loram |
| | 2r | 17.12.91 | **Farnborough T** | A | L | 3-4 | Holmes, Loram, Colcombe |
| 1992-93 (D3) | 1 | 14.11.92 | **Yeovil Town** (Conf) | H | L | 2-5 | Foster, Herd |
| 1993-94 (D3) | 1 | 13.11.93 | **Slough Town** (Conf) | A | W | 2-1 | Sale, Moore |
| | 2 | 04.12.93 | **Sutton Utd** (IL) | H | L | 0-1 | |
| 1994-95 (D3) | 1 | 12.11.94 | **Kidderminster H** (Conf) | A | D | 1-1 | Hathaway |
| | 1r | 23.11.94 | **Kidderminster H** | H | W | 1-0 | Hancox |
| | 2 | 03.12.94 | **Enfield** (IL) | A | D | 1-1 | Okorie |
| | 2r | 13.12.94 | **Enfield** | H | L | 0-1 | |
| 1995-96 (D3) | 1 | 11.11.95 | **Leyton Orient** (D3) | H | W | 1-0 | Byng |
| | 2 | 02.12.95 | **Walsall** (D2) | H | D | 1-1 | Hathaway |
| | 2r | 12.12.95 | **Walsall** | A | L | 4-8aet | Hawthorne, Barrow, Gore, Mateu |
| 1996-97 (D3) | 1 | 16.11.96 | **Luton Town** (D2) | H | L | 0-1 | |
| 1997-98 (D3) | 1 | 15.11.97 | **Luton Town** (D2) | A | W | 1-0 | Gibbs (p) |
| | 2 | 06.12.97 | **Watford** (D2) | H | D | 1-1 | Gurney |
| | 2r | 16.12.97 | **Watford** | A | L | 1-2aet | Clayton |
| 1998-99 (D3) | 1 | 14.11.98 | **Worcester City** (SL) | A | W | 1-0 | Partridge |
| | 2 | 05.12.98 | **Bournemouth** (D2) | H | L | 0-1 | |
| 1999-00 (D3) | 1 | 30.10.99 | **Southend Utd** (D3) | H | W | 1-0 | O'Brien |
| | 2 | 21.11.99 | **Forest Green R** (Conf) | A | W | 3-0 | Brandon, Hill, Donaldson |
| | 3 | 11.12.99 | **QPR** (D1) | A | D | 1-1 | O'Brien |

| | | | | | | | |
|---|---|---|---|---|---|---|---|
| | 3r | 21.12.99 | **QPR** | H | L | 2-3 | Bedeau, Thomas |
| 2000-01 (D3) | 1 | 18.11.00 | **Southend Utd** (D3) | H | D | 1-1 | Ford (p) |
| | 1r | 28.11.00 | **Southend Utd** | A | L | 1-2aet | Chalqi |
| 2001-02 (D3) | | 17.11.01 | **Northampton Town** (D2) | H | L | 1-2 | Hill |
| 2002-03 (D3) | 1 | 16.11.02 | **Borehamwood** (IL) | H | W | 5-0 | Russell (p), Gritton 2, Osei-Kuffour, Fowler |
| | 2 | 07.12.02 | **Blackpool** (D2) | A | L | 1-3 | Gritton |

# TOTTENHAM HOTSPUR

*Formed 1882 as Hotspur FC (not connected to earlier Hotspur FC who played around the Highbury and Barnsbury areas). Tottenham Hotspur 1885. FA Cup and League double 1961. FA Cup winners: 1901 (as a Southern League club) 1921, 1961, 1962, 1967, 1981, 1982, 1991. Runners-up: 1987; Record FA Cup win: 13-2 v Crewe Alexandra, 4th round replay, 03.02.1960. Record FA Cup defeat: 0-5 v Stoke, 1st round, 01.02.1896; 1-6 v Huddersfield Town, 6th round, 03.03.1928, 1-6 v Newcastle United, 3rd round replay, 22.12.1999.*

| | | | | | | | |
|---|---|---|---|---|---|---|---|
| 1894-95 | | | 1q West Herts (H) 3-2; 2q Wolverton (H) 5-3; 3q Clapton (A) 4-0; 4q Luton Town (H) 2-2; 4qr Luton Town (A) 0-4 | | | | |
| 1895-96 (SL) | | | 1q Luton Town (A) 2-1; 2q Vampires (A) L 2-4 FA declared match void because Vampires' pitch was improperly marked' 2qr Vampires (H) 2-1; 3q Ilford (A) 5-1; 4q Old St Stephens (H) 2-1 | | | | |
| | 1 | 01.02.96 | **Stoke** (D1) | A | L | 0-5 | |
| 1896-97 (SL) | | | 1q Old St Stephens (H) 4-0; 2q Maidenhead (H) 6-0; 3q Luton Town (A) 0-3 | | | | |
| 1897-98 (SL) | | | 1q 2nd Coldstream Guards (H) 7-0; 2q Luton Town (H) 3-4 | | | | |
| 1898-99 (SL) | | | 3q Wolverton (H) 4-0; 4q Clapton (A) 1-1; 4qr Clapton (H) 2-1; 5q Luton Town (H) 1-1; 5qr Luton Town (A) 1-1; 5q 2r Luton Town at Tufnell Park 2-0 | | | | |
| | 1 | 28.01.99 | **Newton Heath** (D2) | H | D | 1-1 | Joyce |
| | 1r | 01.02.99 | **Newton Heath** | A | W | 5-3 | Jones, McNaught, Smith, Hartley, Joyce |
| | 2 | 11.02.99 | **Sunderland** (D1) | H | W | 2-1 | Cameron, Bradhsaw |
| | 3 | 25.02.99 | **Stoke** (D1) | A | L | 1-4 | Bradshaw |
| 1899-00 (SL) | 1 | 27.01.00 | **Preston North End** (D1) | A | L | 0-1 | |
| 1900-01 (SL) | 1 | 09.02.01 | **Preston North End** | H | D | 1-1 | Brown |
| | 1r | 13.02.01 | **Preston North End** | A | W | 4-2 | Brown 3, Cameron |
| | 2 | 23.02.01 | **Bury** (D1) | H | W | 2-1 | Brown 2 |
| | 3 | 23.03.01 | **Reading** (SL) | A | D | 1-1 | Kirwan |
| | 3r | 28.03.01 | **Reading** | H | W | 3-0 | Brown 2, Copeland |
| | SF | 08.04.01 | **WBA** (D1) *played at Villa Park* | | W | 4-0 | Brown 4 |
| | F | 20.04.01 | **Sheffield Utd** (D1) *played at Crystal Palace* | | D | 2-2 | Brown 2 |
| | Fr | 27.04.01 | **Sheffield Utd** *played at Burnden Park, Bolton* | | W | 3-1 | Cameron, Smith, Brown |
| 1901-02 (SL) | 1 | 25.01.02 | **Southampton** (SL) | H | D | 1-1 | Copeland |
| | 1r | 29.01.02 | **Southampton** | A | D | 2-2aet | Hughes 2 |
| | 1 2r | 03.02.02 | **Southampton** *played at Elm Park, Reading* | | L | 1-2 | Kirwan |
| 1902-03 (SL) | 1 | 07.02.03 | **WBA** (D1) | H | D | 0-0 | |
| | 1r | 11.02.03 | **WBA** | A | W | 2-0 | Dryburgh (p), Woodward |
| | 2 | 21.02.03 | **Bristol City** (D2) | H | W | 1-0 | Woodward |
| | 3 | 07.03.03 | **Aston Villa** (D1) | H | L | 2-3 | Woodward, Copeland |
| 1903-04 (SL) | 1 | 06.02.04 | **Everton** (D1) | A | W | 2-1 | Woodward, Balmer og |
| | 2 | 20.02.04 | **Aston Villa** (D1) *abandoned after 38 minutes following a pitch invasion* | H | - | 0-1ab | |
| | 2r | 25.02.04 | **Aston Villa** (D1) | A | W | 1-0 | J Jones |
| | 3 | 05.03.04 | **Sheffield Wed** (D1) | H | D | 1-1 | J Jones |
| | 3r | 09.03.04 | **Sheffield Wed** | A | L | 0-2 | |
| 1904-05 (SL) | 1 | 04.02.05 | **Middlesbrough** (D1) | A | D | 1-1 | Glen |
| | 1r | 09.02.05 | **Middlesbrough** | H | W | 1-0 | O'Hagan |
| | 2 | 18.02.05 | **Newcastle Utd** (D1) | H | D | 1-1 | Walton |
| | 2r | 22.02.05 | **Newcastle Utd** | A | L | 0-4 | |
| 1905-06 (SL) | 1 | 13.01.06 | **Burnley** (D2) | H | W | 2-0 | Woodward, Kyle |
| | 2 | 03.02.06 | **Reading** (SL) | H | W | 3-2 | Bull, Walton, Kyle |
| | 3 | 24.02.06 | **Birmingham** (D1) | H | D | 1-1 | Kyle |

| | | | | | | | |
|---|---|---|---|---|---|---|---|
| | 3r | 28.02.06 | **Birmingham** | A | L | 0-2aet | |
| 1906-07 (SL) | 1 | 12.01.07 | **Hull City** (D2) | H | D | 0-0 | |
| | 1r | 17.01.07 | **Hull City** | A | - | 0-0ab | |
| | | | *abandoned after 100 minutes – bad light* | | | | |
| | 1 2r | 21.01.07 | **Hull City** (D2) | H | W | 1-0 | Chapman |
| | 2 | 02.02.07 | **Blackburn Rovers** (D1) | A | D | 1-1 | Walton |
| | 2r | 07.02.07 | **Blackburn Rovers** | H | D | 1-1aet | Reid |
| | 2 2r | 11.02.07 | **Blackburn Rovers** | | W | 2-1 | Walton, Reid |
| | | | *played at Villa Park* | | | | |
| | 3 | 23.02.07 | **Notts County** (D1) | A | L | 0-4 | |
| 1907-08 (SL) | 1 | 11.01.08 | **Everton** (D1) | A | L | 0-1 | |
| 1908-09 (D2) | 1 | 16.01.09 | **Manchester City** (D2) | A | W | 4-3 | Morris (p), Minter 2, R.Steel |
| | 2 | 06.02.09 | **Fulham** (D2) | H | W | 1-0 | R.Steel |
| | 3 | 20.02.09 | **Burnley** (D2) | H | D | 0-0 | |
| | 3r | 24.02.09 | **Burnley** | A | L | 1-3 | Coquet (p) |
| 1909-10 (D1) | 1 | 15.01.10 | **Plymouth Argyle** (SL) | A | D | 1-1 | Humphreys |
| | 1r | 19.01.10 | **Plymouth Argyle** | H | W | 7-1 | Minter, Humphreys 3, R Steel 2, Middlemiss 2 |
| | 2 | 05.02.10 | **Chelsea** (D1) | A | W | 1-0 | Humphreys |
| | 3 | 19.02.10 | **Swindon Town** (SL) | A | L | 2-3 | Minter, R.Steel |
| 1910-11 (D1) | 1 | 14.01.11 | **Millwall Athletic** (SL) | H | W | 2-1 | Minter, Carmichael og |
| | 2 | 04.02.11 | **Blackburn Rovers** (D1) | A | D | 0-0 | |
| | 2r | 09.02.11 | **Blackburn Rovers** | H | L | 0-2 | |
| 1911-12 (D1) | 1 | 13.01.12 | **WBA** (D1) | A | L | 0-3 | |
| 1912-13 (D1) | 1 | 11.01.13 | **Blackpool** (D2) | H | D | 1-1 | Rance |
| | 1r | 16.01.13 | **Blackpool** | A | W | 6-1 | Tattersall 2, Cantrell 2, Steel, Middlemiss |
| | 2 | 01.02.13 | **Reading** (SL) | A | L | 0-1 | |
| 1913-14 (D1) | 1 | 10.01.14 | **Leicester Fosse** (D2) | A | D | 5-5 | Walden, Minter, Cantrell, Bliss 2 |
| | 1r | 15.01.14 | **Leicester Fosse** | H | W | 2-0 | Walden, Bliss |
| | 2 | 31.01.14 | **Manchester City** (D1) | A | L | 1-2 | Bliss |
| 1914-15 (D1) | 1 | 09.01.15 | **Sunderland** (D1) | H | W | 2-1 | Walden, Bliss |
| | 2 | 30.01.15 | **Norwich City** (SL) | A | L | 2-3 | Cantrell, Lansdale og |
| 1919-20 (D2) | 1 | 10.01.20 | **Bristol Rovers** (SL) | A | W | 4-1 | Cantrell 3, Bliss |
| | 2 | 31.01.20 | **West Stanley** (NEL) | H | W | 4-0 | Banks, Wilson 2, Bliss |
| | 3 | 21.02.20 | **West Ham Utd** (D2) | H | W | 3-0 | Wilson 2, Grimsdell |
| | 4 | 06.03.20 | **Aston Villa** (D1) | H | L | 0-1 | |
| 1920-21 (D1) | 1 | 08.01.21 | **Bristol Rovers** (D3) | H | W | 6-2 | Clay (p), Smith, Walden, Seed, Cantrell, Bliss |
| | 2 | 29.01.21 | **Bradford City** (D1) | H | W | 4-0 | Banks, Seed 3 |
| | 3 | 19.02.21 | **Southend Utd** (D3) | A | W | 4-1 | Banks, Seed, Cantrill, Bliss |
| | 4 | 05.03.21 | **Aston Villa** (D1) | H | W | 1-0 | Banks |
| | SF | 19.03.21 | **Preston North End** (D1) | | W | 2-1 | Bliss 2 |
| | | | *played at Hillsborough* | | | | |
| | F | 23.04.21 | **Wolverhampton W** (D2) | | W | 1-0 | Dimmock |
| | | | *played at Stamford Bridge* | | | | |
| 1921-22 (D1) | 1 | 07.01.22 | **Brentford** (3S) | A | W | 2-0 | Seed, Cantrell |
| | 2 | 28.01.22 | **Watford** (3S) | H | W | 1-0 | Bliss |
| | 3 | 18.02.22 | **Manchester City** (D1) | H | W | 2-1 | Wilson, Bliss |
| | 4 | 04.03.22 | **Cardiff City** (D1) | A | D | 1-1 | Seed |
| | 4r | 09.03.22 | **Cardiff City** | H | W | 2-1 | Wilson, Dimmock |
| | SF | 25.03.22 | **Preston North End** (D1) | | L | 1-2aet | Seed |
| | | | *played at Hillsborough* | | | | |
| 1922-23 (D1) | 1 | 13.01.23 | **Worksop Town** (ML) | H | D | 0-0 | |
| | 1r | 15.01.23 | **Worksop Town** | A | W | 9-0 | Seed, Lindsay 4, Handley 3, Dimmock |
| | | | *played at White Hart Lane* | | | | |
| | 2 | 03.02.23 | **Manchester Utd** (D2) | H | W | 4-0 | Lindsay, Handley 3 |
| | 3 | 24.02.23 | **Cardiff City** (D1) | A | W | 3-2 | Seed, Lindsay, Handley |
| | 4 | 10.03.23 | **Derby County** (D2) | H | L | 0-1 | |
| 1923-24 (D1) | 1 | 12.01.24 | **Crystal Palace** (D2) | A | L | 0-2 | |

| | | | | | | | | | |
|---|---|---|---|---|---|---|---|---|---|
| 1924-25 | (D1) | 1 | 10.01.25 | **Northampton Town** (3S) | H | W | 3-0 | Seed, Lindsay, Elkes |
| | | 2 | 31.01.25 | **Bolton Wanderers** (D1) | H | D | 1-1 | Seed |
| | | 2r | 04.02.25 | **Bolton Wanderers** | A | W | 1-0 | Lane |
| | | 3 | 21.02.25 | **Blackburn Rovers** (D1) | H | D | 2-2 | Lane, Dimmock |
| | | 3r | 26.02.25 | **Blackburn Rovers** | A | L | 1-3 | Dimmock |
| 1925-26 | (D1) | 3 | 09.01.26 | **West Ham Utd** (D1) | H | W | 5-0 | Dimmock 3, Osborne 2 |
| | | 4 | 30.01.26 | **Manchester Utd** (D1) | H | D | 2-2 | Thompson, Lindsay |
| | | 4r | 03.02.26 | **Manchester Utd** | A | L | 0-2 | |
| 1926-27 | (D1) | 3 | 08.01.27 | **West Ham Utd** (D1) | A | L | 2-3 | Handley, Dimmock |
| 1927-28 | (D1) | 3 | 14.01.28 | **Bristol City** (D2) | A | W | 2-1 | O'Callaghan, Osborne |
| | | 4 | 28.01.28 | **Oldham Athletic** (D2) | H | W | 3-0 | Handley, O'Callaghan, Dimmock |
| | | 5 | 18.02.28 | **Leicester City** (D1) | A | W | 3-0 | O'Callaghan 2, Dimmock |
| | | 6 | 03.03.28 | **Huddersfield Town** (D1) | A | L | 1-6 | O'Callaghan |
| 1928-29 | (D2) | 3 | 12.01.29 | **Reading** (D2) | A | L | 0-2 | |
| 1929-30 | (D2) | 3 | 11.01.30 | **Manchester City** (D1) | H | D | 2-2 | Osborne, Cook |
| | | 3r | 15.01.30 | **Manchester City** | A | L | 1-4 | Thompson |
| 1930-31 | (D2) | 3 | 10.01.31 | **Preston North End** (D2) | H | W | 3-1 | Harper, Cook, Dimmock |
| | | 4 | 24.01.31 | **WBA** (D2) | A | L | 0-1 | |
| 1931-32 | (D2) | 3 | 09.01.32 | **Sheffield Wed** (D1) | H | D | 2-2 | Hunt, W Evans |
| | | 3r | 13.01.32 | **Sheffield Wed** (D1) | A | L | 1-3 | Hunt (p) |
| 1932-33 | (D2) | 3 | 14.01.33 | **Oldham Athletic** (D2) | A | W | 6-0 | O'Callaghan, Hunt 3, W Evans, Brunskill og |
| | | 4 | 28.01.33 | **Luton Town** (3S) | A | L | 0-2 | |
| 1933-34 | (D1) | 3 | 13.01.34 | **Everton** (D1) | H | W | 3-0 | Howe, Hunt, W Evans |
| | | 4 | 27.01.34 | **West Ham Utd** (D2) | H | W | 4-1 | Hunt 2, W Evans 2 |
| | | 5 | 17.02.34 | **Aston Villa** (D1) | H | L | 0-1 | |
| 1934-35 | (D1) | 3 | 12.01.35 | **Manchester City** (D1) | H | W | 1-0 | W Evans |
| | | 4 | 26.01.35 | **Newcastle Utd** (D2) | H | W | 2-0 | GS Hunt 2 |
| | | 5 | 16.02.35 | **Bolton Wanderers** (D2) | H | D | 1-1 | W Evans |
| | | 5r | 20.02.35 | **Bolton Wanderers** | A | D | 1-1aet | GS Hunt |
| | | 5 2r | 25.02.35 | **Bolton Wanderers** *played at Villa Park* | | L | 0-2 | |
| 1935-36 | (D2) | 3 | 11.01.36 | **Southend Utd** (3S) | H | D | 4-4 | Sargent 2, Morrison 2 |
| | | 3r | 15.01.36 | **Southend Utd** | A | W | 2-1 | Sargent, W Evans |
| | | 4 | 25.01.36 | **Huddersfield Town** (D1) | H | W | 1-0 | Howe |
| | | 5 | 15.02.36 | **Bradford Park A** (D2) | A | D | 0-0 | |
| | | 5r | 17.02.36 | **Bradford Park A** | H | W | 2-1 | GS Hunt 2 |
| | | 6 | 29.02.36 | **Sheffield Utd** (D2) | A | L | 1-3 | Morrison |
| 1936-37 | (D2) | 3 | 16.01.37 | **Portsmouth** (D1) | A | W | 5-0 | Morrison 3, Duncan, Miller |
| | | 4 | 30.01.37 | **Plymouth Argyle** (D2) | H | W | 1-0 | McCormick |
| | | 5 | 20.02.37 | **Everton** (D1) | A | D | 1-1 | McCormick |
| | | 5r | 22.02.37 | **Everton** | H | W | 4-3 | Meek, Morrison 3 |
| | | 6 | 06.03.37 | **Preston North End** (D1) | H | L | 1-3 | Duncan |
| 1937-38 | (D2) | 3 | 08.01.38 | **Blackburn Rovers** (D2) | H | W | 3-2 | Sargent, Gibbons 2 |
| | | 4 | 22.01.38 | **New Brighton** (3N) | A | D | 0-0 | |
| | | 4r | 26.01.38 | **New Brighton** | H | W | 5-2 | Morrison 2, Gibbons 2, Lyman |
| | | 5 | 12.02.38 | **Chesterfield** (D2) | A | D | 2-2 | Gibbons, Miller |
| | | 5r | 16.02.38 | **Chesterfield** | H | W | 2-1 | Sargent, Morrison |
| | | 6 | 05.03.38 | **Sunderland** (D1) | H | L | 0-1 | |
| 1938-39 | (D2) | 3 | 07.01.39 | **Watford** (3S) | H | W | 7-1 | Ward (p), Sargent, GW Hall 2, Duncan, Miller 2 |
| | | 4 | 21.01.39 | **West Ham Utd** (D2) | A | D | 3-3 | Sargent, Morrison, Duncan |
| | | 4r | 30.01.39 | **West Ham Utd** | H | D | 1-1aet | Sargent |
| | | 4 2r | 02.02.39 | **West Ham Utd** *played at Highbury* | | L | 1-2 | Morrison |
| 1945-46 | (D2) | 3 1L | 05.01.46 | **Brentford** (D1) | H | D | 2-2 | Burgess, AE Hall |
| | | 3 2L | 10.01.46 | **Brentford** | A | L | 0-2 | |
| 1946-47 | (D2) | 3 | 11.01.47 | **Stoke City** (D1) | H | D | 2-2 | Ludford, Bennett |
| | | 3r | 15.01.47 | **Stoke City** | A | L | 0-1 | |
| 1947-48 | (D2) | 3 | 10.01.48 | **Bolton Wanderers** (D1) | A | W | 2-0aet | Duquemin 2 |
| | | 4 | 24.01.48 | **WBA** (D2) | H | W | 3-1 | Cox, Duquemin 2 |

| | | | | | | | | |
|---|---|---|---|---|---|---|---|---|
| | | 5 | 07.02.48 | **Leicester City** (D2) | H | W | 5-2 | Cox (p), Duquemin 3, South og |
| | | 6 | 28.02.48 | **Southampton** (D2) | A | W | 1-0 | Bennett |
| | | SF | 13.03.48 | **Blackpool** (D1) | | L | 1-3aet | Duquemin |
| | | | | *played at Villa Park* | | | | |
| 1948-49 | (D2) | 3 | 08.01.49 | **Arsenal** (D1) | A | L | 0-3 | |
| 1949-50 | (D2) | 3 | 07.01.50 | **Stoke City** (D1) | A | W | 1-0 | Baily |
| | | 4 | 28.01.50 | **Sunderland** (D1) | H | W | 5-1 | Walters 2, Bennett 2, Medley |
| | | 5 | 11.02.50 | **Everton** (D1) | A | L | 0-1 | |
| 1950-51 | (D1) | 3 | 06.01.51 | **Huddersfield Town** (D1) | A | L | 0-2 | |
| 1951-52 | (D1) | 3 | 12.01.52 | **Scunthorpe Utd** (3N) | A | W | 3-0 | Baily, Duquemin 2 |
| | | 4 | 02.02.52 | **Newcastle Utd** (D1) | H | L | 0-3 | |
| 1952-53 | (D1) | 3 | 10.01.53 | **Tranmere Rovers** (3N) | A | D | 1-1 | Bennett |
| | | 3r | 12.01.53 | **Tranmere Rovers** | H | W | 9-1 | McClellan 3, Duquemin 2, Hollis 2, Baily 2 |
| | | 4 | 31.01.53 | **Preston North End** (D1) | A | D | 2-2 | Withers 2 |
| | | 4r | 04.02.53 | **Preston North End** | H | W | 1-0 | Duquemin |
| | | 5 | 14.02.53 | **Halifax Town** (3N) | A | W | 3-0 | Bennett 2, Duquemin |
| | | 6 | 28.02.53 | **Birmingham City** (D2) | A | D | 1-1 | Bennett |
| | | 6r | 04.03.53 | **Birmingham City** | H | D | 2-2aet | Bennett, Duquemin |
| | | 6 2r | 09.03.53 | **Birmingham City** | | W | 1-0 | Walters |
| | | | | *played at Molineux* | | | | |
| | | SF | 21.03.53 | **Blackpool** (D1) | | L | 1-2 | Duquemin |
| | | | | *played at Villa Park* | | | | |
| 1953-54 | (D1) | 3 | 09.01.54 | **Leeds Utd** (D2) | A | D | 3-3 | Walters, Bennett 2 |
| | | 3r | 13.01.54 | **Leeds Utd** | H | W | 1-0 | Bennett |
| | | 4 | 30.01.54 | **Manchester City** (D1) | A | W | 1-0 | Bennett |
| | | 5 | 20.02.54 | **Hull City** (D2) | A | D | 1-1 | Bennett |
| | | 5r | 24.02.54 | **Hull City** | H | W | 2-0 | Walters, Baily |
| | | 6 | 13.03.54 | **WBA** (D1) | A | L | 0-3 | |
| 1954-55 | (D1) | 3 | 08.01.55 | **Gateshead AFC** (3N) | A | W | 2-0 | Brooks 2 |
| | | 4 | 29.01.55 | **Port Vale** (D2) | H | W | 4-2 | Gavin, Duquemin, Brooks 2 |
| | | 5 | 19.02.55 | **York City** (3N) | A | L | 1-3 | Robb |
| 1955-56 | (D1) | 3 | 07.01.56 | **Boston Utd** (ML) | H | W | 4-0 | Duquemin, Smith 2, Robb |
| | | 4 | 28.01.56 | **Middlesbrough** (D2) | H | W | 3-1 | Norman, Dunmore, Robb |
| | | 5 | 18.02.56 | **Doncaster Rovers** (D2) | A | W | 2-0 | Brooks, Smith |
| | | 6 | 03.03.56 | **West Ham Utd** (D2) | H | D | 3-3 | Harmer (p), Duquemin, Robb |
| | | 6r | 08.03.56 | **West Ham Utd** | A | W | 2-1 | Harmer, Duquemin |
| | | SF | 17.03.56 | **Manchester City** (D1) | | L | 0-1 | |
| | | | | *played at Villa Park* | | | | |
| 1956-57 | (D1) | 3 | 05.01.57 | **Leicester City** (D2) | H | W | 2-0 | Blanchflower, Robb |
| | | 4 | 26.01.57 | **Chelsea** (D1) | H | W | 4-0 | Medwin, Harmer, Smith, Stokes |
| | | 5 | 16.02.57 | **Bournemouth** (3S) | A | L | 1-3 | Medwin |
| 1957-58 | (D1) | 3 | 04.01.58 | **Leicester City** (D1) | H | W | 4-0 | Medwin, Smith 2, Stokes |
| | | 4 | 25.01.58 | **Sheffield Utd** (D2) | H | L | 0-3 | |
| 1958-59 | (D1) | 3 | 10.01.59 | **West Ham Utd** (D1) | H | W | 2-0 | Smith, Jones |
| | | 4 | 24.01.59 | **Newport County** (D3) | H | W | 4-1 | Smith 2, Dunmore 2 |
| | | 5 | 14.02.59 | **Norwich City** (D3) | H | D | 1-1 | Jones |
| | | 5r | 18.02.59 | **Norwich City** | A | L | 0-1 | |
| 1959-60 | (D1) | 3 | 09.01.60 | **Newport County** (D3) | A | W | 4-0 | Blanchflower, R Smith, Allen 2 |
| | | 4 | 30.01.60 | **Crewe Alexandra** (D4) | A | D | 2-2 | Allen, Jones |
| | | 4r | 03.02.60 | **Crewe Alexandra** | H | W | 13-2 | Harmer, Smith 4, Allen 5, Jones 3 (1p) |
| | | 5 | 20.02.60 | **Blackburn Rovers** (D1) | H | L | 1-3 | Jones |
| 1960-61 | (D1) | 3 | 07.01.61 | **Charlton Athletic** (D2) | H | W | 3-2 | Allen 2, Dyson |
| | | 4 | 28.01.61 | **Crewe Alexandra** (D4) | H | W | 5-1 | Mackay, Jones, Smith, Allen, Dyson |
| | | 5 | 18.02.61 | **Aston Villa** (D1) | A | W | 2-0 | Jones, Neil og |
| | | 6 | 04.03.61 | **Sunderland** (D2) | A | D | 1-1 | Jones |
| | | 6r | 08.03.61 | **Sunderland** | H | W | 5-0 | Mackay, Smith, Allen, Dyson 2 |
| | | SF | 18.03.61 | **Burnley** (D1) | | W | 3-0 | Jones, Smith 2 |
| | | | | *played at Villa Park* | | | | |
| | | F | 06.05.61 | **Leicester City** (D1) | | W | 2-0 | Smith, Dyson |
| | | | | *played at Wembley Stadium* | | | | |

| | | | | | | | |
|---|---|---|---|---|---|---|---|
| 1961-62 (D1) | 3 | 06.01.62 | **Birmingham City** (D1) | A | D | 3-3 | Greaves 2, Jones |
| | 3r | 10.01.62 | **Birmingham City** | H | W | 4-2 | Medwin 2, Allen, Greaves |
| | 4 | 27.01.62 | **Plymouth Argyle** (D2) | A | W | 5-1 | Medwin, White, Greaves 2, Jones |
| | 5 | 17.02.62 | **WBA** (D1) | A | W | 4-2 | Smith 2, Greaves 2 |
| | 6 | 10.03.62 | **Aston Villa** (D1) | H | W | 2-0 | Blanchflower, Jones |
| | SF | 31.03.62 | **Manchester Utd** (D1) *played at Hillsborough* | | W | 3-1 | Medwin, Greaves, Jones |
| | F | 05.05.62 | **Burnley** (D1) *played at Wembley Stadium* | | W | 3-1 | Greaves, Smith, Blanchflower (p) |
| 1962-63 (D1) | 3 | 16.01.63 | **Burnley** (D1) | H | L | 0-3 | |
| 1963-64 (D1) | 3 | 04.01.64 | **Chelsea** (D1) | H | D | 1-1 | Dyson |
| | 3r | 08.01.64 | **Chelsea** | A | L | 0-2 | |
| 1964-65 (D1) | 3 | 09.01.65 | **Torquay Utd** (D4) | A | D | 3-3 | Norman, Gilzean 2 |
| | 3r | 18.01.65 | **Torquay Utd** | H | W | 5-1 | Greaves 3, Robertson, Gilzean |
| | 4 | 30.01.65 | **Ipswich Town** (D2) | H | W | 5-0 | Greaves 3 (1p), Gilzean 2 |
| | 5 | 20.02.65 | **Chelsea** (D1) | A | L | 0-1 | |
| 1965-66 (D1) | 3 | 22.01.66 | **Middlesbrough** (D2) | H | W | 4-0 | Mackay 2 (1p), Saul 2 |
| | 4 | 12.02.66 | **Burnley** (D1) | H | W | 4-3 | Gilzean 3, Saul |
| | 5 | 05.03.66 | **Preston North End** (D2) | A | L | 1-2 | Greaves |
| 1966-67 (D1) | 3 | 28.01.67 | **Millwall** (D2) | A | D | 0-0 | |
| | 3r | 01.02.67 | **Millwall** | H | W | 1-0 | Gilzean |
| | 4 | 18.02.67 | **Portsmouth** (D2) | H | W | 3-1 | Greaves, Gilzean 2 |
| | 5 | 11.03.67 | **Bristol City** (D2) | H | W | 2-0 | Greaves 2 (1p) |
| | 6 | 08.04.67 | **Birmingham City** (D2) | A | D | 0-0 | |
| | 6r | 12.04.67 | **Birmingham City** | H | W | 6-0 | Venables 2, Greaves 2, Saul, Gilzean |
| | SF | 29.04.67 | **Nottingham Forest** (D1) *played at Hillsborough* | | W | 2-1 | Greaves, Saul |
| | F | 20.05.67 | **Chelsea** (D1) *played at Wembley Stadium* | | W | 2-1 | Robertson, Saul |
| 1967-68 (D1) | 3 | 27.01.68 | **Manchester Utd** (D1) | A | D | 2-2 | Chivers 2 |
| | 3r | 31.01.68 | **Manchester Utd** | H | W | 1-0aet | Robertson |
| | 4 | 17.02.68 | **Preston North End** (D2) | H | W | 3-1 | Greaves 2, Chivers |
| | 5 | 09.03.68 | **Liverpool** (D1) | H | D | 1-1 | Greaves |
| | 5r | 12.03.68 | **Liverpool** | A | L | 1-2 | Jones |
| 1968-69 (D1) | 3 | 04.01.69 | **Walsall** (D3) | A | W | 1-0 | Greaves |
| | 4 | 25.01.69 | **Wolverhampton W** (D1) | H | W | 2-1 | Johnson, Greaves |
| | 5 | 12.02.69 | **Aston Villa** (D2) | H | W | 3-2 | Greaves 2 (1p), England |
| | 6 | 01.03.69 | **Manchester City** (D1) | A | L | 0-1 | |
| 1969-70 (D1) | 3 | 03.01.70 | **Bradford City** (D3) | A | D | 2-2 | Greaves, Morgan |
| | 3r | 07.01.70 | **Bradford City** | H | W | 5-0 | Greaves 2, Pearce 2, Morgan |
| | 4 | 24.01.70 | **Crystal Palace** (D1) | H | D | 0-0 | |
| | 4r | 28.01.70 | **Crystal Palace** | A | L | 0-1 | |
| 1970-71 (D1) | 3 | 02.01.71 | **Sheffield Wed** (D2) | H | W | 4-1 | Mullery (p), Gilzean 2, Peters |
| | 4 | 23.01.71 | **Carlisle Utd** (D2) | A | W | 3-2 | Gilzean, Peters, Neighbour |
| | 5 | 13.02.71 | **Nottingham Forest** (D1) | H | W | 2-1 | Gilzean, Chivers |
| | 6 | 06.03.71 | **Liverpool** (D1) | A | D | 0-0 | |
| | 6r | 16.03.71 | **Liverpool** | H | L | 0-1 | |
| 1971-72 (D1) | 3 | 15.01.72 | **Carlisle Utd** (D2) | H | D | 1-1 | Gilzean |
| | 3r | 18.01.72 | **Carlisle Utd** | A | W | 3-1 | Chivers 2, Gilzean |
| | 4 | 05.02.72 | **Rotherham Utd** (D3) | H | W | 2-0 | Gilzean, Peters |
| | 5 | 26.02.72 | **Everton** (D1) | A | W | 2-0 | Gilzean, Peters |
| | 6 | 18.03.72 | **Leeds Utd** (D1) | A | L | 1-2 | Pratt |
| 1972-73 (D1) | 3 | 13.01.73 | **Margate** (SL) | A | W | 6-0 | Chivers 2, Knowles, Pratt, Pearce, Peters |
| | 4 | 03.02.73 | **Derby County** (D1) | A | D | 1-1 | Chivers |
| | 4r | 07.02.73 | **Derby County** | H | L | 3-5aet | England (p), GIlzean, Chivers |
| 1973-74 (D1) | 3 | 05.01.74 | **Leicester City** (D1) | A | L | 0-1 | |
| 1974-75 (D1) | 3 | 04.01.75 | **Nottingham Forest** (D2) | A | D | 1-1 | Chivers |
| | 3r | 08.01.75 | **Nottingham Forest** | H | L | 0-1 | |
| 1975-76 (D1) | 3 | 03.01.76 | **Stoke City** (D1) | H | D | 1-1 | Duncan |
| | 3r | 24.01.76 | **Stoke City** | A | L | 1-2 | Perryman |

| | | | | | | | |
|---|---|---|---|---|---|---|---|
| 1976-77 (D1) | 3 | 08.01.77 | **Cardiff City** (D2) | A | L | 0-1 | |
| 1977-78 (D2) | 3 | 07.01.78 | **Bolton Wanderers** (D2) | H | D | 2-2 | Hoddle, Duncan |
| | 3r | 10.01.78 | **Bolton Wanderers** | A | L | 1-2aet | Taylor (p) |
| 1978-79 (D1) | 3 | 10.01.79 | **Altrincham** (NPL) | H | D | 1-1 | Taylor (p) |
| | 3r | 16.01.79 | **Altrincham** | A | W | 3-0 | Lee 3 |
| | | | *played at Maine Road* | | | | |
| | 4 | 12.02.79 | **Wrexham** (D2) | H | D | 3-3 | Hoddle, Jones, Roberts og |
| | 4r | 21.02.79 | **Wrexham** | A | W | 3-2aet | Jones 3 |
| | 5 | 28.02.79 | **Oldham Athletic** (D2) | H | W | 1-0 | Perryman |
| | 6 | 10.03.79 | **Manchester Utd** (D1) | H | D | 1-1 | Ardiles |
| | 6r | 14.03.79 | **Manchester Utd** | A | L | 0-2 | |
| 1979-80 (D1) | 3 | 05.01.80 | **Manchester Utd** (D1) | H | D | 1-1 | Ardiles |
| | 3r | 09.01.80 | **Manchester Utd** | A | W | 1-0aet | Ardiles |
| | 4 | 26.01.80 | **Swindon Town** (D3) | A | D | 0-0 | |
| | 4r | 30.01.80 | **Swindon Town** | H | W | 2-1 | Armstrong 2 |
| | 5 | 16.02.80 | **Birmingham City** (D2) | H | W | 3-1 | Hoddle 2 (1p), Armstrong |
| | 6 | 08.03.80 | **Liverpool** (D1) | H | L | 0-1 | |
| 1980-81 (D1) | 3 | 03.01.81 | **QPR** (D2) | A | D | 0-0 | |
| | 3r | 07.01.81 | **QPR** | H | W | 3-1 | Galvin, Hoddle, Crooks |
| | 4 | 24.01.81 | **Hull City** (D3) | H | W | 2-0 | Archibald, Brooke |
| | 5 | 14.02.81 | **Coventry City** (D1) | H | W | 3-1 | Hughton, Ardiles, Archibald |
| | 6 | 07.03.81 | **Exeter City** (D3) | H | W | 2-0 | Miller, Roberts |
| | SF | 11.04.81 | **Wolverhampton W** (D1) | | D | 2-2aet | Archibald, Hoddle |
| | | | *played at Hillsborough* | | | | |
| | SFr | 15.04.81 | **Wolverhampton W** | | W | 3-0 | Crooks 2, Villa |
| | | | *played at Highbury* | | | | |
| | F | 09.05.81 | **Manchester City** (D1) | | D | 1-1aet | Hutchison og |
| | | | *played at Wembley Stadium* | | | | |
| | Fr | 14.05.81 | **Manchester City** | | W | 3-2 | Villa 2, Crooks |
| | | | *played at Wembley Stadium* | | | | |
| 1981-82 (D1) | 3 | 02.01.82 | **Arsenal** (D1) | H | W | 1-0 | Crooks |
| | 4 | 23.01.82 | **Leeds Utd** (D1) | H | W | 1-0 | Crooks |
| | 5 | 13.02.82 | **Aston Villa** (D1) | H | W | 1-0 | Falco |
| | 6 | 06.03.82 | **Chelsea** (D2) | A | W | 3-2 | Archibald, Hoddle, Hazard |
| | SF | 03.04.82 | **Leicester City** (D2) | | W | 2-0 | Crooks, Wilson og |
| | | | *played at Villa Park* | | | | |
| | F | 22.05.82 | **QPR** (D2) | | D | 1-1 | Hoddle |
| | | | *played at Wembley Stadium* | | | | |
| | Fr | 27.05.82 | **QPR** | | W | 1-0 | Hoddle(p) |
| | | | *played at Wembley Stadium* | | | | |
| 1982-83 (D1) | 3 | 08.01.83 | **Southampton** (D1) | H | W | 1-0 | Hazard |
| | 4 | 29.01.83 | **WBA** (D1) | H | W | 2-1 | Gibson, Crooks |
| | 5 | 19.02.83 | **Everton** (D1) | A | L | 0-2 | |
| 1983-84 (D1) | 3 | 07.01.84 | **Fulham** (D2) | A | D | 0-0 | |
| | 3r | 11.01.84 | **Fulham** | H | W | 2-0 | Roberts, Archibald |
| | 4 | 28.01.84 | **Norwich City** (D1) | H | D | 0-0 | |
| | 4r | 01.02.84 | **Norwich City** | A | L | 1-2 | Falco |
| 1984-85 (D1) | 3 | 05.01.85 | **Charlton Athletic** (D2) | H | D | 1-1 | Crooks |
| | 3r | 23.01.85 | **Charlton Athletic** | A | W | 2-1 | Falco, Galvin |
| | 4 | 27.01.85 | **Liverpool** (D1) | A | L | 0-1 | |
| 1985-86 (D1) | 3 | 04.01.86 | **Oxford Utd** (D1) | A | D | 1-1 | Chiedozie |
| | 3r | 08.01.86 | **Oxford Utd** | H | W | 2-1aet | Waddle, C Allen |
| | 4 | 25.01.86 | **Notts County** (D3) | A | D | 1-1 | C Allen |
| | 4r | 29.01.86 | **Notts County** | H | W | 5-0 | Chiedozie, C Allen, Falco, Waddle, Hoddle |
| | 5 | 04.03.86 | **Everton** (D1) | H | L | 1-2 | Falco |
| 1986-87 (D1) | 3 | 10.01.87 | **Scunthorpe Utd** (D4) | H | W | 3-2 | Mabbutt, Claesen, Waddle |
| | 4 | 31.01.87 | **Crystal Palace** (D2) | H | W | 4-0 | Mabbutt, O'Reilly og, C Allen (p), Claesen |
| | 5 | 21.02.87 | **Newcastle Utd** (D1) | H | W | 1-0 | C Allen (p) |
| | 6 | 15.03.87 | **Wimbledon** (D1) | A | W | 2-0 | Waddle, Hoddle |

| | | | | | | | |
|---|---|---|---|---|---|---|---|
| | SF | 11.04.87 | **Watford** (D1) | | W | 4-1 | Hodge 2, C Allen, P Allen |
| | | | *played at Villa Park* | | | | |
| | F | 16.05.87 | **Coventry City** (D1) | | L | 2-3aet | C Allen, Mabbutt |
| | | | *played at Wembley Stadium* | | | | |
| 1987-88 (D1) | 3 | 09.01.88 | **Oldham Athletic** (D2) | A | W | 4-2 | C Allen 2, Thomas, Waddle |
| | 4 | 30.01.88 | **Port Vale** (D3) | A | L | 1-2 | Ruddock |
| 1988-89 (D1) | 3 | 07.01.89 | **Bradford City** (D2) | A | L | 0-1 | |
| 1989-90 (D1) | 3 | 06.01.90 | **Southampton** (D1) | H | L | 1-3 | Howells |
| 1990-91 (D1) | 3 | 05.01.91 | **Blackpool** (D4) | A | W | 1-0 | Stewart |
| | 4 | 26.01.91 | **Oxford Utd** (D2) | H | W | 4-2 | Mabbutt, Lineker, Gascoigne 2 |
| | 5 | 16.02.91 | **Portsmouth** (D2) | A | W | 2-1 | Gascoigne 2 |
| | 6 | 10.03.91 | **Notts County** (D2) | H | W | 2-1 | Craig Short og, Gascoigne |
| | SF | 14.04.91 | **Arsenal** (D1) | | W | 3-1 | Gascoigne, Lineker 2 |
| | | | *played at Wembley Stadium* | | | | |
| | F | 18.05.91 | **Nottingham Forest** (D1) | | W | 2-1aet | Stewart, Walker og |
| | | | *played at Wembley Stadium* | | | | |
| 1991-92 (D1) | 3 | 05.01.92 | **Aston Villa** (D1) | A | D | 0-0 | |
| | 3r | 14.01.92 | **Aston Villa** | H | L | 0-1 | |
| 1992-93 (PL) | 3 | 02.01.93 | **Marlow** (IL) | A | W | 5-1 | Sheringham, Barmby 2, Samways 2 |
| | | | *played at White Hart Lane* | | | | |
| | 4 | 24.01.93 | **Norwich City** (PL) | A | W | 2-0 | Sheringham 2 |
| | 5 | 14.02.93 | **Wimbledon** (PL) | H | W | 3-2 | Anderton, Sheringham, Barmby |
| | 6 | 07.03.93 | **Manchester City** (PL) | A | W | 4-2 | Nayim 3, Sedgley |
| | SF | 04.04.93 | **Arsenal** (PL) | | L | 0-1 | |
| | | | *played at Wembley Stadium* | | | | |
| 1993-94 (PL) | 3 | 08.01.94 | **Peterborough Utd** (D1) | A | D | 1-1 | Dozell |
| | 3r | 19.01.94 | **Peterborough Utd** | H | D | 1-1aet | Barmby |
| | | | *Tottenham Hotspur won 5-4 on penalties* | | | | |
| | 4 | 29.01.94 | **Ipswich Town** (PL) | A | L | 0-3 | |
| 1994-95 (PL) | 3 | 07.01.95 | **Altrincham** (Conf) | H | W | 3-0 | Rosenthal, Sheringham, Nethercott |
| | 4 | 29.01.95 | **Sunderland** (D1) | A | W | 4-1 | Klinsmann 2 (1p), Mabbutt, Sheringham |
| | 5 | 18.02.95 | **Southampton** (PL) | H | D | 1-1 | Klinsmann |
| | 5r | 01.03.95 | **Southampton** | A | W | 6-2aet | Rosenthal 3, Anderton, Barmby, Sheringham |
| | 6 | 11.03.95 | **Liverpool** (PL) | A | W | 2-1 | Klinsmann, Sheringham |
| | SF | 09.04.95 | **Everton** (PL) | | L | 1-4 | Klinsmann (p) |
| | | | *played at Elland Road* | | | | |
| 1995-96 (PL) | 3 | 06.01.96 | **Hereford Utd** (D3) | A | D | 1-1 | Rosenthal |
| | 3r | 17.01.96 | **Hereford Utd** | H | W | 5-1 | Sheringham 3, Armstrong 2 |
| | 4 | 27.01.96 | **Wolverhampton W** (D1) | H | D | 1-1 | Wilson |
| | 4r | 07.02.96 | **Wolverhampton W** | A | W | 2-0 | Rosenthal, Sheringham |
| | 5 | 19.02.96 | **Nottingham Forest** (PL) | A | - | 0-0ab | |
| | | | *abandoned after 15 minutes – blizzard* | | | | |
| | 5 | 28.02.96 | **Nottingham Forest** | A | D | 2-2 | Armstrong 2 |
| | 5r | 09.03.96 | **Nottingham Forest** | H | D | 1-1aet | Sheringham |
| | | | *Nottingham Forest won 3-1 on penalties* | | | | |
| 1996-97 (PL) | 3 | 05.01.97 | **Manchester Utd** (PL) | A | L | 0-2 | |
| 1997-98 (PL) | 3 | 05.01.98 | **Fulham** (D2) | H | W | 3-1 | Clemence, Calderwood, Taylor og |
| | 4 | 24.01.98 | **Barnsley** (PL) | H | D | 1-1 | Campbell |
| | 4r | 04.02.98 | **Barnsley** (PL) | A | L | 1-3 | Ginola |
| 1998-99 (PL) | 3 | 02.01.99 | **Watford** (D1) | H | W | 5-2 | Iversen 2, Anderton (p), Nielsen, Fox |
| | 4 | 23.01.99 | **Wimbledon** (PL) | A | D | 1-1 | Ginola |
| | 4r | 02.02.99 | **Wimbledon** | H | W | 3-0 | Sinton, Nielsen 2 |
| | 5 | 13.02.99 | **Leeds Utd** (PL) | A | D | 1-1 | T.Sherwood |
| | 5r | 24.02.99 | **Leeds Utd** | H | W | 2-0 | Anderton, Ginola |
| | 6 | 16.03.99 | **Barnsley** (D1) | A | W | 1-0 | Ginola |
| | SF | 11.04.99 | **Newcastle Utd** (PL) | | L | 0-2aet | |
| | | | *played at Old Trafford* | | | | |
| 1999-00 (PL) | 3 | 12.12.99 | **Newcastle Utd** (PL) | H | D | 1-1 | Iversen |
| | 3r | 22.12.99 | **Newcastle Utd** | A | L | 1-6 | Ginola |

| | | | | | | | | |
|---|---|---|---|---|---|---|---|---|
| 2000-01 | (PL) | 3 | 06.01.01 | **Leyton Orient** (D3) | A | W | 1-0 | Doherty |
| | | 4 | 07.02.01 | **Charlton Athletic** (PL) | A | W | 4-2 | Rufus og, Anderton, Leonhardsen, Rebrov |
| | | 5 | 17.02.01 | **Stockport County** (D1) | H | W | 4-0 | King, Davies 2, Flynn og |
| | | 6 | 11.03.01 | **West Ham Utd** (PL) | A | W | 3-2 | Rebrov 2, Doherty |
| | | SF | 08.04.01 | **Arsenal** (PL) *played at Old Trafford* | | L | 1-2 | Doherty |
| 2001-02 | (PL) | 3 | 16.01.02 | **Coventry City** (D1) | A | W | 2-0 | Poyet, Ferdinand |
| | | 4 | 05.02.02 | **Bolton Wanderers** (PL) | H | W | 4-0 | Anderton (p), Iversen, Etherington, Barness og |
| | | 5 | 17.02.02 | **Tranmere Rovers** (D2) | H | W | 4-0 | Ziege, Poyet 2, Sheringham |
| | | 6 | 10.03.02 | **Chelsea** (PL) | H | L | 0-4 | |
| 2002-03 | (PL) | 3 | 04.01.03 | **Southampton** (PL) | A | L | 0-4 | |

## TOW LAW TOWN

*Formed 1890. First entered FA Cup: 1891-92. FA Vase runners-up: 1998. League club beaten: Mansfield Town. Members of the Northern League.*

| | | | | | | | | |
|---|---|---|---|---|---|---|---|---|
| 1967-68 | (NL) | 1 | 09.01.67 | **Mansfield Town** (D3) *abandoned at half-time – blizzard* | H | - | 0-0ab | |
| | | 1 | 13.01.67 | **Mansfield Town** | H | W | 5-1 | Brown 2 (1p), Cairns, Henderson, Hunt |
| | | 2 | 15.01.68 | **Shrewsbury Town** (D3) | H | D | 1-1 | Henderson |
| | | 2r | 18.01.68 | **Shrewsbury Town** | A | L | 2-6 | Brown, Elliott |
| 1968-69 | (NL) | 1 | 16.11.68 | **Mansfield Town** (D3) | A | L | 1-4 | Hunt |
| 1984-85 | (NL) | 1 | 17.11.84 | **Bradford City** (D3) | A | L | 2-7 | Blair 2 |
| 1989-90 | (NL) | 1 | 18.11.89 | **Bishop Auckland** (NPL) | A | L | 0-2 | |

## TRANMERE ROVERS

*Formed 1884 as Belmont FC. Tranmere Rovers 1885. First entered FA Cup: 1891-92. FA Cup best performance: 5th round, 1968. Welsh FA Cup winners: 1935. Runners-up: 1934. Record FA Cup win: 13-0 v Oswestry United, 1st qualifying round, 1914-15. In Competition Proper: 9-0 v AP Leamington, 1st round, 24.11.1979. Record FA Cup defeat: 1-9 v Tottenham Hotspur 3rd round replay, 14.01.1953. Note: Tranmere's record for 1919-20 shows them competing in two leagues. In October 1919 Tranmere resigned from the Cheshire County League and joined the Central League, taking over the fixtures of Leeds City Reserves after Leeds City were disbanded by the FA.*

| | | |
|---|---|---|
| 1891-92 | (Liv) | 1q Northwich V (H) 1-5 |
| 1892-93 | (LC) | 1q Newtown (A) scratched |
| 1893-94 | (LC) | 2q Stockport County (A) 1-2 |
| 1894-95 | (WDL) | P Northwich V (A) 1-3 |
| 1895-96 | (LWDL) | P Crewe Alexandra (A) 1-2 |
| 1896-97 | (LWDL) | 2q Warrington St Elphins (H) 5-1; Int. Buckley Town (A) 0-2 |
| 1897-98 | (TC) | did not enter |
| 1898-99 | (TC) | did not enter |
| 1899-00 | (LAll) | 1q South Liverpool (A) 0-1 |
| 1900-01 | (TC) | 1q White Star Wanderers (H) 0-1 |
| 1901-02 | (TC) | did not enter |
| 1902-03 | (TC) | did not enter |
| 1903-04 | (TC) | 2q Port Sunlight (H) 3-1; 3q Oswestry Utd (H) D 2-2; 3qr Oswestry Utd (A) 1-2 |
| 1904-05 | (TC) | 2q Port Sunlight (H) 1-3 |
| 1905-06 | (TC) | 1q Chirk (A) 1-1; 1qr Chirk (H) 0-1 |
| 1906-07 | (TC) | 1q Wrexham (A) 1-2 |
| 1907-08 | (TC) | P Rhyl (A) 2-0; 1q Chester (A) 4-0; 2q Witton Albion (A) 1-4 |
| 1908-09 | (TC) | did not enter |
| 1909-10 | (TC) | P Chester (H) 6-0; 1q Whitchurch (H) 4-2; 2q Oswestry Utd (H) 5-1; 3q Shrewsbury Town (H) 0-2 |
| 1910-11 | (LC) | 1q Witton Albion (H) scratched |
| 1911-12 | (LC) | did not enter |
| 1912-13 | (LC) | 1q Oswestry Utd (A) 4-2; 1q Harrowby (A) 1-2 |
| 1913-14 | (LC) | P Lostock Gralam (H) 6-1; 1q Chester (A) 1-2 |
| 1914-15 | (LC) | P Northwich V (H) 2-2; Pr Northwich V (A) 3-2; 1q Oswestry Utd (H) 13-0; 2q Chester (H) 5-1; 3q Wrexham (A) 1-1; 3qr Wrexham (H) 0-1 |
| 1919-20 | (CC/CL) | 1q Crewe Alexandra (A) 0-1 |

| | | | | | | | | |
|---|---|---|---|---|---|---|---|---|
| 1920-21 (CL) | | | 4q Southport (H) 1-0; 5q Rochdale (A) 0-1 | | | | | |
| 1921-22 (3N) | | | 4q Altrincham (A) 4-4; 4qr Altrincham (H) 2-4 | | | | | |
| 1922-23 (3N) | | | 4q Wellington St Georges (A) 1-2 | | | | | |
| 1923-24 (3N) | | | 4q Ellesmere Port (H) 1-0; 5q Coventry City (A) 2-2; 5qr Coventry City (H) 3-2; 6q Gillingham (A) 0-1 | | | | | |
| 1924-25 (3N) | | | 4q Crewe Alexandra (H) 1-1; 4qr Crewe Alexandra (A) 2-0; 5q Southport (H) 0-0; 5qr Southport (A) 0-1 | | | | | |
| 1925-26 (3N) | 1 | 28.11.25 | **Crewe Alexandra** (3N) | H | D | 0-0 | | |
| | 1r | 02.12.25 | **Crewe Alexandra** | A | L | 1-2aet | Proctor | |
| 1926-27 (3N) | 1 | 27.11.26 | **Southport** (3N) | A | D | 1-1 | Marquis | |
| | 1r | 02.12.26 | **Southport** | H | L | 1-2 | Littehales | |
| 1927-28 (3N) | 1 | 26.11.27 | **Shirebrook** (ML) | A | W | 3-1 | Waring 2, Charlton | |
| | 2 | 10.12.27 | **Halifax Town** (3N) | H | W | 3-1 | Bamber, Rimmer 2 (1p) | |
| | 3 | 14.01.28 | **Nottingham Forest** (D2) | A | L | 0-1 | | |
| 1928-29 (3N) | 1 | 24.11.28 | **Rotherham Utd** (3N) | H | W | 2-1 | Flanagan, Beswick | |
| | 2 | 08.12.28 | **Bradford City** (3N) | H | L | 0-1 | | |
| 1929-30 (3N) | 1 | 30.11.29 | **York City** (3N) | A | D | 2-2 | Meston, Waterston | |
| | 1r | 05.12.29 | **York City** | H | L | 0-1 | | |
| 1930-31 (3N) | 1 | 29.11.30 | **Gateshead AFC** (3N) | H | D | 4-4 | Dixon 2, Urmson, Lewis . | |
| | 1r | 03.12.30 | **Gateshead AFC** | A | L | 2-3 | Watts, Urmson | |
| 1931-32 (3N) | 1 | 28.11.31 | **West Stanley** (NEL) | H | W | 3-0 | Dixon, Urmson, Whitehurst | |
| | 2 | 12.12.31 | **Bristol Rovers** (3S) | H | W | 2-0 | Meston, Dixon | |
| | 3 | 09.01.32 | **Chelsea** (D1) | H | D | 2-2 | Dixon, Watts | |
| | 3r | 13.01.32 | **Chelsea** | A | L | 3-5 | Whitehurst 2, Watts | |
| 1932-33 (3N) | 1 | 26.11.32 | **New Brighton** (3N) | H | W | 3-0 | Whitehurst, Urmson, Dixon | |
| | 2 | 10.12.32 | **Bristol City** (3S) | A | D | 2-2 | Urmson, Whitehurst | |
| | 2r | 14.12.32 | **Bristol City** | H | W | 3-2 | Watts 2, Dixon | |
| | 3 | 14.01.33 | **Notts County** (D2) | H | W | 2-1 | Urmson, Whitehurst | |
| | 4 | 28.01.33 | **Leeds Utd** (D1) | H | D | 0-0 | | |
| | 4r | 01.02.33 | **Leeds Utd** | A | L | 0-4 | | |
| 1933-34 (3N) | 1 | 25.11.33 | **Newark Town** (ML) | H | W | 7-0 | Bell 4, Urmson, EW Spencer 2 | |
| | 2 | 09.12.33 | **Bournemouth** (3S) | A | W | 4-2 | Woodward 2, Bell, Pearson | |
| | 3 | 13.01.34 | **Southend Utd** (3S) | H | W | 3-0 | Urmson, Watts, Woodward | |
| | 4 | 27.01.34 | **Liverpool** (D1) | A | L | 1-3 | Meacock | |
| 1934-35 (3N) | 1 | 24.11.34 | **Stalybridge Celtic** (CC) | H | W | 3-1 | Baker 2, Urmson | |
| | 2 | 08.12.34 | **Mansfield Town** (3N) | A | L | 2-4 | Burgin 2 | |
| 1935-36 (3N) | 1 | 30.11.35 | **Carlisle Utd** (3N) | H | W | 3-0 | Woodward 2, Urmson | |
| | 2 | 14.12.35 | **Scunthorpe Utd** (ML) | H | W | 6-2 | Bell 3, Urmson 2, Eden | |
| | 3 | 11.01.36 | **Notts County** (3S) | A | D | 0-0 | | |
| | 3r | 15.01.36 | **Notts County** | H | W | 4-3 | Woodward 2, MacDonald, Bell | |
| | 4 | 25.01.36 | **Barnsley** (D2) | H | L | 2-4 | Urmson, Bell | |
| 1936-37 (3N) | 1 | 28.11.36 | **Oldham Athletic** (3N) | A | L | 0-1 | | |
| 1937-38 (3N) | 1 | 27.11.37 | **Carlisle Utd** (3N) | H | W | 2-1 | Duff, Buckley | |
| | 2 | 11.12.37 | **Hartlepools Utd** (3N) | H | W | 3-1 | Waring, Dellow, Buckley | |
| | 3 | 08.01.38 | **Portsmouth** (D1) | H | L | 1-2 | Dellow | |
| 1938-39 (D2) | 3 | 10.01.39 | **Grimsby Town** (D1) | A | L | 0-6 | | |
| 1945-46 (3N) | 1 1L | 17.11.45 | **South Liverpool** (CC) | A | D | 1-1 | Rosenthal | |
| | 1 2L | 24.11.45 | **South Liverpool** | H | W | 6-1 | Atkinson, Ashcroft 2, Rosenthal, Williamson | |
| | 2 1L | 08.12.45 | **Rochdale** (3N) | H | W | 3-1 | Atkinson, Bell, Rosenthal | |
| | 2 2L | 15.12.45 | **Rochdale** | A | L | 0-3 | | |
| 1946-47 (3N) | 1 | 30.11.46 | **Oldham Athletic** (3N) | A | L | 0-1 | | |
| 1947-48 (3N) | 1 | 29.11.47 | **Stalybridge Celtic** (CC) | H | W | 2-0 | Bridges, Harlock | |
| | 2 | 13.12.47 | **Chester** (3N) | H | L | 0-1 | | |
| 1948-49 (3N) | 1 | 27.11.48 | **Darlington** (3N) | H | L | 1-3 | Gould | |
| 1949-50 (3N) | 1 | 26.11.49 | **Halifax Town** (3N) | H | W | 2-1 | Wheeler, Wood | |
| | 2 | 10.12.49 | **Port Vale** (3S) | A | L | 0-1 | | |
| 1950-51 (3N) | 1 | 25.11.50 | **Cleator M Celtic** (WCL) *played at Workington* | A | W | 5-0 | Iceton 2, Williamson, Wheeler, Bainbridge | |
| | 2 | 09.12.50 | **York City** (3N) | A | L | 1-2 | Bainbridge (p) | |

| | | | | | | | | |
|---|---|---|---|---|---|---|---|---|
| 1951-52 | (3N) | 1 | 24.11.51 | **Goole Town** (ML) | H | W | 4-2 | Atkinson 3, Iceton |
| | | 2 | 15.12.51 | **Blyth Spartans** (NEL) | H | D | 1-1 | Sowden (og) |
| | | 2r | 19.12.51 | **Blyth Spartans** | A | - | 1-1ab | Atkinson |
| | | | | *abandoned after 115 minutes – bad light* | | | | |
| | | 2 2r | 03.01.52 | **Blyth Spartans** | | D | 2-2aet | Rosenthal 2 |
| | | | | *played at Brunton Park, Carlisle* | | | | |
| | | 2 3r | 07.01.52 | **Blyth Spartans** | | W | 5-1 | Tilson 2, Bainbridge, Williams, Rosenthal |
| | | | | *played at Goodison Park* | | | | |
| | | 3 | 12.01.52 | **Huddersfield Town** (D1) | A | W | 2-1 | Tilston, Rosenthal |
| | | 4 | 02.02.52 | **Chelsea** (D1) | A | L | 0-4 | |
| 1952-53 | (3N) | 1 | 22.11.52 | **Ashington** (NEL) | H | W | 8-1 | Atkinson 6, Done 2 |
| | | 2 | 06.12.52 | **Hartlepools Utd** (3N) | H | W | 2-1 | Done 2 |
| | | 3 | 10.01.53 | **Tottenham Hotspur** (D1) | H | D | 1-1 | Iceton |
| | | 3r | 12.01.53 | **Tottenham Hotspur** | A | L | 1-9 | Done |
| 1953-54 | (3N) | 1 | 21.11.53 | **Gateshead AFC** (3N) | A | W | 2-1 | Done 2 |
| | | 2 | 12.12.53 | **Accrington Stanley** (3N) | A | D | 2-2 | Williams, Done |
| | | 2r | 16.12.53 | **Accrington Stanley** | H | W | 5-1 | Williams 2, Done 3 |
| | | 3 | 09.01.54 | **Leyton Orient** (3S) | H | D | 2-2 | Bainbridge, Done |
| | | 3r | 14.01.54 | **Leyton Orient** | A | L | 1-4 | Atkinson |
| 1954-55 | (3N) | 1 | 20.11.54 | **Rochdale** (3N) | H | D | 3-3 | Done 2, Rosenthal |
| | | 1r | 23.11.54 | **Rochdale** | A | L | 0-1 | |
| 1955-56 | (3N) | 1 | 19.11.55 | **Easington C Wel** (Wear) | A | W | 2-0 | Speakman 2 |
| | | 2 | 10.12.55 | **Barrow** (3N) | H | L | 0-3 | |
| 1956-57 | (3N) | 1 | 17.11.56 | **Bishop Auckland** (NL) | A | L | 1-2 | Davies |
| 1957-58 | (3N) | 1 | 16.11.57 | **Witton Albion** (CC) | H | W | 2-1 | Williams, Eglington |
| | | 2 | 07.12.57 | **Durham City** (NL) | A | W | 3-0 | Eglington, Dodd, Williams |
| | | 3 | 04.01.58 | **Notts County** (D2) | A | L | 0-2 | |
| 1958-59 | (3N) | 1 | 15.11.58 | **Bishop Auckland** (NL) | H | W | 8-1 | Eglington, K Williams 4, Green, Rowley, Finney |
| | | 2 | 06.12.58 | **Doncaster Rovers** (D3) | H | L | 1-2 | Rowley |
| 1959-60 | (D3) | 1 | 14.11.59 | **Chester** (D4) | H | L | 0-1 | |
| 1960-61 | (D3) | 1 | 05.11.60 | **Bury** (D3) | H | W | 1-0 | Williams |
| | | 2 | 30.11.60 | **York City** (D4) | H | D | 1-1 | Williams |
| | | 2r | 05.12.60 | **York City** | A | L | 1-2 | Rowley |
| 1961-62 | (D4) | 1 | 04.11.61 | **Gateshead AFC** (NRL) | H | L | 2-3 | Arnell, Frye |
| 1962-63 | (D4) | 1 | 03.11.62 | **Chester** (D4) | A | W | 2-0 | Jones, Hickson |
| | | 2 | 24.11.62 | **Doncaster Rovers** (D4) | A | W | 4-1 | Hickson 2, Manning 2 |
| | | 3 | 05.01.63 | **Chelsea** (D2) | H | D | 2-2 | King, Jones |
| | | 3r | 30.01.63 | **Chelsea** | A | L | 1-3 | Hickson |
| 1963-64 | (D4) | 1 | 16.11.63 | **Doncaster Rovers** (D4) | A | L | 0-3 | |
| 1964-65 | (D4) | 1 | 14.11.64 | **Lincoln City** (D4) | H | D | 0-0 | |
| | | 1r | 18.11.64 | **Lincoln City** | A | L | 0-1 | |
| 1965-66 | (D4) | 1 | 13.11.65 | **Stockport County** (D4) | H | L | 0-1 | |
| 1966-67 | (D4) | 1 | 26.11.66 | **Wigan Athletic** (CC) | H | D | 1-1 | Parnell |
| | | 1r | 28.11.66 | **Wigan Athletic** | A | W | 1-0 | Williams |
| | | 2 | 07.01.67 | **Barrow** (D4) | A | L | 1-2 | Yardley |
| 1967-68 | (D3) | 1 | 09.12.67 | **Rochdale** (D4) | H | W | 5-1 | Yardley, Williams, Hudson 3, Fletcher |
| | | 2 | 06.01.68 | **Bradford Park A** (D4) | A | W | 3-2 | Stevens, Yardley (p), McNamee |
| | | 3 | 27.01.68 | **Huddersfield Town** (D2) | H | W | 2-1 | Beamish, Williams |
| | | 4 | 17.02.68 | **Coventry City** (D1) | A | D | 1-1 | A King |
| | | 4r | 21.02.68 | **Coventry City** | H | W | 2-0 | Hudson, Yardley |
| | | 5 | 09.03.68 | **Everton** (D1) | A | L | 0-2 | |
| 1968-69 | (D3) | 1 | 16.11.68 | **Southport** (D3) | H | L | 0-1 | |
| 1969-70 | (D3) | 1 | 15.11.69 | **Chesterfield** (D4) | H | W | 3-0 | Yardley 2, Beamish |
| | | 2 | 06.12.69 | **Port Vale** (D4) | A | D | 2-2 | Beamish, Scott |
| | | 2r | 08.12.69 | **Port Vale** | H | W | 3-1 | Smith (p), Scott, Broadie |
| | | 3 | 03.01.70 | **Portsmouth** (D2) | A | W | 2-1 | MacNamee, Beamish |
| | | 4 | 24.01.70 | **Northampton Town** (D4) | H | D | 0-0 | |
| | | 4r | 27.01.70 | **Northampton Town** | A | L | 1-2 | Smith |
| 1970-71 | (D3) | 1 | 21.11.70 | **Scunthorpe Utd** (D4) | H | D | 1-1 | Gill |

| | | | | | | | |
|---|---|---|---|---|---|---|---|
| | 1r | 24.11.70 | **Scunthorpe Utd** | A | D | 0-0aet | |
| | 12r | 30.11.70 | **Scunthorpe Utd** | | L | 0-1aet | |
| | | | *played at Goodison Park* | | | | |
| 1971-72 (D3) | 1 | 20.11.71 | **Skelmersdale Utd** (NPL) | A | W | 4-0 | Crossley 2, King, Moore |
| | 2 | 11.12.71 | **Mansfield Town** (D3) | A | D | 2-2 | Crossley, Storton |
| | 2r | 15.12.71 | **Mansfield Town** | H | W | 4-2 | Brodie, Beamish, Moore, Crossley |
| | 3 | 15.01.72 | **Charlton Athletic** (D2) | A | D | 0-0 | |
| | 3r | 17.01.72 | **Charlton Athletic** | H | W | 4-2 | Beamish, Storton, Crossley, Moore |
| | 4 | 05.02.72 | **Stoke City** (D1) | H | D | 2-2 | Yeats, Beamish |
| | 4r | 09.02.72 | **Stoke City** | A | L | 0-2 | |
| 1972-73 (D3) | 1 | 18.11.72 | **South Liverpool** (NPL) | A | W | 2-0 | Flood, Moore |
| | 2 | 09.12.72 | **Bradford City** (D4) | A | L | 1-2 | Young |
| 1973-74 (D3) | 1 | 24.11.73 | **Bury** (D4) | H | W | 2-1 | Tynan, Moore |
| | 2 | 15.12.73 | **Doncaster Rovers** (D4) | A | L | 0-3 | |
| 1974-75 (D3) | 1 | 23.11.74 | **Farsley Celtic** (YL) | A | W | 2-0 | Coppell, Tynan |
| | | | *played at Elland Road* | | | | |
| | 2 | 14.12.74 | **Rochdale** (D4) | A | D | 1-1 | Hanvey og |
| | 2r | 16.12.74 | **Rochdale** | H | W | 1-0 | Crossley |
| | 3 | 04.01.75 | **Peterborough Utd** (D3) | A | L | 0-1 | |
| 1975-76 (D4) | 1 | 22.11.75 | **Coventry Sporting** (WMRL) | A | L | 0-2 | |
| | | | *played at Highfield Road* | | | | |
| 1976-77 (D3) | 1 | 20.11.76 | **Peterborough Utd** (D3) | H | L | 0-4 | |
| 1977-78 (D3) | 1 | 26.11.77 | **Hartlepool Utd** (D4) | H | D | 1-1 | Allen |
| | 1r | 29.11.77 | **Hartlepool Utd** | A | L | 1-3 | James (p) |
| 1978-79 (D3) | 1 | 25.11.78 | **Boston Utd** (NPL) | H | W | 2-1 | McAuley, Moore |
| | 2 | 16.12.78 | **Sheffield Wed** (D3) | H | D | 1-1 | Moore |
| | 2r | 19.12.78 | **Sheffield Wed** | A | L | 0-4 | |
| 1979-80 (D4) | 1 | 24.11.79 | **AP Leamington** (APL) | H | W | 9-0 | Jones og, Lumby 3, O'Neill 2 (1p), Evans 2,Beamish |
| | 2 | 15.12.79 | **Rochdale** (D4) | H | D | 2-2 | Evans, Peplow |
| | 2r | 18.12.79 | **Rochdale** | A | L | 1-2 | Beamish |
| 1980-81 (D4) | 1 | 22.11.80 | **York City** (D4) | H | D | 0-0 | |
| | 1r | 25.11.80 | **York City** | A | W | 2-1aet | Craven, Beamish |
| | 2 | 13.12.80 | **Huddersfield Town** (D3) | H | L | 0-3 | |
| 1981-82 (D4) | 1 | 21.11.81 | **Bury** (D4) | H | D | 1-1 | Brown |
| | 1r | 24.11.81 | **Bury** | A | L | 1-3 | Williams |
| 1982-83 (D4) | 1 | 20.11.82 | **Scarborough** (APL) | H | W | 4-2 | Kerr, O.Brown 3 |
| | 2 | 11.12.82 | **Telford Utd** (APL) | A | D | 1-1 | Brown (p) |
| | 2r | 14.12.82 | **Telford Utd** | H | W | 2-1 | Aspinall, Griffiths |
| | 3 | 08.01.83 | **Wolverhampton W** (D2) | H | L | 0-1 | |
| 1983-84 (D4) | 1 | 19.11.83 | **Bolton Wanderers** (D3) | H | D | 2-2 | Aspinall, Powell |
| | 1r | 22.11.83 | **Bolton Wanderers** | A | L | 1-4aet | Allen |
| 1984-85 (D4) | 1 | 17.11.84 | **Bangor City** (NPL) | A | D | 1-1 | McMullen |
| | 1r | 20.11.84 | **Bangor City** | H | W | 7-0 | Clayton 2, Clarke 3, Anderson, Edwards |
| | 2 | 08.12.84 | **Hull City** (D3) | H | L | 0-3 | |
| 1985-86 (D4) | 1 | 16.11.85 | **Chesterfield** (D3) | H | D | 2-2 | Worthington (p), Rodaway |
| | 1r | 19.11.85 | **Chesterfield** | A | W | 1-0 | Muir |
| | 2 | 07.12.85 | **Bury** (D3) | H | D | 1-1 | Morrissey |
| | 2r | 10.12.85 | **Bury** | A | L | 1-2 | Anderson |
| 1986-87 (D4) | 1 | 15.11.86 | **Spennymoor Utd** (NL) | A | W | 3-2 | Muir 3 (2p) |
| | 2 | 06.12.86 | **Bolton Wanderers** (D3) | A | L | 0-2 | |
| 1987-88 (D4) | 1 | 14.11.87 | **Port Vale** (D3) | H | D | 2-2 | Martindale, Muir |
| | 1r | 16.11.87 | **Port Vale** | A | L | 1-3 | Muir |
| 1988-89 (D4) | 1 | 19.11.88 | **Preston North End** (D3) | A | D | 1-1 | Atkins og |
| | 1r | 22.11.88 | **Preston North End** | H | W | 3-0 | Muir 3 |
| | 2 | 10.12.88 | **Northwich V** (Conf) | A | W | 2-1 | Muir (p), Steel |
| | 3 | 07.01.89 | **Reading** (D3) | H | D | 1-1 | Vickers |
| | 3r | 11.01.89 | **Reading** | A | L | 1-2 | Muir |
| 1989-90 (D3) | 1 | 18.11.89 | **Preston North End** (D3) | A | L | 0-1 | |
| 1990-91 (D3) | 1 | 17.11.90 | **Halesowen Town** (SL) | A | W | 2-1 | Morrissey, Steel |

| | | | | | | | |
|---|---|---|---|---|---|---|---|
| | 2 | 08.12.90 | **Scunthorpe Utd** (D4) | A | L | 2-3 | Vickers, Irons |
| 1991-92 (D2) | 1 | 16.11.91 | **Runcorn** (Conf) | H | W | 3-0 | Irons, Aldridge 2 |
| | 2 | 07.12.91 | **York City** (D4) | A | D | 1-1 | Morrissey |
| | 2r | 17.12.91 | **York City** | H | W | 2-1 | Aldridge, Irons |
| | 3 | 04.01.92 | **Oxford Utd** (D2) | A | L | 1-3 | Malkin |
| 1992-93 (D1) | 3 | 02.01.93 | **Oldham Athletic** (PL) | A | D | 2-2 | Aldridge (p), Nevin |
| | 3r | 12.01.93 | **Oldham Athletic** | H | W | 3-0 | Vickers, Morrissey 2 |
| | 4 | 23.01.93 | **Ipswich Town** (PL) | H | L | 1-2 | Nevin |
| 1993-94 (D1) | 3 | 08.01.94 | **Oxford Utd** (D1) | A | L | 0-2 | |
| 1994-95 (D1) | 3 | 07.01.95 | **Bury** (D3) | A | D | 2-2 | Muir 2 |
| | 3r | 18.01.95 | **Bury** | H | W | 3-0 | O'Brien, Muir, Malkin |
| | 4 | 29.01.95 | **Wimbledon** (PL) | H | L | 0-2 | |
| 1995-96 (D1) | 3 | 06.01.96 | **QPR** (PL) | H | L | 0-2 | |
| 1996-97 (D1) | 3 | 14.01.97 | **Carlisle Utd** (D3) | A | L | 0-1 | |
| 1997-98 (D1) | 3 | 13.01.98 | **Hereford Utd** (Conf) | A | W | 3-0 | Jones 2, Hill |
| | 4 | 24.01.98 | **Sunderland** (D1) | H | W | 1-0 | Parkinson |
| | 5 | 14.02.98 | **Newcastle Utd** (PL) | A | L | 0-1 | |
| 1998-99 (D1) | 3 | 02.01.99 | **Ipswich Town** (D1) | H | L | 0-1 | |
| 1999-00 (D1) | 3 | 11.12.99 | **West Ham Utd** (PL) | H | W | 1-0 | Henry |
| | 4 | 08.01.00 | **Sunderland** (D1) | H | W | 1-0 | Allison |
| | 5 | 29.01.00 | **Fulham** (D1) | A | W | 2-1 | Allison, Kelly |
| | 6 | 20.02.00 | **Newcastle Utd** (PL) | H | L | 2-3 | Allison, G.Jones |
| 2000-01 (D1) | 3 | 06.01.01 | **Portsmouth** (D1) | A | W | 2-1 | Yates, Parkinson |
| | 4 | 27.01.01 | **Everton** (PL) | A | W | 3-0 | Yates 2, Koumas |
| | 5 | 17.02.01 | **Southampton** (PL) | A | D | 0-0 | |
| | 5r | 20.02.01 | **Southampton** | H | W | 4-3 | Rideout 3, Barlow |
| | 6 | 11.03.01 | **Liverpool** (PL) | H | L | 2-4 | Yates, Allison |
| 2001-02 (D2) | 1 | 17.11.01 | **Brigg Town** (NCoE) | H | W | 4-1 | Navarro, Price 2, Flynn |
| | 2 | 08.12.01 | **Carlisle Utd** (D3) | H | W | 6-1 | Koumas 3, Price, Barlow (p), Yates |
| | 3 | 08.01.02 | **Southend Utd** (D3) | A | W | 3-1 | Allison, Price, Flynn |
| | 4 | 27.01.02 | **Cardiff City** (D2) | H | W | 3-1 | Rideout, Flynn, Koumas |
| | 5 | 17.02.02 | **Tottenham Hotspur** (PL) | A | L | 0-4 | |
| 2002-03 (D2) | 1 | 16.11.02 | **Cardiff City** (D2) | H | D | 2-2 | Barlow, Haworth |
| | 1r | 26.11.02 | **Cardiff City** | A | L | 1-2 | Mellon |

## TROJANS

*Formed 1869. Entered FA Cup 1873-74 and 1876-77 but never quite managed to play a match,. Based at Leyton using the Cowley Arms pub as their headquarters.*

| | | | |
|---|---|---|---|
| 1873-74 | 1 | Farningham | - |
| | | *Farningham scratched. Trojans walkover* | |
| | 2 | Wanderers | - |
| | | *Trojans scratched. Wanderers walkover* | |
| 1876-77 | 1 | Sheffield FC | - |
| | | *Trojans scratched. Sheffield FC walkover* | |

## TROWBRIDGE TOWN

*Formed 1880. Entered FA Cup: 1895-96 – 1997-98. Folded 1999. A junior Trowbridge Town club formed 2002 is now playing in local minor leagues.*

| | | | | | | | |
|---|---|---|---|---|---|---|---|
| 1945-46 (WL) | 1 1L | 17.11.45 | **Exeter City** (3S) | H | L | 1-3 | Blake |
| | 1 2L | 24.11.45 | **Exeter City** | A | L | 2-7 | Stratton, Powell |
| 1947-48 (WL) | 1 | 29.11.47 | **Brighton** (3S) | H | D | 1-1aet | Greenland |
| | 1r | 06.12.47 | **Brighton** | A | L | 0-5 | |
| 1957-58 (WL) | 1 | 16.11.57 | **Southend Utd** (3S) | H | L | 0-2 | |
| 1963-64 (SL) | 1 | 16.11.63 | **Coventry City** (D3) | H | L | 1-6 | Skeen |

## TUNBRIDGE WELLS UNITED

*Formed 1886 as Tunbridge Wells FC. Tunbridge Wells Rangers 1903. First entered FA Cup: 1905-06. After a number of name changes the club appeared in the Competition Proper as Tunbridge Wells United in 1954-55 and 1961-62. The present club, Tunbridge Wells, dates from 1967 when the old club was reformed. Members of the Kent League.*

**as Tunbridge Wells Rangers**

| | | | | | | | |
|---|---|---|---|---|---|---|---|
| 1905-06 (SL) | 1 | 13.01.06 | **Norwich City** (SL) | A | D | 1-1 | L Parke |

| | | | | | | | |
|---|---|---|---|---|---|---|---|
| | 1r | 17.01.06 | **Norwich City** | H | L | 0-5 | |
| 1929-30 (SL) | 1 | 30.11.29 | **Bath City** (SL) | H | L | 1-3 | Millard |
| 1930-31 (KL) | 1 | 29.11.30 | **Kingstonian** (IL) | H | W | 3-0 | Thirlaway, Richards, Mackie |
| | 2 | 13.12.30 | **Carlisle Utd** (3N) | A | L | 2-4 | Naimby, Morley |
| 1931-32 (KL) | 1 | 28.11.31 | **Brentford** (3S) | H | D | 1-1 | Spencer |
| | 1r | 02.12.31 | **Brentford** | A | L | 1-2 | Moore |
| 1936-37 (KL) | 1 | 28.11.36 | **Bath City** (SL) | A | W | 2-1 | T Dougan, Iles |
| | 2 | 12.12.36 | **Accrington Stanley** (3N) | A | L | 0-1 | |
| 1937-38 (KL) | 1 | 27.11.37 | **Brighton** (3S) | A | L | 1-5 | Emerson |
| 1938-39 (KL) | 1 | 26.11.38 | **Walthamstow Ave** (AL) | A | L | 1-4 | Robinson |
| **as Tunbridge Wells United** | | | | | | | |
| 1954-55 (KL) | 1 | 20.11.54 | **Brighton** (3S) | A | L | 0-5 | |
| 1961-62 (SL) | 1 | 04.11.61 | **Aldershot** (D4) | A | L | 1-3 | Hall |

## TURTON

*Formed 1872. Entered FA Cup: 1879-80 – 1900-01. Played at Chapeltown, Bolton and were one of a number of strong Bolton teams of the time. Charles Sagar, who played for Bury in the 1900 and 1903 FA Cup finals, joined from Turton in 1898.*

| | | | | | | | |
|---|---|---|---|---|---|---|---|
| 1879-80 | 1 | 25.10.79 | **Brigg Town** | H | W | 7-0 | H Haworth 3, P Toothill 2, T Bentley, Hamer |
| | 2 | 13.12.79 | **Nottingham Forest** | H | L | 0-6 | |
| 1880-81 | 1 | 16.10.80 | **Brigg Britannia** | H | W | 5-0 | |
| | 2 | 18.12.80 | **Astley Bridge** | A | W | 3-0 | Waddicar 2, G Haworth |
| | 3 | 08.01.81 | **Sheffield Wed** | H | L | 0-2 | |
| 1881-82 | 1 | 29.10.81 | **Astley Bridge** | A | D | 2-2 | |
| | 1r | 12.11.81 | **Astley Bridge** | H | D | 1-1 | |
| | 1 2r | 19.11.81 | **Astley Bridge** *played at Great Lever* | | D | 3-3 | |
| | 1 3r | 26.11.81 | **Astley Bridge** | H | W | 2-0 | H Howarth, J Howarth |
| | 2 | 03.12.81 | **Bootle** | H | W | 4-0 | Bentley 2, Hamer, J Howarth |
| | 3 | 17.12.81 | **Darwen** | A | L | 1-4 | J Howarth |
| 1883-84 | 1 | 20.10.83 | **Hurst** | A | L | 0-3 | |

## TYNE ASSOCIATION

*North-East amateurs who entered the FA Cup twice in 1879-80 and 1886-87.*

| | | | | | | | |
|---|---|---|---|---|---|---|---|
| 1879-80 | 1 | 01.11.79 | **Blackburn Rovers** | A | L | 1-5 | Bruce |
| 1886-87 | 1 | 30.10.86 | **Redcar** | A | L | 0-4 | |

## UNITED HOSPITAL

*Formed 1867. Played their home matches in south London.*

| | | | | | | |
|---|---|---|---|---|---|---|
| 1882-83 | 1 | 04.11.82 | **London Olympic** | H | W | 3-0 |
| | 2 | 30.11.82 | **Windsor Home Park** | A | L | 1-3 |

## UNITED LONDON SWIFTS

| | | | | | | |
|---|---|---|---|---|---|---|
| 1885-86 | 1 | 24.10.85 | **Upton Park** | A | L | 2-4 |

## UNITY FC

| | | | | | | |
|---|---|---|---|---|---|---|
| 1878-79 | 1 | | Remnants *Unity FC scratched. Remnants walkover* | | | - |

## UPTON PARK

*Formed 1866. One of the 15 original entrants in the first FA Cup competition in 1871-72. Based in Upton Park, east London. They were stalwarts of the amateur game and were directly involved in a showdown over amateurism which led to the professionals of Preston North End being disqualified from the FA Cup in 1884. Upton Park also played as the Great Britain team in the 1900 Olympic Games in Paris and won the gold medal. They were FA Cup quarter-finalists four times – 1877, 1878, 1882 and 1884. Entered the FA Cup: 1871-72 – 1910-11.*

| | | | | | | |
|---|---|---|---|---|---|---|
| 1871-72 | 1 | 11.11.71 | **Clapham Rovers** | H | L | 0-3 |
| 1872-73 | 1 | 26.10.72 | **1st Surrey Rifles** | A | L | 0-2 |
| 1873-74 | 1 | 29.10.73 | **Oxford University** | A | L | 0-4 |
| 1874-75 | 1 | 24.10.74 | **Barnes** | H | L | 0-3 |
| 1875-76 | 1 | 23.10.75 | **Southall Park** | H | W | 1-0 |
| | 2 | | Sheffield FC *Upton Park scratched. Sheffield FC walkover* | | | - |

| | | | | | | | |
|---|---|---|---|---|---|---|---|
| 1876-77 | 1 | 28.10.76 | **Leyton FC** | H | W | 7-0 | Bastard, W Spreckley, Wild, others 4 |
| | 2 | 09.12.76 | **Barnes** | H | W | 1-0 | |
| | 3 | 24.01.77 | **Marlow** | H | D | 2-2 | Bastard, Winterbottom |
| | 3r | 27.01.77 | **Marlow** | H | W | 1-0 | |
| | 4 | 24.02.77 | **Oxford University** | A | D | 0-0 | |
| | 4r | 10.03.77 | **Oxford University** | H | L | 0-1 | |
| 1877-78 | 1 | 07.11.77 | **Rochester** | H | W | 3-0 | D Hunter 2, J Hunter |
| | 2 | 08.12.77 | **Reading** | H | W | 1-0 | |
| | 3 | 19.01.78 | **Remnants** | H | W | 3-0 | D Hunter, J Hunter, H Williams |
| | 4 | 09.03.78 | **Old Harrovians** | A | L | 1-3 | J Hunter |
| 1878-79 | 1 | 30.10.78 | **Saffron Walden** | H | W | 5-0 | Mitchell 2, J Hunter, W Williams, AN Other |
| | 2 | 04.01.79 | **Barnes** | A | L | 2-3 | Bastard, J Hunter |
| 1879-80 | 1 | 15.11.79 | **Remnants** | A | D | 1-1 | EC Bambridge |
| | 1r | 25.11.79 | **Remnants** | H | W | 5-2 | EC Bambridge 2, Mitchell, others 2 |
| | 2 | 23.12.79 | **Royal Engineers** | A | L | 1-4 | Garnett-Clarke |
| 1880-81 | 1 | 13.11.80 | **Mosquitoes** | H | W | 8-1 | |
| | 2 | 18.12.80 | **Weybridge Swallows** | A | W | 3-0 | Mitchell, Winterbottom, Barnard |
| | 3 | | bye | | | | |
| | 4 | 12.02.81 | **Clapham Rovers** | H | L | 4-5 | Mitchell, others 3 |
| 1881-82 | 1 | 22.10.81 | **St Albans (1877)** | H | W | 3-0 | Bastard, Lafone, Mitchell |
| | 2 | 26.11.81 | **Hanover Utd** | A | W | 3-1 | |
| | 3 | | bye | | | | |
| | 4 | 21.01.82 | **Hotspur FC** | H | W | 5-0 | Barnett, Bastard, Mitchell, others 2 |
| | 5 | 07.02.82 | **Sheffield Wed** | A | L | 0-6 | |
| 1882-83 | 1 | | bye | | | | |
| | 2 | 30.11.82 | **Swifts** | A | D | 2-2 | Bastard, Lafone |
| | 2r | 02.12.82 | **Swifts** | H | L | 2-3 | Mitchell 2 |
| 1883-84 | 1 | 10.11.83 | **Acton** | H | W | 2-0 | Brearley, Hewitt |
| | 2 | | bye | | | | |
| | 3 | 22.12.83 | **Reading** | A | W | 6-1 | |
| | 4 | 19.01.84 | **Preston North End** | A | D | 1-1 | Mitchell |
| | | | *FA disqualified Preston for professionalism. Upton Park advanced* | | | | |
| | 5 | 09.02.84 | **Blackburn Rovers** | H | L | 0-3 | |
| 1884-85 | 1 | 08.11.84 | **West End** | A | D | 3-3 | |
| | | | *West End scratched before replay took place. Upton Park walkover* | | | | |
| | 2 | 06.12.84 | **Reading** | H | W | 3-1 | Lafone, Pellatt, Bastard |
| | 3 | 03.01.85 | **Old Wykehamists** | A | L | 1-2 | |
| 1885-86 | 1 | 24.10.85 | **Utd London Swifts** | H | W | 4-2 | |
| | 2 | 21.11.85 | **Old Carthusians** | A | L | 0-6 | |
| 1886-87 | 1 | 23.10.86 | **1st Surrey Rifles** | H | W | 9-0 | |
| | 2 | 20.11.86 | **Marlow** | A | L | 0-4 | |

## UPTON RANGERS

| | | | | | | | |
|---|---|---|---|---|---|---|---|
| 1883-84 | 1 | 10.11.83 | **Old Wykehamists** | H | L | 0-7 | |

## UXBRIDGE

*Formed 1871. First entered FA Cup: 1873-74. FA Amateur Cup runners-up: 1898. Members of the Isthmian League.*

| | | | | | | | |
|---|---|---|---|---|---|---|---|
| 1873-74 | 1 | 28.10.73 | **Gitanos FC** | H | W | 3-0 | Clark, Turner, AN Other |
| | 2 | 26.11.73 | **Royal Engineers** | A | L | 1-2 | |
| 1874-75 | 1 | | Windsor Home Park | | | - | |
| | | | *Uxbridge scratched. Windsor Home Park walkover* | | | | |
| 1883-84 | 1 | 03.11.83 | **Rochester** | A | L | 1-2 | |
| 1884-85 | 1 | 08.11.84 | **Hotspur FC** | H | L | 1-3 | |
| 1885-86 | 1 | 31.10.85 | **Old Wykehamists** | A | L | 0-5 | |

## VAUXHALL MOTORS (ELLESMERE PORT)

*Formed 1987. First entered FA Cup: 1999-2000. League club beaten: QPR (on penalties). The second club to represent Vauxhall Motors in the FA Cup competition following the Luton-based Vauxhall Motors club which reached the first round in 1947-48. Members of the Northern Premier League.*

| | | | | | | | |
|---|---|---|---|---|---|---|---|
| 2002-03 (NPL) | 1 | 16.11.02 | **QPR** (D2) | H | D | 0-0 | |
| | | | *played at Deva Stadium, Chester* | | | | |

| | | | | | | | | |
|---|---|---|---|---|---|---|---|---|
| | | 1r | 26.11.02 | **QPR** | A | D | 1-1aet | Brazier |
| | | | | *Vauxhall Motors won 4-3 on penalties* | | | | |
| | | 2 | 07.12.02 | **Macclesfield T** (D3) | A | L | 0-2 | |

# VAUXHALL MOTORS (LUTON)

*Formed 1932. Entered FA Cup: 1933-34 – 1991-92. Reformed 1963. Folded 1991.*

| | | | | | | | | |
|---|---|---|---|---|---|---|---|---|
| 1947-48 | (SPT) | 1 | 29.11.47 | **Walsall** (3S) | H | L | 1-2 | Sharp |
| | | | | *played at Kenilworth Road* | | | | |

# VS RUGBY

*Formed in 1956 as Valley Sports Rugby. First entered FA Cup: 1976-77. FA Vase winners: 1983. Now known as Rugby United. Members of the Southern League.*

| | | | | | | | | |
|---|---|---|---|---|---|---|---|---|
| 1984-85 | (SL) | 1 | 17.11.84 | **Northampton Town** (D4) | A | D | 2-2 | Crawley 2 |
| | | 1r | 21.11.84 | **Northampton Town** | H | L | 0-1 | |
| 1985-86 | (SL) | 1 | 16.11.85 | **Orient** (D4) | H | D | 2-2 | Downes 2 |
| | | 1r | 19.11.85 | **Orient** | A | L | 1-4 | Gorman |
| 1986-87 | (SL) | 1 | 15.11.86 | **Bristol City** (D3) | A | L | 1-3 | Lane (p) |
| 1987-88 | (SL) | 1 | 14.11.87 | **Atherstone Utd** (SL) | H | D | 0-0 | |
| | | 1r | 17.11.87 | **Atherstone Utd** | A | W | 2-0 | Ross, Conway |
| | | 2 | 05.12.87 | **Bristol Rovers** (D3) | H | D | 1-1 | Ingram |
| | | 2r | 17.12.87 | **Bristol Rovers** | A | L | 0-4 | |
| 1992-93 | (SL) | 1 | 14.11.92 | **Solihull Borough** (SL) | A | D | 2-2 | Button, Green |
| | | 1r | 25.11.92 | **Solihull Borough** | H | W | 2-1aet | Green, Smith |
| | | 2 | 09.12.92 | **Marlow** (IL) | H | D | 0-0 | |
| | | 2r | 15.12.92 | **Marlow** | A | L | 0-2 | |
| 1993-94 | (SL) | 1 | 13.11.93 | **Brentford** (D2) | H | L | 0-3 | |
| | | 4 | 24.01.59 | **Sheffield Utd** (D2) | H | L | 0-2 | |

# WALKER CELTIC

*Entered FA Cup: 1919-20 – 1938-39. Newcastle-based Non-League club.*

| | | | | | | | | |
|---|---|---|---|---|---|---|---|---|
| 1937-38 | (NEL) | 1 | 27.11.37 | **Bradford City** (3N) | H | D | 1-1 | Haftoe |
| | | 1r | 01.12.37 | **Bradford City** | A | L | 3-11 | Allison 2, Cotterill |

# WALSALL

*Formed in 1888 when Walsall Swifts (formed 1877) and Walsall Town (formed 1879) amalgamated as Walsall Town Swifts. Walsall Swifts and Walsall Town both played in the Competition Proper (see separate records) Walsall Town Swifts became plain Walsall in the summer of 1896. Best FA Cup performance: 5th round 1939, 1975, 1978 Record FA Cup win: 12-0 v Warmley, 1st qualifying round, 27.09.1890 in Competition Proper: 6-1 v Leytonstone, 1st round, 30.11.1946; 6-1 v Margate 1st round replay, 24.11.1955 Record FA Cup defeat: 0-7 v Worcester City, 1st qualifying 11.10.1913 in Competition Proper: 0-6 v Aston Villa, 1st round, 13.01.1912.*

**as Walsall Town Swifts**

| | | | | | | | | |
|---|---|---|---|---|---|---|---|---|
| 1888-89 | | 1 | 02.02.89 | **Sheffield Heeley** | H | W | 5-1 | Shaw 2, Cope, Gray, Morely |
| | | 2 | 16.02.89 | **Wolverhampton W** (D1) | A | L | 1-6 | Gray |
| 1889-90 | (FAI) | | | 1q Wellington St Georges (H) 3-0; 2q Warwick County (A) 1-1aet; 2qr Warwick County (H) 2-0; 3q Burton Swifts (A) 6-1; 4q Small Heath (A) 0-4 | | | | |
| 1890-91 | (FAI) | | | 1q Warmley (A) 12-0; 2q Burslem Port Vale (A) 3-2; 3q Wednesbury OA (H) 5-3; 4q Kidderminster H (A) 0-3 | | | | |
| 1891-92 | (FAI) | | | 1q Wednesbury OA (H) 7-2; 2q Burton Swifts (H) 2-4 | | | | |
| 1892-93 | (D2) | | | 1q Derby Junction (H) 1-0aet; 2q Stourbridge (H) 7-0; 3q Burton Swifts (H) 1-3 | | | | |
| 1893-94 | (D2) | | | 1q Wellington St Georges (A) 3-0; 2q Stourbridge (A) 3-1; 3q Brierley Hill Alliance (H) 1-2 | | | | |
| 1894-95 | (D2) | | | 1q Burton W (A) 0-3 | | | | |
| 1895-96 | (ML) | | | 1q Dresden U (H) 1-0; 2q Redditch (H) 4-0; 3q Wrockwardine Wood (A) 1-3 | | | | |

**as Walsall**

| | | | | | | | | |
|---|---|---|---|---|---|---|---|---|
| 1896-97 | (D2) | | | 3q Dresden U (H) 11-0; 4q Burton Swifts (H) 1-1; 4qr Burton Swifts (A) 0-1 | | | | |
| 1897-98 | (D2) | 1 | 29.01.98 | **Newton Heath** (D2) | A | L | 0-1 | |
| 1898-99 | (D2) | | | 3q Druids (A) 1-2 | | | | |
| 1899-00 | (D2) | | | 3q Kidderminster H (H) 6-1; 4q Wellington T (H) 2-1; 5q Small Heath (A) 0-0; 5qr Small Heath (H) 2-0 | | | | |
| 1899-00 | (D2) | 1 | 27.01.00 | **WBA** (D1) | H | D | 1-1 | Dailly |
| | | 1r | 01.02.00 | **WBA** | A | L | 1-6 | Martin (p) |

| | | | | | | | | |
|---|---|---|---|---|---|---|---|---|
| 1900-01 | (D2) | | | 3q Shrewsbury T (A) 1-1; 3qr Shrewsbury T (H) 1-0; 4q Chirk (A) 1-0; 5q Wellington T (H) 6-0; Int Chesterfield (A) 0-3 | | | | |
| 1901-02 | (ML) | | | 3q Brierley Hill All (A) 1-1; 3qr Brierley Hill All.(H) 2-1; 4q Berwick R, Coventry (H) 0-0; 4q Berwick R (H) 2-1; 5q Burslem Port Vale (A) 2-1; Int New Brompton (H) 2-0 | | | | |
| 1901-02 | (ML) | 1 | 25.01.02 | **Burnley** (D2) | H | W | 1-0 | Colley |
| | | 2 | 08.02.02 | **Bury** (D1) | H | L | 0-5 | |
| 1902-03 | (ML) | | | 2q Brierley Hill All. (H) 0-2 | | | | |
| 1903-04 | (BDL) | | | 3q Coventry C (A) 4-2; 4q Stafford R (A) 2-1; 5q Shrewsbury T (A) 0-1 | | | | |
| 1904-05 | (BDL) | | | 1q Brierley Hill All. (H) 3-0; 2q Coventry C (A) 0-2 | | | | |
| 1905-06 | (BDL) | | | 4q Stockport Co (H) 3-3; 4qr Stockport Co (A) 0-5 | | | | |
| 1906-07 | (BDL) | | | 1q Brierley Hill All. (H) 0-3 | | | | |
| 1907-08 | (BDL) | | | 1q Stafford R (H) 2-5 | | | | |
| 1908-09 | (BDL) | | | P Worcester C (A) 2-0; 1q Kidderminster H (A) 1-2 | | | | |
| 1909-10 | (BDL) | | | P Cannock (H) 1-2 | | | | |
| 1910-11 | (BDL) | | | P Willenhall Swifts (H) 1-0; 1q Hednesford T (A) 3-4 | | | | |
| 1911-12 | (BDL) | | | 4q Stoke (H) 2-1; 5q Accrington S (H) 2-1 | | | | |
| 1911-12 | (BDL) | 1 | 13.01.12 | **Aston Villa** (D1) | A | L | 0-6 | |
| 1912-13 | (BDL) | | | 4q Crewe Alex (H) 2-1; 5q Halifax T (H) 0-0; 5qr Halifax T (A) 0-1 | | | | |
| 1913-14 | (BDL) | | | P Stafford R (H) 1-0; 1q Worcester C (A) 0-7 | | | | |
| 1914-15 | (BDL) | | | ExP Willenhall Pickwick (H) 4-0; P Cannock (H) 2-1; 1q Hednesford T (H) 3-1; 2q Cradley Heath St Lukes (H) 5-2; 3q Stoke (H) 1-0; 4q Wrexham (H) 2-1; 5q Shrewsbury T (A) 1-2 | | | | |
| 1919-20 | (BDL) | | | 4q Worcester C (H) 3-1; 5q Hednesford T (A) 2-4 | | | | |
| 1920-21 | (BDL) | | | P Birmingham Corporation Tramways (H) 3-0; 1q Shrewsbury T (A) 0-1 | | | | |
| 1921-22 | (3N) | | | 4q Shrewsbury T (A) 1-0; 5q Chesterfield (H) 2-0; 6q Mansfield T (A) 1-1; 6qr Mansfield T (H) 4-0 | | | | |
| 1921-22 | (3N) | 1 | 07.01.22 | **Bradford City** (D1) | H | D | 3-3 | Butler, Groves, Reid |
| | | 1r | 11.01.22 | **Bradford City** | A | L | 0-4 | |
| 1922-23 | (3N) | | | 5q Wellington St Georges (A) 5-0; 6q Wigan Borough (H) 1-3 | | | | |
| 1923-24 | (3N) | | | 5q Stalybridge Celtic (H) 3-1; 6q Aberdare A (A) 0-1 | | | | |
| 1924-25 | (3N) | | | 5q Coventry C (H) 1-2 | | | | |
| 1925-26 | (3N) | 1 | 28.11.25 | **Grimsby Town** (3N) | H | L | 0-1 | |
| 1926-27 | (3N) | 1 | 27.11.26 | **Bradford Park A** (3N) | H | W | 1-0 | White |
| | | 2 | 11.12.26 | **Mansfield Town** (ML) | H | W | 2-0 | White, Sarvis |
| | | 3 | 08.01.27 | **Corinthians** | H | L | 0-4 | |
| 1927-28 | (3S) | 1 | 26.11.27 | **Bristol Rovers** (3S) | A | L | 2-4 | White, Groves |
| 1928-29 | (3S) | 1 | 24.11.28 | **Worcester City** (BDL) | H | W | 3-1 | Groves, N Thompson, Gough |
| | | 2 | 08.12.28 | **Sittingbourne** (SL) | H | W | 2-1 | Gough, Moffatt |
| | | 3 | 12.01.29 | **Middlesbrough** (D2) | H | D | 1-1 | N Thompson |
| | | 3r | 21.01.29 | **Middlesbrough** (D2) | A | L | 1-5 | Gough |
| 1929-30 | (3S) | 1 | 30.11.29 | **Exeter City** (3S) | H | W | 1-0 | Roe |
| | | 2 | 14.12.29 | **Newport County** (3S) | A | W | 3-2 | A Walters 3 |
| | | 3 | 11.01.30 | **Swansea Town** (D2) | H | W | 2-0 | Eyres, A Walters |
| | | 4 | 25.01.30 | **Aston Villa** (D1) | A | L | 1-3 | Johnson |
| 1930-31 | (3S) | 1 | 29.11.30 | **Bournemouth** (3S) | H | W | 1-0 | Eyres |
| | | 2 | 13.12.30 | **Newport County** (3S) | H | W | 4-0 | Cooper 3, Bartley |
| | | 3 | 10.01.31 | **Blackburn Rovers** (D1) | A | D | 1-1 | Eyres |
| | | 3r | 15.01.31 | **Blackburn Rovers** | H | L | 0-3 | |
| 1931-32 | (3N) | 1 | 28.11.31 | **Darlington** (3N) | A | L | 0-1 | |
| 1932-33 | (3N) | 1 | 26.11.32 | **Mansfield Town** (3N) | H | W | 4-1 | Lee 2, Taylor, Ball |
| | | 2 | 10.12.32 | **Hartlepools Utd** (3N) | H | W | 2-1 | Lee, Ball |
| | | 3 | 14.01.33 | **Arsenal** (D1) | H | W | 2-0 | Alsop, Sheppard (p) |
| | | 4 | 28.01.33 | **Manchester City** (D1) | A | L | 0-2 | |
| 1933-34 | (3N) | 1 | 25.11.33 | **Spennymoor Utd** (NEL) | H | W | 4-0 | Woolhouse 2, Alsop, Sheppard |
| | | 2 | 09.12.33 | **Clapton Orient** (3S) | H | D | 0-0 | |
| | | 2r | 14.12.33 | **Clapton Orient** | A | L | 0-2 | |
| 1934-35 | (3N) | 1 | 24.11.34 | **Crewe Alexandra** (3N) | A | W | 2-1 | Alsop 2 |
| | | 2 | 08.12.34 | **Watford** (3S) | A | D | 1-1 | Alsop |
| | | 2r | 13.12.34 | **Watford** | H | W | 1-0 | Ball |
| | | 3 | 12.01.35 | **Southampton** (D2) | H | L | 1-2 | Alsop |

| | | | | | | | | |
|---|---|---|---|---|---|---|---|---|
| 1935-36 | (3N) | 1 | 30.11.35 | **Lincoln City** (3N) | H | W | 2-0 | Collins, Evans |
| | | 2 | 14.12.35 | **Chesterfield** (3N) | A | D | 0-0 | |
| | | 2r | 19.12.35 | **Chesterfield** | H | W | 2-1 | Richmond, Bate |
| | | 3 | 11.01.36 | **Newcastle Utd** (D2) | H | L | 0-2 | |
| 1936-37 | (3S) | 1 | 28.11.36 | **Scunthorpe Utd** (ML) | H | W | 3-0 | Evans 3 (1p) |
| | | 2 | 12.12.36 | **Yeovil & Petters Utd** (SL) | H | D | 1-1 | Woolhouse |
| | | 2r | 17.12.36 | **Yeovil & Petters Utd** | A | W | 1-0 | Bulger |
| | | 3 | 16.01.37 | **Barnsley** (D2) | H | W | 3-1 | Evans 2, Harwood |
| | | 4 | 30.01.37 | **Grimsby Town** (D1) | A | L | 1-5 | Evans |
| 1937-38 | (3S) | 1 | 27.11.37 | **Gateshead AFC** (3N) | H | W | 4-0 | Dodd 2, Shelton, Simpson |
| | | 2 | 11.12.37 | **Watford** (3S) | A | L | 0-3 | |
| 1938-39 | (3S) | 1 | 26.11.38 | **Carlisle Utd** (3N) | H | W | 4-1 | Bambrick 3, Alsop |
| | | 2 | 10.12.38 | **Clapton Orient** (3S) | H | W | 4-2 | Bambrick, Bulger, Simpson, Hancocks |
| | | 3 | 07.01.39 | **Newport County** (3S) | A | W | 2-0 | Bambrick, Alsop |
| | | 4 | 21.01.39 | **Notts County** (3S) | A | D | 0-0 | |
| | | 4r | 26.01.39 | **Notts County** | H | W | 4-0 | Alsop 4 |
| | | 5 | 11.02.39 | **Huddersfield Town** (D1) | A | L | 0-3 | |
| 1945-46 | (3S) | 1 1L | 17.11.45 | **Shrewsbury Town** (ML) | A | L | 0-5 | |
| | | 1 2L | 24.11.45 | **Shrewsbury Town** | H | W | 4-1 | Mullard, Bennett, Talbot, Alsop |
| 1946-47 | (3S) | 1 | 30.11.46 | **Leytonstone** (IL) | A | W | 6-1 | Wilshaw 2, Davies 2, Maund, Darby |
| | | 2 | 14.12.46 | **Ipswich Town** (3S) | H | D | 0-0 | |
| | | 2r | 18.12.46 | **Ipswich Town** | A | W | 1-0 | Lishman |
| | | 3 | 11.01.47 | **Liverpool** (D1) | H | L | 2-5 | Kelly, Wilshaw |
| 1947-48 | (3S) | 1 | 29.11.47 | **Vauxhall M (Luton)** (SPT) *played at Kenilworth Road* | A | W | 2-1 | Maund, Welsh (p) |
| | | 2 | 13.12.47 | **Norwich City** (3S) | A | D | 2-2aet | McGowan, Lishman |
| | | 2r | 20.12.47 | **Norwich City** | H | W | 3-2 | Crutchley, Wilshaw, Lishman |
| | | 3 | 10.01.48 | **Coventry City** (D2) | A | L | 1-2 | Lishman |
| 1948-49 | (3S) | 1 | 27.11.48 | **Bristol Rovers** (3S) | H | W | 2-1 | Chapman, Aldred |
| | | 2 | 11.12.48 | **Gainsborough T** (ML) | H | W | 4-3 | Chapman 2, Walters, Condie |
| | | 3 | 08.01.49 | **Fulham** (D2) | A | W | 1-0aet | Devlin |
| | | 4 | 29.01.49 | **Luton Town** (D2) | A | L | 0-4 | |
| 1949-50 | (3S) | 1 | 26.11.49 | **Mansfield Town** (3N) | A | L | 1-4 | Skidmore |
| 1950-51 | (3S) | 1 | 25.11.50 | **Newport County** (3S) | A | L | 2-4 | Corbett 2 |
| 1951-52 | (3S) | 1 | 24.11.51 | **Reading** (3S) | A | L | 0-1 | |
| 1952-53 | (3S) | 1 | 22.11.52 | **Newport County** (3S) | A | L | 1-2 | Giles |
| 1953-54 | (3S) | 1 | 21.11.53 | **Bath City** (SL) | A | W | 3-0 | Allsopp, Dean, Morris |
| | | 2 | 02.12.53 | **Crewe Alexandra** (3N) | H | W | 3-0 | Holding 2, G.Jones |
| | | 3 | 09.01.54 | **Lincoln City** (D2) | A | D | 1-1 | Finlay |
| | | 3r | 14.01.54 | **Lincoln City** | H | D | 1-1aet | Morris |
| | | 3 2r | 18.01.54 | **Lincoln City** *played at the City Ground, Nottingham* | | L | 1-2 | Finlay |
| 1954-55 | (3S) | 1 | 20.11.54 | **Shrewsbury Town** (3S) | H | W | 5-2 | Richards 2, Meek, Morris, Dorman |
| | | 2 | 11.12.54 | **Wrexham** (3N) | A | W | 2-1 | Richards 2 |
| | | 3 | 08.01.55 | **Chelsea** (D1) | A | L | 0-2 | |
| 1955-56 | (3S) | 1 | 19.11.55 | **Margate** (KL) | A | D | 2-2 | Morris, McLaren |
| | | 1r | 24.11.55 | **Margate** | H | W | 6-1 | Walsh 3, Richards 2, McLaren |
| | | 2 | 10.12.55 | **Southampton** (3S) | H | W | 2-1 | Morris, Moore |
| | | 3 | 07.01.56 | **Port Vale** (D2) | H | L | 0-1 | |
| 1956-57 | (3S) | 1 | 17.11.56 | **Newport County** (3S) | H | L | 0-1 | |
| 1957-58 | (3S) | 1 | 16.11.57 | **Brighton** (3S) | A | L | 1-2 | Tarrant |
| 1958-59 | (D4) | 1 | 15.11.58 | **QPR** (D3) | H | L | 0-1 | |
| 1959-60 | (D4) | 1 | 14.11.59 | **Swindon Town** (D3) | A | W | 3-2 | Davies 2, Richards |
| | | 2 | 05.12.59 | **Peterborough Utd** (ML) | H | L | 2-3 | Richards, Billingham |
| 1960-61 | (D3) | 1 | 05.11.60 | **Yeovil Town** (SL) | H | L | 0-1 | |
| 1961-62 | (D2) | 3 | 06.01.62 | **Bristol City** (D3) | A | D | 0-0 | |
| | | 3r | 09.01.62 | **Bristol City** | H | W | 4-1 | Richards 2, Taylor, Hodgkisson |
| | | 4 | 27.01.62 | **Fulham** (D1) | A | D | 2-2 | Richards 2 (1p) |
| | | 4r | 30.01.62 | **Fulham** | H | L | 0-2 | |

| | | | | | | | | |
|---|---|---|---|---|---|---|---|---|
| 1962-63 | (D2) | 3 | 06.03.63 | **Manchester City** (D1) | H | L | 0-1 | |
| 1963-64 | (D3) | 1 | 16.11.63 | **Southport** (D4) | A | L | 1-2 | Newton |
| 1964-65 | (D3) | 1 | 14.11.64 | **Bristol Rovers** (D3) | H | L | 0-2 | |
| 1965-66 | (D3) | 1 | 13.11.65 | **Swansea Town** (D3) | H | W | 6-3 | Clarke 2 (1p), Summers, Kirby 2, Satchwell |
| | | 2 | 04.12.65 | **Aldershot** (D4) | A | W | 2-0 | Taylor, Clarke |
| | | 3 | 22.01.66 | **Stoke City** (D1) | A | W | 2-0 | Kirby, Clarke (p) |
| | | 4 | 12.02.66 | **Norwich City** (D2) | A | L | 2-3 | Kirby, Taylor |
| 1966-67 | (D3) | 1 | 26.11.66 | **St Neots Town** (Met) | H | W | 2-0 | Baker, Taylor |
| | | 2 | 07.01.67 | **Gillingham** (D3) | H | W | 3-1 | Taylor 2, Baker |
| | | 3 | 28.01.67 | **Bury** (D2) | A | L | 0-2 | |
| 1967-68 | (D3) | 1 | 09.12.67 | **Leytonstone** (IL) | A | W | 1-0 | Watson |
| | | 2 | 06.01.68 | **Exeter City** (D4) | A | W | 3-1 | Meath, Watson, Simpson |
| | | 3 | 27.01.68 | **Crystal Palace** (D2) | H | D | 1-1 | Taylor |
| | | 3r | 31.01.68 | **Crystal Palace** | A | W | 2-1 | Simpson, Jackson |
| | | 4 | 17.02.68 | **Liverpool** (D1) | H | D | 0-0 | |
| | | 4r | 19.02.68 | **Liverpool** | A | L | 2-5 | Watson 2 |
| 1968-69 | (D3) | 1 | 16.11.68 | **Leytonstone** (IL) | A | W | 1-0 | Baker |
| | | 2 | 07.12.68 | **St Albans City** (IL) | A | D | 1-1 | Trevis |
| | | 2r | 10.12.68 | **St Albans City** | H | W | 3-1 | Gibbs og, Watson, Wilson |
| | | 3 | 04.01.69 | **Tottenham Hotspur** (D1) | H | L | 0-1 | |
| 1969-70 | (D3) | 1 | 15.11.69 | **Orient** (D3) | H | D | 0-0 | |
| | | 1r | 17.11.69 | **Orient** | A | W | 2-0 | Woodward, Taylor |
| | | 2 | 06.12.69 | **Brighton** (D3) | A | D | 1-1 | Bennett |
| | | 2r | 09.12.69 | **Brighton** | H | D | 1-1aet | Taylor |
| | | 2 2r | 15.12.69 | **Brighton** *played at Highfield Road* | | D | 0-0aet | |
| | | 2 3r | 17.12.69 | **Brighton** *played at Craven Cottage* | | W | 2-1 | Taylor 2 |
| | | 3 | 03.01.70 | **Crystal Palace** (D1) | A | L | 0-2 | |
| 1970-71 | (D3) | 1 | 21.11.70 | **Plymouth Argyle** (D3) | H | W | 3-0 | Morris 2, Woodward |
| | | 2 | 12.12.70 | **Brentford** (D4) | A | L | 0-1 | |
| 1971-72 | (D3) | 1 | 20.11.71 | **Dagenham** (AL) | H | W | 4-1 | Woodward, Wright, Taylor, Morris |
| | | 2 | 11.12.71 | **Brighton** (D3) | A | D | 1-1 | Woodward |
| | | 2r | 14.12.71 | **Brighton** | H | W | 2-1 | Train, Wright |
| | | 3 | 15.01.72 | **Bournemouth** (D3) | H | W | 1-0 | Wright |
| | | 4 | 05.02.72 | **Everton** (D1) | A | L | 1-2 | Evans |
| 1972-73 | (D3) | 1 | 18.11.72 | **Kettering Town** (SL) | H | D | 3-3 | Morris 2, Woodward |
| | | 1r | 22.11.72 | **Kettering Town** | A | W | 2-1 | Atthey, C.Jones |
| | | 2 | 12.12.72 | **Charlton Athletic** (D3) | H | L | 1-2 | Morris |
| 1973-74 | (D3) | 1 | 24.11.73 | **Swansea City** (D4) | H | W | 1-0 | Andrews |
| | | 2 | 15.12.73 | **Plymouth Argyle** (D3) | A | L | 0-1 | |
| 1974-75 | (D3) | 1 | 27.11.74 | **Ashford Town** (SL) | A | W | 3-1 | Buckley 2, Fry |
| | | 2 | 14.12.74 | **Newport County** (D4) | A | W | 3-1 | Taylor, Wright, Buckley |
| | | 3 | 04.01.75 | **Manchester Utd** (D2) | A | D | 0-0 | |
| | | 3r | 07.01.75 | **Manchester Utd** | H | W | 3-2aet | Wright, Buckley 2 (1p) |
| | | 4 | 25.01.75 | **Newcastle Utd** (D1) | H | W | 1-0 | Andrews |
| | | 5 | 15.02.75 | **Birmingham City** (D1) | A | L | 1-2 | Taylor |
| 1975-76 | (D3) | 1 | 22.11.75 | **Huddersfield Town** (D4) | H | L | 0-1 | |
| 1976-77 | (D3) | 1 | 20.11.76 | **Bradford City** (D4) | H | D | 0-0 | |
| | | 1r | 24.11.76 | **Bradford City** | A | W | 2-0 | Taylor, Wright |
| | | 2 | 11.12.76 | **Chesterfield** (D3) | A | D | 1-1 | Hunter og |
| | | 2r | 14.12.76 | **Chesterfield** | H | D | 0-0aet | |
| | | 2 2r | 21.12.76 | **Chesterfield** *played at the Baseball Ground, Derby* | | W | 1-0 | Wright |
| | | 3 | 08.01.77 | **Manchester Utd** (D1) | A | L | 0-1 | |
| 1977-78 | (D3) | 1 | 26.11.77 | **Dagenham** (IL) | H | W | 1-0 | Wood |
| | | 2 | 17.12.77 | **Port Vale** (D3) | H | D | 1-1 | Wood |
| | | 2r | 19.12.77 | **Port Vale** | A | W | 3-1 | King, Shelton, Bates |
| | | 3 | 07.01.78 | **Swansea City** (D4) | H | W | 4-1 | Buckley 3, King |
| | | 4 | 28.01.78 | **Leicester City** (D1) | H | W | 1-0 | Evans |

| | | | | | | | |
|---|---|---|---|---|---|---|---|
| | 5 | 18.02.78 | **Arsenal** (D1) | A | L | 1-4 | Buckley |
| 1978-79 (D3) | 1 | 25.11.78 | **Torquay Utd** (D4) | H | L | 0-2 | |
| 1979-80 (D4) | 1 | 24.11.79 | **Stockport County** (D4) | H | W | 2-0 | Penn, Paul |
| | 2 | 15.12.79 | **Halifax Town** (D4) | H | D | 1-1 | Buckley (p) |
| | 2r | 18.12.79 | **Halifax Town** | A | D | 1-1aet | Buckley |
| | 2 2r | 24.12.79 | **Halifax Town** | A | L | 0-2aet | |
| 1980-81 (D3) | 1 | 22.11.80 | **Stafford Rangers** (APL) | H | W | 3-0 | Buckley, Penn, S Waddington |
| | 2 | 13.12.80 | **Carlisle Utd** (D3) | A | L | 0-3 | |
| 1981-82 (D3) | 1 | 21.11.81 | **Blyth Spartans** (NL) | A | W | 2-1 | Macken, Caswell |
| | 2 | 02.01.82 | **Peterborough Utd** (D4) | A | L | 1-2 | Butler og |
| 1982-83 (D3) | 1 | 20.11.82 | **Kettering Town** (APL) | H | W | 3-0 | Kearns, Preece, Buckley |
| | 2 | 11.12.82 | **North Shields** (NL) | A | W | 3-0 | Round, Buckley, Caswell |
| | 3 | 08.01.83 | **Birmingham City** (D1) | H | D | 0-0 | |
| | 3r | 11.01.83 | **Birmingham City** | A | L | 0-1aet | |
| 1983-84 (D3) | 1 | 19.11.83 | **Bournemouth** (D3) | A | L | 0-4 | |
| 1984-85 (D3) | 1 | 17.11.84 | **Stockport County** (D4) | A | W | 2-1 | Shakespeare, Kelly |
| | 2 | 08.12.84 | **Chesterfield** (D4) | H | W | 1-0 | Mower |
| | 3 | 05.01.85 | **York City** (D3) | A | L | 0-3 | |
| 1985-86 (D3) | 1 | 16.11.85 | **Preston North End** (D4) | H | W | 7-3 | Naughton 3, Elliott, Childs 2, O'Kelly |
| | 2 | 08.12.85 | **Port Vale** (D4) | A | D | 0-0 | |
| | 2r | 10.12.85 | **Port Vale** | H | W | 2-1 | Cross, Hawker |
| | 3 | 04.01.86 | **Manchester City** (D1) | H | L | 1-3 | O'Kelly (p) |
| 1986-87 (D3) | 1 | 15.11.86 | **Chesterfield** (D3) | H | W | 2-0 | Shakespeare, Mower |
| | 2 | 06.12.86 | **Port Vale** (D3) | H | W | 5-0 | Shakespeare 2(2p), Naughton, Cross, Christie |
| | 3 | 10.01.87 | **Charlton Athletic** (D1) | A | W | 2-1 | Kelly, Shakespeare |
| | 4 | 31.01.87 | **Birmingham City** (D2) | H | W | 1-0 | Cross |
| | 5 | 21.02.87 | **Watford** (D1) | H | D | 1-1 | Christie (p) |
| | 5r | 24.02.87 | **Watford** | A | D | 4-4aet | Christie 2, Cross, Hawker |
| | 5 2r | 02.03.87 | **Watford** | H | L | 0-1 | |
| 1987-88 (D3) | 1 | 14.11.87 | **Southend Utd** (D3) | A | D | 0-0 | |
| | 1r | 17.11.87 | **Southend Utd** | H | W | 2-1 | Jones 2 (2ps) |
| | 2 | 05.12.87 | **Gillingham** (D3) | A | L | 1-2 | Kelly |
| 1988-89 (D2) | 3 | 07.01.89 | **Brentford** (D3) | H | D | 1-1 | Pritchard |
| | 3r | 10.01.89 | **Brentford** | A | L | 0-1 | |
| 1989-90 (D3) | 1 | 18.11.89 | **Telford Utd** (Conf) | A | W | 3-0 | Rimmer, Bertschin, Forbes |
| | 2 | 09.12.89 | **Rotherham Utd** (D3) | H | W | 1-0 | Rimmer |
| | 3 | 06.01.90 | **Hereford Utd** (D4) | A | L | 1-2 | Bertschin |
| 1990-91 (D4) | 1 | 17.11.90 | **Aylesbury Utd** (IL) | A | W | 1-0 | McDonald |
| | 2 | 08.12.90 | **Swansea City** (D3) | A | L | 1-2 | Hutchings |
| 1991-92 (D4) | 1 | 16.11.91 | **Yeovil Town** (Conf) | A | D | 1-1 | Tolson |
| | 1r | 27.11.91 | **Yeovil Town** | H | L | 0-1aet | |
| 1992-93 (D3) | 1 | 14.11.92 | **Rotherham Utd** (D2) | A | L | 0-4 | |
| 1993-94 (D3) | 1 | 13.11.93 | **Wrexham** (D2) | A | D | 1-1 | Lightbourne |
| | 1r | 23.11.93 | **Wrexham** | H | W | 2-0 | Lightbourne, McDonald |
| | 2 | 04.12.93 | **Scunthorpe Utd** (D3) | H | D | 1-1 | Wright |
| | 2r | 14.12.93 | **Scunthorpe Utd** | A | D | 0-0aet | |
| | | | *Scunthorpe Utd won 7-6 on penalties* | | | | |
| 1994-95 (D3) | 1 | 12.11.94 | **Rochdale** (D3) | H | W | 3-0 | Lightbourne, Butler 2 |
| | 2 | 03.12.94 | **Preston North End** (D3) | A | D | 1-1 | Wilson |
| | 2r | 13.12.94 | **Preston North End** | H | W | 4-0 | Houghton, Wilson, Lightbourne 2 |
| | 3 | 07.01.95 | **Leeds Utd** (PL) | H | D | 1-1 | Marsh |
| | 3r | 17.01.95 | **Leeds Utd** | A | L | 2-5aet | O'Connor (p), Wetherall og |
| 1995-96 (D2) | 1 | 10.11.95 | **Burnley** (D2) | A | W | 3-1 | Bradley, Wilson, Houghton |
| | 2 | 02.12.95 | **Torquay Utd** (D3) | A | D | 1-1 | Lightbourne |
| | 2r | 12.12.95 | **Torquay Utd** | H | W | 8-4aet | Marsh 2, Lightbourne 2, Wilson, Bradley, O'Connor, Houghton |
| | 3 | 06.01.96 | **Wigan Athletic** (D3) | H | W | 1-0 | Pender og |
| | 4 | 13.02.96 | **Ipswich Town** (D1) | A | L | 0-1 | |
| 1996-97 (D2) | 1 | 16.11.96 | **Northwich V** (Conf) | A | D | 2-2 | Wilson, Lightbourne |
| | 1r | 26.11.96 | **Northwich V** | H | W | 3-1 | Lightbourne 2, Wilson (p) |

| | | | | | | | |
|---|---|---|---|---|---|---|---|
| | 2 | 07.12.96 | **Burnley** (D2) | H | D | 1-1 | Lightbourne |
| | 2r | 17.12.96 | **Burnley** | A | - | 1-0ab | Lightbourne |
| | | | *abandoned at halftime – floodlight failure* | | | | |
| | 2r | 23.12.96 | **Burnley** (D2) | A | D | 1-1aet | Viveash |
| | | | *Burnley won 4-2 on penalties* | | | | |
| 1997-98 (D2) | 1 | 15.11.97 | **Lincoln Utd** (NPL) | H | W | 2-0 | Watson, Boli |
| | 2 | 06.12.97 | **Macclesfield T** (D3) | A | W | 7-0 | Boli 2 (1p), Porter 2, Viveash, Hodge 2 (1p) |
| | 3 | 13.01.98 | **Peterborough Utd** (D3) | A | W | 2-0 | Watson 2 |
| | 4 | 24.01.98 | **Manchester Utd** (PL) | A | L | 1-5 | Boli |
| 1998-99 (D2) | 1 | 14.11.98 | **Gresley Rovers** (SL) | H | W | 1-0 | Roper |
| | 2 | 05.12.98 | **Preston North End** (D2) | A | L | 0-2 | |
| 1999-00 (D1) | 3 | 11.12.99 | **Gillingham** (D2) | H | D | 1-1 | Robbins (p) |
| | 3r | 08.01.00 | **Gillingham** | A | L | 1-2aet | Larusson |
| 2000-01 (D2) | 1 | 18.11.00 | **Exeter City** (D3) | H | W | 4-0 | Matias, Hall, Leitao, Barras |
| | 2 | 08.12.00 | **Barnet** (D3) | H | W | 2-1 | Tillson 2 |
| | 3 | 06.01.01 | **West Ham Utd** (PL) | H | L | 2-3 | Wrack, Angell |
| 2001-02 (D1) | 3 | 08.01.02 | **Bradford City** (D1) | H | W | 2-0 | Bennett, Angell |
| | 4 | 26.01.02 | **Charlton Athletic** (PL) | A | W | 2-1 | Leitao 2 |
| | 5 | 16.02.02 | **Fulham** (PL) | H | L | 1-2 | Byfield |
| 2002-03 (D1) | 3 | 04.01.03 | **Reading** (D1) | H | D | 0-0 | |
| | 3r | 14.01.03 | **Reading** | A | D | 1-1aet | Wrack |
| | | | *Walsall won 4-1 on penalties* | | | | |
| | 4 | 25.01.03 | **Wimbledon** (D1) | H | W | 1-0 | Zdrilic |
| | 5 | 15.02.03 | **Sheffield Utd** (D1) | A | L | 0-2 | |

## WALSALL SWIFTS

*Formed 1877. Entered FA Cup: 1882-83 – 1887-88. They reached the last 16 of the FA Cup in 1885. Walsall Swifts amalgamated with Walsall Town to form Walsall FC in 1888.*

| | | | | | | | |
|---|---|---|---|---|---|---|---|
| 1882-83 | 1 | 21.10.82 | **Aston Villa** | A | L | 1-4 | T Farmer |
| 1883-84 | 1 | 10.11.83 | **Aston Villa** | H | L | 1-5 | J Farmer |
| 1884-85 | 1 | 08.11.84 | **Stafford Road** | A | D | 0-0 | |
| | 1r | 17.11.84 | **Stafford Road** | H | W | 2-1 | Jefferies 2 |
| | 2 | 06.12.84 | **Derby St Lukes** | A | W | 1-0 | Davis |
| | 3 | 10.01.85 | **Birmingham St G** | A | W | 3-2 | Aldridge, Morely, Richards og |
| | 4 | 24.01.85 | **Notts County** | H | L | 0-4 | |
| 1885-86 | 2 | 14.11.85 | **Derby Midland** | A | W | 3-1 | Higgins, Webster 2 |
| | 3 | 12.12.85 | **Wolverhampton W** | A | L | 1-2 | T Farmer |
| 1886-87 | | | did not enter | | | | |
| 1887-88 | 1 | 15.10.87 | **Wolverhampton W** | H | L | 1-2 | Higgins |

## WALSALL TOWN

*Formed 1879. Merged with Walsall Swifts to form Walsall FC 1888.*

| | | | | | | | |
|---|---|---|---|---|---|---|---|
| 1882-83 | 1 | 21.10.82 | **Staveley** | H | W | 4-1 | Arblaster, Harrison, Hill, Tonks |
| | 2 | 02.12.82 | **Stafford Road** | H | W | 4-1 | Bird 2, Bradbury 2 |
| | 4 | 27.01.83 | **Aston Villa** | A | L | 1-2 | Hill |
| 1883-84 | 1 | 10.11.83 | **Birmingham Calthorpe** | A | W | 9-0 | Bird 4, Collington 2, Brettle, Harrison, Ashe |
| | 2 | 01.12.83 | **Wednesbury Town** | H | D | 2-2 | Arblaster 2 |
| | 2r | 06.12.83 | **Wednesbury Town** | A | L | 0-6 | |
| 1884-85 | 1 | 08.11.84 | **Derby County** | A | W | 7-0 | Cope 2, Bird 2, Shaw, Hunter, Ashe |
| | 2 | 06.12.84 | **Aston Villa** | H | L | 0-2 | |
| 1885-86 | 1 | 17.10.85 | **Aston Villa** | H | L | 0-5 | |
| 1886-87 | 1 | 30.10.86 | **Derby St Lukes** | A | D | 3-3 | Bradbury 2, Davis |
| | 1r | 13.11.86 | **Derby St Lukes** | H | W | 6-1 | Bradbury 2, Davis 2, Cox, Wilson |
| | 2 | | bye | | | | |
| | 3 | 11.12.86 | **Birmingham St G** | H | L | 2-7 | Bradbury, Wilson |
| 1887-88 | 1 | 15.10.87 | **Birmingham St G** | H | L | 1-2 | Webster |

# WALTHAMSTOW AVENUE

*Formed 1901. Entered FA Cup: 1921-22 – 1987-88. FA Amateur Cup winners: 1952, 1961. Merged with Leytonstone-Ilford to form Redbridge Forest 1989. League clubs beaten: Northampton Town, Watford, Stockport County, Gillingham, Queens Park Rangers.*

| | | | | | | | | |
|---|---|---|---|---|---|---|---|---|
| 1930-31 | (AL) | 1 | 29.11.30 | **Watford** (3S) | H | L | 1-5 | Lewis |
| 1934-35 | (AL) | 1 | 24.11.34 | **QPR** (3S) | A | L | 0-2 | |
| 1935-36 | (AL) | 1 | 30.11.35 | **Bournemouth** (3S) | H | D | 1-1 | Lewis |
| | | 1r | 04.12.35 | **Bournemouth** | A | L | 1-8 | Vincent |
| 1936-37 | (AL) | 1 | 28.11.36 | **Northampton Town** (3S) | H | W | 6-1 | Davis 3, Magner, Vincent 2 |
| | | 2 | 12.12.36 | **Exeter City** (3S) | H | - | 1-1ab | Lewis |
| | | | | *abandoned after 65 minutes – fog* | | | | |
| | | 2 | 17.12.36 | **Exeter City** | H | L | 2-3 | Matthews 2 |
| 1937-38 | (AL) | 1 | 27.11.37 | **Westbury Utd** (Wilts) | A | W | 3-1 | Magner, Lewis, Matthews |
| | | 2 | 11.12.37 | **Southend Utd** (3S) | H | L | 0-1 | |
| 1938-39 | (AL) | 1 | 26.11.38 | **Tunbridge Wells R** (KL) | H | W | 4-1 | Groves, Foreman, Magner, Kitson |
| | | 2 | 10.12.38 | **Stockport County** (3N) | A | D | 0-0 | |
| | | 2r | 15.12.38 | **Stockport County** | H | L | 1-3 | Vincent |
| 1945-46 | (IL) | 1 1L | 17.11.45 | **Sutton Utd** (AL) | A | W | 4-1 | Groves, Green 3 |
| | | 1 2L | 24.11.45 | **Sutton Utd** | H | W | 7-2 | Groves 4, Davsis 2, Insole |
| | | 2 1L | 08.12.45 | **Brighton** (3S) | H | D | 1-1 | Groves |
| | | 2 2L | 15.12.45 | **Brighton** | A | L | 2-4 | Davis 2 |
| 1948-49 | (IL) | 1 | 27.11.48 | **Cambridge Town** (SPT) | H | W | 3-2 | Lewis 2, Strather |
| | | 2 | 11.12.48 | **Oldham Athletic** (3N) | H | D | 2-2aet | Lewis, O'Connell |
| | | 2r | 18.12.48 | **Oldham Athletic** | A | L | 1-3 | Butterworth |
| 1949-50 | (IL) | 1 | 26.11.49 | **Northampton Town** (3S) | A | L | 1-4 | Tyrell |
| 1950-51 | (IL) | 1 | 25.11.50 | **Mansfield Town** (3N) | A | L | 0-1 | |
| 1952-53 | (AL) | 1 | 22.11.52 | **Wimbledon** (IL) | H | D | 2-2 | Bailey, Hall |
| | | 1r | 26.11.52 | **Wimbledon** | A | W | 3-0 | Lewis 2, Bailey |
| | | 2 | 06.12.52 | **Watford** (3S) | H | D | 1-1 | Croker og |
| | | 2r | 10.12.52 | **Watford** | A | W | 2-1aet | Camis, Lucas |
| | | 3 | 10.01.53 | **Stockport County** (3N) | H | W | 2-1 | Lucas 2 |
| | | 4 | 31.01.53 | **Manchester Utd** (D1) | A | D | 1-1 | Lewis |
| | | 4r | 05.02.53 | **Manchester Utd** | H | L | 2-5 | Lewis 2 |
| | | | | *played at Highbury* | | | | |
| 1953-54 | (IL) | 1 | 21.11.53 | **Gillingham** (3S) | H | W | 1-0 | Groves |
| | | 2 | 12.12.53 | **Ipswich Town** (3S) | A | D | 2-2 | R Walker, J Richards |
| | | 2r | 16.12.53 | **Ipswich Town** | H | L | 0-1 | |
| 1954-55 | (IL) | 1 | 20.11.54 | **QPR** (3S) | A | D | 2-2 | Anderson, Julians |
| | | 1r | 25.11.54 | **QPR** | H | D | 2-2aet | Bee 2 |
| | | 1 2r | 29.11.54 | **QPR** | | W | 4-0 | Julians, Paris, Anderson 2 |
| | | | | *played at Highbury* | | | | |
| | | 2 | 11.12.54 | **Darlington** (3N) | H | L | 0-3 | |
| 1956-57 | (IL) | 1 | 17.11.56 | **Crystal Palace** (3S) | A | L | 0-2 | |
| 1957-58 | (IL) | 1 | 16.11.57 | **Coventry City** (3S) | A | L | 0-1 | |
| 1959-60 | (IL) | 1 | 14.11.59 | **Bournemouth** (D3) | H | L | 2-3 | Harvey, Lewis (p) |
| 1960-61 | (IL) | 1 | 05.11.60 | **QPR** (D3) | A | L | 2-3 | Harvey (p), Minall |
| 1961-62 | (IL) | 1 | 04.11.61 | **Romford** (SL) | H | L | 2-3 | Stone, Minall |
| 1967-68 | (IL) | 1 | 09.12.67 | **Kidderminster H** (WMRL) | H | W | 2-1 | Jackson, Ford (p) |
| | | 2 | 06.01.68 | **Bournemouth** (D3) | H | L | 1-3 | Jackson |

# WALTON & HERSHAM

*Formed 1945 when Walton FC (1896) and Hersham FC (1926) amalgamated. First entered FA Cup as Walton & Hersham 1945-46. FA Amateur Cup winners: 1973. League clubs beaten: Exeter City, Brighton. Members of the Isthmian League.*

| | | | | | | | | |
|---|---|---|---|---|---|---|---|---|
| 1957-58 | (AL) | 1 | 16.11.57 | **Southampton** (3S) | H | L | 1-6 | Sheehan |
| 1969-70 | (AL) | 1 | 15.11.69 | **Barnet** (SL) | H | L | 0-1 | |
| 1970-71 | (AL) | 1 | 21.11.70 | **Telford Utd** (SL) | H | L | 2-5 | Longfield, Edwards |
| 1972-73 | (IL) | 1 | 18.11.72 | **Exeter City** (D4) | H | W | 2-1 | Woffinden, Koskett |
| | | 2 | 09.12.72 | **Margate** (SL) | H | L | 0-1 | |
| 1973-74 | (IL) | 1 | 24.11.73 | **Brighton** (D3) | H | D | 0-0 | |
| | | 1r | 28.11.73 | **Brighton** | A | W | 4-0 | Perkins, Foskett 3 |

| | | | | | | | |
|---|---|---|---|---|---|---|---|
| | 2 | 15.12.73 | **Hereford Utd** (D3) | A | L | 0-3 | |
| 1975-76 (IL) | 1 | 22.11.75 | **Crystal Palace** (D3) | A | L | 0-1 | |
| 1994-95 (IL) | 1 | 21.11.94 | **Swansea City** (D2) | H | L | 0-2 | |

# WANDERERS

*Developed out of the Forest School club which was formed around 1859. Wanderers were one of the 15 original entrants in the FA Cup in the 1871-72 season and were the first FA Cup winners in 1872. They won all five FA Cup finals they played in, including a hat-trick of wins in 1876, 1877 and 1878. Under the rules of the time they were allowed to keep the trophy after winning it three years in succession, but handed it back to the FA with the proviso that no club should be allowed to keep it after a hat-trick of wins. Disbanded at the end of the 1881-82 season. FA Cup winners: 1872, 1873, 1876, 1877, 1878.*

| | | | | | | | |
|---|---|---|---|---|---|---|---|
| 1871-72 | 1 | 11.11.71 | **Harrow Chequers** | | | - | |
| | | | *Harrow Chequers scratched. Wanderers walkover* | | | | |
| | 2 | 16.12.71 | **Clapham Rovers** | A | W | 3-1 | Pelham, others 2 |
| | 3 | 20.01.72 | **Crystal Palace (1861)** | H | D | 0-0 | |
| | | | *Both teams qualified for semi-finals* | | | | |
| | SF | 05.03.72 | **Queen's Park, Glasgow** | | D | 0-0 | |
| | | | *played at Kennington Oval – Queen's Park scratched before the replay. Wanderers gained walkover into the final* | | | | |
| | F | 16.03.72 | **Royal Engineers** | | W | 1-0 | MP Betts |
| | | | *played at Kennington Oval* | | | | |
| 1872-73 | As holders under the rules in opersation they were exempt until the cup final | | | | | | |
| | F | 23.03.73 | **Oxford University** | | W | 2-0 | Kinnaird, Wollaston |
| | | | *played at Lillie Bridge* | | | | |
| 1873-74 | 1 | | Southall Park | | | - | |
| | | | *Southall Park scratched. Wanderers walkover* | | | | |
| | 2 | | Trojans | | | - | |
| | | | *Trojans scratched. Wanderers walkover* | | | | |
| | 3 | 06.12.73 | **Oxford University** | H | D | 1-1 | Maddison |
| | 3r | 31.01.74 | **Oxford University** | A | L | 0-1 | |
| 1874-75 | 1 | 10.10.74 | **Farningham** | H | W | 16-0 | Kingsford 5, Wollaston 4, Alcock 2, Chenery 2, Heron 2, Kenrick |
| | 2 | 21.11.74 | **Barnes** | H | W | 5-0 | Alcock 3, Kenrick, Wollaston |
| | 3 | 30.01.75 | **Oxford University** | H | L | 1-2 | Rawson og |
| 1875-76 | 1 | 23.10.75 | **1st Surrey Rifles** | H | W | 5-0 | Kenrick 2, Maddison 2, Alcock |
| | 2 | 11.12.75 | **Crystal Palace (1861)** | H | W | 3-0 | Wollaston 2, F Heron |
| | 3 | 29.01.76 | **Sheffield FC** | H | W | 2-0 | F Heron 2 |
| | SF | 26.02.76 | **Swifts** | | W | 2-1 | Birley, Wollaston |
| | | | *played at Kennington Oval* | | | | |
| | F | 11.03.76 | **Old Etonians** | | D | 1-1 | Edwards |
| | | | *played at Kennington Oval* | | | | |
| | Fr | 18.03.76 | **Old Etonians** | | W | 3-0 | Wollaston, Hughes 2 |
| | | | *played at Kennington Oval* | | | | |
| 1876-77 | 1 | | Saffron Walden | | | - | |
| | | | *Saffron Walden scratched. Wanderers walkover* | | | | |
| | 2 | 16.12.76 | **Southall Park** | H | W | 6-0 | |
| | 3 | 20.01.77 | **Pilgrims** | H | W | 3-0 | Maddison, Wollaston, AN Other |
| | 4 | | bye | | | | |
| | SF | 20.03.77 | **Cambridge University** | | W | 1-0 | Heron |
| | | | *played at Kennington Oval* | | | | |
| | F | 24.03.77 | **Oxford University** | | W | 2-1aet | Kenrick, Lindsay |
| | | | *played at Kennington Oval* | | | | |
| 1877-78 | 1 | 07.11.77 | **Panthers** | H | W | 9-1 | Heron 4, Wace 2, Wylie 2, Kenrick |
| | 2 | 15.12.77 | **High Wycombe** | A | W | 9-0 | Wace 2, Wollaston 2, Wylie 2, Denton, Kinnaird, og |
| | 3 | 12.01.78 | **Barnes** | H | D | 1-1 | Denton |
| | 3r | 26.01.78 | **Barnes** | H | W | 4-1 | Kinnaird, Wollaston, Wylie, AN Other |
| | 4 | 16.02.78 | **Sheffield FC** | H | W | 3-0 | Denton, Wace, Wylie |
| | SF | | bye | | | | |
| | F | 23.03.78 | **Royal Engineers** | | W | 3-1 | Kenrick 2, Kinnaird |
| | | | *played at Kennington Oval* | | | | |
| 1878-79 | 1 | 09.11.78 | **Old Etonians** | H | L | 2-7 | Kenrick, AN Other |

| | | | | | | | | |
|---|---|---|---|---|---|---|---|---|
| 1879-80 | 1 | 15.11.79 | **Rochester** | A | W | 6-0 | |
| | 2 | 10.01.80 | **Old Carthusians** | H | W | 1-0 | Wace |
| | 3 | 24.01.80 | **Old Etonians** | A | L | 1-3 | Wace |
| 1880-81 | 1 | | Rangers FC, London | | | - | |
| | | | *Wanderers scratched. Rangers FC walkover* | | | | |
| 1881-82 | 1 | | St Barts Hospital | | | - | |
| | | | *Wanderers scratched. St Bart's walkover* | | | | |

## WARE

*Formed 1892. First entered FA Cup: 1926-27. Members of the Isthmian League.*

| | | | | | | | |
|---|---|---|---|---|---|---|---|
| 1968-69 (AL) | 1 | 16.11.68 | **Luton Town** (D3) | A | L | 1-6 | Francis |

## WARWICK COUNTY

*Formed 1876. Entered FA Cup: 1887-88 – 1890-91. Played at Edgbaston cricket ground, Birmingham. Made FA Cup history when they beat Stoke 2-1 in a first qualifying round match on October 6, 1888 to become the first Non-League club to beat a Football League club, just a month into the League's first season.*

| | | | | | | | |
|---|---|---|---|---|---|---|---|
| 1887-88 | 1 | 15.10.87 | **Birmingham Excelsior** | A | L | 1-4 | |
| | | | *FA ordered replay after protest* | | | | |
| | 1r | 22.10.87 | **Birmingham Excelsior** | H | L | 0-5 | |

## WATERLOOVILLE

*Formed 1905. Entered FA Cup: 1966-67 – 1997-98. Merged with Havant Town 1998 to form Havant & Waterlooville. Members of the Southern League. See also Havant & Waterlooville.*

| | | | | | | | |
|---|---|---|---|---|---|---|---|
| 1968-69 (SL) | 1 | 16.11.68 | **Kettering Town** (SL) | H | L | 1-2 | Goodall |
| 1976-77 (SL) | 1 | 20.11.76 | **Wycombe W** (IL) | H | L | 1-2 | Robson |
| 1983-84 (SL) | 1 | 19.11.83 | **Northampton Town** (D4) | A | D | 1-1 | Hore |
| | 1r | 23.11.83 | **Northampton Town** | H | D | 1-1aet | Holland |
| | 12r | 28.11.83 | **Northampton Town** | A | L | 0-2 | |
| 1988-89 (SL) | 1 | 19.11.88 | **Aylesbury Utd** (Conf) | H | L | 1-4 | Whittingham |

## WATFORD

*Formed 1898. First entered FA Cup as Watford FC 1898-99. FA Cup runners-up: 1984. Record FA Cup win: 10-0 v Leighton Cee Springs, 3rd qualifying round, 1900-01; 10-0 v Bournemouth Amateurs, 4th qualifying round, 1913-14. In Competition Proper: 10-1 v Lowestoft Town, 1st round, 27.11.1926. Record FA Cup defeat: 0-10 v Wolverhampton Wanderers, 1st round replay, 24.01.1912. Watford FC trace their roots back to the original premier club in Hertfordshire, Herts Rangers, formed in 1865. By the time the FA Cup began in 1871, the principal clubs in Watford were Herts Rangers and Watford Rovers and their records in the Competition Proper are included under their names. By the 1890s the two principal clubs in the town were Watford St Mary's and West Herts FC. They both entered the FA Cup, neither club reaching the Competition Proper. They finally merged to form Watford in 1898 which is where this record begins.*

| | | | | | | | |
|---|---|---|---|---|---|---|---|
| 1898-99 (SL) | | | P Chesham Town (H) 1-0; 1q Chesham Generals (H) 4-0; 2q Lowestoft Town (H) 2-0; 3q Luton Town (A) 2-2; 3qr Luton Town (H) 0-1 | | | | |
| 1899-00 (SL) | | | 1q Hitchin Town (H) 7-1; 2q Wolverton LNW (H) 1-0; 3q Crouch End Vampires (A) 3-0; 4q Luton Town (A) 2-3 | | | | |
| 1900-01 (SL) | | | 3q Leighton CS (H) 10-0; 4q QPR (H) 1-1; 4qr QPR (A) 1-4 | | | | |
| 1901-02 (SL) | | | 3q West Hampstead (A) 2-1; 4q Luton Town (H) 1-2 | | | | |
| 1902-03 (SL) | | | 3q Fulham (H) 1-1; 3qr Fulham (A) 0-3 | | | | |
| 1903-04 (SL) | | | 3q Redhill (A) 6-1; 4q Luton Town (A) 1-4 | | | | |
| 1904-05 (SL) | | | 3q Biggleswade (H) 7-1; 4q Grays Utd (A) 3-1; 5q Hitchin Town (H) 2-0; 6q Lincoln City (H) 1-1; 6qr Lincoln City (A) 1-2 | | | | |
| 1905-06 (SL) | | | 4q Southport (H) 3-1 | | | | |
| | 1 | 13.01.06 | **Worcester City** (BDL) | A | W | 6-0 | Reid 3, Richardson, Eames, Kelly |
| | 2 | 03.02.06 | **Woolwich Arsenal** (D1) | A | L | 0-3 | |
| 1906-07 (SL) | | | 5q Stockton (A) 2-0 | | | | |
| | 1 | 12.01.07 | **Southampton** (SL) | A | L | 1-2 | Soar |
| 1907-08 (SL) | 1 | 11.01.08 | **Gainsborough T** (D2) | A | L | 0-1 | |
| 1908-09 (SL) | | | 5q West Stanley (H) 4-1 | | | | |
| | 1 | 16.01.09 | **Leicester Fosse** (D1) | H | D | 1-1 | Cleaver |
| | 1r | 20.01.09 | **Leicester Fosse** | A | L | 1-3 | Maclaine |
| 1909-10 (SL) | | | 4q Bromley (H) 8-1; 5q Wycombe W (A) 4-0 | | | | |
| | 1 | 15.01.10 | **Woolwich Arsenal** (D1) | A | L | 0-3 | |
| 1910-11 (SL) | | | 4q Ilford (H) 3-2; 5q Clapton (H) 6-0 | | | | |

| | | | | | | | | |
|---|---|---|---|---|---|---|---|---|
| | | 1 | 14.01.11 | **Barnsley** (D2) | H | L | 0-2 | |
| 1911-12 | (SL) | | | 4q Custom House (A) 5-0; 5q Barrow (H) 2-2; 5qr Barrow (A) 2-1 | | | | |
| | | 1 | 13.01.12 | **Wolverhampton W** (D2) | H | D | 0-0 | |
| | | 1r | 24.01.12 | **Wolverhampton W** | A | L | 0-10 | |
| 1912-13 | (SL) | | | 4q Brentford (A) 0-0; 4qr Brentford (H) 5-1; 5q Chesterfield (A) 1-3 | | | | |
| 1913-14 | (SL) | | | 4q Bournemouth FC (H) 10-0; 5q Gillingham (A) 0-1 | | | | |
| 1914-15 | (SL) | | | 6q Rochdale (A) 0-2 | | | | |
| 1919-20 | (SL) | | | 6q Southend Utd (A) 0-1 | | | | |
| 1920-21 | (D3) | 1 | 08.01.21 | **Exeter City** (D3) | H | W | 3-0 | Hoddinott 2, Waterall |
| | | 2 | 29.01.21 | **Preston North End** (D1) | A | L | 1-4 | Hoddinott |
| 1921-22 | (3S) | 1 | 07.01.22 | **Blackpool** (D2) | A | W | 2-1 | Pagnam 2 |
| | | 2 | 28.01.22 | **Tottenham Hotspur** (D1) | A | L | 0-1 | |
| 1922-23 | (3S) | 1 | 13.01.23 | **Cardiff City** (D1) | A | D | 1-1 | Pagnam |
| | | 1r | 17.01.23 | **Cardiff City** | H | D | 2-2 | Smith, Pagnam |
| | | 1 2r | 22.01.23 | **Cardiff City** *played at Villa Park* | | L | 1-2 | Stephenson |
| 1923-24 | (3S) | 1 | 12.01.24 | **Middlesbrough** (D1) | A | W | 1-0 | Stephenson |
| | | 2 | 02.02.24 | **Exeter City** (3S) | A | D | 0-0 | |
| | | 2r | 07.02.24 | **Exeter City** | H | W | 1-0 | Poole |
| | | 3 | 23.02.24 | **Newcastle Utd** (D1) | H | L | 0-1 | |
| 1924-25 | (3S) | 1 | 10.01.25 | **Brighton** (3S) | H | D | 1-1 | C White |
| | | 1r | 14.01.25 | **Brighton** | A | L | 3-4 | Andrews, Pagnam, Prior |
| 1925-26 | (3S) | 1 | 28.11.25 | **Brighton** (3S) | A | D | 1-1 | Pagnam |
| | | 1r | 02.12.25 | **Brighton** | H | W | 2-0 | Prior, Swan |
| | | 2 | 12.12.25 | **Swansea Town** (D2) | A | L | 2-3 | Pagnam, Prior |
| 1926-27 | (3S) | 1 | 27.11.26 | **Lowestoft Town** (N&S) | H | W | 10-1 | Warner 3, Foster og, Swan 3, Fletcher, Daniels, Edmonds |
| | | 2 | 11.12.26 | **Brighton** (3S) | H | L | 0-1 | |
| 1927-28 | (3S) | 1 | 30.11.27 | **Brighton** | H | L | 1-2 | Parker |
| 1928-29 | (3S) | 1 | 24.11.28 | **Leyton FC** (AL) | A | W | 2-0 | McPherson, Barnett |
| | | 2 | 08.12.28 | **Merthyr Town** (3S) | H | W | 2-0 | Barnett, McPherson |
| | | 3 | 12.01.29 | **Preston North End** (D2) | H | W | 1-0 | Barnett |
| | | 4 | 26.01.29 | **Bournemouth** (3S) | A | L | 4-6 | Barnett 2, Sheppard 2 |
| 1929-30 | (3S) | 1 | 30.11.29 | **Ilford** (IL) | A | W | 3-0 | McPherson 3 |
| | | 2 | 14.12.29 | **Plymouth Argyle** (3S) | H | D | 1-1 | Woodward |
| | | 2r | 18.12.29 | **Plymouth Argyle** | A | L | 0-3 | |
| 1930-31 | (3S) | 1 | 29.11.30 | **Walthamstow Ave** (AL) | A | W | 5-1 | James 3, Woolliscroft, Lindsay |
| | | 2 | 13.12.30 | **Luton Town** (3S) | H | W | 3-1 | James, Woolliscroft, Barnett |
| | | 3 | 10.01.31 | **Oldham Athletic** (D2) | A | W | 3-1 | Barnett, Miller, James |
| | | 4 | 26.01.31 | **Brighton** (3S) | H | W | 2-0 | James 2 |
| | | 5 | 14.02.31 | **Birmingham** (D1) | A | L | 0-3 | |
| 1931-32 | (3S) | 1 | 28.11.31 | **Thames** (3S) | A | D | 2-2 | White 2 |
| | | 1r | 01.12.31 | **Thames** | H | W | 2-1 | White 2 |
| | | 2 | 12.12.31 | **Gainsborough T** (ML) | A | W | 5-2 | White 3, Lowe 2 |
| | | 3 | 09.01.32 | **Fulham** (3S) | H | D | 1-1 | Woodward |
| | | 3r | 14.01.32 | **Fulham** | A | W | 3-0 | Lowe, James, O'Brien (p) |
| | | 4 | 23.01.32 | **Bristol City** (D2) | H | W | 2-1 | Lowe, Barnett |
| | | 5 | 13.02.32 | **Bradford Park A** (D2) | H | W | 1-0 | James |
| | | 6 | 27.02.32 | **Newcastle Utd** (D1) | A | L | 0-5 | |
| 1932-33 | (3S) | 3 | 14.01.33 | **Southend Utd** (3S) | H | D | 1-1 | James |
| | | 3r | 18.01.33 | **Southend Utd** | A | L | 0-2 | |
| 1933-34 | (3S) | 1 | 25.11.33 | **Reading** (3S) | H | L | 0-3 | |
| 1934-35 | (3S) | 1 | 24.11.34 | **Corinthians** | H | W | 2-0 | O'Brien, Rattray |
| | | 2 | 08.12.34 | **Walsall** (3N) | H | D | 1-1 | Carter |
| | | 2r | 13.12.34 | **Walsall** | A | L | 0-1 | |
| 1935-36 | (3S) | 1 | 30.11.35 | **Nunhead** (IL) | A | W | 4-2 | Wright 2, Barnett, Fletcher |
| | | 2 | 14.12.35 | **Rotherham Utd** (3N) | A | D | 1-1 | Devan |
| | | 2r | 18.12.35 | **Rotherham Utd** | H | W | 1-0 | Devan |
| | | 3 | 11.01.36 | **Southall** (AL) | A | W | 4-1 | Barnett 3, Fletcher |
| | | 4 | 25.01.36 | **Leicester City** (D2) | A | L | 3-6 | McPherson 3 (1p) |
| 1936-37 | (3S) | 1 | 28.11.36 | **Ipswich Town** (SL) | A | L | 1-2 | Davies (p) |

| | | | | | | | |
|---|---|---|---|---|---|---|---|
| 1937-38 (3S) | 1 | 27.11.37 | **Cheltenham Town** (SL) | H | W | 3-0 | Wipfler, Lewis, Jones |
| | 2 | 11.12.37 | **Walsall** (3S) | H | W | 3-0 | Barnett, Johnson, Walters |
| | 3 | 08.01.38 | **Sunderland** (D1) | A | L | 0-1 | |
| 1938-39 (3S) | 1 | 26.11.38 | **Northampton Town** (3S) | H | W | 4-1 | Jones, Barnett, Davies, Evans |
| | 2 | 10.12.38 | **Scunthorpe Utd** (ML) | A | W | 2-1 | Dunderdale, Jones |
| | 3 | 07.01.39 | **Tottenham Hotspur** (D2) | A | L | 1-7 | Dunderdale |
| 1945-46 (3S) | 1 1L | 17.11.45 | **Southend Utd** (3S) | H | D | 1-1 | Davies |
| | 1 2L | 24.11.45 | **Southend Utd** | A | W | 3-0 | Lewis 2, Gray |
| | 2 1L | 08.12.45 | **Bromley** (AL) | A | W | 3-1 | Jezzard, Sheen og, Gray |
| | 2 2L | 15.12.45 | **Bromley** | H | D | 1-1 | Gray |
| | 3 1L | 05.01.46 | **Nottingham Forest** (D2) | A | D | 1-1 | Blagg og |
| | 3 2L | 09.01.46 | **Nottingham Forest** | H | D | 1-1aet | Lewis |
| | 3r | 16.01.46 | **Nottingham Forest** *played at White Hart Lane* | | W | 1-0aet | Blagg og |
| | 4 1L | 26.01.46 | **Birmingham City** (D2) | A | L | 0-5 | |
| | 4 2L | 30.01.46 | **Birmingham City** | H | D | 1-1 | Gray |
| 1946-47 (3S) | 1 | 30.11.46 | **Wellington Town** (CC) | A | D | 1-1 | Dunderdale |
| | 1r | 04.12.46 | **Wellington Town** | H | W | 1-0 | Dunderdale |
| | 2 | 14.12.46 | **Port Vale** (3S) | H | D | 1-1 | Beckett |
| | 2r | 17.12.46 | **Port Vale** | A | L | 1-2 | R Evans |
| 1947-48 (3S) | 1 | 29.11.47 | **Torquay Utd** (3S) | H | D | 1-1aet | Usher |
| | 1r | 06.12.47 | **Torquay Utd** | A | L | 0-3 | |
| 1948-49 (3S) | 1 | 27.11.48 | **Leytonstone** (IL) *abandoned after 63 minutes – fog* | A | - | 1-1ab | Nolan |
| | 1 | 04.12.48 | **Leytonstone** | A | L | 1-2 | Leslie |
| 1949-50 (3S) | 1 | 26.11.49 | **Bromley** (AL) | A | W | 2-1 | Hartburn, T Jones |
| | 2 | 10.12.49 | **Netherfield** (LC) | H | W | 6-0 | Thomas 2, Hartburn, Brown, Oliver (p), K Richardson og |
| | 3 | 07.01.50 | **Preston North End** (D2) | H | D | 2-2 | Thomas, Oliver |
| | 3r | 11.01.50 | **Preston North End** | A | W | 1-0 | Thomas |
| | 4 | 28.01.50 | **Manchester Utd** (D1) | H | L | 0-1 | |
| 1950-51 (3S) | 1 | 25.11.50 | **Norwich City** (3S) | A | L | 0-2 | |
| 1951-52 (3S) | 1 | 24.11.51 | **Aylesbury Utd** (Del) | A | W | 5-0 | Thompson 2, Haig 2, Cook |
| | 2 | 15.12.51 | **Hartlepools Utd** (3N) | H | L | 1-2 | Thompson |
| 1952-53 (3S) | 1 | 22.11.52 | **Leytonstone** (IL) | A | W | 2-0 | Thompson 2 |
| | 2 | 06.12.52 | **Walthamstow Ave** (AL) | A | D | 1-1 | Meadows |
| | 2r | 10.12.52 | **Walthamstow Ave** | H | L | 1-2aet | Collins |
| 1953-54 (3S) | 1 | 21.11.53 | **Nuneaton B** (BDL) | A | L | 0-3 | |
| 1954-55 (3S) | 1 | 20.11.54 | **Corby Town** (ML) | A | W | 2-0 | P Walker, E.Smith |
| | 2 | 11.12.54 | **Carlisle Utd** (3N) | A | D | 2-2 | Cook 2 |
| | 2r | 15.12.54 | **Carlisle Utd** | H | W | 4-1 | Cook 2, Adams, Bowie |
| | 3 | 08.01.55 | **Doncaster Rovers** (D2) | H | L | 1-2 | Cook |
| 1955-56 (3S) | 1 | 19.11.55 | **Ramsgate Athletic** (KL) | H | W | 5-3 | Hernon, Graham 3, Brown |
| | 2 | 10.12.55 | **Bedford Town** (SL) | A | L | 2-3 | Farquhar og, Cook |
| 1956-57 (3S) | 1 | 17.11.56 | **Newport (IOW)** (HL) | A | W | 6-0 | Meadows, Graham 2, Walker, Cook 2 |
| | 2 | 08.12.56 | **Ipswich Town** (3S) | H | L | 1-3 | Graham |
| 1957-58 (3S) | 1 | 16.11.57 | **Plymouth Argyle** (3S) | A | L | 2-6 | Cook, Meadows |
| 1958-59 (D4) | 1 | 15.11.58 | **Reading** (D3) | H | D | 1-1 | Gavin, Catleugh |
| | 1r | 19.11.58 | **Reading** | A | W | 2-0 | Gavin, Catleugh |
| | 2 | 06.12.58 | **Torquay Utd** (D4) | A | L | 0-2 | |
| 1959-60 (D4) | 1 | 14.11.59 | **Cheltenham Town** (SL) | A | D | 0-0 | |
| | 1r | 17.11.59 | **Cheltenham Town** | H | W | 3-0 | Uphill 3 |
| | 2 | 05.12.59 | **Wycombe W** (IL) | H | W | 5-1 | Uphill 2, Holton 2 (1p), McNeice |
| | 3 | 09.01.60 | **Birmingham City** (D1) | H | W | 2-1 | Uphill, Holton |
| | 4 | 30.01.60 | **Southampton** (D3) | A | D | 2-2 | Holton, Page og |
| | 4r | 02.02.60 | **Southampton** | H | W | 1-0 | Hartle |
| | 5 | 20.02.60 | **Sheffield Utd** (D2) | A | L | 2-3 | Holton 2 |
| 1960-61 (D3) | 1 | 05.11.60 | **Brentford** (D3) | H | D | 2-2 | Bunce, Holton |
| | 1r | 08.11.60 | **Brentford** | A | W | 2-0 | Fairbrother, Benning |
| | 2 | 26.11.60 | **Crystal Palace** (D4) | A | D | 0-0 | |
| | 2r | 29.11.60 | **Crystal Palace** | H | W | 1-0 | Bunce |

| | | | | | | | |
|---|---|---|---|---|---|---|---|
| | 3 | 07.01.61 | **Rotherham Utd** (D2) | A | L | 0-1 | |
| 1961-62 (D3) | 1 | 04.11.61 | **Southend Utd** (D3) | A | W | 2-0 | Gregory 2 |
| | 2 | 25.11.61 | **Romford** (SL) | A | W | 3-1 | Harmer (p), Brown, Bunce |
| | 3 | 06.01.62 | **Preston North End** (D2) | A | L | 2-3 | Nicholas, Fairbrother |
| 1962-63 (D3) | 1 | 03.11.62 | **Poole Town** (SL) | H | D | 2-2 | Howfield, Chung |
| | 1r | 06.11.62 | **Poole Town** | A | W | 2-1 | Gregory, Harris |
| | 2 | 24.11.62 | **Southend Utd** (D3) | A | W | 2-0 | Harris, Chung |
| | 3 | 20.02.63 | **Rotherham Utd** (D2) | H | W | 2-0 | Howfield, Harris |
| | 4 | 27.02.63 | **Southampton** (D2) | A | L | 1-3 | Ward |
| 1963-64 (D3) | 1 | 16.11.63 | **Peterborough Utd** (D3) | A | D | 1-1 | Oliver |
| | 1r | 19.11.63 | **Peterborough Utd** | H | W | 2-1aet | Oliver, Livesey |
| | 2 | 07.12.63 | **Newport County** (D4) | A | L | 0-2 | |
| 1964-65 (D3) | 1 | 14.11.64 | **Reading** (D3) | A | L | 1-3 | Nicholas |
| 1965-66 (D3) | 1 | 13.11.65 | **Corinthian Casuals** (IL) | A | W | 5-1 | Brace 2, Welbourne, Owen 2 |
| | 2 | 04.12.65 | **Southend Utd** (D3) | A | L | 1-2 | Holton |
| 1966-67 (D3) | 1 | 26.11.66 | **Southend Utd** | H | W | 1-0 | Farrall |
| | 2 | 07.01.67 | **Enfield** (IL) | A | W | 4-2 | Farrall 2, Melling, Garbett |
| | 3 | 28.01.67 | **Liverpool** (D1) | H | D | 0-0 | |
| | 3r | 01.02.67 | **Liverpool** | A | L | 1-3 | Melling |
| 1967-68 (D3) | 1 | 09.12.67 | **Lowestoft Town** (ECL) | A | W | 1-0 | Owen |
| | 2 | 06.01.68 | **Hereford Utd** (SL) | H | W | 3-0 | Eddy, Hale 2 |
| | 3 | 27.01.68 | **Sheffield Utd** (D1) | H | L | 0-1 | |
| 1968-69 (D3) | 1 | 16.11.68 | **Cheltenham Town** (SL) | A | W | 4-0 | Eddy (p), Hale, Garbett, Endean |
| | 2 | 07.12.68 | **Brentford** (D4) | H | W | 1-0 | Garbett |
| | 3 | 04.01.69 | **Port Vale** (D4) | H | W | 2-0 | Scullion, Endean |
| | 4 | 25.01.69 | **Manchester Utd** (D1) | A | D | 1-1 | Scullion |
| | 4r | 03.02.69 | **Manchester Utd** | H | L | 0-2 | |
| 1969-70 (D2) | 3 | 03.01.70 | **Bolton Wanderers** (D2) | A | W | 2-1 | Endean 2 |
| | 4 | 24.01.70 | **Stoke City** (D1) | H | W | 1-0 | Franks |
| | 5 | 07.02.70 | **Gillingham** (D3) | H | W | 2-1 | Lugg 2 |
| | 6 | 21.02.70 | **Liverpool** (D1) | H | W | 1-0 | Endean |
| | SF | 14.03.70 | **Chelsea** (D1) | | L | 1-5 | Garbett |
| | | | *played at White Hart Lane* | | | | |
| | 3/4 | 10.04.70 | **Manchester Utd** (D1) | | L | 0-2 | |
| | | | *played at Highbury* | | | | |
| 1970-71 (D2) | 3 | 06.01.71 | **Reading** (D3) | H | W | 5-0 | Scullion, Endean 3, Eddy (p) |
| | 4 | 23.01.71 | **Oxford Utd** (D2) | A | D | 1-1 | Wigg |
| | 4r | 27.01.71 | **Oxford Utd** | H | L | 1-2 | Wigg |
| 1971-72 (D2) | 3 | 15.01.72 | **Notts County** (D3) | H | L | 1-4 | Wigg |
| 1972-73 (D3) | 1 | 18.11.72 | **Guildford City** (SL) | H | W | 4-2 | Wigg, Butler, Welbourne, Kenning (p) |
| | 2 | 09.12.72 | **Aldershot** (D4) | H | W | 2-0 | Lees, Farley |
| | 3 | 13.01.73 | **Sheffield Utd** (D1) | H | L | 0-1 | |
| 1973-74 (D3) | 1 | 24.11.73 | **Chelmsford City** (SL) | H | W | 1-0 | Morrissey |
| | 2 | 15.12.73 | **Bournemouth** (D3) | H | L | 0-1 | |
| 1974-75 (D3) | 1 | 23.11.74 | **Colchester Utd** (D3) | H | L | 0-1 | |
| 1975-76 (D4) | 1 | 22.11.75 | **Brighton** (D3) | H | L | 0-3 | |
| 1976-77 (D4) | 1 | 20.11.76 | **Gillingham** (D3) | A | W | 1-0 | Mayes |
| | 2 | 11.12.76 | **Hillingdon Borough** (SL) | A | W | 3-2 | Bond (p), Mercer, Coffill |
| | 3 | 08.01.77 | **Northwich V** (NPL) | A | L | 2-3 | Mercer, Bond |
| 1977-78 (D4) | 1 | 26.11.77 | **Hendon** (IL) | H | W | 2-0 | Garner, Mercer |
| | 2 | 17.12.77 | **Colchester Utd** (D3) | H | W | 2-0 | Jenkins, Mercer |
| | 3 | 07.01.78 | **West Ham Utd** (D1) | A | L | 0-1 | |
| 1978-79 (D3) | 1 | 25.11.78 | **Dagenham** (IL) | H | W | 3-0 | Jenkins 3 |
| | 2 | 16.12.78 | **Southend Utd** (D3) | H | D | 1-1 | Jenkins |
| | 2r | 18.12.78 | **Southend Utd** | A | L | 0-1 | |
| 1979-80 (D2) | 3 | 05.01.80 | **QPR** (D2) | A | W | 2-1 | Bolton (p), Rostron |
| | 4 | 26.01.80 | **Harlow Town** (IL) | H | W | 4-3 | Poskett, Patching 2, Bolton |
| | 5 | 16.02.80 | **Wolverhampton W** (D1) | A | W | 3-0 | Poskett 2, Blissett |
| | 6 | 08.03.80 | **Arsenal** (D1) | H | L | 1-2 | Poskett |
| 1980-81 (D2) | 3 | 03.01.81 | **Colchester Utd** (D3) | A | W | 1-0 | Poskett |
| | 4 | 24.01.81 | **Wolverhampton W** (D1) | H | D | 1-1 | Armstrong |
| | 4r | 27.01.81 | **Wolverhampton W** | A | L | 1-2 | Poskett |

| | | | | | | | |
|---|---|---|---|---|---|---|---|
| 1981-82 (D2) | 3 | 02.01.82 | **Manchester Utd** (D1) | H | W | 1-0 | Lohman |
| | 4 | 23.01.82 | **West Ham Utd** (D1) | H | W | 2-0 | Armstrong, Callaghan |
| | 5 | 13.02.82 | **Leicester City** (D2) | A | L | 0-2 | |
| 1982-83 (D1) | 3 | 08.01.83 | **Plymouth Argyle** (D3) | H | W | 2-0 | Rostron, Blissett |
| | 4 | 29.01.83 | **Fulham** (D2) | H | D | 1-1 | Lohman |
| | 4r | 01.02.83 | **Fulham** | A | W | 2-1 | Lohman, Barnes |
| | 5 | 19.02.83 | **Aston Villa** (D1) | A | L | 1-4 | Blissett (p) |
| 1983-84 (D1) | 3 | 07.01.84 | **Luton Town** (D1) | A | D | 2-2 | Barnes, Johnston (p) |
| | 3r | 10.01.84 | **Luton Town** | H | W | 4-3 | Callaghan, Reilly, Barnes, Johnston |
| | 4 | 28.01.84 | **Charlton Athletic** (D2) | A | W | 2-0 | Johnston, Reilly |
| | 5 | 18.02.84 | **Brighton** (D2) | H | W | 3-1 | Reilly, Johnston, Jackett |
| | 6 | 10.03.84 | **Birmingham City** (D1) | A | W | 3-1 | Barnes 2, Taylor |
| | SF | 14.04.84 | **Plymouth Argyle** (D3) | | W | 1-0 | Reilly |
| | | | *played at Villa Park* | | | | |
| | F | 19.05.84 | **Everton** (D1) | | L | 0-2 | |
| | | | *played at Wembley Stadium* | | | | |
| 1984-85 (D1) | 3 | 05.01.85 | **Sheffield Utd** (D2) | H | W | 5-0 | Blissett 4 (1p), Taylor |
| | 4 | 26.01.85 | **Grimsby Town** (D2) | A | W | 3-1 | Blissett 2, Gilligan |
| | 5 | 04.03.85 | **Luton Town** (D1) | A | D | 0-0 | |
| | 5r | 06.03.85 | **Luton Town** | H | D | 2-2aet | Taylor, Terry |
| | 5 2r | 09.03.85 | **Luton Town** | A | L | 0-1 | |
| 1985-86 (D1) | 3 | 04.01.86 | **Coventry City** (D1) | A | W | 3-1 | West 2, Jackett |
| | 4 | 25.01.86 | **Manchester City** (D1) | A | D | 1-1 | Jackett |
| | 4r | 03.02.86 | **Manchester City** | H | D | 0-0aet | |
| | 4 2r | 06.02.86 | **Manchester City** | A | W | 3-1 | Smillie, Barnes, Sterling |
| | 5 | 05.03.86 | **Bury** (D3) | H | D | 1-1 | Barnes |
| | 5r | 08.03.86 | **Bury** | A | W | 3-0 | Callaghan, West, Sterling |
| | 6 | 11.03.86 | **Liverpool** (D1) | A | D | 0-0 | |
| | 6r | 17.03.86 | **Liverpool** | H | L | 1-2aet | Barnes |
| 1986-87 (D1) | 3 | 10.01.87 | **Maidstone Utd** (Conf) | H | W | 3-1 | Falco 2, Allen |
| | 4 | 01.02.87 | **Chelsea** (D1) | H | W | 1-0 | Blissett |
| | 5 | 21.02.87 | **Walsall** (D3) | A | D | 1-1 | Bardsley |
| | 5r | 24.02.87 | **Walsall** | H | D | 4-4aet | Jackett (p), Blissett, Barnes 2 |
| | 5 2r | 02.03.87 | **Walsall** | A | W | 1-0 | Dornan og |
| | 6 | 14.03.87 | **Arsenal** (D1) | A | W | 3-1 | Blissett 2, Barnes |
| | SF | 11.04.87 | **Tottenham Hotspur** (D1) | | L | 1-4 | Allen |
| | | | *played at Villa Park* | | | | |
| 1987-88 (D1) | 3 | 09.01.88 | **Hull City** (D2) | H | D | 1-1 | Allen |
| | 3r | 12.01.88 | **Hull City** | A | D | 2-2aet | Jackett (p), Allen |
| | 3 2r | 18.01.88 | **Hull City** | H | W | 1-0 | Allen |
| | 4 | 30.01.88 | **Coventry City** (D1) | A | W | 1-0 | Senior |
| | 5 | 20.02.88 | **Port Vale** (D3) | A | D | 0-0 | |
| | 5r | 23.02.88 | **Port Vale** | H | W | 2-0 | Senior, Porter |
| | 6 | 12.03.88 | **Wimbledon** (D1) | A | L | 1-2 | Allen |
| 1988-89 (D2) | 3 | 07.01.89 | **Newcastle Utd** (D1) | A | D | 0-0 | |
| | 3r | 10.01.89 | **Newcastle Utd** | H | D | 2-2aet | Redfearn 2 (1p) |
| | 3 2r | 16.01.89 | **Newcastle Utd** | A | D | 0-0aet | |
| | 3 3r | 18.01.89 | **Newcastle Utd** | H | W | 1-0aet | Roeder og |
| | 4 | 28.01.89 | **Derby County** (D1) | H | W | 2-1 | Holden, Redfearn |
| | 5 | 19.02.89 | **Nottingham Forest** (D1) | H | L | 0-3 | |
| 1989-90 (D2) | 3 | 06.01.90 | **Wigan Athletic** (D3) | H | W | 2-0 | Roeder, Hodges |
| | 4 | 27.01.90 | **Sheffield Utd** (D2) | A | D | 1-1 | Penrice |
| | 4r | 30.01.90 | **Sheffield Utd** | H | L | 1-2 | Porter (p) |
| 1990-91 (D2) | 3 | 05.01.91 | **Shrewsbury Town** (D3) | A | L | 1-4 | Falconer |
| 1991-92 (D2) | 3 | 04.01.92 | **Swindon Town** (D2) | A | L | 2-3 | Blissett 2 |
| 1992-93 (D1) | 3 | 02.01.93 | **Wolverhampton W** (D1) | H | L | 1-4 | Nogan |
| 1993-94 (D1) | 3 | 08.01.94 | **West Ham Utd** (PL) | A | L | 1-2 | Porter (p) |
| 1994-95 (D1) | 3 | 07.01.95 | **Scarborough** (D3) | A | D | 0-0 | |
| | 3r | 17.01.95 | **Scarborough** | H | W | 2-0 | Hessenthaler, Holdsworth |
| | 4 | 28.01.95 | **Swindon Town** (D1) | H | W | 1-0 | Hessenthaler |
| | 5 | 18.02.95 | **Crystal Palace** (PL) | H | D | 0-0 | |
| | 5r | 01.03.95 | **Crystal Palace** | A | L | 0-1aet | |

| | | | | | | | | |
|---|---|---|---|---|---|---|---|---|
| 1995-96 | (D1) | 3 | 06.01.96 | **Wimbledon** (PL) | H | D | 1-1 | Mooney |
| | | 3r | 17.01.96 | **Wimbledon** | A | L | 0-1 | |
| 1996-97 | (D2) | 1 | 17.11.96 | **Northampton Town** (D3) | A | W | 1-0 | Bazeley |
| | | 2 | 07.12.96 | **Ashford Town** (SL) | H | W | 5-0 | Connolly 3, Bazeley 2 |
| | | 3 | 21.01.97 | **Oxford Utd** (D1) | H | W | 2-0 | White, Connolly |
| | | 4 | 05.02.97 | **Manchester City** (D1) | A | L | 1-3 | Noel-Williams |
| 1997-98 | (D2) | 1 | 15.11.97 | **Barnet** (D3) | A | W | 2-1 | Rosenthal 2 |
| | | 2 | 06.12.97 | **Torquay Utd** (D3) | A | D | 1-1 | Noel-Williams |
| | | 2r | 16.12.97 | **Torquay Utd** | H | W | 2-1aet | Noel-Williams 2 |
| | | 3 | 03.01.98 | **Sheffield Wed** (PL) | H | D | 1-1 | Kennedy |
| | | 3r | 14.01.98 | **Sheffield Wed** | A | D | 0-0aet | |
| | | | | *Sheffield Wed won 5-3 on penalties* | | | | |
| 1998-99 | (D1) | 3 | 02.01.99 | **Tottenham Hotspur** (PL) | A | L | 2-5 | T Johnson, Kennedy |
| 1999-00 | (PL) | 3 | 11.12.99 | **Birmingham City** (D1) | H | L | 0-1 | |
| 2000-01 | (D1) | 3 | 06.01.01 | **Everton** (PL) | H | L | 1-2 | Mooney |
| 2001-02 | (D1) | 3 | 05.01.02 | **Arsenal** (PL) | H | L | 2-4 | Noel-Williams, Gayle |
| 2002-03 | (D1) | 3 | 04.01.03 | **Macclesfield T** (D3) | A | W | 2-0 | Helguson, Pennant |
| | | 4 | 25.01.03 | **WBA** (PL) | H | W | 1-0 | Helguson |
| | | 5 | 15.02.03 | **Sunderland** (PL) | A | W | 1-0 | Smith (p) |
| | | 6 | 09.03.03 | **Burnley** (D1) | H | W | 2-0 | Smith, Glass |
| | | SF | 13.04.03 | **Southampton** (PL) | | L | 1-2 | Gayle |
| | | | | *played at Villa Park* | | | | |

# WATFORD ROVERS

*Formed 1881. Entered FA Cup: 1886-87 – 1891-92. For a brief history of the development of senior football in the town see Watford.*

| | | | | | | | | |
|---|---|---|---|---|---|---|---|---|
| 1886-87 | | 1 | 23.10.86 | **Swindon Town** | H | L | 0-1 | |
| 1887-88 | | 1 | 15.10.87 | **Chesham** | A | L | 2-4 | |
| | | | | *FA ordered replay after protest* | | | | |
| | | 1r | 22.10.87 | **Chesham** | A | W | 3-1 | |
| | | 2 | 05.11.87 | **Old Carthusians** | H | L | 1-3 | Coles |

# WATH ATHLETIC

*Entered FA Cup: 1899-1900 – 1934-35.*

| | | | | | | | | |
|---|---|---|---|---|---|---|---|---|
| 1925-26 | (ML) | 1 | 28.11.25 | **Chesterfield** (3N) | H | L | 0-5 | |

# WEALDSTONE

*Formed 1889. First entered FA Cup: 1913-14. FA Trophy winners: 1985. FA Amateur Cup winners: 1966. League clubs beaten: Hereford United, Reading. Members of the Isthmian League.*

| | | | | | | | | |
|---|---|---|---|---|---|---|---|---|
| 1949-50 | (AL) | 1 | 26.11.49 | **Port Vale** (3S) | A | L | 0-1 | |
| 1965-66 | (IL) | 1 | 13.11.65 | **Millwall** (D3) | A | L | 1-3 | Cooley |
| 1966-67 | (IL) | 1 | 26.11.66 | **Nuneaton B** (SL) | H | L | 0-2 | |
| 1968-69 | (IL) | 1 | 16.11.68 | **St Albans City** (IL) | H | D | 1-1 | Lindsay (p) |
| | | 1r | 19.11.68 | **St Albans City** | A | L | 0-1 | |
| 1975-76 | (SL) | 1 | 22.11.75 | **Aldershot** (D3) | A | L | 3-4 | Duck 2 (1p), Lewis |
| 1976-77 | (SL) | 1 | 20.11.76 | **Reading** (D3) | A | L | 0-1 | |
| 1977-78 | (SL) | 1 | 26.11.77 | **Hereford Utd** (D3) | H | D | 0-0 | |
| | | 1r | 29.11.77 | **Hereford Utd** | A | W | 3-2 | Ferry 2, Moss |
| | | 2 | 17.12.77 | **Reading** (D4) | H | W | 2-1 | Furphy, Duck (p) |
| | | 3 | 07.01.78 | **QPR** (D1) | A | L | 0-4 | |
| 1978-79 | (SL) | 1 | 25.11.78 | **Enfield** (IL) | H | L | 0-5 | |
| 1979-80 | (SL) | 1 | 24.11.79 | **Southend Utd** (D3) | H | L | 0-1 | |
| 1982-83 | (APL) | 1 | 20.11.82 | **Swindon Town** (D4) | A | L | 0-2 | |
| 1983-84 | (APL) | 1 | 19.11.83 | **Enfield** (APL) | H | D | 1-1 | Graves |
| | | 1r | 22.11.83 | **Enfield** | A | D | 2-2aet | Byatt (p), Graves |
| | | 1 2r | 28.11.83 | **Enfield** | H | W | 2-0 | N.Cordice, Graves |
| | | 2 | 10.12.83 | **Colchester Utd** (D4) | A | L | 0-4 | |
| 1985-86 | (APL) | 1 | 16.11.85 | **Reading** (D3) | A | L | 0-1 | |
| 1986-87 | (Conf) | 1 | 15.11.86 | **Swansea City** (D4) | H | D | 1-1 | Wallace |
| | | 1r | 20.11.86 | **Swansea City** | A | - | 1-2ab | Doyle (p) |
| | | | | *abandoned after 54 minutes – waterlogged pitch* | | | | |
| | | 1r | 24.11.86 | **Swansea City** (D4) | A | L | 1-4 | Donnellan |

# WEDNESBURY OLD ATHLETIC

*Formed 1874. Entered FA Cup: 1881-82 – 1892-93. Played at Wood Green Lane, Wednesbury.*

| | | | | | | | |
|---|---|---|---|---|---|---|---|
| 1881-82 | 1 | 05.11.81 | **Birmingham St G** | H | W | 9-1 | |
| | 2 | 03.12.81 | **Small Heath Alliance** | H | W | 6-0 | Morley 3, Roberts, Reeves, AN Other |
| | 3 | | bye | | | | |
| | 4 | 21.01.82 | **Aston Villa** | H | W | 4-2 | G Woodcock 2, G Holden, Morl |
| | 5 | 11.02.82 | **Blackburn Rovers** | A | L | 1-3 | Growcutt |
| 1882-83 | 1 | 04.11.82 | **Chesterfield Spital** | A | W | 7-1 | Morley 3, Woodcock, Growcutt, G Holden, AN Other |
| | 2 | 18.11.82 | **Aston Villa** | A | L | 1-4 | Morley |
| 1883-84 | 1 | 10.11.83 | **Birmingham St G** | H | W | 5-0 | |
| | 2 | 01.12.83 | **Wolverhampton W** | H | W | 4-2 | Bayliss, Holden, D Tonks 2 |
| | 3 | 29.12.83 | **Aston Villa** | H | L | 4-7 | Bayliss 2, Holden, E Tonks |
| 1884-85 | 1 | 08.11.84 | **Derby Midland** | A | W | 2-1 | |
| | 2 | 06.12.84 | **WBA** | A | L | 2-4 | |
| 1885-86 | 1 | 31.10.85 | **Burton Swifts** | H | W | 5-1 | |
| | 2 | 21.11.85 | **WBA** | A | L | 2-3 | Knight, Taylor |
| 1886-87 | 1 | 30.10.86 | **Aston Villa** | A | L | 0-13 | |
| 1887-88 | 1 | 15.10.87 | **WBA** | A | L | 1-7 | |

# WEDNESBURY STROLLERS

*Formed 1875. Entered FA Cup: 1878-79 – 1881-82. Played at Wood Green Lane, Wednesbury and also at The Trapezium Ground.*

| | | | | | | | |
|---|---|---|---|---|---|---|---|
| 1878-79 | 1 | 02.11.78 | **Oxford University** | A | L | 0-7 | |
| 1879-80 | 1 | 08.11.79 | **Stafford Road** | A | L | 0-2 | |
| 1880-81 | 1 | 30.10.80 | **Aston Villa** | A | L | 3-5 | |
| 1881-82 | 1 | 05.11.81 | **Stafford Road** | H | W | 3-1 | B Knowles, Bryan, Byrne |
| | 2 | 24.11.81 | **Notts County** | A | L | 2-5 | Parker 2, AN Other |
| | | | *FA ordered replay after protest* | | | | |
| | 2r | 10.12.81 | **Notts County** | | L | 1-11 | B Knowles |
| | | | *played at Derby Cricket Ground* | | | | |

# WEDNESBURY TOWN

*Entered FA Cup for these two seasons only.*

| | | | | | | |
|---|---|---|---|---|---|---|
| 1883-84 | 1 | 10.11.83 | **WBA** | A | W | 2-0 |
| | 2 | 01.12.83 | **Walsall Town** | A | D | 2-2 |
| | 2r | 06.12.83 | **Walsall Town** | H | W | 6-0 |
| | 3 | 29.12.83 | **Derby Midland** | H | W | 1-0 |
| | 4 | 19.01.84 | **Old Westminsters** | A | L | 0-5 |
| 1884-85 | 1 | 03.11.84 | **Aston Villa** | A | L | 1-4 |

# WELLING UNITED

*Formed 1963. First entered FA Cup: 1978-79. League club beaten: Gillingham. Members of the Southern League.*

| | | | | | | | | |
|---|---|---|---|---|---|---|---|---|
| 1986-87 | (Conf) | 1 | 15.11.86 | **Maidstone Utd** (Conf) | H | D | 1-1 | Abbott (p) |
| | | 1r | 24.11.86 | **Maidstone Utd** | A | L | 1-4 | Reynolds |
| 1987-88 | (Conf) | 1 | 23.11.87 | **Carshalton Athletic** (IL) | H | W | 3-2 | Gaston og, Booker, Abbott |
| | | 2 | 05.12.87 | **Bath City** (Conf) | H | L | 0-1 | |
| 1988-89 | (Conf) | 1 | 19.11.88 | **Bromsgrove R** (SL) | H | W | 3-0 | Booker, Robbins, White |
| | | 2 | 10.12.88 | **Bath City** (SL) | A | D | 0-0 | |
| | | 2r | 14.12.88 | **Bath City** | H | W | 3-2 | Robbins, Burgess, Handford |
| | | 3 | 07.01.89 | **Blackburn Rovers** (D2) | H | L | 0-1 | |
| 1989-90 | (Conf) | 1 | 18.11.89 | **Gillingham** (D4) | A | D | 0-0 | |
| | | 1r | 22.11.89 | **Gillingham** | H | W | 1-0 | Hone |
| | | 2 | 09.12.89 | **Reading** (D3) | A | D | 0-0 | |
| | | 2r | 13.12.89 | **Reading** | H | D | 1-1aet | Glover |
| | | 2 2r | 19.12.89 | **Reading** | A | D | 0-0aet | |
| | | 2 3r | 22.12.89 | **Reading** | H | L | 1-2 | Robbins |
| 1990-91 | (Conf) | 1 | 17.11.90 | **Swansea City** (D3) | A | L | 2-5 | Francis, Robbins |
| 1991-92 | (Conf) | 1 | 16.11.91 | **Leyton Orient** (D3) | A | L | 1-2 | Berry |
| 1996-97 | (Conf) | 1 | 16.11.96 | **Cambridge Utd** (D3) | A | L | 0-3 | |
| 1998-99 | (Conf) | 1 | 14.11.98 | **Bristol Rovers** (D2) | A | L | 0-3 | |

| | | | | | | | | |
|---|---|---|---|---|---|---|---|---|
| 1999-00 | (Conf) | 1 | 30.10.99 | **Lincoln City** (D3) | A | L | 0-1 | |
| 2001-02 | (SL) | 1 | 17.11.01 | **Reading** (D2) | A | L | 0-1 | |

## WELLINGBOROUGH TOWN

*Formed 1867. First entered FA Cup: 1892-93.*

| | | | | | | | | |
|---|---|---|---|---|---|---|---|---|
| 1928-29 | (UCL) | 1 | 24.11.28 | **Bristol Rovers** (3S) | A | L | 1-2 | Shipley |
| 1965-66 | (UCL) | 1 | 13.11.65 | **Aldershot** (D4) | A | L | 1-2 | B.Daldy |

## WELLINGTON ST GEORGES

*Entered FA Cup: 1886-87 – 1929-30. League club beaten: Tranmere Rovers.*

| | | | | | | | | |
|---|---|---|---|---|---|---|---|---|
| 1886-87 | | 1 | 30.10.86 | **Derby Junction** | H | L | 0-1 | |
| 1887-88 | | 1 | 15.10.87 | **Over Wanderers** | A | L | 1-3 | |
| 1922-23 | | | | 4q Tranmere Rovers (3N) H 2-1; 5q Walsall (3N) A 0-5 | | | | |

## WELTON ROVERS

*Formed 1887. First entered FA Cup: 1906-07. Members of the Western League.*

| | | | | | | | | |
|---|---|---|---|---|---|---|---|---|
| 1964-65 | (WL) | 1 | 14.11.64 | **Weymouth** (SL) | H | D | 1-1 | Prosser |
| | | 1r | 18.11.64 | **Weymouth** | A | L | 3-4 | Henderson 2, Allen |
| 1966-67 | (WL) | 1 | 26.11.66 | **Bournemouth** (D3) | A | L | 0-3 | |

## WEMBLEY

*Formed 1946. First entered FA Cup: 1949-50. Members of the Isthmian League.*

| | | | | | | | | |
|---|---|---|---|---|---|---|---|---|
| 1980-81 | (IL) | 1 | 22.11.80 | **Enfield** (IL) | A | L | 0-3 | |

## WEST AUCKLAND TOWN

*Formed 1892. First entered FA Cup: 1905-06. FA Amateur Cup runners-up: 1961. Members of the Northern League.*

| | | | | | | | | |
|---|---|---|---|---|---|---|---|---|
| 1959-60 | (NL) | 1 | 14.11.59 | **Stockport County** (D4) | H | L | 2-6 | Curtis, Carter |
| 1961-62 | (NL) | 1 | 04.11.61 | **Barnsley** (D3) | H | D | 3-3 | Skelton, Hopper, Bloomfield (p) |
| | | 1r | 08.11.61 | **Barnsley** | A | L | 0-2 | |
| 1998-99 | (NL) | 1 | 14.11.98 | **Yeovil Town** (Conf) | A | D | 2-2 | Milroy, Adamson |
| | | 1r | 24.11.98 | **Yeovil Town** | H | D | 1-1aet | Milroy |
| | | | | *Yeovil won 5-3 on penalties* | | | | |

## WEST BROMWICH ALBION

*Formed 1879. Founder Members of the Football League 1888. FA Cup winners: 1888, 1892, 1931, 1954, 1968; Runners-up: 1886, 1887, 1895, 1912, 1935. In 1931 WBA became the first club to win promotion from Division Two and the FA Cup in the same season. Record FA Cup win: 10-1 v Chatham, 3rd round, 20.03.89; Record FA Cup defeat: 0-5 v Leeds Utd, 4th round, 18.02.67.*

| | | | | | | | | |
|---|---|---|---|---|---|---|---|---|
| 1883-84 | | 1 | 10.11.83 | **Wednesbury Town** | H | L | 0-2 | - |
| 1884-85 | | 1 | 25.10.84 | **Derby Junction** | A | W | 7-1 | Bayliss 2, G Bell 2, Aston 2, Loach |
| | | 2 | 06.12.84 | **Wednesbury Old A** | H | W | 4-2 | Aston 2, Woodhall, Taylor og |
| | | 3 | 03.01.85 | **Aston Villa** | A | D | 0-0 | |
| | | 3r | 10.01.85 | **Aston Villa** | H | W | 3-0 | Loach 2, Bayliss |
| | | 4 | 24.01.85 | **Druids** | H | W | 1-0 | Loach |
| | | 5 | | bye | | | | |
| | | 6 | 21.02.85 | **Blackburn Rovers** | H | L | 0-2 | |
| 1885-86 | | 1 | 31.10.85 | **Aston Unity** | H | W | 4-1 | T Green 2, Woodhall 2 |
| | | 2 | 21.11.85 | **Wednesbury Old A** | H | W | 3-2 | Loach 2, G Bell |
| | | 3 | | bye | | | | |
| | | 4 | 02.01.86 | **Wolverhampton W** | H | W | 3-1 | G Bell, T Green, Loach |
| | | 5 | 23.01.86 | **Old Carthusians** | H | W | 1-0 | T Green |
| | | 6 | 13.02.86 | **Old Westminsters** | H | W | 6-0 | Bayliss 3, G Bell 2, Woodhall |
| | | SF | 06.03.86 | **Small Heath Alliance** | | W | 4-0 | Loach 2, Woodhall 2 |
| | | | | *played at Aston Lower Grounds, Birmingham* | | | | |
| | | F | 03.04.86 | **Blackburn Rovers** | | D | 0-0 | |
| | | | | *played at Kennington Oval* | | | | |
| | | Fr | 10.04.86 | **Blackburn Rovers** | | L | 0-2 | |
| | | | | *played at Derby Racecourse Ground* | | | | |
| 1886-87 | | 1 | 30.10.86 | **Burton Wanderers** | H | W | 5-0 | T Green 2, Bayliss 2, Holden, Paddock |
| | | 2 | 20.11.86 | **Derby Junction** | H | W | 2-1 | G Bell, Roberts |
| | | 3 | | bye | | | | |

| | | | | | | | | |
|---|---|---|---|---|---|---|---|---|
| | | 4 | 15.01.87 | **Birmingham St G** | A | W | 1-0 | T Green |
| | | 5 | 29.01.87 | **Lockwood Bros** | A | W | 1-0aet | Woodhall |
| | | | | *FA ordered replay following protests* | | | | |
| | | 5r | 12.02.87 | **Lockwood Bros** | | W | 2-1 | T Green, Paddock |
| | | | | *played at Derby Cricket Ground* | | | | |
| | | 6 | 19.02.87 | **Notts County** | A | W | 2-1 | Bayliss 2, T Green, Woodhall |
| | | SF | 05.03.87 | **Preston North End** | | W | 3-1 | Pearson 2, Paddock |
| | | | | *played at Trent Bridge* | | | | |
| | | F | 02.04.87 | **Aston Villa** | | L | 0-2 | |
| | | | | *played at Kennington Oval* | | | | |
| 1887-88 | | 1 | 15.10.87 | **Wednesbury Old A** | H | W | 7-1 | Bayliss 3, Wilson 2, Pearson, Horton |
| | | 2 | 05.11.87 | **Birmingham St G** | H | W | 1-0 | Bayliss |
| | | 3 | 26.11.87 | **Wolverhampton W** | H | W | 2-0 | Bassett, Wilson |
| | | 4 | | bye | | | | |
| | | 5 | 07.01.88 | **Stoke** | H | W | 4-1 | Bayliss 4 |
| | | 6 | 28.01.88 | **Old Carthusians** | H | W | 4-2 | Pearson 2, Wilson 2 |
| | | SF | 18.02.88 | **Derby Junction** | | W | 3-0 | Bayliss, Wilson, Woodhall |
| | | | | *played at Victoria Ground, Stoke* | | | | |
| | | F | 24.03.88 | **Preston North End** | | W | 2-1 | Bayliss, Woodhall |
| | | | | *played at Kennington Oval* | | | | |
| 1888-89 | (D1) | 1 | 02.02.89 | **Small Heath** | A | W | 3-2 | W Perry, Wilson, Pearson |
| | | 2 | 16.02.89 | **Burnley** (D1) | H | W | 5-1 | Bayliss 2, Bassett, Wilson, W Perry |
| | | 3 | 02.03.89 | **Chatham** | A | W | 10-1 | Wilson 3, Bayliss 2, Bassett 2, Timmins, W Perry, Conquer og |
| | | SF | 16.03.89 | **Preston North End** (D1) | | L | 0-1 | |
| | | | | *played at Bramall Lane* | | | | |
| 1889-90 | (D1) | 1 | 18.01.90 | **Accrington FC** (D1) | A | L | 1-3 | Wilson |
| | | | | *FA ordered match to be replayed after protest* | | | | |
| | | 1 | 25.01.90 | **Accrington FC** (D1) | A | L | 0-3 | |
| 1890-91 | (D1) | 1 | | Old Westminsters | | | - | |
| | | | | *Old Westminsters scratched. WBA walkover* | | | | |
| | | 2 | 31.01.91 | **Birmingham St G** (FAll) | A | W | 3-0 | Nicholls, Dyer, C Perry |
| | | 3 | 14.02.91 | **Sheffield Wed** (FAll) | A | W | 2-0 | Groves, Pearson |
| | | SF | 28.02.91 | **Blackburn Rovers** (D1) | | L | 2-3 | Groves, Pearson |
| | | | | *played at Victoria Ground, Stoke* | | | | |
| 1891-92 | (D1) | 1 | 16.01.92 | **Old Westminsters** | A | W | 3-2 | McLeod, Pearson, Reynolds |
| | | 2 | 30.01.92 | **Blackburn Rovers** (D1) | H | W | 3-1 | Pearson 2, Geddes |
| | | 3 | 13.02.92 | **Sheffield Wed** (FAll) | A | W | 2-1 | C Perry, Nicholls |
| | | SF | 27.02.92 | **Nottingham Forest** (FAll) | | D | 1-1 | Geddes |
| | | | | *played at Molineux* | | | | |
| | | SFr | 05.03.92 | **Nottingham Forest** | | D | 0-0 | Bassett |
| | | | | *played at Molineux* | | | | |
| | | SF 2r | 09.03.92 | **Nottingham Forest** | | W | 6-2 | Geddes 3, Bassett, Groves, C Perry |
| | | | | *played at the Racecourse Ground, Derby* | | | | |
| | | F | 19.03.92 | **Aston Villa** (D1) | | W | 3-0 | Geddes, Nicholls, Reynolds |
| | | | | *played at Kennington Oval* | | | | |
| 1892-93 | (D1) | 1 | 21.01.93 | **Everton** (D1) | A | L | 1-4 | Pearson |
| 1893-94 | (D1) | 1 | 27.01.94 | **Blackburn Rovers** (D1) | H | L | 2-3 | McLeod 2 |
| 1894-95 | (D1) | 1 | 02.02.95 | **Small Heath** (D1) | A | W | 2-1 | McLeod, Banks |
| | | 2 | 16.02.95 | **Sheffield Utd** (D1) | A | D | 1-1 | Bassett |
| | | 2r | 20.02.95 | **Sheffield Utd** | H | W | 2-1 | Hutchinson, Foulke og |
| | | 3 | 02.03.95 | **Wolverhampton W** (D1) | H | W | 1-0 | McLeod |
| | | SF | 16.03.95 | **Sheffield Wed** (D1) | | W | 2-0 | Hutchinson, Williams (p) |
| | | | | *played at Derby Cricket Ground* | | | | |
| | | F | 20.04.95 | **Aston Villa** (D1) | | L | 0-1 | |
| | | | | *played at Crystal Palace* | | | | |
| 1895-96 | (D1) | 1 | 01.02.96 | **Blackburn Rovers** (D1) | A | W | 2-1 | J.Richards, W.Richards |
| | | 2 | 15.02.96 | **Grimsby Town** (D2) | A | D | 1-1 | McLeod |
| | | 2r | 20.02.96 | **Grimsby Town** | H | W | 3-0 | McLeod, W.Richards |
| | | 3 | 29.02.96 | **Derby County** (D1) | A | L | 0-1 | |
| 1896-97 | (D1) | 1 | 30.01.97 | **Luton Town** (D2) | A | W | 1-0 | Flewitt |

| | | | | | | | | |
|---|---|---|---|---|---|---|---|---|
| | | 2 | 13.02.97 | **Liverpool** (D1) | H | L | 1-2 | Watson |
| 1897-98 | (D1) | 1 | 29.01.98 | **New Brighton Tower** (LL) | H | W | 2-0 | Garfield, Flewitt |
| | | 2 | 12.02.98 | **Sheffield Wed** (D1) | H | W | 1-0 | Flewitt |
| | | 3 | 26.02.98 | **Nottingham Forest** (D1) | H | L | 2-3 | Williams, Bassett |
| 1898-99 | (D1) | 1 | 28.01.99 | **South Shore** (LL) | H | W | 8-0 | Bassett 3, Jones 2, W Richards, Garfield, Barrow og |
| | | 2 | 11.02.99 | **Bury** (D1) | H | W | 2-1 | W Richards 2 |
| | | 3 | 25.02.99 | **Liverpool** (D1) | H | L | 0-2 | |
| 1899-00 | (D1) | 1 | 27.01.00 | **Walsall** (D2) | A | D | 1-1 | Roberts |
| | | 1r | 01.02.00 | **Walsall** | H | W | 6-1 | Jones 2, Brett, Roberts, Richards, Simmons |
| | | 2 | 17.02.00 | **Liverpool** (D1) | A | D | 1-1 | Simmons |
| | | 2r | 21.02.00 | **Liverpool** | H | W | 2-1 | Dunn, Chadburn |
| | | 3 | 24.02.00 | **Southampton** (SL) | A | L | 1-2 | Simmons |
| 1900-01 | (D1) | 1 | 26.01.01 | **Manchester City** (D1) | H | W | 1-0 | Garfield |
| | | 2 | 23.02.01 | **Woolwich Arsenal** (D2) | A | W | 1-0 | Garfield |
| | | 3 | 23.03.01 | **Middlesbrough** (D2) | A | W | 1-0 | Buck |
| | | SF | 08.04.01 | **Tottenham Hotspur** (SL) *played at Villa Park* | | L | 0-4 | |
| 1901-02 | (D2) | 1 | 25.01.02 | **Bury** (D1) | A | L | 1-5 | Simmons |
| 1902-03 | (D1) | 1 | 07.02.03 | **Tottenham Hotspur** (SL) | A | D | 0-0 | |
| | | 1r | 11.02.03 | **Tottenham Hotspur** | H | L | 0-2 | |
| 1903-04 | (D1) | 1 | 06.02.04 | **Nottingham Forest** (D1) | H | D | 1-1 | Simmons |
| | | 1r | 13.02.04 | **Nottingham Forest** | A | L | 1-3 | Smith |
| 1905-06 | (D2) | 1 | 13.01.06 | **Everton** (D1) | A | L | 1-3 | Haywood |
| 1906-07 | (D2) | 1 | 12.01.07 | **Stoke** (D1) | H | D | 1-1 | Broad |
| | | 1r | 17.01.07 | **Stoke** | A | D | 2-2aet | Rankin, Randle |
| | | 1 2r | 21.01.07 | **Stoke** *played at Villa Park* | | W | 2-0 | Pheasant, Dilly (p) |
| | | 2 | 02.02.07 | **Norwich City** (SL) | H | W | 1-0 | Simmons |
| | | 3 | 23.02.07 | **Derby County** (D1) | H | W | 2-0 | Jordan, Buck |
| | | 4 | 09.03.07 | **Notts County** (D1) | H | W | 3-1 | Jordan 2, Buck |
| | | SF | 23.03.07 | **Everton** (D1) *played at Burnden Park* | | L | 1-2 | Haywood |
| 1907-08 | (D2) | 1 | 11.01.08 | **Birmingham** (D1) | H | D | 1-1 | Wilcox |
| | | 1r | 15.01.08 | **Birmingham** | A | W | 2-1 | Wilcox, Jordan |
| | | 2 | 01.02.08 | **Southampton** (SL) | A | L | 0-1 | |
| 1908-09 | (D2) | 1 | 16.01.09 | **Bolton Wanderers** (D2) | H | W | 3-1 | Garraty, Harris (p), Buck |
| | | 2 | 06.02.09 | **Bradford City** (D1) | H | L | 1-2 | Garraty |
| 1909-10 | (D2) | 1 | 15.01.10 | **Clapton Orient** (D2) | H | W | 2-0 | Pailor 2 |
| | | 2 | 05.02.10 | **Bristol City** (D1) | A | D | 1-1 | Pailor |
| | | 2r | 09.02.10 | **Bristol City** | H | W | 4-2 | Hewitt 2, Pailor, Simpson |
| | | 3 | 19.02.10 | **Barnsley** (D2) | A | L | 0-1 | |
| 1910-11 | (D2) | 2 | 04.02.11 | **Derby County** (D2) | A | L | 0-2 | |
| | | 2 | 14.01.11 | **Fulham** (D2) | H | W | 4-1 | Bowser 2, Wollaston, Lloyd |
| 1911-12 | (D1) | 1 | 13.01.12 | **Tottenham Hotspur** (D1) | H | W | 3-0 | Bowser, Deacey, Wright |
| | | 2 | 03.02.12 | **Leeds City** (D2) | A | W | 1-0 | Bowser |
| | | 3 | 24.02.12 | **Sunderland** (D1) | A | W | 2-1 | Pailor 2 |
| | | 4 | 09.03.12 | **Fulham** (D2) | H | W | 3-0 | Bowser 2, Wright |
| | | SF | 30.03.12 | **Blackburn Rovers** (D1) *played at Anfield* | | D | 0-0 | |
| | | SFr | 03.04.12 | **Blackburn Rovers** *played at Hillsborough* | | W | 1-0aet | Pailor |
| | | F | 20.04.12 | **Barnsley** (D2) *played at Crystal Palace* | | D | 0-0 | |
| | | Fr | 24.04.12 | **Barnsley** *played at Bramall Lane* | | L | 0-1aet | |
| 1912-13 | (D1) | 1 | 13.01.13 | **West Ham Utd** (SL) | H | D | 1-1 | Wright |
| | | 1r | 16.01.13 | **West Ham Utd** | A | D | 2-2aet | Gregory, Bowser |
| | | 1 2r | 22.01.13 | **West Ham Utd** *played at Stamford Bridge* | | L | 0-3 | |

| | | | | | | | |
|---|---|---|---|---|---|---|---|
| 1913-14 (D1) | 1 | 10.01.14 | **Grimsby Town** (D2) | H | W | 2-0 | Edwards, Morris |
| | 2 | 31.01.14 | **Leeds City** (D2) | A | W | 2-0 | Bentley, Jephcott |
| | 3 | 21.02.14 | **Aston Villa** (D1) | A | L | 1-2 | Bowser |
| 1914-15 (D1) | 1 | 09.01.15 | **Hull City** (D2) | A | L | 0-1 | |
| 1919-20 (D1) | 1 | 10.01.20 | **Barnsley** (D2) | H | L | 0-1 | |
| 1920-21 (D1) | 1 | 08.01.21 | **Notts County** (D2) | A | L | 0-3 | |
| 1921-22 (D1) | 1 | 07.01.22 | **Chelsea** (D1) | H | W | 4-2 | Blagden 2, Davies, Crisp |
| | 2 | 28.01.22 | **Liverpool** (D1) | A | W | 1-0 | Davies |
| | 3 | 18.02.22 | **Notts County** (D2) | H | D | 1-1 | Davies (p) |
| | 3r | 22.02.22 | **Notts County** | A | L | 0-2 | |
| 1922-23 (D1) | 1 | 13.01.23 | **Stalybridge Celtic** (3N) | H | D | 0-0 | |
| | 1r | 17.01.23 | **Stalybridge Celtic** | A | W | 2-0 | Davies, Morris |
| | 2 | 03.02.23 | **Sunderland** (D1) | H | W | 2-1 | Morris, Jones |
| | 3 | 24.02.23 | **Charlton Athletic** (3S) | A | L | 0-1 | |
| 1923-24 (D1) | 1 | 12.01.24 | **Millwall Athletic** (3S) | A | W | 1-0 | Carter |
| | 2 | 02.02.24 | **Corinthians** | H | W | 5-0 | Morris, Reed, Carter, Davies 2 (1p) |
| | 3 | 23.02.24 | **Wolverhampton W** (3N) | H | D | 1-1 | Wilson |
| | 3r | 27.02.24 | **Wolverhampton W** | A | W | 2-0 | Wilson, Gregory |
| | 4 | 08.03.24 | **Aston Villa** (D1) | H | L | 0-2 | |
| 1924-25 (D1) | 1 | 10.01.25 | **Luton Town** (3S) | H | W | 4-0 | James 3, Wilson |
| | 2 | 31.01.25 | **Preston North End** (D1) | H | W | 2-0 | James, Wilson |
| | 3 | 21.02.25 | **Aston Villa** (D1) | H | D | 1-1 | Carter |
| | 3r | 25.02.25 | **Aston Villa** | A | W | 2-1 | Gregory, James |
| | 4 | 07.03.25 | **Sheffield Utd** (D1) | A | L | 0-2 | |
| 1925-26 (D1) | 3 | 09.01.26 | **Bristol City** (3S) | H | W | 4-1 | Glidden 2 (1p), Carter, Byers |
| | 4 | 29.01.26 | **Aston Villa** (D1) | H | L | 1-2 | Carter |
| 1926-27 (D1) | 3 | 08.01.27 | **Hull City** (D2) | A | L | 1-2 | Howarth |
| 1927-28 (D2) | 3 | 14.01.28 | **Arsenal** (D1) | A | L | 0-2 | |
| 1928-29 (D2) | 3 | 12.01.29 | **Grimsby Town** (D2) | A | D | 1-1 | Cookson |
| | 3r | 16.01.29 | **Grimsby Town** | H | W | 2-0 | Cookson, Chambers |
| | 4 | 26.01.29 | **Middlesbrough** (D2) | H | W | 1-0 | Cookson |
| | 5 | 16.02.29 | **Bradford Park A** (D2) | H | W | 6-0 | Cookson 4, Glidden, Carter |
| | 6 | 02.03.29 | **Huddersfield Town** (D1) | H | D | 1-1 | Glidden |
| | 6r | 06.03.29 | **Huddersfield Town** | A | L | 1-2 | Wood |
| 1929-30 (D2) | 3 | 11.01.30 | **Wrexham** (3N) | A | L | 0-1 | |
| 1930-31 (D2) | 3 | 10.01.31 | **Charlton Athletic** (D2) | H | D | 2-2 | Wood, Sandford |
| | 3r | 14.01.31 | **Charlton Athletic** | A | D | 1-1aet | Carter |
| | 3 2r | 19.01.31 | **Charlton Athletic** *played at Villa Park* | | W | 3-1 | Carter, Wood, WG Richardson |
| | 4 | 24.01.31 | **Tottenham Hotspur** (D2) | H | W | 1-0 | Wood |
| | 5 | 14.02.31 | **Portsmouth** (D1) | A | W | 1-0 | WG Richardson |
| | 6 | 28.02.31 | **Wolverhampton W** (D2) | H | D | 1-1 | WG Richardson |
| | 6r | 04.03.31 | **Wolverhampton W** | A | W | 2-1 | Wood, WG Richardson |
| | SF | 14.03.31 | **Everton** (D2) *played at Old Trafford* | | W | 1-0 | Glidden |
| | F | 25.04.31 | **Birmingham** (D1) *played at Wembley Stadium* | | W | 2-1 | WG Richardson 2 |
| 1931-32 (D1) | 3 | 09.01.32 | **Aston Villa** (D1) | H | L | 1-2 | WG Richardson |
| 1932-33 (D1) | 3 | 14.01.33 | **Liverpool** (D1) | H | W | 2-0 | Wood, WG Richardson |
| | 4 | 28.01.33 | **West Ham Utd** (D2) | A | L | 0-2 | |
| 1933-34 (D1) | 3 | 13.01.34 | **Chelsea** (D1) | A | D | 1-1 | Robbins |
| | 3r | 17.01.34 | **Chelsea** | H | L | 0-1 | |
| 1934-35 (D1) | 3 | 12.01.35 | **Port Vale** (D2) | H | W | 2-1 | Gale, WG Richardson |
| | 4 | 26.01.35 | **Sheffield Utd** (D2) | H | W | 7-1 | WG Richardson 3, Sandford 2, Carter, Gale |
| | 5 | 16.02.35 | **Stockport County** (3N) | A | W | 5-0 | WG Richardson 2, Carter, Gale, Boyes |
| | 6 | 02.03.35 | **Preston North End** (D1) | H | W | 1-0 | Gale |
| | SF | 16.03.35 | **Bolton Wanderers** (D2) *played at Elland Road* | | D | 1-1 | WG Richardson |
| | SFr | 20.03.35 | **Bolton Wanderers** *played at the Victoria Ground, Stoke* | | W | 2-0 | WG Richardson, Sandford (p) |

| | | | | | | | | |
|---|---|---|---|---|---|---|---|---|
| | | F | 27.04.35 | **Sheffield Wed** (D1) | | L | 2-4 | Sandford, Boyes |
| | | | | *played at Wembley Stadium* | | | | |
| 1935-36 | (D1) | 3 | 11.01.36 | **Hull City** (D2) | H | W | 2-0 | Wood, WG Richardson |
| | | 4 | 29.01.36 | **Bradford Park A** (D2) | A | D | 1-1 | Robbins |
| | | 4r | 03.02.36 | **Bradford Park A** | H | D | 1-1aet | Sandford (p) |
| | | 4 2r | 10.02.36 | **Bradford Park A** | | L | 0-2 | |
| | | | | *played at Old Trafford* | | | | |
| 1936-37 | (D1) | 3 | 16.01.37 | **Spennymoor Utd** (NEL) | H | W | 7-1 | Sandford 2, WG Richardson 2, Wood, Jones, Mahon |
| | | 4 | 30.01.37 | **Darlington** (3N) | H | W | 3-2 | WG Richardson 3 |
| | | 5 | 20.02.37 | **Coventry City** (D2) | A | W | 3-2 | Boyes, Mahon 2 |
| | | 6 | 06.03.37 | **Arsenal** (D1) | H | W | 3-1 | Mahon 2, WG Richardson |
| | | SF | 10.04.37 | **Preston North End** (D1) | | L | 1-4 | Robbins |
| | | | | *played at Highbury* | | | | |
| 1937-38 | (D1) | 3 | 08.01.38 | **Newcastle Utd** (D2) | H | W | 1-0 | WG Richardson |
| | | 4 | 22.01.38 | **York City** (3N) | A | L | 2-3 | WG Richardson, Pinder og |
| 1938-39 | (D2) | 3 | 07.01.39 | **Manchester Utd** (D1) | H | D | 0-0 | |
| | | 3r | 11.01.39 | **Manchester Utd** | A | W | 5-1 | Jones 2, Witcomb, Clarke, WG Richardson |
| | | 4 | 21.01.39 | **Portsmouth** (D1) | A | L | 0-2 | |
| 1945-46 | (D2) | 3 1L | 05.01.46 | **Cardiff City** (3S) | A | D | 1-1 | Connelly |
| | | 3 2L | 09.01.46 | **Cardiff City** | H | W | 4-0 | Clarke 2, Newsome 2 |
| | | 4 1L | 26.01.46 | **Derby County** (D1) | A | L | 0-1 | |
| | | 4 2L | 30.01.46 | **Derby County** | H | L | 1-3 | Clarke |
| 1946-47 | (D2) | 3 | 11.01.47 | **Leeds Utd** (D1) | H | W | 2-1 | Barlow, Walsh |
| | | 4 | 25.01.47 | **Charlton Athletic** (D1) | H | L | 1-2 | Elliott |
| 1947-48 | (D2) | 3 | 10.01.48 | **Reading** (3S) | H | W | 2-0 | Finch, Drury |
| | | 4 | 24.01.48 | **Tottenham Hotspur** (D2) | A | L | 1-3 | Rowley |
| 1948-49 | (D2) | 3 | 08.01.49 | **Lincoln City** (D2) | A | W | 1-0 | Barlow |
| | | 4 | 29.01.49 | **Gateshead AFC** (3N) | A | W | 3-1aet | Walsh 2, A.Smith |
| | | 5 | 12.02.49 | **Chelsea** (D1) | H | W | 3-0 | Walsh 3 |
| | | 6 | 26.02.49 | **Wolverhampton W** (D1) | A | L | 0-1 | |
| 1949-50 | (D1) | 3 | 07.01.50 | **Cardiff City** (D2) | A | D | 2-2 | C Williams, Inwood |
| | | 3r | 11.01.50 | **Cardiff City** | H | L | 0-1 | |
| 1950-51 | (D1) | 3 | 06.01.51 | **Derby County** (D1) | A | D | 2-2 | Lee, Barlow |
| | | 3r | 10.01.51 | **Derby County** | H | L | 0-1 | |
| 1951-52 | (D1) | 3 | 12.01.52 | **Bolton Wanderers** (D1) | H | W | 4-0 | Lee 2, Allen, Griffin |
| | | 4 | 06.02.52 | **Gateshead AFC** (3N) | A | W | 2-0 | Allen 2 |
| | | | | *played at St James' Park* | | | | |
| | | 5 | 23.02.52 | **Blackburn Rovers** (D2) | A | L | 0-1 | |
| 1952-53 | (D1) | 3 | 10.01.53 | **West Ham Utd** (D2) | A | W | 4-1 | Lee, Ryan, Allen, Nicholls |
| | | 4 | 31.01.53 | **Chelsea** (D1) | A | D | 1-1 | Nicholls |
| | | 4r | 04.02.53 | **Chelsea** | H | D | 0-0aet | |
| | | 4 2r | 09.02.53 | **Chelsea** | | D | 1-1aet | Dudley |
| | | | | *played at Villa Park* | | | | |
| | | 4 3r | 11.02.53 | **Chelsea** | | L | 0-4 | |
| | | | | *played at Highbury* | | | | |
| 1953-54 | (D1) | 3 | 09.01.54 | **Chelsea** (D1) | H | W | 1-0 | Greenwood og |
| | | 4 | 30.01.54 | **Rotherham Utd** (D2) | H | W | 4-0 | Nicholls, Allen, Ryan |
| | | 5 | 20.02.54 | **Newcastle Utd** (D1) | H | W | 3-2 | Allen 3 |
| | | 6 | 13.03.54 | **Tottenham Hotspur** (D1) | H | W | 3-0 | Barlow, Nicholls 2 |
| | | SF | 27.03.54 | **Port Vale** (D3) | | W | 2-1 | Dudley, Allen (p) |
| | | | | *played at Villa Park* | | | | |
| | | F | 01.05.54 | **Preston North End** (D1) | | W | 3-2 | Allen 2 (1p), Griffin |
| | | | | *played at Wembley Stadium* | | | | |
| 1954-55 | (D1) | 3 | 08.01.55 | **Bournemouth** (3S) | A | W | 1-0 | Williams |
| | | 4 | 29.01.55 | **Charlton Athletic** (D1) | H | L | 2-4 | Williams 2 |
| 1955-56 | (D1) | 3 | 07.01.56 | **Wolverhampton W** (D1) | A | W | 2-1 | Griffin, Lee |
| | | 4 | 28.01.56 | **Portsmouth** (D1) | H | W | 2-0 | Lee, Allen (p) |
| | | 5 | 18.02.56 | **Birmingham City** (D1) | H | L | 0-1 | |
| 1956-57 | (D1) | 3 | 05.01.57 | **Doncaster Rovers** (D2) | A | D | 1-1 | Robson |

| | | | | | | | |
|---|---|---|---|---|---|---|---|
| | 3r | 09.01.57 | **Doncaster Rovers** | H | W | 2-0 | Allen 2 |
| | 4 | 26.01.57 | **Sunderland** (D1) | H | W | 4-2 | Kevan 2, Horobin, Allen (p) |
| | 5 | 16.02.57 | **Blackpool** (D1) | A | D | 0-0 | |
| | 5r | 20.02.57 | **Blackpool** | H | W | 2-1 | Kevan, Allen |
| | 6 | 02.03.57 | **Arsenal** (D1) | H | D | 2-2 | Allen, Wills og |
| | 6r | 05.03.57 | **Arsenal** | A | W | 2-1 | Whitehouse, Kevan |
| | SF | 23.03.57 | **Aston Villa** (D1) *played at Molineux* | | D | 2-2 | Whitehouse 2 |
| | SFr | 28.03.57 | **Aston Villa** *played at St Andrews* | | L | 0-1 | |
| 1957-58 (D1) | 3 | 04.01.58 | **Manchester City** (D1) | H | W | 5-1 | Allen 2, Griffin, Barlow, Ewing og |
| | 4 | 25.01.58 | **Nottingham Forest** (D1) | H | D | 3-3 | Allen, Kevan, Robson |
| | 4r | 28.01.58 | **Nottingham Forest** | A | W | 5-1 | Kevan, Whitehouse, Griffin, Robson, Howe (p) |
| | 5 | 15.02.58 | **Sheffield Utd** (D2) | A | D | 1-1 | Allen |
| | 5r | 19.02.58 | **Sheffield Utd** | H | W | 4-1 | Kevan 2, Alen (p), Robson |
| | 6 | 01.03.58 | **Manchester Utd** (D1) | H | D | 2-2 | Allen, Horobin |
| | 6r | 05.03.58 | **Manchester Utd** | A | L | 0-1 | |
| 1958-59 (D1) | 3 | 19.01.59 | **Sheffield Wed** (D2) | A | W | 2-0 | Jackson, Hogg |
| | 4 | 24.01.59 | **Brentford** (D3) | H | W | 2-0 | Kevan 2 |
| | 5 | 14.02.59 | **Blackpool** (D1) | A | L | 1-3 | Robson |
| 1959-60 (D1) | 3 | 09.01.60 | **Plymouth Argyle** (D2) | H | W | 3-2 | Kevan 3 |
| | 4 | 30.01.60 | **Bolton Wanderers** (D1) | H | W | 2-0 | Jackson, Burnside |
| | 5 | 20.02.60 | **Leicester City** (D1) | A | L | 1-2 | Kennedy |
| 1960-61 (D1) | 3 | 07.01.61 | **Lincoln City** (D2) | A | L | 1-3 | Burnside |
| 1961-62 (D1) | 3 | 06.01.62 | **Blackpool** (D1) | A | D | 0-0 | |
| | 3r | 10.01.62 | **Blackpool** | H | W | 2-1 | Burnside, Smith |
| | 4 | 27.01.62 | **Wolverhampton W** (D1) | A | W | 2-1 | Clark 2 |
| | 5 | 17.02.62 | **Tottenham Hotspur** (D1) | H | L | 2-4 | Kevan, Smith |
| 1962-63 (D1) | 3 | 05.01.63 | **Plymouth Argyle** (D2) | A | W | 5-1 | Kevan 2, Smith, Cram, Newman og |
| | 4 | 06.03.63 | **Nottingham Forest** (D1) | H | D | 0-0 | |
| | 4r | 11.03.63 | **Nottingham Forest** | A | L | 1-2aet | Smith |
| 1963-64 (D1) | 3 | 04.01.64 | **Blackpool** (D1) | H | D | 2-2 | Clark, Howe (p) |
| | 3r | 08.01.64 | **Blackpool** | A | W | 1-0 | Fenton |
| | 4 | 25.01.64 | **Arsenal** (D1) | H | D | 3-3 | Fenton, Kaye, Jones |
| | 4r | 29.01.64 | **Arsenal** | A | L | 0-2 | |
| 1964-65 (D1) | 3 | 09.01.65 | **Liverpool** (D1) | H | L | 1-2 | Astle |
| 1965-66 (D1) | 3 | 22.01.66 | **Bolton Wanderers** (D2) | A | L | 0-3 | |
| 1966-67 (D1) | 3 | 28.01.67 | **Northampton Town** (D2) | A | W | 3-1 | Astle, Clark, Brown |
| | 4 | 18.02.67 | **Leeds Utd** (D1) | A | L | 0-5 | |
| 1967-68 (D1) | 3 | 27.01.68 | **Colchester Utd** (D3) | A | D | 1-1 | Brown (p) |
| | 3r | 31.01.68 | **Colchester Utd** | H | W | 4-0 | Astle 2, Kaye, Clark |
| | 4 | 17.02.68 | **Southampton** (D1) | H | D | 1-1 | Brown |
| | 4r | 21.02.68 | **Southampton** | A | W | 3-2 | Astle 2, Brown |
| | 5 | 09.03.68 | **Portsmouth** (D2) | A | W | 2-1 | Astle, Clark |
| | 6 | 30.03.68 | **Liverpool** (D1) | H | D | 0-0 | |
| | 6r | 08.04.68 | **Liverpool** | A | D | 1-1aet | Astle |
| | 6 2r | 18.04.68 | **Liverpool** *played at Maine Road* | | W | 2-1 | Astle, Clark |
| | SF | 27.04.68 | **Birmingham City** (D2) *played at Villa Park* | | W | 2-0 | Astle, Brown |
| | F | 18.05.68 | **Everton** (D1) *played at Wembley Stadium* | | W | 1-0aet | Astle |
| 1968-69 (D1) | 3 | 04.01.69 | **Norwich City** (D2) | H | W | 3-0 | Rees, Astle (p), Forbes |
| | 4 | 25.01.69 | **Fulham** (D2) | A | W | 2-1 | Hartford, Rees |
| | 5 | 12.02.69 | **Arsenal** (D1) | H | W | 1-0 | Brown |
| | 6 | 01.03.69 | **Chelsea** (D1) | A | W | 2-1 | Brown, Astle |
| | SF | 29.03.69 | **Leicester City** (D1) *played at Hillsborough* | | L | 0-1 | |
| 1969-70 (D1) | 3 | 03.01.70 | **Sheffield Wed** (D1) | A | L | 1-2 | Brown |
| 1970-71 (D1) | 3 | 02.01.71 | **Scunthorpe Utd** (D4) | H | D | 0-0 | |

| | | | | | | | | |
|---|---|---|---|---|---|---|---|---|
| | | 3r | 11.01.71 | **Scunthorpe Utd** | A | W | 3-1 | Brown 2, Astle |
| | | 4 | 23.01.71 | **Ipswich Town** (D1) | H | D | 1-1 | Suggett |
| | | 4r | 26.01.71 | **Ipswich Town** | A | L | 0-3 | |
| 1971-72 | (D1) | 3 | 15.01.72 | **Coventry City** (D1) | H | L | 1-2 | Brown |
| 1972-73 | (D1) | 3 | 13.01.73 | **Nottingham Forest** (D2) | H | D | 1-1 | Winfield og |
| | | 3r | 16.01.73 | **Nottingham Forest** | A | - | 1-1ab | Hartford |
| | | | | *abandoned after 80 minutes – fog* | | | | |
| | | 3r | 22.01.73 | **Nottingham Forest** | A | D | 0-0aet | |
| | | 3 2r | 29.01.73 | **Nottingham Forest** | | W | 3-1 | Cantello, Hartford, Suggett |
| | | | | *played at Filbert Street* | | | | |
| | | 4 | 03.02.73 | **Swindon Town** (D2) | H | W | 2-0 | T Brown, Cantello |
| | | 5 | 24.02.73 | **Leeds Utd** (D1) | A | L | 0-2 | |
| 1973-74 | (D2) | 3 | 05.01.74 | **Notts County** (D2) | H | W | 4-0 | T Brown 3, Johnston |
| | | 4 | 27.01.74 | **Everton** (D1) | A | D | 0-0 | |
| | | 4r | 30.01.74 | **Everton** | H | W | 1-0 | T Brown |
| | | 5 | 16.02.74 | **Newcastle Utd** (D1) | H | L | 0-3 | |
| 1974-75 | (D2) | 3 | 04.01.75 | **Bolton Wanderers** (D2) | A | D | 0-0 | |
| | | 3r | 08.01.75 | **Bolton Wanderers** | H | W | 4-0 | Cantello, Wile, Shaw, Mayo |
| | | 4 | 25.01.75 | **Carlisle Utd** (D1) | A | L | 2-3 | T Brown (p), Nisbett |
| 1975-76 | (D2) | 3 | 03.01.76 | **Carlisle Utd** (D2) | H | W | 3-1 | T Brown 2 (1p), A Brown |
| | | 4 | 24.01.76 | **Lincoln City** (D4) | H | W | 4-2 | T Brown, Martin, B Robson |
| | | 5 | 14.02.76 | **Southampton** (D2) | H | D | 1-1 | T Brown |
| | | 5r | 17.02.76 | **Southampton** | A | L | 0-4 | |
| 1976-77 | (D1) | 3 | 08.01.77 | **Manchester City** (D1) | A | D | 1-1 | Johnston |
| | | 3r | 11.01.77 | **Manchester City** | H | L | 0-1 | |
| 1977-78 | (D1) | 3 | 07.01.78 | **Blackpool** (D2) | H | W | 4-1 | Johnston 2, Regis, T Brown (p) |
| | | 4 | 28.01.78 | **Manchester Utd** (D1) | A | D | 1-1 | Johnston |
| | | 4r | 01.02.78 | **Manchester Utd** | H | W | 3-2aet | Regis 2, T Brown |
| | | 5 | 22.02.78 | **Derby County** (D1) | A | W | 3-2 | Regis 2, Johnston |
| | | 6 | 11.03.78 | **Nottingham Forest** (D1) | H | W | 2-0 | Martin, Regis |
| | | SF | 08.04.78 | **Ipswich Town** (D1) | | L | 1-3 | T Brown (p) |
| | | | | *played at Highbury* | | | | |
| 1978-79 | (D1) | 3 | 09.01.79 | **Coventry City** (D1) | A | D | 2-2 | Cunningham, A Brown |
| | | 3r | 15.01.79 | **Coventry City** | H | W | 4-0 | Batson, T Brown 2, A Brown |
| | | 4 | 26.02.79 | **Leeds Utd** (D1) | A | D | 3-3 | Cunningham, A Brown, Regis |
| | | | | *played at The Hawthorns* | | | | |
| | | 4r | 01.03.79 | **Leeds Utd** | H | W | 2-0aet | Wile, A Brown |
| | | 5 | 10.03.79 | **Southampton** (D1) | H | D | 1-1 | A Brown |
| | | 5r | 12.03.79 | **Southampton** | A | L | 1-2aet | Cunningham |
| 1979-80 | (D1) | 3 | 05.01.80 | **West Ham Utd** (D2) | H | D | 1-1 | Regis |
| | | 3r | 08.01.80 | **West Ham Utd** | A | L | 1-2 | T Brown |
| 1980-81 | (D1) | 3 | 03.01.81 | **Grimsby Town** (D2) | H | W | 3-0 | B Robson, Cowdrill, Barnes |
| | | 4 | 24.01.81 | **Middlesbrough** (D1) | A | L | 0-1 | |
| 1981-82 | (D1) | 3 | 02.01.82 | **Blackburn Rovers** (D2) | H | W | 3-2 | Whitehead, Mackenzie, King (p) |
| | | 4 | 23.01.82 | **Gillingham** (D3) | A | W | 1-0 | Statham |
| | | 5 | 13.02.82 | **Norwich City** (D2) | H | W | 1-0 | Regis |
| | | 6 | 06.03.82 | **Coventry City** (D1) | H | W | 2-0 | Regis, Owen |
| | | SF | 03.04.82 | **QPR** (D2) | | L | 0-1 | |
| | | | | *played at Highbury* | | | | |
| 1982-83 | (D1) | 3 | 08.01.83 | **QPR** (D2) | H | W | 3-2 | Owen 2 (1p), Eastoe |
| | | 4 | 29.01.83 | **Tottenham Hotspur** (D1) | A | L | 1-2 | Whitehead |
| 1983-84 | (D1) | 3 | 07.01.84 | **Rotherham Utd** (D3) | A | D | 0-0 | |
| | | 3r | 11.01.84 | **Rotherham Utd** | H | W | 3-0 | Thompson, Morley 2 |
| | | 4 | 01.02.84 | **Scunthorpe Utd** (D3) | H | W | 1-0 | Forsyth |
| | | 5 | 18.02.84 | **Plymouth Argyle** (D3) | H | L | 0-1 | |
| 1984-85 | (D1) | 3 | 05.01.85 | **Orient** (D3) | A | L | 1-2 | Cross |
| 1985-86 | (D1) | 3 | 13.01.86 | **Sheffield Wed** (D1) | A | D | 2-2 | Reilly, Statham |
| | | 3r | 16.01.86 | **Sheffield Wed** | H | L | 2-3 | Hunt, Thomas |
| 1986-87 | (D2) | 3 | 10.01.87 | **Swansea City** (D4) | A | L | 2-3 | Anderson, Lewis og |
| 1987-88 | (D2) | 3 | 09.01.88 | **Wimbledon** (D1) | A | L | 1-4 | Thorn og |
| 1988-89 | (D2) | 3 | 07.01.89 | **Everton** (D1) | H | D | 1-1 | Anderson |

| | | | | | | | | |
|---|---|---|---|---|---|---|---|---|
| | 3r | 11.01.89 | **Everton** | A | L | 0-1 | |
| 1989-90 (D2) | 3 | 06.01.90 | **Wimbledon** (D1) | H | W | 2-0 | G Robson, Bartlett |
| | 4 | 27.01.90 | **Charlton Athletic** (D1) | H | W | 1-0 | Ford |
| | 5 | 17.02.90 | **Aston Villa** (D1) | H | L | 0-2 | |
| 1990-91 (D2) | 3 | 05.01.91 | **Woking** (IL) | H | L | 2-4 | West, Bradley |
| 1991-92 (D3) | 1 | 16.11.91 | **Marlow** (IL) | H | W | 6-0 | Strodder, Goodman, Shakespeare 2 (1p), McNally, Robson |
| | 2 | 09.12.91 | **Leyton Orient** (D3) | A | L | 1-2 | Williams |
| 1992-93 (D2) | 1 | 14.11.92 | **Aylesbury Utd** (IL) | H | W | 8-0 | Donovan 3, McNally, Taylor, G Robson, Raven, Hamilton |
| | 2 | 06.12.92 | **Wycombe W** (Conf) | A | D | 2-2 | Bradley, Taylor |
| | 2r | 15.12.92 | **Wycombe W** | H | W | 1-0 | Taylor |
| | 3 | 02.01.93 | **West Ham Utd** (D1) | H | L | 0-2 | |
| 1993-94 (D1) | 1 | 14.11.93 | **Halifax Town** (Conf) | A | L | 1-2 | Hunt |
| 1994-95 (D1) | 3 | 07.01.95 | **Coventry City** (PL) | A | D | 1-1 | Ashcroft (p) |
| | 3r | 18.01.95 | **Coventry City** | H | L | 1-2 | Raven |
| 1995-96 (D1) | 3 | 06.01.96 | **Crewe Alexandra** (D2) | A | L | 3-4 | Hunt, Raven, Coldicott |
| 1996-97 (D1) | 3 | 04.01.97 | **Chelsea** (PL) | A | L | 0-3 | |
| 1997-98 (D1) | 3 | 13.01.98 | **Stoke City** (D1) | H | W | 3-1 | Sneekes 2, Kilbane |
| | 4 | 24.01.98 | **Aston Villa** (PL) | A | L | 0-4 | |
| 1998-99 (D1) | 3 | 02.01.99 | **Bournemouth** (D2) | A | L | 0-1 | |
| 1999-00 (D1) | 3 | 11.12.99 | **Blackburn Rovers** (D1) | H | D | 2-2 | Hughes, Evans |
| | 3r | 22.12.99 | **Blackburn Rovers** | A | L | 0-2aet | |
| 2000-01 (D1) | 3 | 06.01.01 | **Derby County** (PL) | A | L | 2-3 | Taylor, Hughes |
| 2001-02 (D1) | 3 | 05.01.02 | **Sunderland** (PL) | A | W | 2-1 | Clement (p), T Johnson |
| | 4 | 26.01.02 | **Leicester City** (PL) | H | W | 1-0 | Clement (p) |
| | 5 | 16.02.02 | **Cheltenham Town** (D3) | H | W | 1-0 | Dichio |
| | 6 | 10.03.02 | **Fulham** (PL) | H | L | 0-1 | |
| 2002-03 (PL) | 3 | 04.01.03 | **Bradford City** (D1) | H | W | 3-1 | Dichio 3 |
| | 4 | 25.01.03 | **Watford** (D1) | A | L | 0-1 | |

## WEST END

*Formed 1868. Entered FA Cup: 1879-80 – 1884-85. Played at Womholt Farm, Uxbridge, near the Princess Alice pub in Uxbridge Road.*

| | | | | | | | |
|---|---|---|---|---|---|---|---|
| 1879-80 | 1 | | Swifts | | | - | |
| | | | *Swifts scratched. West End walkover* | | | | |
| | 2 | 06.12.79 | **Hotspur FC** | H | W | 1-0 | |
| | 3 | | bye | | | | |
| | 4 | 07.02.80 | **Old Etonians** | A | L | 1-5 | Elmslie |
| 1880-81 | 1 | 06.11.80 | **Hanover Utd** | H | W | 1-0 | Harkness |
| | 2 | 11.12.80 | **Marlow** | A | L | 0-4 | |
| 1881-82 | 1 | 29.10.81 | **Remnants** | H | W | 3-2 | Elmslie 2, Black |
| | 2 | 26.11.81 | **Reading** | A | D | 1-1 | |
| | | | *FA disqualified West End. Reading advanced* | | | | |
| 1882-83 | 1 | 04.11.82 | **Hendon (1874)** | H | L | 1-3 | |
| 1883-84 | 1 | 10.11.83 | **Maidenhead** | A | W | 1-0 | Cooper |
| | 2 | 01.12.83 | **Reading** | A | L | 0-1 | |
| 1884-85 | 1 | 08.11.84 | **Upton Park** | H | D | 3-3 | |
| | | | *West End scratched before replay took place. Upton Park walkover* | | | | |

## WEST HAM UNITED

*Formed 1895 as Thames Ironworks. West Ham United 1900. FA Cup winners: 1964, 1975, 1980. Runners-up: 1923. FA Cup Record Win: 8-1 v Chesterfield, 1st round, 10.01.1914. Record FA Cup defeat: 0-6 v Manchester United, 4th round, 26.01.2003.*

**as Thames Ironworks**

| | |
|---|---|
| 1897-98 (Lon) | P Redhill (H) 3-0; 1q Royal Engineers Training Battalion (H) 2-1; 2q St Albans (A) 0-2 |
| 1898-99 (SL) | 1q Royal Engineers Training Battalion (H) 2-0; 2q Brighton Utd (A) 0-0; 2qr Brighton Utd (H) 1-4 |
| 1899-00 (SL) | P Royal Engineers (H) 6-0; 1q Grays Utd (A) 4-0; 2q Sheppey Utd (H) 4-2; 3q Dartford (A) 7-0; 4q New Brompton (A) 0-0; 4qr New Brompton (H) 2-0; 5q Millwall Athletic (H) 1-2 |

**as West Ham Utd**

| | | | | | | | | |
|---|---|---|---|---|---|---|---|---|
| 1900-01 (SL) | | | 3q Olympic FC (H) 1-0; 4q New Brompton (A) 1-1; 4qr New Brompton (H) 4-1; 5q Clapton (H) 1-1; 5qr Clapton (A) 3-2; Int Liverpool (H) 0-1 | | | | |
| 1901-02 (SL) | | | 3q Leyton (A) 1-0; 4q Grays Utd (H) 1-2 | | | | |
| 1902-03 (SL) | | | Int Lincoln City (A) 0-2 | | | | |
| 1903-04 (SL) | | | 3q Brighton (H) 4-0; 4q Clapton (A) 3-0; 5q Chatham (A) 5-0; Int Fulham (H) 0-1 | | | | |
| 1904-05 (SL) | | | 6q Brighton (H) 1-2 | | | | |
| 1905-06 (SL) | 1 | 13.01.06 | **Woolwich Arsenal** (D1) | A | D | 1-1 | Kitchen |
| | 1r | 18.01.06 | **Woolwich Arsenal** | H | L | 2-3 | Bridgeman, Watson |
| 1906-07 (SL) | 1 | 12.01.07 | **Blackpool** (D2) | H | W | 2-1 | Stapley, Winterhalder |
| | 2 | 02.02.07 | **Everton** (D1) | H | L | 1-2 | Stapley |
| 1907-08 (SL) | 1 | 11.01.08 | **Rotherham Town** (ML) | H | W | 1-0 | Blackburn |
| | 2 | 01.02.08 | **Newcastle Utd** (D1) | A | L | 0-2 | |
| 1908-09 (SL) | 1 | 16.01.09 | **QPR** (SL) | A | D | 0-0 | |
| | 1r | 20.01.09 | **QPR** | H | W | 1-0 | Shea |
| | 2 | 06.02.09 | **Leeds City** (D2) | A | D | 1-1 | Miller |
| | 2r | 11.02.09 | **Leeds City** | H | W | 2-1aet | Shea 2 |
| | 3 | 20.02.09 | **Newcastle Utd** (D1) | H | D | 0-0 | |
| | 3r | 24.02.09 | **Newcastle Utd** | A | L | 1-2 | Shea |
| 1909-10 (SL) | 1 | 15.01.10 | **Carlisle Utd** (LC) | H | D | 1-1 | Blackburn |
| | 1r | 20.01.10 | **Carlisle Utd** | H | W | 5-0 | Blackburn 2, Shea, Webb, Randall |
| | 2 | 05.02.10 | **Wolverhampton W** (D2) | A | W | 5-1 | Shea 2, Webb 3 |
| | 3 | 19.02.10 | **QPR** (SL) | A | D | 1-1 | Webb |
| | 3r | 24.02.10 | **QPR** | H | L | 0-1aet | |
| 1910-11 (SL) | 1 | 14.01.11 | **Nottingham Forest** (D1) | H | W | 2-1 | Shea 2 |
| | 2 | 04.02.11 | **Preston North End** (D1) | H | W | 3-0 | Webb 3 |
| | 3 | 25.02.11 | **Manchester Utd** (D1) | H | W | 2-1 | Shea, Caldwell |
| | 4 | 11.03.11 | **Blackburn Rovers** (D1) | H | L | 2-3 | Butcher 2 |
| 1911-12 (SL) | 1 | 03.01.12 | **Gainsborough T** (D2) | H | W | 2-1 | Webb, Harrison |
| | 2 | 03.02.12 | **Middlesbrough** (D1) | A | D | 1-1 | Harrison |
| | 2r | 08.02.12 | **Middlesbrough** | H | W | 2-1 | Ashton, Harrison |
| | 3 | 24.02.12 | **Swindon Town** (SL) | H | D | 1-1 | Butcher |
| | 3r | 28.02.12 | **Swindon Town** | A | L | 0-4 | |
| 1912-13 (SL) | 1 | 13.01.13 | **WBA** (D1) | A | D | 1-1 | Harrison |
| | 1r | 16.01.13 | **WBA** | H | D | 2-2aet | Hilsdon 2 |
| | 1 2r | 22.01.13 | **WBA** | | W | 3-0 | Hilsdon 2, Denyer |
| | | | *played at Stamford Bridge* | | | | |
| | 2 | 01.02.13 | **Aston Villa** (D1) | A | L | 0-5 | |
| 1913-14 (SL) | 1 | 10.01.14 | **Chesterfield** (ML) | H | W | 8-1 | Puddefoot 5, Bailey, Leafe, Ashton |
| | 2 | 31.01.14 | **Crystal Palace** (SL) | H | W | 2-0 | Bailey 2 |
| | 3 | 21.01.14 | **Liverpool** (D1) | H | D | 1-1 | Puddefoot |
| | 3r | 25.01.14 | **Liverpool** | A | L | 1-5 | Puddefoot |
| 1914-15 (SL) | 1 | 09.01.15 | **Newcastle Utd** (D1) | H | D | 2-2 | Leafe 2 |
| | 1r | 16.01.15 | **Newcastle Utd** | A | L | 2-3 | Casey, Leafe |
| 1919-20 (D2) | 1 | 10.01.20 | **Southampton** (SL) | A | D | 0-0 | |
| | 1r | 15.01.20 | **Southampton** | H | W | 3-1 | Puddefoot 2, Butcher |
| | 2 | 31.01.20 | **Bury** (D2) | H | W | 6-0 | Puddefoot 3, Bailey, Butcher, Smith |
| | 3 | 21.02.20 | **Tottenham Hotspur** (D2) | A | L | 0-3 | |
| 1920-21 (D2) | 1 | 08.01.21 | **Sheffield Wed** (D2) | A | L | 0-1 | |
| 1921-22 (D2) | 1 | 07.01.22 | **Swansea Town** (3S) | A | D | 0-0 | |
| | 1r | 11.01.22 | **Swansea Town** | H | D | 1-1aet | Watson |
| | 1 2r | 16.01.22 | **Swansea Town** | | L | 0-1 | |
| | | | *played at Ashton Gate* | | | | |
| 1922-23 (D2) | 1 | 13.01.23 | **Hull City** (D2) | A | W | 3-2 | Watson 2, Moore |
| | 2 | 03.02.23 | **Brighton** (3S) | A | D | 1-1 | Watson |
| | 2r | 07.02.23 | **Brighton** | H | W | 1-0 | Moore |
| | 3 | 24.02.23 | **Plymouth Argyle** (3S) | H | W | 2-0 | Moore, Richards |
| | 4 | 10.03.23 | **Southampton** (D2) | A | D | 1-1 | Watson |
| | 4r | 14.03.23 | **Southampton** | H | D | 1-1aet | Watson |
| | 4 2r | 19.03.23 | **Southampton** | | W | 1-0 | Brown |
| | | | *played at Villa Park* | | | | |

| | | | | | | | | |
|---|---|---|---|---|---|---|---|---|
| | | SF | 24.03.23 | **Derby County** (D2) *played at Stamford Bridge* | | W | 5-2 | Brown 2, Moore 2, Ruffell |
| | | F | 28.04.23 | **Bolton Wanderers** (D1) *played at Wembley Stadium* | | L | 0-2 | |
| 1923-24 | (D1) | 1 | 12.01.24 | **Aberdare Athletic** (3S) | H | W | 5-0 | Brown 2, Henderson, Moore, Williams |
| | | 2 | 02.02.24 | **Leeds Utd** (D2) | H | D | 1-1 | Kay |
| | | 2r | 06.02.24 | **Leeds Utd** | A | L | 0-1 | |
| 1924-25 | (D1) | 1 | 14.01.25 | **Arsenal** (D1) | H | D | 0-0 | |
| | | 1r | 21.01.25 | **Arsenal** | A | D | 2-2aet | Ruffell 2 |
| | | 1 2r | 26.01.25 | **Arsenal** *played at Stamford Bridge* | | W | 1-0 | Kay |
| | | 2 | 31.01.25 | **Nottingham Forest** (D1) | A | W | 2-0 | Ruffell, Yews |
| | | 3 | 21.02.25 | **Blackpool** (D2) | H | D | 1-1 | Watson |
| | | 3r | 25.02.25 | **Blackpool** | A | L | 0-3 | |
| 1925-26 | (D1) | 3 | 09.01.26 | **Tottenham Hotspur** (D1) | A | L | 0-5 | |
| 1926-27 | (D1) | 3 | 08.01.27 | **Tottenham Hotspur** | H | W | 3-2 | Watson 3 |
| | | 4 | 29.01.27 | **Brentford** (3S) | H | D | 1-1 | Ruffell |
| | | 4r | 02.02.27 | **Brentford** | A | L | 0-2 | |
| 1927-28 | (D1) | 3 | 14.01.28 | **Portsmouth** (D1) | A | W | 2-0 | Gibbins, Ruffell |
| | | 4 | 28.01.28 | **Huddersfield Town** (D1) | A | L | 1-2 | Gibbins |
| 1928-29 | (D1) | 3 | 12.01.29 | **Sunderland** (D1) | H | W | 1-0 | Earle |
| | | 4 | 26.01.29 | **Corinthians** | H | W | 3-0 | Earle, Watson, Hughes |
| | | 5 | 16.02.29 | **Bournemouth** (3S) | A | D | 1-1 | Yews |
| | | 5r | 20.02.29 | **Bournemouth** | H | W | 3-1 | Barrett, Yews, og |
| | | 6 | 02.03.29 | **Portsmouth** (D1) | A | L | 2-3 | Barrett 2 |
| 1929-30 | (D1) | 3 | 11.01.30 | **Notts County** (D2) | H | W | 4-0 | Watson 2, Barrett, Gibbins |
| | | 4 | 25.01.30 | **Leeds Utd** (D1) | H | W | 4-1 | Watson 4 |
| | | 5 | 15.02.30 | **Millwall** (D2) | H | W | 4-1 | Watson 2, Gibbins, Yews |
| | | 6 | 01.03.30 | **Arsenal** (D1) | H | L | 0-3 | |
| 1930-31 | (D1) | 3 | 10.01.31 | **Chelsea** (D1) | H | L | 1-3 | Gibbins |
| 1931-32 | (D1) | 3 | 09.01.32 | **Charlton Athletic** (D2) | A | W | 2-1 | Watson 2 |
| | | 4 | 23.01.32 | **Chelsea** (D1) | A | L | 1-3 | Weldon |
| 1932-33 | (D2) | 3 | 14.01.33 | **Corinthians** | A | W | 2-0 | Pollard, Watson |
| | | 4 | 28.01.33 | **WBA** (D1) | H | W | 2-0 | Watson, Wilson |
| | | 5 | 18.02.33 | **Brighton** (3S) | A | D | 2-2 | Musgrave, Watson |
| | | 5r | 22.02.33 | **Brighton** | H | W | 1-0 | Morton |
| | | 6 | 04.03.33 | **Birmingham** (D1) | H | W | 4-0 | Wilson, Morton, Pollard, Barkas og |
| | | SF | 18.03.33 | **Everton** (D1) *played at Molineux* | | L | 1-2 | Watson |
| 1933-34 | (D2) | 3 | 13.01.34 | **Bradford City** (D2) | H | W | 3-2 | Watson 2, Goulden |
| | | 4 | 27.01.34 | **Tottenham Hotspur** (D1) | A | L | 1-4 | Watson |
| 1934-35 | (D2) | 3 | 12.01.35 | **Stockport County** (3N) | H | D | 1-1 | Mills |
| | | 3r | 16.01.35 | **Stockport County** | A | L | 0-1 | |
| 1935-36 | (D2) | 3 | 11.01.36 | **Luton Town** (3S) | H | D | 2-2 | Mangnall, Ruffell |
| | | 3r | 15.01.36 | **Luton Town** | A | L | 0-4 | |
| 1936-37 | (D2) | 3 | 16.01.37 | **Bolton Wanderers** (D1) | H | D | 0-0 | |
| | | 3r | 20.01.37 | **Bolton Wanderers** | A | L | 0-1 | |
| 1937-38 | (D2) | 3 | 08.01.38 | **Preston North End** (D1) | A | L | 0-3 | |
| 1938-39 | (D2) | 3 | 07.01.39 | **QPR** (3S) | A | W | 2-1 | Foxall, Morton |
| | | 4 | 21.01.39 | **Tottenham Hotspur** (D2) | H | D | 3-3 | Foxall 2, Macauley |
| | | 4r | 30.01.39 | **Tottenham Hotspur** | A | D | 1-1aet | Foxall |
| | | 4 2r | 02.02.39 | **Tottenham Hotspur** *played at Highbury* | | W | 2-1 | Foxall, Macauley |
| | | 5 | 11.02.39 | **Portsmouth** (D1) | A | L | 0-2 | |
| 1945-46 | (D2) | 3 1L | 05.01.46 | **Arsenal** (D1) | H | W | 6-0 | Hall 2, Wood 2, Bainbridge, Foreman |
| | | 3 2L | 09.01.46 | **Arsenal** | A | L | 0-1 | |
| | | 4 1L | 26.01.46 | **Chelsea** (D1) | A | L | 0-2 | |
| | | 4 2L | 30.01.46 | **Chelsea** | H | W | 1-0 | Hall |
| 1946-47 | (D2) | 3 | 11.01.47 | **Leicester City** (D2) | H | L | 1-2 | Woodgate |
| 1947-48 | (D2) | 3 | 10.01.48 | **Blackburn Rovers** (D1) | A | D | 0-0aet | |

| | | | | | | | | |
|---|---|---|---|---|---|---|---|---|
| | | 3r | 17.01.48 | **Blackburn Rovers** | H | L | 2-4aet | Parsons, Stephens |
| 1948-49 | (D2) | 3 | 08.01.49 | **Luton Town** (D2) | A | L | 1-3 | Wade |
| 1949-50 | (D2) | 3 | 07.01.50 | **Ipswich Town** (3S) | H | W | 5-1 | Woodgate 2, Gazzard, Wade, Robinson |
| | | 4 | 28.01.50 | **Everton** (D1) | H | L | 1-2 | McGowan |
| 1950-51 | (D2) | 3 | 06.01.51 | **Cardiff City** (D2) | H | W | 2-1 | Barrett, Gazzard |
| | | 4 | 27.01.51 | **Stoke City** (D1) | A | L | 0-1 | |
| 1951-52 | (D2) | 3 | 12.01.52 | **Blackpool** (D1) | H | W | 2-1 | Andrews, O'Farrell |
| | | 4 | 02.02.52 | **Sheffield Utd** (D2) | H | D | 0-0 | |
| | | 4r | 06.02.52 | **Sheffield Utd** | A | L | 2-4 | Woodgate, Gazzard |
| 1952-53 | (D2) | 3 | 10.01.53 | **WBA** (D1) | H | L | 1-4 | Kearns |
| 1953-54 | (D2) | 3 | 09.01.54 | **Huddersfield Town** (D1) | H | W | 4-0 | Hooper 2, Sexton, Dixon |
| | | 4 | 30.01.54 | **Blackpool** (D1) | H | D | 1-1 | Dixon |
| | | 4r | 03.02.54 | **Blackpool** (D1) | A | L | 1-3 | Sexton |
| 1954-55 | (D2) | 3 | 08.01.55 | **Port Vale** (D2) | H | D | 2-2 | Bennett, Hooper |
| | | 3r | 10.01.55 | **Port Vale** | A | L | 1-3 | Hooper |
| 1955-56 | (D2) | 3 | 07.01.56 | **Preston North End** (D1) | H | W | 5-2 | Foan 3, Dare 2 |
| | | 4 | 28.01.56 | **Cardiff City** (D1) | H | W | 2-1 | Dare, Dick |
| | | 5 | 18.02.56 | **Blackburn Rovers** (D2) | H | D | 0-0 | |
| | | 5r | 23.02.56 | **Blackburn Rovers** | A | W | 3-2 | Dick 2, Hooper |
| | | 6 | 03.03.56 | **Tottenham Hotspur** (D1) | A | D | 3-3 | Dick 3 |
| | | 6r | 08.03.56 | **Tottenham Hotspur** | H | L | 1-2 | Dare |
| 1956-57 | (D2) | 3 | 05.01.57 | **Grimsby Town** (D2) | H | W | 5-3 | Smith 2, Lewis, Dick, Musgrove |
| | | 4 | 26.01.57 | **Everton** (D1) | A | L | 1-2 | Dare |
| 1957-58 | (D2) | 3 | 04.01.58 | **Blackpool** (D1) | H | W | 5-1 | Keeble 3, Dick 2 |
| | | 4 | 25.01.58 | **Stockport County** (3N) | H | W | 3-2 | Lewis 2, Keeble |
| | | 5 | 15.02.58 | **Fulham** (D2) | H | L | 2-3 | Grice, Bond |
| 1958-59 | (D1) | 3 | 10.01.59 | **Tottenham Hotspur** (D1) | A | L | 0-2 | |
| 1959-60 | (D1) | 3 | 09.01.60 | **Huddersfield Town** (D2) | A | D | 1-1 | Dick |
| | | 3r | 13.01.60 | **Huddersfield Town** | H | L | 1-5 | Musgrove |
| 1960-61 | (D1) | 3 | 07.01.61 | **Stoke City** (D2) | H | D | 2-2 | Dunmore, Dick |
| | | 3r | 11.01.61 | **Stoke City** | A | L | 0-1 | |
| 1961-62 | (D1) | 3 | 06.01.62 | **Plymouth Argyle** (D2) | A | L | 0-3 | |
| 1962-63 | (D1) | 3 | 04.02.63 | **Fulham** (D1) | H | D | 0-0 | |
| | | 3r | 20.02.63 | **Fulham** | A | W | 2-1 | Boyce, Byrne |
| | | 4 | 04.03.63 | **Swansea Town** (D2) | H | W | 1-0 | Boyce |
| | | 5 | 16.03.63 | **Everton** (D1) | H | W | 1-0 | Byrne |
| | | 6 | 30.03.63 | **Liverpool** (D1) | A | L | 0-1 | |
| 1963-64 | (D1) | 3 | 04.01.64 | **Charlton Athletic** (D2) | H | W | 2-0 | Hurst, Brabrook, Sissons |
| | | 4 | 25.01.64 | **Leyton Orient** (D2) | A | D | 1-1 | Brabrook |
| | | 4r | 29.01.64 | **Leyton Orient** | H | W | 3-0 | Hurst 2, Byrne |
| | | 5 | 15.02.64 | **Swindon Town** (D2) | A | W | 3-1 | Hurst 2, Byrne |
| | | 6 | 29.02.64 | **Burnley** (D1) | H | W | 3-2 | Byrne 2, Sissons |
| | | SF | 14.03.64 | **Manchester Utd** (D1) *played at Hillsborough* | | W | 3-1 | Boyce 2, Hurst |
| | | F | 02.05.64 | **Preston North End** (D2) *played at Wembley Stadium* | | W | 3-2 | Sissons, Hurst, Boyce |
| 1964-65 | (D1) | 3 | 09.01.65 | **Birmingham City** (D1) | H | W | 4-2 | Hurst 2, Byrne, Sissons |
| | | 4 | 30.01.65 | **Chelsea** (D1) | H | L | 0-1 | |
| 1965-66 | (D1) | 3 | 22.01.66 | **Oldham Athletic** (D3) | A | D | 2-2 | Burnett, Hurst |
| | | 3r | 24.01.66 | **Oldham Athletic** | H | W | 2-1 | Hurst, Brabrook |
| | | 4 | 12.02.66 | **Blackburn Rovers** (D1) | H | D | 3-3 | Bloomfield, Hurst, Sissons |
| | | 4r | 16.02.66 | **Blackburn Rovers** | A | L | 1-4 | Hurst |
| 1966-67 | (D1) | 3 | 28.01.67 | **Swindon Town** (D3) | H | D | 3-3 | Hurst 3 |
| | | 3r | 31.01.67 | **Swindon Town** | A | L | 1-3 | Sissons |
| 1967-68 | (D1) | 3 | 27.01.68 | **Burnley** (D1) | A | W | 3-1 | Peters 2, Dear |
| | | 4 | 17.02.68 | **Stoke City** (D1) | A | W | 3-0 | Sissons 2, Hurst |
| | | 5 | 09.03.68 | **Sheffield Utd** (D1) | H | L | 1-2 | Dear |
| 1968-69 | (D1) | 3 | 04.01.69 | **Bristol City** (D2) | H | W | 3-2 | Peters 2, Hunt |
| | | 4 | 25.01.69 | **Huddersfield Town** (D2) | A | W | 2-0 | Peters, Hurst |
| | | 5 | 26.02.69 | **Mansfield Town** (D3) | A | L | 0-3 | |

| | | | | | | | |
|---|---|---|---|---|---|---|---|
| 1969-70 (D1) | 3 | 03.01.70 | **Middlesbrough** (D2) | A | L | 1-2 | Stephenson |
| 1970-71 (D1) | 3 | 02.01.71 | **Blackpool** (D1) | A | L | 0-4 | |
| 1971-72 (D1) | 3 | 15.01.72 | **Luton Town** (D2) | H | W | 2-1 | Hurst, Best |
| | 4 | 09.02.72 | **Hereford Utd** (SL) | A | D | 0-0 | |
| | 4r | 14.02.72 | **Hereford Utd** | H | W | 3-1 | Hurst 3 |
| | 5 | 26.02.72 | **Huddersfield Town** (D1) | A | L | 2-4 | Robson, Best |
| 1972-73 (D1) | 3 | 13.01.73 | **Port Vale** (D3) | A | W | 1-0 | Holland |
| | 4 | 03.02.73 | **Hull City** (D2) | A | L | 0-1 | |
| 1973-74 (D1) | 3 | 05.01.74 | **Hereford Utd** (D3) | H | D | 1-1 | Holland |
| | 3r | 09.01.74 | **Hereford Utd** | A | L | 1-2 | Best |
| 1974-75 (D1) | 3 | 04.01.75 | **Southampton** (D2) | A | W | 2-1 | Lampard, Gould |
| | 4 | 25.01.75 | **Swindon Town** (D3) | H | D | 1-1 | Jennings |
| | 4r | 28.01.75 | **Swindon Town** | A | W | 2-1 | Brooking, Holland |
| | 5 | 15.02.75 | **QPR** (D1) | H | W | 2-1 | Holland, Robson |
| | 6 | 08.03.75 | **Arsenal** (D1) | A | W | 2-0 | A Taylor 2 |
| | SF | 05.04.75 | **Ipswich Town** (D1) | | D | 0-0 | |
| | | | *played at Villa Park* | | | | |
| | SFr | 09.04.75 | **Ipswich Town** | | W | 2-1 | A Taylor 2 |
| | | | *played at Stamford Bridge* | | | | |
| | F | 03.05.75 | **Fulham** (D2) | | W | 2-0 | A Taylor 2 |
| | | | *played at Wembley Stadium* | | | | |
| 1975-76 (D1) | 3 | 03.01.76 | **Liverpool** (D1) | H | L | 0-2 | |
| 1976-77 (D1) | 3 | 08.01.77 | **Bolton Wanderers** (D2) | H | W | 2-1 | Jennings, Pike |
| | 4 | 29.01.77 | **Aston Villa** (D1) | A | L | 0-3 | |
| 1977-78 (D1) | 3 | 07.01.78 | **Watford** (D4) | H | W | 1-0 | Robson |
| | 4 | 28.01.78 | **QPR** (D1) | H | D | 1-1 | Bonds |
| | 4r | 31.01.78 | **QPR** | A | L | 1-6 | Robson |
| 1978-79 (D2) | 3 | 09.01.79 | **Newport County** (D4) | A | L | 1-2 | Robson |
| 1979-80 (D2) | 3 | 05.01.80 | **WBA** (D1) | A | D | 1-1 | Pearson |
| | 3r | 08.01.80 | **WBA** | H | W | 2-1 | Pike, Brooking |
| | 4 | 26.01.80 | **Orient** (D2) | A | W | 3-2 | Stewart 2, og |
| | 5 | 16.02.80 | **Swansea City** (D3) | H | W | 2-0 | Allen, Cross |
| | 6 | 08.03.80 | **Aston Villa** (D1) | H | W | 1-0 | Stewart |
| | SF | 12.04.80 | **Everton** (D1) | | D | 1-1 | Pearson |
| | | | *played at Villa Park* | | | | |
| | SFr | 16.04.80 | **Everton** | | W | 2-1 | Devonshire, Lampard |
| | | | *played at Elland Road* | | | | |
| | F | 10.05.80 | **Arsenal** (D1) | | W | 1-0 | Brooking |
| | | | *played at Wembley Stadium* | | | | |
| 1980-81 (D2) | 3 | 03.01.81 | **Wrexham** (D2) | H | D | 1-1 | Stewart |
| | 3r | 06.01.81 | **Wrexham** | A | D | 0-0aet | |
| | 3 2r | 19.01.81 | **Wrexham** | A | L | 0-1aet | |
| 1981-82 (D1) | 3 | 02.01.82 | **Everton** (D1) | H | W | 2-1 | Bonds, Cross |
| | 4 | 23.01.82 | **Watford** (D2) | A | L | 0-2 | |
| 1982-83 (D2) | 3 | 08.01.83 | **Manchester Utd** (D1) | A | L | 0-2 | |
| 1983-84 (D1) | 3 | 07.01.84 | **Wigan Athletic** (D3) | H | W | 1-0 | Stewart |
| | 4 | 28.01.84 | **Crystal Palace** (D2) | A | D | 1-1 | Swindlehurst |
| | 4r | 31.01.84 | **Crystal Palace** | H | W | 2-0 | Barnes, Pike |
| | 5 | 18.02.84 | **Birmingham City** (D1) | A | L | 0-3 | |
| 1984-85 (D1) | 3 | 05.01.85 | **Port Vale** (D4) | H | W | 4-1 | Goddard 3, Dickens |
| | 4 | 04.02.85 | **Norwich City** (D1) | H | W | 2-1 | Stewart, Pike |
| | 5 | 04.03.85 | **Wimbledon** (D2) | A | D | 1-1 | Cottee |
| | 5r | 06.03.85 | **Wimbledon** | H | W | 5-1 | Cottee 3, Dickens, Allen |
| | 6 | 09.03.85 | **Manchester Utd** (D1) | A | L | 2-4 | Allen, Hogg og |
| 1985-86 (D1) | 3 | 05.01.86 | **Charlton Athletic** (D2) | A | W | 1-0 | Cottee |
| | 4 | 25.01.86 | **Ipswich Town** (D1) | H | D | 0-0 | |
| | 4r | 04.02.86 | **Ipswich Town** | A | D | 1-1aet | Cottee |
| | 4 2r | 06.02.86 | **Ipswich Town** | A | W | 1-0aet | Cottee |
| | 5 | 05.03.86 | **Manchester Utd** (D1) | H | D | 1-1 | McAvennie |
| | 5r | 09.03.86 | **Manchester Utd** | A | W | 2-0 | Pike, Stewart |
| | 5 2r | 12.03.86 | **Sheffield Wed** (D1) | A | L | 1-2 | Cottee |

| | | | | | | | |
|---|---|---|---|---|---|---|---|
| 1986-87 (D1) | 3 | 10.01.87 | **Orient** (D4) | A | D | 1-1 | Hilton |
| | 3r | 31.01.87 | **Orient** | H | W | 4-1 | Parris, Keen, McAvennie, Cottee |
| | 4 | 09.02.87 | **Sheffield Utd** (D2) | H | W | 4-0 | McAvennie 2, Gale, Robson |
| | 5 | 21.02.87 | **Sheffield Wed** (D1) | A | D | 1-1 | McAvennie |
| | 5r | 25.02.87 | **Sheffield Wed** | H | L | 0-2 | |
| 1987-88 (D1) | 3 | 09.01.88 | **Charlton Athletic** (D1) | H | W | 2-0 | Brady, Cottee |
| | 4 | 30.01.88 | **QPR** (D1) | A | L | 1-3 | Cottee |
| 1988-89 (D1) | 3 | 08.01.89 | **Arsenal** (D1) | H | D | 2-2 | Dickens, Bould (og) |
| | 3r | 11.01.89 | **Arsenal** | A | W | 1-0 | Rosenior |
| | 4 | 28.01.89 | **Swindon Town** (D2) | A | D | 0-0 | |
| | 4r | 01.02.89 | **Swindon Town** | H | W | 1-0 | Rosenior |
| | 5 | 18.02.89 | **Charlton Athletic** (D1) | A | W | 1-0 | Slater |
| | 6 | 18.03.89 | **Norwich City** (D1) | H | D | 0-0 | |
| | 6r | 22.03.89 | **Norwich City** | A | L | 1-3 | Ince |
| 1989-90 (D2) | 3 | 06.01.90 | **Torquay Utd** (D4) | A | L | 0-1 | |
| 1990-91 (D2) | 3 | 05.01.91 | **Aldershot** (D4) | A | D | 0-0 | |
| | | | *played at Upton Park* | | | | |
| | 3r | 16.01.91 | **Aldershot** | H | W | 6-1 | Morley 2, Slater, Parris, Bishop, Quinn |
| | 4 | 26.01.91 | **Luton Town** (D1) | A | D | 1-1 | Parris |
| | 4r | 30.01.91 | **Luton Town** | H | W | 5-0 | Parris, Bishop, McAvennie, Morley 2 |
| | 5 | 16.02.91 | **Crewe Alexandra** (D3) | H | W | 1-0 | Quinn |
| | 6 | 11.03.91 | **Everton** (D1) | H | W | 2-1 | Foster, Slater |
| | SF | 14.04.91 | **Nottingham Forest** (D1) | | L | 0-4 | |
| | | | *played at Villa Park* | | | | |
| 1991-92 (D1) | 3 | 04.01.92 | **Farnborough T** (Conf) | A | D | 1-1 | Dicks |
| | | | *played at Upton Park* | | | | |
| | 3r | 14.01.92 | **Farnborough T** | H | W | 1-0 | Morley |
| | 4 | 25.01.92 | **Wrexham** (D4) | H | D | 2-2 | Dicks, Morley |
| | 4r | 04.02.92 | **Wrexham** | A | W | 1-0 | Foster |
| | 5 | 15.02.92 | **Sunderland** (D2) | A | D | 1-1 | Small |
| | 5r | 26.02.92 | **Sunderland** | H | L | 2-3 | C Allen 2 |
| 1992-93 (D1) | 3 | 02.01.93 | **WBA** (D2) | A | W | 2-0 | C Allen, Robson |
| | 4 | 24.01.93 | **Barnsley** (D1) | A | L | 1-4 | Morley (p) |
| 1993-94 (PL) | 3 | 08.01.94 | **Watford** (D1) | H | W | 2-1 | M Allen, Marsh |
| | 4 | 29.01.94 | **Notts County** (D1) | A | D | 1-1 | Jones |
| | 4r | 09.02.94 | **Notts County** | H | W | 1-0aet | Chapman |
| | 5 | 19.02.94 | **Kidderminster H** (Conf) | A | W | 1-0 | Chapman |
| | 6 | 14.03.94 | **Luton Town** (D1) | H | D | 0-0 | |
| | 6r | 23.03.94 | **Luton Town** | A | L | 2-3 | M Allen, Bishop |
| 1994-95 (PL) | 3 | 07.01.95 | **Wycombe W** (D2) | A | W | 2-0 | Cottee, Brown |
| | 4 | 28.01.95 | **QPR** (PL) | A | L | 0-1 | |
| 1995-96 (PL) | 3 | 06.01.96 | **Southend Utd** (D1) | H | W | 2-0 | Moncur, Hughes |
| | 4 | 07.02.96 | **Grimsby Town** (D1) | H | D | 1-1 | Dowie |
| | 4r | 14.02.96 | **Grimsby Town** | A | L | 0-3 | |
| 1996-97 (PL) | 3 | 04.01.97 | **Wrexham** (D2) | A | D | 1-1 | Porfirio |
| | 3r | 25.01.97 | **Wrexham** | H | L | 0-1 | |
| 1997-98 (PL) | 3 | 03.01.98 | **Emley** (NPL) | H | W | 2-1 | Lampard, Hartson |
| | 4 | 25.01.98 | **Manchester City** (D1) | A | W | 2-1 | Berkovic, Lomas |
| | 5 | 14.02.98 | **Blackburn Rovers** (PL) | H | D | 2-2 | Kitson, Berkovic |
| | 5r | 25.02.98 | **Blackburn Rovers** | A | D | 1-1aet | Hartson |
| | | | *West Ham won 5-4 on penalties* | | | | |
| | 6 | 08.03.98 | **Arsenal** (PL) | A | D | 1-1 | I Pearce |
| | 6r | 17.03.98 | **Arsenal** | H | D | 1-1aet | Hartson |
| | | | *Arsenal won 4-3 on penalties* | | | | |
| 1998-99 (PL) | 3 | 02.01.99 | **Swansea City** (D3) | H | D | 1-1 | Dicks |
| | 3r | 13.01.99 | **Swansea City** | A | L | 0-1 | |
| 1999-00 (PL) | 3 | 11.12.99 | **Tranmere Rovers** (D1) | A | L | 0-1 | |
| 2000-01 (PL) | 3 | 06.01.01 | **Walsall** (D2) | A | W | 3-2 | Lampard, Kanoute 2 |
| | 4 | 28.01.01 | **Manchester Utd** (PL) | A | W | 1-0 | Di Canio |
| | 5 | 17.02.01 | **Sunderland** (PL) | A | W | 1-0 | Kanoute |
| | 6 | 11.03.01 | **Tottenham Hotspur** (PL) | H | L | 2-3 | S Pearce, Todorov |

| | | | | | | | | |
|---|---|---|---|---|---|---|---|---|
| 2001-02 | (PL) | 3 | 06.01.02 | **Macclesfield T** (D3) | A | W | 3-0 | Defoe 2, Cole |
| | | 4 | 26.01.02 | **Chelsea** (PL) | A | D | 1-1 | Kanoute |
| | | 4r | 06.02.02 | **Chelsea** | H | L | 2-3 | Defoe 2 |
| 2002-03 | (PL) | 3 | 04.01.03 | **Nottingham Forest** (D1) | H | W | 3-2 | Defoe 2, Cole |
| | | 4 | 26.01.03 | **Manchester Utd** (PL) | A | L | 0-6 | |

# WEST MANCHESTER

| | | | | | | | | |
|---|---|---|---|---|---|---|---|---|
| 1887-88 | | 1 | 15.10.87 | **Fleetwood Rangers** | A | L | 1-4 | |

# WEST STANLEY

*Formed 1889. Entered FA Cup: 1903-04 – 1950-51. Based in County Durham. Originally known as Oakey's Lillywhites. On February 16, 1909 168 miners were killed in one of Britain's worst ever colliery disasters at West Stanley. Folded 1959.*

| | | | | | | | | |
|---|---|---|---|---|---|---|---|---|
| 1919-20 | (NEL) | | | 6q Rotherham County (D2) 1-0; | | | | |
| | | 1 | 10.01. | **Gillingham** (SL) | H | W | 3-1 | Walton, Bohill, Hall |
| | | 2 | 31.01. | **Tottenham Hotspur** (D2) | A | L | 0-4 | |
| 1925-26 | (NEL) | 1 | 28.11.25 | **Rochdale** (3N) | A | - | 1-1ab | Agar |
| | | | | *abandoned at half-time – ground unplayable* | | | | |
| | | 1r | 01.12.25 | **Rochdale** | A | L | 0-4 | |
| 1931-32 | (NEL) | 1 | 28.11.31 | **Tranmere Rovers** (3N) | A | L | 0-3 | |

# WESTBURY UNITED

*Formed 1921. First entered FA Cup: 1921-22. Members of the Western League.*

| | | | | | | | | |
|---|---|---|---|---|---|---|---|---|
| 1937-38 | (Wilts) | 1 | 27.11.37 | **Walthamstow Ave** (AL) | H | L | 1-3 | Butler |

# WESTON-SUPER-MARE

*Formed 1899. First entered FA Cup: 1911-12. Members of the Southern League.*

| | | | | | | | | |
|---|---|---|---|---|---|---|---|---|
| 1961-62 | (WL) | 1 | 04.11.61 | **Bridgwater Town** (WL) | A | D | 0-0 | |
| | | 1r | 09.11.61 | **Bridgwater Town** | H | L | 0-1 | |
| 1993-94 | (SL) | 1 | 13.11.93 | **Woking** (Conf) | A | D | 2-2 | Elson, Bowering |
| | | 1r | 23.11.93 | **Woking** | H | L | 0-1 | |

# WEYBRIDGE SWALLOWS

| | | | | | | | | |
|---|---|---|---|---|---|---|---|---|
| 1880-81 | | 1 | 13.11.80 | **Henley FC** | H | W | 3-1 | |
| | | 2 | 18.12.80 | **Upton Park** | H | L | 0-3 | |

# WEYMOUTH

*Formed 1890. First entered FA Cup: 1893-94. League clubs beaten: Merthyr Town, Aldershot, Shrewsbury Town, Newport County, Cardiff City. Members of the Southern League.*

| | | | | | | | | |
|---|---|---|---|---|---|---|---|---|
| 1924-25 | (SL) | | | 5q Merthyr Town (3S) (H) 3-2; 6q Bristol Rovers (3S) (A) 0-0; 6qr Bristol Rovers (H) 0-2 | | | | |
| 1925-26 | (SL) | 1 | 28.11.25 | **Newport County** (3S) | H | L | 0-1 | |
| 1926-27 | (SL) | 1 | 27.11.26 | **Reading** (D2) | A | D | 4-4 | Caswell, Pilunger, Gibb, Rugg |
| | | 1r | 01.12.26 | **Reading** | A | L | 0-5 | |
| 1948-49 | (WL) | 1 | 27.11.48 | **Chelmsford City** (SL) | H | W | 2-1 | Gallacher, Anderson |
| | | 2 | 11.12.48 | **Yeovil Town** (SL) | H | L | 0-4 | |
| 1949-50 | (SL) | 1 | 26.11.49 | **Aldershot** (3S) | H | D | 2-2 | Northover, Haynes |
| | | 1r | 30.11.49 | **Aldershot** | A | W | 3-2 | Northover (p), Johnson, McGowan |
| | | 2 | 10.12.49 | **Hereford Utd** (SL) | H | W | 2-1 | Haynes, Johnston |
| | | 3 | 07.01.50 | **Manchester Utd** (D1) | A | L | 0-4 | |
| 1951-52 | (SL) | 1 | 24.11.51 | **Brush Sports** (BDL) | A | W | 3-2 | Massart, McCarter, Rowell |
| | | 2 | 15.12.51 | **Bristol Rovers** (3S) | A | L | 0-2 | |
| 1952-53 | (SL) | 1 | 22.11.52 | **Colchester Utd** (3S) | H | D | 1-1 | Rowell |
| | | 1r | 27.11.52 | **Colchester Utd** | A | L | 0-4 | |
| 1953-54 | (SL) | 1 | 21.11.53 | **Bedford Town** (SL) | H | W | 2-0 | Easton, Massart |
| | | 2 | 12.12.53 | **Leyton Orient** (3S) | A | L | 0-4 | |
| 1955-56 | (SL) | 1 | 19.11.55 | **Salisbury City** (WL) | H | W | 3-2 | Stocker 2, Hobbs |
| | | 2 | 10.12.55 | **Southend Utd** (3S) | H | L | 0-1 | |
| 1956-57 | (SL) | 1 | 17.11.56 | **Shrewsbury Town** (3S) | H | W | 1-0 | Henderson |
| | | 2 | 08.12.56 | **Southampton** (3S) | A | L | 2-3 | Easton 2 |
| 1958-59 | (SL) | 1 | 15.11.58 | **Coventry City** (D4) | H | L | 2-5 | Gallard 2 |
| 1960-61 | (SL) | 1 | 05.11.60 | **Torquay Utd** (D3) | H | L | 1-3 | Ayre (p) |
| 1961-62 | (SL) | 1 | 04.11.61 | **Barnet** (AL) | H | W | 1-0 | Court (p) |

| | | | | | | | | |
|---|---|---|---|---|---|---|---|---|
| | | 2 | 25.11.61 | **Newport County** (D3) | H | W | 1-0 | Court |
| | | 3 | 06.01.62 | **Morecambe** (LC) | A | W | 1-0 | Fogg |
| | | 4 | 27.01.62 | **Preston North End** (D2) | A | - | 0-0ab | |
| | | | | *abandoned after 14 minutes – fog* | | | | |
| | | 4 | 29.01.62 | **Preston North End** (D2) | A | L | 0-2 | |
| 1963-64 | (SL) | 1 | 16.11.63 | **Bedford Town** (SL) | H | D | 1-1 | Robertson |
| | | 1r | 21.11.63 | **Bedford Town** | A | L | 0-1 | |
| 1964-65 | (SL) | 1 | 14.11.64 | **Welton Rovers** (WL) | A | D | 1-1 | Hutchinson |
| | | 1r | 18.11.64 | **Welton Rovers** | H | W | 4-3 | Hutchinson 2, Spratt, Hannigan |
| | | 2 | 05.12.64 | **Bristol Rovers** (D3) | A | L | 1-4 | Spratt |
| 1965-66 | (SL) | 1 | 13.11.65 | **Bournemouth** (D3) | A | D | 0-0 | |
| | | 1r | 17.11.65 | **Bournemouth** | H | L | 1-4 | Camp |
| 1967-68 | (SL) | 1 | 09.12.67 | **Orient** (D3) | H | L | 0-2 | |
| 1968-69 | (SL) | 1 | 16.11.68 | **Yeovil Town** (SL) | H | W | 2-1 | Glover (p), Bennett |
| | | 2 | 07.12.68 | **Swansea Town** (D4) | H | D | 1-1 | Etteridge |
| | | 2r | 10.12.68 | **Swansea Town** | A | L | 0-2 | |
| 1969-70 | (SL) | 1 | 15.11.69 | **Northampton Town** (D4) | A | D | 0-0 | |
| | | 1r | 19.11.69 | **Northampton Town** | H | L | 1-3 | Allen |
| 1970-71 | (SL) | 1 | 21.11.70 | **Southend Utd** (D4) | A | L | 0-7 | |
| 1971-72 | (SL) | 1 | 20.11.71 | **Cambridge Utd** (D4) | A | L | 1-2 | Pound |
| 1973-74 | (SL) | 1 | 24.11.73 | **Merthyr Tydfil** (SL) | H | L | 0-1 | |
| 1974-75 | (SL) | 1 | 23.11.74 | **Peterborough Utd** (D3) | A | D | 0-0 | |
| | | 1r | 04.12.74 | **Peterborough Utd** | H | D | 3-3aet | Oakes og, Dorrington, Brown |
| | | 1 2r | 09.12.74 | **Peterborough Utd** | A | L | 0-3 | |
| 1975-76 | (SL) | 1 | 22.11.75 | **Gillingham** (D3) | H | L | 0-2 | |
| 1976-77 | (SL) | 1 | 20.11.76 | **Hitchin Town** (IL) | H | D | 1-1 | Robson |
| | | 1r | 23.11.76 | **Hitchin Town** | A | D | 2-2aet | Keirs, O'Rourke |
| | | 1 2r | 29.11.76 | **Hitchin Town** | | D | 3-3aet | Courtney, McCafferty, Henderson |
| | | | | *played at Aldershot* | | | | |
| | | 1 3r | 02.12.76 | **Hitchin Town** | | L | 1-3 | Keirs (p) |
| | | | | *played at Salisbury* | | | | |
| 1977-78 | (SL) | 1 | 26.11.77 | **Gillingham** (D3) | A | D | 1-1 | Courtney |
| | | 1r | 30.11.77 | **Gillingham** | H | L | 0-1 | |
| 1978-79 | (SL) | 1 | 25.11.78 | **Aldershot** (D4) | A | D | 1-1 | Hawkins |
| | | 1r | 29.11.78 | **Aldershot** | H | L | 0-2 | |
| 1980-81 | (APL) | 1 | 22.11.80 | **Swindon Town** (D3) | A | L | 2-3 | Iannone, Dove (p) |
| 1981-82 | (APL) | 1 | 21.11.81 | **Northampton Town** (D4) | H | D | 0-0 | |
| | | 1r | 24.11.81 | **Northampton Town** | A | L | 2-6 | Finnigan 2 |
| 1982-83 | (APL) | 1 | 20.11.82 | **Maidstone Utd** (APL) | H | W | 4-3 | Morrell, Peter, Bourne, Pearson |
| | | 2 | 11.12.82 | **Cardiff City** (D3) | A | W | 3-2 | Iannone, Finnegan, Pearson |
| | | 3 | 08.01.83 | **Cambridge Utd** (D2) | A | L | 0-1 | |
| 1984-85 | (APL) | 1 | 17.11.84 | **Millwall** (D3) | H | L | 0-3 | |
| 1985-86 | (APL) | 1 | 16.11.85 | **Chelmsford City** (SL) | A | L | 0-1 | |

# WHITBURN

*Formed 1882. Entered FA Cup: 1887-88 – 1909-10. Folded 1973. More than 50 men born in the Co Durham village of Whitburn played for League clubs including three who played in cup finals: Jimmy Seed (Tottenham Hotspur 1921) and Billy Henderson and John Young (both West Ham United 1923).*

| | | | | | | | | |
|---|---|---|---|---|---|---|---|---|
| 1887-88 | | 1 | 15.10.87 | **Middlesbrough** | A | L | 0-4 | |

# WHITBY TOWN

*Formed 1926. First entered FA Cup: 1950-51. FA Vase winners: 1997. FA Amateur Cup runners-up: 1965. League club beaten: Halifax Town. Members of the Northern Premier League.*

| | | | | | | | | |
|---|---|---|---|---|---|---|---|---|
| 1969-70 | (NL) | 1 | 15.11.69 | **York City** (D4) | A | L | 0-2 | |
| 1983-84 | (NL) | 1 | 19.11.83 | **Halifax Town** (D4) | A | W | 3-2 | Hampton, Linacre, Sills |
| | | 2 | 10.12.83 | **Wigan Athletic** (D3) | A | L | 0-1 | |
| 1984-85 | (NL) | 1 | 17.11.84 | **Chesterfield** (D4) | H | L | 1-3 | Granycome |
| 1985-86 | (NL) | 1 | 16.11.85 | **South Liverpool** (NPL) | H | W | 1-0 | Hankin |
| | | 2 | 07.12.85 | **York City** (D3) | A | L | 1-3 | Watson |
| 1986-87 | (NL) | 1 | 15.11.86 | **Doncaster Rovers** (D3) | H | D | 2-2 | Hedley, Graham |
| | | 1r | 18.11.86 | **Doncaster Rovers** | A | L | 2-3 | Humphries og, Hedley |
| 1996-97 | (NL) | 1 | 17.11.96 | **Hull City** (D3) | H | D | 0-0 | |

| | | | | | | | | |
|---|---|---|---|---|---|---|---|---|
| | | 1r | 26.11.96 | **Hull City** | A | L | 4-8aet | Pitman 3(2p), Robinson |
| 2001-02 | (NPL) | 1 | 17.11.01 | **Plymouth Argyle** (D3) | H | D | 1-1 | Gildea |
| | | 1r | 27.11.01 | **Plymouth Argyle** | A | L | 2-3 | Burt, Robinson |

## WHITLEY BAY

*Formed 1897. First entered FA Cup: 1908-09. FA Vase winners: 2002. League clubs beaten: Scarborough, Preston North End. Members of the Northern League.*

| | | | | | | | | |
|---|---|---|---|---|---|---|---|---|
| 1989-90 | (NPL) | 1 | 18.11.89 | **Scarborough** (D4) | A | W | 1-0 | Scott |
| | | 2 | 09.12.89 | **Preston North End** (D3) | H | W | 2-0 | Robinson, Todd |
| | | 3 | 06.01.90 | **Rochdale** (D4) | A | L | 0-1 | |
| 1990-91 | (NPL) | 1 | 17.11.90 | **Tamworth** (SL) | A | W | 6-4 | Briggs 2, Chandler, Barker 2, Ferris |
| | | 2 | 12.12.90 | **Barrow** (Conf) | H | L | 0-1 | |

## WHYTELEAFE

*Formed 1946. First entered FA Cup: 1969-70. Members of the Isthmian League.*

| | | | | | | | | |
|---|---|---|---|---|---|---|---|---|
| 1999-00 | (IL) | 1 | 30.10.99 | **Chester City** (D3) | H | D | 0-0 | |
| | | 1r | 09.11.99 | **Chester City** | A | L | 1-3 | Lunn |

## WIGAN ATHLETIC

*Formed 1932. First entered FA Cup: 1933-34. FA Cup best performance: 4th round, 1980, 1986. FA Trophy Runners-up: 1973. Record FA Cup win: 6-1 v Carlisle Utd, 1st round, 24.11.1934; 5-0 v Darlington, 2nd round, 06.12.1986. Record FA Cup defeat: 0-5 v Chelsea, 3rd round replay, 26.01.1985.*

| | | | | | | | | |
|---|---|---|---|---|---|---|---|---|
| 1934-35 | (CC) | 1 | 24.11.34 | **Carlisle Utd** (3N) | A | W | 6-1 | Armes 2, Roberts 2, Scott, H Robson |
| | | 2 | 08.12.34 | **Torquay Utd** (3S) | H | W | 3-2 | Roberts 2, Scott |
| | | 3 | 12.01.35 | **Millwall** (3S) | H | L | 1-4 | Roberts |
| 1935-36 | (CC) | 1 | 30.11.35 | **Rotherham Utd** (3N) | H | L | 1-2 | Felton |
| 1936-37 | (CC) | 1 | 28.11.36 | **Burton Town** (ML) | A | L | 1-5 | Wallbanks |
| 1937-38 | (CC) | 1 | 27.11.37 | **South Liverpool** (LC) | H | L | 1-4 | Thomas |
| 1953-54 | (LC) | 1 | 21.11.53 | **Scarborough** (ML) | H | W | 4-0 | Lomax, Livesey, Hindle, Lyon |
| | | 2 | 12.12.53 | **Hereford Utd** (SL) | H | W | 4-1 | Lyon, Livesey 2, Hughes og |
| | | 3 | 09.01.54 | **Newcastle Utd** (D1) | A | D | 2-2 | Lyon, Livesey |
| | | 3r | 13.01.54 | **Newcastle Utd** | H | L | 2-3 | Lomax 2 |
| 1954-55 | (LC) | 1 | 20.11.54 | **Barnsley** (3N) | A | L | 2-3 | Penk, Hindle |
| 1956-57 | (LC) | 1 | 17.11.56 | **Goole Town** (ML) | H | L | 1-2 | A McLean |
| 1957-58 | (LC) | 1 | 16.11.57 | **Southport** (3N) | A | W | 2-1 | Buckle, Banks |
| | | 2 | 07.12.57 | **Mansfield Town** (3N) | H | D | 1-1 | Hitchen |
| | | 2r | 11.12.57 | **Mansfield Town** | A | L | 1-3 | Buckle |
| 1962-63 | (CC) | 1 | 03.11.62 | **Gateshead AFC** (NRL) | A | L | 1-2 | Bradbury |
| 1964-65 | (CC) | 1 | 14.11.64 | **Stockport County** (D4) | A | L | 1-2 | Lyon |
| 1965-66 | (CC) | 1 | 13.11.65 | **Doncaster Rovers** (D4) | A | D | 2-2 | Lyon, Crompton |
| | | 1r | 17.11.65 | **Doncaster Rovers** | H | W | 3-1 | Lyon 3 |
| | | 2 | 04.12.65 | **Chester** (D4) | A | L | 1-2 | Llewellyn |
| 1966-67 | (CC) | 1 | 26.11.66 | **Tranmere Rovers** (D4) | A | D | 1-1 | Lyon |
| | | 1r | 28.11.66 | **Tranmere Rovers** | H | L | 0-1 | |
| 1969-70 | (NPL) | 1 | 15.11.69 | **Port Vale** (D4) | H | D | 1-1 | Sutherland |
| | | 1r | 18.11.69 | **Port Vale** | A | D | 2-2aet | Fleming, Fielding |
| | | 1 2r | 24.11.69 | **Port Vale** | | L | 0-1aet | |
| | | | | *played at Old Trafford* | | | | |
| 1970-71 | (NPL) | 1 | 21.11.70 | **S Shields (1936)** (NPL) | A | D | 1-1 | Temple |
| | | 1r | 23.11.70 | **S Shields (1936)** | H | W | 2-0 | Temple, Todd |
| | | 2 | 12.12.70 | **Peterborough Utd** (D4) | H | W | 2-1 | Davies, Fleming (p) |
| | | 3 | 02.01.71 | **Manchester City** (D1) | A | L | 0-1 | |
| 1971-72 | (NPL) | 1 | 20.11.71 | **Halifax Town** (D3) | H | W | 2-1 | Sutherland, Oates |
| | | 2 | 11.12.71 | **Wrexham** (D3) | A | L | 0-4 | |
| 1972-73 | (NPL) | 1 | 18.11.72 | **Grimsby Town** (D3) | A | L | 1-2 | Oates (p) |
| 1973-74 | (NPL) | 1 | 24.11.73 | **Huddersfield Town** (D3) | A | L | 0-2 | |
| 1974-75 | (NPL) | 1 | 23.11.74 | **Shrewsbury Town** (D4) | A | D | 1-1 | King |
| | | 1r | 25.11.74 | **Shrewsbury Town** | H | W | 2-1 | Gore, Jackson |
| | | 2 | 14.12.74 | **Mansfield Town** (D4) | H | D | 1-1 | B Foster og |
| | | 2r | 16.12.74 | **Mansfield Town** | A | L | 1-3 | King |
| 1975-76 | (NPL) | 1 | 22.11.75 | **Matlock Town** (NPL) | H | W | 4-1 | Rodgers 2, Wilkinson, Worswick |
| | | 2 | 13.12.75 | **Sheffield Wed** (D3) | A | L | 0-2 | |

| | | | | | | | | |
|---|---|---|---|---|---|---|---|---|
| 1976-77 | (NPL) | 1 | 20.11.76 | **Matlock Town** (NPL) | A | L | 0-2 | |
| 1977-78 | (NPL) | 1 | 26.11.77 | **York City** (D4) | H | W | 1-0 | Wilkie |
| | | 2 | 17.12.77 | **Sheffield Wed** (D3) | H | W | 1-0 | Whittle |
| | | 3 | 07.01.78 | **Birmingham City** (D1) | A | L | 0-4 | |
| 1978-79 | (D4) | 1 | 25.11.78 | **Bury** (D3) | H | D | 2-2 | Gore, Houghton |
| | | 1r | 28.11.78 | **Bury** | A | L | 1-4 | Moore |
| 1979-80 | (D4) | 1 | 24.11.79 | **Blackpool** (D3) | A | D | 1-1 | Methven |
| | | 1r | 28.11.79 | **Blackpool** | H | W | 2-0 | Gore, Corrigan |
| | | 2 | 24.12.79 | **Northwich V** (NPL) | A | - | 3-0ab | Quinn, Gore, Methven |
| | | | | *abandoned after 65 minutes – fog* | | | | |
| | | 2 | 05.01.80 | **Northwich V** | A | D | 2-2 | Hinnigan, Gore |
| | | 2r | 07.01.80 | **Northwich V** | H | W | 1-0 | Brownbill |
| | | 3 | 14.01.80 | **Chelsea** (D2) | A | W | 1-0 | Gore |
| | | 4 | 26.01.80 | **Everton** (D1) | A | L | 0-3 | |
| 1980-81 | (D4) | 1 | 22.11.80 | **Chesterfield** (D3) | H | D | 2-2 | Houghton 2 |
| | | 1r | 25.11.80 | **Chesterfield** | A | L | 0-2 | |
| 1981-82 | (D4) | 1 | 21.11.81 | **Hartlepool Utd** (D4) | H | D | 2-2 | Methven, Quinn |
| | | 1r | 25.11.81 | **Hartlepool Utd** | A | L | 0-1 | |
| 1982-83 | (D3) | 1 | 21.11.82 | **Telford Utd** (APL) | H | D | 0-0 | |
| | | 1r | 23.11.82 | **Telford Utd** | A | L | 1-2 | Butler |
| 1983-84 | (D3) | 1 | 19.11.83 | **Bradford City** (D3) | A | D | 0-0 | |
| | | 1r | 28.11.83 | **Bradford City** | H | W | 4-2 | Taylor 2, Bruce 2 |
| | | 2 | 10.12.83 | **Whitby Town** (NL) | H | W | 1-0 | Taylor (p) |
| | | 3 | 07.01.84 | **West Ham Utd** (D1) | A | L | 0-1 | |
| 1984-85 | (D3) | 1 | 17.11.84 | **Wrexham** (D4) | A | W | 2-0 | Langley, Newell |
| | | 2 | 08.12.84 | **Northwich V** (APL) | H | W | 2-1 | Newell, Johnson (p) |
| | | 3 | 05.01.85 | **Chelsea** (D1) | A | D | 2-2 | Jewell, Newell |
| | | 3r | 26.01.85 | **Chelsea** | H | L | 0-5 | |
| 1985-86 | (D3) | 1 | 16.11.85 | **Doncaster Rovers** (D3) | H | W | 4-1 | Lowe 2, Newell, Aspinall |
| | | 2 | 07.12.85 | **Runcorn** (Conf) | A | D | 1-1 | Knowles |
| | | 2r | 10.12.85 | **Runcorn** | H | W | 4-0 | Methven, Newell 2, Jones og |
| | | 3 | 04.01.86 | **Bournemouth** (D3) | H | W | 3-0 | Methven, Kelly, Aspinall |
| | | 4 | 25.01.86 | **Southampton** (D1) | A | L | 0-3 | |
| 1986-87 | (D3) | 1 | 15.11.86 | **Lincoln City** (D4) | H | W | 3-1 | Griffiths, Lowe 2 |
| | | 2 | 06.12.86 | **Darlington** (D3) | A | W | 5-0 | Jewell 2, Campbell 2, Thompson |
| | | 3 | 19.01.87 | **Gillingham** (D3) | H | W | 2-1 | Campbell, Thompson |
| | | 4 | 31.01.87 | **Norwich City** (D1) | H | W | 1-0 | Jewell |
| | | 5 | 21.02.87 | **Hull City** (D2) | H | W | 3-0 | Thompson, Jewell, Campbell |
| | | 6 | 15.03.87 | **Leeds Utd** (D2) | H | L | 0-2 | |
| 1987-88 | (D3) | 1 | 14.11.87 | **Altrincham** (Conf) | A | W | 2-0 | Campbell, Butler |
| | | 2 | 05.12.87 | **Wolverhampton W** (D4) | H | L | 1-3 | Hilditch |
| 1988-89 | (D3) | 1 | 19.11.88 | **Hartlepool Utd** (D4) | A | L | 0-2 | |
| 1989-90 | (D3) | 1 | 19.11.89 | **Mansfield Town** (D3) | H | W | 2-0 | Page, Hilditch |
| | | 2 | 09.12.89 | **Carlisle Utd** (D4) | H | W | 2-0 | Johnson, Griffiths |
| | | 3 | 06.01.90 | **Watford** (D2) | A | L | 0-2 | |
| 1990-91 | (D3) | 1 | 17.11.90 | **Carlisle Utd** (D4) | H | W | 5-0 | Griffiths 2, Woods, Rimmer 2 |
| | | 2 | 08.12.90 | **Hartlepool Utd** (D4) | H | W | 2-0 | Page, Griffiths |
| | | 3 | 05.01.91 | **Coventry City** (D1) | A | D | 1-1 | Patterson |
| | | 3r | 09.01.91 | **Coventry City** | H | L | 0-1 | |
| 1991-92 | (D3) | 1 | 16.11.91 | **Scarborough** (D4) | A | W | 2-0 | Pilling, Worthington |
| | | 2 | 07.12.91 | **Stockport County** (D3) | H | W | 2-0 | Griffiths, Powell |
| | | 3 | 05.01.92 | **Notts County** (D1) | A | L | 0-2 | |
| 1992-93 | (D2) | 1 | 14.11.92 | **Carlisle Utd** (D3) | H | W | 3-1 | Williams og, Dalziel og, Powell |
| | | 2 | 02.01.93 | **Bury** (D3) | A | L | 0-1 | |
| 1993-94 | (D3) | 1 | 12.11.93 | **Leek Town** (NPL) | A | D | 2-2 | Skipper, Morton |
| | | 1r | 30.11.93 | **Leek Town** | H | W | 3-0 | McKearney (p), Diskin og, Duffy |
| | | 2 | 04.12.93 | **Scarborough** (D3) | H | W | 1-0 | Gavin |
| | | 3 | 08.01.94 | **Grimsby Town** (D1) | A | L | 0-1 | |
| 1994-95 | (D3) | 1 | 12.11.94 | **Spennymoor Utd** (NPL) | H | W | 4-0 | Leonard, Carragher 2, Kilford |
| | | 2 | 03.12.94 | **Altrincham** (Conf) | A | L | 0-1 | |
| 1995-96 | (D3) | 1 | 11.11.95 | **Runcorn** (Conf) | A | D | 1-1 | Bignall |

| | | | | | | | |
|---|---|---|---|---|---|---|---|
| | 1r | 21.11.95 | **Runcorn** | H | W | 4-2 | Leonard, Diaz, Martinez, Thomson og |
| | 2 | 02.12.95 | **Barrow** (NPL) | A | W | 4-0 | Diaz, Martinez, Black 2 |
| | 3 | 06.01.96 | **Walsall** (D2) | A | L | 0-1 | |
| 1996-97 (D3) | 1 | 16.11.96 | **Blackpool** (D2) | A | L | 0-1 | |
| 1997-98 (D2) | 1 | 15.11.97 | **Carlisle Utd** (D2) | A | W | 1-0 | Jones |
| | 2 | 06.12.97 | **York City** (D2) | H | W | 2-1 | Martinez, Lee |
| | 3 | 03.01.98 | **Blackburn Rovers** (PL) | A | L | 2-4 | Lee, Lowe |
| 1998-99 (D2) | 1 | 14.11.98 | **Blackpool** (D2) | H | W | 4-3 | Greenall, Haworth, Barlow, Lowe |
| | 2 | 05.12.98 | **Notts County** (D2) | A | D | 1-1 | Lowe |
| | 2r | 15.12.98 | **Notts County** | H | D | 0-0aet | |
| | | | *Notts County won 4-2 on penalties* | | | | |
| 1999-00 (D2) | 1 | 30.10.99 | **Cambridge City** (SL) | A | W | 2-0 | Barlow 2 |
| | 2 | 20.11.99 | **Wycombe W** (D2) | A | D | 2-2 | Haworth 2 |
| | 2r | 30.11.99 | **Wycombe W** | H | W | 2-1 | Liddell, Haworth |
| | 3 | 11.12.99 | **Wolverhampton W** (D1) | H | L | 0-1 | |
| 2000-01 (D2) | 1 | 18.11.00 | **Dorchester Town** (SL) | H | W | 3-1 | Roberts, Bidstrup, McIvor og |
| | 2 | 12.12.00 | **Notts County** (D2) | H | D | 1-1 | Ashcroft |
| | 2r | 19.12.00 | **Notts County** | A | L | 1-2aet | Kilford |
| 2001-02 (D2) | 1 | 17.11.01 | **Canvey Island** (IL) | H | L | 0-1 | |
| 2002-03 (D2) | 1 | 16.11.02 | **Hereford Utd** (Conf) | A | W | 1-0 | Green |
| | 2 | 07.12.02 | **Luton Town** (D2) | H | W | 3-0 | Ellington 2, Flynn |
| | 3 | 04.01.03 | **Stoke City** (D1) | A | L | 0-3 | |

## WIGAN BOROUGH

*Members of the Football League 1921-1932. First entered FA Cup: 1922-23. Resigned from the Football League and folded, October 1932.*

| | | | | | | | |
|---|---|---|---|---|---|---|---|
| 1921-22 (3N) | | | did not enter | | | | |
| 1922-23 (3N) | | | 4q Eccles U (H) 4-0; 5q Southport (A) 1-1; 5qr Southport (H) 3-1; 6q Walsall (A) 3-1 | | | | |
| | 1 | 13.01.23 | **Bath City** (SL) | H | W | 4-1 | Fare, Spencer, Dennison, Eatock |
| | 2 | 03.02.23 | **QPR** (3S) | H | L | 2-4 | Findlay, A Williams |
| 1923-24 (3N) | | | 5q Nelson (H) 1-1; 5qr Nelson (A) 1-0; 6q Northampton Town (H) 0-6 | | | | |
| 1924-25 (3N) | | | 5q Bradford PA (H) 0-1 | | | | |
| 1925-26 (3N) | 1 | 02.12.25 | **Nelson FC** (3N) | H | W | 3-0 | Fenner, Riddell, Sayer |
| | 2 | 12.12.25 | **Crewe Alexandra** (3N) | A | D | 2-2 | Sayer, Dickinson |
| | 2r | 16.12.25 | **Crewe Alexandra** | H | W | 2-1 | Fenner 2 |
| | 3 | 09.01.26 | **Stoke City** (D2) | H | L | 2-5 | Sayer, Glover |
| 1926-27 (3N) | 1 | 01.12.26 | **Barrow** (3N) | H | D | 2-2 | McGuire 2 |
| | 1r | 06.12.26 | **Barrow** | A | W | 1-0 | Dickinson |
| | 2 | 11.12.26 | **Crewe Alexandra** (3N) | A | L | 1-4 | Dickinson |
| 1927-28 (3N) | 1 | 26.11.27 | **Rhyl (Welsh)** | A | L | 3-4 | Fenner 2, Dixon |
| 1928-29 (3N) | 1 | 24.11.28 | **Ashington** (3N) | H | W | 2-0 | Lievesley, Mandy |
| | 2 | 08.12.28 | **Grantham Town** (ML) | H | W | 2-1 | Lievesley, Hughton |
| | 3 | 12.01.29 | **Sheffield Wed** (D1) | H | L | 1-3 | Lievesley |
| 1929-30 (3N) | 1 | 30.11.29 | **Lincoln City** (3N) | A | L | 1-3 | Smith |
| 1930-31 (3N) | 1 | 29.11.30 | **Wrexham** (3N) | A | L | 0-2 | |
| 1931-32 (3N) | 1 | 28.11.31 | **Burton Town** (BDL) | | | - | |
| | | | *Wigan Borough had folded before the match was played. Burton Town walkover* | | | | |

## WIGAN COUNTY

*Entered FA Cup: 1897-98 – 1899-1900 playing 12 matches but only one in the Competition Proper. They were the first of the three Wigan clubs to play at Springfield Park.*

| | | | | | | | |
|---|---|---|---|---|---|---|---|
| 1897-98 (LL) | 1 | 29.01.98 | **Manchester City** (D2) | | L | 0-1 | |

## WILLENHALL TOWN

*Formed 1953. First entered FA Cup: 1977-78. FA Vase Runners-up: 1981. Members of the Midland Football Alliance.*

| | | | | | | | |
|---|---|---|---|---|---|---|---|
| 1981-82 (WMRL) | 1 | 21.11.81 | **Crewe Alexandra** (D4) | H | L | 0-1 | |

## WILLINGTON

*Formed 1906 as Willington Temperance. Willington 1911. First entered FA Cup: 1910-11. FA Amateur Cup winners: 1950. Runners-up: 1939. Members of the Northern League.*

| | | | | | | | |
|---|---|---|---|---|---|---|---|
| 1945-46 (NL) | 1 1L | 17.11.45 | **Bishop Auckland** (NL) | H | L | 0-5 | |

| | | | | | | | | | |
|---|---|---|---|---|---|---|---|---|---|
| | | 12L | 24.11.45 | **Bishop Auckland** | A | W | 2-0 | Graham, Lawton |
| 1950-51 | (NL) | 1 | 25.11.50 | **Rochdale** (3N) | A | L | 1-3 | Dodd |
| 1973-74 | (NL) | 1 | 24.11.73 | **Blackburn Rovers** (D3) | H | D | 0-0 | |
| | | 1r | 03.12.73 | **Blackburn Rovers** | A | L | 1-6 | B Newton (p) |

# WIMBLEDON

*Formed 1889 as Wimbledon Old Centrals. Wimbledon 1905. First entered FA Cup: 1906-07. FA Cup winners: 1988. FA Amateur Cup winners: 1963. Runners-up: 1935, 1947. Wimbledon and Old Carthusians are the only clubs to win both the FA Cup and the Amateur Cup. Record FA Cup win: 15-2 v Polytechnic FC, preliminary round, 21.09.1929. In Competition Proper: 7-2 v Windsor & Eton, 1st round, 22.11.1980. Record FA Cup defeat: 0-6 v Fulham, 1st round replay, 03.12.1930.*

| | | | | | | | | |
|---|---|---|---|---|---|---|---|---|
| 1929-30 | (IL) | 1 | 30.11.29 | **Northfleet Utd** (SL) | H | L | 1-4 | Dowden |
| 1930-31 | (IL) | 1 | 30.11.30 | **Fulham** (3S) | A | D | 1-1 | Dowden |
| | | 1r | 03.12.30 | **Fulham** | H | L | 0-6 | |
| 1931-32 | (IL) | 1 | 28.11.31 | **Norwich City** (3S) | H | L | 1-3 | Dowden |
| 1934-35 | (IL) | 1 | 24.11.34 | **Leyton FC** (AL) | H | D | 1-1 | Batchelor |
| | | 1r | 29.11.34 | **Leyton FC** | A | W | 1-0 | Wright |
| | | 2 | 08.12.34 | **Southend Utd** (3S) | H | L | 1-5 | Turner |
| 1947-48 | (IL) | 1 | 29.11.47 | **Mansfield Town** (3N) | H | L | 0-1 | |
| 1952-53 | (IL) | 1 | 22.11.52 | **Walthamstow Ave** (AL) | A | D | 2-2 | Stewart, Stannard |
| | | 1r | 26.11.52 | **Walthamstow Ave** | H | L | 0-3 | |
| 1962-63 | (IL) | 1 | 03.11.62 | **Colchester Utd** (D3) | H | W | 2-1 | Brown, Reynolds |
| | | 2 | 24.11.62 | **Bristol City** (D3) | A | L | 1-2 | Peters og |
| 1963-64 | (IL) | 1 | 16.11.63 | **Bexley Utd** (SL) | A | W | 5-1 | Reynolds 2, Brown, Williams, Keats |
| | | 2 | 07.12.63 | **Bath City** (SL) | H | D | 2-2 | Brown, Reynolds |
| | | 2r | 12.12.63 | **Bath City** | A | L | 0-4 | |
| 1965-66 | (SL) | 1 | 13.11.65 | **Gravesend & N** (SL) | H | W | 4-1 | Cooke 3, O'Rourke |
| | | 2 | 04.12.65 | **Folkestone** (SL) | H | L | 0-1 | |
| 1966-67 | (SL) | 1 | 26.11.66 | **Grantham Town** (ML) | A | L | 1-2 | Cooke |
| 1967-68 | (SL) | 1 | 09.12.67 | **Romford** (SL) | H | W | 3-0 | Hodges 2 (1p), Hobbs |
| | | 2 | 06.01.68 | **Bristol Rovers** (D3) | H | L | 0-4 | |
| 1969-70 | (SL) | 1 | 15.11.69 | **Hillingdon Borough** (SL) | A | L | 0-2 | |
| 1970-71 | (SL) | 1 | 21.11.70 | **Peterborough Utd** (D4) | A | L | 1-3 | Cooke |
| 1973-74 | (SL) | 1 | 24.11.73 | **King's Lynn** (SL) | A | L | 0-1 | |
| 1974-75 | (SL) | 1 | 23.11.74 | **Bath City** (SL) | H | W | 1-0 | Mahon |
| | | 2 | 14.12.74 | **Kettering Town** (SL) | H | W | 2-0 | Cooke, Mahon (p) |
| | | 3 | 04.01.75 | **Burnley** (D1) | A | W | 1-0 | Mahon |
| | | 4 | 25.01.75 | **Leeds Utd** (D1) | A | D | 0-0 | |
| | | 4r | 10.02.75 | **Leeds Utd** | H | L | 0-1 | |
| | | | | *played at Selhurst Park* | | | | |
| 1975-76 | (SL) | 1 | 22.11.75 | **Nuneaton B** (SL) | A | W | 1-0 | Connell |
| | | 2 | 13.12.75 | **Brentford** (D4) | H | L | 0-2 | |
| 1976-77 | (SL) | 1 | 20.11.76 | **Wokingham Town** (IL) | H | W | 1-0 | Connell |
| | | 2 | 14.12.76 | **Leatherhead** (IL) | A | W | 3-1 | Bryant, Marlowe 2 |
| | | 3 | 08.01.77 | **Middlesbrough** (D1) | H | D | 0-0 | |
| | | 3r | 11.01.77 | **Middlesbrough** | A | L | 0-1 | |
| 1977-78 | (D4) | 1 | 26.11.77 | **Enfield** (IL) | A | L | 0-3 | |
| 1978-79 | (D4) | 1 | 25.11.78 | **Gravesend & N** (SL) | A | D | 0-0 | |
| | | 1r | 28.11.78 | **Gravesend & N** | H | W | 1-0 | Cork |
| | | 2 | 16.12.78 | **Bournemouth** (D4) | H | D | 1-1 | Denny |
| | | 2r | 28.12.78 | **Bournemouth** | A | W | 2-1aet | Cork, Parsons |
| | | 3 | 09.01.79 | **Southampton** (D1) | H | L | 0-2 | |
| 1979-80 | (D3) | 1 | 24.11.79 | **Gillingham** (D3) | A | D | 0-0 | |
| | | 1r | 27.11.79 | **Gillingham** | H | W | 4-2 | Leslie 2, Parsons, Dziadulewicz |
| | | 2 | 18.12.79 | **Portsmouth** (D4) | H | D | 0-0 | |
| | | 2r | 24.12.79 | **Portsmouth** | A | D | 3-3aet | Lewington, Denny 2 |
| | | 2 2r | 05.01.80 | **Portsmouth** | H | L | 0-1 | |
| 1980-81 | (D4) | 1 | 22.11.80 | **Windsor & Eton** (AL) | H | W | 7-2 | M Smith 2, Hubbick 3, Cunningham, Cork |
| | | 2 | 13.12.80 | **Swindon Town** (D3) | H | W | 2-0 | Denny, Leslie |
| | | 3 | 03.01.81 | **Oldham Athletic** (D2) | H | D | 0-0 | |
| | | 3r | 06.01.81 | **Oldham Athletic** | A | W | 1-0 | Cork |

| | | | | | | | |
|---|---|---|---|---|---|---|---|
| | 4 | 24.01.81 | **Wrexham** (D2) | A | L | 1-2 | Denny |
| 1981-82 (D3) | 1 | 21.11.81 | **Bedford Town** (SL) | A | W | 2-0 | Suddaby, Ketteridge |
| | 2 | 15.12.81 | **Enfield** (APL) | A | L | 1-4 | Brown (p) |
| 1982-83 (D4) | 1 | 20.11.82 | **Northampton Town** (D4) | A | D | 2-2 | Leslie, Entwistle |
| | 1r | 23.11.82 | **Northampton Town** | H | L | 0-2 | |
| 1983-84 (D3) | 1 | 19.11.83 | **Orient** (D3) | H | W | 2-1 | Cork 2 |
| | 2 | 10.12.83 | **Brentford** (D3) | A | L | 2-3 | Peters, Downes |
| 1984-85 (D2) | 3 | 05.01.85 | **Burnley** (D3) | H | W | 3-1 | Evans, Fishenden 2 (1p) |
| | 4 | 26.01.85 | **Nottingham Forest** (D1) | A | D | 0-0 | |
| | 4r | 30.01.85 | **Nottingham Forest** | H | W | 1-0 | Fishenden |
| | 5 | 04.03.85 | **West Ham Utd** (D1) | H | D | 1-1 | Evans |
| | 5r | 06.03.85 | **West Ham Utd** | A | L | 1-5 | Fishenden |
| 1985-86 (D2) | 3 | 04.01.86 | **Millwall** (D2) | A | L | 1-3 | Gage |
| 1986-87 (D1) | 3 | 10.01.87 | **Sunderland** (D2) | H | W | 2-1 | Sanchez, Hodges |
| | 4 | 31.01.87 | **Portsmouth** (D2) | H | W | 4-0 | Fashanu 2, Blake og, Sayer |
| | 5 | 22.02.87 | **Everton** (D1) | H | W | 3-1 | Hodges, Fashanu, Sayer |
| | 6 | 15.03.87 | **Tottenham Hotspur** (D1) | H | L | 0-2 | |
| 1987-88 (D1) | 3 | 09.01.88 | **WBA** (D2) | H | W | 4-1 | Fashanu, Wise, Turner, Fairweather |
| | 4 | 30.01.88 | **Mansfield Town** (D3) | A | W | 2-1 | Cork, Phelan |
| | 5 | 20.02.88 | **Newcastle Utd** (D1) | A | W | 3-1 | Gibson, Gayle, Fashanu |
| | 6 | 12.03.88 | **Watford** (D1) | H | W | 2-1 | Young, Fashanu |
| | SF | 09.04.88 | **Luton Town** (D1) | | W | 2-1 | Fashanu (p), Wise |
| | | | *played at White Hart Lane* | | | | |
| | F | 14.05.88 | **Liverpool** (D1) | | W | 1-0 | Sanchez |
| | | | *played at Wembley Stadium* | | | | |
| 1988-89 (D1) | 3 | 07.01.89 | **Birmingham City** (D2) | A | W | 1-0 | Gibson |
| | 4 | 28.01.89 | **Aston Villa** (D1) | A | W | 1-0 | Jones |
| | 5 | 18.02.89 | **Grimsby Town** (D4) | H | W | 3-1 | Fashanu, Phelan, Wise |
| | 6 | 19.03.89 | **Everton** (D1) | A | L | 0-1 | |
| 1989-90 (D1) | 3 | 06.01.90 | **WBA** (D2) | A | L | 0-2 | |
| 1990-91 (D1) | 3 | 05.01.91 | **Aston Villa** (D1) | A | D | 1-1 | McGee |
| | 3r | 09.01.91 | **Aston Villa** | H | W | 1-0aet | Cork |
| | 4 | 26.01.91 | **Shrewsbury Town** (D3) | A | L | 0-1 | |
| 1991-92 (D1) | 3 | 04.01.92 | **Bristol City** (D2) | A | D | 1-1 | Fashanu |
| | 3r | 14.01.92 | **Bristol City** | H | L | 0-1 | |
| 1992-93 (PL) | 3 | 02.01.93 | **Everton** (PL) | H | D | 0-0 | |
| | 3r | 12.01.93 | **Everton** | A | W | 2-1 | Fashanu, Earle |
| | 4 | 23.01.93 | **Aston Villa** (PL) | A | D | 1-1 | Elkins |
| | 4r | 03.02.93 | **Aston Villa** | H | D | 0-0aet | |
| | | | *Wimbledon won 6-5 on penalties* | | | | |
| | 5 | 14.02.93 | **Tottenham Hotspur** (PL) | A | L | 2-3 | Dobbs, Cotterill |
| 1993-94 (PL) | 3 | 08.01.94 | **Scunthorpe Utd** (D3) | H | W | 3-0 | Holdsworth 3 |
| | 4 | 29.01.94 | **Sunderland** (D1) | H | W | 2-1 | Scales, Fashanu |
| | 5 | 20.02.94 | **Manchester Utd** (PL) | H | L | 0-3 | |
| 1994-95 (PL) | 3 | 07.01.95 | **Colchester Utd** (D3) | H | W | 1-0 | Harford |
| | 4 | 29.01.95 | **Tranmere Rovers** (D1) | A | W | 2-0 | Leonhardsen, Earle |
| | 5 | 19.02.95 | **Liverpool** (PL) | A | D | 1-1 | Clarke |
| | 5r | 28.02.95 | **Liverpool** | H | L | 0-2 | |
| 1995-96 (PL) | 3 | 06.01.96 | **Watford** (D1) | A | D | 1-1 | Leonhardsen |
| | 3r | 17.01.96 | **Watford** | H | W | 1-0 | Clarke |
| | 4 | 07.02.96 | **Middlesbrough** (PL) | A | D | 0-0 | |
| | 4r | 13.02.96 | **Middlesbrough** | H | W | 1-0 | Holdsworth |
| | 5 | 17.02.96 | **Huddersfield Town** (D1) | A | D | 2-2 | Ekoku 2 |
| | 5r | 28.02.96 | **Huddersfield Town** | H | W | 3-1 | Ekoku, Goodman 2 |
| | 6 | 09.03.96 | **Chelsea** (PL) | A | D | 2-2 | Earle, Holdsworth |
| | 6r | 20.03.96 | **Chelsea** | H | L | 1-3 | Goodman |
| 1996-97 (PL) | 3 | 14.01.97 | **Crewe Alexandra** (D2) | A | D | 1-1 | Perry |
| | 3r | 24.01.97 | **Crewe Alexandra** | H | W | 2-0 | Earle, Holdsworth |
| | 4 | 25.01.97 | **Manchester Utd** (PL) | A | D | 1-1 | Earle |
| | 4r | 04.02.97 | **Manchester Utd** | H | W | 1-0 | Gayle |
| | 5 | 15.02.97 | **QPR** (D1) | H | W | 2-1 | Gayle, Earle |

| | | | | | | | |
|---|---|---|---|---|---|---|---|
| | 6 | 09.03.97 | **Sheffield Wed** (PL) | A | W | 2-0 | Earle, Holdsworth |
| | SF | 13.04.97 | **Chelsea** (PL) | | L | 0-3 | |
| | | | *played at Highbury* | | | | |
| 1997-98 (PL) | 3 | 04.01.98 | **Wrexham** (D2) | H | D | 0-0 | |
| | 3r | 13.01.98 | **Wrexham** | A | W | 3-2 | M.Hughes 2, Gayle |
| | 4 | 24.01.98 | **Huddersfield Town** (D1) | A | W | 1-0 | Ardley |
| | 5 | 14.02.98 | **Wolverhampton W** (D1) | H | D | 1-1 | Euell |
| | 5r | 25.02.98 | **Wolverhampton W** | A | L | 1-2 | Jones |
| 1998-99 (PL) | 3 | 02.01.99 | **Manchester City** (D2) | H | W | 1-0 | Cort |
| | 4 | 23.01.99 | **Tottenham Hotspur** (PL) | H | D | 1-1 | Earle |
| | 4r | 02.02.99 | **Tottenham Hotspur** | A | L | 0-3 | |
| 1999-00 (PL) | 3 | 11.12.99 | **Barnsley** (D1) | H | W | 1-0 | Cort |
| | 4 | 08.01.00 | **Fulham** (D1) | A | L | 0-3 | |
| 2000-01 (PL) | 3 | 06.01.01 | **Notts County** (D2) | H | D | 2-2 | Ardley, Karlsson |
| | 3r | 27.01.01 | **Notts County** | A | W | 1-0aet | Anderssen |
| | 4 | 06.02.01 | **Middlesbrough** (PL) | A | D | 0-0 | |
| | 4r | 13.02.01 | **Middlesbrough** | H | W | 3-1aet | Ardley (p), Euell, Hunt |
| | 5 | 17.02.01 | **Wycombe W** (D2) | A | D | 2-2 | Williams, Agyemang |
| | 5r | 20.02.01 | **Wycombe W** | H | D | 1-1aet | Ainsworth |
| | | | *Wycome W won 8-7 on penalties* | | | | |
| 2001-02 (D1) | 3 | 08.01.02 | **Middlesbrough** (PL) | H | D | 0-0 | |
| | 3r | 15.01.02 | **Middlesbrough** | A | L | 0-2 | |
| 2002-03 (D1) | 3 | 04.01.03 | **Rotherham Utd** (D1) | A | W | 3-0 | Shipperley, McAnuff, Morgan |
| | 4 | 25.01.03 | **Walsall** (D1) | A | L | 0-1 | |

## WIMBORNE TOWN

*Formed 1878. First entered FA Cup: 1924-25. FA Vase winners: 1992. Members of the Wessex League.*

| | | | | | | | |
|---|---|---|---|---|---|---|---|
| 1982-83 (WL) | 1 | 20.11.82 | **Aldershot** (D4) | A | L | 0-4 | |

## WINDSOR & ETON

*Formed 1892. First entered FA Cup: 1892-93. Members of the Isthmian League.*

| | | | | | | | |
|---|---|---|---|---|---|---|---|
| 1925-26 (AL) | 1 | 28.11.25 | **Charlton Athletic** (3S) | A | L | 2-4 | Norris 2 |
| 1980-81 (AL) | 1 | 22.11.80 | **Wimbledon** (D4) | A | L | 2-7 | McCulloch, Hill |
| 1982-83 (IL) | 1 | 20.11.82 | **Brentford** (D3) | H | L | 0-7 | |
| | | | *played at Griffin Park* | | | | |
| 1983-84 (IL) | 1 | 19.11.83 | **Burton Albion** (NPL) | A | W | 2-1 | Hill, Baron |
| | 2 | 13.12.83 | **Bournemouth** (D3) | H | D | 0-0 | |
| | 2r | 19.12.83 | **Bournemouth** | A | L | 0-2 | |
| 1984-85 (IL) | 1 | 17.11.84 | **Gillingham** (D3) | A | L | 1-2 | Yates |
| 1985-86 (IL) | 1 | 16.11.85 | **Torquay Utd** (D4) | H | D | 1-1 | Woods |
| | 1r | 19.11.85 | **Torquay Utd** | A | L | 0-3 | |
| 1991-92 (IL) | 1 | 16.11.91 | **Woking** (IL) | H | - | 1-1ab | Gilman |
| | | | *abandoned after 69 minutes – fog* | | | | |
| | 1 | 26.11.91 | **Woking** (IL) | H | L | 2-4 | Gilman 2 |

## WINDSOR HOME PARK

*Entered FA Cup: 1872-73 – 1874-75.*

| | | | | | | | |
|---|---|---|---|---|---|---|---|
| 1872-73 | 1 | 26.10.72 | **Reigate Priory** | H | W | 4-2 | EH Bambridge, GF Bambridge, Gardiner, AN Other |
| | 2 | 23.11.72 | **South Norwood** | A | L | 0-1 | |
| | | | *FA ordered replay after match ended before 90 minutes were played* | | | | |
| | 2r | 07.12.72 | **South Norwood** | H | W | 3-0 | Clark, Gardiner, F Heron |
| | 3 | 21.12.72 | **Maidenhead** | H | L | 0-1 | |
| 1874-75 | 1 | | Uxbridge | | | - | |
| | | | *Uxbridge scratched. Windsor Home Park walkover* | | | | |
| | 2 | | Oxford University | | | - | |
| | | | *Windsor Home Park scratched. Oxford University walkover* | | | | |
| 1880-81 | 1 | 13.11.80 | **Grey Friars** | A | D | 0-0 | |
| | 1r | 20.11.80 | **Grey Friars** | H | L | 1-3 | |
| 1881-82 | 1 | 22.10.81 | **Reading Minster** | H | L | 0-1 | |
| 1882-83 | 1 | 04.11.82 | **Acton** | H | W | 3-0 | |
| | 2 | 30.11.82 | **United Hospital** | H | W | 3-1 | |

| | | | | | | | | |
|---|---|---|---|---|---|---|---|---|
| | | 3 | 06.01.83 | **Clapham Rovers** | H | L | 0-3 | |
| 1883-84 | | 1 | 10.11.83 | **Royal Engineers** | H | W | 5-3 | Dear 2, Cheeseman, Harrison, Smith |
| | | 2 | 01.12.83 | **Old Wykehamists** | H | L | 0-1 | |
| 1884-85 | | 1 | | Chatham | | | - | |
| | | | | *Windsor Home Park scratched. Chatham walkover* | | | | |

## WINSFORD UNITED

*Formed 1883 as Over Wanderers. Changed name to Winsford United 1899. First competed in FA Cup as Winsford United 1899-1900. Members of the North West Counties League. See also Over Wanderers.*

| | | | | | | | | |
|---|---|---|---|---|---|---|---|---|
| 1975-76 | (CC) | 1 | 22.11.75 | **Peterborough Utd** (D3) | A | L | 1-4 | Chadwick |
| 1991-92 | (NPL) | 1 | 16.11.91 | **Wrexham** (D4) | A | L | 2-5 | Esdaile 2 |
| 1997-98 | (NPL) | 1 | 15.11.97 | **Chester City** (D3) | A | L | 1-2 | Steele |

## WISBECH TOWN

*Formed 1920. First entered FA Cup: 1923-24. League club beaten: Colchester United. Members of the Eastern Counties League.*

| | | | | | | | | |
|---|---|---|---|---|---|---|---|---|
| 1945-46 | (UCL) | 1 1L | 17.11.45 | **Ipswich Town** (3S) | H | L | 0-3 | |
| | | 1 2L | 24.11.45 | **Ipswich Town** | A | L | 0-5 | |
| 1957-58 | (ML) | 1 | 16.11.57 | **Colchester Utd** (3S) | H | W | 1-0 | Pye |
| | | 2 | 07.12.57 | **Reading** (3S) | A | L | 1-2 | Downie |
| 1958-59 | (SL) | 1 | 15.11.58 | **Newport County** (D3) | H | D | 2-2 | Marshall, Sewell |
| | | 1r | 17.11.58 | **Newport County** | A | L | 1-4aet | Pye |
| 1959-60 | (SL) | 1 | 14.11.59 | **Wycombe W** (IL) | A | L | 2-4 | Elliott, Moore |
| 1964-65 | (SL) | 1 | 14.11.64 | **Brentford** (D3) | H | L | 0-2 | |
| 1965-66 | (SL) | 1 | 13.11.65 | **Brighton** (D3) | A | L | 1-10 | Lawrence |
| 1995-96 | (ECL) | 1 | 11.11.95 | **Kingstonian** (IL) | A | L | 1-5 | McLaughlin |
| 1996-97 | (ECL) | 1 | 16.11.96 | **St Albans City** (IL) | H | L | 1-2 | Munns |
| 1997-98 | (SL) | 1 | 15.11.97 | **Billericay Town** (IL) | A | W | 3-2 | Munns, Ward, McLaughlin |
| | | 2 | 06.12.97 | **Bristol Rovers** (D2) | H | L | 0-2 | |

## WITNEY TOWN

*Formed 1885. First entered FA Cup: 1923-24. Reformed 2002 as Witney United. Members of the Hellenic League.*

| | | | | | | | | |
|---|---|---|---|---|---|---|---|---|
| 1971-72 | (Hel) | 1 | 20.11.71 | **Romford** (SL) | H | L | 0-3 | |

## WITTON

*Entered FA Cup: 1884-85 – 1890-91. A separate club from Witton Albion (formed 1887).*

| | | | | | | | | |
|---|---|---|---|---|---|---|---|---|
| 1884-85 | | 1 | | Clitheroe | | | - | |
| | | | | *Clitheroe scratched. Witton walkover* | | | | |
| | | 2 | | bye | | | | |
| | | 3 | 22.12.84 | **Blackburn Rovers** | A | L | 1-5 | |
| 1885-86 | | 1 | 17.10.85 | **Accrington FC** | A | L | 4-5 | |
| 1886-87 | | 1 | 23.10.86 | **Oswaldtwistle Rovers** | A | W | 3-2 | |
| | | 2 | 13.11.86 | **Preston North End** | A | L | 0-6 | |
| 1887-88 | | 1 | 15.10.87 | **Oswaldtwistle Rovers** | A | W | 4-3 | |
| | | 2 | 05.11.87 | **Distillery, Belfast** | A | W | 4-2 | Cunliffe 2, Hothersall, Turner |
| | | 3 | 26.11.87 | **Darwen** | A | D | 1-1 | Horsfield |
| | | 3r | 03.12.87 | **Darwen** | | L | 0-2 | |
| | | | | *played at Blackburn* | | | | |
| 1888-89 | | 1 | 02.02.89 | **Aston Villa** (D1) | A | L | 2-3 | Grimshaw, Turner |

## WITTON ALBION

*Formed 1887. First entered FA Cup: 1907-08. FA Trophy runners-up: 1992. League club beaten: Halifax Town. Members of the Northern Premier League.*

| | | | | | | | | |
|---|---|---|---|---|---|---|---|---|
| 1948-49 | (CC) | 1 | 27.11.48 | **Gainsborough T** (ML) | A | L | 0-1 | |
| 1949-50 | (CC) | 1 | 26.11.49 | **Mossley** (CC) | H | L | 0-1 | |
| 1950-51 | (CC) | 1 | 25.11.50 | **Nelson FC** (LC) | H | L | 1-2 | Williams |
| 1951-52 | (CC) | 1 | 24.11.51 | **Gainsborough T** (ML) | H | W | 2-1 | Christopher, Cowden |
| | | 2 | 15.12.51 | **Workington** (3N) | H | D | 3-3 | Thompson 2, Dale |
| | | 2r | 20.12.51 | **Workington** | A | L | 0-1 | |
| 1953-54 | (CC) | 1 | 21.11.53 | **Nelson FC** (LC) | H | W | 4-1 | Yearsley, McCann, Jones, Dale |
| | | 2 | 12.12.53 | **Grimsby Town** (3N) | H | D | 1-1 | Yearsley |
| | | 2r | 15.12.53 | **Grimsby Town** | A | L | 1-6 | Jones |
| 1957-58 | (CC) | 1 | 16.11.57 | **Tranmere Rovers** (3N) | A | L | 1-2 | Duthie |

| | | | | | | | | | |
|---|---|---|---|---|---|---|---|---|---|
| 1966-67 | (CC) | 1 | 26.11.66 | **Bradford Park A** (D4) | A | L | 2-3 | McDonald, Cunliffe |
| 1990-91 | (NPL) | 1 | 17.11.90 | **Bolton Wanderers** (D3) | H | L | 1-2 | Thomas |
| 1991-92 | (Conf) | 1 | 16.11.91 | **Halifax Town** (D4) | H | D | 1-1 | Thomas |
| | | 1r | 27.11.91 | **Halifax Town** | A | W | 2-1aet | Thomas, Grimshaw |
| | | 2 | 07.12.91 | **Preston North End** (D3) | A | L | 1-5 | Flynn |
| 1992-93 | (Conf) | 1 | 14.11.92 | **Bury** (D3) | A | L | 0-2 | |
| 1993-94 | (Conf) | 1 | 13.11.93 | **Lincoln City** (D3) | H | L | 0-2 | |
| 1994-95 | (NPL) | 1 | 12.11.94 | **Chester City** (D2) | A | L | 0-2 | |
| 1995-96 | (NPL) | 1 | 11.11.95 | **Telford Utd** (Conf) | A | L | 1-2 | Watson |

# WOKING

*Formed 1889. First entered FA Cup: 1903-04. FA Trophy winners: 1994, 1995, 1997. League clubs beaten: WBA, Barnet (2), Cambridge United. Members of The Conference.*

| | | | | | | | | |
|---|---|---|---|---|---|---|---|---|
| 1907-08 | (WS) | 1 | 11.01.08 | **Bolton Wanderers** (D1) | A | L | 0-5 | |
| 1926-27 | (IL) | 1 | 27.11.26 | **Charlton Athletic** (3S) | H | L | 1-3 | Price |
| 1928-29 | (IL) | 1 | 24.11.28 | **Newport County** (3S) | A | L | 0-7 | |
| 1958-59 | (IL) | 1 | 15.11.58 | **Southampton** (D2) | A | L | 1-4 | Hebdon |
| 1968-69 | (IL) | 1 | 16.11.68 | **Brentford** (D4) | A | L | 0-2 | |
| 1978-79 | (IL) | 1 | 25.11.78 | **Barnet** (SL) | A | D | 3-3 | James, Love, Field |
| | | 1r | 28.11.78 | **Barnet** | H | D | 3-3aet | Cosham, Alexander, Morton |
| | | 1 2r | 05.12.78 | **Barnet** | | W | 3-0 | Love, James, Morton |
| | | | | *played at Griffin Park* | | | | |
| | | 2 | 16.12.78 | **Swansea City** (D3) | A | D | 2-2 | Love, Cottrell |
| | | 2r | 19.12.78 | **Swansea City** | H | L | 3-5aet | Morton, Field, Barrett |
| 1986-87 | (IL) | 1 | 15.11.86 | **Chelmsford City** (SL) | H | D | 1-1 | Lansley |
| | | 1r | 17.11.86 | **Chelmsford City** | A | L | 1-2 | Morris |
| 1988-89 | (IL) | 1 | 19.11.88 | **Cambridge Utd** (D4) | H | L | 1-4 | S Wye |
| 1989-90 | (IL) | 1 | 18.11.89 | **Slough Town** (IL) | A | W | 2-1 | Buzaglo, Mulvaney |
| | | 2 | 09.12.89 | **Cambridge Utd** (D4) | A | L | 1-3 | Mulvaney |
| 1990-91 | (IL) | 1 | 17.11.90 | **Kidderminster H** (Conf) | H | D | 0-0 | |
| | | 1r | 21.11.90 | **Kidderminster H** | A | D | 1-1aet | Baron |
| | | 1 2r | 26.11.90 | **Kidderminster H** | A | W | 2-1 | Clement, Russell |
| | | 2 | 08.12.90 | **Merthyr Tydfil** (Conf) | H | W | 5-1 | Biggins 3, L Wye, Buzaglo |
| | | 3 | 05.01.91 | **WBA** (D2) | A | W | 4-2 | Buzaglo 3, Worsfold |
| | | 4 | 27.01.91 | **Everton** (D1) | A | L | 0-1 | |
| | | | | *played at Goodison Park* | | | | |
| 1991-92 | (IL) | 1 | 16.11.91 | **Windsor & Eton** (IL) | A | - | 1-1ab | Baron |
| | | | | *abandoned after 69 minutes – fog* | | | | |
| | | 1 | 26.11.91 | **Windsor & Eton** (IL) | A | W | 4-2 | Milton, Mitchell, Biggins, Friel |
| | | 2 | 07.12.91 | **Yeovil Town** (Conf) | H | W | 3-0 | Friel 3 |
| | | 3 | 04.01.92 | **Hereford Utd** (D4) | H | D | 0-0 | |
| | | 3r | 14.01.92 | **Hereford Utd** | A | L | 1-2aet | Pratt |
| 1992-93 | (Conf) | 1 | 14.11.92 | **Nuneaton B** (SL) | H | W | 3-2 | Clement, Biggins, Carroll |
| | | 2 | 05.12.92 | **Brighton** (D2) | A | D | 1-1 | S Wye |
| | | 2r | 16.12.92 | **Brighton** (D2) | H | L | 1-2 | Senior |
| 1993-94 | (Conf) | 1 | 13.11.93 | **Weston-Super-Mare** (SL) | H | D | 2-2 | Wye, S Dennis |
| | | 1r | 23.11.93 | **Weston-Super-Mare** | A | W | 1-0 | Clement |
| | | 2 | 04.12.93 | **Kidderminster H** (Conf) | A | L | 0-1 | |
| 1994-95 | (Conf) | 1 | 12.11.94 | **Barnet** (D3) | A | D | 4-4 | Fielder, Dennis, Walker, Steele |
| | | 1r | 22.11.94 | **Barnet** | H | W | 1-0 | Tucker |
| | | 2 | 04.12.94 | **Marlow** (IL) | A | L | 1-2 | Tucker |
| 1995-96 | (Conf) | 1 | 11.11.95 | **Barnet** (D3) | A | D | 2-2 | Hay, Steele |
| | | 1r | 21.11.95 | **Barnet** | H | W | 2-1aet | Hay, Steele |
| | | 2 | 02.12.95 | **Enfield** (IL) | A | D | 1-1 | Walker |
| | | 2r | 12.12.95 | **Enfield** | H | W | 2-1 | Hay 2 |
| | | 3 | 06.01.96 | **Swindon Town** (D2) | A | L | 0-2 | |
| 1996-97 | (Conf) | 1 | 15.11.96 | **Millwall** (Conf) | H | D | 2-2 | Foster, Walker (p) |
| | | 1r | 26.11.96 | **Millwall** | A | W | 1-0 | Walker |
| | | 2 | 07.12.96 | **Cambridge Utd** (D3) | A | W | 2-0 | Walker, Taylor |
| | | 3 | 25.01.97 | **Coventry City** (PL) | A | D | 1-1 | Thompson |
| | | 3r | 04.02.97 | **Coventry City** | H | L | 1-2 | Steele |
| 1997-98 | (Conf) | 1 | 15.11.97 | **Southend Utd** (D2) | H | L | 0-2 | |

| | | | | | | | | |
|---|---|---|---|---|---|---|---|---|
| 1998-99 | (Conf) | 1 | 14.11.98 | **Scunthorpe Utd** (D3) | H | L | 0-1 | |
| 2000-01 | (Conf) | 1 | 18.11.00 | **Carlisle Utd** (D3) | A | L | 1-5 | West |

# WOKINGHAM TOWN

*Formed 1875. First entered FA Cup: 1958-59. Members of the Isthmian League.*

| | | | | | | | | |
|---|---|---|---|---|---|---|---|---|
| 1976-77 | (IL) | 1 | 20.11.76 | **Wimbledon** (SL) | A | L | 0-1 | |
| 1982-83 | (IL) | 1 | 20.11.82 | **Cardiff City** (D3) | H | D | 1-1 | Torrance |
| | | 1r | 23.11.83 | **Cardiff City** | A | L | 0-3 | |

# WOLVERHAMPTON WANDERERS

*Formed 1879 when St Lukes (1877) and Goldthorn (1876) amalgamated as Wolverhampton Wanderers. FA Cup winners: 1893, 1908, 1949, 1960. Runners-up: 1889, 1896, 1921, 1939. Record FA Cup win: 14-0 v Crosswell's Brewery, 2nd round, 13.11.1886. Record FA Cup defeat: 0-6 v Rotherham, 1st round, 16.11.1985.*

| | | | | | | | | |
|---|---|---|---|---|---|---|---|---|
| 1883-84 | | 1 | 27.10.83 | **Long Eaton R** | H | W | 4-1 | Brodie 2, J Griffiths 2 |
| | | 2 | 01.12.83 | **Wednesbury Old A** | A | L | 2-4 | Brodie 2 |
| 1884-85 | | 1 | 08.11.84 | **Derby St Lukes** | H | D | 0-0 | |
| | | 1r | 22.11.84 | **Derby St Lukes** | A | L | 2-4aet | Brodie, Brazier |
| 1885-86 | | 1 | 31.10.85 | **Derby St Lukes** | H | W | 7-0 | Brodie 2, H Aston 2, H Wood, Horton, J Aston |
| | | 2 | 21.11.85 | **Stafford Road** | H | W | 4-2 | J Aston 2, H Aston, H Wood |
| | | 3 | 12.12.85 | **Walsall Swifts** | H | W | 2-1 | Brodie, Lowder |
| | | 4 | 02.01.86 | **WBA** | A | L | 1-3 | H Aston |
| 1886-87 | | 1 | 30.10.86 | **Matlock Town** | H | W | 6-0 | Brodie 2, B Griffiths 2, Allen, Hunter |
| | | 2 | 13.11.86 | **Crosswell's Brewery** | H | W | 14-0 | T Hunter 4, Brodie 3, Knight 3, B Griffiths 2, Allen, Law og |
| | | 3 | 11.12.86 | **Aston Villa** | A | D | 2-2 | Brodie, B Griffiths |
| | | 3r | 15.01.87 | **Aston Villa** | H | D | 1-1aet | Brodie |
| | | 3 2r | 22.01.87 | **Aston Villa** | H | D | 3-3aet | B Griffiths 2, Knight |
| | | 3 3r | 29.01.87 | **Aston Villa** | A | L | 0-2 | |
| 1887-88 | | 1 | 15.10.87 | **Walsall Swifts** | A | W | 2-1 | Hunter, Smallwood og |
| | | 2 | 05.11.87 | **Aston Shakespeare** | H | W | 3-0 | Hunter, Shaw, B Griffiths |
| | | 3 | 26.11.87 | **WBA** | A | L | 0-2 | |
| 1888-89 | (D1) | 1 | 02.02.89 | **Old Carthusians** | H | W | 4-3 | Wood 2, Wykes, Mason |
| | | 2 | 16.02.89 | **Walsall Town Swifts** | H | W | 6-1 | Knight 3, Hunter, Lowder, Brodie |
| | | 3 | 02.03.89 | **Sheffield Wed** | H | W | 3-0 | Wykes 2, Fletcher |
| | | SF | 16.03.89 | **Blackburn Rovers** (D1) *played at Alexandra Road, Crewe* | | D | 1-1 | Wykes |
| | | SFr | 23.03.89 | **Blackburn Rovers** *played at Alexandra Road, Crewe* | | W | 3-1 | Allen, Hunter, Wood |
| | | F | 30.03.89 | **Preston North End** (D1) *played at Kennington Oval* | | L | 0-3 | |
| 1889-90 | (D1) | 1 | 18.01.90 | **Old Carthusians** | H | W | 2-0 | Wood 2 |
| | | 2 | 01.02.90 | **Small Heath** (FAll) | H | W | 2-1 | Fletcher, Speller og |
| | | 3 | 15.02.90 | **Stoke** (D1) *FA ordered match to be replayed after Stoke protested about the pitch* | H | W | 4-0 | Worrall 2, Brodie, Wood |
| | | 3 | 22.02.90 | **Stoke** (D1) | H | W | 8-0 | Brodie 5, Wood 2, Allen |
| | | SF | 08.03.90 | **Blackburn Rovers** (D1) *played at Derby Racecourse Ground* | | L | 0-1 | |
| 1890-91 | (D1) | 1 | 17.01.91 | **Long Eaton R** (ML) | A | W | 2-1aet | Wood 2 |
| | | 2 | 31.01.91 | **Accrington FC** (D1) | A | W | 3-2aet | Worrall, Wood, Booth |
| | | 3 | 14.02.91 | **Blackburn Rovers** (D1) | A | L | 0-2 | |
| 1891-92 | (D1) | 1 | 16.01.92 | **Crewe Alexandra** (FAll) | H | D | 2-2aet | Devey, Wykes |
| | | 1r | 23.01.92 | **Crewe Alexandra** | A | W | 4-1 | Baker 2, Wykes |
| | | 2 | 30.01.92 | **Sheffield Utd** (NL) | H | W | 3-1 | Baker 2, Topham |
| | | 3 | 13.02.92 | **Aston Villa** (D1) | H | L | 1-3 | Topham |
| 1892-93 | (D1) | 1 | 21.01.93 | **Bolton Wanderers** (D1) | A | D | 1-1aet | Johnston |
| | | 1r | 28.01.93 | **Bolton Wanderers** | H | W | 2-1 | Wood, Wykes |
| | | 2 | 04.02.93 | **Middlesbrough** (NL) | H | W | 2-1aet | Wykes, Butcher |
| | | 3 | 18.02.93 | **Darwen** (D2) | H | W | 5-0 | Topham 2, Wykes, Butcher, Griffin |
| | | SF | 04.03.93 | **Blackburn Rovers** (D1) *played at Town Ground, Nottingham* | | W | 2-1 | Topham, Butcher |

| | | | | | | | |
|---|---|---|---|---|---|---|---|
| | F | 25.03.93 | **Everton** (D1) | | W | 1-0 | Allen |
| | | | *played at Fallowfield, Manchester* | | | | |
| 1893-94 (D1) | 1 | 27.01.94 | **Aston Villa** (D1) | A | L | 2-4 | Wood, Butcher |
| 1894-95 (D1) | 1 | 02.02.95 | **Darwen** (D2) | A | D | 0-0 | |
| | 1r | 06.02.95 | **Darwen** | H | W | 2-0 | Wykes, Griffin |
| | 2 | 16.02.95 | **Stoke** (D1) | H | W | 2-0 | Wykes 2 |
| | 3 | 02.03.95 | **WBA** (D1) | A | L | 0-1 | |
| 1895-96 (D1) | 1 | 01.02.96 | **Notts County** (D1) | H | D | 2-2 | Henderson, Malpass |
| | 1r | 05.02.96 | **Notts County** | A | W | 4-3 | Wood 2, Beats, Black |
| | 2 | 15.02.96 | **Liverpool** (D2) | H | W | 2-0 | Wood, Owen |
| | 3 | 29.02.96 | **Stoke** (D1) | H | W | 3-0 | Tonks, Henderson, Malpass |
| | SF | 21.03.96 | **Derby County** (D1) | | W | 2-1 | Tonks, Malpass |
| | | | *played at Perry Barr, Birmingham* | | | | |
| | F | 18.04.96 | **Sheffield Wed** (D1) | | L | 1-2 | Black |
| | | | *played at Crystal Palace* | | | | |
| 1896-97 (D1) | 1 | 30.01.97 | **Millwall Athletic** (SL) | A | W | 2-1 | Tonks, Beats |
| | 2 | 13.02.97 | **Blackburn Rovers** (D1) | A | L | 1-2 | Beats |
| 1897-98 (D1) | 1 | 29.01.98 | **Notts County** (D1) | A | W | 1-0 | Beats |
| | 2 | 12.02.98 | **Derby County** (D1) | H | L | 0-1 | |
| 1898-99 (D1) | 1 | 28.01.99 | **Bolton Wanderers** (D1) | H | D | 0-0 | |
| | 1r | 01.02.99 | **Bolton Wanderers** | A | W | 1-0 | Blackett |
| | 2 | 11.02.99 | **Derby County** (D1) | A | L | 1-2 | Beats |
| 1899-00 (D1) | 1 | 27.01.00 | **QPR** (SL) | A | D | 1-1 | Miller |
| | 1r | 31.01.00 | **QPR** | H | L | 0-1aet | |
| 1900-01 (D1) | 1 | 09.02.01 | **New Brighton Tower** (D2) | H | W | 5-1 | Wooldridge 3, Bowen 2 |
| | 2 | 23.02.01 | **Notts County** (D1) | A | W | 3-2 | Harper 2, Beats |
| | 3 | 23.03.01 | **Sheffield Utd** (D1) | H | L | 0-4 | |
| 1901-02 (D1) | 1 | 25.01.02 | **Bolton Wanderers** (D1) | H | L | 0-2 | |
| 1902-03 (D1) | 1 | 07.02.03 | **Bury** (D1) | A | L | 0-1 | |
| 1903-04 (D1) | 1 | 06.02.04 | **Stockton** (NL) | A | W | 4-1 | Smith 2, Wooldridge, Logan og |
| | 2 | 20.02.04 | **Derby County** (D1) | A | D | 2-2 | Whitehouse, Wooldridge |
| | 2r | 24.02.04 | **Derby County** | H | D | 2-2aet | Baynham, Miller |
| | 2 2r | 29.02.04 | **Derby County** | | L | 0-1 | |
| | | | *played at Villa Park* | | | | |
| 1904-05 (D1) | 1 | 04.02.05 | **Sunderland** (D1) | A | D | 1-1 | Wooldridge |
| | 1r | 08.02.05 | **Sunderland** | H | W | 1-0 | J Smith |
| | 2 | 18.02.05 | **Southampton** (SL) | H | L | 2-3 | J Smith, Bevin |
| 1905-06 (D1) | 1 | 13.01.06 | **Bishop Auckland** (NL) | A | W | 3-0 | Baynham, Smith, Pedley |
| | 2 | 03.02.06 | **Bradford City** (D2) | A | L | 0-5 | |
| 1906-07 (D2) | 1 | 12.01.07 | **Sheffield Wed** (D1) | A | L | 2-3 | Wooldridge, Pedley |
| 1907-08 (D2) | 1 | 11.01.08 | **Bradford City** (D2) | A | D | 1-1 | Shelton |
| | 1r | 15.01.08 | **Bradford City** | H | W | 1-0 | Hedley |
| | 2 | 01.02.08 | **Bury** (D1) | H | W | 2-0 | Radford 2 |
| | 3 | 22.02.08 | **Swindon Town** (SL) | H | W | 2-0 | Harrison, Hedley |
| | 4 | 07.03.08 | **Stoke** (D2) | A | W | 1-0 | Radford |
| | SF | 28.03.08 | **Southampton** (SL) | | W | 2-0 | Radford, Hedley |
| | | | *played at Stamford Bridge* | | | | |
| | F | 25.04.08 | **Newcastle Utd** (D1) | | W | 3-1 | Hunt, Hedley, Harrison |
| | | | *played at Crystal Palace* | | | | |
| 1908-09 (D2) | 1 | 16.01.09 | **Crystal Palace** (SL) | H | D | 2-2 | Radford 2 |
| | 1r | 21.01.09 | **Crystal Palace** | A | L | 2-4aet | Hedley, Radford |
| 1909-10 (D2) | 1 | 15.01.10 | **Reading** (SL) | H | W | 5-0 | Blunt 4, Harrison |
| | 2 | 05.02.10 | **West Ham Utd** (SL) | H | L | 1-5 | Wooldridge |
| 1910-11 (D2) | 1 | 14.01.11 | **Accrington Stanley** (LC) | H | W | 2-0 | Hedley |
| | 2 | 04.02.11 | **Manchester City** (D2) | H | W | 1-0 | A Needham |
| | 3 | 25.02.11 | **Chelsea** (D2) | H | L | 0-2 | |
| 1911-12 (D2) | 1 | 13.01.12 | **Watford** (SL) | A | D | 0-0 | |
| | 1r | 24.01.12 | **Watford** | H | W | 10-0 | Halligan 3, J Needham 2, Brooks 2, Hedley, Young, Harrison |
| | 2 | 03.02.12 | **Lincoln City** (CL) | H | W | 2-1 | Hedley, Groves |
| | 3 | 24.02.12 | **Blackburn Rovers** (D1) | A | L | 2-3 | Halligan 2 |

| | | | | | | | |
|---|---|---|---|---|---|---|---|
| 1912-13 (D2) | 1 | 18.01.13 | **London Cal** (IL) | H | W | 3-1 | Halligan 2, J Needham |
| | 2 | 01.02.13 | **Bradford Park A** (D2) | A | L | 0-3 | |
| 1913-14 (D2) | 1 | 10.01.14 | **Southampton** (SL) | H | W | 3-0 | J Needham, Howell, Groves |
| | 2 | 31.01.14 | **Sheffield Wed** (D1) | H | D | 1-1 | Howell |
| | 2r | 04.02.14 | **Sheffield Wed** | A | L | 0-1 | |
| 1914-15 (D2) | 1 | 09.01.15 | **Reading** (SL) | A | W | 1-0 | Harrison |
| | 2 | 30.01.15 | **Sheffield Wed** (D1) | A | L | 0-2 | |
| 1919-20 (D2) | 1 | 10.01.20 | **Blackburn Rovers** (D1) | A | D | 2-2 | Richards 2 |
| | 1r | 15.01.20 | **Blackburn Rovers** | H | W | 1-0 | Lea |
| | 2 | 31.01.20 | **Cardiff City** (SL) | H | L | 1-2 | Harrison |
| 1920-21 (D2) | 1 | 08.01.21 | **Stoke** (D2) | H | W | 3-2 | Edmonds 2, Burrill |
| | 2 | 29.01.21 | **Derby County** (D1) | A | D | 1-1 | Wightman og |
| | 2r | 03.02.21 | **Derby County** | H | W | 1-0 | Richards |
| | 3 | 19.02.21 | **Fulham** (D2) | A | W | 1-0 | Potts |
| | 4 | 05.03.21 | **Everton** (D1) | A | W | 1-0 | Edmonds |
| | SF | 19.03.21 | **Cardiff City** (D2) *played at Anfield* | | D | 0-0 | |
| | SFr | 23.03.21 | **Cardiff City** *played at Old Trafford* | | W | 3-1 | Richards, Edmonds, Brooks |
| | F | 23.04.21 | **Tottenham Hotspur** (D1) *played at Stamford Bridge* | | L | 0-1 | |
| 1921-22 (D2) | 1 | 07.01.22 | **Preston North End** (D1) | A | L | 0-3 | |
| 1922-23 (D2) | 1 | 13.01.23 | **Merthyr Town** (3S) | A | W | 1-0 | Fazackerley |
| | 2 | 03.02.23 | **Liverpool** (D1) | H | L | 0-2 | |
| 1923-24 (3N) | 1 | 12.01.24 | **Darlington** (3N) | H | W | 3-1 | Phillipson 2, Lees |
| | 2 | 02.02.24 | **Charlton Athletic** (3S) | A | D | 0-0 | |
| | 2r | 07.02.24 | **Charlton Athletic** | H | W | 1-0 | Fazackerley |
| | 3 | 23.02.24 | **WBA** (D1) | A | D | 1-1 | Fazackerley |
| | 3r | 27.02.24 | **WBA** | H | L | 0-2 | |
| 1924-25 (D1) | 1 | 10.01.25 | **Hull City** (D2) | A | D | 1-1 | Edwards |
| | 1r | 15.01.25 | **Hull City** | H | L | 0-1aet | |
| 1925-26 (D2) | 3 | 09.01.26 | **Arsenal** (D1) | H | D | 1-1 | Phillipson |
| | 3r | 13.01.26 | **Arsenal** | A | L | 0-1 | |
| 1926-27 (D2) | 3 | 08.01.27 | **Carlisle Utd** (NEL) | A | W | 2-0 | Lees, Weaver |
| | 4 | 29.01.27 | **Nottingham Forest** (D2) | H | W | 2-0 | Phillipson, Weaver |
| | 5 | 19.02.27 | **Hull City** (D2) | H | W | 1-0 | Lees |
| | 6 | 05.03.27 | **Arsenal** (D1) | A | L | 1-2 | Phillipson |
| 1927-28 (D2) | 3 | 14.01.28 | **Chelsea** (D2) | H | W | 2-1 | Phillipson, Baxter |
| | 4 | 28.01.28 | **Sheffield Utd** (D1) | A | L | 1-3 | Phillipson |
| 1928-29 (D2) | 3 | 12.01.29 | **Mansfield Town** (ML) | H | L | 0-1 | |
| 1929-30 (D2) | 3 | 11.01.30 | **Oldham Athletic** (D2) | A | L | 0-1 | |
| 1930-31 (D2) | 3 | 10.01.31 | **Wrexham** (3N) | H | W | 9-1 | Hartill 4, Phillips 3, J Deacon, Hollingsworth |
| | 4 | 24.01.31 | **Bradford City** (D2) | A | D | 0-0 | |
| | 4r | 28.01.31 | **Bradford City** | H | W | 4-2 | Bottrill 2, Hartill, J Deacon |
| | 5 | 14.02.31 | **Barnsley** (D2) | A | W | 3-1 | Hartill, Barraclough, J Deacon |
| | 6 | 28.02.31 | **WBA** (D2) | A | D | 1-1 | Shaw og |
| | 6r | 04.03.31 | **WBA** | H | L | 1-2 | J Deacon |
| 1931-32 (D2) | 3 | 09.01.32 | **Luton Town** (3S) | A | W | 2-1 | Lowton, Phillips |
| | 4 | 23.01.32 | **Preston North End** (D2) | A | L | 0-2 | |
| 1932-33 (D1) | 3 | 14.01.33 | **Derby County** (D1) | H | L | 3-6 | Crook 2, Lowton |
| 1933-34 (D1) | 3 | 13.01.34 | **Newcastle Utd** (D1) | H | W | 1-0 | Phillips |
| | 4 | 27.01.34 | **Derby County** (D1) | A | L | 0-3 | |
| 1934-35 (D1) | 3 | 12.01.35 | **Notts County** (D2) | H | W | 4-0 | Hartill, Phillips, Brown, Martin |
| | 4 | 26.01.35 | **Sheffield Wed** (D1) | H | L | 1-2 | Hartill |
| 1935-36 (D1) | 3 | 11.01.36 | **Leeds Utd** (D1) | H | D | 1-1 | Wrigglesworth |
| | 3r | 15.01.36 | **Leeds Utd** | A | L | 1-3 | Morris |
| 1936-37 (D1) | 3 | 16.01.37 | **Middlesbrough** (D1) | H | W | 6-1 | Galley, Clayton, Smalley, Ashall 2, B Jones |
| | 4 | 30.01.37 | **Sheffield Utd** (D2) | H | D | 2-2 | Clayton, Johnson og |
| | 4r | 04.02.37 | **Sheffield Utd** | A | W | 2-1 | Clayton, Ashall |

| | | | | | | | | |
|---|---|---|---|---|---|---|---|---|
| | | 5 | 20.02.37 | **Grimsby Town** (D1) | A | D | 1-1 | Galley |
| | | 5r | 24.02.37 | **Grimsby Town** | H | W | 6-2 | Clayton 2, Ashall 2, B Jones, Westcott |
| | | 6 | 06.03.37 | **Sunderland** (D1) | H | D | 1-1 | B Jones |
| | | 6r | 10.03.37 | **Sunderland** | A | D | 2-2aet | Galley, Thompson |
| | | 6 2r | 15.03.37 | **Sunderland** | | L | 0-4 | |
| | | | | *played at Hillsborough* | | | | |
| 1937-38 | (D1) | 3 | 08.01.38 | **Swansea Town** (D2) | A | W | 4-0 | Westcott 3, B Jones |
| | | 4 | 22.01.38 | **Arsenal** (D1) | H | L | 1-2 | B Jones |
| 1938-39 | (D1) | 3 | 07.01.39 | **Bradford Park A** (D2) | H | W | 3-1 | Westcott 2, McIntosh |
| | | 4 | 21.01.39 | **Leicester City** (D1) | H | W | 5-1 | Westcott 2, Maguire 2, Dorsett |
| | | 5 | 11.02.39 | **Liverpool** (D1) | H | W | 4-1 | Westcott, McIntosh, Burton, Dorsett |
| | | 6 | 04.03.39 | **Everton** (D1) | H | W | 2-0 | Westcott 2 |
| | | SF | 25.03.39 | **Grimsby Town** (D1) | | W | 5-0 | Westcott 4, Galley |
| | | | | *played at Old Trafford* | | | | |
| | | F | 29.04.39 | **Portsmouth** (D1) | | L | 1-4 | Dorsett |
| | | | | *played at Wembley Stadium* | | | | |
| 1945-46 | (D1) | 3 1L | 05.01.46 | **Lovell's Athletic** (Welsh) | A | W | 4-2 | Davies 2, Galley, Crook |
| | | 3 2L | 09.01.46 | **Lovell's Athletic** | H | W | 8-1 | Galley 3, Wright 2, King, Dunn, Mullen |
| | | 4 1L | 26.01.46 | **Charlton Athletic** (D1) | A | L | 2-5 | Chatham 2 |
| | | 4 2L | 30.01.46 | **Charlton Athletic** | H | D | 1-1 | Wright |
| 1946-47 | (D1) | 3 | 11.01.47 | **Rotherham Utd** (3N) | H | W | 3-0 | Westcott, Hancocks, Pye |
| | | 4 | 25.01.47 | **Sheffield Utd** (D1) | H | D | 0-0 | |
| | | 4r | 29.01.47 | **Sheffield Utd** | A | L | 0-2 | |
| 1947-48 | (D1) | 3 | 10.01.48 | **Bournemouth** (3S) | A | W | 2-1 | Mullen 2 |
| | | 4 | 24.01.48 | **Everton** (D1) | H | D | 1-1aet | Westcott |
| | | 4r | 31.01.48 | **Everton** | A | L | 2-3aet | Westcott 2 |
| 1948-49 | (D1) | 3 | 08.01.49 | **Chesterfield** (D2) | H | W | 6-0 | Hancocks, Pye 2, Mullen, Smyth 2 |
| | | 4 | 29.01.49 | **Sheffield Utd** (D1) | A | W | 3-0 | Hancocks 2, Dunn |
| | | 5 | 12.02.49 | **Liverpool** (D1) | H | W | 3-1 | Dunn, Smyth, Mullen |
| | | 6 | 26.02.49 | **WBA** (D2) | H | W | 1-0 | Mullen |
| | | SF | 26.03.49 | **Manchester Utd** (D1) | | D | 1-1aet | Smyth |
| | | | | *played at Hillsborough* | | | | |
| | | SFr | 02.04.49 | **Manchester Utd** (D1) | | W | 1-0 | Smyth |
| | | | | *played at Goodison Park* | | | | |
| | | F | 30.04.49 | **Leicester City** (D2) | | W | 3-1 | Pye 2, Smyth |
| | | | | *played at Wembley Stadium* | | | | |
| 1949-50 | (D1) | 3 | 07.01.50 | **Plymouth Argyle** (D2) | A | D | 1-1 | Smyth |
| | | 3r | 11.01.50 | **Plymouth Argyle** | H | W | 3-0 | Smyth, Swinbourne, Hancocks |
| | | 4 | 28.01.50 | **Sheffield Utd** (D2) | H | D | 0-0 | |
| | | 4r | 31.01.50 | **Sheffield Utd** | A | W | 4-3 | Hancocks 2, Smyth, Mullen |
| | | 5 | 11.02.50 | **Blackpool** (D1) | H | D | 0-0 | |
| | | 5r | 15.02.50 | **Blackpool** | A | L | 0-1 | |
| 1950-51 | (D1) | 3 | 06.01.51 | **Plymouth Argyle** (3S) | A | W | 2-1 | Dunn, Walker |
| | | 4 | 27.01.51 | **Aston Villa** (D1) | H | W | 3-1 | Walker, Swinbourne, Mullen |
| | | 5 | 10.02.51 | **Huddersfield Town** (D1) | H | W | 2-0 | Dunn 2 |
| | | 6 | 24.02.51 | **Sunderland** (D1) | A | D | 1-1 | Walker |
| | | 6r | 28.02.51 | **Sunderland** | H | W | 3-1 | Dunn, Swinbourne, Walker |
| | | SF | 10.03.51 | **Newcastle Utd** (D1) | | D | 0-0aet | |
| | | | | *played at Hillsborough* | | | | |
| | | SFr | 14.03.51 | **Newcastle Utd** | | L | 1-2 | Walker |
| | | | | *played at Leeds Road, Huddersfield* | | | | |
| 1951-52 | (D1) | 3 | 12.01.52 | **Manchester City** (D1) | A | D | 2-2 | Broadbent, Whitfield |
| | | 3r | 16.01.52 | **Manchester City** | H | W | 4-1 | Mullen 2, Short 2 |
| | | 4 | 02.02.52 | **Liverpool** (D1) | A | L | 1-2 | Mullen |
| 1952-53 | (D1) | 3 | 10.01.53 | **Preston North End** (D1) | A | L | 2-5 | Wilshaw, Smith |
| 1953-54 | (D1) | 3 | 09.01.54 | **Birmingham City** (D2) | H | L | 1-2 | Wilshaw |
| 1954-55 | (D1) | 3 | 08.01.55 | **Grimsby Town** (3N) | A | W | 5-2 | McDonald, Swinbourne, Smith, Wilshaw 2 |
| | | 4 | 29.01.55 | **Arsenal** (D1) | H | W | 1-0 | Swinbourne |

| | | | | | | | |
|---|---|---|---|---|---|---|---|
| | 5 | 19.02.55 | **Charlton Athletic** (D1) | H | W | 4-1 | Wilshaw 3, Hancocks |
| | 6 | 12.03.55 | **Sunderland** (D1) | A | L | 0-2 | |
| 1955-56 (D1) | 3 | 07.01.56 | **WBA** (D1) | H | L | 1-2 | Slater |
| 1956-57 (D1) | 3 | 05.01.57 | **Swansea Town** (D2) | H | W | 5-3 | Bonson 2, Broadbent, Flowers, Mullen |
| | 4 | 26.01.57 | **Bournemouth** (3S) | H | L | 0-1 | |
| 1957-58 (D1) | 3 | 04.01.58 | **Lincoln City** (D2) | A | W | 1-0 | Mullen |
| | 4 | 25.01.58 | **Portsmouth** (D1) | H | W | 5-1 | Mason, Broadbent 2, Mullen, Rutter og |
| | 5 | 15.02.58 | **Darlington** (3N) | H | W | 6-1 | Murray 3, Broadbent 2, Mason |
| | 6 | 01.03.58 | **Bolton Wanderers** (D1) | A | L | 1-2 | Mason |
| 1958-59 (D1) | 3 | 10.01.59 | **Barrow** (D4) | A | W | 4-2 | Lill, Booth, Deeley 2 |
| | 4 | 24.01.59 | **Bolton Wanderers** (D1) | H | L | 1-2 | Hennin og |
| 1959-60 (D1) | 3 | 09.01.60 | **Newcastle Utd** (D1) | A | D | 2-2 | Flowers, Clamp (p) |
| | 3r | 13.01.60 | **Newcastle Utd** | H | W | 4-2 | Murray, Deeley, Flowers, Horne |
| | 4 | 30.01.60 | **Charlton Athletic** (D2) | H | W | 2-1 | Horne, Broadbent |
| | 5 | 20.02.60 | **Luton Town** (D1) | A | W | 4-1 | Mason 2, Murray, Clamp |
| | 6 | 12.03.60 | **Leicester City** (D1) | A | W | 2-1 | Broadbent, Chalmers og |
| | SF | 26.03.60 | **Aston Villa** (D2) | | W | 1-0 | Deeley |
| | | | *played at The Hawthorns* | | | | |
| | F | 07.05.60 | **Blackburn Rovers** (D1) | | W | 3-0 | Deeley 2, McGrath og |
| | | | *played at Wembley Stadium* | | | | |
| 1960-61 (D1) | 3 | 07.01.61 | **Huddersfield Town** (D2) | H | D | 1-1 | Kirkham |
| | 3r | 11.01.61 | **Huddersfield Town** | A | L | 1-2 | Murray |
| 1961-62 (D1) | 3 | 08.01.62 | **Carlisle Utd** (D4) | H | W | 3-1 | Wharton 2, Broadbent |
| | 4 | 27.01.62 | **WBA** (D1) | H | L | 1-2 | Murray |
| 1962-63 (D1) | 3 | 29.01.63 | **Nottingham Forest** (D1) | A | L | 3-4 | Stobart 2, Broadbent |
| 1963-64 (D1) | 3 | 04.01.64 | **Arsenal** (D1) | A | L | 1-2 | Wharton |
| 1964-65 (D1) | 3 | 09.01.65 | **Portsmouth** (D2) | A | D | 0-0 | |
| | 3r | 12.01.65 | **Portsmouth** | H | W | 3-2 | McIlmoyle 2, Crawford |
| | 4 | 30.01.65 | **Rotherham Utd** (D2) | H | D | 2-2 | Crawford, Flowers |
| | 4r | 02.02.65 | **Rotherham Utd** | A | W | 3-0 | Woodruff, Wharton, Wagstaffe |
| | 5 | 20.02.65 | **Aston Villa** (D1) | A | D | 1-1 | Woodruff |
| | 5r | 24.02.65 | **Aston Villa** | H | D | 0-0aet | |
| | 5 2r | 01.03.65 | **Aston Villa** | | W | 3-1 | McIlmoyle 3 |
| | | | *played at The Hawthorns* | | | | |
| | 6 | 10.03.65 | **Manchester Utd** (D1) | H | L | 3-5 | McIlmoyle 2, Knowles |
| 1965-66 (D2) | 3 | 22.01.66 | **Altrincham** (CC) | H | W | 5-0 | Hunt 2, McImoyle, Woodruff, Dewar og |
| | 4 | 12.02.66 | **Sheffield Utd** (D1) | H | W | 3-0 | Knowles 2, McIlmoyle |
| | 5 | 05.03.66 | **Manchester Utd** (D1) | H | L | 2-4 | Wharton 2 |
| 1966-67 (D2) | 3 | 28.01.67 | **Oldham Athletic** (D3) | A | D | 2-2 | Thomson, Bailey |
| | 3r | 01.02.67 | **Oldham Athletic** | H | W | 4-1 | Woodfield, Wharton, Hunt, McIlmoyle |
| | 4 | 18.02.67 | **Everton** (D1) | H | D | 1-1 | Wharton |
| | 4r | 21.02.67 | **Everton** | A | L | 1-3 | Wharton |
| 1967-68 (D1) | 3 | 27.01.68 | **Rotherham Utd** (D2) | A | L | 0-1 | |
| 1968-69 (D1) | 3 | 04.01.69 | **Hull City** (D2) | A | W | 3-1 | Dougan 2, Wignall |
| | 4 | 25.01.69 | **Tottenham Hotspur** (D1) | A | L | 1-2 | Wagstaffe |
| 1969-70 (D1) | 3 | 03.01.70 | **Burnley** (D1) | A | L | 0-3 | |
| 1970-71 (D1) | 3 | 02.01.71 | **Norwich City** (D2) | H | W | 5-1 | McCalliog 2, Gould 2, Hibbitt |
| | 4 | 23.01.71 | **Derby County** (D1) | A | L | 1-2 | Richards |
| 1971-72 (D1) | 3 | 15.01.72 | **Leicester City** (D1) | H | D | 1-1 | McCalliog |
| | 3r | 19.01.72 | **Leicester City** | A | L | 0-2 | |
| 1972-73 (D1) | 3 | 13.01.73 | **Manchester Utd** (D1) | H | W | 1-0 | Bailey |
| | 4 | 03.02.73 | **Bristol City** (D2) | H | W | 1-0 | Richards |
| | 5 | 24.02.73 | **Millwall** (D2) | H | W | 1-0 | Richards |
| | 6 | 17.03.73 | **Coventry City** (D1) | H | W | 2-0 | Richards, Hibbitt |
| | SF | 07.04.73 | **Leeds Utd** (D1) | | L | 0-1 | |
| | | | *played at Maine Road* | | | | |
| | 3/4 | 18.08.73 | **Arsenal** (D1) | A | W | 3-1 | Dougan 2, McCalliog |
| 1973-74 (D1) | 3 | 05.01.74 | **Leeds Utd** (D1) | H | D | 1-1 | Richards |
| | 3r | 09.01.74 | **Leeds Utd** | A | L | 0-1 | |
| 1974-75 (D1) | 3 | 04.01.75 | **Ipswich Town** (D1) | H | L | 1-2 | Richards |
| 1975-76 (D1) | 3 | 03.01.76 | **Arsenal** (D1) | H | W | 3-0 | Hibbitt, Bell, Richards |

| | | | | | | | | |
|---|---|---|---|---|---|---|---|---|
| | | 4 | 24.01.76 | **Ipswich Town** (D1) | A | D | 0-0 | |
| | | 4r | 27.01.76 | **Ipswich Town** | H | W | 1-0 | Gould |
| | | 5 | 14.02.76 | **Charlton Athletic** (D2) | H | W | 3-0 | Richards 3 |
| | | 6 | 06.03.76 | **Manchester Utd** (D1) | A | D | 1-1 | Richards |
| | | 6r | 09.03.76 | **Manchester Utd** | H | L | 2-3aet | Richards, Kindon |
| 1976-77 | (D2) | 3 | 08.01.77 | **Rotherham Utd** (D3) | H | W | 3-2 | Richards. S.Daley |
| | | 4 | 29.01.77 | **Ipswich Town** (D1) | A | D | 2-2 | Richards 2 |
| | | 4r | 02.02.77 | **Ipswich Town** | H | W | 1-0 | Richards |
| | | 5 | 26.02.77 | **Chester** (D3) | H | W | 1-0 | Hibbitt |
| | | 6 | 19.03.77 | **Leeds Utd** (D1) | H | L | 0-1 | |
| 1977-78 | (D1) | 3 | 07.01.78 | **Exeter City** (D3) | A | D | 2-2 | Carr, M.Daly |
| | | 3r | 10.01.78 | **Exeter City** | H | W | 3-1 | S Daley, Hibbitt, Richards |
| | | 4 | 28.01.78 | **Arsenal** (D1) | A | L | 1-2 | Hibbitt |
| 1978-79 | (D1) | 3 | 09.01.79 | **Brighton** (D2) | A | W | 3-2 | S Daley, Bell, Williams og |
| | | 4 | 27.01.79 | **Newcastle Utd** (D2) | A | D | 1-1 | Hibbitt |
| | | 4r | 22.02.79 | **Newcastle Utd** | H | W | 1-0 | Bell |
| | | 5 | 26.02.79 | **Crystal Palace** (D2) | A | W | 1-0 | Patching |
| | | 6 | 10.03.79 | **Shrewsbury Town** (D3) | H | D | 1-1 | Rafferty |
| | | 6r | 13.03.79 | **Shrewsbury Town** | A | W | 3-1 | Rafferty, Carr, Daniel |
| | | SF | 31.03.79 | **Arsenal** (D1) | | L | 0-2 | |
| | | | | *played at Villa Park* | | | | |
| 1979-80 | (D1) | 3 | 05.01.80 | **Notts County** (D2) | A | W | 3-1 | Richards, Berry, Carr |
| | | 4 | 26.01.80 | **Norwich City** (D1) | H | D | 1-1 | Gray |
| | | 4r | 30.01.80 | **Norwich City** | A | W | 3-2 | Richards, Berry, Eves |
| | | 5 | 16.02.80 | **Watford** (D2) | H | L | 0-3 | |
| 1980-81 | (D1) | 3 | 03.01.81 | **Stoke City** (D1) | A | D | 2-2 | Bell, Eves |
| | | 3r | 06.01.81 | **Stoke City** | H | W | 2-1 | Hibbitt, Eves |
| | | 4 | 24.01.81 | **Watford** (D2) | A | D | 1-1 | Richards |
| | | 4r | 27.01.81 | **Watford** | H | W | 2-1 | Richards, Parkin |
| | | 5 | 14.02.81 | **Wrexham** (D2) | H | W | 3-1 | Bell 2, Richards |
| | | 6 | 07.03.81 | **Middlesbrough** (D1) | A | D | 1-1 | Gray |
| | | 6r | 10.03.81 | **Middlesbrough** | H | W | 3-1aet | Richards, Eves, Bell |
| | | SF | 11.04.81 | **Tottenham Hotspur** (D1) | | D | 2-2aet | Carr, Hibbitt (p) |
| | | | | *played at Hillsborough* | | | | |
| | | SFr | 15.04.81 | **Tottenham Hotspur** | | L | 0-3 | |
| | | | | *played at Highbury* | | | | |
| 1981-82 | (D1) | 3 | 02.01.82 | **Leeds Utd** (D1) | H | L | 1-3 | Gray |
| 1982-83 | (D2) | 3 | 08.01.83 | **Tranmere Rovers** (D4) | A | W | 1-0 | Hibbitt |
| | | 4 | 29.01.83 | **Aston Villa** (D1) | A | L | 0-1 | |
| 1983-84 | (D1) | 3 | 07.01.84 | **Coventry City** (D1) | A | D | 1-1 | Clarke |
| | | 3r | 10.01.84 | **Coventry City** | H | D | 1-1aet | Eves |
| | | 3 2r | 16.01.84 | **Coventry City** | A | L | 0-3 | |
| 1984-85 | (D2) | 3 | 05.01.85 | **Huddersfield Town** (D2) | H | D | 1-1 | Pender |
| | | 3r | 23.01.85 | **Huddersfield Town** | A | L | 1-3 | Ainscow |
| 1985-86 | (D3) | 1 | 16.11.85 | **Rotherham Utd** (D3) | A | L | 0-6 | |
| 1986-87 | (D4) | 1 | 15.11.86 | **Chorley** (NPL) | A | D | 1-1 | Mutch |
| | | | | *played at Burnden Park* | | | | |
| | | 1r | 18.11.86 | **Chorley** | H | D | 1-1aet | Forman |
| | | 1 2r | 24.11.86 | **Chorley** | | L | 0-3 | |
| | | | | *played at Burnden Park* | | | | |
| 1987-88 | (D4) | 1 | 14.11.87 | **Cheltenham Town** (Conf) | H | W | 5-1 | Bull 3, Downing, Vaughan |
| | | 2 | 05.12.87 | **Wigan Athletic** (D3) | A | W | 3-1 | Gallagher, Dennison, Robinson |
| | | 3 | 09.01.88 | **Bradford City** (D2) | A | L | 1-2 | Sinnott og |
| 1988-89 | (D3) | 1 | 19.11.88 | **Grimsby Town** (D4) | A | L | 0-1 | |
| 1989-90 | (D2) | 3 | 06.01.90 | **Sheffield Wed** (D1) | H | L | 1-2 | Bull |
| 1990-91 | (D2) | 3 | 05.01.91 | **Cambridge Utd** (D3) | H | L | 0-1 | |
| 1991-92 | (D2) | 3 | 04.01.92 | **Nottingham Forest** (D1) | A | L | 0-1 | |
| 1992-93 | (D1) | 3 | 02.01.93 | **Watford** (D1) | A | W | 4-1 | Holdsworth og, Downing, Mutch, Bull |
| | | 4 | 24.01.93 | **Bolton Wanderers** (D2) | H | L | 0-2 | |
| 1993-94 | (D1) | 3 | 08.01.94 | **Crystal Palace** (PL) | H | W | 1-0 | D Kelly |
| | | 4 | 29.01.94 | **Port Vale** (D2) | A | W | 2-0 | Blades, Keen |

| | | | | | | | |
|---|---|---|---|---|---|---|---|
| | 5 | 19.02.94 | **Ipswich Town** (PL) | H | D | 1-1 | Kelly |
| | 5r | 02.03.94 | **Ipswich Town** | A | W | 2-1 | Mills, Thompson |
| | 6 | 13.03.94 | **Chelsea** (PL) | A | L | 0-1 | |
| 1994-95 (D1) | 3 | 07.01.95 | **Mansfield Town** (D3) | A | W | 3-2 | D Kelly, Denison, Mills |
| | 4 | 30.01.95 | **Sheffield Wed** (PL) | A | D | 0-0 | |
| | 4r | 08.02.95 | **Sheffield Wed** | H | D | 1-1aet | D Kelly |
| | | | *Wolverhampton W won 4-3 on penalties* | | | | |
| | 5 | 18.02.95 | **Leicester City** (PL) | H | W | 1-0 | D Kelly |
| | 6 | 11.03.95 | **Crystal Palace** (PL) | A | D | 1-1 | Cowans |
| | 6r | 22.03.95 | **Crystal Palace** | H | L | 1-4 | D Kelly |
| 1995-96 (D1) | 3 | 06.01.96 | **Birmingham City** (D1) | A | D | 1-1 | Bull |
| | 3r | 17.01.96 | **Birmingham City** | H | W | 2-1 | Ferguson, Bull |
| | 4 | 27.01.96 | **Tottenham Hotspur** (PL) | A | D | 1-1 | Goodman |
| | 4r | 07.02.96 | **Tottenham Hotspur** | H | L | 0-2 | |
| 1996-97 (D1) | 3 | 04.01.97 | **Portsmouth** (D1) | H | L | 1-2 | Ferguson |
| 1997-98 (D1) | 3 | 14.01.98 | **Darlington** (D3) | A | W | 4-0 | Freedman, Paatelainen 2, Ferguson |
| | 4 | 24.01.98 | **Charlton Athletic** (D1) | A | D | 1-1 | Richards |
| | 4r | 03.02.98 | **Charlton Athletic** | H | W | 3-0 | Curle (p), Naylor, Paatelainen |
| | 5 | 14.02.98 | **Wimbledon** (PL) | A | D | 1-1 | Paatelainen |
| | 5r | 25.02.98 | **Wimbledon** | H | W | 2-1 | Robinson, Freedman |
| | 6 | 07.03.98 | **Leeds Utd** (PL) | A | W | 1-0 | Goodman |
| | SF | 05.04.98 | **Arsenal** (PL) | | L | 0-1 | |
| | | | *played at Villa Park* | | | | |
| 1998-99 (D1) | 3 | 02.01.99 | **Bolton Wanderers** (D1) | A | W | 2-1 | Keane 2 |
| | 4 | 24.01.99 | **Arsenal** (PL) | H | L | 1-2 | Flo |
| 1999-00 (D1) | 3 | 11.12.99 | **Wigan Athletic** (D2) | A | W | 1-0 | Robinson |
| | 4 | 08.01.00 | **Sheffield Wed** (PL) | A | D | 1-1 | Sedgley |
| | 4r | 18.01.00 | **Sheffield Wed** | H | D | 0-0aet | |
| | | | *Sheffield Wed won 4-3 on penalties* | | | | |
| 2000-01 (D1) | 3 | 06.01.01 | **Nottingham Forest** (D1) | A | W | 1-0 | Proudlock |
| | 4 | 27.01.01 | **Wycombe W** (D2) | A | L | 1-2 | Robinson |
| 2001-02 (D1) | 3 | 05.01.02 | **Gillingham** (D1) | H | L | 0-1 | |
| 2002-03 (D1) | 3 | 05.01.03 | **Newcastle Utd** (PL) | H | W | 3-2 | Ince, Kennedy, Ndah |
| | 4 | 25.01.03 | **Leicester City** (D1) | H | W | 4-1 | Ndah 2, Miller 2 |
| | 5 | 16.02.03 | **Rochdale** (D3) | H | W | 3-1 | Ndah, Miller, Proudlock |
| | 6 | 09.03.03 | **Southampton** (PL) | A | L | 0-2 | |

## WOMBWELL TOWN

*Entered FA Cup: 1920-21 – 1932-33*

| | | | | | | | |
|---|---|---|---|---|---|---|---|
| 1930-31 (ML) | 1 | 29.11.30 | **Wellington Town** (BDL) | A | D | 0-0 | |
| | 1r | 04.12.30 | **Wellington Town** | H | L | 0-3 | |

## WOOD GRANGE

| | | | | | | | |
|---|---|---|---|---|---|---|---|
| 1876-77 | 1 | 08.11.76 | **Panthers** | A | L | 0-3 | |
| 1877-78 | 1 | 27.10.77 | **High Wycombe** | A | L | 0-4 | |

## WOODFORD BRIDGE

*Formed 1880. Entered FA Cup for these three seasons. Played at the Woodfrod Bridge field, near the White Hart pub, Woodford Essex.*

| | | | | | | | |
|---|---|---|---|---|---|---|---|
| 1881-82 | 1 | 22.10.81 | **Reading Abbey** | H | D | 1-1 | Overton |
| | 1r | 12.11.81 | **Reading Abbey** | A | L | 1-2 | |
| 1882-83 | 1 | 21.10.82 | **Royal Engineers** | A | L | 1-3 | Bullard |
| 1883-84 | 1 | 03.11.83 | **Romford (1876)** | A | L | 0-3 | |

## WOODFORD TOWN

*Formed 1937. First entered FA Cup: 1946-47. Members of the Essex Senior League.*

| | | | | | | | |
|---|---|---|---|---|---|---|---|
| 1986-87 (SL) | 1 | 15.11.86 | **Orient** (D4) | H | L | 0-1 | |

## WOODFORD WELLS

*Formed 1869. Entered the FA Cup for three seasons in the 1870s. Played at Monkham Lane, Woodford, Essex.*

| | | | | | | | |
|---|---|---|---|---|---|---|---|
| 1873-74 | 1 | 11.10.73 | **Reigate Priory** | H | W | 3-2 | Fraser 2, E Beauchamp |
| | 2 | 22.11.73 | **Swifts** | A | L | 1-2 | R Beauchamp |
| 1874-75 | 1 | 31.10.74 | **High Wycombe** | H | W | 1-0 | W Spreckley |

| | | | | | | | | |
|---|---|---|---|---|---|---|---|---|
| | | 2 | 05.12.74 | **Southall Park** | H | W | 3-0 | Wild 2, Bouch |
| | | 3 | 23.01.75 | **Shropshire W** | A | D | 1-1aet | Powell |
| | | 3r | 06.02.75 | **Shropshire W** | H | L | 0-2 | |
| 1875-76 | | 1 | 06.11.75 | **Panthers** | A | L | 0-1 | |

## WORCESTER CITY

*Formed 1902. First entered FA Cup: 1905-06. League clubs beaten: Millwall, Liverpool, Plymouth Argyle, Wrexham, Aldershot. Members of the Southern League.*

| | | | | | | | | |
|---|---|---|---|---|---|---|---|---|
| 1905-06 | (BDL) | 1 | 13.01.06 | **Watford** (SL) | H | L | 0-6 | |
| 1925-26 | (BDL) | 1 | 28.11.25 | **Kettering Town** (SL) | H | D | 0-0 | |
| | | 1r | 03.12.25 | **Kettering Town** | A | D | 0-0aet | |
| | | 1 2r | 07.12.25 | **Kettering Town** | | L | 0-2 | |
| | | | | *played at St Andrews* | | | | |
| 1928-29 | (BDL) | 1 | 24.11.28 | **Walsall** (3S) | A | L | 1-3 | Byers |
| 1950-51 | (SL) | 1 | 25.11.50 | **Hartlepools Utd** (3N) | H | L | 1-4 | Jackman |
| 1957-58 | (SL) | 1 | 16.11.57 | **Aldershot** (3S) | A | D | 0-0 | |
| | | 1r | 21.11.57 | **Aldershot** | H | D | 2-2aet | Bryceland, Knowles |
| | | 1 2r | 25.11.57 | **Aldershot** | | L | 2-3aet | Quigley, Bryceland |
| | | | | *played at St Andrews* | | | | |
| 1958-59 | (SL) | 1 | 15.11.58 | **Chelmsford City** (SL) | A | D | 0-0 | |
| | | 1r | 20.11.58 | **Chelmsford City** | H | W | 3-1 | Gosling, Brown, Skuse |
| | | 2 | 06.12.58 | **Millwall** (D4) | H | W | 5-2 | Brown 2, Skuse, Knowles 2 |
| | | 3 | 15.01.59 | **Liverpool** (D2) | H | W | 2-1 | Skuse, White og |
| | | 4 | 24.01.59 | **Sheffield Utd** (D2) | H | L | 0-2 | |
| 1960-61 | (SL) | 1 | 05.11.60 | **Coventry City** (D3) | H | L | 1-4 | Phillips (p) |
| 1978-79 | (SL) | 1 | 25.11.78 | **Plymouth Argyle** (D3) | H | W | 2-0 | Phelps, Williams |
| | | 2 | 16.12.78 | **Newport County** (D4) | A | D | 0-0 | |
| | | 2r | 18.12.78 | **Newport County** | H | L | 1-2 | Phelps |
| 1982-83 | (APL) | 1 | 20.11.82 | **Macclesfield T** (NPL) | A | W | 5-1 | Moss 2, Tuohy 3 |
| | | 2 | 11.12.82 | **Wrexham** (D3) | H | W | 2-1 | Moss 2 |
| | | 3 | 08.01.83 | **Coventry City** (D1) | A | L | 1-3 | Moss (p) |
| 1983-84 | (APL) | 1 | 19.11.83 | **Aldershot** (D4) | A | D | 1-1 | Moss |
| | | 1r | 21.11.83 | **Aldershot** | H | W | 2-1 | Moss 2 |
| | | 2 | 10.12.83 | **Maidstone Utd** (APL) | A | L | 2-3 | Moss 2 (1p) |
| 1987-88 | (SL) | 1 | 14.11.87 | **Yeovil Town** (IL) | H | D | 1-1 | Ferguson |
| | | 1r | 18.11.87 | **Yeovil Town** | A | L | 0-1 | |
| 1998-99 | (SL) | 1 | 14.11.98 | **Torquay Utd** (D3) | H | L | 0-1 | |
| 2001-02 | (SL) | 1 | 17.11.01 | **Rushden & D** (D3) | H | L | 0-1 | |

## WORKINGTON

*Formed 1884. Reformed 1921. First entered FA Cup: 1887-88. Members of the Football League: 1951-1977. Members of the Northern Premier League.*

| | | | | | | | | |
|---|---|---|---|---|---|---|---|---|
| 1887-88 | | 1 | 15.10.87 | **Bootle** | A | L | 0-6 | |
| 1908-09 | (NEL) | 1 | 19.01.09 | **Bradford City** (D1) | A | L | 0-2 | |
| 1909-10 | (NEL) | 1 | 15.01.10 | **Manchester City** (D2) | H | L | 1-2 | Swan |
| 1926-27 | (NEL) | 1 | 27.11.26 | **Crook Town** (NL) | H | L | 1-2 | Gillfillan |
| 1927-28 | (NEL) | 1 | 26.11.27 | **Bradford City** (3N) | A | L | 0-6 | |
| 1930-31 | (NEL) | 1 | 29.11.30 | **Nelson FC** (3N) | A | L | 0-4 | |
| 1932-33 | (NEL) | 1 | 26.11.32 | **Scunthorpe Utd** (ML) | H | W | 5-1 | Bruce 2, James, Maidment, Charlton |
| | | 2 | 10.12.32 | **Halifax Town** (3N) | A | L | 1-2 | James |
| 1933-34 | (NEL) | 1 | 25.11.33 | **Southport** (3N) | H | W | 1-0 | Stanger |
| | | 2 | 09.12.33 | **Newport County** (3S) | H | W | 3-1 | Charlton, James, Miller |
| | | 3 | 13.01.34 | **Gateshead AFC** (3N) | H | W | 4-1 | Lincoln 2, Charlton 2 |
| | | 4 | 27.01.34 | **Preston North End** (D2) | H | L | 1-2 | Holdcroft og |
| 1934-35 | (NEL) | 1 | 24.11.34 | **Birmingham CT** (BC) | H | W | 2-0 | Thornton, Charlton |
| | | 2 | 08.12.34 | **Northampton Town** (3S) | A | D | 0-0 | |
| | | 2r | 13.12.34 | **Northampton Town** | H | L | 0-1 | |
| 1935-36 | (NEL) | 1 | 30.11.35 | **New Brighton** (3N) | A | W | 3-1 | Boyd 3 |
| | | 2 | 14.12.35 | **Kidderminster H** (BDL) | H | W | 5-1 | Boyd 4, Maidment |
| | | 3 | 11.01.36 | **Bradford Park A** (D2) | A | L | 2-3 | Carruthers, Sewell |
| 1937-38 | (NEL) | 1 | 27.11.37 | **New Brighton** (3N) | A | L | 0-5 | |
| 1938-39 | (NEL) | 1 | 26.11.38 | **Mansfield Town** (3S) | H | D | 1-1 | Pearce |

| | | | | | | | | |
|---|---|---|---|---|---|---|---|---|
| | | 1r | 30.11.38 | **Mansfield Town** | A | L | 1-2 | Pearce |
| 1946-47 | (NEL) | 1 | 30.11.46 | **South Liverpool** (CC) | A | L | 1-2 | Pope |
| 1947-48 | (NEL) | 1 | 29.11.47 | **Lincoln City** (3N) | A | W | 2-0 | Armstrong, Oakes |
| | | 2 | 13.12.47 | **Crewe Alexandra** (3N) | H | L | 1-2 | Oakes |
| 1948-49 | (NEL) | 1 | 27.11.48 | **Stockport County** (3N) | H | L | 0-3 | |
| 1951-52 | (3N) | 1 | 24.11.51 | **Blackhall Colliery** (NEL) | A | W | 5-2 | Maxfield, Simmonds, Dick, McDowall, Mullen |
| | | 2 | 15.12.51 | **Witton Albion** (CC) | A | D | 3-3 | Simmonds 2, Maxfield |
| | | 2r | 20.12.51 | **Witton Albion** | H | W | 1-0 | Simmonds |
| | | 3 | 12.01.52 | **Liverpool** (D1) | A | L | 0-1 | |
| 1952-53 | (3N) | 1 | 22.11.52 | **Chesterfield** (3N) | A | L | 0-1 | |
| 1953-54 | (3N) | 1 | 21.11.53 | **Ferryhill Athletic** (NL) | H | W | 3-0 | Stokoe, Simmonds, McAlone |
| | | 2 | 12.12.53 | **Stockport County** (3N) | A | L | 1-2 | Cameron |
| 1954-55 | (3N) | 1 | 20.11.54 | **Hyde Utd** (CC) | H | W | 5-1 | Bertolini, Whittle 3, Dailey |
| | | 2 | 11.12.54 | **Leyton Orient** (3S) | A | W | 1-0 | Bertolini |
| | | 3 | 08.01.55 | **Luton Town** (D2) | A | L | 0-5 | |
| 1955-56 | (3N) | 1 | 19.11.55 | **Scarborough** (ML) | H | W | 4-2 | Dailey 2, Dunlop, Whittle |
| | | 2 | 10.12.55 | **Bradford Park A** (3N) | A | L | 3-4 | Mitchell, Bertolini, Dunlop |
| 1956-57 | (3N) | 1 | 17.11.56 | **Mansfield Town** (3N) | A | D | 1-1 | Dailey |
| | | 1r | 20.11.56 | **Mansfield Town** | H | W | 2-1 | Bertolini, Dailey |
| | | 2 | 08.12.56 | **Goole Town** (ML) | A | D | 2-2 | Dailey, Finlay |
| | | 2r | 12.12.56 | **Goole Town** | H | L | 0-1 | |
| 1957-58 | (3N) | 1 | 16.11.57 | **Crook Town** (NL) | H | W | 8-1 | Brown, Bertolini 2, Kinloch, Currie 2, Purdon, Steward og |
| | | 2 | 07.12.57 | **Oldham Athletic** (3N) | A | W | 5-1 | Robson 2, Currie, Chisholm, Purdon (p) |
| | | 3 | 04.01.58 | **Manchester Utd** (D1) | H | L | 1-3 | Colbridge |
| 1958-59 | (D4) | 1 | 15.11.58 | **Accrington Stanley** (D3) | A | L | 1-5 | Alexandra |
| 1959-60 | (D4) | 1 | 14.11.59 | **Southport** (D4) | A | D | 2-2 | Morrison, Brownlee |
| | | 1r | 18.11.59 | **Southport** | H | W | 3-0 | Booth, Harburn, McGarry |
| | | 2 | 05.12.59 | **Halifax Town** (D3) | H | W | 1-0 | Rollo (p) |
| | | 3 | 09.01.60 | **Crewe Alexandra** (D4) | A | L | 0-2 | |
| 1960-61 | (D4) | 1 | 05.11.60 | **Stockport County** (D4) | A | L | 0-1 | |
| 1961-62 | (D4) | 1 | 04.11.61 | **Worksop Town** (ML) | H | W | 2-0 | Haasz, McGarry |
| | | 2 | 25.11.61 | **Gateshead AFC** (NRL) | A | W | 2-0 | Haasz, Kirkup |
| | | 3 | 06.01.62 | **Nottingham Forest** (D1) | H | L | 1-2 | McGarry |
| 1962-63 | (D4) | 1 | 03.11.62 | **North Shields** (NEL) | A | D | 2-2 | Commons, Swindells |
| | | 1r | 08.11.62 | **North Shields** | H | W | 7-2 | Carr 4, Commons, Kirkup, Swindells |
| | | 2 | 24.11.62 | **Hull City** (D3) | A | L | 0-2 | |
| 1963-64 | (D4) | 1 | 16.11.63 | **Halifax Town** (D4) | H | W | 4-1 | Martin, Moran 2, Carr |
| | | 2 | 07.12.63 | **Port Vale** (D3) | A | L | 1-2 | Moran |
| 1964-65 | (D3) | 1 | 14.11.64 | **Rochdale** (D4) | H | W | 2-0 | Carr, Moran |
| | | 2 | 05.12.64 | **South Liverpool** (LC) | A | W | 2-0 | Moran 2 |
| | | 3 | 09.01.65 | **Bolton Wanderers** (D2) | A | L | 1-4 | Moran |
| 1965-66 | (D3) | 1 | 13.11.65 | **Hartlepools Utd** (D4) | A | L | 1-3 | Lowes |
| 1966-67 | (D3) | 1 | 26.11.66 | **S Shields (1936)** (NRL) | A | W | 4-1 | Griffin 2 (1p), Tinnion, Oliver |
| | | 2 | 11.01.67 | **Bradford Park A** (D4) | A | L | 1-3 | Oliver |
| 1967-68 | (D4) | 1 | 09.12.67 | **Ryhope Coll W** (Wear) | A | W | 1-0 | Spratt |
| | | 2 | 06.01.68 | **Doncaster Rovers** (D4) | A | D | 1-1 | Tinnion |
| | | 2r | 10.01.68 | **Doncaster Rovers** | H | L | 1-2aet | Tinnion |
| 1968-69 | (D4) | 1 | 16.11.68 | **Scunthorpe Utd** (D4) | H | W | 2-0 | Tinnion, Griffith |
| | | 2 | 07.12.68 | **Port Vale** (D4) | A | D | 0-0 | |
| | | 2r | 11.12.68 | **Port Vale** | H | L | 1-2 | Griffith |
| 1969-70 | (D4) | 1 | 15.11.69 | **Rochdale** (D3) | H | W | 2-1 | Tyrer, Martin |
| | | 2 | 06.12.69 | **Rotherham Utd** (D3) | A | L | 0-3 | |
| 1970-71 | (D4) | 1 | 21.11.70 | **Scarborough** (NPL) | A | W | 3-2 | Spratt 2, Goodfellow |
| | | 2 | 12.12.70 | **Chesterfield** (D3) | A | D | 0-0 | |
| | | 2r | 16.12.70 | **Chesterfield** | H | W | 3-2 | Goodfellow, Ogilvie, Massie |
| | | 3 | 02.01.71 | **Brentford** (D4) | H | L | 0-1 | |
| 1971-72 | (D4) | 1 | 20.11.71 | **Southport** (D4) | A | W | 3-1 | Dunleavy og, Spencer, Goodfellow |
| | | 2 | 11.12.71 | **Bury** (D4) | H | L | 1-3 | Spratt (p) |
| 1972-73 | (D4) | 1 | 18.11.72 | **Stockport County** (D4) | A | L | 0-1 | |

| | | | | | | | | |
|---|---|---|---|---|---|---|---|---|
| 1973-74 | (D4) | 1 | 24.11.73 | **Bradford City** (D4) | A | L | 0-2 | |
| 1974-75 | (D4) | 1 | 23.11.74 | **Darlington** (D4) | A | L | 0-1 | |
| 1975-76 | (D4) | 1 | 22.11.75 | **Rochdale** (D4) | H | D | 1-1 | Heslop |
| | | 1r | 25.11.75 | **Rochdale** | A | L | 1-2aet | Geidmintis |
| 1976-77 | (D4) | 1 | 20.11.76 | **Bury** (D3) | A | L | 0-6 | |
| 1977-78 | (NPL) | 1 | 26.11.77 | **Grimsby Town** (D4) | H | L | 0-2 | |
| 1978-79 | (NPL) | 1 | 25.11.78 | **Rotherham Utd** (D3) | A | L | 0-3 | |
| 1979-80 | (NPL) | 1 | 24.11.79 | **Chester** (D3) | A | L | 1-5 | Diamond |
| 1980-81 | (NPL) | 1 | 22.11.80 | **Carlisle Utd** (D3) | H | D | 0-0 | |
| | | 1r | 01.12.80 | **Carlisle Utd** | A | L | 1-4 | Gill |
| 1981-82 | (NPL) | 1 | 21.11.81 | **Huddersfield Town** (D3) | H | D | 1-1 | Reach |
| | | 1r | 24.11.81 | **Huddersfield Town** | A | L | 0-5 | |
| 1982-83 | (NPL) | 1 | 20.11.82 | **Doncaster Rovers** (D3) | H | L | 1-2 | Gill |

## WORKSOP TOWN

*Formed 1880. First entered FA Cup: 1893-94. League clubs beaten: Nelson, Grimsby Town, Chesterfield, Coventry City, Bradford City. Members of the Northern Premier League.*

| | | | | | | | | |
|---|---|---|---|---|---|---|---|---|
| 1907-08 | (ML) | 1 | 11.01.08 | **Chelsea** (D1) | A | L | 1-9 | Richardson |
| 1921-22 | (ML) | | | 6q Nelson (3N) (H) 2-1 | | | | |
| | | 1 | 07.01.22 | **Southend Utd** (3S) | H | L | 1-2 | Lawrie |
| 1922-23 | (ML) | | | 5q Grimsby Town (3N) (A) 2-0; 6q Chesterfield (3N) H 1-0 | | | | |
| | | 1 | 13.01.23 | **Tottenham Hotspur** (D1) | A | D | 0-0 | |
| | | 1r | 15.01.23 | **Tottenham Hotspur** | H | L | 0-9 | |
| | | | | *played at White Hart Lane* | | | | |
| 1925-26 | (ML) | 1 | 28.11.25 | **Coventry City** (3N) | H | W | 1-0 | Spink |
| | | 2 | 12.12.25 | **Chesterfield** (3N) | H | L | 1-2 | Tremelling |
| 1926-27 | (ML) | 1 | 27.11.26 | **York City** (ML) | A | - | 1-1ab | Tremelling |
| | | | | *abandoned after 58 minutes – fog* | | | | |
| | | 1 | 01.12.26 | **York City** (ML) | A | L | 1-4 | Boulton |
| 1955-56 | (ML) | 1 | 19.11.55 | **Skegness Town** (Lincs) | A | W | 4-0 | Rooth, Dean, Scotson og, Rhodes |
| | | 2 | 10.12.55 | **Bradford City** (3N) | A | D | 2-2 | Mosby, McCall |
| | | 2r | 15.12.55 | **Bradford City** | H | W | 1-0 | Mosby |
| | | 3 | 07.01.56 | **Swindon Town** (3S) | A | L | 0-1 | |
| 1961-62 | (ML) | 1 | 04.11.61 | **Workington** (D4) | A | L | 0-2 | |
| 1978-79 | (NPL) | 1 | 25.11.78 | **Barnsley** (D4) | A | L | 1-5 | Woods |
| 2001-02 | (NPL) | 1 | 17.11.01 | **Bournemouth** (D2) | A | L | 0-3 | |

## WORTHING

*Formed 1886. First entered FA Cup: 1899-1900. Members of the Isthmian League.*

| | | | | | | | | |
|---|---|---|---|---|---|---|---|---|
| 1936-37 | (SCL) | 1 | 28.11.36 | **Yeovil & Petters Utd** (SL) | A | L | 3-4 | Ockenden, Thorlby, Varndell |
| 1982-83 | (IL) | 1 | 20.11.82 | **Dartford** (SL) | H | W | 2-1 | Lelliot, Cornwell |
| | | 2 | 11.12.82 | **Oxford Utd** (D3) | A | L | 0-4 | |
| 1994-95 | (IL) | 1 | 12.11.94 | **Bournemouth** (D2) | A | L | 1-3 | Mintram |
| 1999-00 | (IL) | 1 | 30.10.99 | **Rotherham Utd** (D3) | A | L | 0-3 | |

## WREXHAM

*Formed 1873 (the oldest club in Wales). FA Cup best performance: 6th round, 1974, 1978, 1997. Welsh FA Cup winners: 23 times; Runners-up 22 times. Were the first winners of the Welsh Cup in 1878. Record FA Cup win: 9-1v Wellington St Georges, preliminary round, 1910-11; In Competition Proper: 6-0 v Gateshead Utd, 1st round, 20.11.1976; 6-0 v Charlton, 3rd round, 5.1.1980. Record FA Cup defeat: 1-9 v Wolverhampton W, 3rd round, 10.01.1931.*

| | | | | | | | | |
|---|---|---|---|---|---|---|---|---|
| 1888-89 | | | | 1q Davenham (H)3-0; 2q Northwich V (H) 3-2; 3q Chirk (H) 2-1aet; 4q Chester (A) 3-2 | | | | |
| | | 1 | 02.02.89 | **Swifts** | A | L | 1-3 | Wilding |
| 1889-90 | | | | 2q Northwich V (A) 1-3 | | | | |
| 1890-91 | (TC) | | | 2q Nantwich Town (H) 2-3 | | | | |
| 1891-92 | (TC) | | | 2q Chester (A) 4-2; 3q Crewe Alexandra (A) 1-3 | | | | |
| 1892-93 | (TC) | | | 1q Liverpool Caledonians (A) 1-7 | | | | |
| 1893-94 | (TC) | | | 1q Barnton Rovers (A) 4-3aet; 2q Nantwich Town (A) 3-2; 3q Stockport Co (A) 2-3 | | | | |
| 1894-95 | (TC) | | | 1q Stalybridge Rovers (A) 3-2; 2q Macclesfield (H) 7-1; 3q Glossop (H) 1-2 | | | | |
| 1895-96 | (TC) | | | 1q Newtown (H) 3-1; 2q Crewe Alexandra (H) 3-3aet; 2qr Crewe Alex (A) 2-5 | | | | |
| 1896-97 | (TC) | | | 1q Rock Ferry (H) 0-4 | | | | |

| | | | | | | | | |
|---|---|---|---|---|---|---|---|---|
| 1897-98 | (TC) | | | 1q Warrington St Elphins (A) 3-0; 2q Chirk (A) 2-2; 2qr Chirk (H) 2-0; 3q Crewe Alex (A) 1-4 | | | | |
| 1898-99 | (TC) | | | 1q Chester (H) 3-2; 2q South Liverpool (A) 2-4 | | | | |
| 1899-00 | (TC) | | | 2q Llandudno Swifts (A) 2-1; 3q Dudley Town (H) 3-2; 4q Small Heath (A) 1-6 | | | | |
| 1900-01 | (TC) | | | 3q Stockport County (A) 2-6 | | | | |
| 1901-02 | (TC) | | | 2q Chirk (A) 2-0; 3q Oswestry Utd (A) 2-1; 4q PortVale (H) 2-1ab; 4qr Port Vale (H) 0-0; 4q 2r Port Vale (A) 1-3 | | | | |
| 1902-03 | (TC) | | | 3q Nantwich Town (H) 3-0; 4q Glossop (A) 0-4 | | | | |
| 1903-04 | (TC) | | | 2q Oswestry Utd (A) 0-2 | | | | |
| 1904-05 | (TC) | | | 3q Crewe Alexandra (A) 3-0; 4q Earlestown (A) 2-0; 5q Stockport County (A) 0-4 | | | | |
| 1905-06 | (BDL) | | | P Rhyl (H) 1-4 | | | | |
| 1906-07 | (BDL) | | | P Rhyl (H) 7-0; 1q Tranmere Rovers (H) 2-1; 2q Oswestry Utd (H) 3-1; 3q Whitchurch (H) 3-2; 4q Kidderminster (A)1-2 | | | | |
| 1907-08 | (BDL) | | | 1q Oswestry Utd (H) 0-1 | | | | |
| 1908-09 | (BDL) | | | P Welshpool (H) 6-1; 1q Whitchurch (A) 3-0; 2q Nantwich Town (A) 4-2; 3q Chester (A) 3-1; 4q Hednesford Town (A) 2-1; 5q Oxford City (H) 7-0 | | | | |
| | | 1 | 16.01.09 | **Exeter City** (SL) | H | D | 1-1 | Smith |
| | | 1r | 20.01.09 | **Exeter City** | A | L | 1-2 | Rankin |
| 1909-10 | (BDL) | | | 4q Coventry City (A) 0-3 | | | | |
| 1910-11 | (BDL) | | | P Wellington St Georges (H) 9-1; 1q Chester (A )0-3 | | | | |
| 1911-12 | (BDL) | | | P Harrowby (A) 1-1; Pr Harrowby walkover; 1q Witton Albion (H) 4-2; 2q South Liverpool (H) 4-3; 3q Chester (H) 1-4 | | | | |
| 1912-13 | (BDL) | | | P Chester (H) 2-0; 1q Wellington Town (A) 1-1; 1qr Wellington Town (H) 2-2; 1q 2r Wellington Town (A) 3-0; 2q Northwich V (A) 1-5 | | | | |
| 1913-14 | (BDL) | | | P Witton Albion (A) 5-0; 1q Connah's Quay (A) 2-1; 2q South Liverpool (H) 1-1; 2qr South Liverpool (A) 0-1 | | | | |
| 1914-15 | (BDL) | | | P South Liverpool (H) 2-1; 1q Skelmersdale Utd (H) 2-1; 2q Nantwich Town (H) 4-2; 3q Tranmere Rovers (H) 1-1; 3qr Tranmere R (A) 1-0; 4q Walsall (A) 1-2 | | | | |
| 1919-20 | (BDL) | | | 1q Marlborough OB (H) 8-0; 2q Crewe Alexandra (A) 3-3; 2qr Crewe Alex (H) 0-1 | | | | |
| 1920-21 | (BDL) | | | P Northwich V (H) 3-0; 1q Prescott W (H)7-0; 2q Presscot (H) 2-0; 3q Buckley Utd (A) 0-1 | | | | |
| 1921-22 | (3N) | | | 4q Burton All Saints (H) 4-0; 5q Crewe Alexandra (H) 5-0; 6q Newport County (H) 0-0; 6qr Newport County (A) 0-3 | | | | |
| 1922-23 | (3N) | | | 5q Port Vale (A) 2-0; 6q Hartlepools Utd (H) 1-0 | | | | |
| | | 1 | 13.01.23 | **Bristol City** (3S) | A | L | 1-5 | Jackson |
| 1923-24 | (3N) | | | 5q Port Vale (H) 5-1; 6q Accrington Stanley (A) 0-1 | | | | |
| 1924-25 | (3N) | | | 5q Barrow (A) 0-4 | | | | |
| 1925-26 | (3N) | 1 | 28.11.25 | **Accrington Stanley** (3N) | A | L | 0-4 | |
| 1926-27 | (3N) | 1 | 27.11.26 | **New Brighton** (3N) | H | D | 1-1 | Miles |
| | | 1r | 01.12.26 | **New Brighton** | | D | 2-2 | Smith, Regan |
| | | 1 2r | 06.12.26 | **New Brighton** | | W | 3-1 | Longmuir 2, Smith |
| | | | | *played at Anfield* | | | | |
| | | 2 | 11.12.26 | **Rhyl (Welsh)** | A | L | 1-3 | Griffiths |
| 1927-28 | (3N) | 1 | 26.11.27 | **Durham City** (3N) | A | D | 1-1 | Gunson |
| | | 1r | 30.11.27 | **Durham City** | H | W | 4-0 | Gunson 2, Woodhouse 2 |
| | | 2 | 10.12.27 | **Carlisle Utd** (NEL) | H | W | 1-0 | C Smith |
| | | 3 | 14.01.28 | **Swansea Town** (D2) | H | W | 2-1 | Gunson, Longmuir |
| | | 4 | 28.01.28 | **Birmingham** (D1) | H | L | 1-3 | Thomson |
| 1928-29 | (3N) | 1 | 24.11.28 | **Carlisle Utd** (3N) | H | L | 0-1 | |
| 1929-30 | (3N) | 1 | 30.11.29 | **South Shields** (3N) | A | W | 4-2 | Mays 2, Woodhouse, Bamford |
| | | 2 | 14.12.29 | **Manchester Central** (LC) | A | W | 1-0 | Mays |
| | | 3 | 11.01.30 | **WBA** (D2) | H | W | 1-0 | Mays |
| | | 4 | 25.01.30 | **Bradford City** (D2) | H | D | 0-0 | |
| | | 4r | 27.01.30 | **Bradford City** | A | L | 1-2 | Bamford |
| 1930-31 | (3N) | 1 | 29.11.30 | **Wigan Borough** (3N) | H | W | 2-0 | Taylor, Mustard |
| | | 2 | 13.12.30 | **Wellington Town** (BDL) | A | W | 4-2 | Bamford 3, Lewis |
| | | 3 | 10.01.31 | **Wolverhampton W** (D2) | A | L | 1-9 | Bamford |
| 1931-32 | (3N) | 1 | 28.11.31 | **Gateshead AFC** (3N) | A | L | 2-3 | Lewis, Bamford |
| 1932-33 | (3N) | 1 | 26.11.32 | **Spennymoor Utd** (NEL) | H | W | 3-0 | Frewin, Bamford 2 |
| | | 2 | 10.12.32 | **Brighton** (3S) | A | D | 0-0 | |
| | | 2r | 14.12.32 | **Brighton** | H | L | 2-3 | Bamford, Frewin |

| | | | | | | | | |
|---|---|---|---|---|---|---|---|---|
| 1933-34 (3N) | 1 | 25.11.33 | **Carlisle Utd** (3N) | A | L | 1-2 | Bryant |
| 1934-35 (3N) | 1 | 24.11.34 | **Rochdale** (3N) | H | W | 4-1 | Findlay, Fryer 2, Rogers |
| | 2 | 08.12.34 | **Reading** (3S) | A | L | 0-3 | |
| 1935-36 (3N) | 1 | 30.11.35 | **Barrow** (3N) | A | L | 1-4 | Fryer |
| 1936-37 (3N) | 1 | 28.11.36 | **Blyth Spartans** (NEL) | A | W | 2-0 | Jones, Burgon |
| | 2 | 12.12.36 | **Gillingham** (3S) | H | W | 2-0 | Lapham, Jones |
| | 3 | 16.01.37 | **Manchester City** (D1) | H | L | 1-3 | Burgon |
| 1937-38 (3N) | 1 | 27.11.37 | **Oldham Athletic** (3N) | H | W | 2-1 | Burgon, Fraser |
| | 2 | 11.12.37 | **Bradford City** (3N) | H | L | 1-2 | Burditt |
| 1938-39 (3N) | 1 | 26.11.38 | **Port Vale** (3S) | H | L | 1-2 | Burditt |
| 1945-46 (3N) | 1 1L | 17.11.45 | **Crewe Alexandra** (3N) | A | L | 2-4 | Lloyd 2 |
| | 1 2L | 24.11.45 | **Crewe Alexandra** | H | W | 3-0 | Hayward, Wainwright, Jones |
| | 2 1L | 08.12.45 | **Shrewsbury Town** (ML) | A | W | 1-0 | Hewitt |
| | 2 2L | 15.12.45 | **Shrewsbury Town** | H | D | 1-1 | Heywood |
| | 3 1L | 05.01.46 | **Blackpool** (D1) | H | L | 1-4 | Haycock |
| | 3 2L | 09.01.46 | **Blackpool** | A | L | 1-4 | McLarty |
| 1946-47 (3N) | 1 | 30.11.46 | **Marine** (LC) | H | W | 5-0 | Boothway 4, Brown |
| | 2 | 14.12.46 | **Lincoln City** (3N) | A | D | 1-1 | McLarty |
| | 2r | 18.12.46 | **Lincoln City** | H | D | 3-3aet | Boothway 2, McLarty |
| | 2 2r | 23.12.46 | **Lincoln City** *played at Maine Road* | | L | 1-2 | Gardiner |
| 1947-48 (3N) | 1 | 29.11.47 | **Halifax Town** (3N) | H | W | 5-0 | Beynon 2, Tunnicliffe 2, Jones |
| | 2 | 13.12.47 | **Colchester Utd** (SL) | A | L | 0-1 | |
| 1948-49 (3N) | 1 | 27.11.48 | **Oldham Athletic** (3N) | H | L | 0-3 | |
| 1949-50 (3N) | 1 | 26.11.49 | **Grantham Town** (ML) | H | W | 4-1 | Grainger, Sharp, Tunnicliffe, Booth |
| | 2 | 10.12.49 | **Southend Utd** (3S) | H | D | 2-2 | Tunnicliffe 2 |
| | 2r | 14.12.49 | **Southend Utd** | A | L | 0-2 | |
| 1950-51 (3N) | 1 | 25.11.50 | **Accrington Stanley** (3N) | H | W | 1-0 | Beynon |
| | 2 | 09.12.50 | **Bristol City** (3S) | A | L | 1-2 | Lawrence |
| 1951-52 (3N) | 1 | 24.11.51 | **Halifax Town** (3N) | H | W | 3-0 | Hope 2, Bannan |
| | 2 | 15.12.51 | **Leyton Orient** (3S) | H | D | 1-1 | Tunnicliffe |
| | 2r | 19.12.51 | **Leyton Orient** | A | L | 2-3 | Lawrence, Bannan |
| 1952-53 (3N) | 1 | 22.11.52 | **Beighton MW** (YL) *played at Millmoor, Rotherham* | A | W | 3-0 | Hughes 2, Bannan |
| | 2 | 06.12.52 | **Great Yarmouth T** (ECL) | A | W | 2-1 | Bannan 2 |
| | 3 | 10.01.53 | **Stoke City** (D1) | A | L | 1-2 | Tilston |
| 1953-54 (3N) | 1 | 21.11.53 | **Horden Coll Wel** (NEL) | A | W | 1-0 | Hughes |
| | 2 | 12.12.53 | **Brighton** (3S) | H | D | 1-1aet | Bannan |
| | 2r | 16.12.53 | **Brighton** | A | D | 1-1aet | Wright |
| | 2 2r | 21.12.53 | **Brighton** *played at Selhurst Park* | | W | 3-1 | Bannan, Richards, Hewitt |
| | 3 | 09.01.54 | **Scunthorpe Utd** (3N) | H | D | 3-3 | Tapscott, Bannon 2 |
| | 3r | 14.01.54 | **Scunthorpe Utd** | A | L | 1-3 | Hubbard og |
| 1954-55 (3N) | 1 | 20.11.54 | **Netherfield** (LC) | A | D | 3-3 | Hewitt 2, Green |
| | 1r | 24.11.54 | **Netherfield** | H | W | 4-0 | Hewitt, Jackson, Betts 2 |
| | 2 | 11.12.54 | **Walsall** (3S) | H | L | 1-2 | D Jackson |
| 1955-56 (3N) | 1 | 19.11.55 | **Accrington Stanley** (3N) | A | L | 1-3 | Richards (p) |
| 1956-57 (3N) | 1 | 17.11.56 | **Crewe Alexandra** (3N) | A | D | 2-2 | Thompson 2 |
| | 1r | 20.11.56 | **Crewe Alexandra** | H | W | 2-1 | Thompson, Hewitt |
| | 2 | 08.12.56 | **Scunthorpe Utd** (3N) | A | D | 0-0 | |
| | 2r | 12.12.56 | **Scunthorpe Utd** | H | W | 6-2aet | Anderson, Thompson 2, Hewitt, G Jones, D Jones |
| | 3 | 05.01.57 | **Reading** (3S) | H | D | 1-1 | B Evans |
| | 3r | 09.01.57 | **Reading** | A | W | 2-1 | Anderson, Hewitt |
| | 4 | 26.01.57 | **Manchester Utd** (D1) | H | L | 0-5 | |
| 1957-58 (3N) | 1 | 16.11.57 | **Accrington Stanley** (3N) | H | L | 0-1 | |
| 1958-59 (D3) | 1 | 15.11.58 | **Darlington** (D4) | H | L | 1-2 | Murray |
| 1959-60 (D3) | 1 | 14.11.59 | **Blyth Spartans** (ML) | H | W | 2-1 | Hewitt 2 |
| | 2 | 05.12.59 | **Grimsby Town** (D3) | A | W | 3-2 | Weston 2, Jobling og |
| | 3 | 09.01.60 | **Leicester City** (D1) | H | L | 1-2 | Weston |
| 1960-61 (D4) | 1 | 05.11.60 | **Bangor City** (CC) | A | L | 0-1 | |
| 1961-62 (D4) | 1 | 04.11.61 | **Barrow** (D4) | H | W | 3-2 | Davies, Metcalf 2 |

| | | | | | | | |
|---|---|---|---|---|---|---|---|
| | 2 | 25.11.61 | **Rochdale** (D4) | A | W | 2-1 | Metcalf, Bennion |
| | 3 | 10.01.62 | **Norwich City** (D2) | A | L | 1-3 | Davies |
| 1962-63 (D3) | 1 | 03.11.62 | **Southport** (D4) | A | D | 1-1 | Whitehouse |
| | 1r | 07.11.62 | **Southport** | H | W | 3-2 | R Barnes 2, Whitehouse |
| | 2 | 24.11.62 | **Barrow** (D4) | H | W | 5-2 | Whitehouse 3, Griffiths, R Barnes |
| | 3 | 09.01.63 | **Liverpool** (D1) | H | L | 0-3 | |
| 1963-64 (D3) | 1 | 16.11.63 | **Altrincham** (CC) | A | - | 2-1ab | Metcalfe, Griffiths |
| | | | *abandoned after 76 minutes – fog* | | | | |
| | 1 | 20.11.63 | **Altrincham** | A | D | 0-0 | |
| | 1r | 26.11.63 | **Altrincham** | H | W | 3-0 | T Jones, Metcalfe 2 |
| | 2 | 07.12.63 | **Hull City** (D3) | H | L | 0-2 | |
| 1964-65 (D4) | 1 | 14.11.64 | **Macclesfield T** (CC) | A | W | 2-1 | McMillan 2 |
| | 2 | 05.12.64 | **Southport** (D4) | H | L | 2-3 | K Barnes (p), King |
| 1965-66 (D4) | 1 | 13.11.65 | **South Liverpool** (LC) | H | W | 4-1 | King 3 (1p), Jones |
| | 2 | 04.12.65 | **Hartlepools Utd** (D4) | A | L | 0-2 | |
| 1966-67 (D4) | 1 | 26.11.66 | **Chesterfield** (D4) | H | W | 3-2 | Garrick, Lloyd, Oldfield |
| | 2 | 07.01.67 | **Shrewsbury Town** (D3) | A | L | 1-5 | McMillan |
| 1967-68 (D4) | 1 | 09.12.67 | **Bradford City** (D4) | A | L | 1-7 | Weston |
| 1968-69 (D4) | 1 | 16.11.68 | **Oldham Athletic** (D3) | H | W | 4-2 | Griffiths 2, Moir, Kinsey |
| | 2 | 07.12.68 | **Chesterfield** (D4) | A | L | 1-2 | Charnley |
| 1969-70 (D4) | 1 | 15.11.69 | **Spennymoor Utd** (NL) | A | W | 4-1 | Ingle, Griffiths, Kinsey, Smith |
| | 2 | 06.12.69 | **Hartlepool** (D4) | A | W | 1-0 | Evans |
| | 3 | 03.01.70 | **Norwich City** (D2) | A | W | 2-1 | May, Griffiths |
| | 4 | 24.01.70 | **Liverpool** (D1) | A | L | 1-3 | R.Smith |
| 1970-71 (D3) | 1 | 21.11.70 | **Mansfield Town** (D3) | A | L | 0-2 | |
| 1971-72 (D3) | 1 | 20.11.71 | **Bradford City** (D3) | H | W | 5-1 | Moir, Provan, Whittle 2, McBurney |
| | 2 | 11.12.71 | **Wigan Athletic** (NPL) | H | W | 4-0 | Moir, Kinsey 2, Whittle |
| | 3 | 15.01.72 | **Orient** (D2) | A | L | 0-3 | |
| 1972-73 (D3) | 1 | 18.11.72 | **Darlington** (D4) | A | D | 1-1 | Tinnion |
| | 1r | 22.11.72 | **Darlington** | H | W | 5-0 | Smallman 3, Thomas, Whittle |
| | 2 | 09.12.72 | **Port Vale** (D3) | A | L | 0-1 | |
| 1973-74 (D3) | 1 | 24.11.73 | **Shrewsbury Town** (D3) | H | D | 1-1 | Tinnion |
| | 1r | 27.11.73 | **Shrewsbury Town** | A | W | 1-0 | Davies |
| | 2 | 15.12.73 | **Rotherham Utd** (D4) | H | W | 3-0 | Davies 2, Wilkinson og |
| | 3 | 05.01.74 | **Crystal Palace** (D2) | A | W | 2-0 | Sutton, Smallman |
| | 4 | 26.01.74 | **Middlesbrough** (D2) | H | W | 1-0 | Smallman |
| | 5 | 16.02.74 | **Southampton** (D1) | A | W | 1-0 | Smallman |
| | 6 | 09.03.74 | **Burnley** (D1) | A | L | 0-1 | |
| 1974-75 (D3) | 1 | 23.11.74 | **Mansfield Town** (D4) | A | L | 1-3 | Whittle |
| 1975-76 (D3) | 1 | 22.11.75 | **Mansfield Town** (D3) | A | D | 1-1 | Madden og |
| | 1r | 24.11.75 | **Mansfield Town** | H | D | 1-1aet | Ashcroft |
| | 12r | 08.12.75 | **Mansfield Town** | | L | 1-2 | Dwyer |
| | | | *played at Villa Park* | | | | |
| 1976-77 (D3) | 1 | 20.11.76 | **Gateshead Utd** (NPL) | H | W | 6-0 | Ashcroft 2, Lees, Shinton 3 (1p) |
| | 2 | 11.12.76 | **Goole Town** (NPL) | H | D | 1-1 | Whittle |
| | 2r | 14.12.76 | **Goole Town** | A | W | 1-0 | Shinton |
| | 3 | 08.01.77 | **Sunderland** (D1) | A | D | 2-2 | Ashcroft, Whittle |
| | 3r | 12.01.77 | **Sunderland** | H | W | 1-0 | Ashcroft |
| | 4 | 29.01.77 | **Cardiff City** (D2) | A | L | 2-3 | Whittle, Ashcroft |
| 1977-78 (D3) | 1 | 26.11.77 | **Burton Albion** (SL) | H | W | 2-0 | Shinton, McNeil |
| | 2 | 17.12.77 | **Preston North End** (D3) | A | W | 2-0 | Davis, McNeil |
| | 3 | 07.01.78 | **Bristol City** (D1) | A | D | 4-4 | Shinton 2, Merrick og, McNeil |
| | 3r | 09.01.78 | **Bristol City** | H | W | 3-0 | Thomas, McNeil, Whittle |
| | 4 | 28.01.78 | **Newcastle Utd** (D1) | A | D | 2-2 | McNeil 2 |
| | 4r | 06.02.78 | **Newcastle Utd** | H | W | 4-1 | McNeil 2, Shinton, Cartwright |
| | 5 | 18.02.78 | **Blyth Spartans** (NL) | H | D | 1-1 | McNeil |
| | 5r | 27.02.78 | **Blyth Spartans** | | W | 2-1 | Whittle (p), McNeil |
| | | | *played at St James' Park* | | | | |
| | 6 | 11.03.78 | **Arsenal** (D1) | H | L | 2-3 | McNeil, Sutton |
| 1978-79 (D2) | 3 | 01.02.79 | **Stockport County** (D4) | H | W | 6-2 | Cegielski, McNeil 2, Lyons, Cartwright, Shinton |
| | 4 | 12.02.79 | **Tottenham Hotspur** (D1) | A | D | 3-3 | Shinton, Lyons 2 (1p) |

| | | | | | | | | |
|---|---|---|---|---|---|---|---|---|
| | | 4r | 21.02.79 | **Tottenham Hotspur** | H | L | 2-3aet | Davis, McNeil |
| 1979-80 | (D2) | 3 | 05.01.80 | **Charlton Athletic** (D2) | H | W | 6-0 | Edwards, Vinter 3, McNeil 2 |
| | | 4 | 26.01.80 | **Carlisle Utd** (D3) | A | D | 0-0 | |
| | | 4r | 29.01.80 | **Carlisle Utd** | H | W | 3-1 | McNeil 2, Jones |
| | | 5 | 16.02.80 | **Everton** (D1) | A | L | 2-5 | Vinter |
| 1980-81 | (D2) | 3 | 03.01.81 | **West Ham Utd** (D2) | A | D | 1-1 | Davis |
| | | 3r | 06.01.81 | **West Ham Utd** | H | D | 0-0aet | |
| | | 3 2r | 19.01.81 | **West Ham Utd** | H | W | 1-0aet | McNeil |
| | | 4 | 24.01.81 | **Wimbledon** (D4) | H | W | 2-1 | Fox, McNeil |
| | | 5 | 14.02.81 | **Wolverhampton W** (D1) | A | L | 1-3 | Fox |
| 1981-82 | (D2) | 3 | 02.01.82 | **Nottingham Forest** (D1) | A | W | 3-1 | Dowman, Vinter, McNeil |
| | | 4 | 23.01.82 | **Chelsea** (D2) | A | D | 0-0 | |
| | | 4r | 26.01.82 | **Chelsea** | H | D | 1-1aet | McNeil |
| | | 4 2r | 01.02.82 | **Chelsea** | H | L | 1-2 | Vinter |
| 1982-83 | (D3) | 1 | 20.11.82 | **Holbeach Utd** (UCL) | A | W | 4-0 | Keay, Gregory, Savage, Muldoon |
| | | | | *played at London Road, Peterborough* | | | | |
| | | 2 | 11.12.82 | **Worcester City** (APL) | A | L | 1-2 | Hunt |
| 1983-84 | (D4) | 1 | 19.11.83 | **Sheffield Utd** (D3) | H | L | 1-5 | Coleman |
| 1984-85 | (D4) | 1 | 17.11.84 | **Wigan Athletic** (D3) | H | L | 0-2 | |
| 1985-86 | (D4) | 1 | 16.11.85 | **Bolton Wanderers** (D3) | H | W | 3-1 | Keay, Hencher, Cunnington |
| | | 2 | 07.12.85 | **Notts County** (D3) | A | D | 2-2 | Gregory, Horne |
| | | 2r | 10.12.85 | **Notts County** | H | L | 0-3 | |
| 1986-87 | (D4) | 1 | 15.11.86 | **Hartlepool Utd** (D4) | H | W | 2-1 | Buxton, Charles |
| | | 2 | 06.12.86 | **Rochdale** (D4) | A | W | 4-1 | Steel, Massey 2, Horne |
| | | 3 | 10.01.87 | **Chester City** (D3) | H | L | 1-2 | Steel |
| 1987-88 | (D4) | 1 | 14.11.87 | **Rochdale** (D4) | A | W | 2-0 | Carter, Buxton |
| | | 2 | 05.12.87 | **Bolton Wanderers** (D4) | H | L | 1-2 | Hinnigan |
| 1988-89 | (D4) | 1 | 19.11.88 | **Runcorn** (Conf) | A | D | 2-2 | Bowden, Cooper |
| | | 1r | 22.11.88 | **Runcorn** | H | L | 2-3 | Kearns 2 |
| 1989-90 | (D4) | 1 | 18.11.89 | **Carlisle Utd** (D4) | A | L | 0-3 | |
| 1990-91 | (D4) | 1 | 17.11.90 | **Halifax Town** (D4) | A | L | 2-3 | Preece 2 |
| 1991-92 | (D4) | 1 | 16.11.91 | **Winsford Utd** (NPL) | H | W | 5-2 | Connolly, Watkin 3, Thomas |
| | | 2 | 07.12.91 | **Telford Utd** (Conf) | A | W | 1-0 | Watkin |
| | | 3 | 04.01.92 | **Arsenal** (D1) | H | W | 2-1 | Thomas, Watkin |
| | | 4 | 25.01.92 | **West Ham Utd** (D1) | A | D | 2-2 | Phillips, L Jones |
| | | 4r | 04.02.92 | **West Ham Utd** | H | L | 0-1 | |
| 1992-93 | (D3) | 1 | 14.11.92 | **Crewe Alexandra** (D3) | A | L | 1-6 | Bennett |
| 1993-94 | (D2) | 1 | 13.11.93 | **Walsall** (D3) | H | D | 1-1 | Watkin |
| | | 1r | 23.11.93 | **Walsall** | A | L | 0-2 | |
| 1994-95 | (D2) | 1 | 12.11.94 | **Stockport County** (D2) | H | W | 1-0 | Watkin |
| | | 2 | 03.12.94 | **Rotherham Utd** (D2) | H | W | 5-2 | Connolly 2, Bennett, Hughes, Watkin |
| | | 3 | 07.01.95 | **Ipswich Town** (PL) | H | W | 2-1 | Durkan, Bennett (p) |
| | | 4 | 28.01.95 | **Manchester Utd** (PL) | A | L | 2-5 | Durkan, Cross |
| 1995-96 | (D2) | 1 | 11.11.95 | **Hull City** (D2) | A | D | 0-0 | |
| | | 1r | 21.11.95 | **Hull City** | H | D | 0-0aet | |
| | | | | *Wrexham won 3-1 on penalties* | | | | |
| | | 2 | 02.12.95 | **Chesterfield** (D2) | H | W | 3-2 | Watkin, Hunter, Connolly (p) |
| | | 3 | 06.01.96 | **Peterborough Utd** (D2) | A | L | 0-1 | |
| 1996-97 | (D2) | 1 | 16.11.96 | **Colwyn Bay** (NPL) | A | D | 1-1 | Hughes |
| | | 1r | 26.11.96 | **Colwyn Bay** | H | W | 2-0 | Hughes 2 |
| | | 2 | 07.12.96 | **Scunthorpe Utd** (D3) | H | D | 2-2 | Morris, Watkin |
| | | 2r | 17.12.96 | **Scunthorpe Utd** | A | W | 3-2aet | Hughes, Morris, Watkin (p) |
| | | 3 | 04.01.97 | **West Ham Utd** (PL) | H | D | 1-1 | Hughes |
| | | 3r | 25.01.97 | **West Ham Utd** | A | W | 1-0 | Russell |
| | | 4 | 04.02.97 | **Peterborough Utd** (D2) | A | W | 4-2 | Ward, Watkin, Russell 2 |
| | | 5 | 15.02.97 | **Birmingham City** (D1) | A | W | 3-1 | Hughes, Humes, Connolly |
| | | 6 | 09.03.97 | **Chesterfield** (D2) | A | L | 0-1 | |
| 1997-98 | (D2) | 1 | 15.11.97 | **Rochdale** (D3) | A | W | 2-0 | N Roberts, Connolly |
| | | 2 | 05.12.97 | **Chester City** (D3) | A | W | 2-0 | Connolly 2 |
| | | 3 | 04.01.98 | **Wimbledon** (PL) | A | D | 0-0 | |
| | | 3r | 13.01.98 | **Wimbledon** | H | L | 2-3 | Connolly 2 |

| | | | | | | | |
|---|---|---|---|---|---|---|---|
| 1998-99 (D2) | 1 | 14.11.98 | **Peterborough Utd** (D3) | H | W | 1-0 | Brammer |
| | 2 | 05.12.98 | **York City** (D2) | H | W | 2-1 | Roberts (p), Connolly |
| | 3 | 02.01.99 | **Scunthorpe Utd** (D3) | H | W | 4-3 | Logan og, Connolly 3 |
| | 4 | 23.01.99 | **Huddersfield Town** (D1) | H | D | 1-1 | Connolly |
| | 4r | 03.02.99 | **Huddersfield Town** | A | L | 1-2 | Russell |
| 1999-00 (D2) | 1 | 30.10.99 | **Kettering Town** (Conf) | H | D | 1-1 | N Roberts (p) |
| | 1r | 10.11.99 | **Kettering Town** | A | W | 2-0 | S Roberts, Williams |
| | 2 | 20.11.99 | **Rochdale** (D3) | H | W | 2-1 | N Roberts, Faulconbridge |
| | 3 | 11.12.99 | **Middlesbrough** (PL) | H | W | 2-1 | Gibson, Ferguson |
| | 4 | 08.01.00 | **Cambridge Utd** (D2) | H | L | 1-2 | Connolly |
| 2000-01 (D2) | 1 | 18.11.00 | **Rotherham Utd** (D2) | H | L | 0-1 | |
| 2001-02 (D2) | 1 | 18.11.01 | **Hereford Utd** (Conf) | A | L | 0-1 | |
| 2002-03 (D3) | 1 | 16.11.02 | **Darlington** (D3) | H | L | 0-2 | |

# WREXHAM OLYMPIC

*Entered FA Cup: 1883-84 – 1887-88, a separate club from Wrexham FC.*

| | | | | | | | |
|---|---|---|---|---|---|---|---|
| 1883-84 | 1 | | Liverpool Ramblers | | | - | |
| | | | *Liverpool Ramblers scratched. Wrexham Olympic walkover* | | | | |
| | 2 | 01.12.83 | **Oswestry Town** | H | L | 3-4 | W Davies 2, AN Other |
| 1884-85 | 1 | 18.10.84 | **Goldenhill** | H | W | 1-0 | |
| | 2 | 29.11.84 | **Chirk** | A | L | 1-4 | |
| 1885-86 | 1 | 31.10.85 | **Leek** | A | L | 3-6 | |
| 1886-87 | 1 | 23.10.86 | **Crewe Alexandra** | H | L | 1-4 | T Roberts |
| 1887-88 | 1 | | bye | | | | |
| | 2 | 05.11.87 | **Davenham** | H | L | 1-2 | Groom |

# WYCOMBE WANDERERS

*Formed 1884. A separate club from the old High Wycombe which played in the FA Cup from 1873-78. First entered FA Cup: 1894-95. FA Cup best performance: Semi-finals 2001 (as a Second Division club). FA Amateur Cup winners: 1931. Runners-up: 1937. FA Trophy winners: 1991, 1993. Promoted to the Football League: 1993. League clubs beaten as a Non-League club: Newport County, Bournemouth, Colchester United.*

| | | | | | | | |
|---|---|---|---|---|---|---|---|
| 1932-33 (IL) | 1 | 26.11.32 | **Gillingham** (3S) | A | D | 1-1 | Simmons |
| | 1r | 30.11.32 | **Gillingham** | H | L | 2-4 | Brain, Braisher |
| 1955-56 (IL) | 1 | 19.11.55 | **Burton Albion** (BDL) | H | L | 1-3 | Bates |
| 1957-58 (IL) | 1 | 16.11.57 | **Dorchester Town** (WL) | A | L | 2-3 | Rockell, Reardon |
| 1958-59 (IL) | 1 | 15.11.58 | **Northampton Town** (D4) | A | L | 0-2 | |
| 1959-60 (IL) | 1 | 14.11.59 | **Wisbech Town** (SL) | H | W | 4-2 | Trott 2, Bates, Rockell |
| | 2 | 05.12.59 | **Watford** (D4) | A | L | 1-5 | D Atkins |
| 1960-61 (IL) | 1 | 05.11.60 | **Kettering Town** (SL) | H | L | 1-2 | Thomas |
| 1961-62 (IL) | 1 | 04.11.61 | **Ashford Town** (SL) | H | D | 0-0 | |
| | 1r | 08.11.61 | **Ashford Town** | A | L | 0-3 | |
| 1962-63 (IL) | 1 | 03.11.62 | **Maidenhead** (CRN) | A | W | 3-0 | Hay, Horseman 2 |
| | 2 | 24.11.62 | **Gravesend & N** (SL) | A | L | 1-3 | Thomas (p) |
| 1965-66 (IL) | 1 | 13.11.65 | **Guildford City** (SL) | A | D | 2-2 | Samuels, Worley |
| | 1r | 17.11.65 | **Guildford City** | H | L | 0-1 | |
| 1966-67 (IL) | 1 | 26.11.66 | **Bedford Town** (SL) | H | D | 1-1 | Samuels |
| | 1r | 30.11.66 | **Bedford Town** | A | D | 3-3aet | Bates, Horeseman, Merrick |
| | 1 2r | 05.12.66 | **Bedford Town** | H | - | 1-1ab | Samuels |
| | | | *abandoned after 90 minutes – ground unfit* | | | | |
| | 1 3r | 08.12.66 | **Bedford Town** (SL) | A | L | 2-3 | Horseman 2 |
| 1970-71 (IL) | 1 | 21.11.70 | **Slough Town** (AL) | H | D | 1-1 | Horseman |
| | 1r | 24.11.70 | **Slough Town** | A | L | 0-1 | |
| 1973-74 (IL) | 1 | 24.11.73 | **Newport County** (D4) | H | W | 3-1 | Perrin 2, Evans |
| | 2 | 15.12.73 | **Peterborough Utd** (D4) | H | L | 1-3 | Pritchard |
| 1974-75 (IL) | 1 | 23.11.74 | **Cheltenham Town** (SL) | H | W | 3-1 | Horseman (p), Hallfield, Birdseye |
| | 2 | 14.12.74 | **Bournemouth** (D3) | H | D | 0-0 | |
| | 2r | 18.12.74 | **Bournemouth** | A | W | 2-1 | Horseman, Perrin |
| | 3 | 04.01.75 | **Middlesbrough** (D1) | H | D | 0-0 | |
| | 3r | 07.01.75 | **Middlesbrough** | A | L | 0-1 | |
| 1975-76 (IL) | 1 | 22.11.75 | **Bedford Town** (SL) | H | D | 0-0 | |
| | 1r | 24.11.75 | **Bedford Town** | A | D | 2-2aet | Delaney, Horseman |
| | 1 2r | 01.12.75 | **Bedford Town** | H | W | 2-1 | Bullock, Evans |

| | | | | | | | | |
|---|---|---|---|---|---|---|---|---|
| | | 2 | 13.12.75 | **Cardiff City** (D3) | A | L | 0-1 | |
| 1976-77 | (IL) | 1 | 20.11.76 | **Waterlooville** (SL) | A | W | 2-1 | Priestley, Kennedy |
| | | 2 | 11.12.76 | **Reading** (D3) | H | L | 1-2 | Pearson |
| 1977-78 | (IL) | 1 | 26.11.77 | **Minehead** (SL) | A | L | 0-2 | |
| 1978-79 | (IL) | 1 | 25.11.78 | **Maidstone Utd** (SL) | A | L | 0-1 | |
| 1979-80 | (IL) | 1 | 24.11.79 | **Croydon** (IL) | H | L | 0-3 | |
| 1980-81 | (IL) | 1 | 22.11.80 | **Bournemouth** (D4) | H | L | 0-3 | |
| 1981-82 | (IL) | 1 | 21.11.81 | **Hendon** (IL) | A | D | 1-1 | Vircavs |
| | | 1r | 24.11.81 | **Hendon** | H | W | 2-0 | Kennedy, Glynn |
| | | 2 | 15.12.81 | **Barnet** (APL) | A | L | 0-2 | |
| 1982-83 | (IL) | 1 | 20.11.82 | **Bristol Rovers** (D3) | A | L | 0-1 | |
| 1983-84 | (IL) | 1 | 19.11.83 | **Chelmsford City** (SL) | A | D | 0-0 | |
| | | 1r | 22.11.83 | **Chelmsford City** | H | L | 1-2 | Glynn |
| 1985-86 | (APL) | 1 | 16.11.85 | **Colchester Utd** (D4) | H | W | 2-0 | West, Read |
| | | 2 | 07.12.85 | **Chelmsford City** (SL) | H | W | 2-0 | Reed, McMahon |
| | | 3 | 04.01.86 | **York City** (D3) | A | L | 0-2 | |
| 1990-91 | (Conf) | 1 | 17.11.90 | **Boston Utd** (Conf) | A | D | 1-1 | Evans |
| | | 1r | 21.11.90 | **Boston Utd** | H | W | 4-0 | West 2, Ryan, Creaser |
| | | 2 | 12.12.90 | **Peterborough Utd** (D4) | H | D | 1-1 | Blackler |
| | | 2r | 17.12.90 | **Peterborough Utd** | A | L | 0-2 | |
| 1991-92 | (Conf) | 1 | 16.11.91 | **Kettering Town** (Conf) | A | D | 1-1 | Carroll |
| | | 1r | 27.11.91 | **Kettering Town** | H | L | 0-2 | |
| 1992-93 | (Conf) | 1 | 14.11.92 | **Merthyr Tydfil** (Conf) | H | W | 3-1 | Scott, Carroll, Stapleton |
| | | 2 | 06.12.92 | **WBA** (D2) | H | D | 2-2 | Creaser, Thompson |
| | | 2r | 15.12.92 | **WBA** | A | L | 0-1 | |
| 1993-94 | (D3) | 1 | 14.11.93 | **Bristol Rovers** (D2) | A | W | 2-1 | Langford, Carroll |
| | | 2 | 04.12.93 | **Cambridge Utd** (D2) | H | W | 1-0 | Hemmings |
| | | 3 | 08.01.94 | **Norwich City** (PL) | H | L | 0-2 | |
| 1994-95 | (D2) | 1 | 12.11.94 | **Chelmsford City** (SL) | H | W | 4-0 | Stapleton 2, Bell, Ryan |
| | | 2 | 03.12.94 | **Hitchin Town** (IL) | A | W | 5-0 | Garner 3, Ryan, Bell |
| | | 3 | 07.01.95 | **West Ham Utd** (PL) | H | L | 0-2 | |
| 1995-96 | (D2) | 1 | 13.11.95 | **Gillingham** (D3) | H | D | 1-1 | Patterson |
| | | 1r | 21.11.95 | **Gillingham** | A | L | 0-1 | |
| 1996-97 | (D2) | 1 | 16.11.96 | **Colchester Utd** (D3) | A | W | 2-1 | De Souza, Williams |
| | | 2 | 07.12.96 | **Barnet** (D3) | A | D | 3-3 | McGavin, Williams 2 |
| | | 2r | 17.12.96 | **Barnet** | H | W | 3-2 | Williams, Carroll, De Souza |
| | | 3 | 05.01.97 | **Bradford City** (D1) | H | L | 0-2 | |
| 1997-98 | (D2) | 1 | 15.11.97 | **Basingstoke Town** (IL) | H | D | 2-2 | Cornforth 2 (1p) |
| | | 1r | 25.11.97 | **Basingstoke Town** | A | D | 2-2aet | McGavin 2 |
| | | | | *Basingstoke won 5-4 on penalties* | | | | |
| 1998-99 | (D2) | 1 | 14.11.98 | **Chesterfield** (D2) | H | W | 1-0 | Scott |
| | | 2 | 05.12.98 | **Plymouth Argyle** (D3) | H | D | 1-1 | Baird |
| | | 2r | 15.12.98 | **Plymouth Argyle** | A | L | 2-3 | Read, Carroll |
| 1999-00 | (D2) | 1 | 30.10.99 | **Oxford City** (IL) | H | D | 1-1 | Simpson |
| | | 1r | 09.11.99 | **Oxford City** | A | - | 1-1ab | Simpson |
| | | | | *abandoned – fire broke out at the end of 90 minutes before the penalty shoot-out started* | | | | |
| | | 1 2r | 16.11.99 | **Oxford City** (IL) | A | W | 1-0 | Brown |
| | | | | *played at Manor Ground, Oxford* | | | | |
| | | 2 | 20.11.99 | **Wigan Athletic** (D2) | H | D | 2-2 | Devine, Ryan |
| | | 2r | 30.11.99 | **Wigan Athletic** | A | L | 1-2 | Baird |
| 2000-01 | (D2) | 1 | 18.11.00 | **Harrow Borough** (IL) | H | W | 3-0 | Bates 2, Simpson |
| | | 2 | 10.12.00 | **Millwall** (D2) | A | D | 0-0 | |
| | | 2r | 19.12.00 | **Millwall** | H | W | 2-1 | Rammell, McCarthy |
| | | 3 | 06.01.01 | **Grimsby Town** (D1) | H | D | 1-1 | McCarthy |
| | | 3r | 16.01.01 | **Grimsby Town** | A | W | 3-1 | McCarthy, Simpson, Rogers |
| | | 4 | 27.01.01 | **Wolverhampton W** (D1) | H | W | 2-1 | Rammell, Parkin |
| | | 5 | 17.02.01 | **Wimbledon** (PL) | H | D | 2-2 | Simpson, Brown |
| | | 5r | 20.02.01 | **Wimbledon** | A | D | 1-1aet | Carroll |
| | | | | *Wycome Wanderers won 8-7 on penalties* | | | | |
| | | 6 | 10.03.01 | **Leicester City** (PL) | A | W | 2-1 | McCarthy, Essendoh |

| | | | | | | | | |
|---|---|---|---|---|---|---|---|---|
| | | SF | 08.04.01 | **Liverpool** (PL) | | L | 1-2 | Ryan |
| | | | | *played at Villa Park* | | | | |
| 2001-02 | (D2) | 1 | 16.11.01 | **Hayes** (Conf) | A | W | 4-3 | Rammell 2, Currie 2 |
| | | 2 | 08.12.01 | **Notts County** (D2) | H | W | 3-0 | Bulman, Walker, Currie |
| | | 3 | 08.01.02 | **Fulham** (PL) | H | D | 2-2 | Brown (p), McSporran |
| | | 3r | 15.01.02 | **Fulham** | A | L | 0-1 | |
| 2002-03 | (D2) | 1 | 16.11.02 | **Brentford** (D2) | H | L | 2-4 | Rammell, Brown |

# YEADING

*Formed 1965. First entered FA Cup: 1986-87. FA Vase winners: 1990. Members of the Isthmian League.*

| | | | | | | | | |
|---|---|---|---|---|---|---|---|---|
| 1993-94 | (IL) | 1 | 13.11.93 | **Gillingham** (D3) | H | D | 0-0 | |
| | | | | *played at Hayes FC* | | | | |
| | | 1r | 30.11.93 | **Gillingham** | A | L | 1-3 | James |
| 1994-95 | (IL) | 1 | 12.11.94 | **Colchester Utd** (D3) | H | D | 2-2 | Hippolyte, Graham |
| | | 1r | 22.11.94 | **Colchester Utd** | A | L | 1-7 | McKinnon (p) |

# YEOVIL TOWN

*Formed 1895 as Yeovil Casuals. Changed name to Yeovil Town 1907 and then merged with Petters United to form Yeovil and Petters United in 1919. Reverted to Yeovil Town in 1946. First entered FA Cup in 1907-08. FA Trophy winners 2002. Promoted to Football League 2003. Yeovil Town are the most famous of all FA Cup giant-killers, beating 20 League clubs and reaching the Competition Proper 49 times before finally being promoted to the Football League in 2003. Their most famous exploit was reaching the FA Cup fifth round in 1948-49 beating then powerful Sunderland along the way. League clubs beaten as a Non-League club: Bournemouth (2), Crystal Palace (2), Exeter City, Brighton, Bury, Sunderland, Southend (2), Walsall (2), Brentford, Cambridge United, Torquay United, Hereford United, Fulham, Northampton Town, Colchester United, Blackpool.*

**as Yeovil & Petters Utd**

| | | | | | | | | |
|---|---|---|---|---|---|---|---|---|
| 1924-25 | (SL) | | | 4q Bournemouth (3S) (H) 3-2; 5q Bristol R (3S) (H) 2-4 | | | | |
| 1928-29 | (SL) | 1 | | **Plymouth Argyle** (3S) | A | L | 1-4 | Rowlands |
| 1931-32 | (SL) | 1 | 28.11.31 | **Hayes** (AL) | H | W | 3-1 | Rankin, Davin, Molloy |
| | | 2 | 12.12.31 | **Fulham** (3S) | A | D | 0-0 | |
| | | 2r | 17.12.31 | **Fulham** | H | L | 2-5 | Davin, McNeill |
| 1932-33 | (SL) | 1 | 26.11.32 | **Dartford** (SL) | A | D | 0-0 | |
| | | 1r | 01.12.32 | **Dartford** | H | W | 4-2 | Lewis 3, Parkin |
| | | 2 | 10.12.32 | **Chester** (3N) | A | L | 1-2 | Lewis |
| 1934-35 | (SL) | 1 | 24.11.34 | **Crystal Palace** (3S) | H | W | 3-0 | McNeil, Owens og, Page |
| | | 2 | 08.12.34 | **Exeter City** (3S) | H | W | 4-1 | Smith, Page, Crewe 2 |
| | | 3 | 12.01.35 | **Liverpool** (D1) | H | L | 2-6 | McNeil 2 |
| 1935-36 | (SL) | 1 | 30.11.35 | **Newport (IOW)** (HL) | H | L | 0-1 | |
| 1936-37 | (SL) | 1 | 28.11.36 | **Worthing** (SCL) | H | W | 4-3 | Halliday, Doncaster, Payne, Attley |
| | | 2 | 12.12.36 | **Walsall** (3S) | A | D | 1-1 | Doncaster |
| | | 2r | 17.12.36 | **Walsall** | H | L | 0-1 | |
| 1937-38 | (SL) | 1 | 27.11.37 | **Ipswich Town** (SL) | H | W | 2-1 | Kirk, Attley |
| | | 2 | 11.12.37 | **Gainsborough T** (ML) | H | W | 2-1 | Halliday 2 |
| | | 3 | 08.01.38 | **Manchester Utd** (D2) | A | L | 0-3 | |
| 1938-39 | (SL) | 1 | 26.11.38 | **Brighton** (3S) | H | W | 2-1 | Graham, Laing |
| | | 2 | 10.12.38 | **Folkestone** (SL) | A | D | 1-1 | Graham |
| | | 2r | 15.12.38 | **Folkestone** | H | W | 1-0 | Green |
| | | 3 | 07.01.39 | **Sheffield Wed** (D2) | A | D | 1-1 | Carter |
| | | 3r | 12.01.39 | **Sheffield Wed** | H | L | 1-2 | |
| 1945-46 | (SL) | 1 1L | 17.11.45 | **Bristol City** (3S) | H | D | 2-2 | Hamilton 2 |
| | | 1 2L | 24.11.45 | **Bristol City** | A | L | 0-3 | |

**as Yeovil Town**

| | | | | | | | | |
|---|---|---|---|---|---|---|---|---|
| 1946-47 | (SL) | 1 | 30.11.46 | **Peterborough Utd** (ML) | H | D | 2-2 | Gore, Sibley (p) |
| | | 1r | 05.12.46 | **Peterborough Utd** | A | L | 0-1 | |
| 1948-49 | (SL) | 1 | 27.11.48 | **Romford** (IL) | H | W | 4-0 | Bryant 2, Hamilton, Hargreaves |
| | | 2 | 11.12.48 | **Weymouth** (WL) | A | W | 4-0 | Bryant 2, Hamilton, Hargreaves |
| | | 3 | 08.01.49 | **Bury** (D2) | H | W | 3-1 | Hargreaves, Wright, Hamilton |
| | | 4 | 29.01.49 | **Sunderland** (D1) | H | W | 2-1aet | Stock, Bryant |
| | | 5 | 12.02.49 | **Manchester Utd** (D1) | A | L | 0-8 | |
| | | | | *played at Maine Road* | | | | |
| 1949-50 | (SL) | 1 | 26.11.49 | **Romford** (IL) | H | W | 4-1 | Wright, Foulds, Mansley 2 |
| | | 2 | 10.12.49 | **Gillingham** (SL) | H | W | 3-1 | Wright, Foulds, Mansley |

| | | | | | | | | |
|---|---|---|---|---|---|---|---|---|
| | | 3 | 07.01.50 | **Chesterfield** (D2) | A | L | 1-3 | Mansley |
| 1952-53 | (SL) | 1 | 22.11.52 | **Brighton** (3S) | H | L | 1-4 | Finley |
| 1953-54 | (SL) | 1 | 21.11.53 | **Norwich City** (3S) | H | L | 0-2 | |
| 1955-56 | (SL) | 1 | 19.11.55 | **Aldershot** (3S) | H | D | 1-1 | Elder |
| | | 1r | 23.11.55 | **Aldershot** | A | D | 1-1aet | Reid |
| | | 1 2r | 28.11.55 | **Aldershot** | | L | 0-3 | |
| | | | | *played at The Dell, Southampton* | | | | |
| 1956-57 | (SL) | 1 | 17.11.56 | **Peterborough Utd** (ML) | H | L | 1-3 | McCaffrey |
| 1957-58 | (SL) | 1 | 16.11.57 | **Guildford City** (SL) | A | D | 2-2 | Travis, Alexander |
| | | 1r | 21.11.57 | **Guildford City** | H | W | 1-0 | Travis |
| | | 2 | 07.12.57 | **Bath City** (SL) | H | W | 2-0 | Alexander, Baldwin |
| | | 3 | 04.01.58 | **Fulham** (D2) | A | L | 0-4 | |
| 1958-59 | (SL) | 1 | 15.11.58 | **Southend Utd** (D3) | A | D | 0-0 | |
| | | 1r | 20.11.58 | **Southend Utd** | H | W | 1-0 | Dennis |
| | | 2 | 06.12.58 | **Colchester Utd** (D3) | A | D | 1-1 | Earl |
| | | 2r | 11.12.58 | **Colchester Utd** | H | L | 1-7 | |
| 1960-61 | (SL) | 1 | 05.11.60 | **Walsall** (D3) | A | W | 1-0 | Taylor |
| | | 2 | 26.11.60 | **Bournemouth** (D3) | A | L | 1-3 | Kelly |
| 1961-62 | (SL) | 1 | 04.11.61 | **Notts County** (D3) | A | L | 2-4 | Taylor, Foley |
| 1962-63 | (SL) | 1 | 03.11.62 | **Dartford** (SL) | H | W | 3-2 | Tayor, Foley, Coughin |
| | | 2 | 24.11.62 | **Swindon Town** (D3) | H | L | 0-2 | |
| 1963-64 | (SL) | 1 | 16.11.63 | **Southend Utd** (D3) | H | W | 1-0 | Foley |
| | | 2 | 07.12.63 | **Crystal Palace** (D3) | H | W | 3-1 | Taylor 2, Pound |
| | | 3 | 04.01.64 | **Bury** (D2) | H | L | 0-2 | |
| 1965-66 | (SL) | 1 | 13.11.65 | **Brentford** (D3) | A | L | 1-2 | Harding |
| 1966-67 | (SL) | 1 | 26.11.66 | **Oxford Utd** (D3) | H | L | 1-3 | Muir |
| 1967-68 | (SL) | 1 | 13.12.67 | **Margate** (SL) | H | L | 1-3 | Vowles |
| 1968-69 | (SL) | 1 | 16.11.68 | **Weymouth** (SL) | A | L | 1-2 | Harris |
| 1969-70 | (SL) | 1 | 15.11.69 | **Shrewsbury Town** (D3) | H | L | 2-3 | Housley, Davies |
| 1970-71 | (SL) | 1 | 21.11.70 | **Aveley** (AL) | H | W | 1-0 | Clancy |
| | | 2 | 12.12.70 | **Bournemouth** (D4) | A | W | 1-0 | Myers |
| | | 3 | 06.01.71 | **Arsenal** (D1) | H | L | 0-3 | |
| 1972-73 | (SL) | 1 | 18.11.72 | **Brentford** (D3) | H | W | 2-1 | Weller, Myers |
| | | 2 | 09.12.72 | **Plymouth Argyle** (D3) | H | L | 0-2 | |
| 1975-76 | (SL) | 1 | 22.11.75 | **Millwall** (D3) | H | D | 1-1 | Brown |
| | | 1r | 25.11.75 | **Millwall** | A | D | 2-2aet | Cotton, Housley |
| | | 1 2r | 03.12.75 | **Millwall** | | L | 0-1 | |
| | | | | *played at Recreation Ground, Aldershot* | | | | |
| 1978-79 | (SL) | 1 | 25.11.78 | **Barking** (IL) | H | L | 0-1 | |
| 1979-80 | (APL) | 1 | 24.11.79 | **Enfield** (IL) | A | W | 1-0 | Green |
| | | 2 | 15.12.79 | **Slough Town** (IL) | H | W | 1-0 | Williams |
| | | 3 | 05.01.80 | **Norwich City** (D1) | H | L | 0-3 | |
| 1980-81 | (APL) | 1 | 22.11.80 | **Farnborough T** (IL) | H | W | 2-1 | Morrall, Ritchie |
| | | 2 | 13.12.80 | **Colchester Utd** (D3) | A | D | 1-1 | Green |
| | | 2r | 17.12.80 | **Colchester Utd** | H | L | 0-2 | |
| 1981-82 | (APL) | 1 | 21.11.81 | **Dagenham** (APL) | A | D | 2-2 | Green, Brown |
| | | 1r | 25.11.81 | **Dagenham** | H | L | 0-1aet | |
| 1982-83 | (APL) | 1 | 20.11.82 | **Chesham Utd** (IL) | A | W | 1-0 | Bell |
| | | 2 | 11.12.82 | **Southend Utd** (D3) | A | L | 0-3 | |
| 1983-84 | (APL) | 1 | 19.11.83 | **Harrow Borough** (IL) | H | L | 0-1 | |
| 1984-85 | (APL) | 1 | 17.11.84 | **Torquay Utd** (D4) | A | L | 0-2 | |
| 1985-86 | (IL) | 1 | 16.11.85 | **Hereford Utd** (D4) | H | L | 2-4 | Smith, McGinlay |
| 1987-88 | (IL) | 1 | 14.11.87 | **Worcester City** (SL) | A | D | 1-1 | Pearson |
| | | 1r | 18.11.87 | **Worcester City** | H | W | 1-0 | McGinlay |
| | | 2 | 05.12.87 | **Cambridge Utd** (D4) | A | W | 1-0 | Wallace |
| | | 3 | 09.01.88 | **QPR** (D1) | H | L | 0-3 | |
| 1988-89 | (SL) | 1 | 19.11.88 | **Merthyr Tydfil** (SL) | H | W | 3-2 | Wallace 2, Doherty |
| | | 2 | 10.12.88 | **Torquay Utd** (D4) | H | D | 1-1 | Randall |
| | | 2r | 14.12.88 | **Torquay Utd** | A | L | 0-1 | |
| 1989-90 | (Conf) | 1 | 18.11.89 | **Maidstone Utd** (D4) | A | L | 1-2 | Spencer |
| 1990-91 | (Conf) | 1 | 17.11.90 | **Brentford** (D3) | A | L | 0-5 | |

| | | | | | | | | |
|---|---|---|---|---|---|---|---|---|
| 1991-92 | (Conf) | 1 | 16.11.91 | **Walsall** (D4) | H | D | 1-1 | Wilson |
| | | 1r | 27.11.91 | **Walsall** | A | W | 1-0aet | Cooper |
| | | 2 | 07.12.91 | **Woking** (IL) | A | L | 0-3 | |
| 1992-93 | (Conf) | 1 | 14.11.92 | **Torquay Utd** (D3) | A | W | 5-2 | Batty 3 (2ps), Wilson 2 |
| | | 2 | 05.12.92 | **Hereford Utd** (D3) | H | D | 0-0 | |
| | | 2r | 15.12.92 | **Hereford Utd** | A | W | 2-1 | Sanderson, Coates |
| | | 3 | 03.01.93 | **Arsenal** (PL) | H | L | 1-3 | Batty (p) |
| 1993-94 | (Conf) | 1 | 14.11.93 | **Fulham** (D2) | H | W | 1-0 | Wallace |
| | | 2 | 04.12.93 | **Bromsgrove R** (Conf) | H | L | 0-2 | |
| 1998-99 | (Conf) | 1 | 14.11.98 | **West Auckland T** (NL) | H | D | 2-2 | Patmore, Hannigan |
| | | 1r | 24.11.98 | **West Auckland T** | A | D | 1-1aet | Dale |
| | | | | *Yeovil won 5-3 on penalties* | | | | |
| | | 2 | 05.12.98 | **Northampton Town** (D2) | H | W | 2-0 | Thompson, Patmore |
| | | 3 | 02.01.99 | **Cardiff City** (D3) | A | D | 1-1 | Dale |
| | | 3r | 12.01.99 | **Cardiff City** | H | L | 1-2aet | Hayfield |
| 1999-00 | (Conf) | 1 | 30.10.99 | **Reading** (D2) | A | L | 2-4 | Foster, Eaton |
| 2000-01 | (Conf) | 1 | 18.11.00 | **Colchester Utd** (D2) | H | W | 5-1 | Patmore 2, Belgrave, Skiverton, Way (p) |
| | | 2 | 10.12.00 | **Blackpool** (D2) | A | W | 1-0 | Crittenden |
| | | 3 | 06.01.01 | **Bolton Wanderers** (D1) | A | L | 1-2 | Patmore |
| 2002-03 | (Conf) | 1 | 16.11.02 | **Cheltenham Town** (D2) | H | L | 0-2 | |

## YORK CITY

*Formed 1922. Best FA Cup performance: semi-finals 1955 (as a Third Division club); Record FA Cup win: 6-0 v South Shields, 1st round, 16.11.1968; Record FA Cup defeat: 0-7 v Liverpool, 5th round replay, 20.02.1985.*

| | | | | | | | | |
|---|---|---|---|---|---|---|---|---|
| 1923-24 | (ML) | | | ExP Castleford & Allerton (H) 2-1; P Cudworth (A) 1-0; 1q Mexborough Town (H) 1-1; 1qr Mexborough T (A) 1-1aet; 1q 2r Mexborough Town 1-3 at Doncaster | | | | |
| 1924-25 | (ML) | | | ExP Guiseley (H) 1-0; P Horsforth (H) 7-1; 1q Wombwell (H) 1-2 | | | | |
| 1925-26 | (ML) | | | P Maltby Main (H) 5-3; 1q Wombwell (H) 5-0; 2q Castleford Town (H) 3-0; 3q Wath Athletic (A) 1-4 | | | | |
| 1926-27 | (ML) | | | 1q Guisborough Belmont (H) 5-0; 2q South Bank (H) 4-0; 3q Whitby U (H) 0-0; 3qr Whitby Utd (H) 2-1; 4q Ilkeston Town (A) 5-1 | | | | |
| | | 1 | 27.11.26 | **Worksop Town** (ML) | H | - | 1-1ab | Flood |
| | | | | *abandoned after 58 minutes – fog* | | | | |
| | | 1 | 01.12.26 | **Worksop Town** | H | W | 4-1 | Merritt 2, Rany, Harvey |
| | | 2 | 11.12.26 | **Grimsby Town** (D2) | A | L | 1-2 | Harvey |
| 1927-28 | (ML) | | | 1q Whitby Utd (H) 4-0; 2q Scarborough (H) 1-1; 2qr Scarborough (A) 4-0; 3q Stockton Malleable (H) 7-1; 4q Shildon (A) 1-1; 4qr Shildon (H) 1-2 | | | | |
| 1928-29 | (ML) | | | 1q Stockton (H) 7-1; 2q Normanby Mangnesite (H) 2-1; 3q Bridlington (H) 3-0; 4q Jarrow (A) 0-0; 4qr Jarrow (H) 2-2aet; 4q 2r Jarrow 3-2 at St James' Park | | | | |
| | | 1 | 24.11.28 | **Barrow** (3N) | H | L | 0-1 | |
| 1929-30 | (3N) | | | 4q Scaborough (A) 3-1 | | | | |
| | | 1 | 30.11.29 | **Tranmere Rovers** (3N) | H | D | 2-2 | Fenoughty 2 |
| | | 1r | 05.12.29 | **Tranmere Rovers** | A | W | 1-0 | Fenoughty |
| | | 2 | 14.12.29 | **Southend Utd** (3S) | A | W | 4-1 | Davies, Gardiner, Fenoughty 2 |
| | | 3 | 11.01.30 | **Newcastle Utd** (D1) | A | D | 1-1 | Gardiner |
| | | 3r | 15.01.30 | **Newcastle Utd** | H | L | 1-2 | Evans |
| 1930-31 | (3N) | 1 | 29.11.30 | **Gresley Rovers** (BC) | H | W | 3-1 | Evans, Laycock, Kelly |
| | | 2 | 13.12.30 | **Nelson FC** (3N) | A | D | 1-1 | Brewis |
| | | 2r | 17.12.30 | **Nelson FC** | H | - | 2-0ab | Laycock, Kelly |
| | | | | *abandoned because of fog* | | | | |
| | | 2r | 18.12.30 | **Nelson FC** | H | W | 3-2 | Laycock 2, Sharp |
| | | 3 | 10.01.31 | **Sheffield Utd** (D1) | A | D | 1-1 | Laycock |
| | | 3r | 14.01.31 | **Sheffield Utd** | H | L | 0-2 | |
| 1931-32 | (3N) | 1 | 28.11.31 | **New Brighton** (3N) | A | L | 1-3 | McDonald |
| 1932-33 | (3N) | 1 | 26.11.32 | **Scarborough** (ML) | H | L | 1-3 | Spooner |
| 1933-34 | (3N) | 1 | 25.11.33 | **Hartlepools Utd** (3N) | H | L | 2-3 | Lax, Jenkinson |
| 1934-35 | (3N) | 1 | 24.11.34 | **Burton Town** (BDL) | A | W | 3-2 | Hathway, Jenkins, Dando |
| | | 2 | 08.12.34 | **New Brighton** (3N) | H | W | 1-0 | Speed |
| | | 3 | 12.01.35 | **Derby County** (D1) | H | L | 0-1 | |
| 1935-36 | (3N) | 1 | 30.11.35 | **Burton Town** (ML) | H | L | 1-5 | Lindsay (p) |
| 1936-37 | (3N) | 1 | 28.11.36 | **Hull City** (3N) | H | W | 5-2 | Thompson 2, Agar 3 |

| | | | | | | | |
|---|---|---|---|---|---|---|---|
| | 2 | 12.12.36 | **Southend Utd** (3S) | A | D | 3-3 | Spooner, Thompson 2 |
| | 2r | 16.12.36 | **Southend Utd** | H | W | 2-1aet | Comrie, Spooner |
| | 3 | 16.01.37 | **Bradford City** (D2) | A | D | 2-2 | Comrie, Spooner |
| | 3r | 20.01.37 | **Bradford City** | H | W | 1-0 | Nicol |
| | 4 | 30.01.37 | **Swansea Town** (D2) | A | D | 0-0 | |
| | 4r | 03.02.37 | **Swansea Town** | H | L | 1-3 | Hathway |
| 1937-38 (3N) | 1 | 27.11.37 | **Halifax Town** (3N) | H | D | 1-1 | Hughes |
| | 1r | 01.12.37 | **Halifax Town** | A | W | 1-0 | Baines |
| | 2 | 11.12.37 | **Clapton Orient** (3S) | A | D | 2-2 | Scott, Comrie |
| | 2r | 15.12.37 | **Clapton Orient** | H | W | 1-0 | Hughes |
| | 3 | 08.01.38 | **Coventry City** (D2) | H | W | 3-2 | Spooner, Hughes, Earl |
| | 4 | 22.01.38 | **WBA** (D1) | H | W | 3-2 | Baines 3 |
| | 5 | 12.02.38 | **Middlesbrough** (D1) | H | W | 1-0 | Spooner |
| | 6 | 05.03.38 | **Huddersfield Town** (D1) | H | D | 0-0 | |
| | 6r | 09.03.38 | **Huddersfield Town** | A | L | 1-2 | Baines |
| 1938-39 (3N) | 3 | 11.01.39 | **Millwall** (D2) | H | L | 0-5 | |
| 1945-46 (3N) | 1 1L | 17.11.45 | **Halifax Town** (3N) | A | L | 0-1 | |
| | 1 2L | 24.11.45 | **Halifax Town** | H | W | 4-2 | Lee, Gledhill, Scott 2 |
| | 2 1L | 08.12.45 | **Bishop Auckland** (NL) | A | W | 2-1 | Madison, Winters |
| | 2 2L | 15.12.45 | **Bishop Auckland** | H | W | 3-0 | Winters, Brennan, Robbins |
| | 3 1L | 05.01.46 | **Chesterfield** (D2) | A | D | 1-1 | Mahon |
| | 3 2L | 09.01.46 | **Chesterfield** | H | W | 3-2aet | Kidd og, Winters 2 |
| | 4 1L | 26.01.46 | **Sheffield Wed** (D2) | A | L | 1-5 | Scott |
| | 4 2L | 30.01.46 | **Sheffield Wed** | H | L | 1-6 | Allen |
| 1946-47 (3N) | 1 | 04.12.46 | **Scunthorpe Utd** (ML) | H | L | 0-1 | |
| 1947-48 (3N) | 1 | 29.11.47 | **Rochdale** (3N) | H | L | 0-1 | |
| 1948-49 (3N) | 1 | 27.11.48 | **Runcorn** (CC) | H | W | 2-1 | Brigham, Rudd |
| | 2 | 11.12.48 | **Southport** (3N) | A | D | 2-2aet | Ivey, A Patrick |
| | 2r | 18.12.48 | **Southport** | H | L | 0-2 | |
| 1949-50 (3N) | 1 | 26.11.49 | **Gateshead AFC** (3N) | A | L | 1-3 | Birch |
| 1950-51 (3N) | 1 | 25.11.50 | **Bishop Auckland** (NL) | A | D | 2-2 | M.Patrick, Brennen |
| | 1r | 29.11.50 | **Bishop Auckland** | H | W | 2-1 | A Patrick 2 |
| | 2 | 09.12.50 | **Tranmere Rovers** (3N) | H | W | 2-1 | A Patrick 2 |
| | 3 | 06.01.51 | **Bolton Wanderers** (D1) | A | L | 0-2 | |
| 1951-52 (3N) | 1 | 24.11.51 | **Bradford Park A** (3N) | H | D | 1-1 | A Patrick |
| | 1r | 28.11.51 | **Bradford Park A** | A | D | 1-1aet | A Patrick |
| | 1 2r | 03.12.51 | **Bradford Park A** *played at Elland Road* | | L | 0-4 | |
| 1952-53 (3N) | 1 | 22.11.52 | **Barrow** (3N) | H | L | 1-2 | A Patrick |
| 1953-54 (3N) | 1 | 21.11.53 | **Barnsley** (3N) | A | L | 2-5 | Dunmore, Fenton |
| 1954-55 (3N) | 1 | 20.11.54 | **Scarborough** (ML) | H | W | 3-2 | Wilkinson, Bottom, Spence |
| | 2 | 11.12.54 | **Dorchester Town** (WL) | A | W | 5-2 | Bottom 3, Wilkinson, Fenton |
| | 3 | 08.01.55 | **Blackpool** (D1) | A | W | 2-0 | Storey, Fenton |
| | 4 | 29.01.55 | **Bishop Auckland** (NL) | A | W | 3-1 | Storey, Bottom 2 |
| | 5 | 19.02.55 | **Tottenham Hotspur** (D1) | H | W | 3-1 | Wilkinson 2, Fenton |
| | 6 | 12.03.55 | **Notts County** (D2) | A | W | 1-0 | Bottom |
| | SF | 26.03.55 | **Newcastle Utd** (D1) *played at Hillsborough* | | D | 1-1 | Bottom |
| | SFr | 30.03.55 | **Newcastle Utd** *played at Roker Park* | | L | 0-2 | |
| 1955-56 (3N) | 1 | 19.11.55 | **Rochdale** (3N) | A | W | 1-0 | Wilkinson |
| | 2 | 10.12.55 | **Mansfield Town** (3N) | H | W | 2-1 | Bottom, Hughes |
| | 3 | 07.01.56 | **Swansea Town** (D2) | A | W | 2-1 | Colbridge, Bottom |
| | 4 | 28.01.56 | **Sunderland** (D1) | H | D | 0-0 | |
| | 4r | 01.02.56 | **Sunderland** | A | L | 1-2 | Fenton |
| 1956-57 (3N) | 1 | 17.11.56 | **Southport** (3N) | A | D | 0-0 | |
| | 1r | 20.11.56 | **Southport** | H | W | 2-1 | Wragg, Wilkinson |
| | 2 | 08.12.56 | **Hull City** (3N) | A | L | 1-2 | Bottom |
| 1957-58 (3N) | 1 | 16.11.57 | **Chesterfield** (3N) | H | W | 1-0 | Fenton |
| | 2 | 07.12.57 | **S Shields (1936)** (NEL) | A | W | 3-1 | Wilkinson 2, Bottom |
| | 3 | 08.01.58 | **Birmingham City** (D1) | H | W | 3-0 | Bottom, Wragg, Wilkinson |

| | | | | | | | | |
|---|---|---|---|---|---|---|---|---|
| | | 4 | 25.01.58 | **Bolton Wanderers** (D1) | H | D | 0-0 | |
| | | 4r | 29.01.58 | **Bolton Wanderers** | A | L | 0-3 | |
| 1958-59 | (D4) | 1 | 15.11.58 | **Bury** (D3) | A | - | 0-0ab | |
| | | | | *abandoned after 60 minutes* | | | | |
| | | 1 | 18.11.58 | **Bury** | A | L | 0-1 | |
| 1959-60 | (D3) | 1 | 14.11.59 | **Barrow** (D4) | H | W | 3-1 | Addison, Edgar, Hughes |
| | | 2 | 05.12.59 | **Crook Town** (NL) | A | W | 1-0 | Edgar |
| | | 3 | 09.01.60 | **Bournemouth** (D3) | A | L | 0-1 | |
| 1960-61 | (D4) | 1 | 05.11.60 | **Bradford Park A** (D4) | H | D | 0-0 | |
| | | 1r | 09.11.60 | **Bradford Park A** | A | W | 2-0 | Wilkinson, Addison |
| | | 2 | 30.11.60 | **Tranmere Rovers** (D3) | A | D | 1-1 | Wilkinson |
| | | 2r | 05.12.60 | **Tranmere Rovers** | H | W | 2-1 | Wilkinson 2 |
| | | 3 | 07.01.61 | **Norwich City** (D2) | H | D | 0-0 | Hughes |
| | | 3r | 11.01.61 | **Norwich City** | A | L | 0-1 | |
| 1961-62 | (D4) | 1 | 04.11.61 | **Bradford City** (D4) | A | L | 0-1 | |
| 1962-63 | (D4) | 1 | 03.11.62 | **Rochdale** (D4) | H | D | 0-0 | |
| | | 1r | 06.11.62 | **Rochdale** | A | W | 2-1 | Wragg, Wilkinson |
| | | 2 | 24.11.62 | **Crewe Alexandra** (D4) | H | W | 2-1 | Wragg, Wilkinson |
| | | 3 | 13.02.63 | **Southampton** (D2) | A | L | 0-5 | |
| 1963-64 | (D4) | 1 | 16.11.63 | **Carlisle Utd** (D4) | H | L | 2-5 | Wilkinson 2 |
| 1964-65 | (D4) | 1 | 14.11.64 | **Bangor City** (CC) | H | W | 5-1 | Provan, Aimson 3, Weddle |
| | | 2 | 05.12.64 | **Chesterfield** (D4) | A | L | 1-2 | Aimson |
| 1965-66 | (D3) | 1 | 13.11.65 | **S Shields (1936)** (NRL) | A | L | 1-3 | Aimson (p) |
| 1966-67 | (D4) | 1 | 26.11.66 | **Morecambe** (LC) | H | D | 0-0 | |
| | | 1r | 05.12.66 | **Morecambe** | A | D | 1-1aet | Spencer |
| | | 1 2r | 08.12.66 | **Morecambe** | | W | 1-0 | Spencer |
| | | | | *played at Maine Road* | | | | |
| | | 2 | 07.01.67 | **Middlesbrough** (D3) | A | D | 1-1 | Provan |
| | | 2r | 11.01.67 | **Middlesbrough** | H | D | 0-0aet | |
| | | 2 2r | 16.01.67 | **Middlesbrough** | | L | 1-4 | Horrey |
| | | | | *played at St James' Park* | | | | |
| 1967-68 | (D4) | 1 | 09.12.67 | **Doncaster Rovers** (D4) | H | L | 0-1 | |
| 1968-69 | (D4) | 1 | 16.11.68 | **S Shields (1936)** (NPL) | A | W | 6-0 | Ross 3, MacDougall 2, Baker (p) |
| | | 2 | 07.12.68 | **Morecambe** (NPL) | H | W | 2-0 | MacDougall 2 |
| | | 3 | 04.01.69 | **Stoke City** (D1) | H | L | 0-2 | |
| 1969-70 | (D4) | 1 | 15.11.69 | **Whitby Town** (NL) | H | W | 2-0 | Aimson, Sibbald (p) |
| | | 2 | 06.12.69 | **Bangor City** (NPL) | A | D | 0-0 | |
| | | 2r | 10.12.69 | **Bangor City** | H | W | 2-0 | Mahon, Boyer |
| | | 3 | 03.01.70 | **Cardiff City** (D2) | H | D | 1-1 | Boyer |
| | | 3r | 12.01.70 | **Cardiff City** | A | D | 1-1aet | Taylor |
| | | 3 2r | 15.01.70 | **Cardiff City** | | W | 3-1aet | Swallow 2, Aimson |
| | | | | *played at St Andrews* | | | | |
| | | 4 | 24.01.70 | **Middlesbrough** (D2) | A | L | 1-4 | Boyer |
| 1970-71 | (D4) | 1 | 21.11.70 | **Tamworth** (WMRL) | A | D | 0-0 | |
| | | 1r | 23.11.70 | **Tamworth** | H | W | 5-0 | Aimson 3, Boyer, Hewitt |
| | | 2 | 12.12.70 | **Boston Utd** (NPL) | A | W | 2-1 | Davidson, Mackie (p) |
| | | 3 | 02.01.71 | **Bolton Wanderers** (D2) | H | W | 2-0 | Davidson 2 |
| | | 4 | 23.01.71 | **Southampton** (D1) | H | D | 3-3 | Hewitt, Aimson, McMahon |
| | | 4r | 01.02.71 | **Southampton** | A | L | 2-3 | Aimson, Johanneson |
| 1971-72 | (D3) | 1 | 20.11.71 | **Grimsby Town** (D4) | H | W | 4-2 | Rathbone og, Henderson, Swallow, McMahon |
| | | 2 | 11.12.71 | **Rotherham Utd** (D3) | A | D | 1-1 | Rowles |
| | | 2r | 13.12.71 | **Rotherham Utd** | H | L | 2-3aet | McMahon, Chambers |
| 1972-73 | (D4) | 1 | 18.11.72 | **Mansfield Town** (D4) | H | W | 2-1 | Rowles, Seal |
| | | 2 | 09.12.72 | **Bangor City** (NPL) | A | W | 3-2 | Rowles, Burrows, Pollard |
| | | 3 | 13.01.73 | **Oxford Utd** (D2) | H | L | 0-1 | |
| 1973-74 | (D3) | 1 | 24.11.73 | **Mansfield Town** (D4) | H | D | 0-0 | |
| | | 1r | 10.12.73 | **Mansfield Town** | A | L | 3-5 | Jones 2, Swallow |
| 1974-75 | (D2) | 3 | 04.01.75 | **Arsenal** (D1) | A | D | 1-1 | Seal |
| | | 3r | 07.01.75 | **Arsenal** | H | L | 1-3aet | Lyons |
| 1975-76 | (D2) | 3 | 03.01.76 | **Hereford Utd** (D3) | H | W | 2-1 | Seal, Hosker |

| | | | | | | | | |
|---|---|---|---|---|---|---|---|---|
| | | 4 | 24.01.76 | **Chelsea** (D2) | H | L | 0-2 | |
| 1976-77 | (D3) | 1 | 20.11.76 | **Dudley Town** (WMRL) | A | D | 1-1 | Cave |
| | | 1r | 23.11.76 | **Dudley Town** | H | W | 4-1 | Holmes 2 (1p), Cave, Pollard |
| | | 2 | 11.12.76 | **Rotherham Utd** (D3) | A | D | 0-0 | |
| | | 2r | 14.12.76 | **Rotherham Utd** | H | D | 1-1aet | Holmes (p) |
| | | 2 2r | 21.12.76 | **Rotherham Utd** | A | L | 1-2aet | Hinch |
| 1977-78 | (D4) | 1 | 26.11.77 | **Wigan Athletic** (NPL) | A | L | 0-1 | |
| 1978-79 | (D4) | 1 | 25.11.78 | **Blyth Spartans** (NL) | H | D | 1-1 | Pugh |
| | | 1r | 28.11.78 | **Blyth Spartans** | A | W | 5-3 | Ford, Clements, Wellings 2, Staniforth |
| | | 2 | 16.12.78 | **Scarborough** (NPL) | H | W | 3-0 | Faulkner, Staniforth 2 |
| | | 3 | 09.01.79 | **Luton Town** (D2) | H | W | 2-0 | Staniforth, Randall |
| | | 4 | 27.01.79 | **Nottingham Forest** (D1) | A | L | 1-3 | Wellings |
| 1979-80 | (D4) | 1 | 24.11.79 | **Mossley** (NPL) | H | W | 5-2 | Randall, Eccles, Lorimer, Byrne, Macdonald (p) |
| | | 2 | 15.12.79 | **Bury** (D3) | A | D | 0-0 | |
| | | 2r | 18.12.79 | **Bury** | H | L | 0-2 | |
| 1980-81 | (D4) | 1 | 22.11.80 | **Tranmere Rovers** (D4) | A | D | 0-0 | |
| | | 1r | 25.11.80 | **Tranmere Rovers** | H | L | 1-2aet | Byrne |
| 1981-82 | (D4) | 1 | 21.11.81 | **Stafford Rangers** (APL) | A | W | 2-1 | Ford, Walwyn |
| | | 2 | 12.12.81 | **Altrincham** (APL) | H | D | 0-0 | |
| | | 2r | 02.01.82 | **Altrincham** | A | L | 3-4 | Pollard 2, Walwyn |
| 1982-83 | (D4) | 1 | 20.11.82 | **Bury** (D4) | H | W | 3-1 | Hood, Ford, Walwyn |
| | | 2 | 11.12.82 | **Hartlepool Utd** (D4) | A | D | 1-1 | Pollard |
| | | 2r | 14.12.82 | **Hartlepool Utd** | H | W | 4-0 | Hood, Pollard, Byrne, Ford |
| | | 3 | 08.01.83 | **Crystal Palace** (D2) | A | L | 1-2 | Walwyn |
| 1983-84 | (D4) | 1 | 19.11.83 | **Macclesfield T** (NPL) | A | D | 0-0 | |
| | | 1r | 22.11.83 | **Macclesfield T** | H | W | 2-0 | Sbragia, Byrne |
| | | 2 | 13.12.83 | **Rochdale** (D4) | H | L | 0-2 | |
| 1984-85 | (D3) | 1 | 17.11.84 | **Blue Star** (Wear) | H | W | 2-0 | Walwyn, Houchen |
| | | 2 | 08.12.84 | **Hartlepool Utd** (D4) | A | W | 2-0 | MacPhail, Houchen |
| | | 3 | 05.01.85 | **Walsall** (D3) | H | W | 3-0 | Butler, Walwyn, Hay |
| | | 4 | 26.01.85 | **Arsenal** (D1) | H | W | 1-0 | Houchen (p) |
| | | 5 | 16.02.85 | **Liverpool** (D1) | H | D | 1-1 | Sbragia |
| | | 5r | 20.02.85 | **Liverpool** | A | L | 0-7 | |
| 1985-86 | (D3) | 1 | 16.11.85 | **Morecambe** (NPL) | H | D | 0-0 | |
| | | 1r | 19.11.85 | **Morecambe** *played at Maine Road* | A | W | 2-0 | Sbragia, Walwyn |
| | | 2 | 07.12.85 | **Whitby Town** (NL) | H | W | 3-1 | Ford, Walwyn, Pearce |
| | | 3 | 04.01.86 | **Wycombe W** (APL) | H | W | 2-0 | Walwyn 2 |
| | | 4 | 25.01.86 | **Altrincham** (APL) | H | W | 2-0 | Banton, Ford |
| | | 5 | 15.02.86 | **Liverpool** (D1) | H | D | 1-1 | Ford |
| | | 5r | 18.02.86 | **Liverpool** | A | L | 1-3aet | Canham |
| 1986-87 | (D3) | 1 | 15.11.86 | **Crewe Alexandra** (D4) | H | W | 3-1 | Mills, Banton, Walwyn |
| | | 2 | 06.12.86 | **Caernarfon Town** (NPL) | A | D | 0-0 | |
| | | 2r | 09.12.86 | **Caernarfon Town** | H | L | 1-2 | Canham |
| 1987-88 | (D3) | 1 | 14.11.87 | **Burton Albion** (SL) | H | D | 0-0 | |
| | | 1r | 18.11.87 | **Burton Albion** | A | W | 2-1 | Hood (p), Mills |
| | | 2 | 05.12.87 | **Hartlepool Utd** (D4) | H | D | 1-1 | Wilson |
| | | 2r | 09.12.87 | **Hartlepool Utd** | A | L | 1-3 | Banton |
| 1988-89 | (D4) | 1 | 19.11.88 | **Halifax Town** (D4) | A | L | 0-1 | |
| 1989-90 | (D4) | 1 | 18.11.89 | **Grimsby Town** (D4) | H | L | 1-2 | Warburton |
| 1990-91 | (D4) | 1 | 17.11.90 | **Darlington** (D4) | A | D | 1-1 | Canham |
| | | 1r | 19.11.90 | **Darlington** | H | W | 1-0 | Canham |
| | | 2 | 17.12.90 | **Mansfield Town** (D3) | A | L | 1-2 | Pepper |
| 1991-92 | (D4) | 1 | 16.11.91 | **Bridlington Town** (NPL) | A | W | 2-1 | Blackstone 2 |
| | | 2 | 07.12.91 | **Tranmere Rovers** (D2) | H | D | 1-1 | Hall |
| | | 2r | 17.12.91 | **Tranmere Rovers** | A | L | 1-2 | McCarthy |
| 1992-93 | (D3) | 1 | 14.11.92 | **Stockport County** (D2) | H | L | 1-3 | Canham |
| 1993-94 | (D2) | 1 | 13.11.93 | **Burnley** (D2) | A | D | 0-0 | |
| | | 1r | 30.11.93 | **Burnley** | H | L | 2-3 | Canham, McCarthy |

| | | | | | | | | |
|---|---|---|---|---|---|---|---|---|
| 1994-95 | (D2) | 1 | 12.11.94 | **Rotherham Utd** (D2) | H | D | 3-3 | Naylor 2, McCarthy |
| | | 1r | 22.11.94 | **Rotherham Utd** | A | L | 0-3 | |
| 1995-96 | (D2) | 1 | 12.11.95 | **Notts County** (D2) | H | L | 0-1 | |
| 1996-97 | (D2) | 1 | 16.11.96 | **Hartlepool Utd** (D3) | A | D | 0-0 | |
| | | 1r | 26.11.96 | **Hartlepool Utd** | H | W | 3-0 | Pepper, Himsworth, Tolson |
| | | 2 | 07.12.96 | **Preston North End** (D2) | A | W | 3-2 | Barras, Tolson, Moyes og |
| | | 3 | 13.01.97 | **Hednesford Town** (Conf) | A | L | 0-1 | |
| 1997-98 | (D2) | 1 | 15.11.97 | **Southport** (Conf) | A | W | 4-0 | Rowe 2, Bolland og, Pouton |
| | | 2 | 06.12.97 | **Wigan Athletic** (D2) | A | L | 1-2 | Rowe |
| 1998-99 | (D2) | 1 | 14.11.98 | **Enfield** (IL) | A | D | 2-2 | Cresswell 2 |
| | | 1r | 24.11.98 | **Enfield** | H | W | 2-1 | Jordan, Cresswell |
| | | 2 | 05.12.98 | **Wrexham** (D2) | A | L | 1-2 | Jordan |
| 1999-00 | (D3) | 1 | 30.10.99 | **Hereford Utd** (Conf) | A | L | 0-1 | |
| 2000-01 | (D3) | 1 | 19.11.00 | **Radcliffe Borough** (NPL) | A | W | 4-1 | Potter, Bullock, McNiven, Jordan |
| | | | | *played at Gigg Lane, Bury* | | | | |
| | | 2 | 09.12.00 | **Reading** (D2) | H | D | 2-2 | McNiven, Mathie |
| | | 2r | 19.12.00 | **Reading** | A | W | 3-1 | Agnew, Alcide, Iwelumo |
| | | 3 | 06.01.01 | **Leicester City** (PL) | A | L | 0-3 | |
| 2001-02 | (D3) | 1 | 17.11.01 | **Colchester Utd** (D2) | A | D | 0-0 | |
| | | 1r | 27.11.01 | **Colchester Utd** | H | D | 2-2aet | Brass, Potter |
| | | | | *York City won 3-2 on penalties* | | | | |
| | | 2 | 08.12.01 | **Reading** (D2) | H | W | 2-0 | Richardson, Potter |
| | | 3 | 05.01.02 | **Grimsby Town** (D1) | A | D | 0-0 | |
| | | 3r | 15.01.02 | **Grimsby Town** | H | W | 1-0 | Neilson og |
| | | 4 | 26.01.02 | **Fulham** (PL) | H | L | 0-2 | |
| 2002-03 | (D3) | 1 | 26.11.02 | **Swansea City** (D3) | H | W | 2-1 | Duffield 2 |
| | | 2 | 07.12.02 | **Brentford** (D2) | H | L | 1-2 | Bullock |

## YORKSHIRE AMATEURS

*Formed 1918. First entered FA Cup: 1925-26. Members of the Northern Counties East League.*

| | | | | | | | | |
|---|---|---|---|---|---|---|---|---|
| 1931-32 | (YL) | 1 | 28.11.31 | **Carlisle Utd** (3N) | H | L | 1-3 | S Craven |
| 1945-46 | (YL) | 1 1L | 17.11.45 | **Lincoln City** (3N) | H | W | 1-0 | Melling |
| | | 1 2L | 24.11.45 | **Lincoln City** | A | L | 1-5 | Lyon |

# HEAD TO HEADS

This section provides an at-a-glance record of the meetings between any two Premier League or Football League clubs who were members of those leagues in 2003 – therefore it includes Exeter City and Shrewsbury Town who were relegated from Division Three and Yeovil Town and Doncaster Rovers who were promoted from The Conference. To use the tables, choose the two clubs you want to see meetings between – and look under the name of the club which alphabetically comes first between them.

For example, Arsenal's record against Tottenham Hotspur only appears under Arsenal, while Tottenham's record against West Ham only appears under Tottenham.

Using the Arsenal-Tottenham example there have been five meetings between the clubs starting with a Round 3 meeting in 1948-49 that was a home game for Arsenal.

Matches where one or both clubs were later disqualified are not included. Matches declared void are also not included.

Details of those games will be found in the main results section. Clubs are listed under the name they are known today and the tables include the matches when one or both clubs played under a former name.

The symbols used represent:

| | |
|---|---|
| 1 | Round One etc |
| IR | Some League clubs met in the Intermediate Round, last used in 1904/05 |
| SF | Semi-final |
| F | Final |
| 1r 2retc | first and second replays and so on |
| aet | extra time |
| ab | match abandoned in extra time |
| p | home club won on penalties |
| q | away club won on penalties |
| N | Played on neutral ground |

As stated elsewhere, this section of the book was produced by the Tony Brown, whose many brilliant, statistical works includes *The FA Cup Complete Results*, A Soccer Data publication. The original version of the results reproduced here appeared in that publication..

## Arsenal

**v Aston Villa**

| | | | |
|---|---|---|---|
| 1926 | 5 | A | 1-1 |
| 1926 | 5r | H | 2-0 |
| 1928 | 5 | H | 4-1 |
| 1929 | 6 | A | 0-1 |
| 1931 | 3 | H | 2-2 |
| 1931 | 3r | A | 3-1 |
| 1934 | 6 | H | 1-2 |
| 1954 | 3 | H | 5-1 |
| 1956 | 4 | H | 4-1 |
| 1974 | 4 | H | 1-1 |
| 1974 | 4r | A | 0-2 |
| 1983 | 6 | H | 2-0 |

**v Barnsley**

| | | | |
|---|---|---|---|
| 1907 | 4 | A | 2-1 |
| 1936 | 6 | H | 4-1 |
| 1952 | 4 | H | 4-0 |
| 1987 | 5 | H | 2-0 |

**v Birmingham City**

| | | | |
|---|---|---|---|
| 1892 | 1 | A | 1-5 |
| 1930 | 4 | H | 2-2 |
| 1930 | 4r | A | 1-0 |
| 1956 | 6 | H | 1-3 |
| 1967 | 5 | A | 0-1 |
| 1968 | 5 | H | 1-1 |
| 1968 | 5r | A | 1-2 |

**v Blackburn Rovers**

| | | | |
|---|---|---|---|
| 1901 | 1 | H | 2-0 |
| 1926 | 4 | H | 3-1 |
| 1928 | SF | N | 0-1 |
| 1966 | 3 | A | 0-3 |
| 2001 | 6 | H | 3-0 |

**v Blackpool**

| | | | |
|---|---|---|---|
| 1953 | 6 | H | 1-2 |
| 1970 | 3 | H | 1-1 |
| 1970 | 3r | A | 2-3 |
| 2000 | 3 | H | 3-1 |

**v Bolton Wanderers**

| | | | |
|---|---|---|---|
| 1895 | 1 | A | 0-1 |
| 1912 | 1 | A | 0-1 |
| 1938 | 3 | H | 3-1 |
| 1967 | 4 | A | 0-0 |
| 1967 | 4r | H | 3-0 |
| 1980 | 5 | A | 1-1 |
| 1980 | 5r | H | 3-0 |
| 1983 | 3 | H | 2-1 |
| 1994 | 4 | A | 2-2 |
| 1994 | 4r | H | 1-3aet |

**v Bradford City**

| | | | |
|---|---|---|---|
| 1914 | 1 | A | 0-2 |
| 1962 | 3 | H | 3-0 |
| 1973 | 4 | H | 2-0 |

**v Brentford**

| | | | |
|---|---|---|---|
| 1903 | IR | A | 1-1 |
| 1903 | IRr | H | 5-0 |

**v Brighton & HA**

| | | | |
|---|---|---|---|
| 1935 | 3 | A | 2-0 |
| 1980 | 4 | H | 2-0 |
| 1988 | 4 | A | 2-1 |

**v Bristol City**

| | | | |
|---|---|---|---|
| 1905 | 1 | H | 0-0 |
| 1905 | 1r | A | 0-1 |
| 1907 | 2 | H | 2-1 |
| 1920 | 2 | A | 0-1 |

**v Bristol Rovers**

| | | | |
|---|---|---|---|
| 1904 | IR | A | 1-1 |
| 1904 | IRr | H | 1-1 |
| 1904 | IRr2 | N | 1-0 |
| 1907 | 3 | H | 1-0 |
| 1936 | 3 | A | 5-1 |
| 1967 | 3 | A | 3-0 |

**v Burnley**

| | | | |
|---|---|---|---|
| 1896 | 1 | A | 1-6 |
| 1898 | 1 | A | 1-3 |
| 1937 | 5 | A | 7-1 |
| 1950 | 5 | H | 2-0 |
| 1953 | 5 | A | 2-0 |

**v Bury**

| | | | |
|---|---|---|---|
| 1953 | 4 | H | 6-2 |
| 1959 | 3 | A | 1-0 |

**v Cambridge Utd**

| | | | |
|---|---|---|---|
| 1991 | 6 | H | 2-1 |

**v Cardiff City**

| | | | |
|---|---|---|---|
| 1924 | 2 | A | 0-1 |
| 1927 | F | N | 0-1 |
| 1955 | 3 | H | 1-0 |
| 1969 | 3 | A | 0-0 |
| 1969 | 3r | H | 2-0 |
| 1980 | 3 | A | 0-0 |
| 1980 | 3r | H | 2-1 |

**v Carlisle Utd**

| | | | |
|---|---|---|---|
| 1951 | 3 | H | 0-0 |
| 1951 | 3r | A | 4-1 |
| 1973 | 5 | A | 2-1 |
| 2001 | 3 | A | 1-0 |

**v Charlton Athletic**

| | | | |
|---|---|---|---|
| 1956 | 5 | A | 2-0 |
| 1969 | 4 | H | 2-0 |

**v Chelsea**
1915 2 A 0-1
1930 3 H 2-0
1931 4 A 1-2
1939 3 A 1-2
1947 3 A 1-1
1947 3r H 1-1aet
1947 3r2 N 0-2
1950 SF N 2-2
1950 SFr N 1-0aet
1952 SF N 1-1
1952 SFr N 3-0
1973 6 A 2-2
1973 6r H 2-1
2001 5 H 3-1
2002 F N 2-0
2003 6 H 2-2
2003 6r A 3-1

**v Chesterfield**
1937 3 A 5-1

**v Colchester Utd**
1959 4 A 2-2
1959 4r H 4-0

**v Coventry City**
1975 4 A 1-1
1975 4r H 3-0
1977 4 H 3-1

**v Crystal Palace**
1934 4 H 7-0
1998 5 H 0-0
1998 5r A 2-1

**v Darlington**
1965 3 A 2-0

**v Derby County**
1891 1 H 1-2
1899 1 H 0-6
1934 5 H 1-0
1949 4 A 0-1
1972 5 A 2-2
1972 5r H 0-0aet
1972 5r2 N 1-0
1999 6 H 1-0

**v Doncaster Rovers**
1953 3 H 4-0

**v Everton**
1910 2 A 0-5
1928 4 H 4-3
1981 3 A 0-2

**v Fulham**
1904 1 H 1-0

**v Gillingham**
1898 Q5 H 4-2
1900 Q3 H 1-1
1900 Q3r A 0-0
1900 Q3r2 N 2-2aet
1900 Q3r3 N 1-1
1900 Q3r4 N 0-1
2002 5 H 5-2

**v Grimsby Town**
1907 1 A 1-1
1907 1r H 3-0
1936 SF N 1-0
1986 3 A 4-3

**v Huddersfield Town**
1930 F N 2-0
1932 6 A 1-0

**v Hull City**
1908 1 H 0-0
1908 1r A 1-4
1930 SF N 2-2
1930 SFr N 1-0

**v Ipswich Town**
1978 F N 0-1
1993 6 A 4-2

**v Leeds Utd**
1950 6 H 1-0
1972 F N 0-1
1983 4 H 1-1
1983 4r A 1-1aet
1983 4r2 H 2-1
1991 4 H 0-0
1991 4r A 1-1aet
1991 4r2 H 0-0aet
1991 4r3 A 2-1
1993 4 H 2-2
1993 4r A 3-2aet
1997 4 H 0-1

**v Leicester City**
1922 3 H 3-0
1935 4 A 1-0
1971 6 A 0-0
1971 6r H 1-0
1973 3 H 2-2
1973 3r A 2-1
1975 5 H 0-0
1975 5r A 1-1aet
1975 5r2 A 1-0aet
2000 4 H 0-0
2000 4r A 0-0p

**v Leyton Orient**
1911 1 A 2-1
1952 5 A 3-0
1972 6 A 1-0
1978 SF N 3-0

**v Liverpool**
1913 2 H 1-4
1923 1 A 0-0
1923 1r H 1-4
1927 5 H 2-0
1936 4 A 2-0
1950 F N 2-0
1963 5 H 1-2
1964 5 H 0-1
1971 F N 2-1aet
1980 SF N 0-0
1980 SFr N 1-1aet
1980 SFr2 N 1-1aet
1980 SFr3 N 1-0
2001 F N 1-2
2002 4 H 1-0

**v Luton Town**
1902 IR H 1-1
1902 IRr A 2-0
1924 1 H 4-1
1934 3 A 1-0
1952 6 A 3-2
1986 5 A 2-2
1986 5r H 0-0aet
1986 5r2 A 0-3

**v Manchester City**
1904 2 H 0-2
1932 SF N 1-0
1971 5 A 2-1

**v Manchester Utd**
1906 4 A 3-2
1937 4 H 5-0
1951 5 A 0-1
1962 4 A 0-1
1979 F N 3-2
1983 SF N 1-2
1988 5 H 2-1
1999 SF N 0-0aet
1999 SFr N 1-2aet
2003 5 A 2-0

**v Mansfield Town**
1929 4 H 2-0

**v Middlesbrough**
1930 5 A 2-0
1977 5 A 1-4
1983 5 A 1-1
1983 5r H 3-2
1984 3 A 2-3
1998 4 A 2-1
2002 SF N 1-0

**v Millwall**
1893 Q3 H 3-2
1894 Q3 H 2-0
1897 Q5 A 2-4
1909 2 H 1-1
1909 2r A 0-1
1988 3 H 2-0
1994 3 A 1-0
1995 3 A 0-0
1995 3r H 0-2

**v Newcastle Utd**
1902 1 H 0-2
1906 SF N 0-2
1932 F N 1-2
1936 5 A 3-3
1936 5r H 3-0
1952 F N 0-1
1998 F N 2-0
2002 6 A 1-1
2002 6r H 3-0

**v Northampton Town**
1951 4 H 3-2
1958 3 A 1-3

**v Norwich City**
1952 3 A 5-0
1954 4 H 1-2
1974 3 A 1-0

**v Nottingham Forest**
1979 5 A 1-0
1988 6 H 1-2
1993 5 H 2-0

**v Notts County**
1977 3 A 1-0
1979 4 H 2-0

**v Oxford United**
1963 3 H 5-1
2003 3 H 2-0

**v Peterborough**
1965 4 A 1-2

**v Plymouth Argyle**
1932 4 H 4-2
1987 4 H 6-1

**v Port Vale**
1927 4 A 2-2
1927 4r H 1-0
1998 3 H 0-0
1998 3r A 1-1q

**v Portsmouth**
1932 5 A 2-0
1971 4 A 1-1
1971 4r H 3-2

**v Preston North End**
1922 4 H 1-1
1922 4r A 1-2aet
1938 5 H 0-1
1957 5 A 3-3
1957 5r H 2-1
1999 3 A 4-2

**v QPR**
1921 1 A 0-2
1922 1 H 0-0
1922 1r A 2-1
1990 4 H 0-0
1990 4r A 0-2
2001 4 A 6-0

**v Reading**
1935 5 A 1-0
1972 4 A 2-1
1987 3 A 3-1

**v Rochdale**
1920 1 H 4-2

**v Rotherham Utd**
1960 3 A 2-2
1960 3r H 1-1aet
1960 3r2 N 0-2
1986 4 H 5-1

**v Sheffield Utd**
1903 1 H 1-3
1927 3 A 3-2
1936 F N 1-0
1959 5 H 2-2
1959 5r A 0-3
1978 3 A 5-0
1996 3 H 1-1
1996 3r A 0-1
1999 5r H 2-1
2003 SF N 1-0

**v Sheffield Wed**
1894 1 H 1-2
1907 SF N 1-3
1935 6 A 1-2
1950 3 H 1-0
1963 4 H 2-0
1979 3 A 1-1
1979 3r H 1-1aet
1979 3r2 N 2-2aet
1979 3r3 N 3-3aet
1979 3r4 N 2-0
1993 F N 1-1aet
1993 Fr N 2-1aet

**v Shrewsbury Town**
1968 3 A 1-1
1968 3r H 2-0
1991 5 A 1-0

**v Southampton**
1927 SF N 2-1
1979 6 A 1-1
1979 6r H 2-0
2003 F N 1-0

**v Stoke City**
1928 6 H 4-1
1929 3 H 2-1
1957 3 H 4-2
1971 SF N 2-2
1971 SFr N 2-0
1972 SF N 1-1
1972 SFr N 2-1
1990 3 A 1-0

**v Sunderland**
1893 1 A 0-6
1906 3 H 5-0
1961 3 A 1-2
1973 SF N 1-2
1991 3 H 2-1
1997 3 H 1-1
1997 3r A 2-0

**v Swansea City**
1926 6 A 1-2
1950 4 H 2-1
1968 4 A 1-0

**v Swindon Town**
1911 2 A 0-1
1929 5 A 0-0
1929 5r H 1-0
1972 3 A 2-0

**v Tottenham Hotspur**
1949 3 H 3-0
1982 3 A 0-1
1991 SF N 1-3
1993 SF N 1-0
2001 SF N 2-1

**v Walsall**
1933 3 A 0-2
1978 5 H 4-1

**v Watford**
1906 2 H 3-0
1910 1 H 3-0
1980 6 A 2-1
1987 6 H 1-3
2002 3 A 4-2

**v West Bromwich Albion**
1901 2 H 0-1
1928 3 H 2-0
1937 6 A 1-3
1957 6 A 2-2
1957 6r H 1-2
1964 4 A 3-3
1964 4r H 2-0
1969 5 A 0-1

**v West Ham Utd**
1906 1 H 1-1
1906 1r A 3-2
1925 1 A 0-0
1925 1r H 2-2aet
1925 1r2 N 0-1
1930 6 A 3-0
1946 3 A 0-6
1946 3s H 1-0
1975 6 H 0-2
1980 F N 0-1
1989 3 A 2-2
1989 3r H 0-1
1998 6 H 1-1
1998 6r A 1-1q

**v Wolverhampton W**
1926 3 A 1-1
1926 3r H 1-0
1927 6 H 2-1
1938 4 A 2-1
1955 4 A 0-1
1964 3 H 2-1
1976 3 A 0-3
1978 4 H 2-1
1979 SF N 2-0
1998 SF N 1-0
1999 4 A 2-1

**v Wrexham**
1978 6 A 3-2
1992 3 A 1-2

**v Yeovil Town**
1971 3 A 3-0
1993 3 A 3-1

**v York City**
1975 3 H 1-1
1975 3r A 3-1aet
1985 4 A 0-1

## Aston Villa

**v Barnsley**
1903 2 H 4-1
1995 3 A 2-0

**v Birmingham City**
1888 2 A 4-0
1901 3 A 0-0
1901 3r H 1-0aet

**v Blackburn Rovers**
1889 3 A 1-8
1923 1 H 0-1
1930 5 H 4-1
1980 5 A 1-1
1980 5r H 1-0
1990 3 A 2-2
1990 3r H 3-1
2003 3 H 1-4

**v Blackpool**
1938 4 H 4-0

**v Bolton Wanderers**
1907 2 A 0-2
1949 3 H 1-1aet
1949 3r A 0-0aet
1949 3r2 H 2-1aet
1994 5 A 0-1
2000 SF N 0-0p

**v Bradford City**

| | | | |
|---|---|---|---|
| 1933 | 3 | A | 2-2 |
| 1933 | 3r | H | 2-1 |
| 1935 | 3 | H | 1-3 |

**v Brentford**

| | | | |
|---|---|---|---|
| 1953 | 4 | H | 0-0 |
| 1953 | 4r | A | 2-1 |

**v Brighton & HA**

| | | | |
|---|---|---|---|
| 1955 | 3 | A | 2-2 |
| 1955 | 3r | H | 4-2 |

**v Bristol City**

| | | | |
|---|---|---|---|
| 1900 | 2 | H | 5-1 |
| 1921 | 1 | H | 2-0 |
| 1957 | 5 | H | 2-1 |
| 1963 | 3 | A | 1-1 |
| 1963 | 3r | H | 3-2 |
| 1982 | 4 | A | 1-0 |

**v Bristol Rovers**

| | | | |
|---|---|---|---|
| 1961 | 3 | A | 1-1 |
| 1961 | 3r | H | 4-0 |
| 1980 | 3 | A | 2-1 |
| 1993 | 3 | H | 1-1 |
| 1993 | 3r | A | 3-0 |

**v Burnley**

| | | | |
|---|---|---|---|
| 1907 | 1 | A | 3-1 |
| 1924 | SF | N | 3-0 |
| 1928 | 3 | A | 2-0 |
| 1937 | 3 | H | 2-3 |
| 1947 | 3 | A | 1-5 |
| 1951 | 3 | H | 2-0 |
| 1957 | 6 | A | 1-1 |
| 1957 | 6r | H | 2-0 |
| 1959 | 6 | H | 0-0 |
| 1959 | 6r | A | 2-0 |
| 1974 | 5 | A | 0-1 |

**v Bury**

| | | | |
|---|---|---|---|
| 1903 | SF | N | 0-3 |
| 1905 | 2 | H | 3-2 |

**v Cambridge Utd**

| | | | |
|---|---|---|---|
| 1980 | 4 | A | 1-1 |
| 1980 | 4r | H | 4-1 |

**v Cardiff City**

| | | | |
|---|---|---|---|
| 1927 | 3 | A | 1-2 |
| 1929 | 3 | H | 6-1 |
| 1949 | 4 | H | 1-2 |

**v Charlton Athletic**

| | | | |
|---|---|---|---|
| 1938 | 5 | A | 1-1 |
| 1938 | 5r | H | 2-2aet |
| 1938 | 5r2 | N | 4-1 |
| 1962 | 5 | H | 2-1 |
| 1970 | 3 | H | 1-1 |
| 1970 | 3r | A | 0-1 |

**v Chelsea**

| | | | |
|---|---|---|---|
| 1920 | SF | N | 3-1 |
| 1946 | 5 | A | 1-0 |
| 1946 | 5s | H | 1-0 |
| 1959 | 4 | A | 2-1 |
| 1960 | 4 | A | 2-1 |
| 1987 | 3 | H | 2-2 |
| 1987 | 3r | A | 1-2aet |
| 2000 | F | N | 0-1 |

**v Chesterfield**

| | | | |
|---|---|---|---|
| 1934 | 3 | A | 2-2 |
| 1934 | 3r | H | 2-0 |

**v Coventry City**

| | | | |
|---|---|---|---|
| 1946 | 3 | A | 1-2 |
| 1946 | 3s | H | 2-0 |
| 1965 | 3 | H | 3-0 |
| 1998 | 5 | H | 0-1 |

**v Crewe Alexandra**

| | | | |
|---|---|---|---|
| 1928 | 4 | H | 3-0 |
| 1989 | 3 | A | 3-2 |

**v Crystal Palace**

| | | | |
|---|---|---|---|
| 1913 | 3 | H | 5-0 |
| 1962 | 3 | H | 4-3 |

**v Darlington**

| | | | |
|---|---|---|---|
| 2000 | 3 | H | 2-1 |

**v Derby County**

| | | | |
|---|---|---|---|
| 1886 | 2 | A | 0-2 |
| 1889 | 2 | H | 5-3 |
| 1895 | 1 | H | 2-1 |
| 1896 | 1 | A | 2-4 |
| 1898 | 1 | A | 0-1 |
| 1910 | 2 | H | 6-1 |
| 1913 | 1 | A | 3-1 |
| 1922 | 1 | H | 6-1 |
| 1946 | 6 | H | 3-4 |
| 1946 | 6s | A | 1-1 |
| 1992 | 4 | A | 4-3 |
| 1997 | 4 | A | 1-3 |

**v Doncaster Rovers**

| | | | |
|---|---|---|---|
| 1955 | 4 | A | 0-0 |
| 1955 | 4r | H | 2-2aet |
| 1955 | 4r2 | N | 1-1aet |
| 1955 | 4r3 | N | 0-0ab |
| 1955 | 4r4 | N | 1-3 |

**v Everton**

| | | | |
|---|---|---|---|
| 1897 | F | N | 3-2 |
| 1905 | SF | N | 1-1 |
| 1905 | SFr | N | 2-1 |
| 1953 | 6 | H | 0-1 |
| 1959 | 5 | A | 4-1 |
| 1973 | 3 | A | 2-3 |
| 1978 | 3 | A | 1-4 |
| 2000 | 6 | A | 2-1 |

**v Exeter City**

| | | | |
|---|---|---|---|
| 1914 | 2 | A | 2-1 |
| 1915 | 1 | H | 2-0 |
| 1994 | 3 | A | 1-0 |

**v Fulham**

| | | | |
|---|---|---|---|
| 1905 | 3 | H | 5-0 |
| 1999 | 4 | H | 0-2 |

**v Grimsby Town**

| | | | |
|---|---|---|---|
| 1994 | 4 | A | 2-1 |

**v Huddersfield Town**

| | | | |
|---|---|---|---|
| 1920 | F | N | 1-0aet |
| 1921 | 3 | H | 2-0 |
| 1930 | 6 | H | 1-2 |
| 1936 | 3 | H | 0-1 |
| 1962 | 4 | H | 2-1 |

**v Hull City**

| | | | |
|---|---|---|---|
| 1908 | 2 | H | 3-0 |
| 1926 | 3 | A | 3-0 |
| 1956 | 3 | H | 1-1 |
| 1956 | 3r | A | 2-1 |
| 1999 | 3 | H | 3-0 |

**v Ipswich Town**

| | | | |
|---|---|---|---|
| 1939 | 3 | H | 1-1 |
| 1939 | 3r | A | 2-1 |
| 1975 | 5 | A | 2-3 |
| 1981 | 3 | A | 0-1 |
| 1996 | 5 | A | 3-1 |

**v Leeds Utd**

| | | | |
|---|---|---|---|
| 1924 | 3 | H | 3-0 |
| 1960 | 3 | H | 2-1 |
| 1988 | 3 | A | 2-1 |
| 2000 | 5 | H | 3-2 |

**v Leicester City**

| | | | |
|---|---|---|---|
| 1905 | 1 | H | 5-1 |
| 1966 | 3 | H | 1-2 |
| 1977 | 3 | A | 1-0 |
| 2001 | 4 | H | 1-2 |

**v Leyton Orient**

| | | | |
|---|---|---|---|
| 1929 | 4 | H | 0-0 |
| 1929 | 4r | A | 8-0 |

**v Liverpool**

| | | | |
|---|---|---|---|
| 1897 | SF | N | 3-0 |
| 1914 | SF | N | 0-2 |
| 1967 | 4 | A | 0-1 |
| 1985 | 3 | A | 0-3 |
| 1988 | 4 | H | 0-2 |
| 1992 | 6 | A | 0-1 |
| 1996 | SF | N | 0-3 |

**v Luton Town**

| | | | |
|---|---|---|---|
| 1922 | 2 | H | 1-0 |
| 1957 | 3 | A | 2-2 |
| 1957 | 3r | H | 2-0 |

**v Manchester City**

| | | | |
|---|---|---|---|
| 1900 | 1 | A | 1-1 |
| 1900 | 1r | H | 3-0 |
| 1910 | 3 | H | 1-2 |
| 1915 | 2 | A | 0-1 |
| 1934 | SF | N | 1-6 |
| 1938 | 6 | H | 3-2 |
| 1995 | 4 | A | 0-1 |

**v Manchester Utd**

| | | | |
|---|---|---|---|
| 1906 | 3 | A | 1-5 |
| 1908 | 3 | H | 0-2 |
| 1911 | 2 | A | 1-2 |
| 1920 | 2 | A | 2-1 |
| 1948 | 3 | H | 4-6 |
| 1957 | F | N | 2-1 |
| 1963 | 4 | A | 0-1 |
| 1977 | 6 | A | 1-2 |
| 2002 | 3 | H | 2-3 |

**v Middlesbrough**

| | | | |
|---|---|---|---|
| 1950 | 3 | H | 2-2 |
| 1950 | 3r | A | 0-0aet |
| 1950 | 3r2 | N | 0-3 |
| 1953 | 3 | H | 3-1 |
| 1957 | 4 | A | 3-2 |

**v Millwall**

| | | | |
|---|---|---|---|
| 1900 | 3 | A | 1-1 |
| 1900 | 3r | H | 0-0aet |
| 1900 | 3r2 | N | 1-2 |
| 1901 | 1 | H | 5-0 |
| 1946 | 4 | A | 4-2 |

| | | | |
|---|---|---|---|
| 1946 | 4s | H | 9-1 |
| 1968 | 3 | H | 3-0 |
| 1986 | 4 | H | 1-1 |
| 1986 | 4r | A | 0-1 |

v **Newcastle Utd**

| | | | |
|---|---|---|---|
| 1895 | 2 | H | 7-1 |
| 1897 | 1 | H | 5-0 |
| 1905 | F | N | 2-0 |
| 1924 | F | N | 0-2 |
| 1952 | 3 | A | 2-4 |
| 2001 | 3 | A | 1-1 |
| 2001 | 3r | H | 1-0 |

v **Northampton Town**

| | | | |
|---|---|---|---|
| 1983 | 3 | A | 1-0 |

v **Norwich City**

| | | | |
|---|---|---|---|
| 1938 | 3 | A | 3-2 |
| 1984 | 3 | H | 1-1 |
| 1984 | 3r | A | 0-3 |

v **Nottingham Forest**

| | | | |
|---|---|---|---|
| 1881 | 2 | A | 2-1 |
| 1882 | 1 | H | 4-1 |
| 1895 | 3 | H | 6-2 |
| 1899 | 1 | A | 1-2 |
| 1901 | 2 | H | 0-0 |
| 1901 | 2r | A | 3-1aet |
| 1909 | 1 | A | 0-2 |
| 1959 | SF | N | 0-1 |
| 1979 | 3 | A | 0-2 |
| 1996 | 6 | A | 1-0 |

v **Notts County**

| | | | |
|---|---|---|---|
| 1881 | 3 | A | 3-1 |
| 1882 | 3 | H | 2-2aet |
| 1882 | 3r | A | 2-2aet |
| 1882 | 3r2 | H | 4-1 |
| 1883 | 5 | A | 3-4 |
| 1890 | 2 | A | 1-4 |
| 1897 | 2 | H | 2-1 |
| 1921 | 2 | A | 0-0 |
| 1921 | 2r | H | 1-0 |
| 1922 | 4 | A | 2-2 |
| 1922 | 4r | H | 3-4aet |
| 1982 | 3 | A | 6-0 |
| 1997 | 3 | A | 0-0 |
| 1997 | 3r | H | 3-0 |

v **Oldham Athletic**

| | | | |
|---|---|---|---|
| 1910 | 1 | A | 2-1 |
| 1913 | SF | N | 1-0 |
| 1975 | 3 | A | 3-0 |
| 1990 | 6 | A | 0-3 |

v **Peterborough**

| | | | |
|---|---|---|---|
| 1961 | 4 | A | 1-1 |
| 1961 | 4r | H | 2-1 |

v **Plymouth Argyle**

| | | | |
|---|---|---|---|
| 1906 | 2 | H | 0-0 |
| 1906 | 2r | A | 5-1 |

v **Port Vale**

| | | | |
|---|---|---|---|
| 1925 | 1 | H | 7-2 |
| 1960 | 5 | A | 2-1 |
| 1977 | 5 | H | 3-0 |
| 1990 | 4 | H | 6-0 |

v **Portsmouth**

| | | | |
|---|---|---|---|
| 1911 | 1 | A | 4-1 |
| 1929 | SF | N | 0-1 |
| 1932 | 4 | A | 1-1 |
| 1932 | 4r | H | 0-1 |
| 1986 | 3 | A | 2-2 |
| 1986 | 3r | H | 3-2aet |
| 1998 | 3 | A | 2-2 |
| 1998 | 3r | H | 1-0 |

v **Preston North End**

| | | | |
|---|---|---|---|
| 1888 | 5 | H | 1-3 |
| 1897 | 3 | A | 1-1 |
| 1897 | 3r | H | 0-0 |
| 1897 | 3r2 | N | 3-2 |
| 1938 | SF | N | 1-2 |
| 1939 | 4 | A | 0-2 |
| 1960 | 6 | H | 2-0 |
| 1967 | 3 | A | 1-0 |

v **QPR**

| | | | |
|---|---|---|---|
| 1920 | 1 | H | 2-1 |
| 1969 | 3 | H | 2-1 |

v **Reading**

| | | | |
|---|---|---|---|
| 1912 | 2 | H | 1-1 |
| 1912 | 2r | A | 0-1 |
| 1929 | 5 | A | 3-1 |
| 1930 | 3 | H | 5-1 |

v **Rotherham Utd**

| | | | |
|---|---|---|---|
| 1953 | 5 | A | 3-1 |
| 1959 | 3 | H | 2-1 |
| 1968 | 4 | H | 0-1 |

v **Sheffield Utd**

| | | | |
|---|---|---|---|
| 1901 | SF | N | 2-2 |
| 1901 | SFr | N | 0-3 |
| 1965 | 4 | A | 2-0 |
| 1975 | 4 | H | 4-1 |
| 1996 | 4 | A | 1-0 |

v **Sheffield Wed**

| | | | |
|---|---|---|---|
| 1894 | 3 | A | 2-3aet |
| 1914 | 4 | A | 1-0 |

v **Southampton**

| | | | |
|---|---|---|---|
| 1969 | 4 | A | 2-2 |
| 1969 | 4r | H | 2-1 |
| 1976 | 3 | A | 1-1 |
| 1976 | 3r | H | 1-2aet |
| 2000 | 4 | H | 1-0 |

v **Southend Utd**

| | | | |
|---|---|---|---|
| 1972 | 1 | A | 0-1 |

v **Stockport County**

| | | | |
|---|---|---|---|
| 1908 | 1 | H | 3-0 |

v **Stoke City**

| | | | |
|---|---|---|---|
| 1891 | 2 | A | 0-3 |
| 1902 | 1 | A | 2-2 |
| 1902 | 1r | H | 1-2aet |
| 1904 | 1 | A | 3-2 |
| 1914 | 1 | H | 4-0 |
| 1922 | 3 | A | 0-0 |
| 1922 | 3r | H | 4-0 |
| 1958 | 3 | A | 1-1 |
| 1958 | 3r | H | 3-3aet |
| 1958 | 3r2 | N | 0-2 |

v **Sunderland**

| | | | |
|---|---|---|---|
| 1892 | SF | N | 4-1 |
| 1894 | 2 | A | 2-2aet |
| 1894 | 2r | H | 3-1 |
| 1895 | SF | N | 2-1 |
| 1903 | 1 | H | 4-1 |
| 1913 | F | N | 1-0 |
| 1920 | 3 | H | 1-0 |
| 1933 | 4 | H | 0-3 |
| 1934 | 4 | H | 7-2 |

v **Swansea City**

| | | | |
|---|---|---|---|
| 1924 | 2 | A | 2-0 |
| 1925 | 2 | A | 3-1 |

v **Swindon Town**

| | | | |
|---|---|---|---|
| 1992 | 5 | A | 2-1 |

v **Torquay Utd**

| | | | |
|---|---|---|---|
| 1971 | 1 | A | 1-3 |

v **Tottenham Hotspur**

| | | | |
|---|---|---|---|
| 1903 | 3 | A | 3-2 |
| 1904 | 2 | H | 0-1 |
| 1920 | 4 | A | 1-0 |
| 1921 | 4 | A | 0-1 |
| 1934 | 5 | A | 1-0 |
| 1961 | 5 | H | 0-2 |
| 1962 | 6 | A | 0-2 |
| 1969 | 5 | A | 2-3 |
| 1982 | 5 | A | 0-1 |
| 1992 | 3 | H | 0-0 |
| 1992 | 3r | A | 1-0 |

v **Walsall**

| | | | |
|---|---|---|---|
| 1912 | 1 | H | 6-0 |
| 1930 | 4 | H | 3-1 |

v **Watford**

| | | | |
|---|---|---|---|
| 1983 | 5 | H | 4-1 |

v **West Bromwich Albion**

| | | | |
|---|---|---|---|
| 1885 | 3 | H | 0-0 |
| 1885 | 3r | A | 0-3 |
| 1887 | F | N | 2-0 |
| 1892 | F | N | 0-3 |
| 1895 | F | N | 1-0 |
| 1914 | 3 | H | 2-1 |
| 1924 | 4 | A | 2-0 |
| 1925 | 3 | A | 1-1 |
| 1925 | 3r | H | 1-2 |
| 1926 | 4 | A | 2-1 |
| 1932 | 3 | A | 2-1 |
| 1957 | SF | N | 2-2 |
| 1957 | SFr | N | 1-0 |
| 1990 | 5 | A | 2-0 |
| 1998 | 4 | H | 4-0 |

v **West Ham Utd**

| | | | |
|---|---|---|---|
| 1913 | 2 | H | 5-0 |
| 1977 | 4 | H | 3-0 |
| 1980 | 6 | A | 0-1 |

v **Wimbledon**

| | | | |
|---|---|---|---|
| 1989 | 4 | H | 0-1 |
| 1991 | 3 | H | 1-1 |
| 1991 | 3r | A | 0-1aet |
| 1993 | 4 | H | 1-1 |
| 1993 | 4r | A | 0-0p |

v **Wolverhampton W**

| | | | |
|---|---|---|---|
| 1887 | 3 | H | 2-2aet |
| 1887 | 3r | A | 1-1aet |
| 1887 | 3r2 | A | 3-3aet |
| 1887 | 3r3 | H | 2-0 |
| 1892 | 3 | A | 3-1 |

| | | | |
|---|---|---|---|
| 1894 | 1 | H | 4-2 |
| 1951 | 4 | A | 1-3 |
| 1960 | SF | N | 0-1 |
| 1965 | 5 | H | 1-1 |
| 1965 | 5r | A | 0-0aet |
| 1965 | 5r2 | N | 1-3 |
| 1983 | 4 | H | 1-0 |

# Barnsley

v **Birmingham City**

| | | | |
|---|---|---|---|
| 1912 | 1 | A | 0-0 |
| 1912 | 1r | H | 3-0 |
| 1936 | 3 | H | 3-3 |
| 1936 | 3r | A | 2-0 |
| 1988 | 4 | H | 0-2 |

v **Blackburn Rovers**

| | | | |
|---|---|---|---|
| 1913 | 2 | H | 2-3 |
| 1929 | 3 | A | 0-1 |
| 1956 | 4 | H | 0-1 |
| 2002 | 3 | H | 1-1 |
| 2002 | 3r | A | 1-3 |

v **Blackpool**

| | | | |
|---|---|---|---|
| 1910 | 1 | A | 1-1 |
| 1910 | 1r | H | 6-0 |
| 1949 | 3 | H | 0-1 |
| 1982 | 3 | H | 0-2 |
| 2003 | 1 | H | 1-4 |

v **Bolton Wanderers**

| | | | |
|---|---|---|---|
| 1912 | 3 | A | 2-1 |
| 1988 | 3 | H | 3-1 |
| 1998 | 3 | H | 1-0 |

v **Bournemouth**

| | | | |
|---|---|---|---|
| 1999 | 4 | H | 3-1 |

v **Bradford City**

| | | | |
|---|---|---|---|
| 1912 | 4 | H | 0-0 |
| 1912 | 4r | A | 0-0aet |
| 1912 | 4r2 | H | 0-0aet |
| 1912 | 4r3 | N | 3-2aet |
| 1921 | 1 | A | 1-3 |
| 1925 | 2 | H | 0-3 |
| 1960 | 1 | H | 3-3 |
| 1960 | 1r | A | 1-2 |
| 1961 | 2 | A | 2-1 |
| 1974 | 2 | H | 1-1 |
| 1974 | 2r | A | 1-2 |
| 1983 | 3 | A | 1-0 |

v **Brentford**

| | | | |
|---|---|---|---|
| 1959 | 3 | A | 0-2 |

v **Brighton & HA**

| | | | |
|---|---|---|---|
| 1924 | 1 | H | 0-0 |
| 1924 | 1r | A | 0-1 |
| 1953 | 3 | H | 4-3 |
| 1985 | 4 | H | 2-1 |

v **Bristol City**

| | | | |
|---|---|---|---|
| 1931 | 3 | H | 4-1 |

v **Bristol Rovers**

| | | | |
|---|---|---|---|
| 1910 | 2 | H | 4-0 |
| 1999 | 5 | H | 4-1 |

v **Burnley**

| | | | |
|---|---|---|---|
| 1911 | 2 | A | 0-2 |

v **Bury**

| | | | |
|---|---|---|---|
| 1907 | 3 | H | 1-0 |
| 1964 | 4 | H | 2-1 |
| 1986 | 3 | A | 0-2 |

v **Cambridge Utd**

| | | | |
|---|---|---|---|
| 1983 | 4 | A | 0-1 |

v **Cardiff City**

| | | | |
|---|---|---|---|
| 1957 | 4 | A | 1-0 |
| 1967 | 3 | H | 1-1 |
| 1967 | 3r | A | 1-2 |

v **Carlisle Utd**

| | | | |
|---|---|---|---|
| 1962 | 2 | H | 1-2 |

v **Chelsea**

| | | | |
|---|---|---|---|
| 1989 | 3 | H | 4-0 |

v **Chesterfield**

| | | | |
|---|---|---|---|
| 1901 | Q5 | H | 1-5 |
| 1903 | Q4 | H | 3-2 |
| 1963 | 2 | H | 2-1 |
| 1968 | 1 | A | 0-2 |
| 1972 | 2 | H | 0-0 |
| 1972 | 2r | A | 0-1 |
| 1974 | 1 | A | 0-0 |
| 1974 | 1r | H | 2-1 |

v **Colchester Utd**

| | | | |
|---|---|---|---|
| 1952 | 3 | H | 3-0 |

v **Crewe Alexandra**

| | | | |
|---|---|---|---|
| 1906 | 1 | A | 1-1 |
| 1906 | 1r | H | 4-0 |
| 1927 | 3 | H | 6-1 |

v **Darlington**

| | | | |
|---|---|---|---|
| 1969 | 2 | A | 0-0 |
| 1969 | 2r | H | 1-0aet |
| 1970 | 1 | A | 0-0 |
| 1970 | 1r | H | 2-0 |

v **Derby County**

| | | | |
|---|---|---|---|
| 1897 | 1 | A | 1-8 |

v **Doncaster Rovers**

| | | | |
|---|---|---|---|
| 1899 | Q4 | A | 2-1 |
| 1901 | Q3 | H | 2-1 |

v **Everton**

| | | | |
|---|---|---|---|
| 1909 | 1 | A | 1-3 |
| 1910 | SF | N | 0-0 |
| 1910 | SFr | N | 3-0 |
| 1915 | 1 | A | 0-3 |
| 1963 | 3 | H | 0-3 |
| 1989 | 5 | H | 0-1 |

v **Gillingham**

| | | | |
|---|---|---|---|
| 1913 | 1 | A | 0-0 |
| 1913 | 1r | H | 3-1 |

v **Grimsby Town**

| | | | |
|---|---|---|---|
| 1899 | Q5 | H | 0-0 |
| 1899 | Q5r | A | 1-2 |
| 1900 | Q4 | A | 2-3 |
| 1904 | IR | A | 0-2 |
| 1966 | 2 | H | 1-1 |
| 1966 | 2r | A | 0-2aet |
| 1978 | 2 | A | 0-2 |

v **Hartlepool Utd**

| | | | |
|---|---|---|---|
| 1980 | 1 | H | 5-2 |

v **Huddersfield Town**

| | | | |
|---|---|---|---|
| 1947 | 3 | A | 4-3 |
| 1961 | 4 | A | 1-1 |
| 1961 | 4r | H | 1-0 |
| 1978 | 1 | H | 1-0 |

v **Hull City**

| | | | |
|---|---|---|---|
| 1958 | 3 | A | 1-1 |
| 1958 | 3r | H | 0-2 |

v **Ipswich Town**

| | | | |
|---|---|---|---|
| 1990 | 4 | H | 2-0 |

v **Leeds Utd**

| | | | |
|---|---|---|---|
| 1991 | 3 | H | 1-1 |
| 1991 | 3r | A | 0-4 |
| 2001 | 3 | A | 0-1 |

v **Leicester City**

| | | | |
|---|---|---|---|
| 1912 | 2 | H | 1-0 |
| 1961 | 6 | A | 0-0 |
| 1961 | 6r | H | 1-2 |
| 1969 | 3 | H | 1-1 |
| 1969 | 3r | A | 1-2 |
| 1990 | 3 | A | 2-1 |
| 1993 | 3 | A | 2-2 |
| 1993 | 3r | H | 1-1p |

v **Lincoln City**

| | | | |
|---|---|---|---|
| 1897 | Q5 | A | 2-1 |
| 1900 | Q3 | H | 1-0 |
| 1901 | Q4 | H | 1-0 |
| 1902 | Q5 | H | 0-0 |
| 1902 | Q5r | A | 1-3aet |
| 1903 | 1 | H | 2-0 |
| 1966 | 1 | A | 3-1 |

v **Liverpool**

| | | | |
|---|---|---|---|
| 1895 | 1r | A | 0-4 |
| 1906 | 2 | A | 0-1 |
| 1914 | 1 | A | 1-1 |
| 1914 | 1r | H | 0-1 |
| 1985 | 6 | H | 0-4 |

v **Luton Town**

| | | | |
|---|---|---|---|
| 1933 | 3 | H | 0-0 |
| 1933 | 3r | A | 0-2 |
| 1961 | 5 | H | 1-0 |

v **Manchester City**

| | | | |
|---|---|---|---|
| 1948 | 3 | A | 1-2 |
| 1993 | 5 | A | 0-2 |

v **Manchester Utd**

| | | | |
|---|---|---|---|
| 1938 | 4 | H | 2-2 |
| 1938 | 4r | A | 0-1 |
| 1964 | 5 | H | 0-4 |
| 1998 | 5 | A | 1-1 |
| 1998 | 5r | H | 3-2 |

v **Mansfield Town**

| | | | |
|---|---|---|---|
| 1970 | 3 | A | 2-3 |

v **Middlesbrough**

| | | | |
|---|---|---|---|
| 1981 | 5 | A | 1-2 |

v **Millwall**

| | | | |
|---|---|---|---|
| 1925 | 1 | A | 0-0 |
| 1925 | 1r | H | 2-1 |

v **Newcastle Utd**

| | | | |
|---|---|---|---|
| 1910 | F | N | 1-1 |
| 1910 | Fr | N | 0-2 |
| 1946 | 3 | A | 2-4 |
| 1946 | 3s | H | 3-0 |
| 1998 | 6 | A | 1-3 |

v **Northampton Town**

| | | | |
|---|---|---|---|
| 1926 | 1 | A | 1-3 |
| 1951 | 3 | A | 1-3 |

v **Norwich City**

| | | | |
|---|---|---|---|
| 1922 | 1 | H | 1-1 |
| 1922 | 1r | A | 2-1 |
| 1954 | 2 | A | 1-2 |
| 1992 | 3 | A | 0-1 |

v **Nottingham Forest**

| | | | |
|---|---|---|---|
| 1907 | 1 | A | 1-1 |
| 1907 | 1r | H | 2-1 |
| 1957 | 5 | H | 1-2 |

v **Oldham Athletic**

| | | | |
|---|---|---|---|
| 1922 | 2 | H | 3-1 |
| 1994 | 5 | A | 0-1 |
| 1996 | 3 | H | 0-0 |
| 1996 | 3r | A | 1-2 |
| 1997 | 3 | H | 2-0 |

v **Plymouth Argyle**

| | | | |
|---|---|---|---|
| 1905 | IR | A | 0-2 |
| 1908 | 1 | A | 0-1 |
| 1920 | 2 | A | 1-4 |
| 1953 | 4 | A | 0-1 |
| 1994 | 4 | A | 2-2 |
| 1994 | 4r | H | 1-0 |

v **Port Vale**

| | | | |
|---|---|---|---|
| 1905 | Q6 | H | 0-0 |
| 1905 | Q6r | A | 2-1 |
| 1928 | 3 | A | 0-3 |
| 1957 | 3 | H | 3-3 |
| 1957 | 3r | A | 1-0 |
| 1967 | 2 | H | 1-1 |
| 1967 | 2r | A | 3-1 |
| 1977 | 2 | A | 0-3 |

v **Portsmouth**

| | | | |
|---|---|---|---|
| 1907 | 2 | H | 1-0 |

v **Preston North End**

| | | | |
|---|---|---|---|
| 1922 | 3 | H | 1-1 |
| 1922 | 3r | A | 0-3 |
| 1935 | 3 | A | 0-0 |
| 1935 | 3r | H | 0-1 |
| 1947 | 4 | A | 0-6 |

v **QPR**

| | | | |
|---|---|---|---|
| 1910 | 4 | H | 1-0 |
| 1997 | 4 | A | 2-3 |

v **Reading**

| | | | |
|---|---|---|---|
| 1961 | 3 | A | 1-1 |
| 1961 | 3r | H | 3-1aet |
| 1985 | 3 | H | 4-3 |

v **Rochdale**

| | | | |
|---|---|---|---|
| 1964 | 2 | H | 3-1 |
| 1969 | 1 | H | 0-0 |
| 1969 | 1r | A | 1-0 |
| 1972 | 1 | A | 3-1 |

v **Rotherham Utd**

| | | | |
|---|---|---|---|
| 1946 | 4 | H | 3-0 |
| r1946 | 4s | A | 1-2 |
| 1979 | 2 | H | 1-1 |
| 1979 | 2r | A | 1-2 |
| 1981 | 2 | A | 1-0 |

v **Scunthorpe Utd**

| | | | |
|---|---|---|---|
| 1964 | 3 | A | 2-2 |
| 1964 | 3r | H | 3-2aet |

v **Sheffield Utd**

| | | | |
|---|---|---|---|
| 1990 | 5 | A | 2-2 |
| 1990 | 5r | H | 0-0aet |
| 1990 | 5r2 | H | 0-1aet |

v **Sheffield Wed**

| | | | |
|---|---|---|---|
| 1923 | 2 | A | 1-2 |
| 1931 | 4 | H | 2-1 |
| 1984 | 3 | A | 0-1 |

v **Southampton**

| | | | |
|---|---|---|---|
| 1985 | 5 | A | 2-1 |

v **Southend Utd**

| | | | |
|---|---|---|---|
| 1938 | 3 | A | 2-2 |
| 1938 | 3r | H | 2-1 |

v **Stockport County**

| | | | |
|---|---|---|---|
| 1939 | 3 | H | 1-2 |
| 1950 | 3 | A | 2-4 |
| 1964 | 1 | H | 1-0 |

v **Stoke City**

| | | | |
|---|---|---|---|
| 1936 | 5 | H | 2-1 |
| 1989 | 4 | A | 3-3 |
| 1989 | 4r | H | 2-1 |

v **Swansea City**

| | | | |
|---|---|---|---|
| 1927 | 4 | H | 1-3 |

v **Swindon Town**

| | | | |
|---|---|---|---|
| 1903 | IR | H | 4-0 |
| 1912 | SF | N | 0-0 |
| 1912 | SFr | N | 1-0 |
| 1923 | 1 | A | 0-0 |
| 1923 | 1r | H | 2-0 |
| 1999 | 3 | A | 0-0 |
| 1999 | 3r | H | 3-1 |

v **Torquay Utd**

| | | | |
|---|---|---|---|
| 1981 | 3 | H | 2-1 |

v **Tottenham Hotspur**

| | | | |
|---|---|---|---|
| 1998 | 4 | A | 1-1 |
| 1998 | 4r | H | 3-1 |
| 1999 | 6 | H | 0-1 |

v **Tranmere Rovers**

| | | | |
|---|---|---|---|
| 1936 | 4 | A | 4-2 |

v **Walsall**

| | | | |
|---|---|---|---|
| 1937 | 3 | A | 1-3 |

v **Watford**

| | | | |
|---|---|---|---|
| 1911 | 1 | A | 2-0 |

v **West Bromwich Albion**

| | | | |
|---|---|---|---|
| 1910 | 3 | H | 1-0 |
| 1912 | F | N | 0-0 |
| 1912 | Fr | N | 1-0aet |
| 1920 | 1 | A | 1-0 |

v **West Ham Utd**

| | | | |
|---|---|---|---|
| 1993 | 4 | H | 4-1 |

v **Wigan Athletic**

| | | | |
|---|---|---|---|
| 1955 | 1 | H | 3-2 |

v **Wimbledon**

| | | | |
|---|---|---|---|
| 2000 | 3 | A | 0-1 |

v **Wolverhampton W**

| | | | |
|---|---|---|---|
| 1931 | 5 | H | 1-3 |

v **York City**

| | | | |
|---|---|---|---|
| 1954 | 1 | H | 5-2 |

# Birmingham City

v **Blackburn Rovers**

| | | | |
|---|---|---|---|
| 1933 | 4 | H | 3-0 |
| 1935 | 5 | A | 2-1 |

v **Blackpool**

| | | | |
|---|---|---|---|
| 1938 | 3 | H | 0-1 |
| 1951 | SF | N | 0-0 |
| 1951 | SFr | N | 1-2 |
| 1967 | 3 | H | 2-1 |

v **Bolton Wanderers**

| | | | |
|---|---|---|---|
| 1894 | 1 | H | 3-4 |
| 1930 | 3 | H | 1-0 |
| 1955 | 4 | H | 2-1 |

v **Bradford City**

| | | | |
|---|---|---|---|
| 1932 | 3 | H | 1-0 |

v **Brentford**

| | | | |
|---|---|---|---|
| 1991 | 2 | H | 1-3 |

v **Brighton & HA**

| | | | |
|---|---|---|---|
| 1915 | 2 | A | 0-0aet |
| 1915 | 2r | H | 3-0 |

v **Bristol City**

| | | | |
|---|---|---|---|
| 1951 | 5 | H | 2-0 |
| 1966 | 3 | H | 3-2 |

v **Burnley**

| | | | |
|---|---|---|---|
| 1893 | 1 | A | 0-2 |
| 1901 | 2 | H | 1-0 |
| 1935 | 6 | A | 2-3 |
| 1979 | 3 | H | 0-2 |

v **Bury**

| | | | |
|---|---|---|---|
| 1896 | 1 | H | 1-4 |
| 1963 | 3 | H | 3-3 |
| 1963 | 3r | A | 0-2 |

v **Cardiff City**

| | | | |
|---|---|---|---|
| 1974 | 3 | H | 5-2 |

v **Carlisle Utd**

| | | | |
|---|---|---|---|
| 1957 | 3 | A | 3-3 |
| 1957 | 3r | H | 4-0 |

v **Charlton Athletic**

| | | | |
|---|---|---|---|
| 1934 | 4 | H | 1-0 |

v **Chelsea**

| | | | |
|---|---|---|---|
| 1925 | 1 | H | 2-0 |
| 1929 | 4 | A | 0-1 |
| 1931 | 6 | H | 2-2 |
| 1931 | 6r | A | 3-0 |
| 1953 | 5 | A | 4-0 |
| 1968 | 6 | H | 1-0 |
| 1970 | 3 | A | 0-3 |
| 1975 | 4 | A | 1-0 |

v **Cheltenham Town**

| | | | |
|---|---|---|---|
| 1991 | 1 | H | 1-0 |

v **Colchester Utd**

| | | | |
|---|---|---|---|
| 1990 | 2 | A | 2-0 |

v **Coventry City**

| | | | |
|---|---|---|---|
| 1935 | 3 | H | 5-1 |
| 1981 | 4 | A | 2-3 |

v **Crewe Alexandra**

| | | | |
|---|---|---|---|
| 1998 | 3 | A | 2-1 |

v **Crystal Palace**

| | | | |
|---|---|---|---|
| 1915 | 1 | H | 2-2 |
| 1915 | 1r | H | 3-0aet |
| 1983 | 4 | A | 0-1 |

v **Darlington**

| | | | |
|---|---|---|---|
| 1920 | 2 | H | 4-0 |

v **Derby County**

| | | | |
|---|---|---|---|
| 1886 | 3 | H | 4-2 |
| 1903 | 1 | A | 1-2 |
| 1946 | SF | N | 1-1 |
| 1946 | SFr | N | 0-4aet |
| 1951 | 4 | A | 3-1 |
| 1978 | 4 | A | 1-2 |

v **Doncaster Rovers**

| | | | |
|---|---|---|---|
| 1955 | 5 | H | 2-1 |

v **Everton**

| | | | |
|---|---|---|---|
| 1920 | 1 | H | 2-0 |
| 1939 | 5 | H | 2-2 |
| 1939 | 5r | A | 1-2 |
| 2000 | 4 | A | 0-2 |

v **Fulham**

| | | | |
|---|---|---|---|
| 1947 | 3 | A | 2-1 |
| 1952 | 3 | A | 1-0 |
| 1959 | 4 | H | 1-1 |
| 1959 | 4r | A | 3-2 |
| 1975 | SF | N | 1-1 |
| 1975 | SFr | N | 0-1aet |
| 2003 | 3 | A | 1-3 |

v **Gillingham**

| | | | |
|---|---|---|---|
| 1988 | 3 | A | 3-0 |

v **Grimsby Town**

| | | | |
|---|---|---|---|
| 1926 | 3 | H | 2-0 |
| 1932 | 4 | A | 1-2 |

v **Huddersfield Town**

| | | | |
|---|---|---|---|
| 1914 | 2 | H | 1-0 |
| 1923 | 1 | A | 1-2 |
| 1924 | 1 | A | 0-1 |
| 1971 | 3 | A | 1-1 |
| 1971 | 3r | H | 0-2 |
| 1972 | 6 | H | 3-1 |

v **Hull City**

| | | | |
|---|---|---|---|
| 1955 | 3 | A | 2-0 |

v **Ipswich Town**

| | | | |
|---|---|---|---|
| 1954 | 4 | A | 0-1 |
| 1972 | 4 | H | 1-0 |
| 1982 | 3 | H | 2-3 |
| 1987 | 3 | A | 1-0 |

v **Kidderminster H**

| | | | |
|---|---|---|---|
| 1994 | 3 | H | 1-2 |

v **Leeds Utd**

| | | | |
|---|---|---|---|
| 1972 | SF | N | 0-3 |
| 1977 | 4 | H | 1-2 |
| 1998 | 5 | A | 2-3 |

v **Leicester City**

| | | | |
|---|---|---|---|
| 1892 | Q1 | A | 6-2 |
| 1910 | 1 | H | 1-4 |
| 1934 | 5 | H | 1-2 |
| 1949 | 3 | H | 1-1aet |
| 1949 | 3r | A | 1-1aet |
| 1949 | 3r2 | H | 1-2 |
| 1961 | 5 | H | 1-1 |
| 1961 | 5r | A | 1-2 |
| 1966 | 4 | H | 1-2 |
| 1999 | 3 | A | 2-4 |

v **Leyton Orient**

| | | | |
|---|---|---|---|
| 1952 | 4 | H | 0-1 |
| 1956 | 4 | A | 4-0 |
| 1968 | 4 | H | 3-0 |
| 1990 | 1 | A | 1-0 |

v **Lincoln City**

| | | | |
|---|---|---|---|
| 1969 | 3 | H | 2-1 |

v **Liverpool**

| | | | |
|---|---|---|---|
| 1907 | 1 | A | 1-2 |
| 1920 | 3 | A | 0-2 |
| 1925 | 3 | A | 1-2 |
| 1931 | 3 | A | 2-0 |
| 1947 | 6 | A | 1-4 |
| 1995 | 3 | H | 0-0 |
| 1995 | 3r | A | 1-1p |
| 2002 | 3 | A | 0-3 |

v **Luton Town**

| | | | |
|---|---|---|---|
| 1921 | 1 | A | 1-2 |
| 1975 | 3 | A | 1-0 |

v **Manchester City**

| | | | |
|---|---|---|---|
| 1899 | 1 | H | 3-2 |
| 1913 | 1 | A | 0-4 |
| 1927 | 3 | H | 4-1 |
| 1929 | 3 | H | 3-1 |
| 1947 | 5 | H | 5-0 |
| 1951 | 3 | H | 2-0 |
| 1955 | 6 | H | 0-1 |
| 1956 | F | N | 1-3 |
| 2001 | 3 | A | 2-3 |

v **Manchester Utd**

| | | | |
|---|---|---|---|
| 1904 | IR | A | 1-1 |
| 1904 | IRr | H | 1-1aet |
| 1904 | IRr2 | N | 1-1aet |
| 1904 | IRr3 | N | 1-3 |
| 1928 | 5 | A | 0-1 |
| 1951 | 6 | H | 1-0 |
| 1957 | SF | N | 0-2 |
| 1969 | 5 | H | 2-2 |
| 1969 | 5r | A | 2-6 |

v **Middlesbrough**

| | | | |
|---|---|---|---|
| 1933 | 5 | A | 0-0 |
| 1933 | 5r | H | 3-0 |
| 1959 | 3 | A | 1-0 |
| 1975 | 6 | H | 1-0 |
| 1980 | 4 | H | 2-1 |

v **Millwall**

| | | | |
|---|---|---|---|
| 1957 | 5 | A | 4-1 |

v **Newcastle Utd**

| | | | |
|---|---|---|---|
| 1906 | 4 | H | 2-2 |
| 1906 | 4r | A | 0-3aet |

v **Norwich City**

| | | | |
|---|---|---|---|
| 1985 | 3 | H | 0-0 |
| 1985 | 3r | A | 1-1aet |
| 1985 | 3r2 | H | 1-1aet |
| 1985 | 3r3 | A | 0-1 |

v **Nottingham Forest**

| | | | |
|---|---|---|---|
| 1957 | 6 | H | 0-0 |
| 1957 | 6r | A | 1-0 |
| 1959 | 5 | H | 1-1 |
| 1959 | 5r | A | 1-1aet |
| 1959 | 5r2 | N | 0-5 |
| 1961 | 3 | A | 2-0 |
| 1988 | 5 | H | 0-1 |

v **Notts County**

| | | | |
|---|---|---|---|
| 1897 | 1 | H | 1-2 |
| 1948 | 3 | H | 0-2 |

v **Oldham Athletic**

| | | | |
|---|---|---|---|
| 1911 | 1 | H | 1-1 |
| 1911 | 1r | A | 0-2 |
| 1915 | 3 | H | 2-3 |
| 1953 | 3 | A | 3-1 |
| 1990 | 3 | H | 1-1 |
| 1990 | 3r | A | 0-1 |

v **Port Vale**

| | | | |
|---|---|---|---|
| 1889 | Q2 | H | 3-2 |
| 1898 | Q3 | A | 1-2 |
| 1899 | Q5 | H | 7-0 |
| 1931 | 4 | H | 2-0 |
| 1964 | 3 | H | 1-2 |
| 1972 | 3 | H | 3-0 |

v **Portsmouth**

| | | | |
|---|---|---|---|
| 1902 | IR | A | 1-2 |
| 1905 | 1 | H | 0-2 |
| 1909 | 1 | H | 2-5 |
| 1946 | 3 | H | 1-0 |
| 1946 | 3s | A | 0-0 |
| 1947 | 4 | H | 1-0 |
| 1972 | 5 | H | 3-1 |
| 1976 | 3 | A | 1-1 |
| 1976 | 3r | H | 0-1 |
| 1977 | 3 | H | 1-0 |

v **Preston North End**

| | | | |
|---|---|---|---|
| 1906 | 1 | H | 1-0 |
| 1933 | 3 | H | 2-1 |

v **QPR**

| | | | |
|---|---|---|---|
| 1914 | 3 | H | 1-2 |
| 1974 | 4 | A | 0-2 |

v **Reading**

| | | | |
|---|---|---|---|
| 1993 | 1 | A | 0-1 |

v **Rotherham Utd**

| | | | |
|---|---|---|---|
| 1961 | 4 | H | 4-0 |
| 1967 | 4 | A | 0-0 |
| 1967 | 4r | H | 2-1 |

v **Scunthorpe Utd**

| | | | |
|---|---|---|---|
| 1995 | 2 | H | 0-0 |
| 1995 | 2r | A | 2-1 |

v **Sheffield Utd**

| | | | |
|---|---|---|---|
| 1934 | 3 | H | 2-1 |
| 1953 | 4 | A | 1-1 |
| 1953 | 4r | H | 3-1 |
| 1984 | 3 | A | 1-1 |
| 1984 | 3r | H | 2-0 |

v **Sheffield Wed**

| | | | |
|---|---|---|---|
| 1892 | 2 | A | 0-2 |
| 1969 | 4 | A | 2-2 |
| 1969 | 4r | H | 2-1 |

v **Southampton**

| | | | |
|---|---|---|---|
| 1927 | 4 | A | 1-4 |
| 1935 | 4 | A | 3-0 |
| 1980 | 3 | H | 2-1 |

v **Southend Utd**

| | | | |
|---|---|---|---|
| 1914 | 1 | H | 2-1 |
| 1957 | 4 | A | 6-1 |

v **Stockport County**

| | | | |
|---|---|---|---|
| 1925 | 2 | H | 1-0 |
| 1997 | 4 | H | 3-1 |
| 1998 | 4 | H | 2-1 |

v **Stoke City**

| | | | |
|---|---|---|---|
| 1899 | 2 | A | 2-2 |
| 1899 | 2r | H | 1-2 |
| 1901 | 1 | A | 1-1 |
| 1901 | 1r | H | 2-1aet |
| 1906 | 2 | A | 1-0 |
| 1937 | 3 | A | 1-4 |

v **Sunderland**

| | | | |
|---|---|---|---|
| 1931 | SF | N | 2-0 |
| 1946 | 5 | A | 0-1 |
| 1946 | 5s | H | 3-1 |
| 1956 | SF | N | 3-0 |
| 1981 | 3 | H | 1-1 |
| 1981 | 3r | A | 2-1aet |
| 1984 | 4 | A | 2-1 |

v **Swansea City**

| | | | |
|---|---|---|---|
| 1950 | 3 | A | 0-3 |

v **Swindon Town**

| | | | |
|---|---|---|---|
| 1973 | 3 | A | 0-2 |

v **Torquay Utd**

| | | | |
|---|---|---|---|
| 1956 | 3 | A | 7-1 |
| 1992 | 1 | A | 0-3 |

v **Tottenham Hotspur**

| | | | |
|---|---|---|---|
| 1906 | 3 | A | 1-1 |
| 1906 | 3r | H | 2-0aet |
| 1953 | 6 | H | 1-1 |
| 1953 | 6r | A | 2-2aet |
| 1953 | 6r2 | N | 0-1 |
| 1962 | 3 | H | 3-3 |
| 1962 | 3r | A | 2-4 |
| 1967 | 6 | H | 0-0 |
| 1967 | 6r | A | 0-6 |
| 1980 | 5 | A | 1-3 |

v **Walsall**

| | | | |
|---|---|---|---|
| 1890 | Q4 | H | 4-0 |
| 1900 | Q5 | H | 0-0 |
| 1900 | Q5r | A | 0-2 |
| 1975 | 5 | H | 2-1 |
| 1983 | 3 | A | 0-0 |
| 1983 | 3r | H | 1-0aet |
| 1987 | 4 | A | 0-1 |

v **Watford**

| | | | |
|---|---|---|---|
| 1931 | 5 | H | 3-0 |
| 1946 | 4 | H | 5-0 |
| 1946 | 4s | A | 1-1 |
| 1960 | 3 | A | 1-2 |
| 1984 | 6 | H | 1-3 |
| 2000 | 3 | A | 1-0 |

v **West Bromwich Albion**

| | | | |
|---|---|---|---|
| 1886 | SF | N | 0-4 |
| 1889 | 1 | H | 2-3 |
| 1895 | 1 | H | 1-2 |
| 1908 | 1 | A | 1-1 |
| 1908 | 1r | H | 1-2 |
| 1931 | F | N | 1-2 |
| 1956 | 5 | A | 1-0 |
| 1968 | SF | N | 0-2 |

v **West Ham Utd**

| | | | |
|---|---|---|---|
| 1933 | 6 | A | 0-4 |
| 1965 | 3 | A | 2-4 |
| 1984 | 5 | H | 3-0 |

v **Wigan Athletic**

| | | | |
|---|---|---|---|
| 1978 | 3 | H | 4-0 |

v **Wimbledon**

| | | | |
|---|---|---|---|
| 1989 | 3 | H | 0-1 |

v **Wolverhampton W**

| | | | |
|---|---|---|---|
| 1890 | 2 | A | 1-2 |
| 1954 | 3 | A | 2-1 |
| 1996 | 3 | H | 1-1 |
| 1996 | 3r | A | 1-2 |

v **Wrexham**

| | | | |
|---|---|---|---|
| 1900 | Q4 | H | 6-1 |
| 1928 | 4 | A | 3-1 |
| 1997 | 5 | H | 1-3 |

v **York City**

| | | | |
|---|---|---|---|
| 1958 | 3 | A | 0-3 |

# Blackburn Rovers

v **Blackpool**

| | | | |
|---|---|---|---|
| 1925 | 4 | H | 1-0 |
| 1960 | 4 | H | 1-1 |
| 1960 | 4r | A | 3-0 |

v **Bolton Wanderers**

| | | | |
|---|---|---|---|
| 1882 | 2 | H | 6-2 |
| 1929 | 6 | H | 1-1 |
| 1929 | 6r | A | 1-2 |
| 1936 | 3 | H | 1-1 |
| 1936 | 3r | A | 1-0aet |
| 1946 | 3 | A | 0-1 |
| 1946 | 3s | H | 1-3 |
| 1958 | SF | N | 1-2 |
| 1961 | 4 | A | 3-3 |
| 1961 | 4r | H | 4-0 |
| 2001 | 5 | A | 1-1 |
| 2001 | 5r | H | 3-0 |

v **Bournemouth**

| | | | |
|---|---|---|---|
| 1993 | 3 | H | 3-1 |

v **Bradford City**

| | | | |
|---|---|---|---|
| 1910 | 2 | A | 2-1 |
| 1911 | SF | N | 0-3 |
| 1936 | 4 | A | 1-3 |

v **Brentford**

| | | | |
|---|---|---|---|
| 1989 | 5 | H | 0-2 |

v **Brighton & HA**

| | | | |
|---|---|---|---|
| 1962 | 3 | A | 3-0 |

v **Bristol City**

| | | | |
|---|---|---|---|
| 1951 | 3 | A | 1-2 |

v **Bristol Rovers**

| | | | |
|---|---|---|---|
| 1931 | 4 | H | 5-1 |
| 1954 | 3 | A | 1-0 |
| 1975 | 3 | H | 1-2 |

v **Burnley**

| | | | |
|---|---|---|---|
| 1913 | 4 | H | 0-1 |
| 1952 | 6 | H | 3-1 |
| 1959 | 4 | H | 1-2 |
| 1960 | 6 | A | 3-3 |
| 1960 | 6r | H | 2-0 |

v **Bury**

| | | | |
|---|---|---|---|
| 1914 | 2 | H | 2-0 |
| 1929 | 5 | H | 1-0 |

v **Cardiff City**

| | | | |
|---|---|---|---|
| 1925 | SF | N | 1-3 |
| 1958 | 5 | A | 0-0 |
| 1958 | 5r | H | 2-1 |

v **Carlisle Utd**

| | | | |
|---|---|---|---|
| 1967 | 3 | H | 1-2 |

v **Charlton Athletic**

| | | | |
|---|---|---|---|
| 1947 | 5 | A | 0-1 |
| 1977 | 3 | A | 1-1 |
| 1977 | 3r | H | 2-0 |
| 1994 | 4 | A | 0-0 |
| 1994 | 4r | H | 0-1 |
| 1999 | 3 | H | 2-0 |

v **Chelsea**

| | | | |
|---|---|---|---|
| 1909 | 2 | H | 2-1 |
| 1931 | 5 | A | 0-3 |
| 1984 | 3 | H | 1-0 |

v **Chesterfield**

| | | | |
|---|---|---|---|
| 1961 | 3 | A | 0-0 |
| 1961 | 3r | H | 3-0 |

v **Coventry City**

| | | | |
|---|---|---|---|
| 1980 | 4 | H | 1-0 |
| 1997 | 4 | H | 1-2 |

v **Crewe Alexandra**

| | | | |
|---|---|---|---|
| 1973 | 2 | H | 0-1 |
| 1993 | 4 | A | 3-0 |

v **Darlington**

| | | | |
|---|---|---|---|
| 1975 | 2 | H | 1-0 |

v **Derby County**

| | | | |
|---|---|---|---|
| 1892 | 1 | H | 4-1 |
| 1894 | 3 | A | 4-1 |
| 1902 | 1 | H | 0-2 |
| 1903 | 2 | A | 0-2 |
| 1904 | 3 | A | 1-2 |
| 1912 | 2 | A | 2-1 |
| 1929 | 4 | H | 1-1 |
| 1929 | 4r | A | 3-0 |
| 1932 | 4 | A | 2-3 |
| 1977 | 5 | A | 1-3 |
| 2001 | 4 | H | 0-0 |
| 2001 | 4r | A | 5-2 |

v **Everton**

| | | | |
|---|---|---|---|
| 1895 | 2 | A | 1-1 |
| 1895 | 2r | H | 2-3 |
| 1897 | 3 | A | 0-2 |
| 1898 | 1 | A | 0-1 |
| 1930 | 4 | H | 4-1 |
| 1957 | 3 | A | 0-1 |
| 1958 | 4 | A | 2-1 |
| 1971 | 3 | A | 0-2 |
| 1974 | 3 | A | 0-3 |
| 1986 | 4 | A | 1-3 |

v **Exeter City**

| | | | |
|---|---|---|---|
| 1928 | 4 | A | 2-2 |
| 1928 | 4r | H | 3-1 |

v **Fulham**

| | | | |
|---|---|---|---|
| 1921 | 1 | H | 1-1 |
| 1921 | 1r | A | 0-1 |
| 1962 | 6 | A | 2-2 |
| 1962 | 6r | H | 0-1 |
| 1964 | 4 | H | 2-0 |
| 1980 | 3 | H | 1-1 |
| 1980 | 3r | A | 1-0 |

v **Grimsby Town**

| | | | |
|---|---|---|---|
| 1890 | 2 | H | 3-0 |
| 1964 | 3 | H | 4-0 |

**v Huddersfield Town**

| | | | |
|---|---|---|---|
| 1922 | 3 | H | 1-1 |
| 1922 | 3r | A | 0-5 |
| 1928 | F | N | 3-1 |
| 1939 | 6 | A | 1-1 |
| 1939 | 6r | H | 1-2 |

**v Hull City**

| | | | |
|---|---|---|---|
| 1947 | 3 | H | 1-1 |
| 1947 | 3r | A | 3-0 |
| 1949 | 3 | H | 1-2aet |
| 1952 | 4 | H | 2-0 |
| 1954 | 4 | H | 2-2 |
| 1954 | 4r | A | 1-2 |

**v Ipswich Town**

| | | | |
|---|---|---|---|
| 1996 | 3 | A | 0-0 |
| 1996 | 3r | H | 0-1aet |

**v Kidderminster H**

| | | | |
|---|---|---|---|
| 1980 | 1 | A | 2-0 |

**v Leicester City**

| | | | |
|---|---|---|---|
| 1908 | 1 | A | 0-2 |
| 1965 | 3 | A | 2-2 |
| 1965 | 3r | H | 1-2 |

**v Leyton Orient**

| | | | |
|---|---|---|---|
| 1959 | 3 | H | 4-2 |
| 1977 | 4 | H | 3-0 |
| 1978 | 4 | A | 1-3 |

**v Lincoln City**

| | | | |
|---|---|---|---|
| 1933 | 3 | A | 5-1 |
| 1973 | 1 | A | 2-2 |
| 1973 | 1r | H | 4-1 |

**v Liverpool**

| | | | |
|---|---|---|---|
| 1899 | 1 | A | 0-2 |
| 1904 | 1 | H | 3-1 |
| 1935 | 4 | H | 1-0 |
| 1950 | 3 | H | 0-0 |
| 1950 | 3r | A | 1-2 |
| 1958 | 6 | H | 2-1 |
| 1979 | 4 | A | 0-1 |
| 1983 | 3 | H | 1-2 |
| 1991 | 3 | H | 1-1 |
| 1991 | 3r | A | 0-3 |
| 2000 | 4 | A | 1-0 |

**v Luton Town**

| | | | |
|---|---|---|---|
| 1953 | 3 | A | 1-6 |
| 1976 | 3 | A | 0-2 |

**v Manchester City**

| | | | |
|---|---|---|---|
| 1907 | 1 | H | 2-2 |
| 1907 | 1r | A | 1-0 |
| 1914 | 3 | H | 1-2 |
| 1934 | 3 | A | 1-3 |
| 1969 | 5 | H | 1-4 |

**v Manchester Utd**

| | | | |
|---|---|---|---|
| 1893 | 1 | H | 4-0 |
| 1894 | 2 | A | 0-0aet |
| 1894 | 2r | H | 5-1 |
| 1909 | 3 | A | 1-6 |
| 1912 | 4 | A | 1-1 |
| 1912 | 4r | H | 4-2aet |
| 1928 | 6 | H | 2-0 |
| 1985 | 5 | H | 0-2 |

**v Middlesbrough**

| | | | |
|---|---|---|---|
| 1911 | 3 | A | 3-0 |
| 1914 | 1 | H | 3-0 |
| 1935 | 3 | A | 1-1 |
| 1935 | 3r | H | 1-0 |
| 1962 | 5 | H | 2-1 |
| 1963 | 3 | H | 1-1 |
| 1963 | 3r | A | 1-3 |
| 2002 | 5 | A | 0-1 |

**v Millwall**

| | | | |
|---|---|---|---|
| 1979 | 3 | H | 2-1 |
| 2002 | 4 | A | 1-0 |

**v Newcastle Utd**

| | | | |
|---|---|---|---|
| 1910 | 3 | A | 1-3 |
| 1928 | 3 | H | 4-1 |
| 1952 | SF | N | 0-0 |
| 1952 | SFr | N | 1-2 |
| 1993 | 5 | H | 1-0 |
| 1995 | 3 | A | 1-1 |
| 1995 | 3r | H | 1-2 |
| 1999 | 5 | A | 0-0 |
| 1999 | 5r | H | 0-1 |
| 2000 | 5 | H | 1-2 |

**v Northampton Town**

| | | | |
|---|---|---|---|
| 1913 | 1 | H | 7-2 |
| 1930 | 3 | H | 4-1 |
| 1956 | 3 | A | 2-1 |

**v Norwich City**

| | | | |
|---|---|---|---|
| 1912 | 1 | H | 4-1 |
| 1966 | 5 | A | 2-2 |
| 1966 | 5r | H | 3-2 |

**v Nottingham Forest**

| | | | |
|---|---|---|---|
| 1880 | 3 | A | 0-6 |
| 1904 | 2 | H | 3-1 |
| 1952 | 3 | A | 2-2 |
| 1952 | 3r | H | 2-0 |
| 1986 | 3 | A | 1-1 |
| 1986 | 3r | H | 3-2 |

**v Notts County**

| | | | |
|---|---|---|---|
| 1884 | SF | N | 1-0 |
| 1891 | F | N | 3-1 |
| 1894 | SF | N | 0-1 |
| 1909 | 1 | A | 1-0 |
| 1981 | 3 | A | 1-2 |
| 1992 | 4 | A | 1-2 |

**v Oldham Athletic**

| | | | |
|---|---|---|---|
| 1925 | 1 | H | 1-0 |

**v Oxford Utd**

| | | | |
|---|---|---|---|
| 1964 | 5 | A | 1-3 |
| 1985 | 4 | A | 1-0 |

**v Port Vale**

| | | | |
|---|---|---|---|
| 1928 | 5 | H | 2-1 |
| 1947 | 4 | H | 2-0 |
| 1972 | 1 | H | 1-1 |
| 1972 | 1r | A | 1-3 |
| 1997 | 3 | H | 1-0 |

**v Portsmouth**

| | | | |
|---|---|---|---|
| 1900 | 1 | A | 0-0 |
| 1900 | 1r | H | 1-1aet |
| 1900 | 1r2 | H | 5-0 |
| 1925 | 2 | H | 0-0 |
| 1925 | 2r | A | 0-0aet |
| 1925 | 2r2 | N | 1-0 |
| 1969 | 4 | H | 4-0 |
| 1985 | 3 | A | 0-0 |
| 1985 | 3r | H | 2-1 |
| 1987 | 3 | A | 0-2 |
| 1988 | 3 | H | 1-2 |
| 1994 | 3 | H | 3-3 |
| 1994 | 3r | A | 3-1 |

**v Preston North End**

| | | | |
|---|---|---|---|
| 1900 | 2 | A | 0-1 |
| 1926 | 3 | H | 1-1 |
| 1926 | 3r | A | 4-1 |

**v Reading**

| | | | |
|---|---|---|---|
| 1913 | 3 | A | 2-1 |

**v Rotherham Utd**

| | | | |
|---|---|---|---|
| 1958 | 3 | A | 4-1 |

**v Sheffield Utd**

| | | | |
|---|---|---|---|
| 1897 | 1 | H | 2-1 |
| 1961 | 5 | A | 1-2 |
| 1993 | 6 | H | 0-0 |
| 1993 | 6r | A | 2-2p |

**v Sheffield Wed**

| | | | |
|---|---|---|---|
| 1881 | 2 | H | 0-4 |
| 1882 | SF | N | 0-0 |
| 1882 | SFr | N | 5-1 |
| 1890 | F | N | 6-1 |
| 1903 | 1 | H | 0-0 |
| 1903 | 1r | A | 1-0 |
| 1905 | 1 | H | 1-2 |
| 1960 | SF | N | 2-1 |
| 1966 | 6 | H | 1-2 |
| 1989 | 4 | H | 2-1 |
| 1998 | 4 | A | 3-0 |

**v Shrewsbury Town**

| | | | |
|---|---|---|---|
| 1978 | 3 | H | 2-1 |

**v Southampton**

| | | | |
|---|---|---|---|
| 1948 | 4 | A | 2-3 |
| 1984 | 5 | H | 0-1 |

**v Southend Utd**

| | | | |
|---|---|---|---|
| 1911 | 1 | H | 5-1 |
| 1939 | 4 | H | 4-2 |

**v Stockport County**

| | | | |
|---|---|---|---|
| 1969 | 3 | H | 2-0 |

**v Stoke City**

| | | | |
|---|---|---|---|
| 1906 | 1 | A | 0-1 |
| 1962 | 4 | A | 1-0 |

**v Sunderland**

| | | | |
|---|---|---|---|
| 1890 | 1 | H | 4-2aet |
| 1893 | 3 | H | 3-0 |
| 1939 | 5 | A | 1-1 |
| 1939 | 5r | H | 0-0e |
| 1939 | 5r2 | N | 1-0 |
| 1960 | 3 | A | 1-1 |
| 1960 | 3r | H | 4-1 |
| 1999 | 4 | H | 1-0 |
| 2003 | 4 | H | 3-3 |
| 2003 | 4r | A | 2-2p |

**v Swansea City**

| | | | |
|---|---|---|---|
| 1915 | 1 | A | 0-1 |
| 1939 | 3 | H | 2-0 |
| 1955 | 3 | H | 0-2 |

**v Swindon Town**

| | | | |
|---|---|---|---|
| 1922 | 2 | A | 1-0 |
| 1968 | 3 | A | 0-1 |
| 1970 | 3 | H | 0-4 |
| 1984 | 4 | A | 2-1 |

v **Tottenham Hotspur**

| | | | |
|---|---|---|---|
| 1907 | 2 | H | 1-1 |
| 1907 | 2r | A | 1-1e |
| 1907 | 2r2 | N | 1-2 |
| 1911 | 2 | H | 0-0 |
| 1911 | 2r | A | 2-0 |
| 1925 | 3 | A | 2-2 |
| 1925 | 3r | H | 3-1 |
| 1938 | 3 | A | 2-3 |
| 1960 | 5 | A | 3-1 |

v **Walsall**

| | | | |
|---|---|---|---|
| 1931 | 3 | H | 1-1 |
| 1931 | 3r | A | 3-0 |

v **West Bromwich Albion**

| | | | |
|---|---|---|---|
| 1885 | 6 | A | 2-0 |
| 1886 | F | N | 0-0 |
| 1886 | Fr | N | 2-0 |
| 1891 | SF | N | 3-2 |
| 1892 | 2 | A | 1-3 |
| 1894 | 1 | A | 3-2 |
| 1896 | 1 | H | 1-2 |
| 1912 | SF | N | 0-0 |
| 1912 | SFr | N | 0-1aet |
| 1952 | 5 | H | 1-0 |
| 1982 | 3 | A | 2-3 |
| 2000 | 3 | A | 2-2 |
| 2000 | 3r | H | 2-0aet |

v **West Ham Utd**

| | | | |
|---|---|---|---|
| 1911 | 4 | A | 3-2 |
| 1948 | 3 | H | 0-0aet |
| 1948 | 3r | A | 4-2aet |
| 1956 | 5 | A | 0-0 |
| 1956 | 5r | H | 2-3 |
| 1966 | 4 | A | 3-3 |
| 1966 | 4r | H | 4-1 |
| 1998 | 5 | A | 2-2 |
| 1998 | 5r | H | 1-1q |

v **Wigan Athletic**

| | | | |
|---|---|---|---|
| 1998 | 3 | H | 4-2 |

v **Wolverhampton W**

| | | | |
|---|---|---|---|
| 1889 | SF | N | 1-1 |
| 1889 | SFr | N | 1-3 |
| 1890 | SF | N | 1-0 |
| 1891 | 3 | H | 2-0 |
| 1893 | SF | N | 1-2 |
| 1897 | 2 | H | 2-1 |
| 1912 | 3 | H | 3-2 |
| 1920 | 1 | H | 2-2 |
| 1920 | 1r | A | 0-1 |
| 1960 | F | N | 0-3 |

# Blackpool

v **Bolton Wanderers**

| | | | |
|---|---|---|---|
| 1896 | 2 | H | 0-2 |
| 1912 | 2 | A | 0-1 |
| 1927 | 3 | H | 1-3 |
| 1953 | F | N | 4-3 |
| 1957 | 3 | A | 3-2 |
| 1990 | 1 | H | 2-1 |

v **Bournemouth**

| | | | |
|---|---|---|---|
| 1989 | 3 | H | 0-1 |

v **Bradford City**

| | | | |
|---|---|---|---|
| 1973 | 3 | A | 1-2 |

v **Bristol City**

| | | | |
|---|---|---|---|
| 1905 | IR | A | 1-2 |
| 1959 | 4 | A | 1-1 |
| 1959 | 4r | H | 1-0 |

v **Burnley**

| | | | |
|---|---|---|---|
| 1976 | 3 | H | 1-0 |
| 1990 | 3 | H | 1-0 |

v **Bury**

| | | | |
|---|---|---|---|
| 1892 | Q3 | A | 5-5 |
| 1892 | Q3r | H | 4-3 |
| 1979 | 2 | A | 1-3 |
| 1989 | 2 | H | 3-0 |

v **Charlton Athletic**

| | | | |
|---|---|---|---|
| 1951 | 3 | A | 2-2 |
| 1951 | 3r | H | 3-0 |
| 2002 | 3 | A | 1-2 |

v **Chelsea**

| | | | |
|---|---|---|---|
| 1972 | 3 | H | 0-1 |

v **Cheltenham Town**

| | | | |
|---|---|---|---|
| 1934 | 3 | A | 3-1 |

v **Chesterfield**

| | | | |
|---|---|---|---|
| 1968 | 3 | H | 2-1 |

v **Colchester Utd**

| | | | |
|---|---|---|---|
| 1948 | 5 | H | 5-0 |

v **Coventry City**

| | | | |
|---|---|---|---|
| 1969 | 3 | A | 1-3 |

v **Crewe Alexandra**

| | | | |
|---|---|---|---|
| 1912 | 1 | A | 1-1 |
| 1912 | 1r | H | 2-2 |
| 1912 | 1r2 | N | 2-1 |

v **Crystal Palace**

| | | | |
|---|---|---|---|
| 1906 | 1 | H | 1-1 |
| 1906 | 1r | A | 1-1aet |
| 1906 | 1r2 | N | 1-0 |
| 2003 | 3 | H | 1-2 |

v **Darlington**

| | | | |
|---|---|---|---|
| 1921 | 1 | A | 2-2 |
| 1921 | 1r | H | 2-1 |

v **Derby County**

| | | | |
|---|---|---|---|
| 1920 | 1 | H | 0-0 |
| 1920 | 1r | A | 4-1 |
| 1923 | 1 | A | 0-2 |
| 1977 | 3 | H | 0-0 |
| 1977 | 3r | A | 2-3 |

v **Doncaster Rovers**

| | | | |
|---|---|---|---|
| 1950 | 4 | H | 2-1 |
| 1981 | 2 | A | 1-2 |

v **Fulham**

| | | | |
|---|---|---|---|
| 1936 | 4 | A | 2-5 |
| 1948 | 6 | A | 2-0 |
| 1951 | 6 | H | 1-0 |
| 1957 | 4 | H | 6-2 |

v **Gillingham**

| | | | |
|---|---|---|---|
| 1914 | 1 | A | 0-1 |

v **Grimsby Town**

| | | | |
|---|---|---|---|
| 1991 | 1 | H | 2-0 |
| 1992 | 1 | H | 2-1 |

v **Huddersfield Town**

| | | | |
|---|---|---|---|
| 1933 | 4 | H | 2-0 |
| 1953 | 4 | H | 1-0 |
| 1991 | 2 | A | 2-0 |
| 1996 | 3 | A | 1-2 |

v **Hull City**

| | | | |
|---|---|---|---|
| 1930 | 4 | A | 1-3 |
| 1931 | 3 | A | 2-1 |
| 1971 | 4 | A | 0-2 |
| 1992 | 2 | H | 0-1 |

v **Leeds Utd**

| | | | |
|---|---|---|---|
| 1948 | 3 | H | 4-0 |

v **Leicester City**

| | | | |
|---|---|---|---|
| 1935 | 3 | A | 1-2 |

v **Lincoln City**

| | | | |
|---|---|---|---|
| 1979 | 1 | H | 2-1 |

v **Liverpool**

| | | | |
|---|---|---|---|
| 1950 | 6 | A | 1-2 |

v **Luton Town**

| | | | |
|---|---|---|---|
| 1937 | 3 | A | 3-3 |
| 1937 | 3r | H | 1-2 |
| 1954 | 3 | H | 1-1 |
| 1954 | 3r | A | 0-0aet |
| 1954 | 3r2 | N | 1-1aet |
| 1954 | 3r3 | N | 2-0 |
| 1959 | 6 | H | 1-1 |
| 1959 | 6r | A | 0-1 |

v **Manchester City**

| | | | |
|---|---|---|---|
| 1956 | 3 | A | 1-2 |
| 1966 | 3 | H | 1-1 |
| 1966 | 3r | A | 1-3 |
| 1984 | 3 | H | 2-1 |
| 1988 | 4 | H | 1-1 |
| 1988 | 4r | A | 1-2 |

v **Manchester Utd**

| | | | |
|---|---|---|---|
| 1892 | Q4 | A | 4-3 |
| 1897 | Q5 | A | 2-2 |
| 1897 | Q5r | H | 1-2 |
| 1908 | 1 | A | 1-3 |
| 1911 | 1 | A | 1-2 |
| 1948 | F | N | 2-4 |

v **Mansfield Town**

| | | | |
|---|---|---|---|
| 1951 | 5 | H | 2-0 |
| 1960 | 3 | H | 3-0 |
| 1970 | 4 | H | 0-2 |

v **Middlesbrough**

| | | | |
|---|---|---|---|
| 1946 | 4 | H | 3-2 |
| 1946 | 4s | A | 2-3aet |
| 1946 | 4r | N | 0-1aet |
| 1987 | 1 | A | 0-3 |

v **Newcastle Utd**

| | | | |
|---|---|---|---|
| 1906 | 3 | A | 0-5 |
| 1909 | 2 | A | 1-2 |
| 1932 | 3 | H | 1-1 |
| 1932 | 3r | A | 0-1 |
| 1951 | F | N | 0-2 |

v **Norwich City**

| | | | |
|---|---|---|---|
| 1963 | 3 | A | 1-1 |
| 1963 | 3r | H | 1-3aet |

v **Oldham Athletic**

| | | | |
|---|---|---|---|
| 1928 | 3 | H | 1-4 |
| 1998 | 2 | A | 1-2 |

v **Oxford Utd**

| | | | |
|---|---|---|---|
| 1984 | 4 | A | 1-2 |

**v Plymouth Argyle**
1929 3 A 0-3
1975 3 A 0-2

**v Port Vale**
1933 3 H 2-1
1954 5 A 0-2
1994 1 A 0-2

**v Preston North End**
1920 2 A 1-2
1983 2 A 1-2
1995 1 A 0-1

**v QPR**
1982 4 H 0-0
1982 4r A 1-5
1990 5 H 2-2
1990 5r A 0-0aet
1990 5r2 A 0-3

**v Rochdale**
1993 1 H 1-1
1993 1r A 0-1aet
2002 2 H 2-0

**v Scunthorpe Utd**
1961 3 A 2-6
1988 3 A 0-0
1988 3r H 1-0
1989 1 H 2-1

**v Sheffield Utd**
1892 1 H 0-3
1893 1 H 1-3
1906 2 A 2-1
1915 1 H 1-2
1924 1 H 1-0
1939 3 H 1-2
1968 4 A 1-2

**v Sheffield Wed**
1947 3 A 1-4
1953 3 A 2-1

**v Southampton**
1924 2 A 1-3
1953 5 H 1-1
1953 5r A 2-1
1959 3 A 2-1
1974 3 A 1-2
1976 4 A 1-3

**v Southend Utd**
1921 2 A 0-1
1950 3 H 4-0

**v Stockport County**
1930 3 H 2-1
1951 4 H 2-1

**v Stoke City**
1934 4 A 0-3
1949 4 A 1-1aet
1949 4r H 0-1
1965 3 A 1-4
2000 1 H 2-0

**v Sunderland**
1933 5 A 0-1

**v Swansea City**
1926 3 H 0-2

**v Torquay Utd**
1990 4 H 1-0
2003 2 H 3-1

**v Tottenham Hotspur**
1913 1 A 1-1
1913 1r A 1-6
1948 SF N 3-1aet
1953 SF N 2-1
1991 3 H 0-1

**v Watford**
1922 1 H 1-2

**v West Bromwich Albion**
1957 5 H 0-0
1957 5r A 1-2
1959 5 H 3-1
1962 3 H 0-0
1962 3r A 1-2
1964 3 A 2-2
1964 3r H 0-1
1978 3 A 1-4

**v West Ham Utd**
1907 1 A 1-2
1925 3 A 1-1
1925 3r H 3-0
1952 3 A 1-2
1954 4 A 1-1
1954 4r H 3-1
1958 3 A 1-5
1971 3 H 4-0

**v Wigan Athletic**
1980 1 H 1-1
1980 1r A 0-2
1997 1 H 1-0
1999 1 A 3-4

**v Wolverhampton W**
1950 5 A 0-0
1950 5r H 1-0

**v Wrexham**
1946 3 A 4-1
1946 3s H 4-1

**v Yeovil Town**
2001 2 H 0-1

**v York City**
1955 3 H 0-2

# Bolton Wanderers

**v Bournemouth**
1926 4 A 2-2
1926 4r H 6-2

**v Bradford City**
1992 2 H 3-1
1996 3 A 3-0

**v Brentford**
1976 3 A 0-0
1976 3r H 2-0

**v Brighton & HA**
1907 1 H 3-1
1934 4 A 1-1
1934 4r H 6-1
1992 4 H 2-1

**v Bristol City**
1903 1 H 0-5
1979 3 A 1-3

**v Bristol Rovers**
1905 1 H 1-1
1905 1r A 3-0
1969 4 H 1-2

**v Burnley**
1914 3 A 0-3
1915 3 H 2-1aet
1988 1 A 1-0

**v Bury**
1895 2 H 1-0
1896 3 H 2-0
1922 1 H 1-0
1960 3 A 1-1
1960 3r H 4-2

**v Cambridge Utd**
2000 5 A 3-1

**v Cardiff City**
1927 5 H 0-2
1973 4 H 2-2
1973 4r A 1-1aet
1973 4r2 N 1-0
2000 3 H 1-0

**v Carlisle Utd**
1931 3 H 1-0

**v Charlton Athletic**
1923 4 A 1-0
1933 3 A 5-1
1946 SF N 0-2
1973 3 A 1-1
1973 3r H 4-0
2000 6 H 1-0

**v Chelsea**
1920 1 H 0-1
1972 4 A 0-3

**v Chesterfield**
1911 1 H 0-2
1989 1 H 0-0
1989 1r A 3-2
1991 2 A 4-3
1997 4 H 2-3

**v Coventry City**
1950 3 A 2-1
1987 3 A 0-3

**v Crewe Alexandra**
1896 1 A 4-0
1967 3 H 1-0

**v Crystal Palace**
1982 4 A 0-1

**v Derby County**
1897 2 A 1-4
1901 1 H 1-0
1904 SF N 1-0
1982 3 H 3-1
1993 5 A 1-3

**v Everton**
1888 1r A 2-2
1888 1r2 H 1-1
1907 3 A 0-0
1907 3r H 0-3
1908 3 H 3-3
1908 3r A 1-3aet
1935 6 A 2-1
1953 SF N 4-3

| | | | |
|---|---|---|---|
| 1994 | 3 | H | 1-1 |
| 1994 | 3r | A | 3-2aet |

**v Fulham**

| | | | |
|---|---|---|---|
| 1953 | 3 | H | 3-1 |

**v Grimsby Town**

| | | | |
|---|---|---|---|
| 1897 | 1 | A | 0-0 |
| 1897 | 1r | H | 3-3aet |
| 1897 | 1r2 | N | 3-2 |
| 1933 | 4 | H | 2-1 |
| 2000 | 4 | A | 2-0 |

**v Huddersfield Town**

| | | | |
|---|---|---|---|
| 1923 | 3 | A | 1-1 |
| 1923 | 3r | H | 1-0 |
| 1925 | 1 | H | 3-0 |
| 1929 | SF | N | 3-1 |
| 1956 | 3 | H | 3-0 |
| 1976 | 4 | A | 1-0 |

**v Hull City**

| | | | |
|---|---|---|---|
| 1915 | 4 | H | 4-2 |
| 1924 | 1 | A | 2-2 |
| 1924 | 1r | H | 4-0 |
| 1961 | 3 | A | 1-0 |
| 1985 | 1 | A | 1-2 |

**v Leeds Utd**

| | | | |
|---|---|---|---|
| 1923 | 2 | H | 3-1 |
| 1927 | 4 | A | 0-0 |
| 1927 | 4r | H | 3-0 |
| 1950 | 4 | A | 1-1 |
| 1950 | 4r | H | 2-3aet |
| 1996 | 4 | H | 0-1 |

**v Leicester City**

| | | | |
|---|---|---|---|
| 1929 | 5 | A | 2-1 |

**v Lincoln City**

| | | | |
|---|---|---|---|
| 1994 | 2 | A | 3-1 |

**v Liverpool**

| | | | |
|---|---|---|---|
| 1894 | 3 | H | 3-0 |
| 1924 | 2 | H | 1-4 |
| 1929 | 4 | A | 0-0 |
| 1929 | 4r | H | 5-2aet |
| 1934 | 5 | A | 3-0 |
| 1946 | 4 | H | 5-0 |
| 1946 | 4s | A | 0-2 |
| 1954 | 3 | H | 1-0 |
| 1965 | 5 | H | 0-1 |
| 1993 | 3 | H | 2-2 |
| 1993 | 3r | A | 2-0 |

**v Luton Town**

| | | | |
|---|---|---|---|
| 1898 | 1 | A | 1-0 |
| 1928 | 3 | H | 2-1 |
| 1953 | 5 | A | 1-0 |
| 1973 | 5 | H | 0-1 |
| 1997 | 3 | A | 1-1 |
| 1997 | 3r | H | 6-2 |

**v Manchester City**

| | | | |
|---|---|---|---|
| 1898 | 2 | H | 1-0 |
| 1904 | F | N | 0-1 |
| 1905 | 2 | A | 2-1 |
| 1922 | 2 | H | 1-3 |
| 1926 | F | N | 1-0 |
| 1933 | 5 | H | 2-4 |
| 1937 | 5 | H | 0-5 |
| 1947 | 4 | H | 3-3 |
| 1947 | 4r | A | 0-1 |

**v Manchester Utd**

| | | | |
|---|---|---|---|
| 1958 | F | N | 2-0 |
| 1962 | 3 | A | 1-2 |
| 1991 | 4 | A | 0-1 |

**v Mansfield Town**

| | | | |
|---|---|---|---|
| 1978 | 4 | H | 1-0 |
| 1984 | 2 | H | 2-0 |

**v Middlesbrough**

| | | | |
|---|---|---|---|
| 1906 | 1 | A | 0-3 |
| 1939 | 3 | A | 0-0 |
| 1939 | 3r | H | 0-0aet |
| 1939 | 3r2 | N | 0-1 |
| 1946 | 5 | H | 1-0 |
| 1946 | 5s | A | 1-1 |
| 1978 | 5 | A | 0-2 |

**v Millwall**

| | | | |
|---|---|---|---|
| 1915 | 2 | H | 0-0aet |
| 1915 | 2r | A | 2-2aet |
| 1915 | 2r2 | H | 4-1 |
| 1955 | 3 | H | 3-1 |

**v Newcastle Utd**

| | | | |
|---|---|---|---|
| 1894 | 2 | A | 2-1 |
| 1905 | 3 | H | 0-2 |
| 1951 | 4 | A | 2-3 |
| 1976 | 5 | H | 3-3 |
| 1976 | 5r | A | 0-0aet |
| 1976 | 5r2 | N | 1-2 |

**v Northampton Town**

| | | | |
|---|---|---|---|
| 1935 | 3 | A | 2-0 |
| 1969 | 3 | H | 2-1 |

**v Norwich City**

| | | | |
|---|---|---|---|
| 1923 | 1 | A | 2-0 |
| 1937 | 4 | H | 1-1 |
| 1937 | 4r | A | 2-1aet |

**v Nottingham Forest**

| | | | |
|---|---|---|---|
| 1926 | 6 | A | 2-2 |
| 1926 | 6r | H | 0-0aet |
| 1926 | 6r2 | N | 1-0 |
| 1959 | 6 | A | 1-2 |
| 1968 | 3 | A | 2-4 |
| 1981 | 3 | A | 3-3 |
| 1981 | 3r | H | 0-1aet |

**v Notts County**

| | | | |
|---|---|---|---|
| 1884 | 4 | A | 2-2aet |
| 1884 | 4r | H | 1-2 |
| 1894 | F | N | 1-4 |
| 1908 | 2 | A | 1-1 |
| 1908 | 2r | H | 2-1aet |
| 1915 | 1 | H | 2-1 |
| 1953 | 4 | H | 1-1 |
| 1953 | 4r | A | 2-2aet |
| 1953 | 4r2 | N | 1-0 |

**v Oldham Athletic**

| | | | |
|---|---|---|---|
| 1913 | 1 | A | 0-2 |
| 1929 | 3 | H | 2-0 |
| 1994 | 6 | H | 0-1 |

**v Oxford Utd**

| | | | |
|---|---|---|---|
| 1954 | 4 | A | 4-2 |

**v Plymouth Argyle**

| | | | |
|---|---|---|---|
| 1935 | 4 | A | 4-1 |

**v Port Vale**

| | | | |
|---|---|---|---|
| 1914 | 1 | H | 3-0 |
| 1989 | 2 | H | 1-2 |

**v Portsmouth**

| | | | |
|---|---|---|---|
| 1929 | F | N | 2-0 |
| 1934 | 6 | H | 0-3 |
| 1954 | 5 | H | 0-0 |
| 1954 | 5r | A | 2-1 |
| 1995 | 3 | A | 1-3 |

**v Preston North End**

| | | | |
|---|---|---|---|
| 1888 | 2 | A | 1-9 |
| 1890 | 3 | A | 3-2 |
| 1921 | 1 | A | 0-2 |
| 1932 | 3 | A | 0-0 |
| 1932 | 3r | H | 2-5 |
| 1958 | 3 | A | 3-0 |
| 1959 | 5 | H | 2-2 |
| 1959 | 5r | A | 1-1aet |
| 1959 | 5r2 | N | 1-0 |
| 1964 | 4 | H | 2-2 |
| 1964 | 4r | A | 1-2 |
| 1965 | 4 | A | 2-1 |
| 1966 | 4 | H | 1-1 |
| 1966 | 4r | A | 2-3 |

**v Reading**

| | | | |
|---|---|---|---|
| 1901 | 2 | H | 0-1 |
| 1904 | 1 | A | 1-1 |
| 1904 | 1r | H | 3-2 |
| 1992 | 3 | H | 2-0 |
| 1993 | 2 | H | 4-0 |

**v Scunthorpe Utd**

| | | | |
|---|---|---|---|
| 1959 | 3 | A | 2-0 |
| 2001 | 4 | H | 5-1 |

**v Sheffield Utd**

| | | | |
|---|---|---|---|
| 1890 | 2 | H | 13-0 |
| 1902 | 2 | A | 1-2 |
| 1904 | 3 | A | 2-0 |
| 1915 | SF | N | 1-2 |
| 1923 | SF | N | 1-0 |
| 1956 | 4 | H | 1-2 |
| 1963 | 3 | A | 1-3 |

**v Sheffield Wed**

| | | | |
|---|---|---|---|
| 1890 | SF | N | 1-2 |
| 1892 | 1r | A | 1-4 |
| 1894 | SF | N | 2-1 |
| 1896 | SF | N | 1-1 |
| 1896 | SFr | N | 1-3 |
| 1900 | 1 | A | 0-1 |
| 1954 | 6 | A | 1-1 |
| 1954 | 6r | H | 0-2 |

**v Shrewsbury Town**

| | | | |
|---|---|---|---|
| 1973 | 2 | H | 3-0 |

**v Southampton**

| | | | |
|---|---|---|---|
| 1898 | 3 | H | 0-0 |
| 1898 | 3r | A | 0-4 |
| 1904 | 2 | H | 4-1 |
| 1974 | 4 | A | 3-3 |
| 1974 | 4r | H | 0-2aet |
| 1992 | 5 | H | 2-2 |
| 1992 | 5r | A | 2-3aet |

**v Stockport County**

| | | | |
|---|---|---|---|
| 1910 | 1 | A | 1-4 |
| 1947 | 3 | H | 5-1 |
| 2002 | 3 | A | 4-1 |

v **Stoke City**

| | | | |
|---|---|---|---|
| 1928 | 4 | A | 2-4 |
| 1946 | 6 | A | 2-0 |
| 1946 | 6s | H | 0-0 |
| 1958 | 5 | H | 3-1 |
| 1974 | 3 | H | 3-2 |

v **Sunderland**

| | | | |
|---|---|---|---|
| 1895 | 3 | A | 1-2 |
| 1931 | 4 | H | 1-1 |
| 1931 | 4r | A | 1-3 |
| 1980 | 3 | A | 1-0 |
| 1984 | 3 | H | 0-3 |
| 2003 | 3 | H | 1-1 |
| 2003 | 3r | A | 0-2aet |

v **Swansea City**

| | | | |
|---|---|---|---|
| 1926 | SF | N | 3-0 |

v **Swindon Town**

| | | | |
|---|---|---|---|
| 1914 | 2 | H | 4-2 |

v **Torquay Utd**

| | | | |
|---|---|---|---|
| 1972 | 3 | H | 2-1 |

v **Tottenham Hotspur**

| | | | |
|---|---|---|---|
| 1925 | 2 | A | 1-1 |
| 1925 | 2r | H | 0-1 |
| 1935 | 5 | A | 1-1 |
| 1935 | 5r | H | 1-1aet |
| 1935 | 5r2 | N | 2-0 |
| 1948 | 3 | H | 0-2aet |
| 1978 | 3 | A | 2-2 |
| 1978 | 3r | H | 2-1aet |
| 2002 | 4 | A | 0-4 |

v **Tranmere Rovers**

| | | | |
|---|---|---|---|
| 1984 | 1 | A | 2-2 |
| 1984 | 1r | H | 4-1aet |
| 1987 | 2 | H | 2-0 |

v **Watford**

| | | | |
|---|---|---|---|
| 1970 | 3 | H | 1-2 |

v **West Bromwich Albion**

| | | | |
|---|---|---|---|
| 1909 | 1 | A | 1-3 |
| 1935 | SF | N | 1-1 |
| 1935 | SFr | N | 0-2 |
| 1952 | 3 | A | 0-4 |
| 1960 | 4 | A | 0-2 |
| 1966 | 3 | H | 3-0 |
| 1975 | 3 | H | 0-0 |
| 1975 | 3r | A | 0-4 |

v **West Ham Utd**

| | | | |
|---|---|---|---|
| 1923 | F | N | 2-0 |
| 1937 | 3 | A | 0-0 |
| 1937 | 3r | H | 1-0 |
| 1977 | 3 | A | 1-2 |

v **Wolverhampton W**

| | | | |
|---|---|---|---|
| 1893 | 1 | H | 1-1aet |
| 1893 | 1r | A | 1-2 |
| 1899 | 1 | A | 0-0 |
| 1899 | 1r | H | 0-1 |
| 1902 | 1 | A | 2-0 |
| 1958 | 6 | H | 2-1 |
| 1959 | 4 | A | 2-1 |
| 1993 | 4 | A | 2-0 |
| 1999 | 3 | H | 1-2 |

v **Wrexham**

| | | | |
|---|---|---|---|
| 1986 | 1 | A | 1-3 |
| 1988 | 2 | A | 2-1 |

v **Yeovil Town**

| | | | |
|---|---|---|---|
| 2001 | 3 | H | 2-1 |

v **York City**

| | | | |
|---|---|---|---|
| 1951 | 3 | H | 2-0 |
| 1958 | 4 | A | 0-0 |
| 1958 | 4r | H | 3-0 |
| 1971 | 3 | A | 0-2 |

# Boston Utd

v **Bury**

| | | | |
|---|---|---|---|
| 1984 | 1 | H | 0-3 |

v **Chesterfield**

| | | | |
|---|---|---|---|
| 1975 | 1 | A | 1-3 |

v **Crewe Alexandra**

| | | | |
|---|---|---|---|
| 1936 | 1 | A | 2-4 |
| 1983 | 1 | H | 3-1 |

v **Darlington**

| | | | |
|---|---|---|---|
| 1958 | 2 | A | 3-5 |

v **Derby County**

| | | | |
|---|---|---|---|
| 1956 | 2 | A | 6-1 |
| 1974 | 3 | A | 0-0 |
| 1974 | 3r | H | 1-6 |

v **Hartlepool Utd**

| | | | |
|---|---|---|---|
| 1972 | 2 | H | 2-1 |

v **Leyton Orient**

| | | | |
|---|---|---|---|
| 1968 | 2 | H | 1-1 |
| 1968 | 2r | A | 1-2 |

v **Lincoln City**

| | | | |
|---|---|---|---|
| 1976 | 1 | H | 0-1 |

v **Northampton Town**

| | | | |
|---|---|---|---|
| 2003 | 1 | A | 2-3 |

v **Oldham Athletic**

| | | | |
|---|---|---|---|
| 1953 | 1 | H | 1-2 |

v **Peterborough**

| | | | |
|---|---|---|---|
| 1955 | Q4 | A | 2-1 |

v **Portsmouth**

| | | | |
|---|---|---|---|
| 1972 | 3 | H | 0-1 |

v **Rotherham Utd**

| | | | |
|---|---|---|---|
| 1981 | 1 | H | 0-4 |

v **Scunthorpe Utd**

| | | | |
|---|---|---|---|
| 1939 | Q4 | A | 1-2 |
| 1947 | Q4 | A | 1-4 |
| 1954 | 1 | A | 0-9 |

v **Sheffield Utd**

| | | | |
|---|---|---|---|
| 1983 | 2 | H | 1-1 |
| 1983 | 2r | A | 1-5 |

v **Tottenham Hotspur**

| | | | |
|---|---|---|---|
| 1956 | 3 | A | 0-4 |

v **Tranmere Rovers**

| | | | |
|---|---|---|---|
| 1979 | 1 | A | 1-2 |

v **Wycombe W**

| | | | |
|---|---|---|---|
| 1991 | 1 | H | 1-1 |
| 1991 | 1r | A | 0-4 |

v **York City**

| | | | |
|---|---|---|---|
| 1971 | 2 | H | 1-2 |

# Bournemouth

v **Bradford City**

| | | | |
|---|---|---|---|
| 1936 | 3 | A | 0-1 |
| 1948 | 2 | H | 1-0 |
| 1960 | 4 | A | 1-3 |

v **Brentford**

| | | | |
|---|---|---|---|
| 1926 | 2 | A | 2-1 |
| 1992 | 2 | H | 2-1 |
| 1996 | 2 | H | 0-1 |
| 1997 | 1 | A | 0-2 |

v **Brighton & HA**

| | | | |
|---|---|---|---|
| 1988 | 3 | A | 0-2 |
| 1994 | 1 | H | 4-2 |

v **Bristol City**

| | | | |
|---|---|---|---|
| 1927 | 2 | A | 1-1 |
| 1927 | 2r | H | 2-0 |
| 1939 | 1 | H | 2-1 |
| 1965 | 2 | H | 0-3 |
| 1996 | 1 | H | 0-0 |
| 1996 | 1r | A | 1-0 |
| 1998 | 2 | H | 3-1 |
| 2000 | 2 | H | 0-2 |

v **Bristol Rovers**

| | | | |
|---|---|---|---|
| 1928 | 2 | H | 6-1 |
| 1939 | 2 | A | 3-0 |
| 1964 | 1 | H | 1-3 |
| 1969 | 2 | H | 0-0 |
| 1969 | 2r | A | 0-1 |

v **Burnley**

| | | | |
|---|---|---|---|
| 1961 | 3 | A | 0-1 |
| 1966 | 3 | H | 1-1 |
| 1966 | 3r | A | 0-7 |

v **Cambridge Utd**

| | | | |
|---|---|---|---|
| 1973 | 1 | H | 5-1 |

v **Charlton Athletic**

| | | | |
|---|---|---|---|
| 1974 | 1 | H | 1-0 |
| 1981 | 2 | A | 1-2 |

v **Cheltenham Town**

| | | | |
|---|---|---|---|
| 1993 | 2 | A | 1-1 |
| 1993 | 2r | H | 3-0 |

v **Colchester Utd**

| | | | |
|---|---|---|---|
| 1951 | 1 | H | 1-0 |
| 1973 | 2 | H | 0-0 |
| 1973 | 2r | A | 2-0 |
| 1978 | 1 | A | 1-1 |
| 1978 | 1r | H | 0-0aet |
| 1978 | 1r2 | N | 1-4 |
| 1980 | 2 | A | 0-1 |

v **Coventry City**

| | | | |
|---|---|---|---|
| 1928 | 1 | A | 2-2 |
| 1928 | 1r | H | 2-0 |
| 1963 | 1 | A | 0-1 |

v **Crewe Alexandra**

| | | | |
|---|---|---|---|
| 2003 | 3 | H | 0-0 |
| 2003 | 3r | A | 2-2q |

v **Derby County**

| | | | |
|---|---|---|---|
| 1947 | 3 | H | 0-2 |

v **Doncaster Rovers**

| | | | |
|---|---|---|---|
| 2003 | 1 | H | 2-1 |

v **Everton**

| | | | |
|---|---|---|---|
| 1937 | 3 | A | 0-5 |

**v Exeter City**

| | | | |
|---|---|---|---|
| 1947 | 1 | H | 4-2 |
| 1961 | 1 | A | 1-1 |
| 1961 | 1r | H | 3-1 |

**v Fulham**

| | | | |
|---|---|---|---|
| 1930 | 3 | A | 1-1 |
| 1930 | 3r | H | 0-2 |

**v Gillingham**

| | | | |
|---|---|---|---|
| 1991 | 1 | H | 2-1 |
| 2001 | 3 | H | 2-3 |

**v Hartlepool Utd**

| | | | |
|---|---|---|---|
| 1989 | 4 | A | 1-1 |
| 1989 | 4r | H | 5-2 |

**v Huddersfield Town**

| | | | |
|---|---|---|---|
| 1998 | 3 | H | 0-1 |

**v Ipswich Town**

| | | | |
|---|---|---|---|
| 1953 | 1 | A | 2-2 |
| 1953 | 1r | H | 2-2aet |
| 1953 | 1r2 | N | 2-3 |
| 1992 | 4 | A | 0-3 |

**v Leeds Utd**

| | | | |
|---|---|---|---|
| 1939 | 3 | A | 1-3 |

**v Leyton Orient**

| | | | |
|---|---|---|---|
| 1974 | 3 | A | 1-2 |
| 1987 | 2 | H | 0-1 |

**v Liverpool**

| | | | |
|---|---|---|---|
| 1927 | 3 | H | 1-1 |
| 1927 | 3r | A | 1-4 |
| 1968 | 3 | H | 0-0 |
| 1968 | 3r | A | 1-4 |

**v Luton Town**

| | | | |
|---|---|---|---|
| 1970 | 1 | H | 1-1 |
| 1970 | 1r | A | 1-3 |

**v Manchester Utd**

| | | | |
|---|---|---|---|
| 1949 | 3 | A | 0-6 |
| 1957 | 6 | H | 1-2 |
| 1984 | 3 | H | 2-0 |
| 1985 | 3 | A | 0-3 |
| 1989 | 5 | H | 1-1 |
| 1989 | 5r | A | 0-1 |

**v Mansfield Town**

| | | | |
|---|---|---|---|
| 1937 | 2 | A | 3-0 |

**v Middlesbrough**

| | | | |
|---|---|---|---|
| 1984 | 4 | A | 0-2 |

**v Newcastle Utd**

| | | | |
|---|---|---|---|
| 1973 | 3 | A | 0-2 |
| 1992 | 3 | H | 0-0 |
| 1992 | 3r | A | 2-2q |

**v Northampton Town**

| | | | |
|---|---|---|---|
| 1950 | 4 | H | 1-1 |
| 1950 | 4r | A | 1-2 |
| 1958 | 2 | A | 1-4 |
| 1968 | 1 | H | 2-0 |

**v Notts County**

| | | | |
|---|---|---|---|
| 2000 | 1 | A | 1-1 |
| 2000 | 1r | H | 4-2 |

**v Oldham Athletic**

| | | | |
|---|---|---|---|
| 1955 | 2 | H | 1-0 |

**v Oxford Utd**

| | | | |
|---|---|---|---|
| 1982 | 3 | H | 0-2 |

**v Peterborough**

| | | | |
|---|---|---|---|
| 1980 | 1 | A | 2-1 |
| 2002 | 2 | A | 0-1 |

**v Plymouth Argyle**

| | | | |
|---|---|---|---|
| 1995 | 2 | A | 1-2 |

**v Portsmouth**

| | | | |
|---|---|---|---|
| 1991 | 4 | A | 1-5 |

**v Preston North End**

| | | | |
|---|---|---|---|
| 1994 | 3 | A | 1-2 |
| 1967 | 2 | A | 0-2 |

**v Reading**

| | | | |
|---|---|---|---|
| 1926 | 3 | H | 2-0 |
| 1956 | 1 | A | 0-1 |
| 1982 | 1 | H | 1-0 |

**v Scunthorpe Utd**

| | | | |
|---|---|---|---|
| 1954 | 2 | A | 0-1 |

**v Sheffield Utd**

| | | | |
|---|---|---|---|
| 1990 | 3 | A | 0-2 |

**v Sheffield Wed**

| | | | |
|---|---|---|---|
| 1928 | 3 | A | 0-3 |
| 1932 | 4 | A | 0-7 |

**v Southampton**

| | | | |
|---|---|---|---|
| 1954 | 1 | A | 1-1 |
| 1954 | 1r | H | 3-1 |

**v Southend Utd**

| | | | |
|---|---|---|---|
| 1952 | 1 | A | 1-6 |
| 1972 | 2 | H | 2-0 |
| 1983 | 1 | H | 0-2 |
| 2003 | 2 | A | 1-1 |
| 2003 | 2r | H | 3-2 |

**v Stoke City**

| | | | |
|---|---|---|---|
| 2003 | 4 | A | 0-3 |

**v Swansea City**

| | | | |
|---|---|---|---|
| 2001 | 1 | H | 2-0 |

**v Swindon Town**

| | | | |
|---|---|---|---|
| 1927 | 1 | H | 1-1 |
| 1927 | 1r | A | 4-3 |
| 1957 | 2 | A | 1-0 |

**v Torquay Utd**

| | | | |
|---|---|---|---|
| 1930 | 1 | H | 2-0 |
| 1933 | 1 | A | 0-0 |
| 1933 | 1r | H | 2-2aet |
| 1933 | 1r2 | N | 2-3 |
| 1999 | 2 | A | 1-0 |

**v Tottenham Hotspur**

| | | | |
|---|---|---|---|
| 1957 | 5 | H | 3-1 |

**v Tranmere Rovers**

| | | | |
|---|---|---|---|
| 1934 | 2 | H | 2-4 |

**v Walsall**

| | | | |
|---|---|---|---|
| 1931 | 1 | A | 0-1 |
| 1972 | 3 | A | 0-1 |
| 1984 | 1 | H | 4-0 |

**v Watford**

| | | | |
|---|---|---|---|
| 1929 | 4 | H | 6-4 |
| 1974 | 2 | A | 1-0 |

**v West Bromwich Albion**

| | | | |
|---|---|---|---|
| 1955 | 3 | H | 0-1 |
| 1999 | 3 | H | 1-0 |

**v West Ham Utd**

| | | | |
|---|---|---|---|
| 1929 | 5 | H | 1-1 |
| 1929 | 5r | A | 1-3 |

**v Wigan Athletic**

| | | | |
|---|---|---|---|
| 1986 | 3 | A | 0-3 |

**v Wimbledon**

| | | | |
|---|---|---|---|
| 1979 | 2 | A | 1-1 |
| 1979 | 2r | H | 1-2aet |

**v Wolverhampton W**

| | | | |
|---|---|---|---|
| 1948 | 3 | H | 1-2 |
| 1957 | 4 | A | 1-0 |

**v Wycombe W**

| | | | |
|---|---|---|---|
| 1975 | 2 | A | 0-0 |
| 1975 | 2r | H | 1-2 |
| 1981 | 1 | A | 3-0 |

**v Yeovil Town**

| | | | |
|---|---|---|---|
| 1925 | Q4 | A | 2-3 |
| 1961 | 2 | H | 3-1 |
| 1971 | 2 | H | 0-1 |

**v York City**

| | | | |
|---|---|---|---|
| 1960 | 3 | H | 1-0 |

# Bradford City

**v Brentford**

| | | | |
|---|---|---|---|
| 1955 | 3 | A | 1-1 |
| 1955 | 3r | H | 2-2aet |
| 1955 | 3r2 | N | 0-1 |

**v Brighton & HA**

| | | | |
|---|---|---|---|
| 1959 | 3 | A | 2-0 |

**v Bristol City**

| | | | |
|---|---|---|---|
| 1920 | 4 | A | 0-2 |

**v Burnley**

| | | | |
|---|---|---|---|
| 1911 | 4 | H | 1-0 |
| 1960 | 5 | H | 2-2 |
| 1960 | 5r | A | 0-5 |

**v Bury**

| | | | |
|---|---|---|---|
| 1968 | 2 | H | 2-3 |
| 1992 | 1 | A | 1-0 |

**v Carlisle Utd**

| | | | |
|---|---|---|---|
| 1952 | 1 | H | 6-1 |
| 1980 | 3 | A | 2-3 |

**v Charlton Athletic**

| | | | |
|---|---|---|---|
| 1990 | 3 | A | 1-1 |
| 1990 | 3r | H | 0-3 |

**v Chelsea**

| | | | |
|---|---|---|---|
| 1912 | 2 | H | 2-0 |

**v Chesterfield**

| | | | |
|---|---|---|---|
| 1904 | Q4 | A | 1-2 |
| 1938 | 3 | H | 1-1 |
| 1938 | 3r | A | 1-1aet |
| 1938 | 3r2 | N | 0-2 |
| 1976 | 1 | H | 1-0 |

**v Crewe Alexandra**

| | | | |
|---|---|---|---|
| 1954 | 1 | A | 0-0 |
| 1954 | 1r | H | 0-1 |
| 1978 | 1 | H | 0-1 |
| 2000 | 3 | A | 2-1 |

**v Darlington**

| | | | |
|---|---|---|---|
| 1906 | Q4 | A | 4-0 |
| 1915 | 1 | A | 1-0 |
| 1966 | 1 | A | 2-3 |
| 1980 | 2 | A | 1-0 |

**v Derby County**

| | | | |
|---|---|---|---|
| 1925 | 1 | A | 1-0 |
| 1927 | 3 | H | 2-6 |
| 1936 | 5 | H | 0-1 |
| 1957 | 1 | A | 1-2 |

**v Doncaster Rovers**

| | | | |
|---|---|---|---|
| 1929 | 1 | H | 4-1 |
| 1949 | 1 | H | 4-3 |

**v Everton**

| | | | |
|---|---|---|---|
| 1906 | 3 | A | 0-1 |
| 1915 | 4 | H | 0-2 |
| 1960 | 3 | H | 3-0 |
| 1987 | 4 | H | 0-1 |
| 1997 | 4 | A | 3-2 |

**v Gillingham**

| | | | |
|---|---|---|---|
| 1911 | 1 | A | 1-0 |
| 2000 | 4 | A | 1-3 |

**v Grimsby Town**

| | | | |
|---|---|---|---|
| 1911 | 3 | H | 1-0 |
| 1970 | 1 | H | 2-1 |
| 1999 | 3 | H | 2-1 |

**v Hartlepool Utd**

| | | | |
|---|---|---|---|
| 1975 | 1 | A | 0-1 |

**v Huddersfield Town**

| | | | |
|---|---|---|---|
| 1930 | 5 | A | 1-2 |
| 1993 | 2 | H | 0-2 |

**v Hull City**

| | | | |
|---|---|---|---|
| 1962 | 2 | A | 2-0 |
| 1989 | 4 | H | 1-2 |

**v Ipswich Town**

| | | | |
|---|---|---|---|
| 1953 | 2 | H | 1-1 |
| 1953 | 2r | A | 1-5 |
| 1986 | 3 | A | 4-4 |
| 1986 | 3r | H | 0-1aet |

**v Lincoln City**

| | | | |
|---|---|---|---|
| 1970 | 2 | H | 3-0 |
| 1971 | 2 | A | 2-2 |
| 1971 | 2r | H | 2-2aet |
| 1971 | 2r2 | N | 1-4 |

**v Liverpool**

| | | | |
|---|---|---|---|
| 1907 | 3 | A | 0-1 |
| 1924 | 1 | A | 1-2 |

**v Luton Town**

| | | | |
|---|---|---|---|
| 1974 | 4 | A | 0-3 |

**v Macclesfield**

| | | | |
|---|---|---|---|
| 1971 | 1 | H | 3-2 |
| 1998 | 3 | A | 0-2 |

**v Manchester Utd**

| | | | |
|---|---|---|---|
| 1923 | 1 | H | 1-1 |
| 1923 | 1r | A | 0-2 |

**v Mansfield Town**

| | | | |
|---|---|---|---|
| 1955 | 1 | H | 3-1 |
| 1959 | 1 | A | 4-3 |
| 1983 | 2 | A | 1-1 |
| 1983 | 2r | H | 3-2 |
| 1985 | 2 | H | 2-1 |

**v Middlesbrough**

| | | | |
|---|---|---|---|
| 1915 | 2 | H | 1-0 |
| 1931 | 3 | A | 1-1 |
| 1931 | 3r | H | 2-1 |
| 2001 | 3 | H | 0-1 |

**v Millwall**

| | | | |
|---|---|---|---|
| 1905 | IR | H | 1-4 |
| 1914 | 2 | A | 0-1 |

**v Newcastle Utd**

| | | | |
|---|---|---|---|
| 1911 | F | N | 0-0 |
| 1911 | Fr | N | 1-0 |
| 1913 | 1 | A | 0-1 |
| 1963 | 3 | H | 1-6 |
| 1999 | 4 | A | 0-3 |

**v Norwich City**

| | | | |
|---|---|---|---|
| 1911 | 2 | H | 2-1 |
| 1915 | 3 | H | 1-1aet |
| 1915 | 3r | A | 0-0aet |
| 1915 | 3r2 | N | 2-0 |
| 1976 | 5 | A | 2-1 |

**v Nottingham Forest**

| | | | |
|---|---|---|---|
| 1926 | 3 | A | 0-1 |

**v Notts County**

| | | | |
|---|---|---|---|
| 1910 | 1 | H | 4-2 |
| 1922 | 2 | H | 1-1 |
| 1922 | 2r | A | 0-0aet |
| 1922 | 2r2 | N | 0-1 |
| 1946 | 1 | A | 2-2 |
| 1946 | 1s | H | 1-2 |

**v Oldham Athletic**

| | | | |
|---|---|---|---|
| 1951 | 1 | H | 2-2 |
| 1951 | 1r | A | 1-2 |
| 1956 | 1 | H | 3-1 |
| 1963 | 1 | A | 5-2 |
| 1987 | 3 | A | 1-1 |
| 1987 | 3r | H | 5-1 |

**v Oxford Utd**

| | | | |
|---|---|---|---|
| 1988 | 4 | H | 4-2 |

**v Port Vale**

| | | | |
|---|---|---|---|
| 1964 | 1 | H | 1-2 |
| 1967 | 1 | H | 1-2 |
| 1979 | 1 | H | 1-0 |
| 1981 | 1 | A | 2-4 |
| 1983 | 1 | A | 1-0 |

**v Portsmouth**

| | | | |
|---|---|---|---|
| 1920 | 1 | H | 2-0 |
| 1929 | 4 | A | 0-2 |
| 1988 | 5 | A | 0-3 |

**v Preston North End**

| | | | |
|---|---|---|---|
| 1920 | 3 | A | 3-0 |
| 1959 | 4 | A | 2-3 |
| 1993 | 1 | H | 1-1 |
| 1993 | 1r | A | 5-4 |
| 1996 | 2 | H | 2-1 |

**v QPR**

| | | | |
|---|---|---|---|
| 1912 | 1 | A | 0-0 |
| 1912 | 1r | H | 4-0 |

**v Reading**

| | | | |
|---|---|---|---|
| 1907 | 1 | H | 2-0 |

**v Rochdale**

| | | | |
|---|---|---|---|
| 1960 | 2 | A | 1-1 |
| 1960 | 2r | H | 2-1 |

**v Rotherham Utd**

| | | | |
|---|---|---|---|
| 1928 | 2 | H | 2-3 |
| 1976 | 2 | A | 3-0 |

**v Scunthorpe Utd**

| | | | |
|---|---|---|---|
| 1958 | 3 | A | 0-1 |
| 1982 | 1 | A | 0-1 |
| 1995 | 1 | H | 1-1 |
| 1995 | 1r | A | 2-3aet |

**v Sheffield Utd**

| | | | |
|---|---|---|---|
| 1920 | 2 | H | 2-1 |

**v Sheffield Wed**

| | | | |
|---|---|---|---|
| 1997 | 5 | H | 0-1 |

**v Shrewsbury Town**

| | | | |
|---|---|---|---|
| 1976 | 3 | A | 2-1 |
| 1991 | 1 | H | 0-0 |
| 1991 | 1r | A | 1-2 |

**v Southampton**

| | | | |
|---|---|---|---|
| 1925 | 3 | A | 0-2 |
| 1930 | 3 | H | 4-1 |
| 1976 | 6 | H | 0-1 |

**v Stockport County**

| | | | |
|---|---|---|---|
| 1929 | 3 | H | 2-0 |
| 1935 | 4 | H | 0-0 |
| 1935 | 4r | A | 2-3aet |
| 1979 | 2 | A | 2-4 |

**v Sunderland**

| | | | |
|---|---|---|---|
| 1909 | 3 | H | 0-1 |

**v Tottenham Hotspur**

| | | | |
|---|---|---|---|
| 1921 | 2 | A | 0-4 |
| 1970 | 3 | H | 2-2 |
| 1970 | 3r | A | 0-5 |
| 1989 | 3 | H | 1-0 |

**v Tranmere Rovers**

| | | | |
|---|---|---|---|
| 1929 | 2 | A | 1-0 |
| 1973 | 2 | H | 2-1 |

**v Walsall**

| | | | |
|---|---|---|---|
| 1922 | 1 | A | 3-3 |
| 1922 | 1r | H | 4-0 |
| 1977 | 1 | A | 0-0 |
| 1977 | 1r | H | 0-2 |
| 2002 | 3 | A | 0-2 |

**v West Bromwich Albion**

| | | | |
|---|---|---|---|
| 1909 | 2 | A | 2-1 |
| 2003 | 3 | A | 1-3 |

**v West Ham Utd**

| | | | |
|---|---|---|---|
| 1934 | 3 | A | 2-3 |

**v Wigan Athletic**

| | | | |
|---|---|---|---|
| 1984 | 1 | H | 0-0 |
| 1984 | 1r | A | 2-4 |

**v Wolverhampton W**

| | | | |
|---|---|---|---|
| 1906 | 2 | H | 5-0 |
| 1908 | 1 | H | 1-1 |
| 1908 | 1r | A | 0-1 |
| 1931 | 4 | H | 0-0 |
| 1931 | 4r | A | 2-4 |
| 1988 | 3 | H | 2-1 |

**v Wrexham**

| | | | |
|---|---|---|---|
| 1930 | 4 | A | 0-0 |
| 1930 | 4r | H | 2-1 |
| 1938 | 2 | A | 2-1 |
| 1968 | 1 | H | 7-1 |
| 1972 | 1 | A | 1-5 |

**v Wycombe W**

| | | | |
|---|---|---|---|
| 1997 | 3 | A | 2-0 |

v **York City**

| | | | |
|---|---|---|---|
| 1937 | 3 | H | 2-2 |
| 1937 | 3r | A | 0-1 |
| 1962 | 1 | H | 1-0 |

# Brentford

v **Brighton & HA**

| | | | |
|---|---|---|---|
| 1929 | 1 | H | 4-1 |
| 1975 | 2 | A | 0-1 |
| 1988 | 1 | H | 0-2 |

v **Bristol City**

| | | | |
|---|---|---|---|
| 1906 | 1 | H | 2-1 |
| 1946 | 4 | A | 1-2 |
| 1946 | 4s | H | 5-0 |

v **Bristol Rovers**

| | | | |
|---|---|---|---|
| 1986 | 1 | H | 1-3 |
| 1987 | 1 | A | 0-0 |
| 1987 | 1r | H | 2-0 |

v **Burnley**

| | | | |
|---|---|---|---|
| 1949 | 5 | H | 4-2 |
| 1965 | 3 | A | 1-1 |
| 1965 | 3r | H | 0-2 |
| 2003 | 4 | H | 0-3 |

v **Cambridge Utd**

| | | | |
|---|---|---|---|
| 1995 | 1 | A | 2-2 |
| 1995 | 1r | H | 1-2 |

v **Cardiff City**

| | | | |
|---|---|---|---|
| 1931 | 3 | H | 2-2 |
| 1931 | 3r | A | 2-1 |
| 1947 | 3 | H | 1-0 |
| 1971 | 4 | A | 2-0 |
| 1987 | 2 | A | 0-2 |
| 1994 | 2 | H | 1-3 |

v **Carlisle Utd**

| | | | |
|---|---|---|---|
| 1908 | 1 | A | 2-2 |
| 1908 | 1r | H | 1-3aet |

v **Charlton Athletic**

| | | | |
|---|---|---|---|
| 1946 | 6 | A | 3-6 |
| 1946 | 6s | H | 1-3 |
| 1996 | 4 | A | 2-3 |

v **Chelsea**

| | | | |
|---|---|---|---|
| 1950 | 3 | H | 0-1 |

v **Colchester Utd**

| | | | |
|---|---|---|---|
| 1977 | 2 | A | 2-3 |
| 1982 | 2 | H | 1-1 |
| 1982 | 2r | A | 0-1 |
| 1990 | 1 | H | 0-1 |
| 1998 | 1 | H | 2-2 |
| 1998 | 1r | A | 0-0p |

v **Crystal Palace**

| | | | |
|---|---|---|---|
| 1907 | 3 | A | 1-1 |
| 1907 | 3r | H | 0-1 |
| 1912 | 1 | H | 0-0 |
| 1912 | 1r | A | 0-4 |
| 1957 | 2 | H | 1-1 |
| 1957 | 2r | A | 2-3aet |

v **Derby County**

| | | | |
|---|---|---|---|
| 1937 | 4 | A | 0-3 |
| 2003 | 3 | H | 1-0 |

v **Exeter City**

| | | | |
|---|---|---|---|
| 1959 | 1 | H | 3-2 |
| 1960 | 2 | A | 1-3 |
| 1979 | 1 | A | 0-1 |
| 1982 | 1 | H | 2-0 |

v **Fulham**

| | | | |
|---|---|---|---|
| 1938 | 3 | H | 3-1 |
| 1981 | 2 | A | 0-1 |

v **Gillingham**

| | | | |
|---|---|---|---|
| 1927 | 2 | A | 1-1 |
| 1927 | 2r | H | 1-0 |
| 1971 | 1 | H | 2-1 |
| 1984 | 3 | A | 3-5 |
| 1992 | 1 | H | 3-3 |
| 1992 | 1r | A | 3-1 |

v **Grimsby Town**

| | | | |
|---|---|---|---|
| 1993 | 3 | H | 0-2 |

v **Huddersfield Town**

| | | | |
|---|---|---|---|
| 1920 | 1 | A | 1-5 |
| 1921 | 1 | H | 1-2 |
| 1937 | 3 | H | 5-0 |

v **Hull City**

| | | | |
|---|---|---|---|
| 1934 | 3 | A | 0-1 |
| 1954 | 3 | H | 0-0 |
| 1954 | 3r | A | 2-2aet |
| 1954 | 3r2 | N | 2-5 |
| 1971 | 5 | A | 1-2 |

v **Leeds Utd**

| | | | |
|---|---|---|---|
| 1953 | 3 | H | 2-1 |

v **Leicester City**

| | | | |
|---|---|---|---|
| 1936 | 3 | A | 0-1 |
| 1947 | 4 | H | 0-0 |
| 1947 | 4r | A | 0-0aet |
| 1947 | 4r2 | N | 1-4 |
| 1949 | 6 | H | 0-2 |

v **Leyton Orient**

| | | | |
|---|---|---|---|
| 1956 | 2 | A | 1-4 |
| 1962 | 3 | H | 1-1 |
| 1962 | 3r | A | 1-2 |
| 1967 | 2 | A | 0-0 |
| 1967 | 2r | H | 3-1 |

v **Lincoln City**

| | | | |
|---|---|---|---|
| 1906 | 2 | H | 3-0 |

v **Liverpool**

| | | | |
|---|---|---|---|
| 1906 | 3 | A | 0-2 |
| 1989 | 6 | A | 0-4 |

v **Luton Town**

| | | | |
|---|---|---|---|
| 1910 | Q4 | H | 2-1 |
| 1952 | 4 | A | 2-2 |
| 1952 | 4r | H | 0-0aet |
| 1952 | 4r2 | N | 2-3aet |

v **Manchester City**

| | | | |
|---|---|---|---|
| 1932 | 4 | A | 1-6 |
| 1989 | 4 | H | 3-1 |
| 1997 | 3 | H | 0-1 |

v **Manchester Utd**

| | | | |
|---|---|---|---|
| 1928 | 3 | A | 1-7 |
| 1938 | 5 | H | 2-0 |

v **Middlesbrough**

| | | | |
|---|---|---|---|
| 1907 | 2 | H | 1-0 |
| 1948 | 4 | H | 1-2 |
| 1949 | 3 | H | 3-2aet |
| 1964 | 3 | H | 2-1 |

v **Millwall**

| | | | |
|---|---|---|---|
| 1958 | 1 | A | 0-1 |

v **Newcastle Utd**

| | | | |
|---|---|---|---|
| 1939 | 3 | H | 0-2 |
| 1955 | 4 | A | 2-3 |

v **Northampton Town**

| | | | |
|---|---|---|---|
| 1976 | 1 | H | 2-0 |
| 1985 | 2 | H | 2-2 |
| 1985 | 2r | A | 2-0 |

v **Norwich City**

| | | | |
|---|---|---|---|
| 1931 | 2 | H | 1-0 |
| 1932 | 2 | H | 4-1 |
| 1996 | 3 | A | 2-1 |

v **Nottingham Forest**

| | | | |
|---|---|---|---|
| 1909 | 2 | A | 0-1 |

v **Notts County**

| | | | |
|---|---|---|---|
| 1965 | 2 | H | 4-0 |

v **Oldham Athletic**

| | | | |
|---|---|---|---|
| 1927 | 3 | A | 4-2 |
| 1985 | 3 | A | 1-2 |
| 1991 | 3 | A | 1-3 |
| 1999 | 2 | A | 1-1 |
| 1999 | 2r | H | 2-2q |

v **Oxford Utd**

| | | | |
|---|---|---|---|
| 1962 | 1 | H | 3-0 |
| 1964 | 4 | A | 2-2 |
| 1964 | 4r | H | 1-2 |

v **Peterborough**

| | | | |
|---|---|---|---|
| 1989 | 2 | A | 0-0 |
| 1989 | 2r | H | 3-2 |

v **Plymouth Argyle**

| | | | |
|---|---|---|---|
| 1904 | IR | H | 1-1 |
| 1904 | IRr | A | 1-4 |
| 1929 | 2 | H | 0-1 |
| 1935 | 3 | H | 0-1 |
| 1970 | 1 | H | 0-0 |
| 1970 | 1r | A | 0-2 |
| 1974 | 1 | A | 1-2 |
| 2000 | 1 | H | 2-2 |
| 2000 | 1r | A | 1-2aet |

v **Portsmouth**

| | | | |
|---|---|---|---|
| 1924 | Q6 | H | 1-1 |
| 1924 | Q6r | A | 0-1aet |
| 1931 | 4 | H | 0-1 |
| 1938 | 4 | H | 2-1 |

v **Preston North End**

| | | | |
|---|---|---|---|
| 1911 | 1 | H | 0-1 |
| 1938 | 6 | H | 0-3 |

v **QPR**

| | | | |
|---|---|---|---|
| 1905 | Q6 | A | 2-1 |
| 1946 | 5 | A | 3-1 |
| 1946 | 5s | H | 0-0 |
| 1952 | 3 | H | 3-1 |

v **Reading**

| | | | |
|---|---|---|---|
| 1905 | IR | H | 1-1 |
| 1905 | IRr | A | 0-2 |
| 1927 | 5 | A | 0-1 |
| 1933 | 1 | A | 2-3 |
| 1966 | 2 | A | 0-5 |

v **Rotherham Utd**

| | | | |
|---|---|---|---|
| 1948 | 3 | A | 3-0 |

v **Scunthorpe Utd**

| | | | |
|---|---|---|---|
| 2002 | 2 | A | 2-3 |

v **Southend Utd**
1912 Q5 A 1-0
1914 Q5 H 1-1
1914 Q5r A 0-2
1930 1 A 0-1

v **Stockport County**
1951 3 A 1-2

v **Sunderland**
1967 3 A 2-5

v **Swansea City**
1972 1 A 1-1
1972 1r H 2-3

v **Swindon Town**
1978 2 A 1-2
1980 1 A 1-4
1983 2 A 2-2
1983 2r H 1-3aet

v **Torquay Utd**
1949 4 H 1-0

v **Tottenham Hotspur**
1922 1 H 0-2
1946 3 A 2-2
1946 3s H 2-0

v **Walsall**
1971 2 H 1-0
1989 3 A 1-1
1989 3r H 1-0

v **Watford**
1913 Q4 H 0-0
1913 Q4r A 1-5
1961 1 A 2-2
1961 1r H 0-2
1969 2 A 0-1

v **West Bromwich Albion**
1959 4 A 0-2

v **West Ham Utd**
1927 4 A 1-1
1927 4r H 2-0

v **Wimbledon**
1976 2 A 2-0
1984 2 H 3-2

v **Wycombe W**
1904 Q5 H 4-1
1906 Q4 H 4-0
2003 1 A 4-2

v **Yeovil Town**
1966 1 H 2-1
1973 1 A 1-2
1991 1 H 5-0

v **York City**
2003 2 A 2-1

# Brighton & HA

v **Bristol City**
1951 4 A 0-1
1952 1 H 1-2
1965 1 A 0-1

v **Bristol Rovers**
1905 IR H 1-2

v **Burnley**
1961 4 H 3-3
1961 4r A 0-2

v **Bury**
1938 3 A 0-2

v **Cardiff City**
1921 2 H 0-0
1921 2r A 0-1
1971 3 A 0-1

v **Chelsea**
1933 3 H 2-1
1967 4 H 1-1
1967 4r A 0-4
1973 3 H 0-2

v **Cheltenham Town**
1936 1 H 0-0
1936 1r A 6-0
1971 1 H 4-0

v **Chesterfield**
1951 3 H 2-1

v **Colchester Utd**
1964 1 H 0-1

v **Coventry City**
1911 2 H 0-0
1911 2r A 0-2
1954 1 H 5-1

v **Crystal Palace**
1933 1 A 2-1
1977 1 H 2-2
1977 1r A 1-1aet
1977 1r2 N 0-1

v **Darlington**
1912 1 A 1-2

v **Derby County**
1946 5 H 1-4
1946 5s A 0-6
1961 3 H 3-1

v **Doncaster Rovers**
1932 2 H 5-0

v **Everton**
1913 2 H 0-0
1913 2r A 0-1aet
1924 2 H 5-2

v **Fulham**
1936 3 A 1-2
1996 2 A 0-0
1996 2r H 0-0q

v **Gillingham**
1905 Q4 A 1-0
1976 2 A 1-0

v **Grimsby Town**
1930 3 H 1-1
1930 3r A 1-0

v **Hartlepool Utd**
1948 2 A 1-1aet
1948 2r H 2-1

v **Huddersfield Town**
1922 2 H 0-0
1922 2r A 0-2

v **Hull City**
1985 3 H 1-0
1986 4 A 3-2

v **Ipswich Town**
1950 1 A 1-2
1951 2 H 2-0

v **Kidderminster H**
1969 1 H 2-2
1969 1r A 1-0

v **Leeds Utd**
1989 3 H 1-2

v **Leicester City**
1931 3 A 2-1

v **Leyton Orient**
1914 2 H 3-1
1999 1 A 2-4

v **Lincoln City**
1915 1 H 2-1

v **Liverpool**
1908 2 A 1-1
1908 2r H 0-3
1983 5 A 2-1
1984 4 H 2-0
1991 4 A 2-2
1991 4r H 2-3

v **Luton Town**
1920 Q6 H 0-1
1990 3 H 4-1

v **Manchester City**
1924 3 H 1-5
1983 4 H 4-0

v **Manchester Utd**
1909 1 A 0-1
1981 3 A 2-2
1981 3r H 0-2
1983 F N 2-2aet
1983 Fr N 0-4
1993 4 A 0-1

v **Mansfield Town**
1980 3 A 2-0

v **Middlesbrough**
1906 2 H 1-1
1906 2r A 1-1aet
1906 2r2 N 1-3

v **Millwall**
1957 1 H 1-1
1957 1r A 1-3

v **Newcastle Utd**
1930 5 A 0-3
1983 3 H 1-1
1983 3r A 1-0
1986 3 A 2-0

v **Northampton Town**
1928 2 A 0-1
1969 2 H 1-2
1988 2 A 2-1

v **Norwich City**
1946 3 A 2-1
1946 3s H 4-1
1947 1 A 2-7
1953 2 H 2-0
1955 2 A 0-0
1955 2r H 5-1
1956 2 H 1-2
1958 2 A 1-1
1958 2r H 1-2
1983 6 H 1-0
2003 3 A 1-3

**v Notts County**

| | | | |
|---|---|---|---|
| 1978 | 4 | H | 1-2 |

**v Oldham Athletic**

| | | | |
|---|---|---|---|
| 1914 | 1 | A | 1-1 |
| 1914 | 1r | H | 1-0aet |
| 1921 | 1 | H | 4-1 |
| 1990 | 4 | A | 1-2 |

**v Oxford Utd**

| | | | |
|---|---|---|---|
| 1982 | 4 | H | 0-3 |

**v Peterborough**

| | | | |
|---|---|---|---|
| 1986 | 5 | A | 2-2 |
| 1986 | 5r | H | 1-0 |
| 2000 | 1 | A | 1-1 |
| 2000 | 1r | H | 3-0 |

**v Plymouth Argyle**

| | | | |
|---|---|---|---|
| 2000 | 2 | A | 0-0 |
| 2000 | 2r | H | 1-2 |

**v Port Vale**

| | | | |
|---|---|---|---|
| 1932 | 3 | H | 1-2 |

**v Portsmouth**

| | | | |
|---|---|---|---|
| 1913 | 1 | A | 2-1 |
| 1930 | 4 | A | 1-0 |
| 1948 | 3 | A | 1-4 |
| 1993 | 3 | H | 1-0 |

**v Preston North End**

| | | | |
|---|---|---|---|
| 1908 | 1 | H | 1-1 |
| 1908 | 1r | A | 1-1 |
| 1908 | 1r2 | N | 1-0 |
| 1960 | 5 | A | 1-2 |
| 2002 | 3 | H | 0-2 |

**v QPR**

| | | | |
|---|---|---|---|
| 1935 | 2 | A | 2-1 |
| 1937 | 1 | A | 1-5 |

**v Rotherham Utd**

| | | | |
|---|---|---|---|
| 1960 | 4 | A | 1-1 |
| 1960 | 4r | H | 1-1aet |
| 1960 | 4r2 | N | 6-0 |

**v Rushden & Diamonds**

| | | | |
|---|---|---|---|
| 2002 | 2 | H | 2-1 |

**v Scunthorpe Utd**

| | | | |
|---|---|---|---|
| 1991 | 3 | H | 3-2 |
| 2001 | 2 | A | 1-2 |

**v Sheffield Utd**

| | | | |
|---|---|---|---|
| 1922 | 1 | H | 1-0 |
| 1987 | 3 | A | 0-0 |
| 1987 | 3r | H | 1-2 |

**v Sheffield Wed**

| | | | |
|---|---|---|---|
| 1914 | 3 | A | 0-3 |
| 1927 | 3 | A | 0-2 |
| 1983 | SF | N | 2-1 |

**v Shrewsbury Town**

| | | | |
|---|---|---|---|
| 2002 | 1 | H | 1-0 |

**v Southampton**

| | | | |
|---|---|---|---|
| 1910 | 1 | H | 0-1 |
| 1925 | 2 | A | 0-1 |
| 1986 | 6 | H | 0-2 |

**v Southend Utd**

| | | | |
|---|---|---|---|
| 1963 | 1 | A | 1-2 |
| 1968 | 1 | H | 1-0 |
| 1976 | 3 | A | 1-2 |

**v Swansea City**

| | | | |
|---|---|---|---|
| 1968 | 2 | A | 1-2 |
| 1984 | 3 | H | 2-0 |

**v Swindon Town**

| | | | |
|---|---|---|---|
| 1906 | 1 | H | 3-0 |
| 1934 | 3 | H | 3-1 |

**v Walsall**

| | | | |
|---|---|---|---|
| 1958 | 1 | H | 2-1 |
| 1970 | 2 | H | 1-1 |
| 1970 | 2r | A | 1-1aet |
| 1970 | 2r2 | N | 0-0aet |
| 1970 | 2r3 | N | 1-2 |
| 1972 | 2 | H | 1-1 |
| 1972 | 2r | A | 1-2 |

**v Watford**

| | | | |
|---|---|---|---|
| 1925 | 1 | A | 1-1 |
| 1925 | 1r | H | 4-3 |
| 1926 | 1 | H | 1-1 |
| 1926 | 1r | A | 0-2 |
| 1927 | 2 | A | 1-0 |
| 1928 | 1 | A | 2-1 |
| 1931 | 4 | A | 0-2 |
| 1976 | 1 | A | 3-0 |
| 1984 | 5 | A | 1-3 |

**v West Ham Utd**

| | | | |
|---|---|---|---|
| 1904 | Q3 | A | 0-4 |
| 1905 | Q6 | A | 2-1 |
| 1923 | 2 | H | 1-1 |
| 1923 | 2r | A | 0-1 |
| 1933 | 5 | H | 2-2 |
| 1933 | 5r | A | 0-1aet |

**v Wolverhampton W**

| | | | |
|---|---|---|---|
| 1979 | 3 | H | 2-3 |

**v Wrexham**

| | | | |
|---|---|---|---|
| 1933 | 2 | H | 0-0 |
| 1933 | 2r | A | 3-2aet |
| 1954 | 2 | A | 1-1 |
| 1954 | 2r | H | 1-1aet |
| 1954 | 2r2 | N | 1-3 |

**v Yeovil Town**

| | | | |
|---|---|---|---|
| 1939 | 1 | A | 1-2 |
| 1953 | 1 | A | 4-1 |

# Bristol City

**v Bristol Rovers**

| | | | |
|---|---|---|---|
| 1902 | Q4 | A | 1-1ab |
| 1902 | Q4r | H | 2-3 |
| 1925 | 1 | A | 1-0 |
| 1946 | 2 | H | 4-2 |
| 1946 | 2s | A | 2-0 |
| 1958 | 5 | H | 3-4 |
| 1968 | 3 | H | 0-0 |
| 1968 | 3r | A | 2-1 |
| 1984 | 2 | A | 2-1 |
| 1985 | 2 | H | 1-3 |

**v Bury**

| | | | |
|---|---|---|---|
| 1909 | 2 | H | 2-2 |
| 1909 | 2r | A | 1-0 |
| 1935 | 3 | H | 1-1 |
| 1935 | 3r | A | 2-2aet |
| 1935 | 3r2 | N | 2-1 |

**v Cambridge Utd**

| | | | |
|---|---|---|---|
| 1990 | 5 | H | 0-0 |
| 1990 | 5r | A | 1-1aet |
| 1990 | 5r2 | A | 1-5 |

**v Cardiff City**

| | | | |
|---|---|---|---|
| 1915 | 1 | H | 2-0 |
| 1920 | 3 | H | 2-1 |
| 1924 | 3 | A | 0-3 |
| 1938 | 2 | A | 1-1 |
| 1938 | 2r | H | 0-2 |

**v Carlisle Utd**

| | | | |
|---|---|---|---|
| 1981 | 4 | A | 1-1 |
| 1981 | 4r | H | 5-0 |

**v Charlton Athletic**

| | | | |
|---|---|---|---|
| 1960 | 3 | H | 2-3 |
| 1994 | 5 | H | 1-1 |
| 1994 | 5r | A | 0-2 |

**v Chelsea**

| | | | |
|---|---|---|---|
| 1949 | 3 | H | 1-3 |
| 1990 | 4 | H | 3-1 |

**v Chesterfield**

| | | | |
|---|---|---|---|
| 1997 | 3 | A | 0-2 |
| 2001 | 1 | A | 1-0 |

**v Colchester Utd**

| | | | |
|---|---|---|---|
| 1952 | 2 | A | 1-2 |

**v Coventry City**

| | | | |
|---|---|---|---|
| 1953 | 1 | A | 0-2 |
| 1976 | 3 | A | 1-2 |

**v Crewe Alexandra**

| | | | |
|---|---|---|---|
| 1911 | 1 | H | 0-3 |

**v Crystal Palace**

| | | | |
|---|---|---|---|
| 1936 | 1 | H | 0-1 |
| 1948 | 2 | H | 0-1aet |
| 1949 | 1 | A | 1-0aet |
| 1979 | 4 | A | 0-3 |

**v Derby County**

| | | | |
|---|---|---|---|
| 1909 | SF | N | 1-1 |
| 1909 | SFr | N | 2-1 |
| 1923 | 2 | H | 0-3 |
| 1930 | 3 | A | 1-5 |
| 1934 | 3 | H | 1-1 |
| 1934 | 3r | A | 0-1aet |
| 1980 | 3 | H | 6-2 |
| 1981 | 3 | A | 0-0 |
| 1981 | 3r | H | 2-0 |

**v Doncaster Rovers**

| | | | |
|---|---|---|---|
| 1959 | 3 | A | 2-0 |
| 1964 | 3 | A | 2-2 |
| 1964 | 3r | H | 2-0 |

**v Everton**

| | | | |
|---|---|---|---|
| 1915 | 2 | A | 0-4 |
| 1956 | 3 | A | 1-3 |
| 1995 | 4 | H | 0-1 |
| 1999 | 3 | H | 0-2 |

**v Exeter City**

| | | | |
|---|---|---|---|
| 1964 | 2 | A | 2-0 |
| 1986 | 2 | H | 1-2 |

**v Fulham**

| | | | |
|---|---|---|---|
| 1990 | 2 | H | 2-1 |

**v Gillingham**

| | | | |
|---|---|---|---|
| 1904 | IR | A | 1-1 |
| 1904 | IRr | H | 5-2 |
| 1935 | 1 | H | 2-0 |
| 1947 | 2 | H | 1-2 |

**v Grimsby Town**

| | | | |
|---|---|---|---|
| 1908 | 1 | H | 0-0 |
| 1908 | 1r | A | 1-2 |
| 1920 | 1 | A | 2-1 |

**v Hartlepool Utd**

| | | | |
|---|---|---|---|
| 1989 | 3 | A | 0-1 |

**v Huddersfield Town**

| | | | |
|---|---|---|---|
| 1920 | SF | N | 1-2 |
| 2001 | 3 | A | 2-0 |

**v Hull City**

| | | | |
|---|---|---|---|
| 1974 | 3 | H | 1-1 |
| 1974 | 3r | A | 1-0 |

**v Ipswich Town**

| | | | |
|---|---|---|---|
| 1977 | 3 | A | 1-4 |
| 1980 | 4 | H | 1-2 |

**v Leeds Utd**

| | | | |
|---|---|---|---|
| 1968 | 5 | A | 0-2 |
| 1974 | 5 | H | 1-1 |
| 1974 | 5r | A | 1-0 |

**v Leicester City**

| | | | |
|---|---|---|---|
| 1961 | 4 | A | 1-5 |
| 1992 | 4 | A | 2-1 |
| 2001 | 5 | A | 0-3 |
| 2003 | 3 | A | 0-2 |

**v Leyton Orient**

| | | | |
|---|---|---|---|
| 1983 | 1 | A | 1-4 |
| 2002 | 1 | H | 0-1 |

**v Liverpool**

| | | | |
|---|---|---|---|
| 1910 | 1 | H | 2-0 |
| 1913 | 1 | A | 0-3 |
| 1925 | 2 | H | 0-1 |
| 1929 | 3 | H | 0-2 |
| 1974 | 6 | H | 0-1 |
| 1994 | 3 | H | 1-1 |
| 1994 | 3r | A | 1-0 |

**v Luton Town**

| | | | |
|---|---|---|---|
| 1993 | 3 | A | 0-2 |

**v Manchester Utd**

| | | | |
|---|---|---|---|
| 1909 | F | N | 0-1 |

**v Mansfield Town**

| | | | |
|---|---|---|---|
| 2000 | 1 | H | 3-2 |

**v Middlesbrough**

| | | | |
|---|---|---|---|
| 1903 | IR | H | 3-1 |
| 1968 | 4 | A | 1-1 |
| 1968 | 4r | H | 2-1 |

**v Millwall**

| | | | |
|---|---|---|---|
| 1998 | 1 | H | 1-0 |

**v Northampton Town**

| | | | |
|---|---|---|---|
| 1912 | 1 | A | 0-1 |
| 1982 | 2 | H | 3-0 |

**v Norwich City**

| | | | |
|---|---|---|---|
| 1909 | 3 | H | 2-0 |
| 1924 | 1 | A | 1-0 |
| 1991 | 3 | A | 1-2 |

**v Nottingham Forest**

| | | | |
|---|---|---|---|
| 1922 | 1 | H | 0-0 |
| 1922 | 1r | A | 1-3 |
| 1950 | 1 | A | 0-1 |
| 1981 | 5 | A | 1-2 |
| 1992 | 5 | A | 1-4 |

**v Notts County**

| | | | |
|---|---|---|---|
| 1932 | 3 | A | 2-2 |
| 1932 | 3r | H | 3-2 |
| 1958 | 4 | A | 2-1 |
| 1984 | 3 | A | 2-2 |
| 1984 | 3r | H | 0-2 |

**v Peterborough**

| | | | |
|---|---|---|---|
| 1982 | 3 | A | 1-0 |

**v Plymouth Argyle**

| | | | |
|---|---|---|---|
| 1961 | 3 | A | 1-0 |
| 1987 | 3 | H | 1-1 |
| 1987 | 3r | A | 1-3aet |

**v Portsmouth**

| | | | |
|---|---|---|---|
| 1935 | 4 | A | 0-0 |
| 1935 | 4r | H | 2-0 |
| 1973 | 3 | A | 1-1 |
| 1973 | 3r | H | 4-1 |

**v Preston North End**

| | | | |
|---|---|---|---|
| 1905 | 2 | H | 0-0 |
| 1905 | 2r | A | 0-1 |
| 1935 | 5 | H | 0-0 |
| 1935 | 5r | A | 0-5 |
| 1972 | 3 | A | 2-4 |

**v QPR**

| | | | |
|---|---|---|---|
| 1914 | 1 | A | 2-2 |
| 1914 | 1r | H | 0-2aet |

**v Reading**

| | | | |
|---|---|---|---|
| 1899 | Q5 | H | 3-2 |
| 1901 | IR | A | 1-1 |
| 1901 | IRr | H | 0-0ab |
| 1901 | IRr2 | N | 1-2 |

**v Rotherham Utd**

| | | | |
|---|---|---|---|
| 1935 | 2 | A | 2-1 |
| 1954 | 3 | H | 1-3 |
| 1957 | 3 | H | 4-1 |

**v Sheffield Utd**

| | | | |
|---|---|---|---|
| 1904 | 1 | H | 1-3 |
| 1965 | 3 | H | 1-1 |
| 1965 | 3r | A | 0-3 |
| 1975 | 3 | A | 0-2 |

**v Sheffield Wed**

| | | | |
|---|---|---|---|
| 1924 | 2 | A | 1-1 |
| 1924 | 2r | H | 2-0 |
| 2000 | 3 | A | 0-1 |

**v Southampton**

| | | | |
|---|---|---|---|
| 1898 | Q3 | A | 0-2 |
| 1909 | 1 | H | 1-1 |
| 1909 | 1r | A | 2-0 |
| 1967 | 4 | H | 1-0 |
| 1971 | 3 | A | 0-3 |

**v Southend Utd**

| | | | |
|---|---|---|---|
| 1955 | 1 | H | 1-2 |
| 1989 | 1 | H | 3-1 |

**v Stockport County**

| | | | |
|---|---|---|---|
| 1994 | 4 | A | 4-0 |

**v Stoke City**

| | | | |
|---|---|---|---|
| 1995 | 3 | H | 0-0 |
| 1995 | 3r | A | 3-1aet |

**v Sunderland**

| | | | |
|---|---|---|---|
| 1899 | 1 | H | 2-4 |
| 1964 | 4 | A | 1-6 |

**v Swansea City**

| | | | |
|---|---|---|---|
| 1946 | 3 | H | 5-1 |
| 1946 | 3s | A | 2-2 |
| 1949 | 2 | H | 3-1 |
| 1997 | 1 | A | 1-1 |
| 1997 | 1r | H | 1-0 |

**v Swindon Town**

| | | | |
|---|---|---|---|
| 1986 | 1 | A | 0-0 |
| 1986 | 1r | H | 4-2 |
| 1990 | 3 | H | 2-1 |

**v Torquay Utd**

| | | | |
|---|---|---|---|
| 1954 | 1 | A | 3-1 |
| 1982 | 1 | H | 0-0 |
| 1982 | 1r | A | 2-1 |
| 1988 | 2 | H | 0-1 |

**v Tottenham Hotspur**

| | | | |
|---|---|---|---|
| 1903 | 2 | A | 0-1 |
| 1928 | 3 | H | 1-2 |
| 1967 | 5 | A | 0-2 |

**v Tranmere Rovers**

| | | | |
|---|---|---|---|
| 1933 | 2 | H | 2-2 |
| 1933 | 2r | A | 2-3 |

**v Walsall**

| | | | |
|---|---|---|---|
| 1962 | 3 | H | 0-0 |
| 1962 | 3r | A | 1-4 |

**v Watford**

| | | | |
|---|---|---|---|
| 1932 | 4 | A | 1-2 |

**v West Bromwich Albion**

| | | | |
|---|---|---|---|
| 1910 | 2 | H | 1-1 |
| 1910 | 2r | A | 2-4 |
| 1926 | 3 | A | 1-4 |

**v West Ham Utd**

| | | | |
|---|---|---|---|
| 1969 | 3 | A | 2-3 |

**v Wimbledon**

| | | | |
|---|---|---|---|
| 1963 | 2 | H | 2-1 |
| 1992 | 3 | H | 1-1 |
| 1992 | 3r | A | 1-0 |

**v Wolverhampton W**

| | | | |
|---|---|---|---|
| 1973 | 4 | A | 0-1 |

**v Wrexham**

| | | | |
|---|---|---|---|
| 1923 | 1 | H | 5-1 |
| 1951 | 2 | H | 2-1 |
| 1978 | 3 | H | 4-4 |
| 1978 | 3r | A | 0-3 |

**v Yeovil Town**

| | | | |
|---|---|---|---|
| 1946 | 1 | A | 2-2 |
| 1946 | 1s | H | 3-0 |

## Bristol Rovers

**v Burnley**

| | | | |
|---|---|---|---|
| 1909 | 1 | H | 1-4 |
| 1958 | 4 | H | 2-2 |
| 1958 | 4r | A | 3-2 |

**v Cambridge Utd**

| | | | |
|---|---|---|---|
| 1972 | 2 | H | 3-0 |

**v Cardiff City**

| | | | |
|---|---|---|---|
| 1933 | 1 | A | 1-1 |
| 1933 | 1r | H | 4-1 |
| 2001 | 1 | A | 1-5 |

**v Charlton Athletic**

| | | | |
|---|---|---|---|
| 1927 | 2 | H | 4-1 |
| 1959 | 3 | H | 0-4 |
| 1979 | 4 | H | 1-0 |

**v Chelsea**

| | | | |
|---|---|---|---|
| 1955 | 4 | H | 1-3 |
| 1976 | 3 | A | 1-1 |
| 1976 | 3r | H | 0-1 |

**v Chesterfield**

| | | | |
|---|---|---|---|
| 1908 | 2 | H | 2-0 |

**v Coventry City**

| | | | |
|---|---|---|---|
| 1964 | 2 | A | 2-1 |

**v Crewe Alexandra**

| | | | |
|---|---|---|---|
| 1991 | 3 | H | 0-2 |

**v Crystal Palace**

| | | | |
|---|---|---|---|
| 1929 | 2 | A | 1-3 |

**v Derby County**

| | | | |
|---|---|---|---|
| 1975 | 4 | A | 0-2 |
| 2002 | 3 | A | 3-1 |

**v Doncaster Rovers**

| | | | |
|---|---|---|---|
| 1956 | 4 | H | 1-1 |
| 1956 | 4r | A | 0-1 |
| 1960 | 3 | H | 0-0 |
| 1960 | 3r | A | 2-1 |

**v Everton**

| | | | |
|---|---|---|---|
| 1913 | 3 | H | 0-4 |
| 1969 | 5 | A | 0-1 |

**v Exeter City**

| | | | |
|---|---|---|---|
| 1922 | Q5 | H | 0-0 |
| 1922 | Q5r | A | 2-0 |
| 1924 | Q5 | A | 2-2 |
| 1924 | Q5r | H | 0-1 |
| 1997 | 1 | H | 1-2 |
| 1999 | 2 | A | 2-2 |
| 1999 | 2r | H | 5-0 |

**v Fulham**

| | | | |
|---|---|---|---|
| 1948 | 4 | A | 2-5 |
| 1958 | 6 | A | 1-3 |
| 1971 | 1 | A | 2-1 |
| 1982 | 1 | H | 1-2 |

**v Gillingham**

| | | | |
|---|---|---|---|
| 1932 | 1 | H | 5-1 |
| 1933 | 2 | H | 1-1 |
| 1933 | 2r | A | 3-1 |
| 1951 | 2 | H | 2-2 |
| 1951 | 2r | A | 1-1aet |
| 1951 | 2r2 | N | 2-1 |
| 1998 | 1 | H | 2-2 |
| 1998 | 1r | A | 2-0 |
| 2002 | 4 | A | 0-1 |

**v Grimsby Town**

| | | | |
|---|---|---|---|
| 1910 | 1 | A | 2-0 |

**v Huddersfield Town**

| | | | |
|---|---|---|---|
| 1953 | 3 | A | 0-2 |

**v Hull City**

| | | | |
|---|---|---|---|
| 1911 | 1 | H | 0-0 |
| 1911 | 1r | A | 0-1aet |
| 1951 | 5 | H | 3-0 |
| 1957 | 3 | A | 4-3 |

**v Ipswich Town**

| | | | |
|---|---|---|---|
| 1978 | 5 | H | 2-2 |
| 1978 | 5r | A | 0-3 |
| 1979 | 5 | A | 1-6 |
| 1985 | 3 | H | 1-2 |
| 1998 | 3 | H | 1-1 |
| 1998 | 3r | A | 0-1 |

**v Leeds Utd**

| | | | |
|---|---|---|---|
| 1972 | 3 | A | 1-4 |

**v Leicester City**

| | | | |
|---|---|---|---|
| 1937 | 3 | H | 2-5 |
| 1986 | 3 | H | 3-1 |

**v Leyton Orient**

| | | | |
|---|---|---|---|
| 1930 | 3 | A | 0-1 |
| 1953 | 1 | A | 1-1 |
| 1953 | 1r | H | 1-0 |
| 1995 | 2 | A | 2-0 |
| 1999 | 4 | H | 3-0 |

**v Liverpool**

| | | | |
|---|---|---|---|
| 1992 | 4 | H | 1-1 |
| 1992 | 4r | A | 1-2 |

**v Luton Town**

| | | | |
|---|---|---|---|
| 1901 | IR | A | 2-1 |
| 1951 | 4 | A | 2-1 |
| 1967 | 2 | H | 3-2 |
| 1986 | 4 | A | 0-4 |
| 1995 | 3 | A | 1-1 |
| 1995 | 3r | H | 0-1 |

**v Manchester Utd**

| | | | |
|---|---|---|---|
| 1935 | 3 | H | 1-3 |
| 1956 | 3 | H | 4-0 |
| 1964 | 4 | A | 1-4 |

**v Mansfield Town**

| | | | |
|---|---|---|---|
| 1958 | 3 | H | 5-0 |

**v Middlesbrough**

| | | | |
|---|---|---|---|
| 1902 | 1 | A | 1-1 |
| 1902 | 1r | H | 1-0aet |

**v Millwall**

| | | | |
|---|---|---|---|
| 1902 | IR | A | 1-1 |
| 1902 | IRr | H | 1-0 |
| 1903 | IR | H | 2-2 |
| 1903 | IRr | A | 0-0ab |
| 1903 | IRr2 | N | 0-2 |
| 1907 | 2 | H | 3-0 |

**v Newcastle Utd**

| | | | |
|---|---|---|---|
| 1951 | 6 | A | 0-0 |
| 1951 | 6r | H | 1-3 |

**v Northampton Town**

| | | | |
|---|---|---|---|
| 1908 | 1 | A | 1-0 |
| 1920 | Q6 | A | 2-2 |
| 1920 | Q6r | H | 3-2 |
| 1936 | 1 | A | 0-0 |
| 1936 | 1r | H | 3-1 |
| 1974 | 2 | A | 2-1 |

**v Norwich City**

| | | | |
|---|---|---|---|
| 1913 | 2 | H | 1-1 |
| 1913 | 2r | A | 2-2aet |
| 1913 | 2r2 | N | 1-0 |
| 1964 | 3 | H | 2-1 |

**v Nottingham Forest**

| | | | |
|---|---|---|---|
| 1974 | 3 | A | 3-4 |
| 1977 | 3 | A | 1-1 |
| 1977 | 3r | H | 1-1aet |
| 1977 | 3r2 | N | 0-6 |

**v Notts County**

| | | | |
|---|---|---|---|
| 1913 | 1 | H | 2-0 |

**v Oldham Athletic**

| | | | |
|---|---|---|---|
| 1936 | 2 | A | 1-1 |
| 1936 | 2r | H | 4-1 |
| 1962 | 3 | H | 1-1 |
| 1962 | 3r | A | 0-2 |

**v Peterborough**

| | | | |
|---|---|---|---|
| 1939 | 1 | H | 4-1 |
| 1953 | 2 | A | 1-0 |
| 1969 | 1 | H | 3-1 |

**v Plymouth Argyle**

| | | | |
|---|---|---|---|
| 1983 | 2 | H | 2-2 |
| 1983 | 2r | A | 0-1 |
| 1992 | 3 | H | 5-0 |
| 2002 | 2 | A | 1-1 |
| 2002 | 2r | H | 3-2 |

**v Port Vale**

| | | | |
|---|---|---|---|
| 1963 | 1 | H | 0-2 |

**v Portsmouth**

| | | | |
|---|---|---|---|
| 1900 | Q4 | H | 1-1 |
| 1900 | Q4r | A | 0-4 |
| 1912 | 1 | H | 1-2 |
| 1927 | 3 | H | 3-3 |
| 1927 | 3r | A | 0-4 |
| 1955 | 3 | H | 2-1 |

**v Preston North End**

| | | | |
|---|---|---|---|
| 1914 | 1 | A | 2-5 |
| 1952 | 3 | H | 2-0 |
| 1957 | 4 | H | 1-4 |
| 1960 | 4 | H | 3-3 |
| 1960 | 4r | A | 1-5 |
| 1981 | 3 | A | 4-3 |
| 2000 | 1 | H | 0-1 |

**v QPR**

| | | | |
|---|---|---|---|
| 1907 | 1 | H | 0-0 |
| 1907 | 1r | A | 1-0 |
| 1931 | 3 | H | 3-1 |
| 1938 | 1 | H | 1-8 |

**v Reading**

| | | | |
|---|---|---|---|
| 1899 | Q3 | H | 0-1 |
| 1901 | 1 | A | 0-2 |
| 1923 | Q5 | A | 1-0 |
| 1966 | 1 | A | 2-3 |
| 1990 | 1 | H | 1-1 |
| 1990 | 1r | A | 1-1aet |
| 1990 | 1r2 | H | 0-1 |

**v Rochdale**

| | | | |
|---|---|---|---|
| 2003 | 2 | H | 1-1 |
| 2003 | 2r | A | 2-3 |

**v Rotherham Utd**

| | | | |
|---|---|---|---|
| 1999 | 3 | A | 1-0 |

**v Sheffield Wed**

| | | | |
|---|---|---|---|
| 1906 | 1 | A | 0-1 |

**v Shrewsbury Town**

| | | | |
|---|---|---|---|
| 1988 | 3 | A | 1-2 |

**v Southampton**

| | | | |
|---|---|---|---|
| 1908 | 3 | A | 0-2 |
| 1978 | 4 | H | 2-0 |
| 1981 | 4 | A | 1-3 |

**v Southend Utd**

| | | | |
|---|---|---|---|
| 1915 | 1 | H | 0-0 |
| 1915 | 1r | A | 0-3 |
| 1952 | 4 | A | 1-2 |

**v Stockport County**

| | | | |
|---|---|---|---|
| 1931 | 2 | H | 4-2 |
| 1965 | 3 | H | 0-0 |
| 1965 | 3r | A | 2-3 |

**v Stoke City**

| | | | |
|---|---|---|---|
| 1902 | 2 | H | 0-1 |

**v Sunderland**

| | | | |
|---|---|---|---|
| 1978 | 3 | A | 1-0 |

**v Swansea City**

| | | | |
|---|---|---|---|
| 1922 | Q6 | A | 0-2 |
| 1948 | 3 | H | 3-0 |
| 1979 | 3 | A | 1-0 |
| 1986 | 2 | A | 2-1 |

**v Swindon Town**

| | | | |
|---|---|---|---|
| 1901 | Q5 | H | 5-1 |
| 1902 | Q5 | A | 1-0 |
| 1946 | 1 | A | 0-1 |
| 1946 | 1s | H | 4-1 |
| 1950 | 1 | A | 0-1 |

**v Torquay Utd**

| | | | |
|---|---|---|---|
| 1927 | 1 | A | 1-1 |
| 1927 | 1r | H | 1-0 |

**v Tottenham Hotspur**

| | | | |
|---|---|---|---|
| 1920 | 1 | H | 1-4 |
| 1921 | 1 | A | 2-6 |

**v Tranmere Rovers**

| | | | |
|---|---|---|---|
| 1932 | 2 | A | 0-2 |

**v Walsall**

| | | | |
|---|---|---|---|
| 1928 | 1 | H | 4-2 |
| 1949 | 1 | A | 1-2 |
| 1965 | 1 | A | 2-0 |

**v Wimbledon**

| | | | |
|---|---|---|---|
| 1968 | 2 | A | 4-0 |

**v Wycombe W**

| | | | |
|---|---|---|---|
| 1983 | 1 | H | 1-0 |
| 1994 | 1 | H | 1-2 |

**v Yeovil Town**

| | | | |
|---|---|---|---|
| 1925 | Q5 | A | 4-2 |

# Burnley

**v Bury**

| | | | |
|---|---|---|---|
| 1900 | 1 | H | 0-1 |
| 1934 | 3 | H | 0-0 |
| 1934 | 3r | A | 2-3 |
| 1937 | 4 | H | 4-1 |
| 1956 | 3 | A | 1-0 |
| 1980 | 4 | A | 0-1 |
| 1982 | 2 | A | 1-1 |
| 1982 | 2r | H | 2-1aet |

**v Cambridge Utd**

| | | | |
|---|---|---|---|
| 1995 | 3 | A | 4-2 |

**v Cardiff City**

| | | | |
|---|---|---|---|
| 1926 | 3 | A | 2-2 |
| 1926 | 3r | H | 0-2 |

**v Carlisle Utd**

| | | | |
|---|---|---|---|
| 1983 | 3 | A | 2-2 |
| 1983 | 3r | H | 3-1 |

**v Charlton Athletic**

| | | | |
|---|---|---|---|
| 1947 | F | N | 0-1aet |
| 1949 | 3 | H | 2-1aet |
| 1994 | 3 | A | 0-3 |

**v Chelsea**

| | | | |
|---|---|---|---|
| 1927 | 5 | A | 1-2 |
| 1956 | 4 | H | 1-1 |
| 1956 | 4r | A | 1-1aet |
| 1956 | 4r2 | N | 2-2aet |
| 1956 | 4r3 | N | 0-0aet |
| 1956 | 4r4 | N | 0-2 |
| 1970 | 4 | A | 2-2 |
| 1970 | 4r | H | 1-3aet |
| 1978 | 4 | A | 2-6 |

**v Cheltenham Town**

| | | | |
|---|---|---|---|
| 2002 | 4 | A | 1-2 |

**v Chesterfield**

| | | | |
|---|---|---|---|
| 1933 | 5 | H | 1-0 |
| 1938 | 4 | A | 2-3 |
| 1957 | 3 | H | 7-0 |
| 1984 | 2 | A | 2-2 |
| 1984 | 2r | H | 3-2 |

**v Coventry City**

| | | | |
|---|---|---|---|
| 1911 | 3 | H | 5-0 |
| 1947 | 4 | H | 2-0 |
| 1952 | 4 | H | 2-0 |
| 2000 | 4 | A | 0-3 |

**v Crewe Alexandra**

| | | | |
|---|---|---|---|
| 1891 | 1 | H | 4-2 |

**v Crystal Palace**

| | | | |
|---|---|---|---|
| 1909 | 2 | A | 0-0 |
| 1909 | 2r | H | 9-0 |
| 1983 | 5 | A | 0-0 |
| 1983 | 5r | H | 1-0 |

**v Darlington**

| | | | |
|---|---|---|---|
| 1999 | 1 | N | 2-3 |

**v Derby County**

| | | | |
|---|---|---|---|
| 1914 | 2 | H | 3-2 |
| 1932 | 3 | H | 0-4 |
| 1969 | 3 | H | 3-1 |
| 1992 | 3 | H | 2-2 |
| 1992 | 3r | A | 0-2 |
| 2000 | 3 | A | 1-0 |

**v Doncaster Rovers**

| | | | |
|---|---|---|---|
| 1992 | 1 | H | 1-1 |
| 1992 | 1r | A | 3-1 |

**v Everton**

| | | | |
|---|---|---|---|
| 1892 | 1r | A | 3-1 |
| 1898 | 3 | H | 1-3 |
| 1925 | 1 | A | 1-2 |
| 1962 | 5 | H | 3-1 |
| 1967 | 3 | H | 0-0 |
| 1967 | 3r | A | 1-2 |

**v Exeter City**

| | | | |
|---|---|---|---|
| 1911 | 1 | H | 2-0 |

**v Fulham**

| | | | |
|---|---|---|---|
| 1912 | 1 | A | 1-2 |
| 1924 | 2 | H | 0-0 |
| 1924 | 2r | A | 1-0aet |
| 1927 | 4 | A | 4-0 |
| 1962 | SF | N | 1-1 |
| 1962 | SFr | N | 2-1 |
| 1978 | 3 | H | 1-0 |
| 2003 | 5 | A | 1-1 |
| 2003 | 5r | H | 3-0 |

**v Grimsby Town**

| | | | |
|---|---|---|---|
| 1927 | 3 | H | 3-1 |
| 1974 | 3 | A | 2-0 |
| 2003 | 3 | A | 2-2 |
| 2003 | 3r | H | 4-0 |

**v Hartlepool Utd**

| | | | |
|---|---|---|---|
| 1952 | 3 | H | 1-0 |

**v Huddersfield Town**

| | | | |
|---|---|---|---|
| 1915 | 1 | H | 3-1 |
| 1922 | 1 | H | 2-2 |
| 1922 | 1r | A | 2-3 |
| 1924 | 3 | H | 1-0 |
| 1957 | 5 | A | 2-1 |
| 1964 | 5 | H | 3-0 |
| 1972 | 3 | H | 0-1 |

**v Hull City**

| | | | |
|---|---|---|---|
| 1921 | 3 | A | 0-3 |

**v Leicester City**

| | | | |
|---|---|---|---|
| 1921 | 1 | A | 7-3 |

**v Leyton Orient**

| | | | |
|---|---|---|---|
| 1962 | 4 | H | 1-1 |
| 1962 | 4r | A | 1-0 |

**v Lincoln City**

| | | | |
|---|---|---|---|
| 1905 | IR | H | 1-1 |
| 1905 | IRr | A | 2-3 |
| 1960 | 3 | A | 1-1 |
| 1960 | 3r | H | 2-0 |
| 1977 | 3 | H | 2-2 |
| 1977 | 3r | A | 1-0 |
| 1997 | 1 | H | 2-1 |

**v Liverpool**

| | | | |
|---|---|---|---|
| 1914 | F | N | 1-0 |
| 1947 | SF | N | 0-0aet |
| 1947 | SFr | N | 1-0 |
| 1952 | 5 | H | 2-0 |
| 1963 | 4 | H | 1-1 |
| 1963 | 4r | A | 1-2aet |
| 1969 | 4 | A | 1-2 |
| 1973 | 3 | H | 0-0 |
| 1973 | 3r | A | 0-3 |
| 1979 | 5 | A | 0-3 |
| 1995 | 4 | H | 0-0 |
| 1995 | 4r | A | 0-1 |
| 1997 | 3 | A | 0-1 |

**v Luton Town**

| | | | |
|---|---|---|---|
| 1935 | 4 | H | 3-1 |
| 1947 | 5 | A | 0-0 |
| 1947 | 5r | H | 3-0 |

**v Manchester City**

| | | | |
|---|---|---|---|
| 1931 | 3 | H | 3-0 |
| 1933 | 6 | H | 0-1 |
| 1991 | 3 | H | 0-1 |

**v Manchester Utd**

| | | | |
|---|---|---|---|
| 1901 | 1 | A | 0-0 |
| 1901 | 1r | H | 7-1 |
| 1909 | 4 | H | 2-3 |
| 1910 | 1 | H | 2-0 |
| 1954 | 3 | H | 5-3 |
| 1965 | 5 | A | 1-2 |

**v Mansfield Town**

| | | | |
|---|---|---|---|
| 1935 | 3 | H | 4-2 |

v **Middlesbrough**
1913 3 H 3-1
1947 6 A 1-1
1947 6r H 1-0aet

v **Newcastle Utd**
1895 1 A 1-2
1954 4 H 1-1
1954 4r A 0-1
1974 SF N 0-2

v **Nottingham Forest**
1935 5 A 0-0
1935 5r H 3-0

v **Notts County**
1891 2 A 1-2
1894 1 A 0-1
1939 3 A 1-3
1950 3 A 4-1

v **Oldham Athletic**
1974 4 A 4-1

v **Oxford Utd**
1971 3 A 0-3
1984 3 H 0-0
1984 3r A 1-2

v **Port Vale**
1898 2 H 3-0
1950 4 H 2-1
1977 4 A 1-2
1981 2 H 1-1
1981 2r A 0-2

v **Portsmouth**
1953 3 A 1-1
1953 3r H 3-1
1959 5 H 1-0

v **QPR**
1921 2 H 4-2
1962 3 H 6-1

v **Reading**
1903 IR A 0-1
1965 4 A 1-1
1965 4r H 1-0

v **Rochdale**
1994 2 H 4-1

v **Rotherham Utd**
1949 4 A 1-0
1964 3 H 1-1
1964 3r A 3-2
1986 2 A 1-4
1992 2 H 2-0
1998 1 A 3-3
1998 1r H 0-3
2000 2 H 2-0

v **Scunthorpe Utd**
1990 2 A 2-2
1990 2r H 1-1aet
1990 2r2 H 5-0
2001 3 H 2-2
2001 3r A 1-1p

v **Sheffield Utd**
1890 1 A 1-2
1899 1 H 2-2
1899 1r A 1-2
1914 SF N 0-0
1914 SFr N 1-0
1929 3 H 2-1
1933 4 H 3-1
1936 3 H 0-0
1936 3r A 1-2
1962 6 A 1-0
1993 3 A 2-2
1993 3r H 2-4

v **Sheffield Wed**
1893 2 A 0-1
1930 3 A 0-1
1935 SF N 0-3
1938 3 A 1-1
1938 3r H 3-1
1961 6 A 0-0
1961 6r H 2-0
1983 6 H 1-1
1983 6r A 0-5

v **Shrewsbury Town**
1982 4 A 0-1
1993 2 H 1-1
1993 2r A 2-1
1995 1 H 2-1

v **Southampton**
1908 1 H 1-2

v **Southend Utd**
1915 2 H 6-0

v **Stockport County**
1959 3 A 3-1
1990 1 H 1-1
1990 1r A 2-1

v **Stoke City**
1892 2 H 1-3
1896 2 H 1-1
1896 2r A 1-7
1946 3 A 1-3
1946 3s H 2-1
1980 3 H 1-0
1991 2 H 2-0

v **Sunderland**
1897 1 A 0-1
1913 SF N 0-0
1913 SFr N 2-3
1914 4 A 0-0
1914 4r H 2-1
1920 2 H 1-1
1920 2r A 0-2
1923 1 A 1-3
1953 4 H 2-0
1955 3 A 0-1
1979 4 H 1-1
1979 4r A 3-0

v **Swansea City**
1958 3 H 4-2
1960 4 A 0-0
1960 4r H 2-1
1961 5 H 4-0

v **Swindon Town**
1910 2 A 0-2
1924 4 A 1-1
1924 4r H 3-1
1929 4 H 3-3
1929 4r A 2-3
1933 3 A 2-1
1948 3 H 0-2
1983 4 H 3-1

v **Tottenham Hotspur**
1906 1 A 0-2
1909 3 A 0-0
1909 3r H 3-1
1961 SF N 0-3
1962 F N 1-3
1963 3 A 3-0
1966 4 A 3-4

v **Walsall**
1902 1 A 0-1
1996 1 H 1-3
1997 2 A 1-1
1997 2r H 1-1p

v **Watford**
2003 6 A 0-2

v **West Bromwich Albion**
1889 2 A 1-5

v **West Ham Utd**
1964 6 A 2-3
1968 3 H 1-3

v **Wimbledon**
1975 3 H 0-1
1985 3 A 1-3

v **Wolverhampton W**
1970 3 H 3-0

v **Wrexham**
1974 6 H 1-0

v **York City**
1994 1 H 0-0
1994 1r A 3-2

# Bury

v **Cardiff City**
2000 2 H 0-0
2000 2r A 0-1aet

v **Charlton Athletic**
1928 3 A 1-1
1928 3r H 4-3

v **Chesterfield**
1954 3 A 0-2
1997 1 A 0-1

v **Crewe Alexandra**
1995 2 A 2-1

v **Crystal Palace**
1913 2 A 0-2
1965 3 A 1-5

v **Darlington**
1929 3 A 6-2
1936 3 A 3-2
1981 1 A 2-0

v **Derby County**
1903 F N 6-0
1924 1 A 1-2

| | | | |
|---|---|---|---|
| 1950 | 4 | H | 2-2 |
| 1950 | 4r | A | 2-5 |

**v Doncaster Rovers**

| | | | |
|---|---|---|---|
| 1973 | 1 | A | 1-3 |
| 1976 | 1 | H | 4-2 |

**v Everton**

| | | | |
|---|---|---|---|
| 1897 | 2 | A | 0-3 |
| 1912 | 2 | A | 1-1 |
| 1912 | 2r | A | 0-6 |
| 1933 | 4 | A | 1-3 |

**v Exeter City**

| | | | |
|---|---|---|---|
| 1931 | 4 | H | 1-2 |

**v Fulham**

| | | | |
|---|---|---|---|
| 1939 | 3 | A | 0-6 |
| 1981 | 3 | H | 1-1 |
| 1981 | 3r | A | 0-0aet |
| 1981 | 3r2 | N | 0-1 |

**v Gillingham**

| | | | |
|---|---|---|---|
| 1907 | 2 | H | 1-0 |

**v Grimsby Town**

| | | | |
|---|---|---|---|
| 1953 | 3 | A | 3-1 |
| 1971 | 1 | A | 1-0 |
| 1975 | 2 | A | 1-1 |
| 1975 | 2r | H | 2-1 |

**v Hartlepool Utd**

| | | | |
|---|---|---|---|
| 1960 | 1 | H | 5-0 |
| 1968 | 1 | A | 3-2 |

**v Huddersfield Town**

| | | | |
|---|---|---|---|
| 1930 | 3 | H | 0-0 |
| 1930 | 3r | A | 1-3 |
| 1969 | 3 | H | 1-2 |

**v Hull City**

| | | | |
|---|---|---|---|
| 1914 | 1 | A | 0-0 |
| 1914 | 1r | H | 2-1 |

**v Leeds Utd**

| | | | |
|---|---|---|---|
| 1936 | 4 | A | 2-3 |
| 1966 | 3 | A | 0-6 |

**v Leicester City**

| | | | |
|---|---|---|---|
| 1895 | 1 | H | 4-1 |
| 1910 | 2 | A | 2-3 |
| 1948 | 3 | A | 0-1 |
| 1976 | 4 | A | 0-1 |

**v Leyton Orient**

| | | | |
|---|---|---|---|
| 1968 | 3 | A | 0-1 |
| 1979 | 3 | A | 2-3 |

**v Lincoln City**

| | | | |
|---|---|---|---|
| 1972 | 1 | A | 2-1 |
| 1981 | 2 | H | 2-0 |
| 2002 | 1 | A | 1-1 |
| 2002 | 1r | H | 1-1q |

**v Liverpool**

| | | | |
|---|---|---|---|
| 1980 | 5 | A | 0-2 |

**v Luton Town**

| | | | |
|---|---|---|---|
| 1923 | 1 | H | 2-1 |

**v Manchester City**

| | | | |
|---|---|---|---|
| 1932 | 6 | H | 3-4 |
| 1938 | 4 | A | 1-3 |
| 1963 | 4 | A | 0-1 |

**v Manchester Utd**

| | | | |
|---|---|---|---|
| 1928 | 4 | H | 1-1 |
| 1928 | 4r | A | 0-1 |
| 1929 | 4 | A | 1-0 |
| 1993 | 3 | A | 0-2 |

**v Mansfield Town**

| | | | |
|---|---|---|---|
| 1970 | 1 | H | 2-2 |
| 1970 | 1r | A | 0-2 |
| 1975 | 4 | H | 1-2 |

**v Middlesbrough**

| | | | |
|---|---|---|---|
| 1976 | 3 | A | 0-0 |
| 1976 | 3r | H | 3-2 |

**v Millwall**

| | | | |
|---|---|---|---|
| 1908 | 1 | H | 2-1 |
| 1912 | 1 | H | 2-1 |
| 1926 | 4 | H | 3-3 |
| 1926 | 4r | A | 0-2 |
| 1975 | 3 | H | 2-2 |
| 1975 | 3r | A | 1-1aet |
| 1975 | 3r2 | N | 2-0 |

**v Newcastle Utd**

| | | | |
|---|---|---|---|
| 1896 | 2 | A | 3-1 |
| 1904 | 1 | H | 2-1 |
| 1911 | 1 | A | 1-6 |
| 1951 | 3 | A | 1-4 |

**v Nottingham Forest**

| | | | |
|---|---|---|---|
| 1900 | SF | N | 1-1 |
| 1900 | SFr | N | 3-2aet |
| 1906 | 1 | H | 1-1 |
| 1906 | 1r | A | 2-6 |
| 1933 | 3 | H | 2-2 |
| 1933 | 3r | A | 2-1 |

**v Notts County**

| | | | |
|---|---|---|---|
| 1900 | 2 | A | 0-0 |
| 1900 | 2r | H | 2-0 |
| 1903 | 3 | H | 1-0 |
| 1905 | 1 | H | 1-0 |
| 1971 | 2 | H | 1-1 |
| 1971 | 2r | A | 0-3 |

**v Oldham Athletic**

| | | | |
|---|---|---|---|
| 1960 | 2 | H | 2-1 |

**v Plymouth Argyle**

| | | | |
|---|---|---|---|
| 1915 | 1 | H | 1-1 |
| 1915 | 1r | A | 2-1 |
| 2003 | 1 | H | 0-3 |

**v Portsmouth**

| | | | |
|---|---|---|---|
| 1957 | 3 | H | 1-3 |

**v Preston North End**

| | | | |
|---|---|---|---|
| 1985 | 1 | A | 3-4 |
| 1987 | 1 | A | 1-5 |

**v QPR**

| | | | |
|---|---|---|---|
| 1937 | 3 | H | 1-0 |

**v Reading**

| | | | |
|---|---|---|---|
| 1986 | 4 | A | 1-1 |
| 1986 | 4r | H | 3-0 |

**v Rochdale**

| | | | |
|---|---|---|---|
| 1946 | 3 | H | 3-3 |
| 1946 | 3s | A | 4-2 |
| 1980 | 3 | A | 1-1 |
| 1980 | 3r | H | 3-2 |

**v Rotherham Utd**

| | | | |
|---|---|---|---|
| 1926 | 3 | A | 3-2 |
| 1950 | 3 | H | 5-4 |
| 1952 | 3 | A | 1-2 |
| 1972 | 3 | H | 1-1 |
| 1972 | 3r | A | 1-2 |
| 1990 | 1 | A | 0-0 |
| 1990 | 1r | H | 1-2 |

**v Scunthorpe Utd**

| | | | |
|---|---|---|---|
| 1958 | 2 | A | 0-2 |
| 1984 | 2 | A | 0-2 |
| 1988 | 1 | A | 1-3 |

**v Sheffield Utd**

| | | | |
|---|---|---|---|
| 1900 | 3 | A | 2-2 |
| 1900 | 3r | H | 2-0 |
| 1903 | 2 | A | 1-0 |
| 1904 | 2 | H | 1-2 |
| 1932 | 4 | H | 3-1 |
| 1962 | 3 | H | 0-0 |
| 1962 | 3r | A | 2-2aet |
| 1962 | 3r2 | N | 0-2 |
| 1998 | 3 | A | 1-1 |
| 1998 | 3r | H | 1-2 |

**v Sheffield Wed**

| | | | |
|---|---|---|---|
| 1901 | 1 | A | 1-0 |
| 1978 | 1 | A | 0-1 |

**v Shrewsbury Town**

| | | | |
|---|---|---|---|
| 1977 | 2 | H | 0-0 |
| 1977 | 2r | A | 1-2 |

**v Southampton**

| | | | |
|---|---|---|---|
| 1900 | F | N | 4-0 |
| 1902 | 3 | H | 2-3 |
| 1913 | 1 | A | 1-1 |
| 1913 | 1r | H | 2-1 |
| 1923 | 3 | H | 0-0 |
| 1923 | 3r | A | 0-1 |
| 1947 | 3 | A | 1-5 |

**v Stockport County**

| | | | |
|---|---|---|---|
| 1893 | Q2 | H | 8-1 |
| 1999 | 3 | H | 0-3 |

**v Stoke City**

| | | | |
|---|---|---|---|
| 1898 | 1 | H | 1-2 |
| 1920 | 1 | H | 2-0 |
| 1923 | 2 | H | 3-1 |
| 1932 | 5 | H | 3-0 |
| 1955 | 3 | H | 1-1 |
| 1955 | 3r | A | 1-1ab |
| 1955 | 3r2 | N | 3-3aet |
| 1955 | 3r3 | N | 2-2aet |
| 1955 | 3r4 | N | 2-3aet |

**v Sunderland**

| | | | |
|---|---|---|---|
| 1925 | 1 | H | 0-3 |
| 1946 | 4 | A | 1-3 |
| 1946 | 4s | H | 5-4aet |

**v Swansea City**

| | | | |
|---|---|---|---|
| 1921 | 1 | A | 0-3 |
| 1927 | 3 | A | 1-4 |
| 1932 | 3 | H | 2-1 |
| 1934 | 4 | H | 1-1 |
| 1934 | 4r | A | 0-3 |

**v Swindon Town**

| | | | |
|---|---|---|---|
| 1967 | 4 | A | 1-2 |

**v Torquay Utd**

| | | | |
|---|---|---|---|
| 1931 | 3 | H | 1-1 |
| 1931 | 3r | A | 2-1aet |

**v Tottenham Hotspur**
1901 2 A 1-2

**v Tranmere Rovers**
1961 1 A 0-1
1974 1 A 1-2
1982 1 A 1-1
1982 1r H 3-1
1986 2 A 1-1
1986 2r H 2-1
1995 3 H 2-2
1995 3r A 0-3

**v Walsall**
1902 2 A 5-0
1967 3 H 2-0

**v Watford**
1986 5 A 1-1
1986 5r H 0-3

**v West Bromwich Albion**
1899 2 A 1-2
1902 1 H 5-1

**v West Ham Utd**
1920 2 A 0-6

**v Wigan Athletic**
1979 1 A 2-2
1979 1r H 4-1
1993 2 A 1-1
1993 2r H 1-0

**v Wolverhampton W**
1903 1 H 1-0
1908 2 A 0-2

**v Yeovil Town**
1949 3 A 1-3
1964 3 A 2-0

**v York City**
1959 1 H 1-0
1980 2 H 0-0
1980 2r A 2-0
1983 1 A 1-3

# Cambridge Utd

**v Colchester Utd**
1971 2 A 0-3
1977 1 H 1-1
1977 1r A 0-2

**v Coventry City**
1992 3 A 1-1
1992 3r H 1-0

**v Crystal Palace**
1990 6 H 0-1
2000 3 H 2-0

**v Darlington**
1990 3 H 0-0
1990 3r A 3-1

**v Derby County**
1984 3 H 0-3

**v Doncaster Rovers**
1982 3 A 1-2

**v Exeter City**
1987 1 A 1-1
1987 1r H 2-0
1991 1 A 2-1

**v Fulham**
1991 2 A 0-0
1991 2r H 2-1

**v Gillingham**
1974 1 H 3-2

**v Macclesfield**
1999 2 A 1-4

**v Mansfield Town**
1975 3 A 0-1

**v Middlesbrough**
1991 4 H 2-0

**v Millwall**
1990 4 A 1-1
1990 4r H 1-0aet
2003 3 H 1-1
2003 3r A 2-3

**v Northampton Town**
2003 2 H 2-2
2003 2r A 1-0

**v Norwich City**
1981 3 A 0-1

**v Notts County**
2002 1 H 1-1
2002 1r A 0-2

**v Oldham Athletic**
1974 3 H 2-2
1974 3r A 3-3aet
1974 3r2 N 1-2

**v Peterborough**
1985 1 H 0-2
1995 2 A 2-0

**v Plymouth Argyle**
1978 2 A 0-1
1989 3 A 0-2
1998 1 A 0-0
1998 1r H 3-2aet

**v Reading**
1994 1 H 0-0
1994 1r A 2-1

**v Rochdale**
2001 1 H 2-1

**v Sheffield Wed**
1983 5 H 1-2
1991 5 H 4-0
1993 3 H 1-2

**v Shrewsbury Town**
1979 3 A 1-3

**v Swindon Town**
1992 4 H 0-3
1996 1 A 1-4

**v Torquay Utd**
1955 1 A 0-4

**v Wolverhampton W**
1991 3 A 1-0

**v Wrexham**
2000 4 A 2-1

**v Wycombe W**
1994 2 A 0-1

**v Yeovil Town**
1988 2 H 0-1

# Cardiff City

**v Charlton Athletic**
1938 3 A 0-5
1939 3 H 1-0
1950 4 A 1-1
1950 4r H 2-0
1963 3 A 0-1
1965 3 H 1-2

**v Chelsea**
1921 4 H 1-0
1927 6 A 0-0
1927 6r H 3-2

**v Cheltenham Town**
1939 1 A 1-1
1939 1r H 1-0
2001 2 H 3-1

**v Coventry City**
2003 3 H 2-2
2003 3r A 0-3

**v Crewe Alexandra**
1939 2 H 1-0
2001 3 H 1-1
2001 3r A 1-2

**v Darlington**
1925 1 H 0-0
1925 1r A 0-0aet
1925 1r2 N 2-0
1927 4 A 2-0

**v Derby County**
1949 5 A 1-2

**v Everton**
1977 5 H 1-2

**v Exeter City**
1913 Q4 H 5-1
1976 1 H 6-2
1986 1 A 1-2

**v Fulham**
1925 2 H 1-0

**v Gillingham**
1924 1 H 0-0
1924 1r A 2-0
1985 3 A 1-2
1997 2 H 0-2

**v Grimsby Town**
1937 3 H 1-3

**v Hull City**
1989 3 H 1-2

**v Ipswich Town**
1978 3 H 0-2
1984 3 H 0-3

**v Leeds Utd**
1950 5 A 1-3
1956 3 A 2-1
1957 3 A 2-1
1958 3 A 2-1
1964 3 H 0-1
1972 5 H 0-2
1975 3 A 1-4
2002 3 H 2-1

v **Leicester City**

| | | | |
|---|---|---|---|
| 1923 | 2 | A | 1-0 |
| 1925 | 4 | H | 2-1 |
| 1981 | 3 | A | 0-3 |

v **Leyton Orient**

| | | | |
|---|---|---|---|
| 1932 | 2 | H | 4-0 |
| 1958 | 4 | H | 4-1 |
| 1976 | 3 | A | 1-0 |
| 2000 | 1 | A | 1-1 |
| 2000 | 1r | H | 3-1 |

v **Liverpool**

| | | | |
|---|---|---|---|
| 1928 | 4 | H | 2-1 |
| 1930 | 3 | A | 2-1 |

v **Luton Town**

| | | | |
|---|---|---|---|
| 1994 | 5 | H | 1-2 |

v **Manchester City**

| | | | |
|---|---|---|---|
| 1924 | 4 | A | 0-0 |
| 1924 | 4r | H | 0-1aet |
| 1961 | 3 | H | 1-1 |
| 1961 | 3r | A | 0-0aet |
| 1961 | 3r2 | N | 0-2aet |
| 1967 | 4 | H | 1-1 |
| 1967 | 4r | A | 1-3 |
| 1982 | 3 | A | 1-3 |
| 1994 | 4 | H | 1-0 |

v **Manchester Utd**

| | | | |
|---|---|---|---|
| 1922 | 1 | A | 4-1 |

v **Middlesbrough**

| | | | |
|---|---|---|---|
| 1962 | 3 | A | 0-1 |
| 1994 | 3 | H | 2-2 |
| 1994 | 3r | A | 2-1aet |

v **Millwall**

| | | | |
|---|---|---|---|
| 1987 | 3 | A | 0-0 |
| 1987 | 3r | H | 2-2aet |
| 1987 | 3r2 | H | 1-0 |

v **Newcastle Utd**

| | | | |
|---|---|---|---|
| 1926 | 4 | H | 0-2 |
| 1939 | 4 | H | 0-0 |
| 1939 | 4r | A | 1-4 |

v **Northampton Town**

| | | | |
|---|---|---|---|
| 938 | 1 | A | 2-1 |

v **Norwich City**

| | | | |
|---|---|---|---|
| 1959 | 4 | A | 2-3 |

v **Nottingham Forest**

| | | | |
|---|---|---|---|
| 1922 | 3 | H | 4-1 |
| 1928 | 5 | A | 1-2 |

v **Notts County**

| | | | |
|---|---|---|---|
| 1925 | 3 | A | 2-0 |

v **Oldham Athletic**

| | | | |
|---|---|---|---|
| 1920 | 1 | H | 2-0 |
| 1949 | 3 | A | 3-2 |
| 1998 | 3 | H | 1-0 |

v **Peterborough**

| | | | |
|---|---|---|---|
| 1954 | 3 | H | 3-1 |
| 1988 | 1 | A | 1-2 |

v **Plymouth Argyle**

| | | | |
|---|---|---|---|
| 1959 | 3 | A | 3-0 |

v **Port Vale**

| | | | |
|---|---|---|---|
| 1954 | 4 | H | 0-2 |
| 1960 | 3 | H | 0-2 |
| 1966 | 3 | H | 2-1 |
| 2002 | 2 | H | 3-0 |

v **QPR**

| | | | |
|---|---|---|---|
| 1990 | 3 | H | 0-0 |
| 1990 | 3r | A | 0-2 |

v **Reading**

| | | | |
|---|---|---|---|
| 1927 | SF | N | 3-0 |
| 1935 | 1 | H | 1-2 |
| 1998 | 4 | H | 1-1 |
| 1998 | 4r | A | 1-1p |

v **Rushden & Diamonds**

| | | | |
|---|---|---|---|
| 1996 | 1 | A | 3-1 |

v **Scunthorpe Utd**

| | | | |
|---|---|---|---|
| 1973 | 3 | A | 3-2 |

v **Sheffield Utd**

| | | | |
|---|---|---|---|
| 1925 | F | N | 0-1 |
| 1972 | 3 | A | 3-1 |
| 1999 | 4 | A | 1-4 |

v **Sheffield Wed**

| | | | |
|---|---|---|---|
| 1948 | 3 | H | 1-2aet |

v **Southampton**

| | | | |
|---|---|---|---|
| 1921 | 3 | A | 1-0 |
| 1922 | 2 | A | 1-1 |
| 1922 | 2r | H | 2-0 |
| 1928 | 3 | H | 2-1 |

v **Southend Utd**

| | | | |
|---|---|---|---|
| 1913 | Q5 | H | 0-3 |
| 1976 | 4 | A | 1-2 |

v **Stoke City**

| | | | |
|---|---|---|---|
| 1968 | 3 | A | 1-4 |
| 1987 | 4 | A | 1-2 |

v **Sunderland**

| | | | |
|---|---|---|---|
| 1921 | 1 | A | 1-0 |
| 1930 | 4 | A | 1-2 |
| 1972 | 4 | H | 1-1 |
| 1972 | 4r | A | 1-1aet |
| 1972 | 4r2 | N | 3-1 |

v **Swansea City**

| | | | |
|---|---|---|---|
| 1914 | Q4 | A | 0-2 |
| 1992 | 1 | A | 1-2 |

v **Swindon Town**

| | | | |
|---|---|---|---|
| 1937 | 2 | H | 2-1 |
| 1952 | 3 | H | 1-1 |
| 1952 | 3r | A | 0-1aet |
| 1979 | 3 | A | 0-3 |
| 1996 | 2 | A | 0-2 |

v **Tottenham Hotspur**

| | | | |
|---|---|---|---|
| 1922 | 4 | H | 1-1 |
| 1922 | 4r | A | 1-2 |
| 1923 | 3 | H | 2-3 |
| 1977 | 3 | H | 1-0 |

v **Tranmere Rovers**

| | | | |
|---|---|---|---|
| 2002 | 4 | A | 1-3 |
| 2003 | 1 | A | 2-2 |
| 2003 | 1r | H | 2-1 |

v **Watford**

| | | | |
|---|---|---|---|
| 1923 | 1 | H | 1-1 |
| 1923 | 1r | A | 2-2aet |
| 1923 | r1r2 | N | 2-1 |

v **West Bromwich Albion**

| | | | |
|---|---|---|---|
| 1946 | 3 | H | 1-1 |
| 1946 | 3s | A | 0-4 |
| 1950 | 3 | H | 2-2 |
| 1950 | 3r | A | 1-0 |

v **West Ham Utd**

| | | | |
|---|---|---|---|
| 1951 | 3 | A | 1-2 |
| 1956 | 4 | A | 1-2 |

v **Wolverhampton W**

| | | | |
|---|---|---|---|
| 1920 | 2 | A | 2-1 |
| 1921 | SF | N | 0-0 |
| 1921 | SFr | N | 1-3 |

v **Wrexham**

| | | | |
|---|---|---|---|
| 1977 | 4 | H | 3-2 |

v **Wycombe W**

| | | | |
|---|---|---|---|
| 1976 | 2 | H | 1-0 |

v **Yeovil Town**

| | | | |
|---|---|---|---|
| 1999 | 3 | H | 1-1 |
| 1999 | 3r | A | 2-1aet |

v **York City**

| | | | |
|---|---|---|---|
| 1970 | 3 | A | 1-1 |
| 1970 | 3r | H | 1-1aet |
| 1970 | 3r2 | N | 1-3aet |

# Carlisle Utd

v **Chelsea**

| | | | |
|---|---|---|---|
| 1969 | 3 | A | 0-2 |

v **Cheltenham Town**

| | | | |
|---|---|---|---|
| 1934 | 2 | H | 1-2 |

v **Chesterfield**

| | | | |
|---|---|---|---|
| 1959 | 2 | H | 0-0 |
| 1959 | 2r | A | 0-1 |

v **Coventry City**

| | | | |
|---|---|---|---|
| 1909 | Q5 | A | 1-1 |
| 1909 | Q5r | H | 1-1 |
| 1909 | Q5r2 | N | 3-1 |

v **Crewe Alexandra**

| | | | |
|---|---|---|---|
| 1911 | Q5 | A | 1-1 |
| 1911 | Q5r | H | 3-4 |
| 1930 | 2 | H | 4-2 |
| 1992 | 1 | H | 1-1 |
| 1992 | 1r | A | 3-5aet |

v **Crystal Palace**

| | | | |
|---|---|---|---|
| 1966 | 3 | H | 3-0 |

v **Darlington**

| | | | |
|---|---|---|---|
| 1908 | Q4 | H | 7-0 |
| 1932 | 2 | H | 0-2 |
| 1956 | 1 | A | 0-0 |
| 1956 | 1r | H | 0-0aet |
| 1956 | 1r2 | N | 1-3 |
| 1957 | 2 | H | 2-1 |
| 1962 | 1 | A | 4-0 |
| 1982 | 1 | A | 2-2 |
| 1982 | 1r | H | 3-1 |
| 1995 | 2 | H | 2-0 |
| 1997 | 2 | H | 1-0 |

v **Doncaster Rovers**

| | | | |
|---|---|---|---|
| 1928 | 1 | H | 2-1 |

v **Everton**

| | | | |
|---|---|---|---|
| 1930 | 3 | H | 2-4 |
| 1968 | 4 | H | 0-2 |

v **Fulham**

| | | | |
|---|---|---|---|
| 1909 | 1 | A | 1-4 |
| 1975 | 6 | H | 0-1 |

v **Grimsby Town**

| | | | |
|---|---|---|---|
| 1908 | 2 | A | 2-6 |

**v Hartlepool Utd**

| | | | |
|---|---|---|---|
| 1927 | 1 | H | 6-2 |
| 1963 | 1 | H | 2-1 |
| 1999 | 1 | A | 1-2 |

**v Huddersfield Town**

| | | | |
|---|---|---|---|
| 1973 | 3 | H | 2-2 |
| 1973 | 3r | A | 1-0 |
| 1982 | 3 | H | 2-3 |

**v Hull City**

| | | | |
|---|---|---|---|
| 1933 | 2 | H | 1-1 |
| 1933 | 2r | A | 1-2aet |
| 1979 | 2 | H | 3-0 |
| 1980 | 1 | H | 3-3 |
| 1980 | 1r | A | 2-0 |

**v Ipswich Town**

| | | | |
|---|---|---|---|
| 1967 | 4 | A | 0-2 |
| 1979 | 3 | A | 2-3 |

**v Kidderminster H**

| | | | |
|---|---|---|---|
| 2001 | 2 | A | 2-0 |

**v Leeds Utd**

| | | | |
|---|---|---|---|
| 1950 | 3 | H | 2-5 |

**v Leicester City**

| | | | |
|---|---|---|---|
| 1985 | 4 | A | 0-1 |

**v Leyton Orient**

| | | | |
|---|---|---|---|
| 1937 | 2 | H | 4-1 |

**v Lincoln City**

| | | | |
|---|---|---|---|
| 1929 | 2 | H | 0-1 |
| 1950 | 1 | H | 1-0 |
| 2003 | 1 | H | 2-1 |

**v Liverpool**

| | | | |
|---|---|---|---|
| 1974 | 4 | A | 0-0 |
| 1974 | 4r | H | 0-2 |
| 1977 | 4 | A | 0-3 |
| 1989 | 3 | H | 0-3 |

**v Macclesfield**

| | | | |
|---|---|---|---|
| 1988 | 1 | A | 2-4 |

**v Manchester Utd**

| | | | |
|---|---|---|---|
| 1978 | 3 | H | 1-1 |
| 1978 | 3r | A | 2-4 |

**v Mansfield Town**

| | | | |
|---|---|---|---|
| 1975 | 5 | A | 1-0 |
| 1981 | 3 | A | 2-2 |
| 1981 | 3r | H | 2-1 |

**v Middlesbrough**

| | | | |
|---|---|---|---|
| 1970 | 5 | H | 1-2 |

**v Newcastle Utd**

| | | | |
|---|---|---|---|
| 1968 | 3 | A | 1-0 |

**v Nottingham Forest**

| | | | |
|---|---|---|---|
| 1970 | 3 | A | 0-0 |
| 1970 | 3r | H | 2-1 |

**v Notts County**

| | | | |
|---|---|---|---|
| 1987 | 1 | A | 1-1 |
| 1987 | 1r | H | 0-3 |

**v Peterborough**

| | | | |
|---|---|---|---|
| 1986 | 4 | A | 0-1 |

**v Port Vale**

| | | | |
|---|---|---|---|
| 1961 | 2 | A | 1-2 |

**v Preston North End**

| | | | |
|---|---|---|---|
| 1964 | 5 | A | 0-1 |
| 1975 | 3 | A | 1-0 |
| 1996 | 1 | H | 1-2 |

**v QPR**

| | | | |
|---|---|---|---|
| 1964 | 3 | H | 2-0 |
| 1986 | 3 | H | 1-0 |

**v Rochdale**

| | | | |
|---|---|---|---|
| 1960 | 1 | A | 2-2 |
| 1960 | 1r | H | 1-3aet |

**v Scunthorpe Utd**

| | | | |
|---|---|---|---|
| 1953 | 1 | A | 0-1 |
| 2003 | 2 | A | 0-0 |
| 2003 | 2r | H | 0-1 |

**v Sheffield Utd**

| | | | |
|---|---|---|---|
| 1947 | 3 | A | 0-3 |
| 1973 | 4 | H | 2-1 |

**v Sheffield Wed**

| | | | |
|---|---|---|---|
| 1980 | 2 | H | 3-0 |
| 1997 | 4 | H | 0-2 |

**v Shrewsbury Town**

| | | | |
|---|---|---|---|
| 1966 | 4 | A | 0-0 |
| 1966 | 4r | H | 1-1aet |
| 1966 | 4r2 | N | 3-4aet |

**v Southend Utd**

| | | | |
|---|---|---|---|
| 1908 | Q5 | H | 4-0 |
| 1971 | 3 | A | 3-0 |

**v Stockport County**

| | | | |
|---|---|---|---|
| 1937 | 1 | H | 2-1 |
| 1955 | 1 | A | 1-0 |

**v Sunderland**

| | | | |
|---|---|---|---|
| 1974 | 3 | H | 0-0 |
| 1974 | 3r | A | 1-0 |
| 1994 | 3 | A | 1-1 |
| 1994 | 3r | H | 0-1aet |
| 1995 | 3 | A | 1-1 |
| 1995 | 3r | H | 1-3 |

**v Swansea City**

| | | | |
|---|---|---|---|
| 1937 | 3 | A | 0-1 |

**v Swindon Town**

| | | | |
|---|---|---|---|
| 1950 | 2 | H | 2-0 |
| 1984 | 3 | H | 1-1 |
| 1984 | 3r | A | 1-3 |

**v Tottenham Hotspur**

| | | | |
|---|---|---|---|
| 1971 | 4 | H | 2-3 |
| 1972 | 3 | A | 1-1 |
| 1972 | 3r | H | 1-3 |

**v Tranmere Rovers**

| | | | |
|---|---|---|---|
| 1936 | 1 | A | 0-3 |
| 1938 | 1 | A | 1-2 |
| 1997 | 3 | H | 1-0 |
| 2002 | 2 | A | 1-6 |

**v Walsall**

| | | | |
|---|---|---|---|
| 1939 | 1 | A | 1-4 |
| 1981 | 2 | H | 3-0 |

**v Watford**

| | | | |
|---|---|---|---|
| 1955 | 2 | H | 2-2 |
| 1955 | 2r | A | 1-4 |

**v West Bromwich Albion**

| | | | |
|---|---|---|---|
| 1975 | 4 | H | 3-2 |
| 1976 | 3 | A | 1-3 |

**v West Ham Utd**

| | | | |
|---|---|---|---|
| 1910 | 1 | A | 1-1 |
| 1910 | 1r | A | 0-5 |

**v Wigan Athletic**

| | | | |
|---|---|---|---|
| 1935 | 1 | H | 1-6 |
| 1990 | 2 | A | 0-2 |
| 1991 | 1 | A | 0-5 |
| 1993 | 1 | A | 1-3 |
| 1998 | 1 | H | 0-1 |

**v Wolverhampton W**

| | | | |
|---|---|---|---|
| 1927 | 3 | H | 0-2 |
| 1962 | 3 | A | 1-3 |

**v Wrexham**

| | | | |
|---|---|---|---|
| 1928 | 2 | A | 0-1 |
| 1929 | 1 | A | 1-0 |
| 1934 | 1 | H | 2-1 |
| 1980 | 4 | H | 0-0 |
| 1980 | 4r | A | 1-3 |
| 1990 | 1 | H | 3-0 |

**v York City**

| | | | |
|---|---|---|---|
| 1964 | 1 | A | 5-2 |

## Charlton Athletic

**v Chelsea**

| | | | |
|---|---|---|---|
| 1963 | 4 | H | 0-3 |
| 1995 | 3 | A | 0-3 |

**v Colchester Utd**

| | | | |
|---|---|---|---|
| 1984 | 3 | A | 1-0 |

**v Coventry City**

| | | | |
|---|---|---|---|
| 1937 | 3 | A | 0-2 |
| 1968 | 3 | A | 0-3 |
| 2000 | 5 | A | 3-2 |

**v Crystal Palace**

| | | | |
|---|---|---|---|
| 1969 | 3 | H | 0-0 |
| 1969 | 3r | A | 2-0 |

**v Darlington**

| | | | |
|---|---|---|---|
| 1923 | Q6 | H | 2-1 |

**v Derby County**

| | | | |
|---|---|---|---|
| 1946 | F | N | 1-4aet |
| 1962 | 4 | H | 2-1 |

**v Everton**

| | | | |
|---|---|---|---|
| 1959 | 4 | H | 2-2 |
| 1959 | 4r | A | 1-4aet |
| 1991 | 3 | H | 1-2 |

**v Exeter City**

| | | | |
|---|---|---|---|
| 1935 | 1 | H | 2-2 |
| 1935 | 1r | A | 2-5 |
| 2003 | 3 | H | 3-1 |

**v Fulham**

| | | | |
|---|---|---|---|
| 1946 | 3 | H | 3-1 |
| 1946 | 3s | A | 1-2 |
| 1950 | 3 | H | 2-2 |
| 1950 | 3r | A | 2-1 |
| 1958 | 4 | A | 1-1 |
| 1958 | 4r | H | 0-2 |
| 1981 | 4 | A | 2-1 |
| 2003 | 4 | A | 0-3 |

**v Gillingham**

| | | | |
|---|---|---|---|
| 1934 | 2 | H | 1-0 |

**v Huddersfield Town**

| | | | |
|---|---|---|---|
| 1926 | 3 | H | 0-1 |
| 1958 | 3 | A | 2-2 |
| 1958 | 3r | H | 1-0 |

**v Hull City**
1953 3 A 1-3
1971 3 A 0-3

**v Ipswich Town**
1981 5 A 0-2
1983 3 H 2-3

**v Leeds Utd**
1938 4 H 2-1
1993 3 A 1-1
1993 3r H 1-3

**v Leyton Orient**
1936 3 A 0-3
1982 3 A 0-1

**v Liverpool**
1996 5 A 1-2

**v Luton Town**
1952 3 A 0-1

**v Manchester City**
1923 1 A 2-1

**v Manchester Utd**
1948 5 N 0-2
1994 6 A 1-3

**v Middlesbrough**
1930 4 A 1-1
1930 4r H 1-1aet
1930 4r2 N 0-1aet
1957 3 A 1-1
1957 3r H 2-3
1965 4 H 1-1
1965 4r A 1-2

**v Newcastle Utd**
1947 SF N 4-0
1948 3 H 2-1
1997 3 H 1-1
1997 3r A 1-2aet

**v Northampton Town**
923 Q5 H 2-0

**v Nottingham Forest**
1998 3 H 4-1

**v Notts County**
1978 3 H 0-2

**v Oldham Athletic**
1989 3 H 2-1

**v Peterborough**
1975 2 A 0-3

**v Plymouth Argyle**
1981 3 A 2-1

**v Port Vale**
1934 3 H 2-0

**v Portsmouth**
1929 3 A 1-2
1954 3 A 3-3
1954 3r H 2-3aet
1976 4 H 1-1
1976 4r A 3-0

**v Preston North End**
1923 2 H 2-0
1946 5 A 1-1
1946 5s H 6-0
1947 6 H 2-1
1966 3 H 2-3

**v QPR**
1925 Q6 A 1-1
1925 Q6r H 1-2
1926 2 A 1-1
1926 2r H 1-0
1930 3 H 1-1
1930 3r A 3-0
1970 4 H 2-3
2000 4 H 1-0

**v Rochdale**
1947 3 H 3-1
1955 3 A 3-1

**v Scunthorpe Utd**
1962 3 H 1-0

**v Sheffield Utd**
1967 3 H 0-1
1992 4 H 0-0
1992 4r A 1-3

**v Sheffield Wed**
1976 3 H 2-1
1996 3 H 2-0

**v Stockport County**
1948 4 H 3-0

**v Swindon Town**
1956 4 H 2-1
2000 3 H 2-1

**v Tottenham Hotspur**
1961 3 A 2-3
1985 3 A 1-1
1985 3r H 1-2
2001 4 H 2-4

**v Tranmere Rovers**
1972 3 H 0-0
1972 3r A 2-4

**v Walsall**
1973 2 A 2-1
1987 3 H 1-2
2002 4 H 1-2

**v Watford**
1984 4 H 0-2

**v West Bromwich Albion**
1923 3 H 1-0
1931 3 A 2-2
1931 3r H 1-1aet
1931 3r2 N 1-3
1947 4 A 2-1
1955 4 A 4-2
1990 4 A 0-1

**v West Ham Utd**
1932 3 H 1-2
1964 3 A 0-3
1986 3 H 0-1
1988 3 A 0-2
1989 5 H 0-1

**v Wolverhampton W**
1924 2 H 0-0
1924 2r A 0-1
1946 4 H 5-2
1946 4s A 1-1
1955 5 A 1-4
1960 4 A 1-2
1976 5 A 0-3
1998 4 H 1-1
1998 4r A 0-3

**v Wrexham**
1980 3 A 0-6

# Chelsea

**v Chesterfield**
1911 2 H 4-1
1950 5 A 1-1
1950 5r H 3-0

**v Crewe Alexandra**
1961 3 H 1-2
1990 3 H 1-1
1990 3r A 2-0

**v Crystal Palace**
1906 Q3 A 1-7
1926 4 A 1-2
1970 5 A 4-1
1971 3 A 2-2
1971 3r H 2-0
1976 5 H 2-3

**v Darlington**
1958 4 H 3-3
1958 4r A 1-4aet

**v Derby County**
1947 4 H 2-2
1947 4r A 0-1aet
1953 3 A 4-4
1953 3r H 1-0aet
1983 4 A 1-2
1988 3 A 3-1

**v Doncaster Rovers**
1958 3 A 2-0

**v Everton**
1915 SF N 2-0
1929 3 H 2-0
1938 3 H 0-1
1949 4 H 2-0
1956 5 A 0-1
1992 4 H 1-0

**v Exeter City**
1951 4 A 1-1
1951 4r H 2-0

**v Fulham**
1936 5 H 0-0
1936 5r A 2-3
1939 4 H 3-0
1951 5 H 1-1
1951 5r A 0-3
2002 SF N 1-0

**v Gillingham**
2000 6 H 5-0
2001 4 A 4-2

**v Grimsby Town**
1939 6 H 0-1
1996 5 A 0-0
1996 5r H 4-1

**v Hartlepool Utd**
1956 3 A 1-0
1964 4 H 1-2
1967 3 A 2-1
1983 3 A 1-1
1983 3r H 2-0

**v Hull City**

| | | | |
|---|---|---|---|
| 1909 | 1 | A | 1-1 |
| 1909 | 1r | H | 1-0 |
| 1910 | 1 | H | 2-1 |
| 1966 | 6 | H | 2-2 |
| 1966 | 6r | A | 3-1 |
| 1982 | 3 | H | 0-0 |
| 1982 | 3r | A | 2-0 |
| 1992 | 3 | A | 2-0 |
| 2000 | 3 | A | 6-1 |

**v Ipswich Town**

| | | | |
|---|---|---|---|
| 1968 | 3 | H | 3-0 |
| 1973 | 4 | H | 2-0 |

**v Leeds Utd**

| | | | |
|---|---|---|---|
| 1937 | 3 | H | 4-0 |
| 1952 | 5 | A | 1-1 |
| 1952 | 5r | H | 1-1aet |
| 1952 | 5r2 | N | 5-1 |
| 1966 | 4 | H | 1-0 |
| 1967 | SF | N | 1-0 |
| 1970 | F | N | 2-2aet |
| 1970 | Fr | N | 2-1aet |

**v Leicester City**

| | | | |
|---|---|---|---|
| 1920 | 3 | H | 3-0 |
| 1946 | 3 | H | 1-1 |
| 1946 | 3s | A | 2-0 |
| 1997 | 5 | A | 2-2 |
| 1997 | 5r | H | 1-0aet |
| 2000 | 5 | H | 2-1 |

**v Leyton Orient**

| | | | |
|---|---|---|---|
| 1957 | 3 | A | 2-0 |
| 1972 | 5 | A | 2-3 |
| 1978 | 5 | A | 0-0 |
| 1978 | 5r | H | 1-2 |

**v Lincoln City**

| | | | |
|---|---|---|---|
| 1907 | 1 | A | 2-2 |
| 1907 | 1r | H | 0-1aet |

**v Liverpool**

| | | | |
|---|---|---|---|
| 1932 | 6 | A | 2-0 |
| 1962 | 3 | A | 3-4 |
| 1965 | SF | N | 0-2 |
| 1966 | 3 | A | 2-1 |
| 1978 | 3 | H | 4-2 |
| 1982 | 5 | H | 2-0 |
| 1986 | 4 | H | 1-2 |
| 1997 | 4 | H | 4-2 |

**v Luton Town**

| | | | |
|---|---|---|---|
| 1927 | 3 | H | 4-0 |
| 1935 | 3 | H | 1-1 |
| 1935 | 3r | A | 0-2 |
| 1994 | SF | N | 2-0 |

**v Manchester City**

| | | | |
|---|---|---|---|
| 1915 | 3 | A | 1-0 |
| 1948 | 4 | A | 0-2aet |
| 1971 | 4 | H | 0-3 |

**v Manchester Utd**

| | | | |
|---|---|---|---|
| 1908 | 2 | A | 0-1 |
| 1950 | 6 | H | 2-0 |
| 1963 | 5 | A | 1-2 |
| 1979 | 3 | A | 0-3 |
| 1988 | 4 | A | 0-2 |
| 1994 | F | N | 0-4 |
| 1996 | SF | N | 1-2 |
| 1998 | 3 | H | 3-5 |
| 1999 | 6 | A | 0-0 |
| 1999 | 6r | H | 0-2 |

**v Middlesbrough**

| | | | |
|---|---|---|---|
| 1993 | 3 | A | 1-2 |
| 1997 | F | N | 2-0 |
| 2003 | 3 | H | 1-0 |

**v Millwall**

| | | | |
|---|---|---|---|
| 1914 | 1 | A | 0-0 |
| 1914 | 1r | H | 0-1 |
| 1937 | 4 | A | 0-3 |
| 1985 | 4 | H | 2-3 |
| 1995 | 4 | A | 0-0 |
| 1995 | 4r | H | 1-1q |

**v Newcastle Utd**

| | | | |
|---|---|---|---|
| 1911 | SF | N | 0-3 |
| 1915 | 4 | H | 1-1aet |
| 1915 | 4r | A | 1-0aet |
| 1932 | SF | N | 1-2 |
| 1950 | 4 | H | 3-0 |
| 1959 | 3 | A | 4-1 |
| 1996 | 3 | H | 1-1 |
| 1996 | 3r | A | 2-2q |
| 2000 | SF | N | 2-1 |

**v Northampton Town**

| | | | |
|---|---|---|---|
| 1965 | 3 | H | 4-1 |

**v Norwich City**

| | | | |
|---|---|---|---|
| 1936 | 3 | A | 1-1 |
| 1936 | 3r | H | 3-1 |
| 1968 | 4 | H | 1-0 |
| 2002 | 3 | A | 0-0 |
| 2002 | 3r | H | 4-0 |

**v Nottingham Forest**

| | | | |
|---|---|---|---|
| 1934 | 4 | H | 1-1 |
| 1934 | 4r | A | 3-0 |
| 2000 | 4 | H | 2-0 |

**v Notts County**

| | | | |
|---|---|---|---|
| 1955 | 5 | A | 0-1 |

**v Oldham Athletic**

| | | | |
|---|---|---|---|
| 1999 | 3 | A | 2-0 |

**v Oxford Utd**

| | | | |
|---|---|---|---|
| 1991 | 3 | H | 1-3 |
| 1994 | 5 | A | 2-1 |
| 1999 | 4 | A | 1-1 |
| 1999 | 4r | H | 4-2 |

**v Peterborough**

| | | | |
|---|---|---|---|
| 1965 | 6 | H | 5-1 |
| 2001 | 3 | H | 5-0 |

**v Plymouth Argyle**

| | | | |
|---|---|---|---|
| 1921 | 3 | A | 0-0 |
| 1921 | 3r | H | 0-0aet |
| 1921 | 3r2 | N | 2-1 |
| 1926 | 3 | A | 2-1 |
| 1936 | 4 | H | 4-1 |

**v Portsmouth**

| | | | |
|---|---|---|---|
| 1929 | 5 | H | 1-1 |
| 1929 | 5r | A | 0-1 |
| 1997 | 6 | A | 4-1 |

**v Preston North End**

| | | | |
|---|---|---|---|
| 1969 | 4 | A | 0-0 |
| 1969 | 4r | H | 2-1 |
| 2002 | 5 | H | 3-1 |

**v QPR**

| | | | |
|---|---|---|---|
| 1970 | 6 | A | 4-2 |
| 1974 | 3 | H | 0-0 |
| 1974 | 3r | A | 0-1 |
| 1996 | 4 | A | 2-1 |

**v Reading**

| | | | |
|---|---|---|---|
| 1921 | 1 | A | 0-0 |
| 1921 | 1r | H | 2-2aet |
| 1921 | 1r2 | H | 3-1 |

**v Rochdale**

| | | | |
|---|---|---|---|
| 1951 | 3 | A | 3-2 |

**v Sheffield Utd**

| | | | |
|---|---|---|---|
| 1912 | 1 | H | 1-0 |
| 1915 | F | N | 0-3 |
| 1952 | 6 | A | 1-0 |
| 1967 | 5 | H | 2-0 |
| 1992 | 5 | H | 1-0 |

**v Sheffield Wed**

| | | | |
|---|---|---|---|
| 1913 | 2 | H | 1-1 |
| 1913 | 2r | A | 0-6 |
| 1932 | 5 | A | 1-1 |
| 1932 | 5r | H | 2-0 |
| 1939 | 5 | H | 1-1 |
| 1939 | 5r | A | 0-0aet |
| 1939 | 5r2 | N | 3-1 |
| 1966 | SF | N | 0-2 |
| 1967 | 6 | H | 1-0 |
| 1968 | 5 | A | 2-2 |
| 1968 | 5r | H | 2-0 |
| 1973 | 5 | A | 2-1 |
| 1975 | 3 | H | 3-2 |
| 1994 | 4 | H | 1-1 |
| 1994 | 4r | A | 3-1aet |
| 1999 | 5 | A | 1-0 |

**v Shrewsbury Town**

| | | | |
|---|---|---|---|
| 1966 | 5 | H | 3-2 |
| 1986 | 3 | A | 1-0 |
| 2003 | 4 | A | 4-0 |

**v Southampton**

| | | | |
|---|---|---|---|
| 1923 | 2 | H | 0-0 |
| 1923 | 2r | A | 0-1 |
| 1924 | 1 | H | 1-1 |
| 1924 | 1r | A | 0-2 |
| 1977 | 3 | A | 1-1 |
| 1977 | 3r | H | 0-3aet |
| 1981 | 3 | A | 1-3 |

**v Southend Utd**

| | | | |
|---|---|---|---|
| 1913 | 1 | H | 5-2 |

**v Stoke City**

| | | | |
|---|---|---|---|
| 1934 | 5 | A | 1-3 |
| 1969 | 5 | H | 3-2 |
| 2003 | 5 | A | 2-0 |

**v Sunderland**

| | | | |
|---|---|---|---|
| 1992 | 6 | H | 1-1 |
| 1992 | 6r | A | 1-2 |

**v Swindon Town**

| | | | |
|---|---|---|---|
| 1911 | 4 | H | 3-1 |
| 1915 | 1 | H | 1-1 |
| 1915 | 1r | H | 5-2aet |
| 1920 | 2 | H | 4-0 |
| 1921 | 2 | A | 2-0 |

v **Tottenham Hotspur**

| | | | |
|---|---|---|---|
| 1910 | 2 | H | 0-1 |
| 1957 | 4 | A | 0-4 |
| 1964 | 3 | A | 1-1 |
| 1964 | 3r | H | 2-0 |
| 1965 | 5 | H | 1-0 |
| 1967 | F | N | 1-2 |
| 1982 | 6 | H | 2-3 |
| 2002 | 6 | A | 4-0 |

v **Tranmere Rovers**

| | | | |
|---|---|---|---|
| 1932 | 3 | A | 2-2 |
| 1932 | 3r | H | 5-3 |
| 1952 | 4 | H | 4-0 |
| 1963 | 3 | A | 2-2 |
| 1963 | 3r | H | 3-1 |

v **Walsall**

| | | | |
|---|---|---|---|
| 1955 | 3 | H | 2-0 |

v **Watford**

| | | | |
|---|---|---|---|
| 1970 | SF | N | 5-1 |
| 1987 | 4 | A | 0-1 |

v **West Bromwich Albion**

| | | | |
|---|---|---|---|
| 1922 | 1 | H | 2-4 |
| 1934 | 3 | H | 1-1 |
| 1934 | 3r | A | 1-0aet |
| 1949 | 5 | A | 0-3 |
| 1953 | 4 | H | 1-1 |
| 1953 | 4r | A | 0-0aet |
| 1953 | 4r2 | N | 1-1aet |
| 1953 | 4r3 | N | 4-0 |
| 1954 | 3 | A | 0-1 |
| 1969 | 6 | H | 1-2 |
| 1997 | 3 | H | 3-0 |

v **West Ham Utd**

| | | | |
|---|---|---|---|
| 1931 | 3 | A | 3-1 |
| 1932 | 4 | H | 3-1 |
| 1946 | 4 | H | 2-0 |
| 1946 | 4s | A | 0-1 |
| 1965 | 4 | A | 1-0 |
| 2002 | 4 | H | 1-1 |
| 2002 | 4r | A | 3-2 |

v **Wigan Athletic**

| | | | |
|---|---|---|---|
| 1980 | 3 | H | 0-1 |
| 1985 | 3 | H | 2-2 |
| 1985 | 3r | A | 5-0 |

v **Wimbledon**

| | | | |
|---|---|---|---|
| 1996 | 6 | H | 2-2 |
| 1996 | 6r | A | 3-1 |
| 1997 | SF | N | 3-0 |

v **Wolverhampton W**

| | | | |
|---|---|---|---|
| 1911 | 3 | A | 2-0 |
| 1928 | 3 | A | 1-2 |
| 1994 | 6 | H | 1-0 |

v **Wrexham**

| | | | |
|---|---|---|---|
| 1982 | 4 | H | 0-0 |
| 1982 | 4r | A | 1-1aet |
| 1982 | 4r2 | A | 2-1 |

v **York City**

| | | | |
|---|---|---|---|
| 1976 | 4 | A | 2-0 |

# Cheltenham Town

v **Gillingham**

| | | | |
|---|---|---|---|
| 2000 | 1 | H | 1-1 |
| 2000 | 1r | A | 2-3 |

v **Hull City**

| | | | |
|---|---|---|---|
| 1948 | 2 | A | 2-4 |

v **Kidderminster H**

| | | | |
|---|---|---|---|
| 1948 | Q4 | A | 4-2 |

v **Lincoln City**

| | | | |
|---|---|---|---|
| 1999 | 1 | H | 0-1 |

v **Oldham Athletic**

| | | | |
|---|---|---|---|
| 2002 | 3 | H | 2-1 |
| 2003 | 2 | A | 2-1 |

v **Peterborough**

| | | | |
|---|---|---|---|
| 1997 | 1 | A | 0-0 |
| 1997 | 1r | H | 1-3aet |

v **Reading**

| | | | |
|---|---|---|---|
| 1951 | 1 | A | 1-3 |
| 1957 | 1 | H | 1-2 |
| 1998 | 3 | H | 1-1 |
| 1998 | 3r | A | 1-2 |

v **Sheffield Utd**

| | | | |
|---|---|---|---|
| 2003 | 3 | A | 0-4 |

v **Shrewsbury Town**

| | | | |
|---|---|---|---|
| 2001 | 1 | H | 4-1 |

v **Watford**

| | | | |
|---|---|---|---|
| 1938 | 1 | A | 0-3 |
| 1960 | 1 | H | 0-0 |
| 1960 | 1r | A | 0-3 |
| 1969 | 1 | H | 0-4 |

v **West Bromwich Albion**

| | | | |
|---|---|---|---|
| 2002 | 5 | A | 0-1 |

v **Wolverhampton W**

| | | | |
|---|---|---|---|
| 1988 | 1 | A | 1-5 |

v **Wycombe W**

| | | | |
|---|---|---|---|
| 1975 | 1 | A | 1-3 |

v **Yeovil Town**

| | | | |
|---|---|---|---|
| 1937 | Q4 | A | 2-3 |
| 1951 | Q4 | A | 4-2 |
| 1967 | Q4 | H | 3-3 |
| 1967 | Q4r | A | 1-3 |
| 1979 | Q4 | H | 1-2 |
| 2003 | 1 | A | 2-0 |

# Chesterfield

v **Colchester Utd**

| | | | |
|---|---|---|---|
| 1959 | 3 | A | 0-2 |
| 1910 | Q5 | H | 5-2 |

v **Darlington**

| | | | |
|---|---|---|---|
| 1928 | 1 | A | 1-4 |
| 1933 | 4 | A | 2-0 |
| 1979 | 1 | A | 1-1 |
| 1979 | 1r | H | 0-1 |
| 1992 | 1 | A | 1-2 |

v **Derby County**

| | | | |
|---|---|---|---|
| 1907 | 1 | A | 1-1 |
| 1907 | 1r | H | 1-1ab |
| 1907 | 1r2 | N | 0-4 |
| 1948 | 3 | A | 0-2 |

v **Doncaster Rovers**

| | | | |
|---|---|---|---|
| 1927 | 2 | A | 1-0 |
| 1961 | 1 | H | 3-3 |
| 1961 | 1r | A | 1-0 |
| 1962 | 1 | A | 4-0 |
| 1975 | 2 | H | 1-0 |

v **Everton**

| | | | |
|---|---|---|---|
| 1906 | 2 | A | 0-3 |

v **Fulham**

| | | | |
|---|---|---|---|
| 1910 | 1 | H | 0-0 |
| 1910 | 1r | A | 1-2 |
| 1927 | 3 | A | 3-4 |

v **Grimsby Town**

| | | | |
|---|---|---|---|
| 1900 | Q5 | A | 2-3 |
| 1924 | Q6 | H | 0-0 |
| 1924 | Q6r | A | 0-2 |
| 1925 | Q5 | A | 2-1 |
| 1973 | 2 | A | 2-2 |
| 1973 | 2r | H | 0-1 |
| 1980 | 1 | A | 1-1 |
| 1980 | 1r | H | 2-3 |
| 1998 | 2 | A | 2-2 |
| 1998 | 2r | H | 0-2 |

v **Hartlepool Utd**

| | | | |
|---|---|---|---|
| 1955 | 1 | A | 0-1 |
| 1956 | 2 | H | 1-2 |

v **Huddersfield Town**

| | | | |
|---|---|---|---|
| 1929 | 3 | H | 1-7 |
| 1982 | 2 | H | 0-1 |
| 1990 | 2 | H | 0-2 |

v **Leyton Orient**

| | | | |
|---|---|---|---|
| 1906 | 1 | A | 0-0 |
| 1906 | 1r | H | 3-0 |
| 1926 | 3 | H | 0-1 |

v **Lincoln City**

| | | | |
|---|---|---|---|
| 1904 | Q3 | A | 2-0 |
| 1923 | Q4 | H | 2-0 |

v **Liverpool**

| | | | |
|---|---|---|---|
| 1932 | 4 | H | 2-4 |

v **Macclesfield**

| | | | |
|---|---|---|---|
| 1993 | 1 | A | 0-0 |
| 1993 | 1r | H | 2-2q |

v **Middlesbrough**

| | | | |
|---|---|---|---|
| 1895 | 1 | A | 0-4 |
| 1930 | 3 | H | 1-1 |
| 1930 | 3r | A | 3-4 |
| 1947 | 4 | A | 1-2 |
| 1950 | 4 | H | 3-2 |
| 1997 | SF | N | 3-3aet |
| 1997 | SFr | N | 0-3 |

v **Newcastle Utd**

| | | | |
|---|---|---|---|
| 1896 | 1 | H | 0-4 |

v **Norwich City**

| | | | |
|---|---|---|---|
| 1952 | 2 | A | 1-3 |

v **Nottingham Forest**

| | | | |
|---|---|---|---|
| 1913 | 1 | H | 1-4 |
| 1932 | 3 | H | 5-2 |
| 1997 | 5 | H | 1-0 |

v **Notts County**

| | | | |
|---|---|---|---|
| 1931 | 1 | H | 1-2 |
| 1988 | 1 | A | 3-3 |
| 1988 | 1r | H | 0-1 |

v **Oldham Athletic**

| | | | |
|---|---|---|---|
| 1961 | 2 | H | 4-4 |
| 1961 | 2r | A | 3-0 |
| 1962 | 2 | H | 2-2 |
| 1962 | 2r | A | 2-4aet |
| 1972 | 1 | H | 3-0 |

**v Oxford Utd**
1964 3 A 0-1

**v Peterborough**
1965 3 H 0-3
1981 3 A 1-1
1981 3r H 1-2
1983 1 H 2-2
1983 1r A 1-2

**v Port Vale**
1930 2 H 2-0

**v Portsmouth**
1905 IR A 0-0
1905 IRr A 0-2
1969 3 A 0-3

**v Preston North End**
1982 1 H 4-1

**v Reading**
1902 IR A 1-2

**v Rochdale**
1929 1 H 3-2
1994 1 H 0-1

**v Scunthorpe Utd**
1977 1 A 2-1

**v Sheffield Utd**
1981 2 A 1-1
1981 2r H 1-0

**v Sheffield Wed**
1933 3 A 2-2
1933 3r H 4-2
1954 4 A 0-0
1954 4r H 2-4

**v Shrewsbury Town**
1953 2 A 0-0
1953 2r H 2-4
1990 1 A 3-2

**v Southend Utd**
1939 3 H 1-1
1939 3r A 3-4aet
1954 2 A 2-1
2002 2 H 1-1
2002 2r A 0-2

**v Stockport County**
1905 Q6 H 2-0
1963 1 H 4-1

**v Stoke City**
1972 3 A 1-2

**v Sunderland**
1947 3 H 2-1
1975 3 A 0-2

**v Swindon Town**
1935 3 A 1-2

**v Tottenham Hotspur**
1938 5 H 2-2
1938 5r A 1-2

**v Tranmere Rovers**
1970 1 A 0-3
1986 1 A 2-2
1986 1r H 0-1

**v Walsall**
1901 IR H 3-0
1922 Q5 A 0-2
1936 2 H 0-0
1936 2r A 1-2
1977 2 H 1-1
1977 2r A 0-0aet
1977 2r2 N 0-1
1985 2 A 0-1
1987 1 A 0-2

**v Watford**
1913 Q5 H 3-1

**v West Ham Utd**
1914 1 A 1-8

**v Wigan Athletic**
1981 1 A 2-2
1981 1r H 2-0

**v Wolverhampton W**
1949 3 A 0-6

**v Wrexham**
1967 1 A 2-3
1969 2 H 2-1
1996 2 A 2-3
1997 6 H 1-0

**v Wycombe W**
1999 1 A 0-1

**v Yeovil Town**
1950 3 H 3-1

**v York City**
1946 3 H 1-1
1946 3s A 2-3aet
1958 1 A 0-1
1965 2 H 2-1

# Colchester Utd

**v Darlington**
1979 3 A 1-0

**v Derby County**
1977 4 H 1-1
1977 4r A 0-1

**v Everton**
1971 6 A 0-5
1969 2 H 0-1

**v Exeter City**
1992 1 H 0-0
1992 1r A 0-0p
1995 2 A 2-1

**v Fulham**
1989 1 A 1-0

**v Gillingham**
1985 2 H 0-5
1993 2 A 1-1
1993 2r H 2-3

**v Huddersfield Town**
1948 3 H 1-0

**v Leeds Utd**
1971 5 H 3-2

**v Leyton Orient**
1991 2 H 0-0
1991 2r A 1-4

**v Manchester Utd**
1979 5 H 0-1

**v Millwall**
1954 1 H 1-1
1954 1r A 0-4

**v Newcastle Utd**
1982 3 A 1-1
1982 3r H 3-4aet

**v Oxford Utd**
1979 1 H 4-2

**v Peterborough**
1962 1 A 3-3
1962 1r H 2-2aet
1962 1r2 N 0-3
1967 2 H 0-3
1974 1 H 2-3

**v Plymouth Argyle**
1980 1 H 1-1
1980 1r A 1-0aet
1988 3 A 0-2

**v Port Vale**
1952 1 H 3-1

**v Portsmouth**
1981 1 H 3-0

**v QPR**
1960 1 H 2-3
1964 2 H 0-1
1966 1 H 3-3
1966 1r A 0-4

**v Reading**
1947 1 A 0-5
1949 1 H 2-4
1955 1 A 3-3
1955 1r H 1-2
1980 3 A 0-2
1991 1 H 2-1

**v Rochdale**
1971 4 A 3-3
1971 4r H 5-0

**v Rotherham Utd**
1953 3 A 2-2
1953 3r H 0-2

**v Sheffield Utd**
1989 4 A 3-3
1989 4r H 0-2

**v Shrewsbury Town**
1972 1 H 1-4
1989 3 A 3-0

**v Southend Utd**
1957 1 H 1-4
1985 1 A 2-2
1985 1r H 3-2aet

**v Swansea City**
1989 2 H 2-2
1989 2r A 3-1
2000 1 A 1-2

**v Torquay Utd**
1956 1 A 0-2
1965 2 A 0-2
1968 1 A 1-1
1968 1r H 2-1
1983 1 H 0-2
1984 1 A 2-1

**v Watford**
1975 1 A 1-0
1978 2 A 0-2
1981 3 H 0-1

v **West Bromwich Albion**

| | | | |
|---|---|---|---|
| 1968 | 3 | H | 1-1 |
| 1968 | 3r | A | 0-4 |

v **Wimbledon**

| | | | |
|---|---|---|---|
| 1963 | 1 | A | 1-2 |
| 1995 | 3 | A | 0-1 |

v **Wrexham**

| | | | |
|---|---|---|---|
| 1948 | 2 | H | 1-0 |

v **Wycombe W**

| | | | |
|---|---|---|---|
| 1986 | 1 | A | 0-2 |
| 1997 | 1 | H | 1-2 |

v **Yeovil Town**

| | | | |
|---|---|---|---|
| 1959 | 2 | H | 1-1 |
| 1959 | 2r | A | 7-1 |
| 1981 | 2 | H | 1-1 |
| 1981 | 2r | A | 2-0 |
| 2001 | 1 | A | 1-5 |

v **York City**

| | | | |
|---|---|---|---|
| 2002 | 1 | H | 0-0 |
| 2002 | 1r | A | 2-2p |

# Coventry City

v **Crewe Alexandra**

| | | | |
|---|---|---|---|
| 1934 | 1 | H | 3-0 |
| 1966 | 4 | A | 1-1 |
| 1966 | 4r | H | 4-1 |

v **Crystal Palace**

| | | | |
|---|---|---|---|
| 1908 | 1 | H | 2-4 |

v **Derby County**

| | | | |
|---|---|---|---|
| 1974 | 4 | H | 0-0 |
| 1974 | 4r | A | 1-0aet |
| 1997 | 5 | A | 2-3 |
| 1998 | 4 | H | 2-0 |

v **Everton**

| | | | |
|---|---|---|---|
| 1910 | 4 | H | 0-2 |
| 1966 | 5 | A | 0-3 |
| 1969 | 4 | A | 0-2 |
| 1999 | 5 | A | 1-2 |

v **Exeter City**

| | | | |
|---|---|---|---|
| 1931 | 2 | A | 1-1 |
| 1931 | 2r | H | 1-2 |
| 1956 | 1 | H | 0-1 |

v **Fulham**

| | | | |
|---|---|---|---|
| 1929 | 1 | H | 1-4 |

v **Gillingham**

| | | | |
|---|---|---|---|
| 1962 | 1 | H | 2-0 |

v **Grimsby Town**

| | | | |
|---|---|---|---|
| 1973 | 4 | H | 1-0 |

v **Hartlepool Utd**

| | | | |
|---|---|---|---|
| 1935 | 2 | A | 4-0 |

v **Huddersfield Town**

| | | | |
|---|---|---|---|
| 1955 | 3 | A | 3-3 |
| 1955 | 3r | H | 1-2aet |

v **Hull City**

| | | | |
|---|---|---|---|
| 1972 | 4 | H | 0-1 |
| 1973 | 5 | H | 3-0 |

v **Kidderminster H**

| | | | |
|---|---|---|---|
| 1896 | Q2 | A | 0-0 |
| 1896 | Q2r | H | 2-1 |
| 1903 | Q5 | H | 2-2 |
| 1903 | Q5r | A | 2-4 |

v **Leeds Utd**

| | | | |
|---|---|---|---|
| 1981 | 3 | A | 1-1 |
| 1981 | 3r | H | 1-0 |
| 1987 | SF | N | 3-2aet |

v **Leicester City**

| | | | |
|---|---|---|---|
| 1952 | 3 | A | 1-1 |
| 1952 | 3r | H | 4-1 |
| 1999 | 4 | A | 3-0 |

v **Leyton Orient**

| | | | |
|---|---|---|---|
| 1932 | 1 | H | 2-2 |
| 1932 | 1r | A | 0-2 |
| 1973 | 3 | A | 4-1 |

v **Lincoln City**

| | | | |
|---|---|---|---|
| 1927 | 2 | H | 1-1 |
| 1927 | 2r | A | 1-2 |
| 1963 | 3 | A | 5-1 |

v **Liverpool**

| | | | |
|---|---|---|---|
| 1961 | 3 | A | 2-3 |
| 1970 | 3 | H | 1-1 |
| 1970 | 3r | A | 0-3 |
| 1998 | 3 | A | 3-1 |

v **Luton Town**

| | | | |
|---|---|---|---|
| 1920 | 1 | A | 2-2 |
| 1920 | 1r | H | 0-1 |
| 1948 | 4 | A | 2-3 |

v **Macclesfield**

| | | | |
|---|---|---|---|
| 1999 | 3 | H | 7-0 |

v **Manchester City**

| | | | |
|---|---|---|---|
| 1982 | 4 | A | 3-1 |
| 1985 | 3 | H | 2-1 |
| 1996 | 4 | H | 2-2 |
| 1996 | 4r | A | 1-2 |
| 2001 | 4 | A | 0-1 |

v **Manchester Utd**

| | | | |
|---|---|---|---|
| 1912 | 2 | H | 1-5 |
| 1913 | 1 | A | 1-1 |
| 1913 | 1r | H | 1-2 |
| 1963 | 6 | H | 1-3 |
| 1985 | 4 | A | 1-2 |
| 1987 | 4 | A | 1-0 |

v **Middlesbrough**

| | | | |
|---|---|---|---|
| 1978 | 3 | A | 0-3 |

v **Millwall**

| | | | |
|---|---|---|---|
| 1963 | 2 | A | 0-0 |
| 1963 | 2r | H | 2-1 |
| 1977 | 3 | H | 1-0 |

v **Newcastle Utd**

| | | | |
|---|---|---|---|
| 1967 | 3 | H | 3-4 |
| 1976 | 4 | H | 1-1 |
| 1976 | 4r | A | 0-5 |
| 1994 | 3 | A | 0-2 |

v **Northampton Town**

| | | | |
|---|---|---|---|
| 1931 | 1 | A | 2-1 |
| 1955 | 1 | A | 1-0 |
| 1990 | 3 | A | 0-1 |

v **Norwich City**

| | | | |
|---|---|---|---|
| 1930 | 1 | A | 3-3 |
| 1930 | 1r | H | 2-0 |
| 1975 | 3 | H | 2-0 |
| 1983 | 4 | H | 2-2 |
| 1983 | 4r | A | 1-2aet |
| 1993 | 3 | A | 0-1 |
| 1995 | 4 | H | 0-0 |
| 1995 | 4r | A | 1-3aet |
| 2000 | 3 | A | 3-1 |

v **Nottingham Forest**

| | | | |
|---|---|---|---|
| 1910 | 3 | H | 3-1 |

v **Notts County**

| | | | |
|---|---|---|---|
| 1925 | 1 | H | 0-2 |

v **Oldham Athletic**

| | | | |
|---|---|---|---|
| 1980 | 3 | A | 1-0 |

v **Oxford Utd**

| | | | |
|---|---|---|---|
| 1982 | 5 | H | 4-0 |

v **Plymouth Argyle**

| | | | |
|---|---|---|---|
| 1953 | 3 | A | 1-4 |
| 1959 | 2 | H | 1-3 |
| 1996 | 3 | A | 3-1 |

v **Port Vale**

| | | | |
|---|---|---|---|
| 1914 | Q4 | A | 1-3 |

v **Portsmouth**

| | | | |
|---|---|---|---|
| 1910 | 2 | A | 1-0 |
| 1963 | 4 | A | 1-1 |
| 1963 | 4r | H | 2-2aet |
| 1963 | 4r2 | N | 2-1 |

v **Preston North End**

| | | | |
|---|---|---|---|
| 1910 | 1 | A | 2-1 |

v **QPR**

| | | | |
|---|---|---|---|
| 1961 | 2 | A | 2-1 |
| 1974 | 5 | H | 0-0 |
| 1974 | 5r | A | 2-3 |

v **Reading**

| | | | |
|---|---|---|---|
| 1933 | 2 | A | 2-2 |
| 1933 | 2r | H | 3-3aet |
| 1933 | 2r2 | N | 0-1 |

v **Rochdale**

| | | | |
|---|---|---|---|
| 1921 | Q6 | H | 1-1 |
| 1921 | Q6r | A | 1-2 |
| 1971 | 3 | A | 1-2 |
| 2003 | 4 | A | 0-2 |

v **Rotherham Utd**

| | | | |
|---|---|---|---|
| 1934 | 2 | A | 1-2 |

v **Scunthorpe Utd**

| | | | |
|---|---|---|---|
| 1935 | 1 | H | 7-0 |
| 1936 | 1 | H | 1-1 |
| 1936 | 1r | A | 2-4 |
| 1955 | 2 | H | 4-0 |

v **Sheffield Utd**

| | | | |
|---|---|---|---|
| 1998 | 6 | H | 1-1 |
| 1998 | 6r | A | 1-1p |

v **Sheffield Wed**

| | | | |
|---|---|---|---|
| 1911 | 1 | A | 2-1 |
| 1974 | 3 | A | 0-0 |
| 1974 | 3r | H | 3-1 |
| 1982 | 3 | H | 3-1 |
| 1984 | 4 | A | 2-3 |
| 1987 | 6 | A | 3-0 |

v **Southampton**
1912 1 A 2-0
1960 1 H 1-1
1960 1r A 1-5
1991 4 H 1-1
1991 4r A 0-2

v **Stoke City**
1987 5 A 1-0

v **Sunderland**
1930 3 H 1-2
1951 3 A 0-2
1963 5 H 2-1

v **Swindon Town**
1957 1 A 1-2
1966 3 A 2-1
2001 3 A 2-0

v **Torquay Utd**
1949 3 A 0-1
1988 3 H 2-0

v **Tottenham Hotspur**
1981 5 A 1-3
1987 F N 3-2aet
2002 3 H 0-2

v **Tranmere Rovers**
1924 Q5 H 2-2
1924 Q5r A 2-3aet
1968 4 H 1-1
1968 4r A 0-2

v **Walsall**
1904 Q3 H 2-4
1905 Q2 H 2-0
1925 Q5 A 2-1
1948 3 H 2-1

v **Watford**
1986 3 H 1-3
1988 4 H 0-1

v **West Bromwich Albion**
1937 5 H 2-3
1972 3 A 2-1
1979 3 H 2-2
1979 3r A 0-4
1982 6 A 0-2
1995 3 H 1-1
1995 3r A 2-1

v **Wigan Athletic**
1991 3 H 1-1
1991 3r A 1-0

v **Wolverhampton W**
1973 6 A 0-2
1984 3 H 1-1
1984 3r A 1-1aet
1984 3r2 H 3-0

v **Wrexham**
1910 Q4 H 3-0

v **York City**
1938 3 A 2-3

# Crewe Alexandra

v **Darlington**
1933 2 H 0-2
1950 1 A 2-2
1950 1r H 1-0
1967 2 H 2-1
1994 1 H 4-2

v **Derby County**
1888 5 H 1-0
1948 4 H 0-3
1986 1 A 1-5

v **Doncaster Rovers**
1970 1 A 1-1
1970 1r H 0-1
1971 1 H 0-0
1971 1r A 3-1

v **Everton**
2002 5 A 0-0
2002 5r H 1-2

v **Gillingham**
1936 2 H 2-1

v **Grimsby Town**
1911 2 H 1-5
1967 1 H 1-1
1967 1r A 1-0

v **Hartlepool Utd**
1937 2 H 1-1
1937 2r A 2-1
1979 2 H 0-1

v **Hull City**
1958 1 A 1-2
1964 1 A 2-2
1964 1r H 0-3
1997 2 A 5-1

v **Kidderminster H**
1997 1 H 4-1

v **Leeds Utd**
1994 3 A 1-3

v **Lincoln City**
1910 Q4 H 2-1
1952 1 H 2-4
1962 1 H 2-0
1988 1 A 1-2
1991 1 A 4-1

v **Liverpool**
1992 3 H 0-4

v **Luton Town**
1973 3 A 0-2

v **Macclesfield**
1894 Q3 H 3-2
1994 2 H 2-1

v **Mansfield Town**
1996 2 H 2-0
2003 2 H 3-0

v **Middlesbrough**
1888 6 A 2-0

v **Millwall**
1949 2 H 3-2

v **Oldham Athletic**
1939 1 A 2-2
1939 1r H 1-0
1950 2 H 1-1
1950 2r A 0-0aet
1950 2r2 N 0-3
1955 1 A 0-1

v **Oxford Utd**
1999 3 H 1-3

v **Plymouth Argyle**
1937 3 H 0-2
1951 2 H 2-2
1951 2r A 0-3

v **Port Vale**
1900 Q4 H 2-2
1900 Q4r A 1-3
1904 Q3 H 0-0
1904 Q3r A 1-2
1915 Q4 H 1-1
1915 Q4r A 2-5
1962 2 H 1-1
1962 2r A 0-3
2003 1 A 1-0

v **Preston North End**
1888 SF N 0-4
1977 1 H 1-1
1977 1r A 2-2aet
1977 1r2 N 0-3

v **QPR**
1931 2 H 2-4

v **Rochdale**
1937 1 H 5-1
1961 1 H 1-1
1961 1r A 2-1
1984 1 A 0-1

v **Rotherham Utd**
1947 1 A 0-2
1976 1 A 1-2
1991 4 H 1-0
2002 4 A 4-2

v **Scunthorpe Utd**
1966 1 H 3-0
1982 2 H 1-3

v **Sheffield Utd**
1948 3 H 3-1

v **Sheffield Wed**
1936 3 H 1-1
1936 3r A 1-3aet
2002 3 H 2-1

v **Southampton**
1996 4 A 1-1
1996 4r H 2-3

v **Stockport County**
1894 Q4 A 0-0aet
1894 Q4r H 1-2
1901 Q4 A 3-1
1902 Q4 A 2-3
1924 Q5 A 0-1
1928 2 H 2-0
1960 2 A 0-0
1960 2r H 2-0
2001 4 H 0-1

v **Stoke City**
1886 1 A 2-2
1886 1r H 1-0aet
1887 2 H 6-4aet

v **Sunderland**
1949 3 H 0-2

**v Tottenham Hotspur**

| | | | |
|---|---|---|---|
| 1960 | 4 | H | 2-2 |
| 1960 | 4r | A | 2-13 |
| 1961 | 4 | A | 1-5 |

**v Tranmere Rovers**

| | | | |
|---|---|---|---|
| 1896 | PR | H | 2-1 |
| 1920 | Q1 | H | 1-0 |
| 1925 | Q4 | A | 1-1 |
| 1925 | Q4r | H | 0-2 |
| 1926 | 1 | A | 0-0 |
| 1926 | 1r | H | 2-1aet |

**v Walsall**

| | | | |
|---|---|---|---|
| 1913 | Q4 | A | 1-2 |
| 1935 | 1 | H | 1-2 |
| 1954 | 2 | A | 0-3 |

**v West Bromwich Albion**

| | | | |
|---|---|---|---|
| 1996 | 3 | H | 4-3 |

**v West Ham Utd**

| | | | |
|---|---|---|---|
| 1991 | 5 | A | 0-1 |

**v Wimbledon**

| | | | |
|---|---|---|---|
| 1997 | 3 | H | 1-1 |
| 1997 | 3r | A | 0-2 |

**v Wolverhampton W**

| | | | |
|---|---|---|---|
| 1892 | 1 | A | 2-2aet |
| 1892 | 1r | H | 1-4 |

**v Wrexham**

| | | | |
|---|---|---|---|
| 1892 | Q3 | H | 3-1 |
| 1896 | Q2 | A | 3-3aet |
| 1896 | Q2r | H | 5-2 |
| 1898 | Q3 | H | 4-1 |
| 1905 | Q3 | H | 0-3 |
| 1920 | Q2 | H | 3-3 |
| 1920 | Q2r | A | 1-0 |
| 1922 | Q5 | A | 0-5 |
| 1946 | 1 | H | 4-2 |
| 1946 | 1s | A | 0-3 |
| 1957 | 1 | H | 2-2 |
| 1957 | 1r | A | 1-2 |
| 1993 | 1 | H | 6-1 |

**v York City**

| | | | |
|---|---|---|---|
| 1963 | 2 | A | 1-2 |
| 1987 | 1 | A | 1-3 |

# Crystal Palace

**v Everton**

| | | | |
|---|---|---|---|
| 1907 | 4 | H | 1-1 |
| 1907 | 4r | A | 0-4 |
| 1911 | 1 | H | 0-4 |
| 1922 | 1 | A | 6-0 |
| 1931 | 4 | H | 0-6 |
| 1972 | 3 | H | 2-2 |
| 1972 | 3r | A | 2-3 |

**v Fulham**

| | | | |
|---|---|---|---|
| 1907 | 2 | A | 0-0 |
| 1907 | 2r | H | 1-0 |

**v Gillingham**

| | | | |
|---|---|---|---|
| 1952 | 1 | H | 0-1 |

**v Grimsby Town**

| | | | |
|---|---|---|---|
| 1908 | 3 | A | 0-1 |

**v Hartlepool Utd**

| | | | |
|---|---|---|---|
| 1978 | 3 | A | 1-2 |
| 1993 | 3 | A | 0-1 |

**v Huddersfield Town**

| | | | |
|---|---|---|---|
| 1929 | 5 | A | 2-5 |
| 1990 | 4 | H | 4-0 |

**v Hull City**

| | | | |
|---|---|---|---|
| 1921 | 2 | H | 0-2 |
| 1925 | 2 | A | 2-3 |

**v Ipswich Town**

| | | | |
|---|---|---|---|
| 1958 | 3 | H | 0-1 |

**v Leeds Utd**

| | | | |
|---|---|---|---|
| 1930 | 3 | A | 1-8 |
| 1965 | 6 | H | 0-3 |
| 1967 | 3 | A | 0-3 |
| 1976 | 4 | A | 1-0 |
| 1997 | 3 | H | 2-2 |
| 1997 | 3r | A | 0-1 |
| 2003 | 5 | H | 1-2 |

**v Leicester City**

| | | | |
|---|---|---|---|
| 1984 | 3 | H | 1-0 |
| 1992 | 3 | A | 0-1 |
| 1998 | 4 | H | 3-0 |

**v Leyton Orient**

| | | | |
|---|---|---|---|
| 1982 | 5 | H | 0-0 |
| 1982 | 5r | A | 1-0 |

**v Lincoln City**

| | | | |
|---|---|---|---|
| 1995 | 3 | H | 5-1 |

**v Liverpool**

| | | | |
|---|---|---|---|
| 1938 | 3 | H | 0-0 |
| 1938 | 3r | A | 1-3aet |
| 1977 | 3 | A | 0-0 |
| 1977 | 3r | H | 2-3 |
| 1990 | SF | N | 4-3aet |
| 2003 | 4 | H | 0-0 |
| 2003 | 4r | A | 2-0 |

**v Luton Town**

| | | | |
|---|---|---|---|
| 1906 | Q4 | H | 1-0 |
| 1929 | 3 | A | 0-0 |
| 1929 | 3r | H | 7-0 |
| 1986 | 3 | H | 1-2 |

**v Manchester City**

| | | | |
|---|---|---|---|
| 1921 | 1 | H | 2-0 |
| 1926 | 5 | A | 4-11 |
| 1981 | 3 | A | 0-4 |

**v Manchester Utd**

| | | | |
|---|---|---|---|
| 1990 | F | N | 3-3aet |
| 1990 | Fr | N | 0-1 |
| 1995 | SF | N | 2-2aet |
| 1995 | SFr | N | 0-2 |

**v Mansfield Town**

| | | | |
|---|---|---|---|
| 1963 | 2 | H | 2-2 |
| 1963 | 2r | A | 2-7 |

**v Middlesbrough**

| | | | |
|---|---|---|---|
| 1979 | 3 | A | 1-1 |
| 1979 | 3r | H | 1-0 |

**v Millwall**

| | | | |
|---|---|---|---|
| 1922 | 2 | H | 0-0 |
| 1922 | 2r | A | 0-2 |
| 1929 | 4 | A | 0-0 |
| 1929 | 4r | H | 5-3 |
| 1951 | 1 | H | 1-4 |
| 1957 | 3 | A | 0-2 |
| 1976 | 2 | A | 1-1 |
| 1976 | 2r | H | 2-1 |
| 1985 | 3 | A | 1-1 |
| 1985 | 3r | H | 1-2 |

**v Newcastle Utd**

| | | | |
|---|---|---|---|
| 1907 | 1 | A | 1-0 |
| 1920 | 1 | A | 0-2 |
| 1947 | 3 | A | 2-6 |
| 1988 | 3 | A | 0-1 |
| 1999 | 3 | A | 1-2 |
| 2002 | 3 | A | 0-2 |

**v Northampton Town**

| | | | |
|---|---|---|---|
| 926 | 3 | A | 3-3 |
| 1926 | 3r | H | 2-1 |

**v Norwich City**

| | | | |
|---|---|---|---|
| 1914 | 1 | H | 2-1 |
| 1927 | 1 | H | 0-0 |
| 1927 | 1r | A | 0-1 |
| 1934 | 1 | H | 3-0 |

**v Nottingham Forest**

| | | | |
|---|---|---|---|
| 1965 | 5 | H | 3-1 |
| 1987 | 3 | H | 1-0 |
| 1991 | 3 | H | 0-0 |
| 1991 | 3r | A | 2-2aet |
| 1991 | 3r2 | A | 0-3 |
| 1995 | 4 | A | 2-1 |

**v Notts County**

| | | | |
|---|---|---|---|
| 1924 | 2 | H | 0-0 |
| 1924 | 2r | A | 0-0aet |
| 1924 | 2r2 | N | 0-0aet |
| 1924 | 2r3 | N | 2-1 |

**v Plymouth Argyle**

| | | | |
|---|---|---|---|
| 1908 | 2 | A | 3-2 |
| 1975 | 2 | A | 1-2 |

**v Port Vale**

| | | | |
|---|---|---|---|
| 1948 | 1 | H | 2-1 |
| 1996 | 3 | H | 0-0 |
| 1996 | 3r | A | 3-4aet |

**v Portsmouth**

| | | | |
|---|---|---|---|
| 1962 | 1 | H | 3-0 |
| 1990 | 3 | H | 2-1 |

**v QPR**

| | | | |
|---|---|---|---|
| 1923 | 1 | A | 0-1 |
| 1939 | 1 | H | 1-1 |
| 1939 | 1r | A | 0-3 |
| 1946 | 3 | A | 0-0 |
| 1946 | 3s | H | 0-0ab |
| 1946 | 3r | N | 0-1 |
| 1982 | 6 | A | 0-1 |

**v Reading**

| | | | |
|---|---|---|---|
| 1931 | 3 | H | 1-1 |
| 1931 | 3r | A | 1-1aet |
| 1931 | 3r2 | N | 2-0 |
| 1932 | 1 | A | 1-0 |
| 1953 | 1 | H | 1-1 |
| 1953 | 1r | A | 3-1 |

**v Rochdale**

| | | | |
|---|---|---|---|
| 1990 | 5 | H | 1-0 |

**v Scunthorpe Utd**

| | | | |
|---|---|---|---|
| 1960 | 3 | A | 0-1 |
| 1998 | 3 | H | 2-0 |

**v Sheffield Utd**

| | | | |
|---|---|---|---|
| 1959 | 3 | A | 0-2 |

**v Sheffield Wed**

| | | | |
|---|---|---|---|
| 1973 | 4 | A | 1-1 |
| 1973 | 4r | H | 1-1aet |
| 1973 | 4r2 | N | 2-3 |

**v Shrewsbury Town**

| | | | |
|---|---|---|---|
| 1959 | 2 | H | 2-2 |
| 1959 | 2r | A | 2-2aet |
| 1959 | 2r2 | N | 4-1 |

**v Southampton**

| | | | |
|---|---|---|---|
| 1956 | 1 | H | 0-0 |
| 1956 | 1r | A | 0-2 |
| 1958 | 2 | H | 1-0 |
| 1965 | 4 | A | 2-1 |
| 1973 | 3 | H | 2-0 |
| 1976 | SF | N | 0-2 |

**v Southend Utd**

| | | | |
|---|---|---|---|
| 1937 | 1 | H | 1-1 |
| 1937 | 1r | A | 0-2 |

**v Stockport County**

| | | | |
|---|---|---|---|
| 1934 | 2 | A | 2-1 |

**v Stoke City**

| | | | |
|---|---|---|---|
| 1989 | 3 | A | 0-1 |

**v Sunderland**

| | | | |
|---|---|---|---|
| 1912 | 2 | H | 0-0 |
| 1912 | 2r | A | 0-1aet |
| 1976 | 6 | A | 1-0 |
| 2001 | 3 | A | 0-0 |
| 2001 | 3r | H | 2-4aet |

**v Swansea City**

| | | | |
|---|---|---|---|
| 1980 | 3 | A | 2-2 |
| 1980 | 3r | H | 3-3aet |
| 1980 | 3r2 | N | 1-2 |

**v Swindon Town**

| | | | |
|---|---|---|---|
| 1910 | 1 | H | 1-3 |
| 1924 | 3 | H | 1-2 |
| 1928 | 2 | A | 0-0 |
| 1928 | 2r | H | 1-2 |
| 1955 | 1 | A | 2-0 |

**v Tottenham Hotspur**

| | | | |
|---|---|---|---|
| 1924 | 1 | H | 2-0 |
| 1970 | 4 | A | 0-0 |
| 1970 | 4r | H | 1-0 |
| 1987 | 4 | A | 0-4 |

**v Walsall**

| | | | |
|---|---|---|---|
| 1968 | 3 | A | 1-1 |
| 1968 | 3r | H | 1-2 |
| 1970 | 3 | H | 2-0 |

**v Watford**

| | | | |
|---|---|---|---|
| 1961 | 2 | H | 0-0 |
| 1961 | 2r | A | 0-1 |
| 1995 | 5 | A | 0-0 |
| 1995 | 5r | H | 1-0aet |

**v West Ham Utd**

| | | | |
|---|---|---|---|
| 1914 | 2 | A | 0-2 |
| 1984 | 4 | H | 1-1 |
| 1984 | 4r | A | 0-2 |

**v Wolverhampton W**

| | | | |
|---|---|---|---|
| 1909 | 1 | A | 2-2 |
| 1909 | 1r | H | 4-2 |
| 1979 | 5 | H | 0-1 |
| 1994 | 3 | A | 0-1 |
| 1995 | 6 | H | 1-1 |
| 1995 | 6r | A | 4-1 |

**v Wrexham**

| | | | |
|---|---|---|---|
| 1974 | 3 | H | 0-2 |

**v Yeovil Town**

| | | | |
|---|---|---|---|
| 1935 | 1 | A | 0-3 |
| 1964 | 2 | A | 1-3 |

**v York City**

| | | | |
|---|---|---|---|
| 1983 | 3 | H | 2-1 |

# Darlington

**v Doncaster Rovers**

| | | | |
|---|---|---|---|
| 1960 | 2 | A | 2-3 |

**v Gillingham**

| | | | |
|---|---|---|---|
| 2000 | 2 | A | 1-3w |

**v Grimsby Town**

| | | | |
|---|---|---|---|
| 1886 | 2 | A | 0-8 |
| 1952 | 1 | A | 0-4 |
| 1953 | 1 | H | 2-3 |
| 1961 | 1 | H | 2-0 |
| 1969 | 1 | H | 2-0 |

**v Hartlepool Utd**

| | | | |
|---|---|---|---|
| 1910 | Q2 | A | 1-0 |
| 1911 | Q1 | H | 1-1 |
| 1911 | Q1r | A | 1-0 |
| 1948 | 1 | A | 0-1 |
| 1955 | 3 | A | 1-1 |
| 1955 | 3r | H | 2-2aet |
| 1955 | 3r2 | N | 0-2 |
| 1965 | 2 | A | 0-0 |
| 1965 | 2r | H | 4-1 |
| 1992 | 2 | H | 1-2 |
| 1996 | 1 | A | 4-2 |

**v Huddersfield Town**

| | | | |
|---|---|---|---|
| 1980 | 1 | H | 1-1 |
| 1980 | 1r | A | 1-0 |

**v Hull City**

| | | | |
|---|---|---|---|
| 1947 | 2 | H | 1-2 |
| 1961 | 2 | H | 1-1 |
| 1961 | 2r | A | 1-1aet |
| 1961 | 2r2 | N | 1-1ab |
| 1961 | 2r3 | N | 0-0aet |
| 1961 | 2r4 | N | 0-3 |
| 1993 | 1 | H | 1-2 |

**v Kidderminster H**

| | | | |
|---|---|---|---|
| 2002 | 1 | A | 1-0 |

**v Leyton Orient**

| | | | |
|---|---|---|---|
| 1949 | 2 | H | 1-0 |
| 1977 | 3 | H | 2-2 |
| 1977 | 3r | A | 0-0aet |
| 1977 | 3r2 | N | 0-3 |

**v Lincoln City**

| | | | |
|---|---|---|---|
| 1963 | 1 | A | 1-1 |
| 1963 | 1r | H | 1-2 |

**v Liverpool**

| | | | |
|---|---|---|---|
| 1928 | 3 | A | 0-1 |

**v Luton Town**

| | | | |
|---|---|---|---|
| 2001 | 2 | H | 0-0 |
| 2001 | 2r | A | 0-2 |

**v Manchester City**

| | | | |
|---|---|---|---|
| 1922 | 1 | A | 1-3 |
| 1999 | 2 | H | 1-1 |
| 1999 | 2r | A | 0-1aet |

**v Mansfield Town**

| | | | |
|---|---|---|---|
| 1987 | 1 | H | 2-1 |

**v Middlesbrough**

| | | | |
|---|---|---|---|
| 1895 | Q3 | H | 0-1 |
| 1985 | 3 | A | 0-0 |
| 1985 | 3r | H | 2-1 |

**v Northampton Town**

| | | | |
|---|---|---|---|
| 1912 | 2 | H | 1-1 |
| 1912 | 2r | A | 0-2 |
| 1932 | 3 | H | 1-1 |
| 1932 | 3r | A | 0-2 |

**v Norwich City**

| | | | |
|---|---|---|---|
| 1920 | Q6 | H | 5-0 |
| 1958 | 3 | A | 2-1 |

**v Notts County**

| | | | |
|---|---|---|---|
| 1989 | 1 | H | 1-2 |

**v Oldham Athletic**

| | | | |
|---|---|---|---|
| 1966 | 2 | H | 0-1 |

**v Peterborough**

| | | | |
|---|---|---|---|
| 2002 | 3 | H | 2-2 |
| 2002 | 3r | A | 0-2 |

**v Plymouth Argyle**

| | | | |
|---|---|---|---|
| 1984 | 4 | A | 1-2 |

**v Port Vale**

| | | | |
|---|---|---|---|
| 1914 | Q5 | A | 2-2 |
| 1914 | Q5r | H | 1-1ab |
| 1914 | Q5r2 | N | 0-1 |
| 1954 | 1 | H | 1-3 |
| 1972 | 2 | A | 0-1 |

**v QPR**

| | | | |
|---|---|---|---|
| 1933 | 3 | H | 2-0 |

**v Reading**

| | | | |
|---|---|---|---|
| 1925 | Q6 | A | 1-0 |

**v Rochdale**

| | | | |
|---|---|---|---|
| 1913 | Q5 | A | 1-1 |
| 1913 | Q5r | H | 0-1 |
| 1928 | 2 | H | 2-1 |
| 1958 | 1 | A | 2-0 |
| 1971 | 2 | H | 0-2 |
| 1986 | 1 | A | 1-2 |
| 1996 | 2 | A | 2-2 |
| 1996 | 2r | H | 0-1 |

**v Rotherham Utd**

| | | | |
|---|---|---|---|
| 1949 | 3 | A | 2-4 |
| 1951 | 1 | H | 2-7 |

**v Scunthorpe Utd**

| | | | |
|---|---|---|---|
| 1965 | 1 | A | 2-1 |
| 1974 | 1 | A | 0-1 |
| 1983 | 1 | H | 0-1 |

**v Sheffield Utd**

| | | | |
|---|---|---|---|
| 1911 | 1 | A | 1-0 |

**v Sheffield Wed**

| | | | |
|---|---|---|---|
| 1920 | 1 | H | 0-0 |
| 1920 | 1r | A | 2-0 |
| 1977 | 2 | H | 1-0 |

**v Shrewsbury Town**

| | | | |
|---|---|---|---|
| 1968 | 1 | A | 0-3 |

**v Stockport County**

| | | | |
|---|---|---|---|
| 1935 | 2 | A | 2-3 |
| 1967 | 1 | H | 0-0 |
| 1967 | 1r | A | 1-1aet |
| 1967 | 1r2 | N | 4-2 |

**v Sunderland**

| | | | |
|---|---|---|---|
| 1988 | 1 | A | 0-2 |

**v Swindon Town**

| | | | |
|---|---|---|---|
| 1911 | 3 | H | 0-3 |

**v Tranmere Rovers**

| | | | |
|---|---|---|---|
| 1949 | 1 | A | 3-1 |

**v Walsall**

| | | | |
|---|---|---|---|
| 1932 | 1 | H | 1-0 |

**v West Bromwich Albion**

| | | | |
|---|---|---|---|
| 1937 | 4 | A | 2-3 |

**v Wigan Athletic**

| | | | |
|---|---|---|---|
| 1987 | 2 | H | 0-5 |

**v Wolverhampton W**

| | | | |
|---|---|---|---|
| 1924 | 1 | A | 1-3 |
| 1958 | 5 | A | 1-6 |
| 1998 | 3 | H | 0-4 |

**v Wrexham**

| | | | |
|---|---|---|---|
| 1959 | 1 | A | 2-1 |
| 1973 | 1 | H | 1-1 |
| 1973 | 1r | A | 0-5 |
| 2003 | 1 | A | 2-0 |

**v York City**

| | | | |
|---|---|---|---|
| 1991 | 1 | H | 1-1 |
| 1991 | 1r | A | 0-1 |

# Derby County

**v Everton**

| | | | |
|---|---|---|---|
| 1890 | 1 | A | 2-11 |
| 1897 | SF | N | 2-3 |
| 1898 | SF | N | 3-1 |
| 1911 | 3 | H | 5-0 |
| 1935 | 5 | A | 1-3 |
| 1939 | 3 | H | 0-1 |
| 1950 | 6 | H | 1-2 |
| 1971 | 5 | A | 0-1 |
| 1976 | 3 | H | 2-1 |
| 1977 | 6 | A | 0-2 |
| 1995 | 3 | A | 0-1 |

**v Exeter City**

| | | | |
|---|---|---|---|
| 1931 | 3 | A | 2-3 |

**v Fulham**

| | | | |
|---|---|---|---|
| 1936 | 6 | A | 0-3 |

**v Gillingham**

| | | | |
|---|---|---|---|
| 1986 | 3 | A | 1-1 |
| 1986 | 3r | H | 3-1aet |
| 1997 | 3 | A | 2-0 |

**v Hartlepool Utd**

| | | | |
|---|---|---|---|
| 1985 | 1 | A | 1-2 |

**v Huddersfield Town**

| | | | |
|---|---|---|---|
| 1999 | 5 | A | 2-2 |
| 1999 | 5r | H | 3-1 |

**v Leeds Utd**

| | | | |
|---|---|---|---|
| 1962 | 3 | A | 2-2 |
| 1962 | 3r | H | 3-1 |
| 1968 | 3 | A | 0-2 |
| 1973 | 6 | H | 0-1 |
| 1975 | 5 | H | 0-1 |
| 1996 | 3 | H | 2-4 |

**v Leicester City**

| | | | |
|---|---|---|---|
| 1894 | 2 | A | 0-0aet |
| 1894 | 2r | H | 3-0 |
| 1909 | 2 | A | 2-0 |

**v Leyton Orient**

| | | | |
|---|---|---|---|
| 1963 | 4 | A | 0-3 |
| 1975 | 3 | A | 2-2 |
| 1975 | 3r | H | 2-1 |

**v Lincoln City**

| | | | |
|---|---|---|---|
| 1902 | 2 | A | 3-1 |
| 1907 | 2 | H | 1-0 |

**v Liverpool**

| | | | |
|---|---|---|---|
| 1898 | 3 | H | 1-1 |
| 1898 | 3r | A | 5-1 |
| 1908 | 1 | A | 2-4 |
| 1947 | 5 | A | 0-1 |
| 1964 | 3 | A | 0-5 |
| 1976 | 4 | H | 1-0 |

**v Luton Town**

| | | | |
|---|---|---|---|
| 1946 | 3 | A | 6-0 |
| 1946 | 3s | H | 3-0 |
| 1993 | 4 | A | 5-1 |

**v Manchester City**

| | | | |
|---|---|---|---|
| 1932 | 5 | A | 0-3 |
| 1933 | SF | N | 2-3 |
| 1950 | 3 | A | 5-3 |
| 1955 | 3 | H | 1-3 |

**v Manchester Utd**

| | | | |
|---|---|---|---|
| 1896 | 2 | A | 1-1 |
| 1896 | 2r | H | 5-1 |
| 1897 | 3 | H | 2-0 |
| 1948 | SF | N | 1-3 |
| 1960 | 3 | H | 2-4 |
| 1966 | 3 | H | 2-5 |
| 1976 | SF | N | 0-2 |
| 1983 | 5 | H | 0-1 |

**v Middlesbrough**

| | | | |
|---|---|---|---|
| 1921 | 1 | H | 2-0 |
| 1948 | 5 | A | 2-1 |
| 1952 | 3 | A | 2-2 |
| 1952 | 3r | H | 0-2 |
| 1958 | 3 | A | 0-5 |
| 1997 | 6 | H | 0-2 |

**v Millwall**

| | | | |
|---|---|---|---|
| 1903 | SF | N | 3-0 |
| 1910 | 1 | H | 5-0 |
| 1927 | 4 | H | 0-2 |
| 1928 | 3 | A | 2-1 |
| 1937 | 5 | A | 1-2 |

**v Newcastle Utd**

| | | | |
|---|---|---|---|
| 1906 | 2 | H | 0-0 |
| 1906 | 2r | A | 1-2 |
| 1911 | 4 | A | 0-4 |
| 1912 | 1 | H | 3-0 |
| 1924 | 2 | H | 2-2 |
| 1924 | 2r | A | 2-2aet |
| 1924 | 2r2 | N | 2-2aet |
| 1924 | 2r3 | A | 3-5 |
| 1976 | 6 | H | 4-2 |
| 1991 | 3 | A | 0-2 |

**v Northampton Town**

| | | | |
|---|---|---|---|
| 1909 | 1 | A | 1-1 |
| 1909 | 1r | H | 4-2 |
| 1914 | 1 | H | 1-0 |
| 1950 | 5 | H | 4-2 |

**v Norwich City**

| | | | |
|---|---|---|---|
| 1967 | 3 | A | 0-3 |
| 1984 | 5 | H | 2-1 |

**v Nottingham Forest**

| | | | |
|---|---|---|---|
| 1898 | F | N | 1-3 |
| 1909 | 4 | H | 3-0 |
| 1928 | 4 | H | 0-0 |
| 1928 | 4r | A | 0-2 |
| 1936 | 4 | H | 2-0 |
| 1983 | 3 | H | 2-0 |

**v Notts County**

| | | | |
|---|---|---|---|
| 1929 | 3 | H | 4-3 |
| 1972 | 4 | H | 6-0 |

**v Oldham Athletic**

| | | | |
|---|---|---|---|
| 1994 | 3 | A | 1-2 |

**v Peterborough**

| | | | |
|---|---|---|---|
| 1963 | 3 | H | 2-0 |
| 1973 | 3 | A | 1-0 |

**v Plymouth Argyle**

| | | | |
|---|---|---|---|
| 1909 | 3 | H | 1-0 |
| 1911 | 1 | H | 2-1 |
| 1965 | 3 | A | 2-4 |
| 1984 | 6 | A | 0-0 |
| 1984 | 6r | H | 0-1 |
| 1999 | 3 | A | 3-0 |

**v Port Vale**

| | | | |
|---|---|---|---|
| 1990 | 3 | A | 1-1 |
| 1990 | 3r | H | 2-3 |

**v Portsmouth**

| | | | |
|---|---|---|---|
| 1902 | 3 | A | 0-0 |
| 1902 | 3r | H | 6-3 |
| 1904 | 1 | A | 5-2 |
| 1926 | 3 | H | 0-0 |
| 1926 | 3r | A | 1-1aet |
| 1926 | 3r2 | N | 2-0 |
| 1949 | 6 | A | 1-2 |

**v Preston North End**

| | | | |
|---|---|---|---|
| 1905 | 1 | H | 0-2 |
| 1954 | 3 | H | 0-2 |
| 1959 | 3 | H | 2-2 |
| 1959 | 3r | A | 2-4aet |
| 1970 | 3 | A | 1-1 |
| 1970 | 3r | H | 4-1 |
| 1979 | 3 | A | 0-3 |

**v QPR**

| | | | |
|---|---|---|---|
| 1948 | 6 | A | 1-1aet |
| 1948 | 6r | H | 5-0 |
| 1970 | 5 | A | 0-1 |
| 1973 | 5 | H | 4-2 |

**v Sheffield Utd**

| | | | |
|---|---|---|---|
| 1899 | F | N | 1-4 |
| 1902 | SF | N | 1-1 |
| 1902 | SFr | N | 1-1aet |

| | | | |
|---|---|---|---|
| 1902 | SFr2 | N | 0-1 |
| 1970 | 4 | H | 3-0 |
| 1986 | 4 | A | 1-0 |

**v Sheffield Wed**

| | | | |
|---|---|---|---|
| 1891 | 2 | H | 2-3 |
| 1893 | 1r2 | A | 2-4 |
| 1923 | 3 | H | 1-0 |
| 1986 | 5 | H | 1-1 |
| 1986 | 5r | A | 0-2 |
| 1987 | 3 | A | 0-1 |
| 1993 | 6 | H | 3-3 |
| 1993 | 6r | A | 0-1 |

**v Shrewsbury Town**

| | | | |
|---|---|---|---|
| 1972 | 3 | H | 2-0 |

**v Southampton**

| | | | |
|---|---|---|---|
| 1899 | 3 | A | 2-1 |
| 1989 | 3 | H | 1-1 |
| 1989 | 3r | A | 2-1aet |
| 1998 | 3 | H | 2-0 |

**v Southend Utd**

| | | | |
|---|---|---|---|
| 1926 | 4 | A | 1-4 |
| 1933 | 4 | A | 3-2 |
| 1976 | 5 | H | 1-0 |
| 1978 | 3 | H | 3-2 |

**v Stockport County**

| | | | |
|---|---|---|---|
| 1993 | 3 | H | 2-1 |

**v Stoke City**

| | | | |
|---|---|---|---|
| 1899 | SF | N | 3-1 |
| 1903 | 3 | H | 3-0 |
| 1938 | 3 | H | 1-2 |

**v Sunderland**

| | | | |
|---|---|---|---|
| 1900 | 1 | H | 2-2 |
| 1900 | 1r | A | 0-3 |
| 1933 | 6 | H | 4-4 |
| 1933 | 6r | A | 1-0aet |

**v Swansea City**

| | | | |
|---|---|---|---|
| 1935 | 4 | H | 3-0 |
| 1999 | 4 | A | 1-0 |

**v Tottenham Hotspur**

| | | | |
|---|---|---|---|
| 1923 | 4 | A | 1-0 |
| 1973 | 4 | H | 1-1 |
| 1973 | 4r | A | 5-3aet |

**v Watford**

| | | | |
|---|---|---|---|
| 1989 | 4 | A | 1-2 |

**v West Bromwich Albion**

| | | | |
|---|---|---|---|
| 1896 | 3 | H | 1-0 |
| 1907 | 3 | A | 0-2 |
| 1911 | 2 | H | 2-0 |
| 1946 | 4 | H | 1-0 |
| 1946 | 4s | A | 3-1 |
| 1951 | 3 | H | 2-2 |
| 1951 | 3r | A | 1-0 |
| 1978 | 5 | H | 2-3 |
| 2001 | 3 | H | 3-2 |

**v West Ham Utd**

| | | | |
|---|---|---|---|
| 1923 | SF | N | 2-5 |

**v Wolverhampton W**

| | | | |
|---|---|---|---|
| 1896 | SF | N | 1-2 |
| 1898 | 2 | A | 1-0 |
| 1899 | 2 | H | 2-1 |
| 1904 | 2 | H | 2-2 |
| 1904 | 2r | A | 2-2aet |
| 1904 | 2r2 | N | 1-0 |
| 1921 | 2 | H | 1-1 |
| 1921 | 2r | A | 0-1 |
| 1933 | 3 | A | 6-3 |
| 1934 | 4 | H | 3-0 |
| 1971 | 4 | H | 2-1 |

**v York City**

| | | | |
|---|---|---|---|
| 1935 | 3 | A | 1-0 |

# Doncaster Rovers

**v Everton**

| | | | |
|---|---|---|---|
| 1939 | 4 | A | 0-8 |
| 1985 | 4 | A | 0-2 |

**v Fulham**

| | | | |
|---|---|---|---|
| 1948 | 3 | A | 0-2 |

**v Grimsby Town**

| | | | |
|---|---|---|---|
| 1893 | Q2 | H | 1-1 |
| 1893 | Q2r | A | 1-2 |
| 1900 | Q3 | A | 1-3 |
| 1990 | 2 | A | 0-1 |

**v Hartlepool Utd**

| | | | |
|---|---|---|---|
| 1993 | 1 | H | 1-2 |

**v Huddersfield Town**

| | | | |
|---|---|---|---|
| 1965 | 3 | H | 0-1 |
| 1979 | 1 | H | 2-1 |
| 1995 | 1 | H | 1-4 |

**v Hull City**

| | | | |
|---|---|---|---|
| 1981 | 3 | A | 0-1 |

**v Leyton Orient**

| | | | |
|---|---|---|---|
| 1954 | 5 | A | 1-3 |

**v Lincoln City**

| | | | |
|---|---|---|---|
| 1892 | Q1 | A | 1-3 |
| 1902 | Q4 | A | 0-1 |
| 1974 | 1 | H | 1-0 |

**v Liverpool**

| | | | |
|---|---|---|---|
| 1969 | 3 | A | 0-2 |
| 1974 | 3 | A | 2-2 |
| 1974 | 3r | H | 0-2 |

**v Mansfield Town**

| | | | |
|---|---|---|---|
| 1925 | Q4 | H | 3-2 |
| 1950 | 2 | H | 1-0 |
| 1980 | 2 | H | 1-2 |
| 1982 | 1 | A | 1-0 |
| 1984 | 1 | A | 0-3 |
| 1996 | 1 | A | 2-4 |

**v Middlesbrough**

| | | | |
|---|---|---|---|
| 1952 | 4 | A | 4-1 |

**v Millwall**

| | | | |
|---|---|---|---|
| 1930 | 4 | A | 0-4 |

**v Northampton Town**

| | | | |
|---|---|---|---|
| 1933 | 2 | A | 1-0 |

**v Norwich City**

| | | | |
|---|---|---|---|
| 1925 | 1 | H | 1-2 |
| 1982 | 4 | A | 1-2 |

**v Nottingham Forest**

| | | | |
|---|---|---|---|
| 1936 | 3 | H | 1-2 |
| 1956 | 3 | H | 3-0 |

**v Notts County**

| | | | |
|---|---|---|---|
| 1931 | 2 | H | 0-1 |
| 1964 | 2 | H | 1-1 |
| 1964 | 2r | A | 2-1 |
| 1969 | 1 | H | 1-0 |
| 1990 | 1 | H | 1-0 |

**v Oldham Athletic**

| | | | |
|---|---|---|---|
| 1947 | 2 | A | 2-1 |

**v Peterborough**

| | | | |
|---|---|---|---|
| 1983 | 2 | A | 2-5 |

**v Plymouth Argyle**

| | | | |
|---|---|---|---|
| 1954 | 4 | A | 2-0 |

**v Port Vale**

| | | | |
|---|---|---|---|
| 1980 | 1 | A | 3-1 |

**v Portsmouth**

| | | | |
|---|---|---|---|
| 1947 | 3 | H | 2-3 |
| 1952 | 5 | A | 0-4 |

**v Preston North End**

| | | | |
|---|---|---|---|
| 1998 | 1 | A | 2-3 |

**v QPR**

| | | | |
|---|---|---|---|
| 1985 | 3 | H | 1-0 |

**v Reading**

| | | | |
|---|---|---|---|
| 1950 | 3 | A | 3-2 |
| 1973 | 3 | A | 0-2 |

**v Rochdale**

| | | | |
|---|---|---|---|
| 1931 | 1 | A | 2-1 |
| 1985 | 1 | A | 2-1 |

**v Rotherham Utd**

| | | | |
|---|---|---|---|
| 1926 | 2 | H | 0-2 |
| 1946 | 1 | H | 0-1 |
| 1946 | 1s | A | 1-2 |
| 1951 | 3 | A | 1-2 |
| 1988 | 1 | H | 1-1 |
| 1988 | 1r | A | 0-2 |

**v Rushden & Diamonds**

| | | | |
|---|---|---|---|
| 1999 | 2 | H | 0-0 |
| 1999 | 2r | A | 2-4 |

**v Scunthorpe Utd**

| | | | |
|---|---|---|---|
| 1915 | Q2 | A | 0-1 |
| 2002 | 1 | H | 2-3 |

**v Sheffield Utd**

| | | | |
|---|---|---|---|
| 1938 | 3 | H | 0-2 |
| 1989 | 2 | H | 1-3 |

**v Shrewsbury Town**

| | | | |
|---|---|---|---|
| 1977 | 1 | H | 2-2 |
| 1977 | 1r | A | 3-4 |
| 1978 | 1 | H | 0-1 |
| 1979 | 2 | H | 0-3 |
| 1994 | 1 | A | 1-1 |
| 1994 | 1r | H | 1-2aet |

**v Southend Utd**

| | | | |
|---|---|---|---|
| 1999 | 1 | A | 1-0 |

**v Stockport County**

| | | | |
|---|---|---|---|
| 1972 | 1 | H | 1-2 |
| 1997 | 1 | A | 1-2 |

**v Stoke City**

| | | | |
|---|---|---|---|
| 1930 | 3 | H | 1-0 |

**v Sunderland**

| | | | |
|---|---|---|---|
| 1954 | 3 | A | 2-0 |

**v Swansea City**

| | | | |
|---|---|---|---|
| 1968 | 3 | H | 0-2 |

**v Tottenham Hotspur**

| | | | |
|---|---|---|---|
| 1956 | 5 | H | 0-2 |

**v Tranmere Rovers**

| | | | |
|---|---|---|---|
| 1959 | 2 | A | 2-1 |
| 1963 | 2 | H | 1-4 |
| 1964 | 1 | H | 3-0 |
| 1974 | 2 | H | 3-0 |

v **Watford**
1955 3 A 2-1

v **West Bromwich Albion**
1957 3 H 1-1
1957 3r A 0-2

v **Wigan Athletic**
1966 1 H 2-2
1966 1r A 1-3
1986 1 A 1-4

v **York City**
1968 1 A 1-0

# Everton

v **Exeter City**
1986 3 H 1-0
2000 3 A 0-0
2000 3r H 1-0

v **Fulham**
1926 3 H 1-1
1926 3r A 0-1
1948 5 A 1-1aet
1948 5r H 0-1
1975 5 H 1-2

v **Gillingham**
1984 4 H 0-0
1984 4r A 0-0aet
1984 4r2 A 3-0

v **Grimsby Town**
1931 5 H 5-3
1935 3 H 6-3
1948 3 A 4-1

v **Hull City**
1927 4 A 1-1
1927 4r H 2-2aet
1927 4r2 N 2-3aet
1951 3 A 0-2
1964 3 A 1-1
1964 3r H 2-1

v **Ipswich Town**
1953 3 H 3-2
1969 3 H 2-1
1980 6 H 2-1
1985 6 H 2-2
1985 6r A 1-0
1999 4 H 1-0

v **Leeds Utd**
1933 5 H 2-0
1964 4 A 1-1
1964 4r H 2-0
1965 4 A 1-1
1965 4r H 1-2
1968 SF N 1-0
1985 3 A 2-0

v **Leicester City**
1933 3 A 3-2
1968 6 A 3-1

v **Leyton Orient**
1912 1 A 2-1
1952 3 A 0-0
1952 3r H 1-3
2002 4 H 4-1

v **Liverpool**
1902 1 A 2-2
1902 1r H 0-2
1905 1 A 1-1
1905 1r H 2-1
1906 SF N 2-0
1911 2 H 2-1
1932 3 H 1-2
1950 SF N 0-2
1955 4 H 0-4
1967 5 H 1-0
1971 SF N 1-2
1977 SF N 2-2
1977 SFr N 0-3
1981 4 H 2-1
1986 F N 1-3
1988 5 H 0-1
1989 F N 2-3aet
1991 5 A 0-0
1991 5r H 4-4aet
1991 5r2 H 1-0

v **Luton Town**
1933 6 H 6-0
1985 SF N 2-1aet
1986 6 A 2-2
1986 6r H 1-0

v **Manchester City**
1933 F N 3-0
1949 3 H 1-0
1956 6 A 1-2
1962 4 H 2-0
1966 6 A 0-0
1966 6r H 0-0aet
1966 6r2 N 2-0
1969 SF N 0-1
1981 6 H 2-2
1981 6r A 1-3

v **Manchester Utd**
1903 2 H 3-1
1909 2 A 0-1
1953 5 H 2-1
1957 5 A 0-1
1966 SF N 1-0
1969 6 A 1-0
1983 6 A 0-1
1985 F N 0-1aet
1995 F N 1-0

v **Middlesbrough**
1910 1 A 1-1
1910 1r H 5-3
1971 4 H 3-0
1978 4 A 2-3
1988 4 H 1-1
1988 4r A 2-2aet
1988 4r2 H 2-1
1990 3 A 0-0
1990 3r H 1-1aet
1990 3r2 H 1-0
2002 6 A 0-3

v **Millwall**
1903 3 A 0-1
1973 4 H 0-2

v **Newcastle Utd**
1906 F N 1-0
1921 3 H 3-0
1995 6 H 1-0
1998 3 H 0-1
1999 6 A 1-4

v **Norwich City**
1989 SF N 1-0
1995 5 H 5-0

v **Nottingham Forest**
1893 2 H 4-2
1896 1 A 2-0
1899 2 H 0-1
1953 4 H 4-1
1967 6 A 2-3

v **Notts County**
1954 3 H 2-1
1984 6 A 2-1

v **Oldham Athletic**
1908 2 A 0-0
1908 2r H 6-1
1912 3 A 2-0
1913 4 H 0-1
1990 5 A 2-2
1990 5r H 1-1aet
1990 5r2 A 1-2aet

v **Plymouth Argyle**
1931 3 A 2-0
1975 4 A 3-1
1989 4 A 1-1
1989 4r H 4-0

v **Port Vale**
1956 4 A 3-2
1996 4 H 2-2
1996 4r A 1-2

v **Portsmouth**
1903 1 H 5-0

v **Preston North End**
1893 SF N 2-2
1893 SFr N 0-0
1893 SFr2 N 2-1
1924 1 H 3-1
1928 3 A 3-0
1936 3 H 1-3
1946 3 A 1-2
1946 3s H 2-2aet
2000 5 H 2-0

v **QPR**
1915 3 N 2-1
1950 3 A 2-0

v **Sheffield Utd**
1896 2 H 3-0
1901 2 A 0-2
1907 1 H 1-0
1925 3 A 0-1
1961 3 H 0-1
1970 3 A 1-2

v **Sheffield Wed**
1893 3 H 3-0
1895 3 A 0-2
1896 3 A 0-4
1906 4 H 4-3
1907 F N 1-2

| | | | |
|---|---|---|---|
| 1921 | 2 | H | 1-1 |
| 1921 | 2r | A | 1-0 |
| 1937 | 4 | H | 3-0 |
| 1947 | 4 | A | 1-2 |
| 1954 | 5 | A | 1-3 |
| 1965 | 3 | H | 2-2 |
| 1965 | 3r | A | 3-0 |
| 1966 | F | N | 3-2 |
| 1986 | SF | N | 2-1aet |
| 1988 | 3 | A | 1-1 |
| 1988 | 3r | H | 1-1aet |
| 1988 | 3r2 | H | 1-1aet |
| 1988 | 3r3 | A | 5-0 |
| 1990 | 4 | A | 2-1 |

**v Shrewsbury Town**

| | | | |
|---|---|---|---|
| 1983 | 4 | H | 2-1 |
| 1984 | 5 | H | 3-0 |
| 2003 | 3 | A | 1-2 |

**v Southampton**

| | | | |
|---|---|---|---|
| 1900 | 1 | A | 0-3 |
| 1901 | 1 | A | 3-1 |
| 1905 | 3 | H | 4-0 |
| 1908 | 4 | H | 0-0 |
| 1908 | 4r | A | 2-3 |
| 1981 | 5 | A | 0-0 |
| 1981 | 5r | H | 1-0aet |
| 1984 | SF | N | 1-0aet |
| 1987 | 3 | H | 2-1 |

**v Southend Utd**

| | | | |
|---|---|---|---|
| 1947 | 3 | H | 4-2 |
| 1955 | 3 | H | 3-1 |
| 1992 | 3 | H | 1-0 |

**v Stockport County**

| | | | |
|---|---|---|---|
| 1913 | 1 | H | 5-1 |
| 1921 | 1 | H | 1-0 |
| 1996 | 3 | H | 2-2 |
| 1996 | 3r | A | 3-2 |

**v Stoke City**

| | | | |
|---|---|---|---|
| 1890 | 2 | A | 2-4 |
| 1894 | 1 | A | 0-1 |
| 1898 | 2 | A | 0-0 |
| 1898 | 2r | H | 5-1 |
| 1905 | 2 | A | 4-0 |
| 1977 | 3 | H | 2-0 |
| 1984 | 3 | A | 2-0 |
| 2002 | 3 | A | 1-0 |

**v Sunderland**

| | | | |
|---|---|---|---|
| 1891 | 1 | A | 0-1 |
| 1910 | 3 | H | 2-0 |
| 1925 | 2 | A | 0-0 |
| 1925 | 2r | H | 2-1 |
| 1935 | 4 | A | 1-1 |
| 1935 | 4r | H | 6-4 |
| 1938 | 4 | H | 0-1 |
| 1958 | 3 | A | 2-2 |
| 1958 | 3r | H | 3-1 |
| 1959 | 3 | H | 4-0 |
| 1964 | 5 | A | 1-3 |
| 1966 | 3 | H | 3-0 |
| 1979 | 3 | A | 1-2 |

**v Swansea City**

| | | | |
|---|---|---|---|
| 1954 | 4 | H | 3-0 |

**v Swindon Town**

| | | | |
|---|---|---|---|
| 1912 | 4 | A | 1-2 |
| 1963 | 4 | A | 5-1 |
| 1977 | 4 | A | 2-2 |
| 1977 | 4r | H | 2-1 |
| 1997 | 3 | H | 3-0 |

**v Tottenham Hotspur**

| | | | |
|---|---|---|---|
| 1904 | 1 | H | 1-2 |
| 1908 | 1 | H | 1-0 |
| 1934 | 3 | A | 0-3 |
| 1937 | 5 | H | 1-1 |
| 1937 | 5r | A | 3-4 |
| 1950 | 5 | H | 1-0 |
| 1972 | 5 | H | 0-2 |
| 1983 | 5 | H | 2-0 |
| 1986 | 5 | A | 2-1 |
| 1995 | SF | N | 4-1 |

**v Tranmere Rovers**

| | | | |
|---|---|---|---|
| 1968 | 5 | H | 2-0 |
| 2001 | 4 | H | 0-3 |

**v Walsall**

| | | | |
|---|---|---|---|
| 1972 | 4 | H | 2-1 |

**v Watford**

| | | | |
|---|---|---|---|
| 1984 | F | N | 2-0 |
| 2001 | 3 | A | 2-1 |

**v West Bromwich Albion**

| | | | |
|---|---|---|---|
| 1893 | 1 | H | 4-1 |
| 1906 | 1 | H | 3-1 |
| 1907 | SF | N | 2-1 |
| 1931 | SF | N | 0-1 |
| 1968 | F | N | 0-1aet |
| 1974 | 4 | H | 0-0 |
| 1974 | 4r | A | 0-1 |
| 1989 | 3 | A | 1-1 |
| 1989 | 3r | H | 1-0 |

**v West Ham Utd**

| | | | |
|---|---|---|---|
| 1907 | 2 | A | 2-1 |
| 1933 | SF | N | 2-1 |
| 1950 | 4 | A | 2-1 |
| 1957 | 4 | H | 2-1 |
| 1963 | 5 | A | 0-1 |
| 1980 | SF | N | 1-1 |
| 1980 | SFr | N | 1-2 |
| 1982 | 3 | A | 1-2 |
| 1991 | 6 | A | 1-2 |

**v Wigan Athletic**

| | | | |
|---|---|---|---|
| 1980 | 4 | H | 3-0 |

**v Wimbledon**

| | | | |
|---|---|---|---|
| 1987 | 5 | A | 1-3 |
| 1989 | 6 | H | 1-0 |
| 1993 | 3 | A | 0-0 |
| 1993 | 3r | H | 1-2 |

**v Wolverhampton W**

| | | | |
|---|---|---|---|
| 1893 | F | N | 0-1 |
| 1921 | 4 | H | 0-1 |
| 1939 | 6 | A | 0-2 |
| 1948 | 4 | A | 1-1aet |
| 1948 | 4r | H | 3-2aet |
| 1967 | 4 | A | 1-1 |
| 1967 | 4r | H | 3-1 |

**v Wrexham**

| | | | |
|---|---|---|---|
| 1980 | 5 | H | 5-2 |

# Exeter City

**v Fulham**

| | | | |
|---|---|---|---|
| 1970 | 1 | H | 2-0 |

**v Gillingham**

| | | | |
|---|---|---|---|
| 1936 | 1 | H | 0-4 |

**v Grimsby Town**

| | | | |
|---|---|---|---|
| 1924 | 1 | H | 1-0 |
| 1932 | 3 | A | 1-4 |
| 1949 | 3 | A | 1-2 |
| 1951 | 3 | A | 3-3 |
| 1951 | 3r | H | 4-2 |

**v Hull City**

| | | | |
|---|---|---|---|
| 1938 | 2 | H | 1-2 |

**v Ipswich Town**

| | | | |
|---|---|---|---|
| 1952 | 2 | A | 0-4 |

**v Kidderminster H**

| | | | |
|---|---|---|---|
| 1993 | 1 | H | 1-0 |

**v Leeds Utd**

| | | | |
|---|---|---|---|
| 1929 | 3 | H | 2-2 |
| 1929 | 3r | A | 1-5 |
| 1931 | 5 | H | 3-1 |

**v Leicester City**

| | | | |
|---|---|---|---|
| 1937 | 4 | H | 3-1 |
| 1981 | 4 | A | 1-1 |
| 1981 | 4r | H | 3-1 |

**v Leyton Orient**

| | | | |
|---|---|---|---|
| 1988 | 1 | A | 0-2 |
| 1994 | 2 | A | 1-1 |
| 1994 | 2r | H | 2-2p |

**v Liverpool**

| | | | |
|---|---|---|---|
| 1950 | 4 | A | 1-3 |

**v Luton Town**

| | | | |
|---|---|---|---|
| 1960 | 3 | H | 1-2 |
| 1967 | 1 | H | 1-1 |
| 1967 | 1r | A | 0-2 |

**v Manchester Utd**

| | | | |
|---|---|---|---|
| 1969 | 3 | H | 1-3 |

**v Millwall**

| | | | |
|---|---|---|---|
| 1950 | 1 | A | 5-3 |
| 1955 | 1 | A | 2-3 |
| 1981 | 2 | A | 1-0 |

**v Newcastle Utd**

| | | | |
|---|---|---|---|
| 1981 | 5 | A | 1-1 |
| 1981 | 5r | H | 4-0 |

**v Northampton Town**

| | | | |
|---|---|---|---|
| 1927 | 2 | H | 1-0 |
| 1934 | 1 | A | 0-2 |
| 1948 | 1 | H | 1-1aet |
| 1948 | 1r | A | 0-2 |
| 1970 | 2 | A | 1-1 |
| 1970 | 2r | H | 0-0aet |
| 1970 | 2r2 | N | 1-2 |
| 1998 | 1 | H | 1-1 |
| 1998 | 1r | A | 1-2 |

**v Norwich City**

| | | | |
|---|---|---|---|
| 1990 | 3 | H | 1-1 |
| 1990 | 3r | A | 0-2 |

**v Oldham Athletic**

| | | | |
|---|---|---|---|
| 1937 | 3 | H | 3-0 |

**v Peterborough**

| | | | |
|---|---|---|---|
| 1996 | 1 | H | 0-1 |

**v Plymouth Argyle**

| | | | |
|---|---|---|---|
| 1909 | 2 | A | 0-2 |
| 1957 | 1 | H | 0-2 |
| 1983 | 1 | A | 0-2 |

| | | | |
|---|---|---|---|
| 1997 | 2 | A | 1-4 |

**v Port Vale**

| | | | |
|---|---|---|---|
| 1953 | 1 | A | 1-2 |

**v Portsmouth**

| | | | |
|---|---|---|---|
| 1914 | 1 | A | 4-0 |
| 1992 | 3 | H | 1-2 |

**v Preston North End**

| | | | |
|---|---|---|---|
| 1937 | 5 | A | 3-5 |

**v Reading**

| | | | |
|---|---|---|---|
| 1911 | Q4 | A | 1-1 |
| 1911 | Q4r | H | 1-0 |

**v Rotherham Utd**

| | | | |
|---|---|---|---|
| 1928 | 3 | A | 3-3 |
| 1928 | 3r | H | 3-1 |

**v Rushden & Diamonds**

| | | | |
|---|---|---|---|
| 2003 | 2 | H | 3-1 |

**v Shrewsbury Town**

| | | | |
|---|---|---|---|
| 1964 | 1 | H | 2-1 |
| 1965 | 2 | H | 1-2 |

**v Southampton**

| | | | |
|---|---|---|---|
| 1925 | 1 | A | 1-3 |

**v Southend Utd**

| | | | |
|---|---|---|---|
| 1933 | 1 | A | 1-1 |
| 1933 | 1r | H | 0-1 |
| 1977 | 1 | H | 1-1 |
| 1977 | 1r | A | 1-2aet |

**v Stoke City**

| | | | |
|---|---|---|---|
| 1910 | Q5 | A | 0-0 |
| 1910 | Q5r | H | 1-1aet |
| 1910 | Q5r2 | N | 1-2 |
| 1956 | 3 | H | 0-0 |
| 1956 | 3r | A | 0-3 |

**v Sunderland**

| | | | |
|---|---|---|---|
| 1931 | 6 | A | 1-1 |
| 1931 | 6r | H | 2-4 |

**v Swansea City**

| | | | |
|---|---|---|---|
| 1926 | 1 | H | 1-3 |
| 1971 | 1 | A | 1-4 |
| 1972 | 2 | A | 0-0 |
| 1972 | 2r | H | 0-1 |
| 1992 | 2 | H | 0-0 |
| 1992 | 2r | A | 2-1 |
| 1993 | 2 | H | 2-5 |

**v Swindon Town**

| | | | |
|---|---|---|---|
| 1951 | 2 | H | 3-0 |

**v Torquay Utd**

| | | | |
|---|---|---|---|
| 1929 | 2 | A | 1-0 |
| 1939 | 1 | A | 1-3 |

**v Tottenham Hotspur**

| | | | |
|---|---|---|---|
| 1981 | 6 | A | 0-2 |

**v Walsall**

| | | | |
|---|---|---|---|
| 1930 | 1 | A | 0-1 |
| 1968 | 2 | H | 1-3 |
| 2001 | 1 | A | 0-4 |

**v Watford**

| | | | |
|---|---|---|---|
| 1921 | 1 | A | 0-3 |
| 1924 | 2 | H | 0-0 |
| 1924 | 2r | A | 0-1 |

**v Wolverhampton W**

| | | | |
|---|---|---|---|
| 1978 | 3 | H | 2-2 |
| 1978 | 3r | A | 1-3 |

**v Wrexham**

| | | | |
|---|---|---|---|
| 1909 | 1 | A | 1-1 |
| 1909 | 1r | H | 2-1aet |

**v Yeovil Town**

| | | | |
|---|---|---|---|
| 1935 | 2 | A | 1-4 |

# Fulham

**v Gillingham**

| | | | |
|---|---|---|---|
| 1988 | 1 | A | 1-2 |
| 1995 | 2 | A | 1-1 |
| 1995 | 2r | H | 1-2aet |

**v Grimsby Town**

| | | | |
|---|---|---|---|
| 1954 | 3 | A | 5-5 |
| 1954 | 3r | H | 3-1 |

**v Hartlepool Utd**

| | | | |
|---|---|---|---|
| 1962 | 3 | H | 3-1 |
| 1999 | 2 | H | 4-2 |

**v Huddersfield Town**

| | | | |
|---|---|---|---|
| 1972 | 4 | A | 0-3 |
| 1976 | 3 | H | 2-3 |

**v Hull City**

| | | | |
|---|---|---|---|
| 1913 | 1 | H | 0-2 |
| 1960 | 3 | H | 5-0 |
| 1975 | 3 | H | 1-1 |
| 1975 | 3r | A | 2-2aet |
| 1975 | 3r2 | N | 1-0 |

**v Ipswich Town**

| | | | |
|---|---|---|---|
| 1957 | 3 | A | 3-2 |

**v Leicester City**

| | | | |
|---|---|---|---|
| 1922 | 2 | A | 0-2 |
| 1923 | 1 | A | 0-4 |
| 1960 | 4 | A | 1-2 |
| 1974 | 4 | H | 1-1 |
| 1974 | 4r | A | 1-2aet |

**v Leyton Orient**

| | | | |
|---|---|---|---|
| 1954 | 4 | A | 1-2 |

**v Lincoln City**

| | | | |
|---|---|---|---|
| 1921 | 2 | A | 0-0 |
| 1921 | 2r | H | 1-0 |

**v Liverpool**

| | | | |
|---|---|---|---|
| 1912 | 2 | H | 3-0 |
| 1926 | 4 | H | 3-1 |
| 1934 | 3 | A | 1-1 |
| 1934 | 3r | H | 2-3aet |

**v Luton Town**

| | | | |
|---|---|---|---|
| 1903 | Q5 | A | 1-6 |
| 1904 | Q5 | H | 3-1 |
| 1905 | Q6 | H | 4-0 |
| 1908 | 1 | A | 8-3 |
| 1929 | 2 | H | 0-0 |
| 1929 | 2r | A | 1-4 |
| 1964 | 3 | H | 4-1 |
| 2000 | 3 | H | 2-2 |
| 2000 | 3r | A | 3-0 |

**v Macclesfield**

| | | | |
|---|---|---|---|
| 1968 | 3 | H | 4-2 |

**v Manchester City**

| | | | |
|---|---|---|---|
| 1908 | 3 | A | 1-1 |
| 1908 | 3r | H | 3-1 |
| 1914 | 1 | A | 0-2 |

**v Manchester Utd**

| | | | |
|---|---|---|---|
| 1905 | IR | A | 2-2 |
| 1905 | IRr | H | 0-0aet |
| 1905 | IRr2 | N | 1-0 |
| 1908 | 4 | H | 2-1 |
| 1926 | 6 | H | 1-2 |
| 1958 | SF | N | 2-2 |
| 1958 | SFr | N | 3-5 |
| 1979 | 4 | H | 1-1 |
| 1979 | 4r | A | 0-1 |
| 1999 | 5 | A | 0-1 |
| 2001 | 3 | H | 1-2 |

**v Millwall**

| | | | |
|---|---|---|---|
| 1937 | 3 | A | 0-2 |
| 1951 | 4 | A | 1-0 |
| 1965 | 3 | H | 3-3 |
| 1965 | 3r | A | 0-2 |

**v Newcastle Utd**

| | | | |
|---|---|---|---|
| 1908 | SF | N | 0-6 |
| 1910 | 2 | A | 0-4 |
| 1956 | 4 | H | 4-5 |
| 1961 | 3 | A | 0-5 |

**v Northampton Town**

| | | | |
|---|---|---|---|
| 1912 | 3 | H | 2-1 |
| 1993 | 1 | A | 1-3 |

**v Norwich City**

| | | | |
|---|---|---|---|
| 1908 | 2 | H | 2-1 |

**v Nottingham Forest**

| | | | |
|---|---|---|---|
| 1905 | 2 | H | 1-0 |
| 1906 | 2 | H | 1-3 |
| 1930 | 4 | A | 1-2 |
| 1975 | 4 | H | 0-0 |
| 1975 | 4r | A | 1-1aet |
| 1975 | 4r2 | H | 1-1aet |
| 1975 | 4r3 | A | 2-1 |

**v Notts County**

| | | | |
|---|---|---|---|
| 1926 | 5 | A | 1-0 |
| 1956 | 3 | A | 1-0 |

**v Oldham Athletic**

| | | | |
|---|---|---|---|
| 1983 | 3 | A | 2-0 |

**v Peterborough**

| | | | |
|---|---|---|---|
| 1959 | 3 | H | 0-0 |
| 1959 | 3r | A | 1-0 |

**v Plymouth Argyle**

| | | | |
|---|---|---|---|
| 1922 | 1 | A | 1-1 |
| 1922 | 1r | H | 1-0 |
| 1997 | 1 | A | 0-5 |

**v Port Vale**

| | | | |
|---|---|---|---|
| 1962 | 5 | H | 1-0 |

**v Portsmouth**

| | | | |
|---|---|---|---|
| 1931 | 3 | H | 0-2 |
| 1968 | 4 | H | 0-0 |
| 1968 | 4r | A | 0-1 |

**v Preston North End**

| | | | |
|---|---|---|---|
| 1955 | 3 | H | 2-3 |
| 1974 | 3 | H | 1-0 |

**v QPR**

| | | | |
|---|---|---|---|
| 1900 | Q1 | A | 0-3 |
| 1901 | Q3 | A | 0-7 |
| 1904 | Q3 | A | 1-1 |
| 1904 | Q3r | H | 3-1 |
| 1906 | 1 | H | 1-0 |
| 1972 | 3 | A | 1-1 |

1972 3r H 2-1
1979 3 H 2-0

v **Reading**
1905 1 H 0-0
1905 1r A 0-0aet
1905 1r2 N 1-0aet
1981 1 A 2-1

v **Sheffield Utd**
1936 SF N 1-2
1966 3 A 1-3
1967 4 H 1-1
1967 4r A 1-3
1986 3 A 0-2

v **Sheffield Wed**
1951 3 H 1-0
1973 3 A 0-2
1985 3 H 2-3

v **Shrewsbury Town**
1996 3 H 1-1
1996 3r A 1-2

v **Southampton**
1915 2 H 2-3aet
1999 3 A 1-1
1999 3r H 1-0

v **Southend Utd**
1998 2 H 1-0

v **Stockport County**
1907 1 H 0-0
1907 1r H 2-1

v **Sunderland**
1935 3 A 2-3
1969 3 A 4-1

v **Swansea City**
1996 1 H 7-0

v **Swindon Town**
1920 1 H 1-2
1925 1 A 2-1
1977 3 H 3-3
1977 3r A 0-5
1987 3 H 0-1

v **Tottenham Hotspur**
1909 2 A 0-1
1984 3 H 0-0
1984 3r A 0-2
1998 3 A 1-3

v **Tranmere Rovers**
2000 5 H 1-2

v **Walsall**
1949 3 H 0-1aet
1962 4 H 2-2
1962 4r A 2-0
2002 5 A 2-1

v **Watford**
1903 Q3 A 1-1
1903 Q3r H 3-0
1932 3 A 1-1
1932 3r H 0-3
1983 4 A 1-1
1983 4r H 1-2

v **West Bromwich Albion**
1911 1 A 1-4
1912 4 A 0-3
1969 4 H 1-2
2002 6 A 1-0

v **West Ham Utd**
1904 IR A 1-0
1958 5 A 3-2
1963 3 A 0-0
1963 3r H 1-2
1975 F N 0-2

v **Wimbledon**
1931 1 H 1-1
1931 1r A 6-0
2000 4 H 3-0

v **Wolverhampton W**
1921 3 H 0-1

v **Wycombe W**
2002 3 A 2-2
2002 3r H 1-0

v **Yeovil Town**
1932 2 H 0-0
1932 2r A 5-2
1958 3 H 4-0
1994 1 A 0-1

v **York City**
2002 4 A 2-0

# Gillingham

v **Huddersfield Town**
1993 3 H 0-0
1993 3r A 1-2

v **Ipswich Town**
1985 4 A 2-3

v **Leeds Utd**
2003 4 H 1-1
2003 4r A 1-2

v **Leyton Orient**
1948 1 H 1-0
1961 3 H 2-6
1969 1 A 1-1
1969 1r H 2-1

v **Liverpool**
1914 2 A 0-2

v **Luton Town**
1965 2 A 0-1
1969 2 A 1-3

v **Manchester City**
1908 2 A 1-1
1908 2r H 1-2

v **Millwall**
1895 Q3 H 0-2
1896 Q1 H 0-1
1958 2 A 1-1
1958 2r H 6-1

v **Northampton Town**
1906 1 H 2-1
1921 Q6 A 1-3
1983 2 H 1-1
1983 2r A 2-3
1986 1 H 3-0

v **Nottingham Forest**
1958 3 A 0-2

v **Oldham Athletic**
1922 1 H 1-3
1982 3 H 2-1
1999 1 A 0-2

v **Peterborough**
1970 4 H 5-1
1978 2 H 1-1
1978 2r A 0-2
1989 1 H 3-3
1989 1r A 0-1aet

v **Plymouth Argyle**
1928 1 H 2-1
1959 1 A 2-2
1959 1r H 1-4
1972 1 H 3-2
1982 1 A 0-0
1982 1r H 1-0
1994 2 A 0-2

v **Port Vale**
1963 3 H 2-4

v **QPR**
1948 3 H 1-1aet
1948 3r A 1-3
1964 1 A 1-4

v **Reading**
1955 2 H 1-1
1955 2r A 3-5
1973 1 H 1-2
1979 1 A 0-0
1979 1r H 1-2aet
1996 3 A 1-3

v **Rochdale**
1915 1 A 0-2
1948 2 A 1-1aet
1948 2r H 3-0
1952 2 H 0-3

v **Sheffield Wed**
1995 3 H 1-2
2000 5 H 3-1
2003 3 H 4-1

v **Shrewsbury Town**
1956 1 H 1-1
1956 1r A 1-4aet

v **Southampton**
1899 1 H 0-1
1906 2 H 0-0
1906 2r A 0-1

v **Southend Utd**
1926 2 A 0-1
1928 2 H 2-0
1961 2 H 3-2
1970 1 A 0-0
1970 1r H 2-1

v **Stockport County**
1953 2 A 1-3

v **Stoke City**
1928 3 A 1-6

v **Sunderland**
1908 1 H 3-1

**v Swansea City**

| | | | |
|---|---|---|---|
| 1920 | Q6 | H | 1-1 |
| 1920 | Q6r | A | 1-1 |
| 1920 | Q6r2 | N | 0-0 |
| 1920 | Q6r3 | N | 3-1 |
| 1947 | 3 | A | 1-4 |
| 1960 | 3 | H | 1-4 |
| 1972 | 3 | A | 0-1 |

**v Swindon Town**

| | | | |
|---|---|---|---|
| 1938 | 1 | H | 3-4 |

**v Torquay Utd**

| | | | |
|---|---|---|---|
| 1929 | 1 | H | 0-0 |
| 1929 | 1r | A | 1-5 |
| 1960 | 2 | H | 2-2 |
| 1960 | 2r | A | 2-1 |

**v Tranmere Rovers**

| | | | |
|---|---|---|---|
| 1924 | Q6 | H | 1-0 |

**v Walsall**

| | | | |
|---|---|---|---|
| 1902 | IR | A | 0-2 |
| 1967 | 2 | A | 1-3 |
| 1988 | 2 | H | 2-1 |
| 2000 | 3 | A | 1-1 |
| 2000 | 3r | H | 2-1aet |

**v Watford**

| | | | |
|---|---|---|---|
| 1914 | Q5 | H | 1-0 |
| 1970 | 5 | A | 1-2 |
| 1977 | 1 | H | 0-1 |

**v West Bromwich Albion**

| | | | |
|---|---|---|---|
| 1982 | 4 | H | 0-1 |

**v West Ham Utd**

| | | | |
|---|---|---|---|
| 1900 | Q4 | H | 0-0 |
| 1900 | Q4r | A | 0-2 |
| 1901 | Q4 | H | 1-1 |
| 1901 | Q4r | A | 1-4 |

**v Wigan Athletic**

| | | | |
|---|---|---|---|
| 1987 | 3 | A | 1-2 |

**v Wimbledon**

| | | | |
|---|---|---|---|
| 1980 | 1 | H | 0-0 |
| 1980 | 1r | A | 2-4 |

**v Wolverhampton W**

| | | | |
|---|---|---|---|
| 2002 | 3 | A | 1-0 |

**v Wrexham**

| | | | |
|---|---|---|---|
| 1937 | 2 | A | 0-2 |

**v Wycombe W**

| | | | |
|---|---|---|---|
| 1933 | 1 | H | 1-1 |
| 1933 | 1r | A | 4-2 |
| 1996 | 1 | A | 1-1 |
| 1996 | 1r | H | 1-0 |

**v Yeovil Town**

| | | | |
|---|---|---|---|
| 1950 | 2 | A | 1-3 |

# Grimsby Town

**v Hartlepool Utd**

| | | | |
|---|---|---|---|
| 1936 | 3 | A | 0-0 |
| 1936 | 3r | H | 4-1 |
| 1979 | 1 | A | 0-1 |

**v Huddersfield Town**

| | | | |
|---|---|---|---|
| 1975 | 1 | H | 1-0 |
| 1990 | 3 | A | 1-3 |

**v Hull City**

| | | | |
|---|---|---|---|
| 1949 | 4 | H | 2-3 |

**v Ipswich Town**

| | | | |
|---|---|---|---|
| 1983 | 4 | A | 0-2 |
| 1993 | 5 | A | 0-4 |

**v Leeds Utd**

| | | | |
|---|---|---|---|
| 1998 | 4 | A | 0-2 |

**v Leicester City**

| | | | |
|---|---|---|---|
| 1963 | 3 | H | 1-3 |

**v Leyton Orient**

| | | | |
|---|---|---|---|
| 1934 | 3 | H | 1-0 |

**v Lincoln City**

| | | | |
|---|---|---|---|
| 1885 | 3 | H | 1-0 |
| 1886 | 1 | A | 2-0 |
| 1888 | 3 | H | 2-0 |
| 1889 | Q1 | H | 1-1aet |
| 1889 | Q1r | A | 1-1aet |
| 1889 | Q1r2 | N | 3-1 |
| 1893 | Q4 | H | 5-0 |
| 1894 | Q2 | A | 5-2 |
| 1895 | Q1 | A | 3-0 |
| 1896 | Q3 | A | 4-2 |
| 1899 | Q4 | H | 2-1 |
| 1912 | Q4 | A | 2-3 |
| 1952 | 2 | A | 1-3 |

**v Liverpool**

| | | | |
|---|---|---|---|
| 1894 | 1 | A | 0-3 |
| 1932 | 5 | A | 0-1 |
| 1947 | 4 | A | 0-2 |
| 1980 | 3 | A | 0-5 |

**v Luton Town**

| | | | |
|---|---|---|---|
| 1950 | 3 | A | 4-3 |
| 1996 | 3 | H | 7-1 |

**v Manchester City**

| | | | |
|---|---|---|---|
| 1936 | 5 | H | 3-2 |
| 1959 | 3 | H | 2-2 |
| 1959 | 3r | A | 2-1 |
| 1966 | 4 | A | 0-2 |

**v Manchester Utd**

| | | | |
|---|---|---|---|
| 1931 | 4 | H | 1-0 |

**v Mansfield Town**

| | | | |
|---|---|---|---|
| 1962 | 1 | A | 2-3 |

**v Middlesbrough**

| | | | |
|---|---|---|---|
| 1886 | 3 | A | 1-2 |
| 1901 | IR | H | 0-1 |
| 1936 | 6 | H | 3-1 |
| 1989 | 3 | A | 2-1 |

**v Millwall**

| | | | |
|---|---|---|---|
| 1939 | 4 | A | 2-2 |
| 1939 | 4r | H | 3-2 |
| 1982 | 3 | A | 6-1 |

**v Newcastle Utd**

| | | | |
|---|---|---|---|
| 1903 | 1 | H | 2-1 |
| 1906 | 1 | A | 0-6 |
| 1908 | 4 | A | 1-5 |
| 1982 | 4 | A | 2-1 |

**v Northampton Town**

| | | | |
|---|---|---|---|
| 1915 | 1 | H | 0-3 |

**v Norwich City**

| | | | |
|---|---|---|---|
| 1921 | 1 | H | 1-0 |
| 1995 | 3 | H | 0-1 |
| 1998 | 3 | H | 3-0 |

**v Nottingham Forest**

| | | | |
|---|---|---|---|
| 1887 | 2 | A | 2-2 |
| 1887 | 2r | H | 0-1 |
| 1898 | 1 | A | 0-4 |
| 1900 | 1 | A | 0-3 |
| 1959 | 4 | A | 1-4 |

**v Notts County**

| | | | |
|---|---|---|---|
| 1903 | 2 | H | 0-2 |
| 1922 | 1 | H | 1-1 |
| 1922 | 1r | A | 0-3 |
| 1985 | 3 | A | 2-2 |
| 1985 | 3r | H | 4-2 |

**v Port Vale**

| | | | |
|---|---|---|---|
| 1936 | 4 | A | 4-0 |

**v Portsmouth**

| | | | |
|---|---|---|---|
| 1902 | 1 | H | 1-1 |
| 1902 | 1r | A | 0-2 |
| 1933 | 3 | H | 3-2 |
| 1934 | 4 | A | 0-2 |
| 1950 | 4 | A | 0-5 |
| 1956 | 3 | A | 1-3 |
| 1966 | 3 | H | 0-0 |
| 1966 | 3r | A | 3-1 |
| 1984 | 3 | A | 1-2 |

**v Preston North End**

| | | | |
|---|---|---|---|
| 1889 | 2 | H | 0-2 |
| 1899 | 1 | A | 0-7 |
| 1904 | 1 | A | 0-1 |
| 1973 | 3 | H | 0-0 |
| 1973 | 3r | A | 1-0 |

**v QPR**

| | | | |
|---|---|---|---|
| 1982 | 5 | A | 1-3 |

**v Reading**

| | | | |
|---|---|---|---|
| 1928 | 3 | A | 0-4 |
| 1947 | 3 | A | 2-2 |
| 1947 | 3r | H | 3-1 |
| 1989 | 4 | H | 1-1 |
| 1989 | 4r | A | 2-1 |

**v Rochdale**

| | | | |
|---|---|---|---|
| 1954 | 1 | H | 2-0 |

**v Rotherham Utd**

| | | | |
|---|---|---|---|
| 1989 | 2 | H | 3-2 |

**v Scunthorpe Utd**

| | | | |
|---|---|---|---|
| 1983 | 3 | A | 0-0 |
| 1983 | 3r | H | 2-0 |

**v Sheffield Utd**

| | | | |
|---|---|---|---|
| 1892 | Q3 | H | 1-2 |
| 1939 | 5 | A | 0-0 |
| 1939 | 5r | H | 1-0 |
| 1958 | 3 | A | 1-5 |
| 1980 | 2 | H | 2-0 |

**v Sheffield Wed**

| | | | |
|---|---|---|---|
| 1913 | 1 | A | 1-5 |
| 1997 | 3 | A | 1-7 |

**v Shrewsbury Town**

| | | | |
|---|---|---|---|
| 1998 | 1 | A | 1-1 |
| 1998 | 1r | H | 4-0 |

**v Southampton**

| | | | |
|---|---|---|---|
| 1921 | 2 | H | 1-3 |
| 1955 | 2 | H | 4-1 |
| 1978 | 3 | H | 0-0 |
| 1978 | 3r | A | 0-0aet |
| 1978 | 3r2 | N | 1-4 |

v **Stockport County**
1909 1 H 0-2
1965 2 A 0-1
2000 3 H 3-2

v **Stoke City**
1905 1 A 0-2
1987 3 H 1-1
1987 3r A 1-1aet
1987 3r2 A 0-6

v **Sunderland**
1946 3 H 1-3
1946 3s A 1-2

v **Swansea City**
1993 4 A 0-0
1993 4r H 2-0

v **Swindon Town**
1938 3 H 1-1
1938 3r A 1-2aet

v **Tranmere Rovers**
1939 3 H 6-0

v **Walsall**
1926 1 A 1-0
1937 4 H 5-1

v **Watford**
1985 4 H 1-3

v **West Bromwich Albion**
1896 2 H 1-1
1896 2r A 0-3
1914 1 A 0-2
1929 3 H 1-1
1929 3r A 0-2
1981 3 A 0-3

v **West Ham Utd**
1957 3 A 3-5
1996 4 A 1-1
1996 4r H 3-0

v **Wigan Athletic**
1973 1 H 2-1
1994 3 H 1-0

v **Wimbledon**
1989 5 A 1-3

v **Wolverhampton W**
1937 5 H 1-1
1937 5r A 2-6
1939 SF N 0-5
1955 3 H 2-5
1989 1 H 1-0

v **Wrexham**
1960 2 H 2-3

v **Wycombe W**
2001 3 A 1-1
2001 3r H 1-3

v **York City**
1927 2 H 2-1
1972 1 A 2-4
1990 1 A 2-1
2002 3 H 0-0
2002 3r A 0-1

# Hartlepool Utd

v **Huddersfield Town**
1966 3 A 1-3
1990 1 H 0-2

v **Hull City**
1982 2 A 0-2

v **Ipswich Town**
1978 4 A 1-4
1992 3 A 1-1
1992 3r H 0-2

v **Leeds Utd**
1979 3 H 2-6

v **Lincoln City**
1964 1 H 0-1
1975 2 H 0-0
1975 2r A 0-1
1983 1 H 3-0

v **Luton Town**
1988 3 H 1-2

v **Macclesfield**
1986 1 A 2-1
1994 1 A 0-2
1998 1 H 2-4

v **Manchester City**
1976 3 A 0-6

v **Manchester Utd**
1957 3 H 3-4

v **Mansfield Town**
1936 1 A 3-2
1954 1 H 1-1
1954 1r A 3-0

v **Millwall**
2000 1 H 1-0

v **Newcastle Utd**
1925 1 A 1-4

v **Northampton Town**
1954 2 A 1-1
1954 2r H 1-0aet

v **Norwich City**
1950 2 H 1-1
1950 2r A 1-5

v **Nottingham Forest**
1955 4 H 1-1
1955 4r A 1-2aet

v **Notts County**
1989 2 H 1-0

v **Oldham Athletic**
1951 2 H 1-2

v **Port Vale**
1995 1 A 0-6

v **QPR**
1939 2 H 0-2

v **Rochdale**
1915 Q5 A 0-2
1947 2 A 1-6
1959 1 H 1-1
1959 1r A 3-3aet
1959 1r2 N 2-1

v **Rotherham Utd**
1937 1 A 4-4
1937 1r H 2-0
1969 1 H 1-1
1969 1r A 0-3
1984 1 A 0-0
1984 1r H 0-1aet

v **Scunthorpe Utd**
1930 1 A 0-1
1973 1 H 0-0
1973 1r A 0-0aet
1973 1r2 N 1-2aet
1981 1 A 1-3
2001 1 A 1-3

v **Sheffield Utd**
1993 4 A 0-1

v **Shrewsbury Town**
1967 1 A 2-5
1992 1 H 3-2

v **Southend Utd**
2003 1 A 1-1
2003 1r H 1-2

v **Stockport County**
1931 1 H 2-3
1958 2 A 1-2
1976 1 H 3-0

v **Stoke City**
1954 3 A 2-6

v **Swansea City**
1921 Q6 A 0-3

v **Swindon Town**
2002 1 A 1-2

v **Tranmere Rovers**
1938 2 A 1-3
1953 2 A 1-2
1978 1 A 1-1
1978 1r H 3-1

v **Walsall**
1933 2 A 1-2

v **Watford**
1952 2 A 2-1

v **Wigan Athletic**
1982 1 A 2-2
1982 1r H 1-0
1989 1 H 2-0
1991 2 A 0-2

v **Wrexham**
1923 Q6 A 0-1
1966 2 H 2-0
1970 2 H 0-1
1987 1 A 1-2

v **York City**
1934 1 A 3-2
1983 2 H 1-1
1983 2r A 0-4
1985 2 H 0-2
1988 2 A 1-1
1988 2r H 3-1
1997 1 H 0-0
1997 1r A 0-3

# Huddersfield Town

**v Hull City**
1938 3 H 3-1

**v Ipswich Town**
1959 3 A 0-1

**v Leeds Utd**
1929 4 H 3-0
1931 3 A 0-2
1939 4 A 4-2

**v Leyton Orient**
1982 4 H 1-1
1982 4r A 0-2

**v Lincoln City**
1911 Q4 H 1-1
1911 Q4r A 0-1
1928 3 H 4-2
1995 2 A 0-1

**v Liverpool**
1920 4 H 2-1
1938 5 A 1-0
1955 5 A 2-0
2000 3 H 0-2

**v Luton Town**
1960 4 H 0-1
1985 4 A 0-2

**v Manchester City**
1926 4 A 0-4
1988 3 H 2-2
1988 3r A 0-0aet
1988 3r2 H 0-3

**v Manchester Utd**
1912 1 A 1-3
1924 2 A 3-0
1963 3 A 0-5

**v Mansfield Town**
1977 1 H 0-0
1977 1r A 1-2
2002 2 A 0-4

**v Middlesbrough**
1928 5 H 4-0

**v Millwall**
1922 4 H 3-0
1923 2 A 0-0
1923 2r H 3-0
1927 3 A 1-3
1992 3 H 0-4

**v Newcastle Utd**
1920 2 A 1-0
1955 6 H 1-1
1955 6r A 0-2aet

**v Northampton Town**
1934 4 H 0-2

**v Norwich City**
1987 3 A 1-1
1987 3r H 2-4

**v Nottingham Forest**
1939 3 H 0-0
1939 3r A 3-0

**v Notts County**
1922 SF N 3-1
1938 4 H 1-0

**v Notts County**
1984 4 H 1-2

**v Oldham Athletic**
1932 3 A 1-1
1932 3r H 6-0

**v Peterborough**
1957 4 H 3-1
1996 4 H 2-0

**v Plymouth Argyle**
1920 3 H 3-1
1934 3 A 1-1
1934 3r H 6-2
1964 3 A 1-0
1966 4 A 2-0

**v Port Vale**
1976 2 H 2-1
1994 2 A 0-1

**v Portsmouth**
1935 3 A 1-1
1935 3r H 2-3
1939 SF N 1-2

**v Preston North End**
1922 F N 1-0
1932 5 H 4-0
1938 F N 0-1aet
1951 4 A 2-0

**v QPR**
1932 4 H 5-0
1949 3 A 0-0aet
1949 3r H 5-0
1984 3 H 2-1
1997 3 A 1-1
1997 3r H 1-2
1999 3 A 1-0

**v Reading**
1986 3 H 0-0
1986 3r A 1-2aet

**v Rochdale**
1989 1 H 1-1
1989 1r A 4-3
1992 2 A 2-1

**v Rotherham Utd**
1962 3 H 4-3

**v Scunthorpe Utd**
1993 1 A 0-0
1993 1r H 2-1aet

**v Sheffield Utd**
1913 1 H 3-1
1928 SF N 2-2
1928 SFr N 0-0aet
1928 SFr2 N 1-0
1930 4 H 2-1
1946 3 H 1-1
1946 3s A 0-2
1957 3 H 0-0
1957 3r A 1-1aet
1957 3r2 N 2-1
1989 3 H 0-1

**v Sheffield Wed**
1930 SF N 2-1
1966 5 H 1-2

**v Shrewsbury Town**
1981 3 H 0-3

**v Southend Utd**
1993 4 H 1-2

**v Stoke City**
1971 4 A 3-3
1971 4r H 0-0aet
1971 4r2 N 0-1

**v Sunderland**
1938 SF N 3-1
1950 3 A 0-6

**v Swansea City**
1965 4 A 0-1

**v Swindon Town**
1913 2 H 1-2
2003 1 A 0-1

**v Torquay Utd**
1955 4 A 1-0

**v Tottenham Hotspur**
1928 6 H 6-1
1936 4 A 0-1
1951 3 H 2-0

**v Tranmere Rovers**
1952 3 H 1-2
1968 3 A 1-2
1981 2 A 3-0

**v Walsall**
1939 5 H 3-0
1976 1 A 1-0

**v West Bromwich Albion**
1929 6 A 1-1
1929 6r H 2-1

**v West Ham Utd**
1928 4 H 2-1
1954 3 A 0-4
1960 3 H 1-1
1960 3r A 5-1
1969 4 H 0-2
1972 5 H 4-2

**v Wigan Athletic**
1974 1 H 2-0

**v Wimbledon**
1996 5 H 2-2
1996 5r A 1-3
1998 4 H 0-1

**v Wolverhampton W**
1951 5 A 0-2
1961 3 A 1-1
1961 3r H 2-1
1985 3 A 1-1
1985 3r H 3-1

**v Wrexham**
1999 4 A 1-1
1999 4r H 2-1

**v York City**
1938 6 A 0-0
1938 6r H 2-1

# Hull City

**v Kidderminster H**
1965 1 A 4-1

**v Leicester City**
1925 3 H 1-1
1925 3r A 1-3
1928 3 H 0-1
1978 3 H 0-1

**v Leyton Orient**
1963 3 A 1-1
1963 3r H 0-2aet

**v Lincoln City**
1965 2 H 1-1
1965 2r A 1-3
1995 1 H 0-1

**v Liverpool**
1989 5 H 2-3

**v Luton Town**
1999 2 A 2-1

**v Macclesfield**
2000 1 A 0-0
2000 1r H 4-0
2003 1 H 0-3

**v Manchester City**
1930 5 A 2-1
1934 4 H 2-2
1934 4r A 1-4
1970 3 H 0-1

**v Manchester Utd**
1949 6 H 0-1
1952 3 A 2-0

**v Mansfield Town**
1932 1 H 4-1

**v Middlesbrough**
1922 1 H 5-0
1948 3 H 1-3
1968 3 A 1-1
1968 3r H 2-2aet
1968 3r2 N 0-1

**v Newcastle Utd**
1911 3 A 2-3
1913 2 H 0-0
1913 2r A 0-3
1930 6 A 1-1
1930 6r H 1-0
1935 3 H 1-5
1990 3 H 0-1

**v Northampton Town**
1915 2 H 2-1

**v Norwich City**
1972 3 A 3-0

**v Nottingham Forest**
1922 2 A 0-3
1966 4 H 2-0

**v Notts County**
1991 3 H 2-5

**v Oldham Athletic**
1906 Q4 H 2-1
1911 2 H 1-0
1912 1 A 1-1
1912 1r H 0-1
2002 2 H 2-3

**v Plymouth Argyle**
1930 3 A 4-3
1976 3 H 1-1
1976 3r A 4-1
1986 3 H 2-2
1986 3r A 1-0

**v Port Vale**
1958 2 A 2-2
1958 2r H 4-3aet
1977 3 H 1-1
1977 3r A 1-3aet

**v Portsmouth**
1967 3 H 1-1
1967 3r A 2-2aet
1967 3r2 N 1-3

**v Preston North End**
1921 4 H 0-0
1921 4r A 0-1

**v Reading**
1906 1 H 0-1
1949 2 H 0-0aet
1949 2r A 2-1

**v Rochdale**
1982 1 A 2-2
1982 1r H 2-2aet
1982 1r2 N 1-0aet

**v Rotherham Utd**
1939 1 H 4-1
1951 4 H 2-0
1984 2 A 1-2
1993 2 A 0-1

**v Scunthorpe Utd**
1938 1 H 4-0

**v Sheffield Utd**
1983 1 H 1-1
1983 1r A 0-2

**v Sheffield Wed**
1958 4 A 3-4

**v Shrewsbury Town**
1987 3 A 2-1

**v Southampton**
1915 3 A 2-2aet
1915 3r H 4-0
1966 3 H 1-0

**v Stockport County**
1950 4 A 0-0
1950 4r H 0-2
1959 1 H 0-1
1973 3 A 0-0
1973 3r H 2-0aet

**v Stoke City**
1932 3 A 0-3
1949 5 A 2-0
1971 6 H 2-3
1972 5 A 1-4

**v Sunderland**
1920 1 A 2-6
1933 3 H 0-2
1976 4 A 0-1

**v Swansea City**
1987 4 A 1-0

**v Tottenham Hotspur**
1907 1 A 0-0
1907 1r H 0-0aet
1907 1r2 A 0-1
1954 5 H 1-1
1954 5r A 0-2
1981 4 A 0-2

**v Tranmere Rovers**
1985 2 A 3-0

**v Watford**
1988 3 A 1-1
1988 3r H 2-2aet
1988 3r2 A 0-1

**v West Bromwich Albion**
1915 1 H 1-0
1927 3 H 2-1
1936 3 A 0-2

**v West Ham Utd**
1923 1 H 2-3
1973 4 H 1-0

**v Wigan Athletic**
1987 5 A 0-3

**v Wolverhampton W**
1925 1 H 1-1
1925 1r A 1-0aet
1927 5 A 0-1
1969 3 H 1-3

**v Wrexham**
1964 2 A 2-0
1996 1 H 0-0
1996 1r A 0-0p

**v York City**
1937 1 A 2-5
1957 2 H 2-1

# Ipswich Town

**v Leeds Utd**
1975 6 H 0-0
1975 6r A 1-1aet
1975 6r2 N 0-0aet
1975 6r3 N 3-2
1990 3 A 1-0

**v Leicester City**
1963 4 A 1-3

**v Leyton Orient**
1951 1 A 2-1
1979 4 H 0-0
1979 4r A 2-0

**v Liverpool**
1974 5 A 0-2
1975 4 H 1-0
1979 6 H 0-1
1992 5 H 0-0
1992 5r A 2-3aet

v **Luton Town**

| | | | |
|---|---|---|---|
| 1959 | 5 | H | 2-5 |
| 1962 | 3 | H | 1-1 |
| 1962 | 3r | A | 1-1aet |
| 1962 | 3r2 | N | 5-1 |
| 1982 | 4 | A | 3-0 |

v **Manchester City**

| | | | |
|---|---|---|---|
| 1967 | 5 | A | 1-1 |
| 1967 | 5r | H | 0-3 |
| 1981 | SF | N | 0-1aet |
| 2002 | 4 | H | 1-4 |

v **Manchester Utd**

| | | | |
|---|---|---|---|
| 1958 | 4 | A | 0-2 |
| 1970 | 3 | H | 0-1 |
| 1974 | 4 | A | 1-0 |
| 1988 | 3 | H | 1-2 |

v **Mansfield Town**

| | | | |
|---|---|---|---|
| 1963 | 3 | A | 3-2 |

v **Millwall**

| | | | |
|---|---|---|---|
| 1978 | 6 | A | 6-1 |

v **Newcastle Utd**

| | | | |
|---|---|---|---|
| 1971 | 3 | A | 1-1 |
| 1971 | 3r | H | 2-1 |

v **Norwich City**

| | | | |
|---|---|---|---|
| 1962 | 4 | A | 1-1 |
| 1962 | 4r | H | 1-2 |
| 1983 | 5 | A | 0-1 |

v **Nottingham Forest**

| | | | |
|---|---|---|---|
| 1981 | 6 | A | 3-3 |
| 1981 | 6r | H | 1-0 |
| 1989 | 3 | A | 0-3 |
| 1997 | 3 | A | 0-3 |

v **Oldham Athletic**

| | | | |
|---|---|---|---|
| 1954 | 3 | H | 3-3 |
| 1954 | 3r | A | 1-0 |
| 1964 | 3 | H | 6-3 |

v **Peterborough**

| | | | |
|---|---|---|---|
| 1956 | 1 | A | 1-3 |
| 1960 | 3 | H | 2-3 |
| 1972 | 3 | A | 2-0 |

v **Plymouth Argyle**

| | | | |
|---|---|---|---|
| 1993 | 3 | H | 3-1 |

v **Preston North End**

| | | | |
|---|---|---|---|
| 1954 | 5 | A | 1-6 |
| 1980 | 3 | A | 3-0 |

v **QPR**

| | | | |
|---|---|---|---|
| 1946 | 2 | A | 0-4 |
| 1946 | 2s | H | 0-2 |

v **Reading**

| | | | |
|---|---|---|---|
| 1891 | Q1 | H | 2-0 |
| 1954 | 1 | H | 4-1 |

v **Sheffield Utd**

| | | | |
|---|---|---|---|
| 1974 | 3 | H | 3-2 |
| 1998 | 4 | H | 1-1 |
| 1998 | 4r | A | 0-1 |
| 2003 | 4 | A | 3-4 |

v **Sheffield Wed**

| | | | |
|---|---|---|---|
| 1985 | 5 | H | 3-2 |

v **Shrewsbury Town**

| | | | |
|---|---|---|---|
| 1967 | 3 | H | 4-1 |
| 1981 | 4 | A | 0-0 |
| 1981 | 4r | H | 3-0 |
| 1982 | 5 | A | 1-2 |
| 1984 | 4 | A | 0-2 |

v **Southampton**

| | | | |
|---|---|---|---|
| 1961 | 3 | A | 1-7 |
| 1991 | 3 | A | 2-3 |
| 2000 | 3 | H | 0-1 |

v **Stoke City**

| | | | |
|---|---|---|---|
| 1959 | 4 | A | 1-0 |
| 1964 | 4 | H | 1-1 |
| 1964 | 4r | A | 0-1 |
| 1971 | 5 | A | 0-0 |
| 1971 | 5r | H | 0-1 |

v **Sunderland**

| | | | |
|---|---|---|---|
| 2001 | 4 | A | 0-1 |

v **Swindon Town**

| | | | |
|---|---|---|---|
| 1948 | 1 | A | 2-4 |
| 1965 | 3 | A | 2-1 |
| 1994 | 3 | A | 1-1 |
| 1994 | 3r | H | 2-1aet |

v **Torquay Utd**

| | | | |
|---|---|---|---|
| 1939 | 2 | H | 4-1 |
| 1947 | 1 | H | 2-0 |

v **Tottenham Hotspur**

| | | | |
|---|---|---|---|
| 1965 | 4 | A | 0-5 |
| 1994 | 4 | H | 3-0 |

v **Tranmere Rovers**

| | | | |
|---|---|---|---|
| 1993 | 4 | A | 2-1 |
| 1999 | 3 | A | 1-0 |

v **Walsall**

| | | | |
|---|---|---|---|
| 1947 | 2 | A | 0-0 |
| 1947 | 2r | H | 0-1 |
| 1996 | 4 | H | 1-0 |

v **Watford**

| | | | |
|---|---|---|---|
| 1937 | 1 | H | 2-1 |
| 1957 | 2 | A | 3-1 |

v **West Bromwich Albion**

| | | | |
|---|---|---|---|
| 1971 | 4 | A | 1-1 |
| 1971 | 4r | H | 3-0 |
| 1978 | SF | N | 3-1 |

v **West Ham Utd**

| | | | |
|---|---|---|---|
| 1950 | 3 | A | 1-5 |
| 1975 | SF | N | 0-0 |
| 1975 | SFr | N | 1-2 |
| 1986 | 4 | A | 0-0 |
| 1986 | 4r | H | 1-1aet |
| 1986 | 4r2 | H | 0-1aet |

v **Wolverhampton W**

| | | | |
|---|---|---|---|
| 1975 | 3 | A | 2-1 |
| 1976 | 4 | H | 0-0 |
| 1976 | 4r | A | 0-1 |
| 1977 | 4 | H | 2-2 |
| 1977 | 4r | A | 0-1 |
| 1994 | 5 | A | 1-1 |
| 1994 | 5r | H | 1-2 |

v **Wrexham**

| | | | |
|---|---|---|---|
| 1995 | 3 | A | 1-2 |

v **Yeovil Town**

| | | | |
|---|---|---|---|
| 1938 | 1 | A | 1-2 |

# Kidderminster H

v **Luton Town**

| | | | |
|---|---|---|---|
| 1903 | IR | A | 0-3 |

v **Millwall**

| | | | |
|---|---|---|---|
| 1981 | 1 | H | 1-1 |
| 1981 | 1r | A | 0-1 |

v **Oldham Athletic**

| | | | |
|---|---|---|---|
| 1907 | 1 | A | 0-5 |

v **Peterborough**

| | | | |
|---|---|---|---|
| 1966 | 1 | A | 1-2 |

v **Plymouth Argyle**

| | | | |
|---|---|---|---|
| 1999 | 1 | A | 0-0 |
| 1999 | 1r | H | 0-0q |

v **Preston North End**

| | | | |
|---|---|---|---|
| 1994 | 4 | H | 1-0 |

v **Rushden & Diamonds**

| | | | |
|---|---|---|---|
| 2003 | 1 | H | 2-2 |
| 2003 | 1r | A | 1-2 |

v **Shrewsbury Town**

| | | | |
|---|---|---|---|
| 1933 | Q1 | A | 1-5 |
| 1936 | Q2 | H | 2-2 |
| 1936 | Q2r | A | 2-1 |

v **Swansea City**

| | | | |
|---|---|---|---|
| 1990 | 1 | H | 2-3 |

v **Torquay Utd**

| | | | |
|---|---|---|---|
| 1995 | 1 | H | 1-1 |
| 1995 | 1r | A | 0-1 |

v **Walsall**

| | | | |
|---|---|---|---|
| 1900 | Q3 | A | 1-6 |
| 1909 | Q1 | H | 2-1 |

v **West Ham Utd**

| | | | |
|---|---|---|---|
| 1994 | 5 | H | 0-1 |

v **Wigan Athletic**

| | | | |
|---|---|---|---|
| 1975 | Q4 | A | 0-4 |

v **Wrexham**

| | | | |
|---|---|---|---|
| 1907 | Q4 | H | 2-1 |

# Leeds Utd

v **Liverpool**

| | | | |
|---|---|---|---|
| 1925 | 1 | A | 0-3 |
| 1965 | F | N | 1-2aet |
| 1972 | 4 | A | 0-0 |
| 1972 | 4r | H | 2-0 |
| 1996 | 6 | H | 0-0 |
| 1996 | 6r | A | 0-3 |
| 2001 | 4 | H | 0-2 |

v **Luton Town**

| | | | |
|---|---|---|---|
| 1959 | 3 | A | 1-5 |

v **Manchester City**

| | | | |
|---|---|---|---|
| 1928 | 3 | A | 0-1 |
| 1967 | 6 | H | 1-0 |
| 1977 | 5 | H | 1-0 |
| 1978 | 3 | H | 1-2 |
| 2000 | 4 | A | 5-2 |

v **Manchester Utd**

| | | | |
|---|---|---|---|
| 1951 | 4 | A | 0-4 |
| 1965 | SF | N | 0-0 |
| 1965 | SFr | N | 1-0 |
| 1970 | SF | N | 0-0 |
| 1970 | SFr | N | 0-0aet |
| 1970 | SFr2 | N | 1-0 |

1977 SF N 1-2
1992 3 H 0-1
1995 5 A 1-3

**v Mansfield Town**
1970 5 H 2-0

**v Middlesbrough**
1926 3 A 1-5
1946 3 H 4-4
1946 3s A 2-7
1951 3 H 1-0
1963 4 A 2-0

**v Newcastle Utd**
1931 4 H 4-1
1933 3 A 3-0

**v Norwich City**
1935 4 A 3-3
1935 4r H 1-2
1973 3 A 1-1
1973 3r H 1-1aet
1973 3r2 N 5-0
1977 3 H 5-2

**v Nottingham Forest**
1963 5 A 0-3
1968 4 H 2-1
1980 3 H 1-4
1989 4 A 0-2

**v Notts County**
1976 3 A 1-0

**v Oldham Athletic**
1995 4 H 3-2

**v Oxford Utd**
1994 4 A 2-2
1994 4r H 2-3aet
1998 3 H 4-0

**v Peterborough**
1974 4 A 4-1
1986 3 A 0-1

**v Plymouth Argyle**
1973 4 H 2-1

**v Port Vale**
1996 5 H 0-0
1996 5r A 2-1
2000 3 H 2-0

**v Portsmouth**
1923 1 A 0-0
1923 1r H 3-1
1997 5 H 2-3
1999 4 A 5-1

**v Preston North End**
1934 3 H 0-1
1983 3 H 3-0

**v QPR**
1932 3 A 1-3
1987 5 H 2-1

**v Rochdale**
1952 3 A 2-0

**v Rotherham Utd**
1971 3 A 0-0
1971 3r H 3-2

**v Rushden & Diamonds**
1999 3 A 0-0
1999 3r H 3-1

**v Scunthorpe Utd**
1984 3 H 1-1
1984 3r A 1-1aet
1984 3r2 A 2-4
2003 3 A 2-0

**v Sheffield Utd**
1936 5 A 1-3
1968 6 H 1-0
2003 6 A 0-1

**v Sheffield Wed**
1961 3 A 0-2
1969 3 A 1-1
1969 3r H 1-3

**v Shrewsbury Town**
1965 5 H 2-0

**v Stoke City**
1924 1 H 1-0
1963 3 H 3-1

**v Sunderland**
1927 3 H 3-2
1967 5 A 1-1
1967 5r H 1-1aet
1967 5r2 N 2-1
1973 F N 0-1

**v Swansea City**
1970 3 H 2-1

**v Swindon Town**
1922 1 A 1-2
1970 6 A 2-0
1971 4 H 4-0
1987 4 A 2-1

**v Torquay Utd**
1955 3 H 2-2
1955 3r A 0-4

**v Tottenham Hotspur**
1954 3 H 3-3
1954 3r A 0-1
1972 6 H 2-1
1982 4 A 0-1
1999 5 H 1-1
1999 5r A 0-2

**v Tranmere Rovers**
1933 4 A 0-0
1933 4r H 4-0

**v Walsall**
1995 3 A 1-1
1995 3r H 5-2aet

**v West Bromwich Albion**
1947 3 A 1-2
1967 4 H 5-0
1973 5 H 2-0
1979 4 A 3-3
1979 4r A 0-2aet

**v West Ham Utd**
1924 2 A 1-1
1924 2r H 1-0
1930 4 A 1-4

**v Wigan Athletic**
1987 6 A 2-0

**v Wimbledon**
1975 4 H 0-0
1975 4r N 1-0

**v Wolverhampton W**
1936 3 A 1-1
1936 3r H 3-1
1973 SF N 1-0
1974 3 A 1-1
1974 3r H 1-0
1977 6 A 1-0
1982 3 A 3-1
1998 6 H 0-1

# Leicester City

**v Leyton Orient**
1922 1 H 2-0
1963 5 A 1-0
1964 3 H 2-3
1972 4 H 0-2

**v Lincoln City**
1929 3 A 1-0
1934 3 H 3-0
1959 3 H 1-1
1959 3r A 2-0

**v Liverpool**
1906 1 A 1-2
1963 SF N 1-0
1965 6 H 0-0
1965 6r A 0-1
1969 5 H 0-0
1969 5r A 1-0
1970 5 A 0-0
1970 5r H 0-2
1974 SF N 0-0
1974 SFr N 1-3

**v Luton Town**
1949 5 A 5-5aet
1949 5r H 5-3
1956 3 A 4-0
1959 4 H 1-1
1959 4r A 1-4
1974 5 A 4-0

**v Manchester City**
1920 2 H 3-0
1966 5 A 2-2
1966 5r H 0-1
1967 3 A 1-2
1968 4 A 0-0
1968 4r H 4-3
1969 F N 0-1
1989 3 A 0-1
1994 3 A 1-4
1996 3 H 0-0
1996 3r A 0-5

**v Manchester Utd**
1963 F N 1-3
1976 5 H 1-2

**v Mansfield Town**
1938 3 A 2-1
1969 6 A 1-0
2002 3 H 2-1

**v Middlesbrough**
1911 2 A 0-0
1911 2r H 1-2aet
1927 3 A 3-5
1936 5 A 1-2
1954 3 A 0-0

| | | | |
|---|---|---|---|
| 1954 | 3r | H | 3-2 |
| 1965 | 5 | A | 3-0 |

v **Millwall**

| | | | |
|---|---|---|---|
| 1934 | 4 | A | 6-3 |
| 1969 | 4 | A | 1-0 |
| 1985 | 5 | A | 0-2 |
| 1991 | 3 | A | 1-2 |

v **Newcastle Utd**

| | | | |
|---|---|---|---|
| 1910 | 4 | A | 0-3 |
| 1925 | 2 | A | 2-2 |
| 1925 | 2r | H | 1-0 |
| 1932 | 5 | A | 1-3 |
| 1947 | 5 | A | 1-1 |
| 1947 | 5r | H | 1-2 |

v **Northampton Town**

| | | | |
|---|---|---|---|
| 1905 | Q5 | A | 2-2 |
| 1905 | Q5r | H | 2-0 |
| 1998 | 3 | H | 4-0 |

v **Norwich City**

| | | | |
|---|---|---|---|
| 1913 | 1 | H | 1-4 |
| 1954 | 5 | A | 2-1 |
| 1963 | 6 | A | 2-0 |
| 1979 | 3 | H | 3-0 |
| 1997 | 4 | H | 2-1 |

v **Nottingham Forest**

| | | | |
|---|---|---|---|
| 1901 | 1 | A | 1-5 |

v **Notts County**

| | | | |
|---|---|---|---|
| 1926 | 3 | A | 0-2 |
| 1953 | 3 | H | 2-4 |
| 1971 | 3 | H | 2-0 |
| 1983 | 3 | H | 2-3 |

v **Oldham Athletic**

| | | | |
|---|---|---|---|
| 1979 | 4 | A | 1-3 |

v **Oxford Utd**

| | | | |
|---|---|---|---|
| 1961 | 3 | H | 3-1 |
| 1971 | 5 | H | 1-1 |
| 1971 | 5r | A | 3-1aet |
| 1975 | 3 | H | 3-1 |
| 1988 | 3 | A | 0-2 |

v **Plymouth Argyle**

| | | | |
|---|---|---|---|
| 1965 | 4 | H | 5-0 |

v **Port Vale**

| | | | |
|---|---|---|---|
| 1932 | 4 | A | 2-1 |

v **Portsmouth**

| | | | |
|---|---|---|---|
| 1908 | 2 | A | 0-1 |
| 1934 | SF | N | 1-4 |
| 1949 | SF | N | 3-1 |
| 1995 | 4 | A | 1-0 |

v **Preston North End**

| | | | |
|---|---|---|---|
| 1934 | 6 | A | 1-0 |
| 1938 | 4 | A | 0-2 |
| 1949 | 4 | H | 2-0 |
| 1951 | 3 | H | 0-3 |
| 1954 | 6 | H | 1-1 |
| 1954 | 6r | A | 2-2aet |
| 1954 | 6r2 | N | 1-3 |

v **QPR**

| | | | |
|---|---|---|---|
| 1974 | 6 | A | 2-0 |
| 1987 | 3 | A | 2-5 |

v **Reading**

| | | | |
|---|---|---|---|
| 1928 | 4 | A | 1-0 |

v **Rotherham Utd**

| | | | |
|---|---|---|---|
| 1955 | 3 | A | 0-1 |
| 1968 | 5 | A | 1-1 |
| 1968 | 5r | H | 2-0aet |

v **Sheffield Utd**

| | | | |
|---|---|---|---|
| 1900 | 1 | A | 0-1 |
| 1930 | 3 | A | 1-2 |
| 1950 | 3 | A | 1-3 |
| 1961 | SF | N | 0-0 |
| 1961 | SFr | N | 0-0aet |
| 1961 | SFr2 | N | 2-0aet |
| 1976 | 3 | H | 3-0 |

v **Sheffield Wed**

| | | | |
|---|---|---|---|
| 1924 | 1 | A | 1-4 |
| 1948 | 4 | H | 2-1 |

v **Shrewsbury Town**

| | | | |
|---|---|---|---|
| 1982 | 6 | H | 5-2 |

v **Southampton**

| | | | |
|---|---|---|---|
| 1898 | 1 | A | 1-2 |
| 1911 | 1 | H | 3-1 |
| 1970 | 4 | A | 1-1 |
| 1970 | 4r | H | 4-2aet |
| 1982 | 3 | H | 3-1 |

v **Southend Utd**

| | | | |
|---|---|---|---|
| 1997 | 3 | H | 2-0 |

v **Stoke City**

| | | | |
|---|---|---|---|
| 1925 | 1 | H | 3-0 |
| 1939 | 3 | H | 1-1 |
| 1939 | 3r | A | 2-1 |
| 1954 | 4 | A | 0-0 |
| 1954 | 4r | H | 3-1 |
| 1956 | 4 | H | 3-3 |
| 1956 | 4r | A | 1-2 |
| 1962 | 3 | H | 1-1 |
| 1962 | 3r | A | 2-5 |

v **Sunderland**

| | | | |
|---|---|---|---|
| 1907 | 1 | A | 1-4 |
| 1970 | 3 | H | 1-0 |

v **Swansea City**

| | | | |
|---|---|---|---|
| 1915 | Q6 | A | 0-1 |
| 1929 | 4 | H | 1-0 |

v **Torquay Utd**

| | | | |
|---|---|---|---|
| 1971 | 4 | H | 3-0 |

v **Tottenham Hotspur**

| | | | |
|---|---|---|---|
| 1914 | 1 | H | 5-5 |
| 1914 | 1r | A | 0-2 |
| 1928 | 5 | H | 0-3 |
| 1948 | 5 | A | 2-5 |
| 1957 | 3 | A | 0-2 |
| 1958 | 3 | A | 0-4 |
| 1961 | F | N | 0-2 |
| 1974 | 3 | H | 1-0 |
| 1982 | SF | N | 0-2 |

v **Walsall**

| | | | |
|---|---|---|---|
| 1978 | 4 | A | 0-1 |

v **Watford**

| | | | |
|---|---|---|---|
| 1909 | 1 | A | 1-1 |
| 1909 | 1r | H | 3-1 |
| 1936 | 4 | H | 6-3 |
| 1982 | 5 | H | 2-0 |

v **West Bromwich Albion**

| | | | |
|---|---|---|---|
| 1905 | IR | A | 5-2 |
| 1960 | 5 | H | 2-1 |
| 1969 | SF | N | 1-0 |
| 2002 | 4 | A | 0-1 |

v **West Ham Utd**

| | | | |
|---|---|---|---|
| 1947 | 3 | A | 2-1 |

v **Wolverhampton W**

| | | | |
|---|---|---|---|
| 1939 | 4 | A | 1-5 |
| 1949 | F | N | 1-3 |
| 1960 | 6 | H | 1-2 |
| 1972 | 3 | A | 1-1 |
| 1972 | 3r | H | 2-0 |
| 1995 | 5 | A | 0-1 |
| 2003 | 4 | A | 1-4 |

v **Wrexham**

| | | | |
|---|---|---|---|
| 1960 | 3 | A | 2-1 |

v **Wycombe W**

| | | | |
|---|---|---|---|
| 2001 | 6 | H | 1-2 |

v **York City**

| | | | |
|---|---|---|---|
| 2001 | 3 | H | 3-0 |

# Leyton Orient

v **Lincoln City**

| | | | |
|---|---|---|---|
| 2002 | 2 | H | 2-1 |

v **Liverpool**

| | | | |
|---|---|---|---|
| 1960 | 3 | A | 1-2 |

v **Luton Town**

| | | | |
|---|---|---|---|
| 1931 | 1 | A | 2-2 |
| 1931 | 1r | N | 2-4 |
| 1981 | 3 | H | 1-3 |

v **Manchester City**

| | | | |
|---|---|---|---|
| 1920 | 1 | A | 1-4 |
| 1926 | 6 | H | 1-6 |

v **Middlesbrough**

| | | | |
|---|---|---|---|
| 1926 | 4 | H | 4-2 |
| 1936 | 4 | A | 0-3 |
| 1978 | 6 | A | 0-0 |
| 1978 | 6r | H | 2-1 |

v **Millwall**

| | | | |
|---|---|---|---|
| 1915 | 1 | A | 1-2 |
| 1923 | 1 | H | 0-2 |

v **Newcastle Utd**

| | | | |
|---|---|---|---|
| 1909 | 1 | A | 0-5 |
| 1926 | 5 | H | 2-0 |
| 1930 | 4 | A | 1-3 |

v **Norwich City**

| | | | |
|---|---|---|---|
| 1966 | 3 | H | 1-3 |
| 1978 | 3 | H | 1-1 |
| 1978 | 3r | A | 1-0 |

v **Nottingham Forest**

| | | | |
|---|---|---|---|
| 1914 | 1 | H | 2-2 |
| 1914 | 1r | A | 1-0 |
| 1925 | 1 | A | 0-1 |
| 1971 | 4 | A | 1-1 |
| 1971 | 4r | H | 0-1 |
| 1988 | 4 | H | 1-2 |

v **Notts County**

| | | | |
|---|---|---|---|
| 1947 | 1 | H | 1-2 |

v **Oldham Athletic**

| | | | |
|---|---|---|---|
| 1986 | 3 | A | 2-1 |
| 1992 | 3 | A | 1-1 |
| 1992 | 3r | H | 4-2aet |

v **Plymouth Argyle**

| | | | |
|---|---|---|---|
| 1956 | 3 | H | 1-0 |

**v Port Vale**

| | | | |
|---|---|---|---|
| 1921 | Q6 | H | 1-0 |
| 1927 | 3 | H | 1-1 |
| 1927 | 3r | A | 1-5 |
| 1954 | 6 | H | 0-1 |

**v Portsmouth**

| | | | |
|---|---|---|---|
| 1974 | 4 | A | 0-0 |
| 1974 | 4r | H | 1-1aet |
| 1974 | 4r2 | N | 0-2 |
| 1992 | 4 | A | 0-2 |
| 2002 | 3 | A | 4-1 |

**v Reading**

| | | | |
|---|---|---|---|
| 1958 | 3 | H | 1-0 |
| 1993 | 2 | A | 0-3 |

**v Sheffield Wed**

| | | | |
|---|---|---|---|
| 1961 | 5 | H | 0-2 |
| 1986 | 4 | A | 0-5 |

**v Southampton**

| | | | |
|---|---|---|---|
| 1929 | 3 | A | 0-0 |
| 1929 | 3r | H | 2-1 |
| 1961 | 4 | A | 1-0 |
| 1965 | 3 | A | 1-3 |
| 1985 | 4 | H | 0-2 |

**v Southend Utd**

| | | | |
|---|---|---|---|
| 1908 | Q3 | H | 1-1 |
| 1908 | Q3r | A | 1-3 |
| 1950 | 1 | H | 0-2 |
| 1991 | 1 | H | 3-2 |

**v Stockport County**

| | | | |
|---|---|---|---|
| 1988 | 3 | A | 2-1 |

**v Sunderland**

| | | | |
|---|---|---|---|
| 1913 | 1 | A | 0-6 |
| 1971 | 3 | A | 3-0 |

**v Swansea City**

| | | | |
|---|---|---|---|
| 1924 | 1 | A | 1-1 |
| 1924 | 1r | H | 1-1aet |
| 1924 | 1r2 | N | 1-2 |
| 1988 | 2 | H | 2-0 |

**v Swindon Town**

| | | | |
|---|---|---|---|
| 1928 | 3 | A | 1-2 |
| 1991 | 3 | H | 1-1 |
| 1991 | 3r | A | 0-1 |

**v Torquay Utd**

| | | | |
|---|---|---|---|
| 1937 | 1 | H | 2-1 |
| 1938 | 1 | A | 2-1 |
| 1985 | 2 | H | 3-0 |
| 1996 | 1 | A | 0-1 |

**v Tottenham Hotspur**

| | | | |
|---|---|---|---|
| 2001 | 3 | H | 0-1 |

**v Tranmere Rovers**

| | | | |
|---|---|---|---|
| 1954 | 3 | A | 2-2 |
| 1954 | 3r | H | 4-1 |

**v Walsall**

| | | | |
|---|---|---|---|
| 1934 | 2 | A | 0-0 |
| 1934 | 2r | H | 2-0 |
| 1939 | 2 | A | 2-4 |
| 1970 | 1 | A | 0-0 |
| 1970 | 1r | H | 0-2 |

**v West Bromwich Albion**

| | | | |
|---|---|---|---|
| 1910 | 1 | A | 0-2 |
| 1985 | 3 | H | 2-1 |
| 1992 | 2 | H | 2-1 |

**v West Ham Utd**

| | | | |
|---|---|---|---|
| 1964 | 4 | H | 1-1 |
| 1964 | 4r | A | 0-3 |
| 1980 | 4 | H | 2-3 |
| 1987 | 3 | H | 1-1 |
| 1987 | 3r | A | 1-4 |

**v Wimbledon**

| | | | |
|---|---|---|---|
| 1984 | 1 | A | 1-2 |

**v Wrexham**

| | | | |
|---|---|---|---|
| 1952 | 2 | A | 1-1 |
| 1952 | 2r | H | 3-2aet |
| 1972 | 3 | H | 3-0 |

**v York City**

| | | | |
|---|---|---|---|
| 1938 | 2 | H | 2-2 |
| 1938 | 2r | A | 0-1 |

# Lincoln City

**v Liverpool**

| | | | |
|---|---|---|---|
| 1909 | 1 | A | 1-5 |
| 1955 | 3 | H | 1-1 |
| 1955 | 3r | A | 0-1aet |

**v Luton Town**

| | | | |
|---|---|---|---|
| 1932 | 2 | H | 2-2 |
| 1932 | 2r | A | 1-4 |
| 2000 | 2 | A | 2-2 |
| 2000 | 2r | H | 0-1 |

**v Macclesfield**

| | | | |
|---|---|---|---|
| 1969 | 1 | A | 3-1 |

**v Manchester City**

| | | | |
|---|---|---|---|
| 1905 | 1 | H | 1-2 |

**v Manchester Utd**

| | | | |
|---|---|---|---|
| 1902 | IR | A | 2-1 |

**v Mansfield Town**

| | | | |
|---|---|---|---|
| 1938 | 2 | A | 1-2 |
| 1976 | 2 | A | 2-1 |
| 1988 | 2 | A | 3-4 |

**v Middlesbrough**

| | | | |
|---|---|---|---|
| 1887 | 2 | A | 1-1 |
| 1887 | 2r | H | 2-0 |
| 1920 | 1 | A | 1-4 |

**v Millwall**

| | | | |
|---|---|---|---|
| 1921 | 1 | A | 3-0 |

**v Northampton Town**

| | | | |
|---|---|---|---|
| 1922 | Q5 | H | 1-2 |
| 1924 | Q5 | A | 1-5 |

**v Nottingham Forest**

| | | | |
|---|---|---|---|
| 1947 | 3 | H | 0-1 |

**v Oldham Athletic**

| | | | |
|---|---|---|---|
| 1937 | 2 | H | 2-3 |

**v Peterborough**

| | | | |
|---|---|---|---|
| 1957 | 3 | A | 2-2 |
| 1957 | 3r | H | 4-5aet |

**v Plymouth Argyle**

| | | | |
|---|---|---|---|
| 1914 | 1 | A | 1-4 |

**v Port Vale**

| | | | |
|---|---|---|---|
| 1975 | 1 | A | 2-2 |
| 1975 | 1r | H | 2-0 |
| 1982 | 1 | H | 2-2 |
| 1982 | 1r | A | 0-0aet |
| 1982 | 1r2 | A | 0-2 |
| 1984 | 1 | A | 2-1 |

**v Portsmouth**

| | | | |
|---|---|---|---|
| 1939 | 3 | A | 0-4 |
| 1952 | 3 | A | 0-4 |

**v Preston North End**

| | | | |
|---|---|---|---|
| 1890 | 2 | A | 0-4 |
| 1927 | 3 | H | 2-4 |
| 1954 | 4 | H | 0-2 |
| 1978 | 1 | A | 2-3 |

**v QPR**

| | | | |
|---|---|---|---|
| 1930 | 2 | A | 1-2 |

**v Rochdale**

| | | | |
|---|---|---|---|
| 1938 | 1 | A | 1-1 |
| 1938 | 1r | H | 2-0 |
| 1990 | 2 | A | 0-3 |

**v Rotherham Utd**

| | | | |
|---|---|---|---|
| 1927 | 1 | H | 2-0 |
| 1946 | 2 | A | 1-2 |
| 1946 | 2s | H | 1-1 |
| 1965 | 3 | A | 1-5 |

**v Scunthorpe Utd**

| | | | |
|---|---|---|---|
| 1967 | 1 | H | 3-4 |

**v Sheffield Utd**

| | | | |
|---|---|---|---|
| 1892 | Q2 | A | 1-4 |
| 1961 | 4 | A | 1-3 |
| 1964 | 3 | H | 0-4 |
| 1984 | 2 | H | 0-0 |
| 1984 | 2r | A | 0-1 |

**v Sheffield Wed**

| | | | |
|---|---|---|---|
| 1980 | 1 | A | 0-3 |

**v Southampton**

| | | | |
|---|---|---|---|
| 1953 | 3 | H | 1-1 |
| 1953 | 3r | A | 1-2 |

**v Southend Utd**

| | | | |
|---|---|---|---|
| 1956 | 3 | H | 2-3 |

**v Stockport County**

| | | | |
|---|---|---|---|
| 1906 | 1 | H | 4-2 |
| 1912 | 1 | H | 2-0 |
| 1992 | 1 | A | 1-3 |
| 1996 | 1 | A | 0-5 |

**v Stoke City**

| | | | |
|---|---|---|---|
| 1908 | 1 | A | 0-5 |
| 1911 | Q5 | A | 0-4 |

**v Sunderland**

| | | | |
|---|---|---|---|
| 1999 | 3 | H | 0-1 |

**v Swindon Town**

| | | | |
|---|---|---|---|
| 1935 | 2 | A | 3-4 |
| 1975 | 3 | A | 0-2 |

**v Torquay Utd**

| | | | |
|---|---|---|---|
| 1971 | 3 | A | 3-4 |

**v Tranmere Rovers**

| | | | |
|---|---|---|---|
| 1965 | 1 | A | 0-0 |
| 1965 | 1r | H | 1-0 |

**v Walsall**

| | | | |
|---|---|---|---|
| 1936 | 1 | A | 0-2 |
| 1954 | 3 | H | 1-1 |
| 1954 | 3r | A | 1-1aet |
| 1954 | 3r2 | N | 2-1 |

**v Watford**

| | | | |
|---|---|---|---|
| 1905 | Q6 | A | 1-1 |
| 1905 | Q6r | H | 2-1 |

**v West Bromwich Albion**

| | | | |
|---|---|---|---|
| 1949 | 3 | H | 0-1 |
| 1961 | 3 | H | 3-1 |
| 1976 | 4 | A | 2-3 |

**v West Ham Utd**

| | | | |
|---|---|---|---|
| 1903 | IR | H | 2-0 |

**v Wigan Athletic**

| | | | |
|---|---|---|---|
| 1987 | 1 | A | 1-3 |

**v Wolverhampton W**

| | | | |
|---|---|---|---|
| 1912 | 2 | A | 1-2 |
| 1958 | 3 | H | 0-1 |

**v Wrexham**

| | | | |
|---|---|---|---|
| 1947 | 2 | H | 1-1 |
| 1947 | 2r | A | 3-3aet |
| 1947 | 2r2 | N | 2-1 |

# Liverpool

**v Luton Town**

| | | | |
|---|---|---|---|
| 1920 | 2 | A | 2-0 |
| 1939 | 3 | H | 3-0 |
| 1987 | 3 | A | 0-0 |
| 1987 | 3r | H | 0-0aet |
| 1987 | 3r2 | A | 0-3 |

**v Manchester City**

| | | | |
|---|---|---|---|
| 1956 | 5 | A | 0-0 |
| 1956 | 5r | H | 1-2 |
| 1973 | 4 | H | 0-0 |
| 1973 | 4r | A | 0-2 |
| 1988 | 6 | A | 4-0 |
| 2001 | 5 | H | 4-2 |
| 2003 | 3 | A | 1-0 |

**v Manchester Utd**

| | | | |
|---|---|---|---|
| 1898 | 2 | A | 0-0 |
| 1898 | 2r | H | 2-1 |
| 1903 | 1 | A | 1-2 |
| 1921 | 1 | H | 1-1 |
| 1921 | 1r | A | 2-1 |
| 1948 | 4 | N | 0-3 |
| 1960 | 4 | H | 1-3 |
| 1977 | F | N | 1-2 |
| 1979 | SF | N | 2-2 |
| 1979 | SFr | N | 0-1 |
| 1985 | SF | N | 2-2aet |
| 1985 | SFr | N | 1-2 |
| 1996 | F | N | 0-1 |
| 1999 | 4 | A | 1-2 |

**v Middlesbrough**

| | | | |
|---|---|---|---|
| 1977 | 6 | H | 2-0 |

**v Millwall**

| | | | |
|---|---|---|---|
| 1896 | 1 | H | 4-1 |
| 1989 | 4 | A | 2-0 |

**v Newcastle Utd**

| | | | |
|---|---|---|---|
| 1899 | 2 | H | 3-1 |
| 1908 | 3 | A | 1-3 |
| 1913 | 3 | H | 1-1 |
| 1913 | 3r | A | 0-1 |
| 1921 | 2 | A | 0-1 |
| 1924 | 4 | A | 0-1 |
| 1974 | F | N | 3-0 |
| 1984 | 3 | H | 4-0 |

**v Northampton Town**

| | | | |
|---|---|---|---|
| 1958 | 4 | H | 3-1 |

**v Norwich City**

| | | | |
|---|---|---|---|
| 1909 | 2 | H | 2-3 |
| 1937 | 3 | A | 0-3 |
| 1951 | 3 | A | 1-3 |
| 1986 | 3 | H | 5-0 |
| 1990 | 4 | A | 0-0 |
| 1990 | 4r | H | 3-1 |

**v Nottingham Forest**

| | | | |
|---|---|---|---|
| 1895 | 2 | H | 0-2 |
| 1897 | 3 | H | 1-1 |
| 1897 | 3r | A | 1-0 |
| 1948 | 3 | H | 4-1 |
| 1949 | 3 | A | 2-2aet |
| 1949 | 3r | H | 4-0 |
| 1980 | 4 | A | 2-0 |
| 1988 | SF | N | 2-1 |
| 1989 | SF | N | 3-1 |

**v Notts County**

| | | | |
|---|---|---|---|
| 1901 | 1 | A | 0-2 |
| 1949 | 4 | H | 1-0 |

**v Oldham Athletic**

| | | | |
|---|---|---|---|
| 1907 | 2 | A | 1-0 |
| 1962 | 4 | A | 2-1 |
| 1977 | 5 | H | 3-1 |

**v Oxford Utd**

| | | | |
|---|---|---|---|
| 1972 | 3 | A | 3-0 |

**v Port Vale**

| | | | |
|---|---|---|---|
| 1964 | 4 | H | 0-0 |
| 1964 | 4r | A | 2-1aet |
| 1999 | 3 | A | 3-0 |

**v Portsmouth**

| | | | |
|---|---|---|---|
| 1992 | SF | N | 1-1aet |
| 1992 | SFr | N | 0-0p |

**v Preston North End**

| | | | |
|---|---|---|---|
| 1894 | 2 | H | 3-2 |
| 1962 | 5 | H | 0-0 |
| 1962 | 5r | A | 0-0aet |
| 1962 | 5r2 | N | 0-1 |

**v QPR**

| | | | |
|---|---|---|---|
| 1914 | 4 | H | 2-1 |
| 1990 | 6 | A | 2-2 |
| 1990 | 6r | H | 1-0 |

**v Rochdale**

| | | | |
|---|---|---|---|
| 1996 | 3 | H | 7-0 |

**v Rotherham Utd**

| | | | |
|---|---|---|---|
| 2001 | 3 | H | 3-0 |

**v Scunthorpe Utd**

| | | | |
|---|---|---|---|
| 1956 | 4 | H | 3-3 |
| 1956 | 4r | A | 2-1aet |
| 1958 | 5 | A | 1-0 |

**v Sheffield Utd**

| | | | |
|---|---|---|---|
| 1899 | SF | N | 2-2 |
| 1899 | SFr | N | 4-4 |
| 1899 | SFr2 | N | 0-1 |
| 1915 | 2 | A | 0-1 |
| 1923 | 3 | H | 1-2 |
| 1938 | 4 | A | 1-1 |
| 1938 | 4r | H | 1-0 |

**v Sheffield Wed**

| | | | |
|---|---|---|---|
| 1907 | 4 | A | 0-1 |

**v Shrewsbury Town**

| | | | |
|---|---|---|---|
| 1996 | 4 | A | 4-0 |

**v Southampton**

| | | | |
|---|---|---|---|
| 1902 | 2 | A | 1-4 |
| 1906 | 4 | H | 3-0 |
| 1924 | 3 | A | 0-0 |
| 1924 | 3r | H | 2-0 |
| 1925 | 4 | A | 0-1 |
| 1926 | 3 | A | 0-0 |
| 1926 | 3r | H | 1-0 |
| 1971 | 5 | H | 1-0 |
| 1986 | SF | N | 2-0aet |
| 1990 | 5 | H | 3-0 |

**v Southend Utd**

| | | | |
|---|---|---|---|
| 1957 | 3 | A | 1-2 |
| 1958 | 3 | H | 1-1 |
| 1958 | 3r | A | 3-2 |
| 1979 | 3 | A | 0-0 |
| 1979 | 3r | H | 3-0 |

**v Stockport County**

| | | | |
|---|---|---|---|
| 1915 | 1 | H | 3-0 |
| 1939 | 4 | H | 5-1 |
| 1950 | 5 | A | 2-1 |
| 1965 | 4 | H | 1-1 |
| 1965 | 4r | A | 2-0 |

**v Stoke City**

| | | | |
|---|---|---|---|
| 1900 | 1 | A | 0-0 |
| 1900 | 1r | H | 1-0 |
| 1975 | 3 | H | 2-0 |
| 1983 | 4 | H | 2-0 |
| 1988 | 3 | A | 0-0 |
| 1988 | 3r | H | 1-0 |

**v Sunderland**

| | | | |
|---|---|---|---|
| 1922 | 1 | A | 1-1 |
| 1922 | 1r | H | 5-0 |
| 1961 | 4 | H | 0-2 |
| 1982 | 4 | A | 3-0 |
| 1992 | F | N | 2-0 |

**v Swansea City**

| | | | |
|---|---|---|---|
| 1936 | 3 | H | 1-0 |
| 1964 | 6 | H | 1-2 |
| 1971 | 4 | H | 3-0 |
| 1982 | 3 | A | 4-0 |
| 1990 | 3 | A | 0-0 |
| 1990 | 3r | H | 8-0 |

**v Tottenham Hotspur**

| | | | |
|---|---|---|---|
| 1968 | 5 | A | 1-1 |
| 1968 | 5r | H | 2-1 |
| 1971 | 6 | H | 0-0 |
| 1971 | 6r | A | 1-0 |
| 1980 | 6 | A | 1-0 |
| 1985 | 4 | H | 1-0 |
| 1995 | 6 | H | 1-2 |

**v Tranmere Rovers**

| | | | |
|---|---|---|---|
| 1934 | 4 | H | 3-1 |
| 2001 | 6 | A | 4-2 |

**v Walsall**

| | | | |
|---|---|---|---|
| 1947 | 3 | A | 5-2 |
| 1968 | 4 | A | 0-0 |
| 1968 | 4r | H | 5-2 |

**v Watford**

| | | | |
|---|---|---|---|
| 1967 | 3 | A | 0-0 |
| 1967 | 3r | H | 3-1 |
| 1970 | 6 | A | 0-1 |
| 1986 | 6 | H | 0-0 |
| 1986 | 6r | A | 2-1aet |

**v West Bromwich Albion**

| | | | |
|---|---|---|---|
| 1897 | 2 | A | 2-1 |
| 1899 | 3 | A | 2-0 |
| 1900 | 2 | H | 1-1 |
| 1900 | 2r | A | 1-2 |
| 1922 | 2 | H | 0-1 |
| 1933 | 3 | A | 0-2 |
| 1965 | 3 | A | 2-1 |
| 1968 | 6 | A | 0-0 |
| 1968 | 6r | H | 1-1aet |
| 1968 | 6r2 | N | 1-2 |

**v West Ham Utd**

| | | | |
|---|---|---|---|
| 1901 | IR | A | 1-0 |
| 1914 | 3 | A | 1-1 |
| 1914 | 3r | H | 5-1 |
| 1963 | 6 | H | 1-0 |
| 1976 | 3 | A | 2-0 |

**v Wimbledon**

| | | | |
|---|---|---|---|
| 1988 | F | N | 0-1 |
| 1995 | 5 | H | 1-1 |
| 1995 | 5r | A | 2-0 |

**v Wolverhampton W**

| | | | |
|---|---|---|---|
| 1896 | 2 | A | 0-2 |
| 1923 | 2 | A | 2-0 |
| 1939 | 5 | A | 1-4 |
| 1949 | 5 | A | 1-3 |
| 1952 | 4 | H | 2-1 |

**v Wrexham**

| | | | |
|---|---|---|---|
| 1963 | 3 | A | 3-0 |
| 1970 | 4 | H | 3-1 |

**v Wycombe W**

| | | | |
|---|---|---|---|
| 2001 | SF | N | 2-1 |

**v Yeovil Town**

| | | | |
|---|---|---|---|
| 1935 | 3 | A | 6-2 |

**v York City**

| | | | |
|---|---|---|---|
| 1985 | 5 | A | 1-1 |
| 1985 | 5r | H | 7-0 |
| 1986 | 5 | A | 1-1 |
| 1986 | 5r | H | 3-1aet |

# Luton Town

**v Manchester City**

| | | | |
|---|---|---|---|
| 1936 | 4 | A | 1-2 |
| 1938 | 5 | H | 1-3 |
| 1953 | 4 | A | 1-1 |
| 1953 | 4r | H | 5-1 |
| 1955 | 5 | H | 0-2 |
| 1961 | 4 | H | 3-1 |
| 1969 | 3 | A | 0-1 |

**v Manchester Utd**

| | | | |
|---|---|---|---|
| 1983 | 4 | H | 0-2 |

**v Middlesbrough**

| | | | |
|---|---|---|---|
| 1892 | 1 | H | 0-3 |

**v Millwall**

| | | | |
|---|---|---|---|
| 1903 | 1 | A | 0-3 |
| 1909 | 1 | H | 1-2 |
| 1978 | 4 | A | 0-4 |
| 1985 | 6 | H | 1-0 |
| 1989 | 3 | A | 2-3 |

**v Newcastle Utd**

| | | | |
|---|---|---|---|
| 1973 | 4 | A | 2-0 |
| 1981 | 4 | A | 1-2 |
| 1994 | 4 | A | 1-1 |
| 1994 | 4r | H | 2-0 |

**v Northampton Town**

| | | | |
|---|---|---|---|
| 1911 | 1 | A | 1-5 |
| 1961 | 3 | H | 4-0 |

**v Norwich City**

| | | | |
|---|---|---|---|
| 1928 | 2 | H | 6-0 |
| 1959 | SF | N | 1-1 |
| 1959 | SFr | N | 1-0 |
| 1976 | 4 | A | 0-2 |

**v Nottingham Forest**

| | | | |
|---|---|---|---|
| 1959 | F | N | 1-2 |
| 1971 | 3 | A | 1-1 |
| 1971 | 3r | H | 3-4 |

**v Notts County**

| | | | |
|---|---|---|---|
| 1912 | 1 | H | 2-4 |
| 1947 | 3 | H | 6-0 |

**v Oldham Athletic**

| | | | |
|---|---|---|---|
| 1978 | 3 | H | 1-1 |
| 1978 | 3r | A | 2-1 |

**v Peterborough**

| | | | |
|---|---|---|---|
| 1983 | 3 | H | 3-0 |

**v Plymouth Argyle**

| | | | |
|---|---|---|---|
| 1948 | 3 | A | 4-2 |

**v Port Vale**

| | | | |
|---|---|---|---|
| 1974 | 3 | A | 1-1 |
| 1974 | 3r | H | 4-2 |

**v Portsmouth**

| | | | |
|---|---|---|---|
| 1922 | 1 | A | 1-1 |
| 1922 | 1r | H | 2-1 |
| 1951 | 3 | H | 2-0 |
| 1988 | 6 | H | 3-1 |

**v Preston North End**

| | | | |
|---|---|---|---|
| 1895 | 1 | H | 0-2 |
| 1921 | 3 | H | 2-3 |

**v QPR**

| | | | |
|---|---|---|---|
| 1900 | Q5 | H | 1-1 |
| 1900 | Q5r | A | 1-4 |
| 1901 | Q5 | H | 3-0 |
| 1902 | Q5 | H | 2-0 |
| 1903 | Q3 | A | 3-0 |
| 1930 | 1 | H | 2-3 |
| 1948 | 5 | A | 1-3 |
| 1987 | 4 | H | 1-1 |
| 1987 | 4r | A | 1-2 |
| 1988 | 5 | A | 1-1 |
| 1988 | 5r | H | 1-0 |
| 2001 | 3 | H | 3-3 |
| 2001 | 3r | A | 1-2aet |

**v Reading**

| | | | |
|---|---|---|---|
| 1964 | 2 | H | 2-1 |

**v Rochdale**

| | | | |
|---|---|---|---|
| 1911 | Q5 | A | 1-1 |
| 1911 | Q5r | H | 3-2 |

**v Rotherham Utd**

| | | | |
|---|---|---|---|
| 1955 | 4 | A | 5-1 |

**v Rushden & Diamonds**

| | | | |
|---|---|---|---|
| 2001 | 1 | H | 1-0 |

**v Sheffield Utd**

| | | | |
|---|---|---|---|
| 1991 | 3 | A | 3-1 |
| 1992 | 3 | A | 0-4 |

**v Southampton**

| | | | |
|---|---|---|---|
| 1915 | 1 | A | 0-3 |
| 1988 | 4 | H | 2-1 |
| 1995 | 4 | H | 1-1 |
| 1995 | 4r | A | 0-6 |

**v Southend Utd**

| | | | |
|---|---|---|---|
| 1909 | Q5 | H | 1-1 |
| 1909 | Q5r | A | 4-2 |
| 1929 | 1 | H | 5-1 |
| 1965 | 1 | H | 1-0 |
| 1994 | 3 | H | 1-0 |
| 2002 | 1 | A | 2-3 |

**v Stockport County**

| | | | |
|---|---|---|---|
| 1933 | 2 | A | 3-2 |
| 1958 | 3 | A | 0-3 |

**v Stoke City**

| | | | |
|---|---|---|---|
| 1985 | 3 | H | 1-1 |
| 1985 | 3r | A | 3-2 |

**v Sunderland**

| | | | |
|---|---|---|---|
| 1907 | 2 | H | 0-0 |
| 1907 | 2r | A | 0-1 |
| 1937 | 4 | H | 2-2 |
| 1937 | 4r | A | 1-3 |
| 1965 | 3 | H | 0-3 |
| 1973 | 6 | A | 0-2 |

**v Swansea City**

| | | | |
|---|---|---|---|
| 1947 | 4 | H | 2-0 |

**v Swindon Town**

| | | | |
|---|---|---|---|
| 1892 | Q1 | H | 4-3 |
| 1932 | 1 | A | 5-0 |
| 1938 | 4 | H | 2-1 |
| 1952 | 5 | H | 3-1 |
| 1963 | 3 | H | 0-2 |
| 1968 | 2 | A | 2-3 |
| 1980 | 3 | H | 0-2 |
| 1982 | 3 | H | 2-1 |

**v Torquay Utd**

| | | | |
|---|---|---|---|
| 1997 | 1 | A | 1-0 |
| 1998 | 1 | H | 0-1 |

**v Tottenham Hotspur**

| | | | |
|---|---|---|---|
| 1895 | Q4 | A | 2-2 |
| 1895 | Q4r | H | 4-0 |
| 1896 | Q1 | H | 1-2 |
| 1897 | Q5 | H | 3-0 |
| 1898 | Q4 | A | 4-3 |
| 1899 | Q5 | A | 1-1 |
| 1899 | Q5r | H | 1-1 |
| 1899 | Q5r2 | N | 0-2 |
| 1933 | 4 | H | 2-0 |

**v Walsall**

| | | | |
|---|---|---|---|
| 1949 | 4 | H | 4-0 |

**v Watford**

| | | | |
|---|---|---|---|
| 1899 | Q3 | H | 2-2 |
| 1899 | Q3r | A | 1-0 |
| 1900 | Q4 | H | 3-2 |
| 1902 | Q4 | A | 2-1 |
| 1904 | Q4 | H | 4-1 |
| 1931 | 2 | A | 1-3 |

1984 3 H 2-2
1984 3r A 3-4aet
1985 5 H 0-0
1985 5r A 2-2aet
1985 5r2 H 1-0

**v West Bromwich Albion**
1897 1 H 0-1
1925 1 A 0-4

**v West Ham Utd**
1936 3 A 2-2
1936 3r H 4-0
1949 3 H 3-1
1972 3 A 1-2
1991 4 H 1-1
1991 4r A 0-5
1994 6 A 0-0
1994 6r H 3-2

**v Wigan Athletic**
2003 2 A 0-3

**v Wimbledon**
1988 SF N 1-2

**v Wolverhampton W**
1932 3 H 1-2
1960 5 H 1-4

**v York City**
1979 3 A 0-2

# Macclesfield

**v Oxford Utd**
2001 1 H 0-1

**v Port Vale**
1985 1 H 1-2
1988 3 A 0-1

**v Rochdale**
1913 Q1 H 3-5
1997 1 H 0-2

**v Rotherham Utd**
1988 2 H 4-0

**v Scunthorpe Utd**
1970 1 H 1-1
1970 1r A 2-4

**v Sheffield Wed**
1976 1 A 1-3

**v Shrewsbury Town**
1888 1 H 1-3

**v Stockport County**
1968 1 A 1-1
1968 1r H 2-1
1993 2 H 0-2

**v Swansea City**
2002 2 H 4-1

**v Walsall**
1998 2 H 0-7

**v Watford**
2003 3 H 0-2

**v West Ham Utd**
2002 3 H 0-3

**v Wigan Athletic**
1968 Q4 A 1-1
1968 Q4r H 3-0

**v Wrexham**
1895 Q2 A 1-7
1965 1 H 1-2

**v York City**
1984 1 H 0-0
1984 1r A 0-2

# Manchester City

**v Manchester Utd**
1892 Q1 A 1-5
1926 SF N 3-0
1955 4 H 2-0
1970 4 A 0-3
1987 3 A 0-1
1996 5 A 1-2

**v Middlesbrough**
1904 3 H 0-0
1904 3r A 3-1
1972 3 H 1-1
1972 3r A 0-1
1992 3 A 1-2
1997 5 H 0-1

**v Millwall**
1932 3 A 3-2
1937 6 A 0-2
1938 3 A 2-2
1938 3r H 3-1
1990 3 H 0-0
1990 3r A 1-1aet
1990 3r2 A 1-3

**v Newcastle Utd**
1924 SF N 0-2
1955 F N 1-3
1957 3 A 1-1
1957 3r H 4-5aet
1969 4 A 0-0
1969 4r H 2-0
1975 3 H 0-2
1977 4 A 3-1
1995 5 A 1-3
2002 5 A 0-1

**v Norwich City**
1939 3 A 5-0
1963 5 H 1-2
1981 4 H 6-0

**v Nottingham Forest**
1902 2 H 0-2
1924 1 H 2-0
1974 4 A 1-4
1978 4 A 1-2

**v Notts County**
1962 3 A 1-0
1991 5 A 0-1
1995 3 A 2-2
1995 3r H 5-2

**v Oldham Athletic**
1912 2 H 0-1

**v Oxford Utd**
1974 3 A 5-2

**v Peterborough**
1981 5 A 1-0

**v Plymouth Argyle**
1988 5 H 3-1

**v Port Vale**
1991 4 A 2-1

**v Portsmouth**
1934 F N 2-1
1936 3 H 3-1

**v Preston North End**
1897 1 A 0-6
1902 1 H 1-1
1902 1r A 0-0aet
1902 1r2 A 4-2aet
1903 1 A 1-3
1912 1 A 1-0
1915 1 A 0-0
1915 1r H 3-0
1925 1 A 1-4
1948 5 H 0-1

**v QPR**
1993 4 A 2-1

**v Reading**
1968 3 H 0-0
1968 3r A 7-0
1993 3 H 1-1
1993 3r A 4-0

**v Rotherham Utd**
1979 3 H 0-0
1979 3r A 4-2

**v Sheffield Utd**
1906 1 A 1-4
1914 4 H 0-0
1914 4r A 0-0aet
1914 4r2 N 0-1
1939 4 A 0-2

**v Sheffield Wed**
1904 SF N 3-0
1934 5 A 2-2
1934 5r H 2-0

**v Shrewsbury Town**
1965 3 H 1-1
1965 3r A 1-3
1979 4 A 0-2

**v Southampton**
1910 2 A 5-0
1960 3 H 1-5

**v Southend Utd**
1956 4 A 1-0

**v Stoke City**
1911 1 A 2-1
1928 5 H 0-1
1934 6 H 1-0
1973 3 H 3-2
1976 4 A 0-1

**v Sunderland**
1904 1 H 3-2
1913 2 A 0-2
1928 4 A 2-1
1955 SF N 1-0
1973 5 H 2-2
1973 5r A 1-3
1983 3 A 0-0
1983 3r H 2-1

**v Swindon Town**
1910 4 A 0-2
1930 4 A 1-1

| | | | |
|---|---|---|---|
| 1930 | 4r | H | 10-1 |
| 1953 | 3 | H | 7-0 |
| 1964 | 3 | A | 1-2 |
| 2002 | 3 | H | 2-0 |

v **Tottenham Hotspur**

| | | | |
|---|---|---|---|
| 1909 | 1 | H | 3-4 |
| 1914 | 2 | H | 2-1 |
| 1922 | 3 | A | 1-2 |
| 1930 | 3 | A | 2-2 |
| 1930 | 3r | H | 4-1 |
| 1935 | 3 | A | 0-1 |
| 1954 | 4 | H | 0-1 |
| 1956 | SF | N | 1-0 |
| 1969 | 6 | H | 1-0 |
| 1981 | F | N | 1-1aet |
| 1981 | Fr | N | 2-3 |
| 1993 | 6 | H | 2-4 |

v **Walsall**

| | | | |
|---|---|---|---|
| 1933 | 4 | H | 2-0 |
| 1963 | 3 | A | 1-0 |
| 1986 | 3 | A | 3-1 |

v **Watford**

| | | | |
|---|---|---|---|
| 1986 | 4 | H | 1-1 |
| 1986 | 4r | A | 0-0aet |
| 1986 | 4r2 | H | 1-3 |
| 1997 | 4 | H | 3-1 |

v **West Bromwich Albion**

| | | | |
|---|---|---|---|
| 1901 | 1 | A | 0-1 |
| 1958 | 3 | A | 1-5 |
| 1977 | 3 | H | 1-1 |
| 1977 | 3r | A | 1-0 |

v **West Ham Utd**

| | | | |
|---|---|---|---|
| 1998 | 4 | H | 1-2 |

v **Wigan Athletic**

| | | | |
|---|---|---|---|
| 1971 | 3 | H | 1-0 |

v **Wimbledon**

| | | | |
|---|---|---|---|
| 1999 | 3 | A | 0-1 |

v **Wolverhampton W**

| | | | |
|---|---|---|---|
| 1911 | 2 | A | 0-1 |
| 1952 | 3 | H | 2-2 |
| 1952 | 3r | A | 1-4 |

v **Wrexham**

| | | | |
|---|---|---|---|
| 1937 | 3 | A | 3-1 |

# Manchester Utd

v **Middlesbrough**

| | | | |
|---|---|---|---|
| 1894 | 1 | H | 4-0 |
| 1933 | 3 | H | 1-4 |
| 1961 | 3 | H | 3-0 |
| 1970 | 6 | A | 1-1 |
| 1970 | 6r | H | 2-1 |
| 1971 | 3 | H | 0-0 |
| 1971 | 3r | A | 1-2 |
| 1972 | 5 | H | 0-0 |
| 1972 | 5r | A | 3-0 |
| 1999 | 3 | H | 3-1 |
| 2002 | 4 | A | 0-2 |

v **Millwall**

| | | | |
|---|---|---|---|
| 1953 | 3 | A | 1-0 |

v **Newcastle Utd**

| | | | |
|---|---|---|---|
| 1909 | SF | N | 1-0 |
| 1990 | 5 | A | 3-2 |
| 1999 | F | N | 2-0 |

v **Northampton Town**

| | | | |
|---|---|---|---|
| 1970 | 5 | A | 8-2 |

v **Norwich City**

| | | | |
|---|---|---|---|
| 1906 | 2 | H | 3-0 |
| 1959 | 3 | A | 0-3 |
| 1967 | 4 | H | 1-2 |
| 1991 | 5 | A | 1-2 |
| 1994 | 4 | A | 2-0 |

v **Nottingham Forest**

| | | | |
|---|---|---|---|
| 1935 | 4 | A | 0-0 |
| 1935 | 4r | H | 0-3 |
| 1947 | 4 | H | 0-2 |
| 1981 | 4 | A | 0-1 |
| 1989 | 6 | H | 0-1 |
| 1990 | 3 | A | 1-0 |

v **Notts County**

| | | | |
|---|---|---|---|
| 1904 | 1 | A | 3-3 |
| 1904 | 1r | H | 2-1 |

v **Oldham Athletic**

| | | | |
|---|---|---|---|
| 1913 | 3 | A | 0-0 |
| 1913 | 3r | H | 1-2 |
| 1951 | 3 | H | 4-1 |
| 1990 | SF | N | 3-3aet |
| 1990 | SFr | N | 2-1aet |
| 1994 | SF | N | 1-1aet |
| 1994 | SFr | N | 4-1 |

v **Oxford Utd**

| | | | |
|---|---|---|---|
| 1976 | 3 | H | 2-1 |
| 1989 | 4 | H | 4-0 |

v **Peterborough**

| | | | |
|---|---|---|---|
| 1976 | 4 | H | 3-1 |

v **Plymouth Argyle**

| | | | |
|---|---|---|---|
| 1913 | 2 | A | 2-0 |
| 1924 | 1 | H | 1-0 |
| 1932 | 3 | A | 1-4 |
| 1974 | 3 | H | 1-0 |

v **Port Vale**

| | | | |
|---|---|---|---|
| 1920 | 1 | A | 1-0 |
| 1926 | 3 | A | 3-2 |
| 1929 | 3 | A | 3-0 |

v **Portsmouth**

| | | | |
|---|---|---|---|
| 1901 | IR | H | 3-0 |
| 1907 | 1 | A | 2-2 |
| 1907 | 1r | H | 1-2 |
| 1934 | 3 | H | 1-1 |
| 1934 | 3r | A | 1-4 |
| 1950 | 5 | H | 3-3 |
| 1950 | 5r | A | 3-1 |
| 2003 | 3 | H | 4-1 |

v **Preston North End**

| | | | |
|---|---|---|---|
| 1890 | 1 | A | 1-6 |
| 1946 | 4 | H | 1-0 |
| 1946 | 4s | A | 1-3 |
| 1948 | 6 | H | 4-1 |
| 1962 | 6 | A | 0-0 |
| 1962 | 6r | H | 2-1 |
| 1966 | 6 | A | 1-1 |
| 1966 | 6r | H | 3-1 |
| 1972 | 4 | A | 2-0 |

v **QPR**

| | | | |
|---|---|---|---|
| 1977 | 4 | H | 1-0 |
| 1989 | 3 | H | 0-0 |
| 1989 | 3r | A | 2-2aet |
| 1989 | 3r2 | H | 3-0 |
| 1991 | 3 | H | 2-1 |
| 1995 | 6 | H | 2-0 |

v **Reading**

| | | | |
|---|---|---|---|
| 1912 | 3 | A | 1-1 |
| 1912 | 3r | H | 3-0 |
| 1927 | 3 | A | 1-1 |
| 1927 | 3r | H | 2-2aet |
| 1927 | 3r2 | N | 1-2 |
| 1936 | 3 | A | 3-1 |
| 1937 | 3 | H | 1-0 |
| 1955 | 3 | A | 1-1 |
| 1955 | 3r | H | 4-1 |
| 1996 | 4 | A | 3-0 |

v **Rochdale**

| | | | |
|---|---|---|---|
| 1986 | 3 | H | 2-0 |

v **Rotherham Utd**

| | | | |
|---|---|---|---|
| 1966 | 4 | H | 0-0 |
| 1966 | 4r | A | 1-0aet |

v **Sheffield Utd**

| | | | |
|---|---|---|---|
| 1990 | 6 | A | 1-0 |
| 1993 | 5 | A | 1-2 |
| 1994 | 3 | A | 1-0 |
| 1995 | 3 | A | 2-0 |

v **Sheffield Wed**

| | | | |
|---|---|---|---|
| 1904 | 2 | A | 0-6 |
| 1915 | 1 | A | 0-1 |
| 1925 | 1 | A | 0-2 |
| 1958 | 5 | H | 3-0 |
| 1960 | 5 | H | 0-1 |
| 1961 | 4 | A | 1-1 |
| 1961 | 4r | H | 2-7 |
| 1962 | 5 | H | 0-0 |
| 1962 | 5r | A | 2-0 |

v **Southampton**

| | | | |
|---|---|---|---|
| 1897 | 2 | A | 1-1 |
| 1897 | 2r | H | 3-1 |
| 1963 | SF | N | 1-0 |
| 1964 | 3 | A | 3-2 |
| 1972 | 3 | A | 1-1 |
| 1972 | 3r | H | 4-1aet |
| 1976 | F | N | 0-1 |
| 1977 | 5 | A | 2-2 |
| 1977 | 5r | H | 2-1 |
| 1992 | 4 | A | 0-0 |
| 1992 | 4r | H | 2-2q |
| 1996 | 6 | H | 2-0 |

v **Stoke City**

| | | | |
|---|---|---|---|
| 1895 | 1 | H | 2-3 |
| 1931 | 3 | A | 3-3 |
| 1931 | 3r | H | 0-0aet |
| 1931 | 3r2 | N | 4-2 |
| 1936 | 4 | A | 0-0 |
| 1936 | 4r | H | 0-2 |
| 1965 | 4 | A | 0-0 |
| 1965 | 4r | H | 1-0 |
| 1967 | 3 | H | 2-0 |
| 1972 | 6 | H | 1-1 |
| 1972 | 6r | A | 1-2aet |

v **Sunderland**

| | | | |
|---|---|---|---|
| 1926 | 5 | A | 3-3 |
| 1926 | 5r | H | 2-1 |
| 1964 | 6 | H | 3-3 |
| 1964 | 6r | A | 2-2aet |

| | | | |
|---|---|---|---|
| 1964 | 6r2 | N | 5-1 |
| 1986 | 4 | A | 0-0 |
| 1986 | 4r | H | 3-0 |
| 1996 | 3 | H | 2-2 |
| 1996 | 3r | A | 2-1 |

**v Swindon Town**

| | | | |
|---|---|---|---|
| 1914 | 1 | A | 0-1 |
| 1930 | 3 | H | 0-2 |

**v Tottenham Hotspur**

| | | | |
|---|---|---|---|
| 1899 | 1 | A | 1-1 |
| 1899 | 1r | H | 3-5 |
| 1923 | 2 | A | 0-4 |
| 1926 | 4 | A | 2-2 |
| 1926 | 4r | H | 2-0 |
| 1962 | SF | N | 1-3 |
| 1968 | 3 | H | 2-2 |
| 1968 | 3r | A | 0-1aet |
| 1979 | 6 | A | 1-1 |
| 1979 | 6r | H | 2-0 |
| 1980 | 3 | A | 1-1 |
| 1980 | 3r | H | 0-1aet |
| 1997 | 3 | H | 2-0 |

**v Walsall**

| | | | |
|---|---|---|---|
| 1898 | 1 | H | 1-0 |
| 1975 | 3 | H | 0-0 |
| 1975 | 3r | A | 2-3aet |
| 1977 | 3 | H | 1-0 |
| 1998 | 4 | H | 5-1 |

**v Watford**

| | | | |
|---|---|---|---|
| 1950 | 4 | A | 1-0 |
| 1969 | 4 | H | 1-1 |
| 1969 | 4r | A | 2-0 |
| 1982 | 3 | A | 0-1 |

**v West Bromwich Albion**

| | | | |
|---|---|---|---|
| 1939 | 3 | A | 0-0 |
| 1939 | 3r | H | 1-5 |
| 1958 | 6 | A | 2-2 |
| 1958 | 6r | H | 1-0 |
| 1978 | 4 | H | 1-1 |
| 1978 | 4r | A | 2-3aet |

**v West Ham Utd**

| | | | |
|---|---|---|---|
| 1911 | 3 | A | 1-2 |
| 1964 | SF | N | 1-3 |
| 1983 | 3 | H | 2-0 |
| 1985 | 6 | H | 4-2 |
| 1986 | 5 | A | 1-1 |
| 1986 | 5r | H | 0-2 |
| 2001 | 4 | H | 0-1 |
| 2003 | 4 | H | 6-0 |

**v Wimbledon**

| | | | |
|---|---|---|---|
| 1994 | 5 | A | 3-0 |
| 1997 | 4 | H | 1-1 |
| 1997 | 4r | A | 0-1 |

**v Wolverhampton W**

| | | | |
|---|---|---|---|
| 1949 | SF | N | 1-1aet |
| 1949 | SFr | N | 0-1 |
| 1965 | 6 | A | 5-3 |
| 1966 | 5 | A | 4-2 |
| 1973 | 3 | A | 0-1 |
| 1976 | 6 | H | 1-1 |
| 1976 | 6r | A | 3-2aet |

**v Wrexham**

| | | | |
|---|---|---|---|
| 1957 | 4 | A | 5-0 |
| 1995 | 4 | H | 5-2 |

**v Yeovil Town**

| | | | |
|---|---|---|---|
| 1938 | 3 | H | 3-0 |
| 1949 | 5 | H | 8-0 |

# Mansfield Town

**v Middlesbrough**

| | | | |
|---|---|---|---|
| 1967 | 3 | H | 2-0 |

**v Northampton Town**

| | | | |
|---|---|---|---|
| 1947 | 1 | A | 0-2 |
| 1949 | 2 | H | 2-1aet |

**v Nottingham Forest**

| | | | |
|---|---|---|---|
| 1953 | 3 | H | 0-1 |

**v Oldham Athletic**

| | | | |
|---|---|---|---|
| 1948 | 2 | A | 1-0 |
| 1964 | 1 | A | 2-3 |
| 1966 | 1 | H | 1-3 |
| 1998 | 1 | A | 1-1 |
| 1998 | 1r | H | 0-1 |

**v Oxford Utd**

| | | | |
|---|---|---|---|
| 1965 | 1 | A | 1-0 |
| 2002 | 1 | H | 1-0 |

**v Peterborough**

| | | | |
|---|---|---|---|
| 2001 | 1 | H | 1-1 |
| 2001 | 1r | A | 0-4 |

**v Plymouth Argyle**

| | | | |
|---|---|---|---|
| 1978 | 3 | H | 1-0 |

**v Port Vale**

| | | | |
|---|---|---|---|
| 1986 | 1 | H | 1-1 |
| 1986 | 1r | A | 0-1 |

**v Preston North End**

| | | | |
|---|---|---|---|
| 1949 | 3 | A | 1-2 |
| 1988 | 1 | A | 1-1 |
| 1988 | 1r | H | 4-2 |
| 1991 | 1 | A | 1-0 |
| 1992 | 1 | H | 0-1 |
| 1994 | 1 | H | 1-2 |

**v Rochdale**

| | | | |
|---|---|---|---|
| 1981 | 1 | H | 3-1 |

**v Rotherham Utd**

| | | | |
|---|---|---|---|
| 1969 | 2 | A | 2-2 |
| 1969 | 2r | H | 1-0 |
| 1985 | 1 | H | 2-1 |

**v Scunthorpe Utd**

| | | | |
|---|---|---|---|
| 1921 | Q4 | A | 1-0 |
| 1967 | 2 | H | 2-1 |
| 1971 | 2 | A | 0-3 |
| 1974 | 2 | H | 1-1 |
| 1974 | 2r | A | 0-1 |

**v Sheffield Utd**

| | | | |
|---|---|---|---|
| 1951 | 4 | A | 0-0 |
| 1951 | 4r | H | 2-1 |
| 1969 | 3 | H | 2-1 |
| 1989 | 1 | H | 1-1 |
| 1989 | 1r | A | 1-2 |

**v Sheffield Wed**

| | | | |
|---|---|---|---|
| 1946 | 3 | H | 0-0 |
| 1946 | 3s | A | 0-5 |
| 1967 | 4 | A | 0-4 |
| 1991 | 3 | H | 0-2 |

**v Shrewsbury Town**

| | | | |
|---|---|---|---|
| 1970 | 2 | A | 2-1 |
| 1979 | 1 | H | 0-2 |
| 1993 | 1 | A | 1-3 |

**v Southend Utd**

| | | | |
|---|---|---|---|
| 1969 | 4 | H | 2-1 |

**v Stockport County**

| | | | |
|---|---|---|---|
| 1956 | 1 | H | 2-0 |
| 1983 | 1 | H | 3-2 |
| 1997 | 2 | H | 0-3 |

**v Stoke City**

| | | | |
|---|---|---|---|
| 1948 | 3 | H | 2-4 |

**v Swansea City**

| | | | |
|---|---|---|---|
| 1951 | 3 | H | 2-0 |

**v Tranmere Rovers**

| | | | |
|---|---|---|---|
| 1935 | 2 | H | 4-2 |
| 1972 | 2 | H | 2-2 |
| 1972 | 2r | A | 2-4 |

**v Walsall**

| | | | |
|---|---|---|---|
| 1922 | Q6 | H | 1-1 |
| 1922 | Q6r | A | 0-4 |
| 1927 | 2 | A | 0-2 |
| 1933 | 1 | A | 1-4 |
| 1950 | 1 | H | 4-1 |

**v West Ham Utd**

| | | | |
|---|---|---|---|
| 1969 | 5 | H | 3-0 |

**v Wigan Athletic**

| | | | |
|---|---|---|---|
| 1958 | 2 | A | 1-1 |
| 1958 | 2r | H | 3-1 |
| 1975 | 2 | A | 1-1 |
| 1975 | 2r | H | 3-1 |
| 1990 | 1 | A | 0-2 |

**v Wimbledon**

| | | | |
|---|---|---|---|
| 1948 | 1 | A | 1-0 |
| 1988 | 4 | H | 1-2 |

**v Wolverhampton W**

| | | | |
|---|---|---|---|
| 1929 | 3 | A | 1-0 |
| 1995 | 3 | H | 2-3 |

**v Wrexham**

| | | | |
|---|---|---|---|
| 1971 | 1 | H | 2-0 |
| 1975 | 1 | H | 3-1 |
| 1976 | 1 | H | 1-1 |
| 1976 | 1r | A | 1-1aet |
| 1976 | 1r2 | N | 2-1 |

**v York City**

| | | | |
|---|---|---|---|
| 1956 | 2 | A | 1-2 |
| 1973 | 1 | A | 1-2 |
| 1974 | 1 | A | 0-0 |
| 1974 | 1r | H | 5-3 |
| 1991 | 2 | H | 2-1 |

# Middlesbrough

**v Millwall**

| | | | |
|---|---|---|---|
| 1904 | 1 | A | 2-0 |
| 1913 | 1 | A | 0-0 |
| 1913 | 1r | H | 4-1 |
| 1927 | 5 | A | 2-3 |
| 1969 | 3 | H | 1-1 |
| 1969 | 3r | A | 0-1 |
| 1972 | 4 | A | 2-2 |
| 1972 | 4r | H | 2-1 |

**v Newcastle Utd**

| | | | |
|---|---|---|---|
| 1893 | 1 | A | 3-2 |
| 1896 | Q2 | A | 1-4 |
| 1898 | Q5 | H | 0-2 |
| 1901 | 1 | H | 3-1 |

**v Northampton Town**

| | | | |
|---|---|---|---|
| 1907 | 1 | H | 4-2 |

**v Nottingham Forest**

| | | | |
|---|---|---|---|
| 1938 | 4 | A | 3-1 |
| 1947 | 5 | A | 2-2 |
| 1947 | 5r | H | 6-2 |
| 1993 | 4 | A | 1-1 |
| 1993 | 4r | H | 0-3 |

**v Notts County**

| | | | |
|---|---|---|---|
| 1908 | 1 | A | 0-2 |
| 1920 | 2 | A | 0-1 |
| 1955 | 3 | H | 1-4 |
| 1983 | 4 | H | 2-0 |
| 1984 | 5 | A | 0-1 |
| 1987 | 2 | A | 1-0 |
| 1996 | 3 | A | 2-1 |

**v Oldham Athletic**

| | | | |
|---|---|---|---|
| 1923 | 1 | A | 1-0 |
| 1965 | 3 | H | 6-2 |

**v Peterborough**

| | | | |
|---|---|---|---|
| 1975 | 5 | A | 1-1 |
| 1975 | 5r | H | 2-0 |

**v Plymouth Argyle**

| | | | |
|---|---|---|---|
| 1973 | 3 | A | 0-1 |
| 1991 | 3 | H | 0-0 |
| 1991 | 3r | A | 2-1 |

**v Portsmouth**

| | | | |
|---|---|---|---|
| 1932 | 3 | H | 1-1 |
| 1932 | 3r | A | 0-3 |
| 1980 | 3 | A | 1-1 |
| 1980 | 3r | H | 3-0 |
| 1992 | 5 | A | 1-1 |
| 1992 | 5r | H | 2-4 |

**v Preston North End**

| | | | |
|---|---|---|---|
| 1892 | 2 | H | 1-2 |
| 1904 | 2 | A | 3-0 |
| 1909 | 1 | A | 0-1 |
| 1927 | 4 | A | 3-0 |
| 1987 | 3 | H | 0-1 |

**v QPR**

| | | | |
|---|---|---|---|
| 1913 | 2 | H | 3-2 |
| 1947 | 3 | A | 1-1 |
| 1947 | 3r | H | 3-1 |
| 1982 | 3 | A | 1-1 |
| 1982 | 3r | H | 2-3aet |
| 1998 | 3 | A | 2-2 |
| 1998 | 3r | H | 2-0 |

**v Sheffield Utd**

| | | | |
|---|---|---|---|
| 1923 | 2 | H | 1-1 |
| 1923 | 2r | A | 0-3 |

**v Sheffield Wed**

| | | | |
|---|---|---|---|
| 1895 | 2 | A | 1-6 |
| 1912 | 1 | H | 0-0 |
| 1912 | 1r | A | 2-1 |
| 1960 | 3 | A | 1-2 |
| 1992 | 4 | A | 2-1 |

**v Shrewsbury Town**

| | | | |
|---|---|---|---|
| 1962 | 4 | A | 2-2 |
| 1962 | 4r | H | 5-1 |

**v Southampton**

| | | | |
|---|---|---|---|
| 1906 | 3 | A | 1-6 |
| 1936 | 3 | H | 1-0 |
| 1986 | 3 | H | 1-3 |

**v Stockport County**

| | | | |
|---|---|---|---|
| 1938 | 3 | H | 2-0 |

**v Stoke City**

| | | | |
|---|---|---|---|
| 1933 | 4 | H | 4-1 |
| 1958 | 4 | A | 1-3 |

**v Sunderland**

| | | | |
|---|---|---|---|
| 1888 | 3 | H | 2-2 |
| 1934 | 3 | A | 1-1 |
| 1934 | 3r | H | 1-2 |
| 1939 | 4 | H | 0-2 |
| 1975 | 4 | H | 3-1 |

**v Swansea City**

| | | | |
|---|---|---|---|
| 1981 | 3 | A | 5-0 |
| 1995 | 3 | A | 1-1 |
| 1995 | 3r | H | 1-2 |

**v Tottenham Hotspur**

| | | | |
|---|---|---|---|
| 1905 | 1 | H | 1-1 |
| 1905 | 1r | A | 0-1 |
| 1956 | 4 | A | 1-3 |
| 1966 | 3 | A | 0-4 |

**v Walsall**

| | | | |
|---|---|---|---|
| 1929 | 3 | A | 1-1 |
| 1929 | 3r | H | 5-1 |

**v Watford**

| | | | |
|---|---|---|---|
| 1924 | 1 | H | 0-1 |

**v West Bromwich Albion**

| | | | |
|---|---|---|---|
| 1901 | 3 | H | 0-1 |
| 1929 | 4 | A | 0-1 |
| 1981 | 4 | H | 1-0 |

**v West Ham Utd**

| | | | |
|---|---|---|---|
| 1912 | 2 | H | 1-1 |
| 1912 | 2r | A | 1-2 |
| 1970 | 3 | H | 2-1 |

**v Wimbledon**

| | | | |
|---|---|---|---|
| 1977 | 3 | A | 0-0 |
| 1977 | 3r | H | 1-0 |
| 1996 | 4 | H | 0-0 |
| 1996 | 4r | A | 0-1 |
| 2001 | 4 | H | 0-0 |
| 2001 | 4r | A | 1-3aet |
| 2002 | 3 | A | 0-0 |
| 2002 | 3r | H | 2-0 |

**v Wolverhampton W**

| | | | |
|---|---|---|---|
| 1893 | 2 | A | 1-2aet |
| 1937 | 3 | A | 1-6 |
| 1981 | 6 | H | 1-1 |
| 1981 | 6r | A | 1-3aet |

**v Wrexham**

| | | | |
|---|---|---|---|
| 1974 | 4 | A | 0-1 |
| 2000 | 3 | A | 1-2 |

**v Wycombe W**

| | | | |
|---|---|---|---|
| 1975 | 3 | A | 0-0 |
| 1975 | 3r | H | 1-0 |

**v York City**

| | | | |
|---|---|---|---|
| 1938 | 5 | A | 0-1 |
| 1967 | 2 | H | 1-1 |
| 1967 | 2r | A | 0-0aet |
| 1967 | 2r2 | N | 4-1 |
| 1970 | 4 | H | 4-1 |

# Millwall

**v Newcastle Utd**

| | | | |
|---|---|---|---|
| 1957 | 4 | H | 2-1 |

**v Northampton Town**

| | | | |
|---|---|---|---|
| 1929 | 3 | H | 1-1 |
| 1929 | 3r | A | 2-2aet |
| 1929 | 3r2 | N | 2-0 |
| 1946 | 3 | A | 2-2 |
| 1946 | 3s | H | 3-0 |
| 1956 | 1 | A | 1-4 |
| 1962 | 1 | A | 0-2 |

**v Norwich City**

| | | | |
|---|---|---|---|
| 1992 | 4 | A | 1-2 |

**v Nottingham Forest**

| | | | |
|---|---|---|---|
| 1909 | 3 | A | 1-3 |
| 1972 | 3 | H | 3-1 |

**v Notts County**

| | | | |
|---|---|---|---|
| 1920 | 1 | A | 0-2 |
| 1978 | 5 | H | 2-1 |

**v Oldham Athletic**

| | | | |
|---|---|---|---|
| 1926 | 3 | H | 1-1 |
| 1926 | 3r | A | 1-0 |

**v Oxford Utd**

| | | | |
|---|---|---|---|
| 1954 | 2 | H | 3-3 |
| 1954 | 2r | A | 0-1 |
| 1996 | 3 | H | 3-3 |
| 1996 | 3r | A | 0-1 |

**v Plymouth Argyle**

| | | | |
|---|---|---|---|
| 1907 | 1 | H | 2-0 |
| 1952 | 1 | H | 1-0 |

**v Port Vale**

| | | | |
|---|---|---|---|
| 1947 | 3 | H | 0-3 |
| 1965 | 2 | H | 4-0 |

**v Portsmouth**

| | | | |
|---|---|---|---|
| 1982 | 1 | A | 1-1 |
| 1982 | 1r | H | 3-2aet |

**v Preston North End**

| | | | |
|---|---|---|---|
| 1903 | 2 | H | 4-1 |
| 1948 | 3 | H | 1-2 |

**v QPR**

| | | | |
|---|---|---|---|
| 1900 | 2 | A | 2-0 |
| 1951 | 3 | A | 4-3 |
| 1995 | 5 | A | 0-1 |

**v Reading**

| | | | |
|---|---|---|---|
| 1933 | 3 | H | 1-1 |
| 1933 | 3r | A | 2-0 |
| 1935 | 4 | A | 0-1 |
| 1961 | 1 | A | 2-6 |

**v Rotherham Utd**

| | | | |
|---|---|---|---|
| 1978 | 3 | A | 1-1 |
| 1978 | 3r | H | 2-0 |

**v Scunthorpe Utd**

| | | | |
|---|---|---|---|
| 1952 | 2 | H | 0-0 |
| 1952 | 2r | A | 0-3 |
| 1970 | 3 | A | 1-2 |

| | | | |
|---|---|---|---|
| 1974 | 3 | H | 1-1 |
| 1974 | 3r | A | 0-1 |
| 2002 | 3 | H | 2-1 |

**v Sheffield Utd**

| | | | |
|---|---|---|---|
| 1895 | 1 | A | 1-3 |
| 1914 | 3 | H | 0-4 |

**v Sheffield Wed**

| | | | |
|---|---|---|---|
| 1906 | 2 | A | 1-1 |
| 1906 | 2r | H | 0-3 |
| 1991 | 4 | H | 4-4 |
| 1991 | 4r | A | 0-2 |

**v Shrewsbury Town**

| | | | |
|---|---|---|---|
| 1965 | 4 | H | 1-2 |
| 1980 | 3 | H | 5-1 |

**v Southampton**

| | | | |
|---|---|---|---|
| 1900 | SF | N | 0-0 |
| 1900 | SFr | N | 0-3 |
| 1905 | 1 | A | 1-3 |
| 1927 | 6 | H | 0-0 |
| 1927 | 6r | A | 0-2 |
| 1986 | 5 | A | 0-0 |
| 1986 | 5r | H | 0-1 |
| 2003 | 4 | A | 1-1 |
| 2003 | 4r | H | 1-2aet |

**v Southend Utd**

| | | | |
|---|---|---|---|
| 1993 | 3 | A | 0-1 |

**v Stoke City**

| | | | |
|---|---|---|---|
| 1936 | 3 | H | 0-0 |
| 1936 | 3r | A | 0-4 |
| 1971 | 3 | A | 1-2 |

**v Sunderland**

| | | | |
|---|---|---|---|
| 1937 | SF | N | 1-2 |

**v Swansea City**

| | | | |
|---|---|---|---|
| 1922 | 3 | H | 4-0 |
| 1926 | 5 | H | 0-1 |
| 1999 | 1 | A | 0-3 |

**v Swindon Town**

| | | | |
|---|---|---|---|
| 1984 | 2 | H | 2-3 |

**v Tottenham Hotspur**

| | | | |
|---|---|---|---|
| 1911 | 1 | A | 1-2 |
| 1967 | 3 | H | 0-0 |
| 1967 | 3r | A | 0-1 |

**v West Bromwich Albion**

| | | | |
|---|---|---|---|
| 1924 | 1 | H | 0-1 |

**v West Ham Utd**

| | | | |
|---|---|---|---|
| 1900 | Q5 | A | 2-1 |
| 1930 | 5 | A | 1-4 |

**v Wigan Athletic**

| | | | |
|---|---|---|---|
| 1935 | 3 | A | 4-1 |

**v Wimbledon**

| | | | |
|---|---|---|---|
| 1986 | 3 | H | 3-1 |

**v Wolverhampton W**

| | | | |
|---|---|---|---|
| 1897 | 1 | H | 1-2 |
| 1973 | 5 | A | 0-1 |

**v Wycombe W**

| | | | |
|---|---|---|---|
| 2001 | 2 | H | 0-0 |
| 2001 | 2r | A | 1-2 |

**v Yeovil Town**

| | | | |
|---|---|---|---|
| 1976 | 1 | A | 1-1 |
| 1976 | 1r | H | 2-2aet |
| 1976 | 1r2 | N | 1-0 |

**v York City**

| | | | |
|---|---|---|---|
| 1939 | 3 | A | 5-0 |

# Newcastle Utd

**v Northampton Town**

| | | | |
|---|---|---|---|
| 1911 | 2 | H | 1-1 |

**v Northampton Town**

| | | | |
|---|---|---|---|
| 1911 | 2r | H | 1-0 |
| 1987 | 3 | H | 2-1 |

**v Norwich City**

| | | | |
|---|---|---|---|
| 1963 | 4 | A | 0-5 |

**v Nottingham Forest**

| | | | |
|---|---|---|---|
| 1908 | 1 | H | 2-0 |
| 1921 | 1 | H | 1-1 |
| 1921 | 1r | H | 2-0 |
| 1931 | 3 | H | 4-0 |
| 1955 | 5 | A | 1-1 |
| 1955 | 5r | H | 2-2aet |
| 1955 | 5r2 | H | 2-1aet |
| 1967 | 4 | A | 0-3 |
| 1974 | 6r | N | 0-0 |
| 1974 | 6r2 | N | 1-0 |
| 1985 | 3 | A | 1-1 |
| 1985 | 3r | H | 1-3aet |
| 1991 | 4 | H | 2-2 |
| 1991 | 4r | A | 0-3 |
| 1997 | 4 | H | 1-2 |

**v Notts County**

| | | | |
|---|---|---|---|
| 1927 | 3 | H | 8-1 |

**v Oldham Athletic**

| | | | |
|---|---|---|---|
| 1950 | 3 | A | 7-2 |

**v Peterborough**

| | | | |
|---|---|---|---|
| 1962 | 3 | H | 0-1 |
| 1978 | 3 | A | 1-1 |
| 1978 | 3r | H | 2-0 |
| 2002 | 4 | A | 4-2 |

**v Plymouth Argyle**

| | | | |
|---|---|---|---|
| 1905 | 1 | H | 1-1 |
| 1905 | 1r | A | 1-1 |
| 1905 | 1r2 | N | 2-0 |
| 1955 | 3 | A | 1-0 |
| 1958 | 3 | A | 6-1 |

**v Port Vale**

| | | | |
|---|---|---|---|
| 1993 | 3 | H | 4-0 |

**v Portsmouth**

| | | | |
|---|---|---|---|
| 1924 | 1 | A | 4-2 |
| 1952 | 6 | A | 4-2 |

**v Preston North End**

| | | | |
|---|---|---|---|
| 1898 | 1 | A | 2-1 |
| 1922 | 2 | A | 1-3 |
| 1937 | 3 | A | 0-2 |
| 1939 | 5 | H | 1-2 |
| 1987 | 4 | H | 2-0 |

**v QPR**

| | | | |
|---|---|---|---|
| 1976 | 3 | A | 0-0 |
| 1976 | 3r | H | 2-1 |

**v Reading**

| | | | |
|---|---|---|---|
| 1900 | 1 | H | 2-1 |
| 1969 | 3 | H | 4-0 |
| 1990 | 4 | A | 3-3 |
| 1990 | 4r | H | 4-1 |

**v Rotherham Utd**

| | | | |
|---|---|---|---|
| 1953 | 4 | H | 1-3 |
| 1993 | 4 | A | 1-1 |
| 1993 | 4r | H | 2-0 |

**v Scunthorpe Utd**

| | | | |
|---|---|---|---|
| 1958 | 4 | H | 1-3 |
| 1974 | 4 | H | 1-1 |
| 1974 | 4r | A | 3-0 |

**v Sheffield Utd**

| | | | |
|---|---|---|---|
| 1894 | 1 | H | 2-0 |
| 1902 | 3 | H | 1-1 |
| 1902 | 3r | A | 1-2 |
| 1914 | 1 | H | 0-5 |
| 1947 | 6 | A | 2-0 |
| 1961 | 6 | H | 1-3 |
| 1977 | 3 | A | 0-0 |
| 1977 | 3r | H | 3-1 |
| 1998 | SF | N | 1-0 |
| 2000 | 4 | H | 4-1 |

**v Sheffield Wed**

| | | | |
|---|---|---|---|
| 1905 | SF | N | 1-0 |
| 1915 | 3 | A | 2-1 |
| 1936 | 4 | A | 1-1 |
| 1936 | 4r | H | 3-1 |
| 1956 | 3 | A | 3-1 |
| 1966 | 4 | H | 1-2 |
| 1981 | 3 | H | 2-1 |

**v Southampton**

| | | | |
|---|---|---|---|
| 1898 | 2 | A | 0-1 |
| 1900 | 2 | A | 1-4 |
| 1923 | 1 | H | 0-0 |
| 1923 | 1r | A | 1-3 |
| 1927 | 5 | A | 1-2 |
| 1947 | 4 | H | 3-1 |
| 1970 | 3 | A | 0-3 |

**v Stockport County**

| | | | |
|---|---|---|---|
| 1961 | 4 | H | 4-0 |

**v Stoke City**

| | | | |
|---|---|---|---|
| 1910 | 1 | A | 1-1 |
| 1910 | 1r | H | 2-1 |
| 1951 | 5 | A | 4-2 |
| 1956 | 5 | H | 2-1 |
| 1961 | 5 | H | 3-1 |

**v Sunderland**

| | | | |
|---|---|---|---|
| 1902 | 2 | H | 1-0 |
| 1909 | 4 | H | 2-2 |
| 1909 | 4r | A | 3-0 |
| 1913 | 4 | A | 0-0 |
| 1913 | 4r | H | 2-2aet |
| 1913 | 4r2 | H | 0-3 |
| 1956 | 6 | H | 0-2 |

**v Swansea City**

| | | | |
|---|---|---|---|
| 1915 | 2 | H | 1-1aet |
| 1915 | 2r | A | 2-0 |
| 1952 | 5 | A | 1-0 |
| 1953 | 3 | H | 3-0 |
| 1965 | 3 | A | 0-1 |
| 1995 | 4 | H | 3-0 |

**v Swindon Town**

| | | | |
|---|---|---|---|
| 1910 | SF | N | 2-0 |
| 1929 | 3 | A | 0-2 |
| 1988 | 4 | H | 5-0 |

**v Torquay Utd**

| | | | |
|---|---|---|---|
| 1979 | 3 | H | 3-1 |

**v Tottenham Hotspur**

| | | | |
|---|---|---|---|
| 1905 | 2 | A | 1-1 |
| 1905 | 2r | H | 4-0 |
| 1935 | 4 | A | 0-2 |
| 1952 | 4 | A | 3-0 |
| 1987 | 5 | A | 0-1 |
| 1999 | SF | N | 2-0aet |
| 2000 | 3 | A | 1-1 |
| 2000 | 3r | H | 6-1 |

**v Tranmere Rovers**

| | | | |
|---|---|---|---|
| 1998 | 5 | H | 1-0 |
| 2000 | 6 | A | 3-2 |

**v Walsall**

| | | | |
|---|---|---|---|
| 1936 | 3 | A | 2-0 |
| 1975 | 4 | A | 0-1 |

**v Watford**

| | | | |
|---|---|---|---|
| 1924 | 3 | A | 1-0 |
| 1932 | 6 | H | 5-0 |
| 1989 | 3 | H | 0-0 |
| 1989 | 3r | A | 2-2aet |
| 1989 | 3r2 | H | 0-0aet |
| 1989 | 3r3 | A | 0-1aet |

**v West Bromwich Albion**

| | | | |
|---|---|---|---|
| 1938 | 3 | A | 0-1 |
| 1954 | 5 | A | 2-3 |
| 1974 | 5 | A | 3-0 |

**v West Ham Utd**

| | | | |
|---|---|---|---|
| 1908 | 2 | H | 2-0 |
| 1909 | 3 | A | 0-0 |
| 1909 | 3r | H | 2-1 |
| 1915 | 1 | A | 2-2 |
| 1915 | 1r | H | 3-2 |

**v Wigan Athletic**

| | | | |
|---|---|---|---|
| 1954 | 3 | H | 2-2 |
| 1954 | 3r | A | 3-2 |

**v Wimbledon**

| | | | |
|---|---|---|---|
| 1988 | 5 | H | 1-3 |

**v Wolverhampton W**

| | | | |
|---|---|---|---|
| 1908 | F | N | 1-3 |
| 1934 | 3 | A | 0-1 |
| 1951 | SF | N | 0-0 |
| 1951 | SFr | N | 2-1 |
| 1960 | 3 | H | 2-2 |
| 1960 | 3r | A | 2-4 |
| 1979 | 4 | H | 1-1 |
| 1979 | 4r | A | 0-1 |
| 2003 | 3 | A | 2-3 |

**v Wrexham**

| | | | |
|---|---|---|---|
| 1978 | 4 | H | 2-2 |
| 1978 | 4r | A | 1-4 |

**v York City**

| | | | |
|---|---|---|---|
| 1930 | 3 | H | 1-1 |
| 1930 | 3r | A | 2-1 |
| 1955 | SF | N | 1-1 |
| 1955 | SFr | N | 2-0 |

# Northampton Town

**v Norwich City**

| | | | |
|---|---|---|---|
| 1952 | 1 | A | 2-3 |

**v Nottingham Forest**

| | | | |
|---|---|---|---|
| 1910 | 2 | H | 0-0 |
| 1910 | 2r | A | 0-1 |
| 1966 | 3 | H | 1-2 |

**v Notts County**

| | | | |
|---|---|---|---|
| 1946 | 2 | H | 3-1 |
| 1946 | 2s | A | 0-1 |

**v Oxford Utd**

| | | | |
|---|---|---|---|
| 1996 | 2 | A | 0-2 |

**v Peterborough**

| | | | |
|---|---|---|---|
| 1947 | 2 | A | 1-1 |
| 1947 | 2r | H | 1-1aet |
| 1947 | 2r2 | N | 8-1 |
| 1973 | 1 | A | 0-1 |
| 1981 | 1 | H | 1-4 |
| 1987 | 1 | H | 3-0 |
| 1995 | 1 | A | 0-4 |

**v Port Vale**

| | | | |
|---|---|---|---|
| 1962 | 3 | A | 1-3 |

**v Portsmouth**

| | | | |
|---|---|---|---|
| 1979 | 1 | A | 0-2 |

**v Preston North End**

| | | | |
|---|---|---|---|
| 1934 | 5 | A | 0-4 |
| 1947 | 3 | H | 1-2 |

**v Reading**

| | | | |
|---|---|---|---|
| 1922 | 1 | H | 3-0 |

**v Rochdale**

| | | | |
|---|---|---|---|
| 1990 | 4 | A | 0-3 |

**v Rotherham Utd**

| | | | |
|---|---|---|---|
| 1975 | 2 | A | 1-2 |
| 1993 | 3 | H | 0-1 |
| 2001 | 2 | A | 0-1 |

**v Sheffield Utd**

| | | | |
|---|---|---|---|
| 1902 | 1 | H | 0-2 |

**v Sheffield Wed**

| | | | |
|---|---|---|---|
| 1910 | 1 | H | 0-0 |
| 1910 | 1r | A | 1-0 |

**v Shrewsbury Town**

| | | | |
|---|---|---|---|
| 2000 | 1 | A | 1-2 |

**v Southampton**

| | | | |
|---|---|---|---|
| 1921 | 1 | H | 0-0 |
| 1921 | 1r | A | 1-4 |
| 1934 | 3 | A | 1-1 |
| 1934 | 3r | H | 1-0 |
| 1950 | 3 | H | 1-1 |
| 1950 | 3r | A | 3-2 |
| 1957 | 1 | A | 0-2 |

**v Southend Utd**

| | | | |
|---|---|---|---|
| 1932 | 2 | H | 3-0 |
| 1987 | 2 | A | 4-4 |
| 1987 | 2r | H | 3-2 |

**v Stoke City**

| | | | |
|---|---|---|---|
| 1922 | 2 | H | 2-2 |
| 1922 | 2r | A | 0-3 |

**v Sunderland**

| | | | |
|---|---|---|---|
| 1928 | 3 | A | 3-3 |
| 1928 | 3r | H | 0-3 |
| 1964 | 3 | A | 0-2 |

**v Swansea City**

| | | | |
|---|---|---|---|
| 1989 | 1 | A | 1-3 |

**v Swindon Town**

| | | | |
|---|---|---|---|
| 1953 | 2 | A | 0-2 |

**v Torquay Utd**

| | | | |
|---|---|---|---|
| 1934 | 2 | H | 3-0 |
| 1948 | 2 | H | 1-1aet |
| 1948 | 2r | A | 0-2 |
| 1950 | 2 | H | 4-2 |
| 1960 | 1 | A | 1-7 |
| 1963 | 1 | H | 1-2 |
| 1975 | 1 | A | 1-0 |
| 2002 | 1 | A | 2-1 |

**v Tottenham Hotspur**

| | | | |
|---|---|---|---|
| 1925 | 1 | A | 0-3 |

**v Tranmere Rovers**

| | | | |
|---|---|---|---|
| 1970 | 4 | A | 0-0 |
| 1970 | 4r | H | 2-1 |

**v Watford**

| | | | |
|---|---|---|---|
| 1939 | 1 | A | 1-4 |
| 1997 | 1 | H | 0-1 |

**v West Bromwich Albion**

| | | | |
|---|---|---|---|
| 1967 | 3 | H | 1-3 |

**v Wimbledon**

| | | | |
|---|---|---|---|
| 1983 | 1 | H | 2-2 |
| 1983 | 1r | A | 2-0 |

**v Wycombe W**

| | | | |
|---|---|---|---|
| 1959 | 1 | H | 2-0 |

**v Yeovil Town**

| | | | |
|---|---|---|---|
| 1999 | 2 | A | 0-2 |

# Norwich City

**v Nottingham Forest**

| | | | |
|---|---|---|---|
| 1915 | 1 | A | 4-1 |
| 1965 | 3 | A | 0-1 |
| 1991 | 6 | H | 0-1 |

**v Notts County**

| | | | |
|---|---|---|---|
| 1925 | 2 | A | 0-4 |
| 1992 | 5 | H | 3-0 |

**v Oxford Utd**

| | | | |
|---|---|---|---|
| 1955 | 1 | H | 4-2 |

**v Port Vale**

| | | | |
|---|---|---|---|
| 1989 | 3 | A | 3-1 |

**v Portsmouth**

| | | | |
|---|---|---|---|
| 1950 | 3 | A | 1-1 |
| 1950 | 3r | H | 0-2 |

**v QPR**

| | | | |
|---|---|---|---|
| 1910 | 1 | H | 0-0 |
| 1910 | 1r | A | 0-3 |
| 1947 | 2 | H | 4-4 |
| 1947 | 2r | A | 0-2 |

**v Reading**

| | | | |
|---|---|---|---|
| 1909 | 1 | N | 0-0 |
| 1909 | 1r | A | 1-1aet |
| 1909 | 1r2 | N | 3-2aet |
| 1960 | 1 | H | 1-1 |
| 1960 | 1r | A | 1-2 |

**v Rochdale**

| | | | |
|---|---|---|---|
| 1925 | Q6 | H | 1-0 |
| 1976 | 3 | H | 1-1 |
| 1976 | 3r | A | 0-0aet |
| 1976 | 3r2 | H | 2-1 |

**v Scunthorpe Utd**

| | | | |
|---|---|---|---|
| 1961 | 4 | A | 4-1 |

v **Sheffield Utd**

| | | | |
|---|---|---|---|
| 1959 | 6 | A | 1-1 |
| 1959 | 6r | H | 3-2 |
| 1962 | 5 | A | 1-3 |
| 1989 | 5 | H | 3-2 |
| 1997 | 3 | H | 1-0 |

v **Sheffield Wed**

| | | | |
|---|---|---|---|
| 1908 | 1 | H | 2-0 |
| 1935 | 5 | H | 0-1 |
| 1967 | 5 | H | 1-3 |
| 1999 | 3 | A | 1-4 |
| 2001 | 3 | A | 1-2 |

v **Southampton**

| | | | |
|---|---|---|---|
| 1927 | 3 | A | 0-3 |
| 1992 | 6 | A | 0-0 |
| 1992 | 6r | H | 2-1aet |
| 2003 | 5 | A | 0-2 |

v **Southend Utd**

| | | | |
|---|---|---|---|
| 1923 | Q5 | A | 2-2 |
| 1923 | Q5r | H | 2-1 |

v **Stockport County**

| | | | |
|---|---|---|---|
| 1924 | Q6 | H | 2-0 |

v **Stoke City**

| | | | |
|---|---|---|---|
| 1982 | 3 | A | 1-0 |

v **Sunderland**

| | | | |
|---|---|---|---|
| 1911 | 1 | H | 3-1 |
| 1951 | 5 | A | 1-3 |
| 1956 | 3 | A | 2-4 |
| 1961 | 5 | H | 0-1 |
| 1968 | 3 | H | 1-1 |
| 1968 | 3r | A | 1-0 |
| 1992 | SF | N | 0-1 |

v **Swansea City**

| | | | |
|---|---|---|---|
| 1983 | 3 | H | 2-1 |

v **Swindon Town**

| | | | |
|---|---|---|---|
| 1931 | 1 | H | 2-0 |
| 1959 | 2 | A | 1-1 |
| 1959 | 2r | H | 1-0 |
| 1988 | 3 | A | 0-0 |
| 1988 | 3r | H | 0-2 |
| 1991 | 4 | H | 3-1 |

v **Torquay Utd**

| | | | |
|---|---|---|---|
| 1949 | 2 | A | 1-3 |

v **Tottenham Hotspur**

| | | | |
|---|---|---|---|
| 1915 | 2 | H | 3-2 |
| 1959 | 5 | A | 1-1 |
| 1959 | 5r | H | 1-0 |
| 1984 | 4 | A | 0-0 |
| 1984 | 4r | H | 2-1 |
| 1993 | 4 | H | 0-2 |

v **Walsall**

| | | | |
|---|---|---|---|
| 1948 | 2 | H | 2-2aet |
| 1948 | 2r | A | 2-3 |
| 1966 | 4 | H | 3-2 |

v **Watford**

| | | | |
|---|---|---|---|
| 1951 | 1 | H | 2-0 |

v **West Bromwich Albion**

| | | | |
|---|---|---|---|
| 1907 | 2 | A | 0-1 |
| 1969 | 3 | A | 0-3 |
| 1982 | 5 | A | 0-1 |

v **West Ham Utd**

| | | | |
|---|---|---|---|
| 1985 | 4 | A | 1-2 |
| 1989 | 6 | A | 0-0 |
| 1989 | 6r | H | 3-1 |

v **Wigan Athletic**

| | | | |
|---|---|---|---|
| 1987 | 4 | A | 0-1 |

v **Wimbledon**

| | | | |
|---|---|---|---|
| 1932 | 1 | A | 3-1 |

v **Wolverhampton W**

| | | | |
|---|---|---|---|
| 1971 | 3 | A | 1-5 |
| 1980 | 4 | A | 1-1 |
| 1980 | 4r | H | 2-3 |

v **Wrexham**

| | | | |
|---|---|---|---|
| 1962 | 3 | H | 3-1 |
| 1970 | 3 | H | 1-2 |

v **Wycombe W**

| | | | |
|---|---|---|---|
| 1994 | 3 | A | 2-0 |

v **Yeovil Town**

| | | | |
|---|---|---|---|
| 1954 | 1 | A | 2-0 |
| 1980 | 3 | A | 3-0 |

v **York City**

| | | | |
|---|---|---|---|
| 1961 | 3 | A | 1-1 |
| 1961 | 3r | H | 1-0 |

# Nottingham Forest

v **Notts County**

| | | | |
|---|---|---|---|
| 1879 | 1 | A | 3-1aet |
| 1880 | 1 | H | 4-0 |
| 1884 | 2 | A | 0-3 |
| 1888 | 3 | H | 2-1 |
| 1894 | 3 | H | 1-1aet |
| 1894 | 3r | A | 1-4 |

v **Oldham Athletic**

| | | | |
|---|---|---|---|
| 1913 | 2 | A | 1-5 |

v **Oxford Utd**

| | | | |
|---|---|---|---|
| 1996 | 4 | H | 1-1 |
| 1996 | 4r | A | 3-0 |
| 2000 | 3 | H | 1-1 |
| Oxford Utd | | | |
| 2000 | 3r | A | 3-1 |

v **Peterborough**

| | | | |
|---|---|---|---|
| 1976 | 3 | H | 0-0 |
| 1976 | 3r | A | 0-1 |

v **Plymouth Argyle**

| | | | |
|---|---|---|---|
| 1954 | 3 | A | 0-2 |
| 1967 | 3 | H | 2-1 |
| 1995 | 3 | H | 2-0 |

v **Portsmouth**

| | | | |
|---|---|---|---|
| 1957 | 4 | A | 3-1 |
| 1974 | 5 | H | 1-0 |
| 1992 | 6 | A | 0-1 |
| 1999 | 3 | H | 0-1 |

v **Preston North End**

| | | | |
|---|---|---|---|
| 1892 | 3 | H | 2-0 |
| 1900 | 3 | A | 0-0 |
| 1900 | 3r | H | 1-0 |
| 1964 | 3 | H | 0-0 |
| 1964 | 3r | A | 0-1 |
| 1969 | 3 | A | 0-3 |

v **QPR**

| | | | |
|---|---|---|---|
| 1934 | 3 | H | 4-0 |
| 1978 | 5 | A | 1-1 |
| 1978 | 5r | H | 1-1aet |
| 1978 | 5r2 | H | 3-1 |

v **Reading**

| | | | |
|---|---|---|---|
| 1903 | 1 | H | 0-0 |
| 1903 | 1r | A | 6-3aet |
| 1960 | 3 | H | 1-0 |

v **Rotherham Utd**

| | | | |
|---|---|---|---|
| 1930 | 3 | A | 5-0 |
| 1951 | 2 | A | 1-3 |

v **Sheffield Utd**

| | | | |
|---|---|---|---|
| 1899 | 3 | H | 0-1 |
| 1905 | 1 | H | 2-0 |
| 1910 | 1 | H | 3-2 |
| 1923 | 1 | H | 0-0 |
| 1923 | 1r | A | 0-0aet |
| 1923 | 1r2 | N | 1-1aet |
| 1923 | 1r3 | N | 0-1 |
| 1928 | 6 | A | 0-3 |
| 1937 | 3 | H | 2-4 |
| 1955 | 3 | A | 3-1 |
| 1960 | 4 | A | 0-3 |
| 2002 | 3 | A | 0-1 |

v **Sheffield Wed**

| | | | |
|---|---|---|---|
| 1883 | 3 | H | 2-2 |
| 1883 | 3r | A | 2-3 |
| 1885 | 3 | A | 2-1 |
| 1888 | 5 | H | 2-4 |
| 1897 | 1 | A | 1-0 |
| 1906 | 3 | A | 1-4 |
| 1930 | 6 | H | 2-2 |
| 1930 | 6r | A | 1-3 |
| 1962 | 4 | H | 0-2 |
| 1994 | 3 | A | 1-1 |
| 1994 | 3r | H | 0-2 |

v **Shrewsbury Town**

| | | | |
|---|---|---|---|
| 1915 | Q6 | H | 6-1 |

v **Southampton**

| | | | |
|---|---|---|---|
| 1895 | 1 | A | 4-1 |
| 1898 | SF | N | 1-1 |
| 1898 | SFr | N | 2-0 |
| 1902 | SF | N | 1-3 |
| 1938 | 3 | H | 3-1 |
| 1963 | 6 | H | 1-1 |
| 1963 | 6r | A | 3-3e |
| 1963 | 6r2 | N | 0-5 |
| 1977 | 4 | H | 3-3 |
| 1977 | 4r | A | 1-2 |
| 1984 | 3 | H | 1-2 |
| 1991 | 5 | A | 1-1 |
| 1991 | 5r | H | 3-1 |
| 1993 | 3 | H | 2-1 |

v **Southend Utd**

| | | | |
|---|---|---|---|
| 1926 | 5 | A | 1-0 |

v **Stockport County**

| | | | |
|---|---|---|---|
| 1950 | 2 | H | 0-2 |

v **Stoke City**

| | | | |
|---|---|---|---|
| 1902 | 3 | H | 2-0 |
| 1903 | 2 | H | 0-0 |
| 1903 | 2r | A | 0-2 |
| 1996 | 3 | A | 1-1 |
| 1996 | 3r | H | 2-0 |

v **Sunderland**

| | | | |
|---|---|---|---|
| 1891 | 3 | A | 0-4 |
| 1897 | 2 | A | 3-1 |
| 1900 | 2 | H | 3-0 |
| 1930 | 5 | A | 2-2 |
| 1930 | 5r | H | 3-1 |
| 1965 | 4 | A | 3-1 |

v **Swansea City**

| | | | |
|---|---|---|---|
| 1929 | 3 | H | 1-2 |

v **Swindon Town**

| | | | |
|---|---|---|---|
| 1926 | 4 | H | 2-0 |
| 1967 | 5 | H | 0-0 |
| 1967 | 5r | A | 1-1aet |
| 1967 | 5r2 | N | 3-0 |
| 1978 | 3 | H | 4-1 |

v **Torquay Utd**

| | | | |
|---|---|---|---|
| 1951 | 1 | H | 6-1 |

v **Tottenham Hotspur**

| | | | |
|---|---|---|---|
| 1967 | SF | N | 1-2 |
| 1971 | 5 | A | 1-2 |
| 1975 | 3 | H | 1-1 |
| 1975 | 3r | A | 1-0 |
| 1991 | F | N | 1-2aet |
| 1996 | 5 | H | 2-2 |
| 1996 | 5r | A | 1-1q |

v **Tranmere Rovers**

| | | | |
|---|---|---|---|
| 1928 | 3 | H | 1-0 |

v **Watford**

| | | | |
|---|---|---|---|
| 1946 | 3 | H | 1-1 |
| 1946 | 3s | A | 1-1aet |
| 1946 | 3r | N | 0-1aet |
| 1989 | 5 | A | 3-0 |

v **West Bromwich Albion**

| | | | |
|---|---|---|---|
| 1892 | SF | N | 1-1 |
| 1892 | SFr | N | 1-1 |
| 1892 | SFr2 | N | 2-6 |
| 1898 | 3 | A | 3-2 |
| 1904 | 1 | A | 1-1 |
| 1904 | 1r | H | 3-1 |
| 1958 | 4 | A | 3-3 |
| 1958 | 4r | H | 1-5 |
| 1963 | 4 | A | 0-0 |
| 1963 | 4r | H | 2-1aet |
| 1973 | 3 | A | 1-1 |
| 1973 | 3r | H | 0-0aet |
| 1973 | 3r2 | N | 1-3 |
| 1978 | 6 | A | 0-2 |

v **West Ham Utd**

| | | | |
|---|---|---|---|
| 1911 | 1 | A | 1-2 |
| 1925 | 2 | H | 0-2 |
| 1991 | SF | N | 4-0 |
| 2003 | 3 | A | 2-3 |

v **Wimbledon**

| | | | |
|---|---|---|---|
| 1985 | 4 | H | 0-0 |
| 1985 | 4r | A | 0-1 |

v **Wolverhampton W**

| | | | |
|---|---|---|---|
| 1927 | 4 | A | 0-2 |
| 1963 | 3 | H | 4-3 |
| 1992 | 3 | H | 1-0 |
| 2001 | 3 | H | 0-1 |

v **Wrexham**

| | | | |
|---|---|---|---|
| 1982 | 3 | H | 1-3 |

v **York City**

| | | | |
|---|---|---|---|
| 1979 | 4 | H | 3-1 |

# Notts County

v **Oldham Athletic**

| | | | |
|---|---|---|---|
| 1967 | 1 | A | 1-3 |
| 1991 | 4 | H | 2-0 |

v **Peterborough**

| | | | |
|---|---|---|---|
| 1963 | 1 | H | 0-3 |
| 1981 | 4 | H | 0-1 |

v **Plymouth Argyle**

| | | | |
|---|---|---|---|
| 1923 | 1 | A | 0-0 |
| 1923 | 1r | H | 0-1 |
| 1949 | 3 | A | 1-0aet |

v **Port Vale**

| | | | |
|---|---|---|---|
| 1907 | 2 | A | 2-2 |
| 1907 | 2r | H | 5-0 |
| 1949 | 1 | H | 2-1 |
| 1971 | 1 | H | 1-0 |
| 1988 | 2 | A | 0-2 |

v **Portsmouth**

| | | | |
|---|---|---|---|
| 1952 | 4 | H | 1-3 |
| 1975 | 3 | H | 3-1 |

v **Preston North End**

| | | | |
|---|---|---|---|
| 1907 | 1 | H | 1-0 |
| 1998 | 2 | A | 2-2 |
| 1998 | 2r | H | 1-2aet |

v **QPR**

| | | | |
|---|---|---|---|
| 1924 | 1 | A | 2-1 |
| 1975 | 4 | A | 0-3 |

v **Reading**

| | | | |
|---|---|---|---|
| 1902 | 1 | H | 1-2 |
| 1979 | 3 | H | 4-2 |

v **Rochdale**

| | | | |
|---|---|---|---|
| 1950 | 2 | A | 2-1 |
| 1997 | 2 | H | 3-1 |

v **Rotherham Utd**

| | | | |
|---|---|---|---|
| 1970 | 1 | H | 0-3 |

v **Sheffield Utd**

| | | | |
|---|---|---|---|
| 1891 | 1 | A | 9-1 |
| 1928 | 3 | H | 2-3 |
| 1931 | 4 | A | 1-4 |
| 1999 | 3 | A | 1-1 |
| 1999 | 3r | H | 3-4aet |

v **Sheffield Wed**

| | | | |
|---|---|---|---|
| 1883 | 4 | A | 4-1 |
| 1889 | 2 | A | 2-3 |
| 1890 | 3r2 | N | 1-2 |
| 1895 | 1 | A | 1-5 |
| 1914 | 1 | A | 2-3 |
| 1955 | 4 | A | 1-1 |
| 1955 | 4r | H | 1-0aet |

v **Southampton**

| | | | |
|---|---|---|---|
| 1899 | 2 | H | 0-1 |
| 1903 | 1 | H | 0-0 |
| 1903 | 1r | A | 2-2aet |
| 1903 | 1r2 | N | 2-1aet |
| 1951 | 3 | H | 3-4 |

v **Southend Utd**

| | | | |
|---|---|---|---|
| 1966 | 1 | A | 1-3 |

v **Stoke City**

| | | | |
|---|---|---|---|
| 1891 | 3 | H | 1-0 |
| 1986 | 3 | A | 2-0 |

v **Sunderland**

| | | | |
|---|---|---|---|
| 1891 | SF | N | 3-3 |
| 1891 | SFr | N | 2-0 |
| 1892 | 1r | A | 0-4 |
| 1906 | 1 | A | 0-1 |
| 1973 | 3 | H | 1-1 |
| 1973 | 3r | A | 0-2 |
| 1993 | 3 | H | 0-2 |

v **Swansea City**

| | | | |
|---|---|---|---|
| 1931 | 3 | H | 3-1 |
| 1934 | 3 | A | 0-1 |

v **Swindon Town**

| | | | |
|---|---|---|---|
| 1911 | 1 | A | 1-3 |
| 1912 | 2 | A | 0-2 |
| 1947 | 2 | H | 2-1 |
| 1948 | 4 | A | 0-1 |

v **Torquay Utd**

| | | | |
|---|---|---|---|
| 1936 | 2 | H | 3-0 |

v **Tottenham Hotspur**

| | | | |
|---|---|---|---|
| 1907 | 3 | H | 4-0 |
| 1986 | 4 | H | 1-1 |
| 1986 | 4r | A | 0-5 |
| 1991 | 6 | A | 1-2 |

v **Tranmere Rovers**

| | | | |
|---|---|---|---|
| 1933 | 3 | A | 1-2 |
| 1936 | 3 | H | 0-0 |
| 1936 | 3r | A | 3-4 |
| 1958 | 3 | H | 2-0 |

v **Walsall**

| | | | |
|---|---|---|---|
| 1939 | 4 | H | 0-0 |
| 1939 | 4r | A | 0-4 |

v **Watford**

| | | | |
|---|---|---|---|
| 1972 | 3 | A | 4-1 |

v **West Bromwich Albion**

| | | | |
|---|---|---|---|
| 1887 | 6 | H | 1-4 |
| 1907 | 4 | A | 1-3 |
| 1921 | 1 | H | 3-0 |
| 1922 | 3 | A | 1-1 |
| 1922 | 3r | H | 2-0 |
| 1974 | 3 | A | 0-4 |

v **West Ham Utd**

| | | | |
|---|---|---|---|
| 1930 | 3 | A | 0-4 |
| 1994 | 4 | H | 1-1 |
| 1994 | 4r | A | 0-1aet |

v **Wigan Athletic**

| | | | |
|---|---|---|---|
| 1992 | 3 | H | 2-0 |
| 1999 | 2 | H | 1-1 |
| 1999 | 2r | A | 0-0q |
| 2001 | 2 | A | 1-1 |
| 2001 | 2r | H | 2-1aet |

v **Wimbledon**

| | | | |
|---|---|---|---|
| 2001 | 3 | A | 2-2 |
| 2001 | 3r | H | 0-1aet |

v **Wolverhampton W**

| | | | |
|---|---|---|---|
| 1896 | 1 | A | 2-2 |
| 1896 | 1r | H | 3-4 |
| 1898 | 1 | H | 0-1 |
| 1901 | 2 | H | 2-3 |
| 1935 | 3 | A | 0-4 |
| 1980 | 3 | H | 1-3 |

v **Wrexham**
1986 2 H 2-2
1986 2r A 3-0

v **Wycombe W**
2002 2 A 0-3

v **Yeovil Town**
1962 1 H 4-2

v **York City**
1955 6 H 0-1
1996 1 A 1-0

## Oldham Athletic

v **Peterborough**
2001 2 A 1-1
2001 2r H 0-1

v **Plymouth Argyle**
1977 3 H 3-0

v **Port Vale**
1953 2 A 3-0

v **Preston North End**
2000 3 A 1-2

v **Reading**
1934 3 A 2-1
1995 3 A 3-1

v **Rochdale**
1915 2 H 3-0
1971 1 A 0-2

v **Sheffield Utd**
1915 4 H 0-0aet
1915 4r A 0-3

v **Sheffield Wed**
1930 4 H 3-4
1934 4 H 1-1
1934 4r A 1-6
1935 3 A 1-3
1985 4 A 1-5

v **Shrewsbury Town**
1984 3 A 0-3

v **Southend Utd**
1952 2 A 0-5

v **Stoke City**
1959 3 A 1-5
1979 3 A 1-0
1994 4 H 0-0
1994 4r A 1-0

v **Sunderland**
1924 1 H 2-1
1976 3 A 0-2

v **Swansea City**
2000 2 H 1-0

v **Swindon Town**
1924 2 A 0-2
1996 4 A 0-1

v **Tottenham Hotspur**
1928 4 A 0-3
1933 3 H 0-6
1979 5 H 0-1
1988 3 H 2-4

v **Tranmere Rovers**
1937 1 H 1-0
1947 1 H 1-0
1993 3 H 2-2
1993 3r A 0-3

v **Watford**
1931 3 H 1-3

v **West Ham Utd**
1966 3 H 2-2
1966 3r A 1-2

v **Wimbledon**
1981 3 A 0-0
1981 3r H 0-1

v **Wolverhampton W**
1930 3 H 1-0
1967 3 H 2-2
1967 3r A 1-4

v **Wrexham**
1938 1 A 1-2
1949 1 A 3-0
1969 1 A 2-4

## Oxford Utd

v **Peterborough**
1959 2 A 2-4
1984 1 H 2-0

v **Plymouth Argyle**
1981 2 A 0-3
1990 3 A 1-0

v **Port Vale**
1966 1 H 2-2
1966 1r A 2-3
1964 6 H 1-2

v **QPR**
1973 4 H 0-2

v **Reading**
1984 2 A 1-1
1984 2r H 3-0

v **Sheffield Wed**
1984 5 H 0-3

v **Shrewsbury Town**
1985 3 A 2-0
2000 2 A 2-2
2000 2r H 2-1aet

v **Southampton**
1969 3 H 1-1
1969 3r A 0-2
1990 4 A 0-1

v **Stockport County**
1954 3 A 0-0
1954 3r H 1-0

v **Stoke City**
1970 3 H 0-0
1970 3r A 2-3

v **Sunderland**
1989 3 A 1-1
1989 3r H 2-0
1992 4 H 2-3

v **Swansea City**
1993 3 A 1-1
1993 3r H 2-2q

v **Swindon Town**
2003 2 H 1-0

v **Torquay Utd**
1983 3 H 1-1
1983 3r A 1-2

v **Tottenham Hotspur**
1986 3 H 1-1
1986 3r A 1-2aet
1991 4 A 2-4

v **Tranmere Rovers**
1992 3 H 3-1
1994 3 H 2-0

v **Watford**
1971 4 H 1-1
1971 4r A 2-1
1997 3 A 0-2

v **Wycombe W**
1953 Q3 H 6-2

v **Yeovil Town**
1967 1 A 3-1

v **York City**
1973 3 A 1-0

## Peterborough

v **Plymouth Argyle**
1970 2 H 2-0
1993 2 A 2-3
1997 3 A 1-0

v **Port Vale**
1991 3 A 1-2

v **Portsmouth**
1961 3 A 2-1
1968 3 H 0-1

v **QPR**
1965 2 A 3-3
1965 2r H 2-1

v **Reading**
1992 2 H 0-0
1992 2r A 0-1

v **Rochdale**
2003 1 A 2-3

v **Rotherham Utd**
1970 3 A 1-0

v **Sheffield Utd**
1962 4 H 1-3

v **Sheffield Wed**
1960 4 A 0-2

v **Shrewsbury Town**
1960 1 H 4-3
1966 2 A 2-3

v **Southend Utd**
1974 3 H 3-1
1979 1 A 2-3

v **Sunderland**
1967 4 A 1-7

v **Swansea City**
1965 5 H 0-0
1965 5r A 2-0
1990 2 A 1-3
1998 1 A 4-1

v **Swindon Town**

| | | | |
|---|---|---|---|
| 1956 | 2 | A | 1-1 |
| 1956 | 2r | H | 1-2aet |

v **Torquay Utd**

| | | | |
|---|---|---|---|
| 1949 | 1 | H | 0-1 |
| 1953 | 1 | H | 2-1 |
| 1958 | 1 | H | 3-3 |
| 1958 | 1r | A | 0-1 |
| 1961 | 2 | A | 3-1 |
| 1962 | 2 | A | 4-1 |

v **Tottenham Hotspur**

| | | | |
|---|---|---|---|
| 1994 | 3 | H | 1-1 |
| 1994 | 3r | A | 1-1p |

v **Tranmere Rovers**

| | | | |
|---|---|---|---|
| 1975 | 3 | H | 1-0 |
| 1977 | 1 | A | 4-0 |

v **Walsall**

| | | | |
|---|---|---|---|
| 1960 | 2 | A | 3-2 |
| 1982 | 2 | H | 2-1 |
| 1998 | 3 | H | 0-2 |

v **Watford**

| | | | |
|---|---|---|---|
| 1964 | 1 | H | 1-1 |
| 1964 | 1r | A | 1-2aet |

v **Wigan Athletic**

| | | | |
|---|---|---|---|
| 1971 | 2 | A | 1-2 |

v **Wimbledon**

| | | | |
|---|---|---|---|
| 1971 | 1 | H | 3-1 |

v **Wrexham**

| | | | |
|---|---|---|---|
| 1996 | 3 | H | 1-0 |
| 1997 | 4 | H | 2-4 |
| 1999 | 1 | A | 0-1 |

v **Wycombe W**

| | | | |
|---|---|---|---|
| 1974 | 2 | A | 3-1 |
| 1991 | 2 | A | 1-1 |
| 1991 | 2r | H | 2-0 |

v **Yeovil Town**

| | | | |
|---|---|---|---|
| 1947 | 1 | A | 2-2 |
| 1947 | 1r | H | 1-0 |
| 1957 | 1 | A | 3-1 |

# Plymouth Argyle

v **Preston North End**

| | | | |
|---|---|---|---|
| 1913 | 1 | H | 2-0 |
| 2000 | 4 | H | 0-3 |

v **Reading**

| | | | |
|---|---|---|---|
| 1920 | 1 | H | 2-0 |
| 1969 | 1 | A | 0-1 |
| 2000 | 3 | A | 1-1 |
| 2000 | 3r | H | 1-0 |

v **Rochdale**

| | | | |
|---|---|---|---|
| 1921 | 1 | H | 2-0 |

v **Sheffield Wed**

| | | | |
|---|---|---|---|
| 1904 | 1 | H | 2-2 |
| 1904 | 1r | A | 0-2 |
| 1968 | 3 | A | 0-3 |

v **Shrewsbury Town**

| | | | |
|---|---|---|---|
| 1988 | 4 | H | 1-0 |

v **Southend Utd**

| | | | |
|---|---|---|---|
| 1984 | 1 | A | 0-0 |
| 1984 | 1r | H | 2-0aet |

v **Stockport County**

| | | | |
|---|---|---|---|
| 1936 | 3 | A | 3-2 |
| 2003 | 2 | A | 3-0 |

v **Sunderland**

| | | | |
|---|---|---|---|
| 1912 | 1 | A | 1-3 |
| 1914 | 2 | A | 1-2 |
| 1939 | 3 | A | 0-3 |

v **Swansea City**

| | | | |
|---|---|---|---|
| 1921 | 2 | A | 2-1 |
| 1925 | 1 | A | 0-3 |

v **Swindon Town**

| | | | |
|---|---|---|---|
| 1904 | Q5 | H | 2-0 |
| 1909 | 1 | H | 1-0 |

v **Torquay Utd**

| | | | |
|---|---|---|---|
| 1957 | 2 | A | 0-1 |

v **Tottenham Hotspur**

| | | | |
|---|---|---|---|
| 1910 | 1 | H | 1-1 |
| 1910 | 1r | A | 1-7 |
| 1937 | 4 | A | 0-1 |
| 1962 | 4 | H | 1-5 |

v **Walsall**

| | | | |
|---|---|---|---|
| 1971 | 1 | A | 0-3 |
| 1974 | 2 | H | 1-0 |

v **Watford**

| | | | |
|---|---|---|---|
| 1930 | 2 | A | 1-1 |
| 1930 | 2r | H | 3-0 |
| 1958 | 1 | H | 6-2 |
| 1983 | 3 | A | 0-2 |
| 1984 | SF | N | 0-1 |

v **West Bromwich Albion**

| | | | |
|---|---|---|---|
| 1960 | 3 | A | 2-3 |
| 1963 | 3 | H | 1-5 |
| 1984 | 5 | A | 1-0 |

v **West Ham Utd**

| | | | |
|---|---|---|---|
| 1923 | 3 | A | 0-2 |
| 1962 | 3 | H | 3-0 |

v **Wolverhampton W**

| | | | |
|---|---|---|---|
| 1950 | 3 | H | 1-1 |
| 1950 | 3r | A | 0-3 |
| 1951 | 3 | H | 1-2 |

v **Wycombe W**

| | | | |
|---|---|---|---|
| 1999 | 2 | A | 1-1 |
| 1999 | 2r | H | 3-2 |

v **Yeovil Town**

| | | | |
|---|---|---|---|
| 1929 | 1 | A | 4-1 |
| 1973 | 2 | A | 2-0 |

# Port Vale

v **QPR**

| | | | |
|---|---|---|---|
| 1954 | 3 | A | 1-0 |
| 1960 | 2 | A | 3-3 |
| 1960 | 2r | H | 2-1 |

v **Scunthorpe Utd**

| | | | |
|---|---|---|---|
| 1960 | 4 | A | 1-0 |
| 1985 | 2 | H | 4-1 |

v **Sheffield Utd**

| | | | |
|---|---|---|---|
| 1898 | 1 | A | 1-1 |
| 1898 | 1r | H | 2-1aet |
| 1963 | 4 | H | 1-2 |

v **Sheffield Wed**

| | | | |
|---|---|---|---|
| 1937 | 3 | A | 0-2 |

v **Shrewsbury Town**

| | | | |
|---|---|---|---|
| 1958 | 1 | H | 2-1 |
| 1969 | 1 | A | 1-1 |
| 1969 | 1r | H | 3-1 |
| 1982 | 3 | A | 0-1 |

v **Southampton**

| | | | |
|---|---|---|---|
| 1904 | 1 | A | 0-3 |
| 1994 | 3 | A | 1-1 |
| 1994 | 3r | H | 1-0 |

v **Southend Utd**

| | | | |
|---|---|---|---|
| 1939 | 2 | H | 0-1 |

v **Stockport County**

| | | | |
|---|---|---|---|
| 1904 | Q4 | A | 0-0 |
| 1904 | Q4r | H | 6-0 |
| 1974 | 1 | A | 1-0 |
| 1982 | 2 | H | 4-1 |

v **Stoke City**

| | | | |
|---|---|---|---|
| 1888 | 1 | A | 0-1 |
| 1922 | 1 | H | 2-4 |
| 1951 | 3 | A | 2-2 |
| 1951 | 3r | H | 0-1 |
| 1993 | 1 | A | 0-0 |
| 1993 | 1r | H | 3-1 |

v **Sunderland**

| | | | |
|---|---|---|---|
| 1936 | 3 | A | 2-2 |
| 1936 | 3r | H | 2-0 |
| 1962 | 4 | A | 0-0 |
| 1962 | 4r | H | 3-1 |
| 1992 | 3 | A | 0-3 |

v **Swansea City**

| | | | |
|---|---|---|---|
| 1915 | Q5 | A | 0-1 |
| 1961 | 3 | A | 0-3 |

v **Swindon Town**

| | | | |
|---|---|---|---|
| 1907 | Q5 | A | 2-1 |

v **Torquay Utd**

| | | | |
|---|---|---|---|
| 1959 | 1 | A | 0-1 |

v **Tottenham Hotspur**

| | | | |
|---|---|---|---|
| 1955 | 4 | A | 2-4 |
| 1988 | 4 | H | 2-1 |

v **Tranmere Rovers**

| | | | |
|---|---|---|---|
| 1950 | 2 | H | 1-0 |
| 1970 | 2 | H | 2-2 |
| 1970 | 2r | A | 1-3 |
| 1988 | 1 | A | 2-2 |
| 1988 | 1r | H | 3-1 |

v **Walsall**

| | | | |
|---|---|---|---|
| 1891 | Q2 | H | 2-3 |
| 1902 | Q5 | H | 1-2 |
| 1956 | 3 | A | 1-0 |
| 1978 | 2 | A | 1-1 |
| 1978 | 2r | H | 1-3 |
| 1986 | 2 | H | 0-0 |
| 1986 | 2r | A | 1-2 |
| 1987 | 2 | A | 0-5 |

v **Watford**

| | | | |
|---|---|---|---|
| 1947 | 2 | A | 1-1 |
| 1947 | 2r | H | 2-1 |
| 1969 | 3 | A | 0-2 |
| 1988 | 5 | H | 0-0 |
| 1988 | 5r | A | 0-2 |

v **West Bromwich**

| | | | |
|---|---|---|---|
| 1935 | 3 | A | 1-2 |
| 1954 | SF | N | 1-2 |

v **West Ham Utd**

| | | | |
|---|---|---|---|
| 1955 | 3 | A | 2-2 |
| 1955 | 3r | H | 3-1 |
| 1973 | 3 | H | 0-1 |
| 1985 | 3 | A | 1-4 |

v **Wigan Athletic**

| | | | |
|---|---|---|---|
| 1970 | 1 | A | 1-1 |
| 1970 | 1r | H | 2-2aet |
| 1970 | 1r2 | N | 1-0aet |

v **Wolverhampton W**

| | | | |
|---|---|---|---|
| 1994 | 4 | H | 0-2 |

v **Wrexham**

| | | | |
|---|---|---|---|
| 1902 | Q4r | A | 0-0 |
| 1902 | Q4r2 | H | 3-1 |
| 1923 | Q5 | H | 0-2 |
| 1924 | Q5 | A | 1-5 |
| 1939 | 1 | A | 2-1 |
| 1973 | 2 | H | 1-0 |

# Portsmouth

v **Preston North End**

| | | | |
|---|---|---|---|
| 1930 | 3 | H | 2-0 |
| 1939 | 6 | H | 1-0 |
| 1948 | 4 | H | 1-3 |

v **Reading**

| | | | |
|---|---|---|---|
| 1902 | 2 | A | 1-0 |
| 1927 | 4 | A | 1-3 |
| 1979 | 2 | H | 0-1 |
| 1997 | 4 | H | 3-0 |

v **Scunthorpe Utd**

| | | | |
|---|---|---|---|
| 1954 | 4 | A | 1-1 |
| 1954 | 4r | H | 2-2aet |
| 1954 | 4r2 | N | 4-0 |
| 1963 | 3 | H | 1-1 |
| 1963 | 3r | A | 2-1 |

v **Sheffield Utd**

| | | | |
|---|---|---|---|
| 1960 | 3 | A | 0-3 |
| 1971 | 3 | H | 2-0 |
| 1988 | 4 | H | 2-1 |

v **Sheffield Wed**

| | | | |
|---|---|---|---|
| 1905 | 2 | A | 1-2 |
| 1909 | 2 | H | 2-2 |
| 1909 | 2r | A | 0-3 |
| 1949 | 4 | H | 2-1 |

v **Shrewsbury Town**

| | | | |
|---|---|---|---|
| 1910 | 1 | H | 3-0 |

v **Southampton**

| | | | |
|---|---|---|---|
| 1906 | 1 | A | 1-5 |
| 1984 | 4 | H | 0-1 |
| 1996 | 3 | A | 0-3 |

v **Stockport County**

| | | | |
|---|---|---|---|
| 1949 | 3 | H | 7-0 |

v **Stoke City**

| | | | |
|---|---|---|---|
| 1908 | 3 | H | 0-1 |
| 1964 | 3 | A | 1-4 |

v **Sunderland**

| | | | |
|---|---|---|---|
| 2000 | 3 | A | 0-1 |

v **Swansea City**

| | | | |
|---|---|---|---|
| 1934 | 5 | A | 1-0 |
| 1959 | 3 | H | 3-1 |
| 1972 | 4 | H | 2-0 |
| 1978 | 2 | H | 2-2 |
| 1978 | 2r | A | 1-2 |

v **Swindon Town**

| | | | |
|---|---|---|---|
| 1900 | Q3 | H | 2-1 |
| 1974 | 3 | H | 3-3 |
| 1974 | 3r | A | 1-0 |
| 1989 | 3 | H | 1-1 |
| 1989 | 3r | A | 0-2 |

v **Tottenham Hotspur**

| | | | |
|---|---|---|---|
| 1937 | 3 | H | 0-5 |
| 1967 | 4 | A | 1-3 |
| 1991 | 5 | H | 1-2 |

v **Tranmere Rovers**

| | | | |
|---|---|---|---|
| 1938 | 3 | A | 2-1 |
| 1970 | 3 | H | 1-2 |
| 2001 | 3 | H | 1-2 |

v **West Bromwich Albion**

| | | | |
|---|---|---|---|
| 1931 | 5 | H | 0-1 |
| 1939 | 4 | H | 2-0 |
| 1956 | 4 | A | 0-2 |
| 1968 | 5 | H | 1-2 |

v **West Ham Utd**

| | | | |
|---|---|---|---|
| 1928 | 3 | H | 0-2 |
| 1929 | 6 | H | 3-2 |
| 1939 | 5 | H | 2-0 |

v **Wimbledon**

| | | | |
|---|---|---|---|
| 1980 | 2 | A | 0-0 |
| 1980 | 2r | H | 3-3aet |
| 1980 | 2r2 | A | 1-0 |
| 1987 | 4 | A | 0-4 |

v **Wolverhampton W**

| | | | |
|---|---|---|---|
| 1939 | F | N | 4-1 |
| 1958 | 4 | A | 1-5 |
| 1965 | 3 | H | 0-0 |
| 1965 | 3r | A | 2-3 |
| 1997 | 3 | A | 2-1 |

# Preston North End

v **QPR**

| | | | |
|---|---|---|---|
| 1968 | 3 | A | 3-1 |

v **Reading**

| | | | |
|---|---|---|---|
| 1894 | 1 | H | 18-0 |

v **Rochdale**

| | | | |
|---|---|---|---|
| 2003 | 3 | H | 1-2 |

v **Scunthorpe Utd**

| | | | |
|---|---|---|---|
| 1976 | 1 | H | 2-1 |
| 1984 | 1 | A | 0-1 |

v **Sheffield Utd**

| | | | |
|---|---|---|---|
| 1899 | 2 | H | 2-2 |
| 1899 | 2r | A | 1-2 |
| 1936 | 4 | H | 0-0 |
| 1936 | 4r | A | 0-2 |
| 2002 | 4 | H | 2-1 |

v **Sheffield Wed**

| | | | |
|---|---|---|---|
| 1888 | 6 | A | 3-1 |
| 1905 | 3 | H | 1-1 |
| 1905 | 3r | A | 0-3 |
| 1947 | 5 | A | 2-0 |
| 1954 | SF | N | 2-0 |
| 1957 | 3 | H | 0-0 |
| 1957 | 3r | A | 2-2aet |
| 1957 | 3r2 | N | 5-1 |
| 1992 | 3 | H | 0-2 |

v **Shrewsbury Town**

| | | | |
|---|---|---|---|
| 1994 | 2 | A | 1-0 |

v **Southampton**

| | | | |
|---|---|---|---|
| 1979 | 4 | H | 0-1 |

v **Stockport County**

| | | | |
|---|---|---|---|
| 1920 | 1 | H | 3-1 |
| 1998 | 3 | H | 1-2 |
| 2001 | 3 | H | 0-1 |

v **Stoke City**

| | | | |
|---|---|---|---|
| 1891 | 1 | A | 0-3 |
| 1897 | 2 | H | 2-1 |
| 1937 | 4 | H | 5-1 |
| 1960 | 3 | A | 1-1 |
| 1960 | 3r | H | 3-1 |

v **Sunderland**

| | | | |
|---|---|---|---|
| 1895 | 2 | A | 0-2 |
| 1896 | 1 | A | 1-4 |
| 1909 | 2 | H | 1-2 |
| 1914 | 3 | A | 0-2 |
| 1937 | F | N | 1-3 |
| 1955 | 4 | H | 3-3 |
| 1955 | 4r | A | 0-2 |
| 1963 | 3 | H | 1-4 |

v **Swansea City**

| | | | |
|---|---|---|---|
| 1961 | 4 | A | 1-2 |
| 1964 | SF | N | 2-1 |

v **Swindon Town**

| | | | |
|---|---|---|---|
| 1935 | 4 | A | 2-0 |

v **Tottenham Hotspur**

| | | | |
|---|---|---|---|
| 1900 | 1 | H | 1-0 |
| 1901 | 1 | A | 1-1 |
| 1901 | 1r | H | 2-4 |
| 1921 | SF | N | 1-2 |
| 1922 | SF | N | 2-1 |
| 1931 | 3 | A | 1-3 |
| 1937 | 6 | A | 3-1 |
| 1953 | 4 | H | 2-2 |
| 1953 | 4r | A | 0-1 |
| 1966 | 5 | H | 2-1 |
| 1968 | 4 | A | 1-3 |

v **Tranmere Rovers**

| | | | |
|---|---|---|---|
| 1989 | 1 | H | 1-1 |
| 1989 | 1r | A | 0-3 |
| 1990 | 1 | H | 1-0 |

v **Walsall**

| | | | |
|---|---|---|---|
| 1986 | 1 | A | 3-7 |
| 1995 | 2 | H | 1-1 |
| 1995 | 2r | A | 0-4 |
| 1999 | 2 | H | 2-0 |

v **Watford**

| | | | |
|---|---|---|---|
| 1921 | 2 | H | 4-1 |
| 1929 | 3 | A | 0-1 |
| 1950 | 3 | A | 2-2 |
| 1950 | 3r | H | 0-1 |
| 1962 | 3 | H | 3-2 |

v **West Bromwich Albion**

| | | | |
|---|---|---|---|
| 1887 | SF | N | 1-3 |
| 1888 | F | N | 1-2 |
| 1889 | SF | N | 1-0 |
| 1925 | 2 | A | 0-2 |
| 1935 | 6 | A | 0-1 |
| 1937 | SF | N | 4-1 |
| 1954 | F | N | 2-3 |

v **West Ham Utd**

| | | | |
|---|---|---|---|
| 1911 | 2 | A | 0-3 |
| 1938 | 3 | H | 3-0 |
| 1956 | 3 | A | 2-5 |
| 1964 | F | N | 2-3 |

v **Wolverhampton W**

| | | | |
|---|---|---|---|
| 1889 | F | N | 3-0 |
| 1922 | 1 | H | 3-0 |
| 1932 | 4 | H | 2-0 |
| 1953 | 3 | H | 5-2 |

v **Wrexham**

| | | | |
|---|---|---|---|
| 1978 | 2 | H | 0-2 |

v **York City**

| | | | |
|---|---|---|---|
| 1997 | 2 | H | 2-3 |

# QPR

v **Reading**

| | | | |
|---|---|---|---|
| 1908 | 1 | H | 1-0 |

v **Scunthorpe Utd**

| | | | |
|---|---|---|---|
| 1932 | 2 | A | 4-1 |

v **Sheffield Utd**

| | | | |
|---|---|---|---|
| 1923 | 4 | H | 0-1 |

v **Sheffield Wed**

| | | | |
|---|---|---|---|
| 1967 | 3 | A | 0-3 |

v **Shrewsbury Town**

| | | | |
|---|---|---|---|
| 1953 | 1 | H | 2-2 |
| 1953 | 1r | A | 2-2aet |
| 1953 | 1r2 | N | 1-4 |
| 1954 | 1 | H | 2-0 |
| 1966 | 3 | H | 0-0 |
| 1966 | 3r | A | 0-1 |
| 1977 | 3 | H | 2-1 |

v **Southampton**

| | | | |
|---|---|---|---|
| 1946 | 4 | A | 1-0 |
| 1946 | 4s | H | 4-3 |
| 1959 | 2 | H | 0-1 |
| 1992 | 3 | A | 0-2 |

v **Southend Utd**

| | | | |
|---|---|---|---|
| 1910 | 2 | A | 0-0 |
| 1910 | 2r | H | 3-2 |
| 1956 | 1 | A | 0-2 |
| 1975 | 3 | A | 2-2 |
| 1975 | 3r | H | 2-0 |

v **Stockport County**

| | | | |
|---|---|---|---|
| 1925 | 1 | H | 1-3 |
| 1994 | 3 | A | 1-2 |

v **Stoke City**

| | | | |
|---|---|---|---|
| 1948 | 4 | H | 3-0 |

v **Sunderland**

| | | | |
|---|---|---|---|
| 1957 | 3 | A | 0-4 |

v **Swansea City**

| | | | |
|---|---|---|---|
| 1914 | 2 | A | 2-1 |
| 1963 | 3 | A | 0-2 |
| 2002 | 1 | A | 0-4 |

v **Swindon Town**

| | | | |
|---|---|---|---|
| 1908 | 2 | A | 1-2 |
| 1938 | 2 | A | 1-2 |
| 1971 | 3 | H | 1-2 |
| 1993 | 3 | H | 3-0 |

v **Torquay Utd**

| | | | |
|---|---|---|---|
| 1933 | 2 | A | 1-1 |
| 1933 | 2r | H | 3-1 |
| 2000 | 3 | H | 1-1 |
| 2000 | 3r | A | 3-2 |

v **Tottenham Hotspur**

| | | | |
|---|---|---|---|
| 1981 | 3 | H | 0-0 |
| 1981 | 3r | A | 1-3 |
| 1982 | F | N | 1-1aet |
| 1982 | Fr | N | 0-1 |

v **Tranmere Rovers**

| | | | |
|---|---|---|---|
| 1996 | 3 | A | 2-0 |

v **Walsall**

| | | | |
|---|---|---|---|
| 1959 | 1 | A | 1-0 |

v **Watford**

| | | | |
|---|---|---|---|
| 1901 | Q4 | A | 1-1 |
| 1901 | Q4r | H | 4-1 |
| 1980 | 3 | H | 1-2 |

v **West Bromwich Albion**

| | | | |
|---|---|---|---|
| 1982 | SF | N | 1-0 |
| 1983 | 3 | A | 2-3 |

v **West Ham Utd**

| | | | |
|---|---|---|---|
| 1909 | 1 | H | 0-0 |
| 1909 | 1r | A | 0-1 |
| 1910 | 3 | H | 1-1 |
| 1910 | 3r | A | 1-0aet |
| 1939 | 3 | H | 1-2 |
| 1975 | 5 | A | 1-2 |
| 1978 | 4 | A | 1-1 |
| 1978 | 4r | H | 6-1 |
| 1988 | 4 | H | 3-1 |
| 1995 | 4 | H | 1-0 |

v **Wimbledon**

| | | | |
|---|---|---|---|
| 1997 | 5 | A | 1-2 |

v **Wolverhampton W**

| | | | |
|---|---|---|---|
| 1900 | 1 | H | 1-1 |
| 1900 | 1r | A | 1-0aet |

v **Yeovil Town**

| | | | |
|---|---|---|---|
| 1988 | 3 | A | 3-0 |

# Reading

v **Sheffield Utd**

| | | | |
|---|---|---|---|
| 1998 | 5 | A | 0-1 |

v **Sheffield Wed**

| | | | |
|---|---|---|---|
| 1929 | 4 | H | 1-0 |
| 1966 | 3 | H | 2-3 |

v **Shrewsbury Town**

| | | | |
|---|---|---|---|
| 1971 | 2 | A | 2-2 |
| 1971 | 2r | H | 1-0 |

v **Southampton**

| | | | |
|---|---|---|---|
| 1894 | Q3 | H | 2-1 |
| 1895 | Q2 | A | 2-5 |
| 1896 | Q3 | A | 0-3 |
| 1897 | Q4 | H | 1-4 |
| 1988 | 3 | H | 0-1 |
| 1997 | 3 | H | 3-1 |

v **Southend Utd**

| | | | |
|---|---|---|---|
| 1925 | Q5 | H | 2-1 |
| 1927 | 2 | H | 3-2 |
| 1974 | 2 | A | 0-2 |

v **Stoke City**

| | | | |
|---|---|---|---|
| 1913 | 1 | A | 2-2 |
| 1913 | 1r | H | 3-0 |
| 1999 | 1 | H | 0-1 |

v **Sunderland**

| | | | |
|---|---|---|---|
| 1973 | 4 | A | 1-1 |
| 1973 | 4r | H | 1-3 |
| 1990 | 3 | H | 2-1 |

v **Swansea City**

| | | | |
|---|---|---|---|
| 1927 | 6 | A | 3-1 |
| 1952 | 3 | H | 0-3 |
| 1980 | 4 | A | 1-4 |

v **Swindon Town**

| | | | |
|---|---|---|---|
| 1893 | Q3 | A | 1-2 |
| 1894 | Q4 | A | 2-0 |
| 1898 | Q3 | H | 0-0 |
| 1898 | Q3r | A | 2-3 |
| 1958 | 1 | H | 1-0 |
| 1963 | 1 | A | 2-4 |
| 1975 | 1 | A | 0-4 |

v **Torquay Utd**

| | | | |
|---|---|---|---|
| 1926 | 1 | A | 1-1 |
| 1926 | 1r | H | 1-1aet |
| 1926 | 1r2 | N | 2-0 |
| 1969 | 2 | H | 0-0 |
| 1969 | 2r | A | 2-1 |

v **Tottenham Hotspur**

| | | | |
|---|---|---|---|
| 1901 | 3 | H | 1-1 |
| 1901 | 3r | A | 0-3 |
| 1906 | 2 | A | 2-3 |
| 1913 | 2 | H | 1-0 |
| 1929 | 3 | H | 2-0 |

v **Tranmere Rovers**

| | | | |
|---|---|---|---|
| 1989 | 3 | A | 1-1 |
| 1989 | 3r | H | 2-1 |

v **Walsall**

| | | | |
|---|---|---|---|
| 1952 | 1 | H | 1-0 |
| 2003 | 3 | A | 0-0 |
| 2003 | 3r | H | 1-1q |

v **Watford**

| | | | |
|---|---|---|---|
| 1934 | 1 | A | 3-0 |
| 1959 | 1 | A | 1-1 |
| 1959 | 1r | H | 0-2 |
| 1965 | 1 | H | 3-1 |
| 1971 | 3 | A | 0-5 |

v **West Bromwich Albion**

| | | | |
|---|---|---|---|
| 1948 | 3 | A | 0-2 |

v **Wolverhampton W**

| | | | |
|---|---|---|---|
| 1910 | 1 | A | 0-5 |
| 1915 | 1 | H | 0-1 |

v **Wrexham**

| | | | |
|---|---|---|---|
| 1935 | 2 | H | 3-0 |
| 1957 | 3 | A | 1-1 |
| 1957 | 3r | H | 1-2 |

v **Wycombe W**

| | | | |
|---|---|---|---|
| 1900 | Q3 | A | 8-0 |
| 1977 | 2 | A | 2-1 |

v **Yeovil Town**

| | | | |
|---|---|---|---|
| 2000 | 1 | H | 4-2 |

v **York City**

| | | | |
|---|---|---|---|
| 2001 | 2 | A | 2-2 |
| 2001 | 2r | H | 1-3 |
| 2002 | 2 | A | 0-2 |

# Rochdale

v **Rotherham Utd**

| | | | |
|---|---|---|---|
| 1996 | 1 | H | 5-3 |
| 1999 | 2 | H | 0-0 |
| 1999 | 2r | A | 0-4 |

v **Scunthorpe Utd**

| | | | |
|---|---|---|---|
| 1932 | 1 | A | 1-2 |
| 1957 | 1 | A | 0-1 |
| 1980 | 1 | H | 2-1 |
| 1986 | 2 | A | 2-2 |
| 1986 | 2r | H | 2-1 |
| 1991 | 1 | H | 1-1 |
| 1991 | 1r | A | 1-2aet |

v **Stockport County**

| | | | |
|---|---|---|---|
| 1911 | Q4 | H | 0-0 |
| 1911 | Q4r | A | 0-0 |
| 1911 | Q4r2 | N | 1-0 |
| 1933 | 1 | H | 0-2 |
| 1946 | 1 | A | 2-1 |
| 1946 | 1s | H | 1-1 |

v **Swindon Town**

| | | | |
|---|---|---|---|
| 1913 | 1 | H | 0-2 |

v **Tranmere Rovers**

| | | | |
|---|---|---|---|
| 1921 | Q5 | H | 1-0 |
| 1946 | 2 | A | 1-3 |
| 1946 | 2s | H | 3-0 |
| 1955 | 1 | A | 3-3 |
| 1955 | 1r | H | 1-0 |
| 1968 | 1 | A | 1-5 |
| 1975 | 2 | H | 1-1 |
| 1975 | 2r | A | 0-1 |
| 1980 | 2 | A | 2-2 |
| 1980 | 2r | H | 2-1 |

v **Walsall**

| | | | |
|---|---|---|---|
| 1995 | 1 | A | 0-3 |

v **Watford**

| | | | |
|---|---|---|---|
| 1915 | Q6 | H | 2-0 |

v **Wolverhampton W**

| | | | |
|---|---|---|---|
| 2003 | 5 | A | 1-3 |

v **Wrexham**

| | | | |
|---|---|---|---|
| 1935 | 1 | A | 1-4 |
| 1962 | 2 | H | 1-2 |
| 1987 | 2 | H | 1-4 |
| 1988 | 1 | H | 0-2 |
| 1998 | 1 | H | 0-2 |
| 2000 | 2 | A | 1-2 |

v **York City**

| | | | |
|---|---|---|---|
| 1948 | 1 | A | 1-0 |
| 1956 | 1 | H | 0-1 |
| 1963 | 1 | A | 0-0 |
| 1963 | 1r | H | 1-2 |
| 1984 | 2 | A | 2-0 |

# Rotherham Utd

v **Scunthorpe Utd**

| | | | |
|---|---|---|---|
| 1930 | 2 | A | 3-3 |
| 1930 | 2r | H | 5-4 |
| 1947 | 2 | H | 4-1 |
| 1956 | 3 | H | 1-1 |
| 1956 | 3r | A | 2-4 |
| 1992 | 1 | A | 1-1 |
| 1992 | 1r | H | 3-3p |
| 1997 | 1 | A | 1-4 |

v **Sheffield Wed**

| | | | |
|---|---|---|---|
| 1934 | 3 | H | 0-3 |

v **Shrewsbury Town**

| | | | |
|---|---|---|---|
| 1983 | 3 | A | 1-2 |

v **Southampton**

| | | | |
|---|---|---|---|
| 2002 | 3 | H | 2-1 |

v **Southend Utd**

| | | | |
|---|---|---|---|
| 1966 | 3 | H | 3-2 |

v **Stockport County**

| | | | |
|---|---|---|---|
| 1973 | 2 | H | 0-1 |
| 1991 | 1 | H | 1-0 |
| 1994 | 1 | H | 1-2 |

v **Sunderland**

| | | | |
|---|---|---|---|
| 1982 | 3 | H | 1-1 |
| 1982 | 3r | A | 0-1 |
| 1998 | 3 | H | 1-5 |

v **Swansea City**

| | | | |
|---|---|---|---|
| 1952 | 4 | A | 0-3 |
| 1991 | 3 | A | 0-0 |
| 1991 | 3r | H | 4-0 |

v **Tottenham Hotspur**

| | | | |
|---|---|---|---|
| 1972 | 4 | A | 0-2 |

v **Tranmere Rovers**

| | | | |
|---|---|---|---|
| 1929 | 1 | A | 1-2 |

v **Walsall**

| | | | |
|---|---|---|---|
| 1990 | 2 | A | 0-1 |
| 1993 | 1 | H | 4-0 |

v **Watford**

| | | | |
|---|---|---|---|
| 1936 | 2 | H | 1-1 |
| 1936 | 2r | A | 0-1 |
| 1961 | 3 | H | 1-0 |
| 1963 | 3 | A | 0-2 |

v **West Bromwich Albion**

| | | | |
|---|---|---|---|
| 1954 | 4 | A | 0-4 |
| 1984 | 3 | H | 0-0 |
| 1984 | 3r | A | 0-3 |

v **Wigan Athletic**

| | | | |
|---|---|---|---|
| 1936 | 1 | A | 2-1 |

v **Wimbledon**

| | | | |
|---|---|---|---|
| 2003 | 3 | H | 0-3 |

v **Wolverhampton W**

| | | | |
|---|---|---|---|
| 1947 | 3 | A | 0-3 |
| 1965 | 4 | A | 2-2 |
| 1965 | 4r | H | 0-3 |
| 1968 | 3 | H | 1-0 |
| 1977 | 3 | A | 2-3 |
| 1986 | 1 | H | 6-0 |

v **Wrexham**

| | | | |
|---|---|---|---|
| 1974 | 2 | A | 0-3 |
| 1995 | 2 | A | 2-5 |
| 2001 | 1 | A | 1-0 |

v **York City**

| | | | |
|---|---|---|---|
| 1972 | 2 | H | 1-1 |
| 1972 | 2r | A | 3-2aet |
| 1977 | 2 | H | 0-0 |
| 1977 | 2r | A | 1-1aet |
| 1977 | 2r2 | H | 2-1aet |
| 1995 | 1 | A | 3-3 |
| 1995 | 1r | H | 3-0 |

# Rushden & Diamonds

v **Scunthorpe Utd**

| | | | |
|---|---|---|---|
| 2000 | 1 | H | 2-0 |

v **Sheffield Utd**

| | | | |
|---|---|---|---|
| 2000 | 3 | A | 1-1 |
| 2000 | 3r | H | 1-1q |

v **Shrewsbury Town**

| | | | |
|---|---|---|---|
| 1999 | 1 | H | 1-0 |

# Scunthorpe Utd

v **Sheffield Wed**

| | | | |
|---|---|---|---|
| 1970 | 4 | A | 2-1 |
| 1979 | 1 | H | 1-1 |
| 1979 | 1r | A | 0-1 |

v **Shrewsbury Town**

| | | | |
|---|---|---|---|
| 1996 | 2 | H | 1-1 |
| 1996 | 2r | A | 1-2 |

v **Stockport County**

| | | | |
|---|---|---|---|
| 1949 | 2 | H | 0-1 |
| 1970 | 2 | A | 0-0 |
| 1970 | 2r | H | 4-0 |
| 1978 | 1 | A | 0-3 |

v **Sunderland**

| | | | |
|---|---|---|---|
| 1953 | 3 | A | 1-1 |
| 1953 | 3r | H | 1-2 |
| 1988 | 2 | H | 2-1 |

v **Swindon Town**

| | | | |
|---|---|---|---|
| 1970 | 5 | A | 1-3 |

v **Tottenham Hotspur**

| | | | |
|---|---|---|---|
| 1952 | 3 | H | 0-3 |
| 1987 | 3 | A | 2-3 |

v **Tranmere Rovers**

| | | | |
|---|---|---|---|
| 1936 | 2 | A | 2-6 |
| 1971 | 1 | A | 1-1 |
| 1971 | 1r | H | 0-0aet |
| 1971 | 1r2 | N | 1-0aet |
| 1991 | 2 | H | 3-2 |

v **Walsall**

| | | | |
|---|---|---|---|
| 1937 | 1 | A | 0-3 |
| 1994 | 2 | A | 1-1 |
| 1994 | 2r | H | 0-0p |

v **Watford**

| | | | |
|---|---|---|---|
| 1939 | 2 | H | 1-2 |

v **West Bromwich Albion**

| | | | |
|---|---|---|---|
| 1971 | 3 | A | 0-0 |
| 1971 | 3r | H | 1-3 |
| 1984 | 4 | A | 0-1 |

v **Wimbledon**

| | | | |
|---|---|---|---|
| 1994 | 3 | A | 0-3 |

v **Wrexham**

| | | | |
|---|---|---|---|
| 1954 | 3 | A | 3-3 |
| 1954 | 3r | H | 3-1 |
| 1957 | 2 | H | 0-0 |
| 1957 | 2r | A | 2-6aet |
| 1997 | 2 | A | 2-2 |
| 1997 | 2r | H | 2-3aet |
| 1999 | 3 | A | 3-4 |

v **York City**

| | | | |
|---|---|---|---|
| 1947 | 1 | A | 1-0 |

# Sheffield Utd

v **Sheffield Wed**

| | | | |
|---|---|---|---|
| 1900 | 2 | H | 1-1 |
| 1900 | 2r | A | 2-0 |
| 1925 | 2 | H | 3-2 |
| 1928 | 5 | A | 1-1 |
| 1928 | 5r | H | 4-1 |
| 1954 | 3 | A | 1-1 |
| 1954 | 3r | H | 1-3 |
| 1960 | 6 | H | 0-2 |
| 1993 | SF | N | 1-2aet |

v **Southampton**

| | | | |
|---|---|---|---|
| 1902 | F | N | 1-1 |
| 1902 | Fr | N | 2-1 |
| 1925 | SF | N | 2-0 |
| 1963 | 5 | A | 0-1 |
| 2001 | 3 | A | 0-1 |

v **Southend Utd**

| | | | |
|---|---|---|---|
| 1920 | 1 | H | 3-0 |
| 1935 | 3 | A | 4-0 |
| 1952 | 5 | A | 2-1 |

v **Stockport County**

| | | | |
|---|---|---|---|
| 1926 | 3 | H | 2-0 |
| 1981 | 1 | A | 0-0 |
| 1981 | 1r | H | 3-2aet |

v **Stoke City**

| | | | |
|---|---|---|---|
| 1946 | 4 | A | 0-2 |
| 1946 | 4s | H | 3-2 |
| 1947 | 5 | A | 1-0 |
| 1983 | 3 | H | 0-0 |
| 1983 | 3r | A | 2-3 |

v **Sunderland**

| | | | |
|---|---|---|---|
| 1893 | 2 | H | 1-3 |
| 1901 | 1 | A | 2-1 |
| 1909 | 1 | H | 2-3 |
| 1926 | 4 | H | 1-2 |
| 1931 | 5 | A | 1-2 |
| 1956 | 5 | H | 0-0 |
| 1956 | 5r | A | 0-1 |

v **Swansea City**

| | | | |
|---|---|---|---|
| 1933 | 3 | A | 3-2 |
| 1964 | 4 | H | 1-1 |
| 1964 | 4r | A | 0-4 |

v **Swindon Town**

| | | | |
|---|---|---|---|
| 1908 | 1 | A | 0-0 |
| 1908 | 1r | H | 2-3aet |
| 1921 | 1 | A | 0-1 |

v **Tottenham Hotspur**

| | | | |
|---|---|---|---|
| 1901 | F | N | 2-2 |
| 1901 | Fr | N | 1-3 |
| 1936 | 6 | H | 3-1 |
| 1958 | 4 | A | 3-0 |

v **Walsall**

| | | | |
|---|---|---|---|
| 2003 | 5 | H | 2-0 |

v **Watford**

| | | | |
|---|---|---|---|
| 1960 | 5 | H | 3-2 |
| 1968 | 3 | A | 1-0 |
| 1973 | 3 | A | 1-0 |
| 1985 | 3 | A | 0-5 |
| 1990 | 4 | H | 1-1 |
| 1990 | 4r | A | 2-1 |

v **West Bromwich Albion**

| | | | |
|---|---|---|---|
| 1895 | 2 | H | 1-1 |
| 1895 | 2r | A | 1-2 |
| 1925 | 4 | H | 2-0 |
| 1935 | 4 | A | 1-7 |
| 1958 | 5 | H | 1-1 |
| 1958 | 5r | A | 1-4 |

v **West Ham Utd**

| | | | |
|---|---|---|---|
| 1952 | 4 | A | 0-0 |
| 1952 | 4r | H | 4-2 |
| 1968 | 5 | A | 2-1 |
| 1987 | 4 | A | 0-4 |

v **Wolverhampton W**

| | | | |
|---|---|---|---|
| 1892 | 2 | A | 1-3 |
| 1901 | 3 | A | 4-0 |
| 1928 | 4 | H | 3-1 |
| 1937 | 4 | A | 2-2 |
| 1937 | 4r | H | 1-2 |
| 1947 | 4 | A | 0-0 |
| 1947 | 4r | H | 2-0 |
| 1949 | 4 | H | 0-3 |
| 1950 | 4 | A | 0-0 |
| 1950 | 4r | H | 3-4 |
| 1966 | 4 | A | 0-3 |

v **Wrexham**

| | | | |
|---|---|---|---|
| 1984 | 1 | A | 5-1 |

v **York City**

| | | | |
|---|---|---|---|
| 1931 | 3 | H | 1-1 |
| 1931 | 3r | A | 2-0 |

# Sheffield Wed

v **Shrewsbury Town**

| | | | |
|---|---|---|---|
| 1963 | 3 | A | 1-1 |
| 1963 | 3r | H | 2-1 |

v **Southampton**

| | | | |
|---|---|---|---|
| 1896 | 1 | A | 3-2 |
| 1907 | 2 | A | 1-1 |
| 1907 | 2r | H | 3-1 |
| 1949 | 3 | H | 2-1 |
| 1984 | 6 | H | 0-0 |
| 1984 | 6r | A | 1-5 |
| 2001 | 4 | A | 1-3 |

v **Southend Utd**

| | | | |
|---|---|---|---|
| 1983 | 3 | A | 0-0 |
| 1983 | 3r | H | 2-2aet |
| 1983 | 3r2 | H | 2-1 |
| 1993 | 5 | H | 2-0 |

v **Stockport County**

| | | | |
|---|---|---|---|
| 1977 | 1 | H | 2-0 |
| 1999 | 4 | H | 2-0 |

v **Stoke City**

| | | | |
|---|---|---|---|
| 1894 | 2 | H | 1-0 |
| 1899 | 1 | H | 2-2 |
| 1899 | 1r | A | 0-2 |
| 1909 | 1 | H | 5-0 |
| 1946 | 5 | A | 0-2 |
| 1946 | 5s | H | 0-0 |

v **Sunderland**

| | | | |
|---|---|---|---|
| 1896 | 2 | H | 2-1 |
| 1898 | 1 | A | 1-0 |
| 1902 | 1 | H | 0-1 |
| 1907 | 3 | H | 0-0 |
| 1907 | 3r | A | 1-0 |
| 1972 | 3 | A | 0-3 |
| 1993 | 4 | H | 1-0 |

v **Swansea City**

| | | | |
|---|---|---|---|
| 1962 | 3 | H | 1-0 |

v **Swindon Town**

| | | | |
|---|---|---|---|
| 1928 | 4 | A | 2-1 |
| 1968 | 4 | H | 2-1 |

v **Torquay Utd**

| | | | |
|---|---|---|---|
| 1983 | 4 | A | 3-2 |
| 1989 | 3 | H | 5-1 |

v **Tottenham Hotspur**

| | | | |
|---|---|---|---|
| 1904 | 3 | A | 1-1 |
| 1904 | 3r | H | 2-0 |
| 1932 | 3 | A | 2-2 |
| 1932 | 3r | H | 3-1 |
| 1971 | 3 | A | 1-4 |

v **Tranmere Rovers**

| | | | |
|---|---|---|---|
| 1979 | 2 | A | 1-1 |
| 1979 | 2r | H | 4-0 |

v **Watford**

| | | | |
|---|---|---|---|
| 1998 | 3 | A | 1-1 |
| 1998 | 3r | H | 0-0p |

v **West Bromwich Albion**

| | | | |
|---|---|---|---|
| 1891 | 3 | H | 0-2 |
| 1892 | 3 | A | 1-2 |
| 1895 | SF | N | 0-2 |
| 1898 | 2 | A | 0-1 |
| 1935 | F | N | 4-2 |
| 1959 | 3 | H | 0-2 |
| 1970 | 3 | H | 2-1 |
| 1986 | 3 | H | 2-2 |
| 1986 | 3r | A | 3-2 |

v **West Ham Utd**

| | | | |
|---|---|---|---|
| 1921 | 1 | H | 1-0 |
| 1986 | 6 | H | 2-1 |
| 1987 | 5 | H | 1-1 |
| 1987 | 5r | A | 2-0 |

v **Wigan Athletic**

| | | | |
|---|---|---|---|
| 1976 | 2 | H | 2-0 |
| 1978 | 2 | A | 0-1 |

v **Wimbledon**

| | | | |
|---|---|---|---|
| 1997 | 6 | H | 0-2 |

v **Wolverhampton W**

| | | | |
|---|---|---|---|
| 1889 | 3 | A | 0-3 |
| 1896 | F | N | 2-1 |
| 1907 | 1 | H | 3-2 |
| 1914 | 2 | A | 1-1 |
| 1914 | 2r | H | 1-0 |
| 1915 | 2 | H | 2-0 |
| 1935 | 4 | A | 2-1 |

| | | | |
|---|---|---|---|
| 1990 | 3 | A | 2-1 |
| 1995 | 4 | H | 0-0 |
| 1995 | 4r | A | 1-1p |
| 2000 | 4 | H | 1-1 |
| 2000 | 4r | A | 0-0q |

v **Yeovil Town**

| | | | |
|---|---|---|---|
| 1939 | 3 | H | 1-1 |
| 1939 | 3r | A | 2-1 |

v **York City**

| | | | |
|---|---|---|---|
| 1946 | 4 | H | 5-1 |
| 1946 | 4s | A | 6-1 |

## Shrewsbury Town

v **Southampton**

| | | | |
|---|---|---|---|
| 1953 | 4 | H | 1-4 |

v **Stockport County**

| | | | |
|---|---|---|---|
| 1948 | 2 | A | 1-1ab |
| 1948 | 2r | H | 2-2aet |
| 1948 | 2r2 | N | 2-3aet |
| 1978 | 2 | H | 1-1 |
| 1978 | 2r | A | 2-1 |

v **Stoke City**

| | | | |
|---|---|---|---|
| 1914 | Q4 | A | 0-2 |

v **Swindon Town**

| | | | |
|---|---|---|---|
| 1961 | 2 | A | 1-0 |

v **Torquay Utd**

| | | | |
|---|---|---|---|
| 1956 | 2 | H | 0-0 |
| 1956 | 2r | A | 1-5 |
| 1963 | 2 | H | 2-1 |
| 1966 | 1 | H | 2-1 |

v **Tranmere Rovers**

| | | | |
|---|---|---|---|
| 1910 | Q3 | A | 2-0 |

v **Walsall**

| | | | |
|---|---|---|---|
| 1901 | Q3 | H | 1-1 |
| 1901 | Q3r | A | 0-1 |
| 1904 | Q5 | H | 1-0 |
| 1915 | Q5 | H | 2-1 |
| 1921 | Q1 | H | 1-0 |
| 1922 | Q4 | H | 0-1 |
| 1946 | 1 | H | 5-0 |
| 1946 | 1s | A | 1-4 |
| 1955 | 1 | A | 2-5 |

v **Watford**

| | | | |
|---|---|---|---|
| 1991 | 3 | H | 4-1 |

v **Wigan Athletic**

| | | | |
|---|---|---|---|
| 1975 | 1 | H | 1-1 |
| 1975 | 1r | A | 1-2 |

v **Wimbledon**

| | | | |
|---|---|---|---|
| 1991 | 4 | H | 1-0 |

v **Wolverhampton W**

| | | | |
|---|---|---|---|
| 1979 | 6 | A | 1-1 |
| 1979 | 6r | H | 1-3 |

v **Wrexham**

| | | | |
|---|---|---|---|
| 1946 | 2 | H | 0-1 |
| 1946 | 2s | A | 1-1 |
| 1967 | 2 | H | 5-1 |
| 1974 | 1 | A | 1-1 |
| 1974 | 1r | H | 0-1 |

v **Yeovil Town**

| | | | |
|---|---|---|---|
| 1970 | 1 | A | 3-2 |

## Southampton

v **Southend Utd**

| | | | |
|---|---|---|---|
| 1952 | 3 | A | 0-3 |
| 1960 | 2 | H | 3-0 |
| 1995 | 3 | H | 2-0 |

v **Stoke City**

| | | | |
|---|---|---|---|
| 1933 | 3 | A | 0-1 |

v **Sunderland**

| | | | |
|---|---|---|---|
| 1931 | 3 | A | 0-2 |
| 1932 | 3 | A | 0-0 |
| 1932 | 3r | H | 2-4 |
| 1937 | 3 | H | 2-3 |
| 1948 | 3 | H | 1-0 |
| 1951 | 4 | A | 0-2 |
| 1962 | 3 | H | 2-2 |
| 1962 | 3r | A | 0-3 |
| 1985 | 3 | H | 4-0 |

v **Swindon Town**

| | | | |
|---|---|---|---|
| 1897 | Q5 | H | 8-2 |
| 1898 | Q4 | A | 3-1 |
| 1948 | 5 | H | 3-0 |
| 1996 | 5 | A | 1-1 |
| 1996 | 5r | H | 2-0 |

v **Tottenham Hotspur**

| | | | |
|---|---|---|---|
| 1902 | 1 | A | 1-1 |
| 1902 | 1r | H | 2-2aet |
| 1902 | 1r2 | N | 2-1 |
| 1948 | 6 | H | 0-1 |
| 1983 | 3 | A | 0-1 |
| 1990 | 3 | A | 3-1 |
| 1995 | 5 | A | 1-1 |
| 1995 | 5r | H | 2-6aet |
| 2003 | 3 | H | 4-0 |

v **Tranmere Rovers**

| | | | |
|---|---|---|---|
| 2001 | 5 | H | 0-0 |
| 2001 | 5r | A | 3-4 |

v **Walsall**

| | | | |
|---|---|---|---|
| 1935 | 3 | A | 2-1 |
| 1956 | 2 | A | 1-2 |

v **Watford**

| | | | |
|---|---|---|---|
| 1907 | 1 | H | 2-1 |
| 1960 | 4 | H | 2-2 |
| 1960 | 4r | A | 0-1 |
| 1963 | 4 | H | 3-1 |
| 2003 | SF | N | 2-1 |

v **West Bromwich Albion**

| | | | |
|---|---|---|---|
| 1900 | 3 | H | 2-1 |
| 1908 | 2 | H | 1-0 |
| 1968 | 4 | A | 1-1 |
| 1968 | 4r | H | 2-3 |
| 1976 | 5 | A | 1-1 |
| 1976 | 5r | H | 4-0 |
| 1979 | 5 | A | 1-1 |
| 1979 | 5r | H | 2-1aet |

v **West Ham Utd**

| | | | |
|---|---|---|---|
| 1920 | 1 | H | 0-0 |
| 1920 | 1r | A | 1-3 |
| 1923 | 4 | H | 1-1 |
| 1923 | 4r | A | 1-1aet |
| 1923 | 4r2 | N | 0-1 |
| 1975 | 3 | H | 1-2 |

v **Wigan Athletic**

| | | | |
|---|---|---|---|
| 1986 | 4 | H | 3-0 |

v **Wimbledon**

| | | | |
|---|---|---|---|
| 1979 | 3 | A | 2-0 |

v **Wolverhampton W**

| | | | |
|---|---|---|---|
| 1905 | 2 | A | 3-2 |
| 1908 | SF | N | 0-2 |
| 1914 | 1 | A | 0-3 |
| 2003 | 6 | H | 2-0 |

v **Wrexham**

| | | | |
|---|---|---|---|
| 1974 | 5 | H | 0-1 |

v **York City**

| | | | |
|---|---|---|---|
| 1963 | 3 | H | 5-0 |
| 1971 | 4 | A | 3-3 |
| 1971 | 4r | H | 3-2 |

## Southend Utd

v **Swansea City**

| | | | |
|---|---|---|---|
| 1922 | 2 | H | 0-1 |
| 1949 | 1 | H | 1-2aet |
| 1976 | 1 | H | 2-0 |

v **Swindon Town**

| | | | |
|---|---|---|---|
| 1951 | 1 | H | 0-3 |
| 1969 | 3 | A | 2-0 |

v **Torquay Utd**

| | | | |
|---|---|---|---|
| 1931 | 1 | H | 0-1 |
| 1932 | 1 | A | 3-1 |
| 1958 | 2 | A | 1-1 |
| 1958 | 2r | H | 2-1 |
| 1978 | 1 | A | 2-1 |
| 2000 | 1 | A | 0-1 |
| 2001 | 1 | A | 1-1 |
| 2001 | 1r | H | 2-1aet |

v **Tottenham Hotspur**

| | | | |
|---|---|---|---|
| 1921 | 3 | H | 1-4 |
| 1936 | 3 | A | 4-4 |
| 1936 | 3r | H | 1-2 |

v **Tranmere Rovers**

| | | | |
|---|---|---|---|
| 1934 | 3 | A | 0-3 |
| 2002 | 3 | H | 1-3 |

v **Walsall**

| | | | |
|---|---|---|---|
| 1988 | 1 | H | 0-0 |
| 1988 | 1r | A | 1-2 |

v **Watford**

| | | | |
|---|---|---|---|
| 1920 | Q6 | H | 1-0 |
| 1933 | 3 | A | 1-1 |
| 1933 | 3r | H | 2-0 |
| 1946 | 1 | A | 1-1 |
| 1946 | 1s | H | 0-3 |
| 1962 | 1 | H | 0-2 |
| 1963 | 2 | H | 0-2 |
| 1966 | 2 | H | 2-1 |
| 1967 | 1 | A | 0-1 |
| 1979 | 2 | A | 1-1 |
| 1979 | 2r | H | 1-0 |

v **West Ham Utd**

| | | | |
|---|---|---|---|
| 1996 | 3 | A | 0-2 |

v **Wimbledon**

| | | | |
|---|---|---|---|
| 1935 | 2 | A | 5-1 |

v **Wrexham**

| | | | |
|---|---|---|---|
| 1950 | 2 | A | 2-2 |
| 1950 | 2r | H | 2-0 |

v **Yeovil Town**

| | | | |
|---|---|---|---|
| 1959 | 1 | H | 0-0 |
| 1959 | 1r | A | 0-1 |
| 1964 | 1 | A | 0-1 |
| 1983 | 2 | H | 3-0 |

v **York City**

| | | | |
|---|---|---|---|
| 1930 | 2 | H | 1-4 |
| 1937 | 2 | H | 3-3 |
| 1937 | 2r | A | 1-2 |

# Stockport County

v **Stoke City**

| | | | |
|---|---|---|---|
| 1997 | 3 | A | 2-0 |

v **Torquay Utd**

| | | | |
|---|---|---|---|
| 1948 | 3 | H | 3-0 |

v **Tottenham Hotspur**

| | | | |
|---|---|---|---|
| 2001 | 5 | A | 0-4 |

v **Tranmere Rovers**

| | | | |
|---|---|---|---|
| 1894 | Q2 | H | 2-1 |
| 1966 | 1 | A | 1-0 |

v **Walsall**

| | | | |
|---|---|---|---|
| 1906 | Q4 | A | 3-3 |
| 1906 | Q4r | H | 5-0 |
| 1980 | 1 | A | 0-2 |
| 1985 | 1 | H | 1-2 |

v **West Bromwich Albion**

| | | | |
|---|---|---|---|
| 1935 | 5 | H | 0-5 |

v **West Ham Utd**

| | | | |
|---|---|---|---|
| 1935 | 3 | A | 1-1 |
| 1935 | 3r | H | 1-0 |
| 1958 | 4 | A | 2-3 |

v **Wigan Athletic**

| | | | |
|---|---|---|---|
| 1965 | 1 | H | 2-1 |
| 1992 | 2 | A | 0-2 |

v **Wrexham**

| | | | |
|---|---|---|---|
| 1894 | Q3r | H | 7-0 |
| 1901 | Q3 | H | 6-2 |
| 1905 | Q5 | H | 4-0 |
| 1979 | 3 | A | 2-6 |
| 1995 | 1 | A | 0-1 |

v **York City**

| | | | |
|---|---|---|---|
| 1993 | 1 | A | 3-1 |

# Stoke City

v **Sunderland**

| | | | |
|---|---|---|---|
| 1892 | 3 | H | 2-2aet |
| 1892 | 3r | A | 0-4 |
| 1932 | 4 | A | 1-1 |
| 1932 | 4r | H | 1-1aet |
| 1932 | 4r2 | N | 2-1aet |
| 1952 | 3 | A | 0-0 |
| 1952 | 3r | H | 3-1 |
| 1976 | 5 | H | 0-0 |
| 1976 | 5r | A | 1-2 |

v **Swansea City**

| | | | |
|---|---|---|---|
| 1926 | 4 | A | 3-6 |
| 1935 | 3 | A | 1-4 |
| 1955 | 4 | A | 1-3 |
| 1964 | 5 | H | 2-2 |
| 1964 | 5r | A | 0-2 |
| 1999 | 2 | A | 0-1 |

v **Swindon Town**

| | | | |
|---|---|---|---|
| 1949 | 3 | A | 3-1 |
| 1952 | 4 | A | 1-1 |
| 1952 | 4r | H | 0-1 |

v **Tottenham Hotspur**

| | | | |
|---|---|---|---|
| 1896 | 1 | H | 5-0 |
| 1899 | 3 | H | 4-1 |
| 1947 | 3 | A | 2-2 |
| 1947 | 3r | H | 1-0 |
| 1950 | 3 | H | 0-1 |
| 1976 | 3 | A | 1-1 |
| 1976 | 3r | H | 2-1 |

v **Tranmere Rovers**

| | | | |
|---|---|---|---|
| 1972 | 4 | A | 2-2 |
| 1972 | 4r | H | 2-0 |

v **Walsall**

| | | | |
|---|---|---|---|
| 1912 | Q4 | A | 1-2 |
| 1915 | Q3 | A | 0-1 |
| 1966 | 3 | H | 0-2 |

v **Watford**

| | | | |
|---|---|---|---|
| 1970 | 4 | A | 0-1 |

v **West Bromwich Albion**

| | | | |
|---|---|---|---|
| 1888 | 5 | A | 1-4 |
| 1907 | 1 | A | 1-1 |
| 1907 | 1r | H | 2-2aet |
| 1907 | 1r2 | N | 0-2 |
| 1998 | 3 | A | 1-3 |

v **West Ham Utd**

| | | | |
|---|---|---|---|
| 1951 | 4 | H | 1-0 |
| 1961 | 3 | A | 2-2 |
| 1961 | 3r | H | 1-0 |
| 1968 | 4 | H | 0-3 |

v **Wigan Athletic**

| | | | |
|---|---|---|---|
| 2003 | 3 | H | 3-0 |

v **Wolverhampton W**

| | | | |
|---|---|---|---|
| 1890 | 3r | A | 0-8 |
| 1895 | 2 | A | 0-2 |
| 1896 | 3 | A | 0-3 |
| 1908 | 4 | H | 0-1 |
| 1921 | 1 | A | 2-3 |
| 1981 | 3 | H | 2-2 |
| 1981 | 3r | A | 1-2 |

v **Wrexham**

| | | | |
|---|---|---|---|
| 1953 | 3 | H | 2-1 |

v **York City**

| | | | |
|---|---|---|---|
| 1969 | 3 | A | 2-0 |

# Sunderland

v **Swansea City**

| | | | |
|---|---|---|---|
| 1937 | 5 | H | 3-0 |
| 1955 | 5 | A | 2-2 |
| 1955 | 5r | H | 1-0 |

v **Swindon Town**

| | | | |
|---|---|---|---|
| 1913 | 3 | H | 4-2 |

v **Tottenham Hotspur**

| | | | |
|---|---|---|---|
| 1899 | 2 | A | 1-2 |
| 1915 | 1 | A | 1-2 |
| 1938 | 6 | A | 1-0 |
| 1950 | 4 | A | 1-5 |
| 1961 | 6 | H | 1-1 |
| 1961 | 6r | A | 0-5 |
| 1995 | 4 | H | 1-4 |

v **Tranmere Rovers**

| | | | |
|---|---|---|---|
| 1998 | 4 | A | 0-1 |
| 2000 | 4 | A | 0-1 |

v **Watford**

| | | | |
|---|---|---|---|
| 1938 | 3 | H | 1-0 |
| 2003 | 5 | H | 0-1 |

v **West Bromwich Albion**

| | | | |
|---|---|---|---|
| 1912 | 3 | H | 1-2 |
| 1923 | 2 | A | 1-2 |
| 1957 | 4 | A | 2-4 |
| 2002 | 3 | H | 1-2 |

v **West Ham Utd**

| | | | |
|---|---|---|---|
| 1929 | 3 | A | 0-1 |
| 1992 | 5 | H | 1-1 |
| 1992 | 5r | A | 3-2 |
| 2001 | 5 | H | 0-1 |

v **Wimbledon**

| | | | |
|---|---|---|---|
| 1987 | 3 | A | 1-2 |
| 1994 | 4 | A | 1-2 |

v **Wolverhampton W**

| | | | |
|---|---|---|---|
| 1905 | 1 | H | 1-1 |
| 1905 | 1r | A | 0-1 |
| 1937 | 6 | A | 1-1 |
| 1937 | 6r | H | 2-2aet |
| 1937 | 6r2 | N | 4-0 |
| 1951 | 6 | H | 1-1 |
| 1951 | 6r | A | 1-3 |
| 1955 | 6 | H | 2-0 |

v **Wrexham**

| | | | |
|---|---|---|---|
| 1977 | 3 | H | 2-2 |
| 1977 | 3r | A | 0-1 |

v **Yeovil Town**

| | | | |
|---|---|---|---|
| 1949 | 4 | A | 1-2aet |

York City

| | | | |
|---|---|---|---|
| 1956 | 4 | A | 0-0 |
| 1956 | 4r | H | 2-1 |

# Swansea City

v **Walsall**

| | | | |
|---|---|---|---|
| 1930 | 3 | A | 0-2 |
| 1966 | 1 | A | 3-6 |
| 1974 | 1 | A | 0-1 |
| 1978 | 3 | A | 1-4 |
| 1991 | 2 | H | 2-1 |

v **Watford**

| | | | |
|---|---|---|---|
| 1926 | 2 | H | 3-2 |

v **West Bromwich Albion**

| | | | |
|---|---|---|---|
| 1987 | 3 | H | 3-2 |

v **West Ham Utd**

| | | | |
|---|---|---|---|
| 1922 | 1 | H | 0-0 |
| 1922 | 1r | A | 1-1aet |
| 1922 | 1r2 | N | 1-0 |
| 1963 | 4 | A | 0-1 |
| 1980 | 5 | A | 0-2 |
| 1999 | 3 | A | 1-1 |
| 1999 | 3r | H | 1-0 |

v **Wolverhampton W**

| | | | |
|---|---|---|---|
| 1938 | 3 | H | 0-4 |
| 1957 | 3 | A | 3-5 |

v **Wrexham**

| | | | |
|---|---|---|---|
| 1928 | 3 | A | 1-2 |

v **York City**

| | | | |
|---|---|---|---|
| 1937 | 4 | H | 0-0 |
| 1937 | 4r | A | 3-1 |
| 1956 | 3 | H | 1-2 |
| 2003 | 1 | A | 1-2 |

# Swindon Town

v **Torquay Utd**

| | | | |
|---|---|---|---|
| 1952 | 2 | H | 3-3 |
| 1952 | 2r | A | 1-1aet |
| 1952 | 2r2 | N | 3-1 |
| 1980 | 2 | A | 3-3 |
| 1980 | 2r | H | 3-2 |

v **Tottenham Hotspur**

| | | | |
|---|---|---|---|
| 1910 | 3 | H | 3-2 |
| 1980 | 4 | H | 0-0 |
| 1980 | 4r | A | 1-2 |

v **Walsall**

| | | | |
|---|---|---|---|
| 1960 | 1 | H | 2-3 |

v **Watford**

| | | | |
|---|---|---|---|
| 1992 | 3 | H | 3-2 |
| 1995 | 4 | A | 0-1 |

v **West Bromwich Albion**

| | | | |
|---|---|---|---|
| 1973 | 4 | A | 0-2 |

v **West Ham Utd**

| | | | |
|---|---|---|---|
| 1912 | 3 | A | 1-1 |
| 1912 | 3r | H | 4-0 |
| 1964 | 5 | H | 1-3 |
| 1967 | 3 | A | 3-3 |
| 1967 | 3r | H | 3-1 |
| 1975 | 4 | A | 1-1 |
| 1975 | 4r | H | 1-2 |
| 1989 | 4 | H | 0-0 |
| 1989 | 4r | A | 0-1 |

v **Wimbledon**

| | | | |
|---|---|---|---|
| 1981 | 2 | A | 0-2 |

v **Wolverhampton W**

| | | | |
|---|---|---|---|
| 1908 | 3 | A | 0-2 |

v **Yeovil Town**

| | | | |
|---|---|---|---|
| 1902 | Q3 | H | 4-0 |
| 1903 | Q3 | A | 4-0 |
| 1963 | 2 | A | 2-0 |

# Torquay Utd

v **Tottenham Hotspur**

| | | | |
|---|---|---|---|
| 1965 | 3 | H | 3-3 |
| 1965 | 3r | A | 1-5 |

v **Walsall**

| | | | |
|---|---|---|---|
| 1979 | 1 | A | 2-0 |
| 1996 | 2 | H | 1-1 |
| 1996 | 2r | A | 4-8aet |

v **Watford**

| | | | |
|---|---|---|---|
| 1948 | 1 | A | 1-1aet |
| 1948 | 1r | H | 3-0 |
| 1959 | 2 | H | 2-0 |
| 1998 | 2 | H | 1-1 |
| 1998 | 2r | A | 1-2aet |

v **West Ham Utd**

| | | | |
|---|---|---|---|
| 1990 | 3 | H | 1-0 |

v **Wigan Athletic**

| | | | |
|---|---|---|---|
| 1935 | 2 | A | 2-3 |

v **Yeovil Town**

| | | | |
|---|---|---|---|
| 1924 | Q3 | A | 1-1 |
| 1924 | Q3r | H | 2-1 |
| 1926 | Q4 | H | 3-1 |
| 1985 | 1 | H | 2-0 |
| 1989 | 2 | A | 1-1 |
| 1989 | 2r | H | 1-0 |
| 1993 | 1 | H | 2-5 |

# Tottenham Hotspur

v **Tranmere Rovers**

| | | | |
|---|---|---|---|
| 1953 | 3 | A | 1-1 |
| 1953 | 3r | H | 9-1 |
| 2002 | 5 | H | 4-0 |

v **Walsall**

| | | | |
|---|---|---|---|
| 1969 | 3 | A | 1-0 |

v **Watford**

| | | | |
|---|---|---|---|
| 1922 | 2 | H | 1-0 |
| 1939 | 3 | H | 7-1 |
| 1987 | SF | N | 4-1 |
| 1999 | 3 | H | 5-2 |

v **West Bromwich Albion**

| | | | |
|---|---|---|---|
| 1901 | SF | N | 4-0 |
| 1903 | 1 | H | 0-0 |
| 1903 | 1r | A | 2-0 |
| 1912 | 1 | A | 0-3 |
| 1931 | 4 | A | 0-1 |
| 1948 | 4 | H | 3-1 |
| 1954 | 6 | A | 0-3 |
| 1962 | 5 | A | 4-2 |
| 1983 | 4 | H | 2-1 |

v **West Ham Utd**

| | | | |
|---|---|---|---|
| 1920 | 3 | H | 3-0 |
| 1926 | 3 | H | 5-0 |
| 1927 | 3 | A | 2-3 |
| 1934 | 4 | H | 4-1 |
| 1939 | 4 | A | 3-3 |
| 1939 | 4r | H | 1-1aet |
| 1939 | 4r2 | N | 1-2 |
| 1956 | 6 | H | 3-3 |
| 1956 | 6r | A | 2-1 |
| 1959 | 3 | H | 2-0 |
| 2001 | 6 | A | 3-2 |

v **Wimbledon**

| | | | |
|---|---|---|---|
| 1987 | 6 | A | 2-0 |
| 1993 | 5 | H | 3-2 |
| 1999 | 4 | A | 1-1 |
| 1999 | 4r | H | 3-0 |

v **Wolverhampton W**

| | | | |
|---|---|---|---|
| 1921 | F | N | 1-0 |
| 1969 | 4 | H | 2-1 |
| 1981 | SF | N | 2-2aet |
| 1981 | SFr | N | 3-0 |
| 1996 | 4 | H | 1-1 |
| 1996 | 4r | A | 2-0 |

v **Wrexham**

| | | | |
|---|---|---|---|
| 1979 | 4 | H | 3-3 |
| 1979 | 4r | A | 3-2aet |

v **York City**

| | | | |
|---|---|---|---|
| 1955 | 5 | A | 1-3 |

# Tranmere Rovers

v **West Ham Utd**

| | | | |
|---|---|---|---|
| 2000 | 3 | H | 1-0 |

v **Wigan Athletic**

| | | | |
|---|---|---|---|
| 1967 | 1 | H | 1-1 |
| 1967 | 1r | A | 1-0 |

v **Wimbledon**

| | | | |
|---|---|---|---|
| 1995 | 4 | H | 0-2 |

v **Wolverhampton W**

| | | | |
|---|---|---|---|
| 1983 | 3 | H | 0-1 |

v **Wrexham**

| | | | |
|---|---|---|---|
| 1907 | Q1 | A | 1-2 |
| 1915 | Q3 | A | 1-1 |
| 1915 | Q3r | H | 0-1 |

v **York City**

| | | | |
|---|---|---|---|
| 1930 | 1 | A | 2-2 |
| 1930 | 1r | H | 0-1 |
| 1951 | 2 | A | 1-2 |
| 1961 | 2 | H | 1-1 |
| 1961 | 2r | A | 1-2 |
| 1981 | 1 | H | 0-0 |
| 1981 | 1r | A | 2-1aet |
| 1992 | 2 | A | 1-1 |
| 1992 | 2r | H | 2-1 |

# Walsall

v **Watford**

| | | | |
|---|---|---|---|
| 1935 | 2 | A | 1-1 |
| 1935 | 2r | H | 1-0aet |
| 1938 | 2 | A | 0-3 |
| 1987 | 5 | H | 1-1 |
| 1987 | 5r | A | 4-4aet |
| 1987 | 5r2 | H | 0-1 |

v **West Bromwich Albion**

| | | | |
|---|---|---|---|
| 1900 | 1 | H | 1-1 |
| 1900 | 1r | A | 1-6 |

v **West Ham Utd**

| | | | |
|---|---|---|---|
| 2001 | 3 | H | 2-3 |

v **Wigan Athletic**

| | | | |
|---|---|---|---|
| 1996 | 3 | H | 1-0 |

v **Wimbledon**

| | | | |
|---|---|---|---|
| 2003 | 4 | H | 1-0 |

v **Wolverhampton W**

| | | | |
|---|---|---|---|
| 1889 | 2 | A | 1-6 |

v **Wrexham**

| | | | |
|---|---|---|---|
| 1915 | Q4 | H | 2-1 |
| 1955 | 2 | A | 2-1 |
| 1994 | 1 | A | 1-1 |
| 1994 | 1r | H | 2-0 |

v **Yeovil Town**

| | | | |
|---|---|---|---|
| 1937 | 2 | H | 1-1 |
| 1937 | 2r | A | 1-0 |
| 1961 | 1 | H | 0-1 |
| 1992 | 1 | A | 1-1 |
| 1992 | 1r | H | 0-1aet |

v **York City**

| | | | |
|---|---|---|---|
| 1985 | 3 | A | 0-3 |

# Watford

**v West Bromwich Albion**

| | | | |
|---|---|---|---|
| 2003 | 4 | H | 1-0 |

**v West Ham Utd**

| | | | |
|---|---|---|---|
| 1978 | 3 | A | 0-1 |
| 1982 | 4 | H | 2-0 |
| 1994 | 3 | A | 1-2 |

**v Wigan Athletic**

| | | | |
|---|---|---|---|
| 1990 | 3 | H | 2-0 |

**v Wimbledon**

| | | | |
|---|---|---|---|
| 1988 | 6 | A | 1-2 |
| 1996 | 3 | H | 1-1 |
| 1996 | 3r | A | 0-1 |

**v Wolverhampton W**

| | | | |
|---|---|---|---|
| 1912 | 1 | H | 0-0 |
| 1912 | 1r | A | 0-10 |
| 1980 | 5 | A | 3-0 |
| 1981 | 4 | H | 1-1 |
| 1981 | 4r | A | 1-2 |
| 1993 | 3 | H | 1-4 |

**v Wycombe W**

| | | | |
|---|---|---|---|
| 1910 | Q5 | A | 4-0 |
| 1960 | 2 | H | 5-1 |

# West Bromwich A

**v West Ham Utd**

| | | | |
|---|---|---|---|
| 1913 | 1 | H | 1-1 |
| 1913 | 1r | A | 2-2aet |
| 1913 | 1r2 | N | 0-3 |
| 1933 | 4 | A | 0-2 |
| 1953 | 3 | A | 4-1 |
| 1980 | 3 | H | 1-1 |
| 1980 | 3r | A | 1-2 |
| 1993 | 3 | H | 0-2 |

**v Wimbledon**

| | | | |
|---|---|---|---|
| 1988 | 3 | A | 1-4 |
| 1990 | 3 | H | 2-0 |

**v Wolverhampton W**

| | | | |
|---|---|---|---|
| 1886 | 4 | H | 3-1 |
| 1888 | 3 | H | 2-0 |
| 1895 | 3 | H | 1-0 |
| 1924 | 3 | H | 1-1 |
| 1924 | 3r | A | 2-0 |
| 1931 | 6 | H | 1-1 |
| 1931 | 6r | A | 2-1 |
| 1949 | 6 | A | 0-1 |
| 1956 | 3 | A | 2-1 |
| 1962 | 4 | A | 2-1 |

**v Wrexham**

| | | | |
|---|---|---|---|
| 1930 | 3 | A | 0-1 |

**v Wycombe W**

| | | | |
|---|---|---|---|
| 1993 | 2 | A | 2-2 |
| 1993 | 2r | H | 1-0 |

**v York City**

| | | | |
|---|---|---|---|
| 1938 | 4 | A | 2-3 |

# West Ham Utd

**v Wigan Athletic**

| | | | |
|---|---|---|---|
| 1984 | 3 | H | 1-0 |

**v Wimbledon**

| | | | |
|---|---|---|---|
| 1985 | 5 | A | 1-1 |
| 1985 | 5r | H | 5-1 |

**v Wolverhampton W**

| | | | |
|---|---|---|---|
| 1910 | 2 | A | 5-1 |

**v Wrexham**

| | | | |
|---|---|---|---|
| 1981 | 3 | H | 1-1 |
| 1981 | 3r | A | 0-0aet |
| 1981 | 3r2 | A | 0-1aet |
| 1992 | 4 | H | 2-2 |
| 1992 | 4r | A | 1-0 |
| 1997 | 3 | A | 1-1 |
| 1997 | 3r | H | 0-1 |

**v Wycombe W**

| | | | |
|---|---|---|---|
| 1995 | 3 | A | 2-0 |

# Wigan Athletic

**v Wolverhampton W**

| | | | |
|---|---|---|---|
| 1988 | 2 | H | 1-3 |
| 2000 | 3 | H | 0-1 |

**v Wrexham**

| | | | |
|---|---|---|---|
| 1972 | 2 | A | 0-4 |
| 1985 | 1 | A | 2-0 |

**v Wycombe W**

| | | | |
|---|---|---|---|
| 2000 | 2 | A | 2-2 |
| 2000 | 2r | H | 2-1 |

**v York City**

| | | | |
|---|---|---|---|
| 1978 | 1 | H | 1-0 |
| 1998 | 2 | H | 2-1 |

# Wimbledon

**v Wolverhampton W**

| | | | |
|---|---|---|---|
| 1998 | 5 | H | 1-1 |
| 1998 | 5r | A | 1-2 |

**v Wrexham**

| | | | |
|---|---|---|---|
| 1981 | 4 | A | 1-2 |
| 1998 | 3 | H | 0-0 |
| 1998 | 3r | A | 3-2 |

**v Wycombe W**

| | | | |
|---|---|---|---|
| 2001 | 5 | A | 2-2 |
| 2001 | 5r | H | 2-2q |

# Wolverhampton Wanderers

**v Wrexham**

| | | | |
|---|---|---|---|
| 1931 | 3 | H | 9-1 |
| 1981 | 5 | H | 3-1 |
| 2001 | 4 | A | 1-2 |

# Wrexham

**v York City**

| | | | |
|---|---|---|---|
| 1999 | 2 | H | 2-1 |

# Wycombe Wanderers

**v York City**

| | | | |
|---|---|---|---|
| 1986 | 3 | A | 0-2 |

# FACTS & FEATS

# FA CUP FINAL RESULTS AND LINE-UPS

Capital Letters like this [S] after a player's name signify that the player was a full international *when the final was played.*

Small letters like this [s] signify that the player won a full cap *after the final was played.*

Thus Billy Bremner who was not capped until a few days after Leeds played Liverpool in the 1965 cup final is shown as [s] for 1965 but [S] for 1970, 1972 and 1973.

A 'c' before a player's name signifies the team captain.

## 1872

### Wanderers 1 (Betts)

Edward Bowen, c-Charles William Alcock [e], Alexander George Bonsor [e], Reginald de Courtenay Welch [e]; 1-Morton Peto Betts [e], William Crake,Thomas C Hooman, Edgar Lubbock, Albert Thompson, Robert Walpole Sealy Vidal[e], Charles Henry Reynolds Wollaston[e]. Note: Betts played under thepseudonym 'A.H. Chequer' on the day of the match.

### Royal Engineers 0

Capt William Merriman; Capt Francis Marindin; Lieut George Addison, Lieut Edmund Cresswell, Lieut Hugh Mitchell, Leiut Henry Renny-Tailyour[s], Lieut Henry Rich, Lieut Alfred GeorgeGoodwyn [e], Lieut Herbert Muirhead, Lieut Edmond Cotter, Lieut Adam Bogle

## 1873

### Wanderers 2 (Wollaston, Kinnaird)

Edward Bowen; Albert Thompson, Reginald de Courtenay Welch [E], c-Hon Arthur Kinnaird [S], Leonard Sidgwick Howell [E], Charles Henry Reynolds Wollaston [e], Julian Sturgis, Rev Henry H Stewart, William Stanley Kenyon-Slaney [E], Robert Kennett Kingsford [e], Aexander George Bonsor [E]

### Oxford University 0

Arnold Kirke-Smith; Andrew Leach, Charles Mackarness, Francis Hornby Birley [e], Charles Longman, Frederick Brunning Chappell-Maddison[E], Harold Dixon, Walter Paton, Robert Walpole Sealy Vidal [E], WE Sumner, Cuthbert John Ottaway [E]

March 29; 3,000; A Stair

## 1874

### Oxford University 2 (Mackarness, Patton)

Charles Neapean; Charles Mackarness, Francis Hornby Birley[E], Frederick Thomas Green [e], Robert Walpole Sealy Vidal [E], c-Cuthbert John Ottaway [E], Robert Benson, Frederick Patton, William Stepney Rawson [e], Frederick Brunning Chappell-Maddison [E], Rev Arthur H Johnson

### Royal Engineers 0

Capt William Merriman; c-Major Francis Marindin, Lieut George W Addison, Gerald Onslow, Lieut Henry G Oliver, Lieut Thomas Digby, Lieut Henry Renny- Tailyour [S], Lieut Herbert Edward Rawson [e], Lieut JE Blackman [S] Lieut Charles Wood, Lieut Pelham von Donop [E]

March 14; 2,000; A Stair

## 1875

### Royal Engineers 1 (Renny-Tailyour)

c-Capt William Merriman; Lieut George Sim, Lieut Gerald Onslow, Lieut (later Sir) Richard Ruck, Lieut Pelham Von Donop, Lieut Charles Wood, Lieut Herbert Edward Rawson [E], Lieut William Stafford, Capt Henry Renny-Tailyour [S], Lieut Alexander Mein, Lieut Cecil Vernon Wingfield-Stratford [e]

### Old Etonians 1 (Bonsor)

AG Thompson; Robert Benson, Edgar Lubbock, Francis Wilson, c-Hon Arthur Kinnaird [S], (Sir) James Stronge, Frederick Patton, Charles Farmer, Alexander George Bonsor [E], Cuthbert John Ottaway [E], William Kenyon-Slaney [E]

March 13; 2,000; CW Alcock. After extra time

### Replay

### Royal Engineers 2 (Renny-Tailyour, Stafford)

c-Capt William Merriman; Lieut George Sim, Lieut Gerald Onslow, Lieut (later Sir) Richard Ruck, Lieut Pelham Von Donop, [E] Lieut Charles Wood, Lieut Herbert Edward Rawson [E], Lieut William Stafford, Capt Henry Renny-Tailyour [S], Lieut Alexander Mein, Lieut Cecil Vernon Wingfield-Stratford [e]

### Old Etonians 0

Capt Edward Drummond-Moray; c-Hon Arthur Kinnaird, (Sir) James Stronge, Thomas Hammond, Alfred Lubbock, Frederick Patton, Matthew Farrer, Alexander George Bonsor [E], Edgar Lubbock, Francis Wilson, Charles Farmer

March 16; 3,000; CW Alcock

## 1876

### Wanderers 1 (Edwards)

William D O Greig; Alfred Hugh Stratford [E], William Lindsay, Frederick Brunning Chappel-Maddison [E], Francis Hornby Birley [E], Charles Henry Reynolds Wollaston [E], Charles Francis William Heron [E], George Hubert Hugh Heron [E], John Edwards [E], Jarvis Kenrick, Thomas Hughes

### Old Etonians 1 (Bonsor)

Quintin Hogg; Rev James E C Welldon, Hon Edward Lyttleton [e], Albert Thompson, c-Hon Arthur Kinnaird [S], C Meysey, William Stanley Kenyon-Slaney [E], Hon Alfred Lyttleton [e], Julian Sturgis, Alexander George Bonsor [E], Herbert Allene

March 11; 3,500; WS Rawson. After extra time

### Replay

### Wanderers 3 (Wollaston, Hughes 2)

William D O Greig, Alfred Hugh Stratford [E], William Lindsay, Frederick Brunning Chappel-Maddison [E], Francis Hornby Birley [E], Charles Henry Reynolds Wollaston [E], Charles Francis William Heron [E], George Hubert Hugh Heron [E], John Edwards [E], Jarvis Kenrick, Thomas Hughes

### Old Etonians 0

Quintin Hogg, Edgar Lubbock, Hon Edward Lyttleton, Matthew Farrer, c-Hon Arthur Kinnaird [S], (Sir) James Stronge, William Stanley Kenyon-Slaney, Hon Alfred Lyttleton [e], Julian Sturgis, Alexander George Bonsor, Herbert Allene

March 18; 1,500; WS Rawson

## 1877

### Wanderers 2 (Kenrick,Lindsay)

Hon Arthur Kinnaird [S]; c-Francis Hornby Birley, Charles Denton, Frederick Thomas Green [E], George Hubert Hugh Heron [E], Thomas Hughes, Jarvis Kenrick, William Lindsay[E], Alfred Hugh Stratford [E], Henry Wace [e], Charles Henry Reynolds Wollaston [E]

### Oxford University 1 (Kinnaird og)

Edward Allington; John Bain [E], Owen Dunnell, Rev James H Savory, Arthur Todd, Evelyn Waddington, Rev Philip H Fernandez, Arnold Frank Hills [e] Henry Otter, c-Edward Hagarty Parry [e], William Stepney Rawson [E]

March 24; 3,000; SH Wright, After extra time

## 1878

### Wanderers 3 (Kinnaird, Kenrick 2)

(Sir) James Kirkpatrick; Alfred Hugh Stratford [E], William Lindsay [E], c-Hon Arthur Kinnaird [S], Frederick Thomas Green [E], Charles Henry Reynolds Wollaston [E], George Hubert Hugh Heron [E], John George Wylie [E],Henry Wace [E], Charles A Denton, Jarvis Kenrick

### Royal Engineers 1 (from a rush)

Lovick B Friend; James Cowan, (Sir) William Morris, Charles Mayne, Frederick Heath, Charles Haynes, M Lindsay, c- Robert Hedley, (Sir) Francis Bond, Horace Hutton Barnet [e], Oliver Ruck

March 23; 4,500; SR Bastard

## 1879

### Old Etonians 1 (Clerke)

John Purvis Hawtrey [e]; Edward Christian, Lindsay Bury [E], c-Hon Arthur Kinnaird [S], Edgar Lubbock, Charles Clerke, Norman Pares, Harry Chester Goodhart [e], Herbert Whitfield [E], John Chevalier, H Mark Beaufoy

### Clapham Rovers 0

Reginald Halsey Birkett [e]; c-Robert Andrew Muter Macindoe Ogilvie [E], Edgar Field [E], Norman Coles Bailey [E], James Frederick McLeod Prinsep [e], Frederick Rawson, Arthur J Stanley, Stanley Scott, Herbert Bevington, Edward Growse, Cecil Keith-Falconer

March 29; 5,000; CW Alcock

## 1880

### Clapham Rovers 1 (Lloyd-Jones)

Reginald Halsey Birkett [E]; c- Robert Andrew Muter Macindoe Ogilvie, Edgar Field, Vincent Weston, Norman Coles Bailey [E], Arthur J Stanley, Harold Brougham, Francis John Sparkes [E], F Barry, Edward Ram, Clopton Lloyd-Jones

### Oxford University 0

Percival Chase Parr [e]; Claude William Wilson [E], Robert King, Francis Phillips, Bertram Rogers, c-Reginald T Heygate, Rev George B Childs, John Eyre, (Dr) Francis Crowdy, EH Hill, John B Lubbock (later Lord Avebury)

April 10; 6,000; Major Marindin

### 1881

**Old Carthusians 3** (Page, Wynyard, Parry)

Leonard F Gillett; Walter Norris, (Sir) Elliott Colvin, James Frederick McLeod Prinsep [E], (Sir) Joseph Vintcent, Walter Hansell, Lewis Richards, William Page, Edward Wynyard, c- Edward Hagarty Parry [E], Alexander Todd

**Old Etonians 0**

John Frederick Peel Rawlinson [e]; Charles Foley, Thomas French, c-Hon Arthur Kinnaird [S], R Bryan Farrer, Reginald Heber Macauley [E], Harry Chester Goodhart [e], Herbert Whitfield [E], Philip Novelli, William Anderson, John Chevallier

April 9; 4,000; W Pierce-Dix

### 1882

**Old Etonians 1** (Macauley)

John Frederick Peel Rawlinson [E]; Thomas French, Percy de Paravicini (e), c-Hon Arthur Kinnaird [S], Charles Foley, Philip Novelli, Arthur Tempest Blakiston Dunn [e], Reginald Heber Macauley [E], Harry Chester Goodhart [e], John Chevallier, William Anderson

**Blackburn Rovers 0**

Roger Howarth; Hugh McIntyre [S], Fergus Suter, c-Freddie Hargreaves [E], Harold Sharples, Jack Hargreaves, Geoffrey Avery, James Brown [E], Thomas Strachan, Jimmy Douglas [S], John Duckworth

March 25; 6,500; JC Clegg

### 1883

**Blackburn Olympic 2** (Matthews, Costley)

Thomas Hacking; James Ward, c-Sam Warburton, Thomas Gibson, William Astley, John Hunter [E], Thomas Dewhurst, Alfred Matthews, George Wilson, Jimmy Costley, John Yates [e]

**Old Etonians 1** (Goodhart)

John Frederick Peel Rawlinson [E]; Thomas French, Percy de Paravicini [E], c-Hon Arthur Kinnaird [S], Charles Foley, Arthur Tempest Blakiston Dunn [E], Herbert Bainbridge, John Chevallier, William Anderson, Harry Chester Goodhart [E], Reginald Heber Macauley [E]

March 31; 8,000; Major Marindin

### 1884

**Blackburn Rovers 2** (Sowerbutts, Forrest)

Herbie Arthur [e]; Fergus Suter, Joseph Beverley [E], c-Hugh McIntyre [S], James Forrest [E], Jack Hargreaves, James Brown [E], Jock Inglis [S] Joe Sowerbutts, Jimmy Douglas [S], Joseph Lofthouse [e]

**Queen's Park 1** (Christie)

George Gillespie [S]; John MacDonald [s], Walter Arnott [S], John Gow [s], c- Charles Campbell [S], David Allan, William Harrower [S], (Dr) John Smith [S], William Anderson [S], William Watt [s], Robert Christie [S]

March 29; 4,000; Major Marindin

### 1885

**Blackburn Rovers 2** (Forrest, Brown)

Herbie Arthur [E]; Richard Turner, Fergus Suter, George Haworth [e], Hugh McIntyre [S], James Forrest [E], Joe Sowerbutts, Joe Lofthouse [E], Jimmy Douglas [S], c-James Brown [E], Howard Fecitt

**Queen's Park 0**

George Gillespie [S]; Walter Arnott [S], William MacLeod, John MacDonald [s], c Charles Campbell [S], William Sellar [S], William Anderson [S], N McWhammel, Alexander Hamilton [S], David Allan, Woodville Gray [s]

April 4; 12,500; Major Marindin

### 1886

**Blackburn Rovers 0**

Herbie Arthur [E]; Richard Turner, Fergus Suter, Joseph Heyes, James Forrest [E], Hugh McIntyre [S], Jimmy Douglas [S], Thomas Strachan, Joe Sowerbutts, Howard Fecitt, c-James Brown [E]

**West Bromwich Albion 0**

Bob Roberts [e]; Harry Green, Harry Bell, Ezra Horton, Charlie Perry [e], George Timmins, George Woodhall [e], Tom Green, c-Jimmy Bayliss, Arthur Loach, George Bell

April 3; 15,000; Major Marindin

### Replay

**Blackburn Rovers 2** (Sowerbutts, Brown)
Herbie Arthur [E]; Richard Turner, Fergus Suter, Nat Walton, Jimmy Forrest [E],Hugh McIntyre [S], Jimmy Douglas [S], Thomas Strachan, Joe Sowerbutts, Howard Fecitt, c-James Brown [E]

**West Bromwich Albion 0**
Bob Roberts [e]; Harry Green, Harry Bell, Ezra Horton, Charlie Perry [e], George Timmins, George Woodhall [e], Tom Green, c-Jimmy Bayliss, Arthur Loach, George Bell
April 10; 12,000; Major Marindin

### 1887

**Aston Villa 2** (Hodgetts, Hunter)
Jimmy Warner; Frank Coulton, Harry Simmonds, Harry Yates, Frankie Dawson, Jack Burton, Richmond Davis, Albert Brown, c-Archie Hunter, Howard Vaughton [E], Dennis Hodgetts [e]

**West Bromwich Albion 0**
Bob Roberts [E]; Harry Green, Albert Aldridge [e], Ezra Horton, Charlie Perry [e], George Timmins, George Woodhall [e], Tom Green, c-Jimmy Bayliss [e], John Paddock, Tom Pearson
April 2; 15,500; Major Marindin

### 1888

**West Bromwich Albion 2** (Bayliss), Woodhall)
Bob Roberts [E]; Albert Aldridge [e], Harry Green, Ezra Horton, Charlie Perry [e], George Timmins, George Woodhall [E], Billy Bassett [e], c-Jimmy Bayliss, James Wilson, Tom Pearson

**Preston North End 1** (Dewhurst)
(Dr) Robert Mills-Roberts [W]; Rob Howarth [E],Bob Holmes [e], Nicholas Ross, David Russell [s], Jack Gordon, Jimmy Ross, John Goodall [E], Fred Dewhurst [E], George Drummond, John Graham [S]
March 24; 19,000; Major Marindin

### 1889

**Preston North End 3** (Dewhurst, Ross, Thomson)
(Dr) Robert Mills-Roberts [W]; Rob Howarth [E], Bob Holmes [E], George Drummond, David Russell [s], Johnny Graham [S], Jack Gordon, John Goodall [E], c-Fred Dewhurst [E], Sam Thompson, Jimmy Ross

**Wolverhampton Wanderers 0**
Jack Baynton; Dick Baugh [E], Charlie Mason [E], Albert Fletcher [E], Harry Allen [E], Arthur Lowder [E], Tommy Hunter, David Wykes, c-John Brodie [e], Harry Wood [e], Tom Knight
March 30; 22,000; Major Marindin

### 1890

**Blackburn Rovers 6** (Lofthouse, Jack Southworth, Walton, Townley 3)
Jack Horne; James Southworth, John Forbes [S], Jack Barton [E], George Dewar [S], Jimmy Forrest [E], Joe Lofthouse [E] Harry Campbell [S], Jack Southworth, Nat Walton [E], Billy Townley [E]

**Sheffield Wednesday 1** (Bennett)
John Smith; Haydn Morley, Edward Brayshaw [E], Jack Dungworth, Billy Betts [E], George Waller, Billy Ingram, Harry Woolhouse, Michael Bennett, Albert Mumford, Tom Cawley
March 29; 20,000; Major Marindin

### 1891

**Blackburn Rovers 3** (Dewar, Jack Southworth, Townley)
Rowland Pennington; Tom Brandon [s], c- John Forbes [S], John Barton [E], George Dewar [S], Jimmy Forrest [E], Joe Lofthouse [E], Nat Walton, Jack Southworth, Combe Hall, Billy Townley [E]

**Notts County 1** (Oswald)
James Thraves; Alex Ferguson, John Hendry, Archibald Osborne, David Calderhead [S], Alf Shelton [E], Andrew McGregror, Thomas McInnes c-Jack Oswald [S], William Locker, Harry Daft [E]
March 21; 23,000; CJ Hughes

### 1892

**West Bromwich Albion 3** (Geddes, Nicholls, Reynolds)
Joe Reader [e]; Mark Nicholson, Thomas McCulloch, Jack Reynolds [E/IRE], c- Charlie Perry, Willie Groves [S], Billy Bassett [E], Roddie McLeod, Sam Nicholls, Tom Pearson, Jasper Geddes

**Aston Villa 0**
Jimmy Warner; Billy Evans, Gersham Cox, Harry Devey, Jimmy Cowan [s], John Baird, Charlie Athersmith [E], Jack Devey [E], c-Billy Dickson [S], Dennis Hodgetts [E], Lewis Campbell
March 19; 32,810; JC Clegg

## 1893

### Wolverhampton Wanderers 1 (Allen)

Billy Rose [E]; Dick Baugh [E], George Swift, Billy Malpass, c-Harry Allen [E], George Kinsey [E], Dick Topham [E], David Wykes, Joe Butcher, Alf Griffin, Harry Wood [E]

### Everton 0

Richard Williams; Bob Kelso, Bob Howarth [E], Richard Boyle, Johnny Holt [E], Alex Stewart, Alex Latta, Patrick Gordon, Alan Maxwell, Edgar Chadwick [E], Alf Milward [E]
March 25; 45,000; CJ Hughes

## 1894

### Notts County 4 (Watson, Logan 3)

George Toone [E]; Theo Harper, Jack Hendry, Charles Bramley, c-David Calderhead [S], Alf Shelton [E], Arthur Watson, Sam Donnelly, Jimmy Logan [S] Daniel Bruce [S], Harry Daft [E]

### Bolton Wanderers 1 (Cassidy)

John Sutcliffe [E]; John Somerville, c- Di Jones [W], Harry Gardiner, Alex Paton, Achie Hughes, Robert Tannahill, Jim Wilson, Jimmy Cassidy, Handel Bentley, Joe Dickenson
March 31; 37,000; CJ Hughes

## 1895

### Aston Villa 1 (Chatt)

Tom Wilkes; Howard Spencer [e], Jimmy Welford, Jack Reynolds [E/IRE], Jimmy Cowan [s], George Russell, Charlie Athersmith [E] Bob Chatt, Jack Devey [E], Dennis Hodgetts [E], Steve Smith [E]

### West Bromwich Albion 0

Joe Reader [E]; Billy Williams [e], Jack Horton, Tom Perry [e], Tom Higgins, Jack Taggart [i], Billy Bassett [E], Roddie McLeod, William Richards, Tom Hutchinson, Jack Banks
April 20; 42,560; J Lewis

## 1896

### Sheffield Wednesday 2 (Spikesley 2)

Joe Massey; Jack Earp, Ambrose Langley, Harry Brandon, Tom Crawshaw [E], Bob Petrie, Archie Brash, Alex Brady, Laurie Bell, Harry Davis, Fred Spikesley [E]

### Wolverhampton Wanderers 1 (Black)

Billy Tennant; Dick Baugh [E], Tom Dunn, Billy Owen, Billy Malpass, Hill Griffiths, Joe Tonks, Charlie Henderson, Billy Beats [e], Harry Wood [E], David Black [S]
April 18; 48,836; Lt Simpson

## 1897

### Aston Villa 3 (Campbell, Wheldon, Crabtree)

Jimmy Whitehouse; Howard Spencer [E], Jack Reynolds [E/IRE], Albert Evans, Jimmy Cowan [S], Jimmy Crabtree [E], Charlie Athersmith [E], Jack Devey [E], Johnny Campbell [s], Fred Wheldon [E], John Cowan

### Everton 2 (Bell, Boyle)

Bob Menham; Peter Meechan [S], David Storrier [s], Richard Boyle, Johnny Holt [E], Billy Stewart, Jack Taylor [S], Jack Bell [S], Abe Hartley, Edgar Chadwick [E], Alf Milward [E]
April 10; 65,891; J Lewis

## 1898

### Nottingham Forest 3 (Capes 2, McPherson)

Dan Allsop; Archie Ritchie [S], Adam Scott, c-Frank Forman [e], John McPherson [S], Willie Wragg, Tom McInnes, Charlie Richards [E], Len Benbow, Arthur Capes [e], Billy Spouncer [e]

### Derby County 1 (Bloomer)

Jack Fryer; Jimmy Methven, Joe Leiper, Jack Cox [E], Archie Goodall [ire], James Turner, John Goodall [E], Steve Bloomer [E], John Boag, Jimmy Stevenson, Hugh McQueen
April 16; 62,017; J Lewis

## 1899

### Sheffield United 4 (Bennett, Beers, Almond, Priest)

Willie Foulke [E]; Harry Thickett [E], Peter Boyle [ire], Harry Johnson [e], Tom Morren [E], Ernest 'Nudger' Needham [E], Walter Bennett, Walter Beers, George Hedley [e], Jack Almond, Fred Priest [e]

### Derby County 1 (Boag)

Jack Fryer; Jimmy Methven, Jonathan Staley, Jack Cox [E], Robert Paterson, Johnny May [s], Thomas Arkesden, Steve Bloomer [E], John Boag, Billy McDonald, Harry Allen
April 15; 73,833; A Scragg

## 1900

**Bury 4** (McLuckie 2, Wood, Plant)
Fred Thompson; Jack Darroch, Tommy Davidson, Jack Pray, Joe Leeming, George Ross, Billy Richards, Willie Wood, Jasper McLuckie, Charlie Sagar [E], Jack Plant [E]

**Southampton 0**
Jack Robinson [E]; Peter Meechan [S], Peter Durber, Sam Meston, Arthur Chadwick [E], Bob Petrie, Arthur Turner [E], Jimmy Yates, Joe Farrell, Harry Wood [E], Alf Milward [E]
April 21; 68,945; A Kingscott

## 1901

**Tottenham Hotspur 2** (Brown 2)
George Clawley; Harry Erentz, Sandy Tait, Tom Morris, Ted Hughes [W], c-Jack Jones [W], Tom Smith, John Cameron [S], Sandy Brown, David Copeland, Jack Kirwan [IRE]

**Sheffield United 2** (Priest, Bennett)
Willie Foulke [E]; Harry Thickett [E], Peter Boyle [IRE], Harry Johnson [E], Tom Morren [E], c-Ernest 'Nudger' Needham [E], Walter Bennett [E], Charles 'Oakey' Field, George Hedley [E], Fred Priest [E], Bert Lipsham [e]
April 20; 110,820; A Kingscott

**Replay**

**Tottenham Hotspur 3** (Cameron, Smith, Brown)
George Clawley; Harry Erentz, Sandy Tait, Tom Morris, Ted Hughes [W], c-Jack Jones [W], Tom Smith, John Cameron [S], Sandy Brown, David Copeland, Jack Kirwan [IRE]

**Sheffield United 1** (Priest)
Willie Foulke [E]; Harry Thickett [E], Peter Boyle [IRE], Harry Johnson [E], Tom Morren [E], c-Ernest 'Nudger' Needham [E], Walter Bennett [E], Charles 'Oakey' Field, George Hedley [E], Fred Priest [E], Bert Lipsham [e]
April 27; 20,470; A Kingscott

## 1902

**Sheffield United 1** (Common)
Willie Foulke [E]; Harry Thickett [E], Peter Boyle [IRE], c-Ernest 'Nudger' Needham [E], Bernie Wilkinson [e], Harry Johnson [E], Walter Bennett [E] Alf Common [e], George Hedley [E], Fred Priest [E], Bert Lipsham [E]

**Southampton 1** (Wood)
Jack Robinson [E]; Charles Burgess 'CB' Fry [E], George Molyneux [e], Sam Meston, Tommy Bowman, Albert Lee [e], Arthur Turner [E], c-Harry Wood [E] Arthur Brown, Edgar Chadwick [E], Joe Turner
April 19; 76,914; T Kirkham

**Replay**

**Sheffield United 2** (Hedley, Barnes)
Willie Foulke [E]; Harry Thickett[E], Peter Boyle [IRE], c-Ernest 'Nudger' Needham [E], Bernie Wilkinson [e], Harry Johnson [E], Billy Barnes, Alf Common [e], George Hedley [E], Fred Priest [E], Bert Lipsham [E]

**Southampton 1** (Brown)
Jack Robinson [E]; Charles Burgess 'CB' Fry [E], George Molyneux [e], Sam Meston, Tommy Bowman, Albert Lee [e], Arthur Turner [E], c-Harry Wood [E] Arthur Brown, Edgar Chadwick [E], Joe Turner
April 26; 33,068; T Kirkham

## 1903

**Bury 6** (Leeming 2, Ross, Sagar, Wood, Plant)
Hugh Monteith; Jimmy Lindsey, James McEwen, John Johnston, Frank Thorpe, c-George Ross, Billy Richards, Willie Wood, Charlie Sagar [E] Joe Leeming, Jack Plant [E]

**Derby County 0**
Jack Fryer; Jimmy Methven, Charlie Morris [W], Ben Warren [e], Archie Goodall [IRE], Johnny May [s], Joe Warrington, Charlie York, John Boag, Billy Richards [e], George Davis [e]
April 18; 63,102; J Adams

## 1904

**Manchester City 1** (Meredith)
Jack Hillman [E]; Johnny McMahon, Herbert Burgess [E], Sam Frost, Tom Hynds, Sam Ashworth, Billy Meredith [W], George Livingstone [s], Billy Gillespie, 'Sandy' Turnbull, Frank Booth [e]

**Bolton Wanderers 0**
Dai Davies [W]; Walter Brown, Bob Struthers, Bob Clifford, Sam Greenhalgh, Archie Freebairn, David Stokes, Sam Marsh, Billy Yenson, Walter White [s], Archie Taylor
April 23; 61,374; AJ Barker

## 1905

### Aston Villa 2 (Hampton 2)

Billy George [E]; c-Howard Spencer [E], Freddie Miles, Joe Pearson, Alex Leake [E], Jack Windmill, Billy Brawn [E], Billy Garratty [E], Harry Hampton [e], Joe Bache [E], Alf Hall [e]

### Newcastle United 0

Jimmy Lawrence [s]; Andy McCombie [S], Jack Carr [E], Alex Gardner, Andy Aitken [S], Peter McWilliam [S], Jock Rutherford [E], Jimmy Howie [S], Bill Appleyard, Colin Veitch [e], Bert Gosnell [e]
April 15; 101,117; PR Harrower

## 1906

### Everton 1 (Young)

Billy Scott [IRE]; Jack Crelley, Walter Balmer [E], Harry Makepeace [E], Jack Taylor [S], Walter Abbott [E], Jack Sharp [E], Hugh Bolton, Alex Young [S], Jimmy Settle [S], Harold Hardman

### Newcastle United 0

Jimmy Lawrence [s]; Andy McCombie [S], Jack Carr [E], Alex Gardner, Andy Aitken [S], Peter McWilliam [S], Jock Rutherford [E], Jimmy Howie [S], Ronald Orr [S], Colin Veitch [E], Bert Gosnell [E]
April 21; 75,609; F Kirkham

## 1907

### Sheffield Wednesday 2 (Stewart, Simpson)

Jack Lyall [S]; Billy Layton, Harry Burton, Tom Brittleton [e], Tom Crawshaw [E], Billy Bartlett, Harry Chapman, Frank Bradshaw [e], Andrew Wilson [S], Jimmy Stewart [E], George Simpson

### Everton 1 (Sharp)

Billy Scott [IRE]; Walter Balmer [E], Bob Balmer, Harry Makepeace [E], Jack Taylor [S], Walter Abbott [E], Jack Sharp [E], Hugh Bolton, Alex Young [S], Jimmy Settle [E], Harold Hardman
April 20; 84,594; N Whittaker

## 1908

### Wolverhampton Wanderers 3 (Hunt, Hedley, Harrison)

Tommy Lunn; Jack Jones, Ted Collins, Rev Kenneth Hunt [e], Billy Wooldridge, Albert Bishop, Billy Harrison, Jack Shelton, George Hedley [E], Walter Radford, Jack Pedley

### Newcastle United 1 (Howie)

Jimmy Lawrence [s]; Billy McCracken [IRE], Dick Pudan, Alex Gardner, Colin Veitch [E], Peter McWilliam [S], Jock Rutherford [E], Jimmy Howie [S], Bill Appleyard, Finlay Speedie [S], George Wilson [S]
April 25; 74,697; TP Campbell

## 1909

### Manchester United 1 (Sandy Turnbull)

Harry Moger; George Stacey, Vince Hayes, Dick Duckworth, c-Charlie Roberts [E], Alexander 'Sandy' Bell, Billy Meredith [W], Harold Halse [e], Jimmy Turnbull, Sandy Turnbull, George Wall [E]

### Bristol City 0

Harry Clay; Archie Annan, Joe Cottle [E], Pat Hanlin, Billy Wedlock [E], Arthur Spear, Fred Staniforth, Bob Hardy, Sammy Gilligan, Andy Burton, Frank Hilton
April 24; 71,401; J Mason

## 1910

### Newcastle United 1 (Rutherford)

Jimmy Lawrence [s]; Billy McCracken [IRE], Tony Whitson, c-Colin Veitch [E], Wilf Low [s], Peter McWilliam [S], Jock Rutherford [E], Jimmy Howie [S], Sandy Higgins [S], Albert Shepherd [E], George Wilson [S]

### Barnsley 1 (Tufnell)

Fred Mearns; Dickie Downs [e], Harry Ness, Bob Glendinning, c-Tommy Boyle [e], George Utley [e], Harry Tufnell, George Lillycrop, Ernie Gadsby, Tom Forman, Wilf Bartrop
April 23; 77,747; JT Ibbotson

**Replay**

### Newcastle United 2 (Shepherd 2, 1pen)

Jimmy Lawrence [s]; Billy McCracken [IRE], Jack Carr [E], c-Colin Veitch [E], Wilf Low [s], Peter McWilliam [S], Jock Rutherford [E], Jimmy Howie [S], Sandy Higgins [S], Albert Shepherd [E], George Wilson [S]

### Barnsley 0

Fred Mearns; Dickie Downs [e], Harry Ness, Bob Glendinning, c-Tommy Boyle [e], George Utley [e], Harry Tufnell, George Lillycrop, Ernie Gadsby, Tom Forman, Wilf Bartrop
April 28; 69,000; JT Ibbotson

## 1911

### Bradford City 0

Mark Mellors; Bob Campbell, David Taylor, George Robinson, Willie Gildea, James McDonald, Peter Logan, c-Jimmy Speirs [S], Frank O'Rourke [S], Archie Devine [S], Frank Thompson

### Newcastle United 0

Jimmy Lawrence [S]; Billy McCracken [IRE], Tony Whitson, c-Colin Veitch [E], Wilf Low [S], David Willis, Jock Rutherford [E], George Jobey, Jimmy Stewart [E], Sandy Higgins [S], George Wilson [S]
April 22; 69,068; JH Pearson

### Replay

### Bradford City 1 (Speirs)

Mark Mellors; Bob Campbell, David Taylor, George Robinson, Bob Torrance, James McDonald, Peter Logan, c-Jimmy Speirs [S], Frank O'Rourke [S], Archie Devine [S], Frank Thompson

### Newcastle United 0

Jimmy Lawrence [S]; Billy McCracken [IRE], Tony Whitson, c-Colin Veitch [E], Wilf Low [S], David Willis, Jock Rutherford [E], George Jobey, Jimmy Stewart [E], Sandy Higgins [S], George Wilson [S]
April 26; 58,000; JH Pearson

## 1912

### Barnsley 0

Jack Cooper; Dickie Downs [e], Archie Taylor, Bob Glendinning, Phil Bratley, George Utley [e], Wilf Bartrop, Harry Tufnell, George Lillycrop, George Travers, Jimmy Moore

### West Bromwich Albion 0

Hubert Pearson; Arthur Cook, Jesse Pennington [E], George Baddeley, Freddie Buck, Bob McNeal [e], Claude Jephcott, Harry Wright, Bob Pailor, Sid Bowser [e], Ben Shearman
April 20; 54,556; JR Shumacher

### Replay

### Barnsley 1 (Tufnell)

Jack Cooper; Dickie Downs [e], Archie Taylor, Bob Glendinning, Phil Bratley, George Utley [e], Wilf Bartrop, Harry Tufnell, George Lillycrop, George Travers, Jimmy Moore

### West Bromwich Albion 0

Hubert Pearson; Arthur Cook, Jesse Pennington [E], George Baddeley, Freddie Buck, Bob McNeal [e], Claude Jephcott, Harry Wright, Bob Pailor, Sid Bowser [e], Ben Shearman
April 24; 38,555; JR Schumacher. After extra time

## 1913

### Aston Villa 1 (Barber)

Sam Hardy [E]; Tommy Lyons, Tommy Weston, Tommy Barber, Jimmy Harrop, Jimmy Leach, Charlie Wallace [E], Harold Halse [E], Harry Hampton [E], Clem Stephenson [e], Joe Bache [E]

### Sunderland 0

Joe Butler; Charlie Gladwin, Harry Ness, Frank Cuggy [E], Charlie Thomson [S], Harry Low, Jackie Mordue [E], Charlie Buchan [E], Jimmy Richardson, George Holley [E], Harry Martin [e]
April 19; 120,081; A Adams

## 1914

### Burnley 1 (Freeman)

Ronnie Sewell [e]; Tom Bamford, David Taylor, George Halley, c-Tommy Boyle [E], Billy Watson [E], Billy Nesbit, Dick Lindley, Bert Freeman [E], Teddy Hodgson, Eddie Mosscrop [E]

### Liverpool 0

Kenny Campbell [e]; Ephraim Longworth [e], Bob Pursell, Tom Fairfoul, Bob Ferguson, Donald McKinley [s], Jackie Sheldon, Arthur Metcalfe, Tom Miller [s], Billy Lacey [IRE], Jimmy Nicholl
April 25; 72,778; HS Bamlett

## 1915

### Sheffield United 3 (Simmons, Fazackerly, Kitchen)

Harold Gough [e]; Billy Cook, Jack English, Albert Sturgess [E], Bill Brelsford, c-George Utley [E], Jim Simmons, Stan Fazackerly, Joe Kitchen, Wally Masterman, Bob Evans [E]

### Chelsea 0

Jimmy Molyneux; Walter Bettridge, Jack Harrow [e], Fred Taylor, Tommy Logan [S], Andy Walker, Harry Ford, Harold Halse [E], Bob Thomson, Jimmy Croal [S], Bobby McNeil
April 24; 49,557; HH Taylor

### 1920

**Aston Villa 1** (Kirton)

Sam Hardy [E]; Tom Smart [e], Tommy Weston, c-Andy Ducat [E], Frank Barson [E], Frank Moss [e], Charlie Wallace [E], Billy Kirton [e], Billy Walker [e], Clem Stephenson [e], Arthur Dorrell [E]

**Huddersfield Town 0**

Alex Mutch; James Wood, Freddie Bullock [e], Charlie Slade, Tommy Wilson [e], Billy Watson, George Richardson, Frank Mann, Sam Taylor, Jack Swann, Ernie Islip

April 24; 50,018; JT Howcroft. After extra time

### 1921

**Tottenham Hotspur 1** (Dimmock)

Alex Hunter; Tommy Clay [E], Bob McDonald, Bert Smith [E], Charlie Walters, c-Arthur Grimsdell [E], Jimmy Banks, Jimmy Seed [e], Jimmy Cantrell, Bert Bliss [E], Jimmy Dimmock [E]

**Wolverhampton Wanderers 0**

Noel George; Maurice Woodward, George Marshall, Valentine Gregory, Joe Hodnett, Alf Riley, Tancy Lea, Frank Burrill, Eddie Edmonds, Arthur Potts, Sammy Brooks

April 23; 72,805; S Davies

### 1922

**Huddersfield Town 1** (Smith pen)

Alex Mutch; James Wood, Sam Wadsworth [E], Charlie Slade, Tommy Wilson [e], Billy Watson, George Richardson, Frank Mann, Ernie Islip, Clem Stephenson [e], Billy Smith [E]

**Preston North End 0**

James Mitchell [e]; Tom Hamilton, Alex Doolan, Tom Duxbury, Joe McCall [E], Johnny Williamson, Archie Rawlings [E], Frank Jefferis [E], Billy Roberts [e], Roland Woodhouse, Peter Quinn

April 29; 53,000; JWP Fowler

### 1923

**Bolton Wanderers 2** (Jack, JR Smith)

Dick Pym [e]; Bob Haworth, Alex Finney, Harry Nuttall [e], Jimmy Seddon [e], Billy Jennings [W], Billy Butler [e], David Jack [e], Jack 'JR' Smith, c-Joe Smith [E], Ted Vizard [W]

**West Ham United 0**

Ted Hufton [e]; Billy Henderson, Jack Young, Sid Bishop [e], c-George Kay, Jack Tresadern [E], Dick Richards [W], Billy Brown [e], Vic Watson [E], Billy Moore [e], Jimmy Ruffell [e]

April 28; 126,047; DH Asson

### 1924

**Newcastle United 2** (Harris, Seymour)

Bill Bradley; Billy Hampson, c-Frank Hudspeth [e], Peter Mooney, Charlie Spencer [E], Willie Gibson, James Low, Billy Cowan [S], Neil Harris [S], Tommy McDonald, Stan Seymour

**Aston Villa 0**

Tommy Jackson; Tom Smart [E], Tommy Mort [E], Frank Moss [E], (Dr) Victor Milne, George Blackburn [e], Dick York [E], Billy Kirton [E], Len Capewell, c-Billy Walker[E], Arthur Dorrell [E]

April 26; 91,695; WE Russell

### 1925

**Sheffield United 1** (Tunstall)

Charles Sutcliffe; Bill Cook, Ernest Milton, Harry Pantling [E], Seth King, George Green [e], Dave Mercer [E], Tommy Boyle, Harry Johnson, c-Billy Gillespie [NI], Fred Tunstall [E]

**Cardiff City 0**

Tom Farquharson [NI]; Jimmy Nelson [S], Jimmy Blair [S], Harry Wake, c-Fred Keenor [W], Billy Hardy, Billy Davies [W], Jimmy Gill, Joe Nicholson, Harry Beadles [W], Jack Evans [W]

April 25; 91,763; GN Watson

### 1926

**Bolton Wanderers 1** (Jack)

Dick Pym [E]; Bob Haworth, Harry Greenhalgh, Harry Nuttall [e], Jimmy Seddon [E], Billy Jennings [W], Billy Butler [E], Jack 'JR' Smith, David Jack [E], c-Joe Smith [E], Ted Vizard [W]

**Manchester City 0**

Jim Goodchild; Sam Cookson, Philip McCloy [S], Charlie Pringle [S], Sam Cowan [e], c-Jimmy McMullan [S], Billy Austin [E], Tommy Browell, Frank Roberts [E], Tommy Johnson [e], George Hicks

April 24; 91,447; I Baker

## 1927
### Cardiff City 1 (Ferguson)
Tom Farquharson [NI]; Jimmy Nelson [S], Tommy Watson [NI], c-Fred Keenor [W], Tommy Sloan [NI], Billy Hardy, Ernie Curtis, Sam Irving [NI], Hughie Ferguson, Len Davies [W], George McLachlan
### Arsenal 0
Dan Lewis [W]; Tom Parker [E], Andy Kennedy [NI], Alf Baker [e], Jack Butler [E], Bob John [W], Joe Hulme [E], c -Charlie Buchan [E], Jimmy Brain, Billy Blythe, Sid Hoar
April 23; 91,206; WF Bunnell

## 1928
### Blackburn Rovers 3 (Roscamp 2, McLean)
Jock Crawford; Jock Hutton [S], Herbert Jones [E], c-Harry Healless [E], Willie Rankin, Austin Campbell [e], George Thornewell, Syd Puddefoot [E], Jack Roscamp, Tommy McLean, Arthur Rigby [E]
### Huddersfield Town 1 (Jackson)
Billy Mercer; Roy Goodall, Ned Barkas, Levi Redfern, Tommy Wilson [E], David Steele [S], Alex Jackson [S], Bob Kelly [E], George Brown [E], c-Clem Stephenson [E], Billy Smith [E]
April 21; 92,041; TG Bryan

## 1929
### Bolton Wanderers 2 (Butler, Blackmore)
Dick Pym [E]; Bob Haworth, Alex Finney, Fred Kean [E], c-Jimmy Seddon [E], Harry Nuttall [E], Billy Butler [E], Jim McClelland, Harold Blackmore, George Gibson, Willie Cook [s]
### Portsmouth 0
John Gilfillan; Alex Mackie [NI], Thomas Bell, Jimmy Nichol, Johnny McIlwaine, David Thackeray, Fred Forward, Jack Smith, Jack Weddle, David Watson, Fred Cook
April 27; 92,576; A Josephs

## 1930
### Arsenal 2 (James, Lambert)
Charlie Preedy; c-Tom Parker [E], Eddie Hapgood [e], Alf Baker, Bill Seddon, Bob John [W], Joe Hulme [E], David Jack [E], Jack Lambert, Alex James [S], Cliff Bastin [e]
### Huddersfield Town 0
Hugh Turner [e]; Roy Goodall, Bonwell Spence, Jimmy Naylor, c-Tommy Wilson, Austin Campbell [E], Alex Jackson [S], Bob Kelly [E], Harry Davies, Harry Raw, Billy Smith [E]
April 26; 92,488; T Crew

## 1931
### West Bromwich Albion 2 (WG Richardson 2)
Harold Pearson [e]; George Shaw [e], Bert Trentham, Tommy Magee [E], Bill Richardson, Jimmy Edwards, c-Tommy Glidden, Joe Carter [E], Billy 'WG' Richardson [e], Teddy Sandford [e], Stan Wood
### Birmingham 1 (Bradford)
Harry Hibbs [E]; George Liddell, c-Ned Barkas, Jimmy Cringan, George Morrall, Alec Leslie, George Briggs, Johnny Crosbie [S], Joe Bradford [E], Bob Gregg, Ernie Curtis
April 25; 92,406; AH Kingscott

## 1932
### Newcastle United 2 (Allen 2)
Albert McInroy [E]; c-Jimmy Nelson [S], David Fairhurst [e], Roddie McKenzie, Dave Davidson, Sam Weaver [E], Jimmy Boyd [s], Jimmy Richardson [e], Jack Allen, Harry McMenemy, Tommy Lang
### Arsenal 1 (John)
Frank Moss [e]; c-Tom Parker [E], Eddie Hapgood [e], Charlie Jones [W], Herbie Roberts [E], George Male [e], Joe Hulme [E], David Jack [E], Jack Lambert, Cliff Bastin [E], Bob John [W]
April 23; 92,298; WP Harper

## 1933
### Everton 3 (Stein, Dean, Dunn)
Ted Sagar [e]; Billy Cook, Warney Cresswell [E], Cliff Britton [e], Tommy White [E], Jock Thomson [S], Albert Geldard [E], Jimmy Dunn, c-Dixie Dean [E], Tommy Johnson [E], Jimmy Stein
### Manchester City 0
Len Langford; Sydney Cann, Billy Dale, (Sir) Matt Busby [s], c-Sam Cowan [E], Jackie Bray [e], Ernie Toseland, Bobby Marshall, Alec Herd, Jimmy McMullan [S], Eric Brook [E]
April 29; 92,950; E Wood

## 1934
### Manchester City 2 (Tilson 2)
Frank Swift [e]; Laurie Barnett, Billy Dale, (Sir) Matt Busby [s], c-Sam Cowan [E], Jackie Bray [e], Ernie Toseland, Bobby Marshall, Fred Tilson [e], Alec Herd, Eric Brook [E]
### Portsmouth 1 (Rutherford)
John Gilfillan; Alex Mackie [NI], Billy Smith, Jimmy Nichol, c-Jim Allen [E], David Thackeray, Fred Worrall [e], Jack Smith, Jack Weddle, Jim Easson [S], Sep Rutherford
April 28; 93,258; (Sir) Stanley Rous

## 1935
### Sheffield Wednesday 4 (Rimmer 2, Palethorpe, Hooper)
Jack Brown [E]; Joe Nibloe [S], Ted Catlin [e], Wilf Sharp, Walter Millership, Horace Burrows [E], Mark Hooper, Jack Surtees, Jackie Palethorpe, c-Ronnie Starling [E], Ellis Rimmer [E]
### West Bromwich Albion 2 (Boyes, Sandford)
Harold Pearson [E]; George Shaw [E], Bert Trentham, Jimmy Murphy [W], Bill Richardson, Jimmy Edwards, c-Tommy Glidden, Joe Carter [E], Billy 'WG' Richardson [e], Ted Sandford [E], Wally Boyes [e]
April 27; 93,204; AE Fogg

## 1936
### Arsenal 1 (Drake)
Alex Wilson; George Male [E], Eddie Hapgood [E], Jack Crayston [E], Herbie Roberts [e], Wilf Copping [E], Joe Hulme [E], Ray Bowden [E], Ted Drake [E], c-Alex James [S], Cliff Bastin [E]
### Sheffield United 0
Jack Smith; c-Harry Hooper, Charlie Wilkinson, Ernie Jackson, Tom Johnson, Archie McPherson, Harold Barton, Bobby Barclay [E], Jock Dodds, Jack Pickering [E], Bertie Williams
April 25; 93,384; H Nattrass

## 1937
### Sunderland 3 (Gurney, Carter, Burbanks)
Johnny Mapson; Jimmy Gorman, Alex Hall, Charlie Thomson [s], Bert Johnston [s], Alex McNab [S], Len Duns, c-Raich Carter [E], Bobby Gurney [E], Patsy Gallacher [S], Eddie Burbanks
### Preston North End 1 (Frank O'Donnell)
Mick Burns; Len Gallimore, Andy Beattie [S], Bill Shankly [s], c-Billy Tremelling, Jimmy Milne, Jim Dougal [s], Joe Beresford [E], Frank O'Donnell [S], Willie Fagan, Hugh O'Donnell
May 1; 93,495; RG Rudd

## 1938
### Preston North End 1 (Mutch pen)
Harry Holdcroft [E]; Len Gallimore, Andy Beattie [S], Bill Shankly [S], c-Tom Smith [S], Bob Batey, Dickie Watmough, George Mutch [S], Bud Maxwell, Bobby Beattie [s], Hugh O'Donnell
### Huddersfield Town 0
Bob Hesford; Ben Craig, Reg Mountford, Ken Willingham [E], c-Alf Young [E], Eddie Boot, Joe Hulme [E], Jimmy Issac, Willie MacFadyen [S], Bobby Barclay [E], Pat Beasley [e]
April 30; 93,497; AJ Jewell. After extra time

## 1939
### Portsmouth 4 (Parker 2, Barlow, Anderson)
George Walker; Lew Morgan, Bill Rochford, c-Jimmy Guthrie, Tommy Rowe, Guy Wharton, Fred Worrall [E], Jimmy McAlinden [NI], Jock Anderson, Bert Barlow, Cliff Parker
### Wolverhampton Wanderers 1 (Dorsett)
Robert Scott; Billy Morris [E], Jack Taylor, Tom Galley [E], c-Stan Cullis [E], Joe Gardiner, Stan Burton, Alex McIntosh, Dennis Westcott, Dickie Dorsett, Teddy Maguire
April 29; 99,370; T Thompson

## 1946
### Derby County 4 (Stamps 2. Doherty, B Turner og)
Vic Woodley [E]; c-Jack Nicholas, Jack Howe [e], Jim Bullions, Leon Leuty, Chick Musson, Reg Harrison, Raich Carter [E], Jack Stamps, Peter Doherty [NI], Dally Duncan [S]
### Charlton Athletic 1 (B Turner)
Sam Bartram; Harold Phipps, Jack Shreeve, Bert Turner [W], John Oakes, Bert Johnson, Leslie Fell, Albert Brown, Arthur Turner, c-Don Welsh [E], Chris Duffy
April 27; 98,000; ED Smith. After extra time

## 1947

### Charlton Athletic 1 (Duffy)

Sam Bartram; Peter Croker, Jack Shreeve, Bert Johnson, Harold Phipps, Bill Whittaker, Gordon Hurst, Tommy Dawson, Bill Robinson, c-Don Welsh [E], Chris Duffy

### Burnley 0

Jim Strong; Arthur Woodruff, Harold Mather, Reg Attwell, c-Alan Brown, George Bray, Jack Chew, Billy Morris [W], Ray Harrison, Harry Potts, Peter Kippax
April 26; 99,000; JM Wiltshire. After extra time

## 1948

### Manchester United 4 (Rowley 2, Pearson, Anderson)

Jack Crompton; c-Johnny Carey [NI/IRE], John Aston, John Anderson, Allenby Chilton [e], Henry Cockburn [E], Jimmy Delaney [S], Johnny Morris [e], Jack Rowley [e], Stan Pearson [E], Charlie Mitten

### Blackpool 2 (Shimwell pen, Mortensen)

Joe Robinson; Eddie Shimwell [e], Johnny Crosland, c-Harry Johnston [E], Eric Hayward, Hugh Kelly [s], (Sir) Stanley Matthews [E], Alex Munro [S], Stan Mortensen [E], George Dick, Walter Rickett
April 24; 99,000; CJ Barrick

## 1949

### Wolverhampton Wanderers 3 (Pye 2, Smyth)

Bert Williams [e]; Roy Pritchard, Terry Springthorpe [usa] Wally Crook, Bill Shorthouse, c-Billy Wright [E], Johnny Hancocks [E], Sammy Smyth [NI], Jesse Pye [e], Jimmy Dunn, Jimmy Mullen [E]

### Leicester City 1 (Griffiths)

Gordon Bradley; Horace Jelly, Alec Scott, Walter Harrison, c-Norman Plummer, John King, Mal Griffiths [W], Jack Lee [e], Jim Harrison, Ken Chisholm, Charlie Adam
April 30; 99,500; RA Mortimer

## 1950

### Arsenal 2 (Lewis 2)

George Swindin; Laurie Scott [E], Walley Barnes [W], Alex Forbes [S], Leslie Compton [e], c-Joe Mercer [E], Freddie Cox, Jimmy Logie [s], Peter Goring, Reg Lewis, Denis Compton

### Liverpool 0

Cyril Sidlow [W]; Ray Lambert [W], Eddie Spicer, c-Phil Taylor [E], Laurie Hughes [e], Bill Jones [e], Jimmy Payne, Kevin Baron, Albert Stubbins, Willie Fagan, Billy Liddell [S]
April 29; 100,000; H Pearce

## 1951

### Newcastle United 2 (Milburn 2)

Jack Fairbrother; Bobby Cowell, Bobby Corbett, c-Joe Harvey, Frank Brennan [S], Charlie Crowe, Tommy Walker, Ernie Taylor [e], Jackie Milburn [E], Jorge 'George' Robledo [CH], Bobby Mitchell [s]

### Blackpool 0

George Farm [s]; Eddie Shimwell [E], Tom Garrett [e], c-Harry Johnston [E], Eric Hayward, Hugh Kelly [s], (Sir) Stanley Matthews [E], Jackie Mudie [s], Stan Mortensen [E], Bill Slater [e], Bill Perry [e]
April 28; 100,000; W Ling

## 1952

### Newcastle United 1 (G Robledo)

Ronnie Simpson [s]; Bobby Cowell, Alf McMichael [NI], c-Joe Harvey, Frank Brennan [S], Eduardo 'Ted' Robledo, Tommy Walker, Billy Foulkes [W], Jackie Milburn [E], Jorge 'George' Robledo [CH], Bobby Mitchell [S]

### Arsenal 0

George Swindin; Walley Barnes [W], Lionel Smith [E], Alex Forbes [S], Ray Daniel [W] c-Joe Mercer [E], Freddie Cox, Jimmy Logie [s], Cliff Holton, Doug Lishman, Don Roper
May 3; 100,000; A Ellis

## 1953

### Blackpool 4 (Mortensen 3, Perry)

George Farm [S]; Eddie Shimwell [E], Tom Garrett [E], Ewan Fenton, c-Harry Johnston [E], Cyril Robinson, (Sir) Stanley Matthews [E], Ernie Taylor [e], Stan Mortensen [E], Jackie Mudie [s], Bill Perry [e]

### Bolton Wanderers 3 (Lofthouse, Moir, Bell)

Stan Hanson; John Ball, Ralph Banks, Johnny Wheeler [e], Malcolm Barass [E], Eric Bell, Doug Holden [e], c-Willie Moir [S], Nat Lofthouse [E], Harold Hassall [E], Bobby Langton [E]
May 2; 100,000; M Griffiths

## 1954

### West Bromwich Albion 3 (Allen 2 [1pen], Griffin)

Jim Sanders; Joe Kennedy, c-Len Millard, Jimmy Dudley, Jimmy Dugdale, Ray Barlow, Frank Griffin, Reg Ryan [IRE/NI], Ronnie Allen [E], Johnny Nicholls [E], George Lee

### Preston North End 2 (Morrison, Wayman)

George Thompson; Willie Cunningham [s], Joe Walton, Tommy Docherty [S], Joe Marston, Willie Forbes, c-(Sir) Tom Finney [E], Bob Foster, Charlie Wayman, Jimmy Baxter, Angus Morrison
May 1; 100,000; A Luty

## 1955

### Newcastle United 3 (Milburn, Mitchell, Hannah)

Ronnie Simpson [s]; Bobby Cowell, Ron Batty, c-Jimmy Scoular [S], Bob Stokoe, Tom Casey [NI], Len White, Jackie Milburn [E], Vic Keeble, George Hannah, Bobby Mitchell [S]

### Manchester City 1 (Johnstone)

Bert Trautmann; Jimmy Meadows [E], Roy Little, Ken Barnes, Dave Ewing, c-Roy Paul [W], Bill Spurdle, Joe Hayes, Don Revie [E], Bobby Johnstone [S], Fionan Fagan [RI]
May 7; 100,000; R Leafe

## 1956

### Manchester City 3 (Hayes, Dyson, Johnstone)

Bert Trautmann; Bill Leivers, Roy Little, Ken Barnes, Dave Ewing, c-Roy Paul [W], Bobby Johnstone [S], Joe Hayes, Don Revie [E], Jack Dyson, Roy Clarke [W]

### Birmingham City 1 (Kinsey)

Gil Merrick [E]; Jeff Hall [E], Ken Green, John Newman, Trevor Smith [e], c-Len Boyd, Gordon Astall [e], Noel Kinsey [W], Eddy Brown, Peter Murphy, Alex Govan
May 5; 100,000; A Bond

## 1957

### Aston Villa 2 (McParland 2)

Nigel Sims; Stan Lynn, Peter Aldis, Stan Crowther, Jimmy Dugdale, Pat Saward [RI], Les Smith, Jackie Sewell [E], Bill Myerscough, c-Johnny Dixon, Peter McParland [NI]

### Manchester United 1 (Taylor)

Ray Wood [E]; Bill Foulkes [E], c-Roger Byrne [E], Eddie Colman, Jackie Blanchflower [NI], Duncan Edwards [E], John Berry [E], Liam Whelan [RI], Tommy Taylor [E], (Sir) Bobby Charlton [e], David Pegg [e]
May 4; 100,000; F Coultas

## 1958

### Bolton Wanderers 2 (Lofthouse 2)

Eddie Hopkinson [E]; Roy Hartle, Tommy Banks, Derek Hennin, John Higgins Bryan Edwards, Brian Birch, Dennis Stevens, c-Nat Lofthouse [E], Ray Parry [e], Doug Holden [e]

### Manchester United 0

Harry Gregg [NI]; c-Bill Foulkes [E], Ian Greaves, Freddie Goodwin, Ron Cope, Stan Crowther, Alex Dawson, Ernie Taylor [E], (Sir) Bobby Charlton [E], Dennis Viollet [e], Colin Webster [W]
May 3; 100,000; J Sherlock

## 1959

### Nottingham Forest 2 (Dwight, Wilson)

Chick Thomson; Bill Whare, Joe McDonald [S], Jeff Whitefoot, Bobby McKinlay, c-Jack Burkitt, Roy Dwight, John Quigley, Tommy Wilson, Billy Gray, Stuart Imlach [S]

### Luton Town 1 (Pacey)

Ron Baynham [E]; Brendan McNally [ri], Ken Hawkes, John Groves, c-Syd Owen [E], Dave Pacey, Billy Bingham [NI], Allan Brown [S], Bob Morton, George Cummins [RI], Tony Gregory
May 2; 100,000; J Clough

## 1960

### Wolverhampton Wanderers 3 (McGrath og, Deeley 2)

Malcolm Finlayson; George Showell, Gerry Harris, Eddie Clamp [E], c-Bill Slater, Ron Flowers [E], Norman Deeley [E], Barry Stobart, Jimmy Murray, Peter Broadbent [E], Des Horne

### Blackburn Rovers 0

Harry Leyland; John Bray, Dave Whelan, c-Ronnie Clayton [E], Matt Woods, Mick McGrath [RI], Louis Bimpson, Peter Dobing, Derek Dougan [NI], Bryan Douglas [E], Alastair McLeod
May 7; 100,000; K Howley

## 1961

### Tottenham Hotspur 2 (Smith, Dyson)

Bill Brown [S]; Peter Baker, Ron Henry [e], c-Danny Blanchflower [NI], Maurice Norman [e], Dave Mackay [S], Cliff Jones [W], John White [S], Bobby Smith [E], Les Allen, Terry Dyson

### Leicester City 0

Gordon Banks [e]; Len Chalmers, Richie Norman, Frank McLintock [s], Ian King, Colin Appleton, Howard Riley, c-Jimmy Walsh, Hugh McIlmoyle, Ken Keyworth, Albert Cheesebrough
May 6; 100,000; J Kelly

## 1962

### Tottenham Hotspur 3 (Greaves, Smith, Blanchflower pen)

Bill Brown [S]; Peter Baker, Ron Henry [e], c-Danny Blanchflower [NI], Maurice Norman [e], Dave Mackay [S], Terry Medwin [W], John White [S], Bobby Smith [E], Jimmy Greaves [E], Cliff Jones [W]

### Burnley 1 (Robson)

Adam Blacklaw [s]; John Angus [E], Alex Elder [NI], c-Jimmy Adamson, Tommy Cummings, Brian Miller [E], John Connelly [E], Jimmy McIlroy [NI], Ray Pointer [E], Jimmy Robson, Gordon Harris [e]
May 5; 100,000; J Finney

## 1963

### Manchester United 3 (Law, Herd 2)

David Gaskell; Tony Dunne [RI], c-Noel Cantwell [RI], Pat Crerand [S], Bill Foulkes [E], Maurice Setters, Johnny Giles [RI], Albert Quixall [E], David Herd [S], Denis Law [S], (Sir) Bobby Charlton [E]

### Leicester City 1 (Keyworth)

Gordon Banks [E]; John Sjoberg, Richie Norman, Frank McLintock [s], Ian King, c-Colin Appleton, Howard Riley, Graham Cross, Ken Keyworth, David Gibson, Mike Stringfellow
May 25; 100,000; K Aston

## 1964

### West Ham United 3 (Sissons, Hurst, Boyce)

Jim Standen; John Bond, Jack Burkett, Eddie Bovington, Ken Brown [E], c-Bobby Moore [E], Peter Brabrook [E], Ronnie Boyce, Johnny Byrne [E], (Sir) Geoff Hurst [e], Johnny Sissons

### Preston North End 2 (Holden, Dawson)

Alan Kelly [RI]; George Ross, c-Nobby Lawton, Jim Smith, Tony Singleton, Howard Kendall, David Wilson, Alec Ashworth, Alex Dawson, Alan Spavin, Doug Holden [E]
May 2; 100,000; A Holland

## 1965

### Liverpool 2 (Hunt, St John)

Tommy Lawrence [S]; Chris Lawler [e], Gerry Byrne [E], Geoff Strong, c-Ron Yeats [S], Willie Stevenson, Ian Callaghan [e], Roger Hunt [E], Ian St John [S], Tommy Smith [e], Peter Thompson [E]

### Leeds United 1 (Bremner)

Gary Sprake [W]; Paul Reaney [e], Willie Bell [s], Billy Bremner [s], Jack Charlton [E], Norman Hunter [e], Johnny Giles [RI], Jim Storrie, Alan Peacock [E], c-Bobby Collins [S], Albert Johanneson
May 1; 100,000; W Clements. After extra time

## 1966

### Everton 3 (Trebilcock 2, Temple)

Gordon West [e]; Tommy Wright [e], Ray Wilson [E], Jimmy Gabriel [S], c-Brian Labone [E], Brian Harris, Alex Scott [S], Mike Trebilcock, Alex Young [S], Colin Harvey [e], Derek Temple [E]

### Sheffield Wednesday 2 (McCalliog, Ford)

Ron Springett [E]; Wilf Smith, c-Don Megson, Peter Eustace, Sam Ellis, Gerry Young [E], Graham Pugh, Johnny Fantham [E], Jim McCalliog [s], David Ford, Johnny Quinn
May 14; 100,000; JK Taylor

## 1967

### Tottenham Hotspur 2 (Robertson, Saul)

Pat Jennings [NI]; Joe Kinnear [RI], Cyril Knowles [e], Alan Mullery [E], Mike England [W], c-Dave Mackay [S], Jimmy Robertson [S], Jimmy Greaves [E], Alan Gilzean [S], Terry Venables [E], Frank Saul. Unused sub: Cliff Jones [W]

### Chelsea 1 (Tambling)

Peter Bonetti [E]; Allan Harris, Eddie McCreadie [S], John Hollins [e], Marvin Hinton, c-Ron Harris, Charlie Cooke [S], Tommy Baldwin, Tony Hateley, Bobby Tambling [E], John Boyle. Unused sub: Joe Kirkup
May 20; 100,000; K Dagnal

## 1968

### West Bromwich Albion 1 (Astle)

John Osborne; Doug Fraser [s], c-Graham Williams [W], Tony Brown [e], John Talbut, John Kaye, Graham Lovett, Ian Collard, Jeff Astle [e] Bobby Hope [s], Clive Clark.. Substitution: Dennis Clarke replaced John Kaye 91st min

### Everton 0

Gordon West [e]; Tommy Wright [e], Ray Wilson [E], Howard Kendall, c-Brian Labone [E], Colin Harvey [e], Jimmy Husband, Alan Ball [E], Joe Royle [e], John Hurst, Johnny Morrissey. Unused sub: Roger Kenyon
May 18; 100,000; L Callaghan. After extra time

## 1969

### Manchester City 1 (Young)

Harry Dowd: c-Tony Book, Glyn Pardoe, Mike Doyle [e], Tommy Booth, Alan Oakes, Mike Summerbee [E], Colin Bell [E], Francis Lee [E], Neil Young, Tony Coleman. Unused sub: Dave Connor

### Leicester City 0

Peter Shilton [e]; Peter Rodrigues [W], c-David Nish [e], Bobby Roberts, Alan Woollett, Graham Cross, Rodney Fern, David Gibson [S], Andy Lochhead, Allan Clarke [e], Len Glover. Substitution: Malcolm Manley replaced Len Glover 70th min
April 26; 100,000; G McCabe

## 1970

### Chelsea 2 (Houseman, Hutchinson)

Peter Bonetti [E]; David Webb, Eddie McCreadie [S], John Hollins [E], John Dempsey [RI], c-Ron Harris, Tommy Baldwin, Peter Houseman, Peter Osgood [E], Ian Hutchinson, Charlie Cooke [S]. Substitution: Marvin Hinton replaced Ron Harris 91st min

### Leeds United 2 (Charlton, Jones)

Gary Sprake [W]; Paul Madeley [e], Terry Cooper [E], c-Billy Bremner [S], Jack Charlton [E], Norman Hunter [E], Peter Lorimer [S], Allan Clarke [e], Mick Jones [E], Johnny Giles [RI], Eddie Gray [S] Unusued sub: Mick Bates
April 11; 100,000; E Jennings. After extra time

### Replay

### Chelsea 2 (Osgood, Webb)

Peter Bonetti [E], David Webb, Eddie McCreadie [S], John Hollins [E], John Dempsey [RI], c-Ron Harris, Tommy Baldwin, Peter Houseman, Peter Osgood [E], Ian Hutchinson, Charlie Cooke [S]. Substitution: Marvin Hinton replaced Peter Osgood 105th min

### Leeds United 1 (Jones)

David Harvey [s]; Paul Madeley [e], Terry Cooper [E], c-Billy Bremner [S], Jack Charlton [E], Norman Hunter [E], Peter Lorimer [S], Allan Clarke [e], Mick Jones [E], Johnny Giles [RI], Eddie Gray [S] Unusued sub: Mick Bates
April 29; 62,078; E Jennings. After extra time

## 1971

### Arsenal 2 (Kelly, George)

Bob Wilson [s]; Pat Rice [NI], Bob McNab [E], Peter Storey [E], c-Frank McLintock [S] Peter Simpson, George Armstrong, George Graham [s], John Radford [E], Ray Kennedy [e], Charlie George [e]. Substitution: Eddie Kelly replaced Peter Storey 70th min

### Liverpool 1 (Heighway)

Ray Clemence [e]; Chris Lawler [e], Alec Lindsay [e], c-Tommy Smith [e], Larry Lloyd [e], Emlyn Hughes [E], Ian Callaghan [E], Alun Evans, Steve Heighway [RI], John Toshack [W], Brian Hall. Substitution: Peter Thompson [E] replaced Alun Evans 70th min
May 8; 100,000; N Burtenshaw. After extra time

## 1972

### Leeds United 1 (Clarke)

David Harvey [s]; Paul Reaney [E], Paul Madeley [E], c-Billy Bremner [S], Jack Charlton [E], Norman Hunter [E], Peter Lorimer [S], Allan Clarke [E], Mick Jones [E], Johnny Giles [RI], Eddie Gray [S]. Unused sub: Mick Bates

### Arsenal 0

Geoff Barnett; Pat Rice [NI], Bob McNab [E], Peter Storey [E], c-Frank McLintock [S], Peter Simpson, George Armstrong, Alan Ball [E], Charlie George [e], John Radford [E], George Graham [S]. Substitution: Ray Kennedy [e] replaced John Radford 80th min
May 6; 100,000; DW Smith

## 1973

### Sunderland 1 (Porterfield)

Jim Montgomery; Dick Malone, Ron Guthrie, Mick Horswill, Dave Watson [e], Richie Pitt, c-Bobby Kerr, Billy Hughes [s], Vic Halom, Ian Porterfield, Dennis Tueart [e]. Unused sub: David Young

### Leeds United 0

David Harvey [S]; Paul Reaney [E], Trevor Cherry [e], c-Billy Bremner [S], Paul Madeley [E], Norman Hunter [E], Peter Lorimer [S], Allan Clarke [E], Mick Jones [E], Johnny Giles [RI], Eddie Gray [S]. Substitution: Terry Yorath [W] replaced Eddie Gray 75th min

May 5; 100,000; K Burns

## 1974

### Liverpool 3 (Keegan 2, Heighway)

Ray Clemence [E]; Tommy Smith [E], Alec Lindsay [e], Phil Thompson [e], Peter Cormack [S], c-Emlyn Hughes [E], Kevin Keegan [E], Brian Hall, Steve Heighway [RI], John Toshack [W], Ian Callaghan [E]. Unused sub: Chris Lawler

### Newcastle United 0

Iam McFaul [NI]; Frank Clark, Alan Kennedy [e], Terry McDermott [e], Pat Howard, c-Bobby Moncur [S], Jimmy Smith [S], Tommy Cassidy [NI], Malcolm Macdonald [E], John Tudor, Terry Hibbitt. Substitution: Tommy Gibb replaced Jimmy Smith 70th min

May 4; 100,000; GC Kew

## 1975

### West Ham United 2 (Taylor 2)

Mervyn Day; John McDowell, Tommy Taylor, Kevin Lock, Frank Lampard [E], c-Billy Bonds, Graham Paddon, Trevor Brooking [E], Billy Jennings, Alan Taylor, Pat Holland. Unused sub: Bobby Gould

### Fulham 0

Peter Mellor; John Cutbush, John Lacy, Bobby Moore [E], John Fraser, c-Alan Mullery [E], Jim Conway [RI], Alan Slough, John Mitchell, Viv Busby, Les Barrett. Unused sub: Barry Lloyd

May 3; 100,000; P Partridge

## 1976

### Southampton 1 (Stokes)

Ian Turner; c-Peter Rodrigues [W], David Peach, Nick Holmes, Mel Blyth, Jim Steele, Paul Gilchrist, Mick Channon [E], Peter Osgood [E], Jim McCalliog [S], Bobby Stokes. Unused sub: Hugh Fisher

### Manchester United 0

Alex Stepney [E]; Alex Forsyth [S], Stewart Houston [S], Gerry Daly [RI], Brian Greenhoff [e], c-Martin Buchan [S], Steve Coppell [e], Sammy McIlroy [NI], Stuart Pearson [e], Lou Macari [S], Gordon Hill [e]. Substitution: David McCreery [ni] replaced Gordon Hill 66th min

May 1; 100,000; C Thomas

## 1977

### Manchester United 2 (Pearson, J Greenhoff)

Alex Stepney [E]; Jimmy Nicholl [NI], Arthur Albiston [s], Sammy McIlroy [NI], Brian Greenhoff [E], c-Martin Buchan [S], Steve Coppell [e], Jimmy Greenhoff, Stuart Pearson [E], Lou Macari [S], Gordon Hill [E]. Substitution: David McCreery [NI] Replaced Gordon Hill 81st min

### Liverpool 1 (Case)

Ray Clemence [E]; Phil Neal [E], Joey Jones [W], Tommy Smith [E], Ray Kennedy [E], c-Emlyn Hughes [E], Kevin Keegan [E], Jimmy Case, Steve Heighway [RI], David Johnson [E], Terry McDermott [e]. Substitution: Ian Callaghan [E] replaced David Johnson 64th min

May 21; 100,000; R Matthewson

## 1978

### Ipswich Town 1 (Osborne)

Paul Cooper; George Burley [s], c-Mick Mills [E], Brian Talbot [E], Allan Hunter [NI], Kevin Beattie [E], Roger Osborne, John Wark [s], Paul Mariner [E], David Geddis, Clive Woods. Substitution: Mick Lambert replaced Roger Osborne 79th min

### Arsenal 0

Pat Jennings [NI]; c-Pat Rice [NI], Sammy Nelson [NI], David Price, Willie Young, David O'Leary [RI], Liam Brady [RI], Alan Hudson [E], Malcolm Macdonald [E], Frank Stapleton [RI], Alan Sunderland [e]. Substitution: Graham Rix [e] replaced Liam Brady 65th min

May 6; 100,000; D Nippard

## 1979

### Arsenal 3 (Talbot, Stapleton, Sunderland)

Pat Jennings [NI]; c-Pat Rice [NI], Sammy Nelson [NI], Brian Talbot [E], David O'Leary [RI], Willie Young, Liam Brady [RI], Alan Sunderland [e], Frank Stapleton [RI], David Price, Graham Rix [e]. Substitution: Steve Walford replaced Graham Rix 83rd min

### Manchester United 2 (McQueen, McIlroy)

Gary Bailey [e]; Jimmy Nicholl [NI], Arthur Albiston [s], Sammy McIlroy [NI], Gordon McQueen [S], c-Martin Buchan [S], Steve Coppell [E], Jimmy Greenhoff, Joe Jordan [S], Lou Macari [S], Mickey Thomas [W]. Unused sub: Brian Greenhoff

May 12; 100,000; R Challis

## 1980

### West Ham United 1 (Brooking)

Phil Parkes [E]; Ray Stewart [s], Frank Lampard [E], c-Billy Bonds, Alvin Martin [e], Alan Devonshire [e], Paul Allen, Stuart Pearson [E], David Cross, Trevor Brooking [E], Geoff Pike. Unused sub: Paul Brush

### Arsenal 0

Pat Jennings [NI]; c-Pat Rice [NI], John Devine [RI], Brian Talbot [E], David O'Leary [RI], Willie Young, Liam Brady [RI], Alan Sunderland [e], Frank Stapleton [RI], David Price, Graham Rix [e]. Substitution: Sammy Nelson [NI] replaced John Devine 61st min

May 10; 100,000; G Courtney

## 1981

### Tottenham Hotspur 1 (Hutchinson og)

Milija Aleksic; Chris Hughton [RI], Paul Miller, Graham Roberts [e], c-Steve Perryman [e], Ricardo Villa [ARG], Ossie Ardiles [ARG], Steve Archibald [S], Tony Galvin [RI], Glenn Hoddle [E], Garth Crooks. Substitution: Garry Brooke replaced Ricardo Villa 68th min

### Manchester City 1 (Hutchinson)

Joe Corrigan [E]; Ray Ranson, Bobby McDonald, Nicky Reid, c-Paul Power, Tommy Caton, Dave Bennett, Gerry Gow, Steve Mackenzie, Tommy Hutchison [S] Kevin Reeves [E]. Substitution: Tony Henry replaced Tommy Hutchison 82nd min

May 9; 100,000; K Hackett. After extra time

**Replay**

### Tottenham Hotspur 3 (Villa 2, Crooks)

Milija Aleksic; Chris Hughton [RI], Paul Miller, Graham Roberts [e], c-Steve Perryman [e], Ricardo Villa [ARG], Ossie Ardiles [ARG], Steve Archibald [S], Tony Galvin [RI], Glenn Hoddle [E], Garth Crooks. Unused sub: Garry Brooke

### Manchester City 2 (Mackenzie, Reeves pen)

Joe Corrigan [E]; Ray Ranson, Bobby McDonald, Nicky Reid, c-Paul Power, Tommy Caton, Dave Bennett, Gerry Gow, Steve Mackenzie, Tommy Hutchison [S] Kevin Reeves [E]. Substitution: Dennis Tueart replaced Bobby McDonald 79th min

May 14; 92,000; K Hackett

## 1982

### Tottenham Hotspur 1 (Hoddle)

Ray Clemence [E]; Chris Hughton [RI], Paul Miller, Paul Price [W], Mickey Hazard, c-Steve Perryman [e], Graham Roberts [e], Steve Archibald [S], Tony Galvin [RI], Glenn Hoddle [E], Garth Crooks. Substitution: Garry Brooke replaced Mickey Hazard 104th min

### Queens Park Rangers 1 (Fenwick)

Peter Hucker; Terry Fenwick [e], Ian Gillard [E], Gary Waddock [RI], Bob Hazell, c-Glenn Roeder, Tony Currie [E], Mike Flanagan, Clive Allen [e], Simon Stainrod, John Gregory [e]. Substitution: Gary Micklewhite replaced Clive Allen 50th min

May 22; 100,000; C White. After extra time

**Replay**

### Tottenham Hotspur 1 (Hoddle pen)

Ray Clemence [E]; Chris Hughton [RI], Paul Miller, Paul Price [W], Mickey Hazard, c-Steve Perryman [e], Graham Roberts [e], Steve Archibald [S], Tony Galvin [RI], Glenn Hoddle [E], Garth Crooks. Substitution: Garry Brooke replaced Mickey Hazard 67th min

### Queens Park Rangers 0

Peter Hucker; Terry Fenwick [e], Ian Gillard [E], Gary Waddock [RI], Bob Hazell, Warren Neill, c-Tony Currie [E], Mike Flanagan, Gary Micklewhite, Simon Stainrod, John Gregory [e]. Substitution: Steve Burke replaced Gary Micklewhite 84th min

May 27; 90,000; C White

## 1983

### Manchester United 2 (Stapleton, Wilkins)

Gary Bailey [e]; Mike Duxbury [e], Kevin Moran [RI], Gordon McQueen [S], Arthur Albiston [S], Alan Davies [w], Ray Wilkins [E], c-Bryan Robson [E], Arnold Muhren [NETH], Frank Stapleton [RI], Norman Whiteside [NI]. Unused sub: Ashley Grimes

### Brighton & Hove Albion 2 (Smith, Stevens)

Graham Moseley; Chris Ramsey, Gary A Stevens [e], Graham Pearce, Steve Gatting, Neil Smillie, Jimmy Case, c-Tony Grealish [RI], Gary Howlett [RI], Michael Robinson [RI], Gordon Smith. Substitution: Gerry Ryan [RI] replaced Chris Ramsey 56th min

May 21; 100,000; AW Grey, After extra time

**Replay**

### Manchester United 4 (Robson 2, Whiteside, Muhren pen)

Gary Bailey [e]; Mike Duxbury [e], Kevin Moran [RI], Gordon McQueen [S], Arthur Albiston [S], Alan Davies [w], Ray Wilkins [E], c-Bryan Robson [E], Arnold Muhren [NETH], Frank Stapleton [RI], Norman Whiteside [NI]. Unused sub: Ashley Grimes

### Brighton & Hove Albion 0

Graham Moseley; Gary A Stevens [e], Graham Pearce, c-Steve Foster, Steve Gatting, Neil Smillie, Jimmy Case, c-Tony Grealish [RI], Gary Howlett [RI], Michael Robinson [RI], Gordon Smith. Substitution: Gerry Ryan [RI] replaced Gary Howlett 74th min

May 26; 100,000; AW Grey

## 1984

### Everton 2 (Sharp, Gray)

Neville Southall [W]; Gary M Stevens [e], John Bailey, c-Kevin Ratcliffe [W], Derek Mountfield, Peter Reid [e], Trevor Steven [e], Adrian Heath, Graeme Sharp [s], Andy Gray [S], Kevin Richardson. Unused sub: Alan Harper

### Watford 0

Steve Sherwood; David Bardsley, Neil Price, c-Les Taylor, Steve Terry, Lee Sinnott, Nigel Callaghan, Maurice Johnston [S], George Reilly, Kenny Jackett [W], John Barnes [E]. Substitution: Paul Atkinson replaced Neil Price 58th min

May 19; 100,000; J Hunting

## 1985

### Manchester United 1 (Whiteside)

Gary Bailey [E]; John Gidman [E], Arthur Albiston [S], Norman Whiteside [NI], Paul McGrath [RI], Kevin Moran [RI], c-Bryan Robson [E], Gordon Strachan [S], Mark Hughes [W], Frank Stapleton [RI], Jesper Olsen [DEN]. Substitution: Mike Duxbury [E] replaced Arthur Albiston 91st min Kevin Moran sent off 77th min

### Everton 0

Neville Southall [W]; Gary M Stevens [e], Pat Van den Hauwe [W], c-Kevin Ratcliffe [W], Derek Mountfield, Peter Reid [e], Trevor Steven [E], Graeme Sharp [s], Andy Gray [S], Paul Bracewell [e], Kevin Sheedy [RI]. Unused sub: Alan Harper

May 18; 100,000; P Willis. After extra time

## 1986

### Liverpool 3 (Rush 2, Johnston)

Bruce Grobbelaar [ZIM]; Mark Lawrenson [RI], Jim Beglin [RI], Steve Nicol [S], Ronnie Whelan [RI], c-Alan Hansen [S], Kenny Dalglish [S], Craig Johnston, Ian Rush [W], Jan Molby [DEN], Kevin MacDonald. Unused sub: Steve McMahon

### Everton 1 (Lineker)

Bobby Mimms; Gary M Stevens [E], Pat Van den Hauwe [W], c-Kevin Ratcliffe [W], Derek Mountfield [e], Peter Reid [E], Trevor Steven [E], Gary Lineker [E], Graeme Sharp [S], Paul Bracewell [E], Kevin Sheedy [RI]. Substitution: Adrian Heath replaced Gary M Stevens 65th min

May 10; 98,000; A Robinson

## 1987

### Coventry City 3 (Bennett, Houchen, Mabbutt og)

Steve Ogrizovic; David Phillips [W], Greg Downs, Lloyd McGrath, c-Brian Kilcline, Trevor Peake, Dave Bennett, Micky Gynn, Cyrille Regis [E], Keith Houchen, Nick Pickering [E]. Substitution: Graham Rodger replaced Brian Kilcline 88th min. Unused sub: Steve Sedgley

### Tottenham Hotspur 2 (Allen, Mabbutt)

Ray Clemence [E]; Chris Hughton [RI] Mitchell Thomas, Steve Hodge [E], c-Richard Gough [S], Gary Mabbutt [E], Clive Allen [E], Paul Allen, Chris Waddle [E], Glenn Hoddle [E], Ossie Ardiles [ARG]. Substitutions: Gary A Stevens [E] replaced Ossie Ardiles 91st min; Nico Claesen [BEL] replaced Chris Hughton 97th min

May 16; 98,000; N Midgley. After extra time

## 1988

### Wimbledon 1 (Sanchez)

c-Dave Beasant [e]; Clive Goodyear, Terry Phelan, Vinnie Jones [w], Eric Young [w], Andy Thorn, Terry Gibson Alan Cork, John Fashanu [e], Lawrie Sanchez [NI], Dennis Wise [e]. Substitutions: Laurie Cunningham [E] replaced Alan Cork 56th min; John Scales (e) replaced Terry Gibson 63rd min

### Liverpool 0

Bruce Grobbelaar [ZIM]; Gary Gillespie [S], Gary Ablett, Steve Nicol [S], Nigel Spackman, c-Alan Hansen [S], Peter Beardsley [E], John Aldridge [RI], Ray Houghton [RI], John Barnes [E], Steve McMahon [E]. Substitutions: Craig Johnston replaced John Aldridge 63rd min; Jan Molby [DEN] replaced Nigel Spackman 72nd min

May 14; 98,203; B Hill

## 1989

### Liverpool 3 (Aldridge, Rush 2)

Bruce Grobbelaar [ZIM]; Gary Ablett, Steve Staunton [RI], Steve Nichol [S], c-Ronnie Whelan [RI], Alan Hansen [S], Peter Beardsley [E], John Aldridge [RI] Ray Houghton [RI], John Barnes [E], Steve McMahon [E]. Substitutions: Ian Rush [W] replaced John Aldridge 72nd min; Barry Venison replaced Steve Staunton 91st min

### Everton 2 (McCall 2)

Neville Southall [W]; Neil McDonald, Pat Van den Hauwe [W], c-Kevin Ratcliffe [W], Dave Watson [E], Paul Bracewell [E], Pat Nevin [S], Trevor Steven [E], Tony Cottee [E], Graeme Sharp [S], Kevin Sheedy [RI]. Substitutions: Stuart McCall [S] replaced Paul Bracewell 58th min; Ian Wilson [S] replaced Kevin Sheedy 77th min

May 20; 82,500; J Worrall. After extra time

## 1990

### Manchester United 3 (Robson, Hughes 2)

Jim Leighton [S]; Paul Ince [e], Lee Martin, Steve Bruce, Mike Phelan [e], Gary Pallister [E], c-Bryan Robson [E], Neil Webb [E], Brian McClair [S], Mark Hughes [W], Danny Wallace [E]. Substitutions: Clayton Blackmore replaced Lee Martin 88th min; Mark Robins replaced Gary Pallister 93rd min

### Crystal Palace 3 (O'Reilly, Wright 2)

Nigel Martyn [e]; John Pemberton, Richard Shaw, Andy Gray [e], Gary O'Reilly, Andy Thorn, Phil Barber, c-Geoff Thomas [e], Mark Bright, John Salako [e], Alan Pardew. Substitutions: Ian Wright replaced Phil Barber 69th min; David Madden replaced Andy Gray 117th min

May 12; 80,000; A Gunn. After extra time

**Replay**

### Manchester United 1 (Martin)

Les Sealey; Paul Ince [e], Lee Martin, Steve Bruce, Mike Phelan [e], Gary Pallister [E], c-Bryan Robson [E], Neil Webb [E], Brian McClair [S], Mark Hughes [W], Danny Wallace [E]. Unused subs: Mark Robins, Clayton Blackmore

### Crystal Palace 0

Nigel Martyn [e]; John Pemberton, Richard Shaw, Andy Gray [e], Gary O'Reilly, Andy Thorn, Phil Barber, c-Geoff Thomas [e], Mark Bright, John Salako [e], Alan Pardew. Substitutions: Ian Wright [e] replaced Phil Barber 64th min; David Madden replaced John Salako 79th min

May 17; 80,000; A Gunn

## 1991

### Tottenham Hotspur 2 (Stewart, Walker og)

Erik Thorstvedt [NOR]; Justin Edinburgh, Pat Van den Hauwe [W], Steve Sedgley, David Howells, c-Gary Mabbutt [E], Paul Stewart [e], Paul Gascoigne [E], Vinny Samways, Gary Lineker [E], Paul Allen. Substitutions: Nayim replaced Paul Gascoigne 18th min; Paul Walsh [E] Replaced Vinny Samways 82nd min

### Nottingham Forest 1 (Pearce)

Mark Crossley; Gary Charles [e], c-Stuart Pearce [E], Des Walker [E], Steve Chettle, Roy Keane [RI], Gary Crosby, Garry Parker, Nigel Clough [E], Lee Glover, Ian Woan. Substitutions: Steve Hodge [E] replaced Ian Woan 62nd min; Brian Laws replaced Lee Glover 108th min

May 18; 80,000; R Milford. After extra time

## 1992

### Liverpool 2 (Thomas, Rush)

Bruce Grobbelaar [ZIM]; Rob Jones [E], David Burrows, Steve Nicol [S], Jan Molby [DEN], c-Mark Wright [E], Dean Saunders [W], Ray Houghton [RI], Ian Rush[W], Steve McManaman [e], Michael Thomas [E]. Unused subs: Mike Marsh, Mark Walters [e]

### Sunderland 0

Tony Norman; Gary Owers, Kevin Ball, Gary Bennett, Anton Rogan, David Rush, c-Paul Bracewell [E], Peter Davenport, Gordon Armstrong, John Byrne, Brian Atkinson. Substitutions: Paul Hardyman replaced David Rush 69th min; Warren Hawke replaced Gordon Armstrong 77th min

May 9; 80,000; P Don

## 1993

### Arsenal 1 (Wright)

David Seaman [E]; Lee Dixon [E], Nigel Winterburn [E], Andy Linighan, c-Tony Adams [E], John Jensen [DEN], Paul Davis, Ray Parlour [e], Paul Merson [E], Kevin Campbell, Ian Wright [E]. Substitutions: Alan Smith [E] replaced Ray Parlour 66th min; David O'Leary [RI] replaced Ian Wright 90th min

### Sheffield Wednesday 1 (Hirst)

Chris Woods [E]; Roland Nilsson [SWE] Nigel Worthington [NI], Carlton Palmer [E], David Hirst [E], c-Viv Anderson [E], Chris Waddle [E], Paul Warhurst, Mark Bright, John Sheridan, John Harkes [USA]. Substitutions: Graham Hyde replaced Viv Anderson 85th min; Chris Bart-Williams replaced Chris Waddle 112th min

May 15; 79,347; K Barratt. After extra time

**Replay**

### Arsenal 2 (Wright, Linighan)

David Seaman [E]; Lee Dixon [E], Nigel Winterburn [E], Andy Linighan, c-Tony Adams [E], John Jensen [DEN], Paul Davis, Alan Smith [E], Paul Merson [E], Kevin Campbell, Ian Wright [E]. Substitution: David O'Leary [RI] replaced Ian Wright 81st min. Unused sub: Ian Selley

### Sheffield Wednesday 1 (Waddle)

Chris Woods [E]; Roland Nilsson [SWE], Nigel Worthington [NI], c-Carlton Palmer [E], David Hirst [E], Danny Wilson [RI], Chris Waddle [E], Paul Warhurst, Mark Bright, John Sheridan, John Harkes [USA]. Substitutions: Graham Hyde replaced Danny Wilson 62nd min; Chris Bart-Williams replaced Roland Nilsson 118th min

May 20; 62,267; K Barratt. After extra time

## 1994

### Manchester United 4 (Cantona 2 [2pens], Hughes, McClair)

Peter Schmeichel [DEN]; Paul Parker [E], c-Steve Bruce, Gary Pallister [E], Denis Irwin [RI], Andrei Kanchelskis [CIS/UKR] Roy Keane [RI], Paul Ince [E], Ryan Giggs [W], Eric Cantona [F], Mark Hughes [W]. Substitutions: Lee Sharpe [E] replaced Denis Irwin 84th min; Brian McClair [S] replaced Andrei Kanchelskis 84th min. Unused sub: Gary Walsh (gk)

### Chelsea 0

Dimitri Kharine [RUS]; Steve Clarke, Frank Sinclair [JAM], Jacob Kjeldberg [DEN], Erland Johnsen [NOR], Craig Burley [s], John Spencer [s], Eddie Newton, Mark Stein, Gavin Peacock, c-Dennis Wise [E] Substitutions Glenn Hoddle [E] replaced Craig Burley 65th min; Tony Cascarino [RI] replaced Mark Stein 78th min. Unused sub: Kevin Hitchcock (gk)

May 14; 79,634; D Elleray

## 1995

### Everton 1 (Rideout)

Neville Southall [W]; Matt Jackson, Andy Hinchcliffe, Gary Ablett, c-Dave Watson [E], Joe Parkinson, David Unsworth [e], Barry Horne [W], Graham Stuart, Paul Rideout, Anders Limpar [SWE]. Substitutions: Duncan Ferguson [S] replaced Paul Rideout 51st min; Daniel Amokachi [NIG] replaced Anders Limpar 69th min. Unused sub: Jason Kearton (gk)

### Manchester United 0

Peter Schmeichel [DEN]; Gary Neville [e], Dennis Irwin [RI], c-Steve Bruce, Lee Sharpe [E], Gary Pallister [E], Roy Keane [RI], Paul Ince [E], Brian McClair [S], Mark Hughes [W], Nicky Butt [e]. Substitutions: Ryan Giggs [W] replaced Steve Bruce 46th min; Paul Scholes [e] replaced Lee Sharpe 72nd min. Unused sub: Gary Walsh (gk)

May 20; 79,592; G Ashby

## 1996

### Manchester United 1 (Cantona)

Peter Schmeichel [DEN]; Denis Irwin [RI], Phil Neville [e], David May, Roy Keane [RI], Gary Pallister [E], c-Eric Cantona [F], David Beckham [e], Andy Cole [E], Nicky Butt [e], Ryan Giggs [W]. Substitutions: Paul Scholes [e] replaced Andy Cole 65th min; Gary Neville [e] replaced David Beckham 89th min. Unused sub: Lee Sharpe [E]

### Liverpool 0

David James [e]; Jason McAteer, John Scales [E], Mark Wright [E], Phil Babb [RI], Rob Jones [E], Steve McManaman [E], John Barnes [E], Jamie Redknapp [E], Stan Collymore [E], Robbie Fowler [E]. Substitutions: Ian Rush [W] replaced Stan Collymore 74th min; Michael Thomas [E] replaced Rob Jones 85th min. Unused sub: Tony Warner {gk)

May 11; 79,007; D Gallagher

## 1997

### Chelsea 2 (Di Matteo, Newton)

Frode Grodas [NOR]; Dan Petrescu [ROM], Scott Minto, Frank Sinclair [jam], Frank Lebouef [F], Steve Clarke, Gianfranco Zola [ITA], Roberto Di Matteo [ITA], Eddie Newton, Mark Hughes [W], c-Dennis Wise [E]. Substitution: Gianluca Vialli [ITA] replaced Gianfranco Zola 89th min. Unused subs: Kevin Hitchcock (gk), Andy Myers

### Middlesbrough 0

Ben Roberts; Clayton Blackmore [W], Curtis Fleming [RI], Phil Stamp, c-Nigel Pearson, Gianluca Festa, Emerson [BRA], Robbie Mustoe, Fabrizio Ravanelli [ITA], Juninho [BRA], Craig Hignett. Substitutions: Mickel Beck [DEN] replaced Fabrizio Ravanelli 24th min; Steve Vickers replaced Robbie Mustoe 29th min; Vladimir Kinder [SVK], replaced Craig Hignett 74th min

May 17; 79,160; S Lodge

## 1998

### Arsenal 2 (Overmars, Anelka)

David Seaman [E]; Lee Dixon [E], Nigel Winterburn [E], Patrick Vieira [F], Martin Keown [E], c-Tony Adams [E], Ray Parlour [e], Nicolas Anelka [F], Emmanuel Petit [F], Christopher Wreh [LIB], Marc Overmars [NETH]. Substitution: David Platt [E] replaced Christopher Wreh 63rd min. Unused subs: Alex Manninger [AUT] (gk); Steve Bould [E], Ian Wright [E], Gilles Grimandi

### Newcastle United 0

Shay Given [RI]; Alessandro Pistone, Stuart Pearce [E], David Batty [E], Nikos Dabizas [GRE], Steve Howey [E], Rob Lee [E], Warren Barton [E], Alan Shearer [E], Temuri Ketsbaia [GEO], Gary Speed [W]. Substitutions: Andreas Andersson [SWE] replaced Stuart Pearce 72nd min; Steve Watson replaced Warren Barton 77th min; John Barnes [E] replaced Temuri Ketsbaia 85th min. Unused subs: Shaka Hislop [TT] (gk); Philippe Albert [BEL]

May 16; 79,183; P Durkin

## 1999

### Manchester United 2 (Sheringham, Scholes)

Peter Schmeichel [DEN]; Gary Neville [E], Ronny Johnsen [NOR], David May, Phil Neville [E], David Beckham [E], Paul Scholes [E], c-Roy Keane [RI], Ryan Giggs [W], Andy Cole [E], Ole-Gunnar Solskjaer [NOR]. Substitutions: Teddy Sheringham [E] replaced Roy Keane 9th min; Dwight Yorke [TT] replaced Andy Cole 61st min; Jaap Stam [NETH] replaced Paul Scholes 77th min. Unused subs: Jesper Blomqvist [SWE], Raimund Van Der Gouw

### Newcastle United 0

Steve Harper; Andrew Griffin, Laurent Charvet, Nikos Dabizas [GRE], Didier Domi, Rob Lee [E], Dietmar Hamann [GER], Gary Speed [W], Nolberto Solano [PER], Temuri Ketsbaia [GEO], Alan Shearer [E]. Substitutions: Duncan Ferguson [S] replaced Dietmar Hamann 46th min; Silvio Maric [CRO] replaced Nolberto Solano 68th min; Stephen Glass [S] replaced Temuri Ketsbaia 79th min. Unused subs: Shay Given [RI](gk); Warren Barton [E]

May 22; 79,101; P Jones

## 2000

### Chelsea 1 (Di Matteo)

Ed de Goey [NETH]; Mario Melchiot [NETH] Marcel Desailly [F], Frank Lebouef [F], Celestine Babayaro [NIG], Roberto di Matteo [ITA], c-Dennis Wise [E], Didier Deschamps [F], Gustavo Poyet [URU], George Weah [LIB], Gianfranco Zola [ITA]. Substitutions: Tore Andre Flo [NOR] replaced George Weah 87th min; Jody Morris replaced Gianfranco Zola 90th min. Unused subs: Carlo Cudicini (gk), John Terry (e), Jon Harley

### Aston Villa 0

David James [E]; Ugo Ehiogu [E], c-Gareth Southgate [E], Gareth Barry [e], Mark Delaney [W], Ian Taylor, George Boateng [neth], Paul Merson [E], Alan Wright, Dion Dublin [E], Benito Carbone. Substitutions: Steve Stone [E] replaced Ian Taylor 79th min; Julian Joachim replaced Benito Carbone 79th min; Lee Hendrie [E] replaced Alan Wright 88th min. Unused subs: Peter Enckelman (gk); JLloyd Samuel

May 20; 78,217; G Poll

## 2001

### Liverpool 2 (Owen 2)

Sander Westerveld [NETH]; Markus Babbel [GER], Stephane Henchoz [SWI], c-Sami Hyypia [FIN], Jamie Carragher [E], Danny Murphy [e], Dietmar Hamann [GER], Stephen Gerrard [E], Vladimir Smicer [CZ], Emile Heskey [E], Michael Owen [E]. Substitutions: Gary McAllister [S] replaced Dietmar Hamann 60th min; Robbie Fowler [E] replaced Vladimir Smicer 77th min; Patrick Berger [CZ] replaced Danny Murphy 77th min. Unused subs: Pegguy Arphexad (gk); Gregory Vignal

### Arsenal 1 (Ljungberg)

David Seaman [E]; Lee Dixon [E], Martin Keown [E], c-Tony Adams [E], Ashley Cole [E], Fredrik Ljungberg [SWE], Gilles Grimandi, Patrick Vieira [F], Robert Pires [F], Thierry Henry [F], Sylvain Wiltord [F]. Substitutions: Ray Parlour [E] replaced Sylvain Wiltord 76th min; Nwankwo Kanu [NIG] replaced Fredrik Ljungberg 85th min; Dennis Bergkamp [NETH] replaced Lee Dixon 90th min. Unused subs: Alex Manninger [AUT] (gk); Lauren [CAM]

May 12; 72,500; S Dunn

## 2002

### Arsenal 2 (Parlour, Ljungberg)

David Seaman [E]; Lauren [CAM], Sol Campbell [E], c-Tony Adams [E], Ashley Cole [E], Ray Parlour [E], Sylvain Wiltord [F], Patrick Vieira [F], Fredrik Ljungberg [SWE], Dennis Bergkamp [NETH], Thierry Henry [F]. Substitutions: Edu replaced Dennis Bergkamp 72nd min; Nwankwo Kanu [NIG] Replaced Thierry Henry 81st min; Martin Keown [ENG] replaced Sylvain Wiltord 90th min. Unused subs: Richard Wright [E] (gk); Lee Dixon [E]

### Chelsea 0

Carlo Cudicini; Mario Melchiot [NETH], c-Marcel Desailly [F], William Gallas, Celestine Babayaro [NIG], Jesper Gronkjaer [DEN], Frank Lampard [E], Emmanuel Petit [F], Graeme Le Saux [E], Jimmy Floyd Hasselbaink [NETH], Eidur Gudjohnsen [ISL]. Substitutions: John Terry (e) replaced Celestine Babayaro 46th min; Gianfranco Zola [ITA] replaced Jimmy Floyd Hasselbaink 68th min; Boudewijn Zenden [NETH] replaced Mario Melchiot 77th min. Unused subs: Ed de Goey {NETH] (gk); Slavisa Jokanovic [YUG]

May 4; 73,963; M Riley

## 2003

### Arsenal 1 (Pires)

c-David Seaman [E]; Lauren [CAM], Oleg Luzhny [UKR], Martin Keown [E], Ashley Cole [E], Freddie Ljungberg [SWE], Ray Parlour [E], Gilberto Silva [BRA], Robert Pires [FRA], Dennis Bergkamp [NETH], Thierry Henry [FRA]. Substitution: Sylvain Wiltord [FRA] replaced Dennis Bergkamp 77th min. Unused subs: Stuart Taylor (gk); Nwankwo Kanu [NIG], Kolo Toure [CIV] Giovanni van Bronckhorst [NETH]

### Southampton 0

Antti Niemi [FIN]; Chris Baird [ni], Michael Svensson [SWE], Claus Lundekvam [NOR], Wayne Bridge [E], Paul Telfer [S], Anders Svensson [SWE], Matthew Oakley, Chris Marsden, James Beattie [E], Brett Ormerod. Substitutions: Paul Jones [W] replaced Antti Niemi 66th min; Fabrice Fernandes replaced Chris Baird 87th min; Jo Tessem [NOR] replaced Anders Svensson 75th min. Unused subs: Paul Williams, Danny Higginbotham

May 17; 73,726; G Barber

Abbreviations: ARG-Argentina; AUT-Austria; BEL-Belgium; BRA-Brazil; CAM-Cameroon; CH-Chile; CIS-Commonwealth of Independent States; CIV-Ivory Coast; CZ-Czech Republic; CRO-Croatia; DEN-Denmark; E-England; F-France; FIN-Finland; GEO-Georgia; GER-Germany; GRE-Greece; IRE-Ireland; ISL-Iceland; ITA-Italy; JAM-Jamaica; LIB-Liberia; NETH-Netherlands, NI-Northern Ireland; NIG-Nigeria; NOR-Norway; PER-Peru; RI-Republic of Ireland, ROM-Romania; RUS-Russia; S-Scotland; SVK-Slovakia; SWE-Sweden; SWI-Switzerland; TT-Trinidad & Tobago; UKR-Ukraine; URU-Uruguay; USA-United States of America; W-Wales; YUG-Yugoslavia (from February 2003 renamed Republic of Serbia and Montenegro)

# FA CUP RECORDS

### Biggest Victory (any round)

Preston North End 26, Hyde FC 0, FA Cup 1st round proper, October 15 1887

### The other Biggest Winning Margins in FA Cup history:

1890-91 1q Staveley 19 Sheffield Walkley 0
1893-94 R1 Preston North End 18 Reading 0
1901-02 PR Norwich CEYMS 18 Bury St Edmunds 0
1902-03 3q St Helen's Recreation 18 Rhyl 0
1925-26 PR Windsor & Eton 18 Henley Town 0
1953-54 1q Ferryhill Athletic 18 Skinnigrove Works 0

### Other Matches with an Aggregate of 18 goals or More:

1933-34 EP Oswestry Town 19 Badsey Rangers 3
1914-15 PR Lancaster Town 17 Appleby 2
2002-03 PR Stocksbridge Park Steels 17 Oldham Town 1
1927-28 1q Newark Town 15 Basford United 3
1938-39 1q Burton Town 16 Sandiacre Excelsior Foundry 2

### Biggest Win in FA Cup final

Bury 6, Derby County 0, at Crystal Palace, April 18 1903

### Biggest Win in FA Cup Semi-final

Newcastle United 6, Fulham 0, at Anfield, March 28 1908

### Most Goals in FA Cup Match Competition Proper:

9 goals: Ted MacDougall for Bournemouth v Margate, 1st round, November 20 1971

### Qualifying Competition:

10 goals: Chris Marron, for South Shields v Radcliffe Welfare United, preliminary round, September 26 1947. South Shields won 13-0.
10 goals: Paul Jackson for Stocksbridge Park Steels v Oldham Town, preliminary round, August 31, 2002. Stocksbridge won 17-1 in front of a crowd of 110 people.

## Most Goals in a Season

**19 Jimmy Ross, Preston North End 1887-88**

Ross has traditionally been credited with scoring a record 20 goals in the 1887-88 season, but strictly speaking only 19 counted. He 'lost' one goal when Preston's 6-1 win over Everton in a second round match on November 26, 1887 was declared void by the FA after Everton were expelled from the competition for playing seven ineligible players against Bolton in the first round.

## Most FA Cup Goals in Career:

**49 Henry 'Harry' Cursham, Notts County, 1877-1888**

Harry Cursham scored 48 goals in the Competition Proper and one in a fourth qualifying round match against Staveley on December 8, 1888.

## 20th Century

44 Ian Rush (Liverpool 39, Chester City 4, Newcastle United 1) 1979-1998

41 Denis Law (Huddersfield Town 3, Manchester City 2, Manchester United 34, Manchester City 2) 1957-74.

Law's overall total would have been 47 but the six goals he scored for Manchester City in a fourth round tie at Luton Town on January 28, 1961, were expunged from the records after the match was abandoned in the 69th minute because of a waterlogged pitch. Luton beat Manchester City 3-1 when the match was re-staged. Law scored City's solitary goal.

## Most FA Cup Appearances:

88 Ian Callaghan (Liverpool 79, Swansea City 7, Crewe Alexandra 2)

87 John Barnes (Watford 31, Liverpool 51, Newcastle United 5)

86 Stanley Matthews (Stoke City 37, Blackpool 49)

84 Peter Shilton (Leicester City 30, Stoke City 7, Nottingham Forest 18, Southampton 17, Derby County 10, Plymouth Argyle 1, Leyton Orient 1)

84 Bobby Charlton (Manchester United 80, Preston North End 4)

## Youngest Player in FA Cup in any Round

Andy Awford, 15 years 88 days as a substitute for Worcester City v Borehamwood 3rd qualifying round, October 10 1987.
Worcester City won 3-1

### In Competition Proper

Lee Holmes, 15 years 277 days, for Derby County v Burnley, Round 3 at Griffin Park, January 4, 2003. Holmes replaced Adam Murray after 77 minutes. Burnley won 1-0.

### Youngest Player in an FA Cup final

James Frederick McLeod Prinsep, 17 years, 245 days for Clapham Rovers v Old Etonians, March 29 1879

### Youngest Player in a Wembley Final

Paul Allen, 17 years, 256 days for West Ham United v Arsenal, May 10 1980

### Youngest FA Cup final Scorer

Norman Whiteside, 18 years, 18 days, Manchester United v Brighton & HA, May 26 1983

### Youngest FA Cup final Captain

David Nish, 21 years, 212 days, Leicester City v Manchester City, April 26 1969

### Youngest FA Cup final Goalkeeper

Peter Shilton, 19 years, 220 days, Leicester City v Manchester City, April 26 1969

### Oldest Player in FA Cup in any Round

Billy Meredith, 49 years, 8 months, Manchester City v Newcastle United, semi-final, March 29 1924

Almost 20 years earlier he had scored the winning goal when Manchester City beat Bolton Wanderers 1-0 in the 1904 cup final.

### Oldest Player in an FA Cup final

Walter (Billy) Hampson, 41 years, 257 days, Newcastle United v Aston Villa, April 26 1924

It is believed some players in the 1870s may have been over 40 years old when they played in the final but their birth dates have never been verified.

### Oldest Goalkeeper in an FA Cup final

David Seaman, 39 years 241 days, Arsenal v Southampton, May 17, 2003, also making Seaman the third oldest player ever to appear in the cup final.

### Oldest Scorer in Wembley FA Cup final

Bert Turner, Charlton Athletic v Derby County, 36 years 312 days, April 27 1946.

He also scored an own goal in the same match.

## FA Cup Wins

When Wimbledon beat Liverpool in the cup final on May 14, 1988 they became the 42nd different team to win the cup.

Manchester United have won the cup a record 10 times from 15 appearances, followed by Arsenal with 9 wins from 16 and Tottenham Hotspur 8 wins from 9.

## Summary of FA Cup Wins

Manchester United 10, Arsenal 9, Tottenham Hotspur 8, Aston Villa 7, Blackburn Rovers 6, Liverpool 6, Newcastle United 6, Everton 5, Wanderers 5, West Bromwich Albion 5, Bolton Wanderers 4, Manchester City 4, Sheffield United 4, Wolverhampton W 4, Chelsea 3, Sheffield Wednesday 3, West Ham United 3, Bury 2, Nottingham Forest 2, Old Etonians 2, Preston North End 2, Sunderland 2, Barnsley 1, Blackburn Olympic 1, Blackpool 1, Bradford City 1, Burnley 1, Cardiff City 1, Charlton Athletic 1, Clapham Rovers 1, Coventry City 1, Derby County 1, Huddersfield Town 1, Ipswich Town 1, Leeds United 1, Notts County 1, Old Carthusians 1, Oxford University 1, Portsmouth 1, Royal Engineers 1, Southampton 1, Wimbledon 1

## FA Cup final Appearances

When Middlesbrough played Chelsea in 1997 they became the 53rd different club to have appeared in the cup final.

Arsenal 16, Manchester United 15, Newcastle United 13, Everton 12, Liverpool 12, Aston Villa 10, West Bromwich Albion 10, Tottenham Hotspur 9, Blackburn Rovers 8, Manchester City 8, Wolverhampton W 8, Bolton Wanderers 7, Chelsea 7, Preston North End 7, Old Etonians 6, Sheffield United 6, Sheffield Wednesday 6, Huddersfield Town 5, Wanderers* 5, Derby County 4, Leeds United 4, Leicester City 4, Oxford University 4, Royal Engineers 4, Southampton 4, Sunderland 4, West Ham United 4, Blackpool 3, Burnley 3, Nottingham Forest 3, Portsmouth 3, Barnsley 2, Birmingham City 2, Bury* 2, Cardiff City 2, Charlton Athletic 2, Clapham Rovers 2, Notts County 2, Queens Park, Glasgow 2, Blackburn Olympic* 1, Bradford City* 1, Brighton & HA 1, Bristol City 1, Coventry City* 1, Crystal Palace 1, Fulham 1, Ipswich Town* 1, Luton Town 1, Middlesbrough 1, Old Carthusians* 2, Queen's Park Rangers 1, Watford 1, Wimbledon* 1, (*undefeated),

## Unbeaten in Finals

5 Wanderers (1872, 1873, 1876, 1877, 1878)
2 Bury (1900, 1903)
1 Blackburn Olympic (1883)
Bradford City (1911)
Coventry City (1987)
Ipswich Town (1978)
Old Carthusians (1881)
Wimbledon (1988)

Tottenham Hotspur won the first six finals they contested with victories in 1901, 1921, 1961, 1962, 1981 and 1982. The sequence ended when they lost 3-2 (aet) to Coventry on May 16, 1987.

## Finalists Who Have Never Won

4 Leicester City (1949, 1961, 1963, 1969)
2 Birmingham City (1931, 1956)
Queen's Park, Glasgow (1884, 1885)
1 Brighton & HA (1983)
Bristol City (1909)
Crystal Palace (1990)
Fulham (1975)
Luton Town (1959)
Middlesbrough (1997)
Queens Park Rangers (1982)
Watford (1984)

## FA Cup finalists from Outside the Top Division

When Second Division Sunderland met Liverpool in the 1992 final, they became the 23rd club from outside the top flight to reach the final since the League was founded in 1888.

Of those only eight clubs have gone on to win the cup, the last being West Ham in 1980.

There has never been a final in which both clubs came from outside the top division.

1890 runners-up Sheffield Wednesday (1st, Football Alliance)
1894 winners Notts County (3rd, Div 2)
1900 runners-up Southampton (3rd, Southern League)
1901 winners Tottenham Hotspur (5th, Southern League)
1902 runners-up Southampton (3rd, Southern League)
1904 runners-up Bolton Wanderers (7th, Div 2)
1908 winners Wolverhampton W (9th, Div 2)
1910 runners-up Barnsley (9th, Div 2)
1912 winners Barnsley (6th, Div 2)
1920 runners-up Huddersfield Town (2nd, Div 2)
1921 runners-up Wolverhampton W (15th, Div 2)
1923 runners-up West Ham (2nd, Div 2)
1931 winners West Bromwich Albion (2nd, Div 2)
1936 runners-up Sheffield United (3rd, Div 2)
1947 runners-up Burnley (2nd, Div 2)
1949 runners-up Leicester C (19th, Div 2)
1964 runners-up Preston North End (3rd, Div 2)
1973 winners Sunderland (6th, Div 2)
1975 runners-up Fulham (9th, Div 2)
1976 winners Southampton (6th, Div 2)
1980 winners West Ham (7th, Div 2)
1982 runners-up QPR (5th, Div 2)
1992 runners-up Sunderland (18th, Div 2)

West Bromwich Albion (1931) remain the only team to have won promotion from the Second Division and the FA Cup in the same season. Huddersfield Town also won promotion and reached the FA Cup final in the same season

– 1919-20 – but they lost the final. West Ham United (1923) and Burnley (1947) also gained promotion and lost in the final in the same season.

West Ham's four finals have all featured a club from the old Division Two. In 1923 and 1980 they were in the Second Division themselves while in 1964 they beat Preston and in 1975 Fulham, both in the Second Division.

## Relegated Finalists

Four clubs have been relegated from the top flight and appeared in the cup final in the same season

1926 Manchester City (lost 0-1 to Bolton)
1969 Leicester City (lost 0-1 to Manchester City)
1983 Brighton & HA (lost 0-4 to Manchester United after 2-2 draw)
1997 Middlesbrough (lost 0-2 to Chelsea)

In 1915 Chelsea finished one from bottom in the First Division and also reached the final but they were saved from playing in the Second Division by the First World War and were not relegated. When the First Division was extended in 1919-20, Chelsea retained their place in Division One.

## Losers to Winners

The following clubs all experienced the disappointment of losing the final one year, only to come back and win the cup the following season.

1873 Oxford Uni (lost 2-0 to Wanderers)
1874 Oxford Uni (beat Royal Engineers 2-0)

1874 Royal Engineers (lost 2-0 to Oxford Uni)
1875 Royal Engineers (beat Old Etonians 2-0 after a 1-1 draw)

1879 Clapham Rovers (lost 1-0 to Old Etonians)
1880 Clapham Rovers (beat Oxford Uni 1-0)

1881 Old Etonians (lost 3-0 to Old Carthusians)
1882 Old Etonians (beat Blackburn Rovers 1-0)

1887 WBA (lost 2-0 to Aston Villa)
1888 WBA (beat Preston NE 2-1)
1888 Preston NE (lost 2-1 to WBA)
1889 Preston NE (beat Wolverhampton W 3-0)

1901 Sheffield Utd (lost 3-1 to Tottenham after 2-2 draw)
1902 Sheffield Utd (beat Southampton 2-1 after 1-1 draw)
1933 Manchester City (lost 3-0 to Everton)
1934 Manchester City (beat Portsmouth 2-1)

1937 Preston NE (lost 3-1 to Sunderland)
1938 Preston NE (beat Huddersfield 1-0 aet)

1946 Charlton Ath (lost 4-1 to Derby Co aet)
1947 Charlton At (beat Burnley 1-0 aet)

1955 Manchester City (lost 3-1 to Newcastle Utd)
1956 Manchester City (beat Birmingham City 3-1)

1976 Manchester Utd (lost 1-0 to Southampton)
1977 Manchester United (beat Liverpool 2-1)

1978 Arsenal (lost 1-0 to Ipswich)
1979 Arsenal (beat Manchester Utd 3-2)

1988 Liverpool (lost 1-0 to Wimbledon)
1989 Liverpool (beat Everton 3-2)

1995 Manchester United (lost 1-0 to Everton)
1996 Manchester United (beat Liverpool 1-0)

2001 Arsenal (lost 2-1 to Liverpool)
2002 Arsenal (beat Chelsea 2-0)

## Winners to Losers

Arsenal are the only club to have twice returned to the final as holders and lose the cup, an unwanted record they achieved when they became the first club to play in three successive Wembley finals (1978-79-80).

The only other club to have played in three successive finals winning in only the middle year are Old Etonians (beaten 1881, winners 1882, beaten 1883).

Seven holders have returned to the final the following season and lost:

1882 Old Etonians (beat Blackburn Rovers 1-0)
1883 Old Etonians (lost 2-1 to Blackburn Olympic aet)

1906 Everton (beat Newcastle United 1-0)
1907 Everton (lost 2-1 to Sheffield Wednesday)

1910 Newcastle United (beat Barnsley 2-0 after 1-1 draw)
1911 Newcastle United (lost 1-0 to Bradford City after 0-0 draw)

1971 Arsenal (beat Liverpool 2-1 after extra time)
1972 Arsenal (lost 1-0 to Leeds United)
1972 Leeds United (beat Arsenal 1-0)
1973 Leeds United (lost 1-0 to Sunderland)

1979 Arsenal (beat Manchester United 3-2)
1980 Arsenal (lost 1-0 to West Ham)

1994 Manchester United (beat Chelsea 4-0)
1995 Manchester United (lost 1-0 to Everton)

## Successive wins

Only Wanderers and Blackburn Rovers have won the cup three years in succession – and only five clubs have won the cup in successive seasons.

By a strange coincidence three of them have achieved that feat more than once:

| | |
|---|---|
| Wanderers | 1872 and 1873; 1876, 1877 and 1878 |
| Blackburn Rovers | 1884, 1885 and 1886; 1890 and 1891 |
| Newcastle United | 1951 and 1952 |
| Tottenham Hotspur | 1961 and 1962; 1981 and 1982. |
| Arsenal | 2002 and 2003 |

## Successive Finals

No club has yet appeared in four successive FA Cup finals, although Wanderers and Newcastle United both reached five finals in seven season spells between 1872-1878 and 1905-1911 respectively.

The following clubs have appeared in three successive finals and the (W) or (L) shows how they fared:

Wanderers 1876 (W), 1877 (W), 1878 (W)
Old Etonians 1881 (L), 1882 (W), 1883 (L)
Blackburn Rovers 1884 (W), 1885 (W), 1886 (W)
West Bromwich Albion 1886 (L), 1887 (L), 1888 (W)
Arsenal 1978 (L), 1979 (W), 1980 (L)
Everton 1984 (W), 1985 (L), 1986 (L)
Manchester United 1994 (W), 1995 (L), 1996 (W)
Arsenal 2001 (L), 2002 (W), 2003 (W)

## Successive defeats

Newcastle United are the only club to have twice lost finals in successive seasons:

Old Etonians 1875, 1876
Queens Park, Glasgow 1884, 1885
West Bromwich Albion 1886, 1887
Derby County 1898, 1899
Newcastle United 1905, 1906
Manchester United 1957, 1958
Everton 1985, 1986
Newcastle United 1998, 1999

Derby County lost three finals in six seasons between 1898 and 1903.

## Same Time Next Year

The only occasion that the same two clubs contested the final in successive years was in 1884 and 1885.

1884 Blackburn Rovers 2 Queens Park, Glasgow 1
1885 Blackburn Rovers 2 Queens Park, Glasgow 0

## Met Before

The only clubs to have met each other in three finals are Aston Villa and West Bromwich Albion; Arsenal and Liverpool; Arsenal and Newcastle United. The following lists all the repeat finals

1872 Wanderers 1, Royal Engineers 0
1878 Wanderers 3, Royal Engineers 1

1873 Wanderers 2, Oxford University 0
1877 Wanderers 2, Oxford University 1 (aet)

1884 Blackburn Rovers 2, Queen's Park, Glasgow 1
1885 Blackburn Rovers 2, Queen's Park, Glasgow 0

1887 Aston Villa 2, WBA 0
1892 WBA 3, Aston Villa 0
1895 Aston Villa 1, WBA 0

1888 WBA 2, Preston NE 1
1954 WBA 3, Preston NE 2

1904 Manchester City 1, Bolton Wanderers 0
1926 Bolton Wanderers 1, Manchester City 0

1905 Aston Villa 2, Newcastle United 0
1924 Newcastle United 2, Aston Villa 0

1907 Sheffield Wed 2, Everton 1
1966 Everton 3, Sheffield Wed 2

1922 Huddersfield Town 1, Preston NE 0
1938 Preston NE 1, Huddersfield Town 0 (aet)

1932 Newcastle United 2, Arsenal 1
1952 Newcastle United 1, Arsenal 0
1998 Arsenal 2, Newcastle United 0

1950 Arsenal 2, Liverpool 0
1971 Arsenal 2, Liverpool 1 (aet)
2001 Liverpool 2 Arsenal 1

1977 Manchester United 2 Liverpool 1
1996 Manchester United 1 Liverpool 0

1985 Manchester United 1 Everton 0
1995 Everton 1 Manchester United 0

1986 Liverpool 3, Everton 1
1989 Liverpool 3, Everton 2 (aet)

## FA Cup final Venues

| | |
|---|---|
| 1872 | Kennington Oval |
| 1873 | Lillie Bridge, London |
| 1874-1892 | Kennington Oval |
| 1886 | Replay at The Racecourse, Derby |
| 1893 | Fallowfield, Manchester |
| 1894 | Goodison Park |
| 1895-1914 | Crystal Palace |
| 1901 | Replay at Burnden Park, Bolton |
| 1910 | Replay at Goodison Park |
| 1911 | Replay at Old Trafford |
| 1912 | Replay at Bramall Lane, Sheffield |
| 1915 | Old Trafford |
| 1920-22 | Stamford Bridge |
| 1923-2000 | Wembley Stadium |
| 1970 | Replay at Old Trafford |
| 1981 | Replay at Wembley Stadium |
| 1982 | Replay at Wembley Stadium |
| 1983 | Replay at Wembley Stadium |
| 1990 | Replay at Wembley Stadium |
| 1993 | Replay at Wembley Stadium |
| 2001 to date | Millennium Stadium, Cardiff |

## FA Cup final Dates

In 1963 the cup final was 'postponed' by the FA from the original scheduled date of May 4 to May 25. The reason was because of the 'big freeze' winter of 1962-63 which played havoc with that season's fixture list.

Only two other finals in the competition's history have been decided later in the year than May 25. On May 26, 1983 Manchester United beat Brighton in a replay. On May 27, 1982 Tottenham beat Queens Park Rangers in a replay and this remains the latest date in the year on which the cup final has been decided.

## Crowds

The official record crowd for the cup final is 126,047 for the first Wembley final between Bolton Wanderers and West Ham United in 1923 – but the true attendance at that match will never be known and contemporary reports say as many as 200,000 may have been inside Wembley that afternoon.

That was the last time spectators could pay at the gate at a cup final, although there was cash admission available at the 1982 replay between Tottenham Hotspur and Queens Park Rangers. There have been four 100,000 plus crowds at the final:

1901 Tottenham Hotspur v Sheffield United, Crystal Palace – 110,820
1905 Aston Villa v Newcastle United, Crystal Palace: 101,117
1913 Aston Villa v Sunderland, Crystal Palace: 120,081
1923 Bolton Wanderers v West Ham United, Wembley, 126,047* (*official attendance)

The biggest crowd for an FA Cup match, apart from the final itself was the 84,569 who watched the sixth round tie on March 3, 1934 between Manchester City, the eventual FA Cup winners, and Stoke City. Manchester City won 1-0.

## FA Cup Miscellany

### Enough to Make You Dizzy

Stan 'Dizzy' Burton set a unique record in 1939. On April 29 he played for Wolves in the FA Cup final against Portsmouth and five days later he was transferred to West Ham United. Two days after that he made his debut for the Hammers against Manchester City in a Second Division match to become the only player to play for one club in the FA Cup final and then for another club in a league match in the same season.

## Lowest Crowds

An official crowd figure of 'nil' was recorded when Norwich City played Bradford City in a third round second replay at Sincil Bank, Lincoln on the afternoon of March 3, 1915, 19 years to the day before the Manchester City-Stoke City match.

Norwich played Bradford behind locked doors so that production at a local armaments factory was not disrupted. However, it is estimated that at least 1,000 people managed to gain admittance to watch Bradford's 2-0 win.

On January 16, 1985 Leicester City played Burton Albion behind closed doors in a third round replay at Highfield Road, Coventry where the official attendance was again "nil". Leicester had won Burton's "home" match at Filbert Street 6-1 but the FA ordered the match to be replayed because Burton's goalkeeper had been hit by a missile. Leicester won the replayed match at Coventry 1-0.

On November 25, 1992 Peterborough United beat Kingstonian 9-1 at home in a First Round replay after drawing the first match 1-1. But the FA ordered the match to be replayed because Kingstonian's goalkeeper Adrian Blake had been hit by missiles. Peterborough won the replay behind closed doors 1-0.

## Longest Unbeaten Run in FA Cup History

Blackburn Rovers. 23 matches. After losing 1-0 to Darwen on December 2, 1882 they went unbeaten in their following 23 ties which included 20 successive victories.

The run ended when they lost 2-0 to Scottish club Renton in a first round replay on November 27, 1886.

Arsenal, having won the FA Cup in 2002 and 2003 begin the 2003-04 season unbeaten in 14 successive ties and are bidding to become the first team to appear in four successive finals.

23 Blackburn Rovers Nov.1883-Nov.1886 (does not include one walkover)
21 Arsenal Jan.1979-May 1980
18 Tottenham Hotspur Jan.1981-Feb.1983
17 Arsenal Jan.1971-May 1972
16 Newcastle United Jan.1951-Jan.1953
Wanderers Oct. 1875-Nov.1878
15 Newcastle United Jan.1910-April 1911
Arsenal Jan.1998-April 1999
14 Tottenham Hotspur Jan.1961-Jan.1963
Derby County Jan.1946-Feb.1947
Barnsley Jan.1912-Feb.1913
Leeds United Jan.1972-May 1973
WBA Jan.1968-April 1969
Arsenal* Jan 2002-May 2003

13 Everton Jan.1905-Mar 1906
Sunderland Jan.1937-Mar 1938
Manchester United Jan.1948-Mar 1949
Blackpool Jan.1953-Feb.1954
Liverpool Jan.1989-April 1990
Manchester United Jan.1994-May 1995
12 Blackburn Rovers Jan.1890-Jan.1892
Manchester United Mar 1963-Mar 1964

**Arsenal's current unbeaten run at end of the 2002-03 season.*

The best unbeaten run by a Non-League club is Basingstoke Town who were unbeaten in 16 matches from the 1st qualifying round in 1997-98 through to the 4th qualifying round in 1998/99, although the run does include one drawn match lost on penalties. Wanderers also went 16 games unbeaten (not including byes or walkovers).

## Longest Run Without a Win

Leeds United. 16 matches.

After beating Bradford Park Avenue 2-0 in the Fourth Round on February 2, 1952, Leeds did not win another FA Cup match until March 6, 1963 when they beat Stoke City 3-1 in a third round match.

Rochdale went 13 matches without a win between 1927 and 1945. After beating Crook Town 8-2 in a First Round match on November 26, 1927, Rochdale did not win another cup match until November 17, 1945 when they beat Stockport County 2-1 in a First Round, First Leg match. In fact, Rochdale's win over Crook was their only FA Cup win between 1925 and 1945.

The longest run without a win by a Non-League club is 27 by Marlow. They failed to win a match from 1900-01 to 1926-27 inclusive.

## Longest Run Without a Draw

32 Middlesbrough 1887-88 – 1899-00
30 Leicester City 1925-26 – 1937-38

## Longest Run Without a Home Defeat

32 Sheffield Wednesday 1922-23 – 1945-46
28 Everton 1976-77 – 1986-87

## Longest Run Without an Away Win (including neutral grounds)

24 Millwall 1951-52 – 1971-72
24 Stoke City 1971-72 – 1992-93

## Longest Run Without Conceding a Goal

12 Bradford City 1910-11 – 1911-12

Bradford went 12 matches without conceding a goal from the third round on February 25, 1911 when they beat Grimsby Town 1-0 until a second replay in the fourth round against Barnsley on March 21, 1912 when they lost 3-2. During the run they won the cup for the only time in their history.

## Most Games Needed to Win the FA Cup

Barnsley played a record number of 12 matches (and over 20 hours of football) to win the cup in 1912. Half of those 12 matches ended in 0-0 draws. Arsenal needed 11 matches when they won the cup in 1979, including five in the third round against Sheffield Wednesday.

## Longest Round in FA Cup History

The Third Round of the 1962-63 season was the longest in the history of the FA Cup.

It was originally scheduled to be played on January 5, but only three matches went ahead then with WBA winning 5-1 at Plymouth; Sunderland winning 4-1 at Preston and Tranmere Rovers drawing 2-2 at home to Chelsea.

The round was eventually completed on Monday, March 11 when Middlesbrough beat Blackburn Rovers 3-1 in a replay at Ayresome Park – two days after the original date of the sixth round.

The round lasted 66 days. There were 22 different playing days, and a total of 261 postponements. Sixteen attempts were made to play the tie between Birmingham and Bury which was actually started once and then abandoned. When it was finally played, it ended in a replay.

It was as a result of the chaos caused by the weather and especially the complete lack of soccer on January 5, that the Pools Panel was formed and they sat on four successive Saturdays through January and February to assess the results.

For the record of a round unlikely to be repeated in either its duration or the chaos it caused, this was the breakdown of the 261 postponements:

*Tie, postponements, date played*

| | | |
|---|---|---|
| Lincoln C v Coventry C | 15 | Mar 7 |
| Birmingham v Bury *(plus one abandonment)* | 14 | Mar 5 |
| Sheffield U v Bolton | 14 | Mar 6 |
| Walsall v Manchester C | 14 | Mar 6 |
| Bradford C v Newcastle | 12 | Mar 7 |
| Gillingham v Port Vale | 12 | Feb 27 |
| Leeds U v Stoke C | 12 | Mar 6 |
| Manchester U v Huddersfield T | 12 | Mar 4 |
| Watford v Rotherham U | 12 | Feb 20 |
| Norwich v Blackpool | 11 | Mar 4 |
| Blackburn R v Middlesbrough | 10 | Mar 5 |
| Charlton A v Cardiff C | 10 | Feb 18 |
| Leyton Orient v Hull C | 10 | Feb 11 |
| Shrewsbury v Sheffield W | 10 | Feb 21 |
| Southampton v York C | 9 | Feb 13 |
| Arsenal v Oxford U | 7 | Jan 30 |
| Derby Co v Peterborough | 7 | Feb 4 |

| | | |
|---|---|---|
| Swansea T v QPR | 7 | Jan 26 |
| West Ham U v Fulham | 7 | Feb 4 |
| Carlisle v Gravesend | 5 | Jan 29 |
| Nottingham F v Wolves | 5 | Jan 29 |
| Luton T v Swindon T | 4 | Jan 26 |
| Portsmouth v Scunthorpe U | 4 | Jan 26 |
| Barnsley v Everton | 2 | Jan 15 |
| Bristol C v Aston Villa | 2 | Jan 16 |
| Tottenham H v Burnley | 2 | Jan 16 |
| Grimsby v Leicester C | 1 | Jan 7 |
| Mansfield T v Ipswich T | 1 | Jan 9 |
| Wrexham v Liverpool | 1 | Jan 9 |
| Plymouth A v WBA | 0 | Jan 5 |
| Preston NE v Sunderland | 0 | Jan 5 |
| Tranmere Rv Chelsea | 0 | Jan 5 |
| **Replays** | | |
| Aston Villa v Bristol C | 11 | Mar 7 |
| Scunthorpe U v Portsmouth | 10 | Mar 7 |
| Chelsea v Tranmere R | 5 | Jan 30 |
| Fulham v West Ham U | 3 | Feb 20 |
| Blackpool v Norwich C | 0 | Mar 6 |
| Bury v Birmingham | 0 | Mar 7 |
| Hull C v Leyton Orient | 0 | Feb 19 |
| Middlesbrough v Blackburn R | 0 | Mar 11 |
| Sheffield W v Shrewsbury T | 0 | Mar 7 |
| **Total** 261 | | |

## Marathon Ties

Marathon ties used to be a quirky, loveable feature of the FA Cup that helped define its unique appeal but they ended in 1991-92 when the FA introduced penalty shoot-outs to decide ties still level after one replay and extra time.

The last 'high-profile' marathon tie was the 1980 semi-final between Arsenal and Liverpool. It began with a 0-0 draw at Hillsborough on April 12, 1980 and was followed by a 1-1 draw after extra time at Villa Park on April 16, a 1-1 draw (aet), back at Villa Park on April 28 and was finally resolved when Arsenal won 1-0 at Highfield Road on May 1 – just nine days before the FA Cup final which Arsenal lost 1-0 to West Ham.

The following ties are now unlikely ever to be equalled for their duration, although new records could still be set in the qualifying rounds:

| | | | |
|---|---|---|---|
| 1971-72 | Alvechurch v Oxford City 4th qualifying round | | |
| | *6 matches* | *11 hrs* | *Alvechurch won 1-0* |
| 1924-25 | Leyton FC v Ilford 3rd qualifying round | | |
| | *5 matches.* | *9 hrs 40mins* | *Leyton won 2-0* |
| 1924-25 | Barrow v Gillingham 6th qualifying round | | |
| | *5 matches* | *9 hrs 30mins* | *Barrow won 2-1* |
| 1954-55 | Stoke City v Bury Round 3 | | |
| | *5 matches.* | *9 hrs 22mins* | *Stoke won 3-2* |
| | (Record for Competition Proper) | | |
| 1899-90 | New Brompton v Woolwich Arsenal 3rd qualifying round | | |
| | *5 matches* | *9 hrs* | *New Brompton won 1-0* |
| 1955-56 | Chelsea v Burnley Round 4 | | |
| | *5 matches* | *9 hrs* | *Chelsea won 2-0* |
| 1978-79 | Arsenal v Sheffield Wed Round 3 | | |
| | *5 matches* | *9 hrs* | *Arsenal won 2-0* |
| 1973-74 | Falmouth Town v Bideford 3rd qualifying round | | |
| | *5 matches* | *9 hrs* | *Bideford won 2-1* |
| 1954-55 | Doncaster Rovers v Aston Villa Round 4 | | |
| | *5 matches* | *8 hrs 30mins* | *Doncaster won 3-1* |
| 1960-61 | Hull City v Darlington Round 2 | | |
| | *5 matches* | *8 hrs 30mins* | *Hull won 3-0* |

As well as marathon ties ending in 1991-92, the FA decided that, from 1999, there would be no FA Cup final replays. In the event of a draw after extra time, the match would be decided on penalties.

## 'Quickest' FA Cup Winners

In complete contrast to the above, the 'quickest' winners in FA Cup history were Manchester United in 1963.

It took United just 82 days from them playing their first match in the competition to winning the final. Because of the 'big freeze' that winter, Manchester United did not meet Huddersfield Town in the third round until March 4 following 12 postponements. They went on to win the final against Leicester City on May 25, just 82 days later.

# FA Cup Non-Runners

Manchester United were not the first club to fail to enter the FA Cup in 1999-2000. A number of League clubs have been declared FA Cup Non-Runners either through their failure to send in an entry form by the deadline date or because they refused to compete. In the early days the FA regularly heard protests, disqualified clubs and declared matches void with replays ordered. But these are the most notable examples of senior clubs that missed out on the FA Cup:

### Aston Villa – 1879-80

Villa scratchedand played in a Birmingham Senior Cup match instead of facing the students of Oxford University in a second round tie.

### Sheffield Wednesday – 1886-87

Failed to enter by the deadline date.

### Everton – 1888-89

Everton had been disqualified from the FA Cup the previous season because of professionalism and withdrew in 1888-89, the first season of the new Football League, after being drawn to play Ulster away in a first qualifying round match.

### Sunderland – 1888-89

Although not one of the founder members of the Football League in 1888-89, Sunderland were still one of the most prominent clubs in the country, but they withdrew rather than face bitter rivals Sunderland Albion.

### Clapton Orient – 1906-07

Failed to enter by the deadline date.

### Leeds United – 1919-20

Leeds United, formed in 1919 as the successors to Leeds City, did not enter the FA Cup in their first season when they were members of the Midland League.

### Birmingham – 1921-22

Failed to enter by the deadline date.

### Charlton Athletic – 1921-22

Withdrew after their election to the Third Division South rather than play in the qualifying rounds.

### Halifax Town – 1921-22

Like Charlton, Halifax became members of the Football League for the first time in 1921 joining the Third Division North and withdrew rather than play in the qualifying rounds.

### Wigan Borough – 1921-22

Also became members of the Football League (Division Three North) in 1921-22 but refused to play in the qualifying rounds.

### Doncaster Rovers – 1923-24

Elected to Division Three North in 1923-24, Doncaster had already been paired with Fryston Colliery in a preliminary round match and withdrew rather than play against the works team.

### Bournemouth 1923-24

Bournemouth were elected to Division Three South in 1923-24, but had already been drawn in the preliminary round of the qualifying competition. They scratched rather than play the Portsea Gas Company.

### Queens Park Rangers – 1926-27

Failed to enter by the deadline date.

### Durham City – 1926-27

Members of the Third Division North at the time, Durham did not enter by the deadline date.

### Torquay United – 1927-28

Torquay United were elected to the Third Division South in 1927-28 but withdrew rather than play in the qualifying rounds.

### Nelson – 1928-29

Members of the Third Division North at the time, Nelson did not enter by the deadline date.

### Newport County – 1931-32

After 10 seasons in Third Division South, Newport County were not re-elected for the 1931-32 season and spent a year in the Southern League before winning back their Football League place at the start of the 1932-33 season. They did not enter the FA Cup in their Southern League season while they were also being investigated for alleged financial irregularities regarding a lottery scheme.

### Wigan Borough – 1931-32

Wigan were drawn to play Burton Albion in a first round match on November 28, 1931, but folded and left the Football League (Third Division North) before the match took place. Burton were given a bye to the second round.

### Brighton – 1932-33

Entered the FA Cup on time – but forgot to tick the box which gave them exemption from the qualifying rounds. Rather than pull out they played them. See their club section for the devastating results.

### Hull City – 1945-46

Did not enter as their ground was unfit following war damage.

### New Brighton – 1945-46

New Brighton, then in the Third Division North, also withdrew from the FA Cup because their ground was not yet ready to stage match after the war.

### Shrewsbury Town – 1950-51

Like Charlton, Halifax, Bournemouth, Doncaster and Torquay before them, Shrewsbury Town refused to enter after being elected to the Football League (Division Three South) rather than play in the qualifying rounds.

### Maidstone United – 1992-93

Entered on time, but by November 1992 when the First Round was being staged, Maidstone had gone into liquidation and resigned from the Football League on the eve of the season. That left an odd number of teams in the First Round and Swansea City were handed a bye.

### Manchester United – 1999-2000

The most famous and controversial FA Cup exit of all. Manchester United became the first FA Cup holders not to defend their trophy and the first League club since Shrewsbury Town in 1950-51 to withdraw from the FA Cup when they succumbed to Government and FA pressure to take part in the inaugural FIFA Club World Championship in Brazil in January 2000 as reigning European Champions. It was argued that their participation in the competition in Brazil was a vital ingredient in England's bid to win the right to stage the 2006 World Cup finals which was being decided by FIFA in the summer of 2000.

The FA argued they could not expect to win a bid to stage the World Cup if they did not support FIFA's other tournaments. In the event the English bid failed miserably. It seems, though, there was no reason why Manchester United could not have taken part in both competitions. The tournament in Brazil took place for two weeks in January 2000. The third round of the FA Cup that season was staged in the middle week of December 1999. The fourth round in the second weekend of January and the fifth round in the last week of January.

Assuming they came through the third round, United's fourth round match could easily have been postponed – or United could have played a reserve side – and still beaten most teams in the lower divisions with their second string.

United's decision not to take part created an odd number in the third round draw– 63 teams and not 64 -- and Darlington, who had lost 3-1 to Gillingham in a Second Round tie, were re-instated in the competition as the result of winning a ìlucky losers' draw. They were paired with Aston Villa and lost 2-1.

# FA Cup Final Players

A total of 1,925 players have appeared in the 136 cup final matches (including replays) between 1872 and 2003.

### Appeared in Most FA Cup finals

| | | | |
|---|---|---|---|
| 9 | Arthur Kinnaird | Wanderers | 1873 (W) 1877 (W) 1878 (W); |
| | | Old Etonians | 1875 (L) 1876 (L) 1879 (W) 1881 (L) 1882 (W) 1883 (L) |
| 5 | Charles Wollaston | Wanderers | 1872 (W) 1873 (W) 1876 (W) 1877 (W) 1878 (W) |
| | Jimmy Forrest | Blackburn Rovers | 1884 (W) 1885 (W) 1886 (W) 1890 (W) 1891 (W) |
| | Harry Wood | Wolverhampton W | 1889 (L) 1893 (W) 1896 (L) |
| | | Southampton | 1900 (L) 1902 (L) |
| | Jimmy Lawrence | Newcastle United | 1905 (L) 1906 (L) 1908 (L) 1910 (W) 1911 (L) |
| | Jock Rutherford | Newcastle United | 1905 (L) 1906 (L) 1908 (L) 1910 (W) 1911 (L) |
| | Colin Veitch | Newcastle United | 1905 (L) 1906 (L) 1908 (L) 1910 (W) 1911 (L) |
| | Joe Hulme | Arsenal | 1927 (L) 1930 (W) 1932 (L) 1936 (W) |
| | | Huddersfield Town | 1938 (L) |
| | Johnny Giles | Manchester United | 1963 (W) |
| | | Leeds United | 1965 (L) 1970 (L) 1972 (W) 1973 (L) |
| | Pat Rice | Arsenal | 1971 (W) 1972 (L) 1978 (L) 1979 (W) 1980 (L) |
| | Ray Clemence | Liverpool | 1971 (L) 1974 (W) 1977 (L) |
| | | Tottenham Hotspur | 1982 (W) 1987 (L) |
| | Frank Stapleton | Arsenal | 1978 (L) 1979 (W) 1980 (L) |
| | | Manchester United | 1983 (W) 1985 (W) |
| | Mark Hughes | Manchester United | 1985 (W) 1990 (W) 1994 (W) 1995 (L) |
| | | Chelsea | 1997 (W) |
| | John Barnes | Watford | 1984 (L) |
| | | Liverpool | 1988 (L) 1989 (W) 1996 (L) |
| | | Newcastle United | 1998 (L) |

| | | |
|---|---|---|
| Roy Keane | Nottingham Forest | 1991 (L) |
| | Manchester United | 1994 (W) 1995 (L) 1996 (W) 1999 (W) |
| David Seaman | Arsenal | 1993 (W) 1998 (W) 2001 (L) 2002 (W) 2003 (W) |
| Ray Parlour | Arsenal | 1993 (D) 1998 (W) 2001 (L) 2002 (W) 2003 (W) |

**Notes:**

Arthur Kinnaird played in 11 cup final matches including the replays of 1875 and 1876.
Jimmy Forrest played in six cup final matches (replay 1886)
Charles Wollaston played in six cup final matches (replay 1876)
Johnny Giles played in six cup final matches (replay 1970)
Ray Clemence played in six cup final matches (replay 1982)
Frank Stapleton played in six cup final matches (replay 1983)
Mark Hughes played in six cup final matches (replay 1983)
David Seaman played in six cup final matches (replay 1993)
Ray Parlour played in the drawn cup final against Sheffield Wednesday in 1993, but did not play in the replay which Arsenal won, hence a (D) is shown in his record above.
Glenn Hoddle also played in six cup final matches. He played for Tottenham Hotspur in the replayed finals of both 1981 and 1982, and the final of 1987. His sixth appearance was for Chelsea in 1994.
John Barnes is the only player to be on the losing side with three different teams at Wembley: Watford (1984), Liverpool (1988 and 1996) and Newcastle United (1998).

## Most Winners Medals

| | | | |
|---|---|---|---|
| 5 | Charles Wollaston | Wanderers | 1872, 1873, 1876, 1877, 1878 |
| | Arthur Kinnaird | Wanderers | 1873, 1877, 1878 |
| | | Old Etonians | 1879, 1882 |
| | Jimmy Forrest | Blackburn Rovers | 1884, 1885, 1886, 1890, 1891 |
| 4 | Joe Lofthouse | Blackburn Rovers | 1884, 1885, 1886, 1891 |
| | Mark Hughes | Manchester United | 1985, 1990, 1994 |
| | | Chelsea | 1997 |
| | David Seaman | Arsenal | 1993, 1998, 2002, 2003 |
| | Ray Parlour | Arsenal | 1993*, 1998, 2002, 2003 |

**Notes:**

The Hon Arthur Kinnaird, who later became president of the FA, played in nine of the first 11 cup finals. As well as winning five times he was winning captain four times, twice with Wanderers in 1873 and 1878 and twice with the Old Etonians in 1879 and 1882.
Mark Hughes was the only player to collect four FA Cup winners medals at Wembley.
Ray Parlour collected a winners medal in 1993 despite only playing in the original match against Sheffield Wednesday which was drawn. He did not play in the replay.

## Most Losers Medals

| | | | |
|---|---|---|---|
| 4 | Arthur Kinnaird | Old Etonians | 1875, 1876, 1881, 1883 |
| | Harry Wood | Wolverhampton W | 1889, 1896 |
| | | Southampton | 1900, 1902 |
| | Jimmy Lawrence | Newcastle United | 1905, 1906, 1908, 1911 |
| | Jock Rutherford | Newcastle United | 1905, 1906, 1908, 1911 |
| | Colin Veitch | Newcastle United | 1905, 1906, 1908, 1911 |
| | Paul Bracewell | Everton | 1985, 1986, 1989 |
| | | Sunderland | 1992 |
| | John Barnes | Watford | 1984 |
| | | Liverpool | 1988, 1996 |
| | | Newcastle United | 1998 |

## Winners Medals with Different Clubs

| | | | | |
|---|---|---|---|---|
| Gary Ablett | Liverpool | 1989 | Everton | 1995 |
| Paul Allen | West Ham Utd | 1980 | Tottenham Hotspur | 1991 |
| Francis Birley | Oxford Uni | 1874 | Wanderers | 1876, 1877 |
| Raich Carter | Sunderland | 1937 | Derby County | 1946 |
| Fredk Chappell-Maddison | Oxford Uni | 1874 | Wanderers | 1876 |
| Ray Clemence | Liverpool | 1974 | Tottenham Hotspur | 1982 |

| | | | | |
|---|---|---|---|---|
| Jim Dugdale | WBA | 1954 | Aston Villa | 1957 |
| Johnny Giles | Manchester Utd | 1963 | Leeds Utd | 1972 |
| Frederick Green | Oxford Uni | 1874 | Wanderers | 1877, 1878 |
| Harold Halse | Manchester Utd | 1909 | Aston Villa | 1913 |
| George Hedley | Sheffield Utd | 1899,1902 | Wolverhampton W | 1908 |
| Mark Hughes | Manchester Utd | 1985, 1990, 1994 | Chelsea | 1997 |
| David Jack | Bolton W | 1923, 1926 | Arsenal | 1930 |
| Pat Jennings | Tottenham | 1967 | Arsenal | 1979 |
| Arthur Kinnaird | Wanderers | 1873, 1877, 1878 | Old Etonians | 1879, 1882 |
| Edgar Lubbock | Wanderers | 1872 | Old Etonians | 1879 |
| Billy Meredith | Manchester City | 1904 | Manchester Utd | 1909 |
| Jimmy Nelson | Cardiff City | 1927 | Newcastle Utd | 1932 |
| Peter Osgood | Chelsea | 1970 | Southampton | 1976 |
| Stuart Pearson | Manchester Utd | 1977 | West Ham Utd | 1980 |
| Jack Reynolds | WBA | 1892 | Aston Villa | 1895, 1897 |
| Frank Stapleton | Arsenal | 1979 | Manchester Utd | 1983, 1985 |
| Clem Stephenson | Aston Villa | 1920 | Huddersfield | 1922 |
| Brian Talbot | Ipswich | 1978 | Arsenal | 1979 |
| David Taylor | Bradford City | 1911 | Burnley | 1914 |
| Ernie Taylor | Newcastle Utd | 1951 | Blackpool | 1953 |
| Sandy Turnbull | Manchester City | 1904 | Manchester Utd | 1909 |
| George Utley | Barnsley | 1912 | Sheffield Utd | 1915 |
| RWS Vidal | Wanderers | 1872 | Oxford Uni | 1874 |
| Dennis Wise | Wimbledon | 1988 | Chelsea | 1997, 2000 |

## Winners Medals With Different Clubs In Successive Years

| | | | | |
|---|---|---|---|---|
| Arthur Kinnaird | Wanderers | 1878 | Old Etonians | 1879 |
| Brian Talbot | Ipswich | 1978 | Arsenal | 1979 |

### Losers Medals With Different Clubs In Successive Years

| | | | | |
|---|---|---|---|---|
| Allan Clarke | Leicester City | 1969 | Leeds Utd | 1970 |

## Losers Medals With Different Clubs

| | | | | |
|---|---|---|---|---|
| Clive Allen | QPR | 1982 | Tottenham Hotspur | 1987 |
| Alan Ball | Everton | 1968 | Arsenal | 1972 |
| Bobby Barclay | Sheffield Utd | 1936 | Huddersfield Town | 1938 |
| Ted Barkas | Huddersfield | 1928 | Birmingham | 1931 |
| John Barnes | Watford | 1984 | Liverpool | 1988 |
| | Liverpool | 1996 | | |
| | Newcastle Utd | 1998 | | |
| Paul Bracewell | Everton | 1985, 1986, 1989 | Sunderland | 1992 |
| Mark Bright | Crystal Palace | 1990 | Sheffield Wed | 1993 |
| Charlie Buchan | Sunderland | 1913 | Arsenal | 1927 |
| Jimmy Case | Liverpool | 1977 | Brighton & HA | 1983 |
| Edgar Chadwick | Everton | 1893, 1897 | Southampton | 1902 |
| Allan Clarke | Leicester City | 1969 | Leeds Utd | 1970, 1973 |
| Ray Clemence | Liverpool | 1971, 1977 | Tottenham Hotspur | 1987 |
| Alex Dawson | Manchester Utd | 1958 | Preston NE | 1964 |
| Willie Fagan | Preston NE | 1937 | Liverpool | 1950 |
| John Goodall | Preston NE | 1888 | Derby County | 1898 |
| Glenn Hoddle | Tottenham Hotspur | 1987 | Chelsea | 1994 |
| Steve Hodge | Tottenham Hotspur | 1987 | Nottingham Forest | 1991 |
| Doug Holden | Bolton Wanderers | 1953 | Preston NE | 1964 |
| Bob Howarth | Preston NE | 1888 | Everton | 1893 |
| Joe Hulme | Arsenal | 1927, 1932 | Huddersfield Town | 1938 |
| David James | Liverpool | 1996 | Aston Villa | 2000 |
| Roy Keane | Nottingham Forest | 1991 | Manchester Utd | 1995 |
| Howard Kendall | Preston NE | 1964 | Everton | 1968 |
| Ray Kennedy | Arsenal | 1972 | Liverpool | 1977 |

| | | | | |
|---|---|---|---|---|
| Malcolm Macdonald | Newcastle Utd | 1974 | Arsenal | 1978 |
| Terry McDermott | Newcastle Utd | 1974 | Liverpool | 1977 |
| Frank McLintock | Leicester City | 1961, 1963 | Arsenal | 1972 |
| Peter Meechan | Everton | 1897 | Southampton | 1900 |
| Alf Milward | Everton | 1893, 1997 | Southampton | 1900 |
| Henry Ness | Barnsley | 1910 | Sunderland | 1913 |
| Cuthbert Ottaway | Oxford University | 1873 | Old Etonians | 1875 |
| Stuart Pearce | Nottingham Forest | 1991 | Newcastle Utd | 1998 |
| Nigel Pearson | Sheffield Wed | 1993 | Middlesbrough | 1997 |
| Gary Stevens | Brighton & HA | 1983 | Tottenham Hotspur | 1987 |
| Chris Waddle | Tottenham Hotspur | 1987 | Sheffield Wed | 1993 |
| Harry Wood | Wolverhampton W | 1889, 1996 | Southampton | 1900, 1903 |

## Winners and Losers With Different Clubs

Nearly 50 players have gained winners and losers medals with different clubs. These are the players to have done so since 1923. This list only makes reference to a player who has won and lost with different teams and does not include where a player has won and lost in the final with the same team. For example, it does not include Paul Allen's winning appearance with Tottenham in 1991, or Pat Jennings winning appearance with Arsenal in 1979. Those details are included in the adjacent lists which specify players who have won the FA Cup with different teams, or lost with different teams.

| | *Winning Club* | | *Losing Club* | |
|---|---|---|---|---|
| Gary Ablett | Everton | 1995 | Liverpool | 1988 |
| Paul Allen | West Ham Utd | 1980 | Tottenham Hotspur | 1987 |
| John Barnes | Liverpool | 1989 | Watford | 1984 |
| | | | Newcastle Utd | 1998 |
| Dave Bennett | Coventry City | 1987 | Manchester City | 1981 |
| Austin Campbell | Huddersfield Town | 1930 | Blackburn Rovers | 1928 |
| Allan Clarke | Leeds Utd | 1972 | Leicester City | 1969 |
| Ray Clemence | Liverpool | 1974 | Liverpool | 1971, 1977 |
| | Tottenham Hotspur | 1982 | Tottenham Hotspur | 1987 |
| Stan Crowther | Aston Villa | 1957 | Manchester Utd | 1958 |
| Ernie Curtis | Cardiff City | 1927 | Birmingham | 1931 |
| Duncan Ferguson | Everton | 1995 | Newcastle Utd | 1999 |
| Johnny Giles | Manchester Utd | 1963 | Leeds Utd | 1965, 1970, 1973 |
| Dietmar Hamann | Liverpool | 2001 | Newcastle Utd | 1999 |
| Glenn Hoddle | Tottenham Hotspur | 1981, 1982 | Chelsea | 1994 |
| Doug Holden | Bolton Wanderers | 1958 | Preston NE | 1964 |
| Mark Hughes | Chelsea | 1997 | Manchester Utd | 1995 |
| Joe Hulme | Arsenal | 1930, 1936 | Huddersfield | 1938 |
| David Jack | Bolton Wanderers | 1923, 1926 | Arsenal | 1932 |
| Pat Jennings | Tottenham Hotspur | 1967 | Arsenal | 1978, 1980 |
| Tommy Johnson | Everton | 1933 | Manchester City | 1926 |
| Roy Keane | Manchester Utd | 1994, 1996, 1999 | Nottingham Forest | 1991 |
| Ray Kennedy | Arsenal | 1971 | Liverpool | 1977 |
| Gary Lineker | Tottenham Hotspur | 1991 | Everton | 1986 |
| Edgar Lubbock | Wanderers | 1872 | Old Etonians | 1875, 1876 |
| Jim McCalliog | Southampton | 1976 | Sheffield Wed | 1966 |
| Frank McLintock | Arsenal | 1971 | Leicester City | 1961, 1963 |
| Paul Merson | Arsenal | 1993 | Aston Villa | 2000 |
| Bobby Moore | West Ham Utd | 1964 | Fulham | 1975 |
| Alan Mullery | Tottenham Hotspur | 1967 | Fulham | 1975 |
| Jimmy Nelson | Newcastle Utd | 1932 | Cardiff City | 1925 |
| Stuart Pearson | West Ham Utd | 1980 | Manchester Utd | 1976 |
| Peter Rodrigues | Southampton | 1976 | Leicester City | 1969 |
| John Scales | Wimbledon | 1988 | Liverpool | 1996 |
| Bill Slater | Wolverhampton W | 1960 | Blackpool | 1951 |
| Frank Stapleton | Manchester Utd | 1983, 1985 | Arsenal | 1978, 1980 |
| Brian Talbot | Ipswich Town | 1978 | Arsenal | 1980 |

| | | | | |
|---|---|---|---|---|
| Ernie Taylor | Newcastle Utd | 1951 | Manchester Utd | 1958 |
| | Blackpool | 1953 | | |
| Andy Thorn | Wimbledon | 1988 | Crystal Palace | 1990 |
| Dennis Tueart | Sunderland | 1973 | Manchester City | 1981 |
| Pat Van den Hauwe | Tottenham Hotspur | 1991 | Everton | 1985, 1986, 1989 |
| Dennis Wise | Wimbledon | 1988 | Chelsea | 1994 |
| Ian Wright | Arsenal | 1993 | Crystal Palace | 1990 |

## Played For and Against the Same Club in the FA Cup final

| | *Year* | *Played For* | *Against* |
|---|---|---|---|
| Gary Ablett | 1989 (W) | Liverpool | Everton |
| | 1995 (W) | Everton | Manchester Utd |
| Clive Allen | 1982 (L) | QPR | Tottenham Hotspur |
| | 1987 (L) | Tottenham Hotspur | Coventry City |
| Francis Birley | 1873 (L) | Oxford University | Wanderers |
| | 1877 (W) | Wanderers | Oxford University |
| Alexander Bonsor | 1872 (W) | Wanderers | Royal Engineers |
| | 1873 (W) | Wanderers | Oxford University |
| | 1876 (L) | Old Etonians | Wanderers |
| Austin Campbell | 1928 (W) | Blackburn Rovers | Huddersfield Town |
| | 1930 (L) | Huddersfield Town | Arsenal |
| Fredk Chappell-Maddison | 1873 (L) | Oxford University | Wanderers |
| | 1876 (W) | Wanderers | Old Etonians |
| Stan Crowther | 1957 (W) | Aston Villa | Manchester Utd |
| | 1958 (L) | Manchester Utd | Bolton Wanderers |
| Steve Hodge | 1987 (L) | Tottenham Hotspur | Coventry City |
| | 1991 (L) | Nottingham Forest | Tottenham Hotspur |
| Mark Hughes | 1994 (W) | Manchester Utd | Chelsea |
| | 1997 (W) | Chelsea | Middlesbrough |
| Joe Hulme | 1930 (W) | Arsenal | Huddersfield Town |
| | 1938 (L) | Huddersfield Town | Preston NE |
| Tommy Johnson | 1926 (L) | Manchester City | Bolton Wanderers |
| | 1933 (W) | Everton | Manchester City |
| Ray Kennedy | 1971 (W) | Arsenal | Liverpool |
| | 1977 (L) | Liverpool | Manchester Utd |
| William Kenyon-Slaney | 1873 (W) | Wanderers | Oxford University |
| | 1876 (L) | Old Etonians | Wanderers |
| Arthur Kinnaird | 1873 (W) | Wanderers | Oxford University |
| | 1876 (L) | Old Etonians | Wanderers |
| | 1877 (W) | Wanderers | Oxford University |
| | 1878 (W) | Wanderers | Royal Engineers |
| Edgar Lubbock | 1872 (W) | Wanderers | Royal Engineers |
| | 1876 (L) | Old Etonians | Wanderers |
| Terry McDermott | 1974 (L) | Newcastle Utd | Liverpool |
| | 1977 (L) | Liverpool | Manchester Utd |
| Bobby Moore | 1964 (W) | West Ham Utd | Preston NE |
| | 1975 (L) | Fulham | West Ham Utd |
| Emmanuel Petit | 1998 (W) | Arsenal | Newcastle Utd |
| | 2002 (L) | Chelsea | Arsenal |
| Jack Reynolds | 1892 (W) | WBA | Aston Villa |
| | 1895 (W) | Aston Villa | WBA |
| John Scales | 1988 (W) | Wimbledon | Liverpool |
| | 1996 (L) | Liverpool | Manchester Utd |
| Frank Stapleton | 1978 (L) | Arsenal | Ipswich Town |
| | 1979 (W) | Arsenal | Manchester Utd |
| | 1980 (L) | Arsenal | West Ham Utd |
| | 1983 (W) | Manchester Utd | Brighton & HA |
| | 1985 (W) | Manchester Utd | Everton |
| Clem Stephenson | 1920 (W) | Aston Villa | Huddersfield Town |

| | | | |
|---|---|---|---|
| | 1922 (W) | Huddersfield Town | Preston NE |
| | 1928 (L) | Huddersfield Town | Blackburn Rovers |
| Brian Talbot | 1978 (W) | Ipswich Town | Arsenal |
| | 1979 (W) | Arsenal | Manchester Utd |
| | 1980 (L) | Arsenal | West Ham Utd |
| Ernie Taylor | 1951 (W) | Newcastle Utd | Blackpool |
| | 1953 (W) | Blackpool | Bolton Wanderers |
| Albert Thompson | 1872 (W) | Wanderers | Royal Engineers |
| | 1873 (W) | Wanderers | Oxford University |
| | 1876 (L) | Old Etonians | Wanderers |
| Julian Sturgis | 1873 (W) | Wanderers | Royal Engineers |
| | 1876 (L) | Old Etonians | Wanderers |
| RWS Vidal | 1872 (W) | Wanderers | Royal Engineers |
| | 1873 (L) | Oxford University | Wanderers |

## Played For Three Different Clubs in the FA Cup final

| | | |
|---|---|---|
| John Barnes | Watford | 1984 (L) |
| | Liverpool | 1988 (L) and 1989 (W) |
| | Newcastle Utd | 1998 (L) |
| Harold Halse | Manchester Utd | 1909 (W) |
| | Aston Villa | 1913 (W) |
| | Chelsea | 1915 (L) |
| Ernie Taylor | Newcastle Utd | 1951 (W) |
| | Blackpool | 1953 (W) |
| | Manchester United | 1958 (L) |

## Played Against the Same Opposition in the FA Cup final for Different Clubs

Only 13 men have done this – and only three of them won in both matches against the same opposition – Frederick Green, Jimmy Nelson and Robert Vidal.
Only one man lost to the same opposition playing for different teams – Paul Bracewell.
Both of Duncan Ferguson's appearances against Manchester United were as a substitute.

| | | *played for* | *played against* |
|---|---|---|---|
| John Barnes | 1984 (L) | Watford | Everton |
| | 1989 (W) | Liverpool | Everton |
| Dave Bennett | 1981 (L) | Manchester City | Tottenham Hotspur |
| | 1987 (W) | Coventry City | Tottenham Hotspur |
| Robert Benson | 1874 (W) | Oxford University | Royal Engineers |
| | 1875 (L) | Old Etonians | Royal Engineers |
| Paul Bracewell | 1986 (L) | Everton | Liverpool |
| | 1989 (L) | Everton | Liverpool |
| | 1992 (L) | Sunderland | Liverpool |
| Jimmy Case | 1977 (L) | Liverpool | Manchester United |
| | 1983 (L) | Brighton & HA | Manchester United |
| Duncan Ferguson | 1995 (W) | Everton | Manchester United |
| | 1999 (L) | Newcastle United | Manchester United |
| Frederick Green | 1874 (W) | Oxford University | Royal Engineers |
| | 1878 (W) | Wanderers | Royal Engineers |
| Arthur Kinnaird | 1875 (L) | Old Etonians | Royal Engineers |
| | 1878 (W) | Wanderers | Royal Engineers |
| Edgar Lubbock | 1872 (W) | Wanderers | Royal Engineers |
| | 1875 (L) | Old Etonians | Royal Engineers |
| Jimmy Nelson | 1927 (W) | Cardiff City | Arsenal |
| | 1932 (W) | Newcastle United | Arsenal |
| James Prinsep | 1879 (L) | Clapham Rovers | Old Etonians |
| | 1881 (W) | Old Carthusians | Old Etonians |
| Ernie Taylor | 1953 (W) | Blackpool | Bolton Wanderers |
| | 1958 (L) | Manchester United | Bolton Wanderers |
| RWS Vidal | 1872 (W) | Wanderers | Royal Engineers |
| | 1874 (W) | Oxford University | Royal Engineers |

## Played for Two Clubs in the Same Season

Stan Crowther, who played for Aston Villa against Manchester United in the 1957 cup final, played for both Villa and Manchester United in the 1957-58 season. He was signed by United after the Munich Air Crash in February 1958 and was allowed by the FA to play for United in cup ties, even through he had already played for Villa earlier in the competition.

## Winning Double

Martin Buchan is the only player to have captained FA Cup winning teams in both England and Scotland. He was Aberdeen's captain when they beat Celtic 3-1 in the 1970 Scottish cup final and was United's skipper when they beat Liverpool 2-1 at Wembley in 1977.

## Four-medal Haul

In recent years a number of overseas players have added FA Cup medals to those already won in their own countries before moving to England, but Jimmy Delaney still holds a unique record by winning Scottish, English, Northern Irish and Republic of Ireland cup medals. He won the Scottish FA Cup with Celtic in 1937, the FA Cup with Manchester United in 1948, the Northern Irish FA Cup with Derry City in 1954 and was runner-up with Cork City in the Irish FA Cup in 1956.

## Amateurs in the FA Cup final

It is now more than a century since the strictly amateur teams of London and the Home Counties dominated the FA Cup. From the first final in 1872 until 1881 all ten finals were all-amateur affairs, with Blackburn Rovers the first northern professional side to reach the final in 1882 when they lost 1-0 to Old Etonians, the last "hurrah" for the landed gentry of the day.

In 1883 Blackburn Olympic beat Old Etonians to become the first northern side to win the cup, and the amateurs' hey-day was over.

Only four amateurs played in the final at Wembley between 1923-2000:

**1924 – (Dr) Victor Milne, Aston Villa**

The first amateur to play at Wembley, Victor Milne played at centre-half in the Aston Villa team beaten 2-0 by Newcastle United. He was born in 1897, the year Villa won the cup and league double.

**1946 – Arthur Turner, Charlton Athletic**

Not to be confused with Bert Turner who scored for both sides in the 1946 cup final, Arthur Turner was a 22-year-old RAF officer who played at centre-forward for Charlton in the match. He owns a unique record of being the only cup finalist who never played in a single League match for his club. He played for Charlton during the transitional season of 1945-46 when there was no League football, but did eventually make more than 50 League appearances for Colchester after their election to the League in 1950.

**1947 – Peter Kippax, Burnley**

Winger Peter Kippax played for Burnley in the 1947 cup final – and a year later was in the British team that finished fourth in the soccer tournament in the 1948 Olympic Games.

## Four Consecutive Appearances

Five players appeared in four consecutive FA cup finals for The Wanderers – 1876 plus replay, 1877 and 1878. They were Hubert Heron, Jarvis Kenrick, William Lindsay Alfred Stratford and Charles Wollaston.

Seven Blackburn Rovers players also appeared in four consecutive cup final matches in 1884, 1885, 1886 and the 1886 replay. They were Herby Arthur, Jimmy Brown, James Douglas, Jimmy Forrest, Hugh McIntyre, Fergus Suter and Joe Sowerbutts.

Three clubs played four FA Cup finals in successive years in the 20th century: Sheffield United (1901 and replay, 1902 and replay), Newcastle United (1910 and replay 1911 and replay) and Tottenham Hotspur (1981 and replay and 1982 and replay).

Eight Sheffield United players appeared in all four games: Willie Foulke, Harry Thickett, Peter Boyle, Harry Johnson, Ernest "Nudger" Needham, George Hedley, Fred Priest and Bert Lipsham.

Seven Newcastle players appeared in all four of their matches in 1910 and 1911: Jimmy Lawrence, Billy McCracken, Colin Veitch, Wilf Low, Jock Rutherford, Alex Higgins and George Wilson.

Eight Spurs players appeared in all their four matches in 1981 and 1982: Chris Hughton, Paul Miller, Graham Roberts, Steve Perryman, Steve Archibald, Tony Galvin, Glenn Hoddle and Garth Crooks.

Garry Brooke missed the 1981 replay but played in the three other matches as a substitute – the only man to appear in three cup finals as a substitute.

He was a talented left-winger who scored on his league debut for Burnley against Coventry in August 1946, having earlier been a guest player for Charlton, Grimsby, Manchester United, West Ham, Fulham, Liverpool, Hearts and Hibs during the war.

The 1947 cup final marked a watershed in his career. Before the final was played he was selected for the full England squad for a game against France at Highbury. Had he played he would have been the first amateur to play for the full England side since AG "Baishe" Bower appeared against Wales in 1927. But unfortunately he was taken ill on the eve of the cup final and gave a very disappointing performance. He collapsed on the Monday following the final and although he made a full recovery, his England chance was gone.

He left Burnley for Liverpool in January 1949 and made one league appearance for Liverpool against Birmingham City two months later.

As well as representing Britain in the 1948 Olympics, he also played twice for the Football League and was an outstanding cricketer, playing for Burnley in the Lancashire League in the late 1940s and early 1950s.

**1951 – Bill Slater, Blackpool**

In 1960 Bill Slater captained Wolves to victory in the cup final against Blackburn Rovers, and was also voted Footballer of the Year. It was his second cup final appearance.

His first came in 1951, the day before his 24th birthday when he was a late call-up for the injured Allan Brown and played in the Blackpool side beaten 2-0 by Newcastle. He was still an amateur at the time, and did not turn professional until the 1953-54 season. Like Peter Kippax, he also represented Great Britain in the Olympics, playing in the 1952 Games in Helsinki. He won 20 England amateur caps and 12 at full international level.

The only other amateurs to have played in the cup final in the 20th century were:

CB Fry (Southampton 1902), Sam Ashworth (Manchester City 1904), Dai Davies (Bolton 1904); Harold Hardman (Everton 1906 and 1907), Reverend Kenneth Hunt (Wolverhampton W 1908) and James Mitchell (Preston NE 1922).

Rev Hunt was the only amateur to score a cup final goal in the 20th century, opening the scoring for Wolves when they beat Newcastle United 3-1 at the Crystal Palace.

Davies and Mitchell were the only amateurs to play in goal during the 20th century.

Only two men have won FA Cup and FA Amateur Cup winners' medals. Bob Chatt was in Aston Villa's winning team in 1895 and was later re-instated as an amateur, winning the FA Amateur Cup with Stockton in 1899. Tom Morren, who played once and scored once for England in 1898, won an FA Amateur Cup winners medal with Middlesbrough in 1895 and was Sheffield United's centre-half when they won the FA Cup in 1899.

# FA Cup Final Relatives

There are many instances of members of the same family playing league and cup football and relatives, sometimes even distant ones, have appeared in the cup final with surprising regularity.

## Father and Son

Peter Boyle won FA Cup winners medals with Sheffield United in 1899 and 1902. His son Tommy won a winners medal with Sheffield United in 1925.

Remarkably, Harry Johnson also won FA Cup winners medals with Sheffield United in 1899 and 1902 and his son Harry also won a winners medal with Sheffield United in 1925.

Another son, Tommy, was Sheffield United's centre-half when they lost to Arsenal in 1936.

Hubert Pearson was West Bromwich Albion's goalkeeper when they lost the 1912 FA Cup final to Barnsley. His son Harold Pearson was West Brom's goalkeeper, gaining a winners medal in 1931 and a runners-up medal in 1935. (Also see Cousins).

Les Allen won a cup winners medal for Tottenham in 1961. His son Clive played against Tottenham in the 1982 cup final and for Tottenham in the 1987 final. (Also see Cousins and Uncles and Nephews)

Alec Herd played for Manchester City in the 1933 and 1934 cup finals.

His son David played for Manchester United in the 1963 cup final. Matt Busby, who was a team-mate of Alec in 1933 and 1934, was United's manager in 1963.

Jimmy Dunn played for Everton against Manchester City in 1933 and his son Jimmy played in the 1949 final for Wolves against Leicester City.

Brian Clough was the manager of the Nottingham Forest team that reached the 1991 cup final. His son Nigel was in the team.

Frank Lampard senior and his son Frank junior have both played against Arsenal in the FA Cup final. Frank senior was in the West Ham team that beat Fulham 2-0 in 1975 and Arsenal 1-0 in 1980. Frank junior played against Arsenal in 2002 but his Chelsea team lost 2-0.

## Father-in-law and Son-in-law

Billy Meredith won cup winners medals with Manchester City in 1904 and Manchester United in 1909. His son-in-law Charlie Pringle was in the Manchester City team beaten by Bolton Wanderers in 1926.

Dally Duncan played for Derby County in 1946 against Charlton. His son-in-law Don Revie, the future manager of Leeds and England, played for Manchester City in 1955 and 1956.

## Brothers

There have been a number of cases of brothers playing in the cup final, but only one pair of brothers have played against each other in the same match. In 1874, Herbert Rawson played for the Royal Engineers and his brother William was in the Oxford University team. Oxford won 2-0.

The only pairs of brothers to have played together in an FA Cup winning team and also for England are Frederick and Hubert Heron of Wanderers and Gary and Phil Neville of Manchester United.

On March 4, 1876 the Heron brothers played for England against Scotland and two weeks later played for Wanderers against Old Etonians in the cup final. Scotland won the international 3-0 but Wanderers won the cup final 3-0 after a replay.

Gary and Philip Neville became the first pair of brothers to play for England since the days of Bobby and Jack Charlton in a 3-0 friendly win over China in Beijing on May 23, 1996, 12 days after they both played in the Manchester United team that beat Liverpool 1-0 in the cup final.

Although Philip played for the full 90 minutes, Gary only made a fleeting appearance in that game as an 89th minute substitute for David Beckham. Both Gary and Philip played for the full 90 minutes against Newcastle United in the 1999 cup final which Manchester United won 2-0 to win the double for the third time. Gary had also played in the 1994 cup final against Chelsea when United won the double for the first time.

Bobby and Jack Charlton last played together for England in a World Cup first round match against Czechoslovakia on June 11, 1970 in Guadalajara, Mexico. Like the Heron brothers and the Neville brothers, the Charltons also won the FA Cup, Bobby with Manchester United in 1963 and Jack with Leeds United in 1972.

### Walter and Bob Balmer

Played as full-backs for Everton in their losing 1907 cup final to Sheffield Wednesday. Walter, the older brother, also played in the 1906 cup final when Everton beat Newcastle United

### Ralph and Tommy Banks

Ralph played left-back for Bolton in the 1953 FA Cup final against Blackpool while Tommy played left-back for Bolton in the 1958 final against Manchester United.

### George and Harry Bell

Played for West Bromwich Albion when they lost to Blackburn Rovers in 1886.

### Dave and Gary Bennett

Dave played in two cup finals against Tottenham in 1981, losing with Manchester City and in 1987 when he won with Coventry City. Brother Gary played in the Sunderland team beaten by Liverpool in 1992.

### Jackie and Danny Blanchflower

Jackie could have been a member of the first club in the 20th century to win the double – Danny was. Jackie was in the Manchester United team that went into the 1957 FA Cup final against Aston Villa as champions needing only victory in the cup final to secure the double. But United were beaten 2-1 with Jackie being forced to play in goal after Ray Wood was injured early in the match. Danny skippered the great Tottenham Hotspur side to The Double when they beat Leicester 2-0 in 1961. He also skippered Spurs to victory in the cup final the following year, scoring a penalty in the 3-1 win over Burnley.

### Jack and George Bray

Jack played for Manchester City when they were beaten by Everton in 1933 but gained a winners medal a year later when Manchester City returned to Wembley and beat Portsmouth. His brother George, nine years his junior, was in the Burnley team beaten by Charlton in 1947.

### Bobby and Jack Charlton

Bobby played for Manchester United in the 1957, 1958 and 1963 cup finals, Jack played for Leeds United in 1965, 1970 and 1972. Both played in two losing finals before picking up a winners medal.

### Dennis and Leslie Compton

Dennis and Leslie Compton played together for Arsenal when they beat Liverpool 2-0 in the 1950 cup final. Dennis was one of England's greatest ever cricketers and both played county championship cricket for Middlesex. As well as his 78 Test appearances for England, Dennis also played in 11 Wartime soccer internationals – but never played for England in an official international. Leslie was England's oldest-ever debutant at 38 when he played against Wales at Roker Park in November 1950.

### Archie and John Goodall

Archie and John Goodall played together in the Derby team beaten 3-1 by Nottingham Forest in 1898. John also played for Preston in 1888 and 1889, while Archie made a further appearance for Derby in 1903.

**Brian and Jimmy Greenhoff**
Brian and Jimmy followed the Comptons (1950) and the Robledos (1952) as the third pair of brothers to play together in a winning cup final team in the 20th century when Manchester United beat Liverpool 2-1 in 1977 with Jimmy scoring the winning goal after 55 minutes. Brian also played for United when they lost 1-0 to Southampton in 1976, while Jimmy was in the United team beaten 3-2 by Arsenal in 1979.

**Fred and Jack Hargreaves**
Fred and Jack Hargreaves played together in the Blackburn Rovers team beaten 1-0 in the 1882 final by Old Etonians at Kennington Oval. Jack also played in the winning Blackburn side of 1884.

**Allan and Ron Harris**
Allan and Ron were in the Chelsea side beaten 2-1 by Tottenham Hotspur in the 1967 FA cup final. Ron, the beaten skipper in 1967, returned triumphant with Chelsea in 1970 when he skippered them to victory in the replayed final against Leeds United at Old Trafford.

**Hubert and Frederick Heron**
The Heron brothers (see above) played together for Wanderers in 1876. Hubert also played in the 1877 and 1878 finals.

**Ezra and Jack Horton**
Ezra and Jack both played for West Bromwich Albion. Ezra played in the finals of 1886, 1887 and 1888. Jack played in 1895.

**Harry and Tommy Johnson**
Brothers Harry (1925) and Tommy (1936) both played for Sheffield United in the FA cup final as their father, Harry snr, had done in 1899 and 1902.

**Alfred and Edward Lyttleton**
The Hon. Alfred and The Hon. and Rev. Edward played in the Old Etonians team beaten by Wanderers in 1876.

**Gary and Phil Neville**
Gary and Philip Neville (see above) became the second set of brothers to win the FA Cup with Manchester United after the Greenhoffs, in 1996 when United beat Liverpool. However Gary only played for the last few minutes of the game after coming on as an 89th minute substitute. They did both play the whole match when Manchester United beat Newcastle United in 1999. Gary also played in the 1994 cup final when Manchester United beat Chelsea.

**Frank and Hugh O'Donnell**
The careers of Frank and Hugh O'Donnell spanned the Second World War. They played together in the Preston team which lost the 1937 cup final to Sunderland. Hugh was in the team a year later which beat Huddersfield to win the cup.

**Charles and Thomas Perry**
Five Perry brothers played for West Bromwich Albion in the 1880s and 1890s – Charles, Edward, Thomas, Walter and William. Charles played in the cup finals of 1886, 1888, 1892 and 1897. Tom played in 1895.

**Herbert and William Rawson**
Lieutenant Herbert Rawson and his brother William (see above) are the only brothers to have played against each other in the cup final when they were on opposing sides in 1874. William played for the winning Oxford University team who beat his brother's Royal Engineers side 2-0 at Kennington Oval. Herbert gained a winners medal when the Royal Engineers beat the Old Etonians in the replayed final of 1875. William also made a further appearance in the Oxford University team beaten 2-1 by the Wanderers in 1877.

**Ted and George Robledo**
Edward and George – or rather Eduardo and Jorge – Robledo of Chile played together when Newcastle United beat Arsenal in the 1952 FA cup final with George scoring the only goal. George, a Chile international, also played in the 1951 final.

**Billy and Jack Smith**
Billy and Jack Smith played together in the Portsmouth side beaten by Manchester City in 1934. Jack had also played in the 1929 Pompey side beaten by Bolton Wanderers.

**John and Charles Sutcliffe**
John and Charles own a remarkable brotherly record that is unlikely ever to be beaten – they appeared in cup finals 31 years apart! John, the last man to play for England at both Rugby Union and football, was born on April 14, 1868 and Charles on October 7, 1890. Charles was just three when John played in goal for the Bolton Wanderers team that lost 4-1 to Notts County in the 1894 cup final. He later played for Millwall, Manchester United and Plymouth Argyle where he finally retired as a player aged 44 before becoming a coach at Southend.
Charles was signed by Herbert Chapman for Leeds City in the summer of 1919 but never played for them before they were expelled from the League the following October. He eventually made his league debut for Rotherham County and in 1925 was in goal when Sheffield United beat Cardiff City 1-0 in the third FA cup final at Wembley.

## Cousins

The most recent case of cousins playing together in the cup final was in 1987 when Clive and Paul Allen appeared for the Tottenham side beaten 3-2 by Coventry City – after Clive had given

# FA Cup Miscellany
## The Scots, Irish and Welsh

Clubs from Northern Ireland and Scotland competed alongside English and Welsh clubs in the early days of the competition.

Queen's Park were the most successful Scottish club, reaching the finals of 1884 and 1885, while Rangers reached the semi-final in 1887. The seven Scottish clubs who took part in the 1870s and 1880s were: Cowlairs, Heart of Midlothian, Partick Thistle, Queen's Park, Rangers, Renton and Third Lanark.

More than 100 years later Gretna also took part in the Competition Proper as members of the Northern League. They later joined the Scottish League.

Three clubs from Northern Ireland took part in the Competition Proper: Cliftonville, Linfield Athletic and Distillery. Ulster and Belfast YMCA were among others who took part in qualifying round matches.

Cardiff City are one of two teams from outside England to reach the final (Queen's Park being the others) – but the only ones to win the FA Cup. Runners-up in 1925, they beat Arsenal in 1927.

Spurs a great start with a second minute goal – his 49th of the season.

Paul had become the youngest player to appear in a Wembley final, and the second youngest of all time when he played for West Ham against Arsenal in 1980.

In 2002 Frank Lampard played for Chelsea in the cup final against Arsenal. His cousin Jamie Redknapp had played for Liverpool against Manchester United in 1996 (see Father and Son).

Christopher Wreh, the French Under-21 international who played for Arsenal when they beat Newcastle United 2-0 in 1998 to win the double, is a first cousin of George Weah, the Liberian international, who played for Chelsea when they beat Aston Villa 1-0 in 2000.

In 1931 Harry Hibbs, the England goalkeeper was playing for Birmingham and his cousin, Harold Pearson was at the other end of the field, in goal for West Bromwich Albion. (see father and son/uncle and nephew).

Other examples of cousins being involved in the cup final include:

Dennis Stevens (Bolton Wanderers 1958) and Duncan Edwards (Manchester U 1957); Glyn Pardoe and Alan Oakes (both played for Manchester City 1969); Arthur Chadwick (Southampton 1900) and Edgar Chadwick (Everton 1893, 1897, Southampton, 1902); Jim Baxter and Willie Cunningham (both played for Preston NE, 1954).

Jackie Milburn (Newcastle 1951, 1952 and 1955) and Bobby and Jack Charlton (see brothers) were second cousins. Bobby and Jack's mother Cissie, was Jackie Milburn's first cousin.

### Uncles And Nephews

George Burley won a winners medal with Ipswich Town in 1978. His nephew Craig was in the Chelsea team beaten by Manchester United in 1994.

Les Allen, his son Clive and his nephew Paul all played for Tottenham in cup finals. Les was in the Tottenham team that beat Leicester City 2-0 in 1961 to become the first club in the 20th century to win the double. Clive played for Spurs in 1987 after playing against them in 1982 while nephew Paul played for Spurs in 1991 after playing for West Ham in 1980.

Hubert Pearson (WBA 1912) and Harry Hibbs (Birmingham 1931) were uncle and nephew. Both played in goal and both lost (see cousins).

Brothers Jack and George Bray (see above) played in Wembley finals for Manchester City and Burnley. Their nephew John was in the Blackburn Rovers side beaten 3-0 by Wolverhampton Wanderers in 1960.

Frank Lampard senior is Jamie Redknapp's uncle; while Harry Redknapp is Frank junior's uncle.

### Other connections

There are many other famous cup final family connections. Some of the more interesting:

Herbert Chapman managed Arsenal to three FA Cup finals (1927, 1930 and 1932). His younger brother Harry played for Sheffield Wednesday when they beat Everton 2-1 in the 1907 final.

Roy Dwight, who scored, and then broke his leg playing for Nottingham Forest in the 1959 cup final, was the uncle of singer Elton John, whose original name was Reginald Dwight. Elton John was the Watford chairman when they reached the final in 1984.

Cyrille Regis, who played for Coventry when they won the cup in 1987 is a cousin of former international sprinter John Regis who played a handful of matches for Arsenal's youth and reserve teams.

Bobby Cram never made it to the cup final, but was in the Colchester United team which beat Leeds United 3-2 in one of the most famous giant-killing acts of all time in 1971. He is the uncle of former world record holder and world champion athlete Steve Cram, arguably Sunderland's most famous fan.

Sir Stanley Matthews father Jack, was a

featherweight title contender before the Second World War. Sir Stan's son Stanley junior, won the Boys Singles Championship at Wimbledon in 1962.

Amanda Brown, the daughter of Ken Brown, who played for West Ham in the 1964 cup final, was also a tennis professional.

TV presenter Gaby Logan, the daughter of Terry Yorath who came on as a late substitute for Leeds United in the 1973 cup final against Sunderland was a former international rhythmic gymnast who took part in the Commonwealth Games.

Tracy Neville, the sister of Gary and Philip Neville, is an English netball international.

Cliff Jones, who played for Tottenham in 1961 and 1962 and was Tottenham's unused substitute in 1967, is a cousin of journalist and former professional footballer Ken Jones.

The father of Emlyn Hughes who played for Liverpool in the 1971, 1974 and 1977 finals was a Rugby League international.

The father of Terry Dyson (Tottenham 1961) was a jockey.

Ritchie Woodhall, who shouted "Up The Baggies" on the medal rostrum when he won an Olympic Light Middleweight boxing bronze at Seoul in 1988 is the great-great-great-grandson of George "Spry" Woodhall, who scored England's 100th goal in 1888. He also played in three FA Cup finals for West Bromwich Albion in 1886, 1887 and 1888.

Steve Gatting, who played for Brighton in the 1983 final is the brother of former England Test captain Mike Gatting.

Michael Owen's father Terry was a professional footballer whose 13-year career was mainly spent in the lower divisions (Bradford City, Chester, Cambridge, Rochdale and Port Vale) -- but he did make two appearances in the old First Division in the 1967-68 season – for Everton.

Boudewijn Zenden, who played for Chelsea in 2002 against Arsenal, is the son of a Dutch judo international.

Carlo Cudicini, Chelsea's goalkeeper in 2002, is the son of goalkeeper Fabio Cudicini who won the European Cup with AC Milan in 1969. His other honours include winning the European Cup Winners' Cup with Milan in 1968, the Italian Cup with Milan in 1969 and with Roma in 1964.

Keith Peacock made history as the first substitute in the Football League on August 21, 1965. His son Gavin was in the Chelsea side beaten 4-0 by Manchester United in the 1994 cup final.

Peter Croker, who won a winners medal with Charlton in 1947, was the brother of Ted Croker, himself a former professional and who was later the chief executive of the Football Association.

## Third-Fourth Place Matches

At the start of the 1970s it was decided to replace the traditional eve-of-final England v Young England matches by holding "third-placed playoffs" between the losing semi-finalists.

The idea was quite well supported the first time it was played – probably only due to the large number of Manchester United supporters even then, but was dropped after only a few seasons.

These are the details:

**1969-70 Manchester United 2, Watford 0. Highbury. April 10, 1970**

The first of these games attracted a crowd of 15,000 to neutral Highbury on the night before the FA Cup final between Chelsea and Leeds United and saw Brian Kidd score twice to give United victory.

**Stoke City 3, Everton 2. Selhurst Park. May 7, 1971**

Only 5,031 turned up the night before Arsenal met Liverpool in the cup final. John Ritchie scored twice and Mike Bernard the other as Stoke won after being 2-1 down at halftime. Alan Whittle and Alan Ball scored for Everton.

**1971-72 Birmingham City 0, Stoke City 0. St Andrews. August 5, 1972.**

Held over from the end of the previous season, this was actually the first FA Cup match decided by penalties. Birmingham beat Stoke 4-3 in the shootout. Trevor Francis, interviewed over 30 years later by *The Independent* and asked what he remembered of the game, replied he had absolutely no recollection of it whatsoever.

**1972-73 Arsenal 1, Wolverhampton Wanderers 3. Highbury. August 18, 1973**

This was also held over until the start of the following season. Brendan Hornsby scored for Arsenal, Jim McCalliog and Derek Dougan (2) scored for Wolves.

**1973-74 Leicester City 0, Burnley 1. Filbert Street. May 9, 1974**

The last of the third-fourth place matches took place five days after the cup final. While 100,000 had watched Liverpool beat Newcastle at Wembley, not surprisingly, only 4,000 turned up for this non-event settled by a first half goal from Ray Hankin. It was not held again.

## FA Cup final Cricketers and Rugby Players

Many professional footballers have played First Class cricket, very few ever played first class football and rugby.

Henry Renny-Tailyour therefore holds a unique place in the annals of all three sports. He played in three FA Cup finals for the Royal Engineers (1872, 1874, 1875 when he also scored), played first class cricket for Kent and was capped at full international level for Scotland at both rugby union (1872) and football (1873).

Charles Burgess 'CB' Fry also occupies a special place. Born one month after the first FA Cup final in 1872, he played for Southampton in the 1902 FA Cup final, made one international appearance for England at football, captained England at Test cricket as well as playing first class cricket for Sussex and Hampshire. He also played first class rugby union for Oxford University, Blackheath and the Barbarians.

On March 4, 1893 he equalled the world record for the long jump with a leap of 7.17 metres (23 feet 6 inches) at a meeting at Oxford and later in life was offered the throne of Albania. He died at the age of 84 in September 1956 and is buried at Repton in Derbyshire close to his old Repton School.

Gary Lineker did not play first class cricket but he did play for an invitational side against Germany at Lords in 1992. He scored one run before being dismissed. When asked about the experience afterwards, he replied, "it's always nice to score one against the Germans..."

The following players all appeared in the FA Cup final and played first class cricket:

| | *Final Appearance(s)* | | *Cricket Counties* |
|---|---|---|---|
| Charles Alcock | The Wanderers | 1872 | Essex |
| Morton Peto Betts | The Wanderers | 1872 | Middlesex, Kent & England |
| Edgar Lubbock | The Wanderers | 1872 | Kent |
| | Old Etonians | 1875 | |
| | | 1876 | |
| | | 1879 | |
| Alfred Lyttleton | Old Etonians | 1876 | Middlesex, Worcs & England |
| Edward Lyttleton | Old Etonians | 1876 | Middlesex & Worcs |
| William Kenyon-Slaney | The Wanderers | 1873 | MCC |
| | Old Etonians | 1875 | |
| | | 1876 | |
| Cuthbert Ottaway | Oxford University | 1873 | Kent & Middlesex |
| | | 1874 | |
| | Old Etonians | 1875 | |
| Charles Nepean | Oxford University | 1874 | Middlesex |
| Francis Birley | Oxford University | 1873 | Lancashire & Surrey |
| | | 1874 | |
| | The Wanderers | 1876 | |
| | | 1877 | |
| Henry Renny-Tailyour | Royal Engineers | 1872 | Kent |
| | | 1874 | |
| | | 1875 | |
| Herbert Whitfield | Old Etonians | 1879 | Sussex |
| | | 1881 | |
| Edward Wynyard | Old Carthusians | 1881 | Hampshire |
| Percy de Paravicini | Old Etonians | 1882 | Middlesex |
| | | 1883 | |
| John Goodall | Preston NE | 1888 | Derbyshire |
| | | 1889 | |
| | Derby County | 1898 | |
| Harry Daft | Notts County | 1891 | Nottinghamshire |
| | | 1894 | |
| John Devey | Aston Villa | 1892 | Warwickshire |
| | | 1895 | |
| | | 1897 | |

| | | | |
|---|---|---|---|
| Ernest 'Nudger' Needham | Sheffield United | 1899<br>1901<br>1902 | Derbyshire |
| Willie Foulke | Sheffield United | 1899<br>1901<br>1902 | Derbyshire |
| Charles Burgess 'CB' Fry | Southampton | 1902 | Sussex, Hampshire & England |
| Billy George | Aston Villa | 1905 | Warwickshire |
| Jack Sharp | Everton | 1906<br>1907 | Lancashire & England |
| Harry Makepeace | Everton | 1906<br>1907 | Lancashire & England |
| Andy Ducat | Aston Villa | 1920 | Surrey & England |
| Joe Hulme | Arsenal | 1930<br>1936 | Middlesex |
| Ted Drake | Arsenal | 1936 | Hampshire |
| Raich Carter | Sunderland<br>Derby County | 1937<br>1946 | Derbyshire |
| Jack Lee | Leicester City | 1949 | Leicestershire |
| Dennis Compton | Arsenal | 1950 | Middlesex & England |
| Leslie Compton | Arsenal | 1950 | Middlesex |
| Phil Taylor | Liverpool | 1950 | Gloucestershire |
| Don Roper | Arsenal | 1952 | Hampshire |
| Jack Dyson | Manchester City | 1956 | Lancashire |
| Fred Goodwin | Manchester United | 1958 | Lancashire |
| Jim Standen | West Ham United | 1964 | Worcestershire |
| Geoff Hurst | West Ham United | 1964 | Essex |
| Graham Cross | Leicester City | 1963<br>1969 | Leicestershire |

**Harry Makepeace holds a unique record. He is the only man to:**

- win an FA Cup winners medal – Everton 1906
- win a League Championship medal – Everton 1915
- be capped as a soccer international – 4 England caps 1906-1912
- win a County Cricket Championship medal – Lancashire 1926, 1927, 1928, 1930
- and be capped as a cricket international – 4 England caps vs Australia, 1920/21.

Geoff Hurst played in the same Essex Schools XI as Bobby Moore, was a regular for Essex Seconds for three summers in the early 1960s and played in one County Championship match for Essex against Lancashire at Liverpool in 1962 without scoring in either innings, although he did take two catches in the match.

Jim Standen, West Ham's goalkeeper in the 1964 cup final, won a County Championship medal with Worcestershire in 1964 and took 313 wickets for them between 1960 and 1970. He also topped the first class county bowling averages with 64 wickets at a cost of 13 runs in their championship winning season of 1964.

Andy Ducat played county cricket for Surrey from 1906 to 1931 and scored 23,373 runs in 428 first class matches. He played one Test match for England, against Australia in 1921. He died while playing at Lords in 1942 suffering a heart attack when batting for the Surrey Home Guard against the Sussex Home Guard.

## The FA Cup final and Rugby Union

Only three men played in the FA Cup final and were also capped at full international level at rugby union: Henry Renny-Tailyour (see above). He played rugby for Scotland against England in 1872, he also played in the 1873 Scotland team against England and played in three FA Cup finals for the Royal Engineers scoring in the 1875 replay.

Reginald Hasley Birkett played in goal for Clapham Rovers in the FA Cup finals of 1879 and 1880 and also won four full caps for England at rugby playing three times against Scotland and once against Ireland between 1871-72 and 1876-77.

John Sutcliffe played in goal for Bolton Wanderers in the 1894 final and was also capped for England at rugby, playing against the Maoris in 1888-89. He played his club rugby at the time for Heckmondwike.

## Cup Finalists born outside Britain and the Republic of Ireland

*This list only contains players who appeared in a cup final or replay and does not include unused substitutes.*

**Argentina:** Osvaldo Ardiles (Tottenham Hotspur 1981 and replay, 1987), Ricardo Villa (Tottenham Hotspur 1981 and replay)
**Australia:** Joe Marston (Preston North End 1954)
**Belgium:** Nico Claesen (Tottenham Hotspur 1987), Pat Van den Hauwe (Everton 1985, 1986, 1989; Tottenham Hotspur 1991)
**Brazil:** Emerson (Middlesbrough 1997); Juninho (Middlesbrough 1997), Edu (Arsenal 2002), Gilberto Silva (Arsenal 2003)
**Cameroon:** Lauren (Arsenal 2002, 2003)
**Canada:** Edward Parry (Oxford University 1877; Old Carthusians 1881), Jimmy Nichol (Manchester United 1977)
**Ceuta** (Spanish protectorate in Morocco): Nayim (Mohamed Ali Amar) (Tottenham Hotspur 1991)
**Chile:** Eduardo 'Ted' Robledo (Newcastle United 1952), Jorge 'George' Robledo (Newcastle United 1951, 1952)
**Croatia:** Silvio Maric (Newcastle United 1999)
**Czech Republic:** Vladimir Smicer (Liverpool 2001), Patrick Berger (Liverpool 2001)
**Denmark:** Jesper Olsen (Manchester United 1985), Jan Molby (Liverpool 1986, 1988, 1992), John Jensen (Arsenal 1993 and replay), Peter Schmeichel (Manchester United 1994, 1995, 1996, 1999), Jakob Kjeldberg (Chelsea 1994), Mickel Beck (Middlesbrough 1997), Jesper Gronkjaer (Chelsea 2002)
**Finland:** Sami Hyypia (Liverpool 2001), Antti Niemi (Southampton 2003)
**France:** Eric Cantona (Manchester United 1994, 1996), Frank Lebouef (Chelsea 1997, 2000), Nicolas Anelka (Arsenal 1998), Emmanuel Petit (Arsenal 1998, Chelsea 2002), Patrick Vieira (Arsenal 1998, 2001, 2002), Laurent Charvet (Newcastle United 1999), Didier Domi (Newcastle United 1999), Marcel Desailly (Chelsea 2000, 2002), Didier Deschamps (Chelsea 2000), Gilles Grimandi (Arsenal 2001), Robert Pires (Arsenal 2001, 2003), Thierry Henry (Arsenal 2001, 2002,2003), Sylvain Wiltord (Arsenal 2001, 2002, 2003), William Gallas (Chelsea 2002), Fabrice Fernandes (Southampton 2003)
**French Guyana:** Cyrille Regis (Coventry City 1987)
**Georgia:** Temuri Ketsbaia (Newcastle United 1998, 1999)
**Germany:** Bert Trautmann, (Manchester City 1955, 1956), Wilf Smith (Sheffield Wednesday 1966), Dave Phillips (Coventry City 1987), Dietmar Hamann (Newcastle 1999, Liverpool 2001), Markus Babbel (Liverpool 2001)
**Greece:** Nikos Dabizas (Newcastle United 1998, 1999)
**Iceland:** Eidur Gudjohnsen (Chelsea 2002)
**India:** Alfred George Goodwyn (Royal Engineers 1872). William Stanley Kenyon-Slaney (Wanderers 1873; Old Etonians 1875, 1876), William Lindsay (Wanderers, 1876, 1877, 1878), James Frederick McLeod Prinsep (Clapham Rovers, 1879; Old Carthusians 1881), Charlie Preedy (Arsenal 1930)
**Italy:** Albert Sturgess (Sheffield United 1915), Gianluca Festa (Middlesbrough 1997), Fabrizio Ravanelli (Middlesbrough 1997), Gianluca Vialli (Chelsea 1997), Gianfranco Zola (Chelsea 1997, 2000, 2002), Alessandro Pistone (Newcastle United 1998), Roberto Di Matteo (Chelsea 1997, 2000), Benito Carbone (Aston Villa 2000), Carlo Cudicini (Chelsea 2002)
**Jamaica:** Bob Hazell (QPR 1982 and replay), John Barnes (Watford 1984; Liverpool 1988, 1989, 1996, Newcastle United 1998)
**Liberia:** Christopher Wreh (Arsenal 1998), George Weah (Chelsea 2000)
**Mauritius:** Herbert Rawson (Royal Engineers 1874, 1875), (brother William was born in South Africa)
**Myanmar** (Burma): Charlie Mitten (Manchester United 1948)
**Netherlands:** Arnold Muhren (Manchester United 1983 and replay), Marc Overmars (Arsenal 1998), Jaap Stam (Manchester United 1999). Ed De Goey (Chelsea 2000), Mario Melchiot (Chelsea 2000, 2002), George Boateng (Aston Villa 2000), Sander Westerveld (Liverpool 2001), Dennis Bergkamp (Arsenal 2001, 2002, 2003), Jimmy Floyd Haselbaink (Chelsea 2002), Boudewijn Zenden (Chelsea 2002)
**Nigeria:** John Salako (Crystal Palace 1990 and replay), Daniel Amokachi (Everton 1995), Celestine Babayaro (Chelsea 2000, 2002), Nwankwo Kanu (Arsenal 2001, 2002)
**Norway:** Eric Thorstvedt (Tottenham Hotspur 1991), Erland Johnsen (Chelsea 1994), Tore-Andre Flo (Chelsea 2000), Frode Grodas (Chelsea 1997), Ronny Johnsen (Manchester United 1999), Ole-Gunnar Solskjaer (Manchester United 1999), Jo Tessem (Southampton 2003), Claus Lundekvam (Southampton 2003)
**Peru:** Nolberto Solano (Newcastle United 1999)
**Romania:** Dan Petrescu (Chelsea 1997)
**Russia:** Dmitri Kharine (Chelsea 1994)
**Sierra Leone:** Chris Bart-Williams (Sheffield

Wednesday 1993 and replay)
**Singapore:** Nigel Callaghan (Watford 1984), Eric Young (Wimbledon 1988)
**Slovakia:** Vladimir Kinder (Middlesbrough 1997)
**South Africa:** William Rawson (Oxford University 1874, 1877), Sandy Bell (Manchester U 1909), Tony Whitson (Newcastle U 1910, 1911). Bill Perry (Blackpool 1951, 1953), Des Horne (Wolverhampton Wanderers 1960), Albert Johanneson (Leeds U 1965), Craig Johnston (Liverpool 1986, 1988), Bruce Grobbelaar (Liverpool 1986, 1988, 1989, 1992), Mark Stein (Chelsea 1994)
**Sri Lanka** (Ceylon): Jack Butler (Arsenal 1927)
**Sweden:** Richard Gough (Tottenham Hotspur 1987), Roland Nilsson (Sheffield Wednesday 1993 and replay), Anders Limpar (Everton 1995), Anders Andersson (Newcastle 1998), Freddie Ljunberg (Arsenal 2001, 2002, 2003), Anders Svensson (Southampton 2003), Michael Svensson (Southampton 2003), (Anders and Michael Svensson are not related)
**Switzerland:** Stephane Henchoz (Liverpool 2001)
**Tobago:** Dwight Yorke (Manchester United 1999)
**Ukraine:** Andrei Kanchelskis (Manchester United 1994), Oleg Luzhny (Arsenal 2003)
**United States:** John Harkes (Sheffield Wednesday 1993 and replay)
**Uruguay:** Gustavo Poyet (Chelsea 2000)
**Note:** Terry Springthorpe (Wolves 1949) was later capped by the USA but was English.

# FA Cup final Managers

*The following 14 men have played in, and then managed FA Cup winning teams:*

| | *As A Player* | *As A Manager* |
|---|---|---|
| Peter McWilliam | Newcastle United 1910 | Tottenham Hotspur 1921 |
| Billy Walker | Aston Villa 1920 | Sheffield Wednesday 1935 |
| | | Nottingham Forest 1959 |
| Jimmy Seed | Tottenham Hotspur 1921 | Charlton Athletic 1947 |
| Joe Smith | Bolton Wanderers 1923 | Blackpool 1953 |
| | Bolton Wanderers 1926 | |
| Stan Seymour | Newcastle United 1924 | Newcastle United 1951 |
| | | Newcastle United 1952 |
| Matt Busby | Manchester City 1934 | Manchester United 1948 |
| | | Manchester United 1963 |
| Bill Shankly | Preston North End 1938 | Liverpool 1965 |
| | | Liverpool 1974 |
| Joe Mercer | Arsenal 1950 | Manchester City 1969 |
| Bob Stokoe | Newcastle United 1955 | Sunderland 1973 |
| Don Revie | Manchester City 1956 | Leeds United 1972 |
| Terry Venables | Tottenham Hotspur 1967 | Tottenham Hotspur 1991 |
| George Graham | Arsenal 1971 | Arsenal 1993 |
| Kenny Dalglish | Liverpool 1986 | Liverpool 1986 (player-manager) |
| | | Liverpool 1989 |
| Gianluca Vialli | Chelsea 1997 | Chelsea 2000 |

**Managed most FA Cup final teams**
6 Frank Watt, Newcastle United 1905, 1906, 1908, 1910, 1911, 1924

**Managed most FA Cup winning teams**

| | |
|---|---|
| 4 wins | Sir Alex Ferguson, Manchester United 1990, 1994, 1996, 1999 |
| 3 wins | John Nicholson, Sheffield United 1902, 1915, 1925 |
| | Charles Foweraker, Bolton Wanderers 1923, 1926, 1929 |
| | Bill Nicholson, Tottenham Hotspur 1961, 1962, 1967 |
| | Arsene Wenger, Arsenal 1998, 2002, 2003 |

**Winning FA Cup final managers since the start of the Football League in 1888-89.**
An asterisk shown by a name indicates that the man concerned was largely the administrative head of the club which operated without a recognised team manager. The last club to win the FA Cup without a recognised coach or manager was Preston North End in 1938

| | | |
|---|---|---|
| 1889 | Preston North End | William Sudell* |
| 1890 | Blackburn Rovers | Thomas Mitchell* |
| 1891 | Blackburn Rovers | Thomas Mitchell* |
| 1892 | WBA | Louis Ford* |

| | | |
|---|---|---|
| 1893 | Wolverhampton W | Jack Addenbrooke |
| 1894 | Notts County | Tom Harris* |
| 1895 | Aston Villa | George Ramsey* |
| 1896 | Sheffield Wed | Arthur Dickinson* |
| 1897 | Aston Villa | George Ramsey* |
| 1898 | Nottingham Forest | Harry Hallam* |
| 1899 | Sheffield Utd | JB Wolstinholm* |
| 1900 | Bury | HS Hamer |
| 1901 | Tottenham Hotspur | John Cameron |
| 1902 | Sheffield Utd | John Nicholson |
| 1903 | Bury | HS Hamer |
| 1904 | Manchester City | Tom Maley |
| 1905 | Aston Villa | George Ramsey* |
| 1906 | Everton | Will Cuff* |
| 1907 | Sheffield Wed | Arthur Dickinson* |
| 1908 | Wolverhampton W | Jack Addenbrooke |
| 1909 | Manchester Utd | Ernest Mangnall |
| 1910 | Newcastle Utd | Frank Watt |
| 1911 | Bradford City | Peter O'Rourke |
| 1912 | Barnsley | Arthur Fairclough |
| 1913 | Aston Villa | George Ramsey* |
| 1914 | Burnley | John Haworth |
| 1915 | Sheffield Utd | John Nicholson |
| 1920 | Aston Villa | George Ramsey* |
| 1921 | Tottenham Hotspur | Peter McWilliam |
| 1922 | Huddersfield Town | Herbert Chapman |
| 1923 | Bolton Wanderers | Charles Foweraker |
| 1924 | Newcastle Utd | Frank Watt |
| 1925 | Sheffield Utd | John Nicholson |
| 1926 | Bolton Wanderers | Charles Foweraker |
| 1927 | Cardiff City | Fred Stewart |
| 1928 | Blackburn Rovers | Bob Crompton |
| 1929 | Bolton Wanderers | Charles Foweraker |
| 1930 | Arsenal | Herbert Chapman |
| 1931 | WBA | Fred Everiss |
| 1932 | Newcastle Utd | Andy Cunningham |
| 1933 | Everton | Tom McIntosh* |
| 1934 | Manchester City | Wilf Wild |
| 1935 | Sheffield Wednesday | Billy Walker |
| 1936 | Arsenal | George Allison |
| 1937 | Sunderland | Johnny Cochrane |
| 1938 | Preston North End | no manager |
| 1939 | Portsmouth | Jack Tinn |
| 1946 | Derby County | Stuart McMillan |
| 1947 | Charlton Athletic | Jimmy Seed |
| 1948 | Manchester Utd | Matt Busby |
| 1949 | Wolverhampton W | Stan Cullis |
| 1950 | Arsenal | Tom Whittaker |
| 1951 | Newcastle Utd | Stan Seymour |
| 1952 | Newcastle Utd | Stan Seymour |
| 1953 | Blackpool | Joe Smith |
| 1954 | WBA | Vic Buckingham |
| 1955 | Newcastle Utd | Dugald Livingstone |
| 1956 | Manchester City | Les McDowall |
| 1957 | Aston Villa | Eric Houghton |
| 1958 | Bolton Wanderers | Bill Ridding |
| 1959 | Nottingham Forest | Billy Walker |
| 1960 | Wolverhampton W | Stan Cullis |
| 1961 | Tottenham Hotspur | Bill Nicholson |
| 1962 | Tottenham Hotspur | Bill Nicholson |
| 1963 | Manchester Utd | Matt Busby |
| 1964 | West Ham Utd | Ron Greenwood |
| 1965 | Liverpool | Bill Shankly |
| 1966 | Everton | Harry Catterick |
| 1967 | Tottenham Hotspur | Bill Nicholson |
| 1968 | WBA | Alan Ashman |
| 1969 | Manchester City | Joe Mercer |
| 1970 | Chelsea | Dave Sexton |
| 1971 | Arsenal | Bertie Mee |
| 1972 | Leeds Utd | Don Revie |
| 1973 | Sunderland | Bob Stokoe |
| 1974 | Liverpool | Bill Shankly |
| 1975 | West Ham Utd | John Lyall |
| 1976 | Southampton | Lawrie McMenemy |
| 1977 | Manchester Utd | Tommy Docherty |
| 1978 | Ipswich Town | Bobby Robson |
| 1979 | Arsenal | Terry Neill |
| 1980 | West Ham Utd | John Lyall |
| 1981 | Tottenham Hotspur | Keith Burkinshaw |
| 1982 | Tottenham Hotspur | Keith Burkinshaw |
| 1983 | Manchester Utd | Ron Atkinson |
| 1984 | Everton | Howard Kendall |
| 1985 | Manchester Utd | Ron Atkinson |
| 1986 | Liverpool | Kenny Dalglish |
| 1987 | Coventry City | John Sillett |
| 1988 | Wimbledon | Bobby Gould |
| 1989 | Liverpool | Kenny Dalglish |
| 1990 | Manchester Utd | Alex Ferguson |
| 1991 | Tottenham Hotspur | Terry Venables |
| 1992 | Liverpool | Graeme Souness |
| 1993 | Arsenal | George Graham |
| 1994 | Manchester Utd | Alex Ferguson |
| 1995 | Everton | Joe Royle |
| 1996 | Manchester Utd | Alex Ferguson |
| 1997 | Chelsea | Ruud Gullit |
| 1998 | Arsenal | Arsene Wenger |
| 1999 | Manchester Utd | Alex Ferguson |
| 2000 | Chelsea | Gianluca Vialli |
| 2001 | Liverpool | Gerard Houllier |
| 2002 | Arsenal | Arsene Wenger |
| 2003 | Arsenal | Arsene Wenger |

## Losing FA Cup final managers since the start of the Football League in 1888-89

| | | |
|---|---|---|
| 1889 | Wolverhampton W | Jack Addenbrooke |
| 1890 | Sheffield Wed | Arthur Dickinson* |
| 1891 | Notts County | Edwin Browne* |
| 1892 | Aston Villa | George Ramsey* |
| 1893 | Everton | Dick Molyneux* |
| 1894 | Bolton Wanderers | John Bentley* |
| 1895 | WBA | Edward Stephenson* |
| 1896 | Wolverhampton W | John Addenbrooke |
| 1897 | Everton | Dick Molyneux* |
| 1898 | Derby County | Harry Newbould* |
| 1899 | Derby County | Harry Newbould* |

| | | |
|---|---|---|
| 1900 | Southampton | E Arnfield* |
| 1901 | Sheffield Utd | John Nicholson |
| 1902 | Southampton | E Arnfield* |
| 1903 | Derby County | Harry Newbould |
| 1904 | Bolton Wanderers | John Somerville* |
| 1905 | Newcastle Utd | Frank Watt |
| 1906 | Newcastle Utd | Frank Watt |
| 1907 | Everton | Will Cuff* |
| 1908 | Newcastle Utd | Frank Watt |
| 1909 | Bristol City | Harry Thickett |
| 1910 | Barnsley | Arthur Fairclough |
| 1911 | Newcastle Utd | Frank Watt |
| 1912 | WBA | Fred Everiss |
| 1913 | Sunderland | Robert Kyle |
| 1914 | Liverpool | Tom Watson |
| 1915 | Chelsea | David Calderhead |
| 1920 | Huddersfield Town | Ambrose Langley |
| 1921 | Wolverhampton W | Jack Addenbrooke |
| 1922 | Preston North End | Vincent Hayes |
| 1923 | West Ham Utd | Syd King |
| 1924 | Aston Villa | George Ramsey* |
| 1925 | Cardiff City | Fred Stewart |
| 1926 | Manchester City | no manager |
| 1927 | Arsenal | Herbert Chapman |
| 1928 | Huddersfield Town | Jack Chaplin |
| 1929 | Portsmouth | Jack Tinn |
| 1930 | Huddersfield Town | Clem Stephenson |
| 1931 | Birmingham | Leslie Knighton |
| 1932 | Arsenal | Herbert Chapman |
| 1933 | Manchester City | Wilf Wild |
| 1934 | Portsmouth | Jack Tinn |
| 1935 | WBA | Fred Everiss |
| 1936 | Sheffield Utd | Ted Davison |
| 1937 | Preston North End | Tommy Muirhead |
| 1938 | Huddersfield Town | Clem Stephenson |
| 1939 | Wolverhampton W | Frank Buckley |
| 1946 | Charlton Athletic | Jimmy Seed |
| 1947 | Burnley | Cliff Britton |
| 1948 | Blackpool | Joe Smith |
| 1949 | Leicester City | John Duncan |
| 1950 | Liverpool | George Kay |
| 1951 | Blackpool | Joe Smith |
| 1952 | Arsenal | Tom Whittaker |
| 1953 | Bolton Wanderers | Bill Ridding |
| 1954 | Preston North End | Scott Symon |
| 1955 | Manchester City | Les McDowall |
| 1956 | Birmingham City | Arthur Turner |
| 1957 | Manchester Utd | Matt Busby |
| 1958 | Manchester Utd | Matt Busby |
| 1959 | Luton Town | no manager |
| 1960 | Blackburn Rovers | Dally Duncan |
| 1961 | Leicester City | Matt Gillies |
| 1962 | Burnley | Harry Potts |
| 1963 | Leicester City | Matt Gillies |
| 1964 | Preston North End | Jimmy Milne |
| 1965 | Leeds Utd | Don Revie |
| 1966 | Sheffield Wed | Alan Brown |
| 1967 | Chelsea | Tommy Docherty |
| 1968 | Everton | Harry Catterick |
| 1969 | Leicester City | Frank O'Farrell |
| 1970 | Leeds Utd | Don Revie |
| 1971 | Liverpool | Bill Shankly |
| 1972 | Arsenal | Bertie Mee |
| 1973 | Leeds Utd | Don Revie |
| 1974 | Newcastle Utd | Joe Harvey |
| 1975 | Fulham | Alec Stock |
| 1976 | Manchester Utd | Tommy Docherty |
| 1977 | Liverpool | Bob Paisley |
| 1978 | Arsenal | Terry Neill |
| 1979 | Manchester Utd | Dave Sexton |
| 1980 | Arsenal | Terry Neill |
| 1981 | Manchester City | John Bond |
| 1982 | QPR | Terry Venables |
| 1983 | Brighton & HA | Jimmy Melia |
| 1984 | Watford | Graham Taylor |
| 1985 | Everton | Howard Kendall |
| 1986 | Everton | Howard Kendall |
| 1987 | Tottenham Hotspur | David Pleat |
| 1988 | Liverpool | Kenny Dalglish |
| 1989 | Everton | Colin Harvey |
| 1990 | Crystal Palace | Steve Coppell |
| 1991 | Nottingham Forest | Brian Clough |
| 1992 | Sunderland | Malcolm Crosby |
| 1993 | Sheffield Wed | Trevor Francis |
| 1994 | Chelsea | Glenn Hoddle |
| 1995 | Manchester Utd | Alex Ferguson |
| 1996 | Liverpool | Roy Evans |
| 1997 | Middlesbrough | Bryan Robson |
| 1998 | Newcastle Utd | Kenny Dalglish |
| 1999 | Newcastle Utd | Ruud Gullit |
| 2000 | Aston Villa | John Gregory |
| 2001 | Arsenal | Arsene Wenger |
| 2002 | Chelsea | Claudio Ranieri |
| 2003 | Southampton | Gordon Strachan |

## Foreign Managers and Coaches

Ruud Gullit, the former Dutch international, was the first foreigner to steer a side to victory in the FA Cup final when Chelsea beat Middlesbrough 2-0 in 1997. Player-manager at the time, he made one appearance during their victorious cup run, coming on as an 87th minute substitute in a 2-2 draw at Leicester City in the fifth round. He was also manager of Newcastle United when they reached the FA Cup final in 1999

When Chelsea won the FA Cup in 2000, Italian Gianluca Vialli, restricted to a two-minute substitute appearance by Gullit in 1997, was Chelsea's manager. He was officially Chelsea's player-manager in 2000, but did not make any league or FA Cup appearances during the campaign.

Arsene Wenger was the first French manager to guide his side to FA Cup success when Arsenal beat Newcastle United 2-0 in 1998 to win the double. Wenger won the cup and league double again with Arsenal in 2002 and the FA cup again in 2003.

Gerard Houllier became the second French manager to win the FA Cup when his Liverpool team beat Wenger's Arsenal 2-1 in the 2001 final. It was the first time that both finalists had foreign managers, which was also the case in 2002 when Frenchman Wenger opposed Chelsea's Italian boss Claudio Ranieri.

### Managers' Doubles

*Only two men have managed different FA Cup winning sides:*

| | |
|---|---|
| Billy Walker | Sheffield Wednesday 1935 |
| | Nottingham Forest 1959 |
| Herbert Chapman | Huddersfield Town 1922 |
| | Arsenal 1930 |

Kenny Dalglish (Liverpool) and George Graham (Arsenal) won the FA Cup and League double with one club – and then managed that club to victory in the FA Cup final. Dalglish achieved his feat as player-manager of Liverpool in 1986 and then as manager in 1989.

Graham won the double with Arsenal in 1971, and the FA Cup as manager in 1993. He also became the first manager to win the domestic cup double in the same season as Arsenal also won the League Cup in 1993.

Joe Mercer won the League Championship as a player with Everton (1939) and with Arsenal (1948 and 1953). He also won the FA Cup as Arsenal skipper (1950) and won both the League Championship (1968) and FA Cup (1969) again as the manager of Manchester City.

### Player-managers

The only player-managers to appear in the cup final are Kenny Dalglish (Liverpool 1986) and Glenn Hoddle (Chelsea 1994). Dalglish played for the whole of the final against Everton which Liverpool won 3-1. Hoddle came on as a 65th minute substitute for Chelsea (replacing Craig Burley) in their 4-0 defeat to Manchester United in 1994.

Other FA Cup final player-managers (technically according to their player registrations being valid at the start of the season in question) have been: Trevor Francis (Sheffield Wednesday 1993); Bryan Robson (Middlesbrough 1997), Ruud Gullit (Chelsea 1997) and Gianluca Vialli (Chelsea 2000).

Francis made one league appearance (plus four as a substitute) but did not play in any FA Cup matches in the 1992-93 season. Robson made one league appearance but none in the cup for Middlesbrough during the 1996-97 season while Vialli did not make any appearances in either League or cup for Chelsea during 1999-2000.

### Youngest Manager

The youngest FA Cup final manager was Stan Cullis, who was 33 years 187 days old when he was in charge of the Wolverhampton Wanderers team that beat Leicester City to win the FA Cup in 1949. He had been in the Wolves team beaten in the 1939 final by Portsmouth.

### Manager of English and Scottish FA Cup Winning Teams

Only two men have achieved this: Jimmy Cochrane (Kilmarnock 1929 and Sunderland 1937) and Sir Alex Ferguson (Aberdeen 1982, 1983, 1984 and 1986 and Manchester United, 1990, 1994, 1996 and 1999).

# FA Cup Scorers

### Individual Scoring Records

Henry 'Harry' Cursham is the highest individual scorer in the history of the FA Cup with 49 goals for Notts County between 1877 and 1888. He actually scored 51 FA Cup goals in his career, but two were annulled from the records when the FA ordered an 1881 second round match between Notts County and Wednesbury Strollers to be replayed after Notts County had won the original game 5-3. Harry duly showed his indignation to that by scoring six in an 11-1 win in the replayed game.

He scored 48 goals in the Competition Proper and one in a qualifying round game for his official tally of 49.

Harry Cursham was the first great goalscorer of the English game, pre-dating the far more famous Steve Bloomer by some 15 years. But he has tended to be over-looked because almost all his scoring exploits took place in the decade before the Football League was formed. In fact, he did play League football for Notts County, making nine appearances and scoring twice during the first three league seasons.

He also scored five goals in his eight England appearances – including the first hat-trick by any player in the Home International series. He did that in his last game for England, an 8-1 win over Ireland in February 1884. His brothers Arthur and Charles also played for Notts County while Arthur played for England six times, scoring once.

Harry Cursham later played for Corinthians,

Thursday Wanderers (Sheffield) and Grantham and also played two first class cricket matches for Nottinghamshire, a trial in 1880 and as captain of the side against South Africa in 1904.

He was born on November 27, 1859 and died on August 6, 1941, aged 81.

## FA Cup all-time top scorers

49 Henry 'Harry' Cursham Notts County (49)
44 Ian Rush Chester City (4), Liverpool (39), Newcastle United (1)
41 Denis Law Huddersfield Town (3), Manchester City (2), Manchester United (34), Manchester City (2).
38 Allan Clarke Walsall (4), Fulham (5), Leeds United (25), Leicester City (1), Barnsley (3)
36* Jimmy Ross Preston North End (36)
*Ross's record does not include the goal in the match against Everton in 1887-88 which was later declared void by the FA.

## FA Cup final all-time top scorers

5 Ian Rush, Liverpool 1986 (2) 1989 (2), 1992 (1)
4 Billy Townley, Blackburn R 1890 (3), 1891 (1)
Stan Mortensen, Blackpool 1948 (1), 1953 (3)
Ian Wright, Crystal P 1990 (2); Arsenal 1993 (1), 1993rep (1)
3 Jarvis Kenrick, Wanderers 1877 (1), 1878 (2)
Fred Priest, Sheffield United 1899 (1), 1901 (1), 1902rep (1)
Sandy Brown, Tottenham H 1901 (2), 1901 replay (1)
Jimmy Logan, Notts County 1894 (3)
Jackie Milburn, Newcastle United 1951 (2), 1955 (1)
Nat Lofthouse, Bolton Wanderers 1953 (1), 1958 (2)
Bryan Robson, Manchester United 1983rep (2), 1990 (1)
Mark Hughes, Manchester United 1990 (2), 1994 (1)
Eric Cantona, Manchester United 1994 2 (2pens), 1996 (1)

## FA Cup final Hat-tricks

Only three men have ever scored a hat-trick in the cup final:
Billy Townley, Blackburn Rovers 1890 v Sheffield Wednesday (W 6-1)
Jimmy Logan, Notts County, 1894 v Everton (W 4-1)
Stan Mortensen, Blackpool 1953 v Bolton Wanderers (W 4-3)

Sandy Brown of Tottenham Hotspur scored three goals in the 1901 cup final: two against Sheffield United in the drawn final (2-2) and one in the replay which Tottenham won 3-1.

## Scored in Successive FA Cup finals

| | |
|---|---|
| Alexander Bonsor | 1875 Old Etonians (1) 1876 Old Etonians (1) |
| Jarvis Kenrick | 1877 Wanderers (1) 1878 Wanderers (2) |
| Jimmy Forrest | 1884 Blackburn R (1) 1885 Blackburn R (1) |
| James Brown | 1885 Blackburn R (1) 1886rep Blackburn R (1) |
| Billy Townley | 1890 Blackburn R (3) 1891 Blackburn R (1) |
| Jack Southworth | 1890 Blackburn R (1) 1891 Blackburn R (1) |
| Bobby Johnstone | 1955 Manchester C (1) 1956 Manchester C (1) |
| Bobby Smith | 1961 Tottenham H (1) 1962 Tottenham H (1) |
| Freddie Ljungberg | 2001 Arsenal (1) 2002 Arsenal (1) |

## Scored in three FA Cup final Matches (including replays)

Only three men have achieved this:

| | |
|---|---|
| Fred Priest | Sheffield United 1899 (1), 1901 (1), 1902rep (1) |
| Ian Rush | Liverpool 1986 (2), 1989 (2), 1992 (1) |
| Ian Wright | Crystal Palace 1990 (2), Arsenal 1993 (1), 1993rep (1) |

## Scored for Different Clubs in the FA Cup final

Only three men have achieved this:

| | |
|---|---|
| George Hedley | Sheffield United 1902 (1); Wolverhampton W 1908 (1) |
| Frank Stapleton | Arsenal 1979 (1); Manchester Utd 1983 (1) |
| Ian Wright | Crystal Palace 1990 (2); Arsenal 1993 (1) 1993rep (1) |

## Individual Scoring Record in Competition Proper

9 goals: Ted MacDougall for Bournemouth v Margate, 1st round, November 20, 1971

## Individual Scoring Record in Any FA Cup Match

Qualifying Competition:
10 goals: Chris Marron, for South Shields v Radcliffe Welfare United, Preliminary round, September 26, 1947. South Shields won 13-0.
10 goals: Paul Jackson for Stocksbridge Park Steels v Oldham Town, Preliminary round, August 31, 2002. Stocksbridge won 17-1.

## Individual scoring record in one season

19 – Jimmy Ross, Preston North End 1887-88
As following:

| | | | | *Ross's goals* |
|---|---|---|---|---|
| Oct 15 1887 | R1 v Hyde | won | 26-0 | 8 |
| Nov 26 | R2 v Everton | won | 6-1 | 1* |
| Dec 3 | R3 v Halliwell | won | 4-0 | 2 |
| Dec 10 | R4 v Bolton W | won | 9-1 | 6 |
| Jan 7 1888 | R5 v Aston V | won | 3-1 | 1 |
| Jan 30 | R6 v Sheffield W | won | 3-1 | 1 |
| Feb 18 | SF v Crewe Alex | won | 4-0 | 1 |
| Mar 24 | F v WBA | lost | 1-2 | 0 |

*Match declared void by FA.

Preston's 26-0 win over Hyde is the biggest win in FA Cup history. Preston were so confident of winning the final they asked if they could pose with the trophy before the match. Naturally, after that they were deservedly beaten. However they came back strongly winning the first ever cup and league double in 1889 with Ross scoring one of their goals in the 3-0 FA Cup final win over Wolves.

## Seven Goal Loser

Wilfred (Billy) Minter scored seven goals for St Albans City in a replayed FA Cup Fourth Qualifying round tie against Dulwich Hamlet on November 22, 1922. Dulwich won 8-7 – the only FA Cup tie ever to finish with that scoreline – and Minter became the only player in FA Cup history to score seven goals in one match and finish on the losing side.

## Successive Scoring

Dixie McNeill of Wrexham scored in 10 successive FA Cup rounds (18 goals) between November 26, 1977 and January 29, 1980.
Stan Mortensen of Blackpool scored in 16 out of 17 rounds (25 goals) between January 5, 1946 and January 27, 1951.

## Six or More Goals in One Match in Competition Proper

| | | | |
|---|---|---|---|
| 9 (1p) | Ted MacDougall | Bournemouth 11 Margate 0 | Nov 29 1971 |
| 8 | Jimmy Ross | Preston NE 26 Hyde 0 | Oct 15 1887 |
| 6 | Henry 'Harry' Cursham | Notts Co 11 Wednesbury Str 1 | Dec 12 1881 |
| | Jimmy Ross | Preston NE 9 Bolton W 1 | Dec 10 1887 |
| | Tommy Becton | Preston NE 18 Reading 0 | Jan 27 1894 |
| | George Hilsdon | Chelsea 9 Worksop Town 1 | Jan 11 1908 |
| | Ronnie Rooke | Fulham 6 Bury 0 | Jan 7 1939 |
| | Harold Atkinson | Tranmere Rovers 8 Ashington 1 | Nov 22 1952 |
| | George Best | Northampton T 2 Manchester Utd 8 | Feb 7 1970 |
| | Ted MacDougall | Bournemouth 8 Oxford City 1 | Nov 23 1970 |
| | Duane Darby | Hull City 8 Whitby Town 4 (aet) | Nov 26 1996 |
| * | Denis Law | Luton Town 1 Manchester City 6 | Jan 28 1961 |

**(Goals annulled when the match was abandoned after 69 minutes)*

## Five Goal Hauls Since 1945-46

| | | |
|---|---|---|
| Harry Brooks | Aldershot 7 Reading 3 | Nov 24 1945 |
| Harry Brooks | Aldershot 7 Newport (IOW) 0 | Dec 8 1945 |
| Les Eyre | Norwich City 7 Brighton & HA 2 | Nov 30 1946 |
| Hugh Billington | Luton Town 6 Notts County 0 | Jan 11 1947 |
| Jack Rowley | Manchester United 8 Yeovil Town 0 | Feb 12 1949 |
| Jack Shaw | Darlington 2 Rotherham United 7 | Nov 25 1950 |
| Ron Heckman | Leyton Orient 7 Lovell's Athletic 1 | Nov 19 1955 |
| George Bromilow | Southport 6 Ashton United 1 | Nov 19 1955 |
| Ron Saunders | Gillingham 10 Gorleston 1 | Nov 16 1957 |
| Les Allen | Tottenham Hotspur 13 Crewe Alex 2 | Feb 3 1960 |
| John Atyeo | Bristol City 11 Chichester City 0 | Nov 5 1960 |
| Jack Swindells | Altrincham 6 Scarborough 0 | Nov 13 1965 |
| Andy Lochhead | Burnley 7 Bournemouth 0 | Jan 25 1966 |
| Billy Best | Southend United 10 Brentwood Town 1 | Dec 7 1968 |
| *Tony Philliskirk | Peterborough 9 Kingstonian 1 | Nov 25 1992 |

**(Goals annulled when FA ordered match to be replayed after Kingstonian goalkeeper was hit by a coin thrown by Peterborough fans)*

**Note:** There are 30 instances of players scoring five goals in one FA Cup match before World War Two.

## Hat-tricks or Better in Successive Rounds Since 1945-46

| | | | |
|---|---|---|---|
| **Harry Brooks** | | | |
| 5 goals | R1 2L | Aldershot 7 Reading 3 | Nov 24 1945 |
| 5 goals | R2 1L | Aldershot 7 Newport (IOW) 0 | Dec 8 1945 |
| **Jack Shaw** | | | |
| 5 goals | R1 | Darlington 2 Rotherham Utd 7 | Nov 25 1950 |
| 3 goals | R2 | Rotherham United 3 Nottingham F 1 | Dec 9 1950 |
| **Ian Lawson** | | | |
| 4 goals | R3 | Burnley 7 Chesterfield 0 | Jan 5 1957 |
| 3 goals | R4 | Burnley 9 New Brighton 0 | Jan 26 1957 |
| **Derek Pace** | | | |
| 3 goals | R4 | Sheffield United 3 Nottingham F 0 | Jan 30 1960 |
| 3 goals | R5 | Sheffield United 3 Watford 2 | Feb 20 1960 |
| **Jimmy Greaves** | | | |
| 3 goals | R3rep | Tottenham Hotspur 5 Torquay Utd 1 | Jan 18 1965 |
| 3 goals | R4 | Tottenham Hotspur 5 Ipswich Town 0 | Jan 30 1965 |
| **Gary Moore** | | | |
| 3 goals | R1 | Southend Utd 9 King's Lynn 0 | Nov 16 1968 |
| 4 goals | R2 | Southend Utd 10 Brentwood Town 1 | Dec 7 1968 |
| **Billy Best** | | | |
| 3 goals | R1 | Southend Utd 9 King's Lynn 0 | Nov 16 1968 |
| 5 goals | R2 | Southend Utd 10 Brentwood Town 1 | Dec 7 1968 |
| **Dave Gwyther** | | | |
| 3 goals | R2 | Swansea City 6 Telford Utd 2 | Dec 12 1970 |
| 3 goals | R3 | Swansea City 6 Rhyl 1 | Jan 2 1971 |
| **Guy Whittingham** | | | |
| 3 goals | R3 | Portsmouth 5 Barnet 0 | Jan 5 1991 |
| 4 goals | R4 | Portsmouth 5 Bournemouth 1 | Jan 26 1991 |

**Note:** Clarke of Barrow scored hat-tricks in successive FA Cup matches in the two legs of the second round against Carlisle United on December 8 and 15, 1945. Barrow won the first leg 4-2 and the second leg 4-3.

Moore and Best of Southend are the only two players to both score successive hat-tricks in successive rounds for the same club. Between them they scored 15 of Southend's 19 goals in the two matches. Best's hat-trick against Brentwood was scored in three minutes, and is the fastest hat-trick on record in the Competition Proper.

**Fifteen players scored hat-tricks in successive rounds before the Second World War.**
The most noteworthy was Steve Bloomer who scored three in Derby County's 8-1 first round win over Barnsley on January 30, 1897 and another three in their 4-1 win over Bolton Wanderers in the second round two weeks later.

## Fastest Goal by a Substitute in the FA Cup final

Teddy Sheringham replaced the injured Roy Keane after 9 minutes of the 1999 FA Cup final and scored in the 11th minute, 96 seconds later, to put Manchester United 1-0 up against Newcastle United. Manchester United won 2-0 to complete the second leg of their League, FA Cup and European Cup treble.

## Fastest goal from a Penalty in the FA Cup final

Glenn Hoddle scored the fastest goal from a penalty in an FA Cup final after six minutes of the 1982 replay between Tottenham Hotspur and Queens Park Rangers. It was the only goal of the game and only the third time in FA Cup history the final was decided by a single goal from the penalty spot. The only other occasions were in 1922 when Huddersfield Town beat Preston NE and in 1938 when Preston NE beat Huddersfield Town.

## Fastest FA Cup Goal

The fastest goal in FA Cup history was scored by George Edwards of Aston Villa after 13 seconds of their third round tie against Manchester United at Villa Park on January 10, 1948. An astonishing game ended with eventual cup winners Manchester United beating Aston Villa 6-4 after leading 5-1 at one stage.

Billy Best's hat-trick for Southend against

Brentwood Town on December 7, 1968 is the quickest on record in the Competition Proper. All the goals came in a three-minute spell.

Andy Locke of Nantwich is credited with a hat-trick in 2 minutes 20 seconds during a First Qualifying round match against Droylesden on September 9, 1995. Nantwich won 3-0.

It is claimed that Preston scored six goals in seven minutes during their record 26-0 First Round win over Hyde on October 15, 1887.

## Goalscoring goalkeeper

Former QPR and Welsh international goalkeeper Tony Roberts made FA Cup history on October 27, 2001 when he became the first goalkeeper to score from open play in the competition. Playing for Dagenham and Redbridge at Basingstoke in the Fourth Qualifying round he scored with a last-minute equaliser to force a 2-2 draw and a replay which Dagenham won 3-0. They were eventually beaten by Ipswich Town in the Third Round.

## FA Cup final own goals

There have been relatively few own goals credited in the FA Cup final for the obvious reason that most scorers would claim the goal themselves and ignore any deflections the ball may have taken. But this collection lists the undoubted unfortunates to suffer the player's ultimate nightmare of scoring an own goal in the cup final:

**1877 Arthur Kinnaird The Wanderers.**
Scored own goal to put Oxford University 1-0 up. The Wanderers recovered to win 2-1.

**1946 Bert Turner Charlton Athletic.**
Turner deflected a shot from Derby's Dally Duncan into his own net after Peter Doherty had headed on a cross from Jack Stamps. That gave Derby a 1-0 lead after 85 minutes. A minute later Turner scored Charlton's equaliser from a free-kick. Derby won 4-1 after extra time.

**1960 Mick McGrath Blackburn Rovers.**
After 41 minutes Barry Stobbart of Wolves crossed low and hard into the Rovers' goalmouth. Goalkeeper Harry Leyland dived from his goal attempting to stop the cross reaching Norman Deeley, when McGrath, trying to intercept, turned the ball behind his own goalkeeper and into the net. Wolves won 3-0.

**1981 Tommy Hutchison Manchester City.**
Hutchison had given City a 29th minute lead over Tottenham Hotspur with a great diving header and City still led by that goal after 79 minutes when Spurs were awarded a free-kick just outside City's penalty area. Glenn Hoddle curled the ball beyond the City wall, but the ball struck Hutchison, who had broken off from behind the wall, and the deflection *(cont. p808)*

## Fastest FA Cup final Goals

At least five goals have been scored in the first minute of the FA Cup final, and the fastest on record is Bob Chatt's 40-second goal for Aston Villa which proved to be the only goal of the 1895 cup final against West Bromwich Albion, the first final played at the Crystal Palace.

Some sources give the scorer as Jack Devey, who may have got a deflection off goalkeeper Joe Reader's legs – but every modern publication either officially or semi-officially endorsed by Aston Villa FC credits Chatt as the scorer.

| | | | | |
|---|---|---|---|---|
| 40secs | Bob Chatt | Aston Villa v WBA | 1-0 | April 20 1895 |
| 42secs | Roberto Di Matteo | Chelsea v Middlesbrough | 2-0 | May 17 1997 |
| 45secs | Jackie Milburn | Newcastle U v Manchester C | 3-1 | May 7 1955 |
| 50secs | Fred Spiksley | Sheffield W v Wolves | 2-1 | Apr 18 1896 |
| 55secs | James Roscamp | Blackburn R v Huddersfield | 3-1 | Apr 21 1928 |
| 2min | George Hedley | Sheffield U v Southampton | 2-1r | Apr 26 1902 |
| 2min | Harry Hampton | Aston Villa v Newcastle U | 2-0 | Apr 15 1905 |
| 2min | David Jack | Bolton W v West Ham U | 2-0 | Apr 28 1923 |
| 2min | Jackie Palethorpe | Sheffield W v WBA | 4-2 | Apr 27 1935 |
| 2min | Nat Lofthouse | Bolton W v Blackpool | 3-4 | May 2 1953 |
| 2min | Clive Allen | Tottenham H v Coventry C | 2-3 | May 16 1987 |
| 3min | Joe Hayes | Manchester C v Birmingham C | 3-1 | May 5 1956 |
| 3min | Nat Lofthouse | Bolton W v Manchester U | 2-0 | May 3 1958 |
| 3min | Jimmy Greaves | Tottenham H v Burnley | 3-1 | May 5 1962 |

**Note:** David Jack's goal for Bolton against West Ham in 1923 was the first goal ever scored in the cup final at Wembley.

## Latest FA Cup Final Goals

With penalties less than a minute away, Andy Linighan of Arsenal scored the latest goal to decide any FA Cup final in 1993. The match was deep into injury time at the end of extra time at the end of the replay when Linighan headed in a corner to give Arsenal a 2-1 victory over Sheffield Wednesday. Referee Keren Barratt blew for time after 44 seconds of further playing time.

Previously the latest goal had been in the replayed final of 1912 when Harry Tufnell scored two minutes before the end of extra time to give Barnsley a 1-0 win over West Bromwich Albion after the teams had drawn the first match 0-0.

The latest goal in the cup final itself came in the 119th minute of the 1938 final when George Mutch scored with his famous penalty to give Preston NE a 1-0 extra time win over Huddersfield Town.

| | | | | |
|---|---|---|---|---|
| **Replay – extra time** | | | | |
| 119min 16secs | Andy Linighan | Arsenal v Sheffield Wed | 2-1 | May 20 1993 |
| 118min | Harry Tufnell | Barnsley v WBA | 1-0 | Apr 24 1912 |
| **Final – extra time** | | | | |
| 119min | George Mutch | Preston NE v Huddersfield | 1-0 | Apr 30 1938 |
| 115min | Terry Fenwick | QPR v Tottenham Hotspur | 1-1 | May 22 1982 |
| 114min | Chris Duffy | Charlton A v Burnley | 1-0 | Apr 26 1947 |
| 113min | Ian St John | Liverpool v Leeds Utd | 2-1 | May 1 1965 |
| 113min | Mark Hughes | Manchester Utd v Crystal Palace | 3-3 | May 12 1990 |
| 111min | Charlie George | Arsenal v Liverpool | 2-1 | May 8 1971 |
| 110min | Glenn Hoddle | Tottenham Hotspur v QPR | 1-1 | May 22 1982 |
| **Final – normal time** | | | | |
| 90 min | Bill Perry | Blackpool v Bolton W | 4-3 | May 2 1953 |
| 90 min | Ronnie Boyce | West Ham Utd v Preston NE | 3-2 | May 2 1964 |
| 89 min | Fred Priest | Sheffield Utd v Derby County | 4-1 | Apr 15 1899 |
| 89 min | George Simpson | Sheffield Wed v Everton | 2-1 | Apr 20 1907 |
| 89 min | Stan Mortensen | Blackpool v Bolton W | 4-3 | May 2 1953 |
| 89 min | Ellis Rimmer | Sheffield Wed v WBA | 4-2 | Apr 27 1935 |
| 89 min | Geoff Hurst | West Ham Utd v Preston NE | 3-2 | May 2 1964 |
| 89 min | Alan Sunderland | Arsenal v Manchester Utd | 3-2 | May 12 1979 |
| 89 min | Stuart McCall | Everton v Liverpool | 2-3 | May 20 1989 |
| 88 min | Archie Hunter | Aston Villa v WBA | 2-0 | Apr 2 1887 |
| 88 min | Harry Wood | Southampton v Sheffield Utd | 1-1 | Apr 19 1902 |
| 88 min | Joe Kitchen | Sheffield U v Chelsea | 3-0 | Apr 24 1915 |
| 88 min | Jack Lambert | Arsenal v Huddersfield | 2-0 | Apr 26 1930 |
| 88 min | Norman Deeley | Wolves v Blackburn Rovers | 3-0 | May 7 1960 |
| 88 min | Kevin Keegan | Liverpool v Newcastle | 3-0 | May 4 1974 |
| 88 min | Sammy McIlroy | Manchester Utd v Arsenal | 2-3 | May 12 1979 |
| 88 min | Michael Owen | Liverpool v Arsenal | 2-1 | May 12 2001 |

## FA Cup Miscellany

### Travelling Forest

Nottingham Forest are the only club to have been drawn to play FA Cup matches in all four home countries.

In 1885 they drew their semi-final with Queen's Park at Derby and then lost the replay in the grounds of the Merchiston Castle School in Edinburgh.

In February 1889 they drew 2-2 at home with Linfield Athletic in a first round match. By the time they got to Belfast for the replay, Linfield had announced they had scratched from the competition and Forest gained a walkover. They played a friendly instead, which Linfield won 3-1.

In February 1922 Forest completed the set of all four home countries when they lost 4-1 in a third round match at Cardiff City.

### Scored in Every Round

Unless a team went from the preliminary round of the FA Cup to the final, no-one can actually score in "every" round of the cup. Pedantry dispensed with then, these are the 12 men who have scored in every round possible in one season from the time their club enters through to the final.

| *Year* | *Player* | *Club* | *A* | *B* | *C* | *D* | *Result* |
|---|---|---|---|---|---|---|---|
| 1887 | Archie Hunter | Aston Villa | 10 | 7 | 11 | 40 | Won |
| 1901 | Sandy Brown | Tottenham H | 8 | 7 | 15 | 20 | Won |
| 1905 | Harry Hampton | Aston Villa | 6 | 5 | 7 | 18 | Won |
| 1929 | Harold Blackmore | Bolton W | 8 | 6 | 7 | 17 | Won |
| 1935 | Ellis Rimmer | Sheffield W | 6 | 6 | 8 | 15 | Won |
| 1937 | Frank O'Donnell | Preston NE | 6 | 6 | 11 | 20 | Lost |
| 1948 | Stan Mortensen | Blackpool | 6 | 6 | 10 | 20 | Lost |
| 1951 | Jackie Milburn | Newcastle U | 8 | 6 | 8 | 18 | Won |
| 1953 | Nat Lofthouse | Bolton W | 8 | 7 | 8 | 16 | Lost |
| 1954 | Charlie Wayman | Preston NE | 8 | 6 | 7 | 20 | Lost |
| 1968 | Jeff Astle | WBA | 10 | 7 | 9 | 17 | Won |
| 1970 | Peter Osgood | Chelsea | 8 | 6 | 8 | 25 | Won |

Key: A – Total FA Cup games played by the club;
B – Number of games in which the player scored
C – His total goals
D – Club's total goals

Hunter completed his 'set' at Kennington Oval, Brown completed his at the Crystal Palace (and he also scored in the replayed final at Burnden Park, Bolton), Hampton completed his at the Crystal Palace. Blackmore, Rimmer, O'Donnell, Mortensen, Milburn, Lofthouse, Wayman and Astle all scored in the final at Wembley. Osgood scored in the replayed final at Old Trafford.

gave City keeper Joe Corrigan no chance. The match ended 1-1. Spurs won the replay 3-2.

**1987 Gary Mabbutt Tottenham Hotspur.**
A speculative shot-cum-cross from Lloyd McGrath six minutes into extra time caught Mabbutt on the left knee and the ball looped high over stranded Spurs keeper Ray Clemence and into the back of the net for Coventry's 3-2 winner. Mabbutt had scored a scrappy goal (which some at first credited as an own goal by Coventry skipper Brian Kilcline) to give Spurs a 2-1 lead after 40 minutes. Mabbutt thus became the third player after Turner and Hutchison to score for both sides in the final, but at least he had something to celebrate four years later.

**1991 Des Walker Nottingham Forest.**
Walker had played and scored for Spurs as a junior – but he would rather forget the only senior goal he ever scored for the club. It came four minutes into extra time with Nottingham Forest and Spurs level at 1-1. A corner by Nayim was touched on by Paul Stewart, and Walker in attempting to clear from a Spurs player headed the ball high into his own net. The Spurs player waiting to pounce on the end of the cross ? None other than Gary Mabbutt. That proved to be the winning goal for Spurs who beat Nottingham Forest 2-1 for what was then a record eighth victory in the competition.

## FA Cup Miscellany

### Medal Mix Ups

In 1914 the FA Cup final medals were inscribed 'English Cup' instead of 'FA Cup'. In 1992, Sunderland, beaten by Liverpool in the final were handed the winners medals and Liverpool were given the runners-up medals in error. The players exchanged them afterwards.

In 1970 David Webb failed to collect his winners medal after scoring the winning goal for Chelsea against Leeds United in the replay at Old Trafford. He had swapped his shirt with a Leeds player and a jobsworth refused to let him up into the directors' box where the presentation was taking place believing that he was a Leeds player. He received it afterwards in the dressing room.

# FA CUP FINAL GOALSCORING CHART

This chart shows the order in which the goals were scored in every cup final. Some of the times of goals scored in the early years are untraced

| | | 1st | 2nd | 3rd | 4th | 5th |
|---|---|---|---|---|---|---|
| **1872** | **Wanderers 1 Royal Engineeers 0** | Betts *1-0* | | | | |
| **1873** | **Wanderers 2 Oxford Univ 0** | Wollaston *1-0* | Kinnaird *2-0* | | | |
| **1874** | **Oxford Univ 2 R Engineers 0** | Mackarness *1-0* | Patton *2-0* | | | |
| **1875** | **R Engineers 1 Old Etonians 1**aet | Bonsor *30 0-1* | Renny-Tailyour *40 1-1* | | | |
| **Rep** | **R Engineers 2 Old Etonians 0** | Renny-Tailyour *1-0* | Stafford *2-0* | | | |
| **1876** | **Wanderers 1 Old Etonians 1** | Edwards *35 1-0* | Bonsor *50 1-1* | | | |
| **Rep** | **Wanderers 3 Old Etonians 0** | Wollaston *1-0* | Hughes *2-0* | Hughes *3-0* | | |
| **1877** | **Wanderers 2 Oxford Univ 1**aet | Kinnaird og *0-1* | Kenrick *1-1* | Lindsay *2-1* | | |
| **1878** | **Wanderers 3 R Engineers 1** | Kenrick *5 1-0* | "rush" *1-1* | Kinnaird *2-1* | Kenrick *3-1* | |
| **1879** | **Old Etonians 1 Clapham R 0** | Clerke *65 1-0* | | | | |
| **1880** | **Clapham R 1 Oxford Univ 0** | Lloyd-Jones *80 1-0* | | | | |
| **1881** | **O Carthusians 3 O Etonians 0** | Page *1-0* | Wynyard *2-0* | Parry *3-0* | | |
| **1882** | **Old Etonians 1 Blackburn R 0** | Macauley *8 1-0* | | | | |
| **1883** | **Blackburn Oly 2 Old Etonians 1** | Goodhart *30 0-1* | Matthews *1-1* | Costley *2-1* | | |
| **1884** | **Blackburn R 2 Queen's Park 1** | Sowerbutts *1-0* | Forrest *2-0* | Christie *2-1* | | |
| **1885** | **Blackburn R 2 Queen's Park 0** | Forrest *14 1-0* | Brown *58 2-0* | | | |
| **1886** | **Blackburn R 0 WBA 0** | | | | | |
| **Rep** | **Blackburn R 2 WBA 0** | Sowerbutts *1-0* | Brown *2-0* | | | |

| | | 1st | 2nd | 3rd | 4th | 5th | 6th | 7th |
|---|---|---|---|---|---|---|---|---|
| **1903** | **Bury 6 Derby Co 0** | Ross<br>*20 1-0* | Sagar<br>*48 2-0* | Leeming<br>*56 3-0* | Wood<br>*57 4-0* | Plant<br>*59 5-0* | Leeming<br>*75 6-0* | |
| **1904** | **Manchester C 1 Bolton W 0** | Meredith<br>*23 1-0* | | | | | | |
| **1905** | **Aston Villa 2 Newcastle U 0** | Hampton<br>*2 1-0* | Hampton<br>*76 2-0* | | | | | |
| **1906** | **Everton 1 Newcastle U 0** | Young<br>*75 1-0* | | | | | | |
| **1907** | **Sheffield W 2 Everton 1** | Stewart<br>*21 1-0* | Sharp<br>*38 1-1* | Simpson<br>*89 2-1* | | | | |
| **1908** | **Wolves 3 Newcastle U 1** | Hunt<br>*40 1-0* | Hedley<br>*43 2-0* | Howie<br>*73 1-2* | Harrison<br>*85 3-1* | | | |
| **1909** | **Manchester U 1 Bristol C 0** | Turnbull<br>*22 1-0* | | | | | | |
| **1910** | **Newcastle U 1 Barnsley 1** | Tufnell<br>*37 0-1* | Rutherford<br>*83 1-1* | | | | | |
| **Rep** | **Newcastle U 2 Barnsley 0** | Shepherd<br>*52 1-0* | Shepherd<br>*62p 2-0* | | | | | |
| **1911** | **Bradford C 0 Newcastle U 0** | | | | | | | |
| **Rep** | **Bradford C 1 Newcastle U 0** | Speirs<br>*15 1-0* | | | | | | |
| **1912** | **Barnsley 0 WBA 0** | | | | | | | |
| **Rep** | **Barnsley 1 WBA 0**aet | Tufnell<br>*118 1-0* | | | | | | |
| **1913** | **Aston Villa 1 Sunderland 0** | Barber<br>*75 1-0* | | | | | | |
| **1914** | **Burnley 1 Liverpool 0** | Freeman<br>*58 1-0* | | | | | | |
| **1915** | **Sheffield U 3 Chelsea 0** | Simmons<br>*36 1-0* | Fazackerley<br>*84 2-0* | Kitchen<br>*88 3-0* | | | | |
| **1920** | **A Villa 1 Huddersfield T 0**aet | Kirton<br>*100 1-0* | | | | | | |
| **1921** | **Tottenham H 1 Wolves 0** | Dimmock<br>*53 1-0* | | | | | | |

| | | 1st | 2nd | 3rd | 4th | 5th | 6th | 7th |
|---|---|---|---|---|---|---|---|---|
| **1887** | **Aston Villa 2 WBA 0** | Hodgetts<br>*1-0* | Hunter<br>*88 2-0* | | | | | |
| **1888** | **WBA 2 Preston NE 1** | Bayliss<br>*8 1-0* | Dewhurst<br>*52 1-1* | Woodall<br>*77 2-1* | | | | |
| **1889** | **Preston NE 3 Wolves 0** | Dewhurst<br>*15 1-0* | Ross<br>*25 2-0* | Thompson<br>*70 3-0* | | | | |
| **1890** | **Blackburn R 6 Sheffield W 1** | Townley<br>*6 1-0* | Walton<br>*35 2-0* | Townley<br>*3-0* | J Southworth<br>*4-0* | Mumford<br>*4-1* | Townley<br>*5-1* | Lofthouse<br>*6-1* |
| **1891** | **Blackburn R 3 Notts Co 1** | Dewar<br>*8 1-0* | J Southworth<br>*30 2-0* | Townley<br>*35 3-0* | Oswald<br>*70 1-3* | | | |
| **1892** | **WBA 3 Aston Villa 0** | Geddes<br>*4 1-0* | Nicholls<br>*27 2-0* | Reynolds<br>*55 3-0* | | | | |
| **1893** | **Wolves 1 Everton 0** | Allen<br>*60 1-0* | | | | | | |
| **1894** | **Notts Co 4 Bolton W 1** | Watson<br>*18 1-0* | Logan<br>*29 2-0* | Logan<br>*67 3-0* | Logan<br>*70 4-0* | Cassidy<br>*87 1-4* | | |
| **1895** | **Aston Villa 1 WBA 0** | Chatt<br>*1 1-0* | | | | | | |
| **1896** | **Sheffield W 2 Wolves 1** | Spiksley<br>*1 1-0* | Black<br>*8 1-1* | Spiksley<br>*18 2-1* | | | | |
| **1897** | **Aston Villa 3 Everton 2** | Campbell<br>*18 1-0* | Bell<br>*23 1-1* | Boyle<br>*28 1-2* | Wheldon<br>*35 2-2* | Crabtree<br>*44 3-2* | | |
| **1898** | **Nottm F 3 Derby Co 1** | Capes<br>*19 1-0* | Bloomer<br>*31 1-1* | Capes<br>*42 2-1* | McPherson<br>*86 3-1* | | | |
| **1899** | **Sheffield U 4 Derby Co 1** | Boag<br>*0-1* | Bennett<br>*1-1* | Beers<br>*2-1* | Almond<br>*3-1* | Priest<br>*4-1* | | |
| **1900** | **Bury 4 Southampton 0** | McLuckie<br>*9 1-0* | W Wood<br>*16 2-0* | McLuckie<br>*23 3-0* | Plant<br>*80 4-0* | | | |
| **1901** | **Tottenham H 2 Sheffield U 2** | Priest<br>*10 0-1* | Brown<br>*23 1-1* | Brown<br>*51 2-1* | Bennett<br>*52 2-2* | | | |
| **Rep** | **Tottenham H 3 Sheffield U 1** | Priest<br>*40 0-1* | Cameron<br>*52 1-1* | Smith<br>*76 2-1* | Brown<br>*87 3-1* | | | |
| **1902** | **Sheffield U 1 Southampton 1** | Common<br>*55 1-0* | H Wood<br>*88 1-1* | | | | | |
| **Rep** | **Sheffield U 2 Southampton 1** | Hedley<br>*2 1-0* | Brown<br>*70 1-1* | Barnes<br>*79 2-1* | | | | |

| | | 1st | 2nd | 3rd | 4th | 5th | 6th | 7th |
|---|---|---|---|---|---|---|---|---|
| **1939** | **Portsmouth 4, Wolves 1** | Barlow *29 1-0* | Anderson *43 2-0* | Parker *46 3-0* | Dorsett *54 3-1* | Parker *71 4-1* | | |
| **1946** | **Derby Co 4 Charlton A 1**aet | Bert Turner *85og 1-0* | Bert Turner *86 1-1* | Doherty *92 2-1* | Stamps *97 3-1* | Stamps *106 4-1* | | |
| **1947** | **Charlton A 1 Burnley 0**aet | Duffy *114 1-0* | | | | | | |
| **1948** | **Manchester U 4 Blackpool 2** | Shimwell *12p 0-1* | Rowley *28 1-1* | Mortensen *35 1-2* | Rowley *70 2-2* | Pearson *80 3-2* | Anderson *82 4-2* | |
| **1949** | **Wolves 3 Leicester C 1** | Pye *13 1-0* | Pye *42 2-0* | Griffiths *46 2-1* | Smyth *47 3-1* | | | |
| **1950** | **Arsenal 2 Liverpool 0** | Lewis *18 1-0* | Lewis *63 2-0* | | | | | |
| **1951** | **Newcastle U 2 Blackpool 0** | Milburn *50 1-0* | Milburn *55 2-0* | | | | | |
| **1952** | **Newcastle U 1 Arsenal 0** | G Robledo *84 1-0* | | | | | | |
| **1953** | **Blackpool 4 Bolton W 3** | Lofthouse *2 1-0* | Mortensen *35 1-1* | Moir *39 1-2* | Bell *55 1-3* | Mortensen *68 2-3* | Mortensen *89 3-3* | Perry *90 4-3* |
| **1954** | **WBA 3 Preston NE 2** | Allen *21 1-0* | Morrison *22 1-1* | Wayman *51 1-2* | Allen *63p 2-2* | Griffin *87 3-2* | | |
| **1955** | **Newcastle U 3 Manchester C 1** | Milburn *1 1-0* | Johnstone *44 1-1* | Mitchell *53 2-1* | Hannah *60 3-1* | | | |
| **1956** | **Manchester C 3 Birmingham C 1** | Hayes *3 1-0* | Kinsey *15 1-1* | Dyson *65 2-1* | Johnstone *68 3-1* | | | |
| **1957** | **Aston V 2 Manchester U 1** | McParland *68 1-0* | McParland *73 2-0* | Taylor *83 2-1* | | | | |
| **1958** | **Bolton W 2 Manchester U 0** | Lofthouse *3 1-0* | Lofthouse *50 2-0* | | | | | |
| **1959** | **Nottingham F 2 Luton T 1** | Dwight *10 1-0* | Wilson *14 2-0* | Pacey *62 2-1* | | | | |
| **1960** | **Wolves 3 Blackburn R 0** | McGrath *41og 1-0* | Deeley *67 2-0* | Deeley *88 3-0* | | | | |
| **1961** | **Tottenham H 2 Leicester C 0** | Smith *70 1-0* | Dyson *77 2-0* | | | | | |
| **1962** | **Tottenham H 3 Burnley 1** | Greaves *3 1-0* | Robson *50 1-1* | Smith *51 2-1* | Blanchflower *80p 3-1* | | | |

| | | 1st | 2nd | 3rd | 4th | 5th | 6th | 7th |
|---|---|---|---|---|---|---|---|---|
| **1922** | **Huddersfield T 1 Preston NE 0** | Smith<br>*67p 1-0* | | | | | | |
| **1923** | **Bolton W 2 West Ham 0** | Jack<br>*2 1-0* | JR Smith<br>*53 2-0* | | | | | |
| **1924** | **Newcastle U 2 Aston V 0** | Harris<br>*83 1-0* | Seymour<br>*85 2-0* | | | | | |
| **1925** | **Sheffield U 1 Cardiff C 0** | Tunstall<br>*30 1-0* | | | | | | |
| **1926** | **Bolton W 1 Manchester C 0** | Jack<br>*76 1-0* | | | | | | |
| **1927** | **Cardiff C 1 Arsenal 0** | Ferguson<br>*74 1-0* | | | | | | |
| **1928** | **Blackburn R 3 Huddersfield T 1** | Roscamp<br>*1 1-0* | McLean<br>*22 2-0* | Jackson<br>*55 2-1* | Roscamp<br>*85 3-1* | | | |
| **1929** | **Bolton W 2 Portsmouth 0** | Butler<br>*79 1-0* | Blackmore<br>*87 2-0* | | | | | |
| **1930** | **Arsenal 2 Huddersfield T 0** | James<br>*16 1-0* | Lambert<br>*88 2-0* | | | | | |
| **1931** | **WBA 2 Birmingham 1** | Richardson<br>*25 1-0* | Bradford<br>*57 1-1* | Richardson<br>*58 2-1* | | | | |
| **1932** | **Newcastle U 2 Arsenal 1** | John<br>*15 0-1* | Allen<br>*38 1-1* | Allen<br>*72 2-1* | | | | |
| **1933** | **Everton 3 Manchester C 0** | Stein<br>*41 1-0* | Dean<br>*52 2-0* | Dunn<br>*80 3-0* | | | | |
| **1934** | **Manchester C 2 Portsmouth 1** | Rutherford<br>*26 0-1* | Tilson<br>*73 1-1* | Tilson<br>*87 2-1* | | | | |
| **1935** | **Sheffield W 4 WBA 2** | Palethorpe<br>*2 1-0* | Boyes<br>*21 1-1* | Hooper<br>*70 2-1* | Sandford<br>*75 2-2* | Rimmer<br>*85 3-2* | Rimmer<br>*89 4-2* | |
| **1936** | **Arsenal 1 Sheffield U 0** | Drake<br>*75 1-0* | | | | | | |
| **1937** | **Sunderland 3 Preston NE 1** | O'Donnell<br>*44 0-1* | Gurney<br>*52 1-1* | Carter<br>*70 2-1* | Burbanks<br>*87 3-1* | | | |
| **1938** | **Preston NE 1 Huddersfield T 0** | Mutch<br>*119p 1-0* | | | | | | |

| | | 1st | 2nd | 3rd | 4th | 5th | 6th | 7th |
|---|---|---|---|---|---|---|---|---|
| **1980** | **West Ham 1 Arsenal 0** | Brooking<br>*13 1-0* | | | | | | |
| **1981** | **Tottenham H 1 Manchester C 1**aet | Hutchison<br>*29 0-1* | Hutchison<br>*79og 1-1* | | | | | |
| **Rep** | **Tottenham H 3 Manchester C 2** | Villa<br>*8 1-0* | McKenzie<br>*11 1-1* | Reeves<br>*50p 1-2* | Crooks<br>*60 2-2* | Villa<br>*76 3-2* | | |
| **1982** | **Tottenham H 1, QPR 1**aet | Hoddle<br>*110 1-0* | Fenwick<br>*115 1-1* | | | | | |
| **Rep** | **Tottenham H 1 QPR 0** | Hoddle<br>*6p 1-0* | | | | | | |
| **1983** | **Manchester U 2 Brighton 2**aet | Smith<br>*14 0-1* | Stapleton<br>*55 1-1* | Wilkins<br>*72 2-1* | Stevens<br>*87 2-2* | | | |
| **Rep** | **Manchester U 4 Brighton 0** | Robson<br>*25 1-0* | Whiteside<br>*30 2-0* | Robson<br>*44 3-0* | Muhren<br>*62p 4-0* | | | |
| **1984** | **Everton 2 Watford 0** | Sharp<br>*38 1-0* | Gray<br>*51 2-0* | | | | | |
| **1985** | **Manchester U 1 Everton 0**aet | Whiteside<br>*100 1-0* | | | | | | |
| **1986** | **Liverpool 3 Everton 1** | Lineker<br>*28 0-1* | Rush<br>*57 1-1* | Johnston<br>*63 2-1* | Rush<br>*84 3-1* | | | |
| **1987** | **Coventry C 3 Tottenham H 2**aet | Allen<br>*2 0-1* | Bennett<br>*9 1-1* | Mabbutt<br>*40 1-2* | Houchen<br>*63 2-2* | Mabbutt<br>*96og 3-2* | | |
| **1988** | **Wimbledon 1 Liverpool 0** | Sanchez<br>*37 1-0* | | | | | | |
| **1989** | **Liverpool 3 Everton 2**aet | Aldridge<br>*4 1-0* | McCall<br>*89 1-1* | Rush<br>*94 2-1* | McCall<br>*102 2-2* | Rush<br>*104 3-2* | | |
| **1990** | **Manchester U 3 Crystal P 3**aet | O'Reilly<br>*19 0-1* | Robson<br>*35 1-1* | Hughes<br>*62 2-1* | Wright<br>*70 2-2* | Wright<br>*92 2-3* | Hughes<br>*113 3-3* | |
| **Rep** | **Manchester U 1 Crystal P 0** | Martin<br>*59 1-0* | | | | | | |
| **1991** | **Tottenham H 2 Nottm F 1**aet | Pearce<br>*15 0-1* | Stewart<br>*53 1-1* | Walker<br>*94og 2-1* | | | | |
| **1992** | **Liverpool 2 Sunderland 0** | Thomas<br>*47 1-0* | Rush<br>*68 2-0* | | | | | |

| | | 1st | 2nd | 3rd | 4th | 5th | 6th | 7th |
|---|---|---|---|---|---|---|---|---|
| **1963** | **Manchester U 3 Leicester C 1** | Law<br>*30 1-0* | Herd<br>*57 2-0* | Keyworth<br>*80 2-1* | Herd<br>*85 3-1* | | | |
| **1964** | **West Ham 3 Preston NE 2** | Holden<br>*9 0-1* | Sissons<br>*10 1-1* | Dawson<br>*40 1-2* | Hurst<br>*89 2-2* | Boyce<br>*90 3-2* | | |
| **1965** | **Liverpool 2 Leeds U 1**aet | Hunt<br>*93 1-0* | Bremner<br>*95 1-1* | St John<br>*113 2-1* | | | | |
| **1966** | **Everton 3 Sheffield W 2** | McCalliog<br>*4 0-1* | Ford<br>*57 0-2* | Trebilcock<br>*59 1-2* | Trebilcock<br>*64 2-2* | Temple<br>*80 3-2* | | |
| **1967** | **Tottenham H 2 Chelsea 1** | Robertson<br>*40 1-0* | Saul<br>*67 2-0* | Tambling<br>*85 2-1* | | | | |
| **1968** | **WBA 1 Everton 0**aet | Astle<br>*93 1-0* | | | | | | |
| **1969** | **Manchester C 1 Leicester C 0** | Young<br>*24 1-0* | | | | | | |
| **1970** | **Chelsea 2 Leeds U 2**aet | Charlton<br>*21 0-1* | Houseman<br>*41 1-1* | Jones<br>*84 1-2* | Hutchinson<br>*86 2-2* | | | |
| **Rep** | **Chelsea 2 Leeds U 1**aet | Jones<br>*35 0-1* | Osgood<br>*78 1-1* | Webb<br>*104 2-1* | | | | |
| **1971** | **Arsenal 2 Liverpool 1**aet | Heighway<br>*91 0-1* | Kelly<br>*101 1-1* | George<br>*111 2-1* | | | | |
| **1972** | **Leeds U 1 Arsenal 0** | Clarke<br>*53 1-0* | | | | | | |
| **1973** | **Sunderland 1 Leeds U 0** | Porterfield<br>*30 1-0* | | | | | | |
| **1974** | **Liverpool 3 Newcastle U 0** | Keegan<br>*57 1-0* | Heighway<br>*74 2-0* | Keegan<br>*88 3-0* | | | | |
| **1975** | **West Ham 2 Fulham 0** | Taylor<br>*60 1-0* | Taylor<br>*64 2-0* | | | | | |
| **1976** | **Southampton 1 Manchester U 0** | Stokes<br>*82 1-0* | | | | | | |
| **1977** | **Manchester U 2 Liverpool 1** | Pearson<br>*50 1-0* | Case<br>*52 1-1* | J Greenhoff<br>*55 2-1* | | | | |
| **1978** | **Ipswich T 1 Arsenal 0** | Osborne<br>*77 1-0* | | | | | | |
| **1979** | **Arsenal 3 Manchester U 2** | Talbot<br>*12 1-0* | Stapleton<br>*43 2-0* | McQueen<br>*86 2-1* | McIlroy<br>*88 2-2* | Sunderland<br>*89 3-2* | | |

| | | 1st | 2nd | 3rd | 4th | 5th | 6th | 7th |
|---|---|---|---|---|---|---|---|---|
| **1993** | **Arsenal 1 Sheffield W 1**aet | Wright *20 1-0* | Hirst *61 1-1* | | | | | |
| **Rep** | **Arsenal 2 Sheffield W 1**aet | Wright *34 1-0* | Waddle *68 1-1* | Linighan *119 2-1* | | | | |
| **1994** | **Manchester U 4 Chelsea 0** | Cantona *60p 1-0* | Cantona *66p 2-0* | Hughes *69 3-0* | McClair *90 4-0* | | | |
| **1995** | **Everton 1 Manchester U 0** | Rideout *30 1-0* | | | | | | |
| **1996** | **Manchester U 1 Liverpool 0** | Cantona *85 1-0* | | | | | | |
| **1997** | **Chelsea 2 Middlesbrough 0** | Di Matteo *42secs 1-0* | Newton *83 2-0* | | | | | |
| **1998** | **Arsenal 2 Newcastle U 0** | Overmars *23 1-0* | Anelka *70 2-0* | | | | | |
| **1999** | **Manchester U 2 Newcastle U 0** | Sheringham *11 1-0* | Scholes *53 2-0* | | | | | |
| **2000** | **Chelsea 1 Aston V 0** | Di Matteo *73 1-0* | | | | | | |
| **2001** | **Liverpool 2 Arsenal 1** | Ljungberg *72 0-1* | Owen *83 1-1* | Owen *88 2-1* | | | | |
| **2002** | **Arsenal 2 Chelsea 0** | Parlour *70 1-0* | Ljungberg *80 2-0* | | | | | |
| **2003** | **Arsenal 1 Southampton 0** | Pires *38 1-0* | | | | | | |

# THE OLDEST AND YOUNGEST CUP FINALISTS

The following lists those players known to have played in the FA Cup final after their 36th birthdays. It is possible that some players aged 36 and over may have appeared in some of the early finals, but their dates of birth have never been verified.

Arsenal goalkeeper David Seaman (2001, 2002 and 2003) played in three FA Cup finals after he was 36, while former Arsenal keeper George Swindin (1950 and 1952) played in two Cup finals after he was 36.

Seaman also became the oldest goalkeeper to play in the cup final with Arsenal in 2003 – making him the third oldest cup finalist of all time.

Ray Clemence has the longest span between his first FA Cup final and his last. He first appeared in 1971 for Liverpool against Arsenal and made his final appearance for Tottenham against Coventry 16 years later.

Joe Mercer became the oldest man to captain a team in the FA Cup final with Arsenal in 1952. He has also captained them in 1950. Glenn Hoddle is one of only two men to appear in the cup final as a player/manager with Chelsea in 1994.

## The Oldest Cup Finalists

*Many players on this list also appeared in Cup finals before they were 36.*

| | | | |
|---|---|---|---|
| Walter (Billy) Hampson | 1924 | Newcastle Utd | 41 years 257 days |
| John Oakes | 1946 | Charlton Athletic | 40 years 226 days |
| David Seaman (gk) | 2003 | Arsenal | 39 years 241 days |
| George Baddeley | 1912 | WBA | 38 years 11mths |
| Ray Clemence (gk) | 1987 | Tottenham Hotspur | 38 years 284 days |
| David Seaman (gk) | 2002 | Arsenal | 38 years 228 days |
| Warney Cresswell | 1933 | Everton | 38 years 175 days |
| George Swindin (gk) | 1952 | Arsenal | 38 years 89 days |
| Jimmy McMullan | 1933 | Manchester City | 38 years 34 days |
| Billy Evans | 1892 | Aston Villa | 38 years 31 days |
| Frank Jefferis | 1922 | Preston NE | 37 years 300 days |
| Joe Mercer (capt) | 1952 | Arsenal | 37 years 268 days |
| David Seaman (gk) | 2001 | Arsenal | 37 years 234 days |
| Archie Goodall | 1903 | Derby County | 37 years 8 months |
| Leslie Compton | 1950 | Arsenal | 37 years 229 days |
| John Osborne (gk) | 1968 | WBA | 37 years 210 days |
| Stanley Matthews | 1953 | Blackpool | 37 years 152 days |
| Stan Hanson (gk) | 1953 | Bolton W | 37 years 126 days |
| Syd Owen (capt) | 1959 | Luton Town | 37 years 63 days |
| Lee Dixon | 2001 | Arsenal | 37 years 56 days |
| James Kirkpatrick | 1878 | Wanderers | 37 years 1 day |
| Edward Bowen (gk) | 1873 | Wanderers | 36 years 364 days |
| Jack Charlton | 1972 | Leeds Utd | 36 years 363 days |
| Jimmy Blair | 1925 | Cardiff City | 36 years 349 days |
| William Merriman (gk) | 1875 | Royal Engineers | 36 years 348 days |
| Ted Vizard | 1926 | Bolton W | 36 years 321 days |
| Bert Turner | 1946 | Charlton Athletic | 36 years 312 days |
| Joe Smith (capt) | 1926 | Bolton W | 36 years 302 days |
| Neville Southall (gk) | 1995 | Everton | 36 years 245 days |
| Glenn Hoddle (p/m) | 1994 | Chelsea | 36 years 198 days |
| Bob Kelly | 1930 | Huddersfield Town | 36 years 161 days |
| Gary McAllister | 2001 | Liverpool | 36 years 138 days |
| Dick Pym (gk) | 1929 | Bolton W | 36 years 85 days |
| George Swindin (gk) | 1950 | Arsenal | 36 years 84 days |
| Danny Blanchflower (capt) | 1962 | Tottenham Hotspur | 36 years 84 days |
| Don Welsh (capt) | 1947 | Charlton Athletic | 36 years 60 days |
| Jack Brown (gk) | 1935 | Sheffield Wed | 36 years 39 days |
| Stuart Pearce | 1998 | Newcastle Utd | 36 years 22 days |
| Alex Munro | 1948 | Blackpool | 36 years 18 days |

**(note:** in all case only the players whose birthdates have been verified are included)

## Youngest Cup Finalists

James Frederick McLeod Prinsep, who was born in India on July 27, 1861, played for Clapham Rovers against Old Etonians in the cup final on March 29, 1879, becoming the youngest ever cup finalist at the age of 17 years 245 days – 11 days younger than Paul Allen when he played for West Ham 101 years later.

Although he gained only a loser's medal in 1879, he collected a winners medal two years later when he played for Old Carthusians in their 3-0 victory over Old Etonians. He was 19 years and 256 days old.

But even then, as early as 1881, he was not the first teenager to play in two cup finals. That honour fell to Robert Walpole Sealy Vidal who played for Wanderers against Royal Engineers in the first FA Cup final in 1872 as an 18-year-old and for Oxford University, against Wanderers in 1873. He also played for Oxford University when they beat Royal Engineers 2-0 in the 1874 final.

Three players appear twice in the list of teenage finalists: James Prinsep (1879 and 1881), Robert Walpole Sealy Vidal (1872 and 1873) and David McCreery (1976 and 1977).

McCreery is the only teenager to have played in two Wembley FA Cup finals – coming on as a substitute in both 1976 and 1977. Johnny Mapson, Sunderland's goalkeeper in their winning 1937 team is the 'oldest' teenager, turning 20 the day after the final.

The youngest goalkeeper to play in any FA Cup final is Peter Shilton, who was 19 years 220 days old when he made his only final appearance for Leicester in 1969.

| | | | |
|---|---|---|---|
| James Prinsep | 1879 | Clapham Rovers | 17 years 245 days |
| Paul Allen | 1980 | West Ham Utd | 17 years 256 days |
| Howard Kendall | 1964 | Preston NE | 17 years 345 days |
| Walter Norris | 1881 | Old Carthusians | 18 years 1 day |
| James Ward | 1883 | Blackburn Rovers | 18 years 3 days |
| Norman Whiteside | 1983 | Manchester Utd | 18 years 14 days |
| Cliff Bastin | 1930 | Arsenal | 18 years 43 days |
| Alex Dawson | 1958 | Manchester Utd | 18 years 71 days |
| Cecil Keith-Falconer | 1879 | Clapham Rovers | 18 years 169 days |
| Robert Vidal | 1872 | Wanderers | 18 years 195 days |
| William Sellar | 1885 | Queens Park | 18 years 195 days |
| Johnny Sissons | 1964 | West Ham Utd | 18 years 215 days |
| Tommy Caton | 1981 | Manchester City | 18 years 215 days |
| David McCreery | 1976 | Manchester Utd | 18 years 228 days |
| Edward Growse | 1879 | Clapham Rovers | 18 years 264 days |
| Lee Sinnott | 1984 | Watford | 18 years 312 days |
| Chris Bart-Williams | 1993 | Sheffield Wed | 18 years 333 days |
| Joe Lofthouse | 1884 | Blackburn Rovers | 18 years 349 days |
| Albert Geldard | 1933 | Everton | 19 years 18 days |
| Alfred Lyttleton | 1876 | Old Etonians | 19 years 33 days |
| Nicolas Anelka | 1998 | Arsenal | 19 years 33 days |
| Joe Royle | 1968 | Everton | 19 years 40 days |
| Billy Bassett | 1888 | WBA | 19 years 57 days |
| Gareth Barry | 2000 | Aston Villa | 19 years 86 days |
| Billy Williams | 1895 | WBA | 19 years 90 days |
| Joe Hayes | 1955 | Manchester City | 19 years 106 days |
| Philip Neville | 1996 | Manchester Utd | 19 years 110 days |
| Malcolm Manley | 1969 | Leicester City | 19 years 146 days |
| Dickie Dorsett | 1939 | Wolverhampton W | 19 years 147 days |
| Joseph Vintcent | 1881 | Old Carthusians | 19 years 148 days |
| William Rawson | 1874 | Oxford University | 19 years 151 days |
| Steve Mackenzie | 1981 | Manchester City | 19 years 167 days |
| Tommy Booth | 1969 | Manchester City | 19 years 168 days |
| Warren Neill | 1982 | QPR | 19 years 182 days |
| Graham Cross | 1963 | Leicester City | 19 years 191 days |
| Bobby Charlton | 1957 | Manchester Utd | 19 years 205 days |
| Robert WS Vidal | 1873 | Oxford University | 19 years 208 days |
| Peter Shilton (gk) | 1969 | Leicester City | 19 years 220 days |
| Bertram Rogers | 1880 | Oxford University | 19 years 228 days |

| | | | |
|---|---|---|---|
| Jim McCalliog | 1966 | Sheffield Wed | 19 years 233 days |
| James Brown | 1882 | Blackburn Rovers | 19 years 237 days |
| Howard Spencer | 1895 | Aston Villa | 19 years 240 days |
| William Anderson | 1881 | Old Etonians | 19 years 240 days |
| Sam Ellis | 1966 | Sheffield Wed | 19 years 244 days |
| Frederick Rawson | 1879 | Clapham Rovers | 19 years 245 days |
| Alan Kennedy | 1974 | Newcastle Utd | 19 years 246 days |
| David McCreery | 1977 | Manchester Utd | 19 years 248 days |
| David Bardsley | 1984 | Watford | 19 years 251 days |
| Percy De Paravacini | 1882 | Old Etonians | 19 years 253 days |
| Wilf Smith | 1966 | Sheffield Wed | 19 years 253 days |
| James FM Prinsep | 1881 | Old Carthusians | 19 years 256 days |
| Evelyn Waddington | 1877 | Oxford University | 19 years 262 days |
| Roy Keane | 1991 | Nottingham Forest | 19 years 253 days |
| Ray Kennedy | 1971 | Arsenal | 19 years 284 days |
| Ernie Curtis | 1927 | Cardiff City | 19 years 307 days |
| Mervyn Day (gk) | 1975 | West Ham Utd | 19 years 311 days |
| Arthur Albiston | 1977 | Manchester Utd | 19 years 311 days |
| Johnny Mapson (gk) | 1937 | Sunderland | 19 years 364 days |

## The Oldest FA Cup final Scorers

Even though the careers of players today are longer than they were in the past, it is still a relatively rare occurrence for a player to score a goal in the cup final after his 30th birthday. Only the 33 men listed below have done so.

It is nearly 60 years since Bert Turner became the oldest man to score in the final, and in recent years only Tommy Hutchison has come close to overhauling Turner's record, or of passing Danny Blanchflower and Jack Charlton in the all-time list of older scorers.

Coincidentally, though, Hutchison, who played for Manchester City in the 1981 final against Tottenham, did equal one feat that Turner performed in the 1946 final. Both men scored for both sides and were the only ones to do so in a final at Wembley.

Turner put through his own goal after 80 minutes to give Derby the lead – but made amends 60 seconds later with Charlton's equaliser. Derby won 4-1 in extra time.

Hutchison scored with a header to put Manchester City ahead against Spurs in the 29th minute of the 100th Cup final in 1981 – but 10 minutes from time he deflected Glenn Hoddle's free-kick into his own net for the equaliser. Tottenham went on to win the first final to be replayed at Wembley 3-2 five days later.

| | | | |
|---|---|---|---|
| Bert Turner | 1946 | Charlton Athletic | 36 years 312 days |
| Bert Turner (og) | 1946 | Derby County | 36 years 312 days |
| Danny Blanchflower (pen) | 1962 | Tottenham Hotspur | 36 years 84 days |
| Jack Charlton | 1970 | Leeds Utd | 34 years 338 days |
| Tommy Hutchison (og) | 1981 | Tottenham Hotspur | 33 years 229 days |
| Tommy Hutchison | 1981 | Manchester City | 33 years 229 days |
| Doug Holden | 1964 | Preston NE | 33 years 217 days |
| Teddy Sheringham | 1999 | Manchester Utd | 33 years 50 days |
| Arnold Muhren (pen) | 1983 | Manchester Utd | 32 years 358 days |
| Peter Doherty | 1946 | Derby County | 32 years 326 days |
| Nat Lofthouse (2) | 1958 | Bolton W | 32 years 248 days |
| Jimmy Dunn | 1933 | Everton | 32 years 155 days |
| Bryan Robson | 1990 | Manchester Utd | 32 years 121 days |
| Bob John | 1932 | Arsenal | 32 years 80 days |
| George Ross | 1903 | Bury | 32 years 67 days |
| Charlie Wayman | 1954 | Preston NE | 31 years 350 days |
| Stan Mortensen (3) | 1953 | Blackpool | 31 years 341 days |
| Trevor Brooking | 1980 | West Ham Utd | 31 years 221 days |
| Willie Moir | 1953 | Bolton W | 31 years 13 days |
| Fred Tilson (2) | 1934 | Manchester City | 31 years 9 days |
| Jackie Milburn | 1955 | Newcastle Utd | 30 years 361 days |

| | | | |
|---|---|---|---|
| Stan Seymour | 1924 | Newcastle Utd | 30 years 345 days |
| Jimmy Greenhoff | 1977 | Manchester Utd | 30 years 336 days |
| Paul Rideout | 1995 | Everton | 30 years 279 days |
| Bobby Mitchell | 1955 | Newcastle Utd | 30 years 264 days |
| John Aldridge | 1989 | Liverpool | 30 years 244 days |
| Ian Rush | 1992 | Liverpool | 30 years 202 days |
| Bobby Gurney | 1937 | Sunderland | 30 years 200 days |
| Mark Hughes | 1994 | Manchester Utd | 30 years 194 days |
| Brian McClair | 1994 | Manchester Utd | 30 years 157 days |
| Joe Bradford | 1931 | Birmingham | 30 years 93 days |
| Mal Griffiths | 1949 | Leicester City | 30 years 53 days |
| Reg Lewis (2) | 1950 | Arsenal | 30 years 53 days |
| Jimmy Howie | 1908 | Newcastle Utd | 30 years 37 days |
| Angus Morrison | 1954 | Preston NE | 30 years 5 days |

## The Youngest FA Cup Final Scorers

When Norman Whiteside scored for Manchester United against Brighton in the 1983 cup final replay he became the youngest player ever to score in a cup final, and obviously the youngest to score in a Wembley final. He is also the sixth youngest player to score in a Wembley FA Cup final, earning that distinction when he scored in the 1985 final to give Manchester Utd a 1-0 victory over Everton, the club he later joined.

The previous youngest scorer at Wembley was West Ham's Johnny Sissons who scored in his side's win over Preston in 1964. Remarkably, Geoff Hurst and Ronnie Boyce, West Ham's other scorers in that match, all feature among the 22 youngest players to have scored in a cup final at Wembley.

James Forrest of Blackburn held the record for the youngest scorer in the cup final from 1884 until 1939 when Dicky Dorsett became the youngest player to score at Wembley – a record he then held until 1964. Sandy Brown's two entries represent his goals in the 1901 FA Cup final and the replay a week later.

| | | | |
|---|---|---|---|
| Norman Whiteside | 1983 | Manchester Utd | 18 years 18 days |
| Johnny Sissons | 1964 | West Ham Utd | 18 years 216 days |
| Nicolas Anelka | 1998 | Arsenal | 19 years 33 days |
| Dicky Dorsett | 1939 | Wolverhampton W | 19 years 147 days |
| Steve Mackenzie | 1981 | Manchester City | 19 years 172 days |
| Jim McCalliog | 1966 | Sheffield Wed | 19 years 234 days |
| James Forrest | 1884 | Blackburn Rovers | 19 years 277 days |
| Harry Hampton (2) | 1905 | Aston Villa | 19 years 359 days |
| Edward Wynyard | 1881 | Old Carthusians | 20 years 8 days |
| Norman Whiteside | 1985 | Manchester Utd | 20 years 11 days |
| Gary Stevens | 1983 | Brighton & HA | 20 years 56 days |
| William Stafford | 1875 | Royal Engineers | 20 years 87 days |
| Eddie Kelly | 1971 | Arsenal | 20 years 90 days |
| Joe Hayes | 1956 | Manchester City | 20 years 106 days |
| Jimmy Dimmock | 1921 | Tottenham Hotspur | 20 years 139 days |
| Charlie George | 1971 | Arsenal | 20 years 210 days |
| William Anderson | 1882 | Old Etonians | 20 years 219 days |
| James Forrest | 1885 | Blackburn Rovers | 20 years 283 days |
| David Ford | 1966 | Sheffield Wed | 21 years 73 days |
| Ronnie Boyce | 1964 | West Ham Utd | 21 years 118 days |
| Michael Owen (2) | 2001 | Liverpool | 21 years 148 days |
| Mike Trebilcock (2) | 1966 | Everton | 21 years 166 days |
| Alan Taylor (2) | 1975 | West Ham Utd | 21 years 170 days |
| Charles Clerke | 1879 | Old Etonians | 21 years 201 days |
| Ian Hutchinson | 1970 | Chelsea | 21 years 250 days |
| Jack Dyson | 1956 | Manchester City | 21 years 303 days |
| Alf Common | 1902 | Sheffield Utd | 21 years 329 days |
| WG Richardson (2) | 1931 | WBA | 21 years 330 days |

| | | | |
|---|---|---|---|
| Sandy Brown (2) | 1901 | Tottenham Hotspur | 22 years 13 days |
| Sandy Brown | 1901rep | Tottenham Hotspur | 22 years 20 days |
| Jimmy Greaves | 1962 | Tottenham Hotspur | 22 years 74 days |
| Lee Martin | 1990 | Manchester Utd | 22 years 101 days |
| Geoff Hurst | 1964 | West Ham Utd | 22 years 147 days |
| Jimmy Robertson | 1967 | Tottenham Hotspur | 22 years 155 days |
| David Pacey | 1959 | Luton Town | 22 years 212 days |
| Frank Stapleton | 1979 | Arsenal | 22 years 306 days |

## Oldest Cup Final Goalkeepers

David Seaman became the oldest goalkeeper in FA Cup final history when he played for Arsenal against Southampton in 2003 aged 39 years 241 days. The following lists all the goalkeepers to have played in the cup final on or after their 34th birthdays.

| | | | |
|---|---|---|---|
| David Seaman | 2003 | Arsenal | 39 years 241 days |
| Ray Clemence | 1987 | Tottenham Hotspur | 38 years 283 days |
| David Seaman | 2002 | Arsenal | 38 years 228 days |
| George Swindin | 1952 | Arsenal | 38 years 89 days |
| David Seaman | 2001 | Arsenal | 37 years 234 days |
| John Osborne | 1968 | WBA | 37 years 210 days |
| Stan Hanson | 1953 | Bolton W | 37 years 126 days |
| James Kirkpatrick | 1878 | Wanderers | 37 years 1 day |
| Edward Bowen | 1873 | Wanderers | 36 years 364 days |
| William Merriman | 1875 | Royal Engineers | 36 years 348 days |
| Sam Hardy | 1920 | Aston Villa | 36 years 275 days |
| Neville Southall | 1995 | Everton | 36 years 245 days |
| Dickie Pym | 1929 | Bolton W | 36 years 85 days |
| George Swindin | 1950 | Arsenal | 36 years 84 days |
| Jack Brown | 1935 | Sheffield Wed | 36 years 39 days |
| Peter Schmeichel | 1999 | Manchester Utd | 35 years 183 days |
| Vic Woodley | 1946 | Derby County | 35 years 0 days |
| Pat Jennings | 1980 | Arsenal | 34 years 333 days |
| Alex Stepney | 1977 | Manchester Utd | 34 years 245 days |
| David Seaman | 1998 | Arsenal | 34 years 238 days |
| Bruce Grobbelaar | 1992 | Liverpool | 34 years 216 days |
| Cyril Sidlow | 1950 | Liverpool | 34 years 154 days |
| Gil Merrick | 1956 | Birmingham City | 34 years 100 days |
| Tony Norman | 1992 | Sunderland | 34 years 75 days |
| Arthur Goodchild | 1926 | Manchester City | 34 years 0 days |

## Youngest Cup Final Goalkeepers

Peter Shilton set records throughout his playing career, but he only played in one FA Cup final. Still, he managed to set a record as the youngest ever FA Cup final goalkeeper even if he did end the day with a runners-up medal after his Leicester City side lost 1-0 to Manchester City in 1969.

| | | | |
|---|---|---|---|
| Peter Shilton | 1969 | Leicester City | 19 years 220 days |
| Mervyn Day | 1975 | West Ham Utd | 19 years 311 days |
| Johnny Mapson | 1937 | Sunderland | 19 years 364 days |
| Gary Sprake | 1965 | Leeds Utd | 20 years 28 days |
| Frank Swift | 1934 | Manchester City | 20 years 123 days |
| Gary Bailey | 1979 | Manchester Utd | 20 years 277 days |
| Ronnie Simpson | 1952 | Newcastle Utd | 21 years 205 days |
| Ben Roberts | 1997 | Middlesbrough | 21 years 328 days |
| Pat Jennings | 1967 | Tottenham Hotspur | 21 years 342 days |
| Bob Hesford | 1938 | Huddersfield Town | 22 years 17 days |
| David Harvey | 1970 | Leeds Utd (replay) | 22 years 81 days |

| | | | |
|---|---|---|---|
| Eddie Hopkinson | 1958 | Bolton W | 22 years 186 days |
| Peter Hucker | 1982 | QPR | 22 years 206 days |
| Bobby Mimms | 1986 | Everton | 22 years 210 days |
| David Gaskell | 1963 | Manchester Utd | 22 years 232 days |
| Ray Clemence | 1971 | Liverpool | 22 years 277 days |
| George Walker | 1939 | Portsmouth | 22 years 344 days |
| Harold Pearson | 1931 | WBA | 22 years 352 days |
| Gordon West | 1966 | Everton | 23 years 21 days |
| Ted Sagar | 1933 | Everton | 23 years 81 days |

# Guests of Honour Since 1923

King George V was the first reigning monarch to attend the FA Cup final when he saw Burnley beat Liverpool 1-0 at Crystal Palace in 1914. Although the 1958 programme welcomes the Queen and the Duke of Edinburgh as the Royal Guests of Honour, the Queen did not actually attend the match as she was suffering from a bad cold and presumably watched Bolton Wanderers beat Manchester United 2-0 on her television.

Since the final moved to Wembley in 1923, the principal guests of honour have been:

1923 King George V, The Duke of Devonshire
1924 Duke of York
1925 Duke of York
1926 King George V
1927 King George V
1928 King George V and Queen Mary
1929 Prince of Wales
1930 King George V
1931 Duke of Gloucester
1932 King George V and Queen Mary
1933 Duke of York
1934 King George V
1935 Prince of Wales
1936 Sir Charles Clegg, FA President
1937 King George VI and Queen Elizabeth
1938 King George VI
1939 King George VI
1946 King George VI, Queen Elizabeth, Princess Elizabeth
1947 Duke and Duchess of Gloucester
1948 King George VI
1949 Princess Elizabeth and Duke of Gloucester
1950 King George VI
1951 King George VI and Queen Elizabeth
1952 Sir Winston Churchill
1953 Queen Elizabeth II
1954 Queen Mother and Princess Margaret
1955 Queen Elizabeth II, Duke of Edinburgh, Princess Margaret
1956 Queen Elizabeth II and Duke of Edinburgh
1957 Queen Elizabeth II and Duke of Edinburgh
1958 Duke of Edinburgh
1959 Queen Elizabeth II and Duke of Edinburgh
1960 Duke and Duchess of Gloucester
1961 Duchess of Kent
1962 Queen Elizabeth II and Duke of Edinburgh
1963 Queen Elizabeth II and Duke of Edinburgh
1964 Earl of Harewood
1965 Queen Elizabeth Ii and Duke of Edinburgh
1966 Princess Margaret
1967 Duke and Duchess of Kent
1968 Princess Alexandra
1969 Princess Anne
1970 Princess Margaret
1970r Dr Andrew Stephen, Chairman of the FA
1971 Duke and Duchess of Kent
1972 Queen Elizabeth II and Duke of Edinburgh
1973 Duke of Kent
1974 Princess Anne and Duke of Kent
1975 Duke and Duchess of Kent
1976 Queen Elizabeth II and Duke of Edinburgh
1977 Duke and Duchess of Kent
1978 Princess Alexandra
1979 Prince of Wales
1980 Duke and Duchess of Kent
1981 Queen Mother
1981r Prince Michael of Kent
1982 Princess Anne
1982r Duke of Kent
1982 Duke of Kent
1983 Duke of Kent
1983r Princess Michael of Kent
1984 Duke and Duchess of Kent
1985 Duke of Kent
1986 Duchess of Kent
1987 Duchess of Kent
1988 Princess of Wales
1989 Duke and Duchess of Kent
1990 Duke and Duchess of Kent
1990r Duke and Duchess of Kent
1991 Prince and Princess of Wales, Duke and Duchess of Kent
1992 Duke and Duchess of Kent
1993 Duke and Duchess of Kent
1993r Duchess of Kent
1994 Duchess of Kent
1995 Prince of Wales, Duke of Kent
1996 Duke and Duchess of Kent

| | |
|---|---|
| 1997 | Duke and Duchess of Kent |
| 1998 | Duke and Duchess of Kent |
| 1999 | Prince of Wales, Duke and Duchess of Kent |
| 2000 | Duke of Kent |
| 2001 | Duke of Kent |
| 2002 | Lennart Johansson, President of UEFA |
| 2003 | Sir Bobby Robson |

# FA Cup and Non-League Clubs

Since the League football began in 1888, only three clubs from outside the League have reached the FA Cup final. Sheffield Wednesday, then known as The Wednesday, were the first to do so in 1890, followed by Southampton (1900 and 1902) and Tottenham Hotspur (1901).

Spurs are the only Non-League club to have won the FA Cup.

Since the re-organisation of the competition in 1925 only five Non-League clubs have reached Round Five – the last 16. Kidderminster Harriers were the last to do so in 1994.

## Non-League FA Cup Winners

| | | |
|---|---|---|
| Tottenham H | (SL) | 1900-01 |

## Non-League Beaten Finalists

| | | |
|---|---|---|
| Sheffield Wed | (FAll) | 1889-90 |
| Southampton | (SL) | 1899-1900 |
| Southampton | (SL) | 1901-02 |

## Non-League Beaten Semi-Finalists

| | | |
|---|---|---|
| Nottingham F | (FAll) | 1891-92 |
| Southampton | (SL) | 1897-98 |
| Millwall | (SL) | 1899-1900 |
| Millwall | (SL) | 1902-03 |
| Southampton | (SL) | 1907-08 |
| Swindon Town | (SL) | 1909-10 |
| Swindon Town | (SL) | 1911-12 |

## Non-League Clubs in the Last Eight

| | | |
|---|---|---|
| Birmingham St G | (FAll) | 1888-89 |
| Chatham | (n/af) | 1888-89 |
| Sheffield Wed | (FAll) | 1888-89 |
| Bootle | (FAll) | 1889-90 |
| Nottingham F | (FAll) | 1890-91 |
| Stoke | (FAll) | 1890-91 |
| Sheffield Wed | (FAll) | 1890-91 |
| Sheffield Wed | (FAll) | 1891-92 |
| Middlesbrough Iron | (NL) | 1892-93 |
| Southampton | (SL) | 1898-99 |
| Tottenham H | (SL) | 1898-99 |
| Reading | (SL) | 1900-01 |
| Portsmouth | (SL) | 1901-02 |
| Tottenham H | (SL) | 1902-03 |
| Tottenham H | (SL) | 1903-04 |
| Southampton | (SL) | 1904-05 |
| Fulham | (SL) | 1904-05 |
| Southampton | (SL) | 1905-06 |
| Crystal Palace | (SL) | 1906-07 |
| Coventry City | (SL) | 1909-10 |
| QPR | (SL) | 1909-10 |
| Swindon | (SL) | 1910-11 |
| West Ham | (SL) | 1910-11 |
| QPR | (SL) | 1913-14 |

Since the competition was reorganised in 1925 the best performances by Non-League clubs have been the following who all reached Round Five – the last 16.

| | | |
|---|---|---|
| Colchester U | (SL) | 1947-48 |
| Yeovil Town | (SL) | 1948-49 |
| Blyth Spartans | (NL) | 1977-78 |
| Telford United | (APL) | 1984-85 |
| Kidderminster H | (Conf) | 1993-94 |

In 1919-20, Cardiff City and Plymouth Argyle, then both in the Southern League, reached the Third Round, the equivalent of today's Fifth Round, the last 16.

## Biggest Wins By Non-League Clubs Against League Clubs

| | | | | |
|---|---|---|---|---|
| 18.11.1905 | 3q | 7-1 | Crystal Palace (SL) | v Chelsea (D2) |
| 24.02.1906 | 3 | 6-1 | Southampton (SL) | v Middlesbrough (D1) |
| 24.11.1934 | 1 | 1-6 | Carlisle United (3N) | v Wigan Athletic (CC) |
| 28.11.1936 | 1 | 6-1 | Walthamstow Ave (AL) | v Northampton T (3S) |
| 10.12.1955 | 1 | 1-6 | Derby Co (3N) | v Boston Utd (ML) |
| 07.12 1957 | 1 | 6-1 | Hereford Utd (SL) | v QPR (3S) |
| 21.11.1970 | 1 | 6-1 | Barnet (SL) | v Newport County (D4) |

## Biggest Wins By League Clubs Against Non-League Clubs

*(note this table only includes matches played since the formation of the Football League in 1888)*

| | | | | |
|---|---|---|---|---|
| 27.01.1894 | 1 | 18-0 | Preston (D1) | v Reading (n/af) |
| 01.02.1890 | 2 | 13-0 | Bolton W (D1) | v Sheffield Utd |

| | | | | |
|---|---|---|---|---|
| 17.01.1891 | 1 | 13-1 | Aston Villa (D1) | v Casuals (n/af) |
| 02.02.1897 | 1r | 12-1 | Bury (D1) | v Stockton (NL) |
| 13.01.1906 | 1 | 11-0 | Aston Villa (D1) | v Kings Lynn (N&S) |
| | 1 | 11-0 | Bristol City (D3) | v Chichester City (SCL) |
| 20.11.1971 | 1 | 11-0 | Bournemouth (D3) | v Margate (SL) |
| 02.02.1895 | 1 | 11-1 | Sunderland (D1) | v Fairfield (LL) |
| | 3 | 11-1 | Arsenal (D1) | v Darwen (LC) |
| 11.11.1995 | 1 | 11-2 | Shrewsbury Town (D2) | v Marine (NPL) |
| 01.02.1937 | 1r | 11-3 | Bradford City (D2) | v Walker Celtic (NEL) |
| 24.01.1912 | 1r | 10-0 | Wolverhampton W (D2) | v Watford (SL) |

Nottingham Forest's 14-0 victory over Clapton in January 1891 is still the biggest away win in the cup since the formation of the Football League, but occurred when Nottingham Forest were members of the Football Alliance. Wolves' 14-0 win over Crosswell's Brewery in 1886 is not included as it took place two years before the League's formation.

## Other Big Wins: League Clubs Against Non-League Clubs in Qualifying Rounds

| | | | | |
|---|---|---|---|---|
| 13.10.1894 | 1q | 13-0 | Leicester Fosse (D2) | v Notts Olympic |
| 12.10.1895 | 1q | 13-0 | Lincoln City (D2) | v Peterborough Club |
| 14.10.1893 | 1q | 12-0 | Woolwich Arsenal (D2) | v Ashford United |
| | 1q | 12-0 | Brighton & HA (3S) | v Shoreham |
| | 4q | 12-1 | Gainsborough Trinity (D2) | v Weymouth |
| | 3q | 11-0 | Walsall (D2) | v Dresden United |
| | 1q | 11-0 | Leeds City (D2) | v Morley |
| 17.10.1908 | 2q | 11-0 | Bradford Park Avenue (D2) | v Denby Dale |
| 14.12.1912 | 5q | 11-1 | Glossop North End (D2) | v Southall |

## Victories By Non-League Clubs Over the League Champions

*Four Non-League clubs have beaten the League champions in the FA Cup.*

| | | |
|---|---|---|
| 17.01.1891 | 1 | Stoke (FAll) 3, Preston North End 0 |
| 05.03.1900 | 3 2r | Millwall Athletic (SL) 2, Aston Villa 1 |
| | | *match played at Reading after two drawn games* |
| 08.02.1902 | 2 | Southampton (SL) 4, Liverpool 1 |
| 09.01.1915 | 1 | Swansea Town (SL) 1, Blackburn Rovers 0 |

Stoke's win came less than two years after Preston had won the double – Millwall's win over Aston Villa less than three years after Villa had won the double.

## Victories By Non-League Clubs Over the FA Cup Holders

| | | |
|---|---|---|
| 23.02.1901 | 2 | Tottenham H (SL) 2, Bury 1 |
| 03.02.1902 | 1 | Southampton (SL) 2, Tottenham H (SL) 1 |
| | | *match played at Reading after two drawn games* |
| 11.01.1908 | 1 | Norwich City (SL) 2, Sheffield Wed 0 |
| 21.01.1909 | 1r | Crystal Palace (SL) 4, Wolverhampton W 2 |
| | | *after a 2-2 draw* |

## Victories By Non-League Clubs Over Top Division Clubs

From the formation of the Football League in 1888 until the re-organisation of the competition in 1925, there were 83 victories by Non-League clubs over top division clubs, the majority of these were recorded by Southern League clubs who regularly beat clubs from both the old First and Second Divisions of the Football League.

The most notable victories achieved by non-Southern League clubs over Division One clubs during this period were:

| | | |
|---|---|---|
| 14.01.1911 | 1 | Bristol City 0, Crewe Alexandra (BDL) 3 |
| 14.01.1911 | 1 | Sheffield United 0, Darlington (NEL) 1 |
| 14.01.1920 | 2r | Sheffield Wed 0, Darlington (NEL) 2 |
| 12.01.1924 | 1 | Corinthians (n/af) 1, Blackburn Rovers 0 |
| **Since World War Two:** | | |
| 10.01.1948 | 3 | Colchester United (SL) 1, Huddersfield Town 0 |

| | | |
|---|---|---|
| 29.01.1949 | 4 | Yeovil Town (SL) 2, Sunderland 1aet |
| 05.02.1972 | 3r | Hereford United (SL) 2, Newcastle United 1 |
| 04.01.1975 | 3 | Burnley 0, Wimbledon (SL) 1 |
| 14.01.1986 | 3 | Birmingham City 1, Altrincham (Conf) 2 |
| 07.01.1989 | 3 | Sutton United (Conf) 2, Coventry City 1 |

## Non-League Clubs Victories Over Clubs From Old Second Division (new First Division) Since 1948

| | | |
|---|---|---|
| 24.01.1948 | 4 | Colchester United (SL) 3, Bradford PA 2 |
| 08.01.1949 | 3 | Yeovil Town (SL) 3, Bury 1 |
| 02.01.1955 | 3r | Bishop Auckland (NL) 3, Ipswich Town 0 |
| 03.01.1957 | 3 | Notts County 1, Rhyl Athletic (CC) 3 |
| 09.01.1957 | 3r | Lincoln City 4, Peterborough United (ML) 5aet |
| 15.01.1959 | 3 | Worcester City (SL) 2, Liverpool 1 |
| 09.01.1960 | 3 | Ipswich Town 2, Peterborough United (ML) 3 |
| 04.01.1964 | 3 | Newcastle United 1, Bedford Town (SL) 2 |
| 06.02.1978 | 4 | Stoke City 2, Blyth Spartans (NL) 3 |
| 05.01.1980 | 3r | Harlow Town (IL) 1, Leicester City 0 |
| 05.01.1991 | 3 | West Bromwich Albion 2, Woking (IL) 4 |
| 04.11.1993 | 1 | Halifax Town (Conf) 2 West Bromwich Albion 1 |
| 08.01.1994 | 3 | Birmingham City 1, Kidderminster H (Conf) 2 |
| 03.01.1998 | 3 | Swindon Town 1, Stevenage Borough (Conf) 2 |

## Non-League Clubs Progression (since 1925)

The Top 20 Non-League FA Cup records since 1924-25 based on number of appearances in the Competition Proper:

| | *Competition Proper: Appearances* | *R1* | *R2* | *R3* | *R4* | *R5* | *Victories over FL clubs* |
|---|---|---|---|---|---|---|---|
| Yeovil Town | 49 | 24 | 12 | 12 | - | 1 | 20 |
| Kettering Town | 46 | 33 | 9 | 3 | 1 | - | 14 |
| Telford United | 34 | 24 | 7 | 1 | 1 | 1 | 11 |
| Scarborough | 34 | 22 | 8 | 4 | - | - | 9 |
| Boston United | 32 | 22 | 6 | 4 | - | - | 5 |
| Enfield | 31 | 13 | 14 | 3 | 1 | - | 11 |
| Weymouth | 31 | 21 | 7 | 2 | 1 | - | 5 |
| Bath City | 30 | 13 | 11 | 6 | - | - | 11 |
| Blyth Spartans | 29 | 17 | 10 | 1 | - | 1 | 8 |
| Barnet | 29 | 20 | 4 | 5 | - | - | 2 |
| Altrincham | 28 | 12 | 8 | 7 | 1 | - | 16 |
| Hereford United | 28 | 12 | 11 | 4 | 1 | - | 12 |
| Chelmsford City | 28 | 18 | 8 | 1 | 1 | - | 3 |
| Gainsborough T | 26 | 12 | 13 | 1 | - | - | 5 |
| Wycombe W | 26 | 16 | 8 | 2 | - | - | 3 |
| Dartford | 26 | 17 | 7 | 2 | - | - | 3 |
| Grantham Town | 25 | 13 | 9 | 3 | - | - | 2 |
| Northwich V | 24 | 13 | 9 | - | 1 | 1 | 6 |
| Bishop Auckland | 23 | 13 | 9 | - | 1 | - | 3 |
| Kidderminster H | 23 | 20 | 2 | - | - | 1 | 2 |

**Notes:**

1] Victories over League Clubs include only matches played when the clubs listed above were not members of the Football League and their opponents were in the Football League at the time the match was played.

2] Victories over League clubs include those in the qualifying rounds of the competition. League clubs regularly played in the qualifying rounds from the 1890s until reorganisation in 1925.

3] Northwich Victoria's Fifth Round appearance occurred in 1884.

## Most Victories Over Football League Clubs in One Season:

1900-01 Tottenham H (SL)
1984-85 Telford United (APL)

The largest representation of Non-League clubs in the Third Round since the competition was re-organised in 1925 is six in 1978. They were Blyth Spartans (NL), Enfield (IL), Scarborough (NPL), Tilbury (IL), Wealdstone (SL) and Wigan Athletic (NPL). Blyth Spartans and Enfield were drawn to play each other. Blyth won 1-0.

The highest number to reach the Fourth Round is three in 1957 and 1975. In 1957 Rhyl (CC), New Brighton (LC) and Peterborough United (ML) reached the last 32, while Wimbledon (SL), Stafford Rangers (NPL) and Leatherhead (IL) did so in 1975.

It is now more than 50 years (1951) since no Non-League club reached the Third Round. The last time only one did so was in 1969 when Kettering Town (SL) were the sole survivors losing 2-1 at home to Bristol City after a 1-1 draw at Ashton Gate.

## Non League Top 20

**Yeovil Town**
Seasons in Competition Proper: 49
Best Performance: Fifth Round 1948-49
Victories over Football League clubs: 20
1924-25 4q Bournemouth H 3-2; 1934-35 R1 Crystal Palace H 3-0; R2 Exeter City H 4-1; 1938-39 R1 Brighton H 2-1; 1948-49 R3 Bury H 3-1; R4 Sunderland H 2-1aet; 1958-59 R1 Southend United H 1-0 after 0-0 draw; 1960-61 R1 Walsall A 1-0; 1963-64 R1 Southend United H 1-0; R2 Crystal Palace H 3-1; 1970-71 R2 Bournemouth A 1-0; 1972-73 R1 Brentford H 2-1; 1987-88 R2 Cambridge United A 1-0; 1991-92 R1 Walsall A 1-0aet after 1-1 draw; 1992-93 R1 Torquay United A 5-2; R2 Hereford A 2-1 after 0-0 draw; 1993-94 R1 Fulham H 1-0; 1998-99 R2 Northampton H 2-0; 2000-01 R1 Colchester United H 5-1; R2 Blackpool A 1-0

**Kettering Town**
Seasons in Competition Proper: 46
Best Performance: Fourth Round 1988-89 and 1991-92
Victories over Football League clubs: 14
1895-96 3q Loughborough Town H 2-1; 4q Leicester Fosse A 2-1; 1896-97 5q Leicester Fosse H 2-1; 1898-99 4q Loughborough Town H 2-1; 5q Leicester Fosse A 2-1 after 1-1 draw; 1900-01 R1 Chesterfield A 2-1aet after 1-1 draw; 1961-62 R1 Swindon Town H 3-0 after 2-2 draw; 1963-64 R1 Millwall A 3-2 after 1-1 draw; 1974-75 R1 Swansea City H 3-1 after 1-1 draw; 1976-77 R1 Oxford United A 1-0 after 1-1 draw; 1988-89 R2 Bristol Rovers H 2-1; R3 Halifax Town A 3-2 after 1-1 draw; 1991-92 R2 Maidstone United A 2-1; 2000-01 R1 Hull City A 1-0 after 0-0 draw

**Telford United**
Seasons in Competition Proper: 34
Best Performance: Fifth Round 1984-85
Victories over Football League clubs: 11
1982-83 R1 Wigan Athletic H 2-1 after 0-0 draw; 1983-84 R1 Stockport County H 3-0; R2 Northampton Town H 3-2 after 1-1 draw; R3 Rochdale H 4-1; 1984-85 R1 Lincoln City H 2-1 after 1-1 draw; R2 Preston A 4-1; R3 Bradford City H 2-1; R4 Darlington H 3-0 after draw; 1985-86 R1 Stockport County A 1-0; 1986-87 R1 Burnley H 3-0; 1991-92 R1 Stoke City H 2-1 after 0-0 draw

**Scarborough**
Seasons in Competition Proper: 34
Best Performance: Third Round: 1930-31, 1937-38 1975-76, 1977-78
Victories over Football League clubs: 9
1930-31 R2 Lincoln City H 6-4; 1932-33 R1 York City A 3-1; 1937-38 R1 Darlington A 2-0; 1964-65 R1 Bradford City H 1-0; 1972-73 R1 Oldham Athletic H 2-1 after 1-1 draw; 1973-74 R1 Crewe Alex H 2-1 after 0-0 draw; 1975-76 R2 Preston H 3-2; 1977-78 R1 Rochdale H 4-2; R2 Crewe Alex H 2-0 after 0-0 draw

**Boston United**
Seasons in Competition Proper: 32
Best Performance: Third Round 1925-26, 1955-56, 1971-72, 1973-74
Victories over Football League clubs: 5
1925-26 R2 Bradford PA H 1-0; 1955-56 R2 Derby County A 6-1; 1970-71 R1 Southport A 2-0; 1971-72 R2 Hartlepools H 2-1; 1982-83 R1 Crewe Alex H 3-1 01.02.1890 2q 13-0 Bolton W (D1) v Sheffield U

**Enfield**
Seasons in Competition Proper: 31
Best Performance: Fourth Round 1980-81
Victories over Football League clubs: 11
1977-78 R1 Wimbledon H 3-0; R2 Northampton Town A 2-0; 1980-81 R2 Hereford United H 2-0; R3 Port Vale H 3-0 after 1-1 draw; 1981-82 R2 Wimbledon H 4-1; 1984-85 R1 Exeter City H 3-0 after 2-2 draw; 1988-89 R1 Leyton Orient A 1-0 after 1-1 draw and 2-2aet draw; 1991-92 R1 Aldershot A 1-0; 1994-95 R1 Cardiff City H 1-0; R2 Torquay United A 1-0 after 1-1 draw; 1999-2000 R1 Chesterfield A 2-1

**Weymouth**
Seasons in Competition Proper: 31
Best Performance: Fourth Round 1961-62
Victories over Football League clubs: 5
1924-25 5q Merthyr Town H 3-2; 1949-50 R1 Aldershot A 3-2 after 2-2 draw; 1956-57 R1 Shrewsbury Town H 1-0; 1961-62 R2 Newport County H 1-0; 1982-83 R2 Cardiff City A 3-2

**Bath City**
Seasons in Competition Proper: 30
Best Performance: Third Round: 1931-32, 1934-35 1959-60, 1963-64 1987-88, 1993-94
Victories over Football League clubs: 11
1920-21 5q Merthyr Town H 1-0 after 0-0 draw; 1922-23 5q Exeter City A 2-1; 6q Barrow H 2-0 after 2-2 draw; 1931-32 R2 Crystal Palace
H 2-1; 1952-53 R1 Southend United H 3-1; 1957-58 R1 Exeter City H 2-1; 1959-60 R1 Millwall H 3-1; R2 Notts County A 1-0; 1965-66 R1 Newport County H 2-0; 1992-93 R1 Cardiff City A 3-2; 1993-94 R2 Hereford United H 2-1

**Blyth Spartans**
Seasons in Competition Proper: 29
Best Performance: Fifth Round 1977-78
Victories over Football League clubs: 8
1922-23 5q Ashington H 2-1; 6q Gillingham A 4-1; 1925-26 R1 Hartlepools U 2-1 at Roker Park after 2-2 draw, 1-1aet draw and 1-1aet draw; 1971-72 R1 Crewe Alex A 1-0; R2 Stockport County H 1-0; 1977-78 R2 Chesterfield H 1-0; R4 Stoke City A 3-2; 1995-96 Bury A 2-0

**Barnet**
Seasons in Competition Proper: 29
Best Performance: Third Round 1964-65, 1970-71, 1972-73, 1981-82, 1990-91
Victories over Football League clubs: 2
1970-71 R1 Newport County H 6-1; 1990-91 R2 Northampton Town A 1-0 after 0-0 draw

**Altrincham**
Seasons in Competition Proper: 28
Best Performance: Fourth Round 1985-86
Victories over Football League clubs: 16
1921-22 4q Tranmere Rovers A 4-2 after 4-4 draw; 1965-66 R2 Rochdale A 3-1; 1973-74 R1 Hartlepool H 2-0; 1974-75 R1 Scunthorpe United H 3-1 after 1-1 draw; 1979-80 R1 Crewe Alex H 3-0; R2 Rotherham United A 2-0; 1980-81 R2 Scunthorpe United H 1-0 after 0-0 draw; 1981-82 R1 Sheffield United H 3-0 after 2-2 draw; R2 York City H 4-3 after 0-0 draw; 1982-83 R1 Rochdale H 2-1; 1984-85 R1 Blackpool A 1-0; 1985-86 R2 Blackpool A 2-1; R3 Birmingham City A 2-1; 1988-89 R1 Lincoln City H 3-2; 1992-93 R1 Chester City H 2-0 after 1-1 draw; 1994-95 R2 Wigan Athletic H 1-0

**Hereford United**
Seasons in Competition Proper: 28
Best Performance: Fourth Round 1971-72
Victories over Football League clubs: 12
1953-54 R1 Exeter City H 2-0 after 1-1 draw; 1956-57 R1 Aldershot H 3-2; 1957-58 R2 QPR H 6-1; 1965-66 R2 Millwall H 1-0; 1970-71 R1 Northampton Town A 2-1 after 2-2 draw; 1971-72 R2 Northampton Town at The Hawthorns 2-1aet after 0-0 draw and 2-2aet draw; R3 Newcastle United H 2-1aet after 2-2 draw; 1997-98 R1 Brighton H 2-1; R2 Colchester United 5-4pens after 1-1 draw and 1-1aet draw; 1999-2000 R1 York City H 1-0; R2 Hartlepools U H 1-0; 2001-02 R1 Wrexham H 1-0

**Chelmsford City**
Seasons in Competition Proper: 28
Best Performance: Fourth Round 1938-39
Victories over Football League clubs: 3
1938-39 R2 Darlington H 3-1; R3 Southampton H 4-1; 1967-68 R1 Oxford United at Griffin Park 1-0 after 3-3 draw and 3-3aet draw

**Gainsborough Trinity**
Seasons in Competition Proper: 26
Best Performance: Third Round 1886-87
Victories over Football League clubs: 5
1928-29 R1 Crewe Alex H 3-1; 1931-32 R1 Crewe Alex H 1-0 after 2-2 draw; 1937-38 R1 Port Vale H 2-1aet after 1-1 draw; 1938-39 R1 Gateshead H 2-1; 1945-46 R1 2nd leg Mansfield Town 4-2aet (Gainsborough lost 4-5 on aggregate)

**Wycombe Wanderers**
Seasons in Competition Proper: 26
Best Performance: Third Round 1974-75, 1985-86
Victories over Football League clubs: 3
1973-74 R1 Newport County H 3-1; 1974-75 R2 Bournemouth A 2-1 after 0-0 draw; 1985-86 R1 Colchester United H 2-0

**Dartford**
Seasons in Competition Proper: 26
Best Performance: Third Round 1935-36, 1936-37
Victories over Football League clubs: 3
1935-36 R1 Cardiff City A 3-0; 1961-62 R1 Exeter City H 2-1 after 3-3 draw 1968-69 R1 Aldershot A 3-1

**Grantham Town**
Seasons in Competition Proper: 25
Best Performance: Third Round 1883-84, 1886-87, 1973-74
Victories over Football League clubs: 2
1970-71 R1 Stockport County H 2-1; 1973-74 R2 Rochdale 5-3aet after 1-1 draw

**Northwich Victoria**
Seasons in Competition Proper: 24
Best Performance: Quarter-finals 1883-84
Victories over Football League clubs: 6
1976-77 R1 Rochdale 2-1 at Maine Road after 0-0aet draw and 1-1 draw; R2 Peterborough United H 4-0; R3 Watford H 3-2; 1982-83 R1 Chester City 3-1aet after 1-1 draw; 1984-85 R1 Crewe Alex H 3-1; 2000-01 R1 Bury H 1-0 after 1-1 draw

**Bishop Auckland**
Seasons in Competition Proper: 23
Best Performance: Fourth Round 1954-55
Victories over Football League clubs: 3
1954-55 R2 Crystal Palace A 4-2; R3 Ipswich Town H 3-0 after 2-2 draw; 1956-57 R1 Tranmere Rovers H 2-1

**Kidderminster Harriers**
Seasons in Competition Proper: 23
Best Performance: Fifth round 1993-94
Victories over Football League clubs: 2
1993-94 R3 Birmingham City A 2-1; R4 Preston H 1-0.

## League Clubs Beaten by Non-League Clubs

16 times – Crewe Alexandra
14 times – Exeter City
13 times – Halifax Town
12 times – Rochdale
11 times – Stockport County, Aldershot

## League Clubs Unbeaten by Non-League Opposition Since 1925

Arsenal, Aston Villa, Blackburn Rovers, Bolton Wanderers, Charlton, Chelsea, Everton, Leeds United, Manchester City, Manchester United, Middlesbrough, Nottingham Forest, Portsmouth, Tottenham H, West Ham.

Leeds United are the only Football League club never to have lost to a Non-League club in the FA Cup. Many clubs, like Arsenal, Portsmouth and Spurs were beaten by Non-League opposition when they were Non-League clubs themselves. Manchester United lost to Southern League Fulham in the Intermediate Round in 1904-05.

## Non-League Clubs With Most Consecutive Appearances In Round One

17 times – Hereford United (1955-1972)
Hereford only failed to reach the First Round once in the 24 years between 1948 and 1972 when they were elected to the Football League. In 1954-55 they were beaten by Nuneaton in the fourth qualifying round.

15 times – Rhyl Athletic (1948-1963)
11 times – Wycombe Wanderers (1973-1983)
- Enfield (1976-1986)
- Altrincham (1978-1988)

## Non-League Clubs to Have Reached the Fourth Round, (last 32) and beyond, or the old Second Round equivalent, since the Football League was expanded to 86 clubs in 1921.

**Note:** Corinthians, who did not play in a League, were exempted until the third round.

| *Season* | *Club* | *Lge* | *Round* | *Matches played* |
|---|---|---|---|---|
| 1923-24 | Corinthians | | 2 | 1, Blackburn R 1-0; 2, WBA 0-5 |
| 1925-26 | Corinthians | | 3 | 3, Manchester C 3-3; 3r Manchester C 0-4 |
| 1926-27 | Corinthians | | 4 | 3, Walsall 4-0; 4 Newcastle U 1-3 |
| 1928-29 | Corinthians | | 4 | 3, Norwich C 5-0; 4 West Ham 0-3 |
| | Mansfield T | ML | 4 | 1, Shirebrook 4-2; 2, Barrow 2-1; 3, Wolverhampton W 1-0; 4, Arsenal 0-2 |
| 1933-34 | Workington | NEL | 4 | 1, Southport 1-0; 2, Newport Co 3-1; 3, Gateshead 4-1; 4, Preston NE 1-2 |
| 1938-39 | Chelmsford C | SL | 4 | 1, Kidderminster 4-0; 2, Darlington 3-1; 3, Southampton 4-1; 4, Birmingham 0-6 |
| 1947-48 | Colchester U | SL | 5 | 1, Banbury Spencer 2-1; 2, Wrexham 1-0; 3, Huddersfield T 1-0; 4, Bradford PA 3-2; 5, Blackpool 0-5 |
| 1948-49 | Yeovil T | SL | 5 | 1, Runcorn 2-1; 2, Weymouth 4-0; 3, Bury 3-1; 4, Sunderland 2-1aet; 5, Manchester U 0-8 |
| 1952-53 | Walthamstow A | IL | 4 | 1, Wimbledon 2-2, 3-0; 2, Watford 1-1, 2-1; 3, Stockport Co 2-1; 4, Manchester U 1-1, 2-5 |

| | | | | |
|---|---|---|---|---|
| 1953-54 | Headington Utd | SL | 4 | 1, Harwich & P 3-2; 2, Millwall 3-3, 1-0; 3, Stockport Co 0-0, 1-0 4, Bolton W 2-4 |
| 1954-55 | Bishop Auckland | NL | 4 | 1, Kettering 5-1; 2, Crystal P 4-2 3, Ipswich T 2-2, 3-0; 4, York 1-3 |
| 1956-57 | Rhyl | CC | 4 | 1, Scarborough 3-2; ,2 Bishop Auckland 3-1; 3, Notts Co 3-1; 4, Bristol C 0-3 |
| | New Brighton | LC | 4 | 1, Stockport Co 3-3, 3-2; 2, Derby Co 3-1; 3, Torquay U 2-1; 4, Burnley 0-9 |
| | Peterborough U | ML | 4 | 1, Yeovil T 3-1; 2, Bradford PA 3-0; 3, Lincoln C 2-2, 5-4; 4, Huddersfield T 1-3 |
| 1958-59 | Worcester City | SL | 4 | 1, Chelmsford C 0-0, 3-1; 2, Millwall 5-2; 3, Liverpool 2-1; 4, Sheffield U 0-2 |
| 1959-60 | Peterborough U | ML | 4 | 1, Shrewsbury T 4-3; 2, Walsall 3-2; 3, Ipswich T 3-2; 4, Sheffield W 0-2 |
| 1961-62 | Weymouth | SL | 4 | 1, Barnet 1-0; 2, Newport Co 1-0; 3, Morecambe 1-0; 4, Preston NE 0-2 |
| 1962-63 | Gravesend & N | SL | 4 | 1, Exeter C 3-2; 2, Wycombe 3-1; 3, Carlisle U 1-0; 4, Sunderland 1-1, 2-5 |
| 1963-64 | Bedford Town | SL | 4 | 1, Weymouth 1-1, 1-0; 2, Chelmsford 1-0; 3, Newcastle U 2-1; 4, Carlisle 0-3 |
| 1965-66 | Bedford Town | SL | 4 | 1, Exeter C 2-1; 2, Brighton 1-1,2-1; 3, Hereford 2-1; 4, Everton 0-3 |
| 1969-70 | Sutton United | IL | 4 | 1, Dagenham 1-0; 2, Barnet 2-0; 3, Hillingdon 0-0,4-1; 4, Leeds U 0-6 |
| 1971-72 | Hereford United | SL | 4 | 1, Kings Lynn 0-0, 1-0; 2, Northampton T 0-0, 2-2, 2-1; 3, Newcastle U 2-2, 2-1; 4, West Ham 0-0, 1-3 |
| 1974-75 | Wimbledon | SL | 4 | 1, Bath 1-0; 2, Kettering 2-0; 3, Burnley 1-0; 4, Leeds 0-0, 0-1 |
| | Stafford Rangers | NPL | 4 | 1, Stockport Co 0-0, 1-0; 2, Halifax 2-1; : 3, Rotherham 0-0, 2-0; 4, Peterborough 1-2 |
| | Leatherhead | IL | 4 | 1, Bishops Stortford 0-0,2-0; 2, Colchester 1-0; 3, Brighton 1-0; 4, Leicester C 2-3 |
| 1975-76 | Tooting & M. | IL | 4 | 1, Romford 1-0; 2, Leatherhead 0-0,2-1; 3, Swindon 2-2, 2-1; 4, Bradford C 1-3 |
| 1976-77 | Northwich Victoria | NPL | 4 | 1, Rochdale 1-1,0-0,2-1; 2, Peterborough 4-0; 3, Watford 3-2; 4, Oldham 1-3 |
| 1977-78 | Blyth Spartans | NL | 5 | 1, Burscough 1-0; 2, Chesterfield 1-0; 3, Enfield 1-0; 4, Stoke C 3-2; 5, Wrexham 1-1, 1-2 |
| 1979-80 | Harlow Town | IL | 4 | 1, Leytonstone 2-1; 2, Southend 1-1,1-0; 3, Leicester 1-1, 1-0; 4, Watford 3-4 |
| 1980-81 | Enfield | IL | 4 | 1, Wembley 3-0; 2, Hereford U 2-0; 3, Port Vale 1-1, 3-0; 4, Barnsley 1-1, 0-3 |
| 1983-84 | Telford United | APL | 4 | 1, Stockport 3-0; 2, Northampton 1-1, 3-2; 3, Rochdale 4-1; 4, Derby Co 2-3 |

| | | | | |
|---|---|---|---|---|
| 1984-85 | Telford United | APL | 5 | 1, Lincoln C 1-1, 2-1; 2, Preston 4-1; 3, Bradford C 2-1; 4, Darlington 1-1, 3-0; 5, Everton 0-3 |
| 1985-86 | Altrincham | Conf | 4 | 1, Chorley 2-0; 2, Blackpool 2-1 3, Birmingham C 2-1; 4, York C 0-2 |
| 1988-89 | Sutton United | Conf | 4 | 1, Dagenham 4-0; 2, Aylesbury 1-0; 3, Coventry C 2-1; 4, Norwich C 0-8 |
| | Kettering | Conf | 4 | 1, Dartford 2-1; 2, Bristol R 2-1; 3, Halifax 1-1,3-2; 4, Charlton 1-2 |
| 1990-91 | Woking | IL | 4 | 1, Kidderminster 0-0,1-1, 2-1; 2, Merthyr T 5-1; 3, WBA 4-2; 4, Everton 0-1 |
| 1993-94 | Kidderminster H | Conf | 5 | 1, Kettering 3-0; 2, Woking 1-0; 3, Birmingham C 2-1; 4, Preston 1-0; 5, West Ham 0-1 |
| 1996-97 | Hednesford Town | Conf | 4 | 1, Southport 2-1; 2, Blackpool 1-0; 3, York 1-0; 4, Middlesbrough 2-3 |
| 1997-98 | Stevenage Borough | Conf | 4 | 1, Carshalton 0-0, 5-0; 2, Cambridge U 1-1, 2-1; 3, Swindon 2-1; 4 Newcastle 1-1, 1-2 |
| 2000-01 | Kingstonian | Conf | 4 | 1, Brentford 3-1; 2, Southport 2-1; 3, Southend 1-0; 4, Bristol City 1-1, 0-1 |
| 2002-03 | Dagenham & R | Conf | 4 | 1, Havant & Waterlooville 3-2; 2, Crawley 2-1; 3, Plymouth 2-2, 2-0; 4, Norwich 0-1 |
| 2002-03 | Farnborough Town | Conf | 4 | 1, Harrogate T 5-1; 2, Southport 3-0; 3, Darlington 3-2; 4, Arsenal 1-5 |

# FA Cup Semi-Finals

It is one of the cup's oldest cliches, but even so ... the only people who usually do remember the beaten FA Cup semi-finalists are the fans of the defeated team. The loneliest place in football is the dressing room of a team that has just lost the semi-final, so near yet so far from the final, cup final dreams shattered after having journeyed so far.

Probably as a result of being so close to the final, semi-final records have also been largely over-looked as attention is quickly focused on the big day itself.

**This section contains some usually hard-to-find semi-final stats.**

## Most Semi-Final Appearances

Everton and Arsenal have made a record number of 23 appearances in the semi-finals, Everton reaching the cup final 12 times, Arsenal 16.

## Full list of all semi-final appearances

Arsenal 23, Everton 23, Manchester United 22, Liverpool 21, Aston Villa 19, West Bromwich Albion 19, Tottenham Hotspur 17, Blackburn Rovers 16, Newcastle United 16, Sheffield Wednesday 16, Chelsea 15, Wolverhampton W 14, Bolton Wanderers 13, Derby County 13, Sheffield United 13, Nottingham Forest 12, Southampton 11, Sunderland 11, Manchester City 10, Preston North End 10, Birmingham City 9, Burnley 8, Leeds United 8, Huddersfield Town 7, Leicester City 7, Fulham 6, Old Etonians 6, Oxford University 6, West Ham United 6, Notts County 5, Portsmouth 5, The Wanderers 5, Luton Town 4, Queens Pk (Glasgow) 4, Royal Engineers 4, Watford 4, Blackpool 3, Cardiff City 3, Clapham Rovers 3, Crystal Palace 3, Ipswich Town 3, Millwall 3, Norwich City 3, Old Carthusians 3, Oldham Athletic 3, Stoke City 3, The Swifts 3, Barnsley 2, Blackburn Olympic 2, Bristol City 2, Bury 2, Charlton Athletic 2, Grimsby Town 2, Middlesbrough 2, Swansea City 2, Swindon Town 2, Wimbledon 2, Bradford City 1, Brighton & HA 1, Cambridge University1, Chesterfield 1, Coventry City 1, Crewe Alexandra 1 , Crystal P (1861) 1, Darwen 1, Derby Junction 1, Glasgow Rangers 1, Hull City 1, Marlow 1, Old Harrovians 1, Leyton Orient 1, Plymouth Argyle 1, Port Vale

1, QPR 1, Reading 1, Shropshire Wanderers 1, Wycombe Wanderers 1, York City 1 (replay appearances not included in the totals)
Only eight clubs from outside the top two divisions have reached the FA Cup semi-finals since the Football League was increased from two to three divisions in 1920-21:
1937 Millwall (3S); 1954 Port Vale (3N); 1955 York City (3N); 1959 Norwich City (D3); 1976 Crystal Palace (D3); 1984 Plymouth Argyle (D3); 1997 Chesterfield (D2); 2001 Wycombe Wanderers (D2).
All of them lost in the semi-finals.

## Non-League Semi-finalists since the formation of the Football League

1890 Sheffield Wednesday (Football Alliance) 1892 Nottingham Forest (Football Alliance); 1898 Southampton (Southern League; 1900 Southampton (Southern League), Millwall (Southern League); 1901 Tottenham Hotspur (Southern League); 1902 Southampton (Southern League); 1903 Millwall (Southern League); 1908 Southampton (Southern League); 1910 Swindon Town (Southern League); 1912 Swindon Town (Southern League).
Sheffield Wednesday (1890), Southampton (1900 and 1902) and Tottenham Hotspur (1901) all reached the final.

## Record Semi-final Score

Newcastle United 6 Fulham 0
at Anfield, March 28, 1908
Other big scores:
Manchester City 6 Aston Villa 1
at Huddersfield, March 17 1934
WBA 6, Nottingham F 2,
at Racecourse Ground, Derby, March 9 1892

## Aggregate in One Match

**8 goals:**
WBA 6, Nottingham F 2,
at Racecourse Ground, Derby, March 9 1892
Sheffield U 4, Liverpool 4 (replay)
at Burnden Park, Bolton, March 23 1899
Manchester U 5, Fulham 3 (replay)
at Highbury, March 26 1958
**7 goals:**
Manchester City 6 Aston Villa 1
at Huddersfield, March 17 1934
West Ham 5, Derby County 2
at Stamford Bridge, March 24 1923
Bolton W 4, Everton 3
at Maine Road, Manchester, March 21 1953
Crystal Palace 4, Liverpool 3aet
at Villa Park, April 8 1990

## Aggregate in One Semi-final Tie

**13 goals**
Sheffield United v Liverpool, 1899
The sides met four times before Sheffield United reached the FA Cup final.
**The details:**
*(The 13-goal total does not include the one in the abandoned match)*
March 18 1899 City Ground, Nottingham:
Sheffield U 2, Liverpool 2
March 23 1899 Burnden Park, Bolton:
Sheffield U 4, Liverpool 4 (replay)
March 27 1899 Fallowfield, Manchester
Sheffield U 0, Liverpool 1 (2nd replay)
(abandoned 45 minutes – after pitch invasions and darkness)
March 30 1899 Baseball Ground, Derby:
Sheffield U 1, Liverpool 0 (2nd replay)
**12 goals**
West Bromwich Albion v Nottingham Forest
February 27 1892 Molineux, Wolverhampton:
WBA 1, Nottingham F 1
March 5 1892 Molineux, Wolverhampton:
WBA 1, Nottingham F 1 (replay)
March 9 1892 Racecourse Ground, Derby:
WBA 6, Nottingham F 2 (2nd replay)
**12 goals**
Manchester United v Fulham
March 22 1958 Villa Park, Birmingham:
Manchester U 2, Fulham 2
March 26 1958 Highbury, London:
Manchester U 5, Fulham 3 (replay)

## Combined Aggregate from both Semi-final ties:

**17 goals**
1891-92: Aston Villa 4, Sunderland 1 – 5 goals
WBA v Nottingham F (see above) – 12 goals
**17 goals**
1898-99: Sheffield U v Liverpool (see above) – 13 goals
Derby County 3, Stoke 1 – 4 goals
**16 goals**
1989-90 Crystal Palace 4, Liverpool 3aet – 7 goals
Manchester U 3, Oldham A 3aet – 6 goals
Manchester U 2, Oldham A 1aet – 3 goals

## Abandoned Semi-finals

Only two semi-finals have been abandoned. The first was on March 27, 1899 when the game between Liverpool and Sheffield U at Fallowfield was called off at half-time because of fans invading the pitch and darkness. The next was on April 15 1989 when Liverpool's match with Nottingham Forest was called off after only six minutes as a result of the Hillsborough Disaster.

## Semi-final Sendings Off

March 26 1930 Arthur Childs (Hull City) v Arsenal, replay at Villa Park
April 8 1978 – Mick Martin (WBA) v Ipswich Town at Highbury
April 12 1980 – Brian Kidd (Everton) v West Ham at Villa Park
April 14 1991 Tony Gale (West Ham) v Nottingham Forest at Villa Park
April 9 1995 – Roy Keane (Manchester United) v Crystal Palace at Villa Park
April 9 1995 – Darren Patterson (Crystal Palace) v Manchester United at Villa Park
April 13 1997 – Vladimir Kinder (Middlesbrough) v Chesterfield at Old Trafford
April 11 1999 – Nelson Vivas (Arsenal) v Manchester United at Villa Park
April 14 1999 – Roy Keane (Manchester United) v Arsenal at Villa Park
April 2 2000 – Mark Delaney (Aston Villa) v Bolton Wanderers at Wembley

Roy Keane of Manchester United is the only player to be sent off twice in FA Cup semi-finals.

## Semi-final Scorers

Only 11 men have scored three or more goals in one match in the 305 semi-final matches played up to and including the 2002-03 season, and no-one has scored a hat-trick since 1958 when Alex Dawson scored three in Manchester United's 5-3 replay win over Fulham at Highbury.

## The list of Semi-final Hat-tricks or Better

4 goals
Sandy Brown, Tottenham H 4, WBA 0 at Villa Park, April 8 1901
Fred Tilson, Manchester C 6, Aston Villa 1 at Huddersfield, March 17 1934
Dennis Westcott, Wolverhampton W 5, Grimsby T 0 at Old Trafford, March 251939
3 goals
Harry Goodhart, Old Etonians 5, Marlow 0 at Kennington Oval, March 4 1882
John Smith, Queens Park (Glasgow) 4, Blackburn Olympic 1 at Trent Bridge, March 1 1884
Alf Geddes, WBA 6, Nottingham F, 2nd rep at Racecourse Ground, Derby, March 9, 1892
Steve Bloomer, Derby County 3, Stoke 1 at Molineux, March 18 1899
Jack Weddle, Portsmouth 4, Leicester C 1 at St Andrews, March 17 1934
Stan Pearson, Manchester U 3, Derby Co 1 at Hillsborough, March 13, 1948
Stan Mortensen, Blackpool 3, Tottenham H 1 (aet) at Villa Park, March 13 1948
Alex Dawson, Manchester U 5, Fulham 3, replay at Highbury, March 26 1958

Fred Tilson's four for Manchester City against Aston Villa and Jack Weddle's hat-trick for Portsmouth against Leicester were both scored on the same day. Stan Pearson's hat-trick for Manchester United against Derby and Stan Mortensen's hat-trick for Blackpool against Spurs were also scored on the same day.

## Semi-final Joy and Despair

Old Etonians reached the semi-final six times and made it through to the FA Cup final six times – although in 1880-81 they gained a bye to the final.

The Wanderers reached the semi-final five times and reached five cup finals – although because of walk-overs and byes they only ever played two semi-final matches.

More recently, Blackpool have a 100 per cent record in the semis, winning all three they have played in 1948, 1951 and 1953, although they needed a replay to beat Birmingham City in 1951.

Newcastle have won 13 of their 16 semi-finals, Manchester City have won eight of their 10; Huddersfield have won five out of seven, and West Ham four out of six.

Barnsley, Bury and Charlton Athletic have all appeared in two semi-finals and won both of them while Bradford City, Brighton & HA, Coventry City and QPR have all won the one semi-final they have played.

In contrast, Derby County have a poor semi-final record losing nine out of 13, while Nottingham Forest also have a poor semi-final record, having played in 12 and only won three times.

Birmingham City, who played their first semi-final as Small Heath, have won only two of their nine semis. Everton have lost more semi-finals than any other club – 11 – although they have also reached the Final 12 times as well.

## Semi-finalists Who Have Never Reached the Final

(number of their semi-final appearances in brackets)
Millwall (3), Oldham Athletic (3), Norwich City (3), Stoke City (3), The Swifts (3), Grimsby Town (2), Swansea City (2), Swindon Town (2), Cambridge University (1), Chesterfield (1), Crewe Alexandra (1), Crystal Palace (1861) 1, Darwen (1), Derby Junction (1), Glasgow R (1), Hull City (1), Marlow (1), Old Harrovians (1), Leyton Orient (1), Plymouth Argyle (1), Port Vale (1), Reading (1), Shropshire Wanderers (1), Wycombe Wanderers (1), York City (1).

## Attendances

The record attendance at an FA Cup semi-final is 80,407 for the replay between Derby County and Birmingham at Maine Road, Manchester on March 28, 1946. This was the biggest crowd for a mid-week FA Cup game in England until the cup final replay between Tottenham Hotspur and Manchester City at Wembley Stadium on Thursday, May 14 1981 attracted a gate of 92,000.

The lowest crowd for a semi-final since the War was the 17,987 for the replay between Manchester United and Crystal Palace at Villa Park on April 12, 1995. Part of the reason for the low attendance was due to Palace asking their fans to boycott the match following the death of a Palace fan on the day of the original game three days earlier.

A total of 169,163 watched the four games comprising the 1980 semi-final between Arsenal and Liverpool which Arsenal finally won 1-0 after draws of 0-0, 1-1 and 1-1.

## The Year of No Semi-finals.

Since the FA Cup started in 1871 there have been five occasions when only one semi-final was played (1877, 1878, 1879, 1880, 1881) when one team received a bye into the Final. But in 1873 no semi-finals were played. Oxford University got a bye into the Final after Queen's Park, Glasgow scratched, while under the rules in operation in 1872-73, Wanderers were exempt until the final, having won the cup the previous year.

## FA Cup finalists Without Winning a Semi-Final

In 1871-72, Wanderers drew their semi-final 0-0 with Queen's Park, then advanced to the final after Queen's Park scratched from the replay so they reached the final without winning their semi-final. In 1873 and 1878 the Wanderers also reached the final after semi-final byes.

In 1873 and 1877 Oxford University had semi-final byes while Clapham Rovers reached the finals of 1879 and 1880 after semi-final byes. Old Etonians were the last team to gain a semi-final bye in 1881.

In 1992 Liverpool became the first team to reach the final after winning a penalty shoot-out, knocking out Portsmouth after draws of 1-1 at Highbury and 0-0 at Villa Park, both after extra time.

Liverpool won the penalty shoot-out 3-1 after the second drawn game. Aston Villa reached the 2000 final after a 4-1 penalty shootout win over Bolton Wanderers at Wembley after the teams had drawn 0-0 after extra time.

## FA Cup Miscellany

### The FA Cup Comes to Town

On November 22, 1952 THREE FA Cup first round matches all took place a stone's throw from each other in East London when Leyton Orient, Leytonstone and Leyton were all drawn at home. Leyton Orient, then in the southern section of the Third Division, drew 1-1 at home with Bristol Rovers; Leytonstone, then in the Isthmian League lost 2-0 at home to Watford and Leyton, then in the Athenian League drew 0-0 at home with Southern League Hereford. Both Leyton Orient and Leyton lost their replays. Leyton never played another home match in the Competition Proper, while Leytonstone did not play at home in the Competition Proper for another 13 years.

# SEMI-FINAL RESULTS

*Venues and attendances (where known) season-by-season from 1871-72 – 2002-03.*
*Eventual FA Cup winners in capital letters.*

**1871-72**

| | | |
|---|---|---|
| Feb 17 | Kennington Oval | Royal Engineers 0 Crystal Palace 0 |
| Mar 9 | Kennington Oval | Royal Engineers 3 Crystal Palace 0 |
| Mar 5 | Kennington Oval | WANDERERS 0 Queen's Park (Glasgow) 0 |
| | | WANDERERS w/o Queen's Park (Glasgow) scr |

**1872-73**

| | | |
|---|---|---|
| | | WANDERERS bye |
| | | Oxford University w/o Queen's Park (Glasgow) scr |

**1873-74**

| | | |
|---|---|---|
| Jan 28 | Kennington Oval | Royal Engineers 2 Swifts 0 |
| Feb 28 | Kennington Oval | OXFORD UNIVERSITY 1 Clapham Rovers 0 |

| | | | |
|---|---|---|---|
| **1874-75** | | | |
| Feb 27 | Kennington Oval | | Old Etonians 1 Shropshire Wanderers 0 |
| Feb 27 | Kennington Oval | | ROYAL ENGINEERS 1 Oxford University 1 |
| Mar 5 | Kennington Oval | | ROYAL ENGINEERS 1 Oxford University 0aet |
| **1875-76** | | | |
| Feb 19 | Kennington Oval | | Old Etonians 1 Oxford University 0 |
| Feb 26 | Kennington Oval | | WANDERERS 2 Swifts 1 |
| **1876-77** | | | |
| Mar 20 | Kennington Oval | | WANDERERS 1 Cambridge University 0<br>Oxford University bye |
| **1877-78** | | | |
| Mar 16 | Kennington Oval | | Royal Engineers 2 Old Harrovians 1<br>WANDERERS bye |
| **1878-79** | | | |
| Mar 22 | Kennington Oval | 700 | OLD ETONIANS 2 Nottingham F 1<br>Clapham Rovers bye |
| **1879-80** | | | |
| Mar 27 | Kennington Oval | 2,000 | Oxford University 1 Nottingham F 0<br>CLAPHAM ROVERS bye |
| **1880-81** | | | |
| Mar 26 | Kennington Oval | 2,000 | OLD CARTHUSIANS 4 Darwen 1<br>Old Etonians bye |
| **1881-82** | | | |
| Mar 4 | Kennington Oval | | OLD ETONIANS 5 Marlow 0 |
| Mar 6 | Huddersfield | 6,000 | Blackburn Rovers 0 Sheffield W 0 |
| Mar 15 | Manchester | 10,000 | Blackburn Rovers 5 Sheffield W 1 |
| **1882-83** | | | |
| Mar 17 | Manchester | 2,500 | BLACKBURN OLYMPIC 4 Old Carthusians 0 |
| Mar 17 | Kennington Oval | | Old Etonians 2 Notts County 1 |
| **1883-84** | | | |
| Mar 1 | Lower Grounds | 15,000 | BLACKBURN ROVERS 1 Notts County 0 |
| Mar 1 | Trent Bridge | | Queen's Park (Glasgow) 4 Blackburn Olympic 1 |
| **1884-85** | | | |
| Mar 7 | Trent Bridge | 2,000 | BLACKBURN ROVERS 5 Old Carthusians 1 |
| Mar 14 | Derby CC | 10,000 | Queen's Park (Glasgow) 1 Nottingham F 1 |
| Mar 28 | Edinburgh | 10,000 | Queen's Park (Glasgow) 3 Nottingham F 0 |
| **1885-86** | | | |
| Mar 6 | Lower Grounds | 4,100 | West Bromwich Albion 4 Small Heath 0 |
| Mar 13 | Derby CC | 'large' | BLACKBURN ROVERS 2 Swifts 1 |
| **1886-87** | | | |
| Mar 5 | Crewe | 10,000 | ASTON VILLA 3 Glasgow Rangers 1 |
| Mar 5 | Trent Bridge | 16,068 | West Bromwich Albion 3 Preston NE 1 |
| **1887-88** | | | |
| Feb 18 | Anfield | 10,000 | Preston NE 4 Crewe Alexandra 0 |
| Feb 18 | Stoke | 5,996 | WEST BROMWICH ALBION 3 Derby Junction 0 |
| **1888-89** | | | |
| Mar 16 | Bramall Lane | 22,688 | PRESTON NE 1 West Bromwich Albion 0 |
| Mar 16 | Crewe | 15,000 | Wolverhampton W 1 Blackburn Rovers 1 |
| Mar 23 | Crewe | 9,900 | Wolverhampton W 3 Blackburn Rovers 1 |
| **1889-90** | | | |
| Mar 8 | Derby Racecourse | 14,788 | BLACKBURN ROVERS 1 Wolverhampton W 0 |
| Mar 8 | Perry Barr | 12,000 | Sheffield W 2 Bolton W 1 |

| | | | |
|---|---|---|---|
| **1890-91** | | | |
| Feb 28 | Stoke | 21,774 | BLACKBURN ROVERS 3, West Bromwich Albion 2 |
| Feb 28 | Bramall Lane | 22,000 | Notts County 3 Sunderland 3 |
| Mar 11 | Bramall Lane | 13,147 | Notts County 2 Sunderland 0 |
| **1891-92** | | | |
| Feb 27 | Bramall Lane | 25,000 | Aston Villa 4 Sunderland 1 |
| Feb 27 | Molineux | 21,076 | WEST BROMWICH ALBION 1 Nottingham F 1 |
| Mar 5 | Molineux | 15,930 | WEST BROMWICH ALBION 1 Nottingham F 1 |
| Mar 9 | Derby Racecourse | 8,024 | WEST BROMWICH ALBION 6 Nottingham F 2 |
| **1892-93** | | | |
| Mar 4 | Town Ground | 25,000 | WOLVERHAMPTON W 2 Blackburn Rovers 1 |
| Mar 4 | Bramall Lane | 26,000 | Everton 2 Preston NE 2 |
| Mar 16 | Ewood Park | 15,000 | Everton 0 Preston NE 0 aet |
| Mar 20 | Trent Bridge | 18,000 | Everton 2 Preston NE 1 |
| **1893-94** | | | |
| Mar 10 | Fallowfield | 22,000 | Bolton W 2 Sheffield W 1 |
| Mar 10 | Bramall Lane | 22,000 | NOTTS CO 1 Blackburn Rovers 0 |
| **1894-95** | | | |
| Mar 16 | Ewood Park | 14,000 | ASTON VILLA 2 Sunderland 1 |
| Mar 16 | Derby CC | 25,013 | West Bromwich Albion 2 Sheffield W 0 |
| **1895-96** | | | |
| Mar 21 | Perry Barr | 35,000 | Wolverhampton W 2 Derby Co 1 |
| Mar 21 | Goodison Park | | SHEFFIELD W 1 Bolton W 1 |
| Mar 28 | Town Ground | | SHEFFIELD W 3 Bolton W 1 |
| **1896-97** | | | |
| Mar 20 | Bramall Lane | 30,000 | ASTON VILLA 3 Liverpool 0 |
| Mar 20 | Stoke | 25,000 | Everton 3 Derby Co 2 |
| **1897-98** | | | |
| Mar 19 | Molineux | 29,893 | Derby Co 3 Everton 1 |
| Mar 19 | Bramall Lane | 30,000 | NOTTINGHAM F 1 Southampton 1 |
| Mar 23 | Crystal Palace | 12,000 | NOTTINGHAM F 2 Southampton 0 |
| **1898-99** | | | |
| Mar 18 | Molineux | 24,385 | Derby Co 3 Stoke 1 |
| Mar 18 | City Ground | 21,000 | SHEFFIELD U 2 Liverpool 2 |
| Mar 23 | Burnden Park | 20,000 | SHEFFIELD U 4 Liverpool 4 aet |
| Mar 27 | Fallowfield | 30,000 | SHEFFIELD U 0 Liverpool 1 |
| | *(Abandoned at halftime due to crowd trouble and darkness)* | | |
| Mar 30 | Baseball Ground | 17,000 | SHEFFIELD U 1 Liverpool 0 |
| **1899-00** | | | |
| Mar 24 | Crystal Palace | 34,760 | Southampton 0 Millwall 0 |
| Mar 28 | Elm Park | 10,000 | Southampton 3 Millwall 0 |
| Mar 24 | Stoke | 18,000 | BURY 1 Nottingham F 1 |
| Mar 29 | Bramall Lane | 11,200 | BURY 3 Nottingham F 2aet |
| **1900-01** | | | |
| Apr 6 | City Ground | 31,000 | Sheffield U 2 Aston Villa 2 |
| Apr 11 | Baseball Ground | 23,000 | Sheffield U 3 Aston Villa 0 |
| Apr 8 | Villa Park | 34,979 | TOTTENHAM HOTSPUR 4 West Bromwich Albion 0 |
| **1901-02** | | | |
| Mar 15 | White Hart Lane | 30,000 | Southampton 3 Nottingham F 1 |
| Mar 15 | The Hawthorns | 33,603 | SHEFFIELD U 1 Derby Co 1 |
| Mar 20 | Molineux | 13,284 | SHEFFIELD U 1 Derby Co 1 |
| Mar 27 | City Ground | 15,000 | SHEFFIELD U 1 Derby Co 0 |
| **1902-03** | | | |
| Mar 21 | Goodison Park | 45,000 | BURY 3 Aston Villa 0 |

| | | | |
|---|---|---|---|
| Mar 21 | Villa Park | 40,500 | Derby Co 3 Millwall 0 |
| **1903-04** | | | |
| Mar 19 | Molineux | 20,187 | Bolton W 1 Derby Co 0 |
| Mar 19 | Goodison Park | 53,000 | MANCHESTER C 3 Sheffield W 0 |
| **1904-05** | | | |
| Mar 25 | Hyde Road | 40,000 | Newcastle U 1 Sheffield W 0 |
| Mar 25 | Stoke | 35,000 | ASTON VILLA 1 Everton 1 |
| Mar 29 | Trent Bridge | 25,000 | ASTON VILLA 2 Everton 1 |
| **1905-06** | | | |
| Mar 31 | Stoke | 19,964 | Newcastle U 2 Woolwich Arsenal 0 |
| Mar 31 | Villa Park | 37,000 | EVERTON 2 Liverpool 0 |
| **1906-07** | | | |
| Mar 23 | St Andrews | 36,000 | SHEFFIELD WED 3 Woolwich Arsenal 1 |
| Mar 23 | Burnden Park | 32,381 | Everton 2 West Bromwich Albion 1 |
| **1907-08** | | | |
| Mar 28 | Stamford Bridge | 44,696 | WOLVERHAMPTON W 2 Southampton 0 |
| Mar 28 | Anfield | 45,571 | Newcastle U 6 Fulham 0 |
| **1908-09** | | | |
| Mar 27 | Bramall Lane | 40,118 | MANCHESTER U 1 Newcastle U 0 |
| Mar 27 | Stamford Bridge | 34,000 | Bristol C 1 Derby Co 1 |
| Mar 31 | St Andrews | 27,600 | Bristol C 2 Derby Co 1 |
| **1909-10** | | | |
| Mar 26 | White Hart Lane | 33,000 | NEWCASTLE U 2 Swindon T 0 |
| Mar 26 | Elland Road | 36,000 | Barnsley 0 Everton 0 |
| Mar 31 | Old Trafford | 55,000 | Barnsley 3 Everton 0 |
| **1910-11** | | | |
| Mar 25 | Bramall Lane | 36,479 | BRADFORD C 3 Blackburn Rovers 0 |
| Mar 25 | St Andrews | 40,000 | Newcastle U 3 Chelsea 0 |
| **1911-12** | | | |
| Mar 30 | Anfield | 30,063 | West Bromwich Albion 0 Blackburn Rovers 0 |
| Apr 3 | Hillsborough | 20,050 | West Bromwich Albion 1 Blackburn Rovers 0aet |
| Mar 30 | Stamford Bridge | 48,057 | BARNSLEY 0 Swindon T 0 |
| Apr 3 | Meadow Lane | 18,000 | BARNSLEY 1 Swindon T 0 |
| **1912-13** | | | |
| Mar 29 | Ewood Park | 22,616 | ASTON VILLA 1 Oldham A 0 |
| Mar 29 | Bramall Lane | 33,656 | Sunderland 0, Burnley 0 |
| Apr 2 | St Andrews | 30,000 | Sunderland 3, Burnley 2 |
| **1913-14** | | | |
| Mar 28 | White Hart Lane | 27,464 | Liverpool 2 Aston Villa 0 |
| Mar 28 | Old Trafford | 55,812 | BURNLEY 0 Sheffield U 0 |
| Apr 1 | Goodison Park | 27,266 | BURNLEY 1 Sheffield U 0 |
| **1914-15** | | | |
| Mar 27 | Ewood Park | 22,500 | SHEFFIELD U 2 Bolton W 1 |
| Mar 27 | Villa Park | 22,000 | Chelsea 2 Everton 0 |
| **1919-20** | | | |
| Mar 27 | Bramall Lane | 47,800 | ASTON VILLA 3 Chelsea 1 |
| Mar 27 | Stamford Bridge | 35,000 | Huddersfield T 2 Bristol C 1 |
| **1920-21** | | | |
| Mar 19 | Hillsborough | 44,688 | TOTTENHAM HOTSPUR 2 Preston NE 1 |
| Mar 19 | Anfield | 48,000 | Wolverhampton W 0 Cardiff C 0 |
| Mar 23 | Old Trafford | 45,000 | Wolverhampton W 3 Cardiff C 1 |
| **1921-22** | | | |
| Mar 25 | Turf Moor | 49,727 | HUDDERSFIELD T 3 Notts County 1 |

| | | | |
|---|---|---|---|
| Mar 25 | Hillsborough | 50,000 | Preston NE 2 Tottenham Hotspur 1 aet |
| **1922-23** | | | |
| Mar 24 | Old Trafford | 72,000 | BOLTON W 1 Sheffield U 0 |
| Mar 24 | Stamford Bridge | 50,795 | West Ham 5 Derby Co 2 |
| **1923-24** | | | |
| Mar 29 | St Andrews | 50,039 | NEWCASTLE U 2 Manchester C 0 |
| Mar 29 | Bramall Lane | 54,531 | Aston Villa 3 Burnley 0 |
| **1924-25** | | | |
| Mar 28 | Meadow Lane | 20,100 | Cardiff C 3 Blackburn Rovers 1 |
| Mar 28 | Stamford Bridge | 65,745 | SHEFFIELD U 2 Southampton 0 |
| **1925-26** | | | |
| Mar 27 | White Hart Lane | 25,476 | BOLTON W 3 Swansea T 0 |
| Mar 27 | Bramall Lane | 46,450 | Manchester C 3 Manchester U 0 |
| **1926-27** | | | |
| Mar 26 | Molineux | 39,476 | CARDIFF C 3 Reading 0 |
| Mar 26 | Stamford Bridge | 52,133 | Arsenal 2 Southampton 1 |
| **1927-28** | | | |
| Mar 24 | Filbert St | 25,633 | BLACKBURN ROVERS 1 Arsenal 0 |
| Mar 24 | Old Trafford | 69,260 | Huddersfield T 2 Sheffield U 2 aet |
| Mar 26 | Goodison Park | 53,749 | Huddersfield T 0 Sheffield U 0 aet |
| Apr 2 | Maine Road | 69,360 | Huddersfield T 1 Sheffield U 0 |
| **1928-29** | | | |
| Mar 23 | Anfield | 39,000 | BOLTON W 3 Huddersfield T 1 |
| Mar 23 | Highbury | 36,147 | Portsmouth 1 Aston Villa 0 |
| **1929-30** | | | |
| Mar 22 | Old Trafford | 69,292 | Huddersfield T 2 Sheffield W 1 |
| Mar 22 | Elland Road | 47,549 | ARSENAL 2 Hull C 2 |
| Mar 26 | Villa Park | 46,200 | ARSENAL 1 Hull C 0 |
| **1930-31** | | | |
| Mar 14 | Old Trafford | 69,241 | WEST BROMWICH ALBION 1 Everton 0 |
| Mar 14 | Elland Road | 43,572 | Birmingham 2 Sunderland 0 |
| **1931-32** | | | |
| Mar 12 | Huddersfield | 36,709 | NEWCASTLE U 2 Chelsea 1 |
| Mar 12 | Villa Park | 50,377 | Arsenal 1 Manchester City 0 |
| **1932-33** | | | |
| Mar 18 | Molineux | 37,936 | EVERTON 2 West Ham 1 |
| Mar 18 | Huddersfield | 51,961 | Manchester C 3 Derby Co 2 |
| **1933-34** | | | |
| Mar 17 | Huddersfield | 45,473 | MANCHESTER C 6 Aston Villa 1 |
| Mar 17 | St Andrews | 66,544 | Portsmouth 4 Leicester C 1 |
| **1934-35** | | | |
| Mar 16 | Villa Park | 56,625 | SHEFFIELD W 3 Burnley 0 |
| Mar 16 | Elland Road | 49,605 | West Bromwich Albion 1 Bolton W 1 |
| Mar 20 | Stoke | 49,110 | West Bromwich Albion 2 Bolton W 0 |
| **1935-36** | | | |
| Mar 21 | Huddersfield | 63,210 | ARSENAL 1 Grimsby T 0 |
| Mar 21 | Molineux | 51,568 | Sheffield U 2 Fulham 1 |
| **1936-37** | | | |
| Apr 10 | Huddersfield | 62,813 | SUNDERLAND 2 Millwall 1 |
| Apr 10 | Highbury | 42,636 | Preston NE 4 West Bromwich Albion 1 |
| **1937-38** | | | |
| Mar 26 | Bramall Lane | 65,129 | PRESTON NE 2 Aston Villa 1 |
| Mar 26 | Ewood Park | 47,904 | Huddersfield T 3 Sunderland 1 |

**1938-39**

| | | | |
|---|---|---|---|
| Mar 25 | Highbury | 60,053 | PORTSMOUTH 2 Huddersfield T 1 |
| Mar 25 | Old Trafford | 76,962 | Wolverhampton W 5 Grimsby T 0 |

**1945-46**

| | | | |
|---|---|---|---|
| Mar 23 | Hillsborough | 65,000 | DERBY CO 1 Birmingham C 1 |
| Mar 27 | Maine Road | 80,407 | DERBY CO 4 Birmingham C 0 aet |
| Mar 23 | Villa Park | 70,819 | Charlton A 2 Bolton W 0 |

**1946-47**

| | | | |
|---|---|---|---|
| Mar 29 | Elland Road | 47,978 | CHARLTON A 4 Newcastle U 0 |
| Mar 29 | Ewood Park | 53,000 | Burnley 0 Liverpool 0 aet |
| Apr 12 | Maine Road | 72,000 | Burnley 1 Liverpool 0 |

**1947-48**

| | | | |
|---|---|---|---|
| Mar 13 | Hillsborough | 60,000 | MANCHESTER U 3 Derby Co 1 |
| Mar 13 | Villa Park | 70,687 | Blackpool 3 Tottenham Hotspur 1 aet |

**1948-49**

| | | | |
|---|---|---|---|
| Mar 26 | Hillsborough | 62,250 | WOLVERHAMPTON W 1 Manchester U 1 aet |
| Apr 2 | Goodison Park | 72,500 | WOLVERHAMPTON W 1 Manchester U 0 |
| Mar 26 | Highbury | 62,000 | Leicester C 3 Portsmouth 1 |

**1949-50**

| | | | |
|---|---|---|---|
| Mar 18 | White Hart Lane | 67,752 | ARSENAL 2 Chelsea 2 |
| Mar 22 | White Hart Lane | 66,482 | ARSENAL 1 Chelsea 0 aet |
| Mar 25 | Maine Road | 72,000 | Liverpool 2, Everton 0 |

**1950-51**

| | | | |
|---|---|---|---|
| Mar 10 | Hillsborough | 62,250 | NEWCASTLE U 0 Wolverhampton W 0aet |
| Mar 14 | Huddersfield | 47,349 | NEWCASTLE U 2 Wolverhampton W 1 |
| Mar 10 | Maine Road | 72,000 | Blackpool 0 Birmingham C 0 |
| Mar 14 | Goodison Park | 70,114 | Blackpool 2 Birmingham C 1 |

**1951-52**

| | | | |
|---|---|---|---|
| Mar 29 | Hillsborough | 65,000 | NEWCASTLE U 0 Blackburn Rovers 0 aet |
| Apr 2 | Elland Road | 53,930 | NEWCASTLE U 2 Blackburn Rovers 1 |
| Apr 5 | White Hart Lane | 68,084 | Arsenal 1 Chelsea 1 |
| Apr 7 | White Hart Lane | 57,450 | Arsenal 3 Chelsea 0 |

**1952-53**

| | | | |
|---|---|---|---|
| Mar 21 | Villa Park | 68,221 | BLACKPOOL 2, Tottenham Hotspur 1 |
| Mar 21 | Maine Road | 75,213 | Bolton W 4 Everton 3 |

**1953-54**

| | | | |
|---|---|---|---|
| Mar 27 | Villa Park | 68,221 | WEST BROMWICH ALBION 2 Port Vale 1 |
| Mar 27 | Maine Road | 75,000 | Preston NE 2 Sheffield W 0 |

**1954-55**

| | | | |
|---|---|---|---|
| Mar 26 | Hillsborough | 65,000 | NEWCASTLE U 1 York C 1 |
| Mar 30 | Roker Park | 59,239 | NEWCASTLE U 2 York C 0 |
| Mar 26 | Villa Park | 58,498 | Manchester C 1 Sunderland 0 |

**1955-56**

| | | | |
|---|---|---|---|
| Mar 17 | Villa Park | 69,788 | MANCHESTER C 1 Tottenham Hotspur 0 |
| Mar 17 | Hillsborough | 65,107 | Birmingham C 3 Sunderland 0 |

**1956-57**

| | | | |
|---|---|---|---|
| Mar 23 | Molineux | 55,549 | ASTON VILLA 2 West Bromwich Albion 2 |
| Mar 28 | St Andrews | 58,000 | ASTON VILLA 1 West Bromwich Albion 0 |
| Mar 23 | Hillsborough | 65,107 | Manchester U 2 Birmingham C 0 |

**1957-58**

| | | | |
|---|---|---|---|
| Mar 22 | Maine Road | 74,800 | BOLTON W 2 Blackburn Rovers 1 |
| Mar 22 | Villa Park | 69,746 | Manchester U 2 Fulham 2 |
| Mar 26 | Highbury | 38,258 | Manchester U 5 Fulham 3 |

| | | | |
|---|---|---|---|
| **1958-59** | | | |
| Mar 14 | Hillsborough | 65,107 | NOTTINGHAM F 1 Aston Villa 0 |
| Mar 14 | White Hart Lane | 63,433 | Luton T 1 Norwich C 1 |
| Mar 17 | St Andrews | 49,500 | Luton T 1 Norwich C 0 |
| **1959-60** | | | |
| Mar 26 | The Hawthorns | 55,596 | WOLVERHAMPTON W 1 Aston V 0 |
| Mar 26 | Maine Road | 74,135 | Blackburn Rovers 2 Sheffield W 1 |
| **1960-61** | | | |
| Mar 18 | Villa Park | 69,968 | TOTTENHAM HOTSPUR 3 Burnley 0 |
| Mar 18 | Elland Road | 52,095 | Leicester C 0 Sheffield U 0 |
| Mar 23 | City Ground | 43,500 | Leicester C 0 Sheffield U 0 aet |
| Mar 27 | St Andrews | 37,190 | Leicester C 2 Sheffield U 0 aet |
| **1961-62** | | | |
| Mar 31 | Hillsborough | 65,000 | TOTTENHAM HOTSPUR 3 Manchester U 1 |
| Mar 31 | Villa Park | 59,989 | Burnley 1 Fulham 1 |
| Apr 9 | Filbert Street | 35,000 | Burnley 2 Fulham 1 |
| **1962-63** | | | |
| Apr 27 | Villa Park | 65,000 | MANCHESTER U 1 Southampton 0 |
| Apr 27 | Hillsborough | 65,000 | Leicester C 1 Liverpool 0 |
| **1963-64** | | | |
| Mar 14 | Hillsborough | 65,000 | WEST HAM 3 Manchester U 1 |
| Mar 14 | Villa Park | 63,000 | Preston NE 2 Swansea T 1 |
| **1964-65** | | | |
| Mar 27 | Villa Park | 67,686 | LIVERPOOL 2 Chelsea 0 |
| Mar 27 | Hillsborough | 65,000 | Leeds U 0 Manchester U 0 aet |
| Mar 31 | City Ground | 46,300 | Leeds U 1 Manchester U 0 |
| **1965-66** | | | |
| Apr 23 | Burnden Park | 60,000 | EVERTON 1 Manchester U 0 |
| Apr 23 | Villa Park | 61,321 | Sheffield W 2 Chelsea 0 |
| **1966-67** | | | |
| Apr 29 | Hillsborough | 55,000 | TOTTENHAM HOTSPUR 2 Nottingham F 1 |
| Apr 29 | Villa Park | 62,378 | Chelsea 1 Leeds U 0 |
| **1967-68** | | | |
| Apr 27 | Villa Park | 60,831 | WEST BROMWICH ALBION 2 Birmingham C 0 |
| Apr 27 | Old Trafford | 63,000 | Everton 1 Leeds U 0 |
| **1968-69** | | | |
| Mar 22 | Villa Park | 63,025 | MANCHESTER C 1 Everton 0 |
| Mar 29 | Hillsborough | 53,207 | Leicester C 1 West Bromwich Albion 0 |
| **1969-70** | | | |
| Mar 14 | White Hart Lane | 55,209 | CHELSEA 5 Watford 1 |
| Mar 14 | Hillsborough | 55,000 | Leeds U 0 Manchester U 0 |
| Mar 23 | Villa Park | 62,500 | Leeds U 0 Manchester U 0 aet |
| Mar 26 | Burnden Park | 56,000 | Leeds U 1 Manchester U 0 |
| **1970-71** | | | |
| Mar 27 | Hillsborough | 55,000 | ARSENAL 2 Stoke C 2 |
| Mar 31 | Villa Park | 62,500 | ARSENAL 2 Stoke C 0 |
| Mar 27 | Old Trafford | 62,144 | Liverpool 2 Everton 1 |
| **1971-72** | | | |
| Apr 15 | Hillsborough | 55,000 | LEEDS U 3 Birmingham C 0 |
| Apr 15 | Villa Park | 56,576 | Arsenal 1 Stoke C 1 |
| Apr 19 | Goodison Park | 38,970 | Arsenal 2 Stoke C 1 |

| | | | |
|---|---|---|---|
| **1972-73** | | | |
| Apr 7 | Hillsborough | 55,000 | SUNDERLAND 2 Arsenal 1 |
| Apr 7 | Maine Road | 52,505 | Leeds United 1 Wolverhampton W 0 |
| **1973-74** | | | |
| Mar 30 | Old Trafford | 60,000 | LIVERPOOL 0 Leicester C 0 |
| Apr 3 | Villa Park | 55,619 | LIVERPOOL 3 Leicester C 1 |
| Mar 30 | Hillsborough | 55,000 | Newcastle U 2 Burnley 0 |
| **1974-75** | | | |
| Apr 5 | Villa Park | 58,000 | WEST HAM 0 Ipswich T 0 |
| Apr 9 | Stamford Bridge | 45,344 | WEST HAM 2 Ipswich T 1 |
| Apr 5 | Hillsborough | 55,000 | Fulham 1 Birmingham C 1 |
| Apr 9 | Maine Road | 35,025 | Fulham 1 Birmingham C 0 aet |
| **1975-76** | | | |
| Apr 3 | Stamford Bridge | 52,810 | SOUTHAMPTON 2 Crystal Palace 0 |
| Apr 3 | Hillsborough | 55,000 | Manchester U 2 Derby Co 0 |
| **1976-77** | | | |
| Apr 23 | Hillsborough | 55,000 | MANCHESTER U 2 Leeds U 1 |
| Apr 23 | Maine Road | 52,637 | Liverpool 2 Everton 2 |
| Apr 27 | Maine Road | 52,579 | Liverpool 3 Everton 0 |
| **1977-78** | | | |
| Apr 8 | Highbury | 50,922 | IPSWICH T 3 West Bromwich Albion 1 |
| Apr 8 | Stamford Bridge | 49,098 | Arsenal 3 Leyton Orient 0 |
| **1978-79** | | | |
| Mar 31 | Villa Park | 46,244 | ARSENAL 2 Wolverhampton W 0 |
| Mar 31 | Maine Road | 52,524 | Manchester U 2 Liverpool 2 |
| Apr 4 | Goodison Park | 53,069 | Manchester U 1 Liverpool 0 |
| **1979-80** | | | |
| Apr 12 | Villa Park | 47,685 | WEST HAM 1 Everton 1 |
| Apr 16 | Elland Road | 40,720 | WEST HAM 2 Everton 1 aet |
| Apr 12 | Hillsborough | 50,174 | Arsenal 0 Liverpool 0 |
| Apr 16 | Villa Park | 40,679 | Arsenal 1 Liverpool 1 aet |
| Apr 28 | Villa Park | 42,975 | Arsenal 1 Liverpool 1 aet |
| May 1 | Highfield Road | 35,335 | Arsenal 1 Liverpool 0 |
| **1980-81** | | | |
| Apr 11 | Hillsborough | 50,174 | TOTTENHAM HOTSPUR 2 Wolverhampton W 2 aet |
| Apr 15 | Highbury | 52,539 | TOTTENHAM HOTSPUR 3 Wolverhampton W 0 |
| Apr 11 | Villa Park | 46,537 | Manchester C 1 Ipswich T 0 aet |
| **1981-82** | | | |
| Apr 3 | Villa Park | 46,606 | TOTTENHAM HOTSPUR 2 Leicester C 0 |
| Apr 3 | Highbury | 45,015 | Queens Park Rangers 1 West Bromwich Albion 0 |
| **1982-83** | | | |
| Apr 16 | Villa Park | 46,535 | MANCHESTER U 2 Arsenal 1 |
| Apr 16 | Highbury | 54,000 | Brighton & HA 2 Sheffield W 1 |
| **1983-84** | | | |
| Apr 14 | Highbury | 46,587 | EVERTON 1 Southampton 0 aet |
| Apr 14 | Villa Park | 43,858 | Watford 1 Plymouth A 0 |
| **1984-85** | | | |
| Apr 13 | Goodison Park | 51,690 | MANCHESTER U 2 Liverpool 2 aet |
| Apr 17 | Maine Road | 45,775 | MANCHESTER U 2 Liverpool 1 |
| Apr 13 | Villa Park | 45,289 | Everton 2 Luton T 1 aet |
| **1985-86** | | | |
| Apr 5 | White Hart Lane | 44,605 | LIVERPOOL 2 Southampton 0 aet |
| Apr 5 | Villa Park | 47,711 | Everton 2 Sheffield W 1 aet |

| | | | |
|---|---|---|---|
| **1986-87** | | | |
| Apr 12 | Hillsborough | 51,372 | COVENTRY C 3 Leeds U 2 aet |
| Apr 11 | Villa Park | 46,151 | Tottenham Hotspur 4 Watford 1 |
| **1987-88** | | | |
| Apr 9 | White Hart Lane | 25,963 | WIMBLEDON 2 Luton T 1 |
| Apr 9 | Hillsborough | 51,627 | Liverpool 2 Nottingham F 1 |
| **1988-89** | | | |
| Apr 15 | Hillsborough | 53,000 | LIVERPOOL 0 Nottingham F 0 |
| | *(The Hillsborough Disaster. Abandoned after six minutes)* | | |
| May 7 | Old Trafford | 38,000 | LIVERPOOL 3 Nottingham F 1 |
| Apr 15 | Villa Park | 46,553 | Everton 1 Norwich C 0 |
| **1989-90** | | | |
| Apr 8 | Maine Road | 44,026 | MANCHESTER U 3 Oldham A 3 aet |
| Apr 11 | Maine Road | 35,005 | MANCHESTER U 2 Oldham A 1 aet |
| Apr 8 | Villa Park | 38,389 | Crystal P 4 Liverpool 3 aet |
| **1990-91** | | | |
| Apr 14 | Wembley | 77,893 | TOTTENHAM HOTSPUR 3 Arsenal 1 |
| Apr 14 | Villa Park | 40,041 | Nottingham F 4 West Ham 0 |
| **1991-92** | | | |
| Apr 5 | Hillsborough | 40,102 | Sunderland 1 Norwich C 0 |
| Apr 5 | Highbury | 41,889 | LIVERPOOL 1 Portsmouth 1 aet |
| Apr 13 | Villa Park | 40,077 | LIVERPOOL 0 Portsmouth 0 aet |
| | | | *(LIVERPOOL won 3-1 on penalties)* |
| **1992-93** | | | |
| Apr 4 | Wembley | 76,263 | ARSENAL 1 Tottenham Hotspur 0 |
| Apr 3 | Wembley | 75,364 | Sheffield W 2 Sheffield U 1 aet |
| **1993-94** | | | |
| Apr 10 | Wembley | 56,399 | MANCHESTER U 1 Oldham A 1 aet |
| Apr 13 | Maine Road | 32,211 | MANCHESTER U 4 Oldham A 1 |
| Apr 9 | Wembley | 59,989 | Chelsea 2 Luton T 0 |
| **1994-95** | | | |
| Apr 9 | Elland Road | 38,226 | EVERTON 4 Tottenham Hotspur 1 |
| Apr 9 | Villa Park | 38,256 | Manchester U 2 Crystal P 2 aet |
| Apr 12 | Villa Park | 17,987 | Manchester U 2 Crystal P 0 |
| **1995-96** | | | |
| Mar 31 | Villa Park | 38,421 | MANCHESTER U 2 Chelsea 1 |
| Mar 31 | Old Trafford | 39,021 | Liverpool 3 Aston Villa 0 |
| **1996-97** | | | |
| Apr 13 | Highbury | 32,674 | CHELSEA 3 Wimbledon 0 |
| Apr 13 | Old Trafford | 49,640 | Middlesbrough 3 Chesterfield 3 aet |
| Apr 22 | Hillsborough | 30,339 | Middlesbrough 3 Chesterfield 0 |
| **1997-98** | | | |
| Apr 5 | Villa Park | 39,372 | ARSENAL 1 Wolverhampton W 0 |
| Apr 5 | Old Trafford | 53,452 | Newcastle U 1 Sheffield U 0 |
| **1998-99** | | | |
| Apr 11 | Villa Park | 39,217 | MANCHESTER U 0 Arsenal 0 aet |
| Apr 14 | Villa Park | 30,223 | MANCHESTER U 2 Arsenal 1 aet |
| Apr 11 | Old Trafford | 53,609 | Newcastle U 2 Tottenham Hotspur 0 aet |
| **1999-2000** | | | |
| Apr 9 | Wembley | 73,876 | CHELSEA 2 Newcastle U 1 |
| Apr 2 | Wembley | 62,828 | Aston V 0 Bolton W 0 aet |
| | | | *(Aston V won 4-1 on penalties)* |

| | | | |
|---|---|---|---|
| **2000-01** | | | |
| Apr 8 | Villa Park | 40,037 | LIVERPOOL 2 Wycombe W 1 |
| Apr 8 | Old Trafford | 63,541 | Arsenal 2 Tottenham H 1 |
| **2001-02** | | | |
| Apr 14 | Old Trafford | 61,168 | ARSENAL 1 Middlesbrough 0 |
| Apr 14 | Villa Park | 36,147 | Chelsea 1 Fulham 0 |
| **2002-03** | | | |
| Apr 13 | Old Trafford | 59,170 | ARSENAL 1 Sheffield U 0 |
| Apr 13 | Villa Park | 42,602 | Southampton 2 Watford 1 |

# Semi-Final Venues

Complete breakdown of all the semi-final venues and matches played there.

In all 42 different venues have been used for semi-final matches, including a school ground in Edinburgh, a ground on a racecourse in Derby, three cricket grounds, a rugby ground and Wembley Stadium.

Villa Park has played host to more semi-final matches and replays than any other ground – 52 followed by Hillsborough which has staged 33 semi-finals and replays.

## Birmingham

### Aston Lower Grounds

| | | |
|---|---|---|
| 1884 | March 1 | Blackburn Rovers 1 Notts County 0 |
| 1886 | March 6 | West Bromwich Albion 4 Small Heath 0 |

### Perry Barr

| | | |
|---|---|---|
| 1890 | March 8 | Sheffield Wednesday 2 Bolton Wanderers 1 |
| 1896 | March 21 | Wolverhampton Wanders 2 Derby County 1 |

### Villa Park

| | | |
|---|---|---|
| 1901 | April 8 | Tottenham Hotspur 4 West Bromwich Albion 0 |
| 1903 | March 21 | Derby County 3 Millwall 0 |
| 1906 | March 31 | Everton 2 Liverpool 0 |
| 1915 | March 27 | Chelsea 2 Everton 0 |
| 1930 | March 26 | Arsenal 1 Hull City 0 (replay) |
| 1932 | March 12 | Arsenal 1 Manchester City 0 |
| 1935 | March 16 | Sheffield Wednesday 3 Burnley 0 |
| 1946 | March 23 | Charlton Athletic 2 Bolton Wanderers 0 |
| 1948 | March 13 | Blackpool 3 Tottenham Hotspur 1aet |
| 1953 | March 21 | Blackpool 2 Tottenham Hotspur 1 |
| 1954 | March 27 | West Bromwich Albion 2 Port Vale 1 |
| 1955 | March 26 | Manchester City 1 Sunderland 0 |
| 1956 | March 17 | Manchester City 1 Tottenham Hotspur 0 |
| 1958 | March 22 | Manchester United 2 Fulham 2 |
| 1961 | March 18 | Tottenham Hotspur 3 Burnley 0 |
| 1962 | March 31 | Burnley 1 Fulham 1 |
| 1963 | April 27 | Manchester United 1 Southampton 0 |
| 1964 | March 14 | Preston North End 2 Swansea Town 1 |
| 1965 | March 27 | Liverpool 2 Chelsea 0 |
| 1966 | April 23 | Sheffield Wednesday 2 Chelsea 0 |
| 1967 | April 29 | Chelsea 1 Leeds United 0 |
| 1968 | April 27 | West Bromwich Albion 2 Birmingham City 0 |
| 1969 | March 22 | Manchester City 1 Everton 0 |
| 1970 | March 23 | Leeds United 0 Manchester United 0aet (replay) |
| 1971 | March 31 | Arsenal 2 Stoke City 0 (replay) |
| 1972 | April 15 | Arsenal 1 Stoke City 1 |
| 1974 | April 3 | Liverpool 3 Leicester City 1 (replay) |
| 1975 | April 5 | West Ham United 0 Ipswich Town 0 |
| 1979 | March 31 | Arsenal 2 Wolverhampton Wanderers 0 |

| | | |
|---|---|---|
| 1980 | April 12 | West Ham United 1 Everton 1 |
| 1980 | April 16 | Arsenal 1 Liverpool 1aet (replay) |
| 1980 | April 28 | Arsenal 1 Liverpool 1aet (second replay) |
| 1981 | April 11 | Manchester City 1 Ipswich Town 0aet |
| 1982 | April 3 | Tottenham Hotspur 2 Leicester City 0 |
| 1983 | April 16 | Manchester United 2 Arsenal 1 |
| 1984 | April 14 | Watford 1 Plymouth Argyle 0 |
| 1985 | April 13 | Everton 2 Luton Town 1aet |
| 1986 | April 5 | Everton 2 Sheffield Wednesday 1aet |
| 1987 | April 11 | Tottenham Hotspur 4 Watford 1 |
| 1989 | April 15 | Everton 1 Norwich City 0 |
| 1990 | April 8 | Crystal Palace 4 Liverpool 3aet |
| 1991 | April 14 | Nottingham Forest 4 West Ham United 0 |
| 1992 | April 13 | Liverpool 0 Portsmouth 0aet (replay) |
| | | *(Liverpool won 3-1 on penalties* |
| 1995 | April 9 | Manchester United 2 Crystal Palace 2aet |
| 1995 | April 12 | Manchester United 2 Crystal Palace 0 (replay) |
| 1996 | March 31 | Manchester United 2 Chelsea 1 |
| 1998 | April 5 | Arsenal 1 Wolverhampton Wanderers 0 |
| 1999 | April 11 | Manchester United 0 Arsenal 0aet |
| 1999 | April 14 | Manchester United 2 Arsenal 1aet (replay) |
| 2001 | April 8 | Liverpool 2 Wycombe Wanderers 1 |
| 2002 | April 14 | Chelsea 1 Fulham 0 |
| 2003 | April 13 | Southampton 2 Watford 1 |

**The Hawthorns**

| | | |
|---|---|---|
| 1902 | March 15 | Sheffield United 1 Derby County 1 |
| 1960 | March 26 | Wolverhampton Wanderers 1 Aston Villa 0 |

**St Andrews**

| | | |
|---|---|---|
| 1907 | March 23 | Sheffield Wednesday 3 Woolwich Arsenal 1 |
| 1909 | March 31 | Bristol City 2 Derby County 1 (replay) |
| 1911 | March 25 | Newcastle United 3 Chelsea 0 |
| 1913 | April 12 | Sunderland 3 Burnley 2 (replay) |
| 1924 | March 29 | Newcastle United 2 Manchester City 0 |
| 1934 | March 17 | Portsmouth 4 Leicester City 1 |
| 1957 | March 28 | Aston Villa 1 West Bromwich Albion 0 (replay) |
| 1959 | March 18 | Luton Town 1 Norwich City 0 (replay) |
| 1961 | March 27 | Leicester City 2 Sheffield United 0aet (second replay) |

## Blackburn

**Ewood Park**

| | | |
|---|---|---|
| 1893 | March 16 | Everton 0 Preston North End 0aet (replay) |
| 1895 | March 16 | Aston Villa 2 Sunderland 1 |
| 1913 | March 29 | Aston Villa 1 Oldham Athletic 0 |
| 1915 | March 27 | Sheffield United 2 Bolton Wanderers 1 |
| 1938 | March 26 | Huddersfield Town 3 Sunderland 1 |
| 1947 | March 29 | Burnley 0 Liverpool 0aet |

## Bolton

**Burnden Park**

| | | |
|---|---|---|
| 1899 | March 23 | Sheffield United 4 Liverpool 4 (replay) |
| 1907 | March 23 | Everton 2 West Bromwich Albion 1 |
| 1966 | April 23 | Everton 1 Manchester United 0 |
| 1970 | March 26 | Leeds United 1 Manchester United 0 (second replay) |

## Burnley

**Turf Moor**

| | | |
|---|---|---|
| 1922 | March 25 | Huddersfield Town 3 Notts County 1 |

## Coventry
### Highfield Road
| | | |
|---|---|---|
| 1980 | May 1 | Arsenal 1 Liverpool 0 (third replay) |

## Crewe
### Alexandra Road
| | | |
|---|---|---|
| 1889 | March 16 | Wolverhampton Wanderers 1 Blackburn Rovers 1 |
| 1889 | March 23 | Wolverhampton Wanderers 3 Blackburn Rovers 1 (replay) |

### Nantwich Road
| | | |
|---|---|---|
| 1887 | March 5 | Aston Villa 3 Glasgow Rangers 1 |

## Derby
### Baseball Ground
| | | |
|---|---|---|
| 1899 | March 30 | Sheffield United 1 Liverpool 0 (second replay) |
| 1901 | April 11 | Sheffield United 3 Aston Villa 0 (replay) |

### Cricket Ground
| | | |
|---|---|---|
| 1885 | March 14 | Queen's Park (Glasgow) 1 Nottingham Forest 1 |
| 1886 | March 13 | Blackburn Rovers 2 Swifts 1 |
| 1895 | March 16 | West Bromwich Albion 2 Sheffield Wednesday 0 |

### Racecourse Ground
| | | |
|---|---|---|
| 1890 | March 8 | Blackburn Rovers 1 Wolverhampton Wanderers 0 |
| 1892 | March 9 | West Bromwich Albion 6 Nottingham Forest 2 (second replay) |

## Edinburgh
### Merchiston Castle School
| | | |
|---|---|---|
| 1885 | March 28 | Queen's Park, Glasgow 3 Nottingham Forest 0 (replay) |

## Huddersfield
### Leeds Road
| | | |
|---|---|---|
| 1932 | March 12 | Newcastle United 2 Chelsea 1 |
| 1933 | March 18 | Manchester City 3 Derby County 2 |
| 1934 | March 17 | Manchester City 6 Aston Villa 1 |
| 1936 | March 21 | Arsenal 1 Grimsby Town 0 |
| 1937 | April 10 | Sunderland 2 Millwall 1 |
| 1951 | March 14 | Newcastle United 2 Wolverhampton Wanderers 1 (replay) |

### St John's Rugby Ground
| | | |
|---|---|---|
| 1882 | March 6 | Blackburn Rovers 0 Sheffield Wednesday 0 |

## Leeds
### Elland Road
| | | |
|---|---|---|
| 1910 | March 26 | Barnsley 0 Everton 0 |
| 1930 | March 22 | Arsenal 2 Hull City 2 |
| 1931 | March 14 | Birmingham 2 Sunderland 0 |
| 1935 | March 16 | West Bromwich Albion 1 Bolton Wanderers 1 |
| 1947 | March 29 | Charlton Athletic 4 Newcastle United 0 |
| 1952 | April 2 | Newcastle United 2 Blackburn Rovers 1 |
| 1961 | March 18 | Leicester City 0 Sheffield United 0 |
| 1980 | April 16 | West Ham United 2 Everton 1aet |
| 1995 | April 9 | Everton 4 Tottenham Hotspur 1 |

## Leicester
### Filbert Street
| | | |
|---|---|---|
| 1928 | March 24 | Blackburn Rovers 1 Arsenal 0 |
| 1962 | April 9 | Burnley 2 Fulham 1 (replay) |

## Liverpool
### Anfield
| | | |
|---|---|---|
| 1888 | Feb 18 | Preston North End 4 Crewe Alexandra 0 |
| 1908 | March 28 | Newcastle United 6 Fulham 0 |
| 1912 | March 30 | West Bromwich Albion 0 Blackburn Rovers 0 |
| 1921 | March 19 | Wolverhampton Wanderers 0 Cardiff City 0 |
| 1929 | March 23 | Bolton Wanderers 3 Huddersfield Town 1 |

### Goodison Park

| | | |
|---|---|---|
| 1896 | March 21 | Sheffield Wednesday 1 Bolton Wanderers 1 |
| 1903 | March 21 | Bury 3 Aston Villa 0 |
| 1904 | March 19 | Manchester City 3 Sheffield Wednesday 0 |
| 1914 | April 1 | Burnley 1 Sheffield United 0 (replay) |
| 1928 | March 26 | Huddersfield Town 0 Sheffield United 0aet (replay) |
| 1949 | April 2 | Wolverhampton Wanders 1 Manchester United 0 (replay) |
| 1951 | March 14 | Blackpool 2 Birmingham City 1 (replay) |
| 1972 | April 19 | Arsenal 2 Stoke City 1 |
| 1979 | April 4 | Manchester United 1 Liverpool 0 (replay) |
| 1985 | April 13 | Manchester United 2 Liverpool 2aet |

## London

### Crystal Palace

| | | |
|---|---|---|
| 1898 | March 23 | Nottingham Forest 2 Southampton 0 (replay) |
| 1900 | March 24 | Southampton 0 Millwall 0 |

### Highbury

| | | |
|---|---|---|
| 1929 | March 23 | Portsmouth 1 Aston Villa 0 |
| 1937 | April 10 | Preston North End 4 West Bromwich Albion 1 |
| 1939 | March 25 | Portsmouth 2 Huddersfield Town 1 |
| 1949 | March 26 | Leicester City 3 Portsmouth 1 |
| 1958 | March 26 | Manchester United 5 Fulham 3 (replay) |
| 1978 | April 8 | Ipswich Town 3 West Bromwich Albion 1 |
| 1981 | April 15 | Tottenham Hotspur 3 Wolverhampton Wanderers 0 (replay) |
| 1982 | April 3 | Queens Park Rangers 1 West Bromwich Albion 0 |
| 1983 | April 16 | Brighton & Ha 2 Sheffield Wednesday 1 |
| 1984 | April 14 | Everton 1 Southampton 0aet |
| 1992 | April 5 | Liverpool 1 Portsmouth 1aet |
| 1997 | April 13 | Chelsea 3 Wimbledon 0 |

### Kennington Oval

| | | |
|---|---|---|
| 1872 | Feb 17 | Royal Engineers 0 Crystal Palace 0 |
| 1872 | March 5 | The Wanderers 0 Queens Park (Glasgow)0 |
| 1872 | March 9 | Royal Engineers 3 Crystal Palace 0 (replay) |
| 1874 | Jan 28 | Royal Engineers 2 Swifts 0 |
| 1874 | Feb 28 | Oxford University 1 Clapham Rovers 0 |
| 1875 | Feb 27 | Old Etonians 1 Shropshire Wanderers 0 |
| 1875 | Feb 27 | Royal Engineers 1 Oxford University 1 |
| 1875 | March 5 | Royal Engineers 1 Oxford University 0aet (replay) |
| 1876 | Feb 19 | Old Etonians 1 Oxford University 0 |
| 1876 | Feb 26 | The Wanderers 2 Swifts 1 |
| 1877 | March 20 | The Wanderers 1 Cambridge University 0 |
| 1878 | March 16 | Royal Engineers 2 Old Harrovians 1 |
| 1879 | March 22 | Old Etonians 2 Nottingham Forest 1 |
| 1880 | March 27 | Oxford University 1 Nottingham Forest 0 |
| 1881 | March 26 | Old Carthusians 4 Darwen 1 |
| 1882 | March 4 | Old Etonians 5 Marlow 0 |
| 1883 | March 17 | Old Etonians 2 Notts County 1 |

### Stamford Bridge

| | | |
|---|---|---|
| 1908 | March 28 | Wolverhampton Wanderers 2 Southampton 0 |
| 1909 | March 27 | Bristol City 1 Derby County 1 |
| 1912 | March 30 | Barnsley 0 Swindon Town 0 |
| 1920 | March 27 | Huddersfield Town 2 Bristol City 1 |
| 1923 | March 24 | West Ham United 5 Derby County 2 |
| 1925 | March 28 | Sheffield United 2 Southampton 0 |
| 1927 | March 26 | Arsenal 2 Southampton 1 |
| 1975 | April 9 | West Ham United 2 Ipswich Town 1 (replay) |
| 1976 | April 3 | Southampton 2 Crystal Palace 0 |
| 1978 | April 8 | Arsenal 3 Leyton Orient 0 |

**Wembley Stadium**

| | | |
|---|---|---|
| 1991 | April 14 | Tottenham Hotspur 3 Arsenal 1 |
| 1993 | April 3 | Sheffield Wednesday 2 Sheffield United 1aet |
| 1993 | April 4 | Arsenal 1 Tottenham Hotspur 0 |
| 1994 | April 9 | Chelsea 2 Luton Town 0 |
| 1994 | April 10 | Manchester United 1 Oldham Athletic 1aet |
| 2000 | April 2 | Aston Villa 0 Bolton Wanderers 0aet *(Aston Villa 4-1 on penalties)* |
| 2000 | April 9 | Chelsea 2 Newcastle United 1 |

**White Hart Lane**

| | | |
|---|---|---|
| 1902 | March 15 | Southampton 3 Nottingham Forest 1 |
| 1910 | March 26 | Newcastle United 2 Swindon Town 0 |
| 1914 | March 28 | Liverpool 2 Aston Villa 0 |
| 1926 | March 27 | Bolton Wanderers 3 Swansea Town 0 |
| 1950 | March 18 | Arsenal 2 Chelsea 2 |
| 1950 | March 22 | Arsenal 1 Chelsea 0aet (replay) |
| 1952 | April 5 | Arsenal 1 Chelsea 1 |
| 1952 | April 7 | Arsenal 3 Chelsea 0 (replay) |
| 1959 | March 14 | Luton Town 1 Norwich City 1 |
| 1970 | March 14 | Chelsea 5 Watford 1 |
| 1986 | April 5 | Liverpool 2 Southampton 0aet |
| 1988 | April 9 | Wimbledon 2 Luton Town 1 |

## Manchester

**Fallowfield**

| | | |
|---|---|---|
| 1894 | March 10 | Bolton Wanderers 2 Sheffield Wednesday 1 |
| 1899 | March 27 | Sheffield United 0 Liverpool 1 (second replay) *(abandoned at half-time due to crowd trouble and darkness)* |

**Hyde Road**

| | | |
|---|---|---|
| 1905 | March 25 | Newcastle United 1 Sheffield Wednesday 0 |

**Maine Road**

| | | |
|---|---|---|
| 1928 | April 2 | Huddersfield Town 1 Sheffield United 0 (second replay) |
| 1946 | March 27 | Derby County 4 Birmingham City 0aet (replay) |
| 1947 | April 12 | Burnley 1 Liverpool 0 (replay) |
| 1950 | March 25 | Liverpool 2 Everton 0 |
| 1951 | March 10 | Blackpool 0 Birmingham City 0 |
| 1953 | March 21 | Bolton Wanderers 4 Everton 3 |
| 1954 | March 27 | Preston North End 2 Sheffield Wednesday 0 |
| 1958 | March 22 | Bolton Wanderers 2 Blackburn Rovers 1 |
| 1960 | March 26 | Blackburn Rovers 2 Sheffield Wednesday 1 |
| 1973 | April 7 | Leeds United 1 Wolverhampton Wanderers 0 |
| 1975 | April 9 | Fulham 1 Birmingham City 0aet (replay) |
| 1977 | April 23 | Liverpool 2 Everton 2 |
| 1977 | April 27 | Liverpool 3 Everton 0 (replay) |
| 1979 | March 31 | Manchester United 2 Liverpool 2 |
| 1985 | April 17 | Manchester United 2 Liverpool 1 (replay) |
| 1990 | April 8 | Manchester United 3 Oldham Athletic 3aet |
| 1990 | April 11 | Manchester United 2 Oldham Athletic 1aet (replay) |
| 1994 | April 13 | Manchester United 4 Oldham Athletic 1 (replay) |

**Old Trafford**

| | | |
|---|---|---|
| 1910 | March 31 | Barnsley 3 Everton 0 (replay) |
| 1914 | March 28 | Burnley 0 Sheffield United 0, |
| 1921 | March 23 | Wolverhampton Wanderers 3 Cardiff City 1 (replay) |
| 1923 | March 24 | Bolton Wanderers 1 Sheffield United 0 |
| 1928 | March 24 | Huddersfield Town 2 Sheffield United 2aet |
| 1930 | March 22 | Huddersfield Town 2 Sheffield Wednesday 1 |
| 1931 | March 14 | West Bromwich Albion 1 Everton 0 |

| | | |
|---|---|---|
| 1939 | March 25 | Wolverhampton Wanderers 5 Grimsby Town 0 |
| 1968 | April 27 | Everton 1 Leeds United 0 |
| 1971 | March 27 | Liverpool 2 Everton 1 |
| 1974 | March 30 | Liverpool 0 Leicester City 0 |
| 1989 | May 7 | Liverpool 3 Nottingham Forest 1 |
| 1996 | March 31 | Liverpool 3 Aston Villa 0 |
| 1997 | April 13 | Middlesbrough 3 Chesterfield 3aet |
| 1998 | April 5 | Newcastle United 1 Sheffield United 0 |
| 1999 | April 11 | Newcastle United 2 Tottenham Hotspur 0aet |
| 2001 | April 8 | Arsenal 2 Tottenham Hotspur 1 |
| 2002 | April 14 | Arsenal 1 Middlesbrough 0 |
| 2003 | April 13 | Arsenal 1 Sheffield United 0 |

**Whalley Range**

| | | |
|---|---|---|
| 1882 | March 15 | Blackburn Rovers 5 Sheffield Wednesday 1 (replay) |
| 1883 | March 17 | Blackburn Olympic 4 Old Carthusians 0 |

## Nottingham

**City Ground**

| | | |
|---|---|---|
| 1899 | March 18 | Sheffield United 2 Liverpool 2 |
| 1901 | April 6 | Sheffield United 2 Aston Villa 2 |
| 1902 | March 27 | Sheffield United 1 Derby County 0 (second replay) |
| 1961 | March 23 | Leicester 0 Sheffield United 0aet (replay) |
| 1965 | March 31 | Leeds United 1 Manchester United 0 (replay) |

**Meadow Lane**

| | | |
|---|---|---|
| 1912 | April 3 | Barnsley 1 Swindon Town 0 (replay) |
| 1925 | March 28 | Cardiff City 3 Blackburn Rovers 1 |

**Town Ground**

| | | |
|---|---|---|
| 1893 | March 4 | Wolverhampton Wanderers 2 Blackburn Rovers 1 |
| 1896 | March 28 | Sheffield Wednesday 3 Bolton Wanderers 1 (replay) |

**Trent Bridge**

| | | |
|---|---|---|
| 1884 | March 1 | Queens Park (Glasgow) 4 Blackburn Olympic 1 |
| 1885 | March 7 | Blackburn Rovers 5 Old Carthusians 1 |
| 1887 | March 5 | West Bromwich Albion 3 Preston North End 1 |
| 1893 | March 20 | Everton 2 Preston North End 1 (second replay) |
| 1905 | March 29 | Aston Villa 2 Everton 1 (replay) |

## Reading

**Elm Park**

| | | |
|---|---|---|
| 1900 | March 28 | Southampton 3 Millwall 0 (replay) |

## Sheffield

**Bramall Lane**

| | | |
|---|---|---|
| 1889 | March 16 | Preston North End 1 West Bromwich Albion 0 |
| 1891 | Feb 28 | Notts County 3 Sunderland 3 |
| 1891 | March 11 | Notts County 2 Sunderland 0 (replay) |
| 1892 | Feb 27 | Aston Villa 4 Sunderland 1 |
| 1893 | March 4 | Everton 2 Preston North End 2 |
| 1894 | March 10 | Notts County 1 Blackburn Rovers 0 |
| 1897 | March 20 | Aston Villa 3 Liverpool 0 |
| 1898 | March 19 | Nottingham Forest 1 Southampton 1 |
| 1900 | March 29 | Bury 3 Nottingham Forest 2aet (replay) |
| 1909 | March 27 | Manchester United 1 Newcastle United 0 |
| 1911 | March 25 | Bradford City 3 Blackburn Rovers 0 |
| 1913 | March 29 | Sunderland 0 Burnley 0 |
| 1920 | March 27 | Aston Villa 3 Chelsea 1 |
| 1924 | March 29 | Aston Villa 3 Burnley 0 |
| 1926 | March 27 | Manchester City 3 Manchester United 0 |
| 1938 | March 26 | Preston North End 2 Aston Villa 1 |

**Hillsborough**

| | | |
|---|---|---|
| 1912 | April 3 | West Bromwich Albion 1 Blackburn Rovers 0aet (replay) |

| | | |
|---|---|---|
| 1921 | March 19 | Tottenham Hotspur 2 Preston North End 1 |
| 1922 | March 25 | Preston North End 2 Tottenham Hotspur 1aet |
| 1946 | March 23 | Derby County 1 Birmingham City 1 |
| 1948 | March 13 | Manchester United 3 Derby County 1 |
| 1949 | March 26 | Wolverhampton Wanderers 1 Manchester United 1aet |
| 1951 | March 10 | Newcastle United 0 Wolverhampton Wanderers 0aet |
| 1952 | March 29 | Newcastle United 0 Blackburn Rovers 0aet |
| 1955 | March 26 | Newcastle United 1 York City 1 |
| 1956 | March 17 | Birmingham City 3 Sunderland 0 |
| 1957 | March 23 | Manchester United 2 Birmingham City 0 |
| 1959 | March 14 | Nottingham Forest 1 Aston Villa 0 |
| 1962 | March 31 | Tottenham Hotspur 3 Manchester United 1 |
| 1963 | April 27 | Leicester City 1 Liverpool 0 |
| 1964 | March 14 | West Ham United 3 Manchester United 1 |
| 1965 | March 27 | Leeds United 0 Manchester United 0aet |
| 1967 | April 29 | Tottenham Hotspur 2 Nottingham Forest 1 |
| 1969 | March 29 | Leicester City 1 West Bromwich Albion 0 |
| 1970 | March 14 | Leeds United 0 Manchester United 0 |
| 1971 | March 27 | Arsenal 2 Stoke City 2 |
| 1972 | April 15 | Leeds United 3 Birmingham City 0 |
| 1973 | April 7 | Sunderland 2 Arsenal 1 |
| 1974 | March 30 | Newcastle United 2 Burnley 0 |
| 1975 | April 5 | Fulham 1 Birmingham City 1 |
| 1976 | April 3 | Manchester United 2 Derby County 0 |
| 1977 | April 23 | Manchester United 2 Leeds United 1 |
| 1980 | April 12 | Arsenal 0 Liverpool 0 |
| 1981 | April 11 | Tottenham Hotspur 2 Wolverhampton Wanderers 2aet |
| 1987 | April 12 | Coventry City 3 Leeds United 2aet |
| 1988 | April 9 | Liverpool 2 Nottingham Forest 1 |
| 1989 | April 15 | Liverpool 0 Nottingham Forest 0 *(abandoned after six minutes, Hillsborough disaster)* |
| 1992 | April 5 | Sunderland 1 Norwich City 0 |
| 1997 | April 22 | Middlesbrough 3 Chesterfield 0 (replay) |

## Stoke

**Victoria Ground**

| | | |
|---|---|---|
| 1888 | Feb 18 | West Bromwich Albion 3 Derby Junction 0 |
| 1891 | Feb 28 | Blackburn Rovers 3 West Bromwich Albion 2 |
| 1897 | March 20 | Everton 3 Derby County 2 |
| 1900 | March 24 | Bury 1 Nottingham Forest 1 |
| 1905 | March 25 | Aston Villa 1 Everton 1 |
| 1906 | March 31 | Newcastle United 2 Woolwich Arsenal 0 |
| 1935 | March 20 | West Bromwich Albion 2 Bolton Wanderers 0 (replay) |

## Sunderland

**Roker Park**

| | | |
|---|---|---|
| 1955 | March 30 | Newcastle United 2 York City 0 (replay) |

## Wolverhampton

**Molineux**

| | | |
|---|---|---|
| 1892 | Feb 27 | West Bromwich Albion 1 Nottingham Forest 1 |
| 1892 | March 5 | West Bromwich Albion 1 Nottingham Forest 1 (replay) |
| 1898 | March 19 | Derby County 3 Everton 1 |
| 1899 | March 18 | Derby County 3 Stoke 1 |
| 1902 | March 20 | Sheffield United 1 Derby County 1 (replay) |
| 1904 | March 19 | Bolton Wanderers 1 Derby County 0 |
| 1927 | March 26 | Cardiff City 3 Reading 0 |
| 1933 | March 18 | Everton 2 West Ham United 1 |
| 1936 | March 21 | Sheffield United 2 Fulham 1 |
| 1957 | March 23 | Aston Villa 2 West Bromwich Albion 2 |

# Semi-Final Appearances at a Glance by Current League Clubs

A guide to where clubs have played their semi-finals. The result shown refers to the semi-final match played and where the number of matches are greater than appearances this is because all replays are included.

**Arsenal** (23 appearances, 32 matches)

| | |
|---|---|
| Elland Road | 1930 [D] |
| Filbert Street | 1928 [L] |
| Goodison Park | 1972 replay [W] |
| Highfield Road | 1980 3rd replay [W] |
| Hillsborough | 1971 [D] 1973 [L] 1980 [D] |
| Leeds Road, Huddersfield | 1936 [W] |
| Stamford Bridge | 1927 [W] 1978 [W] |
| St Andrews | 1907 [L] |
| Old Trafford | 2001 [W] 2002 [W] 2003 [W] |
| Victoria Ground, Stoke | 1906 [L] |
| Villa Park | 1930 replay [W] 1932 [W] 1971 replay [W] 1972 [D] 1979 [W] 1980 replay [D], 1980 2nd replay [D] 1983 [L] 1998 [W] 1999 [D] 1999 replay [L] |
| Wembley Stadium | 1991 [L] 1993 [W] |
| White Hart Lane | 1950 [D] 1950 replay [W] 1952 [D] 1952 replay [W] |

**Everton** (23 apps, 29 matches)

| | |
|---|---|
| Bramall Lane | 1893 [D] |
| Burnden Park | 1907 [W] 1966 [W] |
| Elland Road | 1910 [D] 1980 replay [L] 1995 [W] |
| Ewood Park | 1893 replay [D] |
| Highbury | 1984 [W] |
| Maine Road | 1950 [L] 1953 [L] 1977 [D] 1977 replay [L] |
| Molineux | 1898 [L] 1933 [W] |
| Old Trafford | 1910 replay [L] 1931 [L] 1968 [W] 1971 [L] |
| Trent Bridge | 1893 second replay [W] 1905 replay [L] |
| Victoria Ground | 1897 [W] 1905 [D] |
| Villa Park | 1906 [W] 1915 [L] 1969 [L] 1980 [D] 1985 [W] 1986 [W] 1989 [W] |

**Manchester United** (22 apps, 33 matches)

| | |
|---|---|
| Bramall Lane | 1909 [W] 1926 [L] |
| Burnden Park | 1966 [L] 1970 2nd replay [L] |
| City Ground | 1965 replay [L] |
| Goodison Park | 1949 replay [L] 1979 replay [W] 1985 [D] |
| Highbury | 1958 replay [W] |
| Hillsborough | 1948 [W] 1949 [D] 1957 [W] 1962 [L] 1964 [L] 1965 [D] 1970 [D] 1976 [W] 1977 [W] |
| Maine Road | 1979 [D] 1985 replay [W] 1990 [D] 1990 replay [W], 1994 replay [W] |
| Villa Park | 1958 [D] 1963 [W] 1970 replay [D] 1983 [W], 1995 [D], 1995 replay [W], 1996 [W], 1999 [D], 1999 replay [W] |
| Wembley Stadium | 1994 [D] |

**Liverpool** (21 apps, 31 matches)
(Overall match total does not include abandoned matches of 1899 and 1989)

| | |
|---|---|
| Baseball Ground | 1899 2nd replay [L] |
| Bramall Lane | 1897 [L] |
| Burnden Park | 1899 replay [D] |
| City Ground | 1899 [D] |
| Ewood Park | 1947 [D] |
| Fallowfield | 1899 2nd replay [abandoned] |
| Goodison Park | 1979 replay [L] 1985 [D] |
| Highbury | 1992 [D] |
| Highfield Road | 1980 3rd replay [L] |
| Hillsborough | 1963 [L] 1980 [D] 1988 [W] 1989 [abandoned] |
| Maine Road | 1950 [W] 1977 [D] 1977 replay [W] 1979 [D] 1985 replay [L] |
| Old Trafford | 1971 [W] 1974 [D] 1989 |

## FA Cup Miscellany

### Keeping It in the Family – One

Billy Meredith is the oldest player to appear in the FA Cup proper. He was 49 years 8 months old when he played for Manchester City against Newcastle in the cup semi-final on March 29, 1924.

In fact his career spanned so many years that he even played in the same Manchester City team as his own son-in-law. Charlie Pringle married Meredith's eldest daughter Lily, and Pringle and Meredith played in two League matches for City in the twilight of the Welsh wizard's career.

In 1904 Meredith scored City's goal when they beat Bolton 1-0 to win the final. Pringle was in the City side that lost the 1926 FA Cup final to Bolton.

| | |
|---|---|
| | re-arranged match [W] 1996 [W] |
| Villa Park | 1906 [L] 1965 [W] 1974 replay [W] 1980 replay [D] 1980 2nd replay [D] 1990 [L] 1992 replay [W] 2001 [W] |
| White Hart Lane | 1914 [W] 1986 [W] |

**WBA** (19 apps, 23 matches)

| | |
|---|---|
| Anfield | 1912 [D] |
| Aston Lower Grounds | 1886 [W] |
| Bramall Lane | 1889 [L] |
| Burnden Park | 1907 [L] |
| Derby Racecourse Ground | 1892 2nd replay [W] |
| Elland Road | 1935 [D] |
| Highbury | 1937 [L] 1978 [L] 1982 [L] |
| Hillsborough | 1912 replay [W] 1969 [L] |
| Molineux | 1892 [D], 1892 replay [D] 1957 [D] |
| Old Trafford | 1931 [W] |
| St Andrews | 1957 replay [L] |
| Trent Bridge | 1887 [W] |
| Victoria Ground | 1888 [W] 1891 [L] 1935 replay [W] |
| Villa Park | 1901 [L] 1954 [W] 1968 [W] |

**Aston Villa** (19 apps, 22 matches)

| | |
|---|---|
| Baseball Ground | 1901 replay [L] |
| Bramall Lane | 1892 [W] 1897 [W] 1920 [W] 1924 [W] 1938 [L] |
| City Ground | 1901 [D] |
| Ewood Park | 1895 [W] 1913 [W] |
| Goodison Park | 1903 [L] |
| The Hawthorns | 1960 [L] |
| Highbury | 1929 [L] |
| Hillsborough | 1959 [L] |
| Leeds Road | 1934 [L] |
| Molineux | 1957 [D] |
| Nantwich Road | 1887 [W] |
| Old Trafford | 1996 [L] |
| St Andrews | 1957 replay [W] |
| Trent Bridge | 1905 replay [W] |
| Victoria Ground | 1905 [D] |
| Wembley Stadium | 2000 [W] |
| White Hart Lane | 1914 [L] |

**Tottenham Hotspur** (17 apps, 18 matches)

| | |
|---|---|
| Elland Road | 1995 [L] |
| Highbury | 1981 replay [W] |
| Hillsborough | 1921 [W] 1922 [L] 1962 [W] 1967 [W] 1981 [D] |
| Old Trafford | 1999 [L] 2001 [L] |
| Villa Park | 1901 [W] 1948 [L] 1953 [L] 1956 [L] 1961 [W] 1982 [W] 1987 [W] |
| Wembley Stadium | 1991 [W] 1993 [L] |

**Blackburn Rovers** (16 apps, 20 matches)

| | |
|---|---|
| Alexandra Road | 1889 [D] 1889 replay [L] |
| Anfield | 1912 [D] |
| Aston Lower Grounds | 1884 [W] |
| Bramall Lane | 1894 [L] 1911 [L] |
| Derby Cricket Ground | 1886 [W] |
| Derby Racecourse | 1890 [W] |
| Elland Road | 1952 replay [L] |
| Filbert Street | 1928 [W] |
| Hillsborough | 1912 replay [L] 1952 [D] |
| Maine Road | 1958 [L] 1960 [W] |
| Meadow Lane | 1925 [L] |
| Trent Bridge | 1885 [W] |
| St Johns, Huddersfield | 1882 [D] |
| Town Ground, Nottingham | 1893 [L] |
| Whalley Range | 1882 replay [W] |
| Victoria Ground | 1891 [W] |

**Newcastle United** (16 apps, 19 matches)

| | |
|---|---|
| Anfield | 1908 [W] |
| Bramall Lane | 1909 [L] |
| Elland Road | 1947 [L] 1952 replay [W] |
| Hillsborough | 1951 [D] 1952 [D] 1955 [D] 1974 [W] |
| Hyde Road | 1905 [W] |
| Leeds Road | 1932 [W] 1951 replay [W] |
| Old Trafford | 1998 [W] 1999 [W] |
| Roker Park | 1955 replay [W] |
| St Andrews | 1911 [W] 1924 [W] |
| Victoria Ground | 1906 [W] |
| Wembley Stadium | 2000 [L] |
| White Hart Lane | 1910 [W] |

**Sheffield Wed** (16 apps, 18 matches)

| | |
|---|---|
| Derby Cricket Ground | 1895 [L] |
| Fallowfield | 1894 [L] |

## FA Cup Miscellany

### Keeping It in the Family – Two

A number of today's clubs were formed when two or more local teams amalgamated. Some of those early rivalries include:

Newcastle East End beat Newcastle West End 3-0 in a second qualifying round match in 1891. They amalgamated the following summer to form Newcastle United.

Rotherham County met Rotherham Town four times between 1906 and 1913 in qualifying round matches. They eventually merged with each other in 1925 to form Rotherham United.

| | |
|---|---|
| Goodison Park | 1896 [D] 1904 [L] |
| Highbury | 1983 [L] |
| Hyde Road | 1905 [L] |
| Maine Road | 1954 [L] 1960 [L] |
| Old Trafford | 1930 [L] |
| Perry Barr | 1890 [W] |
| St Andrews | 1907 [L] |
| St Johns | 1882 [D] |
| Town Ground, Nottingham | 1896 replay [W] |
| Villa Park | 1935 [W] 1966 [W] 1986 [L] |
| Wembley Stadium | 1993 [W] |
| Whalley Range | 1882 replay [L] |

**Chelsea** (15 apps, 17 matches)

| | |
|---|---|
| Bramall Lane | 1920 [L] |
| Highbury | 1997 [W] |
| Leeds Road | 1932 [L] |
| St Andrews | 1911 [L] |
| Villa Park | 1915 [W] 1965 [L] 1966 [L] 1967 [W] 1996 [L] 2002 [W] |
| Wembley Stadium | 1994 [W], 2000 [W] |
| White Hart Lane | 1950 [D] 1950 replay [L] 1952 [D] 1952 replay [L] 1970 [W] |

**Wolverhampton W** (14 apps, 19 matches)

| | |
|---|---|
| Anfield | 1921 [D] |
| Alexandra Road | 1889 [D], 1889 replay [W] |
| Derby Racecourse Ground | 1890 [L] |
| Goodison Park | 1949 replay [W] |
| The Hawthorns | 1960 [W] |
| Highbury | 1981 replay [L] |
| Hillsborough | 1949 [D] 1951 [D] 1981 [D] |
| Leeds Road | 1951 replay [L] |
| Maine Road | 1973 [L] |
| Old Trafford | 1921 replay [W] 1939 [W] |
| Perry Barr | 1896 [W] |
| Stamford Bridge | 1908 [W] |
| Town Ground, Nottingham | 1893 [W] |
| Villa Park | 1979 [L] 1998 [L] |

**Sheffield United** (13 apps, 23 matches)
(Overall match total does not include abandoned match of 1899)

| | |
|---|---|
| Baseball Ground | 1899 2nd replay [W] 1901 replay [W] |
| Burnden Park | 1899 replay [D] |
| City Ground | 1899 [D] 1901 [D] 1902 2nd replay [W] 1961 replay [D] |
| Elland Road | 1961 [D] |
| Ewood Park | 1915 [W] |
| Fallowfield | 1899 2nd replay [abandoned] |
| Goodison Park | 1914 replay [L] 1928 replay [D] |
| The Hawthorns | 1902 [D] |
| Maine Road | 1928 2nd replay [L] |
| Molineux | 1902 replay [D] 1936 [W] |
| Old Trafford | 1914 [D] 1923 [L] 1928 [D] 1998 [L] 2003 [L] |
| Stamford Bridge | 1925 [W] |
| St Andrews | 1961 2nd replay [L] |
| Wembley Stadium | 1993 [L] |

**Derby County** (13 apps, 17 matches)

| | |
|---|---|
| City Ground | 1902 2nd replay [L] |
| Hillsborough | 1946 [D] 1948 [L] 1976 [L] |
| Leeds Road | 1933 [L] |
| The Hawthorns | 1902 [D] |
| Maine Road | 1946 replay [W] |
| Molineux | 1898 [W] 1899 [W] 1902 replay [D] 1904 [L] |
| Perry Barr | 1896 [L] |
| Stamford Bridge | 1909 [D] 1923 [L] |
| St Andrews | 1909 replay [L] |
| Victoria Ground | 1897 [L] |
| Villa Park | 1903 [W] |

**Bolton Wanderers** (13 apps, 15 matches)

| | |
|---|---|
| Anfield | 1929 [W] |
| Elland Road | 1935 [D] |
| Ewood Park | 1915 [L] |
| Goodison Park | 1896 [D] |
| Fallowfield | 1894 [W] |
| Maine Road | 1953 [W] 1958 [W] |
| Molineux | 1904 [W] |
| Old Trafford | 1923 [W] |
| Perry Barr | 1890 [L] |
| Town Ground, Nottingham | 1896 replay [L] |
| Victoria Ground | 1935 replay [L] |
| Villa Park | 1946 [L] |
| Wembley Stadium | 2000 [L] |
| White Hart Lane | 1926 [W] |

**Nottingham Forest** (12 apps, 17 matches)
(Overall match total does not include abandoned match of 1989)

| | |
|---|---|
| Bramall Lane | 1898 [D] 1900 replay [L] |
| Crystal Palace | 1898 replay [W] |
| Derby Cricket Ground | 1885 [L] |
| Derby Racecourse Ground | 1892 2nd replay [L] |
| Hillsborough | 1959 [W] 1967 [L] 1988 [L] 1989 [abandoned] |
| Kennington Oval | 1879 [L] 1880 [L] |
| Merchiston Castle School Edinburgh | 1885 replay [L] |
| Molineux | 1892 [D] 1892 replay [D] |
| Old Trafford | 1989 [L] |
| Victoria Ground | 1900 [D] |
| Villa Park | 1991 [W] |
| White Hart Lane | 1902 [L] |

**Sunderland** (11 apps, 13 matches)

| | |
|---|---|
| Bramall Lane | 1891 [D] 1891 replay [L] 1892 [L] 1913 [D] |

# FA Cup Miscellany

## Home From Home, Away From Home

Manchester United's Old Trafford ground was so badly damaged by bombs during the Second World War, that in the immediate post-war seasons, they played their home matches at neighbouring Maine Road, and so technically at least, they became the first, and so far only, team to win the cup playing all their matches away from home.

They also set another record that season as the only team to have won the trophy by beating six top flight (old First Division) teams in every round with victories over Aston Villa, Liverpool, Charlton Athletic, Preston North End, Derby County and Blackpool.

Arsenal achieved a remarkable record when they reached the finals in both 1971 and 1972 without once being drawn at home in either year – although they did draw matches at Portsmouth and Leicester in 1971 and at Derby in 1972 so they did in fact play some matches at Highbury. But when Arsenal won the FA Cup in 1950 they did not leave London, being drawn at home in every round before playing two semi-final matches against Chelsea at White Hart Lane and then the final at Wembley.

In 1980-81 and 1981-82 when Tottenham won the FA Cup in successive seasons they played a total of 16 matches – and only two of them were outside London – their semi-final against Wolves at Hillsborough in 1981 which was replayed at Highbury, and their semi-final against Leicester City in 1982 which was at Villa Park.

Luton Town also had a remarkable run of being drawn at home for 11 successive rounds from January 1949 until until January 1953. The only away matches they played in that period were replays.

Birmingham City became the first team to reach the cup final after being drawn away in every round in 1956, while Sheffield Wednesday were the last team to reach the final in this manner in 1966.

| | |
|---|---|
| Elland Road | 1931 [L] |
| Ewood Park | 1895 [L] 1938 [L] |
| Hillsborough | 1956 [L] 1973 [W] 1992 [W] |
| Leeds Road | 1937 [W] |
| St Andrews | 1913 replay [W] |
| Villa Park | 1955 [L] |

**Southampton** (11 apps, 13 matches)

| | |
|---|---|
| Bramall Lane | 1898 [D] |
| Crystal Palace | 1898 replay [L] 1900 [D] |
| Elm Park, Reading | 1900 replay [W] |
| Highbury | 1984 [L] |
| Stamford Bridge | 1908 [L] 1925 [L] 1927 [L] 1976 [W] |
| Villa Park | 1963 [L] 2003 [W] |
| White Hart Lane | 1902 [W] 1986 [L] |

**Preston North End** (10 apps, 12 matches)

| | |
|---|---|
| Anfield | 1888 [W] |
| Bramall Lane | 1889 [W] 1893 [D] 1938 [W] |
| Ewood Park | 1893 replay [D] |
| Highbury | 1937 [W] |
| Hillsborough | 1921 [L] 1922 [W] |
| Maine Road | 1954 [W] |
| Trent Bridge | 1887 [L] 1893 second replay [L] |
| Villa Park | 1964 [W] |

**Manchester City** (10 apps, 10 matches)

| | |
|---|---|
| Bramall Lane | 1926 [W] |
| Goodison Park | 1904 [W] |
| Huddersfield | 1933 [W] 1934 [W] |
| St Andrews | 1924 [L] |
| Villa Park | 1932 [L] 1955 [W] 1956 [W] 1969 [W] 1981 [W] |

**Birmingham City** (9 apps, 12 matches)

| | |
|---|---|
| Elland Road | 1931 [W] |
| Goodison Park | 1951 replay [L] |
| Hillsborough | 1946 [D] 1956 [W] 1957 [L] 1972 [L] 1975 [D] |
| Lower Grounds Aston | 1886 [L] |
| Maine Road | 1946 replay [L] 1951 [D] 1975 replay [L] |
| Villa Park | 1968 [L] |

**Burnley** (8 apps, 12 matches)

| | |
|---|---|
| Bramall Lane | 1913 [D] 1913 replay [L] 1924 [L] |
| Ewood Park | 1947 [D] |
| Filbert Street | 1962 replay [W] |
| Goodison Park | 1914 replay [W] |
| Hillsborough | 1974 [L] |
| Maine Road | 1947 replay [W] |
| Old Trafford | 1914 [D] |
| St Andrews | 1913 replay [L] |
| Villa Park | 1935 [L] 1961 [L] 1962 [D] |

**Leeds United** (8 apps, 10 apps)

| | |
|---|---|
| Burnden Park | 1970 2nd replay [W] |
| City Ground | 1965 replay [W] |
| Hillsborough | 1965 [D] 1970 [D] 1972 [W] 1977 [L] 1987 [L] |
| Maine Road | 1973 [W] |
| Old Trafford | 1968 [L] |
| Villa Park | 1967 [L] 1970 replay [D] |

**Leicester City** (7 apps, 10 matches)

| | |
|---|---|
| City Ground | 1961 replay [D] |

| | |
|---|---|
| Elland Road | 1961 [D] |
| Highbury | 1949 [W] |
| Hillsborough | 1963 [W] 1969 [W] |
| Old Trafford | 1974 [D] |
| St Andrews | 1934 [L] 1961 2nd replay [W] |
| Villa Park | 1974 replay [L] 1982 [L] |

**Huddersfield Town** (7 apps, 9 matches)

| | |
|---|---|
| Anfield | 1929 [L] |
| Ewood Park | 1938 [W] |
| Goodison Park | 1928 replay [D] |
| Highbury | 1939 [L] |
| Maine Road | 1928 2nd replay [W] |
| Old Trafford | 1928 [D] 1930 [W] |
| Stamford Bridge | 1920 [W] |
| Turf Moor | 1922 [W] |

**Fulham** (6 apps, 9 matches)

| | |
|---|---|
| Anfield | 1908 [L] |
| Filbert Street | 1962 replay [L] |
| Highbury | 1958 replay [L] |
| Hillsborough | 1975 [D] |
| Maine Road | 1975 replay [W] |
| Molineux | 1936 [L] |
| Villa Park | 1958 [D] 1962 [D] 2002 [L] |

**West Ham United** (6 apps 8 matches)

| | |
|---|---|
| Elland Road | 1980 replay [W] |
| Hillsborough | 1964 [W] |
| Molineux | 1933 [L] |
| Stamford Bridge | 1923 [W] 1975 replay [W] |
| Villa Park | 1975 [D] 1980 [D] 1991 [L] |

**Notts County** (5 apps, 6 matches)

| | |
|---|---|
| Aston Lower Grounds | 1884 [L] |
| Bramall Lane | 1891 [D] 1891 replay [W] 1894 [W] |
| Kennington Oval | 1883 [L] |
| Turf Moor | 1922 [L] |

**Portsmouth** (5 apps, 6 matches)

| | |
|---|---|
| Highbury | 1929 [W] 1939 [W] 1949 [L] 1992 [D] |
| St Andrews | 1934 [W] |
| Villa Park | 1992 replay [L] |

**Luton Town** (4 apps, 5 matches)

| | |
|---|---|
| St Andrews | 1959 replay [W] |
| Villa Park | 1985 [L] |
| Wembley Stadium | 1994 [L] |
| White Hart Lane | 1959 [D] 1988 [L] |

**Watford** (4 apps, 4 matches)

| | |
|---|---|
| Villa Park | 1984 [W], 1987 [L] 2003 [L] |
| White Hart Lane | 1970 [L] |

**Stoke City** (3 apps, 5 matches)

| | |
|---|---|
| Goodison Park | 1972 replay [L] |
| Hillsborough | 1971 [D] |
| Molineux | 1899 [L] |
| Villa Park | 1971 replay [L], 1972 [D] |

**Oldham Athletic** (3 apps, 5 matches)

| | |
|---|---|
| Ewood Park | 1913 [L] |
| Maine Road | 1990 [D], 1990 replay [L], 1994 replay [L] |
| Wembley Stadium | 1994 [D] |

**Blackpool** (3 apps, 4 matches)

| | |
|---|---|
| Goodison Park | 1951 replay [W] |
| Maine Road | 1951 [D] |
| Villa Park | 1948 [W], 1953 [W] |

**Cardiff City** (3 apps, 4 matches)

| | |
|---|---|
| Anfield | 1921 [D] |
| Meadow Lane | 1925 [W] |
| Molineux | 1927 [W] |
| Old Trafford | 1921 replay [L] |

**Crystal Palace** (3 apps, 4 matches)

| | |
|---|---|
| Stamford Bridge | 1976 [L] |
| Villa Park | 1990 [W] 1995 [D] 1995 replay [L] |

**Ipswich Town** (3 apps, 4 matches)

| | |
|---|---|
| Highbury | 1978 [W] |
| Stamford Bridge | 1975 replay [L] |
| Villa Park | 1975 [D] 1981 [L] |

**Millwall** (3 apps, 4 matches)

| | |
|---|---|
| Crystal Palace | 1900 [D] |
| Elm Park | 1900 replay [L] |
| Leeds Road | 1937 [L] |
| Villa Park | 1903 [L] |

**Norwich City** (3 apps, 4 matches)

| | |
|---|---|
| Hillsborough | 1992 [L] |
| St Andrews | 1959 replay [L] |
| Villa Park | 1989 [L] |
| White Hart Lane | 1959 [D] |

**Barnsley** (2 apps, 4 matches)

| | |
|---|---|
| Elland Road | 1910 [D] |
| Meadow Lane | 1912 replay [W] |
| Old Trafford | 1910 replay [W] |
| Stamford Bridge | 1912 [D] |

**Middlesbrough** (2 apps, 3 matches)

| | |
|---|---|
| Hillsborough | 1997 replay [W] |
| Old Trafford | 1997 [D] 2002 [L] |

**Bristol City** (2 apps, 3 matches)

| | |
|---|---|
| Stamford Bridge | 1909 [D] 1920 [L] |
| St Andrews | 1909 replay [W] |

**Bury** (2 apps, 3 matches)

| | |
|---|---|
| Bramall Lane | 1900 replay [W] |
| Goodison Park | 1903 [W] |
| Victoria Ground | 1900 [D] |

**Swindon Town** (2 apps, 3 matches)

| | |
|---|---|
| Meadow Lane | 1912 replay [L] |
| Stamford Bridge | 1912 [D] |

# FA Cup Miscellany

## You Are What You Eat!

In 1926 Bolton's players openly took "nerve powder" before their 1-0 FA Cup final win over Manchester City,

While in 1939, Wolves players allegedly took a monkey gland potion before playing Portsmouth in the final. If they did – and it is doubtful – it didn't do them much good. They lost 4-1 in one of the biggest FA Cup final upsets of all time.

White Hart Lane 1910 [L]

**Charlton Athletic** (2 apps, 2 matches)
Elland Road 1947 [W]
Villa Park 1946 [W]

**Grimsby Town** (2 apps, 2 matches)
Leeds Road, Huddersfield 1936 [L]
Old Trafford 1939 [L]

**Swansea City** (2 apps, 2 matches)
Villa Park 1964 [L]
White Hart Lane 1926 [L]

**Wimbledon** (2 apps, 2 matches)
Highbury 1997 [L]
White Hart Lane 1988 [W]

**Chesterfield** (1 app, 2 matches)
Old Trafford 1997 [D]
Hillsborough 1997 replay [L]

**Hull City** (1 app, 2 matches)
Elland Road 1930 [D]
Villa Park 1930 replay [L]

**York City** (1 app, 2 matches)
Hillsborough 1955 [D]
Roker Park 1955 replay [L]

**Bradford City** (1 app)
Bramall Lane 1911 [W]

**Brighton & HA** (1 app)
Highbury 1983 [W]

**Coventry City** (1 app)
Hillsborough 1987 [W]

**Crewe Alexandra** (1 app)
Anfield 1888 [L]

**Leyton Orient** (1 app)
Stamford Bridge 1978 [L]

**Plymouth Argyle** (1 app)
Villa Park 1984 [L]

**Port Vale** (1 app)
Villa Park 1954 [L]

**Queens Park Rangers** (1 app)
Highbury 1982 [W]

**Reading** (1 app)
Molineux 1927 [L]

**Wycombe Wanderers** (1 app)
Villa Park 2001 [L]

## Drawn Semi-Finals

Before the days of penalty shootouts after one drawn semi-final, there were several years when the semi-finals took several weeks to settle.

The most notable occasion in modern times was in 1979-80 when Arsenal and Liverpool met four times before Arsenal reached the final:

April 12 Arsenal 0 Liverpool 0 at Hillsborough
April 16 Arsenal 1 Liverpool 1aet at Villa Park
April 28 Arsenal 1 Liverpool 1aet at Villa Park
May 1 Arsenal 1 Liverpool 0 at Highfield Road, Coventry.
Arsenal lost the final just nine days later to West Ham.

The following ties were settled at the third attempt, after two replays:
Sheffield United were involved in four semi-final marathons.
1891-92 WBA v Nottingham F (1-1, 1-1, 6-2)
1892-93 Everton v Preston NE (2-2, 0-0aet, 2-1)
1898-99 Sheffield Utd v Liverpool (2-2, 4-4, 1-0) (not including one abandoned match)
1901-02 Sheffield Utdv Derby C (1-1, 1-1aet, 1-0)
1927-28 Huddersfield T v Sheffield Utd (2-2aet, 0-0aet, 1-0)
1960-61 Leicester C v Sheffield Utd (0-0, 0-0aet, 2-0aet)
1969-70 Leeds Utd v Manchester Utd (0-0, 0-0aet, 1-0)

There were seven occasions when both semi-finals ended in draws:
1871-72; 1899-1900; 1911-12; 1950-51; 1951-52; 1974-75 and 1979-80

There have been five occasions when clubs have twice met in the semi-finals and twice needed to replay to settle the tie:
Arsenal v Chelsea 1949-50 (2-2, 1-0aet) 1951-52 (1-1, 3-0)
Leeds Utd v Manchester Utd 1964-65 (0-0, 1-0) 1969-70 (0-0, 0-0aet, 1-0)
Arsenal v Stoke City 1970-71 (2-2, 2-0) 1971-72 (1-1, 2-1)
Manchester Utd v Liverpool 1978-79 (2-2, 1-0) 1984-85 (2-2aet, 2-1)
Manchester Utd v Oldham Ath. 1989-90 (3-3aet, 2-1aet) 1993-94 (1-1aet, 4-1)

# FA Cup Final Penalties

Only 14 penalties have been awarded in the FA Cup final since penalty kicks were incorporated into the Laws of the Game in 1891-92 and of those 14, eleven have been scored.

Charlie Wallace of Aston Villa was the first to miss with a penalty in 1913. In 1988 John Aldridge became the first to fail from the spot at Wembley while Gary Lineker also failed to score at Wembley in 1991.

Only three finals have ended in a 1-0 scoreline decided by a penalty:

1922 Huddersfield Town 1 Preston North End 0
1938 Preston North End 1 Huddersfield Town 0
1982 Tottenham Hotspur 1 Queens Park Rangers 0 (replay)

The 1982 replay was decided by a sixth minute penalty scored by Tottenham's Glenn Hoddle – the quickest penalty awarded in the final. George Mutch's penalty in the 1938 final was awarded in the last minute of extra time – the latest any penalty has been awarded in the final.

The only players to score penalties and end up on the losing side are Eddie Shimwell (Blackpool 1948) and Kevin Reeves (Manchester City 1981 replay). Despite missing their penalties Charlie Wallace (1913) and Gary Lineker (1991) both ended up on the winning side.

In 1988 Wimbledon's Dave Beasant not only became the first goalkeeper to captain a side in the final, but also the first goalkeeper to save a penalty in a Wembley FA Cup final. Mark Crossley of Nottingham Forest became the second goalie to save a Wembley FA Cup final penalty in 1991.

Eric Cantona of Manchester United became the first player to score two penalties in the final during his side's 4-0 win over Chelsea in 1994. Manchester United's Dutch midfielder Arnold Muhren (1983 replay) is the only other overseas player to score a final penalty.

## The Penalty Dramas

**1910 replay Newcastle Utd 2 Barnsley 0**

The replayed final of 1910 was a roughhouse of a match. Newcastle were the main culprits and early in the match Newcastle's Scottish international forward Sandy Higgins flattened the Barnsley keeper Fred Mearns who had to be stopped by teammates and the referee from a retaliatory attack on the Scot.

Barnsley's right-back Dickie Downs was taken off after being kicked in the stomach at one stage, but after all of Newcastle's physical play, it was Barnsley who conceded the first penalty ever awarded in an FA Cup final when Higgins was tripped in the box.

Albert Shepherd had put Newcastle 1-0 ahead in the 52nd minute and made it 2-0 after 62 minutes from the penalty spot.

**1913 Aston Villa 1 Sunderland 0**

The 1913 final was the first between the two clubs who had finished first and second in the League. Sunderland, the champions were going for the double, last achieved by Aston Villa in 1897, and the match attracted a then world record crowd of 120,081 to the old Crystal Palace.

The penalty was awarded in the first half when Villa's Clem Stephenson was sent sprawling in the box. Charlie Wallace, Villa's England forward, who was born in Co. Durham, stepped up to take the penalty against the club from the north-east – and blasted his attempt wide. Villa recovered and won 1-0 with a second half header from Tommy Barber – just as Stephenson had famously dreamt the night before.

**1922 Huddersfield Town 1 Preston NE 0**

A dour final at Stamford Bridge became the first to be decided by a penalty when England winger Billy Smith scored the only goal from the spot after 67 minutes to give Huddersfield their only FA Cup success.

Smith, a tall, leggy player with fine control, was bundled over by Preston full-back Tom Hamilton, but most observers were convinced the foul had taken place outside the penalty area. Either way, Smith took the penalty and gave James Mitchell, the only bespectacled amateur to play in goal in a final, no chance.

**1938 Preston NE 1 Huddersfield Town 0**

Sixteen years after Huddersfield beat Preston 1-0 with a penalty deciding the outcome, Preston gained their revenge beating Huddersfield 1-0 with the deciding goal also coming from the spot.

One of the most famous penalties of all time was awarded in the last minute of extra time – just as fans were leaving Wembley and BBC commentator Tom Woodroofe promised to "eat my hat" if anyone scored. No sooner were the words uttered when George Mutch, Preston's Scottish international inside-right advanced on goal. The challenge from England centre-half Alf Young – which may or may not have been inside the box – resulted in Mutch falling on to the bone-hard ground and referee AJ Jewell awarding a penalty.

The one surprising aspect of this penalty is why Bill Shankly did not take it. The future Liverpool manager regularly took penalties for Preston and eight of the 13 goals he scored for them in 300 matches were from the spot. Mutch was surprised as well, and wrote later: "I was dazed. I did not even understand that a penalty had been awarded. They handed me the ball, I placed it automatically . I wondered hazily why none of them seemed anxious to take the kick. I took it more casually than I would at morning practice."

He also blasted it past Bob Hesford in the Huddersfield goal, off the crossbar and into the back of the net for the winner.

**1948 Manchester United 4 Blackpool 2**

Eddie Shimwell became the first man to score a penalty in the final and end up on the losing side. The incident came after 12 minutes when Stan Mortensen was tackled from behind by Manchester United's lanky centre-half Allenby Chilton and was pitched headlong into the penalty area.

The referee, CJ Barrick, had been left some way behind by Mortensen's burst of speed, and later newsreel footage suggested, once again, the foul had occurred outside the box. Shimwell fired the penalty under goalkeeper Jack Crompton's body as he fell to his right and Blackpool were 1-0 up. Although United equalised, Blackpool were back in front by the interval but then conceded three goals in the second half to become the first team to lead twice and then lose the final.

**1954 WBA 3 Preston NE 2**

A year after Stanley Matthews finally won a winners medal with Blackpool, much of the attention in the build-up to the 1954 FA Cup final was focused on the other giant of the era – Preston's Tommy Finney. And with just under half-an-hour remaining it looked as though Finney might succeed just as Matthews had done.

Although West Brom had taken a 21st minute lead through Ronnie Allen, Preston had regained the initiative with an almost immediate equaliser from Angus Morrison and a second from Charlie Wayman (51) to put them 2-1 up.

But the match began to turn in West Brom's favour 12 minutes later. Ray Barlow brushed aside two tackles as he moved towards Preston's goal – but was brought down by the third from future Manchester United cup-winning manager Tommy Docherty.

The day before the final, the players had visited the stadium and Allen had watched the penalty spot to the left of the Royal Box, being painted on the pitch. Now he placed the ball on the spot and prepared to beat Preston keeper George Thompson. A momentary delay to pat down a divot just heightened the tension before Allen struck. Thompson – 35 years before Dave Beasant eventually managed it – almost became the first goalie to save a Wembley final penalty. He got a hand to the ball – but could not divert it away from goal. That made it 2-2 with 28 minutes to go and Frank Griffin stole Finney's glory with a late winner.

**1962 Tottenham Hotspur 3 Burnley 1**

Danny Blanchflower had captained Tottenham to the double the previous year and his 80th minute penalty in 1962 clinched Spurs second successive FA Cup victory with a 3-1 victory over Burnley.

Jimmy Greaves had put Spurs ahead after only three minutes while Jimmy Robson had equalised for Burnley with Wembley's 100th FA Cup final goal five minutes after half-time. Spurs were back in front one minute later when Bobby Smith scored for the second successive final – it was to be 40 years before that feat was equalled by Arsenal's Freddie Ljungberg – and while the 'chessboard' final ebbed and flowed, Spurs never looked like losing.

They sealed the match with 10 minutes to go. John White, who was to die so tragically young two years later when he was struck by lightning on a golf course, floated a cross into the middle. Smith challenged for the ball with Burnley goalkeeper Adam Blacklaw, and while a linesman flagged for a foul on Blacklaw, the

**The Penalty Takers**

| | | | |
|---|---|---|---|
| 1910 replay | Albert Shepherd | Newcastle Utd | scored |
| 1913 | Charlie Wallace | Aston Villa | missed |
| 1922 | Billy Smith | Huddersfield T | scored |
| 1938 | George Mutch | Preston NE | scored |
| 1948 | Eddie Shimwell | Blackpool | scored |
| 1954 | Ronnie Allen | WBA | scored |
| 1962 | Danny Blanchflower | Tottenham H | scored |
| 1981 replay | Kevin Reeves | Manchester C | scored |
| 1982 replay | Glenn Hoddle | Tottenham H | scored |
| 1983 replay | Arnold Muhren | Manchester Utd | scored |
| 1988 | John Aldridge | Liverpool | saved |
| 1991 | Gary Lineker | Tottenham H | saved |
| 1994 | Eric Cantona | Manchester Utd | scored |
| 1994 | Eric Cantona | Manchester Utd | scored |

ball ran loose to Terry Medwin. The Spurs winger's shot was handled on the line by Tommy Cummings and referee, Jim Finney, having allowed play to continue, had no option this time but to stop it for a penalty.

Blanchflower a study of cool concentration, sent Blacklaw the wrong way from the spot and Spurs became only the second team in the 20th century after Newcastle United in 1951 and 1952, to win the cup in successive seasons.

**1981 replay Tottenham H 3 Manchester C 2**

Kevin Reeves became the first player for 33 years to score a final penalty and finish on the losing side. The penalty came in the 50th minute of the replayed 100th final which had ended in a 1-1 draw the previous Saturday.

Now, on May 14, 1981 the first ever replayed final at Wembley was taking place on a sunlit spring evening beneath the Twin Towers. Ricky Villa, who had had such a poor game on the Saturday that he had been substituted, put Spurs ahead after just eight minutes of the re-match. Three minutes later Steve Mackenzie had equalised with an outstanding goal for City – and, with 50 minutes gone, City were about to take the lead.

Referee Keith Hackett ruled that Dave Bennett, chasing a long hopeful ball, had been sandwiched between Spurs defenders Graham Roberts and Chris Hughton and pointed to the spot. Reeves blasted the ball high to the left and wide of Spurs goalkeeper Milija Aleksic who at least went the right way but had no chance of saving a superbly taken penalty.

But Spurs recovered. Garth Crooks equalised after 70 minutes and Ricky Villa finished off City in the 76th minute with his brilliant, individual mazy run, the best goal ever scored in the FA Cup final at Wembley.

**1982 replay Tottenham H 1 QPR 0**

For the second successive year Tottenham had reached the final, and for the second successive year the match had gone to a replay. Now for the second successive year a penalty had been awarded in the replay – but this time it was for Spurs rather than against them.

The decision came after only six minutes – the quickest penalty yet awarded in the final, after Tony Currie tripped Graham Roberts following a run of more than 50 yards from his own half by the Spurs defender. There was no argument from the Rangers players and Hoddle made no mistake from the penalty spot.

Just like Danny Blanchflower 20 years earlier, Hoddle sent QPR keeper Peter Hucker the wrong way, and Spurs were on their way to victory. It was also only the third time after the finals of 1922 and 1938 that a single penalty decided the final. Spurs matched their predecessors of 1961 and 1962 and Newcastle of 1951 and 1952 by retaining the cup.

**1983 replay Manchester Utd 4 Brighton & HA 0**

The third successive FA Cup final at Wembley to go to a replay and the third successive replay in which a penalty was awarded. Sir Matt Busby thoroughly enjoyed his 74th birthday as United crushed Brighton 4-0 in the replay after drawing 2-2 in the original game five days previously.

United already had the match won by the time the penalty was awarded. Captain Bryan Robson had opened the scoring after 25 minutes, Norman Whiteside made it 2-0 after 30 minutes and Robson put United 3-0 up a minute before half-time.

After 62 minutes, United were on the attack yet again, and Seagulls defender Gary Stevens, who had scored Brighton's 87th minute equaliser on the Saturday, was facing yet another threat from Robson. With neither player giving an inch, Stevens basically wrestled Robson off the ball – and was immediately penalised.

So Robson now had the chance of becoming the first player since Stan Mortensen 30 years previously to score a hat-trick in the final. Instead he declined the appeals of all his team-mates to take the penalty and handed the ball to Dutchman Arnold Muhren who duly took his opportunity and became the first overseas player to score a penalty in the final.

**1988 Wimbledon 1 Liverpool 0**

John Aldridge had scored 30 goals for Liverpool – including 11 penalties – as Liverpool cantered to the league championship in 1987-88. They came to the final looking for their second double in three years and were odds-on favourites to win – but the match had not gone according to plan.

Wimbledon had taken a surprise lead through a Lawrie Sanchez header after 37 minutes and Liverpool had found it harder and harder to break down some stubborn Dons' defending.

But after 61 minutes it looked as though Liverpool had finally stolen a way through. Clive Goodyear was adjudged by referee Brian Hill to have brought Aldridge down although television replays afterwards clearly showed him playing the ball, not the man. Aldridge picked himself up, placed the ball on the spot and sent it high to goalkeeper Dave Beasant's left.

That was no surprise to the Wimbledon keeper. "I had watched videos of his penalties and they nearly always went to the same position," Beasant said afterwards. "I had done my homework."

He had indeed. Beasant, hurling his 6ft 4ins frame in the right direction became the first goalkeeper for 75 years not to be beaten by a cup final penalty and the first to save an FA Cup final penalty at Wembley.

Half-an-hour later he made more history when he became the first goalkeeper captain to receive the cup.

Liverpool returned to the final a year later – and at least there was some consolation for the inconsolable Aldridge of 1988. He scored after only four minutes of the 1989 final as Liverpool beat Everton 3-2.

**1991 Tottenham H 2 Nottingham F 1**

If it's Tottenham Hotspur in the final a penalty cannot be far behind. In 1962 Danny Blanchflower scored for Spurs, in 1981 Kevin Reeves scored against Spurs, in 1982 Glenn Hoddle scored for Spurs and in 1991 Gary Lineker missed for Spurs.

The England captain became the second player to miss a Wembley FA Cup final penalty – and Mark Crossley the second goalkeeper to save one – after 33 minutes of the 1991 match.

The penalty came with Spurs trailing 1-0 after Stuart Pearce's free-kick which followed Paul Gascoigne's infamous tackle on Gary Charles.

Lineker thought he had equalised after 23 minutes when he stabbed home a cross from Nayim – but the goal was wrongly disallowed for offside. And now he was presented with a second chance to pull Spurs back in the game. Paul Stewart sent Lineker clear of the Nottingham Forest defence with a perfectly weighted ball. Lineker controlled it, and just as he was rounding the 21-year-old Crossley, the Forest goalie tripped him up.

That season was the first in which goalkeepers faced an automatic red card for deliberatly preventing a goalscoring opportunity, but referee Roger Milford allowed Crossley to stay on.

Lineker had already scored a penalty against Crossley in the first leg of the League Cup semi-final the previous February, and now had a great opportunity to bring Spurs back into the match, but Crossley anticipated well, diving to his left to force Lineker's shot high over the goal and away for a corner. However, Crossley and his team mates were beaten in the end by a Paul Stewart equaliser and a Des Walker own goal as Spurs came back to win the cup 2-1 for what was a record eighth time.

**1994 Manchester Utd 4 Chelsea 0**

Alex Ferguson led Manchester United to the double for the first time in 1994 just three months after Sir Matt Busby died at the age of 84 after a short illness. How Sir Matt would have loved this – or at least the second half after Chelsea had more than held their own in driving rain for the opening 45 minutes.

The game turned in nine minutes midway through the second half as Eric Cantona became the first man to score two penalties in the cup final – after 60 and 66 minutes – and Mark Hughes added another after 69 minutes. Brian McClair made it 4-0 just before the end. Cantona had been suffering with back trouble in the first half and Ferguson had considered substituting him. On such decisions, the cup is won or lost.

United finally broke down Chelsea's resistance after an hour when Ryan Giggs skirted past Steve Clarke on the right, eluded Craig Burley and then prodded the ball through to Denis Irwin just inside the Chelsea penalty area. Irwin's touch was enough to trick Eddie Newton into a lunge which spectacularly upended the Irishman and forced referee David Elleray into awarding the penalty. No argument.

Cantona sent goalkeeper Dimitri Kharine the wrong way from the spot, and six minutes later scored from the spot again – into the same corner. This time the penalty was less conclusive and the Chelsea players were furious.

It came after 66 minutes when Mark Hughes split the Chelsea defence with a long ball out of the centre circle. Andrei Kanchelskis and Frank Sinclair chased after the ball – leaving everyone else – including Elleray trailing behind. Sinclair nudged the Ukrainian who tumbled in the box – although TV replays showed the offence took place outside the area. Still, Elleray pointed to the spot again, brushed aside the Chelsea protests and Cantona converted.

The Frenchman had scored a hat-trick at Wembley for Leeds in the Charity Shield in 1992 and had a golden opportunity to score a cup final hat-trick near the end, but with only Kharine to beat again in open play, he fluffed his chance. Still, neither he, nor anyone else associated with United was complaining.

## FA Cup Miscellany

### Strange FA Cup Goal

One of the strangest goals scored in the cup's history came in a second round match on February 8, 1902 between Lincoln City and Derby County. With the score at 0-0, Derby kicked off the second half and their forward and half-back lines surrounded the player with the ball preventing any Lincoln player getting near it.

They guided the ball into the Lincoln goal area before Ben Warren scored the first of a hat-trick in Derby's 3-1 win.

# Penalty Shootouts

The FA decided in 1991 that FA Cup ties would be decided by penalties if, after one replay, the teams were still level at the end of extra time. The FA later ruled that penalty shoot-outs would apply after a single drawn match in the semi-finals and final.

This development ended the multiple replay system that had been a feature of the FA Cup since its inception. The following lists all the penalty shoot-outs since they were introduced in 1991-92.

However, the first penalty shoot-out in FA Cup history actually took place on August 5, 1972 when Birmingham City beat Stoke City 4-3 on penalties at St Andrews after their third place play-off match had ended in a 0-0 draw.

## Penalty shootouts since 1991-92

*(asterisk indicates home team)*

| | | |
|---|---|---|
| 1991-92 | | |
| Nov 26 1991 | r1 | Exeter City* 4 Colchester United 2 (0-0, 0-0 draws) |
| Nov 26 1991 | r1 | Rotherham United* 7 Scunthorpe United 6 (1-1, 3-3) |
| Jan 22 1992 | r3 | Bournemouth 4 Newcastle United* 3 (0-0, 2-2) |
| Feb 5 1992 | r4 | Southampton 4 Manchester United* 2 (0-0, 2-2) |
| April 13 1992 | SF | Liverpool 3 Portsmouth 1 (1-1, 0-0) *at Villa Park* |
| 1992-93 | | |
| Nov 25 1992 | r1 | Macclesfield 3 Chesterfield* 2 (0-0, 2-2) |
| Dec 5 1992 | r1 | Marlow 4 Salisbury City* 3 (3-3, 2-2) |
| Jan 12 1993 | r3 | Swansea City 5 Oxford United* 4 (1-1, 2-2) |
| Jan 20 1993 | r3 | Barnsley 5* Leicester City 4 (2-2, 1-1) |
| Feb 3 1993 | r4 | Wimbledon* 6 Aston Villa 5 (1-1, 0-0) |
| Mar 16 1993 | r6 | Sheffield United* 5 Blackburn Rovers 3 (0-0, 2-2) |
| 1993-94 | | |
| Nov 29 1993 | r1 | Stalybridge Celtic 4 Marine* 2 (1-1, 4-4) |
| Dec 14 1993 | r2 | Exeter City* 5 Leyton Orient 4 (1-1, 2-2) |
| Dec 14 1993 | r2 | Scunthorpe United* 7 Walsall 6 (1-1, 0-0) |
| Jan 19 1994 | r3 | Tottenham Hotspur* 5 Peterborough United 4 (1-1, 1-1) |
| 1994-95 | | |
| Nov 22 1994 | r1 | Bury* 4 Bishop Auckland 2 (0-0, 1-1) |
| Jan 18 1995 | r3 | Liverpool* 2 Birmingham City 0 (0-0, 1-1) |
| Feb 8 1995 | r4 | Millwall 5 Chelsea* 4 (0-0, 1-1) |
| Feb 8 1995 | r4 | Wolverhampton W* 4 Sheffield Wed 3 (0-0, 1-1) |
| 1995-96 | | |
| Nov 21 1995 | r1 | Wrexham* 3 Hull City 1 (0-0, 0-0) |
| Nov 21 1995 | r1 | Sutton United* 3 Kidderminster Harriers 2 (2-2, 1-1) |
| Dec 14 1995 | r2 | Fulham 4 Brighton & HA* 1 (0-0, 0-0) |
| Jan 17 1996 | r3 | Chelsea 4 Newcastle United* 2 (1-1, 2-2) |
| Mar 9 1996 | r5 | Nottingham Forest 3 Tottenham Hotspur* 1 (2-2, 1-1) |
| 1996-97 | | |
| Nov 25 1996 | r1 | Ashford Town 4 Dagenham & Redbridge* 3 (2-2, 1-1) |
| Nov 26 1996 | r1 | Sudbury Town 4 Brighton & HA* 3 (0-0, 1-1) |
| Dec 23 1996 | r2 | Burnley* 4 Walsall 2 (1-1, 1-1) |
| 1997-98 | | |
| Nov 25 1997 | r1 | Colchester United* 4 Brentford 2 (2-2, 0-0) |
| Nov 25 1997 | r1 | Emley* 3 Morecambe 1 (1-1, 3-3) |
| Nov 25 1997 | r1 | Basingstoke Town* 5 Wycombe Wanderers 4 (2-2, 2-2) |
| Nov 26 1997 | r1 | Darlington 4 Solihull Borough* 2 (1-1, 3-3) |
| Dec 16 1997 | r2 | Hereford United* 5 Colchester United 4 (1-1, 1-1) |

| | | |
|---|---|---|
| Dec 16 1997 | r2 | Northampton Town 4 Basingstoke Town* 3 (1-1, 0-0) |
| Dec 17 1997 | r2 | Emley* 4 Lincoln City 3 (2-2, 3-3) |
| Jan 14 1998 | r3 | Arsenal 4 Port Vale* 3 (0-0, 1-1) |
| Jan 14 1998 | r3 | Sheffield Wednesday* 5 Watford 3 (1-1, 0-0) |
| Feb 3 1998 | r4 | Reading* 4 Cardiff City 3 (1-1, 1-1) |
| Feb 25 1998 | r5 | West Ham United 5 Blackburn Rovers* 4 (2-2, 1-1) |
| Mar 17 1998 | r6 | Arsenal 4 West Ham United* 3 (1-1, 1-1) |
| Mar 17 1998 | r6 | Sheffield United* 3 Coventry City 1 (1-1, 1-1) |
| 1998-99 | | |
| Nov 24 1998 | r1 | Macclesfield 9 Slough Town* 8 (2-2, 1-1) |
| Nov 24 1998 | r1 | Yeovil Town 5 West Auckland Town* 3 (2-2, 1-1) |
| Dec 01 1998 | r1 | Plymouth Argyle 5 Kidderminster Harriers* 4 (0-0, 0-0) |
| Dec 15 1998 | r2 | Notts County 4 Wigan Athletic* 2 (1-1, 0-0) |
| Dec 15 1998 | r2 | Oldham Athletic 4 Brentford* 2 (1-1, 2-2) |
| 1999-2000 | | |
| Dec 21 1999 | r3 | Sheffield United 6 Rushden & Diamonds* 5 (1-1, 1-1) |
| Jan 18 2000 | r4 | Sheffield Wednesday 4 Wolverhampton W* 3 (1-1, 0-0) |
| Jan 19 2000 | r4 | Leicester City* 6 Arsenal 5 (0-0, 0-0) |
| April 2 2000 | SF | Aston Villa 4 Bolton Wanderers 1 (0-0) *at Wembley Stadium* |
| 2000-01 | | |
| Jan 23 2001 | r3 | Scunthorpe United* 5 Burnley 4 (2-2, 1-1) |
| Feb 20 2001 | r5 | Wycombe Wanderers 8 Wimbledon* 7 (2-2, 1-1) |
| 2001-02 | | |
| Nov 27 2001 | r1 | York City* 3 Colchester United 2 (0-0, 2-2) |
| Nov 27 2001 | r1 | Lincoln City 3 Bury* 2 (1-1, 1-1) |
| Nov 28 2001 | r1 | Macclesfield 11 Forest Green Rovers* 10 (2-2, 1-1) |
| 2002-03 | | |
| Nov 26 2002 | r1 | Vauxhall Motors 4 Queens Park Rangers* 3 (0-0, 1-1) |
| Nov 27 2002 | r1 | Oldham Athletic 5 Burton Albion* 4 (2-2, 2-2) |
| Jan 14 2003 | r3 | Walsall 4 Reading* 1 (0-0, 1-1) |
| Jan 14 2003 | r3 | Bournemouth 3 Crewe Alexandra* 1 (0-0, 2-2) |
| Feb 5 2003 | r4 | Sunderland* 3 Blackburn Rovers 0 (3-3, 2-2) |

**Notes:** Macclesfield have been involved in the two highest penalty shoot-outs, beating Forest Green Rovers 11-10 in 2001-02 and Slough Town 9-8 in 1998-99.

Wolverhampton Wanderers and Sheffield Wednesday are the only teams to have needed two penalty shoot-outs to decide their ties after two drawn matches. Wolves beat Sheffield Wednesday 4-3 on penalties in a fourth round tie in 1994-95; Sheffield Wednesday beat Wolves 4-3 on penalties in a fourth round tie in 1999-2000.

Liverpool (1992) and Aston Villa (2000) have both progressed to the FA Cup final after winning semi-final shoot-outs. Liverpool became the first team to win the FA Cup after winning a penalty shoot-out en route to the final. Arsenal became the first club to win the FA Cup after winning two penalty shoot-outs in earlier rounds (1998).

A penalty shoot-out was abandoned before it started on November 9, 1999 when a fire broke out under a stand at Oxford City after they had drawn their replay with Wycombe Wanderers 1-1 after extra time. Wycombe won a second replay 1-0 at Oxford United's ground the following week.

## FA Cup Miscellany

### H-Connection

When Wolves beat Newcastle United 3-1 in the 1908 Cup Final, the Wolves goals were scored by Kenneth Hunt, George Hedley and Billy Harrison and Newcastle's goal by Jimmy Howie. The four scorers were the four on the field whose surnames began with the letter H.

# The Double

The FA Cup and League Championship double has been achieved on 10 occasions and these are the records of the double-winning teams

## 1888-89 Preston North End

| Champions: | P | W | D | L | F | A | Pts |
|---|---|---|---|---|---|---|---|
| | 22 | 18 | 4 | 0 | 74 | 15 | 40 |

FA Cup Record

| | | |
|---|---|---|
| Round 1 | Bootle (a) | won 3-0 |
| Round 2 | Grimsby Town (a) | won 2-0 |
| Round 3 | Birmingham St G (h) | won 2-0 |
| Semi-final | WBA (n) | won 1-0 |
| Final | Wolverhampton W (n) | won 3-0 |

Preston are the only club to win the double without losing a league match or conceding a goal in their FA Cup run.

## 1896-97 Aston Villa

| Champions: | P | W | D | L | F | A | Pts |
|---|---|---|---|---|---|---|---|
| | 22 | 18 | 4 | 0 | 74 | 15 | 40 |

FA Cup Record:

| | | |
|---|---|---|
| Round 1 | Newcastle United (h) | won 5-0 |
| Round 2 | Notts County (h) | won 2-1 |
| Round 3 | Preston NE (a) | drew 1-1 |
| Round 3 rep | Preston NE (h) | drew 0-0 |
| Round 3 2 rep | Preston North End (n) | won 3-2 |
| Semi-final | Liverpool (n) | won 3-0 |
| Final | Everton (n) | won 3-2 |

Aston Villa had also won the FA Cup in 1895 and been champions in 1896. Aston Villa later 'prevented' three other clubs winning the double. In 1905 they beat League Champions Newcastle United in the cup final, in 1913 they beat League champions Sunderland in the cup final and in 1957 they beat League champions Manchester United in the cup final. However, in 1961, they were beaten by Spurs in the fifth round of the FA Cup and Spurs went on to do the double.

## 1960-61 Tottenham Hotspur

| Champions: | P | W | D | L | F | A | Pts |
|---|---|---|---|---|---|---|---|
| | 42 | 31 | 4 | 7 | 115 | 55 | 66 |

FA Cup Record:

| | | |
|---|---|---|
| Round 3 | Charlton Athletic (h) | won 3-2 |
| Round 4 | Crewe Alexandra (h) | won 5-1 |
| Round 5 | Aston Villa (a) | won 2-0 |
| Round 6 | Sunderland (a) | drew 1-1 |
| Round 6 rep | Sunderland (h) | won 5-0 |
| Semi-final | Burnley (n) | won 3-0 |
| Final | Leicester City (n) | won 2-0 |

Tottenham became the first club for 64 years and the first in the 20th century to win the double. Tottenham set a number of records in 1960-61: winning their first 11 league games of the season, winning most league matches (31), securing most away wins (16) and equalling Arsenal's 1930-31 record of 66 points. They also retained the FA Cup the following season.

## 1970-71 Arsenal

| Champions: | P | W | D | L | F | A | Pts |
|---|---|---|---|---|---|---|---|
| | 42 | 29 | 7 | 6 | 71 | 29 | 65 |

FA Cup Record:

| | | |
|---|---|---|
| Round 3 | Yeovil Town (a) | won 3-0 |
| Round 4 | Portsmouth (a) | drew 1-1 |
| Round 4 rep | Portsmouth (h) | won 3-2 |
| Round 5 | Manchester City (a) | won 2-1 |
| Round 6 | Leicester City (a) | drew 0-0 |
| Round 6 rep | Leicester City (h) | won 1-0 |
| Semi-final | Stoke City (n) | drew 1-1 |
| Semi-final rep | Stoke City (n) | won 2-1 |
| Final | Liverpool (n) | won 2-1aet |

Arsenal played 64 competitive matches during the season including eight in the European Fairs Cup (now the UEFA Cup) and five in the League Cup.

## 1985-86 Liverpool

| Champions: | P | W | D | L | F | A | Pts |
|---|---|---|---|---|---|---|---|
| | 42 | 26 | 10 | 6 | 89 | 37 | 88 |

FA Cup Record:

| | | |
|---|---|---|
| Round 3 | Norwich City (h) | won 5-0 |
| Round 4 | Chelsea (a) | won 2-1 |
| Round 5 | York City (a) | drew 1-1 |
| Round 5 rep | York City (h) | won 3-1aet |
| Round 6 | Watford (h) | drew 0-0 |
| Round 6 rep | Watford (a) | won 2-1aet |
| Semi-final | Southampton (n) | won 2-0aet |
| Final | Everton (n) | won 3-1 |

Kenny Dalglish became the first player-manager to win the double. Liverpool also reached the semi-finals of the League Cup.

## 1993-94 Manchester United

| Champions: | P | W | D | L | F | A | pts |
|---|---|---|---|---|---|---|---|
| | 42 | 27 | 11 | 4 | 80 | 38 | 92 |

FA Cup Record:

| | | |
|---|---|---|
| Round 3 | Sheffield United (a) | won 1-0 |
| Round 4 | Norwich City (a) | won 2-0 |
| Round 5 | Wimbledon (a) | won 3-0 |
| Round 6 | Charlton Athletic (h) | won 3-1 |
| Semi-final | Oldham Ath (n) | drew 1-1aet |
| Semi-final rep | Oldham Ath (n) | won 4-1 |
| Final | Chelsea (n) | won 4-0 |

Manchester United took their tally of major trophies to six in five seasons and Alex Ferguson became the first man to win the double in both England and Scotland (Aberdeen 1984)

### 1995-96 Manchester United

| Champions: | P | W | D | L | F | A | Pts |
|---|---|---|---|---|---|---|---|
| | 38 | 25 | 7 | 6 | 73 | 35 | 82 |

FA Cup Record:

| | | |
|---|---|---|
| Round 3 | Sunderland (h) | drew 2-2 |
| Round 3 rep | Sunderland (a) | won 2-1 |
| Round 4 | Reading (a) | won 3-0 |
| Round 5 | Manchester City (h) | won 2-1 |
| Round 6 | Southampton (h) | won 2-0 |
| Semi-final | Chelsea (n) | won 2-1 |
| Final | Liverpool (n) | won 1-0 |

Manchester United became the first club to win the double twice and also established a new all-time record of nine FA Cup victories.

### 1997-98 Arsenal

| Champions: | P | W | D | L | F | A | Pts |
|---|---|---|---|---|---|---|---|
| | 38 | 23 | 9 | 6 | 68 | 33 | 78 |

FA Cup Record:

| | | |
|---|---|---|
| Round 3 | Port Vale (h) | drew 0-0 |
| Round 3 rep | Port Vale (a) (Arsenal won 4-3 on penalties) | drew 1-1aet |
| Round 4 | Middlesbrough (a) | won 2-1 |
| Round 5 | Crystal Palace (h) | drew 0-0 |
| Round 5 rep | Crystal Palace (a) | won 2-1 |
| Round 6 | West Ham Utd (h) | drew 1-1 |
| Round 6 rep | West Ham Utd (a) (Arsenal won 4-3 on penalties) | drew 1-1aet |
| Semi-final | Wolverhampton W (n) | won 1-0 |
| Final | Newcastle United (n) | won 2-0 |

Arsenal clinched the title with 10 straight wins at the end of the season before winning the cup and the second double in their history.

### 1998-99 Manchester United

| Champions: | P | W | D | L | F | A | Pts |
|---|---|---|---|---|---|---|---|
| | 38 | 22 | 13 | 3 | 80 | 37 | 79 |

FA Cup Record:

| | | |
|---|---|---|
| Round 3 | Middlesbrough (h) | won 3-1 |
| Round 4 | Liverpool (h) | won 2-1 |
| Round 5 | Fulham (h) | won 1-0 |
| Round 6 | Chelsea (h) | drew 0-0 |
| Round 6 rep | Chelsea (a) | won 2-0 |
| Semi-final | Arsenal (n) | drew 0-0 |
| Semi-final rep | Arsenal (n) | won 2-1aet |
| Final | Newcastle Utd (n) | won 2-0 |

Manchester United took both the title and the FA Cup back from Arsenal to win the double for the third time – before completing the treble by winning the Champions League final against Bayern Munich in Barcelona.

## The Double – Near Misses

(The figure in parentheses for League Championship runners-up shows how many points behind the champions that team finished)

| *Season* | *Club* | *League* | *FA Cup* |
|---|---|---|---|
| 1904-05 | Newcastle Utd | Champions | Runners-up |
| 1912-13 | Sunderland | Champions | Runners-up |
| 1956-57 | Manchester Utd | Champions | Runners-up |
| 1976-77 | Liverpool | Champions | Runners-up |
| 1984-85 | Everton | Champions | Runners-up |
| 1987-88 | Liverpool | Champions | Runners-up |
| 1903-04 | Manchester City | Runners-up (-3) | Winners |
| 1912-13 | Aston Villa | Runners-up (-4) | Winners |
| 1947-48 | Manchester Utd | Runners-up (-7) | Winners |
| 1953-54 | WBA | Runners-up (-4) | Winners |
| 1959-60 | Wolverhampton W | Runners-up (-1) | Winners |
| 1971-72 | Leeds Utd | Runners-up (-1) | Winners |
| 1973-74 | Liverpool | Runners-up (-5) | Winners |
| 1988-89 | Liverpool | Runners-up (gd) | Winners |
| 2002-03 | Arsenal | Runners-up (-5) | Winners |
| 1927-28 | Huddersfield Town | Runners-up (-2) | Runners-up |
| 1931-32 | Arsenal | Runners-up (-2) | Runners-up |
| 1938-39 | Wolverhampton W | Runners-up (-4) | Runners-up |
| 1961-62 | Burnley | Runners-up (-3) | Runners-up |
| 1964-65 | Leeds Utd | Runners-up (ga) | Runners-up |
| 1969-70 | Leeds Utd | Runners-up (-9) | Runners-up |
| 1985-86 | Everton | Runners-up (-2) | Runners-up |
| 1994-95 | Manchester Utd | Runners-up (-1) | Runners-up |
| 2000-01 | Arsenal | Runners-up (-10) | Runners-up |

*notes: ga: goal average; gd: goal difference. Three points for a win from 1981-82.*

### 2001-02 Arsenal

| Champions: | P | W | D | L | F | A | Pts |
|---|---|---|---|---|---|---|---|
| | 38 | 26 | 9 | 3 | 79 | 36 | 87 |

FA Cup Record:

| | | |
|---|---|---|
| Round 3 | Watford (a) | won 4-2 |
| Round 4 | Liverpool (h) | won 1-0 |
| Round 5 | Gillingham (h) | won 5-2 |
| Round 6 | Newcastle United (a) | drew 1-1 |
| Round 6 rep | Newcastle United (h) | won 3-0 |
| Semi-final | Middlesbrough (n) | won 1-0 |
| Final | Chelsea (n) | won 2-0 |

Arsenal matched Manchester United's achievement with a third double – and became the first English champions since the first double winners Preston in 1889 to win the title unbeaten away from home. This was the only occasion the League Championship was secured after the FA Cup had been won.

### Other Doubles – and Better

Liverpool were the first English club to win three major titles in one season. In 1983-84 they won the League Championship, the European Cup and the League Cup. In 2001, Liverpool achieved another treble with victories in the FA Cup, the UEFA Cup and the League Cup.

Manchester United in 1999 were the first English club to win the FA Cup, the League Championship and the European Cup/ Champions League in the same season.

Liverpool won the League Championship and European Cup in 1977 but were beaten by Manchester United in the FA Cup final.

In 1993 Arsenal became the first club to win the FA Cup and the League Cup in the same season. They beat Sheffield Wednesday in both finals, the first time both finals have been between the same two clubs. Liverpool equalled Arsenal's domestic cup double in 2001.

West Bromwich Albion completed a unique double in 1931 when they won promotion from the old Second Division to the First Division and also won the FA Cup in the same season.

The only FA Cup finals to be contested between the clubs finishing first and second in the title race were in 1912-13 and 1985-86. In 1913 Aston Villa defeated Sunderland 1-0 in the FA Cup final, but Sunderland won the title. In 1986 Liverpool finished champions, Everton were runners-up and Liverpool also beat Everton 3-1 in the cup final.

## Right Place, Right Time

When Chris Baird was named in the Southampton team to face Arsenal in the 2003 FA Cup final many neutrals were hearing his name for the first time. Which was not surprising as the Northern Ireland Under-21 international had made just three appearances for Southampton – and two of those were as a substitute in the weeks before the game.

Baird's appearance highlighted how lucky some players can – and might not be – as far as the FA Cup final is concerned. Baird was making only his fourth first team appearance for the Saints against Arsenal – while some of the most famous footballers of all never played in the FA Cup final at all.

The list includes three of England's 1966 World Cup winners who otherwise had long, successful careers. George Cohen, Nobby Stiles and Martin Peters all missed out on an FA Cup final appearance as did George Best, Johnny Haynes, John Charles, Terry Butcher and Southampton's own Matthew Le Tissier, who all played more than 400 league and cup matches in their careers and were among those to miss out on a cup final appearance.

This list represents those players who made less than 20 league appearances for the club they appeared for in the FA Cup final.

Les Sealey, the first on-loan player to appear in an FA Cup final, subsequently signed for United and played 31 league matches for them before moving on to Aston Villa, but had only played two league matches before appearing at Wembley. He replaced Jim Leighton in United's goal for the replayed 1990 final against Crystal Palace.

George Weah is the only other on-loan FA Cup finalist. He joined Chelsea from AC Milan in January 2000 and scored five goals for them in a total of 11 league and four cup appearances.

Arthur Turner was an RAF officer who became the first amateur to play in the FA Cup final since 1924 when Charlton reached the final in 1946. An inside or centre-forward, he scored seven goals in nine appearances as Charlton reached the first post-war final. There was no League football in the 1945-46 season, and he had moved on by the time the League re-started in 1946-47. He later did play in the League for Colchester United.

Laurie Cunningham had a short spell at Wimbledon towards the end of his career. When he came on as a substitute for them in the 1988 final against Liverpool he completed a rare double as he had also played for Real Madrid against Liverpool in the 1981 European Cup Final in Paris. He was killed in a car crash in Spain on July 15, 1989.

Alan Davies was one of Manchester United's outstanding players when they beat Brighton in 1983 and was tipped for a bright future. But af-

**FA Cup final, League Appearances**

| | | |
|---|---|---|
| Arthur Turner | Charlton 1946 | 0 |
| Les Sealey* | Manchester U 1990 | 2 |
| Chris Baird | Southampton 2003 | 3 (1+2sub) |
| Laurie Cunningham | Wimbledon 1988 (sub) | 6 |
| Alan Davies | Manchester U 1983 | 7 (6+1sub) |
| Neil Price | Watford 1984 | 8 (7+1sub) |
| George Weah* | Chelsea 2000 | 11 (9+2sub) |
| Mike Trebilcock | Everton 1966 | 11 |
| Paul Atkinson | Watford 1984 | 11 (8+3sub) |
| Stan Crowther | Manchester U 1958 | 13 |
| Allan Harris | Chelsea 1967 | 14 |
| Jim Bullions | Derby County 1946 | 17 |

ter only seven league appearances for United he moved on to Newcastle and had spells at Swansea City and Bradford City and loan periods at Charlton Athletic and Carlisle United. He played 11 times for Wales, but committed suicide, aged just 30, on February 4, 1992.

Mike Trebilcock was signed by Everton manager Harry Catterick from Plymouth Argyle on New Year's Eve 1965. He played seven League matches for Everton before the 1966 FA Cup final and made four appearances in two seasons following it before a move to Portsmouth and then Torquay United. But he will always be remembered at Goodison Park for the two goals he scored for Everton in their 3-2 win over Sheffield Wednesday in 1966.

Allan Harris was in his second spell at Chelsea, He had earlier made 70 league appearances between 1960 and 1964.

Stan Crowther joined Manchester United after the Munich air crash and spent 10 months at Old Trafford before joining Chelsea. He was granted special dispensation by the FA to play in the cup for United as he had already played for Aston Villa in the 1957-58 season. He had also played for Aston Villa against Manchester United the previous year.

# The Wembley Hoodoo 1952-1965

When Arsenal's Welsh international fullback Walley Barnes tore his knee ligaments chasing Newcastle's Bobby Mitchell during the 1952 FA Cup final, he did not know what he was starting.

Barnes was the first victim of what became known as the Wembley Hoodoo. Between 1952 and 1965 there were nine serious injuries which left one side – usually the losers – either with 10 men or with the unfortunate victim hobbling out on the wing, getting the odd touch now and again but in reality a spectator. The hoodoo was attributed to the turf itself, and in hindsight that may have an element of truth. One school of thought suggests that players in the 1950s, perhaps not as fit or as agile as players today and with their heavier footwear were more prone to have accidents on Wembley's lush turf.

Whatever the reason, the record books might show a very different story if substitutes had been allowed in the 1950s and early 1960s, but they were not permitted in competitive football in England until 1965. So until then teams had to make do with 10 fully fit men, re-organise and hope for the best. There will always be injuries and accidents in all matches, but at least the jinx years of the 1950s and early 60s seem to be over.

**1952 Walley Barnes, Arsenal, injured knee.**
Two weeks before the 1951 FA Cup final Wilf Mannion broke a cheek-bone while playing for England against Scotland at Wembley, the first serious incident of its kind at the stadium in the 1950s. There were no injuries in the final itself, but the jinx struck in the final the following year.

With almost 30 minutes played Barnes was pursuing Newcastle's Bobby Mitchell deep in Arsenal's half. He turned sharply to stay with Mitchell, but caught his studs in the turf and tore the ligaments behind his left knee. Although he limped on for a few minutes with heavy bandaging he was in too much agony and had to leave the field.

Ten-man Arsenal held out for almost an hour but Newcastle won 1-0 with a goal from George Robledo to become the first club in the 20th century to win the cup in successive years. Barnes injury was so bad he missed Arsenal's entire 1952-53 championship-winning season, and did not play again until September 1953.

**1953 Eric Bell, Bolton Wanderers, injured leg.**
After 15 minutes of the 'Matthews Final' Bolton's left half Eric Bell twisted his leg and pulled a muscle that had been troubling him before the match. He went out to the wing, and although he actually scored with a header, leaping off his good leg to put Bolton 3-1 ahead of Blackpool after 55 minutes, Bolton's reshuffled midfield ultimately could not cope with Matthews inspired brilliance. Blackpool won 4-3.

**1955 Jimmy Meadows, Manchester City, injured knee**

The injury to Manchester City right-back Jimmy Meadows was so spookily similar to that of Walley Barnes three years previously, that it's no surprise people thought there was a hoodoo at work on cup final day.

Just like Barnes, Meadows was chasing a Newcastle player deep inside his own half. That Newcastle player was again Bobby Mitchell, the player Barnes had been after in 1952. At almost exactly the same place that Barnes turned sharply so did Meadows. And just as Barnes tore his knee ligaments, so did Meadows.

Meadows left the field just as Barnes had done, but Meadows' story had a sadder ending. Barnes eventually recovered, but Meadows, 24, who had just won his first England cap never played again. Newcastle beat Manchester City 3-1.

**1956 Bert Trautmann, Manchester City, broken neck**

A year after losing to Newcastle, Manchester City returned to Wembley and beat Birmingham City to win the cup for the first time since 1934. All the scoring had been completed when, 15 minutes from time, City's German goalkeeper Bert Trautmann dived at the feet of Birmingham inside forward Peter Murphy – and broke his neck. Trautmann continued playing in extreme pain, holding the posts and the goal netting to stay on his feet. The full extent of the injury was not revealed until an X-ray after the match but at least he made a full recovery from an injury that could have killed him. Manchester City won 3-1.

**1957 Ray Wood, Manchester United, fractured cheekbone**

Manchester United arrived at Wembley in 1957 looking to become the first team in the 20th century team to win the double. The 'Busby Babes' had already clinched the championship and were favourites to beat an Aston Villa side that had finished 10th in the First Division. But after six minutes the fates conspired against United.

Goalkeeper Ray Wood had safely gathered a header from Villa's Peter McParland, who suddenly charged at Wood in a way unthinkable today. Wood's cheekbone was fractured and his effective contribution to United's cup-winning effort was over.

Jackie Blanchflower took over in goal and kept the sun out of his eyes with a cap he borrowed from a photographer sitting behind the touchline. Wood returned to the wing, departed again, came back to play in goal for the final few minutes but ended with a runners-up medal as United's Double dream died. Aston Villa won 2-1.

**1959 Roy Dwight, Nottingham Forest, broken leg**

Roy Dwight's one and only cup final appearance lasted just 30 minutes, but in that time, he managed to score a great goal, break his leg, and effectively end his career.

Dwight, who later regained fame simply for being Elton John's uncle, opened the scoring for Forest with a superb left foot drive after 10 minutes. Forest went 2-0 up through Tommy Wilson before Dwight was injured in a collision with Luton's Brendan McNally. Dwight finished the match having his leg set in a local hospital, listening to the commentary on the radio. Twenty five years after his uncle's cup final exploits, Elton John was at the final in his role as Watford chairman and saw his team lose to Everton. But at least Roy Dwight earned a winners medal as Forest became the first side with 10 men to win the cup at Wembley.

**1960 David Whelan, Blackburn Rovers, broken leg**

The 1960 final was virtually decided in a three-minute spell just before half-time. Wolves, who had missed out on winning the championship for the third successive year by just a single point, were already dominating the final when an own goal by Blackburn's Mick McGrath gave them the lead.

If that wasn't bad enough for Rovers, worse was to follow. A minute later left-back David Whelan made an innocuous challenge on winger Norman Deeley, and broke his right leg. Deeley scored twice in the second half, while Whelan's career was effectively over. He never played for Rovers again, and after a short spell with Crewe he knew he would never be the player he was before the injury and decided to retire. After quitting the game he went into business, became a millionaire and retained his involvement with the game as a dynamic chairman of Wigan Athletic.

**1961 Len Chalmers, Leicester City, leg injury**

In 1957 Manchester United's hopes of becoming the first side in the 20th century to win the double wilted when they lost goalkeeper Ray Wood with a fractured cheekbone after only six minutes of their cup final against Aston Villa. Four years later Tottenham did finally become the first team of the century to win the double – this time helped by the Wembley hoodoo afflicting their opponents.

After 19 minutes Leicester full-back Len Chalmers was injured in a tackle with Les Allen and left the field before returning to limp out the rest of the match on the left wing. In an ironic twist, when Wood was injured in 1957 Jackie

Blanchflower went in goal. Four years later it was Jackie's brother Danny who lifted the cup as Spurs won the double. Late goals from Bobby Smith and Terry Dyson gave Spurs a 2-0 victory over Leicester who had a hoodoo all of their own at the original Wembley, having lost all four FA Cup finals they played there.

**1965 Gerry Byrne, Liverpool, fractured collar-bone**

After only three minutes of the 1965 final between Liverpool and Leeds United, the Leeds captain Bobby Collins collided with Liverpool full-back Gerry Byrne who sustained a broken collar-bone. Byrne refused to come off, shrugging off the injury – or at least not letting on how badly he was hurt. His was a truly heroic performance as Liverpool won an intense, close game 2-1 to lift the cup for the first time in their history. Byrne played a key role in Liverpool's success largely nullifying the influence of Johnny Giles for long periods. Three minutes into extra time he also played a key role in Liverpool's winning goal, crossing for Roger Hunt to score the winner.

He was only the third man injured during the years of the hoodoo to play for the winning side following Bert Trautmann in 1956 and Roy Dwight (1959) and won everlasting respect from the Liverpool fans for his performance.

On May 29, 1965 the Football League's agm approved the use of substitutes because of injury, a decision ratified by the FA on July 3, 1965. West Bromwich Albion's Dennis Clarke was the first substitute used in the final when he replaced John Kaye at the start of extra time in 1968. Ironically, after all that had gone on during the 1950s and 60s, it was a tactical switch and not one made because of injury.

# The FA Cup Trophies

The current FA Cup trophy, first won by Liverpool in 1992, is the fourth to be awarded since the competition began in 1871.

**The First FA Cup, awarded 1872-1895.**

The first FA Cup trophy was made by the firm of Martin, Hall and Co early in 1872 and bore little relation to today's classic trophy. Made of silver, it stood less than 18 inches high, could hold little more than a couple of pints and cost £20 to manufacture. It had a footballer figurine at the top and was known as the 'Little Tin Idol'.

It was won by Wanderers three years in succession between 1876-78 and under the rules of the competition they were entitled to keep it, but they handed it back to the FA with the proviso that no other team could retain it if they won it three times.

When Blackburn Rovers won the cup three years running between 1884-86, the FA awarded them a commemorative shield.

The last winners of the first FA Cup trophy were Aston Villa in 1895. They had the trophy put on display in the window of a football outfitters called William Shillcock whose shop was at 73, Newtown Row, Birmingham. On the night of September 11, 1895, the cup was stolen and never recovered, despite a reward of £10 being offered for it. Villa were later fined £25 by the FA and a new trophy was made.

But although the FA Cup disappeared, the mystery of what happened to it never went away. More than 60 years later, in 1958, 82-year-old Harry Burge, who had spent more than 46 years in prison for various offences, claimed to have been one of the men responsible for the theft.

His 'confession,' which he sold to the *Sunday Pictorial*, was that he and two accomplices melted the cup down for counterfeit half-crowns and he claimed he was part of the gang because he was small enough to slide through a grating and get to the trophy. However he claimed to have gained access to the shop by forcing a back door with a jemmy – a major discrepancy which conflicted with widely reported evidence at the time that access was gained through the roof.

Then in 1975 68-year-old Edwin Tranter told the *Birmingham Evening Mail* that his grandfather Joseph Piecewright was involved.

"He was a bit of a rogue and was sent to prison for making counterfeit florins on the fireplace hob at home. My guess is they were from the melted down FA Cup," he said.

## FA Cup Miscellany

### Suspended FA Cup final Captains

There was an unhappy sequence in the early 1980s when three captains all missed playing in the cup final because of suspension. In 1982 Glenn Roeder missed QPR's replay against Tottenham, in 1983 Steve Foster of Brighton missed the final against Manchester United but played in the replay and in 1984 Wilf Rostron was suspended at the time Watford played Everton. In each case their team lost.

Another 20 years was to pass before evidence that could be as reliably substantiated as possible came to light. *Claret & Blue*, Aston Villa's club magazine, obtained detailed information in 1995 from Mrs Violet Stait, a sprightly 80-year-old and the surviving daughter-in-law of John 'Stosher' Stait, whose nickname came from a truly remarkable Victorian moustache.

In January 1995 *Claret & Blue* published the most credible and informative details yet of how the crime took place and who did it – backed up by checking old records of the families living in the area at the time who were said to be involved. Their checks matched the stories passed down through the years.

Mrs Stait, who married Stosher's late son Jack in 1935, told *Claret & Blue* that her husband told her his father was "one of the men who stole the cup," adding: "I've known since I got married. I was 21 at the time. He used to say to me 'Our Dad pinched that cup out of Shillcock's window.'"

After exhaustive checks, *Claret & Blue*, and later the BBC came to the conclusion that Stait was one of a group of four unemployed men who hatched the plot in a long-demolished pub called the Old Paul Pry. They broke into Shillcock's shop through grating in the roof and effectively lifted the cup and walked out with it through the front door. It was then broken up and melted down in a wash-house in a backyard off Newtown Row with coal stolen from the nearby coal merchants, Thomas Billson in Brewery Street.

However, their crime did not pay. According to *Claret & Blue*: "The four unfortunate conspirators had been double-crossed by their pre-arranged receiver from the jewellery quarter who gave them only half-a-crown (12.5 pence) each for their pains."

Despite the offer of a reward the cup disappeared for ever – but at least the crime gave Villa fans something to taunt their Birmingham neighbours with through the years. "We've LOST the cup more times that you've won it,"they claim. Cruel – but very accurate.

### The Second FA Cup, awarded 1896-1910

Sheffield Wednesday were the first winners of the new cup in 1896 and Newcastle United the last winners in 1910 and there was little difference in the size and style of the second FA Cup from the first. This was because the silversmiths who made it, Messrs Vaughton's of Birmingham, had exact miniature replicas to work from, commissioned by Wolverhampton Wanderers when they won the competition in 1893. One of the Vaughton company's directors was Howard Vaughton who played for Aston Villa when they won the cup in 1887.

In 1910 the FA discovered that the design of the cup had been pirated and they ordered a new one should be commissioned. The second cup was presented to Lord Kinnaird by the Council of the Football Association to mark his 21 years as president.

Aston Villa, Bury, Sheffield United and Sheffield Wednesday each won this cup twice with seven other teams winning it once.

### The Third FA Cup, awarded 1911-1991

The FA had the design of the third cup registered and copyrighted, one of the best moves they ever made. The third cup was a far more imposing trophy than the first two and today is one of the most famous sporting prizes in the world.

A large number of companies submitted designs for the new trophy, but the FA wisely chose the one submitted by Messrs Fattorini and Sons of Bradford. This cup was 19 inches high, excluding the plinth and weighed 175 ounces. By coincidence the first winners of the new cup were Bradford City – the only time they reached the final.

This trophy cost 50 guineas to make. The last winners of the third trophy were Tottenham Hotspur who won it for a record seventh time in 1991 – their eighth victory in all. Manchester United won it six times, Arsenal and Newcastle four times and another 29 teams also had the joy of lifting it.

### The Fourth Cup, awarded since 1992.

The current FA Cup trophy is an exact replica of the third trophy and the first winners were Liverpool whose name was never inscribed on the first two cups.

But on Sunday morning, May 10, 1992, just 17 hours after the team held the cup aloft at Wembley, former Liverpool captain Phil Thompson, the club's reserve team coach, dropped the lid as he left the team's London hotel for the journey home. It smashed on the ground, was badly dented and did not fit back onto its rim properly.

Manchester United have taken this trophy back to Old Trafford three times, while Arsenal have won it for the third time in 2003 and Chelsea have won it twice.

## FA Cup Miscellany

### Stokoe 2, Revie 0

In 1955 Bob Stokoe was centre-half in the Newcastle Utd team that beat Manchester City – with Don Revie at centre-forward – to win the cup. In 1973 Stokoe was the manager of Sunderland when they beat Leeds. His opposing manager was Revie who didn't have a lot of cup luck. A nosebleed kept him out of the Leicester City team in 1949. But he was manager when Leeds won the cup in 1972.

# FA Cup Shocks

### 1. Third Round
### Walsall 2, Arsenal 0
### January 14, 1933

When Arsenal were drawn to play Walsall in the third round of the FA Cup, the outcome seemed a foregone conclusion. Arsenal were top of the First Division and would go on to win the title. Walsall were mired in the middle of Division Three North and had not won a match for a month.

But Arsenal manager Herbert Chapman badly under-estimated the underdogs. Proving that there is nothing new in football, Chapman rested internationals Eddie Hapgood, Bob John and Jack Lambert, claiming they were ill or injured, and also left out winger Joe Hulme, who was having a poor spell.

In their place came three young debutants – Tommy Black, Charlie Walsh and Billy Warnes, while reserve centre-half Norman Sidey had played just once for the first team. Warnes was an amateur international who had come from Isthmian League Woking. Walsh was a centre-forward and Black had recently joined the club from a Scottish junior team.

Arsenal's regular first-team had cost some £30,000 to assemble, Walsall's £70. Arsenal spent more on their boots than Walsall had spent on their entire team – but by the end of that particular 90 minutes at Walsall's old Fellows Park ground, the boot was very definitely on the 'other' foot.

The pitch was cloying and narrow and Walsall started the match so vigorously Arsenal were awarded 10 free-kicks in the first 10 minutes. The Arsenal youngsters were soon floundering in the mud, against the aggressive steely old pros in the Walsall side, and with the entire occasion.

Walsall sensed blood and spilled the first drop of Arsenal's after an hour when Gilbert Alsop opened the scoring by heading a cross past Frank Moss. Five minutes later Black completed a black day in the Black Country from both a personal and collective point of view when he brought down Alsop in the box, and Billy Sheppard made it 2-0 from the penalty spot.

Arsenal failed to respond and never looked like saving the match. Chapman was furious with himself for under-estimating the opposition and with the players who, he believed, had let the side down and he took swift action.

Tommy Black was transferred to Plymouth the following week, Charlie Walsh went to Brentford at the end of the month and Billy Warnes left for Norwich at the end of the season.

That was the last FA Cup defeat Chapman suffered because less than a year later, on January 6, 1934, the architect of the modern Arsenal club was dead of pneumonia. He laid the foundations for the first great era in Arsenal's history but did not live to see them complete a hat-trick of league championships (1933, 1934 and 1935) or their FA Cup victory of 1936 or their league title of 1938. As for Walsall, they lost 4-0 to Manchester City in Round 4 – but they have maintained their reputation as giant-killers as Arsenal will testify. Fifty years later, in November 1983, Walsall beat the Gunners again, 2-1 at Highbury in the League Cup.

Walsall: Cunningham; Bennett, Bird, Reed, Leslie, Salt, Coward, Ball, Alsop, Sheppard, Lee
Arsenal: Moss; Male, Black, Hill, Roberts, Sidey, Warnes, Jack, Walsh, James, Bastin
Scorers: Walsall: Alsop 60, Sheppard 65pen
Crowd: 11,150

### 2. Fourth Round
### Yeovil Town 2, Sunderland 1aet 2.
### January 29, 1949

The most famous victory by a Non-League side over League opposition. Yeovil, whose weekly wage bill was less than £100 a week, were lying sixth from bottom in the Southern League when First Division Sunderland, assembled at a cost of £80,000, came to Somerset.

To put things into context, their star player Len Shackleton had joined Sunderland from Newcastle United for a British transfer record fee of £20,500 the previous year, and the following season they missed out on the league title by just two points.

But Yeovil, whose part-time players worked in aircraft or glove factories, pubs and offices, rose to the occasion on their sloping Huish pitch and won 2-1 with goals from player-manager Alec Stock and an extra-time winner from Eric Bryant.

Yeovil were inspired by a crowd of 17,000 and went ahead through Stock after 26 minutes. Sunderland equalised through John Robinson with 15 minutes remaining, but Bryant secured the victory in the 14th minute of extra time after a mistake by Shackleton who played a loose ball into open space. Yeovil's Ray Wright seized on it and pushed it on for Bryant to race onto and lash it past Johnny Mapson to score. Yeovil lost 8-0 at Manchester United in the fifth round but their place in FA Cup folklore was assured.

Yeovil Town: Dyke; Hickman, Davies, Keeton, Blizzard, Collins, Hamilton, Stock, Bryant, Wright, Hargreaves
Sunderland: Mapson; Stelling, Ramsden, Watson, Hall, Wright, Duns, Robinson, Turnbull, Shackleton, Reynolds
Scorers: Yeovil: Stock 26, Bryant 104; Sunderland Robinson 75.
Crowd: 17,000

## 3. Fifth Round
## Colchester Utd 3, Leeds Utd 2
## February 13, 1971

Fourth Division Colchester United raced into a 3-0 lead after 55 minutes against Don Revie's great side of the period. Leeds had been League champions in 1969, were runners-up in both the League and FA Cup in 1970 and would go on to win the cup in 1972. In 1973 they would reach the cup final again as well as the European Cup Winners Cup final.

But they had no answer to an inspired Colchester side who scored the greatest victory in their history.

Ray Crawford, who claimed to have the Indian sign over Leeds, having scored eight goals against them in the past, struck against them again – twice in the opening 28 minutes. His first after 18 minutes was a free header after Leeds goalkeeper Gary Sprake missed a cross and his second 10 minutes later was hooked home on the ground after beating Paul Reaney to a high cross then falling on to the loose ball. Simmons made it 3-0 after 55 minutes when he took advantage of a mix-up between Sprake and Reaney to nod home into an empty net.

Revie changed tactics, moving Allan Clarke into midfield and pushing Johnny Giles into attack – and it nearly paid off. Norman Hunter headed Leeds back into the match from a Peter Lorimer corner after 60 minutes and 15 minutes later Giles made it 3-2. But somehow Colchester, who had never lost to a First Division side at Layer Road, held for a remarkable win.

Before the match Colchester boss Dick Graham said he would scale the walls of Colchester Castle if his side won. True to his word, he did. Their run ended in the quarter-finals when they lost 5-0 at Everton.

Colchester United: Smith; Hall, Cram, Gilchrist, Garvey, Kurila, Lewis, Simmons, Mahon, Crawford, Gibbs
Leeds United: Sprake; Reaney, Cooper, Bates, Charlton, Hunter, Lorimer, Clarke, Jones, Giles, Madeley
Scorers: Colchester: Crawford 18, 28, Simmons 55; Leeds: Hunter 60, Giles 75
Crowd: 16,000

## 4. Third Round Replay
## Hereford Utd 2, Newcastle Utd 1aet
## February 5, 1972

It is often over-looked now, but Hereford's staggering victory over Newcastle came in a replay after the Southern League side had held their First Division opponents to a 2-2 draw at St James' Park.

Hereford's victory was the first by a Non-League side over First Division opposition since Yeovil's famous 1949 win over Sunderland. If Newcastle fans had laughed at Sunderland's loss down the years, they were now humbled by a comparable embarrassment of their own.

Hereford had done superbly to hold Newcastle in the first match on January 24. The replay was postponed because of incessant rain in the area and Newcastle spent 10 days in a local hotel with nowhere suitable to train as Hereford's pitch became more and more of a quagmire.

Eventually the game went ahead on fourth round day. Newcastle centre-forward Malcolm Macdonald had told the local press Hereford had had their moment of glory in the first game and he would score 10 in the replay. Not for the first time was he to be proved wrong.

He did however head Newcastle into the lead after 85 minutes but if Newcastle thought they had killed off Hereford they were wrong.

Four minutes later Hereford were level, equalising with one of the most famous goals in FA Cup history – Ronnie Radford's 35-metre rocket shot.

As he remembered later: "We were kicking down the slope in the second half, we preferred it that way – and even when they scored we wouldn't lie down. We had such a terrific team spirit. I won the ball in midfield and played a one-two with Brian Owen. The return pass came off Brian's shin.

"It sat there just waiting to be hit. Colin Addison shouted: 'My ball, Raddy,' but then he slipped so I went for it. I just hit it and it flew in. I'd done it before and since but the difference was it was on TV. Once we'd equalised Newcastle had gone. After all, a few minutes earlier they thought they'd won it."

The ball flew into the top corner of Newcastle's net and hordes of youths in 1970s army surplus clothing ran onto the pitch. The event now enshrined in local lore as 'The Invasion of the Parkas' only inspired Hereford to greater strengths.

The match moved into extra time and Ricky George, who had come on for Roger Griffiths after 80 minutes, slithered the ball past Newcastle goalkeeper Iam McFaul and inside the far post with 102 minutes played. Hereford held out for a truly astonishing victory.

In the next round they forced West Ham to a replay before losing 3-1 – but their exploits were suitably rewarded when they were elected into the Football League a few months later.

Hereford United: Potter; Griffiths (George 80), Mallender, Jones, McLaughlin, Addison, Gough, Tyler, Meadows, Owen, Radford

Newcastle United: McFaul; Craig, Clark, Nattrass, Howard, Moncur, Busby, Green, Macdonald, Tudor, Hibbitt

Scorers: Hereford: Radford 88, George 102; Newcastle: Macdonald 85

Crowd: 15,000

## 5. FA Cup Final Sunderland 1, Leeds United 0 May 5, 1973

Leeds returned to Wembley a year after beating Arsenal in the 1972 FA Cup final as probably the hottest favourites of all time. They left the stadium as the victims of the biggest FA Cup final upset of all time.

At one stage in the season Second Division Sunderland were facing the prospect of relegation to the Third Division for the first time in their history but new manager Bob Stokoe averted that danger and soon had them climbing up the table and progressing in the cup.

Leeds were again challenging for First Division honours – and although their league campaign eventually saw them finish third, they fancied their chances against a Sunderland team without one full international.

There were three highlights for Wearside fans that afternoon – Ian Porterfield's 30th minute goal – Jim Montgomery's 70th minute double-save and the way Stokoe, wearing his overcoat and trilby, sprinted to hug Montgomery at the finish – .

The goal came from a Billy Hughes corner on the left which Dave Watson nodded on. Porterfield, unmarked six metres out, killed the ball on his left thigh and crashed it into the roof of the net with his right. 1-0 to Sunderland.

The double-save came when Leeds were dominating the game. Paul Reaney crossed for Trevor Cherry who headed firmly at the far corner. But Montgomery reacted in a flash to palm the ball away – but only as far as Peter Lorimer, the man with the hardest shot in the game. The Scot unleashed all his power but Montgomery, still on the ground, threw up an arm, the ball hit the bar and bounced away safely. At that moment Leeds must have known it was all over.

At the final whistle Stokoe leapt off the bench and ran towards Montgomery having outwitted Leeds manager Don Revie at Wembley for the second time in a cup final. In 1955 Stokoe's Newcastle had beaten Revie's Manchester City 3-1 in the final. Stokoe was victorious again as Sunderland became the first Second Division side to win the trophy for 42 years. But there was more disappointment for Leeds to come. Eleven days later they lost 1-0 to AC Milan in the European Cup Winners Cup final in Salonika.

Sunderland: Montgomery; Malone, Guthrie, Horswill, Watson, Pitt, Kerr, Hughes, Halom, Porterfield, Tueart

Leeds United: Harvey; Reaney, Cherry, Bremner, Madeley, Hunter, Lorimer, Clarke, Jones, Giles, Eddie Gray (Yorath 75)

Scorer: Sunderland: Porterfield 30

Crowd: 100,000

## 6. FA Cup Final Wimbledon 1, Liverpool 0 May 14, 1988

A month before the final, Liverpool destroyed Nottingham Forest 5-0 at Anfield with a display of some of the best football ever seen from an English club side.

On April 23 they clinched the championship with a win over Tottenham and went on to finish the season losing only two League matches.

Nothing it seemed would stop them winning the double for the second time in three seasons.

Wimbledon, a League side for only 11 seasons had other ideas – and frequently expressed them in various unorthodox ways as befitting a team nicknamed the 'Crazy Gang' and including in their line-up such diverse talents as Dennis Wise, Vinny Jones and John Fashanu.

They had been one of the few teams to take a point off Liverpool in the League, drawing with them the previous November, and refused to be intimidated under the Twin Towers. A Lawrie Sanchez header after 37 minutes was the only goal of an astonishing final, best summed up for Liverpool by John Aldridge's missed penalty after 61 minutes – the first in a cup final at Wembley.

Wimbledon goalkeeper Dave Beasant had studied Aldridge's penalty technique and his homework proved decisive. He knew Aldridge almost always put his penalties to the keeper's left – and that's exactly what he did again. Beasant guessed right – and wrote himself into FA Cup history not only for being the first goalkeeper to save a Wembley FA Cup final penalty, but for being the first goalie to skipper his side to victory in the final too.

Liverpool had had chances in the first half and had even had a goal disallowed for reasons best known only to the referee. But Wimbledon had prevented Liverpool from playing their usual game and ruffled them. Sanchez's goal after 37 minutes was enough to separate the teams at the finish as Wimbledon celebrated the greatest day in their history – just 25 years after winning the FA Amateur Cup final at Wembley.

It was a particularly sweet moment for Wimbledon manager Bobby Gould too. Always upset at being left on the bench when West Ham beat Fulham in the 1975 final, Gould finally had a Cup Final win he could really enjoy.

Wimbledon: Beasant; Goodyear, Phelan, Jones, Young, Thorn, Gibson (Scales 63), Cork (Cunningham 56), Fashanu, Sanchez, Wise

Liverpool: Grobbelaar; Gillespie, Ablett, Nichol, Spackman,(Molby 72), Hansen, Beardsley, Aldridge (Rush 63), Houghton, Barnes, McMahon

Scorer: Wimbledon: Sanchez 37

Crowd: 98,203

## 7. Third Round
## Burnley 0, Wimbledon 1
## January 4, 1975

Wimbledon's FA Cup win in 1988 was a culmination of a journey that in a real sense began at Turf Moor on a January day 13 years earlier.

Wimbledon, then in the Southern League, were attempting what no side had done since Darlington, then of the North Eastern League, won 2-0 at Sheffield Wednesday 55 years earlier, That is to beat a First Division side on their own ground.

But Wimbledon knew a thing or two about giant-killing. Mickey Mahon, now a geography teacher, had been in the Colchester side that beat Leeds in 1971 and Dave Bassett, Dave Donaldson and Billy Edwards had all been in the Walton and Hersham team which had knocked out Brighton 4-0 in 1973.

At the time the match was played Burnley, coached by Jimmy Adamson, their skipper in the 1962 FA Cup final against Tottenham, were seventh in the First Division, top scorers with 45 goals. Wimbledon were third in the Southern League.

While Burnley were naturally sharper and fitter, Wimbledon were more inspired – none indeed more so than goalkeeper Dickie Guy who had a brilliant match making four outstanding saves in the first half alone. The only goal came in the 49th minute when Mahon, following up, scored with a well-taken left-foot shot into the corner of the net.

Wimbledon's run continued with a fourth round tie against Leeds, the reigning League champions. Guy earned himself a permanent place in cup folklore when he saved Peter Lorimer's 83rd minute penalty in a 0-0 draw. The replay, at Crystal Palace. was watched by 46,000 who saw Leeds win 1-0 after future Wimbledon boss Dave Bassett deflected the ball past Guy for the only goal of the game.

Burnley: Stevenson; Newton, Thomson (Morris), Ingham, Waldron, Noble, Flynn, Hankin, Fletcher, Collins, James

Wimbledon: Guy; Stockley, Bryant, Donaldson, Edwards, Bassett, Cooke, Rice, Connell, Somers, Mahon

Scorer: Wimbledon: Mahon 49

Crowd: 19,683

## 8. Third Round
## Sutton United 2, Coventry City 1
## January 7, 1989

Less than 18 months previously Coventry City had won the cup for the first time in their history and they took the field at Gander Green Lane in Surrey against Conference League side Sutton United with seven members of their cup winning team in the line-up.

But this was to be a day to forget for the Sky Blues as the 8,000 fans crammed into the ground were about to see one of the great cup upsets. Sutton's manager, the pipe-smoking Barrie Williams, a former English teacher who liked to quote Shakespeare and Kipling in his programme notes, had noticed that Coventry had a weakness on set-pieces and he set out to exploit it fully.

Coventry arrived in good heart. The previous week they had crushed Sheffield Wednesday 5-0 and were fifth in the First Division – but Sutton made a mockery of the difference between the teams and went ahead four minutes before half-time when Tony Rains, playing his 613th match for the club, headed home a Mickey Stephens corner at the far post.

David Phillips brought Coventry level after 52 minutes before Sutton went 2-1 up in the 58th minute after another Stephens corner. This time the scorer was 22-year-old bricklayer Matthew Hanlan as Sutton became only the sixth Non-League club since the war to knock out a Firs Division club. Among those celebrating was Sutton centre-back Vernon Pratt whose brother Bradley was to complete something of a family double two years later when he played in the Woking side that won 4-2 at West Bromwich Albion.

Sutton United: Roffey; Jones, Rains, Golley, V.Pratt, Rogers, Stephens, Dawson, Dennis, McKinnon, Hanlan

Coventry City: Ogrizovic; Borrows, Phillips, Sedgley, Kilcline, Peake, Bennett, Speedie, Regis (Houchen), McGrath, Smith

Scorers: Sutton: Rains 41, Hanlan 58; Coventry: Phillips 52

### 9. Second Round
### Derby County 1, Boston United 6
### December 10, 1955

Six men in the Boston United team that travelled to Derby for this famous second round tie knew all about the Baseball Ground – they were all ex-Derby County players.

They were Reg Harrison, who played for Derby in the 1946 cup final, Geoff Hazledene and his brother Don, the Boston skipper, Ray Wilkins, Dave Miller and goalkeeper Ray Middleton. They were all seeing out their careers in the Midland League while Derby had slipped from the heights they reached just after World War II and were now in the Third Division North.

Even so, not many people in the 23,000 crowd expected anything other than a Derby win but by half-time the Non-League side were 3-1 ahead and they added another three without reply in the second half. In the next round Boston lost 4-0 at Tottenham, but there was a coincidental postscript to the Derby-Boston match years later.

On January 9, 1974 Boston and Derby were drawn together again... and Derby won 6-1 at Boston in a replayed third round tie.

Derby County: Webster, Barrowcliffe, Upton, Mays, McDonnell, Ryan, Cresswell, Parry, Todd, Pye, Powell

Boston United: Middleton; Robinson, Snade, D Hazledene, Miller, Lowder, Harrison, G Hazledene, Wilkins, Birkbeck, Howlett

Scorers: Derby: Pye 36pen; Boston: Wilkins 26, 76, G.Hazledene 33, 61, 64 Birkbeck 42

Crowd: 23,757

### 10. Third Round
### Wrexham 2, Arsenal 1
### January 4, 1992

For the second time a lowly team whose name began with a 'W' humbled Arsenal in the FA Cup. For the first time the team finishing bottom of the Football League the previous season knocked out the League champions.

With only eight minutes remaining though, it seemed Arsenal were set for the fourth round having led since the 43rd minute through an Alan Smith goal.

But then the match was turned on its head. After 82 minutes David O'Leary was penalised for a foul on veteran Gordon Davies some 20 metres from goal and 37-year-old Mickey Thomas who had played for Manchester United against Arsenal in the 1979 cup final, prepared to take it. Perhaps he was thinking to himself "Have this for 1979" because the ball flew straight past David Seaman and into the top right hand corner of the net. It wasn't the first time, or the last, that Seaman would fail to stop a long-range effort from going in and it wasn't the first time Seaman had been left cursing the cup. He was Birmingham's goalkeeper when they lost at home to Altrincham six years earlier.

Two minutes later and Arsenal were out. They failed to deal with a Wrexham attack, Tony Adams allowing 20-year-old Steve Watkin a shot which Seaman failed to stop, giving Wrexham a totally unexpected victory. They went out in the next round, losing to West Ham in a replay.

Arsenal took the experience to heart and made the best of a bad job. The following season they became the first club to win both the FA Cup and the League Cup in the same season.

Wrexham: O'Keefe; Thackeray, Hardy, Carey, Thomas, Sertori, Davies, Owen, Connolly, Watkin, Phillips

Arsenal: Seaman; Dixon, Winterburn, Hillier, O'Leary, Adams, Rocastle, K.Campbell, Smith, Merson, Carter (Groves)

Scorers: Wrexham: Thomas 82, Watkin 84; Arsenal: Smith 43

Crowd: 13,343

### 11. Third Round
### West Bromwich Albion 2, Woking 4
### January 5, 1991

The name of Tim Buzaglo did not mean a great deal to the football world before this match but he became one of the cup's unlikeliest heroes as Isthmian League Woking demolished Second Division West Bromwich Albion, their long cup-tradition counting for nothing.

Buzaglo had made more of a mark in cricket playing for Gibraltar, but he was the inspiration behind this astonishing victory – the first by a Non-League side away to a Second Division side for 13 years.

He not only sent WBA crashing out but his goals also signalled the end of The Hawthorns career for old cup hero, Brian Talbot, back-to-back Cup winner with Ipswich Town and Arsenal in 1978 and 1979. Talbot was sacked as Albion's manager three days after this defeat. The Baggies ended the season relegated to Division Three.

But they started the better side against Woking with Colin West heading them ahead after 35 minutes. Woking had started slowly – and did not get into their stride until the last half-hour – and then all hell broke loose.

Buzaglo equalised with a well-worked goal after 60 minutes and six minutes later Woking went 2-1 up with a second goal from the off-duty cricketer who headed into the empty net after West Brom keeper Melvyn Rees failed to clear.

He made it 3-1 after 71 minutes after Bradley Pratt, whose brother Vernon had played in the Sutton side that knocked out Coventry two years earlier, started the move that led to the goal. The ball was headed on and Buzaglo crashed a searing left-foot shot into the net. Woking made it 4-1 two minutes from time when substitute Worsfold scored with his first touch. Darren Bradley was booed by his own fans when he brought the score back to 2-4 in the dying minutes. Buzaglo was carried off the field shoulder high by both Albion and Woking fans afterwards. It's the sort of thing you read about in *Roy of the Rovers*. But it actually happened.

Woking were drawn at home to Everton in the next round, switched the tie to Goodison Park and gave a good account of themselves before losing 1-0 in front of a crowd of nearly 35,000.

WBA; Rees; Bradley, Strodder, Roberts, Harbey (Palmer), Ford, Robson, McNally, Shakespeare, West, Bannister
Woking: Read; Mitchell, B Pratt, Cowler, Baron, S Wye, Brown, L Wye, Biggins, Buzaglo, Franks (Worsfold)
Scorers: WBA: West 35, Bradley 89; Woking: Buzaglo 60, 66, 71, Worsfold 88
Crowd: 15,100

### 12. Third Round Birmingham City 1, Altrincham 2 January 14, 1986

In some ways this tie made history even before it was played as First Division Birmingham went into the match as the underdogs against the men from the Alliance Premier League. In that sense was it a shock? Well of course it was because even the most blinkered Birmingham fan could not really have expected his team to lose. But they did.

Birmingham had not won for 16 matches, had scored only four times in those matches, had no money for new players and manager Ron Saunders and everyone else knew the club were destined for relegation which duly arrived three months later.

Before then though Altrincham dug the knife in a bit further, mastering a blustery wind far better than Birmingham. The first shock duly arrived after 62 minutes – Birmingham scored through winger Robert Hopkins.

But Altrincham were soon level with Ronnie Ellis prodding home the equaliser. Then, 10 minutes after scoring at the right end, Hopkins put through his own goal after a mix-up with future Arsenal and England goalkeeper David Seaman.

The match, originally scheduled to take place on January 4 was postponed until January 14, but Altrincham were soon brought back to reality 11 days later when they lost 2-0 at Third Division York in the fourth round. Still, their victory over Birmingham was the first by a Non-League side away to a First Division side since Wimbledon beat Burnley in 1975 and marked a new low point in Birmingham's far from outstanding FA Cup record.

Birmingham City: Seaman; Ranson, Dicks, Hagan, Armstrong, Kuhl, Roberts, Wright, Kennedy, Platnauer, Hopkins
Altrincham: Wealands; Gardner, Densmore, Johnson, Cuddy, Conning, Ellis, Davison, Reid, Chesters, Anderson
Scorers: Birmingham: Hopkins 62; Altrincham: Ellis 65, Hopkins 72og.
Crowd: 6,636

# The War Years

The 1915 FA Cup final between Sheffield United and Chelsea, played on April 24, 1915 is unique as it is the only cup final played during a World War. Known as the 'Khaki Cup Final' because of the large number of servicemen in the crowd at Old Trafford, it was played on a day well in keeping with the times – the weather was bleak and murky and there was none of the exuberance from the crowd usually seen at the final. Sheffield United won 3-0.

Regional tournaments were staged from the 1915-16 to the 1918-19 seasons before the return of peacetime soccer in 1919-20, but there were no 'Wartime Cup Finals' during World War One.

During World War Two a number of Cup finals were played.

**1939-40 League Cup Final**
West Ham 1 (Small), Blackburn R 0
June 8, 1940 Wembley 42,399

**1940-41 League Cup Final**
Arsenal 1 (D Compton), Preston NE 1 (McLaren)
May 10, 1941, Wembley, 60,000

**1940-41 League Cup Final Replay**
Preston 2 (R Beattie 2), Arsenal 1 (og)
May 31, 1941 Ewood Park 45,000

**1941-42 League Cup Final**
First leg
Sunderland 2 (Stubbins, Carter), Wolves 2 (Westcott 2)
May 23, 1942, Roker Park, 35,000

Second Leg
Wolves 4 (Rowley 2, Westcott, Broome), Sunderland 1 (Carter)
May 30, 1942, Molineux, 43,038

**1941-42 London Cup Final**
Brentford 2 (Smith 2), Portsmouth 0
May 30, 1942, Wembley, 72,000

**1941-42 Cup Winners Cup Final**
Brentford 1 (Collett), Wolves 1 (Mullen)
June 6, 1942, Stamford Bridge, 20,174

**League South Cup Final**
Arsenal 7 (Lewis 4, Drake 2, D Compton), Charlton 1 (Green)
May 1, 1943, Wembley, 75,000

**1942-43 League North Cup Final**
First Leg
Blackpool 2 (Finan, Burbanks), Sheffield W 2 (Cockroft, Robinson)
May 1, 1943, Bloomfield Road, 28,000
Second Leg
Sheffield W 1 (Robinson), Blackpool 2 (Dodds, Gardner)
May 8, 1943,Hillsborough, 42,657

**1942-43 Cup Winners Cup Final**
Blackpool 4 (Dix, Burbanks, Dodds, Finan), Arsenal 2 (Lewis, D. Compton)
May 15, 1943,Stamford Bridge, 55,195

**1943-44 League South Cup Final**
Charlton 3 (Revell 2, Welsh), Chelsea 1 (Payne pen)
April 15, 1944, Wembley, 85,000

**1943-44 League North Cup Final**
First Leg
Blackpool 2 (Dodds 2), Aston Villa 1 (Goffin)
April 29, 1944, Bloomfield Road, 28,000
Second Leg
Aston Villa 4 (Broome 2, Edwards, Iverson), Blackpool 2 (Dix, Pearson)
May 6, 1944, Villa Park, 55,000

**Cup Winners Cup Final**
Aston Villa 1 (Houghton), Charlton 1 (Revell)
May 20, 1944, Stamford Bridge, 38,540

**1944-45 League South Cup Final**
Chelsea 2 (McDonald, Wardle), Millwall 0,
April 7, 1945, Wembley, 90,000

**1944-45 League North Cup Final**
First Leg
Bolton Wanderers 1 (Lofthouse), Manchester United 0
May 19, 1945, Burnden Park, 40,000
Second Leg
Manchester United 2 (Wrigglesworth, Bryant), Bolton 2 (Barrass 2)
May 26, 1945, Maine Road, 57,395

**1944-45 Cup Winners Cup Final**
Bolton 2 (Hunt, Hamlett), Chelsea 1 (Rooke)
June 2, 1945 Stamford Bridge 35,000

A Wartime Cup for clubs in the west of England and Wales was also staged in the later years of World War Two.
The winners were: 1942-43: Swansea Town; 1943-44 Bath City; 1944-45 Bath City.

# FA Cup Firsts

### 1. The First FA Cup Final
The First FA Cup final was played on March 16, 1872 when the Wanderers met Royal Engineers at the Kennington Oval in front of a 2,000 crowd who paid 1/- (5p) each for the privilege.

### 2. The First Goal In FA Cup History
The first four matches in the history of the FA Cup were played on Saturday, November 11, 1871, and the results were:
Barnes 2, Civil Service 0
Crystal Palace 0, Hitchin 0
Maidenhead 2, Marlow 0
Upton Park 0, Clapham Rovers 3
The first goal on that historic day was scored by Jarvis Kenrick who went on to score twice in Clapham Rovers win over Upton Park.

He later played in three winning finals for the Wanderers, scoring a total of three cup final goals.

### 3. The First Goal Scored In the FA Cup Final
The Wanderers won the first FA Cup final with a goal scored by Morton Peto Betts who was playing for the Wanderers under the pseudonym 'A.H. Chequer' as he was actually a member of the Harrow Chequers club which had scratched when due to play the Wanderers in the first round.

### 4. The First Player to Score Twice in an FA Cup Final
Thomas Hughes, who scored two of the three goals in the 1876 replay was the first man to score more than one goal in the final.

### 5. The First Own-Goal in the FA Cup Final
Lord Kinnaird 'achieved' this is 1877 – but the

fact was lost for more than a century. Playing in goal for the Wanderers against Oxford University he stepped over the goal-line with the ball and Oxford were credited with a goal.

The Wanderers won the match 2-1 but Oxford's goal somehow became 'lost' due to confusing reports of the match in the press and until relatively recently the result of that final was shown as a 2-0 win for the Wanderers.

### 6. The First Player to Score in Successive FA Cup Finals

Alexander George Bonsor became the first player to score in successive finals with goals in both 1875 and 1876 for Old Etonians. He had already played in the 1872 and 1873 finals for the Wanderers without scoring but finished with a winners medal both times. However in both 1875 and 1876 the Old Etonians lost, first to the Royal Engineers and then the Wanderers.

### 7. The First Player to Score in Three Successive FA Cup Finals

Jimmy Brown of Blackburn Rovers scored the first goal in the 1884 final when Blackburn beat Queen's Park 2-1. He scored again in the 1885 final when Blackburn beat Queen's Park 2-0 and became the first player to score in three successive finals when he scored Blackburn's first in the replay of the 1886 final at the Racecourse Ground, Derby, when West Bromwich Albion were beaten 2-0.

### 8. The First Player to Score in Every Round of The FA Cup

Archie Hunter of Aston Villa was the first player to score in every round his team played in 1886-87 although Villa had a bye in Round Four. Sandy Brown of Tottenham Hotspur, in 1900-01 scored in all rounds.

### 9. The First Wembley FA Cup FinalGoal

David Jack of Bolton scored the first FA Cup final goal at Wembley, three minutes after the start of the match against West Ham. He also scored the fifth Wembley FA Cup final goal three years later when Bolton beat Manchester City 1-0 in 1926. The 215th and last FA Cup final goal at the original Wembley was scored by Roberto Di Matteo of Chelsea which secured their 1-0 win over Aston Villa on May 20, 2000.

### 10. The First Player to Score Twice in a Wembley FA Cup final

Jimmy Roscamp of Blackburn Rovers became the first man to score twice in the same Cup Final at Wembley in his team's 3-1 win over Huddersfield Town in 1928.

### 11. The First FA Cup FinalHat-trick

Billy Townley of Blackburn Rovers scored three goals when his side beat Sheffield Wednesday (known simply as The Wednesday at the time) 6-1 in the 1890 cup final at Kennington Oval.

### 12. The First (and Only) Hat-trick in a Wembley FA Cup Final

In 1953 Stan Mortensen of Blackpool became the first (and only) player to score a hat-trick in an FA Cup final at the original Wembley when his side beat Bolton Wanderers 4-3 in the 'Matthews Final' of 1953.

### 13. The First Player to Score for the Losing Side at Wembley

Strangely, from 1910, when Newcastle beat Barnsley 2-0 in the FA Cup final replay, until 1927 when Cardiff beat Arsenal 1-0, the losing side failed to score a goal. Thus the first man to score at Wembley and end up on the losing side was Alex Jackson of Huddersfield Town, who scored his side's solitary goal when they lost 3-1 to Blackburn Rovers.

### 14. The First Player to Score for Both Sides in the FA Cup Final

Bert Turner of Charlton Athletic achieved this particular first in 1946. With 10 minutes left to play between Derby County and Charlton Athletic the score was still 0-0 and extra time looked certain. Then Turner deflected a clearance into his own net to put Derby 1-0 ahead. Less than a minute later he equalised for Charlton with a free-kick – which also took a slight deflection off Derby's Peter Doherty. It was 1-1 at the end of normal time so extra time was needed after all. Doherty also scored for Derby in extra time – but it is Turner who is credited with a goal for each side. Derby won 4-1.

### 15. The First Player to Score a Penalty In The FA Cup Final

Albert Shepherd of Newcastle United took and scored the first penalty awarded in the FA Cup final. The goal came in the replay of the 1910 Cup Final between Newcastle and Barnsley at Goodison Park. Shepherd scored both goals as Newcastle won 2-0.

### 16. The First Player to Score a Penalty in the FA Cup final at Wembley

George Mutch of Preston scored the first penalty awarded in an FA Cup final at Wembley when he successfully converted a 119th minute spot-kick to give his team a 1-0 victory over Huddersfield Town on April 30, 1938.

### 17. The First Player to Miss a Penalty in the FA Cup Final

Charlie Wallace of Aston Villa missed a penalty

in the 1913 final between League champions Sunderland, and Villa, who finished second in the table. The 1913 final was the first between the two clubs finishing first and second in the top division.

### 18. The First Player to Miss a Penalty in The FA Cup final At Wembley

John Aldridge of Liverpool became the first player to miss a penalty in the FA Cup final at Wembley when Dave Beasant of Wimbledon dived to save his 61st minute spot-kick in the 1988 FA Cup final. Wimbledon won the match 1-0. In 1991 Gary Lineker of Tottenham Hotspur became the only other player to have a penalty saved at the original Wembley Stadium when his spot-kick was saved by Mark Crossley of Nottingham Forest. Spurs recovered to win 2-1 after extra time.

### 19. The First Player to Score Two Penalties in the FA Cup Final

Eric Cantona of Manchester United became the first player to score two penalties in a cup final with spot-kick goals after 60 and 66 minutes of the 1994 Final against Chelsea. United won 4-0.

### 20. The First Player to Score in Successive FA Cup finals at Wembley

Bobby Johnstone of Manchester City scored in both 1955 when Manchester City lost 3-1 to Newcastle United and in 1956 when Manchester City beat Birmingham City 3-1.

### 21. The First Goalkeeper to Score a Goal in the FA Cup

Former QPR and Welsh international goalkeeper Tony Roberts became the first goalie to score in the FA Cup when he joined the attack and fired home a low shot to give Dagenham and Redbridge a last-minute equaliser and a 2-2 draw with Basingstoke in a fourth round qualifying tie on October 27, 2001. Dagenham and Redbridge won the replay 3-0 and eventually reached the Third Round where they lost to Ipswich.

### 22. The First FA Cup final Substitute

The 1967 final between Tottenham Hotspur and Chelsea was the first in which a substitute was named in a 12-man squad.

Tottenham's no.12 was Cliff Jones who had played in the 1961 and 1962 cup-winning teams while Chelsea's No.12 was Joe Kirkup, who two years previously had played in the West Ham side that beat TSV Munich 1860 to win the European Cup Winners Cup at Wembley.

But neither man had the honour of being the first substitute in the FA Cup final. A year later West Bromwich Albion's Dennis Clarke became the first substitute used in the FA Cup final when he replaced John Kaye at the start of extra time against Everton. WBA won 1-0 with a goal from Jeff Astle.

### 23. The First Substitute to Score in the FA Cup Final

Eddie Kelly of Arsenal came on for the injured Peter Storey after 70 minutes of the 1971 final against Liverpool and became the first substitute to score in an FA Cup final when he equalised for the Gunners in the 11th minute of extra time.

The following day most newspapers credited George Graham with the goal. It was only after TV cameras behind the goal later proved that Kelly, and not Graham, got the final touch on the ball, was the goal credited to Kelly.

### 24. The First Substitute to Score Twice in the FA Cup Final

Stuart McCall of Everton was the first – by two minutes from Ian Rush of Liverpool. Both McCall and Rush came on as substitutes during the 1989 FA Cup final. McCall scored his first goal in the last minute of normal time to make the score 1-1 and force extra time.

Rush put Liverpool 2-1 ahead in the fourth minute of extra time, and eight minutes later McCall scored his second to make the score 2-2 and become the first substitute to score twice in the cup final. Two minutes after McCall's second, Rush scored his second with six minutes of extra time remaining to become the second substitute to score two goals in the cup final.

### 25. The First Goalkeeping Substitution in the FA Cup Final

Southampton's Welsh international Paul Jones became the first goalkeeper to come on as a substitute in an FA Cup final when he replaced Finnish international teammate Antti Niemi, injured after 64 minutes of the 2003 final against Arsenal.

### 26. The First Club to Reach Two FA Cup Finals

The Wanderers won the first final in 1872 and were handed a bye to the second final. In 1873 they beat Oxford University 2-0 to also become the first club to win the FA Cup in successive years.

### 27. The First Club to Win Three FA CupFinals

The Wanderers won the cup for the third time after a replay in 1876 when they beat the Old Etonians at Kennington Oval. Under the rules of the competition at the time they were entitled to keep the cup after a third win, but handed it back to the FA.

### 28. The First All-English Team to Win the FA Cup

West Bromwich Albion were the first club to win the FA Cup with a team composed of English-born players in 1888. Every player was locally-born and their combined wage bill was about £10 a week. Since then Bolton (1958), Manchester City (1969) and West Ham (1975) have won with all-English teams.

### 29. The First Non-English Team to Win the FA Cup

The Liverpool team which beat Everton to win the FA Cup final in 1986 technically did not contain any 'English' players. Ten of the 11 players in the side were full internationals – but none of them played for England. The only English link was Mark Lawrenson who was born in Preston but who played for the Republic of Ireland.

The line-up with their countries was: Bruce Grobbelaar (Zimbabwe); Mark Lawrenson (Rep. Ireland), Jim Beglin (Rep. Ireland), Steve Nicol (Scotland), Ronnie Whelan (Rep. Ireland), Alan Hansen (Scotland), Kenny Dalglish (Scotland), Craig Johnston (born in South Africa), Ian Rush (Wales), Jan Molby (Denmark), Kevin Macdonald (born in Scotland).

Kenny Dalglish was the first-player manager to win the cup, and he of course, was Scottish.

### 30. The First Player to Win the FA Cup in England and Scotland

Harry Campbell appeared in the Renton team that won the Scottish FA Cup in 1888 and played for Blackburn Rovers when they won the FA Cup two years later. Jimmy Welford, who played for Aston Villa when they beat West Bromwich Albion 1-0 in the 1895 FA Cup final became the first Englishman to appear in winning teams on both sides of the border when he played for the Celtic team which beat Rangers 2-0 in the 1899 Scottish FA Cup final.

### 31. The First Man to Manage English and Scottish FA Cup Winning Teams

Johnny Cochrane became the first man to manage FA Cup winning teams in England and Scotland. He guided St Mirren to victory in the Scottish Cup final in 1926 and Sunderland to victory in the FA Cup final in 1937. Sir Alex Ferguson emulated this achievement in 1990 with Manchester United. He was Aberdeen manager when they won the Scottish Cup in 1982, 1983, 1984 and 1986.

### 32. The First Man to Manage Two FA Cup Winning Teams

Herbert Chapman became the first man to manage two different teams to victory in the FA Cup final with Huddersfield Town in 1922 and Arsenal, who beat Huddersfield in 1930. In recognition of his links with both clubs, the 1930 final was the first at which the finalists walked on to the pitch together.

### 33. The First Man to Play In and then Manage a Winning Team in the FA Cup Final

Peter McWilliam picked up a winners medal as a player when Newcastle United beat Barnsley in the 1910 FA Cup final. He was the manager of Tottenham Hotspur when they beat Wolverhampton Wanderers to win the cup in 1921 when he became the first man to achieve this particular double.

### 34. The First Man to Play For and then Manage the Same Club to Victory In the FA Cup Final

The first man to perform this feat was Stan Seymour who played in the Newcastle United team which beat Aston Villa 2-0, and then managed the club when they won the cup in 1951 and 1952. Seymour also scored one of Newcastle's goals in 1924.

### 35. The First Manager from Outside the British Isles to Win the FA Cup

Dutchman Ruud Gullit became the first man from outside the British Isles to coach or manage the FA Cup winners when his Chelsea side beat Middlesbrough in 1997.

### 36. The First Final Featuring Two Managers from Outside the British Isles

The 2001 FA Cup final between Liverpool and Arsenal was the first in which both teams were managed by men from overseas. It resulted in a victory for Liverpool's French manager Gerard Houllier over Arsenal's French manager Arsene Wenger. In 2002 Wenger's Arsenal won the cup against a Chelsea team managed by Italian Claudio Ranieri.

### 37. The First Non-League Club to Reach the FA Cup Final

Before the foundation of the Football League in 1888 of course all the finalists were non-league, but the first side to reach the final after the formation of the League was Sheffield Wednesday, (then known as The Wednesday), who were playing in the Football Alliance.

They reached the 1890 final and lost 6-1 to Blackburn Rovers who finished third in the Football League that season. Sheffield Wednesday joined the Football League two years later.

### 38. The First Non-League Club to Win the FA Cup

Tottenham Hotspur became the first, and so far only club from outside the Football or Premier Leagues to win the cup since league football began in 1888. Spurs, then in the Southern League, won in 1901 beating Sheffield United 3-1 in a replay at Burnden Park, Bolton, after a 2-2 draw at Crystal Palace.

### 39. The First Non-League Club to Beat the FA Cup Holders

En route to winning the FA Cup in 1901, Tottenham Hotspur, then in the Southern League met First Division Bury, the reigning cup holders, in a second round match on 23 February. Spurs won the tie 2-1. The very next season, still a Non-League side themselves Spurs were knocked out by Southern League opposition, losing to Southampton in the first round.

### 40. The First Club to Win the FA Cup and League Double

Preston North End won the inaugural Football League championship in 1888-89 without losing a match and won the FA Cup the same season without conceding a goal.

### 41. The First Club to Finish Runners-up in the FA Cup and League

Huddersfield Town were the best team in the League in the 1920s when they won three successive titles from 1924-26. Their only success in the cup came in 1922 when they beat Preston 1-0. In 1928 they reached the final again but were beaten 3-1 by Blackburn Rovers. They also finished second in the League behind Everton and became the first side to finish as runners-up in the race for both major honours in the same season.

### 42. The First Second Division Club to Win the FA Cup

The Second Division of the Football League was formed for the 1892-93 season and the following year, in 1894, the first Second Division team won the FA Cup. Notts County, who finished third in the Second Division and missed out on promotion to the first by losing in the Test Matches to Liverpool, beat Bolton Wanderers 4-1 in the final at Goodison Park. Jimmy Logan scored the second FA Cup final hat-trick.

### 43. The First Second Division Club to Win Promotion and the FA Cup in the Same Season

West Bromwich Albion became the first Second Division club to win at Wembley and the first to win a cup and promotion double when they beat Birmingham 2-1 in the all-Midland final of 1931. No other club has been promoted to the top flight and won the FA Cup in the same season since then.

### 44. The First Team to Reach the FA Cup final and be Relegated in the Same Season

Chelsea finished second from bottom of the First Division in 1914-15, the last season before the First World War. But their cup form was in marked contrast to their League form and they reached the FA Cup final, only to lose 3-0 to Sheffield United. But for the war, they would have been relegated, but they kept their place in the First Division when it was expanded from 20 to 22 clubs in 1919.

In 1926 Manchester City finished one from bottom of the First Division and also reached the cup final. There was no war to save them and they went down.

### 45. The First Club from Outside England to Win the FA Cup

When Cardiff City beat Arsenal 1-0 in the 1927 Cup Final they became the first, and so far only non-English club to win the FA Cup final. The only other non-English club to reach the final is Queen's Park Glasgow, who finished as runners-up to Blackburn Rovers in both 1884 and 1885.

### 46. The First FA Cup Match Played on Christmas Day

Only one FA Cup match has been played on Christmas Day and that was in 1888 when Linfield beat Cliftonville 7-0 in a fourth qualifying round second replay. On Boxing Day 1881 Hotspur FC beat Reading Minster 2-0 in a third round match.

### 47. The First Wembley FA Cup Final

The first Wembley FA Cup final was played on April 28, 1923 when First Division Bolton Wanderers beat West Ham United of the Second Division 2-0. The official attendance is recorded as 126,047 but an estimated 200,000 fans were in the stadium by the time the match kicked off.

### 48. The First Team to Score First and Lose the FA Cup Final at Wembley

In 1932 Bob John put Arsenal ahead against Newcastle United after 15 minutes but Newcastle came back to win the cup 2-1 thanks to two goals from Jack Allen.

### 49. The First Reigning Monarch to Attend the FA Cup Final

King George V became the first reigning monarch to attend the final when he saw Burnley beat Liverpool 1-0 in the 1914 final at Crystal Palace. He obviously enjoyed himself because he also attended the finals of 1921, 1923, 1926, 1927, 1928, 1930, 1932, and 1934.

### 50. The First Winning Team to Put Their Ribbons on the FA Cup

One of the great traditions of the FA Cup did not actually start until the competition was almost 30 years old. But the first club to put their ribbons the trophy after winning it were Tottenham Hotspur at their post-match celebration in 1901.

Before the final both sets of ribbons are attached to the trophy – with the losing club's colours removed before the presentation.

### 51. The First Wembley FA Cup Final to Go to a Replay

It was not until 1970 and the 42nd final that the first Wembley Cup Final ended in a draw after extra time. On April 11, 1970 Chelsea and Leeds drew 2-2, with Chelsea winning the replay 2-1 at Old Trafford on April 29. That was also the first FA Cup final to be played at night under floodlights.

### 52. The First FA Cup final Replayed at Wembley

The first Wembley final to be replayed at Wembley was the 1981 match between Tottenham Hotspur and Manchester City. The first game ended in a 1-1 draw on May 9, and was replayed on Thursday, May 14 with Spurs winning 3-2. It was the first final to be replayed since 1970 and was the first of three successive finals (1981, 1982 and 1983) which all ended in draws.

### 53. The First Player Sent Off In an FA Cup Final

It was not until the 116th final match, including replays, that a player was sent off. The unlucky man was Kevin Moran of Manchester United who was dismissed by referee Peter Willis for a late tackle on Everton's Peter Reid on May 18, 1985. Manchester United, although reduced to 10 men, went on to win the match 1-0.

### 54. The First Time an Entire Round was Postponed

At least one match scheduled to take place in every round of the FA Cup did so from the start of the competition in 1871 for the next 98 years. Even during the 'big freezes' of 1947 and 1963 some matches took place on their original dates. But on February 8, 1969, all eight Round Five matches were postponed because of the weather.

### 55. The First FA Cup Tie Played on a Sunday

With rounds of the FA Cup now spread over three days because of broadcasting demands, it seems strange to think that until January 6, 1974, no FA Cup match had ever been played on a Sunday. The first to take place on a Sunday was a third round match between Cambridge United and Oldham Athletic which ended in a 2-2 draw.

### 56. The First £1 Million Gate Receipt at the FA Cup Final

The first FA Cup final match to produce £1 million in takings at the gate was the 1985 match between Manchester United and Everton, which was also Britain's first £1m gate.

However, the 1980 final between West Ham and Arsenal was the first to generate £1 million in overall receipts. Ticket receipts (£730,000) added to TV rights fees and other revenues produced more than £1m in revenue for the first time.

The first final for which receipts are reliably known is the 1885 final which produced a gate of £442. Since then the following ticket sale milestones have been reached (single matches only, not including combined totals of original matches and replays):

| | | |
|---|---|---|
| First £1,000 | 1891 | Blackburn R v Notts County (£1,454) |
| First £10,000 | 1921 | Tottenham H v Wolverhampton W (£13,414) |
| First £100,000 | 1966 | Everton v Sheffield Wed (£109,691) |
| First £500,000 | 1978 | Ipswich v Arsenal (£500,000) |
| First £1m | 1985 | Manchester U v Everton (£1.1m) |
| First £2m | 1990 | Manchester U v Crystal P (£2m) |
| First £3m | 2000 | Chelsea v Aston Villa (£3.1m) |

### 57. The First Third Division Side to Reach the Semi-finals

No side from the old Third Division of the Football League ever reached the final. The first to reach the semi-finals were Millwall in 1937 where they were beaten 2-1 to the eventual winners, Sunderland.

### 58. The First Female Referee

Miss Kim George, a 28-year-old maths teacher from Bognor, became the first woman to officiate in the history of the cup when she refereed a preliminary round tie on September 3, 1988 between Shoreham and Eastbourne. Eastbourne won 3-1.

### 59. The First FA Employee Sent Off in the FA Cup

Mark Osikoya, a marketing executive at the FA whose responsibility as brand manager was to ensure that AXA got as much publicity as possible for their FA Cup sponsorship, certainly achieved that and more in August 2001. Playing for Walton Casuals in an extra-preliminary round match at Saltdean United, he became the first FA employee to be sent off in an FA Cup match after fouling an opponent and abusing a linesman. He was later banned for 10 weeks.

### 60. The First Club To Win the FA Amateur Cup and FA Cup

Old Carthusians won the FA Cup in 1881 and the Amateur Cup in 1894 and 1897. Since then only Wimbledon have repeated that feat winning the Amateur Cup in the FA's Centenary Year of 1963 and the FA Cup in the Football League's Centenary Year of 1988. The FA Amateur Cup was discontinued in 1974. The only other current professional club who could emulate them are Middlesbrough who won the Amateur Cup in 1895 and 1898 and lost to Chelsea in 1997 in their only FA Cup final appearance.

### 61. The First Goalkeeper to Captain an FA Cup Winning Team

Dave Beasant of Wimbledon had a memorable day on May 14, 1988 when he became the first goalkeeper to captain his team to victory in the FA Cup. During the match he became the first goalkeeper to save a penalty in a Wembley FA Cup final when he palmed away John Aldridge's 61st minute spot-kick.

### 62. The First FA Cup final to be Broadcast

The first FA Cup match to be broadcast by radio was the 1926 final between Bolton Wanderers and Manchester City which was relayed only to public halls in both Bolton and Manchester, but it was not a public radio broadcast as such. The first to be broadcast publicly by the BBC was the fourth round match between Corinthians and Newcastle United at Crystal Palace on Saturday, January 29, 1927. The first final to be transmitted to the public was the 1927 match between Cardiff City and Arsenal.

### 63. The First FA Cup final to be Televised Live

The 1937 FA Cup final between Sunderland and Preston North End was partially televised, but the first final to be televised live in its entirety was the 1938 final in which Preston beat Huddersfield 1-0 with George Mutch scoring the deciding goal from the penalty spot in the last minute of extra time. The TV audience was estimated at about 10,000. The attendance at Wembley was 93,000.

### 64. The First Player in The 20th Century to Win the FA Cup with Different Clubs in Successive Seasons

Brian Talbot was the first, and only player in the 20th century to win the FA Cup with different clubs in successive seasons. He was in the Ipswich team which beat Arsenal 1-0 in 1978 and in the Arsenal team which beat Manchester United 3-2 in 1979.

### 65. The First FA Cup finals Featuring Numbers – and Names

The 1933 final between Everton and Manchester City was the first in which the players wore numbered shirts – with Everton wearing numbers 1-11 and Manchester City 12-22. The 1993 final between Arsenal and Sheffield Wednesday was the first in which the players wore their names on the back of their shirts.

### 66. The First FA Cup Penalty Shoot-outs

Penalty shoot-outs were introduced to settle ties after a second drawn match from the 1991-92 season. The first tie to be decided on penalties was the First Round match between Rotherham United and Scunthorpe United on November 26, 1991. After the first match ended in a 1-1 draw, the replay at Rotherham finished 3-3 after extra time. Rotherham won 7-6 on penalties.

The following day Exeter City beat Colchester United 4-2 on penalties after they had drawn their two First Round matches. Colchester thus became the first team to be knocked out of the cup without conceding a goal. The other penalty shoot-outs in the 1991-92 season came in the third round when Bournemouth beat Newcastle 4-3 on penalties; in the fourth round when Southampton beat Manchester United 4-2 and in the semi-finals when Liverpool beat Portsmouth 3-1.

However the first ever FA Cup match to be decided on penalties was a third-place play-off match between Birmingham City and Stoke City at St Andrew's on August 5, 1972. The match ended 0-0 and Birmingham won 4-3 on penalties.

### 67. The First FA Cup Final to be Played 'Indoors'

The 2003 Cup Final between Arsenal and Southampton at Cardiff's Millennium Stadium became the first to be played 'indoors' when the retractable roof was closed for the match.